BRITANNICA
Book of the Year
1970

Encyclopædia Britannica, Inc.

WILLIAM BENTON
Publisher

Chicago, Toronto, London, Geneva, Sydney, Tokyo, Manila

Library of Congress Catalog Number: 38–12082
International Standard Book Number: 0–85229–144–2

BRITANNICA BOOK OF THE YEAR

(Trademark Reg. U.S. Pat. Off.)
Printed in U.S.A.

THE UNIVERSITY OF CHICAGO

The Britannica Book of the Year is published with the editorial advice of the faculties of The University of Chicago

William Benton

A Message from the Publisher

1970—THRESHOLD OF AN EPOCH?

In our search for the significance and pattern of the past, can we begin to comprehend the future more clearly? The desire to do so is understandable in all of us.

Does the tapestry of history sometimes seem to suggest the edge of an epoch—the place where one age stops and another starts—even though there is never such a clear-cut breaking point? Indeed, in each year of the '60s as we took up our *Britannica Book of the Year,* it was our humbling experience to feel that we stood at the edge of a new epoch. We felt that we were alive at that point in history when man knew that—because of an event of his own doing—things would never again be as they were.

This is the impact upon us of the rush of modern science. Here is the glimpse of the future. For have we not—in the words of H. G. Wells—stood upon a footstool and laughed and reached out our hands amid the stars?

Now we enter a new decade which promises to be the most exciting in all of history. When man stepped down onto the surface of the moon last year, all men thrilled not only to an immediate sense of the epochal but also to the visceral grasp of a new perspective of what is to come. What were national boundaries in the face of this human achievement? The fabulous venture was made possible by a chemical discovery from ancient China, by a law of physics first defined by an Englishman, by a research team pioneered by a German scientist, and by a sense of urgency born, after Sputnik, of the competition between the U.S. and the U.S.S.R. Thus the lunar landing should be considered the common heritage of all humanity.

Part of that heritage is the anticipation of an epoch in the making.

One of the pleasures of the Britannica Yearbook is the fact that the minutiae proliferate right along with the cosmic: that the military budget of Andorra during 1969 remained at 300 pesetas, or five dollars, a year—to be spent only for "ceremonial salutes"—and that the first annual International Bicycle Race of Antarctica, three miles across the polar ice cap, was won by New Zealand.

Of more importance is the quickening pace in microbiology, and most particularly in genetic research. You will find in the 1970 Yearbook a recounting of the fact that science has isolated for the first time what is thought to be the basic chemical unit of heredity, the gene, and that we are gaining insight into the "transportation system" by which DNA* is transferred from one cell to another—sometimes by riding piggyback on a virus! It is such research that someday may lead not only to new methods of conquering disease but to the knowledge of how to grow not only specific *cells* but specific *limbs*—a "new" arm, perhaps to replace one that has been amputated—or how to induce entire organs to regenerate of their own accord, making such operations as heart transplants unnecessary. Indeed, it is not inconceivable that science may learn how to "duplicate" an entire human being. Can you conceive sporting events as contests between geneticists to see which nation can turn out entire Olympic teams patterned after world record holders?

On a more ominous level, science may also discover how to send a genetic message—perhaps riding on a virus—that would tamper with the genes of an entire population. For instance, such a genetic message might make an "enemy" population lethally sensitive to some common phenomenon, like pollen, or carbon dioxide—thus turning the air, in effect, into a deadly gas.

Microbiology thus stands today at the same fateful threshold as physics did in 1940—but events are moving more swiftly today than they did then. H. W. Thorpe, a scientist at Cambridge University, observed that today's genetic explorations "are as epoch-making for mankind as any that have preceded them. They rank at least as high, if not higher, in importance than the discovery of fire, or agriculture, the development of printing and the discovery of the wheel." Arthur Koestler put it more dramatically: "The biological time bomb is about to go off in our face."

In this—in the possibility that we may even turn mankind into a monster of some new and unfathomable kind—we can see a reprise of the past, particularly of 1945. That was when the physicists began debating—too late for the people of Hiroshima and Nagasaki—the implications of nuclear fission. Geneticists are now just beginning to examine the implications of their own work. Sir Macfarlane Burnet, a 1960 Nobel laureate and an expert in tissue transplant, said: "It is a hard thing for an experimental scientist to accept, but it is becoming all too evident that there are dangers in knowing what should not be known."

---

* Deoxyribonucleic acid, the "building block" of heredity.

Thus we find that today, as always, the greatest and most perplexing problems of science are ethical and moral and philosophical, and not merely scientific. For science is caught up in the ultimate paradox of mankind: it rewards man's impulse toward omnipotence at the same time that it torments him with his human limitations.

At Britannica, it is our hope always to help you remain aware of this more subtle, less tangible, but most important dimension in mankind's affairs: man's sense of responsibility—his ability to shape his achievements to the imperatives of his age. We are removed in time, but not far in spirit, from those contradictions that led Machiavelli, in distinguishing between *fortuna* and *virtu* in *The Prince*, to argue that half of man's actions are ruled by chance and the other half are governed by man himself. We can see something of this in the vast feeling of frustration that now sweeps the world in the emerging '70s, a feeling impressive not only for its force but for its diversity: the Soviets are frustrated with the Chinese, the Romanians with the Soviets; the pope is frustrated with his bishops, the bishops with their priests; fathers are frustrated with their sons, and vice versa. There is, in all this, much of the classic challenge to age and authority—the feeling, on the one hand, that seniority possesses a particular wisdom and the rebellious certainty, on the other, that it does not. My own feeling —after reading not only the Yearbooks but other publications of Britannica (among them Britannica's *Perspectives*)—is that much of the conflict of today's world is also rooted in an even more traditional dilemma—that of whether morality and law should stand above power.

We at Britannica try to remain sensitive to the fact that the world is a seething laboratory of sociological as well as of scientific change, and that some of the most challenging problems of our times involve the secrets not only of nature but of human nature. We may find, in the perspective of history, that the equation involving justice and power—some might say justice *v.* power—has been a more delicate and perplexing one than that involving $e = mc^2$.*

In this 1970 Yearbook, for instance, you will clearly see evidence of the effort the black peoples of the world are making to find a place in justice *and* a place of power. Note particularly the major feature article by Jomo Kenyatta, who has led Kenya from the status of British colony to a role among the nations of the world. Early last summer I asked President Kenyatta to write the article, and he complied with a moving, informative account of the travail and the rewards of a people struggling first to control their own destiny and then to build a democratic society out of a heritage of tribalism and colonialism. The article becomes even more significant because of events that have taken place in Kenya since we received the original draft. Since then, Kenya has been embroiled in political turmoil—turmoil touched off by a political assassination; turmoil that President Kenyatta is even now struggling to control. I asked the President to deal with the current situation through an addition to his original article. He graciously obliged. As a result the reader of this *Britannica Book of the Year* has a rare insight into a major political crisis in a key African country. The final result of the current struggle in Kenya can have a profound effect on the future of all of Africa because of the sensitive nature of the affairs of that troubled continent. Readers of the *Book of the Year* now have the privilege of an inside look at that crisis.

Moreover, the impact of the black social movement is reflected throughout the *Book of the Year* across a wide range of the year's activities and events in the United States and Great Britain as well as in Africa. It is reflected in the articles on philosophy, economics, education—and particularly and dominantly in the articles reviewing religion. In one of the most powerful movements in all history, the blacks are rising out of their past not only to form nations in Africa and cultures in Europe and America but also to find an eminent place in the activities that fuel the history of mankind. This black movement of our time is different from the development of the great nonwhite cultures that have preceded it, partly, perhaps, in that it is encountering greater resistance. The black effort today affects all hemispheres and all peoples, and it has been made highly visible by the technological advances of communication and transportation. As my late friend Adlai Stevenson, a Britannica director, once said, "Our difficulties are the price of our blessings. . . ."

It is always important not only that new ideas be heard but that they be debated and challenged, if only to test the vitality of those that can endure. Out of such strife comes the creative tension that helps give every epoch its own identity and integrity.

Yet of the events and the conflicts and the new ideas mirrored in the Britannica and its Yearbooks, none seems to me to quench the essential optimism of the age.

"The only deadly sin I know of is cynicism," said Henry Stimson. In this moment when again an epoch seems to be emerging, as at earlier great moments of history, we of Britannica see major achievements, we watch the world pursue great visions. We stand at the edge of the epoch advancing before us in this new decade, and we tremble with exasperation—and anticipation. One day people may look back on our era and envy us the expectation and even the anguish of our age. Shall we not welcome it, this unfolding future, while we are seeking to understand it?

Wm Benton

* The key equation by which Einstein postulated the interrelation of energy and matter.

How to Use the Book of the Year

The *Britannica Book of the Year* is carefully planned for ready availability of reference material.

Three devices aid the reader to find information he seeks in the main section, which begins on page 65: first and most important, the Index; second, hundreds of cross-reference entries grouped alphabetically in the margins of the pages for quick and convenient information; and third, inserted frequently in or after articles, the suggestion to *"see also"* other specific articles for further related information.

The reader will be repaid richly if he learns more of the contents than just the answers to an occasional reference question about an event of the year. In the pages of this volume, including the special articles which begin on page 17, there are many features to be noted.

The first thing to catch the attention of the reader as he thumbs through the volume will be the many pictures and other illustrations. These include many of the outstanding news photographs of the year, gathered from all over the world, and they constitute a remarkable pictorial record of the year's events.

OTHER FEATURES OF SPECIAL INTEREST:

- A list of the authors of the articles in the *Book of the Year* . . . starts on page 7.
- Calendar of major religious and national holidays scheduled or expected to occur in 1970 . . . is on page 50.
- Chronology of 1969 — the major events of the past year listed day by day as they happened . . . starts on page 51.
- Obituaries — sketches of scores of prominent individuals who died in 1969 . . . starts on page 578.
- Biographies of many prominent living figures whose activities dominated the news in 1969 . . . starts on page 137. Government officials are named in articles on their countries. Hundreds of other persons are mentioned in articles.
- Statistical data of all types, the latest available, appear in many articles.

Above all, remember to use the Index (starting on page 803) whenever you wish information in the *Book of the Year*. The alphabetical arrangement of the book enables a reader to find subjects easily; the Index tells not only where articles appear but often guides the reader to other related subjects.

Before using the Index be sure to read the instructions that precede it.

Contents

Editorial Staff

CONTRIBUTORS

Initials and names of contributors to the Britannica Book of the Year *with the articles written by them. The arrangement is alphabetical by initials.*

A.C.Ge./Geography
ARCH C. GERLACH. Chief Geographer, U.S. Geological Survey, Washington, D.C. Editor, *The Professional Geographer*, 1951–54.

A.D.Bu./Honduras
ALLEN D. BUSHONG. Associate Professor of Geography, University of South Carolina.

A.D.C.H./Industrial Review *(in part)*
ALAN DAVID CHRISTIE HAMILTON. Director, Technical Division, International Paints (Holdings) Ltd., London.

A.Dr./Industrial Review *(in part)*
ALFRED DAWBER. Chairman and Editorial Director, Emmott and Company, Ltd.; Kennedy Press Ltd., technical publishers, Manchester. Editor, *Textile Manufacturer*. Compiler of *Mechanical World Year Book; Electrical Year Book.*

Ad.T./Literature *(in part)*
ADRIEN THERIO. Professor of Lettres Françaises, University of Ottawa. Author of *L'Humour au Canada français; Soliloque en hommage à une femme.*

A.D.Wi./Biography *(in part)*; **Sweden**
ALAN DAVID WILSON. Assistant Editor, *Sweden Now.*

Ae.B./Literature *(in part)*
ANNIE J. M. BRIERRE. Literary Critic, *Les Nouvelles Littéraires; La Revue des Deux Mondes; France—U.S.A.* Author of *Ninon de Lenclos.*

A.F.D./Merchandising *(in part)*
ALTON F. DOODY. Professor of Marketing, College of Administrative Science, Ohio State University. Author of *Retailing Management; Marketing in America: Settlement to Civil War* (vol. 1).

A.G./Malta
ALBERT GANADO. Lawyer, Malta.

A.G.A./Investment, International; Trade, International *(in part)*
ALAN GORDON ARMSTRONG. Research Officer, Department of Applied Economics, Cambridge University; Fellow of Selwyn College, Cambridge.

A.G.Bl./Music *(in part)*
ALAN GEOFFREY BLYTH. Music Critic, London.

A.G.R./Religion *(in part)*
ARTHUR GUY REYNOLDS. Registrar and Associate Professor of Church History, Emmanuel College, Toronto.

A.J.A.M./Turkey
ANDREW JAMES ALEXANDER MANGO. Orientalist and broadcaster.

A.J.Z./European Unity
ARNOLD J. ZURCHER. Professor of Comparative Politics, Graduate School of Arts and Sciences, New York University.

Al.Ma./Engineering Projects *(in part)*
ALDO MARCELLO. Civil Engineer.

A.P.Kl./Religion *(in part)*
ALFRED PAUL KLAUSLER. Executive Secretary, Associated Church Press. Author of *Censorship, Obscenity and Sex; Growth in Worship.*

A.R.A./Cricket
ARTHUR REX ALSTON. Broadcaster and Journalist. Author of *Taking the Air; Over to Rex Alston; Test Commentary; Watching Cricket.*

Ar.C.B./Indonesia
ARNOLD C. BRACKMAN. Writer and Consultant on Asian Affairs. Author of *Indonesian Communism: A History; Southeast Asia's Second Front.*

A.R.G.G./Australia; Biography *(in part)*; **Nauru**
ANTHONY ROYSTON GRANT GRIFFITHS. Lecturer in History, Flinders University of South Australia.

A.R.R./Money and Banking
ALAN RAYMOND ROE. Research Officer, Department of Applied Economics, University of Cambridge.

A.R.W./Panama
ALMON ROBERT WRIGHT. Retired Senior Historian, U.S. Department of State.

A.S./Museums and Galleries *(in part)*
ANDREW SZPAKOWSKI. Program Specialist, Monuments and Museums Section, UNESCO, Paris.

A.S.M./Medicine *(in part)*
ABRAHAM SAMUEL MARKOWITZ. Director, Department of Experimental Immunology, Hektoen Institute for Medical Research; Professor of Microbiology, University of Illinois Medical School.

A.Th./Libraries
ANTHONY THOMPSON. General Secretary, International Federation of Library Associations. Author of *Vocabularium Bibliothecarii; Library Buildings of Britain and Europe.*

A.Tl./Industrial Review *(in part)*
ARTHUR TATTERSALL. Cotton Trade Expert and Statistician, Manchester, Eng.

A.T.M./Historical Studies
ALEXANDER TAYLOR MILNE. Secretary and Librarian, Institute of Historical Research, University of London. Compiler of *Writings on British History* (annual).

A.W.Bs./Japan
ARDATH WALTER BURKS. Professor and Director, International Programs, Rutgers University, New Brunswick, N.J. Author of *The Government of Japan; East Asia: China, Korea, Japan.*

A.W.O./Nicaragua
ARDEN W. OHL. Instructor of Geography, Modesto (Calif.) Junior College.

A.W.Wo./Medicine *(in part)*
ALAN WALLER WOODRUFF. Wellcome Professor of Clinical Tropical Medicine, University of London, Physician, Hospital for Tropical Diseases, London. Co-author of *Recent Advances in Tropical Medicine.*

Ay.K./Literature *(in part)*
(THOMAS) ANTHONY KERRIGAN. Editor and translator of *Selected Works* of Miguel de Unamuno (10 vol.). Author of *At the Front Door of the Atlantic.*

B.Ar./Ireland
BRUCE ARNOLD. Free-lance Journalist and Writer, Dublin.

B.B.Mo./Medicine *(in part)*
BERTRAM B. MOSS, M.D. Clinical Director, Division of Gerontology, Chicago Medical School; Medical Administrator, Jewish Home for Aged and Park View Home for Aged. Author of *Caring for the Aged.*

B.C.N./Fuel and Power *(in part)*
BRUCE CARLTON NETSCHERT. Director, National Economic Research Associates, Inc., Washington, D.C. Author of *The Future Supply of Oil and Gas;* Co-author of *Energy in the American Economy: 1850-1975.*

B.D./Biography *(in part)*
BRENDA DAVIES. Head of Information Department, British Film Institute.

Be.N./Track and Field Sports *(in part)*
BERT NELSON. Publisher, *Track and Field News.*

B.Gr./Music *(in part)*
BENNY GREEN. Jazz Critic, *Observer*, London; Record Reviewer, British Broadcasting Corporation. Author of *The Reluctant Art; Blame It on My Youth; 58 Minutes to London; Jazz Decade.* Contributor to *Encyclopedia of Jazz.*

B.N.D./Trade, International *(in part)*
BARRIE NICHOLAS DAVIES. Director, Statistical Division, Economic Commission for Europe, Geneva.

C.C.O./Engineering Projects *(in part)*; **Industrial Review** *(in part)*
CARTER CLARKE OSTERBIND. Director, Bureau of Economic and Business Research, University of Florida. Co-author of *Florida's Older People.*

Cd.H./Religion *(in part)*
CLIFFORD HAIGH. Editor, *The Friend*, London.

C.E.R./Timber
CHARLES EDGAR RANDALL. Assistant Editor, *Journal of Forestry.* Author of *Famous Trees; Our Forests.*

C.F.Sa./Finland
CARL FREDRIK SANDELIN. Foreign News Editor, Finnish News Agency. President, Society of Swedish-speaking Writers in Finland.

C.H.J./U.S. Supplement: *Church Membership Table.*
CONSTANT HERBERT JACQUET, JR. Director of Research Library and Research Associate, National Council of Churches. Editor, *Yearbook of American Churches*, 1970.

C.J.Ay./Motor Sports *(in part)*
CYRIL J. AYTON. Editor, *Motorcycle Sport*, London.

C.L.Be./Conservation (*in part*)
CHARLES LEOFRIC BOYLE. Lieutenant-Colonel, R.A. (ret'd). Chairman, Survival Service Commission, International Union for Conservation of Nature and Natural Resources, 1958–63; Secretary, Fauna Preservation Society, London, 1950–63.

C.L.F.W./Biological Sciences (*in part*)
CHRISTOPHER LEONARD FRANK WOODCOCK. Lecturer on Biology and Associate in Electron Microscopy, Department of Biology, Harvard University.

C.M.Jo./Bowling and Lawn Bowls (*in part*)
CLARENCE MEDLYCOTT JONES. Editor, *World Bowls; Lawn Tennis.* Author of *Winning Bowls; The Watney Book of Bowls.* Co-author of *Tackle Bowls My Way; Bryant on Bowls.*

Co.L./Biography (*in part*)
COLIN LEGUM. Commonwealth Correspondent, *Observer*, London. Author of *Must We Lose Africa?; Bandung, Cairo and Accra; Congo Disaster; Pan-Africanism—A Short Political Guide.* Co-author of *Attitude to Africa; South Africa: Crisis for the West; The Bitter Choice.* Editor of *Africa—A Handbook to the Continent.*

C.R.C./Biography (*in part*)
C(HARLES) RICHARD CORRIGAN. Environment and Resources Editor, *The National Journal.*

Da.J.R./Cinema (*in part*)
DAVID JULIEN ROBINSON. Film Critic, *The Financial Times.* Author of *Buster Keaton; Hollywood in the Twenties; The Great Funnies—A History of Screen Comedy.*

D.A.S.J./Employment, Wages, and Hours
DUDLEY ANTHONY STEPHENSON JACKSON. Research Officer, Department of Applied Economics, University of Cambridge.

D.Az./Literature (*in part*)
DINA ABRAMOWICZ. Librarian, Yivo Institute for Jewish Research Library, New York, N.Y.

D.B.J.F./Football (*in part*)
DAVID BROUGH JAMES FROST. Rugby Union Correspondent, *Guardian*, London.

D.D./Economics
DUDLEY DILLARD. Professor and Head, Department of Economics, University of Maryland. Author of *The Economics of John Maynard Keynes; Economic Development of the North Atlantic Community.*

Dd.H./Inter-American Affairs
DAVID HUELIN. Manager, Economic Intelligence Department, Bank of London and South America Ltd., London.

De.C./Industrial Design
DENNIS CHEETHAM. Lecturer in Liberal Studies, School of Graphics, City of Leicester Polytechnic, Eng.

D.F.C./Metallurgy
DONALD FREDERIC CLIFTON. Professor of Metallurgy, University of Idaho.

D.Fo./Biography (*in part*)**; Migration, International** (*in part*)
DAVID FOUQUET. Staff Writer, *Congressional Quarterly.*

D.H.C.P.-B./Sailing
DOUGLAS HEXTALL CHEDZEY PHILLIPS-BIRT. Associate Member of the Royal Institution of Naval Architects. Consulting naval architect. Yachting correspondent, *Observer*, London. Author of *Sailing Yacht Design; Motor Yacht and Boat Design; The Waters of Wight.*

D.J.I./Medicine (*in part*)
DWIGHT J. INGLE. Professor of Physiology and Professor, the Ben May Laboratory for Cancer Research, The University of Chicago. Author of *Physiological and Therapeutic Effects of Corticotropin (ACTH) and Cortisone; Principles of Research in Biology and Medicine.* Editor of *Perspectives in Biology and Medicine.*

D.J.Ro./Peru
DAVID JONATHAN ROBINSON. Economic Research Officer, Bank of London and South America Ltd., London.

D.K.R.P./Sporting Record
DAVID KEMSLEY ROBIN PHILLIPS. Contributor, *World Sports.* Editor, *World Sports Olympic Games Report.* Co-compiler of *Guinness Book of Olympic Records.*

D.K.Wi./Chronology (*in part*)
DAVID K. WILLIS. Tokyo Correspondent, *The Christian Science Monitor*, Tokyo.

D.L.Bi./Insurance (*in part*)
DAVID LYNN BICKELHAUPT. Professor of Insurance, College of Administrative Science, Ohio State University. Author of *Transition to Multiple-Line Insurance Companies.* Co-author of *General Insurance.*

D.L.McE./Dentistry
DONALD L. McELROY. Associate Dean, College of Dentistry, University of Illinois. Co-author of *Handbook of Oral Diagnosis and Treatment Planning.*

D.L.R./Industrial Review (*in part*)
DENNIS LIONEL RIDER. Director, Glass Manufacturers' Federation, London.

D.M.L.F./Canada
DAVID M. L. FARR. Professor of History, Carleton University, Ottawa. Author of *The Colonial Office and Canada, 1867–1887; Two Democracies; The Canadian Experience.*

D.P.B./Industrial Review (*in part*)
DONALD P. BURKE. Senior Editor, *Chemical Week.*

D.Wn./Burma; Dependent States (*in part*)**; Nepal**
DOROTHY WOODMAN. Contributor on Asian Affairs, *New Statesman*, London. Author of *Himalayan Frontiers; The Republic of Indonesia; The Making of Burma.*

E.A.J.D./Transportation (*in part*)
ERNEST ALBERT JOHN DAVIES. Editor, *Traffic Engineering and Control* (monthly); *Roads and Their Traffic; Traffic Engineering Practice.*

E.B.Br./Religion (*in part*)
EDWIN BLAINE BRONNER. Professor of History and Curator of the Quaker Collection, Haverford College, Haverford, Pa. Author of *William Penn's Holy Experiment.* Editor, *American Quakers Today; An English View of American Quakerism.*

E.B.Nn./Rubber
EDWIN BOHANNON NEWTON. Former Manager, Advanced Rubber Technology, B.F. Goodrich Company, Brecksville, O.

E.Di./Austria
ELFRIEDE DIRNBACHER. Austrian Civil Servant.

E.G.Es./Fuel and Power (*in part*)
ERIC GEORGE ELLIS. Petroleum Technologist and Consultant. Author of *Lubricant Testing; Fundamentals of Lubrication.*

E.Gn./Uruguay
ERNST CLARK GRIFFIN. National Defense Education Act Title IV Fellow, Michigan State University.

E.H.Ha./Vital Statistics (*in part*)
EVELYN HUNTINGTON HALPIN. Writer and consultant on vital statistics and accident prevention programs.

Ei.K./Cities and Urban Affairs (*in part*)
EISSE KALK. Research Officer, International Union of Local Authorities, The Hague, Neth.

El.G.B./Philately and Numismatics (*in part*)
ELSTON GORDON BRADFIELD. Editor Emeritus, *The Numismatist.* Co-editor, *Selections from The Numismatist.* Editor, *Introduction to Numismatics; Franklin and Numismatics.*

E.St./Medicine (*in part*)
ERWIN STENGEL. Emeritus Professor of Psychiatry in the University of Sheffield, Eng.

E.T.Ch./Medicine (*in part*)
EMIL THEODORE CHANLETT. Professor of Sanitary Engineering, Department of Environmental Sciences and Engineering, School of Public Health, University of North Carolina. Contributor to *Air Pollution.*

Ev.R./Domestic Arts and Sciences
EVELYN GITA ROSE. Home economics consultant; Broadcaster; Food Historian; Vice-Chairman, Association of Home Economists of Great Britain; Cookery Editor, *Jewish Chronicle.* Contributor to *Home Economics; Guardian*, London. Author of *More Fun with Your Food; The Jewish Home.*

E.W.M./Religion (*in part*)
ERIK W. MODEAN. Director, News Bureau, Lutheran Council in the U.S.A.

F.A.Ri./Archaeology (*in part*)
FRANCIS ALLEN RIDDELL. State Archaeologist for California.

F.Br./Boxing
FRANK BUTLER. Sports Editor, *News of the World*, London.

F.Dd./Algeria
FRANÇOIS DURIAUD. Reuters correspondent, Algiers.

F.F.R./Fuel and Power (*in part*)
FRANK FERDINAND ROXBOROUGH. Lecturer in Mining Engineering, University of Newcastle upon Tyne.

F.G./Italy
FABIO GALVANO. London Correspondent, *Epoca*, Milan.

F.H.Ka./Religion (*in part*)
FREDERIK HERMAN KAAN. Information Secretary, World Alliance of Reformed Churches, Geneva, Switz.

F.H.Li./Religion (*in part*)
FRANKLIN HAMLIN LITTELL. Professor, Department of Religion, Temple University, Philadelphia, Pa. Author of *The Origins of Sectarian Protestantism; From State Church to Pluralism.*

F.H.Sk./Fuel and Power (*in part*)**; Mining** (*in part*)**; U.S. Supplement:** *Mining Table; Power: Mineral Fuels Table*
FRANK H. SKELDING. President, AMDEC Corp. (mineral consultants).

F.I.Or./Astronautics (*in part*)
FREDERICK I. ORDWAY. Director, Science and Technology Applications and Evaluation Research Institute, University of Alabama in Huntsville. Author of *Life in Other Solar Systems.* Co-author of *History of Rocketry and Space Travel; Basic Astronautics; International Missile and Spacecraft Guide.*

F.J.C.R./Medicine *(in part)*
FRANCIS JOHN CALDWELL ROE. Reader in Experimental Pathology, Institute of Cancer Research, University of London; Associate Pathologist, Royal Marsden Hospital, London. Author of *Biology of Cancer; The Prevention of Cancer.*

F.J.Se./Medicine *(in part)*
FREDRICK J. STARE, M.D. Professor of Nutrition and Chairman, Department of Nutrition, Harvard School of Public Health. Author of syndicated newspaper column "Food and Your Health."

F.L./Swimming
FRANK LITSKY. Assistant to the Sports Editor, the *New York Times;* Co-editor, the *New York Times Official Sports Record Book 1965, 1967, 1968, 1969.*

F.L.Lr./Medicine *(in part)*
FRANCIS LOEFFLER LEDERER, M.D. Emeritus Professor of Otolaryngology, Former Head of the Department of Otolaryngology, University of Illinois College of Medicine, Chicago. Author of *Diseases of the Ear, Nose and Throat.*

F.N.He./Zoos and Botanical Gardens *(in part)*
FRANK NIGEL HEPPER. Principal Scientific Officer, Herbarium, Royal Botanic Gardens, Kew, Eng. Editor of *Flora of West Tropical Africa* (vol. ii and iii).

F.P.P./Fairs and Shows
FREDERICK P. PITTERA. Chairman, International Exposition Consultants Co. Member, Board of Trustees, New York Institute of Technology. Member, Board of Governors, National Business and Professional Council. Director, New Nations Exposition and Development Corporation. Author of *The Art and Science of International Fairs and Exhibitions; The Fairs of the United States and Canada.*

F.S.Rl./Biological Sciences *(in part)*
SIR FREDERICK STRATTEN RUSSELL. Director, Plymouth Laboratory, Marine Biological Association of the United Kingdom, 1945–65. Author of *The Medusae of the British Isles.* Co-author of *The Seas.*

F.W.N./Medicine *(in part)*
FRANK W. NEWELL. Professor of Ophthalmology, The University of Chicago. Author of *Ophthalmology, Principles and Concepts.* Editor, *Transactions of Glaucoma Conferences,* vol. i-v.

F.W.Rr./Meteorology
FRANCIS W. REICHELDERFER. Aeronautical and Marine Meteorology Consultant. Former Chief, Weather Bureau, U.S. Department of Commerce, Washington, D.C.

G.A.A./Dominican Republic
GUSTAVO ARTHUR ANTONINI. Assistant Professor, Department of Geography, College of Social Sciences, University of Puerto Rico, Rio Piedras.

G.A.Po./Profits
GERALD A. POLLACK. Vice-President, Corporate Development, Bendix Corp., Southfield, Mich. Author of *Perspectives on the U.S. International Financial Position.*

G.C./Literature *(in part)*
GIOVANNI CARSANIGA. Lecturer in Italian, University of Sussex, Eng.

G.C.Cu./Jamaica
GLORIA CLARE CUMPER. Chairman, Council of Voluntary Social Services; Member, Judicial Services Commission, Kingston, Jamaica.

G.C.Ho./Merchandising *(in part)*
GRAHAM CHARLES HOCKLEY. Lecturer, Department of Economics, University College, Cardiff. Author of *Monetary Policy and Public Finance.* Co-author of *The Wealth of the Nation: The Balance Sheet of the United Kingdom, 1957–61.*

G.C.L./Ethiopia
GEOFFREY CHARLES LAST. Adviser, Imperial Ethiopian Ministry of Education and Fine Arts, Addis Ababa. Author of *A Regional Survey of Africa; A Geography of Ethiopia.* Co-author of *A History of Ethiopia in Pictures.*

Gd.Sn./Information Science and Technology
GERARD SALTON. Professor of Computer Science, Cornell University. Author of *Information Organization and Retrieval.*

Ge.Me./Television and Radio *(in part)*
GEORGE MELLY. Television and radio critic, *Observer,* London. Author of *Owning Up.*

Ge.S.L./Medicine *(in part)*
GERALD S. LAZARUS. Research Fellow in Dermatology, Harvard Medical School; Clinical Fellow in Dermatology, Massachusetts General Hospital, Boston.

G.F.R./Industrial Review *(in part)*
GEORGE FRANK RAY. Senior Research Fellow, National Institute of Economic and Social Research, London.

G.H.St./Yugoslavia
GEOFFREY HOWARD STERN. Lecturer in International Relations, London School of Economics and Political Science. Author of *50 Years of Communism.*

G.H.v.E./Netherlands
GERRIT HENDRIK van ES. Associate, Institute for Political Science, University of Amsterdam.

G.O.K.B./Migration, International *(in part)*
GUNTHER O. K. BEIJER. Secretary, Social Sciences Council, Royal Netherlands Academy of Sciences and Letters, Amsterdam. Author of *National Rural Manpower; Adjustment to Industry; Rural Migrants in Urban Setting; Some Aspects of Migration Problems in the Netherlands.*

Go.M./Industrial Review *(in part)*
GORDON MINNES. Secretary, Canadian Pulp and Paper Association.

G.P./Literature *(in part)*
GABRIEL PREIL. Writer. Hebrew and Yiddish poet. Author of *Israeli Poetry in Peace and War; Nof Shemesh Ukhfor* ("Landscape of Sun and Frost"); *Ner Mul Kokhavim* ("Candle Against the Stars"); *Mapat Erev* ("Map of Evening"); *Lieder* ("Poems"); *Haesh Vehadmama* ("The Fire and the Silence").

G.P.M.H./Medicine *(in part)*
GERARD P. M. HORSTEN. Professor of General Neurophysiology, University of Nijmegen, Neth. Executive Chief Editor, Excerpta Medica Foundation.

G.R.De./Economic Planning *(in part)*
GEOFFREY RICHARD DENTON. Reader in Economics, University of Reading, Eng. Co-author of *Economic Planning and Policies in Britain, France and Germany.* Editor of *Economic Integration in Europe.*

G.S.Mo./Zoos and Botanical Gardens *(in part)*
GEORGE SAUL MOTTERSHEAD. Director-Secretary, Chester Zoo, Chester, Eng.

G.U./Thailand
GOVINDAN UNNY. Thailand Correspondent, Agence France-Presse, Bangkok.

Ha.Fr./Contract Bridge
HAROLD FRANKLIN. Editor, *English Bridge Quarterly.* Bridge Correspondent, *Yorkshire Post; Yorkshire Evening Post.* Broadcaster. Author of *Best of Bridge on the Air.*

H.A.Ru./Medicine *(in part)*
HOWARD A. RUSK, M.D. Chairman, Department of Rehabilitation Medicine, New York University Medical Center, New York City. Contributing Editor, the *New York Times.* Author of *Rehabilitation Medicine.*

H.A.Ta./Transportation *(in part)*
HAROLD ANTHONY TAYLOR. Air Transport Editor, *Flight International,* London, 1964–69.

H.B./Hockey *(in part)*; **Ice Skating; Skiing**
HOWARD BASS. Winter Sports Correspondent, *The Daily Telegraph,* London; *The Christian Science Monitor,* Boston. Author of *The Sense in Sport; This Skating Age; The Magic of Skiing; Winter Sports.*

H.C.Cl./Literature *(in part)*
HENRY CUMMINGS CAMPBELL. Chief Librarian, Toronto Public Library, Toronto.

H.D.M./Engineering Projects *(in part)*
HORACE DENTON MORGAN. Senior Partner, Sir William Halcrow and Partners, London.

H.Du./Historic Buildings
HIROSHI DAIFUKU. Chief, Section for the Development of the Cultural Heritage, UNESCO, Paris.

He.B.H./Food *(in part)*
HENRY BERNARD HAWLEY. Consultant, Human Nutrition and Food Science, Sherborne, Eng.

He.Se./Medicine *(in part)*
SIR HERBERT (JOHN) SEDDON. Professor of Orthopedics, University of London, 1965–67. Author of *Nerve Injuries.*

H.Go./Biography *(in part)*; **Chess**
HARRY GOLOMBEK. British Chess Champion, 1947, 1949, and 1955. Chess Correspondent, *The Times* and *Observer,* London. Author of *Penguin Handbook on the Game of Chess; Modern Opening Chess Strategy.*

H.H.Sa./Propaganda
HOWLAND H. SARGEANT. President, Radio Liberty Committee. Author of *The Representation of the United States Abroad.*

Hi.S./Housing
HIDEHIKO SAZANAMI. Chief, Urban Facilities Research Group, Building Research Institute, Ministry of Construction, Tokyo. Author of *Housing in Metropolitan Areas.*

H.J.Kl./Prisons and Penology
HUGH JOHN KLARE. Secretary, Howard League for Penal Reform, London. Author of *Anatomy of Prison.* Editor of *Changing Concepts of Crime and Its Treatment.*

H.Ko./Communist Movement
HANS KOHN. Emeritus Professor of History, City College of New York. Author of *Prologue to Nation-States: the French and German Experiences 1789-1815.*

H.L.En./Conservation *(in part)*
HERBERT LEESON EDLIN. Publications Officer, Forestry Commission of Great Britain. Author of *Trees, Woods and Man; Wayside and Woodland Trees; Man and Plants.*

H.M.F.M./Industrial Review *(in part)*
HUGH MICHAEL FINER MALLETT. Editor, *Weekly Wool Chart,* Bradford, Eng.

Ho.S./Biography *(in part)*; **Literature** *(in part)*
HOWARD SERGEANT. Lecturer and writer. Editor of *Outposts,* London. Author of *The Cumberland Wordsworth; Tradition in the Making of Modern Poetry.*

H.R.L./Publishing *(in part)*
HERBERT R. LOTTMAN. Contributing Editor, *Publishers' Weekly;* contributor to *New York Times Book Review, Cultural Affairs,* and other periodicals. Author of *Detours from the Grand Tour.*

H.R.Mo./Music *(in part)*
HAZEL ROMOLA MORGAN. Assistant to Administrative Manager, International Sales Division, E.M.I. Records, London.

H.R.Sh./Agriculture *(in part)*; **Food** *(in part)*; **U.S. Supplement:** *Principal Crops Table*
HARVEY R. SHERMAN. Research Associate, Legislative Reference, Library of Congress.

H.Sa./Biological Sciences *(in part)*
HAROLD SANDON. Formerly Professor of Zoology, University of Khartoum, Sudan. Author of *The Protozoan Fauna of the Soil; The Food of Protozoa; An Illustrated Guide to the Fresh-water Fishes of the Sudan; Essays on Protozoology.*

H.S.N./Fisheries
HAROLD STANLEY NOEL. Editor, *World Fishing*, London.

H.T.Ch./China; Taiwan
HUNG-TI CHU. Expert in Far Eastern Affairs. UN Area Specialist and Chief of Asia-Africa Section and Trusteeship Council Section, 1946–67; Professor of Government, Texas Tech University, Lubbock, 1968–69.

H.Y.S.P./Biography *(in part)*; **India**
HOLENARASIPUR Y. SHARADA PRASAD. Director of Information, Prime Minister's Secretariat, New Delhi.

I.C.C./Argentina
IVOR CECIL COFFIN. Economic Research Officer, Bank of London and South America Ltd., London.

I.H.M./Alcoholic Beverages *(in part)*
IRVING H. MARCUS. Editor-Publisher, *Wines and Vines.* Author of *Dictionary of Wine Terms.*

I.Ka./Mathematics
IRVING KAPLANSKY. Professor, Department of Mathematics, The University of Chicago.

I.M.L./Somalia
IOAN MYRDDIN LEWIS. Professor of Anthropology, London School of Economics, University of London. Author of *Peoples of the Horn of Africa; The Modern History of Somaliland.*

I.Pr./Stock Exchanges *(in part)*
IRVING PFEFFER. Professor of Insurance and Finance, Graduate School of Business Administration, University of California at Los Angeles. Author of *Insurance and Economic Theory; The Financing of Small Business.*

I.S.F./Development, Economic
IRVING S. FRIEDMAN. The Economic Adviser to the President of the International Bank for Reconstruction and Development. Author of *Exchange Controls and The International Monetary System; U.S. Foreign Economic Policy.*

ITU/Telecommunications *(in part)*
INTERNATIONAL TELECOMMUNICATION UNION, Geneva.

Ja.C.C./Molecular Biology *(in part)*
JAMES CLINTON COPELAND. Assistant Geneticist, Division of Biological and Medical Research, Argonne National Laboratory, Argonne, Ill.

Ja.Co./Horse Racing *(in part)*
JAMES COLEMAN. Columnist, Southam Newspapers, Canada.

Ja.E.M./Motor Sports *(in part)*
JAMES EDWARD MARTENHOFF. Boating Editor, *Miami* (Fla.) *Herald.* Author of *How to Buy a Better Boat; Handbook of Skin and Scuba Diving.*

Ja.G.S./Medicine *(in part)*
JAMES G. SHAFFER. Associate Dean and Professor of Microbiology, the Chicago Medical School. Author of *Amebiasis: A Biomedical Problem.*

J.A.He./Antarctica *(in part)*
JOHN ARNFIELD HEAP. Sometime member of the British Antarctic Survey.

J.A.Kr./Chemistry *(in part)*
JAMES ALISTAIR KERR. Lecturer, University of Birmingham, Eng.

Ja.Ma./Television and Radio *(in part)*
JAMES MAGEE. Assistant Editor, European Broadcasting Union, Geneva.

J.A.O'L./Biography *(in part)*
JEREMIAH ALOYSIUS O'LEARY. Latin America Correspondent, *Washington Evening Star*, Washington, D.C. Author of *Dominican Action—1965.*

Ja.R.E./Belgium
JAN ROBERT ENGELS. Editor, *P.V.V. Flitsen* (Journal of the Belgian Party for Freedom and Progress).

J.B.A./Religion *(in part)*
JACOB BERNARD AGUS. Rabbi, Beth El Congregation, Baltimore, Md. Visiting Professor of Religion, Temple University, Philadelphia, Pa. Author of *The Evolution of Jewish Thought; The Meaning of Jewish History.*

J.B.Be./Industrial Review *(in part)*; **Transportation** *(in part)*
JOHN BERESFORD BENTLEY. Staff Writer, *Flight International.* Editor, *Air-Cushion Vehicles.*

J.Be./Baseball *(in part)*
JACK BRICKHOUSE. Manager of Sports, WGN, Inc., Chicago. Publisher of *Jack Brickhouse's Major League Baseball Record Book.*

Jb.K./Molecular Biology *(in part)*
JACOB KASTNER. Associate Physicist and Group Leader, Radiation Dosimetry Group, Radiological Physics Division, Argonne National Laboratory, Argonne, Ill. Author of *The Natural Radiation Environment.*

J.B.Kr./Medicine *(in part)*
JOSEPH BARNETT KIRSNER, M.D. Louis Black Professor of Medicine, The University of Chicago School of Medicine.

J.B.St./Religion *(in part)*
J. BUROUGHS STOKES. Manager, Committees on Publication, the First Church of Christ, Scientist, Boston.

J.C.G.B./Costa Rica; Venezuela
JOHN C. G. BROOKS. Editor, *Fortnightly Review*, Bank of London and South America Ltd., London.

J.C.Y./Chemistry *(in part)*
JOHN COLIN YOUNG. Lecturer in Chemistry, University College of Wales.

Je.Ho./Baseball *(in part)*; **Basketball** *(in part)*; **Biography** *(in part)*; **Football** *(in part)*
JEROME HOLTZMAN. Sportswriter, the *Chicago Sun-Times.*

J.E.I./Biography *(in part)*
JOHN EDWARD INGLE. Law and Justice Editor, *National Journal.*

J.E.McK./Sociology
JAMES EDWARD McKEOWN. Professor and Chairman, Department of Sociology, DePaul University, Chicago. Co-editor of *The Changing Metropolis.* Author of *Study Guide for Economics; Study Guide for Sociology.* Co-author of *A Study of Integrated Living in Chicago.*

J.E.Pa./Literature *(in part)*
JOSÉ EMILIO PACHECO. Associate Editor, *La Cultura en México.* Author of *Morirás lejos; Antología del modernismo.*

Je.Wi./Medicine *(in part)*
JELIA C. WITSCHI. Assistant in Nutrition, Department of Nutrition, Harvard School of Public Health.

J.Fa./Engineering Projects *(in part)*
J. FAUCHART. Ingénieur des Ponts et Chaussées, Service Central d'Études Techniques des Routes et Autoroutes du Ministère de l'Equipement et du Logement, Paris.

J.F.Ba./Biography *(in part)*
JOHN FREDERICK BARTON. Asian Affairs Correspondent, United Press International, Washington, D.C.

J.F.Ss./Veterinary Medicine
J. FREDERICK SMITHCORS. Associate Editor, American Veterinary Publications, Inc., Santa Barbara, Calif. Author of *Evolution of the Veterinary Art; The American Veterinary Profession.*

J.G.M./Consumer Expenditures
JAMES GEORGE MORRELL. Chairman, James Morrell and Associates Ltd.; Economic Adviser to a number of leading companies; Economic Editor, *Management Today.*

J.Gr./Religion *(in part)*
JOHN GRACE. National Chief Secretary and Lieut. Commissioner, Salvation Army.

J.G.S.M./Gardening *(in part)*
JOHN GRAHAM SCOTT MARSHALL. Horticultural Consultant.

J.H.Bo./Biological Sciences *(in part)*
JEFFERY HUGH BOSWALL. Producer of Sound and Television Programs, British Broadcasting Corporation Natural History Unit, Bristol, Eng.

J.J.A./Bowling and Lawn Bowls *(in part)*
JOHN J. ARCHIBALD. Sportswriter, the *St. Louis Post-Dispatch.* Author of *Bowling for Boys and Girls.*

J.J.Ac./Fuel and Power *(in part)*
JOSEPH JOHN ACCARDO. Washington Editor, Chilton Publications; Columnist, *Gas.*

J.J.Gm./Advertising *(in part)*
JARLATH JOHN GRAHAM. Editor, *Advertising Age.*

J.J.Sm./Bolivia; Paraguay
JOHN JERVIS SMITH. Research Officer, Economic Intelligence Department, Bank of London and South America Ltd., London.

J.K./Biography *(in part)*; **Israel**
JON KIMCHE. Editor, *The New Middle East.* Expert on Middle East Affairs, *Evening Standard*, London. Author of *The Second Arab Awakening: The Middle East, 1914–1969.*

J.Ki./Museums and Galleries *(in part)*
JOSHUA B. KIND. Associate Professor of Art History, Northern Illinois University, De Kalb. Midwest Correspondent, *Art News.* Author of *Rouault; Titian.*

J.Kn./France
JEAN MARCEL KNECHT. Assistant Foreign Editor, *Le Monde*, Paris. Formerly Permanent Correspondent in Washington and Vice-President of the Association de la Presse Diplomatique Française.

J.K.R./Agriculture *(in part)*
JOHN KERR ROSE. Senior Specialist in Natural Resources and Conservation, Legislative Reference Service, Library of Congress, Washington, D.C.

J.L.Re./Oceanography
JOSEPH LEE REID. Research Oceanographer, Scripps Institution of Oceanography, La Jolla, Calif. Author of *Intermediate Waters of the Pacific Ocean.*

J.Me./Religion *(in part)*
JOHN MEYENDORFF. Professor of Church History and Patristics, St. Vladimir's Seminary; Professor of History, Fordham University, New York City; Adjunct-Professor of Religion, Columbia University. Author of *The Orthodox Church.*

J.M.Ka./Religion *(in part)*
JOSEPH M. KITAGAWA. Professor of History of Religions, The University of Chicago. Author of *Religions of the East; Religion in Japanese History.*

J.M.Th./Toys and Games
JOHN MICHAEL THEWLIS. Industrial Journalist.

J.N.B./Religion *(in part)*
JOHN NICHOLLS BOOTH. Minister, The Unitarian Church of Long Beach, Calif.; co-founder Japan Free Religious Association. Author of *The Quest for Preaching Power; Introducing Unitarian Universalism.*

Jn.Ky./Religion *(in part)*
JOHN KIELTY. Secretary, General Assembly, Unitarian and Free Christian Churches, London.

Jn.M./Social Services
JOHN MOSS. Barrister-at-Law. Author of *Hadden's Health and Welfare Services Handbook.* Editor of *Local Government Law and Administration.*

J.No./Theatre *(in part)*
JULIUS NOVICK. Assistant Professor of English, New York University, New York City; Guest Lecturer, Drama Division of the Juilliard School. Dramatic Critic for the *Village Voice* and "The Humanist" (TV); Contributor to *The Nation;* the *New York Times.* Author of *Beyond Broadway: The Quest for Permanent Theatres.*

Jo.A./Religion *(in part)*
JOSEPH ANDERSON. Secretary to the First Presidency, Church of Jesus Christ of Latter-day Saints (Mormons), Salt Lake City, Utah.

Jo.A.A./Libya
JOHN ANTHONY ALLAN. Lecturer in Geography, School of Oriental and African Studies, University of London.

Jo.A.K./New Zealand
JOHN ARNOLD KELLEHER. Editor, the *Dominion,* Wellington, N.Z.

Jo.B.W./Biography *(in part);* **Cycling**
JOHN BORLAND WADLEY. Editor, *International Cycle Sport.*

Jo.Hn./Ceylon
JOHN HOCKIN. Formerly London Editor, *Times of Ceylon,* Colombo.

Jo.H.S./Nuclear Energy
JOHN H. STUMPF. Special Projects Editor, Atomic Industrial Forum, Inc.

Jo.N./Mountaineering
JOHN NEILL. Chemical Engineer. Author of Climbers' Club Guides: *Cwm Silyn and Tremadoc, Snowdon South;* Alpine Club Guide: *Selected Climbs in the Pennine Alps.*

Jo.W.McL./Medicine *(in part)*
JOHN WATT McLAREN. Radiologist in charge of the X-Ray Department, St. Thomas's Hospital, London. Editor of *Modern Trends in Diagnostic Radiology,* Series 1, 2, and 3.

J.S.Sw./Molecular Biology *(in part)*
JAMES STOUDER SWEET. Science Editor, Office of Planning and Development, Northwestern University, Evanston, Ill. Executive Editor, *Rand McNally Illustrated Atlas of Today's World* (1967). Author of *Poverty in the USA* (pamphlet). Co-author of *Poverty amid Affluence.*

J.T.B./Cinema *(in part)*
JOHN TEAL BOBBITT. Writer and Producer of Encyclopædia Britannica Films: *The Bill of Rights of the United States; The Congress; The Constitution of the United States; The Declaration of Independence by the Colonies; The Supreme Court.*

J.T.G./Psychology
JOHN T. GOODMAN. Assistant Professor of Psychiatry (Psychology), Department of Psychiatry, McMaster University, Hamilton, Ont.

Ju.W./Alcoholic Beverages *(in part)*
JULIUS WILE. Senior Vice-President, Julius Wile Sons & Co., Inc., New York City. Vice-President, New England Distillers, Inc., Teterboro, N.J. Vice-Chairman, Wine Conference of America. Lecturer on wines, School of Hotel Administration, Cornell University.

J.W.Ma./Alcoholic Beverages *(in part)*
JOHN WILLIAM MAHONEY. Secretary, Wine and Spirit Association of Great Britain; Wine Development Board; Director, Society of Friends of Wine, London. Author of *A Guide to Good Wine* (Introduction); *Wines; Spirits and Liqueurs.*

J.W.Mw./Chronology *(in part)*
JOSEPH W. MARLOW. Lawyer.

Jy.L./Postal Services *(in part)*
JERRY LIPSON. Reporter with the *Chicago Daily News.*

K.de la B./Arctic Regions
KENNETH de la BARRE. Director, Montreal Office, Arctic Institute of North America.

K.F.C./Philately and Numismatics *(in part)*
KENNETH FRANCIS CHAPMAN. Editor, *Stamp Collecting;* Philatelic Correspondent, *The Times,* London. Author of *Good Stamp Collecting.*

K.H.W./Religion *(in part)*
KENNETH H. WOOD. Editor, *The Review and Herald.* Author of *Meditations for Moderns.* Co-author of *His Initials Were F.D.N.*

K.I./Congo, Democratic Republic of the; Dependent States *(in part);* **Equatorial Guinea; Kenya; Malawi; Rhodesia; Tanzania; Uganda; Zambia**
KENNETH INGHAM. Professor of Modern History, University of Bristol, Eng. Author of *Reformers in India.*

K.J.Z./Medicine *(in part)*
KEVIN JEROME ZILKHA. Consultant Neurologist, King's College Hospital; Consultant Physician, The National Hospital, London.

K.K.Mi./Basketball *(in part)*
KEITH KIRKMAN MITCHELL. Lecturer, Department of Physical Education, Leeds University; Hon. General Secretary, Amateur Basket Ball Association.

K.L.O./Rowing
KEITH LANGFORD OSBORNE. Editor, *Rowing,* 1961–63. Hon. Editor, *British Rowing Almanack,* 1961–.

K.Ra./Medicine *(in part)*
KAREL RASKA, M.D. Director, Division of Communicable Diseases, World Health Organization, Geneva.

K.R.P./Literature *(in part)*
KARIN ROSAMUND PETHERICK. Crown Princess Louise Lecturer in Swedish, University College, London.

K.Sm./Albania; Biography *(in part);* **Bulgaria; Economic Planning** *(in part);* **Hungary; Intelligence Operations; Mongolia; Poland; Political Parties; Romania**
KAZIMIERZ MACIEJ SMOGORZEWSKI. Writer on contemporary history. Founder and Editor, *Free Europe,* London. Author of *The United States and Great Britain; Poland's Access to the Sea.*

L.C.Br./Cities and Urban Affairs *(in part)*
LEWIS CHARLES BRAITHWAITE. Research Associate, Centre for Urban and Regional Studies, University of Birmingham, Eng.

L.Ch./Fuel and Power *(in part)*
LUCIEN CHALMEY. Adviser, Union Internationale des Producteurs et Distributeurs d'Énergie Électrique, Paris.

L.F.R.W./Afghanistan; Iran; Pakistan
LAURENCE FREDERIC RUSHBROOK WILLIAMS, C.B.E. Fellow of All Souls College, Oxford University, 1914–21; Professor of Modern Indian History, Allahabad, India, 1914–19. Author of *India Under the Company and the Crown; The State of Pakistan; What About India?; Kutch in History and Legend.* Editor of *Handbook to India, Pakistan, Burma, and Ceylon.*

L.H./South Africa
LOUIS HOTZ. Formerly editorial writer, the *Johannesburg* (S.Af.) *Star.* Co-author and contributor to *The Jews in South Africa: A History.*

L.H.Jo./Telecommunications *(in part)*
LAURENCE HENRY JOHN. Producer, Science Unit, British Broadcasting Corporation (radio).

L.H.No./Geology
LAURENCE H. NOBLES. Professor of Geology and Associate Dean, College of Arts and Sciences, Northwestern University, Evanston, Ill.

L.Ke./Cooperatives
LOTTE KENT. Editor, *Cooperative News Service,* International Cooperative Alliance, London.

L.M.Gd./Antarctica *(in part)*
LAURENCE M. GOULD. Professor of Geology, University of Arizona. Chairman, Committee on Polar Research, National Academy of Sciences. Author of *Cold: The Record of an Antarctic Sledge Journey.*

L.M.M./Seismology
LEONARD M. MURPHY. Chief, Seismology Division, Coast and Geodetic Survey, Environmental Science Services Administration, U.S. Department of Commerce, Washington, D.C.

L.O.T./Biography *(in part);* **Tennis**
LANCELOT OLIVER TINGAY. Lawn Tennis Correspondent, *Daily Telegraph,* London.

L.R.Bu./Education
LEONARD RALPH BUCKLEY. Formerly Assistant Editor, *The Times Educational Supplement,* London.

M.A.G./Literature *(in part)*
MICHAEL A. GONZALEZ. Research student preparing Ph.D. thesis on the Mexican novel.

M.A.K./Economy, World; Payments and Reserves, International
MIROSLAV A. KRIZ. Vice-President, First National City Bank, New York City. Author of *The Price of Gold; Gold in World Monetary Affairs Today; Gold: Barbarous Relic or Useful Instrument?*

Ma.Ka./Music *(in part)*
MAUD KARPELES. Hon. President, International Folk Music Council, Kingston, Ont. Author of *Cecil Sharp: His Life and Works; Folk Songs from Newfoundland.* Editor of *Journal of the International Folk Music Council,* vol. i–xiii and xvi; *English Folk Songs from the Southern Appalachians.*

M.By./Industrial Review (*in part*); **Transportation** (*in part*)
MICHAEL BAILY. Shipping and Transport Correspondent, *The Times*, London.

M.C.G.I./Medicine (*in part*)
MARTIN C. G. ISRAËLS. Director, Department of Clinical Haematology, University and Royal Infirmary, Manchester. Author of *Atlas of Bone Marrow Pathology; Diagnosis and Treatment of Blood Diseases.*

M.C.MacD./Agriculture (*in part*); **Transportation** (*in part*)
MALCOLM CHARLES MacDONALD. Director, Econtel Research Ltd., London. Editor, *Factual Series; Business Cycle Series.*

M.Ct./Laos
MAX COIFFAIT. Correspondent, Agence France-Presse, Vientiane, Laos.

M.D.Bu./Publishing (*in part*)
M. DALLAS BURNETT. Associate Professor of Communications, Brigham Young University, Provo, Utah.

M.E./Electronics
MARCELINO ELECCION. Editor and Staff Writer, Institute of Electrical and Electronics Engineers.

M.F.B.B./Parks
MERVYN FRANCIS BERNARD BELL. Secretary, Countryside Commission.

M.Fd./Medicine (*in part*)
MAXWELL FINLAND, M.D. George Richards Minot Professor of Medicine, Harvard University. Emeritus Epidemiologist, Boston City Hospital.

M.F.F./Income, National
MICHAEL FREDERICK FULLER. Lecturer in Economic and Social Statistics, Eliot College, University of Kent at Canterbury.

M.Fi./Medicine (*in part*)
MORRIS FISHBEIN. Editor of *Medical World News.* Emeritus Professor, The University of Chicago; University of Illinois, College of Medicine. Author of *Modern Home Remedies and How to Use Them; Handy Home Medical Adviser; Concise Medical Encyclopedia.*

M.F.S./Switzerland
MELANIE F. STAERK. Executive Head, Press Service, Swiss National Commission for UNESCO.

Mi.G.M./Industrial Review (*in part*)
MICHAEL G. MESSER. District Editor, *The Oil and Gas Journal.*

M.Mr./Barbados; Botswana; Burundi; Commonwealth of Nations; Dependent States (*in part*)**; Ghana; Lesotho; Maldives, Republic of; Mauritius; Nigeria; Rwanda; Swaziland**
MOLLY MORTIMER. Journalist on Commonwealth and International Affairs. Author of *Trusteeship in Practice; Kenya.*

M.M.Tu./Race Relations (*in part*)
MELVIN MARVIN TUMIN. Professor of Sociology and Anthropology, Princeton University. Author of *Social Class and Social Change in Puerto Rico; Social Stratification; Crimes of Violence in the U.S.*

M.N.Y./Religion (*in part*)
M. NORVEL YOUNG. President, Pepperdine College, Los Angeles. Editor, *Twentieth Century Christian* and *Power for Today.* Author of *Churches of Today.*

Mo.M./Greece
MARIO (S.) MODIANO. Athens Correspondent, *The Times*, London.

M.Pan./Prices
MILIVOJE PANIĆ. Economic Adviser, National Economic Development Office, London.

M.Pl./Industrial Review (*in part*)
MAURICE PLATT. Consulting Engineer. Formerly Director of Engineering, Vauxhall Motors, Ltd. Author of *Elements of Automobile Engineering.*

M.Pu./Mexico; Spain
MANUEL PULGAR. Senior Economic Research Officer, Bank of London and South America Ltd., London.

M.R.-R./Literature (*in part*)
MARCEL REICH-RANICKI. Literary critic, *Die Zeit.* Author of *Deutsche Literatur in West und Ost; Literarisches Leben in Deutschland; Wer schreibt, provoziert; Literatur der kleinen Schritte; Die Ungeliebten.*

M.R.S./Astronautics (*in part*)**; Biography** (*in part*)
MITCHELL R. SHARPE. Science writer. Author of *Living in Space: The Environment of the Astronaut; Yuri Gagarin, First Man in Space.* Co-author of *Applied Astronautics; Basic Astronautics.*

M.S.R./Malaysia; Singapore
MAHINDER SINGH RANDHAVA. Sub-editor, *The Straits Times*, Kuala Lumpur, Malaysia.

M.W.Wi./El Salvador
MURAT WILLIS WILLIAMS. U.S. Ambassador, retired. Formerly ambassador to El Salvador.

M.W.Wo./Religion (*in part*)
REVEREND MAX W. WOODWARD. British Secretary, World Methodist Council.

Mx.B./Vatican City State (*in part*)
MAX BERGERRE. Deputy Director, Vatican Affairs Department, Agence France-Presse, Rome.

Mx.H./Biography (*in part*)
MAX HARRELSON. Chief of United Nations Bureau, The Associated Press.

My.B.B./Western Samoa
MARY BEATRICE BOYD. Senior Lecturer in History, Victoria University of Wellington, N.Z.

N.Cr./Biography (*in part*)**; Germany** (*in part*)
NORMAN CROSSLAND. Bonn Correspondent, *Guardian.*

N.D.McW./Track and Field Sports (*in part*)
NORRIS DEWAR McWHIRTER. Television commentator, British Broadcasting Corporation, London. Compiler, *Guinness Book of Records.*

N.H.K./Religion (*in part*)
NATHAN HOMER KNORR. President, Watch Tower Bible and Tract Society of Pennsylvania.

Ni.B./Literature (*in part*)
NIELS BARFOED. Editor of *Vindrosen.* Literary Critic, *Politiken*, Copenhagen. Author of *Den tøvende dag* (poems); *Ajourføringer* (essays on literature).

N.M.H./Law (*in part*)
NEVILLE MARCH HUNNINGS. Senior Research Officer, British Institute of International and Comparative Law, London. Author of *Film Censors and the Law.*

N.R.U./Commodities, Primary
NORMAN RICHARD URQUHART. Assistant Vice-President, in charge of Commodity Section, First National City Bank, New York City.

N.Si./Horse Racing (*in part*)
NOEL SIMPSON. Managing Director, Sydney Bloodstock Proprietary Ltd., Sydney, Austr.

O.F.K./Norway
OLE FERDINAND KNUDSEN. Editor, *Norway Exports*, Oslo.

O.H.H./Guatemala
OSCAR H. HORST. Professor of Geography, Western Michigan University.

O.K./Industrial Review (*in part*)
ORLAND BENJAMIN KILLIN. Associate Professor of Industrial Education and Technology, Eastern Washington State College.

O.Pl./Medicine (*in part*)
OGLESBY PAUL, M.D. Chief, Division of Medicine, Passavant Memorial Hospital, Chicago, Ill. Professor of Medicine, Northwestern University Medical School, Chicago.

Ot.P./Czechoslovakia; Union of Soviet Socialist Republics
OTTO PICK. Reader in International Relations, University of Surrey.

O.Tr./Biography (*in part*)**; Theatre** (*in part*)
OSSIA TRILLING. Vice-President, International Association of Theatre Critics. Co-editor and contributor, *International Theatre.* Contributor, *The Times*, London.

P.A.H./Religion (*in part*)
THE REV. PETER ANTHONY HEBBLETHWAITE, S.J. Editor, *The Month.* Author of *Bernanos; The Council Fathers and Atheism; Understanding the Synod.*

P.A.St./Astronomy
PETER ALBERT STRITTMATTER. Staff member, Institute for Theoretical Astronomy, University of Cambridge.

P.A.W.-T./Biography (*in part*)**; Golf**
PERCY AINSWORTH WARD-THOMAS. Golf Correspondent, *Guardian*, Manchester.

P.Bs./Art Sales (*in part*)
PIERRE BERÈS. Managing Director, Hermann Publishing Company, Paris. Founder and Editor in Chief, *Sciences.* Expert in rare books.

P.B.St./Publishing (*in part*)
PHYLLIS B. STECKLER. Director of Bibliography, R. R. Bowker Company. Editor of *Textbooks in Print; Children's Books for Schools and Libraries; Book Publishing Record Annual Cumulatives.*

Pe.B./Medicine (*in part*)
PETER BEEDLE. Assistant Secretary, Home Office, London.

P.F.Y./Mining (*in part*)
PAUL FREDERICK YOPES. Mining Engineer, Bureau of Mines, U.S. Department of the Interior, Washington, D.C.

P.Gl./Religion (*in part*)
PAUL GLIKSON. Secretary, Division of Jewish Demography and Statistics, Institute of Contemporary Jewry, The Hebrew University, Israel.

Ph.D./Cameroon; Central African Republic; Chad; Congo, People's Republic of the; Dahomey; Dependent States (*in part*)**; Gabon; Guinea; Ivory Coast; Malagasy Republic; Mali; Mauritania; Niger; Senegal; Togo; Tunisia; Upper Volta**
PHILIPPE DECRAENE. Member of editorial staff, *Le Monde*, Paris. Editor in Chief, *Revue française d'Études politiques africaines.* Research assistant at the Centre d'Études des Relations Internationales de l'Institut d'Études Politiques de Paris. Author of *Le Panafricanisme; Tableau des Partis Politiques Africains.*

Ph.K./Biography (*in part*)**; Labour Unions** (*in part*)
PHILIP KOPPER. Free-lance writer, Washington, D.C.

P.J.T./Medicine *(in part)*
PETER JOHN TAYLOR. Physician in charge, Information and Advisory Service, Trades Union Congress Centenary Institute of Occupational Health, University of London. Author of *Absenteeism—Causes and Control.*

P.L.W./Dance *(in part)*
PETER LANCELOT WILLIAMS. Editor, *Dance and Dancers.*

P.Md./Iraq; Jordan; Kuwait; Lebanon; Middle East; Saudi Arabia; Southern Yemen; Syria; United Arab Republic; Yemen
PETER (JOHN) MANSFIELD. Former Middle East Correspondent, *Sunday Times,* London. Free-lance writer on Middle East affairs.

P.M.Ha./Cities and Urban Affairs *(in part)*
PHILIP MORRIS HAUSER. Professor of Sociology and Director, Population Research Center, The University of Chicago. Editor of *Urbanization in Latin America.*

P.M.Re./Industrial Review *(in part)*
PHILIP MORTON ROWE. Press Officer, British Man-Made Fibres Federation, Manchester.

Pr.K./Sudan
PETER KILNER. Editor, *Arab Report and Record.*

P.Sh./Tourism
PETER SHACKLEFORD. Research Officer, International Union of Official Travel Organizations, Geneva.

P.Ss./Insurance *(in part)*
PERCY STEBBINGS. Insurance Correspondent of *Investors' Chronicle; Post Magazine,* London.

P.V.-P./Biography *(in part)*
PIERRE VIANSSON-PONTÉ. Political News Editor, *Le Monde,* Paris. Author of *Les Gaullistes; The King and His Court.*

P.W.Ga./Industrial Review *(in part)*
PETER WILLIAM GADDUM. Chairman, H. T. Gaddum and Company Ltd., Silk Merchants, Macclesfield, Cheshire, Eng. Author of *Silk—How and Where It Is Produced.*

P.W.He./Cosmetics; Fashion and Dress
PHYLLIS WEST HEATHCOTE. Paris Correspondent on women's topics, *Guardian,* Manchester.

P.W.Mi./Biological Sciences *(in part)*
PETER WALLACE MILES. Reader in Entomology, University of Adelaide, Austr.

R.A.Cr./Literature *(in part)*
ROBERT A. CROMIE. Columnist, the *Chicago Tribune.*

R.A.Kl./Medicine *(in part)*
ROBERT A. KLOBNAK. Director, Department of Public Relations, American Osteopathic Association.

Ra.Pa./Philippines
RAFAEL PARGAS. Computer Operator, National Geographic Society, Washington, D.C.

Ra.R./Dependent States *(in part)*; **Guyana; Trinidad and Tobago**
RANDOLPH RICHARD RAWLINS. Journalist and broadcaster. Research Associate, Instituto para la Integración de América Latina, Buenos Aires.

R.B.Gt./Medicine *(in part)*
ROBERT BENJAMIN GREENBLATT, M.D. Professor and Chairman, Department of Endocrinology, Medical College of Georgia, Augusta. Author of *Office Endocrinology; The Hirsute Female; Ovulation.*

R.B.Le./Colombia; Ecuador
RAYMOND BASIL LEWRY. Senior Research Officer, Bank of London and South America Ltd., London.

R.C.Pe./Industrial Review *(in part)*
ROBIN CHARLES PENFOLD. Public relations executive, Carl Byoir and Associates Ltd., London. Author of *A Journalist's Guide to Plastics.*

R.D.A.G./United Nations *(in part)*
RICHARD D. A. GREENOUGH. Chief English writer, Press Division, UNESCO, Paris. Author of *Africa Prospect; Children's Progress.*

R.d'E./Brazil
RAUL d'ECA. Formerly Fulbright Visiting Lecturer on American History, University of Minas Gerais, Belo Horizonte, Braz. Co-author of *Latin American History.*

R.D.Ho./Andorra; Liechtenstein; Luxembourg; Monaco; San Marino
ROBERT DAVID HODGSON. Assistant Geographer, U.S. Department of State, Washington, D.C. Author of *The Changing Map of Africa.*

R.E.E.H./Religion *(in part)*
REUBEN ELMORE ERNEST HARKNESS. Emeritus Professor of History of Christianity, Crozer Seminary, Chester, Pa. Professor of History of World Religions, History of Christianity, Baptist History, Ellen Cushing Junior College, Bryn Mawr, Pa.

R.F.Br./Medicine *(in part)*
R. F. BRIDGMAN, M.D. Chief Medical Officer, Organization of Medical Care, World Health Organization, Geneva.

R.F.G.C./Religion *(in part)*
RALPH FORMAN GODLEY CALDER. Secretary, Overseas Appointments Bureau, Christian Education Movement, London.

R.F.Mi./Philately and Numismatics *(in part)*
RICHARD F. MILLER. Director, Division of Language and Literature, Eastern Washington State College.

R.F.Sa./Anthropology
RICHARD FRANK SALISBURY. Professor of Anthropology, McGill University. Author of *From Stone to Steel; Vunamami: Economic Transformation in a Traditional Society.*

R.H.Be./Hockey *(in part)*
RICHARD HERBERT BEDDOES. Sports Columnist, the *Toronto Globe and Mail.*

R.H.Tr./Stock Exchanges *(in part)*
ROBERT H. TRIGG. Manager, Institutional Research, New York Stock Exchange.

R.Hy./Peace Movements
RICHARD HATHAWAY. Teaching Faculty, History and International Studies, Goddard College, Plainfield, Vt.; Member, Board of Editors, *Current.*

Ri.W./Biography *(in part)*; **Liberia; United States**
RICHARD WORSNOP. Writer, Editorial Research Reports, Washington, D.C.

R.J.B./Archaeology *(in part)*
ROBERT J. BRAIDWOOD. Professor of Old World Prehistory, the Oriental Institute and the Department of Anthropology, The University of Chicago.

R.J.Fe./Motor Sports *(in part)*
ROBERT JOSEPH FENDELL. New York Editor, *Automotive News.* Automobile Columnist for *Action.* Scriptwriter for *Speed Sport News* syndicated radio series.

R.J.Ra./Defense
ROBERT JOHN RANGER. Lecturer in Politics, University of Aberdeen.

R.K.R./Medicine *(in part)*
RICHARD K. RICHARDS, M.D. Professor of Pharmacology, Northwestern University Medical School, Chicago. Editor of *Clinical Evaluation of Drugs.*

R.L.A./Biography *(in part)*
ROBERT LOUIS ASHER. Staff writer, *Washington Post.* Contributor to *Ten Blocks from the White House.*

R.L.F./Religion *(in part)*
ROBERT LOUIS FRIEDLY. Director, Office of Communication, Christian Church (Disciples of Christ), Indianapolis, Ind.

R.L.Hs./Hockey *(in part)*
RICHARD LYNTON HOLLANDS. Hockey Correspondent. Editor, *Hockey News,* London. Co-author of *Hockey.*

R.L.R./Religion *(in part)*
ROGER LEWIS ROBERTS. Editorial Consultant, *Church Times,* London.

R.L.Ro./Chile
ROBERT L. ROSS. Vice-President, Adela Investment Co., Washington, D.C.

R.M.Gn./Horse Racing *(in part)*
ROBERT MARSHALL GOODWIN. Assistant Editor, London, *Encyclopædia Britannica.*

R.M.My./Television and Radio *(in part)*
ROBERT M. MYERS. Assistant Secretary, American Radio Relay League, Inc., Newington, Conn.

R.M.Sm./Economic Planning *(in part)*
RAMASWAMY MEENATCHI SUNDRUM. Director, Development Programs Study Group, World Bank. Author of *Long-Term Projections for Economic and Social Development.*

Rn.C./Biography *(in part)*; **Cuba; Haiti; Portugal**
ROBIN CHAPMAN. Economic Research Officer, Bank of London and South America Ltd., London.

R.N.S./United Nations *(in part)*
RICHARD N. SWIFT. Head, Department of Politics, New York University, New York City. Author of *International Law: Current and Classic.* Editor of *Annual Review of United Nations Affairs.*

Ro.Go./Vietnam *(in part)*
ROBERT GORALSKI. NBC News Pentagon Correspondent.

Ro.P.H./U.S. Supplement: *Major Legislation Table*
ROBERT PIERPONT HEY. Staff Correspondent, Washington Bureau, *The Christian Science Monitor.*

R.Pn./Alcoholic Beverages *(in part)*
RENE PROTIN. Director, International Vine and Wine Office, Paris.

R.R.No./Biological Sciences *(in part)*
RONALD RICHARDS NOVALES. Associate Professor of Biological Sciences, Northwestern University, Evanston, Ill. Member, Editorial Board, *American Zoologist.*

R.S.Mi./Engineering Projects *(in part)*
RAYMOND SPENCER MILLARD. Deputy Director, Road Research Laboratory, Ministry of Transport, Crowthorne, Berkshire, Eng.

R.V.M./Religion *(in part)*
ROBERT V. MOSS. President, United Church of Christ, New York City; President, American Association of Theological Schools, 1966–68. Author of *The Life of Paul; We Believe; As Paul Sees Christ.*

R.W.Cr./Television and Radio *(in part)*
RUFUS WILLIAM CRATER. Editorial Director, *Broadcasting,* New York City.

R.W.Sm./Religion (*in part*)
REUBEN WILLIAM SMITH. Assistant Professor of Islamic History, The University of Chicago.

R.W.T./Religion (*in part*)
RONALD WILLIAM THOMSON. Assistant General Secretary, Baptist Union of Great Britain and Ireland. Author of *Heroes of the Baptist Church; William Carey; The Service of Our Lives; A Pocket History of the Baptists.*

S.Aa./Denmark
STENER AARSDAL. Economic Editor, *Børsen.* Press Officer, Chamber of Commerce, Copenhagen.

S.A.F./Medicine (*in part*)
STANLEY ANTHONY FELDMAN. Consultant Anesthetist, Westminster Hospital; Adviser, Postgraduate Studies, Royal College of Surgeons, London. Author of *Tracheostomy and Artificial Ventilation.* Co-author of *Principles of Resuscitation.*

S.B.P./Physics
STUART BEAUMONT PALMER. Lecturer, Department of Applied Physics, University of Hull.

Se.H./Political Science
SERGE HURTIG. Director of Studies and Research, Foundation Nationale des Sciences Politiques; Professor, Paris Institute of Political Studies. Former Secretary General, International Political Science Association.

S.E.S./Germany (*in part*)
STEPHAN E. SCHATTMANN. Economist, London.

S.G.J./Crime (*in part*)
SVEND GRAM JENSEN. Research Associate, Institute of Criminal Science, University of Copenhagen.

Sh.P./Race Relations (*in part*)
SHEILA CAFFYN PATTERSON. Research Fellow, Centre for Multi-Racial Studies, University of Sussex, Brighton. Author of *Colour and Culture in South Africa; The Last Trek; Dark Strangers; Immigrants in Industry.*

Si.P./Words and Meanings, New (*in part*)
SIMEON POTTER. Emeritus Professor of English Language and Philology, University of Liverpool. Author of *Our Language; Language in the Modern World; Modern Linguistics.*

S.Mi./Architecture; Art Exhibitions
SANDRA MILLIKIN. Assistant Curator of Drawings, Royal Institute of British Architects, London.

S.M.Mc./Philosophy
STERLING M. McMURRIN. E. E. Ericksen Distinguished Professor of Philosophy, Dean of the Graduate School, University of Utah. Co-author of *A History of Philosophy.*

S.M.Q./Medicine (*in part*)
SHEILA MARGARET QUINN. Executive Director, International Council of Nurses, Geneva.

S.Mu./Biography (*in part*)
STEPHANIE MULLINS. Historian.

Sn.H./Morocco
STEPHEN HUGHES. Reuters Correspondent, Morocco.

S.Pa./Furs
SANDY PARKER. Fur Editor, *Women's Wear Daily.*

S.S.G./Medicine (*in part*)
SYDNEY S. GELLIS, M.D. Professor and Chairman, Department of Pediatrics, Tufts University School of Medicine, and Pediatrician-in-chief, Tufts-New England Medical Center, Boston. Author of *Current Pediatric Therapy.* Editor, *Year Book of Pediatrics.*

S.Tf./Television and Radio (*in part*)
SOL TAISHOFF. President, Editor and Publisher, *Broadcasting,* Washington, D.C.

St.F.B./Horse Racing (*in part*)
STANLEY F. BERGSTEIN. Executive Secretary, Harness Tracks of America Inc.; Vice President, United States Trotting Association.

T.B.F./Medicine (*in part*)
THOMAS B. FITZPATRICK. Edward Wigglesworth Professor of Dermatology and Head, Department of Dermatology, Harvard Medical School; Chief, Dermatology Service, Massachusetts General Hospital, Boston.

T.C.J.C./Industrial Review (*in part*)
THOMAS CHARLES JOHN COGLE. Technical Editor, *Electrical Review.*

T.J.F./Biography (*in part*)
THOMAS J(OHN) FOLEY. Correspondent, Washington Bureau, *Los Angeles Times.* Contributor to *Six Days in June.*

T.J.S.G./Cambodia; Korea; Southeast Asia; Vietnam (*in part*)
THAYIL JACOB SONY GEORGE. Assistant Editor, *Far Eastern Economic Review,* Hong Kong. Author of *Krishna Menon, a Biography.*

T.L.T.L./Medicine (*in part*)
THOMAS LOFTUS TOWNSHEND LEWIS. Obstetric Surgeon, Guy's Hospital; Surgeon, Queen Charlotte's Maternity Hospital; Surgeon, Chelsea Hospital for Women. Author of *Progress in Clinical Obstetrics and Gynaecology;* (jointly) *The Queen Charlotte's Textbook of Obstetrics.*

T.M.R./Savings and Investment
TADEUSZ MIECZYSLAW RYBCZYNSKI. Economist, Lazard Brothers, London.

Tm.S./Gardening (*in part*)
TOM STEVENSON. Garden Columnist, *Baltimore News American; Washington Post; Washington Post-Los Angeles Times News Service.* Author of *Pruning Guide for Trees, Shrubs and Vines; Lawn Guide; Gardening for the Beginner.*

To.S./Literature (*in part*)
TORBJØRN STØVERUD. W.P. Ker Senior Lecturer in Norwegian, University College, London.

T.R.Sh./Speleology
TREVOR ROYLE SHAW. Commander, Royal Navy. Vice-President, British Speleological Association.

T.Sc./Alcoholic Beverages (*in part*)
TILMAN SCHMITT. Brewery Engineer. Editor of *Brauwelt; Brauwissenschaft.*

T.W./Biography (*in part*)**; Football** (*in part*)
TREVOR WILLIAMSON. Sports sub-editor, *Daily Telegraph,* London.

T.W.Me./Engineering Projects (*in part*)
T. W. MERMEL. Assistant to Commissioner for Research and Chief, General Engineering Division, Bureau of Reclamation, U.S. Department of the Interior, Washington, D.C. Chairman, Committee on World Register of Dams, International Commission on Large Dams. Author of *Register of Dams in the United States.*

Va.K./Iceland
VALDIMAR KRISTINSSON. Editor of *Fjármálatidindi.*

V.A.McK./Medicine (*in part*)
VICTOR ALMON McKUSICK. Professor of Medicine, Epidemiology, and Biology, Johns Hopkins University, Baltimore, Md. Author of *Heritable Disorders of Connective Tissue; On the X Chromosome of Man; Human Genetics; Mendelian Inheritance in Man.*

V.F.Ra./Tobacco
VIVIAN FOSTER RAVEN. Editor, *Tobacco.*

V.G.C.B./Photography
VICTOR GORDON CHARLES BLACKMAN. Staff photographer, *Daily Express,* London. Columnist, *Amateur Photographer.*

V.Gr./Crime (*in part*)
VAGN GREVE. Research Associate, Institute of Criminal Science, University of Copenhagen.

V.J.P./Cyprus
VERNON JOHN PARRY. Reader in the History of the Near and Middle East, School of Oriental and African Studies, University of London. Contributor to *New Cambridge Modern History; Cambridge History of Islam; Encyclopaedia of Islam.*

V.L.A./Labour Unions (*in part*)
VICTOR LEONARD ALLEN. Senior Lecturer in Industrial Economics, University of Leeds. Author of *Power in Trade Unions; Trade Union Leadership; Trade Unions and the Government; Militant Trade Unionism; International Bibliography of Trade Unionism.*

V.W.P./Crime (*in part*)**; Police** (*in part*)
VIRGIL W. PETERSON. Executive Director, Chicago Crime Commission. Author of *Gambling—Should It Be Legalized?; Barbarians in Our Midst.*

W.A.Ha./Publishing (*in part*)
WILLIAM A. HACHTEN. Professor, School of Journalism, University of Wisconsin.

W.A.Ka./Publishing (*in part*)
WILLIAM A. KATZ. Professor, School of Library Science, State University of New York. Author of *Introduction to Reference Magazines for Libraries.*

Wa.Ls./Art Sales (*in part*)
WILMA LAWS. Journalist, London. Member, International Association of Art Critics.

W.A.P.M./Commercial Policies; Industrial Review (*in part*)
WILLIAM ARTHUR PEETE MANSER. Consultant, International Iron and Steel Institute, Brussels; Economic Adviser, Baring Brothers and Co., Ltd., London.

W.B./Horse Racing (*in part*)
WILLIAM BONIFACE. Sports writer, the *Baltimore Sun,* Baltimore, Md.

W.B.Mi./Religion (*in part*)
WILLIAM B. MILLER. Manager, Department of History, United Presbyterian Church, U.S.A.

W.C.Bo./Motor Sports (*in part*)
WILLIAM CHARLES BODDY. Editor, *Motor Sport.* Full Member, Guild of Motoring Writers. Author of *The Story of Brooklands; The 200 Mile Race; The World's Land Speed Record; Continental Sports Cars; The Sports Car Pocketbook; The Bugatti Story.*

W.D.Hd./Law (*in part*)
WILLIAM D. HAWKLAND. Provost and Professor of Law, School of Law, State University of New York, Buffalo. Author of *Sales Under Uniform Commercial Code; Cases on Bills and Notes; Commercial Paper; Transactional Guide of the Uniform Commercial Code; Cases on Sales and Security.*

W.D.Hi./Telecommunications (*in part*)
WILLIAM DALE HICKMAN, JR. Washington (D.C.) News Correspondent, McGraw-Hill Publications. Author of *Talking Moons, the Story of Communications Satellites.*

W.Ei./Populations and Areas (*in part*)
WARREN WOLFF EISENBERG. Administrative Assistant to Rep. William J. Green.

W.H.Is./Gambia, The; Sierra Leone
(WILLIAM) HAROLD INGRAMS. Former Adviser on Overseas Information, Colonial Office, London. Author of *Arabia and the Isles; Hong Kong; Seven Across the Sahara; Uganda; The Yemen Imams: Rulers and Revolution.*

WHO/Medicine *(in part)*
WORLD HEALTH ORGANIZATION, Geneva.

W.H.Ta./Religion *(in part)*
WINSTON HOWARTH TAYLOR. Director, Washington Office, Commission on Public Relations and Methodist Information. Author of *Angels Don't Need Public Relations; Ending Racial Segregation in the Methodist Church; Toward an Inclusive Church.*

W.H.Ts./Biography *(in part)*; **United Kingdom**
WILLIAM HARFORD THOMAS. Managing Editor, *Guardian*, London and Manchester.

Wi.L.F./Conservation *(in part)*
WILLIAM L. FIRST. Legislative Assistant to Rep. Thomas S. Foley (Dem., Wash.).

W.Le./Government Finance
WILFRED LEWIS, JR. Chief Economist, National Planning Association. Author of *Federal Fiscal Policy in the Postwar Recessions.*

W.L.We./ Biography *(in part)*; **Literature** *(in part)*
WILLIAM LESLIE WEBB. Literary Editor, *Guardian*, London and Manchester.

W.P./Religion *(in part)*
WILLIAM ASHWORTH PRATT. Director, Salvation Army International Information Services, London.

W.P.Ja./Industrial Review *(in part)*
W. PINCUS JASPERT. Technical editorial consultant. Editor of *Encyclopaedia of Type Faces.*

W.S.Cl./Medicine *(in part)*
WILLIAM STRATTON CLARK. President, Arthritis Foundation, New York City.

W.So./Africa
WALLACE SOKOLSKY. Assistant Professor, History Department, Bronx Community College, the New School for Social Research, New York University, Division of Adult Education. Co-author of *Contemporary Civilization; African Nationalism in the Twentieth Century.*

W.Te./Dance *(in part)*
WALTER TERRY. Dance Critic, *Saturday Review.* Author of *The Dance in America; The Ballet Companion; Miss Ruth: The "More Living Life" of Ruth St. Denis.*

W.Vö./Religion *(in part)*
WALTER ALFRED VÖLKNER. Minister, Evangelical Lutheran Church of Tanzania, Northern Diocese, Kibaya, Tanzania.

W.W.E./Vital Statistics *(in part)*
WINSTON WALLACE EHRMANN. Dean and Professor of Sociology, Cornell College, Iowa. Author of *Premarital Dating Behavior.*

Y.S./Bowling and Lawn Bowls *(in part)*
YRJÖ SARAHETE. Secretary, Fédération Internationale des Quilleurs, Helsinki, Fin.

AUTHORS OF THE SPECIAL REPORTS IN THE 1970 BOOK OF THE YEAR

AGRICULTURE
(Locust Plague: A Danger Averted)
P. T. Haskell
Director
Anti-Locust Research Centre
London

ANTHROPOLOGY
(The Primitive Tribes of South America)
Conrad Gorinsky
Lecturer, Department of Biochemistry
St. Bartholomew's Hospital Medical College
University of London

CANADA
(Trudeau's Foreign Policy: An Early Appraisal)
James Eayrs
Professor, Department of Political Economy
University of Toronto

CINEMA
(The Cinema and Censorship)
John Trevelyan
Secretary
British Board of Film Censors
London

CITIES AND URBAN AFFAIRS
(Indestructible Trash)
Gladwin Hill
National Environmental Correspondent
The New York Times

DEFENSE
(The Military Under Fire)
Robert Sherrill
Washington Correspondent
The Nation

DEVELOPMENT, ECONOMIC
(The Crisis in International Development)
Irving S. Friedman
Economic Adviser to the President of
the International Bank for Reconstruction and Development
Washington, D.C.

ECONOMIC PLANNING
(Economic Background for Czechoslovakia's Crisis)
Ota Sik
Former Deputy Premier of Czechoslovakia
and Director, Economic Institute of
the Czechoslovak Academy of Sciences
Professor, Institute of Applied Economics
Basel University

EDUCATION
(Man's Fundamental Right to Read)
Bruce Felknor
Former Executive Director of the U.S.
Fair Campaign Practices Committee
New York City

FASHION AND DRESS
(The End of the Gray Flannel Suit)
Antony King Deacon
Men's Fashion Editor
The Times
London

LIBRARIES
(The American Library in Paris)
Robert Faherty
Correspondent
Chicago Daily News
Paris

MEDICINE
(Cold as a Treatment for Disease)
Sir James Fraser
Fellow of the Royal College of Surgeons of Edinburgh
Professor of Clinical Science in Surgery
University of Southampton

SOUTHEAST ASIA
(United States Foreign Policy in East Asia)
Hans J. Morgenthau
Albert A. Michelson Distinguished Service Professor
of Political Science and Modern History
The University of Chicago

SPORTING RECORD
(Do Amateurs Exist in Sports?)
William Barry Furlong
Author and Journalist
Chicago

UNITED STATES
(The Conglomerate Phenomenon)
Joel E. Segall
Professor of Finance
Graduate School of Business
The University of Chicago

During the past several years the *Britannica Book of the Year* has brought its readers major feature articles by such world statesmen as former presidents Lyndon B. Johnson of the United States and Rómulo Betancourt of Venezuela, the former prime minister of Japan, Shigeru Yoshida, and Prime Minister Harold Wilson of the United Kingdom. The opinions of the authors, like those of President Jomo Kenyatta of Kenya, whose article "The Emergence of Kenya" prefaces this edition, have been presented as personal points of view and do not necessarily represent the views of the publisher or editors of *Encyclopædia Britannica*.

►

BLACK STAR

THE EMERGENCE OF KENYA

by JOMO KENYATTA

Jomo Kenyatta was elected president of the Republic of Kenya after that former British colony won independence in 1963. He had served previously as prime minister of the self-governing state. A dynamic African political leader for 40 years, President Kenyatta has been highly influential in the achievements his country has made during the past six years. It is with understandable pride that he outlines for readers of the 1970 *Britannica Book of the Year* the advances his country has made, the agonies his people have suffered, and his hopes for the future of Kenya.

A FOREWORD

by Waldemar Nielson

President, African-American Institute
New York City

Over the past quarter of a century, the political map of the world—particularly the third world—has been redrawn drastically, reflecting a train of historic events brought about by a remarkable generation of nationalist and revolutionary leaders, from Mao Tse-tung and Marshal Tito to Habib Bourguiba and Jomo Kenyatta. The distinctive fact about this group of men, now growing elderly, has been the completeness of their involvement in the political, social, and economic transformation of their countries. They began as subversives and agitators; they rose to the leadership of movements that eventually achieved political power; and then, shifting from an oppositional role, they became the responsible heads of established governments.

Of the African leaders who have played a prominent role in the decolonization of that vast continent, Kenyatta occupies a place of special prestige. Not as fiery as Nkrumah of Ghana, as cunning as Houphouët-Boigny of Ivory Coast, or as creative as Nyerere of Tanzania, he outranks them all as a figure on the world scene, partly by the longevity of his career in the struggle for African rights and partly by the sheer force of his personality. Now nearly 80 (the exact date of his birth is not known), Kenyatta has devoted his whole life to politics and the liberation of his country. In the early 1920s he was already general secretary of the Kikuyu Central Association, the action arm of the politically most dynamic tribe in East Africa. In those years he formulated the fundamental African case against the European occupation of the Kenya Highlands and traveled to England as a petitioner for his people. In the early 1930s he returned to England and stayed for 15 years, studying, writing, and campaigning for African independence. In 1938 he published his now classic book *Facing Mount Kenya,* a study of the tribal life of the Kikuyu and of its disruption by the invasion of the white man. He traveled extensively in Europe and studied for a time in the Soviet Union at Moscow University.

On returning to Kenya after World War II, he became president of a new African political party, the Kenya African Union. By 1948 he had become so menacing to the interests of the white settlers that they were demanding his deportation. In October 1952 he and several other African leaders were detained on charges of incitement to violence and in April 1953 he was convicted and sentenced to seven years' imprisonment. By the time of the Kenya Constitutional Conference in London in January 1960, he had become the symbol and personification of the independence struggle and his release had become a major issue in Kenya politics.

The postwar wave of independence in Africa, which began in the north and by 1960 had swept through West Africa, was delayed in reaching East Africa because of the determined resistance of the large number of white settlers living in the area. But in December 1963, Kenya finally became independent and Kenyatta assumed the powers of head of government of the new nation.

Kenya, at the time it first hoisted its own flag, enjoyed certain advantages compared with the other new African nations in terms of climate, resources, and inherited economic infrastructure. But fundamentally it was confronted with the full range of problems that faced most of the others—boundary problems with neighbouring states; the tragic lack of trained manpower; tribal rivalries; vulnerability to foreign interference and subversion; heavy dependence on the export of primary products in an increasingly competitive world market; and a general fragility of new economic arrangements and institutions.

Unlike a growing number of the others, however, Kenya has not been overwhelmed by its difficulties. Under the driving and disciplinary leadership of Kenyatta, Kenya in the first six years of independence has made a rather impressive start. Skillful political compromises, combined with Kenyatta's enormous personal prestige, gave the country an effective degree of political unity. The politically explosive land question was dealt with by a cooperative program with the British, through which white settlers were bought out and the properties transferred to African hands. An early army mutiny was put down, and effective measures were subsequently taken to ensure the loyalty of the officers and the troops to the new government. In political matters a degree of political opposition was allowed to exist, the press was relatively

JOHN MOSS FROM BLACK STAR

free, and insofar as a race relations problem remained, it was largely between Africans and Asians, not Africans and Europeans.

In contrast to many other African countries, therefore, the pace of economic development was not interrupted by independence. In the six years from 1963 through 1969, the average growth of Kenya's gross national product exceeded 5%. African farm production steadily increased, eventually outstripping the levels previously reached by European farmers. By the late 1960s, Kenya, though faced with such serious problems as unemployment, growing corruption in government, and increasing tribal tensions, was still one of the most impressive examples of progress and unity in Africa.

In its general philosophy, Kenya had not followed the approach of many of the former French colonies in continued dependence on their former colonizer, nor the lead of others such as Tanzania, which ruptured old relationships and put its trust in "self-reliance." Instead, Kenya held to a more moderate independent course—maintaining cooperative relations with Britain while actively seeking aid and private investment from various new foreign sources. As its program began to show positive results, it attracted greater interest on the part of the other African states, which were groping for solutions to their own urgent development problems. Moreover, the influence of Kenya's example extended to the South, where the white-minority regimes in Rhodesia, the Portuguese colonies, and South Africa found the country's success a challenge to their claim that the African is inherently incapable of managing his own economic and political affairs.

But more recently—and particularly since mid-1969—a shadow has begun to fall across the bright image of the new Kenya.

Kenyatta suffered terribly during his seven years of imprisonment, and rumours about his health have circulated periodically since. Beginning in 1967, signs of Kenyatta's failing strength became apparent, and thereafter political maneuvering for the succession to the presidency began in earnest. Since then, factions have formed that are determined to block the road to power for their opponents and to preempt it for themselves. One of the strongest of these is a group of young Kikuyu, some of them members of Kenyatta's Cabinet. When Tom Mboya, a member of the less powerful Luo tribe and generally regarded as the most able individual in the Kenyatta government, was assassinated for political motives in July 1969, the finger of suspicion pointed to certain prominent Kikuyu politicians, and ugly tribal disorders were triggered in several regions of the country.

Kenyatta, despite his age and physical condition, has not thus far been willing to redistribute his presidential powers. In response to the disorders that followed Mboya's death, he has taken strong measures.

Over the years, one of the main elements of Kenyatta's political strength has been the fact that the majority of Africans saw him as the only leader able to rise above tribal rivalries and unite the country. Now that tribalism has begun to be rekindled, he must quench that danger once again if the political unity of Kenya is to be maintained and if a major part of the accomplishments of his remarkable political career are not to be ruined.

If he succeeds and if the stability and progress of the nation can be preserved, then the significance of the achievement will be enormous. Many of the new nations of Africa are now at the point of the first great post-independence conjuncture of economic and political crises. Their development programs are sagging and their political discontents and disunity have reached the flash point. These accumulating difficulties have in turn served to help the morale of the embattled white-minority regimes of the South by providing a semblance of credibility to their insistence on the economic and political incompetence of the black man.

More than ever Africa needs its models of achievement. Ghana and Guinea have long since fallen into serious difficulty; Nigeria has been disrupted by a brutal civil war. History, therefore, has placed on Kenya—along with a few other newly independent African nations—the heavy responsibility of continuing to show the way in the cause to which men such as Kenyatta have devoted their lives.

THE POLITICAL APPROACH TO NATION BUILDING

By Dec. 12, 1963, when Kenya became fully independent, I had had more than 40 years in public life—some of them spent uncomfortably—to reflect on and prepare for the manifold tasks of constructive national leadership. I was not sorry to have had that opportunity.

Those who may have glanced through my most recent book, *Suffering Without Bitterness,* will have some inkling of the 40-year story that preceded Kenyan independence. In this presentation, I shall move onward from that familiar ground instead of pointlessly recrossing it. Revenge has always struck me as a form of human debasement that has no place in dynamic leadership, and surely the common message of all the great religions is that only through forgiveness can humanity aspire to hope. Thus, in 1963, my people responded to the immediate need: to forget the tribulations of the past for the sake of the future.

When Kenya achieved independence, along with many of its sister nations, a kind of vacuum could have ensued, a countrywide inertia in both the practical and the psychological sense. The people of Kenya were uplifted by the attainment of *Uhuru* and the raising of our flag, but they were also deprived of the sustaining ambition that, for so many years, had inspired so much effort and sacrifice. It seemed to me that the first task of a vigorous leadership must be to counter any tendency to drift, by ensuring that the people understood all that our independence meant and everything that Kenya had to do. A new president or prime minister in a country such as the United States or Britain does not have to confront this kind of basic challenge. But in a newly emergent and barely developed state, especially in Africa, it is necessary to anticipate and to take steps to alleviate the feeling of anticlimax.

Leading Mau Mau guerrillas: I shall move onward from that familiar ground.

UPI COMPIX

During the final period before independence, I had never pretended to Kenya's people that *Uhuru* and Utopia were synonymous. What I had tried to make clear was that human dignity in freedom could be—and must be—the launching platform from which our country would rise to higher levels of economic advancement and social justice. I was anxious that our people should be armed against false ideas that the going would be easy. Thinking of all this now, six years later, I am confirmed in the belief that, once this danger of depression has been overcome, the people concerned will have acquired a wisdom and a strength sufficient to ward off any other peril.

The institution that led Kenya into organized independence was KANU, the Kenya African National Union. A "national front" in both word and fact, this party gave to our people a sense of commitment and a sense of belonging. Its election manifesto outlined fundamental aims and realistic purposes, not in the language of political hyperbole, but in terms of ideas and priorities and methods to which every ordinary family could respond.

We in KANU have always upheld the principle of government by the people. Unreservedly committed to democracy, the KANU government will shortly place an account of its stewardship before the people in a general election. I am an absolute believer in this process, and not solely on grounds of morality in public life. Welding together many tribes—not to mention races and creeds—into a single nation can be a turbulent process. The KANU government was born out of the aspirations of the people and their yearnings for a better life, but no government can succeed in translating these hopes into reality without the confidence of the people and without the constant refreshment of the strange mystique (perhaps unique to Africa) by which leadership and people can think and move as one.

There are occasional reports these days that KANU has become disheartened or disorganized or is split into cliques. Such assertions can be upsetting to those who have the well-being of our republic at heart. But I have noticed once or twice that the more erudite an observer or critic is reputed to be, the more likely is it that he will bypass or underestimate factors of resilience—the capacity to rise to an occasion—that in Africa are commonplace.

Let me put it this way. It would be unusual for any major party within a free society to be without its factions or its disagreements. This is especially true in a young country, where so much dynamism has been unleashed. But a party must never simply exist, like a cabbage in the ground. Politics must be volatile if it is to be vigorous, and without this kind of vigour a national party would fail to produce fresh ideas or to bring forth new leaders. What counts, ultimately, is knowing when to churn things up and when to close the ranks.

One of the fundamentals that concerned my government in its earliest period was the formulation of the constitution. In long-established states, a constitution may lie forgotten in some dusty archive, or it may merely reflect unwritten tenets of national routine and mentality. But in Africa a constitution is important. It is something personal to a country. It must be the means of clearly codifying ideas and procedures, structures and powers, disciplines and possibilities. And it can inspire perennial scrutiny in a country where every citizen, irrespective of his daily trade or craft, is a constitutional lawyer on the side.

We had to move in stages, amending, over a period of time, the original constitution that had come into force at the time of independence. The first essential was to provide for rule on the foundation of law. I am in complete agreement with all that the British people—before Rhodesia—used to teach and believe: that the rule of law is the only proper basis for the conduct of affairs and the worthwhile advancement of society. Secondly, we embodied within the constitution all that was required for the establishment and functioning of meaningful democracy. Some aspects of these clauses, in regard to election procedures, have recently come under critical review. This is a healthy sign that our democracy in Kenya has not become insipid.

The third need was to include adequate safeguards, covering not only such material matters as the sanctity of property or land, but also the whole aggregation of human freedoms and rights. It is my opinion that, without such entrenched provisions, there can be no guarantee that governments will conduct themselves with justice and propriety. Finally, in the republican constitution (Kenya became a republic a year after independence), we contrived to enshrine the principle of national unity, eliminating the complex stipulations that had emerged from the old fears among tribes, races, and economic classes.

Whatever the kind of constitution, it is still possible for a government to grow remote from the people. In this event, democracy becomes a sham. To obviate this threat, we have vested in our Parliament rights and duties that make this elected body the supreme instrument of the state. Direct representatives of the people, within the National Assembly, have the right of final sanction for all our country's laws. Further control over the conduct of the government is exercised by Parliament through its duty to allocate—or approve submitted allocations of—all public funds.

There is more to life, mercifully, than systems and documentation. Many other formidable needs loomed before us at independence. Among my reflections then was that I should make a forthright response to any sign of patronage from the advanced industrial states. It is not always realized that a new and developing nation must spend a long time working through stages of initial planning, construction, and social readjustment just to reach the starting line. In the beginning it lacks the infrastructures that sophisticated countries have had for generations.

And so the work of economic and social development began. From the viewpoint of political leadership, it was necessary to accommodate many distractions: the tendencies of sectional groups to hide behind slogans; the substitution of imported dogma for apposite thought; sudden eddies of emotion that hid all socioeconomic reality; eccentric or irrelevant concepts, championed most frequently by young men both within and outside Parliament. But always we managed to preserve the critical driving force of national unity. With Kenya in the vanguard of African progress, unity had to mean not merely consolidation against outside threats but also recognition by all the people of our mutual need within the developing state.

The first and most difficult phase of nation building is now successfully behind us. Our flag and our motto are no longer curiosities, but have become unaffected symbols of nationhood. We have created the administrative structures and the basic economic apparatus needed for a thriving state. The Republic of Kenya, freed from so many earlier distractions, is on the way toward providing higher living standards and making life for our people everywhere worthwhile. This could only have happened through the living spirit of what we call *Ujamaa,* or familyhood.

IAN BERRY FROM MAGNUM

Shortly after being released from prison in 1961: To forget the tribulations of the past for the sake of the future.

Independence Day ceremony (left and following page), Dec. 12, 1963: All the noble charters and declarations of history have sprung from one paramount truth—that men have the right to be free.

JOHN MOSS FROM BLACK STAR

Some visitors from the steel-and-concrete bastions of overseas states, fresh from their smog and subways and thrombosis, tend to look on the African people as "unsophisticated." I am generally prompted to wonder: what exactly does this mean? If such a stricture implies lack of familiarity with electronic gadgets, or Chopin's music, or the wines of Alsace, then—for the little this is worth—it may be justified. Yet the citizens of Kenya are mature in other ways, in ways that matter, to an extent that people of foreign origin often find quite hard to understand.

This country, in its short span of nationhood, has faced numerous threats. Certainly, in our economic strivings, we have encountered setbacks and disappointments of many kinds. It has been difficult for many of our people, whether in urban or in rural settings, to wait—to go on waiting—for relief from economic hardships and social pressures. But their faith has never broken. As a people with roots in the land, they have known that the planting and the cultivating must be done before there can be any harvest.

One of the most difficult tasks in politics is to persuade people to face up to unpopular realities. It is natural for men to be impatient. It is fully understandable that all the longed-for fruits of independence—including such basics as the banishment of poverty, illiteracy, and disease—should be desired here and now, especially by the landless and the unemployed. But my government can truly declare that, given so many limitations, nothing more could have been done than has been done. This is a political government, elected and maintained by the people. Our duty is to the people and I have always insisted that we should never attempt to hide realities from them. Only in this way can national integrity be defended.

This creates a dilemma for our "familyhood democracy." Many unpleasant truths—for example, those that affect unemployment—must be recognized clearly and stated courageously. These truths reflect conditions that are by no means unique to Kenya, but of course they are unpalatable to the people, especially those whose futile search for employment builds into major frustration. It follows that a government deliberately geared to such frankness spotlights, of its own volition, situations that are tailor-made for exploitation by an irresponsible opposition. Yet I am certain that this method is right. Political techniques cannot be proved, like mathematical theorems, but our methods have maintained a climate of stability in Kenya at a time when instability would have cast the country back.

Let me conclude these general reflections by saying something more about stability, this time in relation to the paramount importance we currently attach to the transference into local (overwhelmingly African) hands of the greatest possible proportion of economic enterprise and the conduct of affairs. It is true that this springs from the government's fundamental policy: the pursuit of social justice. But it may also be surmised that, without manifest and predominant economic participation by the Kenyan people, stability might sooner or later be threatened.

The aim of our policies is to establish the vast majority of our people on their own land, in their own houses, with their own businesses, with an executive and/or shareholding stake in some major enterprise, or in solid and satisfying jobs. When this is done, stability can be preserved. Possession and the prospect of retaining possession are the cornerstones of self-respect, and as I read all human experience, this alone can maintain stability.

AFRICAN SOCIALISM

Every state has—and certainly is entitled to have—its own ideas as to whether the road to progress should be mapped out in advance, or whether it should follow routes dictated by day-to-day palliatives and pressures.

With regard to Kenya, I have always been convinced that there must be a long-term commitment, buttressed by an underlying philosophy, to policies and programs aimed at specific, declared objectives. It seems to me that momentum can be lost and the

KEYSTONE

fervour of nationhood endangered by experiments with different systems.

Kenya is a country of tremendous potential, but when independence dawned it was exploited and maladjusted. If the process of disciplined nation building was to proceed, it was important that the people should have no doubts about the aims of their society. It was no time to window shop among different theories, and neither the Eastern nor the Western system seemed suited to the country's needs. What the time demanded was a political purpose and a practical technique of our own designing.

Out of this challenge emerged what we call African Socialism. It is important to understand just how this was formulated, and—at least broadly—what it means. Published as a document that has attracted some international attention, this whole proposition expresses feelings about human worth and human brotherhood that have always been embodied in the African way of life. But the presentation of African Socialism did not stop there.

One of the many conclusions I have reached, after half a century in public life, is that empty gestures may provide emotional satisfaction, but they will not feed or educate the people. It is right that even the smallest nations should place a high value on their dignity, but there is no point in taking flamboyant but impractical stands that bear little relation to the facts of life. African Socialism in Kenya, therefore, had to be—and was—adapted to reality. The social aims and economic practices underlying it had to be tailored to existing world patterns.

To be acceptable, however, the entire philosophy had to be truly African. It could not be some disguised and diluted version of an ideology in vogue elsewhere, although we have never hesitated to adopt, from others, useful or compatible techniques. There are two essential African traditions that have influenced African Socialism and, through it, our political approach and progress. One is democracy—not as the facade of respectability that many nations have professed, but in its literal meaning. The other is what we describe as mutual social responsibility, translated into individual and corporate obligations and rights.

The African concept of democracy has always included procedures designed to forestall the seizure and entrenchment of political influence by persons or groups armed with economic power. In this our traditions of democracy have customarily differed from those of capitalist societies. Furthermore, African thinking and practice have always enabled every mature citizen to participate fully and equally in political affairs, and here we have differed from Communism. The sharp class divisions that once existed in Europe never had a parallel in traditional African society. Rather, one of the problems in contemporary Africa has been to prevent antagonistic classes from emerging. Kenya has had the special problem of confronting and smoothing out artificial class barriers that have arisen almost exclusively on the foundation of race.

(Parenthetically, it has been interesting to observe how world political systems have been forced to adapt themselves both to social protest and to technological change. As far as the West is concerned, there have been moves away from strict capitalism toward more genuine democracy; significant dilution of private property rights; increased state responsibility for social services and economic planning; and more progressive taxation policies. Even in the East there have been signs of adaptability, expressed through various forms of ownership, wage differentials, and management incentives, and the utilization of interest rates.)

Since December 1964, when Kenya became a republic, it has been convincingly demonstrated that African Socialism is appropriate for our developing society. In the hard arena of public affairs, where facts count for more than opinions, it has proved successful. But above all, in my view, it has provided purposeful inspiration. There is an ingrained sense of mutual endeavour and concern within African society, and from this has come a dedication, not to any ideology or to any absurd ambition for aggrandisement and power, but to the welfare of mankind.

It is possible to sound hypocritical when uttering such words.

There is too much grubbiness in any country to allow it to claim a halo. But I do observe that, here in Kenya, our goals and principles have given fresh heart to many men and a sense of self-respect to whole communities. On the world stage, Kenya is a single small state, though perhaps one with growing prestige. Yet I sometimes wonder if more powerful nations might not—with some advantage to their people—just glance at Kenya and ponder all that we have set in train.

THE DANGERS OF TRIBALISM

There is no denying that advanced and long-established nations have their problems. Any objective study of history since 1870—and indeed of contemporary newspapers—must indicate that this is so. But I doubt whether these problems are as volatile as those of the new and developing states. Within rational limits, it is possible in advanced countries to take a few fundamentals for granted. This would almost always be disastrous under African conditions, although it may be hoped that, with the passage of time, greater stability will develop.

No African leader can afford to regard his country's unity as

Traditional dance group celebrating independence: Every man has the right to take pride in the culture and customs of his tribe.

JOHN MOSS FROM BLACK STAR

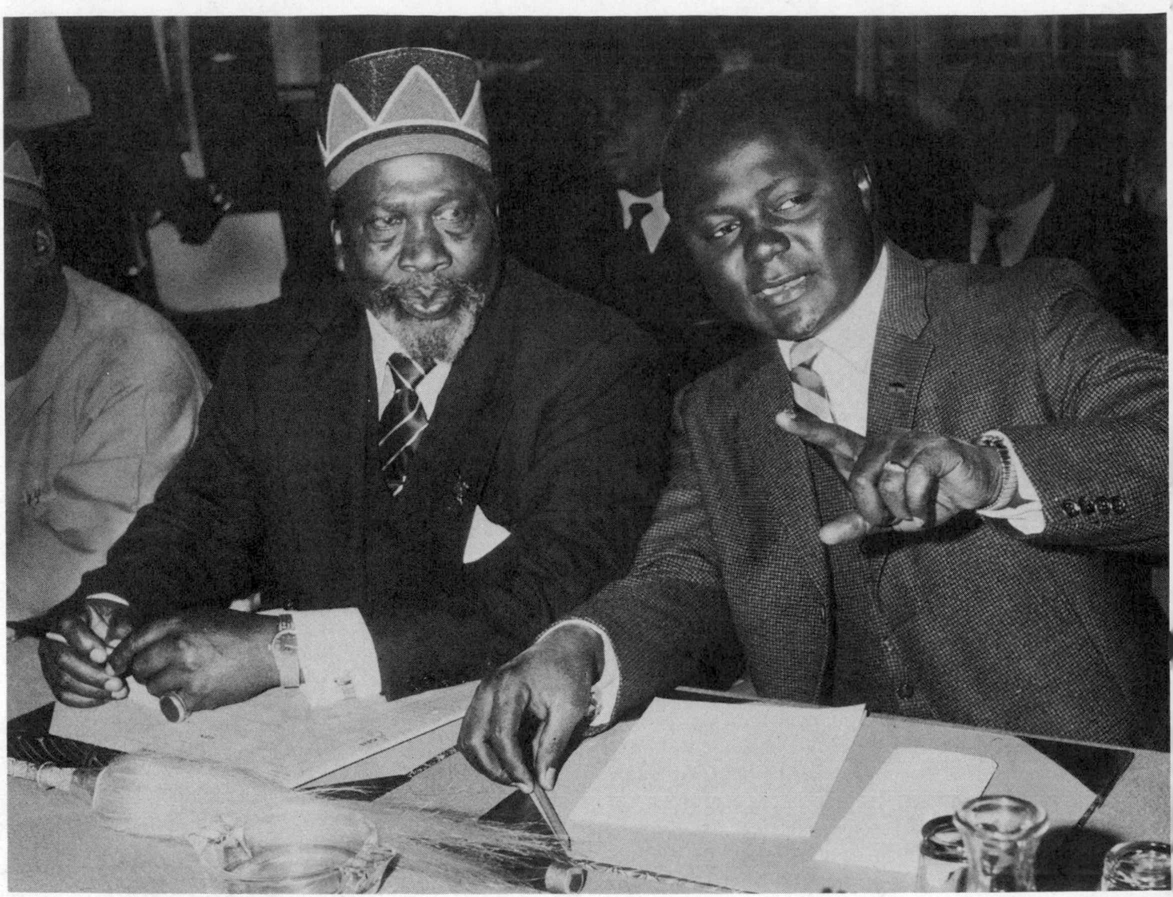

With the minister of economic planning, Tom Mboya: The whole purpose of economic development must be to produce the substance underlying the ideals of society.
KEYSTONE

necessarily enduring. On the contrary, the more entrenched national unity becomes, the more furious and inventive may be the agencies that seek to undermine it. We have had to face the fact that, outside Kenya, there are individuals and institutions hostile toward the perpetuation, under an African government, of good order and social progress in a country of measurable strategic and economic significance. Sometimes by subtle means, but more often as a cash transaction, they have recruited men who were prepared to forsake patriotism for dreams of power or profit. Internally there have also been forces of disunity, aroused or propagated by those who will always be tribalists at heart.

Anyone who has studied my speeches over the years will find that I have continually exhorted Kenya's people to preserve the strength and fervour of national unity at all costs. This has not been for lack of anything fresh to say, but because it is so essential to prevent complacency, to point out the dangers of foreign ideological ambitions and the weakness—even wickedness—of tribalism. Both influences have been present in Kenya. Only constant vigilance can guard against them.

Tribalism is sometimes described as the most dangerous, or at any rate the most explosive, of all the political perils besetting independent Africa. I would not wholly agree with such an assessment, partly because I have encountered fallacies in so many generalizations and partly because tribalism will respond—is already responding—to the cures of education and maturity. But let there be no illusions about the fact that, even today in Kenya, tribal thinking and tribal emotions can and do represent a frequent nagging distraction, an obstinate undercurrent of resentment and disaffection, and a potential danger. This must be both accepted and analyzed.

Before proceeding, however, I must make it plain that lessons drawn in or from Kenya may or may not have bearing on the problems of other states. Ghana, Tanzania, Somalia, the Congo, Uganda, Zambia, Nigeria, Malawi, and many other new nations have much in common with Kenya, many experiences and urges and hazards that we share. Yet, because of differences in historical background, geographic location, ethnic composition, or natural resources, or in nuances of political or social development, neither tribalism nor any other question can be treated as though the same truths apply to all alike.

In Kenya we take the view that every man, to the extent that he feels inclined, has every right to take some pride and interest in the culture and the customs of his tribe. There is encouragement for healthy outward expression of tribal or regional roots—as indeed there is in almost any free nation—through such obvious means as welfare societies, social clubs, or football teams. But all this is far removed from the exploitation of tribalism for political ends.

Even in the British House of Commons, with its procedural background of more than 700 years, childish interventions in debate are not unknown. Therefore, the occasional emergence of ugly petulance in the National Assembly of Kenya should not seem too disheartening or bizarre. When this occurs, it is usually directed at the alleged predominance, at executive levels throughout public life, of members of one certain tribe. Even the most superficial students of Kenya could give this tribe its name, but our purposes will be served adequately by calling it tribe X.

The commonest artillery of tribalism in Kenya is to complain that these X people enjoy undue privileges or powers, within almost every walk of life. Such allegations blink at every fact of Kenya's history. It is a fact that, for a whole generation preceding *Uhuru,* tribe X as an entity and its members as individuals battled for and seized access to educational facilities, both locally and overseas, on a scale that was unknown to other groups. Inevitably, in the early years of our development, these better prepared persons formed the higher cadres of employees and executives, in both the public and the private sectors. Our country could hardly have been allowed to stagnate while we waited for everyone, in every tribe and from every area, to become equally well equipped. Kenya was, in fact, fortunate to have so many persons, irrespective of their origins, who were available and ready to carry the national burden. But there is nothing harder to stem than jealousy, and there are none so blind as those who will not see.

It is grotesque to regard the prominence of any X factor in the conduct of affairs as evidence of deliberate tribalism, especially since it is being constantly diluted by the welcome emergence of more Y and Z participants. Furthermore, since December 1963 Kenya has been building a whole new social fabric. Access to education, from the primary to the postgraduate level, has been provided and assisted throughout the country. No community or area has been neglected. By the middle of the 1970s, or even earlier, men of every tribe will have had ample opportunity to become academically equal to all others, and all will be able to enter rewarding service over the whole spectrum of national need.

Beyond this, however, there are clearly some elements of tribalism that merit the attention of psychiatry. Some of the most fanatic tribalists in our midst are those who find that the world is too much for them. It is not always sufficiently appreciated that industrial and political changes that took shape over nearly two centuries in the older nations have been crammed into 20 years in Africa. Thus, Kenya's rapid and recent emergence as a modern nation has brought transformations—in opportunity and outlook—to which the real tribalists cannot adjust.

Subject to learned opinion, it seems to me that such men are human residue—refugees perhaps—bewildered and unbalanced by the sheer vigour of the progress going on around them. They cling to tribalism not as a tactic, but because they are in need of refuge. Nationhood is too great a concept for them to picture or pursue, and they are driven to reach back into the womb of the past, seeking the protection of the old tribal associations in a misplaced and frantic effort to keep the modern world at bay.

Symptoms of this illness may also be exhibited by those who find themselves struggling for political survival. Fear of losing a parliamentary seat, for example, can lead to a more vicious use of tribalism. Demands, allegations, and irresponsible threats may rise to a hysterical pitch, and the search for advantage or priority for some community or area may become totally divorced from the realities of the area's resources or from sane planning. At the opposite end of the scale, it is not unknown in Africa for a tribal group to attempt to obtain a monopoly over some natural asset that happens to be located in its area. In such a case, the advocates of tribalism, inspired by greed, assault the legitimacy of nationhood while, at the same time, needing and continuing to expect the security and services that only the nation can provide.

In the political context of Kenya, tribalism has been used not merely for self-preservation but as a deliberate part of political strategy. This is the point at which tolerance must be reinforced by strength and political liberties must be measured against the consequences of disaffection. Before strength is brought to bear, however, it must be remembered that while the poison of tribalism may be the first and most obvious weapon used by Kenya's enemies, it is also their last resort and thus a measure of their impotence.

I must repeat that only time will provide the full answer to this problem. Among Kenya's younger men and women especially, what we call the *Harambee* ("pulling together") spirit of nation

Aerial view of Nairobi: There is an enduring myth that Africa is still a place of raw jungles, savage deserts, and primitive tribes.

MOHAMED AMIN FROM KEYSTONE

building is already becoming deeply ingrained. The concept that we are all Kenyans together has rooted and must surely flower. When that happens, I am convinced, tribal arts and cultures will continue to be respected but tribalism as a malady will disappear.

FOREIGN POLICY AND NONALIGNMENT

The fundamental foreign policy of my government is quite easy to define: it rests on the firm belief that international relations ought to be conducted in accordance with the principles of the United Nations Charter. The phrase "ought to be" is employed because Kenya is not naïve enough to anticipate perfection in world society, or to feel unduly aggrieved by its lack. Today the vast majority of smaller nations would gladly subscribe to some codified system of governing international affairs. It is the larger powers, who were principally responsible for the design of the present UN system, that have consistently flouted its most basic provisions. But this does not affect our own conviction that Kenya's foreign policy will be—and world foreign policy should be—rooted in the Charter.

The ideas and purposes implicit in the Charter have the simplicity of greatness. What finer aims could there be than those of enshrining the dignity of man and preserving human rights? No better methods, in pursuit of these objectives, could ever be devised than those stated: to recognize the equality and respect the integrity of member nations; to champion justice under international law; to instill respect for freely entered obligations; and to use world resources in science and technology to combat poverty, illiteracy, sickness, and malnutrition.

Kenya's attitude to the many explosive situations that threaten international peace and security today also springs from the Charter. All member nations are solemnly obliged to settle international disputes by peaceful means, and to refrain from the use or even the threat of force against the territorial integrity and political independence of other states. What more does mankind need?

Yet, despite the wisdom and propriety of these declarations and despite all that mankind has suffered and accomplished, the continuing saga of humanity is still besmirched by nations at war with one another; by appalling disparities between affluence and misery; by smoldering concepts of conquest and occupation; and by violations—often wanton and shameless—of fundamental human rights. Man is a complex animal, sufficiently talented to draw up human commandments approaching the perfection of those that are divine, and yet seemingly incapable of inspiring or contriving any meaningful adherence to their terms.

Of course, day-to-day foreign policy cannot be conducted in the stratosphere of principle or theory. Definite measures have to be taken. In our case, these are built on nonalignment, not as a slogan but as a practical, working policy. A young, developing country must know and must make clear where it stands. From the time of independence, Kenya has been determined not to exchange one form of dominance for another. We have welcomed genuine friendship from any quarter, while having little but contempt for tactical ingratiation. We have responded to all sincere offers of cooperation and assistance, while rebuffing all attempts—however subtle—at blackmail or purchase. I have always told the people that it is better to be poor and free than to be wealthy but kept on a string.

We have never been anything so ordinary as "pro-left" or "pro-right." It is natural that Kenya should detest imperialism, and should associate the whole apparatus of colonialism principally with the West. But it would be absurd if, as an independent and nonaligned country, we were to shrink from maintaining or even enhancing cordial relations with Western countries, on a sensible and satisfying basis of mutual cooperation. At the same time, we have placed no ideological barriers on the flow of trade, and this has meant exploring and opening up new relations with many Eastern countries. But we have never tried to delude ourselves that there is no danger of imperialism—although of a different kind—from the East. Indeed, designs upon Africa—ideological, strategic, and economic—have emanated at least as much from the East as from the West. Alive to all this, we have nonetheless studied the practical working of both socioeconomic systems. If we have adopted some economic techniques from the East, it is not because we necessarily approve of that bloc's policies. Similarly, though we have perpetuated some Western ideas, we should not be simplistically regarded as pro-West.

Political nonalignment in Kenya does not imply any refusal to participate in world affairs, but it does embody a deliberate avoidance of any satellite relationship. Two or three examples here might be useful.

We believe, for instance, that the invasion of Czechoslovakia

Kenyan soldier trains his gun on the Somali border: At times, the relations between Kenya and Somalia have been seriously disturbed.

KEYSTONE

by its Warsaw Pact allies was a clear violation of the sovereignty, political independence, and territorial integrity of that country. It was, in fact, an unpleasant reminder to small states that embarking on a close association with one of the greater powers can turn out to be a hazardous adventure. This whole distressing event tended to undermine further our confidence in the motives of the superpowers, and offered yet another cause for disappointment in the effectiveness of the United Nations Charter.

We have held quite definite opinions on the always dangerous Middle East. As a sovereign member of the United Nations, the State of Israel enjoys the right to exist. We do not appreciate the attitude of permanent belligerency now maintained against Israel by some of its Arab neighbours, and we fervently hope that Israel will be permitted to settle down to a peaceful and constructive existence. On the other hand, my government cannot and will not support the further occupation by Israel of Arab territory brought under its control during the Six-Day War of 1967. The language of the Charter is clear on the question of territorial aggrandisement, and the road to peace does not lie through this occupation of Arab lands.

Kenya has always felt that the war in Vietnam should be condemned as reflecting the arrogance of a big power interfering with and imposing its will upon a smaller country without provocation. This has also been a futile conflict, in which the mighty cannot hope to win through to any conclusion, while the suffering of the Vietnamese people has been senselessly prolonged. In this instance, ideological ambitions have been placed above respect for human life, and a false—almost perverted—sense of national prestige has overridden common sense.

We do not subscribe to any policy of "containing" Communism through the barrel of a gun. Equally, we would condemn any policy seeking to spread Communism through the barrel of a gun. For one thing, both such endeavours must be in gross violation of the Charter. Furthermore, long experience in public affairs has taught me that "solutions" imposed by force of arms will never be permanent, but will merely sow the seeds of conflict.

Finally, I would like to say something about the Commonwealth of Nations. This is a body embracing some 800 million people, or more than a quarter of the world's population. It has real potential for good, but (inevitably) many limitations. It is not held together by any formal treaty obligations, and it has no statutory powers. Its nations and peoples have established a voluntary association, in which they can seek ways of cooperating for the benefit of all and through which they may try to exert some positive influence in world affairs. Sometimes it is impossible for the Commonwealth to take any decisive line on a given issue because its very structure ensures the inclusion of different points of view. There have been moments, notably in regard to Rhodesia, when doors seemed to be closing on the whole idea of a multiracial Commonwealth. In time, however, the Commonwealth generally manages to return to the principles that give it meaning, and I am sure it does no harm for emotions, aroused in times of stress, to be measured against fundamental codes of worthwhile human behaviour.

ECONOMIC APPROACHES—AND SOME PROBLEMS

The whole purpose of economic development must be to produce the substance that will give material form to the ideals of a society. This conception, in Kenya, has strengthened our resolve as we have come to grips with reality.

At the moment a nation achieves independence there is a need for many economic changes, and these must be set in motion without delay. In our case, three such changes seemed to be critical: the countrywide and coordinated transition from a partially subsistence to a wholly monetary economy; an accelerating transition from total dependence on agriculture to a more balanced national development; and a transition, both structural and psychological, from exploitation of our resources for the benefit of others to full use and conservation of these resources to serve human advancement in Kenya.

KEYSTONE

Refugees displaced by border warfare: The young, developing countries of Africa must strive toward solving their problems as members of the same African family.

By the time Kenya had become a republic, some of its basic economic problems could be more closely defined. Our chief concerns at that point were: the redistribution and rapid development of all agricultural land; conservation and utilization, along modern lines, of our vital natural resources; establishment of a basis for the eventual rapid growth of industry and business; attracting capital both domestically and from abroad and designing means to employ this capital in the most socially desirable ways; modifying the tax structure in the interests of equity; guarding (and increasing where possible) reserves of foreign exchange; providing for fuller participation by Africans in an expanding total economy; relieving unemployment and eliminating underemployment; and reconciling the immediate pressures for expanding welfare projects with the need to begin productive endeavours that would yield the wherewithal for future social progress. All this required controls and mechanisms that never existed in Kenya before. Accordingly, we established, within the republican government, an appropriately equipped ministry to design and to issue economic surveys and national development plans.

We were clear in our minds that it was better to move toward economic advancement along flexible rather than doctrinaire lines. We thus determined to permit and encourage various techniques of production and different forms of ownership—state, corporate, cooperative, and individual. My aim from the begin-

JOHN MOSS FROM BLACK STAR

Handing out title deeds to property: Independence creates the need to reconcile traditions with the rigours of modern monetary economy. The million-acre land resettlement program accommodated more than 33,000 families on land bought from former European occupiers.

ning was to create a mixed economy. It was neither practical nor desirable for the government and the public sector to undertake everything that needed to be done, nor was it practical or desirable for private enterprise to bear the whole burden. Each must have its role.

Another issue that had to be confronted was taxation policy. We needed to find means and levels of tax collection that would translate equitable fractions of private savings into public savings and that would conserve and utilize these for the development of the nation and the welfare of the people. Note was taken of the experience of some Western countries, where large individual accumulations of wealth had been amassed before progressive taxes were introduced or—more recently—capital gains were permitted to go untaxed. In conformity with a particular principle of African Socialism, we were determined that taxation measures, while not removing incentive, would make it difficult for those with existing wealth simply to sit back and become more wealthy.

During the initial planning stages, and occasionally since then, my attention has been drawn to the theory that nationalization can resolve all economic and human ills. Some of the advocates of almost-exclusive public ownership have produced arguments that, though flawed, are at least closely reasoned and sincere. The majority, however, have been swept along by slogans without really understanding the issue or the consequences. They think of nationalization as a kind of economic aspirin, guaranteed to clear up all headaches in an hour.

I am not convinced of this myself. If a nation has a limited quantity of public capital, it can of course be employed for the purchase—from others—of existing assets. These assets would then have been nationalized. But how would it benefit Kenya to allocate its severely strained resources in this way? The only change would be in ownership. The country would have no more productive assets than it had before. If I were to tell our urban unemployed, or our struggling families in the countryside, that the government had nationalized some particular industry or company or financial institution, I would not expect them to be filled with joy. Such an action would mean little to them, and would have no beneficial effect on their daily lives.

To carry the argument further, tying up the country's capital in this manner would prevent its use in new enterprises that could have opened up new employment opportunities and provided additional output. It is very probable that the money paid as compensation for nationalized resources, and the people who managed them before nationalization, would leave the country, which would not be of much assistance to us in meeting shortages of skilled manpower or foreign exchange. And it is almost certain that unthinking nationalization would discourage additional private investment.

Nationalization can never be ruled out altogether in a young and developing country, but it should be exercised only when there is a distinctive and clearly attainable social (or even political) objective. There can be a case for nationalization and complete (or at least majority) public ownership when a vital public service has to be provided as part of the government's national responsibility. There can be a case, perhaps, when the need for some particular development is urgent and when its scale is such that private enterprise is reluctant or unable to undertake it. There may be a case when some social objective is being pursued and controls aimed at securing this objective have proved ineffective or unworkable. On balance, however, transfer of existing assets can never be as rewarding as the productive exploitation of new assets. I am convinced that haphazard nationalization has nothing of the vibrancy and continuing promise of voluntary partnership and all-round participation, embracing the government, the private sector, and the people.

All young men and women come to discover, when they go out into the world, that freedom from past controls also means freedom to pay the bills. Much the same applies to a newly emergent state. Along with its other problems in the years that followed independence, Kenya had to establish and maintain overseas diplomatic missions. We had to pay for our admission to the World Bank and the International Monetary Fund. And of course we have had to carry our own defense expenditure, a heavy burden for such a young country.

The winning of independence does not necessarily deprive a country in good standing of the possibility of grants or of access to international loans. But my government and I took the line that, for *Uhuru* to be meaningful, Kenya must aim toward the greatest possible degree of self-sufficiency. We proceeded on the assumption that all recurrent expenditure induced by development, and the greater part of development expenditure itself, should be met from wealth generated through the country's own productive capacity and savings.

By 1965 Kenya was managing to meet all recurrent expenditure from internal resources. Nevertheless, difficult issues of priority have persisted. We have had to weigh stepping up development expenditure against sacrificing further improvements in recurrent services. We have had to consider budgeting reductions in some development targets in order to complete some recurrent-cost objectives. Most of all, we have had to maintain the impetus of national development while facing up to the limitations imposed by recurrent expenditures.

Obviously, there is much more to economic development than

financial planning. We had to embark upon surveys and make long-term assessments of our material resources. Above all, we had to prepare our people for the tasks ahead. Over the years, we have established many new or redesigned institutions, providing technical and vocational training suitable for all types of employment. Concurrently, through training and loan schemes, we have set out to expand and modernize such primary industries as fishing and commercial forestry. All these endeavours, so tragically neglected in the past, are critical ingredients of economic mobilization.

Despite every effort, a young and developing state will go through an inevitable phase in which there is a troublesome degree of unemployment. The causes and factors involved are complex, but it would seem that some unemployment is one of the interim consequences of planned economic and social advancement. The modernization of agriculture, for example, requires some replacement of human labour by machines. But if the process is pursued, a stage will be reached when more intensive working of the land becomes both possible and profitable, creating fresh demands for both skilled and unskilled labour and opening up new opportunities in the agricultural servicing and processing industries. Virtually a new kind of rural economy then comes into being, supported by such improved rural amenities as better housing, schools, health services, water supplies, roads, and electric power. Kenya is entering this rewarding phase now.

Parallels—albeit inexact ones—can be drawn in other fields. It takes a good deal of time to establish an industrial sector of the economy or to build up the flow of tourism, but there comes a moment when the effort will be repaid by abundant opportunity. Rarely can any proposition in economics be expressed in an unqualified manner, but it seems quite certain that an expanding economy is the only effective answer to unemployment. More of Kenya's people are in paid employment—or successful self-employment—today than ever before. Substantial unemployment has persisted, but our whole economy is on the move. We can look to this rapid economic expansion for the answers to many of our problems: the alleviation of unemployment; optimum africanization in all fields; further development of education and welfare services; ambitious district and provincial programs.

It is important that we do all this for ourselves. The Republic of Kenya will never go into the world as a beggar. From the very beginning, the dignity and self-respect of our people have been symbolized by massive achievements in self-help and community-development schemes. Certainly we still need and welcome financial and technical aid from elsewhere, but we have never wanted to be spoon-fed. As we progress further, external aid will merely supplement the labour and the readiness to sacrifice that we ourselves provide.

It must be noted, however, that while we can regulate the negotiation and the use of assistance, we can do nothing about the fact that Kenya's economy is substantially dependent on the world economy as a whole. We have suffered, over the past few years, from shock waves produced by economic setbacks in the major industrial countries and by balance of payments difficulties affecting the principal reserve currencies. The closing of the Suez Canal in 1967 was a significant blow to Kenya. And while the climate of world trade improved in 1968, export prices for our products were generally lower following devaluation of the pound sterling.

Today Kenya has a vigorous economy, but national development must still be sparked by expanding sales of our agricultural output on the world market. Here we confront what amounts to sheer international absurdity. World trade patterns are still based on the futile premise that the prices of all primary products should be kept low and unstable while the prices of capital goods and heavy manufactures from the advanced countries are permitted to rise. This statement can be demonstrated statistically. Over the four-year period 1964–67, the price index for Kenyan exports fell from 100 to 89, while the index for our imports rose from 100 to 105. Kenya confronts falling prices for coffee, tea, sisal, dairy products, meat, maize [corn], and wheat. We are competing with industrialized countries that subsidize their own agriculture—and their agricultural exports—to the point of economic fantasy. And we are faced with the need to alter established trade patterns and tastes, as well as the threat that synthetics will replace sundry food and industrial products.

Kenya is not so naïve as to expect global economic planning, at least in the immediate future. We understand that there will be self-interest and intrigue and ruthless bargaining. Given a fair battlefield on which to fight this economic war, we could —and assuredly would—make our growing presence felt. But under the present system of world price structures, we are expected to enter the battle knowing that the available arms are already monopolized by the enemy.

All our endeavours to diversify the economy, to step up production, to increase productivity, to train and employ more people—all these could come to nought under an international com-

Processing coffee beans: Agriculture is a living craft in which three out of every four of Kenya's families are currently engaged.

AUTHENTICATED NEWS INTERNATIONAL

mercial system based on the shortsighted entrenchment of economic privilege; obsession with profit and self-preservation; and the utter indifference of the overwhelming mass of people in advanced nations toward the young and developing states. Perhaps, one day, the world will crash through this selfishness barrier and enter an era where reality more closely approximates morality, to the practical benefit of all men. It would be no more than just for Kenya's people, after their tremendous endeavours, to reap hard-won rewards in such an environment. As a challenge for mankind, I would rate this as more deeply significant than any excursion into outer space.

AGRICULTURE: LIFEBLOOD OF THE ECONOMY

Much of the injustice—and the resulting unrest—that characterized Kenya in the decades before independence arose over the problem of land. The historical background of the land question is on public record, and it would be impossible as well as unnecessary to summarize it here. What became vital, at independence, was to clarify and then modernize various traditions and ideas on the subject.

Before the advent of the Europeans, there was really no such thing as individual, absolute ownership of land. All land, in an important sense, was tribally owned, and the ultimate right to dispose of it was a matter of tribal concern. Rights to use the available land were, in effect, assigned in perpetuity to various groups within the tribe, subject to the conditions that such resources be properly used and that benefits arising from their use be appropriately distributed. There were built-in safeguards in this system against the possibilities that land would be left idle or would be flagrantly abused, or that benefits from land would be selfishly hoarded. Thus, the rights normally associated with ownership in most Western countries had little if any counterpart in African society.

Independence created the need to reconcile African traditions with the rigours of a modern monetary economy. The new Kenya was obliged to retain—and has retained successfully—the essential stake of African society in the productive resource of land. But it was also necessary to make the ownership of land more explicit if consolidation and planned development were to be carried out. There had to be a form of land ownership that could be legally recognized by the state. Another factor was that development and investment projects required the operation of a credit system, and this in turn required an orderly system of land titles and their registration.

This was one part of the problem. The other basic question concerning land ownership involved the restoration to African hands of substantial areas of the best land in Kenya which (in the African if not the European view) had been stolen and locked away from the African society. It would have been possible, in terms of the power vested in my government, to correct this situation by brigandage, but this would have violated Kenya's attachment to the rule of law. Ignoring questions of value and compensation would merely have answered past injustice with fresh injustice, and this was no answer at all. And, matters of principle aside, it was vital to bring about the transfer in a manner that would not endanger the productivity of the land involved.

Our "million-acre" land resettlement program was virtually completed by mid-1968. It involved no less than 127 individual settlement schemes in various parts of the country, accommodating more than 33,000 families on land bought at fair prices from the former European occupiers. This basic project has been supplemented by other smaller schemes tailored to the circumstances of individual areas or groups—a further 110,000 ac. has recently been made available for settlement of needy families—and by programs involving the transfer of entire large-scale farms to African ownership, whether individual, corporate, or cooperative. It is not correct to say that the entire land resettlement program was politically motivated, although without such an undertaking the political fortunes of the first independent government might possibly have waned. In the event, there was no conflict between government and people over basic necessities, including the need to consider economic as well as social imperatives.

It was vital, in the early years, to correct injustice. That was what the government was for. Something had to be done for the tens of thousands of our people who were landless, unemployed, and almost without hope. But when the principal phases of this massive operation had been completed, the question arose: how shall we continue? Should further large sums of money be spent on settlement projects, or should this money be used for land consolidation, survey and registration of titles, and agrarian development in the former "African areas"? We decided on the second approach, on the grounds that it would increase productivity and output on five times as many acres as the first, and would benefit five times as many African families.

All Kenya's plans for the future were dependent on our ability to obtain maximum production from the land. The core of the KANU manifesto had been the need for a dynamic breakthrough in farming methods in order to finance welfare services for the people. Though it is difficult to measure such things with precision, indications are that at independence one farmer could produce approximately enough food for five persons. In some advanced countries, a single farmer can produce enough to feed himself and 40 others. Our first priority, therefore, was to launch the country on an agrarian revolution, using capital and machinery, modern methods of cultivation, irrigation projects, better seed and better livestock, all supplemented by harder and more skillfully applied work. Today, although there is still some distance to go, Kenyan agriculture has become a far more scientific and successful enterprise. In 1968, the last year for which complete figures are available, gross receipts to farmers in Kenya reached a record £71 million, 5% higher than in the preceding year. One of the most satisfying aspects of this is that more than

Picking tea on a Kericho plantation: One of the most remarkable features of agrarian impulse has been seen in the production of tea, which accounted for 14% of Kenya's gross marketed production in 1968.

AUTHENTICATED NEWS INTERNATIONAL

half of Kenya's gross marketed production (*i.e.*, over and above subsistence) now comes from the small-farm sector.

Our country has a total land area of 142 million ac. This sounds extensive, but in actuality only some 12% of the total is high-potential agricultural land, with sufficient rainfall to support the practices of modern husbandry. Something like 6% is of medium potential, with rainfall that is less abundant and often unreliable. Approximately 73%, including vast areas of arid bush or scrub interspersed with bare plains or semidesert, has to be classified as low-potential land. The remaining 9%, made up of mountains, forest, swamp, or desert, has no agrarian value.

On the face of it, such proportions may seem depressing. Certainly they make our agricultural advances all the more creditable. Three out of every four Kenyan families are currently engaged in agriculture. As a result of their efforts, the annual output of agriculture has increased by more than £20 million since 1963, and something like 60% of our net export earnings have come from agricultural products. Over the period 1967–68, our only substantial nonagricultural exports were petroleum products, soda ash, cement, and—less important but still significant—wood carvings and metal scrap. The predominance of agriculture within Kenya's economy is further demonstrated by the fact that in years of low agricultural income—usually resulting from adverse weather or from a fall in export prices—economic expansion as a whole is correspondingly low.

Later on, I shall discuss diversification of agriculture in some detail. Suffice it to say here that a breakdown of Kenya's gross marketed production indicates that our agrarian sector is already distinguished by variety. High-quality coffee, from small farms as well as from estates, still accounted for 18% of the whole in 1968. Next came slaughter cattle at 17%, reflecting the great expansion of modernized livestock production that has been under way. Also remarkable is the increase in tea production, both on plantations and within the massive smallholder project: tea in 1968 accounted for 14% of the total. Production of wheat and dairy products, backbones of the mixed-farming sector in high-potential areas, each accounted for 9% of marketed output. Maize followed closely with 8%; pyrethrum with 4%; and sugar production—now rapidly expanding following the establishment of two new factories—with 3%. Commodities accounting for at least 1% included such traditional items as cotton, sisal, oilseeds, pulses, wattle, hides and skins, slaughter sheep, wool, pigs, and coconuts, as well as such new and swiftly expanding products as rice, cashew nuts, pineapples (for canning), other fruits and vegetables, and even flowers.

A final point about agriculture concerns the duty of any government to provide for and safeguard the country's food supplies. Basically, in Kenya, this means maize. At independence our nation faced an ever-present threat of famine, and a drought year meant the need for emergency imports or relief supplies. This situation has been wholly remedied, largely as the result of a technological breakthrough in the development of high-yielding hybrid maize. In 1968 some 250,000 tons of maize, surplus to domestic requirements, were exported.

This was not an unmixed blessing, however. The price structure for our farmers is kept as high as we can afford. Therefore, the exported maize had to be subsidized by the government, which purchased it from the growers, through the Marketing Board, at a price exceeding export parity. Nevertheless, it is our belief that maize production for export can be expanded on an economic basis. With this in mind, a bulk handling system, calculated to reduce costs significantly, has been designed and will shortly be installed, and railway rolling stock suitable for cheap and rapid movement to Mombasa will be introduced.

INDUSTRY AND COMMERCE

It is often difficult for financially powerful nations—like the United States and West Germany—to appreciate the economic limitations that can frustrate a young and developing country. Distinguished visitors have sometimes asked me why Kenya

has not undertaken certain economic projects, or why we have not pursued certain aspects of development more rapidly. The only answer I could give is the truth: we have had no option but to proceed on a course of sternly selected priorities, understanding full well that postponement or piecemeal programming of many desirable but less urgent projects is inevitable.

As soon as possible, a country such as Kenya must begin to build an industrial sector on a scale never before envisaged. This sector is needed to provide the final touch to the processes of modernization; to intensify the generation of economic strength and savings; to afford a proper balance for the national economy; and to create employment opportunities, both for trained men and for unskilled labour.

Now well into the second half of its first decade of autonomy, Kenya can and must turn more of its attention toward industrialization and commercial enterprise. We have gained a great deal of experience in the past few years, and have established a number of basic facilities. There seems little doubt that, over the next five years, a great upsurge of industrialization can result if

AUTHENTICATED NEWS INTERNATIONAL

Training program for printers: Foreign investors must provide training facilities for Africans to equip them for service at every level.

the same imaginative effort and public zeal is applied to it that in the past has been applied to agriculture.

To some degree, this process has already begun. In 1967–68, for example, investment in manufacturing industry exceeded the total annual investment in agriculture for the first time. Meanwhile, however, higher levels of domestic income have brought an increasing demand for consumer goods—clothing, radios, chemicals, and the like—that cannot be satisfied by local industries. As a result, imports of such items, which contribute nothing to national economic development, have tended to rise.

Before there can be industrialization, there must be what is called an infrastructure. One element of this is access to abundant and economical power. Kenya is attempting to meet this requirement, and we have already proceeded well beyond the first phase of the large-scale Tana River hydroelectric scheme. This project is part of a national power development plan, for the period up to 1985, based on a total investment of some £250 million.

There is still a lively possibility that oil will be discovered

somewhere in the northeastern sector of Kenya. Active prospecting has continued for some time, and six or seven major holes have been drilled, with findings promising enough to justify further exploration. It would be gratifying to achieve success overnight, but those who are despondent about oil exploration in Kenya might recall that, in Nigeria, intensive drilling continued for 19 years before major deposits were finally found.

So many aspects of economic development depend on good communications. Since *Uhuru,* we have had an immense backlog to make up. By 1968 the old vehicle-breaking dust bath between Nairobi and Mombasa had been replaced by a full tarmac highway, and the last stretches of the international road links with Tanzania and Uganda will soon be brought up to tarmac standard. A new road linking Nairobi with Addis Ababa, Eth., started from both ends, is progressing rapidly. Other major road programs, dependent on access to international finance, are being concentrated on the tea-growing, sugar-growing, and tourist areas.

This infrastructure of roads is supported by long-established railway services—now being modernized—that thread the most productive areas of the country. Mombasa, the greatest port on the eastern coast of Africa, is thus serviced by both road and rail. We found at an early stage that the port facilities at Mombasa would be inadequate to meet our potential trade and traffic needs. Major construction work, including the building of two new deepwater berths, has accordingly been carried out.

The international airport in Nairobi will soon be enlarged significantly, and the Mombasa airport is to be brought up to international standards. Nor have we neglected the need for a network of internal air communications for both passengers and freight. In addition, we are operating a satellite communications system from Nairobi, using the most modern equipment in Africa. Within the past six years, Nairobi has emerged as a commercial and conference centre of world renown.

One of the most important single industrial developments in Kenya has been the siting and operation of the oil refinery at Mombasa. The cement industry, the largest individual user of

KEYSTONE

Grazing elephants: Perhaps nowhere else is there this juxtaposition of 20th-century resources and facilities with such easy access to the pristine thrills of Africa.

electric power in the country, can also be singled out as a major enterprise. In addition, installations exist or have been approved for such industries as vehicle assembly, textiles and clothing of all kinds, brewing, fertilizers, canning of many products, sugar refining, pulp and paper manufacture, chemicals, soap, plastics, electrical engineering, hydraulic equipment, glassware, blankets, grain milling, light bulbs, razor blades, and matches. A notable sign of Kenya's economic buoyancy has been the building boom that we have experienced over the past two or three years.

All these endeavours may be described as the fruits of independence, since before 1963 there was a great reluctance to invest in Kenya on any scale. They may also be considered as the forerunners of an industrial upsurge in Kenya for which there is ample scope and abundant need and which can be served by the exertions of both public and private enterprise.

In the field of public undertaking, my government created, at a fairly early stage, the Development Finance Company of Kenya and the Industrial and Commercial Development Corporation. With slightly different structures and different briefs in terms of scale and sphere of operations, these complementary institutions have become important channels of government participation in industrial projects, in partnership with private capital. Under their own aegis, these two bodies have also launched and financed —or in many cases have assisted through loans or shareholding —business and industrial enterprises of all kinds and sizes, including what we call "industrial estates." Throughout, there has been a clear emphasis on the fullest initiative and participation by the African people.

This, of course, must be a vital consideration. Independence holds no meaning if the economy continues to be almost wholly activated by foreign capital and personnel. We have always made it clear that industrial investment from overseas is both valuable and welcome. Legislation has been passed to encourage and protect external capital and enterprise. But foreign investors are expected to understand and comply with the spirit of mutual social responsibility that is so much a part of our African tradition. They should—indeed, they must—give expression to this spirit by making shares available to willing African buyers; by employing Africans in managerial posts whenever suitably qualified persons can be found; and by providing training facilities for Africans to equip them for service in posts at all technical and executive levels.

My government is determined that Africans must be fully integrated into the commercial and industrial life of the nation. The keywords here, however, are discretion and sanity. There would be no point in shock tactics or ill-considered regulations that could damage the existing or potential fabric of our national economy. Neither would facile solutions serve the purpose. The simple transfer of a business from one man to another, for instance, would not necessarily expand the business or be the best way to develop the country.

The increasing numbers of our citizens who are qualified to play a full part in our industrial and commercial life must have their rightful opportunity to do so. But there is no question of undermining the assurances and freedoms that have been given to private enterprise. To a commendable extent, the industrial and commercial communities have appreciated the government's purpose in working rapidly toward optimum africanization. Our aims will remain, but the means selected will neither discourage nor disrupt private enterprise, and will not inhibit the presence and contribution—within Kenya—of high-grade technical and executive skills.

Big game in the Rift Valley: The sustained-yield cropping of wild game is one concept with very great economic potential.

KEYSTONE

TOURISM

In most tropical countries there are problems of ecology and biological fragility, fully examined and understood only within the past 20 years, that need to be approached with the utmost care. Kenya is no exception. Especially outside the high- and medium-potential agricultural areas, special efforts are needed to avoid erosion and other forms of degradation. Of course, the land must be regarded as a productive resource, and neither national nor local interests would be served by permitting it just to lie idle. All modern techniques of scientific resource management must be considered if these arid range areas are to yield the optimum in revenue, employment, and trade.

Among these techniques, catastrophically neglected in colonial times, is the science of wildlife management. The sustained-yield cropping or ranching of wild game has great economic potential, and it has the advantage of improving, rather than endangering, the ecology of the areas where it is practiced. But the chief beneficiary of wildlife management is, of course, the tourist industry. Tourism in Kenya, based on a system of game reserves and full-scale national parks, is abundantly justifying the priority allotted to it in our planning.

In 1968 about 150,000 tourists were welcomed to Kenya, compared with about 20,000 in 1963. This does not include the 15,000 visitors who came on business, many of whom stayed on as tourists or enjoyed a safari on the side. It is confidently anticipated that, with the continuing expansion of package tours and the advent of the jumbo jets, the number of visitors will show further substantial increases. Tourism has become virtually the world's largest single industry, and Kenya has now undertaken a promotion campaign designed to capture a full share of this enterprise.

Our experience has been that people like to come to a stable and rapidly developing country in which they are treated as guests. They enjoy our climate and scenery and the vigour and good humour of our people. Many are attracted by our beautiful beaches, with their opportunities for big-game fishing (some of the best in the world) and marine sports. Others find pleasure in the mountains and the lakes. But it is the wildlife in our incomparable national parks that represents the key attraction.

Nairobi has emerged as an international centre of tourism. The attractions of our capital city and its immediate surroundings would seem to justify its secure place in the global tourist network, but apart from its own merits, Nairobi is the natural point of departure for safaris into the wildlife areas and journeys to the coast. Perhaps nowhere else on earth is there this juxtaposition of 20th-century facilities and easy access to the thrills of pristine Africa.

In terms of the national economy, the most valuable contribution of tourism is foreign exchange. In 1968 the total foreign exchange earnings from this industry amounted to more than £16 million, exceeding the sum brought in by coffee for the first time in Kenya's history. This contribution is critical to the health of our balance of payments. Our current aim is to double the 1968 figure—to £30 million annually—and to this end much is being done to improve the tourism "infrastructure," including accommodations and communications.

Tourism has other economic by-products that are not always sufficiently appreciated. Employment is a good example. When the new Intercontinental Hotel in Nairobi was opened in 1969, 500 new jobs were created immediately. Something similar will happen when the Nairobi Hilton opens for business, in or before 1970. It is difficult to give a precise figure for all the employment (direct and indirect, full-time or seasonal) that is created by tourism, but the total is very substantial. It must include, directly, employment in all the hotels in Nairobi, up-country, and at the coast; in all the safari lodges; and in the large number of travel agencies, as well as by tourist operators with their transport fleets. Indirectly, everything that tourists do and see and buy generates revenue that finances other needs and creates more employment. Tourists in such numbers represent an important market for Kenya's agriculture and for its manufacturing and service industries, again with both direct and indirect effects on employment.

EDUCATION AND MANPOWER NEEDS

Since the financial year 1963–64, in which Kenya's independence fell, expenditure initiated by the government has increased tremendously. Public outlay on the social services has risen 93%, with the greater part going to education.

In a sense, education should not be regarded as a "service." Nothing was more frustrating, in the Kenya of six years ago, than the obstructions resulting from decades of neglect in this field. It may be difficult for advanced countries to appreciate the position of a new nation when the vast majority of its people, through no fault of their own, are uneducated, largely illiterate, almost wholly unqualified for employment. Thus, we approached education not so much as a social service, but as the most gainful economic investment that the nation could make.

Even so, we have been limited in what we could do. Political opportunists have chided the government more than once for not immediately introducing "universal education," but they have never offered rational advice on how this could be managed. All thinking men realized at the outset that, since we were starting with virtually nothing, universal education would remain a dream until we could build enough schools, until teachers had been trained in sufficient numbers, until all the complex administrative machinery had been set up, and until we had generated enough wealth to provide the requisite financing. All that we could do was make steady progress along these lines. Our progress has been described by some competent observers as phenomenal.

More than one and a quarter million children in Kenya are now receiving a full seven-year course in our primary schools. That is a remarkable statistic, and it provides a solid foundation for further advances. The number of secondary schools in the country has risen from 140 to over 600, and the number of secondary-school pupils in attendance from 26,000 to approximately 102,000. About a quarter of all the children who pass their examinations for the Certificate of Primary Education are currently able to go forward into secondary schools. This is admittedly unsatisfactory, but it compares well with the situation in many other developing states. Considered in relation to Kenya's initial resources, it is something of a miracle.

The number of Kenyan students in the University of East Africa has risen, roughly, from 400 to 1,400, and a further substantial increase can be expected shortly, following the creation of new faculties and the expansion of existing departments. The number of students engaged in degree or postgraduate studies overseas has fluctuated through the years, tending to fall as local opportunities expanded. In 1966 some 4,000 Kenyan students were working in universities and colleges in nearly 20 countries,

Physical training in a centre for homeless or delinquent youth: It would be impossible to govern a society in which men were free to follow any inclination.

AUTHENTICATED NEWS INTERNATIONAL

with the greatest numbers in the United States, the United Kingdom, and the Soviet Union.

Turning back to the schools within Kenya, we first had to embark on a "crash program" of education, building up a whole system from our negligible inheritance. But as we enter this new decade, I am convinced that we must begin to place greater emphasis on quality and content and make sterner efforts to use all our resources more effectively. In principle, the high priority given to education must and will be unaffected. In practice, we must pay more attention to the training and upgrading of teachers, to the availability and standards of books and equipment, and to the reshaping of courses and curricula.

As one example of what I mean, agricultural teaching is to be included in the curricula of 30 of our secondary schools—it has already been started in 7—while other schools will offer courses in business administration or domestic science. But the word "quality" must embrace a new spirit as well as an amended content. We live now in the space age of new technology and the almost boundless capacities of science. To meet its challenge, we must sweep aside the old concept of teaching as the dreary recapitulation of outmoded facts, and invest the whole educational process with the eagerness and vitality of topical discovery. Our best teachers, in the vanguard of this kind of change, will be amply assisted. Today, for example, television receivers in Kenya may be linked, through a local system of satellite communications, to many sources of high-quality programming, suitable for visual teaching from the primary to the university level.

From the beginning, we have needed large numbers of men and women in high- and middle-level positions, and while the number of such persons has increased, the need for them has increased even more rapidly. Today, therefore, we are still suffering from grave shortages of qualified personnel: to teach in the fast-growing secondary school system; to train future teachers; to lecture in the university; to consolidate and survey land prior to registration of titles; to carry on agricultural research and man the extension services; to train farm managers and operate national farms; to manage industrial and commercial establishments (especially where government is in partnership with private enterprise); to plan and implement developments in forestry and fishing and wildlife management; to expand water supplies; to man hospitals and health centres; to engineer and construct roads and airfields and irrigation schemes; to administer the affairs of government. The list is almost endless.

This has been a very serious problem. In the earliest years, we received many generous offers from overseas in the field of social services. Concurrently, self-help and community-development schemes, all over the country, were reflecting the new creative impulse among our people. We were faced with the paradox of being able to build new schools and hospitals and health centres while having little or no hope of equipping them with qualified teachers and medical staff. The effect of manpower shortfalls has perhaps fallen most heavily on the public service, since each addition to development expenditure requires more trained persons to administer it properly. Even to seek foreign aid requires highly qualified staff to battle through the bureaucratic jungle of applications.

Engineering students learning welding: Men who have recently risen from the twin bondage of domination and frustration are now defining and demanding their rightful places and their rightful shares in the pattern of human society.

KEYSTONE

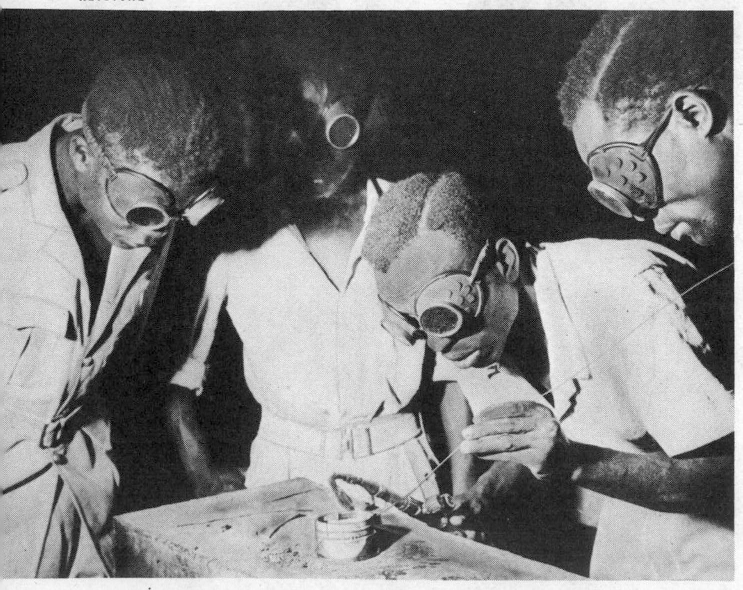

Again, there is the matter of quality. I have always advised our people that Kenya must become—in every sense—a modern state in the wider world society. In this fast-moving world, there is no future in planning or hoping, by 1980, to pass the point that advanced nations had reached in 1964. Throughout the fields of science and technology, and in every other kind of human endeavour, we must catch up and keep up, or else finally be left behind. We must have an inflexible determination to reach and contribute to international standards of skill and of leadership in every profession and craft, as some of our athletes have begun to do already.

A few more words about the public service are in order. Many factors can buttress stability within a country. Some of these touch upon political philosophies, economic policies, or progress toward social objectives. But nothing is more important, in practical terms, than the presence of a mature, impartial, and effective public service.

Certainly nothing has made me more proud, since *Uhuru,* than the solid and dedicated work of our own civil service, embracing all the centralized ministries and departments, the provincial administration, and the Kenya police. There were those who believed that abrupt africanization, up to the highest executive levels, could only lead to disaster. There were those who warned that our ambitions for rapid economic progress and for the creation in Kenya of a whole new social fabric would place too great a strain on a new and untried public service. All these fears have been confounded by the latent talent of our people and by the sense of Kenyan nationalism that has spurred them on.

Today it is possible to discern the sound beginnings of a local civil service tradition. In the first challenging years after independence, the public sector was always in the throes of change. More recently, officers and institutions have found themselves in the more satisfying position of settling down, enjoying the feel of continuity and precedent, and seeing how much, against so many odds, has really been achieved.

There has been loose talk at times about corruption in the civil service. This has undeniably occurred and has been dealt with when discovered. But it has been almost exclusively of the kind that can be described as petty corruption, and it has never been revealed on any large scale. Mankind has not yet been entirely replaced by computers, and our public service is a human machine, staffed and operated by men and women made of flesh and blood. It is unavoidable that, in such a large organization, there should be some instances of human frailty. Some officers in the junior- and medium-level ranks have not been highly educated, or have lacked opportunities for acquiring the values of more widely traveled men. If—possibly against a background of personal difficulties—they are suddenly faced with temptation, a few of them will succumb.

Perspective is the thing. The record of the Kenya Civil Service in this regard will certainly bear comparison with that of any similar institution anywhere in Africa. But even though a thousand officers may carry out responsible tasks and scrupulously handle funds, it is human nature to ignore them and to focus on the thousand-and-first officer, who has yielded to temptation. He is the man who can more easily attract the public gaze, and whose weakness causes suspicion to fall on all his colleagues.

In another field of public service, we have had to ensure that our armed forces in Kenya were so provisioned with modern apparatus that, at all times, they could meet their primary responsibility of defending the integrity of the state. We inherited a basically inadequate army and, at independence, Kenya had no air force and no navy at all. It has been necessary, therefore, to create our own armed services. We have set up a single national Defence Force with shared command and administrative services, in which all units, while mutually respecting each other's technical proficiencies, have become accustomed to planning and working as one team.

Effective control of the armed services, from the chief of defense staff downward, has now passed entirely into Kenyan hands. All branches of the Army have been fully africanized, and total africanization of the Air Force and the Navy is now within reach. This is highly creditable when one bears in mind the complex skills that our young men have had to master.

From the outset it seemed most important to me that the armed services never stand apart from the mainstream of national thought and progress. It has been my task, as commander in chief, to emphasize the complete unity of purpose and interest between the armed forces and the people from whom they spring. As a result, the officers and men of these services have never suffered from a sense of arrogance or—at the other extreme—from a sense of being neglected or forgotten. The ceremonial and civilian-aid contributions that our armed forces have made to nation building are a spectacular addition to their vigilant readiness to perform their primary duty.

NEW HORIZONS FOR THE PEOPLE

Before the attainment of *Uhuru,* Kenya somehow endured beneath the iron fist of social injustice. Instances of this could be found under almost every heading, but three were especially critical. The indigenous people of Kenya had no effective voice in the government of their country or the administration of their daily lives. They were deliberately kept in an uneducated state and were debarred from acquiring practical experience. And they drew hardly any benefit from the growth of the economy.

The very presence of an independent government removed the first of these injustices, and we urgently set about remedying the remaining two. The context of this effort was the belief that freedom is a right, and that without it the basic dignity of man is violated. But if freedom was to be complete and meaningful, our people had to be delivered from the afflictions of poverty, illiteracy, and disease.

These were mammoth tasks for our new country. As we set about them, I emphasized and codified the extension of the African family spirit to the nation as a whole in order to create what we describe as mutual social responsibility. This African tradition is rooted in the self-evident belief that society cannot prosper without the full cooperation of its members. It is reasonable, therefore, that when society does succeed and advance, all its members should share in this prosperity. Translating these approaches into modern terms requires only subtle changes. It has been our hope that the impulse of these philosophies in Kenya might be extended throughout Africa and even beyond.

A great inspirational force had to be mobilized on a countrywide scale. The people had to understand that progress was something they themselves could all help to create. Our forward march could never be left just to those with money to invest or authority to wield. Ideas of this kind had to be disabused, so that the fervour of national patriotism and pride could be maintained. The people had to be persuaded that in any occupation, in any home in any district, the smallest efforts to build and to improve were of importance. The parable of the widow's mite offered a pertinent analogy.

One of the things that became apparent was that solutions to our problems could not always be advanced within the purview of economics alone. Such responses were often too bleak, too clinically indifferent to their effect on people, with their traditions and ambitions and tastes. Not for the first time, it appeared to me that the sociological effects of economic advocacy

KEYSTONE

Handing the national flag to the captain of the Kenya athletic team: Throughout all fields of human endeavour we must catch up and keep up. . . . Some of our athletes have shown the world what might be done.

could benefit from closer study and fuller implementation.

It also became apparent that our efforts to achieve desired objectives for the people could be restricted or diverted by a high rate of population growth. As soon as this factor was properly assessed and appreciated, my government gave full support to family planning endeavours throughout the republic, with mobile clinics operated by professional teams. Apart from their benefits to the individual family, these endeavours were founded on valid national considerations.

It would be impossible to contemplate—or to govern—a society in which there was no discipline and all men were free to follow their own inclinations. Governments both represent and instill a needed discipline, using laws and security forces and administrative regulations. But a discipline that cannot be accepted by the people will not work for long. A valuable part of Christian teaching concerns the values of compassion and tolerance, and also of self-control and the brotherhood of human service.

Often there seems to be a mistaken impression that Christian living removes enjoyment and excitement from life. I do not think this is so. Many of the finest Christian leaders I have met have possessed abundant robustness and humour. It seems to me, on balance, that in enriching a man with a sense of duty and thankfulness, Christian teaching arms him with a kind of humility, which can be far more powerful than arrogance or selfishness or greed.

Having said this, let me observe that the constitution of Kenya gives the people of this country the unqualified right to enjoy freedom of worship. This might be classified as the most fundamental of all freedoms. Such concepts as freedom from hunger or fear, freedom of speech and assembly, are undeniably important, but only freedom of worship is indivisible from the nature of truth and light and the unconquerable spirit of humanity.

Another aim of my government, the expansion of medical institutions, has not been simply a matter of political prudence. A principal objective of my government has been to remove or reverse all aspects of past social injustice, and such an aim can become effective only when politics has deep roots in human compassion. The health of every citizen is therefore of real and immediate importance. Our concept of mutual social responsibility involves recognition that no one lies outside the national perimeter of contribution and need. Beyond this, of course, is the practical point that all the economic strains and challenges of nation building and development demand the efforts of a healthy population.

We have therefore embarked on a substantial and continuing program of building new hospitals, in Nairobi and in provincial and district centres throughout the country. In some cases, existing hospitals could be expanded. The professional advice supplied to the government indicated that, while new construction was of immense value, it was also important to equip hospitals everywhere with more extensive facilities and more modern apparatus. Thus, a high proportion of available resources has been allocated to building new outpatient departments, installing X-ray units, and modernizing operating theatres. Outside the hospitals, a network of health centres has been established on a countrywide scale. We have given considerable priority, as a program in its own right, to maternity treatment and child welfare services. All this activity has been buttressed by urgent and ambitious training schemes, for doctors and for all categories of hospital staff.

Nursing class in a modern hospital: The health of every citizen is of real and immediate importance.

JOHN MOSS FROM BLACK STAR

But there is more to health—in its widest sense—than hospitals and doctors. The precursors of health, and of disease, exist within the conditions of the people's daily living. For this and other reasons, we have been concerned about housing. In many urban areas, the appalling sprawl of slum dwellings and verminous shacks—which we inherited—has been swept away, and blocks of modern flats have been erected. We have been experimenting constantly with the provision of cheap but adequate urban housing, made available under tenant-purchase schemes. Throughout the rural areas, officials and craftsmen have been advising the people on new and better kinds of housing, involving, where appropriate, the use of prefabricated timber components or corrugated iron. More and more women, through government training schemes or through the Maendeleo ya Wanawake organization, have learned at least the basic aspects of hygiene, domestic science, and family care.

In another vital national project, nearly 300 rural piped-water schemes have been planned and completed since independence. This marks another great step forward, not only in directly relieving social hardship, but also in doing away with the unsanitary conditions that are so often responsible for spreading disease. In addition, electricity has been extended to over 20 more townships and rural centres. This is not only of economic significance, but also reflects upon the health and social well-being of the people by opening up the prospect of fuller lives.

Much has been done in a short time, but such tangible endeavours are not all that we have accomplished. Human welfare, especially among the working people, requires some safeguards against unexpected hardships and some provision for old age. We therefore established a National Social Security Fund. Already this fund has accumulated nearly £10 million, representing an important domestic source of investment capital, and it is expected that this figure may reach £20 million by the end of 1971. Workers contributing to the fund are currently entitled to free outpatient treatment in all government hospitals. Further services and benefits can and will be introduced, together with a switch to payment of pensions, rather than bulk sums of money, on retirement.

Tribute should be given here to the contribution that the trade unions have made to our economic expansion and social advancement. The sense of responsibility displayed by these unions has served the cause of industrial peace, which in turn has encouraged investment and all forms of enterprise. Every year since *Uhuru*, there has been a reduction in the number of working days lost to the nation through strikes. The trade unions have recognized that only hard work and growing productivity can fulfill a primary objective of our African Socialism, which is to bring about a rising national income distributed in a more equitable way.

Trade union leaders in the new Kenya have been discovering an important truth: that they must be professional in their judgment and outlook. In the past it might have been sufficient for them to consider only one side of any proposition, whether it concerned wages, terms of service, or hours of work. But in this modern world, and especially in the context of a developing country, trade unionists must also be familiar with the realities of management and productivity.

THE CONTRIBUTION OF AFRICA

In one of my speeches I recall remarking that "All the noble Charters and Declarations of history, and all the Constitutions that enshrine human rights, have sprung from one paramount truth—that men in their spirit and in their striving, under the law, have the right to be free." Such a thought might be dressed up in more vivid rhetoric but, as I look at it again, it seems completely unassailable when put in this straightforward way.

Within the past 10 or 20 years—but a moment of time in the perspective of history—the world has moved sharply away from earlier concepts of colonial patronage or domination. When the United Nations was formed, after World War II, only Ethiopia and Liberia represented what is called "black Africa." Since then, the peoples of many African countries have been freed, with effects that go far beyond mere constitutional freedom from political oppression. The talents and ambitions and cultures of Africa, so long restrained, have taken their place on the international scene. The productive energies of Africa have altered old patterns of economic privilege. The philosophies of Africa have been thrown into the pool of thinking, where ripples can reach out to all mankind.

I have always stood for human dignity in freedom and for the values of tolerance and peace. A generation or so ago these things were considered brash and potentially dangerous by men still obsessed with imperialism and paternalism. Today these same simple aims and beliefs are threatened by new complexities of ideology and power. It seems remarkable to me that limitless propaganda and the paraphernalia of strength should be paraded throughout Africa by the two great rival ideologies, rather like two bull rhinos strutting and puffing and lunging at each other to win the favour of a cow. Neither has had the wit or the humility to realize that what really activates Africa, and what will emerge from Africa, is the greater sanity of simple human values.

With tragic monotony, each new nation born in Africa has become a pawn or a target in the cold war. When some have proved unresponsive, or have stubbornly defended their integrity, certain elements have gone to great lengths to bring government and people into their ideological orbit or under their strategic command. The struggle for independence in many developing states has been overshadowed by the ensuing challenge from outside forces—ambitious for economic dominance, or seeking bridgeheads of power, or tirelessly propagating the appalling concept of perpetual revolution. Some spokesmen of the advanced countries, in the United Nations and elsewhere, have advised African states to reduce their expenditure on defense and reallocate the money saved to education or other forms of productive social service. This we would happily consider if external forces would leave Africa free to concentrate on nation building.

There is an enduring myth about Africa that needs to be dispelled. It has been kept alive by the technical brilliance of Hollywood and its counterparts in Britain, Italy, and elsewhere. The myth, of course, is that Africa is still a place made up exclusively of raw jungles, savage deserts, and primitive or hostile tribes. To us, this appears merely quaint, but it denies perspective to much of mankind. Time and again, visitors to Kenya have told me of their surprise at being driven from an international airport along two-lane highways, catching sight of the National Assembly and the university and modern blocks of government buildings, and ending up (perhaps) in a room in a Hilton hotel. After traveling around Kenya, they have expressed astonishment at the glimpses they have had of modern agriculture, thriving industry, 20th-century schools and hospitals, and hydroelectric undertakings. Leaders in many other African states have doubtless had the same experience.

Perspective and understanding in this physical sense are important if the world is to appreciate what has happened in Africa politically and philosophically. Like many of its sister countries, the Republic of Kenya came into being in a period when the last light from the dying embers of colonialism was throwing into sharp relief the economic and social injustices of half a century. At present the world is still feeling the shock waves of this change. Men who have recently risen from bondage—and others still waiting to emerge—are now defining and demanding their rightful places in human society.

These events have marked a climax, so far at least, to a life spanning a period of turbulent happenings and unforeseen scientific progress. Seventy or so years ago, mankind would have considered as preposterous the very idea of the airplane. Today there are manned vehicles that can penetrate the veils of outer space. Against such a background, mankind has experienced philosophical shocks that are no less startling or meaningful.

People sometimes ask me what Africa really wants: what will be—or should be—the basic purpose of Africa on the world scene. It is not always easy to impress the answers clearly on the minds of those who view the world in terms of money or of missiles. I would say, simply enough, that the objective of Africa is justice. What Africa wants is to sweep aside the aftermath of so many long years of desolation, exploitation, and neglect, and replace this ugly residue with opportunity. Africa is awakening rapidly, but has no thought of conquest or disruption or revenge. In time it will have greater economic strength, but the approach to justice, here and now, must be made first of all through the contribution of a new philosophy. In a society dominated by computers and the soporifics of mass entertainment, advanced nations today seem to have little time to worry and less inclination to think. What Africa must do is to ask where the world is going. And what Africa will champion is the simple idea that, if humanity is to control the way the world is going, we must start from the truism that all men are equal and are equally entitled to respect.

I have never been a preacher, although I have admired many men who have adopted that calling. Their faith is often quite remarkable in its resilience and strength. My own experience in public affairs had equipped me with an attitude that must be described as more cynical, or perhaps as more robust. So frequently, I have seen men shy away from or deliberately distort the values of truth and right. This is a lasting trait of mankind, but moments can still arise when philosophies must be expressed.

My own belief is that we badly need a new social conscience in human relations. Within international bodies, idealistic statements and concepts simply shuffle around the fringes, sometimes in a wistful sort of way. What is required, over and above mere declarations, is the will to end the blackmail of nuclear power, the parading of destructive strength, the confining of human intellect behind bleak walls of ideology, the advancement of self-interest behind a smoke screen of morality.

Jet aircraft and the radio-telephone have made nonsense of the old concepts of distance. Our world is a small place in which all men are close neighbours. But the new technology has outstripped human objectives and ideals, and man himself is still a prisoner of traditional selfishness and apprehension. A philosophy of life that places emphasis on humanity could capture the imagination of the many young people who feel themselves drifting pointlessly.

In terms of scientific advancement, surely the betterment of mankind through economic progress and social justice should be the ultimate aim of all the talent and wealth that is poured into the search for new discoveries. The states of Africa have lagged behind in the contemporary scientific race, but by the same token we have avoided the snares that can so easily entrap the competitors. When Africa does catch up, the philosophies that we will apply to scientific progress may set an example for all humanity. I am not decrying technical progress. My point is simply that mankind would be well advised, before it is too late, to place more emphasis on those applications of science and technology that can solve the massive problems of social injustice and bring new hope to millions of struggling men. There is far more nobility in this than in scientific advances promoted in the cause of prestige or in all the fearsome technology that threatens to destroy the human race.

Independent Africa will have much to contribute. Within our own continent, the pace of events has brought turmoil and the need for adjustment. We have had to create the traditions of discipline, command, and ambition that have activated some nations for centuries, but new philosophy backed by gathering strength is taking its rightful place. It seems to me that few things are more important than that the principles underlying African society should play a greater part in shaping human destiny. What alternative do the powerful nations and blocs have to offer mankind?

THE WORLD FROM THE AFRICAN VIEWPOINT

No country can progress or endure in isolation in the world of today. Each nation must be regarded as one link in a chain of mutual interest. On a practical level, this means that better methods of promoting international trade, of ensuring fair and stable prices for primary products, and of reducing market barriers must be sought and supported by all.

Men's minds are now reaching toward and beyond the year 2000, but many of their political and economic habits belong to the year 1900. For example, there is little evidence of worldwide integration or coordination of economic policies, or of attempts to share the rewards of progress more equitably between rich and poor countries. In fact, the new states of Africa have often found themselves caught in a whirlwind of tendencies—political, economic, and technological—inimical to their purposes and efforts as individual nations.

As we see things from here, there are great regions of the earth where, although certain domestic problems may be both urgent and real, society in general is distinguished by levels of living ranging from comparative abundance to sybaritic affluence. By contrast, in even larger regions the people are suffering from comparative shortage if not from utter deprivation. This is a situation that calls for adjustment, not only on grounds of common sense or equity but also if we are to build the kind of society that all of us should want. There are sufficient resources and talents in the world to banish squalor, if only the will were there.

This gulf, only too apparent in Africa, represents one of the greatest challenges to human survival and advancement. So many countries, often with large and rapidly increasing populations, remain terribly poor. In many of these nations, man's creativeness has long been stifled. Technology is therefore embryonic, great quantities of capital are lacking, and high-level manpower is only now being trained. The simple transference of advanced technology to these countries is not the answer. What is so often required is not the automated end product of one machine, but useful work for thousands and thousands of hands.

Most rich and sophisticated countries appear to be increasingly involved in investing all their savings in their own security. Moreover, they have formed a sort of club, gearing patterns of trade in such a way as to promote commerce among their own members. Their own markets are protected by tariffs or other artificial barriers, while the efforts of developing countries to process their own natural products and to win a more substantial share of the trade in processed goods are systematically nullified.

The increasing use of synthetic substitutes for primary foods and raw materials is already depriving many developing nations of the economic rewards that should accrue from primary production, and is preventing the buildup of investment capital. Countries now advancing on the floodtide of scientific and industrial power should reflect that, in Africa, we have a large segment of world agriculture, on which the economic and vocational needs of uncounted millions depend. Synthetic products cannot be considered as part of "inevitable economic progress." The outpouring of synthetic substitutes for many food products and for such raw materials as sisal, pyrethrum, and cotton must be weighed in the balance of total human sanity. If this headlong rush toward synthetics is not checked, it may be possible for biochemists—supported (or preyed on) by financiers and technicians—to put primary producers in huge areas of the globe out of business. But if the farmers go, mankind is finished.

The output of primary foods and other commodities is both a way of life and the only source of hope for the great bulk of the world's population. To undermine all this effort, to remove this hope, would be a crime against humanity. This fact may carry little weight in the advanced nations, but it is of great practical importance for their own survival, whether they realize it or not. For one thing, to destroy primary production in all the tropical and subtropical areas would obliterate a vast and growing market for capital and consumer goods from the industrial states. Much more ominously, it would bring about a worldwide flood of poverty and hopelessness that could topple walls of complacency and power.

This may seem harsh, but it must be brought to the world's attention. In recent years, the developed nations have adopted a policy of injecting younger and poorer countries with the modern drug (now dwindling in its potency) of aid, while at the same time feeding a thrombosis in the arteries of commerce. Such policies are economically amoral and psychologically unsound. They are what is meant by the word "neocolonialism." And when certain Western nations express hurt surprise over apparent or alleged tendencies in some quarters to turn toward the East, let them reflect on the biblical passage that deals with motes and beams.

Obviously, some aid and assistance to Africa from the world outside has been and must remain of great significance. Nearly all the African states have been severely limited by shortages of domestic savings and the neglect of education. The ability to borrow funds and secure the use of trained personnel from other countries has helped to overcome these limitations. Beyond this, we have been able to examine and adapt from the advanced countries new technological ideas, modern methods of agricultural and industrial organization, and techniques of economic control. All this has provided Africa with the opportunity to leap over many of the hurdles encountered by other societies in the past. We have been able to profit from the experiments—and learn from the mistakes—of other people. Recently the total monetary value of world aid has tended to decline. This is depressing. Although trade and price patterns are of first and most fundamental importance in economic development, aid is nonetheless an important factor.

Another recent trend can be expressed in the formula: "the Lord helps those who help themselves." This I find wholly acceptable. My view has always been that the more Africa can contribute toward its own development, the more aid might justifiably be expected from outside. Donors are understandably attracted to a going concern. Just as too little aid can be frustrating, too much can be burdensome and may even make young countries vulnerable. There are limits to the financing that international institutions and advanced countries can be expected to provide. If our case is that we want a fair and free world economy in which to build up and wield our own strength, then clearly the creation of development capital must rest largely in our hands.

THE UNQUENCHED FIRES OF RACIALISM

In my half century of involvement in human affairs, I have known men of genius and men of scant ability, men of great sobriety and men who were feckless, men who were beyond corruption and men who could be traded, men who got things done and men who wanted things done for them, men who were evil and men who were good. And none of these categories could be correlated with divisions of colour or of race.

Racialism is not only a groundless disease, it is one of the great affronts to human dignity. Never a rational attribute of mankind, it has been used to stir the emotions, to disguise arrogance, to justify domination, to promote political intrigue. Its sham and bigotry have been increasingly exposed, with sacrifice on the part of visionary men. If mankind is to endure and prosper, the malady must be finally conquered, not through the blood and the terrible evil of setting one group against another, but through enlightenment and human service.

What these thoughts lead up to, of course, is the pitiable fact that here in Africa we still have examples of those peculiar kinds of bondage and hypocrisy that are rooted in race. There are still pockets of fascist dictatorship, if that is the most suitable name for it. There are countries in which the will and the rights of the people are suppressed by political and military power, and where an artificial authority is uneasily founded and maintained on the *Herrenvolk* concept (will this never be sufficiently disproved?) of racial divinity.

South Africa provides the most outstanding example of such a system. South African society—to the accompaniment, paradoxically enough, of much professed attachment to the Bible—is based on the theory that the Creation resulted in the emergence of two distinct species of man, one endowed with rights and the other with no claim to any rights whatsoever. Thus it is avowed that the so-called inferior species can never become, and must never be admitted or accepted as being, equal in talent or dignity to the superior product.

The astonishing disregard of logic in such an attitude can lead to situations that are positively ludicrous. Among the Afrikaans people, for example, there are scientists and doctors and businessmen of brilliance who happen to be white. There are also drunkards and criminals and pimps. Among the even-more-indigenous African peoples, there are scholars and physicians and lawyers of brilliance who happen to be black. Yet it has to be maintained that the worst of the white is superior to the best of the black or the entire hopeless system would collapse. There cannot be equal access to responsibilities, opportunities, or rights, lest the whole flimsy sham be revealed. Within every field of human activity—politics, the professions, commerce, sport—there must be separation, so that the illusion of superiority can be kept alive.

Such a system can inspire the most passionate outbursts of condemnation. Fundamentally, of course, it is just silly, but it is also morally very wrong and should have no place in a world where recognition of the common interests of all humanity offers the best hope for survival. Kenya and many of its sister states in Africa have been in the vanguard of condemning this apartheid regime. On the economic front, we have suffered significantly, through loss of markets and in other ways. But such economic gestures, within Africa, have been sincere rather than flamboyant. We have always realized that Kenya (for example), as an individual nation, can never bring more than trifling economic pressure to bear on South Africa, but we have hoped that this African initiative would inspire massive support from other states.

Virtually all the advanced nations have paid fluent lip service to the principle involved whenever South Africa was debated in United Nations councils, but they have continued to uphold the South African regime for reasons of commercial or strategic advantage. Those who support South Africa through investment and trade, while wooing the remainder of Africa with an eye toward potential political and economic support, should reflect on this: it is the apartheid regime today that is in isolation and

Pres. Jomo Kenyatta in 1969: My objective in politics has always been to stand for the purpose of human dignity in freedom, and for the values of tolerance and peace.

MARC & EVELYNE BERNHEIM FROM RAPHO GUILLUMETTE

is being overtaken by events. The purpose of the rest of Africa should be clearly understood. Kenya and its sister states have been seeking to forge world opinion into an effective instrument for the pursuit of human dignity in freedom, but we do not seek revenge or punishment or the disintegration of viable economic structures. In South Africa we want—and inevitably will attain—the reality of justice.

In Kenya we have demonstrated that peoples of different races and tribes can live together harmoniously within the borders of one state. We have established political structures and economic guidelines and social fabrics that are accepted by all and that have served as the precursors of vigorous development. The old conflict between "black" and "white" has been dissolved within the spirit of pulling together that constitutes our national motto: *Harambee*. Two men who happen to be white, for example, are members of my personal staff today. There are some who feared that white racialism in Africa must inevitably be replaced by black racialism. We have shown that this need not be so.

There are men—white men—of rational thought and liberal conscience within South Africa. It is wearisome to hear such men described as Communists. They have paid heed to or have assisted the nationalist struggle simply because they are men of the 20th century who can see beyond the outmoded dogma of race. I only pray now that the South African racialists will not goad the African people there to the point where the nationalist movement is driven to oppose any and all white men as such. But the longer apartheid endures, the more likely such a tragedy becomes, and from a beginning of this sort whole tidal waves of destruction and evil could spread and engulf all mankind.

In the country now known as Rhodesia—but which will become Zimbabwe—there have been trends springing from mimicry of South African ideas. Here the issue is simple. A comparative handful of arrogant men, in what was the self-governing colony of Rhodesia, have established an autonomous apartheid regime, through the process of open revolution against the British Parliament and judiciary and by committing treason against a constitutional monarch.

Viewed against the background of British history, which has not been without its lustre, these events are almost inconceivable. One is tempted to wonder whether this would have been permitted to occur if the protagonists had been black. In the event, through their pathetic ineptitude and condonation by default, the British government and people have become accessories to the offense of overthrowing the law—which is commonly described as revolution. Let me add that, so far as we have been able to discern, Britain has not had significant backing from the governments or nationals of many other states. It is the world at large that has again shrugged off the portents of racial explosion.

A passage on Rhodesia that I wrote nearly two years ago still seems sufficiently appropriate to bear repeating: "What is threatened here is no less than the rule of law itself, the total jurisdiction of the courts of Britain. Should precedent be created, insofar as major crime may pass without the lawful retribution defined and established by society, then the law of the jungle must lie on the outskirts of every city and every village and every home. It would be poignant if Britain, which has in the past bequeathed so much to the world in all the institutions and scruples of law, were to be the springboard of breakdown of this fundamental basis of orderly social behaviour."

We in Africa are not totally unfamiliar with the law of the jungle, but we are convinced that the rule of law is infinitely more wise and valuable. Mankind cannot have it both ways. There cannot be one system for the rich and another for the poor; one for the white and another for the nonwhite. Where do the advanced countries really stand on this issue?

A police state, with all its trappings of restriction and censorship and lies, has been imposed upon Rhodesia by a gang (is there any more accurate word?) of increasingly desperate men. Their removal, now that they have been allowed to become entrenched, will be not without hazard. There may be no limit to the misfortunes they would bring down on Rhodesia's people, black and white alike, rather than surrender. But all this pales into insignificance beside the rotting away of principles and safeguards and beliefs that must ensue unless this treason is defeated by law.

It is sometimes asked: what could Britain do? Not so long ago—when Britain, whatever its other faults or failings, was at least distinguished for dynamism, inventiveness, and courage—such a question would have been unnecessary. The present policy of economic sanctions against Rhodesia is unconvincing, especially when even this is deliberately sabotaged by other nations of both West and East. Equally pointless has been Britain's reluctance to transform the Rhodesian question into an issue of United Nations trusteeship on the ground that it is a purely British problem. Britain is obviously unable to deal with it. Even

UPI COMPIX

MOHAMED AMIN FROM KEYSTONE

With President Kaunda and President Nyerere (above); accepting a gift of friendship from Tanganyika (top): I have always believed strongly in the purposeful encouragement of African unity.

if a policing action is ruled out, her majesty's government could at least give some support to those Europeans in Rhodesia who have clung to their constitutional loyalty and to those others (in commercial and tobacco-growing circles) who see disaster looming through the paper-thin facade of economic confidence held up by Ian Smith.

Britain could also support the African leaders and nationalists through politics, law, and the apparatus of justified harassment. Britain could make it clear that majority rule is inevitable; that a fully representative constitutional conference must and will be held to work out the preparatory stages and timing of independence; and that there must be adequate concern—which other African states would welcome—for economic structures and personal security within Rhodesia. The one thing that Britain should not do is seek refuge in ambiguity, or pretend to itself and others that the forward progress of humanity is possible while a problem of this sort is left unresolved.

All the leaders of independent states in Africa have made it clear that we will never abandon those who are struggling for freedom and human dignity in territories dominated by South Africa, by the rebel regime of Rhodesia, or by Portugal, which still seeks to perpetuate its colonialist grip on Angola, Portuguese Guinea, and Mozambique. The Organization of African Unity has pledged that all its members will work unceasingly for the complete liberation of Africa. This is a resolve that the United Nations should take seriously, since its fulfillment could make the difference between contribution and conflict. No one in history has prevailed for more than a short time against the unquenchable yearning of the human spirit for justice.

AFRICAN UNITY

So many problems are common to the young and developing countries of Africa. I have never discovered an easier solution to these problems than hard and patient toil, coupled with the imaginative utilization of all available resources. Also of value would be more active cooperation rooted in mutual respect between Africa and the more privileged groups of mankind.

Nearly all the struggling states of Africa have severely limited resources—less than they need if they are to advance swiftly beyond the subsistence level. In most cases, these countries have been hampered by rapidly expanding populations, raising the possibility that human problems will multiply more rapidly than solutions. In their early years, these nations have all found themselves grimly battling for a place in the highly competitive arena of world society. Thus it is understandable that many of their approaches and policies have emerged along similar lines.

Before a country can safely and wholeheartedly embark on nation-building programs, there must be no doubts or dangers affecting its national integrity. The carving up of this continent by the colonial powers was based on economic opportunism, strategic advantage, calculated tactics of divide-and-rule, and even jealousy or whim rather than geography or ethnology. Some of the independent states that eventually emerged were therefore tempted—or even bound—to raise frontier issues, having as their objective the redress of past injustice.

This might have led to an explosive situation all over Africa. In many areas there were problems of territorial boundaries, based on economic grievances or on a desire to bring together peoples of a similar ethnic/tribal origin. The Organization of African Unity, founded in the early part of 1963, carried out a survey of this problem. One of the wisest and most effective measures undertaken by this body was to pass a subsequent resolution calling on all member states to respect and accept each other's boundaries as these had been drawn at independence. I supported this resolution from the deepest of convictions and, in the event, it has worked. A series of fratricidal conflicts over the issue of territorial boundaries would have dragged this continent into a future of helpless chaos.

At one time, relations between Kenya and Somalia were quite seriously disturbed by the ethnic consequences of past boundary adjustments. Today our relations with Somalia are cordial and, through diplomatic channels and by exchanges of delegations, we are working toward the greatest possible measure of fruitful cooperation in all socioeconomic fields. No useful purpose would be served by reviewing past conflict in detail, but I am sure that the government of Somalia would support me in singling out one vital point that was implicit in our eventual understanding.

Assisted in the final stages by the good offices of Presidents Kenneth Kaunda of Zambia and Julius Nyerere of Tanzania, Kenya and Somalia were able to demonstrate their capacity to solve problems through a frank and positive approach, as members of the same African family. To my mind this is of great im-

Six African heads of state attending an informal meeting: All the leaders of independent states in Africa have made it clear that we will never abandon those who are struggling for freedom and human dignity.

UPI COMPIX

portance. We must develop and utilize this sense of brotherhood within Africa. As far as possible, we should avoid referring internal questions to international institutions, especially since these institutions are greatly influenced by the very former colonial powers that are responsible for so many of Africa's difficulties.

The Kenya-Somalia dispute was a specific issue, but more general conclusions can be drawn from it. The highest moral principles can be embraced within international diplomacy. There can certainly be initiatives at this level toward meeting the challenges of immoral conduct and stamping out the causes of human misery. But many problems can arise in a particular area in which the gap between local diagnosis and world understanding is quite wide. In such cases it may be difficult for an international body to write and apply the correct prescription. I believe that, at least initially, it is best for local or regional agencies to exert their influence and, if appropriate, apply discipline. Toward this end, goodwill is not lacking in Africa, but smoother machinery needs to be developed.

The future of Africa—as indeed the future of all the world—resides in the young. I have been associated with pan-African movements for a long time. Now the younger generation must seize the opportunity to promote these ideals, and perhaps the best way to begin is by placing in perspective all the geographic and ethnic barriers that for too long have divided mankind. I have noted with satisfaction that students have been seeking ways to transform thought from the ingrained heritage of colonialist concepts toward the fresh vitality of pan-African approaches and endeavours. Below the level of the university, each national system of education in Africa should also emphasize pan-Africanism so as to prepare developing minds for greater future cooperation within the OAU. Of course, education should also promote the endeavours of such bodies as UNESCO to identify and provide for the common needs of all humanity.

I have spoken of safety and integrity, but what is also necessary for full familyhood is understanding. Here again education can help by encouraging the study of Africa's traditional culture. Interest in music, dancing, and folklore can be cultivated among the children of Africa from an early age. As hands become more nimble and minds more flexible, painting and carving and pottery can be added. All our countries have a stake in the culture of Africa. The advantages of closer unity are spoken of today in the jargon of modern development planning, but before there can be true unity there must be a background of mutual appreciation, formed by discovering and sharing our many common elements of history, tradition, and talent.

African unity can be expressed as a political idea: the OAU. It has always seemed to me, however, that this concept should embrace more than just political attitudes, and this opinion has been reinforced in recent years as I have observed the self-interest that has marked the policies of many states. Such an attitude is only natural, of course. The survival of the state must be assured before sacrifices in the cause of unity can in hard practice be contemplated.

It is essential, in my judgment, to broaden the potential basis of African unity by setting realistic targets and opening up endeavours that offer meaningful benefit to all. For example, it would be in the interest of all African states to set up a composite study group on communications and eventually to pool resources so as to build an entirely revitalized communications system within Africa. Great mutual advantages might result if we continued earlier consultations on whether and how to codify and standardize the law, as designed and administered in African societies. Much benefit could arise from the pooling of pure or applied research and the sharing of results. There could and should be a concerted examination of one of Africa's great stumbling blocks, the lack of any common language. African nations that have already made some progress could share techniques with their neighbours. We can learn more from each other than from oversophisticated states outside.

Africa must be opened up in the modern sense, so that practical unity has a chance to take root. The organized development of tourism, for instance, can have a beneficial effect on the economic and social progress of any young nation, and it could be expanded, step by step, by unified activity throughout independent Africa. All over the world, tourism has grown phenomenally in recent years. People in the advanced countries, with more money to spend, have been seeking new pleasures and vivid experiences, and these can be found abundantly in Africa. At the same time, tourists have gained fresh insights into the lives and cultures of their fellow men.

My government in Kenya has been in the vanguard of efforts to develop trade ties with sister states in Africa. There are strong arguments for this kind of innovation. Historically, Africa has received capital goods and manufactured products from the industrial countries while exporting primary food products and raw materials to them in return. Most African states are now broadening the basis of their economies by promoting an industrial sector. They need far wider outlets than are afforded by domestic demand, and the development of markets within the continent of Africa offers the most hopeful long-term prospects.

Between 1966 and 1968, Kenya's exports to African countries outside the East African Community (Kenya, Tanzania, and Uganda) rose by some 40%. This was encouraging, but some difficulties and setbacks were encountered. The lack of communications has already been mentioned, but an even more substantial factor is that most potential African trading partners are developing their economies in similar ways. This being so, export markets for commodities such as canned foods and textiles tend to be lost, before long, to the products of new import-saving industries in the receiving countries. I am certain that through the OAU, and through the Economic Commission for Africa, the ideals of unity in Africa could be greatly strengthened by resolute study of and planning for more effective economic coordination within Africa for the benefit of all.

Similar problems have arisen within agriculture. From the moment of independence in all these countries, governments and farmers alike have been swept along by the impulse toward social justice, which in practice means higher farm income. This has resulted in a stampede toward products likely (on paper at least) to be salable for cash. One result has been an almost desperate dependence on coffee, a crop that is being overproduced in the world as a whole. Diversification programs in tropical and subtropical areas are vitally needed to provide an alternative to this one product.

Coffee is not the only product of which this is true, but a precedent with coffee could be adapted to other commodities. Here is a field in which the pooling of resources, ideas, and experiences within Africa could be of inestimable value. Changes from the "crash-program" approach to agricultural development are inevitable. If we are wise, we can coordinate diversification efforts so as to control these changes and ensure that rural communities and national economies are strengthened.

Sweeping plans, with all their social implications, can be broken down into particular techniques. Again, let me quote an example. Today large transport aircraft are being employed for carrying crops and livestock—even whole breeding herds—between areas of North and South America. In Africa we have hardly begun to use airfreight. Yet its potential is immense, not only within Africa but beyond our shores, where the luxury markets of Europe could be supplied with a wide range of perishable tropical produce.

Great political progress has been made in our continent over the past two decades. The economic battle—for stability and prosperity—is rising to a crescendo now. Capital is needed, and the African Development Bank must and will proceed to make a vital contribution. The creation and employment of this body is another admirable symbol of the growing capacity of African states for self-help and for fruitful cooperation. In both these efforts is found the essential spirit of all that African unity should come to mean.

AN AFTERWORD

ALLEGATIONS OF TRIBAL DISARRAY

Since my main article was written, there have been some events of note in Kenya. Sometimes these events have been strangely misinterpreted in sections of the world press. I have been invited by the publishers to add an epilogue to my article, aimed principally at bringing the story of Kenya up to date but with the attendant opportunity of placing some facts in their correct perspective.

Earlier I dealt with the meaning of tribalism in African affairs. Lately there has been a fresh outbreak of allegations and theorizing, suggesting that the policies of my government—in both the political and the developmental sense—have been motivated by tribal ambitions or even dictated by the desire to inflict some kind of tribal oppression. Nothing could be further from reality. As I have already pointed out, the more tenaciously meaningful national unity is pursued, the more implacable its foes will become. Let me now, once and for all, debunk all these engineered fears and sensational forecasts of tribal conflict within Kenya.

Between the years 1948 and 1952, I spent much time traveling in different parts of the country, building new bridges of unity and understanding between the political nerve centre of Nairobi and all of Kenya's tribes and peoples. I believed and advised then that national unity was the true root of our integrity and strength. During visits to Nyanza or the Coast, to Ukambani or Meru, or in the Rift Valley, I told the people that the fight for human dignity in freedom was one in which all must join, and that the fruits of *Uhuru* would be for all to share. My approaches and convictions, over two ensuing decades, have never changed.

I still like—and manage—to travel into different parts of Kenya, to see for myself the achievements and the problems that are bound up with nation building and to meet the people. But any head of state who is also head of government experiences almost infinite demands on his time. While I am unable nowadays to travel as widely as I would wish, I nonetheless insist on being accessible to all Kenya's people. Today the old bridges of unity have become strong enough to carry two-way traffic. At State House, or at my Gatundu home, therefore, there is a constant flow of leaders and delegations from all parts of the country who have come to visit me. It is important for outside observers to understand what this means, particularly when they have been led astray by absurd descriptions of Kenya as a caldron of potential tribal strife. In October and November 1969, supplementing meetings I had held earlier at the Coast and in Ukambani, a number of important delegations came to see me in Nairobi. They consisted of elders and political leaders, professional men and local dignitaries, farmers and businessmen—a cross-section of the most dynamic and responsible members of these various groups. In each case, we discussed a variety of local projects and needs, the people's hopes and aspirations. But in every case—before these discussions began—these representatives submitted to me a solemn assurance of the personal loyalty of their people and of support for my government. They endorsed and echoed my teaching that national unity is the only foundation of progress. They pledged themselves to work for prosperity and social justice, at peace with all other tribes and communities in the indivisible nation of Kenya.

In each instance, full initiative for the delegations came from the people themselves. None of these meetings took place (even metaphorically) behind locked doors and barbed wire. There was no secrecy about the participants, and no immediate account or subsequent reporting back of the proceedings was in any way censored or restricted. Moreover—and this is a key point—the people of Kenya are enthusiastic enough—even precocious enough—about their politics to strip the veil from any sham and to scoff at mere stage management. We maintain a free press, as well, within this republic. Such letters or editorials as have appeared, following the various meetings, have confirmed or amplified the immediate reports; there have been no cynical references—as would certainly have been the case if concealment had been tried—to any kind of falsity.

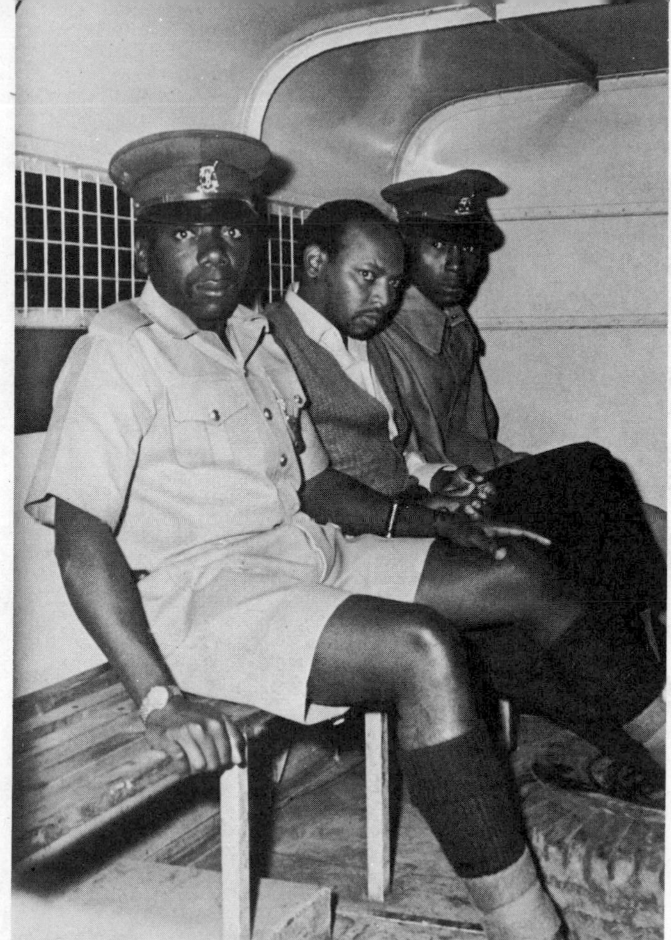

MOHAMED AMIN FROM KEYSTONE

Police escort Nahashon Isaac Njenga Njoroge, accused assassin of Minister of Economic Planning Tom Mboya, to court in Nairobi on Aug. 18, 1969. After the murder the government issued a statement accusing some politicians of using the tragedy to promote their personal ambitions.

One of these delegations consisted of a large and fully representative assembly of the Luo people from Nyanza (followed later by a separate group of Kuria from the southern part of that same province). I could recall, with these Luo elders and dignitaries, how we had worked together—through our respective associations—during the earliest days of Kenya's political struggle. We agreed that national unity was no less vital today than it had been then, and we drew mutual strength from the fact that, despite any disruptive propaganda or subversive effort, it existed still.

These Luo representatives—men of all ages and all vocations—frankly conveyed to me some of the numerous allegations about tribalism that, unless countered, would upset credulous people. There was nothing new in any of them; enemies of stability tend to be conservative about the weapons and tactics they employ. In return, I was at pains to underline and illustrate many of the policies and directives that I had specifically designed to obviate such suspicions and fears. I could also demonstrate, by reference to a list of names and titles, the growing number of prominent Luo (*i.e.*, Kenyans who happened incidentally to be Luo: this point was well taken) who were already holding high posts in the government or public service.

Later, I met representatives of the Kisii people, followed by a large delegation of Somalis from the North Eastern Province and an important group of Abaluhya (and other) leaders from the Western Province. I was also visited by a gathering of the Masai. In every instance, we agreed that tribalism has no place in the government or the nation, and recognized that hard work and local initiative are essential ingredients of economic progress.

MOHAMED AMIN FROM KEYSTONE

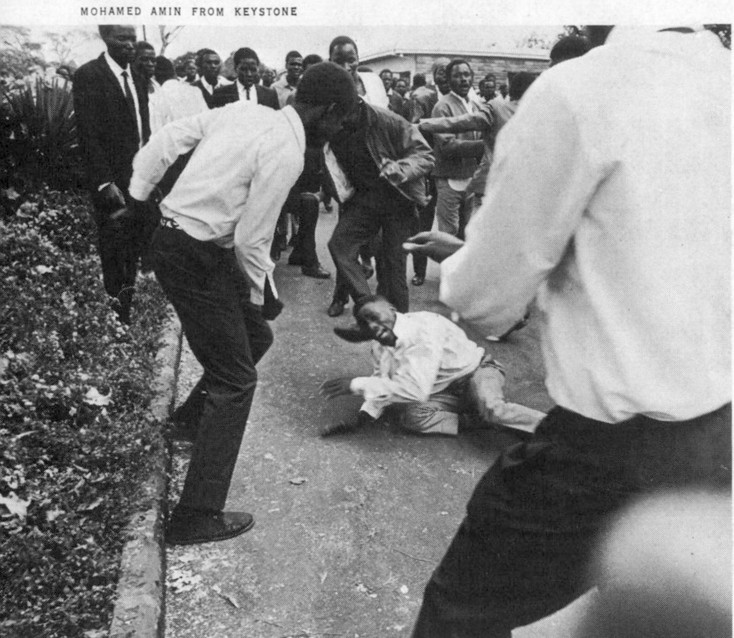

Street fight following the death of Tom Mboya. Rioting was widespread as Luo tribesmen attacked members of the Kikuyu tribe whom they suspected were responsible for the murder.

In each case, as well, we jointly poured scorn on baseless propaganda that certain areas had been "neglected," through forthright and duly publicized discussion of many tangible socioeconomic projects.

The bridges that I sought to build were once frail links between groups of remote and exploited peoples. Now they have become modern arteries of communication, over which flows the stream of national consciousness and thought. The efforts and sacrifices of millions have gone into the shaping of our nationhood. Now and henceforth, national unity must safeguard all that has been won.

As we prepare for our elections, this solidarity has been reflected in the vast attendance and vibrant enthusiasm of the people at the public rallies I have addressed throughout the country. Here is the truth: that under one flag and with one motto—*Harambee*—we have won through from *Uhuru* to real national status. Here is the expression of *Ujamaa* to confound all warped and furtive charges of tribal manipulation.

To say that tribalism is being manifested as official policy in Kenya to secure or perpetuate advantages for some favoured group is a lie. There is no more accurate word. I can only repeat the conclusion advanced in my main article: that tribalism is being—and increasingly will be—dissolved by the solvent of time.

THE BANNING OF THE KPU

Another recent happening in Kenya that inspired much superficial comment overseas was the proscription of the opposition party—the Kenya People's Union—and the detention of about a dozen men who had represented the parliamentary or executive striking force of this movement. Here again, clarity of thought and some regard for reality might prove of value.

Let me first make the point that the KPU did not represent any kind of political threat to my existing government or to the forthcoming KANU government. Any hint that this party had to be banned for such a reason is frankly pathetic.

Neither was the KPU an opposition party in the sense that, in Britain, Conservatives are at loggerheads with Labour or, in the United States, Republicans are opposed to Democrats. In both these cases, there is no question about the fundamental loyalty of the parties concerned. Such true parties may differ quite violently about many things, but when it comes to patriotism and morality, they all subscribe to the principles—even to the conventions—that enable democracy to work while preserving the integrity of the state and enhancing the welfare of the people.

With the KPU in Kenya, the position was quite different. Over a period of two or three years, my government had allotted to this fragmentary group every kind of opportunity to conduct itself in a responsible manner. This tolerance was wholly abused by men, well trained and generously paid, who set out on a calculated program of subversion. Since the latter half of 1967, it had become increasingly apparent that the hard-core leadership of KPU was prepared to destroy—if it seemed necessary to achieve their ends—everything that independence had meant and achieved here in Kenya. They sought untiringly to stir up all the agonies of intertribal conflict. Hardly a parliamentary day went by without one of them referring to a threat of civil war. They moved among the people spreading lies and suspicions and sowing the seeds of an imported dialectic.

Many times my ministers or officials advised me to bring all this to a halt and to consign the perpetrators to a place where they could do no further harm. I resisted this advice, for reasons that were touched upon in my main article. It has always seemed to me that the reasoned rejection of such threats by the people themselves can imbue a young country with a far sterner character than can be achieved when the people are overprotected. In recent months, however, the activities of this group had grown both more ominous and more desperate. Great quantities of seditious literature began to appear in various parts of the country. We were able to trace greater amounts of foreign finance to the KPU leadership than had hitherto been the case. Correspondence was uncovered, between that party and certain foreign diplomats, on the subject of overthrowing the constitutional government of Kenya.

All this had to be taken seriously, but not hysterically. If there had been any remaining benefit of the doubt, it would have been given. But then, when I visited Kisumu in late October, well-rehearsed incitement and hooliganism were openly brought into play. This was something quite different: a deliberate public threat to the integrity—and the purposes—of an independent Kenya, exercised through this challenge to my own resolve and to the strength of the Kenyan government as an entity. The timing, of course, was significant. Here was an "incident" that could have gotten so out of hand as to become Kenya's Sarajevo. It marked the critical phase in the whole program of subversion, with almost everything gambled on a single stroke. It might have plunged the country into chaos and overthrown the apparatus of democracy before an orderly election could be fought and won.

This challenge had to be met—and was met—at once by lawful and effective means. My government is responsible for national integrity, for internal security, and for the whole climate of freedom and opportunity in which the people can pursue their lawful business. All these values have been safeguarded. The fundamental motif of the proscription of the KPU is as simple as that. There comes a time when action is inevitable. My half century of work in Africa and the efforts of all my compatriots for and since *Uhuru* have been preserved against betrayal and misery, and against replacement of the old colonialism by more subtle kinds of human degradation.

The event itself was received by the country without great emotion, but with measurable undertones of relief. Despite some preposterous forecasts in the world press, there have been no outbursts of engineered resentment or disorder in any part of the republic. The *Ujamaa* factor in our nationhood has been cleansed of intrigue, and the people are as one again. Especially in Nyanza Province, the so-called "stronghold" of the KPU, a discernible swing began toward open support for the KANU government and the ideals of unity. In part, this was made possible by the removal of intimidation and the tactics of terrorism, which the KPU leadership had used in that area. But this newly released spirit of Kenyan nationalism echoed and reinforced the sentiments expressed when—as I described above—a representative Luo delegation visited me in Nairobi just a few weeks ago.

There is little more that I personally wish to say about the banning of the KPU. Students and others who are interested in such matters, however, might glean something from a statement that was issued at the time by a party spokesman in our KANU headquarters. To complete the record, I will quote some extracts from this statement here:

. . . . There are some States in which men guilty of subversive or treasonable activity might be shot out of hand. There are other States in which they might be dragged before—and condemned by—the mockery of a so-called People's Court. In this instance, they have merely been lawfully confined, and will have time to reflect that their calculated endeavours to destroy the Kenya nation have finally failed. . . .

. . . . It has been established beyond doubt—as all those present could see for themselves—that the Kisumu disturbances were organised by the KPU leaders, employing certain youth-wingers, in the guise of trained agitators, as their shock-troops. At this moment in our history, it is sad indeed that highly educated men, well versed in political sabotage, should have exploited some illiterate thugs to serve their own destructive ends. No doubt the sponsors felt nothing but contempt for those tricked into abusing their own dignity and risking their own lives. . . .

. . . . Odinga subsequently tried to profess that it is difficult for "aggrieved" people to keep calm. It may well be understandable that calm can be disrupted, when lies and suspicions are constantly utilised to play on the emotions of unsophisticated men. The fact remains that maintenance of law and order is the primary concern of any Government. Thus, over ensuing days, the Kenya Government made it abundantly clear that it is both able and determined to discharge this duty. . . .

. . . . We are all Kenyans. It is well known to us all that only some of the Kisumu people—only a misguided and exploited few of the Luo in Nyanza—were associated with or even knew (in advance) about this outrage. . . .

. . . . Kenyans in our Government or Parliament—who happen to be Luo by origin—have themselves emphasised the fundamental loyalty, the anxiety for peace, and the readiness to work hard, that distinguish the mass of the Luo people of Nyanza. Some have said that Odinga had become the victim, of forces which he could no longer control, or even understand. Oselu-Nyalick has spoken of what he called Odinga's "madness for greatness". Ayodo and Odero-Jowi have solemnly advised the rational and thinking people, among the Luo, to take stock of their role in Kenya's political and economic life. It would have been tragic—although this has now been averted—to allow Odinga's destructive ambitions to drive the Luo into utter isolation. . . .

. . . . Throughout the period of its existence, the KPU had been increasingly revealed in its true colours, as a seditious movement and a superficial Party. It was deserted more and more, by Kenya nationalists who discovered the truth for themselves: by national leaders like Kaggia, Oduya, Kioko, Anyieni and others; and by organisers or spokesmen at branch or district level. Only the hard core remained. . . .

. . . . We are all Kenyans. We all have an equal vested interest in *Ujamaa,* and in the stability of this country. Those who would preach tribalism now are the greatest enemies, both of our past and of our future. Whether born in Kisumu or Kilifi, in Siaya or Samburu, in Migori or Mumias, in Homa Bay or Habaswein, in Nyakach or Nyeri, all of us have a stake in the same nationhood. . . .

. . . . Never again must we be trapped by the vicious doctrine of divide-and-rule. National unity is everything, especially with all foundations of our rapid progress as a modern nation truly laid. We have the fact now of our Republic. Let us reach towards its soul, by setting and then reaching targets—in terms of economic advancement and social justice—that to all but one united and determined people would seem impossible.

KENYA'S ELECTION: GATEWAY TO THE FUTURE

I have emphasized that the KANU government, which has been in charge of Kenya's affairs for the past six years, is committed to democracy. By holding the forthcoming (December) election, therefore, my government is—in effect—presenting itself and all its adherents to the people, and is seeking to obtain a future mandate on the strength of past performance.

When I delivered (June 1969) an address to the nation on Madaraka Day, I stressed the importance of recalling the KANU manifesto of 1963, which had served as the basis for the overwhelming mandate KANU received from the people. I believe it is wise and proper for any government to present and pursue some clearly stated program on all issues of fundamental importance. Unless an administration does this, it may be able—by stretching a few generalizations and ambiguities—to move in directions that the people never really intended but that they find it difficult to influence or alter.

It is not unknown in some countries for a government or a party to try to distort or ignore the promises it has made. Here, the KANU government has brought an exact summary of the 1963 declarations out into the open. I have made it clear that we are not only ready, but are positively insistent, that the subsequent record be matched against the mandate we had. This might seem to be an unusual attitude, but I believe it is an important element of what democracy in practice ought to mean.

Antigovernment riot at Kisumu on Oct. 25, 1969. The incident was seen as a deliberate, planned attempt to disrupt Kenya's democratic apparatus and led to the proscription of the opposition party (KPU) and the detention of a number of party leaders.

UPI COMPIX

To summarize such a complex and comprehensive document as the 1963 election manifesto is not easy, but it can be boiled down to 30 critical points. In order to promote fuller understanding of what, in fact, has been pursued and achieved, I am reproducing these 30 points here. The original KANU government was pledged, by its mandate:

.... to work for the creation of African Socialism in a truly democratic Kenya;

.... to remove all discrimination on racial, tribal, or religious grounds;

.... to build a country wherein men and women could be motivated by a sense of service;

.... to uphold the rule of law, the Bill of Rights, and the independence of the judiciary;

.... to safeguard the personal and property rights—and the safety—of all people;

.... to adopt a republican constitution made appropriate to Kenya's conditions;

.... to preserve the national integrity of Kenya within existing borders;

.... to modernize the system of local government in Kenya;

.... to revitalize education, on a nonracial basis, and to create an expanded system of education calculated to produce good citizens, armed with the knowledge and character to prepare them for careers and conditions in Kenya;

.... to safeguard African culture, and preserve the core of our customs and social patterns;

.... to encourage women to play their full and proper part in a new society;

.... to right the racial disbalance throughout the public service, as well as in commerce and the professions;

.... to promote community development and self-help schemes;

.... to develop all cooperative institutions that were truly supported by the people;

.... to bolster the hard work of the people through a countrywide expansion of health services and hospital facilities;

.... to launch various kinds of housing schemes and assist house builders;

.... to relieve the plight of the landless unemployed through a program of resettlement schemes, supplemented by the promotion of greater agricultural efficiency;

.... to step up agricultural education and extension services for farmers;

.... to proceed rapidly with land consolidation and the registration of titles;

.... to exploit the neglected potential for industrial development in Kenya;

.... to establish technical training facilities at all levels;

.... to encourage private enterprise, and also to make possible—with regard to major projects—a form of investment partnership between overseas capital and public funds;

.... to see that all foreign capital was directed in accordance with national needs;

.... to secure the responsible cooperation of trade unions in nation building;

.... to perfect the processes for the settlement of industrial disputes;

.... to support a modern economy by establishing a central bank and instituting a stock exchange;

.... to build further on the foundations of the East African Common Services;

.... to follow an absolute policy of nonalignment in international affairs;

.... to support the struggles of other African peoples still under colonial or minority rule;

.... to play a constructive part within counsels of the Commonwealth and the United Nations.

All these requirements and commitments represented—in the aggregate—what is sometimes called the people's will. All have been faithfully undertaken or completed by my government. This is the first thing that we have asked our countrywide electorate to consider. In practice, of course, we have gone beyond the bare mandate in many instances, by seizing fresh opportunities or exploiting resources and techniques so as to advance even more rapidly than could have been foreseen in 1963.

This epilogue is necessarily being written some three weeks before Kenya's general election is scheduled to take place. I merely wish now to refute facile suggestions that the absence of any formal opposition party might rob this election of much of its point.

What will emerge during December is a Parliament—and from this a government—freely chosen by all the people. It is already clear, before the official nomination day, that there will be many rival candidates competing for every constituency. This fact is of the greatest significance. These candidates will be men (and one or two women as well) who are representative of all conceivable interests and vocations. While basically adhering to the KANU manifesto about ends, they will express widely different viewpoints about priorities and means. Far more than in 1963, the candidates will be men who have gained in stature through experience in some key sector of modern public life. But all of them will have in common Kenyan nationalism and a readiness to serve the people.

With no sinecure or contrivance to keep them in office, all the ministers and assistant ministers of my past government will be facing full and fierce competition within their own constituencies from men who believe they can do an even better job. In Nyanza men of great talent and unquestioned loyalty have been set free—in the absence of intimidation—to stand on their individual platforms of personality and outlook. Nowhere will I be traveling or speaking to support one candidate against another. The ballot will be scrupulous and secret.

The people may choose. The people must choose. All the anxious thought that has gone into the framing of our constitution and election procedures has been directed to this end. I will and do claim that this election, especially under African conditions, is far more meaningful and democratic than some of the sophisticated undertakings in the advanced nations, bedeviled as they are by the atmosphere of carnival, the hypnotic mass-media propaganda, and the merciless local intrigue, underwritten by opulent party machines.

Out of this election will come changes, at the people's dictate. But we will also have continuity, at the people's wish: preserving the essential principles of unity and stability and building on the foundations of socioeconomic advancement that have been solidly erected.

The election will open a new gateway to Kenya's future, coincident as it will be—significantly—with the publication of a revised and more ambitious development plan. The pace of our national progress must and will quicken, and the patience that has distinguished the period of foundation laying will obtain its reward.

As a final note, let me reaffirm a point that I recently made, in pronouncing that Kenya's aim must be to move more rapidly—though always in an orderly manner—toward full economic independence. This is not to imply that Kenya will no longer welcome investment or initiative from outside, but it does mean that our own government and people must become absolutely paramount in the areas of control and contribution. In fact, our republic has already made remarkable progress toward this target.

We have our own currency and our own financial policy, backed now by strong reserves of foreign exchange. And it is not often realized just how much of the total investment here since *Uhuru* has come from savings and the generation of wealth inside Kenya. Over the past five-year period, the total contribution of the rest of the world to investment in this republic has been no more than 11%.

Starting with almost nothing, we have laid all the basic foundations of economic advancement. We have built the vital infrastructures, including power and communications. We have launched experiments and gained much valuable experience. We have introduced all the mechanisms required to sponsor and regulate the different sectors of a mixed and expanding economy. We have developed secondary education to the extent that enrollment is already 40,000 higher than was thought to be possible by the end of 1970, and we have made enormous strides in equipping our people with the educational basis of further technical or professional training. All this has supported the deliberate and productive policies of africanization, in both the public and the private sector. We have contrived a heartening increase in the utilization of all kinds of health services, and the people everywhere are better fed, better clothed, and better housed than they ever were before.

Overall, this country has made steady and properly planned progress toward greater prosperity. After the election, our task will be both to augment this growing strength and to translate it into social justice for the people everywhere.

BRITANNICA
Book of the Year
1970

1970 Calendar

1969 Chronology of major international events

1969

JANUARY
S	M	T	W	T	F	S
			1	2	3	4
5	6	7	8	9	10	11
12	13	14	15	16	17	18
19	20	21	22	23	24	25
26	27	28	29	30	31	

FEBRUARY
S	M	T	W	T	F	S
						1
2	3	4	5	6	7	8
9	10	11	12	13	14	15
16	17	18	19	20	21	22
23	24	25	26	27	28	

MARCH
S	M	T	W	T	F	S
						1
2	3	4	5	6	7	8
9	10	11	12	13	14	15
16	17	18	19	20	21	22
23	24	25	26	27	28	29
30	31					

APRIL
S	M	T	W	T	F	S
		1	2	3	4	5
6	7	8	9	10	11	12
13	14	15	16	17	18	19
20	21	22	23	24	25	26
27	28	29	30			

MAY
S	M	T	W	T	F	S
				1	2	3
4	5	6	7	8	9	10
11	12	13	14	15	16	17
18	19	20	21	22	23	24
25	26	27	28	29	30	31

JUNE
S	M	T	W	T	F	S
1	2	3	4	5	6	7
8	9	10	11	12	13	14
15	16	17	18	19	20	21
22	23	24	25	26	27	28
29	30					

JULY
S	M	T	W	T	F	S
		1	2	3	4	5
6	7	8	9	10	11	12
13	14	15	16	17	18	19
20	21	22	23	24	25	26
27	28	29	30	31		

AUGUST
S	M	T	W	T	F	S
					1	2
3	4	5	6	7	8	9
10	11	12	13	14	15	16
17	18	19	20	21	22	23
24	25	26	27	28	29	30
31						

SEPTEMBER
S	M	T	W	T	F	S
	1	2	3	4	5	6
7	8	9	10	11	12	13
14	15	16	17	18	19	20
21	22	23	24	25	26	27
28	29	30				

OCTOBER
S	M	T	W	T	F	S
			1	2	3	4
5	6	7	8	9	10	11
12	13	14	15	16	17	18
19	20	21	22	23	24	25
26	27	28	29	30	31	

NOVEMBER
S	M	T	W	T	F	S
						1
2	3	4	5	6	7	8
9	10	11	12	13	14	15
16	17	18	19	20	21	22
23	24	25	26	27	28	29
30						

DECEMBER
S	M	T	W	T	F	S
	1	2	3	4	5	6
7	8	9	10	11	12	13
14	15	16	17	18	19	20
21	22	23	24	25	26	27
28	29	30	31			

1970

THE YEAR 1970 of the Christian Era corresponds to the year of Creation 5730-5731 of the Jewish calendar; to the year 1389-1390 of the Muslim hegira; to the 194th year of the United States; and to the 202nd year of the *Encyclopædia Britannica*.

JANUARY
S	M	T	W	T	F	S
				1	2	3
4	5	6	7	8	9	10
11	12	13	14	15	16	17
18	19	20	21	22	23	24
25	26	27	28	29	30	31

FEBRUARY
S	M	T	W	T	F	S
1	2	3	4	5	6	7
8	9	10	11	12	13	14
15	16	17	18	19	20	21
22	23	24	25	26	27	28

MARCH
S	M	T	W	T	F	S
1	2	3	4	5	6	7
8	9	10	11	12	13	14
15	16	17	18	19	20	21
22	23	24	25	26	27	28
29	30	31				

APRIL
S	M	T	W	T	F	S
			1	2	3	4
5	6	7	8	9	10	11
12	13	14	15	16	17	18
19	20	21	22	23	24	25
26	27	28	29	30		

MAY
S	M	T	W	T	F	S
					1	2
3	4	5	6	7	8	9
10	11	12	13	14	15	16
17	18	19	20	21	22	23
24	25	26	27	28	29	30
31						

JUNE
S	M	T	W	T	F	S
	1	2	3	4	5	6
7	8	9	10	11	12	13
14	15	16	17	18	19	20
21	22	23	24	25	26	27
28	29	30				

JULY
S	M	T	W	T	F	S
			1	2	3	4
5	6	7	8	9	10	11
12	13	14	15	16	17	18
19	20	21	22	23	24	25
26	27	28	29	30	31	

AUGUST
S	M	T	W	T	F	S
						1
2	3	4	5	6	7	8
9	10	11	12	13	14	15
16	17	18	19	20	21	22
23	24	25	26	27	28	29
30	31					

SEPTEMBER
S	M	T	W	T	F	S
		1	2	3	4	5
6	7	8	9	10	11	12
13	14	15	16	17	18	19
20	21	22	23	24	25	26
27	28	29	30			

OCTOBER
S	M	T	W	T	F	S
				1	2	3
4	5	6	7	8	9	10
11	12	13	14	15	16	17
18	19	20	21	22	23	24
25	26	27	28	29	30	31

NOVEMBER
S	M	T	W	T	F	S
1	2	3	4	5	6	7
8	9	10	11	12	13	14
15	16	17	18	19	20	21
22	23	24	25	26	27	28
29	30					

DECEMBER
S	M	T	W	T	F	S
		1	2	3	4	5
6	7	8	9	10	11	12
13	14	15	16	17	18	19
20	21	22	23	24	25	26
27	28	29	30	31		

1971

JANUARY
S	M	T	W	T	F	S
					1	2
3	4	5	6	7	8	9
10	11	12	13	14	15	16
17	18	19	20	21	22	23
24	25	26	27	28	29	30
31						

FEBRUARY
S	M	T	W	T	F	S
	1	2	3	4	5	6
7	8	9	10	11	12	13
14	15	16	17	18	19	20
21	22	23	24	25	26	27
28						

MARCH
S	M	T	W	T	F	S
	1	2	3	4	5	6
7	8	9	10	11	12	13
14	15	16	17	18	19	20
21	22	23	24	25	26	27
28	29	30	31			

APRIL
S	M	T	W	T	F	S
				1	2	3
4	5	6	7	8	9	10
11	12	13	14	15	16	17
18	19	20	21	22	23	24
25	26	27	28	29	30	

MAY
S	M	T	W	T	F	S
						1
2	3	4	5	6	7	8
9	10	11	12	13	14	15
16	17	18	19	20	21	22
23	24	25	26	27	28	29
30	31					

JUNE
S	M	T	W	T	F	S
		1	2	3	4	5
6	7	8	9	10	11	12
13	14	15	16	17	18	19
20	21	22	23	24	25	26
27	28	29	30			

JULY
S	M	T	W	T	F	S
				1	2	3
4	5	6	7	8	9	10
11	12	13	14	15	16	17
18	19	20	21	22	23	24
25	26	27	28	29	30	31

AUGUST
S	M	T	W	T	F	S
1	2	3	4	5	6	7
8	9	10	11	12	13	14
15	16	17	18	19	20	21
22	23	24	25	26	27	28
29	30	31				

SEPTEMBER
S	M	T	W	T	F	S
			1	2	3	4
5	6	7	8	9	10	11
12	13	14	15	16	17	18
19	20	21	22	23	24	25
26	27	28	29	30		

OCTOBER
S	M	T	W	T	F	S
					1	2
3	4	5	6	7	8	9
10	11	12	13	14	15	16
17	18	19	20	21	22	23
24	25	26	27	28	29	30
31						

NOVEMBER
S	M	T	W	T	F	S
	1	2	3	4	5	6
7	8	9	10	11	12	13
14	15	16	17	18	19	20
21	22	23	24	25	26	27
28	29	30				

DECEMBER
S	M	T	W	T	F	S
			1	2	3	4
5	6	7	8	9	10	11
12	13	14	15	16	17	18
19	20	21	22	23	24	25
26	27	28	29	30	31	

RELIGIOUS, NATIONAL, AND OTHER MAJOR HOLIDAYS

January 1970
1 New Year's Day
1 Cameroon, Haiti, Sudan
4 Burma
***6** Epiphany (Twelfth Night)
11 Chad
26 Australia, India

February
2 Candlemas
4 Ceylon
6 New Zealand
10 Shrove Tuesday, Mardi Gras
11 Ash Wednesday
14 St. Valentine's Day
15 First Sunday in Lent
16 Lithuania
24 Estonia
25 Kuwait
27 Dominican Republic

March
3 Morocco
6 Ghana
9 Muslim New Year (1390)
11 Denmark
12 Mauritius
15 Ides of March
17 St. Patrick's Day
17 Ireland
22 Purim (Feast of Lots)
22 Palm Sunday
23 Pakistan
25 Greece
27 Good Friday
29 Easter Sunday

April
1 April Fool's Day
4 Hungary, Senegal
14 Pan American Day
17 Syria
21 Pesach (Passover), 1st day
26 Tanzania
27 Sierra Leone, Togo
29 Japan
30 Netherlands

May
1 International Labour Day
3 Eastern Orthodox Easter
7 Ascension Day
9 Czechoslovakia
11 Israel
11 Laos
14 Paraguay
17 Pentecost
17 Norway
24 Commonwealth Day, U.K.
25 Argentina, Jordan
26 Guyana
27 Afghanistan
***28** Corpus Christi
30 Memorial Day, U.S.
31 South Africa

June
1 Tunisia
2 Italy
10 Shabuoth (Feast of Weeks), 1st day
10 Portugal
11 Kamehameha Day, Polynesian peoples
11 Nepal
12 Philippines
13 Sovereign's Birthday, U.K.
17 Iceland
23 Luxembourg
24 Midsummer Day
30 Congo (Kinshasa)

July
1 Burundi, Canada, Rwanda, Somali Republic
4 United States
5 Venezuela
6 Malawi
12 Orangeman's Day, N.Ire.
14 France, Iraq
15 St. Swithin's Day
18 Spain
20 Colombia
21 Belgium
22 Poland
23 Ethiopia, U.A.R.
26 Liberia, Maldives
28 Peru

August
1 Dahomey, Switzerland
3 Jamaica
6 Bolivia
7 Ivory Coast
9 Singapore
10 Ecuador
15 Korea
17 Gabon, Indonesia
23 Romania
25 Uruguay
31 Malaysia, Trinidad and Tobago

September
6 Swaziland
7 Labor Day, U.S. and Canada
7 Brazil
9 Bulgaria
15 Costa Rica, El Salvador, Guatemala, Honduras, Nicaragua
16 Mexico
18 Chile
21 Malta
22 Mali
23 Saudi Arabia
26 Yemen
30 Botswana

October
1 Rosh Hashana (Jewish New Year, 5731)
1 Cyprus, Nigeria
2 Guinea
4 Lesotho
9 Uganda
10 Yom Kippur (Day of Atonement)
10 China
12 Thanksgiving Day, Canada
14 Malagasy
15 Sukkoth (Feast of Tabernacles), 1st day
24 United Nations Day
24 Zambia
26 Austria, Iran
29 Turkey
31 Ramadân, 1st day
31 Halloween

November
1 All Saints' Day
1 Algeria, Vietnam
3 Panama
7-8 U.S.S.R.
11 Sweden
18 Latvia
22 Lebanon
26 Thanksgiving Day, U.S.
28 Mauritania
29 First Sunday in Advent
29 Yugoslavia
30 Barbados

December
1 Central African Republic
5 Thailand
6 Finland
11 Upper Volta
12 Kenya
18 Niger
23 Hanukkah (Feast of Lights), 1st day
24 Libya
25 Christmas Day
31 New Year's Eve

*Subject to change, in accordance with the Constitution on Sacred Liturgy, promulgated by Ecumenical Council, Vatican II.

Chronology of Events 1969

JANUARY

1

Viet Cong released three U.S. Army prisoners of war in South Vietnam.

New Czechoslovak federal government was inaugurated.

Second round of tariff cuts stipulated by the Kennedy Round agreement went into effect in 11 countries; EEC nations initiated common transport measures.

Biafran leader Col. Odumegwu Ojukwu called for a limited truce to allow relief supplies to reach victims of the Nigerian civil war.

2

Luis A. Ferré succeeded Roberto Sánchez Vilella as governor of Puerto Rico.

Israeli forces were reported to have opened fire on three Lebanese border positions.

3

First session of the 91st U.S. Congress convened; the House of Representatives voted to seat Adam Clayton Powell, Jr. (Dem., N.Y.), fine him $25,000, and strip him of his 22 years of seniority; Sen. Edward M. Kennedy (Mass.) defeated Russell Long (La.) for the post of Democratic whip.

4

Violent fighting erupted in Northern Ireland between Protestant counterdemonstrators and Roman Catholic students on the fourth day of a civil rights march from Belfast to Londonderry.

5

Henry Cabot Lodge was named by Pres.-elect Richard M. Nixon to replace W. Averell Harriman as the chief U.S. negotiator at the Paris peace talks on Vietnam.

6

Government of Kenya began notifying Indian merchants that their retail licenses would not be renewed.

San Francisco State College opened after having been closed for three weeks in the face of continuing student rebellion and a teachers' strike.

7

Czechoslovak Communist Party Presidium removed Josef Smrkovsky from the chairmanship of the National Assembly.

Coalition of opposition parties announced in Dacca that it would boycott Pakistani national elections.

South Vietnamese government announced it had protested continued Communist violations of the Demilitarized Zone to the International Control Commission.

France confirmed that it had barred the sale to Israel of all military equipment and spare parts.

Trial of Sirhan Bishara Sirhan, accused of the murder of Sen. Robert F. Kennedy, opened in Los Angeles, Calif.

U.S.S.R. and France agreed in Paris to double their trade in the next five years.

8

Lebanese Pres. Charles Helou accepted the resignation of Prime Minister Abdullah Yafi and his Cabinet and asked former Prime Minister Rashid Karami to form a new government.

International Committee of the Red Cross announced in Geneva that its relief flights to Biafra had been halted because Equatorial Guinea had banned the importation of diesel fuel.

New Chinese Communist Party draft constitution was reported to designate Defense Minister Lin Piao as Chairman Mao Tse-tung's successor.

Three Soviet and two East German trawlers were seized by a Norwegian gunboat for violating "military waters."

10

Text of a Soviet plan for Middle East peace was published in a Beirut newspaper.

Sweden announced it would extend full diplomatic recognition to North Vietnam.

Saturday Evening Post, founded in 1821, announced plans to suspend publication.

12

New York Jets defeated the Baltimore Colts, 16–7, to win the U.S. professional football championship.

Massive demonstration against British immigration policies was held in London to coincide with the Commonwealth heads of state conference.

13

Czechoslovak journalists agreed to self-censorship in resolving their dispute with the Communist Party.

14

Pres. Lyndon B. Johnson, in his final state of the union message, urged the U.S. to press for peace in Vietnam and the Middle East while continuing his social programs at home.

France pledged it would aid Lebanon if it were attacked by Israel.

South Vietnam proposed that U.S. troops begin a gradual phased withdrawal from that country.

Canadian House of Commons reconvened and began operating under new rules of procedure.

Japanese steel producers and the European Coal and Steel Community announced that they had agreed to restrict steel exports to the U.S.

Sen. Fred R. Harris (Dem., Okla.) was named to succeed Lawrence F. O'Brien as Democratic National Committee chairman.

15

Communiqué closing the Commonwealth heads of state conference noted the opposition of Asian and African members to Britain's policy on Rhodesia.

Pres. Johnson submitted to Congress a budget for fiscal 1970, stipulating that a $3.4 billion surplus was needed to counter inflation.

Denmark, Finland, Norway, and Sweden released plans for a Nordic Economic Union.

16

NATO Defense Planning Committee announced in Brussels the establishment of a NATO Mediterranean fleet.

Brazilian government removed from office 3 Supreme Court justices and 37 federal congressmen.

EEC Executive Commission announced it would institute court proceedings against France for failing to reduce its export subsidy.

Two Soviet Soyuz spacecraft docked in orbit and accomplished the first transfer of men from one space vehicle to another.

Pres. Johnson's annual economic message to Congress cautioned that economic restraint should not be pushed to the point of bringing on a recession.

Jan Palach, a student, burned himself to death publicly in Prague to protest the Soviet occupation of Czechoslovakia.

17

British government White Paper proposed legislation restricting the right to strike.

Reports of political turmoil in China persisted as monitored radio broadcasts denounced Wang En-mao, military commander of Sinkiang Uighur Autonomous Region.

18

South Vietnamese and National Liberation Front delegations joined the U.S. and North Vietnamese teams at the expanded Vietnam peace talks in Paris.

U.S. Secretary of Defense Clark M. Clifford reported that the U.S.S.R.'s store of intercontinental ballistic missiles had increased significantly in the preceding two and a half years.

Bolivian Pres. René Barrientos Ortuño declared a state of siege and suspended constitutional guarantees.

20

Richard M. Nixon was inaugurated as the 37th president of the U.S.

U.S.S.R. affirmed it was ready to begin talks with the U.S. on the control of nuclear missiles.

U.S. Navy court of inquiry on the capture of the USS "Pueblo" opened in Coronado, Calif.

21

Newly inaugurated Delaware Gov. Russell W. Peterson (Rep.) ordered the withdrawal of National Guard troops stationed in Wilmington since April 1968.

22

U.S. Secretary of the Treasury David M. Kennedy stated that the official U.S. gold price would remain $35 per ounce.

French Pres. Charles de Gaulle stated he would serve his full presidential term.

Richard M. Nixon takes his oath as 37th president of the U.S., . . . Jan. 20, 1969.

UPI COMPIX

23

Soviet bloc's Council for Mutual Economic Assistance (Comecon) ended its 22nd session in Berlin in disagreement over several major issues.

U.S. Senate concluded its confirmations of Pres. Nixon's Cabinet appointments by approving the nomination of Walter J. Hickel as secretary of the interior.

24

Chinese chargé d'affaires to the Netherlands Liao Hoshu defected to the West at The Hague.

Spanish government declared a state of exception or emergency, reversing its liberalization policy.

Representatives of France and the Canadian province of Quebec signed three letters of agreement on scientific and economic matters.

Italian Foreign Minister Pietro Nenni announced that his government would recognize the People's Republic of China.

25

U.S. negotiators at the Vietnam peace talks in Paris proposed the restoration of the neutrality of the Demilitarized Zone.

Edward Heath, U.K. Conservative Party leader, called for greater curbs on nonwhite immigration into Britain.

26

Japanese Prime Minister Eisaku Sato declared his determination to have the U.S. restore Okinawa to Japan.

27

Iraq hanged publicly 14 persons, including 9 Jews, charged with spying.

Soviet Foreign Minister Andrei A. Gromyko accused the U.S. of intensifying its military activities in Laos.

North Vietnam charged that U.S. planes had dropped bombs north of the Demilitarized Zone; U.S. State Department denied the charge.

28

U.S. Senate rejected attempts to modify its filibuster rule.

29

Nigerian federal forces launched a "final offensive" against Biafran cities.

Commerce Department announced that the U.S. trade surplus in 1968 had fallen to $726 million.

30

Pres. Nixon directed the Defense Department to develop a plan to end the military draft and create a volunteer army.

North Vietnamese and NLF delegates at the Paris peace talks rejected the U.S. proposal to restore neutrality in the Demilitarized Zone, maintaining that military questions depended on a political settlement.

31

Canadian Secretary of State for External Affairs Mitchell Sharp denounced an exchange of letters between France and Quebec Province that included plans for a joint communications satellite system.

FEBRUARY

1

U.S.S.R. and Peru reestablished diplomatic relations.

Relief airlifts of the International Committee of the Red Cross to refugees in Biafra were resumed from Cotonou, Dahomey.

2

French Pres. de Gaulle called for a spring referendum on constitutional reforms to permit greater regional authority.

3

Al Fatah leader Yasir Arafat was elected chairman of a new executive committee of the Palestine Liberation Organization.

Arab demonstrations and violence occurred for the second day in the Israeli-held city of Gaza.

Mozambique Liberation Front leader Eduardo Chivambo Mondlane was assassinated in Dar es Salaam, Tanzania.

5

Pres. Nixon announced that political patronage was to be eliminated from the U.S. postal service and urged prompt ratification of the treaty to halt the spread of nuclear weapons.

U.S. Federal Communications Commission proposed that cigarette advertising be banned from radio and television.

Italian workers staged a 24-hour strike to support demands for higher government pensions.

Pakistani Pres. Muhammad Ayub Khan announced he had invited opposition leaders to meet with him to discuss demands for constitutional changes.

UN representatives of the Big Four countries began informal preliminary discussions on the possibility of a Middle East peace conference.

6

Peruvian Pres. Juan Velasco Alvarado announced the seizure of all the assets of the International Petroleum Co.

U.S. Defense Department announced that the Sentinel antiballistic missile (ABM) program would be halted for a one-month review.

Al Fatah leader Yasir Arafat announced plans to shift his main guerrilla forces from the U.A.R. and Syria to Jordan.

WIDE WORLD

Anti-U.S. rioting in Istanbul . . . February 16.

7

Caribbean Island of Anguilla voted to break all ties with Britain.

Romanian Communist Party Secretary-General Nicolae Ceausescu reaffirmed Romania's policy of independence and sovereignty.

Czechoslovak Premier Oldrich Cernik announced his country had obtained pledges of $200 million–$300 million in loans for industry.

8

Democratic National Chairman Fred R. Harris announced the establishment of two special commissions on party reform.

Offshore oil well was capped after leaking for 12 days and coating 30 mi. of beaches at Santa Barbara, Calif.

9

Congress Party of Indian Prime Minister Indira Gandhi suffered setbacks in five state assembly elections.

Bank for International Settlements agreed on a program to prevent currency speculation from leading to devaluation.

East Germany announced that West German Federal Assembly members traveling to West Berlin for presidential elections would be barred from crossing East German territory.

10

Canadian Secretary of State for External Affairs Mitchell Sharp announced that Canada would explore the possible establishment of diplomatic relations with China.

Yugoslavia and West Germany signed an industrial, technical, and economic cooperation agreement.

Antipollution guidelines were issued by U.S. Health, Education, and Welfare Secretary Robert H. Finch.

U.A.R. Pres. Gamal Abd-al-Nasser proposed a five-point plan for Middle East peace.

11

Israeli Knesset defeated a no-confidence motion against the government of Prime Minister Levi Eshkol.

Yugoslav Federal Assembly approved the creation of territorial defense, or guerrilla, units throughout the country.

Rioting in Bombay left 43 dead in five days.

12

Canadian federal-provincial conference considering revisions of the constitution adjourned in Ottawa without making any concrete decisions.

Rhodesian nationalist leader Ndabaningi Sithole was convicted of planning to assassinate Prime Minister Ian D. Smith.

13

British Prime Minister Harold Wilson and West German Chancellor Kurt Georg Kiesinger ended a two-day meeting with a declaration of solidarity in efforts to achieve European unity and security.

U.S.S.R. and Japan signed an agreement allowing commercial Japanese planes to fly to Europe across Siberia.

14

Pres. Nixon established a White House Office of Intergovernmental Relations to be headed by Vice-Pres. Spiro T. Agnew.

Peruvian Navy gunboat attacked two U.S. fishing vessels off the coast of Peru.

France refused to attend a special meeting of the Western European Union Council in London, claiming the U.K. request for the meeting was invalid without French consent.

East German and Soviet troops reportedly began maneuvers west of Berlin.

Longest dock strike in New York history ended after 57 days; strikes continued at 20 other U.S. ports.

Twelve-hour strike called by

Pakistan's opposition coalition resulted in violence in West Pakistan cities.

Indian Prime Minister Indira Gandhi named Dinesh Singh to be foreign minister in a major Cabinet revision.

15

Rhodesian Prime Minister Ian D. Smith proposed constitutional changes to prevent black African majority rule.

Willie Mae Rogers resigned her five-day-old appointment as Pres. Nixon's consultant on consumer affairs.

Italian Communist Party Congress closed pledging to continue its independent course.

16

Fighting broke out in Istanbul as 20,000 persons clashed over a visit by ships of the U.S. 6th Fleet.

17

France announced that it was ceasing all participation in the Western European Union.

Anti-inflationary recommendations were submitted to the U.S. Congress by Pres. Nixon's Council of Economic Advisers.

Pakistani Pres. Ayub Khan released a number of political prisoners, including former Foreign Minister Zulfikar Ali Bhutto, and lifted the state of emergency following two weeks of political disturbances.

18

U.S. military spokesman reported there had been no major fighting during the 24 hours of the allies' Tet truce in Vietnam.

U.S. Senate Foreign Relations Committee began hearings on the Sentinel antiballistic missile system.

Israeli commercial airliner was attacked by Arab terrorists as it was about to take off from the Zürich, Switz., airport.

Chinese government canceled the February meeting with the U.S.

19

London School of Economics and Political Science reopened after having been closed for over three weeks because of student disorders.

Pres. Nixon announced his decision to transfer Head Start and Job Corps programs from the Office of Economic Opportunity to established departments.

20

U.K. Defence Minister Denis Healey called on the U.S. to reaffirm its commitment to defend Europe with nuclear weapons.

Pres. Nixon asked Congress for legislation revising the U.S. presidential election procedure.

21

Arab terrorist bomb exploded in a Jerusalem supermarket.

Pakistani Pres. Ayub Khan announced he would not be a candidate in upcoming presidential elections.

British accounts of a meeting between French Pres. de Gaulle and U.K. ambassador to France Christopher Soames reported that de Gaulle had proposed replacing the EEC with new economic and political arrangements.

Western European Union Assembly, meeting in Paris with French delegates attending, endorsed U.K. efforts to encourage consultation within the organization.

22

French Foreign Minister Michel Debré charged Britain had revealed the contents of a confidential meeting by publishing Pres. de Gaulle's plans for the future of Europe.

Brazilian bishops urged prompt democratization of the regime.

23

Pres. Nixon arrived in Brussels, the first stop on an eight-day European tour.

Viet Cong and North Vietnamese troops launched a coordinated series of shellings and ground attacks throughout South Vietnam.

24

Israeli jets bombed two sites in Syria on a road allegedly used by Arab commandos; U.A.R. declared a state of emergency.

Northern Ireland Prime Minister Terence M. O'Neill failed to win a decisive mandate for civil rights reforms in parliamentary elections.

Tanzania, the first country to get U.S. Peace Corps assistance, canceled the program.

25

Australia and New Zealand announced that they would maintain military forces in Malaysia and Singapore after the withdrawal of British forces in 1971.

Arab terrorist bomb severely damaged the British consulate in East Jerusalem.

26

U.A.R. Pres. Nasser warned that another full-scale Middle East war could result if Israel did not withdraw from captured Arab territories.

Pravda article expressed strong U.S.S.R. opposition to Czechoslovak efforts to increase Western trade.

Israeli Prime Minister Levi Eshkol died of a heart attack in Jerusalem; Deputy Prime Minister Yigal Allon was named acting prime minister.

27

Brazilian Pres. Artur da Costa e Silva issued decrees extending government control of political and civil affairs.

28

Equatorial Guinea requested a UN peace-keeping force to counter aggressive acts by Spanish forces.

MARCH

1

Border guards sealed the main access routes to West Berlin for about two hours; Soviet and East German tank convoys were seen along the routes.

Clay L. Shaw was acquitted in New Orleans of charges of conspiring to assassinate U.S. Pres. John F. Kennedy.

Pathet Lao rejected a Laotian government offer to hold talks to end the civil war.

Syrian Defense Minister Lieut. Gen. Hafez al-Assad was reported to have seized control of the government.

2

U.S.S.R. warned it would not guarantee the safety of air traffic to West Berlin.

Anglo-French supersonic aircraft, the Concorde, made its first test flight at Toulouse, France.

Pres. Nixon returned to Washington from his tour of Western Europe.

Soviet and Chinese border forces engaged in heavy fighting over Damansky (Chenpao) Island, disputed territory in the Ussuri River.

3

State of emergency was declared in Equatorial Guinea.

Nigeria confirmed that the Biafran Army had encircled the city of Owerri in a counteroffensive.

4

Violence erupted in Pakistan after two relatively calm weeks.

East German negotiator repeated offers to allow West Berliners greater access to East Berlin in exchange for moving the site of the West German elections.

Demonstrators protesting the Sino-Soviet border clash besieged the U.S.S.R. embassy in Peking for the second day.

Pres. Nixon warned that the U.S. would take appropriate action against new Viet Cong offensive.

5

Gustav Heinemann was elected president of West Germany by federal electors meeting in West Berlin despite Soviet and East German objections.

6

Saigon came under the heaviest and most damaging rocket attack of the current Communist offensive.

U.S. Ambassador Lodge protested the increased Communist attacks on South Vietnam at plenary session of the Paris peace talks.

Arab terrorist bomb exploded in the cafeteria of the Hebrew University in Jerusalem; Israeli security forces destroyed five Arab houses in East Jerusalem.

7

U.S. troops threw back Communist attacks on military outposts in South Vietnam.

8

U.S. military sources reported the incursion of a Marine force into Laos.

UN Secretary-General U Thant announced he was sending a representative to Equatorial Guinea.

9

U.A.R. Armed Forces Chief of Staff Lieut. Gen. Abdel Moneim Riad was killed during the second day of an artillery duel between Israeli and U.A.R. forces across the Suez Canal.

10

James Earl Ray pleaded guilty to the assassination of the Rev. Martin Luther King, Jr., and was sentenced to 99 years in prison in brief court proceedings in Memphis, Tenn.

U.S. Secretary of Defense Melvin R. Laird completed a fact-finding tour of South Vietnam.

Japan announced that its 1968 gross national product of $135 billion was now the second largest in the non-Communist world, surpassing that of West Germany.

11

Nixon administration appointed John N. Irwin as special emissary to explore a resolution of outstanding differences between the U.S. and Peru.

North Korean and U.S. forces exchanged fire in the Korean demilitarized zone.

French Pres. de Gaulle denounced a 24-hour strike of industrial workers as an attempt to "topple the Republic."

Cambodia released four U.S. airmen captured by the Viet Cong in February.

Rafael Caldera became the 43rd president of Venezuela.

12

Gen. Andrew J. Goodpaster was named to succeed Gen. Lyman L. Lemnitzer as supreme allied commander, Europe.

Yugoslav Pres. Tito proposed changes allowing for collective rule for Yugoslavia's Communist Party.

13

Pakistani Pres. Ayub Khan concluded four days of meetings in Rawalpindi with opposition leaders.

Nigeria rejected a Biafran call for a one-month truce to work out plans for a permanent cease-fire.

U.K. emissary to Anguilla reported in London that the Caribbean island was controlled by a "gangster-type element."

Brazilian government undertook its fourth political purge of recent months.

Apollo 9 spacecraft splashed down in the Atlantic Ocean after a ten-day flight testing the lunar module.

U.S. Senate approved the nuclear nonproliferation treaty.

U.S. Ambassador Lodge charged at the Paris peace talks that the continued Communist offensive was an attempt to terrorize the people of South Vietnam into submission.

14

Pres. Nixon asked the U.S. Congress to approve a revised Sentinel antiballistic missile program.

French Pres. de Gaulle and West German Chancellor Kiesinger held their semiannual meeting in Paris.

Israeli jets began an announced series of missions against Arab guerrilla bases by attacking east of the Jordan River.

Pres. Nixon said there was no prospect of a reduction of U.S. forces in Vietnam.

Soviet sources reported that China had halted all shipments across its territory from the U.S.S.R. to North Vietnam.

15

U.S. Marine force moved into the Vietnamese Demilitarized Zone for first time since the November 1968 cease-fire.

Uruguay Pres. Jorge Pacheco Areco lifted many restrictions imposed during a state of emergency in June 1968.

New clashes between Chinese and U.S.S.R. troops along the Ussuri River were reported.

17

Warsaw Treaty Organization member states meeting in Budapest established a combined command for Warsaw Pact forces.

French Council of State charged that Pres. de Gaulle's call for a referendum on reforms was unconstitutional.

Mrs. Golda Meir was sworn in as Israel's fourth prime minister.

Cuba announced it had established an embassy with the Vietnamese National Liberation Front.

19

Anguilla offered no resistance as 100 British paratroops launched a predawn invasion to reestablish British control of the island.

National Liberation Front issued a statement urging its forces to initiate a final, all-out war effort in Vietnam.

20

Communist gunners carried out 65 rocket and mortar attacks throughout South Vietnam.

Sen. Edward M. Kennedy urged that the U.S. adopt a seven-point program to establish better relations with China.

21

Pres. Sékou Touré of Guinea announced that two members of his Cabinet had been arrested as leaders of a conspiracy to overthrow the government.

22

Soviet news agency announced that the frequently postponed World Conference of Communist and Workers' Parties would be held in Moscow on June 5.

British troops in Anguilla . . . March 19

HENRI BUREAU-GAMMA—PIX FROM PUBLIX

Pres. Nixon indicated that the task of dealing with student protests should be left to college authorities.

23

Two major drives by U.S. and South Vietnamese forces were disclosed to have been under way in recent weeks in the A Shau Valley and around Saigon.

24

Jordanian Prime Minister Bahjat al-Talhouni resigned and was replaced by Foreign Minister Abdel Monem Rifai.

25

U.S. and South Vietnam emphasized the need for private talks to break the impasse in the Vietnam peace talks in Paris.

Pakistani Pres. Ayub Khan resigned and turned over power to Gen. Agha Muhammad Yahya Khan, commander in chief of the Army, who proclaimed martial law.

26

Pres. Nixon asked Congress to extend the 10% income tax surcharge for one year.

27

North Vietnamese and National Liberation Front delegations to the Paris peace talks denounced allied overtures for secret peace talks.

British Labour Party candidates were defeated in by-elections for three House of Commons seats.

28

Czechoslovak victory over a U.S.S.R. team in the world championship hockey tournament in Stockholm touched off anti-Soviet demonstrations in Czechoslovak cities.

Dwight D. Eisenhower, 34th president of the U.S., died in Washington, D.C.

29

Pope Paul VI named 33 new cardinals.

30

Israel formally rejected all Big Four proposals on the Middle East that would be contrary to Israel's vital interests.

31

U.K. Prime Minister Wilson completed a five-day visit to Nigeria for talks with Maj. Gen. Yakubu Gowon, leader of the military government; Biafran leader Ojukwu refused to meet with Wilson.

APRIL

1

Ninth Congress of the Chinese Communist Party opened in Peking.

UN Security Council voted to censure Israel for an air attack a week earlier on the Jordanian town of Salt.

U.S. Secretary of Defense Laird announced cuts in the defense budget for fiscal 1970.

2

Iran severed diplomatic relations with Lebanon.

Ghanaian Chief of State Lieut. Gen. Joseph A. Ankrah resigned and was replaced by Brig. Akwasi A. Afrifa.

Pope Paul VI strongly criticized dissidence within the Roman Catholic Church.

Twenty-one Black Panther Party members were charged with plotting to bomb five New York City stores.

Longest U.S. dock strike ended after 103 days with settlements in Galveston and Houston, Tex.

3

Prime Minister Wilson warned that British Cabinet members failing to support government programs would be dismissed.

Big Four UN representatives opened formal discussions in New York City on the Middle East conflict.

U.S. combat deaths in the Vietnam war exceeded those of the Korean War, according to figures issued by the U.S. command in Saigon.

Canadian Prime Minister Pierre Elliott Trudeau announced that his government would begin a phased reduction of the size of its NATO forces.

4

Pres. Nixon announced modest relaxations of controls over U.S. lending and investment abroad.

7

South Vietnamese Pres. Nguyen Van Thieu proposed a six-point program to end the war.

U.S. Secretary of State William P. Rogers announced the indefinite extension of the deadline for the imposition of economic sanctions against Peru for failing to compensate for expropriated U.S.-owned properties.

8

Pres. Nixon earmarked $200 million for clearing and refurbishing riot-damaged areas in 20 U.S. cities.

King Husain of Jordan arrived in Washington, D.C., for talks with Pres. Nixon.

Arab guerrillas and Israeli forces clashed at the ports of Elath and Aqaba on the Gulf of Aqaba; Israel and U.A.R. artillery exchanged heavy fire along the Suez Canal.

Haskell Karp, first person to be kept alive with an artificial heart, died in Houston after receiving a human heart transplant.

General strike paralyzed West Bengal.

9

Greek Prime Minister Georgios

Papadopoulos restored three basic constitutional rights previously held in abeyance.

Student revolt at Harvard University began with the seizure of University Hall by 300 militant students.

10

French Pres. de Gaulle declared he would resign if his referendum on reform was defeated.

Twentieth anniversary of NATO was commemorated in Washington, D.C., ceremonies.

Three Republican U.S. senators left a fact-finding tour of Alaskan villages, charging it was a publicity stunt for Sen. Edward Kennedy.

11

U.S.S.R. proposed the resumption of border negotiations with China.

Sympathy strike throughout Italy protested police handling of residents of Battipaglia who had demonstrated against economic conditions.

Central African Republic Pres. Jean Bedel Bokassa announced that an attempted overthrow of the government had been crushed.

Nixon administration announced a major cutback in the federal Job Corps program.

12

U.S. Federal Trade Commission announced it would require large companies to notify it of mergers 60 days in advance.

Pres. Nixon announced a $4 billion reduction in the revised federal budget for fiscal 1970.

14

Pres. Nixon outlined ten domestic programs he intended to submit to Congress.

Portuguese Premier Marcello Caetano began the first visit by a Portuguese premier to that country's African territories.

15

U.K. Chancellor of the Exchequer Roy Jenkins presented the British budget for fiscal 1969–70, including a wide range of tax increases.

U.S. Navy intelligence plane with 31 men aboard was shot down by two North Korean MiG's off the Korean coast.

16

Antistrike legislation was formally introduced in the British House of Commons.

Summit conference of East and Central African states adopted a manifesto condemning white-ruled regimes in southern Africa.

Chilean Chamber of Deputies rejected Pres. Eduardo Frei Montalva's constitutional reform bill.

17

West German central bank (Bundesbank) was the fifth national monetary agency, along with those of Belgium, Switzerland, the Netherlands, and the U.S., to raise its discount rate in April.

Alexander Dubcek was replaced by Gustav Husak as Czechoslovak Communist Party first secretary.

Sirhan Bishara Sirhan was convicted by a Los Angeles jury of first-degree murder for the slaying of Sen. Robert F. Kennedy.

U.K. Prime Minister Wilson withdrew a bill to reform the House of Lords.

18

U.S. charged at Panmunjom that the North Korean attack on a U.S. plane was a "calculated act of aggression"; Pres. Nixon ordered the resumption of U.S. reconnaissance flights off North Korea.

Bernadette Devlin was elected to the British House of Commons in a Northern Ireland by-election.

19

Iran declared void a 1937 agreement with Iraq on control of the Shatt al Arab river border.

U.A.R. commandos crossed the Suez Canal to attack Israeli positions on the eastern bank.

U.S. presented a squadron of 20 fighter-bombers to the South Vietnamese Air Force.

20

Organization of African Unity talks on Nigerian peace collapsed in Liberia.

Negro students emerged from a Cornell University building they had seized carrying rifles and shotguns.

Bomb attacks on nine post offices and a bus station climaxed a weekend of violence among Roman Catholics, Protestants, and police in Northern Ireland.

21

Pres. Nixon's tax message to Congress called for a 50% reduction in the income tax surcharge in January 1970 and repeal of the 7% investment credit.

U.S. Supreme Court declared unconstitutional state residency requirements for welfare benefits.

British troops began to guard public utilities in Northern Ireland; emergency debate on Ulster crisis began in the House of Commons.

U.S. Navy task force moved into the Sea of Japan.

22

Civil rights leader the Rev. Ralph D. Abernathy began leading marches in Charleston, S.C., supporting a month-old strike by nonprofessional hospital workers.

Nixon administration began discussions of its tax reform proposals with Congress.

UN Secretary-General U Thant reported that a virtual state of war existed between Israel and the U.A.R. along the Suez Canal.

REFERENDUM DU 27 AVRIL 1969
POURCENTAGE DES "OUI" PAR DÉPARTEMENT
TOTAL DES SUFFRAGES DÉCOMPTÉS
INSCRITS :
18.695.781
VOTANTS :
15.052.776
EXPRIMÉS :
14.628.914
OUI :
7.098.989
NON :
7.529.925

LIAISON AGENCY

de Gaulle's reform referendum is lost . . . April 27

23

Pres. Nixon proposed an increased federal attack on organized crime.

Nigerian government said its forces had captured Umuahia, administrative centre of Biafra.

U.A.R. announced it regarded as void the 1967 cease-fire agreement ending the war with Israel.

24

Lebanese Prime Minister Rashid Karami resigned amid criticism of government restrictions against guerrillas using Lebanon as a base for attacks on Israel.

Canadian Transport Minister Paul Hellyer resigned from the Cabinet because of differences on federal housing policy.

26

U.S. Defense Department announced that the task force protecting U.S. reconnaissance flights off North Korea was moving from the Sea of Japan to the Yellow Sea.

27

Bolivian Pres. Barrientos was killed in a helicopter crash; Vice-Pres. Luis Adolfo Siles Salinas became his successor.

French voters rejected reform proposals in a national referendum.

Israeli government eased registration restrictions on Arab businessmen and professionals in East Jerusalem.

28

French Pres. de Gaulle resigned after the defeat of the national referendum; Senate Pres. Alain Poher became interim president.

29

Israeli commandos attacked deep inside the U.A.R., destroying power lines and Nile River bridges.

U.S. congressional hearing revealed a $2.1 billion overcost in the production of an Air Force jet transport, the C-5A Galaxy.

National Guardsmen moved into Cairo, Ill., following three nights of racial unrest.

30

Northern Ireland Prime Minister O'Neill resigned following the Unionist Party's failure to support his reform program.

Cambodian chief of state Prince Norodom Sihanouk withdrew his earlier decision to move toward resuming diplomatic relations with the U.S.

Pres. Nixon asked Congress for authority to consolidate federal programs of aid to the states and cities.

MAY

1

All Soviet bloc countries except East Germany observed May Day with civilian celebrations instead of military parades.

James Chichester-Clark was named prime minister of Northern Ireland.

UN Secretary-General U Thant announced that Middle East envoy Gunnar V. Jarring would not resume mediation efforts for the time being.

State of emergency was declared in Charleston, S.C., as protest marches supporting striking hospital workers continued.

Wildcat strikes throughout Britain protested the government's proposed antistrike legislation.

3

Indian Pres. Zakir Husain died in New Delhi.

4

Black leader James Forman disrupted services at New York City's Riverside Church to press demands that U.S. churches and synagogues pay $500 million as reparations to blacks.

New campaign to control young people was announced in China.

5

Prime Minister Wilson restated British intentions to press for full membership in the EEC at the 20th anniversary meeting of the Council of Europe in London.

6

U.S. Navy Secretary John H. Chafee announced that no disciplinary action would be taken against any of the crew of the "Pueblo" despite a Navy court of inquiry recommendation that two of her officers be court-martialed.

Committee of Ministers of the Council of Europe invited the Greek government to withdraw as it was in violation of the conditions of membership.

Study commissioned by Sen. Edward Kennedy opposed the deployment of the Safeguard antiballistic missile system.

Northern Ireland Prime Minister Chichester-Clark announced amnesty for persons charged with offenses stemming from clashes between Protestants and Roman Catholics.

7

Israeli jets staged the second strike in four days against a guerrilla camp in Jordan.

Indonesia reported its forces had ended a revolt against Indonesian rule among Papuan tribesmen in West New Guinea.

Howard University, Washington, D.C., was closed after students seized eight campus buildings.

8

National Liberation Front presented a ten-point program for an overall solution to the Vietnamese war at the Paris peace talks.

9

U.S. Secretary of State Rogers and South Vietnamese Foreign Ministry said that elements of the NLF peace plan could be a basis for discussion.

Israeli spokesmen, reporting that Israeli commandos had crossed the Jordan River and destroyed 12 Arab guerrilla structures, disclosed that such raids had been occurring for the past year.

Buell G. Gallagher resigned as president of City College of New York after court orders forced the reopening of the school, closed two weeks before during a takeover by black and Puerto Rican students.

Second stage of talks on U.S.-Peruvian relations ended in Washington with no significant agreements.

Roman Catholic Church issued a revised liturgical calendar that eliminated more than 200 saints.

West German Cabinet decided against an upward revaluation of the mark as a wave of currency speculation reached its peak.

11

North Vietnamese and Viet Cong forces launched widespread rocket and ground attacks throughout South Vietnam, the heaviest since the 1968 Tet offensive.

12

Al Fatah leader Arafat reportedly failed to persuade Lebanon to allow the free movement through Lebanon of Syrian-backed guerrillas attacking Israel.

13

Charles Evers, NAACP field secretary, won the Democratic nomination for mayor in Fayette, Miss.

Malaysian Chinese Association announced its withdrawal from the three-party coalition government of Prime Minister Tunku Abdul Rahman following heavy losses in national elections.

Pres. Nixon proposed legislation to revise the military draft system.

Home Secretary James Callaghan was dismissed from Prime Minister Wilson's newly formed "Inner Cabinet" because of his opposition to the antistrike bill.

14

Pres. Nixon proposed an eight-point peace plan that included the mutual withdrawal of U.S., allied, and North Vietnamese troops from South Vietnam.

Canadian House of Commons approved amendments to the Criminal Code that included the liberalization of laws on abortion and homosexual acts.

15

Abe Fortas resigned as an associate justice of the Supreme Court under the pressure of public criticism of his financial dealings.

Rioting broke out in Berkeley, Calif., between police and National Guardsmen and demonstrators protesting the closing of a "People's Park" on a field owned by the University of California.

16

Emergency rule was instituted in Malaysia following four days of fighting between Malay and Chinese groups.

17

Polish Communist Party First Secretary Wladyslaw Gomulka proposed talks with West Germany to establish a permanent Polish border.

Venera 6, second of two U.S.S.R. probes of Venus, entered the planet's atmosphere.

Al Fatah forces raided a fortified Israeli post for the first time since the 1967 war.

18

Brazilian government promulgated its tenth Institutional Act, which extended the sanctions against those deprived of their political and civil rights.

UPI COMPIX

"People's Park" demonstrator confronting National Guard in Berkeley . . . May 15.

19

Sen. Kennedy called for a slowdown in the U.S. space program and the diversion of its funds to domestic problems.

New York Gov. Nelson A. Rockefeller completed a nine-day visit to Central America, the first of four planned fact-finding tours of Latin America for the Nixon administration.

20

Laotian Premier Souvanna Phouma reported he had informed North Vietnam he would halt the bombing of Pathet Lao-held areas by U.S. and Laotian planes if North Vietnamese troops withdrew from Laos.

U.S. and South Vietnamese forces captured Ap Bia Mountain, known as Hamburger Hill, in their 11th attack on the North Vietnamese stronghold.

21

Warren E. Burger, a judge of the U.S. Court of Appeals for the District of Columbia, was nominated by Pres. Nixon to be chief justice of the U.S.

Rhodesian Prime Minister Smith proposed a new constitution that would perpetuate white rule.

U.S. military spokesman in Saigon defended the "Hamburger Hill" offensive against charges by Sen. Kennedy that it was "senseless and irresponsible."

U.S. House of Representatives approved a supplemental appropriations bill that limited federal spending for the first time.

Chilean Pres. Frei called for the extended chileanization of foreign-owned copper firms.

22

Apollo 10 astronauts brought their lunar module, "Snoopy," to within 9.4 mi. of the moon and returned it to the command ship, "Charlie Brown."

Biafran planes staged a surprise attack on the federally held Port Harcourt airport.

Canadian government decided to admit U.S. military deserters on the same basis as other immigrants.

23

Peruvian government canceled the proposed visit of Gov. Rockefeller when the U.S. suspended sales of military equipment in retaliation for Peruvian seizures of U.S. tuna boats.

Canadian Prime Minister Trudeau stated strong objections to the proposed U.S. antiballistic missile system.

24

U.S. Judicial Conference committee met to consider drafting ethics and financial reporting rules for federal judges.

Chinese government expressed readiness to reopen general talks on Sino-Soviet border problems with the U.S.S.R.

25

Coalition government of Sudanese Prime Minister Muhammad Ahmed Mahgoub was overthrown by a leftist military coup; Abubakr Awadallah became prime minister and foreign minister.

South Vietnamese Pres. Thieu assumed leadership of a new six-party coalition, the National Social Democratic Front.

26

Cuban Prime Minister Fidel Castro announced that 1969 sugar production was far short of scheduled goals.

Laotian government troops captured a village near the North Vietnamese frontier in their deepest penetration into Pathet Lao-held territory.

27

Gov. Rockefeller arrived in Bogotá, Colombia, at the start of his second fact-finding tour of Latin America.

Los Angeles Mayor Sam W. Yorty was elected to his third term in a runoff with Negro City Councilman Thomas Bradley.

First shelling attack on the Israeli-held city of Jericho since the 1967 war was staged reportedly by Arab guerrillas.

Alliance for Labor Action, formed by the United Automobile Workers and the International Brotherhood of Teamsters, concluded its founding meeting in Washington, D.C.

Pres. Nixon asked Congress to convert the Post Office Department into a public corporation.

28

Pres. Nixon requested $2.6 billion for foreign aid in fiscal 1970, the smallest request in the history of the program.

Argentinian government imposed a limited state of siege amid student unrest and the threat of a general strike.

Inept supervision of crews completing work at opposite ends of a new nuclear submarine was blamed by a U.S. House Armed Services Committee panel for the sinking of the ship in 35 ft. of water.

U.S. troops were reported to have abandoned Ap Bia Mountain (Hamburger Hill).

29

Czechoslovak Communist Party Central Committee adopted new party guidelines based on orthodox Marxist-Leninist theory.

30

West Germany altered its policy of automatically severing relations with governments extending diplomatic recognition to East Germany.

South Vietnamese Pres. Thieu declared he would oppose a coalition government with the NLF.

Labour protests in Curaçao, Netherlands Antilles, erupted into severe rioting.

31

Gov. Rockefeller shortened to three hours his visit to Bolivia in the face of threats of massive protests.

JUNE

1

Venezuelan Pres. Rafael Caldera requested that Gov. Rockefeller postpone his planned visit to Venezuela.

Interim Pres. Poher and Georges Pompidou were the leading vote-getters in French presidential elections.

Two days of Malay-Chinese clashes in Singapore left two dead.

3

U.S. destroyer "Frank E. Evans" collided with the Australian aircraft carrier "Melbourne" in the South China Sea; 73 U.S. seamen died.

Netherlands Antilles Prime Minister Ciro de Kroon announced that his government had agreed with protesting labour leaders to dissolve Parliament and to call for new elections.

Finance Minister Edgar J. Benson presented an austerity budget for 1969–70 to the Canadian House of Commons.

4

Biafran government pardoned 18 foreign oil workers sentenced to death for aiding the Nigerian war effort.

Six homemade bombs were dropped over Port-au-Prince; Haiti blamed Cuba for the attack.

Chile asked the U.S. to cancel the proposed visit of Gov. Rockefeller because of the threat of strikes and violence.

Argentinian Pres. Juan Carlos Onganía lifted the state of siege and announced the resignation of his Cabinet.

5

British union representatives gave the Trades Union Congress the right to intervene and recommend settlements in wildcat strikes.

6

U.S. Congress Joint Economic Subcommittee began a review of defense costs.

8

Pres. Nixon met with South Vietnamese Pres. Nguyen Van Thieu on Midway Island and announced that 25,000 U.S. troops would be withdrawn from South Vietnam by August 31.

9

U.K. Conservative Member of Parliament Enoch Powell proposed that the government finance the repatriation of black and Asian residents.

U.S. government licensed manufacture and distribution of a vaccine against German measles.

Major U.S. banks raised the prime interest rate from 7½ to 8½%.

South Vietnamese Pres. Thieu reiterated his opposition to a coalition government in a report on the Midway conference.

National Commission on the Causes and Prevention of Violence warned that U.S. legislation proposed to punish students or colleges for campus disorders was likely to spread the conflict.

10

National Liberation Front announced the formation of a Provisional Revolutionary Government of South Vietnam.

UN Security Council voted unanimously to extend the UN peace-keeping force on Cyprus for six more months.

Pope Paul VI addressed the World Council of Churches in Geneva.

11

Bank of Canada raised the bank rate from 7 to 7½%.

Chilean Foreign Minister Gabriel Valdes presented Pres. Nixon with a report outlining Latin America's criticisms of U.S. trade and aid policies.

Chinese Foreign Ministry charged that Soviet troops, tanks, and armoured cars had crossed the border into Sinkiang the previous day.

Royal commission recommended a complete overhaul of the English local government system.

12

Canadian federal-provincial constitutional conference reached agreement on major tax-sharing problems.

WIDE WORLD

Smoke rising over harbour area of Willemstad, Curaçao, during rioting . . . May 30.

13

Communiqué ending talks between U.S.S.R. Foreign Minister Gromyko and U.A.R. Pres. Nasser in Cairo said that a Middle East settlement could only be based on acceptance of the UN Security Council's peace resolution of Nov. 22, 1967.

U.K. House of Commons approved bill liberalizing divorce.

14

U.S.S.R. announced emergency measures to save the 1969 harvest.

15

Georges Pompidou was elected president of France in a runoff election against interim Pres. Poher.

16

Gov. Rockefeller arrived in Brazil on the third of four scheduled trips to Latin America.

17

Representatives of 75 Communist parties concluded their conference in Moscow.

U.S. sources reported that North Vietnamese troops had reoccupied Ap Bia Mountain (Hamburger Hill).

Conservatives won the Republican and Democratic nominations in the New York City mayoral primary; Republican Mayor John V. Lindsay retained a place on the general election ballot as the Liberal Party candidate.

South Korean security forces were reported to have wiped out a band of North Korean commandos about to land in South Korea.

18

Fianna Fail party of Irish Prime Minister John Lynch widened its parliamentary majority in general elections.

British government abandoned its plans to legislate against wildcat strikes.

19

Pres. Nixon said the administration hoped to beat a timetable for withdrawing troops from Vietnam proposed by former Defense Secretary Clifford and that a moratorium on MIRV tests might be offered as part of an arms control agreement with the U.S.S.R.

International Red Cross commissioner general in Nigeria, Auguste R. Lindt, resigned as a result of friction with the government.

20

Spain and U.S. signed an agreement allowing the U.S. to continue to use its military bases in Spain for 15 months more.

Three terrorist bombs exploded

in a street leading to the Wailing Wall in Jerusalem.

Rhodesian voters approved a constitution that perpetuated white rule and the establishment of a separate republic.

Ecuador announced the capture of four U.S. and three Japanese tuna boats for fishing within 200 mi. of its coast.

International Monetary Fund announced approval of an arrangement allowing the U.K. to purchase $1 billion in foreign exchange over a 12-month period.

Internal struggles resulted in factional splits at the Students for a Democratic Society convention in Chicago.

21

Gov. Rockefeller met with Uruguayan leaders in Punta del Este to avoid unrest in Montevideo.

22

Pres. Qahtan al-Shaabi of Southern Yemen resigned and was replaced by a five-man presidential council.

23

Israeli commandos sabotaged Jordan's East Ghor Canal irrigation project.

U.S. Special Forces camp at Ben Het was besieged by North Vietnamese artillery and mortar attacks.

Canadian Defense Minister Leo Cadieux announced plans for a phased cutback of military personnel.

24

Arab saboteurs blew up an oil pipeline in Haifa bay.

Peruvian government approved an agrarian reform law calling for expropriation of all major privately owned land tracts.

Lebanese Pres. Charles Helou ordered Arab guerrillas to leave Lebanon.

Uruguayan Pres. Pacheco reimposed the limited state of siege lifted in March in response to student and worker unrest.

Violence erupted in Montreal during a St. Jean Baptiste Day parade.

British government accepted the resignation of Sir Humphrey Gibbs as governor of Rhodesia; the post was left vacant.

25

Indian government filed protests with Pakistan and China over the construction of a military road linking Kashmir with Tibet.

Dutch chemists identified the chemical that was polluting 200 mi. of the Rhine River as an insecticide used to dust vineyards and fruit trees.

U.S. Senate approved a resolution calling on the executive branch not to commit troops or financial resources to foreign countries without the express approval of Congress.

26

Chilean Pres. Frei announced agreement with the Anaconda Co. on full nationalization of the company's copper mines.

El Salvador severed diplomatic relations with Honduras as a dispute that had resulted in the expulsion of Salvadorean settlers from Honduras was aggravated by rioting during play-offs in the World Soccer Cup competition.

U.S. Federal Reserve Board proposed requirements for its member banks aimed at curbing the flow of Eurodollars.

Nixon administration announced its opposition to an extension of the 1965 Voting Rights Act and presented alternate proposals.

27

South Korean students began violent demonstrations opposing efforts to change the constitution to permit Pres. Park Chung-hee to serve a third term.

Greek Council of State Pres. Michael Stasinopoulos was ousted following the council's cancellation of government dismissals of 21 magistrates.

Health, Education, and Welfare Secretary Finch ended his effort to have John H. Knowles appointed assistant secretary.

Partial settlement of the 14-week Charleston, S.C., hospital workers' strike was reached.

Spanish government suspended ferry service from Spain to British-held Gibraltar.

28

White House announced plans for a visit by Pres. Nixon to five Asian countries and Romania.

30

Argentinian labour leader Augusto Vandor was shot to death in violence surrounding Gov. Rockefeller's fourth Latin-American fact-finding trip.

Morocco formally received control of Ifni from Spain.

Israeli commandos sabotaged the electric power line in the Nile Valley between Cairo and the Aswan Dam.

JULY

1

Israeli national police headquarters was moved from Tel Aviv to East Jerusalem, formerly the Jordanian sector of the city.

Queen Elizabeth II invested her son Prince Charles as prince of Wales and earl of Chester in ceremonies at Caernarvon Castle, Wales.

Big Four UN ambassadors suspended their Middle East peace discussions.

2

U.S. Secretary of State Rogers said that Communist infiltration and combat activities in South Vietnam had decreased since mid-June.

3

U.S. State Department announced it had lifted the ban on credit arms sales to Ecuador and Peru.

Nixon administration reaffirmed the September 1969 deadline for compliance with the 1964 school desegregation order but permitted exceptions for "bona fide" problems.

4

Emergency meeting of the Council of the Organization of American States (OAS) heard charges of aggression by Honduras and El Salvador.

Greek government absolved itself from the constitutional obligation to accept the rulings of the Council of State.

5

Italian Premier Mariano Rumor submitted his coalition government's resignation following a schism in the Socialist Party over cooperation with the Communist Party.

Assassination of Tom Mboya, Kenyan minister of economic affairs, sparked tribal clashes.

6

Gov. Rockefeller completed the last of four Latin-American trips.

7

UN Secretary-General U Thant told the Security Council that open warfare had been resumed along the Suez Canal.

Canadian House of Commons gave final approval to a bill establishing French and English as Canada's official languages.

Honduras reportedly accepted a three-nation mediation committee's proposal for peace with El Salvador.

Roman Catholic Suffragan Bishop of Munich Matthias Defregger was identified as the subject of a Nazi war crimes investigation.

8

Bonny, a pigtail monkey used in a planned 30-day space flight, died 12 hours after being brought down on the ninth day.

U.S. Senate began debate on the proposed deployment of the Safeguard antiballistic missile system.

Yemen Premier Hassan al-Amri was reported to have resigned.

Church of England convocation in London failed to ratify plans for a merger with the Methodist Church.

First U.S. troops to be withdrawn from Vietnam were flown to the U.S.

China charged that Soviet gunboats, troops, and planes had crossed the Amur River into Manchuria.

9

Pres. Nixon ordered a 10% reduction in military and civilian government personnel abroad.

U.S. Justice Department warned the school boards of the city of Chicago and the state of Georgia that they must correct racial imbalances.

Biafra rejected a British proposal for daylight relief flights under federal Nigerian inspection.

10

U.S. State Department confirmed that the U.S. had signed a secret "military contingency" pact with Thailand in 1965.

11

South Vietnamese Pres. Thieu proposed free elections with the National Liberation Front participating.

Boston appeals court reversed the 1968 conviction of Dr. Benjamin Spock for conspiring to counsel draft evasion.

12

Congress Party rejected Prime Minister Indira Gandhi's choice of nominees for the Indian presidency.

Fresh outbreak of violence in Northern Ireland was precipitated by Protestant celebrations marking the anniversary of the Battle of the Boyne.

13

U.A.R. signed an agreement with a French-led consortium to build an oil pipeline that would bypass the Suez Canal.

14

U.S. Justice Department called for accelerated desegregation in 25 Alabama school districts.

Honduras charged that Salvadorean troops had penetrated 40 mi. into its territory.

16

El Salvador claimed the capture of several Honduran towns and called for the surrender of the Honduran Army.

U.S. Apollo 11 spacecraft, carrying three astronauts—civilian Neil Armstrong, Air Force Col. Edwin Aldrin, Jr., and Air Force Lieut. Col. Michael Collins—was launched from Cape Kennedy.

17

Luna 15, Soviet unmanned spacecraft, went into orbit around the moon amid speculation that it might attempt to retrieve lunar samples before Apollo 11.

Canadian Prime Minister Trudeau, on a tour of Canada's Prairie Provinces, was heckled by crowds protesting falling wheat prices.

North Vietnamese and NLF delegations at the Paris peace talks formally rejected the South Vietnamese offer of free elections.

18

UN Security Council heard Zambian complaints of Portuguese raids on its territory.

Norwegian writer-anthropologist Thor Heyerdahl and his crew abandoned their papyrus reed boat, the "Ra," in which they had attempted to prove that ancient Egyptians could have crossed the Atlantic Ocean.

19

Sen. Kennedy reported to Edgartown, Mass., police that he had driven a car that had plunged into a pond on nearby Chappaquiddick Island; the body of a woman passenger was found in the car.

Chad Pres. François Tombalbaye reportedly acknowledged that French troops were aiding government forces against Arab guerrillas.

20

Apollo 11 lunar module, "Eagle," landed on the moon's surface; astronauts Armstrong and Aldrin began a 2¼-hour moon walk.

Israeli jets bombed and strafed U.A.R. military installations on the west bank of the Suez Canal.

21

Apollo 11 ascent stage was blasted off from the moon's surface and linked up with the orbiting command module, "Columbia."

U.S. State Department relaxed trade and travel embargoes applying to China.

Luna 15 crashed into the moon.

Canada announced reductions in some wheat prices, following by three days a similar U.S. action.

22

El Salvador refused to withdraw its troops from Honduras unless the OAS guaranteed acceptance of five conditions.

EEC Council of Ministers accepted a French proposal to consider U.K. membership before the end of 1969.

U.S. Defense Department admitted that lethal nerve gas munitions had been shipped to U.S. overseas forces.

Pres. Nixon ordered a $3.5 billion cut in federal expenditures.

Prince Juan Carlos de Borbón y Borbón was named by Gen. Francisco Franco as his legal successor and heir to the Spanish throne.

24

Apollo 11 crew was greeted by Pres. Nixon after their spacecraft had splashed down in the Pacific Ocean.

U.A.R. and Israeli forces clashed along the Suez Canal in the heaviest battle since the June 1967 war.

U.S. Ambassador Lodge denied a North Vietnamese charge at the Paris peace talks that U.S. troops had invaded Laos.

COURTESY, NASA

Apollo 11 astronaut Aldrin on the moon . . . July 20.

25

Pres. Nixon stated on the island of Guam that while the U.S. would continue its role in the Pacific, peace in Asia must come from Asians.

International Red Cross turned over coordination of Nigerian relief flights to the federal government.

Canadian Parliament adjourned after a closure rule was enforced to press the passage of a package of rules changes.

26

Pres. Nixon arrived in Manila on the first leg of his round-the-world trip.

27

Seven U.S.S.R. warships completed a week-long visit to Havana.

Swedish UN observer was killed during U.A.R.-Israeli fighting along the Suez Canal.

North Vietnam labeled as slanderous charges by Laotian Premier Souvanna Phouma that 60,000 North Vietnamese troops were fighting in Laos.

28

Nixon administration reported a $3.1 billion federal budget surplus for fiscal 1969.

International Monetary Fund announced the completion of ratification of the Special Drawing Rights plan by member nations.

29

El Salvador agreed to a "redeployment" of its troops from Honduras in the face of a threatened OAS embargo.

Yaoundé Convention covering economic association of 18 African nations with the EEC was renewed for five years.

30

OAS foreign ministers approved a peace agreement ending the El Salvador-Honduras "soccer war."

Sen. Kennedy announced he would remain in the Senate despite the controversy surrounding his automobile accident.

Soviet author Anatoli V. Kuznetsov was reported to have defected to Britain.

Pres. Nixon paid a brief, unannounced visit to South Vietnam.

31

Pope Paul VI flew to Uganda and addressed the closing session of the all-Africa bishops' conference.

Mariner 6, U.S. unmanned Mars probe, passed by the planet after photographing its surface.

AUGUST

1

Pope Paul VI met in Uganda with Nigerian and Biafran representatives in an effort to end the Nigerian civil war.

2

South Vietnamese government confirmed the arrests of nearly 50 persons in the previous ten days on suspicion of spying.

Lebanese sources reported that Syrian troops had moved into Jordan.

Pitched battles between Roman Catholics, Protestants, and police began in Belfast, Northern Ireland.

Representatives of the International Grains Arrangement concluded a two-day special meeting in London without announcing a solution to the wheat price war.

Pres. Nixon received the most enthusiastic welcome of his nine-day, eight-nation tour on his arrival in Bucharest, Rom.

3

Israel announced its intention to retain parts of the territory captured in the 1967 war.

Japanese Diet passed legislation increasing the authority of the government to deal with campus disorders.

4

North Vietnam released three U.S. prisoners of war.

U.S. House of Representatives approved a bill extending the 10% income tax surcharge for six months.

5

Nigeria rejected new International Red Cross proposals for inspection of relief flights to Biafra.

Northern Ireland Cabinet announced it had made new emergency plans to cope with rioting.

Mariano Rumor organized a new minority Italian Cabinet composed entirely of Christian Democrats.

Mariner 7, U.S. unmanned spacecraft, recorded its flight across the south polar region of Mars.

6

U.S. Senate narrowly defeated two amendments that would have prohibited deployment of the Safeguard antiballistic missile system.

U.S. command in Saigon announced the arrest of the former commander and seven other members of the U.S. Special Forces (Green Berets) on suspicion of killing a Vietnamese national alleged to be a double agent.

Uruguay General Assembly adopted a resolution nullifying Pres. Pacheco's order that had mobilized striking bank employees into the Army in order to force them back to work.

7

U.K., U.S., and French embassies in Moscow announced an initiative to seek the reduction of tensions over Berlin.

U.S. House of Representatives passed and sent to the Senate an income tax reform and relief bill.

8

France devalued the franc in a surprise move.

Pres. Nixon unveiled plans for an overhaul of the national welfare system.

U.S.S.R.-Chinese border river navigation talks ended.

Communiqué issued by West German Chancellor Kiesinger and Pres. Nixon following two days of talks in Washington, D.C., announced the establishment of a communications "hot line" system between Washington and Bonn.

Australia and New Zealand announced support for the new U.S. policy of conciliation toward China.

10

Currencies of 14 African nations, all former French colonies, were realigned with the devalued franc.

French government ordered a nationwide freeze on prices.

11

Zambian Pres. Kenneth Kaunda announced plans to nationalize Zambia's copper industry.

12

EEC Council of Ministers concluded an emergency meeting in Brussels by suspending France from the uniform agricultural price supports.

Most intense Communist attacks in Vietnam since mid-May were waged against more than 100 cities, towns, and bases.

U.S. wheat prices for Asian and Latin-American markets were lowered in response to Japan's refusal to pay prices that were higher than what Europe was paying.

World Bank raised its lending rate from 6½ to 7%.

Jordanian Prime Minister Rifai resigned and was replaced by Bahjat al-Talhouni.

13

Pres. Nixon outlined a proposal for sharing federal revenues with state and local governments in a special message to Congress.

Apollo 11 astronauts Armstrong, Aldrin, and Collins were honoured by ticker tape parades in New York and Chicago and at a state dinner in Los Angeles.

U.S.S.R. and China reported a new border clash.

Canadian Prime Minister Trudeau announced measures designed to freeze federal spending at current levels.

14

British troops moved into Londonderry to separate Protestant and Catholic rioters at the request of the Northern Ireland government.

15

U.S.–Australian board of inquiry placed major blame on the U.S. destroyer "Frank E. Evans" for its collision with the Australian aircraft carrier "Melbourne."

British government rejected Ireland's proposal for a joint British-Irish peace team in Northern Ireland; Ireland mobilized its reserves and moved regular troops near the Ulster frontier.

17

North Korea announced it had shot down a U.S. Army helicopter with three persons aboard over its territory.

Northern Ireland Prime Minister Chichester-Clark said he would press for reform of Catholic grievances and rejected the possibility of a coalition with the Catholic minority.

Camille, the strongest hurricane to strike the U.S. since 1935, devastated the Mississippi Gulf coast.

18

Pres. Nixon nominated Clement F. Haynsworth, Jr., chief judge of the U.S. Fourth Judicial Circuit, to the U.S. Supreme Court seat vacated by Abe Fortas.

Peruvian officials nationalized nine sugar plantations in accordance with a new agrarian reform law.

19

Fishing rights talks between the U.S. and three South American nations recessed without agreement.

British Army assumed full responsibility for security in Northern Ireland.

Surinam police and Guyanese soldiers clashed over disputed border territory.

20

V. V. Giri was elected president of India in a personal triumph for Prime Minister Indira Gandhi.

Andrew W. Cordier, acting president of Columbia University, agreed to become permanent president.

UN Security Council rejected Ireland's request to consider the Northern Ireland dispute.

21

Bernadette Devlin, Northern Ireland Catholic activist and member of the U.K. Parliament, began a tour of the U.S. to raise funds for riot relief.

U.S. Secretary of Defense Laird announced plans to reduce fiscal 1970 defense spending including personnel cutbacks, deactivation of 100 navy ships, and the closing of some bases.

Al Aqsa Mosque in the old city of Jerusalem was damaged by a fire.

22

British Army called on Northern Ireland's Protestant B Special Constabulary to turn in its weapons in a move to calm Catholic fears.

Israeli police seized an Australian Christian, Michael Rohan, as the person who had set fire to the Al Aqsa Mosque; Israeli Cabinet issued a communiqué protesting Arab charges that Israel was responsible for the fire.

Czechoslovak government issued tighter police controls and emergency laws following four days of massive, orderly demonstrations throughout the country marking the first anniversary of the Soviet-led invasion.

23

Tran Thien Khiem was named to replace Tran Van Huong as premier of Vietnam.

24

U.S. infantry company defied an order to make its sixth attempt in as many days to reach a helicopter shot down in South Vietnam's Que Son Valley.

25

Arab League foreign ministers met in Cairo to consider plans for a "holy war" against Israel.

Zambian Pres. Kaunda declared a state of emergency and took personal control of the ruling United National Independence Party in the face of a political crisis arising from tribal rivalries.

Civil rights coalition shut down ten construction sites in Pittsburgh, Pa., charging unions with discriminatory hiring practices.

27

U.S. State and Defense departments announced a sharp drop in North Vietnamese infiltration of South Vietnam.

Argentinian workers staged their third general strike in three months in defiance of a government ban.

28

U.S. Appeals Court granted an administration request to delay desegregation of 30 Mississippi school districts.

Former Nigerian Pres. Nnamdi Azikiwe withdrew his support of Biafran secession and urged peace talks.

Irish Prime Minister John Lynch proposed negotiations with the U.K. to merge Ireland and Northern Ireland into a single federation.

29

Two Arabs hijacked a U.S. commercial jet bound for Athens and Tel Aviv and diverted it to Damascus, Syria.

British and Northern Ireland governments announced agreement on a series of civil rights reforms for Northern Ireland.

30

Progress Party of Kofi A. Busia won a parliamentary majority in the first free elections in Ghana since 1956.

31

Northern Ireland Catholics refused to remove street barricades in Londonderry until they had evidence that reforms would be carried out.

Brazilian Army, Navy, and Air Force ministers announced they had assumed control of the country while Pres. da Costa e Silva recovered from a stroke.

SEPTEMBER

1

Military officers seized power in Libya by overthrowing the regime of King Idris I.

2

West German Pres. Heinemann called for reconciliation with West Germany's neighbours, especially Poland.

Rock music festival on the Isle of Wight attracted about 250,000 spectators.

Summit meeting to coordinate Arab military activity against Israel opened in Cairo.

3

Israeli forces began heavy strikes against suspected Arab guerrilla concentrations in Lebanon.

French government announced a series of austerity measures designed to protect the devalued franc against inflation.

4

Hanoi Radio reported the death of North Vietnamese Pres. Ho Chi Minh.

U.S. ambassador to Brazil C. Burke Elbrick was kidnapped on a street in Rio de Janeiro.

NAACP announced legal plans to halt work on federally financed construction until more black workers were hired.

U.S. Food and Drug Administration reported it had found the use of birth control pills "safe."

6

Formation of a collective leadership to succeed Ho Chi Minh was announced by Hanoi Radio.

7

Brazilian revolutionaries released U.S. Ambassador Elbrick after their demand that 15 political prisoners be released had been met.

8

Israeli embassies in Bonn and The Hague and the El Al airlines office in Brussels were the targets of bombs thrown by Arab youths.

9

French Pres. Pompidou and West German Chancellor Kiesinger concluded semiannual talks in Bonn that included the expansion of the EEC.

Israeli armoured force crossed the Gulf of Suez and waged a ten-hour attack on U.A.R. coastal positions.

Funeral rites for Ho Chi Minh in Badinh Square, Hanoi, were attended by foreign leaders including U.S.S.R. Premier Aleksei N. Kosygin.

10

Oil leases to sites on Alaska's North Slope were sold in Anchorage for a record total of over $900 million.

OAU heads of state meeting in Addis Ababa called for an end to fighting in Nigeria and immediate peace talks.

11

French national railway service was paralyzed by an engineers' strike.

Cameron Report on Northern Ireland riots upheld Roman Catho-

"LONDON DAILY EXPRESS" FROM PICTORIAL PARADE

Funeral service for Ho Chi Minh in Hanoi . . . September 9.

lic charges of government discrimination and police misconduct.

Soviet Premier Kosygin made a surprise visit to Peking and conferred with Chinese Premier Chou En-lai.

Israel reported it had downed 11 U.A.R. planes over the western coast of the Gulf of Suez in some of the heaviest air combat since the 1967 war.

12

U.S. Army made public the rules under which military personnel were permitted to express their disagreement with national policies.

U.S. Commission on Civil Rights charged that the Nixon administration's recent decisions constituted "a major retreat in the struggle to achieve meaningful school desegregation."

U.S. Senate Judiciary Subcommittee began hearings on federal regulatory agencies.

Nigerian federal government and the International Red Cross signed a plan allowing daytime relief flights to Biafra.

14

Biafra rejected the Red Cross-Nigeria relief flight plan and called for a third party to guarantee its security.

South Korean National Assembly approved constitutional amendment permitting Pres. Park to run for a third term.

Tanker "Manhattan" successfully navigated the Northwest Passage on its search for a commercial route for Alaskan oil.

15

UN Secretary-General U Thant called for the inclusion of China in disarmament talks.

UN Security Council adopted a resolution demanding that Israel rescind all measures aimed at altering the status of Jerusalem.

NASA scientists reported the finding of rare elements and tiny glass spheres in lunar material.

16

U.S. Vice-Pres. Agnew told a Southern governors' conference in Williamsburg, Va., that he opposed plans to bus children to achieve racially balanced schools.

Pres. Nixon announced the withdrawal from South Vietnam of an additional 35,000 U.S. troops.

UN General Assembly convened in New York City and elected as president Miss Angie Brooks of Liberia.

17

Laotian troops were reported to have seized two strategic areas of Laos long held by the Pathet Lao; U.S. Senate passed a proposal barring funds for U.S. combat support in Laos and Thailand.

18

Pres. Nixon, in an address to the General Assembly, appealed to UN members for assistance in bringing about peace in Vietnam.

U.S. House of Representatives approved a proposed constitutional amendment providing for direct election of the president.

U.S. Army announced it would court-martial six of eight Green Berets on charges of murdering a Vietnamese double agent.

Rioting between Muslims and Hindus began in Ahmedabad, India.

19

South Vietnamese Pres. Thieu said his government would not agree to a cease-fire without a political settlement.

Pres. Nixon announced a 50,000-man cut in planned draft calls for the remainder of 1969.

Canada announced it would reduce its forces in Europe from 9,800 to 5,000 men by 1970.

Cuban government announced a new law providing for the extradition of persons who hijacked planes or boats.

20

Foreign ministers of Australia, New Zealand, the Philippines, South Korea, and Thailand announced that their combined force in South Vietnam would not be reduced.

21

North Vietnamese government denounced the U.S. troop withdrawal from South Vietnam as a "perfidious trick."

Operation Intercept, a U.S. effort to halt the flow of drugs from Mexico, went into effect along the U.S.-Mexico border.

22

Street barricades were removed from the Roman Catholic Bogside district of Londonderry, Northern Ireland.

U.S.S.R. informed the U.S. it was not yet prepared to begin strategic arms limitation talks.

Summit conference of 25 Islamic countries to consider consequences of the Al Aqsa Mosque fire opened in Rabat, Mor.

U.S. Supreme Court was asked to overturn the desegregation delay obtained by 30 Mississippi school districts.

23

Pres. Nixon announced the U.S. would proceed with plans for a supersonic airliner.

U.S. Secretary of Labor George P. Shultz ordered into effect the "Philadelphia Plan" designed to increase the employment of minority group members in construction trades.

24

U.S. Republican senators elected Hugh Scott (Pa.) as minority leader and Robert P. Griffin (Mich.) as whip.

Eight persons charged with conspiracy to incite a riot at the 1968 Democratic national convention went on trial in Chicago.

25

Israeli Prime Minister Golda Meir arrived in Washington, D.C., for talks with Pres. Nixon.

Pres. Nixon asked Congress to increase social security benefits by 10% and to provide for future increases linked to cost-of-living increases.

Sen. Charles E. Goodell (Rep., N.Y.) proposed legislation to require the withdrawal of all U.S. troops from Vietnam by the end of 1970.

26

Fighting erupted in Chicago between police and white construction workers protesting government plans to eliminate discrimination in the building trades.

Civilian government of Bolivian Pres. Luis Adolfo Siles Salinas was overthrown; armed forces chief Gen. Alfredo Ovando Candía assumed the presidency.

27

South Vietnamese Pres. Thieu stated that the withdrawal of U.S. troops would take "years and years" because his country had "no ambition" to take over the fighting.

28

Czechoslovak Communist Party Central Committee announced that Alexander Dubcek and Josef Smrkovsky had been dropped from membership; a new, more conservative Cabinet replaced the former government.

West German parliamentary elections gave the Christian Democratic Union 46.1% of the vote and the Social Democratic Party 42.7%; the extreme right-wing National Democratic Party failed to qualify for representation in the Bundestag.

Swedish Prime Minister Tage Erlander announced his resignation as chairman of the Social Democratic Party.

29

U.S.S.R. sources reported that Premier Kosygin had proposed a five-point plan to reduce Sino-Soviet tension at his meeting with Chinese Premier Chou En-lai.

West German government ordered the central bank to permit the mark to be sold freely on foreign exchange markets.

U.S. Secretary of the Army Stanley Resor announced that murder charges against six Green Berets were being dropped.

30

U.S. and Thailand jointly announced that 6,000 U.S. servicemen in Thailand would be withdrawn in the next ten months.

U.S. Senate investigation of alleged irregularities in the operation of Army noncommissioned officers' clubs began.

OCTOBER

1

Chinese Communist Party Chairman Mao Tse-tung, in his first public appearance in over four months, presided at the 20th national day rally in Peking.

Spain severed all telephone and cable service with Gibraltar.

2

Lull in fighting in Vietnam was reflected in the lowest weekly U.S. death toll reported in more than two years.

3

West German Social Democratic and Free Democratic parties announced agreement on a coalition government.

U.A.R. commandos staged one of their largest raids since the 1967 war on Israeli positions in the Sinai Peninsula.

Israeli troops blew up buildings presumed to house Arab guerrillas in two Lebanese villages.

4

Philippines Pres. Ferdinand E. Marcos announced his nation's troops would be withdrawn gradually from South Vietnam.

5

U.K. Prime Minister Wilson announced lower-level Cabinet changes.

6

East German Pres. Walter Ulbricht and U.S.S.R. Communist Party leader Leonid I. Brezhnev stated willingness to cooperate with West Germany in speeches marking East Germany's 20th anniversary.

"LONDON DAILY EXPRESS" FROM PICTORIAL PARADE

British troops in Northern Ireland return sniper's fire . . . October 12.

Bipartisan group of U.S. senators and representatives announced their support of the nationwide antiwar Moratorium planned for October 15.

7

Montreal was "threatened with anarchy" after police and firemen walked off the job in a wage dispute.

U.S. and U.S.S.R. submitted to the Geneva disarmament conference a joint draft treaty to ban nuclear weapons from the ocean floor.

Brazilian armed forces high command announced its choice of Gen. Emílio Garrastazú Médici to become president of Brazil.

8

"Weatherman" faction of the SDS began a planned four days of radical actions to "bring the war home" in Chicago with a rally in Lincoln Park followed by a window-breaking spree through nearby streets.

9

U.S. Department of Health, Education, and Welfare announced that a committee was investigating charges that blacklists barred scientists from serving on advisory panels.

10

South Vietnamese forces assumed full responsibility for the defense of Saigon.

U.S. ended Operation Intercept after Mexico promised to intensify efforts against the production and traffic of marijuana and other drugs.

Israeli Defense Minister Moshe Dayan reported that Israel had successfully defended its positions along the Suez Canal against a U.A.R. summer offensive.

Gen. Lewis B. Hershey was relieved as director of the U.S. Selective Service System after 28 years.

12

British Army sent 600 troops into Belfast to quell intense rioting that had followed publication of a report calling for widespread reforms of Northern Ireland's police forces.

13

Pres. Nixon announced his intention to make a major Vietnam policy address in November and stated he would not be swayed by street demonstrations.

Ota Sik, architect of the 1968 Czechoslovak economic revitalization, was expelled from the Czechoslovak Communist Party.

Israeli Deputy Prime Minister Allon proposed a "home rule" plan for Arabs living on the Israeli-occupied west bank of the Jordan River.

"Cosmic troika" of seven Soviet cosmonauts in three spaceships were orbiting the earth in what was presumed to be an effort to establish a space station.

14

Eric Gordon, with his wife and son, was the third British journalist to be released in October by China.

Philippines requested negotiations to revise the agreement covering U.S. military bases in the Philippines.

Hanoi Radio broadcast an open letter acclaiming the efforts of U.S. antiwar protesters.

Olof Palme succeeded Tage Erlander as prime minister of Sweden.

15

Antiwar Moratorium observances drew massive support throughout the U.S.

Somalian Pres. Abd-i-Rashid Ali Shermarke was assassinated by a national policeman while touring drought-stricken parts of the country.

Canada announced it would ban the controversial hunting of baby seals in the Gulf of St. Lawrence.

Canadian Prime Minister Trudeau notified the French government that it must reach a new understanding on the agreement authorizing its relations with Quebec.

Alexander Dubcek and Josef Smrkovsky were removed from the chairmanships of the Czechoslovak Federal Assembly and Chamber of the People, respectively.

Biafran leader Ojukwu was reported to have notified Gabon Pres. Albert Bongo of his willingness to negotiate peace with Nigeria without preconditions.

16

North Vietnamese negotiators in Paris proposed "private and direct" talks between the U.S. and the Viet Cong; U.S. Ambassador Lodge proposed secret talks among all four participants.

New York Mets defeated the Baltimore Orioles, 5 to 3, to win the 1969 baseball World Series.

17

Arthur F. Burns was named to succeed William McChesney Martin as chairman of the Federal Reserve Board.

Pres. Nixon urged all segments of U.S. society to exercise economic restraint to help curb inflation.

South Korean voters approved a constitutional amendment permitting Pres. Park to run for a third term in 1971.

Divorce reform bill received final approval in the U.K. House of Commons.

18

Lebanese troops clashed with Arab commandos in southern Lebanon.

HEW Secretary Finch ordered the artificial sweetener cyclamate removed from the consumer market by Feb. 1, 1970.

19

U.S. Vice-Pres. Agnew told a Republican dinner audience in New Orleans, La., that the Vietnam Moratorium was "encouraged by an effete corps of impudent snobs who characterize themselves as intellectuals."

20

International Labour Organization was awarded the 1969 Nobel Peace Prize.

Nixon administration proposed reductions in the penalties for possession and use of narcotics.

China and the U.S.S.R. opened border negotiations in Peking.

Nigerian Radio denounced the Biafran offer to negotiate peace.

21

Syria closed its borders with Lebanon and threatened stronger measures to stop Lebanese Army antiguerrilla attacks.

Willy Brandt was elected chancellor of West Germany.

Somalian Army and police seized power in a bloodless coup.

22

Lebanese Prime Minister Karami resigned for the second time in six months and disassociated himself from the government attacks on Palestinian guerrillas.

U.A.R. jets began attacking Israeli positions in the Sinai Peninsula following a buildup of Israeli forces in the area.

23

U.S. Army Sgt. Maj. William O. Wooldridge invoked the Fifth Amendment in testimony before the final session of a Senate investigation of alleged corruption in the operation of army service clubs.

24

West Germany's new government revalued the mark in its first major act.

South Vietnamese Pres. Thieu decreed an economic austerity program to reduce government deficits and avoid a currency devaluation.

25

U.S. and U.S.S.R. announced they would hold preliminary strategic arms limitation talks (SALT) in Helsinki, Fin., in November.

Australian elections reduced substantially the parliamentary majority of the Liberal-Country Party coalition government.

Commando force crossed from Syria into Lebanon and occupied a village.

26

Cease-fire between Lebanese troops and Al Fatah commandos was reportedly in effect as U.A.R. Pres. Nasser sent a personal envoy as mediator.

27

Pres. Jomo Kenyatta of Kenya placed opposition leader Oginga Odinga and 7 colleagues under house arrest on charges of organizing an antigovernment demonstration in which 11 persons were killed.

Canadian Prime Minister Trudeau claimed Canadian sovereignty of all Canadian Arctic waters, not just those within the three-mile limit recognized by the U.S.

28

Pres. Nixon warned Congress that he might not be able to submit a budget in January 1970 unless it speeded up action on appropriations bills.

Israeli United Labour Party was returned to power in national elections but lost its absolute majority.

Roman Catholic synod of bishops closed after taking steps to decentralize the church's governing authority.

29

Spanish Cabinet changes affecting 13 posts gave prominence to the technocrat faction of the Franco regime, consisting chiefly of members of the Catholic lay organization Opus Dei.

U.S. Supreme Court ruled unanimously that 30 Mississippi school districts must integrate at once.

30

U.S. combat deaths in Vietnam were reported to have exceeded 100 the previous week for the first time in five weeks.

Kenyan government outlawed the Kenya People's Union opposition party, charging it with subversion.

31

Warsaw Pact foreign ministers called for an all-European security conference in early 1970.

U.S. Marine Lance Cpl. Raffael Minichiello hijacked a Trans World Airlines jetliner over California and forced it to fly 6,900 mi. to Rome.

Pres. Nixon said that social and economic progress in Latin America would depend on initiatives by the Latin Americans.

NOVEMBER

1

National Commission on the Causes and Prevention of Violence issued a report asking for drastic revision of the U.S. system of justice.

India's ruling Congress Party formally split into two factions.

2

Six men charged with hijacking commercial airliners to Cuba returned voluntarily to the U.S.

3

Pres. Nixon revealed that secret peace initiatives had been rejected by North Vietnam and disclosed a plan to withdraw U.S. combat troops on an orderly but secret schedule.

Lebanon and Palestinian commando negotiators announced an accord in Cairo to end their fighting and to provide for cooperation between their forces in Lebanon.

Canadian Secretary of State for External Affairs Sharp announced that seven diplomatic missions abroad would be closed for economic reasons.

4

Republican Party candidates won gubernatorial elections in New Jersey and Virginia; mayors Lindsay of New York City and Carl B. Stokes of Cleveland, O., were reelected; Negro mayoral candidates lost in five large U.S. cities.

South Vietnamese troops clashed with North Vietnamese forces near Duc Lap in their biggest battle in four months.

Brazilian police killed Carlos Marighela, reportedly head of the revolutionary National Liberation Action, in a gun battle in São Paulo.

5

U.S. District Judge Julius J. Hoffman sentenced Black Panther leader Bobby G. Seale, one of the codefendants in the "Chicago eight" conspiracy trial, to four years in prison for contempt of court.

NATO deputy foreign ministers rejected a Warsaw Pact proposal for an early all-European security conference.

6

U.S. Senate approved and sent to Pres. Nixon a $20.7 billion military authorization bill that included initial authorization for the Safeguard antiballistic missile system.

U.A.R. Pres. Nasser appeared to rebuff reports of a U.S.-U.S.S.R. plan for Middle East peace by declaring the Arab states had no alternative but to fight for recovery of their territories.

North Vietnamese delegate Xuan Thuy charged at the Paris peace talks that Pres. Nixon's disclosure of secret peace moves was "a betrayal of a promise" and a "perfidious trick."

7

Canadian Finance Minister Benson presented the government's White Paper on tax reform to the House of Commons.

Defense posts around Saigon came under Communist attack for the first time since May 1968.

European Free Trade Association reaffirmed readiness to negotiate integration with the EEC.

8

U.A.R. Navy reportedly shelled Israeli positions in the northern Sinai Peninsula.

9

Prince Philip disclosed that the British royal family would soon be operating with a deficit unless Parliament increased the queen's allowance.

10

Nixon administration released Gov. Rockefeller's policy report based on his Latin-American trips.

Israel reported that all U.A.R. ground-to-air missile sites along the Suez Canal had been destroyed by continuous Israeli air attacks.

Communiqué closing the Arab League defense meeting in Cairo accused the U.S. of blocking peace efforts and pledged full support for Palestinian commandos.

11

UN General Assembly rejected for the 20th time a motion to seat Communist China.

Philippines Pres. Marcos was reelected by an overwhelming majority.

12

U.S. Army announced that 1st Lieut. William L. Calley, Jr., had been charged with murder in connection with the reported slaying of an undetermined number of South Vietnamese civilians during a military operation in March 1968 in Song My.

Israeli Defense Minister Dayan announced new, sterner reprisal measures against Arab residents of occupied territories because of increased guerrilla attacks against occupation rule.

Soviet novelist Aleksandr I. Solzhenitsyn was confirmed to have been expelled from the Soviet Writers Union.

13

"March against death," in which 46,000 persons carried names of U.S. soldiers killed in Vietnam past the White House, began.

South Vietnamese opposition leader Gen. Duong Van Minh called for a national referendum on vietnamization.

North Vietnamese troops staged their heaviest assault in a year against U.S. forces in the Demilitarized Zone.

U.S. Vice-Pres. Agnew charged the three major U.S. television networks with a lack of responsible news coverage.

14

Apollo 12 spacecraft was successfully launched in a rainstorm from Cape Kennedy, Fla.

France reversed its 15-year policy of nuclear independence by announcing it would build atomic plants based on U.S. designs.

15

Antiwar protesters, estimated at more than 250,000, staged a peaceful march and rally in Washington, D.C.

Mexican Secretary of the Interior Luis Echevarría Alvarez was formally endorsed as the candidate of the Partido Revolucionario Institucional for the 1970 presidential election.

16

Two Israeli ships were damaged by explosive charges in Elath, on the Gulf of Aqaba.

Allied planes and artillery bombed North Vietnamese gun positions in Cambodia.

17

U.S. and U.S.S.R. began strategic arms limitation talks in Helsinki.

Israeli jets waged their most sustained air attack against Jordanian targets since the 1967 war.

Greek government instituted a new press code including prison terms and fines for press offenses.

Demonstrations throughout Japan planned to prevent Prime Minister Sato from visiting the U.S. to negotiate the return of Okinawa resulted in 1,700 arrests.

Indian Prime Minister Indira Gandhi defeated a censure motion presented by the opposing Congress Party faction.

19

U.S. astronauts Charles Conrad, Jr., and Alan L. Bean landed on the moon in the Apollo 12 lunar module and began the first of two scheduled moon walks.

20

U.S. Vice-Pres. Agnew extended his charges of news management to the press.

White House announced that Henry Cabot Lodge had resigned as chief U.S. negotiator at the Paris peace talks; no immediate replacement was named.

Nixon administration ordered an end to the use of the pesticide DDT in residential areas within 30 days.

Three Palestinian guerrillas were killed and six wounded in the first clash with Lebanese troops since the November 3 truce agreement.

21

U.S. Defense Department announced that another 24 men were under investigation in connection with the alleged massacre at Song My in 1968.

Japanese Prime Minister Sato and Pres. Nixon agreed in Washington, D.C., to the return to Japan in 1972 of Okinawa and the other U.S.-held Ryukyu Islands.

U.S. Senate refused, by a vote of 55 to 45, to confirm Pres. Nixon's nomination of Clement F. Haynsworth, Jr., to be a Supreme Court justice.

22

South Vietnamese Defense Ministry denied reports of the massacre of civilians in Song My by U.S. troops as "totally untrue."

Harvard Medical School scientists reported they had isolated a single gene in an elegant experiment.

23

Congo (Brazzaville) ordered its troops on alert after Pres. Joseph Mobutu of the Congo (Kinshasa) said his country could occupy Brazzaville at will.

Israeli jets pounded U.A.R. installations between Qantara and the city of Suez following two days of U.A.R. commando raids on Israeli positions.

24

U.S.S.R. Pres. Nikolai Podgorny and Pres. Nixon ratified the nuclear nonproliferation treaty at ceremonies in Moscow and Washington.

U.S. military authorities released a captured enemy document stating that nearly 2,900 South Vietnamese had been "eliminated" during the Communist occupation of Hue during the 1968 Tet offensive.

25

Pres. Nixon ordered the destruction of U.S. germ warfare stocks.

West Germany formally proposed talks aimed at improving relations with Poland.

26

Pres. Nixon signed legislation providing for a draft lottery.

Border dispute between Saudi Arabia and Southern Yemen erupted into fighting around an outpost claimed by both countries.

Biafra was reported to have asked Switzerland to mediate the Nigerian civil war.

27

Arab terrorists threw a hand grenade into the Athens office of Israel's El Al airlines, injuring 15 persons.

28

West Germany signed the nuclear nonproliferation treaty after receiving assurances on its interpretation from the U.S. and U.S.S.R.

29

South Vietnamese military court convicted four men, including a former special assistant to Pres. Thieu, of high treason and 37 others of lesser charges of espionage.

National Party of New Zealand Prime Minister Keith J. Holyoake won its fourth successive parliamentary election.

DECEMBER

1

Order of selection for draft in 1970 was determined by a lottery held at the U.S. Selective Service System headquarters in Washington, D.C.

U.S. military command reported that the 60,000 troops to be withdrawn by Dec. 15, 1969, had left Vietnam.

2

U.S. Army board of inquiry began closed hearings in Washington, D.C., on the alleged massacre of South Vietnamese civilians in Song My.

EEC leaders agreed to open negotiations on U.K. membership during 1970.

U.S. House of Representatives endorsed Pres. Nixon's plan to negotiate a "just peace" in Vietnam.

3

North Korea released three U.S. helicopter crewmen captured when their aircraft was shot down in August.

Israeli commandos attacked an Arab guerrilla base in Lebanon in retaliation for an Arab ambush of an Israeli patrol in the Golan Heights.

Two-pronged offensive by federal Nigerian forces against remaining Biafran strongholds was reportedly under way.

4

Two Black Panther leaders were killed in a police raid on a Chicago apartment.

U.S. planes bombed North Vietnamese troops inside Cambodia for the second consecutive day.

White House Conference on Food, Nutrition, and Health voted to ask the government for emergency action against hunger.

5

NATO Council of Ministers expressed receptiveness to the Warsaw Pact proposal for an all-European security conference.

U.S. Senate approved a 15% increase in social security benefits as part of a tax reform bill.

6

Coordinated exchange of prisoners between Israel and Syria and the U.A.R. was accomplished.

Brazilian Army command forbade the publication of reports of torture of political prisoners and the genocide of Brazilian Indians.

8

Soviet Foreign Minister Gromyko met with West German ambassador to Moscow Helmut Allardt to begin talks on a mutual renunciation of force.

9

U.S. Secretary of State Rogers called on Israel to withdraw from Arab territories in return for a binding peace agreement.

10

Dahomey Pres. Émile Derlin Zinsou was ousted by army leaders.

Pres. Nixon requested that the appropriation for the National Foundation on the Arts and the Humanities be nearly doubled, to $40 million, in fiscal 1971.

Canadian federal-provincial conference on constitutional reform ended in disagreement on several issues.

11

Israeli jets downed three Syrian MiG's within sight of Damascus.

North Vietnamese chief negotiator Thuy boycotted the Paris peace talks to protest their "sabotage" by the U.S. failure to name a replacement for Ambassador Lodge.

Chinese and U.S. diplomats held their first formal meeting in two years in Warsaw to discuss the resumption of ambassadorial talks.

12

U.S.S.R. and U.A.R. concluded a high-level conference in Moscow.

National Commission on the Causes and Prevention of Violence issued its final report calling for the diversion of at least $20 billion a year from defense to domestic spending.

Greece withdrew from the Council of Europe as it became clear the country would be suspended for abrogating democratic freedoms.

U.S. Justice Department announced it would investigate the December 4 slaying of two Black Panther leaders by Chicago police.

Bomb explosion in Milan's National Bank of Agriculture killed 14 persons and injured over 90; three bombs also exploded in Rome.

14

South Vietnamese troops initiated eight scattered engagements with Communist forces.

15

Pres. Nixon announced a third reduction of U.S. troops in Vietnam despite reports of increased enemy infiltration.

Ouster of Brig. Gen. Omar Torrijos as the power behind Panama's ruling junta was proclaimed by National Guard leaders.

Greek Prime Minister Papadopoulos ruled out the possibility of early elections.

UN General Assembly voted endorsement of the U.S.-U.S.S.R. proposal to ban nuclear weapons from the ocean floor.

16

France, Britain, and the U.S. sent identical notes to the U.S.S.R. Foreign Ministry requesting talks on the status of Berlin.

Australian Prime Minister John Gorton announced tentative plans for a partial troop withdrawal from South Vietnam.

U.S. Defense Secretary Laird stated that 1970 draft calls could be reduced by 25,000 men as a result of announced troop reductions.

Brig. Gen. Torrijos returned triumphantly to Panama to resume control.

17

UN General Assembly adjourned its 24th session.

Pres. Nixon urged Congress to stop raising expenditure and cutting taxes simultaneously.

Television wedding of Tiny Tim (Herbert Khaury) and Miss Vicky (Victoria Budinger) drew the largest audience ever recorded for a late evening talk show.

18

France was reported to have agreed to sell over 50 Mirage jets to Libya.

U.S. plans for Israeli-Jordanian aspects of a Middle East peace treaty was submitted to France, Britain, and the U.S.S.R.

Newark, N.J., Mayor Hugh J. Addonizio was indicted by a U.S. grand jury on extortion, conspiracy, and tax evasion charges.

House of Lords approved a bill abolishing capital punishment permanently in the U.K.

19

U.S. State Department liberalized rules governing trade with China.

Uganda Pres. Milton Obote was shot leaving a political rally in Kampala.

20

U.S. planes bombed suspected enemy concentrations in the A Shau Valley for the first time in two months.

Sino-Soviet border talks in Peking were reported to be making no progress.

21

Correspondence between East German Pres. Ulbricht and West German Pres. Heinemann agreeing to a meeting in 1970 was made public.

Israeli jets staged a five-hour raid on artillery, mortar, and rocket positions in Jordan.

22

U.S. and U.S.S.R. agreed to begin full-scale SALT negotiations in Vienna in April 1970.

U.S. Congress passed the final version of the Tax Reform Act of 1969.

Poland expressed a willingness to begin talks with West Germany.

Bernadette Devlin was found guilty of inciting to riot and riotous behaviour during Catholic-Protestant clashes in Londonderry in August.

23

Formal agreement was announced on the withdrawal of all U.S. personnel from Wheelus Air Force Base in Libya.

First session of the 91st U.S. Congress adjourned after deferring until 1970 final action on the controversial appropriations for foreign aid and the Labor and HEW departments.

Arab summit conference in Rabat, Mor., ended in a dispute over increasing financial aid to anti-Israeli activities.

25

Israeli jets and commandos raided U.A.R. positions on the Gulf of Suez in the heaviest strike since the 1967 war.

Five gunboats originally sold to Israel and later placed under French embargo left Cherbourg Harbour under mysterious conditions.

26

U.S. Vice-Pres. Agnew left Washington, D.C., for a 23-day, ten-nation Asian tour.

Texas billionaire H. Ross Perot said in Bangkok that North Vietnam had refused to allow the delivery of two planeloads of gifts intended for U.S. war prisoners.

27

French government ordered an inquiry into the presumed sale to a Norwegian firm of five gunboats that were sighted passing through the Strait of Gibraltar into the Mediterranean.

Liberal-Democratic Party of Prime Minister Sato won a decisive victory in Japanese parliamentary elections.

30

U.S. negotiators at the Paris peace talks submitted a list of 1,406 men missing in action and asked that their status as prisoners be confirmed.

Pres. Nixon signed the tax reform bill and pledged to take steps to prevent an unbalanced budget for fiscal 1971.

International Monetary Fund announced approval of an agreement covering the purchase of newly mined South African gold.

31

French government suspended two officials and ordered the recall of the Israeli embassy staff that had certified the contract supposedly selling Israel's interest in five gunboats to a Norwegian firm; the gunboats entered the port of Haifa, Israel.

U.S. Army Staff Sgt. David Mitchell was the second person ordered to stand trial on murder charges in connection with the alleged massacre in Song My.

(D. K. Wi.; J. W. Mw.)

"ONE SMALL STEP..."

Man's lunar landing July 20, 1969.

Advertising

Europe. The controversy over cigarette advertising took another turn in the U.K. in 1969 with the decision by the British Broadcasting Corporation (BBC) to ban cigarette advertising from its publications as of July 1 because of the accumulation of medical evidence about the effects of cigarette smoking. The publications most affected, *Radio Times* (with a circulation of just over 4.3 million) and *The Listener,* had carried cigarette advertising worth about £500,000 a year.

The BBC in its announcement to the manufacturers pointed out that advertising space would still be available for tobacco products other than cigarettes. Expenditure on cigarette advertising, however, had continued to increase, in spite of the ban on television advertising in 1965. A new development during the year was the marketing by Carreras of a new brand, Cambridge, with trading stamps.

The introduction in November in the U.K. of colour transmissions on the two major television channels (*see* TELEVISION AND RADIO) produced a flurry of activity among agencies to produce colour commercials for Independent Television, in spite of the small number of viewers with colour sets. The increase in the television levy on advertising receipts announced in the budget took effect from July 1.

Advertising expenditure in the U.K. in 1968 was £494 million. A survey conducted on behalf of the Advertising Association showed that advertising for branded consumer goods in the private sector accounted for only £234 million of this total. The remaining £260 million was taken up by such categories as government and national boards, trade and technical, retail store, classified, and financial and industrial advertising. The total expenditure on advertising represented 1.8% of total consumers' expenditure and 1.4% of the gross national product (GNP). The level of expenditure as a proportion of either consumers' expenditure or GNP had remained virtually constant during the previous ten years.

Display advertising expenditure as a proportion of consumers' expenditure had decreased significantly while expenditure in other directions (classified and financial, and in trade and technical journals) increased proportionately. Display advertising, which in 1960 had represented 79% of all advertising, accounted for only 71% of the total in 1968. The breakdown of expenditure by type revealed that in 1968 the amount spent on display was £179 million (1967: £165 million); classified other than trade and technical, £87 million (£72 million); financial, £10 million (£7 million); trade and technical journals, £44 million (£41 million); television, £132 million (£124 million); and other media, £42 million (£41 million).

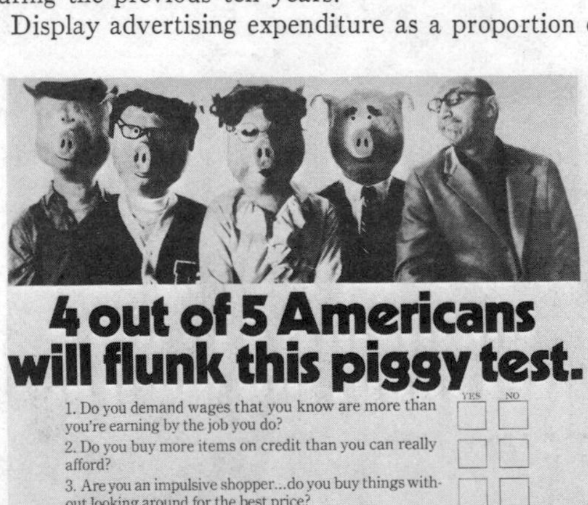

Advertisement created by the Benton and Bowles agency as part of a 1969 all-media public-service campaign to combat inflation.

COURTESY, BENTON AND BOWLES

Of those commercial groups that spent most heavily on advertising, the top three percentage increases compared with 1967 were in publishing, where expenditure rose by 54% to £10.2 million; in financial advertising, which increased by 37% to £17.2 million; and in cigarettes and tobacco, which at £14.4 million showed an increase of 22%. In money terms the most important sectors were food and nonalcoholic drinks at £68 million (1967: £64.3 million), household stores at £34.5 million (£30.7 million), and cosmetics and toiletries at £20.6 million (£18.2 million).

The Television Advertising Congress in London in September considered the problems of commercial television in Europe, where almost every commercial station was subject to government domination and where prospective advertisers found the queues long. Already there was considerable viewing overlap between countries. In Switzerland an estimated 30% of the German-speaking population tuned into West German television, while many Belgians watched the commercial channels of their neighbours, having none of their own. A private company in Luxembourg, the Compagnie Luxembourgeoise de Télédiffusion, claimed viewership on 600,000 sets, of which only 40,000 were in Luxembourg.

In France the level of advertising remained well below that of the U.K., and of other members of the EEC with the exception of Italy. There were a great many small agencies although concentration had resulted in the two chief agencies, Havas Conseil and Publicis, handling 20% of the total French advertising expenditure. The slow growth of advertising in France was attributed to the structure of French business, still dominated by small and innately conservative family concerns. Advertising expenditure in 1967 rose by 5% to Fr. 3,980,000,000. This represented an average expenditure per head of around Fr. 77 (compared with Austria, Fr. 91; U.K., Fr. 150; West Germany, Fr. 220; and U.S., Fr. 419).

Television advertising, allowed in France for the first time on a restricted scale in 1968, was unlikely to make immediate inroads into the major media. The cost of a 30-second advertisement was around Fr. 700,000. Anticipated revenue was Fr. 170 million in 1969, or less than 5% of all advertising revenue. The press still dominated the scene, although from 1962 to 1968 the share of advertising held by the press had fallen from 66 to 58.4%. In 1960 periodicals had accounted for only 35% of total press receipts from advertising, but by 1969 the positions had been reversed, with periodical advertising accounting for 65% of the total. Direct mail and poster advertising were reported to be reviving, after a fall from favour.

In West Germany advertising expenditure increased by 12.5% to DM. 2,940,000,000. The amount spent on newspaper advertising increased by 20.7% to DM. 739.5 million and that on magazines by 14.7% to DM.

1.5 billion. Expenditure on television advertising dropped by 2% to DM. 546.9 million, while expenditure on radio commercials rose by 17.5% to DM. 152 million.

Market research methods came under public suspicion when one of West Germany's leading research firms, Günter Wickert, announced that 87% of the population was against revaluation of the mark, many on the ground that foreign pressure was largely behind the move. When published in the press, the findings were attacked by experts who maintained that the majority of people were completely incapable of realizing the implications of revaluation. Other more innocent findings, such as the disclosure that eight out of ten German males wore their best suit on a Sunday, seemed slightly less credible after this incident. (X.)

North America. The year 1969 was one in which the U.S. economy was constantly aware of the spectre of inflation. As the year started, estimates of expenditures for the advertising industry were, for the most part, cautious. Since 1960 there had been a steady annual increase in the dollars invested in advertising and it was to turn out that 1969 would continue this trend. A gain in ad volume of at least 7% over 1968 was estimated; this meant that the $18.3 billion figure posted in 1968 would rise to over $19.6 billion in 1969.

All of the seven major media in the U.S.—television, magazines, newspapers, radio, business publications, outdoor, and direct mail—estimated increases in their national advertising volume for 1969 as compared with 1968. In all, the seven anticipated an aggregate of $9.6 billion in national advertising dollars (local advertising expenditures were not included in their figures), as compared with an aggregate of $8.8 billion invested in national advertising during 1968.

Newspapers saw a national ad volume of some $1.1 billion, up from about $990 million in 1968, or a gain of 11.1%. Network television expected a grand total for 1969 of $1.7 billion in ad volume, up a healthy 13.3% from $1.5 billion in 1968; spot television anticipated a similar $200 million gain in national ad volume, moving from $1.1 billion in 1968 to $1.3 billion in 1969, an increase of 18.2%. Magazines would post a 4.2% gain for 1969, moving from the previous year's $1,190,000,000 to a new plateau of $1,240,000,000. Business publications, which had amassed total national ad dollars of $781.3 million in 1968, anticipated a 3.9% boost to $811.8 million in 1969. Network radio expected to close out 1969 with a total slightly in excess of, or about the same as, the previous year's figure of $52.5 million. Spot radio, the only category not expecting an increase in ad dollars, was estimated to hold even at the $332 million figure it reached in 1968. The outdoor advertising industry predicted an 8.4% increase, from $155 million to $168 million. Direct mail, the largest of all the media in dollar volume, saw an increase of 7.4%, from $2.7 billion to $2.9 billion.

In 1969 the "consumer" and "consumerism" still were very much in the limelight. One of the biggest investigations undertaken by Congress on behalf of the consumer involved "giveaway" or sweepstakes promotions. Such promotions were carried on by the oil companies, supermarket chains, major soap and detergent makers, and magazines, among others. Ever since their inception these games had come under fire as being deceptive (and in some cases downright fraudulent), particularly because only a small number of the prizes were ever awarded.

Employee recruiting ad prepared by the Deutsch, Shea & Evans agency for General Electric's Aircraft Engine Group. The advertisement appeared in the March 1969 issue of "Ebony."

COURTESY, AIRCRAFT ENGINE GROUP, GENERAL ELECTRIC CORP.

After a long-drawn-out investigation, the House Small Business Committee released findings in mid-November showing that the "preselected winner" ("you may already have won a prize") type of sweepstakes promotion awarded an average of only 10% of the prizes offered in the advertising and that most of the prizes awarded were small. A number of advertisers using "preselected" types of sweepstakes indicated at hearings that they either were moving toward sweepstakes programs that would award all of the prizes offered or were dropping the sweepstakes form of promotion.

Another major move during the year that affected a great number of consumers was the ban placed suddenly on the use of cyclamates as a low-calorie sweetening agent in foods and beverages by Health, Education, and Welfare Secretary Robert H. Finch. Although it was later eased somewhat, at least in relation to diet foods, the ban was a major blow to the soft-drink manufacturers, some of whom depended on low-calorie beverages for as much as 25% of their sales. Nevertheless, in a very short time soft-drink bottlers were on the market with newly formulated noncyclamate diet drinks, most of which contained substantially more calories than the variety with cyclamates although they were still far lower in calories than the regular sugar-sweetened drinks. In many cases ads for the new products, stressing the advantages of the alternative sweetening agents, appeared within a few days of Finch's announcement.

Cigarette advertising, long a hotly debated topic on the U.S. scene, was even more in the spotlight during 1969. The Cigarette Labeling and Advertising Act, passed by Congress in 1965, had required that a caution notice be placed on all cigarette packages, and preempted the Federal Trade Commission from acting on cigarette health claims until July 1, 1969. The FTC gave every indication that it would seek stronger wording of the health warning and also would require warnings in cigarette advertising. After the deadline had passed for new legislation, and with the tobacco industry, Congress, and the broadcasting industry all seeking new solutions, in late July the cigarette makers came up with a proposal: they would remove all cigarette advertising from radio and television by no

Aden: *see* Southern Yemen

later than September 1970. Many anticigarette forces, however, sought an earlier date.

One of the chief concerns expressed by anticigarette forces was the disposition of the estimated $220 million per year being spent on cigarette advertising on radio and television. They hoped to keep any substantial portion of that expenditure from being transferred to other media.

There was a good deal of questioning among advertising people as to the eventual outcome of banning a particular product from certain selected media. If cigarettes were injurious to health, they asked, why should they not be banned from all advertising media? Others, however, maintained that it was wrong to forbid any advertising for a product that was manufactured and sold legally. Although the radio and television media were the only ones presently facing an outright embargo of cigarette advertising, several newspapers, including the *New York Times,* announced during 1969 that they would no longer accept cigarette advertising. Some magazines also announced a similar ad ban and several radio and television stations decided to drop cigarette ads without waiting for the outcome of the hassle between Congress, the tobacco industry, and the media.

KEYSTONE

Gaily decorated bus in London on Aug. 14, 1969, was the first London Transport central bus painted a colour other than red since World War II. The idea of painting a bus as a tourist attraction originated with the Silexine paint company.

The 125 leading advertisers in the U.S. invested $4,830,000,000 in advertising and promotion during 1968, according to the annual tabulation of *Advertising Age*. This was an increase of 6.4% over the $4,540,000,000 invested in 1967. Procter & Gamble remained the perennial leader by a substantial margin—but its overall expenditure dropped from an estimated $280 million in 1967 to $270 million in 1968. General Motors once again held the no. 2 spot, but showed a sharp increase in expenditure from $184 million the year before to $214 million in 1968. The next eight members of the top ten, in decreasing order, were General Foods, Colgate-Palmolive, Ford Motor Co., Sears, Roebuck & Co., Bristol-Myers, American Home Products, Warner-Lambert, and R. J. Reynolds. All showed increases in ad expenditures from 1967 to 1968 except Bristol-Myers, whose expenditure dropped off from $121 million in 1967 to $114.3 million in 1968.

The largest single redesigning program ever undertaken was announced in October 1969 by the Coca-Cola Co., the 14th largest U.S. advertiser with a total 1968 expenditure of $74 million. The face-lifting was to affect everything associated with the company from bottle caps to advertising, but would incorporate the trademarks, red colour, and bottle shape that research had shown consumers identified with the company. The new look was to be unveiled first in the U.S. and then in the 131 other countries where the product was sold. Estimates of the cost of at least the beginnings of the changeover for the next three years were between $12 million and $15 million.

The 600 U.S. advertising agencies included in the annual agency billings report in *Advertising Age* billed a total of $8.9 billion in 1968, compared with $8.3 billion reported the previous year by 564 agencies. The $25 million mark was topped by 56 of the agencies, led once again by J. Walter Thompson Co., whose 1968 billings were $638 million in the U.S. and overseas. Other leaders, in declining order of billing, were McCann-Erickson ($478.5 million); Young & Rubicam ($472.6 million); Ted Bates & Co. ($334 million); Batten Barton Durstine & Osborn ($319.5 million); Foote, Cone & Belding ($271.4 million); Leo Burnett Co. ($265.1 million); Doyle Dane Bernbach ($254.1 million); Grey Advertising ($207 million); and Ogilvy & Mather ($205 million).

There was a noticeable cutback in personnel among agencies during 1968. Whereas nine of the ten largest agencies showed increases in billing from the previous year, seven of those nine had cutbacks in personnel. Reasons for these cutbacks varied, but there was no question that the profit pinch that agencies had begun to feel in the past few years was the answer in many cases. Still another factor was the continuing increase in television billings; agencies required fewer employees per million dollars of television billing than they did per million dollars of print billing.

Advertising agency profits showed what was termed a "modest improvement" in 1968, according to figures on annual costs and profits released by the American Association of Advertising Agencies. Net profit after taxes averaged 3.97% of gross income, which was up from the 1967 figure of 3.57% but down from the 4.98% profit shown in 1966. Gross income, taken as a percentage of billings, amounted to 0.76% in 1968, compared with 0.69% the previous year and 0.98% in 1966. The "modest" profit improvement was attributed primarily to a substantial increase in billing, resulting in a proportionate decrease in overhead costs.

The much more rapid movement of major agencies into overseas markets was the big agency story in 1969. In May, Chicago's giant Leo Burnett Co. acquired the major agency parts of London Press Exchange's extensive holdings, which at the time were billing some $85 million. Combined billings of Burnett and LPE for 1969 were expected to total $375 million. In the wake of the Burnett-LPE announcement came news that Needham, Harper & Steers ($120 million in billings), S. H. Benson Ltd. in London ($70 million), and Havas Conseil in France ($54 million) were working on some sort of joint development of their international facilities that would be a working combine with total billings of nearly $250 million. A month later Sullivan, Stauffer, Colwell & Bayles announced the purchase of a minority interest in Lintas, the giant London-based shop owned by Unilever. Based on 1968 billings—$107.7 million for SSC&B and $155.9 million for Lintas—the combined operation was estimated to be billing in the area of $300 million by the end of 1969.

Advertising activity in Canada during 1969 picked up pace smartly, and unless some unforeseen economic setbacks were encountered was likely to continue to do so into the 1970s. The estimated rise in ad revenues for the year was 7%, or $967.2 million, as compared with $902.1 million in 1968. More than $500 million of the 1969 total came from expenditures made by the 189 companies that were members of the Association of Canadian Advertisers. The overall expenditure broken down by media was: daily newspapers, $295 million; catalogs and direct mail, $212 million; television, $129.8 million; radio, $100 million; outdoor, car cards, signs, $68 million; weeklies (semi- and tri-), $45 million; directories, $42 million; business publications, $30 million; general magazines, $23.5 million; weekend supplements, $16 million; and farm publications, $5 million.

Canada's top advertiser in 1968 was General Motors, with an expenditure of $8,319,000. Second was Procter & Gamble, with $6,105,000, followed by General Foods, Imperial Tobacco Co. of Canada, Canadian Breweries, Ford Motor Co. of Canada, Colgate-Palmolive, Lever Bros., Kraft Foods, and Air Canada.

In the summer of 1969 the Canadian Department of Consumer and Corporate Affairs declared war on misleading advertising. The department prepared a list of offenses and announced that it would soon get some test cases under way. Among the areas to be covered were misleading statements of fact regarding costs and prices, unsupported claims of performance, deceptive use of contests, "free" offers that were not in fact free, bait and switch offers, contests with no prizes available, and phony direct mail "directory" solicitations. (J. J. GM.)

See also Industrial Review; Merchandising; Telecommunications; Television and Radio.

Afghanistan

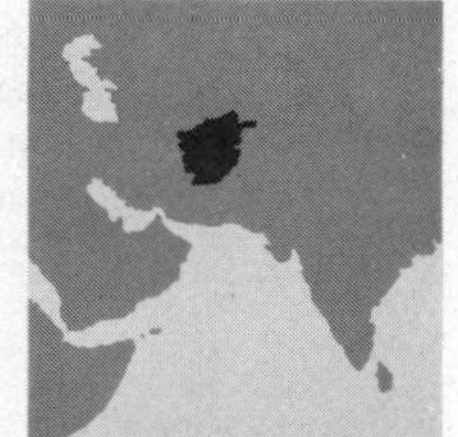

A constitutional monarchy in central Asia, Afghanistan is bordered by the U.S.S.R., China, West Pakistan, and Iran. Area: about 252,000 sq. mi. (652,000 sq.km.). Pop. (1969 est.): 16,515,886, including Pathans, Tadzhiks, Uzbeks, Hazaras. Cap. and largest city: Kabul (metro. area pop., 1969 est., 472,313). Language: Persian and Pashto. Religion: Muslim. King, Mohammad Zahir Shah; prime minister in 1969, Noor Ahmad Etemadi.

Domestically, 1969 was a year of quiet administrative and economic progress. The division of powers among the executive, the legislature, and the judiciary laid down in the 1964 constitution, although virtually completed in 1968, entailed much detailed work in its precise application to existing institutions. This was especially true in the judicial field, where the structure and functions of the lower courts, previously shaped largely by tradition, were found to need considerable alteration. The changes necessitated in this, as in other branches of the administration, were effected with little friction, due to the popularity of the prime minister and to the steady support which he received from the king.

In September Afghanistan held its second free parliamentary election since the introduction of the constitution in 1964. Many conservative local landowners who had shunned the first election campaigned for office and won seats. Often they won at the expense of more liberal, national-minded incumbents; the new Parliament, thus, was expected to be more conservative than the previous one.

Afghanistan, however, did not escape the worldwide spread of radical ideas among the student population, and in July the government found it necessary to close Kabul University temporarily because of student unrest. Secondary schools in the capital were also shut, but there were no serious disturbances.

In the economic field, the policy of mobilizing local resources to replace by degrees the massive foreign aid furnished by the U.S. and the U.S.S.R. continued in accordance with Afghan determination to avoid undue dependence on external help. The main difficulty lay in the shortage of capital for investment in the private sector; and in spite of the inducements proffered by the government—tax-free starting years, protective tariffs, customs-free import of capital goods—growth was slow.

In foreign affairs, the traditional Afghan desire to preserve complete autonomy regardless of external aid and to maintain friendly relations with other countries remained dominant. India's desire for close relations was shown by a visit from Prime Minister Indira Gandhi and by Indian aid in the restoration of the Bamian antiquities. In May Soviet Premier Aleksei N. Kosygin arrived to attend the country's 50th independence day celebrations. Relations with Pakistan and with its new government after the fall

AFGHANISTAN

Education. Public schools only (1967–68): primary, pupils 447,347, teachers 6,932; secondary, pupils 54,397, teachers 3,667; vocational, pupils 7,320, teachers 562; teacher training, students 6,296, teachers 418; higher (at Universities of Kabul and Nangrahar), students 3,642, teaching staff 612.

Finance. Monetary unit: afghani, with a par value of 45 afghanis to U.S. $1 (108 afghanis = £1 sterling) and a free rate (Sept. 1, 1969) of 76.30 afghanis to U.S. $1 (182 afghanis = £1). Budget (1966–67 est.): revenue 4,284,000,000 afghanis; expenditure 2,929,000,000 afghanis (excluding 1,728,000,000 afghanis development expenditure). Money supply: (March 1969) 5,931,000,000 afghanis; (March 1968) 5,529,000,000 afghanis.

Foreign Trade. (1967–68) Imports 10,453,700,000 afghanis (including 5,448,600,000 afghanis loan and grant imports); exports 5,017,600,000 afghanis. Import sources: U.S.S.R. 13%; Japan 8%; U.S. 5%; India 5%. Export destinations: U.S.S.R. 33%; India 16%; U.K. 16%; U.S. 8%; Pakistan 8%. Main exports: fruit and nuts 39%; karakul (Persian lamb) skins 21%; cotton 12%; carpets 8%; wool 7%.

Transport and Communications. Roads (motorable; 1966) *c.* 6,700 km. Motor vehicles in use (1967): passenger 27,600; commercial 15,308. Air traffic (1967): 84,839,000 passenger-km.; freight 5,298,000 net ton-km. Telephones (Jan. 1968) *c.* 9,800. Radio receivers (Dec. 1965) 200,000.

Agriculture. Production (in 000; metric tons): cotton, lint (1967) 23, (1966) 21; sugar, raw value (1966–67) *c.* 8, (1965–66) *c.* 11; rice (1966), 337 (1965) 380; wheat (1966) 2,033, (1965) 2,282; corn (1966) 720, (1965) 720; barley (1966) 375, (1965) 380; wool, greasy (1962) *c.* 24. Livestock (in 000; 1967–68): cattle *c.* 3,665; sheep 21,000 (including *c.* 6,000 karakul); horses *c.* 300; asses *c.* 1,200; goats *c.* 3,200; camels *c.* 300; chickens (1954) 40,000.

Industry. Production (in 000; metric tons; 1967–68): coal 152; electricity (kw-hr.) 357,000; cement 124; salt 32; cotton yarn 0.9; cotton fabrics (m.) 64,000.

Aerospace Industry: *see* Astronautics; Defense; Industrial Review; Transportation

Afars and Issas, French Territory of: *see* Dependent States of Pres. Muhammad Ayub Khan were correct rather than cordial because of continued Afghan support for the promotion of "Pakhtunistan." This support again became vocal when the Pakistan government incorporated the states of Dir, Swat, and Chitral, hitherto domestically autonomous, into the administrative structure of West Pakistan, in accordance, it was claimed, with the wishes of the states' peoples. The resulting resentment in Afghanistan did not last, and the country's policy of friendly neutrality toward both the Communist and non-Communist worlds continued smoothly. (L. F. R. W.)

Africa

The mood of Africa during 1969 ran the gamut from sadness over the continued killing in the Nigerian-Biafran war to elation at the first Pan-African Cultural Festival in July. Contrasts abounded. Several coups d'etat continued the pattern of recent years, but Ghana held national elections three years after the military had seized power from Kwame Nkrumah. The Congo achieved some measure of economic and tribal stability, but tribalism flared in Kenya. South Africa developed surface-to-air missiles, while continuing to keep television out of the country. The British were criticized for not doing something more tangible about white-dominated Rhodesia but only four African states paid their "liberation dues" for 1968–69 to harass the white-controlled southern nations. Cognizant of "the winds of change," Spain relinquished control of the small enclave of Ifni to Morocco on June 30, but at the other end of the continent a new political party was formed dedicated to even more extreme apartheid (racial separation policies) in South Africa.

Nigerian-Biafran War. Despite efforts of the Organization of African Unity (OAU), Pope Paul VI, former Nigerian Pres. Nnamdi Azikiwe, and others to end the war that had begun in July 1967, Nigerian and Biafran positions, both political and military, remained fundamentally the same. Casualties including civilians since the beginning of the war were about two million. Biafrans lost their capital of Umuahia in mid-April but shortly afterward succeeded in taking Owerri by siege from the central government. In fact, the small Biafran air force attacked oil installations held by the central government. Biafran strategy appeared to be to secure a stalemate.

A severe psychological blow was dealt Biafrans when the hero of Nigerian nationalism, Nnamdi Azikiwe, first president of federal Nigeria and an Ibo as well, returned from the U.K. in September and said that he would appeal to his fellow tribesmen to give up their secession and join again in a united Nigeria. He insisted that they had no reason to fear genocide at the hands of federal troops. There was no evidence, according to an international team that toured Nigerian-held territory, that the several hundred thousand Ibos there were objects of genocide. Biafrans, however, pointed to an air raid on the town of Umuohiagu on February 7, in which 200–300 people were killed and hundreds more wounded, and they reacted coolly to Azikiwe's change of position.

Evidence of this mutual suspicion was found in the tangled web of negotiations concerning Red Cross flights into Biafra. After a Nigerian Air Force plane shot down a Red Cross plane on June 5, the latter suspended its relief airlift. Two months later the Nigerian government agreed to its renewal only to have the Biafrans reject the terms of the accord. Food came to Biafra from several international sources, and during the summer an average of four planes a night carried in excess of 150 tons of arms a week to the Biafrans. Bitter at the British for their aid to the federal government and grateful to the French for their help, many Biafrans began to embrace French culture. At the year's end there seemed to be little likelihood of an end to the tragic war.

Coups and Plots. On May 25 young army officers seized power in the Sudan and proclaimed a one-party socialist state with Col. Gafaar Muhammad al-Nimeiry heading the Revolutionary Council. Ousted Pres. Ismail al-Azhari, who had been the Sudan's first prime minister in 1956, died in August before he could be questioned about charges of governmental corruption. One-third of the new ministers were avowed Communists. Secession of the nation's three southern provinces, which had been in rebellion for several years, was not tolerated by the new regime. But this did not deter the formation of a new military-led provisional government in the south, known as the Anyidi revolutionary government and pledged to continue the war. On July 28 Sudan's prime minister, Abubakr Awadallah, charged that the United States was attempting to sabotage his government. The Revolutionary Council deposed Awadallah in late September, and al-Nimeiry took his place as prime minister. No shift in national policy seemed indicated by this move.

In a bloodless coup on September 1, a revolutionary council deposed 79-year-old King Idris I of Libya (who was in Turkey at the time) and proclaimed the Libyan Socialist Republic. A policy of Arab nationalism and socialism was announced for the world's third largest oil-exporting country, though existing agreements were to be honoured. The U.S. and Britain, nonetheless, were told that their military base leases would not be renewed. The regime promised a more equitable distribution of wealth, which in a decade had increased from a per capita income of $100 to $1,100 per year.

On October 15 Abd-i-Rashid Ali Shermarke, president of Somalia since June 1967, was assassinated. Six days later, less than 24 hours after his funeral, an Army-inspired national revolutionary council took control of the government, arrested Prime Minister Muhammad Hajì Ibrahim Egal, and said it would work to eliminate corruption and institute socialism. As in the case of the Libyan coup, foreign commitments were to be respected. Political parties, which in March had participated in a democratic election, were banned. One reason for the revolution may have been the displeasure felt by many Somalis in regard to the border agreement with Kenya and Ethiopia worked out by the Shermarke-Egal regime.

Several former French colonies experienced threats to their regimes during the year, though most were unsuccessful. An exception was the overthrow of Dahomey's first civilian president in several years, Émile Derlin Zinsou, by army officers in December. In May Zinsou had announced the arrest of 20 members of the Dahomean Democratic Union for plotting to overthrow him, and a former head of state, Alphonse Alley, had been sentenced on October 4 to ten years' imprisonment for having tried to kidnap the army chief. On April 12, Pres. Jean Bedel Bokassa of the Central African Republic announced the foiling of a coup by army officers. In Guinea Pres. Sékou Touré announced on March 21 that two members of his

Cabinet had been arrested for trying to seize control of the government. By mid-May Touré had purged the Army of dissident officers and had announced the death sentence for 12 opponents. A state of emergency was declared in Senegal on June 11, after a long period of labour and student unrest. In Algeria 56 defendants were accused in March of conspiring against the four-year regime of Pres. Houari Boumédienne. Four months later their number had grown to 180.

Elsewhere, in Malawi eight men were hanged for their part in a plot against the government the previous year. In the Watutsi-dominated land of Burundi a plan by the rival Bahutus to gain control of the state was thwarted on September 17, when 20 prominent persons were arrested. And in Tanzania six persons were arrested on October 11 for undermining law and order while Pres. Julius Nyerere was in Moscow.

Quite evidently, many African nations were going through a "time of troubles," compounded of inflated hopes for a better life, personal ambition, different economic philosophies, and tribal rivalry.

Tribal Friction. African nationalism in the aftermath of independence was sufficiently strong to keep most states together, and also, ironically, to inhibit closer union among them. In the process of weaving together national unity, however, the still-potent forces of tribal allegiance plagued many states. In addition to the tragic fighting in Nigeria, old antagonisms continued in different parts of the continent. The civil war in Chad, which pitted northern Muslims against the government and which had taken thousands of lives during the past few years, did not end. In Eritrea, which had been incorporated into Ethiopia in 1962, an intermittent guerrilla war appeared to grow more intense with two hijackings of Ethiopian airplanes.

In the aftermath of the assassination of Kenya's minister for economic affairs, Tom Mboya, disorders broke out that reflected and exacerbated tension between the Kikuyu (Kenya's largest tribe) and Luo. Although a Luo, Mboya had stood for national unity. Fearing that their influence might wane, some Kikuyu revived tribal oath taking. Pres. Jomo Kenyatta (*see* BIOGRAPHY), a Kikuyu, was criticized for letting the oath taking occur on his property. Disorders broke out on October 25 at Kisumu, when Kenyatta opened a Soviet-financed hospital; 11 persons were killed and 78 wounded. As a consequence, former Vice-Pres. Oginga Odinga, a Luo who led the opposition Kenya People's Union, was placed under house arrest. Differences between Kenyatta and Odinga were partly political and partly a reflection of tribal distrust.

Tribal consciousness also contributed to the electoral victory of Kofi Busia's Progress Party in Ghana on August 29. His leading opponent, Komla A. Gbedemah, received almost all of his support from the Ewes, while Busia (*see* BIOGRAPHY) got his from the Akan-speaking peoples.

Deaths of Leaders. More than passing interest was evoked by the deaths of several noted Africans. As if symbolizing the end of an era of conflict in the Congo (Kinshasa), two key figures in the early years of that nation's independence died. Former Pres. Joseph Kasavubu, a rival of the late Patrice Lumumba in 1960–61, who had been deposed in 1965 by Gen. Joseph Mobutu, died on March 24. Moise Tshombe, whom Kasavubu had dismissed from office, was declared dead in Algeria on June 30, two years after he was kidnapped over the Mediterranean and made a prisoner in Algeria. He was reported to have died of a heart attack; some suspicions were aroused over the circumstances of his death. The chameleonlike Tshombe, who served as the prime minister of the Congo in 1964–65, aroused strong feelings, both for and against him, throughout Africa. His detractors thought it appropriate that he was buried in Belgium.

"LONDON DAILY EXPRESS" FROM PICTORIAL PARADE

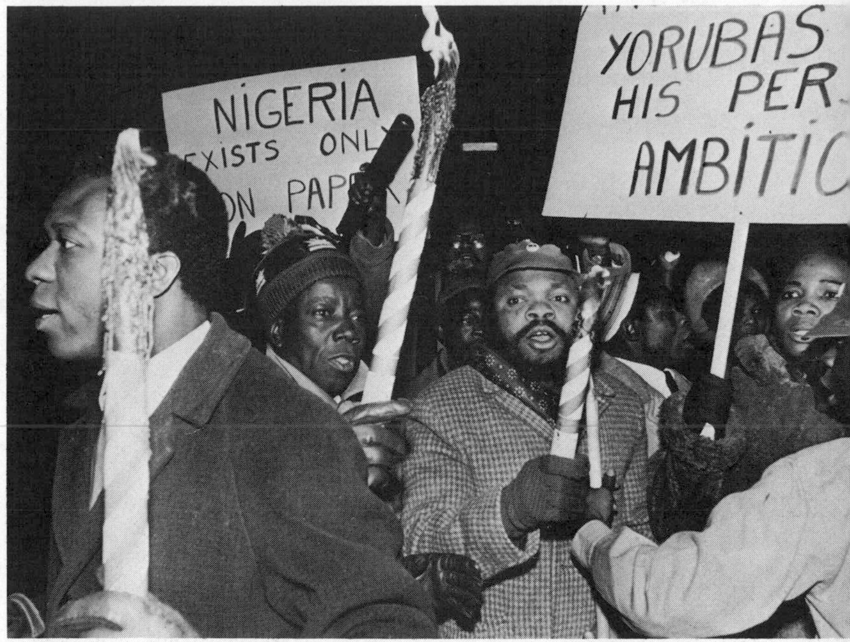

Biafrans protesting British arms sales to Nigeria war-danced through central London beating bongo drums and carrying torches, July 1, 1969. Police prevented the group from reaching Nigeria House.

A young African of articulate presence and international reputation, Kenya's minister of economic affairs, Tom Mboya, was killed on July 5, in downtown Nairobi. The assassination of the 38-year-old secretary-general of the governing Kenya African National Union and potential successor to President Kenyatta touched off tribal rioting of 30,000 people at his funeral. Another death of political significance for Africa was that of Eduardo Chivambo Mondlane, leader of the anti-Portuguese liberation front (FRELIMO), in Mozambique. On February 3, he was killed by a bomb in Dar es Salaam. As mentioned above, A. A. Shermarke, president of Somalia, was killed on October 15, and Sudan's ousted president, Ismail al-Azhari, died on August 26. On September 28 Nicolas Grunitzky, ousted as Togo's president in January 1967, died after a road accident. For additional information on these men, *see* OBITUARIES.

Elections. The most important election in Africa during the year occurred in Ghana. After three years of military rule following the overthrow of Pres. Kwame Nkrumah in February 1966, Kofi A. Busia was sworn in as prime minister on September 3. Having won 105 of 140 seats in the National Assembly, his Progress Party took over a country burdened with a formidable debt of $900 million. On October 17 Busia told the UN that his government could not afford to accept the debts incurred by his predecessors. Whatever its difficulties, as the first nation to have a civilian government gain power from a military regime through parliamentary elections, Ghana again provided a model for Africa.

On Dec. 19, 1968, Zambians voted in their first general election since independence. Pres. Kenneth Kaunda's United National Independence Party remained in power, with 81 of 105 legislative seats. In the first election since independence in 1966, voters in Botswana returned Pres. Seretse Khama's Botswana Democratic Party to power. The December parliamentary elections in Kenya resulted in the defeat of more than 70 incumbents of the 158-seat Assembly, including five government ministers. And, although they were later nullified by the coup in October, Somalia did hold parliamentary elections in late March.

The Southern Tier. Whites continued their domination over the southern portion of Africa with comparatively little change. Rhodesia, which had unilaterally broken with the U.K. in November 1965, held a referendum in June that favoured a white-dominated republic.

In South Africa, white domination secured further official sanction for its authority when a new Bureau of State Security (BOSS) received powers over the admission of evidence in court, thus making it practically immune from public control. Illustrative of the restrictive atmosphere in the country was the conviction of Laurence Gandar, editor in chief of the *Rand Daily Mail,* in July on charges of having published information about brutality in prisons without "reasonably verifying" the data. The new Reconstituted National Party of South Africa, formed in October, was dedicated to even more extreme apartheid than was already being practiced.

The Portuguese continued their military operations against the Africans in Angola and Mozambique, buoyed by the murder of Mondlane and the defection of Lazaro Kavandame, who for four years had led a guerrilla group in Mozambique. But the rebels claimed to have won control over one-fifth of Mozambique and in October were told that Sweden would contribute money to their cause. The rich oil finds off Cabinda (Angola) and the signing of final contracts with a South African consortium to build the Cahorabassa hydroelectric project on the Zambezi River in Mozambique indicated that Portugal intended to remain in control of both territories.

"LONDON DAILY EXPRESS" FROM PICTORIAL PARADE

Pres. Jomo Kenyatta of Kenya (top) met with Pres. Philibert Tsiranana of the Malagasy Republic (bottom) in Nairobi in April 1969 to discuss their countries' relations with Rhodesia and South Africa.

Regional Organizations. The OAU met in Addis Ababa, Eth., in September. Delegates from 41 nations discussed the Nigerian-Biafran war, economic sanctions and guerrilla operations against the white-dominated governments of southern Africa, and Israel's occupation of part of the United Arab Republic. Elected chairman of the conference was Ahmadou Ahidjo, president of the Cameroon. U Thant, secretary-general of the UN, addressed the meeting and appealed to the OAU to help end the war in Nigeria. On that issue the OAU maintained its policy of recognizing the original boundaries of Nigeria, from which Biafra had seceded in May 1967. The OAU's consultative committee on Nigeria met several times during the year to discuss the war and seek means to end it.

In December 1968, the Central African Republic had withdrawn from the Union of Central African States, which had also included the Congo (Kinshasa) and Chad. The organization, which had been founded early in 1968, had not proved economically advantageous to its members and went out of existence. The Central African Republic then rejoined the Central African Customs and Economic Union, other members of which were Congo (Brazzaville), Chad, Cameroon, and Gabon.

Economic Developments. On June 27 the European Common Market agreed to give $900 million in aid over five years to 18 African states (most of them former colonies of France). This continued previous arrangements, and, although less than what the Africans requested, was expected to be of great importance to their economies. In another instance of mutual accommodation, the Congo (Kinshasa) and the European Common Market signed an $18 million agreement on July 13 to begin financing a hydroelectric dam on the Inga rapids of the Congo River. And on September 25 the Congo (Kinshasa) and the Belgian mining company Union Minière came to an understanding of their three-year dispute over the seizure of the company's assets. In Zambia, too, an accord was reached in October with two mining companies which had been nationalized in August. The copper companies, worth approximately $1.2 billion, would allow 51% of their shares to be taken over by the Zambian government. The Zambians (as did other Africans) wanted the quickest possible "africanization" of jobs but recognized that for a long time to come they would need outside skills and capital. Neither Niger, with its newly found uranium, nor Botswana, with its recently discovered diamonds, could hope to extract the riches by themselves.

CAMERA PRESS—PIX FROM PUBLIX

Reporter Benjamin Pogrund (left) and editor in chief Laurence Gandar (right) of the "Rand Daily Mail" leave Rand Supreme Court in Johannesburg on July 10, 1969, after being convicted under the South African Prisons Act of publishing false information about prisons.

Other Developments. Among other African events during 1969 were Pope Paul VI's visit to Uganda at the end of July (the first by any reigning pontiff), and the election of Miss Angie Brooks (*see* BIOGRAPHY) of Liberia to be the 24th president of the UN General Assembly. Nigerian playwright Wole Soyinka, a strong critic of continuing the Nigeria-Biafra war, was released from prison. The Ghanaian government released Soviet trawlers after detaining them for spying.

Despite their problems Africans took great pride in their coming together in Algiers (July 21–August 1) for the first Pan-African Cultural Festival. They sought to express the common threads of their heritage and future common interests. (W. So.)

See also Dependent States; Migration, International; Refugees; articles on the various political units.

ENCYCLOPÆDIA BRITANNICA FILMS. *Life in the Sahara* (1953); *Egypt and the Nile* (1954); *East Africa (Kenya, Tanganyika, Uganda)* (1962); *The Suez Canal* (1962); *Continent of Africa (Lands Below the Sahara)* (1963); *The Republic of South Africa* (1963); *West Africa (Nigeria)* (1963); *The Nile Valley and Its People* (1964); *Oasis* (1965).

Agriculture

The world's farmers—with the assistance of nature—again provided a bountiful harvest in 1969, although in most areas it was not of record proportions. There was winter damage in parts of Eurasia, drought in some areas, and famine in such disorganized places as Biafra. However, 1969 was a third year of significant progress in the Indian subcontinent and some other less developed areas that had been on the brink of disaster in the mid-1960s. World production of cereals, including rice, reached a record level in 1968–69, and world production of fats and oils was forecast at an all-time high of 41 million tons in 1969. A deficiency of animal protein, particularly in some less developed countries, continued to be a major problem, but proposals to increase the harvest of foods from the sea and to convert high-protein oilseeds into human food were more discussed than activated.

Substantial surpluses of some major agricultural items became all too evident, causing a shift in attention from the need for increased production to problems of storage, prices, distribution, and the maintenance of healthy trade patterns and viable rural economies. There was a significant reduction in world trade in agricultural products in 1968–69. Some experts even suggested the rapid agricultural growth of less developed countries would not be absorbed internally and would result in additional surpluses being thrown on the world market. Experience with grains, especially wheat under the International Grains Arrangement, and with coffee, butter, and perhaps sugar surpluses suggested the necessity of dealing with underlying factors of production, rather than merely attempting to maintain prices within predetermined ranges. The World Bank doubled its efforts to stimulate agricultural production in less developed areas, and various national and international groups appeared to be moving beyond the hortatory to possibly more effective attention to the population spiral.

NORTH AMERICA

United States. Agricultural production in 1969 attained a new record index level of 121 (1957–59 = 100), compared with 120 in 1968 and 118 in 1967. Though production was adequate-to-surplus across a broad spectrum, the demands of an affluent society for red meats elevated prices in that sector to uncommon levels, whereas prices for most crops were comparatively depressed. Farm income improved despite sharply rising costs, with most of the increase going to the livestock sector. Exports declined and surpluses accumulated, but for the most part remained below record levels.

In legislative terms, 1969 was a quiet year. In addition to rapidly advancing agricultural technology, problems of revitalizing the rural economy, corporation farming, tax-loss farming, and the quality of the environment (with special reference to pesticide contamination) received much attention. The American Farm Bureau Federation, the largest of the farm organizations, celebrated its 50th year.

Crops. Production in 1969 was again at new record high levels; an "all-crops" index of 120 (1957–59 = 100) exceeded the previous record of 119 set in 1968. Because of official diversion programs, only 300 million ac. were planted for harvest, 2% or 6.8 million ac. less than in 1968; it was estimated that 288,373,000 ac. would be harvested, compared with 293,862,000 ac. a year earlier. The composite index of yield per acre covering 28 leading crops was a record 130, compared with 128 in 1968.

Food-grain production (wheat, rice, and rye) was indicated at 49.1 million tons—an index of 130, compared with 141 in 1968. The 1969 wheat allotment of 51.6 million ac. was down 13% from a year earlier; some 47,546,000 ac. were harvested, 14% fewer than in 1968, and production was down 7% to 1,456,299,000 bu. Yield per acre averaged 30.6 bu., a new record. Included in the total were 1,149,976,000 bu. of winter wheat (down 6% from the record crop of 1968) and a record 104,643,000 bu. of durum (up 7%). Other spring wheat, later than normal in several major growing areas, was down 17% to 201,680,000 bu. Rice production was indicated at 90,168,000 cwt., 14% less than the record 1968 crop. Allotted acreage was reduced to 2,160,542, 10% below 1968, and about 2,130,000 ac. were harvested with an average yield of 4,233 lb. per ac. The rye crop was up 38% to 32,028,000 bu., harvested from 1,354,000 ac. Acreage increased by 34.5% over 1968, and yield per acre was a new record high 23.7 bu. Popcorn production was 538,435,000 lb., compared with 466,346,000 lb. in 1968.

Production of feed grains (corn, oats, barley and grain sorghums) was indicated at 171 million tons, 2% more than in 1968, but below the 1967 record. Total acreage, largely restrained by official programs, declined by 1%, but oats acreage rose 6%. Corn (maize) was indicated at 4,444,199,000 bu. from 54,758,000 ac., compared with 4,374,840,000 bu. from 55,707,000 ac. in 1968. Yield was a record 81.2 bu. per ac. Oats, a dwindling crop since World War II, rallied in 1969 to 938,153,000 bu. from 18,343,000 ac., the largest crop since 1963. Barley production was 415,898,000 bu., only slightly below the 418,168,000 bu. of 1968; the average yield of 44.4 bu. per ac. was a new record. Sorghum grain production also set a new record of 757,322,000 bu., 3% above 1968. Only 13,699,000 ac. were harvested—about 2% less than in 1968—but the average yield of 55.3 bu. per ac. was the second highest ever recorded.

Forage was generally abundant. The total hay crop of 127,480,000 tons from 63,026,000 ac. exceeded the 125,588,000 tons of 1968 and was slightly larger than the 1967 record. Alfalfa accounted for 74,818,000 tons of the total; clover and timothy for 23,888,000 tons; wild hay for 8,604,000 tons; and lespedeza for 1,997,000 tons.

Oilseed production totaled about 39.4 million tons, 1% more than in 1968 and 15% above 1967. Soy-

Table I. Index Numbers of Volume of Agricultural Production

Average 1952–56 = 100

Region	Total agricultural production			Per capita food production		
	1968*	1967	1948–52	1968*	1967	1948–52
Western Europe	145	143	84	130	129	86
North America	126	124	93	107	107	99
Latin America	144	147	88	100	104	96
Oceania	164	144	90	129	110	102
Far East (excl. China and Japan)	148	141	87	106	103	94
Near East (excl. Israel)	156	153	84	107	108	92
Africa (excl. South Africa)	141	139	87	96	96	97
Eastern Europe and U.S.S.R.	174	167	82	148	142	88
Other developed countries (Japan, South Africa, and Israel)	162	165	81	140	145	87
All above regions	147	143	87	114	113	93

*Preliminary.

Source: Food and Agriculture Organization of the United Nations, *The State of Food and Agriculture, 1969* (1969).

Path winding through 15-ft. snowdrifts was cleared by ranchers in Alberta, Canada, so cattle could reach haystacks during a subzero cold spell in February 1969.

"CALGARY HERALD"

beans were indicated at 1,094,466 bu., cottonseed at 4,245,000 tons, and flaxseed at 36,094,000 bu. Peanuts harvested for nuts were indicated at a record high 2,570,460,000 lb. from 1,437,000 ac., compared with 2,542,841,000 lb. in 1968. The 1969 cotton crop of 10,036,000 bales was substantially below the 10,948,000 bales of 1968, but larger than the very short 1967 crop. Indicated acreage under relaxed restrictions was up 10.5%, but the yield of 429 bu. per ac. was down sharply. U.S. production accounted for approximately one-fifth of the estimated world crop of 52,285,000 bales.

U.S. sugar production reached a new record index of 175, compared with 162 in 1968. The sugar-beet crop was a record 27,961,000 tons, 10% more than the previous record set in 1968 and 45% more than in 1967. Production of sugarcane for sugar and seed was indicated at 22,845,000 tons, down 8%.

Total production of all types of tobacco was indicated at 1,799,447,000 lb., 5% more than in 1968 but 9% below 1967. Following a year of reduced acreage and reduced yields, the 923,000 ac. harvested represented an increase of nearly 5% over 1968. Acreage for the flue-cured type was up 9% and the indicated crop was 1,058,000,000 lb. Production of the Burley type was indicated at 574 million lb. and the Maryland type crop at 31.9 million lb. Fresh vegetable supplies in 1969 were down for most types; sweet corn, melons, and lettuce were among the exceptions. Production of the principal vegetable crops for processing was down by 22% from 1968. Dry field peas were indicated at 4,862,000 cwt., 30% above 1968, and dry edible beans at 18,777,000 cwt., up 6%. The important fall potato crop was forecast at 231,209,000 cwt., compared with 220,924,000 cwt. in 1968, and the total crop was 305,141,000, cwt., compared with 294,192,000 cwt. Sweet potato production totaled 13,687,000 cwt., compared with 13,763,000 cwt. a year earlier.

Indicated tonnage of deciduous fruits was 11% above 1968 and 26% above 1967. The apple crop was forecast at a record 158,645,000 bu., peaches at 78,648,000 bu., pears at 710,750 tons; and grapes at 3,828,000 tons. California plums and prunes were the only deciduous fruits indicated as falling short of 1968. Production of edible tree nuts was indicated at 343,800 tons, 25% more than in 1968; the almond crop of 114,000 tons was the largest of record. The 1969–70 production of citrus fruits promised to be nearly 9% larger than the 1968–69 production of 183,850,000 boxes of all oranges, 55 million of grapefruit, 16.6 million of lemons, 700,000 of limes, 1.8 million of tangelos, 5,320,000 of tangerines, and 4.5 million of temple oranges.

Livestock. Production of all livestock and products rose 1% in 1969, to an index level 19% above the 1957–59 average. Meat animals increased 1% to an index of 124; dairy products declined 1% to 97; and poultry and eggs rose 3% to 138. The livestock sector of the economy, with a value of about $20,192,443,000 at the beginning of the year, accounted for $13.4 billion (against $12.1 billion in 1968) of the $20,535,000,000 total cash receipts from farming during the first half of 1969.

Cattle and calves numbered 109,661,000 head on Jan. 1, 1969, compared with 109,152,000 head a year earlier. The 1969 calf crop was estimated at 44,473,000 head (44,102,000 head in 1968). Of the total, beef animals, at 88,051,000 head, accounted for all of the expansion. Dairy cattle totaled 21,610,000 head, compared with 22,251,000 head a year earlier, and the 14,123,000 cows and heifers two years of age and over represented a decline of about half a million head. Record numbers of cattle were moved through feed yards for fattening; as of July 1, 1969, some 10,397,000 head were on feed.

The long attrition of the dairy herd finally resulted in some decline in milk production, despite abundant feed and pasture, improved management, and improved stock. Milk production for the first eight months of 1969 was 80,035,000,000 lb., compared with 81,214,000,000 lb. for the same months of 1968.

Hogs were an enigma in 1969. On January 1, 57,205,000 head were reported on U.S. farms—up from 54,265,000 head a year earlier—and the March report indicated further expansion. With hog prices high and the corn-hog price ratio highly favourable, the pig crop in the ten Corn Belt states had risen 2% from December 1968 to February 1969, and producers' intentions were to increase the number of sows farrowing after March by 5–6%. However, the June report indicated a sharp decline in the spring pig crop, with March–May farrowings down 8%. Later reports substantiated this drop without fully explaining it, and indicated that the total 1969 pig crop would fall somewhat short of the 94.5 million pigs saved in 1968. Nor was any large increase in prospect for the later summer-autumn 1969 pig crop or for the spring crop of 1970. One result was that prices continued at uncommonly high levels far into the autumn.

Sheep numbers continued their long decline, reaching 21,111,000 head as of Jan. 1, 1969, down 5% from a year earlier. The 1969 lamb crop of 13,561,000 head was 6% below 1968. Wool production, indicated at 200 million lb. greasy basis, was down 5.9%. The decline was blamed on labour costs, restricted size of operation, and greater profits from cattle.

The January 1969 total of 420,204,000 chickens on farms was down from 425,158,000 head a year earlier. Of the total, 363,481,000 head were classed as potential layers, compared with 374,129,000 head a year earlier. Fewer layers and a reduced rate of lay lowered egg production by 2% in the first eight months of 1969, to 46,119,000,000. Larger production was expected during the autumn, however. Prices were near those of a year earlier. With consumer demand for broiler meat strong, production rose by perhaps 7% above the 2,514,870,000 head produced in 1968. Broiler meat output in federally inspected processing plants in the first seven months of 1969 totaled 3.7 billion lb., 8% more than a year earlier. Prices were up about 7%. Early intentions to raise 109,582,000 head of turkeys in 1969, about 3% more than in 1968, were not carried out; the number would approximate that of 1968, but because of 1.8 million more head of heavy types, more meat would be produced.

Colonies of bees in the United States totaled 4,731,000 on July 1, down moderately from 4,764,000 a year earlier. Early indications were for a honey crop significantly larger than the small 200 million lb. of 1968.

Farm Prices, Costs, Income, and Finances. The index of prices received by farmers in mid-September 1969 was 275 (1910–14 = 100), down from the 1969 high of 284 in June but above the 268 of September 1968. All crops had declined to 214 from 231 a year earlier, while livestock and products had risen to 328 from 300 during the same period. Tobacco was up substantially, feeds were off moderately, and cotton and fruit were down sharply. During part of the year, corn exceeded wheat in price for the first time since 1947. The increase in the livestock sector derived largely from meat-animal prices; dairy products and wool rose moderately while poultry and eggs fell.

The parity index of prices paid by farmers for commodities and services was 374 in September 1969 (1910–14 = 100), up from 356 in September 1968 and near the all-time high of 375 set in June 1969. Prices paid for farm family living items rose to 354 from 338 and production items to 304 from 292. Interest stood at 577 (518 a year earlier), taxes at 1,020 (951), and wage rates at 1,010 (922). The number of hired farm workers for the week ended August 30 was 1,676,000, 7% below a year earlier and the lowest on record.

The parity ratio was 74, one point off from a year earlier; the newer adjusted parity ratio, which included government payments, was 79, down from 81 in September 1968. The farmer's share of the consumer's dollar cost of the retail "market basket" in August was 41%, up from the 1968 average of 39%. In July the index of retail food cost was 126.7 (1957–59 = 100), compared with 120 a year earlier; meanwhile, the more inclusive consumer price index had moved from 121.5 in July 1968 to 128.2.

Cash receipts from farm marketings during the first half of 1969 rose to a record $19.9 billion, compared with $18.3 billion for the corresponding period of 1968. Volume marketed increased 2% and prices averaged 5.5% higher. Livestock and products, at $13.4 billion, accounted for most of the increase. For most crops, increased volume outweighed lower prices, but potato prices were so low that portions of the crop were plowed under in protest. Production expenses on an annual basis were estimated at a seasonally adjusted $38.4 billion, an increase of $2.5 billion from the 1968 rate. The realized gross, based on the first half of 1969, was estimated at an annual rate, seasonally adjusted, of about $54 billion, compared with $50.5 billion in 1968.

Realized net farm income, estimated at an annual rate (seasonally adjusted), was $1 billion above the $14.6 billion of 1968. Realized net farm income per farm in 1968 was $4,841, up $300 from 1968 but below the record $5,044 of 1966. Disposable personal income for the farm population, at a record $2,163 per capita in 1968, was still only 73% as much as the per capita income of the nonfarm population.

The value of all U.S. farm assets on Jan. 1, 1969, was estimated at $297.9 billion, 5% higher than a year earlier. Real estate had advanced by 4.6%, other physical assets by 6.6%, and financial assets by 3.5%. Liabilities, at $55.4 billion, had increased by 9.9%; farm mortgage debt was up 9%. Commodity Credit Corporation (CCC) loans to farmers rose 62% to $2.3 billion.

Trade and Stocks. An eased food situation in parts of the world and a prolonged strike of longshoremen reduced U.S. farm exports for the second consecutive year—to $5,741,000,000, compared with $6,312,000,000 in 1967–68. Cotton, wheat, feed grains, rice, and vegetable oils contributed heavily to the decline.

UPI COMPIX

Junked cars line a levee to prevent erosion and flooding of fertile farmland in the Tulare Lake Basin, California, in April 1969.

Table II. Tobacco Production of the Principal Producing Countries

In 000 lb.

Country	Indicated 1969	1968	Average 1960–64	Average 1955–59
Argentina	107,454	135,834	106,262	72,932
Brazil	409,202	334,793	336,211	306,009
Bulgaria	...	...	211,393	171,578
Burma	94,797	119,048	88,212	90,944
Canada	237,340	218,807	196,295	165,770
China	...	...	1,399,820	1,687,600
Colombia	96,980	91,490	76,950	80,389
Dom. Rep.	46,297	36,155	61,729	43,021
France	110,230	117,018	92,090	120,416
Greece	178,919	194,368	218,741	199,945
Hungary	...	59,524	48,192	61,940
India	765,437	812,836	736,399	596,366
Indonesia	220,500	231,500	159,596	153,267
Italy	167,285	163,425	125,595	168,220
Japan	389,328	426,365	333,382	315,506
Korea, South	176,368	153,654	76,291	59,708
Mexico	136,906	101,412	96,364	74,277
Pakistan	400,000	410,000	212,912	238,568
Philippines	171,606	194,159	152,708	95,277
Rhodesia	137,300	132,180	226,233	193,406
Thailand	89,252	87,014	64,750	56,126
Turkey	321,100	356,325	278,771	261,081
U.S.S.R.	570,000	562,200	368,206	438,715
United States	1,799,447	1,712,299	2,178,400	1,913,757
Yugoslavia	92,593	96,561	84,965	97,253

Source: U.S. Department of Agriculture.

Table III. Cotton Production of the Principal Producing Countries

In 000 500-lb. bales

Country	Indicated 1969	1968	1967	Average 1960–64	Average 1935–39
Argentina	475	520	335	552	289
Brazil	3,500	3,300	2,700	2,235	1,956
China	6,600	6,800	7,000	5,040	2,855
Colombia	700	640	465	335	23
Greece	450	335	441	377	77
India	5,200	4,900	5,300	4,741	5,348*
Iran	750	690	528	494	171
Mexico	2,000	2,450	2,000	2,206	334
Pakistan	2,500	2,450	2,390	1,656	...
Peru	425	425	460	632	379
Spain	300	350	297	427	10
Sudan	1,000	960	900	675	248
Syria	650	705	580	656	28
Turkey	1,850	2,000	1,800	1,091	249
U.S.S.R.	9,500	9,300	9,300	7,370	3,430
U.A.R.	2,200	2,005	2,005	2,037	1,893
United States	10,036	10,948	7,458	14,795	13,149

*Includes Pakistan.
Source: U.S. Department of Agriculture.

Table IV. Orange (Including Tangerine) Production in Principal Producing Countries

In 000 boxes

Country	1968*	1967	Average 1960–64
Algeria	11,500	11,800	11,647
Argentina	25,699	23,772	21,540
Brazil†	49,779	49,183	27,020
Greece	11,810	6,607	7,646
Israel	27,715	29,144	16,536
Italy	52,441	45,308	30,650
Japan	85,145	61,685	38,314
Mexico	28,313	27,778	23,478
Morocco	23,080	24,446	15,493
South Africa	16,350	15,830	13,939
Spain	54,517	65,390	51,191
Turkey	14,850	14,204	8,522
U.A.R.	...	12,950	10,336
United States	238,626	166,018	145,937

*Preliminary.
†State of São Paulo only.
Source: U.S. Department of Agriculture.

Commercial sales for dollars totaled $4.8 billion, down from $5 billion a year earlier. Food for Peace programs took $900 million ($1.3 billion in the previous year).

Imports of agricultural products into the U.S. during 1968–69 rose to $4,931,000,000, up 6% from the $4,656,000,000 of 1967–68. Supplementary (competitive or partially competitive) products increased to $3,072,000,000 from $2,845,000,000, and complementary (noncompetitive) products to $1,859,000,000 from $1,811,000,000. During the first seven months of 1969, red meat imports rose to 918,810,000 lb. from 863,947,000 lb. a year earlier, causing some alarm among U.S. producers of beef and lamb.

Grain stocks on July 1, 1969, were larger than a year earlier, except for corn and rye. The four feed grains totaled 79 million tons, moderately larger than a year earlier. Carry-over of old-crop wheat was 811 million bu.; including a 69% larger supply of durum, the total was 50% above 1968 and the largest since 1965. Carry-over stocks of soybeans on September 1 were a record 322 million bu. The CCC reported that as of June 30, 1969, investment in price-support loans had risen to $3,334,025,000 from $2,268,217,000 a year earlier and inventories to $1,244,452,000 from $912,697,000.

Legislation and Administration. For the most part, 1969 was a year of inquiry and suggestion in preparation for general agricultural legislation to extend or replace the act of 1965, due to expire at the end of 1970. Proposed major legislation, offered jointly by a coalition of 22 farm organizations, in large part would extend the existing program. More spectacularly, a tractor caravan of the United Grain Farmers of America journeyed to Washington urging "Parity, not Charity."

Limitation of farm program payments to farmers was much discussed but, as passed by Congress in late November, the USDA appropriation for fiscal 1970 carried no such provision. Net total new budget authority provided by the bill was approximately $7.3 billion, a reduction of slightly more than $700 million from fiscal 1969. In early November, Congress approved funds totaling $610 million for Food Stamp Program operations in fiscal 1970, an increase of $270 million from a year earlier.

Secretary of Labor George P. Shultz opposed giving agricultural workers the right to organize under the National Labor Relations Act, proposing instead a special three-man Farm Labor Relations Board to handle farm labour problems. The United Farm Workers Organizing Committee continued its grape boycott efforts and raised an issue as to the effect of pesticides on farm workers. (*See* LABOUR UNIONS.) In November the government ordered a virtual halt to the use of DDT by 1971.

Canada. Even more than most of the world's grain producers, Canadian farmers were noticeably in distress during 1969. The cause was a crisis of abundance. To cope with this problem, acreage planted to wheat in the Prairie Provinces was reduced by 15% to 24,968,000, and a record 28.8 million ac. were held in summer fallow. On official recommendation, more acreage was planted to feed grains; the barley harvest was 389.2 million bu., compared with 325.4 million bu. in 1968, and oats totaled 386.4 million bu., compared with 362.5 million bu. Acreage sown to flaxseed was up 60%. The record 2 million ac. planted to the comparatively new rapeseed crop would produce about 37.6 million bu. (19.4 million bu. in 1968).

The 1969 growing season was favourable in the Prairie Provinces, although wet weather reduced some eastern crops. The Canadian wheat crop was officially forecast at 684,276,000 bu., compared with 649.8 million bu. in 1968 and a 1958–67 average of about 560 million bu. Meanwhile, in contrast to the mid-1960s, the world faced a wheat glut. New records had been set in 1967–68 and 1968–69, although world wheat production in 1969–70 was down about 5.1% to 293.5 million tons. World trade in wheat and flour (grain equivalent) declined in 1968–69 to about 1,730,000,000 bu., some 10% below a year earlier and the lowest level since 1962–63. Among the results was an increase in carry-over stocks in major exporting countries to about 2 billion bu. at the end of the 1968–69 season, some 620 million bu. more than a year earlier. Another result was a severe decline in wheat prices. The struggle for limited export markets led to a "wheat war," with successive competitive reductions taking prices down to about the 1942 level. This violated the minimums set in the International Grains Arrangement, which was not suspended, though several discussion conferences were held.

With production continuing at a high level and wheat exports slowed, Canadian stocks accumulated to a record high of about 830 million bu., double the level of 1966 and 16% above the previous high set in 1957. In September a sale of 86.2 million bu. of wheat to China for $135 million was announced, but at about the same time it was indicated that the U.S.S.R. had bought only 201 million bu. under a three-year contract that called for the purchase of 336 million bu. by July 31, 1969. Realized net income of Canadian farmers from farming operations amounted to $1,597,100,000 in 1968, 3.2% below 1967 and 8.3% below the record $1,742,500,000 of 1966. The Wheat Board was not able to call on farmers for deliveries, and 1968–69 wheat delivery schedules of five bushels per acre were extended on a limited basis for 1969–70. The resulting shortage of cash in growers' hands was in part relieved by interest-free advances on the new crop, even though outstanding advances had not been fully repaid.

Among other crops, flue-cured tobacco exports, mostly to the U.K., increased to 46.4 million lb. in 1968 from 41.3 million lb. in 1967. The average price was a high $1.07 per pound. British Columbia's fruit was reported to have been hit hard by the 1968–69 winter. The apple crop for all of Canada was an average one of 21.8 million bu., compared with 20.1 million bu. in 1968. Major livestock numbers declined, in part because of high demand for meat at good prices. Canada's cattle and calf slaughter for the first half of 1969 fell 4% below the corresponding period of 1968, and hog slaughter was off 13%. Parliament approved legislation limiting financial losses to farmers from pesticide residues. A farmer using registered pesticides properly would be compensated by the government if a residue problem should lead to a sales ban against his product. Starting in 1970, Ontario would ban DDT use, with some exceptions.

LATIN AMERICA

Improved growing conditions indicated a sharp recovery for agriculture over important regions of Latin America in 1969. Early estimates pointed to good crops in Argentina, Brazil, Colombia, and Venezuela and significant recovery in Peru and Ecuador. Total agricultural output in Latin America in 1968 was reported by the USDA at an index of 129 (1957–

59 = 100), a decline from 130 a year earlier. At the same time, a 3% increase in population lowered per capita food supplies from an index of 108 in 1967 to only 104. Production in Mexico and Central America continued upward to new record levels, but dry weather in South America lowered output in some important producing areas.

Mexico. Total agricultural output in Mexico rose to a record index of 156 in 1968, nearly 5% more than in 1967, and the outlook was for a further increase of 2% in 1969. Food production in 1968 rose from 156 to 166 and per capita food supplies rose nearly 3%. Wheat production in 1968 fell to 1,793,000 tons from 2,058,000 in 1967, but rice production at 455,000 tons (rough basis) was up 6%. Increased acreage and good moisture raised the 1968 corn harvest 8% to a record 9.2 million tons. Strong demand for feed grains encouraged expansion of sorghum in the lower central plateau region; acreage rose about 8% and production more than 35%. Improved pasture conditions resulted in recovery of the livestock sector. Cattle numbers were little changed, but marketing of heavier weights raised beef and veal production about 10%.

Cotton plantings for the 1969 harvest were estimated at nearly 20% below 1968. Estimated 1968–69 sugar production was up slightly to 2,570,000 short tons and 1969 tobacco production was forecast at a high 162 million lb.

Expansion of Mexico's agricultural exports in 1968 was aided by improved cotton supplies. Sugar exports rose 14%, reflecting a larger quota in the U.S. market, and coffee shipments were up nearly 20%. Wheat and corn exports dropped sharply from high 1967 levels, but exports of Mexican horticultural crops to the U.S. continued to rise.

Central America. Agricultural conditions in Central America through mid-1969 were generally favourable, although Hurricane Francelia in September was reported to have damaged the Honduran coffee crop. Food production in 1968 stood at an index of 150, more than 7% above a year earlier. A 10% decline in coffee output offset gains in food production, so that total agricultural output rose less than 1%. Rice production, reflecting increased use of improved varieties, was up 7% to 457,000 tons. Corn production rose 8% to 1,742,000 tons, and grain sorghum 7% to 259,000 tons. Expectations of higher prices led to a 4% increase in 1968–69 cotton acreage, but volcanic damage lowered production in Nicaragua and this, together with some yield reduction in Guatemala, offset gains in other producing countries; output of 231,000 tons was 2% above 1967.

As a result of government crop-diversion policies, the coffee crop was down to 360,000 tons from 399,000. Production of sugar at 707,000 tons, less than 2% above 1967, reflected credit and other restrictions used to reduce acreage in Guatemala and Costa Rica. Output of bananas, at 3,060,000 tons, was up 10%. Regional output of livestock products rose nearly 4% in 1968.

Heavier supplies of principal commodities led to a rise in Central America's agricultural exports. Coffee exports, spurred by the record crop of 1967 and large export quotas, increased 19%. Shipments of bananas were estimated at 26% above a year earlier, and meat exports rose 11%. Imports of wheat were up 3% and of corn, 14%, but rice imports declined sharply.

South America. Adverse weather reduced Brazil's agricultural output about 2% in 1968, from a 1967 index of 135. A sharply lower coffee crop was partially offset by a 15% increase in cotton production. The index of per capita food production declined more than 3% below 1967 levels. Production of rice increased about 3% above 1967, to an estimated 5.3 million tons, despite the effects of dry weather; a further increase was forecast for 1969. The 1968–69 wheat crop rose 90% to 700,000 metric tons. Dry weather, particularly in São Paulo, reduced prospects for the 1969 corn crop to 11.5 million tons, compared with 12.5 million a year earlier. The important bean crop was down 22% in 1968. Favourable growing conditions resulted in a record 1967–68 crop of 2.7 million bales of cotton, more than a third higher than in 1966–67; the 1968–69 cotton crop was forecast at 3.2 million bales. Beef production in 1968 rose 3% to 1,550,000 tons, despite poor pasture conditions. Agricultural exports were encouraged by increased supplies and by the currency devaluation of 1968. Coffee exports, which accounted for 42% of the total, were up 15% and cotton shipments rose 25%. Weather conditions improved in 1969; output of most crops resumed a strong upward trend, although 1969 corn production was lower than a year earlier. The 1968 drought and frosts in July 1969 were expected to reduce the 1969–70 coffee crop.

The USDA's second estimate of the 1969–70 world coffee crop was for production of 65,130,000 bags (132.3 lb. each), 7% more than in 1968–69; exportable production was estimated at 47,139,000 bags. The estimate, however, was based largely on early prospects for a substantial increase in Brazilian production. One estimate placed the damage to Brazil's crop at 6 million bags or more, but Brazilian Coffee Institute stocks of 20 million bags were thought to be adequate to cover any deficit in production. World exports of green coffee in 1968 were estimated at a record 54,183,000 bags, an increase of 8% over a year earlier. South American producing nations shipped 50.8% of the total and the African share rose to 30.1%. Exchange earnings by the 41 coffee-producing nations were reported at $2.4 billion, 9% more than in 1967.

In March the International Coffee Council approved a resolution proposing the establishment, on the basis of world demand, of individual production goals for exporting countries in the 1972–73 coffee year, in order to bring about long-term equilibrium between production and consumption. The resolution also proposed a desired level of stocks to be held by each exporting nation. The council approved a total world quota of 46 million bags for the 1969–70 coffee year, which began October 1, compared with the adjusted quota of 47.8 million bags in 1968–69. The official ceiling price of 38.67 cents per pound was to be increased to 39.67 cents on Jan. 1, 1970.

Adverse weather reduced Argentina's agricultural output 11% in 1968. The index of total production was 111, compared with 119 in 1967. The food production index fell from 124 to 115, and the per capita food production index from 108 to 98. Grain acreage had been increased 7% in 1968 on the strength of favourable price expectations, but early drought lowered the corn crop by 18% and dry, hot weather at harvest time reduced wheat production by 20%. Indications were for a slight recovery in 1969, with increased feed-grain, rice, and citrus production. The early outlook was for a 10% increase in corn production and a 65% increase for sorghum grains. The

continued on page 81

Table V. Honey Production in Specified Countries
In 000,000 lb.

Country	1968*	Average 1960–64
Argentina	31	47
Australia†	44	41
Austria	12	10
Brazil	16	17
Canada	33	35
Chile	12	14
France	18	32
Germany, West	23	26
Guatemala	5	5
Italy	15	15
Japan	18	15
Mexico	80	60
New Zealand	12	12
Spain	21	20
United States	200	253
Yugoslavia	8	8

*Preliminary.
†Crop year beginning July of previous year.
Source: U.S. Department of Agriculture.

SPECIAL REPORT

LOCUST PLAGUE: A DANGER AVERTED

By P. T. Haskell

During 1968 and early 1969 the press, especially in Africa and Asia, was filled with reports of a threatened plague of the desert locust, which began late in 1967, gathered momentum in 1968, and was brought under control in 1969. What are these plagues, how do they develop, and how are they controlled?

Locusts are insects of the order Orthoptera, the "straight-winged insects," so-called for their two pairs of long narrow wings. They are cousins of the grasshoppers but differ from them in two important characteristics. The first is their gregariousness; locusts react to, and are stimulated by, the presence of other locusts, and they behave so as to keep together in a crowd. Since they can multiply at a high rate—each female can lay 200–300 eggs in her lifetime and these offspring all stay together—their populations can reach enormous numbers. The second important characteristic of locusts is their urge to migrate, always to be on the move. Even in the early stages, when the young locusts have no wings and are called hoppers, this locomotor urge causes them to march over the country at two to three miles an hour. When they become adult and develop wings, they migrate by flying—still, however, maintaining their gregariousness and thus moving in great masses or swarms, the typical and dangerous manifestation of locusts.

Locusts have threatened man's crops since the beginning of agriculture, as is witnessed by carvings on tombs of the 6th dynasty (*c.* 2345–2181 B.C.) at Saqqarah in Egypt and by the account of the "eighth plague" in the Book of Exodus (about 1300 B.C.). Through the ages locusts have taken their toll. In 125 B.C. a locust invasion of North Africa, then the granary of the Roman Empire, resulted in the deaths of some 800,000 people from starvation; in 1931 approximately 20% of the subsistence crops in Kenya were destroyed; and in 1954–55 damage estimated at $14 million was done to citrus crops in Morocco in six weeks. Even worse, in Ethiopia in 1958 locusts attacked the cereal crops and destroyed the food of a million people for a year.

How can locusts do such damage? First, research shows that each adult locust, which weighs two or three grams, can eat its own weight in food every 24 hours. Next, a locust swarm measuring about one square kilometre can contain between 50 million and 100 million insects. Thus, by simple arithmetic, a dense swarm measuring 100 sq.km. can eat more than 10,000 metric tons of food every day.

Add the power of rapid movement to this destructive potential, and one has a dangerous pest that is very difficult to control. The crowds of young locusts, called hopper bands, may move some 20 or 30 mi. before they become adult and form flying swarms, but then their speed of movement is dramatically increased. Although a locust can fly at a maximum speed of some 12–15 mph, the swarm as a whole moves with the wind and so can cover 50 or 100 mi. a day.

There are about a dozen or so species of swarming locust in the world, every major land mass except North America having at least one. In the 1920s, when locust infestation was worldwide, the British government set up a small scientific unit to investigate the problem and see how it could be controlled. From this modest beginning grew the present Anti-Locust Research Centre in London, the largest unit of its kind in the world and a recognized centre of research and information on locusts and grasshoppers. Formerly under the Colonial Office, it later became a scientific unit of the U.K. Ministry of Overseas Development.

Migration and Breeding. Since 1929 the centre, in collaboration with scientists from many countries, has carried out extensive research to establish the details of the life and movements of the most harmful locust species. As a result of this work, two major types of locust were recognized: the "outbreak area" type and the "invasion area" type. An example of the first is the African migratory locust, *Locusta migratoria migratorioides,* which caused enormous damage over vast areas of Africa from the late 1920s to 1941. During the height of that infestation, swarms of locusts had invaded almost the entire southern two-thirds of the continent. Research showed, however, that the swarms initiating this invasion all came from a small outbreak area situated on the floodplains of the Niger River. Even when all the swarms of the migratory locust had disappeared from the rest of Africa, large populations could still be found there. The theory was proposed that, when the locust population in this area increased, swarms of the insects migrated to favourable areas outside. There they bred, more swarms were produced, and these flew farther on and invaded more territory, thus spreading the plague. The swarms could not maintain themselves indefinitely outside the outbreak area and hence they eventually died out, but a residual population remained in the Niger floodplain that obviously might be capable of starting another plague.

The suggested solution was to set up an international control organization inside this area, to keep watch on the permanent population with a view toward controlling any increase. Accordingly, in 1949 the governments of Britain, France, and Belgium initiated the International African Migratory Locust Organisation (OICMA), which as of 1969 was financed by no less than 20 independent African countries. The correctness of the outbreak area theory has been vindicated by the fact that no swarms of this locust have escaped from the outbreak area since OICMA was set up. This success underlined two important points. First, the locust problem is an international one, because locusts ignore frontiers, flying from one country to another and perhaps back again. Second, the basis of any control work must be a scientific study of the movements of the locust. These principles were successfully applied to another outbreak area species in Africa, the red locust, which has its breeding grounds in Tanzania and Zambia and other Central African countries. The International Red Locust Control Service (IRLCS) was set up in 1940, and since that time no swarms of this locust have escaped.

The other variety of locust, the invasion area type, is exemplified by the desert locust, *Schistocerca gregaria.* This is the biblical locust, and it can inhabit the vast region stretching from the Atlantic Ocean across northern Africa and the Middle East to the Bay of Bengal. Unlike the migratory and red locusts, this species has no restricted outbreak area; it can live and breed anywhere within this region of approximately 29 million sq.km.—one-fifth of the world's land surface. In the invasion area of this locust live some 300 million people of about 55 nations, and most of them rely on subsistence agriculture. To them, locust invasion can mean hunger and perhaps famine, and so it is not surprising that international interest in the control of the desert locust is very great.

Since 1929 the Anti-Locust Research Centre has maintained an intelligence service on this insect, receiving reports of its occurrence by radio, cable, and letter throughout the year. From analysis of these reports it has been found that the swarm movements are not haphazard but show a seasonal pattern. As has been noted, swarms move with the wind, generally at a speed lower than the wind speed. A most important consequence of this for the locusts is that they eventually drift into zones of low-level wind convergence, which are areas where rain is likely to fall. Thus, although the desert locust lives mainly in arid and

COURTESY, ANTI-LOCUST RESEARCH CENTRE, LONDON

Swarm of desert locusts in Morocco during the plague of 1954. In a six-week period citrus crops valued at $14 million were destroyed.

semiarid areas, swarms usually arrive at the rainy season, and this is the only time when conditions are right for successful breeding, since the eggs must be laid in moist soil and need considerable water for their development. This also ensures that the emerging hoppers have green vegetation available for feeding. In the desert locust area the major weather phenomena are seasonal, and since the major migration patterns are linked with them, it has been possible to work out the seasonal movements of the locust. This information provides a basis for forecasting when particular countries can expect to be invaded. Another important consequence of swarm movement with the wind is that knowledge of wind speed and direction in an area that contains swarms enables the probable movement of those swarms to be forecast, an obvious requirement for efficient control.

Plague and Recession Periods. The desert locust population shows long-term fluctuations; periods characterized by large populations and many swarms and hopper bands are called plague periods. During these periods young swarms, which may cover an aggregate area of 1,000 sq.km., leave their breeding areas and migrate to others, where they can give rise to hopper band infestations over hundreds of thousands of square kilometres. The opposite of plague periods are recession periods, during which the locust population is very low and consists mostly of insects scattered over very large areas. These scattered populations occur in definite ecological regions, called the recession area. A locust outbreak or upsurge occurs when the low populations in the recession area breed, increase in numbers, and form swarms that fly out and colonize the invasion area. If this cycle of events is not recognized and interrupted in its early stages, then the swarms breed, more swarms are formed, and a new plague develops.

The desert locust had been in recession during 1962–67; in early 1967 locust numbers were apparently as low as at any time on record, but it is now clear that the sequence of events that led to the new upsurge had already started. It seems likely that there were four separate outbreaks contributing significantly to the upsurge: in Oman; in Saudi Arabia and Yemen; in Sudan, Ethiopia, and the U.A.R.; and in Algeria and Niger. The main reason for this buildup was the rainfall, which was not only unusually heavy and widespread in Africa and the Middle East but which occurred in a succession of seasons. As a result, there was successful breeding by successive locust populations, producing a rapid rise in numbers and an alarming situation. By May 1969, however, the numbers of locusts had dramatically fallen and the immediate danger was over. How was this brought about?

International Locust Control. It is clear from what has been said that locust control is an international problem, and indeed it can be thought of as a paramilitary operation in which two factors are all-important: intelligence and firepower.

Modern research has provided adequate and mobile firepower. It is obvious that the control force has to be as mobile as the locusts, and this means using light aircraft. The firepower is supplied by modern insecticides, together with special rotary atomizers, fitted to the aircraft, which produce a curtain of insecticide in the form of tiny drops. So powerful are these chemicals that one gallon can kill two million locusts. Furthermore, locust scientists have developed the technique of ultra-low-volume spraying, so that as little as one-quarter pint of spray is used to the acre. This is not only cheaper and more efficient than high-volume spraying, but also safer from the point of view of man and his domestic animals.

But how can this firepower be efficiently deployed? Only by intelligence of the enemy, and it is here that international cooperation plays such an important role. The coordination of this effort has been undertaken by the United Nations Food and Agriculture Organization (FAO), which holds regular meetings of the countries concerned to establish policy and coordinate activities. With the help of the United Nations Development Program (UNDP), a large research program has been undertaken, one result of which has been the formation (1961) of the Desert Locust Information Service. This service acts as the central intelligence unit. It is operated as part of the Anti-Locust Research Centre in London and is responsible for issuing to all countries concerned a monthly summary of the desert locust position, together with a forecast of the movements and invasions expected. It also issues special warnings of important developments. In December 1967 it was able to give no less than four months' warning of the impending locust upsurge, thus enabling the threatened countries to order supplies of insecticide, move their aircraft control units to the most advantageous positions, and make other necessary preparations.

The actual organization of control activities is regionally based. In some areas the various countries have joined together under FAO regional commissions; India, Pakistan, Iran, and Afghanistan form one such grouping. Elsewhere, independent regional control bodies have been set up; for example, the Desert Locust Control Organization for Eastern Africa, which covers Tanzania, Kenya, Uganda, Ethiopia, Somalia, Sudan, and the French Territory of Afars and Issas (Djibouti).

All these organizations have expert personnel as well as aircraft and equipment. In 1967, however, after five years of locust recession, many of them had inadequate supplies of insecticide, equipment needed replacing, and they often required the services of additional experts such as entomologists or pilots. Through the international locust machinery this dangerous situation was brought to the attention of UNDP, FAO, and various donor countries such as the U.K., the U.S., France, Canada, and West Germany, which were asked to provide additional assistance. In response to this appeal more than $1 million worth of equipment, insecticides, and personnel were poured into the fight, making it possible for the regional organizations to mount large-scale aerial spraying operations against the invading swarms. At this point nature also gave a helping hand. Because of the weather situation, the most important locust populations were concentrated in two areas, Ethiopia and Sudan, and Morocco, and in both areas control campaigns killed a large proportion of the insects. Thus, the locust populations were greatly reduced and, since the rain partially failed, breeding by the survivors was negligible. Locust numbers dropped as dramatically in early 1969 as they had risen in 1968.

This international campaign affords clearer evidence than had hitherto been available of the power of modern techniques of survey, forecasting, and control, and it augurs well for the future. However, it is also clear that the organization and machinery are neither completely adequate nor foolproof. The key to the whole edifice is international cooperation, without which no useful work can be done. It is heartening and hopeful to note that countries of opposing ideologies were brought together, frontier problems were overcome, nationals of many countries worked side by side, and massive international aid was provided—all in response to the challenge offered by one of man's oldest and most dangerous enemies.

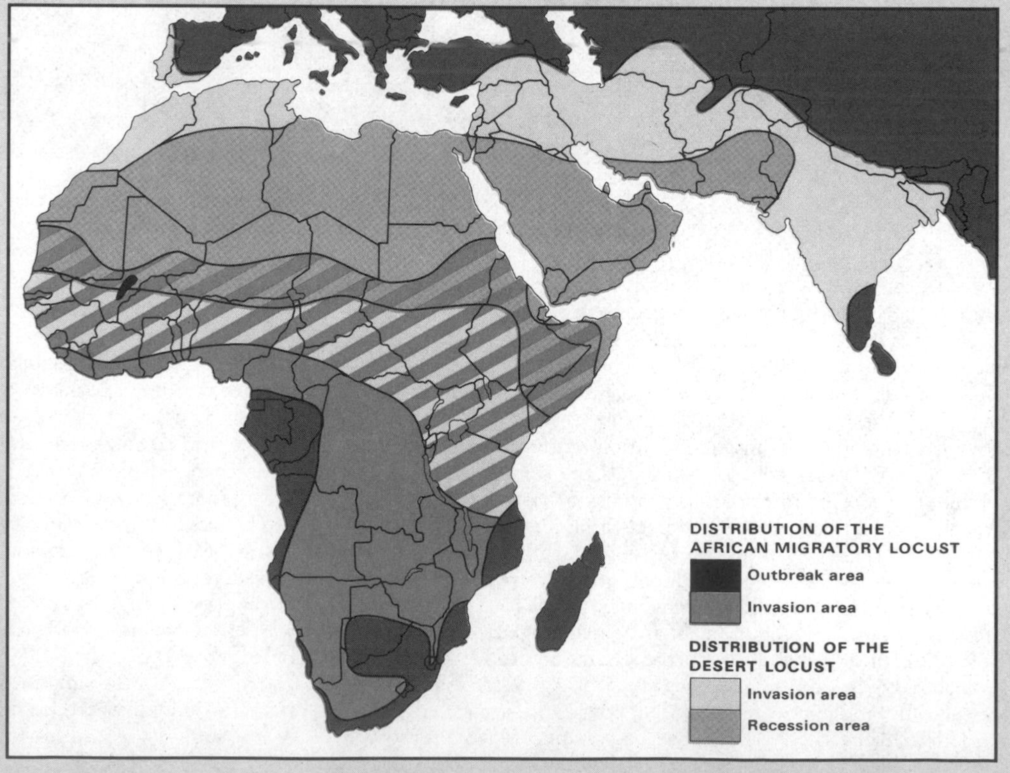

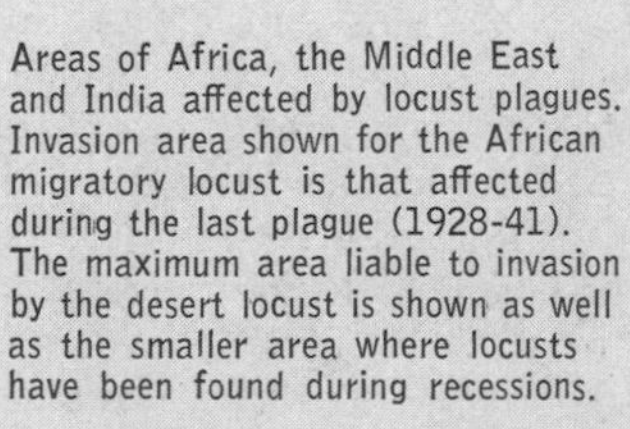
Areas of Africa, the Middle East and India affected by locust plagues. Invasion area shown for the African migratory locust is that affected during the last plague (1928-41). The maximum area liable to invasion by the desert locust is shown as well as the smaller area where locusts have been found during recessions.

continued from page 77
1969 wheat situation was reported as improved, with production forecast at 255 million bu. Cattle numbers rose to 51.5 million in mid-1968; beef and veal production, at 2.6 million tons, was about 1% above a year earlier. Agricultural exports fell in 1968; corn exports were down by nearly a third and meat shipments by almost a fifth. Wheat exports were 13% above a year earlier.

Uruguay's early-harvest crops suffered reduced yields from drought in 1968, but later crops and pastures benefited from improved moisture. The index of agricultural production, at 108, was 11% higher than in 1967. Drought led to increased livestock slaughter early in the year, and the trend continued as demand remained strong; beef production was 20% above 1967. The 1968–69 wheat crop was estimated at 484,000 tons, more than twice the amount harvested a year earlier, and gains were registered in the production of other cereals.

Drought in Paraguay throughout much of 1968 resulted in lowered output of sugarcane, soybeans, corn, and fruit. The total index of production fell to 117 from 126 a year earlier. Production of refined sugar was down 16% and corn production, at 180,000 tons, was down by more than a third. With price levels unfavourable, livestock producers refused to deliver more than 170,000 head of cattle, although the government-fixed beef slaughter quota for export packers was 250,000 head. A 5% increase in acreage sown to principal crops in Chile, combined with good growing conditions for most cereals, helped raise the index of total agricultural production in that country to 120, about 4% above 1967. The outlook for 1969 production was for a 15% decline, resulting from continued drought. Agricultural exports increased in 1968. Food imports also rose, however, as stocks were built up to offset anticipated drought-induced shortages.

Colombia's agricultural output rose to a record index of 128 in 1968, some 6% above 1967; the index of food production advanced more than 6%. High support prices encouraged an increase in wheat acreage and production was 50% more than in 1967. Coffee exports were 7% above a year earlier. Severe drought lowered Peru's total agricultural output 2% in 1968; food production fell nearly 6% below the record 1967 level. The highland wheat crop was down more than 20% and corn production fell 12% below the record 638,000 tons produced in 1967. Output of livestock products was also adversely affected. Indications in early 1969 pointed to a continued reduction of food crops, caused by shortages of irrigation water in the coastal region. Pres. Juan Velasco Alvarado announced in June that the government would nationalize all major landholdings. In late August the government assumed control of the W. R. Grace & Co. sugar properties, which included some 25,000 ac. in plantations and a sugar-processing plant. The end of a three-year drought in Bolivia's uplands contributed to partial recovery of agriculture; total output rose 3% in 1968, to an index of 110. Bolivia's wheat harvest was the first good one since 1964. Venezuela's agricultural growth slowed in 1968, with a 3% increase in crops offset by a decline in livestock products. The index of total production rose 1%, to 162, and the food production index, at 173, was unchanged.

Caribbean. The 1968 agricultural situation throughout most of the five Caribbean nations (Cuba, Dominican Republic, Haiti, Jamaica, and Trinidad and Tobago) was affected by unusually dry weather that lasted until midyear, reducing sugar yields and other crops. Production fell in four of the five nations, and only Trinidad and Tobago, with a production index of 120, made a significant gain. For the region as a whole, the index of total production fell to 87, compared with 93 a year earlier, and per capita supplies were reduced about 8%. More adequate moisture pointed to a sharp recovery in 1969, especially in the Dominican Republic and Haiti.

Cuba's total agricultural output was estimated at an index of 80, compared with 87 in 1967. The Castro government continued to focus its agricultural effort on sugar, a commodity facing a heavily glutted world market and low prices. Against the government's 1970 target of a 10 million-ton sugar crop, midyear estimates placed the 1969 harvest at 4.7 million tons, down from 5.2 million tons harvested in 1968. The livestock industry continued to receive attention. The government set a target of 15 million head of cattle for 1980, compared with an estimated 1968 total of 7 million.

World production of sugar in 1968–69 reached a new record of 75,446,000 short tons (raw value), an increase of 3% over the 1967–68 crop and 24% above average. Record or near-record crops in the U.S., the Dominican Republic, France, India, and Australia offset reverses in other areas. The USDA's first estimate for the 1969–70 world sugar crop was for a record 79,362,000 short tons (raw value), exceeding 1968–69 by 5%. World sugar trade declined slightly in 1968. Exports amounted to 20 million tons (raw value), compared with 20.2 million tons a year earlier.

Sugar prices fell to less than 3.25 cents per pound in September 1969, but the market firmed after a meeting of the International Sugar Council, held in London to discuss ways to prevent further declines. Among the measures agreed on were stoppage of all imports by members from nonmembers and a ban on any redistribution of shortfalls in quota allocations.

Guatemalan coffee drying on a concrete patio is turned at intervals to expose all beans to the sun.

COURTESY, "FOREIGN AGRICULTURE"

World Production and Trade of Principal Grains

In 000 metric tons

	Wheat			Barley			Oats			Rye			Corn (Maize)			Rice		
	Production		Imports— Exports+	Production		Imports— Exports+	Production		Imports— Exports+	Production		Imports— Exports+	Production		Imports— Exports+	Production		Imports— Exports+
	1948-52 average	1968	1965–68 average	1948-52 average	1968	1965–68 average	1948-52 average	1968	1965–68 average	1948-52 average	1968	1965–68 average	1948-52 average	1968	1965–68 average	1948-52 average	1968	1965–68 average
World total	170,858	333,939	−c.52,750* +c.52,850*	59,227	126,809	−c.7,200* +c.7,070*	61,719	55,699	−c.1,410* +c.1,440*	36,967	32,404	−c.660* +c.630*	139,416	250,734	−c.25,300* +c.25,550*	167,336	283,514	−c.7,580* +c.7,470*
EUROPE																		
Austria	348	1,045	−60	210	770	−213	274	324	−383	343	413	−49	120	399	−265 +1†	—	—	−39†
Belgium	525	855	−541‡ +198†‡	244	574	−453‡ +43†‡	483	314	−81‡ +1†‡	221	87	−22‡ +2†‡	3	3§	−933‡ +133‡	—	—	−40‡ +7†‡
Bulgaria	1,776	2,549	−232† +205†	332	807	−67† +1†	148	76	−6†	240	24	−13†	720	1,768	−53† +115†	37	39	−22† +7†
Czechoslovakia	1,493	3,128	−1,141	1,046	c.2,093	−338† +16†	961	968§	−3†	1,110	689§	−43†	316	421§	−224† +1†	—	—	−83† +4†
Denmark	285	464	−14 +77†	1,708	5,047	−336 +219	922	861	−52 +16	365	131	−27	—	—	−199 +1†	—	—	−7†
Finland	263	516	−57 +15†	201	774	−29†	718	1,064	−8† +13†	201	134	−34 +2†	—	—	−27	—	—	−14†
France	7,791	14,842	−643 +3,582	1,534	9,062	−1† +2,250	3,392	2,506	−4† +78	573	333	+23	452	5,174	−564 +1,299	46	91	−110 +31
Germany, East	1,243	2,050	−1,287† +2†	593	c.1,950	−207†	1,188	845§	—	2,516	c.1,950	−56† +2†	5	1§	−239†	—	—	−51†
Germany, West	2,669	6,198	−1,695 +128†	1,402	4,974	−1,462 +26	2,523	2,893	−474 +36	3,066	3,186	−52 +8	20	197§	−2,440 +177	—	—	−157 +19†
Greece	894	1,515	−19 +254†	211	487	−17	119	c.108	—	47	9	—	225	375	−215	39	108	−4† +15†
Hungary	1,909	3,137	−180† +49†	654	906	−211†	216	97§	−2†	732	c.238	—	2,068	3,764	−63† +68†	40	41	−31† +5†
Ireland	327	406	−272	163	740	−37	616	c.271	−20	4	1§	—	—	—	−123	—	—	−2†
Italy	7,170	9,590	−1,075 +15	258	258	−948 +2†	495	390	−210 +3†	123	75	−2†	2,306	3,988	−4,710 +222	723	639	−5† +129
Netherlands	324	679	−774 +307	201	389	−218 +550	419	321	−99 +92	455	239	−77 +14	26	—	−2,130 +21†	—	—	−65 +17†
Norway	58	11§	−359	109	621	−68	170	176	−14	2	4	−41	—	—	−93	—	—	−6†
Poland	1,833	4,655	−1,342	1,061	1,500	−397 +59	2,238	2,818§	−25†	6,374	8,523	−35†	c.24	14§	−497†	—	—	−65
Portugal	499	797	−309	96	95	−7†	124	143	—	162	197	—	421	529	−251	114	153	−30† +1†
Romania	2,778	4,848	+323†	412	c.425	—	367‖	163§	—	177‖	48	+24†	2,495‖	7,105	+440†	35‖	69§	−33†
Spain	3,625	5,480	−54	1,909	3,441	−394	519	539	−1†	482	364	−2†	520	1,473	−2,220	280	363	+88
Sweden	677	1,059	−62 +260	231	1,776	−4 +84†	804	1,523	+137	258	207	−45 +14	—	—	−49	—	—	−11†
Switzerland	260	373	−402	55	112	−360	68	32§	−153	34	65	−1	6	22§	−190	—	—	−21† +1†
U.S.S.R.	35,759¶	96,200	−6,979† +2,234†	6,354♀	26,100	+1,179†	13,005♀	11,581§	+11†	17,961♀	c.13,000	+156†	5,751‖	8,800	+363†	202♀	1,047	+4†
United Kingdom	2,397	3,571	−4,104 +3†	2,061	8,408	−177 + 681	2,852	1,250	−18 +1†	52	c.11	−7†	—	—	−3,509 +10†	—	—	−115 +1†
Yugoslavia	2,171	4,363	−761	323	450	−3† +61†	286	295	+2	248	138	—	3,078	6,810	+396	5	18	−27†
ASIA																		
Burma	4¶	67§	−2δ	—	—	—	—	—	—	—	—	—	30‖	60§	+18*	5,481	8,485	+837
Cambodia	—	—	—	—	—	—	—	—	—	—	—	—	57	154	+93*	1,635¶	3,251	+277
China	15,913‖	c.27,000	−5,812†	c.12,360	c.18,000	−12† +1†	c.1,540	c.2,000	−21†	—	—	—	c.14,082	c.24,000	−46† +195†	58,188‖	c.92,000	−82† +932†
India	6,087	16,567	−6,354	2,384	3,469	—	—	—	−1δ	—	—	—	2,165	c.6,500	−94†	33,383	c.58,500	−617 +3†
Indonesia	—	—	—	—	—	—	—	—	—	—	—	—	1,535¶	2,527§	—	9,441¶	15,249	−440†
Iran	c.1,879‖	c.4,977	−152□	c.767	1,160	−1†	—	—	—	—	—	—	6¶	c.15§	—	424	957	−17† +6†
Iraq	448	1,361	−132 +15 †	722	931	+96*	—	—	—	—	—	—	14	4§	—	203	325	−1†
Japan	1,375	c.1,012	−3,941	2,020	1,021	−580	119	93	−18	6	c.1□	−72	57	51	−4,034	12,736	18,765	−640
Korea, South	139	345	−588	c.846	c.2,084	−56†	4	—	—	36	25	—	14	60§	−2†	3,385	4,286	−9† +3†
Lebanon	51	48	−240* +1†	25	13□	−63† +5†	2	c.2□	—	—	—	—	12	5§	−47† +1†	1	—	−20† +1†
Malaysia	—	—	−114†	—	—	—	—	—	−1†	—	—	—	8□	c.10§	−61†	670◇	1,061§	−362† +34†
Pakistan	3,685	6,477	−1,598	150	121	—	—	—	—	—	—	—	384	629	—	12,399	19,515	−96 +135
Philippines	—	—	−439	—	—	—	—	—	−2†	—	—	—	695	1,619	−1†	2,767	4,789	−239
Syria	761	600	−123* +9*	321	512	+99*	6	3	−6†	—	—	—	31	9§	−7† +2†	13	2§	−30†
Thailand	—	—	−27†	—	—	—	—	—	—	—	—	—	31	c.1,300	+1,041*	6,846	10,895	+1,478
Turkey	4,770	9,602	−168	2,270	3,560	−5†	326	450	—	500	820	+24	747	1,000	—	109	233§	+5†
Vietnam, South	—	—	...	—	—	...	—	—	...	—	—	...	30¶	34§	−8♀	2,395◇	4,366	−530
AFRICA																		
Algeria	996	1,532	−535† +38†	808	536	−20† +4†	137	32§	−5†	1¶	—	—	6	3□	−2†	—	5§	−2†
Kenya	101▲	159▲	15†	8▲	14□▲	—	5	1§	—	—	—	—	93▲	c.140§▲	−112† +48*	c.6	16§	−2†
Morocco	786	2,556	−553*	1,481	3,215	−14† +2	51	c.25	+1	4	1§	—	302	c.240	−12† +19	8¶	43	+2†
South Africa	555▲	1,225▲	−285	41▲	39▲	+3†	79♀	c.143	—	10‖	7	—	2,400▲	5,089▲	−136† +1,330	c.6	c.2□	−73 +1†
Tunisia	452	383	−241 +26	218	130	−36 +5	14	c.9□	−2†	—	—	—	4+	c.4□+	−12†	—	—	—
United Arab Republic	1,113	1,518	−1,487 +2†	123	c.105	−2† +2†	—	—	—	—	—	—	1,378	2,297	−159 +1†	971	2,586	+420
NORTH AND CENTRAL AMERICA																		
Canada	13,443	17,686	+11,310	4,245	7,084	+828	6,220	5,591	+159	469	331	+175	388	2,051	−631 +8†	—	—	−47†
Mexico	534	1,894	−1† +254	160	180	−30	47	61§	−7†	—	—	—	3,090	9,360	−6 +1,087	173	455	−14†
United States	31,065	42,740	−20 +18,444⊕	5,843	9,104	−146 +974	18,970	13,492	−44 +230	524	590	−38 +80	74,308	111,125	−25 +14,652⊕	1,925	4,777	−18 +1,663
SOUTH AMERICA																		
Argentina	5,175	5,900	+4,050	656	556	+165	743	490	+243	526	360	+31	2,839	6,560	+3,441	137	283	+50†
Bolivia	37◇	c.60§	−12δ	39	57	—	2¶	c.10□	—	—	—	—	163◇	c.250§	—	20¶	63§	—
Brazil	498	749	−2,333	15	c.30	−33	9	21§	−13	17	17§	—	5,841	13,030	−3† +714	2,921	6,932	+179
Chile	928	1,220	−405*	79	157	+1†	80	115§	+1†	5	8	—	68	321	−20†	75	93	−25†
Colombia	124	c.130	−198*	50	c.115	—	—	—	−6†	—	—	—	733	c.1,000§	+1†	248	784	—
Peru	146	c.150	−512	208	c.170	−14	c.2	1§	—	—	—	—	275	590	−5† +1†	191	400	−52†
Uruguay	469	c.250	+105†	23	c.42	+2†	44	c.33§	+5†	—	—	—	141	c.69	−3†	41	116§	+32†
Venezuela	5¶	2§	−596*	—	—	—	—	—	−9*	—	—	—	303	604§	−27†	41	295	−4† +35†
OCEANIA																		
Australia	5,161	14,687	+6,057	531	1,538	+297	560	1,666	+287	12	10§	—	126	193	—	63	221	−15† +86
New Zealand	139	442	−93	49	219	—	49	42	—	2‖	—	—	10	18§	—	—	—	−4†

Note: (—) indicates quantity nil or negligible; (. . .) indicates quantity not known; (c.) indicates provisional or estimated.
*1965–67 average.
†1965–66 average.
‡Belgium-Luxembourg economic union.
§1967.
‖Average of 4 years.
¶Average of 3 years.
♀1950.
δ1964–65 average.
□1966.
◇Average of 2 years.
▲Farms and estates only.
+Incl. sorghum.
⊕Incl. foreign aid shipments.

Sources: FAO *Production Yearbook 1968; FAO Trade Yearbook 1967; FAO Monthly Bulletin of Agricultural Economics and Statistics.*

(M.C. Mac D.)

Angry farmers from Le Lude, France, destroy apple trees in the orchard of a local industrialist, March 28, 1969. The farmers were protesting the owner's intention of marketing his produce in competition with theirs.

KEYSTONE

WESTERN EUROPE

Early indications were that agricultural production in 1969 would approximate the 1968 record index of 131 (1957–59 = 100), for a third consecutive year of high agricultural output. Production of grains was reduced overall. Wheat was down about 100 million bu. to 1,650,000,000 bu., oats fell to 819 million bu. from 872 million, and barley, grown on a larger acreage than in 1968, was about the same at 1,735,000,000 bu. Only the corn crop was larger. The current cycle of livestock expansion apparently peaked. Cattle numbers were up less than 1%, hog numbers were little changed, and even the recent sharp upward trend in broiler production slowed. Serious problems of overproduction and marketing continued with respect to butter, dry skim milk, wheat, and some fruits, and the EEC agricultural policy encountered some difficulties.

United Kingdom and Ireland. Despite efforts to step up production and reduce imports, provisional results of the June 1969 agricultural censuses indicated that British agricultural production was barely holding steady, with some reduction in crops offset by a slow expansion in livestock. Total U.K. grain production was indicated at about 13.6 million tons, 3% higher than in 1968 but 5.5% below the record 14.4 million-ton crop of 1967. Both autumn and spring sowings were reduced by difficult weather, and 440,000 ac. were left fallow. The acreage in fodder crops was also lowered substantially. The area in horticultural crops was increased, but fruit prospects were reduced by pollination failures. Cattle were indicated at 12,440,000 head, 2.5% more than a year earlier. The 7,850,000 swine on farms represented a 6.5% increase but sheep numbers, at 26,760,000 head, were down 4.5%. A record of nearly 41 million chickens were being grown for meat, but the rate of increase had flattened out. The size of the laying flock also appeared to have stabilized, at about 75 million birds.

The annual review of March 1969 emphasized selective expansion of priority commodities—wheat, barley, beef, and pigs—with lesser increases in fat sheep and potatoes. Assistance to farmers was increased by a gross £41.4 million, partially offset by reductions of £4.6 million in the egg guarantee and £2.5 million in the fertilizer subsidy. Net farming income for 1968–69 was estimated at £500 million, £39.5 million less than in the previous fiscal year, while farming costs were expected to rise by £40.3 million in 1969–70. Refractory trade problems continued. With increasing imports of subsidized cheese and a buildup of stocks threatening the price of domestically produced cheese, foreign suppliers were requested voluntarily to restrict exports of Cheddar. Major foreign suppliers—chiefly Oceania, Ireland, and Canada—agreed to voluntary restrictions on exports through March 1970, with the understanding that New Zealand's quota would not be less than 170,000 tons. Meat exports were increased, but imports of unboned beef, mutton, lamb, and pork and of unprocessed offals from Latin America were banned for fear of foot-and-mouth disease. An attempt by U.K. farmers to displace imported onions—largely from Spain and the Netherlands—was unsuccessful because of consumer preference for the foreign varieties.

Ireland's third program for economic and social development (1969–72) envisaged an annual growth of 1.75% in agricultural production, with growth items most likely to be cattle, milk, hogs, sheep, barley, and horticultural crops. Export markets were expected to take most of the increase. The decline in the farm labour force was expected to continue at the recent rate of 9,000 a year, and total state support to agriculture at the end of the program was projected at more than £100 million (about £80 million in 1968–69). The livestock sector, source of about 85% of Ireland's gross agricultural output, enjoyed a record year in 1968 despite a 16% reduction in beef and veal production. Numbers were increased moderately in

Table VI. Poultry Meat Production in Selected Countries*

In 000,000 lb.

Country	1968†	1967	1966	Average 1955–59
Belgium-Luxembourg	200	223	203	95
France	1,199	1,129	1,076	511
Germany, West	463	450	388	172
Italy	838	829	769	215
Netherlands	470	441	389	96
Total EEC	3,170	3,071	2,825	1,089
Austria	80	76	73	4
Canada	807	818	790	428
Denmark	142	146	149	58
Greece	125	102	90	36
Japan	606	529	434	—
Poland	243	236	229	109
Switzerland	15	15	30	7
United Kingdom	1,149	1,062	974	455
United States	9,140	9,410	8,994	5,480

*On ready-to-cook basis (70% of live weight).
†Preliminary.
Source: U.S. Department of Agriculture, Foreign Agricultural Service.

Table VII. Egg Production in Specified Countries

In 000,000

Country	1968*	1967	1966
Argentina	2,760	2,640	2,520
Australia†	2,500	2,554	2,328
Belgium-Luxembourg	3,438	3,083	2,932
Brazil	9,480	8,750	8,604
Canada	5,481	5,306	5,002
Czechoslovakia	3,017	3,110	3,080
France	10,800	10,300	9,700
Germany, East	3,975	3,995	3,894
Germany, West	14,076	13,802	12,901
Hungary	2,800	2,750	2,436
Italy	9,750	10,465	10,570
Japan	24,715	23,307	18,756
Mexico	5,375	5,356	5,200
Netherlands	3,875	3,695	4,190
Poland	6,415	6,348	6,253
Romania	3,033	2,900	2,814
U.S.S.R.	35,500	33,921	31,700
United Kingdom‡	15,216	14,916	14,412
United States	69,356	70,161	66,484

*Preliminary.
†Year ending June 30 of year shown.
‡Excludes Northern Ireland production consumed locally; year ending May 31.
Source: U.S. Department of Agriculture, Foreign Agricultural Service.

Table VIII. Milk Cows and Milk Production in Specified Countries

	Number of milk cows in 000			Milk production in 000,000 lb.		
Country	1968*	1967	Average 1961–65	1968*	1967	Average 1961–65
Australia	2,794	2,881	3,190	15,340	16,177	15,244
Austria	1,115	1,109	1,122	7,330	7,407	6,743
Belgium	1,065	1,026	1,024	9,283	8,934	8,664
Canada	2,616	2,668	2,930	18,335	18,228	18,404
Denmark	1,295	1,303	1,428	11,303	11,448	11,713
Finland	...	1,041	1,171	...	7,847	8,207
France	10,333	9,817	9,409	68,343	64,716	54,162
Germany, West	5,865	5,858	5,852	48,768	47,877	45,368
Greece	481	492	434	1,239	1,243	1,159
Ireland	1,607	1,568	1,373	8,110	7,652	6,458
Italy	3,430	3,485	3,448	20,723	21,781	21,872
Netherlands	1,830	1,780	1,701	17,017	16,612	15,597
New Zealand	2,165	2,141	2,007	13,080	13,957	12,302
Norway	470	478	568	4,105	3,948	3,666
Sweden	853	873	1,180	7,275	7,315	8,446
Switzerland	929	928	926	7,103	7,202	6,837
United Kingdom	4,399	4,356	4,203	26,476	25,786	24,791
United States	13,022	13,501	16,195	117,281	118,769	125,660

*Preliminary.
Source: U.S. Department of Agriculture, Foreign Agricultural Service.

1969. Sheep numbers continued to decline, despite payment programs to encourage feeding and production of spring lambs. In January 1969 a livestock and meat export promotion board (CBF) was set up to operate mainly in the U.K.

EEC Countries. Agricultural production in the six EEC countries made an excellent showing in 1969. Wheat, at 1,145,400,000 bu., was down from the record 1,186,800,000 bu. of 1968, but the 701.7 million bu. of barley approximated the very large 1968 crop and the oat crop of 436.3 million bu. was off only slightly. Cattle numbers increased to 52,430,000 head from 51,922,000 a year earlier, and hog numbers rose slightly to 42,320,000 head. Meat production in 1968 had increased about 500 million lb.

The very abundance raised problems. By September 1969 the butter surplus was reported at 330,000 tons. The dairy surplus was indicated at 5 to 6 million metric tons of milk equivalents, and was increasing by as much as 1 million tons per year. In July the Council of Ministers postponed setting the butter price for 1969–70, as well as the intervention price for dry skim powder.

In a delayed decision in April the council raised import levies against corn and barley for 1969–70 by about 2.5% as of August 1, thus further reducing the spread between the price of wheat and other grains within the EEC. Price supports and subsidies financed through the European Agricultural Fund had risen from $1.3 billion in 1967–68 to $2.2 billion in 1968–69, with butter support alone costing nearly $600 million. Among reforms considered were a sharp reduction in the support price for butter and the use of some part of the dairy herd in beef production.

There was increasing evidence of serious dislocation within the EEC. The Common Agricultural Policy (CAP) was already in trouble as a result of accumulating surpluses and high support costs. In August the uniform agricultural price policy was suspended for two years to protect French farmers from the effects of devaluation of the franc. In this way it was hoped a rise in food prices in France and a distortion of trade within the EEC resulting from competition by devalued French agricultural products could be prevented. On October 1 the European Commission ruled "illegal" a 5.5% tax on all agricultural imports imposed by the Bonn government to protect West German farmers from low-priced imports after the value of the mark was permitted to "float." Later the tax was allowed to stand on certain farm imports, including grain and dairy products.

Agricultural production in Belgium and the Netherlands made selective advances in 1969, with pork, poultry, and milk making the strongest showings. The Dutch wheat crop exceeded that of 1968 by 3% and barley production totaled 19.5 million bu., compared with 17.9 million bu. in 1968. Agricultural exports from the Netherlands to other EEC countries increased 15% in 1968, to $2.3 billion, while agricultural imports rose 11% to $1,450,000,000.

The large West German grain crop of 18.7 million tons was only slightly below the record 1968 crop of 19.1 million tons; imports, especially from France, also increased, and stocks were at an all-time high. Cattle numbers rose but hogs were cut back.

In the autumn of 1969 French farmers were awaiting the effects of devaluation. The crop season had been generally favourable. The 539 million-bu. wheat crop was down moderately from the record 549.1 million bu. of 1968, and the barley crop was a large 411.7 million bu. Corn, not grown in France on a considerable scale until recent years, was forecast at 216.5 million bu., compared with 205.7 million bu. in 1968. Large grain exports from France, especially of soft wheat in 1968–69 and potentially in 1969–70, were disturbing to major exporting countries and to a degree accounted for the growing ineffectiveness of the International Grains Arrangement. There were also charges that French grains had a competitive advantage in West Germany. After the revaluation of the mark at a fixed parity in October, the EEC ministers agreed to allow West German farmers to receive compensation for lost earnings. The Community contribution would be at least $150 million during a four-year period, against losses estimated at $460 million annually.

Agricultural production continued at favourable levels in Italy in 1969. The important wheat crop totaled 330.7 million bu., lower than the 352.4 million-bu. crop of 1968 but substantially above the 1960–64 average. The 1969 corn crop was forecast at 177.2 million bu., larger by 20 million bu. than in 1968. The 1968–69 orange crop of 1,350,000 tons (52,441,000 boxes) was 10% above the previous year and 25% above average. Sizing was poor, however; difficult marketing and transportation problems were encountered and prices were reduced. In protest, farmers dumped oranges in main streets and blocked roads and railroads. The government made bulk purchases, especially in Sicily.

Other Countries. Free trade in agricultural products, requested by Denmark, remained a major area of disagreement as a proposed treaty defining a Nordic customs union was discussed by Denmark, Norway, Sweden, and Finland. As of mid-July 1968 the number of farms in Denmark had declined to 152,708, about 6,600 less than a year earlier, and farm labourers totaled 43,900, representing a decline of 8,200 in a year's time. Even so, surplus barley production occurred in 1968, permitting exports to Norway for the first time. The 1969 barley crop of 227.4 million bu. was not quite so large. A trend toward self-sufficiency in animal feeds continued, partly because livestock numbers were declining, as EEC market outlets became more and more restricted. About two-thirds of Danish livestock production was exported. Of this, 56% went to the EEC, compared with 92% before the introduction of high EEC import levies.

Sweden reported a sharply lowered wheat harvest, as did Switzerland and Austria. Swedish production of feed grains was also sharply below the abundant 1968 crop. Spain and Portugal reported smaller wheat harvests. Spain produced 177.3 million bu., compared with 201.2 million bu. in 1968, and the Portuguese crop totaled 14.9 million bu. as against 29.3 million bu. Increased agricultural production in Spain had reduced import requirements substantially but had provided little expansion in exports. Exports of most fruits and vegetables were down sharply in 1967–68 and recovered only slightly in 1968–69. However, large exports were indicated from the 433,000 tons of olive oil produced in 1968–69. Commercial almond production in 1969 was estimated at 32,000 tons (shelled basis), substantially lower than the 45,000 tons of 1968.

Both the wheat (65.1 million bu.) and the corn (15.7 million bu.) harvests in Greece in 1969 were indicated as record large. It was expected that 200,000 tons of wheat would be available for export. The barley crop was also larger in 1969, notwithstanding a cutback in acreage from 870,000 in 1968 to 756,000 because of unfavourable weather. A tobacco policy plan for 1970–74 was drafted; the 241 million-lb. production goal for 1970 would include 209 million lb. for export, of which 182.4 million lb. would be of the oriental and 26.5 million lb. of the Burley type. Grower support prices were increased somewhat for sultanas, but lowered for currants. A world shortage of dried fruits was expected to result in higher prices.

AFRICA

Prospects for agriculture throughout Africa were generally good in 1969, although some regions suffered setbacks and others were still recovering from the widespread drought conditions of 1968. Per capita food supplies in 1968 had fallen to an index of 100 (1957–59 = 100) from 103 in 1967. North African cereal crop forecasts indicated a possible grain deficit of 3 million tons in 1969, and the effects of 1968's erratic weather in West Africa were still being felt by subsistence farmers. South Africa's corn crop was hit by drought, but Rhodesia's was record high. Negotiations for renewing the 1964–69 Yaoundé Convention between the EEC and 18 African nations were completed on July 29; trade provisions included the lowering of the EEC external tariff on a number of tropical products and the granting of trade preferences on some African products competing with Community farm products. The threat of the desert locust plague still hung over much of northern and eastern Africa. Losses in 1968 had been kept to a minimum, largely through the efforts of the Desert Locust Control Organization for Eastern Africa. (*See* Special Report.)

North Africa. Cereal crops in North African countries in 1969 appeared to have fallen below the record levels achieved a year earlier. Excessive rain in some areas and drought in others reduced the projected output by as much as 50%. Morocco's wheat crop was forecast at about 1,613,000 metric tons, a third below the 2,411,000-ton harvest of 1968, but there was a large carry-over. High-yielding Mexican wheat, planted on 12,400 ac., did not reach expected levels because of leaf blight. Barley production was down 40% and flood damage reduced the 1969 sugar-beet acreage from 72,270 to 59,250. Algeria's grain crops, affected by excessive rain at harvest time, were expected to be smaller than the 1968 total of 2.1 million tons, about three-fourths of which was wheat and a fifth, barley. Tunisia's subnormal 1968 cereal crop of 519,000 tons was not expected to be matched in 1969, but good yields were reported from 32,000 ac. of new variety Mexican wheat.

In March 1969, Tunisia and Morocco signed five-year agreements as a first step toward full association with the EEC; trade arrangements included a lowering of the EEC common external tariff on Moroccan and Tunisian citrus from 20 to 4%. Morocco's 1968 citrus production of 751,000 tons—over 80% of it oranges—provided 610,000 tons for export. Algerian citrus production was down 5% in 1968, but Tunisia's 1968–69 citrus crop was more than 10% above a year earlier.

Indications were that the U.A.R.'s 1969 grain crop would equal or surpass that of 1968, when 1,518,000 tons of wheat, 2.3 million tons of corn, and 2,350,000 tons of rice were harvested. By mid-July various European countries had contracted to supply more than 2.5 million tons of grains in 1969–70 to supplement 1969 U.A.R. production. The 1969 cotton crop reportedly totaled 2,005,000 bales (480 lb. net), about the same as a year earlier and slightly below the 1960–64 average. Leaf spot disease and leafworm infestation were more successfully controlled by aerial spraying than in previous years. The acreage devoted to cotton for 1969–70 was reported to be 1,730,000, compared with 1,519,000 in 1968–69. Cotton production in Sudan in 1969 was estimated at 209,000 tons, 7% more than a year earlier.

West Africa. A severe shortage of rainfall made 1968 a lean year for subsistence farmers in Mauritania, Mali, Senegal, Upper Volta, and Niger. Senegal's important rice, sorghum, and millet crops were down by one third and the 1968 peanut crop, at 770,000 metric tons, was the smallest in recent years. Prospects for the 1969 peanut crop rose with heavy rains in July, but low prices and the migration of peasants to urban areas militated against a reversal of the downward trend. Mali's 1968 production of millet, sorghum, corn, and rice was 40% below the 990,000-ton harvest of a year earlier. The 1968 sorghum and millet crops in Niger were estimated at less than 1 million tons, down a third from 1967. Cotton production in Chad in 1968–69 reached a record 200,000 bales (480 lb. net).

The Ivory Coast's 1969–70 coffee crop, forecast at 4 million bags, was 14% larger than a year earlier and substantially above the country's quota under the International Coffee Agreement. The Ivory Coast *Plan Palmier* (Palm Plan) and *Plan Cocotier* (Coconut Tree Plan) were expanded. By the end of 1968 some 124,000 ac. had been planted to oil palms under the nine-year-old *Plan Palmier,* and 6,000 ac. of coconut palm plantings had been completed under the *Plan Cocotier,* launched in 1967. West African palm oil production in 1969 was forecast at 891,000 metric tons, an increase of 12% over a year earlier.

Ghana's 1968 cocoa bean crop totaled 340,000 metric tons, compared with 422,000 tons a year earlier. In mid-1969 the Cocoa Marketing Board raised producer prices 1.63 cents per pound for 1968–69 main crop cocoa and instituted a subsidy program for sales of insecticides to cocoa farmers. Ghana also instituted a Cotton Development Board to promote cotton production. Nigeria's 1968–69 cocoa bean production was down sharply from a year earlier, when 235,000 tons were harvested. Beginning with the 1969–70 marketing season (July 11), Nigerian producer prices for Grades I and II beans were increased to 18.75 cents

Water sprinkles a palm grove in the Libyan desert from an irrigation system completed in 1969. The irrigation project, a joint venture of the Libyan government and U.S. industry, was developing water reserves believed to stretch for hundreds of miles below the desert surface.

COURTESY, "FOREIGN AGRICULTURE"

and 16.87 cents per pound, respectively. Nigeria's 1968 peanut crop, at 1,542,000 tons, was 23% above that of a year earlier. Production of subsistence crops in Nigeria was down 2 to 3%, and a severe shortage of seed yams threatened production of that staple in Biafra. The UN Development Program and the FAO called a conference at Monrovia, Liberia, in early September to consider establishment of a rice development project to reduce heavy rice imports into West Africa.

Early estimates for the 1969–70 world cocoa bean crop year, which began October 1, were set by the U.S. Department of Agriculture at 1,335,300 metric tons, about 9% larger than the FAO's 1968–69 estimate of 1,228,700 tons. The 1968–69 world crop had been 9% below a year earlier and 19% below the 1964–65 record. African production had fallen to 861,700 tons from 973,300 in 1967–68, largely because of reduced production in Ghana, Ivory Coast, and Nigeria. (South American production, at 255,300 tons, was 2% smaller than a year earlier.) Grindings for 1969 were forecast at 1,344,000 tons, a slight decline from the 1968 record grind of 1,384,000 tons. Imports of cocoa beans in 1968 totaled 1,045,000 tons, a decline of 5% from 1967. Stocks in the U.S., the world's largest importer, fell to 335,536 bags (132.3 lb. each) by late September 1969, compared with 724,425 bags a year earlier. Supplies were expected to remain short and prices high into the new cocoa year. New York prices for African cocoa beans rose to a high of 48.7 cents per pound in December 1968, but by May 1969 they had fallen back to an average of 44.6 cents. In late June the seven-year attempt to negotiate an International Cocoa Agreement failed again, when Brazil rejected a draft proposal for establishment of a price range between 20 and 29 U.S. cents per pound.

East Africa. Major crops in 1969 in East Africa were expected to equal or surpass 1968, and per capita food supplies registered encouraging growth. Total output in Kenya in 1968 was 7% above 1967, reflecting substantial increases in both corn and wheat acreage. Coffee production in 1969 was expected to exceed the 46,000-ton output of a year earlier. The Kenya Coffee Development Authority accelerated its program to draw subsistence farmers into the cash economy. Tea production in 1968 was up about a fifth, and tea was expected to be Kenya's leading cash crop by 1973. The corn crop was forecast at 1.6 million tons, an increase of 100,000 tons over a year earlier; the gain was the result of increasing use of varietal hybrid seed developed at Kitale. Kenya's transition from a grain-deficit to a grain-surplus country was marked by exports of some 210,000 tons of corn in 1968.

Uganda's agriculture was expected to continue the growth registered in 1968, when total production rose 4%. The Uganda coffee crop for 1969–70 was estimated at about 165,000 tons, somewhat below the above-average 1968 output. Tea production was forecast at 15,500 tons, slightly above the record of a year earlier, and cotton production was expected to rise above the 54,000-ton 1968 harvest. Uganda pursued its diversification program to reduce dependence on cotton and coffee as cash crops. Ethiopia's agriculture in 1968 registered a 2% growth over a year earlier, and further gains were expected in 1969.

Total agricultural output in Tanzania reached an index of 139 in 1968, despite a decline in sisal production. The 1969 crop outlook was good, with increases forecast for coffee, tea, cotton, and corn. Production of sisal was expected to fall to 210,000 tons, some 10,000 tons below 1968. Tanzania received an International Development Association credit of $1.2 million to be used by a subsidiary of Tanzania's National Development Corporation to develop five ranches covering 420,000 ac. Development of the country's livestock potential was being held back by rinderpest and the tsetse fly, by lack of an integrated marketing and transportation system, and by the need for an adequate feeding program to carry cattle through the prolonged dry season.

Exports of vanilla beans from the Malagasy Republic in 1968 totaled 961 metric tons valued at $10.2 million, an increase of 44% over 1967. Clove exports,

Table IX. Cattle and Buffalo Numbers in Major Producing Areas

In 000

Area	Estimated 1969*	1968*	Average 1961–65
North America	163,000	162,000	150,500
Canada	11,475	11,775	11,332
Mexico	24,000	23,628	19,337
United States	109,661	109,152	103,892
South America	190,200	191,800	168,700
Argentina	...	51,465	43,341
Brazil	...	89,992	78,718
Colombia	19,583	18,830	15,780
Venezuela	7,000	6,911	6,580
Western Europe	88,100	87,500	83,400
France	21,918	21,680	20,020
Germany, West	14,045	13,981	13,115
Italy	9,900	9,800	9,292
United Kingdom	12,123	11,996	11,610
Eastern Europe	34,700	35,400	33,000
Poland	...	10,940	9,697
Yugoslavia	5,305	5,737	5,509
U.S.S.R.	95,700	97,200	83,500
Africa	134,400	134,600	128,100
South Africa	...	12,145	12,514
Tanzania	...	...	8,550
Asia	425,600	423,500	395,500
Iran	5,855	5,750	4,782
Japan	...	3,155	3,327
Philippines	5,970	5,805	4,849
Turkey	15,750	15,413	13,783
Oceania	29,200	27,800	25,300
Australia	...	19,218	18,357
New Zealand	8,700	8,247	6,646
World total†	1,160,900	1,159,800	1,068,000

*Preliminary.
†Includes allowance for any missing data for countries shown and for other producing countries not shown.
Source: U.S. Department of Agriculture.

Table X. Hog Numbers in Major Producing Areas

In 000

Area	Estimated 1969*	1968*	Average 1961–65
North America	79,700	77,800	76,100
Canada	5,695	6,058	5,220
Mexico	10,200	9,978	9,170
United States	57,205	55,265	55,544
South America	76,700	78,000	66,700
Argentina	...	3,800	3,388
Brazil	...	63,406	53,126
Western Europe	76,100	76,100	66,300
Denmark	7,769	8,061	7,284
France	10,584	10,693	8,908
Germany, West	18,725	19,033	16,933
Italy	5,500	5,305	4,787
Spain	6,673	6,824	5,870
United Kingdom	7,991	7,633	7,098
Eastern Europe	48,100	49,400	47,000
Germany, East	...	9,254	8,654
Hungary	6,000	6,609	6,216
Poland	...	13,911	13,080
Yugoslavia	5,099	5,865	5,815
U.S.S.R.	49,000	50,900	59,800
Africa	5,500	5,600	5,100
South Africa	...	1,290	...
Asia	171,900	171,300	122,400
Japan	...	5,535	3,474
Philippines	12,000	11,500	9,236
Taiwan	...	3,003	2,917
Oceania	3,000	2,900	2,500
Australia	...	2,056	1,567
World total†	510,000	511,900	445,900

*Preliminary.
†Includes allowance for any missing data for countries shown and for other producing countries not shown.
Source: U.S. Department of Agriculture, Foreign Agricultural Service.

Table XI. Sheep Numbers in Major Producing Areas

In 000

Area	Estimated 1969*	1968*	Average 1961–65
North America	29,600	30,800	37,200
Canada	602	653	911
Mexico	6,600	6,706	6,064
United States	21,111	22,140	29,023
South America	125,900	125,000	121,100
Argentina	...	47,800	48,127
Brazil	...	23,065	19,997
Peru	...	15,100	14,454
Uruguay	...	21,500	21,860
Western Europe	75,500	76,100	79,400
France	9,599	9,510	8,876
Greece	7,800	7,919	8,765
Italy	8,450	8,300	7,956
Spain	16,726	16,648	20,574
United Kingdom	19,732	20,424	20,689
Eastern Europe	44,700	45,500	42,800
Bulgaria	...	9,905	10,070
Romania	14,282	14,380	12,217
Yugoslavia	9,719	10,345	10,232
U.S.S.R.	140,300	138,500	133,900
Africa	133,500	135,300	134,000
Morocco	...	...	14,710
South Africa	...	42,172	39,759
Asia	251,100	249,000	218,600
Iran	34,000	33,000	21,445
Turkey	37,000	35,878	32,863
Oceania	228,500	227,400	211,500
Australia	...	166,972	160,924
New Zealand	60,500	60,474	50,536
World total†	1,029,100	1,027,600	978,500

*Preliminary.
†Includes allowance for any missing data for countries shown and for other producing countries not shown.
Source: U.S. Department of Agriculture, Foreign Agricultural Service.

at 12,425 tons, and black pepper exports, at 3,095 tons, were both more than double the 1967 level.

Total world production of the major hard fibres (sisal, henequen, and abaca) fell to 1,792,200,000 lb. in 1968, 5% less than a year earlier. Output was down in all the major producing countries, although gains were registered by some smaller producers such as Haiti, Angola, and Mozambique. Sisal production, at 1,317,800,000 lb., was down about 5%, as producing nations cut output to meet the export quotas established under the informal arrangement sponsored by the FAO Study Group on Hard Fibers in 1967. Tanzanian sisal production, at 434 million lb., was down 11% and Brazil, the second largest sisal grower, produced 418.9 million lb., about 4% less than a year earlier. Production of both abaca and henequen fell 13%.

Central and Southern Africa. Agricultural production in most sections improved in 1969. Although drought early in the year reduced South Africa's corn crop to slightly less than 5 million tons, conditions improved later and were generally good for winter grains. To ensure sufficient supplies of white corn, South Africa arranged for imports of 735,000 tons from Rhodesia. At the same time, South Africa rescinded its export bans on corn (imposed in November 1968 for white corn and February 1969 for yellow corn) and started to export some yellow corn. Improved weather indicated a record wheat crop, estimated at 1,360,000 tons, and farmers were reportedly shifting acreage from corn to wheat production. South Africa's production of sorghum in 1969 was affected by severe drought early in the year; the low 1969 crop would hardly cover expected domestic requirements for livestock feed and beer production. The 1969 citrus crop was expected to exceed the 1968 record of 622,000 tons. Total fruit exports in 1968 reached an estimated $146.7 million, compared with $123.6 million a year earlier.

Good weather in Rhodesia was expected to result in quality crops of flue-cured and Burley tobacco. The government continued price guarantees for these types in 1969–70, but did not continue supports for the oriental crop. Corn production in Rhodesia, Malawi, and Zambia totaled 1.8 million tons in 1968, 16% below 1967. In 1969, however, Rhodesia anticipated production of over 1 million tons, allowing for sales to South Africa. Rhodesia's 1968–69 cotton crop was estimated at 200,000 bales, a sharp increase over the 1967–68 record.

The Central African Republic cotton crop, at 55,000 to 59,000 tons, also appeared to be a record. Basic food crops in the Congo (Kinshasa) in 1969 were considered to have achieved pre-independence levels; nevertheless, population growth in the intervening years had reduced per capita food production below the 1957–59 average. Malawi's 1968–69 cotton crop was estimated at some 30,000 bales, a third above 1967–68 output. Zambia's 1969 flue-cured tobacco production fell below the 13.5 million lb. estimated earlier in the season and excessive rains resulted in a corn crop below domestic needs for the second successive year.

EASTERN EUROPE AND THE U.S.S.R.

This diverse area reached a new high index of agricultural production in 1968—138 (1957–59 = 100), compared with 133 in 1967—but dropped off moderately in 1969. On a per capita basis, the 1968 index was 123, compared with 119 for the previous year. Higher crop production in some areas presumably was related to improved weather conditions. The livestock situation in early 1969 was described as stagnant, and there was even a reduction in meat supply. There were indications that policy changes since 1963, especially those pertaining to increased availability of fertilizer and machinery, higher levels of agricultural investment, higher prices, incentives to producers, and improved production and marketing practices, were bearing fruit.

Eastern Europe. Midseason forecasts indicated that 1969 was much improved, compared with the drought-troubled situation a year earlier, in the southern countries of Bulgaria, Hungary, Romania, and Yugoslavia. Prospects in the northern countries were not so bright. Overall, an increase of 5% in wheat and feed grains was forecast, with a record large wheat crop of more than 25 million tons and total feed-grain production 7% higher than in 1968. Oilseed production was substantially reduced by a heavy winter kill of the rapeseed crop in Poland and East Germany, but prospects for the sunflower crop were favourable. The outlook for potatoes and sugar beets was only fair and acreage continued to decline. Livestock inventories fell, especially of hogs in Hungary and Yugoslavia; feed stocks were tight and there was some incidence of foot-and-mouth disease.

Early prospects in Yugoslavia were for a grain crop of 13.2 million tons, up from 12 million tons in 1968 and slightly more than the record harvest of 1966. Corn was expected to reach 7.5 million tons, 6% less than the record but enough to supply tonnage for export. Romania was believed to be in a position to export significant quantities of both corn and wheat. Under the New Economic Mechanism introduced in 1968, long-range objectives for Hungarian agriculture were formulated by central planners, but planning and management were the responsibility of the individual producer or farm. Producer prices were revised to make average farms profitable, and some free-market transactions and competition among buyers were introduced. The 1969 wheat crop was 126.8 million bu., substantially larger than the 114.5 million bu. of 1968. Soil-moisture levels were reported below normal in Bulgaria at midsummer, but vegetable and industrial crops, increasingly grown under irrigation, escaped serious damage.

A long, hard winter and a cold spring were followed by late summer drought in Poland and some neighbouring areas, indicating a possible need for grain imports. Wheat production was 152.8 million bu., considerably below the record 171 million bu. of 1968. Other grains, hay and pastures, potatoes, and sugar beets were also affected. East German food-grain crops declined about 10%, but Czechoslovakia had a large wheat crop of 125.3 million bu.

U.S.S.R. Agricultural production in 1969 was below the excellent record of 1968, when the index for total agricultural production stood at 143 (134 in 1967). Winter damage to grain crops, especially fall-sown wheat, stimulated the seeding of a record 51.3 million ha. (126.7 million ac.) to spring wheat and 46.7 million ha. to other spring grains. Wheat production was estimated at about 65 millions tons, 17% below the near-record 2,631,800,000 bu. of 1968. In early October it appeared that one-sixth of the grain area remained to be harvested, mostly in northern Kazakhstan and Siberia. Whether or not that race was lost, the decision was made to fulfill the contract with Canada for about 131 million bu. of wheat.

Rye, possibly a casualty of the affluent society, continued the sharp downtrend apparent throughout the world since 1950. Acreage for harvest in the U.S.S.R., the major producing country, was reduced to 28,714,000, compared with 30,317,000 in 1968 and a 1961–65 average of 40,340,000. Production was indicated as substantially below the 500 million bu. of 1968. (Poland, the second ranking producer, harvested 313 million bu.; these two countries accounted for about two-thirds of world production.) Barley acreage in the U.S.S.R. was increased to 54,362,000, apparently to replace winter-killed crops. Acreage of oats also was increased to 22,239,000; it was expected that the crop would exceed the 668.3 million bu. of 1968. Cotton planting was delayed, but the area seeded was reported as 4% greater than in 1968, partly because government purchase prices for 1969-crop cotton were raised 15%. A large output of 9.5 million bales resulted. Sugar production for 1969–70 was estimated as slightly larger than the 9.7 million tons of 1968–69. Hay and forage crops were retarded by the late spring, but later weather was more favourable. Fruit production, which had been rising sharply in recent years, was expected to be at least equal to that of 1968. Output of livestock products was thought to be limited by summer drought in some areas in 1968, by scarce feeds prior to the 1968 harvest, and by the severe winter of 1968–69. Milk products were near the level of the previous year, but meat production was off by 8 to 10%.

COURTESY, "FOREIGN AGRICULTURE"

Bagged wheat in the Ludhiana marketplace in the Punjab (below) is loaded manually (above) into railroad cars. India harvested a record wheat crop in May 1969.

COURTESY, "FOREIGN AGRICULTURE"

MIDDLE EAST AND INDIA

Middle East. The region experienced an uncommonly good agricultural year in 1968, with the index of agricultural production at 139 (1957–59 = 100); preliminary indications were that 1969 was even better. However, the 1968 index was only 106 on a per capita basis.

Wheat acreage in Turkey rose to 20,509,000 in 1969, up from 20,015,000 in 1968 and well above the 19,243,000-ac. average of the early 1960s. Some 316 million bu. were harvested, against 308 million bu. the previous year. The barley crop also was larger: 165.3 million bu. versus 160.8 million bu. in 1968. The 1968–69 cotton crop was a record 2 million bales, compared with the previous record (1967–68) of 1.8 million bales. Yields averaged 545 lb. per ac., a new high. Exports during the first eight months of the crop year were 713,000 bales, compared with 883,000 during the corresponding period a year earlier. Poor weather lowered the fruit and nut crops. A filbert crop of only 110,000 tons (in-shell basis) was anticipated. Citrus fruits—largely oranges—for export as fresh fruit and processed products continued to be an expanding sector of Israel's agricultural economy. Some 27,715,000 boxes of oranges and tangerines, 7,495,000 boxes of grapefruit, and 1,044,000 boxes of lemons were harvested in 1968–69. Though important in the export market, Israel's production was only a fraction of world production, which in 1968–69 totaled 668,114,000 boxes of oranges and tangerines, 71,985,000 boxes of grapefruit, and 57,851,000 boxes of lemons. In early 1969 more than 550 tons of winter strawberries grown under plastic were flown from Israel to the European market. Cotton acreage, most of it irrigated, was a record 82,000. The 1969 wheat crop was 7.3 million bu., up from the 7 million bu. of 1968 and nearly three times the average of the early 1960s. The barley crop was substantially smaller than in the previous year, however, and Israel continued to have a feed-grain deficit.

Syria harvested 28.7 million bu. of barley, well above average and more than double the 1968 crop. Considerable progress in sheep breeding was reported. Fruit and vegetables were reported to be withering on 500 sq.mi. of farms in Jordan as a result of war damage to irrigation facilities. Lebanon, with an exportable surplus of 140,000 tons of apples for 1968–69 and about the same tonnage of citrus, found markets mainly among neighbouring Arab countries. A ten-year technical assistance program negotiated with the Ford Foundation in 1968 would be directed in part to upgrading wheat production. Rainfall in Iraq was satisfactory for good harvests and total production was up 13% from 1967.

Iran in 1968 achieved a record wheat production of 161.7 million bu., far more than the 2,740,000-ton average of 1961–65. Some 250,000 tons were exportable. Production in 1969 was 154.3 million bu. Barley production also declined moderately—to 55.1 million bu., compared with 58.3 million bu. in 1968. Cotton production in 1968–69 reached a record 665,000 bales. The 1969 almond crop was indicated at 7,000 tons, the same size as in the previous year. Both acreage and production of sugar were being increased sharply in an effort to achieve self-sufficiency.

Pakistan. In 1969, as in 1968, a record wheat harvest brought West Pakistan near to self-sufficiency in this important food grain and raised some problems of storage and distribution. The 1969 harvest was indicated at 252.8 million bu., up from 238,000 bu. in 1968. Only 14,652,000 ac. were harvested in 1969, against 14,977,000 ac. the year before; presumably the higher yield was due to improved varieties. Barley, a much less important crop, rose to 5.6 million bu. from 5 million bu. a year earlier. A severe food shortage developed in some East Pakistani urban areas in early 1969 despite a record large 1968–69 crop of about 19.5 million tons of paddy rice. It was indicated that some 1.4 million tons of grain imports would be needed in 1969. Higher prices in 1969 were expected to encourage jute production in excess of the 1.2 million-ton crop of 1968, some of which was flood damaged. Production of cotton continued an upward trend, as did corn.

India. Though comparatively favourable weather must be given some of the credit, the massive attention accorded to Indian agricultural problems in recent years appeared to be producing significant results. Wheat imports declined from 238 million bu.

in 1967 to about 183 million bu. in 1968. Wheat production again set a new record—661.4 million bu. in 1968–69, compared with 608.8 million bu. a year earlier. Such abundance created new storage, pricing, and distribution problems, and the government set a high procurement target of 132 million bu. Barley, meanwhile, fell to 137.8 million bu., compared with 159.3 million bu. in 1968, apparently as a result of low rainfall in some areas. Food grains other than wheat and rice totaled 27.5 million tons for 1968–69, somewhat below the 28.9 million tons of the previous year. Production of rice for 1968–69 was estimated at more than 39 million tons (milled), down some 2 million tons from 1967–68. About 3.6 million ha. were planted to high-yielding varieties, an increase of more than 40%. A total of 246,000 new pumping sets, 76,000 private tube wells, and 2,000 state tube wells were installed during 1968–69. It was estimated that domestic production of fertilizer might reach a million tons in 1969 (650,000 tons in 1968) and that 100,000 farm tractors might be in use on Indian farms by 1970.

A mounting surplus confronted tea growers and traders of India, Ceylon, and other producing countries. Tea output in 1969 in the main producing countries was 2,321,000,000 lb., 42 million lb. more than in the previous year when world supply had risen about 90 million lb. Consumption, meanwhile, had increased by only 36 million lb., and London prices averaged about *3d.* a pound below a year earlier. India produced about 40% of the total and Ceylon nearly one quarter. Projections to 1975 indicated that half of the anticipated increase would be in those countries, though most new British investment in tea plantations was going into East Africa. Conferences in India, Rome, and Uganda stressed the importance of arriving at an international price-stabilization agreement but did not agree on the new machinery that would be needed. Ceylon made plans to convert some tea land to other crops.

THE FAR EAST

A preliminary view suggested that the Far East experienced an even more fortunate agricultural year in 1969 than in 1968, when production had gained about 3% over 1967. The important rice crop was estimated to have been moderately larger, though data for the Communist areas were highly inadequate. In general, food shortages no longer appeared critical; imports were continued on a less urgent scale, and surplus supplies of some important items appeared.

Record large Japanese rice harvests in 1967 and 1968 resulted in accumulation of milled rice stocks to a level of 5.1 million tons (about eight months' domestic requirements). Measures considered to alleviate the problem included diversion of land to other crops, a limited free market system, maintenance of prices at the 1968 level, and allocation of 1 million tons as livestock feed. The 1969 rice crop was reduced by cold, damp spring weather to an indicated 12.3 million metric tons (milled basis), compared with 13.2 million tons in 1967 and 1968. Despite the surplus, Japanese grain imports rose 8% in 1968–69. Feed-grain imports totaled 8.5 million tons (up 11%) and wheat and flour, 4.2 million tons (up 4%). Rice imports were down 20%. A reduction in the 1969 wheat harvest to 29 million bu., compared with 37.2 million bu. in 1968, suggested a probable expansion of wheat imports in 1969–70.

Winter damage, a cold spring, and flooding in China

Table XII. Sugar Production of the Principal Producing Countries

In 000 short tons, raw value

Country	Forecast 1969–70	1968–69	1967–68	Average 1960–61 to 1964–65
Argentina	1,068	1,019	844	950
Australia	2,365	3,055	2,556	1,806
Brazil	5,048	4,804	4,922	3,815
China	2,200	2,200	2,000	1,026
Colombia	818	784	743	421
Cuba	8,000	5,200	5,500	5,596
Czechoslovakia	1,100	1,005	1,000	1,160
Denmark	335	375	363	341
Dominican Republic	950	920	735	852
France	2,741	2,623	1,905	2,309
Germany, East	1,000	815	820	869
Germany, West	2,193	2,174	2,271	1,980
India	4,978	4,640	3,092	3,694
Indonesia	800	750	716	708
Iran	642	568	504	185
Italy	1,498	1,422	1,804	1,082
Jamaica	476	432	498	524
Mauritius	689	728	658	559
Mexico	2,300	2,220	2,520	1,899
Netherlands	797	792	828	620
Peru	827	678	848	873
Philippines	1,903	1,755	1,759	1,704
Poland	1,700	1,881	2,109	1,693
South Africa	1,740	1,659	2,009	1,233
Spain	952	815	692	560
Taiwan	788	834	975	992
Turkey	695	778	872	639
United Kingdom	1,073	1,075	1,075	988
U.S.S.R.	11,000	11,651	11,503	7,623
United States	5,835	5,904	5,383	4,850
U.S. dependencies*	575	483	645	1,012
Yugoslavia	558	477	540	323
World total	79,362	75,446	73,034	61,035

*Puerto Rico and Virgin Islands of the U.S.
Source: U.S. Department of Agriculture, Foreign Agricultural Service.

Table XIII. Coffee Production (Green) in Principal Producing Countries

In 000 bags, 132.3 lb. each

Country	1969–70*	1968–69	1967–68	Average 1960–61 to 1964–65
Angola	3,350	3,175	3,400	2,910
Brazil	20,000	16,500	23,000	25,840
Cameroon	1,100	1,100	1,100	801
Colombia	7,900	7,900	8,000	7,760
Congo (Kinshasa)	1,100	1,000	1,000	990
Costa Rica	1,300	1,260	1,350	1,056
Ecuador	800	1,000	1,175	751
El Salvador	2,300	1,900	2,400	1,812
Guatemala	1,850	1,650	1,850	1,704
India	1,300	1,280	1,050	1,045
Indonesia	2,000	2,000	2,150	2,016
Ivory Coast	4,000	3,500	4,500	3,185
Kenya	835	775	650	624
Malagasy Republic	800	950	1,100	923
Mexico	3,000	2,800	2,800	2,431
Peru	960	860	880	700
Philippines	750	800	700	631
Tanzania	900	900	740	497
Uganda	2,750	3,150	2,700	2,429
Venezuela	750	750	700	821
Total North America	11,565	10,557	11,567	10,194
Total South America	30,582	27,192	33,891	35,986
Total Africa	18,299	18,144	18,474	15,077
Total Asia and Oceania	4,684	4,724	4,527	4,082
World total	65,130	60,617	68,459	65,339

*Second estimate.
Source: U.S. Department of Agriculture, Foreign Agricultural Service.

Table XIV. World Cocoa Production In Leading Areas*

In 000 metric tons

Area	Forecast 1969–70	1968–69	1967–68	Average 1955–56 to 1959–60
North and Central America	79.3	74.6	76.9	84.8
Dominican Republic	30.0	26.0	30.0	35.4
South America	265.5	255.3	260.9	195.6
Brazil	160.0	160.0	144.7	118.1
Ecuador	55.0	47.0	70.0	41.3
Africa	951.4	861.7	978.0	929.1
Cameroon	100.0	100.0	91.5	79.9
Equatorial Guinea	37.0	37.0	34.0	30.2
Ghana	375.0	341.0	421.6	458.4
Ivory Coast	150.0	144.5	146.8	104.7
Nigeria	245.0	195.0	238.6	217.8
Asia and Oceania	39.1	37.1	33.2	25.7
New Guinea and Papua	29.0	27.0	24.0	14.2
World total	1,335.3	1,228.7	1,349.0	1,235.4

*Crop year, October 1 to September 30.
Source: U.S. Department of Agriculture, Foreign Agricultural Service.

Table XV. Tea Production in Principal Producing Areas

In 000,000 lb.

Area	Forecast 1969	1968	1967	1966	Average 1960–64
World*	2,321	2,270	2,160	2,170	1,909
Asia	2,026	2,007	1,932	1,933	1,753
Ceylon	503	496	487	490	465
India	886	886	843	829	768
Indonesia†	88	88	74	88	97
Japan	190	187	188	183	177
Pakistan	66	63	65	62	54
Taiwan	55	54	54	47	42
U.S.S.R.	120	119	121	124	93
Africa	237	208	179	184	123
South America	58	56	49	53	33

*Excluding China.
†Estate production.
Source: U.S. Department of Agriculture, Foreign Agricultural Service.

Farmer stands in an empty dam (opposite page) and dead sheep lie along a boundary fence (right) in the area south and east of Nyabing, Austr., which was affected by widespread drought in 1969.

"LONDON DAILY EXPRESS" FROM PICTORIAL PARADE

reduced early 1969 crops, especially rice; a good wheat harvest was reported in some areas. Weather conditions appeared to have improved for crops harvested in the autumn, which included about two-thirds of the grain and all industrial crops except rapeseed. Increased inputs such as fertilizer and improved management also apparently contributed to more favourable results. One estimate was that as many as 25 million urban residents were "sent down" to do farm work. Estimated soybean production was 244 million bu., an increase over 1968 but below the 1962–66 average. Feedstuffs appeared to be sufficiently abundant to permit some expansion in livestock production, and preliminary evidence suggested that the new contract with Canada for wheat was probably prompted by price advantage rather than pressing need. Weather conditions in North Korea suggested that 1969 grain crops might exceed the estimated 5.2 million to 5.5 million tons of 1968.

Taiwan continued to serve less developed nations as an example of success in modern agriculture. The land reform appeared highly successful, although there was concern about flight from the farms, especially of the young adults. Grain surpluses were becoming something of a problem. The rice carry-over was twice as large as normal and this, plus a large new crop and restricted export prospects, threatened to create a burdensome situation.

Amid the disorganization of war, South Vietnam attempted to reverse the downtrend in agriculture evident since 1963. The "Land to the Tiller" program would include land titles at the village level, with a maximum of 5 ha. (12.5 ac.) per family. Thai rice production was expanded in 1969 to 14 million tons in an effort to keep exports at the 1.5 million-ton level despite an expanding population. Some 2.4 million tons of all grains were exported in 1968–69, 4% more than in 1967–68. Feed grains, almost wholly corn, contributed 1.3 million tons to the total and rice, 1 million tons. The 1968–69 rice harvest was 12,410,000 tons, up from 11.2 million the previous year but smaller than the 13.5 million tons of 1966–67. Burma, with a large rice crop of 8,186,000 tons in 1968–69, was expected to increase exports to about 600,000 or 700,000 tons. The Sungei Muda Irrigation Scheme, nearing completion in Malaysia, would increase rice production there by 50%.

High-yielding varieties of rice had been adopted rapidly in the Philippines as well as in India and Pakistan. There were problems of consumer acceptance, however, and it appeared that the new varieties would be purchased only at a substantial discount in price. Though reduced by drought, the Philippine crop of 4,576,000 tons in 1968–69 was the same as that of the previous year and substantially larger than the 1961–65 average. Abaca production in 1968 was indicated at 168.7 million lb., down 14% from 1967, which in turn was 13% below 1966. A larger crop in 1969–70 would provide a small export surplus. Firmer prices and the building of new mills suggested that the decline might be ending. Copra exports in the first half of 1969 totaled about 255,000 tons, approximately 5% more than in the corresponding months of 1968. The 1968–69 sugar harvest, reduced by two typhoons and some drought, totaled 1,755,000 tons, and the basic U.S. quota of 1,126,020 tons was supplied with some difficulty.

Indonesian agriculture appeared to be slowly recovering after years of disorganization. The 1968–69 rice crop of 16,308,000 tons was the same as the previous year but nearly one-third larger than the 1961–65 average. As the world's leading pepper exporter, Indonesia provided 82,102,000 lb. in 1967 (46.3 million lb. the year before). The world total was 200,315,000 lb., 33% above the previous year. India's exports, at only 45,999,000 lb., were down by 8.8 million lb., largely because of a seven cents per pound export duty levied by the government. Sarawak increased exports to 43,680,000 lb. from 29,241,000 lb. and Brazilian exports rose to 21,299,000 lb. Prices remained comparatively low during much of 1968 but advanced sharply during part of 1969.

OCEANIA

Australian farm production continued to expand in 1969, with prospects for near-record harvests of wheat and rice. Cattle were reported at record high numbers. Aggressive promotion of both production and exports contributed to a gross value of production in 1968–69 forecast at $4.4 billion, 17% above a year earlier. Severe drought in Queensland in 1969 prompted the state and federal governments to adopt relief measures.

Australia's 1969–70 wheat harvest, which began in December, was forecast at 499,664,000 bu., down

Table XVI. Production of Meats in Principal Producing Countries

In 000,000 lb., carcass-meat basis

Country	Beef and veal 1968*	Beef and veal 1967	Beef and veal Average 1961–65	Pork (excluding lard) 1968*	Pork (excluding lard) 1967	Pork (excluding lard) Average 1961–65	Mutton, lamb, and goat meat 1968*	Mutton, lamb, and goat meat 1967	Mutton, lamb, and goat meat Average 1961–65
Argentina	5,732	5,666	4,913	410	467	384	459	441	345
Australia	1,994	1,937	1,941	333	313	257	1,465	1,314	1,310
Belgium-Luxembourg	545	536	482	772	705	528	8	6	6
Brazil	3,417	3,318	3,095	1,221	1,228	1,022	119	114	106
Canada	1,950	1,823	1,588	1,195	1,180	1,003	20	21	30
Colombia	...	818	837	...	88	95	...	5	5
Denmark	470	477	343	1,578	1,618	1,463	7	6	3
France	4,134	4,041	3,585	2,811	2,883	2,588	310	315	273
Germany, West	2,734	2,632	2,542	4,740	4,332	3,979	24	24	30
Italy	1,671	1,570	1,388	948	968	887	101	88	88
Japan	331	323	400	1,135	1,227	649	3	3	6
Mexico	1,169	1,058	1,046	573	558	453	135	134	129
Netherlands	676	653	617	1,336	1,188	928	19	19	18
New Zealand	760	665	614	84	81	94	1,249	1,148	1,038
Poland	...	1,077	878	...	1,997	1,826	...	...	58
South Africa	880	905	998	142	135	115	342	291	281
Spain	536	474	403	...	950	632	289	295	267
U.S.S.R.	9,740	9,560	6,520	7,440	7,440	6,250	1,760	1,760	1,870
United Kingdom	1,992	2,031	1,978	1,968	1,814	1,796	539	577	559
United States	21,610	21,011	17,862	13,063	12,581	11,863	602	646	755
Yugoslavia	542	527	415	705	681	648	110	110	102

*Preliminary.
Source: U.S. Department of Agriculture.

from the 1968–69 record of 539,600,380 bu. Moisture conditions during July and August were reported as excellent over the wheat belt, with the exception of Western Australia. In March the minister for primary industry warned wheat growers that advance payments were not likely to be continued on quota deliveries to the Australian Wheat Board unless there was a dramatic increase in wheat sales. While the government had no thought of imposing production controls, growers could not rely on government financial support for wheat crops of the order of 500 million bu. Later in March, at a meeting of the Australian Wheat Growers' Federation, growers agreed to press for production quotas limiting output to about 9.5 million tons. New South Wales was the first wheat-producing state to announce details of its 1969–70 delivery quota system; its quota of 123 million bu. would guarantee growers about 50% of their 1968–69 deliveries, with preference being given to wheat producers of long standing.

Wheat and flour exports in fiscal 1968–69 totaled 5,366,000 tons, nearly 1.6 million tons less than in the previous year; China and Japan were the major customers; a contract with China, involving 82 million bu. of wheat valued at $140 million, was the largest ever completed by the Australian Wheat Board. As of July 1969 carry-over stocks totaled 11.2 million tons, compared with 4.3 million tons a year earlier, and unless exports could be increased sharply, they were expected to reach 17 million tons by July 1, 1970. The large carry-over strained storage facilities, and it was clear to the Wheat Board that it would be impossible to accept all the wheat to be delivered under the 1969–70 quota system. The board made special funds available to state wheat boards to provide emergency storage facilities for more than 1.2 million tons. Even so, growers in some areas would have difficulty moving wheat into storage and qualifying for the first advance payment on deliveries.

Australia's 1969–70 rice harvest, mostly grown in New South Wales, was expected to reach a record 284,000 tons of paddy, compared with 225,000 tons in 1968–69. The drought in Queensland reduced the 1969 grain sorghum crop from the 13.5 million bu. of 1968 to perhaps 10 million bu., of which some 4 million bu. was accounted for by a record crop in New South Wales. Production of sunflower seed continued to be encouraged; in 1968–69 crushers arranged with growers to produce 5,000 long tons, but adverse weather resulted in the production of only about 1,500 tons.

Cotton production in 1968–69 was estimated at 170,000 bales (480 lb. net), compared with 150,000 bales in 1967–68. Yields were nearly 4½ times greater than the 1960–64 average. Traditionally a cotton-importing country, Australia for the first time exported 9,500 bales of cotton to Japan in late 1968. Excellent growing conditions produced a record tobacco crop estimated at 33.5 million lb., a 48% increase over the 22.7 million lb. of 1968 and substantially in excess of the marketing quotas. In March the Tobacco Board set the leaf marketing quota for 1970-crop tobacco at 31 million lb. The 1969–70 citrus crop was forecast at 11,755,000 bu., 11% less than the record production in 1968–69 but about equal to 1967–68. Poor weather and disease reduced the 1969 canned fruit pack to its lowest level in four years; the total pack was estimated at 9,510,000 cases, compared with 10,989,000 cases a year earlier.

The livestock industry in 1969 was considered to be fully recovered from the devastating drought of 1965. Cattle numbers on March 31, 1969, were estimated at 20.8 million head, well above the pre-drought high of 19,055,000 head. Dairy herd numbers were the lowest in 14 years, however, since all of the expansion was in beef cattle. Preliminary estimates placed the 1968–69 slaughter at 5.6 million head, about the same as in the preceding two years. Beef and veal production for 1969 was estimated at 905,000 long tons, compared with 890,000 tons in 1968 and 865,000 tons in 1967. Over a fourth of 1968 production moved into the export market. Sheep numbers in 1969 were estimated to have reached a new record, well above the 166.9 million head reported for March 1968. There was an emphasis on lamb production over mutton, and a shift from coarser to finer wool. Hog numbers reached a record 2,056,000 head in 1968, an increase of 14% over 1967.

New Zealand's agriculture underwent further reexamination in 1969, after two years of adjustment that included sharply reduced wool prices, recession and devaluation, and reduced export markets for dairy produce. Low prices for wool and dairy products had decreased total farm income from U.S. $370 million in 1965–66 to $347 million in 1967–68. The long-range agricultural program had been reviewed in August 1968, and production targets had been established calling for annual production increases of 4.5% through 1978–79. The dairy industry was of primary concern in 1969. New Zealand's 620,000 head of cattle (mostly dairy cows) produced about 520,000 tons of dairy products for export, 211,000 tons of which was butter. Reduction of the U.K. butter quota had left the industry searching for markets, and the poor export outlook raised the question of whether New Zealand could afford to continue to expand at the rate called for by the August 1968 conference. Prime Minister Keith Holyoake was reported to be resolutely opposed to direct subsidies. Alternative proposals included incentives to promote diversification to beef production, elimination of weaker dairy units, and a guaranteed price for a production quota. The 1969 budget, presented to Parliament on June 26, contained an incentive plan for beef production, but dairymen protested that it was insufficient to relieve the cost-price squeeze.

Wool production in Oceania, which accounted for about 44% of the world total, was forecast at 2,733,000,000 lb. in 1969, 2.3% above a year earlier. Australia's production, at 1,997,700,000 lb., was up 3% and New Zealand's, at an estimated 735 million lb., was up slightly. With world sheep numbers close to the 1968 record of 1,028,000,000 head, total world production of wool was indicated at about 6,230,100,000 lb., greasy basis (3,600,000,000 lb., clean basis), only slightly more than in the preceding year. The world wool trade in 1968 had recovered from the low levels of a year earlier; exports of tops, yarns, and fabrics totaled 743 million lb., 15% above 1967 and slightly more than the high levels reached in 1966. A 9% rise was recorded for raw-wool exports from the five major producing countries in the Southern Hemisphere during July 1968–April 1969, and a continuation of this trend could move most of the region's 1968–69 surplus production into export channels. However, wool stocks were well above average, largely because of holdover stocks in New Zealand. Prices in 1968–69 were generally steady, at a slightly lower level than a year earlier. Mill use of raw wool in the major manufacturing countries in 1968 and

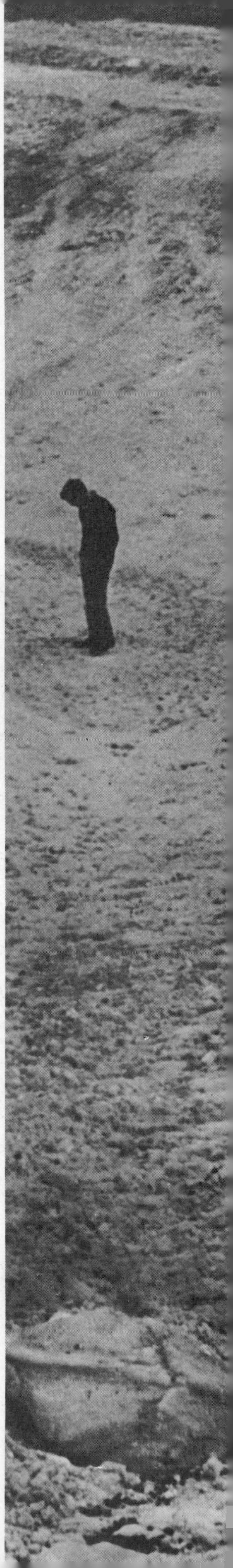

"LONDON DAILY EXPRESS" FROM PICTORIAL PARADE

1969 was estimated at approximately 3,450,000,000 lb. (J. K. R.; H. R. Sh.)

See also Commercial Policies; Commodities, Primary; Conservation; Cooperatives; Fisheries; Food; Gardening; Industrial Review; Prices; Tobacco.

Encyclopædia Britannica Films. *Antibiotics* (1952); *The Story of Rice* (1952); *The Story of Sugar* (1953); *The Middle States* (1955); *Milk* (1955); *Meat—From Range to Market* (1956); *The Wheat Farmer* (1956); *The Corn Farmer* (1960); *DNA: Molecule of Heredity* (1960); *Seed Germination* (1960); *Wheat Country* (1960); *Wheat Rust* (1960); *The Cotton Farmer* (1963); *Cattleman—A Rancher's Story* (1964); *The Dairy Farmer* (1965); *The Great Plains—Land of Risk* (1966); *Interior West: The Land Nobody Wanted* (1966); *The Orange Grower* (1967); *The Sheep Rancher* (1967); *Midwest—Heartland of the Nation* (1968); *Produce—From Farm to Market* (1968).

Albania

A people's republic in the western part of the Balkan Peninsula, Europe, Albania is on the Adriatic Sea, bordered by Greece and Yugoslavia. Area: 11,100 sq.mi. (28,748 sq.km.). Pop. (1967 est.): 1,964,730. Cap. and largest city: Tirane (pop., 1967 est., 169,300). Language: literary Albanian and two spoken dialects, Gheg in the north, Tosk in the south. Religion: Muslim, Orthodox, Roman Catholic. First secretary of the Albanian (Communist) Party of Labour in 1969, Enver Hoxha; president of the Presidium of the People's Assembly, Haxhi Leshi; chairman of the Council of Ministers (premier), Mehmet Shehu.

During 1969 Albania received arms and munitions of Soviet manufacture from China. This was the result of an urgent request from Albania, which was alarmed both by the presence of the Soviet fleet in the Mediterranean and by the 1968 occupation of Czechoslovakia by Warsaw Pact forces. In October 1968 an Albanian delegation headed by Gen. Beqir Balluku, deputy premier and minister of national defense, had visited Peking. At a banquet given by the Albanian ambassador, Premier Chou En-lai had declared that "the 700 million Chinese were determined to give firm support to Albania in every possible way." An agreement signed on November 20 by Chou and Adil Carcani, the Albanian deputy premier, had provided for a substantial expansion of Chinese military and economic aid to Albania.

The first ships with military matériel from China arrived at the Albanian ports of Durres and Vlore in the spring of 1969. At the same time, a strong Chinese military and technical mission reached Albania and began improving the country's roads, railways, and communications. The existing railway lines linking Durres with Tirane and with Peqin were being extended northward to Shkoder and southeastward to Pogradec on the Ohrid Lake. According to Western press reports, six missile bases were being constructed to defend the two main ports and the island of Sazan, where the Soviets had built a submarine base that they had had to abandon in 1961.

The almost permanently bad Albanian-Yugoslav relations improved somewhat, after a particularly tense period at the end of 1968 when Albanians of the Kosovo-Metohija autonomous province of Serbia started separatist demonstrations. Taking into account Marshal Tito's obviously anti-Soviet statement that "the Yugoslav people were prepared to defend their independence at all costs," Enver Hoxha in July 1969 instructed *Zëri i Popullit*, his chief daily newspaper, to state that in spite of their ideological differences with the Yugoslav leadership, the Albanian people "would without hesitation help the Yugoslav peoples in their resistance to an aggression."

On November 8, on the occasion of the 25th anniversary of the establishment of the Albanian People's Republic, the government decided that it would cancel the individual income tax, free agricultural cooperatives in the hilly regions from annual tax and consider the loans accorded to them in 1966 and 1967 as nonredeemable grants, reduce prices of consumer goods, medicines, and some agricultural implements, and increase the prices paid by the state for meat and wool deliveries. (K. Sm.)

ALBANIA

Education. (1965–66) Primary, pupils 361,241, teachers 12,980; secondary, pupils 31,270, teachers 1,189; vocational, pupils 18,574, teachers 718; teacher training, students 5,417, teachers 209; higher (including University of Tirane with 7,284 students), students 12,761, teachers 517.

Finance. Monetary unit: lek, with an official exchange rate of 5 leks to U.S. $1 (12 leks = £1 sterling) and a tourist rate of 12.5 leks to U.S. $1 (30 leks = £1). Budget (1968 est.): revenue 4,250,000,000 leks; expenditure 3,985,000,000 leks.

Foreign Trade. (1964) Imports U.S. $98 million; exports U.S. $66 million. Import sources: China 63%; Czechoslovakia 10%; Poland 8%; East Germany 5%. Export destinations: China 40%; Czechoslovakia 19%; East Germany 10%; Poland 10%. Main exports: fuels, minerals, and metals (including iron ore and chrome ore) 54%; foodstuffs (including wine and fruit) 21%; timber, wool.

Transport and Communications. Roads (motorable; 1960) 3,100 km. Motor vehicles in use (1960 est.): passenger 1,900; commercial (including buses) 3,400. Railways (1966) 151 km. Shipping (1968): merchant vessels 100 gross tons and over 11; gross tonnage 36,550; traffic (1966) goods loaded *c.* 1.3 million metric tons, unloaded *c.* 500,000 metric tons. Telephones (Dec. 1963) 10,150. Radio receivers (Dec. 1967) 135,000. Television receivers (Dec. 1965) *c.* 1,000.

Agriculture. Production (in 000; metric tons; 1966; 1965 in parentheses): wheat *c.* 115 (*c.* 100); corn *c.* 165 (158); rye *c.* 7 (*c.* 7); oats *c.* 16 (*c.* 16); barley (1967) *c.* 9, (1966) *c.* 9; cottonseed (1967) *c.* 16, (1966) *c.* 16; sugar, raw value (1968–69) *c.* 16, (1967–68) *c.* 15; potatoes *c.* 31 (*c.* 33); tobacco *c.* 13 (12); sawn timber (cu.m.; 1964) 142, (1963) 156. Livestock (in 000; Dec. 1967): sheep *c.* 1,700; cattle *c.* 425; pigs *c.* 144; goats (Dec. 1964) 1,199; poultry (Oct. 1964) 1,730.

Industry. Production (in 000; metric tons; 1967): lignite *c.* 340; crude oil 1,091; petroleum products (1965) 392; electricity (kw-hr.) *c.* 555,000; chrome ore (oxide content) 127; iron ore (1966) *c.* 404; copper ore (metal content; 1966) 4; cement (1966) 135; cotton fabrics (m; 1964) 28,000.

Alcoholic Beverages

Beer. World production of beer increased by approximately 23 million hl. (hectolitres) in 1968 to reach 570 million hl., an increase of 4% over the previous year. The growth was greatest in Eastern Europe (over 8%) and in Oceania (over 6%). Increases in Asia (5%), Central and South America (4%), and Western Europe (3.5%) were close to the average; increases were comparatively modest in the U.S. (2%) and Africa (1%).

The most important beer producing countries were, as before, the U.S. (134 million hl.); West Germany (including West Berlin, 79 million hl.); and the U.K. (52.5 million hl.). The world's largest brewery concern, Anheuser Busch Inc. (headquarters at St. Louis, Mo.) produced in its seven breweries 21.5 million hl., more than the total production of France (20 million hl.), Oceania (17 million hl.), Canada (15 million hl.), or the whole of Africa (11 million hl.).

Aircraft:
see Defense; Industrial Review; Transportation

Air Forces:
see Defense

Air Races and Records:
see Sporting Record

"THE TIMES," LONDON

Prospective buyer samples a 1792 vintage wine at Christie's in London before an auction of high-quality wines, held on Oct. 2, 1969.

The Schlitz Brewing Co., the second largest U.S. producer, which already had interests in Spain, established itself in the EEC through acquisition of the Belgian Brasserie de Ghlin. Because it was clearly difficult for foreign firms to get a foothold in the German brewing industry, the acquisition of the West German soft drinks firm of Lehnig AG (which also owned a brewery) by the French Brasserie de Kronenbourg (Strasbourg) was of particular interest. The Skol brand enlarged its distribution area and plants were opened in Brazil and Yugoslavia.

Increasing interest in breweries was being shown by the tobacco manufacturing industry. Rothmans of Pall Mall (U.K.) gained control of Canadian Breweries (Canada's biggest brewery), in which Philip Morris (U.S.) had also shown interest. The West German tobacco firm Reemtsma, which already had a large share in the Henniger group, bought large holdings in Dortmunder Union-Brauerei (West Germany's largest producer) and in Hannen Brauerei. The most important national merger was that of the Dutch breweries Heineken and Amstel, which between them supplied almost 60% of the Netherlands' beer production.

Research continued into the use of enzyme preparations, with unmalted instead of malted grain, and favourable reports on this method were received. The use of hop extracts instead of natural hops had greatly increased. "Pre-isomerized" extracts could also be added after fermentation, a process that reduced the consumption of hops. In the U.K., demand for hops, which had been falling sharply, rose in 1969 and the best hop crop in ten years was forecast. The continuous fermentation method, however, aroused less interest than the possibilities of extensive automation of traditional brewing processes. An example of advanced automation was the Whitbread Brewery in Luton (U.K.), opened in 1969.

The quantity and variety of throwaway packs for beer grew considerably. Already beer was being sold in bottles of hard polyvinyl chloride (PVC). The development of these lighter bottles stimulated the manufacturers of glass bottles to produce lighter, stronger no-return glass bottles. Research continued on still lighter bottles of special glass coated with a very thin film of plastic to make them less easily breakable. Attempts were also being made to alter the nature of the glass itself so that the fragments of throwaway bottles would decompose and serve to enrich the soil. The lightest no-return containers on the market were the Swedish Rigello bottle, a paper-plastic combination weighing about 20 g., and seamless spun aluminum cans weighing about 24 g. (T. Sc.)

Spirits. With some exceptions, world consumption of spirits in 1969 continued its upward trend. However, increased duties and the further imposition of nontariff barriers to imports, particularly by the less prosperous nations, multiplied, and there was an increasing tendency toward virtual state monopoly in African and South American countries. In Eastern European countries, increasing demand for spirits was countered by repressive government measures, principally higher duties. Drunken driving caused concern everywhere and severe legislation was adopted by some countries.

Any serious attempt to cut back spirits consumption was unlikely because so much revenue was derived from duties. In the U.K., revenue annually amounted to about £750 million (spirits about £300 million). Because of further duty increases in 1968, spirits consumption in the U.K. declined in volume by about 5%; almost 90% of the bottle store price represented duty. Export shipments of Scotch whiskey during 1968 rose from 43.1 million proof gallons to 59.2 million. British gin exports also increased, from 4,140,000 proof gallons in 1967 to 5,060,000 in 1968. Many British brand owners, however, had distilleries overseas or had licensed local distillers, so that exports alone did not show a true picture.

New regulations regarding labeling and description were under discussion in the U.S., while in the U.K. a new definition of whiskies, Scotch, Irish, and others, was contained in the Finance Act of 1969. Little progress was made toward the completion of internationally acceptable definitions of different types of spirits by the EEC or the Council of Europe. Further progress was made, however, in the production of potable spirits from industrial bases.

Statistics showed that the highest consumption of spirits per head was in Poland, 5–6 bottles per annum, but, taking all alcoholic beverages into account, France was the top consumer with the U.K. 19th and the U.S. 20th. (J. W. Ma.)

Apparent consumption of distilled spirits in the U.S. in 1968 reached a record high of 345 million gal., 6.4% above 1967. Per capita consumption rose 5.5% to 1.73 gal. Consumption per drinker remained at 3.8 gal. Prohibition was eliminated in 89 areas in 17 U.S. states by local option.

Consumer expenditure for alcoholic beverages for 1968 was $19.7 billion, compared with $18.3 billion in 1967. The U.S. federal excise tax on spirits remained at $10.50 per proof gallon. Federal excise taxes on alcoholic beverages totaled $4,319,536,000 in 1968, or 28.6% of all excise taxes collected; 74.3% of the beverage tax was accounted for by distilled spirits. State and local government revenues from distilled spirits taxes were estimated at $1,320,000,000. During fiscal 1969, U.S. agents seized 4,362 stills producing illicit spirits—1,537 less than in 1968—and 1,964,972 gal. of mash.

A total of 985,641,278 gal. of distilled spirits, including industrial alcohol, were produced in the U.S.

Technicians examine the central control panel of the new Whitbread Brewery, Europe's largest fully automated brewery, in Luton, Eng. Beginning full production in 1969, it was capable of brewing 1,250,000 bbl. a year.

SPORT & GENERAL FROM PICTORIAL PARADE

in fiscal 1969, 8.9% more than in 1968. Whiskey production was up 9.8% to 179,943,428 tax gallons; the increase included 50,795,895 tax gallons of light whiskey distilled at higher than 160 proof, first authorized for production on Jan. 26, 1968. Brandy increased 8.3% to 16,687,227 tax gallons; and rum increased 0.8% to 1,013,839 tax gallons. Total bottlings rose 5.4% to 303,976,850 gal. Vodka exceeded gin bottlings by 27.6%, and production of bottled cocktails continued to rise. Bourbon was the largest selling whiskey in the U.S. and, by virtue of this fact, in the world. Production of bourbon whiskey for fiscal 1968 reached a ten-year high of 126,507,531 gal., an increase of 10.5 million gal. over 1967.

Total imports of spirits into the U.S., at 82,246,000 tax gallons, were up 10.4% in 1968; their value was $454 million, or 78% of alcoholic beverage imports. The percentage of bulk to total whiskey rose from 26.6 to 28.4% for Canadian whiskey and from 24.9 to 26.4% for Scotch. Rum, primarily imported from Puerto Rico and the Virgin Islands, increased 7.9%. Tequila imports rose 20.1% to 698,720 gal. in 1968, and that quantity was equaled during the first nine months of 1969. Total U.S. distilled spirits exports rose 40% to 3,206,862 gal. in 1968; whiskey exports, at 2,023,193 gal., increased 20.2%.

In Canada public revenue from alcoholic beverage taxes rose 10.2% to Can$787,713,000 in fiscal 1968. Consumption of spirits was up 7.9% to 22,946,000 imperial gals. Production rose 13.4% to 70,738,000 imperial tax gallons, imports fell 2%, and exports increased 26%. (JU. W.)

Wine. In 1969 the harvest was smaller than that in the previous year in France and Italy, but it increased in Spain, Austria, and Portugal. Given the importance of the first two countries, it was estimated that wine production as a whole showed a slight decrease in comparison with 1968, when production had reached 278,830,000 hl. Quality varied: it was excellent in Sicily, Spain, in France in the Loire Valley,

Table I. Estimated Consumption of Beer in Selected Countries

In litres* per capita of total population

Country	1964	1965	1966	1967
Belgium†	140.0	140.0	140.0	140.0
Czechoslovakia	124.7	130.0	132.1	129.3
Germany, West	122.3	122.0	125.8	127.2
Luxembourg	130.8	125.7	128.7	121.4
Australia‡	106.8	109.1	113.7	116.8
New Zealand	101.8	103.7	107.3	109.9
Austria	89.9	92.1	98.8	102.6
United Kingdom	89.6	91.5	90.4	93.2
Denmark	83.7	78.5	88.7	91.5
Germany, East	80.3	80.6	81.7	84.5
Switzerland	79.3	74.0	74.8	76.3
Canada§	67.5	67.7	67.7	69.5
Ireland	62.2	66.3	61.7	63.5
United States‡	60.2	60.2	62.1	63.2
Hungary	42.5	44.2	46.4	49.9
Sweden	40.4	40.4	43.3	45.4
Netherlands‖	35.0	37.2	39.0	44.2
France	40.7	39.2	40.4	40.8
Colombia	48.6	37.0	...	38.0
Venezuela	31.0	32.0	...	35.0
Norway	26.5	27.8	28.8	30.0
Finland	24.5	25.1	27.8	29.9
Spain	21.6	23.4	26.4	28.4
Poland	23.9	24.0	25.6	27.7
Mexico	26.3	30.0	...	25.0

*One litre = 1.0567 U.S. quarts = 0.8799 imperial quart.
†Including so-called "household beer."
‡Years ending June 30.
§Years ending March 31.
‖Excluding ships' supplies.

Table II. Estimated Consumption of Potable Distilled Spirits in Selected Countries

In litres* of 100% pure spirit per capita of population

Country	1964	1965	1966	1967
Poland	2.40	2.60	2.80	3.00
Sweden	2.60	2.70	2.65	2.70
United States†	2.36	2.47	2.55	2.67
Yugoslavia	...	2.60	2.80	2.60
France‡	...	...	1.60	2.50
Spain	2.10	2.50	3.21	2.30
Germany, West	2.40	2.72	2.35	2.23
Canada§‖	1.71	1.79	2.03	2.16
Germany, East	1.80	1.90	2.09	2.10
Austria	2.00	2.20	2.00	2.00
Hungary	1.90	1.50	1.75	1.85
Switzerland	...	1.80	...	1.84
Ireland	1.37	1.76	1.66	1.79
Romania	1.50	1.67	...	1.73
Italy	1.50	1.48	1.60	1.70
Netherlands	1.48	1.89	1.44	1.63
Norway	1.29	1.33	1.36	1.42
Finland	1.30	1.40	1.40	1.40
Czechoslovakia	0.96	1.08	1.24	1.32
New Zealand	1.17	1.22	1.22	1.12
South Africa¶	1.00	1.11	1.14	1.11
Belgium	0.93	1.12	0.95	0.96
United Kingdom	0.90	0.83	0.84	0.84
Australia†	0.78	0.90	0.78	0.78

†Years ending June 30.
‡Including alcohol-based aperitifs but excluding liqueur wines.
§Years ending March 31.
‖Reported annual consumption for the years 1961–63.
¶Consumption per capita of whole population, irrespective of colour.

Table III. Estimated Consumption of Wine in Selected Countries

In litres* per capita of total population

Country	1964	1965	1966	1967
France†	124.0	121.1	119.0	120.0
Italy	105.4	111.0	117.0	113.0
Portugal	104.0	108.6	114.5	95.3
Argentina	87.2	85.1	80.2	80.2
Spain	62.8	57.6	68.0	68.0
Chile	54.0	42.4	...	50.0
Switzerland‡	41.0	38.3	39.1	39.1
Greece	37.9	39.2	38.7	38.0
Hungary	34.3	32.8	30.1	34.2
Luxembourg	40.6	30.1	34.9	33.8
Austria	26.0	29.8	30.0	31.9
Romania§	...	29.0	...	29.0
Uruguay	...	25.0	...	26.0
Yugoslavia	25.0	24.8	25.0	25.0
Buglaria	16.7	17.6	20.0	20.0
Czechoslovakia	12.3	11.9	17.1	18.6
Germany, West	18.0	16.8	17.4	15.7
Belgium	9.2	11.2	9.7	10.6
South Africa	9.1	8.7	8.4	9.2
Cyprus	...	12.0	12.0	8.0
U.S.S.R.	5.6	5.8	6.0	7.0
Australia	5.5	6.1	6.8‖	6.8
Sweden	4.2	4.3	4.6	5.0
Poland	4.9	4.8	4.5	4.7
Netherlands	...	...	3.5	4.1

†Excluding cider (23.3 litres per capita in 1963).
‡Excluding cider (11.8 litres per capita annually, 1961–63).
§Estimates based on production of wine.
‖Year ending June 30, 1967.

Source: Produktschap voor Gedistilleerde Dranken, *Hoeveel Alcoholhoudende Dranken Worden er in de Wereld Gedronken?*

Gironde, and Alsace, in Germany in the region of Baden, in Switzerland in the Valais, in Austria, and in Dalmatia; it was average (that is, better than 1968 but inferior to 1967) in central Italy, in southern France (the Midi) and in the Rhône Valley, and in the German Rhinelands.

In France there was a marked decrease in 1969 in production, which fell to 56,637,000 hl. from 65,-170,000 hl. in 1968. The outstanding cause of this decrease was the September rain, which forced wine-growers to bring in the harvest early, particularly in southern France (the Midi). In the Bordeaux region, the red wines had colour and texture, but production was between 30% and 40% less than usual, while white wines were 20% less. In Burgundy, the warm days at the end of September induced a fall in acidity and an increase in sugar content, so that the 1969 vintage was comparable to that of 1964. In the Beaujolais region, harvests were brought in in fine weather, so that the wine was of good quality; nevertheless, it did not produce an outstanding vintage. Quantity was about 20% less than in the previous year. In the Rhône Valley, the vintage was very satisfactory from the point of view of quality, though production was only a little more than half that of a normal year's harvest. In Alsace and in the Champagne country quality was also very good.

The Italian harvest in 1969 was of average size (65 million hl.). Wines of low alcoholic content were better than in the year before, and, generally speaking, the quality of all wines was improved. Alcoholic content rose in comparison with 1968 in Piedmont, Venezia, and Trentino, but it fell in Emilia-Romagna and in central and southern Italy.

According to figures provided by the Statistical Service of the General Technical Secretariat, the Spanish harvest was in the region of 26 million hl., or 1.5 million hl. greater than in the preceding year. This increase was particularly evident in western Andalusia (an increase of 26%) and in the Mancha (an increase of 15%). However, alcoholic contents produced were, on the whole, lower than in the previous year. (R. PN.)

The 1969 vintage in the U.S. was expected to produce wines of generally good quality, with a number of wines warranting a rating of excellent. In parts of the Midwest, the grape crop was disappointingly small, but in California, where almost 80% of U.S. wines were produced, grapes reached excellent maturity, holding a promise of top quality for many varieties. In upstate New York, the second major wine area, the harvest provided enough grapes to indicate production of almost 20 million gal. of wine.

The California crush, totaling 1.9 million tons, was the second largest on record. A heavy production of table wine was clearly indicated by the consumption data of U.S. wines for fiscal 1969. Table wine sales reached 94 million gal., a 15% advance over the previous year, and set a new record for the 17th year in a row. Consumption of sparkling wine was 11.3 million gal., a new high for the 11th straight year. For the "special natural wines," those with dramatic brand names, consumption reached a new high of 17.4 million gal. Only sales of traditional dessert wines (port, sherry, etc.) fell. Total sales of U.S. wines topped the 200 million gal. mark for the first time.

Particularly noteworthy in regards to the 1969 vintage in the U.S. was the spread of mechanical harvesting of grapes. Field crushing was added to the mechanical harvesting pattern. (I. H. M.)

Algeria

A republic on the north coast of Africa, Algeria is bounded by Morocco, Mauritania, Mali, Niger, Libya, and Tunisia. Area: 919,591 sq.mi. (2,381,743 sq.km.). Pop. (1968): 12,943,000. Cap. and largest city: Algiers (pop., 1966, 903,530). Language: Arabic, Berber, French. Religion: Muslim. President in 1969, Col. Houari Boumédienne.

The Algerian government declared 1969 the "year of industry." Of a capital investment budget of nearly $1.3 billion, 56% was devoted to industry. A series of major contracts were signed, mostly with Western concerns, and the first production of cast iron, at the El Hadjar complex in eastern Algeria, coincided with the fourth anniversary of President Boumédienne's regime. Cast iron was to be exported until a Soviet-equipped steel division became fully operational. The initial yearly output of steel was planned to be 400,-000 tons, and it was expected that this would be increased threefold later.

The year's most spectacular contract was signed with the U.S.-owned company El Paso Natural Gas. The company agreed to purchase 10 billion cu.m. of Saharan natural gas annually for 25 years. The first shipments were expected to reach the east coast of the U.S. in 1973.

French, West German, Italian, Japanese, and British firms were awarded contracts for the construction of industrial plants, often financed with loans and export credits, which were to be completed during the country's first four-year development plan, starting in 1970. Meanwhile, efforts to diversify trade suppliers and outlets continued. France, however, remained the main trading partner, accounting for more than 50% of the exchanges.

Along with a consistently favourable trade balance, Algeria had foreign reserves standing at $440 million at the end of February. These, as well as its determination to demonstrate independence, explained why Algeria did not follow suit when the French franc was devalued in August.

Algeria's adherence to the Organization of Petroleum Exporting Countries (OPEC), in July, was expected to reinforce its determination to be represented at all stages of the oil and gas industry, from prospecting to marketing, and to have a major bearing on the revision of the Franco-Algerian state agreements of 1965. Oil and gas revenues were estimated in the 1969 budget at $250 million, a 25% increase as compared with the previous year, when 43 million tons of crude oil were produced.

With the departure from office of French Pres. Charles de Gaulle, Algeria lost an ally who had often given way to its demands. The contact with French authorities was renewed in October when the French foreign minister, Maurice Schumann, returned the visit paid to Paris by his Algerian counterpart, Abdelaziz Bouteflika, 15 months earlier. In the meantime, however, Algeria was reported to have ordered military aircraft from France, thus breaking a Soviet monopoly.

Relations with the Soviet Union continued to develop in the economic and trade fields and were marked at the political level by a state visit paid by Soviet Pres. Nikolai V. Podgorny, one of four Eastern European leaders to be received in Algeria in 1969; the others were Todor Zhivkov of Bulgaria, Marian

Spychalski of Poland, and Marshal Tito of Yugoslavia.

Diplomatic relations broken over the Middle East issue, with the U.S. in June 1967 and with West Germany in May 1965, remained severed, while Algeria's full commitment to support the Palestinian commandos was demonstrated by the visits paid to Algiers by commando leader Yasir Arafat (*see* BIOGRAPHY) and the political and material aid provided to them.

Special emphasis was given to the improvement of relations with bordering North African countries—Morocco, Tunisia, and Libya. In January, President Boumédienne visited Morocco, where a 20-year renewable treaty of cooperation was signed. A similar treaty was signed with Libya before the monarch was overthrown there, but the Algerian president was the first foreign leader to set foot on Libyan soil after the republic was proclaimed, partly to express support to the new leaders and partly to check the influence on them of U.A.R. Pres. Gamal Abd-al-Nasser. Boumédienne spent a few hours in Bengasi on his return from Addis Ababa, Eth., where, as outgoing chairman, he had addressed the sixth summit conference of the 41-nation Organization of African Unity (OAU).

A few weeks earlier Algiers had played host to the OAU-sponsored first Pan-African Cultural Festival, attended by 31 countries and by liberation movements from 6 white-ruled territories.

A Revolutionary Court sitting in the western port of Oran sentenced to death a total of 12 men on conspiracy charges. They included former Chief of Staff Tahar Zbiri, who led an abortive rebellion in December 1967, and Belkacem Krim, a former vice-president of the pre-independence Algerian provisional government. Both men, exiled abroad, were sentenced in their absence.

Meanwhile, President Boumédienne continued encouraging the development of local government. Assemblies were elected in the country's 15 *willayas* (departments), where municipal councils had been installed two years earlier. These developments were to culminate in the election of a national assembly and a president of the republic. (F. DD.)

ALGERIA

Education. (1966–67) Primary, pupils 1,359,518, teachers 30,586; secondary, pupils 96,845, teachers 4,430; vocational, pupils 34,439, teachers 2,618; teacher training, students 4,052, teachers 255; higher (including 3 universities; 1969), students 10,681, teaching staff 816.

Finance. Monetary unit: dinar, with a par value of 4.94 dinars to U.S. $1 (11.85 dinars = £1 sterling). Budget (1968 est.) balanced at 3,539,000,000 dinars.

Foreign Trade. (1967) Imports 3,154,088,000 dinars; exports 3,571,805,000 dinars. Import sources: France 60%; U.S. 8%; U.S.S.R. 5%. Export destinations: France 59%; West Germany 13%; U.K. 6%. Main exports: crude oil 69%; wine 8%; petroleum products 7%.

Transport and Communications. Roads (1965) 35,541 km. Motor vehicles in use (1967): passenger 98,000; commercial (including buses) 80,200. Railways: (1966) 3,945 km.; traffic (1968) 857 million passenger-km., freight 1,232,000,000 net ton-km. Telephones (Dec. 1967) 148,905. Radio receivers (Dec. 1967) *c.* 700,000. Television receivers (Dec. 1966) *c.* 100,000.

Agriculture. Production (in 000; metric tons; 1968; 1967 in parentheses): wheat 1,920 (1,266); barley 534 (299); oats (1967) 32, (1966) 6; potatoes 210 (204); dates (1967) *c.* 140, (1966) 156; figs (1967) 44, (1966) 46; oranges (1967) 381, (1966) 382; tomatoes (1966) *c.* 100, (1965) 80; onions (1966) *c.* 68, (1965) 38; tobacco *c.* 13.6 (*c.* 13.4); olive oil *c.* 19 (*c.* 22); wine 1,005 (645). Livestock (in 000; Nov. 1965): goats *c.* 1,700; sheep (Nov. 1966) *c.* 6,000; cattle (Nov. 1967) 800; asses *c.* 248; mules *c.* 147; horses *c.* 117; camels *c.* 175.

Industry. Production (in 000; metric tons; 1968): crude oil 40,775; natural gas (cu.m.) 3,284,000; electricity (excluding most industrial production; kw-hr.) 1,305,000; iron ore (52% metal content) 3,012; phosphate rock (1967) 350.

Andorra

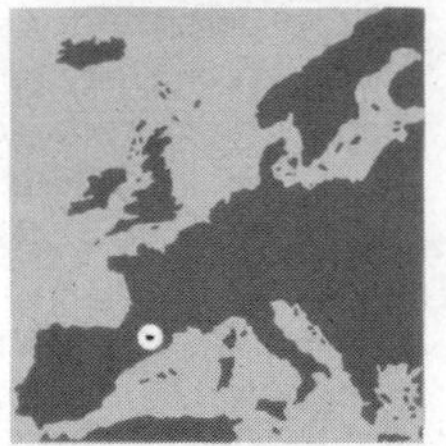

An autonomous principality of Europe, Andorra is in the Pyrenees Mountains between Spain and France. Area: 175 sq.mi. (453 sq.km.). Pop. (1969): 18,233. Cap.: Andorra la Vella (Catalan) or Andorra la Vieja (Spanish) (pop., 1969 parish census, 7,227). Language: chiefly Catalan. Religion: predominantly Roman Catholic. Co-princes: the president of the French Republic and the bishop of Urgel, Spain, represented by their *vegeurs* (provosts) and *batlles* (prosecutors). An elected Council General of 24 members elects the first syndic (*sindic procurador general de les valls d'Andorra*); in 1969, Francesc Escudé-Ferrero.

During 1969 the Council General passed legislation permitting an increase in the foreign capital in Andorran firms from the existing 33⅓% if this was deemed to be in the national interest. Military expenses continued to be budgeted at 300 pesetas ($5) annually for ammunition for ceremonial salutes.

Tourist facilities continued to expand. In 1969 there were 172 modern hotels and similar establishments, half of which remained in operation during the winter sports season. Tourism reached an annual total of 1.5 million visitor-days, and on one day in August over 16,000 foreign vehicles were registered at the frontiers. To control the great increase in traffic, the national police department was augmented to 20 men and a chief.

Tourism, agriculture, commerce, and cigarette manufacturing continued as the main sources of revenue, with the last-named attaining an annual production value of about $800,000. In addition, the French Postal Service granted to Andorra half of the revenues gained from stamps and services in the principality, to be spent on social services. The total alloted for the first year (1968) approximated $1 million.

Both co-princes changed in 1969. Charles de Gaulle was succeeded as president of France by Georges Pompidou, and Bishop Navarri of Urgel resigned. The bishop of Lérida (Spain) would serve as co-prince until the pope filled the vacancy of Urgel.

In December parish elections were held for half of the 24 general councillors, as well as for the first syndic and the subsyndic. (R. D. Ho.)

ANDORRA

Education. (1966–67) Primary (including preprimary), pupils 1,712, teachers 36; secondary, pupils 161, teachers 11.

Finance. Monetary units: French franc and Spanish peseta. No budget and taxes; public treasury is funded by small import, gasoline, and liquor levies and frontier tolls. Exchange and deposit banking is important.

Foreign Trade. (1968) Imports from France Fr. 104,832,000 (U.S. $21,234,000), from Spain, 659,866,726 pesetas (U.S. $10,846,000). Tourism (1967): visitors *c.* 1 million; hotels *c.* 160.

Communications. Radio receivers (Dec. 1967) 5,500. Television receivers (Dec. 1967) 1,400.

Agriculture and Industry. Production: cereals, potatoes, tobacco, wool; hydroelectric generation and export. Livestock (in 000; 1965): sheep *c.* 25; cattle *c.* 3; horses *c.* 1.

Antarctica

Ten nations occupied 34 stations in the Antarctic Treaty area and 7 stations on sub-Antarctic islands in the winter of 1969. At almost all stations synoptic observations were continued for the purpose of meteorology, ionospheric and auroral studies of the upper atmosphere, and geomagnetic and seismic studies of the earth.

In May representatives from Australia, France, the U.S., and the U.S.S.R. met in Paris to lay plans for the International Antarctic Glaciological Project (IAPG), to be carried out over the following decade in the relatively unexplored area of East Antarctica. The fifth Consultative Meeting of Antarctic Treaty Nations was held in Paris, Nov. 18–Dec. 2, 1968. Discussions were held on the issuance of a postage stamp commemorating the tenth anniversary of the signing of the treaty, conservation of marine mammals, telecommunications, and coordination with other governmental bodies with Antarctic interests.

For the second time in two years, volcanic eruptions and earthquakes forced the evacuation by helicopter of Argentinian, British, and Chilean personnel from their stations on Deception Island, near the north end of the Antarctic Peninsula. The British station, graveyard, and whaling station were heavily damaged by mudflows up to seven feet deep. The Chilean station was completely destroyed by a combination of ashfall, mudflow, and scoria five inches to several feet deep. Water vapour and hydrogen sulfide gas were present, and free sulfur was being deposited from numerous small fumaroles and vents. The ground temperature near the Chilean station fluctuated between 50° and 70° C. The Argentinian station was unharmed, but a thin coating of ash lay over it and the surrounding area.

Scientific Programs. According to the terms of the Antarctic Treaty, the continent is reserved for scientific purposes only. International collaboration of scientific programs is fostered by the Scientific Committee on Antarctic Research (SCAR) of the International Council of Scientific Unions (ICSU).

Argentina. The Argentines occupied eight stations in the Antarctic. A new airfield, suitable for use by C-130 Hercules transport aircraft, was tentatively sited on Seymour Island, Antarctic Peninsula. The icebreaker "General San Martin" again participated in the International Weddell Sea Oceanographic Expedition.

Australia. The new Casey Station about one mile across the bay from the old Wilkes Station was officially opened on Feb. 19, 1969. Because of unusually heavy sea ice, resupply of Casey Station was delayed for several weeks until mid-February. Eleven men wintered at Davis Station, on the Ingrid Christensen Coast, which was reopened in February after being closed since 1965. The station was provided with a background music system, and the effect of this music on the winter party would be evaluated as part of the research program. In the mountains of Victoria Land about 150 mi. W of Scott Base, two geologists discovered the well-preserved fossil jawbone of a crossopterygian fish, an ancient fish-reptile of 360 million years ago. The find lent further credence to the continental drift theory, which considers Antarctica as having once been a part of a supercontinent called Gondwanaland.

Belgium. Although Roi Baudouin Base was closed in 1967, the Belgians continued collaboration with the South Africans in the vicinity of Sanae Station. Eight Belgians, with two aircraft, supported the establishment of a South African winter station in the mountains south of Sanae.

Chile. Chile continued to operate the Arturo Prat and Bernardo O'Higgins stations in the Antarctic Peninsula region. Following the destruction of Pedro Aguirre Cerda Station on Deception Island in 1967, a new station was established on Fildes Peninsula, King George Island, near the Soviet Bellingshausen Station. It was visited by Pres. Eduardo Frei Montalva of Chile in February 1969, and the station thereafter bore his name. Also in February, helicopters from the Chilean supply ship "Piloto Pardo" successfully rescued all members of a team of British vulcanologists studying the effects of the eruptions on Deception Island.

France. French activities in the Antarctic continued to be centred at Dumont d'Urville in Terre Adélie. The sea ice conditions made access to the station by the relief ship "Thala Dan" difficult and assistance was required from the "Nella Dan." A teletype link was established between Dumont d'Urville, Mirny, McMurdo, and Kerguélen stations. In winter, academic courses were made available to the staff and contributed much to buoy the spirits of the personnel.

Japan. The outstanding field traverse of the year, under the leadership of Masayoshi Murayama of Japan's State Science Museum, was carried out by a party of 12 which left Syowa Station on Sept. 28, 1968. An accident with a mechanical ice drill required one member of the party to be returned to base. The South Pole was reached on December 19 via the U.S. Plateau Station by a route that provided valuable glaciologic data. The party returned to their station on February 15, having covered a total distance of 3,200 mi.

New Zealand. Eleven men spent the winter at Scott Base and five men, including one American exchange scientist, wintered at Vanda Station in Wright Dry Valley, 80 mi. from Scott Base. A radiotelephone link was established between Vanda and Scott. Six men on a four-vehicle tractor-train moved five tons of huts, fuel, and supplies from Scott to Vanda. Two of the vehicles broke through snowbridges covering hidden crevasses, but were eventually recovered. Large clouds of dust formed by the tractor-train impaired visibility and caused mechanical problems.

Norway. Norway, which did not maintain permanent stations, collaborated with other nations in the scientist-exchange program. A six-man expedition mapped and studied the geology of the Kraul Mountains in Queen Maud Land. Fossil plant leaves were found in geologic strata 150 to 200 million years in age, further supporting the continental drift theory.

South Africa. Fourteen South Africans and eight Belgians departed on the "R.S.A." in January on the second year of their joint expedition. Work was largely centred in the South African Sanae Station and the new winter field site on Borg Massif, about 248 mi. S of Sanae. Meteorological observations and other research were continued at Marion Island, Prince Edward Islands, and Gough Island.

United Kingdom. The British Antarctic Survey carried on research programs at eight stations on the continent, the Antarctic Peninsula, and islands in the Antarctic seas. A six-man party was airlifted to the Shackleton Range, where they conducted ground sur-

Alliance for Progress: *see* Inter-American Affairs
Aluminum: *see* Mining
American Literature: *see* Literature
American Samoa: *see* Dependent States
Anesthesiology: *see* Medicine
Anglican Communion: *see* Religion
Angling: *see* Sporting Record
Angola: *see* Dependent States
Anguilla: *see* Dependent States
Anniversaries: *see* Calendar, 1970, page 50

veys for 40 days in an area encompassing 3,000 sq.mi. A new twin-engine Otter aircraft, with five men aboard, was forced by low fuel and bad weather to land on the Larsen Ice Shelf on the east coast of the Antarctic Peninsula. Helicopters from HMS "Endurance" delivered fuel to the downed aircraft, which returned safely to Adelaide Station. The Otter then flew on to evacuate the five men who had wintered at Fossil Bluff after their aircraft crashed in February 1968.

United States. Nearly 200 scientists and technicians representing 50 institutions participated in the season's fieldwork. Plateau Station, the highest, coldest, and most isolated U.S. station in Antarctica, was closed, after operating since 1965. Attempts to drill into bedrock below the 7,098-ft. hole drilled through the ice at Byrd Station in 1968 were unsuccessful. The International Weddell Sea Oceanographic Expedition was supported by the icebreaker "Glacier." Because of severe ice conditions, the ships were unsuccessful in recovering the four current meter arrays emplaced by the 1968 expedition. The new research vessel "Hero" successfully completed its first season in support of scientists at and around Palmer Station in the Antarctic Peninsula. The "Eltanin" made six cruises in the South Pacific and South Indian oceans. For the first time, C-141 Starlifter jet aircraft made regular scheduled flights to Antarctica. A cargo of penguins, skuas, and seals was airlifted from McMurdo to research laboratories and zoos in the U.S. On November 29, in commemoration of the 40th anniversary of Adm. Richard Byrd's first Antarctic expedition, a U.S. Navy Hercules reenacted his historic first flight over the South Pole. Among the passengers was Laurence Gould, who had been his second in command. In December an Ohio State University team working in the Queen Alexandra Range reported a significant find of Triassic fossils that further substantiated the continental drift theory.

U.S.S.R. Research programs were continued at five Antarctic stations. Transfer of the headquarters of the Soviet expedition from Mirny to Molodezhnaya was carried on. A new addition to the Molodezhnaya base was a rocket launching ground built of steel, aluminum, plastic, and fibre glass and equipped with heated launching pads, enabling rockets to be fired at −40° C and in high winds. A number of M-100 meteorological rockets were launched to heights of 60 mi. In February Soviet scientists carried out a series of powerful explosions along a 250-mi. path in Queen Maud Land to facilitate study of the continent's interior geology. Using aqualungs, Soviet biologists studied marine life in Davis Sea near Mirny. They discovered a wealth of animal life that included sea sponges, starfish, and sea urchins.

Other Activities. In January, 112 tourists visited the Antarctic Peninsula aboard the Chilean naval ship "Aquiles." Air New Zealand applied for permission to initiate DC-8 tourist flights to and from Antarctica starting in 1971. Fourteen stations of six nations (Argentina, France, New Zealand, the U.K., the U.S.S.R., and the U.S.) were competing in the second annual Antarctic International Chess Competition. Moves were transmitted between stations by radio. In 5° F temperatures, New Zealanders won the first International Bicycle Race in Antarctica. U.S. and New Zealand cyclists competed over the hilly, snow-covered three-mile road separating Scott and McMurdo stations. (L. M. Gd.; J. A. He.)

See also Geography.

Anthropology

The flow of fossil material from the Olduvai Gorge excavations in Tanzania of L. S. B. Leakey and his associates continued in 1969. Potassium-argon dating techniques placed specimens well before the earliest previously established date for tool users of 1,750,000 years ago, but analysts differed on whether the newly found specimens were indeed hominid, or members of an undifferentiated hominid-anthropoid group of creatures. Nonetheless, heated discussion of the earliest stages of human social development continued.

Earlier searches of Pleistocene gravels in India by T. D. McCown (*see* Obituaries) had recovered large numbers of Paleolithic tools that must have been of comparable age to those of Olduvai but no fossils of the toolmakers accompanied them. Elwyn Simons and his associates at Yale, although not discovering any new fossil specimens, reevaluated a long-known Indian fossil skull, *Ramapithecus,* and placed it within the range of the hominid creatures that in an African context are termed australopithecines. From its geologic associations this skull was presumed to be much older than the African series and, if this were in fact the case, the whole question of an "African genesis" for man would be thrown open again.

The question of how hominid society evolved was also a major topic of concern. A highly controversial but headline-hitting theory was proposed by Lionel Tiger in *Men in Groups*. Tiger saw the crucial distinction between human and subhuman society as residing in the ability shown by human males to join together for activities that do not provide their own immediate rewards. Males and females may be held together by sexual bonds, which may prove satisfactory to both partners; females may be held together by affective or protective bonds, which again satisfy both partners. But human males distinctively join together for political, social, and economic interaction, and thus provide the potential for long-term planning and cooperation. The establishment of such male bonding, he argued, was crucial to the emergence of human society, and continued to provide the basis for male dominance in political and economic spheres.

The idea of social evolution as a progression of stages based on an underlying technology continued to

continued on page 102

Norwegian anthropologist Thor Heyerdahl's papyrus boat, the "Ra," crosses the Sahara Desert during the first phase of its attempted trip from Morocco to Mexico.

GAMMA—PIX FROM PUBLIX

THE PRIMITIVE TRIBES OF SOUTH AMERICA

By Conrad Gorinsky

In this time of spectacular technological feats and expansionist schemes, it is well to recall that there are still groups of humans isolated from our world, nomadic in a region that is home to them but synonymous with terror to most other human communities in the world. Such a region is Amazonas.

The plight of the South American Indian has recently received some publicity in the world press. Supplementing an already large and horrifying literature documenting past persecution and decimation, these recent reports, both official and academic, reveal that the grisly process unleashed on the Amerindians still threatens their tribal existence—where it survives. That they survive at all is largely the result of geographic remoteness, but they remain prey to Western man and his civilization and are being sought out and hunted from their last refuge in the jungles of Amazonas.

The need now is not for more documentation, but for action on behalf of the Amerindian, for realization that he is not a fossil or an anachronism to be removed in the name of progress. Here is cultural man, an authority on an environment as old as man himself, whose way of life has been the most successful and persistent adaptation man has ever achieved. Modern man, on the other hand, has yet to experience the cost of what his technology has inflicted.

Genocide. On March 14, 1968, a report was published by the Brazilian Ministry of the Interior, based on the findings of an inquiry team headed by Public Attorney Jáder Figueiredo Correia. Attempts were made to bribe the team, and 32 death threats were directed to them. The government admitted that genocide had been perpetrated within its frontiers. The report stated that thousands of Indians had been murdered and that these and other atrocities had been committed or condoned by members of the former Indian Protection Service (SPI). The SPI, founded in 1911 by Marshal Cândido Matiano da Silva Rondon, himself part Indian, was famous for its order of "Die if necessary, but never kill." Yet the head of the service was accused of 42 crimes, including collusion in several murders, the illegal sale of land, and embezzlement. Doubt was expressed whether as many as ten of the service's employees, out of a total of over a thousand, would be fully cleared of guilt.

Rich landowners had attacked and killed Indians, either directly or by hiring gunmen, often shooting them after making them drunk. Tribes were attacked from the air with dynamite or mown down by machine-gun fire. Others were deliberately infected with smallpox or given food poisoned with arsenic and formicides, after which rumours of epidemic outbreaks were started to lull suspicions. Vilma Chiara, curator of the Ethnology Museum in São Paulo, described how business enterprises wishing to sell land would fly the farmers over the areas and allow them to pick out plots. The seller promised to "scour" all the land that had been bought; well-armed men would go in on foot, silently encircle and then machine-gun all the inhabitants.

The view of a former Brazilian senior civil servant expresses the cynicism of those involved: "The Indians are of no interest, they are total savages, they have no law, no religion and live like animals. They even offer their women to anyone who passes by. Put yourself in the position of an official of SPI, living miles away in Amazonas, in miserable conditions, when all he has to do is to rub out a few of these people and he can be in Rio de Janeiro with fast cars, women, and luxury. You would do the same." When asked if there was anyone who cared for the Indians, he replied, "Absolutely no one."

Although the brutal acts in Brazil were clear enough, little could be expected in the way of redress. The inquiry committee has been threatened with a violent process of multiplication—12 new committees were being formed to investigate its findings—indicating that yet another report was in danger of being shelved.

The concept of the SPI, a body unique in South America, arose from Rondon's realization that integration spelled death for the Amerindians; its failure is a tragedy that bodes ill for them. It has been claimed, for example, that Peruvians and Colombians have hunted for Ticuna Indians along the Brazilian rivers. In 1968 some publicity was given to a case of extermination of the Cuiaba Indians, carried out by Colombians and Venezuelans in the frontier region. One of those arrested, Anselmo Nieves Aguirre, cynically confessed to having killed 32 Indians since 1960. Another accomplice remarked, "The Indians are different from the whites, but similar to monkeys." The real reasons for the collective homicide are still obscure and justice has again been slow. However, the effect is familiar: panic was caused among the tribes of a region, forcing them to flee and leave the land open for speculators.

In Peru, on March 18, 1964, some small villages inhabited by Indians of the Cocama tribe were attacked from the air with machine guns, antipersonnel bombs, and napalm. The official version claimed that the operation was in response to an Indian attack on a scientific research expedition. Yet there was no scientist in the expedition, which was in fact on a punitive raid. Other charges were laid against the Indians—that they were smugglers, ferocious opium addicts, Communists, and kidnappers—in order to justify attacks by government forces.

Much more has been suppressed in these and other areas. The process continues, but at an accelerated pace, so that some of these tribes will probably not survive more than a decade. Most tribes, including those that have withdrawn from encroaching civilization—*e.g.*, the Yabarana—are now completely surrounded in relatively small areas and are about to be overrun.

Amerindians are frequently the victims of traditionally unstable South American politics. They are used as scapegoats for ready-made crises or as an easy source of reward, either in terms of the lands they occupy or in the use of the Indians themselves. Paradoxically, on the one hand they are regarded as nonhuman while on the other their labour and their women are sought out.

The Rupununi Indians. On Jan. 2, 1969, an armed uprising, involving some Amerindians, occurred in Guyana (formerly British Guiana). The official death toll was given as seven, including five policemen, but the unofficial count was much higher; the British seconded officer who led the Guyanese Defence Force to quell the uprising admitted that "there has been a great deal of terror." This tragedy contains all the ominous implications for the fate of South American Indians. Guyana as a whole can be regarded as a microcosm of all the factors that are involved.

The Macushi are one of the tribes living in the disputed area along the frontier of Venezuela and Guyana. This tribe is in a particularly vulnerable position because the national boundaries of Brazil, Venezuela, and Guyana cut across their traditional transit areas through the Pacaraima Mountains in the Guyana Shield. According to the 1946 census, there were 1,676 Macushi Indians living in the northern areas of the Rupununi savannas and 2,200 Wapishana Indians in the southern parts. The combined population is given as about 9,000 today. It should be noted that the population was a static 4,000 prior to the advent of DC-3 aircraft, which introduced many new settlers into the area, largely for administrative purposes. The main source of income for the Macushi is the collection of balata (latex), but recently they have accumulated considerable herds of cattle. Income is also derived from the sale of corn, tobacco, and other minor products. The work is seasonal and fits in well with their temperament and economy, for they can work as little or as much as they like and still have time for hunting and field-making in the nearby forest.

These occupations obviously conflict with conventional educational programs and modern organizational requirements. Young Amerindians of the Rupununi savannas are in the precarious position of having been subjected in one generation to a sudden transition from a primitive, self-sufficient tribal society to an aimless, nonproductive, half-educated one. They are schooled at a primary level, and at the expense of their traditional knowledge of self-support gained by experience in the field. These two factors serve to breed frustration in the first instance and starvation in the second. This situation is aggravated by the rise in the number of children, who form the only educated class. This rise is not entirely due to increased medical benefits, for the Amerindians are largely without medical help. Nor is it due to an increased food supply—the savannas have deteriorated rapidly as a result of erosion, caused by the growing frequency of savanna fires; the supply of game is depleted by the greater use of firearms. In addition to these problems the supply of fish has declined with the ecological changes caused by the rise in population density.

Race Relations. Furthermore, the inferior education they have received does not fit the Rupununi Indians for competition with their counterparts on the coast. The net result is that these people have been shown the signs of better things but denied the means of getting them, and this leaves them with no choice but to return to their fields, ill equipped and with a sense of degradation and betrayal. Opportunities for a secondary education are virtually nonexistent. The Amerindians also harbour suspicion of the coastal peoples dating from the past, as noted by the 19th-century explorer Sir Robert Schomburgk: "Mixtures of Indians and Negroes are very rare, the former generally regarding the latter with supreme contempt, even hating them like hereditary enemies." This attitude of the Amerindians toward Africans and later toward East Indians contrasts with the favour shown to Europeans. From early times the Amerindians in Guyana were not enslaved and were treated as equals by Europeans, and they grew accustomed to that special treatment. When their political usefulness ended, a new relationship was formed with the missionaries—again European—who took it as their duty to protect them. The Amerindian thus became conditioned to patronage and handouts, but now he is abandoned in the storm of the developing, independent country.

Respect for the European even took religious forms. In 1845 an Akawaio *piaiman* (witchdoctor) named Awacaipu called a meeting of followers and informed them of the approach of the millennium. When it failed to appear, he told them that only by killing themselves could they be resurrected as white people. About 400 perished before Awacaipu himself was killed. Later, about 1870, a Macushi prophet named Bichiwong claimed to have visited England where he saw God in a dream. There he was given a piece of paper, the front page of the Bible, that had been hidden by the white people and that would give power to the Amerindian. He began the Hallelujah cult, which was taken up by the Arekuna, Patamona, and Akawaio tribes. The Macushi are a mystical people, but they also possess considerable material knowledge. Charles Waterton, Schomburgk, and others visited the Rupununi to collect information about the famed Macushi curare—a preparation that has captured the attention of scientists to the present day, although no comprehensive work on the use of plants by the Macushi or any other tribe has been attempted.

Cultural Invasion. Following the 1969 uprising, some Macushi Indians await trial for murder and treason, unable to afford the estimated U.S. $25,000 required for their defense. The Rupununi tribes feel betrayed, for a number of people trusted by them have been refused access to the area, including Peter D'Aguiar whose minority United Force party championed the Amerindian cause.

An editorial in the newspaper of the ruling party stated:

> Many Guyanese are beginning to recognize the significance of the brainwashing involved in having our Amerindian people singled out for peculiar attention and described as "The Gentle People" or "Children of the Forest" or allied terms of patronage. If the problem is seen mainly as one of isolation, then the needs of the situation become a little clearer—the need for urgent lines of communication with the rest of Guyana; the need to populate the area, to start with the already existing basis for industry—the cattle, the nuts—and to move on from there to build up a complex of industrial units drawing power from Tiboku; to develop in an atmosphere that will completely push aside the centuries old tradition of a special kind of attitude to Rupununi, to the Amerindians, to the "Bush."

Population Control. The Tiboku scheme is a smaller version of the Hudson Institute's proposition to dam the Amazon, which —coupled with the Pan-American Highway and allied projects— has doomed the Amerindian. His fault rests with his success in

Using primitive boat and weapons, a Kamayura Indian of Brazil hunts for food. Many primitive tribes of South America survive only because of their geographic isolation.

"THE TIMES," LONDON

maintaining a characteristically stable and happy society. In 1884 Everard F. Im Thurn estimated the number of Macushis at 1,500, compared with the 1946 census figure of 1,676. The almost static population figures indicate a regulation that is not characteristic of the society that threatens the Amerindians. The irony is that the Tiboku scheme is to be financed by the World Bank, whose president, Robert McNamara, has called for a curb on human population. As yet nothing is known about how these Amerindians have managed to stabilize their societies and why, when their cultures are invaded, there is a population increase, even though diseases such as measles and tuberculosis are simultaneously introduced.

The Lessons for Modern Civilization. The Amerindians can be seen as representing the backstop of humanity which, if removed, will expose mankind to its greatest peril—that of uncontrolled growth. Modern political systems demand increased population densities to control the forums of power, which in turn are used to justify the multiplication of industrial complexes. This supplies a market for Western expertise and satisfies the expansionist needs of developing nations. However, a glance at the population growth curve should make it obvious that there must be a limit.

The future of modern civilization depends on research, but the directions that research takes are dictated by technological needs—a preoccupation that holds great dangers for the survival of man, for if he destroys his environment he destroys himself. Also characteristic of Western culture is its increasing withdrawal from biological awareness and its overpreoccupation with developing and refining a limited number of biotypes, rather than safeguarding the diversity of life forms available and ascertaining their value and extent.

The South American Indian is an undisputed authority on his environment. Some Amerindians are nomadic in an area with the richest botanical speciation in the world. It should be remembered that man is totally dependent on plants for his food and for the air he breathes, and the forested areas of the world are thus particularly important. The Amerindian has already given much of his knowledge to the world, and he should be repaid at least by recognition of this fact.

It should be possible to impress upon the nations that are these peoples' custodians, and upon international opinion as a whole, that primitive peoples have value per se, both now and in the long term, and that there is urgent need to protect their cultures as a legacy for the future. This is a major consideration, for to accept the case that cultural plurality is essential to the survival of man is to go against prevailing opinion. We assume that what is good for one will be good for another. With our political and economic systems now geared to open-ended expansion and global exposure, the converse could also apply—that what is bad for one is equally bad for another. Any mistake made by a standardized global culture at an environmental or genetic level will of necessity affect all of society that is exposed to that influence.

If we are to help the Amerindians, and in turn to learn from them, there is a need, in the first instance, for self-education in the art of communication with a culture that is totally different from our own. An understanding of the Amerindian leads to a better understanding of ourselves. Without communication there is, of course, no sharing of experience, and the absence of this leads to the ignorant tendency to equate "primitive" with "savage." There is a much larger element of fear in the white—and black—man's dealings with primitive peoples than he is prepared to acknowledge: a fear of the unknown, of people who, while obviously human, live in a totally strange world where the distinctions between spiritual and material are unknown, a world whose assumptions and motivations we can scarcely understand.

The areas where Amerindians live could be safeguarded and administered without impeding the progress of the countries involved. There the Amerindian could assimilate those elements of Western culture that are compatible with his own and be free to reject those that are not. Special educational programs could be implemented by national institutes for Amerindian affairs, which would benefit the Amerindian, the nation, and the world at large. For example, given training in such fields as ethnobotany, Amerindians could contribute their expertise to the UNESCO "Man and the Biosphere" program by responsibly exploring and documenting the potential of their environment. Again, the importance to humanity of such information as the long-term effects of drugs used by the Amerindians is inestimable. It is our responsibility to display the depth of understanding that appreciates the value of a reciprocal exchange of knowledge.

An Amerindian Commission? The Amerindian requires a special relationship with international sympathy. To this end, a Commission of Amerindian Affairs, based at the United Nations, should be established. It should hold regular meetings of representatives of the member states on integrated policies to safeguard Amerindian interests, which often spread across national frontiers. New groups such as the International Work Group for Indigenous Affairs and the Primitive Peoples Fund, and more established organizations such as the International Congress of Americanists, the International Union of Anthropological and Ethnological Sciences, and the American Anthropological Association, should be able to set up such a commission and expedite its acceptance by the United Nations.

The Primitive Peoples Fund, formed in March 1969 and launched officially in October, sees South America—and particularly Amazonas—as a priority area. It wishes to act quickly and effectively, but recognizes the dangers of doing so too hastily. Thus, the fund intends first of all to finance and organize research to establish not only which tribes are in most urgent need of help, but how best to help them so that their own wishes are respected. It hopes to send out its own observers and also to set up grants to encourage other anthropologists and scientists, working in related fields, to study endangered tribes and the ways in which they can adapt without compromising their culture or dignity.

Because the very survival of the Amerindian is in jeopardy, a medical service is essential, and this is the best form of aid that can be supplied in the short term. The Amerindians have no immunity to such diseases as measles, influenza, tuberculosis, and smallpox, and there are a number of uncontacted tribes who run the risk of decimation by introduced viral infections. Priority should be given to this, since the immediate objective is to keep the tribes alive following the trauma of initial contact with the overwhelming culture. Government agencies have been unable to meet this need.

It is also vitally important to establish and safeguard the Amerindians' rights to their lands. The fund will form a panel of lawyers, anthropologists, and administrators to draft a legal code setting down the rights of all primitive peoples, and it is hoped that this will be ratified by the United Nations.

However, no action of permanent value can be taken in a vacuum. Indeed, in many cases it might be difficult for the fund to act effectively at all, unless the climate of opinion is changed. It hopes, therefore, to form influential lobbies to press for changes in the law where primitive peoples have few or no rights, and to ensure that what benign laws there are, are upheld.

Details of the Amerindian situation must be open to investigation. The recent refusal of the Guyana government to allow a medical investigation by international organizations, such as the International Red Cross, following reports of an influenza epidemic is an indication of the lack of moral pressure. Agencies are only admitted on invitation by a government, and action is usually prevented on the ground that it would involve interference in the country's internal affairs. Furthermore, since the Amerindian has no lobby at the UN, or within his own country, any possible action on his behalf is dismissed as representing a minority interest by comparison with other, more pressing demands. But if there are to be any Amerindian survivors, the need to arrest the accelerating process of devastation is urgent.

continued from page 98
concern many anthropologists. Controversy over Marvin Harris' work *The Rise of Anthropological Theory,* which rejected as valueless those parts of anthropology that are neither historical nor indicative of an interest in productive technology, provoked a major discussion in the international journal *Current Anthropology*. Julian Steward, in a development of his earlier ideas of how various "levels of sociocultural integration" exist within single nation-states and produce convergences of multilineal evolutionary paths, edited a three-volume collection of studies by his former students or co-workers entitled *Contemporary Change in Traditional Societies.* A supranational "world industrial culture" was seen as effecting a "modernizing" convergence throughout the world.

On a less abstract level, however, interest in ecological studies was sparked by the work of Roy A. Rappaport and his book *Pigs for the Ancestors.* In a thorough quantitative study he showed how, in an agricultural area of New Guinea, local populations of people and pigs vary from group to group and in cycles over time. Crucial points in these cycles followed the performance of rituals for the ancestors. He argued that rituals were ecological regulating mechanisms. Their performance by one group signaled to other groups that the performers had reached certain points in the population cycles. By performing the ceremonies, and slaughtering most pigs, pig overpopulation was corrected and the cycle restarted.

The rising concern of anthropologists with the ways in which humans plan and make decisions was reflected in F. G. Bailey's *Stratagems and Spoils.* Politics can be looked at as a game, in which people compete for valued "prizes" within a framework of publicly acknowledged "normative rules" and utilize a body of private wisdom, formulated as a series of "pragmatic rules." Bailey applied his analytical scheme to British politics during World War I, to French politics after World War II, and to politics among Pathans, and in the Indian state of Orissa. In all cases contestants recruit supporters; "confront" each other with messages about the size of their "teams," and periodically meet in "encounters" where the relative strength of the teams is measured.

Game Theory in the Behavioral Sciences, edited by I. Buchler and H. Nutini, tried to relate complex behaviours to the simple mathematical formulations that describe the strategies of such games as "Chicken." In "Chicken" both players suffer severely if both choose the same collision course, and both suffer slightly if both choose to be "chicken"; yet if one player preempts and carries straight on, he wins, while the one who is "chicken" loses, though not as much as if both had kept on collision course.

Yet a psychologist's (A. Rapoport) study of people actually playing such a game with varying levels of reward and punishment showed that they behave almost, but not exactly, as formal mathematical analysis suggests they rationally should. But difficulties in quantifying the environmental parameters—the rewards and chances involved—usually made a mathematical analysis impracticable. The mathematical games, however, provided formal models in terms of which actual behaviour could be understood.

The giant of European anthropology, Claude Lévi-Strauss, also continued his search for the rules of human thought. Further volumes appeared in his series *Mythologiques.* But while his method was gaining new adherents by its erudition and logical rigour, the first serious criticisms began emerging, notably in a review of the second volume in the *American Anthropologist.* Although the identification of pairs of opposed myth motifs was always possible, and following the "transformations" of each motif into another motif yielded interesting combinations of subsequent oppositions, the review argued, by what criterion can one identify what is a "transformation"?

In professional affairs the most notable retirement from official position, though not from activity, was that of Margaret Mead, from the curatorship at the American Museum of Natural History. The issue of the professional ethics of studying "other peoples" continued to concern anthropologists everywhere. When a previously unknown group of Indians was encountered in Surinam many anthropologists rushed to preserve them from change so that they could be studied; others argued that treating them as museum specimens was completely unethical. (R. F. SA.)

See also Archaeology.

ENCYCLOPÆDIA BRITANNICA FILMS. *Remnants of a Race* (1955); *American Indians of Today* (1957); *Indian Family of Long Ago* (1957); *Indians of Early America* (1957); *Eskimo Family* (1959); *Cave Dwellers of the Old Stone Age* (1960); *Eskimo in Life and Legend (The Living Stone)* (1960); *Prehistoric Man in Northern Europe* (1961); *The Egyptologists* (1967).

The "Ra" sails for Mexico. Thor Heyerdahl patterned the vessel after ancient Egyptian drawings and sailed from Moroccan shores to prove that ancient Egyptians could have discovered the New World. His theory was based on the close resemblance of the great Mexican pyramids to the Egyptian pyramids at Giza.

"PARIS MATCH" FROM PICTORIAL PARADE

Archaeology

Eastern Hemisphere. Unstable political conditions in 1969 tended to curtail field excavations in various Old World regions of traditional archaeological interest, and prospects for the following year did not look generally brighter. There was further concern, in countries with rich archaeological potential such as Italy, Greece, and Turkey, over the continued illicit looting of sites for objects for the antiquities market. In Turkey this even included a substantial theft from the Izmir Museum of Archaeology, and for a time it appeared that the national reaction might be a denial of excavation permits to legitimate foreign archaeologists. A possible further complication—at least as far as the United States was concerned—was retrenchment on the part of foundation sources of archaeological financing.

Pleistocene Prehistory. F. Clark Howell reported that very crude stone tools, fashioned from pebbles, had been identified in the so-called Omo beds in extreme southern Ethiopia. These strata contain the oldest known *Australopithecus* fossils, which are taken as evidence of man's immediate ancestor and approach four million years in age. H. de Lumley released details of a *c.* 300,000-year-old campsite in the French Riviera including the earliest known man-made shelter—a crude oval hut. In the nearby and slightly later cave site of Lazaret, which contained Acheulean flint tools, de Lumley also found evidence of hutlike lean-to structures built against the sides of the cave.

In a review article in *Science,* R. G. Klein, considering the various Mousterian industries of European Russia, noted further evidence of the apparently abrupt replacement of these Middle Paleolithic-

Neanderthal associated industries by industries of the Upper Paleolithic associated with modern-type men. The question of whether modern man and his characteristic Upper Paleolithic tools evolved over a broad front from many Neanderthal populations or in some one relatively restricted area remained unanswered. Near Santander, Spain, L. G. Freeman exposed two human burials of *c.* 30,000 years ago. One skeleton, an adult, was remarkably well preserved. A. W. Louw and R. J. Mason reported on the Bushman Rock-Shelter site in the eastern Transvaal, S.Af. The artifacts of "Middle Stone Age" type there (and in the Cave of the Hearths) had radiocarbon determinations considerably earlier than anticipated, suggesting a general reconsideration of the accepted linear developmental picture of the southern African Paleolithic.

The Near East. In the U.A.R. a cosmic ray detection experiment to locate the suspected burial chamber in the Great Pyramid of the pharaoh Khafre failed. Some 30,000 fragments of relief sculpture from a ruined building of the pharaoh Ikhnaton at Karnak were being photographed and codified in another experiment involving computerized matching of fragments. Thousands of mummified sacred birds and monkeys and a gold-bronze statue of the goddess Isis were recovered at Saqqarah by a British expedition, while a U.S. expedition exposed a first-dynasty palace at Hierakonpolis. U.S., French, and German expeditions continued their long-range research in the Luxor region, and the sarcophagus of Tutankhamen was reopened in an attempt to establish that pharaoh's kinship with another—probably royal—body discovered in 1907.

Work in the Palestinian region was complicated by the political situation. The excavation of sites within gun range on either side of the Jordan had to be abandoned (including Jean Perrot's almost completed work at the important early site of Munhata). Farther back in the west bank territory of occupied Jordan, the Israeli Department of Antiquities allowed three major expeditions to resume work. Thus the American Schools of Oriental Research excavations at Ai and Shechem continued. The Early Bronze Age (*c.* 2750 B.C.) fortifications of Ai were cleared further, and there was some exploration of later levels. A geological survey was continued at Shechem, and Bronze, Iron, and Roman Age buildings were excavated. The impressive Hebrew Union College Biblical and Archaeological School excavation at Gezer continued, and the school also worked on a Middle Bronze Age necropolis and settlement at Tell el-Ful (Gibeah). In Jordan a joint U.S.-Jordanian training excavation, directed by R. H. Dornemann, worked on the citadel of Amman.

In Lebanon an important early 1st millennium B.C. site, Tell el-Ghassil, was under continued excavation by D. C. Baramki of the American University of Beirut. The site contains temples destroyed by fire, probably set by the Assyrians. A large Middle Bronze Age building in Syria was cleared by French excavators at the great coastal site of Ras Shamra (Ugarit). In both Syria and Iraq the political situation tended to discourage excavation, but R. M. Adams of the University of Chicago was able to continue his important surface survey work near Nippur in Iraq, and also to do test excavations on the site of a small Sassanian-early Islamic town.

In contrast to Syria and Iraq, the political stance of Iran was reflected by the number of expeditions from Western countries at work there. Frank Hole of Rice University returned to the Deh Luran plain in lowland Khuzistan, and located a site (Chagha Sefid) with an important linkage over a gap in the 6th millennium B.C. sequence of that area. T. C. Young's Royal Ontario Museum expedition at Godin Tepe, east of Kermanshah, worked on both 1st and 4th millennium B.C. levels, the later yielding the massive architecture of a Median citadel.

In Turkey, also, the long-range excavations of well-established expeditions (such as that of the University of Ankara at Kultepe, of the German Archaeological Institute at Bogazkoy, and the Harvard-Cornell clearances at Sardis) continued. The important Keban salvage effort in central Anatolia got off to a promising start, with U.S., British, and West German excavators joining Turkish archaeologists in about a dozen operations. One of these, that of the University of Chicago at Korucu, directed by M. van Loon, resulted in a 5,000-year sequence, including a remarkably promising series of Hittite levels. Farther south, on the piedmont near Diyarbakir, a joint Istanbul-Chicago expedition under H. Cambel and R. J. Braidwood resumed excavations on the early village site of Cayonu, *c.* 7000 B.C., and P. J. Watson tested a nearby Halafian site. M. Mellink of Bryn Mawr cleared 3rd millennium B.C. architecture and a rich cemetery at Karatas-Semayuk. At Acemhoyuk, N. Ozguc exposed the contents of storage magazines, with more traces of the site's important carved ivories, parts of furniture, and some weapons, all of *c.* 1800 B.C.

The Greco-Roman Regions. T. W. Jacobsen of Indiana University continued his excavations in the important Franchthi cave with its long sequence indicating—for Greece—a transition from the food-collecting to the food-producing stages at *c.* 6000 B.C. A joint University of California at Los Angeles (UCLA)-University of Sheffield (Eng.) excavation at Photolivos in Thrace showed that about 35 ft. of strata contain traces of probably continuous occupation from *c.* 4500 to 2500 B.C. Continuing work at the site should do much to clarify Aegean and southeastern European cultural relationships. In Crete a complete early Minoan village, Myrtos, was exposed and appeared to have been a single building complex. A partially underwater site, Pavlopetri on the island of Elaphonesos, yielded Mycenaean and some earlier pottery. More houses were cleared under the volcanic debris on the island of Thera. Further work at Mycenae itself exposed a group of curious painted clay idols of human females and of snakes.

For the classical age, important architectural clearances were being developed at the site of the harbour city of Knidos in Asia Minor by a Long Island University expedition. Frescoes and stucco, a marble head of a girl, and evidence for the plan of a Corinthian temple were exposed. A Greek ship of about the time of Alexander the Great was examined 90 ft. underwater off Kyrenia in Cyprus. It was about 60 ft. long and had a lead sheathing as protection against worms. A late Roman-Byzantine-period city was under excavation in the Israeli Negev. In Greece itself the long-range U.S. excavations on the Athenian agora continued, and several U.S. universities resumed their programs in the Corinth region. In southern Italy a Brown University expedition worked again at Buccino, a site with prehistoric, 4th century B.C., and imperial Roman remains. Architectural clearance continued at the Etruscan site at Poggio Civitate in Tuscany, where a life-sized standing male sphinx appeared. A remarkable find of Roman pewter vessels was made in a gravel pit in England. A second accidental find, of

KEYSTONE

Royal Navy divers examine amphorae recovered in June 1969 from a Roman vessel that sank in Ognina Bay, Sicily, about 300 B.C. The finds were donated to the National Museum at Syracuse.

Antigua:
see Dependent States

Arabia:
see Dependent States; Kuwait; Middle East; Saudi Arabia; Southern Yemen; Yemen

Arab League:
see Middle East

UPI COMPIX

Gold-bronze statue of the Egyptian fertility goddess Isis holding the child Horus, which rocks back and forth, on her knee. The discovery of the statue, unearthed by Walter Emery near the Saqqarah Pyramid, was announced early in 1969.

slightly earlier age, was a group of gold necklaces discovered near Ipswich.

Late Prehistoric and Historic Europe. Another accidental discovery came from excavations for a parking garage in Bonn, W.Ger. The foundations of the original elector's palace appeared, as well as those of five houses dating to the 13th and 14th centuries A.D. and a variety of contemporary artifacts. In England a corduroy road or swamp causeway of *c.* 3000 B.C. was traced in Somerset. A small carved human figure, taken to be hermaphroditic, was also discovered. G. Eogan cleared a remarkable central chamber in the great megalithic mound at Knowth in the Boyne River Valley in Ireland. A corbeled roof rose over the centre of the chamber above a heavy stone basin, where the cremated bones of chieftains probably were deposited.

Asia and Africa. There was little news of archaeological activity in either continent, outside of the Near Eastern regions. Continuing concern was expressed over the rising water table and the destructive effects of salt encrustation on the brick structures at the great Indus Valley site of Mohenjo-Daro in West Pakistan. A. P. Okladnikov published a new series of the riverside rock drawings of Siberia. There was considerable interest in the yield of the Spirit Cave, Thailand, from which C. F. Gorman of the University of Hawaii reported evidence of food-production as early as 7000 B.C. Another series of rock art was recorded in Western Australia, including roughly engraved full-face human faces, to which no firm date could be assigned. For northwest Africa, an increasing number of radiocarbon determinations appeared to fix the date of the upper Capsian assemblages at the 6th millennium B.C., but there was as yet no evidence of food production at that time. (R. J. B.)

Western Hemisphere. It is generally conceded that man's entry into the New World was from Asia via the Bering Strait to Alaska, at a time when glacial ice had robbed the seas of enough water to draw down the ocean level and the crossing could be made on dry land. Alan L. Bryan, University of Alberta, presented a working hypothesis that man crossed the Beringia land bridge before it was covered during the Woronzofian transgression, between 25,000 and 35,000 years ago, and moved southward by way of an ice-free corridor between the Cordilleran and Keewatin ice sheets. This movement, however, was interrupted when the two masses of ice coalesced about 25,000 years ago. Bryan pointed out that, since man had not developed bifacially flaked projectile points at that time, a reasonable hypothesis is that all American bifacially flaked, stone projectile point traditions evolved south of the coalescent ice sheets from the Large Leaf-shaped Point or Biface Tradition. These traditions moved northward, east of the Rockies and up the Lower Fraser Valley, as the ice sheet receded. Later, about 8,000 years ago, microblade traditions related to the Arctic began expanding southward from the unglaciated Yukon and Alaska, becoming established in central and southern British Columbia approximately 7,500 years ago.

Commenting on Bryan's hypothesis, Vance C. Haynes, Jr., Southern Methodist University, pointed out that, if Bryan's hypothesis is correct, possibly as much as 25,000 years of cultural development had elapsed before emergence of the Llano Complex typified by the fluted Clovis Points. This is more than twice the amount of time that has passed since the Llano Complex and the time of an exponential rise in New World cultures. Haynes further noted that Bryan's hypothesis implies that all cultural developments and technologies older than 8,500 years ago in the New World are the result of independent invention and parallel development in both America and Asia. The explanation for the sudden appearance of Clovis sites throughout central North America after 12,000 years ago may lie in a separate migration from Alaska at that time by people with an already developed technology. If confirmed, this would modify Bryan's hypothesis of independent invention and parallel development of cultural technologies in the New World before 8,500 years ago, for Clovis sites date from before that time.

Alaska and Canada. Under the direction of Roscoe Wilmeth, Canadian National Museum of Man, work was continued at the Potlatch site at Anahim Lake in central British Columbia. Excavations there in 1968 indicated an early historic Chilcotin Indian component and an earlier occupation characterized by microblades. Testing was carried out behind Potlatch House, the major structure, and a small collection of microblades was obtained. Two house structures were excavated, together with several test pits. Both houses were shallow circular basins lacking interior features, differing markedly from the typical Chilcotin winter structures excavated in 1968.

J. V. Wright, National Museum of Canada, excavated an archaeologically rich site discovered by the Hays survey of the Thelon Drainage, Keewatin District, Northwest Territories. The earlier materials recovered indicated that the site, located on the west end of Aberdeen Lake, was occupied by a group whose archaeological assemblage is duplicated throughout the eastern portions of the area. G. F. MacDonald, National Museum of Canada, directed the excavation of sites in the Prince Rupert area of British Columbia. Some 150 burials spanning 5,000 years were recovered from a series of cemeteries at one site. The nonhuman bone content of the midden deposit was collected for osteological evaluation of the prehistoric fauna.

Wendell H. Oswalt of UCLA completed an archaeological survey of Kagati Lake in southwestern Alaska that revealed the existence of five sites with a quantity of large, heavy, bifacial percussion-flaked artifacts. These specimens do not belong to the Denbigh complex, but seemingly predate it. Preliminary evaluation of the assemblage suggested an age greater than 5,000 years.

Plains. Archaeological investigations at Willow Creek Valley south of Calgary, Alta., were conducted by R. M. Getty, University of Calgary; 220 camps, rock alignments, tipi-ring sites, and buffalo jumps were recorded. Brien O. K. Reeves, University of Calgary, directed the second season of investigations at the Waterton Lakes National Park under the sponsorship of the National and Historic Sites Service. New sites included a historic Indian camp of about 1850, a multicomponent kill-campsite, a multicomponent camp revealing a sequence from the Early Prehistoric to the Late Prehistoric period, and a multicomponent fishing station.

Dee C. Taylor, University of Montana, directed investigations at a site near Wilsall, Mont. The site was found by amateurs who discovered 90 artifacts, presumably associated with a human skeleton, while hauling dirt and rock fill from the base of a small buffalo jump. The Iowa State University-National Park Service investigations in the Red Rock and Saylorville reservoir areas along the Des Moines

River, directed by David Gradwohl, yielded a sparse artifact inventory indicative of a Woodland occupation.

Middle America. In a second season of field research in the Lake Yojoa region of northwestern Honduras, Claude F. Baudez and Pierre Becquelin, Centre National de la Récherche Scientifique, Paris, concentrated their excavations at the Los Naranjos site. Three superimposed constructions were disclosed, the first two being of the Eden phase (200 B.C.–A.D. 550) and the last of the Yojoa phase (A.D. 550–950). In the western part of the site a second ball court was excavated near the one dug the previous season. It was constructed in Rio Blanco times (A.D. 950–1250). Near the court was a habitation group consisting of three house platforms and a ceremonial structure laid out around a plaza.

Under the direction of Frederick W. Lange, University of Wisconsin, the Associated Colleges of the Midwest instituted an archaeological survey in northwestern Costa Rica, with headquarters in San José. Material recovered from the 84 sites located demonstrated a relatively long time span of cultural activity in the area. Ceramics range from Zoned Bichrome (300 B.C.–A.D. 300) to the Murillo-type pottery known to have been in use at the time of Spanish contact.

Investigation of cave sites in the Chame region of Panama by Don Crusoe, Florida State University Museum, provided information on the cultural past of that region. Hunting, fishing, gathering, and possibly agriculture formed the basic subsistence pattern of the Monagrillo phase of the Parita sequence (2130 B.C.). The caves were used extensively for burials during the Sarigua-Santa María phase, when ceramic types were manufactured coeval with the ceramic complexes of the sites of Bahía de Chame and Madden. Some sites in the Chame and Madden Lake region appeared to be contemporary with the Cerro Mangote phase of the Azuero Peninsula, thus dating close to 5000 B.C.

Archaeological fieldwork in Campeche, Mex., during 1969, conducted by the Brigham Young University-New World Archaeological Foundation, was restricted to the northern part of the state at the sites of Xcalumkin (Holactún), Dzibilnoac, and Santa Rosa Xtampak. Mapping at Dzibilnoac showed that the site covers about 1.5 million sq.m., with approximately 175 structures thus far identified. All of the standing buildings were constructed during the Late Classic period (A.D. 700–900), but many platforms and mounds of the Late Preclassic period (*c.* 300 B.C.–A.D. 100) are still intact in cornfields or have later structures built on top of them.

South America. Ronald Webber, University of Illinois, worked at two sites near the eastern end of Imaríacocha, Peru. Extensive ceramic collections were made of the Caimito materials that are very closely related to the ceramic style on the Río Napo and are almost certainly ancestral to the ceramics of the modern Cocama. Peter Roe, University of Illinois, and Warren De Boer, University of California at Berkeley, worked at a Peruvian village called Shehuaya where they recovered a vast amount of material related to the Cumancaya tradition.

William L. Allen, University of California at Santa Barbara, assisted by Juan Yangúez-Bernal, University of Illinois, undertook investigations in the Alto Pachitea of Peru. They were able to demonstrate a continuity between the very early Cabichaniqui complex and the Pangotsi complex dated at around 1200 B.C. Christopher B. Donnan, UCLA, and Michael Moseley, Harvard, collaborated on archaeological research in Peru's Moche Valley. The Moseley party had as its primary interest the ruins of Chan Chan, while Donnan's group conducted excavations at a mound near the town of Huanchaco.

Excavations were carried out at the site of Guatacondo, in the Atacama Desert of northern Chile, by Clement W. Meighan and Christopher B. Donnan, UCLA, and Grete Mostny of the National Museum of Chile. The project involved study of a remarkably preserved town with about 180 circular adobe structures and associated cemeteries, apparently dating from the short time, about the beginning of the Christian era, when the region was favourable for agriculture.

Western United States. The Marmes Rock-Shelter site near the confluence of the Palouse and Snake rivers in eastern Washington was flooded in February 1969, in spite of an earthen dike erected to protect the site from the floodwaters of the Lower Monumental Dam reservoir. Radiocarbon age determinations by the U.S. Geological Survey date the Marmes level, containing Marmes Man, at 7890 B.C. ± 300, somewhat later than was originally suggested for this material. Upriver from the Marmes site on the middle Snake River, parties from Washington State and Idaho State universities discovered materials of equal antiquity, culturally comparable to the early Marmes materials. All of these early Snake River materials appeared to be derived from a common source similar to the Lind Coulee materials from central Washington, first described by R. D. Daugherty in 1953.

An Early Man site was recorded by Francis A. Riddell and William H. Olsen, California Department of Parks and Recreation, on the south shore of Tulare Lake in the San Joaquin Valley. The specimens found included a number of points closely analogous to specimens of the fluted point tradition (Clovis-Folsom).

Robert F. Heizer, University of California at Berkeley, continued a long-range study of coprolites (dried human fecal matter) collected over a number of years from Lovelock Cave north of Fallon, Nev. In prehistoric times the area was inhabited by the Paiute Indians, remnants of whom still live in the region. Laboratory analysis demonstrated that the people who left the coprolites ate baked cattail pollen and parched bulrush seeds, raw whole baby birds, and cooked ducks and geese. Occasionally they ate beetles after biting the heads off, and also antelope, bighorn sheep, and squirrel, often including the hair. They also ate small fish such as chub, and one coprolite was found to contain the bones of 51 small chub —more than 3½ lb. of fish—apparently eaten in one meal. (F. A. Ri.)

See also Anthropology.

Encyclopædia Britannica Films. *Carbon Fourteen* (1953); *The Egyptologists* (1967).

1,000-lb. basalt sculpture of an Aztec goddess (above) and a skeleton, dating from the Spanish colonial period, with shackles around the ankles and one knee (below) unearthed in Mexico City during excavation for a new subway system. The finds were reported early in 1969.

COURTESY, ARIEL VALENCIA RAMIREZ

Architecture

The death of two of modern architecture's brilliant pioneers saddened the profession in 1969. Walter Gropius, founder of the Bauhaus and for many years professor at Harvard University, died in July at the age of 86; and, in August, Ludwig Mies van der Rohe, originator of the refined, understated, steel-and-glass type of architecture as exemplified so beautifully in his West Berlin National Gallery of 1968, died in Chicago (*see* OBITUARIES). The influence of these men, together with that of Le Corbusier, who died in 1965, can be seen in countless buildings erected in the 20th century. Gropius' influence was great as a teacher and as a force promoting the application of good design principles to everyday objects. And to Mies's philosophy is owed the skyline of so many of America's cities, today dominated by tall elegant glass skyscrapers illustrative of his dictum that "less is more."

In the United Kingdom the Royal Institute of British Architects awarded its Royal Gold Medal for Architecture for 1969 to a 70-year-old Glasgow architect, Jack Coia, chiefly known as a designer of Roman Catholic churches. Coia, senior partner in the firm of Gillespie, Kidd and Coia, was described as "the most distinguished architect Scotland has produced since Charles Rennie Mackintosh, and the creator of an austere but expressive style based on the vigorous handling of brick." Coia's best churches were those at East Kilbride and at Dennistoun, Glasgow; he also designed a spectacular seminary at Cardross, completed in 1967. In 1966 he was commissioned to design a group of student residential buildings at the University of Hull, Yorkshire, his first buildings outside Scotland.

It was not a spectacular year for new buildings, although plans were going ahead in many quarters for Expo 70, to be held in Osaka, Jap., which promised to be something of an architectural event. The designs for the main festival plaza, featuring a large area covered by a space deck, were completed by Japanese architects Arata Isozaki and Atsushi Ueda. In overall charge of planning was Kenzo Tange.

Museums. Of the year's buildings a surprisingly large number of new museums merited attention. Mies van der Rohe's West Berlin art gallery was followed by two more new West German museums of architectural distinction. Philip Johnson of the U.S. designed the Richard Kaselowsky art gallery at Bielefeld, Westphalia. The building was square in plan with a reinforced concrete frame and oversailing windowless walls on the entrance front.

Roman Catholic Church in Boness, Scot., designed by Jack Coia, recipient of the 1969 Royal Gold Medal for Architecture awarded by the Royal Institute of British Architects.

WILLIAM J. TOOMEY © "THE ARCHITECTS' JOURNAL"

Two of the three units planned for the Wilhelm Lehmbruck museum and sculpture gallery in the Immanuel-Kant Park in Duisburg were completed. The architect was Manfred Lehmbruck, son of the sculptor for whom the museum was named. The main building had a roof supported by an external concrete frame, which left the galleries free of internal columns and allowed for maximum flexibility.

In Oakland, Calif., a new city museum of a most unusual design was built. The structure was underground and gave back the whole site to the community in the form of a parklike terraced podium —a nonbuilding providing a garden environment. The museum, which housed collections devoted to art, natural science, and history, opened in the fall. The architect responsible for this new concept was Kevin Roche of Roche, Dinkeloo and Associates, who designed the Ford Foundation's headquarters in New York City.

Also partly subterranean was the new Sibelius Museum at Turku, Fin., by Woldemar Baeckman. The plan consisted of two major central spaces in the shape of a small concert hall open all around to museum galleries. The exterior was a simple composition of glass and concrete.

São Paulo's first art museum, designed by Lina Bo, the ex-wife of the museum director, opened in March. The design featured a box slung from four concrete piers. The interior was free of columns, with paintings displayed on a series of floor-to-ceiling transparent plastic panels.

At Fishbourne, Sussex, Eng., a new archaeological museum built to house the extensive Roman ruins recently excavated there was designed by architects Carden, Godfrey, and Macfayden. A new underground art gallery was designed by Powell and Moya for Christ Church, Oxford, and built to house the college's priceless collection of paintings, which could not previously be made conveniently available for public viewing. At the Tate Gallery in London a new plan to increase the available space in this badly overcrowded museum was rejected after a widespread public outcry. The plan worked out by architects Llewelyn-Davies, Weeks, Forestier-Walker, and Bor was a compromise that required the destruction of the portico and open space at the entrance and the encasing of the front in a featureless modern design. The model of the plan went on public view, and comment was invited. As a result of a rejection of this solution it was announced later in the year that an adjacent site would be acquired, promising a more satisfactory architectural solution to the Tate's space problems in the future.

Transportation Facilities. At London's Heathrow Airport the No. 1 terminal building opened. The architects were Frederick Gibbers and Partners. The terminal was the third and, to date, the largest of the passenger terminals and was intended to accommodate British short-haul international and domestic flights. Included in the design was a multistory garage for 800 cars.

Transportation was in the architectural news in other ways in 1969. The *Architectural Review* devoted a whole issue (June 1969) to the new Cunard liner "Queen Elizabeth 2." The ship, the nearest thing to a completely man-made total environment, housing a wide range of human activity, was remarkable for the careful attention given to the quality of the design. Dennis Lennon and Partners were responsible for coordinating the interiors, which were the efforts of some of the leading British designers. The ship even carried its own specially designed art gallery.

Churches. In 1969 several new churches excited architectural interest. At the Rhineland pilgrimage site of Neviges in West Germany a new pilgrims' centre to accommodate 7,000 people was under construction. The church, first step in the plans, was designed by architect Gottfried Böhm to seat 800 with standing room for 2,200. It was the second largest sacred structure in the diocese of Cologne, after Cologne cathedral. The structure was reinforced concrete with a polygonal ground plan and a folded plate roof rising in successive peaks to a height of 114 ft.

At Yarzeh, Lebanon, the chapel for the Monastère de l'Unité by Liger Belair was finished but the convent, designed by Pierre el Khoury, was still being built. The centre was conceived by Pope John XXIII as an attempt to further the cause of ecumenism in a country where Muslims and Christians already lived in amity. The site was a wooded hillside, and the chapel was essentially organic in conception. It consisted of a combination of curved forms crowned by a roof of double curvature and by a triangular bell tower. The finish was of rough-shuttered concrete both inside and out, in sympathy with the wild landscape.

The new temple to Maria Madre e Regina designed by Antonio Guacci overlooking the city and gulf of Trieste was constructed on the principle of the triangle, symbol of the Trinity. This system created a honeycomb effect.

Rather different in style was the new church at Fulton, Mo. Sir Christopher Wren's City of London church of St. Mary the Virgin, Aldermanbury, badly bombed in World War II, was reconstructed on the Westminster College campus in Fulton under the supervision of Marshall Sisson of London and Frederick G. Sternberg of St. Louis. It was intended to serve as the student chapel, and a Churchill library and museum were housed in the undercroft.

University Buildings. On the campus of the University of Illinois at Champaign-Urbana, the Krannert Center for the Performing Arts, incorporating five theatres, was designed by Max Abramovitz, architect of the Philharmonic Hall in Lincoln Center, New York City.

At Cornell University the new agronomy building by Ulrich Franzen was hailed as the first distinguished example of modern architecture on that campus. The reinforced concrete structure, clad in rust-coloured weatherproof brick, consisted of a 13-story laboratory building, a two-story administration building, and four stories of teaching laboratories.

Moore and Turnbull, architects of the faculty club for the University of California at Santa Barbara, created an environment intended to reflect the various facets of Los Angeles: neon lights, freeways, motels, Hollywood, and the Hispanic style.

City Buildings. Boston's new city hall was completed. Constructed with concrete columns and cores cast in situ, the project was won in competition in 1962 by architects Kallmann, McKinnell and Knowles, who later worked in collaboration with Campbell, Aldrich and Nutty. The new building was situated on a brick-paved square and bounded on two sides by the raised podium of the Federal Office block and Faneuil Hall. The approved master plan for the Government Center was designed by architect I. M. Pei.

© BERND KIRTZ ABCV

One of three units of the Wilhelm Lehmbruck museum and sculpture gallery in the Immanuel-Kant Park in Duisburg, designed by Manfred Lehmbruck and completed in 1969.

In San Francisco the recently completed Alcoa Building by architects Skidmore, Owings and Merrill was an essay in structural expressionism, with its facades sheathed in exposed diagonal seismic bracing. The Marin County Civic Center in nearby San Rafael, Calif., the last work of Frank Lloyd Wright, was finally completed, ten years after his death, while in Tokyo the new 1,000-room Imperial Hotel to replace Wright's demolished masterpiece was designed by Teitaro Takahashi.

Medical buildings also made news in several countries in 1969. The new 26-story teaching hospital in Rotterdam, Neth., by Van Embden and Choisy became a prominent feature on the city skyline with its clean-looking concrete structure sheathed in panels of white enameled aluminum. A new medical centre at Jyväskylä in central Finland based on U.S. and Canadian models was financed by local physicians and designed by city architects Niilo Hartikainen and Erkki Kantonen. It was literally a "supermarket for health," housing 50 specialists and providing comprehensive treatment facilities. The new Sulaibikhat Women's Hospital, Kuwait, designed by architect John R. Harris, was financed from oil royalties by the Kuwait government.

The new Czechoslovak embassy in London, overlooking Kensington Palace Gardens, was completed. The architects were Jan Sramek, Jan Bocan, and Karel Stepanski of Prague in cooperation with Sir Robert Matthew, Johnson-Marshall and Partners. The L-shaped complex of exposed concrete was decorated

Archery: *see* Sporting Record

with colourful examples of Czechoslovak arts and crafts.

In Manchester, Eng., a new office building, Pall Mall Court in King Street, designed by Harry Teggin of the firm of Brett and Pollen, achieved a striking visual impact by appearing to be an all-black structure. The effect was achieved by the use of coloured and transparent glass and gave the illusion of jet stone. It was a witty solution to the problem of building in a grimy industrial city. (S. Mi.)

See also Cities and Urban Affairs; Engineering Projects; Housing; Industrial Review.

Encyclopædia Britannica Films. *The Living City* (1953); *Art of the Middle Ages* (Humanities Course) (1962); *Athens: The Golden Age* (Humanities Course) (1962); *Chartres Cathedral* (Humanities Course) (1962); *The Louvre* (1966).

SPORT & GENERAL FROM PICTORIAL PARADE

Ken Hedges (left) and Wally Herbert (centre) of the four-man British Trans-Arctic Expedition are welcomed aboard the Royal Navy ice patrol ship HMS "Endurance" by Capt. Peter Buchanan after their 476-day, 3,700-mi. trek across the Arctic via the North Pole ended in June 1969.

Arctic Regions

The year 1969 was a significant one for the Arctic, especially the North American Arctic. The successful traversing of the Northwest Passage through the Canadian Arctic islands by a large commercial vessel assured that the enormous mineral resources of Alaska, the Yukon, and the Northwest Territories would be realized, because they could now be transported economically to world markets. Concurrent with this potentially massive resource development, however, was the general realization, among all the nations bordering on the Arctic, that immediate steps must be taken to protect the delicate northern terrestrial and marine ecological balance from the lasting ill effects of industrial pollution. As the year ended those two factors—resource development and conservation of the environment—held the attention of governments and industrialists alike, and in the case of Canada the government proposed in October a law that would establish and maintain pollution prevention measures and resource development control standards in the nation's northern regions.

The state of Alaska decided in January that it intended to reject all bids on construction of the winter trail to the North Slope (the site on the northern coast of rich petroleum deposits) and that it would build the road itself. The state expected to cut by 25% the time required to build the road by doing its own work.

In May the *Alaska News Review* reported that 343 trucks carrying 7,464 tons of equipment and supplies had used the state's 420-mi. winter-haul road to the North Slope. It also was announced that an estimated 33,000 tons of equipment and supplies were being flown from Anchorage and Fairbanks each month to the Slope, primarily for use by oil companies. The winter-haul road was constructed by the state at an estimated cost of $350,000 and produced no income because there were no tolls or weighing facilities. It was indicated that the road would continue to be open during the next three winters and that tolls might then be charged.

In March the U.S. secretary of the interior announced that the hunting of musk-oxen at Nunivak Island National Wildlife Refuge would not be permitted. The herd on Nunivak, numbering about 750, was originally imported from Greenland in 1936 and numbered 35 at that time.

Areas:
see Populations and Areas; *see also the individual country articles*

In May a romantic chapter in the story of Canada's North ended when two Royal Canadian Mounted Police with their dog teams and sleds returned from the last long spring patrol of the vast northern wilderness. The growth of a network of roads, the building of airports, and the use of snowmobiles all but eliminated the dependence on this mode of travel. The two teams set out from Old Crow in the Yukon, and their last stop was at Aklavik on the Mackenzie River delta, a journey of about 800 mi.

In June the British Trans-Arctic Expedition, led by Wally Herbert, completed what was described as the longest, loneliest walk in the world, having journeyed by dogsled and ice drift from Point Barrow, Alaska, across the North Pole to Small Blackboard Island, Svalbard.

Resources. In September Alaska offered for sale 179 tracts totaling 450,858 ac. of potential oil land on the North Slope. Most of the acres offered were onshore, with only a few offshore tracts available. About 800,000 ac. of unleased land in the same area, much of it offshore, was retained by the state for future sale. In the sale the state collected an estimated $900,220,590 in bonus lease bids for one-third of the oil field. It was the largest such sale of drilling rights in U.S. history. Among the highlights of the sale were the largest bid per acre ever for oil land in the U.S., $28,223, and the largest single bid, $72.2 million for one 2,560-ac. lease. The state of Alaska was to receive $1 per year per acre on the lease price and a share of future production.

It was reported in June that a total of 21 oil rigs were operating on the Alaskan North Slope oil fields in comparison with one a year earlier. Thirteen of the rigs were reported operating in the Prudhoe Bay area. During the same month, Humble Oil and Refining Co. officials stated that Anchorage would probably become a supply base for the firm's Northwest Passage Project, which was a plan to transport Alaskan oil via tanker to markets on the east coast of the U.S. The officials believed that six giant icebreaking tankers of the 250,000-ton deadweight class would be needed by 1975. Each tanker might cost as much as $50 million. If other companies on the North Slope were to follow the same pattern, 25 to 30 supertankers would eventually be operating across the top of the continent.

The tanker SS "Manhattan," the largest commercial vessel built in a U.S. shipyard, sailed from the east coast of the U.S. through the Northwest Passage to Prudhoe Bay on the North Slope, where it arrived in late September. A number of performance tests under varying ice conditions were executed. The entire testing project was estimated to cost $39 million, including the construction of the specially designed 115,000-ton tanker. The vessel proved that a commercially feasible route exists for tankers to carry oil from Alaska's North Slope to the east coast of North America and to Europe.

On many occasions during the historic voyage the Canadian icebreaker "John A. Macdonald" was called upon to free the huge tanker when it became caught in the Arctic ice pack. Experts anticipated that it would be necessary to station icebreakers along the route should it come into general use in the future.

The Atlantic Richfield Co. announced in March a proposed billion dollar pipeline for moving Alaskan crude oil from the North Slope 800 mi. overland. Scheduled to open in 1972, it would carry a maximum of 500,000 bbl. per day. The pipeline's capacity was expected to be increased in the three years following the opening to an eventual 1.2 million bbl. per day.

The Canadian government announced in June that ten airports would be established at remote settlements in the Northwest Territories and the Yukon over the next eight to ten years at a cost of close to $6 million. The objective of the program was to provide year-round transportation to isolated communities and to improve resource development as well as medical, educational, and other services.

Research. In August it was reported that digging conducted at a prospective nuclear test site at Amchitka revealed a culture perhaps 9,000 years old and predating that of the present Aleutian Islanders. An expedition in March sponsored jointly by the National Museum of Man and the National Geographic Society discovered a large Eskimo burial centre of the prehistoric Thule culture. The finding of the 350-year-old site was expected to close many gaps in the understanding of the Thule culture; for example, by answering biological questions about the early Eskimo people and by providing insight into their attitudes and behaviour toward death.

In June a Danish expedition visited the former U.S. ice cap station, Camp Century, which is in the Greenland ice cap about 150 mi. inland from Thule. The under-the-surface camp is entered through a 300-m. shaft sloping down from the snow surface. The purpose of the expedition was to collect ice samples before the shaft is gradually closed by the flow of ice. From an examination of core samples of ice, scientists believed it would be possible to study variations in the climate over the past 100,000 years.

The Soviet newspaper *Gudok* reported in April that "North 69," the largest high-latitude expedition ever to be launched, was beginning its operations. The expedition was to be responsible for the delivery of various supplies to base points from where they would be reshipped to the "North Pole" drifting stations. The expedition's program included the distribution of automatic radio meteorological stations over a wide area of the Arctic seas and the central Polar basin.

It was recorded in May by the Soviet publication *Vodnyy Transport* that the work of the high-latitude expedition "North 21" was coming to an end. The ice station had been established in October 1968 with the help of the icebreaker "Leningrad," which was situated to the northeast of Wrangel Island. During the seven months that the station was operating, scientists performed extensive research work and found that the ice flow had traveled about 600 mi. from east to west.

(K. DE LA B.)

See also Archaeology; Geography.

ENCYCLOPÆDIA BRITANNICA FILMS. *The Arctic—Islands of the Frozen Sea* (1959); *The Face of the High Arctic* (1959); *High Arctic—Life on the Land* (1959); *The High Arctic Biome* (1961); *Life on the Tundra* (1965).

Argentina

The republic of Argentina, occupying the southeastern section of South America, is bounded by Bolivia, Paraguay, Brazil, Uruguay, Chile, and the Atlantic Ocean. It is the second largest Latin-American country, after Brazil, with an area of 1,072,156 sq.mi. (2,776,884 sq.km.), excluding 481,177 sq.mi. of Antarctic and South Atlantic island areas. Pop. (1969 est.): 23,983,000. Cap. and largest city: Buenos Aires (pop., 1969, 3,484,000). Language: Spanish. Religion: mainly Roman Catholic. President in 1969, Juan Carlos Onganía.

Domestic Affairs. The strikes and violent disorders in the large cities of Argentina in May and June of 1969 marked the first serious challenge to the authority of the three-year-old Onganía regime. They also threatened to jeopardize the monetary stability and orderly development of the economy fostered by Adalbert Krieger Vasena since his appointment as minister of economy and labour in January 1967. The May disturbances in Córdoba, Rosario, and elsewhere, in which more than 20 people lost their lives, were sparked by comparatively trivial grievances. They were, however, undoubtedly symptomatic of popular dissatisfaction with the lack of communication between government and community, and with some features of economic and social policy, notably the strictly observed wage freeze.

President Onganía declared that the regime would not bow to violence and would remain faithful to the aims of the so-called Argentinian revolution that it had instituted. A wholesale revision of the administration was undertaken, nevertheless, in June, and many

Youths flee tear gas in Buenos Aires on June 29, 1969, as police disperse demonstrators protesting Nelson Rockefeller's visit.

UPI COMPIX

members of the government, including all the ministers, were replaced. The two key posts of interior and of economy and labour were given to Gen. Francisco Imaz and José María Dagnino Pastore, respectively. They were committed to more or less the same successful economic policies as before, but with the added and difficult task of initiating the "social phase" of the revolution without undermining the country's very real economic progress.

In late June protests against the impending visit to Argentina of U.S. Pres. Richard Nixon's special emissary, Nelson Rockefeller, led to several bomb outrages in Buenos Aires and a call for strike action by the militant antigovernment faction of the union movement. In the midst of this unrest the prominent labour leader Augusto Vandor was murdered in his office by a group of armed men—an incident that prompted the government to adopt emergency powers by declaring a state of siege. Several hundred people were arrested, generally for short periods, and Vandor's rival, the militant Raimundo Ongaro, was held in "protective custody."

Vandor's death provided the government with a good reason for temporarily adopting a more authoritarian attitude, but it also deprived it of what was potentially its most promising contact with organized labour, at a time when it had committed itself to restoring the former machinery of wage-bargaining councils. In July the government appointed an official to supervise the reorganization of the nationwide labour union federation with the object of restoring a united and fully responsible labour movement, but this intrusion by the authorities was strongly resented by union leaders.

The sensitive questions of government-labour relations and social policy gave rise to rumours of differences of opinion within the armed forces. Several senior army officers were disciplined in August for vaguely defined reasons, and some press reports implied a link between the activities of some of these and an abortive and ill-planned coup against the regime, in which armed men succeeded in capturing a Córdoba radio station for a short time on July 31.

The Economy. Indications in 1969 of unrest in the political and social spheres by no means reflected any deterioration in the state of the economy. A loss in gold reserves was noted after the May riots, but for most of the year these remained at a high level of more than $800 million. Imports rose sharply during the year; their value in the first seven months was more than 50% higher than in the comparable period of 1968, largely because of heavy purchases of machinery and metals. The gross domestic product in the first half of the year was 7.1% higher than in January–June 1968, and the construction and manufacturing industries showed increases of 15.4 and 8.8%, respectively.

The growth in imports was partly matched by a fairly buoyant export performance. A notable feature of this was the substantial increase in beef shipments, running at 50% above their 1968 level for much of the year. The value of shipments of beef cuts, as distinct from the more traditional carcasses, indeed showed a 100% increase during January–July as the trade adapted itself in anticipation of the new requirements of the United Kingdom market. The Northumberland Committee set up by the British government to report on the 1967–68 epidemic of foot-and-mouth disease in England and Wales recommended that all imports into the United Kingdom of bone-in beef and unprocessed beef offal from countries where the disease was endemic, including Argentina, should be banned after Oct. 1, 1969. A subsequent announcement by the British government that boneless cuts would attract a customs duty of 5% instead of the former 20% did much to dispel the apprehension of Argentinian exporters.

President Onganía's administration continued in 1969 to exercise firm control over the public finances, and there were strong indications that it would succeed in reducing the annual budget deficit to the projected figure of 43 billion pesos. This would represent a continuation of the downward trend achieved since 1966 when the deficit was 140 billion pesos. In consequence of this and the stringent wage policy, the rate of inflation, which had been running at an annual average of 28% between 1960 and 1967, was reduced to 9.6% in 1968 and promised to be even less in 1969. The fiscal situation was sufficiently strong at the beginning of the year to allow the government to make several tax concessions, such as the abolition of the six-year-old emergency tax and the tax on dividends distributed in Argentina. One controversial innovation was that of a tax on land values. Legislation published in April empowered the central bank to issue, not later than Jan. 1, 1970, a new monetary unit. The new peso would be equivalent to 100 of the existing pesos. (I. C. C.)

ENCYCLOPÆDIA BRITANNICA FILMS. *Argentina* (*People of the Pampa*) (1957).

ARGENTINA

Education. (1966) Primary, pupils 3,449,226, teachers 174,074; secondary (1965), pupils 184,955, teachers 29,287; vocational (1965), pupils 425,588, teachers 59,775; teacher training (1965), students 184,934, teachers 22,066; higher (including 14 universities), students 251,631, teaching staff 16,102.

Finance. Monetary unit: peso, with exchange rates of 350 pesos to U.S. $1 and 840 pesos to £1 sterling. Gold and foreign exchange, central bank: (March 1969) U.S. $712 million; (March 1968) U.S. $641 million. Budget (1969 est.): revenue 977.3 billion pesos; expenditure 1,020,500,000,000 pesos. Gross national product: (1967) 5,156,000,000,000 pesos; (1966) 4,008,000,000,000 pesos. Money supply: (March 1969) 1,402,000,000,000 pesos; (March 1968) 1,125,000,000,000 pesos. Cost of living (Buenos Aires; 1963 = 100): (May 1969) 325; (May 1968) 305.

Foreign Trade. (1968) Imports 409,220,000,000 pesos; exports 478,180,000,000 pesos. Import sources: U.S. 23%; Brazil 12%; West Germany 11%; U.K. 7%; Italy 6%. Export destinations: Italy 14%; U.S. 12%; Netherlands 10%; Brazil 9%; U.K. 8%; Chile 6%; Spain 5%; West Germany 5%. Main exports: meat 24%; corn 10%; wheat 10%; wool 8%; hides and skins 5%.

Transport and Communications. Roads (1968) 215,304 km. Motor vehicles in use (1967): passenger 1,163,100; commercial 629,174. Railways: (1966) 41,182 km.; traffic (1968) 13,779,000,000 passenger-km., freight 13,226,000,000 net ton-km. Air traffic (1967): 1,555,610,000 passenger-km.; freight 25,853,000 net ton-km. Shipping (1968): merchant vessels 100 gross tons and over 315; gross tonnage 1,196,817. Telephones (Dec. 1967) 1,553,789. Radio receivers (Dec. 1967) 8 million. Television receivers (Dec. 1967) 1.9 million.

Agriculture. Production (in 000; metric tons; 1968; 1967 in parentheses): wheat 5,900 (7,320); corn 6,560 (8,510); barley 620 (588); oats 490 (690); potatoes 1,967 (1,797); linseed 580 (385); cotton, lint 73 (87); peanuts 283 (354); oranges 832 (755); apples 470 (516); sunflower seed 940 (1,196); tobacco 59 (63); beef and veal (1967) 2,588, (1966) 2,347; butter (1967) 42, (1966) 45; cheese (1967) 165, (1966) 170; wool, greasy (1967) 190, (1966) 198; quebracho extract (1967) 119, (1966) 113; wine 1,951 (2,817). Livestock (in 000; June 1968): cattle 51,465; sheep (June 1966) *c.* 48,500; pigs *c.* 4,250; chickens (1965–66) 34,000.

Industry. Index of manufacturing (1963 = 100): (1968) 139; (1967) 129. Fuel and power (in 000; 1968): crude oil 17,370 metric tons; coal 472 metric tons; natural gas 5,346,000 cu.m.; electricity (excluding most industrial production) 13,504,000 kw-hr. Production (in 000; metric tons; 1968): cement 4,213; crude steel 1,553; cotton yarn 83; passenger cars (including assembly; units) 132; commercial vehicles (including assembly; units) 48.

Art Exhibitions

To mark the 300th anniversary of the death of Rembrandt, a number of museums organized commemorative exhibitions in 1969. The first of these was "Rembrandt and His Pupils," seen at the Montreal Museum of Fine Arts and the Art Gallery of Ontario in Toronto at the beginning of the year. With 18 paintings by Rembrandt and 90 by his forerunners, pupils, and contemporaries, the successful exhibition was visited by over 220,000 persons. Later in the spring the British Museum mounted a show of Rembrandt's late etchings not often seen together. Also in London, Colnagi held a related print exhibition entitled "The Age of Rembrandt," which included works by other famous 17th-century artists as well: Claude Lorrain, Van Dyck, J. Callot, and others. The grandest exhibition of all was held in the autumn at the Rijksmuseum in Amsterdam and was devoted solely to Rembrandt's works. The three mediums in which he worked were represented by about 20–25 paintings, 120 drawings, and 140–150 etchings. The exhibition, the fifth devoted to Rembrandt to be held in the Rijksmuseum, included many works that had not been seen in Amsterdam before. Particular emphasis was placed on works belonging to the last two decades of the artist's development.

"The Great Age of Fresco: Giotto to Pontormo," which had been seen by over 180,000 persons during its first month at New York's Metropolitan Museum of Art in the fall of 1968, was also shown in Amsterdam and was mounted in London's Hayward Gallery in the spring. Certainly one of the largest and best attended shows of the year, the exhibition of frescoes from Florence was intended as a gesture of gratitude for aid given to that city following the disastrous floods of 1966. It consisted of 70 original frescoes and fresco fragments, many of monumental size, that previously could be examined only with difficulty in dimly lit churches. Modern techniques developed in Florence permitted the removal of the entire pigmented surface of old frescoes. In many cases this was done of necessity in order to arrest decay, but the process also made it possible to expose the *sinopie* or first underdrawings of a mural, and many such preliminary drawings were included in the show and could be studied in relation to the finished design.

"Demonstration in Paris" (Sacco and Vanzetti series, 1931–32) from the Ben Shahn Retrospective Exhibition held Sept. 20–Nov. 16, 1969, at the New Jersey State Museum in Trenton.

COURTESY, NEW JERSEY STATE MUSEUM (OWNED BY MR. AND MRS. SAMUEL PORTER; PHOTOGRAPH BY ERIC POLLITZER)

One of the major winter exhibitions in London in 1968–69 was the Royal Academy's Bicentenary Exhibition, staged to commemorate the 200th anniversary of the founding of that institution. The exhibition was enormous, with over 1,000 items including paintings, sculpture, drawings, prints, miniatures, and medals. The later 19th-century artists were particularly well represented, and it was possible to see many paintings from outside the U.K. rarely lent for exhibition. The majority of the items, however, had been shown at the Academy in the past.

A large retrospective exhibition of the work of the American Abstract Expressionist painter Willem de Kooning (b. 1904) was organized by the Museum of Modern Art in New York and seen in Amsterdam, London, New York, Chicago, and Los Angeles. The show consisted of 147 items dating from the mid-1930s to 1966. It was the first time a full-scale exhibition of the work of this leading postwar American painter had been shown in London.

Another exhibition of work by contemporary American artists seen in London was the "Art of the Real" at the Tate Gallery, organized by the Museum of Modern Art. It included works by Ellsworth Kelly, Tony Smith, and Robert Morris. At London's Whitechapel Gallery the American Helen Frankenthaler had a retrospective show in the spring.

In the summer a comprehensive Pop Art show opened in London at the Hayward Gallery. Artists represented included Peter Blake, R. B. Kitaj, Eduardo Paolozzi, Nicholas Munro, and Roy Lichtenstein. There were 160 items in all, and the exhibition was arranged according to formal themes: household objects, cinema images, comic-strip images, food, clothing, and images drawn from art itself.

The 200th anniversary of the birth of Napoleon was marked by exhibitions at the Grand Palais and the Petit Palais in Paris and at his birthplace in Corsica. The French also honoured two literary figures with exhibitions devoted to Baudelaire at the Petit Palais and to Chateaubriand at the Bibliothèque Nationale in Paris. At the University of Michigan Museum of Art in Ann Arbor, an exhibition in the spring called "The World of Voltaire" featured items representative of artistic and literary life in 18th-century Europe.

Exhibitions in the United States in 1969 covered a wide range of subjects. At the Baltimore (Md.) Museum of Art a large show of masterpieces "From El Greco to Pollock: Early and Late Works" brought together pairs of works by a whole range of artists and included many fine examples. The Metropolitan Museum of Art held an exhibition of Florentine Baroque art in the spring. With 38 paintings and several sculptures, drawings, and prints, all taken from

UPI COMPIX

Exhibit of works by young sculptors was displayed in the spring of 1969 in the Halles of Paris, the former marketplace of the French capital.

Armies:
see Defense

Art:
see Architecture; Art Exhibitions; Art Sales; Dance; Literature; Museums and Galleries; Theatre

American collections, it was the largest show of 17th-century Florentine works ever held. The University of Kansas Art Museum, Lawrence, mounted an exhibition illustrating the history of the mezzotint, organized by the Metropolitan Museum of Art. Forty-five paintings and 16 drawings by William Sidney Mount, founder of the American school of genre painting, were shown at the National Gallery of Art, Washington, D.C. Much of the material was borrowed from the Melville collection of the Suffolk Museum and Carriage House, Stony Brook, N.Y., the largest repository of the artist's work. The show traveled to St. Louis, Mo., the Whitney Museum of American Art in New York, and the De Young Museum in San Francisco.

A monumental exhibition of the graphic art of the 19th-century American artist Winslow Homer, organized by the new Museum of Graphic Art of New York, was circulated to 14 cities. It included all his etchings, important lithographs, and wood engravings, as well as paintings and drawings used as sources. Also organized by the Museum of Graphic Art and seen as well at the Brooklyn Museum was "American Printmaking—The First 150 Years." Covering the period 1670–1821, the show consisted of 112 rare works including the oldest known American print, John Foster's woodcut of Richard Mather, done in 1670.

The Philadelphia Museum of Art featured an important exhibition of Mexican art from the 16th to the 20th century. Many of the works were drawn from the museum's own resources, which included one of the finest public collections of Mexican art in the U.S. In the late spring Harvard's Fogg Art Museum in Cambridge, Mass., held a show entitled "Daumier Sculpture, A Critical and Comparative Study," which brought together many works by Honoré Daumier, the 19th-century French artist noted for his caricatures. Russian state and theatre designs formed the basis for a show at the John and Mable Ringling Museum of Art, Sarasota, Fla., which featured designs by Eugene Berman.

The National Gallery in Washington, D.C., began a series of small, intimate shows of selected paintings from the splendid collection of English art owned by Mr. and Mrs. Paul Mellon. The first of these was devoted to J. M. W. Turner and consisted of 16 extremely fine paintings by that 19th-century English master. The Cloisters in New York, the branch of the Metropolitan Museum of Art devoted to medieval art and architecture, held an important exhibition of art of the Middle Ages from October 1968 to early 1969. The 200 masterpieces were drawn from private collections in the U.S. and Canada and included fine examples of stained glass and illuminated manuscripts. Also in New York, the Guggenheim Museum arranged a show of 125 selected works from the collection of Peggy Guggenheim, after whose uncle the museum was named. Miss Guggenheim's collection was begun in the 1930s and was generally considered to be one of the outstanding collections of 20th-century art in the world. All the great modern artists were represented, including Picasso, Braque, Max Ernst, Alberto Giacometti, Fernand Léger, and Paul Klee.

"Master Prints of Japan, Ukiyo-e Hanga" was the title of an exhibition sponsored by the University of California at Los Angeles Art Council and seen at the Dickson Art Center in Los Angeles. The *Ukiyo-e* or "Floating World" school of Japan produced masterful wood-block prints, depicting simple Japanese pleasures, that were meant for the average man. The show traced the development of the *Ukiyo-e* print from the 17th to the mid-19th century. Because of the extreme fragility of the prints it was not possible for the show to travel.

The University of Texas, Austin, held a spring exhibition of paintings, drawings, and lithographs by Marsden Hartley (1877–1943), a pioneer American artist of the early 20th century. One hundred works dating from 1907 to 1943 were assembled at Austin, many representing seascapes and landscapes of the Maine coast. A Hartley retrospective was also held in New York in the autumn at the Bernard Danenberg Galleries.

In Paris large-scale exhibitions continued to draw crowds as they had in the past few seasons. A show entitled "1,000 Years of Art in Poland" was mounted at the Petit Palais. Polish art, relatively rarely seen in large quantities in the West, is interesting for its successive absorption of German, French, and Russian influences. The exhibition, the largest of its kind ever sent abroad, consisted of 350 works lent by 24 museums, libraries, churches, and other institutions in Poland. The museums of Warsaw and Cracow were particularly well represented.

The exhibition of the graphic works of the Norwegian Expressionist Edvard Munch, mounted in the early spring at the Musée des Arts Décoratifs, was very different in effect. Munch's moving works inspired a new approach to lithography and to colour engraving on wood. In the winter the Institut Néerlandais in Paris held a superb show of 182 17th-century Dutch landscape drawings, all from the collection of Fritz Lugt. The exhibition illustrated the development of landscape drawing in the 17th century and included an outstanding group by Rembrandt and his followers. The drawings were also seen in Brussels, Rotterdam, Neth., and Bern, Switz.

In the summer of 1969 the city of Strasbourg museum organized a second exhibition of modern European art with the support of the Council of Europe, on the theme "The Russian Ballets of Serge de Diaghilev." The Orangerie in Paris was the site in the summer of an exhibition of the work of Edgar Degas, which consisted of paintings, pastels, drawings, prints, and sculpture drawn from the collections of the

Visitor "performing" Andy Warhol's "Dance Steps–Tango" at the Pop Art Exhibition held at the Hayward Gallery, London, in 1969.

"THE TIMES," LONDON

Louvre. The museum at Valenciennes celebrated the 150th anniversary of the birth of the landscape painter Henri Harpignies in that city with an exhibition of his works.

The Musée des Beaux-Arts in Le Havre mounted "Masterpieces from the Hermitage" (Leningrad); artists from Rembrandt to Ingres and including Nicolas Poussin, François Boucher, and J. B. S. Chardin were represented. In return, the Pushkin Museum in Moscow exhibited about 100 paintings on the subject of Romanticism in France which drew crowds in the spring of 1969. The pictures, lent by French museums, represented artists from Jacques-Louis David to J. B. C. Corot, including Eugène Delacroix, Antoine Gros, Jean-Louis Géricault, and Victor Hugo.

In Italy the Palazzo Bianco in Genoa exhibited more than 100 17th- and 18th-century Genoese paintings in the autumn. In Venice an exhibition entitled "From Ricci to Tiepolo," held at the Doge's Palace in the summer, emphasized figure painting and portraiture.

At Mannheim in West Germany brightly coloured abstract canvases by the Danish-born Hamburg artist K. Sönderborg were exhibited in April at the Städtische Kunsthalle. The Staatliche Kunsthalle of Baden-Baden exhibited works by the English sculptor Henry Moore. The Musée d'Ixelles in Brussels organized a show on the theories, projects, and achievements of "modernist" Belgian architects from 1890 to 1940.

Visitors to London were granted the rare opportunity of seeing nearly 200 drawings by Leonardo da Vinci from the queen's collection. These magnificent drawings were on view at the Queen's Gallery, Buckingham Palace, for several months. French paintings from the Mesdag Museum in The Hague came to London and were shown at the Wildenstein Gallery. The collection, formed by the Dutch painter and patron Hendrik Willen Mesdag (1831–1915), included works by C. F. Daubigny, Jean-François Millet, A. J. T. Monticelli, and Corot.

Other shows in London included the Institute of Contemporary Arts' "Fluorescent Chrysanthemum," emphasizing the merging of fine arts and design in the work of 61 Japanese artists, designers, and composers. Many of the works were executed in illuminated plastics. Large, colourful, welded-steel sculptures by British sculptor Anthony Caro formed an Arts Council exhibition at the Hayward Gallery, and the Lefevre Gallery held a Monet loan exhibition of 21 landscapes done before about 1880, all borrowed from British sources. "Baroque in Bohemia" was the title of a magnificent exhibition of Czechoslovakian art at the Victoria and Albert Museum. The show included particularly fine examples of Bohemian Baroque sculpture.

The Tate Gallery held an exhibition of work by the Belgian Surrealist René Magritte, who died in 1967, with 101 strangely fascinating pictures dating from 1926 to 1966. Later in the spring the Tate held a large retrospective of works by the pioneer British modern painter Ben Nicholson. In the autumn the newly appointed U.S. ambassador to London, Walter H. Annenberg, made available to the Tate 32 paintings of the French School from his private collection. These ranged from Baudin to Jean Fautner and included works by Gauguin, Van Gogh, Monet, Cézanne, and Toulouse-Lautrec.

An outstanding show was that devoted to the Pre-Raphaelite artist William Holman Hunt, organized by the Walker Art Gallery, Liverpool, and also seen at the Victoria and Albert Museum. It was the first opportunity since 1907 for enthusiasts of 19th-century British painting to see most of Holman Hunt's pictures together. (S. Mi.)

See also Museums and Galleries; Photography.

Encyclopædia Britannica Films. *The Louvre* (1965); *Michelangelo* (1965); *Meaning in Modern Painting* (1967); *The Artist at Work—Jacques Lipchitz Master Sculptor* (1968); *Henry Moore—The Sculptor* (1969); *Siqueiros—"El Maestro"* (1969).

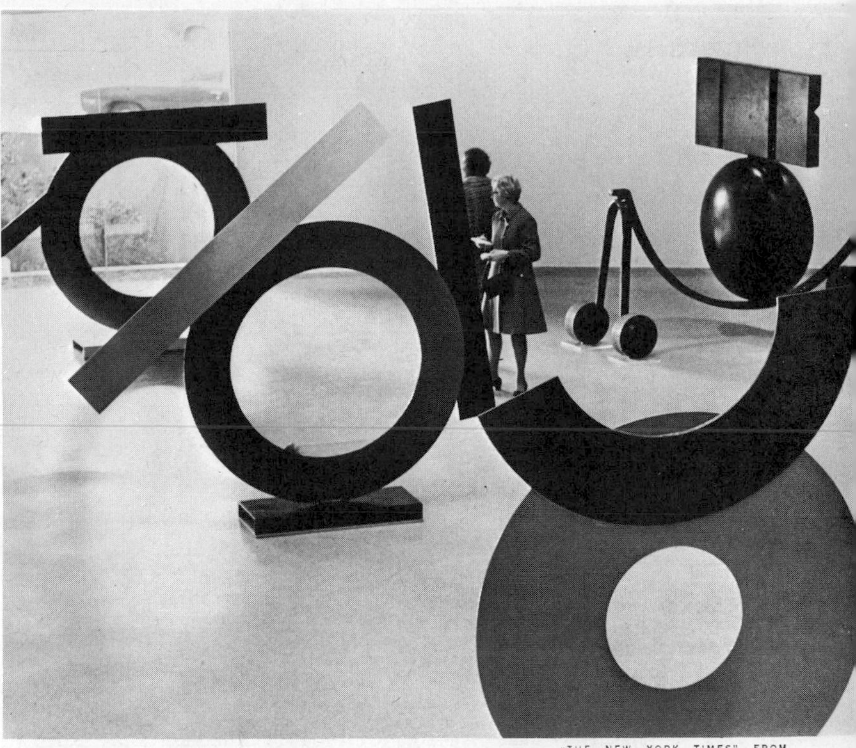

"THE NEW YORK TIMES" FROM WIDE WORLD

Geometrical metal constructions included in the David Smith retrospective exhibition at the Solomon R. Guggenheim Museum in New York City, April 1969.

Art Sales

One more Rembrandt self-portrait passed from private ownership in 1969 when the Norton Simon Museum, Los Angeles, bought an early signed portrait belonging to Col. Heywood-Lonsdale for £483,000 at Christie's in London. At the same sale a ceiling painting by Tiepolo went to the National Gallery, London, for £409,000. The Tiepolo had been listed for years as "whereabouts unknown," when in fact it and four others had remained in their previously known positions on the ceiling of the United Arab Republic's embassy in London.

This sale helped to boost Christie's turnover for the season to a total of £15,239,661, an increase of 21% over 1968. The world record turnover was again held by Sotheby's of London at £25,082,520.

Jewelry played a larger part than usual in the year's sales. In Geneva, Christie's sold the collection of the late Nina Dyer for a total of £538,780. Among the more important pieces were two splendid diamond rings, of which one brought £111,947 (SFr. 1,150,000) and the other, £107,019 (SFr. 1.1 million).

In New York the historic pearl "La Peregrina," weighing 203.84 grains, was bought for $37,000 by the actor Richard Burton. Later in the year he acquired a 69.42-carat diamond from Cartier's; the price was undisclosed, but the jewelry firm had paid a record $1,050,000 for the gem at Parke-Bernet's.

Albrecht Durer's "Stag Beetle," dated 1505, was sold at Sotheby's on June 26, 1969, for £58,000—a world record price for a drawing.

COURTESY, MRS. W. LAWS

That salesroom also held an interesting sale of Renaissance jewelry collected by the late Melvin Gutman. The pieces contained few precious stones, and the value lay in the exquisite craftsmanship. The highest price was $32,000 for a rare 16th-century Scottish gold and enameled necklace. A French enameled gold and jeweled pomander of about 1600, which fetched $31,000, had been bought at Parke-Bernet's in 1943 for $1,800. A 16th-century German enameled gold and bloodstone pendant, bought at Parke-Bernet's in 1950 for $325, went for $23,000.

French Impressionist paintings again rose in price. Camille Pissarro's "Jardin des Tuileries, Matinée de Printemps" sold for $260,000 in New York, while at a sale in Paris held by Ader and Picard, Fr. 1 million was paid for "Bords de Seine à Port-Marly" by Alfred Sisley. A painting by Paul Signac, "Le Port de Portrieux" of 1888, made Fr. 551,000 in Paris and a Monet, "Les Glacons," fetched Fr. 375,000. The same auctioneers, Rheims and Laurin, sold an extremely rare piece of French furniture, a Louis XVI "petite table" by Carlin, for Fr. 510,000.

Interest in old master drawings and water colours increased. Fierce competition for the water-colour drawing "Stag Beetle" by Albrecht Dürer, monogrammed and dated 1505, brought £58,000, paid by the French film actor Alain Delon. Fine old silver was much sought after, and Christie's sold a pair of English engraved tankards (1686) for £56,000. These had made a record price of £17,000 at Christie's in 1963, and the auctioneers reckoned that they had increased in value at the rate of 15*s*. an hour over the ensuing five years.

A sale was held in Florence of some of the remaining treasures of the Talleyrand-Périgord–Ruspoli family: the Ghirlandajo panel depicting St. Peter the Martyr was sold for 100 million lire, and a Roman sculpture of the centaur Chiron for 40 million lire.

Bidding by Japanese collectors helped to raise the prices of Chinese porcelain. London auctioneers began to hold sales in Tokyo, where Christie's sold a large 14th-century blue jar for £25,700, the highest price ever paid for a single piece of porcelain. T'ang figures of horses showed the biggest rise of all. One was sold at Parke-Bernet's for $32,000. (Wa. Ls.)

Book Sales. With so many old libraries being dispersed, it was remarkable that in 1969 a large portion of an 18th-century one was offered for sale nearly intact. The library of Bishop Thomas Percy (1729–1811), editor of the *Reliques of Ancient English Poetry,* had suffered only two losses since his death: some 120 volumes had been given to the Bodleian Library, Oxford, and a U.S. dealer had purchased some others in 1928. The 1,800 remaining titles bound in approximately 880 volumes, with numerous annotations in Percy's handwriting, were purchased at Sotheby's on June 23 for the Queen's University, Belfast, for £90,000.

Continued interest was shown in the various fields of book collecting. The first edition of Marx's *Das Kapital* (1867), inscribed by the author, was sold in London for £2,400. In May, in Paris, a copy of the first edition of Flaubert's *Madame Bovary* (1857) brought Fr. 101,770. A vellum copy of the first edition of Montaigne's *Essais* (1580) was sold in London on March 3 for £3,400.

Scientific books increased in value. At Sotheby's, Joseph Carpue's *An Account of Two Successful Operations for Restoring a Lost Nose* (1816) fetched £1,400 at the dispersal of the books of the Royal Medical Society of Edinburgh. William Gilbert's *De Magnete* (1600) was sold for £1,600 and the rare and beautiful *Nouveau Recueil d'ostéologie et de myologie* by Jacques Gamelin (1779) for £1,100.

Fine bindings were sold in Paris in November 1968. Part I of Johannes Magnus' *Historia de omnibus gothorum sueonumque regibus* of 1555, bound for Henri II, brought Fr. 182,070, and an exquisite 17th-century Le Gascon binding on Pierre Moreau's *Les Sainctes Prières de l'ame Chrétienne* (1649) made Fr. 133,670. Illustrated books also showed an increase. In Bern, Switz., in June, examples of Picasso's work

One of a pair of 18-in. Viennese swans made of lapis lazuli and silver gilt and set with rubies, diamonds, and emeralds. The pair, made about 1870, sold at Sotheby's for £2,350 on March 3, 1969.

SPERRYN'S LTD.

as a book illustrator brought extravagant prices: Ovid's *Metamorphoses* (1931) fetched SFr. 32,200 and Balzac's *Chef d'oeuvre inconnu* (1931) SFr. 20,700.

Illuminated manuscripts appeared in the Phillipps sale where a copy of the 10th-century Persian poet Firdausi's *Shah-Nama* (Book of Kings), written and painted in 1654, made £34,000. Among 14th- and 15th-century manuscripts sold during the year was one by the encyclopaedist Vincent de Beauvais, written and illustrated for Charles V of France (*c.* 1370–80), which fetched £88,000, and a Bologna Bible (*c.* 1430) made for Cardinal Albergati, which brought £85,000.

At Sotheby's in June, some 570 letters from Dr. Johnson's friend Mrs. Thrale brought £8,800 and the manuscript of her *Children's Book or Rather Family Book*, £5,500. A fragment of 26 lines of Goethe's *Faust*, written by the author on a half sheet of paper, was sold for £6,500. A letter by Shelley was sold at Sotheby's for £3,800 by the governors of Harrow School. In Paris the Houghton Library, Harvard University, purchased a manuscript of Stéphane Mallarmé's *Le Livre* for Fr. 22,570; the Bibliothèque Nationale bought a 44-page manuscript of one of Diderot's *Salons* (1761) for Fr. 65,470 and some 16,500 letters from the actress Juliette Drouet to Victor Hugo for Fr. 277,236.

On April 15 in New York, Parke-Bernet's sold one of eight known copies (out of 60 issued) of the first printing of the Constitution of the United States of America, printed at Philadelphia on Aug. 6, 1787, for $155,000; it had belonged to Pierce Butler, delegate from South Carolina to the Constitutional Convention. This world record was surpassed three weeks later when a broadsheet of the Declaration of Independence printed at Philadelphia in 1776, of which 16 copies are known, was sold in Philadelphia by Samuel T. Freeman & Co. to a Texas buyer for $404,000. (P. Bs.)

Astronautics

With the first manned landing on the moon in July and another moon walk in November, 1969 stood out as the most momentous year in the history of astronautics. The full assessment of this triumph of human dedication and ability would have to await the judgment of future generations, but there was no question about its immediate impact.

Manned Space Flight. From the time of its launch on July 16 to the lunar landing on July 20 and through to the return splashdown on July 24, almost every major aspect of the flight of Apollo 11 was witnessed via television or followed on radio by hundreds of millions of people in nearly every part of the globe, China being the chief exception. The pulse of humanity rose with the giant, 363-ft.-high, 6,484,280-lb. Saturn V launch vehicle as it made its flawless flight from Pad 39A before hundreds of thousands of spectators at Cape Kennedy, Fla. So accurate was the translunar insertion that three of the planned enroute trajectory corrections were not necessary. Aboard the Apollo 11 were U.S. astronauts Neil A. Armstrong, Edwin E. Aldrin, Jr., and Michael Collins (*see* BIOGRAPHY). Their enthusiasm was evident from the beginning, as mission commander Armstrong exclaimed "... this Saturn gave us a magnificent ride ... It was beautiful!"

The three astronauts conducted their transposition and docking maneuvers, first turning the command-service module combination around and then extracting the lunar module from its resting place above the Saturn's third stage. The third stage of the Saturn then fired to start the men on their 240,000-mi. journey to the moon. On their arrival the astronauts slowed their spacecraft so that it would go into lunar orbit. Apollo 11 entered first an elliptical 70-to-195-mi. path and then a nearly circular orbit between 62 and 75 mi. above the surface of the moon.

On the morning of July 20 Armstrong and Aldrin crawled from the command module through an interconnecting tunnel into the lunar module. Toward the end of the 12th lunar orbit, the Apollo 11 became two separate craft: the command-service module, henceforth known as "Columbia," piloted by Collins, and the lunar module, nicknamed "Eagle," occupied by Armstrong and Aldrin.

By firing the "Eagle" 's propulsion system, the two astronauts changed from their nearly circular orbit to an elliptical course whose closest approach to the moon was only 50,000 ft. At this low point they again fired their engine, this time to undergo the powered descent initiation maneuver. At about 500 ft. above the surface Armstrong began maneuvering the craft manually (although the main engine continued under automatic control) to avoid landing in a rock-strewn crater.

For about a minute and a half, Armstrong hovered the "Eagle," moving it laterally with the reaction control system until he found a clear area on which to descend. Then the contact light went on inside the cockpit, as the 68-in. probes dangling below "Eagle" 's footpads signaled contact with the ground. One second later the descent rocket engine was cut off, as the astronauts gazed down onto a sheet of lunar soil blown radially in all directions. Armstrong then radioed, "Houston, Tranquillity Base here. The Eagle has landed!"

Six and a half hours later, on July 20, Armstrong stepped out onto the lunar soil with the words, "That's one small step for a man, one giant leap for mankind." He immediately described the surface as "fine and powdery" and said that there was no difficulty in moving about. Aldrin joined his companion about 20 minutes later.

During their more-than-two-hour moon walk, Armstrong and Aldrin set up a device to measure the composition of solar radiation reaching the moon, a device to receive laser beams from astronomical observatories on earth to determine the exact distance of the two bodies from one another, and a passive seismometer to measure moonquakes and meteor impacts long after the astronauts had returned home. They also took about 50 lb. of rock and soil samples and took many photographs, and maintained constant communication with mission control in Houston, Tex. After 21 hr. 37 min. on the moon's surface, the astronauts used "Eagle" 's ascent stage to launch it back into lunar orbit. After various maneuvers "Eagle" once again docked with Collins in "Columbia" and the trip back to earth began soon afterward.

Splashdown of the Apollo 11 occurred in the Pacific Ocean about 900 mi. SW of Hawaii on July 24. The astronauts were immediately placed in quarantine in a van on the recovery ship. From there, they were flown to the Manned Spacecraft Center in Houston, where they were transferred into the large, 58-room Lunar Receiving Laboratory. The quarantine lasted

Association Football: *see* Football

Three photographs from the Apollo 11 mission climaxed by the first manned lunar landing, July 20, 1969. Neil Armstrong and Edwin Aldrin made the descent to the surface; Michael Collins piloted the command module. Above, Apollo 11 landing site photographed from lunar orbit. Right, Edwin Aldrin descending the lunar module ladder to the lunar surface. Far right, Aldrin standing beside the U.S. flag deployed by the astronauts.

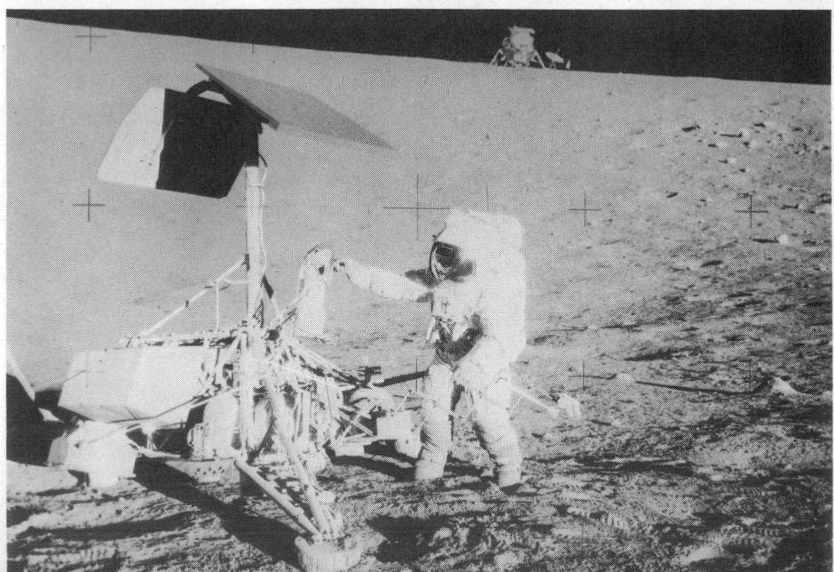

The Apollo 12 mission was highlighted by man's second landing on the moon on Nov. 19–20, 1969. The crew conducted extensive extravehicular activity and scientific experiments. Charles Conrad and Alan Bean explored the lunar surface while Richard Gordon remained in orbit. Above left, one of the astronauts holds a container of lunar soil. Above, S-band antenna deployed near the lunar module and a crewman standing at the Modularized Equipment Storage Assembly. Left, Apollo 12 crew member removing pieces from Surveyor 3 which landed on the moon on April 19, 1967. A television camera and a number of other parts were detached and brought back to earth for scientific examination.

COURTESY, NASA

Major Satellites and Space Probes Launched Oct. 20, 1968—Oct. 20, 1969

Name/country/ launch vehicle/ scientific designation	Launch date, lifetime*	Weight (kg.)†	Shape	Diameter	Length or height	Experiments	Apogee (km.)†	Perigee (km.)†	Period (min.)	Inclination to Equator (degrees)
		Physical characteristics					Initial orbital elements			
Soyuz 2/U.S.S.R./not available/ 1968-93A	10/25/68 10/28/68	5,850 (13,000)	Cylinder with spherical compartment	2.1 m. (7 ft.)	7.5 m. (25 ft.)	Unmanned rendezvous target for Soyuz 3	224 (139)	184 (115)	88.5	51.7
Soyuz 3/U.S.S.R./not available/ 1968-94A	10/26/68 10/30/68	5,850 (13,000)	Cylinder with spherical compartment	2.1 m. (7 ft.)	7.5 m. (25 ft.)	Cosmonaut Georgi Beregovoi rendezvoused with but did not dock with Soyuz 2	224 (140)	204 (127)	88.6	51.4
Pioneer 9/U.S./Thor-Delta/ 1968-100A	11/8/68	66.7 (148)	Cylinder	94 cm. (37 in.)	88 cm. (35 in.)	Obtain data on solar wind, energetic particles, and magnetic fields in space	Solar orbit			—
Zond 6/U.S.S.R./not available/ 1968-101A	11/10/68 11/17/68	‡	Truncated cone	‡	‡	Checkout of navigation and guidance, and reentry systems for future lunar probes	Circled moon and returned to earth			
Proton 4/U.S.S.R./not available/ 1968-103A	11/16/68 7/24/69	16,580 (37,500)	Cylinder	‡	‡	Cosmic ray research	480 (308)	203 (158)	91.75	31.5
HEOS 1/ESRO/Thor-Delta/ 1968-109A	12/5/68	107 (238)	Elongated hexahedron	128 cm. (51.2 in.)	250 cm. (100.4 in.)	Study magnetic fields, solar wind, and cosmic radiation outside earth's magnetosphere	224,000 (139,453)	4,300 (2,696)	6,792.7	28.2
OAO 2/U.S./Atlas-Centaur/ 1968-110A	12/7/68	2,000 (4,446)	Elongated hexahedron	2.1 m. (7 ft.)	3.3 m. (10 ft.)	Study young, hot stars in ultraviolet spectrum; study gases in interplanetary space	776 (485)	770 (479)	89.6	65
ESSA 8/U.S./Thor-Delta/ 1968-114A	12/15/68	132 (290)	Cylinder	107 cm. (42 in.)	56 cm. (22 in.)	Weather satellite	1,460 (910)	1,420 (880)	114.6	101.8
Intelsat 3A/U.S./Thor-Delta/ 1968-116A	12/18/68	290 (642)	Cylinder	140 cm. (56 in.)	107 cm. (41 in.)	Communications satellite	35,600 (22,257)	35,585 (22,244)	1,436	0.71
Apollo 8/U.S./Saturn V/ 1968-118A	12/21/68 12/27/68	28,650 (63,650)	Truncated cone and cylinder	12.3 m. (35.3 ft.)	3.9 m. (12.8 ft.)	First trip of men around the moon to test lunar spacecraft	Flight time: 147 hr. 11 sec.			
Venera 5/U.S.S.R./not available/ 1969-01A	1/5/69 5/16/69	1,130 (2,490)	Tower with detachable sphere	3 m. (12 ft.)	1.2 m. (4 ft.)	Investigate the properties of the Venusian atmosphere	Flight time: 136 days			
Venera 6/U.S.S.R./not available/ 1969-02A	1/10/69 5/17/69	1,130 (2,490)	Tower with detachable sphere	3 m. (12 ft.)	1.2 m. (4 ft.)	Investigate the properties of the Venusian atmosphere	Flight time: 127 days			
Soyuz 4/U.S.S.R./not available/ 1969-04A	1/14/69 1/17/69	5,860 (13,000)	Cylinder with spherical compartment	2.1 m. (7 ft.)	7.5 m. (25 ft.)	Carried cosmonaut V. Shatalov into orbit for rendezvous and docking target for Soyuz 5	224 (139)	204 (127)	88.7	51.7
Soyuz 5/U.S.S.R./not available/ 1969-05A	1/15/69 1/18/69	5,860 (13,000)	Cylinder with spherical compartment	2.1 m. (7 ft.)	7.5 m. (25 ft.)	Carried cosmonauts B. Volynov, Y. Khrunov, and A. Yeliseyev into orbit for docking with Soyuz 4. Two cosmonauts transferred to Soyuz 4 for return.	232 (145)	208 (131)	88.8	51.7
OSO 5/U.S./Thor-Delta/ 1969-06A	1/22/69	288 (641)	Eight-sided box	110 cm. (44 in.)	97.5 cm. (39 in.)	Study solar influence on earth's atmosphere	559 (348)	537 (334)	95.6	32.95
ISIS-1/Canada/Thor-Delta/ 1969-09A	1/30/79	240 (532)	Polyhedron	125 cm. (50 in.)	105 cm. (42 in.)	Study of the earth's ionosphere	3,526 (2,192)	578 (359)	128.4	88.4
Intelsat 3/U.S./Thor-Delta/ 1969-11A	2/6/69	144 (320)	Cylinder	140 cm. (56 in.)	107 cm. (41 in.)	Communications satellite	35,809 (22,237)	35,786 (22,221)	1,436	1.3
Tacomsat 1/U.S./Titan III-C/ 1969-13A	2/9/69	720 (1,600)	Cylinder	2.4 m. (8 ft.)	6 m. (20 ft.)	Military communications satellite	36,044 (22,384)	35,939 (22,320)	1,446.6	0.6
Mariner 6/U.S./Atlas-Centaur/ 1969-14A	2/25/69 7/31/69	382 (850)	Octagon	125 cm. (50 in.)	50 cm. (20 in.)	Mars probe to study surface temperatures, atmospheric composition, and topography	Flight time: 157 days			
ESSA 9/U.S./Thor-Delta/ 1969-16A	2/26/69	138 (308)	Cylinder	107 cm. (42 in.)	56 cm. (22 in.)	Weather satellite	1,505 (937)	1,430 (887)	115.2	101.8
Apollo 9/U.S./Saturn V/ 1969-18A	3/3/69 3/13/69	43,580 (97,500)	Truncated cone and cylinder	3.9 m. (12.8 ft.)	17.7 m. (58.4 ft.)	Checkout of the Apollo spacecraft system, including the lunar module	508 (317)	197 (123)	91.46	33.8
Meteor 1/U.S.S.R./not available/ 1969-29A	3/26/69	‡	Cylinder	1.5 m. (5 ft.)	4.8 m. (16 ft.)	Weather satellite	686 (427)	632 (393)	97.9	81.1
Mariner 7/U.S./Atlas-Centaur/ 1969-30A	3/27/69 8/5/69	382 (850)	Octagon	125 cm. (50 in.)	50 cm. (20 in.)	Mars probe to study surface temperatures, atmospheric composition, and topography	Flight time: 132 days			
Molniya 1L/U.S.S.R./not available/ 1969-35A	4/11/69	1,100 (2,200)	Windmill shape with six vanes	1.7 m. (5.5 ft.)	3.3 m. (11 ft.)	Communications satellite	39,595 (24,700)	483 (251)	712.1	64.9
Nimbus 3/U.S./Thor-Delta/ 1969-37A	4/14/69	570 (1,268)	Conical skeleton with two vanes	1.5 m. (5 ft.)	2.9 m. (9.5 ft.)	Weather satellite	1,133 (706)	1,072 (669)	107.3	99.9
Apollo 10/U.S./Saturn V/ 1969-43A	5/18/69 5/26/69	43,580 (97,500)	Truncated cone and cylinder	3.9 m. (12.8 ft.)	17.7 m. (58.4 ft.)	Last checkout of the Apollo spacecraft system before landing of men on the moon	Orbited moon and returned to earth			
Intelsat 3D/U.S./Thor-Delta/ 1969-45A	5/22/69	144 (320)	Cylinder	140 cm. (56 in.)	107 cm. (41 in.)	Communications satellite	35,801 (22,100)	35,787 (22,098)	1,436.5	0.5
OGO 6/U.S./Thor-Agena D/ 1969-51A	6/5/69	635 (1,410)	Box with booms	82.5 cm. (33 in.)	170 cm. (68 in.)	Orbiting geophysical observatory	1,089 (682)	397 (246)	99.6	82
Explorer 41/U.S./Thor-Delta/ 1969-53A	6/21/69	78 (175)	Octagon with two booms	70 cm. (28 in.)	25 cm. (10 in.)	Interplanetary monitoring platform for solar wind, magnetic fields, cosmic rays	213,849 (110,728)	378 (213)	4,840	83.8
Biosatellite 3/U.S./Thor-Delta/ 1969-56A	6/29/69 7/7/69	690 (1,536)	Conical cylinder	1.5 m. (4.8 ft.)	3 m. (10 ft.)	Test effects of weightlessness on monkey and other life forms	387 (201)	356 (200)	92	33.5
Luna 15/U.S.S.R./not available/ 1969-58A	7/13/69 7/21/69	‡	‡	‡	‡	Check out navigation and guidance systems of lunar landing probe	Flight time: 3 days			
Apollo 11/U.S./Saturn V/ 1969-59A	7/16/69 7/24/69	66.097 (106,608)	Truncated cone and cylinder	3.9 m. (12.8 ft.)	17.7 m. (58.4 ft.)	First landing of men on the moon, astronauts N. Armstrong, E. Aldrin, and M. Collins	Flight time to moon: 4 days			
Molniya 1M/U.S.S.R./not available/ 1969-61A	7/23/69	1,100 (2,200)	Cylinder with conical top	1.2 m. (4 ft.)	3.6 m. (12 ft.)	Communications satellite	39,526 (24,600)	496 (310)	711	64.9
Zond 7/U.S.S.R./not available/ 1969-67A	8/8/69 8/14/69	‡	‡	‡	‡	Check out navigation and guidance systems for future lunar soft-landing probes	Flight time: 6 days			
OSO 6/U.S./Thor-Delta/ 1969-68A	8/9/69	288 (640)	Octagon	110 cm. (44 in.)	97.5 cm. (39 in.)	Study influence of the sun on earth's atmosphere	554 (344)	489 (304)	95.1	32.9
ATS 5/U.S./Thor-Delta/ 1969-69A	8/12/69	330 (660)	Cylinder	140 cm. (56 in.)	180 cm. (72 in.)	Advanced technology satellite	35,956 (24,600)	34,844 (21,600)	1,416.4	2.6
Meteor 2/U.S.S.R./not available/ not available	10/6/69	‡	‡	‡	‡	Weather satellite	690 (431)	630 (394)	97.1	81.2
Soyuz 6/U.S.S.R./not available/ not available	10/11/69 10/16/69	6,000 (13,200)	Cylinder with spherical end	2.1 m. (7 ft.)	9.6 m. (32 ft.)	First of three manned spacecraft launched to form a space station	221 (138)	186 (116)	88.4	51.7
Soyuz 7/U.S.S.R./not available/ not available	10/12/69 10/17/69	6,000 (13,200)	Cylinder with spherical end	2.1 m. (7 ft.)	2.1 m. (7 ft.)	Second of three spacecraft in space station experiment	226 (141)	206 (129)	88.6	51.7
Soyuz 8/U.S.S.R./not available/ not available	10/13/69 10/18/69	6,000 (13,200)	Cylinder with spherical end	2.1 m. (7 ft.)	2.1 m. (7 ft.)	Third of three spacecraft in space station experiment	224 (140)	208 (130)	88.6	51.7
Intercosmos 1/U.S.S.R./not available/ not available	10/14/69	‡	‡	‡	‡	Soviet scientific satellite, first of a new series	640 (400)	259 (162)	93.3	48.4

*All dates are in universal time (UT).
†English units in parentheses: weight in pounds, apogee and perigee in statute miles.
‡Not available.

21 days from the time "Eagle" took off from the moon; during that period, the astronauts were checked for any disease they might have picked up on the moon, and the lunar samples were subjected to preliminary analyses.

Despite low banks of clouds and persistent rain, the year's second manned moon landing mission, Apollo 12, was launched on November 14. Approximately 36.5 seconds after the launch an electrical surge passed through the huge Saturn V rocket and down through the conducting exhaust plume, overloading the circuits and causing a temporary loss of power aboard the spacecraft. Fortunately, the Saturn V itself was not affected, and power was soon restored in the spacecraft by resetting the circuit breakers.

In command of the mission was Charles Conrad, Jr., a former U.S. Navy test pilot who had previously orbited the earth in Gemini 5 and Gemini 11. Command module pilot was Richard F. Gordon, Jr., a former Navy test pilot who had walked in space during the Gemini 11 flight. Lunar module pilot Alan L. Bean, also a former Navy test pilot, was on his first space mission.

Gordon remained in orbit aboard the command module, while Conrad and Bean skillfully brought "Intrepid," the lunar module, down on target on November 19. During their 31½-hour sojourn on the Ocean of Storms plain, the astronauts made two excursions, one 4 hours long and one of 4½ hours. Television coverage was not possible because of equipment failure.

After studying the area in the immediate vicinity of "Intrepid," the astronauts moved out to deploy the Apollo lunar surface experiments package, which was designed to send back to earth, over a period of approximately a year, information on the physics and structure of the surface and subsurface and the effects on the lunar environment of the corpuscular, magnetic, and other phenomena emanating from the sun.

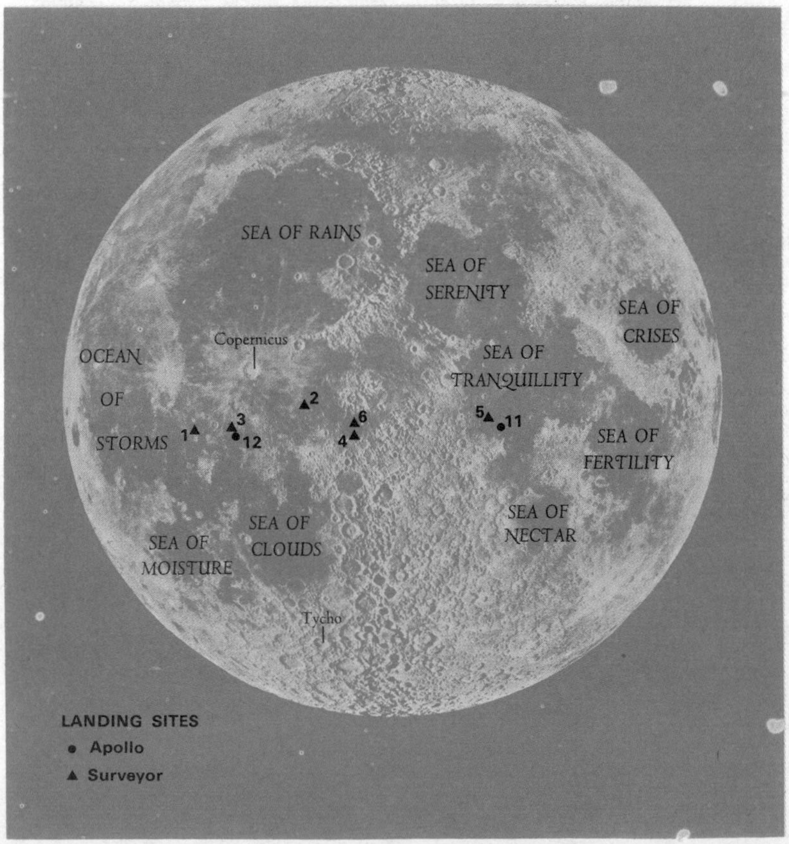

On their second excursion Conrad and Bean strolled and trotted around to several small craters out to a distance of 1,300 ft., and visited the nearby Surveyor 3. They discovered that the spacecraft had changed in colour from white to tan, and that structurally it seemed somewhat brittle.

The lunar module took off from the moon's surface and redocked with the orbiting command module without incident. After the rendezvous and docking were over, the ascent stage of "Intrepid" crashed onto the moon in an experiment to provide a seismic test of its internal structure. To the surprise of the scientific world, the lunar seismometer registered, over a period of nearly an hour, reverberations that were set up by the lunar module. Selenologists and lunar physicists, predicting that the experiment would lead to new interpretations of the lunar interior, suggested that it might be fractured.

Splashdown took place in the Pacific Ocean three miles from the U.S.S. "Hornet" on November 24.

The achievements of Apollo 11 and Apollo 12 had been made possible by the earlier Apollo flights. In December 1968 Apollo 8 with Frank Borman, James Lovell, Jr., and William Anders aboard, had become the first manned spacecraft to travel to the moon and then go into orbit around it. During the ten-day Apollo 9 flight that began on March 3, astronauts James A. McDivitt, David R. Scott, and Russell L. Schweickart performed rendezvous and docking of the lunar module with the command-service module while in earth orbit. The ascent and descent stage propulsion and reaction control systems of the lunar module were exercised, and guidance, navigation, computer, display, and intervehicular communications systems were tested.

So successful was the Apollo 9 mission that it was repeated—in lunar orbit—two months later. Apollo 10 proved the feasibility of rendezvous and docking of the Apollo modules in orbit around the moon and the ability of the lunar module's descent propulsion system to function properly. Thomas P. Stafford and Eugene A. Cernan manned the lunar module, while John W. Young remained in the command vehicle. After Apollo 11, NASA (the U.S. National Aeronautics and Space Administration) firmed its plans for a launch rate of three Apollo missions per year, separated by four-month intervals.

Both NASA and the U.S. Air Force continued to plan ambitious earth-orbital missions during the year, with strong indications that the two government organizations would work closely together. For many years the Air Force had been working on the MOL, or Manned Orbiting Laboratory, program; but on June 10, the Department of Defense announced its cancellation as "a major step" toward trimming the military budget. NASA, for its part, continued to develop the Saturn V Workshop and conducted studies of larger space stations with the hope of realizing operational systems by the mid-1970s. The initial project, the Workshop, was to be a space station made up of a Saturn V S-4B third stage, a multiple docking adapter, an airlock, and a telescope mount.

Despite the acclaim given to the space voyagers, a number of U.S. astronauts decided to leave the program during the year. Michael Collins, the command-module pilot of Apollo 11, joined the State Department. Frank Borman (Apollo 8) resigned to become field director of Advanced Space Stations of NASA, while William A. Anders of the same flight was nominated by U.S. Pres. Richard Nixon to become executive secretary of the National Aeronautics and Space Council in Washington. In September, James A. McDivitt, of Gemini 4 and Apollo 9, became manager of the Apollo Spacecraft Program at the Manned Spacecraft Center, while L. Gordon Cooper, Jr., was named assistant for NASA's space shuttle program at Houston. Earlier in the year a Mercury-Gemini-Apollo veteran, Navy Capt. Walter M. Schirra, Jr., resigned to become president of a Denver industrial firm. Alan Shepard, meanwhile, returned to full astronaut flight status in May. He had undergone an operation to correct a fault that had left him subject to periodic dizzy spells. Shepard was America's first man in space, flying the Mercury Redstone in May 1961. During the year NASA gained the services of seven astronauts transferred from the canceled Manned Orbiting Laboratory program.

Despite its scientific and technical successes, NASA experienced difficulties during the year. First was the matter of finding a qualified person interested in running the space agency. After approaching, and receiving "no's," from a dozen or so candidates, President Nixon appointed Thomas O. Paine to the post—one of the last to be filled in the new administration. The space budget was subject to debate for many months, and only in early November did the U.S. Congress agree on an authorization of $3,715,000,000. During the year, debates grew within the space community concerning an alleged neglect of science in favour of technology. Following Apollo 11, three space agency scientists and a scientist-astronaut resigned amid complaints that future Apollo plans did not include enough science and scientist-astronauts. It was hoped that the appointment of Massachusetts Institute of Technology professor Gene Simmons as chief scientist at NASA's Manned Spacecraft Center would help heal the scientist-engineer rift.

Although no manned space station programs were officially announced by the U.S.S.R., there were many indications during the year that that nation would concentrate in the near future on large-scale earth orbital operations rather than attempt to send a manned spacecraft to the moon. The Soviets began the year by sending two Soyuz spacecraft into orbit in mid-January. Vladimir A. Shatalov went into orbit in Soyuz 4 on January 14, followed the next day by a three-man crew in Soyuz 5 consisting of Boris V. Volynov, Yevgeni V. Khrunov, and a civilian physicist-engineer, Aleksei S. Yeliseyev. After maneuvering in orbit, the two spacecraft rendezvoused and docked on January 16 under the manual control of Shatalov. Once coupled, Yeliseyev and Khrunov passed first into the work compartment and then out of their spacecraft through the hatch. After about an hour in space, they entered Soyuz 4's work compartment and thence into the command area. The Soyuzes were separated about four hours after their initial docking and landed safely.

These flights were followed in mid-October by a second series, this time with three spacecraft involved. Soyuz 6 was lofted into orbit on October 11 carrying cosmonauts Georgi S. Shonin and Valeri N. Kubasov. Then, consecutively, on October 12 and 13, two more spacecraft followed, Soyuz 7 with Anatoly V. Filipchenko, Viktor V. Gorbatko, and Vladislav N. Volkov aboard, and Soyuz 8 with Shatalov (veteran of Soyuz 4) and Yeliseyev (of Soyuz 5).

No sooner was Soyuz 6 in orbit than speculation arose as to the ultimate purpose of the mission. Much of the speculation was based on rumours within the Soviet Union that a major effort had begun leading to the establishment of a permanent space station in earth orbit, reinforced by the fact that the major announced task of Soyuz 6 was to conduct in-space welding experiments. Other assignments were to observe and photograph objects on earth of geographical and geological interest and to make medical tests in space.

Less than 24 hours after Soyuz 6 had gone into orbit, Soyuz 7 was launched with three men aboard. Both craft moved at the same inclination in orbits with very similar perigee-apogee elements. When Kubasov reported, in a live television broadcast from space, that his craft had "no special instruments for docking" or any "automatic systems for close maneuvering," it appeared that no attempts would be made to join the two craft.

Rumours persisted, however, that something spectacular would take place following the launch of Soyuz 8. But nothing unusual seemed to happen as the three spacecraft circled around the earth. The crews were reported to have exchanged information using light indices and visual optical methods, and the Soviet news agency, Tass, did mention that such information was related to the establishment of "long-term orbital laboratories." On October 15 both Soyuz 6 and Soyuz 8 approached "as close as several hundred" metres to their companion Soyuz 7, but there was no rendezvous and docking and the purpose of the mission remained something of a mystery.

Space Carrier Vehicles. The first U.S. carrier vehicle launched during 1969, a Thor-Delta, sent NASA's Orbiting Solar Observatory (OSO) 5 into orbit on January 22. Despite this success, the Delta family was plagued with problems that started back in mid-September 1968 when a loose wire in the first stage's guidance system rate gyro distribution led to pitch-plane oscillations that in turn led to the failure of an Intelsat 3 mission. After that flight, eight successes were registered until July 25, when the carrier again malfunctioned in another Intelsat 3 attempt. This was followed by a failure on August 27 to boost a Pioneer probe into solar orbit. A NASA-industry investigation and review team was immediately set up to find out what had happened to a carrier that, since May 1960, had chalked up 67 successes out of 73 launches, but had suffered half of its failures since the September 1968 Intelsat 3 shot.

Saturn V continued to perform admirably, with only minor difficulties being recorded. In order to suppress the longitudinal oscillation that had occurred late in the firing period of the rocket's second stage in both the Apollo 8 and 9 missions, it was decided to cut off the inner engine 80 seconds early in the Apollo 10 flight. To compensate for the resulting loss of thrust, the four outer engines were set to burn approximately 15 seconds longer.

Saturn V performed equally well on the Apollo 11 mission, sending off the spacecraft on such an accurate trajectory that the initial midcourse correction was not needed. With the successful completion of the Apollo 11 mission, production stretchouts were ordered for the Saturn V, while the Saturn IB was canceled altogether.

Meanwhile, the Soviet Union announced the "serial" production of its standard booster, presumably the carrier employed with varying upper stages beginning with the Vostok series and carrying through to the Soyuz 4, 5, 6, 7, and 8 missions in 1969. Numerous

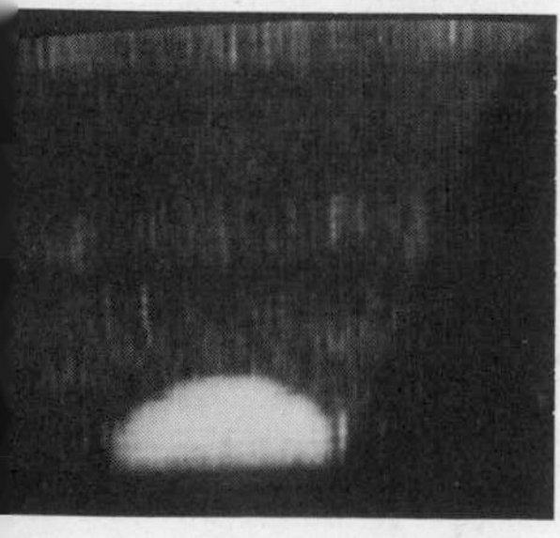

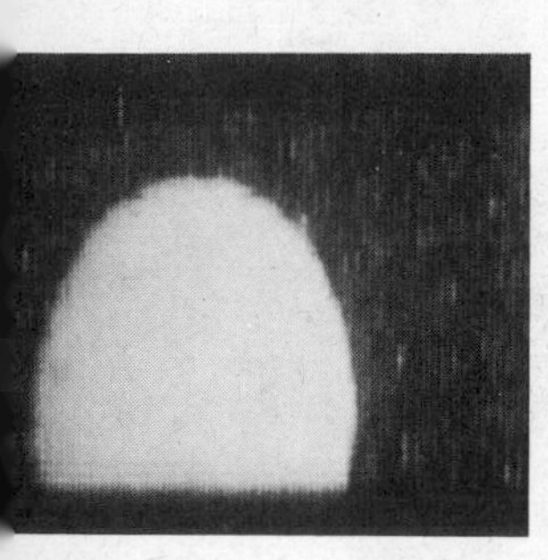

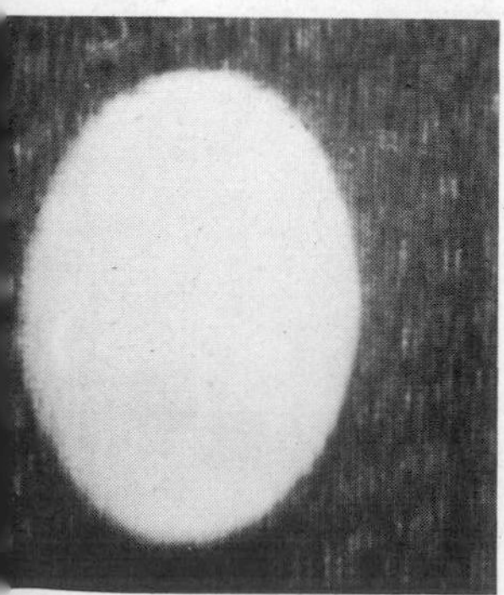

The first pictures of Mars, taken by Mariner 6 and relayed to television screens on July 29, 1969. Each television picture contained 3.9 million bits of information and took five minutes to build, line by line.

UPI COMPIX

pictures of the carrier used to orbit Soyuz were released during the year.

In Western Europe, the ELDO (European Launcher Development Organization) continued to suffer technical and financial difficulties, the technical highlighted by problems with the third stage of the Europa I carrier, and the financial resulting from rising costs and Britain's and Italy's resolve to lower their contributions by 16 and 11 million monetary units, respectively. The deficits were to be borne by increased French, West German, Belgian, and Dutch payments. At a meeting in April in Paris, ELDO agreed to press ahead with plans to launch two second-generation Europa II's from the new equatorial range in French Guiana in 1970 and 1971, and also to qualify the carrier for the French-West German Symphonie communications satellites and possibly scientific payloads. In late summer Britain confirmed the intention announced earlier to withdraw completely from ELDO by the end of 1970 when Europa I development was scheduled to be terminated; nevertheless, the U.K. promised to supply Blue Streak first stages for another five or more years. That stage and France's Coralie second stage functioned well during a Europa I F-8 launch from Woomera, Austr., on July 2, but the German Astris third stage failed to ignite. Because of the malfunction, the 440-lb. Italian satellite payload did not orbit.

Unmanned Satellites. The year 1968 closed with several significant satellite launchings. On November 16, the Soviet Union launched Proton 4, a 17-ton spacecraft instrumented to study very-high-energy cosmic rays. The U.S. on December 5 launched the 238-lb. HEOS 1 (Highly Eccentric Orbit Satellite) for ESRO (European Space Research Organization). The satellite contained experiments by scientists from Belgium, France, West Germany, Italy, and the United Kingdom. They were designed to study interplanetary magnetic fields as well as solar and cosmic ray particles outside the magnetosphere during periods of high solar activity.

On Dec. 7, 1968, the 4,400-lb. OAO 2 (Orbiting Astronomical Observatory) was launched. Placed into a near-circular earth orbit at 485.7 mi., it was the heaviest and most complex automated satellite ever launched by the U.S. In its first 20 days of operation it collected 20 times more data on ultraviolet radiation from stars than had been gathered during 15 years of sounding rocket firings. The satellite had 11 telescopes to observe interstellar dust and the ultraviolet radiation from young, hot stars that could not be observed from the earth. On April 12, 1969, OAO 2 began tumbling in orbit and lost its usefulness.

NASA launched ESSA 8 on Dec. 15, 1968, the 18th successful weather satellite in a series that began with Tiros 1 in 1960. ESSA 8 was placed into a near-circular, polar, sun-synchronous orbit at an altitude of 900 mi. and had two automatic picture transmission cameras that immediately began transmitting cloud-cover photographs to tracking stations in 52 nations.

Both Sweden and the Netherlands announced plans for national satellites to be launched by a U.S. Scout. The Netherlands Ministry of Economic Affairs undertook a design study of a 285-lb. astronomical satellite. The Swedes began design studies for a satellite to investigate the Aurora Borealis and reserved $10 million for the project.

Canada pushed ahead with plans for its own communications satellite. Studies made for its Department of Communications proposed a satellite capable of handling six colour television channels or 6,000 voice channels. With an estimated life of five years, it would be placed into a synchronous orbit above Winnipeg.

The world's largest and most complex military communications satellite was launched by the U.S. on February 9. The 1,600-lb. Tacomsat (Tactical Communications Satellite) was placed into synchronous orbit above the Galapagos Islands in the Pacific Ocean. It provided worldwide military communications from units in the field, ships at sea, and aircraft. The satellite carried a variety of antennae that could transmit signals to radio receivers on earth with antennae as small as one foot in diameter.

On April 14 Nimbus 3 was launched along with a small Secor 13 piggyback geodetic satellite. Nimbus 3, a veritable potpourri of scientific instruments, carried sensors for making cloud-cover pictures of the earth in both daylight and night as well as for taking the temperature at various levels within the atmosphere. Special radio receivers in it were designed to locate small transmitters placed on airplanes, balloons, and even on an elk named Moe wandering through Yellowstone National Park! Nimbus 3 was also the first nonmilitary satellite to carry nuclear power supplies; two Snap 19 plutonium-238-powered batteries backed up its solar-cell power supply.

An unusual astronautical event occurred on April 28. Explorer 34 began reentering the atmosphere over northern Australia and then, suddenly, skipped back out and took up a new orbit. NASA officials said that it was the first time such a thing had happened since satellites began reentering the earth's atmosphere. In April Robert G. Stone of the Goddard Space Flight Center announced that data returned from the Explorer 38 (radio astronomy experiment) satellite, launched on July 4, 1968, showed that the earth sporadically emits very-low-frequency radio waves as does Jupiter. These signals, which cannot penetrate the earth's atmosphere, were detected by the 1,500-ft. antennae of the satellite, which orbited at an altitude of 3,640 mi.

June 7 saw the final, fiery demise of Echo 2, long a familiar sight around the world as it moved across the evening sky. Launched on January 25, 1964, the 135-ft.-diameter balloon was used as a passive communications and geodetic satellite by scientists in many nations. It burned on reentering the atmosphere over Siberia just north of the Sea of Okhotsk after orbiting the earth 28,000 times.

On June 27 the Soviet Union launched its 1,000th payload into orbit since Sputnik 1 in 1957. It was Cosmos 288, a military reconnaissance satellite.

June 29 saw the launch of Biosatellite 3. The 1,536-lb. satellite carried a small pigtail monkey named Bonny. Scheduled for a 30-day stay in orbit, the mission aborted after 8½ days because the monkey had begun to show signs of deterioration. It died less than 12 hours after landing and recovery in the Pacific Ocean. Later autopsy findings showed that the effects of weightlessness upon the monkey had contributed to its death. Apparently ignoring the fact that the monkey had been immobilized for 8½ days, many scientists viewed with alarm the prospects for man in space,

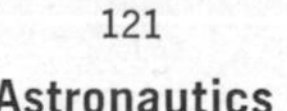

despite the fact that man had spent two weeks in space with no fatal results.

On October 14 the U.S.S.R. announced the beginning of a new series of scientific satellites with the launching of Intercosmos 1. It was a solar observatory satellite that could be monitored by tracking stations in Eastern European nations as well as in the Soviet Union.

Space Probes. As 1968 ended the U.S. launched Pioneer 9 (on November 8) into an orbit around the sun. Among its scientific tasks were monitoring solar activity and giving an early warning of solar flares to Apollo astronauts on the moon. It joined Pioneers 6, 7, and 8 in providing data to the Solar Disturbance Forecast Center, in Boulder, Colo. In addition, it carried instruments to study the solar wind, cosmic ray particles, and electric fields in interplanetary space.

Both Mars and Venus again became targets for probes in 1969. The Soviet Union chose to explore Venus, while the U.S. selected Mars for investigation. Venera 5 was launched on January 5 and was followed by Venera 6 on January 10; the latter was given a different initial velocity and followed a slightly different trajectory to ensure that it would arrive at Venus within a day of the former. Both probes were destined to land on the dark side of Venus.

Like the earlier Venera 4, both probes were two-part craft. The basic vehicle contained the guidance and communications system and solar-cell power supplies. A special soft-landing pod weighing 891 lb. was also carried by each and dropped off to land on the planet, while the main structure continued into a solar orbit. The soft-lander was a 3.3-ft.-diameter sphere with an offset centre of gravity to orient it downward before its parachute deployed.

As the pods descended through the thickening atmosphere of Venus, they transmitted data on its temperature, pressure, and chemical makeup. Venera 5 transmitted for 53 minutes, and Venera 6 for 51 minutes. Each included a radar altimeter to gauge the distance to the surface. The Venera 5 pod drifted until it was 21.6 mi. above the surface, as measured by its radar altimeter, and the Venera 6 pod descended until it was 22.8 mi. high. As heavily protected as they were, the pods could withstand pressures of only 27 atmospheres; thus, they were presumably crushed before they reached the surface. Extrapolating temperature and pressure from this altitude to the surface beneath each probe, Soviet scientists determined that the surface temperature beneath Venera 5 was 986° F and the pressure 140 atmospheres (2,058 lb. per sq.in.). Similarly, the conditions beneath Venera 6 were 752° F and 882 lb. per sq.in. The difference between the values could be accounted for by a very rugged surface, with Venera 5 being over a deep basin and Venera 6 over a plateau.

Mariner 6 was launched toward Mars from Cape Kennedy on February 25. It weighed 850 lb. and was placed on a trajectory that would take it across the face of the planet in its equatorial region at an altitude of 2,000 mi. Instrumentation in the probe consisted of two television cameras (one wide angle and one narrow angle), an infrared spectrometer, an ultraviolet spectrometer, and an infrared radiometer.

The two spectrometers were used to identify components of the Martian atmosphere, and the radiometer to determine the temperature of the planet in various locations. The television cameras took pictures of the surface for topographical studies. Radio waves beamed through the atmosphere permitted scientists to determine the pressure at the surface.

En route to Mars, Mariner 6 reported that the sun radiates only 125.7 w/sq.ft. rather than the previously supposed 129.5 w/sq.ft. Knowing this new value, designers of future spacecraft could build more efficient environmental control systems.

Mariner 6 passed Mars at an altitude of 2,120 mi. on July 30. It took 74 pictures, 24 of them during the nearest approach. The probe lost data from one of the two channels of its infrared spectrometer instrumentation because of a malfunction in the system. However, the remaining channel showed scientists that the Martian atmosphere contained no detectable nitrogen in its upper layers. This finding was discouraging for those who believed that life may exist on Mars. Carbon dioxide, oxygen, and hydrogen were detected.

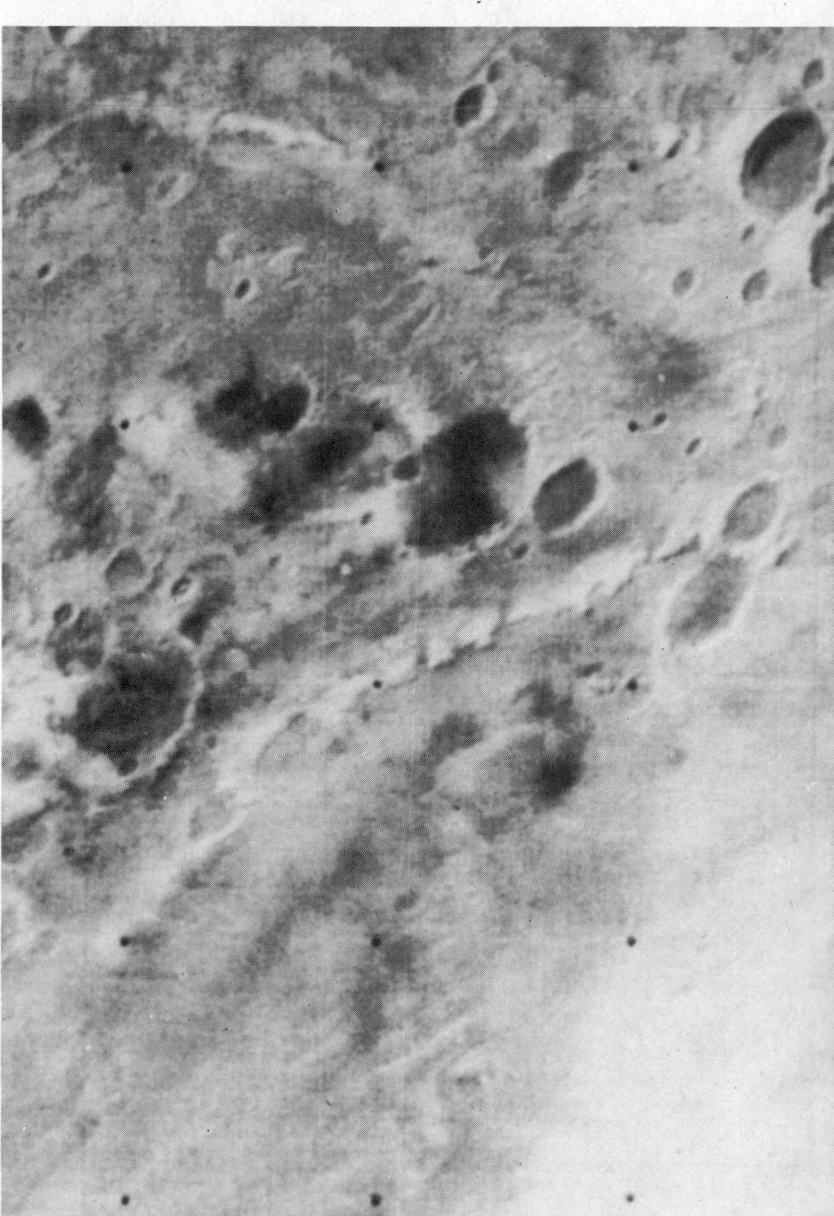

WIDE WORLD

South polar region of Mars as relayed by Mariner 7 on Aug. 6, 1969. A wide variety of crater sizes and forms as well as linear features not related to cratering can be seen.

Mariner 7 was launched on March 27 on a trajectory that took it across the south pole of Mars on August 5. The spacecraft took 91 pictures, 33 of them at the nearest approach. While there was some discrepancy between its measurements and those of Mariner 6, they were in general agreement. Temperature measurements of the planet ranged from −253° F at the south pole to a mild 75° F at the equator. The apparent atmospheric pressure at the planet's surface was reported to be 6.5 millibars, compared with 1,000 millibars at the earth's surface.

Examinations of photographs from both probes showed that Mars had a surface quite different from that of the moon despite the presence of craters. There was extremely rough terrain near the south pole of Mars, with snowdrifts approximately three feet deep; the prominent Hellas feature, in contrast, seemed devoid of craters altogether.

The most controversial and mysterious probe of 1969 was Luna 15, launched on July 13 from the U.S.S.R. Four days later it entered an orbit around the moon ranging between 540 mi. and 150 mi. at an angle of 126° to the moon's equator. On July 18 its onboard propulsion system fired to change the orbit to one of 126 mi. by 34 mi., and the following day found it again altered to 136 mi. by 59 mi. On July 20, the orbit was reshaped to 69 mi. by 10 mi. After these three days of maneuvers it crashed into the lunar surface on July 21 in the Sea of Crises, about 500 mi. NE of the U.S. Apollo 11 base. Since there had been no deployment of Soviet land or sea recovery forces, it seemed that Luna 15 was not designed to return to the earth, despite rumours that it was to have soft-landed, picked up lunar rocks, and returned them to the earth before the astronauts of Apollo 11.

Rocket-Powered Research Vehicle (X-15). Activity in the X-15 program ended as 1968 drew to a close. On Oct. 24, 1968, X-15 No. 1 was flown to 250,000 ft. and to a speed of Mach 5.04 (3,682 mph) by NASA pilot William H. Dana to test certain types of instrumentation and to perform an experiment for the Western Test Range. Dana's flight was the 199th in a series that began on Sept. 17, 1959. It was also the last for the famous experimental craft. A scheduled 200th flight on December 20 was canceled because of bad weather. During the life of the X-15, it made 154 flights at speeds of Mach 4 or greater, 109 flights at speeds of Mach 5 or greater, and 4 flights at greater than Mach 6. (F. I. Or.; M. R. S.)

See also Astronomy; Defense; Industrial Review; Meteorology; Telecommunications; Television and Radio.

Encyclopædia Britannica Films. *Earth Satellites: Explorers of Outer Space* (1958); *Rockets: How They Work* (1958); *First Men into Space* (1962); *Frontiers in Space* (1962); *A Trip to the Planets* (1963); *The Van Allen Radiation Belts* (1963); *Space Probes—Exploring Our Solar System* (1964); *You and the Aerospace Future* (1966).

Eclipses, 1970

Feb. 21	Moon, partial (begins 05:59.3 E.T.*), visible in N. and S. America, Pacific O., New Zealand
March 7	Sun, total (begins 15:04.9 E.T.*), visible in N. and S. America
Aug. 17	Moon, partial (begins 01:07.1 E.T.*), visible in Europe, Africa, Atlantic O., N. and S. America, Antarctica
Aug. 31-Sept. 1	Sun, annular (begins 19:00.6 E.T.*), visible in Australia, Pacific O.

Transit of Mercury, 1970

May 9	Mercury, transit over the disk of the sun (begins 04:20 E.T.*), visible in Alaska, Asia, Australia, Europe, Africa, N. and S. America

Equinoxes and Solstices, 1970

March 21	Vernal equinox (00:57 U.T.†)
June 21	Summer solstice (19:43 U.T.†)
Sept. 23	Autumnal equinox (10:59 U.T.†)
Dec. 22	Winter solstice (06:36 U.T.†)

*Ephemeris Time
†Universal Time
Source: *American Ephemeris and Nautical Almanac, 1970.*

Astronomy

With the probable detection of gravitational radiation, the torrent of new observations on pulsars, and the discovery of formaldehyde in interstellar space, 1969 would in any case have been a most exciting year for astronomers. Above all, however, it will be remembered as the year in which man first set foot on the moon. In so doing, he transformed the moon from an object of astronomical observation into the first celestial body upon which controlled experiments could be done. Some implications of these experiments are discussed below. For a discussion of the moon flight itself, *see* Astronautics.

The Moon. The problem of the composition of the lunar surface, particularly in the large, apparently flat regions known as *maria*, or "seas," long challenged astronomers. Two principal schools of thought on this subject emerged. The first maintained that these seas consisted of deep layers of very fine dust, incapable of bearing any substantial load, and that the moon was a cold, inactive planet that had remained essentially unchanged since its formation. The second school held that the lunar surface was to be understood in terms of volcanic activity, the surface, therefore, being comparatively young and firm and the interior having been hot and active as in the earth.

The question began to be resolved when the U.S. unmanned Surveyors found that the surface of the Sea of Tranquillity was a firm, rock-strewn, dusty desert similar in many respects to a dehydrated earth. Indeed, chemical analysis of samples brought back by the astronauts demonstrated that the lunar surface consists mainly of oxides of silicon, magnesium, and iron just as does the earth's mantle. The abundance of titanium oxide is, however, greater than expected. The rocks are igneous in type, establishing their origin in molten material and providing some evidence that the moon had been volcanically active in the past.

The sensitive seismograph placed on the lunar surface in July by the U.S. astronauts of Apollo 11 did not function as well as had been hoped, but early reports indicated a surprisingly high level of seismic activity. One of the most remarkable events of the Apollo 12 mission occurred when the lunar module was jettisoned to crash land on the moon's surface. The seismic waves that resulted from the impact lasted 55 minutes, in contrast with the one minute a similar impact would cause on the earth. Puzzled scientists began searching for an explanation.

Preliminary results from potassium-argon dating indicated that rock samples from the Sea of Tranquillity are at least three billion to four billion years old. This suggested that very little volcanic activity occurred after an initial burst shortly after the moon formed, presumably 4.5 billion years ago at about the same time as the earth.

The evidence gathered, of course, influenced ideas on the origin of the moon. In particular, the rock dating seemed to argue against suggestions that the moon was once part of the earth and then ejected from it into orbit. It also seemed to raise difficulties for the proposal that the moon was an independent planet captured in a retrograde orbit by the earth's gravitational field and arriving at its present orbit by means of tidal interactions with the earth. If either of those hypotheses were correct, the moon's surface should probably have been in a molten state more recently than indicated by the rock samples, due to the immense dissipation of dynamic energy that would have occurred during the period of close approach. By late 1969 it appeared more probable that the moon was formed out of the same cloud of dust as was the earth, but, being less massive, lost its atmosphere and ceased its surface activity rather quickly. In view, however, of the considerable uncertainties in all these theories it should be emphasized that the question of the present structure of the moon, let alone its origin, was far from settled.

Pulsars. Since the discovery of pulsars (pulsating radio sources) in 1968 by A. Hewish and J. Bell at the Mullard Radio Astronomy Observatory, Cambridge, Eng., more than 40 of these emitters of pulsed radio energy have been discovered. They ranged in period from 0.033 to almost 2 sec. The group at the University of Sydney, Austr., that detected a substantial proportion of the presently known pulsars pointed out that these objects are situated near the galactic plane and may be concentrated toward the spiral arms. The pulsars are thus associated with young stellar populations and may be the remnants of type II supernovas, which are catastrophic explosions of the more massive stars as they reach the end point of nuclear burning. The fact that the pulsar with the shortest known period, NPO520, was found in the Crab Nebula, the debris from a supernova explosion in 1054 A.D., and also that the second fastest pulsar, PSR0833–45 (0.089 sec.), is likewise associated with supernova remnants in Vela supports this hypothesis. Indeed, these two sources yielded particularly important results.

The short periods made it appear unlikely that pulsars were associated with white dwarfs, leaving neutron stars as the only remaining candidates. Since neutron stars are expected to vibrate at much higher frequency than those observed, rotation has become the favoured clock mechanism for the pulsars, a proposal first made by T. Gold of Cornell University. This seems, however, to require a radiation beaming process (like a searchlight) to provide the pulses, but despite many suggestions no generally acceptable mechanism was proposed. On the other hand, with a steady loss of energy, one might expect the rotational speed to decrease, and this phenomenon has been found to occur in most pulsars but most significantly in those with the shortest periods. More startling was the simultaneous discovery, by V. Radhakrishnan and R. Manchester at the Australian National Radio Astronomy Observatory in Parkes and P. Reichley and G. Downs in the U.S. (Jet Propulsion Laboratory, Pasadena, Calif.), of a small but sharp decrease in the period of the Vela pulsar in a matter of a few days, although both before and after this event the period was slowly increasing as expected. This change must, on the present model, be associated with alterations in the basic structure of a neutron star.

In order to gain understanding of the radiation mechanism, considerable study was made of pulse structure, particularly by the groups at Cornell University and at Nuffield Radio Astronomy Laboratories, Jodrell Bank, in England. In some sources the pulses were single but, particularly among those with longer periods, the main pulse may consist of multiple subpulses. F. Drake even provided evidence that these subpulses may themselves be periodic, with time scales of a few milliseconds. Intense polarization was measured, the direction of which was found to change in some cases during the course of a single pulse. The pulse intensity was also demonstrated to vary irregularly with radio frequency, but there was some tentative evidence of periodic amplitude variations at fixed radio frequency, at least in some pulsars. In this aspect of pulsar research, it must be conceded that the observations were well in advance of any theory.

Perhaps the most dramatic discovery in 1969 was the optical identification of the Crab Nebula pulsar by W. Cocke, M. Disney, and D. Taylor at the University of Arizona. The optical source is pulsed in the same way as the radio emission and corresponds to the 15th-magnitude star first suggested as the supernova remnant by R. Minkowski and W. Baade almost 30 years earlier. The optical radiation is polarized, has a stable mean spectrum, and shows no absorption of emission lines. Unfortunately, other pulsars escaped detection at optical wavelengths. On the other hand, the Crab Nebula pulsar was also detected in the infrared region of the spectrum by a group of astronomers at the California Institute of Technology and found to have an intensity consistent with the radio and optical values.

More exciting still was the detection of pulsed X-ray emission from this pulsar by three independent groups in the U.S. The signal again shows a main and secondary pulse, although the difference between them is less marked than at optical wavelengths. They coincide to within one millisecond of their optical counterparts. If some beaming mechanism really is operating, it must be considered extremely fortunate that the earth happens to lie in the right direction to receive signals from the Crab Nebula and quite remarkable that this beaming works equally well over such a range of wavelengths. While there are no observations in direct conflict with the model of beamed radiation from a rotating neutron star, it should be emphasized that, with the knowledge of the pulsars still so limited, the picture could change radically overnight.

Interstellar Matter. With the discovery of plane polarization in radiation from pulsars, these objects became excellent probes for measuring the galactic magnetic field by using the Faraday rotation effect. The interaction of the electromagnetic wave with the interstellar plasma causes the plane of polarization to be rotated by an amount dependent on the frequency of the radiation, the line of sight component of the magnetic field, the interstellar electron density, and the distance to the source. Together with the delay in pulse arrival times at different frequencies, which depends on electron density and distance, these measurements should in the near future provide a wealth of data on the properties of the interstellar medium.

In the meantime, more traditional methods were employed to determine the structure of the galactic magnetic field in the solar neighbourhood. D. Mathewson at Mt. Stromlo Observatory, near Canberra, Austr., combined his own measurements of optical polarization of starlight in the southern sky with those of observers in the Northern Hemisphere to show that the polarization vectors map out a clear pattern in the sky. Since this polarization is due to absorption by elongated dust grains which tend to be aligned by a magnetic field, such measures provide a tracer for the magnetic field structure. In this way Mathewson was able to show that the local galactic magnetic field has a tightly wound helical form, thereby settling a long-standing astronomical controversy. This structure is consistent with results obtained from Faraday rotation studies and from polarization measures of nonthermal radio emission from regions containing the field.

For many years observation of the discrete features in the radio spectrum was limited to the 21-cm. line of neutral hydrogen augmented in 1963 by lines of the OH (hydroxyl) radical at 18 cm. During the last year, however, lines from three additional molecules were detected. First, C. Townes, A. Cheung, and their collaborators at the University of California announced the discovery of emission from the 1.25 cm. transition of ammonia (NH_3) in several interstellar clouds. Shortly afterward emission at 1.35 cm. arising from a rotational transition of water vapour (H_2O) was detected by the same group. Last, but perhaps most remarkable of all, was the detection of interstellar formaldehyde (H_2CO), in both absorption and emission lines, by D. Buhl, P. Palmer, L. Snyder, and B. Zuckerman through a transition at 6.2 cm. All three molecules tend to be found near OH regions

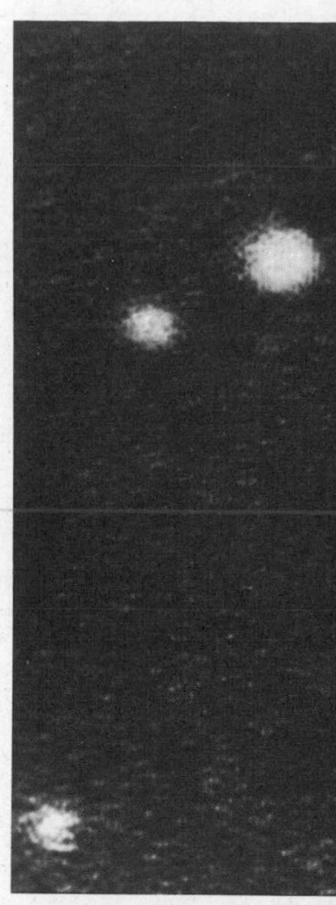

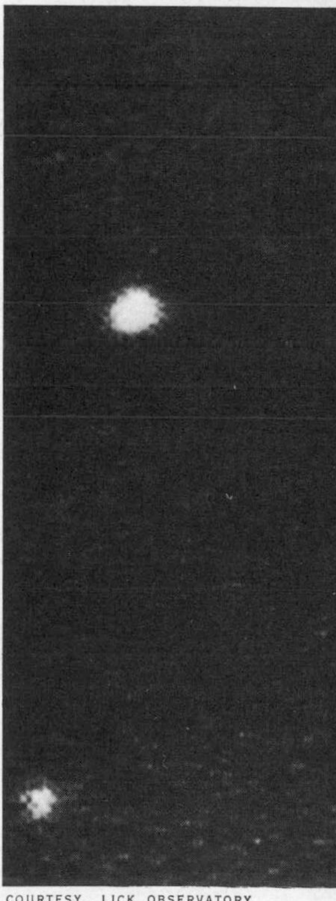

COURTESY, LICK OBSERVATORY

A brilliant pulsar, previously thought to be an ordinary star, flashes on (top) and off (bottom) in these photographs produced by a special rapid scanning technique. The rate of light pulses, 33 per second, is identical to that of the previously observed radio pulses. Photos were released in February 1969.

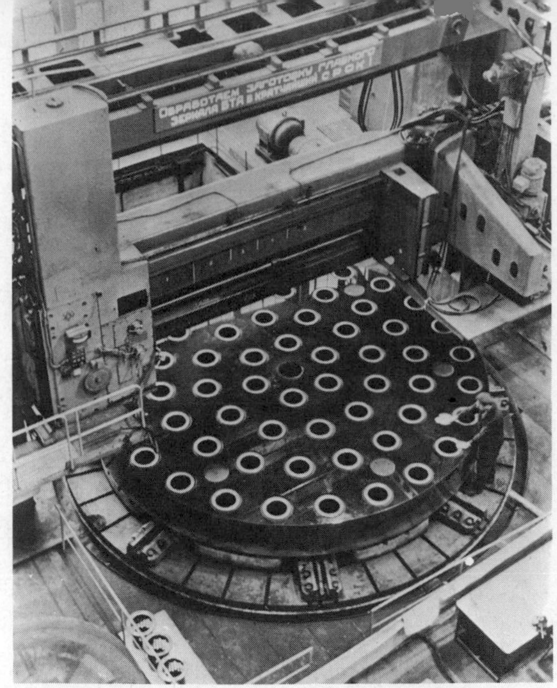

Workman cleans the reflector mirror of a 236.22-in. telescope lens being manufactured at the LOMO optical works in Leningrad in 1969. The telescope, one of the world's largest, was to be installed at the Zelenchuk Observatory.

"LONDON DAILY EXPRESS" FROM PICTORIAL PARADE

and, like OH, the excitation is usually far from thermodynamic equilibrium; that is, some maser-like action is involved. The fact that OH sources themselves are often associated with regions of dust and ionized gas implies a connection with the birth of stars, and the existence in detectable quantities of such complex molecules (particularly H_2CO) in interstellar space has led to some speculation on the origin of life itself. Where and how these molecules form was still an open question at the year's end, but the most likely possibility seemed to be in the atmospheres of very cool stars.

Infrared Astronomy. In order to study physical processes in cool stars, observations are required at infrared wavelengths, where most of the energy is emitted. Progress in this field was retarded by the opacity of the earth's atmosphere to much of this radiation and, even more seriously, by the lack of sensitive detectors for photons of this energy. The latter deficiency was rectified by the design of solid-state detectors cooled in some cases to liquid helium temperatures to reduce thermal noise. It is perhaps worth emphasizing that at room temperature the telescope, dome, and detection windows all radiate at maximum strength at a wavelength of ten microns. The problem is rather similar to attempting optical photometry with bright lights located in the telescope tube. However, by using sophisticated electronic techniques and working either from balloons or through "windows" in the earth's atmosphere, considerable advances have been made, particularly during the last year.

A survey at the wavelength of 2.2 μ was completed by G. Neugebauer and his collaborators at the California Institute of Technology during which a number of sources invisible at optical wavelengths were detected. With a spectrometer designed by F. Gillet and W. Stein at the Universities of California and Minnesota, astronomers from those two institutions studied the infrared spectrum of cool stars, finding evidence of two distinct types of circumstellar emission. From carbon stars, such as R Coronae Borealis, this emission was consistent with black body radiation and presumably arose from carbon grains surrounding the star. More surprising was the probable detection of emission from mineral grains in a number of M stars, for example μ Cep and Mira. The spectral distribution of this radiation closely resembled that expected from oxides of silicon, magnesium, and iron—material common in stony meteorites, in the earth's mantle, and on the lunar surface. R. G. Gilman, at the Goddard Institute of Space Studies, New York, was able to show that if the abundance of oxygen exceeds that of carbon, minerals of the type observed will tend to form in the atmospheres of very cool stars. Although the stars observed are at a later stage of evolution than the sun, it appeared fairly certain that a similar process occurred during the formation of the early solar system; the more refractory mineral grains were left in the neighbourhood of the earth, thus accounting for its composition. In this context it is interesting that emission from mineral grains was also discovered in the Orion Nebula, a region of active star formation.

The galactic centre was the subject of intensive study in the infrared. E. Becklin and Neugebauer showed that between 2–20 μ it was possible to distinguish three distinct sources of radiation from the galactic nucleus. They were: an extended source with an energy distribution similar to K and M stars and presumably due to a large aggregate of such objects; a "pointlike" source, perhaps a cool but extremely luminous star; and a source of about three light-years in extent with a spectral distribution similar to that found in the Seyfert galaxy NGC 1068 by D. E. Kleinmann and F. J. Low. W. Hoffmann and C. Frederick, using a balloon-mounted telescope, reported the detection of an intense and extended source of radiation at 100 μ, but preliminary observations by a group at Rice University, Houston, Tex., failed to confirm this. However, there was no doubt that our own galaxy (a normal spiral) has at its centre a source of infrared and radio emission remarkably similar to that in NGC 1068. Since Seyfert galaxies are known to possess extremely bright, compact cores, these observations could also imply a similar, if less intense, condensation in our galaxy, arising presumably through gravitational contraction as the stars dissipate their kinetic energy in collisions. Indeed, D. Lynden-Bell, Royal Greenwich Observatory in England, suggested that such large but optically undetectable mass concentrations may exist in the centres of many galaxies, thereby accounting for some of the anomalously high observed mass-to-light ratios.

Cosmology. Most cosmological discussion centred on the microwave background radiation, which was generally held to be a relic of the radiation field in the "hot big bang" cosmologies. A necessary condition for this to be the case is that the spectrum be of black body form, which, with the long wavelength measures, would mean a temperature of 3° K. However, the "big bang" interpretation came under fire from a number of sources. F. Hoyle and N. Wickramasinghe, Cambridge University, and V. Reddish, Royal Observatory, Edinburgh, Scot., suggested that the microwave background arises from thermalization of starlight by molecular hydrogen frozen into grains. A. Wolf and G. Burbidge, at the University of California, investigated the possibility that the observed radiation arises from the integrated, Doppler-shifted, infrared emission from galaxies, a proposal that would require almost all galaxies to be strong infrared sources.

By far the most serious threat to the big bang interpretation came from the balloon observations of M. Harwit and J. Houck at Cornell University. On two occasions they measured the intensity of radiation in the wavelength range 0.4–1.3 mm., at which the 3° K black-body spectrum should be decreasing sharply. Instead, they found that the intensity continues to increase toward the shorter wavelengths, as for a "gray body." Although a number of astronomers proposed alternative explanations of this observation, it must, if confirmed by future measurements, cast doubt on the cosmological interpretation of the background radiation field; this interpretation had once appeared to be the strongest argument against the "steady state" cosmologies.

Gravitational Radiation. Although the various cosmologies were as much in doubt as ever, the General Theory of Relativity, upon which they were based, received further support during 1969. From Einstein's theory it was predicted that gravitational radiation should exist and be emitted by bodies whose mass quadrupole (or higher) moment is changing. A group led by J. Weber at the University of Maryland worked for several years to develop the extremely sensitive apparatus required to detect such radiation. Briefly, the method was to look for normal mode oscillations of an elastic body, in this case a suspended rod, excited by the dynamic derivatives of the gravitational potentials. The main difficulty was the elimination of other sources of excitation, particularly those of seismic or electromagnetic origin. Using a number of detectors working in the vicinity of 1,660 Hz. (one Hertz = one cycle per second), Weber claimed that the number of coincidences between signals recorded at different stations was much in excess of those expected from thermal fluctuations. Although the signals were only slightly greater than the thermal noise, the statistical evidence appeared strong enough to indicate that in all probability gravitational radiation had been detected for the first time. The source of this radiation remained unclear, though Weber speculated on its origin in supernova explosions. Certainly, if confirmed, this discovery must be considered a major triumph for the General Theory of Relativity. Its astronomical implications range from the dynamics of pulsars to the evolution of galactic nuclei. (P. A. St.)

See also Astronautics.

ENCYCLOPÆDIA BRITANNICA FILMS. *Planets in Orbit—The Laws of Kepler* (1960); *Stars and Star Systems* (1960); *The Story of Palomar* (1960); *Charting the Universe with Optical and Radio Telescopes* (1963); *A Trip to the Planets* (1963); *The Van Allen Radiation Belts* (1963).

Australia

A federal parliamentary state and a realm of the Commonwealth of Nations, Australia occupies the smallest continent and, with the island state of Tasmania, is the sixth largest country in the world. Area: 2,967,877 sq.mi. (7,686,810 sq.km.). Pop. (1969 est.): 12,295,300. Cap.: Canberra (pop., 1969 est., 119,235). Largest city: Sydney (metro. pop., 1966 census, 2,447,219). Queen, Elizabeth II; governors-general in 1969, Lord Casey and, from April 30, Sir Paul Hasluck; prime minister, John Grey Gorton.

Domestic Affairs. The Liberal government faced a difficult period in 1969, an election year. Though returned to office in October, the Liberal Party's majority was considerably reduced. Prime Minister Gorton had, however, strengthened his position in April after Sir Paul Hasluck (*see* BIOGRAPHY) took up office as Australia's new governor-general. When Hasluck retired from the Ministry of External Affairs, Gorton brought two of his closest supporters into the ministry. Gordon Freeth became minister for external affairs and G. D. Erwin succeeded Freeth as minister for air.

In May the government faced industrial unrest when Clarence Lyle O'Shea, secretary of the Victorian branch of the Tramway and Motor Bus Employees' Association, was fined A$500 by the Commonwealth Industrial Court after failing to appear before it to answer questions on the union's affairs. The union owed A$8,100 in fines for contempt of no-strike orders and a large sum in legal costs, which O'Shea refused to pay in protest against the penal provisions of the Commonwealth Arbitration Act. O'Shea was jailed for a week, during which time train, bus, and power workers went on strike in all states except Tasmania. After O'Shea's release the unions pledged to continue the fight to repeal the penal clauses.

The government was also embarrassed by the controversial prosecution of an officer of the Department of Trade, Graham Pratt, following the leakage of a confidential diplomatic cable and the publication of its contents by a Canberra publisher, Maxwell Newton. After Commonwealth police investigated the affairs of Newton, Pratt was charged with a breach of sec. 70 of the Commonwealth Crimes Act, which declared it an offense for a Commonwealth public servant to make an unauthorized disclosure of information obtained during the course of his duty. The charge against Pratt was later withdrawn by the prosecution. Subsequently a Canberra Supreme Court judge declared invalid warrants under which the house, business premises, and bank of Newton were searched by Commonwealth police in May and June. On the main objection to the warrants, that they were too wide, the judge commented that a warrant could not authorize the seizure of things in general, and ought to refer to a particular offense and to authorize seizure by reference to that offense.

With the federal election due on October 25, the government and the opposition took a keen interest in the state elections and federal by-elections held during 1969. There were state elections in both Tasmania and Queensland in May. The 35-year-old Tasmanian Australian Labor Party (ALP) government was narrowly defeated. Since this was the only ALP ministry left in Australia, the morale of the party suffered a severe blow. The Queensland state election resulted in a swing of 4% to the ALP, but the Liberal-Country Party coalition government was returned. Federal by-elections held in the electorates of Curtin (Western Australia), Bendigo (Victoria), and Gwydir (New South Wales) did not cause any upset. In Curtin the Liberal Party candidate's majority was reduced by 7,000 votes in one of the government's safest seats. The ALP retained Bendigo, and in Gwydir the Country Party candidate was returned.

The ALP prepared for the coming federal election at its midyear annual conference by rewriting a quarter of its platform. The 1969 federal conference decided that a Labor government would give Commonwealth aid to all schools, state and independent, primary, secondary, and technical. Aid to independent schools was a sensitive electoral issue because the Roman Catholic Church had a well-established and extensive system of education. The leader of the ALP, E. G. Whitlam, pledged his party to reform the health

Athletics:
see Baseball; Basketball; Bowling and Lawn Bowls; Boxing; Cricket; Cycling; Football; Golf; Hockey; Ice Skating; Rowing; Skiing; Sporting Record; Swimming; Tennis; Track and Field Sports

Atomic Energy:
see Nuclear Energy

CENTRAL PRESS FROM PICTORIAL PARADE

Australia's new governor-general, Sir Paul Hasluck, and his wife, Alexandra. Sir Paul, formerly Australian minister for external affairs, succeeded Lord Casey in 1969.

and medical benefits system, to abolish penal clauses in the Arbitration Act, to introduce a fair wheat stabilization scheme, and to guarantee an effective minimum price for woolgrowers.

The preelection situation was complicated by the decision of R. J. Turnbull, an Independent senator from Tasmania, to form a new political party. Turnbull said that Australia was losing its democracy. Parliament sat for only 40 days a year, and the time members spent in their constituencies was generally spent on thinking about how to get reelected. Cabinet government, he believed, had become autocratic.

The federal election on October 25 resulted in the return of the Liberal government, but with a majority reduced from 38 to 7 seats. This further weakened the position of Prime Minister Gorton, two of whose Cabinet colleagues, David Fairbairn, minister of national development, and William McMahon, treasurer and deputy leader of the party, decided to contest the leadership. Gorton managed to hold his position in the secret party ballot of November 7 and in the subsequent Cabinet reshuffle McMahon was removed from the treasury and given the post of minister for external affairs, ensuring his frequent absence from the country. Fairbairn was dropped from the Cabinet along with three other ministers.

On June 3 the aircraft carrier "Melbourne," flagship of the Australian Navy, was involved in its second major naval disaster in five years. It collided with the U.S. destroyer "Frank E. Evans" in the South China Sea. The "Evans" was cut in two, the bow section sank, and the aft section was secured to the "Melbourne." The accident was remarkably similar to the one in which the "Melbourne" and the Australian destroyer "Voyager" collided on Feb. 10, 1964.

Foreign Affairs. Southeast Asia policy and relations with the Soviet Union were the chief areas of interest in Australian diplomacy in 1969. On February 25 the prime minister made a policy statement explaining what the Australian government was prepared to do militarily in Malaysia-Singapore after the British withdrawal of troops from the area in 1971. Australia intended to maintain servicemen after the British left and did not plan to set any specific terminal date. Two squadrons of Mirages totaling 42 aircraft were to be stationed at Butterworth in Malaysia and one section was to be left at Tengah in Singapore. In conjunction with New Zealand, Australia planned to maintain a two-battalion organization of ground troops, of which the Australian component would be 1,200 men.

Australian forces were not to be used for the maintenance of civil law and order, which was the responsibility of the government concerned. They would be available, however, subject to the Australian government's prior consent, for use against externally promoted and inspired Communist infiltration and subversion, which the prime minister judged was likely to be the most probable form of aggression in the area.

The government's policy toward the U.S.S.R. was the centre of controversy following a speech made by Minister for External Affairs Freeth to Parliament on August 14. Freeth said that it would be unthinkable for Australia to take any comfort from hostilities between the U.S.S.R. and China. He announced a new conciliatory policy toward the Soviet presence in the Indian Ocean, and looked forward to Soviet cooperation for Asian regional development. Australia and the U.S.S.R. had begun talks on Asian security, he announced, and the talks represented the start of a new era in Soviet-Australian relations. In a major review of Australia's foreign policy, he expressed reservation about the nuclear nonproliferation treaty, and reiterated that the question of reducing Australian forces in Vietnam would depend on the progress of peace negotiations, enemy activity, and South Vietnamese strength.

Freeth's most important remarks concerned Soviet proposals for involvement in Asian security. Freeth quoted the Soviet foreign minister, Andrei A. Gromyko, as having told the Supreme Soviet in July that the prerequisite and potential for an improvement in Soviet relations with Australia existed. L. I. Brezhnev, general secretary of the Soviet Communist Party, had spoken earlier of the need to create a system of collective security in Asia, and it seemed to the Australian Ministry of External Affairs that the Soviet Union was exploring the reactions of other countries before trying to convert the idea into any firm or detailed proposal. Both in Canberra and in Moscow the Australian and Soviet governments had been in contact on matters of bilateral interest and in discussions on wider issues. After the reference to the possibility of Soviet-Australian cooperation in a Southeast Asian nonaggression pact, Freeth warned that any realistic plan for regional security had to take into account the possibility of aggression from outside, the most likely source of aggression being China.

Sen. Vincent C. Gair, federal parliamentary leader of the Democratic Labor Party (DLP)—whose preferences had in part kept the government in office under the Australian preferential voting system—led the at-

AUSTRALIA

Education. (1966) Primary, pupils 1,703,552, teachers 63,200; secondary, pupils 800,778, teachers 42,500; vocational, pupils 145,900; higher (including teacher training), students 145,000, teaching staff (at universities and teacher-training colleges only) 5,660.

Finance. Monetary unit: Australian dollar, with a par value of A$0.89 to U.S. $1 (A$2.14 = £1 sterling). Gold and foreign exchange, official and banks: (May 1969) U.S. $1,536,000,000; (May 1968) U.S. $1,280,000,000. Commonwealth budget (1968–69 est.): revenue A$5,974,000,000; expenditure A$5,999,000,000. Gross national product: (1967–68) A$23,840,000,000; (1966–67) A$22,480,000,000. Money supply: (April 1969) A$4,865,000,000; (April 1968) A$4,488,000,000. Cost of living (1963 = 100): (Jan.–March 1969) 118; (Jan.–March 1968) 115.

Foreign Trade. (1968) Imports A$3,489,900,000; exports A$3,149,500,000. Import sources: U.S. 26%; U.K. 22%; Japan 11%; West Germany 6%; Canada 5%. Export destinations: Japan 23%; U.S. 14%; U.K. 14%; New Zealand 5%. Main exports: wool 24%; wheat 9%.

Transport and Communications. Roads (1967) 911,021 km. (including 97,983 km. main roads). Motor vehicles in use (1968): passenger 3,383,503; commercial (including buses) 908,862. Railways (government; 1968): 40,466 km.; freight traffic 20,490,000,000 net ton-km. Air traffic (1967): 6,412,970,000 passenger-km.; freight 193,124,000 net ton-km. Shipping (1968): merchant vessels 100 gross tons and over 314; gross tonnage 818,247; goods loaded 48 million metric tons, unloaded 32.4 million. Telephones (June 1967) 3,178,278. Radio receivers (June 1968) 2,580,000. Television receivers (June 1968) 2,519,000.

Agriculture. Production (in 000; metric tons; 1968; 1967 in parentheses): wheat 14,571 (7,547); oats 1,774 (719); barley 1,538 (835); corn 193 (191); potatoes 663 (653); sugar, raw value (1968–69) 2,769, (1967–68) 2,372; apples 373 (373); oranges 257 (225); wool, greasy *c.* 805 (802); milk (1967–68) 7,032, (1966–67) 7,512; butter (1967–68) 196, (1966–67) 222; cheese (1967–68) 71, (1966–67) 70; beef and veal (1967–68) 910, (1966–67) 880; mutton and lamb (1967–68) 665, (1966–67) 601; wine 195 (189). Livestock (in 000; March 1968): sheep 166,912; cattle 19,218; pigs 2,056; horses (March 1967) 479; chickens (1965–66) *c.* 21,500.

Industry. Fuel and power (in 000; metric tons; 1968): coal 40,882; lignite 23,290; crude oil 1,767; manufactured gas (cu.m.; 1966–67) 3,330,000; electricity (kw-hr.) 46,508,000. Production (in 000; metric tons; 1968): iron ore (65% metal content) 26,400; bauxite 4,961; pig iron 5,628; crude steel 6,483; zinc 209; copper 85; lead 178; tin 3.7; nickel (1967) 2.1; aluminum 97; cement 3,930; cotton yarn 31; wool yarn 24; gold (troy oz.; 1967) 627; passenger cars (including assembly; units) 345; commercial vehicles (including assembly; units) 73.

tack on the speech. Gair said that Freeth had virtually welcomed the Soviets into the Indian Ocean, and that a military pact with the U.S.S.R. would mean Soviet air, naval, and missile bases near Australian shores. Although the prime minister said that he would not make concessions to the DLP, he nevertheless stated bluntly that Australia was not considering the possibility of defense arrangements with the Soviet Union and tried to cool down the issue.

The Economy. In 1969 Australia's economic boom continued and there was no evidence of a slowdown. There was a general upward trend of wages and prices, labour was scarce, the level of demand was high, and output increased strongly. Residential housing and building activity, a key growth sector in the Australian economy, was high. The volume of rural production was greater than in the previous, drought-affected year.

The minister for primary industry, J. D. Anthony, announced on January 3 that Australia would supply at least 505 million lb. of meat (worth A$180 million) to the U.S. during 1969. The Australian Wheat Board also made substantial sales of wheat, including 2.2 million tons to China, for shipment from February 1969 to March 1970.

A major effect on the Australian economy resulted from the decision of the full bench of the Commonwealth Arbitration Commission to grant equal pay to women. The bench rejected a move by employers to have the equal pay test case dismissed. J. H. Wooten, council for the employer organizations, the Australian Council of Retailers, and the Angliss meat chain, told the Arbitration Court that the implementation of equal pay would cause men to lose marginal awards for skill and would raise living costs. He claimed that the majority of men supporting wives and families would resent the altering of the Australian wage structure to favour men whose wives were working. In the test case, the Australian Council of Trade Unions was seeking the abolition of the 25% gap between male and female basic wage rates in all awards. On June 19 the Arbitration Court accepted the principle that women doing the same work as men ought to receive the same pay. The increase was to be introduced gradually over three years. An important proviso was that the equality of the work had to be determined first.

The mining giant Conzinc-Riotinto of Australia Ltd. (CRA) signed contracts covering the sale to Japan of more than A$1 billion worth of copper from the vast deposits on the New Guinea island of Bougainville. The deal involved the supply of 950,000 tons of copper to Japanese copper smelters during a 15-year period. An opencut mining operation was proposed by CRA, which estimated that the ore deposits amounted to 760 million tons, with a copper content averaging 0.51%.

The copper project caused the government considerable embarrassment. In August there were riots on Bougainville when the Papua-New Guinea administration decided to lease the land on Bougainville belonging to the Rorovana people to CRA, because they considered that this course would cause the least disturbance to the island's community. On August 5 police used tear gas and batons to disperse a crowd of about 65 native villagers from Rorovana who had lined up in front of bulldozers that were ready to clear 175 ac. of land for CRA. There was considerable criticism of the attitude of the minister for external territories, C. E. Barnes. Barnes said that if the CRA copper project was to develop, the land was necessary, and he approved the issue of the lease despite the refusal of the landowners to negotiate. He repeated that the Papua-New Guinea administration would continue to use force against those natives who demonstrated about the acquisition of their land for the project.

Treasurer McMahon presented an election year budget on August 12. It provided major increases in social services, cuts in defense spending, no changes in direct or indirect taxation, and included a new form of state aid, a direct Commonwealth subsidy for all children attending independent schools. The state-aid project was estimated to cost A$24.5 million a year and the new social services, health, unemployment, and repatriation programs rose by A$192 million over the 1967–68 figure to A$1,659,000,000. Foreign aid was up by A$13 million to A$150 million, of which A$76 million was to be spent on the Papua-New Guinea administration. Rural industry was assisted by a program costing A$30 million a year. The decision to cut back defense spending by 5% to A$1,104,000,000 was strongly criticized by the DLP.

Australia joined the international wheat price-cutting war, which threatened to jeopardize the future of the International Grains Arrangement and the stability of the Australian wheat industry. For Asian, Pacific, and South American markets wheat prices were cut by nine cents (Australian) a bushel—a drop of 6% below the internationally fixed minimum price of A$1.68 a bushel. The Australian price cuts were caused by a world glut of wheat. Future benefits to the Australian economy were expected to flow from the firm establishment of the Australian National Line in the trade between Australia and the U.K. and Europe. The Australian National Line entered the Shipping Conference as a first step toward operation in European trade. Australian membership was on the basis of 7.25% of all cargoes, including those suitable for containers. (A. R. G. G.)

See also Dependent States.

ENCYCLOPÆDIA BRITANNICA FILMS. *Australia* (1959); *Changing Matilda: The New Australia* (1965).

Austria

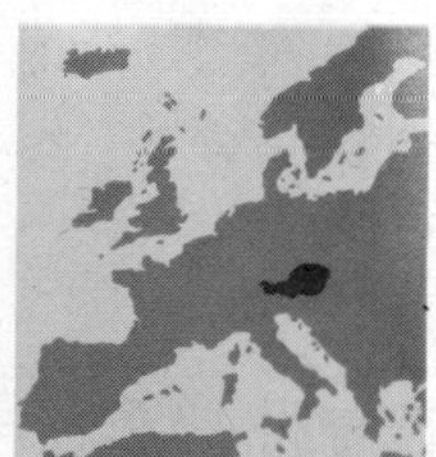

A republic of central Europe, Austria is bounded by Germany, Czechoslovakia, Hungary, Yugoslavia, Italy, Switzerland, and Liechtenstein. Area: 32,374 sq.mi. (83,849 sq.km.). Pop. (1968 est.): 7,349,500. Cap. and largest city: Vienna (pop., 1968 est., 1,642,072). Language: predominantly German. Religion: 89% Roman Catholic. President in 1969, Franz Jonas; chancellor, Josef Klaus.

In the continuing tension that followed the Soviet occupation of Czechoslovakia in 1968, the Austrian government maintained its efforts to exert a stabilizing influence in Central Europe, particularly in the Danube basin, and to prevent a resumption of the cold war in that area. A return to cold war propaganda methods was noted, however. Czechoslovak politicians and mass media constantly warned that "imperialist centres" existed in Austria from which nationalists, Zionists, and representatives of the Vatican would send agents provocateurs and spies to Czechoslovakia to bring about the downfall of the socialist way of life. Such accusations were sharply denied by the Austrian Ministry of the Interior.

The number of refugees entering the country from Czechoslovakia caused serious problems. Between August and October 1968 some 27,000 Czechs were said to have entered Austria. Of these, 20,000 emigrated to other countries, and the 7,000 who stayed in Austria were cared for by charitable organizations. Between June and August 1969, 8,000 Czechoslovaks sought refuge in Austria. At that time, 3,286 refugees from other Eastern European states were being cared for in Austrian camps. Considerable budgetary sums had to be allocated to pay for their upkeep, and great efforts were made to resettle the refugees in other countries as quickly as possible.

A number of high officials of the Czechoslovak secret service had fled the country and divulged the names of several agents of the Eastern bloc working in the West. Thus Austria was able to arrest and sentence a number of persons who were in the pay of foreign intelligence services, particularly that of Czechoslovakia. This caused great public interest, since the agents were mostly employed in the central administration. A parliamentary board of inquiry was set up to investigate the matter.

The Austrian Communist Party experienced an internal crisis following the events in Czechoslovakia. At a party conference in January factions for and against the Soviet move met face to face. Ernst Fischer, one of the best-known members of the old guard, resigned from the party's central committee and became a spokesman for the "revisionists" within the world Communist movement. Fischer was expelled from the party on October 13.

A government reshuffle took place in May. The minister of education, Theodor Piffl-Percevic, an opponent of the referendum on schools discussed below, resigned his post and left Parliament; his place was taken by Alois Mock. Karl Pisa, state secretary of information, also left the government and became deputy secretary-general of the Austrian People's Party (ÖVP). The state secretary in the federal Chancellery, Karl Gruber, was succeeded by Heinrich Neisser.

State elections in Salzburg and Vienna in March and April resulted in losses for the ÖVP; in Salzburg the number of seats it held fell from 15 to 13 and in Vienna from 35 to 30. The Socialist Party of Austria (SPÖ) and the Austrian Freedom Party (FPÖ) both gained, and in Vienna the small party of Franz Olah, former president of the Federation of Trade Unions and former minister of the interior, captured three seats. In Vienna the Communists lost the seats they had previously held. In the state elections in Lower Austria and Vorarlberg in October the ÖVP narrowly retained its absolute majorities.

Olah's success in the elections led to bitter political quarrels. Proceedings had been brought against him for breach of duty, embezzlement, and fraud and in March he was sentenced, in the first instance, to one year's imprisonment. In June, Olah appeared in the council chamber to take his seat in the Vienna legislative assembly. The burgermeister ordered him to leave, but Olah refused to do so on the ground that his conviction had not yet been ratified. He was then forcibly ejected from the chamber, was injured in the process, and subsequently lodged three complaints with the Constitutional Court.

Two proposals were put to public vote during the year. The first, calling for revocation of legislation for the introduction of a compulsory ninth school year, was supported by conservative and Catholic circles and gained 340,000 signatures. The second, calling for a 40-hour week, was supported by the unions and Socialists and 900,000 signatories voted for it. As a result of these referenda, the National Assembly postponed the ninth school year for at least three years and appointed a commission to inquire into school reforms; negotiations were started on the gradual shortening of working hours.

Austria's economy took a strong upward swing in 1968–69, partly as a result of outside influences and partly because of expansionist measures introduced by the government. The growth rate of the gross national product, 4.1% in 1968, was estimated at 7% for 1969. In mid-1969 the nationalized industries were the focus of political controversy. The ÖVP proposed that the Austrian Industrial Corporation (ÖIG), which administered the nationalized industries, be given greatly increased powers of management and finance. The trade unions and the Socialist Party voiced the suspicion that the ÖVP wanted to give the ÖIG these new powers in order to sell the enterprises and thereby denationalize them. In September the trade unions threatened to strike all nationalized industries should such a law be passed and demanded a constitutional guarantee of the maintenance of nationalization.

In May, Lujo Toncic Sorinj, a former foreign minister, was elected secretary-general of the Council of Europe. The Austrian airline, AUA, began transatlantic services in April. (E. Di.)

AUSTRIA

Education. (1966–67) Primary, pupils 812,734, teachers 36,111; secondary, pupils 134,619, teachers 9,055; vocational, pupils 191,671, teachers 12,531; teacher training, students 5,928, teachers 510; higher (including 6 universities), students 49,551, teaching staff, 4,973.

Finance. Monetary unit: schilling, with a par value of 26 schillings to U.S. $1 (62.40 schillings = £1 sterling). Gold and foreign exchange, central bank: (June 1969) U.S. $1,254,000,000; (June 1968) U.S. $1,336,000,000. Budget (1968 est.): revenue 77,787,000,000 schillings; expenditure 82,737,000,000 schillings. Gross national product: (1968) 294.7 billion schillings; (1967) 279.1 billion schillings. Money supply: (May 1969) 64 billion schillings; (May 1968) 59,080,000,000 schillings. Cost of living (1963 = 100): (June 1969) 122; (June 1968) 119.

Foreign Trade (1968) Imports 64,897,000,000 schillings; exports 51,708,000,000 schillings; net foreign exchange receipts from tourism 11,206,000,000 schillings. Import sources: EEC 57% (West Germany 41%, Italy 7%); Switzerland 7%; U.K. 6%. Export destinations: EEC 40% (West Germany 23%, Italy 10%); Switzerland 9%; U.K. 6%; U.S. 5%. Main exports: machinery 18%; iron and steel 12%; textile yarns and fabrics 8%; timber 7%; chemicals 6%; paper and board 5%.

Transport and Communications. Roads (1968) 93,273 km. Motor vehicles in use (1968): passenger 1,053,321; commercial 107,392. Railways: state (1967) 5,923 km.; private (1966) 635 km.; traffic (state only; 1967) 5,934,000,000 passenger-km., freight 8,247,000,000 net ton-km. Air traffic (1968): 312 million passenger-km.; freight 4,309,000 net ton-km. Telephones (Dec. 1967) 1,163,194. Radio receivers (Dec. 1967) 2,146,000. Television receivers (Dec. 1967) 978,000.

Agriculture. Production (in 000; metric tons; 1968; 1967 in parentheses): wheat 926 (1,045); rye 413 (377); barley 770 (772); oats 324 (336); corn 399 (316); potatoes 3,473 (3,049); sugar, raw value (1968–69) 301, (1967–68) 300; apples (1967) 361, (1966) 367; wine 317 (332); timber (cu.m.; 1967) 11,500, (1966) 11,600. Livestock (in 000; Dec. 1967): cattle 2,480; sheep 130; pigs 2,932; horses 66; goats 88; chickens 10,856.

Industry. Fuel and power (in 000; metric tons; 1968): lignite 4,177; coal (1967) 14; crude oil 2,723; natural gas (cu.m.) 1,629,000; electricity (kw-hr.) 25,702,000 (72% hydroelectric in 1967); manufactured gas (Vienna only; cu.m.) 630,000. Production (in 000; metric tons; 1968): iron ore (30% metal content) 3,481; pig iron 2,470; crude steel 3,468; magnesite (1967) 1,535; aluminum 116; copper 18; lead 7; zinc 15; cement 4,552; paper (1967) 761; nitrogenous fertilizers (N content; 1967–68) *c.* 245; cotton yarn 19; woven cotton fabrics 18; wool yarn 13; rayon fibres (1967) 57.

Automobile Industry:
see Industrial Review; Transportation

Automobile Racing:
see Motor Sports

Aviation:
see Defense; Transportation

Bacteriology:
see Medicine

Badminton:
see Sporting Record

Bahama Islands:
see Dependent States

Bahrain:
see Dependent States

Balance of Payments:
see Payments and Reserves, International

Ballet:
see Dance

Banking:
see Money and Banking

Baptists:
see Religion

Barbados

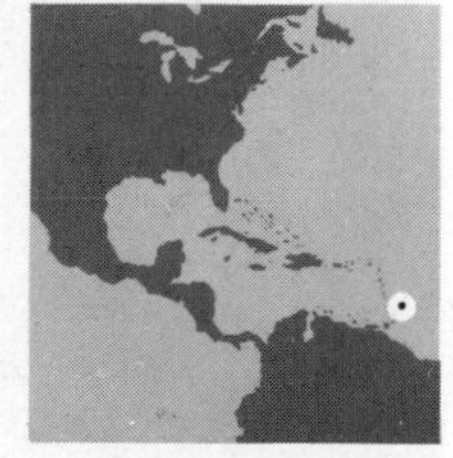

The parliamentary state of Barbados is a member of the Commonwealth of Nations and occupies the most easterly island in the southern Caribbean Sea. Area: 166 sq.mi. (430 sq.km.). Pop. (1969 est.): 252,900, predominantly Negro. Cap. and largest city: Bridgetown (pop., 1969, 12,300). Language: English. Religion: Christian, with Anglicans in the majority. Queen, Elizabeth II; governor-general in 1969, Sir John Stow; prime minister, Errol Walton Barrow.

Following the meeting on regional cooperation of the Commonwealth Caribbean heads of state, which took place in February 1969, and the opening of the Caribbean Secretariat in Guyana in March, the governor-general's opening speech to the new session of Parliament in June pledged Barbados to an all-out effort toward economic integration of the Caribbean and Latin-American countries. Barbados ministers took an active part in all the political and economic conferences of the area, both Commonwealth and American, including the Inter-American Economic and Social Council of the Organization of American States, held for the first time on Commonwealth Caribbean territory in June; the OAS educational conferences held in Argentina and Brazil; and the OAS Economic and Social Council meeting in Trinidad. Barbados acted as host to a Caribbean heads of state meeting on the University of the West Indies in June and was represented at Caribbean Free Trade Area (CARIFTA) meetings in Guyana.

Close relations with Canada were maintained. A state visit from the governor-general of Canada in February was followed by the signing of an agreement with the Canadian Economic and Social Aid program, under which voluntary technical aid is provided by retired technical and business experts. A Cabinet reshuffle early in 1969 involved the creation of new portfolios, most notably for housing and economic affairs.

Barbados continued to enjoy political and economic stability, despite an increasingly dense population (1,500 per sq.mi.) and a still precarious dependence on sugar, which made up 85% of total exports. Tourism, which had been increasing at around 15% a year since 1961, was regarded as a major development priority. Estimated government expenditure for 1969–70 stood at ECar$68 million and revenue at ECar$58 million, leaving a deficit of ECar$10 million to be financed by loans.

Barbados was accepted as the 22nd member of the Inter-American Development Bank in March 1969. Great Britain continued to be Barbados' main trading partner, with about 30% of the total, although inter-island trade, especially into the Jamaican market, was expanding. New investments by the Commonwealth Development Corporation were undertaken in Barbados at the end of 1968. Plans for the expansion of light industry and for further diversification of agriculture were under consideration. (M. MR.)

BARBADOS

Education. (1966–67) Primary, pupils 43,759, teachers (1964–65) 1,241; secondary, pupils 13,241, teachers (1964–65) 497; vocational, pupils 414; teacher training, students 148; higher, students 403, teaching staff (1964–65) 57.

Finance and Trade. Monetary unit: East Caribbean dollar, with a par value of ECar$2 to U.S. $1 (ECar $4.80 = £1 sterling). Budget (1967–68 rev. est.): revenue ECar$52,094,000; expenditure ECar$45,515,-400. Foreign trade (1967): imports ECar$134,311,260 (29% from U.K., 20% from U.S., 13% from Canada, 6% from Venezuela, 5% from Trinidad and Tobago); exports ECar$72,309,480 (42% to U.K., 16% to U.S., 7% to Canada, 6% to Windward Islands). Main exports: sugar 68%; molasses 7%; rum 6%.

Agriculture. Sugar production, raw value (1968–69) 157,000 metric tons, (1967–68) 162,000 metric tons.

Baseball

Professional baseball's 100th anniversary season in 1969 brought with it an "incredibility gap." The New York Mets, perennial doormats of the National League since their birth in 1962, in 1969 climbed to the top of the baseball world. It was a rags-to-riches story in the finest tradition and was one of the most surprising sports developments in history.

Both the National and American leagues expanded from 10 to 12 teams in 1969, and each league was split into two 6-team divisions, Eastern and Western. Because of their ninth-place finish in 1968, Manager Gil Hodges (*see* BIOGRAPHY) and his Mets were held in total disregard in the Eastern Division of the National League by preseason oddsmakers. But between August 14 and October 2, when the divisional competition formally ended, the Mets turned a 9½-game deficit into an 8-game bulge to overhaul and thrash the front-running Chicago Cubs, who had led the division the first 155 days of the season. New York won 38 of its last 49 regular-season games.

The Mets' momentum carried over into the best-of-five National League pennant play-off against the Atlanta Braves, winners of the Western Division. The

Table I. Final Major League Standings, 1969

National League
Eastern Division

Club	W.	L.	Pct.	G.B.	N.Y.	Chi.	Pitt.	St. L.	Phil.	Mon.	Atl.	Cin.	Hou.	L.A.	S.D.	S.F.
New York	100	62	.617	—	—	10	10	12	12	13	8	6	2	8	11	8
Chicago	92	70	.568	8	8	—	7	9	12	10	9	6	8	6	11	6
Pittsburgh	88	74	.543	12	8	11	—	9	8	13	4	7	9	4	10	5
St. Louis	87	75	.537	13	6	9	9	—	11	11	6	4	5	9	8	9
Philadelphia	63	99	.389	37	6	6	10	7	—	7	6	2	4	4	8	3
Montreal	52	110	.321	48	5	8	5	7	11	—	4	4	1	2	4	1

Western Division

Club	W.	L.	Pct.	G.B.	Atl.	S.F.	Cin.	L.A.	Hou.	S.D.	Chi.	Mon.	N.Y.	Phil.	Pitt.	St.L.
Atlanta	93	69	.574	—	—	9	12	9	15	13	3	8	4	6	8	6
San Francisco	90	72	.556	3	9	—	8	13	8	12	6	11	4	9	7	3
Cincinnati	89	73	.549	4	6	10	—	10	9	11	6	8	6	10	5	8
Los Angeles	85	77	.525	8	9	5	8	—	12	12	6	10	4	8	8	3
Houston	81	81	.500	12	3	10	9	6	—	10	4	11	10	8	3	7
San Diego	52	110	.321	41	5	6	7	6	8	—	1	8	1	4	2	4

Ties: Chicago 1, Cincinnati 1.

American League
Eastern Division

Club	W.	L.	Pct.	G.B.	Balt.	Det.	Bos.	Wash.	N.Y.	Clev.	Cal.	Chi.	K.C.	Minn.	Oak.	Sea.
Baltimore	109	53	.673	—	—	11	10	13	11	13	6	9	11	8	8	9
Detroit	90	72	.556	19	7	—	8	7	10	11	7	9	8	6	7	10
Boston	87	75	.537	22	8	10	—	6	11	12	8	5	10	7	4	6
Washington	86	76	.531	23	5	11	12	—	8	15	7	8	5	6	4	5
New York	80	81	.497	28½	7	8	7	10	—	8	9	9	7	2	6	7
Cleveland	62	99	.385	46½	5	7	6	3	9	—	4	4	7	5	5	7

Western Division

Club	W.	L.	Pct.	G.B.	Minn.	Oak.	Cal.	K.C.	Chi.	Sea.	Balt.	Bos.	Clev.	Det.	N.Y.	Wash.
Minnesota	97	65	.599	—	—	13	11	10	13	12	4	5	7	6	10	6
Oakland	88	74	.543	9	5	—	12	10	10	13	4	8	7	5	6	8
California	71	91	.438	26	7	6	—	9	9	9	6	4	8	5	3	5
Kansas City	69	93	.426	28	8	8	9	—	10	10	1	2	5	4	5	7
Chicago	68	94	.420	29	5	8	9	8	—	10	3	7	8	3	3	4
Seattle	64	98	.395	33	6	5	9	8	8	—	3	6	5	2	5	7

Ties: Kansas City 1, New York 1, Seattle 1, California 1.

UPI COMPIX

PICTORIAL PARADE

Mickey Mantle, left, New York Yankee star fielder for 18 years, hangs up his uniform after retirement ceremony in Yankee Stadium, June 8, 1969. Right, Ted Williams returned to baseball to manage the Washington Senators in 1969.

Mets wrecked Atlanta in three straight games by scores of 9–5, 11–6, and 7–4. In the meantime, Baltimore was capturing the American League pennant. The Orioles, champions of the Eastern Division by a staggering margin of 19 games over defending world champion Detroit, beat Western Division titlist Minnesota in the play-offs in another three-game sweep, 4–3 (12 innings), 1–0 (11 innings), and 11–2. This set the stage for the World Series: favoured Baltimore versus the underdog's underdog, the New York Mets. It took the Mets only five games to demolish the Orioles. They lost the Series opener, and then climaxed their remarkable season by reeling off four successive triumphs.

Bowie Kuhn, a lawyer who had been serving as the National League attorney since 1950, became baseball's fifth commissioner in 1969. He succeeded Gen. William Eckert, whose resignation under pressure had been accepted by the club owners in December 1968. From the beginning Kuhn gave vigorous leadership to baseball and found solutions to some of the game's problems, including a threatened strike by the Major League Baseball Players Association.

The threatened players' strike was concerned with pension benefits and took the form of a spring training boycott. The players agreed that they would not sign their 1969 contracts or report to spring training until their pension dispute with the owners was settled. Most of the players, perhaps as many as 95%, supported the boycott and did not join their teams until a new pension contract was agreed upon.

Agreement was reached after an all-night meeting of the players' association on February 24 in New York City. The new contract was for three years and called for the owners to contribute $5,450,000 annually to the players' pension fund. This was an increase of $350,000 over the owners' first offer. During the conflict Kuhn assumed a stance of neutrality and urged both sides to compromise.

Baseball made progress in its effort to put more offense into the game. The strike zone was narrowed, and the height of the pitcher's mound reduced. An average of 8.16 runs was scored in each game, compared with 6.84 in 1968. The combined team batting average for the major leagues jumped from .237 to .248.

To make it easier to hit home runs, six of the major league teams shortened their fences. In addition, some experimenting with the game took place during spring training, including the use of a pinch batter for a pitcher without the pitcher being forced to leave the game. These experiments were not greeted with enthusiasm, however, and were abandoned.

The unofficial major league attendance was 27,253,-387, an increase of more than 4 million from the 1968 season. The increase, however, was principally due to the addition of four new franchises, in Montreal, Seattle, San Diego, and Kansas City. Of the four, only the Montreal Expos had a home gate of more than 1 million, drawing 1,212,608 paid admissions. Twelve of the 24 major league teams drew more than a million spectators, led by the New York Mets who had a home attendance of 2,175,373.

Cub outfielder Billy Williams played in his 896th consecutive game on June 29 to erase the National League record held by Stan Musial of the St. Louis Cardinals. Willie Mays of the San Francisco Giants hit his 600th home run on September 22 to become the only player other than Babe Ruth to reach that level.

Bill Stoneman of the expansion Montreal Expos pitched the first of six no-hit, no-run games in 1969. Jim Maloney of Cincinnati, Don Wilson of Houston, Jim Palmer of Baltimore, Ken Holtzman of the Cubs, and Bob Moose of Pittsburgh also registered no-hit masterpieces.

The Cardinals' Steve Carlton struck out 19 Mets in a nine-inning game to surpass the record of 18 shared by Bob Feller, Sandy Koufax (twice), and Don Wilson. Ironically, the Cardinals lost the game to the Mets, 4–3, another indication of the New Yorkers' unpredictability.

Ted Williams, the last of baseball's .400 hitters (.406 in 1941), came out of retirement to manage the Washington Senators. Under his guidance, the Senators performed with respectability, turning in a record of 86–76 to finish fourth in the American League's Eastern Division. Two more of the greatest stars in the game, center fielder Mickey Mantle of the New York Yankees and pitcher Don Drysdale of the Los Angeles Dodgers, retired because of injuries. Mantle's decision came in the spring after a brilliant career that included 536 home runs. Drysdale quit in August with a lifetime mark of 209–166 and the all-time record for consecutive scoreless innings pitched, $58\frac{2}{3}$.

Four men were added to the Baseball Hall of Fame at Cooperstown, N.Y.: Stan Musial, Roy Campanella, Waite Hoyt, and Stan Coveleski.

Major Leagues. Five of the six teams in the Western Division of the National League entered the stretch run with a shot at the title. The Atlanta Braves finished with a rush to outlast San Francisco by three games and Cincinnati by four. Los Angeles and Houston slumped in the last days.

Left in the lurch by the Mets in the Eastern Division, in addition to Chicago, was St. Louis, the defending league champion. The Cardinals, favoured to win it all again, faded to fourth, 13 games behind. The Mets won 100 games in running up their margin of 8 games over the runner-up Cubs and 12 over third-place Pittsburgh.

Baltimore compiled 109 wins in breezing to American League Eastern Division honours by 19 games over the Detroit Tigers. The Minnesota Twins beat out Oakland by nine games in the Western Division.

The World Series opened in Baltimore, and the Orioles got six-hit pitching from Mike Cuellar to beat the Mets, 4–1. Don Buford led off the Baltimore first inning with a home run to establish the trend. The Orioles put the game away with three runs in the fourth against loser Tom Seaver.

The Mets squared the Series by winning the second game, 2–1, on a run-scoring single by Al Weis in the ninth inning. Jerry Koosman held the Orioles hitless for six innings and led, 1–0, on Donn Clendenon's home run before the Orioles used their only two hits of the game to tie it in the seventh. The losing pitcher was Dave McNally.

The Series switched to Shea Stadium in New York City for the third game, and Mets center fielder Tommie Agee stole the show. His lead-off home run in the first inning triggered a 5–0 Mets win, and his two spectacular catches twice thwarted Baltimore uprisings. Gary Gentry, with fine relief help from Nolan Ryan, got the win over Jim Palmer.

A diving catch by right fielder Ron Swoboda in the ninth inning saved the Mets from disaster in the fourth game. They went on to win in 10 innings, 2–1. The winner was Seaver on a six-hitter, the loser, relief pitcher Dick Hall.

The Mets completed their meteoric rise in the fifth game. They won, 5–3, after trailing, 3–0, to capture the World Series, four games to one. The victory went to Koosman on a five-hitter, and the loss to relief pitcher Eddie Watt. Doubles by Cleon Jones and Swoboda snapped a 3–3 tie in the eighth, and New York added an insurance run on two Baltimore errors. The Orioles had piled up an early 3–0 lead on a two-run home run by starting pitcher McNally and another homer by Frank Robinson. But in the Mets' sixth, plate umpire Lou DiMuro ruled that Jones had been nicked on the foot by a pitched ball. He first called it a ball, but then awarded Jones first base after detecting a shoe-polish stain on the ball. Clendenon then hit a home run to make the score 3–2. The usually light-hitting Weis homered in the seventh to tie the game. Thereafter, the Mets were not to be denied.

Harmon Killebrew of Minnesota won American League home run honours in the wake of a spectacular battle against Washington's Frank Howard and Oakland's Reggie Jackson. Killebrew hit 49, Howard 48, and Jackson 47. Killebrew also drove in the most runs with 140. Rod Carew of Minnesota took the batting title with .332. Carew also tied Pete Reiser's major league record by stealing home plate seven times. Tommy Harper of Seattle led the majors in stolen bases with 73. Detroit pitcher Denny McLain, who won 31 in 1968, paced the league again, this time with a 24–9 record. McLain threw nine shutouts. Other 20-game winners were: Baltimore's Mike Cuellar,

UPI COMPIX

Left, pitcher Phil Niekro of the Atlanta Braves throws first pitch of 1969 National League play-offs to New York Met center fielder Tommie Agee on October 4. Mets won series. Right, Baltimore's Boog Powell scores winning run against Minnesota in American League play-off game of October 5. Catcher George Mitterwald failed to tag runner who was waved home by winning pitcher Dave McNally, in jacket.

WIDE WORLD

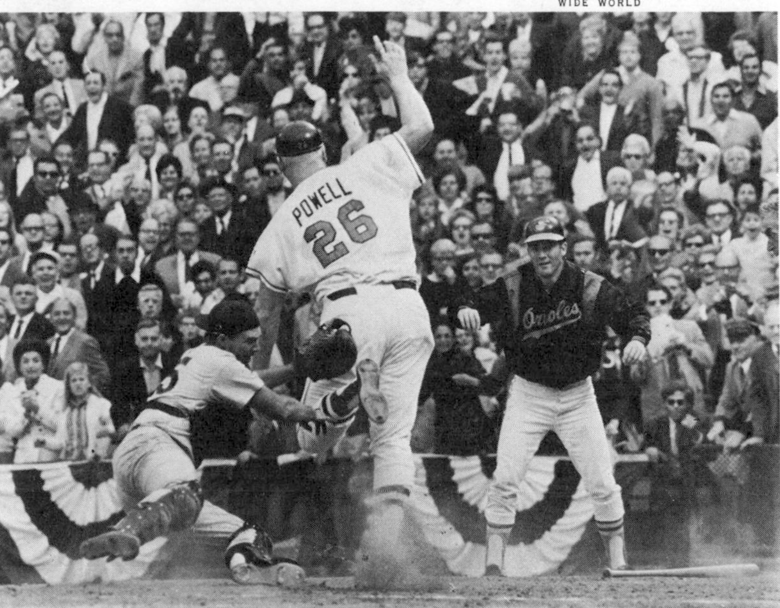

UPI COMPIX

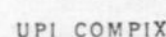

Left, New York Met Donn Clendenon hits a homer over the left field fence on Oct. 15, 1969, to give team a 1–0 lead over the Baltimore Orioles in fourth game of the Series. Right, Mets' Jerry Koosman goes into his stretch against Baltimore in the second game of the Series on October 12.

23–11; Minnesota's Jim Perry, 20–6; Baltimore's Dave McNally, who won his first 15 games, 20–7; Minnesota's Dave Boswell, 20–12; and New York's Mel Stottlemyre, 20–14. Dick Bosman of Washington had the best earned run average with 2.19. Minnesota's Ron Perranoski was credited with a record 31 games saved by his relief pitching.

In the National League, Willie McCovey of San Francisco nosed out Atlanta's Henry Aaron for the home run title. McCovey hit 45 to Aaron's 44. McCovey also paced the runs-batted-in department with 126. Pete Rose of Cincinnati repeated as batting champion with an average of .348. Pittsburgh's Matte Alou collected 231 hits, tops in the majors.

The National League had nine 20-game winners, headed by the 25–7 record of the Mets' Tom Seaver. Other 20-game winners included: Atlanta's Phil Niekro, 23–13; San Francisco's Juan Marichal, 21–11; Chicago's Ferguson Jenkins, 21–15; Los Angeles' Bill Singer, 20–12; St. Louis' Bob Gibson, 20–13; Houston's Larry Dierker, 20–13; Chicago's Bill Hands, 20–14; and Los Angeles' Claude Osteen, 20–15. The best earned run average was posted by Marichal, 2.10. Cincinnati relief pitcher Wayne Granger appeared in a record 90 games.

The Most Valuable Player awards were won by Killebrew in the American League and McCovey in the National. Tom Seaver won the Cy Young Award for best pitcher in the National League, while McLain and Cuellar shared Cy Young honours in the American League. Manager of the Year honours went to Ted Williams in the American League and Gil Hodges in the National League. Rookie-of-the-year honours went to Ted Sizemore of the Los Angeles Dodgers in the National League and Lou Pinella of the Kansas City Royals in the American League.

The National League used two home runs by San Francisco's Willie McCovey and another by Cincinnati's Johnny Bench to spark a 9–3 rout of the American League in the All-Star game at Washington, D.C. The game was played July 23 after being rained out the previous night, the first such postponement in All-Star history. A crowd of 45,259 watched the National Leaguers pile up an 8–2 lead in the first three innings behind winning pitcher Steve Carlton of St. Louis. The loser was Mel Stottlemyre of the Yankees. The victory marked the seventh straight for the National League, which took a 22–17 lead in the series. One game ended in a tie.

A number of managerial changes occurred during the year. Al Lopez of the Chicago White Sox quit in May because of ill health and was replaced by Don Gutteridge. The California Angels fired Bill Rigney late in May, replacing him with Harold ("Lefty") Phillips. Philadelphia's Bob Skinner quit in August and George Myatt led the team until the end of the season; the Phillies later announced that Frank Lucchesi would manage the team in 1970.

In late-season and post-season moves, John McNamara replaced Hank Bauer at Oakland; Danny Murtaugh was named to take over for Larry Shepard at Pittsburgh; and Boston fired Dick Williams in favour of Eddie Kasko. Cincinnati hired George ("Sparky") Anderson after ousting Dave Bristol. Joe Gordon resigned at Kansas City, and Charlie Metro became manager. The Minnesota Twins, in somewhat of a surprise, shelved Billy Martin, who had managed the team to the Western Division title. Bill Rigney replaced Martin. Joe Schultz was fired as the manager at Seattle and was succeeded by Bristol.

Other Leagues. The Pacific Coast League (PCL), after six years of widespread geography (from Hawaii to Indianapolis), had a new look in 1969, its 76th year. The PCL lost Seattle and San Diego to major league expansion and released four other cities to the rejuvenated American Association. New franchises in Eugene, Ore., and Tucson, Ariz., gave the PCL a sound eight-team league. The PCL then divided into Northern and Southern divisions. Tacoma, managed by Whitey Lockman, a former major leaguer, won the Northern Division title. Led by pitcher Archie Reynolds, who finished with a league-leading 2.32 earned run average, Tacoma climaxed its season by defeating Eugene in the play-offs three games to two. The PCL attendance was 1,076,360.

The American Association (AA), dormant since 1962, was reactivated under the leadership of Allie Reynolds, a former New York Yankee pitching star, and the six-team league enjoyed a highly successful comeback season. The Omaha Royals won the championship by a comfortable margin. The AA was scheduled to become an eight-team league in 1970.

The International League (IL) had one of the most exciting pennant races in its long history. Louisville

Table II. Minor League Standings, 1969

Pacific Coast League
Northern Division

Club	W	L	Pct.	G.B.
Tacoma	86	60	.589	—
Vancouver (B.C.)	71	73	.493	14
Spokane	71	73	.493	14
Portland	57	89	.390	29

Southern Division

Club	W	L	Pct.	G.B.
Eugene	88	58	.603	—
Phoenix	75	71	.514	13
Hawaii (Honolulu)	74	72	.507	14
Tucson	60	86	.411	28

Tacoma defeated Eugene three games to two in best-of-five play-off.

International League

Club	W	L	Pct.	G.B.
Tidewater (Portsmouth, Va.)	76	59	.563	—
Louisville	77	63	.550	1½
Syracuse	75	65	.536	3½
Columbus (O.)	74	66	.529	4½
Rochester (N.Y.)	71	69	.507	7½
Toledo	68	72	.486	10½
Buffalo	58	78	.426	18½
Richmond	56	83	.403	22

Play-offs

Semifinals (best of five): Columbus defeated Tidewater three games to one; Syracuse defeated Louisville three games to two. Finals (best of seven): Syracuse defeated Columbus four games to one.

American Association

Club	W	L	Pct.	G.B.
Omaha	85	55	.607	—
Tulsa	79	61	.564	6
Indianapolis	74	66	.529	11
Oklahoma City	62	78	.443	23
Iowa (Des Moines)	62	78	.443	23
Denver	58	82	.414	27

No play-offs.

Mexican League

Club	W	L	Pct.	G.B.
Reynosa	91	63	.591	—
Monterrey	88	63	.583	1½
Jalisco	82	70	.539	8
Veracruz	81	73	.526	10
Mexico City Reds	74	80	.481	17
Puebla	72	82	.468	19
Poza Rica	63	87	.420	26
Mexico City Tigers	60	93	.388	30½

No play-offs.

held first place most of the season, but the chase was so close that five clubs were challenging for the championship. Portsmouth finally emerged with the title the day before the regular season ended. Portsmouth then lost in the play-offs as Syracuse, third in the regular season, defeated Columbus in the finals of the Governors' Cup play-offs. IL attendance was 1,083,250.

Amateur. Arizona State defeated Tulsa, 10–1, on Larry Gura's six-hit pitching to win the College World Series in the 20th annual tournament, at Omaha, Neb., on June 20. Gura wound up with a 19–2 record for the season while Arizona State had 56–11. Arizona State lost its opener to Texas, 5–0, in the double elimination tournament, but then rallied to capture five straight games. (J. Be.; Je. Ho.)

Basketball

United States. *Intercollegiate.* The University of California at Los Angeles (UCLA), led again by Lew Alcindor, a 7-ft. $1\frac{1}{2}$-in. centre, won its third consecutive National Collegiate Athletic Association (NCAA) championship, the first time a school had ever won three years in a row. Additionally, it was the fifth national title for UCLA in the last six years, also a record. The only year missed by UCLA was 1966 when Alcindor was a college freshman and not eligible for varsity competition.

This latest UCLA victory was, to a considerable extent, another personal triumph for Alcindor. He became the first man to be named the outstanding player in NCAA tournament play for three successive years. Indeed, only three others had gained this honour for two consecutive years: Bob Kurland of Oklahoma A and M in 1945–46; Alex Groza, Kentucky, 1948–49; and Jerry Lucas, Ohio State, 1960–61.

During the three years that Alcindor played, UCLA had a combined 88–2 won-and-lost record, losing only to Houston (71–69) on Jan. 20, 1968, in a game which Alcindor played despite an eye injury that impaired his vision; and to the University of Southern California (USC) on March 8, 1969, also by two points (46–44). In the latter game USC played ball control, purposely preventing UCLA and Alcindor from possession.

This loss broke a 41-game UCLA winning streak and triggered speculation that the Bruins were also likely to lose in the postseason NCAA tournament, which began soon thereafter. But UCLA recovered and marched to the title with tournament victories over New Mexico State, Santa Clara, Drake, and Purdue, in that order. Only Drake threw up a big challenge, losing 85–82 in the semifinals.

Purdue, the champion of the Big Ten conference, was expected to give UCLA a strong test in the finals. But the Boilermakers were off their game and sank only 29.3% of their shots from the floor, considerably below the 49.9% average for their previous 27 games. Rick Mount, the Purdue star, missed on 14 consecutive field goal attempts during the first half, although he finished with 28 points, high for the Boilermakers. Alcindor, who played little more than half the game, led all scorers with 37 points and sank 15 out of 20 field goal attempts. UCLA triumphed by the decisive score of 92–72.

Table I. Major College Champions, 1969

League	Team and location	League record	All games
Eastern (Ivy)	Princeton (N.J.)	14-0	19-7
Yankee	Massachusetts (Amherst)	9-1	17-7
Atlantic Coast	North Carolina (Chapel Hill)	12-2	27-5
Southeastern	Kentucky (Lexington)	16-2	23-5
Southern	Davidson (N.C.)	9-0	27-3
Ohio Valley	*Murray State (Ky.)	11-3	22-6
	Morehead State (Ky.)	11-3	18-9
Intercollegiate (Big Ten)	Purdue (West Lafayette, Ind.)	13-1	23-5
Mid-American	Miami (Oxford, O.)	10-2	15-12
Big Eight	Colorado (Boulder)	10-4	21-7
Missouri Valley	*Drake (Des Moines, Ia.)	13-3	26-5
	Louisville (Ky.)	13-3	21-6
Southwest	Texas A and M (College Station)	12-2	18-9
Western A.C.	*Brigham Young (Provo, Utah)	6-4	17-11
	Wyoming (Laramie)	6-4	19-9
AAWU (Pacific Eight)	UCLA (Los Angeles, Calif.)	13-1	29-1
West Coast	Santa Clara (Calif.)	13-1	27-2

*Won play-off for NCAA tournament berth.

Table II. NBA Final Standings and Play-offs, 1969

Eastern Division				Western Division			
Team	W	L	Pct.	Team	W	L	Pct.
Baltimore	57	25	.695	Los Angeles	55	27	.671
Philadelphia	55	27	.671	Atlanta	48	34	.585
New York	54	28	.659	San Francisco	41	41	.500
Boston	48	34	.585	San Diego	37	45	.451
Cincinnati	41	41	.500	Chicago	33	49	.402
Detroit	32	50	.390	Seattle	30	52	.366
Milwaukee	27	55	.329	Phoenix	16	66	.195

Play-offs

Eastern semifinals	Western semifinals
New York 4, Baltimore 0	Los Angeles 4, San Francisco 2
Boston 4, Philadelphia 1	Atlanta 4, San Diego 2
Eastern finals	Western finals
Boston 4, New York 2	Los Angeles 4, Atlanta 1

Championship series

Boston defeated Los Angeles 4 games to 3
Los Angeles 120, Boston 118
Los Angeles 118, Boston 112
Boston 111, Los Angeles 105
Boston 89, Los Angeles 88
Los Angeles 117, Boston 104
Boston 99, Los Angeles 90
Boston 108, Los Angeles 106

WIDE WORLD

UCLA's Lew Alcindor blocks a backhand shot by Drake's Don Draper (right) in the NCAA semifinal championship game at Louisville, Ky., March 20, 1969. UCLA won 85–82.

Pete Maravich, a junior from Louisiana State, won the NCAA's major division scoring championship for the second year in a row. Playing despite injuries, Maravich totaled 1,148 points in 26 games, a record 44.2 average that broke the 43.8 he had set the season before. Maravich had 50 or more points in nine games and dominated to such an extent that he won the scoring title by the widest margin ever, 10.9 points per game. Rick Mount of Purdue was second with 932 points, a 33.3 average, and Calvin Murphy, Niagara, third with 778, a 32.4 average.

Alcindor, not a contender for the scoring championship because he generally did not take enough shots, led in field goal accuracy by sinking 64% of his shots. His three-year shooting percentage was .641, bettering the previous career record of .624 set by Ohio State's Jerry Lucas. Spencer Haywood of Detroit, a sophomore and the nation's fourth highest scorer, won the rebounding title with an average of 21.5 rebounds per game.

Players chosen on the first-string All-American team, as published in the *Official NCAA Basketball Guide,* were Alcindor, UCLA; Haywood, Detroit; Murphy, Niagara; Maravich, Louisiana State; and Mount, Purdue. The second team consisted of Dan Issel, Kentucky; Mike Maloy, Davidson; Bud Ogden, Santa Clara; Charlie Scott, North Carolina; and Jo Jo White, Kansas.

Kentucky Wesleyan (Owensboro) won the NCAA college division tournament, its second in succession, and finished with a 25–5 record. In capturing the title, Wesleyan defeated American International College of Springfield, Mass., in the semifinals, 83–82, and concluded with a 75–71 triumph over Southwest Missouri (Springfield). George Tinsley of Wesleyan was voted the tournament's most valuable player. Temple won the National Invitation Tournament, defeating Boston College 89–76 in the finals.

Professional. The Boston Celtics, a traditional power in the National Basketball Association (NBA), set still another precedent in 1969 by becoming the first team to finish lower than second during the regular season and then come on to win the championship play-offs. It was the 11th NBA title in the last 13 years for the Celtics who, as usual, had excellent team balance; their top scorer, John Havlicek, averaged only 21.6 points and ranked 14th in the league.

Coached by Bill Russell (*see* BIOGRAPHY), who also continued as a player, the Celtics barely managed to qualify for the play-offs by finishing fourth in the Eastern Division behind Baltimore, Philadelphia, and New York in that order. Baltimore, which rose from last to first place in one season, was eliminated by New York in the semifinal play-offs. Boston eliminated Philadelphia in the other Eastern semifinal, then beat New York for the divisional title and climaxed its season by defeating the heavily favoured Western Division champion Los Angeles Lakers in the best of seven series for the league's top honours.

The final series went the full seven games. The Lakers appeared to have the better personnel, including three players of all-star magnitude: Wilt Chamberlain, Elgin Baylor, and Jerry West. The Lakers won the first two games, but the Celtics rallied to win the next two. Los Angeles won the fifth game to take a 3–2 lead in games, but the Celtics again came back to win the next two games and the title. It was the first time that a team won after dropping the first two games.

Jerry West, long-time Laker star, was named the most valuable player in the play-off series, during which he scored a record 556 points for a 30.9 average. The only other player with more than a 17-point average in the play-offs was Boston's Havlicek, who scored 458 points for a 25.4 mark. Bill Russell, Boston's player-coach, was also instrumental in the Celtics' surprise victory.

Keith Erickson of the L.A. Lakers attempts to steal the ball from San Francisco Warrior Nate Thurmond during the first game of the NBA Western Division play-offs, March 26, 1969. Lakers took the series 4 games to 2.

WIDE WORLD

Los Angeles' loss in the play-offs was attributed, at least partially, to the almost season-long friction between star centre Wilt Chamberlain and Bill van Breda Kolff, the Los Angeles coach. Their troubled relationship was apparent in the seventh and final play-off game. Chamberlain took himself out of the game when he wrenched his knee with five minutes remaining. He subsequently asked van Breda Kolff several times to send him back in, but to no avail. The Lakers lost the game 108–106.

It was an unusual season in another respect in that several rookies leaped into immediate prominence. The most outstanding first-year men were Westley Unseld of Baltimore, who won the most valuable player and rookie of the year honours, and Elvin Hayes of San Diego, who won the scoring title, the first rookie to lead the league in point-making since Chamberlain in 1960.

Hayes scored 2,327 points for a 28.4 average, and was also fourth in rebounding. Earl Monroe of Baltimore was second to Hayes in scoring with 2,065 points, a 25.8 average, and Bill Cunningham of Philadelphia was third with 2,034. Unseld was not among the scoring leaders and only had a 13.8 average, but he seldom took field goal attempts, averaging only 11 shots a game. His primary value was in rebounding; his total of 1,491 was second only to Chamberlain's 1,712.

NBA attendance was 4,427,297, up 21% from the previous season. About 10% of this increase was due to the addition of new franchises in Milwaukee and Phoenix, which brought league membership to 14 teams. One regular-season doubleheader, played in Houston's Astrodome, drew 41,163 spectators. Never before in its 23-year history had a crowd half that size paid to see an NBA attraction.

The Oakland Oaks, coached by Alex Hannum, won the championship in the rival American Basketball Association (ABA). The Oaks defeated the Indiana (Indianapolis) Pacers in the final play-off series, four games to one, and immediately following this victory challenged the Boston Celtics, asking them to play for the "world championship." The NBA declined. Later, there were some indications that the NBA and ABA would merge, but such a merger was not in effect when play began in the 1969–70 season.

(JE. HO.)

World Amateur. The tenth Balkan championship for men was played at Izmir, Turk., during December 1968. Two games went into overtime: when Romania played Greece the score at full time was 74 all, but during the extra period Romania went ahead to win 92–82; in the Bulgaria *v.* Romania game the score at the end of regulation playing time was 68 all, and in an exciting finish Bulgaria scraped home 82–80. The tournament winner was Yugoslavia with Romania and Turkey placing second and third, respectively.

Uruguay won the 23rd South American men's championship played in Uruguay during March by beating Brazil, 65–42. The final placings in the tournament were: (1) Uruguay, (2) Brazil, (3) Argentina, (4) Peru, (5) Chile, (6) Colombia, and (7) Paraguay.

The fifth invitation Albert Schweitzer Cup for junior men was played at Mannheim, W.Ger., during April. The competition was particularly fierce between Italy and Czechoslovakia. The first time they met, Italy beat Czechoslovakia fairly convincingly 69–56, and in the second game in the final round Italy again won, 53–50. The final standings were as follows: (1) Italy, (2) Czechoslovakia, (3) Poland, (4) Turkey, (5) Romania, and (6) West Germany.

In the third European championships for girls, staged in West Germany during August, the Soviet women once again demonstrated their superiority. Unbeaten in the qualifying tournament in Cologne, they continued their unbeaten record in the finals. Bulgaria finished second and Yugoslavia third.

The 1968–69 edition of the European Cup for champion clubs produced a memorable final at Barcelona when the Soviet Central Army Team, Moscow TSKA, defeated the defending champions, Real Madrid, 103–99. Real Madrid led at half time, 45–42, and throughout the second half neither club was more than two points ahead. With a few seconds to go Real Madrid was ahead 81–79 when Vladmir Adnrejev collected two points to give the game its first tie, 81 all. At the end of the first period of extra time it was 93 all and at the end of the second period of extra time it was TSKA's cup, 103–99.

The highlight of the season for European basketball was the European men's championship, held in Naples during September. In the preliminary matches perhaps the most interesting game occurred when the U.S.S.R. played Yugoslavia. This was the first time the two teams had met since they played each other in the Olympics, and it was Yugoslavia who won, 73–61. In the final games first and second places were determined when Yugoslavia again played the U.S.S.R.; this time the Soviets were the winners, 81–72, and with this result they gained the championship. The most exciting game took place when Czechoslovakia played Poland to decide third and fourth places. The match was closely contested with neither team more than two or three points ahead at any time. At the final whistle Czechoslovakia won 77–75 for third place.

(K. K. MI.)

ENCYCLOPÆDIA BRITANNICA FILMS. *Basic Elementary Basketball Skills* (1967); *Playing Better Basketball* (1967).

WIDE WORLD

Boston Celtic coach Bill Russell grabs rebound during first game of the NBA Eastern Division play-offs, April 6, 1969, against New York Knickerbockers. Defending champion Celtics won the game 108–100 and went on to win the series and the title.

Belgium

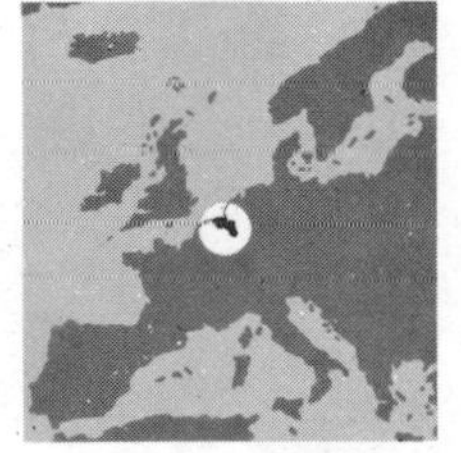

A constitutional monarchy on the North Sea coast of Europe, Belgium is bordered by the Netherlands, Germany, Luxembourg, and France. Area: 11,781 sq.mi. (30,513 sq.km.). Pop. (1969 est.): 9,631,910. Cap.: Brussels (commune pop., 1969 est., 166,920). Largest city: Antwerp (commune pop., 1969 est., 234,099). Language: French and Dutch. Religion: predominantly Roman Catholic. King, Baudouin I; prime minister in 1969, Gaston Eyskens.

In June the government put forward a program, the salient features of which were proposals for cultural autonomy for the Walloon and Flemish communities and for economic decentralization. Cultural autonomy, requested by the Flemish wing of the Social Christians, required a revision of the constitution, but the two coalition parties (Social Christians and Socialists) were unable to obtain the necessary two-thirds majority in both the Senate and the Chamber of Representatives. Though not opposed to cultural autonomy, the Liberals (PLP) considered the government draft proposals unacceptable and drew up their own. These, in turn, were rejected by the government, which suggested that the opposition proposals be introduced in the form of amendments to the government draft. Anticipating a deadlock in the Senate, the government decided on a different interpretation of the procedural rules in order to thwart opposition attempts to block the voting.

Beekeeping: *see* Agriculture

Beer: *see* Alcoholic Beverages

The PLP proposals, submitted to the Special Senate Committee on Constitutional Reform, were all voted down. Calling the government attitude "manipulation," the Liberals decided to boycott the public debate when the government proposals reached the floor of the Senate. The Volksunie (Flemish Nationalist Party), another opposition group, was willing to help the government obtain the required two-thirds majority, provided special voting rules for the protection of minorities' rights (which, in view of the increasing Flemish preponderance within the country, were especially desired by the Walloon wing of the Social Christians) were not introduced as part of the proposed amendments. The government refused and the Volksunie joined the Liberals in their boycott.

When the first votes were taken a third opposition group, the FDR-RW (an alliance of French-language parties in Brussels and Wallonia) helped the government to obtain a two-thirds majority on the revision of certain "technical" articles in the constitution, but not on the "community" articles (relating to cultural autonomy), which it wanted the government to postpone until Parliament reassembled in the fall. Early in September, Eyskens, realizing that the chances of winning approval for the government proposals on cultural autonomy were slim, invited the opposition groups to reexamine community relations and work out solutions likely to get the two-thirds majority required in Parliament. The talks ended in deadlock.

During the debate in the Chamber of Representatives on economic decentralization, which was strongly favoured by the Walloon wing of the Socialists, the size of the Brussels economic area was the subject of heated arguments. Flemish representatives were of the opinion that allowing Brussels to control an economic area beyond the limits of the bilingual agglomeration was another underhand maneuver by French-speaking Belgians to spread French influence over Flemish (unilingual) territory. On the other hand, French-speaking politicians from the capital viewed the existing agglomeration limits as an economic "straightjacket."

The debate revealed widely divergent opinions in the three national parties (Social Christians, Socialists, and Liberals) on the future role and position of Brussels and the surrounding Flemish boroughs. As finally approved in the lower house, the bill on economic decentralization provided for the creation of three economic councils, one for the Flemish part of the country, another for Wallonia, and a third for the centrally located bilingual province of Brabant, the latter sharing its authority with the other two.

Abortive attempts were made to achieve a regrouping of political forces. While Paul Vanden Boeynants, a former prime minister, urged the formation of a new "constellation"—in effect a union of moderates—the PLP leader, Omer Van Audenhove, declared that his party should seek to form the basis of an enlarged "neo-liberal party" in a two-party system. The Socialist leader, Léo Collard, called on all "progressive" forces to join the Socialists, an appeal intended for the Christian Democrats in the Social Christian Party.

Friction related to community relations also marked the discussions on the universities expansion program. After much haggling an agreement was drawn up, providing for funds for the transfer and installation of the French section of the Catholic University of Louvain (Leuven) at a new site at Ottignies in Wallonia, as well as funds for the Flemish section of Brussels University, which became fully autonomous.

Controversy over the value-added tax, due to be introduced on Jan. 1, 1970, culminated in a surprise announcement by the government on September 10 that, because of the international monetary and internal economic situations, the new tax would be postponed for one year—subject to EEC approval. In July industrial activity was 10.6% higher than a year earlier, and unemployment was down to 3.6%. Exports during the first seven months of 1969 reached BFr. 284 billion, a new record and 21.5% more than in the corresponding period of 1968. The cost of living increased by about 4%. On the money market, interest rates climbed to new heights. On September 17 the National Bank raised the discount rate to 7.5%; in December 1968 the rate had risen from 3.75 to 4.5%. At the end of August the bank signed swap agreements with the New York Federal Reserve Bank for $500 million and with the Deutsche Bundesbank for DM. 400 million, designed to enable it to cope with monetary upheavals expected in the fall.

A Belgian government delegation went to The Hague on April 26 to examine, with the Dutch government, possible ways of giving the Benelux Economic Union new impetus. On February 23–24, U.S. Pres. Richard Nixon was in Brussels, the first foreign capital he visited during his term of office. (JA. R. E.)

BELGIUM

Education. Primary, pupils (1966–67) 1,006,425, teachers (1964–65) 38,220; secondary (1965–66), pupils 282,619, teachers (1964–65) 35,348; vocational, pupils (1966–67) 466,149, teachers (1964–65) 39,439; teacher training (1965–66), students 33,112; higher (at 4 universities; 1965–66), students 40,268.

Finance. Monetary unit: Belgian franc, with a par value of BFr. 50 to U.S. $1 (BFr. 120 = £1 sterling). Gold and foreign exchange, central bank: (June 1969) U.S. $2,024,000,000; (June 1968) U.S. $2,056,000,000. Budget (1968 rev. est.): revenue BFr. 250,986,000,000; expenditure BFr. 272,634,000,000. Gross national product: (1967) BFr. 977 billion; (1966) BFr. 916 billion. Money supply: (May 1969) BFr. 382 billion; (May 1968) BFr. 362 billion. Cost of living (1963 = 100): (June 1969) 124; (June 1968) 119.

Foreign Trade. (Belgium-Luxembourg economic union; 1968) Imports BFr. 416.7 billion; exports BFr. 408.2 billion. Import sources: EEC 55% (West Germany 21%, France 15%, Netherlands 15%); U.S. 8%; U.K. 7%. Export destinations: EEC 64% (Netherlands 21%, West Germany 21%, France 19%); U.S. 9%. Main exports: iron and steel 16%; machinery 10%; nonferrous metals 9%; textile yarns and fabrics 9%; motor vehicles 8%; chemicals 8%.

Transport and Communications. Roads (1968) 91,758 km. (including 335 km. expressways in 1967). Motor vehicles in use (1968): passenger 1,806,464; commercial 270,026. Railways: (state only; 1967) 4,336 km.; traffic (1968) 7,908,000,000 passenger-km., freight 6,634,000,000 net ton-km. Air traffic (1968): 1,977,000,000 passenger-km.; freight 125 million net ton-km. Shipping (1968): merchant vessels 100 gross tons and over 218; gross tonnage 932,900. Navigable inland waterways in regular use (1966) 1,595 km. Telephones (Dec. 1967) 1,746,170. Radio receivers (Dec. 1967) 3,190,000. Television receivers (Dec. 1967) 1,801,000.

Agriculture. Production (in 000; metric tons; 1968; 1967 in parentheses): wheat 844 (842); oats 314 (361); barley 583 (623); rye 87 (90); potatoes 1,662 (1,943); flax fibre 18 (17); sugar beets, raw value (1968–69) 589, (1967–68) 579; meat 602 (568); fish catch (1967) 64, (1966) 63. Livestock (in 000; May 1968): cattle 2,805; pigs 2,502; sheep (Dec. 1967) 65; horses (Dec. 1967) 79; chickens (May 1967) 35,030.

Industry. Fuel and power (in 000; 1968): coal 14,800 metric tons; manufactured gas 4,247,000 cu.m.; electricity 26,564,000 kw-hr. Production (in 000; metric tons; 1968): pig iron 10,370; crude steel 11,573; copper 341; lead 110; zinc 251; tin 4.9; cement 5,743; cotton yarn 72; cotton fabrics 69; wool yarn 73; woolen fabrics 35; rayon and acetate yarn 17; rayon and acetate fibres 26.

AGNEW, SPIRO THEODORE

If Vice-Pres. Spiro T. Agnew represented the "silent majority" in the U.S., he himself was not silent during 1969. The relatively obscure former governor of Maryland, propelled by the workings of Richard Nixon's Southern strategy at the 1968 Republican national convention into the traditionally obscure job of vice-president, had confounded the political jokesters of the '68 campaign and become a household word.

Agnew had emerged from the campaign with something of a reputation for finding the inapt remark (as when he called a *Baltimore Sun* newsman a "fat Jap"), but his forays in 1969 were more vitriolic. He came out solidly against dissidents and demonstrators and labeled the leaders of the October 15 anti-Vietnam war Moratorium as, among other things, "an effete corps of impudent snobs." In a nationally televised speech, he accused TV network commentators of being biased in their treatment of the news generally and of Nixon's November 3 Vietnam speech in particular. The network heads—always nervous because they depend on federal licensing—were still quivering when he took out against segments of the liberal Eastern press, specifically the *Washington Post* and the *New York Times*.

Some observers said that he was playing the role Nixon had played when he was Dwight Eisenhower's vice-president—taking the "low road" while the president remained above controversy. Others, pointing to his numerous appearances in the South, felt he was being used to draw potential supporters of former Alabama Gov. George Wallace into the Republican fold. (Wallace gave some colour to this opinion by exhibiting what seemed suspiciously like jealousy.) Agnew himself said he was merely expressing his opinions, and there seemed little doubt that they echoed the opinions of many Americans, disturbed by dissent and the crumbling of old ideals and suspicious of the liberal Establishment. In any case, Agnew seemed to be one more magnet serving to polarize American opinion.

At year's end, Agnew undertook a more usual vice-presidential duty—a ten-nation Asian tour. Born Nov. 9, 1918, Agnew attended Johns Hopkins and, after serving in World War II, received a law degree from the University of Baltimore. He became governor of Maryland in 1966. (PH. K.)

PICTORIAL PARADE
Spiro Theodore Agnew

ALDRIN, EDWIN EUGENE, JR.

U.S. astronaut and member of the first crew to land on the moon, Edwin "Buzz" Aldrin in January 1969 was selected as pilot for the lunar module on the Apollo 11 mission. Apollo 11 lifted off from the Kennedy Space Center, Florida, on July 16, and the lunar module, code-named "Eagle," touched down on the moon on July 20. Aldrin remained in the "Eagle" for several minutes after fellow astronaut Neil Armstrong became the first man to set foot on the moon. After joining him, Aldrin assisted Armstrong in deploying several scientific experiments on the surface of the moon, collecting soil samples and rocks, and evaluating man's ability to adapt to the moon's weak gravity. Before reentering the lunar module Aldrin spent one hour and 44 minutes walking or running on the moon. After a stay of more than $21\frac{1}{2}$ hours on the moon, Aldrin and Armstrong rejoined their companion astronaut, Michael Collins, in the "Columbia" spacecraft orbiting the moon. The Apollo 11 mission ended successfully on July 24 when the "Columbia" splashed into the Pacific Ocean about 1,200 mi. SW of Hawaii.

Aldrin was born in Glen Ridge, N.J., on Jan. 20, 1930. His father was an officer in the U.S. Army Air Corps and held several cross-country speed records for biplanes. Deciding to follow his father's profession, Aldrin received an appointment to the U.S. Military Academy. He graduated third in his class in 1951 and then transferred to the Air Force. A year later he received his wings and during the Korean War flew F-86 jets, completing 66 combat missions and receiving the Distinguished Flying Cross. In October 1963 he was selected to become the first U.S. astronaut with a doctoral degree. On Nov. 11, 1966, as pilot of Gemini 12, he was launched into orbit with command pilot James A. Lovell, Jr., on the last mission in the Gemini series. During the four-day flight, Aldrin spent 5 hours and 32 minutes outside the spacecraft, performing many scientific and engineering tasks. (M. R. S.)

ARAFAT, YASIR

Known variously to his followers as Abu Ammar or just as "the Doctor," Yasir Arafat emerged in the late 1960s as the spokesman of the Al Fatah movement, which was dedicated to overthrowing Israel and regaining its territory for the Palestinian Arabs. Al Fatah was formally constituted in 1965 and obtained support from Arab students at universities in Europe. It survived the Arab defeat by Israel in the 1967 war and in 1968 gained control of Palestine Liberation Organization headquarters in Cairo. At that time Arafat was installed as chairman. During 1969 he greatly increased the budget of the organization and served as de facto representative of the Palestinian Arab commandos in the field. Wearing battle dress and carrying a pistol, he was a dominating figure among the squabbling Arab leaders at the Rabat, Mor., Arab summit in December.

Arafat claimed to have no other politics than the reoccupation of Palestine by the Arabs. Many who know him, however, believed that he was essentially a moderate and would play a decisive role in negotiations for a political settlement between the two antagonists.

Arafat was born into an upper middle-class family of landowners and traders in Ramallah (or possibly Jenin), north of Jerusalem, in 1921.

During the Palestine war of 1948 his family left Palestine for Jordan and Lebanon. Arafat went on to Cairo University, where he graduated with a degree in civil engineering. After the Suez conflict in 1956 he joined the U.A.R. Army as an officer in the Engineering Corps. In 1959 he returned to Beirut, Lebanon, on the invitation of Émile Bustani, the owner of a conglomeration of companies, and then represented Bustani in Kuwait. He parted company from Bustani to join a rival firm in Kuwait in 1961, and after working in Saudi Arabia and the Persian Gulf area, returned to Beirut and seriously concerned himself with Palestinian politics. (J. K.)

PICTORIAL PARADE
Neil Alden Armstrong

PICTORIAL PARADE
Edwin Eugene Aldrin, Jr.

ARMSTRONG, NEIL ALDEN

On July 20, 1969, U.S. astronaut Neil Armstrong stepped out of his spacecraft and became the first man to set foot on the moon. His words on the historic occasion were, "That's one small step for a man, one giant leap for mankind." Armstrong spent 2 hours and 4 minutes walking on the moon. Including time inside the lunar module, he and fellow astronaut Edwin Aldrin spent more than $21\frac{1}{2}$ hours on the moon before rejoining astronaut Michael Collins in the "Columbia" spacecraft orbiting it at an altitude of 69 mi. Armstrong and Aldrin collected samples of the lunar soil and rocks and deployed several scientific experiments on the moon. The Apollo 11 mission ended successfully with a splashdown in the Pacific Ocean on July 24.

Armstrong was born in Wapakoneta, O., on Aug. 5, 1930. His father, Stephen, was an auditor for the state of Ohio, and the family moved frequently before settling in Wapakoneta. As a teen-age youngster Armstrong took flying lessons and in 1946, on his 16th birthday, received his pilot's license before he had obtained his automobile driver's license.

From 1949 to 1952 Armstrong served as an aviator in the U.S. Navy, completing 78 combat missions during the Korean War. After his naval service he returned to his studies at Purdue University, West Lafayette, Ind., where he graduated in 1955 with a degree in aeronautical engineering. For several years after graduation Armstrong flew developmental aircraft, such as the

F-100, F-101, and F-50, and also piloted the X-15 rocket plane on seven of its flights.

In September 1962 Armstrong was selected as the first civilian astronaut. His first assignment was backup command pilot to L. Gordon Cooper for the Gemini 5 mission on Aug. 21, 1965. As command pilot of Gemini 8, on March 16, 1966, Armstrong performed the first docking of two spacecraft in orbit. A malfunction in one of his spacecraft's thrusters caused the mission to be terminated short of its planned three days.

While undergoing Apollo flight training in 1968, Armstrong narrowly escaped death when his lunar landing trainer lost power and crashed. In January 1969 he was selected to be the commander of Apollo 11, the first lunar landing in the U.S. space program. Apollo 11 was launched on July 16, 1969, at 9:32 A.M. EDT from Launch Complex 39 at the Kennedy Space Center in Florida. The lunar module, code-named "Eagle," touched down on the moon at 4:17:40 P.M. EDT on July 20. (M. R. S.)

ATTENBOROUGH, RICHARD

With the motion picture *Oh! What a Lovely War,* which opened to unanimous praise in London in the spring of 1969, Richard Attenborough successfully made the dangerous leap from acting to direction. Although he had formed his own production company, Beaver Films, with Bryan Forbes (*q.v.*) ten years before and had produced several films, he was still known to the public only as an actor.

Attenborough was born in Cambridge, Eng., on Aug. 29, 1923, and made his theatre debut in 1941. He scored a great success as Pinkie, the young criminal, in Graham Greene's *Brighton Rock* in 1943. Before serving in the RAF for three years, he had already made a notable film appearance as the frightened little stoker in Noel Coward's *In Which We Serve* in 1942. It led to a series of similar "simpering baby-faced idiot" roles, which he hated, but the British cinema was still deep in war nostalgia and most young actors found themselves perpetually in uniform.

Occasionally he got out of the rut, repeating his stage triumph in *Brighton Rock,* playing a schoolboy in *The Guinea Pig* and a demented gunman in *The Man Upstairs,* but the real break came with his first film for Beaver Films, which he also co-produced. This was *The Angry Silence,* in which he was a workman ostracized by his workmates for not joining a strike. Once launched in production, he chose his parts with care—the comic Welsh poet in *Only Two Can Play,* the down-at-the-heels barrister in *Dock Brief,* the cowed husband in *Seance on a Wet Afternoon,* the bullying sergeant major in *Guns at Batasi.* His second directorial project was awaited with eager interest. He had long wanted to make a film about Gandhi, but a more likely choice was a film version of Simon Raven's novel *The Feathers of Death.* (B. D.)

BARTON, DEREK H. R.

Sharing the 1969 Nobel Prize for Chemistry with Odd Hassel (*q.v.*) of Norway was Derek H. R. Barton, a professor of organic chemistry at the Imperial College of Science and Technology in London. The two scientists were honoured for their research into the shape—or three-dimensional conformation—of molecules.

An academician for most of his career, Barton was a visiting professor at Harvard University in 1949–50 when a colleague expressed confusion over the inconsistent behaviour of cyclohexanes, a group of hydrocarbons. "It sounded obvious to me that this could be explained by an analysis of the three-dimensional shape of the substance," Barton recalls.

The fact that molecules are three dimensional had been accepted for a century, but chemists still treated cyclohexanes as though they were two-dimensional. Barton and Hassel uncovered the error and determined that these hydrocarbon molecules could "lie" in a variety of positions if the atoms within them were twisted into new configurations.

The work had numerous applications in medical research and the development of new drugs. By 1969 such progress had been made that researchers could predict what properties a substance would acquire even before they changed its conformation in the laboratory. Moreover, the discovery of the double helix of deoxyribonucleic acid (DNA), which carries the genetic code and determines heredity, was made possible through Barton's and Hassel's findings in conformation analysis.

Barton was born in Gravesend, Eng., Sept. 8, 1918. He was educated at Tonbridge School and at Imperial College at the University of London. He taught at several institutions, including Birkbeck College, the Massachusetts Institute of Technology, the University of Illinois, the University of Wisconsin, and the University of Glasgow. He received honorary degrees from the University of Montpellier and the University of Dublin. (PH. K.)

BECKETT, SAMUEL

There was irony and good sense in the selection of Samuel Beckett as Nobel laureate for literature in 1969: irony because the Irish expatriate probably cared less for international distinctions than any other writer; good sense because, as one of the most innovative and influential writers of his generation, he probably deserved the prize most. Still, his selection was somewhat surprising, since the Swedish Academy had shown a penchant in recent years for honouring writers drawn from the ranks of the obscure, the uninfluential, and the political left.

To say that Beckett was apolitical would be an understatement. He was almost monastically insulated from everything except his writing. Undoubtedly his best-known work was *Waiting for Godot* (1952), a full-length play that goaded Western theatre into taking a new direction. Later plays include *Krapp's Last Tape,* a work with one character and a tape recorder; *Endgame,* in which the characters perform in ashcans; and *Play,* which calls for a man and two women to be enclosed in jars. His work presents the inevitable hope of man in the face of inexorable hopelessness—the fact that he must continue to seek though he is irredeemably lost. The final scene in *Waiting for Godot* is an example:

> Vladimir: Well? Shall we go?
> Estragon: Yes, let's go.
> *They do not move.*
> *Curtain.*

Beckett was born in Ireland on April 3, 1906. After graduating from Trinity College he went to Paris in the '20s, came home to teach briefly at Trinity, and in 1937 returned to Paris to stay. His publisher announced he would not go to Stockholm to receive the $73,000 award. "If some gentlemen on the Swedish Academy have decided to give me this prize, there's nothing I can do about it," Beckett was quoted as saying. The Swedish Academy was not likely to take offense. Its official statement read in part: "Beckett has exposed the misery of man in our time through new dramatic and literary forms. His . . . muted minor tone holds liberation for the oppressed and comfort for the distressed." (PH. K.)

BENN, ANTHONY WEDGWOOD

As a result of the British government reshuffle that took place in October 1969, Anthony Wedgwood Benn, minister of technology, was put in charge of an industrial and technological empire embracing the nationalized industries and government interests in aviation, shipping, research, and industrial reconstruction. Benn, at the age of 44, found himself responsible for a department with a staff of 39,000, an annual budget of about £1,500 million, and investment totaling about £900 million annually. This was quite apart from the 963,000 employees of the nationalized industries.

Born April 3, 1925, Benn was educated at Oxford University, receiving an M.A. degree in 1949. When first elected to Parliament in 1950 he was the youngest M.P. His political career, however, was threatened by succession to the peerage of his father, Lord Stansgate, which would exclude him from the House of Commons. When his father died in 1960, Benn had to give up his seat, and though he was reelected by his Bristol constituency he was debarred from sitting in the Commons until the Peerage Act was passed. This law enabled the son of a peer to renounce the succession to his father's title and was the successful culmination of a campaign led by Benn himself.

Youthful in appearance, energetic, and sometimes held to be undiscriminatingly enthusiastic, Benn won a reputation as the government's technological "whiz kid." When the Labour Party government of Harold Wilson was formed in 1964, Benn became postmaster-general. He moved to the Ministry of Technology in 1966, convinced of the potential of technology for the future of the United Kingdom.

Benn was also an acute and ambitious politician, winning a seat on the Labour Party National Executive Committee at the age of 34. He frequently spoke on the larger issues of political strategy, and in major speeches during 1969 outlined his views on the need for industrial reconstruction, the reform of governmental and parliamentary institutions, improved education, and increased participation in decision making. (W. H. Ts.)

BENTON, WILLIAM

Continuing his efforts to promote the use of English, publisher William Benton in 1969 proposed that the wide use of the language in Japan be recognized by the

William Benton

establishment of an International Institute of Intercommunication in that country. Benton had long been interested in this subject, and in 1966 had proposed aggressive promotion of English as a second language in non-English-speaking countries. The former U.S. senator also gave important financial support to efforts to improve television programming in the U.S. He pledged $200,000 from the William Benton Foundation to the work of the National Citizens Committee for Broadcasting in this field.

Benton received two important awards during the year. In the spring the National Conference of Christians and Jews honoured him with its National Human Relations Award and in October he received the Kajima Peace Award from Japan's Kajima Institute of International Peace. Another highlight of the year was a dinner marking the 40th anniversary of the founding of Benton and Bowles, the advertising agency he had established with Chester Bowles three months before the crash of 1929. On February 25, in his capacity of publisher and board chairman of *Encyclopædia Britannica,* he unveiled a new 20-volume reference work, *Annals of America.* To his surprise, he found that the editors had included two of his own pieces of writing among the 2,202 selections: *The Economics of a Free Society,* published in 1944, and his 1951 bill of particulars against the excesses of the late Sen. Joseph McCarthy of Wisconsin. Meanwhile, an unusual art show was running under Benton's cosponsorship in a small gallery at the New York City Center. It was a collection of little-known and rarely seen drawings of the late Reginald Marsh, assembled from the collections of Benton and the widow of the artist, Mrs. Felicia Marsh, who cosponsored the exhibit.

Born in Minneapolis, Minn., April 1, 1900, Benton was graduated from Yale in 1921. After seven years as a partner in Benton and Bowles, he had become a millionaire and left to enter public service. He became a vice-president of the University of Chicago in 1937 and in 1943, in association with the university, he became publisher and chairman of *Encyclopædia Britannica.* He served as assistant secretary of state under Pres. Harry S. Truman, was appointed to the U.S. Senate in 1949 and reelected for a two-year term in 1950, and served as U.S. delegate to UNESCO, 1962–68. He traveled widely and wrote extensively; his books include *The Voice of the Kremlin, This Is the Challenge,* and *The Voice of Latin America.* (Mx. H.)

BEST, GEORGE

Voted association football (soccer) player of the year in 1968 by the Football Writers' Association, George Best achieved further recognition in 1969 when he was selected to play on an all-star Fédération Internationale de Football Association (FIFA) team against Brazil. Because of an injury, however, he was unable to play.

Best was born May 22, 1946, in Belfast, N.Ire. He showed athletic ability early and in 1961 joined a local boys' club to play football. A scout from the Manchester United club saw him play and signed him to a contract. Best made his league debut with Manchester United in 1963. The next year he also began playing for Northern Ireland and by the end of the 1968–69 season had competed for his country 17 times.

Best helped Manchester United win the European Cup in 1968 and, previously, two Football Association championships and two runner-up medals. Off the soccer field he was something of a pop idol. He hoped that the house he was building near Manchester would help him to settle down, but there was little sign of it when his ex-fiancée sued him for breach of promise in December. He was also a successful businessman, running two boutiques and writing a newspaper column. His annual earnings were estimated at about $50,000. (T. W.)

BOND, EDWARD

One of the younger members of Britain's "New Wave" of dramatists, Edward Bond achieved considerable success in 1969: his plays had more performances throughout Europe during the year than did those of any of his "New Wave" contemporaries. Early in 1969, London's Royal Court Theatre, which discovered him in 1960, staged a season of three of his plays in alternating repertory, something unheard of in the case of a living dramatist. Two of his plays went on tour with the Royal Court players in Italy and Yugoslavia, and at the Belgrade Festival *Narrow Road to the Deep North* won a coveted award.

Born to working-class parents in London on July 18, 1934, Bond attended various state schools until he was 14. After working at odd jobs and serving in the Army, he joined the Royal Court's "writers' group." His first play, *The Pope's Wedding,* about solitude and the generation clash, was banned by the British censor. Bond himself said that the reason for this was his unmasked hatred of the cynical Establishment and his frank treatment of man's inhumanity to man. He won the George Devine Award for new writers in 1968.

After the censorship was abolished, Bond came into his own in Britain. Productions of *Saved,* built around the senseless murder of a defenseless infant, *Early Morning,* a pseudohistorical satire, and *Narrow Road to the Deep North,* an exotic anticolonialist drama that "mirrored the colonialism in our hearts," followed. He adapted Anton Chekhov's *The Three Sisters* for the Royal Court and began writing an original drama with the same title about the three daughters of King Lear. Bond's film scripts included *Michael Kolhaas, Blow Up,* and *Laughter in the Dark,* and in 1969 he was hired to write a film of the life of Russian dancer Vaslav Nijinsky. (O. Tr.)

BOULEZ, PIERRE

Pierre Boulez, who had set the music world on its ear more than once with his acerbic tongue and his innovative compositions, was preparing in 1969 to bring new dissonance to "Fun City." In June the New York Philharmonic announced that he would succeed Leonard Bernstein as its music director and resident conductor, taking over in 1971.

Called "the glamour boy of modernism" by the *New York Times,* Boulez had a conducting style that was diametrically opposed to that of the flamboyant Bernstein. On the podium Boulez (it rhymes with "who says") was a brilliant metronomic machine who worked without score or baton and conducted "like a semaphore." More important was the new repertoire he was expected to bring to Philharmonic Hall, and the new, young audience he hoped to attract.

An exponent of serial music, he would probably leave 19th-century works—the orchestra's traditional bread and butter—to guest conductors and concentrate on presenting experimental concerts of modern music. "Let's not have a museum" at Lincoln Center, he said. "Let's have a laboratory." His modernism, however, was that of Schoenberg, Webern, Stravinsky, and Mahler, and he eschewed such gimmickry as electronic composition, which he considered a fad. "Next year," he said, "they'll discover the viola da gamba."

Born in Montbrison, France, March 26, 1925, Boulez won first prize at the Paris Conservatory when, at 20, he displayed "stupefying virtuosity." He spent a decade as music director at Jean-Louis Barrault's Théâtre Marigny, where he first shook the musical Establishment by organizing a startling contemporary concert series, Domaine Musicale. His compositions were banned from the French national radio for 15 years, and he was to declare "there is more stupidity in the French musical community than anywhere else." If he was short of honour in his own country, however, he was highly regarded elsewhere: in Bayreuth, W.Ger., where he brought new interpretative depth to Wagner; in Baden-

HORST TAPPE—PIX FROM PUBLIX

Richard Attenborough

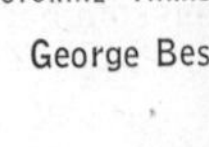

CENTRAL PRESS FROM PICTORIAL PARADE

George Best

HORST TAPPE—PIX FROM PUBLIX

Pierre Boulez

Baden, W.Ger., where he lived and led the prestigious South-West German Radio Orchestra; in London, where he was to direct the BBC Symphony Orchestra; and in the U.S., where he had been the principal guest conductor of George Szell's Cleveland (O.) Orchestra. (PH. K.)

BRANDT, WILLY

The first Social Democrat to head a German government for more than 39 years, Willy Brandt was elected on Oct. 21, 1969, by a majority of three votes in the Bundestag to the West German federal chancellorship. His coalition government of Social Democrats and Free Democrats took office the following day. His party had polled 42.7% in the federal election on September 28 and won 224 seats, an increase of 22 over the election in 1965. Even so he could govern only with the aid of the Free Democrats.

For three years Brandt had served as West Germany's foreign minister in the coalition government of Social Democrats and Christian Democrats led by Kurt Georg Kiesinger. During this period he placed particular emphasis on the need to improve relations with the countries of Eastern Europe. Accordingly, West Germany exchanged diplomatic relations with Romania and resumed diplomatic relations with Yugoslavia after a break of ten years. It also attempted to establish better terms with East Germany but was thwarted by the East Germans' insistence that West Germany must first recognize its Communist regime. One of the first moves by Brandt's government was to "admit the existence of two German states"—but without according diplomatic recognition to East Germany.

Born Herbert Ernst Karl Frahm in Lübeck, Dec. 18, 1913, Brandt assumed his present name after fleeing to Norway from the Nazis in 1933. When Norway fell, he entered Sweden, was granted Norwegian citizenship, and worked as a journalist and resistance supporter. He returned to Germany after the war as press attaché at the Norwegian military mission in Berlin. In 1947 he took German nationality again and resumed an active role in the Social Democratic Party.

Brandt was elected president of Berlin's Chamber of Deputies in 1955, became governing mayor of West Berlin two years later, and won an international reputation for his calm firmness during the crisis situations in the city. Elected deputy chairman of the Social Democratic Party in 1962 and chairman in 1964, he was the party's candidate for the federal chancellorship in 1961 and 1965. (N. CR.)

BROOKS, ANGIE ELIZABETH

Assuming office as president of the 24th session of the UN General Assembly in September 1969, Angie Brooks expressed concern at what she called "the gradual decline of the United Nations in the eyes of public opinion." She avoided a judgment as to whether this image reflected reality or was based on misunderstandings, but she urged delegates of the 126-member body to remember that their job was to work for peace. The 41-year-old lawyer-diplomat, second woman and third African to head the assembly, called upon her fellow diplomats to probe their souls and search deep into their minds "to ascertain whether or not in fact we have given—and are giving—to the United Nations cause the best and the most of ourselves." She further urged them to cherish and cultivate the United Nations as "the best means of international cooperation that has been at mankind's disposal since the beginning of its history." Miss Brooks was elected without opposition.

Born the daughter of a clergyman on Aug. 24, 1928, in Virginia, Liberia, Miss Brooks obtained a number of degrees from U.S. educational institutions, including a B.A. from Shaw University, Raleigh, N.C.; a bachelor of law and master of science from the University of Wisconsin; and doctor of law degrees from Shaw and Howard universities. She also did graduate work in international law at the University College Law School of London University and obtained a doctor of civil law degree from Liberia University.

She became active in UN affairs in 1954 when she first attended an assembly session as a delegate for Liberia. Most of her UN work was connected with dependent territories and trusteeships. Her posts included the chairmanship of the General Assembly's Fourth (Trusteeship) Committee in 1961 and the vice-presidency of the Trusteeship Council in 1966. In Liberia she became assistant attorney general in 1953 and assistant secretary of state in 1958, a post she continued to hold. She established a reputation as a fighter for the rights of African people—especially women. (MX. H.)

BUCHER, LLOYD M.

After 11 months of ordeal in a North Korean prison following the capture of the intelligence ship USS "Pueblo" and its crew in 1968, Navy Comdr. Lloyd M. Bucher, captain of the "Pueblo," faced further agony in 1969 after his return to the U.S.

Shortly after the release of the crew on Dec. 22, 1968, the Navy launched a special court of inquiry into the incident. Opening in Coronado, Calif., on January 20, the inquiry attempted to determine, first, whether Commander Bucher had used all means available to resist capture and whether the crew had adequately performed its duty of preventing the capture of classified material and equipment; and second, whether the crew had any choice but to make false confessions of intrusion and spying on North Korea. Even while the inquiry was going on, critics charged that the Navy had failed to provide for the ship's defense and was seeking scapegoats.

Bucher, who had been wounded during the seizure, told the court that the "Pueblo" was so inadequately armed that to resist would have invited slaughter. In highly emotional testimony, he recalled the extreme torture meted out by the North Koreans and said he had signed statements and confessions after his crew had been threatened with execution. Other crewmen corroborated his testimony.

On May 6 the secretary of the navy announced that the court of inquiry had called for a general court-martial for Bucher and the ship's intelligence officer, and for letters of admonition and reprimand for several Navy officials. However, the secretary decided to set aside the court's recommendation because the crew had "suffered enough." Bucher was assigned to attend the Navy's postgraduate school in Monterey, Calif. (*See* DEFENSE: *Special Report*.)

Bucher was born in Pocatello, Ida., Sept. 1, 1927. Orphaned at an early age, he was educated in various orphanages and at Boys Town, Neb., where he became an outstanding athlete. He joined the Navy and later attended the University of Nebraska on the G.I. Bill. After graduation he joined the Navy submarine service, where he spent his Navy career before assuming command of the "Pueblo" in 1967. (D. FO.)

BURGER, WARREN EARL

"Our history tells us that our Chief Justices have probably had more profound and lasting influence on their times and on the direction of the nation than most Presidents have had," U.S. Pres. Richard M. Nixon said on May 21, 1969. He had just nominated Warren Earl Burger to become the 15th chief justice of the United States, in the hope that Burger would change the speed, if not the direction, charted for the nation by the Supreme Court under its 14th chief justice, Earl Warren. Nixon, who had blamed the "Warren court" for much of the crime problem that was a principal issue in the 1968 presidential campaign, described Burger as the "strict constructionist" needed to return the court to its proper role as interpreter rather than maker of law.

The Senate Judiciary Committee, after a friendly hearing that lasted only one hour and 40 minutes, approved the nomination unanimously on June 3. On June 9 the Senate advised and consented to the nomination by a 74–3 vote.

Burger came to the Supreme Court from the U.S. Circuit Court of Appeals for the District of Columbia, where he was a frequent dissenter on a progressive bench. He did not wear easily the label of "liberal" or "conservative," however. In civil rights cases, for instance, he had no trouble matching strides with his liberal colleagues and with the Supreme Court. It was his criticism of the Warren court's approach to individual liberties in conflict with the criminal process that brought Burger to the attention of President Nixon. While not quarreling with the outcome of most of the celebrated criminal cases, Burger attacked the court's practice of laying down sweeping procedural rules on a case-by-case method. He preferred the court to limit its holdings to the facts of the individual cases and leave rule making to an advisory commission with the time and resources to consider problems in depth.

Burger was born in St. Paul, Minn., on Sept. 17, 1907. He attended the University of Minnesota and obtained his law degree by studying nights at St. Paul College of Law. He practiced law in the firm of Faricy, Burger, Moore, and Costello until 1953, when he went to Washington to become an assistant attorney general during Pres. Dwight D. Eisenhower's first term. Eisenhower appointed Burger to the D.C. circuit court in 1956. (J. E. I.)

BUSIA, KOFI ABREFA

In September 1969, just ten years after he had gone into exile to avoid arrest under Kwame Nkrumah's regime, Kofi Busia became Ghana's new prime minister. As the leader of the parliamentary opposition after Ghana achieved independence in 1957, Busia was a bitter rival of Nkrumah, who was toppled from power by an army coup in 1966.

Busia was born on July 11, 1913. After early promise as a pupil in the schools of the Gold Coast (the British colony that preceded Ghana), he won academic distinction in England by gaining history degrees at London and Oxford universities, as well as a doctorate in social anthropology. He spent 15 years as a teacher and then as the first African administrative officer appointed by the colonial authorities in the Gold Coast.

Although by nature and inclination a scholar rather than a politician, Busia felt irresistibly drawn into public life by the independence struggle. He rapidly rose in the movement to become leader of the United Gold Coast Convention. As a member of the Ghana National Assembly (1957–59), he urgently warned his country against the erosion of democratic standards under

Nkrumah's rule. When he believed he could no longer survive politically in Ghana, he decided to go into exile to campaign against the Nkrumah regime from academic bases in the U.K. and the Netherlands.

Toward the end of 1961 Busia resigned his academic posts to devote himself full-time to politics again, believing that the end of the Nkrumah regime was approaching. But he had to wait almost five years before the military ousted Nkrumah. Busia was then able to return home as vice-chairman and, subsequently, chairman of the political committee of the military-led National Liberation Council. But he did not work well with the military leaders. He therefore resigned as chairman and devoted himself to preparing the way for the emergence of his new Progress Party, which decisively won the national elections in August 1969. (Co. L.)

BUTLER, MICHAEL

But for Michael Butler, hair would still be the stuff of a penitent's shirt and nudity might never have made a hit on Broadway. Butler's *Hair* was the hippie musical that "blew my mind" when he saw it in Greenwich Village. He bought the rights, raised $225,000 (including $90,000 of his own), and hired Tom O'Horgan to remount it on Broadway in the spring of 1968.

Eighteen months later it was still SRO at the Biltmore Theater, productions were on the boards in eight other cities and three foreign countries, and five more companies were being formed. The LP cast recording was at the top of the charts; astrology (as in the hit song "The Age of Aquarius") was a national fad; on-stage nakedness was the theatrical rage; and Butler was looking forward to personal profits of at least $1.5 million a year "for several years."

If success was new to Butler, money certainly was not. As *Life* magazine put it: "He was born with a silver polo mallet in his mouth."

The birth of this scion of the Butler Companies, reportedly one of the nation's largest concentrations of wealth, took place in Chicago on Nov. 26, 1926. His upbringing was apparently chaotic, with a protean cast of stepparents, and his academic career was ubiquitous. He matriculated at a series of schools before making it through Culver Military Academy in 1945. At the University of Virginia he concentrated on fox hunting and at the University of Colorado, on skiing. Forsaking academe, he married three times, safaried in Africa, visited the maharaja of Jaipur, entertained a Hashemite king, chummed with John Kennedy, squired the duchess of Windsor, dropped hundreds of thousands of dollars in real estate, ran for the Illinois state senate, and lost. He was, in a word, a playboy.

Then came *Hair* and a new option on life. It was a hit, and he was its Producer. He saw himself as "a connection" between the old and the new, between young artists and the moneyed Establishment. (Still, for all his alleged liberalism, he barred *Hair*'s two principal writer/actors from the theatre after they improvised on stage.) Butler did not intend to rest on his laurels. Future commitments included producing records, managing a progressive rock group, and making a musical of *Frankenstein,* in which the monster would emerge as "a very beautiful person." (Ph. K.)

CAETANO, MARCELLO

On Sept. 25, 1968, following the illness of António de Oliveira Salazar, Marcello José das Neves Alves Caetano was appointed premier of Portugal. Salazar had held the office since 1932. After assuming his new post Caetano introduced a measure of political freedom, reformed the National Union (the official political party), recalled opponents of the regime from exile, and curbed the powers of the secret police. He visited Brazil, the African overseas provinces, and the United States during 1969 and displayed a more outgoing style of leadership than did his predecessor. He continued to pursue a cautious economic policy, favoured foreign investment and closer ties with Europe, and called for greater autonomy for the overseas provinces. In September 1969 he revised the electoral law to guarantee free elections for the National Assembly on Oct. 26, 1969. In these first significantly contested elections in Portugal since 1926 Caetano and his National Union won an overwhelming victory with 89% of the vote.

Caetano was born of humble parents in Lisbon, Aug. 17, 1906; his father was a primary-school teacher. He was graduated in law at the University of Lisbon in 1929. While there, he caught the attention of Salazar, who became Portugal's finance minister in 1928 and appointed him in 1929 as judicial auditor to the ministry. In 1931 Caetano was closely involved in drawing up Portugal's new constitution, which was approved in 1933. He was regarded as the theoretician behind it.

In 1944 Caetano was given the post of minister for the colonies and was responsible for formulating the law that established the colonies as overseas provinces. In 1949 he was appointed president of the Corporative Chamber, which was responsible for reviewing government legislation. He played at this time a major part in reforming the National Union. In 1955 he became minister attached to the premier and was the effective deputy premier. He was subsequently reported to have disagreed with Salazar over manipulation of the constitution and education policy. As a result Caetano assumed the rectorship of the University of Lisbon in 1959. He resigned in 1962 after police had entered the university precincts, but remained a professor of law. (Rn. C.)

CALDERA RODRIGUEZ, RAFAEL

After trying for two decades to win election to the presidency of Venezuela, Rafael Caldera Rodriguez finally achieved his goal in March 1969. The 53-year-old leader of COPEI, the Social Christian Party, embarked on a five-year term as chief of state for the ten million Venezuelans. His election to office was a first for Venezuela; never before had the country seen an orderly transition of power from one political party to another after a free election. Caldera won a narrow victory over Gonzalo Barrios, candidate of the incumbent Acción Democrática party, and maintained a much wider margin over conservative Miguel Angel Burelli Rivas and liberal Luis Beltrán Prieto Figueroa.

When he assumed the presidency, Caldera became the third consecutive democratically elected president after a long series of dictatorships and unrest. The dictatorial period ended in 1958 when a popular uprising ousted Gen. Marcos Pérez Jiménez.

Caldera was born Jan. 24, 1916, in San Felipe in the mountain state of Yaracuy. His family moved to Caracas when he was nine years old, and he received a Jesuit education that influenced his religious and social philosophy. He graduated from the national university with degrees in law and political science.

AUTHENTICATED NEWS INTERNATIONAL

Willy Brandt

PICTORIAL PARADE

Marcello Caetano

PICTORIAL PARADE

Warren Earl Burger

During the 1930s he founded a conservative Roman Catholic student movement in opposition to Marxist groups. COPEI, however, gradually moved ideologically toward the left as it acquired support over the years from labour and intellectuals.

Caldera was an unsuccessful candidate for the presidency four times and spent time in prison for defying Pérez Jiménez. He made a record as a brilliant lawyer, however, in the years when he was organizing the Social Christians.

As president Caldera's greatest challenges were expected to be to preserve Venezuela against periodic outbreaks by leftist terrorists and to improve marketing agreements for oil, the main source of the nation's wealth. He also inherited a boundary dispute with Guyana in which Venezuela claimed sovereignty over virtually two-thirds of the former British colony. (J. A. O'L.)

CALLAGHAN, (LEONARD) JAMES

As Britain's home secretary, James Callaghan found himself in charge of the intervention from Whitehall in the Ulster troubles in August 1969. Traditionally, the Home Office is something of a political minefield. Callaghan had moved there in November 1967, after three discouraging years at the Treasury that had culminated in the devaluation of sterling. Succeeding the libertarian Roy Jenkins, he brought to his varied responsibilities a more conventional—some might say a more conservative—approach to such matters as control of the immigration of Kenyan Asians, the drug controversy, gambling, political protest demonstrations, and responsibility for the police, though his concern for prison reform and child care was firmly in the humanitarian-reformist Labour tradition.

In 1963 Callaghan had run third, after Harold Wilson and George Brown, in the contest for the leadership of the Labour Party after the death of Hugh Gaitskell. His status in the Labour government had suffered during his years in office since 1964. Early in 1969 he became involved in a sharp dispute with his senior Cabinet colleagues over trade union legislation, and for some months he was dropped from the prime minister's inner Cabinet.

Paradoxically, the Ulster disturbances served to revive Callaghan's political reputation. He took charge at a time when most ministers, including the prime minister, were away on holiday, and with smoothness and decision moved troops to Northern Ireland and placed his own police and civil service advisers alongside the administration in Belfast. When he visited Northern Ireland to see for himself, his relaxed good humour, studied moderation, and gift of the common touch made him widely welcome.

Callaghan's understanding of politics stemmed from continuous membership in the House of Commons since 1945. Born March 27, 1912, in Portsmouth, he worked as a trade union official for a few years in the 1930s. He retained his contacts with the unions and stood rather apart from some of the university-educated intellectuals in the government, though in 1959 he became a visiting fellow of Nuffield College, Oxford. (W. H. Ts.)

CEAUSESCU, NICOLAE

In the four years since March 1965 when, as a virtual unknown, Nicolae Ceausescu became general secretary of the Romanian Workers' Party, he had become a national leader enjoying a personal popularity unparalleled in modern Romania. As president in 1969, his position had been enhanced by his strong stand against the Soviet-led invasion of Czechoslovakia in August 1968 and by his denunciation in February 1969 of the doctrine of "limited sovereignty" that the U.S.S.R. had promulgated to justify the invasion.

The threat of outside interference in early 1969 in the form of pressure for Warsaw Pact troop maneuvers in Romania only served to unify the people behind Ceausescu in parliamentary elections in March and to reinforce their anti-Soviet tendencies. The neutralist role that Ceausescu had been carving for Romania through his insistence that international exchanges and contacts were indispensable to peaceful coexistence culminated in August in the visit of U.S. Pres. Richard M. Nixon, the eighth non-Communist head of state to visit Romania in two years and the first U.S. president to visit a Communist state in peacetime.

Born on Jan. 26, 1918, at Scornicesti, in the foothills of the Carpathian Mountains, Ceausescu joined the illegal Union of Communist Youth at the age of 15. After the liberation he became a member of the Central Committee. He joined the Central Committee Secretariat in 1954, was elected to the Politburo in 1955, and became general secretary after the death of Gheorghe Gheorghiu-Dej on March 19, 1965.

Stepping out of the shadow of his predecessor almost immediately, at the Romanian Communist Party Congress in July 1965 Ceausescu strongly emphasized the principles of national sovereignty and independence as the permanent basis of Romania's international policy. Following this policy, on May 7, 1966, he criticized the old Comintern for having put Soviet interests ahead of all else and even implied that Bessarabia, now part of the U.S.S.R., was historic Romanian land. In January 1967, Romania established diplomatic relations with West Germany and, following the Arab-Israeli war of that year, refused to follow the Warsaw Pact countries in severing diplomatic relations with Israel. In December 1967, Ceausescu took over the post of president of the State Council. (K. Sm.)

CHABAN-DELMAS, JACQUES

France's new premier in 1969 was a man with three faces. To the general public, Jacques Chaban-Delmas was brilliant and quick-witted, but at the same time frivolous and superficial. His political opponents said that he was tenacious and intelligent, but also ambitious and inconstant. His friends claimed that, on the contrary, he was firm and loyal, determined and courageous. No doubt there was some truth and some falsehood in each of these contradictory descriptions.

Chaban-Delmas was born on March 7, 1915, in Paris, served in the Army during the Battle of France and, after France's defeat, became a leader in the Resistance. It was then that he adopted the name "Chaban" to disguise his identity. In November 1946 he was elected Radical-Socialist deputy for the Gironde, and the following year he became mayor of Bordeaux, an office that he still held in 1969.

Deputy Chaban-Delmas' political loyalties were shifting ones. He was a Gaullist with de Gaulle, a radical with Pierre Mendès-France, a man of the centre-right and then of the centre-left. Three times the Fourth Republic made him a minister. He was minister of public works in the Mendès-France government of 1954 and minister of state under the Socialist premier Guy Mollet. In charge of the Ministry of Defense during the Algerian war, he defended the government in his official capacity while at the same time joining with the Gaullists to bring it down. When de Gaulle took power in 1958, he fought for and won the presidency of the National Assembly. His political sense was to serve him well in that post, which he held, without serious opposition, for 11 years.

It was well known that he was bored by this office, the responsibilities of which were more formal than influential since the Gaullists held an absolute majority in the Assembly. As he had formerly joined with Mendès-France and then with Mollet, so now he threw in his lot with Georges Pompidou, whom de Gaulle dropped from the premiership in 1968. Following de Gaulle's retirement and Pompidou's election to the presidency in 1969, Chaban-Delmas became premier—second in command of the new regime. (P. V.-P.)

CHARLES, PRINCE OF WALES

With a few glaring exceptions, Queen Elizabeth II's broadcast plea (Christmas 1957) that her children be allowed privacy to grow up "as normally as possible" had been respected, so her investiture of her son Charles as prince of Wales in Caernarvon Castle on July 1, 1969, symbolized the very real "showing" of the prince, not only to the people of Wales but also to the British public and to the world. The comparatively secluded years of school and of his first terms (from October 1967) at Trinity College, Cambridge, gave place in 1969 to the greater publicity and tension attending his term's studies at the University College of Wales, Aberystwyth, the medieval pageantry of Caernarvon, and his subsequent five-day tour of Wales.

The prince was seen to be attractive, intelligent, amusing, sensitive, and frank. Said to resemble in character his grandfather, King George VI, he shared that king's diffidence but also his courage in overcoming it. This was especially notable when, confronted by demonstrators at Cardiff (June 28, 1968), he deliberately walked across to attempt to speak with them. Perhaps because, as he said, his position "builds up a little bit of a barrier," he got on best with those considerably older or younger than himself. Described by his mother as a "country person," he particularly enjoyed and excelled in field sports and was an excellent swimmer and horseman. He made his first solo airplane flight on Jan. 14, 1969. A lover of music, especially that of the 18th century, he had played the piano, trumpet, and cello. He also showed an interest in acting; his more publicized roles included Richard III (1960), Macbeth (1965), and a dustman (1969).

Born in Buckingham Palace, London, on Nov. 14, 1948, and christened Charles Philip Arthur George, he attended Hill House (pre-preparatory) school in London (1956–57), Cheam (preparatory) School in Berkshire (1957–62), and Gordonstoun in Morayshire (1962–67). He described his two terms (January–May 1966) at Timbertop, a bush outpost of Geelong Grammar School, Victoria, Austr., as "the most wonderful experience I've ever had." In his first terms at Cambridge he took part I of the archaeology and anthropology tripos, and was going on to read history. (S. Mu.)

CHICHESTER-CLARK, JAMES

Circumstance rather than ambition brought James Chichester-Clark to the prime ministership of Northern Ireland in May 1969 at a time of deep unrest in Ulster. He was something of a compromise choice for the leadership of the Ulster Unionists after the fall of the reformist Terence O'Neill. Born Feb. 12, 1923, he had the conventional background of the Ulster landed gentry. For 18 years he had been a regular soldier in the Irish Guards, and his first experience in public affairs was as aide-de-camp to Field Marshal Earl Alexander of Tunis when he was governor-general of Canada. Chichester-Clark entered Ulster politics in 1960 as a Unionist M.P. in the Northern Ireland Parliament, rising to become government chief whip in 1963, leader of the House in 1966, and minister of agriculture in 1967. A reserved, rather retiring person, he remarked of himself, "I was a man with a bit of spare time, and I hoped I could do something useful."

Though he sometimes showed the stereotyped reactions of the Ulster Unionist—in blaming subversive Irish elements for the August rioting, for example—Chichester-Clark took a middle-of-the-road position and counted himself a progressive. The firmness with which he pursued moderate policies antagonized some extremists in his party, but he was able to command a massive vote of confidence from the Unionist Party council at the end of September.

While he rejected the idea of a coalition government as politically impracticable, he tried to bring Protestant and Roman Catholic interests together by setting up a "peace conference" for consultation between the different religious groups and by establishing a tribunal to hear complaints of intimidation or discrimination. "The great majority of the people of Northern Ireland detest the sectarian divisions which have been fomented in recent times," he said. "My duty is to encourage a sense of public responsibility among all sections of the community, and to ensure that the great body of moderate opinion asserts itself." (W. H. Ts.)

CLEAVER, ELDRIDGE

Eldridge Cleaver, whose book *Soul on Ice* (1968) was one of the most cogent explanations of the underlying reasons for cultural alienation of blacks in the United States, spent 1969 in de facto exile. Faced with revocation of his parole from the California prison system, the information minister of the militant Black Panther Party had fled the country late in 1968.

For nearly a year, his movements were veiled. He surfaced in Cuba, but seemed to get a cool reception from Prime Minister Fidel Castro's government. Later he appeared in Algiers and in Moscow, where he argued that the Soviet regime should strenuously support revolutionary movements elsewhere. "We feel the Soviet Union's arsenal is not the private property of the Soviet Union." He told a reporter he could travel freely in Communist countries, using his driver's license and an FBI "wanted" poster instead of a passport. He said he was in close touch with affairs in the United States and intended to continue "functioning in the struggle against the oppressive system there." In a statement late in the year, he urged America's blacks to make common cause with oppressed peoples everywhere.

Cleaver was indeed a revolutionary, but in light of his book, it appeared that he was driven to a revolutionary position when his rational explanations of justifiable minority demands fell on a nation of deaf ears. *Soul on Ice,* according to the *New York Times,* was one of the ten best books of the year. It recounted in the first person the manifestations and implications of both minority status and latent racism inherited from a slave system. It also explained a new syndrome widely seen in liberal circles—the mutual sexual attraction between white women and black men. Cleaver presented a simple cultural thesis: Black women were accessible to their white masters during the period of slavery, but the reverse was not true. In cultural terms, black men were "forbidden fruit" to white women and vice versa. Today, they are acting out repressed cultural desires.

Cleaver, who had brief formal education, began reading extensively during a nine-year prison term for rape. For a time he was affiliated with the Black Muslims and Malcolm X, before breaking with them to join the Black Panthers. (PH. K.)

COLLINS, MICHAEL

A member of the crew of Apollo 11, U.S. astronaut Michael Collins remained in orbit around the moon while Neil Armstrong and Edwin Aldrin descended to its surface. The Apollo 11 mission began with a successful launch on July 16 from the Kennedy Space Center, Florida. On July 20 Collins orbited the moon at 69 mi. while Armstrong and Aldrin made the landing. During successive orbits Collins made repeated attempts to locate the lunar module but without success. He was rejoined in orbit by Armstrong and Aldrin after they had spent more than $21\frac{1}{2}$ hours on the moon. The Apollo 11 mission ended successfully on July 24, 1969, with a splashdown in the Pacific Ocean about 1,200 mi. SW of Hawaii.

Collins was born on Oct. 31, 1930, in Rome, Italy, where his father, Maj. Gen. James L. Collins, was military attaché at the U.S. embassy. After graduating from the U.S. Military Academy, Collins transferred to the Air Force and later became an experimental flight test officer at Edwards Air Force Base, California.

Collins was among a group of 14 astronauts selected by the National Aeronautics and Space Administration in October 1963. After completing his basic training at the Manned Spacecraft Center in Houston, Tex., he was assigned as backup pilot to James Lovell, Jr., who, with Frank Borman, orbited the earth in Gemini 7 for two weeks after being launched on Dec. 4, 1965. Collins' first space flight mission came on July 18, 1966, as pilot of Gemini 10. During its three-day mission, Collins twice left his craft and ventured into space to perform engineering tasks, including the recovery of scientific experiments attached to an Agena vehicle with which Gemini 10 had rendezvoused and docked.

In 1968 Collins was chosen as a crew member for Apollo 8, the first manned spacecraft to orbit the moon and return to earth. However, a bone spur and loose disk pressing on his spinal column necessitated an

UPI COMPIX

Charles, prince of Wales

A.F.P. FROM PICTORIAL PARADE

Michael Collins

BRUNO BARBEY FROM MAGNUM

Eldridge Cleaver

CAMERA PRESS—PIX FROM PUBLIX

James Chichester-Clark

WIDE WORLD

Charles Evers

KEYSTONE

Bernadette Devlin

ERICH LESSING FROM MAGNUM

Charles de Gaulle

operation that removed him from that mission. The Apollo 11 mission was to be his last; late in 1969 Pres. Richard Nixon appointed him assistant secretary of state for public affairs. (M. R. S.)

COOLEY, DENTON A.

Denton Cooley had performed more heart transplants than any other man, but it was his 19th patient who attracted national attention in April 1969. For while Christiaan Barnard of South Africa had performed the first heart transplant and Michael E. DeBakey was the real pioneer in open heart surgery, Cooley was the first to implant an artificial heart in a human patient.

The patient was Haskell Karp, a 47-year-old printing estimator with terminal heart disease. Operating at St. Luke's Episcopal Hospital in Houston, Tex., Cooley discovered that the heart damage was too severe to repair. He cut away part of the diseased heart muscle and replaced it with a synthetic fabric, but the heart would not beat spontaneously. Faced with no other alternative except letting the patient die, Cooley then implanted a mechanical heart made of a silicone plastic.

Acknowledging that the artificial implant was only temporary, Cooley and the patient's family issued a nationwide appeal for a heart donor. One was found in Massachusetts, and her heart was transplanted into Karp's chest 65 hours after the first operation. He died 38 hours later of pneumonia and kidney failure.

The cause of the furor that followed was the suggestion that Cooley had used what was essentially an experimental technique on a human guinea pig. There was also the suspicion that the device had been developed under the auspices of DeBakey, who had received $1.5 million from the National Heart Institute for the purpose. NHI wanted to know whether federal funds had gone into the development of the heart Cooley used and, if so, whether federal guidelines regarding experimental techniques had been observed. It was apparent that DeBakey had not approved Cooley's use of his device, for he was critical of his colleague's actions. Cooley said his device had been developed under a $50,000 grant from the Texas Heart Institute, which he headed, but one of his key assistants had just spent five years on DeBakey's project.

Cooley was born in Houston, Aug. 22, 1920, did his undergraduate work at the University of Texas, and received his M.D. from Johns Hopkins in 1944. Following further training in London, he returned to Houston, where he joined the medical faculty of Baylor University. In 1963 he was named professor of the Baylor College of Medicine, of which DeBakey was president. (Ph. K.)

CROSLAND, (CHARLES) ANTHONY (RAVEN)

In the British government reshuffle in October 1969, Anthony Crosland, at the age of 51, became the head of a new Department of Local Government and Regional Planning, in which the Ministry of Transport was merged with the Ministry of Housing and Local Government and the regional planning functions of the disappearing Department of Economic Affairs were absorbed. His new responsibilities were to include environmental pollution in all forms —the first time that the threat of pollution had received such powerful political recognition. As head of this group of planning departments, Crosland would take direct responsibility for major planning decisions of national consequence, such as the choice of site for a third London airport.

Crosland had made his reputation as one of the intellectuals in the government. Born on Aug. 29, 1918, he had been an Oxford University lecturer in economics before being elected to Parliament in 1950. His book *The Future of Socialism* (1956) established him as a leading theorist in the Labour Party. He moved in the Gaitskell circle of political intellectuals, and excited some suspicion among the Labour rank and file by leading a well-to-do social life in London. Yet egalitarianism was the core of Crosland's political thinking; he joined the Labour Party to fight the class society and social inequality. Though sometimes taken as a playboy, in office he showed himself to be an extremely hard worker.

He held a number of the leading positions in the Wilson governments. Going to the Department of Education and Science in January 1965, he made the decision that no more new universities should be established in the next ten years but that there should be greater development of colleges of higher education and polytechnics. As president of the Board of Trade from August 1967, he was one of the ministers most closely concerned with the export drive and with overseas trade in general. Crosland was a strong advocate of British entry into the EEC, arguing that Britain could find a new sense of direction only in a European context. (W. H. Ts.)

DEFREGGER, MATTHIAS

The Roman Catholic auxiliary bishop of Munich, Matthias Defregger, became a centre of public controversy in 1969 after the disclosure that as a captain in the German Army he had passed on an order to execute the male inhabitants of an Italian village in 1944. Defregger was in command of the intelligence section of an infantry division which in June 1944 was in retreat north of Rome. His unit, in the village of Filetto di Camarda, was attacked by partisans who were after radio equipment. Four soldiers were killed, and the divisional commander, who died later, ordered Defregger to shoot every male in the village as a reprisal.

There seemed to be general agreement that he refused to carry out that order. But the commander insisted on reprisals and, seeing no way out, Defregger passed the order on to a subordinate and set about supervising preparations for the unit's continued retreat. In the meantime 17 villagers were murdered.

Many years after the murders West German lawyers were sifting through files of documents about war crimes in Italy when they came across an incident involving Defregger's old division. The bishop was interviewed. He knew nothing about that case, but he told the lawyers voluntarily about the murders at Filetto. Inquiries were opened, but it was decided not to prosecute since there was at the most evidence that Defregger had committed manslaughter; and, according to the statute of limitations, prosecutions for manslaughter may not be started more than 15 years after the crime was committed. But after a public outcry it was announced that the Frankfurt prosecutor would reopen the case.

Defregger was born in Munich on Feb. 18, 1915. He studied theology after the war and was ordained a priest in 1949. He became one of the closest assistants and advisers of Julius Cardinal Döpfner, the senior prelate of the Roman Catholic Church in West Germany. Cardinal Döpfner strongly defended Defregger from public criticism. Defregger was appointed auxiliary bishop of Munich in 1968. (N. Cr.)

DE GAULLE, CHARLES ANDRÉ JOSEPH MARIE

After 29 years of a public life that began on June 18, 1940, at the microphones of the BBC and more than 10 years of almost royal rule over the French Fifth Republic, Charles de Gaulle suddenly left politics at noon on April 28, 1969, and went on to occupy the place reserved for him in history.

Since the student revolt and the strikes of May–June 1968, a great feeling of unease had hung over France. People felt vaguely that the aging head of state had not grasped the meaning of events. The Gaullist electoral triumph on June 30, 1968, had solved nothing, and the general disquiet was intensified in November by the crisis of the franc.

De Gaulle's reply to this silent questioning was a referendum concerning reforms so varied, ill conceived, and insignificant that, after approving ten major referenda in as many years, the French for the first time answered "no" by 53% of the vote.

De Gaulle had tied his continuation in office to a referendum once too often and, as soon as the results were known, he resigned. A short time afterward he left France for Ireland, where he stayed throughout the campaign for the election of his successor. On his return to his home in Colombey-les-Deux-Églises, he retired behind a wall of silence, refusing to receive anyone except a few close friends and devoting most of his time to writing his new *Memoirs*.

This departure from power countered three commonly made forecasts. First, de Gaulle had acted as a true democrat: rejected by the electorate, he accepted their verdict. Second, the regime he had founded and led survived. The Gaullists remained united, for the time being at least. There was no deluge. Finally, this voluntary retirement was quite clearly final, despite the suspicions of those who saw it only as a political maneuver. At 78, the old man thus added the final touch to the part of his image that was most precious to him: his own historical figure.

Born Nov. 22, 1890, de Gaulle graduated from the École Spéciale Militaire at Saint-Cyr. After the fall of France in World War II, he rallied continued French resistance to Germany from England and formed the first provisional government in France after its liberation. He retired from public life in 1953 but returned in 1958 to become president under a new constitution. (P. V.-P.)

DELBRÜCK, MAX

A biology professor at the California Institute of Technology, Max Delbrück was a member of the informal research team that won the 1969 Nobel Prize for Physiology or Medicine. His colleagues, with whom he had shared data for decades, were Alfred Hershey and Salvador Luria (*qq.v.*).

The work the three men performed was carried out largely between 1940 and 1952. It involved the most basic research into the nature and genetics of viruses. So basic was their work, in fact, that without it James D. Watson (once a student of Delbrück and Luria) and Francis H. C. Crick could not have discovered the structure of the deoxyribonucleic acid (DNA) molecule.

Delbrück, a physicist turned biologist, began his viral research at Vanderbilt University. He developed a method of purifying viruses to study them and discovered that a single virus invades a single bacterial cell. He was joined by Luria; together they studied the interaction between viruses and the bacteria they infect. They discovered that both could mutate, thereby changing their infectious characteristics as well as their immunities. Their findings ultimately enabled others to develop vaccines against virus-caused diseases, such as polio.

Born in Berlin, Sept. 4, 1906, Delbrück received a Ph.D. in physics from the University of Göttingen in 1930. A refugee from Nazi Germany, he did research in Denmark and Switzerland before coming to the U.S. in 1937 to join the Caltech faculty as a Rockefeller Foundation fellow. He moved to Vanderbilt two years later and returned to Caltech in 1947 as a professor of biology.

Having jointly won the Louisa Gross Horowitz Prize with Luria a week earlier, Delbrück donated his half of that $25,000 award to Amnesty International, an independent group that worked in behalf of political prisoners of all countries.

(Ph. K.)

DEVLIN, (JOSEPHINE) BERNADETTE

Acclaimed by some as a latter-day Joan of Arc, "thrown up," as she herself has said, "by the complex of economic, political, and social problems of Northern Ireland," Bernadette Devlin demonstrated in her brief public career much of the obstinate honesty, zeal, and incapacity for compromise that led Joan to the stake. These qualities brought Miss Devlin to trial, and occasionally made her feel personally destroyed. Elected as an independent member of Parliament for Mid-Ulster on April 17, 1969, she took her seat on April 22 and promptly defied convention by making her maiden speech immediately, in an emergency debate then being held on the riots in Londonderry.

Bernadette Devlin campaigned for election on a program of opposition to Unionism, and of "justice for the people." A Roman Catholic, she maintained a nonsectarian approach, urging Catholic and Protestant workers to unite. While repudiating any suggestion that she encouraged violence (she at first tried to restrain the rioters of Londonderry in July and August), she nevertheless believed that, if attacked, people had a right to defend themselves. This was her explanation (October 30–31) to the Scarman Tribunal as to why she carried bricks to the Bogside barricades and organized the throwing of gasoline bombs to form a wall of flame between rioters and police.

Her concern for those rendered homeless by the "troubles" was shown by her fund-raising tour (August 21–September 3) of the U.S., which she cut short on discovering that its organizers were also raising money for the (clandestine) Irish Republican Army. Six months after her election Bernadette, disillusioned with Parliament ("I never wanted to join their bloody club"), yearned to return to her studies and train for work that she felt would be of solid worth. Her life story, *The Price of My Soul,* published on November 3, explained her views. On December 22 she was sentenced to six months' imprisonment for incitement to riotous behaviour, but was granted bail pending an appeal.

Born in Cookstown, Northern Tyrone, on April 23, 1947, she was the third of six children. Her father, a carpenter, died when she was 9, and her mother, largely the source of Bernadette's convinced Christian faith, when she was 19. Entering the Queen's University, Belfast, to study psychology (October 1965), she became involved in 1968 with the then two-year-old Civil Rights Association and took part in its marches. (S. Mu.)

DONLEAVY, JAMES PATRICK

Another of J. P. Donleavy's increasingly self-concerned novels, *The Beastly Beatitudes of Balthazar B,* appeared in 1969. It was met generally with the respectful disappointment that his recent work had produced in hopeful readers. He himself may have gotten more gratification out of his legal triumph in June, when 12 years of litigation with Maurice Girodias' defunct Olympia Press over the rights to his first and best novel, *The Ginger Man,* ended with the case being dismissed.

That bawdy, brilliant first novel still accounted for most of Donleavy's reputation. "The most representative novel of the 1950s," V. S. Naipaul once called it. It was certainly the most imitated for a decade or more, and continued to maintain an influence and audience when other "picaresque" novels and antiheroes were fading. It owed much to James Joyce and to Donleavy's own experience of Dublin, where he royally spent a GI grant at Trinity College, and perhaps something to his friend Brendan Behan, who first read it in manuscript and called it "an act of love for Ireland."

What was entirely Donleavy's own contribution was a peculiar kind of self-parodying dandyism, which grew more peculiar and perhaps less funny in his later work. In 1964 Donleavy described the novelist's art in this way: "You are an actor, writing down the stage directions after you've played the part." Not surprisingly, three of his novels reached the stage.

Born in 1926 of Irish parents in New York City, Donleavy was educated there by Jesuits and Christian Brothers. He joined the U.S. Navy in 1944 and after the war married an English girl and read zoology for a time at Trinity College, Dublin. *The Ginger Man* was published by Girodias in Paris in 1955, and in an expurgated version by Neville Spearman in 1956. It was followed by a play, *Fairy Tales of New York* (1961); the novel *A Singular Man* (1963); *Meet My Maker, the Mad Molecule,* stories and sketches (1964); and the novella *The Saddest Summer of Samuel S* (1966).

(W. L. We.)

EVERS, CHARLES

The drowsy little southwestern Mississippi town of Fayette woke up in the glare of national attention in 1969 when it elected Charles Evers to the $75-a-month job of mayor. Not only had a black man defeated the town's mayor of 20 years, 77-year-old R. J. Allen, but the campaign and victory had served as a touchstone for dozens of other black candidates across the state. Evers, who had succeeded his assassinated brother, Medgar, as field secretary of the National Association for the Advancement of Colored People in 1963, had been working for years to rally Mississippi's black vote.

Building on his experiences as a civil rights worker, businessman (all sorts of enterprises, including Fayette's "Medgar Evers Shopping Center"), and student of national Democratic politics, Charles Evers vowed to end "hate, violence and police brutality." Though about three-fourths of Fayette's citizenry was black, Evers aimed his theme of love and nonviolence at both races, with posters that said "Don't vote for a black man. Or a white man. Just a good man." After the election—which also brought into office an all-black board of aldermen—he repeated his intention to make Fayette a "clean and righteous town," administered without racial favouritism.

For Charles Evers, the achievement was another step in the political-civil rights struggle that he had promised to carry on for his brother. Born Sept. 11, 1922, in Decatur, Miss., Evers received a degree in social science from Alcorn (Miss.) College and, after military service, operated hotel and funeral enterprises in Philadelphia, Miss., before moving to Chicago in 1957 to teach physical education and run a number of businesses. On his return to Mississippi, he organized black voter drives, backed black candidates, and in 1968 ran for Congress, making it as far as a runoff election. After he announced his candidacy for mayor, more than 170 blacks signed up to run for office in the state. (R. L. A.)

FEATHER, VICTOR

Victor Feather became general secretary of the British Trades Union Congress in January 1969, when the trade unions were a centre of sharp political controversy. A TUC official since 1937, he succeeded George Woodcock, whose deputy he had been since 1960.

In order to check the number of strikes, the Labour government had proposed legislation that would require a statutory "cooling-off period" after a strike notice was given, and would impose penalties on trade unionists who broke the law. From the start, Feather was critical of the government's policy. When the government outlined its policy in a White Paper in January, Feather complained of the "mad rush to Parliament for new laws," arguing that a bad atmosphere between management and men could not be dealt with by statute. After several months of stubborn resistance by the unions, the government gave way on penal sanctions in exchange for "a solemn and binding" undertaking by the TUC that it would use all its influence to bring about industrial peace.

Public attention tended to focus on the disputes that were not settled rather than those that were, and Feather by habit and temperament was an unobtrusive, behind-the-scenes operator who did not seek publicity for his successes. However, Barbara Castle, the minister with whom he had clashed over the projected trade union legislation, paid him the compliment of saying that he was "potentially one of the greatest general secretaries of the trade union movement."

Coincidentally, Feather had been much influenced in his youth—in Bradford where he was born in 1908—by Barbara Castle's father, Frank Betts, one of the Labour Party's pioneers. He came of a family dedicated to the Labour movement, and was christened Victor Grayson Hardie, the second and third names being the surnames of leading figures in early Labour Party history. Before joining the TUC he worked as a truck driver in Bradford, and always retained a marked Yorkshire accent. His down-to-earth style could deceive people who were surprised to find that he was a discerning collector of painting and sculpture, and that he was deeply interested in international trade unionism. (W. H. Ts.)

FERRÉ, LUIS ALBERTO

A 65-year-old millionaire industrialist, Luis Alberto Ferré, broke the 28 years of rule of the Popular Democratic Party when he was elected governor of the Commonwealth of Puerto Rico in November 1968. His victory, with 43% of the vote, on the ticket of the New Progressive Party revived the hopes of those islanders who favoured a future as the 51st state of the United States. In a plebiscite only the year before, 60% of the Puerto Ricans voted for continued status as a commonwealth, 39% favoured statehood, and less than 1% desired independence.

Ferré soft-pedaled his statehood beliefs in his victorious campaign over the Popular Democrats and the maverick incumbent governor, Roberto Sánchez Vilella. He was, however, expected to call for another plebiscite on the statehood issue in 1970 and was certain to press for Puerto Rico's admission to the U.S. as a state if the outcome reflected a majority desire for an end to commonwealth status.

Puerto Rico's commonwealth status brought its people U.S. citizenship and military obligation but also meant that they paid no federal income taxes and had no vote in Congress. Ferré acknowledged that statehood would mean a higher tax bill for Puerto Ricans, but he believed that statehood would attract new industries and would also result in improved federal welfare programs and higher wages. He believed that statehood would remove any danger that Puerto Rico, which had a small but violent nationalist faction, would be caught up in any Caribbean-style turmoil. Ferré was born Feb. 17, 1904, in Ponce. His father, Don Antonio Ferré, trained his four sons in a variety of management skills, and together they built a multimillion-dollar empire. Luis was educated at Massachusetts Institute of Technology and became a mechanical engineer. Starting with a small ironworks, the Ferré family built up a complex of seven companies. In 1969 their enterprises manufactured 90% of the island's cement, nearly all of its bottles, and much of its tile and paperboard. (J. A. O'L.)

FINCH, ROBERT HUTCHISON

In the U.S. administration, Secretary of Health, Education, and Welfare Robert Finch was reputedly the man closest to Pres. Richard Nixon. Sometimes that was not enough. During 1969, Finch was bloodied in two highly publicized domestic controversies.

Having brought off a minor coup by securing civil rights leader James Farmer as his principal assistant secretary, Finch apparently pushed his luck by nominating John Knowles, administrator of Massachusetts General Hospital, as assistant secretary for health and scientific affairs. The choice of Knowles, a medical liberal, did not please the conservative and powerful American Medical Association. The AMA solicited the loquacious support of Everett M. Dirksen, the Senate Republican leader, and after a round of internecine battles the job went to Roger Egeberg of California, also a liberal but less of a maverick.

Later, Attorney General John Mitchell let it be known that enforcement of the Supreme Court mandate to desegregate all U.S. school districts would be delayed, HEW policies notwithstanding. Many observers credited the change in policy to the influence of Sen. Strom Thurmond (Rep., S.C.), who had led the Southern delegations at the GOP national convention into the Nixon camp.

Rumours to the contrary, Finch—whose liberal credentials were supported by, among other things, his stand in favour of minimal federal welfare standards—remained in charge of the largest domestic federal organization, a massive agency with an annual budget of $50 billion and more than 100,000 employees. Mastering such a monster was the job Finch had wanted. A friend quoted him as saying, "I want to innovate and make a difference."

Born in Tempe, Ariz., Oct. 9, 1925, Finch was on the staff of Rep. Norris Poulson in Washington when he met a freshman congressman named Nixon who recommended he go to law school. He received his LL.B. from the University of Southern California in 1951 and practiced law before returning to Washington in 1958 as the then vice-president's administrative assistant. He was director of Nixon's ill-fated campaign against John Kennedy and Nixon's confidential adviser when the latter ran unsuccessfully for governor of California. After losing two bids for a House seat, Finch was elected lieutenant governor of California in 1966. He guided Nixon's second presidential campaign and was named HEW secretary in December 1968. (Ph. K.)

FOCCART, JACQUES

Was he the 007 of Gaullism, the *éminence grise* of de Gaulle and then of his successor? Or was the cloak-and-dagger image that Jacques Foccart had acquired over nearly 20 years in political life only a myth? One thing was certain: without wishing to, Jacques Foccart in 1969 represented to French public opinion and to a section of the press the dark and secret side of a movement born in the clandestine days of the Resistance and whose underground activity had always grown parallel to its public existence. In short, Jacques Foccart appeared to be the head of the *barbouzes*—the secret agents of Gaullism.

No one could look more reassuring than this little man of 56, plump and bald, who for 25 years had been seen constantly in de Gaulle's shadow. At most, he seemed a faithful employee, whose job it was, among other things, to coordinate daily the intelligence and police reports that a government normally has at its disposal; an old companion who had become the intermediary carrying the petitions of Gaullists to the general and, in the other direction, the general's orders to his followers. This was his explanation.

The image remained, however. Officially Jacques Foccart was secretary-general for the French Community, responsible for France's relations with the young French-speaking nations of Africa. After becoming president, Georges Pompidou gave Foccart back this post, which the interim president, Alain Poher, had ostentatiously taken away three weeks after de Gaulle's resignation. Who, in fact, was Jacques Foccart? A quiet, conscientious, senior civil servant who had become the innocent victim of rumour and intrigue? Or the masked leader of secret operations? Presumably the real Jacques Foccart was somewhere between.

Foccart was born on Aug. 31, 1913, in Ambrières, Mayenne, and attended the College of the Immaculate Conception at Laval. His profession was that of exporter. Among his many governmental posts were councillor of foreign commerce for France (from 1954); councillor of the French Union on behalf of the Assembly of French Peoples (1952–58); president of the Council (June 1958–January 1959); secretary-general of the Community (March 1960); and secretary-general to the presidency for the Community and for African and Malagasy commerce (from May 1961). (P. V.-P.)

FORBES, BRYAN

Appointed in April 1969 as head of production for the new EMI Associated British Picture Corporation combine at Elstree studios, Bryan Forbes was one of the most important and influential men in British films. He was uniquely qualified for the post, having spent 21 years in the industry as actor, writer, director, and producer.

Forbes was born in London on July 22, 1926, and trained for the stage, making his debut in 1942. After serving three years in the armed forces, he played his first film role, that of a dying gunner, in Michael Powell's *The Small Back Room* in 1948. This was the first of many relaxed and likable portrayals of servicemen in such films as *The Wooden Horse* and *The Colditz Story*.

A brief excursion to Hollywood in 1952 for *The World in His Arms* was followed by Forbes's first chance at film-writing—the script of yet another war film, *Cockleshell Heroes*. Its success led to a number of scripting chores, often rewrite jobs and collaborations that Forbes found frustrating. "Show me a film scripted by seven writers, and I'll show you a lash-up," he said. "A film should have one recognizable signature." With this in mind, he and Richard Attenborough (*q.v.*) set up their own production company, Beaver Films, and their first film, *The Angry Silence* (1959; scripted and co-produced by Forbes), was a critical and financial success.

He wrote two more successful scripts, *The League of Gentlemen* and *Only Two Can Play,* before directing his first film, *Whistle Down the Wind* (1961). This was followed by *The L-Shaped Room, Seance on a Wet Afternoon, King Rat* (made in Hollywood), *The Whisperers,* and *Deadfall,* all of which he wrote and directed. His latest was an all-star version of Giraudoux's *The Madwoman of Chaillot.*

Forbes announced a schedule of 15 productions for Associated British, including several by young newcomers. He described the program as "the most serious and ambitious attempt to revitalize the British film industry in 20 years." At a time when a withdrawal of U.S. capital seemed likely, the continued existence of the industry in the U.K. might depend on his success. (B. D.)

FORMAN, JAMES

The blacks' campaign for economic equality took a new and controversial path that shook the religious community in 1969. The dispute arose in Detroit April 26 when James Forman, a former head of the Student Nonviolent Coordinating Committee (SNCC), delivered a "Black Manifesto" to the National Black Economic Development Conference. He told the conference, sponsored by church and social organizations, that churches and synagogues throughout the U.S. should pay $500 million to the Conference as "reparations" for past exploitation of blacks.

The amount, later raised to $3 billion, would go to finance such projects as a Southern land bank, black publishing and broadcasting facilities, and a black university. The Manifesto also called for a socialistic society run by blacks and recognized the possibility of "armed confrontation and long years of sustained guerrilla warfare inside this country."

During the following months Forman and his followers appeared in churches in New York City and throughout the country making their demands. These demands were also made before bodies of individual denominations and large religious groupings. Although the demands and the resulting publicity prompted some church groups to initiate black or antipoverty programs, most shunned making contributions directly to Forman's organization. Forman was dropped as a director of SNCC "because of his extensive duties with the Black Manifesto."

Forman was born in Chicago, Oct. 5, 1929. He attended public schools there and graduated from Roosevelt University in 1951. After service in the Army he returned to Chicago, joining the Juvenile Research Center and teaching in public schools. He left later studies at the Institute of African Affairs at Boston University to join the civil rights movement, first in Fayette County, Tenn., on behalf of improved conditions for black sharecroppers and voter registration. He became one of the early leaders of SNCC and was named executive secretary in 1961. He lost his leadership position in SNCC in 1966 during a broad shakeup of the organization, which in 1969 changed its name to the Student National Coordinating Committee. (D. Fo.)

FORTAS, ABE

Less than eight months after a U.S. Senate filibuster had blocked his elevation to chief justice of the United States, Associate Justice Abe Fortas resigned from the Supreme Court on May 14, 1969, under a threat of impeachment and amid congressional concern about the ethical conduct of judicial officers generally. Fortas had been a member of the court since 1965, an appointee of Pres. Lyndon B. Johnson. His resignation followed the disclosure in a magazine article in May that he had received in January 1966 a $20,000 fee from the family foundation of Louis E. Wolfson, who was then under investigation by the Securities and Exchange Commission for selling unregistered securities. (Wolfson was later convicted of the charge and sentenced to a year in prison.) Fortas issued a statement on May 4, acknowledging that the Wolfson Foundation had "tendered" the fee but denying that he had "accepted" it, and asserting that the fee was not intended as an inducement to intervene in Wolfson's behalf. (The time between "tender" of the fee and Fortas' nonacceptance was 11 months, during which the $20,000 was deposited in a bank in Fortas' name.)

A number of senators demanded that the associate justice make a "better explanation" of the Wolfson matter or resign from the court. On May 14 Fortas tendered his resignation to the president, who accepted it the next day without comment. Fortas also released a letter he had written the members of the court explaining his resignation. "There has been no wrongdoing on my part," Fortas insisted in the letter. He said he feared, however, that "public controversy" would affect the work and position of the court if he remained a member.

Fortas was born on June 19, 1910, in Memphis, Tenn., and was educated at Southwestern College and Yale University Law School. After several years on the Yale Law School faculty, he went to Washington, D.C., where he held a series of positions in administrative agencies. He entered private practice in 1946 in the firm of Arnold, Fortas & Porter, where he remained until his appointment to the court. As an associate justice, he was regarded as a member of the court's liberal faction. (J. E. I.)

WIDE WORLD
Abe Fortas

KEYSTONE
Jacques Foccart

FRIEDMAN, MILTON

Iconoclastic is the adjective his fellow economists apply to Milton Friedman of the University of Chicago, a non-Keynesian in an age dominated by the economic theories of John Maynard Keynes. Friedman himself once said: "In one sense, we are all Keynesians now; in another, no one is a Keynesian any longer."

A cherished Keynesian thesis holds that most people are better off with a gently rising price level, but in the title essay of *The Optimum Quantity of Money and Other Essays* (1969), Friedman maintains that society is far more likely to be served by a gentle deflation. In brief, Friedman contends that a gentle deflation would lower cash balances that consumers and businesses need to keep on hand. Individuals could substitute consumption or lending for idle balances, and the effect would be more consumption, more lending, and hence an increase in general welfare.

This theory seems to contradict Friedman's basic position that the money supply—controlled by the Federal Reserve Board—should grow at a steady rate of between 3 and 5% a year. Since production increases at about that rate, the Friedman rule implicitly argues for stable prices. But in a final "schizophrenic note" to his new essay, Friedman continues to support the 3 to 5% rule on the ground that an immediate switch to a deflationary policy would be too hard on a previously inflationary economy. Friedman continued his long-running battle with the Federal Reserve Board in 1969. Testifying before the congressional Joint Economic Committee's subcommittee on economy in government, he warned that the country faced "an unnecessarily severe inflation" and high unemployment in 1970 unless the board relaxed its tight-money policy.

Born in Brooklyn, N.Y., on July 31, 1912, Friedman studied at Rutgers, the University of Chicago, and Columbia, joined the University of Chicago in 1946, and became Paul Snowden Russell professor of economics there in 1962. The first of the 12 books bearing his name (alone or in collaboration) appeared in 1943. He served sporadically with the federal government and was an economic adviser to Republican presidential nominees Barry Goldwater in 1964 and Richard Nixon in 1968. (Ri. W.)

FRISCH, RAGNAR

A Norwegian pioneer in the esoteric art of econometrics, Ragnar Frisch shared the first Nobel Prize for Economic Science in 1969 with Jan Tinbergen (*q.v.*) of the Netherlands. The new $73,000 award was endowed by the national Bank of Sweden to commemorate its 300th anniversary.

Frisch and Tinbergen were honoured for developing what had been defined as "the mathematical expression of economic theory." Simplifying their approach, the *New York Times* observed the men "see the essence of economics in systems of equations, not in the verbal formulations of a Smith or Marx." Their techniques had reduced the vagueness of economic analysis so significantly that they were being used by government economic agencies and private organizations the world over.

Frisch's specialty was developing mathematical models that describe specific economic environments. Such models could now be constructed for entire economies to make more accurate prognoses of future trends. The U.S. Federal Reserve Board, in fact, had used econometric techniques for the first time in 1969 to make its annual economic forecasts. Working with the Massachusetts Institute of Technology, the board developed a model comprising 80 equations of variables to describe the nation's economic dynamics. The advantage of such a technique was that the effects of increased federal spending, for instance, or a change in interest rates could be projected with greater certainty. By changing the variables in the equations, the results of alternative economic policies could be studied.

Frisch was born in Oslo on March 3,

1895, and studied at Oslo University. He taught at Yale for a year but returned to his alma mater as professor of social economy and statistics in 1931. He retired from the university in 1965, having been a guiding light of its Institute for Social Economy, a founder of the Econometrics Society, and editor of that organization's journal until 1955. He also served as an economic adviser to various governments, including India and the U.A.R. During World War II, Frisch was among the Oslo University intellectuals imprisoned by the Nazis. One of his cell mates was Odd Hassel who shared the 1969 Nobel Prize for Chemistry.

(PH. K.)

GARRASTAZÚ MÉDICI, EMÍLIO

The third military officer to become president of Brazil since the armed forces ousted the civilian regime in 1964, Gen. Emílio Garrastazú Médici was propelled into the limelight in October 1969 from the relative obscurity of commanding the 3rd Army at Porto Alegre in Brazil's southernmost region. His name was little known, even in Brazil, until Pres. Artur da Costa e Silva, a retired army marshal, suffered a stroke toward the end of the summer and was incapacitated for further service.

The illness of Costa e Silva and the concurrent kidnapping by terrorists of the U.S. ambassador, C. Burke Elbrick, created a volatile situation in Brazil. The three chiefs of the Army, Navy, and Air Force briefly assumed control of the nation and let it be known that the civilian vice-president would not take the reins. Instead, they began a series of urgent meetings to decide on another military man to fill the office of president.

Médici was selected from among five Army generals on the ground of broadest acceptability to the military. Politically, he was regarded as a middle-of-the-roader in military terms, not one of the hard-line rightists who advocated indefinite institutional rule. He had previously remained generally aloof from politics. As with most Brazilian military leaders, however, he was an ultranationalist and a committed enemy of Marxism.

Born in Rio Grande do Sul on Dec. 4, 1905, Médici became an army cadet in 1924. He became widely respected in army circles for his forcefulness. No one could forecast whether he had made up his mind about the sort of government Brazil ought to have in the future. Over the short haul, however, he was likely to continue the present form of government, with an all-powerful military group ruling through a built-in majority in the Congress, or merely by decree.

(J. A. O'L.)

GELL-MANN, MURRAY

Regarded by some as Albert Einstein's scientific successor, Murray Gell-Mann won the 1969 Nobel Prize for Physics. A professor at the California Institute of Technology, he was credited with making understandable order of the seeming chaos that shrouded the world of subatomic physics. The Nobel committee cited his "contributions and discoveries concerning the classification of elementary particles and their interactions" and noted that his work was of "decisive importance."

By the 1950s other researchers had become baffled by the behaviour and relationships of the more than 100 particles and antiparticles that were known to make up the nucleus of the atom. Gell-Mann, then in his 20s, developed his "Strangeness Theory" and explained these particles' energy states by describing how they moved.

Later he deduced "the Eightfold Way" of approximate symmetry by grouping the particles according to categories that had common characteristics. Like the periodic table of the elements, which was defined a century earlier, Gell-Mann's groupings had obvious gaps that enabled him to predict the existence of then unknown particles. In 1964 physicists at the Brookhaven National Laboratory identified Omega Minus, a negatively charged particle with a lifetime of one ten-billionth of a second. Omega Minus completed one of Gell-Mann's groups and convinced the scientific fraternity of his theory's validity. Subsequently, he posited the existence of even smaller particles, called quarks, which he believed were the basic building blocks of the particles that make up the atom's nucleus.

The youngest son of Austrian immigrants, Gell-Mann was born in New York City, Sept. 15, 1929. He entered Yale University on his 15th birthday, earned a Ph.D. degree from the Massachusetts Institute of Technology when he was 22, and, after teaching at the University of Chicago, was named professor of physics at Caltech when he was 26. He became R. A. Millikan professor of theoretical physics there in 1967.

(PH. K.)

GIRI, VARAHAGIRI VENKATA

On being sworn in as India's fourth president on Aug. 24, 1969, V. V. Giri said: "My three illustrious predecessors have been men of intellectual eminence and erudition. I have no such claims to make. I am only a common man, having spent the major part of my life as an active participant in the working-class movement."

Although it was true that Giri was not a scholar, he was a keen student of economic and constitutional affairs. He came to high office with a noteworthy record of achievement in trade unionism and in the struggle for Indian independence.

Giri was born Aug. 10, 1894, at Berhampur. The son of a lawyer, he went to Dublin to study law at the National University. Returning to India in 1916, Giri joined the Indian National Congress, an organization that opposed British rule of India, and also started legal practice. His heart was not in the law, however, but in the politics of breaking the law. He had his first taste of prison in 1922 for taking part in the noncooperation movement led by Gandhi. Giri organized the Bengal Nagpur Railway Union and helped to found the All-India Railwaymen's Federation. The strikes he led earned for him a name as both organizer and negotiator, as well as the presidency of the All-India Trade Union Congress. He was elected to the Indian Legislative Assembly in 1934. In 1937, when the Indian National Congress decided to contest provincial elections, Giri was elected to the Madras Legislative Assembly.

During World War II Giri was in prison with other nationalist leaders of India. When India became independent after the war, he served as high commissioner to Ceylon, where he had to deal with the difficult problem of Indian immigrants. In 1952 he was elected to the national Parliament and joined the Cabinet as minister of labour. He resigned in 1954 and later served as governor of Uttar Pradesh, Kerala, and Mysore. In 1967 he was elected vice-president of India and became ex officio chairman of the Council of States.

When Zakir Husain died on May 3, 1969, Giri became acting president. He offered himself for election as an independent candidate against N. Sanjiva Reddy, the candidate of the Congress Party's parliamentary board, and received the backing of Prime Minister Indira Gandhi. His dramatic victory was hailed as a triumph of the "people's candidate."

(H. Y. S. P.)

GOODPASTER, ANDREW J.

The quiet, efficient adviser to four presidents, Gen. Andrew J. Goodpaster on July 1, 1969, became supreme allied commander, Europe—military commander of the North Atlantic Treaty Organization. He succeeded Gen. Lyman L. Lemnitzer, who retired at the age of 69.

Goodpaster began 1969 in a familiar White House role. He had been summoned in late 1968 to assist President-elect Richard M. Nixon in working out the new administration's Vietnam policy. Since May 1968 he had been intimately involved in the Vietnam problem, first as a member of the U.S. delegation to the Paris peace negotiations, then as deputy to Gen. Creighton W. Abrams, commander of U.S. troops in South Vietnam. On March 12, Nixon ended speculation that a European would succeed Lemnitzer when he announced Goodpaster's appointment.

Goodpaster assumed his new post as the alliance was observing its 20th anniversary, after which any of the 15 members could withdraw by giving a year's notice. Although the Soviet Union's 1968 Czechoslovakian intervention had instilled a new sense of purpose in NATO, the alliance in recent years had been gripped by complacency, fragmentation, and disaffection in a time of prosperity and lessening East-West tensions, and by fear that the war in Vietnam was eroding the U.S. commitment.

The NATO assignment was not unfamiliar to Goodpaster, who had assisted Gen. Dwight D. Eisenhower in establishing the command in 1950. In 1954 he became staff secretary to President Eisenhower. After a short tour of Europe in the early years of the Kennedy administration, he returned to Washington in 1962 as special assistant to the chairman of the Joint Chiefs of Staff. In 1967 he became senior Army member of the UN Military Staff Committee.

Goodpaster was born Feb. 12, 1915, in Granite City, Ill., and attended West Point, where he ranked second in the class of 1939. During World War II he served in North Africa and Italy. He also attended Princeton University, where he received a master's degree in engineering in 1948 and a Ph.D. in political science in 1950.

(D. Fo.)

GRANATELLI, ANTHONY JOSEPH

After more than two decades of frustration, Andy Granatelli in 1969 saw one of his automobiles cross the finish line first at the Indianapolis 500-mi. race. Ironically, when victory came it was with a conventional piston-type car and not with the turbine engine that he had been pioneering. He had entered turbines in the 1967 and 1968 races. In 1967 the turbocar was leading when a ball bearing broke, three laps from the finish. Granatelli entered two turbocars in 1968. Both were in contention but failed near the end of the race.

A controversial figure in U.S. auto racing and also an industrial tycoon, Granatelli was born March 18, 1923, in Dallas, Tex., where his father, Vincent, had emigrated from Italy. A grocer, the elder Granatelli lost his business during the depression of the 1930s and moved his family to Chicago, where he had relatives.

Granatelli and his brothers, Joe and Vincent, Jr., added to the family's meagre finances by starting stalled cars and handling simple auto repair jobs. As the brothers' sophistication with engine design increased, they built hot rods, racing those cars themselves and later selling them to others. Granatelli-owned cars soon became an annual fixture in the Indianapolis 500.

Granatelli and his brothers competed in and promoted races, hauling their cars from town to town. Andy drove for more than a decade but only once at Indianapolis, in 1948, when he crashed into a wall during the qualifying trials. Later, when working for the Studebaker Corp., he set many world and national speed records for passenger production cars at the Bonneville Salt Flats in Utah.

In the early 1960s Granatelli designed and built a team of the world's first successful turbine-powered racing cars. The U.S. Auto Club, after Granatelli's near victory at Indianapolis in 1967, changed its rule on turbine engines and decreed that the air intake be reduced from 23.9 to 15.9 sq.in.; a year later it was decreased further to 11.9. These reductions, Granatelli insisted, made his turbocars ineffective. Thus, in 1969 he withdrew his turbocars and instead entered a record fleet of 11 automobiles at Indianapolis, all piston types.

In the meantime, Granatelli built the Scientifically Tested Products Corp. (STP), originally a division of Studebaker, into a multimillion-dollar enterprise. The initials, which also stood for "scientifically treated petroleum," became well known because of heavy advertising. (JE. HO.)

HASLUCK, SIR PAUL MEERNAA CAEDWALLA

Sir Paul Hasluck left Australia's Department of External Affairs to take up his duties as governor-general in late April 1969. His appointment was well received, although there was criticism because he was the first governor-general to be appointed directly from political office. Suggestions were made that he was chosen because the prime minister, John G. Gorton, wanted to get a potential rival out of the way.

Hasluck's detachment and nonpartisan approach had made him less successful in politics than he might have been. He was inclined to be aloof and donnish, and he refused to canvass his supporters at crucial times when he was in a position to obtain advancement. In 1966, when Prime Minister R. G. Menzies retired, Hasluck was expected to succeed Harold E. Holt as deputy leader of the Liberal Party, but he was outmaneuvered by W. McMahon. His unwillingness to campaign and distaste for intrigue cost him the prime ministership in January 1968, after Holt's death, when the Liberty Party chose Gorton after a close vote.

Yet because of these very qualities, he was well fitted for the role of viceregal head of state. Freed from the inhibitions of party politics, Hasluck began to comment on the Australian community of the future. He thought it very important that writers and artists and younger people in the country try to see the vision of what Australia could be, and try to give expression to that vision.

Born in Fremantle on April 1, 1905, Hasluck was educated at the University of Western Australia. He worked as a journalist (1922) and a university lecturer (1939) before joining the Department of External Affairs (1941). He was the first Australian permanent representative at the UN (1946) and wrote the political volume of the Australian official war history (*The Government and the People, 1939–41,* 1951). He was member of the House of Representatives for the Western Australian electorate of Curtin (1949–69), minister for territories (1951–63), and minister for defense (1963–64). As minister for external affairs (1964–69), he had carried the responsibility of dealing with Australian involvement in Vietnam and the problem of Australia's defense after the projected U.K. withdrawal from Southeast Asia in 1971. (A. R. G. G.)

HASSEL, ODD

A retired Oslo University professor, Odd Hassel, shared the 1969 Nobel Prize for Chemistry with Derek Barton (*q.v.*) of London's Imperial College of Science and Technology. The men were honoured for their work in conformation analysis, the study of how complex molecules are shaped.

During the 1930s and 1940s Hassel studied cyclohexane, a hydrocarbon with a zigzag chain of six carbon atoms that form a ring. His research revealed how these atoms orient themselves with regard to each other. Barton moved on to larger molecules and showed that a specific substance acquires different properties if its composite atoms are arranged in a new manner. Important applications of this knowledge are to be found in the creation of synthetic molecules, such as those that are used in modern drugs.

Hassel was born in Oslo, Nor., May 17, 1897. He studied at the university there and earned his doctorate at Berlin University in 1924. He returned to Oslo University to teach and was director of physical chemistry from 1934 to 1964, when he retired. He was named an honorary fellow of the Chemical Society of London, and was also a former chairman of the Norwegian Chemical Society and a member of the Norwegian Council for Science and Humanities.

During the occupation of Norway by Nazi Germany in World War II, many members of the Oslo University community were imprisoned in a special camp at nearby Grini. Hassel spent two years there and was the cell mate of Ragnar Frisch (*q.v.*), who shared the 1969 Nobel Prize for Economic Science. (PH. K.)

HATHAWAY, DAME SIBYL MARY

At the end of July 1969, Dame Sibyl Hathaway, 85-year-old hereditary ruler of Sark in the Channel Islands, astounded its some 450 inhabitants by announcing that she intended to hand over the administration to Guernsey (of which bailiwick Sark forms a part). She complained that members of the island's parliament, the Court of Chief Pleas, broke laws they had themselves framed, and that she was constantly being appealed to about infringements although, with only one vote in the Chief Pleas, she had no power to redress the situation. It was announced that a small committee would be formed to negotiate a new constitution for Sark with the crown officers of Guernsey, and the bailiff of Guernsey assured the Sarkese that no secret talks had been, or would be, held. The dame's heir, her grandson Michael Beaumont, expressed agreement with her decision.

At the age of 85, the dame had devoted 43 years of sterling service to the island, marked notably by her outstanding leadership during the German occupation (July 1940–May 1945), when her statesmanlike dealings with the enemy authorities did much to mitigate the sufferings of the islanders. Under the circumstances, her wish to shift the burden would appear fully justified.

Born in Guernsey in January 1884, the elder daughter of William Collings, the 20th seigneur of the island since it was first granted (1565) to Sir Helier de Carteret by Queen Elizabeth I, she married Dudley Beaumont (d. 1918) at the age of 17. She succeeded her father in 1926, and in 1929 married Robert W. Hathaway (d. 1954), an American who had become British by naturalization. He was deported to Germany in 1943. The dame made frequent lecture tours in the U.S. After World War II

COURTESY, NATO
Andrew J. Goodpaster

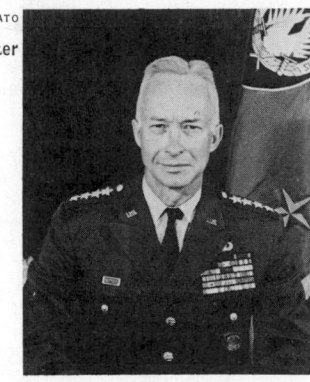

UPI COMPIX
Varahagiri Venkata Giri

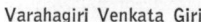

WIDE WORLD
Anthony Joseph Granatelli

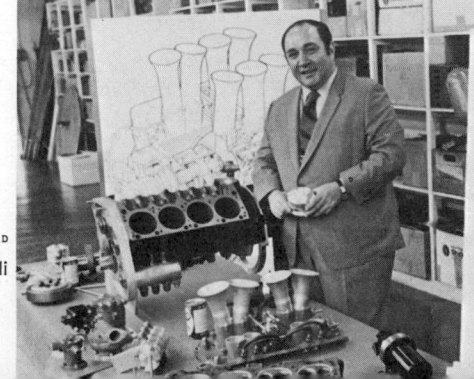

she invited Prince Philip to open (1949) the harbour at La Masseline in Sark, entertaining him and the then Princess Elizabeth, who returned to Sark as queen in 1957. Always known in Sark as *La Dame*, Mrs. Hathaway was created a dame of the British Empire in 1965. Her autobiography, *Dame of Sark*, was published in 1961. (S. Mu.)

HAYAKAWA, S(AMUEL) I(CHIYE)

S. I. Hayakawa first acquired fame as a popularizer of semantics, the science of language. Twenty-five years later, in 1969, he reemerged as a man who was willing to use force when language failed.

In the fall of 1968 the Black Students Union at San Francisco State College had presented a list of "nonnegotiable demands" to the administration: it included admission of all black applicants and the creation of an autonomous department devoted to minority studies. All but the most militant leaders admitted that the demands were too extreme, and many conservatives agreed to the immediate need for a black studies program within the existing academic framework. The strike leaders, however, adopted a policy of disruption, and classes were suspended. California state authorities, led by Gov. Ronald Reagan, demanded that order be restored. The existing college administration was relieved of command and Hayakawa, then a professor with no administrative experience, was named acting president (his appointment was later made permanent).

Hayakawa's approach to the disorders was authoritarian. He banned all meetings that did not carry his endorsement, refused to negotiate with students or with faculty members sympathetic to them, and called in the police in force. Overseeing his first demonstration, he announced over loudspeakers: "This is a warning. All innocent bystanders leave the vicinity. Those of you who want trouble, stay there. The police will see that you get it." Independent observers cataloged numerous accounts of nonparticipants being severely beaten by the police and the scene was repeated many times. But Hayakawa did restore order to the campus, and in so doing became one of the best-known public figures in California. Polls in 1969 showed he was known to more people than former Gov. Edmund G. (Pat) Brown. He was prominently mentioned as a possible candidate for superintendent of public instruction or even senator.

Born of immigrant Japanese parents in Vancouver, B.C., July 18, 1906, Hayakawa received his Ph.D. from the University of Wisconsin in 1935. His teaching career brought him to San Francisco in 1955.

His chief claim to fame was *Language in Action* (1941), a book on semantics, then an infant discipline. Scholars called it a "primer," but it made the Book-of-the-Month Club list and continued to provide its author with what he referred to as "bushels of money." (Ph. K.)

HAYNSWORTH, CLEMENT FURMAN, JR.

Before Aug. 18, 1969, few people outside Greenville, S.C., and the lawyers practicing in the 4th Circuit Court of Appeals had ever heard of Clement F. Haynsworth, Jr. A wealthy Southern aristocrat and a successful fifth-generation lawyer, he had been rewarded in 1957 with a federal judicial appointment for supporting Dwight D. Eisenhower for president. He became a competent, hard-working judge, neither reactionary nor innovative. When Pres. Richard M. Nixon on August 18 nominated him to the Supreme Court, therefore, the dominant reaction was "Who is he?"

Nixon's first Supreme Court nominee, Chief Justice Warren E. Burger, had been confirmed routinely, and it was assumed that Haynsworth would get the same treatment. By the time the Senate Judiciary Committee began hearings on the nomination on September 16, however, it was apparent the nomination faced a battle. Feeling that the judge lacked zeal for their causes, labour and the civil rights groups joined in a serious lobbying effort to stop the nomination. It was suggested that the choice of Haynsworth was part of a "Southern strategy" to court white Southern voters or to pay off Nixon's Southern supporters.

But the nomination was not halted by ideological attacks. Something else was needed, and the opposition found it—Haynsworth had participated as a judge in several cases in which, arguably, his financial interests were linked to those of litigants. In the course of developing these charges and defending against them, the committee and the judge made public all the judge's finances and his tax returns during his years on the bench. The judge's supporters—and the American Bar Association's committee on federal judges—minimized the indiscretions, but they became the means by which the nomination was defeated. The vote, on November 21, was 45–55, with 17 Republicans joining 38 Democrats against. Despite considerable pressure, Nixon supported Haynsworth throughout, and afterward personally congratulated him on his decision to remain on the federal bench.

Haynsworth was born Oct. 30, 1912, in Greenville. A graduate of Furman University, founded by one of his ancestors, and Harvard Law School, he worked in his family's law firm in Greenville until his appointment to the 4th Circuit. (J. E. I.)

HEINEMANN, GUSTAV

The first Social Democratic head of state since the formation of West Germany in 1949, Gustav Heinemann was elected president of the republic on March 5, 1969. In the electoral college, which is composed of all the members of the federal Parliament plus representatives from the Länder (states), he had a majority of six over his Christian Democratic opponent, Gerhard Schröder. Heinemann owed his election to the support of the Free Democrats, and this cooperation between the two parties set the pattern for the government coalition formed after the federal election in September.

The new president, widely respected as a liberal-minded, progressive politician, was one of the founders of the Christian Democratic Union and had been mayor of Essen and minister of justice in North Rhine-Westphalia before joining Konrad Adenauer's government as minister of the interior in 1949. He resigned his government post in 1950 in protest against the policy of German rearmament, and formed a new political party, the "All-German People's Party," which was dedicated to a policy of neutrality in the belief that this was the best way to achieve the reunification of the country.

The party failed and after it was dissolved in 1957 Heinemann joined the Social Democrats. He was made minister of justice when the two principal parties, the Christian Democrats and the Social Democrats, went into a coalition in 1966, and he quickly established a reputation as a reformer.

Born in Schwelm, Westphalia, July 23, 1899, Heinemann served in World War I and afterward studied law, economics, and history at several German universities. He set up a law practice in Essen and subsequently joined the management of a steelworks in the town. During the Hitler era Heinemann was actively engaged in the German Confessing Church, which was a centre of resistance to Nazism. (N. Cr.)

HEMERY, DAVID PETER

For his feats on the track, David Hemery, a tall, blond British athlete, was honoured by the queen when he was made a Member of the Order of the British Empire in the New Year's honours list at the beginning of 1969. His easy striding and natural style had earned him the Olympic gold medal in the 400-m. hurdles the previous October in Mexico City, when he set a world record time of 48.1 sec. in the final.

Born at Cirencester, Gloucestershire, on July 18, 1944, Hemery soon developed a taste for all games at school. Business took the family from England to the United States when Hemery was a teen-ager, and he attended several schools in both countries before going in 1965 to Boston University, where he was graduated with a degree in business administration.

Hemery crossed the Atlantic during his period of study in Boston to compete in the British championships and in a match against the U.S.S.R. in London, and he duly won hurdles events in both meets. In 1966 he was chosen a member of the British team to compete in the Commonwealth Games in Kingston, Jamaica. He won the gold medal in the 120-yd. high hurdles in a British record time of 14.1 sec. and was voted the British Broadcasting Corporation's Sportsman of the Year. By the time of the 1968 Olympics he was in a class by himself in Britain and by the following June he had broken or equaled 16 U.K. records.

During 1969 Hemery switched from the 400 m. back to the shorter distance of 110 m. and also tried his hand at the decathlon, where he was not immediately successful because of deficiencies in the field events. He was selected as a member of the British team to compete in the European championships in Athens, where he finished second in the 110-m. high hurdles. (T. W.)

HERSHEY, ALFRED DAY

In the informal team of U.S. researchers who won the 1969 Nobel Prize for Medicine or Physiology, Alfred Hershey was the one native-born American. His colleagues were Salvador Luria and Max Delbrück (*qq.v.*).

Studying how viruses infect bacteria cells, Hershey built on findings the other two men had made. Specifically, he demonstrated that a virus infects a bacteria cell by injecting its own nucleus into it and leaving its protein shell outside. Using radioisotopes, he demonstrated in 1952 that DNA (deoxyribonucleic acid), which makes up the virus's nucleus, was responsible for genetic mutations in succeeding generations of cells.

The aggregate research of the three men, who worked separately but cooperatively beginning in 1942, was applied in a variety of ways. Without it, vaccines against a host of diseases, including polio, German measles, and mumps, could not have been developed. "Indirectly, the discoveries also bring about an increased understanding of the mechanism of inheritance and of those mechanisms that control the development, growth and function of tissues and organs," the Nobel Prize committee declared when it announced the $75,000 prize.

Born Dec. 4, 1908, in Owosso, Mich., Hershey was educated at Michigan State College, where he earned a bachelor's degree in 1930 and his doctorate four years later. From 1934 to 1950 he taught at Washington University School of Medicine, St. Louis, Mo. He resigned his associate professorship there to work at the Carnegie Institution's genetics research facility on Long Island. In 1962 he was named its director.

Hershey's spare-time activities included woodworking, sailing, and gardening. A *New York Times* profile described him as "a very quiet, withdrawn sort of man who avoids . . . most hectic social activities." (PH. K.)

HEYERDAHL, THOR

In 1947 a descendant of the Vikings inspired armchair adventurers around the world by sailing 4,300 mi. across the Pacific on a balsa raft called "Kon-Tiki." In the summer of 1969 he tackled the Atlantic in a boat made of bulrushes.

Thor Heyerdahl was not motivated solely by an itch for adventure. A Norwegian ethnologist, he sought to prove heretical theories about the migration of ancient peoples. In the first instance he sought to show that Polynesia could have been settled by pre-Inca refugees from South America; in the second, that Inca and Mayan cultures were directly influenced by the Egyptians centuries before Columbus. Heyerdahl posited this to explain certain striking similarities between Egyptian and pre-Columbian cultures. Traditionalists, assuming the two civilizations developed similar practices independently, argued that Egyptians could not have crossed the Atlantic because their reed boats would surely have disintegrated.

Heyerdahl engaged boat builders in Chad (where reed craft are still used), imported Ethiopian papyrus to the U.A.R. (where reeds no longer grow), and built the "Ra," named for the ancient Egyptian sun god, in the shadow of the Pyramids. Tomb paintings and necrological documents provided the blueprint for the 13-ton, 45-ft.-long hull, which was launched from Safi, Mor., on May 25. Heyerdahl's crew included an American, an Italian, an Egyptian, a Mexican, a Russian, and one of the boat builders. This was to test another theory: that men of different backgrounds can cooperate under crisis conditions.

That hypothesis was proved, evidently, because crises occurred and all hands survived. The steering oars broke; the mast fractured; the boat listed because of improper lading. Seas crashed over the stern, which became dangerously waterlogged. Heyerdahl learned too late that a seemingly extraneous line on the tomb drawings represented a rope from the mast to hold the stern above water. Still, "Ra" held together for nearly two months and sailed 2,600 mi. before she was abandoned barely 600 mi. from a Western Hemisphere landfall.

Heyerdahl was born in Larvik, Nor., Oct. 6, 1914, and studied at the University of Oslo. Besides the "Kon Tiki" experiment, his account of which sold 20 million copies, he worked in the Galápagos Islands and British Columbia. He popularized the carved heads of Easter Island in *Aku Aku*. (PH. K.)

HODGES, GILBERT RAY

Leo Durocher's famed admonition that "nice guys finish last" did not hold true for 1969. A "nice guy" finished first—Gil Hodges, a longtime baseball professional who managed the New York Mets to first place in the National League and to a subsequent World Series triumph over the Baltimore Orioles. Deservedly, he was named National League Manager of the Year.

PICTORIAL PARADE

Clement Furman Haynsworth, Jr.

WIDE WORLD

S. I. Hayakawa

GAMMA—PIX FROM PUBLIX

Thor Heyerdahl

The Met victories, achieved against heavy odds, solidified Hodges' growing reputation as one of the best, if not the best, among today's major league managers. Hodges was, indeed, a miracle worker with the Mets. He platooned his players at four different positions, yet brought the Mets home winners despite what almost all the experts insisted was, man-for-man, a somewhat inferior team.

Quiet and modest, Hodges always had been one of the best-liked personalities in professional sports. When he was stricken with a heart attack on Sept. 24, 1968, while finishing his first season as the Mets' manager, his fans prayed for him and sent him hundreds of cards, just as they had done 15 years earlier when he was a player with the old Brooklyn Dodgers and engulfed in a long batting slump.

Hodges was born on April 24, 1924, in Princeton, Ind. He signed his first baseball contract with Brooklyn in 1943 for a $1,000 bonus. Originally a third baseman, he was used as a catcher during his first season in the major leagues. The next year he was switched to first base and developed into one of the best fielding and hitting first basemen in baseball history. In a 16-year major-league playing career he slammed 370 home runs, drove in 1,274 runs, and had a .273 lifetime batting average. He set a National League record by hitting 14 grand slam home runs and in one game, on Aug. 31, 1950, he hit four home runs.

Hodges was a player with the first Mets team, but the Mets released him in May 1963, when he assumed the managership of the Washington Senators. Hodges managed the Senators for 4½ years. Under his tutelage, the Senators won more games each year than they had the year before and had risen to a sixth-place tie in 1967, his last season with the club. The Mets then signed him as their manager. (JE. HO.)

HUGHES, TED

From his first, sudden arrival on the British literary scene, Ted Hughes, winner of the valuable 1969 Florence International Poetry Prize, had always been something of an enigma, and the critics had experienced the utmost difficulty in placing his work. For one thing, there was the manner in which he sprang into the limelight, to be welcomed as "a remarkable poet" by so distinguished a critic as Edwin Muir. Since poets traditionally send their work first to small poetry magazines and then to national periodicals before bringing out a volume, it is extremely rare for a poet of any potentiality to escape the notice of talent scouts. Yet until he won the First Publication Award of the New York Poetry Center (judged by W. H. Auden, Stephen Spender, and Marianne Moore) in 1957, Hughes was practically unknown in Britain. Few of his poems had previously appeared in print and those few almost exclusively in American magazines. When the prizewinning poems were published by Faber later that year under the title of *The Hawk in the Rain*, the volume came as a complete surprise.

Hughes was born at Mytholmroyd, Yorkshire, on Aug. 17, 1930. He served for two years with the RAF before going to Cambridge (Pembroke College), where he graduated in 1954. It was at Cambridge that he met and later married the American poet Sylvia Plath, who died in 1963. After trying a variety of occupations, Hughes visited the United States in 1957 and taught English literature for a time at the University of Massachusetts before returning to Britain.

If Hughes's first book was an immediate success, his second, *Lupercal* (1960), and third, *Selected Poems* (with Thom Gunn, 1962), served to establish his reputation as the most outstanding British poet since Dylan Thomas. *The Earth Owl and Other Moon People* (1963) tended to perplex readers, but *Wodwo* (1967) showed that Hughes had extended his range to create an exciting world of mysterious, savage, half-human creatures, like his "Ghost Crabs." Also a writer of children's stories, Hughes was awarded a Guggenheim fellowship in 1959, the Somerset Maugham Award in 1960, and the Hawthornden Prize in 1961. (HO. S.)

HUSAK, GUSTAV

One of the first persons to call for democratization when Alexander Dubcek replaced Antonin Novotny as first secretary of the Czechoslovak Communist Party in January 1968 was Gustav Husak, a founder of the Slovak Communist Party who had been sentenced to life imprisonment for "bourgeois deviation" during the Stalinist purges of the 1950s. On April 17, 1969, however, when the Central Committee yielded to Soviet pressure to remove Dubcek, Husak became his replacement.

Husak's rise to power was quick. An articulate intellectual, Husak was one of the four deputy premiers under Oldrich Cernik during the liberalization effort, but he joined conservatives in denouncing as illegal the results of the party congress held by the liberals as Warsaw Pact forces were moving into Czechoslovakia in August 1968. In September 1968 he formally emerged as first secretary of the Slovak Communist Party and soon was known to be one of the three officials, along with Cernik and Lubomir Strougal (*q.v.*), to control real power.

Known to be a staunch patriot as well as a conservative, Husak as first secretary was more likely than Dubcek to compromise with the wishes of Moscow. That he was also stern was obvious by May 29, 1969, when he announced a hardening of policies and a reassertion of party dominance in government administration, economy, and culture. Two days later he announced a party purge of "opportunistic elements."

Born on Jan. 10, 1913, in Bratislava, Husak was graduated from the law faculty of Comenius University in 1937. During World War II he was a leader of the Slovak Communist Party's anti-German activities.

On May 4, 1950, he was dismissed from his postwar appointment as chairman of the Board of Commissioners, the Slovak regional government. He was arrested on Feb. 6, 1951, deprived of his seat in the National Assembly, expelled from the party, and accused of spying for the "imperialist powers." He was sentenced to life imprisonment in 1954 and released in May 1960 as a result of an amnesty. While waiting for a review of his trial and rehabilitation, he wrote a history of the Slovak wartime uprising. (K. Sm.)

IACOCCA, LIDO ANTHONY

Henry Ford II thought he had a better idea when he lifted Semon E. (Bunkie) Knudsen from General Motors Corp. in 1968 and installed him as president of the Ford Motor Co. But in 1969 Knudsen's light was doused and the coming thing at Ford's Dearborn, Mich., headquarters was Lee Iacocca.

Iacocca, who brandished long cigars and sideburns and shiny cuff links, had spent the past 23 of his 45 years with the company, working his way from showrooms to the executive suite. When Knudsen arrived, Iacocca was one of three executive vice-presidents, a member of the board, and the company's top style setter. He had helped Ford forget the Edsel disaster by overseeing the design and promotion of the wildly successful Mustang. The new Maverick also bore his brand.

PICTORIAL PARADE
Edward Moore Kennedy

It was no secret around the automobile industry that Iacocca had his eye on the president's job—and that he did not appreciate taking orders from a onetime General Motors man. Iacocca was used to taking orders only from Ford himself. Knudsen, as strong-minded a man as Iacocca, helped bring on the showdown by making early morning visits to the production and styling lines and directing changes without Iacocca's knowledge. As a result of Knudsen's dawn attacks, there were grumblings that some of the company's cars were beginning to look like Pontiacs.

Knudsen's career at Ford ended on Sept. 2, 1969, when Henry Ford told him that things just hadn't worked out. Knudsen, professing bewilderment, announced his firing at a September 11 press conference. At a separate press conference the same day, Ford announced a realignment of the executive structure. Iacocca emerged as the clear winner. Although there would be no title of Ford Motor Co. president for the immediate future, Iacocca kept his executive vice-presidency and board seat and was named president of all the company's North American automobile operations. Asked if he was sorry to see Knudsen go, Iacocca replied that he had never said "no comment" to the press in his life, but he would say "no comment" to that question.

Born in Allentown, Pa., Iacocca won a bachelor of science degree at Lehigh University and a graduate engineering degree at Princeton. He lived in Bloomfield Hills, Mich., also the home of much of General Motors' top brass. (C. R. C.)

JACKLIN, ANTHONY

On July 12, 1969, a few days after his 25th birthday, Tony Jacklin became the first British golfer to win the British Open championship since Max Faulkner in 1951. At Lytham St. Annes he resisted a powerful overseas challenge that included Gary Player of South Africa, the defending champion; Billy Casper and Jack Nicklaus of the U.S.; and Peter Thomson of Australia and won by two strokes. His victory was due in great measure to the skills he had developed playing competitive golf in the United States during the previous three years.

Jacklin first played in a U.S. tournament in 1965 and was quick to realize that if he were to reach the highest class he must compete constantly against the finest players. The following spring he performed well in the Masters tournament at Augusta, Ga. His enjoyment of the occasion and the huge crowds, and his response to the pressure revealed qualities of temperament almost unique among British golf professionals of the postwar generation.

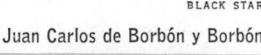

BLACK STAR
Juan Carlos de Borbón y Borbón

In 1967 Jacklin won two major British events and gained a place on the Ryder Cup team. This entitled him to exemption from prequalifying for tournaments in the U.S., and he took advantage of this status to the extent that in 1968 he won almost $60,000 in official prize money. His victory in the Greater Jacksonville Open was the first of consequence by a British golfer in the U.S. since Ted Ray won the U.S. Open in 1920.

Jacklin was born July 7, 1944, and attended school in Scunthorpe, Eng.; after some success as an amateur he became an assistant at Potters Bar, near London. His promise was soon evident but he was inclined to swing his clubs too fast. By the summer of 1969 he had mastered a constant and slower rhythm. This sustained him throughout the British Open and again in September when he played a major part in achieving a tie for Britain against the U.S. in the Ryder Cup matches. (P. A. W.-T.)

JUAN CARLOS DE BORBÓN Y BORBÓN

In what may well have been the most important political event in Spain in 30 years, and perhaps the least surprising, on July 22, 1969, Spanish Chief of State Francisco Franco presented to the Cortes (parliament) a law designating Don Juan Carlos de Borbón y Borbón the future king of Spain. The law granted the 31-year-old grandson of Spain's last king, Alfonso XIII, the titles of prince of Spain and "royal highness" until the death or incapacitation of Franco. It was passed immediately and overwhelmingly by the Cortes. At his formal investiture before the Cortes the following day, the prince swore his loyalty to the principles of Franco's National Movement.

The announcement was the culmination of steps taken to fulfill Franco's 30-year-old promise to restore the monarchy, which had ended when Alfonso left the country in 1931. A 1947 law had abolished the republic and established Spain as a "representative monarchy." Franco picked Juan Carlos as his successor over his father, Don Juan de Borbón y Battenberg, a lifelong opponent of Franco's policies. Beginning in 1948 Juan Carlos was educated in Spain, where he graduated from the military and naval academies and served apprenticeships in all the government ministries under Franco's direct supervision.

More recently, legislation in 1967 provided for succession to the throne, and in December 1968 Prince Carlos Hugo de Borbón-Parma, the Carlist pretender to the throne, was expelled from the country. The move that made Franco's announcement of his successor possible, however, came on Jan. 7, 1969, when Juan Carlos said for the first time that he would accept the throne if offered. Previously he had maintained that his father's claim preceded his own.

Juan Carlos was born in Rome on Jan. 5, 1938. In 1955 he entered the Academia General Militar at Saragossa. He later attended the Escuela Naval Militar at Marín in Pontevedra, the Academia General del Aire at San Javier in Murcia, and the University of Madrid. A jet-fighter and helicopter pilot, Olympic yachtsman, accomplished horseman, and black-belt karate expert, he was married in Athens on May 14, 1962, to Princess Sophia of Greece. They had two daughters, Elena and Cristina, and a son, Felipe. (K. Sm.)

KAPWEPWE, SIMON

Zambia's vice-president, Simon Kapwepwe, deepened his country's political crisis in August 1969 by resigning his office. Later, however, he withdrew his resignation at Pres. Kenneth Kaunda's insistence.

Kapwepwe, a tall, bearded, 47-year-old nationalist veteran, was often portrayed as an ambitious rival to Kaunda, but it seemed more accurate to view him not as a challenger to the president but as wishing to maintain his position as the natural successor if Kaunda should be forced to resign by others. The two men were, in fact, lifelong friends. Both born in Bemba country in northern Zambia (then the British colony of Northern Rhodesia), they went to the same Anglican mission school at Lubwa, where both qualified as teachers. Later, they launched the United National Independence Party, which in 1963 won their country's independence.

Kapwepwe became noted for his volatility and emotional language. Although a fervent nationalist, he never ceased to cultivate his image as the leader of the Bemba people. In this role he contributed to the tribal conflicts that led to President Kaunda's decision to abolish the ruling party's central committee.

Kapwepwe was strongly influenced by the ideas of Mohandas Gandhi during the four years (1951–55) that he spent in India, where he studied journalism. On his return to Northern Rhodesia, he was promptly imprisoned for possessing subversive literature. His militancy led to his being detained again for almost a year in 1959. After Zambia became independent Kapwepwe served his country as minister of agriculture and as foreign minister, becoming vice-president in 1967. (Co. L.)

KENNEDY, DAVID MATTHEW

In a year of rapid inflation and uncertain economic indicators, U.S. Secretary of the Treasury David M. Kennedy occupied one of the more difficult Cabinet posts in the Nixon administration in 1969. It fell to him to justify the administration's policy of "firm restraint," a tightrope walk between—as he told the congressional Joint Economic Committee on February 19—the risks of trying to "stop inflation too abruptly" and the dangers of "doing too little."

Named to the Cabinet after a long and successful career in banking, Kennedy got his first taste of life in the Washington fishbowl when an apparently casual remark, interpreted to mean that the new administration might consider changing the gold price, sent shivers through the world's money markets. Then, as the Senate considered confirmation of his appointment, he found himself under fire because he still owned stock in his former bank, the Continental Illinois National Bank and Trust Co. in Chicago.

These episodes soon paled, however, as Kennedy undertook the politically unpopular task of urging extension of the 10% income tax surcharge and deletion of popular but presumably inflationary provisions from the tax-reform bill before Congress. His most trying moments may have occurred during a September 4 appearance before the Senate Finance Committee, when he "strongly" urged passage of the tax-reform bill, but suggested that it be "improved" to reduce the net loss of federal tax revenue from $2.4 billion to $1.3 billion a year. The "bias in the [present] bill against investment in favor of consumption," he said, "could impede economic growth . . . by curtailing the incentive to make productive investments"—an argument that accorded with Kennedy's known interest in the role of the business community in solving urban problems.

Kennedy was born on July 21, 1905, on a ranch at Randolph, Utah, received his B.A. from Weber College, Ogden, Utah, and his M.A. and LL.B. from George Washington University, Washington, D.C. The first 16 years of his working career were spent with the Federal Reserve Board. He served for two years in the Treasury Department during the Eisenhower administration, and headed a commission under Pres. Lyndon Johnson that produced a major change in the presentation of the federal budget. In 1956 Kennedy became president and in 1959 board chairman of the Continental Illinois. (Rɪ. W.)

KENNEDY, EDWARD MOORE

Sen. Edward M. (Ted) Kennedy (Dem., Mass.), sole heir to his family's tragedy-ridden political magic, found his public career undergoing its stiffest test as a result of an automobile accident on July 18, 1969. The car he was driving veered off a narrow bridge on Chappaquiddick Island, Mass., and plunged into a pond, killing Mary Jo Kopechne, 28, a Washington secretary who had been a passenger in the vehicle.

News of the nighttime death did not become known until the next morning, and the circumstances surrounding it came to light in piecemeal fashion for weeks afterward—causing serious public concern and curiosity about the senator's actions and reactions in the incident. Kennedy pleaded guilty to leaving the scene of an accident, receiving a two-month suspended sentence and a one-year probation. Questions remained, and the senator called in friends and advisers to discuss how the issue should be handled. The result was a dramatic televised explanation in which he told of trying in vain to rescue Miss Kopechne, of experiencing shock, confusion, and even a feeling that perhaps some "awful curse" hung over the Kennedys. He said he would leave his political future in Massachusetts to the voters.

His prospects for reelection to the Senate in 1970 appeared to be little damaged, but uncertainty surrounded his chances of becoming president. Before the accident he had been considered a favourite to win the Democratic nomination in 1972 if he wanted it. Now, any such possibility appeared to be ruled out.

On his return to the senate after a period of seclusion, Kennedy confirmed that he would not seek the presidency in 1972. While legal maneuvering over the holding of an inquest continued, he devoted himself to his Senate duties as majority whip, a post he had won from Sen. Russell B. Long (Dem., La.) in an upset vote in January. As he had done before to the delight of liberals, Kennedy took the leadership in a number of floor battles: against the deployment of the antiballistic missile, against the war in Vietnam, for extensive tax reform, and for funds for the education of American Indians.

Edward Moore Kennedy was born Feb. 22, 1932, in Brookline, Mass., and was educated at Harvard and the University of Virginia Law School. In 1962 he was elected to complete the unexpired Senate term of his brother John in a contest that centred on his political inexperience and kinship to the then-president. He was reelected easily in 1964. (R. L. A.)

KENYATTA, JOMO

Kenya's relative political stability since it achieved independence in 1963 was due almost entirely to the authority of its president, Jomo Kenyatta. Reviled during the Mau Mau insurrection by most of the country's white settlers as "the leader of darkness," Kenyatta subsequently came to be respected by Kenyans of all races, who affectionately called him *Mzee* ("the old man"). But the health of the aging president (his exact age was unknown but he was estimated to be almost 80) came increasingly to be read almost like a temperature chart of the health of his country after the assassination of his lieutenant and heir apparent, Tom Mboya, in July 1969.

The assassination caused the incipient threat of tribal conflict in Kenya to be brought close to the surface. Mboya, a member of the country's second largest tribe, the Luo, was vital to the president's efforts to diminish fears that his own Kikuyu tribe, the country's largest, wished to dominate the government. Kenyatta, though a veteran nationalist, was regarded by many non-Kikuyu as being too narrowly engaged in the affairs of his own tribe. This suspicion was strengthened when the Kikuyu, after Mboya's death, began taking secret oaths pledging loyalty to Kikuyu leadership in the elections due to be held in December. Trouble occurred again late in October when crowds in western Kenya threw rocks at Kenyatta's car and shouted threats at him. In retaliation, the government placed Oginga Odinga, a Luo and head of the opposition in Parliament, under house arrest and banned the opposition party.

Kenyatta was born about 1893 in the Kikuyu tribal area near Nairobi. At the age of about 12 he was virtually adopted by missionaries and had his earliest education in Church of Scotland mission schools. His first entry into politics (having assumed the name of Kenyatta) was as general secretary of the Kikuyu Central Association in 1928, and as editor of its journal. He went to the U.K. in 1929 to defend his tribe's claims to the restoration of land they said had been taken from them under British colonial rule. He was to remain there for 15 years.

During this period Kenyatta studied anthropology at the London School of Economics, wrote a book, *Facing Mount Kenya,* about his own people, and joined the British Labour Party. When he finally returned home in 1946 he was elected president of the Kenya African Union. In 1952 he was arrested for being a leader of the Mau Mau revolt against white colonial rule, a charge he denied then and afterward. Almost nine years later he was granted full release from detention to lead his country, which was then on the eve of its independence. (Co. L.)

KISSINGER, HENRY

U.S. Pres. Richard Nixon's principal adviser on foreign policy, at least in the first year of his administration, was not Secretary of State William Rogers but Henry A. Kissinger of Harvard. A consultant to the Eisenhower, Kennedy, and Johnson administrations, and from 1957 associated with Gov. Nelson Rockefeller of New York, Kissinger was named by Nixon in December 1968 as presidential assistant for national security affairs.

Kissinger's high status in the White House was soon evident. He played a vital role in Nixon's shift from the concept of nuclear "superiority" to that of nuclear "sufficiency"; he was the chief planner of the president's trip to Europe in February; he was a central figure in the administration's effort to reach a negotiated settlement in Vietnam; and he played a vital role in the presidential decision-making process on the Safeguard antiballistic missile system. Kissinger accompanied Nixon to Europe in February, to Midway Island in June for a meeting with South Vietnamese Pres. Nguyen Van Thieu, and to Thailand, India, Pakistan, Romania, and Great Britain in late July and early August.

His eminence as a foreign-policy expert dated from the publication in 1957 of *Nuclear Weapons and Foreign Policy,* in which he argued that American survival depended "not only on our strength, but also on our ability to recognize . . . aggression in all its forms. In the nuclear age, by the time a threat has become unambiguous it may be too late to resist it." The book was written at a time when the "massive [nuclear] retaliation" doctrine of John Foster Dulles held sway. The more flexible Kissinger policy was adopted by Pres. John Kennedy only four years later. Kissinger's ability to serve such varied masters inspired some skepticism, but no one questioned his expertise. Presidential assistant H. R. Haldeman said early in 1969, "When the President is faced with a decision he asks a lot of fast questions, and Henry has always done his homework."

Born in Fürth, Ger., on May 27, 1923, Kissinger emigrated to the U.S. in 1938 with his family to escape Hitler. After serving in World War II, he entered Harvard, receiving his doctorate in 1954. At the time of his appointment as assistant to Nixon, he was a professor in the Harvard department of government. (Ri. W.)

KUZNETSOV, ANATOLI VASILIEVICH

A Soviet Ilyushin Il-62 airliner landed at the London Airport, Heathrow, on July 24, 1969, with two notable passengers on board: Gerald Brooke, who was returning home from Soviet prisons (*see* Intelligence Operations), and Anatoli Vasilievich Kuznetsov, a Soviet writer. Looking at a crowd of newsmen, Brooke joked to Kuznetsov: "That reception committee is for you not for me." Six days later, however, Kuznetsov became front-page news when he was granted asylum in Britain.

Kuznetsov had been planning his escape for years. By suggesting he would write a book on Lenin's stay in Britain, he obtained permission to do research in London with a "translator," actually a secret police agent. On the fifth evening of his stay he managed to get away from his constant companion at a Soho striptease, and to contact David Floyd, a Russian-speaking expert on Communist affairs for the *Daily Telegraph.* Floyd informed the Home Office of Kuznetsov's request to stay in Britain, because he "could not write, sleep, or breathe" in the U.S.S.R. The following day he was granted an unlimited residence permit. He refused all meetings with Soviet embassy officials.

In a series of press and television interviews Kuznetsov revealed, among other things, that in 25 years not one of his writings had been printed in the U.S.S.R. as he had written it. Stating that "Kuznetsov is a dishonest conformist, cowardly author," he said he would now use the name A. Anatol.

Kuznetsov was born in August 1929 in the Kurenevka district of Kiev, Ukraine. At the age of 12 he heard the machine-gun fire of the massacre of an estimated 100,000–200,000 Jews at Babi Yar by occupying German forces. In 1955 Kuznetsov became a member of the Communist Party.

His first book, *Continuation of a Legend: Notes of a Young Person,* appeared in 1957, was translated into more than 30 languages, and made his reputation as a novelist. Kuznetsov sued the French publisher for distorting the work, but after his defection he stated that the French version was the best of the translations, eliminating the distortions added by the Soviet publisher. His other novels were *On a Sunny Day,* a children's book; *At Home; Babii Yar,* a documentary novel of the 1941 massacre; and *The Fire,* which was criticized for its negative view of Soviet life. (K. Sm.)

LAIRD, MELVIN ROBERT

Thrust into a post he originally did not want by a president-elect who would have preferred someone else, Melvin R. Laird in 1969 left the relative freedom of the House of Representatives, where he had hoped to be speaker someday, to become the U.S. secretary of defense in a year marked by skepticism and criticism of the defense establishment. In his 17 years in Congress, Laird had been a leading Republican workhorse, theoretician, and military expert. As the Nixon administration's sombre, determined spokesman for often unpopular defense and foreign policies, he assumed the sort of controversial image held by Secretary of State Dean Rusk in the previous administration.

In a cool, hard style reminiscent of Rusk, Laird dealt with concern over the Vietnam war, inflation, military spending, waste and inefficiency in defense procurement, and adverse publicity about incidents such as the capture of the "Pueblo." During the first half of the year he appeared repeatedly before Congress, television viewers, and live audiences in an effort to sell the Safeguard antiballistic missile (ABM) system to Congress and the nation. He barely succeeded—ABM eventually passed the Senate by the narrowest of margins.

Later in the year, he became the principal defender of U.S. Vietnam policy in the face of renewed public and congressional opposition. Laird was reportedly one of the main architects of the Nixon administration's policy of "vietnamizing" the war. He either inaugurated or expanded a number of major arms programs, but he was also forced to heed the growing clamour by cutting defense spending and reforming purchasing practices.

Born Sept. 1, 1922, in Omaha, Neb., Laird had been a political official virtually all of his adult life. After graduating from Carleton College in Northfield, Minn., and serving in World War II, he was elected to the Wisconsin state senate in 1946 and to the U.S. Congress in 1952. As chairman of the Republican platform committee in 1964, he was instrumental in drafting a controversial platform on behalf of Barry M. Goldwater. In *A House Divided: America's Strategy Gap* (1962), he advocated a firm policy of military superiority and deterrence. (D. Fo.)

LAVER, RODNEY GEORGE

Perhaps the best and certainly the most successful lawn tennis player in history, the left-handed, red-headed Australian Rod Laver captured the imagination of the sporting world in 1969 by winning the Grand Slam—the four major championships of Australia, France, Wimbledon, and the U.S.—for the second time. Among men, only J. Donald Budge of the U.S. had won the Grand Slam before, and that only once—in 1938. Laver played majestically well, excelling in every facet of the game, equipped with every shot, combining power with delicacy of touch, and possessing rare speed of foot, intelligence in court craft, and a temperament that enabled him to rise to his best when the opposition threatened most.

Laver was born Aug. 9, 1938, at Gladstone, Queensland, the son of two tournament lawn tennis players. Introduced early to the game, at 13 he was selected for a coaching course by a Brisbane newspaper. Later he came to the attention of the Australian Davis Cup captain, Harry Hopman, and became a member of the Australian Davis Cup squad at the age of 18. He first toured overseas in 1956, and his first outstanding success was winning the Australian doubles championship with Robert Mark and the Wimbledon mixed doubles with Darlene Hard in 1959. He won the Australian singles in 1960. He was singles runner-up at Wimbledon in 1959 and 1960 and champion in 1961 and 1962.

In 1962 he was champion not only of Wimbledon but also of Australia, Italy, France, West Germany, and the U.S. He became a contracted professional in 1963 and dominated the professional game until the introduction of open tournaments in 1968, when he won the first open Wimbledon championship. In 1969 he was singles champion of Australia, South Africa, France, Wimbledon, and the U.S. His outstanding skill also made him the biggest money winner in tennis. In prize money alone, his success in the U.S. Open in September brought his earnings to more than $100,000 for the season. (L. O. T.)

LINDSAY, JOHN VLIET

In an amazing comeback performance, John V. Lindsay overwhelmed the candidates of the two major political parties to win reelection on Nov. 4, 1969, to a second four-year term as mayor of New York City. The 47-year-old former congressman had been virtually counted out when he failed to win the Republican nomination in the June primary. Not only did his Republican opponent, John Marchi, run ahead of him, but the three front-running candidates in the Democratic primary each received more than double the 105,358 votes cast for him. He refused to concede defeat, however, and began a strenuous campaign as the candidate of the Liberal Party and the newly organized Independent Party.

The contest for what he called the second hardest job in the U.S. cut across party lines on a scale not seen since the days of the late Fiorello La Guardia. Lindsay won the endorsement of such figures as Jacob Javits and Charles Goodell, New York State's Republican senators, and former Supreme Court Justice Arthur J. Goldberg, a leading Democrat. At the last minute, Robert F. Wagner, former Democratic mayor of New York, announced he had voted for Lindsay. The outcome was a victory by about 160,000 votes over his nearest opponent, Democrat Mario Procaccino.

The secret ingredient appeared to be Lindsay's appeal to two classes, the city's intellectuals and its poor, especially its blacks. Both the Democratic and the Republican candidates pitched their campaigns to the conservative middle class. One question left unanswered by the election was Lindsay's future standing in the Republican Party. Announcing after the election that he intended to remain at his post in New York for the full four years, he also insisted that he was still a Republican, despite his election as a Liberal. It was noted by the

New York Times that his "stature as a national figure has been enormously enhanced."

Lindsay was born Nov. 24, 1921, in New York City, was graduated from Yale in 1944, and served in the Navy during World War II before entering law school. He represented New York's 17th congressional district (the "Silk Stocking District") in the U.S. House of Representatives from 1959 until his election as mayor in 1965.

(Mx. H.)

LURIA, SALVADOR EDWARD

Sedgwick professor of biology at the Massachusetts Institute of Technology (MIT), Salvador Luria was one of three cooperating scientists who won the 1969 Nobel Prize for Medicine or Physiology. His colleagues were Alfred Hershey and Max Delbrück (*qq.v.*).

Coming to the United States from his native Italy in 1940, Luria joined Delbrück, who was studying the interaction of viruses and bacteria at Vanderbilt University. Specifically, their research involved bacteriophages, prolific viruses that infect bacterial cells rather than ordinary ones. Together they created models that described mathematically how phages multiply. Their work was to revolutionize modern molecular biology, especially as it relates to viral diseases, which include cancer and the common cold.

After they left Vanderbilt, Luria and Delbrück continued to work in concert. Hershey had joined their cause in 1942 and the three worked as a transcontinental team known as the "Phage Group."

Also interested in the arts, Luria sculpted and taught a world literature course for graduate scientists. This was in keeping with his belief that the purpose of science is to further the humanistic ends of civilization.

Luria was born in Turin, Italy, Aug. 13, 1912. He studied medicine in Italy and then came to the U.S., where he performed research and taught at Columbia University's College of Physicians and Surgeons, the Carnegie Institution, the University of Illinois, and Indiana University. He joined the MIT faculty in 1958. (Ph. K.)

McGOVERN, GEORGE S(TANLEY)

Bolstered by reelection to the Senate and a new prominence brought on by his brief presidential bid the year before, Sen. George S. McGovern (Dem., S.D.) assumed several key roles in the Democratic Party in 1969. He hammered early and hard at the Nixon administration's policies, particularly its failure to bring a prompt end to the war in Vietnam. As chairman of the Senate Select Committee on Nutrition and Human Needs, he held hearings that pointed to the widespread existence of hunger among the U.S. poor.

These activities, coupled with his work for internal Democratic Party reform and his reputation for independent thought, would have been enough to place him with former Vice-Pres. Hubert H. Humphrey and Sen. Edmund S. Muskie (Dem., Me.) on the list of potential Democratic presidential candidates for 1972. But when an automobile accident involving Sen. Edward M. Kennedy (Dem., Mass.) led to a flat statement from the last of the Kennedy brothers that he would not run in 1972, McGovern's political standing took on a new dimension.

The South Dakotan's close ties with the Kennedys had been evident since the 1968 presidential campaign, when he rallied Robert F. Kennedy's followers after the New York senator's assassination. Now he reaffirmed his friendship with Ted Kennedy and, while not discounting a Kennedy

KEYSTONE

Anatoli Vasilievich Kuznetsov

DECLAN HAUN FROM BLACK STAR

George S. McGovern

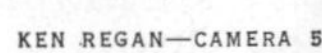

KEN REGAN—CAMERA 5

Norman Mailer

bid after 1972, said "I could become a serious candidate in 1972—I'm not going to rule that out." He would defer judgment until the 1970 elections, he said.

McGovern, who felt that the Democratic Party was in "very serious trouble" as an attraction for a "working majority of the country," laboured vigorously as chairman of the party's Commission on Party Structure and Delegate Selection. He urged reforms that would increase public participation and ensure the selection of convention delegates who reflected the current feeling in the country.

Born in the farm village of Avon, S.D., on July 19, 1922, McGovern served as a pilot in World War II. He graduated in 1945 from Dakota Wesleyan, where later he was a professor of political science and history, and received a Ph.D. in American history and government from Northwestern University in 1953. He served four years in the House of Representatives and a term as director of the Food for Peace program before entering the Senate in 1963.

(R. L. A.)

MAILER, NORMAN

The year 1969 was a vintage one for Norman Mailer—author, celebrity, film maker, nominee to Harvard University's Board of Overseers, and candidate for mayor of New York City. He lost his bid for mayor but won the Long Island University Polk Award, the National Book Award, and the Pulitzer Prize for his personal/political observations of 1967: *The Armies of the Night*. He also reportedly collected approximately $1 million from *Life* magazine to describe his feelings about the U.S. moon landing.

Born in Long Branch, N.J., Jan. 31, 1923, Mailer graduated from Harvard and then attended the Sorbonne. He served in the U.S. Army during World War II and wrote about it in his first novel, the widely acclaimed *The Naked and the Dead* (1948); two later novels, *Barbary Shore* (1951) and *The Deer Park* (1955), were less successful. Mailer then turned to essays and commentary, including *The White Negro* (1958) and *Advertisements for Myself* (1959).

In 1964 he caught fire. Covering the U.S. national political conventions for *Esquire* magazine, he wrote provocative personal appraisals of those events that channeled the nation's course. He proved he could write well even when he was writing very fast. The next year he applied speed writing to fiction, producing *An American Dream* in monthly installments to meet *Esquire* deadlines. In 1966 he wrote *Cannibals and Christians,* and the next year a novel that was nontopical despite its title, *Why Are We in Vietnam?* During those years he also produced, directed, and acted in two films that received mixed notices, *Beyond the Law* and *Wild 90*.

Politically, Mailer called himself a "left conservative," which meant that he considered the possibility of applying radical solutions to contemporary problems while sharing the conservative's lack of faith in centralized government. In practice, this meant that Mailer was in sympathy with the "march on the Pentagon," a four-day event in October 1967 that demonstrated massive opposition to the country's Vietnam war policies. Mailer was invited to participate. He went to Washington, attended some demonstrations, marched on the Pentagon, was thrown in jail, sobered up, and wrote *The Armies of the Night* to recount it all.

After all the prizes were in, Mailer turned his energies to New York City, which he suggested should secede from the state for tax purposes. Running for mayor in the Democratic primary election with former police reporter Jimmy Breslin (who was running for president of the city council), Mailer urged decentralization of the metropolitan government in order to make the city machinery responsive to New Yorkers. Though they stirred up some excitement, Mailer and Breslin lost by the widest of margins. (Ph. K.)

MAXWELL, ROBERT

Robert Maxwell, who described himself in *Who's Who* as self-educated, had built up from scratch Britain's most rapidly expanding publishing empire, Pergamon Press, Ltd. By the end of 1969 he had lost Pergamon to a U.S. conglomerate, Leasco Data Processing Equipment Corp., headed by Saul Steinberg (*q.v.*). At a shareholders' meeting packed with Pergamon employees holding single shares, Maxwell and his seven associates were voted off the board. (*See* PUBLISHING.)

Born Jan Ludvik Hoch in 1923, into a family of Orthodox Jewish farmers in the Carpathian Mountains (then part of Czechoslovakia), he joined the anti-Nazi resistance, escaped to France, and later went to England. As a member of the North Staffordshire Regiment, he took part in the Normandy landings and won a Military Cross. For a time after the end of the war he served in the press censorship department of the allied control commission in Germany.

It was at this stage that his interests turned to publishing, and he became connected with a firm trading in German scientific documents. Leaving the control commission in 1947, he set up the firm of Robert Maxwell and Co. Ltd. in 1948 and later the Pergamon Press. In 1951 he bought the book wholesaling firm of Simpkin Marshall, which subsequently went bankrupt. He built up Pergamon Press mainly on the basis of scientific works (some obtained from Communist countries) and other educational publications, including *Chambers's Encyclopædia,* with an international sales force directed particularly toward the less developed countries. By the time of the Leasco bid in 1969, Pergamon Press was valued at about £25 million.

Meanwhile, however, Maxwell had suffered a number of misfortunes in other ventures. He lost £200,000 in taking over a failing car insurance company. In 1967, 1968, and 1969 he failed in take-over bids for the Butterworth publishing firm and for two newspapers, the *News of the World* and the *Sun.* Though a wealthy self-made man, Maxwell counted himself a Socialist, and became Labour M.P. for Buckingham in 1964. His undisguised ambition made him less than popular with some of his colleagues, but he compelled admiration by taking charge of House of Commons catering and making it pay—an achievement that had eluded his predecessors in the job for many years.

(W. H. Ts.)

MEIR, GOLDA

Few heads of government could boast more varied experience in positions of responsibility than Mrs. Golda Meir, who became prime minister of Israel in 1969. Among the many posts she had held prior to her most recent appointment were ambassador to the Soviet Union, minister of labour, and minister of foreign affairs.

Born in Kiev, Russia, on May 3, 1898, she emigrated with her family to Milwaukee, Wis., in 1906. She grew up in Milwaukee and became a schoolteacher there, but in 1921 she emigrated as a Zionist pioneer to Palestine, then under British control. Within her first seven years there she moved up from membership in the collective settlement of Merhavia, near Nazareth, to a series of posts connected with the Histadrut, the Jewish trade union movement in Palestine. In 1928 she became secretary of the Women's Labour Council and then progressed through the World Zionist Organization and the Jewish Agency for Israel, becoming head of the latter's Political Department in 1946.

Israel gained its independence in 1948 and immediately became embroiled in a war with the Arabs over control of Palestine. During the conflict Mrs. Meir served as military governor of the Jewish sector of Jerusalem. After Israel's triumph in the war Mrs. Meir became her nation's ambassador to the Soviet Union. She returned home in 1949 and served as minister of labour until 1956, when she was named minister of foreign affairs.

In 1966 she retired from the ministry and became secretary-general of Mapai, the Labour Party. She had also retired from that position when the sudden death of Prime Minister Levi Eshkol early in 1969 produced a vacuum in the political life of Israel. It was quickly determined that Mrs. Meir was the only effective candidate for the office, and on March 11 she was charged to form her first government. (J. K.)

MERCKX, EDDY

One of the world's outstanding road-racing cyclists, Eddy Merckx of Belgium enjoyed one of his most successful years in 1969 with victories in the Tour de France, Paris–Nice, Milan–San Remo, Tour of Flanders, Liège–Bastogne–Liège, and Paris–Luxembourg races. He was injured in a racing accident in France on September 9 but resumed competition three weeks later. His 1969 earnings were estimated at more than $190,000.

Merckx was born June 17, 1945, in the Belgian village of Meensel-Kiezegem. From boyhood he desired to be a great cyclist, and at 16 began racing in the Junior category. The next season (1962) Merckx won 24 road races and was coached by prewar Tour de France rider Felicien Vervaecke, who declared that one day his pupil would win both a world championship and the Tour de France.

Both predictions were realized. In 1964 Merckx took the world amateur road title at Sallanches (France), and in 1967 he won the professional championship at Heerlen (Neth.). The Tour de France eluded him until 1969, when he not only won the 2,600-mi. event but captured six stages of it as well.

Among Merckx's other triumphs were: (1966) Milan–San Remo; (1967) Ghent–Wevelgem, Milan–San Remo, Flèche Wallonne, two stages of the Tour of Italy, Criterium des As; (1968) Tour of Sardinia, Paris–Roubaix, Tour of Italy (including four stage wins), Tour of Swiss Romande, and Tour of Catalonia. (Jo. B. W.)

MITCHELL, JOHN NEWTON

John Mitchell, the quiet Wall Street lawyer who became attorney general of the United States after managing Richard M. Nixon's presidential campaign, emerged in 1969 as a powerful influence in the new administration. Though he had only known Nixon for about a year before their two New York firms merged in 1967, Mitchell had gained Nixon's confidence as a totally unemotional but brilliant organizer—a middle-of-the-road pragmatist.

He conferred with the president daily, serving as the chief executive's top-level generalist. His sharpest critics labeled him a strong conservative, but others found him without a hard ideological viewpoint. They attributed his tough talk about "activists," his vigorous law enforcement stands, and his cautions against moving too swiftly on desegregation matters as common-sense compromises between potentially destructive extremes.

His influence surfaced on many fronts: he defended the use of wiretapping in certain cases; he was not opposed to capital punishment; he visited Chief Justice Earl Warren to discuss the case of Justice Abe Fortas, who later resigned; he was instrumental in the appointment of Warren E. Burger to succeed Warren.

As a member of the White House Council for Urban Affairs, he was outspoken on housing and welfare policies. He had a voice in foreign affairs as a member of the National Security Council.

In late October, the Nixon administration —and particularly the Justice Department— suffered a major policy setback. The Supreme Court, by then under Chief Justice Burger, unanimously and bluntly rejected arguments by Mississippi school districts and the administration that deadlines for desegregation plans should be delayed. The court's 1954 call for "all deliberate speed" was replaced by a demand that dual school systems end "at once." It would be up to the president, Mitchell, and the agencies concerned to readjust their position.

The attorney general's cool, stern image tended to cast him as the "heavy" in the administration, but many associates described him as the "go-slow" man who simply objected to sudden changes. Born Sept. 15, 1913, in Detroit, Mitchell attended Fordham University and its law school, graduating in 1938. He served as a Navy commander in World War II before settling into his career as a private attorney. (R. L. A.)

NAMATH, JOSEPH WILLIAM

America has had dozens of major sports celebrities, but none have been quite like Joe Namath, the star quarterback of the New York Jets. Though only 26, he had become almost an instant legend; this was demonstrated by the fact that four books were published about him in 1969, including his autobiography, *I Can't Wait Until Tomorrow . . . 'Cause I Get Better Looking Every Day.*

In addition, Namath had his own television show, had appeared in one motion picture, had several outside business interests, including a food franchising concern, and was given a $10,000 fee for shaving his flowing Fu Manchu mustache in a television commercial. He also became embroiled in controversy and had a brief retirement from professional football in the summer of 1969 when he refused to sell his share of Bachelors III, a nightclub in New York City, which, according to football commissioner Pete Rozelle, was frequented by "undesirables." Rather than sell, Namath, in tears, announced that he would retire from football, stating that he could not play much longer anyway because of his bad legs. Later he relented, sold his nightclub holdings, and was fully reinstated.

Namath was born May 31, 1943, in Beaver Falls, Pa. The fifth child of a Hungarian steelworker, he began playing football at an early age with his three brothers. After high school he received 52 offers from colleges and universities. He chose the University of Alabama, where he won All-American honours, and obtained a record $427,000 bonus contract from the New York Jets of the American Football League (AFL).

Namath led the Jets for the next four seasons and was the star in the 1969 Super Bowl game. A decisive 18–20-point pregame underdog, the Jets scored a 16–7 upset win over the champion Baltimore Colts of the established National Football League (NFL). Namath completed 17 of 28 passes for 206 yd., a Super Bowl record. The Jets' triumph destroyed the myth of NFL superiority and for the first time established the considerably younger AFL as a major professional football league. Namath was named the AFL's Most Valuable Player by the league's coaches. (JE. HO.)

NEWBY, PERCY HOWARD

A novelist surprisingly prolific for one so gifted and serious was rewarded in 1969 when P. H. Newby won the new Booker Prize for his novel *Something to Answer*

A.F.P. FROM PICTORIAL PARADE

Eddy Merckx

DENNIS BRACK FROM BLACK STAR

John Newton Mitchell

Golda Meir

ISRAEL SUN—PIX FROM PUBLIX

PICTORIAL PARADE

Richard Milhous Nixon

For, which had appeared at the end of the previous year. Not all critics agreed, but the judges thought it marked a notable advance in the work of this diffident, dedicated writer, who produced his 17 novels and collections of stories during his spare time from another successful career at the British Broadcasting Corporation (BBC), where since 1958 he had been controller of the Third Programme.

Born in Sussex, Eng., in 1918, Newby went to grammar school in Worcester and to teacher-training college in Cheltenham. During World War II he served in France and North Africa as a stretcher-bearer until shortly after the El Alamein offensive in late 1942, when he was sent to Fouad 1st University, Cairo, to lecture in English literature. He returned to England in 1946 and joined the BBC in 1949. By that time he had already published five novels, one of which, *A Journey to the Interior* (1945), won him a Rockefeller award.

Egypt was a formative experience for Newby. He was fascinated by its landscapes and seascapes, by the extreme candour of Egyptian curiosity, and by the ecstasies of language brought on by the simplest transactions. It became the scene of much of his fiction, and it was natural that Britain's conflict with the U.A.R. over the Suez Canal in 1956 should have been even more traumatic for him than for most Englishmen.

This trouble provided the mainspring for both *A Guest and His Going* (1959) and *Something to Answer For,* but the latter probed more painfully into the relationship between public and private morality. It retained something of the rueful responsiveness to the "muddle" of human experience that Newby seemed to owe to E. M. Forster. What marked the novel especially, however, was the peculiar energy and aptness of its language, something akin to that quality of Joseph Conrad's language and vision that has been called his "energy of registration." Of Newby's earlier novels probably the best, and most Forsterian, was *The Picnic at Sakkara* (1955). (W. L. We.)

NIXON, RICHARD MILHOUS

The president of the United States should be an "activist" who would "bring dissenters into policy discussions" and build his administration on "the broadest possible base," Republican Party presidential nominee Richard M. Nixon declared in a campaign broadcast of Sept. 19, 1968. One year later, President Nixon's performance was being judged by candidate Nixon's standard and, in the opinion of some critics, was falling short of meeting it. The problems besetting the new president basically were those that had plagued his predecessor: the Vietnam war, inflation, and racial unrest.

No discernible progress toward a negotiated settlement of the Vietnam war had been made by the end of 1969. In an effort to break the deadlock in the Paris peace talks, Nixon announced in June that 25,000 U.S. troops would be withdrawn from South Vietnam by August 31. Additional withdrawals of approximately 35,000 and 50,000 troops were announced by the president in September and December.

An eight-point peace plan announced by Nixon in May called for mutual withdrawal of "major portions" of U.S., allied, and North Vietnamese troops from South Vietnam, and for internationally supervised elections to ensure "each significant group in South Vietnam a real opportunity to participate in the political life of the nation." In a speech to the nation on November 3, Nixon called on the "great silent majority" of Americans to support his Vietnam policy.

Two highlights of the president's first year in office were his trips to Europe in February and March and to Asia and Europe in July and August. The latter journey included a two-day visit to Romania, where Nixon received a tumultuous welcome. It was the first trip by a U.S. president to a Communist country in almost 25 years.

Nixon came under fire as a result of his appointment of U.S. Circuit Court Judge Clement F. Haynsworth (*q.v.*) to be an associate justice of the U.S. Supreme Court. It created great controversy throughout the nation and divided Republican members of the Senate, where the appointment was eventually rejected.

On the domestic front, Nixon strove to hold down federal spending in an effort to combat inflation. Such efforts usually are unpopular, and they proved to be so in 1969. Blacks complained that the Nixon administration was basically hostile to black aspirations. But Nixon could claim that his support of proposals to remove poor people from federal income tax rolls, to establish a federal minimum standard of welfare assistance, and to open up more opportunities for blacks in craft unions belied such charges.

Nixon was born Jan. 9, 1913, in Yorba Linda, Calif. He was graduated from Whittier College and from Duke University Law School. After serving in the Navy during World War II, he won election in 1946 as a U.S. representative from California. He was elected to the U.S. Senate four years later, and in 1952 became vice-president on the ticket headed by Dwight D. Eisenhower. Nixon was defeated by John F. Kennedy in the presidential election of 1960. (Ri. W.)

GAMMA—PIX FROM PUBLIX

Georges Jean Raymond Pompidou

CAMERA PRESS—PIX FROM PUBLIX

Ian Richard Kyle Paisley

OVANDO CANDÍA, ALFREDO

Gen. Alfredo Ovando Candía became president of Bolivia on Sept. 26, 1969, by leading a military coup against the constitutional civilian president, Luís Adolfo Siles Salinas. The coup was bloodless, as Ovando avoided casualties by careful planning and an overwhelming show of force. He made his move while Siles Salinas was visiting the eastern city of Santa Cruz. Ovando's troops seized government buildings, communications centres, and the airport at 6 A.M. while most of the country slept and hustled Siles out of the country before there could be any reaction. Most Bolivians accepted the change calmly. Ironically, Ovando had been considered a prohibitive favourite to win the presidency in the regularly scheduled election of May 1970, but evidently he decided he could not afford to wait.

Long considered a friend of the U.S., Ovando in 1969 claimed to be ideologically identified with Peru's socialist-minded military junta, and there was a decidedly left-of-centre hue to his Cabinet. Three weeks after assuming the presidency he decided to expropriate the properties of the Gulf Oil Corp. in Bolivia. This was a surprising and possibly foolhardy move because Gulf was the biggest foreign investor in Bolivia and, at the same time, had not yet completed construction of facilities important to Bolivia's economic future. The oil fields and pipelines seized by Ovando's decree pumped 30,000 bbl. a day for export, but Gulf handled the shipment and marketing. Ovando appointed a commission to decide on compensation for Gulf, but unless the company was satisfied, Bolivia might well find itself with petroleum that it could neither use nor market.

Ovando was born in Cobija, April 6, 1918. His education was a military one, and he had been a soldier since 1936. His main political support came from the Army and the peasants. (J. A. O'L.)

PAISLEY, IAN RICHARD KYLE

For three years before the outbreak of the violent Ulster rioting in August 1969, the Rev. Ian Paisley had been at the heart of the sectarian turmoil that divided Northern Ireland. The voice of extreme Protestant opinion, Paisley had first come to public attention in the mid-1960s as a critic of the ecumenical movement. The self-styled moderator of a breakaway sect called the Free Presbyterian Church of Ulster, Paisley was born in Ballymena, County Antrim, in 1926, and was ordained a minister of this church by his father, who had broken with the Baptists. He had studied at a school of evangelism in South Wales and took a degree at a theological seminary in Rockford, Ill.; an honorary doctorate of divinity was conferred on him by Bob Jones University, Greenville, S.C., in 1966.

A tall, heavily built man, Paisley had a powerful voice, considerable eloquence, and a quick wit in argument. In 1961 his church had only about 1,000 members, but by 1969 it claimed some 10,000 members and had perhaps 200,000 sympathizers. His appeal was aggressively antipapist and hostile to the reforming government of Terence O'Neill, whom he fought at the 1969 general election.

By this time Paisley had earned a demagogic reputation and had twice been sentenced to imprisonment for unlawful assembly. In June 1969 he was refused entry to Switzerland, where he planned to lead a demonstration against the pope's visit to Geneva. Though he denied that he encouraged violence, his speeches were undeniably inflammatory in effect. At the time of the Belfast riots, he was reported as saying, "What we need is another Cromwell." He wanted the citizens of Ireland treated as aliens and said that the British home secretary, James Callaghan, was siding with the Roman Catholic hierarchy against Ulster. There was some evidence, however, that his influence did not match his gifts for publicity. In September, when he called for 100,000 to lobby a meeting of the Northern Ireland Parliament, less than an estimated 5,000 responded. (W. H. Ts.)

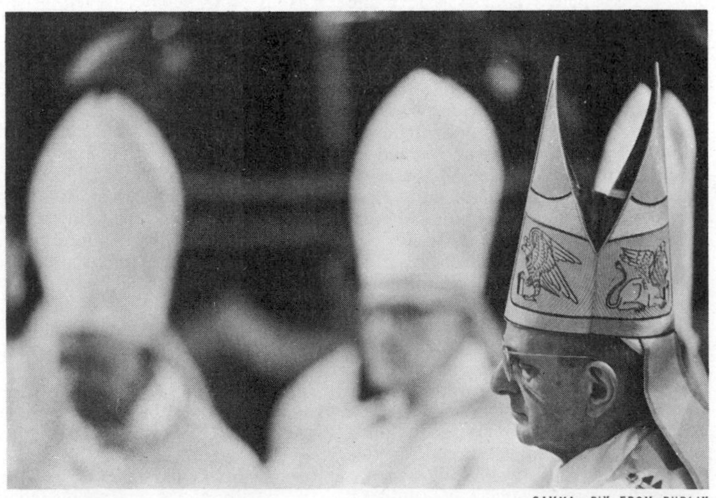

GAMMA—PIX FROM PUBLIX

Paul VI

PALME, OLOF

In October 1969 Olof Palme succeeded Tage Erlander as chairman of the Swedish Social Democratic Labour Party and prime minister of Sweden. His elevation had been expected for some time, and he had frequently been referred to as Erlander's "crown prince."

Palme was born Jan. 30, 1927, in Stockholm. He was educated at a private boarding school and Stockholm University, where, in 1951, he received a law degree. Palme entered Parliament as a Social Democrat in 1958 and joined the government in 1963 as a minister without portfolio. In 1965 he was appointed minister of communications and in 1967 minister of education and ecclesiastical affairs, a post he held until he became prime minister.

Palme's position as prime minister was expected to be strong. The Social Democrats had been in power since 1932 and at the 1968 election received more than 50% of the vote. The three main opposition parties were divided and seemed incapable of working together. It seemed unlikely that there would be any abrupt policy shifts under Palme. He had worked closely with Erlander for more than 15 years and presumably was thinking along the same lines. Palme defined his political aims as: (1) preventing technological advances from creating unreasonable social consequences; (2) working for equality between the different groups in society; (3) working for increased democratization in all spheres giving the people joint responsibility and joint influence; and (4) contributing to the internationalization of Swedish society.

In February 1968, when Sweden's relations with the U.S. were at a low ebb, Palme had attracted attention by taking part in an anti-U.S. demonstration in which the North Vietnamese ambassador to Moscow also participated. In December 1969 he accepted an invitation to speak at Kenyon College,

Gambier, O. (where he received a B.A. in 1948), and also at the National Press Club in Washington. It was expected that he would take this opportunity to initiate an improvement in relations between the two countries. (A. D. Wi.)

PAUL VI

The sixth year of the reign of Pope Paul VI was marked by historic travels and deep concern over challenges to papal authority and church doctrine which the pontiff said periled the life of the church.

The pope emphasized a desire to heal the differences among Christians by flying to Geneva June 10 to pray with Protestants at the World Council of Churches. He called the historic occasion a "truly blessed encounter, a prophetic moment, dawn of a day to come and yet awaited for centuries."

But he also declared that "We do not consider that the question of membership [in the World Council] . . . is so mature that a positive answer could or should be given. The question remains in hypothesis. It contains serious theological and pastoral implications. It thus requires profound study and commits us to a way that honesty recognizes could be long and difficult."

Paul VI also became the first reigning pope to visit the African continent when he made a three-day official visit to Kampala, Uganda, in the summer to preside at a meeting of African bishops and to confer with Pres. Milton Obote and several other African leaders. He pledged that the church would aid the economic development of African nations.

Paul VI criticized priests who left the church, particularly those who renounced their vows of celibacy and married. In April he said the life of the church was periled by the "restless, critical, unruly and demolishing rebellion" of priests and laymen. He said that the rebellion was directed against the church's tradition and authority.

At the synod of bishops, which he convened October 11 in the Sistine Chapel, the pope promised bishops a greater voice in church government, but rejected the liberal contention that he did not have the right to rule the whole church. The pope enlarged the Sacred College to an all-time high of 134 on March 28 by naming 33 new cardinals from 19 countries. Also during the year the pope ordered a simpler style of dress for all church authorities and abolished the traditional red hats for cardinals.

Pope Paul, born Giovanni Battista Montini on Sept. 26, 1897, in Concesio, Italy, was crowned as pontiff on June 30, 1963. (*See* RELIGION: *Roman Catholic Church.*) (J. F. BA.)

PICCARD, JACQUES ERNEST JEAN

Jacques Piccard spent a month in the summer of 1969 shooting what may be the slowest rapids in the world—and possibly the most significant to man. An oceanographer, engineer, and designer, he negotiated the Gulf Stream, the "river in the ocean," for 1,500 mi. in a special 130-ton, $5 million submarine, the "Ben Franklin."

The project was jointly conducted by the U.S. Navy, the National Aeronautics and Space Administration, and the Grumman Aircraft Corp. Its purposes included learning how men behave in a sealed environment over long periods, as well as collecting geophysical and ecological data about the Gulf Stream.

Most dramatically, perhaps, Piccard and his five-man crew discovered that the current is "not merely one flood of water but several swirling, colliding, meandering torrents tumbling northward." Drifting from off West Palm Beach, Fla., to a point 300 mi. from Halifax, N.S., they determined that it flowed faster than expected—about 2 knots overall, but as fast as 3.3 knots in places. They also determined that the Gulf Stream is a sort of marine desert with very little aquatic life—a 30-ft. jellyfish here, a squid that hitched a ride for a day, a swordfish that attacked the ship. Plankton, the microscopic life that forms the basis of the marine food chain, was scarce.

To Piccard, being under water was an old story. He had made innumerable dives, including the deepest on record—in "Trieste," a self-propelled bathyscaphe that he himself designed. In 1960 he and a U.S. Navy officer descended nearly seven miles in the Marianas Trench off Guam. Piccard, a U.S. Navy consultant, spotted marine life there and concluded that the oceans' deepest spot was a dynamic environment and should not be used as a depository for radioactive wastes. The Swiss scientist also designed a mesoscaphe, or middle-depth underwater vehicle, that carried tourists during the Swiss National Exhibition in 1964.

Piccard was born July 28, 1922, in Brussels. His father, Auguste, a physics professor at the University of Brussels and a pioneer in lighter-than-air craft, set an altitude record in the sealed gondola of a balloon that carried him ten miles above the earth. (PH. K.)

POMPIDOU, GEORGES JEAN RAYMOND

The rise of Georges Pompidou to the French presidency in 1969 clearly showed that, although politics may be defined as the art of the possible, it also leaves a considerable amount to obstinacy and luck. In 1962, at the age of 50, this former grammar school teacher was unknown to the general public. When, to the amazement of the country, Charles de Gaulle appointed him premier, he had never held an electoral mandate, had never exercised any governmental responsibility, and had never even set foot in the Chamber of Deputies except in the public gallery.

For six years his prudent conduct of the government, his nerve, and his skill increasingly confirmed his status as a major public figure. He was referred to as the crown prince. During the disturbances of May 1968, when the nation seemed on the point of collapse and de Gaulle himself hesitated, Pompidou held firm, righted the boat, and organized the Gaullist electoral victory. For his pains, he was dismissed.

It was then that luck came to the aid of obstinacy. De Gaulle staked his office on an ill-conceived referendum, was defeated, and stepped down. Just 38 hours after he had retired, Pompidou announced his candidacy. His principal opponent, Alain Poher, president of the Senate and interim president of the republic, was a formidable opponent—the more so because he too was a man of the centre and, in fact, very close to the Gaullist position. In his campaign Pompidou spoke of continuity, but also of change; of loyalty, but also of a determination to remain open-minded. All the public opinion polls and other forecasts put him in the lead, and when the time came he won handily. Less than ten years after first entering politics, he moved into the Elysée as the successor to de Gaulle and president of the republic for seven years.

Pompidou was born on July 5, 1911, at Montboudif in the Cantal. At the end of 1944 he held a post in de Gaulle's Cabinet, and later he became a member of the general's personal staff, while continuing his career in the Conseil d'État and then as a director of the Rothschild Bank. When de Gaulle returned to power in 1958, he made Pompidou director of his Cabinet during the transition between the Fourth and Fifth Republics and appointed him as premier in April 1962. (P. V.-P.)

RAHMAN, TUNKU ABDUL

Tunku Abdul Rahman, who joined rival ethnic factions and widely spread territories into the federation of Malaysia in 1963, found it necessary to use all his talents to hold his riot-torn nation together in 1969. Absolute political power was given to the Malay-dominated National Operations Council after serious riots between Malays and Chinese erupted following the national elections on May 10, during which Rahman's ruling Alliance Party lost parliamentary strength but remained in power. Nearly 200 persons were known to have been killed and hundreds injured in the riots. Although Rahman remained prime minister, his deputy and long-time heir apparent, Tun Abdul Razak, became actual director of the National Operations Council.

Rahman himself narrowly won his parliamentary seat in the ill-fated elections. He carried his home district of Alor Star in northern Malaysia by only 3,504 votes, compared with 11,954 in the 1964 general elections. The Alliance Party, which was based upon cooperation among Malay, Chinese, and Indian organizations, kept control in only 6 of the 13 states in which election contests were held. Western diplomatic circles expressed their belief that the need for imposition of council rule indicated that Malaysia would have to adopt new racial patterns and policies to ease strains between the country's Malays and Chinese.

Born Feb. 8, 1903, Rahman was the seventh child of the reigning sultan of Kedah. His family traced its ancestry back 1,000 years through 9 Hindu and 16 Muslim sultans. At 16, he was sent to England, where he attended Cambridge University and later studied law at the Inner Temple in London. After returning to Malaya he became an officer in the Kedah state civil service in 1931. Malaya gained its independence from the U.K. in 1957, and Rahman was named prime minister, a post he continued to hold after the federation of Malaysia was created in 1963. (J. F. BA.)

ROCKEFELLER, NELSON ALDRICH

New York Gov. Nelson A. Rockefeller devoted most of the summer of 1969 to four violence-marred visits to Latin America as head of a fact-finding mission for Pres. Richard M. Nixon. The president described the assignment as "one of the most vitally important missions ever undertaken by an independent group on behalf of the United States."

Despite protest demonstrations and clashes in which one person was killed in Honduras and three in the Dominican Republic, Rockefeller traveled 43,000 mi. and visited 20 nations. Scheduled visits to Peru, Chile, and Venezuela were canceled at the request of the governments of those countries, and some other visits were curtailed. Nevertheless, Rockefeller concluded at the end of his travels that the mission was worthwhile. His 137-page report was finally made public by the White House on November 10. It warned that poverty, frustration, and political instability in Latin America might lead to more regimes like that of Fidel Castro. Rockefeller's chief recommendation was an increase in U.S. grants to train Latin-American security forces. He also proposed creation of a Western Hemisphere Security Council.

Rockefeller gained the spotlight again by rebuking Sen. Charles E. Goodell—whom he had appointed to fill Robert Kennedy's unexpired Senate term—for proposing legislation that would require the withdrawal of all U.S. troops from Vietnam by the end of 1970. Locally, he promised that the trouble-plagued Long Island Railroad, a state-operated commuter line, would be the best in the country by October 7. On that date, he proclaimed that his promise had been fulfilled, but few commuters agreed. He endorsed—but did not campaign for—the GOP candidate for mayor of New York, John Marchi. John Lindsay's reelection left the city in the hands of a man who, if perhaps closer to Rockefeller ideologically, was a formidable rival politically.

Rockefeller was born at Bar Harbor, Me., July 8, 1908, the son of John D. Rockefeller, Jr. After graduating from Dartmouth College, Hanover, N.H., he was active in family enterprises, serving as president of Rockefeller Center from 1938 to 1945 and from 1948 to 1951. He served as coordinator of inter-American affairs, 1940–44; assistant secretary of state, 1944–45; and special assistant to Pres. Dwight D. Eisenhower, 1954–55. He was elected governor of New York in 1958 and reelected in 1962 and 1966. (Mx. H.)

ROSEN, CARL GUSTAF VON

In August 1968 the veteran Swedish pilot Count Carl Gustaf von Rosen undertook, on behalf of a church relief organization, a hedgehopping daylight flight from the Portuguese island of São Tomé to Biafra. Thus began an involvement with the Biafran cause that repeatedly brought his name into the headlines in the following months. Von Rosen's action was hardly out of character: he had a habit of helping the underdog. In 1935 he assisted Ethiopia against Italy; in 1939–40, Finland against the U.S.S.R. He was also active in the Netherlands in 1940 and in the Congo in 1960.

He was born Aug. 19, 1909, at Helgesta, south of Stockholm, and obtained his flying certificate in 1929. He was a pilot with the Swedish Red Cross in Ethiopia, 1935–36; flight captain with KLM, 1937–39; volunteer in the Finnish Air Force, 1939–40; flight captain with ABA, 1940–46; and colonel in the Ethiopian Air Force 1946–56. From 1957 he was flight captain with Transair Sweden airlines.

In 1968 von Rosen had flown to São Tomé with a cargo of food and medical supplies from the Roman Catholic relief agency Caritas. Appalled at the plight of Biafra, where more than a year of civil war had led to widespread famine, he determined to break the Nigerian blockade. On returning to Sweden, he was summoned by the prime minister to explain his actions. In an effort to rouse world opinion, von Rosen then visited Geneva to talk with relief organizations and later flew to New York, where he attempted to meet UN Secretary-General U Thant. By this time he was firmly committed to Biafra, and it was announced that he would take charge of operations in São Tomé which, it was hoped, would lead to the establishment of an "air bridge" for aid supplies.

The air bridge was a success. Then, in May 1969, events took a dramatic turn. It was reported that von Rosen, together with other Swedish pilots, had attacked the Nigerians in small, Swedish-made aircraft. This led to accusations that he was conducting a "private war," and there was much concern in official circles. Throughout, however, von Rosen stressed that he was motivated only by humanitarian considerations. He returned to Sweden in June, amid great publicity. At about the same time he published a book, *Biafra as I See It,* in which he gave his views on the matter.

(A. D. Wi.)

ROTH, PHILIP

In 1969 Philip Roth did his best to destroy an American institution: the Jewish Mother—or so many of his mother's kind must have thought. His vehicle was *Portnoy's Complaint,* a kosher shaggy dog story exhibiting titanic skill. The book had a first printing of 150,000 copies; Roth's advance check from Random House was $250,000; paperback and book club rights sold for $645,000. It was, in a word, a hit.

The novel comprises the narrative soul-searching on a psychiatrist's couch of one Alexander Portnoy, possibly the most priapismic character in literature. "Acts of exhibitionism, voyeurism, fetishism, autoeroticism and oral coitus are plentiful," says the fictional psychiatrist, describing the patient's newly identified syndrome. "As a consequence of the patient's 'morality,' however, neither fantasy nor act issues in genuine sexual gratification, but rather in overriding feelings of shame and dread of retribution. . . . Many of the symptoms can be traced to the bonds obtaining in the mother-child relationship." The villain of the piece is Mother Portnoy.

Here was a book containing things only the underground pulps or the most erudite literati had described before. Nice readers do not buy the stuff that panders to perverts, nor will they tackle Henry Miller and Joyce, but Roth was a recognized writer. More important, he had written a brilliant, simple, funny book. Many critics praised the work—*Washington Post* book editor Geoffrey Wolff called it the book of his generation—but there was still controversy. Some people would not read *Portnoy* because of the "dirty" words and others bought it because of them. Significantly, perhaps, *Portnoy* was bumped from the top of the best-seller list by a book that titillatingly skirted the matters Roth had the skill and heart to present directly—*The Love Machine* by Jacqueline Susann (*q.v.*).

Roth was born in Newark, N.J. (Portnoy's hometown), on March 19, 1933. He earned degrees at Bucknell and the University of Chicago, taught at Chicago and at the Iowa Writers' Workshop, and was a writer in residence at Princeton. He was a Guggenheim fellow and a member of the National Institute of Arts and Letters. His earlier work included *When She Was Good, Letting Go,* and *Goodbye, Columbus,* which won the National Book Award in 1960 and was made into a successful film in 1969.

(Ph. K.)

RUMOR, MARIANO

Massive strikes for better pay and working conditions and feuding among the Socialists made governing Italy difficult in 1969. In fact, Premier Mariano Rumor presided over two different shaky governments during the year.

On July 5 Rumor, a Christian Democrat, announced the resignation of his six-month-old, centre-left coalition government with the Socialists and Republicans because there had been a major schism within the Socialist Party. While the collapse of the government caused havoc, it constituted political recognition of the instability that had been expressed in Italy for months. President Giuseppe Saragat asked Rumor to try to form another government, but on August 1 Rumor informed Saragat he had failed. Saragat persisted, however, and on August 5 Rumor agreed to form Italy's 30th postwar government, this time consisting entirely of the minority Christian Democrats.

The Socialists, who had formed the major support of Rumor's earlier government, forgot their infighting long enough to announce support of the new Cabinet. The new government was far from a durable political solution to Italy's problems, but was designed to avoid a national election during strife-torn times.

Rumor moved to extend the life of the government by postponing local and regional elections scheduled for November until the spring of 1970.

Rumor, a bachelor, was born on June 6, 1915, in Vicenza in northeastern Italy. He taught literature after graduating from the University of Padua, but after World War II he began a new career as an organizer of the Christian Democratic Party in Vicenza. A rapid climb through party and government ranks followed. In December 1963 he became political secretary when Aldo Moro resigned the top party post to head the first centre-left coalition government.

Following parliamentary elections in May 1968, Moro resigned and Rumor failed to get support for a coalition government from the United Socialist Party. An interim premier, Giovanni Leone, was named and, on Dec. 12, 1968, following a 23-day crisis precipitated by Leone's resignation, Rumor, having this time formed a government, was sworn in as premier. (J. F. Ba.)

RUSSELL, WILLIAM FELTON

During his 13-year career as a player and later coach with the Boston Celtics, Bill Russell, who retired from basketball at the age of 35 in 1969, set many precedents. He was, for example, the only five-time winner of the Podoloff Cup, given annually to the most valuable player in the National Basketball Association (NBA). Additionally, Russell in 1966 became the first black to manage a major professional sports team in the United States.

Yet Russell most likely will be remembered for actually changing the style of basketball. A 6-ft. 10-in. centre, he brought to the game defensive skills that were previously absent, and to the surprise of some fashioned a highly successful career out of blocking shots and rebounding. The blocked shot, previously a minor and seldom-successful tactic, was to become a Russell trademark.

Never a high scorer, Russell averaged only 15.1 points a game as a professional, and in only one game scored as many as 37 points. Nonetheless, he led Boston to 11 league championships and received more individual honours than did his longtime, high-scoring rival in the NBA, Wilt Chamberlain.

Russell was born Feb. 12, 1934, in Monroe, La., where his father worked in a paper bag factory. Hoping to improve conditions for his wife and two sons, the elder Russell moved the family to Oakland, Calif. Although skinny and clumsy as a schoolboy, Russell was tall for his age and managed to win a place on the school basketball team. He improved rapidly and went to San Francisco University on a basketball scholarship. San Francisco, with Russell in the starring role, won two national championships and 55 games in a row. Russell then led the 1956 U.S. Olympic team to a world title, and immediately afterward joined the professional Boston Celtics, sparking them to their first league crown in the NBA. His value to the Celtics was such that they won the league championship in each of his first five years. In 1966 Russell was named the Celtics' player-coach and led the team to two more titles. (Je. Ho.)

SCHEEL, WALTER

With the formation of the West German coalition government of Social Democrats and Free Democrats in October 1969, Walter Scheel was appointed foreign minister and vice-chancellor. As chairman of the Free Democratic Party, he had fought the 1969 federal election campaign with the declared intention of replacing the former grand coalition of the two main parties (Christian Democrats and Social Democrats) with an alliance slightly left of centre.

Under his leadership the Free Democratic Party had provided the small parliamentary opposition to the big coalition and in this role had become increasingly liberal, particularly in its attitude toward East Germany. It proposed that the relationship "between the two German states should be regulated by treaty." In the process the party lost much of its traditional support, polling only 5.7% in the federal election in September, compared with 9.5% in 1965. In the new Parliament it had only 30 seats, compared with a previous total of 49. Nonetheless, by joining the Social Democrats the party was instrumental in forming the new coalition.

Scheel was no newcomer to government office. He had served as minister for economic cooperation, the man responsible for development aid, during 1961–66, first under Konrad Adenauer and then in the government headed by Ludwig Erhard.

Born July 8, 1919, in Solingen, Scheel first worked in banking. He served with the German Air Force during World War II, and afterward went into private business as an economic consultant. He was elected to the Bundestag in 1953 and subsequently became a member of the Common Assembly of the European Coal and Steel Community and of the European Parliament. In 1967 he was elected a vice-president of the Bundestag, and he became chairman of the Free Democratic Party in January 1968. (N. Cr.)

SCHILLER, KARL

Opinion polls taken before the federal election in September 1969 showed that Karl Schiller, the minister of economics, was the most popular politician in West Germany. More than any other man, he was credited with the success of the coalition government in overcoming the economic recession that had brought down the regime of Ludwig Erhard in 1966.

At the time, the economic situation was aggravated by severe problems in the industrial areas of the Ruhr and the Saar, where thousands of miners were out of work. With the aid of public investment budgets and tax incentives, Schiller introduced a policy that sought to combine a market economy with overall economic control. The crisis was gradually removed, and a new period of expansion began without any danger to price stability.

The harmony between Schiller and the finance minister, Franz Josef Strauss (*q.v.*), came to an abrupt end in May 1969, when Schiller advocated a revaluation of the mark. Revaluation became one of the main issues of the election campaign. In the election the Christian Democrats lost control of the government to the Social Democrats and Free Democrats, whose first act was to revalue the mark. Schiller, a Social Democrat, remained minister of economics in the new government.

WIDE WORLD
William Felton Russell

AUTHENTICATED NEWS INTERNATIONAL
Walter Scheel

KEYSTONE
Mariano Rumor

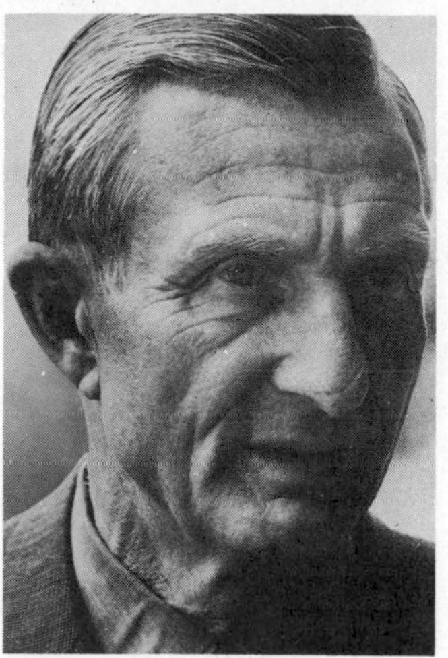
CAMERA PRESS—PIX FROM PUBLIX
Carl Gustaf von Rosen

KEYSTONE
Karl Schiller

Born in Breslau, April 24, 1911, Schiller studied political economy and sociology at several German universities. For a time he was a member of the Nazi Party, but he left on joining the German Army in 1941. In 1939 he had qualified as university teacher at Kiel, and after the war he became visiting professor at Kiel University. In 1947 he was appointed professor of political economy at Hamburg University, where from 1956 to 1958 he served as vice-chancellor. Schiller joined the Social Democratic Party in 1946, and from 1948 to 1953 was senator for economic affairs and transport in Hamburg. In 1961 he was summoned to West Berlin to fill the same post there. He moved to Bonn four years later when he was elected to the Bundestag, and became minister of economics in 1966. (N. Cr.)

SEAVER, (GEORGE) THOMAS

U.S. Pres. Richard M. Nixon, a lifelong sports enthusiast, was host at a White House reception in July 1969 for major league baseball players and officials, in honour of baseball's 100th anniversary. When pitcher Tom Seaver was introduced, President Nixon said: "Oh, I know you. You were winning before the Mets were."

George Thomas Seaver, 25, and the son of a sportsman, was a winner the moment he surfaced in the major leagues in 1967. He won 16 games that season, then a Met record, and was chosen as the National League's Rookie of the Year. He won 16 games the following season and in 1969 led the Mets to their first pennant with a 25–7 record; in addition, he won one game each in the National League play-offs and in the World Series.

A right-hander whose best pitch was a fast ball, Seaver won more games than any other major league pitcher in 1969. His record might have been even better except for an injury. Four of his seven losses were suffered in late July and early August when he was troubled by a sore shoulder. He finished the regular season with ten consecutive victories and was an almost unanimous choice (23 out of 24 votes) for the National League's Cy Young Award. After the season he demonstrated his individuality by advertising in publications his availability for personal appearances and product endorsements.

Seaver was born in Fresno, Calif., Nov. 17, 1944. His father, Charles Seaver, was a champion golfer in California and a member of the United States Walker Cup team in the 1930s. Tom attended the University of Southern California and as a junior won ten games.

The Los Angeles Dodgers picked him in baseball's college draft but did not sign him and Seaver's name went back into the hopper for the next draft. This time he was chosen by the Atlanta Braves, who signed him for $50,000. The signing was not completed before USC had started another season and hence was in violation of baseball's college rule.

William Eckert, then the baseball commissioner, voided the deal. Seaver complained about this to Eckert, who immediately notified the other major league clubs that if they were willing to meet Atlanta's price they could enter a special drawing for the young pitcher. Three clubs responded: the Mets, the Philadelphia Phillies, and the Cleveland Indians. The Mets won the drawing. (Je. Ho.)

SHAW, CLAY L.

A New Orleans jury took only 50 minutes on March 1, 1969, to acquit Clay L. Shaw of conspiring with Lee Harvey Oswald and others to murder U.S. Pres. John F. Kennedy, thereby ending a two-year legal fantasy that brought first fame and then contempt and derision to prosecutor Jim Garrison, and wasted Shaw's comfortable retirement savings. Garrison, the New Orleans district attorney, had arrested Shaw on March 1, 1967, announcing that he had solved the Kennedy case and that he would disprove the Warren Commission's conclusion that Oswald had acted alone in the Nov. 22, 1963, assassination. A New Orleans grand jury indicted Shaw on March 22, 1967. Long before Shaw eventually came to trial on Jan. 21, 1969, however, Garrison's case appeared to be discredited, and there were demands for a federal investigation.

At the time of his arrest, Shaw was in retirement at 54 after serving as managing director of the International Trade Mart, a nonprofit organization he had helped develop to promote trade through the port of New Orleans. He was comfortable in retirement, having done well in business, and his carriage-house home in the French Quarter was a model of restoration in a city with a weakness for past glories. Shaw was named the city's outstanding citizen in 1965. Self-educated (he did not go to college after graduating from a New Orleans high school at 15), Shaw had some success as a playwright, his works being performed principally by high-school and college groups.

The case against Shaw was the testimony of a handful of witnesses attempting to link him with Oswald, a pilot named David Ferrie, and, to a lesser extent, with Jack Ruby, who killed Oswald in the Dallas jail. The witnesses were to claim that Shaw met with Oswald and Ferrie on two occasions in New Orleans and that they formulated a plan to kill Kennedy during those meetings. Shaw insisted, however, that he had "never laid eyes" on Oswald and Ferrie. At the trial Garrison's three main witnesses were not convincing and cast doubt on their own reliability. Undaunted by the acquittal, Garrison two days later charged Shaw with perjury and, despite the fiasco, went on to win reelection to another term as district attorney. (J. E. I.)

SILLS, BEVERLY

It became official in Milan in April 1969: Beverly Sills (née Belle Silverman of Brooklyn) was the greatest living coloratura soprano and possibly one of the greatest ever. For years this had been a well-kept secret among patrons of the New York City Opera, but a performance of Rossini's rarely heard *The Siege of Corinth* at La Scala changed all that. Miss Sills sang so beautifully that the orchestra gave her a standing ovation during rehearsal.

Miss Sills, who was 39 in 1969, made her professional debut on radio at the age of 3 on "Uncle Bob's Rainbow House." Before entering adolescent retirement at 12, "Bubbles Silverman" was known to housewives across the country as "the nightingale of the mountains" on "Our Gal Sunday." Leaving soap opera for grand opera, she studied with Estelle Liebling, who had been Galli-Curci's coach, and made her debut with the New York City Opera in 1954.

During the next several years she developed an astonishingly broad repertoire. She regularly sang all three roles in *Tales of Hoffmann,* Cleopatra in Handel's *Julius Caesar,* Marguerite in *Faust,* Donna Anna in *Don Giovanni,* and the title roles in *La Traviata* and *Lucia di Lammermoor.* Once she sang Violetta 54 times in nine weeks on tour. "My voice was all right," she recalled, "but my feet were killing me."

But her fame properly rested on her dramatic skill, her stage presence, musicality, and her impeccable vocal precision. These talents—and the indefinable matter of being an incomparable interpreter of song—combined to make her the greatest active coloratura. That fact was attested by audiences around the world—everywhere, it seemed, but at New York's Metropolitan Opera. Rudolf Bing, major domo of the Met, conceded that "a number of distinguished singers" have not appeared there. Miss Sills shrugged. "The Met serves three purposes: It raises your fee outside, gives you a springboard and makes your aunts happy." Among the six highest paid performers in the world, Miss Sills did not need a springboard, and if she could find fulfillment outside Lincoln Center, her aunts would be just as pleased.

Critics wrote that Miss Sills's artistic depth increased after personal tragedies. She and her husband, financial writer Peter B. Greenough, had two children, a retarded son and a deaf daughter. (Ph. K.)

SITHOLE, NDABANINGI

The Rev. Ndabaningi Sithole, 48-year-old leader of the Zimbabwe African National Union (ZANU), was sentenced to six years' imprisonment in February 1969 for plotting the murder of the Rhodesian prime minister, Ian Smith, and two of his ministers. Sithole was found guilty of instigating this assassination plot from prison, where he had been detained under emergency regulations since November 1965.

A soft-spoken, determined Congregationalist minister, Sithole was born in 1920 in Matabeleland, Southern Rhodesia, the son of a builder. After a missionary education he completed his higher studies by correspondence courses. At the age of 35 he went to the Andover Newton Theological School at Newton Centre, Mass., where he studied for 3½ years. During this period he wrote *African Nationalism,* which won him considerable fame. He resisted the opportunity to become a U.S. citizen and returned home in 1958 to be ordained as a minister. He was also appointed principal of a primary school.

In 1960 Sithole decided to devote himself fully to politics as a champion of African majority rule for Southern Rhodesia, then a British colony. During the next four years he had more than 50 criminal charges of a political nature preferred against him. In 1963, becoming disillusioned with the existing nationalist party to which he belonged (the Zimbabwe African People's Union), he helped to form a rival liberation group of which he became president-general. Until the unilateral declaration of independence by the white minority in Rhodesia in late 1965, Sithole had been a firm advocate of nonviolent methods of political struggle; then his attitude showed some change. Despite his detention he succeeded by one means or another to encourage resistance to Ian Smith's regime. (Co. L.)

SMOTHERS BROTHERS

Tommy and Dickie Smothers, who beat "Bonanza"'s entire Cartwright clan to the draw in the battle for TV viewers, were dropped in 1969 by some nameless villain who shot them in the back from a CBS conference room. They presented an hour-long comedy, music, and variety show that was designed to appeal to students and young adults and to relate to minority groups. That, apparently, was what dis-

GIL FRIEDBERG—PIX FROM PUBLIX

Beverly Sills

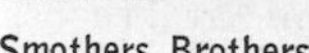

WIDE WORLD

Smothers Brothers

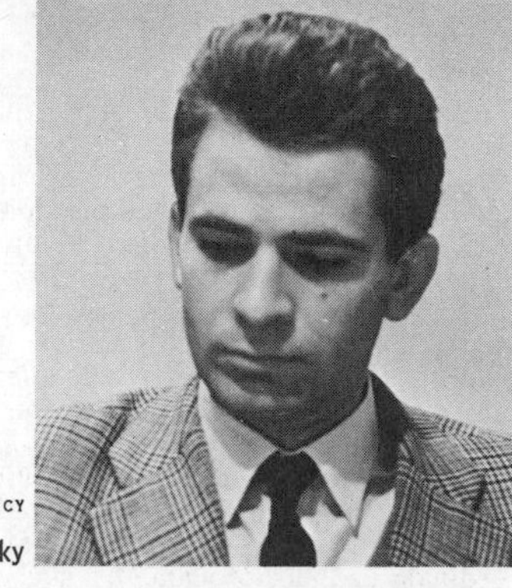

NOVOSTI PRESS AGENCY

Boris Spassky

turbed CBS, although the show attracted at least one-third of Sunday night viewers.

In March the network canceled a specific show, saying that the brothers had not presented the master tape in time for local affiliated stations to preview the program. This fact was disputed, but it appeared that CBS was most concerned about the content: folk singer Joan Baez dedicated a song to her jailed pacifist husband; a monologue by comedian Jackie Mason contained a slightly risqué line.

CBS said the Federal Communications Commission had prohibited some material. The FCC denied it. CBS said a lot of things—about the Senate, about responsibility to the public, about ratings. But it scratched the show for good when a program lampooned U.S. Sen. John O. Pastore (Dem., R.I.), who was investigating TV practices, and a comedian did an offbeat monologue on Jonah and the whale. The consensus among observers was that the network feared the show might offend somebody.

Tom, the spokesman for the pair, argued that the blandness CBS wanted was idiotic. After privately viewing the offending program, the *New York Times* critic said that "there could not be the slightest objection" to it. Nonetheless, the CBS cancellation was final. Since it came too late in the spring for the brothers to negotiate with another network for the fall season, they peddled the show themselves to an ad hoc network of nearly 100 independent stations. It was a success, and they planned later specials.

Thomas Bolyn Smothers III was born at Governors Island, N.Y., Feb. 2, 1937, and Richard was born there Nov. 20, 1939. Their father, an army officer, died a prisoner of the Japanese. After attending San Jose (Calif.) State College, the boys formed a trio that got bottom billing at San Francisco's Purple Onion. One night the main attraction, a flamenco dancer, could not go on, so Tom and Dick expanded their musical show with the dialogue that became their hallmark. (Ph. K.)

SPASSKY, BORIS

When, on April 14, 1969, Boris Spassky played the first game of his challenge chess match against the titleholder, Tigran Petrosian, he lost in a manner that seemed to show that nerves rather than skill were going to dictate the course of the match. Most people thought that once again Petrosian was going to gain the upper hand and retain his title. But Spassky had already shown in the series of Candidates' matches by which he had gained the right to a challenge match that his nerves were of iron and his powers of resilience enormous. By the end of the eighth game of the challenge he was leading by 5–3.

The match seemed as good as over. But Petrosian still had great stamina and fighting spirit and, though seven years older than his rival, he could hardly be termed an old man at age 40. He won both the 10th and 11th games and reduced his opponent's lead to a minimum. Spassky held on for five more draws, won the next game, and, after another draw, the 19th game. When the 23rd game was agreed a draw, Spassky had won the match and the world championship, for the next three years at least.

Looking back, it was clear that almost from the very start Spassky was marked out to be a world chess champion. He was born in Leningrad on Jan. 30, 1937, and by the age of 12 was classed as a candidate master. He was just 16 when he first played in an international tournament, at Bucharest, and tied for fourth place. He again drew world attention by becoming Junior World Champion in 1955.

Two factors were holding him back. He had to devote time and energy to his journalism studies at Leningrad University and his rise coincided with that of Mikhail Tal, the Riga genius who had outstripped Spassky between 1957 and 1960. Gradually, however, he won a series of Candidates' matches and beat Tal in the final, only to lose the challenge match in 1966 to Petrosian. The next three years saw a definite advance in Spassky's style until he was ready to take on Petrosian once again, this time with success.

Away from the chessboard Spassky was quiet yet cheerful and spoke excellent English. He was very much in the tradition of the great world champions, all of whom had varied intellectual gifts. (H. Go.)

STEINBERG, SAUL PHILLIP

"I always knew there was an Establishment," said Saul Steinberg, 30-year-old head of Leasco Data Processing Equipment Corp., "I just used to think I was part of it." In February 1969, however, Leasco's stock fell 34 points in two weeks of dumping by bank trust departments under what could only have been heavy pressure from their biggest Wall Street clients. Steinberg had assumed that his move to take over Chemical Bank, the sixth largest in the U.S., would be accepted as nothing more than a conglomerate expanding its holdings. Instead he was treated as any brash kid would be for moving in where he was not wanted.

Steinberg's methods also came to the attention of the City of London's financial Establishment in 1969 as Leasco moved to acquire for its computers the scientific and technical information—and the entrée into European markets—available at Pergamon Press Ltd., headed by Robert Maxwell (*q.v.*). What began as a friendly merger turned sour when Steinberg questioned Pergamon's profitability, and the City's persuasive powers failed to patch the deal together again. In the end, the combined voting power of stock held by Leasco and a band of insurance companies and pension funds forced Maxwell and his seven associates off the Pergamon board.

Steinberg had started Leasco in 1961 on $25,000 put up by his father. By 1969 the company was a conglomerate with profits of $35.6 million on revenues of $415 million. It had successfully coped with the major pitfall of computer leasing, outdated expensive equipment, by moving into other "problem-solving services," software, time-sharing, and consulting firms, which Steinberg began acquiring in 1967. He also began looking to Europe where less sophisticated competition provided greater growth potential. But the need for cash, which inspired Leasco's swift attack in 1968 on Reliance Insurance Co. of Philadelphia, and unrealized capital gains of $120 million brought Steinberg under the unfriendly eye of Wall Street.

Born on Aug. 13, 1939, in Brooklyn, Steinberg attended the Wharton School of Finance and Commerce (University of Pennsylvania) where he wrote a lengthy paper on the potentials of the computer leasing business. It was rejected as inadequate and mistaken.

STRAUSS, FRANZ JOSEF

As finance minister of West Germany until late October 1969, Franz Josef Strauss spent much of the year up to the federal election in September in the guise of defender of the mark. He was implacably opposed to revaluation, while the Social Democratic economics minister, Karl Schiller (*q.v.*), was in favour of it. This issue caused a wide rift between the two in the months preceding election day. The new government formed by the Social and the Free Democrats after the election favoured the adoption of Schiller's ideas, and the mark was revalued in October. Strauss was replaced as finance minister by Alex Möller, a Social Democrat.

Strauss, since 1961 chairman of the Bavarian Christian Social Union, a party closely affiliated with the Christian Democrats, was regarded as one of the most able men in West German political life, though many people considered him to be dangerous. A staunch European, he wished Europe to become a "third force" in the world with a nuclear capability of its own. But he often displayed nationalistic tendencies and was intolerant of minority opinions.

Strauss was elected to the Bundestag in 1949 and became minister without portfolio in the government of Konrad Adenauer in 1953, subsequently taking over the Ministry for Atomic Affairs. He succeeded Theodor Blank in 1956 as minister for defense and built the West German military into a modern army and one of the most important elements of NATO.

Strauss was forced to resign as minister in 1962 as a result of the so-called "Spiegel affair," in which members of the staff of the magazine *Der Spiegel* were arrested and their offices searched and occupied by federal police after the publication of a report about a NATO exercise. A court later ruled that there was no basis for charges against Strauss that he had misused his authority. In 1966 he was brought back into the government and as finance minister introduced a system of long-term financial planning.

Born in Munich, Sept. 6, 1915, Strauss studied history and classics at the University of Munich. He served in the German armed forces during World War II and was an officer on the eastern front. Before becoming a professional politician, he was a district magistrate. (N. Cr.)

STROUGAL, LUBOMIR

The new deputy first secretary of the Czechoslovak Communist Party, selected on June 3, 1969, was Lubomir Strougal, an unwavering Marxist who had successfully shifted to the winning side of each of Czechoslovakia's power struggles of recent years. Some observers believed that Strougal's appointment to the second most powerful post in Czechoslovakia meant that he would soon succeed Gustav Husak (*q.v.*) as first secretary; others saw it as an effort to bring the ambitious Strougal, a Czech, under direct control of Husak, a Slovak.

Strougal had been agriculture minister and later interior minister while Antonin Novotny was president and party leader. In 1965, as Novotny came under increasing criticism for his Stalinist policies, he switched to a job in the party secretariat and in February 1967 was appointed chairman of a committee on living standards. During the liberalization effort of 1968 Strougal rejoined the government as a deputy premier and chairman of the Supreme Economic Council.

After the Soviet-led invasion of Czechoslovakia in August 1968, Strougal returned to the secretariat. In November 1968, prior to the reorganization of Czechoslovakia into a federation of two semiautonomous Czech and Slovak republics, he was given the post of chairman of the bureau for the management of party work in the Czech lands of Bohemia and Moravia. The new bureau had been created to counterbalance the enhanced position the Slovak Communist Party would have in the new federation.

Strougal quickly transformed the new post into a personal power base. He began a purge of the liberals in the lower levels of the Czech party organizations and was soon considered to be Moscow's choice as Alexander Dubcek's successor. The day of his appointment as deputy first secretary also brought an announcement of the purge of the last major liberal stronghold under his authority, the Prague city organization. The next day Strougal joined Czechoslovakia's delegation to the World Conference of Communist and Workers' Parties in Moscow.

Born on Oct. 19, 1924, in Veseli-nad-Luznici, Strougal graduated as a doctor of law from Prague's Charles University. A Communist Party member from 1945, he was only 35 when he made his first judicious shift from regional party organizer to agriculture minister in 1959. (K. Sm.)

SUENENS, LÉON JOSEF CARDINAL

Cardinal Suenens, primate of Belgium, was already well known from his work at the second Vatican Council as a reformer and an enthusiastic exponent of the doctrine of episcopal "collegiality." The development of his ideas in his book *Coresponsibility in the Church* (1968), further clarified in an interview (May 1969) with the editor of *Informations Catholiques Internationales,* made him a figure of controversy as the highest so-called "rebel" in the Roman Catholic Church. The interview brought a letter of protest from several cardinals of the Roman Curia, but he was openly supported by some cardinals and bishops and by such leading theologians as Hans Küng. In October 1969 he repeated many of his criticisms in Pope Paul's presence at the synod of Bishops held in Rome.

Cardinal Suenens' views stemmed from his theology of the church, which he saw as a dynamic society, the "people of God." Within the church, dialogue must take place on all levels—pope with bishops, bishops with priests and people. Yet the cardinal, in stressing this broad-based view, never suggested that the church was, or could be, a democracy; it remains a monarchy whose absolute ruler is Christ, from whom (and not from below) the bishops receive their mandate, and for whose exclusive service every priest exists. He asserted, indeed, that the papal title of head of the universal church is unique, possessed by divine right by every successor of Peter, but he followed the Pauline doctrine of the interrelation of the members of the body (I Cor. 12) in stressing that the primacy cannot be exercised in separation from the bishops.

Born in Brussels on July 6, 1904, Cardinal Suenens studied for the priesthood in Rome, was ordained on Sept. 4, 1927, and lectured in philosophy at the Malines seminary (1930–39). Consecrated bishop (1945), he was appointed archbishop of Malines-Brussels and primate of Belgium in December 1961, and was made a cardinal in March 1962. He helped prepare the agenda for Vatican II and several of the council documents, notably that *On the Church in the Modern World.* (S. Mu.)

SUSANN, JACQUELINE

Jacqueline Susann was a writer. First she wrote a little book called *Every Night, Josephine* about how she walked her dog. Then she wrote a big book called *Valley of the Dolls,* about the insane world of glamorous show-biz people. The "dolls," while possibly a pun, were the pills these poor celebs took. It might have been called *Vale of the Dollars,* for the book sold ten million copies and the film adaptation grossed $20 million. *Publishers' Weekly* reported that it had sold more copies than any other novel published in the 20th century.

In 1969 she put together *The Love Machine,* a Rube Goldberg construction of unction and sexual innuendos about some cookie cutter characters in television land. It topped the best-seller list and was sold to the movies for a record $1.5 million.

As *Harper's* observed, "There is a built-in audience of ten million for every book she turns out." Miss Susann can tell a story in a simple manner that draws the reader along the way spaghetti leads meat sauce. Furthermore, she writes for a specific audience: *"Valley,"* she said, "showed that a woman in a ranch house with three kids had a better life than what happened up there at the top."

Twenty years earlier, the producers of radio soap operas suggested that "20 million housewives can't be wrong." Miss Susann agreed: "Money is applause." Some unwary critics have tried to make her blush over this kind of thought. During one of her frequent TV appearances, an interviewer asked, "Don't you ever wake up in the middle of the night and realize you haven't done anything that is really artistic?" Miss Susann shot back, "Do you wake up and think you're not Huntley-Brinkley?"

Miss Susann admitted to 42 years, although old theatre programs credited her with nonjuvenile roles on Broadway 30 years earlier. She was once, in fact, the Best Dressed Actress on TV and the girl in the Schiffli embroidery ads. *Who's Who of American Women* described her as follows: "Susann, Jacqueline, author Valley of the Dolls. Address: care Director of Public Relations, Random House, 457 Madison Avenue, N.Y.C., 10022*." The asterisk signifies that the published biography could not be verified. (Ph. K.)

TINBERGEN, JAN

The chairman of the United Nations Committee on Development Planning, Jan Tinbergen of the Netherlands School of Economics, shared the first Nobel Prize for Economic Science in 1969 with a Norwegian colleague, Ragnar Frisch (*q.v.*).

Both men were honoured for their de-

COURTESY, SIMON & SCHUSTER

Jacqueline Susann

velopment of econometrics, which is the mathematical approach to economic theory and a highly systematized approach to applied economics. The discipline they evolved had enabled economists of various specialties to replace vague, conceptual tools with concrete, statistical elements. By making economic analysis a more precise process, they enabled colleagues to make more accurate evaluations of fiscal trends and more cogent predictions of future developments.

An example of the econometric technique was Tinbergen's working model of the Netherlands' economic environment. This incredibly complex system included 27 equations with more than 50 variables representing aspects of the Dutch economy. Since it enabled researchers to evaluate various approaches to economic problems, it had been useful in making short-term analyses as well as in areas of political and economic planning.

In the late 1930s, when he was economic adviser to the League of Nations, Tinbergen studied the economic development of the United States between World War I and the depression. This work had been credited with providing "much of the raw material for later development of business cycle theory and for the application of methods of economic stabilization."

Tinbergen was born in The Hague on April 12, 1903, and studied at the University of Leiden. In 1933 he became professor at the Netherlands School of Economics. He also served on the Netherlands' Central Bureau of Statistics and for years was director of the Central Planning Bureau. He served on the boards of various private corporations and advised a number of governments as well as his own. (PH. K.)

VELASCO ALVARADO, JUAN

Maj. Gen. Juan Velasco Alvarado, president of the revolutionary government of Peru, seized control of that South American nation at the head of a military coup that ousted the elected president, Fernando Belaúnde Terry, on Oct. 3, 1968. Six days later Velasco electrified the Western Hemisphere by announcing the expropriation of $200 million worth of the properties of the U.S.-owned International Petroleum Co. (IPC), an act that caused a deterioration of relations between the U.S. and Peru.

The expropriation prompted the U.S. to begin negotiations with Peru in an effort to obtain compensation for the nationalized properties, but the thinly veiled threat of invocation of the Hickenlooper Amendment by the U.S. failed to bring any move from Velasco to pay for the seized properties. The amendment requires that all economic aid be terminated unless appropriate action is being taken toward achieving compensation.

At the same time, Peruvian naval units continued periodic seizures of U.S. tuna boats fishing within the 200 mi. of Pacific Ocean claimed by Peru as sovereign territory. Relations between Lima and Washington were also not helped by Peru's refusal to permit New York Gov. Nelson A. Rockefeller to visit the nation as part of his mission for U.S. Pres. Richard Nixon in search of a new U.S. policy toward Latin America.

Velasco's government attracted wide Peruvian public support with its seizure of the IPC properties. The move appealed to the intense nationalism growing in Peru as well as other Latin nations in the second half of the 1960s.

Velasco, who was responsive to the sentiments of a neonationalistic group of younger officers, was a cool professional soldier who had shown little interest in politics. He was born June 16, 1909, in Piura, and became a military cadet in 1928 as soon as he was graduated from secondary school at the Liceo San Miguel. From that time he rose steadily in the military ranks. (J. A. O'L.)

WEBSTER, RONALD

Described (March 25, 1969) by Anthony Lee, then British administrator in Anguilla, as having done great service to the island by "putting it on the map," Ronald Webster, who became Anguilla's de facto president (February 1969) following the secession (June 1967) of the West Indian island from the newly established Associated State of St. Kitts-Nevis-Anguilla, remained an enigmatic and highly volatile figure. On March 12, 1969, he violently rejected proposals brought to the island by William Whitlock, a British envoy, and the threatening behaviour of his followers caused Whitlock to leave Anguilla. Whitlock subsequently declared that Webster seemed dominated and intimidated by U.S. businessman Jack Holcomb (who was deported from Anguilla on March 20, following the arrival there of British paratroopers on March 19).

After the British paratroopers landed on Anguilla, Webster went to New York City (March 23) to seek UN support against Britain, and declared that he would have been arrested had he remained in Anguilla. Anthony Lee denied this, and Webster returned on March 27. Following talks with Lord Caradon, Britain's permanent representative at the UN, an agreement was announced by which a British representative would govern Anguilla in consultation with a seven-man council originally set up by Webster in July 1968; and Britain gave an assurance that Anguilla would not be forced into any political association it did not desire. Back in New York, Webster then claimed that the British had double-crossed him; but in Anguilla on April 26 he seemed happier, and favourably disposed toward the new British administrator, John Cumber.

Said to be 53 years old, an Anguillan-born businessman and property owner, Webster appeared adept at concealing details of his career. As of 1969 a Seventh-day Adventist lay preacher, he was thought to have favoured other sects in the past, and to have served at some time in the Dutch armed forces. His emotional reactions and rapid changes of opinion gave weight to the view that, possibly genuinely anxious for the island's welfare and certainly politically naïve, he had been the tool of other men. His issue of postage stamps (1967–68) brought considerable revenue to Anguilla, and he later spoke of issuing a set of coins. (S. MU.)

WILLIAMS, THEODORE SAMUEL (TED)

Organized baseball observed its 100th anniversary in 1969, and it was quite appropriate that, in that same milestone year, Ted Williams returned to the major leagues. After an absence from baseball of eight years, Williams, who repeatedly had insisted he would never want to be a manager, signed a five-year contract to manage the Washington Senators, perennial American League tailenders.

Almost immediately there was speculation that Williams would find managing a totally frustrating experience, as many star players had before him. But Williams succeeded. The Senators, under his prodding, finished with an 86–76 won-and-lost record, the first time in 17 years they had won more games than they had lost. For his efforts, Williams was selected as the American League's Manager of the Year.

Ted Williams was born on Aug. 30, 1918, in San Diego, Calif. In his autobiography, *My Turn at Bat*, a 1969 best seller, Williams told of his youth and of his mother who "had me out with the Salvation Army . . . , and, oh, how I hated that. . . . I'd stand behind the bass drum, trying to hide so none of my friends would see me."

Williams signed his first baseball contract at the age of 17 with the San Diego Padres of the Pacific Coast League. A year later he was purchased by the Boston Red Sox who paid the Padres $25,000 and also gave them five players in exchange.

"PARIS MATCH" FROM PICTORIAL PARADE

Léon Josef Cardinal Suenens

PICTORIAL PARADE

Juan Velasco Alvarado

Williams' claim as one of baseball's best batters was certified in 1941, his third season in the majors, when he hit .406, the first player to hit .400 since 1923. When he retired in 1960, after hitting a home run in his last time at bat, he had compiled a lifetime batting average of .344; had twice won the Triple Crown (best batting average, most home runs, and most runs batted in); and ranked third in home runs with 521, trailing only Babe Ruth and Jimmy Foxx. He was elected to Baseball's Hall of Fame in 1966.

Williams' batting achievements were even more remarkable because he twice left the diamond to serve as a U.S. Marine Corps flyer—in World War II and in the Korean War. He lost five years of baseball because of his service time; many sportswriters estimated that he might have hit as many as 700 home runs (Ruth hit a record 714) if his career had not been interrupted.

(Je. Ho.)

WILLIAMSON, NICOL

Although the view of *The Times*'s critic that Nicol Williamson was the greatest British actor of his generation could be disputed by not a few rival claimants, there was no question that his performance of the title role in *Hamlet,* which Tony Richardson directed on the open stage of London's Round House and which later toured the United States, won him the highest praise everywhere. It could be said that 1969 was the year in which this Scottish actor had arrived.

Born in Hamilton, Scot., on Sept. 14, 1938, Williamson spent his theatrical apprenticeship from the age of 21 at the Dundee Repertory Theatre, working with director Anthony Page. He first attracted critical notice playing important roles in the Royal Shakespeare Company's experimental season at London's Arts Theatre in 1962, and he joined the Royal Court Theatre in the following year. He appeared in several plays, including some by Shakespeare, and scored his first big hit as the egregious Bill Maitland in John Osborne's *Inadmissible Evidence* in 1964. Directed by Page, this play was also made by the same director into a film that won its star universal acclaim in 1969.

Williamson's other film hits also fell into this period. They were (after the earlier *The Bofors Gun*) *Laughter in the Dark* and *The Reckoning,* while the filmed version of Richardson's *Hamlet* was due to be shown in 1970. Williamson also formed his own company to make *Macbeth* in 1970. Among his other memorable stage roles at the Royal Court were the leads in *Kelly's Eye, A Cuckoo in the Nest,* and *The Ginger Man.* In performances at other theatres, his Vladimir in *Waiting for Godot* and Poprishchin in *The Diary of a Madman* called for remarkable feats of physical endurance.

(O. Tr.)

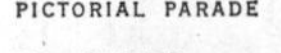
PICTORIAL PARADE

Nicol Williamson

YAHYA KHAN, AGHA MUHAMMAD

When former Pres. Muhammad Ayub Khan bowed to public pressure and resigned his office on March 25, 1969, Gen. Agha Muhammad Yahya Khan assumed the presidency of Pakistan. Ayub Khan's resignation came about amid near anarchy after nearly ten months of serious riots and public discontent with corruption and living standards. At a meeting called by Ayub Khan just before he resigned, commanders of the Air Force and Navy swore loyalty to Yahya Khan. The new president imposed martial law immediately, and was not expected to lift it until after the national elections, which he set for Oct. 5, 1970.

Yahya Khan indicated that he would not be a candidate in the 1970 elections. In a broadcast made March 26, the day following his assumption of power, he said, "My sole aim in imposing martial law is to protect life, liberty, and property of the people and put the administration back on the rails."

The new president concentrated on restoring public order. He made no major changes in foreign policy, continuing Ayub Khan's triangular arrangement based upon friendship with the United States, the Soviet Union, and China. Pakistan also continued its role as a member of the Commonwealth of Nations, the Central Treaty Organization (CENTO), and the Southeast Asia Treaty Organization (SEATO), acting as an observer in the latter.

Yahya Khan was born on Feb. 4, 1917, in Peshawar, on the northwest frontier of then British India, into the historically important Kizilbash family, whose name meant "red turbans." The family was descended from the elite soldiery of Nadir Shah, the Persian ruler who crippled the Mogul Empire and conquered Delhi early in the 18th century.

Yahya Khan was educated at Punjab University and the Indian Military Academy at Dehru Dun. During World War II he served in the Middle East and Italy. When India was partitioned in 1947, he organized the Pakistani Staff College. He became brigadier general at the age of 34, major general at 40, and lieutenant general at 49. In 1958 he played a leading role in the coup that brought Ayub Khan to power. Yahya Khan succeeded Gen. Muhammad Musa as commander in chief of the Pakistan Army on March 29, 1966.

(J. F. Ba.)

WIDE WORLD

Samuel W. Yorty

YORTY, SAMUEL W.

On April 1, 1969, Los Angeles Mayor Sam Yorty's bid for a third term seemed doomed. He had run second in a field of 14 candidates with 183,000 votes, only 26% of the total. Black city councilman Tom Bradley had easily topped the list with 42%. But 56 days later, the scrappy maverick Democrat upset Bradley in a runoff election, having convinced an additional 264,000 Angelenos to vote for him.

Yorty's foes claimed he frightened rather than convinced the voters. Bradley himself accused Yorty of making "a blatant appeal to racial fears and prejudices." Yorty denied this, but his campaign included charges that the black councilman would "no doubt" bring black militants into his administration. In a period when TV news shows were filled with scenes of campus violence, Yorty accused Bradley, a former policeman, of being antipolice.

Yorty's victory, followed shortly by the election of a city detective as mayor of Minneapolis and by New York Mayor John Lindsay's primary loss to a conservative state senator campaigning on a law-and-order platform, was seen by some as proof that 1969 was truly "the year of the cop" in U.S. politics. This analysis failed to hold up in later state and municipal elections, however.

Yorty's success was the latest "up" in an up-and-down political career spanning more than three decades. Elected to the California assembly in 1936 as a crusading liberal, he alienated some of his support when he sponsored a resolution setting up a state committee on un-American activities. A number of election losses followed, but in 1949 he won a special election for his old assembly seat and, the following year, was elected to the U.S. House of Representatives. After losing two bids for the U.S. Senate, he gained the Los Angeles mayoralty in 1961, even though he had lost the support of Democratic leaders by endorsing Richard M. Nixon in the 1960 presidential race.

Born in Lincoln, Neb., Oct. 1, 1909, Yorty moved to Los Angeles shortly after graduating from high school. He worked days and went to prelaw and law schools at night at Southwestern University, the University of Southern California, and the University of California Extension.

(T. J. F.)

Biological Sciences

Opening the new department of molecular biology at Edinburgh University in November 1968, Nobel laureate Jacques Monod foresaw that the "impatient young men" of 10 to 20 years hence would be searching for a new integral approach to biology in which organisms would be described as wholes rather than simply in terms of their component molecules. Monod's concern was echoed by others, including René Dubos in *So Human an Animal.* Organisms as wholes have always been the central concern of classical biology, and the degree to which the newer technological and the older classical biologies might converge toward the future "meta-biology" (Monod's term) would be a useful index of the progress of the science in coming years.

In 1969 several popular lines of research were leading in this direction. Progressing from its earlier preoccupation with bacteria, viruses, and the genetic code, molecular biology increasingly influenced all aspects of cell biology. Nucleic acid and protein specificities played an increasing role in relation to taxonomy and evolution, and R. J. Britten's and E. H. Davidson's ideas concerning sensor, integrator, and productor genes promised to rejuvenate many branches of the life sciences. While work on the mechanism of hormone action and on the roles of proteins and nucleic acids in nerve action and in the higher functions of the brain marked significant advances in understanding the integrative mechanisms in higher animals, the possibility of a breakthrough into the previously baffling problems of the nonlocalized functions of the brain, such as perception of form, came with Dennis Gabor's suggestion of a model based on the hologram and a subsequent alternative model proposed by D. J. Willshaw and others. (*See* MOLECULAR BIOLOGY.)

The two way flow of discoveries and ideas between medicine and biology continued to benefit both sciences. Research in immunology (greatly stimulated by the demands of transplant surgery) and cancer influenced many aspects of cell biology; developments of surgical prostheses required intensive research upon a broad spectrum of problems relating to cartilage, articular mechanisms, etc.; discovery of the mode of action of rifampicin (a modification of fungal rifomycin) on bacterial RNA polymerase and on vaccinia virus was of importance equally to the biologist and to the pathologist.

Evolutionary studies benefited from the very precise dating of events during the Pleistocene resulting from studies of the changes of sea levels, especially in the Atlantic and Baltic. D. R. Pilbeam's work on *Ramapithecus* and R. Leakey's discoveries of Omo I, II, and III in Ethiopia revised the dating of the origins of the hominids and of *Homo sapiens,* respectively. Important discoveries in the Precambrian included a 1,600,000,000-year-old organism from Australia very similar to the present-day alga *Eucapsis.* Even more remarkable, a living microorganism was found in Wales apparently identical with *Kakabekia umbellata,* previously known from the 1,900,000,000-year-old Gunflint deposits near Lake Superior. The special interest of this is that the living organism was found in an environment of low oxygen and high ammonia such as is believed to have been characteristic of the times before the evolution of photosynthetic plants. The spectacular Apollo and Mariner flights, however, strengthened the biologists' traditional skepticism about extraterrestrial life.

UPI COMPIX

Gerald M. Edelman of Rockefeller University displays a model of the chemical structure of the key molecule of immunity. The discovery was announced before the Federation of American Scientists for Experimental Biology, April 14, 1969.

The integral approach was strongly marked in matters of conservation. While the publication of the *Red Book* by James Fisher and others gave an authoritative account of the numerous animals and plants in imminent danger of extermination, the main interest centred less on individual species than on habitats and indeed on the whole terrestrial environment. Projects for the exploitation of the seabed for industrial and military purposes, with the consequent danger of permanent damage to this as yet relatively virgin part of the biosphere, led to a demand for a comprehensive international oceanographic program comparable to the current International Biological Program and the International Hydrological Decade. Several shocking and costly cases of environmental damage by pollution (*e.g.,* the Rhine), destructive exploitation, or acts of war forced the importance of environmental conservation on the public and its statesmen. Consequences of this were the banning in various countries of all use of DDT and UN Secretary-General U Thant's characteristically outspoken memorandum proposing an international conference on the human environment. Events of the year, including growing concern with population problems, were rapidly sweeping human ecology to the centre of the hurly-burly of world politics, and the dominant emphasis on this subject at the rebel students' Free University in California raised hopes that the impatient young men of the day were aware of this.

(H. SA.)

Botany. The 11th International Botanical Congress, held at the University of Washington, stressed the importance of the application of botanical knowledge and methods to the survival and well-being of the human race, particularly in the areas of nutrition, conservation, and pollution. A symposium on the world food supply stressed the urgency of the need to accelerate food production and forecast severe consequences within 15 to 20 years if present trends in population growth and food production continued.

Welcome contrasts to these sombre predictions were reports on advances in food research. The use of plants as sources of protein rather than carbohydrate was outlined and methods of extracting leaf protein were described. From leaf juices, the protein could be coagulated and used for human consumption, and the remaining fluids and fibre utilized for growing microorganisms or as cattle fodder.

Remarkable success in the breeding of new strains

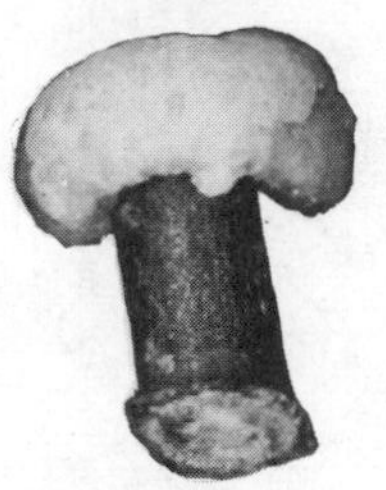

Top, aspen shoot produced artificially from a tiny plug of unspecialized, nonsexual tree cells. A section of aspen stem (centre) produces a mass of undifferentiated cells (bottom) when treated with a complex chemical mixture of nutrients and growth hormones.

COURTESY, THE INSTITUTE OF PAPER CHEMISTRY

of rice was reported from the Rice Research Institute in the Philippines. One strain, IR-8, was reported to yield between 6,000 and 8,000 kg. per ha., compared with an average yield of 1,500 kg. per ha. from the varieties previously grown in tropical Asia. Further improvements in IR-8 were expected to give better cooking, eating, and milling properties and increased resistance to insect and disease attack. The breeding of a higher protein content into rice was also shown to be a possibility for the near future.

Regarding the potential food value of microbial cultures, it was shown that the yield of protein and dietary energy per unit area for algae grown under controlled conditions in ponds could surpass traditional crop plants by 10- to 50-fold. Further, the amount of water needed per unit of protein was similarly increased, and the productivity per worker was up 50- to 100-fold. Capital investment was one-fifth of that for rice, but the power requirement per unit of protein remained about the same as for conventional crops.

The use of microorganisms that could grow on cheap or otherwise waste materials was also discussed. *Hydrogenomonas,* when grown on hydrogen and oxygen (produced electrolytically), carbon dioxide, and urea, needed only 5 to 8% of the electricity required to grow *Chlorella* photosynthetically; *Pseudomonas* or *Methanomonas* could be grown using methane (from natural gas) or methanol as a carbon source; and yeasts grown on normal alkane or gas oil were being grown commercially for cattle feed. It was pointed out that protein from microbial sources could not be expected to replace traditional human foods in the near future since problems of palatability and digestibility were considerable. *Hydrogenomonas* cells, for example, produced severe gastrointestinal upsets in humans.

In molecular botany, progress was reported in understanding the regulation of gene expression in higher plants. Whether the information encoded in a gene is translated or not was known to be dependent on the presence or absence of histone proteins on the chromosomal deoxyribonucleic acid (DNA). Histones, however, were known to attach nonspecifically to DNA and the mechanism for turning on one particular gene was unknown. In 1969 a new class of nucleic acid, chromosomal RNA, was described that could be extracted from chromatin and had the property of hybridizing with part of the chromosomal DNA. RNA could be synthesized in vitro from native chromatin (DNA + histones + chromosomal RNA). After removal of the chromosomal RNA, transcribed RNA could still be made from the DNA template, but it was found to be different from that made by native chromatin. When the chromosomal RNA was added back, however, native-type RNA could again be synthesized.

Another topic that attracted wide interest was the biology of plant membranes, in particular the membranes of plastids. Enrichment of the special pigment molecules that transfer light energy (in the form of excited electrons) to the other components of the photosynthetic system was reported to be accomplished by the action of detergent on membranes of photosynthetic bacteria and on higher plant plastids. The majority of pigment molecules served as light harvesting arrays, passing the collected energy to these reaction centres. In the case of *Rhodospirillum rubrum,* the reaction centre units appeared in the electron microscope as rods of 50 Å by 230 Å, while in higher plants the reaction centres of photosystem I were 80 Å by 140 Å.

The structure of plastid and other membranes as revealed by freeze-fracturing and freeze-etching, a topic of some controversy over the past few years, was partially resolved. It was generally agreed that the particles seen on membranes by these techniques were located on the inside surfaces of the double-layered membrane sheets. From the current theory of the mechanism of freeze-fracturing, it should have been possible to find indentations on the opposing side of a membrane corresponding to the positions of the large particles. No matching indentation sites were reported, however, and it was proposed that a reappraisal of the freeze-fracturing mechanism would have to be made to accommodate this observation.

A further feature of membrane research that was much discussed was the mechanism by which energy in the form of electron transport was converted into chemical energy. Whether this energy conversion took the form of a chemical reaction, a chemosmotic effect via membranes, or was caused by changes in membrane conformation was vigorously debated.

(C. L. F. W.)

Zoology. An advance occurring in the field of animal behaviour in 1969 was the fully documented report of the homing tendency in deer mice (*Peromyscus maniculatus*) made by Jacques Bovet of the University of Calgary, Alta. Bovet displaced the deer mice far from their homesites and then followed the trails they made in the snow. The mice followed a homeward-oriented route, rather than a random one. As was to be expected, however, there was some zigzagging of the route and they ended up covering more than twice the displacement distance to their home. Earlier studies in which mice had greater distances to travel had not disclosed this feature. Also, Bovet's mice may have been highly motivated, in view of the snow and intense cold prevailing during his study. How the mice make their way homeward remained unknown, but visual clues were thought not to be the primary factors, because of the constantly changing environment in the tests.

It had been assumed that responses controlled by the autonomic nervous system were not capable of modification by learning. N. E. Miller and his co-workers at the Rockefeller University, New York City, however, were showing that such responses can be modified by learning, provided an appropriate experimental animal was used. They used rats whose skeletal responses had been paralyzed by curare, so that the effects they observed could not have been the result of increased neuromuscular activity. The responses that were produced by providing appropriate rewards were increased or decreased heart rate, relaxation or contraction of intestinal musculature, increased urine formation by the kidney, and changes in gastric blood flow or blood pressure.

In a typical experiment, if a rat showed a slight increase in its heart rate, it would be rewarded by electrical stimulation of certain areas of the brain known to produce pleasure to the animal. This was then followed by a further increase in heart rate, which was called instrumental learning. If progressively larger changes were required before reward, Miller's group was able to obtain an increase in heart rate averaging 20% in 90 minutes.

The salivation rate of thirsty dogs was also modified by a method such as this, showing that the responses of the animal used by Pavlov for conditioned reflex work could be modified. Curare could not be used in the salivation experiments because of its strong ability to enhance salivation itself. Preliminary work with humans indicated that they too are capable of instrumental learning, although curarization was not possible.

A striking finding in vertebrate zoology occurred in the description by D. Bardack and R. Zangerl of the first fossil lampreys, which were found in Middle Pennsylvanian strata in northeastern Illinois. Some six specimens were examined and a new species, *Mayomyzon pieckoensis,* was named. The fossils lay in a lateral position, with their eyes, gill baskets, livers, and intestinal tracts preserved in the form of dark stains. The cartilaginous elements of the cranial skeleton could also be discerned and were comparable to those found in present-day lampreys, although they differed in relative size and position. *Mayomyzon,* however, reached only one-quarter to one-half the length of comparable stages of living species.

This showed that lampreys had not changed much since the time of the fossils, some 275 million years ago. It might even be possible to prove that they evolved neotenically from the larvae of ostracoderm or preostracoderm fishes. Because the cyclostome fishes (lampreys and hagfishes) are the only living descendants of the most primitive vertebrates, the extinct ostracoderms, this discovery filled an important gap in the fossil record of living vertebrates. Since *Mayomyzon* lacks hagfish characteristics, the hagfishes must have had a separate pre-Pennsylvanian ancestry.

In the field of classification, systematists were becoming increasingly aware that their work was a part of population biology. By studying the diversity among animals, systematists in the past had mainly tried to answer evolutionary and genetic questions. More recently they developed methods of classifying animals for other purposes: numerical (phenetic) classifications, based on relative degrees of similarity and ignoring evolutionary history and, at the other extreme, the cladistic classifications, based on assumed lines of descent while ignoring similarity. Most systematists used both approaches. In addition, there was an increase in the belief that there is value in making numerous classifications as alternate ways of summarizing the same information about the animals, even though it was agreed that there can only be one classification to which the names of animals could be applied. (R. R. No.)

Entomology. In 1969 growing alarm over the accumulation of organic insecticides in the environment prompted Sweden to announce that DDT would be prohibited for agricultural use, barring emergencies, for a two-year trial period and that dieldrin and aldrin would be banned entirely beginning in 1970. Denmark banned DDT, and the U.S. ordered an end to its use in residential areas and planned a virtual halt to all use by 1971. These insecticides persist on vegetation and in soils. When exposed to sunlight, dieldrin and aldrin are converted to "photoisomers" that were reported by M. A. Q. Khan and associates at Rutgers University, New Brunswick, N.J., to have increased toxicity to insects and vertebrates. Ingested DDT and dieldrin accumulate in animal tissues and had caused death or decreased reproduction of wildlife. Perhaps even more ominously, DDT had been reported in Antarctic penguins, thousands of miles from the nearest points of application.

The very persistence of such insecticides, while alarming to conservationists, was nevertheless a boon to farmers. In the U.K. where, as in many other countries, there are some restrictions on the use of insecticides, it was estimated that the outright banning of DDT, dieldrin, and heptachlor would add £1 million to the annual costs of agricultural production to cover alternative methods of pest control.

New methods of insect control that would not contaminate the environment with materials toxic to other forms of life continued to be the aim of many research programs throughout the world. In 1968 attention had focused on "hormone-mimetic" compounds that interfere with the growth and maturation of insects, but by late 1968 and in 1969, the most often reported advances came in the field of "pheromones," substances that are released by insects and affect the behaviour of other individuals of the same species. Manipulation of these chemical communicators could be the means of controlling insect populations or their activities by inhibiting mating, trapping the insects, or repelling them from produce.

D. Schneider and U. Seibt of West Germany's Max-Planck-Institut für Verhaltensphysiologie reported that males of some butterflies dust females with secretions emanating from extrusible, brush-like "hairpencils." The dust contains an aphrodisiac and another factor that acts as a glue, causing the dust to adhere to the female. Males deprived of either factor, although capable of mating, were unable to induce females to accept them.

One or both sexes of a number of insects were now known to produce attractants by which one sex finds the other. Some males also produce a pheromone that is transferred during mating and tends to deter other males from mating subsequently with the same female. In 1968 this phenomenon had been found to occur in the housefly by T. S. Adams and D. R. Nelson of the U.S. Department of Agriculture; in 1969 it was also reported by G. M. Happ of New York University to occur in adults of the mealworm, *Tenebrio molitor.* A similar pheromone produced by the malarial mosquito, *Aedes aegypti,* was found by M. S. Fuchs and associates of the University of Notre Dame to be a protein, and was called by them a monogamy pheromone.

A number of workers had reported in recent years that "alarm" pheromones are secreted by some ants, sucking bugs, and beetles when attacked. These highly

A one by one-half inch mouselike zoological mystery from West Pakistan. The British Museum named the creature "Salpingotus michaelis" in honour of its owner, Michael Fitzgibbon of England. The animal is thought to be a type of jerboa (a small rodent from African deserts with great jumping powers).

"LONDON DAILY EXPRESS" FROM PICTORIAL PARADE

volatile substances cause other individuals to disperse. Conversely, G. B. Pitman and associates of the Boyce Thompson Institute for Plant Research, Inc., Yonkers, N.Y., investigated the "aggregation" pheromones of scolytid beetles that attack pine trees. They reported that both sexes of four species of *Dendroctonus* produced in the hind gut up to four of the same five volatile alicyclic compounds that in various combinations and proportions acted as aggregation pheromones. Similarly, L. Barton-Brown and associates of Australia's Commonwealth Scientific and Industrial Research Organization (CSIRO) reported that egg-laying females of the blowfly *Lucilia cuprina* produce a pheromone that attracts other females. Moreover, contact with other flies tended to increase the number of eggs laid.

An entomological conference at the Agricultural University at Wageningen in the Netherlands was the second international conference on "Insect and Host-plant" in 20 years. Experts from many nations discussed the stimuli that enable insects to find their natural food plants, the factors that limit their choice of food, the factors that make some varieties of plant resistant to the feeding of insects, and the use that plant breeders can make of such factors to develop resistant commercial varieties.

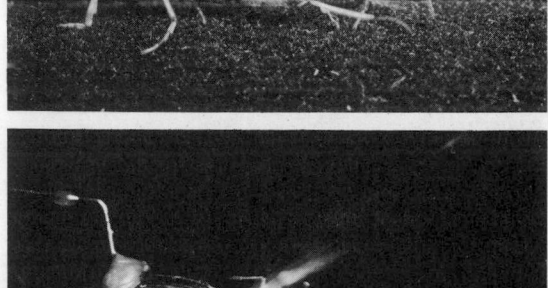

Bombardier beetle repels an ant with a blast of boiling-hot noxious spray. Cornell University scientists recently deciphered the mechanism by which the beetle stores and ejects the mixture of hydroquinones, hydrogen peroxide, and enzymes that comprises the spray.

COURTESY, T. EISNER AND D. ANESHANSLEY, CORNELL UNIVERSITY

Recent advances outlined at the conference included reports that caterpillars that have a range of possible food plants rapidly become conditioned to the species on which they first feed, and thereafter tend to reject other plants within the range. Such induced food preferences were even found to influence the choice by mature females of the plants on which they laid their eggs. A number of naturally occurring "phagostimulant" compounds that elicit feeding responses were reported. Some were of no nutritional value to the insect, while others, such as sugars and amino acids, were of direct importance. The plants on which insects settle and feed were not determined by attractive substances alone. Some plant compounds were actively repellent to some insects, although acceptable or even attractive to others.

At the same time, plants reacted to the feeding of insects by producing toxic phenolic compounds. One theory outlined at the conference sought to relate the evolution of feeding preferences in plant-sucking bugs to the production by the insects of salivary detoxifying systems that, in some instances, had had secondary effects on plant growth and were basically the cause of galls and other malformations of plants.

An unusual item of interest reported in 1969 was the finding by P. Harris and associates of the Canada Department of Agriculture that some bloodsucking mosquitoes can survive and reproduce in the absence of mammalian sources by feeding on the body fluids of caterpillars. These authors speculate that mosquitoes may thus be able to transmit diseases to other insects, just as they do to man and other vertebrates.

(P. W. Mi.)

Ornithology. The discovery of a new and striking swallow, the white-eyed river martin, named *Pseudochelidon sirintarae,* was reported in 1969 from a lake in central Thailand. The only other known member of the genus occurs in western central Africa.

With regard to another unique species, the great albatrosses, Lance Tickell showed that the royal and the wandering albatrosses, almost alone among the 8,700 kinds of bird that exist, have such a protracted breeding cycle that they can rear a chick only every other year.

In a review of the extensive migrations of the Arctic tern, F. Salomonsen showed that the species not only regularly migrates from North Atlantic breeding grounds to the edge of the pack ice south of Australia, but that first-year birds also circumnavigate the continent of Antarctica as well. Admittedly, since they do not breed in their first year, there is additional time for these young birds to make the journey, but even so they display almost unbelievable powers of flight endurance and navigation.

Observations in South Africa by T. J. Cade and G. L. Maclean confirmed beyond doubt that male sand grouse deliver water to their young by soaking the abdominal feathers. Furthermore, these feathers are remarkably specialized in shape and texture to increase their water-holding capacity.

The nighthawk, found over most of North America, normally nests on flat, bare ground in a forest clearing. In 1869 it was first reported nesting on the flat graveled roofs of human habitations. A study by J. T. Armstrong of 13 nighthawk pairs nesting in Detroit showed that this habit was now common. The males performed diving and booming displays over roofs in the centres of their territories and defended their ground from other nighthawks.

That resuscitation measures used on oiled seabirds tended to kill all but the most lightly oiled birds was the conclusion drawn by W. R. P. Bourne in a review of the history and effect of oil pollution on birds. Species that dive for their food were very much more affected than surface feeders, especially wildfowl on inland waters and auks at sea. It was likely that oil pollution was causing serious and permanent reductions in the numbers of certain birds in both the North Atlantic and the eastern Pacific.

Other publications included David Lack's *Ecological Adaptations for Breeding in Birds,* two volumes on *Eagles, Hawks, and Falcons of the World* by Leslie H. Brown and Dean Amadon, and an assessment of scientific research in *Bird Navigation* by G. V. T. Matthews. The avifauna of the whole of South America, nearly 3,000 species, were listed in R. M. de Schauensee's *The Species of Birds of South America and Their Distribution.*

In the field of economic ornithology, a variety of authors discussed *The Problems of Birds as Pests* including: bird strikes on aircraft, bullfinches attacking fruit buds, oystercatchers as pests of shell fisheries, the agricultural status of the rook, and the quelea problem in Africa. The quelea, a weaver sometimes called the locust bird, was probably the greatest avian pest, making serious inroads as it does on grain crops. It might also be the commonest bird in the world; breeding colonies contained millions of nests. Destruction programs were expensive and brought only temporary reductions in the population.

Recordings issued in 1969 included *A Sound-Guide to the Birds of North-west Africa* issued by the French Institute ECHO, a small German disc presenting the song of the wild canary, and a record of avian voices accompanying the book *Bird Song: A World of Music* (in Danish) by Poul Bondesen. Bondesen classified birdsongs into three groups according to their character and composition: the starling group, nonrhythmic songs lacking definite structure; the chaffinch group, short phrases with definite pattern and rhythm; and the skylark group, continuous outpouring song. In addition, recordings of birds' voices were expected to predominate in the new Library of Wildlife Sounds inaugurated in July 1969 at the British Institute of Recorded Sound.

German ornithologist Paul Feindt cleared up an ornithological mystery that had bedeviled the field identification of European crakes for more than a decade. Crakes are birds of marshy places, seldom seen but often heard. Feindt showed that a sound long thought to emanate from Baillon's crake is, in fact, the voice of the female little crake. The true voice of the Baillon's had escaped identification because it is very quiet, and very closely resembles the croaking of the edible frog. By extraordinary coincidence, a similar mystery was solved in North America. A call ascribed in the past with varying degrees of confidence to the black rail or to the yellow rail was proved to belong to the Virginia rail. (J. H. Bo.)

Marine Biology. In 1969 much research was done on the metabolism of plankton organisms. Since the discovery in 1962 that particulate matter could be formed by bubbling air through seawater, the occurrence of inorganic and organic particles in the sea and their size and chemical composition had been much studied. Such particles are formed at the sea surface and carried downward by convection currents. They supplement the living phytoplankton available as food for plankton animals. It was found that this material is present mainly as aggregates in the surface layers, but deeper down small particles and flakes predominate. In deep water particulate matter has probably originated from death and decay of phytoplankton and zooplankton in the upper layers. This was substantiated by chemical analysis, which showed a predominance of polysaccharides that would be resistant to biological attack while sinking.

"THE TIMES," LONDON

Andean flamingo mothers her chick at the Wildfowl Trust, Slimbridge, Gloucestershire, Eng. The chick was believed to be the first Andean flamingo hatched in captivity.

Increased attention was given to the part played by predatory animals in the sea. The way in which the giant spiny starfish, *Acanthaster planci,* feeds on coral was described. It envelops as much of a coral colony as its size will allow, then everts its stomach and spreads it over the coral coenosarc. The coral secretes much mucus and extrudes its mesenterial filaments. After about one hour the polypary layer is already decomposed into semifluid shreds leaving white patches of the coral skeleton exposed. Feeding mostly at night, the starfish attacks corals of all shapes and seems to feed within a fixed territory. In 20 days one starfish stripped 15 colonies of 17 species ranging in size from 5 to 15 cm. In view of the damage done by this animal on the Great Barrier Reef it was evident that it may play an important part in limiting the development of a coral reef.

Another example of predation by starfish was reported south of Tromsø, Nor., where the common starfish, *Asterias rubens,* was seen attacking the Icelandic scallop, *Chlamys islandica.* A concentration of

CHARLES MITCHELL—CANADIAN PRESS

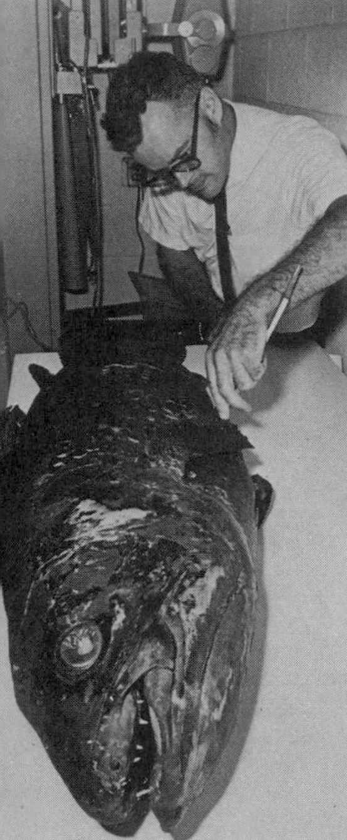

Donald McAllister of the National Museum of Canada examines a 92.4-lb. lobefin caught during 1969 in the Indian Ocean. The fin and pelvic structures of the lobefin are considered an evolutionary step in the development of arms and legs. Until recently the fish was known only by fossils 60 million to 400 million years old.

starfish completely covered an area of sea bottom 10 by 100 m. Their density was 97 individuals per square metre in the centre and 48 per square metre near the edge. The whole swarm moved forward through a bed of scallops, 60 to the square metre, and demolished the lot. Huge quantities of empty shells sometimes found on scallop beds may thus be due to starfish predation rather than to catastrophic changes in salinity and temperature. Among other examples of predation investigated was the destruction of young fishes by jellyfish.

Research on factors governing settlement of sedentary organisms was continued. As with barnacles and tube-building worms, it was found that larvae of the oyster, *Ostrea edulis,* were gregarious and would prefer to settle on surfaces previously treated with water extract of oyster tissues. The larva must make contact with the treated surface before deciding to settle and is not affected by the substance in solution. Pronase, a proteolytic enzyme, destroyed the settlement-inducing activity of the extract.

The structure of the antennular attachment disc of the larva of the acorn barnacle, *Balanus balanoides,* was examined with the scanning electron microscope. Its surface is composed of many microscopic villi by which it can adhere to the substratum rather than by suction. It is used for temporary attachment while the animal explores the substratum, and for permanent cementing at completion of the exploratory phase. An open-ended hair in the axial sense organ is thought to be chemosensory.

In a study of the ability of limpets to withstand desiccation it was pointed out that the very close fit of a shell to its "home" scar on the rock helps to prevent water loss. Animals that are unable to return to their homes are therefore at risk. In this connection experiments on the homing of the chiton *Acanthozostera gemmata* failed to explain how it finds its way. Although on its outward journey it normally browses a path through algae it can still home if displaced. Airborne odours or topographical memory were not thought to be factors in homing.

The ghost crab, *Ocypode ceratophthalma,* is the fastest running crustacean. Maximum speed on sand was observed to be 1.8 m. per sec. and on ship deck 2.4 m. per sec., or about 4 or 5 mph. Sex did not affect speed.

In a study of Antarctic benthos it was found that the development of the free larvae of the starfish *Odontaster viridis* is extremely slow and that they are largely demersal, which, like brooding, is an adaptation for avoiding the rigorous conditions in the surface waters. Fertilization of the egg and development to plutei within the animal were recorded for the first time in the sea urchin *Arbacia punctulata.*

It was found that sharks can appreciate underwater sound. The attractive sound levels were remarkably low and sharks could locate a sound within seconds from over 25 m., the limit of human vision under water. It was thought that sharks might thus find their prey by sound rather than by smell. Some sharks gain lift by their large pectoral fins and forward motion. Such action might disturb prey and there are some species of deep-sea sharks that live near the bottom and probably hover to locate their prey. These all have small pectoral fins and it was found that their large livers contain much squalene. This is not a metabolic reserve; it enables the shark to be almost neutrally buoyant, and is 80% more effective for lift than cod-liver oil.

In 1956 a description was published for the first time of a wormlike animal found in Kiel Bay in 1928. This was *Gnathostomula paradoxa* and it proved to belong to a new phylum of the animal kingdom, the Gnathostomulida. Like the recently discovered phylum Pogonophora, it has now been found that the gnathostomulid worms are widely distributed. By 1969 the phylum consisted of 5 genera and 17 species, occurring in coastal waters of all the oceans and seas of the Northern Hemisphere. The small animals live interstitially in bottom sediments from sandy gravels to muddy sands, but are found mainly in the finer sediments. They appear to be most closely related to the Turbellaria, but also show affinities to the Gastrotricha and Rotatoria.

Chemical composition as an aid to systematic classification was investigated in sponges whose morphological characters are difficult to classify. Twenty species of siliceous sponges, Desmospongiae, from New Zealand were analyzed. Results in general confirmed recognized systematic grouping. Amino acid patterns were found to be distinguishing characteristics down to and including genera, and three species of *Tethys* tested were also thus separable. (F. S. Rl.)

See also Conservation; Gardening; Medicine.

ENCYCLOPÆDIA BRITANNICA FILMS. *Life Along the Waterways* (1952); *The Atom and Biological Sciences* (1953); *Insects* (1953); *Marine Life* (1953); *The Strands Grow* (Part I, "Web of Life Series") (1953); *Life in the Desert* (1954); *Life in the Grasslands (North America)* (1954); *Flowers at Work* (1955); *Life in the Forest* (1955); *Mollusks (Snails, Mussels, Octopuses, and Their Relatives)* (1955); *Plant Traps—Insect Catchers of the Bog Jungle* (1955); *Reptiles* (1955); *Worms—The Annelida* (1955); *Crustaceans (Lobsters, Barnacles, Shrimp, and Their Relatives)* (1956); *Seed Dispersal* (1956); *Spiders* (1956); *The Frog* (1957); *Growth of Seeds* (1957); *Protozoa (One-Celled Animals)* (1957); *Roots of Plants* (1957); *Life in the Sea* (1958); *Microscopic Life: The World of the Invisible* (1958); *Osmosis* (1958); *The EBE Biology Program* (a basic series of 56 films and 51 filmstrips divided into five major units: ecology; plant life; animal life; physiology; and heredity and adaptive change) (1960–69); *Beginnings of Vertebrate Life* (1963); *How Pine Trees Reproduce—Pine Cone Biology* (1963); *Life Between Tides* (1963); *Life Story of the Hummingbird* (1963); *Life Story of the Oyster* (1963); *Life Story of the Sea Star* (1963); *The Marine Biologist* (1963); *Metamorphosis—Life Story of the Wasp* (1963); *Life Story of a Water Flea (Daphnia)* (1965); *Life Story of the Ladybird Beetle* (1965); *Message from a Dinosaur* (1965); *Army Ants: Study In Social Behavior* (1966); *Discovering the Forest* (1966); *Experimenting with Animals (White Rats)* (1966); *The Fish in a Changing Environment* (1966); *Flowering Plants* (1966); *Food from the Sun* (1966); *Green Plants and Sunlight* (1966); *Life Story of a Grasshopper* (1966); *The Marsh Community* (1966); *A Plant Through the Seasons (Apple Tree)* (1966); *Trees and Their Importance* (1966); *Chromosomes of Man* (1967); *Life Story of a Social Insect: The Ant* (1967); *Looking at Mammals* (1967); *Monarch Butterfly Story* (2nd ed., 1967); *Photosynthesis* (2nd ed., 1967); *Water for Living Things* (1967); *Insect Parasitism—The Alder Woodwasp and Its Enemies* (1968); *Radioisotopes: Tools of Discovery* (1969).

Biophysics: *see* Molecular Biology

Birth Statistics: *see* Vital Statistics

Boating: *see* Motor Sports; Rowing; Sailing; Sporting Record

Bobsledding: *see* Sporting Record

Bolivia

A landlocked republic in central South America, Bolivia is bordered by Brazil, Paraguay, Argentina, Chile, and Peru. Area: 424,162 sq.mi. (1,098,581 sq.km.). Pop. (1969 est.): 4.5 million, of whom more than 50% were Indian. Language: officially Spanish. Religion: Roman Catholic. Legal cap.: Sucre (pop., 1966 est., 59,701). Seat of government and largest city: La Paz (pop., 1966 est., 362,298). Presidents in 1969, Gen. René Barrientos Ortuño and, from April

27, Luís Siles Salinas; head of military government from September 26, Gen. Alfredo Ovando Candía.

A politically turbulent year reached its climax on September 26 when a military junta overthrew the civilian government of President Siles and replaced him with General Ovando (*see* BIOGRAPHY), the commander of the nation's armed forces. The coup was bloodless and appeared to mark a trend toward increased nationalism. The national elections scheduled for 1970 were apparently canceled.

The first act of the new regime was to invalidate the legislation that governed the operations of Bolivia Gulf Co., a subsidiary of the U.S.-owned Gulf Oil Corp. In taking this action, General Ovando claimed that the law had not given Bolivia its fair share of the company's profits. The possibility of complete nationalization of the oil company was not ruled out, and Ovando issued a statement in which he pledged that the government would obtain control over the nation's sources of production. On October 17 the government nationalized the company.

Political conflict began early in the year. In January a state of siege was imposed and seven opposition leaders were arrested and exiled to Paraguay following the uncovering of a so-called "subversive plot," said to be financed from Cuba. The crisis provoked resignations by two Cabinet members, although the influential minister of the interior, Capt. David Fernández, was later persuaded to return. Both the government and Comibol, the state mining corporation, came under attack from the church over mining conditions, it being claimed that the government had not honoured past agreements. Urban guerrilla incidents led to reports that a major guerrilla insurgency was being planned under the leadership of Guido "Inti" Peredo (*see* OBITUARIES), chief Bolivian lieutenant of the dead Che Guevara.

BOLIVIA

Education. (1965) Primary, pupils 496,068, teachers 17,841; secondary, pupils 82,927, teachers 3,921; vocational, pupils 8,615, teachers 1,404; teacher training, students 6,605, teachers 461; higher (at 8 universities), students 13,426.

Finance. Monetary unit: peso boliviano (11.88 pesos = U.S. $1; 28.51 pesos = £1 sterling). Gold and foreign exchange, central bank: (May 1969) U.S. $33.5 million; (May 1968) U.S. $38.8 million. Budget (1969 est.) balanced at 1,173,400,000 pesos. Money supply: (March 1969) 1,225,300,000 pesos; (March 1968) 1,107,400,000 pesos. Cost of living (La Paz; 1963 = 100): (Jan. 1967) 129; (Jan. 1966) 117.

Foreign Trade. Imports (1967) U.S. $150.9 million; exports (1968) U.S. $175.7 million. Import sources: U.S. 41%; West Germany 12%; Japan 12%; Argentina 6%; U.K. 5%. Export destinations: U.S. 43%; U.K. 41%; West Germany 5%. Main exports: tin 53%; silver 6%; tungsten 6%.

Transport and Communications. Roads (1966) *c.* 28,000 km. (including *c.* 6,200 km. all-weather). Motor vehicles in use (1967): passenger 21,700; commercial 6,300. Railways (1967) 3,580 km. Air traffic (1967): 61,880,000 passenger-km.; freight 1.4 million net ton-km. Telephones (Jan. 1968) *c.* 29,800. Radio receivers (Dec. 1965) 525,000.

Agriculture. Production (in 000; metric tons; 1967; 1966 in parentheses): corn 224 (249); barley *c.* 60 (*c.* 63); wheat (1966) *c.* 70, (1965) *c.* 70; potatoes 635 (670); cassava (1966) *c.* 170, (1965) 174; sugar, raw value (1968–69) *c.* 112, (1967–68) 104; rubber (exports) *c.* 2.5 (*c.* 2.5). Livestock (in 000; Oct. 1965): sheep *c.* 6,150; cattle *c.* 2,700; pigs *c.* 705; horses *c.* 214; asses 550; goats *c.* 1,200; llamas *c.* 1,500; chickens 2,950.

Industry. Production (in 000; metric tons; 1967): crude oil 1,838; electricity (kw-hr.) 595,000 (81% hydroelectric in 1966); cement 65; tin concentrates (metal content) 28; other metal ores (exports; metal content) lead 20.3, antimony 11.5, zinc 16.7, tungsten 1.9, copper 6.3, silver 0.14.

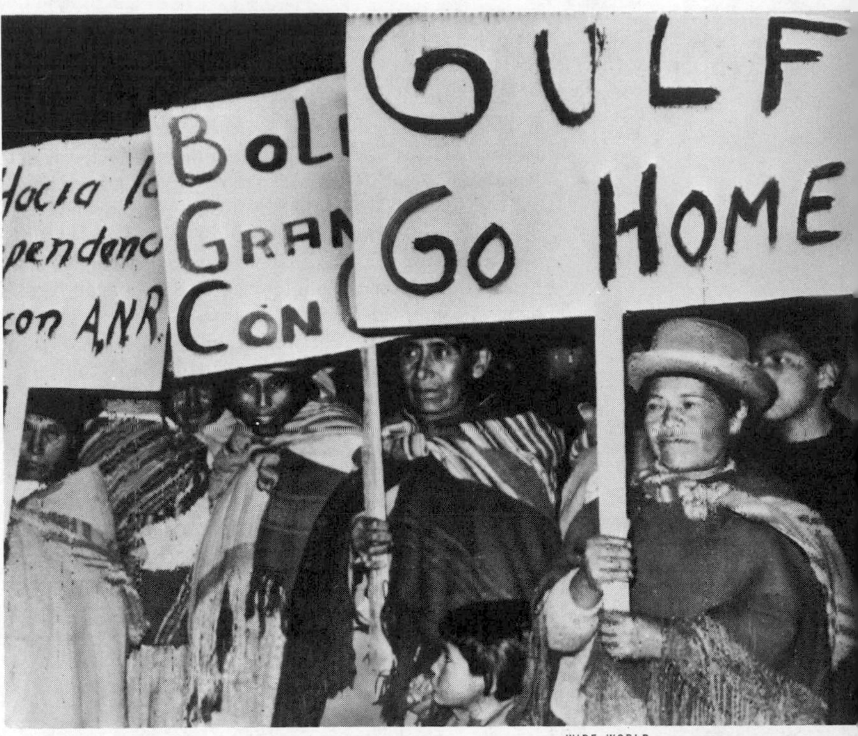

WIDE WORLD

Bolivian women march in front of the presidential palace in La Paz, Oct. 17, 1969. The demonstration in support of the nationalization of the Bolivia Gulf Co. began shortly after government authorities seized the company's holdings.

Army dissatisfaction, especially among junior officers intolerant of the role the U.S. Central Intelligence Agency had allegedly played in Bolivian affairs during Barrientos' administration, urged General Ovando to seize power. To consolidate his position Barrientos looked to the Cochabamba region, despite discontent among peasants over attempts to impose a land tax. On April 27, a week after the state of siege was lifted, Barrientos died in a helicopter crash while touring the Cochabamba region. (*See* OBITUARIES.)

In the absence of General Ovando, then on a visit to the U.S., the deputy army chiefs supported the constitutional successor, civilian Vice-President Siles, whose presidency was endorsed by Ovando on his return. President Siles formed a caretaker government with a number of Ovando nominees in the new Cabinet, declaring that he had no intention of being a candidate in the presidential elections due in May 1970. Until the coup in September General Ovando, a declared candidate, had seemed content to wait to succeed to power by constitutional election.

Bolivians, aware of the nationalization of U.S. oil and copper interests in Peru and Chile, respectively, expressed increasing anti-imperialist sentiments during 1969. Anti-U.S. demonstrations caused the visit on May 31 of U.S. Pres. Richard Nixon's special emissary, Nelson Rockefeller, to be curtailed to a three-hour airport meeting with President Siles.

In 1969 Bolivia's economy strengthened despite the political confusion. Monetary stability was maintained, and international reserves increased due to the firm world price of tin. The policy of economic diversification to reduce the nation's dependence on tin continued, and crude oil exports rose slightly. However, the gradual extinction of oil reserves after 1971 was forecast unless investment in further exploration was forthcoming. Natural gas emerged as a future large earner of foreign exchange, and an agreement was reached to supply gas over the next 20 years to Argentina via a projected Santa Cruz-Yacuiba pipeline, for which a World Bank loan equivalent to $23 million was announced in July. (J. J. SM.)

Bonds:
see Savings and Investment; Stock Exchanges

Books:
see Art Sales; Literature; Publishing

Borneo:
see Indonesia; Malaysia

Botanical Gardens:
see Zoos and Botanical Gardens

Botany:
see Biological Sciences

Botswana

A landlocked republic of southern Africa, Botswana is bounded by South Africa, South West Africa, and Rhodesia. Area: 220,000 sq.mi. (570,000 sq.km.). Pop. (1969 est.): 623,000, almost 99% African. Capital: Gaborone (pop., 1969 est., 14,000). Largest city: Serowe (pop., 1967, 37,350). Language: English (official) and Tswana. Religion: about 85% pagan. President in 1969, Sir Seretse Khama.

Landlocked, drought-ridden, and with a small poverty-stricken population, Botswana in 1969 continued to depend on foreign aid. Economic lifeblood remained in the form of cattle and animal products (90% of total exports). The national herd's estimated expansion to 2.5 million, with an annual export of 200,000 carcasses, was still dependent on new water holes. The Botswana Meat Commission, run by the government and the Commonwealth Development Corporation, continued to play a central role and in 1968 paid record prices, totaling R 8 million, to local producers for 100,000 head of cattle.

"LONDON DAILY EXPRESS" FROM PICTORIAL PARADE

Sculpture produced by native artists at the Lokgaba Centre in Botswana. The centre, established by Peace Corps volunteers, was planned as a self-supporting craft workshop and artists' colony.

The CDC Molopo Ranch project, on the edge of the Kalahari Desert, also showed a record profit on its 20,000 cattle and continued to act as a model for ranching development. Land tenure, as well as water supply, continued to pose difficulties; in the eight tribal territories of 107,497 sq.mi., there was still no written title that could be used as security for loans. The government was compelled in May to ask the World Food Program to extend famine relief for another year.

Hopes for the economic prospects of mining grew steadily after the discovery of copper, nickel, coal, and kimberlite diamond pipes. Provision in the National Development Plan, 1968–73, for the Shashi industrial complex southwest of Francistown called for an estimated R 36 million, more than half of which was to be paid for by an already heavily committed South Africa. The biggest single mining operation, for copper and nickel smelting, was under construction near Francistown by Roan Selection Trust at an estimated cost of R 45 million. Pres. Sir Seretse Khama stated at Totome in August that mining developments would create more than 3,000 new jobs and that the revenue should end dependence on Britain. But he warned that many would still need to work in South Africa.

Despite illness, the president maintained his control over the nation, though he was obliged to warn the House of Chiefs against political activities. He met with the prime minister of South Africa, B. J. Vorster, for the first time, in Johannesburg, and in May agreed to an extradition treaty to counter the infiltration of armed terrorists. The Botswana police force was doubled. It was estimated that refugees (mainly from Angola) had increased 500% in the last half of 1968. The government planned to give genuine refugees "land and seed and the facilities for becoming useful, self-supporting citizens." (M. Mr.)

BOTSWANA

Education. (1967) Primary, pupils 71,577, teachers 1,713; secondary, pupils 1,854, teachers 111; vocational, pupils 91, teachers 13; teacher training, students 310, teachers 18.

Finance and Trade. Monetary unit: South African rand (R 1 = U.S. $1.40; R 1.714 = £1 sterling). Budget (1968–69 est.) balanced at R 14,745,661. Foreign trade (1967): imports R 19,975,281; exports R 9,218,503. Main exports: meat 42%; hides and skins 18%; meat extract 14%; other meat products 11%; live cattle 5%.

Agriculture. Production (in 000; metric tons; 1966; 1965 in parentheses): sorghum *c.* 70 (*c.* 70); corn *c.* 1 (*c.* 1). Livestock (in 000; 1967–68): cattle 1,105; sheep 218; goats 717; poultry 119.

Bowling and Lawn Bowls

During 1969 membership in the Fédération Internationale des Quilleurs (FIQ), the world governing organization of tenpin bowling, increased to 44 countries with the affiliation of the Bahamas, Ecuador, and the Philippines. The number of registered individual bowlers increased from eight million to almost ten million.

The most important amateur tenpin bowling competition of the year was the third European Championship Tournament at Copenhagen in June. A record entry of 136 men and 61 women from 16 different countries filled the lanes for five days and rolled 25 new tournament records. Bowlers from Israel were seen in an international tournament for the first time. A 42-year-old Swede, Bernt Hellström, and a 46-year-old Belgian, Mrs. Nadie Kindermanns, proved that bowling was not a sport only for youngsters. Hellström finished his fight for the individual all-events title with an average of more than 211 for his last eight games, leaving his countryman G. Friman second, more than 250 pins behind. The hardest fight, however, took place in the women's division. With only two games to go the difference between the leading and the third woman was three pins. Mrs. Kindermanns' determination to win was the strongest, and she calmly continued to roll one strike after another till the final frame. The winners were: men's teams of five, (1) U.K., 5,602, (2) Finland, 5,569, (3) Norway, 5,550; men's doubles, (1) Sweden, 2,501, (2) Finland, 2,393, (3) France, 2,340; men's teams of eight, (1) Sweden, 12,030, (2) Finland, 11,957, (3) U.K., 11,821; men's all events, (1) B. Hellström, Swed., 5,725, (2) G. Friman, Swed., 5,472, (3) P. Kittelsen, Nor., 5,463; women's teams of five, (1) U.K., 5,239, (2) West Germany, 5,161, (3) Belgium, 5,141; women's doubles, (1) U.K., 2,375, (2) Finland, 2,278, (3) West Germany, 2,162; women's teams of four, (1) Finland, 4,407, (2) France, 4,350, (3) Sweden, 4,345; women's all events, (1) Nadie Kindermanns, Belg., 4,493, (2) Tuula Kaartinen, Fin., 4,437, (3) Lea Hilokoski, Fin., 4,423.

The most important amateur singles tournament of the season was the International Masters Tournament, with finals in Guadalajara, Mex., in December 1968. This tournament again drew several thousand bowlers in national eliminations throughout the world; 32 national winners were invited to Mexico to bowl for the international masters crown. West German locksmith Fritz Blum, a finalist for the fourth time, fulfilled his ambition to be the best amateur bowler in the world. Second was Jack Kramer of Canada and third, Benjamin Corona of Mexico.

The winners of the Tournament of the Americas in Miami, Fla., were: men's singles, Eddie Jackson, U.S., 3,023; men's all events, Eddie Jackson, U.S., 7,419; men's doubles, Mexico, 3,614; women's singles, Adela Cardozo, Panama, 2,922; women's all events, Grace Werkmeister, U.S., 6,825; women's doubles, Venezuela, 3,488; mixed doubles, U.S., 2,364; mixed foursomes, Mexico, 4,499.

The third Asia International Bowling Tournament took place in December 1968 in Bangkok, Thailand, with bowlers from five countries. The winners were: teams of five, Thailand, 5,517; teams of four, Philippines, 4,290; doubles, Thailand, 2,291; singles, K. Suthides, Thailand, 1,202. (Y. S.)

United States. Billy Hardwick, who feared in December 1968 that his bowling career was ended because of rheumatoid arthritis, made a remarkable medical recovery and became the dominant figure in the Professional Bowlers Association (PBA) tournaments in 1969. Hardwick, a 28-year-old righthander from Louisville, Ky., appeared certain to win the bowler-of-the-year award, bestowed in 1968 upon Jim Stefanich of Joliet, Ill.

With several tournaments remaining, Hardwick had seven firsts. He won the All-Star meet—the national individual championship in Miami, sponsored by the Bowling Proprietors Association of America—and the PBA events in Milwaukee, Wis., Denver, Colo., Redwood City, Calif., Fort Worth, Tex., Grand Rapids, Mich., and Joliet, Ill. His earnings in competition were over $60,000. Jim Godman of Hayward, Calif., captured the $25,000 first prize in the PBA Firestone Tournament of Champions in Akron, O. Wayne Zahn, Atlanta, Ga., won the PBA National in New York City for the second time in three years.

Nelson Burton, Jr., of St. Louis, Mo., was a winner in the American Bowling Congress (ABC) tournament, held in Madison, Wis., compiling a 732 series for the singles title in the Classic Division (for professionals). Don McCune, Munster, Ind., and Jim Stefanich combined for 1,355 to win the doubles. A quintet organized just for the ABC tournament, the Dick Weber Wrist Masters, of Santa Ana, Calif., rolled a six-game total of 6,413 to place first in the team competition. Larry Lichstein, Hartford, Conn., won the Classic all-events title with 2,060 for nine games.

Greg Campbell of St. Louis took the ABC's Regular Division singles championship with 751. Other Regular Division winners were: doubles, Robert Maschmeyer and Charles Guedel, both of Indianapolis, Ind., 1,379; team, PAC Advertising, Lansing, Mich., 3,165; all events, Eddie Jackson, Cincinnati, O., 1,988. Guedel bowled the tournament's highest game, a 299.

There was a surprise in the Masters tournament, held annually in conjunction with the ABC meet, when little-known Jim Chestney of Denver, Colo., defeated professional Barry Asher of Costa Mesa, Calif., in the finals. The 21-year-old Chestney had been beaten earlier in the tournament, and so it was necessary for him to win two four-game matches from previously undefeated Asher. The Denver bowler won by scores of 962–795 and 923–754.

The biggest news among women bowlers in the 1968–69 season was made in South Sioux City, Neb., on Oct. 10, 1968, when Bev Ortner of Galva, Ia., rolled league games of 267, 264, and 287 for 818. This was the highest score ever compiled by a woman in competition sanctioned by the Woman's International Bowling Congress (WIBC).

For the second successive year, Dorothy Fothergill of North Attleboro, Mass., won the women's division of the All-Star meet. Kayoka Suda of Japan was the runner-up.

The WIBC tournament took place in San Diego, Calif. The winners in the Open Division were: singles, Joan Bender, Arvada, Colo., 690; doubles, Gloria Bouvia, Portland, Ore., and Judy Cook, Grandview, Mo., 1,315; team, Fitzpatrick Chevrolet, Concord, Calif., 2,986; all events, Helen Duval, Berkeley, Calif., 1,927. In Division One the winners were: singles, Ann Keerbs, Churdan, Ia., 649; doubles, Bertha Keeney and Joyce Georgeson, both of Wheatridge, Colo., 1,205; team, Bowlorado Lanes, Ft. Collins, Colo., 2,719; all events, Janice Pickle, Tucson, Ariz., 1,743. Ann Feigel of Tucson won the WIBC Queens tournament, defeating the 1967 champion, Mildred Martorella of Rochester, N.Y., 832–765, in the final four-game match.

The 1969 National Duckpin Tournament was held in the Bowl America Westwood Lanes, Bethesda, Md. The winners in the team competition were: men, Snelling and Snelling, Baltimore, Md., 2,057; women, Eudowood Gardens, Baltimore, 1,871; mixed, The Scrubs, Hagerstown, Md., 1,912. In doubles competition the champions were: men, Al Grandy and Jerry Rosen, both of Plainfield, Conn., 885; women, Mary Ann Mitchell and Cathy Dyak, both of Manchester, Conn., 803; mixed, Fran Haas and Don Lopardo, both of Torrington, Conn., 867. Singles winners were: men, William Wall, Washington, D.C., 485; women, Gertha Wilson, Silver Spring, Md., 438. The all-events champions included: men, Sterling Fritz, Baltimore, 1,333; women, Minerva Weisenborn, Baltimore, 1,248. (J. J. A.)

Lawn Bowls. The English Bowling Association (EBA) announced during 1969 that it was willing to promote a world championships series if a sponsor would come forward. This willingness followed the failure by George N. Boulton, president of the International Bowling Board (IBB) and of the New Zealand Bowling Association, to secure backing for a 1972 series in his country. This left the 1970 Commonwealth Games as the next major world meeting of bowlers but, as South Africa and the United States were ineligible, these would be an inadequate substitute.

World champion David Bryant was appointed a Member of the British Empire (MBE) in the 1969 New Year Honours list. This was the beginning of a splendid year for him because he won, in order, the English and British Isles indoor singles championships, the English fours and pairs outdoor championships, and the British Isles outdoor fours championship; he was also runner-up in the British Isles pairs championship. By winning the British Isles fours he

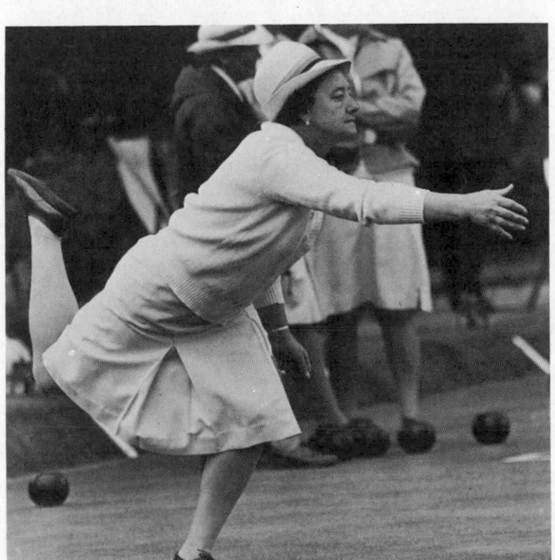

Mrs. I. Hodd, Durham team captain, shows rugged form as she competes in semifinal round of the English Women's Bowling Association Championships at Wimbledon Park, Eng.

CENTRAL PRESS FROM PICTORIAL PARADE

Cambridgeshire skip, Frances Sims, tries body English as she bowls in the English Women's Bowling Association Championships at Wimbledon Park, Eng., in August 1969.

KEYSTONE

added a new title to the many he already possessed, and his English outdoor wins took him ahead of the previous record of seven held by Percy Baker. Bryant's efforts pushed into the shadows the achievements of his club fellow and pupil David Rhys Jones, who, though only 26, had won by August five English titles in three events, four more than Bryant had won at the same age.

England continued to reign supreme indoors by taking the International Team Championship (Hilton Cup) but was defeated by Scotland in the outdoor International Team Championship. In ladies' bowls in England, where 27,000 entries were received for the English Women's Bowling Association Championships, Mavis Steele established a record by winning the singles for the third time.

In Australia Marty Millsom of Footscray, Victoria, defeated the Queensland champion, Keith Poole, 31–23 to capture the national singles championships. In South Africa the first Masters Championship was won by Kelvin Lightfoot, Natal. (C. M. Jo.)

Boxing

The continued absence from the ring of Muhammad Ali, because he had declined on conscientious grounds to be drafted into the U.S. armed forces, left the world heavyweight championship in confusion throughout 1969. Ali's last appearance in the ring was when defending his title successfully against Zora Folley in 1967. His appeal against induction dragged on, and the World Boxing Association (WBA) continued to recognize Jimmy Ellis, Louisville, Ky., as world heavyweight champion while the New York State Athletic Commission and six other states recognized Joe Frazier, Philadelphia. Frazier, undefeated as a professional, defended the New York version of the heavyweight title successfully. After outpointing Oscar Bonavena (Arg.) at Philadelphia in December 1968, he disposed of Dave Zyglewicz (U.S.) in one round the following April and in June stopped leading contender Jerry Quarry (U.S.) in seven rounds. Ellis did not defend his version of the title in 1969. He was scheduled to risk it against Henry Cooper, champion of Europe, Britain, and the Commonwealth, in London in September. The British Boxing Board of Control, however, refused to recognize the fight as a championship affair so the match was made and advertised as being for the WBA championship. However, the fight was canceled when Cooper underwent a cartilage operation.

Cooper, who had successfully defended the European title by knocking out the Italian champion, Piero Tomasoni, in Rome in March, relinquished his British title as a protest against the British boxing authorities' refusal to recognize his proposed fight with Ellis as an official world heavyweight championship. Cooper, who won the British title in January 1959, had held it longer than any heavyweight in history. The British board matched Jack Bodell (Eng.) with Carl Gizzi (Wales) for the title Cooper had given up. Bodell became the champion by beating Gizzi in October. The European Boxing Union declared Cooper's European championship vacant. In December Peter Wieland of West Germany knocked out Bernard Thebault of France to win the title.

Bob Foster (U.S.) remained world light-heavyweight champion, successfully defending the title by beating Frank De Paula (U.S.) in one round and Andy Kendall (U.S.) in four rounds. The middleweight championship remained with Nino Benvenuti (Italy); the Italian outpointed Don Fullmer (U.S.) at San Remo, Italy, beat Fraser Scott (U.S.) in Naples and Luis Rodriguez (U.S.) in Rome. The welterweight championship changed hands when José Napoles (Mex.) stopped Curtis Cokes (U.S.) in 13 rounds in April. Two months later Napoles again beat Cokes in 11 rounds. In October Napoles retained the title by outpointing Emile Griffith (U.S.). Carlos Ortiz (U.S.), who had held the lightweight crown for many years, lost it to Carlos Çruz (Dominican Republic). Cruz in turn lost it to Mando Ramos (U.S.). An Australian born in France, Johnny Famechon, won the world featherweight championship by outpointing José Legra (Spain) in London and successfully defended it against Fighting Harada (Jap.) in Sydney, Austr. Shozo Saijo (Jap.) retained the WBA featherweight title, beating José Luis Pimental (Mex.) in two rounds. Lionel Rose (Austr.) retained the world bantamweight title by outpointing Alan Rudkin (Eng.) in Melbourne, Austr., but then lost it when he was knocked out in the fifth round by Ruben Olivares (Mex.) in Los Angeles. Another Mexican, Efren Torres, captured the flyweight championship from Chartchai Choinoi (Thailand) and defended it successfully against Susumo Hanagata (Jap.). Hiroyuki Ebihara (Jap.) won the WBA version of this title from José Severino (Brazil) and then lost it to Bernabe Villacampo (Philippines).

In Europe a new light-heavyweight champion was crowned when Yvan Preberg (Yugos.) outpointed Eddie Avoth (Wales) for the vacant title at Zagreb, Yugos. Preberg became the only professional cham-

Boxing Champions
as of Dec. 31, 1969

Division	World	Europe	Commonwealth	Britain	Canada	Orient
Heavyweight	Jimmy Ellis, U.S.* Joe Frazier, U.S.	Peter Wieland, W. Ger.	Henry Cooper, Eng.	Jack Bodell, Eng.	George Chuvalo, Ont.	...
Light heavyweight	Bob Foster, U.S.	Yvan Preberg, Yugos.	Bob Dunlop, Austr.	Eddie Avoth, Wales	Al Sparks, Man.	...
Middleweight	Nino Benvenuti, Italy	Tom Bogs, Denmark	vacant	Les McAteer, Eng.	Dave Downey, N.S.	Sung Kap Choi, S. Kor.
Junior middleweight	Fred Little, U.S.*	Gerhart Piaskowy, W. Ger.	...	...	...	Hideo Kanazawa, Jap.
Welterweight	José Napoles, Mex.	Johann Orsolics, Aus.	Ralph Charles, Eng.	Ralph Charles, Eng.	Joe Durelle, Que.	Hisao Minami, Jap.
Junior welterweight	Nicolino Loche, Arg.	Bruno Arcari, Italy	...	Vic Andretti, Eng.	Colin Fraser, Ont.	Chung Kyo Shin, S. Kor.
Lightweight	Mando Ramos, U.S.	vacant	Percy Hayles, Jam.	Ken Buchanan, Scot.	Al Ford, Alta.	Jaguar Kakizawa, Jap.
Junior lightweight	Hiroshi Kobayashi, Jap.	...	...	Jimmy Anderson, Eng.	Les Gillies, N.S.	Saleman Anuchit, Thai.
Featherweight	Johnny Famechon, Austr. Shozo Saijo, Jap.*	Tomaso Galli, Italy	vacant	Jimmy Revie, Eng.	Rocky MacDougall, N.S.	Hurbert Kang, S. Kor.
Bantamweight	Ruben Olivares, Mex.	Salvatore Burruni†	Alan Rudkin, Eng.	Alan Rudkin, Eng.	Jack Burke, N.B.	Takao Sakurai, Jap.
Flyweight	Efren Torres, Mex. Bernabe Villacampo (Phil.)*	Fernando Atzori, Italy	vacant	John McCluskey, Scot.	...	Erbito Salavarria, Phil.

*Recognized as champions only by World Boxing Association.
†Burruni announced in July his intention of retiring but no further steps ensued.

CENTRAL PRESS FROM PICTORIAL PARADE

WIDE WORLD

Left, challenger Alan Rudkin lands a right to the head of world bantamweight champion Lionel Rose. Rose retained his title in the 15-round bout in Melbourne, Austr., Aug. 3, 1969. Right, heavyweight Joe Frazier on the ropes during his match with Jerry Quarry in New York's Madison Square Garden, June 23, 1969. Frazier won on a technical knockout in the seventh round.

pion from a Communist country. The middleweight championship changed hands when Tom Bogs (Denmark), former European light-heavyweight champion, beat the defender, Carlos Duran (Italy), in Copenhagen. A new welterweight champion was also crowned when Johann Orsolics (Aus.) caused a surprise by beating the titleholder, Jean Josselin of France. The European lightweight title, retained by Pedro Carrasco (Spain) in a fight with Miguel Velasquez (Spain), was later declared vacant by the European Boxing Union. The European featherweight championship was taken over by Tomaso Galli (Italy), who defeated Manuel Calvo (Spain). Salvatore Burruni (Italy) retained the European bantamweight title against his French challenger, Pierre Vetroff. The flyweight division, once so popular in Europe and Britain, was very inactive throughout the year. In fact, Fernando Atzori, the Italian holder of the European championship, only defended it once, when he outpointed Kamara Diop (France). In Britain the champion, John McCluskey, also successfully defended his title once—against Tony Barlow (Manchester).

Boxing was not active in the Commonwealth. The vacant light-heavyweight championship was won by the Australian Bob Dunlop. Another Australian, Johnny Famechon (featherweight), relinquished his Commonwealth title after becoming world champion. Lionel Rose, also of Australia, who had lost his world bantamweight title, remained Commonwealth bantam champion but decided to challenge for featherweight honours.

At one time in Britain there was a threat that four reigning champions might all surrender their titles: Henry Cooper gave up the heavyweight crown; Johnny Pritchett relinquished the middleweight championship and announced his retirement from the ring; featherweight Howard Winstone retired; and Ken Buchanan, the Scot who had won the British lightweight title and was undefeated after 33 professional fights, announced his retirement after a difference of opinion with his manager. Later, however, Buchanan was persuaded to change his mind and continued to box. New British champions included Eddie Avoth (Wales), who took the light-heavyweight championship from John "Young" McCormack (Ire.) when he stopped the Irishman in 11 rounds. Jimmy Revie took over Winstone's featherweight crown when he stopped John O'Brien of Scotland in five rounds. Les McAteer, from Birkenhead, Eng., succeeded Johnny Pritchett as middleweight champion when he was matched for the vacant title against Wally Swift. Jimmy Anderson successfully defended the junior lightweight championship by beating Colin Lake, while Vic Andretti retained the junior welterweight crown by stopping former champion Des Rea (Ire.).

All boxing fans were saddened at the premature death of Rocky Marciano (*see* OBITUARIES). (F. BR.)

Brazil

A federal republic in eastern and central South America, Brazil is bounded by the Atlantic Ocean and all the countries of South America except Ecuador and Chile. Area: 3,286,470 sq.mi. (8,511,965 sq.km.). Pop. (1969 est.): 93 million, including (1960 census) Caucasians 60%; mulattoes 26%; Negroes 11%; Amerindians 2%; Asians 1%. Principal cities (metro. pop., 1969 est.): Brasília (cap.) 450,000; Rio de Janeiro 4.4 million; São Paulo 5.8 million. Language: Portuguese. Religion: 93% Roman Catholic. Presidents in 1969, Artur da Costa e Silva and, from October 30, Gen. Emílio Garrastazú Médici.

Domestic Affairs. Two main events dominated the political life of Brazil during 1969: the enforced "recess" of Congress and other legislative bodies throughout the country, which resulted from President Costa e Silva's suspension of constitutional guarantees on Dec. 13, 1968; and the taking over of the responsibilities of the government by the three armed forces ministers after President Costa e Silva suffered a stroke in August.

For some time there had been unrest, political agitation, and terrorist activities throughout the country. These activities took the form of student rallies in which some professional agitators had taken part; vehement critical comments in the news media; bomb throwing and armed attacks against gun-selling shops and banks; and bitter pronouncements in Congress against the regime and the military leaders who backed it.

Late in 1968 Congress refused a presidential request to deprive one of its members of his parliamentary immunities in order to allow his trial for inciting the people against the armed forces. In a memorable session fraught with emotion the government's request was turned down by the Congress. This defeat was considered a serious blow to the prestige of the armed forces. Pressured by military leaders, President Costa e Silva, on Dec. 13, 1968, took a decisive step: after consultation with the National Security Council he signed Institutional Act number 5 giving him special sweeping powers. These included authorization to "recess" the national Congress, the state assemblies, and the municipal legislative bodies for a period to be determined by him. Meanwhile, he would legislate by decree.

On that same day Costa e Silva declared the national Congress in "recess" for an indeterminate period. A few days later a general investigating committee was set up to investigate cases of malfeasance by public officers while in office. On Dec. 31, 1968, the president explained to the nation on television and radio that he had taken such radical measures to prevent the subversion of public order and to preserve the accomplishments of the 1964 revolution.

Then the cancellation of mandates and the suspension of political rights started. A few judges, army officers, and one Cabinet member resigned. Late in January President Costa e Silva signed a new Institutional Act (number 6), reducing the number of members of the Supreme Court of Justice. A military-police committee was created to investigate subversive acts. At the end of February, Act number 7 was signed, suspending elections for legislative or executive offices in the entire country. These elections would be held later, only when considered opportune by the president.

For a while things seemed to have quieted down. But in March, soon after the festivities of Carnival—which in Brazil stop practically every other activity or serious preoccupation—the suspension of political rights of citizens and the dismissals from office started anew: more members of Congress, university teachers, a number of diplomats and employees of the Foreign Ministry, and several army officers were affected. Other Institutional and Complementary Acts were signed by the president in quick succession.

Brazilian political prisoners arrive at the Mexico City airport, Sept. 7, 1969, after being freed in exchange for kidnapped U.S. Ambassador C. Burke Elbrick.

UPI COMPIX

In April, Act number 8 authorized the president to decree administrative reforms of the federal, state, and large-city municipal governments. The conventions of the political parties, previously set for July and September, were postponed.

Meanwhile, as the situation seemed to have cooled off somewhat, the administration took several constructive measures concerning rural and university reforms. Certain changes in the 1967 constitution were considered in order to grant broader powers to the executive. A committee was appointed under the chairmanship of Vice-Pres. Pedro Aleixo to study those changes. In June the vice-president submitted to the president the recommendations of his committee, and it was announced that the president intended to recall the Congress in order to pass on the proposed constitutional amendments. In August the president was given the final draft of the proposed amendments for his approval and submission to the Congress, the reopening of which he was said to be planning to announce on Independence Day (September 7).

However, late in August, President Costa e Silva—a 66-year-old man in apparent good health—suffered a cerebral hemorrhage that left him partially paralyzed on his right side and unable to speak. The military leaders who supported the regime decided that in order to avoid a subversive outbreak they would assume the responsibility for carrying out the measures necessary to maintain the peace and public order and would take steps to guarantee the national security. The nation was informed of this decision in a proclamation that was broadcast and televised on August 31. The decision of the military, it was said, had the consent and approval of the stricken president. A new Institutional Act (number 12) was issued by the three armed forces ministers—Adm. Augusto Hamann Rademaker Grunewald, Gen. Aurélio de Lyra Tavares, and Air Marshal Marcio de Souza e Mello—embodying this decision and authorizing the three ministers to issue the necessary "acts" or decrees for the continuation of the administration.

A few days later (September 4), when the nation had scarcely had time to recover from the shock caused by the president's illness, U.S. Ambassador C. Burke Elbrick was abducted from his limousine by a small group of terrorists. A note called "Manifesto to the Brazilian People" was left in the ambassador's car. It denounced Brazil's regime and the government of the U.S., and demanded the release of 15 leftist prisoners within 48 hours with provision for their safe conduct to one of three mentioned countries. This was to be done in exchange for the ambassador's safe release.

Fearing for the ambassador's safety, the authorities promptly agreed to these demands. The 15 prisoners, mostly student leaders, were released and flown to Mexico, where they arrived September 7. That same day, late in the evening, Ambassador Elbrick was released unharmed except for some slight bruises on his forehead caused by rough handling on the day of the abduction. It was announced in Rio de Janeiro that the authorities knew the identity of the abductors and were taking steps for their immediate arrest. Other arrests of known enemies of the regime were ordered. On September 5 the three ministers signed

Institutional Act number 13, providing that the executive should have the power, on recommendation from the minister of justice or the armed forces, to expel from the country any citizen who was considered "inconvenient," "pernicious," or "dangerous" to the security of Brazil. Several persons were forthwith expelled under this authority.

At the end of September the government leaders faced the problem of deciding whether to maintain the current scheme of government or to replace the stricken president with someone who would rule in his own name. On October 6 they decided to follow the latter course and selected a career army officer, General Garrastazú Médici, as Brazil's new president. The Congress formally elected Médici president on October 25, and he was inaugurated on October 30.

The Economy. Despite these disturbing events the country continued to grow and prosper. The population was estimated to have reached about 93 million, and the large industrial cities continued to grow; the gross national product increased 6% in 1968; inflation was being gradually reduced to 20% a year; and exports of manufactured goods and agricultural products increased and were expected to reach $2 billion by the end of 1969.

Steel production increased 14%, electric power 13%, and automobile production 41%. It was announced that the United States Steel Corp. had entered into an agreement with the large government-controlled iron-ore-exporting Companhia Vale do Rio Doce to develop the enormously rich mineral resources of the Tocantins Valley and the iron ore district of Minas Gerais. (R. D' E.)

ENCYCLOPÆDIA BRITANNICA FILMS. *The Amazon—People and Resources of Northern Brazil* (1957); *Brazil—People of the Highlands* (1957).

BRAZIL

Education. (1966) Primary, pupils 10,695,391, teachers 393,001; secondary, pupils 1,805,247, teachers 99,665; vocational, pupils 412,339, teachers 32,253; teacher training, students 265,626, teachers 25,725; higher (including 43 universities), students 180,109, teaching staff 36,109.

Finance. Monetary unit: new cruzeiro, with an exchange rate (as devalued July 7, 1969) of 4.10 cruzeiros to U.S. $1 (9.82 cruzeiros = £1 sterling). Gold and foreign exchange, official: (May 1969) U.S. $392 million; (May 1968) U.S. $268 million. Budget (1970 est.): revenue 15,874,000,000 cruzeiros; expenditure 16,474,000,000 cruzeiros. Gross national product: (1966) 43,844,000,000 cruzeiros; (1965) 30,405,000,000 cruzeiros. Money supply: (Dec. 1968) 21,460,000,000 cruzeiros; (Dec. 1967) 14,931,000,000 cruzeiros. Cost of living (São Paulo; 1963 = 100): (May 1969) 865; (May 1968) 704.

Foreign Trade. (1968) Imports 6,826,200,000 cruzeiros; exports 4,960,500,000 cruzeiros. Import sources: U.S. 32%; West Germany 11%; Argentina 7%; U.K. 5%. Export destinations: U.S. 33%; West Germany 8%; Argentina 6%; Italy 6%; Netherlands 5%. Main exports: coffee 41%; raw cotton 7%; iron ore 6%.

Transport and Communications. Roads (1965) 803,068 km. (including 36,170 km. main roads). Motor vehicles in use (1967): passenger 1,533,400; commercial (including buses) 953,700. Railways: (1966) 31,961 km.; traffic (1967) 13,517,000,000 passenger-km., freight 19,893,000,000 net ton-km. Air traffic (1967): 3,210,027,000 passenger-km.; freight 94,217,000 net ton-km. Shipping (1968): merchant vessels 100 gross tons and over 398; gross tonnage 1,294,190. Telephones (Jan. 1968) 1,472,677. Radio receivers (Dec. 1968) *c.* 5.5 million. Television receivers (Dec. 1966) *c.* 2.5 million.

Agriculture. Production (in 000; metric tons; 1968; 1967 in parentheses): corn 13,030 (12,824); rice 6,932 (6,792); cassava 28,994 (27,268); potatoes 1,573 (1,467); sweet potatoes (1967) 2,226, (1966) 1,913; cotton, lint 607 (564); coffee (1967) 1,398, (1966) 1,366; cocoa (1966–67) 173, (1965–66) 171; bananas (1967) 5,165, (1966) 4,626; oranges 2,844 (2,701); sisal 356 (319); tobacco (1967) 243, (1966) 228; peanuts 770 (751); sugar, raw value (1968–69) 4,410, (1967-68) 4,376; dry beans 1,780 (2,554); soybeans 751 (716); rubber 22 (21); timber (cu.m.; 1966) *c.* 161,100, (1965) *c.* 156,400; fish catch (1967) 429, (1966) 436. Livestock (in 000; Dec. 1967): cattle 88,762; horses (Dec. 1966) 9,082; pigs 64,734; sheep (Dec. 1966) 22,102; goats (Dec. 1966) 13,957; chickens (Dec. 1966) 255,795.

Industry. Fuel and power (in 000; 1967): coal 1,957 metric tons; crude oil (1968) 7,797 metric tons; natural gas (1968) 983,000 cu.m.; electricity 34,239,000 kw-hr. (85% hydroelectric). Production (in 000; metric tons; 1968): pig iron 3,373; crude steel 4,436; bauxite (1967) 302; iron ore (metal content; 1967) 15,163; manganese ore (metal content; 1967) 598; gold (troy oz.; 1967) 172; cement 7,280; wood pulp (1966) *c.* 750; paper (1966) 720; passenger cars (including assembly; units) 160; commercial vehicles (including assembly; units) 105.

Bulgaria

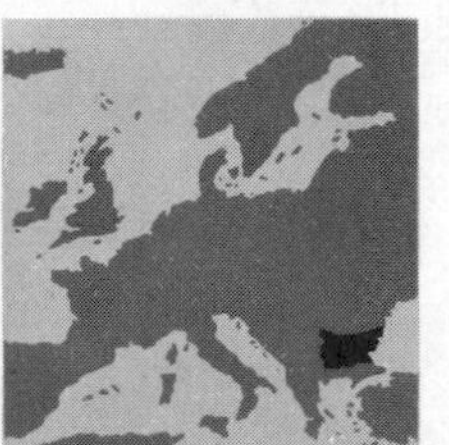

A people's republic of Europe, Bulgaria is situated on the eastern Balkan Peninsula along the Black Sea, bordered by Romania, Yugoslavia, Greece, and Turkey. Area: 42,823 sq.mi. (110,912 sq.km.). Pop. (1967 est.): 8,310,200. Cap. and largest city: Sofia (pop., 1967 est., 825,200). Language: chiefly Bulgarian. First secretary of the Bulgarian Communist Party and chairman of the Council of Ministers (premier) in 1969, Todor Zhivkov; chairman of the Presidium of the National Assembly, Georgi Traikov.

On Sept. 9, 1969, Bulgaria celebrated the 25th anniversary of the Communist revolution in that country. In the presence of dignitaries from all the Communist states, including China and Yugoslavia, Premier Zhivkov expressed "eternal gratitude to the Soviet Union without whose decisive assistance the victory of Sept. 9, 1944, would not have been possible." He added, somewhat ambiguously, that Bulgaria opposed "interference of a country in the home affairs of other countries." Opening the military parade, Gen. Dobri Dzhurov, minister of national defense, eulogized the virtues of Communist unity and criticized "leftist and rightist revisionists"—a statement that led the Chinese delegate to leave the reviewing stand in protest.

During the weeks preceding the anniversary, the Bulgarian press was full of articles illustrating the country's achievements since the end of World War II. In 1968 the national income, calculated per head of population in 1961 prices, was 3.8 times higher than in 1939. The value of industrial production was said to be 30 times that of 1939, and the number of persons employed in industry rose between 1948 and 1967 from 312,000 to 1,150,000. During the same period the number employed in agriculture was reduced by half to about 1.6 million, but agricultural production more than doubled.

This progress was mainly due to Soviet aid. Bulgaria also occupied fourth place among the U.S.S.R.'s trading partners. According to economic agreements signed in Moscow in May, Bulgarian imports of Soviet crude petroleum would rise from 5.5 million to 10 million tons between 1971 and 1975. A pipeline would be built across Romania to carry natural gas from western Siberia to Bulgaria, and by 1975 Bulgaria would receive 3,000,000,000 cu.m. of gas yearly.

In April 1969 Zhivkov paid an official visit to Austria—a visit that had been postponed because of Bulgarian participation in the 1968 invasion of Czechoslovakia. Ivan Bashev, the foreign minister, was absent,

Bridge: *see* Contract Bridge

Bridges: *see* Engineering Projects

British Antarctic Territory: *see* Dependent States

British Commonwealth: *see* Commonwealth of Nations

British Honduras: *see* Dependent States

British Indian Ocean Territory: *see* Dependent States

Broadcasting: *see* Telecommunications; Television and Radio

Brunei: *see* Dependent States

Buddhism: *see* Religion

Budgets, National: *see* Government Finance

Building and Construction Industry: *see* Engineering Projects; Housing; Industrial Review probably because of his indiscreet (though subsequently denied) remarks to a group of visiting Austrian journalists about the possibility of Warsaw Pact forces intervening in other member countries that attempted to follow the Czechoslovak way. In Vienna, Zhivkov spoke of the idea of a European security conference, proposed by the Warsaw Pact powers in Budapest, Hung., March 17.

Bulgaria's relations with Romania were correct. The two governments had been discussing the construction of a dam and a hydroelectric power station on the Danube River, but nothing was decided because of the project's high cost. Following Zhivkov's visit to Turkey in March 1968, relations between the two countries had improved. The Bulgarian-Turkish agreement providing for the reunification of families of Bulgarian citizenship but of Turkish origin came into force on Aug. 19, 1969. Under the agreement, Bulgarian subjects of Turkish nationality having close relatives who had settled in Turkey before 1952 were free to emigrate there. The Turkish minority in Bulgaria was estimated to number somewhat more than 500,000.

Relations with Greece had become cool after the 1967 military coup, but according to Kharlamt Traikov, the Bulgarian deputy foreign minister, Bulgaria was continuing to apply all of the 12 agreements concluded with Greece on July 9, 1964, covering a range of outstanding postwar differences. (K. Sm.)

Bulgarian citizens carry a portrait of former Premier Georgi Dimitrov through the streets of Sofia during a celebration commemorating the 25th anniversary of the end of World War II.

KEYSTONE

BULGARIA

Education. (1966–67) Primary, pupils 1,108,415, teachers 49,485; secondary, pupils 123,145, teachers 7,089; vocational, pupils 266,541, teachers (1965–66) 8,761; teacher training, students 251, teachers (1965–66) 2; higher (including Sofia University with 13,940 students), students 92,807, teaching staff 6,647.

Finance. Monetary unit: lev, with an official exchange rate of 1.17 leva to U.S. $1 (2.81 leva = £1 sterling) and a tourist rate of 2 leva to U.S. $1 (4.80 leva = £1). Budget (1969 est.): revenue 5,052,000,000 leva; expenditure 5,041,000,000 leva.

Foreign Trade. (1968) Imports U.S. $1,759,000,000; exports U.S. $1,611,000,000. Import sources (1967): U.S.S.R. 50%; East Germany 8%; Czechoslovakia 6%. Export destinations (1967): U.S.S.R. 53%; East Germany 8%; Czechoslovakia 6%. Main exports (1967): tobacco and cigarettes 14%; cereals, fruit, and vegetables 7%; clothing 7%; wines and spirits 7%; metals 5%.

Transport and Communications. State roads (1966) 29,233 km. (including 2,418 main roads). Motor vehicles in use (1961): passenger *c.* 9,300; commercial *c.* 20,400. Railways: (1967) 4,158 km.; traffic (1968) 5,708,000,000 passenger-km., freight 12,200,000,000 net ton-km. Air traffic (1966): 506,677,000 passenger-km.; freight 8,678,000 net ton-km. Shipping (1968): merchant vessels 100 gross tons and over 112; gross tonnage 548,102. Telephones (Dec. 1967) 338,446. Radio receivers (Dec. 1967) 2,218,000. Television receivers (Dec. 1967) 420,000.

Agriculture. Production (in 000; metric tons; 1968; 1967 in parentheses): wheat 2,549 (3,254); corn 1,768 (1,971); barley (1967) 985, (1966) 1,064; oats 76 (169); dry peas (1967) 83, (1966) 93; sunflower seed (1967) 478, (1966) 423; cotton, lint *c.* 22 (19); sugar, raw value (1968–69) *c.* 254, (1967–68) *c.* 279; tomatoes (1967) 715, (1966) 751; grapes (1967) 923, (1966) 1,081; apples (1967) 413, (1966) 344; tobacco 114 (118). Livestock (in 000; Jan. 1968): sheep 9,905; cattle 1,363; goats 384; pigs 2,314; horses 224; asses 301; poultry 27,726.

Industry. Index of industrial production (1963 = 100): (1968) 181; (1967) 161. Production (in 000; metric tons; 1968): coal 439; lignite 28,308; crude oil 474; electricity (kw-hr.) 15,450,000; iron ore (32% metal content) 2,642; manganese ore (metal content; 1967) 13; copper concentrates (metal content) 31; lead concentrates (metal content) 86; pig iron 1,110; crude steel 1,460; copper (1967) 33; lead 93; zinc 75; cement 3,512; sulfuric acid 472; soda ash (1967) 218; cotton yarn 70; cotton fabrics (m.) 319,000; wool yarn 20; woolen fabrics (m.) 22,560.

Burma

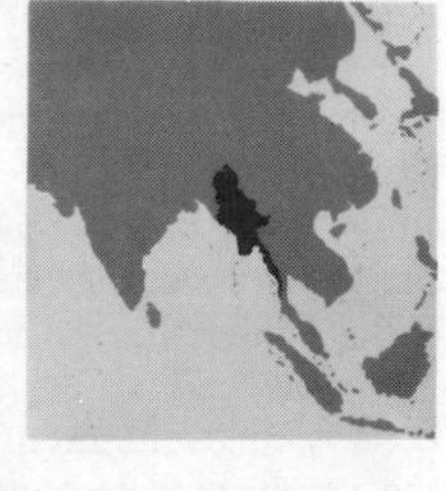

A republic of southeast Asia, Burma is on the Indochinese Peninsula, bordered by East Pakistan, India, Tibet, China, Laos, and Thailand. Area: 269,789 sq.mi. (698,754 sq. km.). Pop. (1969 census): 26,980,000. Cap. and largest city: Rangoon (pop., 1969 census, 1,733,000). Language: Burmese 66%. Religion: Buddhist 84%. Chairman of the Revolutionary Council and prime minister in 1969, Gen. Ne Win.

In November 1968 Gen. Ne Win invited former political leaders to form an advisory board to discuss the means of establishing national unity with a view to drafting a new constitution. The only political party, the Burmese Way to Socialism Programme, was evolving a pattern for a people's democracy. Gen. Ne Win, who had often proclaimed his disbelief in the value for Burma of parliamentary democracy, and the Revolutionary Council hoped that the advisory board would take this evolving pattern into consideration when they produced their ideas in May of 1969.

However, the political rivalries that had for so long bedeviled Burmese life came to the surface again. Former Prime Minister U Nu suggested that he should be given the power by Gen. Ne Win to set up an interim government in consultation with the advisory body. U Nu further suggested that the old parliament should be summoned and the 1947 union constitution revived. A second group suggested the calling of a national unity congress of members of the Revolutionary Council and the peasants' and workers' councils to reexamine the measures taken under the Burmese Way to Socialism Programme, and draw up a new national program, demanding one political party only and the replacement of the existing bureaucracy with people's administration councils. This people's democracy would replace the existing military-controlled regime. Finally, the three-member U Kyaw Nyein group, which agreed with the second group on basic principles, advocated a unitary form of government as opposed to the federal system ultimately envisaged. The end result was stalemate.

After a short visit to India, ostensibly a religious pilgrimage, U Nu began a world tour to mobilize opinion against the regime, demanding the end of military rule and the deposition of Gen. Ne Win, by insurrection if necessary.

The problem of insurgency remained, despite the divisions among the rebel movements and the fact that the most famous Communist leader, Thakin Than Tun, had been killed in an ambush by one of his own lieutenants. Burmese Communists were said to have virtually occupied parts of Kokang state, and in May the Thai foreign minister reported that Chinese forces had construction battalions building strategic roads in the state of Kachin.

The process of nationalization continued. Industries affected included textiles, food, chemicals, porcelain and pottery, metal goods, printing, cinemas, and the increasingly lucrative gemstone prospecting and mining concerns. Accompanying features of a people's democracy included the concepts of the Model Worker, the Socialist Worker Hero, and peasants' and workers' vacation camps visited by officials of the Burmese Way to Socialism Programme. The importance placed by the Revolutionary Council on the development of the health service was reflected in the growing number of hospitals and doctors; there were only 576 hospitals in 1961–62 but the number had increased to 2,013 in 1967–68. During the same period, however, the number of private practitioners had fallen by about 70%, largely as a result of many Indian doctors having left the country.

The economic situation remained uncertain and productivity low. The transition from a foreign-controlled capitalist economy to that of a socialist state, together with the insufficiency of trained labour and the problems of incentives for peasants and workers, posed many unanswered questions. In February the *Working People's Daily* announced that Japan had agreed to extend to Burma a loan of not more than $30 million to finance industrial projects. The loan was to be repaid over 20 years. Also reported, in June, was a UN annual aid grant of $850,000 for 1969–72.

Burma continued to adopt a neutralist policy in international affairs. At the consultative conference of nonaligned countries in Yugoslavia in July, the Burmese delegate spoke against the formation of any third world bloc. Gen. Ne Win and India's prime minister, Indira Gandhi, exchanged visits, while boundary teams demarcated about 240 mi. of the two nations' common frontier. Gen. Ne Win also visited Pakistan, and some improvement in Sino-Burmese relations was said to have accrued from the good offices of Pakistan's former Pres. Muhammad Ayub Khan. Delegations from North Korea and East Germany visited Rangoon. (D. WN.)

ENCYCLOPÆDIA BRITANNICA FILMS. *Burma, People of the River* (1957).

BURMA

Education. (1965–66) Primary, pupils 1,886,335, teachers 36,975; secondary (1964–65), pupils 497,275, teachers 15,631; vocational (1964–65), pupils 2,846, teachers 99; teacher training (1964–65), students 3,138, teachers 145; higher (including universities of Mandalay and Rangoon with 10,791 students), students 31,190, teaching staff 3,264.

Finance. Monetary unit: kyat, with a par value of 4.76 kyats to U.S. $1 (1 kyat = 1*s*. 9*d*. sterling). Gold and foreign exchange, official: (June 1969) U.S. $139 million; (June 1968) U.S. $152 million. Budget (1968–69 est.): revenue 8,116,000,000 kyats; expenditure 8,416,000,000 kyats. Money supply: (Feb. 1969) 2,682,000,000 kyats; (Feb. 1968) 2,496,000,000 kyats. Gross national product: (1963–64) 7,731,000,000 kyats; (1962–63) 8,115,000,000 kyats.

Foreign Trade. (1968) Imports 531.1 million kyats; exports 527 million kyats. Import sources (1967): U.S. 15%; Japan 14%; China 11%; U.K. 11%; Pakistan 6%; West Germany 5%; U.S.S.R. 5%; Australia 5%. Export destinations (1967): India 11%; Ceylon 9%; China 7%; Japan 7%; Indonesia 6%; West Germany 6%; Singapore 6%; U.K. 6%; Denmark 5%; Pakistan 5%. Main exports: rice 35%; teak 30%; oil cakes 5%.

Transport and Communications. Roads (1966) *c*. 25,000 km. (including 12,180 km. all-weather). Motor vehicles in use (1967): passenger 27,900; commercial (including buses) 27,300. Railways: (1966) 4,290 km.; traffic (1968) 2,133,000,000 passenger-km., freight 813 million net ton-km. Air traffic (1968): 98,560,000 passenger-km.; freight 1,720,000 net ton-km. Telephones (Dec. 1967) 21,713. Radio receivers (Dec. 1966) 367,000.

Agriculture. Production (in 000; metric tons; 1968; 1967 in parentheses): rice 8,485 (7,714); rubber (exports) *c*. 9.1 (*c*. 6.1); sesame (1967) 83, (1966) 57; peanuts (1967) 389, (1966) 278; dry beans (1966) 140, (1965) 114; cotton, lint *c*. 21 (21); jute (1967) 18, (1966) 13; tobacco *c*. 42 (41); sugar, raw value (1968–69) *c*. 228, (1967–68) *c*. 217; timber (cu.m.; 1966–67) 5,200, (1965–66) 5,000. Livestock (in 000; March 1968): cattle *c*. 6,750; buffaloes (June 1966) 1,259; pigs *c*. 1,300; goats (June 1966) 607.

Industry. Production (in 000; metric tons; 1968): cement 176; crude oil 740; electricity (excluding most industrial production; kw-hr.) 414,000; lead ore and concentrates (metal content; 1967) 7.7; zinc concentrates (metal content; 1967) 5.2; tin concentrates (metal content) 0.3.

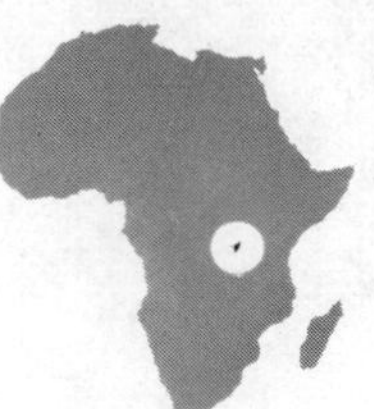

Burundi

A republic of eastern Africa, Burundi is bordered by the Congo, Rwanda, and Tanzania. Area: 10,759 sq.mi. (27,865 sq.km.). Pop. (1969 est.): 3,475,000, mainly Hutu, Tutsi, and Twa. Cap. and largest city: Bujumbura (pop., 1969 est., 105,000). Language: Kirundi and French. Religion: Roman Catholic 40%; Protestant 5%; animist 55%. President in 1969, Michel Micombero.

Following a Cabinet reshuffle, a major political trial of 13 leaders of the old monarchical regime (overthrown in 1966) took place in December 1968. Six former ministers, including the former president of the Legislative Assembly, T. Siryuyumunsi, were sentenced to ten years' imprisonment on charges of writing open letters hostile to the government. The remainder received terms of from three to ten years.

Close relationships were maintained with neighbouring states. During January President Micombero received Pres. Léopold S. Senghor of Senegal in Bujumbura for an exchange of views. In February Burundi applied for membership in the East African Community and also attended the foreign ministers' conference of the East and Central African section of the Economic Commission for Africa (ECA). President Micombero in May attended the second Convention of the Peoples' Revolutionary Movement of the Congo (Kinshasa).

Relations with neighbouring Rwanda had been complicated by the rupture of diplomatic relations between the Congo (Kinshasa) and Rwanda in 1968, but relations were resumed in February 1969. During June 10–12 the foreign ministers of the Congo (Kinshasa) and Burundi met to consider mutual development problems and the formation of a regional group.

Burundi continued to receive considerable external financial aid. In February the European Development

BURUNDI

Education. (1966–67) Primary, pupils 152,962, teachers 3,933; secondary, pupils 2,932, teachers 229; vocational, pupils 1,781, teachers 186; teacher training, students 1,948, teachers 192; higher (including University of Bujumbura), students 268, teaching staff 82.

Finance. Monetary unit: Burundi franc, with a par value of BurFr. 175 to Belgian Fr. 100 (BurFr. 87.50 = U.S. $1; BurFr. 210 = £1 sterling). Budget (1967 est.): revenue BurFr. 1,550,000,000; expenditure BurFr. 1,639,000,000. Gold and foreign exchange, central bank: (March 1969) U.S. $2,270,000; (March 1968) U.S. $2,590,000.

Foreign Trade. (1968) Imports BurFr. 1,994,000,000; exports BurFr. 1,426,000,000. Import sources (1967): Belgium-Luxembourg 24%; U.S. 17%; Japan 14%; Tanzania 12%; West Germany 11%; Kenya 9%. Export destinations (1967): U.S. 79%; U.K. 11%. Main exports: coffee 82%; cotton 9%.

Transport and Communications. Roads (1967) *c*. 6,000 km. (including 80 km. with improved surface). Telephones (Jan. 1967) *c*. 3,000.

Agriculture. Production (in 000; metric tons; 1967; 1966 in parentheses): corn 116 (110); sweet potatoes 757 (743); dry beans 123 (155); bananas 1,311 (1,279); coffee 15 (13). Livestock (in 000; Dec. 1967): cattle 596; sheep 206; goats 434.

Fund of the EEC announced aid to Burundi amounting to $2.8 million for roads and $1 million for the tea industry. The International Monetary Fund granted $4 million as part of a $12 million development plan for the tea industry. (M. Mr.)

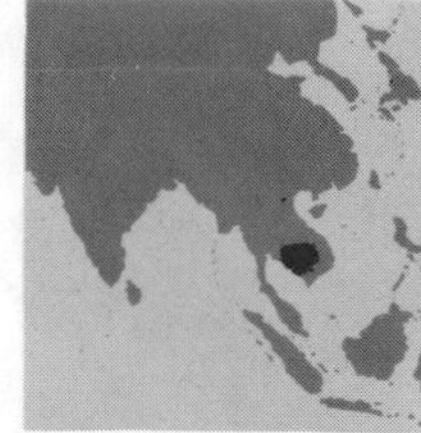

Cambodia

A constitutional monarchy (without a ruling monarch in 1969) of Southeast Asia, Cambodia is the southwest part of the Indochinese Peninsula. Area: 69,898 sq.mi. (181,035 sq.km.). Pop. (1968 est.): 6,557,000, including (est.) Cambodian 85%; Vietnamese 8%; Chinese 6%. Cap.: Phnom Penh (pop., 1962, 393,995). Language: Khmer and French. Religion: Buddhism. Chief of state in 1969, Prince Norodom Sihanouk; premiers, Samdech Penn Nouth until August 13 and Gen. Lon Nol from August 14.

CAMBODIA

Education. (1967–68) Primary, pupils 998,000, teachers (1965–66) 15,711; secondary, pupils 107,000, teachers (1965–66) 3,196; vocational (1965–66), pupils 4,015, teachers 336; teacher training (1965–66), students 945, teachers 77; higher (including 2 universities at Phnom-Penh; 1965–66), students 9,465, teaching staff (universities only) 725.

Finance. Monetary unit: riel (35 riels = U.S. $1; 84 riels = £1 sterling). Budget (1967 est.): revenue 5,440,000,000 riels; expenditure 6,640,200,000 riels.

Foreign Trade. (1967) Imports 3,365,000,000 riels; exports 2,907,000,000 riels. Import sources: France 29%; Japan 16%; China 9%; Singapore 9%; U.K. 5%. Export destinations: Hong Kong 19%; Singapore 10%; France 9%; China 8%; South Vietnam 6%. Main exports: rubber 25%; rice 42%; corn 5%.

Transport and Communications. Roads (1967) 10,826 km. (including 2,600 km. all-weather). Motor vehicles in use (1967): passenger 21,700; commercial 10,600. Railways: (1968) 552 km.; traffic (1967) 142 million passenger-km., freight 66 million net ton-km. Air traffic (1968): 50,880,000 passenger-km.; freight 1,152,000 net ton-km. Waterways (Mekong River: 1967) *c.* 1,400 km. Telephones (Jan. 1968) *c.* 5,900. Radio receivers (Dec. 1967) 1 million. Television receivers (Dec. 1967) *c.* 20,000.

Agriculture. Production (in 000; metric tons; 1968; 1967 in parentheses): rice 3,251 (2,457); rubber 51 (54); dry beans (1967) 29, (1966) 25; corn 154 (150). Livestock (in 000; Dec. 1967): cattle 1,815; buffaloes 856; pigs 1,078.

Cambodia's internal problems in 1969 constrained Prince Sihanouk to take drastic measures to counter the deteriorating economic situation and the increasing threat to Cambodia's independence posed by Communist-backed insurrection within the country and external pressure from Cambodia's neighbours, notably North Vietnam.

At the beginning of the year Sihanouk called for a new orientation of the Cambodian economy, one which would emphasize international cooperation. Subsequently, he mentioned the possibility of joining the World Bank and the International Monetary Fund and said that the government was considering whether to reaccept U.S. economic aid, which had ceased in 1963. On June 11, after earlier rejecting U.S. moves toward reconciliation, Sihanouk announced the resumption of diplomatic relations with the United States following a U.S. note recognizing Cambodian independence, integrity, and neutrality. It was thought that this might result in some U.S. capital investment in Cambodia, and the 12.5% devaluation of the Cambodian riel in August following the devaluation of the French franc was also seen as an encouragement to investors.

In August Sihanouk disclosed that the state was incurring a revenue loss of $330,000 every month, in addition to a budget deficit of $20 million, and warned that years of strict austerity lay ahead. It was announced that Premier Samdech Penn Nouth was retiring for health reasons. The National Assembly voted unanimously for Gen. Lon Nol, a former premier with close contacts in the U.S., to succeed him, Sihanouk having threatened to resign unless a new government could be formed rapidly. Lon Nol announced that the policy of nationalization would be discontinued, and Sihanouk warned the new government that failure to redress the financial situation would lead to dire consequences, including the loss of national independence.

Cambodian vendors display their wares at an international free market on the South Vietnam border. The location of the market shifted from one side of the border to the other depending on the local political situation.

WIDE WORLD

The political threat to Cambodian independence was no less disturbing. In April Cambodia protested to the UN Security Council that the U.S. was defoliating rubber plantations and crops near the border with South Vietnam. In May two U.S. helicopters were shot down over Cambodian territory, bringing renewed protests from Phnom Penh. The Vietnamese Communists reactivated cells in Cambodia to support the Khmer Rouge guerrillas, whose strength was estimated at around 3,000. Sihanouk commented on the improved armament of the guerrillas and on the involvement of North Vietnamese and Viet Cong troops in Cambodia. As the guerrillas began striking at Cambodian Army units, he warned them that they were playing into U.S. hands. Criticizing North Vietnam for infiltrating troops "up to regiment size" into Cambodia, he said that if the Cambodian people had to choose between the Communists and the U.S., they would prefer the latter. Nevertheless, in May diplomatic relations with the South Vietnamese National Liberation Front (political arm of the Viet Cong) were raised to embassy level.

Though relations with Thailand improved, with hints of a possible resumption of diplomatic ties, Phnom Penh accused the Thais in May of trying to create a rebel government in Cambodia, following the capture of armed rebel groups near the Thai border.

The belief that Sihanouk would not jeopardize Cambodian neutrality by turning toward the West received confirmation when, a week after announcing the resumption of relations with the U.S., he received the Chinese ambassador and told him that Cambodia would continue to fight the Americans. In May he extended full diplomatic recognition to East Germany, whereupon the West German government retaliated by ceasing all diplomatic activities in Phnom Penh and announcing that it would give no new aid. Sihanouk explained Cambodia's brand of neutralism in a characteristic statement in August. "When the U.S. does silly things to us," he said, "we have to move a little closer to China. But if the Communists themselves get ugly, they had better take care too. Their provocations will only push us into the other camp."

(T. J. S. G.)

Cameroon

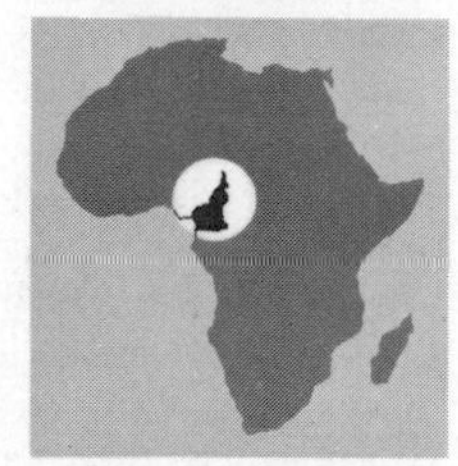

A federal republic of west equatorial Africa on the Gulf of Guinea, Cameroon borders on Nigeria, Chad, the Central African Republic, the Congo (Brazzaville), Gabon, and Equatorial Guinea. Area: 183,591 sq.mi. (475,500 sq.km.). Pop. (1968 est.): 5,493,000, mainly Negrò. Cap.: Yaoundé (pop., 1964 est., 103,015). Largest city: Douala (pop., 1964 est., 159,000). Language: Bantu, Sudanic, French, and English. Religion: mainly animism or tribal beliefs; some Christian and Muslim. President in 1969, Ahmadou Ahidjo.

The political scene remained stable throughout 1969 with no significant changes in government. On March 10, the congress of the Cameroon National Union, the sole authorized party, confirmed state control of all Cameroon's political organizations.

On several occasions during the year President Ahidjo publicly emphasized his hostility to Biafran separatism. In his view the only solution to the conflict between Nigeria and Biafra lay in a compromise that would respect Nigeria's territorial integrity while giving a degree of autonomy to its various regions.

CAMEROON

Education. (1965–66) Primary, pupils 713,603, teachers (including preprimary) 15,719; secondary, pupils 28,529, teachers 1,080; vocational, pupils 10,279; teacher training, students 2,045; higher (including University of Cameroon), students (1966–67) 1,804, teaching staff 134.

Finance. Monetary unit: CFA franc, with a parity of CFA Fr. 50 to the French franc (CFA Fr. 277.71 = U.S. $1; CFA Fr. 666.50 = £1 sterling). Federal budget (1968–69 est.) balanced at CFA Fr. 27.5 billion (including capital expenditure of CFA Fr. 2.9 billion).

Foreign Trade. (1968) Imports CFA Fr. 46,320,000,000; exports CFA Fr. 46,720,000,000. Import sources (1967): France 56%; West Germany 8%; U.S. 5%. Export destinations (1967): France 30%; Netherlands 19%; West Germany 11%; U.S. 11%. Main exports: coffee 27%; cocoa 23%; aluminum 10%; timber 6%.

Transport and Communications. Roads: (East Cameroon; 1968) 44,111 km. (including 5,236 km. main roads); (West Cameroon; 1967) 1,773 km. Railways: (1967) 535 km.; traffic (1968) 149 million passenger-km., freight 206 million net ton-km. Telephones (Jan. 1968) *c.* 4,800. Radio receivers (1968) *c.* 210,000.

Agriculture. Production (in 000; metric tons; 1967; 1966 in parentheses): coffee *c.* 66 (*c.* 63); sweet potatoes (1966) 308, (1965) 345; cassava (1966) 774, (1965) 711; cocoa (1966–67) *c.* 86, (1965–66) *c.* 79; bananas (1966) 117, (1965) *c.* 124; peanuts *c.* 126 (*c.* 125); rubber (exports) 11.8 (12.3); cotton, lint (1968) *c.* 24, (1967) 17; corn (East Cameroon only) 250 (286); dry beans (1966) 21, (1965) 26; millet and sorghum (1966) *c.* 490, (1965) 484; palm kernels (1966) *c.* 21, (1965) *c.* 25; palm oil (1966) *c.* 35, (1965) *c.* 34; timber (cu.m.; 1966) *c.* 5,800, (1965) *c.* 5,800. Livestock (in 000; East Cameroon only; Dec. 1967): cattle 1,850; pigs 250; sheep (Dec. 1965) *c.* 1,150; goats 3,500; poultry 7,500.

Industry. Aluminum production (1968) 45,000 metric tons.

On July 17 the village of Djoum on the frontiers of Cameroon, Gabon, and Congo (Brazzaville) was the scene of an attack by members of the revolutionary underground Union of the Cameroon Peoples (UPC). This single incident was a sudden reminder of the existence of this secret movement, of which nothing had been heard for a year and a half.

On July 29, at the National Assembly in Yaoundé, a second economic agreement was signed between the six members of the European Economic Community and the 18 African associated states. The World Bank loaned $7.9 million and France $3.6 million for further development of Cameroon's palm-oil industry, an attempt to meet the country's internal needs for edible fats. Planting was to cover the eastern forest area, a sparsely populated region ill-suited for other crops. The U.S. Export-Import Bank loaned CFA Fr. 759 million for improving the telecommunications network between Yaoundé and Fort Foreau.

On April 7 the president inaugurated the road from Douala to Tiko on the new bridge over the Mungo River, and on April 8 he opened the railway from Mbanga to Kumba, one of the main links between the country's two provinces. A financial convention was signed on April 22 with the EEC for the second section of the Trans-Cameroon Railway, to go from Belabo to Ngaoundéré, the EEC contributing $20 million. The World Bank granted a similar sum for school construction, road building, and a tea-growing project in the western region. President Ahidjo inaugurated a nurses' training centre in May in Bamenda, and in October the new University Centre for Health Sciences was opened in Yaoundé. (PH. D.)

Canada

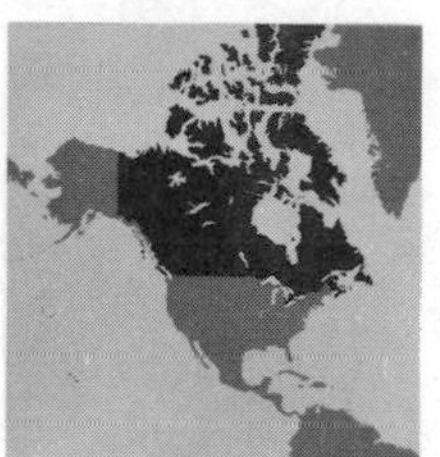

Canada is a federal parliamentary state and member of the Commonwealth of Nations covering North America north of conterminous United States and east of Alaska. Area: 3,851,809 sq.mi. (9,976,196 sq. km.). Pop. (1968 est.): 21,061,000, including (1961) British 43.8%; French 30.4%; other European 22.6%; Indian and Eskimo 1.2%. Cap.: Ottawa (metro. pop., 1968, 518,000). Largest city: Montreal (metro. pop., 1968, 2,527,000). Language (1961): English only 67.4%; French only 19.1%; both 12.2%; neither 1.3%. Religion: Roman Catholic 45.7%; Protestant 47.7%. Queen, Elizabeth II; governor-general in 1969, D. Roland Michener; prime minister, Pierre Elliott Trudeau.

With no dramatic changes in the leadership of the federal government such as had occurred in 1968, Canada experienced a year of political calm in 1969. The year saw the settling into office of a youthful Liberal administration headed by Trudeau, who had succeeded Lester B. Pearson as prime minister on April 20, 1968.

Inevitably the demands of his position changed the style of the unconventional and stimulating figure who had won a great personal triumph in the general election of June 25, 1968. Trudeau as prime minister showed himself to be a careful, even cautious, administrator, concerned in his first year in power to assess and refashion the process of decision making in Ottawa. His changes in governmental machinery emphasized the coordination of policies, not only between federal ministries but between Ottawa and the provinces. Trudeau also sought to arouse a greater public responsiveness to the actions of government and tried,

Business Management: *see* Employment, Wages, and Hours; Industrial Review; Merchandising

Business Review: *see* Economy, World

Butter: *see* Agriculture

with some success, to inspire a "dialogue" between various groups.

Domestic Affairs. The legislative program of the Trudeau administration for the 1968–69 parliamentary session, while extensive, introduced few innovations. Most of the measures had been previously studied or approved by the Pearson government and some of them had already been before Parliament. This was true of the Official Languages Act, which received royal assent before the summer recess and went into force in September. It embodied one of Trudeau's principal approaches to the question of nationalistic division in Canada: to provide a congenial atmosphere for French-speaking Canadians in every part of the country in order to prevent the growth of a "ghetto mentality" among those residing in the province of Quebec.

The act made French and English the official languages of the federal government. It guaranteed access in both languages to federal services—administrative and judicial—in designated bilingual districts including Ottawa. At the crucial second reading of the bill on May 27, almost a quarter of the Conservative members of the House of Commons broke with their leader, Robert Stanfield, to vote against the bill. Most of the dissidents came from ridings in the Prairie Provinces and were led by former Prime Minister John Diefenbaker, whom Stanfield had replaced as party leader in 1967.

Another piece of legislation approved in 1969 had been before Parliament for almost two years. This was a group of controversial amendments to the Criminal Code permitting therapeutic abortions and allowing homosexual acts between consenting adults. New provisions were also inserted to ban harassing telephone calls and to strengthen firearms registration. The first two changes were vigorously opposed by Créditiste members from Quebec who staged a filibuster in an effort to prevent their passage.

In June Parliament gave final assent to an important feature of the new government's communications policy: the establishment of a telecommunications satellite, Telesat Canada, to be built by private firms at a cost of $65 million. The satellite system would offer television and telegraph services throughout Canada in both English and French. It was hoped to put the satellite into orbit by 1971 or 1972, the launching to be carried out by the U.S. on a cost-reimbursable basis.

The government also brought forward proposals to promote housing through granting federal loans to provinces or municipalities to acquire land in advance of housing demands. A nonprofit corporation, Hockey Canada, was also set up to develop a national team that would endeavour to win the world hockey championship for Canada in 1970.

The first legislative session of the 28th Parliament of Canada, which began on Sept. 12, 1968, sat continuously, except for a Christmas recess, until July 25, 1969. After a summer recess the formal end of the first session occurred on October 22 and next day the second session began with a statement of the government's plans for 1969–70. The Trudeau government emphasized the need for a reform of parliamentary procedure. A series of proposals for speeding up the work of Parliament by transferring more of the consideration of legislation to specialized standing committees had been introduced early in the first session. It was expected that the changes would save up to 50 days a year of Parliament's time.

The most crucial section of the new rules was a proposal that the government might, if a committee of party House leaders could not agree on a timetable, lay down a schedule of dates for the progress of legislation through Parliament. The government's timetable could be put to a vote in the House after only two hours of debate. This proposal, Rule 16A, was bitterly opposed by the opposition parties when it was first introduced and put aside just before the Christmas recess. But it was made clear that the Trudeau Cabinet regarded Rule 16A as the key to reforms. The proposal was reintroduced toward the end of the session and debate on the new rules began in earnest on July 7. A filibuster staged by the opposition irritated Trudeau, who was scheduled to make a tour of the Prairie Provinces in mid-July.

Eventually the government announced that it would use a closure motion, which is not debatable and must be voted on immediately, to end the debate. In the Canadian Parliament closure was a dangerous weapon since it could be represented as a denial of the right of parliamentary discussion. In 1956 it had been a major issue in the election campaign that led to the defeat of the Liberal government that had employed it four times. After a debate that lasted until the early hours of the morning, the rules proposal was approved on July 25 by the Liberal Party majority, 142–84. The closing stage of the debate was marked

CANADA

Education. (1966–67) Primary, pupils 3,768,875, teachers 138,398; secondary and vocational, pupils 1,521,646, teachers 83,008; higher (including 34 principal universities), students 372,275, teaching staff 37,561.

Finance. Monetary unit: Canadian dollar, with a par value of Can$1.08 to U.S. $1(Can$2.59 = £1 sterling). Gold and foreign exchange, official: (June 1969) U.S. $2,631,000,000; (June 1968) U.S. $2,581,000,000. Budget (1967–68 actual): revenue Can$9,076,589,447; expenditure Can$9,868,991,666. Gross national product: (1968) Can$67,368,000,000; (1967) Can$61,973,000,000. Money supply: (May 1969) Can$13,210,000,000; (May 1968) Can$11,990,000,000. Cost of living (1963 = 100): (May 1969) 121.

Foreign Trade. (1968) Imports Can$12,358,000,000; exports Can$13,576,000,000. Import sources: U.S. 73%; U.K. 6%; EEC 5%. Export destinations: U.S. 68%; U.K. 9%; EEC 6%. Main exports: motor vehicles 18%; machinery 10%; nonferrous metals 10%; metal ores 9%; newsprint 7%; timber 7%; wheat 5%; wood pulp 5%.

Transport and Communications. Roads (1968) 806,281 km. (including 2,611 km. expressways). Motor vehicles in use (1967): passenger 5,771,900; commercial (including buses) 1,505,000. Railways: (1967) 69,470 km.; traffic (1968) *c.* 4.4 billion passenger-km., freight *c.* 139,500,000,000 net ton-km. Air traffic (1968): 11,690,000,000 passenger-km.; freight 286.3 million net ton-km. Shipping (1968): merchant vessels 100 gross tons and over 1,296; gross tonnage 2,402,983; goods loaded 78,990,000 metric tons, unloaded 49,320,000 metric tons. Telephones (Dec. 1967) 8,345,000. Radio receivers (Dec. 1967) 12,050,000. Television receivers (Dec. 1966) *c.* 5.7 million.

Agriculture. Production (in 000; metric tons; 1968; 1967 in parentheses): wheat 17,686 (16,137); oats 5,591 (4,691); barley 7,084 (5,414); rye 331 (337); corn 2,051 (1,882); potatoes 2,090 (2,130); rapeseed 424 (560); linseed 461 (238); tobacco (1967) 57, (1966) 53; butter 148 (153); cheese 87 (87); timber (cu.m.; 1966) *c.* 114,100, (1965) *c.* 103,600; fish catch (1967) 1,290, (1966) 1,346. Livestock (in 000; June 1967): cattle 9,269; sheep 962; horses 370; pigs 6,012; poultry 80,102.

Industry. Labour force (excluding agriculture; June 1969) 7,817,000. Unemployment: (May 1969) 4.7%; (May 1968) 4.6%. Index of industrial production (1963 = 100): (1968) 137; (1967) 130. Fuel and power (in 000; metric tons; 1968): coal 7,945; lignite 2,042; crude oil 51,177; natural gas (cu.m.) 52,223,000; electricity (kw-hr.) 175,430,000 (80% hydroelectric in 1967). Mineral and metal production (in 000; metric tons; 1968): crude steel 10,206; iron ore (shipments; 55% metal content) 42,064; copper ore (metal content) 552; nickel ore (metal content; 1967) 226; zinc ore (metal content) 1,156; lead ore (metal content) 328; aluminum (exports) 782; asbestos (1967) 1,417; gold (troy oz.) 2,700; silver (troy oz.) 45,000; uranium oxide (1967) 3.4. Other production (in 000; metric tons; 1968): wood pulp 14,670; newsprint 7,285; synthetic rubber 197; passenger cars (units) 835; commercial vehicles (units) 280. Dwelling units completed (1968) 171,000.

PETER BREGG—CANADIAN PRESS

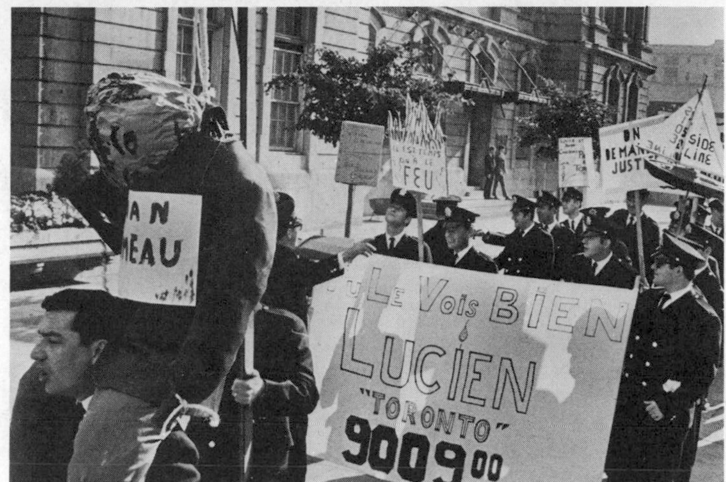

"MONTREAL STAR"

"MONTREAL STAR"

Left, Montreal firemen stage a protest march, Oct. 6, 1969. An arbitrated wage settlement awarded them half the increase they had demanded. Canadian troops guard Montreal City Hall (top left) and looters plunder a downtown store (above) during a strike by the city's police and firemen, Oct. 7–8, 1969.

by harsh words between Prime Minister Trudeau and the leaders of the opposition parties, which did not enhance the reputation of any of the speakers.

There was one important loss from the Trudeau Cabinet in 1969. Paul Hellyer, minister of transport and deputy prime minister, had chaired a task force that toured Canada for three months and recommended a series of sweeping changes in the federal government's role in the housing field. When these proposals were not approved by the Cabinet after two months' consideration, Hellyer resigned on April 24 to dramatize his concern over the lack of progress. Behind this specific issue was Hellyer's feeling that the Trudeau government's theory of federalism blocked decisive action on subjects, such as housing and pollution, that were considered to fall under provincial jurisdiction.

A new ministry, Regional Economic Expansion, was created in 1969 to stimulate economic activity in depressed regions and to work for a more uniform level of incomes across Canada. Jean Marchand, a former labour leader from Quebec and a longtime associate of Trudeau, was given this major portfolio. The former Departments of Forestry and Fisheries were combined into one department, as were the Departments of Trade and Commerce and Industry. A new Department of Communications, with responsibility for the post office and telecommunications, was set up under Eric Kierans.

Canada moved toward a comprehensive national medical insurance plan in 1969, largely completing a process that had begun in 1966 with the passage of federal legislation. The plan had gone into effect in 1968 when British Columbia and Saskatchewan enrolled in it. Nova Scotia, Newfoundland, and Manitoba entered the program on April 1, 1969, Alberta on July 1, and Ontario on October 1. Of the three provinces still outside the scheme, Quebec planned its own physician's insurance coverage, New Brunswick had approved the program but had not yet set a date for entry, and Prince Edward Island had not reached a decision in the matter.

Constitutional Reform. While there were few concrete advances toward the realization of a new federal-provincial structure in 1969, preparations for a reformulation of the constitutional relationship between the federal government and the ten provinces progressed in a less combative manner than in past years. This was partly due to the attitude of the new premier of Quebec, Jean-Jacques Bertrand, who possessed a milder temperament than his predecessor, Daniel Johnson, although he clearly shared the conviction that a "special status" must be found for Quebec in any new constitutional structure. Trudeau continued to stress the importance of guaranteeing individual rights as a means of providing French-speaking Canadians an assured place in the country's society. He pressed for a charter of human rights—linguistic, educational, and judicial—to be entrenched in the Canadian constitution.

The first federal-provincial conference of the year, which was held in Ottawa on February 10–12, took up constitutional issues. Five committees of ministers were appointed to look into language rights, the entrenchment of fundamental human rights in a revised constitution, regional disparities, reform of the federal upper house or Senate, and the status of the Su-

continued on page 189

TRUDEAU'S FOREIGN POLICY: AN EARLY APPRAISAL

By James Eayrs

Modern political science rejects, and rightly, the notion that one man—be his name Lenin or Stalin, Chamberlain or Churchill, Hitler or Mussolini, Nehru or Sukarno, Roosevelt or Kennedy—can make his country's foreign policy just as he pleases. Experts tell us, and correctly, that behind every "output," or policy decision, there lurk a dozen "inputs"—economic capability, military capacity, political structure, competing elites, and the rest—that constrain the would-be foreign-policy-maker-on-horseback. It was Mussolini himself who reminded us, in a moment of clarity, that "there is no such thing as originality in foreign policy."

The most charismatic leader is subject to a hard if not an iron law limiting his scope, making finite his options, bringing down to earth and sometimes burying his lofty conceptions of the public good. Canadian leaders, charismatic or otherwise, have not merely acknowledged such a law, they have groveled in its presence. If one prime minister has said publicly that "Canada is a difficult country to govern," most have said it privately and all have thought it. The precariousness of Canada's economy, the tensions of its culture, the sparseness of its people, the looming proximity of a great, if friendly, power are all invoked as extenuating circumstances. Circumstances—"inputs" in the jargon—these incontestably are; to what degree they are extenuating, historians—not politicians—must judge.

The Case of the Careful Swinger. In the case of Pierre Elliott Trudeau, 15th prime minister of Canada since confederation, a final verdict is premature. The Liberal Party awarded him its leadership in April 1968. The Canadian people voted him their confidence in June 1968—but what a vote of confidence it was! The Liberals gained 155 seats out of 264, with strong support in all parts of the Dominion save the Maritimes—from factory and farm, from those who spoke English and those who spoke French, and from those who spoke Ukrainian (or any of a score of other tongues). Trudeau's was the first majority government in Canada in ten years, and it had been formed by a man who had been virtually unknown only months earlier. He had made few promises, he had given fortune no hostages. As much as democracies ever deliver themselves into a politician's hands, Canada was Trudeau's, to lead it where he would. If Canada is difficult to govern, it would be easier for him than most.

So meteoric a rise, joined to a swashbuckling life-style, led many of his idolators to expect startling things of his government. "He is as tribal as the Beatles," Marshall McLuhan had declaimed impressively if enigmatically, and the sandals, turtleneck, and leather coat worn when he was minister of justice suggested more than mere sartorial novelty. But it was not only the inevitable presence of inputs that doomed such expectations. They had misunderstood their man.

For the new prime minister was no plunger, in foreign policy or anything else. Those who believed the contrary were misled by surface eccentricities of dress and by a deportment that was startling—if to some charming—in one of his age (49) and station. It is instructive to watch him on the apparatus plungers use. First he looks in the pool. Then he tests the water. Then he tests the board. Only after meticulous checking out is the two-and-one-half gainer, or whatever it may be, faultlessly executed. As with diving, so with politics. "In a non-revolutionary society," he wrote some years ago, "no manner of reform can be implanted with sudden universality. Democratic reformers must proceed step by step, convincing little bands of intellectuals here, rallying sections of the working class there, and appealing to the under-privileged in the next place." This is not the cry of a man about to turn his country upside down; it is the creed of a conservative, who makes haste slowly.

"LONDON DAILY EXPRESS" FROM PICTORIAL PARADE

Canadian Prime Minister Pierre Trudeau arriving in London for the Commonwealth Prime Ministers' Conference, April 1, 1969. Despite his reputation as a swinger he proved to be a cautious statesman.

After 18 months in office, the most comprehensive statement of Trudeau's view of the world and Canada's place in it remained the document issued from his office on May 29, 1968, on the eve of the general election. It is more of a don's-eye view than a diplomat's, reflecting one of his several previous callings; it may be none the worse for that.

Trudeau saw then, and generally continued to see, a world in which peace is kept through terror by two superpowers that fortunately were "showing increasing responsibility about unleashing it." As a result, "the threat of major military clash has measurably receded"—though "not the need to ensure that the intricate power balance is maintained by a wide variety of means." It is a world where "international tension is sustained . . . because of localized hostilities, latent disputes, racial discrimination, economic and social distress," in which the focuses of instability, apart from Vietnam, are to be found in the Middle East, in the southern half of Africa, and among the wretched of the earth. It is, finally, a polycentric world: "Although it remains true that there are some fundamental and far-reaching differences between us and the Communist countries, it is no longer true to say that the Communist world is monolithically and implacably opposed to us."

What, in such a world, had Canada to contribute? Not as much as it had in the truly exceptional circumstances just after World War II: "Then we were probably the largest of the small powers. Our currency was one of the strongest. We were the fourth or fifth trading nation and our economy was much stronger than the European currencies. We had one of the very strongest navy and air forces. But now Europe has regained its strength. The Third

World had emerged." That did not mean there was little Canadians could do. It meant rather that they should cut their suits to fit their cloth, bring output into line with inputs. "Realism—that should be the operative word in our definition of international aim. Realism in how we read the world barometer. Realism in how we see ourselves thriving in the climate it forecasts."

All very elementary—but the statement of May 29 contained two hints of major changes in policy. The prime minister could hardly omit China from his *tour d'horizon,* not just because China contained (as it was becoming more fashionable to recognize) one quarter of the human race but also because the prime minister was an old China hand on a modest scale. In 1960 he and a companion had roamed the mainland for a month, and the perceptive book published by these *Deux Innocents en Chine* (as they inaccurately described themselves) on their return heaped scorn on Canadian no less than on U.S. policy. By 1968 the condition of China and of at least one of the report's authors had changed considerably, so scorn is more decorously expressed in the May 29 statement. Nonetheless, Trudeau's views had not altered. China, the "innocent" become prime minister noted,

> continues to be both a colossus and a conundrum. Potentially the People's Republic of China poses a major threat to peace largely because calculation about Chinese ambitions, intentions, capacity to catch up and even about actual developments within China have to be based on incomplete information—which opens up an area of unpredictability. Mainland China's exclusion from the world community stems partly from policies of non-recognition and of seeking to contain Chinese communism through military means, and partly from Peking's own policies and problems. Yet most of the major world issues to which I have referred will not be resolved completely or in any lasting way, unless and until an accommodation has been reached with the Chinese nation.

The other hint of change concerned Canada's defense relations with Western Europe and the United States. "We will take a hard look," the prime minister promised,

> in consultation with our allies, at our military role in NATO and determine whether our present military commitment is still appropriate to the present situation in Europe. We will look at our role in NORAD [North American Air Defense Command] in the light of the technological advances of modern weaponry and of our fundamental opposition to the proliferation of nuclear weapons.

It remains to trace the fate of these initiatives over the first year and a half of Trudeau's government.

The China Question. Recognition of the People's Republic and an exchange of ambassadors between Ottawa and Peking were policies that, for their consummation, required the acquiescence of the mainland government. It would have been possible merely to go through the motions. Recognition could have been offered on terms that the Canadian government knew Peking would not accept—some version, for example, of a "two Chinas" policy that did not involve Canada's turning away from Taiwan. Such a strategy, known to insiders as "negotiating to failure," seems to have been considered during the early months when the government was assessing the reaction of the various interested parties—its own public, the U.S. government, Taiwan, and, of course, any twitch of interest that might emanate from Peking. These soundings taken, the government made up its mind to negotiate to success. "There is no objective of this government," Mitchell Sharp, the secretary of state for external affairs, declared in the House of Commons on Sept. 18, 1968, "I consider more important than this one set forth by the Prime Minister and myself during the election campaign." To reach it would probably mean breaking off diplomatic relations with Taiwan, but in diplomacy, as in business, there is seldom such a thing as a free lunch.

No one could fairly say that the Canadian government was falling over itself in haste when—despite remonstrances from Washington, contrary advice from Canberra, and the anguished pleading of the ambassador to Canada from Taiwan—it revealed, early in 1969, its intention to open direct negotiations with the Peking regime concerning an exchange of ambassadors. The policy had been deferred for 20 years. It had been Canada's intention to follow the example of the United Kingdom, India, and other friendly nations that had recognized the People's Republic within a few months of its proclamation on Oct. 1, 1949. Ottawa had even selected an ambassador who had gone so far as to rent a house in Peking. Like its Commonwealth partners, Canada planned this step not out of admiration for the achievements of Mao Tse-tung but in the spirit of Sir Winston Churchill's dictum that recognition does not confer a compliment, it secures a convenience—the principal convenience being, in Canada's case, a wider market for its grains.

A combination of considerations—the preoccupation of a fledgling foreign office with more pressing concerns (of which the launching of NATO was paramount), uncertainty about Washington's reaction, concern over Peking's failure to respond to recognition by the United Kingdom—caused Ottawa to hesitate. By the time the government of Canada was ready for action, the Chinese had entered the Korean War and had been given (January 1951) the status of "aggressor" by the UN General Assembly. At least once during the next two decades the government warily circled the nettle of recognition, but in the end shrank from grasping it. Early in 1957 the then foreign minister, Lester Pearson, candidly explained why: "We did not consider it worth having a first-class row with the United States over a matter on which public opinion in our own country is strongly divided." He might have added that Canada's nonrecognition policy—which, unlike that of the United States, sprang neither from ideological considerations nor from global realpolitik but rather from what Pearson described as "a calculated weighing of advantages and disadvantages"—offered Canada the best of both worlds. It gave the minimum of offense to the United States while imposing no practical disadvantage upon Canadians wishing to trade with or travel in China. The great wheat sales of the early 1960s confirmed this analysis.

What, then, caused the change? There were several factors: the personal convictions of Trudeau, who was perhaps unique among the leaders of the West in that he had shaken the hand of Mao Tse-tung; the movement of Canadian opinion, particularly in the intellectual community, away from the old golden rule of never aggravating the United States unnecessarily; the realization by the Trudeau government and the Liberal Party that the country had put them in power not to carry on the old policies but to change those policies and that, while no change would be simple, a change on China would be least difficult; and finally, and perhaps above all, the shared realization of policy community and general public alike that the continued isolation of China, over whose deserts the familiar mushroom cloud now rose, was not merely absurd but highly dangerous.

So, in Stockholm in May 1969, formal negotiations were opened between the Chinese and Canadian ambassadors over the terms of mutual recognition. These negotiations continued. They might end in failure, but it was not the intention of the Canadian government that this should occur.

A New Look at NATO. The new China policy would require the agreement of the new China. The new Atlantic policy—if such it might be called—could be carried out despite the hostility of all concerned.

"Hostile" may be an exaggerated description of the NATO governments' reaction on learning that the Trudeau government was reconsidering Canada's 20-year-old commitment to the defense of Western Europe. "Worried" is no exaggeration, however. There was the worry of bureaucracies everywhere when faced by uncertainty and the prospect of change. Western Europe was worried lest a Canadian withdrawal stimulate the Soviet appetite for adventure and, like the first in a row of falling dominoes, lead to retreat all along the line. The United States was worried lest Canada's initiative touch off a new round of domestic isolationism and encourage the demand that U.S. troops be recalled from overseas. Some Americans were shocked as well as worried. "If Canada actually thinks of getting out of NATO," a prominent senator was quoted as saying, "it would be a betrayal. Our people would never forget it."

PETER BREGG—CANADIAN PRESS

Canadian Communist Party members demonstrate before Parliament March 12, 1969, to protest Canada's involvement in NATO. In April the government announced its decision concerning the alliance.

The simplest interpretation of this and other intemperate expressions by certain U.S. congressmen is that they were intended to influence the Canadian foreign policy review in the direction of the status quo. To the extent that the apprehension was genuine, rather than feigned for this purpose, it arose through unfamiliarity with the Trudeau style of policy formation. The prime minister's caution and conservatism do not stop him from keeping his direst options open until the moment of decision, nor do they inhibit his posing questions in a manner that, in a politician, often seems provocative to the point of perversity. He could ask a mining community looking to him for better housing if it has thought of the day when the ore body would give out. With the same directness, he more than once stated that a possible outcome of the foreign policy review would be a neutral Canada.

A special reason for keeping Atlantic options open was to preserve the credibility of the foreign policy review, particularly among some of those invited to take part in it. Canadian foreign policy is ordinarily made by the Canadian foreign office, and the Department of External Affairs had its own foreign policy review ready for the new prime minister. Examining its own performance, it unsurprisingly found it good. To secure a more detached appraisal, and to fulfill his election promise of "participatory democracy," Trudeau sought the advice of academics and intellectuals outside government circles. The outsiders approached their assignment in a properly skeptical spirit, and the prime minister's insouciant hints that radical foreign policy change could be just around the corner may have been intended to reassure them that they were participants in a review, not a charade.

The invasion of Czechoslovakia by troops of the Soviet Union and several Eastern European countries in August 1968 could not help but affect the foreign policy review. Those favouring the continuation of Canada's European commitments—they included the Department of External Affairs and the Ministry of National Defence and their spokesmen in the Cabinet—felt that their case had been greatly strengthened, and in the public mind it was. The prime minister was concerned that this new "input" should not bring the process of reexamination to a halt or bias unduly those engaged upon it. "Do the events in Czechoslovakia and perhaps the Mediterranean lead me to believe that NATO should be strengthened? I'd say you could argue just as easily to the contrary—that because of Czechoslovakia we have concrete evidence that the Soviet Union is weaker now than it was before; it can no longer count on Czechoslovakia as a solid ally in a military conflict."

By April 1969 the debate had gone on a year, the debaters were beginning to repeat themselves, and no consensus was in sight. The country was still confused, albeit on a higher level of confusion. An impending NATO meeting in Washington commemorating the 20th anniversary of the alliance seemed an opportune time to bring a divided Cabinet to decision. The Cabinet, more deeply divided than had been supposed, met longer than had been expected.

On April 3 the prime minister made his long-awaited announcement. Canada would remain a member of the alliance: "The Government has rejected any suggestion that Canada assume a nonaligned or neutral role in world affairs." But it would begin pulling back from Europe: "The Canadian Government intends, in consultation with Canada's allies, to take early steps to bring about a planned and phased reduction of the size of the Canadian forces in Europe."

So mousey a change, following such mountainous labour, invited scorn. A mocking editorial called it "a cannon trick performed by circus clowns." But, as the prime minister pointed out, this was not the promised new Atlantic policy but only the initial phase thereof. First came the setting of the course; later, in Phase II, the timing and the tempo would be determined. Trudeau would not be rushed in this. It was his manner to take one thing at a time and as much time as might be needed for that one thing; when that one thing was his country's foreign policy, he conceded that much time was needed. "Some people think it is taking too long," he observed on April 12, 1969. "But it will take longer, because you only re-examine your foreign policy once in a generation."

The results of the reexamination were announced on September 19. Canada's NATO forces in Europe were to be cut in half by the fall of 1970. The brigade group of some 6,000 men and the air division of some 4,000 men in West Germany would be phased out. A land force of 2,800 men and an air element of 2,200 men would be combined under a single headquarters in southern Germany for an interim period of three years. By January 1972 it was planned that no Canadian armed forces in Europe would have access to nuclear weapons. Throughout the foreign policy review Trudeau had maintained a pose of impartiality, "letting a hundred flowers blossom and a hundred schools of thought contend"—but if this was the correct way of handling contradictions among his people, it did not mean that he had no thoughts of his own. Once or twice he allowed these to be glimpsed. "We are not threatened by communism or fascism or even by atomic bombs," the prime minister told the students of Queen's University at Kingston, Ont., on Nov. 8, 1968, "as much as we are by the fact that very large sections of the world go to bed hungry every night and large sections of our society do not find fulfillment in our society. I am less worried about what is over the Berlin Wall than about Chicago and what might happen in our great cities in Canada."

He was not the first to worry about the safety of the cities. "Should war come again," Mackenzie King had reflected sombrely in October 1945, "the atomic bomb would be the weapon and Canada the scene of battle." Pierre Trudeau was preoccupied more with the threat of race war and class war than with that of nuclear war. Still, continental defense was posing problems. In May 1968 the prime minister could write with some complacency of the diminishing threat of a major military clash, of the growing stability of the power balance. That was before he became aware of the ways in which ballistic missile defense (BMD) and the multiple independently targeted reentry vehicle (MIRV) might disturb that balance. His government had promised a reconsideration of its role in NORAD, the combined U.S.-Canada air defense command created in 1958 against the threat of bomber attack on North America, "in the light of the technological advances of modern weaponry." But were BMD and MIRV advances or regressions? The prime minister had his views on that, as on most other things, but he deemed it prudent not to take his stand until the government and people of the United States had taken theirs.

continued from page 185

preme Court and the judiciary. Meetings between Justice Minister John Turner and the provincial attorneys general resulted in the disappearance of fears that the Official Languages Bill would be challenged in the courts by some western provinces.

At a second conference on June 11–12, the discussion centred on a more acceptable distribution of taxing and spending powers between the two levels of government. It was agreed in principle that the central and provincial governments should have access to all tax fields; that every effort should be made to avoid the taxpayer having to meet taxation on his income, property, or purchases from more than one province; and that taxing powers should not be exercised in such a way as to create "tax barriers" to interprovincial trade, a problem that could only be dealt with through regular meetings of federal and provincial financial officials. In answer to provincial charges that they were often committed to heavy expenditures through the federal initiation of "shared cost" programs without their consent, Ottawa promised that it would not embark on programs of this sort without establishing that there was a national consensus. The task of formulating the detailed arrangements for these principles of action was turned over to continuing committees.

Provincial Affairs. Two provinces held general elections in 1969, one of which overturned the sitting government. In Manitoba E. R. Schreyer led the New Democratic Party to a narrow victory on June 25 over a Conservative administration that had been in power since 1958. The NDP won 28 of the 57 seats in the legislature; the Conservatives won 22. Later, a Liberal member announced he would vote with the NDP, giving the party a one-vote majority. The victory marked the second occasion in Canada when a socialist party had gained control of a provincial government.

The election in British Columbia on August 27 resulted in the sixth consecutive victory for W. A. C. Bennett and his Social Credit Party, which won 47% of the popular vote and 39 out of 55 seats in the chamber. The New Democratic Party declined to 11 members and five Liberals were elected. A summer of industrial unrest was believed to have been a powerful factor in the victory of the Bennett government.

Foreign Affairs. The most important new departure of the Trudeau government in 1969 came in defense policy, where it was decided that Canada would begin to reduce its military commitment to the North Atlantic Treaty Organization (*see* Special Report). This force amounted, in 1969, to four armoured infantry brigades totaling 6,000 men and an air force division of 3,800 men and cost the government $150 million a year to maintain. There had been doubts for some years about the military value of the Canadian forces in European defense planning. One of the first acts of the Trudeau government was to initiate a thorough appraisal of Canada's foreign and defense policies. On April 3 the prime minister announced that a phased reduction of Canadian forces in Europe would begin in 1970. No details of the reductions were given immediately since Trudeau stated that procedures would have to be worked out in consultation with the defense planning committee of NATO. He confirmed that there had been heated discussions in the Cabinet on the issue—"strong men have strong opinions"—but that the decision had been reached without any resignations.

The April 3 statement placed the protection of Canadian sovereignty at the head of the list of Canadian military priorities. At present the U.S. provided a large share of Canada's protection. "If any part of that can be supplied by us rather than by the Americans, we will want to do it," Trudeau stated. At a meeting of NATO ministers in Washington held on April 10–11 to commemorate the 20th anniversary of the alliance, Mitchell Sharp, minister for external affairs, defended Canada's right to decide its defense policy. He indicated that the economic strength of Western Europe had been a factor in leading Canada to feel that it could safely reduce its contributions to NATO.

There was no doubt as well that the growing costs of Canada's military budget had been a major factor in the decision. The current defense expenditure of $1.8 billion (one-sixth of the national budget) was considered inadequate for the support of the 98,000 men serving with NATO and participating in the defense of North America and in peace-keeping operations. It was estimated that spending on defense would have to increase to about $2.5 billion a year to carry out these functions, a rise that the Trudeau administration was not prepared to sanction in its campaign for economy in the public sector. In June, Leo Cadieux, minister of national defense, told the House of Commons that Canada's revised defense posture could be achieved within a defense budget frozen at the level of $1.8 billion for each of the next three years.

The future pattern of Canada's military forces was divulged gradually over the next few months. The armed forces would be cut back to between 80,000 and 85,000 men by 1972, along with a similar reduction in civilian personnel and the closing of some military bases. There would be a reexamination of "command and control activities" in an effort to reduce headquarters staff and to improve the ratio of operational to nonoperational forces. The NATO forces would be halved by the fall of 1970, leaving 5,000 men concentrated in southern Germany in two bases under a single headquarters. Canada would give up its nuclear role in NATO by 1972, with the withdrawal first of the Honest John missiles and then of the CF-104 Starfighters. The result would be a highly flexible "light airmobile force."

Cadieux emphasized that there would be no change in the use of nuclear weapons in Canada under the NORAD arrangements. The aircraft carrier "Bonaventure," recently refitted, would be decommissioned by 1970 and two destroyer escorts would be reduced to training levels. Four destroyers presently under construction would be fitted for helicopters. The government would require 50 new helicopters by 1971 for surveillance of Arctic and coastal waters.

At meetings on March 24–25 between Prime Minister Trudeau and Pres. Richard Nixon in Washington, Trudeau emphasized that Canada was concerned about the danger of an escalation in nuclear weapons following the U.S. decision to build the Safeguard antiballistic missile system and received assurances on the purposes and implementation of the program. Trudeau reported that he had come to the conclusion that the Spartan missiles in the system would not be operating in Canadian airspace and would create no problems for Canada but that the second missile, the shorter range Sprint, might possibly explode in Canadian airspace. The two leaders and their advisers also talked about trade problems and the future disposal of energy resources between the two countries.

The question of Canadian sovereignty in the Arctic archipelago was a subject of discussion in Parliament on several occasions during 1969. It was alleged that the Canadian claim to ownership of the Arctic islands might be challenged by the U.S., which had a strong interest in the free passage of the channels between the islands. The U.S. tanker "Manhattan" had traveled through the Northwest Passage in the late summer to test the feasibility of the route to transport Alaskan oil. The Trudeau government stated that ownership of the Arctic islands and continental shelf rested with Canada, which would also exercise full sovereign control over all the waters between these islands. In late October, however, the prime minister stated that he was not yet prepared to announce the precise Arctic waters that Canada claimed. He disclosed that the government was preparing legislation to prevent the pollution of Arctic waters by commercial interests.

Montreal firemen battle blaze set by rioting students in the new Sir George Williams University building, Feb. 11, 1969. The street below was littered with student records and computer cards thrown by the students.

"MONTREAL GAZETTE"

The quarrel between Canada and France over the latter's disposition to accord the province of Quebec the status of an independent nation received more fuel during 1969. Late in January, Jean-Guy Cardinal, Quebec's minister of education, was received in Paris as a virtual head of state by Pres. Charles de Gaulle and other French officials. He signed an agreement by which Quebec and France promised to study the joint development of a communications satellite system.

In February a joint Canadian-Quebec delegation, headed by a federal minister, attended an educational conference of French-speaking nations in Niamey, Niger. A similar conference in 1968 had been responsible for the suspension of diplomatic relations between Canada and Gabon, but this quarrel was mended in 1969 when Gabon agreed to the Canadian position and diplomatic relations were resumed.

In October two junior ministers of the French government visited Quebec but declined invitations to call on federal officials at Ottawa. This action, which had the effect of reviving tension, was seen as surprising in view of the friendly gestures France had made toward Canada since its new president, Georges Pompidou, had taken office.

The Economy. The performance of the Canadian economy in 1969 reached levels predicted by federal economists the year before. The gross national product rose by an estimated 7% to $77.3 billion on the basis of current prices. About half the increase was in real terms, the rest in price increases. Exports to the U.S. were held back by strikes in mining and transportation and sluggish motor vehicle sales. Agricultural markets were depressed and there was difficulty in disposing of the Canadian wheat crop. Exports to all countries for the first nine months of 1969 amounted to $10,930,600,000, while imports were valued at $10,401,600,000. The trade surplus was only about half that experienced in 1968, a factor that would undoubtedly produce a larger balance of payments deficit.

An effort to restrain public expenditure resulted in a lessening of demand in the economy in 1969. Building starts were down in the early part of the year before gaining strength and there was a decline in inventory investment. Nevertheless, the rate of unemployment was lower than in 1968, standing throughout most of the year at just below 5%. The Bank of Canada rate on loans to the chartered banks was increased to a record-breaking 8% in July.

The federal budget was presented on June 3 and forecast the largest surplus since 1957. Expenditures for the fiscal year 1969–70 were estimated at $11,650,000,000, with revenues at $12,025,000,000. Of the $390 million surplus expected, $125 million was deducted to cover the federal government's share of the operating deficits of Expo 67. This left a predicted surplus of over $250 million.

Finance Minister Edgar Benson stated that inflation was still the major problem in economic policy and that all available forces, public and private, must be deployed against it. He announced that the 3% temporary surtax on personal and corporation income taxes would be extended to the end of 1970 in an effort to reduce purchasing power. In addition, sweeping tariff reductions contemplated under the Kennedy Round would be implemented immediately instead of over the next two and a half years. These would affect $2 billion in imports and would tend to produce lower factory costs for Canadians. The Trudeau administration entered the battle against inflation by announcing in August the freezing of most government expenditures for 1970–71. A prices and incomes commission was set up to coordinate and plan measures against the upward trend of prices and wages. (D. M. L. F.)

ENCYCLOPÆDIA BRITANNICA FILMS. *Canada: The Atlantic Provinces* (1958); *Canada: The Industrial Provinces* (1958); *Canada: The Pacific Provinces* (1958); *Canada: The Prairie Provinces* (1958); *The St. Lawrence Seaway* (1959); *Canada's Royal Canadian Mounted Police* (1963).

Central African Republic

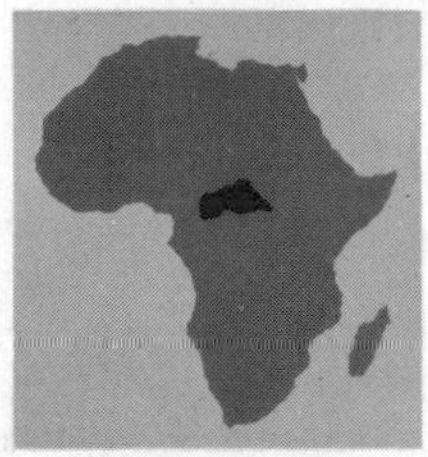

The landlocked Central African Republic is bounded by Chad, Sudan, the Congo republics, and Cameroon. Area: 240,540 sq.mi. (663,000 sq.km.). Pop. (1968 est.): 1,488,000, chiefly Mandja-Baya, Banda, Mbaka, and Azande. Cap. and largest city: Bangui (pop., 1966, 150,000). Official language: French. Religion: mainly animist. President and premier in 1969, Jean Bedel Bokassa.

Following an official visit to France in February, President Bokassa confirmed that he had thwarted an attempted coup d'etat, the second of his presidency. Alexandre Banza, long considered the regime's second in command but in semi-disgrace for more than a year, was shot after a summary trial by the permanent military tribunal; his Ministry of Health was abolished. The execution was followed by rumours concerning the fate of former Pres. David Dacko, whose subsequent trial before the same court was halted on President Bokassa's instruction. Dacko remained under house arrest.

A Cabinet reshuffle in February resulted in the creation of two new ministries—Finance and Foreign Affairs, the president retaining the portfolio of the Interior. In September a company of French parachutists, called for by the president the previous year, was sent home, its presence apparently no longer warranted by the internal situation.

In the field of inter-African relations, lively arguments continued in January between the Central African Republic and the Congo (Kinshasa), where President Bokassa's abandoning of the Union of Central African States in order to rejoin the Central African Customs and Economic Union had caused much resentment. A conciliatory mission to Bangui on behalf of the African and Malagasy Common Organization succeeded in obtaining an agreement to normalize relations between the two countries.

The Central African Republic signed its first trade agreement with Sudan in January; 20,000 head of cattle were bought for Sud£400,000 plus a consignment of wood. In March the World Bank agreed to a loan of $4.2 million for the reconstruction of the road between the capital, Bangui, and Mbaïki in the potentially rich province of Lobaye. The road network, expected to cost $5.6 million, was to be completed by 1972. The European Development Fund in May agreed to finance the construction of the Nola River Port at a cost of $450,000, and the West German government granted a loan of CFA Fr. 383 million to develop a river fleet on the Sangha River for the transport of wood. (PH. D.)

CENTRAL AFRICAN REPUBLIC

Education. (1966–67) Primary, pupils 148,845, teachers 2,504; secondary, pupils 4,668, teachers 208; vocational, pupils 1,220, teachers 152; teacher training, students 195, teachers 20. The University of Bangui was scheduled to open in 1970.

Finance. Monetary unit: CFA franc, with a parity of CFA Fr. 50 to the French franc (CFA Fr. 277.71 = U.S. $1; CFA Fr. 666.50 = £1 sterling). Budget (1968 est.) balanced at CFA Fr. 9.6 billion.

Foreign Trade. (1967) Imports CFA Fr. 10,909,000,000; exports CFA Fr. 7,166,000,000. Import sources: France 61%; West Germany 9%. Export destinations: France 42%; U.S. 30%; Israel 14%. Main exports: diamonds 47%; cotton 23%; coffee 20%.

Agriculture. Production (in 000; metric tons; 1967; 1966 in parentheses): cotton, lint 16 (15); peanuts *c.* 60 (60); sweet potatoes (1966) 40, (1965) 40; cassava (1966) 1,000, (1965) 1,000; coffee 10.5 (9). Livestock (in 000; 1965–66): cattle 450; pigs (1967–68) *c.* 25; sheep *c.* 112; goats 500; chickens 900.

Industry. Diamond production (1967) 521,000 metric carats.

Ceylon

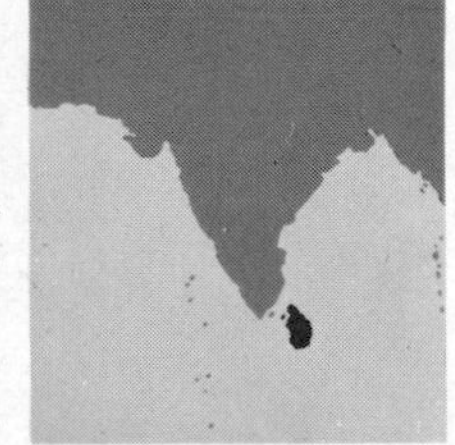

An Asian parliamentary state of the Commonwealth of Nations, Ceylon occupies an island off the southeast coast of peninsular India. Area: 25,332 sq.mi. (65,610 sq.km.). Pop. (1967 est.): 11,701,000, including Sinhalese about 70%; Tamils 22%; Moors 6%. Cap. and largest city: Colombo (pop., 1966, 546,000). Language: Sinhalese (official), Tamil, and English. Religion: mainly Buddhism, with Hindu, Christian, and Muslim minorities. Queen, Elizabeth II; governor-general in 1969, William Gopallawa; prime minister, Dudley Senanayake.

In 1969 Ceylon completed 21 years of independence with an improving record of political stability, a greater degree of national unity, and encouraging economic progress. Broadcasting to the nation on Independence Day, Prime Minister Senanayake said it was Ceylon's good fortune that freedom had been preserved intact. He added, however, that no democratic system was safe without economic stability and that this was only possible with proper development. In Ceylon, where 70% of the people worked on the land, agricultural development had to come first, and the prime minister drew attention to the outstanding success of the national campaign for increased production of home-grown food.

In fact, economic growth in 1968 reached the high rate of 8.3%, compared with 4.4% the previous year. The increase in rice production, in particular, was impressive, and in 1969 the harvest was expected to yield 71 million bu. U. B. Wanninayake, finance minister, also drew attention to the steady increase in the output of the new industrial corporations, which rose from a value of CRs. 70 million in 1965 to CRs. 262 million in 1968. Private industrial production had also advanced, and the growth of investment in construction was particularly noteworthy, with the growth rate for 1968 reaching 27%. While the cost of living index had been steady in 1965 and 1966 but had moved up slightly in 1967, the rise had been sharper in 1968, largely due to the effects of the devaluation of the Ceylon rupee. However, in 1968 the increase in average per capita money income, which amounted to over 16%, more than compensated for the higher living costs.

Unemployment remained a problem and was particularly acute in the case of persons with secondary school and university education but without any specialized skills. This was tragic, the finance minister

Canadian Literature: *see* Literature
Canals: *see* Transportation
Cancer: *see* Medicine
Canning Industry: *see* Food
Canoeing *see* Sporting Record
Cape Verde Islands: *see* Dependent States
Cardiology and Circulation: *see* Medicine
Caroline Islands: *see* Dependent States
Catholic Church: *see* Religion
Cattle: *see* Agriculture
Cave Exploration: *see* Speleology
Cayman Islands: *see* Dependent States
Cement: *see* Mining
Census Data: *see* Populations and Areas; *see also the individual country articles*
Central America: *see* Inter-American Affairs; *articles on the various countries*

CEYLON

Education. (1965–66) Primary, pupils 1,780,559; secondary, pupils 817,508; primary and secondary, teachers 94,564; teacher training, students 5,302, teachers 449; higher (including 2 universities with 4,025 students; 2 additional universities were founded in 1967), students 14,139, teaching staff 563.

Finance. Monetary unit: Ceylonese rupee, with a par value of CRs. 5.95 to U.S. $1 (CRs. 14.29 = £1 sterling). Gold and foreign exchange, official: (June 1969) U.S. $39 million; (June 1968) U.S. $50 million. Budget (1967–68 est.): revenue CRs. 2,049,909,306; expenditure CRs. 2,204,816,231. Gross national product: (1967) CRs. 8,791,000,000; (1966) CRs. 8,217,000,000. Money supply: (March 1969) CRs. 1,893,000,000; (March 1968) CRs. 1,814,000,000.

Foreign Trade. (1968) Imports CRs. 2,173,000,000; exports CRs. 2,035,000,000. Import sources: U.K. 15%; China 11%; U.S. 8%; India 7%; Australia 6%; Japan 5%; West Germany 5%. Export destinations: U.K. 25%; China 10%; U.S. 7%; Australia 5%; South Africa 5%. Main exports: tea 57%; rubber 16%; coconut products 16%.

Transport and Communications. Roads (1968) 20,955 km. Motor vehicles in use (1968): passenger 84,678; commercial 28,186. Railways: (1967) *c.* 1,500 km.; traffic (1966–67) 2,560,000,000 passenger-km., freight 322 million net ton-km. Air traffic (1968): 97.1 million passenger-km.; freight 2.9 million net ton-km. Telephones (Dec. 1967) 51,093. Radio receivers (Dec. 1967) *c.* 425,000.

Agriculture. Production (in 000; metric tons; 1967; 1966 in parentheses): cassava 346 (289); sweet potatoes 73 (63); rice (1968) 1,349, (1967) 1,150; tea 221 (222); rubber (1968) 149, (1967) 143; copra (1966) 230, (1965) 266; cocoa beans 2 (2.6). Livestock (in 000; June 1967): cattle 1,659; sheep 25; buffaloes 765; goats 580; pigs 128; chickens 6,256.

Industry. Production (in 000; metric tons; 1967): cement 189; graphite (exports) 10; electricity (kw-hr.) 581,000.

pointed out, in view of Ceylon's basic shortage of expertise in many fields, from specialist teachers in the schools to skilled technicians in industry.

Meanwhile, there was a slight improvement in the balance of payments position which, in terms of the U.S. dollar, showed a deficit of $61 million in 1968, compared with one of $70 million in 1967. For 1969 export earnings were expected to increase by approximately CRs. 55 million to a total of CRs. 2,030,000,000, including CRs. 1,115,000,000 from tea. This last estimate, CRs. 46 million less than in 1968, reflected the lower prices on markets depressed by the overproduction of tea, running at a rate of about 2% a year over world consumption. For Ceylon, dependent on tea for as much as 60% of its foreign exchange, this posed serious problems only ameliorated in part by improved returns from the two other main export crops, rubber and coconuts.

Two features of the budget were the long overdue grant of salary increases to public servants, costing CRs. 125 million a year, and the levying of new taxation to yield an additional CRs. 106 million.

Ceylon's largest hydroelectric power station, with a capacity of 75 Mw., required to meet the increased demand for electricity for industrial expansion, was opened at Polpitiya in May. The country's first oil refinery went into production in July. (Jo. Hn.)

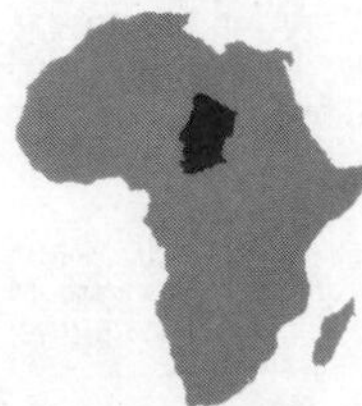

Chad

A landlocked republic of central Africa, Chad is bounded by Libya, Sudan, the Central African Republic, Cameroon, Nigeria, and Niger. Area: 490,750 sq.mi. (1,271,000 sq.km.). Pop. (1968): 3.5 million including Saras, Arabs, and other Africans. Cap. and largest city: Fort-Lamy (pop., 1967 est., 118,000). Official language: French. Religion: Muslim and animist. President and premier in 1969, François Tombalbaye.

Reelected president of the republic for a second seven-year term on June 15, François Tombalbaye had once more to confront the growing guerrilla threat to his French-backed regime. In March he had been compelled to invoke his country's defense pact with France, calling for significant administrative and military aid when the rebellion became too difficult for his 6,000-strong Army to handle. Most of the guerrillas were Arabs, who opposed the domination of Chad by the black men who lived in the southern part of the country.

While the first troop reinforcements were being sent from Corsica to Fort-Lamy, where 1,600 men of the French Overseas Intervention Force were already based, two high-ranking French officials, the former administrator, Pierre Lami, and Brig. Gen. Michel Arnaud, undertook an examination of Chad's administrative structure with the aim of eventually reorganizing it completely. The French soldiers, who at the start gave simple logistical assistance, became directly engaged in the maintenance of order in several districts, notably Borkou, Ennedi, Tibesti, Ouaddï, Guera, and Salamat.

Endeavouring to minimize the seriousness of the situation, the Chad government accused the international press of mounting a campaign against the country by describing as "subversion" what officials termed pure acts of "organized banditry." However, on several occasions reports coming from Chad indicated major clashes between rebels and regular soldiers, and France was considerably embarrassed by the first killing of one of its troops in September.

By the end of the year about 800 men of the French Foreign Legion (the 2nd Overseas Parachute Regiment) were garrisoned at Fort-Lamy, Mongo, Fort-Archambault, and Abéché. In September Brig. Gen. Edouard Cortadellas replaced Brigadier-General Arnaud as special military representative of France in the service of President Tombalbaye, with orders to crush the rebels by April 1970.

On September 27 the authorities reestablished by decree the powers of the traditional chiefs, hoping thus to reassure the discontented population and to protect it from certain administrative abuses condemned by the central government. In spite of all efforts, however, the guerrilla bands, confined at first to the borders with Libya and Sudan, took advantage of the atmosphere of civil war to spread their activities. The problem of who was to succeed President Tombalbaye was ever present, but the internal divisions within Chad's opposition made a calm examination of the alternatives impossible. (Ph. D.)

CHAD

Education. (1966–67) Primary, pupils 172,485, teachers 2,136; secondary, pupils 7,993, teachers 265; vocational, pupils 502, teachers (1965–66) 30; teacher training, students 594, teachers 29.

Finance. Monetary unit: CFA franc, with a parity of CFA Fr. 50 to the French franc (CFA Fr. 277.71 = U.S. $1; CFA Fr. 666.50 = £1 sterling). Budget (1969 est.) balanced at CFA Fr. 12.6 billion. Cost of living (Fort-Lamy; 1963 = 100): (June 1969) 131; (June 1968) 126.

Foreign Trade. (1967) Imports CFA Fr. 9,901,000,000; exports CFA Fr. 6,635,000,000. Import sources: France 46%; U.S. 10%; West Germany 6%; Nigeria 6%. Export destinations: France 57%; Nigeria 8%; Japan 5%. Main exports: cotton 83%; cattle 6%.

Chemistry

Physical and Inorganic. *Nitrogen Fixation Cycle.* The search for coordination complexes (particular types of chemical compounds or ions) that could catalytically reduce nitrogen to ammonia under chemically mild conditions took a considerable step forward in 1969 when E. E. van Tamelen and co-workers at Stanford (Calif.) University discovered a novel industrial pathway to ammonia in which the reaction steps took place at room temperature and atmospheric pressure. This method overcame the major disadvantage of previous complexes in which the bound nitrogen could not be reduced or otherwise chemically transformed into any useful end product.

The key to the new method lay in the catalytic properties of titanium compounds such as titanium diisopropoxide and dicyclopentadienyl titanium that acted repeatedly in a continuous nitrogen fixation-reduction cycle. Such true catalytic behaviour distinguished these compounds from other forms of titanium and other transition elements that had yielded complexes incapable of reduction to ammonia. A typical experiment involved a mixture of commercially available titanium tetraisopropoxide and a reducing agent such as sodium naphthalide in a solvent of tetrahydrofuran or diglyme. The reactants were stirred under an atmosphere of nitrogen at room temperature. The tetravalent titanium compound was reduced by the sodium naphthalide to the divalent form, which bound a molecule of nitrogen. The nitrogen complex was further reduced by additional sodium naphthalide to an ammonia complex; subsequent alcoholic hydrolysis produced ammonia and gave back titanium isopropoxide, which could initiate further reaction.

Metal Strengthening by Electrolysis. To meet the demands of advancing technology for stronger and better metals, scientists at the General Electric Company's Research Center, Schenectady, N.Y., developed a process that strengthened metals by giving them a harder coating. The method, known as metalliding, involved electrolytic reactions carried out in a bath of molten fluoride salts that acted as a "solvent" to diffuse metals and metalloids such as boron and silicon into the surface of other metals and alloys. Metalliding was applied to iron, nickel, aluminum, and titanium, as well as to relatively soft metals such as copper and molybdenum and to the rare earths cerium and scandium.

In the electrolysis, the cathode consisted of the metal to be coated while the anode comprised the metal or the metalloid that was to form the coating. When direct current was passed from the anode to the cathode, anode material traveled to the cathode via the molten fluoride bath, where it diffused into and reacted with the surface of the cathode. The resulting surface composition exhibited radically different properties from those of the original metal; molybdenum, for instance, a relatively soft metal, assumed a surface almost as hard as diamond when boron was diffused into it by the metalliding process.

High-Temperature Thermodynamic Data. Previously inaccessible thermodynamic data for liquid metals and alloys, such as enthalpy increments, were derived from the method of levitation calorimetry developed by J. L. Margrave and his research group at Rice University, Houston, Tex. This technique combined levitation and electromagnetic heating with conventional isothermal drop calorimetry. A small sample (0.5 to 1.5 g.) was placed in a nonuniform, rapidly alternating electromagnetic field; the resulting eddy currents brought about heating and mixing when the sample melted. The sample was supported within the specially designed coils by the magnetic field without the need for a container. The levitation coils, through which cooling water was pumped at high velocity, consisted of copper tubing wound first clockwise and then counterclockwise to obtain the best magnetic field configuration.

After the sample was heated and equilibrated, its temperature was measured with an optical or photoelectric pyrometer. The sample was then allowed to drop into the calorimeter by suddenly removing the magnetic field. The calorimeter contained a lining of the sample material, to avoid a correction for heat gained or lost with some other material after falling into the calorimeter. Yielded by this process were the heats of fusion of refractory metals such as tungsten and tantalum, which previously had to be estimated.

Spectroscopy and Molecular Structure. Two spectroscopic approaches to the study of the inner electronic structures of atoms and molecules provoked considerable interest. D. W. Turner (Balliol College, Oxford) highlighted the technique of photoelectron spectroscopy, which was an adaptation of β-ray spectroscopy, a well-established method in physics. Basically the method measured the electron kinetic energy distributions following photoionization. Provided that the energy of the photon was sufficiently large and that the velocities of the ejected electrons could be analyzed, the electron binding energies or ionization potentials could be determined. Each occupied orbital of the atom or molecule was represented by a group or band of electrons in the photoelectric spectrum, and the order and spacing of these bands reproduced the orbital energy level diagram. The technique proved particularly useful in confirming energy level structures predicted many years earlier by molecular orbital theory.

A commercial spectrometer operating at much higher excitation energies also became available in 1969. The induced electron emission spectrometer was designed to measure both the energy that bound orbital electrons of elements and compounds to their nuclei and the changes in that energy that arose from chemical modifications to the structure. The sample under investigation—gas, solid, or liquid—was placed in the analytical chamber and evacuated before bombardment with soft X rays to dislodge the inner electron shell. The deflected electrons then passed through a uniform electrostatic field that dispersed them according to their energies, which could be measured by multiplier circuits. The instrument had equal sensitivity throughout the entire periodic table, with the exception of hydrogen. (J. A. Kr.)

Organic. The increasingly powerful interplay of theory and techniques led to further impressive advances during the year, especially in synthetic organic chemistry. Cyclopropanone, a simple but highly reactive small ring compound, was extensively investigated by N. J. Turro. The classical structure **1** was shown to be valid, though the carbon-oxygen bond length was relatively short. Reaction of cyclopropanone with hydrogen chloride yielded simple adducts such as **2**, but the strained ring was evidently only just able to resist the attack of acidic reagents, for 2,2-dimethylcyclopropanone was found to be converted to

UPI COMPIX

Derek Barton (above) of the organic chemistry department at the Imperial College of Science and Technology, London, and Odd Hassel (below) of the University of Oslo were joint winners of the 1969 Nobel Prize for Chemistry.

Cheese: *see* Agriculture

Chemical Industry: *see* Industrial Review

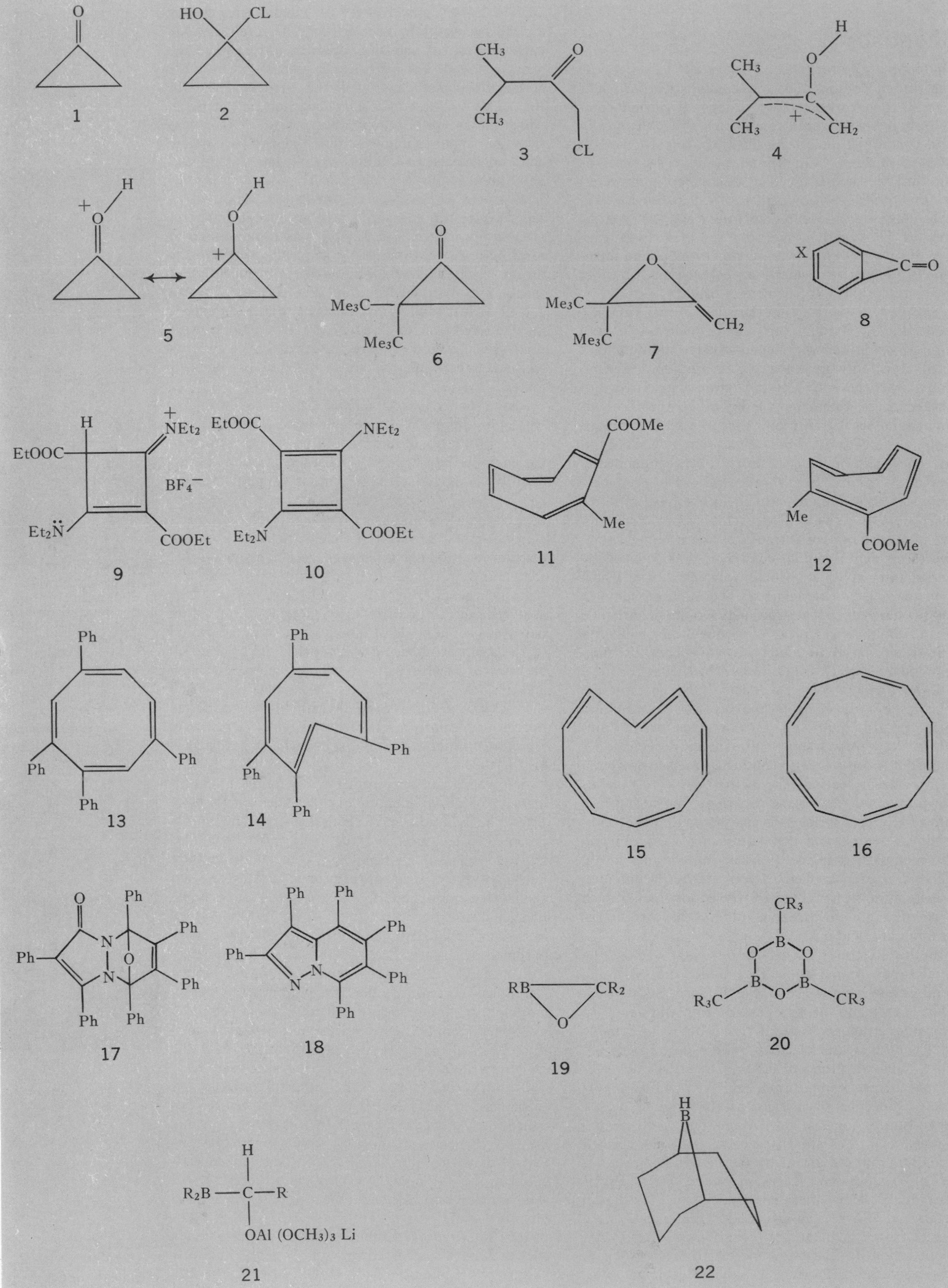

O
1
HO
CL
2
CH3
O
CH3
3
CL
H
CH3
O
C
CH3
+
CH2
4
H
+
O
H
O
+
5
O
Me3C
Me3C
6
O
Me3C
Me3C
CH2
7
X
C=O
8
H
+
NEt2
EtOOC
BF4−
Et2N
COOEt
9
EtOOC
NEt2
Et2N
COOEt
10
COOMe
Me
11
Me
COOMe
12
Ph
Ph
Ph
Ph
13
Ph
Ph
Ph
Ph
14
15
16
O
Ph
Ph
N
O
Ph
N
Ph
Ph
Ph
17
Ph
Ph
Ph
Ph
N
N
Ph
Ph
18
RB
CR2
O
19
CR3
B
O
O
B
B
R3C
O
CR3
20
H
R2B
C
R
OAl (OCH3)3 Li
21
H
B
22

the open-chain adduct **3** by hydrogen chloride. Stabilization of the ring-opened ion **4** by the methyl groups was considered to favour it by comparison with the cation **5** formed on protonation of cyclopropanone itself. A new route to substituted cyclopropanones was developed from the epoxidation of allenes by peracetic acid; 1,1-di-tert-butylallene was transformed in this way into 2,2-di-tert-butylcyclopropanone **6,** no doubt through the epoxide **7,** which spontaneously rearranged to **6.** The presence of the tert-butyl groups much reduced the reactivity of the cyclopropanone system, as is often found on introduction of these large substituents into such strained situations.

A related compound, incorporating a similar small ring, is benzocyclopropenone; (**8,** X = H). The chlorine-substituted derivative (**8,** X = Cl) was detected as an intermediate by trapping in methanol solution, when a mixture of methyl m- and p-chlorobenzoates was obtained. A molecule containing the cyclobutadiene ring system, not dependent on coordination to a transition metal ion for its stability, was reported. Ethyl dimethylaminopropiolate, $EtOOC.C{\equiv}C.NEt_2$, dimerized on treatment with boron trifluoride and phenol to yield a salt **9;** this product evolved hydrogen on treatment with sodium hydride to give **10.**

One of the problems faced a century ago in analyzing the chemistry and structure of benzene was the lack of isomers that were to be expected from substitution on adjacent carbon atoms in a cyclic system of alternating single and double bonds. Although this is no longer relevant to aromatic chemistry, the occurrence of this type of isomerism in similar nonaromatic cyclic compounds is of interest. When methyl 2-methylcyclooctatetraenecarboxylate was examined by proton magnetic resonance spectroscopy, the two positional isomers, **11** and **12,** were shown to be present in a ratio of approximately 17:1 at 27° C, with **11** predominating. Irradiation of the mixture at about −50° C resulted in the photochemical conversion of **11** to **12** until virtually equal amounts of each isomer were then present; 1,2,4,7-tetraphenylcyclooctatetraene was also found to be isomerized by irradiation. In this case, however, it seemed that a change in geometry only was involved, the configuration about one of the double bonds changing from *cis* to *trans.* In the conversion of the isomers **13** to **14** no migration of the double bonds appeared to have taken place.

Proton magnetic resonance evidence was also adduced to show that, contrary to earlier reports, irradiation of *cis*-9,10-dihydronaphthalene at −60° C leads directly to the formation of cyclodecapentaene, among other products. The initial isomer appeared to have the *trans* configuration at one double bond, **15,** and underwent subsequent photochemical transformation into the "all-*cis*" compound, **16.** This isomerization is thus the reverse of the situation encountered with the tetraphenylcyclooctatetraene.

The pyrolysis of the tetraphenylcyclopentadienone adduct **17** of the unstable pyrazolone unexpectedly resulted in the elimination of carbon dioxide, although the two oxygen atoms are well separated in the adduct. A series of rearrangement reactions were thus postulated to account for the approach of the oxygen atoms and the formation of the product, **18.**

The ingenious use of organoboron compounds in organic synthesis, developed by H. C. Brown and his colleagues at Purdue University, West Lafayette, Ind., over the last decade, gained further impetus in two directions. Reaction of carbon monoxide with an organoborane R_3B was found to occur virtually quantitatively at 100°–125° C, and boraepoxides **19** or boroxines **20** could be obtained as intermediates by controlling the experimental conditions.

Further modification of the reaction path resulted from admixture of lithium trimethoxyaluminohydride with the reacting borane. Uptake of carbon monoxide then occurred at 25° C, though neither reagent alone reacted under these conditions. The intermediate, **21,** that resulted could be hydrolyzed to the primary alcohol, RCH_2OH, and oxidized to the aldehyde, RCHO.

In parallel with these carbonylation reactions, an additional extension of the original hydroboration reaction was described. The addition reaction of equimolar quantities of borane and 1,5-cyclooctadiene in tetrahydrofuran, followed by refluxing for one hour, gave 9-borabicyclo [3.3.1] nonane, **22.** This compound was found to be quite exceptionally stable for one containing a boron-hydrogen bond. (J. C. Y.)

See also Industrial Review; Molecular Biology; Physics.

ENCYCLOPÆDIA BRITANNICA FILMS. *Preface to Chemistry* (1954).

Chess

In August 1968, V. Liberson (U.S.S.R.) was an easy first at an international tournament in Debrecen, Hung. Former world champion V. Smyslov (U.S.S.R.) was first at the sixth Rubinstein Memorial Tournament, again held at Polanica Zdroj, Pol. Bent Larsen (Den.) won the U.S. Open at Aspen, Colo., with 11 out of 12, and the Canadian Open with an even more convincing 10½ out of 11. The world champion, Tigran Petrosian (U.S.S.R.), tied for the Moscow Championship with David Bronstein (U.S.S.R.).

First place in the Capablanca Memorial Tournament in Havana, August 30 to September 20, went to R. Cholmov (U.S.S.R.). Bobby Fischer (U.S.) made his only 1968–69 appearance in international chess at Vinkovci, Yugos., where he was first. The Soviet grand master E. Geller was first at an international tournament at Kislovodsk, U.S.S.R., and another Soviet master, J. Sacharov, was first at Varna, Bulg. There was a triple tie for first place at Sombor, Yugos., in October between V. Hort (Czech.), B. Ivkov, and R. Kurajica (both Yugos.).

The 18th Olympiad was held at Lugano, Switz., in October and November, and the U.S.S.R., with a team headed by Petrosian and Boris Spassky, was a convincing first. The U.S., handicapped by the absence of Fischer (who disliked the playing arrangements and departed without playing a single game), was fourth. In November former world champion M. Tal (U.S.S.R.) was first in a tournament at Gori, U.S.S.R. Two strong international tournaments were held from November to December. One, in East Berlin, in memory of Emanuel Lasker, ended in a tie between the East German W. Uhlmann and Bronstein; the other, at Palma de Mallorca, Spain, resulted in a runaway victory for V. Korchnoi (U.S.S.R.). The first international tournament in Greece, held in Athens in December, was won by the Czechoslovak grand master Ludek Pachman. Smyslov was first at the Hastings (Eng.) tournament and the European Junior Championship (a new event) went to K. Maeder (W.Ger.).

In January 1969 a very strong international tournament at Beverwijk, Neth., ended in a tie between former world champion M. Botvinnik and Geller (both U.S.S.R.). The U.S.S.R. Championship, at Alma-Ata, ended in a tie between I. Zaitsev and L. Polugaievsky, the latter easily winning the playoff later. The annual international tournament at Málaga, Spain, was a tie between Pal Benko (U.S.) and Ivkov. In March a match between Larsen and Tal at Eersel, Neth., to decide which of them was to be placed third in the Candidates' events, was won by Larsen. L. Portisch and Smyslov tied for first place in the third international tournament at Monaco in April and an international tournament at Zagreb, Yugos. (April–May), was won by M. Damjanovic (Yugos.).

The match between Petrosian and Spassky, held in Moscow from April to June, saw the end of the former's six-year reign as world champion. Spassky (*see* BIOGRAPHY) won the match comfortably by 12½–10½. The women's world championship match, held at about the same time at Tbilisi, U.S.S.R., and Moscow, ended in an easy victory for the titleholder, Nona Gaprindashvilli.

Sicilian defense (19th game, World Championship Match, Moscow, June 1969).

White B. Spassky	Black T. Petrosian	White B. Spassky	Black T. Petrosian
1 P — K4	P — QB4	13 B — Kt3	R — K1 (e)
2 Kt — KB3	P — Q3	14 K — Kt1	B — B1
3 P — Q4	P X P	15 P — Kt4 (f)	Kt X KtP
4 Kt X P	Kt — KB3	16 Q — Kt2	Kt — B3
5 Kt — QB3	P — QR3	17 R — Kt1	B — Q2
6 B — Kt5	QKt — Q2 (a)	18 P — B5	K — R1 (g)
7 B — QB4	Q — R4	19 QR — KB1	Q — Q1 (h)
8 Q — Q2	P — R3 (b)	20 P X P	P X P (i)
9 B X Kt	Kt X B	21 P — K5	P X P
10 O-O-O	P — K3 (c)	22 Kt — K4	Kt — R4
11 KR — K1	B — K2 (d)	23 Q — Kt6	P X Kt (j)
12 P — B4	O — O	24 Kt-Kt5	resigns (k)

(a) 6 . . ., P — K3 is the normal line here and is indeed safer than the text move. (b) Again, P — K3 is recognized as usual here, but it seems that Petrosian was averse to playing it since he had experienced difficulties after having used it against Ivkov at Bled in 1961. Nevertheless, the move with the RP is bad since it presents White with an easy object of attack on the king side. (c) Geller has suggested here that White's attack might have been met by 9 . . ., P — K4, and if then 10 Kt — B5, B X Kt; 11 P X B, R — B1; 12 B — Kt3, B — K2. (d) Immediately fatal would have been 11 . . ., P — QKt4; 12 B — Kt3, P — Kt5; 13 Kt — Q5; but instead Tal's 11 . . ., B — Q2 followed by O — O — O has much to be said for it. (e) Too slow; better was 13 . . ., B — Q2. (f) A forcing sacrifice that must be accepted, since otherwise there comes P — Kt5. (g) After 18 . . ., P — K4; White retreats with the Kt when he threatens both R X P and Q — Kt6. (h) If 19 . . ., P — K4; 20 KKt — K2, R — K2; 21 Kt — Q5, Kt X Kt; 22 P — B6, Kt X P; 23 R X Kt, and White wins. (i) After 20 . . ., B X P; 21 Kt X B, P X Kt; we get lines similar to that in the game. (j) Or 23 . . ., Kt — B5; 24 R X Kt, P X R; 25 Kt — KB3, Q — Kt3; 26 Kt — K5, B — B3; 27 Q X RPch followed by mate. (k) Since if 24 . . ., P X Kt; 25 Q X Ktch, K — Kt1; 26 Q — B7ch, K — R1; 27 R — B3.

Sicilian defense (International Tournament at Puerto Rico, October 1969)

White L. Kavalek	Black M. Damjanovic	White L. Kavalek	Black M. Damjanovic
1 P — K4	P — QB4	19 Kt X Kt	Q — R2
2 Kt — KB3	Kt — QB3	20 R X P	Q — K6
3 P — Q4	P X P	21 R — Q3	Q — Kt3
4 Kt X P	Q — B2	22 Kt — K4	O — O (d)
5 Kt — Kt5	Q — Kt1	23 Kt — B6ch	K — R1 (e)
6 P — QB4	P — K3	24 B X P	P — Kt3 (f)
7 P — KB4	P — QR3	25 B X P	P X B
8 Kt(Kt5) — B3	Q — R2	26 P — QB5	Q — Kt4
9 P — QR3	B — B4	27 R — R3ch	K — Kt2
10 B — Q3	P — Q3 (a)	28 R — R7ch	K X Kt
11 P — QKt4	B — K6	29 Q — R1ch	P — K4
12 R — R2	Kt — B3	30 P X Pdbch	K — K3
13 R — B1	P — KR4 (b)	31 R X R	Kt X KP
14 B X B	Q X Bch	32 Q — R2ch	Kt — B5 (g)
15 R — K2	Q — Q5	33 R — B4	K — Q4
16 R — Q2 (c)	Q — K6ch	34 Q — K2	B — B4
17 B — K2	Kt X KP	35 Q — Q1ch	K — B3 (h)
18 R — Q3	Kt X Kt	36 Q — B3ch	resigns

(a) Black loses a piece after 10 . . ., B — Kt8; 11 Q — Q2, B X P; 12 Q — KB2. (b) A serious weakening of his king side under the mistaken impression that he is counterattacking; better was P — K4. (c) Threatening to win the QP by 17 B — K2. (d) If 22 . . ., P — K4; 23 P X P, Kt X P; 24 R — Q5, with great advantage to White. (e) Acceptance of the piece leads to mate after 23 . . ., P X Kt; 24 R — Kt3ch, K — R2; 25 B — Q3ch, K — R3; 26 R — R3, etc. (f) In reply to 24 . . ., R — Q1 there comes the elegant 25 B — Kt6! (g) Or 32 . . ., Q — B5; 33 R — K8ch, K — B3; 34 Q X Q, Kt X Q; 35 R(R7) — R8. (h) Now he is mated but 35 . . ., K — K4 or K — K3 would be met by 36 R X Kt. This was the most brilliant game of the whole tournament.

Child Welfare:
see Education; Social Services

In June, Larsen won the second Anderssen Memorial Tournament at Bussum, Neth. Korchnoi won yet another first prize at Luhacovice, Czech. The veteran U.S. grand master Sammy Reshevsky had an outstanding success at Nathanya, Israel. The Netherlands was first at the Clare Benedict European Team Tournament at Adelboden, Switz., in July. Albin Planinc (Yugos.) obtained a surprise victory at the Vidmar Memorial Tournament at Ljubljana, Yugos. There were surprises also at two international tournaments at Lublin, Pol., in July and August: the first was won by the 20-year-old Polish champion, J. Lewi, and the second by the Hungarian L. Barczay. The Asztalos Memorial Tournament at Zalaegerszeg, Hung., was won easily by Mark Taimanov (U.S.S.R.). Equally convincing was Portisch's victory in the IBM International Tournament at Amsterdam. The annual match between the U.S.S.R. and Yugoslavia, at Skopje, Yugos., was won by the U.S.S.R. team by 22–18.

The U.S.S.R. was first at the World Students Team Championship, held at Dresden, E.Ger., in August. The World Junior Championship, held at Stockholm in August, was won by Anatol Karpov (U.S.S.R.). The U.S. Open, at Lincoln, Neb., was again won by Benko. Jonathan Penrose won the British Championship for the tenth time. The annual Varna International Tournament was won in September by N. Krogius (U.S.S.R.). First and second places in the 1969 Capablanca Memorial Tournament at Havana went to the Soviet grand masters Korchnoi and A. Suetin. The U.S.S.R. was first in the fourth Women's Olympiad, held at Lublin. The 37th Soviet Championship, played in Moscow during September and October, ended in a tie between Petrosian and Polugaievsky. This was also a zonal tournament, and the first four (excluding Petrosian, who went straight into the Candidates) qualified for the Interzonal Tournament in 1970. In October Spassky easily won an international tournament at San Juan, P.R. (H. Go.)

Chile

A republic extending along the southern Pacific coast of South America, Chile has an area of 292,257 sq.mi. (756,946 sq.km.), not including its Antarctic claim between 53° and 90° W. It is bounded by Argentina, Bolivia, and Peru. Pop. (1969 est.): 9,565,628. Cap. and largest city: Santiago (pop. of greater Santiago, 1969 metro. est., 2,516,421). Language: Spanish. Religion: predominantly Roman Catholic. President in 1969, Eduardo Frei Montalva.

For the first time in more than 30 years, a mutiny occurred in the Chilean Army. In October the Tacna and Yungay regiments near Santiago mutinied, allegedly in protest against low pay, inadequate equipment, and political promotions. The mutineers were led by recently retired Brig. Gen. Roberto Viaux Marambo. The mutiny resembled a workers' strike more than a rebellion.

Despite this claim, the rebels demanded and received the resignation of the defense minister and the army commander in chief. The mutineers surrendered after less than 24 hours, and no one was fatally injured. The mutiny, nevertheless, threw a new element of uncertainty into the pre-presidential election campaigning, which started shortly after the March parliamentary elections.

The results of the March elections favoured the conservative Nationalist Party, which came back from near oblivion to second place, after the ruling Christian Democratic Party. The Christian Democrats themselves increased their number of seats in the Senate but lost their control in the Chamber of Deputies. The other centre and leftist parties showed little change over the previous elections. The new composition of the Chamber, with the Senate in parentheses, was as follows: Christian Democratic 55 (22), Radical 24 (9), Communist 22 (6), National 34 (5), Socialist 15 (4), Popular Socialist none (2), Social Democratic none (1), and Independent none (1).

Following the elections and as a prelude to the 1970 presidential elections, the Christian Democratic and Radical parties each split into two groups. Jacques Chonchol, one of the authors and administrators of the Chilean agrarian reform, set up his own Movimiento de Accion Popular Unida (MAPU) to attract the left-leaning members of the Christian Democratic Party. Julio Duran, meanwhile, formed the Democratic Radical Party after the Radical Party organization voted to seek closer ties with the leftist parties. This virtually completed the splitting of Chile's traditional political parties.

Six parties announced presidential candidates, including Radomiro Tomic, Christian Democrat; Pablo Neruda, Communist; Sen. Alberto Baltra, Radical; Salvador Allende, Socialist; Jacques Chonchol, MAPU; and Sen. Rafael Tarud, independent. Other candidates were expected to be announced before the parties began negotiating on alliances.

The economy continued to grow by about 4.5% per year. The country's balance of payments improved, and the 1970 budget proposals did not include any provision for foreign loans. On the negative side, inflation accelerated beyond the 30% registered in 1968. The most dynamic forces behind the country's growth and favourable balance of payments were the continuation of record high prices for copper on the London Metal Exchange and the more favourable terms negotiated by the government with the large copper mines.

Those new terms radically increased the government's share in the profits of the mines when the price of copper exceeded 40 cents per pound. Most of the increased revenue was being used by the government to finance its acquisition of shares in the foreign-owned copper mines under the country's "chileanization" program. This program, negotiated in 1968, gave the government increased participation in the large foreign-owned copper mines through the negotiated sale by the parent company of stock in its subsidiary. The most significant purchases during the year under this program included the total purchase of the Andes Copper Mining Company and the Chile Exploration Company, both subsidiaries of the Anaconda Company, for a to-be-audited book value of about $200 million.

The government also embarked on a $100 million development program to expand the country's small and medium mines. Half the program was being financed by an Anglo-Belgian-West German consortium.

Internal communications improved when the government inaugurated its national television network covering the entire country on September 18. Until that date, television had been broadcast city by city.

A rash of bank and supermarket robberies turned out to be the work of the Peking-oriented Movimiento de Izquierda Revolucionaria, a violence-prone splinter group of the leftist parties. Several of the alleged bank robbers were arrested, and the party leadership went underground. (R. L. Ro.)

The world's largest open-pit copper mine, in Chuquicamata, Chile, owned by a subsidiary of the Anaconda Co.

COURTESY, THE ANACONDA COMPANY

CHILE

Education. (1967) Primary, pupils 1,874,414; secondary, pupils 168,208; vocational, pupils 93,006; teacher training (1965), students 6,896, teachers 525; higher (including 8 universities; 1965), students 43,608, teaching staff 8,835.

Finance. Monetary unit: escudo, with (Sept. 1, 1969) a banks' free market exchange rate (for trade and some invisible operations) of 9.51 escudos to U.S. $1 (22.82 escudos = £1 sterling) and a brokers' market rate (for most other transactions) of 10.87 escudos to U.S. $1 (26.06 escudos = £1). Gold and foreign exchange, central bank: (May 1969) U.S. $252.2 million; (May 1968) U.S. $110.6 million. Budget (1969 est.): revenue 10,605,000,000 escudos; expenditure 11,337,000,000 escudos. Gross national product: (1967) 31,419,000,000 escudos; (1966) 24,312,000,000 escudos. Money supply: (Dec. 1968) 4,482,000,000 escudos; (Dec. 1967) 3,241,000,000 escudos. Cost of living (Santiago; 1963 = 100): (June 1969) 459; (June 1968) 346.

Foreign Trade. (1967) Imports U.S. $868.3 million; exports U.S. $909.8 million. Import sources: U.S. 36%; West Germany 13%; Argentina 11%; U.K. 7%; Venezuela 6%. Export destinations: U.S. 18%; Netherlands 14%; U.K. 14%; Japan 12%; Italy 8%; West Germany 8%; France 5%; Belgium-Luxembourg 5%. Main exports: copper bars, ore, and concentrates 78%; iron ore 7%.

Transport and Communications. Roads (1968) 54,520 km. Motor vehicles in use (1968): passenger 195,298; commercial 58,911. Railways: (1967) *c.* 9,000 km.; traffic (principal railways; 1968) 2,085,000,000 passenger-km., freight 2,637,000,000 net ton-km. Air traffic (1968): 601.4 million passenger-km.; freight 49,847,000 net ton-km. Shipping (1968): merchant vessels 100 gross tons and over 130; gross tonnage 268,641. Telephones (Dec. 1967) 289,676. Radio receivers (Dec. 1968) *c.* 1,375,000. Television receivers (Dec. 1968) *c.* 150,000.

Agriculture. Production (in 000; metric tons; 1968; 1967 in parentheses): wheat 1,196 (1,204); barley *c.* 165 (*c.* 120); oats (1967) 115, (1966) 123; corn 321 (362); sugar, raw value (1968–69) *c.* 188, (1967–68) 162; rice 93 (*c.* 89); potatoes 725 (717); dry beans 72 (90); wine (1967) *c.* 489, (1966) 474; wool, greasy (1967) *c.* 23, (1966) *c.* 24; timber (cu.m.; 1967) 6,400, (1966) 6,900; fish catch (1967) 1,053, (1966) 1,383; whale catch (numbers; 1966–67) 744, (1965–66) 1,099. Livestock (in 000; 1967–68): cattle *c.* 3,000; sheep (1965–66) *c.* 6,600; pigs *c.* 1,025; horses (1965–66) *c.* 534.

Industry. Production (in 000; metric tons; 1968): coal 1,474; crude oil 1,760; electricity (kw-hr.) 6,793,000; iron ore (65% metal content) 11,916; pig iron 442; crude steel 526; copper 349; nitrate of soda (1967) 869; iodine (1967) 2.2; molybdenum (metal content; 1967) 4.7; silver (1967) 0.10; gold (troy oz.; 1967) 57; woven cotton fabrics (m.) *c.* 113,000; fish meal (1967) 165.

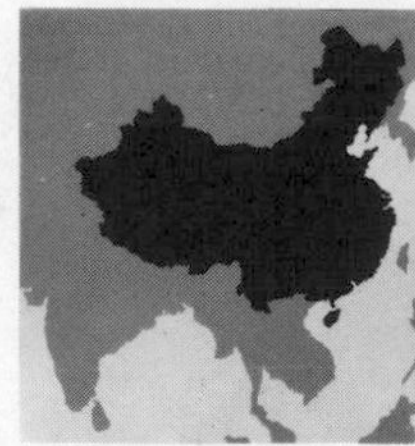

China

The most populous country in the world and the third largest in area, China is bounded by the U.S.S.R., Mongolia, North Korea, North Vietnam, Laos, Burma, India, Bhutan, Sikkim, Nepal, Pakistan, and Afghanistan. From 1949 the country has been divided into the People's Republic of China (Communist) on the mainland and on Hainan and other islands, and the Republic of China (Nationalist) on Taiwan (*see* TAIWAN). Area: 3,691,501 sq.mi. (9,560,988 sq.km.), including Tibet but excluding Taiwan. Pop. of the People's Republic (1969 est.): 750 million, of which about 94% are Han. Cap.: Peking (metro. pop., 1967–68 est., 7 million). Largest city: Shanghai (metro. pop., 1967–68 est., 10 million). Language: Chinese (Mandarin dialect). Chairman of the Communist Party in 1969, Mao Tse-tung; premier, Chou En-lai.

The most significant internal event of the year was the convocation in April of the long-postponed ninth congress of the Chinese Communist Party. It marked the consummation of the protracted Cultural Revolution, which had been directed against traditional and bureaucratic ideas and tendencies, bourgeois individualism, factionalism, and internal and external revisionism, as well as against political opponents of Chairman Mao. By consecrating a purge of the so-called revisionists who had followed the capitalist road, the congress proclaimed the victory of Maoism and acclaimed Mao and his heir-designate, Lin Piao, as the supreme leaders. Nevertheless, the congress failed to solve the problem of internal struggle, as factionalism continued to delay party rebuilding at the provincial level and factional fighting was reported in a number of provinces.

Toward the latter part of the year there was a notable reduction in Mao's personality cult in the official press, which began to emphasize the collective unity of the country's top leadership. This reflected a realignment of political forces, with Premier Chou En-lai taking a prominent role in public and foreign affairs. While Peking propaganda continued with a policy equally antagonistic to United States capitalism and Soviet revisionism, the government itself began to take a more flexible and pragmatic attitude in the conduct of foreign relations and agreed in early October to hold talks with the Soviet Union on the Chinese-Soviet border disputes, which had led to open hostilities.

Domestic Affairs. The convocation of the ninth party congress marked a new chapter in the history of contemporary China under the Communists. Owing largely to the party leaders' conflicting views on internal and external policies, the congress had met only once before since the party came to power in 1949.

The ebb and flow of Mao's leadership and prestige in the party were reflected in the constitution and platform of the party adopted at each recent congress. The seventh congress was held at Yenan in April 1945 when the strength and solidarity of the party as well as Mao's popularity and prestige were at an all-time high. The ideological declaration in the 1945 constitution stated that "the Communist Party of China guides its entire work by the teachings which unite the theories of Marxism-Leninism with the actual practice of Chinese revolution—the thought of Mao Tse-tung." When the eighth congress was convened in 1956, however, the demands of the general public and party leaders for economic, military, administrative, educational, and social modernization conflicted with Mao's theory of perpetual revolution, which even failed to receive majority support in the Central Committee of the party. The ideological provision in the 1956 party constitution merely stated that "the Communist Party of China takes Marxism-Leninism as its guide to action" without reference to the thought of Mao. As a preparatory step to the convening of the ninth congress, a draft constitution of the party was circulated toward the end of 1968.

In comparison with the previous constitution the draft was shorter, simpler, and more general in its provisions. But there were significant alterations emphasizing Mao's thought as the guiding principle in party structure and organizational changes, which included: the limitation of party membership to proletarian and revolutionary elements; the abolition of the office of secretary-general and the Censory Committee; the provision for only one vice-chairman of the party; the reduction of the Central Committee's Standing Committee to five members; and the designation of Lin Piao as Mao's successor, thus depriving the party of the right to elect its own chairman. By these changes collective leadership of and responsibility for the party were replaced or modified by centralization of power in the hands of the Standing Committee, over which Mao and Lin could maintain complete control.

The main tasks of the ninth congress, which took place from April 1 to 24 mostly in closed sessions, were to adopt the draft constitution, approve Lin's

CHINA

Education. Primary, pupils (1959–60) 90 million, teachers (1964) *c.* 2.6 million; secondary (1958–59), pupils 8,520,000; vocational (1958–59), pupils 850,000; teacher training (1958–59), students 620,000; higher (1962–63), students 820,000.

Finance. Monetary unit: jen min piao or people's bank dollar, also called the yuan, with an official exchange rate of 2.46 yuan to U.S. $1 (5.90 yuan = £1 sterling). Budget (1960 draft est.; no later figures published) balanced at 70,020,000,000 yuan. Net aggregate product (1959 at 1952 prices; 1952 in parentheses) 152 billion yuan (61.1 billion yuan).

Foreign Trade. (1967) Imports *c.* U.S. $2 billion; exports *c.* U.S. $1.9 billion. Import sources: Japan *c.* 18%; West Germany *c.* 13%; Australia 12%. Export destinations: Hong Kong *c.* 21%; Japan *c.* 14%; U.S.S.R. *c.* 6%. Main exports: textiles and clothing, metals and ores, rice, meat, tea, coal.

Transport and Communications. Roads (1966) *c.* 550,000 km. (including *c.* 200,000 km. with improved surface). Motor vehicles in use (1967): passenger *c.* 50,000; commercial *c.* 300,000. Railways: (1966) *c.* 36,000 km.; traffic (1959) 45,670,000,000 passenger-km., freight 265,260,000,000 net ton-km. Air traffic (1960): 63,882,000 passenger-km.; freight 1,967,000 net ton-km. Shipping (1968): merchant vessels 100 gross tons and over 239; gross tonnage 765,545. Inland waterways (including Yangtze River; 1966) *c.* 160,000 km. Telephones (1951) 255,000. Radio receivers (Dec. 1966) *c.* 8 million. Television receivers (Dec. 1965) *c.* 100,000.

Agriculture. Production (in 000; metric tons; 1967; 1966 in parentheses): rice *c.* 90,000 (*c.* 88,000); corn *c.* 25,000 (*c.* 24,500); wheat *c.* 28,000 (*c.* 25,700); barley *c.* 16,000 (*c.* 15,500); potatoes *c.* 30,000 (*c.* 29,500); soybeans (1968) *c.* 10,670, (1967) 11,200; peanuts *c.* 2,450 (*c.* 2,360); cotton, lint *c.* 1,518 (*c.* 1,409); jute *c.* 460 (*c.* 450); rapeseed *c.* 1,120 (*c.* 1,120); sugar, raw value (1968–69) *c.* 3,200, (1967–68) *c.* 3,200; tobacco *c.* 850 (*c.* 820); tea *c.* 160 (*c.* 160); oranges, tangerines, and clementines *c.* 600 (*c.* 570); wool, greasy *c.* 79 (*c.* 79); timber (cu.m.; 1966) *c.* 136,000, (1965) 135,000; fish catch (1960) 5,800, (1959) 5,020. Livestock (in 000; 1966–67): cattle *c.* 62,900; sheep *c.* 69,700; pigs *c.* 210,000; goats *c.* 55,000; buffaloes *c.* 30,000; horses *c.* 7,600; asses *c.* 11,000.

Industry. Fuel and power (in 000; metric tons; 1967): coal (including lignite) *c.* 250,000; coke *c.* 12,000; crude oil *c.* 9,000; electricity (kw-hr.; 1960) *c.* 58,500,000. Production (in 000; metric tons; 1967): iron ore (metal content) *c.* 15,400; pig iron *c.* 14,000; crude steel *c.* 12,100; lead *c.* 90; copper *c.* 90; aluminum *c.* 80; bauxite *c.* 350; tungsten concentrates (oxide content) *c.* 10; cement *c.* 11,000; sulfuric acid (1966) *c.* 2,500; chemical fertilizers (1966) *c.* 5,500; cotton yarn (1960) 1,633.

political report, and elect a new Central Committee. The congress was attended by 1,512 delegates (1,026 at the eighth congress), who had been selected by consultation with the revolutionary committees and not by election by provincial and local party congresses as had been done previously. The composition of the delegates to the ninth congress reflected the composition and influence of the revolutionary committees of the 29 administrative areas. One-third of the chairmen and vice-chairmen of these administrative areas, totaling 229 persons, were military leaders, and a large number of them became delegates to the congress. Seventy-one of a total of 176 members of the congress presidium—about three times the number in the eighth congress—were military leaders, while the remainder was made up of party cadres, Cultural Revolutionists, workers, and peasants. The draft constitution was adopted without significant amendments, while Lin's political report, made at the opening meeting, was approved on April 14. The report proclaimed Mao's thought to have an equal status with Marxism-Leninism as the basis for all the actions of the people of China, laid down guidelines in foreign policy in broad terms, and emphasized the importance of unity for the realization of Mao's thought of aiming toward the realization of world Communism by world revolution.

Before closing on April 24 the congress elected a large Central Committee of 279 members (170 full members and 109 alternates), compared with 97 full and 96 alternate members of the previous Central Committee. Only 53 (32 full and 21 alternate) former members were reelected, and 140 failed to make the grade. Of the 32 reelected full members, 21 were military figures, while, altogether, 118 out of the 279 members were in the military services.

At the first session of the new Central Committee on April 28, a 21-member Politburo and a Standing Committee of 5 members were elected. Chairman Mao and his deputy, Defense Minister Lin Piao, headed the list of names on the Standing Committee, and the other three members, listed in the order of the Chinese character or alphabetical order, were Ch'en Pao-ta, Chou En-lai, and K'ang Sheng. The official announcement of these names specifically pointed out that aside from Mao and Lin there was no order of precedence for the other names. Ch'en and K'ang were leaders in the Cultural Revolution and were close and loyal to Mao; only Chou seemed likely to have independent ideas. Including the 5 Standing Committee members, the new Politburo was composed of 21 full members and 4 alternates. Nine of the 21 full members were military men, and more than half of the members were known to be loyal supporters of Mao and Lin.

The result of the congress showed that Mao and his supporters were determined to make sure that their policies and views should be translated into action before Mao's death. While the new party leadership structure was completed in accordance with Mao's wishes, the government still lacked a chief of state to replace the deposed Liu Shao-ch'i. There were no indications concerning the convocation of the National People's Congress to elect a successor to Liu.

Although Mao's efforts to rebuild the Communist Party in his image at the central level met no serious open opposition, the reconstitution of the party at the provincial level proved to be slow and difficult. One reason was that the revolutionary committees, set up during the Cultural Revolution to run local and provincial governments, were not enthusiastic about the establishment of new party branches that would encroach on their newly founded authority. Another problem was that the process of "struggle-criticism-transformation," involving reeducating intellectuals in order to root out bourgeois elements and thus accelerate the construction of Communist society under proletarian dictatorship, had lost its appeal and support after three turbulent years of Cultural Revolution. Furthermore, the rivalry and dissension among the three components of the revolutionary committees (armed forces, Red Guards, party leaders) inevitably delayed the attempts at provincial organization. Toward the end of 1969 various low-level party branches were formed in government departments, educational institutions, factories, and farm collectives, but party organizations for entire provinces had not been established.

The disappearance of the 75-year-old Chairman Mao from public view from May 19 to October 1 caused a great deal of speculation and rumours about his health and capability. On October 1 Mao's reappearance at Peking's T'ien-an-Men Square to preside over the 20th anniversary of Communist rule in China attracted great attention, but Mao made no speech to mark the occasion. Compared with the 10th anniversary celebration in 1959, the 20th anniversary celebration appeared to be a muted affair. However, Peking heralded the occasion by setting off its first underground nuclear test on September 23 and its third three-megaton nuclear explosion in the atmosphere, in the Lop Nor area, on September 29.

Economic Development. While the disruption and damage to industrial and agricultural production caused by the Cultural Revolution had not fully been repaired by 1969, steps had been taken since late 1968 to restore production by issuing a series of directives to stop factional strife and to repair and restore the transport system. Reform measures to improve the economy included: simplification of the administrative organization by reducing the number of departments and their staff; decentralization of the management of industry; participation of workers in management; and the reform of the wage system by reducing wage differentials between highest and lowest levels and by replacing material incentives with Mao-study and ideology. In October the Peking leadership announced a new economic policy and plan with emphasis on agriculture and light industry instead of heavy industry.

Up-to-date statistics remained unavailable. The 1968 agricultural output was below the bumper year of 1967. Grain production in 1967 was estimated at 190 million tons and that of 1968 at slightly less. In September 1969, official publications boasted that the year's wheat and barley harvest had been abundant, and that as a result of the discovery of new deposits and the development of refining and production facilities, China had become self-sufficient in oil.

Foreign Relations. The guidelines of foreign policy adopted by the ninth Party Congress pointed in the following directions: the promotion of good relations among socialist countries friendly to China; the support of revolutionary movements of the oppressed peoples; opposition to capitalist and socialist imperialism, but also coexistence with friendly nonsocialist countries. In the implementation of these directives there was a definite change of attitude and style as evidenced by: restoring diplomatic relations with nearly 20 countries (all but one—in the United Arab Republic—of China's 51 ambassadors had been

Chairman Mao Tse-tung (left) addresses the ninth congress of the Chinese Communist Party in Peking in April 1969. Lin Piao (right) was officially designated as Mao's heir during the congress.

CAMERA PRESS—PIX FROM PUBLIX

recalled during the Cultural Revolution); lifting restrictions on travel by foreign diplomats in China; and releasing British and other foreign correspondents who had been detained during the Cultural Revolution.

With the end of the U.S. bombing of North Vietnam, China early in 1969 withdrew a major portion of its worker-troops stationed in North Vietnam to maintain the railway link between the two countries. After the death of North Vietnam's chief of state, Ho Chi Minh, and following the visit of North Vietnam's Premier Pham Van Dong to Peking in October, China signed a new aid agreement with North Vietnam. Peking recognized the Viet Cong's new provisional revolutionary government in June and continued to give publicity to "liberation struggles" in Laos, Thailand, and Burma. In March Yugoslavia was invited to send an economic mission to China, during which the two nations concluded a trade agreement—the first diplomatic contact between the two in nine years. Peking continued talks with Canada and Italy with a view to recognition. The talks failed to lead to fruition because Peking insisted that Canada and Italy should break diplomatic relations with Nationalist China (Taiwan).

On Nov. 26, 1968, Peking made a surprise suggestion to resume the talks between the Chinese and U.S. ambassadors in Warsaw in February 1969, after the inauguration of U.S. Pres. Richard Nixon. In January, however, Liao Ho-shu, chief of the Chinese diplomatic mission in the Netherlands, defected to the U.S. This led to a protest by China, on February 6, in which Peking charged that the U.S. government, in collusion with the Netherlands, had engineered Liao's defection. On February 19 Peking canceled the ambassadorial talks scheduled for the following day, and by the end of the year had made no effort to resume them.

While the Nixon administration proposed no change in U.S. policy concerning the admission of China to the UN and the defense of Taiwan, it did ease regulations on travel by Americans to China, permitted U.S. citizens abroad to purchase Chinese products up to $100, and, late in the year, announced a relaxation of trade restrictions to permit trade in Chinese goods through third countries. On various occasions U.S. Secretary of State William Rogers reiterated the willingness of the U.S. to ease international tensions and to improve relations with China. Peking appeared to show interest in the U.S. overtures. However, in late October, China charged that a U.S. plane had intruded into China's airspace and had been shot down. According to Peking this was the 19th pilotless high-altitude military reconnaissance plane shot down by the Chinese.

The border disputes between China and the Soviet Union that flared up in 1969 were deeply rooted in historical relations that long antedated Communism. Under the czars of Russia chunks of Chinese territory of about 700,000 sq.mi., including the Amur River basin, the Maritime Territory, and Soviet Central Asia, were annexed by Russia under three unequal treaties in 1858, 1860, and 1864. As a result China and Russia shared a common border of more than 4,000 mi. from Manchuria to central Asia. The deteriorating relations between the two countries, resulting from their differing national interests, ideological conflict, and bitter rivalry for leadership in the world Communist movement, led to increased tension along this frontier. On March 2 fighting broke out at Chen-Pao Island—Damansky Island in Russian—an uninhabited islet in the Ussuri River, which makes up most of the Manchurian border between China and the Soviet Union. Each nation blamed the other as the aggressor. Mutually antagonistic demonstrations spread in both countries. The Soviet embassy in Peking was put under siege, and on March 7 demonstrators in Moscow smashed numerous windows of the Chinese embassy. On March 15 a second major clash occurred at Chen-Pao Island, with casualties on both sides. Following Moscow's repeated suggestions for reopening talks on the border question, Peking accepted on May 12 a Soviet proposal for a meeting of the Joint Commission for Navigation on Boundary Rivers, which met in Khabarovsk, U.S.S.R., on June 18. On August 8 the navigation talks were concluded with the signing of a protocol to improve the shipping situation on border rivers.

In May incidents occurred on the border separating Soviet Kazakhstan and China's Sinkiang Province, where rich oil fields and Chinese nuclear installations were located. Large numbers of Chinese and Soviet troops clashed on June 10 at the Dzungarian Gates on the Sinkiang border. Peking charged that Soviet forces

Christian Churches: *see* Religion
Christian Science: *see* Religion
Churches of Christ: *see* Religion
Church Membership: *see* Religion
Church of England: *see* Religion
Church of Scotland: *see* Religion
Church Unity: *see* Religion
Cigars and Cigarettes: *see* Tobacco

had intruded into Sinkiang, and Moscow contended that Soviet frontier guards had fired in self-defense. In a lengthy speech on June 7 at the World Conference of Communist and Workers' Parties in Moscow, Soviet party chief Leonid I. Brezhnev condemned Mao and the Chinese Communist actions as disrupting the world Communist movement for unity. Diplomatic sources revealed that Moscow had sounded out the reaction of its fellow countries in the Warsaw Pact and of the U.S. concerning the possibility of taking preemptive measures against Peking to destroy its nuclear installations.

Meanwhile, tension and unrest continued on the borders, and on August 13 a new and bloody clash between Chinese and Soviet troops broke out on their central Asian border. Peking and Moscow continued to exchange charges and denunciations. The Chinese protest of August 19 reported 429 border violations in June and July. In reply, on September 10, Moscow charged Peking with 488 frontier violations between June and mid-August.

A dramatic 11th-hour meeting between Premiers Aleksei N. Kosygin and Chou En-lai, perhaps inspired by Ho Chi Minh's "will" urging Communist unity, took place in September. A week earlier Chou had flown to North Vietnam to offer condolences over the death of Ho, but he returned suddenly to Peking on the same day, before Kosygin's arrival in Hanoi for the same purpose. However, on his way home from Ho's funeral, Kosygin made an unexpected but special stop in Peking on September 11 and held a long conference with Chou at the Peking airport. According to reports, Kosygin concretely proposed that the border issues be negotiated at the deputy ministerial level, and that each side drop its campaigns against the other and resume full diplomatic and economic relations. Subsequently, tensions between Peking and Moscow were significantly eased, and on October 7 it was officially confirmed that China and the Soviet Union had agreed to hold talks in Peking. On October 18 a Soviet delegation of 30 persons, led by First Deputy Foreign Minister Vasily V. Kuznetsov, arrived in the Chinese capital. Negotiations began on October 20, but no significant progress had been reported by the year's end.

In its statement of October 7 on the negotiation of border issues, China accepted Sino-Soviet boundary treaties "imposed on China by Tsarist Russian imperialism" as the basis for an overall settlement of the boundary question, and proposed that in order to maintain the status quo of the border and avert armed conflicts, the armed forces of both sides should withdraw from all the disputed areas along the border. Furthermore, the Chinese statement, while recognizing the existence of an ideological gap and "irreconcilable differences of principle" between China and the Soviet Union, stressed that normal state relations between the two countries should be maintained.

(H. T. Ch.)

See also Communist Movement; Propaganda; Taiwan.

ENCYCLOPÆDIA BRITANNICA FILMS. *China Under Communism* (1962); *China: A Portrait of the Land* (1967); *China's Industrial Revolution* (1967); *China's Villages in Change* (1967).

Cinema

In the cinema of 1969 certain characteristics appeared to be practically universal. The relaxation of censorship restrictions that had recently become increasingly evident seemed to have spread to almost every country in the world. (*See* Special Report.) Technically too, 1969 seemed to consolidate and confirm an almost worldwide, if less obvious, revolution that had begun several years earlier. The traditional techniques of film-making that had prevailed since the 1920s, and whose principal characteristic was the preeminence of montage—the effect achieved by the rapid cutting from shot to shot—had been very largely supplanted by a much greater reliance on *mise-en-shot* (set scenes). This revolution in stylistic approach was brought about by a combination of factors, among them the influence of television, and of the larger, more precise screen images achieved by technically developed camera and projection equipment.

Film festivals in 1969 returned to something like normal after the revolutionary demonstrations that had shaken most of the major international film events in 1968. Festivals were at pains to play down the traditional black-tie-and-starlet glamour element; Venice abandoned the award of prizes.

A fringe aspect of cinema activity was the proliferation, particularly in the English-speaking countries, of literature on the cinema. A few years previously publishers would barely look at film books; in 1969 their lists tended to contain many. The shift from fan magazines to serious critical works must to a degree have reflected a change in attitudes and audiences. With the demand for film books went a very much enlarged public interest in the past culture of the cinema, reflected in the popularity of ever-older films on television and the support given to cinematheque and film-archive showings. Among the English-language books published in 1969 special mention should be made of Kevin Brownlow's monumental record of silent cinema artists, *The Parade's Gone By;* Lotte Eisner's study of German Expressionism, *The Haunted Screen;* and Lillian Gish's autobiography, *The Movies, Mr. Griffith and Me.*

The English-Speaking Cinema. *U.S.* In the U.S. production in recent years had been based on a pattern of three principal categories of film: the multimillion dollar "blockbuster"; the moderately expensive film with the built-in box-office value of a big star name or the best-seller property (play or novel) from which it was adapted; and the comparatively cheap, run-of-the-mill program picture, largely sold by association with the middle-range films. In Britain the pattern tended to exclude the "blockbusters," although 1969 brought three striking exceptions in *Isadora, The Battle of Britain,* and *Alfred the Great.*

But the film production, depending a great deal on the intangibles of art and taste, can never be exactly planned or predicted in terms of industrial organization. Several of the most conspicuous of recent successes (whether in terms of massive box-office returns or critical acclaim), from *Bonnie and Clyde* to *The Graduate, If . . . ,* and *Midnight Cowboy,* were films that represented comparatively small initial investments. On the other hand, such a film as *Star!,* on which much faith and cash were pinned, proved a considerable disappointment financially as well as artistically. The success of these films must have been all the more frustrating to those whose concern was to organize the cinema as industry, since each of these box-office hits would be difficult to imitate. Unlike the James Bond or the *Carry On* formulas, imitation, even if it were possible, was unlikely to be profitable.

Midnight Cowboy, with John Schlesinger of the U.K. as director, must be reckoned one of the out-

Annual Cinema Attendance

Country	Total in 000	Per capita
Afghanistan	6,100	0.4
Albania	7,800	4
Algeria	26,900	2.4
Andorra	200	18
Argentina	145,000	7
Austria	65,800	9
Bahrain	1,300	7
Barbados	1,600	7
Belgium	44,700	5
Bolivia	3,200	0.9
Brazil	314,500	4
Brunei	2,200	22
Bulgaria	124,100	15
Burma	218,000	9
Cambodia	10,700	2
Canada	99,900	5
Central African Rep.	500	0.4
Chile	61,400	7
China	4,000,000	6
Colombia	80,100	4
Congo (Brazzaville)	1,700	2
Cuba	49,900	7
Cyprus	8,700	14
Czechoslovakia	128,400	9
Denmark	33,900	7
Dominican Republic	5,300	2
Ecuador	15,100	3
El Salvador	15,100	6
Equatorial Guinea	650	2.5
France	240,700	5
Germany, East	119,000	7
Germany, West	280,000	5
Ghana	13,700	2
Greece	61,200	7
Guatemala	9,700	2
Guyana	4,400	7
Hong Kong	98,500	27
Hungary	104,600	10
India	1,825,000	4
Indonesia	259,600	3
Iran	52,000	3
Iraq	8,300	1
Ireland	38,000	13
Israel	50,300	20
Italy	640,000	12
Japan	372,700	4
Jamaica	1,300	0.7
Jordan	6,100	3
Kenya	7,300	0.8
Korea, South	150,800	5
Kuwait	200	0.9
Lebanon	32,100	14
Liberia	1,400	1.4
Libya	3,400	3
Liechtenstein	70	4
Luxembourg	3,000	9
Macao	5,300	30
Malagasy Rep.	3,300	0.5
Mali	3,700	0.8
Malta	4,000	13
Mauritius	7,700	10
Mexico	346,500	9
Monaco	200	7
Mongolia	1,500	1.5
Morocco	19,400	1.5
Netherlands	34,300	3
New Zealand	26,000	10
Nicaragua	7,500	5
Pakistan	201,500	2
Poland	164,700	5
Portugal	28,300	3
Romania	216,100	11
San Marino	220	12
Senegal	5,200	1.5
Singapore	25,100	14
Somalia	3,200	1
Spain	403,900	13
Sudan	10,100	0.8
Sweden	35,400	5
Switzerland	48,000	7
Syria	21,000	4
Taiwan	67,000	7
Trinidad and Tobago	6,700	8
Turkey	30,000	1
U.S.S.R.	4,200,000	18
U.A.R.	63,300	2
United Kingdom	289,000	5
United States	2,288,000	12
Uruguay	16,500	6
Venezuela	60,000	8
Vietnam, South	24,000	1.5
Western Samoa	200	2
Yugoslavia	114,600	6

Note: Figures given are most recent available.
Source: UNESCO *Statistical Yearbook* (1967).

standingly successful U.S. films of the year, in terms of both critical reception and box office. Adapted from James Leo Herlihy's novel of the same name, it told of the friendship of two lonely drifters in New York City, social outcasts who still managed to retain a little dignity and human warmth in their relationship. The playing of Jon Voight as a slow-witted, unsuccessful gigolo come to town from Texas, and of Dustin Hoffman (the star of *The Graduate*) as a seedy, crippled con man, a second-generation Italian-American, was astonishing; it gave a human solidity to a film that elsewhere, despite shrewd observations of contemporary urban living, tended to be self-indulgently overdecorated.

Jon Voight's film debut took place a year or so earlier in an independently made shoestring-budget film, which only reached the public cinemas late in 1969. Paul Williams' *Out of it*—a seriocomic impression of the pleasures and agonies of high-school life for a boy of above-average intelligence and perceptions but below-average looks and physique—revealed a maturity of vision and accomplishment astonishing for the feature debut of a 23-year-old director. Williams subsequently directed a feature in Britain, *The Revolutionary,* in which Voight, by now reckoned the most remarkable new film actor of 1969, starred.

Another low-budget and independent production that achieved considerable critical and commercial success on both sides of the Atlantic was Dennis Hopper's *Easy Rider,* in which the leading roles were played by the director himself and the producer, Peter Fonda. This was a feeling, despairing impression, by means of a picaresque journey across the U.S., of the confrontation between the hippie dropout and the violence in organized, "respectable" society. Another attempt to look seriously at the hippie subculture was Arthur Penn's *Alice's Restaurant,* based on the song of that name by Arlo Guthrie, who played the leading role in the film.

COURTESY, UNITED ARTISTS

Joe Buck (Jon Voight, left) and Ratso (Dustin Hoffman) dodge New York City traffic in a scene from "Midnight Cowboy."

John Schlesinger was not the only British director to have made an impact in Hollywood, at a time when U.S. money and talent continued by and large to dominate international production. Peter Yates, who had directed a stylish crime film, *Robbery,* in Britain, made an excellent thriller, *Bullitt,* distinguished by its atmospheric use of San Francisco locations and by one of the best automobile chases ever filmed.

The older school of directors and the time-honoured types of motion pictures were not looking their best in 1969. Otto Preminger came up with *Skidoo!,* a zany comedy whose critical reception was worse than cool. George Cukor's version of Laurence Durrell's *Justine* was generally spoken of as a travesty. Carl Foreman produced a portentous Western saga, *MacKenna's Gold,* directed by the Englishman J. Lee Thompson, which was very badly received by critics in the U.S. and Britain. The best musical was *Sweet Charity,* an effective translation to the screen by Bob Fosse of a stage musical that he had also directed in the theatre and that was itself based on a film, Federico Fellini's *Le Notti de Cabiria.*

Westerns apparently retained their perennial appeal. The controversial Sam Peckinpah, an evident admirer of John Ford, directed his most successful film to date in *The Wild Bunch.* A few critics found it undisciplined and ill-proportioned, and noted Peckinpah's failure to equal Ford's great transitions of mood from the tragic and monumental to the intimate and comic. Perhaps Andrew V. McLaglen's *The Undefeated* came nearer to the Fordian tone. Altogether more modest than either, *The Good Guys and The Bad Guys* confirmed the maturing of Burt Kennedy's talent as a director of witty light-comedy Westerns that nevertheless respected both the traditions of the form and the intelligence of the audience.

The U.S. Academy of Motion Picture Arts and Sciences presented its annual Academy Awards in April. *Oliver!,* a musical based on Charles Dickens' novel *Oliver Twist* and also adapted from a stage musical, was voted the best motion picture of 1968. For the first time in the history of the awards there was a tie for best actress, the honours going to Katharine Hepburn for her role in *The Lion in Winter* and Barbra Streisand for *Funny Girl.* Miss Hepburn became the first actress to win the award two years in succession since Luise Rainer in 1936–37. Cliff Robertson won the best actor award for his work in *Charly,* while Jack Albertson was the best supporting actor for *The Subject Was Roses.* Ruth Gordon won best supporting actress for *Rosemary's Baby,* and Sir Carol Reed was named best director for *Oliver!*

Britain. For several years U.S. investment had been a major factor in the prosperity of other film industries, notably that of Britain. The situation had always given rise to certain misgivings at the possibility of partial or full withdrawal of the investment. In late 1969 the prospect seemed nearer and more alarming than at any previous time. An effort at conscious local reorganization of British production was the program announced when Bryan Forbes (*see* BIOGRAPHY) was appointed head of Associated British Pictures Corporation in the spring of 1969. Forbes's plans to introduce new talent and to address a U.S. market were laudable, if perhaps overoptimistic.

In fact there had been a number of promising debuts during the year. Dick Clements partially wrote as well as directed *Otley,* a successful return to zany comedy. The hero, a light-fingered but sympathetic layabout, was played by Tom Courtenay. Waris Hussein came from television to direct a sensitive adaptation of Margaret Drabble's novel *The Millstone,* under the title *A Touch of Love,* about the experiences of an unmarried mother. Anthony Page's film version of John Osborne's *Inadmissible Evidence,* which he had already directed in the theatre with the same star, Nicol Williamson (*see* BIOGRAPHY), was perhaps underrated.

The outstanding feature film of the year, released just before Christmas 1968, was unquestionably Lindsay Anderson's *If . . .*, which earned top honours at the Cannes Film Festival in May. This fantasy of life in an imaginary English public school, which moved into areas of the surreal as it followed the spiritual and imaginative lives of its three boy heroes, caught the imagination of many young people by the way it crystallized feelings of revolt against those parts of organized society that seemed to the young to have become ossified and irrelevant.

Of the large-budget films that were an unusual feature of British production in 1969, *The Battle of Britain* aimed at dignity rather than more vital qualities in its celebration of a heroic moment in British history. It had cost $13 million and several years of effort. Directed by Guy Hamilton, it included a distinguished roster of British players, led by Sir Laurence Olivier and Sir Michael Redgrave. The actor Richard Attenborough (*see* BIOGRAPHY) emerged as a director with notable éclat in *Oh! What a Lovely War*. Originally a radio program of words and songs of World War I, it had been filled out first to a play at Joan Littlewood's Theatre Workshop, and then was adapted to a spectacular film. Despite some dull sections and clumsinesses, the film found brilliant solutions to the problems of adaptation and of finding an equivalent to the methods of stylization used on the stage.

Isadora, directed by Karel Reisz, suffered the fate of many large-budget films and was seen only in a version apparently much abridged by its nervous producers. Vanessa Redgrave's performance was admired for its panache but perhaps fell short of conveying what were the special qualities of the real Isadora Duncan. Other films in the "blockbuster" class were less successful. An ambitious *Alfred the Great,* directed by Clive Donner, foundered for want of a firm script construction; Peter Shaffer's play *The Royal Hunt of the Sun* seemed too flimsy to bear the weight of an expensive production, partly shot on location in Peru.

Other, somewhat less costly play adaptations met with better success. The U.S. director Robert Aldrich's version of *The Killing of Sister George* enjoyed a considerable succès de scandale on account of its graphic depiction of lesbian mores. Most critics agreed that the director weakened the impact of the film by being more curious about his heroines (played by Beryl Reid and Susannah York) as lesbians than as characters. *The Prime of Miss Jean Brodie* owed its success more to Maggie Smith's virtuoso interpretation of Muriel Spark's Scottish schoolmistress than to Ronald Neame's somewhat stodgy and pedestrian direction.

Western Europe. *France*. The generation that came to the fore in the late 1950s—the former "nouvelle vague"—continued to dominate French production. Claude Chabrol's *La Femme infidèle* maintained the brilliant return to form of *Les Biches*. A controlled, funny, enigmatic tale of infidelity, jealousy, and lust, it was set against the comfortable world of a bourgeois home in de Gaulle's self-sufficient France.

Following his less than happy foray into the British cinema, with *One Plus One*, Jean-Luc Godard with *Le gai Savoir* disappointed all but his most dedicated supporters. Originally made for television and then bought back by its director when it was reckoned to be unshowable on that medium, the film set out to depict a contemporary young man and woman receiving their political education from the signs and symbols, pictures and sounds of our times. The juxtapositions —play with words and images—should have been stimulating, but half the time proved simply tedious.

One of the most original French films of the year was Jacques Rivette's *L'Amour fou,* another film that suffered considerably at the hands of its producers and distributors who were alarmed by the great length (4 hr. 12 min.) of the original version. To a large extent improvised, the movie detailed the relationship of a theatre director, currently at work on a production of *Antigone,* and his wife, who suffers feelings of jealousy and exclusion. Eric Rohmer's cool and elegant *Ma Nuit chez Maud* related how a young man, played by Jean-Louis Trintignant, found his philosophical as well as his marital outlook influenced by an encounter with another woman.

Inevitably the event of the year for the French cinema was a new film by the veteran Luis Buñuel. To succeed *Belle de jour* he had made a brilliantly comic, sardonic, and essentially serious exploration in time and space of all the heresies of the Roman Catholic faith; *La Voie lactée* showed the old Surrealist at his most rich and characteristic.

Italy. The most eagerly awaited Italian film was Federico Fellini's *Satyricon*. When it finally appeared at the Venice Film Festival, it turned out to be immensely decorative, but overwhelmingly long and heavy, leaving its premiere audience distinctly bewildered and battered. Staged with immense and elaborate care as it was, Fellini's recreation of ancient Rome lacked the wit, the vitality, and the eroticism of Petronius, on whose picaresque tale it was based.

Pier Paolo Pasolini's enigmatic *Porcile* also made its appearance at Venice. The film consisted of two parallel parables. Somewhere in the 17th century a starving young man becomes a cannibal, and afterward persuades a band of disciples to join him, wandering and marauding, consuming stray travelers. In contemporary West Germany, the son of a rich industrialist who is deeply involved with old Nazi associations has a sexual preference for pigs. The cannibal is left at the end to be devoured by the beasts of the desert; the modern young man is gobbled up by his pig lovers. While one was sometimes left guessing at precise meanings, the sensuous qualities of the film were admirable.

Sweden. Ingmar Bergman's *Shame* was a departure in several ways for the great Swedish director. For one thing the nightmare of the characters was outside themselves rather than within them, in this case being a war that degrades and separates a perfectly ordinary couple. His technique, too, was more informal, with hand-held cameras and improvised dialogue. Another Bergman film, *The Ritual,* was originally made for Swedish television, which gave it, too, a distinctive stylistic character, with extensive use of close-ups and hard black-and-white photography. This was a parable about a cabaret act—two men and a woman— who are arraigned for supposed obscenity. The three of them and the interrogating judge become caught up in a ritualistic game of mutual humiliation.

In *Adalen 31* the young Bo Widerberg brought the same romantic and picturesque qualities he had employed in *Elvira Madigan* to a grimmer subject: a labour demonstration in the early 1930s, when several people were killed. Criticism was divided between praise for the visual elegance and distaste for the film's sentimentality.

Finland. The film industry of Finland continued

continued on page 207

Sir Laurence Olivier as Field Marshal Sir John French stands amid acres of white crosses in the closing scene of "Oh! What a Lovely War," an antiwar musical released in 1969.

COURTESY, PARAMOUNT PICTURES

THE CINEMA AND CENSORSHIP

By John Trevelyan

The years 1968–69 brought significant change in the field of censorship, with marked effects on both the cinema and the live theatre. New demands for freedom of expression in the arts produced increasing pressures on all forms of restraint, and reflections of this could be seen in most parts of the world, with the exception of the totalitarian states, Southeast Asia, and the emergent African countries. It seems likely that this period will ultimately be regarded by social historians as a milestone in the history of censorship.

The United States. Developments in the United States had considerable influence on the position of censorship in the United Kingdom and Western Europe—except Spain and to some extent France—and were on much the same lines as developments in Scandinavia. New freedoms opened new markets. Sex and pornography in books, films, and theatre, which had previously been available only in backstreets or underground, began to spread to areas where formerly they had been found unacceptable. Books and magazines that were formerly on sale only in the 42nd Street district of New York City could now be found in shops and on newsstands in other parts of town; films that had formerly been shown in only a few theatres in the same district went on "theatrical distribution"; sex and nudity in the live theatre, which had formerly been confined to Greenwich Village and off-Broadway theatres, suddenly became acceptable to the main theatre-going public.

In the live theatre *Hair*, a musical show with a cast of young people, which was peppered with four-letter words and had a scene in which several actors removed all their clothes, became a sensational success. The Living Theater, directed by Julian Beck, adopted the same technique, mixed with political protest. Straight plays like *The Beard* showed sexual acts on the stage with dialogue that was totally uninhibited. This led, in 1969, to British drama critic Kenneth Tynan's producing a musical with nudity, sex, and eroticism, called *Oh! Calcutta!*, which stimulated such a demand for tickets that seat prices were soon raised to astronomical heights.

Foreign films, mainly from Scandinavia, fitted into this pattern. A Swedish film, *I, a Woman*, which many people regarded as pornographic, was put on theatrical distribution, leading the way for others. Another Swedish film, *I Am Curious* (*Yellow*), which showed complete frontal nudity (of both sexes) and copulation, was confiscated by the U.S. Customs Service in New York City. A U.S. District Court ruled it obscene, thus justifying Customs, but the verdict was appealed and subsequently reversed by a higher court. This film was eventually shown in its complete form in a New York theatre where it was a huge commercial success, although its main theme, which was related to Swedish politics, could hardly have been an attraction for American audiences. In contrast, a Boston exhibitor was given a short prison sentence for exhibiting the same film, and police action was taken in some other cities and states; the film, however, continued to be distributed.

The mainstream of the U.S. motion picture industry reacted to these developments, and for the first time in nearly 40 years felt it necessary to protect itself from public criticism. Precensorship of films, which until only a few years earlier had been used by a few states and cities, had, after legal battles extending over many years, eventually been judged illegal by the U.S. Supreme Court and had ceased to exist. The only controls left were the law and the film industry's "self-regulation," which had been established in 1930 under Will Hays. This self-regulation was operated from Hollywood by a division of the Motion Picture Association of America—the Production Code Administration—and film producers working for the main companies were bound to observe what was laid down in a document called the "Production Code." The original code, which had been drawn up in 1930, was a restrictive document; in 1966 it was completely revised and considerably shortened by the recently appointed president of the Motion Picture Association, Jack Valenti. In this modified form it remained operative.

Since increasing freedom for film makers produced the risk of further public criticism of the film industry and the risk of harm to children, the Motion Picture Association introduced in November 1968 a system of rating films. Films that were approved by the Production Code Administration were rated as follows: "G"—suitable for general audiences; "M"—suitable for adults, and for children 16 years old and under, with parental discretion advised; "R"—suitable for adults and for 16-year-olds and under who are accompanied by a parent or other adult. In addition to this, films not approved by the Production Code Administration, or not submitted for approval, can be shown under an "X" rating, which recommends that no person under 16 years of age should be admitted to see them.

The operation of this classification is voluntary, although states or cities may produce enforcement legislation and vary the minimum age. In introducing the system, Valenti said that it was motivated by two concerns—a willingness to give film makers greater freedom of expression and a desire that children be safeguarded.

One result of this rating system appears to be that films rated "X" are a special attraction to the public. Two examples are *I Am Curious* (*Yellow*) and *The Killing of Sister George*. Time will show whether the commercial attraction of "X" films is short-lived or enduring. Since the film industry is fighting for survival in the highly competitive field of entertainment, and since many of the major film companies are now subsidiaries of

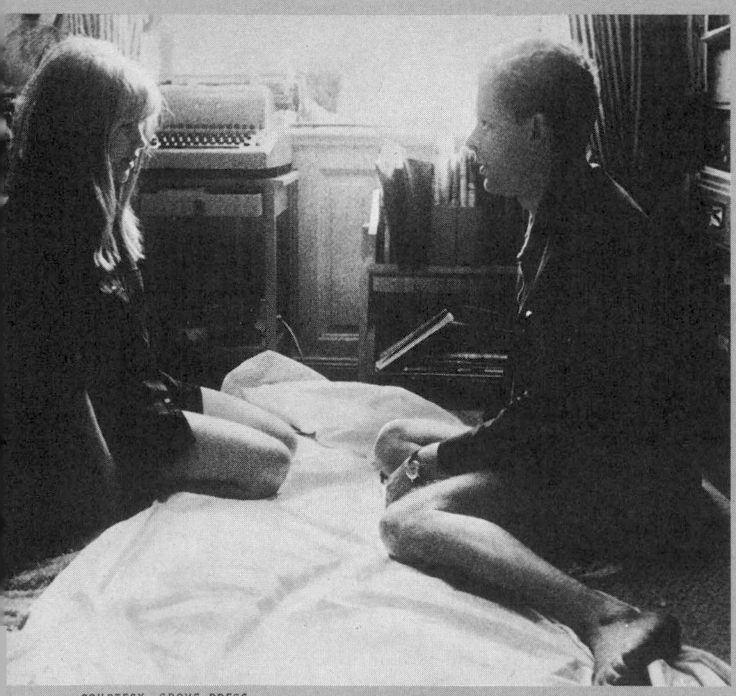

COURTESY, GROVE PRESS

Lena Nyman and Borje Ahlstedt as young lovers in "I Am Curious (Yellow)," a sexually explicit film of 1969, directed by Sweden's Vilgot Sjöman.

giant corporations, it is reasonable to expect that profitability will dictate production policies.

United Kingdom. A highly significant change was the abolition in 1968 of precensorship for the live theatre. Some form of control had existed since the 16th century, and ever since then powers of censorship had rested with the lord chamberlain, an officer of the Royal Household; those powers had been embodied in the Theatres Act of 1843, which was still operative. Following a debate in the House of Lords in February 1966, Parliament set up a joint committee "to review the law and practice relating to the censorship of stage plays," and in June 1967 this committee recommended the total abolition of precensorship and licensing of plays and the repeal of the relevant portions of the 1843 act. Legislation was subsequently introduced in the Theatres Act of 1968. This made possible the production of stage plays that the lord chamberlain would not have licensed, but theatre managements still risked prosecution for showing obscenity.

In the field of books and publications there were also important developments. The Obscene Publications Act of 1959 introduced for the first time in such legislation a defense in terms of literary quality and educational value, but it still retained the definition of obscenity, on the basis of a formula that originated in 1868, as "a tendency to deprave and corrupt." Because the exact meaning of those words had never been defined, in the few cases that have come to the courts juries have been compelled to make subjective judgments and to judge literary quality as it was assessed by expert witnesses. In 1966 Sir Cyril Black, a member of Parliament, having failed to persuade the attorney general to take proceedings in the courts against the publishers of *Last Exit to Brooklyn,* initiated court proceedings as a private citizen. A London magistrate being satisfied that there was a prima facie case, proceedings were taken by the director of public prosecutions. The case was heard in 1967 before a judge and jury, and the publishers were convicted. On subsequent appeal this verdict was reversed. Perhaps as a result of this case, in the summer of 1968 the Arts Council of Great Britain called a conference of writers, publishers, and others directly concerned to consider whether the Obscene Publications Acts of 1959 and 1964 needed to be revised. The conference was clearly of the opinion that they did, and as a result the Arts Council appointed a working party to give the matter detailed consideration. Reporting in July 1969, the working party recommended that obscenity should no longer be regarded as an indictable offense and that all relevant acts of Parliament be repealed. The next step was for Parliament to decide whether or not to implement this by legislation.

In the light of these developments the precensorship of films came under increasing pressure. Since 1912 censorship has been undertaken by an independent body, the British Board of Film Censors. This organization was set up on the initiative of the film industry, with the approval of the government, but is not a governmental body. The board views, and censors when considered necessary, all films to be shown at commercial cinemas; any local authority, however, has the legal right to reverse or modify any decision that the board takes. In effect the local authorities act as "courts of appeal," but only a very few films are the subject of appeal at any given time.

The principal function of the British Board of Film Censors is the protection of children. This is undertaken by classification of films, as follows: "U"—for any adult, or child of not less than 5 years of age; "A"—for any adult, and for children under 16 years of age accompanied by a person over 16; "X"—for any person 16 years of age and above. This system of classification is embodied in regulations and is enforceable at law.

The board has no rules or code and judges each film on its merits; in its decisions it attempts to reflect contemporary public attitudes. In the light of this it has in recent years become increasingly liberal in dealing with scenes of sex, but it has retained a restrictive policy in dealing with scenes of violence. The present category system is now under consideration, and some reconstruction may be expected.

COURTESY, CINERAMA RELEASING CORPORATION

Susannah York (right) comforts Beryl Reid in a scene from "The Killing of Sister George." The "X"-rated 1969 film dealt with the lesbian relationship between an aging TV actress and her young lover.

Denmark. During the 1960s there has been increasing public debate on the subject of pornography. In 1964 the courts acquitted the publishers of *Fanny Hill.* In an effort to establish an interpretation of obscenity, the case was taken to the nation's Supreme Court, where the acquittal was upheld. In 1966 the Permanent Criminal Law Committee recommended, by a majority vote, that legal restrictions on written pornography should be removed, and this was put into effect by the Danish Parliament in 1967. Restrictions on pictorial pornography, however, were retained. There followed a marked decline in sales of written pornography and a corresponding increase in sales of pictorial pornography, a situation that produced for the courts difficulties arising from the uncertain interpretations of obscenity. As a result further legislation was passed, and as of July 1, 1969, all legal restrictions on pictorial pornography were removed, although sales to children under 16 remained illegal. Danish films have become increasingly explicit in their presentation of sex, which appears to be acceptable to the public, and the Danish Parliament in 1969 passed legislation removing all censorship of films for adults (persons of 16 years of age and upward).

Sweden. Film censorship in Sweden has become increasingly permissive with regard to scenes of sex, but has maintained a restrictive policy with scenes of violence. The State Cinema Bureau, a government body responsible for precensorship, has tried to keep sex scenes within what it regards as reasonable limits, but has on occasion been overruled by higher authority. Books and magazines displayed in shop windows and on newsstands, not only in Stockholm but even in small towns, would result in prosecution in most other countries. It is not surprising, therefore, that a commission set up by the Ministry of Education has recommended the abolition of film censorship for movies shown to adult audiences; it seems likely that there will be legislation to that effect in 1970. As in Denmark, censorship of films to be shown to children would be retained.

Italy. In recent years Italy probably produced more sex films than any other country. The increasingly liberal policies of the Ministry of Entertainment's censorship board led to the resignation of several members in protest. Franco Zeffirelli, a motion picture director, publicly condemned the production of salacious and pornographic films, which resulted in his expulsion from the Italian Association of Cinema Authors. The constitutionality of the articles of the Italian Penal Code on obscenity, which defines it as "that which, according to public sentiment, offends public morals," was formally questioned. The Christian Democratic Party has proposed to Parliament an alternative definition as "acts and objects that offend morals according to the sentiments of a good father of a family." While the arguments continue, sex films continue to be produced.

West Germany. In 1968 there was a substantial increase in the production of sex-education films as a result of the great commercial success of a film called *Helga,* which, though made for schools and colleges, proved to be the biggest box-office success since World War II. Since sex education seemed to be a certain commercial success, other films were made on those lines. The educational purpose of these films was emphasized as a justification for their visual content. The Censorship Board appears to have accepted this justification.

Other Countries. In the Netherlands in 1969 a committee—the Advies Commissie voor de Filmkeuring—recommended the abolition of film censorship for adults. The position in Belgium remains unchanged; there is censorship of films to be shown to children, but there has never been censorship of films to be shown to adults. In France the Censorship Commission, essentially under government control, has in recent years tended to reflect less liberal attitudes in the presentation of sex.

In India, although film censorship continues to be more restrictive than in Western countries, a committee recommended in 1969 that "if in telling the story it is logical, relevant or necessary to depict a passionate kiss or a nude human figure, there should be no question of excluding the shot."

Having experienced markedly restrictive governmental censorship before and during World War II, the Japanese replaced it with a system of self-censorship by the industry. This has proven to be more liberal, as regards both sex and violence, than in most other countries. It seemed to be acceptable to filmgoers in Japan, although the liberality created the possibility of further government intervention.

A king, horribly mutilated by war, passes by the fat beggar Francesco in "Satyricon," Federico Fellini's fantasy fable cataloging the debaucheries of ancient Rome. Characters were played by beggars, prostitutes, and madmen from real life.

"PARIS MATCH" FROM PICTORIAL PARADE

The Censorship Debate. Censorship will remain a controversial subject, probably for some years, in most free societies. The chief protagonists in each country will be virtually the same—the liberal intellectual who demands freedom for the artist and freedom of choice for the adult, and the conservative (so-called "reactionary") who believes that the adult does not know what is good or bad for him and must have people to decide this for him. The decisions will not, however, be made by either faction; they will be made by national legislatures—the elected representatives of the people—who will probably accept a sensible compromise, if they can find one, that will give the artist freedom and that will control the pornographer in the interests of society and the individual.

There are in fact two quite different issues: one is legal; the other is social. To suggest that there is only one issue is to cause confusion of thought. The legal issue is concerned with the interpretation in exact terms of such words as "obscenity" and "pornography" and of such phrases as "tend to deprave and corrupt." Unless the law is made specific—so that it can establish exactly what is to be prohibited and punished—it can only lead to confusion and injustice. This must be accepted as a reasonable argument for the repeal, or at least the rewriting, of such laws as are capable of various interpretations. The social issue is concerned with the well-being of the individual and of society. Although research has produced no definite findings about the influence, good or bad, of the mass media, there are indications that people are influenced by what they see and hear and, to perhaps a lesser extent, by what they read. A complete reconciliation of opposing opinions may not be possible, but it should be noted that what may be a correct solution to the legal issue may prove to be wrong with regard to the social issue. The aim, of course, should be to find a way of giving freedom to the artist without doing social or individual harm by giving freedom also to the people who set out to make money by exploiting human weakness.

continued from page 203

its startling recovery of recent years, the new directors being mostly young and concerned with highly contemporary subjects: Timo Bergholm's *Punahilkka* (*Little Red Riding Hood*), for instance, was a sad and funny account of the difficulties experienced by a reform school girl in trying to establish a place for herself in an unsympathetic society.

Eastern Europe. *U.S.S.R.* After several years in which few Soviet films attracted great interest outside their domestic market, several motion pictures of international appeal appeared. Andrei Tarkovski's *Andrei Rublev* was in fact made in 1967, but not released, as the authorities apparently found its picture of medieval Russia too sombre. At the 1969 Cannes Festival, a somewhat mutilated version showed it to be a brooding, visionary glimpse of history, in which Tarkovski was evidently fascinated by the paradox of how a man can be caught up in brutal and barbaric times and yet still produce works of such serenity and joy as Rublev's icons.

Other directors of a younger generation came to the fore. Andrei Konchalovski (director of *The New Teacher*) made a startlingly beautiful adaptation of Ivan Turgenev's novel *A Nest of Gentlefolk*. Larisse Shapitko's *Wings,* with its apparently casual structure, unexpectedly paid tribute to Italian director Michelangelo Antonioni in its study of a misfit—a former wartime flier who cannot adjust to civilian life. In contrast to the respectable dullness of *The Brothers Karamazov,* the last work of the veteran Ivan Pyriev, another adaptation of Fëdor Dostoevski, A. Alov and V. Naumov's *A Bad Joke,* turned out to be a wild and fascinating extravaganza.

Of the older generation, Sergei Yutkevitch made a film that looked back to the adventurous spirit of Soviet art in the 1920s when the director himself was first becoming established in the theatre and the cinema. Based on a fragment from the life of Anton Chekhov, it employed extravagant stylization to striking and delightful effect.

Hungary. In 1969 Hungary found itself with a director of international stature in Miklos Jancso, but the films that he released in 1969 disappointed even his most ardent champions. The characteristic style—entirely abandoning conventional montage film-making for a style dependent on long (often ten-minute) takes and elaborate *mise-en-shot*—had become mannered and even eccentric. The stylistic mannerism emphasized the obsessive quality of the subject matter. *The Confrontation* dealt with the situation of young Hungarians in the post-World War II period of reorganization for socialism. *Sirocco d'Hiver,* a Franco-Hungarian co-production, was about political activists and terrorists in the early 1930s. In both films Jancso employed his now too familiar technique of interpreting his characters' political actions through ritualistic behaviour and action.

Czechoslovakia. Not surprisingly the Czechoslovak cinema was in an apparent state of uncertainty. No new film by Milos Forman, Ivan Passer, Jan Nemec, or Jiri Menzel, the most talented directors to have emerged in the last few years, was seen in 1969. The Czechoslovak films seen at the Venice Festival—a period drama directed by Hynek Bocan (*Cest a Slava*) and a whimsical morality play, Stefan Uher's *Genii* ("The Devils")—were indifferent in quality and noncommittal in content.

Poland. The Polish cinema seemed to have entered upon an uncertain phase also, reflected in the inequality of the latest films of the country's most distinguished director, Andrjez Wajda. After a brilliant impressionistic recapitulated portrait of a deceased actor (unambiguously the subject was the Polish actor Zbigniew Cybulski who was killed a year or so earlier) as seen through the eyes of his friends, Wajda's next film, *The Fly Hunt,* was a slight and tedious tragicomedy about a young man snatched from his natural —and preferred—place as a failure by a young woman who tries to drive him to success.

Latin America. Much interest was focused on the Latin-American cinema, where a new, young, vigorous, and generally militant leftist movement had arisen against the old familiar background of a worn-out commercial industry. Glauber Rocha, a much-admired young Brazilian director, showed his *Antonio das Mortes* at the Cannes Festival, where the audience was divided between those who found its story of bandits and savage slaughter operatic, and those who found it simply heavily melodramatic. The Venice Festival was much enlivened by the appearance of a film by a new Brazilian director, Joaquim Pedro de Andrade's *Macunaima,* an energetic and thoroughly bawdy fantasy of peasant life.

The young Cuban cinema continued to show the vigour of its youthful directors. Humberto Solas' *Lucia* was a showy virtuoso piece, three love stories set in three revolutionary situations. *La Prima Carga al Machete,* telling of the rising of 1868 against the Spanish colonists, also suffered from its showiness.

Meanwhile, the Bolivian director Jorge Sanjines made, in *Yawa Mallku,* an authentic revolutionary film, angrily exposing the gulf between rich and poor in his country, and also the continuing readiness to suppress the Indian races into extinction.

Asia. The most striking of the new young Japanese directors was Nagisa Oshima, who had been making feature films for several years, but only came to prominence outside his own country in 1969 with *Death by Hanging* (made in 1968), *Diary of a Shinjuku Thief,* and *The Boy. Diary of a Shinjuku Thief* was a fantasy that equated the attempts of a boy and girl to discover sexual fulfillment with the political aspirations of their generation. *The Boy* concerned a family that lived by faking road accidents and then blackmailing the unfortunate drivers who were thus framed. The whole affair, the economic uncertainties and moral degradation, was seen through the eyes of a child, the hapless tool of the criminals.

The traditional historical genre of Japanese film-making was maintained by Masahire Shinoda's *Double Suicide,* based, rather surprisingly, on a Banraku puppet play about a love triangle. (DA. J. R.)

Nontheatrical. Nontheatrical motion pictures figured prominently in approximately 70 film festivals of international interest that were held in a number of countries during 1969. Notable among these were the showings at the Edinburgh (Scot.) Film Festival, August 24 to September 12. Also of special distinction were the Venice (Italy) Film Festival held in August, featuring nontheatrical as well as entertainment films, and the International Industrial Film Festival held in Berlin in November. Festivals of importance were also held in Moscow; Brno, Czech.; Cork, Ire.; Trieste, Italy; Melbourne, Austr.; Rio de Janeiro, Braz.; Buenos Aires, Arg.; and New York City.

The growing influence of innovation in nontheatrical film making was indicated by the wide recognition given in festivals outside the U.S. to the U.S.-made film *Why Man Creates,* produced by Saul Bass for

Martine Carol portrays a fading Spanish dancer and courtesan in the 1955 film classic "Lola Montes," which began its first commercial run in U.S. theatres in April 1969.

COURTESY, BRANDON FILMS

Peter Fonda (centre) as Wyatt and Dennis Hopper as Billy in the film "Easy Rider," which probed contemporary youthful values. Film was directed by co-star Hopper.

COURTESY, COLUMBIA PICTURES

Kaiser Aluminum & Chemical Corp. It received seven awards in showings at six festivals.

Nearly 1,000 films were entered in the 11th annual American Film Festival held in New York, May 13 to May 18. This major event gave awards to 41 motion pictures in 46 categories ranging from "Classroom Films for Lower Grades"—won by *The Cow,* produced by Dimension Films—to "Medical Sciences for Professional Audiences," won by *The Dynamic Electrocardiogram of the Middle-Aged Man,* produced by Sturgis-Grant Productions. Though no radical innovations appeared, a widening use of new techniques of film making in all types of productions was revealed.

Reports on trends in U.S. nontheatrical films indicated continued growth. An estimated $1,264,000,000 was spent for films and other audiovisual materials and equipment in 1968, showing a gain of 8%, slightly better than the growth of the preceding year. Schools continued to be the largest segment of the market for films, gaining 6% over the preceding year. In spite of a reduction in federal funds for such purposes, increased purchases of films and other materials pushed up expenditures by schools to $570 million.

The second largest market, business and industry, increased by 9% with a total of $458 million spent.

The output of new motion pictures matched the modest growth of the market. According to estimates, there were 13,750 new films produced in 1968, an increase of 9% over the preceding year. However, there was no increase in the production of films for education. Approximately 1,700 films were produced in this category, the same number as were produced in 1967. (J. T. B.)

See also Photography; Television and Radio.

ENCYCLOPÆDIA BRITANNICA FILMS. *New Tools for Learning* (1952); *The Unique Contribution* (1959); *Project Discovery: A Demonstration in Education* (1965); *Let Them Learn* (1967); *Growing* (1969)—a completely computer-animated film.

Cities and Urban Affairs

The cities of the world were comparatively quiet in 1969. Summer race riots did not occur as expected in the U.S. but religious riots exploded in the Northern Ireland cities of Londonderry and Belfast. There was little evidence, however, that the fundamental problems of urban areas were being solved anywhere in the world, and the spending of an estimated $30 billion to put U.S. astronauts on the moon contrasted with the low priority of resources allocated to urban affairs. With the changeover of administration in the U.S. there was little legislation. But for Britain it was a bumper year; the number of acts passed and the important Maud report on local government reflected official interest in public participation in planning and regional government.

Urban Planning. There was continual public discussion of urban affairs that left no part of "civilization"—physical, social, or economic—unexamined, and this broadened into a consensus that technology had now become a threat to human existence and values. It was felt that city planning was now too important and too difficult to be left to planners, and that there had been too much concentration on the physical planning of new buildings and roads and too little on social relationships and the quality of life. Two new trends of opinion were illustrated by two talks made to planning conferences during the year. John Rex, professor of social theory and institutions at Durham University, attacked the garden city mainstream tradition behind planning for divorcing the suburb from its urban context, and asked not merely for suburban lawns and houses but also for "downtown" streets. Des Wilson, director of Shelter, a U.K. organization to help the homeless, criticized planning for "the group that can afford change rather than the group that needs it," saying the poor could not afford what the planners wanted to plan: "The middle class gets planning for people, the rest get planning for the proletariat."

Despite its faults, however, most critics wanted more planning, though dynamic, flexible, strategic planning rather than the conventional static land-use planning of the past. For instance, Colin Buchanan, in a May report for the British Road Federation, criticized existing policies and asked "whether planning is achieving very much more than tagging along after the event, tidying up as best it can, but not really exercising any significant influence on the course of events." Part of the problem in the U.K. was the lack of regional authorities in places like Birmingham, but even in London, where there was an authority, there was continual conflict between the boroughs and the Greater London Council (GLC). The Greater London Development Plan, published in March, was attacked by one critic for containing no proper policies for overspill, the dispersal of industries and offices, transportation, the function of the central area, or housing densities and patterns.

Housing. As usual housing was a central issue. A new feature in Rome and in London in 1969 was the occupation by "squatting" homeless families of empty office blocks and houses awaiting demolition. Anthony Greenwood, U.K. minister of housing and local government, said the local authorities should use their powers to levy rates on empty property: "I can well understand the bitterness of people on the waiting list who see fine new buildings kept empty while developers wait for bigger rewards."

The reaction of the London boroughs to the squatters varied considerably. Lewisham offered empty houses to any organization that undertook to rehouse the families when the time for demolition came. But Redbridge Council, having itself protested the destruction of 100 houses in a motorway (expressway) scheme, spent thousands of pounds to make uninhabitable empty houses not required for demolition until 1976, when a plan to destroy 1,000 houses in order to change the town centre from residential to commercial and reap the extra rates was to be carried out. In fact, ministry approval for the redevelopment had not even been obtained, and, as the squatters pointed out, the £450 needed to make each house habitable could have been recouped in rents and rates long before any theoretical redevelopment.

Urban Roadways. The other increasingly important issue in every city in the world was whether the quality of life and the homes in the inner areas were to be sacrificed to provide accessibility for the suburbanites. A London Motorway Action Group was formed to oppose the proposed London Motorway Box, which, with other roads, would uproot 45,000 people and cost £1.5 billion. A confidential official study predicted that in 1981 the overall situation would be little changed, except that the worst-affected areas would be in different locations.

A detailed article on the London motorway schemes, "The Motorway Juggernaut" by Nicholas Taylor, appeared in *The Sunday Times* in January. Taylor pointed out that in the Greenwich area four major east-west roads were projected within a mile, and continued: "When the GLC states baldly that increasingly the community as a whole is demanding mobility, it ignores the less trendy fact that the majority will never be 'mobile' in the motorized sense; old people, children, mothers without that second car." It also ignored the "one all-important law" that detailed traffic planning should be based not on "keeping vehicles on the move" but on "delineating the areas within which life is led and activities conducted"; Taylor also pointed out that £100 million could provide a complete new subway line.

United Kingdom. A wide range of urban problems was covered in legislation passed in the U.K. in late 1968 and 1969. The Town and Country Planning Act, passed in October 1968, distinguished between broad structure plans that would require ministry approval and local plans that would not. The structure plan for an area would outline general policy and indicate action areas in which comprehensive treatment was to be expected in the following decade. Formerly the public did not have the right to make representations until the plan was submitted to the minister. Under the new system the authority would have to publish a detailed local survey, release the structure plan in draft form, and give the public proper opportunity to comment before the plan was put into final form and submitted to the minister. Other provisions in the act were new procedures for compulsory purchase and a time limit of five years for planning permissions for development.

The Transport Act of 1968 provided for a massive injection of public money from central and local government into public transport by putting passenger services on the same basis as urban principal roads. As agencies for regional transport planning, Passenger Transport Authorities were set up for Manchester, Merseyside, West Midlands, and Tyneside, and London Transport was taken over by the GLC. One of the first grants was £13 million toward the £17.5 million extension of the London Victoria subway line to Brixton. In addition local authorities were empowered to manage traffic not just for road safety but "to improve or preserve amenity or take account of the needs of pedestrians."

In August the government's White Paper proposal, "Old Houses into New Homes," became law. The main provisions were an increase in the maximum discretionary grant from £400 to £1,000 (£1,200 for the conversion of three or more stories); an increase in the normal total standard grant available by right from £155 to £200; and a new Exchequer grant to local authorities of 50% for environmental improvements on costs of up to £100 per dwelling in newly designated General Improvement Areas.

New York City worker ignores mugging taking place only a few feet away. Psychological studies reported in 1969 showed that crowded environments tend to repress individuals from helping in emergency situations.

CATHERINE URSILLO FROM NANCY PALMER AGENCY

During the year the Ministry of Housing and Local Government published probably the most lavish planning reports on historic towns ever produced—the conservation studies of York by Lord Esher, Bath (central area) by Colin Buchanan, Chichester by the West Sussex County Council, and Chester by Donald Insall. The reports were not merely concerned with the preservation of buildings; they consolidated recent advances in planning ideology and technique such as urban renewal, environmental standards, road hierarchies, the pictorial and sculptural approach to townscape, and consideration of towns within a regional setting.

In all, conservation was seen as part of the normal process of planning, and preservation was combined with detailed suggestions for new buildings of appropriate scale and character. A general objective was to make the historic central areas attractive to live in, and all the surveys emphasized the large number of historic buildings virtually unused above ground floor level. All four reports made recommendations for a national Urban Conservation Service (York) or a Historic Towns Corporation (Chester) with "wide powers to acquire property and to repair, manage, and dispose of it efficiently," but the Bath report rejected the setting up of a National Conservation Authority on the ground that it would separate conservation from other aspects of planning.

The successful creation of an all-purpose pedestrian shopping street in London Street, Norwich—without the provision of alternative traffic routes—demonstrated that local traders need not always fear adverse effects on their business from the exclusion of traffic. In London Street 28 out of 32 shops recorded an increase in trade, in one case by 20%.

Peter Shepheard, president of the Royal Institute of British Architects, at the institute's annual conference in July called for an end to the building of high-rise blocks of flats for families in Britain. "These blocks disrupt the whole life of families. A mother should be able to look out of her flat and shout to her child in the playground. Why should people live piled up like this, when they could live near the ground at the same density, near trees and their children's playgrounds? I have been told it is because architects feel they must be 'with it.'"

After a gas explosion had resulted in the partial collapse of a system-built 22-story block with load-bearing walls in London in May 1968, the government directed that blocks of flats should be capable of resisting explosions of five pounds per square inch (5 psi). Existing blocks needed only to be strengthened to resist 2.5 psi if the gas supply were replaced by electricity. According to a June 1969 report in *The Times,* however, some councils had taken little action. Bristol did not even know how many blocks were affected and Liverpool, with 3,000 flats in 24 blocks to deal with, had not only done no remedial work but had completed four similar blocks and allowed them to be occupied.

In February, the commission of inquiry into a site for a third London airport, chaired by Sir Eustace Roskill, selected four sites for further consideration: Cublington, Buckinghamshire; Foulness (offshore), Essex; Nuthampstead, Hertfordshire; and Thurleigh, Bedfordshire. Significantly Stansted, the government's original choice, was not included. A June report of the Standing Conference on London and South East Regional Planning favoured Foulness on the ground that this was the most suitable of the four areas to take the growth associated with the airport (estimated to be providing 65,000 jobs in the 1990s). The cost of improving the subregional infrastructure would be least at Foulness. Also, because the airport would be over the sea, the 100-sq.mi. area of likely noise nuisance would affect fewer people and limit future development less than for the three inland sites.

The site and foundation works for an airport wholly on reclaimed land would cost £33 million—double that of an inland site—but this might well be offset by combining the airport with a deepwater shipping terminal to rival Rotterdam, Neth. In February a feasibility study into a £130 million scheme to do this was announced by a consortium that included the Port of London Authority and the borough of Southend.

New Towns. In January, 41,000 ac. in central Lancashire were designated as the site of a proposed New Town. The area included Preston with a population of 250,000 (which was expected to double by the end of the century). In February the interim report on the proposed North Buckinghamshire new city of Milton Keynes was published. This project would include the existing towns of Bletchley, Wolverton, and Stony Stratford, and would have 250,000 people in 30 years. The project envisaged a city with a unified health service, schools built on a campus system, and possibly a "dial-it-yourself" minibus service. The essence of the transport system would be motorways, a grid of roads one kilometre apart, and computerized control of traffic lights. The city had a new objective—a wide range of houses varying in price and size both for rent and for sale, and, as at Telford (formerly Dawley), half the homes were to be privately owned. Since many families could not afford a house of Sir Parker Morris standard, the design would enable people to enlarge and upgrade their houses when they became more affluent. (L. C. Br.)

World's 25 Most Populous Cities

		Population				
		City proper			Metropolitan	
Rank	City and country	Most recent census	Estimate	Year	Estimate	Year
1	Tokyo, Japan	8,893,094*	9,035,000	1969	...	...
2	New York, U.S.	7,781,984	8,125,000	1968	11,679,858	1968
3	Shanghai, China†	—	—	—	10,000,000	1967–68
4	London, U.K.‡	—	—	—	7,763,820	1968
5	Peking, China†	—	—	—	7,060,000	1967–68
6	Moscow, U.S.S.R.	5,049,905	6,507,000	1967	8,500,000	1966
7	São Paulo, Brazil	3,164,804	5,000,000	1966	5,685,000	1968
8	Cairo, U.A.R.	4,219,853§	4,769,000	1969	4,904,000	1966
9	Jakarta, Indonesia	2,906,533	4,462,000	1968	4,349,950	1967
10	Leningrad, U.S.S.R.	2,899,955	3,706,000	1967	4,050,000	1965
11	Rio de Janeiro, Brazil	3,223,408	...	...	4,207,000	1968
12	Chicago, U.S.	3,550,404	3,540,000	1969	6,972,000	1969
13	Seoul, S. Korea	3,793,280§	...	...	...	...
14	Buenos Aires, Argentina	2,966,634	3,484,000	1969	7,866,000	1967
15	Mexico City, Mexico	2,832,133	3,483,649	1969	6,815,000	1967
16	Tientsin, China	2,693,831‖	3,278,000	1958	3,800,000	1958
17	Madrid, Spain	2,259,931	3,241,054	1969	2,926,374	1965
18	Osaka, Japan	3,156,222*	3,042,000	1969	...	...
19	Bombay, India	2,771,933	3,077,000	1967	5,368,000	1968
20	Calcutta, India	2,927,289	3,044,000	1967	3,109,000	1968
21	Los Angeles, U.S.	2,481,595	2,940,000	1969	7,168,200	1969
22	Teheran, Iran	2,719,730§	2,840,494	1967	3,114,950	1965
23	Delhi-New Delhi, India	2,359,408	2,760,000	1966	3,470,000	1968
24	Rome, Italy	2,188,160	2,707,189	1969	3,150,900	1965
25	Paris, France	2,790,091¶	2,597,771	1968	8,182,241	1968

*1965. †Municipality. ‡Greater London. §1966. ‖1953. ¶1962.
Rankings based on latest estimates of city proper population. Most recent census refers to 1959, 1960, or 1961, except as footnoted. Berlin, both sectors combined 1968 population 3,231,697, is excluded due to the political as well as physical division of the city.

United States. Chronic and acute urban problems continued to plague metropolitan America during 1969, although overt manifestations of alienation and frustration took somewhat different forms than they had in 1968. Student rebellions on the nation's college campuses, following the Chicago Democratic convention hostilities in August 1968, stole the headlines from the black revolution, and demonstrations were increasingly by whites as well as blacks. In general, blacks abandoned the major riot within large city ghetto areas as an instrument for expressing their hostilities in favour of techniques that could not do as much damage to areas in which they resided; lower middle class whites continued to resent the disorders produced by the blacks, student radicals, and advocates of peace, and they added to disorder by demonstrations of their own. Public employees including teachers, social workers, policemen, firemen, and sanitation workers used the force of illegal strikes in efforts to gain their objectives.

U.S. Department of Justice officials reported that disturbances in urban slums were down some 50% in 1969 from the 1968 level, whether measured by the number of persons involved or by the severity of the riot. The decrease in such disturbances, however, could not be interpreted as a decrease in interracial tensions or in the effort of blacks to improve their lot. Indications of unalleviated interracial tensions included widespread rioting in smaller cities; chronic hostilities in a number of cities, of which Cairo, Ill., was an example; increased sniper and guerrilla tactics; concentration on specific grievances with demonstrations in respect of education, welfare, and construction employment; and increased coalition of factions within the black community including the wide spectrum of organizations ranging from street gangs and various militant organizations including the Black Panther Party to branches of the more traditional and moderate Urban League and National Association for the Advancement of Colored People. The shift away from the big city riot was dramatically illustrated in Chicago by the black who smashed 14 display windows in the Marshall Field & Co. downtown store with the explanation that it was about time that blacks stopped destroying their own neighbourhoods.

For the time being, the problems relating to schools, welfare, and the construction industry were likely to remain the major targets of the blacks. The Lemberg Center for the study of violence at Brandeis University, Waltham, Mass., reported that schools were involved in 79% of the racial disorders from January to May 1969, as contrasted with only 17% during the like period in 1968. The most dramatic example of black student revolt was that at Cornell University

continued on page 213

INDESTRUCTIBLE TRASH

By Gladwin Hill

Just as much of our air in recent years has become saturated with contaminants and our waterways overloaded with pollutants, so have communities throughout the United States and elsewhere suddenly been confronted with "the third pollution": an increasingly formidable cascade of solid waste. Such waste included garbage and other trash from homes, commercial refuse, industrial scrap, the rubbish from construction and demolition, agricultural wastes, and mining debris. Altogether, the total amount generated in the United States, according to the federal Bureau of Solid Waste Management, was 3.5 billion tons a year, 17 tons for every person in the country.

Fortunately, the bulk of this vast mass of refuse—two billion tons of agricultural wastes and one billion tons of mining debris—was widely dispersed outside cities. But that still left approximately 350 million tons a year of urban wastes—more than a ton per person and roughly ten pounds per person per day.

It is axiomatic that material that goes into a community must eventually be removed, or the community will be overwhelmed in debris. But that axiom was widely ignored until recently. Since prehistoric times, refuse traditionally was disposed of by dumping it on the outskirts of communities, with the occasional supplement of burning.

Suddenly, however, this traditional system became uncomfortably inadequate. Population in most communities soared. Also, because higher living standards brought greatly increased consumption of materials of all sorts, the per capita generation of refuse was twice what it was in the 1920s and was expected to double again within the next 20 years.

A significant part of this waste volume came from packaged commodities, particularly prepared foods: packaging and containers accounted for nearly 15% of the national waste load. Ubiquitous roadside litter was a distasteful witness to the annual use, in the U.S. alone, of 60 billion cans and 30 billion bottles.

Meanwhile, affluence virtually eliminated the old-time salvaging and reuse of materials. Junkmen no longer coursed the streets crying "Old rags! . . . Bottles! . . ." as they did in the early years of this century. The changed economics were reflected most conspicuously in the great numbers of derelict automobiles littering both the countryside and city streets. A combination of rising repair costs and declining scrap metal values caused people to abandon cars that might once have gone to salvage. Such cities as New York, Philadelphia, and Chicago had to cope with as many as 30,000 abandoned cars a year—with removal costing up to $30 a car.

Room for disposing of refuse dwindled literally to the vanishing point in many places. Expanding communities impinged on their old "outskirts" until the latter were no longer there. Most vacant land was too valuable to be used for dumps. And the mounting problem of air pollution made the old practice of casual burning intolerable. Los Angeles, where the smog problem first became acute, outlawed backyard incinerators and even closed down its municipal incinerators in the late 1950s.

The problem of what to do with refuse suddenly confronted one community after another. The acuteness of the problem was brought home to the nation in 1968 when San Francisco, with little land left for dumping along the shores of its bay, announced that it was contemplating transporting its garbage and refuse by railroad 375 mi. to a desert area in Lassen County on the Nevada border.

A U.S. Problem. The "solid waste crisis" that came into full prominence in 1969 was centred in the U.S. In less developed countries, where abodes built of old tin cans and cardboard were familiar, one man's trash was often another man's treasure; and in many of these nations what nobody wanted was, because of prevailing customs, discardable anywhere. In the more advanced nations, such as those in Western Europe, the waste disposal problem was less acute for three reasons: merchandise, and, thus, its resulting debris, was not so plentiful; thrifty salvaging was more ingrained (in Great Britain, for instance, the salvaging of paper and metals was still routine); and in some nations, effective disposal methods were more advanced than they were in the United States. Both France and West Germany had sophisticated, fumeless incinerators whose heat was used to generate power.

The United States' solid waste crisis was essentially economic—a sudden convergence, in mathematical terms, of three curves representing growing waste volume, scarcity of urban land, and rising haulage costs. At the 1969 rate of generating waste a year's refuse of 10,000 people was enough to cover an acre of land to a depth of seven feet. There was little urban land left for disposing of this trash, although there were hundreds of thousands of square miles of desert and other wasteland where centuries of the nation's rubbish could be neatly buried. Such land would be difficult to utilize, however, because of the cost of moving refuse to such remote areas.

Typically, it cost a large city about $30 a ton to collect and dispose of refuse. Most of this cost went for collecting. Once municipal refuse was assembled at a central depot, the cost of disposing of it in a dump or landfill was about $5 a ton. Burning the refuse cost more, upward of $7 a ton, which was why dumping remained the prevailing practice. But if the dumping point was distant, disposal costs rose sharply. San Francisco's 375-mi. rail-haul plan was at least temporarily suspended in mid-1969 because the prospective disposal cost was more than $8 a ton, whereas there was still enough relatively close-haul dump land, with a disposal cost of about $6 a ton, to meet the problem for a few more years. The city decided to use this nearby land while developing a long-range disposal plan.

Methods of Disposal. There were only two things that could be done, ultimately, with refuse: burn it or bury it, either on land or in the ocean. Because even scientific burning left a residue of up to 30% of the original volume, there would always be material to be buried. The vast reaches of the ocean are a tempting repository, but they had two limitations: there was no knowledge at present of the ecological consequences of a large-scale infusion of extraneous substances into the ocean; and, obviously, the ocean would be most useful as a disposal area chiefly to coastal communities.

The growing problem of waste impelled the U.S. Congress in 1965 to pass the Solid Wastes Disposal Act. The law created a Bureau of Solid Waste Management in the U.S. Public Health Service and provided for both research financing and grants to states for waste management planning.

Little information about national waste was available. The bureau's first task was to mount a comprehensive survey. It was not scheduled to be completed until 1971, but a preliminary report made late in 1968 presented an illuminating summary of conditions. Among these were that only 64% of the nation's people lived in communities that had refuse collection systems. About half of household wastes were collected by public agencies, and one-third by private collectors; the rest householders disposed of themselves. The bulk of commercial and industrial wastes were handled by private collectors.

About 80% of the United States' collected waste, by weight, went to dumps; about 15% was incinerated; and only about 3%

was salvaged. There were 12,000 dumps in the country and 300 community incinerators. The federal survey classified 94% of the dumps and 70% of the incinerators as "unacceptable" in terms of good sanitation.

The prospect of diminishing waste volume at the source to a degree that would appreciably alleviate the problem seemed nil. The nation's consumption of commodities seemed almost certain to increase, and with it the amount of refuse. An example was the field of fibre-and-plastic "disposables," ranging from bathing suits to bedspreads. A relatively small business in 1969, it was expected to grow into a billion-dollar-a-year industry by 1980.

The possibility of lessening the waste disposal load through salvaging appeared to be small, with one significant qualification: that the day might come when it would not only be worthwhile but also essential to salvage basic materials, not for their intrinsic value, but because reusing them would be the most expeditious way of getting rid of them.

In the meantime, with scrap steel bringing as little as $20 a ton, "tin" cans (actually tin-plated steel) were not worth salvaging under present waste-handling methods. Scrap aluminum was, however, worth ten times as much, and one company paid people in some cities a half cent each for aluminum beverage cans.

In Japan and West Germany up to 90% of paper is regularly salvaged and reused. But in the U.S. the proportion of paper products made from reused paper declined steadily to about 20% in 1969, and recovery of paper from household waste became increasingly impractical. Wastepaper from offices, which once commanded a price, by 1969 in New York City cost up to $37 a ton to be hauled away.

Proposed Disposal Systems. Systematic attacks on the waste problem fell into three areas: collection, processing, and disposal. The chief alternative to truck collection was the idea of moving household refuse through pipes to central disposal points. In Sweden and the U.K. some large apartment developments were equipped with pneumatic-tube systems that carried dry trash as much as a mile and a half. The Walt Disney organization was planning to institute such a system at its new development in Florida.

In a federally sponsored project at the University of Pennsylvania, Iraj Zandi concluded that refuse could be ground up in households, mixed with a small amount of water, and carried through pipes in slurry form to some disposal depot—at long-term costs comparable to those for conventional collection. However, the system would involve a large capital investment, might not obviate conventional collection for nonhousehold refuse, and did not resolve the problem of ultimate disposal. Also, the sewage systems in most places were already overtaxed.

A perennial dream in waste management was the conversion of trash into compost for soil conditioning. This required a rather elaborate mechanical setup for sorting bulky and unassimilable material out of trash, grinding the remainder, and baking it to neutralize organic materials. Its chief drawback was that there would probably be a market for only a very small part of the waste so converted. More than a dozen composting plants were established in the U.S. in recent years, and most of them had to close because of small demand. A few composting plants operated regularly in Europe, but they were also acknowledged to be unprofitable: the loss was charged against the cost of alternative disposal methods.

Concerns in the United States, Japan, and Europe were working on compressing refuse into small, very dense blocks that could then be disposed of more easily, or even used in road and building construction. For the latter purpose, however, engineers of the American Public Works Association expressed reservations about both the cohesion and the sanitary aspects of the blocks.

An alternative to the laborious production of compost or blocks was simply to burn refuse and possibly put the resulting heat to use. Scientific incineration as practiced in Europe, although almost unknown in the United States, appeared to have many advantages and probably would come into wider use. It involved engineering treatment plants precisely so that refuse would be consumed at optimum temperatures with a minimal residue of gases and ash. In West Germany and France—and in an experimental project at Hempstead, N.Y.—the heat from these plants was being used commercially, thus returning a portion of their operating costs.

Incineration, however, also presented problems. One was the tendency of metals, glass, and plastics to melt, clog grates, and thereby interfere with combustion. There was also the question of meeting more rigid municipal air pollution standards: Los Angeles, for instance, did not allow even power plants to burn anything but natural gas except in emergencies.

A number of experimental projects in advanced incineration methods, some federally sponsored, were in progress during 1969. They ranged from flameless "wet oxidation" combustion to gas-fired furnaces that would reduce all refuse to a clean, gravel-like residue.

Incinerators involved large capital investments. Construction costs in the United States for such plants doubled between 1964 and 1969 from $5,000 to $10,000 per daily ton of capacity. Thus, for a big city an installation could mean a cash outlay of more than $20 million.

Future Prospects. For many reasons, therefore, national thinking on ultimate waste disposal continued to centre on dumping. A slow transition began from the old type of haphazard, unsightly dump to the system of "sanitary landfill." This method consisted of compacting each day's deposit of refuse and covering it with a layer of compacted dirt. The end result of this process was, at many locations, more usable land than existed previously. The 70 principal communities of Los Angeles County, which is bordered by low mountains with many undeveloped gulches, disposed of all their refuse this way, at a total cost of only $12 a ton including collection. By the same process, recreational hills were built in Virginia Beach, Va., and a number of other communities.

Topographical and drainage problems make sanitary landfill less than a universal solution. Through 1969 only about 5% of the refuse in the U.S. had been handled that way, although this seemed due less to unsuitability than to public misapprehensions about annoyance and cost.

As simply a physical extension of conventional dumping, the rail-haul disposal system was also beguiling. But there were complications involved in implementing this method. By late 1969, although a half dozen cities had taken preliminary steps toward rail-haul, the system had not materialized anywhere. Like San Francisco, Denver, Colo., backed off from it because of uncertain economics and dependability. Milwaukee, Wis., believed that it had the economics worked out but could not find a community within a feasible distance willing to assume the role of garbage repository.

Using abandoned surface mining pits, of which there were about two million acres in the U.S., seemed like a clever solution. But just as Philadelphia was about to start using such areas 100 mi. distant from the city, state health officials pointed out that old mines were notorious for their acid drainage and water contamination, and that there was insufficient knowledge about how the addition of garbage and refuse might complicate that problem.

A 1969 report of the California Department of Health said: "With but a few notable exceptions, solid waste management practices are unrealistic and clearly inadequate. The five basic deficiencies of the current systems are fragmented authority and lack of cooperation, inadequate planning, inadequate standards, poorly developed technology, and inadequate financing."

The ultimate resolution of these deficiencies, federal experts believed, would require, along with advanced technology, the abandonment of the prevailing community-by-community pattern of waste disposal in favour of regional collaboration.

continued from page 210
in which the blacks finally left the building they had seized bearing arms—and only after they had produced sharp divisions among faculty and administration that led to a change in administration. Insistent efforts to break into the traditionally segregated construction labour unions were manifest in Philadelphia, Pittsburgh, Pa., and Chicago. These efforts led to "backlash," disorderly white union demonstrations that contained the threat of violent physical confrontation. Plans were being evolved for opening the unions and employment to blacks in the construction industry.

Evidence mounted that lower middle class white Americans had heightened their backlash response to increasing pressures for racial equality, growing campus unrest spearheaded by the radical Students for a Democratic Society (SDS), insistent demonstrations for peace in Vietnam, and continued high levels of crime. It was the "forgotten man" who was reported to have helped elect Pres. Richard M. Nixon, who continued his support of California Gov. Ronald Reagan and his strong stand against campus unrest, and who turned increasingly to "law and order" candidates in local elections. Reports from around the nation indicated that whites continued to arm themselves against possible interracial strife. Moreover, these whites were giving increasing signs that they resented the programs being sponsored on behalf of the blacks and were perceiving themselves as a victimized majority. The demonstrations by white construction workers in Pittsburgh and Chicago were among the signs of growing white militancy that presaged more rather than less disorder and that contained important national as well as local political implications.

Campus disorders reached their peak during the year with the greatest violence manifest at the University of California at Berkeley. The hard core "New Left" students in the SDS openly espoused "revolution" and the destruction of "the Establishment," and sought "confrontations" that would maximize the "radicalization" of student bodies. College administrations and faculties varied greatly in their responses and, on the whole, revealed inability to deal with the unprecedented disruptions. By year's end, however, with the prodding of political leaders, legislative enactments, alumni reactions, and adverse general public reaction, there were indications that student disruptions would no longer be greeted with as much tolerance and permissiveness. The role of the SDS in the coming year remained uncertain after the fragmentation of that organization at its annual convention in Chicago. Visible efforts were under way, however, to bring disruption to the secondary schools, especially in black communities.

Strikes by public employees continued to beset city administrations large and small. Teachers, policemen, fire fighters, social workers, and other public employees turned to the strike, formal or informal, to achieve their salary and other objectives. Chicago experienced one teachers' strike and was threatened with another; the "blue flu" afflicted many jurisdictions as policemen and fire fighters sought to improve their situations. Some strikes of public employees had definite racial overtones, as in the case of the prolonged strike of hospital employees in Charleston, S.C. Continued fiscal problems experienced by city governments provided little hope that strikes by public employees would diminish.

Peace demonstrations continued throughout the metropolitan U.S. with and without violence. Such demonstrations gave every indication of becoming part of the American scene as long as the U.S. remained embroiled in Vietnam. Massive peace demonstrations were staged in most large cities on October 15, designed among other things to close the nation's schools, and were followed by a massive peace march in Washington, D.C., on November 15. The trial of the "Chicago eight," the accused leaders of the disorders during the Democratic convention week in Chicago, began in September, and its outcome would undoubtedly affect the future course of demonstrations and official responses to them.

The chaos and disorders afflicting metropolitan America continued to reflect the fact that man had not yet learned how to live in the transformed physical and technological world he had created. The United States was still completing its first half century as an urban nation (in the sense that more than 50% of the population lived in urban places—places of 2,500 persons and over). It was small wonder, therefore, that the nation continued to be faced with the "urban crises"—manifest in physical, economic, social, and governmental problems. It remained to be seen how soon the U.S. could manage to deal effectively with the problems that urbanism as a way of life had generated. (P. M. Ha.)

In January the Office of Economic Opportunity claimed that "an estimated four million Americans climbed above the poverty line in 1968." Pres. Lyndon B. Johnson in his final state of the union message stressed the need to continue and increase the Great Society social programs.

In his last budget President Johnson proposed increases in all federally aided urban programs. The Department of Housing and Urban Development allocation, however, was cut since direct loans for housing had been more than replaced by private financing. In April, President Nixon proposed reductions in all of the programs except anticrime. HUD Secretary George Romney announced in April a major reorganization of the Model Cities program and, in May, proposed a new plan to build low-cost housing for the poor by mass-production methods. Romney estimated that by continuing current rates of construction, "we will fall more than ten million units short of our housing needs."

Another pointer to the future was given by the 300,000-word "master plan" for New York City, the contents of which were reported in the *New York Times* in February. The plan, prepared by the City Planning Commission, set out a development strategy involving a $19 billion, ten-year program to "create" a new middle class out of the city's poor. It also proposed limiting the number of cars permitted to enter midtown Manhattan, and the establishment of community hospitals with doctors assigned to every family in the neighbourhood. (L. C. Br.)

Municipal Government. During 1969 reform of local government structure and functions continued to be of primary concern. In many countries reforms came about under the pressure of new forms of comprehensive planning at the regional level. This was particularly true for many metropolitan areas. It was therefore not surprising that a conference organized by the International Union of Local Authorities

COURTESY, NORWICH CITY COUNCIL

Pedestrians enjoy London Street in Norwich, Eng., from which traffic was excluded in 1969. Almost all shops on the street showed an increase in trade.

COURTESY, CITY OF BOSTON

New experimental traffic sign in Boston uses simplified, colour-coded symbols. The signs were tested under a project funded by U.S. Department of Housing and Urban Development.

(IULA), which was held in Prague, Czech., in the spring of 1969, had as its major theme "Regional Planning and Regional Government in Europe."

Experiments were found to be under way in various new forms of regional government, both at the supralocal and the subnational level. In most countries voluntary associations between local authorities existed for a variety of purposes ranging from cooperation on technical services to supramunicipal planning bodies. The major drawback of such associations was that any decision could be blocked by the unwillingness to cooperate of only one or two member municipalities. Therefore, authorities had been created with more extensive powers, particularly in the field of planning, such as the Greater Hanover Association, the Rijnmond Authority covering the Rotterdam metropolitan area, the Greater London Council, several planning associations in West Germany, and the *communautés urbaines* in France.

In a number of countries, however, there was a need for more comprehensive reform. In some of the smaller European countries, notably Sweden and Denmark, sweeping reforms were taking place through the amalgamation of previously existing authorities into larger, more viable units. In the Benelux countries, a similar process was under way, but on a smaller scale and at a more gradual pace.

At the regional (subnational) level, an interesting difference could be noted between reforms that were taking place in Eastern and in Western European countries. In some of the former, such as Romania, Yugoslavia, and Czechoslovakia, the goal of reform was to abolish the regional level of government, which was felt to be an extension of the central government. On the other hand, in several Western European countries, for example, France, the U.K., and Italy, reforms were aimed at the creation of a regional tier of government that would act as a counterbalance to a dominant central government. The initial attempts of the French Gaullist government to introduce reform legislation by referendum failed in April 1969, perhaps not so much because of the nature of the reform as because Pres. Charles de Gaulle had put his mandate at stake.

In the United Kingdom, the Royal Commission on Local Government, under the chairmanship of Lord Redcliffe-Maud, submitted its long-awaited final report in June. The commission recommended a complete overhaul of English local government. London was excluded from the terms of reference. The commission listed four faults with the existing system: the areas did not fit the pattern of life and work in modern England; the division into town and country made proper planning impossible; services were split within the counties; and many local authorities were too small, too poor, and too short of qualified manpower and technical equipment to function properly.

The Maud report's basic proposals were to create 61 new areas covering town and country, of which 58 would be unitary authorities and three, covering Birmingham, Liverpool, and Manchester, would be two-tier structures of metropolitan government; to group the 61 areas, together with Greater London, into eight provinces with provincial councils; and to create an unspecified number of local councils for towns and villages, the main duty of which would be to provide an opportunity for the expression of public opinion.

These suggestions became the subject of major discussion. Whereas it had long been recognized that the plethora of local government units (currently 1,210 in England) should be reduced to a more rational system, the fear remained that in doing so, government would become too far removed from the citizens. It was this concern that led to the appointment of the Skeffington Committee on Public Participation in Planning in Great Britain, whose report, "People and Planning," was published in the summer of 1969. This report could be considered the most authoritative source of new ideas and proposals on how local government can promote citizen participation, even though the particular emphasis in this instance was on planning.

In addition to conventional publicity methods such as radio, press, and other information sources, new information techniques, which would encourage apathetic citizens to take an active part in formulating and implementing community policies, were suggested in the Skeffington report. Concrete measures proposed included the establishment of community forums that would bring together local organizations such as chambers of commerce, trade unions, churches, political parties, youth groups, and civic societies. Such gatherings could provide the means whereby a two-way flow of information between local government authorities, on the one hand, and the public and its various groupings on the other, could take place. In addition, the publication of such material as maps and plans and the mounting of exhibitions, all of which could be easily understood by the public, were emphasized.

Another proposal was for the appointment by local authorities or by social councils of community development officers who would perform the basic function of developing in "apathetic" citizens a sense of involvement in local affairs. Finally, it was urged that public participation in planning should, in the future, be undertaken on the basis of a clearly defined timetable for information and consultation at various stages. It would have to be realized that if citizens were to be granted the right of effective participation, both they and the authorities would have to accept the costs involved in terms of money, time, and manpower.

The Maud report was accepted by the government and Prime Minister Harold Wilson announced that a bill would be introduced "after thorough consideration."

An ever present concern of local government, local finance, was the subject of the 1969 congress of IULA, which was held in Vienna in June. In a survey covering 33 countries throughout the world, the general rapporteur, A. H. Marshall of the Institute of Local Government Studies of the University of Birmingham, Eng., emphasized that whereas citizens expected increasingly more, better, and nationally uniform services, local governments continued to be faced with inelastic financial resources. New sources of income were needed. These might derive from a fairer distribution of revenue between central and local governments as well as from an expansion of the local tax base to include sources that were new for many local units, such as automobiles and users and personal and business income. Moreover, new methods of financial administration were indicated. For example, present budgeting methods whereby future plans were based primarily on the previous year's income and expenditure might be replaced by a more comprehensive look at present and future needs that could be provided in a system of planning, programming and budgeting (PPBS).

Citizenship:
see Migration, International

Civil Aviation:
see Transportation

Civil Defense:
see Defense

Civil Rights:
see Race Relations

Clothing:
see Fashion and Dress; Furs

Coal:
see Fuel and Power; Mining

Cocoa (Cacao):
see Agriculture

Coffee:
see Agriculture

Coinage:
see Philately and Numismatics

Coke:
see Fuel and Power; Mining

Colleges:
see Education

New budgeting methods were but one aspect of modern management techniques that were receiving ever more attention from efficiency-conscious local governments and their citizens. Whereas immediately after World War II punched cards were considered to be an advanced aid to local administrations, municipal governments now were using, in some instances, third-generation machines covering new system possibilities and with enormous capacity. Municipalities in many countries, either alone or in cooperation with neighbouring local governments or on a regional basis, were using electronic data processing (EDP) for such main groups of functions as personnel and financial administration, population records, land records, and building, documentation, and scientific calculations.

In Denmark, municipalities could become members of one of six regional centres, as well as have the benefit of technical aid from the government's Data Processing Centre. Furthermore, plans were under way for the establishment of the Municipal EDP Council, which would decide the administrative organization of new nationwide applications, the establishment of joint planning and programming and municipal cooperation in nationwide registers, and further consultation on all EDP questions of importance to the municipalities and the regional centres.

In other countries, EDP services were offered by local government associations. The Swedish Town Federation opened a new branch devoted to serving its members in the field of data processing. In the U.S., cooperative arrangements could be divided into three broad classifications: among cities, or between cities and school districts, or between cities and counties; between the local and the state levels of government; and between the federal government and the state with specific information made available to the local governments. In Japan, municipalities tended to use the facilities of private computer centres, although there was a trend toward the joint use of computers by several government authorities. In Israel, a "company for data processing in Israel," which was being financed 40% by the central government and 60% by local governments, aimed eventually to provide EDP services for all 187 municipalities in the country.

The continuing reliance on the computer in local government administration brought problems as well as solutions. Among the former was the need for education of management on all levels in basic computer concepts. An interesting initiative in this regard was taken by the Local Authorities' Management Services and Computer Committee, which was established in 1967 in the U.K. LAMSAC ran a series of computer appreciation courses for local government staff that attracted a large response. In addition, this organization, which was created and designed to work for local government councils, offered advice and assistance on all matters pertaining to management sciences and their use, planned training courses, study groups, and conferences to meet local government needs, provided a comprehensive advisory service on training in organization and methods, work study, and related management techniques and methods, and initiated and coordinated future research in this broad field.

In other countries, municipal training institutes offered a wide range of courses and seminars in local government affairs. In Canada and other countries, the local government officers association and the universities developed correspondence training for various kinds of municipal officers. In the U.S. a special postgraduate study in all aspects of public administration was offered by many universities to help train management-level government employees, particularly city managers. Appointed by local councils, usually on a nonpolitical basis, city managers had as their main responsibility the coordination of local administration and the advising of local councils to whom they were responsible on the drawing up and implementation of development plans. The concept of the coordinating manager was gaining acceptance as a means of increasing administrative efficiency and of making the most effective use of limited financial resources.

A number of new methods had been devised in recent years in the training of higher level local government officers. These included role playing; the in-basket or in-tray exercise, whereby the actual job of the administrator was simulated by requiring the trainee to deal with a series of letters, memoranda, reports, position papers, problems, complaints, and the like, as if he were being confronted by these items in a real work situation; problem analysis; sensitivity training; incident process; programmed learning methods and teaching machines.

In the new decade that was just beginning it was anticipated that a start in some instances, and a continuation in others, of integrated policy planning would become increasingly apparent. With rapidly continuing urbanization, rising costs of personnel and services, more sophisticated management techniques, and increasingly urgent demands by citizens for efficient use of tax money or for involvement in local decision-making, local governments could no longer support administrative departmentalization. Rather, planning would be more and more comprehensive and integrated until its goal would be not just improvements in problem areas or localities but changes in the total living environment. (EI. K.)

See also Architecture; Crime; Historic Buildings; Housing; Parks; Police; Transportation.

ENCYCLOPÆDIA BRITANNICA FILMS. *The Living City* (1953); *Health in Our Community* (1959); *Megalopolis—Cradle of the Future* (1962); *Chicago—Midland Metropolis* (1963); *Operation Bootstrap* (1968); *Problems of Conservation—Air* (1968); *The House of Man, Part II—Our Crowded Environment* (1969); *The South: Roots of the Urban Crisis* (1969).

Colombia

A republic in northwestern South America, Colombia is bordered by Panama, Venezuela, Brazil, Peru, and Ecuador and has coasts on both the Caribbean Sea and the Pacific Ocean. Area: 439,734 sq.mi. (1,138,914 sq.km.). Pop. (1968 est.): 19,829,185. Cap.: Bogotá (pop., 1968, 1,984,599). Language: Spanish. State religion: Roman Catholic (90%). President in 1969, Carlos Lleras Restrepo.

Solid economic and political progress was maintained in 1969 following the government's triumph in December 1968 when Congress approved its vitally important reforms to the constitution. The new amendments provided for government by simple rather than two-thirds majority; the equal distribution of offices between the Liberals and Conservatives (party parity) was to be gradually eliminated; and in time of economic or social stress the executive could declare a state of emergency and rule by decree for a maximum period of 90 days in any one year. According to the constitution, Lleras was due to hold office until August 1970, when he would be succeeded by a Conservative president until 1974 when the National Front arrangement was to end. Elections for departmental assemblies and municipal councils in the midterm year 1972 would not be subject to the National Front's party parity provisions. For one presidential term beyond the National Front period the membership of the Supreme Court and the Council of State would remain under party parity provisions. In December the Conservative convention chose Misael Pastrana Borrero as the man who would rule Colombia for the four-year term beginning in August 1970. Pastrana, who promised to continue the policies of the Lleras administration, was a former Colombian ambassador to the U.S. and former minister of the interior.

The good performance registered in 1968 by the Colombian economy continued unabated in 1969. The rise in the gross national product was expected to reach 6.5% in real terms in 1969, compared with 6% in 1968 and 4% in 1967. The exchange position improved steadily throughout 1968 when net reserves rose by $71.5 million. Despite increased imports in the first five months of 1969, net exchange reserves rose by an additional $15.3 million, bringing the net surplus to $50.5 million, compared with a deficit position of $36.3 million in December 1967. To reduce its dependence upon coffee the Colombian government continued to direct its policy toward the promotion of other exports.

The value of minor exports reached $105 million in the first half of 1969 against $70.2 million in the comparable period of 1968. Increases of more than 100% were recorded for cotton products, rice, emeralds and precious metals, shellfish, textiles, and vegetables. It was estimated that the value of such minor exports would reach a total of $228 million in 1969. The revised estimate took into account expected increases in exports of meat, cotton, and new products.

For the fourth consecutive year the national accounts remained healthy: the cumulative surplus amounted to 1,080,000,000 pesos on June 30. The 1970 budget, submitted to Congress on July 31, amounted to 13,828,000,000 pesos, including 605 million pesos for additional investment expenditure contingent upon congressional approval of increased sales taxes and a higher tax on foreign travel. These increases were part of the recommendations of a special committee headed by Richard A. Musgrave of Harvard University, commissioned by the Colombian government to recommend reform of the country's

AMEX—PIX FROM PUBLIX

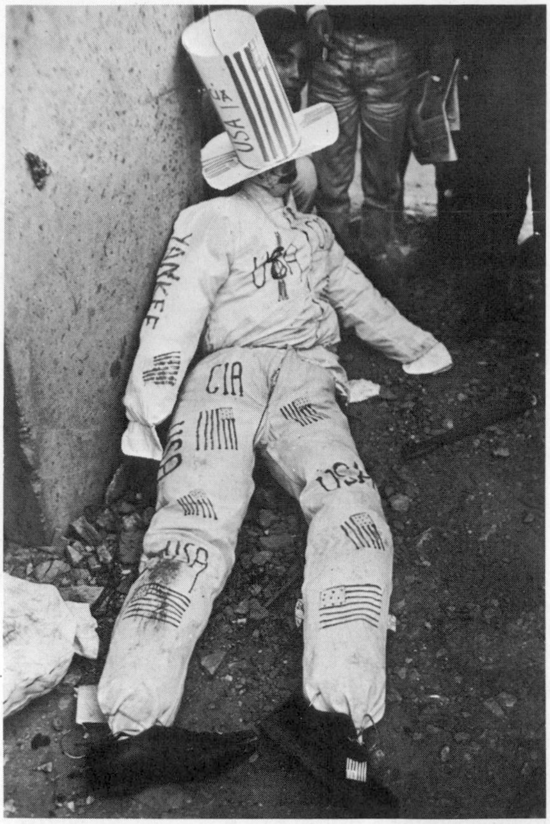

Effigy of Uncle Sam paraded by Colombian students in Bogotá during demonstrations protesting Nelson Rockefeller's visit to Latin America as special envoy of President Nixon.

tax system. The 1969 budget was originally estimated at 11,362,000,000 pesos but rose to 13,023,000,000. Severe credit restrictions continued in force, and the government suspended the rediscount facilities of banks that failed to fulfill their legal cash reserve requirements. Such monetary restraints helped restrict the rise in the cost of living to 4% in the first half of 1969.

The fourth meeting of the Credit Consultative Group for Colombia took place in Paris at the end of January and agreed in principle to grant loans totaling $328 million. Colombia was also granted a loan of $60 million from the U.S. Agency for International Development to finance imports of U.S. goods, and a standby credit of $33,250,000 by the International Monetary Fund: the IMF arrangement was in support of a program aimed at continued strengthening

COLOMBIA

Education. (1966) Primary, pupils 2,408,489, teachers 67,764; secondary, pupils 320,287, teachers 21,332; vocational, pupils 129,562, teachers 8,567; teacher training, students 63,549, teachers 4,627; higher (including 34 universities), students 49,930, teaching staff 8,190.

Finance. Monetary unit; peso, with a free rate (Sept. 1, 1969) of 17.40 pesos to U.S. $1 (41.50 pesos = £1 sterling). Gold and foreign exchange, central bank: (June 1969) U.S. $165 million; (June 1968) U.S. $117 million. Budget (1969 est.) balanced at 11,362,000,000 pesos. Gross national product: (1967) 82,050,000,000 pesos; (1966) 72,360,000,000 pesos. Money supply: (March 1969) 15,438,000,000 pesos; (March 1968) 13,228,000,000 pesos. Cost of living (Bogotá; 1963 = 100): (June 1969) 188; (June 1969) 168.

Foreign Trade. (1967) Imports 6,986,000,000 pesos; exports 6,009,000,000 pesos. Import sources: U.S. 45%; West Germany 10%; U.K. 7%. Export destinations: U.S. 44%; West Germany 13%; Netherlands 7%. Main exports: coffee 59%; crude oil 10%.

Transport and Communications. Roads (1967) *c.* 45,000 km. (including 7,200 km. with improved surface). Motor vehicles in use (1967): passenger 140,200; commercial (including buses) 116,500. Railways: (1966) 3,483 km.; traffic (1968) 351 million passenger-km., freight 1,124,700,000 net ton-km. Air traffic (1968): 1,560,000,000 passenger-km.; freight 60,474,000 net ton-km. Shipping (1968): merchant vessels 100 gross tons and over 47; gross tonnage 208,846. Telephones (Dec. 1967) 734,755. Radio receivers (Dec. 1967) *c.* 2.2 million. Television receivers (Dec. 1966) *c.* 400,000.

Agriculture. Production (in 000; metric tons; 1968; 1967 in parentheses): rice 784 (662); wheat *c.* 125 (*c.* 80); corn (1967) *c.* 1,000, (1966) 940; barley *c.* 115 (*c.* 94); potatoes (1967) *c.* 800, (1966) 762; cassava (1966) 1,625, (1965) 2,213; coffee (1967) *c.* 474, (1966) 405; bananas (1966) 962, (1965) 965; cotton, lint *c.* 130 (*c.* 101); cane sugar, raw value (1968–69) *c.* 700, (1967–68) 663; sugar, panela (1968–69) *c.* 590, (1967–68) *c.* 608; tobacco 41 (42). Livestock (in 000; Dec. 1967): cattle 16,233; sheep (Dec. 1965) 1,702; pigs 2,634; goats (Dec. 1965) 688; horses (Dec. 1965) 951; poultry (Oct. 1965) 21,476.

Industry. Fuel and power (in 000; 1968): crude oil 8,793 metric tons; natural gas 1,212,000 cu.m.; coal (1967) *c.* 3,100 metric tons; electricity (excluding industrial production) *c.* 6,350,000 kw-hr. Production (in 000; metric tons; 1968): crude steel ingots 199; magnesite (1966) 0.2; gold (troy oz.; 1967) 258; salt (1967) 470; cement 2,367.

of Colombia's balance of payments and at increased freedom in its international transactions.

Colombia's external debt service was equivalent to 12.7% of export proceeds in 1968. Taking into account loans to be negotiated in the next four years, the Departamento Administrativo Nacional de Planeación estimated that the percentage would rise from 12.5–13% in 1969 to 16–17% in 1973. Even the latter percentage was well within the country's acceptable indebtedness capacity, which was considered to be 20%.

The Trans-Andean pipeline from Orito to Tumaco was inaugurated on May 10. Initial output was 50,000 bbl. of oil a day, representing more than a quarter of Colombia's total production: it was forecast that within two years the Putumayo oil fields would be producing 100,000 bbl. daily.

A Colombian government contract to participate in the establishment and operation of a motor vehicle assembly plant was won by Renault, among ten bidders from seven countries. Colombia was a signatory, along with Bolivia, Chile, Ecuador, and Peru, of the Andean Subregional Integration Agreement signed in Bogotá on May 26. (R. B. Le.)

Encyclopædia Britannica Films. *Colombia and Venezuela* (1961).

Commercial Policies

World trade grew remarkably in 1968, and the momentum of this growth was carried forward into 1969. Total world exports rose by $22 billion in 1968, an increase of 12%. This compared with a growth of $9 billion in 1967 and stood as a record postwar performance, with the sole possible exception of the year 1950–51. In volume terms, the 1968 increase was probably greater than in any other postwar year. The totals of world trade since 1963, given in the table, illustrate the position.

This high rate of expansion was given impetus by strong economic growth in the major industrial countries, particularly in the United States, and by heightened demand from the less developed countries, whose reserves increased steadily over the year and whose purchasing power was strengthened by heavy U.S. military and other expenditure in the Far East. Trade expansion was divided almost equally between industrialized and less developed countries, with a slight advantage in favour of the former. Exports from industrial countries rose 12–13% and from less developed countries, 8%. Exports from industrial countries to other industrial countries rose 14% and from industrial countries to primary producing countries, 10%.

The underlying trend, despite a slight fall in exports to primary producers, continued strongly upward in the early part of 1969. Efforts to slow down national economic growth, particularly in the U.S. and France, would probably bring about some decline in world trade expansion in the second half, but it was expected that, even so, overall growth for the year would not fall substantially short of that for 1968.

These conditions of generally healthy trade expansion might have been expected to lead to a widespread relaxation of commercial policies. In many of the major countries, however, this was not the case. Official overseas spending continued to give rise to a deficit in the overall payments accounts of Britain and the U.S. France was thought to be in a position of weakened external balance following the May–June riots of 1968, with the capital outflow from July on appearing as a sign of deteriorating external balance account; and the West German visible surplus remained large. The result was various forms of restriction of the free flow of international trade. A system of import quotas and export rebates had been imposed in France in 1968. In the U.K. the import deposit scheme introduced in November 1968 was maintained throughout the year. In West Germany a tax on exports and a rebate on imports, both at the rate of 4%, were introduced in November 1968 and maintained until October 1969. In addition, various measures of domestic economic management were introduced, notably in Britain, France, the U.S., and Denmark, that were designed to reduce the level of home demand and to depress imports.

In August the French franc was devalued, and this was followed in October by the revaluation of the West German mark. These actions, combined with an apparent improvement in the trading accounts of the U.S. and the U.K., led to an easing of the position in the closing months of the year. It should be noted that the constraints on commercial policy mentioned above were confined to the countries of Western Europe and the U.S. On the whole, other regions reflected fairly faithfully the expansive mood of world trade.

Commercial Policies of Industrial Countries. A new antidumping act, under which new powers were conferred on the Board of Trade to determine the fair market price of dumped goods imported from state trading countries, was introduced in the United Kingdom. The fourth reduction in customs duties on U.K. goods entering Ireland came into force as of July 1, under the Anglo-Irish Free Trade Area Agreement of December 1965.

The West German government authorized exporters, particularly to less developed countries, to sell commercial drafts to domestic banks after coverage by official export credit guarantees. The object of this move was to transfer the financing of trade from the exporters to the banks. At the same time, a DM. 250 million ceiling was imposed on the scheme in order to place a check on exports.

Early in the year the U.S. president signed Public Law 90-635, implementing five international conventions. These provided, among other things, for quicker customs handling of container ships and for the temporary duty-free entry of various items of professional equipment. The U.S. Federal Trade Commission proposed the exemption from the Fair Packaging and Labeling Act (requiring the name and place of the manufacturer, packer, or distributor to be displayed) of commodities subject to the Wool Products Labeling Act and the Textile Fiber Products Identification Act. The commission ruled that a number of articles, including household fixtures, household appliances, and automotive replacement parts, were exempt from that provision of the act relating to the location of net quantity statements. In September the president requested the Tariff Commission to institute an inquiry into the effect on the U.S. balance of payments and on employment in the U.S. of the tariff privileges granted on the reentry of U.S. goods shipped abroad for processing, finishing, or assembly. The bulk of the category in question was made up of transportation equipment imports from Canada, West Germany, Sweden, and the U.K.

New antidumping legislation was introduced by

Colonies: *see* Dependent States
Comecon: *see* Economic Planning
Commerce: *see* Commercial Policies; Consumer Expenditures; Economy, World; Merchandising; Trade, International

Canada on Jan. 1, 1969. This brought to an end the previous rule by which antidumping duties were automatically levied whenever the imported price of any particular article appeared lower than the home sale price. In July the full tariff reductions agreed under the Kennedy Round, not formally due to come into force until 1972, were made effective immediately. This was done in an effort to contain the rise in Canadian manufacturing costs.

In December 1968 the Japanese government announced its intention to press ahead with the liberalization of imports and to abolish all quotas within the space of two or three years. At the same time, the government declared that safeguards would be set up to ensure that foreign goods that competed with Japanese goods did not flood the market, and that, moreover, the Japanese government would take account of discrimination practiced on Japanese exports. The announcement was followed ten days later by a conference on the liberalization of trade with the U.S., at the end of which it was stated that decisions had been taken on a substantial number of items. Further negotiations followed for the lifting of restrictions on trade with the U.K.

Policies of the Less Developed Countries. In May 1969 the South African minister of economic affairs announced that the total allocation of import permits for the year would be no less than for 1968. In both Australia and New Zealand there was evidence of a move away from the strong protection hitherto afforded to domestic industries. Both the Tariff Board and the Department of Trade and Industry in Australia spoke in favour of exposing home industries more fully to competition from outside, and this view was warmly echoed in Western Australia. The New Zealand minister of industries and commerce and the minister of customs issued a joint statement saying, among other things, that economic developments over the next ten years would entail a move away from quantitative controls and toward tariffs as a means of home protection.

In keeping with the Brazilian government's new policy of making progressive small changes in the parity of the cruzeiro, the exchange rate was reduced by $1\frac{1}{4}$% on May 13; the new buying rate was 4.025 cruzeiros = U.S. $1 and the selling rate was 4 cruzeiros = $1. Colombia announced an import program of U.S. $51 million per month for the period from April 1969 to March 1970, an increase of 14% over the previous year. Dinesh Singh, incoming minister of external affairs in India, advocated increasing trade with the countries of Africa and Asia, the areas of India's greatest political interest. In the first half of 1969 India received more than $400 million from the developed countries, including a $125 million interest-free, 50-year loan from the International Development Association to assist in the importation of essential materials for production. In the course of the year the finance minister promulgated a series of restrictive criteria under which foreign capital would be allowed into the country. Similar guidelines were issued with respect to collaborative agreements with foreign firms. Under the government's import policy, announced in March, 316 items were totally banned while 129 further items, hitherto admitted without restrictions on actual users, were subjected to severe limitations. A number of trade agreements were concluded with countries in all parts of the world.

Under a voluntary program begun in July, monthly letter of credit facilities for importers were reduced by 30% in the Philippines; this followed a deterioration in the balance of payments. In Iraq an overall allocation of 158 million dinars for imports during 1969 was made under a new import program. Widespread increases in the Iranian commercial benefit tax hit luxury imports and sales of foreign goods competing with domestic industry. In Israel wide-ranging tariff reductions were made on January 1, the government's view being that industry should henceforth hold its own in international competition; some 600 individual products were affected.

Planned Economy Countries. On the whole, established trade attitudes in the planned economy countries were little changed in 1969. The Soviet Union, the major economic entity involved, was basically self-sufficient, with foreign trade accounting for less than 5% of its gross national product. Soviet trade continued to be conducted by state trading organizations, both for exports and for imports. These organizations pursued arbitrary pricing policies, designed on the one hand to secure sales of Soviet products abroad regardless of their price in the home market and, on the other hand, to secure imports of foreign goods, where needed, at prices that would not upset the returns available to domestic industries in the internal market. As in previous years, the U.S.S.R. tended to resort to the outside world only when temporary maladjustments or deficiencies appeared in the planned movement of the domestic economy.

The situation in the other planned economy countries was slightly different since these, on the whole, tended to be more reliant on foreign trade. Here again, however, trade was focused mainly on the Soviet Union, and any inclination to trade on a wider basis was discouraged. Nevertheless, some advances were made toward freer trade relations with other countries. The president of the U.K. Board of Trade stated in April that, in view of the increase in U.K. exports to the Soviet Union and Romania, restrictions on imports into the U.K. from these two countries would be removed on a number of products as of May. The products concerned included machinery, furniture, paper products, chemicals, and plastics. The Board of Trade pointed out that the liberalization would be reconsidered if unsatisfactory policies on pricing, nondiscrimination, and reciprocal purchases of British goods ensued. This decision followed earlier relaxations on imports from Bulgaria, Czechoslovakia, Hungary, and Poland.

A number of treaties for increased trade were concluded during the year between India and various Eastern European countries. It was also reported that trade between Uganda and the U.S.S.R. had increased by 500% since the signing of the 1964 trade agreement.

Trade Policies of International Organizations. It was agreed by all parties to the Kennedy Round that the closing date for the application of the protocol relating to chemicals would be postponed from Jan. 1, 1969, to Jan. 1, 1970. Under this protocol the U.S. was to benefit by supplementary tariff reductions

Total World Exports
In U.S. $000,000,000 f.o.b.

Year	Amount
1963	134.84
1964	151.64
1965	164.40
1966	180.32
1967	189.36
1968	211.32

on chemicals, provided the American Selling Price system of valuation was abolished.

Meanwhile, the General Agreement on Tariffs and Trade (GATT) turned to the question of nontariff obstacles. These were defined as "any government law or practice which is not a tariff which tends to limit the free flow of trade between one country and another." After circulating an inquiry to member governments, GATT drew up an inventory of such nontariff obstacles. They fell under five major headings: (1) specific limitations on imports (quotas, embargoes, import licensing, etc.); (2) government participation in trade (export subsidies, official procurement, limited calls for tender, state trading, state monopolies); (3) customs and administrative entry procedures (countervailing duties, arbitrary classification, antidumping practices, valuation, etc.); (4) standards involving imports and domestic goods (industrial, health, safety, content, labeling, processing, marking, packaging, and certification procedures that impede imports); and (5) restraints on imports by price mechanisms (import deposits, surcharges, port, statistical and excise taxes, credit restrictions, consular fees, stamp taxes, variable levies, border taxes). Having identified the obstacles, GATT then proceeded to determine which practices most seriously affected trade. Again member governments were circularized, and replies were arriving as the year ended.

The European Economic Community confirmed that it would move from its transitional to its final stage at the beginning of 1970, as laid down in the Treaty of Rome. Italy and Belgium stated that they would be unable to introduce the added value consumption tax (TVA) by Jan. 1, 1970, as required by the Community's decision of 1967. The system would be introduced in 1972 and in 1971 in Italy and Belgium, respectively. In accordance with art. 3 of the treaty, the European Commission submitted to the Council of Ministers in July 1969 a draft regulation on the establishment of common rules for EEC exports. In the previous April a similar draft had been submitted on the unification of import policies. The proposal itself referred only to the ceramics industry, but it was accompanied by a general program for common rules over the whole field of Community imports. An agreement on the second phase of Turkey's association with the Six was signed at the end of the year, although some delay before ratification was likely.

In accordance with a major decision taken in 1969, the governments of the European Free Trade Association (EFTA) countries pushed on during the year with the question of interchangeable standards. As of May, national electrical testing stations in all EFTA countries were authorized to accept test reports from similar stations in other countries. A meeting of the Committee of Trade Experts in June examined the possibility of similar arrangements for pressure vessels, agricultural machinery, tractors, industrial trucks, and nonelectrical heating, cooking, and lighting equipment.

A draft treaty for the establishment of the Nordic customs union (Nordek) was produced in mid-July. The draft reflected complete agreement on policies concerning economic matters, capital movements, trade, shipping, industrial and energy matters, the labour market, social affairs, trade legislation and restrictive practices, education, training, research, and aid to less developed countries. However, there were differences of opinion regarding the tariff levels to be adopted for the customs union, and on questions affecting agriculture, fisheries, land transport, and establishment of firms.

With the setting up of the Caribbean Secretariat in Georgetown, Guyana, in March, the 11-member Caribbean Free Trade Agreement was formally set in motion. Steps were being taken to eliminate both tariff and nontariff barriers. The Central American Common Market recorded a 25% increase in trade over the previous year. Costa Rica, however, failed to implement the protocol of San José, under which each member country was required to increase import duties by 30% on all merchandise originating outside the area. Because of an adverse balance of payments, Nicaragua reinstated duties on products from Central American countries. (W. A. P. M.)

See also Agriculture; Commodities, Primary; Development, Economic; Payments and Reserves, International; Trade, International.

Commodities, Primary

The UN Food and Agriculture Organization (FAO) estimated that combined world output (excluding China) of agricultural, fishery, and forestry products in 1968 increased by about 3% (*see* Table I). This was close to the average rate of increase over the preceding ten years and somewhat more than the growth in population. However, in contrast with past years when fishery production tended to grow faster and forestry more slowly, the increases in output in 1968 in the three sectors were approximately equal.

By rising 3% in 1968, overall world food production remained a step ahead of the population growth rate of 2%. In the less developed regions, the growth in food production in 1968, at around 2%, was more modest. This increase followed sharp rises in 1967, which in most cases followed one or two years of poor crops due mainly to unfavourable weather. With their populations continuing to grow at a rate of 2.7% per year, little, if any, increase in per capita food production occurred in most of the less developed regions of the world in 1968.

Looking at the individual regions, the brightest note came from the Far East (excluding Japan and China). Both food and agricultural production rose by 5% with per capita food production almost back to the 1965–66 level. This progress, which reflected a technological breakthrough with new higher-yielding cereal varieties—rather remarkable in view of varying weather conditions—also enabled most major food importing countries in the region to move toward greater self-sufficiency in food grains and to improve their stock position.

Food production results in the other less developed regions were less favourable. Output increased by about 3% in the less developed countries of Africa but in per capita terms was virtually unchanged. Production in the Near East was only fractionally higher with per capita output down about 1%; in Latin America, food output dropped 2% and was mainly attributed to droughts that began in 1967 and lasted in some cases into 1969. Latest available figures showed that population growth in Latin America was rising at 2.9% annually, versus a worldwide rate of 1.9%.

The growth of food production in both Latin America and the Near East remained below the average rates recorded for the preceding decade. Furthermore, these average rates were generally deemed too slow relative to both the growth of population and the growth of demand associated with acceptable economic growth. The estimated increase in demand for food in the less developed countries associated with the growth objectives of FAO's Indicative World Plan was 3.9% a year; the corresponding annual growth rate for agricultural production was 3.5%.

In the more developed regions, agricultural production in 1968 was generally higher than in 1967. Notwithstanding decreases in individual countries arising from unfavourable weather as well as some efforts to restrain output, Western Europe and North America showed increases of 2% each. The increase in Eastern Europe and in the U.S.S.R. was about 5% while Oceania (where 1967 output, particularly in Australia, was trimmed by drought) reported a sharp rise of 15%.

Among other primary commodities—excluding agricultural, fishery, and forestry products—crude petroleum, pig iron, and crude steel, as well as nonferrous metals, benefited by increased world demand, which encouraged higher world production (*see* Table II). Cement, however, continued to be plagued with excess capacity and surplus supplies. World production of natural rubber rose 6% in 1968, reflecting record outputs in Malaysia, Thailand, and Ceylon. World consumption of natural rubber, however, increased by 11% in 1968 and, as in previous years, exceeded production, this time by 5 to 6%. The production deficit in natural rubber was met from stocks, including those held by the governments of Malaysia and the U.S. and by commercial concerns. Meanwhile, world output of synthetic rubber, which increased by 13%, accounted for about 63% of world total new rubber usage in 1968. In the U.S., the synthetic product provided nearly 77% of total new rubber requirements.

Prices and Terms of Trade. Table III shows trends in primary commodity prices during recent years. As usual, there was considerable variation among the various products. In 1968, prices of beef, cocoa, copper, copra, cotton, lead, and newsprint moved higher while declines were recorded for butter, hides, jute, peanuts, sugar, tin, wheat, and zinc.

The value of combined world exports of agricultural, fishery, and forest products increased by about 3% in 1968, largely reflecting a sharp rise in earnings of forest products. World trade in agricultural products remained about the same, as lower prices offset a 3% rise in volume. Some improvement occurred in the trade positions of the less developed countries but was unevenly distributed. Also, much of the recovery followed widespread declines in 1967. In the more developed countries, agricultural export earnings fell for the second consecutive year. As the accompanying chart shows, prices for commodity exports of less developed countries in 1968 were about as favourable as prices for commodity exports from industrial countries. This was in sharp contrast with the mid-1960s when prices for primary commodity exports from less developed countries were less favourable than those of the more developed countries.

Looking at the main agricultural commodities, the value of world exports in 1968 fell slightly from $21.3 billion to $21.1 billion. Oversupply of most temperate-zone products lowered the value of exports from the more developed countries by 3%. Part of this decline was caused by lower food aid shipments rather than by a drop in commercial sales.

Less developed countries registered some increases in export receipts and raised their aggregate earnings by about 2%, compared with an average growth rate of 3% yearly during 1962–66 and a fall of 5% in 1967. The largest absolute additions among agricultural commodities were made by fats and oils, coffee, and cotton with smaller gains by cocoa, rubber, and jute. Textile exports, which rose 3% in the case of cotton and 17% for wool, were leading factors in this upturn. Because of sharply higher prices for cocoa, coconut oil, and cotton—as well as relatively stable prices for coffee and rubber—there was no deterioration in the overall terms of trade for agricultural exporters.

Export earnings from agricultural products in the less developed countries of the Far East fell in 1968 for the fifth consecutive year to their lowest level since 1958. The decline in earnings, reflecting both lower prices and reduced volume, was particularly noticeable for four of the region's principal exports—rice, jute, kenaf, and tea—which accounted for about a third of the total. For rice, the drop in earnings was 19%. The value of sugar and rubber exports was about the same as in 1967. Rubber, which comprised 25% of export earnings, suffered a moderate decline in unit value that was offset by increased volume in line with production from areas replanted with high-yielding varieties.

Latin-American exports of agricultural products increased fractionally in 1968 after two years of decline. Beef and veal shipments were reduced sharply because of the temporary ban on imports of Argentinian beef by the United Kingdom after an outbreak of foot-and-mouth disease in that country. An offsetting factor, however, was larger exports of canned beef at higher prices. Latin-American earnings from coffee increased by 8% as higher prices and quantities were aided by larger exports to the U.S. and to European countries. Export earnings from cereals were down sharply and the value of sugar exports remained unchanged. Banana prices were lower but were compensated by larger volumes exported.

In the Near East, the volume of agricultural exports in 1968 fell slightly but, because of relatively good prices, particularly for rice and cotton (which provide over 60% of the region's export earnings from agriculture), total value rose about 5% over 1967. Exports of fruit expanded further in 1968 and were about 85% above ten years earlier. Rice exports, mostly from the U.A.R., were record high, 30% above 1967, with the rise in value up by about half. Exports of tobacco (mainly from Turkey) declined owing to weak international demand for oriental leaf and strong competition from other exporting countries.

The value of Africa's agricultural exports in 1968 showed a sharp rise of 10%, although still below the level reached in 1964. Most of Africa's major agricultural export products showed increases in both volume and value. A notable exception was peanut oil, for which lower prices more than offset larger shipments, mainly from Nigeria to the U.K. The same was true of palm kernel oil. The volume of cocoa exports (because of reduced crops) fell to a seven-year low but substantially higher prices resulted in export earnings well above the 1967 figure. The upward trend in coffee earnings was maintained as a result of record exports and higher prices.

Commodity Policies. *National Policies.* There was little change in policies relative to agricultural and other commodities in most countries during 1968–69. India's decision to purchase a large quantity of wheat from the U.S. did not indicate a poor harvest. It was part of a definite policy to build up reserves for distribution in areas of scarcities and thereby keep grain prices from soaring to levels out of the reach of people in need. To spread the "green revolution," India hoped to increase its irrigation facilities and to produce more fertilizer. Current fertilizer production was around 1.5 million tons per year, well below 1969 needs of around 3.5 million and the estimated 4.1 million tons required for 1970–71.

The farm price support policies in the European Economic Community (EEC), which cost about $3.5 billion annually, were in a state of flux. Financing of the farm policies and the rules that provide for national contributions were particularly troublesome. About half of the farm budget had been covered by levies on agricultural imports, 90% of which were paid into the fund by the importing member states. The balance was covered with a fixed percentage paid by each EEC member. On the basis of average shares paid in 1968 and 1969, West Germany paid 30.2%; France, 24.9%; Italy, 24.7%; the Netherlands, 11.2%; Belgium, 8.8%; and Luxembourg, 0.2%. As the major food exporter, France was the biggest net beneficiary from the fund while West Germany, as the major importer, contributed the most.

After much disagreement about the system of financing the farm program, EEC ministers in late 1969 agreed on a compromise definite farm financing program, which cleared the way for the U.K. to join the trading bloc. For 1970, the percentages of the total fund to be paid by each country were to be: West Germany, 31.8%; France, 28%; Italy, 21.4%; the Netherlands, 10.35%; Belgium, 8.25%; and Luxembourg, 0.2%. After 1970 any nation's contributions in a given year could not be greater than 101% or less than 98.5% of its contributions in the previous year. Beginning in 1975 and until the end of 1977, each country's contribution would be within 2% of its previous year's contribution.

Except for liberalization of food stamp disposal programs to the needy, U.S. food and agricultural programs underwent little change in 1969. Despite various acreage reduction programs, the 1969 crop harvest was record high. Although exceeded by both 1967 production and the record 1968 output, the 1969 wheat crop exceeded foreseeable distribution in the following year. Coming on top of an increased carryover, this crop dropped prices in some harvests during the harvesting season to 27-year lows. Hoping to reduce future wheat stocks, Secretary of Agriculture Clifford M. Hardin set the acreage allotment for the 1970 wheat crop at a record low, 12% below the 1969-crop allotment. Largely because of booming markets for livestock and livestock products, U.S. overall farm prices in 1969 averaged about 6% above 1968 levels. Although production costs continued at record high levels, realized farm income was appreciably above a year earlier.

Because the Food and Agriculture Act of 1965 had been extended in 1968 through 1970, there was no immediate pressure on the Nixon administration to devise its own farm program. On Sept. 24, 1969, however, Hardin outlined a number of proposals for possible inclusion in a new program, one of which would set aside crop acreage including whole farms. Also proposed was a domestic allotment plan and a diversion plan for crops with substantially lower loan rates to encourage movement of commodities into export markets.

Nationalization of copper mines increased in 1969. On June 26, Anaconda Co., a U.S.-owned copper firm, announced that to avoid expropriation through legislation by the government of Chile it had agreed to the nationalization of its Chilean subsidiaries, the Chile Exploration Co. and the Andes Copper Mining Co. On August 11, the government of Zambia stated that it would take a 51% interest in the mine operating companies of Roan Selection Trust Ltd. and the Zambian branch of the Anglo American Corp. of South Africa, Ltd. In late September, Union Minière du Haut-Katanga and the Congo (Kinshasa) settled their dispute over the government's seizure of the Belgian company's copper mining operations in Katanga in 1967.

International Policies. Increased exportable supplies and reduced import requirements exerted a downward pressure on world wheat prices in 1969. Since the new three-year International Grains Arrangement (IGA) had become effective on July 1, 1968, wheat export prices had been at and even below their respective minimum levels; average prices for most wheats were below those of a year earlier when no agreement was in effect. As the season advanced, an increasing number of sales were made at prices below IGA minimums. In March 1969, the Canadian Wheat Board, in order to safeguard Canada's interest, decided to meet this competition by reducing its wheat export prices below the IGA minimums. The U.S. announced a similar policy, but the wheat price war was continued. Finally, on July 11, at a meeting in Washington, D.C., five IGA exporting members—Canada, Argentina, Australia, the EEC, and the U.S.—announced that for the time being IGA minimum wheat export prices were abandoned. While these developments in themselves did not mean a complete collapse of the IGA, it was obvious that the pact was put to a considerable test.

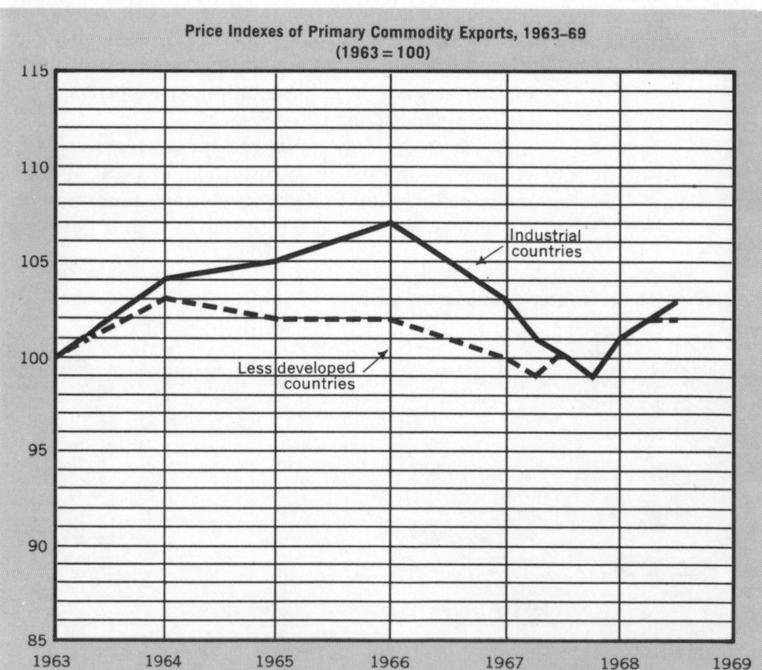

Table 1. Indexes of World Production of Agricultural, Fishery, and Forestry Products

1952–56 average=100

Item	1958	1962	1966	1967	1968
Total production	113	125	137	143	146
Agriculture	114	126	138	143	147
Fisheries	112	135	162	169	176
Forestry	106	113	124	125	128
Population	108	117	127	129	132
Per capita production	105	107	109	110	111
Agriculture	105	108	109	111	112
Fisheries	104	116	128	131	133
Forestry	98	97	98	97	97

Source: Food and Agriculture Organization of the United Nations, *The State of Food and Agriculture, 1969.*

Table II. Indexes of World Production of Certain Raw Materials

1963 average=100

Raw material	1959	1962	1966	1967	1968
Coal*	93	97	105	105	105
Crude petroleum	75	93	125	135	147
Cement	77	95	123	128	136
Pig iron†	77	95	124	130	138
Crude steel	78	93	123	129	137
Copper (smelter)‡	78	98	112	101	113
Zinc‡§	84	97	119	119	132
Lead‡§	88	96	108	110	118
Tin‖	79	101	108	121	127
Aluminum‡§	76	91	131	145	153
Natural rubber	99	103	116	119	126

*Including coal equivalent of brown coal and lignite.
†Including ferroalloys.
‡Excluding the U.S.S.R., East Germany, and North Korea.
§Excluding Czechoslovakia and Romania.
‖Excluding the U.S.S.R. and Eastern Europe.
Source: United Nations, *Monthly Bulletin of Statistics.*

The new International Coffee Agreement (ICA) came into force in October 1968. After two weeks of bitter debate, on Aug. 29, 1969, the Executive Board of the International Coffee Organization (ICO) set initial overall annual export quotas for the 1969–70 season, beginning Oct. 1, 1969, at 46 million bags, against initial quotas of 47.8 million bags for the 1968–69 season. Also, for the 1969–70 season, the ICO set up a special quota reserve of 2 million bags, 500,000 bags above 1968–69, to be distributed depending on the composite price of the four groups of coffee. With the composite price well above the trigger level of 38.67 cents per pound, 500,000 bags of this reserve were distributed to exporters during October–December 1969.

Releases of coffee from the special reserve did not change the upward or downward adjustment of quotas under the modified selectivity system. Floor and ceiling prices, which trigger the upward and downward adjustments, were increased by 1.5 cents per pound. Thus, the price floors and ceilings for 1969–70 for the four groups of coffee were (in U.S. cents per pound): Colombian Mild Arabicas, 40.75 and 44.75; other Mild Arabicas, 38.75 and 42.75; unwashed Arabicas, 36.75 and 40.75; and Robustas, 32 and 36. If the average daily price for any group of coffee for 20 consecutive market days (up from 15 days in 1968–69) was below the floor or above the ceiling of its indicator price range, the quota of each member of that group would be adjusted.

Upward adjustment counts, completed in October 1969, increased quotas of ICA exporters by 1,750,000 bags. After reaching the highest levels in several years during November 1969—reflecting good overall demand in the face of a reduced crop in Brazil (the leading producer) and prospects of an even smaller one in 1970–71—coffee prices slipped a bit in December but remained well above levels of a year earlier.

The sharp rise in coffee prices in late 1969 led to demands by some U.S. coffee interests for a study of the world supply-demand situation to ascertain the conditions required to suspend the ICA temporarily or do away with it altogether. As of Oct. 1, 1969, stocks of coffee held in producing countries were estimated at about 44.5 million bags, off from 55 million a year earlier and the record of nearly 80 million bags as recently as 1966.

The current International Sugar Agreement (ISA), which went into force Jan. 1, 1969, for five years, sought to maintain the world free market price of sugar between a minimum of 3.25 cents per pound (f.o.b. Caribbean port basis) and a maximum of 5.25 cents per pound. After rising to a near five-year high of 4.08 cents in June 1969, the world free sugar price by August had dipped below the minimum target. It remained below 3.25 cents for the balance of 1969, closing the year at around 2.85 cents. The International Sugar Council, therefore, fixed initial export quotas for 1970 at 90% of basic export tonnages in an effort to bring world available supplies and demand into closer balance. Prospects for higher production meant that the task of getting the price above the ISA minimum in 1970 could be difficult.

Inasmuch as demand for tin had been outrunning available supplies (reflecting production difficulties), the price of tin in early December 1969 broke through the International Tin Agreement (ITA) ceiling of about $1.75 per pound. As a result, the International Tin Council (ITC) lifted quotas on tin exports from the producing members of the ITA, effective Jan. 1, 1970. Also, the ITC asked producers to export as much tin as possible before January 1. When the price of tin exceeds the ITA ceiling, the buffer stocks manager is required to sell tin from his supplies. But with demand so strong, tin prices kept rising despite the buffer stock sales. With his supplies dwindling, the buffer stock manager took advantage of an ITA option and withdrew from the market for six weeks "in the interests of producer nations." The U.S., while not a member of the ITA, had a gentleman's agreement with the ITC not to sell its surplus tin, last reported at around 25,000 tons.

After four consecutive seasons of deficit cocoa bean production, preliminary prospects for the 1969–70 season (October 1–September 30) indicated that world crops and consumption would be in rather close balance. Cocoa bean prices remained relatively high, but the six-nation alliance of cocoa-producing countries—Brazil, Cameroon, Ghana, Ivory Coast, Togo, and

Table III. Changes in International Prices of Selected Major Primary Commodities

Commodity, unit, country of origin, and market	Wholesale price in U.S. dollars 1961	1966	1967	1968	July 1969
Beef (100 lb.) U.K. (London)	25.43	34.39	32.74	35.42	38.00
Butter (100 lb.) New Zealand (London)	32.00	37.66	36.60	32.14	32.14
Cocoa (100 lb.) Ghana (N.Y.)	22.60	24.43	29.07	34.40	47.76
Coffee (100 lb.) Brazil (N.Y.)	36.01	40.79	37.93	37.48	37.36
Copper (100 lb.) U.K. (London)	28.69	69.22	51.10	56.09	65.19
Copra (100 lb.) Philippines (London)	6.39	6.46	7.34	8.82	7.39
Cotton (100 lb.) U.A.R. (Liverpool)	45.03	49.96	53.24	58.66	63.40
Hides (100 lb.) Argentina (London)	24.12	32.59	25.26	19.58	25.04
Jute (short tons) Pakistan (London)	393	343	310	280	280
Lead (100 lb.) U.K. (London)	8.04	11.69	10.28	10.91	14.09
Newsprint (short tons) Canada (Quebec)	116.70	119.50	122.40	124.00	128.60
Peanuts (100 lb.) Nigeria (London)	8.88	8.46	8.11	7.49	9.45
Petroleum (bbl.) Venezuela (La Cruz)	2.80	2.80	2.80	2.80	2.80
Rice (100 lb.) Thailand (Bangkok)	8.60	8.30	8.50	8.70	8.40
Rubber (100 lb.) Malaysia (Singapore)	27.29	21.35	17.70	17.33	24.66
Sugar (100 lb.) Caribbean (N.Y. for exp.)	2.91	1.92	2.06	1.98	3.73
Tea (100 lb.) Ceylon-India (N.Y.)	48.80	48.20	45.93	46.00	41.00
Tin (100 lb.) Malaysia (Penang)	110.00	158.10	147.00	138.60	153.30
Tobacco (100 lb.) U.S. (U.S.)	61.50	64.50	65.00	66.50	69.24
Wheat (bu.) Canada (Ft. William)	1.73	1.92	1.90	1.82	1.77
Wool (100 lb.) Australia (Sydney)	50.50	57.20	51.00	51.80	48.20
Zinc (100 lb.) U.K. (London)	9.72	12.75	12.34	11.91	12.86

Source: International Monetary Fund, *International Financial Statistics.*

that the first six years of a child's life are the most crucial years of all for acquiring the ability to learn.

Now there is impressive evidence that your hunch was correct: that psychologists can measure the knowledge, interest and abilities of a six-year-old and predict with astonishing accuracy what his I. Q., achievements, attitudes, values and skills will be when he reaches age sixteen!

Just how this was demonstrated -- with 50,000 subjects, selected and studied over a 55-year period from 1900 to 1955 -- is the subject of a newly published report by the eminent child psychologist, Dr. Benjamin Bloom. It's importance to parents, however, lies not in its statistics but in its implications. If the young child's natural desire to learn is fulfilled -- if he is encouraged to become inquisitive, confident, anxious to acquire information and abilities, ready to explore questions and discover answers, he is almost certain to grow to his full intellectual potential. He will have learned to stretch his mind -- and for the rest of his life he will enjoy a fuller measure of success.

AT LAST -- EDUCATOR-APPROVED, SCIENTIFIC HELP FOR PARENTS WHO WANT SUCCESS FOR THEIR CHILDREN!

Up to now parents have had little real help in finding correct, educator-approved ways to help stretch their young children's minds. (And unfortunately, very few parents have the time to become their children's tutors.) We knew something should be done to harness those bright, questioning little minds -- to encourage thought, to provoke an interest in words, numbers and ideas -- to answer the questions that begin, "Tell me why, Mommy -- ".

Nigeria—in late October requested the UN Conference on Trade and Development to speed up the progress of talks for an international cocoa agreement. Likewise, with the decline in world export earnings from tea (1968 earnings ...

... than solely British responsibilities, and this was reflected in the extension of the activities of the Commonwealth Secretariat, which took over some work of the defunct U.K. Commonwealth Office.

The final communiqué contained no special direc-

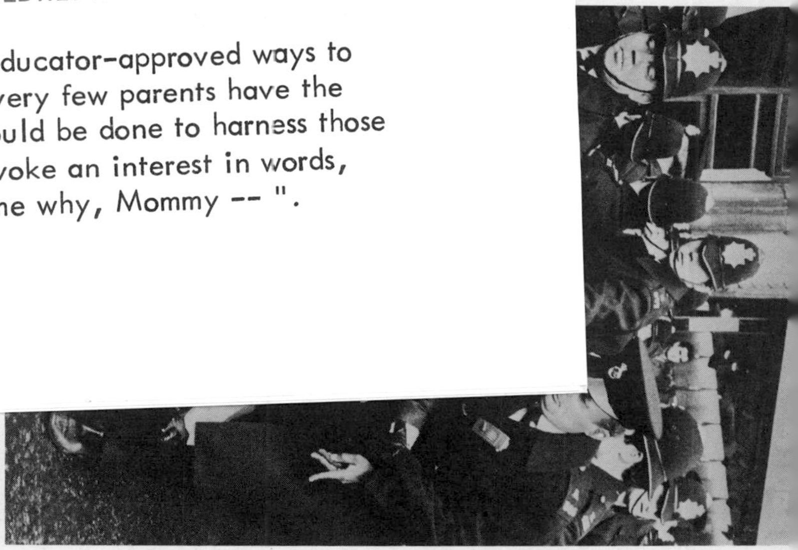

CENTRAL PRESS FROM PICTORIAL PARADE

Police removing demonstrator from Marlborough House in London as the Commonwealth Prime Ministers' Conference began on Jan. 7, 1969. Crowds gathered outside to protest policies relating to Rhodesia and Nigeria.

...re the impor- ...ich and poor ...aid schemes. ..., prime min- ...e conference ...ctive leader- ...n among the

...ed its third ...n mediation ...ibal rivalries ...Ghana, Gen. ... A. Afrifa, ...as itself re- ...led by Kofi ...the govern- ...in the face ...tribes. The ...nomic plan- ...ed the ten- ...o tribes as ... 1963 ap- ...emergency ...of Chinese ...he Tanzam

...white judi- ...stice. The ...ugust: this ...es. Simon ... some ob- ...the ruling ...nda, Kap- ...mbia con- ...Rhodesia. ...n Smith a ...nstitution, ...ference to a South African sphere of influence. Malawi, Botswana, Lesotho, and Swaziland were increasingly closely associated economically with South Africa.

Other Countries. In the Mediterranean the emerging factor was the expansion of Soviet naval power.

Common Market: *see* Commercial Policies; European Unity; *see also* Index *for information on specific common markets*

Continued defense requirements complicated Malta's transfer from a fortress to a viable civilian economy. Terrorist activity continued in Cyprus with the failure of talks between Greeks and Turks to secure a substantive agreement.

In India the government of Indira Gandhi faced increasing internal political dissension. Relations with Pakistan continued to be dominated by the issue of Kashmir and by the two countries' relations with the U.S.S.R. and China. The latter's road-building schemes directed toward India alarmed the Indian government. In Malaysia racial disturbances broke out in May between Malays and Chinese. The defense of the Southeast Asian Commonwealth countries in view of the planned British withdrawal was discussed in June at a conference in Canberra, Austr., attended by Australia, Malaysia, New Zealand, Singapore, and the U.K. Australia, despite some evidence of isolationist leanings, promised to continue financial and technical aid to Southeast Asia after 1971 and, with New Zealand, to maintain forces in the region. A major Commonwealth exercise was planned for 1970 to test the viability of an integrated defense organization in place of British protection.

Canada, with its first majority government for a decade, showed increased confidence both at home and in its overseas dealings. Canada's aid program extended to more than 80 countries, with particular support for the Caribbean. In the latter area Guyana, apart from border disputes with Venezuela and Surinam, faced an internal political confrontation between its two major parties. The republic of Nauru late in 1968 became the Commonwealth's first "special member" with the right to participate in all functional meetings and activities and to receive technical assistance. The Associated States of the West Indies, although they were not fully independent, also took part in Commonwealth activities.

Economic Affairs. The 1969 Prime Ministers' Conference stressed the need to expand Commonwealth trade and develop the existing range of technical cooperation. Commonwealth trade continued to increase at a rate faster than that of world trade in general. After the U.S., the older Commonwealth nations remained the U.K.'s chief trading partners. The Commonwealth Development Corporation, 21 years old in 1969, continued to be one of the most successful organizations of its type. In 1969 it reached its borrowing ceiling of £160 million and consideration was given to raising this limit to £260 million. In 1968 the corporation had successfully fulfilled its objectives of developing local resources in partnership with local organizations and of paying its way. British aid to less developed countries stood at £210 million in 1968. Special assistance was given to Malaysia and Singapore to help compensate for the withdrawal of British forces there. The flow of intra-Commonwealth aid through the Colombo Plan and the Special Commonwealth African Assistance Plan also rose. Britain remained the largest contributor. U.K. technical assistance increased from £33 million to £41 million in 1968, and greater use was made of private consultants. Technical and educational aid was also provided by the Commonwealth Institute and the Commonwealth Foundation. By the end of 1968 the latter had allocated about £450,000 to professional organizations throughout the Commonwealth. (M. Mr.)

See also articles on the various political units.

Commonwealth of Nations

Country	Area (sq.mi.)	Pop. (1966–69 estimate)	Capital	Status	Chief of state and head of government* (as of Dec. 31, 1969)
United Kingdom	94,213	55,282,500	London	Constitutional monarchy	Queen, Elizabeth II Prime minister, Harold Wilson
Australia	2,967,877	12,295,300	Canberra	Federal parliamentary state	Governor-general, Lord Casey Prime minister, John Grey Gorton
Barbados	166	252,900	Bridgetown	Parliamentary state	Governor-general, Sir Winston Scott Prime minister, Errol Walton Barrow
Botswana	220,000	623,000	Gaborone	Republic	President, Sir Seretse Khama
Canada	3,851,809	21,061,000	Ottawa	Federal parliamentary state	Governor-general, D. Roland Michener Prime minister, Pierre Elliott Trudeau
Ceylon	25,332	11,964,000	Colombo	Parliamentary state	Governor-general, William Gopallawa Prime minister, Dudley Senanayake
Cyprus	3,572	622,000	Nicosia	Republic	President, Archbishop Makarios III
Gambia, The	4,000	357,000	Bathurst	Parliamentary state	Governor-general, Alhaji Sir Farimang Singhateh Prime minister, Sir Dawda Jawara
Ghana	92,100	8,376,000	Accra	Republic	President, Kofi Busia
Guyana	83,000	741,978	Georgetown	Parliamentary state	Governor-general, Sir David J. E. Rose Prime minister, Forbes Burnham
India	1,232,560	524,080,000	New Delhi	Federal republic	President, Zakir Husain Prime minister, Mrs. Indira Gandhi
Jamaica	4,244	1,939,649	Kingston	Parliamentary state	Governor-general, Sir Clifford Campbell Prime minister, Hugh L. Shearer
Kenya	224,960	10,504,000	Nairobi	Republic	President, Jomo Kenyatta
Lesotho	11,716	1,018,135	Maseru	Constitutional monarchy	Chief of state, Moshoeshoe II Prime minister, Leabua Jonathan
Malawi	45,747	4,285,000	Zomba	Republic	President, H. Kamuzu Banda
Malaysia	127,581	10,169,179	Kuala Lumpur	Federal constitutional monarchy	*Yang di-pertuan agong*, Tuanku Ismail Nasiruddin Shah ibni al-Marhum Sultan Zainal Abidin Prime minister, Tunku Abdul Rahman
Malta	122	320,764	Valletta	Parliamentary state	Governor-general, Sir Maurice Dorman Prime minister, George Borg Olivier
Mauritius	720	794,750	Port Louis	Parliamentary state	Governor-general, Sir Leonard Williams Prime minister, Sir Seewoosagur Ramgoolam
New Zealand	103,736	2,780,839	Wellington	Parliamentary state	Governor-general, Sir Arthur Porritt Prime minister, Keith J. Holyoake
Nigeria	356,669	64,561,000	Lagos	Federal republic	Head of provisional military government, Yakubu Gowon
Pakistan	365,950	111,829,575	Islamabad	Federal republic	President, Gen. Agha Muhammad Yahya Khan
Sierra Leone	27,699	2,475,000	Freetown	Parliamentary state	Acting governor-general, Justice Banja Tejan–Sie Prime minister, Siaka Stevens
Singapore	225	2,003,800	Singapore	Republic	President, Inche Yusof bin Ishak Prime minister, Lee Kuan Yew
Swaziland	6,704	408,609	Mbabane	Constitutional monarchy	King, Sobhuza II Prime minister, Prince Makhosini Dhlamini
Tanzania	361,821	12,926,000	Dar es Salaam	Republic	President, Julius Nyerere
Trinidad and Tobago	1,980	1,030,000	Port-of-Spain	Parliamentary state	Governor-general, Sir Solomon Hochoy Prime minister, Eric Williams
Uganda	91,076	8,133,000	Kampala	Federal parliamentary state	President and prime minister, Milton Obote
Zambia	290,587	4,143,700	Lusaka	Republic	President, Kenneth Kaunda

*Where Queen Elizabeth II serves as chief of state, her representative (governor-general) is listed.

Communications: *see* Telecommunications; Television and Radio

Communist Movement

At the end of 1969, the Soviet Communist Party's goal of asserting leadership over all Communist states and parties seemed nearer realization than it had a year earlier, though only within narrow limits. To some degree, this was the result of greater elasticity on the part of the Soviet leadership, especially Soviet Premier Aleksei N. Kosygin. The task of the Soviet leadership, however, was made more difficult by the fact that it had to fight on two fronts, in Europe and in Asia.

East-West Conflict. The 20th anniversary of the establishment of the People's Republic of China was celebrated on Oct. 1, 1969, with mass meetings throughout the country. In Peking party chairman Mao Tse-tung and his heir apparent, Lin Piao, were present at the celebration after an unexplained absence of several months from the public eye. The Cultural Revolution was declared ended, and in his main address Lin emphasized unity and hard work. He spoke of the intention of U.S. imperialism and of socialist (meaning Soviet) imperialism to attack China and warned that the Chinese would victoriously defend their country. "We will not attack," he declared, "unless we are attacked."

Unlike the celebration of China's tenth anniversary, which was attended by the then Soviet premier, Nikita S. Khrushchev, and many other leading figures, the 1969 celebration saw few delegations from the outside world. Only the governments of North Korea, North Vietnam, the Provisional Revolutionary Government of South Vietnam, and Cambodia were present from Southeast Asia; Pakistan and Nepal from central Asia; Algeria, the Congo (Brazzaville), Guinea, and Tanzania from Africa; and Albania and Romania from Europe. Mongolia, the oldest Communist state in Asia, was absent and firmly maintained its traditional link with the Soviet Union. On the other hand, Albania, which had broken diplomatic relations with the Soviet government in December 1961, continued to follow a policy of closest cooperation with China. The only European Communist state to maintain good relations with both the Soviet Union and China was Romania, which was represented at the 20th anniversary celebration by Premier Ion Gheorghe Maurer.

Though the rift between Soviet and Chinese Communism could be viewed simply as a rift between Europe and Asia, it was psychologically rooted in Chinese resentment of European interference in China over the last 150 years. Czarist Russia had played a great part in this interference, and it was more successful than its imperialist rivals in retaining and colonizing formerly Chinese—though very sparsely populated—parts of Asia. The Soviet Marxists, on the other hand, felt a superiority as the oldest heirs of revolutionary Marxism who could look back upon an experience in the theory and practice of Marxism-Leninism stretching over half a century.

But the conflict between the two great Communist powers was not only ideological or psychological. It was also a typical conflict of national interest over disputed borders. The Sino-Soviet frontier in Asia is probably the longest anywhere; in some places it is poorly defined, and the treaties ceding Chinese territory have been variously interpreted. Violent border conflicts there are far from unknown. One of the most important occurred in March 1969 around the island that the Soviets call Damansky and the Chinese call Chen-Pao, one of the islands in the Ussuri River which, according to the treaty of 1860, forms the frontier between Chinese Manchuria and the Soviet coastal province. The military conflict opened an unusually bitter chapter in the war of invectives between the two countries. On both sides it provided an opportunity for an appeal to patriotism—an appeal with warlike implications.

The possibility that the several large-scale frontier confrontations of 1969 might actually lead to war brought a change in the Soviet and Chinese attitudes. The ideological antagonism between the two parties might continue, but the U.S.S.R. and China apparently became determined to normalize their relationship and thus avoid the outbreak of open warfare with its unforeseeable consequences. The Vietnamese Communist leader Ho Chi Minh, who died in early September, had asked in his testament for a reconciliation of the two great Communist powers. On September 11, on his return from Ho's funeral, Kosygin surprisingly stopped in Peking where he met with Chinese Premier Chou En-lai. Though the meeting was only a short one, it was the first since February 1965 when, after Khrushchev's fall, the Soviet leadership had suggested a normalization of Sino-Soviet relations. That proposal had been rejected, but by September 1969 internal and external pressures had risen to such a degree that China accepted in principle the invitation to a discussion of the Sino-Soviet border.

On October 7 China officially announced that an agreement had been reached with the Soviet Union to attempt a peaceful settlement of the boundary question through negotiations, and talks between the two countries on the territorial boundary problem began in Peking on October 20. At the time of the announcement, the Chinese government declared that "it has never demanded the return of the territory which czarist Russia had annexed" and solemnly repeated its often-made declaration "that at no time and under no circumstances will China be the first to use nuclear weapons."

Soviet border guards (right) advancing on Chinese soldiers preceding armed clash in March 1969 on territory claimed by both countries. A Soviet photographer was killed in the exchange near the Ussuri River.

TASS FROM SOVFOTO

The rather ambiguous relations between China and North Vietnam showed definite signs of improvement in the early fall. The Soviet Union and Communist China had both supported North Vietnam in the long struggle against the U.S., but the main burden of this support, estimated at $1 billion a year, was borne by the U.S.S.R. (Chinese aid was believed to amount to $200 million a year). A new agreement on Chinese aid to Hanoi for 1970 was signed in the late summer of 1969, before the signing of a similar agreement with the Soviets and the European Communist countries. The North Vietnamese delegation to the celebration of the 20th anniversary was received most warmly.

It should be pointed out that the three Asian Communist governments outside China had followed their own—different—policies. China had claimed no leadership role similar to that which the Soviet Union claimed in Eastern Europe, and Asian Communism had no formal unifying ties comparable to the Warsaw Pact and Comecon. In 1966 the Soviet-Mongolian military alliance had been renewed for 20 years. North Korea under Kim Il Sung emphasized the need for a spirit of independence, self-sufficiency, and self-defense. No delegation from Communist China participated in the celebration of North Korea's 20th anniversary.

Eastern Europe. Within the context of the international Communist movement, the efforts of Soviet leadership in early 1969 were concentrated on two interconnected problems: to keep ideology and policy in the Eastern European countries in line with those of the Soviet Union, and to call a worldwide conference of Communist parties, both in and out of power. The purpose of this Communist summit conference, which met in Moscow in June, was to present a united front in support of the Soviet Union against China. The Soviet Union was only partly successful in achieving its two goals, and this after long efforts and discussions that for a time seemed to threaten the unity of the movement in Eastern Europe.

The varieties of Communism that had arisen in Eastern Europe were based primarily on differences of national interest. It was still impossible to say whether there had been a real breakdown in the solidarity of European Communism. Albania had certainly broken away, and it had seemed for some time that Czechoslovakia, under the leadership of Alexander Dubcek, would follow suit. In view of the strategic position of Czechoslovakia, the Soviets—with the memory of 1938–39 still vivid—apparently feared that Czechoslovakia might declare itself neutral or nonaligned, as Hungary might have done in 1956. They regarded Dubcek as weak, and feared that general freedom of discussion and elections based on a multiparty system might destroy the leading position of the Czechoslovak Communist Party. This fear had led in August 1968 to the invasion of Czechoslovakia by the Soviet Union and four other members of the Warsaw Pact, among which East Germany and Poland felt especially threatened by the liberalization of the Czechoslovak regime and its insistence on complete national sovereignty. This insistence was fully shared by Romania under Nicolae Ceausescu, but the strategic position of Romania was entirely different and Ceausescu, in his domestic policy, followed a line no less rigid than that of the Soviet Union.

Though the invasion of Czechoslovakia aroused deep animosity against the Soviet Union among the Czechoslovaks and was sharply criticized in anti-Communist and even in many Communist countries and parties (among them China and Albania, Romania and Yugoslavia), the Soviet Union avoided any irreversible split by acting with circumspection and restraint. The occupation forces were soon reduced from over 500,000 to about 70,000. By a prolonged process of negotiations and pressure, the Soviet Union brought the official policy of Czechoslovakia more or less in line with Soviet policy. The liberal reforms of 1968 were undone bit by bit, and though no puppet regime was established in Czechoslovakia, in April 1969 Dubcek was replaced as party chief by Gustav Husak, a man of the middle or slightly to the right of the middle.

Both Dubcek and Husak were Slovaks. The Slovaks represent about one-third of the population of Czechoslovakia, and their country is much less highly developed than the Czech lands. It was important to note that, after 50 years of Czechoslovak existence, the Slovaks in 1969 finally achieved a status of full

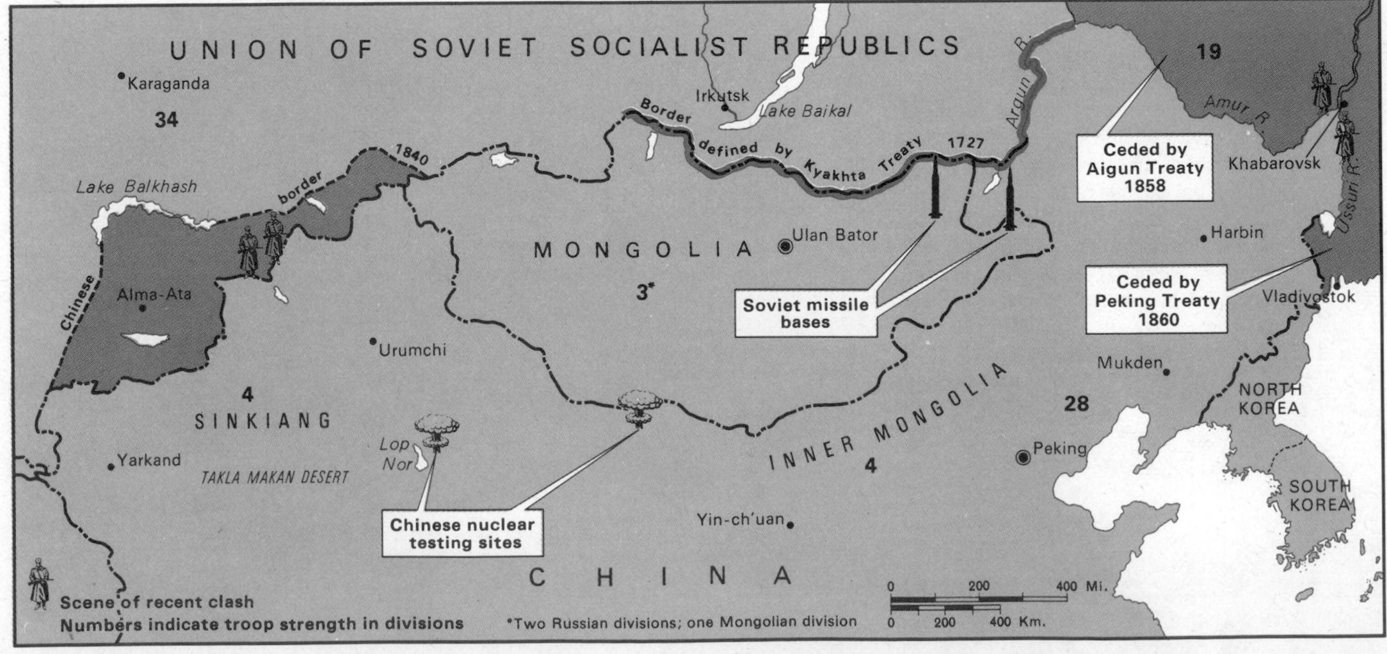

equality with the Czechs. The formerly unitary state of Czechoslovakia was transformed into a federal state of Czechs and Slovaks, with each group having its own Cabinet and parliament. The former National Assembly was to be replaced by a House of Peoples, based on general suffrage, and a House of Nations, in which Czechs and Slovaks would each have 75 representatives.

Normalization in Eastern Europe? At the end of 1969, the various Eastern European Communist governments were following their own lines of development, while trying to maintain good relations within the Communist system. The one exception was Albania, which pursued an extremist course—allied with China, hostile to the Soviet Union and to "revisionist" Yugoslavia. At the beginning of March 1969, at the ninth party congress of the Yugoslav Communist League, Marshal Tito reiterated the statement he had made at his press conference on Nov. 30, 1968, that Yugoslavia would adhere to its long-standing policy of nonalignment with any military bloc and nonrecognition of any spheres of interest. At the press conference Tito had stressed his admiration for Pres. Charles de Gaulle of France and his friendship with Pres. Gamal Abd-al-Nasser of the U.A.R. Within the framework of nonalignment Yugoslavia remained faithful to the Marxist doctrine.

When East Germany celebrated its 20th anniversary in the early fall of 1969, its position seemed stronger than ever before. Walter Ulbricht, the first secretary of the Socialist Unity Party and chairman of the Council of State, who had directed his country's policy from its beginning, could refer to the great economic progress achieved in the last few years. After its reparation payments to the U.S.S.R. had ceased over a decade earlier, East Germany had become the world's seventh ranking nation in industrial output. Equally satisfactory for Ulbricht was the growing strength of his country in the international field. In 1969 his aspirations were helped by the recognition of East Germany as a sovereign independent state by several Arab nations and Cambodia, and by formation of a West German government under Willy Brandt, the leader of the Social Democrats. The Soviet government seemed near its goal of recognition of the existence of "two independent German states with equal rights."

In neighbouring Poland, the cautiously centrist Wladyslaw Gomulka outmaneuvered the leader of the nationalist-Stalinist party faction, led by Gen. Mieczyslaw Moczar. Moczar had long been minister of the interior and thus in control of the police. In his struggle for power, he relied on the veterans of the partisan war in Poland and on arousing anti-Jewish sentiments. However, Gomulka's conviction of the need for close cooperation with the Soviet Union carried the day in the party.

The quiet and cautious reform policy of Janos Kadar in Hungary had brought about economic reforms that made life generally easier for the population. The Bulgarian regime under Todor Zhivkov followed its traditional policy of close cooperation with the Soviet Union, while at the same time emphasizing national culture and art. Finally, the Romanian Communist Party at its tenth congress in August could reap the benefits of Ceausescu's adroit policy. This son of a village cobbler had succeeded in transforming the Romanian party from an elitist group into a national mass movement. He put the progress of the national economy and the improvement of Romania's international ties with all countries into the foreground of his achievements. At the same time, he emphasized that Romania would not abandon Communist orthodoxy and would cooperate above all with Communist and workers' parties. Like Khrushchev at the 20th congress of the Soviet party in February 1956, Ceausescu put the responsibility for all past "Stalinist" mistakes and domestic persecutions on his late predecessor, Gheorghe Gheorghiu-Dej, though Ceausescu had served as his loyal collaborator for many years.

World Communist Meeting. The normalization and the economic recovery of most of the European Communist states finally allowed the realization of Soviet party general secretary Leonid I. Brezhnev's wish for a World Conference of Communist and Workers' Parties. It was held in Moscow, June 5–17, 1969. The Soviets could find satisfaction in that, after several stormy preparatory meetings, the Moscow conference actually occurred, and that so many parties attended and so many of those present accepted a common declaration of purpose. Also on the credit side were openness and publicity of discussion such as had never been practiced in former party congresses. Of the Communist governments, five (China, North Korea, North Vietnam, Albania, Yugoslavia) were not represented and Cuba sent only an observer. Unanimity was achieved on a small number of rather obvious positions—the coordination of plans to celebrate the centenary of Lenin's birth in April 1970, support of the North Vietnamese and the Viet Cong, condemnation of Israeli aggression, and retention of the existing frontiers in Europe.

The meeting ended with a lengthy declaration of the "tasks at the present stage of the struggle against imperialism." The world socialist system of which the statement spoke embraced all 14 Communist-dominated countries, including China, Albania, Yugoslavia, and Cuba. No one was "excommunicated." Obviously the declaration was the result of much compromise. Problems in connection with China and Czechoslovakia were not discussed, and China was supported with regard to its right to Taiwan and a seat in the UN. The relationship among the Communist countries was defined as a "complex historical process," based upon recognition of proletarian internationalism, the equality and sovereignty of each country, and noninterference in each other's internal affairs. It was stressed that the nonparticipation of some parties in the conference would not affect cooperative efforts with those in attendance.

There was no mention of a centre of the world movement—a tacit acceptance of the principle of polycentrism that the late Italian Communist leader Palmiro Togliatti had demanded before his death in 1964. Togliatti's "unity in diversity" had made great strides within world Communism. A return to monolithic Stalinism, at least in the international field, seemed highly improbable, but only the future could show how far the example of the Moscow conference, with its relative freedom of discussion and avoidance of mutual vituperation, would be followed. (H. Ko.)

See also China; Czechoslovakia; Defense; Intelligence Operations; and articles on the various countries.

ENCYCLOPÆDIA BRITANNICA FILMS. *Poland: Land Under Communism* (1960); *Poland and the Soviet Power* (1961); *Berlin: Test for the West* (1962); *China Under Communism* (1962); *The Soviet Challenge (The Industrial Revolution in Russia)* (1962); *Hungary and Communism: Eastern Europe in Change* (1964); *China: A Portrait of the Land* (1967); *China's Industrial Revolution* (1967); *China's Villages in Change* (1967).

Comoro Islands: *see* Dependent States

Congo, Democratic Republic of the

A country of equatorial Africa, the Congo is bounded by the Central African Republic, Sudan, Uganda, Rwanda, Burundi, Tanzania, Zambia, Angola, the Congo (Brazzaville), and the Atlantic Ocean. Area: 905,559 sq.mi. (2,345,409 sq.km.). Pop. (1969 est.): 16,586,000. Cap. and largest city: Kinshasa (metropolitan pop., 1969, 1,052,520). Language: French; Bantu dialects, mainly Swahili and Lingala. Religion: mainly fetishism. President in 1969, Joseph Mobutu.

KEYSTONE

Pres. Joseph Mobutu during a visit to Greece in March 1969 to discuss areas of possible cooperation between the two countries.

The deaths of two men who had played a leading part in the Congo's achievement of independence occurred in 1969. Joseph Kasavubu, one of the pioneers of the country's independence movement and first president of the new nation, died in March. He had withdrawn from public life late in 1965 when General Mobutu seized power. On June 29, two years after being kidnapped and taken to Algeria, Moise Tshombe, former prime minister of the Congo and before that self-styled president of the secessionist Katanga state, also died, still in captivity (*see* OBITUARIES). There was a further echo from the Congo's recent turbulent past on June 10 when General Ngalo, who took part in the rebellion in Kisangani in 1964 and who had been in hiding since 1965, was captured and executed.

Revolt of a different kind occurred on June 4 when soldiers fired on university and high school students demonstrating to demand higher financial grants. Six students were killed, about twice as many injured, and 34 detained. Fifteen of the latter were charged with plotting against the state. As a sequel to these events the Bulgarian ambassador and the French consul general were both expelled in August, having allegedly assisted in the escape from the country of a number of students who were to have given evidence at the trial of their comrades. Diplomatic relations with Bulgaria were also suspended.

In August, President Mobutu reorganized his Cabinet. Among those to be removed from office was Justin Bomboko, who was later appointed ambassador to the U.S. in succession to Cyrille Adoula, who had himself replaced Bomboko as foreign minister.

In the field of foreign relations the year also began in a disturbed fashion. The fourth conference of heads of state of the African and Malagasy Common Organization (OCAM), meeting in Kinshasa late in January, sent a conciliation mission to Brazzaville in an attempt to find some means of renewing relations between the two Congo states, broken off after Mobutu had ordered the execution of Pierre Mulele in October 1968. As a first step Presidents Mobutu and Marien Ngouabi discussed the possibility of reviving trade across the Congo River. In November, however, there was a renewal of tension.

Relations with the Central African Republic, along with the Congo one of the three members of the Union of Central African States (UEAC), founded only the previous April, began to deteriorate in November 1968. In December, Central African Republic Pres. Jean Bedel Bokassa announced that his country would leave the UEAC to rejoin an earlier economic alliance with Cameroon, Congo (Brazzaville), and Gabon. Mobutu believed that this change of heart had been inspired by the French, who feared that the creation of the UEAC would encourage U.S. trade with the countries concerned to the detriment of French interests. In January Mobutu threatened reprisals against the Central African Republic unless it allowed free access of produce to Chad, the other UEAC member. Later the Central African Republic suspended diplomatic relations with Kinshasa.

In contrast to this unsettled state of affairs the economic condition of the Congo seemed healthier than it had been since independence. This was the result of 18 months of steady improvement following the monetary reforms of June 1967. The high prices offered for copper contributed to this success, but another important factor was the reduction in government spending that Mobutu's policy had achieved. The United States had been the chief supporter of the monetary reforms, while Belgium had limited itself primarily to the provision of technical aid. Having balanced its accounts and built up a reasonable surplus, the government believed it could look forward to a period of expansion. Although the overall economic development plan was not complete, it became clear that, whatever program might be pursued, there would be a need for hydroelectric power. Work was therefore started on the first stage of the Inga project, which involved the channeling of part of the waters of the Congo River into the Deuren Valley.

A delegation from the U.K.'s Manchester Chamber of Commerce visited Congo in February when the

CONGO, DEMOCRATIC REPUBLIC OF THE

Education. (1965–66) Primary, pupils 2,066,809, teachers 55,157; secondary, pupils 70,066, teachers (1962–63) 1,875; vocational, pupils 21,635, teachers (1962–63) 863; teacher training, students 26,377, teachers (1962–63) 943; higher (at 3 universities; 1966–67) students 2,925, teaching staff (1964–65) 443.

Finance. Monetary unit: zaire, with an official exchange rate of 0.50 zaire to U.S. $1 (1.20 zaires = £1 sterling) and free market rate (Sept. 1, 1969) of 0.66 zaire to U.S. $1 (1.58 zaires = £1 sterling). Gold and foreign exchange, central bank: (March 1969) U.S. $129,560,000; (March 1968) U.S. $92,810,000. Budget (1968 est.): revenue 125 million zaires; expenditure 114 million zaires. Money supply: (March 1969) 148,990,000 zaires; (March 1968) 112,560,000 zaires. Cost of living (Kinshasa; 1963 = 100): (Dec. 1968) 339; (Dec. 1967) 286.

Foreign Trade. (1967) Imports 132.7 million zaires; exports 220 million zaires. Import sources: Belgium-Luxembourg 23%; U.S. 22%; France 10%; Italy 9%; U.K. 9%; West Germany 9%. Export destinations: Belgium-Luxembourg 48%; Italy 12%; France 11%; U.S. 8%; West Germany 7%; U.K. 6%. Main exports (1966): copper 57%; tin 6%; diamonds 6%; coffee 6%.

Transport and Communications. Roads (1968) 141,298 km. Motor vehicles in use: passenger (1967) *c.* 43,500; commercial (including buses; 1964) 32,900. Railways: (1966) 5,164 km.; traffic (1967) 457 million passenger-km., freight 1,848,000,000 net ton-km. Air traffic (1968): 358.7 million passenger-km.; freight 12,260,000 net ton-km. Inland waterways (including Congo River; 1966) *c.* 13,500 km. Telephones (Dec. 1967) 23,919. Radio receivers (Dec. 1968) *c.* 60,000. Television receivers (Dec. 1968) *c.* 7,000.

Agriculture. Production (in 000; metric tons; 1967; 1966 in parentheses): palm oil *c.* 178 (*c.* 168); palm kernels *c.* 107 (*c.* 102); rubber (exports; 1968) 33, (1967) 30; cotton, lint 8 (7); coffee 60 (54); peanuts *c.* 113 (*c.* 113); rice (1966) 122, (1965) 109; corn *c.* 250 (*c.* 241); sweet potatoes and yams (1966) *c.* 306, (1965) *c.* 298; cassava (1966) 8,116, (1965) 7,247; sugar, raw value (1968–69) *c.* 44, (1967–68) 36; timber (cu.m.; 1966) *c.* 11,500, (1965) *c.* 11,400. Livestock (in 000; Dec. 1966): cattle 750; sheep 565; goats (Dec. 1965) *c.* 2,409; pigs 405.

Industry. Production (in 000; metric tons; 1967): copper 242; coal (1968) 62; zinc 61; tin 1.8; cobalt ore (metal content) 9.7; manganese ore (metal content) 140; gold (troy oz.) 154; diamonds (metric carats) 13,153; electricity (kw-hr.; 1966) 2,926,000.

Congregational Churches: *see* Religion

minister of national economy, Ferdinand Tumba, stated that the government was anxious to promote the establishment of new companies in the country. This visit was followed by an industrial mission from Belgium, led by Prince Albert, head of Belgium's office for foreign trade. This was the first visit by a member of the Belgian ruling family since independence and was an indication of that nation's growing confidence in the Congo's economic future. This confidence was reflected in the interest shown by the Lonrho company in obtaining all or part of the management contract for the Katanga copper mines, held by Union Minière. (K. I.)

Congo, People's Republic of the

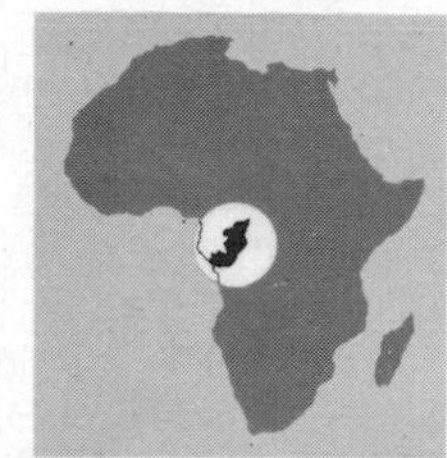

A republic of equatorial Africa, the Congo Republic is bounded by Gabon, Cameroon, the Central African Republic, the Congo (Kinshasa), Angola, and the Atlantic Ocean. Area: 134,749 sq.mi. (349,000 sq.km.). Pop. (1968 est.): 870,000, mainly Bantu Negroes; Europeans 11,000. Cap. and largest city: Brazzaville (pop., 1962 est., 135,632). Language: French and Bantu dialects. Religion: mostly pagan, with a strong Christian minority. President in 1969, Maj. Marien Ngouabi; premier, Maj. Alfred Raoul.

At the beginning of 1969 Maj. Marien Ngouabi, head of the Army and president of the directory of the National Revolutionary Council, became chief of state, replacing Maj. Alfred Raoul. The latter, who had become interim president in September 1968, retained the post of premier.

In February Congolese leaders set in motion a thoroughgoing purge and proceeded to arrest several dozen political personalities and officers. At the same time a decree was published, establishing a Revolutionary Court of Justice in Brazzaville.

A number of political trials took place in Brazzaville in May, June, and July. Two Frenchmen were sentenced for an attempt on the security of the state, one to life imprisonment and the other to ten years. Felix Mouzabakani, former minister of the interior and army commander, was condemned to hard labour for life, while heavy punishments were meted out to other officers, all accused of having attempted to re-establish former Pres. Fulbert Youlou in power. In August four new sentences were announced against persons accused of conspiring with Youlou, who had been ousted in 1963 and was living in exile in Spain.

Although Congolese leaders took every opportunity to proclaim themselves champions of progress, they were not spared confrontation with the demands of various groups within the country. In May students of Brazzaville's centre for higher education vehemently protested against conditions there. Strikes paralyzed Pointe-Noire in July and August.

On December 31 President Ngouabi proclaimed that the nation's new official name would be the People's Republic of the Congo. Also reflecting the leftist orientation of the government were the adoption of the "Internationale" as the national anthem and of a new flag resembling that of the Soviet Union.

In the international arena tension between Israel and the Congo grew, the latter reproaching the Israeli government for aggravating, by its attitude, the situation in the Middle East. On May 15, President Ngouabi paid a five-day official visit to Algeria. An agreement of views was proclaimed on all international matters. Relations with the Congo (Kinshasa) deteriorated in November, when Brazzaville closed its border. (Ph. D.)

CONGO, REPUBLIC OF

Education. (1966–67) Primary, pupils 194,968, teachers 3,264; secondary, pupils 15,939, teachers 512; vocational, pupils 2,931, teachers (1965–66) 132; teacher training, students 562, teachers 50; higher (1965–66), students 840, teaching staff 84.

Finance. Monetary unit: CFA franc, with a parity of CFA Fr. 50 to the French franc (CFA Fr. 277.71 = U.S. $1; CFA Fr. 666.50 = £1 sterling). Budget (1969 est.) balanced at CFA Fr. 15,939,000,000.

Foreign Trade. (1967) Imports CFA Fr. 20,240,000,000; exports CFA Fr. 11,730,000,000. Import sources: France 54%; West Germany 13%. Export destinations: Netherlands 21%; West Germany 18%; U.K. 16%; France 15%; Israel 5%; Congo (Kinshasa) 5%. Main exports: timber 42%; diamonds 34%.

Transport and Communications. Roads (1966) 10,842 km. (including 243 km. with improved surface). Motor vehicles in use (1965): passenger 9,028; commercial 6,830. Railways: (1966) 797 km.; traffic (1967) 128 million passenger-km., freight 396 million net ton-km. Telephones (Dec. 1967) 8,726. Radio receivers (Dec. 1968) 62,000. Television receivers (Dec. 1968) *c.* 1,000.

Agriculture. Production (in 000; metric tons; 1967; 1966 in parentheses): coffee 0.7 (*c.* 0.8); peanuts 17 (20); palm kernels (1966) 6, (1965) 5.6; palm oil (1966) *c.* 7.1, (1965) *c.* 7.1; cassava (1966) *c.* 700, (1965) *c.* 700. Livestock (in 000; 1966–67): cattle *c.* 23; sheep *c.* 50; pigs 18.

Conservation

By 1969 the rapid development of remote sensing, an outcome of space research and scientific reconnaissance for warfare, gave man an extended range of vision to assess the world's land and water resources. Infrared detectors reached the point where aerial observers could pierce clouds of smoke to plot, by the heat emitted, the actual path of a forest fire. Side-looking radar was employed to see through the perpetual cloud cover that had hitherto baffled aerial photography over moist tropical regions. As such physical aids grew more sophisticated, it became possible to identify crop plants from their radiations and even to distinguish healthy and diseased crops.

Improved cameras invented for aerial surveillance by satellites or high-flying aircraft made it possible to record conditions over immense stretches of territory simultaneously and at low cost. In hydrological research, the extent and depth of glaciers and snowfields, which defeated ground exploration, could now be quickly revealed. Even the quality of water was assessable to some degree because of the difference in radiation characteristics between silt-laden rivers and those carrying purer water.

The major problem facing every conservationist, how to assess conditions quickly over vast expanses of terrain, was in sight of solution. With the elaboration of these techniques, skilled interpreters would be able to provide more information within a few hours than had hitherto been possible after months of aerial or ground survey employing only conventional equipment.

Much of this new information was obtained from satellites circling the earth, and was international in character, cutting right across the traditional method of securing facts about each country's resources from

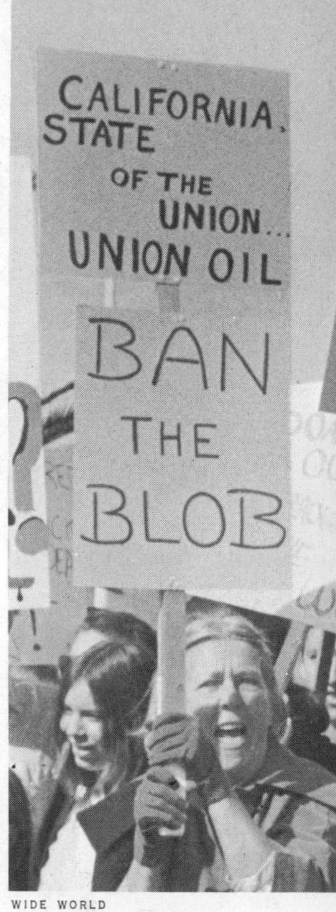

WIDE WORLD

California state worker (below) cleaning oil from Santa Barbara beaches that were fouled by oil from an offshore well. Pickets (above) protest the drilling operations of Union Oil, owner of the leaking well.

WIDE WORLD

D.P.A. FROM PICTORIAL PARADE

Workers scooping dead fish from the Rhine River near Koblenz, W.Ger., in June 1969. An estimated 25 million fish were killed by an insecticide that had been accidentally introduced into the river near Frankfurt.

national surveys that varied widely in extent and accuracy, and were commonly out of date before issue. A better-equipped alien country might now, conceivably, have better forecasts of crop production and timber output than the country itself.

Britain's veteran conservationist, F. Fraser Darling, collaborated with Vladimir Sokolov of the U.S.S.R., Frederick Smith of the U.S., and François Bourlière of France in a study for UNESCO entitled *Impacts of Man on the Biosphere.* According to their report, from the earliest times man had modified his environment. Nomadic pastoralists usually caused steady and irreversible deterioration of grassland to desert, a change that they did not foresee and could not, within the limits of their culture and technology, halt. But both pastoral and arable farmers in the so-called undeveloped countries were able to achieve a harmonious relationship with their environment. Modern techniques, exploiting cash crops for distant markets, could wreck a delicately balanced conservation system far faster than ill-advised husbandry. Man as a world citizen was now obliged to recognize his responsibility to retain desirable environments for himself and his fellows in all countries. But methods of conservation and resource use could not safely be transported from one land to another without fundamental studies of their application to different social and physical surroundings.

Land and Forests. Studies by the Forestry Division of the United Nations Food and Agriculture Organization (FAO) showed that the world would require 30% more timber in 1975 than it did in 1961—an increase of about 20,000,000,000 cu.ft. a year. This caused national forestry authorities everywhere to recast their programs, which hitherto had been based on more modest increases. In Great Britain the Forestry Commission celebrated its 50th anniversary, with 1,800,100 ac. of productive woodland established since 1919. But its economist, A. J. Grayson, calculated that current expansion of forests, running at 70,000 ac. a year, did little more than keep pace with expanding demand, largely for industrial use. Though output of timber would double between 1969 and 1980, consumption would rival this expansion and the proportion of home output would only increase from 10 to 12% or so. In the U.S. Edward P. Cliff, chief of the Department of Agriculture Forest Service, reported that one million acres annually were being restocked on private lands alone. Yet 30 million ac. of unstocked, cutover woodlands needed early replanting to avert future timber famine.

The Australian Forestry Council formulated fresh objectives for commonwealth foresters. It estimated that, by A.D. 2000, Canadian supplies of timber and newsprint would all be absorbed within the North American continent, mainly by the U.S. In common with other countries that had benefited from Canadian exports, Australia was now obliged to plan for self-sufficiency. Planting, now done mechanically with U.S. Lowther machines, was stepped up to 75,000 ac. a year.

Lebanon launched its "Green Plan" as part of the FAO World Food Program. In the highlands, a coordinated plan would safeguard the ancient cedars and promote food production. Intensive agriculture on 15,000 ac. of reclaimed land, supporting a population of 6,000, would be based on fruit- and nut-bearing trees, including olive, almond, apricot, cherry, pear, peach, pistaccio, and plum, together with grapevines. Initial steps were the terracing of the hill slopes and the removal of the ubiquitous goats, age-long enemies of both orchard trees and cedars.

Kenya emerged as a market garden for temperate Europe and a source of fresh farm produce for tropical Africa. Cheap air freight enabled growers to market perishable cut flowers and subtropical fruits in London, Paris, and Hamburg at prices that competed with similar produce from Mediterranean lands and California. The alternative short flight across the African continent made possible deliveries of fresh meat, milk, cream, and cheese to luxury markets in Liberia, Ghana, and Nigeria.

In Australia the Commonwealth Scientific and Industrial Research Organization set up a Rangelands Research Program, headed by R. A. Perry, to investigate the future conservation of the continent's arid and semiarid zones. Surprisingly, this region, occupying 2.2 million sq.mi. in the heart of Australia, was an economic success. It carried 48 million sheep and 4.5 million cattle and produced exports of meat, wool, and hides valued at A$400 million, or 25% of the national export income. Similar grasslands in the Middle East, Asia, and North Africa, where intensive but ill-controlled animal husbandry began around 2000 B.C., had degenerated to steppe and desert by the beginning of the Christian era.

The Australian investigations, based on Deniliquin in New South Wales, which was a winter-rainfall semiarid climate, and on Alice Springs, with its so-called "summer-rainfall" but truly arid climate, would have meteorological, soil-science, botanical, and zoological aspects. Researchers would seek to know how much rain is held by the soil, is used by vegetation, or becomes lost as runoff during brief storms; varying conditions of wind and solar radiation would affect the issue. The life histories of the main grasses and other forage plants would need evaluation to secure adequate reseeding or vegetative spread under grazing pressures. The behaviour of the grazing flocks and herds with respect to food preferences and quantities required, and their physiological reactions to both high temperatures by day and cold by night, would also need fundamental study. Aerial surveys would play a prominent part, a fortunate circumstance being the general freedom from clouds, which elsewhere restrict photography. The results were expected to have applications in other regions of low rainfall, including African deserts, Russian steppes, and American prairies.

In the Netherlands the Institut voor Cultuurtechniek en Waterhuishouding (Institute for Land and Water Management Research) at Wageningen, headed by C. van den Berg, celebrated *A Decade of Research in Land and Water Management* with an explanatory volume. The original impetus behind this institute was the tremendous problem of water supply for Dutch farms, market gardens, and nurseries. The Netherlands has a low rainfall and little high ground. Agricultural water supplies were drawn largely from the Rhine, which was polluted to an increasing degree by chemicals and even common salt. Embanked fields below sea level also suffered from the low-level infiltration of saline water from the North Sea. The desirable concentration of research in intensive horticulture in an industrialized society might be judged by the Netherlands' Westland province, where 80% of the useful surface was under glass. Four-fifths of the rainfall had to be diverted from greenhouse roofs to storage holders for horticultural use and all soil was under close control.

Writing on *Soil Improvement,* G. P. Wind showed that even under intensive Dutch farming methods much soil was only partially used. Physical compaction limited root penetration, and sandy soils were self-compacting even after cultivation. Chemical characteristics such as acidity might confine certain crop roots to limited zones of an otherwise penetrable and fertile soil. Clay soils, when wet, sometimes failed to support the weight of grazing cattle, since a cow's hoof imposes a pressure of 60 psi; penetration of the surface damaged the tissues of the grass plants and could destroy the sward. It was not enough to drain with the latest machinery and fertilize according to a soil chemist's analysis of nutrient deficiency. Conservation demanded exacting inquiries into the behaviour of plant, soil, and stock out in the field before and after treatments.

The Forest Protection Section of the Australian Commonwealth Forest Research Institute, Canberra, pioneered the use of incendiary "bombs" as a fire-control measure. Local conditions made it desirable, on occasion, to start "clean up" fires, under control, on rugged areas of mountain bush, from which an uncontrolled blaze could spread to more valuable forest. Aircraft could rapidly drop scores of small capsules designed to ignite as soon as two chemicals mix, about half a minute after their release from the plane.

B. T. Tatham of Alginate Industries Ltd., writing on "Viscous Water" in the international forestry journal *Unasylva,* outlined a powerful new weapon for forest-fire fighting, developed by Great Britain's Forestry Commission. Sodium alginate, a long-chain polymer extracted from seaweed harvested off Scotland's rugged west coast, raised the viscosity of water and caused it to cling to tree foliage and scrub vegetation, such as gorse and heather. It could be formulated as a dry powder or liquid suspension and effectively mixed with plain water from any source by using a modified centrifugal pump. In contrast to ordinary water, which ran off dry fuel and was largely wasted, every drop of viscous water acted as an effective fire retardant.

In a study entitled "Venezuela's Empty Rain Forests," published in *The Geographical Magazine,* David Harris investigated the critical problem of protein conservation in the Orinoco Basin of South America, where a diminishing population of Guiaca Indians suffered from chronic malnutrition. Although the hot, moist climate promoted dense forest growth, the same factors led to infertile soils. Cultivation was only possible in *conucos* or temporary clearings made with vast labour in mature forest. Manioc, pawpaws, bananas, yams, ocumo, and arrowroot, the Indians' staple crops, provided starch but little protein, since they yielded roots or succulent fruits rather than protein-rich seeds. The virtual extermination of the region's two largest mammals, the tapir and the aquatic manatee, made it impossible to obtain animal protein, other than from small jungle mammals, birds, and river fish.

The age-old equilibrium between Indian culture and a jungle that yielded sparse but perpetual sustenance had been disrupted by European intrusions, with the gun replacing the hunter's blowpipe, and no reversal of the downward trends was in sight. (*See* ANTHROPOLOGY: *Special Report.*) In contrast, the river-valley cultures of Southeast Asia remained vigorous because of their successful protein-rich seed crop, rice; Africans had sorghum, and other American Indians raised corn (maize).

Water. Reviewing hydrological forecasting in the U.S.S.R., V. V. Rahhamanov and A. P. Shastin of the Hydrometeorological Service outlined the great importance of water control to the Soviet economy. The annual outflow of the country's rivers amounted to 4,300 cu.km., or one-ninth of the world total. Many major rivers arise in southern mountains and traverse the hot, arid steppes of Central Asia to reach the plains of Siberia, where they become icebound for much of the year. Irrigation for agriculture, industrial use, power supplies, and navigation all called for accurate forecasts of streamflow. The sampling of winter snow was undertaken on a vast scale with over 3,000 observation points, some in open country, others within forests or deep in mountain ravines.

In Uganda, P. H. Temple of Makerere University College, Kampala, carried out studies of the glaciers on the Ruwenzori Range, 16,791 ft., under the International Hydrological Decade program. These glaciers were unique in their situation virtually on the Equator. Temple found evidence of overall retreat, interrupted locally by pauses and occasional advances. None of these glaciers were major sources of water supply but

COURTESY, POWER AUTHORITY OF THE STATE OF NEW YORK

Cofferdam (top) halting the flow of water over the American portion of Niagara Falls during the summer of 1969. Engineers hoped to find methods of preventing erosion of the falls' rock face.

they could serve as significant indicators of climatic change.

In the state of Kedah the government of Malaysia was constructing the Sungei Muda Irrigation Project, which would allow double-cropping of rice over 400 sq.mi. of coastal land. Though the annual rainfall averaged 90 in., it fell largely in autumn, and only one crop a year had been possible. By constructing a reservoir of 800,000 ac-ft. capacity, and carefully controlling levels by computerized calculations, a second crop would be made possible in the spring.

Thermal pollution increased as a major threat to fish, and indeed to all forms of aquatic life, as more and more electric power plants were constructed in the U.S. While the Federal Water Pollution Control Administration put 93° F as the highest inhabitable temperature for most sorts of fish, biological researchers considered far lower temperatures to be seriously harmful. The practical, but expensive, solution appeared to be the building of great cooling towers that would discharge the waste heat into the atmosphere.

In May a remarkable, large-scale outbreak of marine pollution led to the suspension of phosphorus production by the Electric Company of Canada on the coast of Newfoundland. The British firm of Albright and Wilson had backed this £15 million industrial complex at Long Harbour, which began operations late in 1968. In February 1969 discoloured dead fish were found floating belly up. Later the Canadian federal minister of fisheries, Jack Davis, ordered the plant's closure. At the same time all fishing in one of Newfoundland's richest grounds, Placentia Bay, was suspended because of possible hazards to health while inquiries were pursued to ascertain the actual cause. In July the minister permitted resumption of the plant's operations on a limited scale, following the installation of effluent treatment ponds and a recycling system for waste.

In mid-June a serious international water-supply crisis arose on the lower reaches of the Rhine River. Dead fish, estimated to number 25 million, were found over a long stretch downstream from Mainz in West Germany. Rhine water forms the main supply for the major Dutch cities of Amsterdam, Rotterdam, and The Hague, and the authorities promptly halted abstraction from the river and fell back on storage reservoirs. The Netherlands Institute of Social Health identified the poison as endosulfan, also called Thiodan, an insecticide containing chlorinated hydrocarbon compounds. This was manufactured near Frankfurt, but pollution was first noted well downstream from the plant. It was believed that a moderate quantity, perhaps no more than 220 lb., had seeped out of a lead-plated metal canister that had fallen overboard from a barge. The pollutant took ten days to disappear out to sea. (H. L. En.)

A greatly accelerated public concern about the problems of protecting the quality of the environment was particularly evident in the U.S. in 1969 in the case of water resources. At the beginning of the year, national attention was focused on the problem of water pollution when a leak developed at a Union Oil Company drilling operation in the Santa Barbara Channel off the coast of California. Millions of dollars in damages resulted when the oil blackened miles of scenic coastline and destroyed thousands of fish and birds.

Also pointed out during the year was the fact that pollution in some of the Great Lakes was so severe that it might not be possible to clean up the mess created by industry and man. The nation's rivers, particularly those in the Midwest and the East, were being polluted at an alarming rate. Industry was blamed for a major share of the contamination, but much of the pollution also was caused by untreated domestic sewage dumped into waterways by thousands of communities. While governments could legislate to force industry to comply with water pollution control standards, there was no way to effectively induce the residents of communities to vote in favour of a bond issue to build sewage treatment facilities.

The Interior Department reported in April that all 50 states had submitted acceptable or partially acceptable water quality standards to the federal government under terms of the 1965 Water Quality Act. *Science* magazine, however, reported in August that only 21 of the states had their standards fully approved and about half of those were now considered inadequate and subject to further tightening.

Congress was expected to give final approval to legislation amending the Federal Water Pollution Control Act. The bill would provide federal authority to clean up oil spills regardless of source, with recovery of cost; forbid any federal agency—or those operating on federal leases (such as oil and gas leases)—to pollute waterways; authorize a $50 million revolving fund in the Interior Department for emergency oil cleanup efforts; provide for identification, designation, and cleanup of the discharge of hazardous materials other than oil; extend research authorizations for acid-mine drainage, pollution control in the Great Lakes, and oil pollution; and set up an Office of Environmental Quality in the Executive Office of the President.

Mounting public interest in water pollution control was emphasized in November, when the Senate approved an amended public works appropriations bill that included the largest antipollution expenditure ever passed. More than $1 billion was allocated to clean up the U.S. water supply. This was $400 million above the amount approved by the House and nearly five times what the Nixon administration requested. Meanwhile, the Senate Public Works Committee was considering comprehensive legislation to extend the Solid Waste Disposal Act of 1965 and to authorize more federal funds for the construction of waste treatment facilities and for more research and planning in solid waste disposal. The Federal Water Pollution Control Administration in August reported it was establishing a new program providing for intensive reporting and investigation of fish kills caused by water pollution.

There was considerable discussion about how the cost of water resource development projects would be borne. H. G. Wilm, assistant director for state grants, Water Resources Council, pointed out that a major part of existing and future investment in natural resource development was, and would be, nonfederal. "It has already become true that the federal government cannot afford to pay the share of natural resource development and rehabilitation that it has pledged itself to do," he told the American Society for Public Administration in January. (Wi. L. F.)

Wildlife. In November 1968 representatives of 39 nations met in Rome to consider oil pollution of the sea. Ornithologists J. J. C. Tanis and M. F. Mörzer Bruyns estimated that 150,000 seabirds were killed annually by oil on the eastern side of the Atlantic. The British committee on oil pollution reported the opening of a research unit, under R. B. Clark, department of zoology, University of Newcastle upon

Tyne, to study the treatment and rehabilitation of seabirds, with help from the World Wildlife Fund. Progress toward disposal of oil slicks at sea came with the introduction of the Esso product Corexit, followed, in August 1969, by the Imperial Chemical Industries' Dispersol OS, an emulsifying agent insoluble in water and claimed to be practically harmless to sea life.

Following the Santa Barbara oil leak in February, Ian McMillan, investigator for Defenders of Wildlife, reported that abnormal casualties among elephant seals and infant sea lions on San Miguel Island, part of a proposed national park, might have been caused by the oil. He called for a proper system to gather and disseminate official information on such vital problems as the Santa Barbara disaster.

In June the American Society of Mammalogists considered the situation of marine mammals, including the sea otter, *Enhydra lutris,* which was on the verge of extinction in the early 1900s, but whose population had increased under protection. Demands to stop population growth came from the Californian abalone fishing industry, on the claim that the otters were depleting the abalone stock. Investigation into the population and habits of the otter continued under the University of California and the Fish and Game departments of California and Alaska.

Sightings of sea otters indicated a high survival rate among the 359 otters taken from Amchitka Island, Alaska, and released to repopulate parts of their former range. The colony of northern fur seals discovered on San Miguel Island in 1968 remained under observation. Conservation of the Pacific walrus made progress because reduction in the use of dog teams in the western Arctic lessened demand for meat and because trophy hunters were restricted to one male walrus each year. No improvement was revealed in the situation of the Hawaiian monk seal, *Monachus schauinslandi,* but the population of the northern elephant seal in United States waters showed healthy growth, with a 25% increase of pups over 1968.

In Papua, following an investigation into the crocodile skin industry by H. R. Bustard, partial protection was given to the saltwater crocodile, *Crocodylus porosus,* and to the New Guinea freshwater crocodile, *C. novaeguineae.* In his second investigation into the status of the Nile crocodile, *C. niloticus,* Hugh Cott again stressed the need to prevent visitors from disturbing nesting female crocodiles, who were occupied with maternal duties for nearly six months of the year. In Florida a drive started to stop the slaughter of the endangered American alligator, *Alligator mississippiensis,* in the Everglades National Park, where 40,000 were killed illegally every year.

The Survival Service Commission of the International Union for Conservation of Nature found lack of international cooperation to be a main cause of population declines of marine turtles. Exploitation of adult turtles in Nicaragua threatened protection of breeding colonies in Costa Rica. Surinam and French Guiana protected turtles, but until recently almost all nesting turtles in Guyana had been killed quite legally.

In May the Wild Life Society of Rhodesia reported that the population of the square-lipped (or white) rhinoceros, *Diceros simus,* reached 85, including young born in the national parks. The species had been reintroduced from Natal in 1962 after extermination in Rhodesia 50 years before. There was anxiety, however, about the survival of the slower-breeding black rhinoceros, *Diceros bicornis.* The Zoological Society of Rhodesia said that game ranching, unless strictly controlled, had failed, because the lifting of restrictions on the sale of game meat had given poachers an easy market and because all kinds of killing, such as snares and shooting over water holes at night, were being permitted. Such practices caused waste, especially among newborn young left in the bush while their mothers trekked long distances to water.

In Britain the Mammal Society reported a general, serious decline of the otter except in northwest England and Scotland. The decline was attributed to increased pleasure boat and tourist traffic, increased trapping for the high pelt value (£5 to £7), and to pollution of rivers by pesticides, particularly in wheat-growing districts. Pesticides were also blamed for the death of badgers. Of eight badgers found dead and analyzed at the Nature Conservancy's station at Monks Wood, two killed by automobiles contained average amounts of dieldrin in the liver and six contained hundreds of times more dieldrin in addition to other pesticides. Disregard of the voluntary ban on the use of dieldrin in spring corn dressings was suspected. In May the Royal Society for the Protection of Birds reported the reestablishment of the black-tailed godwit as a breeding bird, the purchase of a reserve on the Ouse Washes to protect this and other marsh birds, and the appointment of a warden to guard them.

In Spain J. A. Valverde reported the acquisition of the Gusdiamar marshes as a nature reserve with the help of the World Wildlife Fund. The reserve covered an area of 13 sq.mi. to the east of the Coto Donana reserve in the Guadalquivir delta. It was also planned to acquire the intervening Hinojos marshes, so as to make a single "National Park of the Marshes."

In July the International Council for Bird Preservation announced that the U.S. had banned the importation of feathers of the gray jungle fowl, *Gallus sonneratii,* an Indian bird threatened with extermination by the demands of fly fishermen for its golden spotted neck feathers or "capes." Following a public appeal launched by the council in cooperation with the World Wildlife Fund, Cousin Island in the Seychelles group was bought and established as a nature reserve.

In New Zealand the Royal Forest and Bird Protection Society reported that the Maori owners of Whakau, Middle, Green, and Korapuki islands had presented them to the crown as nature reserves. The gift of these islands, rich in bird and plant life, extended the Hauraki Gulf Maritime Park. Whakau was especially notable because of the transfer there in 1966 of specimens of the saddleback, one of New Zealand's

Conservationists in 1969 opposed the completion of this partially built jet airport in the heart of Florida's Everglades area. Charging that the construction would upset the ecology of the unique wilderness, they forced a review of the plan.

LARRY HUSTON FROM NANCY PALMER AGENCY

indigenous endangered birds. The proposal to exploit the mineral deposits of Coppermine Island was dropped after preliminary tests had shown that they could not be developed economically. This decision followed local and international protests by naturalists who feared not only the end of this important nature reserve, but also the introduction of rats to this and other islands of the Hen and Chickens group. Stringent regulations were made to protect the Parma wallaby, *Macropus parma,* thought to be extinct in its native Australia but rediscovered on Kawau Island, N.Z., where it had been introduced during the 19th century. (C. L. Be.)

See also Arctic Regions; Biological Sciences; Disasters; Engineering Projects; Fuel and Power; Historic Buildings; Medicine; Mining; Parks; Timber.

Encyclopædia Britannica Films. *Nature's Plan* (1953); *Look to the Land* (1954); *Succession—From Sand Dune to Forest* (1960); *The Cave Community* (1961); *The High Arctic Biome* (1961); *The Community* (1962); *The Grasslands* (1962); *The Temperate Deciduous Forest* (1962); *The Tropical Rain Forest* (1962); *What Is Ecology?* (1962); *The Pond and the City* (1964); *The House of Man: Our Changing Environment* (1965); *Waterfowl: A Resource in Danger* (1965); *Trees and Their Importance* (1966); *Water for Living Things* (1967); *The Everglades: Conserving a Balanced Community* (1968); *Problems of Conservation—Air* (1968); *The House of Man, Part II—Our Crowded Environment* (1969); *Problems of Conservation—Forest and Range* (1969); *Problems of Conservation—Minerals* (1969); *Problems of Conservation—Water* (1969).

Consumer Expenditures

The marked recovery in consumer spending in the major industrialized countries that developed in 1968 was maintained and extended in 1969. Following the check to spending in 1967, notably in the U.S., West Germany, and Britain, a strong expansion in North America contributed to high and inflationary levels of spending in 1968, which spilled over into 1969. In spite of measures aimed at damping down demand, consumer spending around the world showed a substantial increase for 1969 as a whole.

Spending on consumer goods and services in the non-Communist world rose by 9% in value and 4% in volume. Measured in current prices, the increase was above the average of recent years, and it is notable that price increases were well above average. Thus a substantial element of the increase in purchases was due to inflationary pressures, and the rise in the volume of consumption was close to the five-year average. (*See* Table I.)

The evidence of the changes in consumption in the regional groupings from 1965 to 1969 serves as a reminder of the substantial time lag between government action and response in terms of the rate of spending. In the U.S., for example, consumer spending continued to forge ahead in 1969 despite government measures to dampen down the economy.

In West Germany spending leaped ahead in 1969, mainly as a result of the expansionary measures taken by the authorities early in 1968. In France the wage explosion that followed the riots in May 1968 produced an abnormally large rise in incomes in 1969, which was then translated into a substantial increase in consumer spending. It should be noted that the devaluation of the franc during the year and government measures associated with the change would not affect spending until 1970.

The French experience mirrored that of the U.K. following the devaluation of the pound late in 1967. The first effects of devaluation were inflationary, and consumer spending spurted early in 1968. Harsh government measures to cut back consumer spending produced a maximum effect after an interval of nearly a year, so that spending in Britain in volume terms rose by less than 1% in 1969.

The contrasts between regions for spending in both current and fixed prices are shown in Chart 1. Japan is shown separately because of its spectacular rate of growth, unparalleled for a relatively advanced economy with a population of more than 100 million. Total output in Japan in 1969 was second only to that of the U.S. among non-Communist countries, and the rate of growth attained by Japan indicated that it would shortly begin to leave European nations far behind in levels of output and spending. This point is also brought out in Chart 2, which shows the change in consumption per capita between 1963 and 1967. Whereas consumption in volume terms increased by one-third in Japan, consumption per capita in the U.K. increased by only 7%.

Measured in current prices, the discrepancy was even sharper, for consumer prices during this period rose more in Japan than in other major economies. In contrast to North America, where prices rose by 9%, Japanese prices rose by 20%. In Western Europe prices rose by 15%, and for the Organization for Economic Cooperation and Development (OECD) countries as a whole the average rise amounted to 11%.

As can be seen from Chart 1, there was some discrepancy in consumer price movements in 1968 and 1969. In the EEC countries the price rise was lower than average in both years. Price rises were as high as $5\frac{1}{2}$% for both the U.S. and the U.K. in 1969, the rise in the latter being induced in part by the 1967 devaluation. In Japan the price increases again were substantial.

The regional figures mask some important differences between countries, the most notable being the case of West Germany. Because of a dramatic increase in output and output per man in 1968–69, cost and price rises were extremely small. It was not until the second half of 1969 that German consumer prices began to rise at a rate comparable to the international

CHART 1.

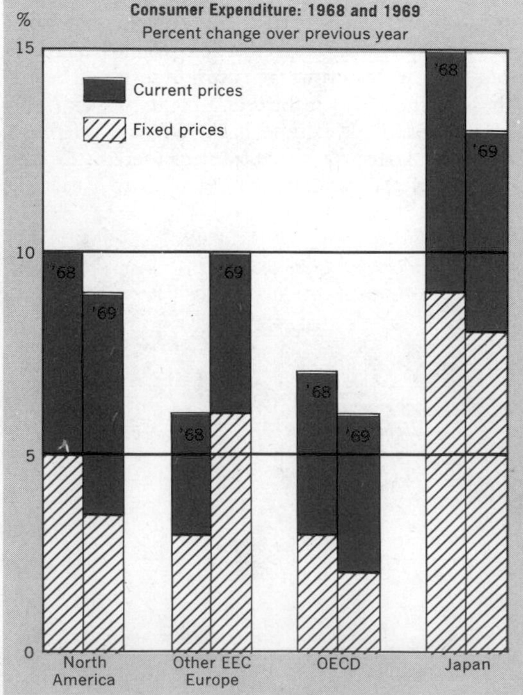

Construction Industry: *see* Engineering Projects; Housing; Industrial Review

Consumer Credit: *see* Money and Banking

average. The fact that German prices were relatively stable in this period as compared with those in competing countries resulted in a disparity in currency values that culminated in the revaluation of the mark at the end of the year.

Australia experienced a strong rise in spending in 1969, originating in part from the vigorous mineral development in progress. In South Africa spending also rose at a good rate, and a significant recovery took place in New Zealand. Developments in Canada were fairly closely in line with those in the U.S., though the growth rate slackened as a result of government measures and the weakness of the world wheat market.

In the U.S.S.R. consumer spending continued to advance at a strong pace, though less rapidly than in 1968. The value of sales increased by about 8%. Personal savings rose at a faster rate, continuing the trend of the preceding few years, and it was notable that production of consumer goods was stepped up in an attempt to meet pent-up demand and to provide incentives for faster growth in labour productivity. Nevertheless, production of cars remained at an extremely low level by comparison with output in Western countries. The construction of the Fiat plant, aimed at meeting part of the car-production deficiency, fell behind schedule. Soviet car production was equal to only 3% of U.S. production (compared with 33% of U.S. production for West Germany and 22% for the U.K.). Considering that the population of the U.S.S.R. was bigger than that of the U.S., the gulf in this form of consumer spending between the two countries was exceptionally wide.

Little was known about developments in China. Production and consumption were disrupted in Czechoslovakia, but elsewhere in Eastern Europe consumption rose substantially. India was benefiting from the devaluation of some years earlier and, more importantly for consumer spending, there was a good increase in grain yields. In countries where agriculture accounts for a large part of total output, consumption is almost impossible to estimate because so much produce is consumed without passing through markets. It seemed certain, however, that the rise in crop yields must have led to a good increase in personal consumption in both India and Pakistan.

CHART 2.

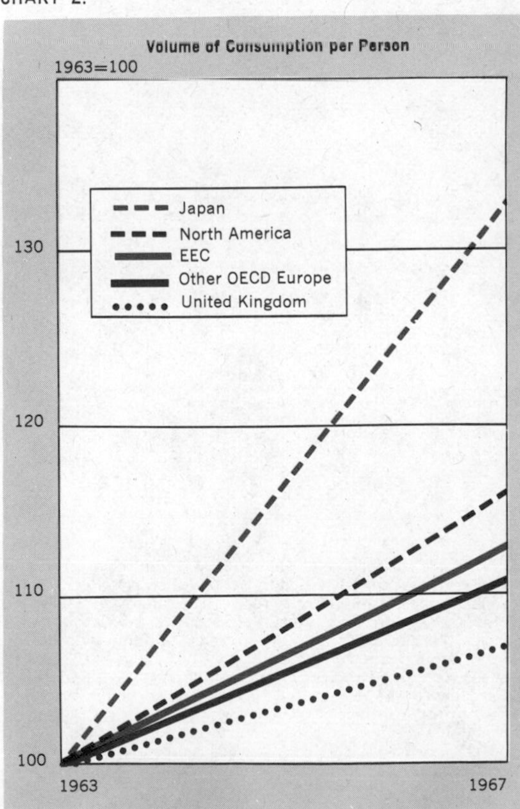

Detailed statistics on the composition of consumer spending are available only after a long delay (1969 national accounts data for the OECD countries as a whole would not be available until 1971). Nevertheless, it is pertinent to examine the trends in spending on the major classes of goods. The most volatile element of spending is for durable goods and appliances. In 1967 there was a pronounced falling off of car sales in the U.S., West Germany, and the U.K. In 1968 there was a large increase in sales, particularly in the U.S. in 1968 and in West Germany in 1969. In the U.K., however, car sales remained static in 1969.

Table II shows the distribution of consumer spending by class of spending for the main OECD groupings. The contrasts are most sharp in the case of food. As income rises, the proportion required for food declines; that is to say, consumption of a fairly wide range of foodstuffs stays roughly the same, regardless of the size of the consumer's income. Thus in a rich country such as the U.S., where income levels are, on the average, two or three times greater than in Western Europe, a much smaller proportion of income is required for basic necessities. Thus only 19% of expenditure was on food in North America, compared with 30% in Europe. Spending on clothing accounted for broadly similar proportions—9% in North America and 11% in Europe—suggesting that clothing can still be regarded as a necessity and that the proportion of consumer spending devoted to clothing declines to some extent as incomes rise.

Spending on housing was in sharp contrast, however. Rent (which for this purpose includes estimates for owner-occupied housing) accounted for 14% of all spending in North America, compared with 10% in Europe. In other words, as incomes rise, spending on housing tends to account for a rising share of consumption. The explanation lies in the fact that housing

Table I. Consumer Expenditure in 1963 Prices

1963=100

Region	1965	1966	1967	1968	1969
North America	113	118	122	128	133
EEC	109	114	118	122	129
OECD Europe	109	113	117	121	125
Japan	117	127	138	150	162
U.K.	106	108	110	113	114

Table II. Expenditure on Various Consumer Items as a Proportion of Total Consumer Expenditure, 1967

Item	North America	EEC	Other OECD Europe
Food	19	31	30
Clothing	9	11	11
Rent	14	10	10
Durables	12	10	8
Other	46	38	41
Total	100	100	100

Table III. Consumer Expenditure in OECD Countries, 1967

Item	Share of total	Per cent increase over previous year
Food	24.7	+4.3
Clothing	10.0	+5.1
Rent	12.2	+7.1
Durables	10.4	+3.5
Other	42.7	+8.3
Total	100.0	+6.3

rapidly ceases to be regarded as a necessary item of shelter and becomes a function of personal wealth and freedom. The area of housing space per person tends to rise with income, as do the housing amenities. In addition, there was a growing trend toward ownership of a second home. A similar trend was apparent for consumer spending on durable goods, with the proportion of total spending going to the purchase of cars, furniture, and appliances rising steadily with the level of income.

A common feature throughout the non-Communist world was the record level of interest rates that developed in response to the world monetary and exchange problems. Against such a background, it was remarkable that consumer spending rose so strongly in 1969. Half the rise was due to inflationary price increases. Nevertheless, the increase of 4% in the volume of spending was a strong development in view of the difficult economic circumstances confronting the U.S., the U.K., and France. (J. G. M.)

Contract Bridge

In an eventful year for contract bridge, pride of place must go to the story of the championship that failed to produce a champion. The European championships were staged in Oslo in late June and early July 1969. An Italian team, which included only two members of their world champion Blue Team, had a runaway victory in the open series. The ladies' series was much more closely contested and with one round to play there were two possible winners, Great Britain and France. Great Britain led by one point and both it and France seemed likely to score a maximum eight points in their final matches against Denmark and Greece, respectively. At half time, however, both were surprisingly down and the French ladies, the first to finish, finally lost 6–2. Their hopes now depended on the Danish ladies winning 7–1, but Denmark had in fact won 5–3.

The British ladies were published as the winners, the celebrations went on into the night, and disillusionment came the following morning. At one of the tables in the Great Britain-Denmark match the time limit had been exceeded by 13 minutes in the first half of the match. Although this had apparently been noted, no action had been taken. Generally, on the first two occasions on which a team was involved in slow play the penalty was in the form of a warning, which was intended to serve as a deterrent. Neither team had been previously warned, but a special rule existed in respect of the final round of the championship and the effect of it was that Great Britain and Denmark became liable to a fine of two victory points.

The day after the championship, the appropriate committee met, found that the time limit had in fact been exceeded by 13 minutes, and penalized Great Britain and Denmark two victory points. This reduced Great Britain to level terms with France, and since France had the better "goal average" it became the winner. The British team appealed, but the decision was upheld. The French team renounced the title but accepted the winners' prizes. The British team was presented with the runner-up prizes, which they courteously returned to the organizing committee. And the records showed that while 13 countries competed in the ladies' championship, not one of them was declared the winner.

The Italian Blue Team, which had held the Bermuda Bowl, the official world championship, continuously since 1957 announced that it would defend it for the last time in May 1969 in Rio de Janeiro. The team went out in a blaze of glory to complete a record that may be unparalleled in any other game or sport. It had won the Bermuda Bowl on ten successive occasions and won the second and third team Olympiads in 1964 and 1968 (the Bermuda Bowl not being played for in Olympic years). Giorgio Belladonna, Massimo d'Alelio, and Pietro Forquet were on all 12 winning teams. Walter Avarelli was missing once only, in 1963. Benito Garozzo joined the team in 1961 and Camillo Pabis Ticci joined in 1963.

The year 1969 also welcomed a new and unexpected challenge. Italy's opponents in Rio de Janeiro were the United States, representing North America; Brazil, the South American champions; France, representing Europe; and Taiwan, making its first world championship appearance as the representative of the Far Eastern Zone. The five competing countries met each other three times in order to qualify two teams for the final. It was generally expected that France and the U.S. would dispute the right to meet Italy in the final. However, Taiwan, a team with no practiced partnerships and little international experience, surprised everybody by reaching the final in convincing style. Though they were no match for the Italians, they ended on a high note, winning the very last hand of the championship, played for them by M. F. Tai and Patrick Huang (*see* box, below).

Of the Eastern European countries, Poland, Czechoslovakia, Hungary, and Yugoslavia were already active participants in international bridge. There was a sizable competition program and a healthy membership in the U.S.S.R., which might reasonably be expected soon to enter into international competition.

Though the British players Terence Reese and

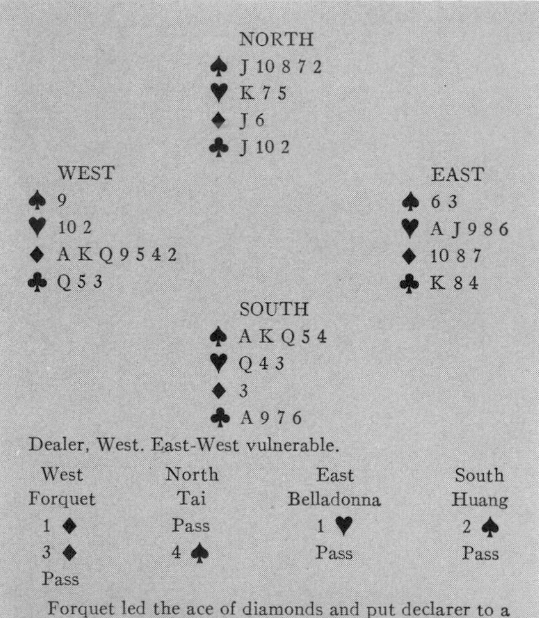

NORTH
♠ J 10 8 7 2
♥ K 7 5
♦ J 6
♣ J 10 2

WEST
♠ 9
♥ 10 2
♦ A K Q 9 5 4 2
♣ Q 5 3

EAST
♠ 6 3
♥ A J 9 8 6
♦ 10 8 7
♣ K 8 4

SOUTH
♠ A K Q 5 4
♥ Q 4 3
♦ 3
♣ A 9 7 6

Dealer, West. East-West vulnerable.

West	North	East	South
Forquet	Tai	Belladonna	Huang
1 ♦	Pass	1 ♥	2 ♠
3 ♦	4 ♠	Pass	Pass
Pass			

Forquet led the ace of diamonds and put declarer to a stern test when he switched to the ten of hearts at trick 2. Without hesitation Huang rose with dummy's king of hearts. East won and returned a heart for declarer's queen. Declarer was now able to cross to dummy on the second round of trumps and lose a club finesse to West, who was unable to lead a further heart, and dummy's third heart was eventually discarded on declarer's long club. After Forquet's excellent switch at trick 2 declarer would have failed in his contract had he played a low heart from the table. Taiwan thus ended the Bermuda Bowl championship with a winning board.

Boris Schapiro were eligible for competition at all levels after a story that had dragged on since they had been accused of cheating in the world championships in Buenos Aires in 1965, Reese himself added a further chapter when he withdrew from the British selection trials at a stage when he seemed certain to qualify. R. Swimer, who had been the British nonplaying captain when Reese and Schapiro were accused of cheating in Buenos Aires, was one of the competitors in the trials. In the course of the trials an action for libel, arising out of the Buenos Aires affair, was heard, and in it Swimer gave evidence at variance with the British Bridge League position (a full acceptance of its own Foster Report and vindication of the two players). Reese expressed himself unable to continue in trials in which Swimer was also a competitor, and several other players withdrew in sympathy with him. The validity of the trials was thereby considerably weakened. There was every prospect that the troubles were now at an end and that Great Britain would be fully represented in the Pairs Olympiad and the European championships in 1970. (HA. FR.)

Cooperatives

During 1969 the process of integration continued within the cooperative movements of a number of countries, in an effort to meet the growing competition from centralized enterprises.

In Austria the Reform Commission submitted a report recommending the establishment of a cooperative structure to reorganize consumer societies, replacing small shops by large self-service units and regrouping central warehouses. A National Cooperative Council was established in France by the central organizations of consumers, workers' productive, low-rent housing, fisheries, and credit cooperatives. For the first time in the history of the French Cooperative Movement, the various branches of cooperation, with the exception of the agricultural sector, were brought together to define their aims and to decide on policy. Progress was made in the implementation of the new policy of centralized planning and coordination in the consumer movement of West Germany. The main feature of the modernization drive was a massive publicity campaign on a national scale, using the COOP symbol for the first time.

A special congress held in March 1969 in the Netherlands rejected an expert committee's proposal that the consumer movement should be organized into one national society. A working party was set up to review the recommended changes. The process of reconstituting the organizational structure of the Polish consumer movement was virtually completed, with new regional cooperatives providing a number of centralized services for local retail societies. In Switzerland the trend toward increased concentration was accelerated during 1969. The annual congress approved changing the name of the Swiss Union of Consumer Cooperatives to COOP Swiss. In the U.K. the number of consumer societies was reduced by 86 to 539 during 1968. Talks on integration of the 100-year-old Cooperative Union with the Cooperative Wholesale Society (CWS)—excluding the Scottish CWS—were initiated.

The International Cooperative Alliance. At the end of 1969, the number of cooperative federations with membership in the ICA totaled 142 in 59 countries. The first youth conference organized by the ICA, held in London in May 1969, discussed the problem of attracting youth to cooperative ideas. A meeting of the ICA Research Officers' Group, held in August in Helsinki, Fin., discussed "Research Techniques for Analysing the Cooperative Image." The 38th International Cooperative Seminar, held in Czechoslovakia in September, discussed the position of a member in a cooperative society.

In May a conference on "Coop Integration," organized by the ICA Committee on Retail Distribution in Stockholm, dealt with the integration of wholesaling and retailing. The first International Seminar for technical executives of building cooperatives, organized by the ICA Committee for Workers' Productive and Artisanal Societies, was held in Genoa, Italy, in March.

The work of the ICA Regional Office and Education Centre for South East Asia was discussed at a meeting of the Advisory Council for South East Asia, held in Teheran, Iran, in March. "Training of Indian Cooperative Personnel Abroad" was the subject of a seminar organized by the Regional Office and the Swedish Cooperative Centre in New Delhi, India, in February. A national seminar on "Consumer Cooperation" was held at the University of Teheran in May with the assistance of the Regional Office. The first international cooperative study course organized by the cooperative movement of Australia and the commonwealth government was held from March 24 to May 7. The course was based on an examination of the establishment and management of cooperatives in rural areas. Cooperative organizations in Southeast Asia participated in the second Asian International Trade Fair, held in Teheran during October.

The work of the ICA Office for East and Central Africa was discussed at meetings of the Cooperative Council in February and March, with representatives from Kenya, Tanzania, and Uganda in attendance. A seminar to bring the leaders of the national organizations in the three countries together was held in Moshi, Tanzania, in April.

The Latin American Institute for Cooperative Integration, supported by the Organization of Cooperatives of America, the International Cooperative Alliance, and Kooperativa Förbundet, Sweden, began operations at the beginning of 1969. The institute initiated two projects: one in Pôrto Alegre, Braz., and the other in El Salvador.

The 24th congress of the International Cooperative Alliance took place in Hamburg, W.Ger., in September. The central theme was "Contemporary Cooperative Democracy" in the free market and in planned economies. The paper presented by the ICA secretariat argued that greater rationalization and centralization were required to meet the pressures of competition, that decision making was increasingly being entrusted to professional management, and that the gap between members and management was thereby widened. Machinery had to be provided for more effective representation of the views of individual members, and members had to be stimulated to participate in the affairs of their cooperative. Reforms of structures were considered a precondition to any improvement in efficiency in the market economy countries. This would allow better operation of democracy within better managed cooperative organizations.

In the planned-economy countries, rationalization continued only up to the limits beyond which the process would hamper member participation. One of the new ways of increasing such participation was the formation of member committees at the shop level.

An International Declaration of Consumer Rights was unanimously adopted by the ICA congress. The declaration, prepared in consultation with the ICA Consumer Working Party, opened with a short statement of rights: (1) a reasonable standard of nutrition, clothing, and housing; (2) adequate standards of safety and a healthy environment free from pollution; (3) access to unadulterated merchandise at fair prices and with reasonable variety and choice; (4) access to relevant information on goods and services and to education on consumer topics; and (5) influence in economic life and democratic participation in its control. Other resolutions receiving approval dealt with intercooperative trade, cooperative housing, cooperative legislation in developing countries, and the role of women in cooperative enterprises. Also adopted were a resolution reaffirming the ICA's strong support for all forthright efforts in the pursuit of peace and a call to member organizations to increase their support of technical assistance programs in the less developed countries through the ICA Development Fund.

Progress in cooperative insurance was reported at one of the conferences that preceded the ICA congress. The ICA Insurance Committee had 57 affiliated members from 25 countries in 1969, and all were expanding their business in spite of increased competition. The Insurance Development Bureau, together with the Reinsurance Bureau, continued to survey the possibilities for cooperative insurance in various countries. Reinsurance contracts in force had risen from 117 in 1952 to nearly 550 in 1969, when the amount of business totaled almost £5 million.

"Collaboration with UN Organizations" and "Cooperative Housing Projects in Developing Countries" were discussed at the ICA Housing Conference. A feasibility study to develop cooperative housing in East Africa was completed by the International Cooperative Housing Development Association, under the auspices of the Economic Commission for Africa (ECA).

The activities of the ICA Agricultural Committee were discussed at the Agricultural Conference. Two studies engaging the committee were on "Cooperative Processing and Marketing for the Development of Agriculture" and "The Financing of Cooperative Enterprise at the International Level." The subcommittee dealing with fisheries cooperatives received the report of a mission to Ceylon, which had carried out a feasibility study on a cooperative fish-canning factory.

Considerable progress in cooperative trade was reported at the annual meeting of the Cooperative Wholesale Committee. Food sales had increased, mainly through the joint use by CWC members of existing buying offices of the Scandinavian Cooperative Wholesale Society in Santos, Braz., and San Francisco and of the English CWS in Sydney, Austr. Purchases in canned fruit had risen from £120,000 in 1966 to £650,000 in 1968, while purchases in the nonfood sector had increased by 83% in the same period.

The International Cooperative Petroleum Association at its annual meeting reported a steadily expanding influence. One of its most remarkable achievements was assisting the government of Ceylon in building its own oil refinery.

Membership and Trade. The latest statistics available showed, for the first time, a decrease in the total number of societies in membership with the ICA —from 611,523 in 1966 to 593,712 in 1967—almost entirely as a result of amalgamation. Membership within these societies had risen 10.82% over 1966—from 230,547,925 to 255,508,443. The largest increase in both number of societies and membership was recorded in the U.S. The largest membership was again reported in the U.S.S.R. (over 56 million), followed by India (over 53 million). Of the total membership, the greatest proportion was in consumer societies (44.14%), followed by credit societies (27.85%), agricultural societies (18.02%), miscellaneous societies (5.21%), building and housing societies (2.33%), workers' productive and artisanal societies (1.9%), and fisheries societies (0.55%).

The total trade of cooperative societies affiliated with the ICA reached $107.3 million in 1967. Consumer societies had a turnover of more than $60,285,000. The total turnover of the international trading federations was somewhat less than in the preceding year. At the end of 1968, 20 cooperative organizations and 15 banks were shareholders in the International Cooperative Bank. Turnover amounted to $88,296,000 in 1968, compared with $66,264,000 in 1967, an increase of 33%.

Other Activities. Continued progress was made in the collaboration between the ICA and the UN. The ICA was classified in the "general" category by the UN Trade and Development Board, and the UN Economic and Social Council (Ecosoc) committee for nongovernmental organizations agreed to assign it Category I status.

A resolution concerning the role of the cooperative movement in economic and social development was approved by Ecosoc in June. A study on "The Role of Cooperatives in the Industrialization of Developing Countries," commissioned by the International Labour Organization, was carried out by the ICA. The second ad hoc consultation on agricultural cooperatives and other farmers' associations in Africa, sponsored by the Food and Agriculture Organization, the International Labour Organization, the ECA, the International Federation of Agricultural Producers, and the ICA, was held in Nairobi, Kenya, in June.

(L. Ke.)

Cosmetics

The year 1969 saw the rediscovery of soap and water as a cleansing agent for the face. At first sight this appeared to be a move in the right direction for the woman who resented the high cost of prestige cleansing creams. Hopes were quickly dispelled, however, when the price of face soaps was announced by such leading firms as Estée Lauder and a new cosmetic-producing group, Clinique. A box of two bars of Estée Lauder Almond Meal Scrub soap carried a price tag of £2 15*s.* ($5), while a "clinically formulated" six-ounce cake of facial soap by Clinique was offered at the astronomical price of £3 6*s.* ($7.50).

Another breakthrough in the cosmetics field, again by Clinique, was the marketing of fragrance-free beauty products. The philosophy behind them was: "We adore perfume but it is Clinique's view that a woman should be free to choose her own fragrance, not have it imposed on her in every cosmetic she chooses." Clinique claimed that its hypoallergenic products were subjected to three forms of medically monitored testing.

Faced with the eternal question in the highly com-

Copper:
see Mining

Corn:
see Agriculture

High fashion makeup introduced by Max Factor in 1969 included the breezy look (bottom), the gallery look (centre), and the star look (top).

petitive beauty business—"What next?"—Revlon answered by concentrating on woman from the neck down. In addition to a "Moon Drops" bath collection of sulfur, seawater, and milk treatments, Revlon put on the market the "Borghese Body Pride" collection, named after the Italian cosmetician Princess Marcella Borghese. It included a body night cream, a leg conditioning lotion, and a cleaning gel, aimed, according to a brochure, "at the woman who understands that nudity is a liberating self-awareness."

"There's nothing so sexy as looking as if you'd just cried," said Mary Quant at the launching of her "bedraggled eyelashes" in the spring of 1969. Despite the decline of the "emphatic eye" vogue, the false eyelash business continued to prosper. The British company Eyelure maintained its dominance over the market. In 1968 Eyelure sold five million pairs of false eyelashes in the U.K. and exported over £750,000 worth, an achievement that won for the company the Queen's Award to Industry and an export gold medal. In 1969 Eyelure was reported to be "revamping a special shape for the important Japanese market."

In the spring of 1969, following its earlier venture into the lipstick and nail polish field, the House of Dior introduced a comprehensive cosmetic range comprising nearly a hundred items with colour coordination as the dominant factor. Singled out was "Eau Tendre" (eye makeup remover), for which the company claimed an effect "similar to that of tears." Carrageen or Irish moss, a form of marine algae, was used by Dorothy Gray as the basic ingredient in a new range of skin foods called "Satura Algene." This "protein to protein" theory in skin treatment was the basic concept behind the "marine" products introduced in Paris by Ingred Millet in the fall of 1968. Of these, the two most important were "Crème Ostrea" (oyster cream) and a mud face-pack called "Marinea."

The trend toward a "healthier," more natural look in makeup continued in 1969. In its spring promotion, Revlon described its Ultima II "Transparent Face Tints" as "see-through, fresh-aired, sunny." The "Miss Ayer" face was said to have the "delicate shades of a watercolour painting." (P. W. HE.)

See also Fashion and Dress.

Costa Rica

A Central American republic, Costa Rica lies between Nicaragua and Panama and has coastlines on the Caribbean Sea and the Pacific Ocean. Area: 19,650 sq.mi. (50,900 sq.km.). Pop. (1968 est.): 1,615,480, including white and mestizo 97.6%. Cap. and largest city: San José (pop., 1968 est., 196,720). Language: Spanish. Religion: predominantly Roman Catholic. President in 1969, José Joaquín Trejos Fernández.

In 1969 Costa Rica continued to progress, despite repeated altercations with its partners in the Central American Common Market. These were caused first by the Legislative Assembly's refusal to ratify the San José Protocol, signed by government representatives of the five member countries on June 1, 1968. This protocol required the imposition for five years of a 30% surcharge on import duties for nonessential goods imported from outside Central America and permitted emergency sales taxes of 10 and 20%, respectively, on semiluxury and luxury goods produced within Central America. The second cause of the difficulties was the government's refusal to permit imports of rice from El Salvador at a time when there was a heavy surplus of Costa Rica's own rather more expensive rice.

In political affairs the impasse between the president (Partido de Unificación Nacional) and the Assembly majority (Partido de Liberación Nacional) continued. The most serious example of this was the

COSTA RICA

Education. (1966–67) Primary, pupils 296,058, teachers 9,354; secondary, pupils 47,828, teachers (1965–66) 1,931; vocational, pupils 6,034, teachers (1965–66) 284; teacher training (1965–66), students 2,108, teachers 22; higher (including University of Costa Rica; 1965–66), students 7,229, teaching staff 617.

Finance. Monetary unit: colón, with a par value of 6.625 colones to U.S. $1 (15.90 colones = £1 sterling). Gold and foreign exchange, central bank: (June 1969) U.S. $30.9 million; (June 1968) U.S. $20.7 million. Budget (1969 est.) balanced at 720 million colones. Gross national product: (1967) 4,486,000,000 colones; (1966) 4,149,000,000 colones. Money supply: (March 1969) 915 million colones; (March 1968) 808.1 million colones. Cost of living (San José; 1963 = 100): (May 1969) 111; (May 1968) 107.

Foreign Trade. (1968) Imports 1,417,400,000 colones; exports 1,141,100,000 colones. Import sources (1967): U.S. 39%; Japan 9%; West Germany 8%; U.K. 7%; El Salvador 6%; Guatemala 6%. Export destinations (1967): U.S. 48%; Nicaragua 8%; West Germany 8%. Main exports: coffee 32%; bananas 26%.

Transport and Communications. Roads (1966) *c.* 10,000 km. (including *c.* 5,000 km. all-weather and 660 km. of Pan-American Highway). Motor vehicles in use (1967): passenger 29,800; commercial (including buses) 15,900. Railways (1967) 703 km. Air traffic (1968): 110.6 million passenger-km.; freight 8,570,000 net ton-km. Telephones (Jan. 1968) 27,498. Radio receivers (Dec. 1965) 130,000. Television receivers (Dec. 1967) 66,000.

Agriculture. Production (in 000; metric tons; 1967; 1966 in parentheses): coffee *c.* 77 (*c.* 73); bananas *c.* 548 (*c.* 523); sugar, raw value (1968–69) 155, (1967–68) 146; dry beans 19 (19); cocoa (1967–68) 7.4, (1966–67) 9. Livestock (in 000): cattle (1967–68) *c.* 1,400; pigs (1965–66) *c.* 146.

Industry. Electricity production (1967) 757 million kw-hr. (92% hydroelectric).

failure to approve the San José Protocol: it was voted down in December 1968 despite votes in its favour by two Assembly committees, both with Liberacionista majorities. Later the Liberacionista candidate for president in the 1970 election, former Pres. José Figueres, called for approval of the Protocol, in an effort to persuade the Assembly majority to reverse its decision.

Of the candidates for the presidential election in February 1970, Figueres was believed to stand ahead of the Unificacionista candidate, former Pres. Mario Echandi Jiménez. This was partly because for 20 years no party had won two consecutive presidential elections and partly because of Figueres' high reputation in the country.

The considerable economic progress of 1968 continued in 1969. Costa Rica's rate of economic growth in 1968 was probably the highest in Latin America—10.2% at current prices or 8% at constant prices. This was attributed partly to the 13% increase in total manufacturing output and partly to the large growth in the quantity of bananas for export. There was also an improvement in public finance and in trade: the budget deficit in 1968 was less than half that of 1967 and promised to be even smaller in 1969. With the expected growth in banana exports, total exports in 1968 rose to $174 million, against only $144 million in 1967. The free rate for the Costa Rican colón continued to appreciate until it reached 6.95 colones per U.S. dollar (selling) in mid-April—only 33 points below the official selling rate.

By August relations with the international lending agencies, which had been poor as a result of Costa Rica's preference for deficit financing and for dual rates of exchange, and also because of the San José Protocol delay, improved sufficiently for the World Bank to lend the nation more than $18 million for the expansion of electric power and telecommunications.

Private foreign capital continued to flow into Costa Rica. Despite the prohibition on the taking of deposits by foreign banks, there was sufficient confidence in Costa Rica's future to induce two large international banks, the Bank of London and Montreal and the First National City Bank of New York, to establish finance companies in San José with the ultimate hope of converting them into bank branches.

The agreement signed in November 1968 between the Aluminum Company of America (Alcoa) and the government for a $71 million investment in the mining of bauxite and its conversion into alumina, near San Isidro del General, was expected to result in a greatly increased foreign exchange income for Costa Rica. (J. C. G. B.)

Cricket

Cotton: *see* Agriculture; Industrial Review
Council for Mutual Economic Assistance: *see* Economic Planning
Council of Europe: *see* European Unity
Credit and Debt: *see* Government Finance; Money and Banking; Payments and Reserves, International

In 1968–69 international cricket was played between West Indies and Australia, West Indies and New Zealand, Pakistan and England, England and West Indies, and England and New Zealand.

Australia v. West Indies. West Indies under G. S. Sobers lost a series in Australia 3–1. After losing the first test, Australia under W. M. Lawry proved far too strong for a side that included some players who were past their prime. Against weak bowling, Lawry, K. D. Walters, and I. M. Chappell scored nine centuries, and Walters achieved a record of 242 and 103 in the fourth test at Adelaide, while G. D. McKenzie and A. N. Connolly (both fast medium) had good support from leg spinner J. W. Gleeson. For West Indies, only Sobers and B. F. Butcher, who made two centuries each, lived up to their batting reputation, and, with W. W. Hall and C. C. Griffith lacking their former speed and accuracy, the bulk of the bowling was done by Sobers (18 wickets) and L. R. Gibbs (24 wickets). To add to the West Indies problems, Sobers was worried with a shoulder injury which affected his bowling.

West Indies won the first test at Brisbane by 125 runs. In the first innings they made 296 (M. C. Carew 83, R. B. Kanhai 94). Australia responded with 284 (Lawry 105, Chappell 117); West Indies then made 353 (C. H. Lloyd 129, Gleeson five for 122), and Sobers (six for 73) and Gibbs (three for 82) bowled Australia out for 240. Australia won the second test at Melbourne by an innings and 30 runs. West Indies, sent in to bat, were bowled out for 200 (McKenzie eight for 71). A partnership of 298 between Lawry (205) and Chappell (165) virtually won the match, Australia making 510, to which West Indies replied with 280 (S. M. Nurse 74, Sobers 67, Gleeson five for 61). Australia also won the third test at Sydney by ten wickets. West Indies made 264 (Lloyd 50, Sobers 49) and 324 (Butcher 101, Kanhai 69); Australia made 547 (Walters 118, I. R. Redpath 80, E. W. Freeman 76) and 42 for no wicket. West Indies fought back in the fourth test at Adelaide. A record 1,764 runs were scored, and West Indies just failed to separate the last Australian pair, so the match was drawn. West Indies made 276 (Sobers 110) and 616 (Butcher 118, Carew 90, Kanhai 80, D. A. J. Holford 80, Connolly five for 122). Australia replied with 533 (Walters 110, Chappell 76, Lawry 62, K. R. Stackpole 62) and 339 for nine (Chappell 96, Lawry 89, Walters 50, Stackpole 50). Australia won the fifth test at Sydney by 382 runs. A partnership of 336 between Lawry (151) and Walters (242) settled the issue, Australia making 619. West Indies replied with 279 (Carew 64, Lloyd 53). Australia in their second innings made 394 for eight declared (Redpath 132, Walters 103), and West Indies, after a blaze of strokes by Sobers (113) and Nurse (137), finally made 352.

New Zealand v. West Indies. West Indies drew a short rubber, winning the first test, losing the second, and drawing the third. A cricket-weary Sobers played a small part, but brilliant batting by Nurse (two centuries) and Carew (one) compensated in part. Reserve fast bowler R. M. Edwards was the chief wicket-taker. For New Zealand B. R. Taylor and B. F. Hastings made one century each, B. E. Congdon, G. R. Dowling (captain), and G. M. Turner all batted steadily, and R. C. Motz was the leading bowler (17 wickets).

West Indies won the first test at Auckland, N.Z., by five wickets. New Zealand made 323 (Taylor 124, Congdon 85) and 297 for eight declared (Dowling 71, V. Pollard 51 not out). West Indies made 276 (Carew 109, Nurse 95), and a brilliant 168 by Nurse, supported by Butcher (78 not out), enabled West Indies to score 348 for five. In the second test New Zealand won a famous victory (only the fifth in their test history) at Wellington, N.Z., by six wickets. West Indies made 297 (Butcher 50, J. L. Hendriks 54 not out, Motz six for 69) to which New Zealand replied with 282 (Turner 74, Congdon 52, Edwards five for 84). Good bowling by Motz, B. W. Yuile, and R. S. Cunis had West Indies out for 148 (Butcher

59), and New Zealand then made 164 for four (Hastings 62 not out). The third test at Christchurch, N.Z., was drawn. West Indies made 417 (Nurse 258, Carew 91, Motz five for 113). New Zealand made 217 and, following on, made 367 for six (Hastings 117 not out, Dowling 76).

Pakistan v. England. After the Marylebone Cricket Club (MCC) tour of South Africa had been canceled, a short tour of Pakistan was arranged but was abandoned because of political riots in Pakistan. All three tests were interrupted by violent spectators and were drawn, with cricketers unable to concentrate. For England M. C. Cowdrey (captain), B. L. D'Oliveira, C. Milburn, and T. W. Graveney each made one century, and D. J. Brown, R. M. C. Cottam, and D. L. Underwood shared most of the wickets. For Pakistan the best batting came from three men playing in English county cricket, Majid Jehangir, Mushtaq Muhammad, and Asif Iqbal. The most effective bowlers were Saeed Ahmad (the captain), Asif Masood, and Intikhab Alam.

England v. West Indies and v. New Zealand. England at home had a successful summer, winning short rubbers against West Indies and New Zealand 2–0 each. England's most successful batsmen were G. Boycott with two centuries against the West Indies, and J. H. Edrich with two against New Zealand. Other centuries were scored by R. Illingworth, the new England captain, and J. H. Hampshire against West Indies, and by P. J. Sharpe against New Zealand. The most successful bowlers were Brown, B. R. Knight, and J. A. Snow against West Indies, while Underwood took 24 New Zealand wickets for only 9.16 each. For West Indies Sobers, once more captain, was not the force of old, either with bat or ball. C. A. Davis made the only century, and Butcher was the most consistent batsman. The medium-paced J. N. Shepherd took most wickets (12), and Sobers took 11. For New Zealand, Hastings, Congdon, and Turner each made over 50 at least once, while the outstanding bowler was slow left-arm H. J. Howarth (8 wickets) supported by Taylor (10), Motz (7), and D. R. Hadlee (6), all fast medium.

Against the West Indies England won the first test at Old Trafford by ten wickets. They made 413 (Boycott 128, Edrich 58, Graveney 75, D'Oliveira 57). West Indies replied with 147, Snow and Brown taking four wickets each. West Indies then made 275 (R. C. Fredericks 64), and England responded with 12 for no wickets. The second test at Lords was drawn. West Indies made 380 (Davis 103, Fredericks 63, S. G. Camacho 67, Snow five for 114). England, after losing their first five wickets for 61, made 344 (Hampshire 107, Illingworth 113, A. P. Knott 53). West Indies declared its second innings at 295 for nine (Lloyd 70, Fredericks 60, Sobers not out 50), and in its second innings England made 295 for seven (Boycott 106, Sharpe 86). England won the third test at Headingley by 30 runs. England made 223 (Edrich 79) and 240 (Sobers five for 42), while West Indies scored 161 and 272 (Butcher 91, Camacho 71).

Against New Zealand, England won the first test at Lords by 230 runs. England made 190 (Illingworth 53) and bowled New Zealand out for 169, Illingworth and Underwood taking four wickets each. In its second innings England made 340 (Edrich 115) and, though Turner carried his bat for 43 not out, New Zealand was bowled out for 131 (Underwood seven for 32). The second test at Trent Bridge was ruined by rain and was drawn. New Zealand made 294 (Hastings 83, Congdon 66), to which England replied with 451 for eight declared (Edrich 155, Sharpe 111). In its second innings New Zealand made 66 for one. England won the third test at the Oval by eight wickets. New Zealand made 150 (Turner 53, Underwood six for 41) and 229 (Hastings 61, Underwood six for 60). England made 242 (Edrich 68) and 138 for two (M. H. Denness 55 not out).

County and National Cricket. Glamorgan won the English County Championship and was undefeated. Gloucestershire placed second and Surrey third. Yorkshire, champions for the previous three years, had a disastrous summer and finished 13th. They had compensation, however, by winning the one-day 60 overs per side competition for the Gillette Cup by beating Derbyshire in the final by 69 runs. A new Sunday competition, the Players Sunday League (40 overs per side), was a great success from the playing and financial viewpoint, and was won by Lancashire, with Hampshire second and Essex third.

Despite a season blessed with abundant sunshine, runs scored and wickets taken were fewer than usual. Serious accidents marred the early days. Cowdrey, the Kent and England captain, snapped an Achilles tendon and missed most of the season, and Milburn, at the height of his powers as a hard-hitting batsman and crowd entertainer, had his career ended by losing an eye in a car accident. Edrich was the only batsman to score more than 2,000 runs, and only Cottam (109 wickets) and four others took 100 or more wickets. Cricketers from overseas again played a leading part, especially the Pakistanis Mushtaq (Northamptonshire), the leading all-rounder (1,831 runs and 78 wickets), and Younis (Surrey; 1,760 runs), and the South African M. J. Proctor (Gloucestershire; 108 wickets). The leading English all-rounders were Illingworth (Leicestershire; 950 runs and 62 wickets) and T. W. Cartwright (Warwickshire; 779 runs and 108 wickets).

South Australia won the Sheffield Shield, and Auckland the Plunket Shield in New Zealand. Transvaal won the Currie Cup in South Africa, and Jamaica the Shell Regional Trophy in West Indies. In India, West Zone won the Duleep Trophy, Bombay the Ranji Trophy, and the State Bank of India retained the Moin-ud-Dowlah Tournament Gold Cup. Lahore won the Qaid-i-Azam Trophy in Pakistan.

World Cricket Championship. A new venture was staged in Australia between eight two-man teams from England, Australia, South Africa, and West Indies. Five rounds were played, each side batting for eight six-ball overs, or till both batsmen were out, and scoring one point for a win. West Indies (Sobers and Hall) won with 9 points. The Pollock brothers, R. G. and P. (South Africa), finished second, and England (Milburn and K. F. Barrington) third. Unfortunately, Barrington collapsed with a heart attack that ended his first-class career. (A. R. A.)

Crime

International collaboration in the field of criminological research continued in 1968–69. That cooperation included the meeting of a UN consultative group in Geneva in August 1968, the Council of Europe's sixth Conference of Directors of Criminological Research Institutes in Strasbourg in November 1968, "contact seminars" arranged by the Scandinavian Research

BEN ROTH AGENCY

'Havana, Havana, Havana. Am I sick of the sight of Havana."
—Waite, "The Sun," London.

Council for Criminology (in Finland in October 1968 and in Norway in August 1969), and an international convention of criminology arranged by the Centro de Estudios Criminológicos in Mendoza, Arg., in June 1969. In 1969 Interpol published the biennial statistical handbook covering the years 1965–66, the most accessible source of international comparison.

Recent studies seemed to confirm a criminological belief that industrialized and highly developed countries rank among those with a high larceny rate and a low murder rate, while less developed countries have a low larceny rate and either a high or a low murder rate. (Murder rates are capable of exceptional fluctuation.) International comparisons are always dangerous; comparisons on a national basis are much more reliable. Studies of national trends, however, such as Franz Császár's survey of the development of juvenile delinquency and adult crime in Austria from 1953 to 1964 and a similar report by the *British Journal of Criminology,* confirmed the trend.

If the increase in recorded crime was not to overwhelm police forces, it was suggested that removing some offenses from the criminal category would permit the police to concentrate on the remaining offenses. The Danish experience with regard to the repeal of the regulations concerning pornography aroused great interest and was under thorough scrutiny in Denmark and abroad. (V. Gr.; S. G. J.)

Major Crimes. *United States.* Serious crimes in the U.S. in 1968 totaled almost 4.5 million, an increase of 17% over 1967, according to the Uniform Crime Reports published by the Federal Bureau of Investigation (FBI). From 1960 to 1968 daytime burglaries of residences rose 247%. A study of offenders released in 1963 revealed that 63% were rearrested within five years with 43% rearrested within one year. During the first six months of 1969, serious crimes in the U.S. increased 9% over the same period in 1968. Violent crimes rose 13% with robbery up 17%, forcible rape 15%, aggravated assault 10%, and murder 8%. Cities of 250,000 and above had an increase in serious crime during the first half of 1969 of 8%; the rise in the suburbs was 11% and in rural areas 8%. The National Automobile Theft Bureau reported that 776,000 cars were stolen in 1968, an increase of 18% over 1967. The auto theft rate had risen 114% since 1960.

The body of Karen Sue Beineman, a freshman at Eastern Michigan University in Ypsilanti, was found in a wooded ravine on the outskirts of nearby Ann Arbor on July 26; she had last been seen riding with a motorcyclist on the afternoon of July 23, 1969. A 22-year-old college senior, John Norman Collins, a motorcycle enthusiast, was arrested on August 1, and charged with her murder. Miss Beineman was the fourth young woman to be murdered in the area since March and the seventh within a two-year period. Three of the women were Eastern Michigan University coeds, two were University of Michigan students, one was a high school dropout, and one a junior-high-school student; all were long-haired brunettes ranging in age from 13 to 23 years. A University of Michigan graduate student, Margaret Phillips, was also found murdered in July. A convicted rapist on whose rehabilitation program she was working was charged with her murder.

The bodies of five persons were discovered in a plush Bel-Air home in Los Angeles on the morning of August 9. Two of the victims, actress Sharon Tate and Jay Sebring, a noted hairdresser, were found inside the home. Sebring had a hood over his head and both had ropes tied around their necks, one of which had been thrown over a beam as if a hanging had been intended. Sprawled on the lawn in front of the house were the stabbed bodies of Abigail Folger, a coffee heiress, and Voityck Frokowski, an amateur photographer. The fifth victim, Steven Parent, was slumped behind the wheel of an automobile. The Bel-Air home had been rented by Miss Tate's husband, director Roman Polanski, who was in Europe working on a movie. In December police arrested several members of a hippie cult after a woman member, in custody in connection with other offenses, allegedly told fellow prisoners that she had witnessed the slayings.

Following a trial lasting almost four months, a Los Angeles jury on April 23 returned a death-penalty verdict against Sirhan Bishara Sirhan, a Jerusalem-born Jordanian, for the assassination of U.S. Sen. Robert F. Kennedy on June 5, 1968. On March 10, 1969, James Earl Ray, an escaped convict, entered a plea of guilty in Memphis, Tenn., to the assassination on April 4, 1968, of the Rev. Martin Luther King, Jr., noted Negro civil rights leader. Ray was sentenced to 99 years in prison. On March 1, following about 40 days of testimony much of which was intended by District Attorney Jim Garrison to discredit the Warren Commission findings, a New Orleans jury deliberated only 50 minutes before acquitting Clay L. Shaw (*see* BIOGRAPHY) of conspiracy in the assassination of Pres. John F. Kennedy.

Numerous airplanes were hijacked again in 1969, mostly in the eastern U.S., and forced to fly to Cuba. The longest hijacking began on October 31 when Raffaele Minichiello, a U.S. Marine and Vietnam veteran, bought a $15.50 ticket for a Trans World Airlines flight from Los Angeles to San Francisco. He forced the plane to fly to Rome, stopping in Denver, Colo., New York City, Bangor, Me., and Shannon Airport, Ireland. Minichiello was captured by Italian police ten miles south of Rome five hours after fleeing from the Rome airport. On November 2, six persons accused of separate air hijackings turned themselves in to FBI agents in Champlain, N.Y., after leaving Cuba on a freighter to Montreal.

Robberies of financial institutions in Washington, D.C. (102 in 1968), were three times greater than in any previous year. On Jan. 8, 1969, two FBI agents, Anthony Palmisano and Edwin R. Woodriffe, were shot to death while seeking bank robbery suspect Billie Austin Bryant, an escaped convict, at the home of his estranged wife. Woodriffe was the first black FBI agent to be killed in line of duty.

During the first eight months of 1969, there were 356 bus robberies in New York City, compared with 244 in 1968. In Chicago there were 57 bus robberies in December 1968, compared with 28 in December 1967. By August 1969, an exact-fare system, which eliminated the need for the driver to carry money, had been installed in buses in at least 34 cities.

In February 1969 the stereotypers' union at the *New York Times* threatened a one-day work stoppage if the "strongest action" was not taken to make the Times Square area safe for persons at night. The police department offered to provide escorts for night workers from their jobs to subway or bus stations. New York City officials and hotelkeepers asserted in January 1969 that prostitution and related crimes were getting out of hand. Blamed was a new law effective Sept. 1, 1967, that reduced the penalty for prostitution. On Sept. 1, 1969, the penalty for prostitution was raised from 15 to 90 days.

The fraudulent use of credit cards became a major crime problem in many cities. In January 1969 witnesses testified to a New York state senate subcommittee that the organized underworld had in some instances bought the cooperation of postal employees who are able to steal large numbers of credit cards from the mail.

Mexico. Dykes Askew Simmons, Jr., the first U.S. citizen ever sentenced to death in Mexico, escaped from a Monterey prison on April 6, 1969, by dressing as a woman and mingling with 400 wives of inmates who had been visiting their husbands. An accomplice drove him across the border at Roma, Tex. On September 24 his body was found in East Fort Worth.

Brazil. C. Burke Elbrick, the U.S. ambassador to Brazil, was released by his abductors on September 7 after 15 political prisoners had been flown to asylum in Mexico. In November Patrick Dolan, son of a U.S. business executive, was found shot to death near São Paulo after he had been kidnapped and a ransom paid. There had been 58 bank robberies in Brazil by August 1969 with a total loot of about $600,000.

Canada. At least 75 slayings occurred in the Montreal area in 1968, an increase of nearly 5% over 1967. In the 15 months prior to May 1969 there had been 41 gang-war killings, more than had occurred during the past 15 years. According to police, Montreal's predominantly Italian underworld oligarchy was being challenged by younger Quebec French Canadians. Montreal was also described as having more bank robberies than any other city in North America —93 in the first six months of 1969 compared with 48 in the same period in 1968.

About 300 persons were in the Montreal Stock Exchange when a bomb explosion injured 27 persons. A bomb that exploded in the store of the Queen's Printer later in February was the tenth blast in Montreal in 1969 and the 60th since August 1968. Many were believed linked to the Quebec separatist movement. Police also seized large caches of dynamite, detonators, and separatist literature in raids in and around Montreal.

The biggest manhunt in Ontario's history followed the kidnapping of Mrs. Henry Radcliffe Nelles near Toronto on September 7. Three days after Mrs. Nelles was freed police arrested six men including a former fiancé of the victim and a Toronto policeman and recovered the $200,000 ransom.

Georges Lemay, whose "wanted" poster was flashed around the world during the first Tel-Star television satellite broadcast, was convicted in Montreal in January 1969 of having masterminded the looting of 273 safety-deposit boxes in a downtown Montreal bank. On May 14 the House of Commons approved sweeping changes in Canada's Criminal Code including the legalization of abortions and some homosexual acts, the liberalization of the law on probation, and the restriction of the use of firearms. Also passed in 1969 was a bill providing all crime victims in Ontario with financial reimbursement for medical and other expenses. Similar laws were in effect in Newfoundland, Saskatchewan, and Alberta.

United Kingdom. Serious crime in England increased nearly 7% in 1968; crimes of violence rose 18.4%. Motorists accounted for about 65% of the convictions for less serious crimes. Throughout the London area, crime increased less than 1% in 1968 but in the financial district it increased about 45% in an outbreak of larcenies from business premises, shops, and warehouses. The annual report of Sir Eric St. Johnston, chief inspector of constabulary, revealed that crime in Britain outside of London increased $8\frac{1}{2}$% in 1968 with indictable offenses exceeding one million for the first time. Offenses showing significant increases were those of violence and narcotic violations. An increase in fraud was attributed to the proliferation of credit trading.

Bandits armed with shotguns hijacked a truck in central London on March 31, 1969, and escaped with a box of gold bullion worth £75,000. Bank employees in northwest London threw chairs, paperweights, and inkstands at robbers armed with ax handles and a shotgun as they fled with their loot in pillowcases. Also in March, three men posing as shopfitters erected a wooden screen in front of a jewelry store window. Ignored by customers entering and leaving the shop, they drilled through the armoured plate glass and,

"PARIS MATCH" FROM PICTORIAL PARADE

Police storming the farm home of André Fourquet, accused of killing a French policeman. The assault so provoked the mentally ill farmer that he killed his two children and committed suicide.

using a twisted wire, eased 25 rings through the hole.

In August Jon Appleby was caught trying to saw his way out of a Leeds jail with hacksaw blades that had been concealed in roast chickens brought to him by his wife and two friends. It was announced in January 1969 that 40 prisoners at Wormwood Scrubs, most of whom were convicted of sex offenses against children, underwent a painless ten-minute operation in which a small pill of synthetic female hormone was inserted under the skin. Prison physicians asserted that this is no longer an experimental approach to sex offenders but could be considered positive treatment.

France. By far the largest jewel theft reported in France for many years occurred on Sept. 10, 1969, when Mrs. Simore Karoff, a U.S. art dealer, discovered that her suitcase containing jewels worth $1.5 million had been forced open and emptied. In Lourdes, Maniel Lozano, sacristan of the underground basilica of the shrine, was arrested with his wife on March 6 on charges of having embezzled between $60,000 and $70,000 in collections during the last ten years. In January Paris police, confounded by reports of a "giant four-armed pickpocket" operating in crowded subway and railroad stations, arrested Mohamed Baouche, a 6-ft. 4-in. Algerian. Upon opening his ankle-length overcoat, they discovered his small 12-year-old nephew inside.

Spain. In September 1969 customs officials at Algeciras were reported making scores of arrests of foreigners for possession of marijuana. Arab drug pushers were allegedly informing Spanish police about their clients and collecting rewards of as much as 80% of the fines imposed on offenders, many of whom were college students.

West Germany. In January 1969 Frankfurt was reported to be the crime centre in West Germany. Robberies had doubled in the past five years and confidence men preyed on wealthy industrialists, air travelers, and visitors to the city's big fairs. Frankfurt's prostitutes were among the biggest earners in the city's underworld; although 1,200 were officially registered, at least four times that number were estimated to be operating illegally. In a Stuttgart court in March former Nazi SS. officer Hans Sohns was convicted of having abetted the murder of 280 slave labourers after using them in a Hitler-ordered exhumation program to destroy evidence of Nazi killings.

Poland. In the biggest counterfeiting operation in Polish history, ten persons were tried in Warsaw for printing and circulating 600,000 bills printed at night in the Warsaw headquarters of the Polish Economic Society. Several persons charged with involvement in nationwide student turmoil in 1968 received prison sentences in 1969.

Switzerland. On Jan. 31, 1969, six members of a religious sect, including a defrocked priest, Josef Stocker, were found guilty in Geneva of causing serious bodily harm to 17-year-old Bernadette Hasler who died after being flogged to "exorcise the devil." Swiss officials reported in March that Andre Hirsch, a former Geneva banker then under arrest, was the brains behind an international heroin smuggling ring in which heroin was concealed in cans of fish products shipped from Spain to New York aboard Swedish freighters.

Italy. In March 1969 the mayors of Palermo and Trapani, in Sicily, testified to a parliamentary anti-Mafia commission that they had encountered no significant difficulties with the Mafia. However, Giovanni Ravalli, who as prefect represented the national government in Palermo, stated that 8,500 inhabitants had been judicially warned about their suspected criminal activities and 1,000 others made to move out of the region. In Trapani, there were 24 murders in 1963 but only 6 each year since.

On September 14 police arrested 14 persons, filed minor charges against 375, and seized 126 guns in a crackdown on the Mafia in western Sicily. They also recovered 20 stolen automobiles, handed out 2,437 traffic tickets, searched 260 homes, 86 persons, and 7,500 automobiles, and checked the ownership of 7,000 head of cattle.

In Ascoli Piceno a trial of 250 persons charged with producing or selling adulterated wine was quashed in July 1969 because the evidence—2.8 million quarts of wine—was stolen. Police discovered that all the wine had been siphoned from the huge storage vats in four locked cellars and replaced with dyed water. Authorities estimated that at least 300 trips by tanker truck were required to haul the wine away. Later, Fabio Lanciotti, a wine-cellar owner, was arrested and confessed he had masterminded the theft.

U.S.S.R. On Jan. 22, 1969, a gunman was arrested after having fired several pistol shots at a procession carrying cosmonauts and Soviet officials to a mass meeting in the Kremlin's Palace of Congresses. The chauffeur of the cosmonauts' car was struck in the head by three bullets and died on January 31. Crime news did not usually appear in the Soviet press but in September a weekend supplement of *Izvestia* disclosed the arrest of a gang of fur thieves that had watched the windows of apartment houses in Moscow for expensive-looking curtains that would indicate the presence of other things of high quality.

India. India was deeply concerned over smuggling that was damaging to its economy. Gift parcels were allegedly being sent by prearrangement from Hong Kong, Tokyo, Bangkok, and other points to individuals in Nepal who accepted them under many names. The parcels were then brought into India duty-free.

Japan. The Metropolitan Police Board announced that 277,000 crimes were reported in Tokyo in 1968, 17,500 more than in 1967. A new record was established in Tokyo on April 9, 1969, when for the 120th consecutive day no serious crime was committed in the city. However, Tokyo police consider only those cases requiring them to establish an investigating team as "serious crimes."

Thailand. Thai officials asserted that the growing sophistication and tighter organization of southern bandits was harming the economy, which depended on rubber production. Some rubber planters had received demands for protection money ranging from $250 to $2,500 and small coconut estates had ceased production because of the demands. (V. W. P.)

See also Law; Police; Prisons and Penology.

Cuba

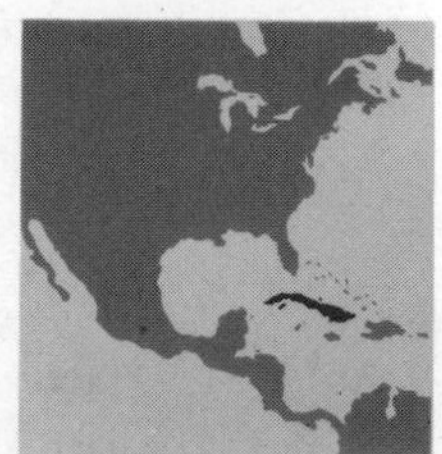

The socialist republic of Cuba occupies the largest island in the Greater Antilles of the West Indies. Area: 42,827 sq.mi. (110,922 sq.km.), including several thousand small islands and cays. Pop. (1967 est.): 7,937,200, including (1953) white 72.8%; mestizo 14.5%; Negro

Crops:
see Agriculture
Cross-country:
see Sporting Record

12.4%. Cap. and largest city: Havana (pop., 1967 est., 1,008,500). Language: Spanish. Religion: predominantly Roman Catholic. President in 1969, Osvaldo Dorticós Torrado; prime minister, Fidel Castro.

In 1969 Cuba remained politically stable but failed to make significant economic progress. The most important developments occurred in relations with the Soviet Union and the attempt to achieve a sugar crop of 10 million tons in 1970, along with the increased diversification of agriculture. Prime Minister Fidel Castro announced on January 2 that plans to industrialize would have to be postponed indefinitely, and that in the future agricultural production would take precedence.

The improvement in Cuban-Soviet relations dating from Castro's expression of support for the Soviet invasion of Czechoslovakia in August 1968 continued in 1969. The Soviet Union supported Cuba's apparent decision to concentrate on promoting economic development rather than on instigating guerrilla revolts elsewhere. Prior to August 1968 the Soviet government had concentrated on fostering commercial and diplomatic ties with existing governments in Latin America that Cuba wished to overthrow by violent means. At the conference of the UN Economic Commission for Latin America (ECLA), held in April in Lima, Peru, the Cuban delegate, while denying that Cuba had modified its attitude on relations with other Latin-American governments, indicated that Cuban support for guerrilla activities was primarily ideological and by example.

The first sign of the improvement in Soviet-Cuban relations was the visit to Havana in January of Kirill V. Novikov, of the Soviet Foreign Ministry, for celebrations of the tenth anniversary of the takeover by the revolutionary government. The 1969 trade agreement between the two countries, signed in February, was the most favourable ever to Cuba, providing for trade and Soviet aid worth $527 million, a 60% increase over the figure for 1967. In July a Soviet naval squadron visited Havana to demonstrate support for the Castro regime. Cuba sent observers to the World Communist Conference held in Moscow in June, after initially indicating that it would not be represented, and declared its support for the Soviet Union.

A Cuban intelligence officer who defected to the U.S. in July stated that Cuba and the Soviet Union had signed a secret agreement in 1968 under which the Cuban government was committed to restricting its criticism of Soviet policies in Latin America and of Moscow-oriented Communist parties in the area. In return the Soviet government was to send 5,000 technicians to help develop agriculture, mining, fishing, nuclear energy, and the armed forces; increase oil supplies; and maintain economic aid at its current level of about $350 million a year.

Sugar rationing was introduced in January. On May 26 Castro announced that the 1969 sugar crop would amount to only 4.7 million tons, and that harvesting of the 1970 crop, the target for which was 10 million tons, was to begin in July immediately after work on the 1969 crop had been completed. Estimated production in 1970, however, was put by observers at only 8 million tons. Great efforts were being made to fulfill the 10 million-ton goal: there was a 50% rise in the area allocated to cane and a tenfold increase in the use of fertilizers; mechanical harvesters were introduced on a large scale; the modernization program for the sugar mills was speeded up; and labour was conscripted from the towns. Work, however, was held up by heavy rains in the provinces of Camagüey and Oriente, and locally manufactured harvesters supplementing those supplied by the Soviet Union frequently broke down.

The government sought to fulfill the ambitious 1970 target (originally set in 1964) for prestige reasons and to meet current export commitments. Cuba was permitted to sell 5 million tons a year at 6 cents a pound to the Soviet Union under an agreement signed in 1964, and its annual quota under the International Sugar Agreement, signed late in 1968, was 2.1 million tons, valued at approximately $94 million. In the previous two years Cuba had preferred to sell sugar on the free market at 2 cents a pound and sales to the Soviet Union lapsed. The 1964 support price agreement was to end in 1970, and Cuba was therefore anxious to sell an increased amount of sugar to the Soviet Union to ensure its favourable renewal.

Progress continued to be made toward the diversification of agriculture. Areas formerly devoted to sugar were given over to rice, citrus fruits, coffee, and tobacco. An ambitious program was drawn up to develop the fishing industry, especially with a view to increasing exports. Trade with Western Europe as a means of avoiding the U.S. trade embargo continued; despite a chronic shortage of foreign exchange, commercial payments were nearly always promptly made.

U.S. press reports in May stated that Cuba wished to arrive at a rapprochement with the U.S., but no firm moves were subsequently made. Cooperation between the two countries was restricted to an agreement in February over the return of hijacked airliners and their original passengers to the U.S. and the management of the flow of refugees from Cuba, which averaged 45,000 a year.

A further indication of the gradual fall in the standard of living since 1959 was the announcement in

CUBA

Education. (1966–67) Primary, pupils 1,253,042, teachers 40,228; secondary, pupils 170,285, teachers 10,196; vocational, pupils 46,376, teachers 3,726; teacher training, students 25,547, teachers 1,438; higher (at 3 universities), students 33,704, teaching staff 4,220.

Finance. Monetary unit: peso, officially at parity with the U.S. dollar (2.40 pesos = £1 sterling). Budget (1966) balanced at 2,718,000,000 pesos.

Foreign Trade. (1967) Imports 1,170,000,000 pesos; exports 875 million pesos. Import sources: U.S.S.R. 58%; China 7%; East Germany 5%. Export destinations: U.S.S.R. 52%; China 11%; Spain 7%; Czechoslovakia 6%; East Germany 5%. Main exports (1966) sugar and products 85%.

Transport and Communications. Roads (1965) 13,340 km. (including 1,144 km. of the Central Highway). Motor vehicles in use (1965): passenger 162,000; commercial (including buses) 103,700. Railways (1966): public 4,591 km.; plantation 12,645 km. Shipping (1968): merchant vessels 100 gross tons and over 104; gross tonnage 237,603. Telephones (Jan. 1968) 238,224. Radio receivers (Dec. 1967) *c.* 1,325,000. Television receivers (Dec. 1967) *c.* 575,000.

Agriculture. Production (in 000; metric tons; 1967; 1966 in parentheses): corn *c.* 120 (*c.* 127); sweet potatoes *c.* 230 (*c.* 240); rice (1968) 182, (1967) 93; sugar, raw value (1968–69) *c.* 5,000, (1967–68) *c.* 5,000; coffee *c.* 27 (*c.* 27); oranges (1966) *c.* 133, (1965) 96; tobacco *c.* 51 (51). Livestock (in 000; 1967): cattle 7,172; pigs 331; sheep 331; goats 468.

Industry. Production (in 000; metric tons; 1967): crude oil 99; copper ore (metal content; 1966) 5.4; nickel ore (metal content; 1966) *c.* 26; manganese ore (metal content; 1966) *c.* 31; chrome ore (oxide content) *c.* 11; cement *c.* 800; petroleum products (1966) 3,835; electricity (kw-hr.; 1966) 3,709,000.

HOWARD HARRISON FROM NANCY PALMER AGENCY

Herding cattle in Cuba's Camagüey Province in the summer of 1969. In an effort to bolster the Cuban economy, the Castro government was attempting to develop the agricultural potential of Camagüey.

May of bread rationing. Supplies of most consumer goods were restricted, and this caused some popular discontent leading, in some cases, to reported small-scale disturbances. In March Castro called for a drive against crime and delinquency and criticized serious deficiencies in the educational system. The government persisted in its efforts to abolish the use of money and encouraged barter operations in rural areas. Urban transport and entertainment facilities became entirely free, and it was intended eventually to abolish all forms of income tax. (RN. C.)

ENCYCLOPÆDIA BRITANNICA FILMS. *The West Indies* (1965).

Cycling

Well satisfied with their gold medals, not one of the 1968 Olympic cycling champions—all Europeans—stayed on to contest the 1968 world amateur championships a month later (November) in Montevideo, Urug. While the latter titleholders must, therefore, be considered consolation champions, it is possible that some of those who won at high-altitude Mexico City might not have succeeded in the near sea-level conditions at Montevideo. The 1968 champions were: *Track:* sprint, Luigi Borghetti (Italy); 1,000-m. time trial, Niels Fredborg (Den.); 4,000-m. team pursuit, Italy; 4,000-m. individual pursuit, Mogens Frey (Den.); tandem sprint, Walter Gorrini and Giordano Turrini (Italy). *Road:* individual 125-m., Vittorio Marcelli (Italy); 100-km. team, Sweden.

Competition in amateur tournaments remained at a high level in 1969 as few of the 1968 Olympic or world champions were tempted to turn professional. Of the outstandingly successful French trio, Pierre Trentin and Daniel Morelon continued to dominate sprint events on the track, but Daniel Rebillard, the surprise individual pursuit winner at the Olympic Games, was a comparative failure back in Europe. On the road, two members of the Olympic champion Dutch quartet, Fedor Den Hertog and Joop Zoetemelk, won major amateur multistage races.

The most spectacular performance of the season was by Den Hertog, who two years previously had been told after a racing accident that he would never cycle again. Den Hertog dominated the 1,500-mi. Tour of Britain (May 24–June 15), winning by 12 minutes over his compatriot Popke Oosterhof, who won 6 of the 15 stages. Despite their individual supremacy the Dutch were beaten in the team competition by Poland. The second Olympic gold medalist from the Netherlands, Zoetemelk, won the 12-day Tour of Yugoslavia (June 29–July 10) and then in September took the 10-day Tour de l'Avenir. British riders achieved their best performances ever in this amateur Tour de France, national amateur champion Brian Jolly wearing the yellow jersey of leadership for two days, and David Rollinson and William Bilsland winning daily stages. By heading the fifth day's racing, Augustin Alcantara (Mex.) became the first non-European to win a stage of the French classic.

Teammates Martyn Roach of London and Bryce Beeston of New Zealand crash near the finish line during the Stoke-on-Trent stage of the Tour of Britain, May 31, 1969. Both recovered and crossed the finish line.

WIDE WORLD

Earlier in the year (May 9–24) Jean-Pierre Danguillaume (France) won the 14-day test that normally follows the Warsaw-Berlin-Prague triangle. In this year of troubled Soviet-Czechoslovak relations, the so-called "Peace Race" cut out Prague altogether, only touched briefly on Czechoslovakian roads near the Polish border, and had no Czechoslovak riders taking part.

Czechoslovakia was, nevertheless, host country for the 1969 world amateur men's and women's championships at Brno in August. The results of these events were: Men: *Track:* sprint, Morelon; 1,000-m. time trial, Gianni Sartori (Italy); tandem sprint, Jurgen Geschke and Werner Otto (E.Ger.); 4,000-m. individual pursuit, Xavier Kurmann (Switz.); 4,000-m. team pursuit, U.S.S.R.; 1-hr. motor-paced, Albertus Boom (Neth.). *Road:* 112-mi. individual, Leif Mortensen (Den.); 100-km. team, Sweden. Women: *Track:* sprint, Galina Tsareva (U.S.S.R.); 3,000-m. pursuit, Raisa Obodovskaya (U.S.S.R.). *Road:* individual 43.2-mi., Audrey McElmury (U.S.).

Highlights of the 1969 championships were the third successive victory of the four remarkable Swedish Pettersen brothers (Tomas, Gösta, Sture, and Erik) in the road team time trial and the success of Mrs. McElmury in the women's road race. Hers was the first world cycling championship won by a U.S. competitor since 1912. In October Frey set a new hour unpaced amateur world record of 47.513 km. (29.52 mi.) in Mexico City.

The world professional track championships were decided at the Sportpaleis in Antwerp, Belg., on August 5–9, the first time a complete world series had been held on an indoor track. Belgian riders, Patrick Sercu (sprint) and Ferdinand Bracke (5,000-m. pursuit), took two titles, the latter beating defending champion Hugh Porter (U.K.) in a sensational final. Jaap Oudkerk (Neth.) won the 100-km. motor-paced championship.

On the nearby Zolder motor-racing circuit Harm Ottenbros (Neth.) was first in the 163-mi. road championship. This was a complete surprise since Ottenbros had played only a minor role in earlier one-day classic and multistage tests. Outstanding in these was Eddy Merckx (*see* BIOGRAPHY) of Belgium, who followed up his third success in the 180-mi. Milan-San Remo race on March 19 with a runaway win in the punishing 160-mi. Tour of Flanders. After these and other successes, with a victory in Liège-Bastogne-Liège (*c.* 160 mi.) for good measure, Merckx was hopeful that his Italian sponsors would "rest" him during the three weeks of the Tour of Italy from May 16 to June 8 to allow him to build up strength for the Tour de France (June 28–July 20). His hopes were not realized, and Merckx was obliged to ride the Italian Tour. After 14 days' racing he was in the lead and in a strong position to repeat his 1968 win. Then he was dramatically expelled from the race following a positive dope test. The automatic one-month suspension from racing meant that he would be unable to ride the Tour de France. Possibly swayed by public opinion that Merckx had been the victim of a "fixed" drink, the Union Cycliste International lifted the suspension and the Belgian was allowed to ride the Tour de France, where his opponents included Felice Gimondi who had won his nation's tour after Merckx's disqualification.

Stung by the Italian incident, Merckx rode powerfully to win the overall contest by 18 minutes over the second man, Roger Pingeon (France). He was first in five of the daily stages, topped the points classification, won the Grand Prix de la Montagne as the best climber, and led the winning trade team. During three weeks Merckx passed ten dope tests and was even appearing voluntarily at the medical centre in his anxiety to prove he was "clean." The 1969 Tour de France saw the emergence of the first Portuguese rider to play a major role in the race, Joaquin Agostinho, who won two stages.

Other national tour results were: Tour of Spain, Pingeon; Tour of Switzerland, Vittorio Adorni (Italy); and Tour of Belgium, Eric de Vlaeminck (Belg.). Notable single-day race winners were: Paris-Roubaix and Bordeaux-Paris, Walter Godefroot (Belg.); Paris-Tours, Hermann Van Springel (Belg.; Van Springel also won the Grand Prix des Nations with 100 km. in 2 hr. 19 min. 16 sec.); Flèche Wallonne, Joseph Huysmans (Belg.); Tour of Lombardy, Gerben Karstens (Neth.).

Many records were broken during the British amateur time trial season. These included 25 mi., Alfred Engers, 51 min. 0 sec.; 50 mi., David Whitehouse, 1 hr. 47 min. 38 sec.; 12 hr., John Watson, 281.88 mi.; 24 hr., Roy Cromack, 507 mi.; women's 50 mi., Beryl Burton, 1 hr. 55 min. 4 sec. Cromack was the first rider to exceed 500 mi. in 24 hours on British roads. A remarkable 24-hour ride took place in September when Australian professional Vic Browne covered 524 mi. in a one-way journey.

British cycling suffered a sad loss during July when 24-year-old Peter Buckley died following a training accident. Born on the Isle of Man, Buckley won the Commonwealth Games road championship in Jamaica, and two weeks before his death became the first native rider to win the Manx International Trophy.

(Jo. B. W.)

Cyprus

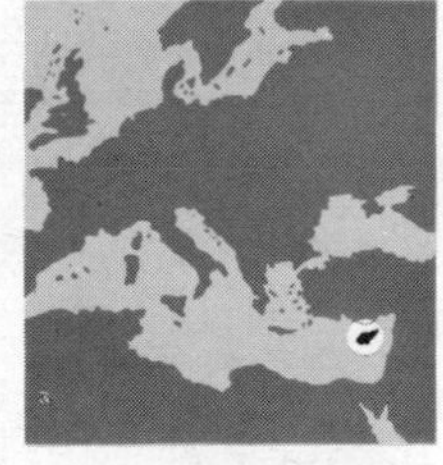

An island republic and a member of the Commonwealth of Nations, Cyprus is in the eastern Mediterranean. Area: 3,572 sq.mi. (9,251 sq.km.). Pop. (1968 est.): 622,000, including Greeks 77%; Turks 18%. Cap. and largest city: Nicosia (pop., 1968 est., 112,000). Language: Greek and Turkish. Religion: Greek Orthodox 77%; Muslim 18.3%. President in 1969, Archbishop Makarios III.

The progress made in negotiations between the Greek Cypriots and the Turkish Cypriots continued to be slow and arduous during 1969. Both sides had presented, in written form, their views on communal administration. Among the Greeks it was felt that the Turks still had in mind a system that would amount to a virtual separation of the two communities. The Turkish Cypriots, it seemed, wanted their villages and their sectors in the towns to be under Turkish councils endowed with control over taxation, police, and public services. As for the Greek Cypriots, their desire was to see the local administration established along lines representing economic and geographic realities, the areas with a predominance of Turks in their population to have also a predominance of Turkish officials in charge of local government. It was over the extent of the autonomous powers to be given to the Turkish Cypriots and over the level at which the central regime would assume control of affairs that the divergence of views was most evident. The Greek Cypriots showed themselves resolute in their wish to avoid all solutions that might approximate the establishment of a "quasi-partition" in the affairs of the island. Although no decisive result emerged from the discussions, there was still hope that a genuine advance would soon be made toward a measure of agreement. Two subcommittees were created, one to examine the problems surrounding the reemployment of Turkish Cypriots in the public services, the other to consider a new law that would allow Greeks and Turks alike to vote on a common electoral roll.

It was made known in October 1968 that the UN force in Cyprus, numbering approximately 4,250 men, was to lose about one quarter of its strength. U Thant, the UN secretary-general, had ordered this reduction in view of the peaceful conditions in the island and also because of a deficit in the contributions needed from member states to maintain the force.

Also in October 1968 there was tension between the governments at Athens and at Nicosia. A report emanating from Greece accused the Cypriot minister of the interior and of defense, Polycarpos Georghadjis, of involvement in the attempt, on Aug. 13, 1968, to kill Georgios Papadopoulos, the Greek prime minister. It was stated in the Cypriot newspaper *Agon* that Greece might wish to sever diplomatic relations with Cyprus and to withdraw its troops from the island if President Makarios did not take action in this matter. Georghadjis then tendered his resignation to the president who, after careful consideration, de-

CYPRUS

Education. (1966–67) Primary, pupils 72,933, teachers 2,176; secondary, pupils 29,782, teachers 1,217; vocational, pupils 4,107, teachers 247; higher, students 308, teaching staff 21.

Finance. Monetary unit: pound, at par with the pound sterling (C£1 = U.S. $2.40). Budget (1968 est.): revenue C£24,093,256; expenditure C£20,859,087. Gold and foreign exchange, monetary authorities: (May 1969) U.S. $154.7 million; (May 1968) U.S. $129 million.

Foreign Trade. (1968) Imports C£70,943,000; exports C£36,959,000. Import sources: U.K. 34%; Italy 11%; West Germany 8%; U.S. 5%. Export destinations: U.K. 37%; West Germany 19%; Netherlands 5%; Italy 5%; U.S.S.R. 5%; Spain 5%. Main exports: copper 20%; citrus fruit 19%; potatoes 12%; iron pyrites 8%.

Transport and Communications. Roads (1967) 8,150 km. (including 1,878 km. with improved surface). Motor vehicles in use (1967): passenger 37,330; commercial 12,795. Air traffic (1968): 65,160,000 passenger-km.; freight 1,490,000 net ton-km. Shipping (1968): merchant vessels 100 gross tons and over 109; gross tonnage 652,588. Telephones (Dec. 1967) 34,137. Radio receivers (Dec. 1967) 146,000. Television receivers (Dec. 1967) 28,000.

Agriculture. Production (in 000; metric tons; 1967; 1966 in parentheses): wheat *c.* 97 (56); potatoes (1966) 134, (1965) 139; olives *c.* 17 (17); grapes (1968) 168, (1967) *c.* 146; oranges (1966) 62, (1965) 56; grapefruit (1966) *c.* 36, (1965) *c.* 27. Livestock (in 000): sheep (1966–67) 380; cattle (1967–68) *c.* 37.

Production (in 000; metric tons; 1967): asbestos 20; copper ore (exports; metal content) 15; chromium ore (oxide content) 10; cement (1968) 241; electricity (excluding most industrial production; kw-hr.; 1968) 454,000.

Curling: *see* Sporting Record

Currency: *see* Money and Banking

Cybernetics: *see* Information Science and Technology

cided to accept it. At Nicosia students and also members of the former EOKA (Union with Greece) organization, in which Georghadjis had once held a prominent role, arranged demonstrations calling for the reinstatement of the minister.

Of possible importance for the future of Cyprus were the visible signs of a movement toward the promotion of organized political parties, that is, over and above the existing pro-Communist front AKEL (Anorthotikon Komma Ergazomenou Laou). After his resignation as minister of the interior and defense, Georghadjis set out to gather his adherents into a Unified Party. There was also some evidence pointing to the emergence of a national front embracing those reluctant to abandon the prospect of a close association between Cyprus and Greece.

With the passage of time the problem of relations with Greece, Turkey, and the U.K. became clearer. The Greek Cypriots, in general, believed that future alliances should not involve the presence in Cyprus of armed forces representing foreign states, and were willing to see the 900 Greek troops stationed on the island under the 1960 agreements return to Greece. The Turkish minority, however, regarded its 600 troops as a guarantee of survival. Greek Cypriot public sentiment appeared to favour an independent, nonaligned Cyprus, perhaps still within the Commonwealth of Nations and perhaps also within the European Common Market. As to relations with the U.K., Cyprus, at some future date, would no doubt raise the question concerning the British bases on the island. On several occasions during the year threats were made to hold large-scale public demonstrations against their retention by Britain, one reason being to express sympathy with the Arabs, whose support for Cyprus was useful in the UN. British forces were an asset, nevertheless, and contributed up to £15 million a year to the economy. One possible solution might be for the U.K. to relinquish its sovereign power over the bases and to lease them thereafter from the Cyprus government as air and communications centres.

(V. J. P.)

Czechoslovakia

A federal socialist republic of central Europe, Czechoslovakia lies between Poland, the U.S.S.R., Hungary, Austria, and Germany. Area: 49,371 sq.mi. (127,870 sq.km.), including Slovakia 18,922 sq.mi. Pop. (1969 est.): 14,418,000 (Slovakia 4.5 million), including (1966) Czech 66%; Slovak 29%. Cap. and largest city: Prague (pop., 1969 est., 1.1 million). First secretaries of the Communist Party of Czechoslovakia in 1969, Alexander Dubcek and, from April 17, Gustav Husak; president; Ludvik Svoboda; premier, Oldrich Cernik.

In January 1969 there was still hope that some of the reforms initiated during 1968 could be salvaged. On January 1 one of the principal administrative changes proposed in Dubcek's program was implemented: Czechoslovakia became a federal state. Henceforth the Czech lands (Bohemia and Moravia) and Slovakia would have regional governments, responsible to regional legislatures, while the responsibilities of the federal government would be limited to defense, foreign affairs, the interior, planning, finance, foreign trade, and labour and welfare. Cernik continued as premier of the new federal government.

These institutional changes did nothing to alleviate public discontent with the state of affairs caused by the Soviet occupation of the country. On January 25 great crowds attended the funeral in Prague of Jan Palach, a student who had set fire to himself as a protest against infringements of national independence. There were no violent anti-Soviet demonstrations, however. On February 25, Jan Zajic committed suicide in the same manner.

Evidence of Soviet pressure on Czechoslovakia was provided by the refusal of the Czechoslovak Communist Party to send a fraternal delegation to the Yugoslav Party Congress in March. This aroused much feeling in Czechoslovakia, where the unequivocal Yugoslav condemnation of the Soviet invasion was still remembered. At the end of March, a new crisis arose when a celebration of the second victory within a week of the Czechoslovak ice hockey team over the Soviets turned into an anti-Soviet demonstration. The Prague office of Aeroflot, the Soviet state airline, was ransacked before a crowd of about 100,000. The Soviets apparently used the incident to justify fresh demands for restrictions, especially the reintroduction of full censorship.

Dubcek's demotion began in earnest in April. On April 17 he resigned as first party secretary, but retained his place in the reduced party Presidium and became chairman of the Federal Assembly. His removal from this post and from the Presidium followed in September, and in October he was expelled from the Central Committee itself. Later he was appointed ambassador to Turkey.

CZECHOSLOVAKIA

Education. (1966–67) Primary, pupils 2,164,432, teachers 97,792; secondary, pupils 111,219, teachers 7,618; vocational, pupils 277,585, teachers 19,615; teacher training, students 9,589, teachers 540; higher (including 9 universities), students 139,059, teaching staff 18,757.

Finance. Monetary unit: koruna, with an official exchange rate of 7.20 koruny to U.S. $1(17.28 koruny = £1 sterling) and a tourist rate of 16.20 koruny to U.S. $1(38.74 koruny = £1). Budget (1969 est.) balanced at 156.2 billion koruny.

Foreign Trade. (1968) Imports 22,155,000,000 koruny; exports 21,638,000,000 koruny. Import sources (1967): U.S.S.R. 36%; East Germany 12%; Poland 7%; Hungary 6%. Export destinations (1967): U.S.S.R. 32%; East Germany 11%; Poland 8%; Hungary 5%. Main exports (1967): machinery 37%; motor vehicles 10%; iron and steel 8%; textiles 8%; chemicals 5%.

Transport and Communications. Roads (1966) *c.* 133,000 km. (including 72,908 km. main roads). Motor vehicles in use (1967): passenger 521,200; commercial (including buses) 165,200. Railways: (1967) 13,332 km. (including 2,165 km. electrified); traffic (1968) 18,960,000,000 passenger-km., freight 56,710,000,000 net ton-km. Air traffic (1968): 776 million passenger-km.; freight 13.6 million net ton-km. Shipping (1968): merchant vessels 100 gross tons and over 8; gross tonnage 74,386. Telephones (Dec. 1967) 1,678,717. Radio receivers (Dec. 1967) 3,844,000. Television receivers (Dec. 1967) 2.6 million.

Agriculture. Production (in 000; metric tons; 1967; 1966 in parentheses): wheat 2,516 (2,247); barley 1,936 (1,608); oats 968 (746); rye 689 (790); potatoes 6,037 (5,846); sugar, raw value (1968–69) *c.* 897, (1967–68) *c.* 842. Livestock (in 000: Jan. 1968): cattle 4,436; pigs 5,601; sheep 770; chickens (Jan. 1967) 28,026.

Industry. Index of industrial production (1963 = 100): (1968) 136; (1967) 129. Production (in 000; metric tons; 1968): coal 26,064; brown coal 74,882; electricity (kw-hr.) 41,395,000; crude oil (1967) 200; iron ore (30% metal content) 1,572; pig iron 6,920; steel 10,554; cement 6,484; sulfuric acid 977; nitrogenous fertilizers (1967) 245; superphosphates (1967) 244; cotton yarn 112; cotton fabrics (m.) 504,000; woolen fabrics (m.) 46,000; silk fabrics (m.; 1967) 666; passenger cars (units) 126; commercial vehicles (units) 51. Dwellings completed (1968) 83,000.

Dubcek's place as first secretary was taken by Gustav Husak (*see* BIOGRAPHY) and, at the beginning of June, the conservative position within the leadership was further strengthened by the appointment of Lubomir Strougal (*see* BIOGRAPHY) to the newly created post of deputy first secretary. Despite promises to the contrary, Dubcek's fall was followed by repressive measures on a fairly large scale. Censorship of the mass media was virtually restored and journalists known as hard-liners were put in charge of leading newspapers and of the news departments of radio and television stations. In April Josef Havlin, a strong supporter of former Pres. Antonin Novotny, was appointed chief censor. Attempts were made to replace professional and mass organizations, which had been active in support of the reforms, with more amenable bodies.

A more serious reaction occurred on the first anniversary of the Soviet invasion: five persons were killed in riots in Prague and Brno as troops with fixed bayonets and police using submachine guns and tear gas dispersed crowds. Over 2,000 arrests followed. The anniversary had been preceded by joint Soviet-Czechoslovak military maneuvers, described as "command-staff exercises."

Dubcek's supporters were steadily weeded out. Josef Smrkovsky, perhaps the most popular of the reformers of 1968, left the party Presidium in April; in September he lost the chairmanship of the lower house of the Federal Assembly and his place on the party Central Committee. Other reformers were dropped from the Central Committee at the same time. Ota Sik (who was living in Switzerland), author of the economic reforms adopted by Dubcek and a deputy premier in 1968, was removed from the Central Committee in May and deprived of his party membership in September. Frantisek Kriegel, formerly chairman of the National Front (which included all political and mass organizations), was expelled from the party in May. The May plenum of the Central Committee was followed by widespread personnel changes in party organizations at all levels in Bohemia and Moravia, culminating in the resignation of the entire Presidium of the Prague City Communist Party Committee. These purges of "progressives" coincided with a policy of rehabilitating the "conservatives," many of whom had been accused of treachery after the Soviet invasion of August 1968. Rehabilitation of persons unjustly persecuted during the Stalin era was not suspended, however. It would have been illogical to do so, since Husak himself was among the most prominent victims of the 1950s.

Meanwhile, the exodus of refugees continued. Most were intellectuals, academics, journalists, and skilled technologists, and their departure represented a brain drain that Czechoslovakia could ill afford. An amnesty offered by President Svoboda in May to all who had left the country "illegally" produced little response. The grace period expired on September 15, and in October some 100,000 exit visas valid for travel to the West were canceled.

The state of the Czechoslovak economy had been one of the prime causes of the leadership crisis that had brought Dubcek to power. In 1968, however, the leadership had been so deeply involved with the need to respond to Soviet demands on the ideological and political fronts that the reforms were never applied. In June 1969 the government dropped the bill on socialist enterprises, which embodied some of the principles of the proposed economic reforms. The general lethargy pervading the country as a result of political disillusionment inevitably had an adverse effect on economic performance. In September the deputy governor of the Czechoslovak State Bank warned in the party daily *Rude Pravo:* "If the decline in working morale and increase in apathy at work continue, it will no longer be possible to avoid economic stagnation."

In October, Husak, Cernik, and President Svoboda went to Moscow; an agreement was reached to increase Soviet shipments of raw materials, especially crude oil, iron ore, and cotton, to Czechoslovakia, and the U.S.S.R. also agreed to supply equipment for a new high-capacity atomic power station. (OT. P.)

See also Economic Planning; Propaganda.

THREE LIONS

Honour guard of students carrying Czechoslovak flag under statue of St. Wenceslas in Prague on Jan. 20, 1969 as crowds pay tribute to Jan Palach who burned himself to death in protest against Soviet intervention.

Young Czechoslovaks gesturing and shouting at Soviet troops as thousands of their countrymen demonstrated on the first anniversary of the 1968 Soviet invasion, August 20.

GAMMA—PIX FROM PUBLIX

Dahomey

A republic of West Africa, Dahomey is located north of the Gulf of Guinea and is bounded by Togo, Upper Volta, Niger, and Nigeria. Area: 43,483 sq.mi. (112,622 sq.km.). Pop. (1968 est.): 2,576,600, mainly Dahomean and allied tribes. Cap.: Porto-Novo (pop., 1968, 81,412). Largest city: Cotonou (pop., 1968 est., 129,140). Language: French and local dialects. Religion: animist, with Christian and Muslim minorities. President in 1969, Émile Derlin Zinsou to December 10; head of the military government from December 10, Lieut. Col. Maurice Kouandete.

Dahomey's year-long flirtation with civilian rule ended in December 1969 with the overthrow of President Zinsou in an apparently bloodless military coup. Throughout the year, Zinsou had had to face the same difficulties as those who had preceded him as head of state—national insolvency and political instability. In April he thwarted a conspiracy aimed at removing him from power, and in July he had a small group of officers arrested, among whom was a former head of state, Lieut. Col. Alphonse Alley. On December 10 he was deposed, and the reins of government were taken over by Lieut. Col. Maurice Kouandete, who had been head of state for a brief period in 1967 following the overthrow of Pres. Christophe Soglo. Zinsou's exact fate was unknown, although reports from Togo indicated that he had been taken to Dahomey's northern interior.

Throughout the year the labour unions had maintained an atmosphere of suppressed agitation, notably at Cotonou, where in June, following a strike of postal and railway workers, teachers, and schoolchildren, troops had compelled strikers to go back to work. Zinsou's attempts at political reorganization had met with numerous obstacles—hostility from certain elements in the Army, the impatience of the unions, and opposition from students and members of the civil service. In February Zinsou visited West Germany, and on March 5 was received by U.S. Pres. Richard Nixon at the White House. A long-term, interest-free loan of $4.6 million was forthcoming from the International Development Association, and an equal amount came from France for agricultural development. (Ph. D.)

DAHOMEY

Education. (1966–67) Primary, pupils 132,690, teachers 3,302; secondary, pupils 10,425, teachers 400; vocational, pupils 733, teachers (1965–66) 72; teacher training, students 322, teachers 27; higher, students 53, teaching staff (1965–66) 5.

Finance. Monetary unit: CFA franc, with a parity of CFA Fr. 50 to the French franc (CFA Fr. 277.71 = U.S. $1; CFA Fr. 666.50 = £1 sterling). Budget (1968 est.): receipts CFA Fr. 8,258,000,000 (including French aid CFA Fr. 600 million); expenditure CFA Fr. 7,757,000,000.

Foreign Trade. (1967) Imports CFA Fr. 11,860,000,000; exports CFA Fr. 3,750,000,000. Import sources: France 45%; Italy 18%. Export destinations: France 35%; Netherlands 15%; U.S. 14%; West Germany 7%; Togo 5%; Nigeria 5%; Belgium-Luxembourg 5%. Main exports: palm oil 40%; cotton 10%; palm nuts and kernels 9%.

Agriculture. Production (in 000; metric tons; 1967; 1966 in parentheses): cassava *c.* 1,120 (*c.* 1,089); peanuts *c.* 27 (*c.* 27); cottonseed *c.* 8 (*c.* 6); sweet potatoes *c.* 604 (*c.* 587); corn *c.* 250 (*c.* 250); palm oil (1966) 43, (1965) 43; palm kernels *c.* 42 (*c.* 47); coffee (1966) *c.* 1.4, (1965) *c.* 1.4. Livestock (in 000; 1966–67): cattle *c.* 450; pigs 272; sheep 421.

Dairy Products: *see* Agriculture

Dams: *see* Engineering Projects

Dance

Indisputably, the ballet event of 1969 was the U.S. debut of the Stuttgart (W.Ger.) Ballet from the Württemberg State Theatre. The company, its repertory, and its personnel were virtually unknown when the curtain went up at the new Metropolitan Opera House at Lincoln Center June 10. When it fell the Stuttgart Ballet had triumphed. The all-important talent energizing the company, whose background included the direction by ballet's greatest artist-reformer of two centuries ago, Jean-Georges Noverre, was that of South African-born John Cranko. In the eight years of his association with Stuttgart, Europeans and, in 1969, Americans discovered him as one of the foremost directors of the day and one of the great choreographers of the century.

The company played only New York City in its debut engagement but returned in the fall for a coast-to-coast tour. The major ballets were Cranko's *Romeo and Juliet,* to the Sergei Prokofiev score and with scenery and costumes by Jürgen Rose; *The Taming of the Shrew,* with a special score by Kurt-Heinz Stolze, based on Scarlatti themes, and scenery and costumes by Elisabeth Dalton; and *Eugene Onegin,* based on the Pushkin tale, with Tchaikovsky music that was not from the opera of the same name and scenery and costumes by Jürgen Rose. The New York engagement was augmented by such one-act works (all choreographed by Cranko) as a classical *Divertissements* from *The Nutcracker* (Tchaikovsky); the demi-caractère *Jeu de Cartes* (Stravinsky); the near-modern dance *Opus 1* (Webern); and the avant-garde *Présence* (Bernd-Alois Zimmermann).

Dancers almost unknown to U.S. balletomanes instantly became as admired and as familiar as American, English, Russian, or Danish dance stars. These included the prima ballerina, Marcia Haydée (from Brazil), Richard Cragun (U.S.), Egon Madsen (Denmark), Heinz Clauss, Susanne Hanke, Birgit Keil (W.Ger.), Judith Reyn (Rhodesia), and the troupe's first mime, Hella Heim, once a student in the Royal Court Theatre of Württemberg and promoted to soloist by command of the last king of Württemberg.

The Royal Ballet's engagement at New York's Metropolitan Opera House and long transcontinental tour marked not only the 20th anniversary of the company's American debut but also the 50th birthday of prima ballerina Dame Margot Fonteyn. Dame Margot again danced the dual role of Odette-Odile in *Swan Lake* and, as she had done 20 years before, played the role of Princess Aurora in *The Sleeping Beauty.*

A new U.S. dance group, the American Ballet Company, was founded in 1969 and directed by Eliot Feld, formerly a principal dancer and a choreographer for the American Ballet Theatre. Feld's company was brought into being through the aid of grants and by being given resident status at the Brooklyn Academy of Music, directed by Harvey Lichtenstein. The company had its debut in the summer at the Festival of Two Worlds in Spoleto, Italy, and its U.S. debut in a two-week engagement in the fall at the Brooklyn Academy of Music.

The American Ballet Theatre, which had danced at the Brooklyn Academy of Music for the first time in December of 1968, returned to that theatre for a two-week season in December. There were two premieres, Michael Smuin's *The Eternal Idol,* suggested

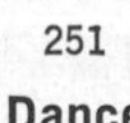

KEYSTONE

Sanson Candelaria as the Roasted Swan in Les Grands Ballets Canadiens' production of "Carmina Burana" in London, May 27, 1969. The performance marked the first appearance in England by the Canadian company.

by a Rodin sculpture and with music of Chopin, and Dennis Nahat's *Brahms Quintet.*

The New York City Ballet, directed by George Balanchine and Lincoln Kirstein, and the resident ballet company at the New York State Theater at Lincoln Center, continued its extensive seasons there, as well as out-of-town appearances and its annual summer repertory engagement at the Saratoga Arts Festival, Saratoga Springs, N.Y. In 1969, new works included Jacques d'Amboise' *Tchaikovsky Suite,* John Clifford's *Fantasies* (Ralph Vaughan Williams), and, most important, the first ballet that Jerome Robbins had created for this company in many years, *Dances at a Gathering* (to piano music of Chopin), which was praised in both New York and Monte Carlo.

In its four years at the New York City Center, the City Center Joffrey Ballet had increased the length of its spring and fall residencies. During 1969 its new works and new productions included two Danish classics from the 19th century, August Bournonville's *Konservatoriet* and *William Tell Variations,* and two new works by Gerald Arpino, the company's principal choreographer: *Animus,* to music of Jacob Druckman, and *The Poppet,* with music by Hans Werner Henze. A major effort was a production of Leonide Massine's *The Three-Cornered Hat,* a ballet dating back to the Diaghilev era of Ballets Russes, with music of de Falla and scenery and costumes by Picasso. Massine himself directed the revival, which starred Luis Fuente.

The Harkness Ballet, founded and produced by Rebekah Harkness, reached its fifth birthday. There was an extensive season in Europe as well as two New York engagements, at the Music Box Theater on Broadway and at the Brooklyn Academy of Music. During the year, Benjamin Harkarvy, for some years associated with the Netherlands Dance Theatre, joined Lawrence Rhodes, the company's principal male dancer, as co-director. The Harkness Ballet had a baby brother during the year when the Harkness Youth Dancers, which had appeared informally in a previous season, was launched as a professional company.

Ballets centred outside of New York that continued and even expanded their annual activities included the San Francisco Ballet, the Boston Ballet, the National Ballet (Washington, D.C.), the Pennsylvania Ballet, the Cincinnati Ballet, and Ballet West, an expansion of the Utah Civic Ballet. The National Ballet pulled an international dance coup by presenting in Washington and Newark, N.J., the first appearances of Dame Margot Fonteyn in the early-19th-century classic *La Sylphide,* choreographed by Bournonville in 1836 and restaged by Elsa Marianne von Rosen. Continuing summertime dance festivals in addition to the one at Saratoga included the venerable Jacob's Pillow Dance Festival, with ballet highlights sharing the season with modern dance and ethnic events; the American Dance Festival at New London, Conn., which introduced ballet into its modern dance programs; the Caramoor Festival at Mt. Kisco, N.Y.; and the Rebekah Harkness Dance Festival in New York City's Central Park.

Among Europe's major events was the Soviet Union's First International Ballet Competition, held in Moscow. The pas de deux gold medal winners from the U.S.S.R. were Nina Sorokina and Yuri Vladimirov, and a silver medalist, representing U.S. ballet, was the Iceland-born principal of the Harkness Ballet, Helgi Tomasson. The year also saw the first Swedish ballet festival to be directed by Denmark's Erik Bruhn, which included Bruhn's *Giselle* and the first European production of Robbins' *Les Nóces.*

Maya Plisetskaya, the Bolshoi Ballet's prima ballerina, was seen outside of her homeland in the first ballet created especially for her, *Carmen,* choreographed by Alberto Alonso and with a score, based on Bizet, by her husband, Rodion Shchedrin. The Kirov Ballet from Leningrad staged *Raymonda* with

Barbara Remington, left, and Pamela Johnson danced the roles of pupils to Paul Sutherland in the Joffrey Ballet's production of "Konservatoriet." The production was staged at the New York City Center in early 1969.

JACK MITCHELL

DOMINIC—PIX FROM PUBLIX

Margot Fonteyn and Rudolf Nureyev dance the parts of doomed lovers in the American premiere of Roland Petit's "Pelléas and Mélisande" at New York's Metropolitan Opera House, May 15, 1969.

Natalia Makarova at the 1969 Vienna Festival, which also featured the only European appearance of the Joffrey Ballet. The West Berlin Opera Ballet, in a plan to extend its choreographic range, invited George Balanchine, Norman Walker, and Bill Evans from the U.S. to stage ballets. (W. TE.)

In the U.K. in 1969 the Arts Council published its *Report on Opera and Ballet in the United Kingdom 1966–1969*. It was found that the U.K. had dance companies of a size and quality to reach out to most geographic and intellectual areas. Of the two large-scale companies for large theatres, the Royal Ballet's Covent Garden company staged a new production in 1969 of the Petipa/Tchaikovsky *The Sleeping Beauty,* produced by Peter Wright with additional choreography by Sir Frederick Ashton.

The only other work for which Ashton was responsible in the 1968–69 period was a semidramatic version of Elgar's *Enigma Variations* with Derek Rencher as Elgar and Svetlana Beriosova as his wife. Kenneth MacMillan revived his *Olympiad* (to Stravinsky's *Symphony in Three Movements*), which he had previously created for the West Berlin Opera Ballet. Roland Petit created *Pelléas and Mélisande* (to Schoenberg music) especially for Margot Fonteyn and Rudolf Nureyev. There was also a revival of the Glazunov/Petipa *Raymonda* Act III, which Nureyev had previously revived for the Royal Ballet's smaller company.

Because it was continually on tour, the smaller company had little time to put on new works. However, during its winter regional tour, Antony Tudor created a new ballet—*Knight Errant* (to Richard Strauss music from *Le Bourgeois Gentilhomme* and *Ariadne auf Naxos*)—mainly for David Wall who, owing to injury, could not appear in the first performances. The company also staged works of two choreographers, both Royal Ballet dancers: Geoffrey Cauley's *In the Beginning* (to Poulenc sonatas) and David Drew's *Intrusion* (to Schubert's Fantasia in F Minor), which had previously been created for students of the Royal Ballet School. It was difficult to say whether the policies of the two Royal Ballet companies would continue unchanged after the retirement in 1970 of the artistic director, Sir Frederick Ashton, who was to be succeeded by John Field and Kenneth MacMillan as co-directors.

London's Festival Ballet continued with its regional touring as well as three European tours—to Italy, France, and Spain—and tours to the Far East and Japan. Its London home had been the converted concert platform of the Royal Festival Hall, but in the summer of 1969 the company had a season in a proper theatre, at the London Coliseum. A new full-length *Coppelia* mounted by Jack Carter was added to the other classics in the repertory, and for the London season John Taras revived his *Piège de Lumière,* originally created for the Marquis de Cuevas company. Also new to the repertory was *Meadow Lark* (to Haydn flute quartets) by Eliot Feld. Jack Carter celebrated the Berlioz centenary with *The Unknown Island* (to a Berlioz song cycle).

Of Britain's medium-sized companies, Ballet Rambert enlarged its already important contemporary repertory with *Embrace Tiger and Return to Mountain* (to a Morton Subotnick score) by U.S. choreographer Glen Tetley. Norman Morrice, co-director of the company with Dame Marie Rambert, created *Pastoral Variée* (to Paul Ben-Hain music). Other members of the company created works that went into the repertory: John Chesworth with *Pawn to King 5* (Pink Floyd music) and Christopher Bruce with *George Frideric* (Handel music). Ballet Rambert also embarked on its first European tours—to Germany, Austria, and Italy.

The Western Ballet had become one of the first regionally based companies by making its home in Glasgow with the Scottish Opera and changing its name to Scottish Theatre Ballet. This was the first step toward the decentralization and regional development that the Arts Council report had recommended. The more distinguished works in the company's existing repertory were being retained and Scottish Theatre Ballet was to continue touring England as well as Scotland and to give regular London seasons at Sadler's Wells.

Among the small-sized companies the Royal Ballet's Ballet for All group continued its tours with a form of lecture-demonstration developed by Peter Brinson, its director. A new addition was the company and demonstration group of the London School of Contemporary Dance whose artistic director was Robert Cohan, one of Martha Graham's principal dancers. The company was strengthened by other Graham dancers including Noemi Lapzeson, Robert Powell, and William Louther. The repertory included several works by Cohan as well as the works of other young British choreographers, and the first London season in September 1969 at The Place, the company's new headquarters, proved that it was a valuable addition to the British scene.

Among the many visiting companies to appear at Sadler's Wells were the Netherlands Dance Theatre, whose large repertory, mainly by Glen Tetley and Hans van Manen, was much admired; the Alwin Nikolais Dance Theatre, whose great impact on audiences was due to the wonderful combination of movement, sound, light, and all kinds of scenic effect, created by Nikolais; the Prague Studio Ballet; and Les Grands Ballets Canadiens, making its first European tour.

In spite of heavy subsidies for the Paris Opéra, the Opéra Comique, and other state institutions, France had made no great contribution to ballet development in recent years. In February the Royal Danish Ballet paid its first visit to France since 1938. The Ministry of Cultural Affairs started to subsidize a number of *"maisons de la culture"* in various major towns. The first to be concerned with dance theatre was in Amiens where, early in 1969, the newly formed Ballet-Théâtre Contemporain gave a number of performances of works by young choreographers.

(P. L. W.)

See also Music; Theatre.

Defense

The reemergence of the strategic arms race between the superpowers was the most important military event of 1969. Compared with the Soviet invasion of Czechoslovakia the previous year, it seemed less dramatic but of far greater long-term significance. Whatever its effects in Europe, the invasion had not impaired U.S. belief in the need for a mutual détente or, more accurately, a working relationship to mitigate the worst consequences of the superpowers' joint dependence on nuclear weapons. This had seemed possible, given strategic stability, but if that stability vanished the consequences would be incalculable. The cold war atmosphere would reappear, because neither side could afford to trust the other's intention. Instead, each would rely on estimated capabilities, using the military approach of considering the worst case as the only prudential guide to action. Fears of an effective disarming first strike might prove self-fulfilling. Resources would be diverted from constructive uses to give less security for more money. The key to the changed strategic equation lay in the interaction between ABM's (antiballistic missiles), MIRV's (multiple independently targeted reentry vehicles), and SALT (strategic arms limitation talks).

The incoming U.S. president required time to evaluate his position on all three, but the delay itself significantly accentuated the problem. Of the three, ABM was the most pressing. The last months of Pres. Lyndon Johnson's administration had seen the Sentinel ABM network develop into a major internal political issue. Protests had come not, as expected, from residents of cities left unprotected by it, but from those cities where ABM's were being installed. Critics of the system thus gained a far wider hearing. They alleged the system could not defend soft targets such as cities. Pres. Richard Nixon's announcement of Sentinel's replacement by the Safeguard system did little to mollify the anti-ABM lobby because it changed only the deployment of the weapons.

Both systems had the same basic components: a long-range, high-speed radar and antimissile missiles. In the U.S. these were MAR (multifunction array radar using electronic switching instead of mechanical rotation to scan the horizon); Spartan (a long-range missile for interception outside the atmosphere); and Sprint (a short-range missile able to hit enemy warheads 20 to 30 mi. from their target). Theoretically, enemy missiles would be picked up soon after launch by PAR (perimeter acquisition radar), which would inform the central control system. The ABM installation assigned to the interception would take over tracking on its tactical missile site radar (MSR) and launch Spartans. The slower moving debris and decoys would be separated by the atmosphere from any remaining warheads, which the Sprint could then destroy. Spartans alone could provide a very limited defense over an area of several hundred miles around their bases, hence the term area defense. Sprint's limited range meant that each battery could give its much greater protection to only a small area—point defense.

The difference between the two ABM systems was their deployment. Sentinel used point defense to protect cities against a Chinese attack, leaving missile and Strategic Air Command (SAC) bases undefended. Safeguard reversed this, removing ABM sites from voters' backyards to missile silos and command and control centres, including Washington, D.C. Being oriented against the U.S.S.R., it gave a limited area defense as well. A slower deployment would have the first two installations guarding Minuteman missiles in Montana by 1973. Costs were higher, at $7 billion, but were spread over a longer period, with Phase I costing only $2.1 billion. Progress in SALT and other spheres could thus be considered before further phases were undertaken.

Senate approval for Safeguard came on August 6, after an exceptionally bitter debate in which the advantages and disadvantages of ABM were fully explored. Opponents argued it was ineffective and destabilizing. A limited, or thin, deployment like Sentinel or Safeguard would be helpless against the sort of attack the Soviet Union could launch by the time it was ready. The radars, without which an ABM is useless, were vulnerable to high-level thermonuclear explosives producing blackout over hundreds of miles. The whole system was so complex that it probably could not function in peacetime, let alone in an attack environment. On the other hand, it was too expensive a premium against the slight danger that the Chinese would decide to initiate a nuclear exchange that would wipe them out in return for destroying one or two U.S. cities. Yet the very weakness of the ABM's made the system more destabilizing. Once a thin system was built, its defects would create irresistible pressures for its expansion into a thick one, able to provide defense against a large-scale Soviet attack. The Soviets would anticipate this and develop countermeasures in the form of increased penetration aids, as the U.S. had done when the Galosh ABM system was installed around Moscow. This had produced MIRV's. So by making their deployment by both sides inevitable, ABM's would start a process the effect of which would be to push both powers off the existing technological plateau and up another step in the arms race.

The proponents of the ABM saw it as the least destabilizing reply to inevitable developments. Time lags meant that a decision had to be taken immediately on how to protect the U.S. strategic offensive forces against the threat the Soviets could pose, in terms of

Deaths:
see Vital Statistics;
see also biographies of prominent persons who died in 1969, listed under Obituaries

Debts, National:
see Government Finance

a preemptive first strike, in 1975. Increasing these forces meant more Minutemen, which might be useless since they would be equally vulnerable to attack, or more Poseidon submarine-launched missiles. These could produce an unbalanced retaliatory force, too easily upset by advances in antisubmarine warfare. Both could create Soviet fears that the U.S. wanted to maintain its superiority in deliverable warheads. Defensive measures could be passive, in the form of increased hardening of missile silos against nuclear explosions, but this was no longer effective against the growing accuracy of attacks. Active defense, in the form of ABM's, thus became the best alternative. ABM had been improved to the state where the cost-exchange ratio (the cost of shooting down an incoming missile compared with the cost of the missile) was approaching unity, making it as economical to use defensive missiles to protect existing ICBM's as to buy more of them. Although ABM would work sufficiently well to be worth buying, it would not work well enough to threaten stability on its own, in the sense that one power might decide a successful first strike could reduce his opponent's retaliatory forces so much that the opponent's second strike could be intercepted by his active defenses (antiaircraft and ABM). Partly, this derived from the uncertainty factor. Attack calculations must always assume that enemy defenses will perform very well against an attack that will go very badly. ABM thus enhanced deterrence by increasing the range of uncertainties facing an attacker. The pro-ABM faction also tended to view MIRV as a far more dangerous development but to deny that it could be stopped by halting ABM.

The connection between the two was that MIRV originated as former U.S. Secretary of Defense Robert S. McNamara's counter to Soviet ABM's. In the U.S. configuration, MIRV consists of a "bus," containing a rocket motor and guidance system, with three separate 200-kiloton warheads. Once in space, the bus separates from the booster rocket and maneuvers to drop each of its warheads on a different target in a different trajectory. It could hit, for example, Moscow, Odessa, and Vladivostok, or New York, Washington, and Los Angeles. It should be particularly effective against missile silos, since these are vulnerable only to direct hits, which means within a quarter of a mile. Each MIRV is more accurate than previous missiles, and since there are three warheads on one missile, there is a good chance that at least one warhead will land on target. The difference is between shooting with a pistol and a shotgun. For the defense, MIRV is an almost insuperable problem. A single-warhead missile is launched in a fixed trajectory that can be calculated soon after launch, enabling defensive missiles to intercept it. The MIRV bus has no fixed course, and each warhead's path can be calculated only after it has been detached.

The time factor means that only point defense can function against MIRV, and even then it has a harder job since the attack can come from any angle. The intermediate MRV (multiple reentry vehicle) is much simpler, consisting of three warheads on the U.S. Navy Polaris A3 or Air Force Minuteman II missile. Since these are not maneuverable and can land only in a relatively narrow area, they are almost as vulnerable to ABM's as single warheads.

MIRV created two main problems. The first was the reestablishment of the superiority of offense by enabling a successful first strike to destroy enough of the adversary's forces to make his retaliation negligible or acceptable. One bomber or one missile with MIRV's could knock out more than one enemy mis-

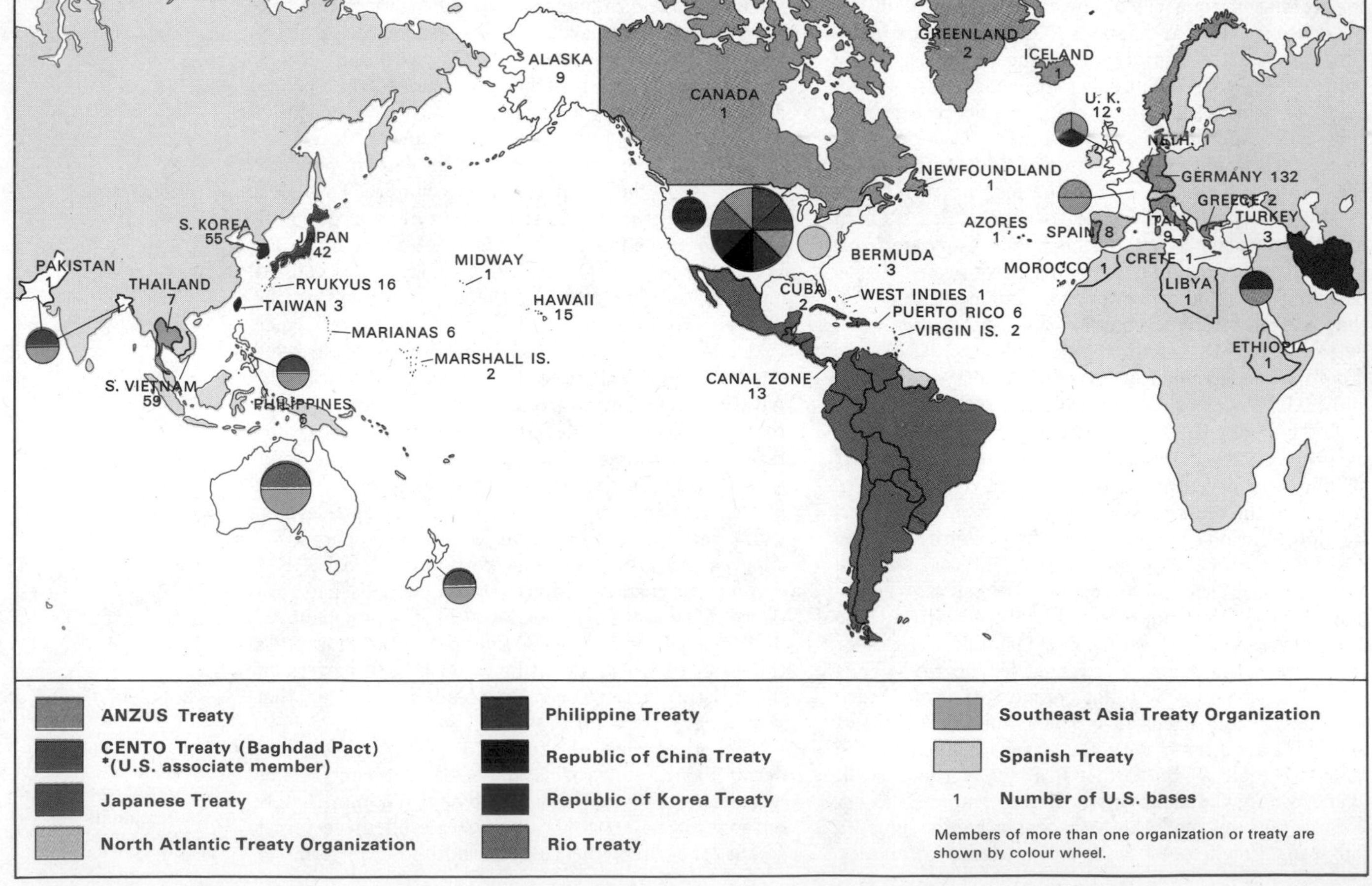

sile, whereas it took an estimated four single-warhead ICBM's to destroy one ICBM in a silo. The second problem was the reduced effectiveness of unilateral verification in army control agreements. Developments in satellite reconnaissance had given the superpowers the ability to detect even quite small installations on each other's territory. An agreement to freeze ICBM's at, say, 1,200 could be monitored without the on-site inspection rejected by the U.S.S.R. Now, however, one missile might have one warhead or MIRV's, and the two could be changed over in hours.

If SALT were to achieve any meaningful results, it seemed imperative that they start at the earliest possible date, before MIRV developed past the stage where it could be controlled. A considerable debate arose between those who said this had already happened and their opponents. The U.S. was about halfway through a two-year program of testing scheduled to end in July 1971, while the Soviets had tested a multiple warhead on their SS-9 missile in April. The question of whether or not it was a MIRV illustrated the dangers the new weapon posed. The U.S. Department of Defense admitted uncertainty but claimed the Soviet missile's performance characteristics were nearer those of a MIRV than an MRV. This supported Secretary of Defense Melvin Laird's earlier testimony that the SS-9 represented a Soviet bid for a first strike capability.

The State Department and the Central Intelligence Agency were less pessimistic. While agreeing that total assurance against MIRV development was impossible, they saw a chance to obtain controls on testing that would slow down deployment. More importantly, such controls would prevent the large-scale continued testing required to establish confidence in a weapon's operational performance, without which neither side could regard its own or the other side's MIRV's as first-strike weapons. The SS-9 (a liquid-fueled missile able to carry one 25-megaton warhead or three 5-megaton ones) was less evidence of Soviet aggressiveness than part of a drive for parity. It had been in service since 1965, and the 200 that were deployed could carry the fractional orbital bombardment system (FOBS), a warhead delivered in a low trajectory less easily spotted by radar and so able to reach U.S. bases before bombers on 15-minute alert could take off. This made it an entirely logical weapon for the Soviet Union, while its continued production could reflect output targets intended to offset any U.S. drive to regain superiority. Although inconclusive, the debate tended to increase support for SALT by demonstrating the dangers in the existing means of trying to deal with the effects of a military technology that seemed increasingly like Frankenstein's monster.

Bureaucratic factors delayed the start of SALT. President Nixon preferred a methodical approach, with the pros and cons of every position spelled out, whereas President Johnson had preferred to leave detailed examination for those areas where agreement seemed possible. The Soviets, in turn, reconsidered their views in the light of the Nixon administration's performance and attitude. Opponents of SALT in the U.S.S.R., strongest in the Army, may also have used the lack of progress as evidence that the U.S. was not serious. Some saw evidence of similar trends in the U.S. However, in late October the Soviets agreed to preliminary talks, which opened on November 17 in Helsinki, Fin. The results were generally considered to be encouraging, and full-scale talks were scheduled to begin early in 1970.

Disarmament. Arms control continued to suffer from the aftermath of the Soviet invasion of Czechoslovakia. The 18-Nation Disarmament Committee (ENDC) session that began on March 18 proved to be the last for the organization as it had been set up in 1962. The lack of meaningful progress, and ENDC's expansion to 26 members, confirmed its change to a negotiating forum to which the superpowers could present proposals they had agreed on between themselves.

Instead of moving forward with the momentum gained by the nonproliferation treaty (NPT), ENDC found itself searching for alternative measures while the NPT was stalled. The Czechoslovak affair had made ratification by the U.S. impossible before the 1968 presidential election, and President Nixon did not obtain the necessary Senate consent until March. He then withheld his consent until Soviet ratification, which was itself being delayed pending West German signature and ratification. West Germany's government, in turn, pleaded the forthcoming September election as a justification for inaction. It was also waiting to see whether the Italians and Japanese would continue to hold out against signing. The new German government of Chancellor Willy Brandt that came to power in October appeared better disposed toward the NPT than its predecessor. In late November the U.S. and the U.S.S.R. ratified the treaty simultaneously in Washington and Moscow. A few days later, West Germany signed, although it indicated that formal ratification must await clarification of the question of what international agency would supervise its nuclear research and development program. The Japanese seemed likely to sign early in 1970. Nevertheless, by the time the requisite 40 states, plus the U.K. (the third nuclear power concerned), had ratified, it seemed likely the delay to the NPT would amount to two years.

Against this unpromising background, ENDC examined four measures. The most important was the Soviet draft treaty on the preservation of the seabed for peaceful uses, banning all military use outside a 12-mi. coastal zone. It focused on a problem that had been under discussion in the UN Committee on the Seabed since a Maltese resolution of 1967 drew attention to the need for action to stop the arms race from spreading to the ocean floor. Of the 17 states present (France continued to abstain from ENDC), 14 supported the Soviets. They were opposed by the U.S., which insisted that total demilitarization of the seabed would pose considerable verification difficulties. The U.S. alternative proposal, put forward on May 22, was for a ban on weapons of mass destruction beyond a three-mile coastal zone. This would preserve intact the extensive U.S. sonar network for tracking Soviet submarines. Two compromise proposals were made. Canada, on May 13, suggested that limited defensive measures be allowed up to 200 mi. from the shoreline. After Japan declared for the U.S. position on July 17, Sweden offered an alternative on July 24, banning all except passive defense installations beyond 12 mi. and all weapons of mass destruction beyond 3 mi. Within the 12-mi. zone the coastal state would have the sole right of verification; outside it, all installations would be open for inspection. In August, however, the U.S.S.R. accepted the principle of the U.S. offer in order to secure an agreement proposing a ban on weapons of mass destruction outside a 12-mi. coastal zone. The U.S. accepted this in September. Since the treaty would ban weapons

BEN ROTH AGENCY

—Vadillo, "Siempre," Mexico.

COURTESY, RCA

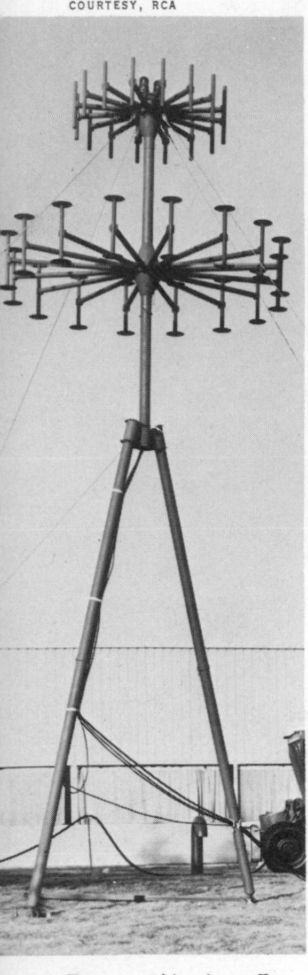

Transportable air traffic control tower developed for the U.S. Air Force can be set up in an hour. It has capabilities equal to those of the largest commercial jetports.

only the superpowers could develop, acceptance of an agreed draft was expected in 1970.

None of the other three proposals before ENDC was expected to take effect. Two were presented each year: a comprehensive test ban treaty (CTB) and a cutoff in the production of fissionable material for weapons purposes. The CTB foundered on the rock of inspection, with the U.S.S.R. insisting that national means of verification were adequate while the U.S. demanded on-site inspection of suspicious events. The Swedish representative, Alva Myrdal, observed, however, that the real issue was the political utility of a ban. This was low, since the 1963 partial test-ban treaty allowed underground testing that gave each side the opportunity to improve its nuclear weapons, while providing a meaningful agreement with no likelihood of cheating. The U.S.S.R. and the U.S. saw little gain and much risk in going further. Hence their coldness to the Swedish draft CTB introduced on April 1: on-site inspection by invitation of the state where suspicious events occurred, with no penalties for failure to issue the invitation. The Soviet counter, on August 20, was the familiar offer of a noninspected ban on tests with a seismic signal of more than 4.75 plus a moratorium on tests below that level. The U.S. continued to reject this, and a CTB seemed as far off as ever. So did the U.S. suggestion for a cutoff in the production of fissionable material for weapons purposes. Its larger stockpile of such material conferred an automatic advantage on the U.S., which did, however, suggest on April 21 that it could be subject to International Atomic Energy Agency inspection, an indication of growing trust in the IAEA.

The British draft convention on biological weapons, introduced on July 10, met with equally little success. It would ban their development, production, or use, thereby strengthening the 1925 Geneva Protocol which forbids only actual bacteriological warfare. The U.S. had never ratified the protocol but, with the Soviet Union, insisted that the best course was to strengthen it rather than to introduce a new convention. The Soviets also opposed any separation of biological and chemical warfare.

On July 3, Japan and Mongolia accepted the invitation of the U.S. and the U.S.S.R., as co-chairmen, to join the conference, which was further enlarged on August 7 by the addition of the Netherlands, Hungary, Argentina, Morocco, Pakistan, and Yugoslavia. The resulting 26-nation conference (including the still-absent France) was renamed the Conference of the Committee on Disarmament (CCDA).

NATO

After reacting sharply to the Soviet invasion of Czechoslovakia at their November 1968 ministerial meeting, the NATO members failed to take any corresponding action to strengthen their defenses, although the Europeans moved close to an agreed doctrine on the use of tactical nuclear weapons. In January the NATO Defense Planning Committee established "on-call" allied naval forces, held available to counter any Soviet naval moves in the Mediterranean. They were soon joined by MARAIRMED, a NATO maritime air command based in Italy.

The NATO ministerial meeting in Washington on April 10–11 celebrated the organization's 20th birthday with a communiqué restating established positions. It reaffirmed adherence to forward defense (meeting an attack on West Germany on its frontiers, not falling back) and determination to protect West Berlin; admitted that mutual force reductions would have to be postponed; and announced a U.S. promise to consult with NATO on SALT.

The session of the NATO Nuclear Planning Group (NPG) held in London on May 29–30 had far more significance for allied strategy. At its previous meeting in October 1968, the group had considered use of nuclear land mines for the purpose of making one or two demonstration explosions early in an attack. Britain and West Germany had elaborated these ideas into a comprehensive strategy. Tactical nuclear weapons could not be used on a large scale in West Germany. Since they were essential to a forward defense, the threshold for use would have to be lowered to a few days in the event of a major attack. The decision to fire would be limited to the state supplying nuclear weapons (the U.S.) and the state providing the base and delivery system, plus the target state if it was a NATO member. These conclusions were broadly accepted by all members (except France) at the NPG meeting at Warrenton, Va., in November and were confirmed by the defense ministers' meeting in December.

This reversed the McNamara doctrine that NATO should acquire the capability for a conventional defense of Europe for up to four weeks. Indeed, for the first time Britain, France, and West Germany had reached an agreed position on the early use of tactical nuclear weapons. Whether the U.S. would accept it seemed another matter—hence the growing interest in the possibilities for Anglo-French nuclear cooperation. Surprisingly, the new U.S. administration seemed inclined to favour the idea, and suggestions were made that it might be prepared to assist with the development of a joint force. In contrast to the previous administration's opposition to all proliferation, it apparently felt that such a force might provide a long-term solution to European fears about the viability of the U.S. commitment to use nuclear weapons in their defense. A report issued by the British Royal United Services Institution concluded that the French were ahead in land-based missiles while Britain had superior warheads (including hydrogen bombs) and guidance systems, offering real gains from collaboration.

These trends toward greater reliance on nuclear weapons were reinforced by Canada's decision to replace its 6,000-man mechanized brigade in Europe with commando-style light air-mobile forces, announced at the NATO defense ministers' session in Brussels just before the NPG meeting. The existing 4,000-man air arm operating six squadrons of CF-104 Starfighter jets would also be cut, although no details were given. The ground forces would lose their nuclear capability, but this might be retained for the existing air element, using U.S. warheads under the existing two-key system. Sharp criticisms of the Canadian withdrawal were made, especially by the British minister of defense, Denis Healey. The Canadian force was more important than its numbers indicated, since it consisted of well-equipped volunteer units in NATO's most vulnerable area, the North German plain. If it were reduced, other small states in NATO might follow suit, thus lowering the nuclear threshold still further.

European cooperation in defense procurement continued to be adversely affected by difficulties in reconciling views on specifications, as with the multi-role combat aircraft (MRCA). The RAF wanted a two-seater strike and reconnaissance plane to fit into the

Approximate Strengths of Regular Armed Forces of the World

Country	Military personnel in 000s: Army	Navy	Air Force	Aircraft carriers	Warships: Submarines*	Cruisers	Destroyers/ Frigates	Total Ships	Aircraft: Bombers†	Fighters	Defense expenditure as % of GNP
I. NATO											
Belgium	78.0	4.4	20.0	—	—	—	—	47	88 FB, 50 B	44	2.4
Canada	37.3	18.3	42.7	1	4	—	22	37	48 FB, 36 B	36	2.5
Denmark	28.0	7.0	10.5	—	4	—	2	43	48 FB	48	2.3
Germany, West	328.0	36.0	101.0	—	11	—	18	135	256 FB	76	3.9
Greece	118.0	18.0	23.0	—	2	—	12	61	105 FB	45	4.3
Italy	313.1	42.4	64.5	—	10	4	22	142	95 FB	105	2.7
Luxembourg	0.56	—	—	—	—	—	—	—	—	—	1.0
Netherlands	82.0	20.0	22.0	—	6	2	16	104	100 FB	50	3.9
Norway	21.0	8.0	9.0	—	15	—	5	56	64 FB	16	3.8
Portugal	148.0	16.5	17.5	—	4	—	13	51	36 FB	12	6.2
Turkey	400.0	40.0	43.0	—	10	—	10	76	360 FB	140	3.9
United Kingdom	198.0	92.0	115.0	4	22, 3N, 3 FBNS	1	27	263	224 FB, 70 B	124	5.3
United States	1,522.0	106.3‡	869.0	22	62, 40N, 41 FBMS	13	229	900	834 FB, 510 SB	1,240	9.2
II. OTHER EUROPEANS											
Austria	46.0	—	4.0	—	—	—	—	—	18 FB	—	1.2
Finland	31.4	2.0	3.0	—	—	—	3	31	30 FB	—	1.8
France	328.0	70.0	105.0	4	19	2	44	162	54 FB, 36 B	120	5.3
Spain	210.0	44.5	35.0	1	4	1	24	84	60 FB	75	2.2
Sweden	49.0	11.6	24.0	—	23	1	16	85	120 FB	288	3.8
Switzerland	19.5	—	7.0	—	—	—	—	—	180 FB	72	2.5
Yugoslavia	180.0	18.0	20.0	—	4	—	3	123	135 FB	150	5.7
III. WARSAW PACT											
Albania	30.0	3.0	5.0	—	4	—	—	32	—	60	N.a.
Bulgaria	125.0	7.0	22.0	—	2	—	2	40	72 FB	144	2.9
Czechoslovakia	175.0	—	5.5	—	—	—	—	—	300 FB	300	5.7
Germany, East	90.0	16.0	31.0	—	—	—	4	127	—	270	5.7
Hungary	90.0	—	7.0	—	—	—	—	—	15 B	110	2.9
Poland	185.0	20.0	70.0	—	5	—	3	128	140 FB, 60 B	450	4.8
Romania	170.0	8.0	15.0	—	—	—	—	46	—	220	3.0
U.S.S.R.	2,000.0	465.0	505.0	2	320, 42N, 18 FBMS	25	92	1,397	1,750 FB, 750 B, 150 SB	4,700	9.3
IV. FAR EAST AND OCEANIA											
Australia	46.7	17.5	29.95	1	3	—	10	41	45 FB	48	4.8
Burma	130.0	6.0	6.5	—	—	—	1	52	15 FB	—	5.1
Cambodia	35.0	1.5‡	2.0	—	—	—	—	18	30 FB	15	6.3
China	2,500.0	141.0	180.0	—	33	—	8	394	...+150 B	...	9.0
Indonesia	275.0	40.0	50.0	—	6	1	18	124	38 FB, 25 B	55	2.1
Japan	169.0	39.0	42.0	—	8	—	40	179	—	500	0.8
Korea, North	350.0	9.5	25.0	—	4	—	—	190	430 FB, 80 B	80	N.a.
Korea, South	550.0	47.0‡	23.0	—	—	—	9	58	45 FB	160	4.5
Laos	63.0	0.4	1.5	—	—	—	—	—	50 FB	—	9.5
Malaysia	38.7	3.0	3.0	—	—	—	2	10	20 FB	—	3.9
New Zealand	5.7	2.9	4.5	—	—	1	4	8	12 FB, 12 B	—	1.9
Philippines	18.0	5.5	9.0	—	—	—	—	32	22 FB	38	1.6
Taiwan	400.0	70.0‡	85.0	—	—	—	11	142	105 FB	210	7.6
Vietnam, North	450.0	2.5	4.5	—	—	—	—	11	68 B	125	...
Vietnam, South	420.5	31.0	21.0	—	—	—	—	56	60 FB	12	12.5
V. MIDDLE EAST, NORTH AFRICA, AND SOUTH ASIA											
Algeria	53.0	2.0	2.0	—	—	—	—	28	33 B	140	6.4
India	848.0	20.0	57.0	1	2	2	15	50	305 FB, 50 B	270	3.6
Iran	200.0	6.0	15.0	—	—	—	2	13	122 FB	50	5.8
Iraq	70.0	2.0	6.0	—	—	—	—	—	90 FB, 18 B	105	11.2
Israel§	11.5/268.0	3.0/7.0	8.0/15.0	—	4	—	2	11	248 FB, 15 B	12	16.1
Jordan	53.0	0.25	1.7	—	—	—	—	—	11	—	14.7
Pakistan	300.0	9.0	15.0	—	1	—	4	20	120 FB, 36 B	60	3.7
South Africa	28.0	2.5	5.0	—	—	—	8	30	60 FB, 24 B	46	2.5
Saudi Arabia	28.0	1.0	5.0	—	—	—	—	—	—	43	11.9
Syria	60.0	1.5	9.0	—	—	—	—	11	90 FB	55	12.6
United Arab Republic	180.0	12.0	15.0	—	12	—	6	63	210 FB, 42 B	100	12.5

Note: Data exclude paramilitary, security, and irregular forces. Naval data exclude vessels of less than 100 tons standard displacement.
*Nuclear hunter-killers (N), Fleet Ballistic Missile Submarines (FBMS).
†Medium and heavy bombers (B), fighter bombers (FB), and strategic bombers (SB).
‡Includes Marine Corps.
§Second figure is fully mobilized strength.
Source: Institute for Strategic Studies, 18 Adam Street, London WC 2, *The Military Balance, 1969–70.*

NATO strategy of graduated response; the West Germans preferred a single-seater ground-support fighter. The memorandum of understanding signed on May 14 established a one-year project-definition phase to be undertaken by the Panavia company, consisting of the British Aircraft Corporation and Messerschmitt-Bölkow, with a one-third share each, plus Fiat (Italy) and Fokker (Netherlands) with one-sixth each. When it entered service in 1975–76, the plane was expected to be twin-engined, with variable geometry wings. Nominal production costs would be $3.6 million apiece; West Germany would take 560, Britain 340, and the Netherlands and Italy 100 each. On July 2 the Dutch dropped out, however, claiming the aircraft could not be in service before 1978 and was too expensive. The Italians took a similar view. Despite these vicissitudes, the Rolls-Royce RB-199 engine was selected for the MRCA-75 on September 5 (in preference to the U.S. Pratt and Whitney model). The Anglo-French Jaguar supersonic trainer and light strike aircraft made better progress, with each country committed to buying 200, in five different versions.

Gen. Lyman L. Lemnitzer retired on July 1 after more than six years as supreme allied commander, Europe (SACEUR), and was succeeded by Gen. Andrew J. Goodpaster (*see* BIOGRAPHY). At the North Atlantic Assembly held in Brussels in October the NATO attitude to the proposed European Security Conference emerged as sympathetic but skeptical.

UNITED STATES

Paradoxically, the most important development in U.S. defense policy was the growth of a politically important opposition to what Pres. Dwight Eisenhower, in his 1961 farewell address, had called "the military-industrial complex." It took the form of a realization that the military was not infallible and resulted in a totally changed attitude toward military requests for appropriations. Where these had previously been passed almost automatically, Congress started demanding more information, refusing many items, reducing others, and insisting on far more stringent checks on cost inflation.

The decisive factor was the Sentinel ABM system,

GAMMA—PIX FROM PUBLIX

U.S. Army tank forces participate in Operation Reforger I near the Czechoslovak border in 1969. During maneuver troops and equipment were flown to Europe for a test of their combat readiness.

which provided an effective political focus for the antimilitary feeling built up by the war in Vietnam. In the winter of 1968 work had begun on the ABM sites to protect Boston and other major cities. Apparently for the first time, their citizens realized they were paying an estimated $5 billion in taxes to have storage areas for nuclear warheads for the Sprint and Spartan missiles in their backyards. Military assurances that accidents with the weapons were impossible were not accepted. The attack on the ABM system gathered strength after the Republican victory in the presidential elections. Traditionally, the Republicans were the promilitary party (although it had been the Democrats who had vastly expanded the armed forces and engaged in the Vietnam war). The Democratic majority in Congress thus had an ideal weapon with which to attack the new administration.

Sentinel's cancellation and its replacement by Safeguard did little to mollify criticism, especially when it later emerged that the $6.6 billion estimate excluded $1.2 billion for the warheads. This intensified the strict examination of the Pentagon's inadequate accounting techniques. Further evidence concerning them was brought to light when the Sub-Committee on Economy in Government of the Joint Economic Committee, under Sen. William Proxmire (Dem., Wis.), issued its report on May 28; it found that the cost of the Air Force C-5A Galaxy jet transport had risen from between $2.9 billion and $3.1 billion to between $4.3 billion and $5.2 billion. This had been concealed by the Air Force to help the Lockheed-Georgia Co. offset its loss on the contract. Various ceilings on cost overheads, established in the original contract, had apparently been waived by the assistant secretary in charge. The Pentagon accounting officer responsible for overseeing the contract, who had revealed these facts to the committee, was punished by transfer to a less responsible position and later discharged. The F-111 fighter-bomber, itself a failure, was revealed to have an electronic brain the cost of which rose from $610 million to $2,520,000,000, an increase concealed from the secretary of defense. The Cheyenne helicopter, before cancellation, overran original estimates by 300%. In December the General Accounting Office revealed that major U.S. weapons systems were overrunning estimates by $20 billion.

Chemical warfare activities within the U.S. increased fear of the military. In May the Army finally admitted responsibility for killing some 6,000 sheep at the Dugway Proving Ground in Utah in March 1968, when a container carrying a lethal nerve gas leaked during a test. Only the wind direction, apparently, had saved Salt Lake City. The resultant concentration on the activities of the Chemical Corps revealed a plan to ship 27,000 tons of nerve gas across the U.S. by train, before encasing it in concrete and dropping it into the Atlantic. The medical team accompanying the train to deal with accidents consisted of one doctor and a small decontamination unit. The episode seemed to many to demonstrate how infatuation with new gadgets could blind the military to any broader implications. Partly as a result of pressure created by these incidents, a complete review of U.S. policy on chemical and biological warfare (CBW) was instituted in June. In November, President Nixon pledged that the U.S. would never use biological weapons and would use chemical weapons only for defensive purposes, although he excepted tear gas and chemical defoliants from the ban. He also ordered the destruction of the existing stock of biological weapons and urged the Senate to approve U.S. ratification of the 1925 Geneva Protocol. Only a few weeks later, however, 200 persons had to be evacuated when a small quantity of nerve gas leaked at Dugway.

The Army came into the spotlight with the revelation by a Senate subcommittee that it had spent over $1 billion on the Sheridan battle tank and its Shillelagh weapons system; neither was satisfactory. In July, Sen. J. William Fulbright's (Dem., Ark.) Foreign Relations Committee discovered the existence of a secret military agreement allegedly committing the U.S. to aid Thailand in the event of the latter being attacked. When asked to produce the agreement for examination, the Pentagon refused, saying the committee members must come over to the Department of Defense if they wished to examine it. This led to accusations that the military was abrogating to itself the State Department's functions while refusing to answer to the legislative branch. Although the agreement was finally made available and turned out to be strictly limited, the impression remained. The arrest of eight Special Forces personnel in Vietnam in August on a charge of murder further increased fears about how far either the legislature or the executive was able to exercise real control over the forces. Subsequently, the release of the eight men was ordered by the secretary of the army on the ground that a fair trial was impossible, since the CIA would not allow its agents to give evidence, but this seemed a flimsy excuse for burying an embarrassing episode. It also appeared to put the CIA above the law. (See *Vietnam,* below.)

The Navy came in for criticism for its handling of intelligence-gathering missions. The decision not to court-martial Cmdr. Lloyd Bucher of the USS "Pueblo" did little to erase the memory that no contingency plans had been made for the vessel's protection, despite warnings that an attack was possible. There was no escort, either with the ship or within range, no air cover, no effective defensive armament, and insufficient provision for the destruction of classified documents or code-breaking equipment. Indeed, Commander Bucher appeared to have had difficulty in informing his superiors that the vessel was under attack. An apparent inability to learn from experience was revealed when, in April, a Navy EC-121 aircraft with functions similar to those of the "Pueblo" was shot down by North Koreans, with the loss of 31 men.

No escorting aircraft had been provided. (*See* Special Report.)

The total effect of these incidents was to weaken faith in the military's technical competence. The president recognized this when, in July, he appointed a distinguished 14-man committee to conduct a complete study of the Pentagon. Neither this nor Secretary Laird's highly publicized economy moves could stave off attacks, however. The final Senate vote on ABM, which approved Safeguard by 51 votes to 49, accurately reflected the hostility to the military.

President Johnson's defense budget for fiscal 1969–70, presented to Congress on January 15, totaled $81.5 billion, a $4.8 billion increase over the previous year. Vietnam was to receive $25.4 billion, a drop of $400 million. Subsequently, a series of cuts was introduced by the Nixon administration. In April the president announced a $1.1 billion overall reduction. On August 21, Secretary Laird specified the first installment of a further $3 billion in cutbacks, including a 100,000-man cut in total manpower (to 3.4 million) and deactivation of over 100 Navy ships, among them the battleship "New Jersey." The major Air Force share in the cuts, announced October 29, included dropping all 86 of the B-58 supersonic bombers, 5 fighter squadrons, and 2 Nike Hercules batteries. With Secretary Laird's statement of the previous day announcing reductions in 307 military bases, this brought the total cuts to $1.7 billion.

Criticism of U.S. involvement in Thailand and Laos also grew. Early in September talks had begun with Thailand on a phased withdrawal of the 49,000 U.S. servicemen stationed there. The war in Vietnam appeared to be spreading into nearby Laos, where 20,000 North Vietnamese troops had helped the Communist Pathet Lao to push past the 1961 cease-fire lines, threatening the populous Mekong Valley. A U.S. military assistance program of $100 million per year seemed to have little effect.

UNITED KINGDOM

The major issues in British defense policy continued to be the implications of the withdrawal from "east of Suez," NATO strategy, and the future of the British nuclear deterrent. The Defence White Paper of February 20 claimed that the major reorientation of Britain's defense effort had been accomplished. The 1969–70 defense budget, at £2,266 million, was £5 million less than the previous year and less than 6% of GNP. After 1971, Britain's military effort would be confined to Europe, although the ability to send a brigade group overseas would be retained. The carrier "Ark Royal," having completed the refit enabling it to operate the Phantoms purchased from the U.S., would rejoin the fleet in 1970 to cover the pullout from Singapore and the Persian Gulf. Together with the other remaining fleet aircraft carrier, HMS "Eagle," it would then be phased out. The two commando-carriers, operating helicopters, could be kept on longer because of their lower operating costs. Unofficial suggestions were made that they might be able to use an improved Harrier V/STOL (vertical/short takeoff and landing) fighter.

But without either carriers or the land-based air cover the canceled F-111 was to have provided, it was clear that no major overseas operations would be contemplated. Thus, although the Conservative opposition claimed it would retain an overseas role for Britain, it would still have to withdraw the forces from Singapore—currently one Gurkha brigade plus one battalion in Brunei; the Far East Air Force with Canberra bombers, Shackleton reconnaissance planes, and Hunter and Lightning fighters; and the modest naval force. This would leave the Hong Kong garrison of one British and one Gurkha brigade, which was scheduled to remain at that strength, and the forces in the Persian Gulf. These were two battalions (about 3,000 men) and the Gulf Air Force at Bahrain with Shackletons and Hunters. The only real possibility seemed a slight change in the pace of withdrawal, possibly with greater assistance being given to Singapore to build up its own forces. This could be helped by the decision, announced by Australian Prime Minister John Gorton on January 3, that Australia would station forces in Singapore.

The serious intercommunal conflict between Malays and Chinese in Malaysia that broke out in May also served to emphasize how fragile was any stability in the area. The downfall of King Idris of Libya in September emphasized the vulnerability of conservative pro-Western monarchs to the forces of Arab nationalism. Prodded by the new government, the British agreed to close the military establishments at El Adem and Tobruk by early 1970 and the U.S. began talks concerning evacuation of Wheelus Air Force Base. Keeping the rulers of Bahrain, Qatar, and the seven Trucial States on their thrones appeared to be an increasingly short-term proposition.

With Britain becoming a purely European power in military terms, Defense Secretary Healey revised his interpretation of NATO strategy at a defense seminar at Munich, W.Ger., in February. Although still called flexible response, it moved toward the West German position by insisting that the Warsaw Pact powers' superiority in numbers and reinforcement capability would compel a relatively early resort to tactical nuclear weapons, probably within two days of a large-scale attack. This might require a change from the pattern of all-volunteer forces with few reserves, appropriate for overseas operations, to some form of selective service, with much greater use of cadre formations on the Swedish model, capable of rapid expansion in an emergency. Britain's reserves were proportionately the lowest in Europe, comprising 40,000 effectives in the Territorial and Army Volunteer Reserves; the further 168,000 in the General Army Reserves were considered useless. Moreover, a recruiting shortfall of 15,000 men in the previous year suggested future difficulties.

Although the forces had been cut by 21,000 to 389,000 at Jan. 1, 1969, and were scheduled to be reduced to 340,000 by 1973, the lack of opportunities for overseas service promised to cause a major drop in recruitment and reenlistment. The Prices and Incomes Board (PIB) June report on service pay scales recommended that, from the 1970 financial year onward, these be replaced by the military salary, which would translate all payments in kind into cash terms, and thus enable more effective comparison with civilian pay. As an interim measure implemented in September, a pay increase totaling £14 million (equal to 3½%) was made, but was distributed along the new lines. The subsequent upswing in recruiting was attributed to the Ulster troubles.

Another historic change was the RAF's relinquishment of its nuclear deterrent role to the Royal Navy's Polaris submarines in July. The remaining 50 Vulcan bombers and Victor tankers were reassigned to NATO in a tactical role, although the Vulcans retained their ability to carry nuclear weapons. Despite the introduction of 100 U.S. Phantoms out of 160 ordered, the RAF remained very short of modern aircraft; apart from Lightning interceptors, it was dependent on planes dating from the mid-1950s. The successive cancellation of the TSR-2 and F-111 bombers threatened to leave a serious gap in the mid-1970s.

The Navy received an eighth nuclear-powered hunter-killer submarine, while work was begun on designing a successor to the excellent Leander-class general purpose frigates. In the longer run, serious doubts were felt about the purpose of maintaining the third largest navy in the world if Britain was indeed transforming itself into a purely European power.

In terms of equipment, the Army made no significant innovations, although the Chieftain main battle tank replaced the Centurion in six of the armoured regiments in the 49,000-strong British Army of the Rhine (BAOR) in West Germany. Under a new agreement signed July 21, the West Germans agreed to pay £106 million, or 80% of the total cost of the BAOR for the 1969–71 financial years. The services participated in two Commonwealth peace-keeping operations, however, besides shouldering much of the thankless burden of the UN peace-keeping operation in Cyprus. In March, 300 troops were sent to the tiny Caribbean island of Anguilla following reports that gangsters were encouraging the island's proclaimed secession from the British associated state of St. Kitts-Nevis-Anguilla. The reports proved to be unfounded, but before they were withdrawn in September the soldiers did much to restore the goodwill toward Britain that had been lost. (*See* DEPENDENT STATES.) In grim contrast to that almost comic operation was the intervention in Northern Ireland in August, following three days of rioting between Catholics and Protestants. The police, regarded by the Catholics as being on the Protestant side, proved unable to establish order and the British government exercised its reserve power under the Act of Union to send in troops. Commanded by Lieut. Gen. Ian Freeland, the first battalion of 600 men quickly grew to some 7,000. Operating under exceptionally difficult conditions, they managed, by the exercise of restraint and tact, to keep the warring factions apart and to restore order. With no political solution in sight, however, the situation remained extremely tense, making it increasingly likely that the Army would have to continue in its paramilitary role for months, if not years. (*See* UNITED KINGDOM.)

British troops in position to meet a mock attack on Gibraltar by Marine commandos, Aug. 9, 1969. The defense exercise was intended as a demonstration to Franco that Britain had no intention of abandoning the Rock.

"LONDON DAILY EXPRESS" FROM PICTORIAL PARADE

FRANCE

President de Gaulle's resignation on April 28, and the subsequent economic difficulties culminating in devaluation of the franc on August 8, threw into doubt the feasibility of defense *à tous azimuts* (in all directions). Under Gen. C.-L.-M. Ailleret, this Gaullist concept had been the basis of the nuclear *force de frappe,* which was to be capable of instant and massive retaliation against any attack from any quarter. Delays in the nuclear program had led to a revision of declared policy, via Gen. M. M. L. Fourquet's April article in the *Revue de Défense Nationale.* This advocated a progressive response in three stages against an attack by the U.S.S.R. The first stage would be conventional forces; then, when they were overcome, tactical nuclear weapons to buy a few hours; and, finally, strategic nuclear and thermonuclear weapons. In essence, this was NATO's strategy, and the article created expectations that France might reassign forces to that organization.

These expectations were strengthened by the slowdown in the development of the *force de frappe* and consequent changes that would have to be made in the five-year defense plan for 1971–75. Although the second French thermonuclear test was still scheduled for the summer of 1970, it seemed likely that the existing Strategic Air Command (CFAS) would have to continue into the 1970s with its 62 Mirage IVA twin-jet bombers and 12 C-135F tankers. Construction of silos and protected command centres for the 27 IRBM missiles in Haute-Provence continued, although developments in MIRV and ABM technology were likely to make these obsolete before completion. Of the fleet ballistic missile submarines (FBMS), four were scheduled for completion between 1970 and 1975. Each would carry 16 missiles, of 1,500-mi. range, and 200-kiloton warheads, comparable to Polaris. More important for the new doctrine of progressive response was the apparently short-range Pluton tactical nuclear weapons system resembling the U.S. Sergeant, which had a range of 75 mi. and a warhead in the kiloton range. Five army divisions were scheduled to receive Pluton by 1976, but the likelihood of delays gave France a strong interest in reacquiring tactical nuclear weapons from the U.S. under the NATO two-key system. There were reports that inquiries had been made as to what nuclear forces might be available in a serious European crisis if the French government were to request them.

On June 29 the French premier, Jacques Chaban-Delmas, indicated French interest in a European nuclear force, consisting of the combined French and British deterrents. The U.K. government responded coolly to this and other proposals for cooperation with France in the nuclear field, but support for the idea was growing. The U.S. government hinted it might drop its opposition to independent deterrents and assist a joint venture to ensure its safety and credibility.

The defense budget was Fr. 27,595,000,000, including certain items of the military nuclear program not shown in the Defense Ministry's budget estimates. The higher figure showed a drop of Fr. 2,559,000,000 or 9% from the comparable figure for the previous year, though expenditure on the nuclear force showed a 5% increase. On September 16 it was proposed that military service be cut from 16 to 12 months, with effect from 1970. French arms sales abroad rose by a staggering 68% to Fr. 3,372,000,000, reflecting the success of France's policy of selling to any customer (except Israel) who could pay. Thus, sales included Mirage jet fighters to Peru after the U.S. had refused to supply such advanced aircraft, and fighters, submarines, helicopters, and small arms to South Africa after the British arms embargo.

The Anglo-French Jaguar jet fighter and trainer proved successful. The Army continued to replace the M-47 Patton tank with the AMX30 medium tank, bringing the total of armoured regiments thus re-equipped to five. The AMX13 light tank and the EBR (heavy) and AML (light) armoured cars were re-armed with 90-mm. guns. French forces continued to play an active role in protecting French interests overseas, notably in Chad. Pres. François Tombalbaye had requested French aid against rebels in his northern provinces in August 1968, and on April 15, 1969, 260 Foreign Legionnaires and Marines were sent as reinforcements. On September 2 the French government announced that 130 conscripts were to be withdrawn, though according to unofficial estimates 700 men had been added in one year to the 900-man garrison at Fort-Lamy. Chad government figures showed 1,126 rebels killed in the first half of 1969. Within France, an air-portable division, with parachute troops and an amphibious brigade, was kept ready to combine with the Navy's two helicopter carriers and two assault ships to provide a more powerful *force d'intervention* if France's control over its former colonies was threatened.

WEST GERMANY

The 1969–70 defense budget of DM. 21.2 billion was only about DM. 8 million more than that of the previous year, although a DM. 2.5 billion increase over the next four years was envisaged. At about 4% of GNP, the budget represented a lower proportionate expenditure than that of the U.S., Britain, France, or Portugal. The Soviet invasion of Czechoslovakia continued to dominate defense planning, but a coherent response was slow to emerge. On Nov. 29, 1968, the defense minister, Gerhard Schröder, painted a gloomy picture. If NATO were at full strength, the Warsaw Pact would still have three times its manpower and firepower, besides the mobility that had surprised the Bundeswehr. Immediate measures included a reversal of the planned drop in the Bundeswehr from its existing 442,000 (including reserves) to 400,000.

The February White Paper on defense in the 1970s showed a significant reassessment of needs. The main task of the Bundeswehr was still to fight a limited, conventional war on the West German frontier, but the new inspector general, Albert Schenz, argued that this required two different types of forces instead of the existing infantry and armour formations. Half of the border was covered by subalpine terrain favourable to defense. This could best be covered by defense-in-depth brigades, a new type of unit equipped for stationary, defensive warfare, less mobile and with less vulnerable supply lines. Initially, two of West Germany's 32 brigades would adopt the new role, their mobile units and tank elements being transferred to the North German plain to form the nucleus of an operational reserve able to stem any breakthrough. With a 15% expansion in the Army and the call-up of reserves doubled, the Bundeswehr was expected to reach 460,000 by the end of 1969. The expansion might ease the shortage of 5,000 officers and 30,000 NCO's.

Whether these additional numbers would alleviate low morale in the Army was uncertain. This became a serious issue in May, when Maj. Gen. Hellmut Grashey, the deputy chief of staff for the Army (who later resigned), claimed that since defense was now assured through deterrence, the Army should concentrate on maintaining internal security and revising its "inner guidance" concept of discipline. Originated by Gen. Graf von Baudissin, this concept replaced the old traditions of blind obedience with reliance on individual thought and conscience, but it produced unsoldierly soldiers. Further morale problems were created by a report on the secret service (May 23). An investigating committee had been established after a series of curious incidents in late 1968, including the mysterious deaths of several high-ranking officers and the theft of a Sidewinder missile. The committee decided against altering the existing three-way division of responsibility between the Office for the Protection of the Constitution, the Federal Intelligence Service, and military counterintelligence. Fortunately, the new Social Democratic defense minister, Helmut Schmidt, enjoyed the confidence of the services.

The decision that election of the new West German president should take place in West Berlin produced a minor crisis. The original Soviet protest of Dec. 23, 1968, was followed on Feb. 9, 1969, by an East German ban on overland travel to West Berlin by those participating in the election. At the end of the month the East Germans increased their inspection of goods in transit to West Berlin, making vague accusations that military matériel was being manufactured there. To this point, the crisis appeared to be building up in the customary pattern, with increasing Soviet and East German pressure being countered by British, French, and U.S. reaffirmations of their rights under the postwar four-power agreements. Yet the election (March 5) of Gustav Heinemann as Heinrich Lübke's successor passed off without incident, as had President Nixon's visit to West Berlin a week earlier.

This uncertainty was reflected in their unwillingness to sign the NPT. The Social Democrats were considerably more favourable toward the treaty, however, and on November 28, about a month after they came to power, West Germany signed—but did not immediately ratify—it.

The Bundestag Budgetary Committee cut requests for additional spending, made in November 1968, by DM. 10 million, leaving DM. 18,790,000,000. Messerschmitt-Bölkow reached agreement with Nord- and Sud-Aviation to cooperate on producing a jet trainer for France and West Germany, the latter to take a total of 500. The Dornier company was developing a German replacement for the Army's French Alouette II helicopter. Arms sales abroad increased; four 1,000-ton submarines were sold to Greece and three to Argentina, 410 Leopard medium tanks to the Netherlands and 80 to Norway (which also bought 12 light submarines), three corvettes to Portugal, and four patrol boats to Saudi Arabia.

VIETNAM

Five years after their major commitment to the war in Vietnam, U.S. forces began a phased withdrawal, starting in July. Together with the death of President Ho Chi Minh in September, this seemed to indicate that the often prematurely heralded end to the conflict might be in sight. Hanoi's intransigence had prevented the equally long-awaited Paris peace talks from producing any effective results, and it was uncertain

continued on page 265

SPECIAL REPORT

THE MILITARY UNDER FIRE

By Robert Sherrill

Outwardly, at least, the ambitions of the U.S. military and the conduct of its friends in industry appeared to be under more relentless criticism in 1969 than at any time since the mid-1930s, when "merchants of death" was the popular description for munitions manufacturers and when 71% of those interviewed in a 1937 Gallup poll said they thought it had been a mistake to fight in World War I. By mid-1969 the pollsters, helping to relive history, found that a majority of people believed that the United States was spending too much on arms (though 92% also admitted they lacked the haziest idea of what the arms budget came to) and a majority felt it had been a mistake to get into the seemingly endless war in Vietnam.

Something had developed between the cocky years of John Kennedy and the first cautious year of Richard Nixon, and that something was a military-bureaucratic-industrial combine over which Congress seemed to have little control, but against which the public had slowly begun to react. The remarkable feature of this opposition was that it represented such a diverse cross section of the public: radical students, liberal professors, liberal and conservative economists, liberal and conservative congressmen (though not many of these last—mainly, like Sen. Harry F. Byrd, Jr., of Virginia, they were critical of the military only for economy reasons), apolitical soldiers, and nonpolitical federal courts.

On every side the tide of pro-militarism, which had been swelling since President Kennedy's historically sharp increase in the 1961 Pentagon budget, began to recede—not far, but enough to leave the admirals and generals at least temporarily stranded and vulnerable to attack. A great part of the trouble rose from the growing alienation between a citizenry that could handle sophisticated dialogue and a military hierarchy that was beginning to bore people with its old arguments. As George C. Wilson, the *Washington Post*'s Pentagon reporter, put it, "Tired old generals and admirals—none of them under 50—are making tired old arguments to a national constituency which considers these fine old men obsolete."

Perhaps the best sign of what was happening came in the cracking of old idols. The storied Special Forces, the especially trained, jungle-fighting Green Berets who had been revitalized during that earlier period of Kennedyesque infatuation with the armed forces, passed into a shadowy phase. When eight Green Berets were arrested in a murky murder case involving a reputed Vietnamese double agent, much of the newspaper coverage pictured the erstwhile heroes as little better than assassins and torturers. The ordinary GI received similar treatment in stories of an alleged massacre of Vietnamese civilians at a village nicknamed "Pinkville" in 1968.

And nothing sounded more antiquated by 1969 than some of the Kennedy era boasting about Pentagon efficiency. It became quite the fashion for newspaper columnists to dig around in old magazines and quote, with appropriate sarcasm, some of the claims of Defense Secretary Robert McNamara and his Whiz Kids. An example was Adam Yarmolinsky, who in March 1967 wrote in the *Atlantic:* "Political administrators on the other side of the Potomac can learn from their friends in the Pentagon how to put their own houses in better order."

Don't Give Up the Ship? If the year had a symbolic episode —in the manner in which it dealt both with heroism and with efficiency—it was the inquiry conducted by the Navy into the conduct of Comdr. Lloyd M. Bucher, his officers and men, who had spent 11 months in a North Korean prison after their ship, the poorly outfitted, 177-ft. USS "Pueblo," was captured while on an intelligence mission off North Korea on Jan. 23, 1968.

If all did not come out in the inquiry, much did. When the North Koreans demanded that Bucher confess that the "Pueblo" had been spying, the alumnus of Boys Town, Neb., decided to play it square and safe, to sign the confession without extended duress (in fact, the day after being imprisoned). He had seen no reason to risk his life and the lives of his men. That was the stuff of a different era when military men laid greater stress on heroics.

As it turned out, Bucher had chosen the very route to the heart of square, safe America, as well as to the heart of the non-Establishment left. Surrendering without firing a shot, signing confessions without being tortured, shaking and quivering and weeping as he testified at the court of inquiry—these were hardly the actions of the fictional military hero. But they were the actions that at this moment in history appealed to both sides of America: to the squares because they were fed up with Washington's refusal to go all out against the Communists and saw no reason for the crew of one ill-equipped ship to pay a price that the desk generals and admirals would not pay; to the sophisticated left—"the liberal magazines and the newspapers and the columnists who saw him as a virtual existential hero" (in the phrase of the *New York Times*'s Bernard Weinraub)—because he had lived for the moment in order to live at all and had thrown over Establishment and storybook values.

"I saw no point in senselessly sending people to their deaths." There was the key Bucher statement. The fact that America not only forgave him but applauded him reveals, as well as any one thing can, the mood of the nation. The decision to abjectly turn over his ship to the enemy, to violate naval regulations ("The commanding officer shall not permit his command to be searched by any person representing a foreign state . . . so long as he has the power to resist"), and to wipe out nearly two centuries of naval tradition—the decision to do these things rather than go down fighting, and thereby coincidentally save the face of the Pentagon, was received by popular opinion as not only the wise but the heroic thing to do.

Bit by bit the bungling of the "Pueblo" episode came to light: the fact that U.S. planes in Osan, South Korea, could have reached the "Pueblo" in 28 minutes but could not have effected a rescue because their bomb racks (for conventional bombs) were in storage in Japan and they were only equipped with atomic bombs; the fact that the message from the National Security Agency to the Navy, warning against sending the "Pueblo," somehow went astray. When Navy Secretary John Chafee announced at the conclusion of the inquiry that he was going to let the matter drop without the further airing that would have come through courts-martial, explaining that he felt Commander Bucher "has suffered enough," there were hoots of skepticism from editors who felt the Navy was simply trying to avoid further embarrassment.

More devastating to the military establishment because of its unexpectedness was the criticism that came from its old friends on the House Armed Services Committee. In a slashing 77-page attack on the Defense Department, a nine-man subcommittee of the HASC cited the capture of the "Pueblo" and the later shooting down of an EC-121 reconnaissance plane by North Korean forces as evidence of "serious deficiencies," requiring a "complete review of our military-civilian command structure and its capability to cope with emergency situations." It categorized the Pentagon's intelligence superstructure as cumbersome and sluggish and laid the blame for the capture of the "Pueblo" not on its officers and crew but on the Pentagon for failing to interpret properly warning signs coming out of North Korea. Perhaps the most startling part of the report, coming as it did from the ordinarily last-ditch HASC, was the recommendation that the military's Code of Conduct be changed to "provide some latitude," so that U.S. servicemen could give more information than just their identity to their captors and thus avoid rough treatment.

The Dissenter as Soldier. For the first time in history there was enough organized opposition within the ranks of the armed services to make headlines. This had been building for several years and from several directions, with the spectrum of dissent ranging from soldiers who did not like the way the Army was set up and who wished to reform it to soldiers who thought a conscript army should be done away with altogether. But even the best known of the reforming organizations, the American Servicemen's Union (seeking: the right to refuse illegal orders; racial equality; free association; trial by jury of peers; election of officers; abolition of the salute and of the requirement to say "sir"; and a federal minimum wage), was not such a revolutionary conception—German soldiers are permitted to unionize; the Israeli soldier rarely has to salute and the atmosphere in many Israeli camps is more that of a democratic family gathering than of a regimented power pyramid.

More revolutionary and more successful in attracting public attention and shaking the Pentagon were the legal attacks on the constitutionality of the Uniform Code of Military Justice, a code originally modeled after the military laws of Rome and old Britain. These attacks usually arose from angry confrontations over the questions of free speech and free association. Among the matters at issue were the off-base GI coffeehouses, established near military camps for off-duty soldiers who preferred debating the merits of U.S. war policies to getting drunk. The coffeehouses had a prim reputation but, judging from the way they were harassed by the military police, the military viewed them as dens of subversion.

Since there were only three coffeehouses, at widely scattered bases, their importance was mainly symbolic. Far more persuasive were the underground GI newspapers—at least two dozen of them—published on and off bases. (*Ultimate Weapon* at Ft. Dix, New Jersey; *Short Times* at Ft. Jackson, South Carolina; *Flag-in-Action* at Ft. Campbell, Kentucky; *FTA* at Ft. Knox, Kentucky; *Fatigue Press* at Ft. Hood, Texas; etc.) Many bloomed and died like flowers in the spring, but some developed a permanence and a circulation that accurately reflected the underlying unhappiness of thousands of young men whose lives had been interrupted to fight an unpopular war. At least three editors of underground newspapers had been court-martialed. And here and there individual protests made the headlines, as when junior officers and enlisted men picketed or paraded or circulated petitions against the war and against the military itself.

Perhaps not as significant but much more frightening to the Pentagon were the rebellions and semirebellions that broke out on various bases: the hundred or so men at Ft. Jackson, black and white, who objected boisterously when officers attempted to suppress their political bull session; the three hundred-odd who rioted at the Ft. Ord, California, stockade because of poor living conditions; the half a hundred at Ft. Dix who rioted in the stockade for similar reasons; and the famous 27 prisoners at the Presidio stockade in San Francisco who sat down in what the Army insisted on calling a mutiny.

Out of this turmoil developed a number of court cases that apparently stood an excellent chance of extending the Bill of Rights —especially the right to freedom of press and speech—to men in uniform. The federal courts set up several curbs on the military. The U.S. Supreme Court ruled that the military cannot court-martial men for activities conducted off base, off duty, and out of uniform—a ruling that could encourage antiwar action on the part of off-duty servicemen. Not so important, but equally symbolic, was the decision forbidding the court-martialing of U.S. civilians who work in war zones such as Vietnam.

Against such a background, it was not surprising that wide publicity was given to a group of soldiers in Vietnam who refused to follow their young commanding officer into action. There were extenuating circumstances—the fighting had been hard, the officer was inexperienced, and the men were soon persuaded by an older officer and a veteran noncom to rejoin the fighting. The Army, playing down the affair, took no action other than to transfer the young officer to a different unit. Yet the incident, minor though it may have been, led many to speak what to the professional military had been the unspeakable: suppose dissent should spread to the front lines. . . .

UPI COMPIX

U.S. soldiers leave court at the close of their court-martial on June 5, 1969, on charges of mutiny arising from their participation in a sit-down demonstration at the San Francisco Presidio stockade in October 1968.

The Pentagon on the Home Front. On college campuses, elements of the student body and faculty continued to demonstrate against the draft, against the ROTC, and against permitting companies engaged in war production, such as Dow Chemical, to use on-campus facilities for recruiting employees. There were some measurable effects—the Pentagon, for example, promised to withdraw ROTC training at Harvard and Dartmouth at the end of the 1969–70 school year.

The most important development, however, was in the campus laboratories, on which the Pentagon depended for about one-third of its research. On one day of simultaneous protest, students and professors at 18 campuses, from Cambridge, Mass., to Berkeley, Calif., held rallies at which laboratory service to the military-industrial complex was deplored. A hundred professors at the Massachusetts Institute of Technology went on a one-day research strike, and classes at the University of Pennsylvania were suspended for the day so that there could be prolonged discussions about the merits and demerits of defense research. For several years many of the important research professors had been so unhappy with "secret" Pentagon work that they had been threatening to refuse any more Pentagon contracts. Some, in fact, had already dropped out. MIT and Stanford, two of the Defense Department's major contractors, decided to cut back on secret work with an eye to phasing it out of their institutional activities altogether.

In Congress critical analyses of the defense budget expanded dramatically. As the *Wall Street Journal* noted editorially, "Never before has the nation seen the strategic arms race debated in such breadth and detail." It is one thing when noncongressional gadflies such as John Kenneth Galbraith denounce the House Armed Services and Appropriations committees as "second lieutenant sycophants of the Pentagon," but it is something else when the chairmen of those two committees, L. Mendel Rivers (Dem., S.C.) and George Mahon (Dem., Tex.), engage in a public quarrel over military spending. Mahon, normally an unquestioning pro-militarist, demanded that the arms budget be cut because "the military has made so many mistakes, it has generated a lack of confidence"; for this, Mahon's wisdom—and by implication his patriotism—was called into question by Rivers,

SENATORIAL PROBES
PENTAGON WASTED BILLION$ & BILLION$ & BILLION$

BEN ROTH AGENCY
"September Morn"
—Pierott.

who accused his colleague of "playing into the hands of the enemies of the military." That clash was only one straw in the wind of congressional disapproval. Another was the obvious gusto with which the Senate Permanent Subcommittee on Investigations dug into a scandal concerning alleged graft in NCO clubs and grilled the former army provost marshal about questionable dealings in arms obtained from police departments.

The deployment of the Safeguard antiballistic missile system passed the Senate by the narrowest of margins, and the long, bitter debate on that issue proved to be only the prelude to an extended harangue over the $20 billion military procurement authorization bill. More time was spent fighting over particular items in the bill (the C-5A cargo plane, the Manned Strategic Aircraft, the F-14A carrier-based fighter, the CVA-69 carrier, the Main Battle Tank) than ever before in modern times. Congress' timetable fell hopelessly behind, but the critics refused to be turned aside by appeals to their patriotism—the kind of appeals that once would have worked automatically.

Plus ça change. And yet, when all was done, could it truly be said that 1969 was a watershed year, after which the militarists' hold on the national budget and on the federal commitment would inevitably decline? Not at all. If it was true, as the *Washington Post* warned, that "the United States is rapidly acquiring at least some of the characteristics of a warfare state," nothing that occurred within the year, nor the accumulation of everything that happened in the year, could be viewed as the beginning of a trend away from that condition. The opposition was noteworthy not because it was impressively large but because it occurred on several levels of society and because it was taking place after half a dozen years in which the only opposition to the Pentagon had come from the "peacenik" organizations, easily identifiable and easily dismissed by the Establishment.

Otherwise, things remained much as they had been. The suddenness with which the assault on the arms budget took place did shake from the defense industry an admission of what many critics had already suspected—that only about $20 billion of the $80 billion budget actually went into the cost of producing armaments; the other three-fourths went into overhead, much of it frivolously sophisticated pork barrel—but the challenge to the industry resulted in few measurable reforms. While the General Accounting Office was now empowered to keep a closer watch on defense contracts, there was clear evidence that in practice it would continue to couch its reports on Pentagon spending (in the GAO's own words) "in constructive terms rather than in terms of the deficiencies being reported." John S. Foster, Jr., director of defense research and engineering for the Pentagon, conceded that "the public has lost patience with us," but—far from being repentant—he struck back with the argument that "this critical attitude" could result in "the nation's losing its technological superiority over the Soviet Union."

The revolt against secret research on the campuses was put down by the soothing voices of Foster and of Lee DuBridge, for 22 years president of the California Institute of Technology and now President Nixon's science adviser, who assured Congress and the campus scientists that the amount of secret research being done had dropped by half (from 8 to 4%) in the last couple of years, and that they hoped to get it down to 1 or 2% or zero very shortly. Nevertheless, 75% of all university research was still supported by the government and most of that by the Pentagon.

As for the U.S. Supreme Court's freeing of the off-duty, off-base, out-of-uniform soldier from the potential rigours of military justice, within 72 hours of that decision the Pentagon had sent a directive to all field commanders to disregard the court and to proceed with justice as usual. Obviously the military meant to fight it out with the court on an ad hoc, case-by-case basis that could effectively block any practical effect of the court's decision for years.

While the revolt against college ROTC drew headlines, statistically it was not an impressive eruption; only about 3% of the 497 ROTC units across the country had experienced any trouble. Meanwhile, the Pentagon could take quiet comfort in the knowledge that, whatever happened on the college level, it was raising a new generation of potential warriors in the nation's high schools, where the Junior ROTC program flourished.

Nothing, really, had changed. In a year of political disillusionment, of economic retrenchment, of stalemate in war, it was inevitable that the people would vent their unhappiness on some part of the Establishment. Uniquely, they did so against the military part. But the Establishment is not called that for nothing. It is very well established, and no part of it more so than the Pentagon.

When auditors from the Bureau of the Budget wish to inspect the records of the Defense Department, they must still go to the Pentagon—Pentagon officials being the only group in Washington who do not deign to bring their records to the bureau. When members of the Senate Foreign Relations Committee wish to inspect secret agreements between the Defense Department and foreign nations, they must still go to the Pentagon, for Pentagon officials will not bring these agreements to the Capitol. The military budget-cutters in the 91st Congress sometimes talked in terms of massive reductions, but they had been around too long to be deluded by their own talk. In the end they felt they had achieved a comparative victory by chipping away less than 5%.

It was a year of protest in which the American people were at least able to say that they had not been totally conditioned to respond as the Pentagon wished. But when one looked beneath the cosmetics, it was still an America carrying the deep intaglio of the military: defense spending at the rate of $1,000 per taxpayer per year, a military budget that bought 15% of the finished products of all U.S. industries, a defense industry that employed 38% of all physicists. When one looked behind the Rotarian handshake and the Welcome Wagon smile, it still appeared to be an America that was, in the biblical phrase, "a nation of fierce countenance."

continued from page 261
whether the war would end with any sort of settlement or just be scaled down. Increasing North Vietnamese operations in neighbouring countries suggested that Southeast Asia would continue to be the scene of fighting, but President Nixon made it clear during his July tour of the area that this would not involve U.S. forces. In the future, countries threatened with subversion would stand or fall largely by their own efforts.

Although pressures within the U.S. made it imperative for the new president to pull U.S. troops out of South Vietnam, it was by no means clear at the start of the year whether the enemy was going to facilitate this or make it more difficult by insisting on an undisguised surrender. On January 16 the 77-day procedural deadlock on the seating of delegations to the peace talks was broken by agreement on a plain, round, green-baize table. The North Vietnamese and the National Liberation Front (NLF), the Viet Cong's political arm, always spoke of four delegations to maintain the fiction of NLF independence. The U.S. and South Vietnamese denied this, referring instead to the two sides.

The North Vietnamese and Viet Cong seemed to have changed to a low-cost, long haul strategy. Instead of North Vietnamese troops engaging U.S. forces in large actions, up to the regimental level, they adopted the tactic of tying down U.S. and South Vietnamese forces by their presence but confining combat to raids with the Viet Cong in commando-style units of company size (not more than 140). Their targets were areas of U.S. and South Vietnamese cooperation (as in the April 20 raid on the major training camp at Lam San). South Vietnamese towns were hit by indiscriminate bombardment, 159 being struck on May 12 in a major coordinated attack. The aim was clearly to undermine the confidence of the South Vietnamese in their government and the government's confidence in a continued U.S. presence. In Mao Tse-tung's classification, this represented a retreat to the second stage of guerrilla war, whereas the previous year had seen a switch to the third, involving large-scale battles to destroy the weakened opponent.

A not-dissimilar change in U.S. strategy suggested that each side was feeling the effects of the very heavy fighting and losses in 1968. Gen. William C. Westmoreland's search-and-destroy operations, involving sweeps through suspected Viet Cong territory by thousands of troops, were dropped by his successor, Gen. Creighton Abrams, who saw U.S. mobility and firepower as better suited to surrounding the enemy after they attacked. In an effort to lessen U.S. casualties, this concept was broadened, under political pressure, to a strategy of protective reaction. By July, U.S. commanders were chafing under what they regarded as excessive restrictions based on a misreading of the military situation. In their view, the post-Tet offensive in early 1969 had been a gambler's last throw. Its failure and the switch in U.S. bombing from North Vietnam to Viet Cong concentrations in the South had broken the enemy's back.

Against this, three incidents, each one relatively insignificant in itself, indicated an apparent inability on the part of the U.S. to secure control of the enemy at acceptable costs. In February, 500 North Vietnamese attacked a camp at Bien Hoh, losing 235 while inflicting casualties described by a U.S. spokesman as "light." But, in miniature, it had the same effect as the Tet offensive, now admitted by General Westmoreland to have been equal to Pearl Harbor in its effective surprise. It proved the U.S. could not provide security anywhere and made a mockery of the computerized "hamlet evaluation system" (HES). Intended to provide evaluations of hamlet security in percentage terms, HES seemed another example of the failure of technology in the Vietnamese war. Then, in May, the U.S. lost 55 killed and 273 wounded in five days of fighting for Ap Bia Mountain, which the troops had nicknamed Hamburger Hill. Sen. Edward Kennedy and other critics claimed the military had wasted soldiers' lives by sending them against entrenched forces in World War I style, and the incident served to underline the inability of U.S. firepower to eliminate casualties, since even B-52s had been used in the operation. Army publicity for the July 2 relief of the Special Forces Camp at Ben Het after a 56-day siege involving Soviet-designed PT-76 tanks proved counterproductive. The 3,000-strong Asian force and its U.S. advisers seemed rather to have demonstrated the inability of the South Vietnamese to fight effectively. The focus on the Special Forces was particularly unfortunate, since the arrest of eight of its members, including the commander, Col. Robert Rheault, on a murder charge occurred at the beginning of August. According to the version given by the defense lawyer, the victim was a South Vietnamese agent who had fallen under suspicion of being a Communist double agent. The CIA had given the defendants orders for his liquidation, euphemistically described as "termination with extreme prejudice." The Army, which was trying to regain control of clandestine operations, saw a chance to destroy the Green Berets as competitors for prestige and funds and arrested the eight, ignoring their rights as military personnel.

Lack of reliable intelligence about losses and changes in strategy prevented any firm estimate of trends for some time. While U.S. estimates put North Vietnamese casualties at 500,000 killed and 250,000 permanently wounded, the North Vietnamese remained able to inflict politically significant casualties on the U.S. forces at will. In the week May 11–17, 430 were killed; by mid-August the weekly death rate had dropped to 96, the lowest figure for two years; then it rose sharply to 300 for the last week in August. These figures played a considerable part in the battle within the U.S. to influence the president's decision on troop withdrawals. At his June meeting with Pres. Nguyen Van Thieu of South Vietnam, he had announced the pullout of 25,000 of the 550,000 U.S. troops. The second cut was to have been decided in August, but was delayed because of the upsurge in fighting.

The military balance appeared to have remained relatively unchanged. Of 550,000 U.S. troops, only 90,000 were combat forces. South Vietnam's general mobilization had provided 35,000 regular troops, plus 220,000 regional defense forces, 170,000 popular forces, and 100,000 paramilitary personnel. Against this were North Vietnamese Army groups totaling 55,000, plus 10,000 with the Viet Cong to bring them up to 55,000. An additional 40,000 regulars served as support troops and there were 70,000 guerrillas. The rate of North Vietnamese infiltration to the South had fallen, and on August 27 the State Department and the Pentagon openly clashed over how this should be interpreted. Dean Rusk, the former secretary of state, and his old department maintained that the lower infiltration rate was significant, especially in conjunction with the withholding of North Vietnamese troops from fighting. Although agreeing that infiltration had dropped, the Pentagon attributed this to the effectiveness of U.S. interdiction and claimed it left relative force levels untouched. North Vietnam had sent 100,000 men south in the first half of 1969, but lost only 93,653 killed in that period as against 119,000 in the same period of the previous year. The Joint Chiefs of Staff recommendation in their National Security Council Memorandum 36 of September 8 was for a phased reduction of U.S. forces to 250,000 in 1972, with a second cut of 30,000.

The death of Pres. Ho Chi Minh (*see* OBITUARIES) on September 3 probably played a significant part in President Nixon's September 16 decision to withdraw a further 35,000 troops. It was widely believed that more withdrawals—or even a cease-fire—might be announced in the president's November 3 address to the nation, which came during a time of heightened antiwar protest in the U.S. He refused to announce any definite timetable, however, although he reemphasized his policy of vietnamization and of seeking to end the war on honourable terms. A pullout of 50,000 men by April 15, 1970, was announced December 15.

As the year ended, however, the U.S. press was concentrating on an incident that—if it actually happened—had occurred nearly two years earlier, in March 1968. According to several men who had taken part in the operation, a large number of civilians, including women and small children, had been massacred by U.S. troops in the district of Song My, a complex of villages nicknamed "Pinkville" by the GI's and generally believed to be a Viet Cong stronghold. The officer in command of the operation—who, however, had not actually entered the village until later—denied that a massacre had taken place. The conflicting evidence remained to be sorted out, presumably at the court-martial of the first lieutenant who had led troops into Song My and possibly of other men as well. Nevertheless, public revulsion over the incident was yet another factor affecting the future of the U.S. involvement.

UPI COMPIX

Helicopter drops supplies to the Duc Lai Special Forces camp 120 mi. NE of Saigon, Nov. 8, 1969. The camp came under attack as North Vietnamese regulars began their winter offensive.

SOVIET UNION

The 1969 Soviet defense budget stood at 17.7 billion rubles, or $42 billion on the basis of real resources in equivalent U.S. prices. Including expenditures listed under other ministries for such items as nuclear warheads, research and development of advanced weapons systems, and military parts of the space program, the true figure was probably nearer $53 billion. This gave a real increase of $3 billion against the official 1 billion rubles. Both figures represented a 6% increase over the 1968 figures—much less than the 15% rise between 1967 and 1968. Since changes in these figures usually reflect the party line on the international situation, they could be taken to indicate a certain degree of stabilization, even though considerable tension existed.

The achievement of numerical parity with the U.S.'s 1,054 strategic missiles was certainly a major advance for a power that had spent the first 23 years of the nuclear age behind its rival in these weapons. Continued production of land-based ICBM's and nuclear-powered submarines carrying 16 missiles similar to Polaris, the latter at the rate of four a year, would give it 1,150 ICBM's and 160 submarine-launched ballistic missiles (SLBM's) by the beginning of 1970. This seemed to indicate a wish to diversify the force while compensating for the close spacing of older missile sites that rendered them vulnerable to attack. In this context, it seemed significant that the total of MRBM's and IRBM's targeted on Western Europe was kept constant at 700.

Development of the Galosh ABM system deployed around Moscow and Leningrad was apparently halted after the completion of 67 out of 140 sites. The main missile, after which the system was named, was similar to the U.S. Spartan, with a range of several hundred miles and a nuclear warhead of one–two megatons. Combined with the types of radars used, it seemed suitable only for limited area defense against U.S. attacks. The halt was subject to two interpretations. It could be taken as evidence that the system was no longer effective against the attacks it now had to face, proving the futility of ABM systems. Alternatively, the delay might be occasioned by slowness in producing a more advanced missile, able to loiter in the vicinity of incoming warheads and give the defense more time to calculate the optimum interception. Those who favoured the latter interpretation also argued that the Tallinn line, an air defense system in Estonia, could be upgraded to have a limited ABM function by connecting it to the ABM radars and control system.

The real difficulty continued to be the lack of information on Soviet strategic doctrine. After the Warsaw Pact meeting at Bucharest in March, there were reports of undefined changes in the command structure giving a greater role to the Eastern European allies. Soviet forces stationed in Czechoslovakia comprised five divisions, part of an overall 20% increase in Soviet troop strength in Eastern Europe. The general expansion of military forces seemed to have been guided less by any coherent doctrine than by the military's ability to obtain political agreement to the ideal solution: more equipment for all services. The unprecedented cancellation of the traditional Red Army parade on May Day suggested that the collective leadership felt impelled to demonstrate its control over the military sphere, thereby implying that it was questioned.

Clashes with Chinese forces on the Ussuri River, starting in March, certainly strengthened the military. Between 100,000 and 200,000 Soviet troops—some eight to ten divisions—had been moved into Mongolia, concentrating at Ulan Bator and Erhlien. Air bases had been built at Omsk, Irkutsk, and Vladivostok, plus a major base at Chita. In the border fighting several Soviets were killed, and tanks and artillery were used. Many observers were reminded of the Russo-Japanese clashes in 1938, culminating in divisional-strength engagements. Fears were increased when, in August, the Soviet Union asked its Warsaw Pact allies what their attitude would be to destruction of the Chinese nuclear installations in Sinkiang by a preemptive (presumably nuclear) strike. Indian reports said the Chinese had already shifted their gaseous diffusion plants to Tibet. Sino-Soviet border talks at the deputy foreign minister level, following Kosygin's September 11 visit to Peking, remained deadlocked.

Naval activity in the Mediterranean and Indian Ocean testified to a growing Soviet interest in translating the second largest navy in the world into political influence. On January 10 two ships visited the port of Hodeika in Yemen. In July a squadron including cruisers and destroyers returned after a 30,000-mi. cruise in the Pacific, during which it visited 30 states. This was followed by fleet exercises in the Mediterranean. By August 26 the usual squadron of 1 heavy cruiser, 8–10 destroyers, 8–10 submarines, and as many support ships had been increased to 61 ships, including the new aircraft carrier-cruiser "Moskva," carrying 20 Ka-20 Harp antisubmarine helicopters. Although 20 ships returned to the Black Sea, a further 14 passed in through Gibraltar to bring the total, with other changes, to 79 in mid-September. The U.A.R. was the centre of Soviet interest, with 5–8 ships based in Salum Bay.

CHINA

Soviet attempts to extend the Brezhnev doctrine to China led to the border incidents between the two countries. The Soviet justification for invading Czechoslovakia had been that when one socialist country endangers the achievements of socialism, all other socialist countries must intervene to protect them. Since this made the Communist Party of the Soviet Union the judge of what constituted orthodox and legitimate Communist governments, it was naturally opposed by the Chinese. The limitation of the conflict, combined with talks at the deputy foreign minister level, suggested an initial willingness to use the clashes as political bargaining counters. Nonetheless, Defense Minister Lin Piao's April report to the ninth party congress devoted 12 paragraphs to denunciation of the U.S.S.R., compared with one against the U.S. In August, Huang Yung-sheng, the Chinese chief of the general staff, spoke of collusion between the U.S. and the Soviet Union.

These developments further enhanced the role of the People's Liberation Army (PLA) as the only viable, organized force left after the collapse of the Communist Party organization. It was entrusted with the task of maintaining order and production in the later stages and the aftermath of the Cultural Revolution. The new-style revolutionary committees established by Mao Tse-tung institutionalized this expanded power of the PLA. The command structure of the armed forces remained basically unchanged, with Lin Piao and Huang Yung-sheng prominent in both domestic and foreign policy developments.

Increases in 1968 apparently brought the regular force up to 3.3 million men, about the same as the Soviet Union's, with an estimated 150 million Chinese available for drafting. These could not be equipped with advanced weapons, though adequate infantry weapons continued to be available. Armour consisted of Soviet-designed T-34 and T-54 tanks, the latter made in China and called the T-59. The Air Force weaknesses were similar, reliance being placed on obsolete MiG-19 and MiG-17 fighters, supplemented by a few MiG-21s and Sa-2 Guideline missiles. Very restricted indigenous oil supplies limited conventional military operations. A moderate buildup of forces in Inner Mongolia took place, however, bringing the total to three field armies, each of three divisions (totaling 108,000 men), plus two more infantry divisions and one tank division. Casualties among Soviet armour in the March clashes on the Ussuri River indicated that some of the three artillery regiments attached to each division had been active.

The classic guerrilla defensive strategy of opposing numbers to technology could not succeed against the threat of a limited Soviet attack against Chinese nuclear installations. Mao Tse-tung and Chou En-lai, his premier who functioned as foreign minister (Chou's post until 1958), therefore relied on their nuclear weapons for deterrence.

During the Cultural Revolution, Marshal Nieh Jung-chen, head of the Science and Technology Commission, Gen. Wang Ping-chang, minister of the Seventh Machine Building Ministry, and Chien San-chiang, director of the Atomic Energy Institute—the troika of China's nuclear program—were severely attacked, but they seemed to have emerged unscathed. Nevertheless, the esprit de corps of the nuclear establishment was damaged, and this development may have been reflected in the mixed results of nuclear tests undertaken in 1968–69. A thermonuclear test on Dec. 24, 1967, had failed, and no more had been attempted until late 1968. Of the two in 1969, the low-yield test on September 23 was the first conducted underground, a fact that was hard to explain, since China had never signed the 1963 nuclear test ban treaty forbidding atmospheric tests. On September 29 a three-megaton hydrogen bomb was exploded, the first to have been air-dropped. The Chinese nuclear stockpile was estimated at 70–100 atomic bombs of the type used against Japan in World War II (20,000 tons) or a smaller number of more powerful weapons. The greatest weakness continued to be in delivery systems. Contrary to expectations, the tests did not include a 3,500-mi. ICBM or even a 700-mi. MRBM to supplement the force of Tu-4s (copies of the World War II U.S. B-29 Superfortress) and obsolete Il-28 twin-jet bombers. Even these could, however, threaten the Soviet border cities of Khabarovsk, Vladivostok, and Alma-Ata, plus the Mongolian capital, Ulan Bator.

INDIA AND PAKISTAN

The 1969–70 Indian defense budget of $1,491,000,000 represented a negligible increase over the previous year and remained below 3% of GNP. A significant change was the increased emphasis given to the Navy and Air Force.

During his visit in March, Marshal Andrei A. Grechko, the Soviet minister of defense, said India would receive all-out support if China attacked it. This was but one sign of increasing Soviet interest in India as the pivot of an anti-China policy that resembled nothing so much as the post-World War II U.S. doctrine of containment of the Soviet Union. Logically enough, Soviet Premier Aleksei N. Kosygin, following in the footsteps of John Foster Dulles, later speculated about the possibility of a collective security pact in Asia. Mrs. Indira Gandhi's government hastily denied Indian interest in the idea, but the defense forces clearly favoured it. In an article in the May 8 issue of an Indian naval journal, an Indian Ocean alliance was suggested, comprising India, Japan, Australia and New Zealand, Malaysia, Thailand, Indonesia, and Burma. Speedy disavowals contrasted with governmental attempts in July to obtain a U.S. and Soviet bilateral guarantee, although there still appeared to be unwillingness to grant naval bases to the Soviet Union.

Nevertheless, Soviet aid continued to be received in considerable quantity. On June 15 it was announced that India would receive two more former Soviet submarines in September and December, bringing the total to four. All would have Soviet-trained crews. In September the Soviet Union supplied an unidentified number of Osa-class patrol boats with Styx short-range missiles, and two of the three Petya-class destroyer escorts promised the previous year were delivered. To house this growing naval strength, the dockyard at Vishakhapatnam was scheduled for completion by the beginning of 1970.

The Air Force share in expansion included MiG-21 interceptors coming off the Soviet-built production lines near Bombay. Some 120 were in service by July. They were joined by 25 of the initial order of 60 Marut 1A fighter-bombers, the first Indian-built and designed jet aircraft (though the design team was led by Kurt Tank of the old German Focke-Wulf firm). Difficulties in finding a suitable engine handicapped its performance and delayed development of the Mark 2 version, intended to have a speed of Mach 2. Of 140 Su-7B fighter-bombers being supplied by the U.S.S.R., only two squadrons (24 aircraft) were operational. Further purchases of the French Alouette III helicopter would bring the total over the 100 mark.

The Indian government's counterinsurgency campaigns in the Nagaland area on the northeastern frontier seemed to be taking effect at last. The capture of Gen. Mowu Angami with 200 of his men seemed to have stopped Peking's attempts to start a guerrilla war in India. A further 250 rebels were killed or captured with Burmese assistance. The forces had the expected Chinese arms: 60-mm. mortars, AK-47 rifles, hand grenades, and rocket launchers. Estimates put the remaining rebel forces at 1,500 in the Naga and Burma hills and 400 in Nagaland itself. In May reports indicated that a considerable number of the 43,000-strong Nagas favoured abandonment of their struggle for independence, largely because of its manifest lack of success. Between March and July, 12 rebels were killed, 450 surrendered, and 570 were captured. Hopes of peace fell in August when seven Indian policemen were killed in one ambush and 14 persons were killed in other incidents. As against this, China was thought to be losing interest in the Nagas, who had proved unwilling to sacrifice themselves with the dedication expected from followers of Chairman Mao.

No progress was made on the Kashmir question, although the Soviet Union made its lack of sympathy for this quarrel increasingly clear and did not intend to let it affect the Soviet policy of supporting India and Pakistan as counters to China. Indian complaints in June that some 50 of the promised 200 T-54/55 tanks ordered by Pakistan in 1968 had arrived were met by a reminder that, since 1965, India had received equipment for two infantry battalions, 250 T-54/55 tanks, and 120 MiG-21s from the U.S.S.R.

Pakistan's defense budget rose again—to $542 million, an increase of $28 million over the previous year. The Navy ordered three Daphne-class submarines from France while the Air Force took delivery of several partially filled orders: 12 out of 18 Mirage III:E interceptors and fighter-bombers and the remaining 9 of 12 TF-104G Starfighters from Belgium. The increase in the MiG-19 establishment to four squadrons may have indicated that the very considerable difficulties experienced in getting them into service with inadequate technical assistance had been overcome, rather than that China had made further deliveries.

MIDDLE EAST

Throughout the year, fighting between Israel and its Arab neighbours increased in violence until a state of permanent war existed along the Suez Canal. The heaviest reprisals failed to halt raids by Arab guerrillas, who injected a new dimension into the conflict by hijacking airliners and attacking those flown by El Al, the Israeli airline. The four-power talks on the Middle East dragged on, with the only agreement being the superpowers' mutual desire to avoid any risk of inadvertent confrontation, provided this did not require any modification of their political goals. Outside arms supplies continued to flow into the area, although the new French government maintained its predecessor's embargo on shipment of the 50 Mirage III's paid for by Israel. The September 1 coup in Libya that deposed King Idris cast doubt on the assurances he had given the U.K. that the Chieftain tanks it was to sell him would not be used against Israel; in December the British Aircraft Corporation, unable to reach agreement with the new government, canceled $288 million in contracts for air defense equipment. Pres. Gamal Abd-al-Nasser's September purge of high-ranking U.A.R. service officers and politicians underlined the endemic instability in the area.

The major problem increasingly seemed to be the breakdown of effective governmental control over the Arab guerrillas, as was shown by the fighting in Lebanon in November, when the government barely succeeded in maintaining its authority. In Jordan, King Husain was reduced to being a nominal ruler, with an Iraqi regiment of 12,000 men and 15,000 guerrillas in his country. Jordan was the main base for Al Fatah, probably the most successful guerrilla group, whose main support and control came from the U.A.R. However, it was the Popular Front for the Liberation of Palestine, operating from Lebanon, that added a new factor of uncertainty to the situation with its attacks on Israeli and other civilian aircraft, and the threat it posed to the Lebanese government. On February 18 the pilot and copilot of a heavily loaded El Al Boeing 720B were wounded in an attack at the Zürich, Switz., airport, in which one of the attackers was killed by an Israeli guard. When massive security precautions were initiated around El Al planes, the guerrillas responded with the hijacking of a U.S. Trans World Airlines Boeing on August 29. On arrival in Damascus, the Israeli passengers were arrested, although the four women among them were quickly released under heavy diplomatic pressure. The seriousness of the threat to civil aviation was much greater than the casualties suggested, since only luck had prevented both aircraft from being totally destroyed. The September 8 bomb attacks on Israeli embassies in Bonn and The Hague and on the El Al office in Brussels suggested growing indiscrimination in Arab attacks.

Israel's strategy of retaliation seemed increasingly inefficient against the guerrillas, while involving the Israelis in precisely the war of attrition that the Arabs had always regarded as their best chance of victory. On February 24 Israeli air strikes against Al Fatah bases at El Hamme and Maisa led to dogfights that cost the Syrians two MiG-17s. Early in March the U.A.R. decided to engage in repeated bombardments of the Israeli side of the Suez Canal, and on March 9 lost its chief of staff, Maj. Gen. Muhammad Abdel Moneim Riad, to Israeli counterfire. Against Israel's 6,000 to 12,000 men and 60 tanks, the U.A.R. concentrated 70,000 troops, 750 tanks, 800 artillery pieces, and 250 aircraft. In April Israel struck at U.A.R. radar in Jordan and electricity supply lines in the Nile Valley in reply to constant harassment by guerrillas. On May 21 three Arab MiG's were downed, one by a U.S.-manufactured Hawk surface-to-air missile, the first kill by this weapon. A few days later the Aramco pipeline, carrying 440,000 bbl. of oil daily from Saudi Arabia across the Golan Heights, was blown up. Israel announced that full repairs would be permitted only if the pipeline was diverted so there would be no danger of escaping oil polluting water supplies. The switch to economic targets on both sides was confirmed by the destruction of Jordan's Ghor irrigation canal on June 23, and of the Haifa oil pipeline the next day.

July saw a sharp escalation in the air war, with the Arabs losing 16 aircraft in the first two weeks, including 7 Syrian MiG's on July 8 in the biggest air battle since the Six-Day War. On July 20 Israel raided the U.A.R. fortress on Green Island, losing 25 killed but destroying four missile sites and radar, artillery, and mortar positions. August and September saw continuing escalation. After Jordan's artillery attacks breached an agreement with Israel, arranged by the U.S. to permit repairs to the Ghor Canal, the canal was cut again on August 10. On August 21 a fire at the Al Aqsa Mosque in Jerusalem, one of the three greatest Muslim religious shrines, brought a call for a jihad (holy war) from the Arabs. On September 9 Israel demonstrated U.A.R. vulnerability in the Gulf of Suez by landing a force that stayed ashore for ten hours, ranging the 50 mi. between El Hafayir and Ras Zafarana. The 3,000 U.A.R. defenders seemed helpless to prevent the destruction of vital radar installations, though some reports suggested they were confused by Israeli use of captured Soviet equipment. The U.A.R.'s reprisal raid cost it 7 MiG-21s, 3 Su-7 fighter-bombers, and 1 MiG-17, against 1 Israeli aircraft. The unusually high losses may have been attributable to the use in action of the first of 50 Phantoms being supplied to Israel by the U.S.

The U.A.R. continued to receive Soviet war supplies, and its forces were stronger than before the Six-Day War. Of 850 medium and heavy tanks, only 150 were now the older T-34s, their replacements being T-54s and T-55s with 100-mm. guns. The Air Force had nearly 50% more fighters, though the U.S.S.R. refused requests for the MiG-23 for fear one might be shot down over Israel and its secrets discovered. They did supply 100 Su-7 fighter-bombers, 100 MiG-21 fighters, and 120 MiG-15 and MiG-17 fighter-bombers. A shipment of 100 amphibious armoured personnel carriers (APC's) suggested preparation for a limited offensive, although the U.S.S.R. continued to exercise strict control over operations by withholding spare parts. The return of some 200 Soviet-trained U.A.R. pilots at the end of September improved the previous ratio of 100 pilots to 400 aircraft. As protection against surprise attack, shelters for 250 fighters and bombers were built, along with additional airfields deep inside the U.A.R. In July the value of Soviet military aid since 1967 was put at approximately $2,054,000,000 for the U.A.R., $411 million for Syria, and $461 million for Iraq.

Despite this, the U.A.R. defense budget was a record $805 million, compared with the preceding year's $690 million. Additional forces in prospect included two armoured brigades to be added to the existing six, one infantry brigade, and two artillery brigades. The Syrians faced a similar increase in spending with a budget of $195 million, against $137 million in 1968. Combat losses of MiG-21s reduced the Syrian Air Force by 5, to 145, which included 20 Su-7 all-weather fighter-bombers. The Army grew by 10,000 men; armour was strengthened by a further 100 T-54/55 tanks, bringing the total to 300. Jordan's 1969 defense budget of $126 million represented 15% of GNP. Army strength remained constant, but more M-47 and M-48 U.S. tanks were received. An 18-plane squadron of Starfighters was still to be formed, a year after delivery of the original order of 30 aircraft had begun.

Israel also suffered from vastly increased defense spending, with a 1969–70 budget of $829 million, $201 million or nearly one-third higher than in the previous year. At 16.1% of GNP (at market prices), it was proportionately the highest in the world. Much of the expenditure went for munitions and equipment expended in the continual fighting. The Air Force received 46 more A-4E Skyhawk fighter-bombers and wished to purchase an additional 80, plus 20 more Phantom F-4 fighter-bombers (besides the original 50 ordered from the U.S.). The Army tried to buy Chieftain tanks from Great Britain but was refused, although some Centurions may have been sold.

SOUTH OF THE SAHARA

Despite the loss of its "capital," Umuahia, on April 22, the small remaining area of Biafra controlled by the secessionist leader Col. Odumegwu Ojukwu continued to hold out against superior federal forces. Hampered by lack of any overall command, the federal government's three divisions suffered from the defects—notably lack of fire-control discipline—to be expected in an army expanded from 10,000 men to 100,000. A fivefold increase in French arms shipments into Biafra by night flights helped to slow the federal encirclement and aided in the destruction of the federal garrison left to hold the Biafran town of Owerri. After Owerri's capture in April and President de Gaulle's resignation, French arms supplies appeared to have been reduced but not eliminated. They were augmented, according to some reports, by an increasing flow from Portugal and South Africa.

With progress on the ground slow and uncertain, the key to a federal victory seemed to lie in establishing an effective blockade in the air. Biafra depended on only two airstrips, at Uli and Uga, 20 mi. apart. This necessarily brought the government into conflict with the organizations flying relief supplies into Biafra, since Colonel Ojukwu rejected all proposals for federal inspection of supplies to verify that they did not include arms. The U.A.R. pilots employed by the Nigerian Air Force proved singularly incompetent and aroused international protest with their indiscriminate bombing of civilians. However, the emergence of a tiny Biafran air force of light planes, led by an elderly Swede, Count Carl Gustav von Rosen (*see* BIOGRAPHY), produced a sharp Soviet reaction. All-weather MiG-19F interceptors and pilots of the East German Air Force were sent out and quickly succeeded in shooting down a DC-7 running in a cargo of rice on the night of June 7. Relief flights ceased, and it seemed likely that arms flights would be strongly curtailed. Meanwhile, deaths from starvation in Biafra rose rapidly.

The year opened with the federal final push on Umuahia, Nuehe, and Orlu. Biafra counterattacked Owerri, cutting it off by February. Both attacks succeeded in April, Umuahia falling on April 22 and Owerri on April 24. The most important feature of the campaign was the federal bombing of virtually undefended targets, brought to the attention of the outside world largely through the reports of Winston Churchill (who, following the example of his famous grandfather, had become a war correspondent). The British government came under such heavy pressure to change its policy of support for the federal side that Prime Minister Harold Wilson felt constrained to announce a flying visit to Nigeria just before the voting on an emergency debate in the Commons. Not surprisingly, his visit, on March 27–31, had no visible effect.

The justification for British policy became clear in the light of estimates that Nigerian oil production would reach 50 million tons by the year's end, and that Nigeria would be among the top ten oil producers by the early 1970s. The Biafrans, realizing the importance of oil, gave priority to guerrilla raids on oil installations. On May 9, 11 European oilmen were killed and 18 captured, although the latter were released on June 5. The oil companies appeared to cut back on operations near Biafran territory, but this seemed unlikely to result in any significant production slowdown. Nevertheless, the increasing vulnerability of the Nigerian forces to guerrilla tactics as they extended their lines of communication was shown by their reinforcement of the two weak brigades in the area north of Port Harcourt to five full brigades. This may well have accounted for the failure of their 6,000-man drive on the Uli airstrip, reported on July 21.

By then, a marked change in federal conduct of the war was under way, with emphasis on the "quick kill" solution, whatever the costs. On June 14, August Lindt, the International Red Cross relief coordinator, was declared persona non grata after relief flights had been suspended three days earlier. At the end of the month the Nigerian government announced it would control all relief, thereby depriving Biafra of some $30 million a year in foreign exchange. The relief agencies protested violently, making it clear they could not afford to maintain their stockpiles and aircraft for very long if there was no prospect of their being used.

While the federal Army retained its superiority in manpower and firepower, the external arms shipments to Biafra made it increasingly hard for the poorly trained government forces to obtain local superiority. Estimates varied, but seemed to indicate French supplies were running at 150 tons per week by February, stopped in April, and resumed in May, only to halt again. They were drawn from a stockpile at Libreville in Gabon, which, with Ivory Coast, had recognized Biafra. Two DC-3s, one DC-4, and one C-46 acted as transports. After May, South Africa and Portugal increasingly replaced France as suppliers, initially at a reduced level but later at a record 175–200 tons a week. The equipment consisted of small arms, automatic weapons, ammunition, and antipersonnel mines of all nationalities, including Soviet weapons captured in the Algerian war of independence. Although the influx of refugees into Biafra's remaining 4,000 sq.mi. of territory apparently enabled the Army to maintain its strength of 30,000, its high morale and efficiency could hardly compensate for the continued shortage of equipment. One rifle to three men remained the rule. Nor did the Biafrans have anything to combat the British Saladin armoured cars that enabled federal troops to dominate the roads.

In the air, however, the Biafrans managed, unbelievably, to achieve a temporary superiority. Their secret weapon was the Swedish Minicon MFI-9B, a light single-seater aircraft fitted with racks for 12 76-mm. French Matra rockets. Five were bought in Sweden and armed in France by Count von Rosen. Von Rosen claimed that, in their first raid on a federal airbase, these planes destroyed or put out of action on the ground two MiG fighters and one Il-28 light bomber. The effect of this can be gauged by earlier reports that the serviceable aircraft in the federal Air Force had been reduced to three Il-28s, six MiG-17s, two damaged Jet Provost fighter-trainers, and one or two Czechoslovak Delfins. Sweden hastily banned the export of further Minicons, but not before another eight had been acquired from their unsuspecting owners. In August and September they were reported as attacking oil installations. The Soviet Union seized the chance to increase its influence in Nigeria and apparently persuaded the government to dismiss its U.A.R. pilots in exchange for East German planes, men, and radar equipment. These seemed likely to establish an unchallengeable air supremacy.

Farther south, 1969 was a quiet year in comparison with 1968. The guerrilla threat to Rhodesia appeared to have been halted by the establishment of semipermanent bases for Rhodesian and South African counterinsurgency patrols in the Zambezi Valley. The guerrilla bases in neighbouring Zambia (which officially denied their existence) housed between 500 and 1,600 trained men, but further recruits were apparently deterred from joining by the prospect of almost certain death or capture. The tactics of sending in small raiding groups having failed, the only alternative was a mass attack. This seemed equally unlikely to produce any results and would dissipate the remaining guerrillas. They faced a Rhodesian Army of 3,400 with an additional 7,000 reservists, plus the paramilitary British South African Police (BSAP) of 6,400 active and 28,500 reserve members. The small Air Force of 80 combat aircraft was designed for a ground attack role. The squadron of Alouette III helicopters might well have received reinforcements from South Africa, since the type was common to both countries. Zambia's vulnerability to any white retaliation circumscribed its support for the guerrillas, though in time this reduced the pressure in Rhodesia for a preemptive strike against Zambian airfields.

The focus of guerrilla activity shifted to the Caprivi Strip, joining South West Africa, Botswana, Rhodesia, Angola, and Zambia. South African forces clashed with small groups of infiltrators and captured the inevitable Soviet and Chinese weapons, including the excellent Avtomat Kalashnikov 47 automatic rifle, by now the hallmark of Communist-supported freedom fighters everywhere. There were no signs that the guerrillas would be any more successful there than in Rhodesia.

In Portugal, Antonio Salazar's illness led to his replacement as head of the government by Marcello Caetano. There seemed no likelihood of a change in Portugal's determination to retain the overseas territories of Mozambique and Angola, especially after the June announcement that vast oil fields had been discovered in northern Angola. The estimated Portuguese defense budget of $321 million was 80% above the 1961 figure. Portugal maintained 122,000 troops in Africa, including 55,000 in Angola, 40,000 in Mozambique, and 27,000 in Portuguese Guinea. The guerrilla movements, shaken by the assassination of one of their principal leaders, Eduardo Mondlane (*see* OBITUARIES), seemed to have made little progress, although they retained control of considerable areas in Mozambique and Angola.

South Africa's record defense budget of $381 million reflected the costs of developing both sophisticated naval forces, including a $21 million submarine base, and special antiguerrilla facilities and training camps. Cooperation with France continued to further progress toward self-sufficiency in arms; the first South African guided missile was launched, and a development program was announced that included Cactus, an advanced surface-to-air missile, and an air-to-air missile. (R. J. RA.)

See also Astronautics; Nuclear Energy; Vietnam.

Denmark

A constitutional monarchy of north central Europe lying between the North and Baltic seas, Denmark includes the Jutland Peninsula and 100 inhabited islands in the Kattegat and Skagerrak straits, the largest being Sjaelland (Zealand) and Fyn. Area (excluding Faeroe Islands and Greenland): 16,597 sq.mi. (43,057 sq.km.). Pop. (1969 est.): 4,873,091. Cap. and largest city: Copenhagen (pop., 1969 est., 833,027). Language: Danish. Religion: the Danish Lutheran Church is the established church. King, Frederik IX; prime minister in 1969, Hilmar Baunsgaard.

With the persistence of inflation, unemployment, and a considerable deficit in the balance of payments, 1969 began in an atmosphere of very cautious optimism. Agricultural exports, which, although displaced by industrial exports as the most important foreign-currency earner, were still a vital part of the economy, met with many obstacles, especially from central European markets.

Despite the relaxation in the autumn of 1968 of regulations that restricted price increases, industrial managements continued to complain that costs were being allowed to run ahead of artificially controlled prices. This resulted in the abolition of remaining restrictions in the old "prices and profits freeze" system, and their replacement by a set of rules of arbitration, whereby the monopoly commission was empowered to dictate a price freeze for 40 days. During that time disputing companies would be able to negotiate price rises with the authorities, thus allowing some measure of control over inflationary wage-price spirals. A labour dispute in May led to a strike by 40,000 agricultural workers, but was brought to an end after an emergency session of the Folketing.

By autumn unemployment had dropped to 1½% of the labour force, and many industries were still complaining of a shortage of manpower. Considerable numbers of Turkish and Yugoslavian workers were imported by the larger shipyards.

During the year the balance of payments situation worsened. Although, initially, exports increased, imports increased far more; for every 75 kroner worth of goods exported, Denmark was importing goods worth 100 kroner. By the end of the year the estimated deficit was between 2.5 and 3 billion kroner.

The value-added tax introduced at 10% in 1967 rose to 12½% in 1968 and remained there during 1969. A pay-as-you-earn taxation system was to be introduced Jan. 1, 1970 (Danes were currently paying their taxes up to 18 months after having earned income). A decline in consumption was predicted for the new year since, although the pay-as-you-earn tax was to be levied at only 95% of the previous tax rate, its effects on wage and salary increases would be felt immediately.

During the crises over the French franc and the West German mark in the spring and summer, a considerable amount of Danish currency flowed into West Germany, partly as pure speculation, and partly in order to make advance payments for imports out of fears of Deutsche Mark revaluation. The effect of this was to force the government on May 12 to raise the bank interest rate to a European record of 9%.

DENMARK

Education. (1966–67) Primary, pupils 523,187; secondary, pupils 179,541, primary and secondary, teachers *c.* 38,350; vocational, pupils 154,243; teacher training, students 11,815; higher (including 4 universities with 31,686 students), students 44,803, teaching staff (1965–66) 6,423.

Finance. Monetary unit: Danish krone, with a par value of 7.50 kroner to U.S. $1 (18 kroner = £1 sterling). Gold and foreign exchange, central bank: (June 1969) U.S. $372 million; (June 1968) U.S. $388 million. Budget (1969–70 est.): revenue 28.5 billion kroner; expenditure 28 billion kroner. Gross national product: (1967) 84,260,000,000 kroner; (1966) 77,080,000,000 kroner. Money supply: (April 1969) 28,070,000,000 kroner; (April 1968) 23.1 billion kroner. Cost of living (1963 = 100): (Feb. 1969) 138; (Feb. 1968) 132.

Foreign Trade. (1968) Imports 24,182,000,000 kroner; exports 19,788,000,000 kroner. Import sources: EEC 33% (West Germany 19%); U.K. 14%; Sweden 15%; U.S. 8%. Export destinations: EEC 23% (West Germany 12%); U.K. 21%; Sweden 15%; U.S. 8%; Norway 7%. Main exports: meat and meat preparations 20% (including bacon 8%); machinery 19%; dairy products 7%.

Transport and Communications. Roads (1966) 61,630 km. (including 102 km. expressways). Motor vehicles in use (1968): passenger 955,300; commercial 254,200. Railways: state (1967) 2,354 km.; private (1966) 1,184 km.; traffic (state only; 1968) 3,224,000,000 passenger-km., freight 1,380,000,000 net ton-km. Air traffic (including Danish part of international operations of Scandinavian Airlines System; 1968): 1,202,400,000 passenger-km.; freight 55.4 million net ton-km. Shipping (1968): merchant vessels 100 gross tons and over 1,140; gross tonnage 3,204,040. Telephones (including Faeroe Islands; Dec. 1967) 1,469,195. Radio licenses (Dec. 1967) 1,588,000. Television licenses (Dec. 1967) 1,182,000.

Agriculture. Production (in 000; metric tons; 1968; 1967 in parentheses): wheat 461 (420); barley 5,059 (4,382); oats 861 (904); rye 131 (118); potatoes 866 (857); sugar, raw value (1968–69) 341, (1967–68) 329; butter 161 (154); cheese 105 (124); pork 773 (791); beef and veal 265 (263); fish catch (1967) 1,070, (1966) 851. Livestock (in 000; July 1968): pigs 8,003; cattle 3,149; sheep (July 1967) 122; horses (July 1967) 42; chickens (July 1967) 18,524.

Industry. Production (in 000; metric tons; 1968): pig iron 78; crude steel 457; cement 2,194; superphosphates (1965) 799; nitrogenous fertilizers (1967–68) 59; manufactured gas (cu.m.) 391,000; electricity (net; excluding most industrial production; kw-hr.) 11,733,000. Merchant vessels launched (100 gross tons and over; 1968) 484,000 gross tons.

Students battle police during demonstration at Copenhagen University against the Danish award of the Sonning Prize to Icelandic author Halldór Laxness. Students objected to business methods of the fund's donor.

NORDFOTO FROM PICTORIAL PARADE

NORDFOTO FROM PICTORIAL PARADE

King Frederik and Queen Ingrid drive through the streets of Copenhagen, as Frederik celebrated his 70th birthday.

This move badly hit the stock market, which had been enjoying a boom, and the effective interest on long-term house mortgages reached 11%. Moreover, while 1968 saw a drain on the gold and currency reserves of 50 million kroner, during the first six months of 1969 the outflow increased to well over 500 million kroner. When reserves began to dry up altogether, the government stopped foreign exchange dealings and introduced emergency measures, approved by the Folketing on May 23. These included an increase in the price of gasoline, a large increase in motor registration charges for cars, trucks, and buses, a new state lottery, increases in passenger airport tax, railway season tickets, and postal and telegraph charges. Just before the increase in the bank rate the country had received a West German loan of DM. 235 million, and on May 19, $45 million was withdrawn from the International Monetary Fund. Prior to the opening of the Folketing in the autumn, Denmark had foreign reserves enough to cover only one month's imports, and the situation was clearly inflationary. Speaking at the opening session of the Folketing on October 7, the prime minister, Hilmar Baunsgaard, indicated his government's intention to reduce the rate of growth in public expenditure and to support agricultural development programs.

Among major projects under discussion in the latter half of the year were the planned construction of bridges between the islands of Sjaelland and Fyn and between Copenhagen and the southern Swedish coast, and the establishment of a new international airport outside Copenhagen. Under prevailing budgetary policy as much as 40% of Danish income was consumed by public enterprise, and the figure was expected to reach 50% in the near future.

A matter of great concern to Denmark in 1969 was its choice of European markets, a choice that would greatly affect the country's future. The so-called Nordek plan for a Scandinavian customs union, originally proposed by the prime minister, met with unanimous resistance from Danish businessmen. The Federation of Danish Industry, the Chamber of Commerce, and the Agricultural Council all opposed the plan, and the liberal agrarian party Venestre, one of the coalition partners in the government, recommended a halt to further negotiations in favour of more vigorous approaches to the European Economic Community (EEC), especially since hopes for the success of the U.K.'s application rose at that time. A poll published by *Berlingske Tidende* on September 28 showed an overwhelming majority in favour of entry to the EEC, but conditional upon entry of the U.K. When confronted with the possibility of entry without the U.K., the majority preferred the Nordek plan.

On July 1 Denmark removed all restrictions on the sale of pictorial pornography to persons over 16; restrictions on written pornography had been abolished in 1967. A "pornography fair," consisting of exhibits, shows, and motion pictures, was held in Copenhagen in October. (S. AA.)

ENCYCLOPÆDIA BRITANNICA FILMS. *Scandinavia—Norway, Sweden, Denmark* (1962).

Dentistry

Recent research findings tended to indicate that dental caries (tooth decay) is an infectious disorder. Research on gnotobiotic (germ-free) and controlled strains of experimental animals demonstrated that dental caries occurs only when a specific strain of cariogenic streptococci are present in the oral environment. It was noted that a lesion in the enamel or dentin (material composing the principal mass of a tooth) occurs only when these cariogenic streptococci colonize on the surface of the enamel or the dentin to form a cariogenic plaque. Thus, an emphasis has been placed on plaque control to prevent caries. The previously held idea that any acidogenic organism could produce caries was no longer defensible. Only those acidogenic organisms that could also produce dextrans (a group of polysaccharides) were caries initiators.

Caries progression in man, according to some competent investigators, consisted of more than a process of demineralization or proteolysis. It appeared, instead, to be made up of complex enzymatic processes, the actions of other aciduric organisms, and the interplay between them. Another well-known but ill-defined factor is the effect of the oral environment and the resistance of the host.

Other caries research findings indicated that demineralized carious dentin may be remineralized outside the living body. A 10% stannous fluoride solution appeared to produce the best results as noted by examination of dentinal matrix under an electron microscope.

Periodontal disease, a disorder involving the supporting structures of the tooth, remained the major contributing factor in adult tooth loss. Some leading investigators concluded that there is a definite relationship between the amount of plaque, oral debris, and calculus (incrustation on a tooth). Although there was evidence of correlation between oral debris and periodontal disease, there was little evidence to show which caused the other. Studies in men and dogs showed that when oral hygiene procedures were discontinued dental plaque developed, followed by gingivitis (inflammation of the gums). Upon the removal of the dental plaque by means of oral hygiene procedures, the gingival inflammatory process subsided. These studies lent support to the hypothesis that dental plaque is an initial cause of gingivitis in men and dogs. Since gingivitis that does not receive treatment invariably develops into periodontitis, it could be concluded that dental plaque is a primary factor in the development of a periodontal condition.

The great need in periodontal disease was to recognize and treat the high incidence of gingivitis that appears in young people. Early treatment would inevitably cut down the advancing destructive process (periodontitis) before it involved the deeper tissues and eventually caused the loss of teeth.

Research concerning derangements of the temporomandibular joint and its associated structures was becoming of increased interest and concern to most dentists. Problems involved in the joint and its associated structures continue to plague the patient as well as the practitioner. Basic as well as clinical research provided the answers to some of these problems, but the investigation as well as the associated literature became so extensive that it was almost impossible for an individual to be knowledgeable in all areas. To help deal with this problem the American Society of Oral Surgeons in conjunction with the American Dental Association held a multidisciplinary conference on the subject of the temporomandibular joint, and the results of the conference were made available to dentists. (D. L. McE.)

Dependent States

New attempts were made during 1969 to find acceptable futures for the remaining—mostly nonviable—dependent territories, the majority of which were British. In accordance with long-established U.K. policy, endorsed by art. 73 of the UN Charter, the British government sought solutions based on self-determination. There was, however, considerable pressure for other solutions from various groups in the UN General Assembly, notably in the cases of Gibraltar, British Honduras, and the Falkland Islands. The Commonwealth Prime Ministers' Conference, the Caribbean Free Trade Area (CARIFTA), and the experience of Anguilla all indicated that joint, regional Commonwealth action was most acceptable in working out stable futures for British dependencies. This replaced the associated status idea (in which full self-government was limited by British responsibility for external affairs) by a Commonwealth status related to the Commonwealth Secretariat and the nearest Commonwealth region, thus relieving the U.K. of any odium as a residual colonial power. Nauru's acceptance as the 29th member of the Commonwealth, with "special status," indicated a convenient solution to the problem of the proliferating ministates. The example of Nauru was likely to be followed in other parts of the world.

Following the 1968 constitutional conference, a new constitution for Gibraltar came into effect in May 1969, which increased domestic responsibility without altering the colony's international status and reiterated Britain's promise that no change would be made without the freely expressed wish of the people. Strong Spanish pressure in June (which included the closing of the La Línea frontier and the Algeciras ferry) contributed to the emergence of the Integration with Britain Party, under Maj. Robert Peliza, as the dominant partner in a coalition government after the July elections. The UN General Assembly resolution demanding the "termination of the colonial situation in Gibraltar by October 1" was rejected by the British government as unacceptable and unrealistic, and the situation remained unresolved. Britain protested to Spain in October over the cutting of telephone links with Gibraltar. Although Spain's economic siege continued, hopes grew that Gibraltar would survive and prosper in the face of the economic reorientation being forced upon it.

CENTRAL PRESS FROM PICTORIAL PARADE

British trooper searches two men on a street in Anguilla, March 19, 1969. After the tiny West Indies island had declared its secession from the associated state of St. Kitts-Nevis-Anguilla, British troops and police landed to quell the brief rebellion.

Africa. After Swaziland achieved independence in 1968, Britain retained no territory in Africa and France very little. Both, like the U.S.S.R. and China in North and East Africa, maintained spheres of influence, however.

French Africa. In the French Territory of Afars and Issas (formerly French Somaliland), a new government came into being without incident at the end of 1968. Political uncertainty persisted, however, despite Somalia's abandonment of its territorial claims, divisions among the opposition groups, and the presence of strong military forces at Djibouti. In July the Liberation Front, from its headquarters at the Somalian capital of Mozadiscio, appealed to the UN to hasten decolonization of the territory.

Portuguese Africa. Eduardo Mondlane, president of the Front for the Liberation of Mozambique (FRELIMO), was killed by a bomb explosion in Dar es Salaam, Tanzania, on February 3 (*see* OBITUARIES). He was succeeded by former Vice-Pres. Uria Simango (first as interim president and then as coordinator of a three-man presidium), but there was a strong possibility that more militant elements might gain control of the movement and that, in any case, Mondlane's policy of international nonalignment would be jeopardized by left-wing sympathizers. Opposition to Portuguese rule certainly did not slacken, in either Mozambique or Angola. Meanwhile, Portugal had committed 40% of its 1968 budget to defense and there was no evidence of a weakening of resolve in Lisbon following the accession of Marcello Caetano to the premiership.

Portuguese economic cooperation with South Africa was extended during the year as the result of an agreement to adapt the waters of the Kunene River for irrigation and power purposes in South West Africa and southern Angola. In July a further agreement was announced for the Cahorabassa hydroelectric plant in northern Mozambique, to be financed mainly by South African and U.S. capital. Work was due to start on this project, the largest dam in Africa, in the autumn,

continued on page 276

DEPENDENT STATES

Territory	Political status	Area (sq.mi.)	Population (1966–69)	Capital	Population of capital*	Government officials
AFRICA						
Afars and Issas	French overseas territory	8,880	126,700	Djibouti	65,000	Governor, Louis Saget
Angola	Portuguese overseas province	481,135	5,397,100	Luanda	300,000	Governor-general, Lieut. Col. Silvino Silvério Marques
Bouvet Island	Norwegian dependency	23	—	—	—	—
British Indian Ocean Territory	British colony	29	850	—	—	Commissioner, Bruce Greatbatch
Cape Verde Islands	Portuguese overseas province	1,557	228,000	Praia (São Tigao)	13,142	Governor, Cmdr. Rosado do Sacramento Monteiro
Comoro Islands	French overseas territory	878	283,000	Moroni (Grande Comore)	11,515	High commissioner, Antoine Colombani
Mozambique	Portuguese overseas province	302,328	7,492,000	Lourenco Marques	183,798	Governor-general, Gen. José Augusto da Costa Almeida
Portuguese Guinea	Portuguese overseas province	13,948	529,000	Bissau	55,958	Governor, Brig. Arnaldo Schulz
Réunion	French overseas *département*	969	435,948	Saint-Denis	72,500	Prefect, Alfred Diefenbacher
Saint Helena	British colony	156	4,722	Jamestown	1,475	Governor, D. A. Murphy; Administrators, Brig. H. McDonald (Ascension), B. Watkins (Tristan da Cunha)
São Tomé and Príncipe	Portuguese overseas province	372	70,773	São Tomé (São Tomé)	5,714	Governor, Maj. A. da Silva Sebastião
Seychelles	British colony	89	49,981	Port Victoria (Mahé)	12,000	Governor, Bruce Greatbatch
South West Africa (Namibia)	†	317,827	610,000	Windhoek	66,810	Administrator, W. C. du Plessis
Spanish Sahara	Spanish African province	102,703	48,607	Aaiún	9,812	Governor-general, Gen. Joaquín Agulla Jiménez-Coronado
ANTARCTICA						
Australian Antarctic Territory	Australian external territory	2,472,000	—	—	—	—
British Antarctic Territory‡	British colony	650,000	86	—	—	High commissioner, Sir Cosmo Haskard
French Southern and Antarctic Lands	French overseas territory	157,874	132	—	—	Administrator, Pierre Rolland
Peter I Island	Norwegian dependency	96	—	—	—	—
Queen Maud Land	Norwegian dependency	—	—	—	—	—
Ross Dependency	New Zealand dependency	160,000	42	—	—	—
ASIA						
Bahrain	British-protected sheikhdom	256	200,800	Manama	89,500	Sheikh, Isa bin Sulman al-Khalifah British political agent, A. D. Parsons
Bhutan	Indian-protected kingdom	18,000	1,000,000	Thimphu		Druk gyalpo (king), Jigme Dorji Wangchuk
Brunei	British-protected sultanate	2,226	115,822	Brunei	17,000	Sultan, Pengiran Muda Mahkota Hassanal Bolkiah
Christmas Island	Australian external territory	52	3,381	—	—	Official representative, J. W. Stokes
Cocos (Keeling) Islands	Australian external territory	5.5	684	—	—	Official representative, C. I. Buffet
Hong Kong	British colony	398	3,987,500	Victoria	621,200	Governor, Sir David Trench
Macao	Portuguese overseas province	6	300,000	Macao	153,630	Governor, Lieut. Col. António Lopez dos Santos
Neutral Zone	Area jointly governed by Kuwait and Saudi Arabia	2,500	. . .	—	—	—
Neutral Zone	Disputed area claimed by Iraq and Saudi Arabia	7,000	. . .	—	—	—
Portuguese Timor	Portuguese overseas province	5,763	580,000	Dili	10,753	Governor, Lieut. Col. José Alberty Correia
Qatar	British-protected sheikhdom	4,000	80,000	Doha	22,500	Sheikh, Ahmad bin Ali bin Abdullah al-Thani British political agent, R. H. M. Boyle
Ryukyu Islands	U.S. civil administration	848	969,000	Naha City (Okinawa)	269,000	High commissioner, Lieut. Gen. Ferdinand T. Unger
Sikkim	Indian-protected kingdom	2,744	191,000	Gangtok	9,000	Chogyal (king), Palden Thondup Namgyal Principal administrative officer, R. N. Haldipur
Trucial States	7 Arab sheikhdoms under British protection	32,278	180,184	—	—	Sheikh for each state British political agent, H. G. Balfour-Paul British political agent, A. T. Lamb
EUROPE						
Faeroe Islands	Self-governing integral part of the realm of Denmark	540	38,214	Thorshavn	9,796	Head of local government, Hakun Djurhuus
Gibraltar	British colony (self-governing)	2.25	26,007	—	—	Governor, Fleet Adm. Sir Varyl Begg; Chief minister, Sir Joshua Hassan
Guernsey	British crown dependency	30	46,182	St. Peter Port	15,706	Lieutenant governor, Sir Charles Coleman; Bailiff, Sir William Arnold
Isle of Man	British crown possession	227	49,958	Douglas	19,269	Lieutenant governor, Sir Ronald Garvey
Jan Mayen	Territory of Norway	144	36	—	—	—
Jersey	British crown dependency	45	64,000	St. Helier	26,594	Lieutenant governor, Sir Michael Villiers; Bailiff, R. H. Le Masurier
Svalbard	Territory of Norway	23,957	2,808	Longyearbyen	857	Administrator, Tollef Landsverk
NORTH AMERICA						
Antigua	British associated state (self-governing)	108	61,000	St. John's	14,000	Governor, Sir Wilfred E. Jacobs; Premier, Vere Cornwall Bird
Bahama Islands	British colony (self-governing)	4,404	148,000	Nassau (New Providence)	89,354	Governor, Sir Francis Cumming-Bruce; Prime minister, Lynden O. Pindling
Bermuda	British colony (self-governing)	21	51,000	Hamilton (Great Bermuda)	3,000	Governor, Lord Martonmere; Government leader, Sir Henry Tucker
British Honduras	British colony (self-governing)	8,866	116,455	Belize	36,677	Governor, Sir John Paul; Prime minister, George C. Price
British Virgin Islands	British colony	59	11,500	Road Town (Tortola)	1,950	Administrator, J. S. Thomson
Canal Zone	U.S. leased territory	647	51,249	Balboa Heights	—	Governor, Brig. Gen. Walter P. Leber
Cayman Islands	British colony	118	10,000	Georgetown (Grand Cayman)	4,000	Administrator, A. C. Long

Territory	Political status	Area (sq.mi.)	Population (1966–69)	Capital	Population of capital*	Government officials
Corn Islands	U.S. leased territory	4	1,872§	—	—	Administrator, U.S. State Department
Dominica	British associated state (self-governing)	290	70,000	Roseau	15,880	Governor, Louis Cools-Lartigue; Premier, E. O. Le Blanc
Greenland	Self-governing integral part of the realm of Denmark	840,000	43,729	Godthaab	6,104	Official representative, N. O. Christenson
Grenada	British associated state (self-governing)	133	104,188	St. George's	8,644	Governor, I. G. Turbott; Premier, E. M. Gairy
Guadeloupe	French overseas *département*	685	317,000	Basse-Terre	15,360	Prefect, Pierre Bolotte
Martinique	French overseas *département*	421	320,030	Fort-de-France	99,051	Prefect, Raphael Petit
Montserrat	British colony	38	14,690	Plymouth	3,500	Administrator, D. R. Gibbs; Chief minister, W. H. Bramble
Netherlands Antilles	Self-governing integral part of the realm of the Netherlands	394	210,521	Willemstad (Curaçao)	43,547	Governor, N. Debrot; Prime minister, E. Jonckheer
Puerto Rico	U.S. commonwealth	3,421	2,749,000	San Juan	504,400	Governor, Roberto Sánchez Vilella
Saint Kitts-Nevis-Anguilla‖	British associated state (self-governing)	138	56,000	Basseterre	15,742	Governor, Sir Frederick Phillips; Premier, R. L. Bradshaw
Saint Lucia	British associated state (self-governing)	238	114,000	Castries	24,587	Governor, Sir Frederick J. Clarke; Premier, John G. M. Compton
Saint-Pierre and Miquelon	French overseas territory	93	5,129¶	Saint-Pierre (Saint-Pierre)	4,501	Governor, Georges Poulet
St. Vincent	British associated state (self-governing)	150	90,000	Kingstown	20,688	Administrator, Hywel George; Chief minister, R. M. Cato
Swan Islands	U.S. unincorporated territory	1	28§	—	—	Administrator, Federal Aviation Administration
Turks and Caicos Islands	British colony	166	6,272	Grand Turk	2,339	Governor, Sir Francis Cumming-Bruce; Administrator, R. E. Wainwright
Virgin Islands of the U.S.	U.S. organized unincorporated territory	133	49,742	Charlotte Amalie (St. Thomas)	13,914	Governor, Ralph Paiewonsky
OCEANIA						
American Samoa	U.S. organized unincorporated territory	79	28,000	Pago Pago (Tutuila)	1,608	Governor, Owen S. Aspinall
British Solomon Islands	British protectorate	11,500	148,000	Honiara (Guadalcanal)	9,000	High commissioner for the Western Pacific, Sir Michael Gass
Canton and Enderbury Islands	British/U.S. condominium	27	370	—	—	British high commissioner for the Western Pacific, Sir Michael Gass; U.S. administrator, Federal Aviation Administration
Central and Southern Line Islands	British dependency	36	—	—	—	High commissioner for the Western Pacific, Sir Michael Gass
Cook Islands	Self-governing territory of New Zealand	88	20,938	Rarotonga	—	High commissioner, R. G. Davis; Prime minister, Albert Henry
Fiji	British colony	7,055	512,062	Suva (Viti Levu)	55,000	Governor, Sir Robert Foster
French Polynesia	French overseas territory	1,543	97,000	Papeete (Tahiti)	30,000	Governor, Pierre Angeli
Gilbert and Ellice Islands	British colony	342	53,517	Tarawa	10,616	High commissioner for the Western Pacific, Sir Michael Gass; Resident commissioner, V. J. Andersen
Guam	U.S. organized unincorporated territory	212	53,744	Agaña	2,200	Governor, Manuel F. S. Guerrero
Heard and McDonald Islands	Australian external territory	113	—	—	—	—
Howland, Baker, and Jarvis Islands	U.S. unincorporated territory	3	—	—	—	Administrator, U.S. Department of the Interior
Johnston and Sand Islands	U.S. unincorporated territory	1	156§	—	—	Administrator, U.S. Department of the Navy
Kingman Reef	U.S. unincorporated territory	♀	—	—	—	Administrator, U.S. Department of the Navy
Midway Islands	U.S. unincorporated territory	2	2,356§	—	—	Administrator, U.S. Department of the Navy
New Caledonia	French overseas territory	7,335	100,500	Nouméa	43,100	Governor, Jean Risterrucci
New Guinea	Australian trust territory	92,160	1,702,280	Port Moresby (on Papua)	41,848	Administrator, Sir Donald Cleland
New Hebrides	British/French condominium	5,700	80,425	Vila	3,100	British high commissioner, Sir Michael Gass; French high commissioner, Jean Risterrucci
Niue Island	New Zealand island territory	100	5,232	—	—	Resident commissioner, L. A. Shanks
Norfolk Island	Australian external territory	13	1,152	—	—	Administrator, Roger B. Nott
Palmyra Island	U.S. unincorporated territory	4	—	—	—	Administrator, U.S. Department of the Interior
Papua	Australian external territory	86,100	606,784	Port Moresby	41,848	Administrator, Sir Donald Cleland
Pitcairn Island	British colony	19	87	Adamstown	—	Governor, Sir Robert Foster
Tokelau Islands	New Zealand island territory	4	1,900	—	—	Administrator (high commissioner in Western Samoa), J. B. Wright
Tonga	British-protected kingdom	270	79,000	Nuku'alofa	15,545	King, Tupou IV; Premier, Prince Tu'ipelehake; British commissioner, A. C. Reid
Trust Territory of the Pacific Islands (Marshall, Caroline, and Mariana Islands)	United States trust territory	687	94,469	Saipan	8,664	High commissioner, W. R. Norwood
Wake Island	U.S. unincorporated territory	3	2,003	—	—	Administrator, Federal Aviation Administration
Wallis and Futuna	French overseas territory	93	7,000¶	Matautu (Uvea)	. . .	Administrator, André Duc Dufayard
SOUTH AMERICA						
Falkland Islands	British colony	6,270	2,132	Stanley	1,115	Governor, Sir Cosmo Haskard
French Guiana	French overseas *département*	35,135	44,392	Cayenne	24,581	Prefect, René Letellier
Surinam	Self-governing part of the realm of the Netherlands	63,251	375,200	Paramaribo	110,867	Governor, H. de Vries; Prime minister, J. A. Pengel

*Most recent available figure.
†On Oct. 27, 1966, the UN General Assembly adopted a resolution to terminate South Africa's mandate and put South West Africa under the direct responsibility of the UN. South Africa considers the resolution illegal and has stated that it intends to continue its jurisdiction over the territory.
‡Includes some territory claimed by Argentina and Chile.
§1960.
‖Following Anguilla's attempted secession from St. Kitts-Nevis in January 1969, a British commissioner was appointed to administer the island pending settlement of its future status.
¶1965.
♀Less than 0.5 sq.mi.
A dash (—) indicates none or negligible; three dots (. . .) indicate not available.

continued from page 273

but the involvement of U.K. and U.S. companies was jeopardized by Rhodesian participation in the scheme, and Swedish participation was withdrawn. UN sanctions forbade member states to allow their nationals to engage in activities calculated to promote the export of any commodities from Rhodesia.

Portugal appeared to have achieved a noteworthy success in Guinea when Rafael Barbosa, president of the African Independence Party for Guinea and the Cape Verde Islands (PAIGC), together with 91 of his supporters, swore loyalty to the Portuguese government on August 5. This followed the defection of the Mozambique African leader Lazaro Kavandame in March, though the importance of this was immediately discounted by a FRELIMO statement that Kavandame had been suspended from the executive committee of the movement in January.

Spanish Africa. On June 30 Spain formally returned to Morocco the enclave of Ifni on the Moroccan Atlantic coast. An agreement between Morocco and Spain had been signed at Fez on January 4, pursuant to a 1966 UN resolution requesting decolonization of the territory. Ifni had been under Spanish occupation since 1934, although it was originally ceded to Spain by the sultan of Morocco in 1860 and the Spanish connection with Ifni went back to 1476. The eventual return to Morocco of the Spanish "plazas" on its Mediterranean coast remained subject to negotiation.

Caribbean. Two colonies, Montserrat and the British Virgin Islands, together with the six associated states, made up the British dependencies in the eastern Caribbean. In 1969 the internal affairs of the associated state of St. Kitts-Nevis-Anguilla attracted world attention and aroused regional concern over the conditions and prospects of the poorer Caribbean territories. The island of Anguilla announced its secession from St. Kitts-Nevis in January. The Anguillan leader Ronald Webster (*see* BIOGRAPHY) forced British officials to leave the island amid accusations that Anguilla's action was the work of U.S. gangster elements. In March, at the request of Premier Robert Bradshaw of St. Kitts-Nevis and with the agreement of the Commonwealth prime ministers, British troops were sent to Anguilla and remained in occupation until September. A commissioner was installed to rule the island pending the recommendation of a Caribbean Commission.

Antigua, Dominica, St. Lucia, and Grenada retained their associate status with Britain. Despite internal political disagreement, St. Vincent achieved this status on October 27, following a June constitutional conference in London. In April a state of emergency was proclaimed on Montserrat following attacks on police. Montserrat had made it clear that it wished to pursue economic development before seeking constitutional advancement. In the Bahamas the government of Lynden Pindling announced that white settlers in Freeport would need work permits in order to remain there. It was thought that the hard-line immigration policy would probably ease, however, as economic expansion created a need for more foreign workers.

In British Honduras the government of George C. Price showed a growing interest in regional institutions, particularly CARIFTA. Interest was also expressed in the Central American Common Market and the Organization of American States. The dispute with Guatemala over that country's claim to "Belize" remained unresolved, in spite of reported continuing diplomatic consultations between the British and Guatemalan governments. In February the Commonwealth Caribbean heads of government declared their backing for member states with border problems.

During the year there was increased pressure from St. Lucia, Grenada, and some other states for some form of regional integration and a Commonwealth treaty of defense with Canada, but no ultimate definition of what constituted an external threat as against a threat to internal security could be agreed upon. The Caribbean Office of the UN Economic Commission for Latin America emphasized the great dependence of the area on tourism and ancillary industries. The poorer states argued that major benefits within CARIFTA went to the more prosperous islands, while

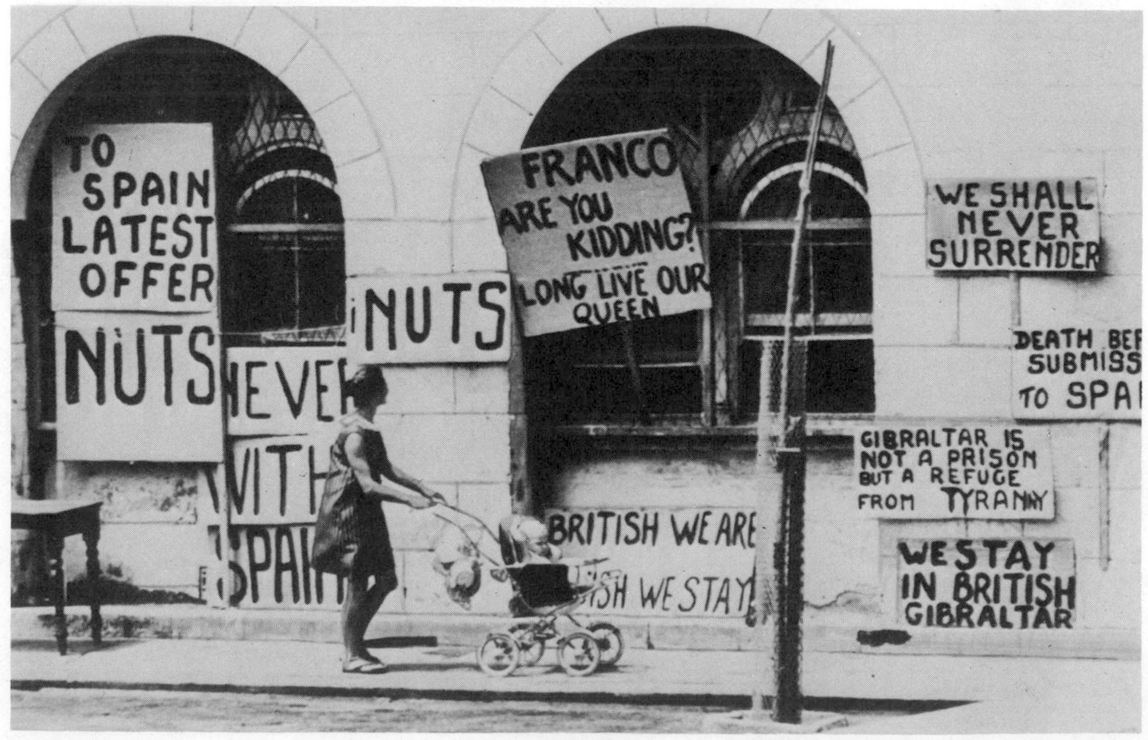

Residents of Gibraltar demonstrated loyalty to British government by raising these signs defying Spanish demands in 1969 that Rock be returned to Spain.

POPPERFOTO FROM PICTORIAL PARADE

AUSTRALIAN EXTERNAL TERRITORY

PAPUA

Education. (1968) Primary, pupils 65,035, teachers 1,733; secondary, pupils 5,140, teachers 213; vocational, pupils 1,160, teachers 88; teacher training, students 533, teaching staff 48.

Finance and Trade. Monetary unit: Australian dollar (A$0.89 = U.S. $1; A$2.14 = £1 sterling). Budget (1967–68): revenue A$49,468,000 (including A$23,140,399 grant by Australian government); expenditure A$49,257,000. Foreign trade (1967–68): imports A$60,554,000 (63% from Australia, 8% from Japan, 6% from U.S., 5% from U.K.); exports A$12,477,000 (79% to Australia, 11% to U.S.). Main exports: rubber 28%; copra 24%.

Agriculture. Production (in 000; metric tons): copra (1966) 15, (1965) 17; rubber (1968) 5.6, (1967) 5.1.

Industry. Gold production (1967) 43 troy oz.

AUSTRALIAN TRUST TERRITORY

NEW GUINEA

Education. (1968) Primary, pupils 144,572, teachers 4,009; secondary, pupils 9,181, teachers 408; vocational, pupils 2,165, teachers 131; teacher training, students 959, teachers 107.

Finance and Trade. Monetary unit: Australian dollar. Budget (1966–67): revenue A$72,709,477 (including A$49,979,402 grant by Australian government); expenditure A$76,762,308. Foreign trade (1966–67): imports A$76,132,000; exports A$44,382,000. Import sources: Australia 53%; Japan 12%; U.S. 6%; U.K. 6%. Export destinations: Australia 40%; U.K. 31%; U.S. 7%; West Germany 7%; Japan 5%. Main exports: coffee beans 23%; cocoa beans 21%; copra 18%; coconut oil 12%; timber 5%; plywood 5%.

Agriculture. Production (in 000; metric tons; 1967; 1966 in parentheses): copra *c.* 65 (93); coconut oil (exports; 1965) 22, (1964) 26; cocoa 25 (21); coffee (1966) *c.* 3.4, (1965) 3.4; timber (cu.m.; 1966–67) *c.* 4,300, (1965–66) *c.* 4,200. Livestock (in 000; March 1967): cattle 35; pigs 4; horses 1.

Industry. Gold production (1967) 27,628 troy oz.

BRITISH COLONIES AND PROTECTORATES

ANTIGUA

Education. (1963–64) Primary, pupils 11,052; secondary, pupils 6,073; primary and secondary, teachers 470; teacher training, students 50, teachers 3.

Finance and Trade. Monetary unit: East Caribbean dollar (ECar$2 = U.S. $1; ECar$4.80 = £1 sterling). Budget (1967 est.): revenue ECar$13,759,496; expenditure ECar$12,632,803. Foreign trade (1967): imports ECar$39,094,190 (29% from U.S., 23% from U.K., 10% from Trinidad and Tobago); exports ECar$4,968,599 (21% to Canada, 9% to U.S., 5% to U.K., 5% to Puerto Rico). Main export petroleum products 85%. Tourism (1967) 59,174 visitors.

BAHAMA ISLANDS

Education. (1965–66) Primary, pupils 21,100, teachers 471; secondary, pupils 7,512, teachers 167; vocational, pupils 525, teachers 17; higher, students 28, teaching staff 3.

Finance and Trade. Monetary unit: Bahamian dollar, with a par value of B$1.02 to U.S. $1 (B$2.45 = £1 sterling). Budget (1968 est.): revenue B$61,609,463; expenditure B$66,230,345. Foreign trade (1967): imports B$160,863,283 (81% from U.S., 11% from U.K., 8% from Canada); exports B$32,270,861 (74% to U.S., 9% to U.K., 6% to Canada). Main exports: cement 19%; rum 14%; pulpwood 12%. Tourism (1967): visitors 576,800; gross receipts (1965) *c.* U.S. $60 million.

Transport and Communications. Shipping (1968): merchant vessels 100 gross tons and over 113; gross tonnage 303,407. Telephones (Jan. 1968) 31,520. Radio receivers (Dec. 1966) 47,000. Television receivers (Dec. 1964) *c.* 4,500.

BERMUDA

Education. (1966–67) Primary, pupils 9,067, teachers 384; secondary, pupils 3,460, teachers 223; vocational, pupils 454, teachers 52.

Finance and Trade. Monetary unit: Bermuda pound, at par with the pound sterling (Ber£1 = U.S. $2.40); British coin (legal tender) and U.S. currency circulate. Budget (1968 est.): revenue Ber£7,898,473; expenditure Ber£9,534,070. Foreign trade: imports (1968) U.S. $73.2 million; exports (1967) U.S. $60.2 million. Import sources: U.S. 45%; U.K. 22%; Canada 9%. Export destinations: U.K. 22%; Australia 13%; U.S. 12%; Netherlands 11%; France 8%; Japan 7%. Main exports: concentrated essences 60%; beauty preparations 10%. Tourism (1967): visitors 237,200; gross receipts U.S. $51.9 million.

Transport and Communications. Shipping (1968): merchant vessels 100 gross tons and over 30; gross tonnage 380,053. Telephones (Jan. 1968) 24,534. Radio receivers (Dec. 1967) 25,000. Television receivers (Dec. 1967) 13,000.

BRITISH HONDURAS

Education. (1966–67) Primary, pupils 29,158, teachers (1965–66) 1,030; secondary, pupils 2,835, teachers (1965–66) 165; vocational, pupils 340, teachers (1965–66) 16; teacher training, students 143, teachers (1965–66) 12; higher (abroad; 1967–68), students 167.

Finance and Trade. Monetary unit: British Honduras dollar (BH$1.67 = U.S. $1; BH$4 = £1 sterling). Budget (1969 est.): revenue BH$27.2 million; expenditure BH$27.4 million. Foreign trade (1967): imports BH$36,951,914; exports BH$20,469,880. Import sources: U.S. 34%; U.K. 30%; Jamaica 7%; Netherlands 5%. Export destinations: U.K. 38%; U.S. 29%; Mexico 13%; Canada 10%. Main exports: sugar 39%; citrus fruits and products 17%; mahogany 5%.

BRITISH SOLOMON ISLANDS

Education. (1967) Primary, pupils 24,378, teachers (1966) 1,046; secondary, pupils 589, teachers 23; vocational, pupils 212, teachers 13; teacher training, students 114, teachers 10.

Finance and Trade. Monetary unit: Australian dollar. Budget (1968 est.) balanced at A$7,711,498 (including U.K. grant-in-aid A$2,196,575). Foreign trade (1968): imports A$9,399,099; exports A$5,554,332. Main exports (1967): copra 74%; timber 22%.

BRITISH VIRGIN ISLANDS

Education. (1966–67) Primary and secondary, pupils 2,450, teachers 125.

Finance and Trade. Monetary unit: U.S. dollar (U.S. $2.40 = £1 sterling). Budget (1967 est.): revenue U.S. $2,013,780 (including U.K. financial aid U.S. $794,216); expenditure U.S. $2,075,559. Foreign trade (1967): imports U.S. $3,890,025; exports U.S. $87,835. Main exports: fish 42%; livestock 34%; fruit 8%.

CAYMAN ISLANDS

Education. (1966–67) Primary, pupils 1,673, teachers (1964–65) 53; secondary, pupils 472, teachers (public schools only) 20.

Finance and Trade. Monetary unit: Jamaica dollar (following conversion to decimal currency on Sept. 8, 1969, Jam$2 = £1 sterling; Jam$0.83 = U.S. $1). Budget (1967 actual): revenue Jam$1,045,154; expenditure Jam$1,014,292. Foreign trade (1967): imports Jam$3,422,816; exports Jam$47,580. Main exports: rope 22%; turtle shell 14%.

Transport. Shipping (1968): merchant vessels 100 gross tons and over 26; gross tonnage 16,749; *c.* 1,100 persons were employed as seamen in U.S. ships in 1960.

DOMINICA

Education. (1965–66) Primary, pupils 17,200, teachers (1963–64) 459; secondary, pupils 1,452, teachers (1963–64) 83; vocational (1963–64), pupils 350, teachers 16.

Finance and Trade. Monetary unit: East Caribbean dollar. Budget (1967 est.): revenue ECar$7,874,949; expenditure ECar$8,303,448. Foreign trade (1966): imports ECar$17,374,715; exports ECar$11,144,021 (90% to U.K. in 1965). Main export (1965) bananas 78%.

FALKLAND ISLANDS

Education. (1967) Primary and secondary, pupils 336, teachers 40.

Finance and Trade. Monetary unit: Falkland Island pound, at par with the pound sterling; British currency also circulates. Budgets: (colony; 1968–69 est.) revenue FI£340,000, expenditure FI£468,500; (dependencies; 1968–69 est.) revenue FI£56,000, expenditure FI£55,000. Foreign trade: (colony; 1967) imports FI£711,335, exports FI£824,187 (mainly wool); (dependencies) imports (1967) FI£12,491, exports (1966) FI£1,368,361 (mainly whale and seal oil).

FIJI

Education. (1967) Primary, pupils 104,971; secondary, pupils 11,153; vocational, pupils 785; teacher training, students 313; teachers, all grades 3,588; higher (medical school), students 168. The University of the South Pacific at Suva opened in 1968; students (1968) 160.

Finance and Trade. Monetary unit: Fiji dollar (F$.871 = U.S. $1; F$2.09 = £1 sterling); the Fiji dollar replaced the former Fiji pound from Jan. 13, 1969 (F$2 = F£1). Budget (1968 est.): revenue F$28,679,000; expenditure F$29,089,000. Foreign trade (1968): imports U.S. $75.4 million (27% from Australia, 22% from U.K., 13% from Japan, 10% from New Zealand, 5% from U.S.); exports U.S. $53.7 million (38% to U.K., 14% to U.S., 12% to Australia, 6% to Canada, 5% to New Zealand). Main exports (1967): sugar 65%; gold 9%; coconut oil 8%. Tourism (1967): visitors 56,000; gross receipts U.S. $12.6 million.

Transport and Communications. Ships entered (1967) vessels totaling 1,655,000 net registered tons; goods loaded (1967) 519,000 metric tons, unloaded 446,000 metric tons. Telephones (Jan. 1968) 12,802. Radio receivers (Dec. 1967) 40,000.

Agriculture and Industry. Production (in 000; metric tons): sugar, raw value (1968–69) *c.* 390, (1967–68) 296; copra (1967) 25, (1966) 26; bananas (1966) 4, (1965) 2; cement (1967) 47; gold (troy oz.; 1967) 111.

GIBRALTAR

Education. (1966–67) Primary, pupils 2,582, teachers 117; secondary, pupils 1,761, teachers 102; vocational, pupils 106, teachers 12.

Finance and Trade. Monetary unit: Gibraltar pound, at par with the pound sterling; British currency also circulates. Budget (1968 est.): revenue Gib£2,212,200; expenditure Gib£2,288,990. Foreign trade (1967): imports Gib£8,244,584; exports Gib£2,614,590. Tourism (1967) 463,642 arrivals.

Transport. Shipping (1968): merchant vessels 100 gross tons and over 17; gross tonnage 59,394. Ships entered (1967) vessels totaling 13,510,796 net registered tons; goods loaded (1966) 3,000 metric tons, unloaded 256,000 metric tons.

GILBERT AND ELLICE ISLANDS

Education. (1967) Primary, pupils 12,576; secondary, pupils 951; primary and secondary, teachers 611; vocational, pupils 108, teachers 5; teacher training, students 89, teachers 11.

Finance and Trade. Monetary unit: Australian dollar. Budget (1968 est.): revenue A$3,857,520; expenditure A$3,595,650. Foreign trade (1967): imports A$3,942,689; exports A$6,200,348. Main exports (1966): phosphates 64%; copra 26%.

GRENADA

Education. (1966–67) Primary, pupils 28,943, teachers (1965–66) 691; secondary, pupils 2,770, teachers (1965–66) 117; teacher training (1965–66), students 33, teachers 5.

Finance and Trade. Monetary unit: Trinidad and Tobago dollar (TT$2 = U.S. $1; TT$4.80 = £1 sterling). Budget (1967 est.) balanced at TT$13,935,772 (including TT$3,400,000 aid and grants). Foreign trade (1967): imports TT$23,895,657; exports *c.* TT$10,195,961. Import sources: U.K. 35%; Canada 11%; U.S. 11%. Export destinations: U.K. 58%; U.S. 5%. Main exports: bananas 33%; cocoa beans 28%; nutmegs 11%; mace 5%.

GUERNSEY

Education. (1967) Primary and secondary, pupils 8,399.

Finance and Trade. Monetary unit: pound sterling. Budget (1967): revenue £4,913,357 (including £134,403 for Alderney); expenditure £4,526,578 (including £116,495 for Alderney). Foreign trade included with U.K. Main exports (1967): tomatoes, flowers, stone. Tourism (1967) 221,834 passengers arrived.

HONG KONG

Education. (1966–67) Primary, pupils 661,957, teachers 20,593; secondary, pupils 206,075; vocational, pupils 11,658; secondary and vocational, teachers 8,526; higher (including University of Hong Kong and Chinese University of Hong Kong with 4,622 students in 1967–68), students 11,343, teaching staff 1,241.

Finance and Trade. Monetary unit: Hong Kong dollar (HK$6.06 = U.S. $1; HK$14.55 =

they derived no benefits from the agricultural protocol —largely inoperative during 1969—that was supposed to ensure markets for agricultural exports. It was reported that at least two associated states were considering substituting association with Trinidad and Tobago for association with Britain. Such a move might give them access to World Bank or Inter-American Development Bank funds, hitherto denied because of their political status.

Following strikes and civil disorders in the Netherlands Antilles in May, a new government drawn from the three socialist parties was formed in December.

Middle East. In the Persian Gulf the British government continued its efforts to assist the local rulers to activate the Federation of Arab Amirates. The defense needs of the federation following British withdrawal from the Gulf in 1971 were the subject of discussions in London. The federation would link Bahrain, Qatar, and the seven Trucial States, Abu Dhabi, Dubai, Sharjah, Fujairah, Ras al Khaimah, Umm al Qaiwain, and Ajman. Britain was reported to be confident that agreement could be reached with Iran, which had laid claim to Bahrain. At discussions among the rulers in Abu Dhabi in October, the ruler

£1 sterling). Budget (1968–69 est.): revenue HK$1,952,324,700; expenditure HK$1,965,353,-000. Foreign trade (1968): imports HK$12,470,-000,000 (22% from Japan, 19% from China, 14% from U.S., 9% from U.K.); exports HK$8,-428,000,000 (34% to U.S., 13% to U.K., 6% to Japan, 5% to West Germany). Main export textiles 48%.

Transport and Communications. Roads (1968) 1,006 km. Railways (1966) 35 km. Shipping (1968): merchant vessels 100 gross tons and over 135; gross tonnage 766,213. Ships entered (1967) vessels totaling 27,651,000 net registered tons; goods loaded (1968) 2,635,000 metric tons, unloaded 9,017,000 metric tons. Telephones (Jan. 1968) 353,912. Radio receivers (Dec. 1967) 623,000. Television receivers (Dec. 1967) 93,000.

ISLE OF MAN

Education. (1968–69) Primary, pupils 3,996; secondary, pupils 3,292; vocational, pupils 1,940.

Finance and Trade. Monetary unit: pound sterling. Budget (major items; 1968–69): revenue £8,951,880; expenditure £10,885,540. Foreign trade included with U.K. Tourism (1968) 494,-699 passengers arrived.

Transport. Roads (1968) *c.* 650 km. Motor vehicles in use (1968): passenger and commercial 15,663; motorcycles 1,875. Railways (1968) 110 km.

Agriculture. Livestock (in 000; 1967): cattle 32; sheep 123; pigs 4; poultry 124.

JERSEY

Education. (1968) Primary and secondary, pupils 9,803.

Finance and Trade. Monetary unit: Jersey pound, at par with the pound sterling. Budget (1967): revenue £12,221,607; expenditure £7,-482,384. Foreign trade included with U.K. Main exports (1967): potatoes, tomatoes, cattle. Tourism (1967) 733,000 passengers arrived.

MONTSERRAT

Education. (1967–68) Primary, pupils 2,908, teachers (1964–65) 89; secondary, pupils 268, teachers (1964–65) 16.

Finance and Trade. Monetary unit: East Caribbean dollar. Budget (1968 est.): revenue ECar$5,603,510; expenditure ECar$5,599,510. Foreign trade (1967): imports ECar$6,923,900; exports ECar$500,000. Main exports: fruit and vegetables 52%; cotton 48%.

ST. HELENA

Education. (1966–67) Primary, pupils 753; secondary, pupils 409; primary and secondary, teachers 60; teacher training (1964–65), students 31, teachers 6.

Finance and Trade. Monetary unit: pound sterling. Budget (1967 actual): revenue £513,-717; expenditure £493,616. Foreign trade (1967): imports £410,037 (56% from U.K., 30% from South Africa); exports £19,234 (44% to U.K., 44% to South Africa). Main export (1966) hemp 75%.

Agriculture. Livestock (1967): cattle 671; sheep 1,175; goats 1,153; pigs 545; poultry 11,-068; donkeys 848; horses 26.

ST. KITTS-NEVIS-ANGUILLA

Education. (1966–67) Primary, pupils 15,460, teachers (1964–65) 453; secondary, pupils 1,653, teachers (1964–65) 68; vocational (1964–65), pupils 300, teachers 4.

Finance and Trade. Monetary unit: East Caribbean dollar. Budget (1966 actual): revenue ECar$6,820,617; expenditure ECar$6,530,756. Foreign trade (1966): imports ECar$15,817,508; exports ECar$8,614,875. Main export sugar 88%.

ST. LUCIA

Education. (1964–65) Primary, pupils 23,417, teachers 688; secondary, pupils 1,032, teachers 56; teacher training, students 40, teachers 7.

Finance and Trade. Monetary unit: East Caribbean dollar. Budget (1966 est.): revenue ECar$10.2 million; expenditure ECar$9.4 million. Foreign trade (1966): imports ECar$28,386,100 (34% from U.K., 10% from Trinidad and Tobago, 7% from Netherlands Antilles); exports ECar$12,108,770 (83% to U.K.). Main exports: bananas 77%; copra 8%; coconut oil 5%.

ST. VINCENT

Education. (1966–67) Primary, pupils 26,992, teachers 1,038; secondary, pupils 2,638, teachers 93; teacher training, students 257, teachers 14.

Finance and Trade. Monetary unit: East Caribbean dollar. Budget (1968 est.): revenue ECar$10,607,355; expenditure ECar$10,749,355. Foreign trade (1966): imports ECar $16,108,057 (32% from U.K., 16% from Trinidad and Tobago, 12% from Canada, 11% from U.S.); exports ECar$6,710,847 (58% to U.K., 13% to Trinidad and Tobago, 11% to Barbados, 7% to U.S.). Main exports: bananas 52%; arrowroot starch 13%.

SEYCHELLES

Education. (1966) Primary, pupils 7,912, teachers 324; secondary, pupils 1,506, teachers 86; vocational, pupils 202, teachers 7; higher, students 47, teaching staff 4.

Finance and Trade. Monetary unit: Seychelles rupee, valued at SRs. 5.56 to U.S. $1 (SRs. 13.33 = £1 sterling). Budget (1968 est.): revenue SRs. 12,558,596 (excluding grant-in-aid, valued at Rs. 2,466,667 in 1967); expenditure SRs. 17,018,596. Foreign trade (1967): imports SRs. 24,595,360 (36% from U.K., 8% from Burma, 6% from Hong Kong, 6% from Kenya); exports SRs. 10,-517,737 (53% to India, 7% to U.K., 5% to West Germany). Main exports: copra 53%; cinnamon bark 29%.

TURKS AND CAICOS ISLANDS

Education. (1967) Government primary, pupils 1,683.

Finance and Trade. Monetary unit: Jamaica dollar. Ordinary budget (1967 est.): revenue £419,853; expenditure £395,286. Foreign trade (1967): imports £356,943; exports £50,692. Main exports (1966): crayfish 66%; salt 22%.

BRITISH-FRENCH CONDOMINIUM

NEW HEBRIDES

Education. (1964) Primary, pupils 12,521, teachers 570; secondary, pupils 1,734, teachers 80; vocational, pupils 104, teachers 7; teacher training, students 70, teachers 5. French educational establishments only (1966): primary, pupils 5,280; secondary, pupils 93; teacher training, students 25.

Finance. Monetary units: Australian dollar and New Hebrides franc (NHFr. 89.76 = U.S. $1; NHFr. 215.44 = £1 sterling; NHFr. 100.54 = A$1). Condominium budget (1968 est.) balanced at A$2,790,000. British administration budget (1968–69 est.) balanced at A$1,846,734. French administration budget (1968 est.): revenue A$1,476,387; expenditure A$4,102,900.

Foreign Trade. (1968) Imports A$9,080,643; exports A$10,432,050. Import sources: Australia 45%; France 15%; Japan 10%; Hong Kong 6%. Export destinations: France 47%; Japan 23%; U.S. 16%; Venezuela 6%. Main exports: copra 53%; fish 23%; manganese ore 14%.

Agriculture and Industry. Production (in 000; metric tons): copra (1966) 35, (1965) 29; manganese ore (metal content; 1967) 35.

BRITISH-PROTECTED STATES

BAHRAIN

Education. (1966–67) Primary, pupils 32,829; teachers (including preprimary; 1965–66) 1,215; secondary, pupils 7,632; vocational, pupils 768; teacher training, students 360; secondary, vocational, and teacher training, teachers (1965–66) 479.

Finance and Trade. Monetary unit: Bahrain dinar, with a par value of 0.48 dinars to U.S. $1 (1.14 dinars = £1 sterling). Budget (1967 est.): revenue 11,184,000 dinars; expenditure 9,260,000 dinars. Foreign trade (excluding oil; 1968): imports 52,021,000 dinars (24% from U.K., 16% from Japan, 12% from U.S., 5% from India, 5% from Pakistan); reexports 18,494,000 dinars (57% to Saudi Arabia, 8% to Qatar, 6% to Abu Dhabi, 6% to Iran, 5% to Dubai). Main export petroleum and products.

Industry. Production (in 000; metric tons): crude oil (1968) 3,768; petroleum products (1967) 11,650.

BRUNEI

Education. (1967–68) Primary, pupils 26,245, teachers 1,191; secondary, pupils 6,641, teachers 393; vocational, pupils 106, teachers 8; teacher training, students 354, teachers 20.

Finance and Trade. Monetary unit: Brunei dollar, with a par value of Br$3.06 to U.S. $1 (Br$7.35 = £1 sterling). Budget (1968 est.): revenue Br$157,973,720; expenditure Br$189 million. Foreign trade (1967): imports Br$137,-662,898; exports Br$248,264,287. Import sources: U.K. 28%; Singapore 17%; U.S. 9%; Japan 7%; China 6%; Thailand 5%. Export destination Sarawak 98%. Main export crude oil 95%.

Agriculture. Production (in 000; metric tons): rice (1966) 3, (1965) 3; rubber (exports; 1968) 0.1, (1967) 0.4. Livestock (in 000; Dec. 1965): cattle 2; pigs 8; goats *c.* 4.

Industry. Production (1967): crude oil 5,099,-000 metric tons; natural gas 217 million cu.m.

QATAR

Education. (1966–67) Primary, pupils 11,740, teachers 604; secondary, pupils 1,928, teachers 137; vocational, pupils 233, teachers 34; teacher training, students 57, teachers 12.

Finance and Trade. Monetary unit: Qatar/Dubai riyal, with a par value of 4.75 riyals to U.S. $1 (11.40 riyals = £1 sterling). Foreign trade: imports (1966) 162,747,821 riyals (15% from U.K., 11% from U.S.); exports (1963) 290 million riyals. Main export crude oil.

Industry. Crude oil production (1968) 16,180,-000 metric tons.

TONGA

Education. (1967) Primary, pupils 16,446, teachers (1966) 609; secondary, pupils 8,702, teachers (1966) 309; teacher training (1966), students 66, teachers 5.

Finance and Trade. Monetary unit: pa'anga, at par with the Australian dollar. Budget (1968–69 est.) balanced at 2,397,815 pa'angas. Foreign trade (1967): imports 5,729,561 pa'angas; exports 3,566,321 pa'angas. Main exports: bananas 45%; copra 39%.

TRUCIAL STATES

Education. Primary-intermediate (1958), pupils *c.* 2,000.

Finance and Trade. Monetary units: Abu Dhabi, Bahrain dinar; other states, Qatar/Dubai of Abu Dhabi, Sheikh Zaid, was elected president of the federation for a two-year period. Abu Dhabi was selected as the provisional capital.

Far East. In contrast with 1967, when Hong Kong had suffered from Communist-organized disturbances, 1968 and 1969 proved both peaceful and profitable for the colony. The economic success of 1968, based largely on textiles and tourists, went on to reach record heights in 1969. A contract signed with Costain Civil Engineering, Ltd., in June enabled work to begin in August on an £18 million seabed tunnel, which would link Hong Kong with the mainland city of Kowloon. Despite local admiration for independent Singapore, there appeared little likelihood of greater self-government while China remained a threat. Chinese tolerance, based on the estimated £250 million in foreign exchange funds that entered China each year through Hong Kong, would be unlikely to continue toward a self-governing territory favourable to Taiwan. Changes in Hong Kong's immigration laws were proposed, the main one being that Commonwealth citizens should be liable to the same restrictions as aliens.

Indian Ocean. The power vacuum in the Indian Ocean and the Persian Gulf caused by British with-

riyal. Budgets (1967 est.): Abu Dhabi *c.* £35 million; other states *c.* £3 million. Foreign trade, Dubai only: imports (1967) 476,895,343 riyals; exports (1966) 56,092,197 riyals. Import sources: Switzerland 19%; Japan 17%; U.K. 15%; U.S. 8%. Export destinations: Persian Gulf states 63%; Ceylon 10%; Saudi Arabia 8%; Muscat and Oman 7%. Main export (excluding oil) dry fish 8%; reexports (entrepôt trade) account for 92% of total. Foreign trade, Abu Dhabi (with U.K. only; 1968): imports £9,550,000; exports £14.5 million.

Industry. Crude oil production (1968) 24,293,000 metric tons.

DANISH REALM

FAEROE ISLANDS

Education. (1966–67) Primary, pupils 6,282; secondary, pupils 1,191; primary and secondary, teachers 299; vocational, pupils 1,032, teachers 88; teacher training, students 80, teachers 12; higher, students 6, teaching staff 4.

Finance and Trade. Monetary unit: Danish krone (7.50 kroner = U.S. $1; 18 kroner = £1 sterling). Foreign trade (1967): imports 186,340,000 kroner; exports 177,810,000 kroner. Import sources: Denmark 73%; U.K. 9%; Norway 6%; Sweden 5%. Export destinations: Italy 22%; Spain 16%; Denmark 10%; U.K. 9%; Sweden 7%; Chile 6%; U.S. 5%; Brazil 5%. Main exports fish and products 77%.

Agriculture and Industry. Fish catch (1967) 173,300 metric tons. Livestock (in 000; June 1966): sheep *c.* 73; horses 1. Electricity production (1966–67) 55 million kw-hr.

GREENLAND

Education. (1966–67) Primary, pupils 7,795; secondary, pupils 712; primary and secondary, teachers 553; teacher training, students 16, teachers (1965–66) 4.

Finance and Trade. Monetary unit: Danish krone. Foreign trade (1967): imports 318,053,000 kroner; exports 91,887,000 kroner. Import source Denmark 93%. Export destinations: Denmark 51%; U.S. 34%. Main exports: fish and products 81%; minerals 13%.

Agriculture. Production: fish catch (in 000; metric tons; 1967) 45, (1966) 44. Livestock (in 000): sheep (Nov. 1965) 40; reindeer (1961) 2.8; sledge dogs (1959) 12.5.

Industry. Production (in 000; metric tons; 1967): coal 32; cryolite (exports) *c.* 68.

FRENCH OVERSEAS DÉPARTEMENTS AND TERRITORIES

COMORO ISLANDS

Education. (1967) Primary, pupils 10,395; secondary, pupils 813; primary and secondary (1966), teachers 218.

Finance and Trade. Monetary unit: CFA franc, with a parity of CFA Fr. 50 to the French franc (CFA Fr. 277.71 = U.S. $1; CFA Fr. 666.50 = £1 sterling). Budget (1969 est.) balanced at CFA Fr. 1,269,000,000. Foreign trade (1968): imports CFA Fr. 1,763,000,000; exports CFA Fr. 1,008,200,000. Import sources (1965): France 47%; Malagasy Republic 17%; Cambodia 10%; Thailand 7%; Argentina 6%. Export destinations (1965): France 47%; U.S. 28%; Malagasy Republic 6%. Main exports: essential oils 37%; vanilla 35%; copra 17%.

FRENCH GUIANA

Education. (1966–67) Primary, pupils 6,739, teachers (including preprimary) 237; secondary, pupils 1,747; vocational, pupils 574; secondary and vocational, teachers 138.

Finance and Trade. Monetary unit: franc, at par with the French (metropolitan) franc (Fr. 5.55 = U.S. $1; Fr. 13.33 = £1 sterling). Budget (1968 est.) balanced at Fr. 57,972,895. Foreign trade (1967): imports Fr. 207,940,000 (72% from France, 13% from U.S.); exports Fr. 18,434,000 (78% to U.S., 11% to France, 5% to Martinique). Main exports: shrimps 76%; timber 5%.

FRENCH POLYNESIA

Education. (1967) Primary, pupils 24,984, teachers (1965) 782; secondary, pupils 5,645, teachers (1965) 204; vocational, pupils 550, teachers (1965) 65; teacher training (1965), students 27, teachers 3.

Finance. Monetary unit: CFP franc, with a parity of CFP Fr. 18.18 to the French franc (CFP Fr. 100.99 = U.S. $1; CFP Fr. 242.36 = £1 sterling). Budget (1967) balanced at CFP Fr. 2,332,000,000.

Foreign Trade. (1967) Imports CFP Fr. 10,229,000,000; exports CFP Fr. 1,184,000,000. Import sources (1966): France 80%; U.S. 8%. Export destinations (1966): France 52%; South Vietnam 23%; New Zealand 9%; Japan 6%. Main exports: phosphates 21%; copra 18%; vanilla 6%. Tourism (1967): visitors 23,600; gross receipts U.S. $4.7 million.

Industry. Phosphate rock production (1966) 177,000 metric tons.

FRENCH TERRITORY OF AFARS AND ISSAS

Education. (1965–66) Primary, pupils 4,082, teachers 117; secondary, pupils 596, teachers 40; vocational, pupils 145, teachers 9; teacher training, students 9, teachers 2.

Finance. Monetary unit: Djibouti franc, with a par value of DjFr. 214.39 to U.S. $1 (DjFr. 38.60 = 1 French franc; DjFr. 514.54 = £1 sterling). Budget (1968 est.) balanced at DjFr. 2 billion.

Foreign Trade. (1967) Imports DjFr. 6,713,000,000; exports DjFr. 604 million. Import sources: Iran 24%; France 18%; U.K. 12%; Ethiopia 7%. Export destinations (1966): France 66%; Aden 5%. Main exports: manufactures, hides. There is a considerable transit trade through Djibouti for Ethiopia.

Transport. Ships entered (1965) vessels totaling 14,834,000 net registered tons; goods loaded (1966) 120,000 metric tons, unloaded 2,078,000 metric tons.

GUADELOUPE

Education. (1966–67) Primary, pupils 65,065, teachers (including preprimary) 1,857; secondary, pupils 15,334; vocational, pupils 2,696; secondary and vocational, teachers 705; teacher training, students 101, teachers 9; higher (1964–65), students 209.

Finance and Trade. Monetary unit: local franc, at par with the French (metropolitan) franc. Budget (1966 est.) balanced at Fr. 228,262,936. Foreign trade (1967): imports Fr. 491,839,000 (72% from France, 10% from U.S.); exports Fr. 160,136,000 (74% to France, 19% to U.S.). Main exports: sugar 50%; bananas 35%; rum 8%.

MARTINIQUE

Education. (1966–67) Primary, pupils 66,664, teachers 2,356; secondary, pupils 23,422; vocational, pupils 1,821; secondary and vocational, teachers 1,077; teacher training, students 258, teachers 5; higher (at Institut Henri Vizioz), students 510, teaching staff (1964) 19.

Finance and Trade. Monetary unit: local franc, at par with the French (metropolitan) franc. Budget (1968 est.) balanced at Fr. 287 million. Foreign trade (1967): imports Fr. 521,152,000 (73% from France, 6% from U.S.); exports Fr. 177,909,000 (91% to France). Main exports: bananas 57%; sugar 16%; rum 11%; canned fruit 9%.

NEW CALEDONIA

Education. (1968) Primary, pupils 22,817, teachers (1966) 819; secondary, pupils 3,295, teachers (1966) 151; vocational, pupils 941, teachers (1966) 80; teacher training (1966), students 33, teachers 12.

Finance. Monetary unit: CFP franc. Budget (1969 est.) balanced at CFP Fr. 3,053,989,000.

Foreign Trade. (1967) Imports CFP Fr. 7,068,000,000; exports CFP Fr. 7.1 billion. Import sources: France 53%; Australia 19%; U.S. 8%. Export destinations: France 52%; Japan 29%; Canada 10%; U.S. 5%. Main exports: nickel castings 46%; nickel matte 28%; nickel 23%.

Transport and Communications. Ships entered (1965) vessels totaling 1,351,000 net registered tons; goods loaded (1966) 1,425,000 metric tons, unloaded 821,000 metric tons. Telephones (Dec. 1967) 6,004. Radio receivers (Dec. 1967) 15,000.

Industry. Production (in 000; metric tons; 1967): iron ore (metal content) 112; chrome ore (oxide content) 0.9; nickel ore (metal content; 1966) 87; electricity (kw-hr.; 1966) 606,000.

RÉUNION

Education. (1967–68) Primary, pupils 115,693, teachers 3,450; secondary, pupils 4,551, teachers 310; vocational (1965–66), pupils 696, teachers 54; teacher training, students 801, teachers 95.

Finance and Trade. Monetary unit: CFA franc. Budget (1969) balanced at CFA Fr. 10.3 billion; French aid (1969) CFA Fr. 1,937,000,000. Foreign trade (1967): imports CFA Fr. 28,720,000,000; exports CFA Fr. 8,990,000,000. Import sources: France 66%; Malagasy Republic 9%. Export destination France 90%. Main exports: sugar 81%; essential oils 11%.

SAINT-PIERRE AND MIQUELON

Education. (1966–67) Primary, pupils 1,155, teachers 63; secondary and vocational, pupils 377, teachers 47.

Finance. Monetary unit: CFA franc. Ordinary budget (1967 est.) balanced at CFA Fr. 590,075,000.

Foreign Trade. (1967) Imports CFA Fr. 1,917,728,000; exports CFA Fr. 684,058,000. Import sources: Canada 48%; France 30%; U.K. 10%; U.S. 6%. Export destinations: U.S. 65%; Canada 17%; France 17%. Main exports: fresh and frozen fish 67%; livestock 17%; dried fish 10%; fish meal 5%.

INDIAN-PROTECTED STATES

BHUTAN

Education. (1966–67) Primary, pupils 12,300, teachers 257; secondary, pupils 2,099, teachers 126; vocational, pupils 51, teachers 6.

Finance and Trade. Monetary unit: Indian rupee (Rs. 7.50 = U.S. $1; Rs. 18 = £1 sterling). Budget (1962 est.) balanced at Rs. 4.2 million (including Rs. 500,000 subsidy from India). Five-year development plan (1961–66) total expenditure (rev. est.) Rs. 153 million, all granted or guaranteed by India. Planned development aid from India (including aid to Sikkim; 1968–69) Rs. 50 million. About 95% of external trade is with India. Main exports (1963–64): timber Rs. 1,250,000; coal Rs. 220,000.

drawal was followed by an expansion of Soviet naval activity, indirectly in support of the Indian Navy. Discussions on the future of the Seychelles were begun in Port Victoria during a September visit by Lord Shepherd, minister of state at the Foreign and Commonwealth Office.

The National Liberation Movement of Comoro (MOLINACO) claimed support from 69% of the islanders. In a sixth anniversary message from Nairobi, Kenya, exiled leader A. A. Noordi alerted members to be prepared for revolution in order to win independence from France. In October there were demonstrations on the island of Mayotte, during which one person was killed and others were wounded. Following the transfer of the capital of the Comoro Islands from Dzaoudzi on Mayotte to Moroni on Grande Comore, the inhabitants of Mayotte demanded the status of an overseas territory and vigorously opposed the government of Said Mohammed Cheikh.

Pacific. *British Pacific Territories.* The South Pacific Conference held its annual meeting at Nouméa, New Caledonia, to discuss its technical and social advancement program, which had a 1969 budget of $1 million contributed by Australia, New Zealand, the

SIKKIM

Education. (1963) Primary and secondary, pupils 11,620.

Finance and Trade. Monetary unit: Indian rupee. Budget (1967–68 est.) revenue *c.* Rs. 12.5 million. Five-year development plan (1967–72) Rs. 90 million, all financed by India. Planned development aid from India (including aid to Bhutan; 1968–69) Rs. 50 million. Foreign trade is mainly with India. Main exports (excluding barter; 1960 est.): cardamom Rs. 5 million; oranges Rs. 1.4 million; potatoes Rs. 400,000.

NETHERLANDS OVERSEAS TERRITORIES

NETHERLANDS ANTILLES

Education. (1966–67) Primary, pupils 41,645, teachers 1,156; secondary, pupils 9,029; vocational, pupils 3,626, teachers 168; teacher training, students 311; secondary and teacher training, teachers 366.

Finance. Monetary unit: Netherlands Antilles guilder or florin, with a parity of 0.52 Netherlands Antilles guilders to the Netherlands guilder (1.89 Netherlands Antilles guilders = U.S. $1; 4.53 Netherlands Antilles guilders = £1 sterling). Budgets: central (1966 est.), revenue 66,689,603 Netherlands Antilles guilders, expenditure 66,-593,089 Netherlands Antilles guilders; Curaçao (1965), revenue 57,195,006 Netherlands Antilles guilders, expenditure 57,697,423 Netherlands Antilles guilders; Aruba (1965), revenue 34,091,426 Netherlands Antilles guilders, expenditure 32,-954,275 Netherlands Antilles guilders. Cost of living (Curaçao; 1963 = 100): (April 1969) 106; (April 1968) 105.

Foreign Trade. (1967) Imports 1,256,193,000 Netherlands Antilles guilders; exports 1,144,839,-000 Netherlands Antilles guilders. Import sources: Venezuela 76%; U.S. 10%. Export destinations: U.S. 44%; Canada 9%; U.K. 6%; Japan 5%. Main export petroleum products 96% (from crude oil imported from Venezuela, accounting for 79% of imports).

Transport and Communications. Roads (1967) 1,183 km. (Curaçao 541 km., Aruba 380 km., Bonaire 209 km., St. Maarten 53 km.). Motor vehicles in use (Aruba and Curaçao; 1967): passenger 26,300; commercial 5,000. Ships entered (Aruba and Curaçao; 1967) vessels totaling 85,917,000 gross registered tons; goods loaded (Aruba and Curaçao; 1966) *c.* 36.3 million metric tons, unloaded *c.* 42.2 million metric tons. Telephones (Dec. 1967) 24,610. Radio receivers (Dec. 1966) 121,000. Television receivers (Dec. 1966) *c.* 25,000.

Industry. Production (in 000; metric tons; 1967): petroleum products 36,530; phosphate rock (exports) 116; electricity (kw-hr.; 1965) 1,080,000.

SURINAM

Education. (1964–65) Primary, pupils 71,397, teachers 2,052; secondary, pupils 10,252, teachers 463; vocational, pupils 1,430, teachers 78; teacher training, students 1,583, teachers 150; higher, students 667, teaching staff 74.

Finance. Monetary unit: Surinam guilder or florin, with a parity of 0.52 Surinam guilders to the Netherlands guilder (1.89 Surinam guilders = U.S. $1; 4.53 Surinam guilders = £1 sterling). Budget (1968 est.): revenue 134,671,000 Surinam guilders; expenditure 137,216,000 Surinam guilders.

Foreign Trade. (1968) Imports 187 million Surinam guilders; exports 214 million Surinam guilders. Main import sources (1967): U.S. 38%; Netherlands 13%; U.K. 6%; Japan 6%; West Germany 6%. Main export destinations (1967): U.S. 52%; West Germany 10%; Netherlands 9%; Canada 7%; Norway 6%; Italy 5%. Main exports (1966) bauxite and aluminum 91%.

Transport and Communications. Roads (1967) 1,560 km. Motor vehicles in use (1967): passenger 8,900; commercial 2,700. Railways (1961) 86 km. Ships entered (1966) vessels totaling 3,906,000 net registered tons; goods loaded (1966) 5,039,000 metric tons, unloaded 644,000 metric tons. Telephones (Dec. 1967) 9,046. Radio receivers (Dec. 1967) 65,000. Television receivers (Dec. 1966) 16,000.

Agriculture. Production (in 000; metric tons; 1967; 1966 in parentheses): rice 118 (112); sugar, raw value (1966) 18, (1965) 19; oranges 11 (10); grapefruit 6 (6); bananas (1966) 25, (1965) 16. Livestock (in 000; Jan. 1967): cattle 47; goats 8; sheep 4; pigs 11.

Industry. Production (in 000; metric tons; 1967): bauxite 5,466; aluminum (exports) 31; stone (1966) 47; gold (troy oz.) 4.5; rum (litres; 1966) 2,523; electricity (kw-hr.) 843,000.

NEW ZEALAND TERRITORIES

COOK ISLANDS

Education. (1966) Primary, pupils 5,072, teachers 268; secondary, pupils 639, teachers 43; teacher training, students 104, teachers 8.

Finance and Trade. Monetary unit: New Zealand dollar (NZ$0.89 = U.S. $1; NZ$2.14 = £1 sterling). Budget (1967–68): revenue NZ$1,-817,000 (excluding NZ$1,869,000 grant-in-aid); expenditure NZ$3,686,000. Foreign trade (1966): imports NZ$3,196,000; exports NZ$1,740,000. Main exports: fruit juice 45%; clothing 23%; citrus fruit 11%; copra 8%.

NIUE ISLAND

Education. (1966) Primary, pupils 1,345, teachers 80; secondary, pupils 260, teachers 14; teacher training (1964), students 32, teachers 5.

Finance and Trade. Monetary unit: New Zealand dollar. Budget (1967–68): revenue NZ$752,673 (excluding NZ$751,200 grants); expenditure NZ$1,560,233. Foreign trade (1967): imports NZ$598,156; exports NZ$103,378. Main exports: copra, bananas.

PORTUGUESE OVERSEAS TERRITORIES

ANGOLA

Education. (1965) Primary, pupils 218,598, teachers 4,835; secondary, pupils 15,248, teachers 708; vocational, pupils 13,912, teachers 807; teacher training, students 936, teachers 77; higher, students 606, teaching staff 73.

Finance and Trade. Monetary unit: Angola escudo, at par with the Portuguese escudo (28.75 escudos = U.S. $1; 69 escudos = £1 sterling). Budget (1968 est.) balanced at 5,164,787,000 escudos. Foreign trade (1967): imports 7,905,-000,000 escudos (35% from Portugal, 17% from West Germany, 13% from U.S., 8% from U.K.); exports 6,837,000,000 escudos (33% to Portugal, 27% to U.S., 10% to Netherlands). Main exports: coffee 53%; diamonds 18%.

Transport. Roads (1967) *c.* 48,000 km. Motor vehicles in use (1967): passenger 55,500; commercial (including buses) 21,900. Railways (1966) 3,110 km. Ships entered (1967) vessels totaling 4,239,000 net registered tons; goods loaded (1967) 1,973,000 metric tons, unloaded 990,000 metric tons.

Agriculture. Production (in 000; metric tons; 1967; 1966 in parentheses): dry beans *c.* 64 (*c.* 64); cottonseed 18 (13); sisal *c.* 59 (*c.* 67); sugar, raw value (1968–69) *c.* 80, (1967–68) 63; coffee *c.* 204 (*c.* 198); palm oil (1966) *c.* 35, (1965) *c.* 32; palm kernels (exports; 1966) 14, (1965) 14; fish catch (1967) 292, (1966) 327. Livestock (in 000; Dec. 1967): sheep 137; goats 715; cattle 2,095; pigs 315.

Industry. Production (in 000; metric tons; 1968): crude oil 548; iron ore (60–65% metal content) 3,219; diamonds (metric carats; 1967) 1,289; salt (1967) 78; fish meal (1967) 40.

CAPE VERDE ISLANDS

Education. (1966–67) Primary, pupils 27,194, teachers 490; secondary, pupils 1,688, teachers 66; vocational, pupils 610, teachers 36.

Finance and Trade. Monetary unit: Cape Verde escudo, at par with the Portuguese escudo. Budget (1968 est.) balanced at 118,952,000 escudos. Foreign trade (1967): imports 258.8 million escudos; exports 30,913,000 escudos.

Transport. Ships entered (1966) vessels totaling 6,709,000 net registered tons; goods loaded (1966) 43,000 metric tons, unloaded 583,000 metric tons.

GUINEA

Education. (1965–66) Primary, pupils 13,449, teachers 245; secondary, pupils 434, teachers 24; vocational, pupils 623, teachers 32.

Finance and Trade. Monetary unit: Guinea escudo, at par with the Portuguese escudo. Budget (1966 est.) balanced at 152,590,000 escudos. Foreign trade (1967): imports 471,851,000 escudos; exports 91,174,000 escudos.

Agriculture. Production (in 000; metric tons): shelled peanuts (1967) 11.2, (1966) 4.8; palm kernels (exports; 1966) *c.* 10, (1965) *c.* 12. Livestock (in 000; 1966–67): cattle 230; pigs 98; sheep 54; goats 144.

MACAO

Education. (1966–67) Primary, pupils 35,520, teachers 916; secondary, pupils 9,177, teachers 562; vocational, pupils 2,276, teachers 123; teacher training, students 114, teachers 26.

Finance and Trade. Monetary unit: patacá (1 patacá = 4.75 escudos; 6.05 patacás = U.S. $1; 14.53 patacás = £1 sterling). Budget (1967 est.) balanced at 46,677,000 patacás. Foreign trade (1967): imports 245,522,000 patacás (60% from Hong Kong, 33% from China); exports 143,168,-200 patacás (23% to Hong Kong, 18% to West Germany, 14% to U.S., 7% to Mozambique, 7% to Portugal, 6% to France, 5% to Italy).

Transport. Ships entered (1966) vessels totaling 5,279,462 net registered tons; goods loaded (1967) 43,000 metric tons, unloaded 277,000 metric tons.

MOZAMBIQUE

Education. (1964) Primary, pupils 358,378, teachers 4,486; secondary, pupils 8,290, teachers 598; vocational, pupils 12,389, teachers 767; teacher training, students 841, teachers 65; higher, students 388, teaching staff 81.

Finance and Trade. Monetary unit: Mozambique escudo, at par with the Portuguese escudo. Budget (1967 rev. est.): revenue 4,595,000,000 escudos; expenditure 4,594,000,000 escudos. Foreign trade (1967): imports 5,726,800,000 escudos (32% from Portugal, 11% from South Africa, 10% from U.K., 8% from West Germany, 5% from Iraq); exports 3,501,500,000 escudos (38% to Portugal, 14% to South Africa, 8% to U.S., 7% to U.K.). Main exports (1966): cashew nuts 19%; cotton 15%; sugar 14%; tea 8%; timber 5%; copra 5%.

Transport. Roads (1966) *c.* 38,000 km. (including *c.* 4,000 km. main roads). Motor vehicles in use (1966): passenger 52,700; commercial (including buses) 11,600. Railways (1966) 3,670 km. Ships entered (1967) vessels totaling 15,-951,000 net registered tons; goods loaded (1967) 8,671,000 metric tons, unloaded 4,020,000 metric tons.

U.K., France, the U.S., and Western Samoa. The value of the Pacific as a tourist area on the Caribbean model increased as U.S. interests began to buy up land in Fiji, the Cook Islands, and the New Hebrides. Opposition in the New Hebrides came from an indigenous political movement that aimed at regaining undeveloped land under European title.

Fiji's preparation for a constitutional conference leading to full self-government continued to be bedeviled by the question of the common electoral roll, in view of the fact that the Indian immigrant population outnumbered indigenous Fijians. Despite good economic prospects for the sugar crop, this same racial problem appeared in the negotiations with Indian cane farmers for the renewal of their contracts in 1970. The left-wing and anti-British attitude of the Indian opposition party hardened the views of the moderate government of Ratu Sir K. K. T. Mara. In New Britain the suggestion that the Rabaul council should be multiracial was rejected. In Tonga the prospects for a major offshore oil drilling program were reported as good. King Taufa'ahau Tupou was said to have asked the British government for an independence conference, to be held probably during 1970.

Agriculture. Production (in 000; metric tons; 1968; 1967 in parentheses): cotton, lint *c.* 44 (32); sisal *c.* 32 (31); sugar, raw value (1968–69) *c.* 215, (1967–68) 200; copra (exports; 1966) 38, (1965) 39; bananas (1966) *c.* 25, (1965) *c.* 25; tea (1967) 14, (1966) 14. Livestock (in 000; Dec. 1966): goats 457; sheep *c.* 107; cattle (Dec. 1967) *c.* 1,200; pigs *c.* 100; asses 16.

Industry. Production (in 000; metric tons; 1967): petroleum products 710; cement 243; electricity (excluding most industrial production; kw-hr.; 1966) 219,000.

SÃO TOMÉ AND PRÍNCIPE ISLANDS

Education. (1964–65) Primary, pupils 6,500, teachers 150; secondary, pupils 398, teachers 19; vocational, pupils 110, teachers 5.

Finance and Trade. Monetary unit: Guinea escudo. Budget (1966 est.) balanced at 74,887,000 escudos. Foreign trade (1967): imports 158,059,000 escudos; exports 226,726,000 escudos.

Agriculture. Production (in 000; metric tons; 1967; 1966 in parentheses): cocoa 10.3 (10.9); copra (1966) 5.5, (1965) 6.3; bananas (1966) *c.* 5, (1965) 3; palm kernels (exports; 1966) *c.* 3.5, (1965) *c.* 3.5; palm oil (1966) *c.* 1.4, (1965) *c.* 1.4. Livestock (in 000; 1967): cattle 3.3; sheep 2.6; pigs 3.7; goats 1.

TIMOR

Education. (1965–66) Primary, pupils 18,488, teachers 462; secondary, pupils 679, teachers 57; vocational, pupils 17, teachers 7.

Finance and Trade. Monetary unit: Timor escudo, at par with the Portuguese escudo. Budget (1966 est.) balanced at 77,904,000 escudos. Foreign trade (1966): imports 141,468,000 escudos; exports 35,416,000 escudos.

Agriculture. Production (in 000; metric tons; 1966; 1965 in parentheses): corn 16 (7); rice 12 (10); sweet potatoes 13 (13); copra *c.* 1 (*c.* 1); coffee 2.1 (2.8). Livestock (in 000; 1965–66): goats 251; pigs 226; buffaloes 124; horses 106; cattle 51; sheep 57.

SOUTH AFRICAN LEAGUE OF NATIONS MANDATE

SOUTH WEST AFRICA (NAMIBIA)

Education. (1966) Primary and secondary, pupils 93,491, teachers 2,970.

Finance and Trade. Monetary unit: South African rand, with a par value of R 0.71 to U.S. $1; (R 1.71 = £1 sterling). Budget (1966–67): revenue R 115,370,000; expenditure R 113,047,000. Foreign trade included in the South African customs union. Main exports (1966): minerals (including diamonds) R 128 million; karakul pelts R 14.5 million.

Agriculture. Production (in 000; metric tons; 1967; 1966 in parentheses): corn *c.* 10 (*c.* 10); millet (1966) *c.* 13, (1965) *c.* 13; beef and veal (1966) 73, (1965) 54; butter *c.* 2 (*c.* 2); fish catch 740 (650). Livestock (in 000; 1966–67): cattle *c.* 2,350; sheep *c.* 3,800; goats *c.* 1,420; poultry (1965–66) *c.* 339.

Industry. Production (in 000; metric tons; 1966): copper ore 37; lead ore (metal content) 102; zinc ore (metal content) 28; tin concentrates (metal content; 1967) 0.7; silver (1967) 0.045; diamonds (metric carats; 1967) *c.* 1,900; electricity (kw-hr.; 1963) 188,000.

SPANISH OVERSEAS PROVINCE

SPANISH SAHARA

Education. Primary (1966–67), pupils 1,869, teachers 47; secondary, pupils 768, teachers 29.

Finance and Trade. Monetary unit: Spanish peseta (70 pesetas = U.S. $1; 168 pesetas = £1 sterling). Budget (1966) balanced at 216 million pesetas. Imports (1966) 156,683,000 pesetas; exports nil.

Agriculture and Industry. Livestock (in 000; 1966): camels 38; goats 54; sheep 9. Electricity production (1967) 5,120,000 kw-hr. Phosphate mining was being developed.

UNITED STATES DEPENDENCIES

AMERICAN SAMOA

Education. (1966–67) Primary, pupils 6,432, teachers 272; secondary and vocational, pupils 2,889, teachers 65.

Finance and Trade. Monetary unit: U.S. dollar. Budget: revenue (1967 est.) $13,149,000 (including U.S. grant $9,149,000); expenditure (1965) $13,010,350. Foreign trade (with U.S. only; 1967): imports $18.1 million; exports $29,921,000. Main export (1964–65) fish (mostly canned tuna) 98%.

Agriculture. Production (in 000; metric tons; 1967; 1966 in parentheses): copra *c.* 0.7 (*c.* 0.7); bananas 1 (1). Livestock (in 000): pigs (April 1966) *c.* 20; chickens (July 1966) *c.* 20.

GUAM

Education. (1966) Primary (including preprimary), pupils 14,170, teachers 459; secondary, pupils 8,387, teachers 336; higher, students 1,476, teaching staff 100.

Finance and Trade. Monetary unit: U.S. dollar. Budget (1965 actual): revenue $28,615,091 (including U.S. grants $3,097,543); expenditure $30,189,542. Foreign trade (1966): imports $40,422,760 (60% from U.S. in 1965); exports $6,741,682 (49% to U.S. in 1965). Main exports: transshipped foodstuffs, scrap metal.

Agriculture and Industry. Main crops: corn, sweet potatoes, taro, cassava. Industrial production (in 000; 1967): stone (metric tons) 464; electricity (excluding most industrial production; kw-hr.) 530,000.

PANAMA CANAL ZONE

Education. (1966–67) Primary, pupils 8,717, teachers 299; secondary and vocational, pupils 5,503, teachers 229; higher, students 1,390, teaching staff 73.

Finance. Monetary unit: U.S. dollar.

Traffic and Trade. (1967–68) Total number of oceangoing vessels passing through the canal 13,199; total cargo tonnage 96,550,165; total tolls collected U.S. $83,907,063. Nationality and number of commercial vessels using the canal: U.S. 1,647; Liberian 1,543; Norwegian 1,498; British 1,453; West German 1,279; Japanese 1,036; Panamanian 519; Netherlands 469; Swedish 466; Greek 444; Danish 434. Foreign trade (1964): imports U.S. $64.7 million; exports U.S. $9.1 million.

PUERTO RICO

Education. (1966–67) Primary, pupils 476,343, teachers 12,890; secondary and vocational, pupils 238,987, teachers 8,480; higher (including 4 universities), students 44,516, teaching staff 3,500.

Finance. Monetary unit: U.S. dollar. Central government budget (1967–68): revenue $926,021,829; expenditure $902,044,799 (U.S. total payments to Puerto Rico $377,544,697). Gross national product: (1967–68) $3,740,000,000; (1966–67) $3,358,200,000. Cost of living (1963 = 100): (May 1969) 119; (May 1968) 116.

Foreign Trade. (1967–68) Imports $1,969,377,926 (80% from U.S.); exports $1,447,132,672 (87% to U.S.). Main exports (1963–64): textiles 24%; sugar 14%. Tourism (1967): visitors 809,400; gross receipts U.S. $161.8 million.

Transport and Communications. Roads (1968) *c.* 9,500 km. Motor vehicles in use (1967): passenger 337,800; commercial (including buses) 65,300. Shipping traffic (1967–68) goods unloaded 26,848,000 tons. Telephones (Dec. 1967) 240,821.

Agriculture. Production (in 000; metric tons; 1967; 1966 in parentheses): bananas 106 (107); coffee 15 (13); sugar, raw value (1968–69) *c.* 726, (1967–68) *c.* 585; tobacco 5.6 (7.5); pineapples 74 (67); oranges 30 (37); grapefruit 10 (12); sweet potatoes 23 (27); milk *c.* 360 (354); beef and veal *c.* 20 (19). Livestock (in 000; Jan. 1968): cattle 497; pigs 184; chickens (Jan. 1966) 3,619.

Industry. Production (in 000; metric tons; 1967): sand and gravel 12,792; stone 6,594; cement (1968) 1,525; electricity (kw-hr.; 1968) 6,182,000.

RYUKYU ISLANDS

Education. (1966–67) Primary, pupils 148,932, teachers 4,378; secondary, pupils 115,754, teachers 4,416; vocational, pupils 11,613, teachers 580; higher (including 3 universities), students 6,051, teaching staff 468.

Finance and Trade. Monetary unit: U.S. dollar. Budget (1968): revenue $104,747,524 (including U.S. grant $10,133,804 and Japanese grant $21,887,586); expenditure $104,507,619. Foreign trade (1967): imports $316 million; exports $90 million. Import sources: Japan 78%; U.S. 15%. Export destinations: Japan 76%; U.S. 8%. Main exports (1966–67): sugar 52%; canned pineapple 20%.

Agriculture. Production (in 000; metric tons; 1966; 1965 in parentheses): rice 12 (10); pineapples 88 (68); sweet potatoes 112 (*c.* 70); sugarcane (1968–69) 220, (1967–68) 221; fish catch (1967) 29, (1966) 25. Livestock (in 000; Dec. 1967): cattle *c.* 20; pigs 167; goats *c.* 40; chickens (Dec. 1966) 1,390.

VIRGIN ISLANDS, U.S.

Education. (1966–67) Primary, pupils 9,626, teachers 395; secondary and vocational, pupils 4,027, teachers 289; higher, students 1,223, teaching staff 60.

Finance and Trade. Monetary unit: U.S. dollar. Budget (2-year; 1967–69 est.): revenue (including grant-in-aid) $49,112,000; expenditure $43,978,486. Foreign trade (1967): imports $172,155,000 (60% from U.S.); exports $92,307,000 (81% to U.S.). Tourism (1967): visitors 554,434; gross receipts *c.* $75 million.

Industry. Stone production (1967) 166,000 metric tons.

UNITED STATES TRUST TERRITORY

CAROLINE, MARIANA, AND MARSHALL ISLANDS

Education. (1966–67) Primary, pupils 26,069, teachers 1,061; secondary, pupils 3,230, teachers 220; vocational, pupils 121, teachers 16; teacher training, students 1,082.

Finance and Trade. Monetary unit: U.S. dollar. Budget (1968 est.) balanced at $24,680,000 (including U.S. grant $24 million). Foreign trade (1968): imports $13.6 million (50% from U.S., 28% from Japan); exports $3 million (27% to Japan). Main exports: copra 83%; scrap metal 10%.

Agriculture. Production (in 000; metric tons; 1966; 1965 in parentheses): copra *c.* 12.5 (12.5); bananas *c.* 3 (*c.* 3); pineapples 110 (93). Livestock (in 000; June 1967): cattle 5; pigs *c.* 22; goats 5; poultry 200.

Australian External Territories. The first year of the new House of Assembly in Papua-New Guinea brought the beginnings of political party development —notably the Melanesian Independence Party, which aimed at attaching Bougainville to the Solomons, and the United Niugini Party, which desired to include West New Guinea. The discovery of new tribes in the West Sepik area in 1969 showed how far the country was from any sort of unified national consciousness. The number of refugees crossing the border from West New Guinea (Irian Barat), coupled with the arrival of Indonesian paratroops to oppose West Irianian rebels, posed problems for Papua-New Guinea. In the interest of maintaining good relations with Indonesia, the Australian government in May played down a shooting incident on the border when Indonesian police pursued refugees from West Irian. The much criticized "act of free choice" in West Irian decided in favour of Indonesia. Djakarta promptly promised development aid and "full autonomy" for West Irian by 1971. (*See* INDONESIA.)

French Pacific Territories. In September several people were injured in disturbances in Nouméa, New Caledonia, involving the police and youths protesting against police investigations following the discovery of subversive pamphlets on the Loyalty Islands. The territorial assembly condemned those responsible, and several persons received heavy prison sentences.

WIDE WORLD

Militiamen and police attempt to restore order on May 30, 1969, to the embattled city of Willemstad, Curaçao, a Netherlands dependency. Mobs of striking refinery workers ran through city, looting and burning.

The island was struck by Tropical Storm Colleen in February. Also in February, nickel workers received the first of two wage increases, demanded following a rise in the world price of nickel. Three new mining companies were said to be planned.

In February a new governor of Tahiti arrived in Papeete. The territorial assembly declared in favour of Tahitian internal self-government.

U.S. Pacific Territories. A report made for the U.S. Economic Development Administration declared that Eastern Samoa would remain "irrevocably linked" with the U.S. Massive economic aid and televised educational programs were increasing U.S. influence. After a two-year attempt to formulate a way of welding into a viable single state 95,000 people scattered over 2,000 islands in more than 3,000 sq.mi. of ocean, 95% of whose revenue came from aid, the Micronesian Political Status Commission reported that it would aim at a self-governing state in free association with the U.S. following a plebiscite. Economic viability rested on U.S. payment for the use of Kwajalein as an antimissile base and suggested ventures on the Nauru football-pool model.

In November U.S. Pres. Richard Nixon and Japanese Prime Minister Eisaku Sato announced agreement on the reversion of Okinawa to Japanese control, subject to "necessary legislative support." Despite its surrender of all title to the Kuril Islands in 1951, Japan continued to claim them, but the U.S.S.R. maintained that its control of the Kurils was an internal matter.

Indian Protected States. *Bhutan.* Bhutan's emergence into the modern world continued throughout 1969. In June the national assembly, the Tsongdu, unanimously passed an amendment to the constitution that made the monarchy dependent on the approval of the people. If the Tsongdu passed a vote of no confidence in the monarch by a two-thirds majority, the monarch was to abdicate in favour of the next member of the ruling Wangchuk dynasty. Voting was to be by secret ballot. The first vote, taken immediately after the amendment was passed, resulted in 133 votes in favour of the monarch, 2 against, and 2 abstentions. Any member could bring a motion of no confidence at any time, and the monarch had to seek a vote of confidence every three years.

Progress continued on the economic front. The Indian Border Roads Organization (DANTAK) widened the country's major road to Thimphu, and telephones and electric power lines were breaking down the isolation of the one million Bhutanese. Under the Colombo Plan, Australia supplied 40 three-ton trucks and the U.K. supplied four Land Rover ambulances and provided technical training. While Bhutan's geographic position made dependence on India inevitable, the country was seeking other sources of economic aid in order to facilitate a policy of nonalignment. There were an estimated 1,000 Indian military personnel in Bhutan as advisers.

Sikkim. The economic development of Sikkim was threatened in December 1968 by greater floods than had ever before been recorded. The Indian government, deeply involved in Sikkimese economic affairs, came to the rescue with an offer of a Rs. 10 million grant-in-aid to repair damaged bridges and roads. When the chogyal visited New Delhi in December, the then deputy prime minister, Morarji Desai, suggested that the government of Sikkim might also accept the services of India's Life Insurance Corporation, the Industrial Credit and Investment Corporation, and the Industrial Finance Corporation. No immediate statement was made on this offer, but the chogyal understood the inevitabilities of economic aid and strategy that his country's geographic position imposed. Democratization was also being discussed, and the issue of a constitutional monarchy was on the program of both the Sikkim National Congress and the Sikkim State Congress.

Indian and Chinese troops still faced each other along Sikkim's frontier with China, and roads leading to the key points still carried arms and munitions rather than trade. The Sino-Soviet dispute was of greater concern to China during 1969 than its border dispute with India, and the result was relative calm for Sikkim. The easier atmosphere permitted more emphasis on programs for education and health, which were still lagging.

Dermatology: *see* Medicine

Economic Aid. Dependent territories, like the rest of the less developed world, found that gross domestic product was not keeping pace with population growth (highest in Asia, Africa, and South America). Increased aid, either bilaterally or via multilateral agencies, was a feature of 1969, particularly in relation to Portuguese Africa and the French spheres of influence. British aid to less developed areas in 1969 totaled over £210 million, of which over 90% went to the Commonwealth. Aid to the dependent territories increased from £12.8 million in 1967–68 to nearly £15 million in 1968–69, with most of it coming via Colonial Welfare and Development and the Commonwealth Development Corporation. The largest commitments were for housing, education, roads, and civil aviation; grants of over £2 million went to British Honduras and over £8 million went to the Pacific territories.

The discovery of offshore oil in Tonga and advances in marine technology gave new hope to small islands surrounded by rich deposits of underwater minerals. The question of national appropriation and exploitation was discussed at the Commonwealth conference at the request of Malta. Further moves toward Commonwealth partnership for the remaining associated and dependent territories were foreshadowed by their participation in Commonwealth technical conferences, particularly those on transport and telecommunications held in London during 1969. Voluntary and private aid and investment continued at a high rate, in both British and other dependent territories.

(PH. D.; K. I.; M. MR.; RA. R.; D. WN.; X.)

See also Africa; Portugal; South Africa; United Nations.

Development, Economic

Measured in terms of the growth of gross domestic product (GDP), 1968, the latest year for which figures were available, was an encouraging year for the less developed countries. Their combined GDP grew at a rate higher than the average of 5% recorded for the period 1960–67. The average growth of per capita income was only 2.5%, however, due largely to the growth of population (also 2.5%). Moreover, the average figures conceal wide regional variations. The per capita income growth rate in Africa and the Western Hemisphere during 1960–67 was only 1.6% and in South Asia, 1.7%. At the other end of the scale, less developed countries in southern Europe showed an improvement of 5.6%. ("Less developed countries" in general refers to all Asian countries except Japan and the Sino-Soviet countries, all African countries except South Africa, all of Latin America, and Cyprus, Greece, Malta, Portugal, Spain, Turkey, and Yugoslavia. The group covers about 1.7 billion people, or more than 70% of the world's population outside the Sino-Soviet countries.)

Prospects for the future were given a new stimulus by the report of the Commission on International Development headed by Lester Pearson, published in October 1969. The commission had been set up by the World Bank to study the effect of external aid over the preceding 20 years and to propose guidelines for the future. The report underlined the growing need for development finance to help the less developed countries maintain a higher growth in per capita income in the face of rising populations and increasing repayment obligations and debt service charges. It recommended raising the level of official development assistance to at least 1% of the developed countries' gross national product by 1975, emphasized the need for funds on concessionary terms, and came down heavily in favour of channeling more aid through multilateral agencies.

Financial Position of Less Developed Countries. The export earnings of less developed countries increased by about 8% in 1968, compared with an average increase of 6.5% during 1961–68. The 1968 rise was relatively small for Latin America but substantial for Asia and Africa. Apart from petroleum-producing countries (among which Libya continued to register the most remarkable gains), South Korea, Israel, Pakistan, Mexico, and Taiwan experienced relatively large gains in exports. India's exports, which had remained rather stagnant for some years, increased by 8% in 1968, and were especially large for nontraditional, manufactured, and semimanufactured products. Latin-American exports grew little in 1967 and 1968: the exports of Argentina and Chile declined, while Brazil's rose by about 15% in 1968 to $1 billion. A general deceleration in export earnings was expected for 1969 in response to measures taken by the industrialized countries to reduce demand.

Domestic savings are a major source of finance for investment in the less developed countries. In the 1960s domestic savings financed 85% of total investment—a major achievement since a high savings rate accomplished at low income levels means a heavy sacrifice. In 1960–67 average capital formation from savings in the less developed countries, expressed as a percentage of gross national product (GNP equals GDP plus net factor payments on foreign investments), was 15, and varied from about 11% throughout Asia, 13.1% in Africa, and 14.8% in the Middle East to 16.3% and 21.5% in Latin America and southern Europe, respectively. The average for industrialized countries in the same period was 21.7%. For a number of less developed countries the proportion of savings out of additional income (usually called the marginal savings ratio) was higher than the average savings/income ratio, suggesting that the average savings ratio over time was also rising. This encouraging performance was due largely to structural reform in fiscal management and investment institutions.

Helped by the inflow of foreign resources, gross investment in most less developed countries was higher than domestic savings. Expressed as a percentage of GNP for the period 1960–67, the average for all less developed countries was 17.8, a figure that again concealed wide regional variations (for example,

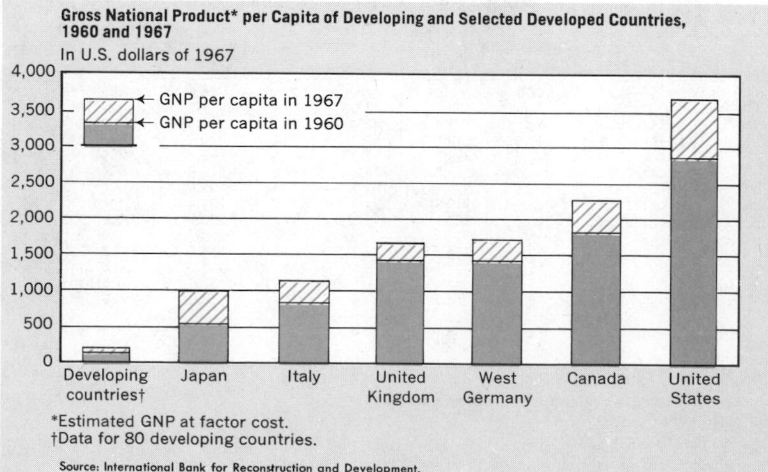

19.8% in the Middle East and 13.9% in South Asia).

Official Financial Assistance. External capital tends to seek out those investment projects that meet high technical, economic, and financial standards, but in the past the lack of managerial, organizational, and technical expertise in less developed countries often hampered the preparation of projects. Individual developed countries as well as international organizations therefore provided technical assistance to less developed countries in order to increase the latter's

continued on page 287

Table I. Economic Indicators for Less Developed Countries, Regional Summary*

Region	Average annual rates of growth (%), 1960–67						Percent of GNP average 1960–67		
	Population	Total GDP	GDP per capita	Exports†	Imports†	Total gross investment	Gross investment	Savings	Current account deficit
Africa	2.4	4.0	1.6	5.4	2.3	4.7	16.7	13.1	3.6
South Asia	2.4	4.1	1.7	1.5	3.0	5.5	13.9	11.3	2.6
East Asia	2.7	5.6	2.8	5.4	7.3	11.4	15.6	11.0	4.6
Southern Europe	1.4	7.1	5.6	13.7	14.0	14.2	24.9	21.5	3.4
Western Hemisphere	2.9	4.5	1.6	4.8	4.6	2.5	17.7	16.3	1.4
Middle East	2.9	7.2	4.2	8.7*	7.2	6.4	19.8	14.8	5.0
Total	2.5	5.0	2.5	6.1	5.7	6.2	17.8	15.0	2.8

*Data are for 80 less developed countries covering approximately 97% of GDP of all less developed countries.

Countries included under each region are as follows:

Africa—Algeria, Angola, Cameroon, Congo (Kinshasa), Ethiopia, Gabon, Ghana, Ivory Coast, Kenya, Libya, Malagasy Republic, Malawi, Mali, Mauritius, Morocco, Niger, Nigeria, Rhodesia, Senegal, Sierra Leone, Sudan, Tanzania, Togo, Tunisia, Uganda, United Arab Republic, Upper Volta, and Zambia (these countries account for 92% of the aggregate GDP of the region); South Asia—Burma, Ceylon, India, and Pakistan (coverage 100%); East Asia—Cambodia, Hong Kong, Indonesia, Korea, Malaysia, Papua and New Guinea, Philippines, Singapore, Thailand, Taiwan, and Vietnam (coverage 94%); southern Europe—Cyprus, Greece, Portugal, Spain, Turkey, and Yugoslavia (coverage 100%); Western Hemisphere—Argentina, Barbados, Bolivia, Brazil, British Honduras, Chile, Colombia, Costa Rica, Dominican Republic, Ecuador, El Salvador, Guatemala, Guyana, Haiti, Honduras, Jamaica, Mexico, Nicaragua, Panama, Paraguay, Peru, Surinam, Trinidad and Tobago, Uruguay, and Venezuela (coverage 99%); Middle East—Iran, Iraq, Israel, Jordan, Lebanon, and Syria (coverage 78%).

†Goods and services at current prices.

Source: International Bank for Reconstruction and Development.

Table II. Trade Balance of Less Developed Countries

In U.S. $000,000,000

Item	1962	1963	1964	1965	1966	1967	1968
Less developed countries							
Exports (f.o.b.)	31.1	33.8	37.1	39.3	42.3	44.0	47.9
Imports (c.i.f.)	−35.5	−37.2	−41.0	−44.2	−48.0	−49.9	−53.3
Trade balance	−4.4	−3.4	−3.9	−4.9	−5.7	−5.9	−5.4
Excluding less developed countries of southern Europe†							
Exports (f.o.b.)	28.7	31.2	34.0	35.9	38.3	39.6	43.3
Imports (c.i.f.)	−31.1	−32.0	−35.2	−37.3	−39.9	−41.8	−44.8
Trade balance	−2.4	−0.8	−1.2	−1.4	−1.6	−2.2	−1.5
Excluding southern Europe and major petroleum exporters†‡							
Exports (f.o.b.)	22.2	24.3	26.2	27.5	29.4	29.7	32.4
Imports (c.i.f.)	−28.3	−29.3	−31.8	−33.4	−35.8	−37.2	−39.5
Trade balance	−6.1	−5.0	−5.6	−5.9	−6.4	−7.5	−7.1

*Greece, Portugal, Spain, Turkey, Yugoslavia.

†Venezuela (June 1968), Saudi Arabia (from 1965; estimated increase of imports: $46 million).

‡Iran, Iraq, Kuwait, Libya, Saudi Arabia, Venezuela.

Source: International Monetary Fund, *International Financial Statistics* (October 1969).

Table III. Total Official and Private Flow of Long-Term Financial Resources (Net)* from DAC Countries to Less Developed Countries and Multilateral Agencies by Country

In U.S. $000,000

Country	Official flows				Private flows			
	1962	1966	1967	1968	1962	1966	1967	1968
Australia	73.8	128.1	167.2	156.8	...	20.0	25.0	30.4
Austria	13.8	36.5	38.8	28.1	17.2	12.8	9.0	45.8
Belgium	69.8	81.1	98.8	93.0	48.4	96.9	65.6†	150.0
Canada	54.4	211.7	213.0	212.8	55.2	55.0	40.9	93.6
Denmark	7.4	26.1	28.0	28.7	7.3	−4.8‡	−3.2‡	45.0
France	977.0	744.8	825.5	855.2	418.2	574.9	515.8	627.7
Ger., W.	467.8	485.9	546.6	595.2	182.2	251.6	593.6	1,039.7
Italy	106.1	121.9	155.9	149.5‡	284.3	509.7	131.4	355.7‡
Japan	168.2	395.4	500.6	507.1	118.0	229.7	296.9	542.2
Netherlands	65.0	93.9	113.5	134.4	49.2	160.2	114.7	141.7
Norway	6.9	13.1	15.5	23.1	−0.1	4.0	14.7	34.6
Portugal	40.8	24.3	46.6	42.0‡	...	15.4	31.8	31.8‡
Sweden	18.5	56.9	59.9	74.0	18.8	51.1	60.8	53.0
Switzerland	4.9	3.2	3.6	18.9	156.2	107.0	130.1	195.8
U.K.	421.0	525.9	498.0	428.3	322.9	413.3	343.4	417.3
U.S.	3,535.5	3,660.0	3,723.0	3,605.0	819.0	1,359.9	1,842.4	2,070.7
Total	6,030.9	6,608.8	7,034.5	6,952.1	2,496.8	3,856.7	4,212.9	5,875.0‡

*Net of loan repayments and private capital repatriation.

†Excluding reinvested earnings.

‡Estimate.

Source: Organization for Economic Cooperation and Development, *Statistical Tables for the 1969 Annual Aid Review* (July 1969).

SPECIAL REPORT

THE CRISIS IN INTERNATIONAL DEVELOPMENT

By Irving S. Friedman

The years since the end of World War II have been notable for the growth of an almost universal commitment to promote the economic and social development of the poorer countries. Never before have so many thought so deeply and striven so hard to organize, in concert, a constructive effort to meet one of the greatest challenges in history: helping 2,000,000,000 persons in over 100 countries achieve the economic and social transformation necessary for their continued survival in viable nations.

This effort has been guided by three main concepts. The first is political: the recognition that a situation where two-thirds of the people live in deep poverty while one-third enjoys varying degrees of affluence cannot be conducive to the long-term peace and stability of the world. The second is humanitarian: that such a situation is basically unjust, and therefore offensive to the human conscience. Third, there is an awareness that the well-being of all is best promoted not by the isolated affluence of the few but by the shared progress of the many. The validity of these concepts has been increasingly accepted within national frontiers, and the postwar efforts at international economic cooperation derive sustenance from the same kind of thinking.

Achievements of the 1960s. It is interesting to examine the results of these efforts so far. They have, on the whole, been fairly encouraging. Some of the poorer countries have made impressive gains; others have lagged behind badly. But, taken as a group, it is no inconsiderable achievement that their economic growth during the 1960s has averaged almost 5% a year—thus approximating the target set by the United Nations when it designated the period as the Decade of Development. Not only is this rate of growth higher than in the 1950s, when it averaged about 4.6%; it is also substantially higher than that achieved by the developed countries in the early stages of their development.

The greatest advance has been in industry. Since 1948 their industrial production has risen, on average, by 7% annually, and the rise has been accompanied by a considerable diversification of industrial activity. Their agricultural production has also increased, although less adequately (by about 3% annually). Not only has the proportion of the population employed in agriculture been falling steadily, but in many countries the modernization of agricultural enterprise is making impressive progress. The improvements in productive capacity have facilitated an expansion of trade. Between 1960 and 1968 the less developed countries increased their annual exports from about $28 billion to $44 billion, while their imports rose from a little over $30 billion to $45.5 billion.

Of even greater significance for the future is the fact that, over the years, the less developed countries have greatly increased their capacity to absorb new investments productively and efficiently. The infrastructure facilities that are essential to economic development—such as roads, railways, electric power plants—have been greatly expanded in many countries. There have been improvements in education and in health services—improvements that are never quite reflected over the short term in national income statistics.

In this connection, a point that bears emphasis is that about 85% of the investment that has made the growth possible has been financed by the less developed countries from their own resources. The remaining 15% of total investment has been financed from abroad in the form of public loans, or grants, or private investment. But, although proportionally small, these investments have represented a vital contribution providing for the importation of machinery, equipment, and other essential ingredients of development. In absolute terms, also, the contribution has been a substantial one. Between 1961 and 1968, the net flow of official resources from 16 more developed countries to less developed countries and multilateral institutions totaled about $51 billion. In 1968, it was $7 billion. In addition, the private flow totaled about $30 billion, reaching close to $6 billion in 1968. Technical assistance programs, both bilateral and multilateral, have also aimed at alleviating the shortage of technical, scientific, and managerial skills that are often as serious an obstacle to economic progress as the shortage of capital. Expansion of trade with the less developed countries has been accomplished by the general lowering of barriers on products of interest to these countries or by negotiating special arrangements such as those of France with its former African colonies.

Although the development effort has scored considerable successes, the problems that remain are formidable. In the less developed countries, too many of the fruits of economic growth continue to be neutralized by growth in population, which has been increasing at an average annual rate of 2.5%. The rise in population not only keeps down living standards when economies are registering significant rates of growth in overall output, but enhances the difficulties in obtaining more domestic savings and causes increased demands for public capital investments. It also has important implications for dealing effectively with the already existing problems of large-scale unemployment and illiteracy.

There have also been weaknesses in following satisfactory economic policies in many less developed countries. In the manufacturing sector, for example, the policy of increasing domestic production of manufactured goods to substitute for goods hitherto imported has frequently created serious problems. The foreign exchange saving has proved to be much less than was expected because of the continuing need for imports of equipment and intermediate goods. Because almost all the less developed countries have small markets, substitution for imports has led either to production in small plants of less than optimum size or to optimum-size plants producing below capacity. In both cases, the result has been high-cost production behind high tariff walls. Not only has it made the balance of payments problems worse, it has negated the dynamic element of growth that could come best from an internationally competitive export sector.

Until quite recently, agricultural production barely kept pace with population growth, and in many areas it even fell behind. Fortunately, however, thanks to a change in government policies, increasing use of fertilizers, and a technological breakthrough in high-yield varieties of wheat and rice, the situation has changed dramatically in the last two years. It is too early to say how deep and how lasting the effect of this Green Revolution will be. It will depend largely on whether the less developed countries continue to show the determination, and to intensify their efforts, to solve their agricultural problems, including those that arise out of the very successes of the technological breakthrough.

Increasing the rate of national savings out of additional income remains an especially important need of public policy in the less developed countries. These savings are the counterpart to the real resources that are needed for investment. But the poorer a country is, the more difficult it is to divert current income away from consumption. There are also many institutional and sociological difficulties in mobilizing savings. In too many countries, social privilege takes the form of an inequitable sharing of the burden of taxation. On the other hand, too much taxation of the most productive and enterprising firms and individuals may dampen the development process. Fortunately, there is enough experience to indicate that greater mobilization of domestic resources can be accomplished by economic policies designed to give proper incentives to thrift and enterprise.

No less important than the formation of material capital are government policies and programs to enhance the growth of human capital, especially by broadening skills and know-how. The scarcity of such assets is often a major constraint on the effective use of other forms of capital.

Finally, the less developed countries have yet to give adequate recognition to the importance of taking measures to increase exports rapidly in order to meet development needs. Growth of exports can provide the foreign exchange required for imports and, further, the mobilization of export earnings for development purposes presents less of a problem to less developed countries than the mobilization of earnings in other sectors of the economy.

Declining Interest in Assistance. The immensity of these problems and the somewhat fitful progress in tackling them has given rise to a feeling of disappointment and frustration in the more developed countries. There are increasing signs in some countries, particularly the U.S., of the weakening of will to help the development efforts of the poor countries. Other developed countries are increasing their programs, but not sufficiently to offset the declines. The origins of a number of development assistance programs can be traced back to the days of the cold war, when assistance was recommended on the ground that it would help build bulwarks against Communism. In other cases, assistance was urged more positively to strengthen democratic institutions in the less developed countries. The spread of neutralism in the third world and the inability of democratic institutions to flourish in an environment of direst poverty and social tension were read by some as indictments of assistance to such countries, or at least as reasons for reduced support.

Arguments have been made in some, though not all, of the developed countries that budgetary or balance of payments difficulties prevent an increase in aid, that the increase would in any case not be justified since so much of the aid already given has been wasted, that too much of the aid has been used for satisfying political whims and building prestige projects, and that the less developed countries must learn to mobilize and use their own resources more effectively before they ask for bigger handouts from the developed countries. The inspiration for such arguments, however, comes largely from the circumstance that a number of the objectives that the developed countries hoped to achieve through their aid programs have not been achieved in the short run. In the process, the long-term objectives have been fading from the public conscience. The real crisis of aid today is that the marriage between the long- and the short-run objectives has not been worked out. Although the objective conditions exist for much more successful development than in the past in most of the less developed countries, the will to help has been greatly weakened.

The danger implicit in the present situation is that, if current trends continue, the gap between the richer and the poorer nations will continue to widen. Although in per capita income terms the growth in the latter has not been far behind, in absolute amounts the growth of the richer nations has been a great deal higher, because they have moved up from a much higher base. Many of the poor countries have not yet reached a per capita income of $100 per annum, while the developed countries include a number whose per capita income is over $2,000 or $3,000. The already dangerous gap between the two is now widening with startling rapidity.

In a world composed of isolated communities, the widening of the gap might not have mattered much. But through spectacular improvements in communications and transport, people in poorer countries have acquired some knowledge and new expectations of the quality of life enjoyed in the richer nations.

The problems of the statistical gap are thus compounded by those of the expectations gap. The more intractable the two become, the more powerfully the leaders of the poorer countries are propelled into a search for explanations and excuses. Not surprisingly, the search finds the reasons for failure in the policies of the richer nations, particularly their aid and trade policies.

Ingredients for a Better Future. What can be done to change current trends and ensure a less discouraging future? The vast array of problems that the less developed countries face within a framework of low economic output and productivity cannot be dealt with effectively unless there is national determination to give the highest political priority to development. Widespread poverty cannot be neglected without threatening the very existence of the countries; the solution is thus not distinct from the problem of national survival. National priorities must reflect these concerns. Moreover, the poorer countries cannot escape the fact that economic development is an all-embracing process.

It is not sufficient that the less developed countries expand their physical capacities—roads and railways, power plants and irrigation works—however important these may be. The commitment to development must be translated into more effective policies and actions. For instance, sustained efforts are required to mobilize domestic savings for investment through better tax systems and an improved framework for savings. Policy measures to curb inflationary pressures and to maintain economic stability can be conducive to growth in real terms as they assist both savings and exports. In addition, policies aimed at establishing and maintaining a realistic rate of exchange can be of great assistance in promoting the growth of exports. In many countries there is scope for improved tax administration. Greater responsiveness to private foreign investors will certainly help. There is also a need for greater receptivity to modern technology in all its forms—not just in the building of factories and infrastructure facilities, but also in the organization of schools, accounting practices, public administration, and corporate management.

Given a readiness to accept changes such as these, there is no reason for any country to conceive a ceiling on its ability to develop, whether that target is a growth rate of 3, 5, or 7%. Nor is there any reason for it to jettison its old cultural values in the transition to modernity; in almost every less developed country, there can be found sectors of activity where the most modern technology has been adapted to and reconciled with the preservation of the cultural heritage.

As far as the developed countries are concerned, there is inadequate realization of the fact that the contribution sought from them is by no means excessive. However large the figures may seem in absolute terms, their contribution to development cannot constitute anything more than a very small fraction of their resources—whether judged by their gross national product, domestic public investment programs, total budgets, total private consumption, exports, or supply of talent. It is estimated that the combined annual GNP of the industrialized countries has increased by more than $750 billion during 1960–68. Over the same period, the increase in the annual flow of official development assistance has been only $1.8 billion; even if private flows—which can fluctuate very widely from year to year—are counted in, it is still only about $4.5 billion. It is estimated that the less developed countries are capable of absorbing—usefully, productively, and efficiently—about $5 billion more of external resources than they are getting. Even if the developed countries were to provide this extra $5 billion in the immediate future, the new total would still be less than 1% of the combined GNP of these countries—the target already accepted by the developed countries and endorsed by the Commission on International Development headed by Lester Pearson.

A contribution of 1% of GNP toward stimulating a development effort that has, on balance, brought promising results can hardly be described as too large. Providing resources of this order on a continuing and more assured basis would not only give a greater impetus to the growth of the less developed countries, it would also bring a tremendous payoff in terms of the future peace and security of the world. Seen in this perspective, the problems of international economic development might command a better understanding. But the difficulty is that a decision on the question as to whether more resources are to be allocated to development assistance or to something else is a decision that is made at the margin. Legislators find even budgetary increases hard to accept because they have to be made at the cost of something else—defense, a space program, or domestic welfare schemes. Moreover, the fact must be recognized that everywhere in the developed world there are urgent needs for large public investments and other expenditures, coupled with rising private investment and consumption. It is in this environment that, to say the least, in some of the major donor countries the priority given to development assistance has not been increasing. In this sense, there is an urgent need to find a new definition of the more developed countries' interests that will redefine domestic priorities and show how national interests are closely interlinked with those of the less developed countries.

Multilateral Aid. The useful role that multilateral organizations can play in the development process has been increasingly recognized over the years. Because of this recognition, a variety of multilateral agencies have been established, such as the World Bank, the International Development Association, the European Development Fund, the European Investment Bank, the Inter-American Development Bank, the Asian Development Bank, and various UN agencies. Contributions channeled through multilateral agencies, however, still remain only about 10% of the total official flow.

While bilateral aid has an important contribution to make to the progress of the poorer countries, there is a strong case for giving greater emphasis to the multilateral approach in order to make the development effort more efficient and productive. The strength of multilateral organizations lies in the fact that economic development is their predominant objective; they are permanent institutions and not apt to be diverted from helping the implementation of sound development strategies by short-run considerations of the sort that influence the administration of bilateral aid. In a multilateral effort, it is also possible to draw not only money but also technical and managerial skills from a wide variety of sources, particularly from the private sector, and to facilitate international competitive bidding for equipment and services that enables the less developed countries to get better value for their money. Since multilateral organizations appraise country economic strategies and policies as well as provide finance according to objective criteria that are known to be in the best interests of the less developed countries, it is easier for them to influence the economic policies and performance of those countries.

The urgent necessity today is for a stronger development effort and for a stronger emphasis on the role of multilateral organizations in this effort. With the impressive economic, scientific, and technological progress of recent times, it is at last within man's power to eliminate poverty and build a better and safer world. The crisis in development is thus a crisis of national priorities within both the developed and the less developed countries—a crisis stemming from a failure to realize existing potentialities, not a crisis resulting from inability to succeed. There is no escaping the urgency and overwhelming importance of the need—or the fact that the job can be done successfully—but these facts are no guarantee that adequate policies will be stubbornly and persistently pursued. Statesmanship and leadership of the highest order are the greatest need in the international development effort. There is evidence that this need will be met as understanding of the problem deepens and widens.

Table IV. Net Flow of Official Bilateral Capital to Less Developed Countries by Type
In U.S. $000,000

Item	1961	1966	1967	1968
Total official bilateral, *net	5,277	6,077	6,299	6,290
Bilateral grants and grant-like contributions	4,034	3,802	3,676	3,411
Grants as a percent of total bilateral	76	63	58	54

*Disbursements.
Source: OECD, *Statistical Tables for 1969 Annual Aid Service* (July 1969).

Table V. Average Financial Terms of Official Bilateral Loan Commitments

Country	Weighted average maturity years			Weighted average interest rates (%)		
	1966	1967	1968	1966	1967	1968
Total bilateral loans*	23.5	23.4	24.8	3.1	3.7	3.3
United States	29.3	28.2	30.0	3.0	3.6	3.5
United Kingdom	23.9	24.1	24.8	1.0	1.1	1.3
France	15.3	15.1	18.0	3.5	3.7	3.7
Germany, West	21.2	19.0	21.2	3.3	4.3	3.9
Italy	8.0	9.3	9.3	3.7	4.0	4.0
Japan	14.1	16.6	18.0	5.2	4.8	3.9

*Countries covered are members of the Development Assistance Committee of the OECD, listed in Table III.
Source: OECD, *Statistical Tables for 1969 Annual Aid Review* (July 1969).

continued from page 284

portfolio of projects and facilitate the inflow of foreign capital. In 1968 technical assistance disbursements by members of the Development Assistance Committee (DAC) of the Organization for Economic Cooperation and Development reached a record $1.5 billion, an increase of 11% over 1967.

According to preliminary estimates of the DAC, the flow of official capital from DAC member countries to less developed countries and to multilateral institutions, net of amortization, amounted to nearly $7 billion in 1968, roughly the same as in 1967. (*See* Table III.) Official assistance thus increased by some $343 million from 1966 and was about $650 million higher than in 1965. The flow of official aid from France rose from $745 million in 1966 to $825 million in 1967 and to $855 million in 1968; official assistance from West Germany increased from $486 million in 1966 to $595 million in 1968; and the flow of official aid from Japan amounted to $395 million in 1966, compared with $507 million in 1968. However, official assistance from the U.S. rose only slightly in 1967 and stabilized at $3,605,000,000 in 1968. The official flow of funds from the U.K. fell in 1968 compared with 1967. The World Bank estimated that the less developed countries could utilize effectively some $4 billion more per year in development finance than had been made available.

While the volume of official assistance remained at about the same level in 1968 as in 1967, the terms of this assistance, according to preliminary DAC data, improved slightly. Average interest rates on loans extended by DAC members rose to 3.7% in 1967, then dropped to about 3.3% in 1968. The average maturity period of bilateral loans, which had hardened from 28.4 years in 1964 to 23.5 years in 1966, remained roughly the same in 1967 and increased a little in 1968. The share of grants in total flows of official assistance continued to decline: in 1968 it was about 54%, compared with 63% in 1966 and 76% in 1961. (*See* Tables IV and V.)

Grant and loan disbursements of the multilateral organizations concerned with providing financial assistance to less developed countries (chiefly the World Bank, the International Development Association [IDA], the European Development Fund, the Inter-American Development Bank, the European Investment Bank, and various UN agencies) were higher in 1968 than in 1967—about $1.2 billion, compared with a little over $1 billion (net of capital subscriptions, bond purchases, and repayments). Loan commitments rose from nearly $1.2 billion to nearly $1.7 billion. Because of tighter financial conditions in the capital markets, the World Bank, in common with other borrowers, found the cost of funds in the market moving generally upward. As a result, borrowing costs of the bank in fiscal 1969 averaged 6.46%, compared with 6.17 and 5.52% in 1967–68 and 1966–67, respectively. The rising cost of borrowing was reflected in the bank's decision to raise its lending rate from 6 to $6\frac{1}{4}$% in January 1968, to $6\frac{1}{2}$% in August 1968, and to 7% as of Aug. 1, 1969. In March 1968 the economically advanced member countries of the IDA, an affiliate of the World Bank that makes low-interest loans (0.75%) with a maturity period of 50 years, had reached agreement on a second general replenishment of the association's resources at the rate of $160 million annually for three years, beginning November 1968. However, the replenishment did not come into force until July 1969.

By mid-1968 the total outstanding debt of 79 less developed countries for which data were available reached $47.5 billion, representing an increase of 6% over the end of 1966 and of 44% over 1964. The increase in total indebtedness had been accompanied by a sharp rise in total debt service payments. (*See* Table VI.) Debt service payments on public and publicly guaranteed external debt of the 79 less developed countries rose by about $500 million in 1966 and by about $188 million in 1967. In percentage terms, the most rapid increases occurred in Africa and South Asia.

Unless the terms of aid became more commensurate with the debt-servicing capacity of the less developed countries, there was a danger that debt crises would become more persistent in the future. The short-term solution to the problem for countries already in difficulty might lie in rescheduling or refinancing arrangements for debt service payments due in the next few years, but the longer-term and more basic solution depended on increasing the magnitude and liberalizing the terms of future aid, together with the implementation of economic policies that would strengthen the ability of countries to service foreign debt and ensure the effective use of all borrowed funds.

Net Flow of Financial Resources from DAC Countries Combined in Relation to Aid Targets
Resource flow to less developed countries and multilateral agencies, net of repayments of principal

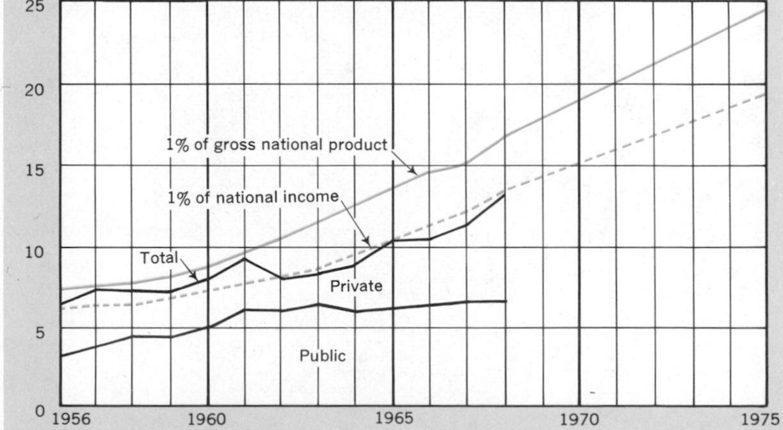

Source: International Bank for Reconstruction and Development.

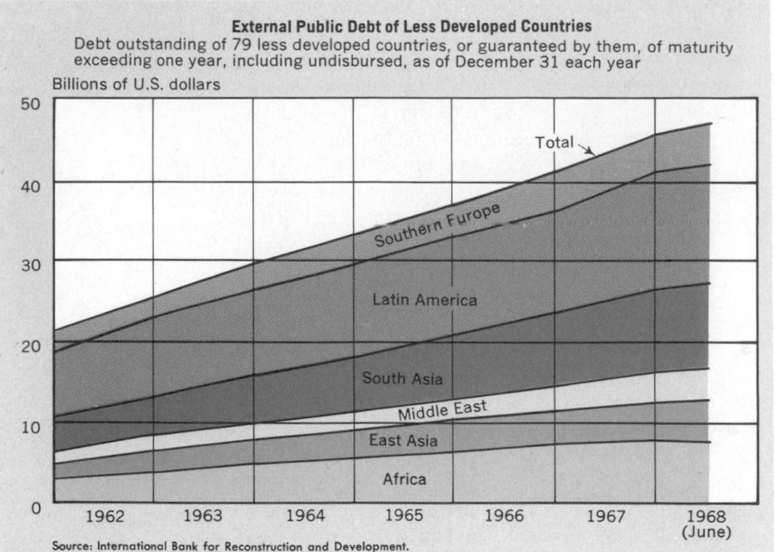

Private Capital Flows. The flow of private capital from DAC countries to less developed countries and multilateral institutions, net of amortization, reached $4.2 billion in 1967 and was tentatively estimated at $5.9 billion in 1968, an increase of more than 40%. Bilateral private capital flows remained at roughly the same level, but the sale of bonds net of redemptions by multilateral institutions in capital markets (other than to official institutions) rose. (*See* INVESTMENT, INTERNATIONAL.)

New Initiatives. The most dramatic change in the field of economic development was in the area of food production. In contrast to 1965 and 1966, when the less developed countries experienced alarming declines in food production per capita, 1967 and 1968 showed a marked improvement. Moreover, there were signs that this recovery was not merely the result of more favourable weather, but was influenced also by widespread application of agricultural inputs, thus reflecting a permanent technological change. Nonetheless, there would be continuing need for imports of food into a number of the less developed countries.

At the second session of the United Nations Conference on Trade and Development (UNCTAD), held in New Delhi, India, in early 1968, it had been decided to continue consideration of the scheme for supplementary financial measures, proposed by the staff of the World Bank. The scheme was designed to protect development programs from the disruptive effects of unexpected export shortfalls by providing supplemental resources to countries that pursue sound economic and financial policies. The Intergovernmental Group on Supplementary Finance, set up by UNCTAD to examine the scheme, came to the conclusion that arrangements for supplementary finance could be designed and that supplementary financial measures should be administered within the World Bank Group in consultation with the International Monetary Fund (IMF). The Intergovernmental Group stressed that in the operation of any supplementary financial measures discretion could be left to the administering agency, which would take into account the development plan and all information relevant to the objectives of supplementary financial measures. UNCTAD agreed with the group's conclusions; it invited the World Bank Group to consider introducing arrangements for supplementary finance.

In the fall of 1967 the boards of governors of the IMF and the World Bank had adopted a resolution that the staffs of the two institutions should prepare a special study concerning possible ways of stabilizing primary product prices. The analytical part of the study, submitted to the governors at the 1968 annual meeting of the two institutions, examined postwar price fluctuations, trends in commodity trade, and their causes; considered measures to improve the level and trend of export earnings; and analyzed measures to deal with fluctuations around the trend. The study attempted to view the commodity problem in the perspective of development efforts and policies. After further studies, the World Bank and the IMF separately made a series of recommendations on specific financial measures and other ways in which the two institutions could assist in helping to find solutions to the problem. A number of these proposals were adopted by the executive directors of the bank in 1969, and a report on them was sent to all member countries. They included proposals to intensify the diversification of production in less developed countries; strengthen the competitiveness of primary products; finance the holding of commodity stocks; help administer and support internal commodity agreements; and improve market access. (I. S. F.)

See also Agriculture; Commodities, Primary; Economic Planning; Industrial Review; Inter-American Affairs; Nuclear Energy; Payments and Reserves, International; Trade, International.

Table VI. External Public Debt Outstanding and Debt Service Payments of Less Developed Countries

In U.S. $000,000,000

Region	Debt outstanding as of Dec. 31 1962	1963	1964	1965	1966	1967	Debt outstanding as of June 30, 1968 Disbursed	Undisbursed*	Total	Service payments 1962	1963	1964	1965	1966	1967	1968†
Africa	4.042	4.971	5.517	6.618	7.379	8.038	6.640	1.314	7.952	0.225	0.494	0.433	0.445	0.463	0.535	0.443
Southern Europe‡	2.478	2.912	3.433	4.051	4.441	4.903	3.791	1.327	5.118	0.222	0.265	0.330	0.407	0.444	0.461	0.506
East Asia	2.812	3.235	3.744	3.906	4.395	4.988	4.253	1.378	5.630	0.264	0.165	0.171	0.206	0.341	0.280	0.369
Middle East	1.667	1.708	1.880	2.446	2.740	3.631	2.392	1.251	3.643	0.210	0.188	0.212	0.182	0.200	0.168	0.162
South Asia§	4.736	5.923	6.881	7.837	9.196	10.118	7.903	2.541	10.444	0.227	0.269	0.359	0.347	0.417	0.486	0.565
Western Hemisphere‖	10.207	10.964	11.720	12.207	12.895	14.521	11.032	3.723	14.754	1.437	1.368	1.672	1.692	1.916	2.039	1.973
Total¶	25.942	29.713	33.175	37.065	41.046	46.199	36.011	11.534	47.542	2.585	2.749	3.177	3.279	3.781	3.969	4.018

*Due to a lack of information on amounts undisbursed for Congo (Kinshasa), Ghana, and Israel, the entire amount outstanding is considered disbursed.
†Projected.
‡Includes private debt of Yugoslavia.
§Does not include suppliers' credits of India.
‖Includes private debt of Brazil.
¶Includes 79 countries as follows: Africa—Botswana, Burundi, Cameroon, Central African Republic, Chad, Congo (Kinshasa), Dahomey, East African Community, Ethiopia, Gabon, Ghana, Guinea, Ivory Coast, Kenya, Lesotho, Liberia, Malagasy Republic, Malawi, Mali, Mauritania, Morocco, Niger, Nigeria, Rhodesia, Rwanda, Senegal, Sierra Leone, Somalia, Sudan, Swaziland, Tanzania, Togo, Tunisia, Uganda, United Arab Republic, Upper Volta, and Zambia; southern Europe—Cyprus, Greece, Malta, Spain, Turkey, and Yugoslavia; East Asia—Indonesia, Korea, Malaysia, Philippines, Singapore, Thailand, and Taiwan; Middle East—Iran, Iraq, Israel, Jordan, and Lebanon; South Asia—Ceylon, India, and Pakistan; Western Hemisphere—Argentina, Bolivia, Brazil, Chile, Colombia, Costa Rica, Dominican Republic, Ecuador, El Salvador, Guatemala, Guyana, Honduras, Jamaica, Mexico, Nicaragua, Panama, Paraguay, Peru, Trinidad and Tobago, Uruguay, and Venezuela.

Note: Items may not add to totals due to rounding.
Source: International Bank for Reconstruction and Development.

Diamonds
see Mining

Disasters

The loss of life and property in disasters during 1969 included the following. (*See also* METEOROLOGY.)

AVIATION

Jan. 5 Gatwick, Eng. Afghan Boeing 727 commercial airliner en route from Kabul to London came into Gatwick Airport through dense fog and just short of the runway rammed into a brick house; 50 persons (including 2 in the house) were killed and 13 injured.
Jan. 6 Bradford, Pa. U.S. Convair 580 propjet flying 1,000 ft. below the regular approach altitude into Bradford Regional Airport plowed into a snow-covered golf course (the second plane to crash in the same area within a two-week period); of the 27 persons aboard 11 were killed.
Jan. 13 Santa Monica Bay, Calif. Scandinavian DC-8 jetliner on a trip from Copenhagen to Los Angeles developed landing-gear trouble in making its descent into Los Angeles International Airport and nosed into the bay; 15 of those aboard drowned, 30 were rescued.
Jan. 18 Off Los Angeles, Calif. U.S. Boeing 727 jet scheduled for Denver and Milwaukee was shattered by a violent explosion moments after takeoff and fell into shark-infested waters; all 38 persons aboard perished.
Feb. 5 Off southern Taiwan. U.S. Air Force Hercules rescue plane on a search mission for eight missing crewmen of the Japanese freighter "Shoka Maru" crashed into the icy sea; 11 airmen were lost and presumed dead, 1 survived.
Feb. 11 South of Manila, Phil. Philippine C-47 plane was reported missing; air and sea search failed to find any sign of the craft or its 20 passengers and crew members.
Feb. 18 Hawthorne, Nev. U.S. DC-3 "gamblers' flight" bound for southern California disappeared over the Sierra Nevada; all 35 persons aboard were presumed dead.
Feb. 24 Near Kaohsiung, Taiwan. Nationalist Chinese twin-engine transport propjet on a regular flight from Kaohsiung to T'ai-pei reported engine trouble and crashed in a sugarcane field; all 36 passengers and crewmen died.
March 16 Maracaibo, Venez. Venezuelan DC-9 jetliner en route from Caracas to Miami at takeoff from Grano de Oro Airport plunged to earth and exploded in a residential area; known dead were 155 persons—74 passengers and the 10 crew members and at least 71 on the ground.
March 20 New Orleans, La. U.S. DC-3 chartered by 24 sportsmen from Memphis for a hunting trip in British Honduras, in making an approach to New Orleans International Airport crashed in heavy fog and burned; 13 hunters and 3 crewmen were killed, 11 others survived.
March 20 Aswan, U.A.R. Special flight of a U.A.R. Ilyushin-18 ended in disaster when the plane crashed at Aswan Airport on its return trip from Mecca to Jiddah, Saudi Arabia; most of the 87 persons who perished were Muslim pilgrims; 14 survivors were injured.
April 2 Near Cracow, Pol. Polish AN-24 en route from Warsaw to Cracow plunged to the ground and killed all 51 persons aboard.
April 16 Near Kinshasa, Congo. Congolese Air Force plane dived into the Congo River in attempting a landing at Ndjili Military Airport; 45 soldiers and members of their families died.
April 23 Near Saigon, South Vietnam. Two U.S. Army helicopter gunships collided in midair, crashed, and killed 16 U.S. and Vietnamese soldiers.
June 4 Near Monterrey, Mex. Mexican Boeing 727 jet bound for Monterrey from Mexico City rammed into Monk's Peak, a rain-soaked Sierra Madre mountainside and killed all 79 passengers and crewmen aboard.
June 5 Western Aleutian Is., Alaska. U.S. Air Force RC-135 reconnaissance plane on a routine mission from Shemya to Eielson Air Force Base near Fairbanks was reported missing about 250 mi. E of Shemya; the 19 men aboard were presumed dead.
July 6 Near Winder, Ga. Small U.S. feeder-line Beechcraft 99 on a flight from Atlanta to Greer, S.C., crashed into a pasture 50 mi. E of Atlanta; all 14 persons aboard were killed.
July 12 Near Simra, Nepal. Nepalese DC-3 aircraft on a flight from Katmandu to Simra lost contact and was believed to be down near the Indian border; all 35 aboard were presumed dead.
July 26 Biskra, Alg. Algerian twin-jet Caravelle chartered in Paris and bound for the oil field of Hassi Messaoud crashed in the Sahara and burned; of the 30 technicians and 7 crewmen aboard, 35 died.
Aug. 4 Valparaiso, Chile. U.S. Navy C-47 transport en route from Santiago to Mendozo, Arg., with U.S. Navy and Air Force personnel aboard was reported to have been forced down in the Andes Mountains during a storm; all 16 persons aboard were presumed dead.
Aug. 26 Moscow, U.S.S.R. Huge Soviet Ilyushin IL-18 with 112 passengers aboard flying from Sochi to Moscow's Vnukovo Airport crash landed and burned after an apparent landing-gear malfunction; an unofficial report listed 15 deaths.
Sept. 8 Eastern Colombia. Colombian C-47 military transport on a village-to-village hop went down in the mountainous countryside and killed all 32 persons aboard.
Sept. 9 Shelbyville, Ind. U.S. twin-engine DC-9 letting down over Weir-Cook Municipal Airport, Indianapolis, collided with a small Piper Cherokee flown by a student pilot; the two aircraft plummeted into a soybean field scattering debris over a wide area including a trailer park; all 82 persons aboard the DC-9 as well as the 1 man in the small plane were killed.
Sept. 12 Antipolo, Phil. Philippine 111 twinjet in approaching Manila International Airport struck a hillside in a housing subdivision and brought death to 45 persons aboard the aircraft; 2 others survived.
Sept. 20 Da Nang Air Base, South Vietnam. Vietnamese DC-4 commercial jet liner en route from Pleiku collided with a U.S. Air Force F-4 Phantom jet as both planes were making final landing approaches to the airport; the F-4 crewmen were unhurt but when the DC-4 fell into a field all 75 Vietnamese aboard as well as 2 persons on the ground were killed.
Sept. 21 Mexico City, Mex. Mexican Boeing 727 on a flight from Chicago with U.S. tourists bound for Mexico City and Acapulco plowed into swampy ground at the end of a runway at the International Airport; 29 of the 118 persons aboard died.
Sept. 26 Central Bolivia. Bolivian DC-6 on a one-hour flight between Santa Cruz and Cochabamba disappeared somewhere in the snowcapped Andes; all 71 persons aboard including members of Bolivia's leading soccer team were presumed dead.
Oct. 2 Gulf of Tonkin. U.S. Navy C-2A Greyhound cargo plane on a routine flight from Cubi Point, Philippines, to the carrier "Constellation" went down for undetermined reasons; all 26 U.S. servicemen drowned.
Nov. 19 Lake George, N.Y. U.S. 227-B twin-engine turboprop nearing its destination at Warren County Airport slammed into an Adirondack peak and burst into flames; all 14 persons aboard were killed.
Nov. 20 Iju, Nigeria. Nigerian VC-10 jet bound for Lagos from London and three minutes away from a scheduled landing at Ikeja Airport crashed into a thickly wooded area, burst into flames, and killed all 87 persons aboard.
Dec. 3 Off La Guaira, Venez. French Boeing 707 jetliner on its way to Paris fell into the Caribbean and exploded minutes after taking off from Caracas; all 62 passengers and crew members died.
Dec. 8 Keratea, Greece. Greek DC-6 airliner flying from Crete to Athens encountered driving rain and hurricane winds that slapped it against a 2,000-ft. mountain 25 mi. SE of Athens Airport killing all 90 persons aboard.
Dec. 22 Nha Trang, South Vietnam. South Vietnamese DC-6B passenger liner exploded and crashed into a group of homes and a school; 22 persons died, 14 others were unaccounted for.
Dec. 22 San Diego, Calif. U.S. Navy F-8 Crusader jet fighter slammed into a hangar, burst into flames, and set off explosions that destroyed eight other jets; 15 men were killed and at least 20 injured.

FIRES AND EXPLOSIONS

Jan. 15 Victoria State, Austr. Week-long bush fires fanned by strong winds raged through thousands of acres of forest and range land; 17 persons were known dead, and 200 homes were destroyed.
Jan. 26 Dunnville, Ont. The 50-room Victoria Hotel was gutted by a fire in which 13 persons died.
Feb. 6 Koriyama, Jap. Fire engulfed a resort hotel and spread through an amusement centre killing 30 persons.
Feb. 19 Bologna, Italy. Four-story apartment building was wrecked by an explosion resulting from a gas leak; 10 persons perished, 17 others were injured.
Feb. 25 New York, N.Y. Ignited by tracing paper, fire in the

Wreckage of Ariana Afghan Airlines Boeing 727, which crashed through homes while landing in the fog at Gatwick Airport, England, on Jan. 5, 1969. At least 52 lives were lost and 13 persons injured.

KEYSTONE

offices of a Fifth Avenue architectural firm brought death to 11 persons and injured 5 others.
March 9 Manila, Phil. Slum apartment building was destroyed by fire; 14 persons died, with damage estimated at $125,000.
April 5 Oakwood Bayou, Ark. Gasoline, used to light a wood-burning stove, set off an explosion and fire in a 14-room home; of 12 family members and friends gathered for an Easter reunion, 10 died.
April 6 Bridgeport, Conn. Early-morning fire swept through an old wooden tenement and trapped the sleeping occupants, of whom at least 11 perished in the flames.
July 10 Near Posen, Mich. Two-story family farmhouse burned to the ground killing 10 members of the 12 in the family.
Dec. 2 Notre-Dame-du-Lac, Que. A three-story wooden home for the aged and infirm was ravished by a fire that killed 38 of the elderly pensioners; 29 persons survived.
Dec. 18 Brooklyn, N.Y. Flash fire, believed to have been started by defective Christmas lights, gutted the top stories of a small frame house as the 27 occupants were sleeping; 10 members of one family (9 children, 1 adult) perished.
Dec. 26 Saffron Walden, Eng. Sixteenth-century Rose and Crown Hotel was swept by fire thought to have started in the television room; 11 persons died and a number of others were injured.

KEYSTONE

Column of smoke rises from the blasting-powder factory at Dottikon, Switz., after a huge explosion killed 15 persons and injured 40 others on Aug. 4, 1969.

MARINE

Jan. 14 Pearl Harbor, Hawaii. U.S. nuclear aircraft carrier "Enterprise" was swept by fire and explosions centred on the flight and hangar decks; 27 men died and 82 others were injured.
Jan. 24 Dacca, Pak. Two boats collided on the Buriganga River dumping the passengers into the water; 50 persons drowned.
Feb. 22 Assiut, U.A.R. A small sailboat in the Nile, overloaded by 62 persons rushing to get home from a funeral, overturned and drowned 40 of the passengers.
March 13 Oregon Inlet, N.C. Soviet 125-ft. fishing trawler sank after colliding with the 36,000-ton Panamanian tanker "Esso Honduras"; as many as 25 Soviet sailors were presumed dead.
April 6 New Orleans, La. Taiwan freighter "Union Faith" passing under the Greater New Orleans Mississippi River bridge collided with the lead barge of a string of oil barges; ensuing explosions and fire sank the "Union Faith"; 25 men were missing and presumed dead.
April 13 Off Kuwait. A small boat loaded with Iranians attempting illegal entry into Kuwait capsized and sank 5 mi. offshore; 30 persons drowned, 5 others were missing.
June 2 South China Sea. U.S. Navy destroyer "Frank E. Evans" on SEATO maneuvers with about 40 other warships misinterpreted an order and was sliced in two by the Australian aircraft carrier "Melbourne"; when the sheared-off forward portion of the "Evans" sank, 74 officers and enlisted men went down with it and were presumed dead, 200 others were rescued.
June 21 Beira, Mozambique. A barge transporting 150 Portuguese troops and their vehicles, en route to reinforce a garrison beleaguered by guerrillas, sank and drowned 108 of the men.
Aug. 9 Near Shikotan I., Jap. Soviet patrol boat collided with a Japanese fishing boat, the cuttlefish Boat No. 13 "Fukuju Maru"; 11 fishermen of the 12-man crew were killed.
Aug. 15 Cairo, U.A.R. A river launch sank in the Nile River and drowned 24 persons, 16 others were saved.
Aug. 18 Évian-Les-Bains, France. The pleasure boat "Fraidieu," loaded with vacationing French teen-age girls, plunged beneath the waters of Lake Geneva and carried 19 persons to their death; 34 others were rescued.
Aug. 25 North of Sydney, Austr. Australian 1,465-ton freighter "Noongah," battling high seas and strong winds, rolled over and sank; 24 missing crewmen were presumed dead, 2 were rescued.
Oct. 8 Near Cape Shiono, Jap. South Korean freighter, the 1,051-ton "Dragon," sank about 20 mi. offshore; 12 seamen were drowned, 8 others were saved by a passing British ship.
Nov. 5 New Jersey Coast. Transatlantic oil tanker, the 629-ft. Liberian "Keo," broke up in heavy seas 120 mi. SE of Nantucket; after a fruitless three-day search by the U.S. Coast Guard, the 36 lost crewmen were presumed dead.
Dec. 24 Barrancabermeja, Colombia. Ferry, overcrowded by families homeward bound for Christmas, collided with four oil barges and sank into the Magdalena River; from 25 to 40 persons drowned.
Dec. 26 NE of Midway I. U.S. munitions ship "Badger State" began to break up in heavy seas and was abandoned by the crew; 1 body was recovered from the rough waters, 25 crewmen were lost and presumed dead, and 14 were rescued.

MINING

Jan. 23 Welkom, S.Af. Explosion of methane gas at the President Steyn gold mine killed 15 miners and injured 13 others; 2 persons were missing.
March 31 Barroteran, Mex. Deadly gases prevented rescuers from reaching miners trapped 800 ft. underground when explosions ripped through no. 2 and no. 3 shafts of a coal mine belonging to Altos Hornos de Mexico; at least 180 miners were given up for dead.
July 7 Jui Feng, Taiwan. Floating coal dust set off an explosion that repercussed through the mine killing 24 miners; 53 others were injured.
Sept. 22 Izuwa, Jap. A cave-in following a coal mine explosion killed 2 miners; 12 others were missing and presumed dead.
Nov. 7 Buffelsfontein, S.Af. Dynamite explosion in a gold mine buried a shaft-blasting team $1\frac{1}{2}$ mi. beneath the surface killing 60 members of the crew and injuring 14 others.
Nov. 14 Salisbury, Rhodesia. An elevator cage broke loose from its cables and plunged 3,500 ft. down a mine shaft killing 20 men.

MISCELLANEOUS

Jan. 1 Indore, India. Rioting between Hindu and Muslim religious groups brought death to 12 persons.
March 12 Singida, Tanzania. Consumption of tainted meat caused 11 persons to die of poisoning.
June 15 San Rafael, Spain. Opening day celebration by 500 patrons of a new restaurant turned to horror as a second-story floor began to sag, the walls quickly crumbled and brought down the roof crushing at least 57 persons; 140 were injured.
Nov. 8–9 Rio de Janeiro, Braz. A hot, sunny weekend combined with rough seas off the beaches caused 35 deaths by drowning; 440 other persons required treatment for dehydration.
Nov. 26 Osaka, Jap. Eleven workers drowned at construction project 64 ft. beneath the Shirinashi River when an air pipe broke loose from a caisson.
Nov. 29 Guadalajara, Mex. The roof of the church of San Luis Gonzago collapsed upon 200 worshipers killing at least 19 persons.
Dec. 25 Bukavu, Congo (Kinshasa). Expected arrival of Pres. Joseph D. Mobutu triggered a stampede among a crowd waiting outside the football stadium; 27 persons were killed and more than 107 others were injured.

NATURAL

Jan. 3 Khurasan Prov., Iran. An earthquake of moderate intensity striking along the Iran-U.S.S.R. border brought death to 50 and injured 300 others; about 800 homes were destroyed.
Jan. 18–26 Southern California. Torrential rains of nine days' duration finally ceased, leaving the area a sea of mud and debris with a death toll of at least 100 persons; more than 9,000 homes were destroyed or damaged and property loss was estimated at $60 million.
Jan. 23 Southern Mississippi. Slashing a mile-wide swath through the hill country at dawn, tornadoes killed 31 persons, injured hundreds of others, and leveled at least 35 buildings.
Feb. 9–10 Northeastern U.S. Two-day storm dumped 15 in. of snow along the eastern seaboard causing a total of 166 deaths (New England 73, New York City 43, New York State 37, New Jersey 11, and Pennsylvania 2); lost business was estimated at about $25 million.
Feb. 23 Celebes Is. An earthquake striking Madjene and the surrounding area killed 64 persons, injured 97 others, and destroyed more than 1,200 buildings.
Feb. 23–26 Southern California. Second downpour of drenching rains within four weeks caused renewed mudslides and flooding; more than 12,500 residents were driven from their homes, with many of the houses sliding down the muddy hillsides; 18 persons died, others were unaccounted for and thought to be buried under mud and debris.
Feb. 24–27 New England-Virginia coast. Heavy 2-to-3-ft.-deep snows covered the eastern states for the second time in a month; 40 deaths in New England and 14 in New York City were attributed to the storm.
Feb. 28 Straits of Gibraltar. Earthquake of great magnitude was felt along the coasts of Portugal, Spain, and Morocco; 13 persons died.
Feb. 28 Central Sulawesi, Indon. Striking without warning, an earthquake killed 64 persons; 100 others were injured and property damage was at least $1.5 million.
March 17 Alagôas State, Braz. A flash flood sweeping through the Mundaú Valley, a drought-stricken area of northeast Brazil, reportedly killed 218 persons and left 50,000 others homeless.
March 28 Western Turkey. A strong earthquake rumbled through an area near Alasehir killing at least 53 persons and injuring 350 others; 2,500 homes and 2 mosques collapsed.
March 29 Northeast Ethiopia. A major earthquake destroyed completely the town of Sardó; 24 persons perished, another 165 were injured, and property damage was estimated at $320,000.
April 4–6 Azerbaijan Prov., Iran. Torrential rains caused flooding that brought death to at least 20 persons.
April 14 East Pakistan. Cities of Dacca and Comilla suffered most heavily as a 90-mph tornado struck the area; at least 540 persons died and more than 1,000 others were injured.
May 17–21 Southern India. Windstorms and tidal waves struck villages along the Bay of Bengal and killed 618 persons in the city of Vijayawada, 20,000 others were homeless; hundreds of cattle died in the floodwaters of the Krishna River in Andhra Pradesh, and crop damage in the rich ricelands was estimated at $40 million.
July 4 Northern Ohio. Sudden violent storm caused high choppy waters on Lake Erie and heavy flooding inland; 41 persons died.
July 6 Northern French coast. Brittany and Normandy resorts were scourged by 100-mph winds off the Atlantic; most of the 23 victims of the storm were vacation sailors.
July 7 Kyushu I., Jap. Week-long rainstorms brought death to 72 persons.

July 22 Kannaman, India. Torrential rains and strong winds striking the village caused the collapse of a new elementary school that killed 15 children and injured 92 others.
July 27 Northern Philippines. Typhoon Viola with 100-mph winds caused rough seas, landslides, and swollen rivers that contributed to the death of 11 persons; 17 others were missing and presumed dead.
Aug. 6 Northern Minnesota. Eight separate twisters writhed through the vacation resort country leaving the heaviest destruction in the Roosevelt Lake area; 14 persons were killed and at least 40 others injured.
Aug. 6–8 South Korea. Heavy monsoon rains pelting the countryside caused landslides centred about Hwachon in the north; 85 persons perished, 15 others were missing, and 12,000 left homeless.
Aug. 17–20 Gulf of Mexico. States of Mississippi, Louisiana, Alabama, and Virginia were ravished by Hurricane Camille, spawned off Cuba August 15 and finally dissipating off the Virginia coast; at least 400 persons were dead or missing and presumed dead; damage was estimated at $1 billion.
Sept. 14 Southern Mexico. Month-long torrential rains and flooding brought death to at least 58 persons.
Sept. 14 South Korea. Southern coastline was heavily battered by the most severe rainstorms in ten years; flooding caused most of the 475 deaths; 407 persons were injured, 78 others missing; property damage was about $61 million.
Sept. 28 Taiwan. Typhoon Elsie raged across the island killing 102 persons, 24 others were missing and 227 injured; crops were heavily damaged.
Sept. 28–Oct. 8 Tunisia. After five years of drought the country was deluged by ten days of torrential rain and flooding, with one-half the land under mud and water; 500 persons were listed as dead; 50,000 homes were destroyed, as were highways, railroads, bridges, and whole villages.
Sept. 30 Cape Province, S.Af. Major earthquake leveled three villages and killed 11 persons, 1,000 others were homeless.
Oct. 1–5 Taiwan. Typhoon Flossie striking within a week of Typhoon. Elsie left 75 dead and 31,000 homeless; damage amounted to millions.
Oct. 13 Biskra, Alg. Continuing flooding over a wide area brought death to 68 persons; 218 others were injured, and more than 100,000 homeless; typhoid, dysentery, and measles added to the misery of the sufferers.
Oct. 19 Morelia, Mex. Workmen assisted by a number of schoolchildren were toiling to rebuild a damaged village church when an earth slide rumbled down to half cover the building; 18 children were buried alive.
Oct. 27 Banja Luka, Yugos. Series of three powerful earthquakes hit the city and surrounding area leaving 22 persons dead, 700 injured, and more than 60,000 others homeless in the midst of thousands of ruined buildings.
Nov. 11 Bay of Bengal, India. Cyclone and tidal wave swept the coastline, tearing up huge trees; at least 23 persons died, 30 others were injured.
Dec. 4 Tunisia. Countrywide seasonal rains of unusual intensity over a two-month period left 542 persons dead, 300,000 homeless, and property damage beyond $40 million.

RAILROAD

Jan. 31 Ch'onan, South Korea. Engineer failed to see a red signal light obscured by blinding snow and rammed his Seoul-bound express into the rear of another passenger train stopped on the tracks; at least 35 persons were killed, 102 others injured.
Feb. 4 Tamil Nadu State, India. As a train glided beneath the girders of a bridge 28 persons died when they were swept off the roof upon which they were riding.
Feb. 7 Violet Town, Austr. Head-on collision of the Sydney-Melbourne passenger express and a freight train, both traveling at 60 mph, brought death to at least 10 persons and injured 85 others.
March 21 São Paulo, Braz. Packed electric train halted by a power failure was plowed into by a locomotive coming to its aid when the power surged on suddenly; 30 to 40 persons were killed and 300 injured.
March 25 La Louvière, Belg. Early morning mist caused two passenger trains to crash head on; 20 persons died and 70 others were injured.
June 21 Near Benares, India. Ten-coach train jumped the tracks as it passed over a bridge across the Maghai River; 69 persons perished and at least 150 others were injured.
June 22 Hanover-Linden, W.Ger. A railroad car loaded with ammunition for the armed forces exploded as the train was stopped at the suburban station; at least 12 firemen and railroad workers were killed, 3 others were missing, and 10 injured.
July 15 Near Cuttack, India. A train filled with pilgrims on their way to Puri for the "juggernaut" festival was halted by a passenger who pulled the emergency brake to get off where there was no stop; before the train could get under way it was rammed from the rear by a speeding freight; at least 81 persons were killed, more than 150 others were injured.

TRAFFIC

Jan. 1 Ismailia, U.A.R. Cairo-to-Suez passenger bus collided with a truck killing 14 riders and injuring 35 others.
Jan. 7 Cairo, U.A.R. A bus swerving to miss an oncoming car smashed through a fence and plunged into the Nile River; 15 passengers perished and 20 others were missing.

UPI COMPIX

Authorities rescue passengers of two crowded commuter trains, which crashed head-on near La Louvière, Belg., on March 25, 1969. Twenty persons were killed and 70 injured.

Jan. 10 Seoul, South Korea. Crowded bus collided with a train at a grade crossing; 18 persons died and 70 were injured, many critically.
Jan. 15 Tuzla, Turk. Zonguldak-to-Istanbul bus toppled off a bridge into the ravine below and brought death to 22 riders; 14 others were injured.
Feb. 5 Near Casablanca, Mor. Collision of a truck and a bus traveling between Safi and Marrakech caused the deaths of 17 persons and injured 17 others.
March 2 Covington, Ga. A drag-racing car pushing 180 mph spun off the track, hurtled into a group of spectators, and killed at least 11 of them; as many as 50 others were injured.
March 17 Fresno, Colombia. Bus accident accounted for 30 deaths; 19 persons were injured.
May 19 Northern Turkey. Passenger bus ran off the highway into a stream killing 18 persons.
May 27 Northern Philippines. Speeding bus overtook a jeep carrying about 30 persons, piled into it, and killed 10 riders; another 15 were injured.
June 4 Corum, Turk. Loaded truck plowed into a group of pedestrians killing 13 and injuring 6 others.
June 21 Central Syria. Truck transporting 35 girls to the harvest fields overturned and killed 25 of the girls.
July 15 Dinant, Belg. Dutch vacationers were dumped into the Meuse River when their tour bus left the road because of faulty brakes; 21 passengers died, 4 others who swam ashore survived.
Sept. 8 Ankara, Turk. Artvin-to-Samsun bus pulling onto the shoulder to make way for a passing truck fell into a 600-ft. ravine; 13 occupants of the bus died and 50 others were seriously injured.
Oct. 2 Casma Province, Peru. Intercity bus collided with a heavily loaded truck and burst into flames; 21 passengers perished and 25 others were severely burned.
Oct. 4 Toumba, Mex. Trolley car sliced through a bus and killed 15 of the bus riders; 2 others were injured.
Oct. 5 Near Madurai, India. Mountain-road collision between a bus and a jeep impelled the bus down the mountainside and killed at least 22 persons; 40 others were injured.
Oct 5 Vranje, Yugos. A bus careened off the road and overturned bringing death to at least 10 riders.
Nov. 1 South of Cairo, U.A.R. Skidding bus landed in an irrigation ditch killing 18 of the 40 passengers.
Dec. 8 Northern Dahomey. A truck carrying 140 refugees from Ghana overturned killing 15 persons and injuring 73 others.
Dec. 12 Bulawayo, Rhodesia. A bus flipped off a bridge and fell 100 ft. into the 20-ft.-deep Gwaai River; 21 persons perished and many others were missing and presumed to have been drowned.
Dec. 17 Guatemala City, Guatemala. Bus collided with an auto and both vehicles were thrown into a 1,200-ft. ravine; 26 persons died, 25 others were injured.
Dec. 23 Erivan, Armenia, U.S.S.R. Details were unavailable concerning a bus crash that reportedly killed as many as 100 persons.
Dec. 29 Southwestern Colombia. Veering off the mountain road between Popayán and Pasto a bus caused the death of at least 10 persons; another 29 were injured.

Domestic Arts and Sciences

Home Economics. In 1969 home economists set about the task of implementing in practical terms the

Disciples of Christ: *see* Religion
Diseases: *see* Medicine
Divorce: *see* Vital Statistics
Docks: *see* Transportation

theme of international cooperation discussed at their conference in Bristol, Eng., in 1968. The Paris-based International Federation of Home Economics (IFHE) appointed a trilingual secretary and a bilingual librarian to its headquarters secretariat to expedite its dealings with member organizations in 61 different countries. In addition, members of the executive committee of the IFHE met in Stuttgart, W.Ger., with senior home economists from the UN Food and Agriculture Organization (FAO) and UNESCO, with a view toward establishing a closer working relationship.

The American Home Economics Association (AHEA) devoted the entire April issue of its journal to the theme of international cooperation, and reported that the current holders of its international scholarships included home economists from New Zealand, Scotland, Ireland, India, Greece, Nepal, the Netherlands, and France. The British Association of Teachers of Domestic Science offered free tuition to six foreign teachers at a refresher course held in Liverpool.

COURTESY, TSAO DESIGNS

"The Tom Edison Lamp," designed by John Gardner and manufactured by TSAO Designs, has self-contained dimmer to alter brightness from fireplace light to high brilliance.

In the field, home economists continued their efforts to raise the standard of family life. In Nigeria home economists from the U.S. Agency for International Development (AID) instituted a program to improve the standard of village life. In Brazil home economists lectured at the third Consumer Education Course in Fortaleza, Ceará, on topics that ranged from consumer credit to economic systems. In the U.S. home economists provided intensive training for the 5,500 aides needed for a nationwide food and nutrition education program aimed at helping low-income families acquire the knowledge and skills necessary to obtain adequate diets.

The nutritional needs of special groups were also recognized in the U.K. by the establishment of a geriatric nutrition unit at Queen Elizabeth College, University of London. This followed voluntary pioneer work done by home economists in the scheme for welfare milk for the elderly.

Much thought was given during 1969 to ways of improving both the standard of home economics education and the image of the profession as a whole. In Poland the home economics committee published plans to cooperate with foreign home economists by exchanging views on the best methods of disseminating skills in home economics. In Algeria improved programs of teacher training were instituted. In the U.K. the Department of Education and Science called a special meeting to discuss the problem of home economics education in post-secondary educational institutions; the University of Surrey was to award an honours degree in home economics. Pennsylvania State University renamed its College of Home Economics a "College of Human Development" and appointed a male social scientist as head.

The rehabilitation of the handicapped continued to engage the interest of home economists. In the U.S., 120 representatives of the profession and the interdisciplinary field of rehabilitation attended an AHEA-sponsored national workshop on "Future Directions for Home Economics in Rehabilitation," while in the U.K., Association of Home Economists (AHE) members collated information on practical aids for the handicapped housewife, to be incorporated in a book prepared by the equipment panel of the Disabled Living Activities group of the Central Council for the Disabled. The AHEA, which was celebrating its 60th anniversary, held its annual meeting in Boston, Mass., on the theme of "Building for the Future"; topics such as family planning, drug addiction, and civil disobedience were discussed.

Also planning for the future, the U.K. Federation for Education in Home Economics set up a working party on "metrication for the housewife," installed a former chairman of the AHE (Barbara Morrison) as convenor, and published its first recommendations —six basic recipes for home economics teaching—in anticipation of the change to the metric system in Britain due to take place by 1975.

Looking toward the next international congress, to be held in Helsinki, Fin., in July 1972, the IFHE published its work plan and priorities for the period July 1968–July 1972. Progress was to be reviewed at a meeting of the permanent international council in Wiesbaden, W.Ger., in 1970.

Food Preparation. The dietetic, nutritional, and hygienic qualities of the ingredients used in food preparation were matters of particular interest to both the domestic and the institutional consumer during 1969. At the same time, the packaging used for these ingredients—and the utensils in which to prepare them—were being designed with the convenience of the cook increasingly in mind.

The "health foods" market continued to expand, with an estimated 100,000 consumers spending £14 million on "whole foods," "compost-grown vegetables," and the like in the U.K. alone. Manufacturers continued to serve the growing market for low-calorie foods by offering slimmer versions of their standard packs containing half the normal number of calories. In the U.K. this continued preoccupation with weight reduction was reflected in a survey that showed sales of flour had fallen by 21% over the preceding decade.

In October the U.S. secretary of health, education, and welfare announced a ban on cyclamate sweeteners in foodstuffs on the ground that research had shown that cyclamates could produce cancer and congenital deformities in rats and chicks. Although the U.S. ban was later relaxed somewhat, other countries, including Sweden, Canada, and the U.K., ordered the withdrawal of cyclamate-sweetened foodstuffs from the market. Other widely used additives appeared to be in line for reexamination in the U.S. No official action was taken, but reports that monosodium glutamate caused brain damage in baby mice led three leading babyfood manufacturers to announce that they would no longer use it in their products.

On the international scene, the Codex Alimentarius Commission set up by the FAO and the World Health Organization (WHO) established committees in several European cities to further its program of setting international standards for 200 items of food in general use. Likely to be of more immediate benefit in food preparation was the research undertaken in many different countries aimed at finding acceptable man-made foods to meet the worldwide shortage of protein. In Nigeria and India, tests were made of a machine that could produce rich yet inexpensive protein from common jungle weeds. Food technologists in Italy succeeded in making a palatable protein biscuit derived from petroleum-based products.

To satisfy the increasing demand of the housewife for high-quality cuts of meat that could be roasted, broiled, or fried, meat tenderized by a special process (which made cheaper cuts suitable for high-quality marketing) was shipped from South Africa to the U.K. The British housewife was also promised (as the result of research at the Meat Research Institute near Bristol) the possibility of buying meat in quality-price-linked categories for the first time.

In the centenary year of the invention of margarine, it was reported that whereas the consumption of premium margarines in the U.S. had increased nearly fivefold in the preceding decade (with the soft, polyunsaturated varieties accounting for nearly half the total sales), butter still remained supreme in the U.K. Yearly consumption in Britain amounted to 19 lb. per capita, compared with 12 lb. of margarine. Although the value of butter marketed in the U.K. during the year reached £200 million, two major suppliers, Australia and Denmark, complained that British butter prices were uneconomic from the point of view of the producer. Whatever the price abroad, however, the Danish butter eater was at least assured of the freshness of the native product; after a vigorous campaign by the Danish consumer council, a new law was passed making the date-stamping of all butter compulsory.

While the U.S. continued to lead the world in the consumption of frozen foods, with per capita consumption of 70½ lb. a year (compared with 27 lb. in Sweden, 13½ lb. in the U.K., and 7½ lb. in West Germany), a new process of freezing by sprays of liquid nitrogen instead of blast freezing in air was reported in the U.K. Interest in the home freezing of foods (as well as the bulk storage of commercially frozen foods) was triggered in Britain by a London symposium at which it was revealed that, though only about 1% of British households had freezers installed, more than 500 firms were already offering bulk supplies of frozen foods direct to the housewife. In Australia, however, the consumers' association described many "freezer-food plans" (in which the appliances and the food with which to stock them were linked in credit-payment plans) as "the nation's biggest food swindle."

Less preparation than ever was involved in the use of many new foods. In Italy campers could buy a new range of self-heating cooked meals. Following in the wake of food research for the space program, a concentrated "space food stick" in chocolate, peanut butter, and tomato flavours was introduced in the U.S. by Pillsbury. In the U.K. a range of peeled, cooked, and vacuum-packed vegetables began to challenge traditional canned varieties.

Trend setters in the packaging field included a wide-necked sauce jar from AB Platmanufaktur of Sweden; a roasting film for meat, rolls, and pastry packs from 3M; and reclosable "zipper" bags for frozen foods and "zip-open cans" from Metal Box. Also noteworthy was the increasing use of nonreturnable, disposable milk cartons (long popular in the U.S.), using materials that ranged from cartonboard (in Japan) to polyethylene (in West Germany).

In cooking utensils the main emphasis was on the use of materials that could be easily maintained and cleaned. The most newsworthy development was the introduction by du Pont of a hard-base Teflon nonstick finish; the most time-saving was a cook-and-serve ware that, in the Wear-Ever Cerama range, incorporated a ceramic exterior finish with a heavy-duty, Teflon-lined aluminum body.

Household Appliances. The 1969 models of appliances showed little radical departure from previous designs, but a clue to future development lay in the various prototype models that were announced. Making use of the most sophisticated materials and processes of modern technology, these promised the housewife an era of space-age cookery with noise and maintenance kept to the minimum. Prototypes included a laser-beam can opener, adjustable to cans of any size or shape; a self-cleaning ultrasonic blender, powered by a fuel cell; and a fuel-cell-powered thermoelectric iron giving instant heat, which was said to remove spots of any kind but which would not scorch fabric.

A new concept of the use of present appliance models was suggested in the design of the winning entry in the first Birds Eye kitchen design competition, arranged in collaboration with the British Council of Industrial Design. It consisted of a single cylindrical unit in which a home freezer, two electric hobs, two gas burners, a microwave oven, a sink, and a dishwasher could be rotated at will.

While the housewife waited for such dreams to become reality, she could choose from a bewildering variety of appliances with ever more sophisticated attachments and design features. In many new stoves, the outstanding feature was the self-cleaning system (available for both electric and gas ranges), which in some cases (the English Electric E70) could be set to operate overnight. More conventional stoves had nonstick oven interiors, using a special finish (first developed for gardening tools) backed with stainless steel. On other stoves, new features included temperature-controlled warming shelves, heat- and time-controlled storage drawers, and broilers that could be converted when necessary into a second oven. Flexibility in use was also to be found in many of the new freezer-refrigerators; in one model it was possible to convert a section from freezer to refrigerator as required.

Though Europe still lagged behind the U.S. in refrigerator ownership, 86% of the homes in Sweden were reported to have refrigerators, compared with 59% in Britain, 73% in France, and 76% in West Germany. The move toward compactness continued: the 1969 model of a five-cubic-foot refrigerator occupied only three square feet, compared with four square feet in 1959.

There was a new feeling for mobility in appliances. Many refrigerators and stoves were being offered with optional casters. A Hoover washer/spin dryer, the Wheelaway, was so compact that its makers claimed it could be used in any room in the house, and in their advertising they compared it with a compact car. Mini-dryers were also introduced; half the size of many dryers, they were designed to fit on a shelf or hang on the wall of a bathroom.

The claim by British manufacturers that Italian washing machines were being dumped in the U.K. was rejected by the Board of Trade on the ground that the price differential was due to the lesser degree of sophistication in the Italian models. The latest U.S. models were more programmed than ever before. In one model, for example, purchasers were offered a permanent-press cycle, automatic prewash, infinite water level control, self-cleaning lint filter, and an automatic bleach and fabric softener.

Britain's Gas Council announced a far-reaching research program aimed at producing low-cost appliances specifically designed for use with natural gas. The low corrosive properties of natural gas would permit the use of cheaper materials and cut the cost of parts replacement and maintenance.

It was in the field of small appliances that the news of most general interest was to be found. Hoover (Great Britain) expressed confidence in the growth potential of this market by announcing plans to boost output by 30%. A U.S. company, National Presto Industries, offered the consumer no less than 26 different electrical appliances. The West got one of its first views of a (Nationalist) Chinese appliance when a convertible table cooker/room heater, designed in Taiwan, went on display in London.

Almost every category of consumer was considered in small-appliance design. A table-top oven for the handicapped, designed by Tricity in cooperation with the Nuffield Orthopaedic Centre, incorporated positive controls with specially extended finger grips and an audible "click" movement, making it possible for oven settings to be "counted" by the blind homemaker. Ideas of more general appeal included a sealer and bag kit by Dazy that heat-sealed food in plastic bags for the home refrigerator or freezer; an electric toothbrush with a bacteria-inhibiting lamp for tumbler or toothbrush; and Cory's infrared food warmer/defroster for mounting under wall cupboards.

Interior Decoration. The major influence on interior decoration in 1969 was to be found in the varied schools of modern art such as Surrealism, abstract lyricism, and geometrical abstract, expressed in fabric design, colour, and form as well as in the use of materials such as steel, aluminum, and plexiglass.

While there was a strong international feeling in interiors everywhere, with designers such as Charles Eames and Jo Colombo in favour in all parts of the world, the basic design ingredients were interpreted in totally different ways from one country to another. Nowhere was this more evident than at the "Design 69 from 22 Countries" exhibition staged in London to coincide with the sixth congress of the International Council of Societies of Industrial Design. The U.S. interpreted its current mood with a Charles Eames chair chosen for "timelessness," while the Argentinian exhibit had been selected for "sobriety and accuracy" and that from the U.K. for "innovation."

In furniture and interior design exhibitions everywhere, the Italians seemed to lead, especially at the Salon du Meuble held in France in January. While much fibreglass and plastic were used (as in vacuum-molded tables in vivid acrylic colours and transparent plexiglass storage units), there was also a strong trend to more traditional materials, such as soft leather, and lacquered chair frames with natural rush seats. Indeed, 90% of the furniture was still based on wood.

In the U.K. this feeling for natural materials and textures was interpreted in a "rugged look," with form and colour set against rugged textures—bare stone walls juxtaposed with well-waxed timber; hessian with brightly lacquered furniture (as shown in Edward Samuel's Irish holiday cottage and the new Queen Elizabeth Hall on the South Bank of the Thames). A feeling for tradition was also evident in a new-found interest in timber beams for both new and old houses.

The "Scandinavian look" of the 1950s was slowly disappearing; individual countries were opting for their own styles, though these often showed a strong Italian influence. This was particularly evident at the May exhibition of furniture in Copenhagen where, though the traditional slim shapes could still be found, a growing number of chairs and couches were shown in bulky, well-padded, round shapes, with pale removable covers in checks or stripes, decorated with loose cushions in gaily coloured and hugely patterned cottons. Oak and lacquered surfaces were replacing teak and rosewood.

In chairs and couches, comfort was all, with designers using soft upholstery materials such as glove leather and dralon. This feeling for softness reached its zenith at the 1969 Milan International Furniture Exhibition, where expanded polyurethane-foam chairs (designed by Gaetano Pesce) were presented in airtight plastic envelopes from which they emerged in a predetermined shape.

There were signs of new inventiveness in the field of domestic lighting, demonstrated by the establishment of Rotaflex Concorde International's Total Environment Workshop, where domestic and industrial lighting problems could be discussed monthly. Never before had there been such a wide range of fittings that were both functional and decorative—as, for example, the "flexi" range designed by Robert Welch for Lumitron. On the other hand, Victorian designs, using such modern materials as metalized plastic and polystyrene, were very popular. Except for use in period rooms, the conventional lampshade was a thing of the past. Instead, table lamps were helmets (Artemide of Italy), eggs (Ceasare Casati), balls, cylinders, mushrooms, and globes.

With antique-furniture prices reaching new heights, the young bought cheap Victoriana instead. Opaline glass, medallions, and stripped pine were popular items in London's King's Road. Older consumers were responsible for a boom in reproduction antique furniture of the Queen Anne, Georgian, and Regency periods.

Colour was the keynote in floor coverings, whether it was the shocking pink, emerald green, and vivid yellow shown at the London Carpet Exhibition or the orange, green, and turquoise of the vinyl-simulated tiles seen in many U.S. kitchens. Geometric and tile designs were still the favourites for "hard" floor coverings, but there was a move toward the more traditional Jacobean and Persian designs for carpets. There was also an increasing use of conventional materials, and the International Wool Secretariat reported that European consumption of carpet wool had reached about £225 million a year—an increase of 10% in a decade.

It was in the bathroom that interior design showed its most exuberant inventiveness during the year. Designers banished the tiled walls and plain plastic accessories that had been in vogue for so long. The influence of Rome and Greece was to be seen in centrally placed baths and sinks set in marble surrounds, and that of the French Empire period in stained glass windows and velvet upholstered chairs.

(Ev. R.)

See also Fashion and Dress; Food; Industrial Design.

ENCYCLOPÆDIA BRITANNICA FILMS. *How to Make a Simple Loom and Weave* (1958); *How to Make a Starch Painting* (1958); *Lines in Relief—Woodcut and Block Printing* (1964); *Cloth—Fiber to Fabric* (1968).

Dominican Republic

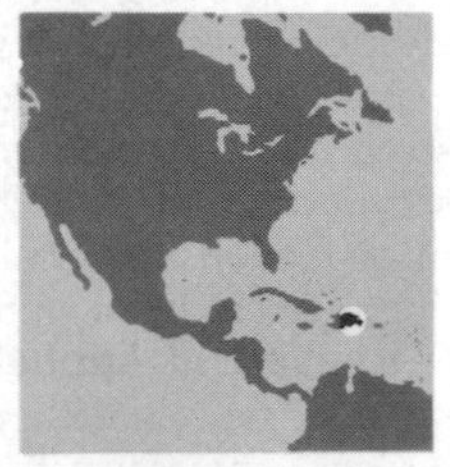

Covering the eastern two-thirds of the Caribbean island of Hispaniola, the Dominican Republic is separated from Haiti, which occupies the western third, by a rugged mountain range. Area: 18,720 sq.mi. (48,484 sq.km.). Pop. (1969 est.): 4,174,490, including European 28%; mestizo and mulatto 60%; Negro 11%. Cap. and largest city: Santo Domingo (pop., 1967 est., 577,371). Language: Spanish. Religion: Roman Catholic. President in 1969, Joaquín Balaguer.

President Balaguer and his Reformist Party ushered in 1969 as "Education Year" and established as primary goals the construction of rural schools and a crash program to eradicate illiteracy among Dominican youth. The need for adequate schooling was highlighted by the government's negotiation with UNICEF to establish a teacher-training program that, if successful, would provide by 1972 approximately 900 elementary school instructors for the hard-pressed western frontier.

After three consecutive years in power and substantial achievements to his credit, President Balaguer announced in June his candidacy for the 1970 presidential elections. Tensions mounted as rival political parties mustered support to oppose the incumbent president. Even within the Reformist Party loyalty was divided after Vice-Pres. Francisco Augusto Lora announced his bid for the coming presidential race and received backing from the Integrated Anti-Reelection Democratic Movement (MIDA) and the United National Revolutionary Front (FRUN). Nonetheless, by midyear Balaguer had retained the support of the National Youth Movement (MNJ), a sizable portion of the influential business community, and the majority of peasant farmers and ranchers.

The leftist-oriented Dominican Revolutionary Party (PRD) retained former Pres. Juan Bosch as its titular head and philosophical mentor, but it was also characterized by division within the rank and file. Bosch maintained his self-imposed exile in Europe throughout the year and continued to preach a doctrine of popular dictatorship which stated that representative democracy was an unworkable political system within the Dominican Republic. The unpopularity of Bosch among the majority of Dominican peasants and an overriding fear that the popular dictatorship system, if adopted, would produce revolution divided the PRD leadership and left the party without a viable candidate.

LAURE AMEX—PIX FROM PUBLIX

Security forces armed with machine guns guard the streets of Santo Domingo to prevent riots during Gov. Nelson Rockefeller's 24-hour visit to the Dominican Republic.

Reaction to Balaguer's drive for reelection prompted moderates to group about former Pres. Héctor García-Godoy in his newly formed National Conciliation Movement (MCN). The Revolutionary Social Christian Party (PRSC), adhering to its platform of offering a middle road between capitalism and socialism, based its bid on the need for sweeping agrarian reform within the republic. Finally, the Quisqueyano Democratic Party (PQD) continued to function as the main support for the aspirations of retired right-wing Brig. Gen. Elías Wessin y Wessin.

Both right- and left-wing extremist groups, intent on eliminating the Balaguer government before 1970, reverted to terrorist acts and fostered a nationwide public transit strike in August that crippled the country for a short time. Throughout the year the Autonomous University of Santo Domingo continued to function as a haven for Communist groups and forces intent on embarrassing the government. Repeated disorders and provocations by students forced its closing innumerable times.

Despite political tensions the moderate policies of President Balaguer continued to provide a stabilizing effect on social and economic conditions throughout the nation. Nelson Rockefeller's visit in early July was without serious incident and gave a substantial boost to Reformist Party morale. By mid-September President Balaguer had demonstrated his faith in the democratic process by repealing the ban on political rallies.

Expansion of irrigation and power facilities received greatest priority within the government's annual development plan and counted as an important objective of the National Development Plan, programmed for the 1970–74 period. The initiation of work on the Tavera and Valdesia dam complexes was given particular emphasis. (G. A. A.)

ENCYCLOPÆDIA BRITANNICA FILMS. *The West Indies* (1965).

DOMINICAN REPUBLIC

Education. (1966–67) Primary, pupils 585,153, teachers 10,850; secondary, pupils 63,627, teachers 2,734; vocational, pupils 25,272, teachers 731; teacher training, students 437, teachers 51; higher (1965–66), students 6,606, teaching staff 414.

Finance. Monetary unit: peso, at parity with the U.S. dollar (2.40 pesos = £1 sterling). Gold and foreign exchange, central bank: (March 1969) U.S. $36.8 million; (March 1968) U.S. $28.1 million. Budget (1967 est.) balanced at 178.2 million pesos. Gross national product: (1967) 1,068,200,000 pesos; (1966) 1,012,400,000 pesos. Money supply: (March 1969) 134.9 million pesos; (March 1968) 113 million pesos. Cost of living (Santo Domingo; 1963 = 100): (June 1969) 101; (June 1968) 105.

Foreign Trade. (1968) Imports 196.8 million pesos; exports 163.5 million pesos. Import sources (1967): U.S. 55%; Japan 7%; West Germany 6%; Trinidad and Tobago 6%. Export destination U.S. (1967) 87%. Main exports: sugar 54%; coffee 11%; cocoa 8%; bauxite 8%; tobacco 7%.

Transport and Communications. Roads (1963) 6,250 km. (including 4,250 km. first class). Motor vehicles (1967): passenger 28,900; commercial (including buses) 13,700. Railways (1965) 220 km. (excluding *c.* 1,600 km. on sugar estates). Telephones (Jan. 1968) 34,234. Radio receivers (Dec. 1967) *c.* 150,000. Television receivers (Dec. 1967) 85,000.

Agriculture. Production (in 000; metric tons; 1968; 1967 in parentheses): rice 169 (147); corn 40 (39); coffee (1967) *c.* 38, (1966) *c.* 30; sugar, raw value (1968–69) *c.* 800, (1967–68) *c.* 710; cassava (1966) *c.* 170, (1965) *c.* 160; peanuts *c.* 50 (45); sweet potatoes (1966) *c.* 100, (1965) *c.* 100; oranges (1967) 57, (1966) 56; bananas (1966) *c.* 220, (1965) *c.* 220; tobacco *c.* 11 (19). Livestock (in 000; June 1968): cattle *c.* 1,100; pigs (June 1967) *c.* 1,250; horses *c.* 255; mules *c.* 85; asses *c.* 145; sheep (June 1967) *c.* 81.

Industry. Production (in 000; metric tons; 1967): bauxite 1,092; cement 310; electricity (kw-hr.) 705,000.

Dominica:
see Dependent States

Draft:
see Defense

Drama:
see Cinema; Theatre

Dress:
see Fashion and Dress; Furs

Drugs:
see Medicine

Dutch Guiana:
see Dependent States

Dutch Overseas Territories:
see Dependent States

Ear, Nose, and Throat Diseases:
see Medicine

Earthquakes:
see Disasters; Seismology

Eastern Orthodox Churches:
see Religion

Economic Planning

One simple definition of the term "economic planning" is that it is a set of policies that together make a coherent strategy for achieving stated objectives. This is true of the indicative planning of the countries of Western Europe; of the plans put into operation by the less developed countries; and of the directive planning of the centrally planned economies. The differences among these three types consist largely in the choice of objectives and in the institutional machinery devised to attain them.

Industrialized Countries. Medium- and long-term economic planning in Western Europe continued during 1969 to be overshadowed by short-term crises and uncertainties. In Britain uncertainty about whether and when the devaluation of November 1967, and its accompanying measures, would finally produce the hoped-for surplus in the balance of payments persisted at least up to August–September, when the trade returns finally showed the prospect of a substantial surplus. In France, the weakness of the franc resulting from the crisis of May 1968 finally resulted in devaluation in August 1969. Speculative pressure in West Germany for a revaluation of the mark forced the authorities to allow a "floating" rate, as a prelude to revaluation, in September 1969. These exchange adjustments, combined with electoral changes (the replacement of Charles de Gaulle by Georges Pompidou and the formation of a Social Democratic-Free Democratic government in West Germany), the continuing international discussion of a new exchange adjustment mechanism, and the disruption of the European Economic Community both by internal problems and by applications for membership, created a climate extremely unfavourable to medium- and long-term planning.

Only in the U.K. did the events of the year provide at least a fairly clear picture of the future status of economic planning. The new planning document, to replace the defunct National Plan of September 1965, was published in February. That *The Task Ahead* was described as a "planning document," not a plan, indicated that the planners and the government had fully recognized the unfortunate results of excessive optimism surrounding the National Plan. It also indicated that the medium-term prospects of the economy could not be assessed until the immediate situation, especially regarding the balance of payments, became clearer. The forecasts, extending only up to 1972, were modest and conditional, and alternative indications for the growth of the economy, dependent on varying assumptions about the development of the balance of payments, helped to create a flexibility far removed from the target-setting of the National Plan. Despite some wild talk of rapid export-led growth following the favourable trade returns of the late summer, the attitude remained cautious throughout the year. The remaining problem was to know whether such a tentative document as *The Task Ahead* could have any worthwhile effect on economic policy and performance.

Meanwhile, work continued on devising a medium-term model of the British economy, which might eventually improve the technical basis of medium-term forecasting. In October the change in attitude toward planning was institutionalized by the abolition of the Department of Economic Affairs (DEA), whose responsibilities for medium- and long-term plans were assumed by the Treasury. Thus was recognized the failure of the attempt in 1964 to give long-term plans more influence by separating them from the Treasury's concern with the short-term and balance of payments situation. The other institutional innovation of 1964, the Ministry of Technology, was strengthened, however, by its taking over from the Board of Trade the sponsorship of the greater part of productive industry and responsibility for the operation of regional policy; it also took over the supervision of the Industrial Reorganisation Corporation from the DEA. The Ministry of Technology thus became the major instrument of a type of planning, the emphasis of which had become industrial and structural rather than economic.

France and West Germany were even more in the grip of short-term uncertainty during 1969 than the U.K. In France work on the preparation of the Sixth Plan was overshadowed by the developing economic crisis that culminated in the August devaluation. As in Britain during 1967–69, so in France it was impossible to draw up a meaningful medium-term plan until the effects of this step were clarified. Meanwhile, emphasis was bound to be placed on plans for shorter periods, similar to the Intermediate Plan and the Stabilization Plan for the early 1960s. The preparatory work for the Sixth Plan had already continued the shift noticeable in the Fifth Plan toward more emphasis on the structure of industry and less on the quantitative targets.

While in the U.K. and in France the problem was whether the balance of payments could be improved in order to allow export-led growth in line with a medium-term plan, in West Germany rapid and stable export-led growth was threatened by inflationary pressure emanating from an undervalued currency, and by the political difficulties in the way of correcting this situation by a revaluation. The assumption of power by the SPD-FDP coalition made revaluation possible following the earlier "floating" of the mark. Although the effects of revaluation would only be seen during 1970 and 1971, steady growth was expected to continue. There was, however, no reason to expect a major shift toward more medium-term planning in West Germany. During the previous government, with Karl Schiller (*see* BIOGRAPHY) as federal minister for economics, some mild aspects of planning had been introduced. But these amounted to little more than using national accounting data to help coordinate governmental policy, with some additional benefit accruing from providing the private sector with a better guide than previously to the likely development of policy and of the economy as a whole. There was no question of using detailed forecasts for individual industries to influence decisions in the private sector, as in earlier British and French planning. With a predominantly Social Democrat government a further shift toward planning was to be expected, although this was unlikely to be dramatic.

With little effective medium-term planning at the national level in 1969, it could not be expected that the EEC would make progress with the development of its medium-term policy program. The second program, published in 1968, filled in some of the industrial detail omitted from the first one in 1966, but no industrial forecasts or targets were attempted, in view of West German opposition. Studies on the necessary elements of a European industrial policy (sectoral policy, science policy, company law, etc.) took place in Brussels during 1969. However, the French devaluation plunged the EEC even deeper into crisis, mainly by its effect on agricultural policy, and with negotiations for membership by Britain and other states pending, 1969 was hardly propitious for the development of EEC planning.

The year was, then, from almost every aspect, a depressing one for medium-term planners. Three trends were distinguishable: continued retreat from the enthusiasm of the early and mid-1960s; confirmation of the vastly greater influence of short-term plans and policies; and the further shift of emphasis within the medium term from quantitative indications to structural adaptations of industries. (G. R. DE.)

Less Developed Countries. The idea that less developed countries should use the planning approach to organize and coordinate their development efforts was widely advocated by economists and various UN and other aid agencies and was accepted by most countries. As a result, by 1969 most of these countries had some sort of document described as a development plan. In recent years, however, there had been increasing concern with the failure of many of these countries to implement their plans. This failure was due to a variety of reasons, but one important one concerned the inherent weaknesses in the plans themselves and in the political and administrative machinery available for their implementation.

The problem of inadequate implementation became most serious in regard to medium-term planning. On the one hand, there was a growing concern that the time period covered by such plans was too short to provide an effective overall strategy of development. On the other hand, this time period was too long for governments of less developed countries to make reliable projections of resources, especially foreign exchange resources from export earnings and external assistance, on which their plans depend so heavily. Furthermore, in some cases, plans had not been seriously formulated with a view to implementation but rather for various propaganda and other purposes. Quite often, plans were drawn up primarily to serve as bases for negotiating foreign aid from bilateral and multilateral sources. A particularly important reason for failure was the fact that the agencies that formulated the plans did not have sufficient authority over the agencies responsible for their implementation.

In view of the growing concern with the difficulties of implementing plans as formulated, two new trends took place in economic planning in the less developed countries. One was toward making economy-wide plans on an annual basis. Such "annual planning" was introduced in India, when its fourth five-year plan had to be delayed for lack of assurance about adequate resources. Other countries also began using this method even in conjunction with their medium-term plans. The other trend was toward making long-term plans that were restricted to particular sectors of the economy, such as education, agriculture, or transport.

National plans also had to be considered in their international aspects. For example, there was a growing awareness that international aid, to be effective, had to be related to the development plan of the recipient country. This led to the practice of review and evaluation of plans by aid agencies such as the World Bank and the U.S. Agency for International Development.

Apart from these trends, there recently was active concern about an international framework for de-

continued on page 300

SPECIAL REPORT

ECONOMIC BACKGROUND FOR CZECHOSLOVAKIA'S CRISIS

By Ota Sik

Even before World War II Czechoslovakia was an industrial country. In 1937 industry contributed 53% of the national income. But like most small industrial countries, prewar Czechoslovakia was largely dependent on other countries for both imports of raw materials and export markets for its products. This raised considerable structural problems for industry and, even before the war, compelled Czechoslovakia to seek a concept of development that would ensure the necessary growth of foreign trade, along with the growth of its national income.

Czechoslovakia's industrial development, therefore, gradually adapted itself to the requirements of international technological progress, though without completely overcoming economic instability and extreme vulnerability during trade depressions. The linking of Czechoslovak industry with the international economy undoubtedly contributed not only to its rapid and effective development, but also to the severity of the crisis during the interwar years.

The Postwar Economy. After the war it was a matter of extreme urgency to reorganize production. Apart from traditional exports of consumer goods, the production and export of machinery, which had been given priority during the war, required further rapid development. Postwar Czechoslovakia had not only the qualified industrial and intellectual potentials for this development, especially in the chemical, electrotechnical, and building industries, but to some extent also the sources of raw materials and facilities for rapid penetration of both traditional and new foreign markets.

Unfortunately, it is not only economic aspects but political structures and aims that determine economic objectives. For the ruling political power to direct economic development against the logic of economics is understandably possible during unusual and relatively short periods. Once political considerations and objectives govern economic development over long periods, the result is repression of basic laws determining this development—the buildup of an ineffective structure of production, lack of balance, and disregard of socioeconomic requirements, and delays in technical and qualitative development of production. All this causes enormous economic losses to society.

For a few years, roughly up to 1951, the Czechoslovak economy was developing very favourably. Along with profound proprietary and socioeconomic changes, effected in conjunction with socialistic development, a new system was worked out to establish the most effective productive structure and its most suitable adjustment to international economic development, with long-term provision of outlets and raw material supplies. Competitive exports to traditional Western markets would need to be increasingly supplemented by exports to new and inexhaustible Eastern markets.

Cooperatives and large nationalized concerns rapidly developed in addition to the private enterprises. By 1949 a mixed type of economy had developed, combining healthy competition with socialist concerns and democratic management systems, and supplemented by democratic planning and control of economic development by the state.

The large national concerns had generally very capable management. Directors were frequently appointed by political parties associated with the National Front; the board of directors appointed the managers; the management was concerned mainly with turnover, commercial development, and profits. These factors prevailed, in a descending tendency, until about 1951–52.

The National Economy Plan, which had a macroeconomic character designed to guide business concerns, represented the economic program of the government and was obligatory only for the organs of government. It was a first attempt at a market economy under macroeconomic planning. The plans were drawn up by commissions representing workers, business concerns, and political and professional organizations. Committees of special representatives and experts were formed to work out the aims and fundamentals of national economic development on a scientific and democratic basis that respected the relative independence of the market and the marketing function of business concerns.

Instructions from Stalin. Government policy, after overcoming postwar inflation, aimed at some market reorganization. But the development of this democratic economic system was interrupted without having attained internal equilibrium and a functioning buying market: in 1947 stress between West and East led to the cold war, and in 1950 the cold war became open war in Korea. This political situation caused a radical change in developments in Czechoslovakia.

The war stress called for an immediate increase of armed forces in the socialist countries, which, from the economic point of view, meant special preference for the heavy industries. Industrialization of the less developed socialist countries, however, was affected not only by the objective danger of war but still more by subjective political conceptions that no longer respected the fundamental economic laws. Unrealistic efforts were made to catch up quickly with the more highly developed capitalist countries in the production of basic commodities, and to speed up the establishment of heavy industry.

Czechoslovakia had to change the orientation and structure of its industry completely to ensure a constantly growing supply of heavy industry products for socialist countries. It was on direct instructions from Stalin in February 1950 that the Czechoslovak authorities decided on a further basic increase of annual industrial output and, in particular, of heavy industry output. Within a short time investments in heavy industry showed an immense increase. This reorientation was bound to change foreign trade basically. While in 1948 the turnover with capitalist and less developed countries was higher than with socialist countries, by 1953 the position had been reversed.

This ill-considered, sudden, and enforced change was disastrous for a small country like Czechoslovakia. It not only meant giving up the basic ideas of economic development but also led to a long-term economic policy that ignored all basic economic laws. The restructuring was realizable only by retarding development of all other branches of the economy—agriculture, light industry, consumer goods, foodstuffs, transport and communications, services, housing, technical development, modernization of production, exploitation of traditional markets, and foreign trade. The new development caused heavy and lasting inflation, inefficiency of productive labour, gradual deterioration of traditional Czechoslovak products, and increasing backwardness of the service industries, which in modern times have considerable influence on the progress of production. This resulted in slowing the rise of the standard of living, and, later, in shortages of consumer goods and other supplies, growing loss of leisure (especially for women), and further deterioration of living conditions.

The New Ideology. Such a fundamental and rapid change could not have been effected without political and ideological preparation. This preparation consisted of actions against many political and economic leaders and was inspired by Stalin's influence in almost all the people's democracies of the time for full harmonization with the political aims of the U.S.S.R. and identification with the aims of world socialism. The process hit Czechoslovakia very deeply and not only deprived the country of a number of prominent politicians and economists but brought into power a set of average and subaverage officials who for many years stifled all political thinking and all possibility of independent dealing with new problems. All pioneers of the postwar development were considered enemies of socialism; many were executed or imprisoned for long periods. All who raised doubts as to their sympathy with the new political line were relieved of their duties.

Only a few economists foresaw the dire consequences of this political and economic policy and most of them were eliminated. Any independent analytical and social science activity was suppressed, and most economic data were classified as secret. Under the influence of one-sided, limited, and untrue information, continuous political pressure, and government repression, the people lost the ability to judge the justice or suitability of the political and economic development, not to mention any changes to improve the economy.

During 1951–52, as the Soviet centralizing bureaucracy system was introduced, business concerns ceased to be independent and became subject to control by economic units. Their market orientation was discarded. Instead of the general business managements, a large number of economic ministries were established, with an even larger number of central administrations. By means of this huge bureaucratic apparatus and mechanically plotted plans, the state determined the output expected from each factory as well as outputs of certain main products, distributed and allotted administratively the outputs of factories and concerns, determined the amount and purpose of all investments, distributed all labour, and supervised productivity of labour and production costs. The state decided the extent, structure, and orientation of foreign trade, calculated the price of all products, and controlled all financial transactions.

Prices ceased to have any actual economic function, even as expressions of the true cost of a given product or market demand for it, and were looked upon as mere accounting units. Owing to official price fixing, some goods produced excessive profits while others produced low profits, or only losses. A high turnover tax was imposed and, in some cases, more than several hundred percent was added to the retail price of some goods while other goods were taxed little or not at all. Prices thus had no actual meaning in relation to production. Some firms were operating at a loss without any fault of theirs, while others were profitable without any merit of their own. Losses did not threaten the existence of the business any more than profits were any special benefit. Premiums introduced to reward firms for increasing their profits thus had no real effect.

The planning centre determined outputs on the basis of gross prices. It became increasingly difficult for firms to meet automatically increased output targets except by making minimum changes in the assortment produced. An increasing number of firms preferred to produce only those goods that, owing to high material costs, were very profitable in relation to the labour costs; this facilitated complying with the planned output. These firms reduced production of goods with low material costs and unfavourable prices. Prices thus had a considerable effect on the microstructure of all planned production, but absolutely no relevance for consumer needs or demand. All factories conceived the idea of wasting materials and means of production without regard to the actual needs of the buyer. The growing quantity of unwanted goods was forced upon consumers either by direct government measures or by economic pressure because other, wanted goods were not available. But stocks of unwanted and unsalable goods grew from year to year.

Growing Economic Disaster. The concern of factories to increase output prevented them from considering quality or any innovations and technological developments. An increasing shortage of foreign exchange and the complete control of foreign trade delayed importation of modern techniques. Hence, all new machinery and equipment were below the international mean level, let alone the international top standard. There was hardly any replacement of old equipment, especially in the consumer and foodstuff industries. The high percentage of old and completely written-off equipment was the main cause of the steady falling off of labour productivity. Steadily, more extensive, burdensome, and less effective investments were required to ensure the planned growth of production; between 1956 and 1965 investments had to be roughly quadrupled in order to secure an unchanged rate of growth of national income. More and more labour was required and had to be recruited from among housewives or workers from minor industries.

Increasing investments for planned growth required a steadily increasing building activity. As there was no priority for the building industry, it had a constant struggle with shortages of labour, equipment, and materials. This widened the span between increasing investments and production, and resulted in slower building and conversion rates and noncompletion of buildings. This in turn resulted in increasing tying-up of material and labour, higher costs, and lower efficiency.

Increasing investment and heavy industry activities necessarily brought about inflationary pressure. While year after year the state braked increases of mean wages, the number of workers in heavy industries, especially at higher wages, was steadily growing. The total wage rolls thus grew rapidly, but buying power decreased because of the shortage especially of services of all kinds and of long-term consumer goods.

There was no remedy to be expected from foreign trade. Falling behind world standards in technological and qualitative development year after year caused increasing losses on foreign markets. The obtainable prices for an increasing number of exported goods not only left no profits, but the same volume of imported goods required a steadily increasing volume of Czechoslovak exports. The loss on foreign trade was not borne by the makers of the goods, who were paid at domestic rates by the State Foreign Trade Monopoly firms. They merely endeavoured to work to the state schedule, which every year called for a larger output to cover the planned imports.

The monopoly firms were allowed to sell imported goods to Czechoslovak buyers at a fixed domestic price sufficient to pay for the export goods supplied. But as the amount paid for exports continually exceeded the total sum due for imports, the monopoly firms were incurring increasing losses. This did not trouble them very much because they were subsidized by the state. But the increasing subsidies lowered the national income and thus the buying power of all the people.

The strains increased, foreign exchange reserves became exhausted, and during the last few years the Czechoslovak trade balance with capitalist countries became passive. Inflation was on the increase but was prevented from becoming open because prices were fixed by the state. During the last few years, however, it had become impossible to prevent a gradual increase of prices. The clearest sign of inflation was the rapidly growing enforced savings of consumers and firms that represented unrealizable buying power and increased stocks of unwanted goods and the number of suspended investments.

The Need for Change. All attempts to change the industrial structure and limit the volume of investments failed because of the opposite tendency of the whole control system and also because of the impossibility of diverting labour, investments, and imports from the heavy industries. Increasingly, the pressure of foreign trade became the decisive factor opposing all attempts at structural changes, apart from the fact that the old control system, by the inertia of its planning and trading, created insurmountable obstacles to any change.

It was thus clear that these "eternal" problems of the Czechoslovak economy, which the central organs attributed to shortcomings of the industrial structure, were inseparable from centralized bureaucratic economic controls that, over the years, had left their imprint on the structure of the economy. Separate structural changes, quick development of modern, effective, and competitive manufacturing equipment, increased production of consumer goods and foodstuffs, increased housing and production of building materials, and modernization of transport and communications would require considerable investments and involve some additional factors such as labour and the relative limitation of heavy industries. Investment capital could be found only by changing the control system and after some relatively appreciable time. The process of change might be accelerated by fairly large foreign loans, purchase of patent licenses, and cooperation with progressive foreign firms; but without a thorough change of the system there would not even be any guarantee that foreign credits, if any, would actually be used for the development of equipment and an effective increase of exports and foreign exchange convertibility of credits.

A plan to change the control system in Czechoslovakia originated about 1963. It met with resistance by the conservative forces, which were tied to the old system by both ideology and interest. The main object was to replace the old control system with a modern macroeconomically planned orientation, supplemented by mainly indirect economy control by the state. The state would concentrate its direct investment activity on the infrastructure. The socialist collective concerns would become independent, changed into materially interested and responsible market units. Elements of a consistent, autonomous political economy system would include: assurance that the workers' cooperatives would not only bear the trading risks but also elect workers' councils as the highest administrative and supervisory organs of their concerns; restoration of the economic function of markets, prices, and money, indirect market regulation by the state, and internal and external competition pressure together with systematic antimonopolistic state control; decentralization of foreign trade activities with cessation of state trade and currency policy; and creation of a capital market based on relatively independent socialistic banking concerns, with convertibility of Czechoslovak currency.

The new control system would presuppose considerable organizational and personnel changes and creation of an entirely new mechanism, with criteria of selection and preparation of economists and political economists. It would be unthinkable without actual democratization of the entire political system.

"Czechoslovak Spring." An increasing number of leading politicians and economists had become convinced during the last few years of the need for economic reforms, which were always opposed by the old political party headed by Pres. Antonin Novotny. The struggle for economic reform thus in due course became a struggle for ousting the Novotny government and finally for introducing a democratic political system. People began to realize that a consistent change of economic development and of the entire control system was unthinkable without corresponding political changes. The objective economic situation thus became a factor that contributed decisively to the political defeat of the Novotny regime and culminated in the "Czechoslovak spring" in which changes toward a better, more efficient economy began to be made.

Military interference and political events in August 1968 prevented implementation of the proposed economic and political reforms and thus also the solution of the accumulated economic problems. The great demoralization of labour, a reaction to these political events, has rendered the economic crisis much more acute and increased inflation. The longer the necessary changes based on actual economic criteria and motives are delayed, the more conflicts and economic losses will result, causing a steady drop in the standard of living in Czechoslovakia.

continued from page 297

velopment plans and strategies. Various agencies of the UN, such as the Committee for Development Planning, were engaged in drawing up a second Development Decade for the '70s. A similar interest underlay the recommendation of the Commission on International Development (the Pearson Commission), which submitted its report in September.

(R. M. SM.)

Centrally Planned Economies. During April 23–26, a special session of the Council for Mutual Economic Assistance (CMEA, or Comecon) was held in Moscow with the participation of first secretaries of the Communist and Workers' parties, and prime ministers of the eight member countries. The formal occasion was the 20th anniversary of the founding of Comecon, but the main purpose was to speed up economic integration of the "socialist world market."

Comecon's achievements were impressive. In 1950 its share in world industrial production was about 18%; by 1967 that proportion had risen to 31%. Under the UN classification the Comecon countries belonged to medium-developed states. In East Germany, Czechoslovakia, and the U.S.S.R. the national yearly income per head averaged between $800 and $1,000, while in Poland, Hungary, Romania, and Bulgaria the corresponding figures ranged from $600 to $800. Only in Mongolia was the average income per head less than $600. In 1967 the share of industry in the formation of national income in the countries of the Comecon bloc (Mongolia excepted) ranged from 46% in Bulgaria to 62% in Czechoslovakia.

The main theme of the April summit meeting was "the examination of problems connected with forms and methods of cooperation among member-countries," a statement somewhat concealing the ideal of economic integration, which some members cherished and others distrusted or frankly opposed. However, the clear realization existed that the outmoded and restrictive procedures prevailing within the bloc had handicapped economic development in the face of the economic and technical challenge from the Western world.

The Soviet, Polish, and Bulgarian leaders supported integration for economic and political reasons. Economically, they emphasized that rapid advancement of the socialist countries was possible only on the basis of industrial specialization and the foundation of a common market; politically, they argued, integration was a logical consequence of the Marxist-Leninist principle of "proletarian internationalism."

The Hungarians insisted that Comecon should be reformed by adopting some of the proven methods of the EEC, with due respect, of course, for the special features of Comecon. They believed that the abolition of quota and barter systems in trade among the Comecon members and the introduction of currency convertibility would be major reforms leading to the establishment of a thriving economic community of the socialist states.

The Romanians, however, categorically rejected integration within the Comecon framework, while arguing that mutual cooperation among the member states would lead to the economic advancement of each country. Romania's resistance to Soviet plans for integration remained firm, on the ground that integration not only curtailed national independence but also introduced Western monopoly relations under the guise of socialism.

The Czechoslovak and East German governments also were not enthusiastically supporting a policy of integration but for a different reason. Their two countries were the most industrialized in the bloc, and their ambition was to produce manufactured goods that could compete in world markets.

These objections resulted in the postponing once more of concrete discussion about integration, and in the continued compromise between the integrationists

Waving black flags, French students demonstrate at the Place de la Bastille in support of labour union wage demands during 24-hour strike in March 1969.

GAMMA—PIX FROM PUBLIX

and those states insisting on full individual rights of decision making. Nevertheless, the summit meeting decided to establish a Comecon Investment Bank; to increase capital contributions of member states to the International Bank for Economic Cooperation (IBEC) which started functioning on Jan. 1, 1964; and to coordinate long-term planning with the five-year programs taking effect from 1971.

Bulgaria. Measures ensuring autonomy for some industrial enterprises, first introduced on Jan. 1, 1967, were applied to all on Jan. 1, 1969. The Bulgarian system of planning, which was similar to that of the U.S.S.R., was justified ideologically in an article in the October 1968 issue of *Novo Vreme,* the monthly organ of the Bulgarian Communist Party. The article attempted to demonstrate that the economic reforms were in harmony with the Leninist principle of "democratic centralism," adding, however, that greater centralism suited Bulgaria better than some other socialist countries.

Hungary. On Jan. 1, 1969, the New Economic Mechanism (NEM) entered its second year. Elaborated by a special committee in which two Politburo members, Rezso Nyers and Bela Biszku, exercised major influence, the Hungarian model of economic planning was a blending of central control at the top with a considerable degree of liberalization at the level of the producing enterprises.

The NEM aroused fewer suspicions in Moscow than had the far-reaching reforms introduced in 1967 in Czechoslovakia under Ota Sik's influence. This was probably because Janos Kadar, first secretary of the Hungarian Communist Party, remembering the events of 1956, handled the situation in Hungary more realistically than had Alexander Dubcek in Czechoslovakia in 1968. Compared with similar reforms in other Eastern European socialist countries, East Germany excepted, the Hungarian economic reform was a large-scale undertaking.

Poland. Following the guidelines for the 1971–75 development plan, adopted in November 1968 by the fifth congress of the Polish United Workers' Party, a plenary session of its Central Committee was held in Warsaw on April 3–4. New methods of planning and investments were discussed. A cautious trend toward more flexible planning, fewer central ministerial directives, more authority for industrial amalgamations, and increased decision making by certain individual enterprises was endorsed.

Boleslaw Jaszczuk, a member of the Politburo and secretary of the Central Committee in charge of national economy, declared in his report that, in order to ensure a high rate of industrial growth, greater importance would be given to more rational management and accelerated technological progress. Furthermore, a change would be made in the structure of production toward a selective grouping into *kombinaty,* or amalgamates, of plants producing such industrial goods as machine tools, electrical and electronic equipment, and chemical products.

At the party's special conference held in Warsaw on May 7, Jozef Kulesza, chairman of the Planning Commission of the Council of Ministers, and Jozef Pajestka, his deputy, explained that the 1971–75 plan was being drafted by a new method. Individual enterprises would first prepare their own suggestions; then a national five-year plan would be assembled based on these findings.

East Germany. The West German Ministry for All-German Affairs published in the summer a report that acknowledged the success of the new East German system of economic planning and management. East German agriculture had recovered from the throes of collectivization and practically met the country's needs in foodstuffs. There was no difference in the cost of basic foods between West and East Germany. In proportion to the populations, the number of households with television sets was the same in both parts of Germany in 1968, but the number of East German families with refrigerators, washing machines, and vacuum cleaners was half that of West Germany.

Czechoslovakia. Hopes that Gustav Husak, new first secretary of the Czechoslovak Communist Party (*see* BIOGRAPHY), would manage to obtain from the U.S.S.R. a large loan in hard currency did not materialize. Jan Tabacek, the federal minister of foreign trade, said in July in an interview published by the Soviet magazine *Novoye Vremya* that Soviet-Czechoslovak trade would be worth $2.2 billion in each direction in 1969, and that during the 1971–75 five-year plan this amount would increase by one-third. Particularly rapid growth was expected in Soviet deliveries of machinery and equipment to Czechoslovakia, and this was to be achieved partly on credit. (*See Special Report.*) (K. SM.)

See also Development, Economic; Government Finance.

Economics

Economics experienced more than normal ferment in 1969. An increasing number of economists felt the need to become professionally involved in vital policy issues. Not that economists had ever been reticent to raise their voices—as Maurice Dobb of Cambridge once said, economists combine the scientific dignity of ethical neutrality with an undiminished capacity for passing judgment on practical affairs. At issue in 1969 was the philosophical and methodological question of whether ethical neutrality is either necessary or desirable. Is or should economics be a "value-free" discipline?

Kenneth Boulding of the University of Colorado, in his presidential address on "Economics as a Moral Science" to the American Economic Association, challenged the view that economics is and should be a value-free science (*American Economic Review,* March 1969). According to Boulding, economics is and must be a moral science in the sense that it involves statements about the rank order of preferences applied to more than one person.

Economists have often looked to the natural sciences for a model methodology. Boulding pointed out that, as the physical and biological sciences become more powerful and are able to change the world as well as describe it, they too are inevitably confronted with moral choices among alternatives. Biological scientists will really understand the evolutionary process only by engaging in it. In economics an ultimate test of the validity of a theory of unemployment, for example, is its ability to indicate what needs to be done to eliminate or reduce unemployment. Boulding asserted: "When knowledge changes the world . . . the concept of value-free science is absurd."

Boulding's criticism of traditional economics was symptomatic of widespread dissatisfaction. One expression of this was the organization by younger economists of the Union for Radical Political Economics, which had 1969 counterparts in most other social sciences. Opposition to the war in Vietnam and a demand for drastic domestic reforms provided the stimulus for these organizations, the members of which wanted to use their professional training to help create a better world.

The Union for Radical Political Economics held meetings at a rump session of the American Economic Association in Philadelphia in December 1968, but boycotted the regular meetings in Chicago. Although its membership was diverse, the dominant group was sympathetic with the New Left. This faction criticized capitalism for its failure to solve such problems as inflation, urban decay, congestion, pollution, and numerous other ills of contemporary society. Some called into question marginal (incremental) analysis as diverting attention from a systematic treatment of larger issues and tending to cast economists in the role of apologists for the status quo. There was a general dislike for the doctrine of consumer sovereignty, which holds that consumer preferences, no matter how bizarre, should be taken as given. These tastes, the young radicals said, are not given but are created by advertising and other techniques of corporate capitalism. The ideas of Karl Marx were viewed sympathetically by many, although Marx's economic analysis did not take them very far in their effort to rewrite the principles of economics.

Another stinging criticism of the "conventional wisdom" of economics came from E. J. Mishan of the London School of Economics and Political Science, one of the leading students of theoretical welfare economics. Continuing a line of analysis from previous writings, Mishan, in an article titled "Economic Priority: Growth or Welfare" (*Political Quarterly,* January 1969), contended that economic growth of the type taking place in the U.K., the U.S., and other modern industrial nations conflicts with social welfare.

Under private enterprise, according to Mishan, the market does not lead to maximum welfare because total costs and benefits are not measured by market prices. Large external diseconomies (social costs not included in private costs) accompany economic growth and lead to a deterioration of the physical environment. For example, automobiles pollute the air, clog city streets, and contribute to the destruction of natural beauty in the countryside. Mishan labeled the private automobile one of the great disasters of the human race.

Mishan characterized the U.S. economy as one in which increasing resources are pressing against limited wants, reversing the traditional economic principle that scarce resources are always insufficient to satisfy unlimited wants. Mishan's conclusions resembled those in J. K. Galbraith's *The Affluent Society,* but Mishan utilized more formal economic analysis and his outlook for the future was more pessimistic. Mishan did, however, believe that steps could be taken to make modern living more bearable. One of his proposals was a charter of amenity rights for the citizen.

A comprehensive view of the management of waste disposal was given by Robert U. Ayres and Allen V. Kneese in an article titled "Production, Consumption, and Externalities" (*American Economic Review,* June 1969). In maximizing their earnings, private businessmen discharge wastes into the atmosphere and into watercourses without cost to themselves. In economic analysis these situations are treated as external diseconomies peculiar to particular firms and industries; that is, they are treated in what economists call a particular equilibrium framework of the firm or industry. Ayres and Kneese argued that waste disposal is so general and so massive in modern society that it should be considered an integral part of the production and consumption process of the economy as a whole; that is, it should be placed within the framework of general equilibrium analysis.

Ayres and Kneese pointed out that the act of economic consumption does not destroy the elements that enter production. The weight of basic materials entering into production in the U.S. in 1965 was estimated at 2.5 billion tons, and the weight of the residuals going back into the environment after consumption was approximately the same. In less developed rural economies waste disposal was not a serious problem—manure and garbage, for example, were recycled into production or were accumulated on the private property of the producer—but in mass urban societies the external diseconomies become progressively more serious as population and the level of output increase. Ad hoc taxes and restrictions are not sufficient to obtain quality management of the environment. Central planning is also needed to provide measures for waste disposal. The authors expressed their general equilibrium model in mathematical form and considered the problems of empirically implementing the model. (*See* CITIES AND URBAN AFFAIRS: *Special Report.*)

In contrast to national income and product accounts, which measure the flow of goods and services through the marketplace, social indicators are concerned with external economies (education, research, health) and external diseconomies (pollution, congestion, noise). Solutions to most of these problems require collective action through governments. If social indicators were developed, they would provide information about national well-being in the several welfare areas, as well as the basis for deciding the direction in which to allocate scarce resources according to national priorities.

In October a committee of scientists sponsored by the National Academy of Sciences and the Social Science Research Council strongly endorsed the idea of an annual social report. The committee urged that the reports begin at once under private auspices financed with foundation and federal grants, and continue in that status until the social indicators could be established on a solid foundation. They recommended that by 1976 the report become a government document drawn up annually for the president by a Council of Social Advisers.

Inflation continued to be the most pressing issue of U.S. economic policy during 1969. Economic policy in the U.S. seemed to have advanced during the 1960s to a stage where high employment could be assured through maintaining aggregate demand by means of fiscal-monetary policy. The unsolved problem was how to prevent an unacceptable rate of price inflation in the face of continuous high-level employment. Economists did not doubt that inflation could be curtailed by rigorous monetary-fiscal restraints, but could inflation be curbed without precipitating a recession? The Nixon administration's Council of Economic Advisers adopted a policy of "gradualism" in curbing the boom and easing into a period of relative price stability.

Concern with inflation stimulated further examination of the so-called Phillips curve, which is a relation between rates of unemployment and rates of inflation (or rates of wage changes). As unemployment in the U.S. fell below 4% in the late 1960s, the rate of retail price inflation rose to politically unacceptable levels—above 5% annually in 1969. In a paper entitled "Improving the Labor Market Trade-Off Between Inflation and Unemployment" (*American Economic Review, Papers and Proceedings,* May 1969), Charles Holt of the University of Wisconsin examined the microeconomic basis of the Phillips curve, which he found in special characteristics of the labour market.

In the U.S. the turnover of labour is extremely high. Holt cited a figure of 30 million layoffs and quits per year in a total labour force of approximately 75 million. As a result, employers must recruit continually. When aggregate demand in the economy is rising, workers anticipate better wages elsewhere and search for higher paying positions, either while still working or after quitting their present jobs. Low-wage employers suffer from high quit rates and long vacancy durations and are under pressure to offer higher money wages or to accept workers of lower qualifications (an indirect form of wage increase). This process of quitting old jobs in order to take new ones generates an upward creep of money wages in the economy as a whole in times of rising aggregate demand. When unemployment is low, workers flowing through the labour market tend to expect and to receive higher wages; when unemployment is high and unemployment periods are long, workers tend to accept lower wages than they had hoped to get. The policy implications of Holt's analysis were to improve labour markets through better information, lower turnover rates, and manpower training, which would give a better match between job vacancies and the workers available to fill them.

The first Nobel Prize in Economics ("prize in economics to the memory of Alfred Nobel" was the official wording) was awarded in 1969. It went to Jan Tinbergen of the Netherlands School of Economics in Rotterdam and Ragnar Frisch of the University of Oslo (*see* BIOGRAPHY), who were cited "for having developed and applied dynamic models for the analysis of economic processes." Both had pioneered in econometrics and mathematical economics and applied powerful analytical tools to economic planning in less developed as well as developed countries. Frisch's special work was in measuring marginal utility, mathematical statistics, mathematical programming, and the theory of production. He was credited with coining the word "econometrics." Tinbergen applied dynamic analysis to business cycles in the U.S. and the U.K. and developed the first large-scale econometric model while working with the League of Nations during the 1930s. (D. D.)

See also Economy, World; Government Finance; Income, National; Merchandising; Money and Banking; Payments and Reserves, International; Trade, International.

Economy, World

The longest business boom ever recorded in the United States and the ebullient, although shorter, booms in Western Europe, Japan, and Canada led to still further increases in output, employment, and incomes in 1969. Rising production in the industrial parts of the world, in turn, provided a strong stimulus to output in countries producing primary commodities, with prices of base metals and rubber at record heights. The result was an unusually large 13% expansion of world trade.

If rapid expansion of national production and of world trade were the only criteria of an efficient and sustainable economic performance, the 1969 record would, indeed, have to be regarded as truly gratifying. This record was, however, marred by serious imbalances, which manifested themselves, domestically, in strong price-cost pressures and, internationally, in severe disturbances in the balances of payments of several of the major nations and in recurrent crises in the foreign exchange markets. (*See* PAYMENTS AND RESERVES, INTERNATIONAL.)

The world's economic performance in 1969 represented the prolongation of the upsurge in economic activity during 1968—an upsurge that was itself a turn-around from the business slowdown in much of the industrial world from mid-1966 through mid-1967. The volume of combined output of the main industrial countries—gross national products (GNP's) in real terms, *i.e.,* after correction for price increases—grew in 1969 by about 5% year on year, against nearly 6% in 1968, according to the Organization for Economic Cooperation and Development (OECD). (*See* Table I.) The rapidity of expansion in world output beginning with 1968 stemmed in large degree from the impetus originating in the U.S., which produces almost half of the world's output of goods and services.

Output increased substantially during 1969 in all industrial countries with the principal exception of the United Kingdom (Table I and Chart 1). Even though Japan did not duplicate its 15% performance of 1968, it topped the world league table of GNP increases. In many countries, 1969 was a year of greater growth than 1968; in some, growth was faster than the average during the past decade. In the course of the year, however, there were signs of a slowdown in output in the U.S. During the first nine months of 1969, "real" GNP in the U.S. grew at an annual rate of only 3.2%, compared with 4.8% during the same period a year earlier.

Industrial production turned downward in the U.S.

Table I. Growth of Real Output in Major Industrial Countries

Country	Annual percent changes in real gross domestic product 1958–67	1968	1969
Japan*	10.7	14.2	12.5
France	5.1	4.2	8.25
Germany, West*	4.8	7.0	7.75
Italy	5.6	5.4	6.0
Canada*	4.7	4.7	5.0
United States*	4.6	4.9	2.75
United Kingdom	3.3	3.6	2.0
Major countries	5.2	5.8	4.75
Denmark	5.0	3.6	7.0
Belgium	4.4	4.0	6.0
Austria	4.3	4.1	5.5
Netherlands	5.0	6.2	5.0
Switzerland	4.9	4.0	4.5
Norway	4.8	3.8	4.5
Sweden	4.5	3.3	4.5
Other industrial countries†	4.7	4.1	5.25
Other OECD countries‡	5.8	5.1	7.5
European OECD countries	4.8	5.0	6.0
All OECD countries	5.2	5.7	5.0

Note: Arranged in descending order of growth of output within each group of countries in 1969.

*As measured by percentage changes in real gross national product (GNP). Both GNP and gross domestic product measure the market value of product attributable to consumption expenditures, gross domestic capital formation (public and private), and net exports of goods and services; GNP also includes net investment income received from abroad.

†Including Finland, Iceland, Ireland, and Luxembourg in addition to the countries listed.

‡Including Greece, Portugal, Spain, and Turkey.

Source: Adapted from OECD, *Economic Outlook* (December 1969).

during the third quarter; it flattened out in the U.K., West Germany, and France, and fell in Italy because of strikes. For the year as a whole, however, industrial output reached an all-time record (Chart 2). Steel experienced an extraordinary boom.

Output expanded because demand, which had been rising since mid-1967 and by 1968 had already been very strong, grew still further—reaching by mid-1969 clearly excessive and inflationary proportions. Italy was a major exception. In many countries, much of the further stimulus to demand in 1969 came from industrial investment. Prominent among the reasons for strong capital expenditures was the rise in unit labour costs and the widespread belief that the rise would persist; but the need to increase capacity for the years ahead was also an essential factor. Private consumption remained strong everywhere. This was not surprising in view of rising employment, higher incomes, and a weakened propensity to save. In the U.S. and the U.K., however, the rate of increase in private consumption slowed down noticeably. It remained stationary, on the whole, in Canada and Japan. It increased in France, West Germany, and Italy. (*See* Table II.)

Public consumption showed a sizable decline in the U.S., remained stationary in the U.K., France, Italy, and Japan, and rose in West Germany and Canada (Table II). In many countries, including the U.K., France, and the U.S., the overall budgetary position was stronger in 1969 than only a year or two previously; but this was the result partly of the growth of tax receipts that followed the rise in output and incomes accompanied by rising prices, and partly of further increases in taxation—increases that, in turn, stimulated wage increases and, hence, consumption. The arms race—not only the race between the U.S. and the U.S.S.R., but the soaring outlays on armaments practically everywhere—was a critical facet in the demands on government budgets.

In the European Common Market countries, as well as in the U.K. and, of course, Japan, much of the expansionary stimulus also came from exports, particularly to the U.S. In West Germany, the business recovery after the 1967 slowdown was achieved largely through exports, which led to a substantial trade surplus.

In the U.S., demand pressures showed signs of easing during the second half of 1969. In Canada, with a dip in output, the margin of unused resources increased. A measure of slack also developed in the U.K. In continental Europe, however, demand pressures increased. The degree of capacity utilization reached an all-time peak in West Germany and the highest level for ten years in France. In Italy, capacity utilization rose somewhat but was still below that of 1963–64; because of this appreciable slack, Italy's situation—characterized also by sizable unemployment—remained different from the situations of other countries.

Prices and Costs. Against the background of strong demand practically everywhere, prices and costs experienced unusually large increases in 1969. The general price level—as measured, in Table III, by the so-called deflators of gross national product—rose at an exceptionally rapid rate in the U.S. France had a third year of sizable price increases; West Germany fared best. Consumer prices showed even greater increases than general price levels. In the U.S., the rise between November 1968 and November 1969 reached 5.8%—in sharp contrast with many years of reasonable stability, which was the envy of the world (Chart 3). In continental Europe, where a lessening of pressure on demand in 1967 was accompanied by an easing of pressure on prices, consumer price increases accelerated. In part, however, the rise was the consequence of the increases in consumer taxes, as in the U.K. and France, and of the changeover to the value-added tax, as in the Netherlands.

Unit labour costs in industry benefited in most countries from the upswing in output and rose distinctly less than consumer prices. The U.S. was an exception; with the scope for cyclical gains in productivity largely exhausted, unit labour costs rose considerably more in the U.S. than in other major industrial countries except France.

CHART 1.

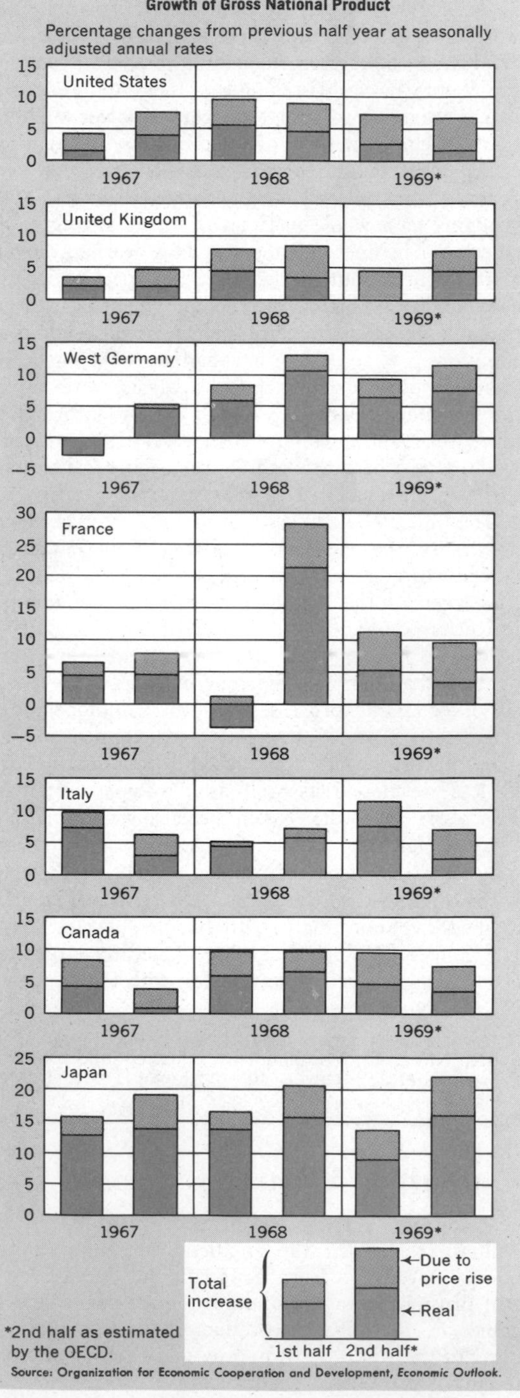

Export prices of manufactures charged by U.S. competitors increased by much less than those of U.S. manufacturers. The British and French competitive position was eased as a result of the devaluations in 1967 and 1969, respectively; and West Germany's position was rendered less competitive by the upvaluation of the mark. In France, West Germany, and the Netherlands, which have the value-added tax system, exports are completely exempted from tax; in many other countries, indirect taxes are refunded at least partly. Inflation, combined with the absence of tax relief for U.S. exporters, thus places U.S. exports at a disadvantage.

Export prices of manufactures invariably rose less than domestic prices. As a result, imported goods became increasingly competitive with domestic goods. Not unnaturally, countries that experienced a particularly buoyant demand provided rapidly rising export outlets to others.

Value of Money. The shrinkage in the value of money accelerated in 1969 almost everywhere (Table IV). The U.S. dollar slipped badly. In the 12 months ended November 1969, it lost 5.5% of its buying power, compared with cuts of 4% in 1968 and 2.7% in 1967. At the 5.5% depreciation rate, the dollar would lose half of its purchasing power in 12 years.

Among Western European countries, the rate of money depreciation accelerated markedly for France, the Netherlands, and Portugal. The loss of domestic purchasing power of the French franc rose from 4.4% in 1968 to 5.8% in 1969. The British pound lost buying power at a rate of 4.9%, compared with 4.5% a year earlier. The West German mark, which for three years in a row had put on one of the best performances, began to depreciate once again, although moderately. Nevertheless, with a 2.7% loss of its buying power in the 12 months ended October 1969, the mark fared better in terms of domestic value than the currency of any industrial country except Switzerland. For Italy, the loss of the buying power of the lira amounted in 1969 to 3.4% from the exceptionally low figure of 1.4% in 1968.

Only a few countries showed a rate of currency shrinkage in 1969 smaller than in 1968; prominent among these were Denmark, Finland, Norway, Spain, and, outside of Europe, Peru and Indonesia. On the other hand, the most pronounced acceleration of the rate of money depreciation occurred in Colombia and Mexico in Latin America, and India and Taiwan in Asia. Chile ranked as the most inflation-prone country.

Inflation exacted its toll in the rise in interest rates, which moved to historic highs (*see* MONEY AND BANKING). In the long-run perspective, interest rates were also pushed up by nonmonetary factors—the growth of population and the quickening pace of technological progress, for instance. But in recent years these growing demands for capital were further stimulated by the bullishness of inflationary spending by both businesses and consumers; and these demands were, in turn, speeded up by attempts to buy before prices and costs rose still further. The resulting pressures on available funds inexorably exerted an upward push on interest rates.

Furthermore, and not unnaturally, savers wanted higher and higher interest rates to compensate for the loss of the buying power of money. With the rise in interest rates, long-term bonds greatly depreciated in value. The market value of the U.S. Treasury 4¼s of 1992/87, issued only seven years before at the highest rate permissible under the legal ceiling applicable to U.S. government long-term bonds, had dropped by the end of December 1969 by about 30%. After allowing for the loss of the purchasing power of the dollar, the real loss suffered by anyone who bought the bonds when they were issued was somewhat over 40%. British Treasury 2½s redeemable after 1975 traded in late December at less than 30 and had, in real terms, only 12% of the value at which they were issued in 1946. The sharp rise in interest rates throughout the world appeared, therefore, much less impressive if allowance was made for the depreciation of money.

Mistrust springing from a sense of the inevitability of further inflation was evidenced by the decline in saving habits—a serious development, since there cannot be economic growth without capital. It was dramatized by the lack of esteem for government bonds and other fixed-interest securities and by the widespread belief that only real estate, stocks, paintings, antiques, etc., could afford protection against the depreciation of money.

Combating Inflation. To combat inflationary pressures, most nations had recourse to monetary and fiscal restraints, as reviewed in other articles of the *Book of the Year*. Delays in taking remedial measures to hold down excessive demand actually intensified

Table II. Growth of Gross National Products and Balances on Current Account in Major Industrial Countries

Country		Real growth rates (Change from previous year) Private consumption	Public consumption	Fixed Investment	GNP*	Current account of balance of payments† ($000,000)
Japan	1967	9.6%	5.5%	17.1%	12.9%	−0.19
	1968	9.4	6.9	22.9	14.2	1.05
	1969	9.0	6.25	19.0	12.5	2.20
France	1967	4.3	6.0	6.0	4.5	0.24
	1968	4.5	4.2	5.6	4.2	−0.86
	1969	7.0	5.0	9.5	8.25	−1.30
Germany, West	1967	0.6	3.3	−7.3	0.0	2.46
	1968	3.6	0.1	7.8	7.0	2.84
	1969	7.0	4.0	15.0	7.75	1.50
Italy	1967	7.2	2.8	10.2	6.5	1.60
	1968	4.3	4.1	7.4	5.4	2.64
	1969	6.0	3.5	10.0	6.0	2.45
Canada	1967	4.8	4.7‡	−1.0§	3.1	−0.50
	1968	4.5	1.1‡	−1.8§	4.7	−0.09
	1969	5.0	3.5‡	5.25§	5.0	−0.65
United States	1967	3.0	11.2‡	−1.4§	2.4	2.18
	1968	5.2	6.0‡	5.5§	4.9	−0.28
	1969	3.0	1.0‡	5.25§	2.75	−0.60
United Kingdom	1967	1.8	4.7	6.8	1.8	−1.03
	1968	2.5	0.5	3.5	3.5	−0.72
	1969	0.5	0.0	0.5	2.0	0.70

Note: Arranged in descending order of growth of GNP in 1969.
*Gross domestic product (GDP) for France, Italy, and the U.K.
†Balance on goods and services plus net transfers.
‡Includes public expenditure for fixed investment.
§Gross private domestic investment.
Source: Adapted from OECD, *Economic Outlook* (July and December 1969).

Table III. The Price Rise in Major Industrial Countries

Country	In percent Annual changes in the GNP deflator* 1958–67	1958–68 Smallest annual rise	1958–68 Largest annual rise	1968	1969
France	3.8	2.5	6.4	5.0	6.5
Japan	4.4	2.6	5.9	4.0	5.0
United States	1.8	1.2	4.0	4.0	4.75
Canada	2.5	0.7	4.5	3.6	4.5
United Kingdom	3.0	1.3	4.9	3.7	4.25
Italy	3.8	−0.5	8.7	1.5	3.25
Germany, West	2.9	0.7	4.3	2.2	3.0
All OECD countries	2.5	2.0	3.8	3.8	4.75

Note: Arranged in descending order of price rises in 1969.
*GNP deflator measures the extent to which changes in gross national product are due to price rises rather than changes in real output.
Source: Adapted from OECD, *Economic Outlook* (December 1969).

inflationary pressures in the U.S. as well as in other countries and were the main reason for the slowness with which most of the economies responded to monetary and fiscal restraints. By year end, however, signs of leveling off became gradually visible in the U.S. In other industrial countries, there was no evidence of a slowdown other than that stemming from constraints on capacity in West Germany and France; but most countries maintained restrictive policies into 1970. If expectations were confirmed that all major industrial nations other than Japan were, in early 1970, on the threshold of seeing results from their disinflationary efforts, some general reduction in rates of economic growth would take place throughout much of the world. Such a development must be viewed as a correction for the past rates of expansion that had become clearly unsustainable and had, of necessity, to be reduced.

There was little sign as 1969 drew to a close of a slowing down of price and wage inflation, however. The process was slow for two reasons. First, demand pressures would calm down only with the passage of time; and second, it would take time for the reduced demand pressures to moderate rises in prices and costs. As demand pressures were reduced, the quickening of cost push became a distinct problem—one that was aggravated by the slowdown in the volume of output, which pushed up unit costs even more. The inflation of the "demand-pull" variety, which is relatively favourable to profits, threatened to be replaced by one of the "cost-push" variety in which rising wages, wage demand, and other costs push against profit margins.

What mattered was that the processes of disinflation be orderly so that they would not cloud business horizons, damage world trade, and, hence, the output and incomes of people everywhere. One danger was that of a cumulative downturn developing unexpectedly as a result of an abrupt downward shift in business confidence in an environment of persistent wage cost-push and a seemingly intractable profit squeeze.

What also mattered was that, once the first round had been won against inflation, the world economy—beset by strong cost-push forces—should not relapse into a new inflationary posture. For the monetary nature of the crisis was only skin-deep. Fundamentally, the crisis was one of modern society—political and social in its very nature. It stemmed from persistent efforts of people and governments everywhere to consume, invest, or otherwise use more goods and services than their national economies were capable of producing.

National Economies. *United States.* For 1969 as a whole, the GNP of the U.S. was officially estimated at $932 billion—7.75% more than in 1968. Of this advance, however, price increases accounted for as much as 4.75%—the worst inflation since 1951. The "real" increase in GNP in 1969 was thus a mere 3%, as against 5% in 1968. The year's performance was the third poorest of the 1960s, better than only 1961 and 1967. At year end, real growth in the economy practically stopped. The pace of price increases began to lose momentum but remained uncomfortably large.

The inflation in 1969 stemmed directly from the sudden and very large expansion in aggregate demand that, in an economy approaching virtually full employment, accompanied the buildup of the military conflict in Vietnam after mid-1965, the launching of new social programs, and the failure to adopt prompt and adequate fiscal and monetary steps to hold down this forced expansion. It is true that, to curb the excessive demand brought about by the large budget deficit itself, taxes were increased in mid-1968; but this belated action was offset by an outburst of personal consumption and private investment spending. These pressures of private demand originated, at least partly, in the seemingly tenacious and deeply imbedded inflationary psychology and were facilitated by a premature easing of monetary restraint. By December 1968, the Federal Reserve Board reapplied monetary restraint to dampen the boom.

The new administration, installed in January 1969, conducted the battle against inflation on a wider front. It supported the monetary restraint and tightened fiscal restraint through extension of the 10% income tax surcharge from July through December 1969, which Congress approved in mid-August, and through elimination of the tax credit on new investment outlays, which Congress passed in December retroactive

Table IV. Depreciation of Money

Country	Indexes of value of money 1958=100		Annual rates of depreciation (percent)		
	1963	1968	'58–'68*	'67–'68	'68–'69†
Guatemala	100	98	0.2	1.9	−2.7
Bolivia	66	48	7.1	4.9	0.7
El Salvador	102	97	0.3	2.5	1.1
Finland	86	62	4.7	7.7	1.4
Venezuela	95	92	0.9	1.0	1.5
Honduras	95	83	1.9	2.2	1.6
South Africa	93	80	2.2	1.8	2.1
Israel	78	61	4.9	2.1	2.2
Luxembourg	95	82	2.0	2.5	2.3
Switzerland	90	76	2.7	2.3	2.4
Austria	87	73	3.0	2.7	2.4
Greece	92	83	1.9	0.4	2.5
Spain	78	54	5.9	4.7	2.6
Germany, West	90	80	2.2	1.6	2.7
Sweden	87	70	3.5	1.9	2.7
Norway	88	72	3.3	3.4	2.8
Australia	92	79	2.2	2.6	2.9
Iran	79	73	3.1	0.7	3.1
Italy	86	72	3.2	1.4	3.4
Peru	68	37	9.6	16.2	3.4
Denmark	82	60	4.9	7.1	3.6
Thailand	101	89	1.2	2.2	3.6
Belgium	94	79	2.3	2.7	3.8
Philippines	86	68	3.8	−0.1	3.8
Turkey	65	47	7.3	5.6	3.8
Morocco	83	79	2.3	0.5	3.8
Canada	94	81	2.2	3.9	4.2
United Kingdom	90	74	2.9	4.5	4.9
New Zealand	90	74	3.0	4.1	4.9
Ecuador	87	72	3.3	4.7	4.9
Pakistan	94	74	2.9	0.2	4.9
Japan	79	62	4.7	5.1	5.3
United States	94	83	1.9	4.0	5.5
Mexico	90	77	2.5	2.2	5.7
France	80	69	3.8	4.4	5.8
Netherlands	90	72	3.2	3.6	6.7
Ireland	91	73	3.1	4.6	7.7
Argentina	20	7	23.8	13.9	7.7
Jamaica	85	75	2.8	3.7	8.0
Yugoslavia	71	34	10.2	6.2	8.5
Portugal	90	72	3.3	5.7	9.7
Taiwan	68	60	5.0	7.3	10.1
India	87	54	5.9	3.1	10.1
Korea	64	32	10.8	9.7	10.4
Colombia	61	37	9.6	5.5	12.2
Indonesia	8	‡	58.9	55.6	12.7
Brazil	15	2	32.1	19.5	19.6
South Vietnam	84	23	13.5	22.0	19.7
Iceland	74	44	7.8	12.0	20.4
Chile	37	11	20.1	21.0	22.5

Note: Depreciation of money is measured by rates of decline in the domestic purchasing power of national currencies (as computed from reciprocals of official cost-of-living or consumer price indexes), not by rates of price inflation. For example, a rate of inflation of 100% is equivalent to a 50% rate of depreciation of buying power of money.
*Compounded annually.
†Latest 12-month period available.
‡Less than one.
Source: First National City Bank, New York, N.Y.

to April. It also endeavoured—firmly, but not quite successfully—to hold down federal expenditures.

In early 1969, the watchword was gradualism—stopping the overheating of the economy quietly and painlessly through a slowdown in the growth in money supply and through a budgetary surplus. The principal purpose of this gradualism was, of course, to spare the economy the shocks of mass bankruptcies and unemployment. While this objective remained valid, the policy of gradualism—or, perhaps, only the word—fell gradually from grace. This was evidenced by the virtual stoppage in the growth of money supply during the second half of 1969, though offset, in part, by increased velocity of money. The stoppage was preceded by a wide swing in the federal budget from a large deficit to a sizable surplus.

The shortcomings of gradualism were plainly visible from the persistence of inflationary expectations due, in good part, to the widespread belief that any business recession would be shallow and short-lived if only because fighting inflation all the way was not regarded as feasible politically. Attitudes like these were, of course, matters of concern to the administration and to the Federal Reserve, which, in the second half of the year, categorically reaffirmed their determination to stop inflation. The obvious stake was to safeguard the dollar which, as already noted, was depreciating at a rate that would have halved its buying power in only 12 years, and to restore the basis for a more nearly balanced, efficient, and genuinely productive growth of the U.S. economy. But political considerations also weighed in the balance—the resentment against inflation among the forgotten middle class citizens who, in the view of political analysts, constituted the hard core of Pres. Richard M. Nixon's support in 1968.

By year end, the pattern of the business slowdown had become visible. Retail sales were flat; auto manufacturers cut down production schedules at an unusually early stage; housing starts declined; industrial production trended downward from midyear after a 5% rise in the preceding 12 months; total after-tax corporate profits were being squeezed; personal income growth slowed; and stock market prices were down. The composite of leading business indicators was flat; in the past it had behaved in similar fashion prior to declines in the pace of economic growth.

In contrast to these signs of a slowdown, plant-and-equipment spending plans of businesses for 1970 showed a further rise, in part because of expected cost increases. Whether businesses would actually carry out investment plans on such a scale, however, remained doubtful. The stagnant retail trade, itself a sign of a falling off in final demand, augured that added capacity, at a time of rapid technological obsolescence, might prove uneconomic, despite the haste to beat higher costs—especially if it became less probable that the higher costs would materialize. Faced with a slippage in profits, rising wage costs, lagging productivity gains, and a possibility of a slowdown in the economy, businesses were expected to review their investment outlays. Cutting productive investment meant less future consumption, housing, and services and, consequently, future pain and turbulence.

Was the United States curbing real growth before it might lick inflation? There was no sure answer to this momentous question. For the ability to forecast and manage a complex economy is limited. A poet—known among economists as Sir Alec Cairncross, who was from 1964 to 1968 head of Her Majesty's Government Economic Service—expressed, in a few verses that deserve to be recorded here for eternity, the predicaments of economic forecasters endeavouring to help economic policy makers:

KEYSTONE

Buyers, eager to convert their francs into stocks, crowd the floor of the Paris Stock Exchange on Aug. 11, 1969, during the first session after government announced the franc's devaluation.

A trend is a trend is a trend
But the question is, will it bend?
Will it alter its course
Through some unforeseen force
And come to a premature end?

The administration and the Federal Reserve cannot, through fine tuning, keep the economy on a straight and narrow path. The best that can be hoped for is that, with common sense and determination on the part of the policy makers, the economy will effect a transition to a socially acceptable rate of price-wage increases without the shocks that slow down economic growth abruptly and, given the potential of the economy, excessively. For a low growth rate means less employment. But a rise in unemployment is no evidence of the success of efforts to contain inflation. It is part of an unwanted cost—a cost that must be alleviated in all ways that help reduce human hardships and, in the longer run, through renewed expansion as well as, with regard to structural unemployment, through better education and training and a more effective matching of those who are unemployed with available jobs.

At the close of 1969, the hope was that, as inflation diminished, real growth would be resumed. While adjustment would be far from painless, it would be manageable. The critical question was whether such an adjustment would cure inflation. Would the policy makers shift from combating inflation to combating recession as soon as first signs of a recession became visible, as in 1966? (A recession is technically defined as two successive quarters of declining real GNP.)

The deep-seated concern that inflation may remain a way of life—even though it is recognized that inflation is corroding the very fabric of the U.S.—rested on day-to-day observation of the hard facts of political, social, and economic life. The first of these was the persistence of the wage spiral—despite the easing pressure of demand that made it more and more difficult for price increases to stick and thus brought about a profit squeeze. Wages and benefits were negotiated in late 1969 for annual increases giving people not only productivity gains but also compensation for past and future inflation. Comprehensive wage-price controls were, as was universally recognized, impossible for political as well as practical reasons. But the administration was urged to appeal to the business community and to labour to maintain prices, wages, and dividends unchanged temporarily until the inflationary psychosis might begin to spend itself and people once again believed that prices could be reasonably stable and interest rates could settle down to more tolerable levels. Only a few years earlier, the Johnson administration had quietly buried price-wage "guidelines" because they had proved unworkable.

The second hard fact of life that aroused concern was the pressure and temptation to ease fiscal restraints. At year end, Congress passed—and the president signed—a tax bill that reduced the tax surcharge to 5% for the first half of the calendar year 1970 and provided tax relief, beginning with the second half, not only by eliminating the surcharge but in many other ways as well. Much of the tax relief was of the sort to encourage consumption, to the detriment of the savings and investment on which economic growth depends.

Tax relief does not necessarily create a deficit in the federal budget since tax receipts rise with the growth of national income. For this to be true presupposes, however, that increases in government expenditures are held down. This is an unrealistic expectation. Along with tax relief, Congress in late 1969 raised social security benefits more liberally than was justified to offset the consequences of past inflation. Substantial increases in government spending are well nigh inevitable to help deal with the problems of the slums, racial strife, schools, drug addiction, teen-age unemployment, medical care, inadequate transportation, traffic congestion, air and water pollution, and unsafe streets.

Despite President Nixon's determination to keep the federal budget for the fiscal year 1970–71 in balance, concern remained over the possibility of slippage into deficit, which would provide new stimulus to the economy even before inflation had been brought under control. Fiscal policy thus threatened once again to assume a more expansive posture—a turnaround that would have a direct impact on spending, infringe on capital markets whose capacity is limited, and add, therefore, to the burden of monetary policy.

The third reason for concern at year end was that businessmen and consumers, fed up to the teeth with tight money, had become disillusioned and impatient with the slow progress of disinflation. Understandably, inflation-conscious, but recession-worried, participants in the economic process looked for easier money.

The slowing pains visible in the economy at year end were almost universally diagnosed as calling for a softening in the posture of severe monetary restrictiveness. The cure appeared difficult and delicate. Despite an extraordinary revival of monetary research, the philosopher's stone that would enable the policy makers to direct and stabilize the economy was not discovered. Besides, the inflation and overheating of 1969 were not minor deviations from the economy's straightforward path that a brief and simple adjustment would correct. In this regard, the experience of the winter of 1966–67—in circumstances that were broadly similar to those of 1969–70—was uppermost in people's minds. Three years earlier the shift from restraint to reexpansion had come too soon and was much too strong and, because of its overstimulative effect on output and incomes, the disinflationary efforts were actually wasted. A drop in GNP for a short time would not cure inflation.

There are thus several sides to the elephant of the U.S. economy. Money matters; but so do wages and productivity, and federal taxes, spending, and borrowing. As far ahead as could be seen at year end, the U.S. economy was being kept going by the forces of demand, both in the private and public sector, that had remained strong. The wage spiral continued unabated. Looking beyond 1970, the economy was faced with an excess, not a deficiency, of demand, and with a seemingly intractable wage-cost push. The practical choice was not one between austerity and freewheeling, but between a moderate slowdown in 1970 or a sharp downturn later on, with unpredictable economic, social, and political consequences.

Canada. The remaining part of this section sketches economic trends, developments, and policies in Canada and the United Kingdom. References to other industrial countries are made elsewhere in the *Book of the Year.* The economic conditions and problems in less developed nations are reviewed under DEVELOPMENT, ECONOMIC.

In Canada, whose economic performance, not too surprisingly, is directly influenced by the U.S., the signs of the deceleration in the real rate of U.S. growth became increasingly apparent. It is true that, as a result of a strong upturn in GNP in the last quarter of 1968 and the first quarter of 1969, the year-to-year increase was still 5%; but the second quarter, in fact, saw a slight fall and, during the remainder of the year, expansion was modest. Industrial production trended downward.

Like the U.S., Canada had an income tax surcharge for more than a year; it also had an additional levy on income—the Social Development Tax—imposed at the beginning of 1969. But, to pay the new taxes, people tended to reduce their rate of saving. The government called for a slower growth in federal spending. Monetary policy was tightened markedly and the money supply, which had increased at an 8% annual rate during the first half of 1969, fell somewhat thereafter.

While prices did not rise as much as in the U.S., wage costs experienced a bigger increase. Unlike in the U.S., efforts were made in Canada to develop an incomes policy. A new Prices and Incomes Commission sought to secure agreement among business, labour, and the professions on a voluntary program of income restraint; the attitude of labour seemed, however, averse to the introduction of guidelines or voluntary restraints on wage increases. In the event that other efforts failed, the government announced that it was considering further tax and tariff measures to combat inflation.

United Kingdom. In the United Kingdom, the economy during 1969 expanded by only 2%; but its balance of payments did well. The long sequence of fiscal and monetary restraints thus brought the growth of domestic demand under better control; only export demand was buoyant. The turnaround was achieved without exacting a socially unacceptable price since unemployment remained roughly stable at 2.6% of the labour force.

When by the end of 1968, a full year after the sterling devaluation, the balance of payments failed to improve, Britain had little choice but to face the practical necessity of slowing down the rate of domestic spending to develop what is known as "a basic" balance of payments surplus (*i.e.,* a surplus on current account and long-term capital transactions), needed to repay indebtedness incurred to finance previous "basic" deficits. To produce the surplus, the government in March 1968 called for a growth in output by 4% and for restrictive fiscal, monetary, and incomes policies to reinforce the effects of the devaluation by cutting back consumption.

By the end of 1968, however, the external basic balance was still in deficit for several reasons, above all because the greater domestic consumption pulled in more imports.

Of necessity, therefore, the government's strategy was revised in late 1968 and early 1969. To hold down consumption, consumer credit was tightened still further and taxes on spending were again raised; to reduce domestic investment, special tax advantages were allowed to lapse and corporate taxes were increased. The cost of imports was raised by ½% as importers were required to make, with the government, six-month interest-free deposits equal to 50% of the value of certain categories of imports.

More generally, the U.K. was committed to the International Monetary Fund—as laid down in May 1969 for the fiscal year ended March 1970—to contain within prescribed limits domestic credit expansion, including the government's own borrowings and foreign lending to the public sector. The containment of government expenditures and the rise in tax receipts permitted, for the first time in recent years, a sizable reduction in government debt, including that held by banks. This turnaround, by lessening the need for the Bank of England to support government bond prices, made possible a restrictive monetary policy relying more on market forces and less on direct credit controls. Besides, tax exemptions granted on capital gains from the sale of government bonds encouraged government bond ownership by nonbank investors.

At long last, the strategy worked. The growth in the economy was slowed down to a more nearly sustainable rate. Personal consumption and investment increased but moderately. Imports were held down and, with a rise in exports, a current account surplus emerged in the second half of 1969.

Incomes policy, moribund for years, was pronounced dead. But its formal demise strengthened, if anything, the awareness that real power affecting the value of the pound very importantly rests in the processes of collective bargaining that determine wages and wage costs.

Looking into 1970, the continuance of Britain's economic miracle appeared to be dependent on three factors: world trade, the expansion of which, at the unusually high rate of 13%, had benefited British exports in 1969; a substantial advance in industrial investment; and a moderation in tax relief and in monetary expansion—moves that, in view of the measure of slack in the economy, the stronger balance of payments, and the approaching parliamentary elections, appeared quite likely.

The Shortage of Capital on the Threshold of the 1970s. Economic growth and prosperity throughout the world during the 1960s exceeded the expectations held by even the greatest optimists. Even in India and Pakistan, two nations among the many haunted by the ghost of Malthus, food output rose with the introduction of high-yielding strains of grains and other technological improvements. In the industrialized world, more and more people enjoyed rising standards of living and leisure. These were remarkable accomplishments—even without worshiping the god of economic growth.

The rub was that masses of people everywhere—in the U.S. and other industrial countries, as well as in the less developed parts of the world—wanted even more goods and services. The world had embarked upon the revolution of rising expectations. The pattern was, however, not at all new since Tocqueville described it more than a century ago: nothing stimulates unrest as much as reform; the removal of some grievances sharpens keenly the awareness of those grievances still remaining.

The shortage of resources was aggravated by political and military insecurity in an unsettled world. The disengagement from Vietnam would not put an end to strains and drains on the U.S. as a de-

CHART 2.

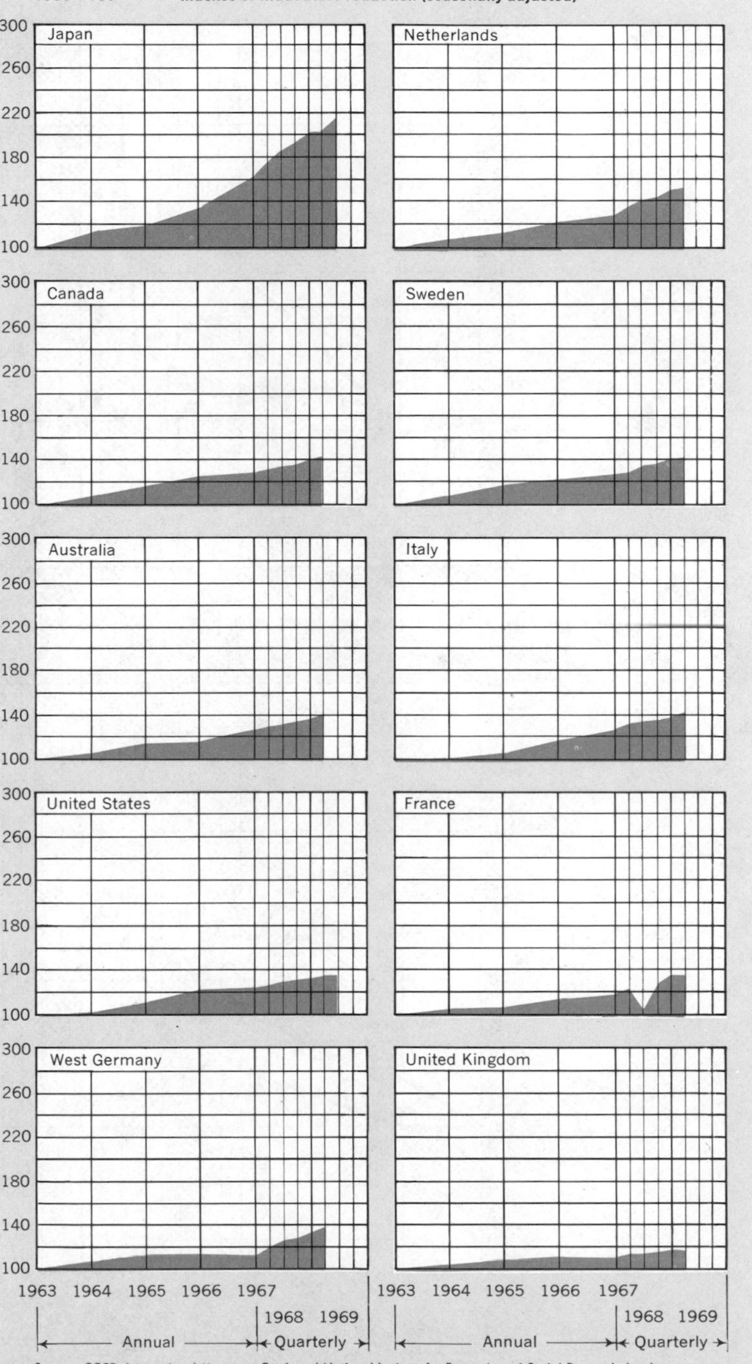

Sources: OECD, International Monetary Fund, and National Institute for Economic and Social Research, London.

pendable power engaged, because of its political and economic weight, in the maintenance of world peace. The U.S. and the U.S.S.R. embarked in November 1969 upon strategic arms limitation talks (SALT); but this contact was to be concerned not with a reduction in the present arms race but with the prevention of another intensification of a race the nature of which was still veiled in the mists of the future. While there was a stalemate between the two superpowers, open rivalry was the case among smaller countries in various parts of the world.

To meet the pressures of consumers and governments for more goods and services, productive capital was needed in ever growing amounts. The need to exploit new scientific discoveries and, far more important quantitatively, to diffuse the application of existing technology throughout the world economy was overwhelming.

CHART 3.

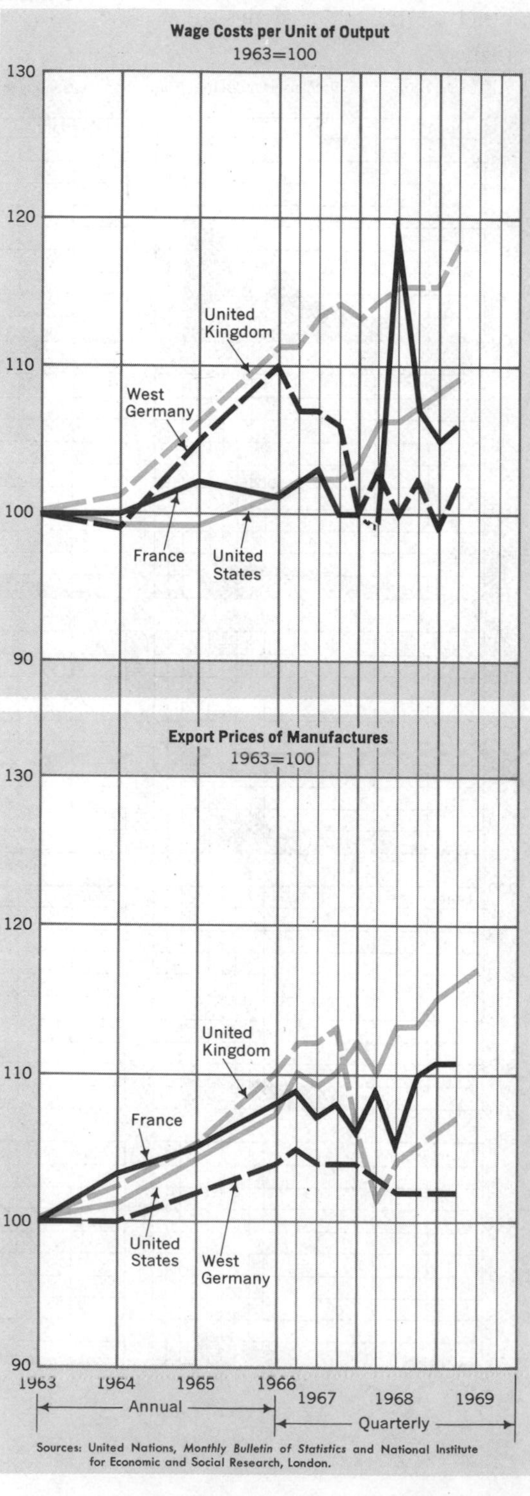

Sources: United Nations, *Monthly Bulletin of Statistics* and National Institute for Economic and Social Research, London.

But demands for capital far outstripped supplies, even in economically advanced countries. For this reason, and also because of disillusionment in the advanced countries about the effectiveness with which scarce capital was being used in some of the less developed countries, flows of development assistance to the poorer nations were (in real if not in monetary terms) well below the amounts hoped for at the beginning of the United Nations Development Decade. On the eve of the 1970s, improved trade opportunities and international investment of multinational corporations thus appeared more powerful forces in promoting economic development than government aid as it had developed over the past 15 years.

For these reasons—not to mention other factors such as the population explosion or the pollution of the planet—the most critical economic problem of the 1970s will be the worldwide shortage of capital. Encouragingly, the failures and mistakes of the past contain the seeds of hope that nations will learn from them. (M. A. K.)

See also Advertising; Agriculture; Economics; Employment, Wages, and Hours; Housing; Income, National; Industrial Review; Labour Unions; Merchandising; Prices; Profits; Stock Exchanges; Trade, International; United States; also articles on various industries.

Ecuador

A republic on the west coast of South America, Ecuador is bounded by Colombia, Peru, and the Pacific Ocean. Area: 109,483 sq.mi. (283,561 sq.km.), including the Galápagos Islands (a dependency of 3,075 sq.mi.) and excluding claimed territory. Pop. (1968 est.): 5,776,100. Cap.: Quito (pop., 1968 est., 483,847). Largest city: Guayaquil (pop., 1968 est., 716,617). Language: Spanish, but Indians speak Quechuan and Jíbaro. Religion: mainly Roman Catholic. President in 1969, José María Velasco Ibarra.

In 1969 Ecuador continued to suffer repercussions both from the previous year's serious drought and from political uncertainties. The combination of these difficulties, plus rising imports and falling exports, was reflected in a dangerous fall in exchange reserves.

The governing ability of José Velasco Ibarra, president for the fifth time at the age of 75, was severely tested. After only three months in office Velasco faced a political crisis when his Cabinet resigned on Dec. 3, 1968. This resignation arose when the Liberals withdrew their support from his administration because of the government's proposed cuts in the civil service. The government was, therefore, increasingly dependent upon support in Congress from the Socialists and Conservatives. Cooperation from the latter subsequently tended to lessen when it became apparent that Velasco favoured improved relations with the U.S.S.R. and Eastern Europe.

In June, Ecuador's relations with the U.S. were strained when nine U.S. tuna-fishing boats were seized. The boats were released after the fishermen had been reminded of Ecuador's claim that its territory included its coastal waters to a width of 200 mi. There was strong reaction in the U.S. Congress, with some members demanding armed escorts for the U.S. tuna fleet. A fishing limits conference was later held in Buenos Aires where the U.S. endeavoured to reach agreement with Peru, Ecuador, Chile, and Argentina over the 200-mi. claim.

The visit of Nelson Rockefeller to Quito at the end of May provoked violent anti-U.S. demonstrations. There were student protests over examination requirements in various centres, and in September municipal unrest led to serious disorders in Quito and Guayaquil.

The Texaco-Gulf Oil group had further successes in its drilling operations in northeast Ecuador. Under a revised agreement with the government, Texaco-Gulf returned to the state 931,450 ha. that it held in excess of the maximum concession of 500,000 ha. permitted under Ecuadorean law. The reduced concession contained the area in which its 13 wells had been drilled. The revised agreement raised royalty payments and surface taxes and called upon the concessionaire to build a pipeline from Lago Agrio to Esmeraldas by the end of 1972. In July the Ministry of Industry and Commerce invited offers from Ecuadorean and foreign companies interested in the development of petroleum deposits in the northeast. The total area of 2.4 million ha. included the 931,000 ha. handed over by the Texaco-Gulf group.

When President Velasco began his four-year term in September 1968, the deficit in the 1969 budget was estimated at 1.4 billion sucres. Early in May 1969 the president obtained Senate approval for the placing on the international market of a $70 million government bond issue, of which $60 million would be used to help finance the 1969 and 1970 budgets. This bond issue, together with new indirect taxes estimated to yield 200 million sucres, prompted hopes that most of the 1969 budget deficit would be covered. The 1970 budget was provisionally estimated at 4,532,000,000 sucres, compared with 4,048,000,000 sucres finally approved for 1969.

Early in 1969 the expansion of the money supply caused apprehension. The Junta Monetaria imposed a drastic increase in the legal cash reserve requirements of commercial banks, from 25 to 30%, to be carried out by stages between February and September. The international reserves of the Banco Central del Ecuador fell from $41.4 million at the end of 1968 to $12 million on June 30, 1969, but rose to $24 million in July: this sharp increase was due to an initial payment of $11 million to the government under the terms of the revised agreement with Texaco-Gulf. On April 7 the International Monetary Fund granted Ecuador a standby credit of $18 million, in support of a stabilization program based on a fiscal policy of restraining expenditure.

The trade picture for 1969 was unfavourable: in the first six months the value of import permits rose by about $5 million, while that of export permits fell by almost $18 million. To help reduce import demand, the government introduced in June drastic increases in prior deposits and a minimum waiting period of 91 days before foreign exchange could be granted for the payment of imports. The government also threatened to curtail imports from those countries with which Ecuador had persistent trade deficits.

Though Ecuador remained the world's largest banana exporter, it was rapidly losing ground to Central American countries. The development of the superior Cavendish strains in Central America meant that Ecuador could no longer depend on its Gros Michel varieties. The government therefore began to encourage the conversion of Gros Michel plantations to the higher-yield and disease-resistant Cavendish strains. To increase Ecuador's competitive position, Velasco reduced the banana export tax 50%, and by mid-1969 Ecuador had gained new markets in Argentina, Uruguay, Bulgaria, and Yugoslavia.

Significant government proposals during 1969 included the establishment of stock exchanges in the form of joint-stock companies, state ownership of the proposed oil pipeline from the Texaco-Gulf deposits to the coast, the establishment of a state oil company, and a 50% government participation in the profits of sugar exports to the U.S. (R. B. LE.)

ECUADOR

Education. (1966–67) Primary, pupils 851,117, teachers 22,388; secondary, pupils 72,638, teachers 6,644; vocational, pupils 46,177, teachers 2,913; teacher training, students 15,492, teachers 838; higher (including 9 universities), students 16,047, teaching staff 1,995.

Finance. Monetary unit: sucre, with a par value of 18 sucres to U.S. $1 (43.20 sucres = £1 sterling) and a free rate (Oct. 13, 1968) of 21.50 sucres to U.S. $1 (51.50 sucres = £1). Gold and foreign exchange, central bank: (June 1969) U.S. $49.7 million; (June 1968) U.S. $60.7 million. Budget (1968 est.) balanced at 4,944,000,000 sucres. Gross national product: (1968) 26,520,000,000 sucres; (1967) 24.4 billion sucres. Money supply: (June 1969) 3,620,000,000 sucres; (June 1968) 3,387,000,000 sucres. Cost of living (Quito; 1965 = 100): (April 1969) 122; (April 1968) 111.

Foreign Trade. (1967) Imports U.S. $167.7 million; exports U.S. $200.1 million. Import sources: U.S. 45%; West Germany 12%; Japan 6%; France 5%; Venezuela 5%. Export destinations: U.S. 42%; West Germany 19%; Italy 8%; Japan 5%. Main exports: bananas 44%; coffee 24%; cocoa 15%; sugar 5%.

Transport and Communications. Roads (1966) 18,345 km. Motor vehicles in use (1967): passenger 19,800; commercial (including buses) 28,100. Railways: (1966) *c.* 1,340 km.; traffic (1967) 53 million passenger-km., freight 66 million net ton-km. Air traffic (1967): 216,744,000 passenger-km.; freight 2,966,000 net ton-km. Telephones (Jan. 1968) *c.* 45,000. Radio receivers (Dec. 1967) 801,000. Television receivers (Dec. 1967) 71,000.

Agriculture. Production (in 000; metric tons; 1967; 1966 in parentheses): corn 231 (177); barley *c.* 105 (*c.* 95); potatoes 403 (390); dry beans 38 (37); coffee 67 (74); cocoa 60 (53); bananas 3,163 (2,956); rice 173 (*c.* 185); cassava 327 (279); oranges 194 (200); sugar, raw value (1968–69) *c.* 204, (1967–68) 208. Livestock (in 000; 1966–67): cattle *c.* 1,800; sheep *c.* 2,040; pigs *c.* 1,700; horses *c.* 230; chickens *c.* 5,370.

Industry. Production (in 000; metric tons; 1967): petroleum products 809; crude oil (1968) 232; electricity (kw-hr.; 1966) *c.* 700,000; cement 430; gold (troy oz.) 6.7; silver (troy oz.) 80.

Education

The rumblings of student power, so much a feature of education in recent years, continued to be heard throughout 1969. In Britain, the U.S., and elsewhere they could be detected in the secondary schools as well as the universities, as militant associations of adolescent pupils began to ape the undergraduates. At the same time, 1969 was a year of recriminations as educators and others examined and reported on specific instances of student unrest. The earlier mood of acknowledging faults and seeking reforms was overtaken by a new tendency to apportion blame.

From the point of view of history, however, the most important fact concerning education in 1969 went almost unnoticed and certainly undiscussed. It

Ecumenical Movement: *see* Religion

MANCHETE FROM PICTORIAL PARADE

More than 10,000 high-school students compete on April 12, 1969, in a scholarship contest at Corintians Gymnasium in São Paulo, Braz. The contest, sponsored by a local radio station, offered university scholarships and a year's trip abroad as prizes.

had nothing to do with student power. It was the revelation that, in spite of the drive for literacy, the number of illiterates in the world was increasing. This emerged in a report published, ironically enough, on International Literacy Day (September 8) by UNESCO. The report, covering 92 member states, showed that although the percentage of illiteracy in the world was being reduced, the increase in population was outstripping the gains. Surveys suggested that out of a world population of 2,335,000,000 adults in 1970, some 810 million would be illiterate if the previous rate of reduction was maintained. This would be an increase of 70 million over 1960.

The report underlined the importance of current campaigns against illiteracy. It was estimated, for instance, that in Iran the 25,000-strong literacy corps, serving as an alternative to military conscription, had taught reading to over one million Iranians between 1963 and 1968. At the same time, the report lent added interest to relevant teaching techniques. Thus, in England, great importance was attached to a new evaluation of i.t.a., the Initial Teaching Alphabet devised by Sir James Pitman, which employs 44 characters, each representing a single sound, instead of the traditional alphabet. The new alphabet, by which children learn to read phonetically, had been on trial in some schools for eight years. Assessing the results, researchers from the Victoria University of Manchester department of education found that in most schools—though not in all—children using i.t.a. had learned to read earlier, more easily, and at a faster rate than similar children using traditional orthography. The evidence suggested that for most children, in most schools, the use of i.t.a. would considerably raise the standard of reading and the rate of scholastic progress, though it seemed likely that the advantage would be lost after the transition to the traditional alphabet.

The need for children to change to normal reading eventually remained the centre of controversy for many teachers, since it was widely held that children should not be taught anything they had to unlearn later. Even so, the Manchester researchers found that use of i.t.a. was spreading. After acknowledging the points about transition, the report said firmly, "The educational and intellectual advantages of a child learning to read fluently at a very early age are very considerable and may affect his whole confidence and future progress."

Quality and Equality. The controversy about i.t.a. could not be separated from a wider controversy about the methods and standards in primary schools, which in turn was linked to vigorous challenges from some quarters to the egalitarian principle in education. In Britain these challenges were intensified by the determination of the Labour government to abolish all selective schools at the secondary level and to replace them by a comprehensive system.

In the U.S., Arthur Jensen, a University of California psychologist, set off debate with an article in the *Harvard Educational Review* in which he emphasized that children differ intellectually and that schools should recognize these differences. Although this in itself ran somewhat counter to the egalitarian strain in American education, what provoked violent reaction was his suggestion that blacks, as a group, lack certain cognitive aspects of intelligence. Thus he called into question the whole theory of compensatory education, whereby blacks and other "culturally deprived" groups are given an enriched educational program to bring them up to standard. Critics pointed out, among other things, that he had based his findings largely on an analysis of IQ tests, which were themselves under fire as being overly weighted toward white, middle-class culture and therefore invalid when used with other groups.

The most important criticism of egalitarianism in Britain came from Lord Snow, himself a former Labour Party minister, who declared at a press conference in New York in April that because of genetic differences it is impractical to regard all mankind as one. "It is fairly certain," he said, "that there are distinctive differences between ethnic and racial groups which can be categorized in terms of a 'gene pool.'" Society had to stand or fall by certain fundamental principles, such as that all men are equal in the sight of God, but this did not mean treating all men as potential 29-ft. long-jumpers.

Lord Snow's remarks were described by Edward Short, the U.K. secretary of state for education and science, as "reminiscent of Dr. Goebbels." They had, however, come soon after the publication in England of *Fight for Education,* a so-called Black Paper, in which a number of the country's well-known intellectuals criticized the permissive and progressive methods currently in vogue. Short saw the paper as part of a massive turn toward reaction. He warned a National Union of Teachers conference that it was an attack on liberal ideas on education generally and declared that its publication marked one of the blackest days for education in a century.

There were other attempts at rebuttal. In a retaliatory pamphlet, *Verdict on the Facts: the Case for Educational Change,* published by the Advisory Centre for Education, it was argued that no country had a finer system of education than Britain. In this pamphlet, as elsewhere, statistics were employed. It was pointed out, for instance, that ordinary-level passes in the General Certificate of Education, taken toward the end of the secondary-school course, increased from 591,753 to 1,323,260 between 1953 and 1965, and advanced (sixth form)-level passes rose from 82,930 to 261,496—an increase in the annual supply of intellectual power to the nation of between 200 and 300%.

continued on page 316

SPECIAL REPORT

MAN'S FUNDAMENTAL RIGHT TO READ

By Bruce Felknor

Only rarely since the invention of movable type has reading been the subject of a truly dramatic gesture. Technological advances have made reading material abundant and educational developments have changed the teaching of reading, but these have been evolutionary rather than revolutionary. But on Sept. 23, 1969, U.S. Commissioner of Education James E. Allen, Jr., staked a breathtaking new claim for reading. He proclaimed a new right, "as fundamental as the right to life, liberty, and the pursuit of happiness—the right to read."

Allen sounded his revolutionary theme before the annual convention of the National Association of State Boards of Education and challenged its members to assume the obligation to provide that right to every child in the U.S. by the end of the 1970s. He stipulated that he was not talking about eliminating the few and dwindling pockets of illiteracy that still exist in the U.S. Rather, his concern was with *functional* illiteracy and the cultural limitations of inability to read well enough to enjoy reading.

"Imagine, if you can," he said, "what your life would be like if you could not read, or if your reading skill were so meager as to limit you to the simplest of writings, and if for you the door to the whole world of knowledge and inspiration . . . had never opened. For more than a quarter of our population this is true. For them education, in a very important way, has been a failure, and they stand as a reproach to all of us." Allen cited "the shocking facts" about reading deficiencies:

One American student in four has "significant reading deficiencies."
Up to half the students in large city school systems read below expectation.
There are still more than three million illiterate U.S. adults.
About half of unemployed persons 16–21 years of age are functionally illiterate.
Three-quarters of New York's juvenile offenders are retarded in reading by two years or more.
In a recent armed forces program 60.2% of the young men tested stood below seventh grade in reading and academic ability.

"The tragedy of these statistics," he declared, "is that they represent a barrier to success that for many young adults produces the misery of a life marked by poverty, unemployment, alienation, and, in many cases, crime." Turning to the majority who have acquired basic reading skills, Allen spoke of a "barrier which limits the fulfillment of their right to read," which exists "when the skill of reading is not accompanied by the desire to read. We fail, therefore, just as much in insuring the right to read when the desire is absent as when the skills are missing."

Thus the commissioner opened a wide field: proclaim the right to read; instill and advance the desire to read; eliminate functional illiteracy among U.S. youth in the decade now beginning; and attack adult illiteracy in the bargain. He urged educators not to get "bogged down in debate over methods" of teaching reading. "It is the *goal* with which we must be concerned," he said.

Allen readily conceded the enormity of the task. "This is education's moon," he said, "the target for the decade ahead." To hit that target, he acknowledged the need for involvement far beyond the educational community: national, state, and local political leaders and legislative bodies; the publishing industry, advertising, and the news media; business and industry in general as well as labour; foundations and civic and community organizations; research and scientific organizations; the worlds of entertainment and sports. Most essential, he suggested, was "the understanding and support of an enlightened and enthusiastic public."

Reaction among educators, publishers, the news media, and in other areas was immediate and enthusiastic. For all their toll of tragedy and war, the 1960s had moved education closer to the top among national priorities than any previous decade. The commissioner of education was now calling for the selection of one basic target for education in the decade ahead, and the troops were willing.

Every subsequent speech delivered by the commissioner for the remainder of 1969 renewed the challenge. He was specific: to the initial audience of the Association of State Boards of Education, and to every subsequent group, he called for action as well as commitment, and for progress reports. "I therefore call upon you to take upon yourselves the obligation of assuring that every child in your state will learn to read, and I request that you begin immediately in your own state to consider how this goal can be achieved, to assemble resources, to plan, and to report back to me what actions you have taken under state leadership so that the school year 1969–70 can be recorded as the year when together we set in motion the nation-wide effort that will erase this intolerable deficit in American education." In November he asked the Council of Chief State School Officers not only for support but to inform him by Feb. 1, 1970, of "the plans of your states to achieve this goal."

Allen promised reports and consultations on the part of the U.S. Office of Education. But he was careful not to promise any massive infusion of new federal funds to support his "moon shot." A week after firing his opening gun, the commissioner told the Citizens Schools Committee of Chicago that "the battle against inflation and our continued involvement in Vietnam make it unlikely that there will be any large increases in federal education funds in the near future." Instead of relying on new federal moneys the commissioner, who came to his post in the spring of 1969 from a distinguished tenure as chief state school officer of New York, counted on a reallocation of priorities in spending federal (and state) funds that are already available. Five titles under the Elementary and Secondary Education Act alone made billions of dollars accessible to state school systems under terms that allowed virtually any proportion to be spent on reading improvement. The commissioner estimated that there was some $50 billion that could feasibly be redirected to make a reality of his "right to read."

For all Allen's caution about the possibilities for federal financial support, the temper of the 91st Congress as it recessed on December 23 seemed more amicable to increasing educational funding than Pres. Richard M. Nixon. At adjournment the House of Representatives had approved a Senate-House conference recommendation to increase educational spending by $1 billion over the White House recommendations of the spring. The Senate, fearing a pocket veto by the president while the two houses were out of session, held off its approval of the legislation until the new session of Congress.

But new money or not, Commissioner Allen's challenge brought wide and eager response. He slated for early 1970 the formation of a national citizens' committee whose honorary chairman would be the first lady, Mrs. Nixon. Volunteers from the business world—not only educational publishers, who had an obvious stake in the program's success, but public-spirited industrialists and others—began to rally at year's end, and a bureau to coordinate efforts was set up in Allen's office in December. President Nixon and Health, Education, and Welfare Secretary Robert Finch gave their blessing. U.S. education had been handed a brand-new agenda for the 1970s. Not an attack on illiteracy per se, as Commissioner Allen was quick to point out, but a much broader and more comprehensive attack on a crucial element of education, economic well-being, and culture, the "right to read" concept concentrated on the ability to read, and to read well, linked inseparably with the desire to read.

KEYSTONE

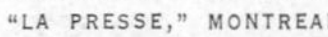
"LA PRESSE," MONTREAL

Above, students at the London School of Economics vote to call a one-day strike to demonstrate their support for five militants who received summonses from the disciplinary board. Above right, Canadian students battle in the street during a French-English language dispute in Montreal Sept. 10, 1969.

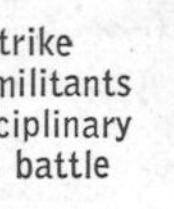

UPI COMPIX

KEYSTONE

Left, students at Zürich (Switz.) University conduct funeral services for student democracy Feb. 2, 1969, after faculty decided against student participation in academic administration. Above, campus police and students play tug-of-war with an anti-ROTC protester at demonstration at Tulane University, New Orleans, La., April 29, 1969.

COURTESY, YALE UNIVERSITY

UPI COMPIX

Above left, James P. Comer, who was appointed associate dean of the Yale Medical School on June 12, 1969, is the first Negro to hold that position. Above right, Angela Davis, a black militant and admitted Communist, was fired from her assistant professorship at UCLA under an old rule prohibiting the hiring of Communists in the California university system despite her apparent popularity with the students.

UPI COMPIX

Above, London elementary and secondary school pupils march on March 2, 1969, in support of School Action Union demands for control of schools by students and teachers, outlawing of corporal punishment, and more pay for teachers. Below, Students for a Democratic Society rally around the statue at Columbia University's Low Library, Feb. 27, 1969.

PICTORIAL PARADE

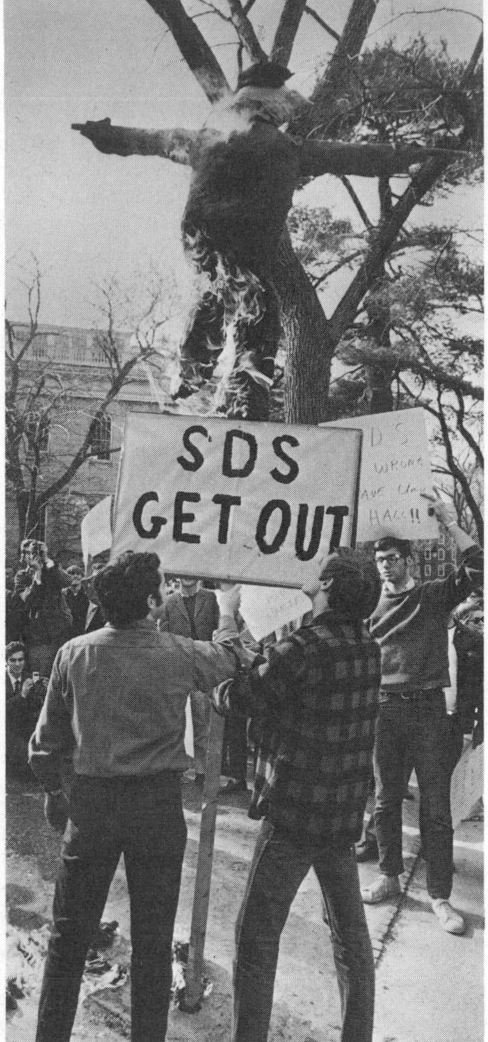

UPI COMPIX

Above, Harvard University students burn an effigy of SDS protesters who had seized University Hall on April 9, 1969. Below, militant Harvard and Radcliffe students picket in front of Memorial Church on April 18, 1969, after erecting crosses in Harvard Yard as a protest against ROTC and the Vietnam war.

WIDE WORLD

Left, Black Panther member counsels a child at a Liberation School held during the summer of 1969 at the Good Shepherd Mission in the Brownsville section of Brooklyn, N.Y. Goals of the school, where students ranged in age from 4 to 14, included political awareness, family unity, the Black Panther program, and obedience to party leaders.

WIDE WORLD

continued from page 312

Led by C. B. Cox of the Victoria University of Manchester, the authors of the Black Paper returned to the attack in the autumn with a second document. "In this Black Paper," they declared,

> we again suggest that if informed, civilized, mature and well balanced citizens are wanted for the future, we must scrutinize most carefully those educationists who teach hatred of authority and contempt of tradition; who nurture ignorance and self-indulgence as a point of principle; and who disregard the claims or indeed the realities of the social world.

On egalitarianism, the Black Paper was unequivocal:

> The frightening aspect of egalitarianism is that while it costs far more to bring into effect than equality of opportunity it disintegrates the standards and structures on which education depends. It is a levelling-down process, actively unjust to brighter children, who become a new under-privileged, and for this same reason dangerous for the nation as a whole.

The minister of education had a different view of the future. In a speech in County Durham in October, he looked forward to the day when secondary schools would be rid of the traditional examination

> which still hangs like a millstone round the necks of the schools, tests what it tests and nothing more. How much more sensible and efficient it would be if the universities, professional bodies and employers based their selection of young people upon a cumulative school record for the whole secondary school life instead of upon the ability to store and reproduce a mass of facts.

Student Power and Teacher Unrest. The arguments about the Black Paper took place in the context of increasing demands from pupils for a greater degree of self-determination. In Canada, for instance, the president of the Ontario Education Association invited high school students to take part in the association's annual convention, and two senior pupils were appointed to Manitoba's Education Advisory Board. In Britain there was some attempt to advance pupil power by ad hoc organizations of senior pupils who attracted attention by public demonstrations. The movement received more formidable support in March, when the National Union of Students launched a campaign to recruit sixth formers to its ranks.

At the same time, warnings were sounded for pupils who took things into their own hands. In France the early part of the year was marked by some unrest in the lycées, with strikes initiated by students on a variety of pretexts. In March, Edgar Faure, the minister of education, warned the principals of lycées throughout France that, when many adolescents of the same age were already at work, these more privileged young people could not be allowed to fail their part of the educational contract and to waste the large sums allotted to them by the community. Those who went on strike would be assumed to have broken their contracts and would be sent home.

It was not pupils alone who were involved in strikes during 1969. Once more the year was marked by dissatisfaction among teachers in many countries over such matters as pay and status, with the dissatisfaction often crystallizing into disruptive action. In England and Wales the major teachers' unions repeatedly brought their grievances before the public. Early in the year, to show its discontent with the way salaries were negotiated, the National Association of Schoolmasters had its members work to rule in selected areas. In some cases this led to suspension of the teachers concerned, whereupon the association retaliated by staging lightning strikes. The dispute was particularly bitter in County Durham. Meanwhile, the National Union of Teachers prepared fresh salary demands, launched a massive publicity campaign to draw public attention, and staged a two-week strike affecting more than 150,000 children in December.

The dissatisfaction of the British teachers was heightened by other factors during the year. Financial stringency led some local education authorities to dispense with part-time teachers—a move that, it was felt, would increase the work of the career teacher. At the same time, the Department of Education and Science decided to do away with the old yardsticks that decreed a maximum of 30 pupils for a secondary class and 40 for a primary class. Because of teacher shortages these regulations had never been strictly applied, and the ministry felt they were unrealistic, especially since, under modern team-teaching techniques, a team of teachers might be engaged with a large number of pupils at once. The disappearance of the safeguard, however, was seen by many teachers as a danger when local authorities were under constant pressure to economize. It was also feared that the local authorities would not be able to employ all the recruits to teaching who were coming out of the training institutions, though the output of these institutions had been specifically increased to reduce class size.

On the credit side, the year saw definite progress toward the setting up of a Teachers' General Council in England and Wales. Long mooted but delayed by disagreements among the unions, the council was intended to represent the teachers as well as the public interest, and was expected to give teachers true professional status by controlling entry to the teaching service and exercising discipline over its members.

There was a similar move in South Africa. A commission of inquiry set up by the government in 1968 proposed that a central professional council for the training of teachers be established, to include representatives of teachers' associations, provincial education departments, and the universities. One of its main tasks should be to promote the prestige of the teaching profession. The commission further proposed that high-school teachers be trained at the universities and primary-school teachers at training colleges, but this proposal was resisted by those who felt that it would split the profession. In Australia efforts were being made to form a single, nationwide teachers' union to replace the separate state unions.

There was trouble elsewhere. In West Germany the state of Baden-Württemberg found itself short 1,300 teachers for the 1968–69 school year. Emergency measures included closing of the smallest rural schools, the recall of some pensioned teachers, and the payment of overtime. About the same time, Mexico had to authorize substantial pay increases for teachers to avert a threatened walkout. In contrast, the Philippines' education department ordered a week's closure for all the public schools in Manila in January so that tempers might cool after the 9,000-strong teaching force had threatened a strike over pay. In Ireland a pay dispute in February closed the secondary schools for three weeks.

More was heard during the year of expatriate teachers, particularly British, who were recruited to the new countries in Africa only to complain that their conditions of service were different from what they had been led to expect, and that they had difficulty in obtaining their correct salaries or in taking their savings out of the country. In Kenya, in particular, several British headmasters and headmistresses with many years of service had their appointments termi-

World Education

Most recent official data

Country	1st level (primary) Students (full-time)	1st level Teachers (full-time)	1st level Total schools	General 2nd level (secondary) Students (full-time)	General 2nd level Teachers (full-time)	General 2nd level Total schools	Vocational 2nd level Students (full-time)	Vocational 2nd level Teachers (full-time)	Vocational 2nd level Total schools	3rd level (higher) Students (full-time)	3rd level Teachers (full-time)	3rd level Total schools	Literacy % of population	Literacy Over age
Afghanistan	474,425	10,245	2,493	68,505	2,506	278	15,620	779	62	5,242	534	5	20.	7–12
Albania	268,542	8,666	2,629	197,015	8,092	932	21,005	637	25	12,436	606	6	...	...
Algeria	1,585,682	36,255	5,222	130,960	5,384	372	46,453	3,132	233	10,681	816	14	...	...
Argentina	3,480,534	180,423	25,609	197,571	30,137	905	689,665	92,257	3,001	265,303	19,788	461	...	...
Australia	1,765,508	62,600	9,880*	889,855	50,700	...	175,000	...	220	162,000	...	210	...	...
Austria	653,759	28,556	4,822	382,131	21,950	1,248	60,669	5,377	412	55,665	7,054	34	100.	...
Barbados	44,752	1,511	136	20,789	987	36	632	20	3	440	40	2	97.0	7
Belgium	988,699	48,720	8,934	304,030	42,044	1,148	360,702	54,045	2,662	91,059	...	428	99.61	20
Bolivia	635,843	22,732	8,193	114,185	4,486	463	10,684	1,671	102	28,593	2,949	29	39.5	15
Botswana	82,187	2,086	280	3,049	161	10	413	35	4	—	—	—	33.9	10
Brazil	10,695,391	393,001	127,355	2,483,212	157,643	6,698	677,965	57,978	2,897	180,109	36,109	609	66.	7–11
Bulgaria	1,095,964	50,746	4,583	107,915	6,665	273	266,807	16,786	586	90,024	6,998	43	91.4	8
Burundi	180,419	4,534	1,004	3,652	295	19	4,692	395	46	348	82	2	...	...
Cameroon	682,748	12,925	3,372	41,768	...	127	13,060	...	52	2,019	...	5	...	...
Canada	4,182,240	163,562	16,334	1,425,381	89,805	2,621	328,525	...	1,185	270,093	18,665	215	98.37	20
Central African Republic	158,435	2,694	754	5,850	245	15	1,522	133	15	—	—	—	13.	10
Chad	178,699	2,406	750	8,222	284	27	1,126	41	8	188	...	...	12.4	10
Chile	1,934,478	38,985	7,184	153,114	10,103	568	69,702	6,507	263	56,491	...	8	16.2	15
Colombia	2,733,432	78,098	27,361	405,778	27,058	2,207	180,926	13,555	1,457	62,844	3,327	62	72.9	15
Congo (Brazzaville)	224,386	3,885	932	1,451	186	4	2,437	281	32	1,381	123	6	...	...
Costa Rica	348,950	11,743	2,479	64,252	2,888	104	5,757	445	16	11,647	816	6	...	...
Cuba	1,460,754	48,994	14,807	186,358	10,703	434	67,753	4,741	140	35,490	4,500	3	...	...
Cyprus	72,466	2,211	562	31,407	1,257	57	4,143	236	11	339	24	4	81.9	7
Czechoslovakia	2,052,526	98,399	10,947	98,918	6,402	343	196,246	14,724	610	100,193	16,403	35	100.	6–15
Dahomey	151,751	3,582	842	13,483	595	66	...	92	7	175	24	1	33.	12
Denmark	506,131	36,530	2,442	127,253	3,480	173	119,329	...	178	56,244	5,800	51	100.	8
Dominican Republic	685,550	12,259	5,155	87,752	3,648	637	2,475	...	10	14,951	1,010	8	64.5	15
Ecuador	813,353	21,713	6,846	62,956	6,004	248	54,312	3,226	259	15,395	1,754	14	69.6	10
El Salvador	516,875	13,406	2,919	57,533	3,051†	492	26,685	...	359	8,199	599	7	51.	10
Equatorial Guinea	38,015	504	297	2,095	56	2	547	52	4	...	...	...	...	...
Ethiopia	513,848	10,416	1,821	89,102	3,349	325	9,493	641	85	3,870	...	9	...	...
Finland	428,926	19,187	5,385	375,549	19,681	1,145	98,781	7,077	745	51,775	5,023	19	...	...
France	7,460,065	257,558	79,484	2,598,644	188,413	9,942	833,492	20,519	2,682	458,409	19,905	518	100.	7
Germany, East	2,487,639*	82,028*	8,051	...	...	...	605,141	...	1,378	110,581	...	44	100.	...
Germany, West	5,982,065	188,817	29,511	1,907,774	81,447	4,068	2,035,090	34,092	4,884	576,811	55,308	3,341	...	...
Ghana	1,420,886	48,641	10,656	53,561	3,145	171	37,121	2,337	211	5,699	682	5	21.	6
Greece	975,869	27,376	10,822	374,616	11,251	909	81,244	6,348	457	58,000	1,192	28	85.	...
Guatemala	484,645	13,432	4,986	43,537	3,699	364	19,541	2,957	388	10,743	...	4	63.	14
Guyana	171,469‡	5,421‡	389‡	16,372‡	705‡	40‡	1,445	...	2	1,006	...	2	85.	10
Haiti	275,192	6,778	1,909	23,047	1,286	75	5,892	383	26	1,313	226	11	...	...
Honduras	373,937	10,396	4,126	33,392	2,515	112	1,212	106	9	2,883	...	1	47.3	10
Hungary	1,254,745	62,523	5,771	125,616	8,086	356	102,613	4,862	230	52,061	9,230	89	96.6	7
Iceland	27,724	1,009	207	15,863	732	131	12,747	245	101	2,099	105	2	99.	8
India	36,470,933	990,352	391,895	28,667,965	932,735	102,755	2,056,011	46,450	223,446	1,967,796	129,618	5,736	30.	...
Indonesia	15,949,109	343,029	61,678	999,485	39,560	5,291	454,349	28,045	2,118	155,077	17,015	190	42.9	10
Iran	2,753,132	85,157	15,556	781,507	24,252	2,067	25,118	2,118	265	58,993	...	78	33.	7
Iraq	1,017,050	47,058	5,137	285,721	9,428	840	12,461	1,444	74	41,189	1,879	59	...	...
Ireland	308,249	15,722	4,917	146,966	7,815	942	4,973	221	111	20,570	1,547	29	100.	...
Israel	564,725	28,943	4,697	72,242	6,819	343	53,827	5,202	267	36,338	5,828	56	...	...
Italy	4,706,180	218,922	40,304	2,380,891	187,301	10,131	1,105,047	95,471	4,464	488,227	17,011	58	91.6	6
Jamaica	347,957	6,177	745	36,731	1,612	58	4,105	216	12	...	...	9	81.9	...
Japan	9,383,190	356,012	25,262	9,565,025†	430,487†	16,280†	...	...	...	1,565,129	89,598	922	...	...
Jordan§	229,691	5,643	748	75,139	3,061	509	2,491	107	8	4,063	196	13	42.	15
Kenya	1,209,680	37,923	6,135	101,361	4,644	601	7,612	544	38	4,563	421	4	60.	16
Korea, South	5,622,816	96,358	5,810	1,441,700	36,653	1,880	235,809	8,970	444	172,830	8,996	127	93.3	11
Kuwait	65,495	2,962	121	51,434	3,562	83	4,828	771	26	1,468	143	6	...	...
Laos	206,998	6,051	3,070	6,669	388	22	5,073	614	16	542	53	3	66.	6
Lebanon	544,475	25,151	2,235	115,541	2,559	400	15,520	1,065	223	36,110	1,833	12	88.	14
Liberia	120,101	3,211	905	12,866	669	85	1,230	106	5	1,213	127	3	8.9	10
Liechtenstein	2,295	77	14	919	63	5	...	...	...	72	6	1	100.	7
Luxembourg	36,700	1,584	444	9,459	438	20	4,700	221	28	...	...	...	99.	7
Malagasy Republic	723,200	9,893	...	62,430	1,260	68	5,570	487	48	3,520	180	10	61.	15
Malaysia	1,658,675	53,356	6,053	574,302	22,247	1,063	3,981	293	13	13,747	1,098	32	...	...
Maldives, Republic of	7,216	19	97	156	58	3	...	...	...	...	...	...	54.67	...
Mali	186,022	5,324	744	1,841	171	6	4,365	418	25	345	90	3	...	...
Malta	55,754	2,631	169	10,820	493	28	1,688	166	6	1,210	219	4	83.5	14
Mauritius	142,959	4,253	332	39,703	1,706	137	1,245	59	5	94	10	1	62.6	5
Mexico	8,156,417	167,926	42,713	932,699	62,432	3,813	170,887	...	443	178,436	...	84	...	...
Morocco	1,135,865	32,729	...	274,102	2,176	...	13,336	11,038	...	10,698	552	...	...	...
Nauru	1,443	93	9	354	24	2	—	—	—	—	—	—	100.	7
Nepal	442,251	16,407	6,631	78,304	3,876	841	4,500	131	25	11,802	819	36	11.5	10
Netherlands	1,509,319	51,977	8,879	537,281	28,200	1,664	390,502	35,000	1,982	153,548	15,500	337	100.	7
New Zealand	509,841	18,555	2,638	179,922	8,788	382	1,355	633	6	26,912	2,166	26	...	...
Nicaragua	268,883	7,585	2,350	32,953	1,497	132	7,137	477	59	6,022	719	2	50.08	10
Nigeria	1,791,309	56,963	8,925	166,577	8,451	858	32,116	2,016	173	3,961	1,007	4	...	...
Norway	387,042	17,117	3,259	231,702	12,156	1,249	74,062	5,126	689	30,508	3,125	32	...	...
Pakistan	7,697,857	184,146	64,888	3,043,185	105,064	10,203	37,018	2,851	248	321,203	12,183	355	...	...
Panama	221,692	7,451	1,519	44,873	2,236	76	22,078	854	111	11,548	360	1	78.3	10
Paraguay	406,342	12,722	2,809	47,326	...	456	...	...	...	...	...	...	25.	10
Peru	2,208,299	62,416	19,587	368,565	22,443	1,248	74,990	7,378	386	79,166	8,579	122	61.1	15
Poland	5,706,270	201,368	26,992	306,135	15,044	1,150	871,897	50,287	9,357	178,145	25,565	76	97.3	7
Rhodesia	720,312	19,117	3,382	45,261	2,471	175	4,060	239	26	1,442	219	4	...	...
San Marino	2,230	114	32	804	57	3	258	...	...	84	...	...	...	...
Saudi Arabia	363,426	16,601	1,686	58,674	3,341	249	7,847	753	50	5,352	410	15	...	...
Sierra Leone	136,824	4,759	939	22,119	1,107	66	1,053	57	4	1,616	355	11	7.	17
Singapore	371,781	12,426	484	147,581	6,817	125	2,912	291	9	8,738	703	5	78.	10
South Africa‖	2,911,178	68,662	12,822	447,705	22,327	1,230	152,041	4,204	217	79,437	6,661	46	...	...
Spain	4,178,686	122,775	118,786	1,119,803	34,669	6,470	329,335	18,217	755	153,991	10,513	37	98.	15
Sudan	496,632	10,430	3,058	130,001	6,468	950	5,813	468	39	10,387	1,096	9	17.1	10
Swaziland	62,082	1,627	358	6,246	300	31	337	45	4	66	21	1	70.7	15
Sweden	622,000	27,700	4,500	379,326	32,600	300	167,980	15,300	800	114,848	...	36	...	...
Switzerland	464,910	21,762	...	290,330	6,583	...	162,571	...	...	40,836	2,773	10	100.	16
Tanzania	795,719	15,862	4,484	27,628	1,287	95	2,832	145	3	6,728	207	20	...	...
Thailand	5,140,636	159,089	26,876	394,419	22,535	1,555	80,010	7,650	...	41,154	4,431	15	70.8	10
Togo	171,436	3,290	837	13,678	538	59	1,499	...	9	50	11	1	35.	15
Trinidad and Tobago	227,296	...	771	45,813	1,867	126	906	79	3	1,701	176	8	76.	15
Tunisia	844,994	16,194	2,131	95,564	...	115	37,353	...	80	7,723	...	2	...	...
Turkey	6,509,633	102,061	33,369	757,883	27,363	1,567	203,512	12,887	881	126,039	6,727	89	68.72	6
Uganda	632,162	...	2,671	43,238	...	124	7,713	...	52	2,179	...	1	...	...
U.S.S.R.	38,343,000	1,449,000	214,290*	4,800,000	251,000	...	3,659,000	134,000	...	2,396,000	201,000	...	...	...
United Arab Republic	3,492,935	89,736	9,005	959,366	39,747	2,527	180,732	14,323	577	177,891	7,748	74	40.3	10
United Kingdom	5,658,468	195,354	28,458	3,496,770	187,179	7,060	259,597	50,084	908	286,383	35,834	236	...	...
United States	31,728,000	1,237,000	88,556	19,596,000†	985,000†	31,203†	...	...	...	7,571,636	481,000	2,483	97.6	14
Vietnam, South	1,968,994	33,221	6,932	470,925	11,528	627	9,323	485	24	31,272	689	10	70.	8–70
Western Samoa	27,596	924	149	9,522	369	57	392	35	4	...	...	...	97.5	10–14
Yugoslavia	2,893,624	109,314	14,067	181,328	9,666	402	458,665	27,025	1,343	143,430	10,600	261	...	...

Note: Third level may include individual faculties within a university. *Primary and secondary combined. †General and vocational combined. ‡Not including private. §Data refer to east bank of Jordan only. ‖Not including Indian.

NORDISK PRESSEFOTO FROM PICTORIAL PARADE

Pupils, aged 6 to 15, "play Indians" during a two-week group-teaching experiment during May 1969 in Maaløv, a suburb of Copenhagen. Teachers and students wore handmade clothes; students attended classes in tepees and made their own meals over a fire.

nated in the summer on one month's notice, instead of the six months to which they claimed to be entitled. It was alleged that their replacement by Africans was a political move related to the coming elections. Subsequently, Kenya faced a widespread strike when its teachers were not paid on time.

Race, Religion, and Sex. In the U.S. the burning issue in 1969 was once more racial desegregation. In July, for example, Gov. Lester Maddox of Georgia was planning to close the state's schools rather than accept government proposals for desegregation. Calling school desegregation a Communist plot, he called for a massive school boycott by white children and proposed that Sunday-school rooms be turned into private schools, which would not be subject to the desegregation plans. He declared that he did not mind if the federal government took away its $75 million annual aid for education—at least Georgia would then be able to run its own schools. At the same time, former Gov. George Wallace of Alabama was making speeches to enthusiastic all-white audiences in which he urged them to use civil disobedience to regain freedom of choice in their children's schooling.

Even where desegregation was not opposed, there were practical difficulties. In Charlotte, N.C., where blacks were enthusiastic about it and the whites were at least acquiescent, the board of education planned to close seven all-black schools in the city and to bus the black pupils to white schools in the suburbs. Blacks mounted a vigorous campaign against this. "Why," asked a spokesman, "should the black students forget school tradition, mascots, honor programs, athletic prominence . . . with no assurance that they will receive anything in return?" White parents had been equally incensed at a suggestion that white children be transported to black schools.

Geodesic domes of plastic and wood constructed by students in September 1969 in a field near University of Massachusetts at Amherst. Occupants of "Free University City" were protesting overcrowding on campus.

WIDE WORLD

The position of the Nixon administration seemed ambivalent. Robert Finch, secretary of health, education, and welfare, decided to postpone the carrying out of desegregation plans for 33 recalcitrant school districts in Mississippi, but his decision was overruled by the Supreme Court. In contrast, the Department of Justice had acted to restrain some school districts in Georgia from dropping their plans. How far the Nixon administration was simply facing realities and to what extent it was motivated by political considerations was a matter for argument, but there was some feeling that valuable psychological momentum was being lost.

In South Africa students at the University of Witwatersrand staged protests in April to mark the tenth anniversary of the legislation that imposed racial segregation on the South African universities. In a lecture there, Lord Butler, former British minister of education, said that student power would not leave South African universities untouched. Even with the government policy as it was, he wondered whether an open university would not have something more to contribute to South Africa. Harry Oppenheimer, chancellor of the University of Cape Town, praised the protesting students and declared that academic freedom in South Africa was virtually synonymous with the right to admit non-Europeans to study and teach at the English-medium universities. Subsequently, 400 students at the all-African university college in Turfloop, Transvaal, complained that they were treated like children and sought to affiliate with the anti-apartheid National Union of South African Students.

In March the council of the University College in Rhodesia announced its unanimous agreement to maintain the nonracial character of the college and to admit students of all races on merit only. In June, however, after Rhodesia's constitutional referendum, Terence Miller resigned as principal of the college, believing, as he said, that the advancement of Africans in general and of educated Africans in particular would be indefinitely postponed. The prospect before the college, he maintained, was likely to be that of a university in enemy-occupied territory, in which the principal would be expected to collaborate in policies that he must in his heart condemn.

In Montreal an educational dispute over English-speaking classes in the suburb of St. Leonard actually led to the reading of the Riot Act. The school board had decided to phase out these classes, to the satisfaction of the militant French element in the neighbourhood. However, the English-speaking residents, many of them of Italian extraction, wanted their children to be taught in English as well as French, since they thought English would be of greater use on a continent where it was the dominant language. It was during a demonstration against this attitude that violence flared in September. The violence was deplored by Prime Minister Pierre Elliott Trudeau, but he pointed out that the federal government could not act since both education and the administration of justice fell within provincial jurisdiction.

Canada, like many other countries, was involved in controversies over religious education. After a four-year inquiry, a committee recommended to the Ontario legislature that moral and ethical instruction of an informal kind should take the place of religious teaching. The singing of the national anthem and the reading of some universal prayer, such as the Lord's Prayer, could still be used to open the school day, but the statutory two half-hour lessons should be abandoned. The committee was not willing to abolish religious studies completely, however. It recognized their cultural value but was against any indoctrination. It recommended that courses in comparative religion be made available, though they should be optional in the higher grades.

In Britain there were mounting demands, particularly from humanist groups, that compulsory religious instruction be taken out of the state schools. The minister of education stood firm against this, partly from his own conviction and partly because research appeared to show that parents wanted the instruction retained. The validity of the research was questioned, however.

A related point finally had been settled in the U.S. at the end of 1968. The Supreme Court struck down the so-called Arkansas "monkey law," which had banned the teaching of the Darwinian theory of evolution in that state's schools. The court held that the law in Arkansas was contrary to the U.S. Constitution, which guarantees religious freedom and makes the guarantee binding on the individual states. The decision left only Mississippi with an antievolution law on its books, and this was expected to be affected.

If evolution came into its own in the U.S., however, there was a backlash over sex. After a period during which the ingenuity of the American educational system in imparting sex instruction had to be studied to be believed, a nationwide reaction appeared to be setting in. It was estimated in the autumn that 15 states were considering legislation to ban sex instruction in schools; Louisiana had already done so and New York had banned the use of state funds for the purpose. Parent groups such as POSSE (Parents Opposed to Sex and Sensitivity Education) and MOMS (Mothers for Moral Stability) became common. Among the protesters were parents who questioned course content and teacher preparation rather than the principle of sex education itself, but their voices tended to be lost amid noisier accusations that sex instruction encouraged lax behaviour and that in any case it was a Communist plot. When Governor Maddox attacked the Communists over school desegregation, he added, "They are destroying America through sex education and not letting teachers pray and read the Bible."

In contrast, the Mexican government actively recommended in 1969 that sex instruction be given in schools, and in Britain the BBC announced plans to give sex instruction for eight- and nine-year-olds on both radio and television in 1970.

Campus Violence. Violence at the university level continued. In January some 8,500 riot police stormed Tokyo University to restore law and order after a year-long student strike. The students had originally demonstrated against out-of-date lectures, unsympathetic professors, and rigid administrative procedures. It had been hoped until the last moment that police action could be avoided, and the university authorities had agreed to a long program of reforms, largely designed to give the students a greater say in affairs. As often happens in student disorders, however, there was an element more interested in social upheaval than in reform, and these militants barricaded themselves in a university building. Damage was estimated at $1 million. The government subsequently took severe action against the university, canceling its next entrance examination. Two months later classes reopening in the university's suburban annex had to be suspended after violent clashes between extremists and more moderate elements in the student body.

In April in the U.S. police were in action at Harvard. This institution had long been thought a model of liberal attitudes; it had been among the first to deny academic credits for membership in the Reserve Officers Training Corps and its president, Nathan Pusey, had been a noted opponent of McCarthyism in the 1950s. Even so, demonstrators led by the militant Students for a Democratic Society occupied the university hall, demanding, among other things, an end to all reserve officer training as well as a reduction of rents in university-owned buildings. A force of 400 policemen cleared the hall and 200 arrests were made. As had happened elsewhere, the police intervention exacerbated some of the more moderate students, and subsequently there was a student strike in protest.

While military affairs had been among the matters of protest at Harvard, observers elsewhere noted a swing from Vietnam to racism as the rallying point for student disturbances. Racial troubles of one sort or another erupted in many U.S. institutions, usually over demands for black subjects in the curriculum and for exclusively black facilities. In April the country was shocked by pictures of rifle-carrying blacks leaving a building they had occupied at Cornell. Later in the year, agitation over the dismissal of a lecturer at the University of California on the ground that she was a Communist was all the more bitter because she was also black. It was said that the blacks wanted recognition of themselves as blacks, with a history and heroes of their own. On the other side, Roy Wilkins, executive director of the National Association for the Advancement of Colored People, declared that the movement was unrealistic, since blacks had to live in what was predominantly a white man's world.

The student troubles in the U.S. excited much comment. In his annual report in July, J. Edgar Hoover, director of the Federal Bureau of Investigation, noted that 225 of the country's institutions of higher learning had had their work disrupted in the previous 12 months through sit-ins or more violent disorders. "Never before in our history," he said, "has there been such a strong Revolutionary Marxist movement of young people so eager to tear down established authority, while it is the immediate goal of the 'new left' to gain complete control of our educational system." Noting that Students for a Democratic Society had instigated much of the unrest, Hoover declared that the American Communist Party and other Marxist groups were seeking to take over this movement. He noted, too, that the Black Panther Party, in his view the most dangerous of the black extremists, was addressing itself to colleges and high schools as well as to the ghettos. Hoover's report reflected a hardening of opinion against student disturbances. An opinion poll in California in the spring showed 72% of Californians strongly in favour of expulsion for all students who challenged and defied the authorities. The poll also suggested that the biggest factor in the increasing popularity of Gov. Ronald Reagan was his firm handling of student riots.

Pres. Richard M. Nixon made a number of comments during the year. In a presidential statement on student unrest, published in March, he condemned violence and intimidation, drew attention to the dangers to intellectual freedom, and declared that when the actions or judgments of the university community were influenced by violence or threats, the community

"TORONTO TELEGRAM"

Critical shortage of space at East End High School in Toronto was solved in 1969 by addition of 35 portable classrooms.

ceased to be a university. He declared, however, that the federal government could not and should not enforce such principles. That was a matter for the university. At the same time he deplored the depersonalization of education and called for more experiments in the university curriculum and more student involvement in the decision-making process.

A month later, in an address to the U.S. Chamber of Commerce, he strongly condemned student revolutionaries and said that the universities should have the backbone to stand up against them. In June, in an address at General Beadle State College, Madison, S.D., he sharply attacked permissive college administrators or professors who either surrendered to extremists or supported them. In the same month, the President's Commission on the Causes and Prevention of Violence urged universities to develop plans for dealing rapidly and effectively with student demonstrations. The commission, under the chairmanship of Milton Eisenhower, president emeritus of Johns Hopkins University, said that while scholarly examination and decision were admirable qualities for the process of education, they would be a prescription for disaster in dealing with naked force. At the same time the commission expressed itself as disturbed at some public reaction. People who wanted to punish the colleges by cutting off funds could unwittingly be helping the radical minority.

In Britain the Select Committee on Education and Science, an official parliamentary commission, reported on student unrest in October after a nine-month inquiry. Discounting as dangerously facile the suggestion that unrest was caused by a few troublemakers, the committee took a clear stand:

> Our institutions of higher education must recognize that changed circumstances brought about by their own expansion, changes in society itself and the need to question long-standing assumptions should compel a ready and sympathetic response to proposals for reappraisal and reform.

Noting the dissatisfaction expressed by students at the obvious inequalities between universities and other institutions of higher education, the committee called for a Higher Education Commission, with statutory powers, whose responsibilities would embrace all institutions of higher education—universities, polytechnics, colleges of education, teacher-training colleges, and art, commercial, and technical colleges. The committee called on the government to consider methods whereby all institutions of higher education could be financed in the same way. It urged that in no circumstances should education authorities use the empty threat of withdrawal of grant in an attempt to discipline students, and it was suggested that newly appointed university and college teachers should receive some organized instruction or guidance on how to teach.

Problems and Policies. In the U.S., the Carnegie Commission on Higher Education, reporting in December 1968, had proposed a massive expansion of the U.S. system to meet the needs of the next decade. Led by Clark Kerr, former president of the University of California, the commission called for a $10 billion annual increase in federal spending on higher education, plus the establishment of 550 new colleges. Kerr pointed out that a boy or girl whose family income was in the top half of the national income range was three times more likely to get a college education than one whose family was in the bottom half. The proposed program was to include federal grants to one million students who could not otherwise afford to go to college, and this grant was to go directly to the student so that the colleges would have to compete for entrants. At the same time the commission recommended that a National Student Loan Bank be set up to make long-term loans without regard to income. A further proposal was for 20 new medical schools and an expansion of existing ones to provide, in all, for 75% more students by 1976.

Pres. Milton Obote of Uganda, in an address to East and Central African students at Kampala in April, declared his support for student power when it was directed against colonialism. Observers commented, however, that he would not tolerate it if it was directed against his own government. In the Congo (Kinshasa) new government regulations imposed stricter state control on the universities. Rectors and vice-rectors were to be appointed by the president and professors and lecturers by the minister of education.

In January the Spanish government used emergency powers to banish a number of professors and lecturers of the University of Madrid to remote villages. In April Georgios Papadopoulos, the Greek prime minister, appealed to the nation's students to abide by the ideals and moral values of Hellenic culture and Christianity and to set an example to the rest of the world. Malaysian Prime Minister Tunku Abdul Rahman said in August that if students preferred to spend their time on rabble-rousing politics they would have cause to regret it. When the Czechoslovak universities opened after the summer vacation, they were required to complete dossiers on the political activities of teachers and students. In West Germany a code of discipline for students was tabled for ratification by the individual state parliaments, and in Mexico the ruling political party appointed a national youth director with specific responsibilities for avoiding student unrest.

Quebec signed a cultural pact with Ontario in June whereby both agreed, where possible, to provide instruction in the appropriate language for French- or English-speaking minorities; educational programs on radio and television were to be exchanged and studies completed in one province were to be recognized in the other. In the same month a complete research unit of nine physicists at Queen's University of Belfast, N.Ire., was reported to be emigrating to York University, Toronto. In Britain preparations continued for the Open University or university of the air, which was expecting 100,000 applicants when it started operations in 1970. At the same time plans were being laid for a new private university free of state involvement. A five-year, £2 million plan to develop the use of computers in British education and technical training was recommended to the government by the National Council for Educational Technology. In East Germany a new faculty of journalism was opened at Leipzig's Karl Marx University, and in India a college of fishery science was established at Bangalore.

(L. R. Bu.)

See also Cinema; Libraries; Medicine; Museums and Galleries; Police; Race Relations; Sociology.

Encyclopædia Britannica Films. *New Tools for Learning* (1952); *Should I Go to College?* (1957); *The Unique Contribution* (1959); *You Can Go a Long Way!* (1961); *George W. Beadle* ("Dialogue for This Decade") (1962); *Sterling McMurrin* ("Dialogue for This Decade") (1962); *Project Discovery: A Demonstration in Education* (1965); *How a Scientist Works* (1967); *The Humanities Films: Their Aims and Uses* (1967); *Project Discovery II: Let Them Learn* (1967); *Suzuki Teaches American Children and Their Mothers* (1967); *Teaching French with Films,* Parts I and II (1967); *Toward Inquiry—Teaching Earth Science* (1967).

Eggs:
see Agriculture
Egypt:
see United Arab Republic
Eire:
see Ireland
Electrical Industries:
see Fuel and Power; Industrial Review: Nuclear Energy

Electronics

The landing of man on the moon was undoubtedly the most spectacular accomplishment of electronics during 1969. The major contributors—the computer and communications technologies—were essential to every phase of the mission. The computer network performed in excess of 50 million calculations per minute, and the communications system provided television coverage of the event to the world.

Computers. As the control source for the approximately 50 rocket engines of the Apollo 11 and 12 spacecraft, or as the heart of the most sophisticated guidance and navigation system ever devised, or in any of the countless other functions of the Apollo missions, the computer amply demonstrated that it was among man's most versatile tools. Less glamorously, however, the computer field in general concentrated on refining its third-generation product rather than on making innovations. The emphasis during the year was on small computers and calculators and on peripheral equipment; the latter grew at twice the pace of the "mainframe" business.

Two decisions of enormous importance to the computer "software" industry were made during the year: the U.S. Court of Customs and Patent Appeals ruled that two Mobil Oil Corp. computer experts (C. D. Prater and J. Wei) could patent a computer program (such software had been previously unpatentable); and the U.S. Internal Revenue Service decided that software could be written off as either a normal business expense or as a capital expenditure.

The industry giant, International Business Machines Corp. (IBM), faced with several antitrust suits that included one by the U.S. Department of Justice, decided in response to "unbundle" or separate the costs of computer software and hardware, previously offered as a package deal. As was expected, the rest of the industry began to follow suit.

In the U.S., Congress approved the use of computers to provide fast and accurate data on federal spending, and the Public Health Service developed a computer program that analyzed electrocardiograms (EKG's) with a false negative-diagnosis rate of less than 1% (an average cardiologist misinterpreted EKG's at a rate of up to 10%). One U.S. firm announced that it would market a synthesizer that would make speech intelligible to computers, while the U.S. Air Force tested a system that planned tactical air operations involving up to 140 squadrons in as many as 60 sorties over 32,000 possible targets, all in 5½ minutes.

In West Germany, hydrographers used a computer to reduce the time needed for plotting river and harbour profiles from months to only days. Also, a computer-run noise-monitoring system warning of high noise levels over residential areas was installed near Stuttgart.

The newest arrival in computer technology took the form of magnetic bubbles 0.00004 in. in diameter and serving in both memory and logic functions. One cubic inch of this material was able to contain several million bits of information.

Communications. As a result of a decision in 1968 by the U.S. Federal Communications Commission (FCC) permitting "foreign attachments" to be connected to the telephone system, the greatest area of activity in the communications field involved "modems," data handling devices between the central processor and user. One of those benefiting from the decision, Xerox, began to offer long-distance transmission of copies of documents, while the Bell system itself began quoting prices for its Picturephone.

The U.S. Federal Aviation Agency (FAA) responded to the crisis of air-traffic congestion in a number of ways that involved electronics. It awarded a $35 million contract for automated radar terminal systems (ARTS 3) at 62 of the nation's busiest airports. In late 1968 the FAA had installed an automatic readout system at Kennedy International Airport (New York); in 1969 it proved invaluable in reducing verbal communication between pilot and flight controller over an area of approximately 4,200 sq.mi. The FAA also approved "area navigation," which provided a straight-line flight path by allowing planes to operate along almost any air route within range of very-high-frequency omnirange ground stations.

If the U.S. Navy had had the digital signaling system that it tested in 1969 on its intelligence ship "Pueblo," it is unlikely that North Korea would have captured the ship. The digital selective calling system not only drastically shortened the time required to establish voice links between ships, but also doubled the channel capacity and provided for authentication of messages.

The year was a good one for radar: the Raytheon Co. introduced a very-narrow-beam millimetre-wave system for missile batteries, battlefield data systems, and front-line communications that was immune to interception or jamming; a French firm developed a system so sensitive that it could spot high-tension wires 1,500 yd. away; the U.S. Army successfully operated a low-level device that detected and charted underground tunnels in Vietnam; and the Aerospace Corp. tested a new millimetre-wave radar that had a ten-mile range resolution of six inches.

Other developments in communications during the year included a locator device that detected downed

A mechanical monster that mimics movements of its operator through advanced electronic control system is tested by General Electric engineer. Quadruped machine was developed by GE under U.S. Army contract.

UPI COMPIX

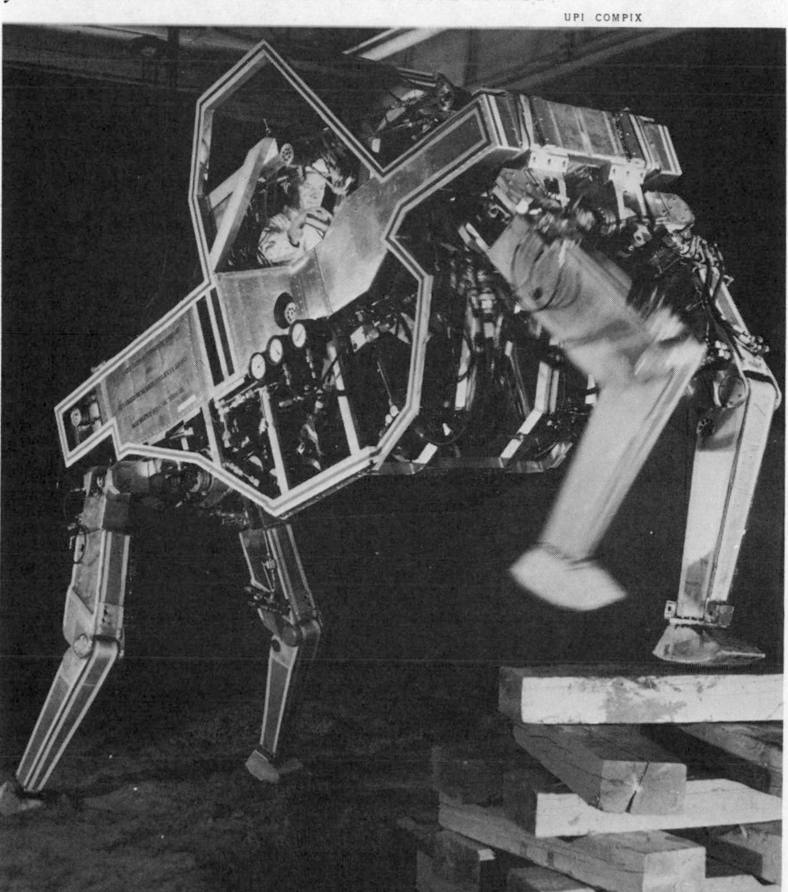

planes even in dense wet foliage. The Bendix Corp. located and actuated offshore distribution pipeline valves by remote sonic signals, and International Telephone and Telegraph Corp. tested a cordless telephone that operated within a distance of 60 ft. from handset to table set.

Semiconductor Technology. There was no question that large-scale integrated (LSI) arrays had finally arrived in 1969. The most complex off-the-shelf bipolar circuit being offered contained 253 gates on a $1\frac{1}{2}$-in. silicon wafer with 156 leads (far in excess of the 100-gate requirement). LSI hybrids, devices containing bipolar and metal oxide semiconductor (MOS) chips and employing thin- and thick-film technology, became the next step in integrated circuit (IC) fabrication. They employed beam leads to obtain reliability, ease of assembly and repair, and automation. By the end of the year the first complete production line for LSI arrays was in operation.

The fast and popular emitter-coupled logic (ECL) was bested in 1969 by a faster digital logic circuit called ECL/tunnel-diode development. Ion-implantation techniques promised to replace the standard diffusion process in forming junctions. The microwave Gunn diode found a new use as a replacement for the backward-wave oscillator tube, while the British Army used the diode to replace the klystron in its solid-state transceiver.

AUTHENTICATED NEWS INTERNATIONAL

U.S. airman operates a computerized centre installed in 1969 at U.S. bases in England and Europe as part of worldwide communications system.

In other developments, a reliable new pressure-sensing transducer was developed for the DC-10 digital air-data computer. A new instrument eliminated costly steps by cutting printed-circuit board masks directly from rough sketches. A solid rechargeable electrolyte battery with almost unlimited shelf life provided flash cubes with a self-contained power supply. Japan built the world's largest power semiconductor—a silicon-controlled rectifier rated at 10,000 v. and 400 amp. and a diode rated at 10,000 v. and 600 amp.

Lasers. The most widely known use of the laser during 1969 was associated with the Early Apollo Scientific Experiments Package (EASEP) deployed by the Apollo 11 crew on the moon's surface. After the astronauts left the Laser Ranging Retro-Reflector experiment (an array of 100 fused-silica corner reflectors), a ruby laser aimed through a 107-in. telescope on earth was able to measure the distance to the moon to an accuracy of 1.5 m.

Other developments during the year included: an yttrium-aluminum-garnet laser with a continuous-wave output of 250 w., used for silicon-wafer dicing, resistor trimming, holography, optics alignment, hole drilling, and underwater detection; a 3-Mw. ruby laser producing as many as nine discrete colours simultaneously; and a high-resolution laser scanning system being used to transmit reconnaissance photos from Vietnam to the Pentagon in minutes. The last-mentioned system was expected to have wide application for news media, hospitals, and weather forecasting.

In France, the world's second most powerful laser was produced. It had an output of 4 trillion watts (4 terawatts—the Sandia Corp. of the U.S. had the most powerful with 10 terawatts). In Japan a laser range finder attained an accuracy of one part per million.

Instrumentation. The most important measures taken in this field followed the publicity given the announcement that 1,200 patients die of accidental electrocutions each year. Responsible medical-instrument manufacturers responded to the news that stray currents (transmitted via the saline solutions used with cardiac catheters) could kill at levels as low as 15 microamperes by incorporating the technique of circuit isolation within their equipment. One company developed a $55 pocket-size instrument that could detect currents as small as 5 microamperes.

Other medical instrumentation included a Doppler-effect blood-pressure monitor and spirometer to measure respiratory parameters, a subtract and dual-channel colour-scanning technique used with a Polaroid camera to detect cancer of the pancreas, and xerographic mammograms to discover breast cancer in women.

What seemed likely to be a major breakthrough in law enforcement took place at 15 sheriff substations throughout Los Angeles County with the first installation of the Ampex Videofile, which stores records, fingerprints, and photographs on videotape, thereby cutting retrieval time for such information from one day to five minutes. In New York City a computer system called "Sprint" (Special Police Radio Inquiry Network) enormously increased police effectiveness by processing emergency calls so that the nearest available manpower and equipment could be dispatched to the scene of the emergency. It could perform this operation within three seconds.

The best hope of finding the alleged Loch Ness monster seemed to lie in a digital sonar that detected one-inch spheres 50-yd. under the Scottish lake. One firm invented a rugged tiltmeter with a resolution of 0.0005 arc second that could detect an earthquake before it began, while another produced an electronic tester more sensitive than a microscope for measuring irregularities on ball bearings. Up to an hour's warning of dangerous approaching storms became possible by means of a U.S. Air Force system that distinguished between harmless and destructive air turbulences; the U.S. Navy began operating a low-light-level television system that could detect submarines from an airplane under starlight conditions.

Industrial and Consumer Electronics. The most dramatic innovations in this area occurred within the automobile industry, although many consumers were unaware of the changes that took place. Most widespread of the innovations was the change from relay-operated voltage regulators to IC designs. Rear-window defrosters, fuel pumps, speedometers, and odometers also went electronic, and turn signals gave way to sequential flashers. Auto makers replaced

PICTORIAL PARADE

Electronic flight director, designed by General Electric to provide visual flight information for aircraft pilots from takeoff to landing. The seven-inch TV screen, mounted on the instrument panel, replaces a large number of indicators.

electromechanical parts with discrete semiconductor devices in ignition systems and tachometers. Engineers also developed an electronic fuel-injection system, an antiskid braking system that uses sensors and a computer to measure and evaluate wheel velocity and road surface conditions, and an automatic speed-control system using a type of electronic memory system to retain the desired speed setting.

Plans were also made for infrared sensors that would provide instantaneous information on velocity and distance of leading and trailing vehicles, with the response being an accelerating or braking of the control car. Finally, work was begun to enable future generations to see the day when drivers on automated highways would be able to switch to an autopilot mode when driving conditions were poor or to relieve fatigue.

The year 1969 saw an increase in colour-television tube brightness of up to 100%, while examination of 4,838 colour sets on Long Island revealed that one out of five still emitted X rays at a level higher than the safe limit of 0.5 milliroentgens per hour at five centimetres from the set. Electronic tuning for radio and television, which received much publicity earlier in the year, did not live up to its press notices, mainly because of its prohibitive cost and poor tracking performance.

In the U.S., Bell Telephone Laboratories, Inc., made a telephone that allowed the deaf to "see" messages in coded flashes of light and the blind to "feel" them in the vibrations of a finger pad. A West German firm marketed a gasless semiconductor heat pump with no moving parts that functioned either to heat or to cool homes, camps, or airborne units; no maintenance was needed for years. The Japanese exported an all-IC "Dick Tracy" type of wristwatch-radio; the Swiss introduced a solid-state stopwatch that contained a light-emitting diode readout. Australia reported developing an electronic taxi meter with a memory that computes and displays the fare; and a British firm advanced the top speed of photographic shutters to 100 million frames per second. (M. E.)

See also Industrial Review; Information Science and Technology; Medicine; Photography; Telecommunications; Television and Radio.

ENCYCLOPÆDIA BRITANNICA FILMS. *Electrons at Work* (1961).

El Salvador

A republic on the Pacific coast of Central America and the smallest country on the isthmus, El Salvador is bounded on the west by Guatemala and on the north and east by Honduras. Area: 8,100 sq.mi. (21,000 sq.km.). Pop. (1968 est.): 3,266,492. Cap. and largest city: San Salvador (pop., 1968 est., 340,544). Language: Spanish. Religion: Roman Catholic. President in 1969, Col. Fidel Sánchez Hernández.

Conflict with Honduras. Hopes for economic and social progress in El Salvador were badly shattered in July by the outbreak of a bloody border war with Honduras. Frivolously called the "soccer war" by the world press when it first drew headlines, the conflict quickly brought death and human tragedy on a scale rarely known in Salvadoran history. Hard-earned government funds were suddenly shifted from national development budgets to immediate military procurement. The carefully built foundations of the Central American Common Market were shaken, and barriers were thrown up to trade, frustrating hopes for a truly integrated economy in the isthmus.

Quarreling over the frontier had been sporadic for some three years, partly because of genuine doubts about the delineation of the border but mainly because of growing difficulties experienced by Salvadoran nationals living in Honduras. These immigrants, numbering about 300,000, had left their overpopulated country in recent decades to seek work or busi-

EL SALVADOR

Education. (1965–66) Primary, pupils 397,810, teachers 11,537; secondary, pupils 38,619, teachers 1,848; vocational, pupils 9,929, teachers 908; teacher training, students 6,288, teachers 368; higher (including 2 universities), students 3,627, teaching staff 619.

Finance. Monetary unit: colón, with a par value of 2.50 colones to U.S. $1 (6 colones = £1 sterling). Gold and foreign exchange, central bank: (June 1969) U.S. $56.5 million; (June 1968) U.S. $64.7 million. Budget (1968 rev. est.) balanced at 218,337,000 colones. Gross national product: (1967) 2,205,000,000 colones; (1966) 2,093,000,000 colones. Cost of living (1963 = 100): (June 1969) 104; (June 1968) 106.

Foreign Trade. (1968) Imports 538.8 million colones; exports 530.3 million colones. Import sources (1967): U.S. 31%; Guatemala 13%; Japan 8%; West Germany 7%; U.K. 6%; Honduras 6%. Export destinations (1967): U.S. 27%; West Germany 22%; Guatemala 16%; Honduras 10%; Japan 8%; Nicaragua 7%; Costa Rica 6%. Main exports: coffee 44%; cotton 7%.

Transport and Communications. Roads (1966) 8,394 km. (including 625 km. of Pan-American Highway). Motor vehicles in use (1967): passenger 30,100; commercial (including buses) 13,700. Railways (1967) *c.* 750 km. Telephones (Jan. 1968) 37,796. Radio receivers (Dec. 1967) *c.* 396,000. Television receivers (Dec. 1967) 45,000.

Agriculture. Production (in 000; metric tons; 1968; 1967 in parentheses): rice 84 (78); corn 235 (189); sorghum 118 (108); coffee (1967) *c.* 138, (1966) 123; cotton, lint *c.* 43 (*c.* 35); sugar, raw value (1968 69) 145, (1967–68) 147. Livestock (in 000; 1966–67): cattle *c.* 925; pigs *c.* 321; horses *c.* 74; chickens *c.* 2,000.

Industry. Production (1968): cement 155,000 metric tons; electricity (excluding most industrial production) *c.* 550 million kw-hr.

ness opportunities in the lightly populated Honduran territory. As their number grew larger and Hondurans recognized them as competitors, the government of El Salvador began to hear tales that Hondurans were mistreating them. Some Salvadoran squatters were displaced early in 1969 under the provisions of a Honduran land-reform law, and the Salvadoran government charged that Honduras was jealous of the harder-working Salvadorans and was trying to exterminate them.

The dispute flared into the open and attracted attention on June 26, when El Salvador broke diplomatic relations. Honduras reciprocated the following day. The immediate cause of the break had been rioting over the results of two international football (soccer) matches. Honduras had won the first match on home grounds, but charged foul play when El Salvador won the second match in San Salvador on June 22.

When the diplomatic break came, the Organization of American States (OAS) sent a mission from its Human Rights Committee to visit the two countries. El Salvador's foreign minister, Francisco José Guerrero, accused Honduras of instigating genocide, and his government produced a film showing mutilated victims of alleged Honduran atrocities. On July 14 regular formations of Salvadoran troops moved into Honduras. Scattered air raids took place using World War II-type fighter planes and even private or sports planes.

Since neither country had total armed forces of more than 6,000 men, fighting was on a minor scale, but it was nonetheless bloody. Honduran forces were unable to stop the initial Salvadoran advance, but the Salvadorans lacked supplies to sustain operations. Five days after fighting started, the OAS arranged a fragile cease-fire, but the Salvadorans already lacked matériel to continue the invasion. Military casualties claimed by each side were not more than 100 killed or wounded, but civilian casualties, especially in the neighbourhood of Nueva Ocotepeque in Honduras, were reported by witnesses to have reached nearly one thousand.

During the cease-fire, withdrawal of forces was delayed because El Salvador continued to press its charge of genocide and demanded guarantees for the protection and safety of the 300,000 Salvadorans in Honduras. Finally, on July 29, El Salvador, under threat of OAS economic sanctions, agreed to what it called a "redeployment" of forces. An OAS observer team of 20 men was sent to patrol the frontier, while efforts for a permanent settlement continued.

The impact of the fighting on Salvadoran political, economic, and social life was enormous. All social classes were brought into the relief effort, first to help feed soldiers at the front and then to cope with a stream of refugees that had reached 38,000 by October and continued at an average rate of about 100 per day. Some refugees had relatives with whom they could live, but many more had to be cared for by the hard-pressed Salvadoran Red Cross.

Of serious long-range consequence was the end to trade between El Salvador and Honduras. In the period after the war the only goods that could cross the Salvadoran-Honduran border were those originating in a third country. The Pan-American Highway, upon which the factories of El Salvador depended to export products to its Common Market partners, was closed by Honduras. In December, in an effort to save the Common Market, the foreign ministers of the member countries agreed that negotiations between Honduras and El Salvador would begin early in 1970.

Internal Affairs. The tragedy of the Salvadorans in Honduras did, however, stimulate some new efforts at land reform in El Salvador. A private industrialist, Francisco de Sola, brought together a group of Salvadoran businessmen to form a corporation to purchase land that could be divided among needy refugees, with corresponding credit and technical assistance. Renewed efforts were undertaken by the government to push through the National Assembly long-pending agricultural land-reform legislation. The success of its efforts would depend upon the determination of the government to face the habitual opposition of the republic's large landowning families.

There were no national elections in 1969, but the country was preparing for crucial elections for the National Assembly in March 1970. The governing Party of National Conciliation (PCN), which had 27 seats (of the total 52), was to be challenged by the Christian Democratic Party (PDC), which had 19, and by the growing National Revolutionary Movement (MNR), a moderate-left organization.

(M. W. Wi.)

Emigration: *see* Migration, International

Employment, Wages, and Hours

The International Labour Organization, in addition to celebrating its 50th anniversary in 1969 and being named to receive the Nobel Peace Prize (*see* Labour Unions), launched the World Employment Programme to combat the world's growing unemployment problems. The insufficiency of jobs was a serious problem for the less developed countries and it was rapidly growing worse in many countries. Thus, the main preoccupation of the ILO's program was "to make productive employment for large numbers of people a major goal of national and international policies for development." The *Report of the Director-General to the International Labour Conference* pointed out that "until recently employment was not effectively recognized as an objective in its own right which must be pursued energetically for social and political as well as for economic reasons. Thus, policies for economic development which did not include employment among their major objectives have resulted in jobs and incomes for only a privileged few."

The magnitude of the problem facing the world in the 1970s is presented in Table I. The population and the labour force of the industrialized nations were expected to expand by 10%, and 55 million more jobs would be required; in the less developed countries population would expand by 20%, and 229 million more jobs would be required if the already precarious unemployment situation was not to deteriorate still further. About one-third of the increase in the labour force would be absorbed in agriculture. Hence it was important that the World Employment Programme direct a larger proportion of aid to agricultural and rural development, in particular to development projects that used a large amount of labour.

Table II indicates how the less developed countries suffered from a shortage of skilled manpower. In the industrialized economies 14% of the labour force was employed in the two top (well educated) grades of employment, whereas for the less developed countries this proportion was only 3%. In less developed countries the labour force was concentrated in agricultural and related activities and only 16% was in what might loosely be termed "industry"; the proportion in the more developed countries, 34%, more than doubled that figure. These statistics indicated the importance of education to the less developed countries, but unfortunately a great deal of their education was elementary and nontechnical and served only to equip workers with sales and low-grade clerical skills rather than with the more needed skills of industrial workers. Therefore, in the World Employment Programme greater emphasis was to be given to projects for vocational training in accordance with long-term forecasts of the skills required by the given country.

The ILO report did not consider the problem of clashes between the World Employment Programme and other objectives of the ILO. It was possible that the establishment of legal minimum wages might not be compatible with maximizing employment; that the promotion of trade unionism might make it more difficult to ensure that the burdens and rewards of development were equitably shared; and that the free international movement of labour might mean that less developed countries would continue to suffer from the brain and skill drain at a time when rapid development demanded a halt to this loss of skilled labour. Finally, the report was not particularly forthright about the population problem, which should not be neglected as a long-term answer to the employment problem. The World Employment Programme, however, represented an important consensus on the need to concentrate on the provision of productive jobs for the world's labour force as a way to increase living standards in the poorer countries and to spread the benefits of such increases more equitably among the population.

Employment and Unemployment. The main contrast between the less developed and the industrialized economies can be seen in Table III: in 1967 the less developed economies had an average increase in population of 2.4% and the industrialized economies had an average increase of 0.9%. This disparity had been the case for many years and was coupled with a corresponding difference in the rates of growth of the labour force. In the less developed economies, agriculture tended to be a backward sector (a survey of 24 less developed economies showed that output per worker in agriculture was, on average, half that per worker in the rest of the economy) and, at the same time, agriculture contained a large proportion of the economically active population (42% on average). In contrast, the more technically advanced agriculture in the industrialized countries contained only 14% of the labour force on average.

Less Developed Economies. One of the main needs of economic development in the poorer countries was to provide jobs in the more advanced sectors of the economy for the rapidly growing labour force. Failure to do so resulted in large increases in the number of unemployed concentrated in shantytowns around the main cities, or in underemployment in the rural areas; either was a large social and economic waste. The rate of growth of employment in manufacturing was often quite high and for the small sample covered in Table III averaged 9.4% in 1967 over 1966. But because this large percentage increase occurred for what was generally only a relatively small part of the labour force, the absolute number of jobs provided was often insufficient. In 1967 the range of changes in unemployment was too wide for the average to be meaningful, but a broader sample provided in the United Nations *Monthly Bulletin of Statistics* (August 1969) indicated that the situation was not deteriorating quite so fast as it had been: the average increase in unemployment in 1966 over 1965 was 17%, whereas in 1968 there was a 5% fall in unemployment from 1967.

Industrial Market Economies. Taken as a whole, 1967 was a year of recession in the industrial market economies with an average fall in manufacturing employment of 1% and an appalling average increase in unemployment of 41.6% (or of 28% excluding the extreme case of West Germany; *see* Table III). By 1968 economic expansion had begun in several countries and by 1969 every country was expanding more rapidly than previously. Consequently, employment everywhere was growing and unemployment falling: in 1969 the average increase in employment was 2.3%, compared with 0.1% for 1968; and the average decrease in unemployment was 10.2%, compared with the 8.5% increase the previous year. (*See* Table IV.)

In 1968 and early 1969 employment in the U.S. expanded and unemployment fell because of unforeseen increases in military spending and difficulties in restraining the rest of the economy through fiscal and monetary measures. In Canada employment fell and unemployment rose in 1968, continuing the trend of the 1967 recession. In the second half of 1968, however, this trend was being reversed, and by mid-1969 manufacturing employment had increased by 3.6% over mid-1968 and the rise in unemployment had been completely halted.

In Western Europe, except in West Germany and the Netherlands, unemployment continued to rise in 1968, but this trend had reversed by mid-1969 and manufacturing employment was increasing as economic activity expanded. In West Germany fiscal policy was expansionary after the deflation of 1966 had corrected the current account balance of payments deficit of 1965. Consequently industrial output increased by 9% in 1968; by mid-1968 there were $3\frac{1}{2}$ times as many unfilled vacancies as unemployed, and foreign workers were again filling the gap.

In France unemployment in 1968 was over a quarter larger than in 1967 (which in turn was a third higher than in 1966) and this was undoubtedly a contributory factor to the social and industrial unrest of 1968. By mid-1969 there had been little change in the situation; both employment and unemployment remained stable, as vigorous expansion was incompatible with the maintenance of the exchange value of the franc. Devaluation in August 1969 might have made expansionary policies possible but because the government was proceeding with extreme caution, there was unlikely to be any immediate marked change in the situation.

In the United Kingdom the government followed a

Table I. Total Population and Labour Force

In 000,000

Item	1960	1970	1980	Increase 1970–80 Numbers	%
Industrialized countries					
Population	994	1,110	1,234	124	10
Labour force	447	498	553	55	10
Less developed countries					
Population	2,003	2,487	3,106	619	20
Labour force	856	1,019	1,248	229	18
Farmers and related workers	595	666	743	77	10
Others (industrial and service)	261	353	505	152	30

Source: International Labour Office, *The World Employment Programme: Report of the Director-General to the International Labour Conference* (1969).

Table II. Occupational Structure of the Labour Force, 1970 (%)

Type of worker	Industrialized countries	Less developed countries
Professional, technical, and related	9	2
Administrative, executive, and managerial	5	1
Clerical	11	3
Sales	8	6
Service, sport, and recreation	9	4
Transport and communications operations	5	2
Farmers, fishermen, hunters, loggers, etc.	19	65
Craftsmen, production process, miners, and labourers not elsewhere specified	34	16

Source: International Labour Office, *The World Employment Programme: Report of the Director-General to the International Labour Conference* (1969).

policy of economic restraint in 1968 "to make devaluation work," that is, to ensure that increased production was exported rather than consumed at home, and to restrain imports of consumption goods. Consequently there was a slight fall in employment and a slight rise in unemployment during 1968. In the first half of 1969, however, the value of exports was 12% higher than in the first half of 1968 and the index of industrial production was 4% higher. This expansion entailed a slight rise in manufacturing employment and a fall in unemployment of 3.8%.

Centrally Planned Economies. The growth rate of employment in the centrally planned economies of Eastern Europe and the Soviet Union tended to decline slightly each year. This might be attributed to the fact that labour supplies were becoming scarcer because of a steady decline over two decades in the rate of population growth rather than to any marked slackening in the rate of growth of output.

This growing scarcity of labour was forcing economic reforms aimed at increasing efficiency in general and labour productivity in particular: only by keeping productivity growth high could a fast rate of growth of output be maintained. In general these reforms aimed at changes in methods of central planning giving more scope for initiative at the lower levels of decision making so that resources could be used more flexibly and hence more efficiently. This enabled enterprises to adopt systems of incentive wage payments aimed at raising labour productivity. Despite these reforms, and perhaps even because of them, there was a general tendency for industrial employment to rise faster than planned, or for productivity to rise by less than was planned, indicating that the reforms had yet to be fully effective. However, an average rate of growth of industrial productivity of 5.4% in 1968 should be considered a fairly satisfactory achievement. (*See* Table V.)

In the U.S.S.R. actual national income grew faster than planned owing to an increase in investment caused by decentralization, which made it easier for enterprises to obtain credit and to reinvest their operating surplus. The output of the construction industry increased substantially, and this meant a faster rate of growth of employment and a lower rate of increase of productivity than had been planned. In Bulgaria the rate of growth of industrial output was rapid despite the depression caused by a poor agricultural harvest. The growth in industrial productivity was very rapid, as the authorities were trying to reduce the outflow of labour from agriculture and to redeploy industrial labour. In Hungary, a new system of economic control was introduced in 1968. There the policy was to restrict the growth of demand so as to ensure that the changeover would not be endangered. The rate of growth of output was low and for various reasons (strict control of wages, a reduction in hours worked) employment expanded faster than planned. Thus, Hungary had a low rate of growth of output per man-year, although output per man-hour expanded by 4.5% in 1968.

Wages. *Industrial Market Economies.* Table VI gives the rates of increase of money and real wages in manufacturing and of consumer prices in the industrial market economies. The average rate of increase of money wages was 7.8% in 1968 and was higher by one percentage point at 8.8% in 1969; the average rate of price increase had risen too, from 3.8% in 1968 to 4.5% in 1969, and consequently there was not much difference in the rate of growth of real wages—3.9% in 1968 and 4.2% in 1969. The higher rates of wage and price increase were due to the expansionary policies generally being followed after the recession of 1967.

In the U.S. output was expanding in the first half of 1968 at an annual rate of 6.4%, but in the second half it accelerated to an annual rate of 10% due to a large increase in federal expenditure on defense and to increased investment. Following this, consumer spending increased, the restraining effects of a tax increase being nullified by the public, which reduced the proportion of income saved to pay the higher taxes, rather than decreasing its consumption. Although consumer spending slackened in 1969, business investment remained high and, with no official moves directly to counteract inflation, the annual rate of price increase rose from 4.2% in 1968 to 5.5% in 1969, thus reducing the rate of growth of real wages. By the end of 1969 credit restraint to combat inflation was expected to entail slower growth and a rise in unemployment.

In West Germany the rate of growth of money wages remained fairly low in 1968 and 1969 and the rate of price increase rose from 1.8 to 2.6%. The

Table III. Employment, Unemployment, and Population

Changes for 1967 over 1966(%)

Country	Employment General	Employment Manufacturing	Unemployment	Population	Economically active population engaged in agriculture (1965)
Less developed:					
Honduras	2.2	14.4	—	2.9	45
Korea, South	2.9	27.1	−11.4	2.4	54
Philippines	10.4	1.4	14.8	3.5	59
Puerto Rico	1.6	4.9	0.0	1.1	19
Singapore	0.4	−1.1	17.7	2.2	7
Taiwan	8.7	—	−24.1	2.6	47
Trinidad	4.2	—	11.1	1.5	19
Uganda	4.4	9.4	—	2.5	89
Average	4.3	9.4	1.4	2.4	42
Industrialized:					
Austria	−1.1	−3.3	5.2	0.5	20
Belgium	−0.5	−2.9	38.7	0.6	6
Canada	3.1	−0.3	18.0	2.0	9
France	—	−1.5	33.3	0.8	18
Germany, West	−3.1	−4.9	188.1	0.4	11
Italy	−0.3	3.5	−10.4	0.7	24
Japan	3.0	5.0	43.2	1.1	27
Netherlands	−0.7	−2.0	94.6	1.2	9
Norway	2.1	1.2	− 4.2	0.9	18
Sweden	−1.2	−4.9	34.4	0.8	12
United Kingdom	−0.7	−2.8	54.8	0.6	4
United States	2.0	1.2	3.5	1.1	6
Average	0.3	−1.0	41.6	0.9	14
Planned economies:					
Bulgaria	3.3	5.1	—	0.6	59
Czechoslovakia	1.2	1.3	—	0.5	16
Germany, East	1.4	1.2	—	0.1	19
Hungary	1.0	2.8	—	0.4	31
Poland	3.8	4.2	—	0.8	42
Romania	4.0	3.8	—	0.7	59
Yugoslavia	−0.7	−0.5	—	1.1	53
Average	2.0	2.6	—	0.6	40

Sources: International Labour Office, *Year Book of Labour Statistics* (1968); United Nations Food and Agriculture Organization, *Production Yearbook* (1967).

WIDE WORLD

The Rev. James Groppi leads a demonstration against the Allen Bradley Co. in Milwaukee, Wis., on Aug. 11, 1969, to protest alleged racial discrimination in hiring practices.

faster rate of price inflation occurred as exports increased strongly in the second half of 1968 and the first half of 1969 and led to increases in investment and a small increase in private consumption. The rate of growth of real wages continued to be low at 2.6% in 1968 and 2.2% in 1969, but the labour force had the compensating advantage of working in a fully employed economy.

In France the rate of growth of money wages was high in both 1968 and 1969 after the strikes of early 1968 and the consequent wage settlements. These resulted in an increase in wages of 4–5% in June and of a further 2½–3% in October for 13 million higher paid workers, an increase of 35% in the minimum legal wage affecting 1–1.5 million workers, and an increase of 56% in wages for 700,000 agricultural workers. These wage increases were followed by a boom in private consumption, and the rate of price inflation increased from 4.6% in 1968 to 6.4% in 1969. Nevertheless, gains in real wages were substantial and the trade gap widened; the volume of imports was a third higher in the first half of 1969 than in the first half of 1968. The increase in wages was paid for by devaluation.

In the Netherlands the rate of growth of money wages was high in both years at 8 and 8.7%, but the rate of price inflation was only 3.7% in 1968 because rapid increases in productivity actually reduced labour costs per unit of output. But early in 1969 prices began to rise at a rate of almost 1% a month because of the new value added tax, and in April the government announced a complete freeze of all prices. These measures were expected to entail a change in the growth rate of real wages for 1969 as a whole.

In the U.K. average earnings in 1968 were 8.6% higher than in 1967, most of this increase occurring in the last quarter of 1967. During 1968 and 1969 there was supposed to be a ceiling of 3½% on wage increases and for the first half of 1968 increases were moderate, but there was a large increase in wages in the second half of 1968 after the railway unions forced the government to consent to a substantial wage increase. Thus, by mid-1969 money wages were 7.9% higher than in mid-1968, the rate of price inflation had increased from 4.7% in 1968 to 5.5% in 1969, and the rate of growth of real wages had declined sharply. The government resorted to monetary and fiscal control, which created more unemployment, in order to reduce consumption so as to restrain imports and ensure that exports continued to expand.

In Japan the rate of growth of money wages was

Table IV. Employment in Manufacturing in Industrialized Countries

Changes over previous year(%)

Country	Employment 1968	Employment 1969*	Unemployment 1968	Unemployment 1969*	Hours worked per week 1968
Canada	−0.8	3.6	21.3	0.3	0
United States	1.6	2.1	−5.4	−1.8	0.3
Japan	2.8	2.5	—	3.5	−0.4
Austria	−1.7	3.2	9.1	−3.9	0.2
Belgium	−2.0	—	21.2	−16.8	—
France	−2.2	0.8	29.6	−3.3	−0.2
Germany, West	1.3	5.9	−29.6	−52.6	2.4
Ireland	2.3	6.3	2.8	−5.4	0
Italy	1.7	4.0	0.7	−5.8	0
Netherlands	−0.9	0.0	−9.3	−32.2	−0.9
Norway	−0.3	0.8	44.7	−5.7	−2.9
Sweden	1.2	0.0	16.0	−4.4	—
United Kingdom	−1.0	0.6	0.3	−3.8	0.5
Average	0.1	2.3	8.5	−10.2	−0.1

*Second quarter over second quarter 1968.
Source: Organization for Economic Cooperation and Development, *Main Economic Indicators* (September 1969).

Table V. Output, Employment, and Productivity in the Planned Economies

Change in 1968 over 1967(%)

Country	Output	Employment	Productivity
Bulgaria	11.8	2.3	9.3
Czechoslovakia	5.2	1.3	3.8
Germany, East	6.1	0.3	5.8
Hungary	4.9	3.8	1.1
Poland	9.3	3.5	5.7
Romania	11.6	4.5	6.8
U.S.S.R.	8.1	3.0	5.0
Average	8.1	2.7	5.4

Source: United Nations Economic Commission for Europe, *Economic Survey of Europe in 1968.*

very high in 1968 and 1969. With only small price increases in both years, there were substantial gains in real wages of 9.8 and 10.9%. This was due to the continuation of the rapid boom based on investment. After a period of trade deficit in 1967, exports (particularly to the U.S. and Far Eastern countries) rose rapidly in 1968 and 1969, thus enabling the boom to be sustained. Despite the very rapid growth of the economy, price increases were fairly moderate because of rapid productivity increases that kept pace with the wage increases. The growth of real gross national product was remarkably high at 10% in 1966, 13% in 1967, 14% in 1968, and a probable 10–12% in 1969. Japan was now the world's third largest industrial nation after the U.S. and the U.S.S.R.

Less Developed Economies. In the less developed countries there was a marked tendency for money wages in manufacturing to rise at a rapid rate. (*See* Table VII.) Price increases also tended to be rapid, but there was nevertheless a tendency for real wages in manufacturing to rise at a faster rate than in the industrialized countries. However, these wage increases accrued to only a small section of the population while everyone bore the burden of rising prices. The effect of this was that real incomes for a large section of the population might well have been falling; that is, the few urban industrially employed rich got richer, and the many rural workers and urban unemployed got poorer. Furthermore, rising wages might well have hampered the growth of employment. Very often the cause of rising wages was simply pressure from militant trade unions, particularly those dealing with large and wealthy foreign-owned companies. These political pressures usually resulted in a spiral of wage increases.

Many governments, in their concern to tackle increasing inequality among their citizens, growing unemployment, and impoverishment of the rural areas, had legislated against trade unions, effectively banning strikes by forcing the parties to submit their unresolved disputes to an industrial court whose rulings were final and legally binding. They also put ceilings on the wage increases to be permitted. But these measures raised the dilemma that by controlling labour costs in this way profits were increased. As it was politically impracticable for governments to hold down the standards of living of their citizens so that shareholders (often foreign) might receive either a bigger dividend or a faster rate of appreciation of their capital (if profits were reinvested in the enterprise), an increasingly common solution was for the government to take the companies concerned into public ownership, so that the benefits of larger profits accrued to the whole community.

Centrally Planned Economies. Increases in the cost of living continued to be very low in the centrally planned economies and rises in money wages were correspondingly moderate. (*See* Table VIII.) Those countries instituting economic reforms seemed to have higher rates of money wage and price increases as enterprises took advantage of the discretion given to them. The impact of the reforms in Czechoslovakia and the U.S.S.R. on money wages is obvious: wage increases in 1968 were about three percentage points higher than in 1967.

Hours. In most industrial countries the length of the working week was gradually being shortened as people took part of their increased incomes in the form of more leisure. In the short run, however, fluctuations in the working week were the result of economic fluctuations. While in the recession of 1967 the length of the working week tended to fall, in 1968 most industrial economies grew more rapidly and there was less short-time work and more overtime available. The length of the working week tended to increase slightly, especially in the U.K. and West Germany. (*See* Table IV.) In other countries the change tended to be negligible, except in Norway where on July 1, 1968, the contractual working week was reduced from 45 to 42½ hours, a fall of about 5%. It was likely that in those countries with high rates of taxation and with adequate provision for social security, workers might increasingly tend to prefer a decrease in the number of hours worked to outright (and taxable) increases in income.

(D. A. S. J.)

See also Economics; Economy, World; Income, National; Industrial Review; Labour Unions; Prices.

ENCYCLOPÆDIA BRITANNICA FILMS. *Working Together* (1952); *Walter P. Reuther* ("Dialogue for This Decade") (1963); *The Industrial Revolution—Beginnings in the United States* (1968); *The Rise of Labor* (1968); *The Industrial Worker* (1969).

Table VI. Money and Real Wages in Manufacturing and Consumer Prices: Industrialized Countries

Changes over previous year(%)

Country	Money wages 1968	Money wages 1969*	Real wages 1968	Real wages 1969*	Prices 1968	Prices 1969
Canada	7.3	7.6	3.0	2.6	4.2	4.8
United States	6.1	6.6	1.8	1.1	4.2	5.5
Japan	15.7	16.5	9.8	10.9	5.4	5.1
Austria	6.9	4.4	4.2	1.0	2.6	3.4
Belgium	5.6	7.3	2.8	3.4	2.7	3.8
Denmark	11.4	—	2.5	—	8.7	—
France	12.4	16.9	7.5	9.9	4.6	6.4
Germany, West	4.4	4.8	2.6	2.2	1.8	2.6
Ireland	8.8	11.9†	3.9	4.8†	4.7	6.7
Italy	3.6	7.3	2.2	5.1	1.4	2.0
Netherlands	8.0	8.7	4.1	0.5	3.7	8.1
Norway	7.5	12.1	4.0	8.5	3.4	3.3
Sweden	6.5	6.7	4.5	4.2	1.9	2.5
Switzerland	4.0	4.7	1.5	2.0	2.5	2.6
United Kingdom	8.6	7.9	3.7	2.3	4.7	5.5
Average	7.8	8.8	3.9	4.2	3.8	4.5

*Second quarter over second quarter 1968.
†First quarter 1969 over first quarter 1968.
Source: Organization for Economic Cooperation and Development, *Main Economic Indicators* (September 1969).

Table VII. Money and Real Wages in Manufacturing and Consumer Prices: Less Developed Countries

Change over previous year(%)

Country	Money wages 1967	Money wages 1968	Real wages 1967	Real wages 1968	Prices 1967	Prices 1968
Ceylon	1.3	—	−0.9	—	2.2	5.9
Chile	27.4	34.2	7.8	5.9	18.2	26.7
Colombia	10.4	10.3	2.0	4.4	8.2	5.7
El Salvador	1.3	—	−0.1	—	1.4	2.6
Ghana	3.2	—	11.3	—	−7.3	10.0
Greece	11.8	7.3	10.0	6.9	1.7	0.4
Guatemala	2.6	2.5	2.1	0.6	0.5	1.9
Korea, South	22.5	26.5	10.5	14.2	10.9	10.8
Mexico	6.0	—	2.9	—	3.0	2.3
Philippines	5.3	—	−1.5	—	6.9	0.7
Puerto Rico	6.9	11.5	2.6	8.5	4.2	2.8
Taiwan	13.4	—	9.7	—	3.3	7.9
Average*	9.3	15.4	4.7	6.8	4.4	6.5

*Average of available statistics.
Source: United Nations, *Monthly Bulletin of Statistics* (August 1969).

Table VIII. Wages and Cost of Living: Planned Economies

Change over previous year(%)

Country	Money wages 1967	Money wages 1968	Real wages 1967	Real wages 1968	Cost of living 1967	Cost of living 1968
Bulgaria	11.0	2.0	—	−3.0	—	5.0
Czechoslovakia	5.5	8.2	3.9	7.0	1.4	1.2
Germany, East	2.4	—	1.1	—	1.3	—
Hungary	4.0	2–2.5*	4.0	2–2.5*	1.0	†
Poland	4.0	3.9	2.5	1.5	1.5	2.4
Romania	2.8	—	2.3	—	0.5	—
U.S.S.R.	4.2	7.5	5.0	—	†	—
Average‡	3.4	4.8	3.1	2.0	1.0	2.2

*Figures given as ranges have been taken at midpoint.
†Negligible.
‡Average of available statistics.
Source: United Nations Economic Commission for Europe, *Economic Survey of Europe in 1968*.

Engineering Projects

Bridges. *Suspension Bridges.* The Lillebælt (Little Belt) suspension bridge in Denmark (spans of 787 ft., 1,968 ft., and 787 ft.) and the Newport Bridge in the U.S. (spans of 688 ft., 1,600 ft., and 688 ft.) were both completed in 1969. The cables for each of these bridges were prefabricated. This method, common in Europe, was new in the U.S. At Newport it allowed considerable time-saving in the construction of the bridge and improved protection against corrosion. The cables were laid in groups of 61 parallel strands which were protected by glass-reinforced resins.

During the year the deck of the Verrazano-Narrows Bridge, New York, was doubled by the addition of a lower level for cars. The bridge was then capable of carrying almost 50 million vehicles a year. Verrazano's record span for a suspension bridge (4,260 ft.) was challenged by two projects: the Humber Bridge (U.K.) with a central span of 4,580 ft., for which government approval was announced in April and which was due for completion in 1976; and the projected suspension bridge between the islands of Honshu and Shikoku, Japan, with a planned maximum span of nearly 5,000 ft. and pylons more than 1,000 ft. high.

Another project close to realization was the Golden Horn Bridge in Istanbul, Turk., more than 5,000 ft. in total length. The bridge would include a single suspended span of 3,254 ft. The cable bridge on the Lower Yarra was under construction near Melbourne, Austr. It was to be 120 ft. wide with spans of 341 ft., 1,166 ft., and 341 ft., carried by a single row of cables resting on two steel pylons rising from a single footing.

Other Metal Bridges. The Baton Rouge cantilever bridge over the Mississippi River, with a main span of 1,233 ft., was completed in 1969 and work began on a cantilever bridge over the Delaware River. The central span of the latter extended 1,643 ft., between outer spans of 823 ft., making it the third largest bridge of its type in the world.

Also in the U.S., a project was under consideration in Portland, Ore., for a bridge with a total length of 2,152 ft., including an arch of 1,255 ft. The bridge would carry two four-lane roadways, one above the other. In Denmark, the Femø Sund Bridge, a 665-ft. bowstring type, was entirely prefabricated and was floated about 40 mi. into position. In South Africa, the Mitchell Bridge in Natal consisted of an arch of 520-ft. span, with a lower deck.

All the above-mentioned bridges consisted of two parallel arches. A more original bridge was being built at Hallein, Aus.: a bowstring to cross the Salzbach in a span of 442 ft.; it was 100 ft. wide and had a single axial arch. The deck consisted of two caisson girders linked by triangulated crosspieces, which ensured wind-bracing. In Belgrade, Yugos., the Sava River was to be crossed by a bridge 6,100 ft. long, of which the central part was to be an inclined-prop steel structure some 1,600 ft. long. The 90-ft.-wide bridge was widely praised for the elegance of its lines.

In 1969 the most interesting girder bridges had widths approaching 100 ft. They were either caisson bridges (for example the Beez Bridge in Belgium with spans of 262 ft., 495 ft., and 262 ft., with a caisson 31 ft. long and 16.5 ft. high) or consisted of two T-shaped girders, as for instance the Kiefersfelden Bridge on the Inn River, Austria, with 541-ft. spans.

NORDISK FROM PICTORIAL PARADE

The Lillebælt bridge, Denmark's first suspension bridge, during construction in 1969. The bridge linked Jutland with the island of Fyn.

The Bay of Guanabara, between Rio de Janeiro and Niteroi, Braz., was to be crossed by a bridge 8½ mi. long. The part crossing the navigable channels, 2,800 ft. long, would be of steel, with spans of 656 ft., 984 ft., and 656 ft.; the deck would consist of two 21½-ft.-wide caissons varying in height from 43 ft. to 25 ft.

Prestressed-Concrete Bridges. The Nusle Valley in Prague, Czech., was crossed by a cantilever bridge 1,590 ft. long in five continuous spans: three central spans of 379 ft. and two outer ones of 224 ft. The deck was a reinforced-concrete caisson of trapezoidal section and had two traffic levels, the upper one for a six-lane highway and the lower one for two railway lines.

In France the Givors Bridge over the Rhône River, with two 360-ft. spans, and the Oissel Bridge on the Seine River, with five 328-ft. spans, were also built as cantilevers with voussoirs cast in situ. In West Germany, a bridge with spans of 262 ft., 496 ft., and 262 ft. was constructed in a similar way but with much longer voussoirs since their cofferings, instead of being suspended, rested on the ground. For bridges of greater length, which had to be completed in a short time, voussoirs were generally prefabricated, the joints being bonded with epoxy resins.

The Chillon viaduct in Switzerland, following Lake Geneva for a distance of nearly 7,000 ft. between 15 ft. and 160 ft. above the ground, consisted of two parallel bridges, each 42 ft. wide and carried on a single caisson, with main spans of 302 ft. and 341 ft. The deck was cantilevered out in prefabricated sec-

Endocrinology: *see* Medicine

tions weighing from 45 to 80 tons, and work proceeded at a rate of about 30 ft. a day.

Prefabrication of girders in prestressed concrete continued to prove the most economical method of construction for crossing distances of between 80 ft. and 160 ft., provided that there were a large number of girders to be prefabricated. In West Germany, the Tienfenbachtal and Phädchensgraben bridges had, respectively, seven spans of 172 ft. and ten spans of 77 ft. In West Pakistan, on the Ravi River, two such bridges, one with seven spans of 144 ft. and one with 12 spans of 132 ft., were constructed. In Lagos, Nigeria, a bridge 4,482 ft. long comprised nine spans, the seven central ones being 200 ft. long each.

Near New York City the 3,000-ft.-long Jamaica Bay viaduct had central prestressed cantilever spans of 130 ft., 265 ft., and 130 ft., with a suspended span of 143 ft. The Como railway bridge in Australia had seven spans of 159 ft. on twin prestressed caisson girders 12 ft. high and 7 ft. wide.

The extension of the Western Avenue freeway in London called for the construction of four curved viaducts, with a total length of more than 2½ mi. These viaducts were built of prefabricated, 7.5-ft.-long segments weighing up to 130 tons and had spans of between 50 and 204 ft.

Two types of transversal section were used to carry expressways 50 ft. in width: a triple-webbed caisson as in the 1,890-ft.-long Döllbach Bridge, near Heilbronn, W.Ger., and a deck (1–1½ ft. thick) with twin longitudinal rectangular or trapezoidal ribs, not cross-beamed, set 29 ft. apart, as in the 3,080-ft.-long Sechselden (W.Ger.) Bridge. (J. FA.)

Buildings. Building construction in 1969 continued to be influenced by social and economic conditions as well as by changing technology and innovations in design. The rising costs of construction brought forth efforts to introduce innovations that would reduce such costs. Thus, in the industrialized nations there was a renewed interest in prefabrication. Mass production of prefabricated sections of buildings was considered in many parts of the world to be a possible way of confronting labour shortages and spiraling costs in the construction of homes as well as other types of buildings. Rapid urbanization and the social problems associated with it brought to the fore the need to utilize fully the vast capabilities of building, engineering, transportation, and technical knowledge in order to provide better community environments in which to live. In the U.S. the condominium offered new legal arrangements that stimulated the construction of individual housing projects of sufficient size to house thousands of people.

It was reported in *Building Construction* that the technology developed by systems builders had produced exciting results in Great Britain. In the London borough of Lambeth an urgently needed urban renewal program was started in 1965. At an early time in the project, systems building techniques were eval-

Major World Dams Under Construction in 1969*

Name of Dam	River	Country	Type†	Height (ft.)	Length of crest (ft.)	Volume content (000 cu.yd.)	Gross capacity of reservoir (000 ac-ft.)
Almendra	Tormes	Spain	AG	649	13,438	3,267	2,025
Aswan, High (Sadd-el Aali)	Nile	U.A.R.	ER	364	12,565	55,809	133,000
Auburn	N.F. American	U.S.	A	680	3,500	6,000	2,500
Ayracik	Yesil Irmak	Turkey	A	551	1,715	1,464	689
Beas	Beas	India	E	380	5,000	44,200	6,600
Cahorabassa	Zambezi	Mozambique	A	525	994	589	129,389
Castaic	Castaic	U.S.	E	340	5,200	44,000	350
Charvak	Chirchik	U.S.S.R.	ER	551	2,499	24,975	1,620
Chirkey	Sulak	U.S.S.R.	A	764	1,109	1,602	2,252
Don Pedro‡	Tuolumne	U.S.	ER	585	1,900	16,760	2,030
Dworshak	Clearwater	U.S.	G	717	3,287	6,500	3,453
Emosson	Barberine	Switzerland	A	590	1,736	1,400	182
Gokcekaya	Sakarya	Turkey	A	518	1,529	850	737
Gran Suarna	Navia	Spain	A	499	1,150	882	567
Idikki	Periyar	India	MA	561	1,201	609	1,182
Ilha Solteira	Paraná	Brazil	EG	262	20,300	32,838	17,172
Inguri	Inguri	U.S.S.R.	A	892	2,198	4,967	891
Kanev	Dnieper	U.S.S.R.	E	82	52,950	49,520	2,125
Kapchagay	Ili	U.S.S.R.	E	164	7,741	10,338	22,761
Keban	Euphrates	Turkey	RG	679	3,598	19,600	25,110
Khantaika	Khantaika	U.S.S.R.	RE	213	21,058	2,452	16,743
Kolnbrein	Malta	Austria	A	607	1,814	1,804	130
Krasnoyarsk	Yenisei	U.S.S.R.	G	407	3,493	5,685	59,425
Las Portas	Camba	Spain	G	498	1,587	977	609
Melones‡	Stanislaus	U.S.	ER	625	1,600	15,970	2,400
Mica	Columbia	Canada	R	800	2,600	42,000	20,000
Montanejos	Mijares	Spain	AG	492	820	163	203
Mratinje	Piva	Yugoslavia	A	722	853	1,019	749
Nagawado	Azusa	Japan	A	508	1,200	865	100
Nurek	Vakhsh	U.S.S.R.	E	1,017	2,390	70,806	8,424
Saratov	Volga	U.S.S.R.	E	131	4,130	19,034	10,854
Sayansk	Yenisei	U.S.S.R.	A	774	3,503	11,916	25,353
Talbingo	Tumut	Australia	R	530	2,300	18,500	747
Tarbela	Indus	Pakistan	ER	485	9,000	186,000	11,100
Toktogul	Naryn	U.S.S.R.	A	705	1,352	3,480	15,800
Ukai	Tapi	India	EG	225	16,164	33,370	6,900
Ust-Ilim	Angara	U.S.S.R.	EG	344	11,695	17,090	48,100
Vilyuy	Vilyuy	U.S.S.R.	ER	213	1,968	3,790	14,985
Zeya	Zeya	U.S.S.R.	G	371	2,312	10,456	55,080
MAJOR WORLD DAMS COMPLETED IN 1968 AND 1969*							
Bennett W.A.C. (Portage Mt.)	Peace	Canada	E	600	6,700	57,200	57,000
Bullards Bar‡	North Yuba	U.S.	A	635	2,200	2,700	930
Cochiti	Rio Grande	U.S.	E	251	28,200	41,100	513
Daniel Johnson (Manicouagan No. 5)	Manicouagan	Canada	MA	703	4,284	2,950	115,000
Guri (first stage)	Caroni	Venezuela	ER	348	2,264	4,917	14,349
Mossyrock	Cowlitz	U.S.	MA	605	1,750	1,240	1,586
Oroville	Feather	U.S.	E	770	6,920	80,310	3,538

*Having a height exceeding 492 ft. (150 m.); or having a total volume content exceeding 20 million cu.yd. (15 million cu.m.); or forming a reservoir exceeding 12 million ac-ft. capacity.
†Type: E=earth; R=rockfill; A=arch; G=gravity; MA=multiple arch.
‡Replacement of present dam.

(T. W. Me.)

uated. As a result of the study, the Wates System was selected. The basis for selection was reported to be the extreme flexibility of the system and the wide experience in contemporary architecture of the firm that had developed it. Many joint planning meetings were held by the architects and the Wates technicians. When the design and terms had been agreed upon, the building project was started, and in 1969 this contract for eight 22-story structures, each of which contained 80 two-story apartments, was nearing completion. Because the eight buildings were located within a few miles of each other, an on-site component manufacturing plant was set up nearby. The structural components were cast in adjustable steel molds. The buildings were erected by two teams of seven men, each team constructing about 200 units per week or about one two-story apartment each day. This was one illustration of the efforts in industrialized nations to introduce prefabrication into the building process.

In the U.S. an organization was formed in 1969 by members of the precast, prestressed concrete industry for the mass production of standardized building components. This program was designed to deliver systems building components for multi-unit housing and industrial and institutional facilities. The components consisted of a complete package for floors, roofs, exterior and interior walls, and structural systems. It was reported that a nationwide study predicted that by 1980, approximately 90% of all federally assisted building would be constructed on a systems basis.

In 1969 the residents in most urban areas of the U.S., as well as in other countries of the world, had little if any recreation space; had difficult access to shops, schools, and community facilities; were confronted with the problem of dangerous street crossings; and had to spend hours each day commuting to work. Efforts to deal with these problems were not new, but evidence of progress toward the solution of them was an interesting part of the building picture in 1969. Community development under way in Finland, Norway, and Sweden achieved notable results. The satellite communities of Stockholm were a good example. The construction of these was begun in 1954 but the most recent one, Skarholmen, opened late in 1968. In this community as well as in the ones built earlier there was a centre for community activities as well as for shops. The centre was surrounded by housing and was connected to the central city of Stockholm by a clean, attractive, efficient subway system.

In the Netherlands, the development of satellite communities in the densely populated area around Amsterdam was the result of planning that had been in process over several centuries, but only since World War II had the General Extension Plan for Amsterdam been implemented. On the western side of the city six suburbs had been built. These communities provided homes for 140,000 people. Three new communities were being built north of Amsterdam to house more than 50,000 people. On the southern side, a city that would house more than 30,000 was in the process of construction in 1969. On the southeastern side of the city, a unique community by the name of Bijlmermeer was being built. The development when completed was to consist of megastructures to house a large proportion of the 125,000 people planned for the community. The solution to traffic problems was sought by routing express traffic on elevated highways, local traffic on semielevated roads, and bicycle paths and footpaths on the surface level with no intersections to be crossed. All parked cars were to be in garages to free space around buildings for parks and recreation areas. Plans such as these revealed the significant progress of the Dutch in combining the construction of homes with community planning. In *Building Research* in 1969, it was reported that new planned communities to improve the environment of urban dwelling were under way in Australia, Brazil, Canada, Denmark, Finland, France, West Germany, Great Britain, India, Israel, Italy, Japan, Mexico, the Netherlands, Norway, Pakistan, Poland, Portugal, Sweden, the U.S.S.R., Venezuela, and Yugoslavia.

In the United States, the University of Utah's new sports arena, a $4.5 million structure, was built with a dome constructed of laminated timber. This was reported to be the largest covered area in the world spanned by a column-free wood structural system. This structure continued a tradition that was started with the Mormon Tabernacle in Salt Lake City. The new large domed structure was designed to be a sports and special events building. The design of the dome provided dignity appropriate to the style of the other buildings on the campus, but had great appeal also because of its economy. The cost of $4.5 million was less than half of the total amount budgeted for the building. It was reported that there were several factors that contributed to the low cost. These related to the costs of both delivery and erection. The shape and weight of the individual members used in the dome simplified handling from the shop where they were made to their final placement in the dome. There was uniformity in the size of members and an almost identical pattern of connections. This meant that assembly operations were repeated over and over again. Thus, the complete shop fabrication resulted in a rapid rate of assembly. The prefabricated decking consisted of 2-in. tongue-and-groove material joined into panels that were nailed into place by automatic tools. The building was recessed into the ground so that two-thirds of the seats were below ground level. Thus they could be poured on the ground and supported by it. (C. C. O.)

Dams. *Europe.* In Spain the 416-ft.-high Alcántara hollow-gravity concrete dam on the Tagus River was completed in 1969. The Almendra Dam on the Tormes River, which was to be Europe's largest pumped-storage plant, was still under construction. The El Grado concrete gravity dam on the Cinca River (height 426 ft., crest length 3,142 ft., volume 1,342,700 cu.yd.) and the Las Portas gravity dam on the Camba River (height 498 ft., crest length 1,587 ft., volume 977,000 cu.yd.) were also under advanced construction.

In France the Grande Maison earthfill dam on the Eau d'Olle River (height 591 ft., crest length 2,329 ft., volume 24,852,000 cu.yd.) was in the early stages of construction. The Quaira della Miniera concrete gravity dam on the Pracomune River in Italy was completed in 1968. In Switzerland construction began on the Emosson arch dam on the Barberine River (height 590 ft., crest length 1,736 ft., volume 1.4 million cu.yd.). It would submerge the old Barberine Dam, built between 1920 and 1930. The two rock abutments of the new dam were not formed by the valley proper but rather by the remains of an enormous glacial barrier protruding from it. Among 12 dams under construction in Yugoslavia were the

Spilje earthfill dam on the Crni Drim River (363 ft. high) and the Tikves earthfill dam on the Crna River (372 ft. high), each with a volume of about 3.5 million cu.yd.

In Greece the 328-ft.-high Kastraki earthfill dam on the Acheloos River, built of river sand and gravel with a central clay core, was completed in January. Under construction in Austria was the Kölubrein arch dam on the Malta River (height 607 ft., crest length 1,814 ft., volume 1,804,000 cu.yd.). The Solina concrete gravity dam on the San River in Poland (height 262 ft., crest length 2,626 ft., volume 3,660,000 cu.yd.) was completed in November 1968. In Sweden the 348-ft.-high Seitevare earth and rockfill dam on the Lule River was also completed late in 1968. The Belmeken (height 308 ft.) and Kamtchia (height 253 ft.) rockfill dams on the Vatcha River in Bulgaria were being built under complex geologic conditions. The Vidraru arch dam on the Arges River in Romania (height 545 ft., crest length 1,000 ft., volume 654,000 cu.yd.) was at an advanced stage of construction.

In the U.S.S.R. the Inguri double-curvature arch dam under construction on the Inguri River (height 892 ft., crest length 2,198 ft., volume 4,967,000 cu.yd.) would, when completed, be the world's highest concrete arch dam. Construction continued on the great Nurek earth dam on the Vakhsh River, due to begin power production in 1973 (height 1,017 ft., base thickness 4,920 ft., crest length 2,390 ft., volume 70,806,000 cu.yd., storage capacity 8,424,000 ac-ft.). Work in the U.S.S.R. also continued on the Toktogul arch dam on the Naryn River (705 ft. high) and on the Ust-Ilim earthfill gravity dam on the Angara River (height 344 ft., crest length 11,695 ft., volume 17,090,000 cu.yd.).

Asia. In India the Srisallam concrete gravity dam on the Krishna River (height 470 ft., crest length 1,680 ft., volume 2,686,000 cu.yd.) was under construction, and work started on the 440-ft.-high Maneri concrete gravity dam on the Bhagirath River and on the 482-ft.-high Thein rockfill dam on the Ravi River. Construction continued on the Nagarjunasagar stone masonry dam. Its reservoir would form the largest man-made lake in India.

In Japan the Nagano rockfill dam on the Kuzuryu River was completed in late 1968. More than 100 dams were under construction in Japan.

North and South America. In the United States dams completed in 1969 included the Amistad earthfill and concrete gravity dam on the Rio Grande in April, the Mossyrock arch dam on the Cowlitz River (height 605 ft., volume 1,240,000 cu.yd.) in May, and, in July, the New Bullards Bar double-curvature arch dam on the North Yuba River, the nation's fourth highest at 635 ft. Construction continued on the Dworshak concrete gravity dam on the Clearwater River in Idaho, the highest concrete gravity dam in the U.S. (height 717 ft., crest length 3,287 ft., volume 6.5 million cu.yd.), due to be completed in 1972. Construction methods utilized on this dam included radio-controlled, high-speed cableways for rapid placement of concrete; a new system of self-raising forms; installation of an underground rock-crushing plant; and an electronically controlled aggregate plant. Also under construction were the 385-ft.-high compacted rockfill with clay core Jocassee Dam on the Keowee River, South Carolina; the New Don Pedro earth and rockfill dam on the Tuolumne River in California (height 585 ft.); and the Libby concrete gravity dam on the Kootenai River, Montana (height 420 ft.). In building the Libby Dam, due for completion in 1972, six gantry cranes placed the concrete, working from a 2,000-ft.-long steel trestle.

In Canada the 600-ft.-high Bennett Dam on the Peace River, British Columbia, was completed late in 1968. The 800-ft.-high Mica rockfill dam on the Columbia River was under construction. This project involved the placing of 42.2 million cu.yd. of fill by a fleet of 120-ton tractor-trailer bottom dumps.

In Brazil the Estreito earth and rockfill dam on the Rio Grande (height 302 ft., volume 6,540,000 cu.yd.) was completed in February. The Paraitinga earthfill dam on the Paraitinga River (height 331 ft., crest length 3,662 ft., volume 9,255,500 cu.yd.) was under construction. In Venezuela the first stage of the Guri earth and rockfill dam with concrete gravity section on the Caroni River (height 348 ft.) was inaugurated in November 1968. One of the world's largest hydroelectric projects, Guri had a generating capacity of 6,000 Mw.

Oceania and Africa. In Tasmania the Gordon River arch dam (height 450 ft.) was under construction. Two dams were under construction in Morocco, the Noubaz Dam on the Dra River (height 230 ft.), which would form a reservoir of more than 400,000 ac-ft., and the Ait-aadel Dam on the Tessaout River (height 262 ft., crest length 1,968 ft.), due for completion in September 1970. (AL. MA.)

Roads. In 1969, important new highway engineering projects were completed in countries throughout the world. The major projects detailed below did not necessarily reflect general trends. There were, however, two such trends worth remarking.

The governments of the less developed countries tended more and more to consider transport in the context of their overall plans for economic and social development, and this led to an increased concentration of effort on developing the network of secondary roads so that agricultural produce and other goods might be delivered more easily and quickly to domestic and foreign markets. In countries that already had a highly developed road system, there was increased concentration on urban transport problems, which resulted in the building of more urban expressways and, more significantly, in a more careful consideration of the interaction between transport and the quality of urban life.

Europe. A new 56-mi. road across Haukeli Mountain, linking east and west Norway, was opened in September 1968. Almost 9 mi. of the road ran through tunnels. Part of the road rose to more than 3,500 ft. above sea level, but the Norwegian road authorities hoped to keep it open all year by using snowplows. The entrances to the tunnels were protected by 262-ft. vaults of concrete, and the road itself was elevated approximately 7 to 10 ft. to allow the snow to be blown off.

In the Netherlands, 34 additional miles of expressways were opened in 1968. The total length of expressways in use by the end of 1968 was 463 mi. In Spain, 35 mi. of high-speed roads were opened in 1968 and 32 mi. more were added in 1969; 79 mi. were planned for 1970. The Mongat–Mataró section of tollway was scheduled to be opened in 1970. It would link the Barcelona–Mongat freeway with the Mataró industrial area along the Mediterranean.

During the year several sections of expressway were opened in Italy. One was the 36-mi. length from

Fano to Ancona. This section completed the 130.5-mi. expressway from Bologna to Ancona. Another was a 9-mi. section of the Salerno–Reggio Calabria expressway. The new section extended from Sala Consilina to Buonabitacolo. The Voghera–Piacenza section of the Turin–Piacenza expressway was also opened to traffic. In Austria, the road authorities completed a new section of the Brenner expressway between Volders and the Brenner Pass. In January an additional 5.9 mi. of the Durham, Eng., A1(M) expressway was opened. The final section, 6.3 mi. long, was opened in September. The 22.4-mi. expressway ran from Aycliffe to the Birtley bypass at Chester-le-Street. Another U.K. project completed during the year was the 4.2-mi. Avonmouth section of the M5 expressway.

North and South America. A 54-mi. length of the BR-277 highway, which ran the 460 mi. from the port of Paranaguá to Foz do Iguaçu, Braz., was opened during the latter part of 1968. The new section, from Paranaguá to Curitiba, was the first phase of an important highway improvement project. A much more substantial section, 334 mi. in length, was completed in 1969. The road formed part of the Pan-American Highway system, the Brazilian portion of which was completely paved.

In Peru, an 84.5-mi. section of the Marginal Forest Highway, linking Juanjui and Tarapoto, was opened toward the end of 1968, and in the same year a 130.5-mi. expressway between Mexico City and Querétaro was completed. In Caracas, Venezuela, an important new interchange was finished during 1969 after five years of work. The interchange, which cost $53 million to build, contained three miles of six-lane roads at four levels and could carry 60,000 vehicles a day. The project served all the main city routes.

The U.S. secretary of transportation, John A. Volpe, announced in 1969 that 27,975 mi. of the 42,500-mi. national interstate system of highways were open to traffic and that another 5,050 mi. were under construction.

Africa. In Botswana, improvements were made to the 24 mi. of road between Ramoutsa and Thamaga, and in Lesotho the Masianokeng-Tsoaing section of the Leabua Highway was tarred. An expressway linking the Idi–Ayunre beltway with the Lagos–Benin road at Ilesha, Nigeria, was opened. In South Africa, the loop road from the border of Mozambique to the border of Angola, running through South Africa and South West Africa, was completed. The finished highway was 3,000 mi. long.

A 19-mi. road from Tiko to Douala, in Cameroon, was opened during the year. The road, known locally as "unification highway," ran through difficult country, including mangrove forests and swamps. Another road extending through inhospitable terrain was the new 280-mi. Timimoun–El Golea road in Algeria. Built at a cost of $14.8 million, it crossed the Sahara Desert and was the first link between Saroua and the Oasis. In Kenya, the 309 mi. of road from Mombasa to Nairobi was blacktopped throughout its length. This work was completed in August 1968.

Asia and Oceania. Israel opened a 9.3-mi. section of the Tel Aviv–Haifa expressway running between Hadera and Zikhron Ya'aqov. In Japan the 215-mi. Tokyo–Nagoya expressway was opened in May. It formed a link with the Nagoya–Kobe expressway to provide a high-speed route to the industrial and very densely populated part of Japan. Because of the difficult nature of the soil (a clay soil of volcanic ashes), special techniques had to be used to stabilize the embankments during and after construction. These included sand compaction piles, counterweight embankments, sand piles, and surcharge methods. The completed road carried an average of more than 16,000 vehicles a day.

A road often described as being the highest in the world was completed during the year. It ran from Leh in the Ladakh area of east Kashmir to Manali in the Himachal Pradesh area of India and rose to 17,493 ft. at its highest point. Pakistan announced the opening of a trade route to China. When completed, the route would cross the Karakoram Range between Hunza state and Sinkiang. In December 1968 in Thailand, a 180-mi. military road from Sattahip to the United States Air Force base at Korat was opened. In Australia the third section of the expressway from Sydney to Newcastle was completed in 1969. (R. S. Mi.)

Tunnels. There was a continued increase in the rate of driving achieved by tunneling machines and in the use of new types of machines. In the U.K., Kinnear Moodie Ltd., using its universal drum digger, broke its 1968 world record for rate of advance of completed tunnel (including erection of permanent lining) by driving and lining 1,215 ft. of 100-in.-diameter tunnel in one week. Both records were achieved in the Wraysbury–Datchett water tunnel for London's Metropolitan Water Board.

A 12-ft.-diameter, 3.9-mi.-long tunnel through the River Mountains, part of the U.S. Bureau of Reclamation's Southern Nevada Water Project, was started in the autumn of 1968 and holed through nine months later. A Jarva Mark 11/14 tunneling machine

One of twin 110-story towers of the World Trade Center under construction in lower Manhattan in 1969. Building was to be world's tallest.

UPI COMPIX

was used; it developed a thrust of 866,000 lb. and could cut a tunnel from 11 to 14 ft. in diameter. The tunnel passed through variable igneous rock ranging from 1,000 psi (pounds per square inch) to 23,000 psi compressive strength. The best drive in one day was 293 ft.

A new type of tunneling machine, the Greenside-McAlpine tunnel heading machine, which could excavate horseshoe-shaped tunnels, was used successfully in the U.K. on the Great Charles Street Tunnel, Birmingham, and on the cooling water tunnels of Hinkley Point nuclear power station, Somerset. Excavation was by cutters mounted on a rotating head. The head was mounted on and traversed along an arm that swung through 180 degrees, thus allowing the head to be applied over the full area of tunnel face.

The continued expansion of the European expressway system maintained the demand for new road tunnels. The world's longest road tunnel, 10⅛ mi., was to be built through the Swiss St. Gotthard Pass between Goschen and Airolo. By June the Swiss government had chosen for the tunnel the design by Electro-Watt Engineering Services Ltd. costing $39.8 million and, in addition, had authorized a $3.7 million bore alongside the tunnel to serve as an emergency escape route. There were to be four ventilation shafts, two vertical and two inclined, the shortest 1,000 ft. and the longest 2,940 ft., varying from 17.4 ft. to 31.2 ft. in diameter. The road was to be two-way, 24.5 ft. wide. Fresh air and exhaust air ducts would be formed in the space between the roadway ceiling and the crown of the tunnel, and the maximum amount of ventilation would be 70,000 cu.ft. per second for traffic up to 1,600 vehicles per hour.

The Rome–Adriatic expressway under construction was eventually to include three mountain tunnels with lengths of 1 km., 4.5 km., and 10 km. Construction of the 10-km. tunnel started in 1969, and completion was scheduled for 1972. The tunnel was to have twin bores, each with a two-lane road, 7.5 m. wide and 4.75 m. high, together with a third bore for fresh air and exhaust ventilation ducts and drainage.

The European road system was greatly improved by the opening of a number of underwater road tunnels, all constructed by the immersed tube method. Amsterdam's road tunnel under the IJ was opened in October 1968. The Scheldt Tunnel at Antwerp, the Limfjord Tunnel in Denmark, and the Heinnord Tunnel near Rotterdam were all opened in 1969. In June a contract was signed for a cross-harbour tunnel in Hong Kong, the first immersed-tube-type road tunnel in Asia.

Two tunnels of great length were at an early stage of construction. In South Africa, all three contracts for the 51-mi.-long Orange–Fish Tunnel had been let; the total cost was £35 million with completion scheduled for 1972. The tunnel was to be lined with concrete, have a diameter of 17.5 ft., a ventilation capacity of 2,000 cu.ft. per second, and would pass through siltstones, mudstones, and bands of dolerite; tunneling boring machines were not being used. The second long tunnel was a 20-ft.-diameter sewer which was to be constructed from a central interceptor 100 ft. below the streets of Mexico City. The city lay on a deep layer of mud within an extinct volcano; the tunnel would pass 30 mi. through the mud and an additional 40 mi. through the rocky rim of the crater to discharge into a mountain lake. (H. D. M.)

ENCYCLOPÆDIA BRITANNICA FILMS. *St. Lawrence Seaway* (1959); *The Panama Canal* (1961); *The Suez Canal* (1962); *Holland: Hold Back the Sea* (1967).

England: *see* United Kingdom

English Literature: *see* Literature

Entertainment: *see* Cinema; Dance; Fairs and Shows; Music; Television and Radio; Theatre

Entomology: *see* Biological Sciences

Environmental Services: *see* Medicine

Epidemics: *see* Medicine

Episcopal Church: *see* Religion

Equatorial Guinea

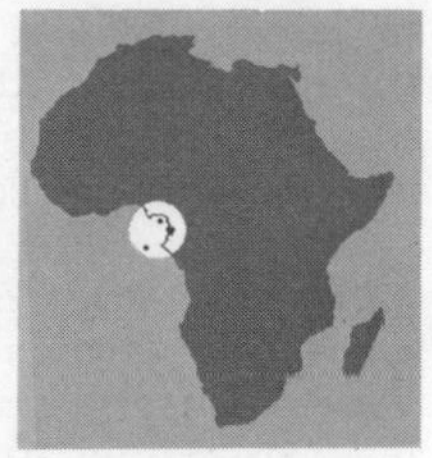

The African republic of Equatorial Guinea consists of Río Muni, which is bordered by Cameroon on the north, Gabon on the east and south, and the Atlantic Ocean on the west; and the offshore islands of Fernando Po and Annobón. Area: 10,830 sq.mi. (28,050 sq.km.). Pop. (1969 est.) 286,000. Cap. and largest city: Santa Isabel, on Fernando Po (pop., 1965 est., 37,152). President in 1969, Francisco Macías Nguma.

After speeches by President Macías demanding economic independence and a reduction of the number of Spanish flags flown in Equatorial Guinea, incidents took place in Bata in the last week of February that led to the death of a Spanish civilian. The Spanish ambassador, Juan Durán Loriga, called out the 260-man civil guard left behind by Spain as a temporary measure following independence. On February 28 Macías complained to Spanish chief of state Francisco Franco that the Spanish ambassador and the consul general had been plotting against his government and using the civil guard as their instrument. On the same day he also wrote to the secretary-general of the UN, U Thant, asking him to send a peace-keeping force to counter Spanish aggression. The Spanish government then advised Spanish civilians in Equatorial Guinea to seek the protection of the consulate general. On March 5 it was reported that there had been an unsuccessful attempt to overthrow the government, and shortly afterward several of the leaders of the abortive coup, including Atanasio N'Dongo, the foreign minister, Bonifacio Ondó Edu, former prime minister, and Saturnino Ibongo, formerly UN representative, were reported dead. Macías then assumed dictatorial powers, accusing Spain of having supported the coup, which the Spanish government firmly denied. By April 5 a majority of the Spaniards had left the country.

Two missions arrived in the country early in March in response to the disturbances. Pres. Houari Boumédienne of Algeria, then president of the Organization of African Unity, sent his personal representative, but after discussions in Bata and in Madrid he was unable to induce Franco to slow down the evacuation

EQUATORIAL GUINEA

Education. (1966–67) Primary, pupils 38,395, teachers 504; secondary, pupils 2,343, teachers 40; vocational (1965–66), pupils 464, teachers 35; teacher training, students 130, teachers 28.

Finance. Monetary unit: peseta Guineana (introduced on Oct. 12, 1969), at par with the Spanish peseta. Budget (1966) balanced at 1,650,623,000 pesetas.

Foreign Trade. (1966) Imports 1,278,000,000 pesetas (58% from Spain in 1965); exports 1,817,000,000 pesetas (97% to Spain in 1965). Main exports (1965): cocoa 44%; coffee 21%; timber 19%.

Transport and Communications. Length of bus routes (1962) 5,002 km.; buses in use 124. Ships entered (1964) 582; cargo unloaded (metric tons; 1966) 102,000, loaded 290,000. Telephones (Jan. 1965) 1,249. Radio receivers (Dec. 1968) *c.* 70,000.

Agriculture. Production (in 000; metric tons; 1967; 1966 in parentheses): coffee 6.6 (6.4); cocoa (1967–68) 33, (1966–67) 39; palm kernels (exports) *c.* 2 (*c.* 2); palm oil *c.* 4 (*c.* 4); timber (exports; 1965) 331. Livestock (in 000; 1966–67): sheep *c.* 26; cattle *c.* 3; pigs *c.* 5; goats *c.* 6.

Industry. Electricity production (1964) 10,212,336 kw-hr.

of skilled Spanish technicians. The second mission, dispatched by U Thant and led by Marcial Tamayo of Bolivia, failed to win the support of Macías for a two-month moratorium on political change to provide an opportunity for the training of Guineans to take over skilled posts. Tamayo's mission did lead to an offer by Spain of $5,760,000 to be used to balance Guinea's budget and to the dispatch of a team of World Health Organization (WHO) experts to Santa Isabel in April.

(K. I.)

Ethiopia

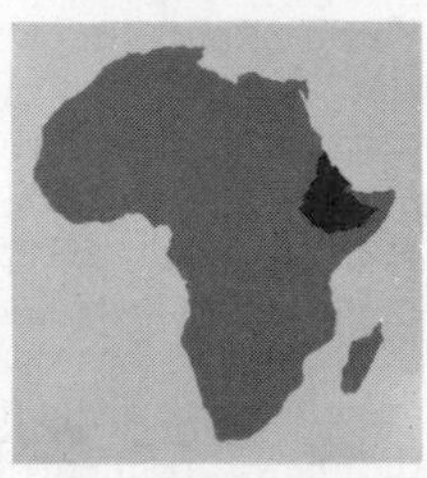

A constitutional monarchy of northeastern Africa, including the formerly autonomous federated state of Eritrea, Ethiopia is bordered by Somalia, the French Territory of Afars and Issas, Kenya, the Sudan, and the Red Sea. Area: 471,776 sq.mi. (1,221,900 sq.km.). Pop. (1968 est.): 23.9 million. Cap. and largest city: Addis Ababa (pop., 1968, 644,100). Language: Amharic (official) and English. Religion: Ethiopian Orthodox (Coptic) Christian 65%; Muslim 30%. Emperor, Haile Selassie I; prime minister in 1969, Aklilu Habte Wold.

A number of Cabinet changes took place in 1969, the most important of which were the switch of the long-time minister of finance, Ato Yilma Deressa, to the Ministry of Commerce, Industry, and Tourism and his replacement by Ato Mamo Tadesse, previously minister of justice, and the replacement of the minister of education, Ato Akalewerk Habte Wold, by Ato Seifu Mahatme Selassie from the Ministry of Public Works. Ato Akalewerk was appointed minister of justice. In a structural change, the previous Ministry of Planning and Development was incorporated as a commission in the prime minister's office, and the vice-minister, Ato Belai, was appointed the first chief commissioner. The fourth of the quadrennial elections to the lower chamber of Parliament also occurred in 1969.

In the economic sphere, Ethiopia still faced difficulties in export trade, partly caused by the closing of the Suez Canal, and was seeking ways to diversify agriculture away from the concentration on coffee cultivation in the south. Discussions took place with the World Bank for the development of a large area in the north, suitable for dry farming, stretching from Humera on the Takkaze (Setit) River southward along the border with Sudan.

There were also considerable agricultural developments in the Arba Minch area at the southern end of Lake Abaya (Margherita). An agreement was signed with the United Nations Development Program (UNDP) and the International Labour Organization (ILO) in August for an Eth$3.8 million industrial training project. In September an Eth$25 million agreement was signed with the United States Agency for International Development for the improvement of facilities at Addis Ababa and Asmara airports to permit the day and night landing of supersonic jets. Some emphasis was placed on the tourist industry, and developments included the opening of the Addis Ababa Hilton Hotel.

Generally, however, the government faced financial problems in 1969 arising from the need to finance necessary economic development projects and also from difficulties in administering the new tax structure in rural areas. A significant financial measure was the initiation of public bids for short-term government treasury bills.

Communications developments included the installation of new radio transmitters in Harar and Asmara and the establishment of a telecommunications link between Addis Ababa and Abidjan, capital of Ivory Coast, which improved the much-needed east-west links in Africa. An agreement was signed for the construction of a new desert highway to link the port of Assab with Addis Ababa. On the other hand, Ethiopian Airlines business was seriously affected by a number of hijacking and bomb incidents, officially attributed to an organization that was based in Syria but probably linked with political extremism in Eritrea.

Other developments included the opening in July of the new St. Paul's Hospital for the Poor, for which capital was provided by West German churches, and the establishment of a National Commission for Education, which was to review the whole education structure and make recommendations for its improvement to the government.

The education system was considerably disrupted at various times during the year by student unrest, but in September, at the beginning of the Ethiopian new year, Haile Selassie declared an amnesty for all students who had been imprisoned or suspended from schools and universities.

Haile Selassie addressed the ILO Conference in Geneva in July, visited the U.S. also in July to discuss economic assistance, and continued to play an important part within the Organization of African Unity in efforts to end the war in Nigeria.

(G. C. L.)

ETHIOPIA

Education. (1966–67) Primary, pupils 409,710, teachers 9,431; secondary (1965–66), pupils 50,438, teachers 1,603; vocational (1965–66), pupils 3,461, teachers 271; teacher training (1965–66), students 1,680, teachers 93; higher (at 2 universities), students 3,096, teaching staff 469.

Finance. Monetary unit: Ethiopian dollar, with a par value of Eth$2.50 to U.S. $1 (Eth$6 = £1 sterling). Gold and foreign exchange, central bank: (June 1969) U.S. $63.9 million; (June 1968) U.S. $69 million. Budget (1968–69 est.): revenue Eth$612 million; expenditure Eth$651.5 million. Money supply: (June 1969) Eth$407.8 million; (June 1968) Eth$385.3 million.

Foreign Trade. (1968) Imports Eth$432.4 million; exports Eth$266 million. Import sources (1967): Italy 19%; West Germany 14%; Japan 14%; U.S. 9%; U.K. 8%. Export destinations (1967): U.S. 43%; Italy 8%; Saudi Arabia 6%; West Germany 5%. Main exports: coffee 58%; hides and skins 9%; cereals 8%; oilseeds 8%.

Transport and Communications. Roads (1968) *c.* 23,000 km. (including 7,304 km. all-weather). Motor vehicles in use (1967): passenger 34,596; commercial 8,563. Railways (1967) 1,087 km. Air traffic (1968): 299 million passenger-km.; freight 18,760,000 net ton-km. Telephones (Dec. 1967) 32,355. Radio receivers (Dec. 1968) *c.* 500,000. Television receivers (Dec. 1966) 5,000.

Agriculture. Production (in 000; metric tons; 1967; 1966 in parentheses): corn *c.* 770 (827); teff and sorghum *c.* 3,350 (3,002); barley 850 (822); wheat *c.* 350 (*c.* 310); linseed *c.* 60 (59); sunflower seed (1966) 34, (1965) 31; sugar, raw value (1968–69) *c.* 73, (1967–68) *c.* 74; chick-peas 173 (170); lentils *c.* 95 (*c.* 98); sweet potatoes *c.* 100 (99); potatoes *c.* 148 (*c.* 145); coffee *c.* 150 (*c.* 150). Livestock (in 000; 1966–67): cattle *c.* 25,758; sheep *c.* 12,100; goats *c.* 11,100; horses 1,361; mules 1,361; asses 3,790; camels *c.* 960; poultry (1965–66) 42,600.

Industry. Production (in 000; metric tons; 1965–66): cotton yarn 7.5; cotton fabrics (sq.m.) 43,000; shoes (pairs; 1967) 609; cement 89; electricity (kw-hr.; 1966–67) 318,000.

Equestrian Events: *see* Sporting Record

Espionage: *see* Intelligence Operations

European Atomic Energy Community: *see* Nuclear Energy

European Coal and Steel Community: *see* Commercial Policies; European Unity

European Economic Community: *see* Commercial Policies; European Unity

European Free Trade Association: *see* Commercial Policies; European Unity

European Unity

In the movement to achieve greater economic and political unity in Europe, an event of primary significance during 1969 was the retirement of Charles de Gaulle (*see* BIOGRAPHY) as president of France. Not without reason, supporters of such unity had considered him the chief obstacle to further progress. His disappearance from the Elysée Palace on April 28 was, therefore, an occasion for jubilation among those who believed it would now be possible to reinstate and implement the maximum agenda for continued development of the European Communities (the European Coal and Steel Community or Schuman Pool; the European Atomic Energy Community or Euratom; and, by far the most important, the European Economic Community or Common Market).

That agenda contained two principal items: first, to enlarge the membership by the admission of Britain, whose application had been twice vetoed by de Gaulle, and also of certain other states that had been waiting in the wings; and, second, to bring about as quickly as possible, in conformity with the Treaty of Rome of 1957, such reformations of the Community institutions and extensions of their powers as would complete their "transitional phase." That phase was to end on December 31 when, according to the treaty, full economic union would have been achieved among the six member states.

KEYSTONE

Queen Elizabeth II addresses the assembly of the Council of Europe at Banqueting House in London on May 5, 1969, during a ceremony marking the 20th anniversary of the organization.

Once de Gaulle had gone, suggestions for getting on with this agenda were quickly forthcoming. As so often in the past, the initiative was taken by Jean Monnet who, despite his four score years, had lost none of his enthusiasm for a federal organization of Western Europe. As spokesman for the Action Committee for the United States of Europe, the most influential private organization supporting "European" solutions, Monnet now recommended the immediate admission of Britain, with the attendant issues to be clarified later, and the admission shortly afterward of the other three applicants: Ireland, Norway, and Denmark. Thus enlarged, the EEC should move as rapidly as possible toward a viable economic union and commit itself to the eventual achievement of political union. At almost the same time, Walter Hallstein, former chairman of the EEC Commission, also serving as a spokesman of the Action Committee, recommended that the Commission (which in 1968 had been expanded to a 14-member "European" body serving all three Communities) should be made responsible to a European parliament, the members of which, in due course, would be elected directly by the people. A popularly controlled decision-making forum, it was hoped, would promote progress toward an economic union and make its operation more acceptable.

In the weeks that followed, it became apparent that the hopes of those who sponsored this post-de Gaulle agenda were likely to be disappointed. To be sure, the new president of France, Georges Pompidou, lacked the charisma of his predecessor. It had been predicted that he would have to deny himself de Gaulle's almost Soviet-like luxury of saying "no" without qualification and, like any ordinary politician, seek a policy of compromise and accommodation on such issues as British membership. Pompidou's shifting of Michel Debré, with his reputation of being more Gaullist than de Gaulle, from the French Foreign Office and his replacement by Maurice Schumann, a traditional "European," seemed to be an earnest of such a policy.

But Pompidou soon made it clear that he was no more likely to compromise seriously any French interest on behalf of European unity than de Gaulle had been. His first rather general observation that the Communities ought to be enlarged was quickly followed by the quite definite statement that France would not support Britain's admission until the Six had agreed among themselves upon a definitive agricultural subsidy policy—presumably one in which France would continue to enjoy the advantages provided by the existing temporary arrangement, under which the Community stabilization fund returned to France's farmers almost twice the amount that France contributed to the fund. A pledge for agreement on agricultural policy was the price exacted by France at the Council of Ministers meeting at The Hague in December, in return for somewhat grudging French acquiescence to the start of negotiations with Britain, probably about the middle of 1970.

This coupling of the French offer to consider enlargement of the Communities with a demand for a prior settlement of the farm subsidy policy served as an all too realistic reminder that the second part of the proposed post-de Gaulle agenda—expediting the effort to make the EEC a true economic union—would also prove difficult. Agricultural policy had been unified in most respects some two years earlier, but the Six had never agreed on a definitive distribution of the cost of the agricultural price subsidy, and solution had been further complicated by national interests that had become vested during the two-year period. Then, too, the existing policy had produced mountainous surpluses, especially in dairy products. Only drastic structural changes in European agriculture, such as were contemplated by the so-called Mansholt plan, were likely to be effective in solving the surplus problem and making future subsidy costs bearable for the governments. Moreover, the Mansholt plan was considered extremely costly, at least at the outset, and unpopular for many reasons.

In addition to agriculture, there were many other areas in which achievement would continue to fall far short of the minimum that would satisfy the concept of economic union. Even the customs union that has been in existence since July 1968 was still hampered by nontariff obstacles to intra-Community trade, and there was no really unified Community commercial policy toward the rest of the world.

Especially disheartening to those who wished to proceed with the work of expanding and improving the Communities, now that de Gaulle was gone, was the evidence that his parochial nationalist spirit lingered on, influencing not only his successors but the leaders of the other five EEC states as well. Each was fearful of concessions already made to Community rule; each hesitated to go further; each wanted to retain the right of national decision making, even in matters that the Rome Treaty clearly intended to be handled on a Community-wide basis by the end of 1969. In short, a neo-Gaullist attitude, hostile to integration, affected all Community members and not merely pre- or post-de Gaulle France. For this reason, progress on the substantive post-de Gaulle agenda was all too likely to be nonexistent or, at best, painfully slow.

Many supporters of European integration cherished the view that, once economic integration had reached a certain limited point, the movement would become essentially irreversible. Integration would then continue inevitably toward complete economic union and, eventually, establishment of a political union of a federal type. Twelve years of experience with the EEC scarcely supported this view; indeed, in certain cases, the evidence pointed to the opposite. Steps already taken to enhance economic integration, however successful, had made the participants fearful of further steps. Hence instead of moving the Communities toward a unified decision-making structure, separate from that of the individual states, the result, all too frequently, had been exactly the reverse. Increasingly the Brussels organization had been reduced to an intergovernmental agency, like the Council of Europe, in which representatives of member states used the Community organs to promote policies that had already been formulated by their respective national governments.

Whether or not this reactionary trend would be reversed would probably receive clarification within the next year. If the EEC could agree on a definitive farm policy and then admit Britain and other applicant states, prospects for further forward movement should brighten. If, thereafter, serious efforts were made to harmonize social, economic, and fiscal policies among member states, and Community organs were given power to administer the sectors of economic life that, under the treaty, they were intended to regulate, the hopes of friends of European unity might be revived. Added confidence in such a revival would be generated if, as a result of admitting Britain and other states to the Communities, impetus was given to providing a greater degree of popular involvement, through elections, in the operation of the Communities, and if their administration was subjected to a parliamentary type of responsibility.

Almost equally helpful to progress would be a Community climate favourable to the creation and operation of transnational European industrial enterprises, and the willingness of entrepreneurs and governments to pool capital and technical expertise and broaden markets. Jean-Jacques Servan-Schreiber's condition that such enterprises be European owned and operated, and not merely expansions of U.S. enterprise, was probably also a desirable if not a necessary condition. Perhaps the principal requirement for further progress was a subjective one, namely, the dedication of a new and younger generation of leaders to the ideals of unity. These new men would have to take over from the postwar generation of leaders, who had grown too old and whose ideals, in any case, had become too deeply compromised by their responsibilities to their own national governments.

Even to enumerate such obvious requirements for further progress as these suggested how considerable was the distance still to be traveled before the Communities reached the goal that the Treaty of Rome expected them to have reached by the end of 1969. It suggested, too, that the forward steps taken since 1957 were not necessarily irreversible.

Western European Union. Continuing procrastination in enlarging the Communities and moving toward further substantive integration had the effect of reviving, at least temporarily, the significance of the lesser institutions concerned with European unity. The Western European Union, for example, came out of the doldrums early in the year because Britain, as one of its seven members (the other six being, rather conveniently, the members of the Communities), thought the WEU might provide it with a bridge to ultimate Community membership. Accordingly, at the annual meeting of the WEU Assembly, Britain suggested that the agenda should include various foreign policy and other items and voiced the hope that the ensuing discussion might yield decisions in which it and the Six would see eye to eye.

What was then still Gaullist France reacted to this British maneuver with Gallic expedition and intensity. Debré, de Gaulle's foreign minister, declared that WEU's agenda was illegal, that France would boycott the meetings, and that, if this sort of thing was not stopped, France would secede from WEU altogether. The WEU had come into being in 1948 as a precursor of NATO, and West Germany and Italy had become members in 1954 following France's rejection of the European Defense Community Treaty. Hence WEU was basically a European security organization, and history was on the side of France in rejecting the British effort to exploit WEU for broad political ends. Nevertheless, thanks to de Gaulle and his attitude toward British membership in the Communities, a more or less moribund European organization had at least made newspaper headlines.

Council of Europe. The much better known and more important 18-member Council of Europe, with headquarters in Strasbourg, France, was more successful in providing a forum for discreetly advancing the

BEN ROTH AGENCY

"Could be a trap, Georges. Try saying 'Oui' and see what happens!" —Emmwood, "London Daily Mail."

cause of enlarged Community membership. During its 20th anniversary meeting in London in May (the Council had been formed by a statute drafted at St. James's Palace, Westminster, May 5, 1949)—a meeting that had been opened by Queen Elizabeth II—British Prime Minister Harold Wilson exploited the occasion to reiterate his government's intention to secure full membership in the EEC. A variety of foreign ministers and other dignitaries from the various European states strongly endorsed the prime minister's policy.

Similar opportunities for advancing the cause of enlarged EEC membership were furnished, from time to time, by the Council's Committee of Ministers and its Consultative Assembly. In May the latter body passed a formal resolution calling on the six EEC states to convene a meeting with the heads of all states seeking membership, tendered its good offices to investigate obstacles to enlarged membership, and offered its assistance in overcoming them. As another part of the 20th anniversary observance, organs of the Council reviewed the two decades of effort to secure cooperative and uniform national action on subjects in various areas—social, cultural, scientific, legal, economic, and administrative, and in the area of "human rights and fundamental freedoms." The resulting record of draft conventions, accepted by the Council's member states, was impressive and constituted a contribution to European unity that was not to be discounted. (*See* GREECE.)

European Free Trade Association. Still another of the lesser European entities, the seven-member European Free Trade Association (EFTA), was also affected by the uncertainty surrounding the matter of enlarging the membership of the Communities. Essentially, EFTA was the handiwork of British diplomatic initiative in 1959, at a time when Britain was rejecting original membership in the EEC in favour of the more limited concept of a free trade union. A decade later, when Britain had changed its mind, some of its EFTA partners—among them Sweden, Switzerland, Austria, and Portugal—did not want to follow its lead. They hoped instead to establish preferential trade links with the Brussels organization, and in the early months of 1969 urged adoption of a plan along this line that the French had proposed and that some other EEC members supported. Britain, however, rebuffed them and insisted on full membership. The United States helped to inter the plan by suggesting that it would violate the policy against discriminatory trade practices of the General Agreement on Tariffs and Trade (GATT).

Subsequently, the Nordic members of EFTA, Denmark, Norway, and Sweden, led by the latter and by Finland (an associate member), considered plans for a trade organization of their own. The result, in July, was a draft treaty for an Organization of Nordic Economic Cooperation (Nordek), which would operate within the confines of EFTA. In December, however, further steps in the formation of Nordek were deferred until after the Finnish elections scheduled for March 1970. The uncertain future of EFTA was paradoxical, since all quantitative indices suggested that it had been successful. Its objective of free trade among its members was reached in 1967, three years ahead of treaty schedule, and intra-EFTA trade had increased some 150% since the organization's inception.

(A. J. Z.)

See also Commercial Policies; Defense; France; Payments and Reserves, International; Trade, International.

Evangelical Churches: *see* Religion

Exchange Rates: *see* Payments and Reserves, International

Exhibitions: *see* Art Exhibitions; Fairs and Shows; Museums and Galleries; Photography

Expeditions, Scientific: *see* Antarctica; Arctic Regions; Mountaineering; Oceanography; Speleology

Faeroe Islands: *see* Dependent States

Fairs and Shows

Virtually all of the world's major fairs and shows closed the 1969 season with substantial increases in attendance and gross revenues as more than a billion people flocked to an estimated 14,500 indoor and outdoor events. Smaller fairs, with less than 200,000 attendance, slipped marginally as a result of stiff competition and high operating costs. Some industry spokesmen in North America even predicted the ultimate demise of the traditional county and district fairs in the U.S. and Canada; state and provincial fairs recorded gains of 17–22% over 1968 while most county and district fairs showed no appreciable improvement, except where admission prices had been raised.

Over 113 million people visited nearly 3,200 fairs in the U.S. and an estimated 800 in Canada, topping the 1968 season by 3 million. A total of one billion (representing multiple visits in some cases) jammed arenas, fun parks, stadiums, and fairs and spent over $1 billion on food and drink alone. North American fairs spent more than $22 million on star attractions. Most fairs raised front gate admissions but approximately 60% operated with free grandstand shows. Admissions ranged from 50 cents to $2. Elsewhere in the world admissions to public fairs were somewhat higher in 1969 than in 1968, except in South America and on the Asian continent.

Amusement and theme parks continued to proliferate in the U.S., Canada, and Europe, with the total estimated at over 16,500. More than two billion people attended fun parks in 1969, and an additional 1.4 billion visited the world's community parks, zoos, and aquariums. Significant gains were also recorded for commercial exhibitions.

The frequency of world's fairs in recent years had made their development and promotion more difficult. Such was the case with Expo 70, Asia's first universal exhibition, scheduled to be held from March 15 through Sept. 13, 1970, near Osaka, Japan. At year's end, after a somewhat inauspicious beginning, Expo 70 was beginning to rise from its 815-ac. site. Among the more than 60 participating nations, the U.S. planned a $4.4 million, elliptical, air-supported, plastic, dome-shaped pavilion housing $10 million worth

Contestant participates in the Great Triumph-Rover Car Painting Competition held in 1969 at the International Automobile Show in New York City's Coliseum.

"THE NEW YORK TIMES"

of exhibits. The Soviet pavilion, dominating the southern end of the fair, was a sharp-edged arrow topped by a huge red star. The Canadians, who as the hosts of Expo 67 came to the fair as veterans, constructed a rectangular building with roofless walls sloping inward at a 45° angle and outside walls covered with mirrors. Expo 70's theme building, surrounded by a 64-ac. Japanese garden, was a vast rectangular roof of aluminum ball-and-joint construction spread over theatre and display halls and covered, but not concealed, by a plastic sheathing. A conical Tower of the Sun rose through the building, which would house exhibits reflecting the fair's official theme, "Progress and Harmony for Mankind."

The inevitable world's fair tower, 396 ft. tall and aptly called Expo-Tower, afforded a dramatic view of the Kita Settsu mountain range to the northwest. Moving sidewalks, a 2.7-mi. monorail, and assorted ground vehicles would help move a projected 50 million visitors (less than 700,000 of whom were expected to come from North America). Advance ticket sales were far from encouraging: less than a million advance tickets were sold at the peak of promotional effort. At 720 yen ($2) for adults and 360 yen ($1) for children, advance tickets were only 23 cents and 12 cents, respectively, below the general admission price.

Cities in the eastern U.S. were competing for the right to host Expo 76, celebrating the bicentenary of the Declaration of Independence. Contenders were Boston, Philadelphia, Miami, and Washington, D.C.

International Trade Fairs. The world's great commercial fair centres boomed in 1969. Attendance by foreign buyers reached an all-time high, and over 80% of the world's 800 international trade fairs reported substantially increased demands for exhibit space. A typical example was the Interhospital Trade Fair held at Düsseldorf, W.Ger., June 19–25, which reported an attendance of 90,000 trade visitors, 20,000 more than in 1968, and 580 exhibitors, compared with 443 a year earlier. The traditional general category trade fairs, such as the Milan (Italy) Samples Fair and the International Samples Fair of Barcelona, Spain, recorded the largest number of exhibitors to date.

Some 74 nations played host to trade fairs in 1969. West Germany continued as the world's key trade fair centre, with the greatest number of fairs occurring at Cologne. The 100th show under the U.S. overseas trade fair program was held in Brussels, March 22–30. Some 4,000 U.S. firms had written sales estimated at over $200 million in 30 countries since the program's inception in 1963. Among the new trade fairs that emerged during the year were those at Kinshasa, Congo; Hobart, Tasmania; and Luanda, Angola.

Fairs. Annual fairs catering to the general public emerged with the highest income and attendance records in their history in 1969, although poor weather lowered attendance in a few cases. The State Fair of Texas at Dallas, which topped the 3 million attendance mark in 1968, fell to 2,992,853 as a result of rain and unseasonable cold, leaving Toronto's Canadian National Exhibition (3,188,500) as North America's only "over 3 million gater." Unfavourable weather at the Minnesota State Fair, St. Paul, reduced attendance from the previous record, but the Michigan State Fair, Detroit, enjoyed its highest paid attendance since 1941 and the highest gross income in its history. Other record setters included the Ohio State Fair,

Selected Major National and International Fairs, 1969

Country and date	Event and place	Attendance
Algeria		
Aug. 29–Sept. 14	International Trade Fair, Algiers	1,200,000
Angola		
Nov. 9–23	Industrial Fair, Luanda	160,000
Argentina		
July 13–Aug. 3	83rd International Agricultural and Industrial Exhibition, Buenos Aires	2,500,000
Australia		
Sept. 5–13	Royal Exhibition, Adelaide	220,000
Austria		
July 26–Aug. 3	International Trade Fair, Dorbin	340,000
Belgium		
Sept. 13–18	International Trade Fair, Ghent	533,000
Bolivia		
September	Agricultural and Trade Fair, Santa Cruz	38,000
Brazil		
Oct. 11–26	Children's Show, São Paulo	200,000
Bulgaria		
Sept. 21–30	25th International Fair, Plovdiv	860,000
Canada		
Aug. 14–Sept. 1	Canadian National Exhibition, Toronto	3,188,500
Aug. 16–Sept. 1	Pacific National Exhibition, Vancouver, B.C.	1,148,861
Aug. 22–31	Central Canada Exhibition, Ottawa	658,550
Congo		
June 30–July 21	International Fair, Kinshasa	600,000
Cyprus		
Sept. 5–28	15th International Cyprus Trade Fair, Nicosia	2,300,000
Czechoslovakia		
Sept. 7–16	International Trade Fair, Brno	1,200,000
Finland		
Sept. 19–28	50th Finnish Industries Fair, Helsinki	68,000
France		
Jan. 1–10	8th International Pleasure Boat Show, Puteaux	250,000
Sept. 18–29	International Trade Fair, Marseilles	1,600,000
May 30–June 8	28th International Aerospace Exhibition, Paris	1,250,000
Germany, East		
Aug. 31–Sept. 7	International Fall Fair, Leipzig	240,000
Germany, West		
Sept. 19–28	German Industries Fair, Berlin	220,000
Sept. 11–21	International Auto Show, Frankfurt	500,000
Greece		
Sept. 7–28	International Trade Fair, Thessaloniki	1,300,000
Hungary		
Sept. 7–28	International Fall Fair, Budapest	400,000
India		
Dec. 21–Jan. 31	Industrial Exhibition, Madras	755,000
Indonesia		
June 14–Aug. 23	International Trade Fair, Jakarta	3,200,000
Iran		
Oct. 5–24	2nd Asian International Trade Fair, Teheran	1,500,000
Iraq		
Oct. 1–31	International Trade Fair, Baghdad	500,000
Italy		
May 24–June 8	24th Mediterranean Fair, Palermo, Sicily	700,000
Oct. 29–Nov. 9	51st International Auto Show, Turin	600,000
Japan		
Nov. 11–16	11th Auto Show, Tokyo	200,000
Malta		
July 1–15	13th International Malta Trade Fair, Naxxar	100,000
Netherlands		
Sept. 19–30	88th Ideal Home Show, The Hague	210,000
Jan. 6–9	International Hotel and Restaurant Fair, Amsterdam	52,000
New Zealand		
Aug. 20–Sept. 6	International Trade Fair, Auckland	230,000
Norway		
Aug. 14–21	3rd Norwegian Fisheries Fair, Trondheim	150,000
Peru		
Nov. 14–30	6th Pacific International Trade Fair, Lima	600,000
Somalia		
Sept. 28–Oct. 12	10th International Trade Fair, Mozadiscio	400,000
South Africa		
Oct. 20–25	Fishing Industries Exhibition, Cape Town	100,000
Spain		
July 1–12	International Samples Fair, Bilbao	1,200,000
April 20–30	International Automobile Salon, Barcelona	400,000
April 15–30	Ibero-American Samples Fair, Seville	558,691
June 1–15	37th International Samples Fair, Barcelona	1,400,000
Surinam		
Sept. 25–Oct. 8	Surinam Trade Fair, Paramaribo	600,000
Sweden		
Sept. 3–14	St. Erik's International Trade Fair, Stockholm	213,000
Switzerland		
Sept. 25–Oct. 5	20th Fall Fair, Zürich	350,000
Syria		
Aug. 25–Sept. 20	16th International Trade Fair, Damascus	1,250,000
Turkey		
Aug. 20–Sept. 20	38th International Trade Fair, Izmir	1,700,000
U.A.R.		
Oct. 2–23	International Fair for Agriculture and Food, Cairo	600,000
United Kingdom		
Oct. 15–25	International Motor Exhibition, London	600,000
Sept. 3–11	International Engineering Exhibition, Glasgow	100,000
U.S.S.R.		
Oct. 15–25	Fruit Growing Machinery and Equipment Show, Kishinev	200,000
Nov. 21–Dec. 2	Machinery and Apparatus for Welding Show, Leningrad	85,000
United States		
Aug. 8–17	Wisconsin State Fair, West Allis	1,022,793
Aug. 23–Sept. 1	Minnesota State Fair, St. Paul	1,376,887
Sept. 12–21	Eastern States Exposition, West Springfield, Mass.	715,523
Sept. 12–21	New Jersey State Fair, Trenton	585,000
Aug. 26–Sept. 1	New York State Fair, Syracuse	550,049
Aug. 22–Sept. 1	Indiana State Fair, Indianapolis	1,009,476
Aug. 22–Sept. 1	Michigan State Fair, Detroit	913,784
Aug. 14–23	Kentucky State Fair, Louisville	498,272
Aug. 27–Sept. 1	Allegheny County Fair, Pittsburgh, Pa.	700,000
Oct. 4–19	State Fair of Texas, Dallas	2,992,853
Aug. 21–Sept. 1	Ohio State Fair, Columbus	2,053,971
Yugoslavia		
Sept. 11–21	International Fall Fair, Zagreb	2,000,000
Zambia		
Aug. 8–11	Zambia Agriculture Show, Lusaka	75,000

Source: Frederick P. Pittera, *Fairs of the World* (1969).

DPA FROM PICTORIAL PARADE

Large Ferris wheel in Westfalen Park greets visitors to the International Federal Garden Show in Dortmund, W.Ger., April 25 to Oct. 12, 1969.

Columbus, and the Pacific National Exhibition, Vancouver, B.C. The Royal Easter Show, Sydney, Austr.; the Indiana State Fair, Indianapolis; the Smithfield Show, London; and the Argentinian Exposición Nacional de Ganadería, Palermo, all had over a million attendance.

Industrial Shows. Appropriations for construction of industrial show and convention facilities rose to new heights in 1969, with over $100 billion committed. Over 17,000 industrial shows were held during the year in more than 80 countries and attendance was believed to have exceeded the 1968 record by 30%. Most exhibit buildings were booked to capacity, even during the off season. New York City's Coliseum reported a 10% increase in new-show commitments.

The traditionally popular auto shows held at Paris, New York, Turin (Italy), Chicago, and London continued to grow in size and attendance; the New York International Automobile Show expanded to four floors of the Coliseum. Boat, sports, and outdoor equipment shows were also high in attendance and number of exhibits, with flower, photography, and home shows coming up rapidly. Notable among the shows held for public attendance only were the International Sport, Camping, and Vacation Show in New York; the ninth annual International Boat Show, Genoa, Italy; and the Swedish Ideal Home Exhibition at Göteborg.

Pop Art painted umbrellas displayed at the Teen-age Fair 69 in Düsseldorf, W.Ger.

DPA FROM PICTORIAL PARADE

Amusement Parks. Almost two billion people flocked to the world's approximately 16,800 amusement facilities in 1969. Revenues were the highest of any recreational activity. Millions of dollars in new amusement ride orders were placed with manufacturers during the year as park operators sought to attract patrons with new ride presentations. Some parks were operating under a policy that required concessionaires to bring new rides each year, forcing many to become ride importers and distributors. Ride prices were higher than ever in the U.S. and Canada. Rockaways (N.Y.) Playland was charging $1 for a roller-coaster ride on weekends; in 1950 the same ride was 35 cents.

More than 360 million North Americans spent an estimated $500 million at over 1,000 U.S. and Canadian theme parks, kiddielands, and general amusement parks and some 1,500 municipal parks, zoos, and aquariums. The few municipally owned and operated parks showed generally poorer revenue returns than their privately owned counterparts. Belgium's ancient woodland Heysel Park at Brussels and the Tivoli Gardens at Copenhagen had the greatest number of visitors in their history.

Carnivals, Rodeos, and Circuses. Over 90% of U.S. and Canadian fairs booked carnival shows in 1969, and rodeos and circuses were also in great demand. The increased interdependence of carnival shows and agricultural fairs had brought new prosperity to small carnival units, which once were nearing extinction as they fled from sheriff to sheriff. Approximately two-thirds of the 600 carnival shows that toured the U.S. and Canada opened earlier in 1969 than in 1968, with the average show season running 28 weeks, compared with 19.5 in 1963. Carnivals in France were having a more difficult time, particularly in and around Paris where, because of traffic congestion, they could operate only on certain holidays.

Rodeos were also increasingly popular as livestock show and fair fixtures. More than 600 shows approved by the Rodeo Cowboy's Association were held in 46 U.S. states and 5 Canadian provinces. Total prize money was over $4 million. An additional 600 events were held in Central and South America, although some were little more than theatrical productions. A standard fixture in Latin America for over 16 years, Tony Aguilar's National Mexican Festival and Rodeo, grossed over $2 million in its second season in the U.S. The first championship rodeo in more than ten years appeared at New York's Madison Square Garden in August.

An estimated 125 new circus units began operation in 1969, bringing the number of circuses touring the world to 425, with 56 units covering fairs and still dates on the North American continent. England's famous Chipperfield Circus, which had moved to South Africa in 1964, returned to tour its former home country. The Jim Beck's, Duffy's, and Fossett circuses reported highly successful dates in Ireland, but they were forced to avoid the troubled areas around Belfast. Mexico's Circo Orrin, a relative newcomer that shared lower Rio Grande Valley dates with the Atayde Bros. Circus, reported exceptional business. Elsewhere, circus acts were being booked in increasing numbers by independent producers for specialized shows. Typical of this trend was Circus Circus, booked into a gambling casino at Las Vegas, Nev. Some venerable circus organizations reported their best show seasons in history, among them the Hamid-Morton Circus, Ringling Bros. and Barnum & Bailey, King Bros., James Bros., Pollack Bros., Mills Bros., Hubert Castle, and Dobritch-International in North America, Circus Knie in Switzerland, and Miranda Orfei Circus in Italy.

Livestock and Horse Shows. Among the thousands of livestock shows held in 1969, North American events emphasized cash, ribbon, and trophy awards for breed categories, as did the venerable shows in Great Britain. Shows held in other regions of Europe and in South America concentrated for the most part on marketing, with on-the-spot sales a prominent part of the events. The majority of state and county fairs in the U.S. and provincial and district fairs in Canada featured livestock and horse shows. Many specialized livestock shows were combined with other types such as dairy shows, while others were merged into nearby annual fairs. Some

20,000 animals and 1,500 exhibitors from 40 U.S. states and Canada participated in the annual Denver National Western Stock Show; over 150,000 persons witnessed this event. In Houston, Tex., a record 501,-827 livestock fanciers and rodeo fans packed that city's Astrodome to witness judging events and a rodeo that offered $103,000 in prize money.

A third of the world's horse shows took place in North America, with approximately 800 sanctioned by the American Horse Show Association. The horse show at New York's Madison Square Garden, the Pennsylvania Farm Show at Harrisburg, the New York State Fair at Syracuse, and the Pin Oak Charity Horse Show, Houston, drew the greatest crowds in history in 1969. (F. P. P.)

See also Architecture; Art Exhibitions.

Fashion and Dress

The accent on fashion in 1969 was again on extreme youth, and older women continued to declare that there was nothing for them in the shops. In the fall, however, it was felt that an era of casual, quiet, and more classic dressing was on the way in: "country-into-town tweeds, unobtrusive colours, well-bred accessories" were reported from Paris by Alison Adburgham in Britain's *Guardian.* The Paris-based International Fashion Office (a branch of the International Wool Secretariat) seemed to be of much the same opinion. Listing "out-of-date" styles, they censured "sensation-seeking and gimmicky garments."

The most significant fashion factor to emerge was the acceptance of trouser outfits as rational everyday wear for every occasion. No longer were there stories in the press of trousered young women being turned away from elegant restaurants. The acceptability of the trouser suit and its derivatives did not mean that pants were as yet in the majority, however. The skirted leg was still the norm, despite mounting pressures from trend-setting sources.

Leading Paris couturier Yves St. Laurent, from whose influence the vogue for trousers could be said to have stemmed, continued to promote them in his spring and fall collections. The Dior-London ready-to-wear fall collection featured more than 50 trouser outfits to one skirt. From San Francisco, "one of the great suit cities of the world," the *Christian Science Monitor* reported that "pants and suits are synonymous this year. Combined they are an answer to the hemline controversy." Serena Sinclair, fashion editor of the *Daily Telegraph*, reported a similar trend in London: "This autumn British fashion is moving resolutely into pants." Evidence of the mounting demand for pants from all age and income groups was the setting up in a London store of a special department to deal exclusively in trouser outfits. As a corrective to the growing trend, Levi Strauss, a firm name that was almost synonymous with pants, announced a nonpant collection consisting of skirts, shirts, and culottes.

A statement by the Mexican-born, Paris-based avant-garde designer Ruben Torres suggested that men were fighting back. Speaking of his skintight pants ("men are going to have to get used to clothes that fit the body") and of the "uplift, aerodynamic" underpants designed to go under them, he said: "My designs are strictly masculine—it means that no woman will be able to wear our trousers." (*See* Special Report.) At issue with this defensive attitude, Paris couturier Jacques Estérel stated that "identification of the sexes in terms of clothes will become a thing of the past." He designed identical tunic and pants outfits for father, mother, and child. "Unisex" clothes were advertised from the walls of London's subway, and the psychological implications of unisex were eagerly discussed.

The vogue for trousers had an inevitable reaction on hemlines, although the hemline controversy remained unresolved. Younger girls were reluctant to abandon the miniskirt, although trousers encroached on the position of the mini with the realization that many a skirt looked smarter with trousers added. By the fall of 1969 the miniskirt had, in fact, begun to lose some of its appeal, although its demise was perhaps overconfidently heralded in some quarters. Without doubt it was the advent of those flaring pants on the fashion scene and the comforting feel of wool flapping around the ankles that opened the way for the long swirling coats of the fall collections in Paris, London, New York, Madrid, and Rome.

Controversial as the new trend appeared at the time, many leading designers were prepared to take it seriously. Victor Joris of Cuddlecoat was reported as having said of the prospects for maxicoats and skirts, "It's just a feeling. . . . I think the time is right." In addition to maxicoats, his fall collection included ankle-length cable-knit vests, cable-knit jump suits, city trouser suits, polo coats over jump suits, suits with ankle-length skirts, and knee-length cardigans over ankle-length sweater skirts or pants. Joris, however, did not see this trend as an indication that all hemlines were coming down. Rather, he regarded the maxi as an extra outfit.

As the battle of the maxi length raged in the fall, designers and buyers alike felt that the "extra-outfit" approach to the new length was the safe one to take. Many international buyers in Paris settled for the maxicoat over a thigh-high skirt. Proportion was the key to the long, flat, clinging look that was typical of fashion throughout the year. In its release sheet on the French ready-to-wear collections, the International Fashion Office reported that the tunic look was the most characteristic. The top of the silhouette continued to lengthen, contrasting with ultrashort skirts or with pants. The latter dictated the proportions for 1970 and gave a new ratio to lengths. "The result of their wide acceptance is a fashion with an entirely different balance."

The International Fashion Office release gave these leads to trouser styling for 1969: "Flat on the hips with no pockets or darts. Less width than last season, maximum at ankle 23 to 25 cm. [9 to $9\frac{7}{8}$ in.] (more widely flared in the case of evening models). Always worn with thick-heeled shoes." Listed as out-of-date were: the classic suit, coordinated dress and coat ensembles, the real cocktail dress (to which should be added the real evening dress), and, as already noted, "sensation-seeking and gimmicky garments."

The most significant coat silhouette was the redingote, featuring a double-breasted cut and buttoned high under wide revers. Other acceptable coat shapes were the perennial trench coat, a wrapover bathrobe style, and those with a side fastening. It was the tunic, however—long, clinging, and teamed with flaring pants or a brief, flared skirt—that could be called the fashion hallmark of 1969. Describing the line, a U.S. fashion writer called it the "cling and fling" look. Continuing its success of previous seasons, the sleeve-

continued on page 344

Falkland Islands:
see Dependent States
Farming:
see Agriculture

SPECIAL REPORT

THE END OF THE GRAY FLANNEL SUIT

By Antony King Deacon

What might be called the "Peacock Revolution" began in 1957 in Carnaby Street, an insignificant back street in the West End of London, when John Stephen, a young shop assistant from Glasgow, opened a boutique there. But the influences that made Carnaby Street a synonym for far-out male fashions and one of London's major tourist attractions, and that caused the conservative menswear industry to reorient itself during the 1960s, could be traced back to the end of World War II.

During the years immediately following the war, Britain was suffering the deprivations and moral staleness characteristic of a nation's postwar life. Food and clothing were still rationed and drabness was everywhere, exemplified by the pervasive "demob suit" issued free to all members of the forces on their discharge. As the 1950s progressed and rationing ended, young men began to experiment with their clothes. The first really cohesive fashion was set by the "Teddy boys," who wore very long jackets, often with velvet collars and lapels, hanging in a straight line from the shoulder to a point about two inches above the knee. Colours were usually dark shades of blue, wine, gray, and brown. Matching trousers—"drainpipes" or "stovepipes"—were cut very tight from top to bottom. Shoes were either long and pointed Italian style or thick crepe-soled suèdes. Hair was cut long in the style of Tony Curtis.

The Teddy boys were superseded in the mid-1950s by the "Rockers," who wore leather jerkins studded with anything that would glitter and sparkle or festooned with small plastic dolls and other trinkets. They wore jeans that they sanded to make them look worn and old and then shrank to size by sitting in them in a bath of cold water.

About 1958 there was an anti-Rocker movement toward tidiness and smart—rather than colourful or showy—clothes: two-piece suits that were well cut and without cuffs; pastel coloured shirts; and slip-on shoes with rounder toes than had previously been worn. The followers of this new fashion were called "Mods," and furious battles between Mods and Rockers became regular occurrences at some seaside resorts.

It was the Mods who were the first customers of Carnaby Street. The country had become more affluent, and young men were now earning higher wages and were able to spend considerably more on their clothes than young Britishers had ever done before. The Mods were interested in dress more from a studied carefulness and a need to be tidy and respectable than from the urge to be fashionable or to wear any kind of "uniform," but they did want their clothes to be entirely different from those worn by their elders.

Carnaby Street supplied this difference. Suddenly the brightest and the craziest was the best. Carnaby Street wooed a huge number of seamstresses and other workers from the Savile Row trade, and the small boutiques made and sold "one-off" garments straight from the sewing machines. The prices were high and the turnover was enormous. In a matter of 18 months practically the whole street was taken over by menswear retailers of an entirely new and revolutionary brand.

It was not until the early '60s that the general menswear industry overcame its initial skepticism toward Carnaby Street,

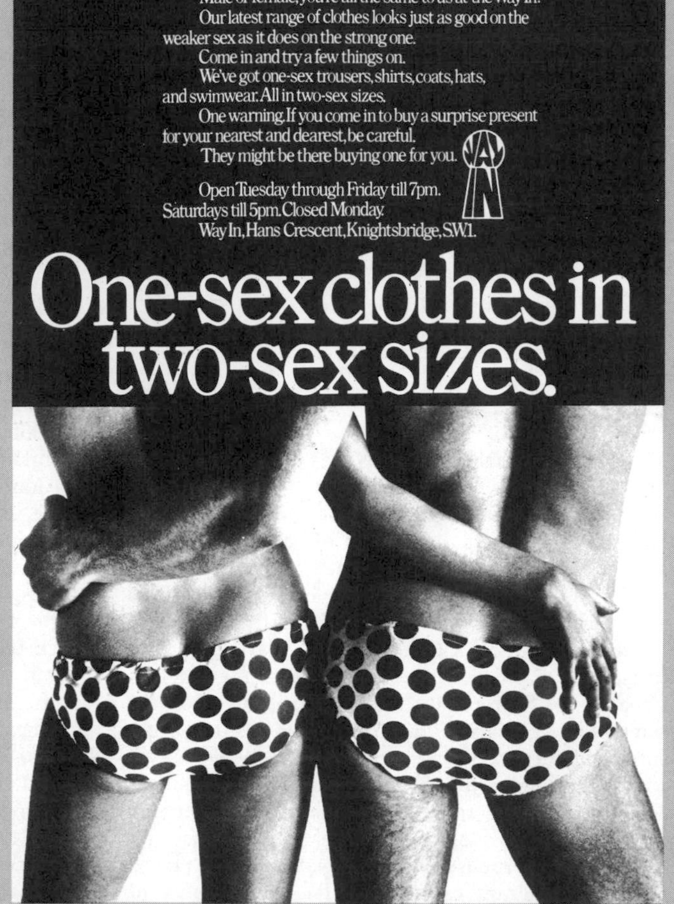
Male or female, you're all the same to us at the Way In.
Our latest range of clothes looks just as good on the weaker sex as it does on the strong one.
Come in and try a few things on.
We've got one-sex trousers, shirts, coats, hats, and swimwear. All in two-sex sizes.
One warning. If you come in to buy a surprise present for your nearest and dearest, be careful.
They might be there buying one for you.
Open Tuesday through Friday till 7pm.
Saturdays till 5pm. Closed Monday.
Way In, Hans Crescent, Knightsbridge, SW1.
One-sex clothes in two-sex sizes.

COURTESY, HARRODS

Advertisement for Harrods "Way In" boutique emphasizes the "unisex" look in men's and women's clothing.

but when it finally got the message of sartorial revolution, it exploded into a frenzy of activity. Soon long-established stores that had previously cultivated an image of staid conservatism were jumping on the bandwagon. Austin Reed opened its "Cue" department of high-fashion, very colourful menswear. Harrods opened the "Way In" on its fourth floor. Aquascutum began its "Club 92." Simpson's had a "Trend" department and Moss Bros. a "One Up" section—all of which were devoted to extreme fashions and aimed at a more discerning market than that centred in Carnaby Street.

To supply the growing demand from an ever widening public, the general menswear industry, the large manufacturing companies, and the chain stores began to experiment with high fashion for men. And as the merchandise became more available, retailers in the provinces and abroad began to buy such Carnaby-type clothing as cheap mohair and worsted suits, bright, colourful shirts with large collars, wide "kipper" ties, and gaudy accessories. At one time the exports of men's high fashion clothes to the United States far exceeded the total of all other types of garment exported to that market. Soon every town in Britain had at least one men's boutique where the young men—and women—could emulate what they saw being worn by such stars as the Beatles and the Rolling Stones in press photographs and on television. For one of the most important single factors in the Peacock Revolution was certainly the fact that pop stars wore outrageous and overstated fashions.

Then two things happened that changed the course of the revolution radically. First, the King's Road, Chelsea, long known as the artists' quarter of London, became the new important area for men's and women's fashions. Small shops such as Granny Takes a Trip and Hung On You opened, and they were immediately followed by branches of Carnaby Street shops and such firms as John Michael and Cecil Gee. Simultaneously, the "drug scene" opened, bringing with it a frenzy of sartorial activity. Boys and girls who were blowing their minds wanted clothes that reflected their total war with society, that had nothing to do with anything that had happened before—that must, in fact, be as wild as their minds. And since a large proportion of the drugs and the drug philosophy came from the East, the clothes sold reflected an Eastern influence—long, flowing caftans, Afghan leather jackets with thick pile wool linings and mirrors sewn into them, shirts with stand-up collars, and wild silk chukhas (silk squares). It took about 18 months for the Eastern influence to reach the large-scale manufacturers, and when it did there was a period of stand-up collar (Nehru) suit jackets (even raincoats were shown with stand-up collars) and, after Lord Snowdon and other prominent men had been seen wearing them, turtleneck shirts that went under the new jackets. Bonsoir, an established shirt and pajama manufacturer, made long cotton caftans for both him and her.

The other major occurrence was the emergence of the designer. Only a few years previously the designer had been someone sitting in a back room of the factory who helped make the coffee when he was not working out a sleeve length or the shape of a lapel. Now everyone was interested in who had designed the new merchandise. Men like Peter Golding, Tom Gilbey, Rupert Lycett-Green (Blades of Savile Row and Madison Avenue), Douglas Haywood, and Michael Fish suddenly became personalities in and out of the industry. Each made a considerable contribution toward calming down the design of menswear, which at the time of the Eastern influences was getting rather out of hand.

Outside Britain the Carnaby Street type of merchandise was soon to become outdated and rejected by discerning and affluent young people. In the United States the designer cult—which in the womenswear field had always been stronger there than in Britain—grew rapidly for menswear. Such men as Oleg Cassini, Bill Blass, and John Weitz began to design clothes under license for large manufacturers. Hardy Amies, a British haute couture designer previously employed by Hepworth's, a U.K. menswear retail chain, signed up with Genesco. In Italy such well-known tailors and women's designers as Valentino, Datti, Angelo Litrico, Bruno Piattelli, Patrick de Barentzen, and Carlo Pallazzi all began to sell their names to large clothing manufacturers and to make their designs available to a mass public. Paris also took up the flag of male fashions as Pierre Cardin, Gilbert Feruch, Ted Lapidus, and Jacques Esterel entered the field.

At the end of the 1960s, fashion in the sense of the "colour of the season" or the "line of the season" had ceased to exist. Both men and women were wearing anything they felt suited them, borrowing freely from the opposite sex. The "unisex" look arrived (advertised by Harrods "Way In" boutique as "One-Sex Clothes in Two-Sex Sizes") and this trend toward a merging of the sexes was emphasized by the wearing of jewelry by men in the form of pendants and rings, the use of handbags that made up for the lack of pocket space in closely fitting garments, and the vast consumption by men of cosmetic preparations—mainly deodorants and after-shave lotions, but soon to include a full range of makeup including eyeliner, face powder, and rouge.

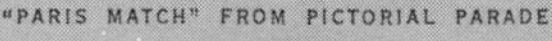
"PARIS MATCH" FROM PICTORIAL PARADE

Left, Scotch plaid greatcoat with ten buttons and large lapels from Diffusion Renoma of France. Ensemble includes the shirt and scarf shown. Below, belted wool jersey jump suit designed by Peter Golding. Right, tailored white leather coat shown by Austin Reed Ltd.

PETER KINNEAR

JOHN ADAMS STUDIOS

continued from page 341

KEYSTONE

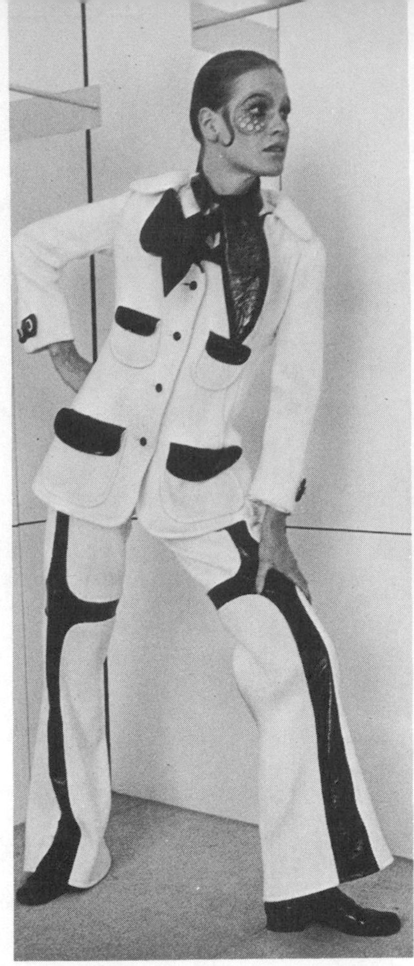

LIAISON

LIAISON

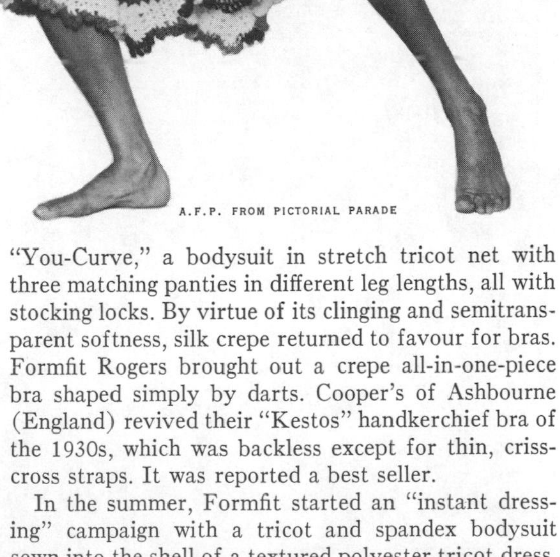

A.F.P. FROM PICTORIAL PARADE

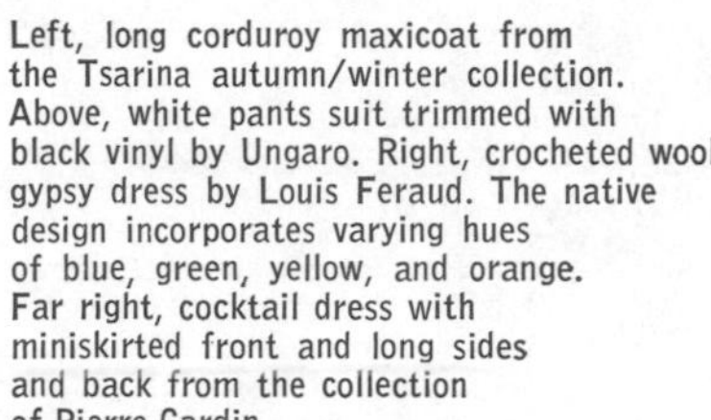

Left, long corduroy maxicoat from the Tsarina autumn/winter collection. Above, white pants suit trimmed with black vinyl by Ungaro. Right, crocheted wool gypsy dress by Louis Feraud. The native design incorporates varying hues of blue, green, yellow, and orange. Far right, cocktail dress with miniskirted front and long sides and back from the collection of Pierre Cardin.

less jumper or pinafore dress worn over a contrasting long-sleeved shirt or sweater was a favourite style. Even in summer, the sleeveless dress was the exception. Shirt sleeves and the still fuller "bishop" sleeve (or, to give it its new label, the "Camelot" sleeve) were typical fashion points.

While the overall look was covered up—long sleeves, high necklines, long skirts, pants, 20-ft.-long mufflers—the see-through look could be said to have reached its permissive limits. The waist-deep V neckline over no-bra breasts and the sheer chiffon blouse over a nude torso were accepted evening wear while, as a result of the lifting of censorship, nudity—male as well as female—was total on the stage. The designers of underwear lost no time in coming to terms with the no-bra cult and with the typically lean, clinging, unstructured style of clothes. A New York correspondent reported: "Fall has a maxi list of mini garments that do their control and camouflage job without making ridges on what's on top." Warner's, the "grandaddy of the bodysuit family," brought out "You-Curve," a bodysuit in stretch tricot net with three matching panties in different leg lengths, all with stocking locks. By virtue of its clinging and semitransparent softness, silk crepe returned to favour for bras. Formfit Rogers brought out a crepe all-in-one-piece bra shaped simply by darts. Cooper's of Ashbourne (England) revived their "Kestos" handkerchief bra of the 1930s, which was backless except for thin, crisscross straps. It was reported a best seller.

In the summer, Formfit started an "instant dressing" campaign with a tricot and spandex bodysuit sewn into the shell of a textured polyester tricot dress. The "bra-dress," hailed as the year's bright notion, was available in most stores. The stretch toweling jump suit, an idea carried over from 1968, was a holiday favourite for 1969. Sleepwear generally was streamlined to a minimum, but renewed interest in ultrafeminine, full-length nightgowns was reported.

The trend in knitwear was toward lanky, hugging effects directly inspired by St. Laurent's vests and tunics. The long, long vest or sweater paired to pants was reported as the "number one look everywhere." Rib-knit "catsuits," strongly featured by Cardin under coats and tunics in his fall collection and used as the basis for almost every Courrèges model at that time, were in heavy demand.

Plain, coloured stockings and tights were de rigueur for all but formal occasions. Shoes remained chunky looking. In the fall, however, a more pointed toe—designed to go with the maxi-length skirt—made its appearance in the collections of leading shoemakers in France and Italy. Heeled ankle boots were shown at the same time and for the same reason.

Renewed interest in hats was evident among teenagers and younger women. The fedora was the favourite shape, but it was the small, neat, bonneted or helmeted head that was typical. This look was introduced to give the illusion of a longer body, which, in the final analysis, was the aim of everything—including long straight hair and higher heels—that happened in the fashion field during 1969. (P. W. HE.)

Finland

The republic of Finland is bordered on the north by Norway, on the west by Sweden and the Gulf of Bothnia, on the south by the Gulf of Finland, and on the east by the U.S.S.R. Area: 130,128 sq.mi. (337,032 sq.km.). Pop. (1969 est.): 4,699,115. Cap. and largest city: Helsinki (pop., 1969 est., 532,310). Language (1960): Finnish 92.4%; Swedish 7.4%. Religion: Lutheran 92.5%; Orthodox 1.3%. President in 1968, Urho Kaleva Kekkonen; prime minister, Mauno Koivisto.

Finland became the 22nd member of the Organization for Economic Cooperation and Development (OECD) at the beginning of 1969. In a survey in July the organization praised developments in Finland since the 1967 devaluation of the markka and forecast continued economic progress and increased exports. The balance of payments had improved in 1968, unemployment decreased, and throughout 1969 there was an expansion of activity. The stabilization program covering the labour market in 1968 and 1969 was renewed for 1970 in order to maintain control of prices and wages. There was a foreign trade surplus of 102 million markkaa in 1968, compared with a deficit of 622 million markkaa in 1967.

The United Kingdom was Finland's number one partner in total trade, followed by Sweden, the Soviet Union, West Germany, and the U.S. The share of the Eastern bloc (including the Soviet Union) in Finland's total imports fell between January and July 1969 to 15.3%, from 21.4% in 1968, and its share of exports to 18.7% from 20.6%. During the corresponding period the EEC accounted for 26.5% of Finland's imports and 23.4% of exports. EFTA's shares were 38.5 and 38.8%, respectively.

On August 26 a new trade agreement with the U.S.S.R. was signed for the period 1971–75. Finland's first nuclear power station was to be delivered by the Soviet Union under an agreement signed on September 9. The power station, to be erected at Loviisa east of Helsinki, would have a capacity of 440 Mw. The U.S.S.R. was to supply the nuclear fuel for a 20-year period, and the power station was expected to be ready for commercial use by June 1976. Orders for the various construction stages were to be placed with the Finnish metal industry.

During the year high-level talks took place between Finland, Denmark, Norway, and Sweden on closer economic cooperation—the so-called Nordek plan—aimed at strengthening the position of the Scandinavian countries in a future integrated Europe. On December 8, however, Finland withdrew from the talks, and the others decided to defer further action until after the Finnish election in March 1970.

At the same time that the Finns were enjoying a stabilized economy, the government felt that the foreign policy of the last decades had stabilized into a neutrality recognized by both East and West. Accordingly, in May it issued a memorandum on the possibility of holding an eventual European security conference in Helsinki. The memorandum was delivered to all governments in Europe and to the governments of the U.S. and Canada. Finnish representatives abroad were instructed to sound out the positions of the concerned nations and consult them on conditions necessary for a preparatory meeting.

On October 25 Helsinki was named as the site for talks between the U.S. and the Soviet Union on the limitation of strategic arms (SALT), which began there on November 17. (*See* DEFENSE.)

European security and international problems on the whole were discussed by President Kekkonen dur-

FINLAND

Education. (1966–67) Primary, pupils 438,057, teachers 19,177; secondary, pupils 367,583, teachers 19,089; vocational, pupils 89,258, teachers 8,077; teacher training, students 2,403, teachers 375; higher (including 7 universities), students 46,289, teaching staff 4,499.

Finance. Monetary unit: markka, with a par value of 4.20 markkaa to U.S. $1 (10.08 markkaa = £1 sterling). Gold and foreign exchange, central bank: (June 1969) U.S. $253.3 million; (June 1968) U.S. $322.8 million. Budget (1969 est.) balanced at 9,199,000,000 markkaa. Gross national product: (1967) 29.9 billion markkaa; (1966) 27,630,000,000 markkaa. Money supply: (May 1969) 2,675,000,000 markkaa; (May 1968) 2,268,000,000 markkaa. Cost of living (1967 = 100): (June 1969) 112; (June 1968) 110.

Foreign Trade. (1968) Imports 6,689,000,000 markkaa; exports 6,870,000,000 markkaa. Import sources: U.S.S.R. 17%; West Germany 15%; Sweden 14%; U.K. 13%; U.S. 5%. Export destinations: U.K. 21%; U.S.S.R. 15%; West Germany 11%; Sweden 10%; U.S. 6%; Netherlands 5%. Main exports: paper 30%; timber 17%; wood pulp 15%.

Transport and Communications. Roads (1968) 71,049 km. (including 102 km. expressways). Motor vehicles in use (1968): passenger 580,999; commercial 97,055. Railways: state (1967) 5,620 km.; private (1966) 74 km.; traffic (state only; 1967) 2,153,000,000 passenger-km., freight (state only; 1968) 5,627,000,000 net ton-km. Air traffic (1968): 439.2 million passenger-km.; freight 7,588,000 net ton-km. Navigable inland waterways (1967) *c.* 6,600 km. Shipping (1968): merchant vessels 100 gross tons and over 399; gross tonnage 1,127,896. Telephones (Dec. 1967) 949,976. Radio receivers (Dec. 1967) 1,663,000. Television receivers (Dec. 1967) 899,000.

Agriculture. Production (in 000; metric tons; 1968; 1967 in parentheses): wheat 516 (507); rye 134 (163); barley 774 (681); oats 1,064 (940); potatoes 908 (881); sugar, raw value (1968–69) *c.* 49, (1967–68) 62; timber (cu.m.; 1967) 41,100, (1966) 41,700; butter 105 (96); fish catch (1967) 74, (1966) 71. Livestock (in 000; June 1968): cattle 2,071; sheep 155; pigs 680; horses 126; chickens (June 1967) 7,284.

Industry. Production (in 000; metric tons; 1968): iron ore (67% metal content) 527; pig iron 1,105; crude steel 695; copper 36; cement 1,478; plywood (cu.m.; 1967) 574; cellulose (1967) 4,083; mechanical wood pulp (1967) 1,664; chemical wood pulp (1967) 4,055; cardboard (1967) 994; newsprint 1,246; other paper (1967) 2,156; electricity (kw-hr.) 17,990,000; manufactured gas (cu.m.) 60,000.

Federated Malay States:
see Malaysia

Feed Grains:
see Agriculture

Fencing:
see Sporting Record

Fernando Po:
see Equatorial Guinea

Festivals:
see Cinema; Music

Fibres:
see Agriculture; Industrial Review

Field Hockey:
see Hockey

Fiji:
see Dependent States

Finance, International:
see Development, Economic; Economy, World; Money and Banking; Payments and Reserves, International

ing a number of visits abroad. He met with French Pres. Charles de Gaulle in Paris on January 17, and with Soviet Premier Aleksei N. Kosygin in Leningrad on May 19–20, paid a state visit to the United Kingdom on July 15–20, and met Kosygin again during an unofficial visit to the Soviet Union from July 27 to August 3. Kekkonen also paid the first-ever Finnish state visits to Romania (September 22–26), Hungary (September 26–October 1), and Czechoslovakia (October 1–4), during which he had talks with Nicolae Ceausescu, Janos Kadar, and Ludvik Svoboda.

King Baudouin and Queen Fabiola of Belgium paid a state visit to Finland on June 16–20 and Soviet Pres. Nikolai V. Podgorny made an official visit on October 14–18.

The major domestic issue in Finland was the split within the 50,000-member Communist Party, which had representatives in both the Cabinet and Parliament through its affiliate, Finland's People's Democratic League (SKDL). Signs of a division had appeared at the time of the Warsaw Pact intervention in Czechoslovakia in August 1968, and the party's 15th congress on April 3–6, 1969, ended in a final clash between the majority, supporting chairman Aarne Saarinen, and the minority of "Stalinists," with former party chairman Aimo Aaltonen as one of its strong men. The opposition left the congress hall and the new Central Committee and Politburo elected by the congress were composed of Saarinen's supporters. Saarinen was reelected for a new three-year period. Ville Pessi, 67, resigned as secretary-general, a post he had held since 1945, and was succeeded by Arvo Aalto, 36. Pessi, however, remained as a member of the Central Committee. The congress also approved a new party program designed to bring about "democratic socialism" by peaceful means.

Shortly before the congress, Saarinen had visited Moscow for talks with Soviet party leaders, who obviously gave their support to him while at the same time hoping for unity within the Finnish party. Reconciliation talks failed, and in September the opposition announced that it would nominate separate candidates for the general election in March 1970. A continued division was expected to result in a setback for the party and the SKDL. In the 1966 elections the SKDL became the third largest group in Parliament (41 seats), behind the Social Democrats (55) and the Centre Party (49). (C. F. SA.)

Fisheries

Although 1969 was not a particularly eventful year for the fisheries industry, general expansion and investment occurred on a great many fronts, especially in the Far East and Oceania. It appeared that the world had really come to grips with the urgent business of winning protein from the sea.

Table I. Whaling: 1967-68 Season

Area and country	Blue whale	Fin whale	Humpback whale	Sei whale	Sperm whale	Others	Percentage assigned under quota agreement*
	Number of whales caught						
Antarctic: pelagic (open sea)							
Japan	...	613	...	7,119	104	...	47
Norway	...	360	...	672	74	...	23
U.S.S.R.	...	1,182	...	2,566	2,390	...	30
Total	...	2,155	...	10,357	2,568	...	...
Outside the Antarctic†	66	3,449	4	10,699	20,961	266	...

Note: No whaling operations from South Georgia during the 1967–68 season.
*Antarctic only.
†1966-67.
Source: Committee for Whaling Statistics, *International Whaling Statistics.*

At long last, the U.S. surveyed its home fisheries, which had been falling further and further behind other nations in vessels and equipment. In a comprehensive report entitled *Our Nation and the Sea,* the U.S. government laid down guidelines for fisheries development and investment. At the same time, it linked fisheries development with oceanographic research aimed at overall exploitation of the ocean and seabed. Indicative of the new U.S. attitude was the commissioning of two new freezer factory trawlers, "Seafreeze Atlantic" and "Seafreeze Pacific."

Among the established high-technology fishing nations of Europe, major expansion was confined to the Communist countries and Ireland. The Soviet fleet grew by 366 vessels to a total of 20,000; one of them, the giant mother ship "Vostok"—the world's largest—carried its own fleet of 70-ft. fibre-glass catcher boats. In 1968, 60% of the Soviet Union's fish were quick-frozen and no less than 1,000,000,000 cans of seafood were produced. Soviet scientists continued to promote international collaboration in research by inviting foreign scientists to join their research vessels in the Mediterranean and the Indian Ocean and by exchanging scientists with the U.S. Bureau of Commercial Fisheries. They announced a major project: making a computer model of world ocean characteristics for fish stock forecasting purposes.

Poland mounted a $13 million research project in collaboration with the UN Food and Agriculture Organization (FAO), with Poland paying most of the bill. The Polish shipbuilding industry continued to export fishing vessels to the U.K., France, Ireland,

Table II. World Fisheries, by Country, Catch, and Value of Catch, 1967*†

Country	Catch in 000 metric tons	Value in U.S. $000
Argentina	241	12,030
Australia	92	49,693
Belgium	64	16,790
Burma	360‡	63,819
Cambodia	163‡	38,384
Canada	1,290	151,688
Chile	1,053	...
Colombia	57‡	8,626
Cuba	63	28,830
Denmark	1,070	91,266
Faeroe Is.	173	...
Finland	74	19,244
France	820	265,358
Germany, East	223‡	...
Germany, West	662	92,834
Hong Kong	87	11,976
Hungary	28	36,380
Iceland	896	...
India	1,400	...
Israel	22	12,587
Italy	337	166,586
Japan	7,814	...
Korea, South	749	...
Malaysia	367	88,555
Mexico	350	75,772
Morocco	258	15,215
Netherlands	315	61,860
Norway	3,214	161,547
Panama	72	7,257
Peru	10,110	117,247
Philippines	769	271,426
Poland	339	...
Portugal	506‡	67,429
South Africa	904	...
South West Africa	740	...
Spain	1,431	325,524
Sweden	338	44,126
Taiwan	458	104,625
Thailand	849	148,296
United Kingdom	1,026	174,659
United States	2,384	...
Venezuela	107	22,949
Vietnam, South	381‡	122,238

*Excludes whaling.
†Some double counting may occur.
‡1966.
Sources: United Nations Food and Agriculture Organization, *Yearbook of Fishery Statistics*, vol. 24.

and other Western nations. Ireland's expansion proceeded, and the government made proposals for a World Fisheries Bank. Dublin was to be the scene of the World Fishing Exhibition in 1971, Ireland's first event of this kind.

While the Eastern European countries continued to expand their fleets, most Western European nations followed more of a standstill policy. With trawler interests still recovering from the previous year's frozen fillet surplus, and Norwegian herring purse seiners in trouble after the failure of the winter herring, there was an inclination to invest in cold stores rather than in vessels.

One of the inhibiting factors in Britain—besides the difficulty of obtaining building subsidies—was fear that the loss of three trawlers in 1968 would lead to changes in design that could require costly modifications. Also, life was uncertain among the "big three" trawler companies—the Ross Group, Associated Fisheries, and Boston Deep Sea Fishing. Despite a previous rejection of a merger by the Monopolies Commission, a marriage was arranged between the trawling fleets of Ross and Associated, with Boston opting out. Soon afterward, Ross was taken over by Imperial Tobacco in a £47 million deal.

In Spain trawler building ended with a flourish when the country's biggest trawler, the 360-ft. "Mino," was completed and left for the South African hake grounds. Following the discovery of good tuna stocks off Angola, five Spanish yards switched to building tuna clippers.

With the massive assault on hake stocks in South African waters by Spain, West Germany, Japan, and the U.S.S.R., South African owners were forced to invest in new, bigger trawlers to work more distant grounds. Two major trawling companies merged and placed a R 6 million order for six large stern trawlers —two from Britain and the rest from home yards.

In Australia and New Zealand, foreign vessels continued to exploit grounds underfished by home fleets. One statement declared that Japan and Taiwan had carried out far more research in Australian waters than had the federal government. Some new vessels were built for the West Coast shrimp fishery. The Gulf of Carpentaria shrimp bonanza showed a falloff following the application of a belated vessel licensing system, but foreign vessels—including some from Kuwait—reaped the richest harvest. After the failure of New Zealand's one effort to establish a distant fishery, U.S. interests were reported to be studying the country's fish resources with an eye to investment, probably in rock lobster. Some 90 Japanese trawlers had been working New Zealand grounds.

Expansion took place in Ghana where, despite past disasters, new stern trawlers were built and shore facilities were set up. India, with ten new ships from the U.S.S.R., was actively exporting shrimp to the U.S. Both North and South Vietnam were planning expansion, and South Korea was buying big factory ships from the Netherlands. Greenland and the Faroes were both investing in large stern trawlers. Mexico planned to build 100 British-equipped shrimp trawlers. There were also signs of a major investment in fisheries by Brazil; surveys of stocks by foreign experts were to be followed by the establishment of shore facilities and fishing fleets.

In the search for new sources of protein, work continued in many countries on the farming of fish, prawns, and eels; a breakthrough was made in stimulating breeding in captivity by the use of hormone extract. Soviet scientists explored the possibility of harvesting krill—the shrimplike creatures that whales eat by the ton—to make edible paste. An FAO conference at Halifax, N.S., discussed the need to define and maintain adequate standards of fish quality—though this was felt by many to mean "to the standards required for the U.S. market." Concern was expressed by the FAO over the increasing threat of river and coastal pollution in many countries, affecting both shellfish beds and fish. According to the FAO, 28 nations claimed international fishing limits of 3 mi.; 31 claimed 12 mi.; and 6, no less than 200 mi.

(H. S. N.)

See also Food.

Food

Food Supplies. The outlook for food supplies in 1969 improved as the world's agriculture appeared to sustain the expansion that had been registered in 1968. Indications pointed to continued growth, but at more modest rates in some areas, especially in cereals, where unusual gains had been made in 1968. Significant progress in production of cereals in the Indian subcontinent and in some other areas seemed assured. Record output of fats and oils in 1969 was forecast.

Total world food supplies in 1968 rose approximately 3% above a year earlier, lessening somewhat the apocalyptic view of famine over large areas of the less developed world. The recovery of agricultural production in many of the poorer nations in 1967 was continued in 1968, and although gains were not spectacular, several elements bolstered the sometimes-flagging hope of observers that developing economies could realize a degree of self-sufficiency in food. Still, the margin between food production and rapid population growth was uncomfortably thin in some countries, and for the less developed regions overall, the year registered no gains above 1967 in per capita food supplies.

Agricultural trade was, for the most part, stagnant in 1968, and excess supplies hung over world markets, depressing prices and discouraging growth. Even more serious, the reemergence of surpluses among the more developed nations threatened to stall market development and expansion of agricultural trade by those less developed nations in which technological advances promised exportable surpluses in the near future. Aid from the developed to the less developed countries continued to expand overall in 1968, but official development assistance declined, and there was evidence, particularly among principal donor countries, of a more critical questioning of the purposes and effectiveness of aid programs.

Food Production. According to the United Nations Food and Agriculture Organization (FAO), total agricultural production in the developed areas of the world (Europe and the U.S.S.R., North America, Oceania, Japan, South Africa, and Israel) in 1968 rose to an index of 147 (1952–56 = 100), 3% or more above a year earlier. A very large increase in output in Oceania raised the index of total production for that area from 144 in 1967 to 164, slightly more than 14%; this gain was offset by weather reverses and production restraints in other parts of the developed world.

In the less developed regions (Latin America, the Far East except Japan, the Near East except Israel, and Africa except South Africa), where marked in-

Fires:
see Disasters; Insurance

Fishing:
see Sporting Record

Floods:
see Conservation; Disasters; Engineering Projects

Folk Music:
see Music

CAMERA PRESS—PIX FROM PUBLIX

GAMMA—PIX FROM PUBLIX

Above, food grain piles up and rots in Gabon in 1969, while private pilots are sought to make the dangerous night airlift into Biafra.

Above right, starving children await their food ration at a relief agency centre in Biafra.

creases in total output were registered in 1967, total agricultural production advanced about 2% in 1968. Of particular interest was the Far East (excluding China), where widespread adoption of new cereal varieties, as well as favourable weather, combined to raise total agricultural output 5% above 1967. Results in the other less developed regions were far less satisfactory; 2% gains were shown for the Near East and Africa. In Latin America, severe and widespread drought reduced total output 2% below the record index of 147 registered in 1967.

The largest gains in world food production in 1968, in terms of commodities, were made in cereals, citrus, and soybeans. The FAO estimated world production of wheat in 1968 at 333,939,000 metric tons, a 14% increase over 1967, due largely to an increase in wheat output in India and Pakistan as well as in North Africa. The world barley crop, at 126,809,000 tons, was 8% higher than a year earlier, and rice output rose to a new record 283,514,000 tons, 4% above the 1967 record. Sugar production, at 75,446,000 short tons, showed only a slight increase for the third consecutive year. Oilseed crops registered a modest 4% increase over 1967, in terms of oil equivalent, reflecting larger production of soybeans and cottonseed in the U.S. and a larger sunflower seed crop in the U.S.S.R. World meat production increased by 2% in 1968, and total milk output was larger, contributing to a further growth in surpluses. A much larger citrus crop in the U.S. and Japan offset Mediterranean losses and raised world production to 29,370,000 tons, almost 15% above 1967. Among the commodities showing a decline in production in 1968 were peanuts (−6%), corn (−6%), coffee (−11%), and apples (−10%).

Food Balance. However impressive the gains in food output, per capita supplies were only 1% more in 1968 than a year earlier. Population growth rates in the less developed areas continued at a rate of 2 to 3% each year, reducing, if not totally negating in some areas, gains in food production. Taking the less developed regions as a whole, per capita food supplies in 1968 remained at an index of 104, unchanged from 1967. Among all the less developed regions, only in the Far East did per capita food production increase in 1968; there, the index rose to 106, a 3% increase over 1967, but still less than the index of 108 registered in 1963.

In other parts of the less developed world, per capita production was lower in 1968 than a year earlier; in Latin America, production was 4% less than in 1967; in the Near East, a 1% decrease was registered; and in Africa, the index at 96 was unchanged from a year earlier. For the less developed regions overall, the index of total food production in 1968 was 14% more than in the 1952–56 period. These food levels compared with an overall 2% increase in per capita food production among the developed regions, where the index registered production gains totaling 28% over the 1952–56 average.

The world's attention again focused on Nigeria in 1969, where that nation's civil war was reported to have been responsible for some 1.5 million deaths from hunger, according to a Red Cross mission's estimate in June. Red Cross efforts to relieve the food situation in the Biafra enclave were interrupted in June by activities of the Nigerian Air Force. In August, news reports indicated that death rates from famine were again rising, after having been reduced from an estimated 6,000 per day in late 1968 by relief measures earlier in 1969. Incidence of kwashiorkor was also reported to have risen at a rapid rate by late August. In the autumn, floods in Tunisia resulted in heavy damage to 1969 crops, and generated relief shipments of food from neighbouring countries, Europe, and the U.S. The U.S. Food for Peace program provided aid valued at $99.6 million to relieve food shortages caused by 53 natural disasters in 1968, including drought-famine situations in Latin America and Africa, widespread flooding in East Pakistan, and a devastating earthquake in Iran in September.

A report by the U.S. Department of Agriculture's Economic Research Service stated that gains in cereal production using the new varieties of wheat and rice might reach a rate of 4 to 6% a year, but that it was unlikely that economic demand would increase much more than 4% unless livestock production could be developed fast enough to use substantial amounts for feed. Georg Borgstrom of Michigan State University cautioned against overoptimism for the potentials of the new varieties, citing their requirements for irrigation water, insecticide sprays, and

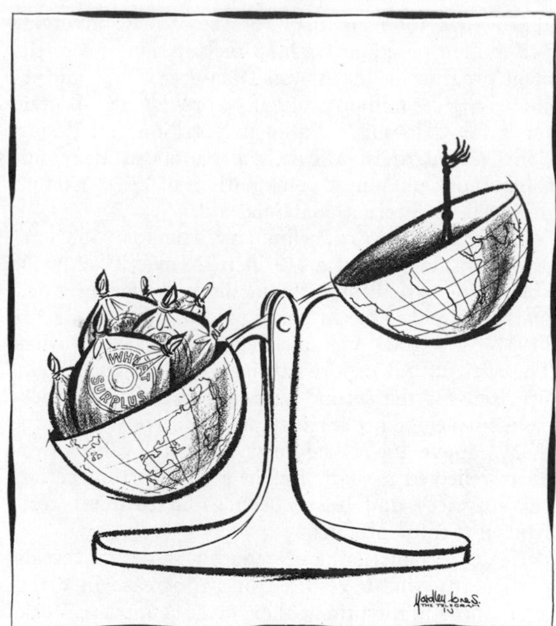

BEN ROTH AGENCY

—Yardley Jones, "Toronto Telegram," Canada.

fertilizers, and their shortcomings as a source of badly needed protein supplies in diet-deficit regions.

A considerable effort continued to improve the protein component of diets, including not only expansion of conventional sources, but the genetic improvement of cereal grains, the fortification of foods with missing essential amino acids, and development of nonconventional sources of protein. Two efforts that showed considerable near-future promise were the continuing development of high-lysine corn and fish protein concentrate (FPC).

Development Assistance. Foreign assistance to agriculture in the less developed regions of the world increased substantially in 1968–69. The FAO reported that loans and grants by the World Bank group of institutions in the year ended June 30, 1969, rose to $1,780,000,000 from $953.5 million a year earlier. Assistance for livestock development projects rose from $55.3 million in 1967–68 to $87 million; for irrigation projects, 1968–69 loans and grants totaled $136 million, as compared with $75 million a year earlier. Grants and loans to expand agricultural credit rose from $13 million to $69 million; and for land settlement and development projects, from $23.7 million in 1967–68 to $67 million in 1968–69.

Under the U.S. Food for Peace program, countries receiving shipments of food were required to set aside 20% of the foreign currencies generated under that program for programs to assist agricultural development; in addition, 5% of such funds were required by a 1968 amendment to the program to be made available for voluntary population control programs, if requested by the recipient nation. The total of such foreign currency agreements signed in calendar 1968 was $263 million, distributed among 25 countries; loans for economic development totaling $91.1 million were provided under the "self-help" features of the Food for Peace program, bringing the total of such loans to $5.7 billion.

Development continued on two newly established centres for tropical agriculture sponsored by the Rockefeller, Ford, and W. K. Kellogg foundations. The Center for Tropical Agriculture, under development in Colombia, was to emphasize forage-beef production in the lowland tropics and serve as a Latin American link to the International Rice Research Institute (Philippines) and the International Maize and Wheat Improvement Center (Mexico). The second new institute, located in Nigeria, was to work on crops and soils of the humid tropics and to serve as a training centre for African nations.

In June, the 34-nation executive council of the FAO approved a two-year budget of $71.3 million, an 18.2% increase over its 1968–69 budget. The increase was seen as another step in FAO's changing course, from that of fact-finding and statistics-gathering toward enlarged emphasis on action programs to improve agricultural productivity. A key point in the new direction of FAO was the enlisting of private enterprise in the development process.

U.S. Developments. In spite of heightened concern, the U.S. had an unclear view of the extent or severity of its malnutrition problem at the start of 1969. In 1968, however, the U.S. Senate had authorized a Select Committee on Nutrition and Human Needs, with Sen. George McGovern (Dem., S.D.) as chairman, to investigate the problem, determine its extent, and recommend needed solutions.

Early in 1969, the Public Health Service reported to the committee on preliminary findings of the first scientific nutritional survey of the U.S., which was planned to cover families in the lowest quarter income brackets in ten states. Arnold Schaefer, director of the project, reported: that 34% of preschool children examined exhibited symptoms of anemia serious enough to warrant medical attention; that goitre was, by World Health Organization standards, endemic in Texas; that growth retardation was common; that vitamin A deficiency afflicted 33% of children under six who were examined; and that some children had rickets, scurvy, beriberi, marasmus, or kwashiorkor—diseases usually associated with famine conditions in less developed areas.

By mid-March, proposals to alleviate hunger abounded, sponsored by both long-time proponents of expanded programs and a considerably enlarged number of legislators, public officials, and organizations come lately to the cause. In a message to Congress in May, Pres. Richard M. Nixon called hunger and malnutrition in the U.S. "embarrassing and intolerable" and called for a $1 billion expansion of the food stamp program. In August, President Nixon's welfare message to Congress included the statement that for dependent families "there will be an orderly substitution of food stamps by the new direct monetary payments." Congress approved an increase in the Food Stamp Program appropriation to $610 million; the Senate also approved reforms in the program, but the matter was still pending when the session ended. Meanwhile, the White House Conference on Food, Nutrition, and Health, held in early December, was used as a forum by representatives of various minority groups to urge action on what they called a "hunger emergency."

Civilian utilization of all U.S. farm commodities produced in 1969 was estimated by the U.S. Department of Agriculture at 76%; 90% of livestock commodities produced went to civilian consumption, as did 34.7% of total crop commodities produced. Per capita consumption of meat products by U.S. civilians in 1969 was estimated at about 1% less than the 182.7 lb. consumed in 1968. Consumption of veal was expected to continue its 15-year decline. Egg consumption, at an estimated 314 per capita, was slightly less than in 1968. Consumption of dairy products continued to trend slowly downward in 1969. Per capita consumption of fresh fruit, reflecting increased production, was expected to rise to new records; a 7% increase raised total use to about 83 lb. The sharpest rise in this category was fresh citrus, up 16% from the 1968 level of 26.1 lb. per capita. No change was expected in per capita consumption of fresh vegetables, cereals, sugar, coffee, tea, or fats and oils; a 5% decline in lard was partially offset by an increase in per capita use of margarine.

Expenditures by U.S. citizens for food in 1969 were expected to rise to a record $105.5 billion or more, as compared with $101 billion in 1968. This would be only about 17% of disposable income, as compared with 17.2% in 1968 and 20% in 1960. Of total expenditures in 1968, foods originating on U.S. farms accounted for $89.5 billion, the farm value of which reached $28.9 billion.

The consumer price index for food in the U.S. in August 1969 was reported at 127.4 (1957–59 = 100), about 5.7% more than a year earlier. Sharp increases in retail food prices brought equally sharp criticism from housewives, especially in the case of retail meat prices. The FAO reported that consumer food prices continued to increase in 1968 in most of the 104 countries for which data were available; prices showed an increase from 1967 of from 1 to 10% in 69 countries; no change in 11 countries; and a decline in 14 countries. In ten countries, retail food prices rose in a range of from 11 to 51% or more over 1967.

Aid Programs. The U.S. Department of Agriculture reported that in 1968 donations of commodities to schools, institutions, and needy persons totaled 1,841,900,000 lb., an increase of 5% over a year earlier. Total donated commodities constituted less than 1% of U.S. total consumption. Participation in the commodity distribution program in April 1969 was reported at 3,163,292 persons in 1,187 counties; an additional 3,205,013 persons received benefits under the food stamp program in 1,438 counties. The Senate Select Committee on Nutrition and Human Needs reported that 469 counties operated neither of the federal food programs as of mid-June.

The U.S. Food for Peace program (Public Law 480), extended through 1970, was responsible for shipments of farm commodities valued at $1,178,000,000 in 1968, as compared with $1,237,000,000 in 1967. Title I sales (sales for foreign currencies) were valued at $539 million, a decline from $736 million a year earlier. Government-to-government donations for disaster relief and economic development, at $101 million, were slightly less than a year earlier, as were donations made through voluntary relief agencies, at $150 million. The new self-help features for utilizing the proceeds of sales for foreign currencies to develop the food production capacity of recipient nations were included in most of the sales agreements made in 1969. Wheat and flour continued to be the main constituents of shipments; India, Turkey, Israel, and Bolivia were the largest markets.

The World Food Program, operated by FAO, was the recipient of contributions from many countries in 1969. A pledge of $8 million for 1969–70 from Sweden made that country the fourth largest contributor to the program, following the U.S., Canada, and Denmark. Requests for WFP aid ran high, and in early May Executive-Director Francisco Aquino called for $400 million in food, cash, and services to meet needs through 1972. In May the organization approved a food aid plan for the U.A.R. involving $45 million to support a land reclamation and settlement program in the Aswan Dam area. Other aid included a $42.2 million program to provide high-protein foods for Colombia's National Nutrition and Education Campaign. In March, the European Economic Community announced contributions of 1,035,000 tons of wheat to international food aid.

Trade and Stocks. Preliminary data for 1968 indicated that, in spite of a 3% increase over 1967 in the volume of agricultural commodities traded in world markets, total value of the trade, at an index of 133 (1957–59 = 100), was unchanged from a year earlier. The agricultural export earnings of developed countries fell for the second successive year, while those of less developed countries were tentatively estimated at 2% above 1967. The decline in total value of exports reflected a sharp fall in earnings from cereals (except rice) and lesser declines in earnings from fruit and dairy products.

Heavy production and reduced trade in cereals, particularly wheat, resulted in an increase in carryover stocks in the principal exporter countries; stocks of wheat on July 1, 1969, among the five largest trading nations were estimated at 2,004,000,000 bu., 45% more than a year earlier. The FAO reported world stocks of butter on Dec. 1, 1968, at 625,200 metric tons, an increase of nearly 30% above a year earlier; stocks totaling 364,900 tons in the EEC countries comprised more than half of world supplies.

(H. R. SH.)

Food Processing and Technology. *Legislation and Control.* As a result of new evidence concerning the long-term effect of large doses of cyclamate in rats, the U.S. Department of Health, Education, and Welfare decided, as a precautionary measure, to prohibit its use. The use of cyclamates in Britain had been kept under continuous review and, although no specific evidence of harmful effects had been found, in view of the American results it was decided that their use should be discontinued. Many other countries followed suit. The U.S. ban was later relaxed to permit use of cyclamates in diet foods, but both the U.S. and the U.K. decided that toxicological investigations should continue.

Reports appeared in the U.S. press of a so-called Chinese restaurant syndrome (headache, dizziness, flushing), which was attributed by some authorities to the excessive use of monosodium glutamate (MSG). Certain types of baby foods were also criticized on the ground that they contained an excessive amount of salt and that use of MSG was unnecessary. Some manufacturers discontinued the use of MSG.

The U.K. Meat Sterilization Regulations were revised to prohibit the importation of meat unfit for human consumption or its removal from a knacker's yard unless sterilized. The alternative procedure of staining was withdrawn. In view of the need to provide patients in intensive care units with sterilized food, a proposal was made to amend the regulations to allow the irradiation of food for such patients. Otherwise little or no progress was made anywhere concerning permissive legislation for the preservation of meat and other foodstuffs by irradiation.

Much attention, especially in the U.S. and Britain, was given to the potential hazards of persistent pesticides and agricultural chemicals entering food chains. In consequence, restrictions were imposed on the use of certain chlorinated hydrocarbons. Anxiety was also expressed concerning the contamination of foods with antibiotic-resistant strains of bacteria due to the extensive use of antibiotic feed supplements. Restrictions on the use of antibiotic feeds were announced by the U.K. minister of agriculture in November.

Dairy Industry. A new dairy was commissioned in Britain, capable of processing 100,000 gal. daily. It was said to have the most advanced control system extant; it was completely automated and provided with closed-circuit television to monitor plant functioning. A Swiss company developed a machine for the production of 1½ litre plastic bottles, including filling and sealing, at the rate of 2,250 containers per hour. The introduction of plastic bottles increased milk sales of another company by 1,000 gal. per day.

A milk substitute for use in tea was developed in Canada, and filled milk products gained ground in the U.S.; 25% of the milk-fat market was lost to margarine, imitation creams, and toppings. The production of milk increased in India but was still only about one quarter of the estimated requirement. A British company developed an instrument for counting cells in milk at high speed, to help in the early diagnosis of mastitis, a major factor adversely affecting milk quality and yields.

Yogurt and related products continued to increase in popularity and to attract innovations; a British company introduced a frozen yogurt and a freeze-dried preparation was developed in Bulgaria. A novel truncated-cone-shaped container was developed in Britain for yogurt. A flavoured dessert cheese, containing fruits, nuts, and cream curd, was produced in the U.S., and the large-scale manufacture of baker's cheese was introduced in Britain. Israel developed a low-calorie ice cream in which sugar was replaced by artificial sweetener. The shortage of calf rennet led to intensified research in many countries to develop substitutes of plant and microbial origin. Successful results were reported from Britain, Denmark, Japan, and the U.S.

Fish Industry. Fish farming continued to make progress, especially in Japan where fish were shepherded to feeding boxes by sonic wave signals and electric shock barriers. Japan had considerable success in bringing sturgeon to maturity in 4 years instead of the normal 17 by dietary and environmental means. This success in breeding gave hope that caviar might be produced commercially. By squeezing the sperm from the male sole and using it to fertilize eggs under laboratory conditions, Japanese scientists increased yields of fish to a point well on the way toward mass production. Japan also carried out considerable sea farming for breeding and producing scallops, salmon, and trout.

Experiments carried out in Scotland showed that plaice and sole could be reared from their eggs at three times the normal rate by making use of the warm water from nuclear power stations. It was also found that flatfish required only one-twentieth of the space formerly thought to be necessary; a cage of 20 by 10 ft. was enough to produce a ton of fish in two years at a low cost. The production of oysters was insufficient to meet the demand in Britain of nearly 300 million per year. A pilot plant was set up near Plymouth for the hatching and raising of oyster larvae and a practicable system was developed for the commercial production of spat; spawning of the oysters was achieved throughout the year.

Work on the culture of oysters was also carried out in the U.S. Temperature-controlled sea water rich in phytoplankton flowed over plastic trays containing the oysters and spawning was controlled by varying the temperature of the water. The larvae were transferred to large tanks and fed with special algae. It was claimed that the growth cycle could be halved by this method. U.S. researchers reported that the shelf life of fresh fish was almost doubled by saturating the refrigerated brine with carbon dioxide.

A milk substitute made entirely from fish was developed in Chile. It was made entirely from hake, although cheaper fish could be used; it had no odour or flavour of fish, was in the form of a white powder, and tasted like milk when reconstituted. It was originally intended for calf food and was said to be cheap to produce, to contain more protein than milk powder, and to be suitable for use in the manufacture of cheese products and ice cream.

Meat Industry. The Polish Meat Research Institute developed a process for producing smoked food, which it claimed was free from any potential danger to the consumer. An extract was prepared from the natural wood smoke, and gas chromatography showed it to be completely free from carcinogens.

Orange peel was introduced as a source of fodder ingredient for cattle in Australia. A process was developed in South Africa whereby 400 lb. of green feed for cattle could be produced hydroponically in a 2,000-gal. tank of water. The use of a fertility drug made it possible to obtain six or seven lambs per litter and an automatic lamb feeding machine was constructed to take full advantage of this. Such developments led to intensified research on the development of suitable ewe milk replacers.

New Zealand developed a food product made from venison for use as a flavouring agent or a beverage.

A.F.P. FROM PICTORIAL PARADE

Abandoning 770-year-old Les Halles, Parisian produce wholesalers move to new quarters at Rungis (above) in early 1969. Top, administrative centre for the new market.

In France an aerosol for the flavouring of fried chicken was developed. A new process for the tenderization of meat was invented in South Africa.

Fruit and Vegetable Industry. The problems of recruiting labour to pick fruit and vegetable products became more acute, and it was stated by a Michigan professor that any crop that could not be picked mechanically was doomed to disappear from the U.S. market. Much attention was therefore given to the development of mechanical harvesters. The development of apple harvesters was regarded as especially urgent. A new machine with rotating rubber-covered arms was devised to move along a row of trees and knock the apples onto a conveyor belt. Another machine was designed to travel along a row of trees where it sensed each trunk electronically in order to remove and collect the apples. Preparations were made to lay out orchards in a different manner to utilize the full benefits of mechanical harvesting and to improve the shape of trees to the same purpose by selective grafting and pruning.

In California a method was devised for drying potatoes and peeling them mechanically. This enabled the skins to be converted into cattle feed and kept them out of the sewage system. A water-soluble xanthan gum, a microbial polysaccharide manufactured from corn sugar, was approved by the U.S. Food and Drug Administration for use in food, chiefly beverages.

The production and export of fruit, vegetables, and preserves increased considerably in Bulgaria and Hungary. Portugal made remarkable progress in tomato processing and became one of the biggest suppliers of canned tomato products. India and Indonesia came to an agreement that gave them a virtual world monopoly of pepper.

Packaging. The use of plastics continued to expand and in the U.S. a roast-in-bag plastic package was introduced for frozen meat and poultry. Shrinkage during cooking was considerably reduced and the poultry acquired a golden brown colour in the oven. A British food company changed completely to a shrink-film pack for all its retail meat and meat products. A machine was developed in the U.K. for the packaging of difficult products, such as crisps (potato chips), nuts, raisins, and sweets, at a rate of 60–100 bags per minute.

In Sweden a new rectangular milk package was developed as an alternative to the familiar tetrahedron; it was adopted by many Swiss dairies. A new disposable plastic package for beer also proved popular. Coloured cartons in which cakes could be baked were developed in Britain; their open tops could be sealed with cellulose films after baking. A glass composition container developed in the U.S. could, it was claimed, be produced three to four times as fast as the conventional glass bottle; its wide mouth and smooth lip enabled it to be used as a drinking glass.

Nutritional Requirements. The problem of providing sufficient protein for the world population continued to engage the attention of food technologists. In New Zealand an edible protein preparation from wool was developed by a process of enzyme and chemical treatment. It was estimated that if the full potential of oilseed protein were realized, it would provide 20 million tons per year. About one quarter of the world production of fish was converted into fish meal for animal feeding; much was exported for this purpose to countries where there was protein deficiency. Conversion of fish meal to protein concentrate suitable for human consumption was achieved, but commercial production was negligible although some was used for food supplementation in Malaysia.

Work on the production of single cell protein from bacteria, algae, yeasts, and fungi continued on the ground that their manufacture would not utilize agricultural land. The biomass from these organisms contained 42–75% protein on a dry basis; such protein usually contained essential amino acids in such proportions as to satisfy the FAO recommendations for human requirements. A factory was built in Scotland to manufacture 4,000 tons of yeast a year, obtained by growth on petroleum hydrocarbons. Work was begun on a process for producing animal feed protein from household waste by microbial fermentation.

A new source of protein in tropical regions was found by Norwegian scientists working in Biafra; it was claimed to help solve some nutritional problems. The cassava plant grows in abundance there but the Biafrans eat only the root, which is very poor in protein. The Norwegians found that the dried leaves contain up to 36% of protein that has all of the essential amino acids except methionine. It was proposed to add this at the rate of 2 g. per kg. of dried leaves (at a cost of $1.86 per ton), thus making the protein quality equivalent to that of meat. The yield of cassava protein per acre was found to be 1,200 lb., compared with 130 lb. for rice and 260 lb. for yams and taro.

Further improvements were made in the U.S. and Japan in the isolation and production of bland soy protein isolates. Such isolates were spun into threads and processed to simulate meat products, often incorporating flavourings, colouring, and other materials; these were formed into chips, slices, or other convenient shapes.

Such products were reported to have considerable similarity to normal foods in respect to texture and flavour. Many new products of various types and of good nutritive value were produced by an expansion-extrusion process in which defatted soybean flour was used as the raw material.

The demand for rice continued to fall in Japan while that for meat increased. A substantial surplus of rice developed, due partly to the fall in demand and partly to increased yields. The demand for meat encouraged Japanese manufacturers to develop a variety of meat substitutes derived from soybeans. A high protein food was developed in Brazil; it was made from full-fat soybean flour, cornstarch, skimmed milk powder, vitamins, and minerals. It was mixed with sugar and water to form a gruel. It was reported to be well accepted because it resembled the traditional Brazilian cereal eaten by children. A high protein biscuit was developed by the Commonwealth Scientific and Industrial Research Organization for children in less developed countries, and plans were made to manufacture it in Zambia. The equivalent of one pint of whole milk was provided by nine biscuits, which were made in various flavours. The milk protein was obtained by co-precipitating the lactalbumin with casein in the presence of calcium salts. It was said to have a high biologic value and to be free from lactose, which may not be well tolerated by many malnourished children. (HE. B. H.)

See also Agriculture; Commodities, Primary; Domestic Arts and Sciences; Fisheries; Prices.

ENCYCLOPÆDIA BRITANNICA FILMS. *Food and People* (1956); *Why Foods Spoil (Molds, Yeasts, Bacteria)* (1957); *Food from the Sun* (1965); *Plankton: Pastures of the Ocean* (1965); *Produce—From Farm to Market* (1968).

Food and Agriculture Organization, United Nations: *see* Food

Food Preparation: *see* Domestic Arts and Sciences

Football

Association Football (Soccer). The two dominant developments of 1969 were the qualifications for the World Cup finals, to be held at four centres in Mexico during June 1970, and the continuing violence both on the field and among spectators before, during, and after matches. The extreme example of such violence was the using of a World Cup qualifying match (played in neutral Mexico) in Group 13 between El Salvador (which won 3–2) and Honduras as a partial excuse for a limited-scale war between the two nations. In the other hemisphere, all-night riots took place at Kirikkale, Turk., between rival groups of fans; 3 people were killed and more than 50 were injured after a match between the local team and Idmanyurdu, of Tarsus, had ended in a 1–1 draw. Most national authorities decided to introduce stiffer penalties and special measures. In the U.S.S.R. one of the stars of the Soviet World Cup squad, Anatoli Banishevsky, was banned for two years following a drunken street brawl, and another, Eduard Streltsev, was expelled from his club, though the sentence was later commuted to a five-match suspension. In Poland, Stefan Florenski was sentenced to a two-year ban for striking a referee, and three others received a suspended sentence of six months during a match between their team, Gornik, and Katowice, in which scuffling had broken out. At a higher level, the Union of European Football Associations (UEFA) ruled that teams whose supporters were unruly during a European competition match would be held responsible and would lose the game 3–0. They warned Manchester United, Rangers of Glasgow, and AC Milan, the European Cup holders, about the behaviour of their fans.

In the World Cup qualifications there were several shocks, the biggest being the elimination of Argentina from the last 16. Group 10 was headed by Peru, with Argentina finishing third and last, although they had been regarded as perhaps the most powerful football nation in South America. Belgium and two former champions, Brazil and Uruguay, together with automatic qualifiers Mexico (host country) and England (current titleholders), had already secured places in the final 16 by early September. North Korea, one of the surprise teams in the previous finals in England in 1966, was ruled out of the competition by the Fédération Internationale de Football Association (FIFA). The North Koreans had objected to the geographic spread of their group, which included Israel and New Zealand; asked to send a representative to attend a meeting in Mexico, they failed to do so and did not suggest an alternative site for their qualifying matches. Accordingly, New Zealand and Israel were to meet to decide who should play the winners of Group 15A for a place in Mexico.

FIFA anticipated that a difference in interpretation of the laws of the game between the European football-playing nations and those of the American continents could lead to trouble in the World Cup finals. Accordingly, the organization sent Ken Aston (England), deputy chairman of its Referees' Committee, on a fact-finding tour of South America as a preliminary step to the laying down of a universal interpretation of laws for the finals.

Inter-Continental Club Championship Cup. This tournament, called by many the world club championship and contested annually by the winners of the South American Club Championship and the holders of the European Cup, had become renowned for its violent outbursts. The 1968 contest between Estudiantes (Argentina) and Manchester United (England), though far tamer than the preceding year's fracas between Celtic (Scotland) and Racing (Argentina), still was marked by the expulsion of some players and was punctuated by fouls. N. Stiles, the Manchester and England halfback, was ordered off the field by Sosa Miranda, the Paraguayan referee, ten minutes from the end of the first leg in the Boca Juniors stadium in Buenos Aires. He and the home midfield player, C. Bilardo, seemed to be having a private running battle, but the Englishman was given his marching orders for protesting against an offside decision, given against him, with a gesture that came in the "ungentlemanly conduct" category. The play in the first leg was well below the normal level of both teams. Estudiantes often had to resort to long-range shooting, while the United attack did little more than sputter. The Argentinians, however, were well practiced in their various ploys from free kicks, and it was from such a move that the only goal came. From a corner, M. Conigliaro scored after 26 minutes. Some while later United got the ball in the net, also following a free kick, but W. Foulkes of United was ruled offside. The Argentinians were then mainly on the attack, but their ideas were too stereotyped for them to add to their tally. During the game A. Stepney, the United goalkeeper, handed a bottle which had been thrown at him from the crowd to the referee, who was also kept busy dealing with the many fouls.

The second leg at Old Trafford, Manchester, on October 16, was little better in regard to fouls, and two players were dismissed from the field a few minutes from the end by the Yugoslav referee C. Zecevic. They were United's G. Best (*see* Biography) and Estudiantes' H. Medina. Three other players, Argentinians, were reprimanded. In the early stages of the game Estudiantes played some good football and deservedly went ahead when J. Veron exploited the free kick to score after six minutes. United was too cautious in its breaks from defense, and this inhibition played into the visitors' hands. However, with the Argentinians making Best the target for most of their attentions and being content to keep the home forwards out, it was not until after the two men had been sent off that W. Morgan tied the score. Although United pressed forward for another goal to take them to a play-off match, it was in vain.

European Cup. The efficiency of its defense and the ability to strike quickly and hard from it enabled AC Milan to regain in 1969 the European Cup, the premier European club trophy. Milan overcame Ajax, of Amsterdam, in Madrid on May 28, winning 4–1. This final game, watched by approximately 50,000 people in the huge Real Madrid stadium, was a personal triumph for Pierino Prati, who scored a hat trick and so joined the elite and small band of footballers who had scored three goals in a European Cup final. The Italians' defense blotted out the Ajax attack and in particular kept a tight rein on J. Cruyff, the leading Dutch player. However, Cruyff did pave the way for his club's goal when he was brought down in the penalty area, after which V. Vasovic hit home the spot kick. But by then Prati had given Milan a two-goal lead, and with A. Sormani adding a third before Prati completed his hat trick the cup was on its way back to Milan's San Siro stadium. Ajax, after

Milan's quick opening strike, had been forced to concentrate on attack and so left themselves somewhat open at the back, a situation which the Italians rapidly exploited.

On its way to the final, AC Milan had eliminated the two immediate past holders of the trophy, the Glasgow club Celtic and Manchester United, while Ajax defeated the free-scoring Benfica (Portugal) team only in a play-off after extra time.

European Cup-Winners' Cup. Slovan Bratislava broke fresh ground when it became the first Czechoslovak team to take a major European trophy, beating Barcelona 3–2 in the final of the European Cup-Winners' Cup tournament at Basel, Switz., on May 21. The Czechoslovakians, playing spirited, skillful soccer, went into the lead in two minutes when R. Cvetler scored, only to have the Spaniards tie them quickly through J. A. Zaldua. But Slovan Bratislava, producing some orthodox power play, gambled on attack. This decision proved right when within half an hour they added two more goals, V. Hrivnak and J. Capkovic being the marksmen, to go in for half time with a 3–1 lead. In the second half Barcelona pounded away at the Slovan goal. These efforts were rewarded when C. Rexach scored in the 52nd minute but, try as they might, Barcelona could not break the Czechoslovak defense again.

E. D. LACEY

Rod Thomas, Swindon (left), beats George Armstrong, Arsenal, to the ball during the Football League Cup final at Wembley on March 15, 1969. Swindon, a third-division team, defeated Arsenal, a first-division team, 3–1.

Slovan had reached the final by narrowly defeating the Scottish team Dunfermline by an aggregate score of 2–1 in the two-match semifinal, but Barcelona was far more convincing in knocking out Cologne 6–3 on aggregate at the same stage.

Inter-Cities Fairs' Cup. Newcastle United defeated the Hungarian team Ujpest Dozsa of Budapest 6–2 in the two-leg final, which had something of a fairy-tale ring about it. The first game at St. James's Park, Newcastle, on May 29, was watched by 60,000 people, and after a stalemate in which the Hungarians' defense easily held United's forwards, R. Moncur, the home captain, switched from defense to attack and scored twice to shake the visitors. J. Scott added another goal to open up a 3–0 gap in the English club's favour. But the Hungarians, who had knocked out the defending champion Leeds in the quarterfinals, were determined to wipe out the deficit on their own ground in Budapest on June 11. So they attacked at the game's onset and were soon two goals in the lead. It looked as if they would succeed, but in the second half Moncur, who had not scored in 30 league games, led the fight back and scored Newcastle's first goal. P. Arentoft, Newcastle's Danish inside forward, and A. Foggon added two more goals to give the English team the trophy and its manager, Joe Harvey, a fitting 50th-birthday present.

British Isles Championship. For the first time this tournament was staged at the end of the season during eight days in May, an experiment that was only partly successful. It was a success in that national team managers were not restricted in their choice of players by club calls. But because the games were televised, crowds were small, the most glaring example being on May 6 when the 135,000-seat Hampden Park stadium in Glasgow attracted only 7,483 spectators to see Scotland draw 1–1 with Northern Ireland.

England again triumphed, winning the tournament outright for the 27th time. They were successful in all three matches, with that against Scotland as the climax before a packed Wembley stadium in London. The English team, playing in the familiar 4–3–3 formation, was far too efficient for Scotland, and with World Cup heroes G. Hurst and M. Peters each scoring twice as against a lone effort by C. Stein in reply, Sir Alf Ramsey's men clinched the title with their victims as runners-up. Earlier, England had beaten Wales 2–1 at Wembley and Northern Ireland 3–1 in Belfast, though the latter game was closer than the score suggested. Wales produced in Ron Davies of Southampton perhaps the outstanding player of the tournament.

Administration. The European Fairs' Cup, formerly the Inter-Cities Fairs' Cup, would in the 1971–72 season come under the aegis of UEFA proper instead of the special committee that formerly administered it. The same authority decided to run a new European Under-23 competition for the 33 member nations, while the finals of the Olympic Games in 1972 would again consist of 16 teams, despite moves by the Olympic authorities to get the number cut to eight.

Two goalkeepers on opposite sides of the globe set milestones in their careers during the year. Dos Santos Neves, known to the soccer world as Gylmar, the Brazilian World Cup star, received his 100th cap when he turned out shortly before his 39th birthday to keep goal against England. During that time he had won two World Cup winners' medals with his country, as well as many other honours. The other was set by Lev Yashin, a legendary Soviet athlete, who played his 300th game for Moscow Dynamo at the end of the season. During his long career, he had captured the public's imagination with his all-black gear and acrobatic saves as well as with his fine sense of sportsmanship.

On November 19, the 29-year-old Brazilian star Pelé (Edson Arantes do Nascimento) scored his 1,000th goal, for Santos, to win 2–1 against Vasco da Gama before 75,000 applauding fans in Rio de Janeiro. Pelé thus set a scoring record for first-class professional football. Brazil issued a postage stamp in his honour.

For national cup and league champions, *see* SPORTING RECORD. (T. W.)

Rugby. *Rugby Union.* During 1968–69 Australia made a major tour of South Africa as well as a short tour of Ireland and Scotland; South Africa made a brief tour of France; and Wales made a short tour of New Zealand, Australia, and Fiji. It was also during this period that the International Board ruled that there was nothing wrong in principle with the squad system of coaching for national teams.

The first of the tours was that of the Australians to Ireland and Scotland in October and November 1968. As with all such short visits, the Australians were given insufficient time after their journey in which to settle down before their first match, and from the point of view of results the tour was not successful. The Australians, captained by P. Johnson from hooker, were beaten by Ireland 10–3 in Dublin and by Scotland 9–3 at Murrayfield. Of the five matches played Australia won two and lost three, scored 38 points, and were scored upon 40 times. It was hoped that the tour would provide valuable experience for the Australians' long trip to South Africa a few months later.

The South Africans' short tour of France also took place in October and November. It was the first tour of France undertaken by an International Board country that did not also include a visit to the British Isles. South Africa won both the international matches of the tour, 12–9 at Bordeaux and 16–11 in Paris, but it was beaten 11–3 by South-West France at Toulouse. South Africa's final record was won 5, lost 1; points for 84, points against 43.

The chief features of the home international championship were the rise of Wales and the fall of France. The Welsh, who the previous season had finished fourth of the five countries, won both the championship and the triple crown. The French finished last, having beaten all four home countries the previous season. Wales, which had adopted the squad system of training and which was coached by Clive Rowlands, the former Welsh captain, started by beating Scotland 17–3 at Murrayfield and Ireland 24–11 at Cardiff. The Welsh were then held to a draw, 8–8, by France in Colombes, but they finished their campaign triumphantly by beating England 30–9 at Cardiff. This was Wales' widest margin of victory in the tournament since 1922, and it gave them their 11th triple crown. Ireland's defeat by Wales was the Irishmen's only setback, for they beat France 17–9 in Dublin, England 17–15 in Dublin, and Scotland 16–0 at Murrayfield and so finished second in the standings. England, with victories by 22–8 over France at Twickenham and 8–3 over Scotland at Twickenham, finished third, while Scotland placed fourth, thanks to beating France 6–3 in Colombes in the first fixture of the championship. France's defeat at Twickenham was its tenth consecutive defeat in international matches. When D. P. Rogers (Bedford) played for England against France at Twickenham, it was his 32nd appearance for his country. He thus beat the record for England caps held since 1927 by Lord Wakefield with 31.

At the annual meeting of the International Board in London in March a revised version of the laws of the game was approved. The laws had been largely rewritten with the aim of simplification and clarification, but no major changes had been made in the rules themselves. Representatives of the home countries reported that the experimental law restricting kicking to touch had proved a success, and the board agreed that the experiment could continue for another season—1969–70—in the Northern Hemisphere. The ruling on the squad system of coaching for national teams had been sought and given because some people believed that Wales, in getting together its squad of players for weekends of coaching, was running the risk of being accused of professionalism.

The short tour by Wales of New Zealand, Australia, and Fiji took place in May and June. It was the first time a side representing Wales had visited these countries. The Welsh fared well in their three provincial matches in New Zealand, drawing with Taranaki and beating both Otago and Wellington, but they were heavily defeated in the two international tests, losing to New Zealand 19–0 and 33–12. Many people, however, believed that the Welsh should not have been expected to play a test as early as the second game of the tour. The key to the New Zealand successes was the tough and skilled play of their forwards, among whom such great players as Colin Meads, Ken Gray, and Brian Lochore were still going strong. In the second test Fergie McCormick, the New Zealand full-back, scored 24 points, thus setting a new world record for the number of points scored by one player in a full international match. The Welsh record in New Zealand was won 2, drawn 1, lost 2, points for 62, points against 76. Wales then played one game in Australia, an international contest which they won 19–16 at Sydney. In this game the clever play of the Welsh backs excited the crowd, and the same was true in Suva where the Welsh beat a representative Fijian team 31–11. This was the first time a team from the home countries had visited Fiji.

Hong Kong and South Korean team members fight for ball in the mud during first Asian Rugby championship tourney in March 1969 at Tokyo's Prince Chichibu Field.

UPI COMPIX

WIDE WORLD

Arkansas tailback Bill Burnett leaps past a Texas linebacker to score in the first period of the game that determined the top-ranked college team, Dec. 6, 1969. Texas rallied in the final quarter to win 15–14.

The Australians were unfortunate in that at the time of their tour of South Africa, in June, July, August, and September, several of their leading players had either turned professional in Rugby League or were not available or were injured. Thus they had to tour without such experienced players as Ken Catchpole, P. Johnson, and John Brass. Their forwards proved no match for the South Africans and the Australians were outplayed in the four-match test series. They did reasonably well in the provincial contests when their quick and lively forwards could avoid being bogged down in a grueling tussle. Their captain, Greg Davis, set a notable example of constructive play in the loose from wing forward. South Africa won the first test 30–11 in Johannesburg, the second 16–9 at Durban, the third 11–3 at Cape Town, and the fourth 19–8 at Bloemfontein. Piet Visagie, South Africa's standoff, scored a record 43 points in the series.

England set an example to other countries by the swiftness with which it took advantage of the International Board's ruling about national squad coaching. At the prompt suggestion of Albert Agar, the chairman of England's selectors, Don White, the former Northampton and England wing forward, was appointed England's first official coach. Then, on August 23 and 24—a week before the new British season opened—a squad of 30 players was given a weekend of intensive coaching.

Southern California's Sandy Durko picks up yardage against Michigan before being tackled by Dan Dierdorf in the Rose Bowl game, Jan. 1, 1970. Southern California won 10–3.

UPI COMPIX

Rugby League. The 1968–69 season was particularly interesting in that a team representing Wales was fielded for the first time since 1963. The Welsh beat England 24–17 at Salford and then went on to lose by no more than 13–17 to France in Paris. Great Britain played its customary two matches against France, winning 34–10 at St. Helens but losing 9–13 at Toulouse. Australia toured New Zealand and tied the test series, 1–1, thus retaining the Trans-Tasman Cup. Australia won the first test 20–10, and New Zealand won the second 18–14. By winning this second test the New Zealanders brought to an end a losing string of 12 matches. (D. B. J. F.)

U.S. Football. The 1969 intercollegiate football season provided some surprises. From the beginning and almost to the end of the season, Ohio State's Buckeyes, a traditional power, were rated best in the nation. The Buckeyes were undefeated, untied, and had won most of their first eight games with such ease that many were sure that they would complete the season without encountering an opponent capable of giving them a genuine challenge. Then came Ohio State's final regular-season game, a battle against Michigan, a longtime rival. Appropriately, the largest crowd to see a college game up to that time, 103,588, was in attendance at Michigan's stadium in Ann Arbor. They watched in surprise as the Wolverines defeated Ohio State's so-called superteam, 24–12. This victory enabled Michigan to tie Ohio State for the Big Ten championship and also qualified Michigan for the Rose Bowl.

Ohio State plunged in the ratings, and undefeated Texas of the Southwest Conference surfaced as the country's best. Two weeks later, Texas closed its regular season against Arkansas, also unbeaten and variously ranked second or third. After three quarters Arkansas' Razorbacks were leading 14–0 and appeared to be about to stage an upset. But Texas rallied in a spectacular surge that gave it a dramatic 15–14 victory.

Texas then closed out the year with a 21–17 triumph over Notre Dame in the Cotton Bowl, the Longhorns again coming from behind with a fourth-quarter blitz. Penn State, challenging Texas for the nation's top ranking, had to struggle and was comparatively unimpressive in defeating Missouri 10–3 in the Orange Bowl. Thus, at the finish, the Associated Press ratings acclaimed Texas first and Penn State second. Other teams in the AP top ten, in order, were Southern California, Ohio State, Notre Dame, Missouri, Arkansas, Mississippi, Michigan, and Louisiana State. In the United Press International poll, which ended with the regular season, Texas was also rated first and Penn State second.

There were many highly publicized individual players, and among them was Steve Owens of Oklahoma who set eight major rushing records and was also chosen as the winner of the Heisman Trophy, awarded annually to the nation's outstanding college player. Mike Phipps, Purdue quarterback, finished second to Owens in the Heisman balloting.

Field-goal kicking continued to increase. According to official statistics compiled by the National Collegiate Sports Service, the number of successful field goals rose 18% over the previous year. There were 669 field goals in 1969 out of 1,402 attempts, a 47.7 ratio of success. All of these 1969 figures established new records. One kicker, Bob Jacobs of Wyoming, booted 18 field goals for a new individual record. Al Limahelu of undefeated San Diego State also emerged as one of the season's kicking stars by making 59 of 60 extra-point attempts, a new record. Limahelu set another record by making 50 consecutive extra points, the most such points in a row without a miss during one season.

San Diego State, which finished with a flawless 11–0 record, became a major team (essentially, for purposes of statistics) in 1969 and won three national statistical championships, including the scoring title, with a 46.4-point average per game. It was the highest major scoring average since the 1956 season. Dennis Shaw, the San Diego State quarterback, put more points on the board than any player for a major college in history. Shaw, running and passing, was responsible for 270 points in the Aztecs' ten regular-season games. This included 39 touchdown passes, an all-time one-season record. The previous mark was 32 by Jerry Rhome of Tulsa in 1964.

Owens of Oklahoma was also among the season's record setters. He broke most of the major rushing marks, including most rushes in one game, 55; most rushes in one season, 358; most rushes per game on the average, 35.8; most rushes during a career, 905; and most yards gained rushing during a career, 3,867. Quarterback Steve Ramsey of North Texas State, a star passer, set four principal records: most yards total offense, career (three years), 6,568; most touchdowns responsible for, running and passing, career, 71; most passes attempted, career, 1,015; and most passes completed, career, 491.

Attendance increased for the 16th consecutive year and was a record 27,626,160 for the 2,820 games played by the 615 major college teams. This did not include any of the postseason All-Star and bowl games, which also drew huge crowds.

As in other recent years there was some racial unrest. Fourteen black players boycotted practice at Indiana University, claiming they were victims of discrimination. Coach John Pont met with them and advised the blacks that another unexcused absence from practice would result in their dismissal from the squad. Only two of the blacks returned.

Militants, both black and white, tried to force the Western Athletic Conference to oust Brigham Young University for alleged racial policies. There was a major incident at the University of Wyoming when 14 black players were dropped from the squad in midseason for wearing armbands to protest the Brigham Young policy.

East. Penn State won the Lambert Trophy, symbolic of Eastern supremacy, for the third consecutive year, tying the record set by the legendary Army teams of Glenn Davis and "Doc" Blanchard in the mid-1940s. The Nittany Lions extended their unbeaten string to 30 games with an 11–0 season. Wesleyan and Delaware shared the Lambert Cup for excellence among the smaller Eastern colleges.

Yale, Princeton, and Dartmouth finished in a three-way tie for the Ivy League title, all with 6–1 records. Yale, led by fullback Bill Primps, defeated Harvard 7–0 in their traditional game, the 86th in the series. Massachusetts won the Yankee League title with a 5–0 record.

Midwest. Ohio State and Michigan shared the Big Ten championship with identical 6–1 records, all as a result of Michigan's climactic upset victory over the Buckeyes. Michigan won the game principally as a result of six pass interceptions. Purdue was third in the conference with a 5–2 record, and Minnesota fourth with 4–3.

Notre Dame finished with an 8–1–1 mark, losing 28–14 to Purdue and tying Southern California 14–14. The Irish broke a 44-year precedent by accepting an invitation to the Cotton Bowl and changed its long-standing policy against postseason games. Explained the Rev. Edmund Joyce, chairman of the faculty board in control of athletics: "The crucial consideration was the urgent need for funds to finance student academic programs and scholarships."

UPI COMPIX

Kansas City quarterback Len Dawson gets good blocking as he drops back to pass against the Minnesota Vikings in the Super Bowl, Jan. 11, 1970. Kansas City won 23–7.

Missouri and Nebraska shared the Big Eight Conference title, both finishing with 6–1 records. Missouri beat Nebraska 17–7 in the first conference game for both teams but subsequently was defeated by Colorado 31–24.

Far West. A 32-yd. pass from Jimmy Jones to Sam Dickerson with 92 seconds left to play gave Southern California a 14–12 triumph over traditional rival UCLA. This victory earned the Trojans the Pacific Eight title and a Rose Bowl invitation. Southern California was 6–0 in the conference and 9–0–1 for the season, the only blemish being its tie with Notre Dame. UCLA and Stanford tied for second in the conference with 5–1–1 records.

South. Tennessee and Louisiana State led the Southeastern Conference but did not fully dominate football in the South. Tennessee handed "Bear" Bryant's Alabama squad its worst defeat, 41–14, but lost to Mississippi 38–0 and finished with a 9–1 record. Louisiana State also lost to Mississippi 26–23. Mississippi, in turn, was beaten by both Kentucky and Houston. South Carolina won the Atlantic Coast Conference title, while Davidson and Richmond shared the Southern Conference championship.

Southwest. Texas' 15–14 victory over Arkansas hinged on one of the most daring plays of the season. Trailing 14–8 with four minutes and 48 seconds remaining, Texas gambled and refused to punt when it had the ball on its 43-yd. line with fourth down and three yards to go. Instead, quarterback James Street threw a deep pass to end Randy Peschel, who caught it and was downed on the 13. Two plays later Texas

Minnesota Vikings' Bill Brown gains five yards against Cleveland in the NFL championship game at Bloomington, Minn., Jan. 4, 1970. Minnesota won 27–7 to become the first expansion team to win a league championship.

UPI COMPIX

scored for a 14–14 tie and then Happy Feller kicked the extra point to give the Longhorns their 19th consecutive victory.

Bowl Games. Southern California defeated Michigan 10–3 in the Rose Bowl before 103,878, the largest crowd ever to see a college game. Texas, led by quarterback James Street and by fullback Steve Worster, defeated Notre Dame 21–17 in the Cotton Bowl. Penn State won 10–3 over Missouri in the Orange Bowl, and Mississippi defeated Arkansas 27–22 in the Sugar Bowl.

Professional. Despite four somewhat dull divisional races, the National Football League (NFL) had another big season at the gate and for the third year in a row topped the 6 million mark in attendance with 6,293,243 paid admissions for regular-season play. The attendance for the American Football League (AFL) was 2,988,069, also a record.

The NFL divisional winners were Dallas (11–2–1) in the Capitol; Cleveland (10–3–1) in the Century; Los Angeles (11–3) in the Coastal; and Minnesota (12–2) in the Central. Minnesota defeated Los Angeles 23–20 for the Western title, and Cleveland crushed Dallas 38–14 in the East. Minnesota then defeated Cleveland 27–7 for top NFL honours and thus became the first expansion team to win a league championship.

The AFL, in an obvious attempt to get additional television revenue, tried a unique divisional play-off system, for one season only, in which the first two teams in each division were given play-off positions. The result was that a second-place team, the Kansas City Chiefs, walked off with the league title.

The New York Jets, the defending AFL champions, won in the East with a 10–4 record but lost 13–6 in play-offs to Kansas City, which finished second in the West. Oakland, the no. 1 team in the West, beat Houston 56–7 in the other first-round game. Then, Kansas City upset Oakland 17–7 for the championship.

Kansas City finished the season with another upset victory by defeating Minnesota 23–7 in the fourth and final Super Bowl game matching the champions of the two rival pro leagues. The game was played on Jan. 11, 1970, before a crowd of 80,898 in New Orleans. A 13-point underdog, Kansas City led all the way and dominated throughout. The Chiefs were ahead 16–0 at the half and had such an aggressive defense that the Vikings did not make a first down by rushing until late in the third period. The Vikings, who usually had a superior running game, were held to only 67 yd. from scrimmage. The individual stars of the game were Kansas City's Len Dawson and Jan Stenerud. Dawson, a veteran quarterback, completed 12 of 17 passes including a 46-yd. touchdown pass to Otis Taylor. Stenerud's field goals accounted for the Chiefs' first nine points.

Quarterback Roman Gabriel, who threw 24 touchdown passes and led the Los Angeles Rams to 11 consecutive victories prior to their loss to Minnesota, was selected the NFL's most valuable player. Calvin Hill, a running back with the Dallas Cowboys, won NFL rookie of the year honours.

Gale Sayers of the Chicago Bears, who suffered a severe knee injury in 1968, returned to his previous form and won the league's rushing title with 1,032 yd. from scrimmage, his second 1,000-yd. season. Place-kicker Fred Cox of Minnesota won the scoring title with 121 points on 43 extra-point kicks and 26 field goals. Sonny Jurgensen of Washington was the league's leading passer.

Daryle Lamonica of Oakland, whose 34 touchdown passes led both leagues, was selected the AFL's most valuable player. Greg Cook of Cincinnati was the AFL rookie of the year and also the top passer with a completion average of 53.8%. Dick Post of San Diego led all AFL rushers with 873 yd., and Jim Turner of the Jets captured the scoring title with 129 points on 32 field goals and 33 extra points.

The two pro leagues completed their merger plans at a marathon 36-hour meeting on May 10. Three NFL clubs, the Baltimore Colts, Cleveland Browns, and Pittsburgh Steelers, were to be transferred in 1970 to the American Conference of the merged league, balancing the two conferences at 13 teams each. All 26 of the teams were to share equally in the revenue from televising the games.

Five former players were installed in the Professional Football Hall of Fame in Canton, O. They were Albert ("Turk") Edwards, Washington Redskin tackle from 1932 to 1940; Leo Nomellini, a tackle who played 174 consecutive games with San Francisco; Earle ("Greasy") Neale, who coached the Philadelphia Eagles to the 1948 NFL title; Ernie Stautner, a defensive tackle who starred for the Pittsburgh Steelers; and Joe ("Jet") Perry, the third best ground gainer in professional football history.

Canadian Football. The Ottawa Rough Riders, led by quarterback Russ Jackson, defeated the Saskatchewan Roughriders 29–11 in the annual Grey Cup game, symbolic of supremacy in the Canadian Football League (CFL). The game was played in Montreal on November 29 before a capacity crowd of 33,172. Jackson threw four touchdown passes, two of which were caught by Ron Stewart on plays covering 80 and 32 yd. He was voted the outstanding player in the game, a fitting climax to his 12-year professional career. In addition, he was also honoured for the third time with the Schenley Award, given annually to the outstanding player in Canada. He retired immediately after the season.

The total regular season attendance for the CFL was 1,447,218, up from the previous season. Ottawa won the Eastern Conference title with an 11–3 record, and Saskatchewan won Western Conference honours with a 13–3 mark. Tommy Joe Coffey led the league in scoring with a record 148 points on 12 touchdowns, 30 extra-point conversions, 13 field goals, and 7 singles. (JE. HO.)

France

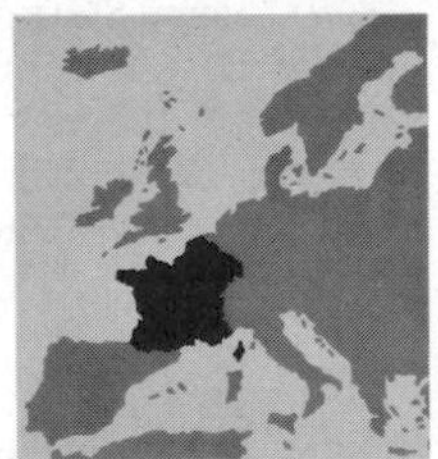

A republic of western Europe and head of the French Community, France is bounded by the English Channel, Belgium, Luxembourg, Germany, Switzerland, Italy, the Mediterranean Sea, Monaco, Spain, Andorra, and the Atlantic Ocean. Area: 211,209 sq.mi. (547,033 sq.km.), including Corsica. Pop. (1969 est.): 50,223,000. Cap. and largest city: Paris (pop., 1968 est., 2,597,771). Language: French. Presidents in 1969, Charles de Gaulle until April 28, Alain Poher (interim president), and, from June 20, Georges Pompidou; premiers, Maurice Couve de Murville and, from June 20, Jacques Chaban-Delmas.

Domestic Affairs. *Departure of de Gaulle.* In France the outstanding event of 1969 was undoubtedly the retirement of President de Gaulle (*see* BIOGRA-

Foreign Aid: *see* Development, Economic

Foreign Credits: *see* Development, Economic; Payments and Reserves, International

Foreign Exchange: *see* Payments and Reserves, International

Foreign Investments: *see* Investment, International

Forests: *see* Conservation; Timber

Formosa: *see* Taiwan

PHY) from the political scene and his replacement by Pompidou (*see* BIOGRAPHY) as president of the French Republic. De Gaulle's former premier thus became the 19th president of the republic and the second of the Fifth Republic.

De Gaulle was president of the Fifth Republic from Jan. 8, 1959, to April 28, 1969, or just over ten years. To understand the significance of his retirement, it is enough to recall the circumstances in which it took place. At the end of 1968, the government had drawn up the draft of a referendum concerning regionalization and the reform of the Senate. This double proposal raised opposition of every sort, and the French people had difficulty in grasping all its implications, so de Gaulle decided, in March, to hurry things along. Against the advice of many of his colleagues, among them Premier Couve de Murville who wanted the referendum to ask two distinct questions, de Gaulle not only joined the two matters together but also—though nothing obliged him to do this—linked his own fate to the result. A negative vote would bring about his departure—and that was what happened.

By the evening of April 27, there could be no doubt as to the verdict of the French people: the "noes" had carried the day in metropolitan France with 11,943,233 votes (53.17% of the votes cast) against 10,515,655 "yes" votes (or 46.82% of the total). Results from the overseas *départements* did not make any noticeable difference in these percentages. From April 28 at midday, de Gaulle ceased to be president of the republic, having announced his decision from Colombey-les-deux-Églises in the following communiqué: "I am ceasing to carry out my responsibilities as president of the republic. This decision takes effect from today, at midday."

At once Poher, president of the Senate, prepared to move into the Élysée, since, according to the constitution, the president of the Senate must perform the functions of president of the republic during the interim period before the election of a new president. This must be held not less than 20 and not more than 35 days after the vacancy occurs. While public opinion reacted with amazement to the hardly credible spectacle of what a U.S. newspaper called "a political suicide enacted before the whole world," Pompidou, without wasting a moment, announced his candidature for the presidency on the following day. Soon he was joined by Poher (for the Centrists), Jacques Duclos (for the Communists), and Gaston Defferre (for the Socialists).

Presidential Election. After a hectic campaign, the first round of the election on June 1 saw Pompidou in the lead, far ahead of his rivals, with 10,051,816 votes (44.46% of the votes cast)—that is to say, with a slightly smaller percentage than de Gaulle had obtained in the first round of the presidential election in 1965. Poher, who was next, took only 5,268,651 votes (23.30%), a little more than the total of votes gained in 1965 by Jean Lecanuet, Jean-Louis Tixier-Vignancour, and Pierre Marcilhacy, all three of whom supported him. He was closely followed by Duclos (21.27%), who thus regained the ground lost by the Communists in 1968, while the Socialist candidate, Defferre, suffered a heavy defeat, obtaining only 5.01% of the vote. The three other candidates—Michel Rocard (Parti Socialiste Unifié), Alain Krivine (Communist League), and Louis Ducatel (right-wing independent)—gained so small a proportion of the vote that they lost their deposits of Fr. 100,000. (These deposits must be made by candidates before

JEAN-PIERRE REY—LIAISON

WIDE WORLD

"THE TIMES," LONDON FROM PICTORIAL PARADE

Left, Pres. Charles de Gaulle speaks to reporters just prior to the April referendum which led to his resignation. Above, a Parisian passes election posters for the seven candidates in the June presidential election.

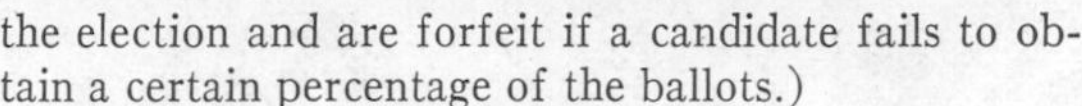

the election and are forfeit if a candidate fails to obtain a certain percentage of the ballots.)

The second round, on June 15, was a runoff, as provided for by the constitution, between the two best-placed candidates. It confirmed the results of the first round, giving Pompidou 11,064,371 votes, or 58.21% of the total poll, against 7,943,118 votes, or 41.78% of the poll, for Poher.

Pompidou carried an absolute majority in 87 *départements,* though he had gained an absolute majority in only 13 *départements* in the first round. Poher also made considerable progress between the first and second rounds, thanks in part to the withdrawal of Defferre (5% of the vote) and also to agreements on the left (including the extreme left). Abstentions were considerable, however, amounting almost to a "third party" since they accounted for 31.14% of the electorate.

The New Government. After taking office on June 20, the new president immediately chose his premier, Chaban-Delmas (*see* BIOGRAPHY), for many years president of the National Assembly. The new government was noticeably different from its predecessor: it had 39 members (compared with 31), of whom 20 were secretaries of state; 11 ministers and secretaries of state were retired, including Couve de Murville, André Malraux, Pierre Messmer, Jean-Marcel Jeanneney, and Edgar Faure. Seven ministers changed their posts, among them Michel Debré (from foreign affairs to defense); Maurice Schumann (from social affairs to foreign affairs); Olivier Guichard (from regional planning to education); and François-Xavier Ortoli (from finance to industrial development).

Among the 20 newcomers were René Pleven (justice), Valéry Giscard d'Estaing (economy and finance), Jacques Duhamel (agriculture), Joseph Fontanet (labour), and Edmond Michelet (cultural affairs). The Ministry of Information was abolished and Léo Hamon became government spokesman.

At first sight the new government appeared less "conformist" than its predecessor. Commentators remarked on the presence in key posts of convinced "Europeans" such as Schumann, Duhamel, and Giscard d'Estaing. The government policy statement by Chaban-Delmas on June 26 before the National Assembly emphasized the defense of the franc, sound financial policy, economic expansion, and social progress. Foreign policy was scarcely mentioned, and some

FRANCE

Education. (1965–66) Primary, pupils 5,523,827, teachers (including preprimary) 263,025; secondary, pupils 2,455,209; vocational, pupils 772,160; secondary and vocational, teachers 189,448; teacher training, students 31,907, teachers 2,033; higher (including 23 universities), students 509,764, teaching staff (universities only; 1964–65) 16,904.

Finance. Monetary unit: franc, with a par value (following the devaluation of Aug. 10, 1969) of Fr. 5.55 to U.S. $1 (Fr. 13.33 = £1 sterling). Gold and foreign exchange, official: (June 1969) U.S. $3,610,000,000; (June 1968) U.S. $5,517,000,000. Budget (1970 est.): revenue Fr. 178,738,000,000; expenditure Fr. 177,788,000,000. Gross national product: (1967) Fr. 572.1 billion; (1966) Fr. 531.9 billion. Money supply: (April 1969) Fr. 214.7 billion; (April 1968) Fr. 192.2 billion. Cost of living (1963 = 100): (June 1969) 124; (June 1968) 115.

Foreign Trade. (1968) Imports Fr. 68.8 billion; exports Fr. 62,590,000,000. Import sources: EEC 47% (West Germany 21%, Belgium-Luxembourg 10%, Italy 9%, Netherlands 6%); U.S. 9%; U.K. 5%. Export destinations: EEC 43% (West Germany 19%, Belgium-Luxembourg 10%, Italy 9%, Netherlands 5%); U.S. 6%; Switzerland 5%; U.K. 5%. Main exports: machinery 17%; chemicals 11%; motor vehicles 9%; iron and steel 8%; textile yarns and fabrics 6%; cereals 6%. Tourism (1967): visitors 12 million; gross receipts U.S. $1,029,000,000.

Transport and Communications. Roads (1968) 784,506 km. (including 1,132 km. expressways). Motor vehicles in use (1968): passenger 11,210,000; commercial 1,748,000. Railways: (1967) 37,320 km.; traffic (state only; 1968) 35,730,000,000 passenger-km., freight 63,036,000,000 net ton-km. Air traffic (1967): 10,151,980,000 passenger-km.; freight 321,406,000 net ton-km. Navigable inland waterways (1967): 10,438 km. (including 7,629 km. in regular use); freight traffic 12,965,000,000 ton-km. Shipping (1968): merchant vessels 100 gross tons and over 1,495; gross tonnage 5,796,360. Telephones (Dec. 1967) 6,999,621. Radio licenses (Dec. 1967) 15,256,000. Television licenses (Dec. 1967) 8,316,000.

Agriculture. Production (in 000; metric tons; 1968: 1967 in parentheses): wheat 14,842 (13,969); rye 333 (343); barley 9,062 (9,713); oats 2,506 (2,784); corn 5,174 (4,111); potatoes 9,977 (10,396); rice 91 (115); rapeseed 449 (429); tomatoes (1967) 596, (1966) 617; onions (1967) 205, (1966) 204; apples 3,923 (4,401); flax fibre 51 (66); sugar, raw value (1968–69) *c.* 2,379, (1967) 1,727; wine 6,331 (6,203); tobacco 51 (47); beef and veal (1967) *c.* 2,116, (1966) 1,735; pork (1967) *c.* 1,678, (1966) 1,332; milk *c.* 30,500 (*c.* 29,000); butter 580 (530); cheese *c.* 575 (645); fish catch (1967) 820, (1966) 805. Livestock (in 000; Oct. 1967): cattle 21,417; sheep 9,510; horses 1,009; pigs 9,746; chickens (laying hens) *c.* 75,000.

Industry. Index of production (1963 = 100): (1968) 125; (1967) 120. Fuel and power (in 000; 1968): coal (metric tons) 41,908; electricity (kw-hr.) 117,380,000; manufactured gas (cu.m.; 1967) 7,367,000. Production (in 000; metric tons; 1968): iron ore (32% metal content) 55,059; bauxite 2,768; pig iron 16,730; crude steel 20,394; aluminum 440; lead 130; zinc 206; cement 26,419; cotton yarn 257; cotton fabrics 199; wool yarn 131; wool fabrics 62; rayon filament yarn 51; rayon staple fibre 67; nylon filament yarn 64; nylon staple fibre 69; sulfuric acid 3,344; superphosphates (1967–68) 1,496; passenger cars (units) 1,832; commercial vehicles (units) 242; petroleum products (1967) 65,108.

people remarked that diplomacy was following political decision making. The day before it heard this policy statement, the Assembly had elected its new president, Achille Peretti (Union pour la Défense de la République), a deputy, mayor of Neuilly-sur-Seine, and already first vice-president.

The new style of the Fifth Republic was also highlighted at Pompidou's first press conference on July 10—exactly one year, to the day, since he had offered his resignation as premier to de Gaulle. In his replies to the 37 questions that he was asked, the new president did not try to evade any issue. His remarks were significant less for the substance of what was said than for the spirit and the style of the saying. However, Pompidou did emphasize his wish to give the French economy an international dimension. The Gaullists and their friends congratulated themselves on the continuation of Gaullist policy, in accordance with promises made during the electoral campaign, while the left maintained its opposition unchanged.

The Council of Paris. In June the Council of Paris, known until 1967 as the Municipal Council of Paris, elected as its president Étienne Royer de Véricourt (Centrist), who took over from Bernard Rocher. Véricourt was elected by 48 votes to 36 for Madeleine Marsin, a Communist. One of the first decisions of the new council was to approve the plan to redevelop Les Halles following the removal of the market to Rungis. (*See* HISTORIC BUILDINGS.) Afterward, it had to consider plans to redevelop the Rond-Point des Champs-Élysées, the Porte Maillot, the Marais, and the Entrepôts de Bercy.

The Economy. *Devaluation.* The first hitch in continuity with the preceding regime was not long in coming. The devaluation of the French franc was arranged in complete secrecy and suddenly announced on August 8 in the evening, at the end of an extraordinary Cabinet meeting. It took effect on the following Sunday at 10 P.M. No minister opposed the principle of this decision. "We are merely pointing out an accomplished fact," Pompidou said on television. He justified this reversal of de Gaulle's decision of Nov. 24, 1968, not to devalue the franc by saying that the operation could succeed "at a low temperature" while in the "feverish" conditions of 1968 it would certainly have failed.

In September the government made public the "accompanying measures" for the devaluation, in line with the following calendar for the restoration of basic stability: (1) January 1970, budgetary stability; (2) April 1970, balance of production and internal demand; (3) July 1970, balance of payments.

In the course of a four-day extraordinary session of Parliament starting on September 16, Chaban-Delmas put forward his plan "designed to drive out of our various systems everything which we still retain from the old demons of inflation." The National Assembly approved it by 369 votes to 85. The minister of the economy and finance set out five essential guidelines: (1) to reduce state demand by a slowing down of expenditure and a return to budgetary stability; (2) to reduce the state of tension in industry; (3) to redirect individual consumption toward savings; (4) to substitute exports for internal demand; and (5) to spread the burden of sacrifice fairly by protecting the weak.

The third part of the three-part recovery plan, after devaluation of the franc and the announcement of the "accompanying measures," was the presentation of the 1970 budget by Giscard d'Estaing, shortly after the normal beginning of the new session of Parliament on October 2. On October 8 the Council of Ministers approved the draft finance bill to be debated by the National Assembly. It provided for an austerity budget, with a 6% rise in public spending but a 9% growth in production. For the first time in many years, the budget allowed for a balance of receipts and expenditure. At the same time, the Bank of France again tightened credit restrictions slightly by raising the bank rate from 7 to 8% (in line with the U.K. and Canada). During his second press conference on September 23, President Pompidou had already defended

Adm. Georges Cabanier, grand chancellor of the Legion of Honour, decorates the newly inaugurated French Pres. Georges Pompidou with the Great Cross of the Legion of Honour at the Élysée Palace, June 20, 1969.

GAMMA—PIX FROM PUBLIX

"PARIS MATCH" FROM PICTORIAL PARADE

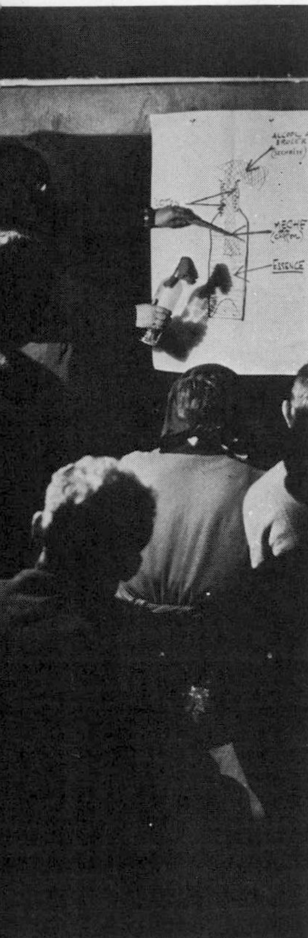

Members of the secret French organization Front de la Liberation de la Bretagne show peasants how to make Molotov cocktails. The group's slogan was "Change the incipient revolt into a revolution."

saving and tried to make every individual citizen responsible for the success or failure of the government's recovery plan.

Industrial Mergers. The year 1969 also saw new developments in the industrial field, with the creation of a chemicals group of world dimensions under the aegis of Rhône-Poulenc, and mergers in the electrical construction industry (CGE, Thomson, Brandt, Alsthom) and in the textiles industry (Pricel, Dolfuss-Mieg). In size, however, these mergers were dwarfed by that announced at the end of July between Saint-Gobain and Pont-à-Mousson under the patronage of the Compagnie Financière de Suez. This new French group was the first with a turnover of more than Fr. 10 billion. Employing between 150,000 and 180,000 persons, it was the largest enterprise in France and the eighth in Europe (coming in front of Nestlé and Fiat); it was probably 45th in the world. Finally, in October, a merger was announced between Sud-Aviation, Nord-Aviation, and the Société d'Études et de Réalisation d'Engins Balistiques (SERB), which from Jan. 1, 1970, would constitute the Société Nationale Aéro-Postale. This would be the second largest European aeronautics enterprise, after Hawker Siddeley, with 40,000 employees and a turnover of Fr. 2 billion.

Foreign Policy. From the beginning of the year, de Gaulle was exceptionally active in the field of foreign affairs. On January 2, Vladimir Kirillin, vice-chairman of the Council of Ministers of the U.S.S.R., arrived in Paris to act as co-president, with Debré, of the "high commission" to develop economic and technical cooperation, created following the journey to Moscow by de Gaulle in June 1966. In spite of the events in Czechoslovakia, de Gaulle carried on his policy of "understanding, cooperation, and relaxation of tension."

On January 10 the premier of Yugoslavia, Mika Spiljak, was welcomed on an official visit. This was the first time since President Tito's visit to France in 1956 that a Yugoslav head of government had come to Paris.

At the beginning of February, Debré's visit to Spain emphasized the common viewpoint of the two countries. The chief aim of the trip was to stimulate French business circles to a greater interest in Spain's industrial development.

After a ministerial-level meeting of the Western European Union (WEU) on February 6–7, at which all the members except France had welcomed proposals for interstate foreign policy consultations, a meeting on the Middle East took place at the ambassadorial level in London on February 14. France found the meeting unnecessary and, beyond refusing to take part, threatened to leave the union. Two further meetings of the council at permanent representative level were boycotted, and the French government expressed fears that WEU discussions might disrupt the work of the EEC. (*See* EUROPEAN UNITY.)

Prior to these events, on February 4, a diplomatic upheaval had occurred between France and Great Britain following an interview that de Gaulle had granted to Christopher Soames, the British ambassador to Paris. During the interview de Gaulle made clear his desire to see a Europe independent of the U.S., the abolition of NATO, and the transformation of the EEC into a loose form of free trade area with an inner political association of the U.K., France, Italy, and West Germany. He made it known that he would welcome a British initiative for talks with France on cooperation toward this end. The British government, however, felt that it was both expedient and honorable to make these proposals known to its allies, especially in view of the imminent visits of U.S. Pres. Richard M. Nixon to Europe and of U.K. Prime Minister Harold Wilson to West Germany.

When the purport of the confidential talk was revealed in London, the French president clearly indicated his intention not to give any further audiences to the British diplomat. Thus, the audience that Pompidou granted to Soames on October 10 was welcomed as a sign of a thaw in relations. However, the WEU crisis was not resolved and France still refused to take part in the work of that organization.

The stalemate in European affairs appeared not only within the WEU, but also on the questions of the enlargement of the Common Market and the political structure of Europe. No progress was made on these matters during 1969, either during the visit to Paris of West German Chancellor Kurt Kiesinger (March 13–14) or during the visit of Pompidou to Bonn in September. Despite the friendliness of these meetings, the proximity of the elections in West Germany (which saw the replacement of Kiesinger by Willy Brandt) and the subsequent revaluation of the mark prevented any substantial progress from being made. At the meeting of the EEC heads of state, held early in December at The Hague, Neth., Pompidou formally withdrew de Gaulle's veto of British entry but otherwise remained close to the Gaullist line regarding enlargement of the Community. France's conditions for opening negotiations with Britain included continuation of the agricultural pricing policy, which would prove extremely expensive for the U.K.

On the other hand, both Paris and Washington were encouraged by the results of President Nixon's visit to France (February 28–March 2). Three private meetings between the U.S. president and de Gaulle helped to give a certain equanimity to relations between the two countries.

Schumann, the minister of foreign affairs, went on a two-day official visit to Algiers on October 2. This was the first time that a French foreign minister had gone to Algeria since it achieved independence seven years earlier. Debré, Schumann's predecessor in the Quai d'Orsay, had twice planned this visit, but had to abandon it—the first time in December 1968, following a breakdown in commercial negotiations, and again in April 1969, after the departure of de Gaulle. Following Schumann's discussions with Pres. Houari Boumédienne and his foreign minister, Abdelaziz Bouteflika, a communiqué was issued announcing the setting up of a "high commission," to meet at least once a year in order to develop cooperation between the two countries.

Afterward, Schumann visited Moscow (October 9–14), where he held talks with the principal Soviet leaders and presided over the opening session of the regular meeting of the Committee for Franco-Soviet Cooperation. A communiqué underlined the wish of both countries to continue their joint studies of world problems. Also raised was the subject of President Pompidou's scheduled journey to the U.S.S.R. in 1970, and an invitation was handed to L. I. Brezhnev, N. V. Podgorny, and A. N. Kosygin to visit Paris. After having accepted the invitation of President Nixon to go to the U.S. in February 1970, President Pompidou thus showed that he would like to maintain, and even reinforce, ties with the Eastern European countries.

(J. KN.)

See also Propaganda.

Fuel and Power

The spectacular discovery of one of the world's largest oil fields in Alaska in 1968 continued to generate exciting news during 1969. Between January and September the oil companies with leases on the North Slope of Alaska, between the Brooks Range and the Arctic Ocean, continued to drill exploratory wells amid great secrecy in preparation for the lease sale held by the state of Alaska on September 10. In that sale the state leased 450,858 ac. for a total sum of $900,220,590, the largest such sale of U.S. state or federal lands in history. During the following weeks it was announced that the year's drilling had resulted in the discovery of at least three other oil fields.

At the same time, plans were being made for transporting the oil to U.S. and world markets. An application was made for construction of a 48-in. pipeline from Prudhoe Bay on Alaska's north coast to Valdez on the south coast. The 800-mi. pipeline would cost an estimated $900 million and would be scheduled for an initial capacity of 500,000 bbl. per day in 1972. Eventual capacity would be 1.2 million bbl. a day.

For the U.S. oil industry 1969 was also memorable as the year in which a long-standing government policy designed to encourage exploration and development of the nation's oil resources was modified. As part of a general tax reform measure, Congress cut the oil depletion allowance from 27½ to 22% (a similar reduction was made for gas and adjustments were made for certain minerals). A Cabinet task force, appointed in March to review the oil-import quota system established in 1959, raised fundamental questions concerning the necessity or even desirability of maintaining the system as a means of providing national security through protection of the domestic oil industry from foreign competition.

A mishap in drilling during January in the Santa Barbara Channel, off the coast of southern California, resulted in the release of an estimated 21,000 gal. of crude oil per day, which contaminated a large stretch of California beaches, both on the mainland and on the adjacent islands. A massive remedial effort extending over several months eventually brought the sea-floor leak under control and cleaned up the beaches. All drilling was temporarily halted and was resumed only under strict new government regulations designed to minimize the chance of recurrence.

Elsewhere in the world, one of the most significant oil discoveries of the year occurred in the northwest corner of the United Arab Republic (U.A.R.), where a large strike of "Libyan-type" oil opened the possibility that the U.A.R. might eventually join the ranks of its fellow countries of North Africa as a major oil producer. Offshore activity continued to dominate exploration efforts almost everywhere, with the continuation of drilling in the North Sea, the Persian Gulf, the Bass Strait south of Australia, and in the Atlantic off equatorial Africa, and new activity in the Adriatic Sea and the South China Sea off Malaysia and the islands of Indonesia. Further work in the Tyumen Province of the Soviet Union established that area as one of the world's great concentrations of oil and gas, especially the latter; and a wholly new gas area was discovered in the Chukot National Okrug west of Anadyr, on the Bering Sea opposite Alaska.

The infant liquefied natural gas (LNG) industry continued to grow at a healthy pace throughout the world. The use of LNG to fuel the engines of standard automobiles and trucks was demonstrated on a commercial basis in California, and plans were announced by utilities on both the east and west coasts of the U.S. to convert their automotive fleets to LNG fuel. Initial LNG deliveries via tanker were begun from Alaska to Japan and from Libya to Spain. The latter involved the largest gas-liquefaction plant yet built.

In March the annual report on oil and gas reserves of the U.S., issued by committees of the oil and gas industries, revealed that in 1968, for the first time since reserve statistics began to be collected in 1946, consumption of natural gas (19.4 trillion cu.ft.) exceeded reserve additions during the year (13.8 trillion cu.ft.). As a result, U.S. gas reserves declined from an estimated 292.9 trillion cu.ft. to 287.3 trillion cu.ft. The reserve report added to the controversy over the policies of the U.S. Federal Power Commission (FPC) in its regulation of the field prices of natural gas. The gas-producing and pipeline industries contended that the ceiling prices set by the FPC in a series of cases extending back to 1960 were too low to encourage the necessary exploration and development of new gas reserves. Supporters of the FPC's policies contended that the prices were adequate and that the decline in the nation's gas reserves was only temporary and would soon be reversed.

Construction was also begun during the year on two experimental plants for the production of synthetic fuels from coal. One plant, at Princeton, N.J., was designed to convert coal to synthetic crude oil, fuel gas, and a solid char fuel. The other, at Rapid City, S.D., was to test the feasibility of converting lignite into synthetic pipeline gas. A third experimental plant, previously constructed, successfully completed its first test run, producing synthetic crude oil from coal in a continuous process.

In Canada a second project for the production of synthetic crude oil from tar sands was approved by the government. The project was to be located at Mildred Lake, Alta., 25 mi. NW of McMurray and 260 mi. NE of Edmonton. Construction was to begin in 1974 and production was scheduled for 1976.

As had become common every year, because of the increasing use of air conditioning, summer heat waves pushed weekly electricity consumption in the U.S. to a new all-time peak of 31,640,000,000 kw-hr. during July. The effect of this new high level of consumption on utility systems was not, however, usual. Because of delays in the construction of many new nuclear power plants, normal reserve-capacity margins did not exist, and large sections of the northeastern U.S. were subject to "brownouts." Under such conditions voltages were reduced slightly, and customers were requested to cut back on usage. Lighting was curtailed in office buildings, and banks of elevators were taken out of service; telephone companies used standby diesel generators.

The first tidal power station in the Soviet Union began operation during the year, and on the Kola Peninsula, within the Arctic Circle, work was proceeding on an extensive program of thermal and hydroelectric power plants; a large-capacity nuclear plant was also under construction in the region. Negotiations were begun between the U.S.S.R. and Japan for the joint construction of a complex of thermal power stations either in eastern Siberia or on the northern tip of Sakhalin Island. Power would be transmitted to Japan via a direct-current line approximately 1,250 mi. long.

(B. C. N.)

COAL

As forecast, the tonnage of coal mined in 1968 was greater than in 1967. The output of 2,050,000,000 metric tons of hard coal was 2.2% above the 1967 figure, thus reversing the momentary halt in expansion of world production. Hard coal production in 1968 was still considerably less than the record output of 2,097,000,000 metric tons achieved in 1966. The output of lignite, however, reached 825 million tons, thus making 1968 a record year in terms of output of coal of all types.

In general, 1968 trends in world coal production followed a pattern similar to that of 1967. A notable exception was the U.S., where output of hard coal fell for the first time since 1961. Production in Western Europe decreased by 5%, but the Eastern European industry (including the U.S.S.R.) showed an increase of 1.3%. The biggest advances in 1968 were made in Asia. This was almost wholly attributed to the recovery of the coal industry in China, where the serious reversals of 1967 seemed to have been halted and production again reached the 300 million-ton mark. Elsewhere in Asia production followed a pattern similar to recent years.

An international survey of the world's reserves of workable fossil fuels reported in 1968 that coal accounted for 88% of the total, petroleum for 3%, oil shale, 6%, and natural gas, 3%.

U.S.S.R. With a total output of 594 million tons in 1968, the Soviet Union remained the world's leading producer. Production of hard coal was 446 million metric tons, an increase of 1.4% over the 1967 figure. The Soviet government proposed stepping up output to 675 million tons in 1970, and a major modernization program was implemented involving both underground- and surface-mining operations. Considerable money was made available for the importation of mining equipment. The proportion of output obtained by opencut methods was to be increased to 30%. In 1969, 22 new pits and opencut workings became operational.

United States. In 1969 the U.S. coal industry was expected to achieve its highest sales level in 20 years, largely because of an increase of 6.5% in demand from power-generating stations. The expected consumption of 568 million tons (including 51 million tons for export) was likely to exceed production. In the first half of 1969 output was down 16 million tons from the corresponding period in 1968, and a serious shortage of coal was forecast. During 1968, 545 million tons of bituminous coal and lignite were produced, a reduction of 4.9 million tons from 1967. This first output reversal experienced in the U.S. since 1961 was attributed almost wholly to the miners' strike of October 1968. Toward the end of 1968 the industry embarked on an expansion program that involved the opening of 75 new collieries. They were expected to add 90 million tons to the industry's annual capacity within five years.

Significant progress was made in 1968 on the industrial conversion of coal into gasoline and gas. The U.S. Office of Coal Research published its final report on the research and development contract with Hydrocarbon Research Inc., which showed that coal-into-oil refineries with capacities of 100,000 bbl. a day could produce gasoline for an estimated consumer price of $5.04 per bbl. A pilot industrial plant in West Virginia proved that gasoline could be derived from coal for 11.5–13.5 cents a gallon.

European Economic Community (EEC). The coal-producing nations of the EEC continued to suffer reductions of output in 1968. Belgium, with an output of 14.8 million metric tons, suffered a 9.9% loss against 1967; France, with 41.9 million tons, a loss of 11.9%; Italy, with 375,000 tons, a loss of 8.5%; and the Netherlands, with 6.6 million tons, a loss of 17.4%. The average decline in production throughout the EEC was 4.7%, the relative stability of West Germany (112 million tons for a decline of only 0.03% from 1967) moderating the high losses of the other four countries. Hard coal production in 1969 was expected to fall again, but the anticipated loss in output of 1.8% was a significant improvement in the recent trend. In spite of the overall drop in output for the Community, France and Italy were expected to record slight increases in 1969.

Underground output per manshift continued to improve, and in 1968 the average for the EEC was 3.064 tons against 2.824 tons in 1967. This increase of 8.5% compared with a 12% reduction in the number of underground workers during the year.

United Kingdom. During the financial year ended March 30, 1969, output was 160.6 million long tons, a reduction of 10.3 million tons from the previous year. National Coal Board (NCB) deep-mined output was 153 million tons, with an additional 6.6 million tons coming from opencut operations. Licensed mines contributed 1 million tons. A total of 55 NCB collieries were closed, involving 27,300 men. Overall output per manshift at the end of the fiscal year increased 9% over the previous year. This improved productivity contrasted with a manpower decrease of 46,000, at 12.6% the highest-ever annual reduction.

Output in 1969–70 was expected to be 155 million tons, and over the same period between 40 and 45 mines were likely to be closed, affecting 25,000–30,000 workers. U.K. coal consumption was increasing, however, with the electric power industry using 30% more coal in the first half of 1969. Exports were also expanding rapidly, and the demand for coke from the domestic steel industry remained strong. Thus, it was possible that fewer mines would close than had been expected.

Poland. In 1968, 127 million tons of hard coal were produced, an increase of 3.1 million over the 1967 output. The production of lignite approached 30 million tons. Increased output was achieved by increased mechanization and reduction in manpower. Underground productivity increased from 2.01 tons per manshift in 1967 to 2.32 tons per manshift in 1968. Coal exports during 1968 reached 26 million tons of hard coal, the highest since 1951 and 2 million tons more than in 1967. The increase was due exclusively to expansion of coal exports to Western countries, which reached 13.5 million tons.

India. The 1968 output of 75 million tons was 4.7 million tons higher than for the preceding year. Capacity and production exceeded consumption, however, and the loss of the 1-million-ton annual export trade with Pakistan meant that coal mine inventories were likely to remain high. Alternative markets were unlikely to absorb the large quantity of low-grade coal available.

Japan. During 1968 Japan produced 46,-569,000 tons of hard coal, a decline of 915,-000 tons from 1967. High production costs led to the continued decline of domestic output. To satisfy the increasing demand, imports rose steeply, increasing nearly 7 million tons over 1967. The Japanese steel industry, anxious to secure supplies of coking coal, completed contracts mainly with the U.S., Australia, Canada, and Poland. A contract was also concluded for the supply of 23 million tons of coking coal from the U.S.S.R. from 1969 to 1975.

Australia. Output increased to 40.8 million tons in 1968. This advance was due to the progress made in developing foreign markets and to the continued domestic demand. Coal exports to Japan reached 12 million tons in 1968, an increase of 3 million tons compared with 1967. Contracts were negotiated for the supply of almost 190 million tons of coal to Japan between 1968 and 1985. The Australian industry was

Actual and Forecast Consumption of Coal as Percentage of All Energy Sources

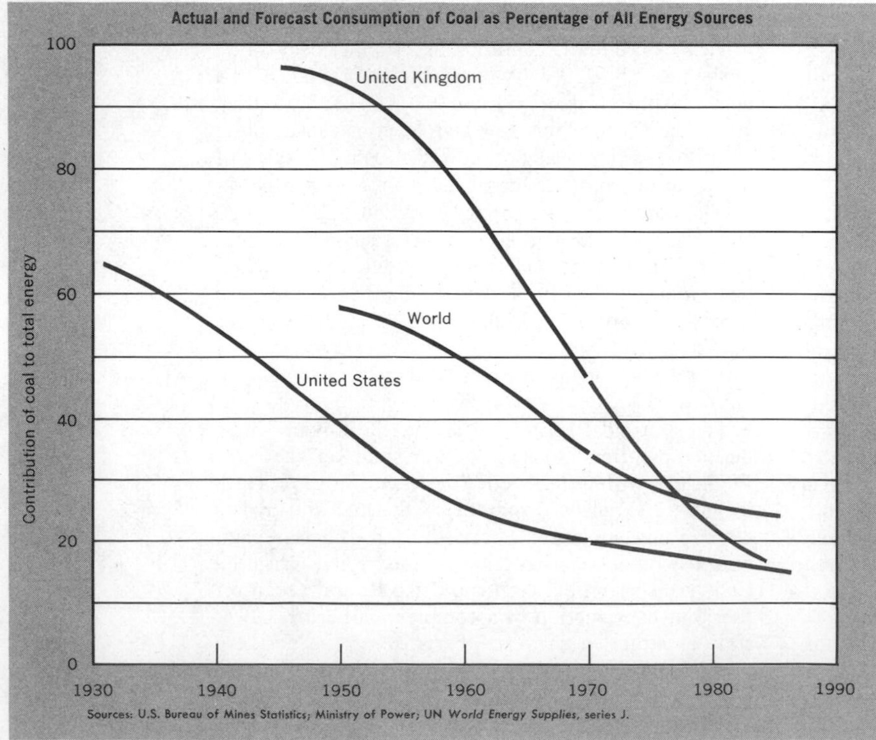

Sources: U.S. Bureau of Mines Statistics; Ministry of Power; UN *World Energy Supplies*, series J.

expected to register significant gains in both production and exports during 1969.

Africa. Coal output during 1968 was 55.4 million metric tons, of which 50.6 million tons was produced by South Africa. Rhodesia's output of 3 million tons was the only significant contribution from the other African coal-producing nations. In South Africa, the coal industry made large gains during 1968 when production rose by 4.8%. With an expanding demand for coal, it was expected that production would increase steadily, particularly since reserves were large and South Africa's energy supply was almost exclusively coal-based.

South America. Coal production during 1968 was 9.8 million tons, a gain of 300,000 tons over 1967. Brazil was the largest producer with 4.6 million tons; Colombia produced 3 million tons; and Chile accounted for 1.5 million tons. Whereas Chile and Colombia remained static, Brazil continued to record a modest annual increase.

Canada. Domestic production fell by 500,000 tons during 1968 to 7.95 million tons. In spite of this reversal the future of the industry looked bright in view of the important new coal-mining developments planned in the western provinces. The first quarter of 1969 saw production increases of more than 1% over the same period of the previous year. During 1968 Canada imported 17,150,000 tons of hard coal from the U.S., whereas Canadian coal exports, mainly to Japan, were little more than 1 million tons.
(F. F. R.)

ELECTRICITY

A marked upward trend in world consumption of electricity appeared in 1968, during which the growth was 8.4%. This tendency was confirmed and became general during 1969, as shown by the following results for the first six months of the year: France +13.3%; West Germany +11%; U.S.S.R. +10%; U.S. +9%; U.K. +8.2%; and Italy +7.9%.

Nuclear-Electric Power. Nuclear power suffered a reaction of unpopularity, especially in the U.S. where the year's first order for a nuclear power station was not placed until April.

Reasons for this slowdown included the lowering of prices of competing sources of power; the difficulties in perfecting high-capacity installations; the backlog in manufacture of equipment; and the rise in construction costs, due partly to a shortage of specialized labour. Glenn T. Seaborg, chairman of the U.S. Atomic Energy Commission, stated that construction costs had doubled in the five years prior to 1969.

The United Kingdom maintained its lead in capacity installed (44.1% of world total), production of electricity during 1968 (28 billion kw-hr. or 33%), and the cumulative production of electricity since the first nuclear power station came into operation (59.5%).

According to the International Atomic Energy Agency (IAEA), the number of power reactors was expected to reach 105 at the beginning of 1970. Located in 15 countries (including those in Eastern Europe), these reactors represented an installed capacity of approximately 20,000 Mw. By 1975 it was expected that 283 nuclear reactors with a total capacity of 130,000 Mw. would be in service in 21 countries.

The first U.S. reactor of 1969 was ordered by the Virginia Electric and Power Co. This was a PWR (pressurized heavy water moderated and cooled reactor) unit of 815 Mw. for the North Anna station, ultimately planned to reach a capacity of 4,000 Mw. In May the Alabama Power Co. ordered a PWR reactor of 820 Mw., and in August the Public Service Electric and Gas Co. ordered two BWR (boiling heavy water moderated and cooled reactor) units of 1,115 Mw. each, although reserving the right to cancel the order for the second unit. The 515-Mw. BWR reactor at Oyster Creek, N.J., ordered in November 1963, finally ran at full capacity in August 1969. The Bolsa Island (California) project, to have comprised two reactors with a capacity of 1,800 Mw., had to be abandoned.

In Canada work began in December 1968 on the Bruce County (Ontario) power station, which was to have a capacity of 3,000 Mw. in four units of 750 Mw. of the heavy-water type. The unit was to be constructed on the site of the Douglas Point station (200 Mw.) where a factory for the production of heavy water was also to be installed. Canada also had under construction the Pickering station at Toronto, the eventual capacity of which would be 2,000 Mw., and the Gentilly station on the St. Lawrence River, a BWR-type reactor (250 Mw.) due for completion in 1971.

The Japanese power program for 1969–70 provided for four nuclear stations: Fukushima (2,784 Mw.); Takahama (826 Mw.); Hamaoka (500 Mw.); and Kashima (460 Mw.). In India, two BWR-type reactors of 190 Mw. each in the Tarapur station came into operation. In addition, India had under construction four reactors of 200 Mw. each of the Canadian heavy-water-and-natural-uranium type.

At the end of its program of magnox-type reactors, the U.K. abandoned this system in favour of the AGR (advanced gas cooled, graphite-moderated reactor) type, and four AGR stations were under construction. A fifth was planned for Heysham, Lancashire, with a capacity of 2,500 Mw.

West Germany, with an installed capacity of 860 Mw., had under construction seven power stations with a total capacity of 2,562 Mw., including three experimental stations. Several projects for nuclear power stations on the banks of the Rhine River were under consideration.

In France the natural-uranium station Saint-Laurent-des-Eaux 1 (480 Mw.) was linked to the distribution network in March 1969. Construction of Saint-Laurent-des-Eaux 2 (515 Mw.) and of Bugey 1 (545 Mw.), of the same type, was under way, but the Fessenheim project on the Rhine was abandoned. France seemed finally to have rejected natural-uranium, graphite-moderated, gas-cooled reactors in favour of light-water units. However, consideration of the heavy-water system (obviating the need for enriched uranium) was proposed.

Italy, which had three nuclear power stations in operation with a total capacity of 622 Mw., planned a fourth of between 600 and 750 Mw. capacity, at Messanone on the Po River. In June the Swedish Sydsvenska company announced that it had ordered a BWR-type reactor of 580 Mw. to be installed at Barsebeck, north of Malmö. This brought to 3,320 Mw. the total capacity either in operation (210 Mw.), under construction (1,950 Mw.), or on order (1,160 Mw.) in that country.

Finland turned to the U.S.S.R. for the construction of the Loviisa power station, to include a PWR-type reactor of 440 Mw., identical to that of the Novo Voronezh station. In Switzerland, the first PWR-type reactor (350 Mw.) at the Beznau power station began to provide electricity in June 1969.

The first Dutch nuclear power station was ordered from West Germany in April 1969. It was to be situated at Borssels, near Vlissingen, and would include a PWR-type reactor of 400–450 Mw., due to go into operation in 1973. Soviet-aided construction of the first Bulgarian nuclear power station, with an initial capacity of 800 Mw., began at Kozloduy.

In 1961 the United Kingdom had put into operation at Dounreay an experimental breeder of 14 Mw., and this provided the necessary information for work to begin on a larger installation with a capacity of 250 Mw., due to go into operation in 1972. France began the construction of its Phénix breeder, also of 250 Mw., due to operate in 1973. Shortly afterward the 300-Mw. breeder which West Germany, Belgium, and the Netherlands were to build jointly was expected to come into service. The U.S. was considering a breeder of a capacity of between 300 and 500 Mw.

It was admitted that the first really competitive breeders would need a capacity of at least 1,000 Mw. At its meeting in Zermatt, Switz., in June, the managing committee of the International Union of Electric Power Producers and Distributors (UNIPEDE) proposed that manufacturers and distributors in the six EEC countries should set up an agreement, under Community auspices, to study a breeder on a commercial scale with a capacity of not less than 1,000 Mw.

Thermoelectricity. Thermoelectric power, currently favoured by a spectacular fall in the price of fossil combustibles, notably of fuel oil, still accounted for the greater part of world power production. In the U.S. the Tennessee Valley Authority in October 1969 brought into service the cross-compound No. 3 group with a capacity of 1,150 Mw. in its Paradise station. The most powerful British power station, that at Drax in Yorkshire, was to initially include three units of 660 Mw., but the Central Electricity Generating Board was considering placing an order

Oblic thermoelectric power plant under construction in Yugoslavia. Six new power plants, including Oblic, entered service in 1969, raising Yugoslavia's production of electricity 16% over the previous year.

AUTHENTICATED NEWS INTERNATIONAL

Installed Capacity and Production of Electric Power in Selected Countries, 1967*

Political division	Hydroelectric power: Operating plants: Installed capacity (000 kw.)	Hydroelectric power: Operating plants: Production (000,000 kw-hr.)	Total electric power: Installed capacity (000 kw.)	Total electric power: Production (000,000 kw-hr.)
World	...	...	...	3,843,600
Afghanistan	212.0	343	227.0	357
Albania	...	203†	...	555
Algeria‡	228§	410	500§	1,191
Argentina	367§	1,225§	5,486‖	15,917‖
Australia	2,893‡	7,802	11,051‡	41,547
Austria	4,287	17,698	6,366	24,439
Belgium	65	238	6,647	23,990
Bolivia	144‖	471‖	215‖	595
Brazil	5,787	29,190	8,042	34,239
Bulgaria	770	2,022	2,865	13,631
Burma	104	286§	262	587§
Cambodia¶‡	—	—	39‖	93
Cameroon	152‖	976‖	168‖	984
Canada	23,353	132,748	32,763	165,625
Central African Republic‡	6.6§	28.2	8.3§	28.2
Ceylon	113‖	399‖	219‖	581
Chad¶‡	—	—	9.8§	26
Chile	720	4,255	1,569	6,892
Colombia	843§	3,721†	1,872‖	6,086‖
Costa Rica	174.7	694	236.3	757
Cuba	—	128♀	1,100‖	3,709‖
Czechoslovakia	1,539	3,717	9,589	38,622
Denmark	...	25	3,255	9,480
Ecuador	67§	260‖	255‖	700‖
El Salvador	109‡	428‡	172	526
Ethiopia	91.8	209	292.0	318‖
Finland	2,070	11,629	4,452	16,760
France	13,722	45,134	31,613	111,637
Gabon‡	—	—	16.0	55.8
Germany, East	630‖	1,060	11,522	59,686
Germany, West	4,591	16,544	45,495	180,712
Ghana	512	1,495	628	1,560
Greece	596‡‖	1,643‡	1,492‖	6,680
Guatemala	25♀‡	116‡‖	131‖	526
Guyana	—	—	80.8	240
Honduras	32‡‖	127‡‖	77‖	204‖
Hong Kong¶‡	—	—	949	3,464
Hungary	21	82	2,060	12,474
Iceland	123‡	664‡	192	706
India	4,918‖	16,799‖	11,442‖	40,411‖
Indonesia‡	284	917	590	1,677
Iran	272‡	636	896‡	4,500
Ireland‡	219‖	798	1,170‖	4,264
Israel¶	—	—	1,002‡	4,728
Italy	14,601	42,949	28,759	96,829
Jamaica	19†‡	140‡‖	260‖	870‖
Japan	17,124	69,655	49,526	244,863
Kenya‡	28.1	201	113.6	339
Korea, South	300‡	953‡	1,083	5,276
Kuwait¶‡	—	—	163†	1,335
Laos¶‡	—	—	10.2‖	24.7
Lebanon‡	198	683	374	907
Liberia	37.5‖	40‖	164‖	339‖
Libya¶‡	—	—	79.8	212
Luxembourg	926‡	913‡	1,163	2,221
Malagasy Rep.	28.7§	96‡	82.4§	152§
Malawi‡	24.6	79.8	38.2	85.2
Malaysia:				
Malaya	139‖	725	502‖	2,642
Sabah¶	—	—	27.1	68
Sarawak¶			35.6	81
Mexico	2,292§	12,246	5,914	20,927
Morocco‡	323	932	438	1,448
Netherlands¶	—	—	8,669	30,056
New Zealand‡	2,273	9,971	2,975	11,600
Nicaragua	59.3§	220‖	135.0‖	335‖
Nigeria	21	141	450	1,112
Norway	10,140‖	52,721	10,272‖	52,814
Pakistan	353‖	1,753‖	1,175‖	3,903‖
Panama	—	—	118.7‡‖	524‖
Paraguay¶	—	—	61.0	205‖
Peru	772‖	3,121	1,412‖	4,583
Philippines	410	1,636‡	1,222‖	5,567‖
Poland	373	994	10,933	51,257
Portugal	1,425	5,498	1,778	5,937
Rhodesia	705‖	4,471	1,191‖	4,952
Romania	811	1,476	5,198	24,769
Rwanda	21.3‖	46.8‖	22.5‖	48.1‖
Singapore¶‡	—	—	464‖	1,425
South Africa	16†	40†	6,560†	36,495
Spain	7,990	22,733	12,645	41,200
Surinam	...	585	232.5	843
Sweden	10,147	49,275	13,293	53,796
Switzerland	8,750	29,730	9,270	30,553
Syria	—	—	254	676
Taiwan	721‡	2,634‡	1,690	8,609
Tanzania‡	41.2‖	178§	71.6‖	297
Thailand	162.9‡‖	1,064‡‖	540.6‖	1,854‖
Trinidad and Tobago¶	—	—	258	1,035
Tunisia	28‡	37‡	209	620
Turkey	731	2,370	2,001	6,167
Uganda	137‡	702‡	165	704‡
U.S.S.R.	24,813	88,571	131,727	587,699
U.A.R.	345‡‖	1,837‡‖	1,681‖	5,895‖
United Kingdom	2,159	5,741	55,732	209,368
United States	48,819	224,894	288,094	1,316,914
Uruguay‡	236‖	1,399‖	488‖	1,841‖
Venezuela	387♂	1,636	2,455	9,479
Vietnam, South‡	163‖	...	439‖	682
Yugoslavia	2,605	10,655	4,480	18,702
Zambia	50	276§	262	604

Figures are for total gross generation of electricity by plants generating primarily for public use and by industrial establishments generating largely for their own use unless otherwise indicated.
*Preliminary. †1964. ‡Electricity from plants generating primarily for public use. §1965. ‖1966. ¶Thermal only. ♀1963. ♂1962.
Source: *United Nations Statistical Yearbook*, 1968. (F.H.Sk.)

in 1970 for a unit of 1,200 to 1,300 Mw. France brought into service in July 1968 the first group of 600 Mw. of the Porcheville station and in May 1969, a group of identical capacity in the Le Havre station.

Hydroelectricity. The rate of construction of hydroelectric installations was decreasing in industrial countries, most of which had exhausted the possibilities of their most promising waterfalls and were turning their attention to pumped storage stations. Only in the less developed countries did worthwhile possibilities exist for the realization of projects capable of harnessing great rivers.

In Africa the Kainji Dam on the Niger River, begun in 1962, was inaugurated in February 1969. The station consisted of four groups of 80 Mw., but eight supplementary groups might later be added to bring the eventual capacity of the station to nearly 1,000 Mw.

The World Bank granted a loan to Ghana to add two groups of 147 Mw. to the station on the Volta River, which would then reach its maximum of 887 Mw. This was expected to meet Ghana's needs until 1977.

In November 1968, the president of Venezuela inaugurated the first stage of the Guri project (eventual capacity up to 6,000 Mw.) on the Caroní River, 400 mi. SE of Caracas. In France the two groups (190 Mw. each) of the Villarodin station were linked to the network in December 1968, as was, in the autumn of 1969, the third group of the Vouglans station on the Ain.

The station at Kastraki on the Acheloos River in Greece began operating in June 1969 with the first of four 80-Mw. groups. An agreement was signed in May between France and Greece for an installation at Polyphyton on the Alcathon River.

A Swedish manufacturer was to equip the Castaic pumped storage station which would have a total capacity of 1,200 Mw. and supply peak-hour power to Los Angeles. The U.K. secretary of state for Scotland authorized a project to build a pumped storage station at Foyers on Loch Ness, to consist of two reversible pump-turbine groups of 150 Mw. each. (L. Ch.)

GAS

In the U.S. consumption of natural gas continued to increase in 1968, while production of new reserves failed to keep pace. For three years, the increase in consumption each year had been about 1 trillion cu.ft. In 1959–68 the increase averaged 850 billion cu.ft. per year.

In 1968, sales totaled 18 trillion cu.ft., 15.7 trillion cu.ft. of which were attributed to the 33 major interstate pipelines. Comparable figures in 1967 were 16.6 trillion cu.ft. and 14:5 trillion cu.ft. Reserves dropped 5.5 trillion cu.ft. at the beginning of 1969 after having gained 3.5 trillion cu.ft. a year earlier. The trend indicated that the current 14:5 ratio of reserves to production would drop to 11 by 1974.

The U.S. gas utility industry expected that by 1975 it would add 7.1 million new customers to the 39.9 million it already served; there would be an additional 5.5 million by 1980 and another 6.2 million by 1985. To serve 64.4 million homes and business enterprises in 1990, 246,000 mi. of new pipeline costing $46 billion would be needed to make up a total network of 1.8 million mi.

Plant investment in the U.S. was slightly more than $3 billion for 1969, a fraction higher than for 1968. Revenues from sales were expected to cross the $9 billion mark, as compared with $8.8 billion and $8.3 billion in 1968 and 1967.

A potential gas supply of 1,220,000,000,000,000 cu.ft. of gas, 420 trillion cu.ft. of which were in Alaska, was estimated to be under the surface of the U.S. To meet future demand, roughly 40,000 exploratory wells were said to be needed each year for the next 30 years. Since 1954, however, an average of 12,000 exploratory wells had been drilled, and exploration in general began a decline in 1956 that continued to 1969.

Two notable events in 1969 offered an opportunity to turn the situation around, however: Alaska accepted bids of more than $900 million on 450,000 ac. of its North Slope oil and gas find near Prudhoe Bay; and in Colorado, a nuclear explosion equal to 40,000 tons of TNT was set off under Battlement Mesa, about 40 mi. NE of Grand Junction, in the hope of freeing natural gas. Not until the spring of 1970, however, could the effectiveness of the latter experiment be determined.

Reduction of the gas depletion allowance from 27½ to 22% as part of the 1969 tax reform bill threatened to reduce the economic incentives for further gas exploration and production in the U.S. In addition, tighter regulations for drilling offshore were imposed following the blowing out of an oil well near Santa Barbara, Calif., and the consequent spread of an oil slick over 800 sq.mi. of the Pacific Ocean.

In spite of the new restrictions the U.S. gas industry continued to expand. The FPC allowed El Paso Natural Gas Co. to build a $118 million pipeline from Texas to southern California. The same company contracted to buy the first large-scale supplies of overseas natural gas for importation into the U.S., agreeing to buy 1 billion cu.ft. of liquefied gas a day over a 25-year period from a government-owned gas company in Algeria.

In Canada, natural gas sales totaled 766 billion cu.ft. in 1968, 9.7% above the 698 billion cu.ft. sold in 1967. Exports to the U.S. amounted to 604 billion cu.ft., a jump of 17.7% over the 1967 total. Imports increased to 80 billion cu.ft. in 1968 from 70 billion cu.ft. in 1967.

The gas find in Alaska threatened to affect gas trade with the U.S., however. Aside from a possible revision of current supply patterns, a transportation dispute also loomed between Canada and the U.S. Humble Oil and Refining Co. of the U.S. was attempting to link Alaska with the Atlantic Coast by icebreaking the Northwest Passage, which, of course, involved Canadian waters.

In Latin America, a vast find was discovered in Trinidad, off the coast of Venezuela. Tests showed an initial flow of more than 300 billion cu.ft. per day. U.S. exploration in Latin America was expected to be more cautious in the future. Rising nationalism, especially in Peru and Ecuador, made U.S. investment in Latin America more risky. According to international law the right of ownership of gas belonged to the country where the gas fields were located, and government take-over of foreign companies usually meant a less-than-value purchase price. (J. J. Ac.)

The financial year of 1968–69 was an outstanding one for the state-run British gas industry. Gas sales reached a record of more than 4.6 billion therms, an increase of 11.1%; massive industrial contracts for the supply of natural gas were negotiated; three major contracts for the supply of North Sea gas were signed in spite of initial difficulties with the conversion program; appliances belonging to 418,000 customers were converted to burn natural gas; and the industry earned a record surplus of £17.5 million, compared with a deficit of £12.9 million in 1967–68.

A highlight of the year was the negotiation of a contract between the Gas Council and Imperial Chemical Industries Ltd. for the sale of about 1 billion therms per year of natural gas for 15 years. The contract was one of the biggest of its kind ever concluded. It doubled the sales of gas to British industry. An important national economic benefit was the estimated annual import saving of approximately £10 million. The bulk of the gas was to be used for ammonia synthesis in the manufacture of fertilizers.

Late in 1968 the British Gas Council concluded agreements with the Shell and Esso groups and with the Gas Council-Amoco Group for supplies of gas from the Leman and Indefatigable North Sea gas fields. The Leman field was believed to be the largest offshore gas field in the world. The gas-containing reservoir of sand had a thickness of up to 800 ft., and extended beneath an area 18 mi. by 5 mi. Leman was estimated to contain about 12 trillion cu.ft. of gas, almost half the total reserve of the North Sea gas fields, which was estimated at around 30 trillion cu.ft. Including the West Sole and Hewett fields, the Gas Council had supply contracts totaling more than 3 billion cu.ft. of gas a day—more than double the existing British gas demand.

A fifth major field was found in the North Sea during the year. Named Viking, it was about 50 mi. NE of the Norfolk coast and was discovered by the Continental Oil Co.-National Coal Board partnership. The field was estimated to contain about 4–5 trillion cu.ft. of gas. Other promising discoveries were made offshore. The only significant onshore natural gas field—at Lockton, near Scarborough—was due to begin producing in the autumn of 1970. Onshore prospecting was stepped up in 1969, but no significant discoveries were announced. New areas for offshore prospecting were offered by the British government, including the Irish Sea.

The year 1969 was the tenth anniversary of the discovery of the huge Groningen gas field in the Netherlands. The discovery of the Groningen field had sparked off the massive and successful search for hydrocarbons in the North Sea. Groningen's estimated reserves were over 58 trillion cu.ft., more than double those of the North Sea gas fields. In the West it was second only to the Hugoton field in the U.S. The search in the North Sea had paid off for Britain; of the other countries Norway had a known discovery near the median line with U.K. waters. The Norwegian sector showed promising signs, but pipelining was not yet a feasible proposition from deep water areas far from land. In the West German sector of the North Sea the gas found was too heavily contaminated with nitrogen to be useful as a fuel. Many of the Dutch sources also revealed a heavy nitrogen content.

Three major distributors, Trans-Canada Pipelines, Westcoast Transmission Co., and Northern Natural Gas Producing Co., launched separate studies concerning the feasibility of pipelines to carry natural gas from fields in the Northwest Territories and eastern Alaska to markets in California, eastern Canada, and the U.S. Middle West. Sales of Canadian gas to the domestic and export markets showed an increase of 17% for the first quarter of 1969 as compared with the corresponding period of 1968. It was believed that gas from the north would be needed within ten years to prevent a shortage, as markets expanded faster than resources could be proved in southern Canada. It was hoped that pipeline proposals would spur exploration and development of the northern fields. Canadian gas exports to the U.S. were running at about 2.2 billion cu.ft. a day, an increase of 200 million cu.ft. a day over 1968.

France in 1969 imported approximately 670 million cu.ft. a day of Groningen gas and in 1970 was to begin bringing in about 350 million cu.ft. a day of Algerian gas to add to the 50 million cu.ft. a day already taken from that country. The Algerian imports were in a liquid form, a method of shipping natural gas pioneered by the British gas industry in the early 1960s.

COURTESY, STANDARD OIL COMPANY (NEW JERSEY)

Liquefied natural gas facility at Marsa el Brega, Libya, completed in 1969. Natural gas is cooled and stored here before being shipped abroad.

The Royal Dutch-Shell group obtained a £650 million order to supply natural gas from its Brunei fields to Japan. The order covered a total quantity of 65 million tons spread over 20 years. Initial deliveries were planned for the winter of 1972–73, and the gas was to be shipped in liquid form in quantities rising to a level of about 520 million cu.ft. a day, the equivalent of almost 4 million tons a year.

These deliveries would significantly increase the total world trade in liquefied natural gas, which had been growing steadily over the previous five years. In 1969 the largest projects were Libya's contract to supply 345 million cu.ft. a day to Italy and Spain and the Algerian order to send 350 million cu.ft. a day to France. The contract between Alaska and Japan entailed quantities of about 140 million cu.ft., while Algeria supplied to the U.K. at a rate of 100 million cu.ft. a day.

The U.S.S.R. continued its efforts to sell more gas abroad. Negotiations with West Germany, France, Finland, and Japan took place during 1969. In 1968 a contract was agreed with Austria for 30 billion cu.m. (1,060,000,000,000 cu.ft.) of gas over a 20-year period and supplies started at the end of 1968. In that year Soviet gas exports rose by 34% to 24.3 billion cu.m. In December 1969, Italy's hydrocarbons monopoly, the Ente Nazionale Idrocarburi (ENI), signed a 20-year agreement to import gas from the U.S.S.R., and there were indications at the end of the year that both West Germany and France would agree to take Soviet supplies via the pipeline that terminated in Bratislava, Czech. According to initial plans, this pipeline would be extended into Bavaria, with spurs to other parts of West Germany and France. West Germany was reported to be negotiating for 52.5 billion cu.m. over 20 years.

The latest figure for the total world reserves of natural gas was 898.3 trillion cu.ft., including 287 trillion in the U.S., 219 trillion in the Middle East, 94 trillion in the U.S.S.R., and 76 trillion in Africa. (X.)

PETROLEUM

The year 1969 was one of considerable transition for the world petroleum industry. The impact of the Arab-Israeli war of 1967 was still felt, and the oil companies turned from the Middle East to find fields of great promise in the coastal regions of West Africa and also on the northernmost coast of Alaska. The year brought a number of new developments in processing technology, many of them in the petrochemical field, and also potentially far-reaching mergers and changes in company ownership. In June, British Petroleum Co. Ltd. announced an agreement for the merger of its principal U.S. subsidiary, BP Oil Corp., with Standard Oil Co. of Ohio (Sohio). This was aimed at increasing BP's marketing outlets for its Alaskan

Alaska's natural resources commissioner, Thomas E. Kelly, (right) announces the closure of mineral rights auction of North Slope oil land, Sept. 10, 1969.

UPI COMPIX

STATE OF ALASKA 23RD OIL AND GAS LEASE SALE
ALASKA MAP SERVICE, INC.

AUTHENTICATED NEWS INTERNATIONAL

Oceangoing tugs tow huge underwater petroleum storage tank, the first of its kind, to a site off Dubai in the Arabian Gulf, where it was submerged in 1969.

oil. In October an attempt was made by the U.S. Department of Justice to declare the BP merger illegal.

Total proved and probable crude oil reserves in the world increased 2.7%; that is, from an estimated 495,947,000,000 bbl. at the end of 1967 to 509,877,000,000 bbl. in 1968. Figures for long-established sources such as the U.S. or Venezuela tended to remain low due to the traditional conservative approach. However, commonly used data for some of the newer producing countries tended to include oil that was not only considered as proved by conservative standards—such as those of the American Petroleum Institute—but also much crude petroleum that such standards would only regard as probable. The gain was partially accounted for by Alaska. A healthy increase was most apparent in the Middle East, mainly in Iran and Saudi Arabia and, to a somewhat lesser extent, in Muscat and Oman and Dubai.

Production. The figure for the total worldwide output of crude oil rose approximately 9.2% in 1968 to an average of 38.5 million bbl. a day. As in previous years practically all of this growth occurred in the Eastern Hemisphere, *i.e.*, 2,729,000 bbl. a day, compared with 519,000 in the Western Hemisphere, where gains were on the whole modest. The U.S., for example, recorded a gain of 302,000 bbl. a day for a rise of 3.4%, whereas the previous year it had increased almost 6%. Venezuela rose only 1.8% to an average of 3,605,000 bbl. a day. Venezuela's position as the world's third largest producing nation was threatened by several Middle East countries, notably Libya.

Greater political stability resulted in Middle East output returning to more normal growth patterns. The total gain for the region, at 1,286,000 bbl. a day, was 12.8% higher than in 1967. The 11,316,000-bbl.-a-day figure for 1968 represented more than 29% of the total world output. Both Saudi Arabia and Iran rose to more than 2.8 million bbl. a day each. Most spectacular for its growth record was Libya, where the 1968 average output was 2.6 million bbl. a day, 49% above that of the previous year; indications were that, barring political disturbance, this figure would be well into the 3-million-bbl.-a-day bracket by the end of 1969. Nigeria finally showed a decline owing to the effects of the continuing civil war. Its production was only 138,000 bbl. a day, compared with 319,000 bbl. a day in 1967. Australia appeared to have begun its long-anticipated rise in production. Its production, however, was moderate in 1968, 37,000 bbl. a day. Indonesia also started to renew its strength, the 1968 average production of 601,000 bbl. a day representing an 18% growth over the previous year. In Eastern Europe the U.S.S.R. maintained its steady rate of growth and rose by 7.3%, thus moving above 6 million bbl. a day for the first time in its history. Other countries in the Communist bloc showed their usual moderate increases.

Consumption. Total world demand for petroleum increased by 6.9% in 1968 to 38,282,000 bbl. a day. In the Eastern Hemisphere it rose by 7.7% to 21,523,000 bbl. a day, while a 6% increase in the Western Hemisphere brought the average figure up to 16,759,000 bbl. a day. Eight countries had a consumption above one million daily barrels: the U.S., the U.S.S.R., Japan, West Germany, the U.K., France, Italy, and Canada.

Processing. Worldwide crude oil refining capacity increased to 42,139,300 bbl. a day, a gain of 4.4 million bbl. a day, or 11.8%, over the capacity at the end of 1967. In the non-Communist part of the world the total was approximately 36.5 million bbl. a day, which represented an 11% increase over 1967. The number of countries with refining capacity in excess of one million barrels per day remained at nine. In order of descending rank they were as follows: U.S., 11,658,000 bbl. a day; U.S.S.R., an estimated 4.7 million bbl. a day; Japan, 2,337,900 bbl. a day; Italy, 2,284,700 bbl. a day; West Germany, 2,116,200 bbl. a day; France, 2,041,500 bbl. a day; U.K., 2,030,800 bbl. a day; Canada, 1,201,900 bbl. a day; and Venezuela, 1,200,500 bbl. a day. In the area of petrochemical manufacturing the total number of operating plants rose to 1,225, a 9.5% increase over 1967. Of this total, there were 463 installations in the Eastern Hemisphere and 762 in the Western Hemisphere.

A new acetylene process was developed by the E. I. du Pont de Nemours Co., details of which were made public for the first time by the du Pont Elastomer Chemicals Department at a joint meeting of the Society of Chemical Industry and the Deutsche Gesellschaft für Chemisches Apparatewese e.V. at Frankfurt am Main, W.Ger. Hydrocarbons, diluted with hydrogen, are pyrolyzed in an essentially continuous plasma produced by magnetic rotation of an electric arc. Dimethylformamide is used in the recovery and purification of the acetylene, which is then fully acceptable for use in the manufacture of neoprene (synthetic rubber). A 50-million-lb.-per-year process plant was put into successful commercial operation at the du Pont installation in Montague, Mich. The arc reactor converted a refinery hydrocarbon cut into acetylene with a yield that depended upon the chain length of the hydrocarbon. Thus, a 75% yield was achieved with butane, but as the chain length increased, the yield dropped to 65%.

Transportation. By the middle of 1968 the worldwide tanker fleet—of 10,000 tons deadweight and larger—had reached 110,142,317 tons deadweight. This was 10.6% higher than the figure recorded for mid-1967. Tankers sailing under the Liberian flag of registry remained most numerous: 624 ships for a total tonnage of 24,933,144 deadweight, or 22.64% of the total. Japan moved back into fourth position ahead of the U.S., having recorded a substantial growth of 18.3% in tonnage. Nowhere was the impact of the giant tanker more evident than in the data published during the year showing trends in ships on order or under construction. Thus at the end of 1967 the average size of new tankers had reached 88,400 tons deadweight, which was 42% larger than those on order one year earlier. New shipbuilding yards were being constructed for larger tankers. About 15 shipyards were designed for tankers of 500,000 tons deadweight, and one yard in Sweden could reportedly build vessels up to 750,000 tons deadweight. Yards with a capability for vessels of one million tons deadweight were in the offing.

(E. G. Es.)

See also Conservation; Engineering Projects; Industrial Review; Mining; Nuclear Energy; Transportation.

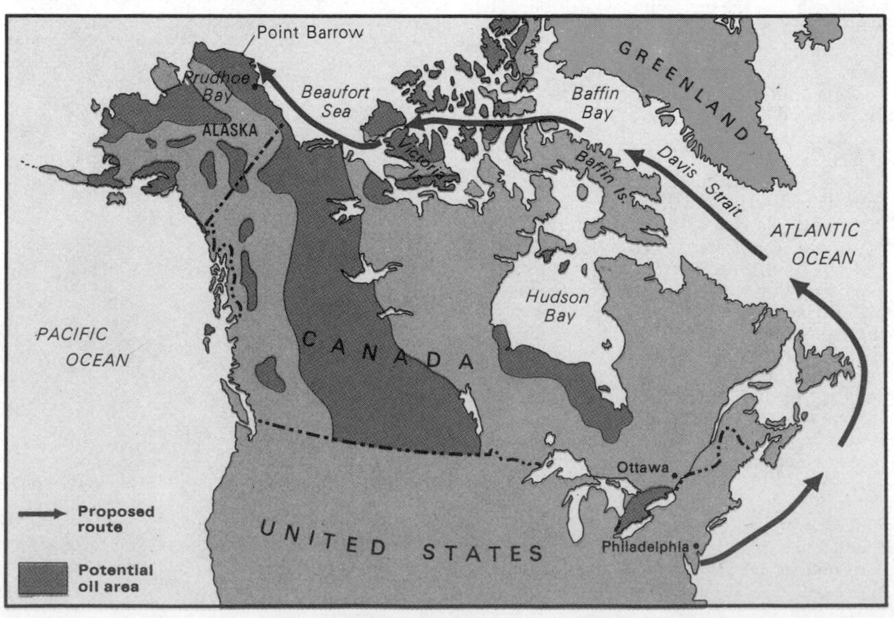

Furs

The U.S. fur industry underwent its most trying year in decades during 1969. Government measures designed to curb inflation resulted in tight money and expensive credit, neither of which was conducive to business in the luxury field. A further factor was the declining stock market, which also dampened willingness to spend for furs.

Tallies on retail sales were incomplete by the year's end, but qualified sources believed the decline would be appreciable—perhaps 10% below the previous year's approximately $400 million. In addition to consumer reticence, retail stores held back in their preparations for the season. The major consideration here was the expensive interest on credit, which forced many stores to channel their investments into merchandise that offered faster turnover prospects.

Renewed interest in hitherto neglected furs, particularly in the lower price ranges, afforded some measure of relief, although sales of inexpensive furs could not compensate for what was lost in big-ticket business. The inexpensive items, commonly referred to as fun furs or young furs, were directed chiefly to the younger market and to young-thinking matrons. They included rabbit, various types of lamb, raccoon, fox, calfskin, bobcat, bassarisk, and muskrat. In addition, furriers did well with assembled furs, crafted from paws, tails, and other discards and sewn together in interesting patterns.

Furs for men continued to make headway; the wall of resistance appeared to be crumbling as more and more men wore furs in public. Interestingly enough, another factor seemed to be the ready acceptance by men of synthetic textile coats that resembled fur.

The dullness that the trade experienced was mostly concentrated in mink, which normally accounted for more than two-thirds of U.S. fur sales volume. Fashion houses catering to wealthy clients enjoyed normal business for the year, but the rank and file—particularly those that concentrated on classic styling and ordinary quality—registered sharp declines. Mink skin prices, however, were higher in 1969 than the year before, with the exception of some of the lighter mutations. Taken as a whole, average prices of mink were up 9%. The explanation was that the skins were sold largely in the first half of the year, before the manufacturing and selling season started.

Prices of other furs also held steady or advanced. An important strengthening factor was the sustained European demand for virtually all species. Retail business was excellent in West Germany, Italy, Switzerland, the U.K., and Scandinavia, and the purchase of furs was steady. This also meant that the bulk of the European mink crop was consumed on that continent, with much less coming to the U.S. than in previous years. Imports of mink into the U.S. totaled about 3.3 million pelts for the seven-month importing season, compared with 4.1 million a year earlier. U.S. production amounted to about 5.5 million skins, more than one million below the preceding year. The number of mink ranches in the U.S. also declined, but figures at the end of the year were still incomplete.

Alaska seal prices reflected market demand more closely than mink, since the second of the semiannual auctions was conducted in a period when business was at its most difficult. Prices for black-dyed seals fell nearly 43%, the sharpest drop recorded, and the average price of blacks was $64.10, a 20-year low. Here, too, the pattern reflected the worldwide fur business picture. Blacks were used largely in the U.S. On the other hand, the colours, usually used in Europe, enjoyed somewhat better demand and showed smaller price declines.

Seal harvesting caused some furore in North America and Europe again in 1969. The methods used in killing the seals in the Pribilof Islands, as well as the whitecoat seals on Prince Edward Island, evoked complaints and demonstrations by humane societies and other groups. In October, Canada announced that it was forbidding the taking of baby seals in the Gulf of St. Lawrence and banning the use of clubs for killing the older pups.

Toward the year's end the leading segments of the U.S. industry, motivated by the poor season, banded together in an American Fur Trade Council to provide a body through which major problems could be processed and positions formulated. (S. Pa.)

See also Fashion and Dress.

Gabon

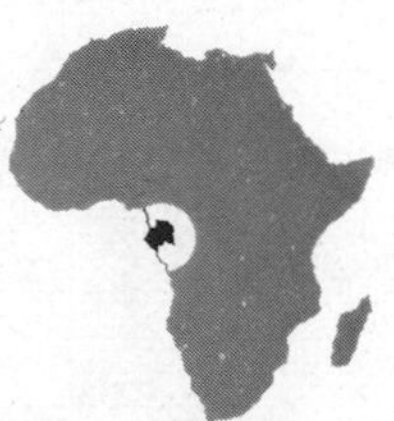

A republic of western equatorial Africa and a member of the French Community, Gabon is bounded by Río Muni, Cameroon, the Congo (Brazzaville), and the Atlantic Ocean. Area: 102,317 sq.mi. (265,000 sq.km.). Pop. (1969 est.): 480,000. Cap. and largest city: Libreville (pop., 1968, 53,000). Language: French and Bantu dialects. Religion: traditional tribal beliefs; Christian minority. President in 1969, Albert Bernard Bongo.

Following the February legislative elections, in which the Gabonese Democratic Party—the only one authorized—gained a practically unanimous majority, President Bongo executed a major administrative reshuffle. He criticized government officials for inefficiency and then issued a set of decrees providing for military intervention in the civil administration, naming three officers to ministerial posts. The decrees also reestablished President Bongo's direct control over all information media, which he had relinquished the previous year. In March an amnesty was granted

GABON

Education. (1967) Primary, pupils 81,125, teachers 2,314; secondary, pupils 5,203, teachers 336; vocational, pupils 1,504, teachers 92; teacher training (1966), students 418, teachers 27; higher, students 364 (students abroad 376).

Finance. Monetary unit: CFA franc, with a parity of CFA Fr. 50 to the French franc (CFA Fr. 277.71 = U.S. $1; CFA Fr. 666.50 = £1 sterling). Budget (1969 est.) balanced at CFA Fr. 13 billion.

Foreign Trade. (1968) Imports CFA Fr. 15,933,000,000; exports CFA Fr. 30,803,000,000. Import sources: France 57%; U.S. 10%; West Germany 8%. Export destinations: France 34%; U.S. 12%; Netherlands Antilles 12%; West Germany 9%. Main exports: crude oil 34%; timber 24%; manganese 21%; uranium 6%.

Transport and Communications. Roads (1968) 5,555 km. Motor vehicles in use (1968): passenger 5,230; commercial 4,490. Railways (1967) *c.* 570 km. Telephones (Jan. 1968) *c.* 4,100. Radio receivers (Dec. 1967) 50,000. Television receivers (Dec. 1964) 1,200.

Agriculture. Production (in 000; metric tons; 1967; 1966 in parentheses): corn *c.* 2 (*c.* 2); coffee *c.* 2.5 (*c.* 2.5); cocoa (1967–68) 4.5, (1966–67) 5.1; bananas *c.* 10 (*c.* 10); timber (cu.m.) *c.* 2,600 (*c.* 2,500). Livestock (in 000; 1966–67): cattle *c.* 4; pigs *c.* 6; sheep *c.* 45; goats *c.* 50.

Industry. Production (in 000; metric tons): crude oil (1968) 4,640; manganese ore (metal content; 1967) 586.

Furniture:
see Domestic Arts and Sciences

to political prisoners who had participated in the attempted coup d'etat of February 1964.

Every effort was made to speed up Gabon's economic development, with the cooperation of France. The latter agreed to financial participation in the construction of a railway planned to connect the iron deposits of the Mekambo region—the exploitation of which was seen as imminent—with the new deepwater port of Owendo. The French government also gave financial assistance for the building of the Kinguele Dam, which would provide Gabon with hydroelectric power. A CFA Fr. 200 million loan from the Central Fund of Economic Cooperation was made to help improve the electric power network.

Continuing his policy of active support for the Biafran secessionists, on his visit to Paris in July President Bongo was assured by French Pres. Georges Pompidou that French aid to Biafra would be maintained. The Gabonese were disquieted by events in Equatorial Guinea, where on March 5 a coup d'etat was attempted. The possibility of anarchy there raised the spectre of instability in the immediate vicinity of Gabon. (PH. D.)

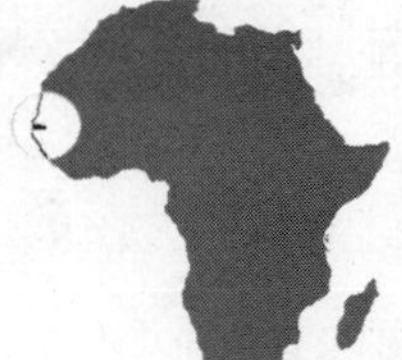

Gambia, The

A small independent parliamentary state and member of the Commonwealth of Nations, The Gambia extends from the Atlantic Ocean along the lower reaches of the Gambia River in West Africa, and is completely surrounded by Senegal. Area: 4,361 sq.mi. (11,295 sq.km.), including 358 sq.mi. of estuarine water. Pop. (1969 est.): 357,000, including (1963) Mandingoes 40.8%; Fulas 13.5%; Woloffs 12.9%; Jolas 6.9%; Sarahulis 6.8%; non-Africans 1.9%. Cap. and largest city: Bathurst (pop., 1967 est., 32,371). Language: English (official). Religion: predominantly Muslim. Queen, Elizabeth II; governor-general in 1969, Alhaji Sir Farimang Singhateh; prime minister, Sir Dawda Jawara.

In 1969 The Gambia's economy was again dependent upon the state of the world peanut market. Production of peanuts in 1968–69 rose by 3% to more than 120,000 tons in spite of poor rainfall.

The finance minister, S. M. Dibba, stated at the annual meeting of the International Monetary Fund and the World Bank in Washington, D.C., October 1968, that the terms of trade in The Gambia had deteriorated progressively during the last 15 years and that the bank had been asked for aid to develop Bathurst Port.

The U.S. government made a loan of $40,000 to the executive committee of the Senegalese-Gambia committee to provide for three U.S. experts to advise on communications between the two countries. President Léopold Senghor of Senegal visited Bathurst in February for the annual meeting of heads of government of the two nations provided for under the 1967 treaty of association.

There was considerable discussion on measures to prevent the extensive smuggling between the two countries, and a committee of experts was set up in April to study the problem. These meetings led to some demonstrations by youths during which stones were thrown at vehicles and at the Senegalese High Commission. Smuggling had become increasingly extensive and blatant. From Senegal smuggling consisted mainly of peanuts that came by truck or boat. This occurred because the Senegalese farmer preferred a cash payment on delivery to a promissory note from the government's agricultural buying organization, even if the latter's rate was higher. The main smuggling from The Gambia to Senegal was in consumer goods, principally cloth, British cigarettes, and transistor radios. Shops in The Gambia were described in the local press as being commonly full of "Senegalese officials and their wives making considerable purchases at prices and qualities they will never have in their republic."

The Gambia was again to consider adopting a republican constitution. There had been a referendum on the question in 1965, but only a small number of the electorate voted and the proposal was defeated by about 700 votes. Sir Dawda Jawara said in August that his government had prepared a draft constitution that would be laid before Parliament and when approved would be submitted to a referendum. On the day of acceptance a republic within the Commonwealth would be proclaimed, probably in April 1970.

(W. H. Is.)

THE GAMBIA

Education. (1967–68) Primary, pupils 15,386, teachers 460; secondary, pupils 5,178, teachers 145; vocational, pupils 162, teachers 14; teacher training, students 136, teachers 10.

Finance and Trade. Monetary unit: Gambian pound, at par with the pound sterling (Gam£1 = U.S. $2.40). Budget (1969–70 est.): revenue Gam£3,173,000; expenditure Gam£3,256,000. Foreign trade (1966–67): imports Gam£7,125,000; exports Gam£6,313,000. Import sources: U.K. 36%; Japan 19%; China 5%; Burma 5%. Export destinations: U.K. 61%; Portugal 21%; Italy 7%; Switzerland 6%. Main exports: peanut oil 37%; peanuts 36%; peanut meal 20%.

Gardening

Interest in the commercial and amenity aspects of gardening was reflected in the number and variety of international conferences held in 1969. Topics ranged from turf-grass research, the popularity of lilies, and the extension of hydroponics to legislation to protect plant breeders. The Euroflor international show held in Dortmund, W.Ger., had as its theme "European Spring." Among the less common plants, which seemed more numerous than at earlier shows, were bromeliads, cacti, aphelandras, and medinillas. The third Floralies exhibition was held in the new 70-ac. park at Bois de Vincennes in Paris. Exhibitions of different kinds that were organized from April to October helped to bring the crowds on repeated visits.

U.S. Department of Agriculture (USDA) reports indicated that air pollution, soil compaction, and salt in the soil, resulting from its heavy use as a road de-icer, had reduced the vitality of shade trees planted in cities—oaks, elms, maples, and planes (sycamores) —to the point where they have become very susceptible to attacks of insects and diseases. Two programs to develop better trees for cities were launched in 1969 by the National Arboretum in conjunction with the USDA Beltsville Research Center. To provide better trees for planting within 10 to 20 years, trees with attractive form, good growth rate, and tolerance of air pollution would be budded (grafted) onto rootstocks with proved tolerance of soil compaction, salt in the soil, and resistance to soil-borne pathogens. In the second, long-range program, a 150-ac. tract at the Beltsville centre was being planted with trees developed by commercial nurseries and research projects. The tract would serve as a major test garden and form the basis of a breeding arboretum for genetics research.

Studies done in the Blue Rock State Forest east of Colombus, O., demonstrated that air pollution was strangling the eastern white pine. Relatively low levels of pollution caused chlorotic dwarf disease, characterized by a sickly, mottled yellow colour and a much smaller size. It was established that sulfur dioxide, ozone, or an interacting mixture of both gases was responsible. Some white pines were known to be genetically resistant to the disease and it was hoped that the discovery of the cause would help in the development of more resistant trees.

Studies at the Florida Citrus Experiment Station resulted in a recommendation that dwarfed citrus trees be substituted for standards in orchards and gardens. Rootstocks that had a dwarfing effect on the scion had been used successfully in commercial plantings in other countries. Pennsylvania State University reported that fruit damage from birds continued to be serious in state orchards. Heavy losses in sweet and sour cherries, plums, and bush and bramble fruits were said to be due mostly to robins, starlings, blackbirds, and cowbirds. Blueberries caged against birds in a small experimental planting averaged 8.5 pints of fruit per plant while uncaged plants averaged less than 0.1 pint.

A rich deep pink hybrid tea rose, First Prize, was the All-America award winner for 1970. The underside of the petals was almost a light red while the upper side was pink, providing a bicolour effect. In the All-British Trials a silver award was given to Red Glow, a marigold entered by W. Atlee Burpee Co., and a bronze award went to Madame Butterfly, an antirrhinum entered by Goldsmith Seed Inc. Seven new vegetables were given 1969 All-America awards. Green Comet, an F_1 hybrid broccoli, received a gold medal and Stonehead, an F_1 hybrid cabbage, received a silver medal. Bronze medals went to Harvester Queen, an F_1 hybrid cabbage; Tokyo Cross, an F_1 hybrid turnip; Snow King, an F_1 hybrid cauliflower; St. Pat Scallop, an F_1 hybrid squash; and Kindred, a winter squash. Cherry Buttons, a buttons-type zinnia, received a silver medal in the 1969 All-America flower awards. Two F_1 cactus-type zinnias, Rosy Future and Torch, Polka Dot, a Vinca rosea, and Snow Ball, a dwarf cornflower, received bronze medals.

Propagating stock of several new plants developed and tested at the U.S. National Arboretum was released during 1969 to commercial nurseries that build up supplies for public sale; the plants included eight hybrid magnolias, four hybrid hollies, eight viburnums, four *Lagerstroemias* (crape myrtles), one pyracantha, and one *Hibiscus rosa-sinensis*. Two new apple varieties, Jonagold and Spijon, were released by the New York State Agricultural Experiment Station, Geneva. These had resulted from crosses made 24 and 25 years before and were selected because of their orchard behaviour, eating quality, and attractive colour after months in storage.

The State Fruit and Vegetable Research Station, Gembloux, Belg., released Manila, a cultivar of salad chicory (witloof) bred for quality, ease of forcing, and high yield potential. West Germany's Max-Planck-Institut released a mutant of the normal mushroom, 59C, which grows in a solid clump without stalk or gills. The Dutch were experimenting with deep freezing to obtain tulips year-round. Old

A.B.C., PARIS

Artificial lake with sculpture and fountain by Giacometti at the third Floralies Internationales at Bois de Vincennes, Paris, April–October 1969.

rhododendrons—some almost lost to cultivation—were returning to popularity in Britain. Mauves, whites, and flowers with a prominent blotch or "eye" tended to be more hardy than their modern relatives.

A new purple raspberry, Amethyst, was introduced by Iowa State University. It was a cross between Robertson and Cuthbert, and bore shiny berries that were sweeter than most red varieties but less sweet than black types. The Scottish Research Institute also released a new raspberry, Glen Cova, that was virus-free, ripened early, and cropped over a long period. A harvesting machine for raspberries developed in Canada vibrated mechanically bent raspberry canes to detach the mature fruit.

Beltsville scientists discovered that the amount of a group of water-soluble pigments known as anthocyanins within cells of day lilies determines whether the flower will be red, violet, or a combination of the two. When only limited amounts or no anthocyanins are present, day lily flowers are yellow or orange because the anthocyanins are masked by other pigments, predominantly yellow or orange carotenoids, the plastids of flower cells. Knowledge of the pigments responsible for day lily colour meant that redder and bluer flowers might soon be available to gardeners.

Cucumber sex expression was modified by foliar applications of Ethrel (2-chloroethane-phosphoric acid) in tests at North Carolina State University. As many as 19 continuous pistillate nodes were produced on monoecious cucumber plants. Studies at the Florida Agricultural Experiment Station showed that a holding solution of quinoline salts (8-hydroxyquinoline citrate) and sucrose could double the vase life and improve the quality of fresh-cut gladioli. The salts were believed to kill stem-clogging bacteria and allow the flower to absorb more water.

An eight-year experiment at Michigan State University indicated that productivity of fatigued land could be improved by deep plowing (20 in. deep). The practice had already been used to break up subsoil layers and improve soil texture with additions of clay and organic matter. Strips of aluminum foil spread on the ground more than doubled yields of vegetables and improved the quality of gladiolus flowers during tests at Beltsville. The foil reflected ultraviolet light from the sun causing flying insects, especially aphids, which often transmit virus diseases that reduce crop yields and which insecticides do not kill rapidly enough, to change their course.

Hollow ceramic rings were being employed at the University of Idaho to determine the location and amount of moisture absorption by potato roots. The rings were placed at different depths in the soil and moisture was supplied to the soil through the rings. By recording the amount of water used by each ring, water use could be determined at various levels in the soil throughout the life of the plant.

Research at several agricultural experiment stations determined that chemical antitranspirants were capable of reducing the transpiration rate when applied to plant foliage, usually as sprays of emulsions of wax, latex, or plastics that dry to form thin transparent films. Since stomata serve as portals for both the loss of water vapour and the intake of carbon dioxide, researchers were trying to determine whether an antitranspirant barrier might not also reduce plant growth. (J. G. S. M.; Tm. S.)

See also Agriculture; Biological Sciences; Zoos and Botanical Gardens.

ENCYCLOPÆDIA BRITANNICA FILMS. *Plant Through the Seasons (Apple Tree)* (1965); *Flowering Plants and Their Parts* (1966); *Green Plants and Sunlight* (1966); *Gardens for Everyone* (1967).

Geography

As the 1960s drew to a close, geographers could look back over a decade of rapid change within the profession. A solid foundation had been laid for further progress in the transition from mere description of the characteristics of areas to analysis of the dynamics and processes by which phenomena become spatially associated. Modern geographic research had gradually developed a frame of reference with two basic components and three subsystems. The basic components were spatial-structural and spatial-interaction elements. The subsystems were human, physical, and activity, with the third serving as the interface between the other two.

The U.S. Army Topographic Command's observation station on Heard Island in the south Indian Ocean. From March to November in severe weather the six-man team photographed the frequent passings of NASA's PAGEOS geodetic satellite to obtain data for greatly improved accuracy in future geographic positioning.

AUTHENTICATED NEWS INTERNATIONAL

This interface constituted a frontier for further geographic research in the 1970s, which was expected to concern itself with the construction and manipulation of models dealing with social organization, change, interaction, and policy. Perhaps the growing interest in social geography reflected the desire of younger people to become more involved in relating public policy to significant social issues, but the growing capacity for bulk data processing and the focusing of geographic research on dynamic processes had also helped to bring about marked changes in the discipline. Among the major new subjects of interest were systems of cities related to different theoretical constructs; public policy issues; and problems such as resources management, race relations, housing, poverty and hunger, transportation, environmental pollution, recovery from disasters, and urban and regional development.

Research into environmental perception and the interactions between man and his environment was being effectively stimulated by the increasing availability of masses of synoptic data gathered by a variety of remote sensing instruments in earth-orbiting satellites. Satellites developed experimentally by the National Aeronautics and Space Administration (NASA) had become operational in the fields of telecommunications and weather observation and were approaching operational status for geodetic measurements and earth resources observations. A large segment of the profession had become involved with the use of remote sensing instrumentation in high-flying aircraft and satellites to view broad areas synoptically, to obtain repetitive coverage that revealed time-lapse changes, and to gather data in otherwise inaccessible areas.

The Association of American Geographers created a Commission on Remote Sensing; the International Geographical Union converted its former Commission on Interpretation of Aerial Photographs to a Commission on Geographical Data Sensing and Processing; the Pan American Institute of Geography and History created a Committee on Remote Sensing and devoted a plenary session of its ninth General Assembly in June 1969 to that subject. An Advisory Committee on the Geographic Applications of Remote Sensing was created in the National Academy of Sciences, and geography departments in more than a score of universities were carrying out remote sensing experiments sponsored jointly by NASA and the Geographical Applications Program of the U.S. Geological Survey. They had been particularly successful in using infrared colour photography and its multispectral components, multilens camera clusters, electronic scanning devices, and radar for pattern recognition and enhancement that improved the validity of maps, graphs, and charts.

Land-use and urban studies completed in 1969 resulted in the production of a 14-category land use map at 1:1,000,000 of a 150,000-sq.mi. strip along the U.S.-Mexico border from California to central Texas, developed from Gemini and Apollo satellite photography, and of a housing and neighbourhood quality analysis of Phoenix, Ariz., and representative segments of metropolitan Los Angeles and Chicago, developed from aircraft imagery. The use of remote sensing techniques and data by geographers was being focused on the analysis of spatial patterns of city systems, urban growth, detection of change in urban functional areas, urban climatology, and interurban as well as regional planning for the improved management of resources in disaster-prone areas and of related transportation linkages and traffic flows.

The increasingly dynamic nature of modern geography had led to a threefold expansion of the profession in ten years. The principal U.S. organization, the Association of American Geographers, had more than 6,000 members in 1969, and the addition of eight member countries to the International Geographical Union (IGU) in 1968, bringing the total to 73, indicated the growing worldwide maturity of the profession. The theme of the 1969 annual meeting of the National Council for Geographic Education was "Geographic Learning for the Future." Employment opportunities for geographers with graduate degrees far exceeded the supply of adequately trained people, and the U.S. Office of Education and the National Science Foundation, in an effort to remedy this situation, were subsidizing special institutes, packaged lesson plans, mechanical aids, and new textbooks.

The plans of the IGU's Canadian organizing committee for the 22nd International Geographical Congress, to be held in Montreal in 1972, included symposia and technical sessions whose breadth of research would exceed even those of the 21st congress (New Delhi, India, 1968). The other international organization in the field of geography, the Pan American Institute of Geography and History, elected Arch C. Gerlach, chief geographer of the U.S. Geological Survey, as its president for 1969–73. (A. C. Ge.)

See also Antarctica; Arctic Regions.

Encyclopædia Britannica Films. *Maps for a Changing World* (1960); *The Earth in Change: The Earth's Crust* (1961); *The Language of Maps* (1964); *If You Could See the Earth* (1967).

Geology

Rocks from the Moon. A new dimension was added to the science of geology in 1969 with the return to earth by the Apollo 11 and Apollo 12 lunar missions of actual samples of material from the lunar surface. Detailed geologic mapping of the visible portions of the moon's surface had been progressing for many years using photographs from earth-based telescopes and from the moon-orbiting flights of the Apollo and Lunar Orbiter series. All of these maps, however, lacked one vital component—positive identification of the types of rock materials involved.

Thus the opportunity to examine, identify, and analyze actual lunar materials was sure to add immeasurably to man's understanding of the nature and origin of the moon and might also help in delineating the origin and early history of the earth as well.

The lunar surface at the Apollo 11 landing site in the Sea of Tranquillity was found to consist of unsorted fragmental debris that ranged in size from particles too fine to be resolved by the naked eye to blocks 0.8 m. in width. This debris forms a layer (somewhat analogous to the soil layer blanketing most of the earth's surface) that is porous and very weakly coherent at the surface. It apparently grades downward into similar but more densely packed material at a depth of about one metre.

Many small craters ranging in diameter from a few centimetres to several tens of metres with a depth of one metre or less dotted the surface in the vicinity of the landing site. All of these craters had rims, walls, and floors of relatively fine-grained material and had evidently been excavated entirely in the lunar soil layer.

WIDE WORLD

Aerial photograph of the Colorado River delta taken for a geologic survey by the U.S. Department of the Interior. The dark area at the bottom is the Gulf of California; the light areas are sand and other deposited material.

Rock fragments at the Apollo 11 landing site had a wide variety of shapes, but most were rounded to subrounded on their upper surfaces. This rounding suggested that one or more processes of erosion were active on the lunar surface. Differential erosion, in which resistant portions of the rock surface are left in raised relief by a general wearing away or ablation, was evident on some specimens. This ablation might have been caused primarily by small-particle bombardment of the surface. Some of the rocks had rounded surfaces produced by the peeling off of closely spaced exfoliation shells. There was no evidence of erosion by surface water.

Tiny deep pits, a fraction of a millimetre to about 2 mm. in diameter, occurred on the rounded surfaces of most rocks. Many of these pits were lined with glass. They clearly had been produced by a process acting on the exposed surface, presumably by the impact of small particles. In addition to glassy pits, thin glass crusts occurred that appeared to be the result of spattering.

Two major groups of rock types were identified in the material collected: crystalline rocks and breccias. The crystalline rocks were volcanic in the sense that they were once lavas or near-surface molten materials. There was, however, no proof that the molten condition was generated in the same fashion as that of terrestrial volcanoes. Fluid material might also have been formed by an impact mechanism as yet unstudied. Many phenomena were observed in the loose material and breccias that strongly suggested melting induced by strong and intense shock.

The major minerals identified could be assigned to known rock-forming mineral groups. Most abundant were the pyroxenes, followed by plagioclase, ilemenite, olivine, and, perhaps, native iron.

The crystalline rocks were dark gray in colour, and most were vesicular (containing small, spherical cavities). They most closely resembled terrestrial microgabbros or basalts. The breccias were mixtures of fragments of different rock types and were gray to dark gray in colour, with specks of white, light gray, and brownish-gray rock fragments. Most were fine grained with angular fragments smaller than 1 cm. in diameter. The fragments consisted of rocks, minerals, and glass.

Thus the fabric and mineralogy of the rocks of the

Garment Industry: *see* Fashion and Dress; Furs

Gas Industry: *see* Fuel and Power

Gastroenterology: *see* Medicine

Gemstones: *see* Mining

Genetics: *see* Medicine; Molecular Biology

Sea of Tranquillity divided them into two genetic groups: (1) fine- and medium-grained crystalline rocks of igneous origin, probably originally deposited as lava flows, but later dismembered and redeposited as impact debris, and (2) breccias of complex history. The absence of secondary hydrated minerals suggested that there has been no surface water in the landing region since the rocks were exposed.

Potassium-argon measurements on these igneous rocks showed that they crystallized three to four billion years ago. These dates were preliminary estimates, but there was a good chance that the time of crystallization of some of the rocks returned by Apollo 11 might be earlier than that of the oldest rocks so far found on earth. This raised new and exciting speculation as to the relation of the origin of the moon to the origin of the earth. (*See* ASTRONOMY.)

The presence of nuclides produced by cosmic rays showed that the rocks studied so far had been within one metre of the lunar surface for at least 100 to 150 million years. This indicated a high degree of stability in recent conditions on the moon.

The chemical composition of the lunar materials was significantly higher in titanium and zirconium than that of terrestrial materials; it was somewhat lower in alkali and volatile elements. No evidence of biological material was found in the samples.

The Apollo 12 astronauts landed in the Ocean of Storms in an area that appeared to be somewhat dustier than the Apollo 11's landing site. Preliminary analyses of the rocks returned indicated that they were similar to those of Apollo 11, although one was thought to have been formed far below the moon's surface and another was entirely covered with glass.

JOIDES Project. Meanwhile, earthbound geologists continued to probe the deep ocean floor in the search for additional data to support recent theories about the evolutionary history of the earth. The JOIDES (Joint Oceanographic Institutions for Deep Earth Sampling) Deep Sea Drilling Project was an outgrowth of the abortive Mohole project. Its primary operational objective was to recover samples of sediment and to make shallow penetration of igneous rocks beneath or within the sediments at many sites in the deep oceans.

A recently elucidated theory, widely in vogue in 1969, suggests that the most significant mechanism in the development of the gross features of the earth's surface is the phenomenon of sea-floor spreading. In this theory the mid-ocean ridge is the point where new earth crust is being formed. Materials extruded upward from the earth's mantle are cooled to form crust that then moves off across the ocean bottom somewhat like a vast conveyor belt before plunging downward back into the mantle in an oceanic trench. If such a process has indeed been operative in the geologic past, then the rocks of the ocean floor close to the Mid-Atlantic Ridge should be significantly younger than those found at some distance from the ridge.

Paleontologists developed techniques of determining the relative ages of deep-sea sediments from the kinds of calcareous fossils imbedded therein. Specific age checkpoints could be established in this time scale by the study of the decay of radioactive isotopes.

An additional aspect of this historical chronology was provided by studies of the remnant magnetism both in the sediments and in the basalts of the ocean floor. Although there was no adequate theory to explain its origin, it had been known for many years that the earth possesses a significant magnetic field. This field tends to influence the magnetic properties of certain sedimentary and volcanic rock types at the time of their formation. Studies of these rocks can then, in turn, reveal the nature of the magnetic field at the time of their formation. Paleomagnetic investigations of sedimentary and volcanic rocks both on land and in the ocean basins showed that there had been several complete reversals of the magnetic field in the geologic past.

The basalts that are formed on the mid-ocean ridges are among the best rock types for the retention of magnetism. As the crust moves slowly outward away from the ridges, these basalts carry their remnant magnetism with them much like a gigantic tape recorder.

It was the crucial nature of the relative ages of portions of the ocean floor to the theory of sea-floor spreading that influenced the decision to make the first leg of the Deep Sea Drilling Project a traverse across the North Atlantic Ocean in late 1968 and early 1969. Only the most preliminary results from this leg were known by the end of 1969, but it had become clear that the closer one came to the Mid-Atlantic Ridge the younger the layer of sediment just on top of the crust. This strongly supported the supposition that the ocean floor crust nearest the ridge had risen to the surface most recently. (L. H. No.)

See also Antarctica; Mining; Oceanography; Seismology; Speleology.

ENCYCLOPÆDIA BRITANNICA FILMS. *Geological Work of Ice* (1960); *The Earth in Change: The Earth's Crust* (1961); *Erosion—Leveling the Land* (1964); *Evidence for the Ice Age* (1964); *Rocks that Form on the Earth's Surface* (1964); *Waves on Water* (1964); *What Makes Clouds?* (1964); *What Makes the Wind Blow?* (1964); *Why Do We Still Have Mountains?* (1964); *The Beach—A River of Sand* (1965); *Rocks that Originate Underground* (1966); *How Solid Is Rock?* (1968); *Reflections on Time* (1969).

Germany

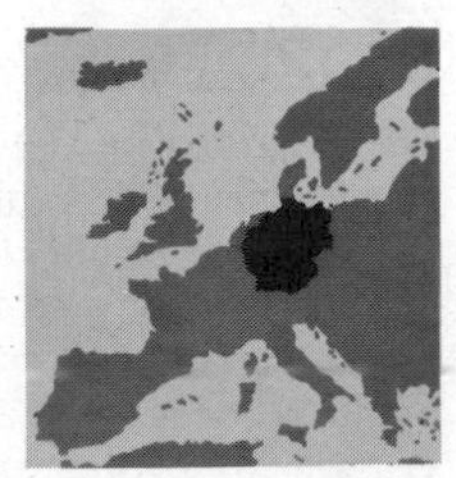

A country of central Europe, Germany was partitioned after World War II into the Federal Republic of Germany (Bundesrepublik Deutschland; West Germany) and the German Democratic Republic (Deutsche Demokratische Republik; East Germany), with a special provisional regime for Berlin. Germany is bordered by Denmark, the Netherlands, Belgium, Luxembourg, France, Switzerland, Austria, Czechoslovakia, and Poland and the North and Baltic seas.

Federal Republic of Germany. Area: 95,964 sq.mi. (248,548 sq.km.). Pop. (1969 est.): 60,463,000. Provisional cap.: Bonn (pop., 1969 est., 138,000). Largest city: Hamburg (pop., 1969 est., 1,822,800). (West Berlin, which is an enclave within East Germany, had a population of 2,141,400 in 1969.) Language: German. Religion: Protestant 50.6%; Roman Catholic 46.3%; Jewish 0.04%. President in 1969, Heinrich Lübke and, from July 1, Gustav Heinemann; chancellors, Kurt Georg Kiesinger and, from October 21, Willy Brandt.

The federal election on Sept. 28, 1969, resulted in the first real switch of political power in the 20-year history of the Federal Republic. For the first time the Social Democrats became the major force in the federal government, their chairman, Willy Brandt (*see* BIOGRAPHY), succeeding Kurt Georg Kiesinger in the chancellorship. Although the Christlich-Demokratische Union (Christian Democratic Union or CDU), with its branch in Bavaria, the Christlich-

German Literature: *see* Literature

Soziale Union (Christian Social Union or CSU), emerged once again from the federal election as the strongest party, it was pushed into opposition. The CDU/CSU polled 46.1% of the total votes (242 seats). The Sozialdemokratische Partei Deutschlands (Social Democratic Party of Germany or SPD), formerly in the "grand coalition" government with the Christian Democrats, polled 42.7% (224 seats). The third largest political party, the Freie Demokratische Partei (Free Democratic Party or FDP), polled only 5.8% (30 seats, a decrease of 19). The extreme right-wing Nationaldemokratische Partei Deutschlands (National Democratic Party of Germany or NPD) polled 4.3%, less than the minimum of 5% necessary for representation in the new parliament.

The chairman of the FDP, Walter Scheel (*see* BIOGRAPHY), who had taken his party on a leftish course, had been openly working for alliance with the SPD and this was undoubtedly the main reason why his party lost so much support. But although the Free Democrats were the losers, they were able to determine the shape of the next government, since neither of the two main parties was in a position to govern alone. The FDP rejected an offer from Kiesinger for a long-term partnership with the Christian Democrats, and instead quickly came to terms with the Social Democrats, promising to support Brandt's candidature for the chancellorship. To secure election as chancellor by the Bundestag, Brandt required at least 249 votes (an overall majority). This meant that at least 25 of the FDP's 30 deputies must vote for him. He was elected—on October 21—with a majority of three votes.

The new government, which had a majority of 12 in the Bundestag over the Christian Democrats, included three FDP ministers, Scheel (foreign), Hans-Dietrich Genscher (interior), and Josef Ertl (agriculture). For the SPD, Helmut Schmidt, formerly the party's parliamentary floor leader, became defense minister, Karl Schiller (*see* BIOGRAPHY) remained minister of economics, and Alex Möller succeeded Franz-Josef Strauss (*see* BIOGRAPHY) at the Finance Ministry.

This cooperation between the SPD and the FDP was a predictable consequence of the presidential election in West Berlin in March, when the Free Democratic members of the electoral college supported the SPD candidate, Gustav Heinemann (*see* BIOGRAPHY), the minister of justice. Heinemann was elected by six votes and became the first Social Democratic head of state since the founding of the Federal Republic. The choice of West Berlin for the election caused loud protests from the East Germans and the U.S.S.R., who claimed this was a violation of the city's four-power status, but the threatened crisis did not materialize.

In his government statement of policy to the Bundestag on October 28, Brandt admitted, through his chief spokesman, Conrad Ahlers, the existence of two German states within one German nation, but said that international recognition of the German Democratic Republic by Bonn was out of the question, since neither state could regard the other as a foreign country. He repeated an offer made by the previous government to negotiate with the East Germans about future cooperation, and agreed that this cooperation could if necessary be regulated by treaty. A positive East German response to this offer came on December 17.

The emphasis of Brandt's policy statement was on the need for domestic reform. The first action of the new government had been to revalue the Deutsche Mark. The Social Democratic members of the grand coalition government had been demanding this since May, but had not been able to overcome the opposition of the Christian Democrats and, more especially, of the finance minister, Strauss. Revaluation was a principal issue in the election campaign.

In June, the partners in the grand coalition reached a compromise on the question of the future prosecution of war criminals. They decided that the statute of limitations for genocide should be abolished, and the existing statute for murder be extended from 20 to 30 years. Originally, the statute of limitations was to apply from the end of 1969.

West Germany's efforts to prevent recognition of East Germany by countries of the uncommitted world received a severe setback during the year; six nations decided to take up diplomatic relations with East Berlin. In most cases there was nothing Bonn could do about it, as most of these countries had not had relations with West Germany since Bonn had recognized Israel in 1965. In the case of neutral Cambodia, however, the West German ambassador was withdrawn and relations were "frozen." This action represented a compromise by the coalition government that did not completely abandon the Hallstein Doctrine whereby West Germany declared it would break off diplomatic relations with countries that recognized East Germany.

In his government statement of policy, Chancellor Brandt said that West Germany was ready to have diplomatic relations and to increase trade links with any country in the world that shared its desire for peaceful cooperation. He emphasized that the government would continue to pursue the policy of its predecessor to improve relations with the U.S.S.R. and other Eastern European countries. He said the government would suggest a date for negotiations with the U.S.S.R. on exchanging nonaggression declarations, and would take up the offer of the Polish government to open talks on a treaty to establish the Oder-Neisse line as Poland's permanent border. Further, it would sign the nuclear nonproliferation treaty subject to the clarification of certain points.

The chancellor underlined his government's loyalty to the North Atlantic Alliance, but added that the

D.P.A. FROM PICTORIAL PARADE

Pres. Gustav Heinemann (left) and Chancellor Willy Brandt, leaders of the Social Democratic Party, which gained control of the government in 1969 for the first time in the 20-year history of the Federal Republic.

GERMANY: Federal Republic

Education. (1966–67) Primary, pupils 5,671,876, teachers 214,433; secondary, pupils 1,658,969, teachers 89,322; vocational, pupils 2,122,467, teachers 84,732; teacher training (1965–66), students 50,134, teachers 2,481; higher (including 36 universities), students 406,831.

Finance. Monetary unit: Deutsche Mark, with a par value (from Oct. 27, 1969) of DM. 3.66 to U.S. $1 (DM. 8.78 = £1 sterling). Gold and foreign exchange, central bank: (June 1969) U.S. $8,788,000,000; (June 1968) U.S. $7,283,000,000. Budget (1968 est.) balanced at DM. 80,657,000,000. Gross national product: (1968) DM. 528.8 billion; (1967) DM. 485.1 billion. Money supply: (April 1969) DM. 84.7 billion; (April 1968) DM. 77.2 billion. Cost of living (1963 = 100): (June 1969) 116; (June 1968) 113.

Foreign Trade. (1968) Imports DM. 80,660,000,000; exports DM. 99,420,000,000. Import sources: EEC 41% (France 12%, Netherlands 11%, Italy 10%, Belgium-Luxembourg 8%); U.S. 10%; U.K. 5%. Export destinations: EEC 38% (France 12%, Netherlands 10%, Italy 8%, Belgium-Luxembourg 7%); U.S. 10%; Switzerland 6%; U.K. 5%. Main exports: machinery 30%; motor vehicles 13%; chemicals 13%; iron and steel 7%.

Transport and Communications. Roads (1968) 405,015 km. (including 3,966 km. autobahns). Motor vehicles in use (1968): passenger 12,045,699; commercial 1,025,366. Railways: federal (1967) 30,007 km. (including 7,269 km. electrified); private (1966) 4,559 km.; traffic (1968) 34,301,000,000 passenger-km., freight 60,159,000,000 net ton-km. Air traffic (1968): 6,007,000,000 passenger-km.; freight 348,548,000 net ton-km. Navigable inland waterways in regular use (1967) 4,454 km.; freight traffic 45,785,000,000 ton-km. Shipping (1968): merchant vessels 100 gross tons and over 2,732; gross tonnage 6,527,946. Telephones (Dec. 1967) 10,321,281. Radio receivers (Dec. 1967) 27.8 million. Television receivers (Dec. 1967) 13,806,000.

Agriculture. Production (in 000; metric tons; 1968; 1967 in parentheses): wheat 6,198 (5,819); rye 3,186 (3,159); barley 4,974 (4,734); oats 2,893 (2,718); potatoes 19,196 (21,294); apples 1,570 (2,238); sugar, raw value (1968–69) 1,974, (1967–68) 2,058; wine 527 (563); milk 22,121 (21,710); butter 537 (518); cheese 437 (416); meat 3,370 (3,137); fish catch (1967) 661, (1966) 657. Livestock (in 000; Dec. 1967): cattle 13,979; pigs 19,022; sheep 811; horses used in agriculture 282; chickens 88,556.

Industry. Index of production (1963 = 100): (1968) 128; (1967) 114. Unemployment: (1968) 1.6%; (1967) 2.1%. Fuel and power (in 000; metric tons; 1968): coal 111,832; lignite 101,515; crude oil 7,982; coke (1967) 35,245; electricity (kw-hr.) 203,934,000; manufactured gas (cu.m.) 19,232,000. Production (in 000; metric tons; 1968): iron ore (32% metal content) 6,446; pig iron 30,523; crude steel 41,151; zinc 203; copper 433; lead 274; aluminum 490; cement 33,089; sulfuric acid 4,200; cotton yarn 254; woven cotton fabrics 186; wool yarn 79; rayon filament yarn 71; rayon staple fibre 191; nylon filament yarn 195; nylon fibre 167; nitrogenous fertilizers (1967–68) 1,559; potash (oxide content; 1967) 2,460; synthetic rubber 245; plastics and resins 3,250; passenger cars (units) 2,862; commercial vehicles (units) 240. Merchant vessels launched (100 gross tons and over; 1968) 1,346,000 gross tons. New dwelling units completed (1968) 519,000.

common interests of West Germany and the U.S. were strong enough "to allow for a more independent German policy within a more active partnership." As to Western Europe, he said the enlargement of the EEC was essential.

In November, in keeping with Brandt's policy declaration, Bonn signed but did not ratify the nuclear nonproliferation treaty. In what was apparently something of a defeat for Walter Ulbricht, the East German president, a meeting of Eastern European leaders held in Moscow in December agreed to speed up efforts to reach an understanding with the Federal Republic. A few days later formal talks on mutual renunciation of force and various other issues began in Moscow between Soviet Foreign Minister Andrei A. Gromyko and the West German ambassador to the U.S.S.R., Helmut Allardt. Moves looking toward rapprochement with Bonn were also made by Poland and Czechoslovakia.

In February, the visit of British Prime Minister Harold Wilson to Bonn and West Berlin coincided with a chorus of Communist protest and threats about the holding of the West German presidential election in West Berlin. Wilson supported the right of the West Germans to elect their head of state in West Berlin. A few days later, U.S. Pres. Richard M. Nixon was in West Berlin, and gave the firmest guarantee of its security heard for some years. (N. Cr.)

German citizens protesting U.S. involvement in Vietnam demonstrating at U.S. embassy in Bad Godesberg, W.Ger., Jan. 10, 1969.

ADN ZENTRALBILD FROM EASTFOTO

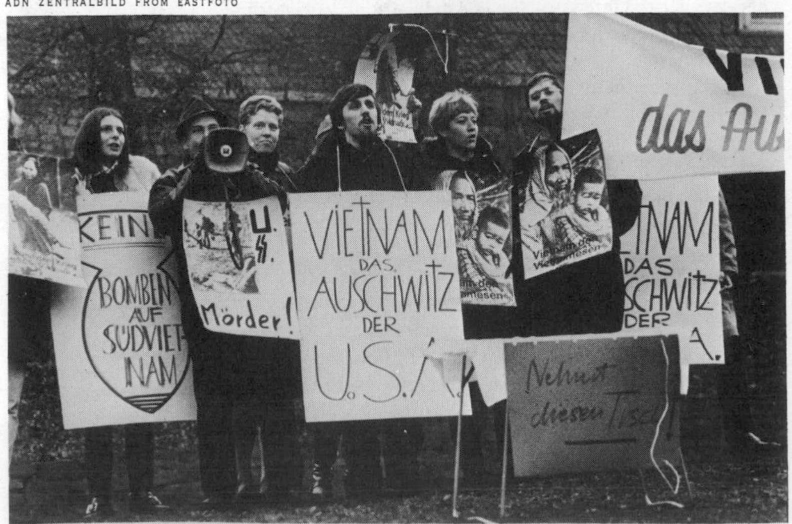

West Berlin. Because of the election of the president of the Federal Republic in the city on March 5, West Berlin was exposed to increased pressure by the German Democratic Republic supported by the U.S.S.R. Diplomatic protests to the Western powers and the Federal Republic denounced the election as a "planned provocation" and a "gross violation of international law." Hints were dropped that West Berliners might receive permits to visit East Berlin at or after Easter if the election did not take place in the city. Harassment began in earnest on February 8 with an East German decree barring overland access to the city to members of the Bundestag and of the armed forces. Joint East German–U.S.S.R. troop maneuvers were held in western and central areas of East Germany at the beginning of March and traffic on the autobahn to West Berlin was interrupted without warning on a number of days. On February 27, when pressure was at its highest, U.S. President Nixon, accompanied by Chancellor Kiesinger and Foreign Minister Brandt, visited the city. Nixon reaffirmed the U.S. guarantee to defend West Berlin.

The election of March 5 passed without incident, but delays to traffic continued throughout the summer, apparently to express disapproval of the city's involvement in the parliamentary election campaign in the Federal Republic. On September 11 Klaus Schütz, the city's governing mayor, was ordered off a train at the Marienborn checkpoint. To honour a long-standing invitation, the newly elected Chancellor Brandt paid a brief, informal visit to the city on October 31, ignoring an East German protest.

To maintain the demilitarized status of Berlin the three Western powers reaffirmed on August 8 that the West Berlin police were entitled to execute arrest warrants issued by West German courts. Thus they were able to deal with military deserters and draft dodgers in West Berlin.

Klaus Schütz was reelected chairman of the Berlin Social Democratic Party on June 1 and visited Warsaw on June 16. The three Western commandants forbade the NPD to hold a congress in the city on October 25.

A Polish LOT airline plane en route from Warsaw to Brussels via East Berlin was hijacked by two young East Germans on October 19 and forced to land at West Berlin's Tegel airport in the French sector. This was the first time a commercial airliner of a Communist country had been hijacked and also the first time an incident of this kind had occurred over Germany. The West Berlin police reported on August 10 that 4,293 East Germans had escaped to West Berlin during the eight years since the borders were sealed on Aug. 13, 1961, while 2,648 others were arrested by East German border guards while trying to escape.

German Democratic Republic. Area: 41,766 sq. mi. (108,174 sq.km.). Pop. (1969 est.): 17,084,101. Cap. and largest city: East Berlin (pop., 1969 est., 1,083,913). Language: German. Religion (1950): Protestant 81.3%; Roman Catholic 11%. First secretary of the Socialist Unity (Communist) Party (SED) and president in 1969, Walter Ulbricht; minister president (premier), Willi Stoph.

History was made when Willy Brandt, the Federal Republic's new chancellor, referred to the German Democratic Republic by its name in his policy statement to the Bundestag on October 28. Until then expressions like "the other part of Germany" had been the rule. There was no question of the Federal Republic being willing to recognize East Germany as a foreign country as understood in international law. But then Walter Ulbricht had ceased of late to demand such recognition. On October 6, at the ceremony in honour of the 20th anniversary of the East German state, he extended to the Federal Republic an offer of "good neighbourly relations on the basis of equality of rights and peaceful coexistence." But his address also contained the familiar demands on Bonn as well as a call for the dissolution of the NPD and the rooting-out of "neo-Nazis" from the administration and the armed forces of the Federal Republic.

The whole tone of Ulbricht's speech was significantly sharper than that of Leonid I. Brezhnev, general secretary of the Communist Party of the U.S.S.R., who was in East Berlin for the occasion. Though he did not disclose any softening of the Soviet position, Brezhnev when commenting on the parliamentary elections in the Federal Republic hailed the defeat of the NPD as "a clear-cut success for democratic forces in the Federal Republic." With talks between Bonn and Moscow going forward on the possible exchange of assurances of nonaggression, the East German attitude showed some signs of thawing when, in December, Berlin responded positively to Brandt's offer of negotiations.

All in all the 20th anniversary year saw some material progress in East Germany's quest for international recognition. When *Neues Deutschland*, the official party organ, reported on July 11 that the U.A.R. had recognized East Germany and agreed to exchange ambassadors, the number of non-Communist countries that had taken this step during the year had increased to six. Southern Yemen had done so on June 30, Sudan on June 27, Syria on June 5, Cambodia on May 8, and Iraq on April 30. The government of the Federal Republic announced on July 23 that the East German national anthem could be played, and the East German flag flown at international sports events in the Federal Republic, including the Olympic Games in Munich in 1972, but that the policy of nonrecognition of East Germany would stand.

D.P.A. FROM PICTORIAL PARADE

East German soldiers block traffic on the autobahn between West Berlin and Helmstedt, March 5, 1969. The blockade was a protest against West German presidential elections held in West Berlin.

The standard of living in the 20th year of the state's existence had risen markedly above prewar levels and was easily the highest in the entire Soviet bloc. The gross social product had increased five times since 1949 and was put at just short of MDN. 260 billion in 1969, compared with MDN. 243 billion in 1968. Average monthly earnings rose 2½ times in the same period.

A steady increase in military expenditure extending well into the 1970s was envisaged in an article on "The Economic Defense Effort of the G.D.R." in the August issue of the economic journal *Wirtschaftswissenschaft*. According to the 1969 economic plan and budget, East Germany spent MDN. 6,350,000,000 during the year on defense—about 8.6% of total state expenditure and an increase of 10% over 1968. The article stated that "it has been estimated that air defense costs alone in the 1970s will be ten times as high as in 1960 [when total defense expenditure was offi-

GERMANY: Democratic Republic

Education. (1966–67) Primary, pupils 2,301,-100, teachers (1963–64) 102,017; secondary, pupils 92,500, teachers 6,300; vocational, pupils 485,000; teacher training, students 14,500; vocational and teacher training, teachers 24,300; higher (including 7 universities), students 108,-656, teaching staff 14,200.

Finance. Monetary unit: "Mark of the German Bank of Issue" (Ostmark), with an official exchange rate of MDN. 2.22 to U.S. $1 (MDN. 5.33 = £1 sterling) and a general rate (Oct. 1969) of MDN. 4.20 to U.S. $1 (MDN. 10.01 = £1). Budget (1968): revenue MDN. 58.9 billion; expenditure MDN. 58.8 billion. Gross material product: (1967) MDN. 101.2 billion; (1966) MDN. 95.7 billion.

Foreign Trade. (1967) Imports MDN. 15,-059,000,000; exports MDN. 15,764,000,000. Import sources: U.S.S.R. 40%; Czechoslovakia 9%; West Germany 9%; Poland 5%. Export destinations: U.S.S.R. 38%; Czechoslovakia 8%; West Germany 8%; Poland 8%; Hungary 5%. Main exports: lignite; chemicals; machinery; transport equipment.

Transport and Communications. Roads (1967) *c.* 160,000 km. (including 46,832 km. main roads and 1,390 km. autobahns). Motor vehicles (1967): passenger 827,000; commercial (including buses) 330,800. Railways: (1967) 15,513 km. (including 1,191 km. electrified); traffic (1968) 16,800,000,000 passenger-km., freight 38,581,000,000 net ton-km. Navigable inland waterways in regular use (1966) 2,519 km.; freight traffic (1967) 2,576,000,000 ton-km. Shipping (1968): merchant vessels 100 gross tons and over 361; gross tonnage 806,074. Telephones (Dec. 1967) 1,780,319. Radio receivers (Dec. 1967) 5,874,000. Television receivers (Dec. 1967) 3,902,000.

Agriculture. Production (in 000; metric tons; 1967; 1966 in parentheses): wheat 2,012 (1,521); rye (1968) *c.* 1,950, (1967) 1,986; barley 1,927 (1,525); oats 845 (703); potatoes 14,065 (12,823); sugar, raw value (1968–69) *c.* 558, (1967–68) 554. Livestock (in 000; Dec. 1967): sheep 1,818; cattle 5,019; pigs 9,254; goats 236; horses used in agriculture 219; poultry (Dec. 1966) 37,070.

Industry. Index of production (1963 = 100): (1968) 136; (1967) 127. Production (in 000; metric tons; 1968): lignite 247,200; coal (1967) 1,787; petroleum products (1967) 5,450; manufactured gas (cu.m.) 4,113,000; electricity (kw-hr.) 63,228,000; iron ore (metal content; 1967) 407; pig iron 2,332; steel (ingots only) 4,373; copper ore (metal content; 1967) 19; potash (oxide content; 1967) 2,206; cement 7,550; sulfuric acid 1,078; nitrogenous fertilizers (1967) 336; superphosphates (1967) 168; synthetic rubber (1967) 110; passenger cars (units; 1967) 111; commercial vehicles (units; 1967) 22; cotton fabrics (sq.m.; 1967) 247,000.

D.P.A. FROM PICTORIAL PARADE

Berlin policeman struggles with youth in front of Hotel am Zoo on eve of the Federal Republic presidential elections of March 1969. Youths gathered to express disapproval of right-wing National Democratic Party of Germany.

cially stated to be a little more than MDN. 1 billion]. Costs for the Army, Navy, and Air Force will increase fourfold."

The Soviet and East German armies were to co-operate more closely on army education, under an agreement signed in East Berlin on January 29. On January 16 it had been reported that discussions on army youth education had also taken place between East German and Polish officials. These talks coincided with an intensified drive for paramilitary training for all young people in East Germany, ostensibly in honour of its 20th anniversary. On September 24 the People's Chamber unanimously approved the signing of the nuclear nonproliferation treaty.

The elections of the SED's executive, which began on March 1 with the first meetings of local party organizations and ended on June 8 with the final Regional Delegates' Conferences, brought few new faces to the fore. Gerald Götting, chairman of the Christian Democratic Union (CDU), was elected president of the People's Chamber on May 12 in the place of Johannes Dieckmann (*see* OBITUARIES).

The year saw the final split of the all-German Evangelical Church, though for several years past the churches of West and East Germany had been unable to meet jointly. On September 10 the Synod of the League of the Evangelical Church in East Germany held its inaugural conference in Potsdam-Hermannswerder. With the signing of the articles of the new League two months previously, the last ties with the Evangelical Church in the Federal Republic had been formally severed.

Colour television based on the French SECAM system began on October 3. To begin with, 4 hours out of a total weekly television output of 21 hours were transmitted in colour.

Trade between the U.S.S.R. and East Germany in 1970 was planned to total 3.3 billion rubles, 7% above the planned level for 1969, according to a protocol signed in East Berlin on October 2 at the conclusion of the visit by a Soviet delegation headed by Nikolai S. Patolichev, minister of foreign trade. In the first half of the year trade between West Germany and East Germany rose by 26% over the corresponding period of 1968. At this rate the Federal Republic was well on its way to replacing Czechoslovakia as East Germany's second most important trading partner.

(S. E. S.)

ENCYCLOPÆDIA BRITANNICA FILMS. *Germany—People of the Industrial West* (1957); *Berlin: Test for the West* (1962).

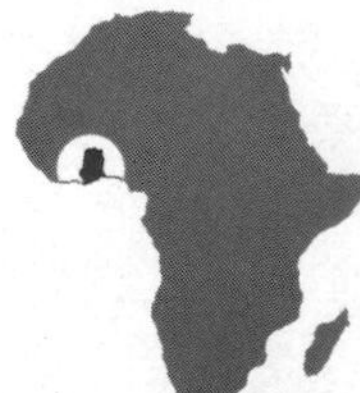

Ghana

A republic of West Africa, Ghana is on the Gulf of Guinea and is bordered by Ivory Coast, Upper Volta, and Togo. Area: 92,100 sq.mi. (238,539 sq.km.). Pop. (1968 est.): 8,376,000. Cap. and largest city: Accra (pop., 1968 est., 615,800). Language: English (official); local Sudanic dialects. Religion: traditional tribal beliefs; Christian and Muslim minorities. Chairmen of the National Liberation Council and of the Executive Council in 1969, Lieut. Gen. Joseph A. Ankrah and, from April 2 to September 30, Brig. Akwasi A. Afrifa (from September 30, the councils were replaced by a three-man Presidential Commission); prime minister from September 30, Kofi Busia.

The long discussions about a return to civilian rule in Ghana were interrupted on April 2, when Lieut. Gen. Joseph Ankrah resigned as chairman of the National Liberation Council and was replaced by 33-year-old Brig. Akwasi A. Afrifa, the commissioner of finance. Ankrah admitted complicity in a fund-raising campaign aimed at supporting his own candidacy for president and was alleged to have accepted money from foreign companies. The removal of a man who had been regarded as above politics and acceptable as a nonexecutive president removed also a centre of national stability. Afrifa, who had been one of the leaders of the 1966 coup that ousted Kwame Nkrumah, had done much as commissioner of finance to restore Ghana's credit and to control government spending. In a nationwide broadcast he declared that the National Liberation Council would continue its mission of eliminating corruption, restoring freedom and justice, returning Ghana to civilian rule, and rebuilding the economy. He announced that the lifting of the ban on political parties would still come into effect on May 1.

The danger from supporters of Kwame Nkrumah continued to be felt in Ghana, and in February the Amissah commission was set up to inquire into the involvement of Air Marshal Michael Otu with an alleged plot for the return of the exiled former president in December 1968, in which two Soviet trawlers detained by the Ghanaians were said to be concerned. Otu was exonerated in September. In January the price for Nkrumah's return to Ghana was raised to £50,000; although still officially co-president of Guinea, he remained virtually under house arrest there and was not encouraged to publicize his views.

There were signs that Guinea might recognize a Ghanaian civil government, a move that might lead to the return of Nkrumah. The final report of the commission headed by Justice Annie Jiagge on the assets of Nkrumah's Convention People's Party (CPP)

GHANA

Education. (1966–67) Primary, pupils 1,292,213, teachers 49,546; secondary, pupils 168,729, teachers 2,832; vocational, pupils 17,587, teachers 775; teacher training, students 16,158, teachers 1,106; higher (at 3 universities), students 4,478, teaching staff 723.

Finance. Monetary unit: new cedi, with a par value of 1.02 cedis to U.S. $1 (2.45 cedis = £1 sterling). Gold and foreign exchange, official: (June 1969) U.S. $109.5 million; (June 1968) U.S. $111.1 million. Budget (1969–70 est.): revenue 375,680,000 cedis; expenditure 302,680,000 cedis. Gross national product: (1967) 1,769,000,000 cedis; (1966) 1,779,000,000 cedis. Money supply: (April 1969) 239.8 million cedis; (April 1968) 222.2 million cedis. Cost of living: (Accra; 1963 = 100): (April 1969) 154; (April 1968) 146.

Foreign Trade. (1968) Imports 314,032,000 cedis; exports 338,782,000 cedis. Import sources: U.K. 28%; U.S. 19%; West Germany 11%; Japan 6%. Export destinations: U.K. 27%; U.S. 18%; Netherlands 11%; West Germany 10%; Japan 7%. Main exports: cocoa 55%; timber 8%; gold 8%; diamonds 5%.

Transport and Communications. Roads (1967) 31,000 km. Motor vehicles in use (1967): passenger 29,200; commercial (including buses) 18,800. Railways (1968): 1,271 km.; traffic 425 million passenger-km., freight 276 million net ton-km. Shipping (1968): merchant vessels 100 gross tons and over 57; gross tonnage 120,486. Telephones (Dec. 1967) 37,225. Radio receivers (Dec. 1966) 555,000. Television receivers (Dec. 1967) 5,000.

Agriculture. Production (in 000; metric tons; 1967; 1966 in parentheses): cassava 1,174 (1,171); sweet potatoes 909 (748); corn 282 (358); millet and sorghum 164 (176); rice 43 (30); peanuts *c.* 61 (*c.* 61); cocoa (exports; 1967–68) 421, (1966–67) 381; timber (cu.m.) 8,600 (7,200); fish catch 110 (79). Livestock (in 000; 1967–68): cattle 662; sheep (1966–67) 486; pigs 77; goats (1966–67) 412.

Industry. Production (in 000; 1967): gold 763 troy oz.; diamonds 2,537 metric carats; manganese ore (metal content) 239 metric tons; bauxite (1968) 284 metric tons; electricity (1968) 2,588,000 kw-hr.

further pinpointed the need to fight corruption.

Afrifa rapidly reorganized the Executive Council, replacing six ministers and creating a new Ministry of Rural Development, headed by I. M. Ofori of the University of Science and Technology, Kumasi. J. W. K. Harlley, chief of police and vice-chairman, retained his posts.

In January the 140-member Constituent Assembly met to discuss the drafting of a new constitution, in accordance with the report of the 1968 constitutional commission. The Assembly, charged with producing a constitution safeguarded against any reemergence of dictatorial rule, was indirectly elected by a number of national bodies, including the Bar Association, House of Chiefs, and the Trades Union Congress, and also had 14 members nominated by the government. The proposed constitution provided for a division of executive power between the prime minister and the president, who was to be indirectly elected, over the age of 50, and would serve for only one term of eight years. The president would be advised by a Council of State, and the Supreme Court was to be the final arbiter of the constitution. For the first three years, however, the constitution ruled that a three-man commission, composed of members of the National Liberation Council, would exercise the powers of president unless the National Assembly voted otherwise. August 29 was announced as election day to allow three weeks for the promised transfer to civilian government by September 30.

The government decree prohibiting former Nkrumah ministers from forming political parties was amended, and former finance minister Komla A. Gbedemah's National Alliance of Liberals presented the strongest challenge to Kofi Busia's Progress Party. The campaign was notable for the total absence of leftist language and a concentration on the personality of the party leader rather than on national issues. Under art. 71 of the new constitution Gbedemah was barred from holding office, as he had been found guilty of public misconduct by the Jiagge commission. The voting resulted in a landslide victory for the Progress Party and its leader, Kofi Busia (*see* BIOGRAPHY), with 105 of the 140 National Assembly seats going to Progress Party candidates. Voting also followed tribal lines with the Progress Party, dominated by the Ashantis, failing to win seats in Gbedemah's Ewe homeland. No Ewe was in the government.

The new government took office under the three-man presidential commission provided by the constitution. It included Afrifa, who resigned from the Army, Harlley, and Maj. Gen. A. K. Okran, chief of the Defense Staff.

Firm political victory did not ensure national stability. There were accusations of election rigging by the defeated National Alliance of Liberals, and tribal conflict took place in Yendi where 19 people were killed in rioting over the choice of a new Dagomba chief.

The budget presented in July revealed a rise in the gross national product of only 1.7% in 1968, while the cost of living had increased by 8%. Unemployment remained one of the most intractable problems. J. H. Mensah, appointed finance commissioner in the National Liberation Council reshuffle in April, became minister of finance and economic affairs in the new government. He emphasized the need for improving agricultural productivity and export performance, and announced measures to encourage agriculture, forestry, fishing, industry, and exports. Whatever benefit Ghana might gain from favourable trends in the cocoa market, the burden of its international debt remained heavy. The new government began discussions with major creditors aimed at refinancing the total debt. (M. MR.)

Golf

The golfing year of 1969 was notable for the fine showing of British players in competition with those of the United States. Tony Jacklin (*see* BIOGRAPHY) became the first British golfer to win the British Open since 1951 when he beat a powerful overseas field, including most of the leading U.S. players, at Royal Lytham St. Annes. The Ryder Cup match at Royal Birkdale ended in a tie, and a young British team came within a sight of victory in the Walker Cup match at Milwaukee, Wis.

In the United States the Open, Masters, and Professional Golfers' Association (PGA) championships produced new winners in Orville Moody, George Archer, and Raymond Floyd; this followed the trend of a year in which many young golfers gained their first success in professional tour events. In Britain Bernard Gallacher won two tournaments and was second in four others, a performance without precedent for a golfer of 20. For only the second time since 1959, Arnold Palmer, Gary Player, and Jack Nicklaus failed to win one of the three major U.S. championships. Only Player, runner-up in the PGA, came close. Throughout the 1960s these three, with Billy Casper, had dominated the money-winning lists. At the end of the season Frank Beard was the leading money winner with $175,223.

WIDE WORLD

Orville Moody holes out on the 18th green to win the U.S. Open championship at the Champions Golf Club in Houston, Tex., June 15, 1969.

Probably the outstanding individual performance was that of Jacklin. Soon after his 25th birthday he took the lead in the third round of the British Open, two strokes ahead of Bob Charles and Christy O'Connor. Nicklaus, five strokes behind, was the nearest American. On the last day Jacklin survived a severe test of his skill and nerve to win by two strokes from Charles. It was the first time since 1937 that a British player had beaten a fully representative world field.

In September Jacklin played a commanding part for Britain in the Ryder Cup. He won four and halved two of his six matches, the finest record in the match. The contest was one of the most remarkable in Ryder Cup history. Britain, inspired by the golf of Jacklin and Peter Townsend, took a 4–3 lead in the two-ball foursomes on the first day; the United States drew level after the four-ball matches, and at this point no fewer than 12 of the 16 games had reached the last green. The climax on the last afternoon was straight from fiction as Jacklin and Nicklaus stood all square on the 18th tee in the final match. Jacklin had defeated Nicklaus easily in the morning and now the countries were even; thus, the Ryder Cup depended on these two—win, lose, or draw. Both played the last hole perfectly and a tie was achieved. An hour before, a U.S. victory had seemed certain, but Gallacher had won five holes out of seven and beaten Lee Trevino; Brian Huggett halved his match after being one down and three to play against Casper; and Jacklin holed a putt of 18 yd. on the 17th to square his game with Nicklaus. Such courage and resolution in finishing by British golfers had been extremely rare on these occasions. The result was particularly encouraging for the future of the Ryder Cup because the U.S. had won 12 of

Gerontology: *see* Medicine; Social Services
Gibraltar: *see* Dependent States
Glass Manufacture: *see* Industrial Review
Gold: *see* Mining; Payments and Reserves, International

"VANCOUVER SUN"

Winner Bob Cox blasts out of a sand trap at the 16th hole in the final round of the Canadian Professional Golfers' Association championship, Aug. 10, 1969.

the previous 13 encounters, and consequently U.S. public interest in the match had seemed to be declining.

Few gave the British much chance in the Walker Cup tournament for amateur players in Milwaukee. The United States led by 4 points after the first day, but, led by Michael Bonallack, the British rallied to within a fraction of victory. Wonderful recovery shots by Allen Miller of the U.S. on the 17th and 18th enabled him to beat Michael King, when he was in danger of losing; while Bruce Critchley and Tom Craddock of the U.K. failed to win their matches after leading until the last holes. This all happened within half an hour, and the U.S. scrambled home by 10–8, with six matches halved. It was, nonetheless, a fine effort by a young British team of which only Bonallack and Rodney Foster had played in the tied match at Baltimore four years previously. Bonallack had retained the British amateur title at Hoylake, defeating U.S. players Dale Morey, in the quarter finals, and William Hyndman by 3 and 2 in the final. The British were unable to make a strong challenge in the

Tony Jacklin grimaces at shot during practice round for the British Open, which he won in July 1969 at Royal Lytham St. Annes.

CENTRAL PRESS FROM PICTORIAL PARADE

United States amateur championship at Oakmont, Pa., in which Steve Melnyk, an outstanding collegiate golfer, gained a commanding victory by five strokes. Marvin Giles was second for the third year in succession.

Each of the major U.S. championships produced stirring finishes. At Augusta, Ga., Archer, the tallest of first-class golfers, prevailed in the Masters after a desperate struggle with five others and finished one stroke ahead of Casper, George Knudson of Canada, and Tom Weiskopf. In the Open at Houston, Tex., Moody likewise resisted a close pursuit, winning by a single stroke from Deane Beman, Al Geiberger, and Bob Rosburg. This was Moody's first victory since turning professional after a career in the Army, but he proved his quality by winning the World Series of Golf at Akron, O., and by helping Lee Trevino to regain the World Cup for the United States in Singapore. Trevino showed wonderful resilience in winning the World Cup individual title, because one week earlier he had suffered one of the most startling collapses in history. In the Alcan Golfer of the Year Tournament at Portland, Ore., he led by six strokes with three holes to play only to lose by one stroke to Casper, who finished with four straight birdies. Failure cost Trevino $40,000, the difference between first and second prize.

For the first time, an important golf occasion was the scene of political demonstrations. On the third day of the PGA championship at Dayton, O., Nicklaus and Player, competing together, suffered considerable interference. Objects were thrown onto greens and tees, including ice from a drink container into Player's face, and a group of demonstrators rushed onto the 10th green. Both golfers behaved with dignity and restraint, and no one was hurt, but conceivably the interruptions cost Player the title. He finished second, a stroke behind Floyd, who played with fine composure in gaining his first major success.

In women's golf Catherine Lacoste of France, the U.S. Open champion in 1967, won the amateur championships of Britain, France, and the U.S. In winning the U.S. title at Irving, Tex., she beat Ann Welts, a three-time champion, and in the final Shelly Hamlin. Miss Lacoste, who clearly had no superior in modern women's golf, later announced that she probably would not defend these titles. Carol Mann and Kathy Whitworth were the most consistent winners on the U.S. professional tour.

During the year it was agreed by the Royal and Ancient Golf Club of St. Andrews and the United States Golf Association that the new continuous putting rule in which a player putts until he holes out would cease to operate from Jan. 1, 1970.

(P. A. W.-T.)

Government Finance

By the end of the 1960s, government finance could no longer be regarded simply as the problem of raising state revenues through taxes or borrowing to finance public expenditures. This traditional "revenue raising" focus had given way to a more sophisticated understanding of the responsibilities of government financial managers. Increasingly, at least for central governments of sovereign states, public finance had become the task of selecting tax, expenditure, and borrowing measures that: (1) provided a desired allocation of national resources between private wants and wants that could be satisfied only through collective action; (2) helped keep the national economy on a stable growth path, avoiding both inflation and unemployment; (3) achieved a more desirable distribution of after-tax income between the various income and social groups in the society than would flow automatically from completely market-oriented production; and (4) generated appropriate incentives or disincentives to private behaviour from the viewpoint of influencing the economy's rate of growth and balance of international payments.

Most of these policies, but especially those concerned with economic stabilization, led to almost continuous review and adjustment of budget and financial policies by national governments, and 1969 was no exception in this respect. Because of the importance of the stabilization function, a review of fiscal developments can be understood only in the context of the price and employment trends in the national economy being reacted to by the fiscal authorities. Moreover, because economic stabilization is a dual responsibility of fiscal policy (*i.e.*, changes in taxes and expenditures) and monetary policy (*i.e.*, credit and interest rate policies by the central bank), government budget policies bear an intimate relation to government monetary policies. (*See* ECONOMY, WORLD: MONEY AND BANKING.)

The United States. The war in Vietnam continued in 1969, as in the four preceding years, to play an important role in U.S. economic developments and in the federal budget. The budget transmitted to Congress by the Johnson administration in January 1969 estimated that military activities in Southeast Asia would require $29 billion, or 16% of the budget, in fiscal 1969 and $25 billion, or 13%, in the 12 months ending June 30, 1970. By 1969, however, defense outlays for Vietnam were no longer rising at the rapid rate of previous years, and a war-related 10% income tax surcharge enacted by Congress in mid-1968 (a year later than initially requested by the president) had begun to take hold in offsetting the expansionary economic impact of the federal budget. Under the combined influences of the surtax, an increase in social security payroll taxes on Jan. 1, 1969, revenue growth under existing taxes, and a hold-down of expenditure growth required by the Congress as a condition for enacting the surtax, the federal budget in the fiscal year ended June 30, 1969, showed a small surplus, as against a massive $25 billion deficit in the previous year. (*See* Table.)

As a result, the federal government switched from being a large borrower of funds from the capital markets in 1968 to being a net supplier, and the publicly held public debt, which had risen $23 billion in fiscal 1968, declined. The surtax, which was initially designed to apply to corporate income for all of 1968 and the first half of 1969, and to personal income from April 1968 through June 30, 1969, took the form of a 10% add-on to income tax liability under regular income taxes for these periods. The increase in social security taxes at the beginning of 1969 (under legislation enacted previously) stepped up the combined employer-employee tax rate from 8.8% of covered payrolls to 9.6%. Meanwhile, monetary policy, which had remained relatively accommodating toward demands for credit during 1968, became sharply restrictive, driving up interest rates and forcing postponement of credit-financed private outlays, particularly new housing. Thus, under the combined impact of budget surpluses and tight money, the economy, which had become quite overheated in 1968, slowed perceptibly during 1969, although without as much relief from inflationary pressures as had been hoped for from these policies.

When the Nixon administration took office in January, the 10% surtax on corporation and individual income taxes was due to expire June 30, and the 7% automobile excise tax and 10% telephone service excise tax were both due to drop to a 5% rate effective Jan. 1, 1970. The Johnson administration had proposed extending all of these tax rates for one additional year on the ground that continuing inflationary pressures would require retention of these fiscal restraints. Outgoing Treasury Secretary Joseph Barr also entered a strong plea for Congress to reform federal income taxes to make them more equitable, pointing out that existing tax loopholes enabled many wealthy individuals to be taxed very lightly or to escape taxes altogether.

In April the Nixon administration issued its review of the budget for fiscal 1970 that had been transmitted in January by Pres. Lyndon Johnson, and promised $4 billion lower expenditures than the earlier estimates, in spite of increased costs for some items. The new administration also expressed its agreement with the need for continuing fiscal restraint. However, instead of recommending extension of the surtaxes at the 10% rate for a full year, it proposed dropping the rates to 5% after six months (*i.e.*, on Jan. 1, 1970) and making up the balance by ending the 7% income tax credit for business investment that had been a controversial feature of the tax code since 1962. The investment credit, which provided a reduction in income tax liability for up to 7% of the cost of new business equipment, had been inaugurated at the request of the Kennedy administration as a means of spurring private investment and the rate of economic growth. The Nixon administration felt that this incentive, which served to reduce income tax payments by about $3 billion per year, was not a particularly high priority use of public funds.

Congress at first responded by extending the surtax for six months only, through the end of 1969, making it clear that any further extension would be considered only in conjunction with far-reaching tax reform. It also clamped a tight ceiling on federal expenditures, the second year in a row in which this device had been used by Congress in an attempt to curtail expenditures by more restrictive means than were already imposed through the regular annual appropriations process. In September the administration presented its revised budget estimates for fiscal 1970. Pointing out that uncontrollable increases for a number of civilian programs threatened the narrow

The Budget of the U.S. Government*

In $000,000,000

Item	Fiscal year ending June 30, 1968 (actual)	1969† (actual)	1970‡ (est.)
Receipts	153.7	187.8	198.8
Outlays			
National defense	80.5	81.3	77.4
Other	98.3	103.5	115.5
Total	178.8	184.8	192.9
Surplus (+) or deficit (−)	− 25.2	+ 3.1	+ 5.9
Gross federal debt held by public (end of period)	290.6	279.5	—

*Detail may not add to totals due to rounding.
†Subject to minor revision in final accounting.
‡Official estimates as of Sept. 17, 1969.
Source: U.S. Bureau of the Budget.

BEN ROTH AGENCY

"The talks are going on. . . ."—Behrendt, "Het Parool," Amsterdam.

estimated surplus, while inflationary pressures in the economy continued to call for a restrictive fiscal policy, the administration announced a further $3 billion cut in military outlays and a $500 million cut in civilian outlays below earlier estimates, on top of the $4 billion cuts announced in April. The revised budget for fiscal 1970 would still allow a $12 billion year-to-year increase in nondefense federal outlays and a budget surplus of $5.9 billion. Major increases over the fiscal 1969 amounts would include $3 billion for employee pay raises; $4.5 billion for the Department of Health, Education, and Welfare; $1.5 billion in interest on the public debt resulting from higher interest rates; and $1.1 billion for programs of the Department of Housing and Urban Development. A little later, the administration announced a work slowdown on 75% of federally financed construction projects, as a further step to try to cool off the still strong inflationary pressures. The estimated budget surplus for fiscal 1970, however, was contingent on the enactment of still pending tax legislation.

The House Ways and Means Committee, under the chairmanship of Wilbur Mills (Dem., Ark.), worked intensively on tax reform for much of the year, and by the end of the summer the House had passed a bill that promised the most thoroughgoing overhaul of the federal income tax structure since 1954. The Senate Finance Committee subsequently diluted some of the House-passed reforms and other changes were made on the Senate floor, but the completed bill, as ironed out in conference committee, was finally passed in late December. The president signed it on December 30, despite some reservations. The law contained the concept of a minimum tax, designed to prevent individuals and corporations from escaping taxation completely; a flat-rate 10% tax was to be applied to income over $30,000 from various sources that had been given preferential treatment under existing legislation. However, income on interest from state and municipal bonds remained tax-exempt. Capital gains (*i.e.*, income from sale of capital assets), long taxed at rates well below those for ordinary income, would be taxed at slightly higher (though still favourable) rates. The 27½% "depletion allowance" write-off for oil and gas producers was trimmed back to 22%. Rules for tax-exempt foundations were tightened, and such foundations were to be subject to an excise tax amounting to 4% of their income. Rules for averaging irregular income for tax purposes were liberalized. The personal exemption was to be raised in stages to $750 in 1973 (from $600) and, over the same period, the standard deduction would be raised to 15% of income or $2,000, whichever was lower (from 10% or $1,000). Provision was made to give tax relief to low-income taxpayers, single persons, and persons with high earned income.

In addition to these reforms of the basic tax structure, social security payments were raised 15% effective Jan. 1, 1970; the anti-inflation surtax was extended to June 30, 1970, at a 5% rate; the 7% investment tax credit was terminated retroactive to April 1969; and automobile and telephone excises were kept at their existing rates of 7 and 10%, respectively, for an additional year beyond Jan. 1, 1970.

Congress also acted in 1969 to extend once again the "temporary" interest equalization tax (IET). The IET, which levies a tax on foreign debt issues sold in the U.S., had been initiated in July 1963 as a device to improve the U.S. balance of payments following a year in which there had been heavy capital outflows as a result of the purchase of foreign securities by U.S. investors. This tax was initially justified on the ground that lower interest rates in the U.S. than abroad and a superior organization of U.S. capital markets, making borrowing easier there, should not be allowed to cause such large capital outflows at a time of balance of payments difficulties. Later, the interest rate differentials between the U.S. and other countries narrowed, and foreign capital markets developed more fully, but the IET had had a substantial favourable balance of payments effect which the U.S. was reluctant to abandon.

Another interesting issue that arose in 1969 was the proposal to shift the federal fiscal year from its July 1–June 30 dating to coincide with the calendar year. Currently, the budget transmitted in January of each year covered the fiscal year starting six months later. With the increase in the size and complexity of the budget over the years, Congress had been taking longer and longer to act on appropriation requests —to the point where few federal agencies were likely to receive their appropriations by the start of the fiscal year and many did not receive their appropriations until the fiscal year was three, four, or even five months old. Making the fiscal year coterminous with the calendar year would give Congress longer to act on appropriations before the fiscal year began.

While considerable effort was devoted in 1969 to finding ways to reduce future federal income tax rates, state and local governments in the U.S. continued to raise tax rates at a very rapid clip. At the local level, this meant primarily increases in property taxes, and at the state level, a broad range of taxes, especially sales and income taxes. As of Oct. 31, 1969, 34 state legislatures had imposed new taxes or increased rates on existing taxes during the year in 75 major tax actions, worth $2.8 billion or 7% of existing revenues. Legislation pending in several other states would raise the year's total to a record $3.7 billion. These developments followed two years of rapid increases in state tax collections associated with economic growth, inflation, and statutory actions, which, combined, had lifted revenues by about one-third between fiscal 1967 and fiscal 1969. Illinois and Maine joined the ranks of states levying personal and corporate income taxes, and the state of Washington tentatively planned to follow suit subject to voter approval in

1970. If the Washington tax was approved, it would bring the number of states levying broad-based personal income taxes to 38 and the number with corporate income taxes to 44. Also in 1969, Vermont became the 45th state to impose a general sales tax.

There was increasing concern in 1969 over the fiscal imbalance between the various levels of government in the U.S., with the federal government having the best revenue sources from the standpoint of automatic revenue response to economic growth and inflation, while state and local governments faced the most rapidly growing demands for new and expanded public services. In particular, the fiscal plight of the large cities, with stagnant tax bases and mushrooming demands for services, became increasingly evident.

One approach toward redressing this fiscal imbalance that had been under discussion for several years was federal revenue sharing; *i.e.*, turning over to states and/or localities a portion of revenues collected under federal income taxes. Revenue sharing received a new impetus in 1969 when the Nixon administration proposed a scheme under which, eventually, 1% of federal personal taxable income (about 5% of federal revenue from personal taxes) would be turned over to state and local governments with rather minimal restrictions on their use. It was expected that the budget to be transmitted by the president in January 1970 would propose an initial start on revenue sharing during fiscal 1971, but it was far from obvious that Congress would agree to such a proposal. Critics of revenue sharing pointed to the remaining large capacity of the federal government to assist states and localities through grants-in-aid for specific expenditure categories, and many felt that the larger measure of federal control implicit in the categorical grant approach was preferable.

With market rates of interest on outstanding government bonds exceeding 6% for most of 1969, the legal interest rate ceiling of $4\frac{1}{4}$% which the U.S. Treasury was authorized to offer on new bonds of longer than seven years' maturity operated effectively to prevent any new long-term debt issues. It had been several years since the government had been able to borrow any significant volume of long-term funds, and the administration finally asked Congress to remove the ceiling altogether. This Congress refused to do, but the House did pass a bill to raise the ceiling on savings-type bonds, purchased by individuals in relatively small amounts, to 5%. In the prevailing tight money and high interest rate conditions of 1969, redemptions of previously issued Treasury savings bonds were running well ahead of new sales.

France. Budgetary actions in France in 1969 were heavily influenced by balance of payments considerations and international speculation against the franc. The civil disturbances in the spring of 1968 had left an aftermath of wage and price increases that threatened the competitive position of French exports, particularly by comparison with West Germany where costs and prices were more stable. Rumours that there would have to be either a devaluation of the franc or an upward revaluation of the West German mark touched off severe currency speculation in November 1968, requiring both countries to make certain policy adjustments as an alternative to altering their exchange rates. In the case of France, planned expenditures for 1969 were cut back from the amounts set forth in the initial budget of October 1968, in which higher wages for civil servants had promised a substantial year-to-year rise. Subsidies for public enterprises were reduced, and a 3% across-the-board cut in the spending of individual ministries other than education was ordered. There was also some cutback in planned military expenditures and in selected government investment projects.

On the tax side, payroll taxes on employers were abolished, while rates on value-added taxes (VAT), really a broad-based sales tax, were increased from a range of 6–20% to 7–25%. This shift in tax burdens from enterprises to households was designed to encourage exports and discourage imports, since import prices would be affected by the higher VAT rates but not by lower payroll tax rates. In December the timing of collections of 1969 income taxes was altered to reduce payments by higher income groups during the first half of the year. As a result of the combined tax and expenditure actions, the forecast 1969 overall budget deficit, including financial transactions, was trimmed from the Fr. 11.7 billion level estimated in October to Fr. 6.4 billion.

Meanwhile, monetary policy was tightened sharply, and foreign exchange controls were reintroduced. Under the combined effects of fiscal and monetary restraint, demand abated somewhat in the first half of 1969. Wage and price rises were still high, however, and the balance of payments remained under pressure from mounting imports and speculative outflows of capital. Plans to cut expenditures in the second half of the year were announced by Finance Minister Valéry Giscard d'Estaing, with the saved funds to be placed in a new countercyclical reserve to be released later if the economy slowed down.

In August the franc was devalued, and new budgetary measures were announced to try to keep the resulting higher import prices from working through to increased domestic costs and prices. Corporate tax payments would be speeded up, depreciation rules for tax purposes tightened, and cutbacks in government spending on agriculture, roads, and bridges put into effect, with the result that the planned budget deficit would be wiped out altogether. Further increases in consumer taxes were resisted, however, on the ground that they might accelerate wage demands and therefore accomplish little in combating inflation. Longer-term measures looked toward creation of an industrial reorganization bank, modernization of the nationalized industries, increasing research and development outlays, and a reduced bureaucracy.

West Germany. In recent years the West German authorities had finally been converted to the modern fiscal policy approach of gearing tax and budget decisions to economic stabilization goals. An attempt to pursue this approach in 1969, however, ran into the difficulty that domestic stabilization and balance of payments objectives posed contradictory requirements.

The West German economy expanded strongly in 1968 and 1969, led by a strong growth of exports that threatened to disrupt the country's record of relatively stable costs and prices. It was clear both to the authorities and to West Germany's trading partners that some reduction of the German export surplus would be beneficial to all concerned. An up-valuation of the mark would work in this direction, and there was considerable speculation during 1968 and most of 1969 that such a revaluation would be undertaken. In the November 1968 currency crisis, the West German authorities avoided revaluing the mark and instead instituted a system of border taxes that increased export prices and reduced import prices by 4%. Coupled with cooperative measures by the French authorities, this temporarily stilled exchange rate speculation. A program was subsequently worked out to apply part of the revenue proceeds of these border taxes toward strengthening those sectors of the economy most affected by this quasi-revaluation.

In the initial budget for 1969, higher wages and salaries and increased defense outlays promised a much faster rate of rise in government spending than in the preceding year. The government also reduced the federal share of income tax receipts from 37 to 35% on condition that the Länder (state) governments pass on one half of the DM. 1 billion involved to the local communes. When inflationary pressures began to increase in the first half of the year, however, cuts in federal expenditure plans amounting to DM. 1.8 billion were announced, and the official economic advisers filed a report recommending that either the mark be revalued or that steps be taken to curb the private investment boom—by reducing tax depreciation allowances or by raising taxes on business investment. Meanwhile, the Länder and communes, which possess considerable fiscal autonomy, were encouraged to devote a substantial portion of their rising tax revenues to debt reduction rather than to expenditure increases, and the federal government planned to do the same.

The difficulty with this approach was that demand-reducing measures could only serve to further strengthen the already too high export surplus. By contrast, an export reduction, if it could be brought about, would serve to reduce inflationary pressures. The West German authorities finally bowed to the inevitable and, after a change of government in the fall, put revaluation of the mark into effect. As part of the revaluation, the 4% border taxes were terminated.

United Kingdom. Britain's fiscal and monetary policies in 1969 were directed toward improving its balance of trade by holding back domestic demand. A sizable devaluation of the pound in the fall of 1967 had been designed to increase Britain's export surplus, but progress during 1968 had been painfully slow, as prices, wages, and imports continued to expand in spite of restrictive budgetary policies.

In the April 1969 budget, taxes were increased once again, and the increase in planned public expenditures was held below the rates of recent years. The corporation tax was raised from 42½ to 45%; contributions of employers under the selective employment tax (SET) were increased; fuel and excise duties were raised; and the purchase tax was extended to some previously exempt commodities. These increases were only partially offset by some modest income tax relief.

An important recent development in the U.K. was the recognition of the difficulty of successfully pursuing restrictive monetary policy while the central bank supported the market for Treasury bonds at relatively stable prices. Under this practice, financial institutions feeling squeezed for funds could replenish their liquidity by selling off Treasury securities without major capital losses. In 1969 the Bank of England progressively lowered the prices at which it stood ready to absorb Treasury securities, thus permitting monetary policy to cooperate more effectively with fiscal policy in restraining demand.

By fall, clear signs of improvement in the British trade balance began to emerge, and the 1970 budget was expected to resume a more expansionary posture.

Great Britain: *see* United Kingdom

Japan. Japan in 1969 was in the midst of a continued strong economic boom which, unlike previous booms, was not accompanied by balance of payments difficulties. The 1969 budget, therefore, was geared to continuing economic expansion. General fund expenditures were scheduled to rise 15.8% over 1968, and investment and loan programs 14%. The budget placed special emphasis on investment in social overhead capital (river control, forestry, roads, ports, harbours, airports, and housing) and also provided for social security liberalization, agricultural improvements, and expansion of educational facilities. With the rapid growth rate generating sharply increased revenues, the budget also provided for a large reduction of income tax equal to 3% of total government revenue. Steps were taken to change the tax formula on profits from sale of land and to tighten tax treatment of expense accounts.

Canada. The Canadian economy is strongly influenced by economic developments in the U.S., so that problems confronting Canadian financial officials often closely parallel those in the U.S. Like the U.S., Canada had been combating excess demand inflation through restrictive budget and monetary policies. The budget presented in October 1968 was directed toward restoring price stability by achieving a balanced budget for fiscal 1969–70. A social development tax at the rate of 2% of taxable income was introduced, and taxes were extended to banks and life insurance companies. A virtual freeze on federal employment was planned, and cooperation was sought with provincial governments in restraining jointly financed expenditures.

In June 1969 revised budget estimates were issued showing a substantial surplus for fiscal 1970, the first surplus of any size in 13 years. With the economy still expanding strongly, extension for another year of the 3% surtax on individual and corporate incomes, introduced at the beginning of 1968, was announced.

Other Countries. A number of countries switched over in 1969 to the value-added tax (VAT) system of indirect taxation. This is a broad-based sales-type tax, levied at each stage of the manufacturing-distribution process against the "value added" at that stage; *i.e.*, excluding from the tax base at that stage the value of purchased raw materials or intermediate products. In theory, a 5% tax applied only to the value added at each stage would add only 5% to final product prices, in contrast to other forms of indirect taxes which may pyramid at successive stages. There had been widespread movement among European countries in recent years to switch over to this form of tax, pioneered by the French. The EEC Council of Ministers had directed member countries to make this change by the beginning of 1970 in the interest of harmonizing national tax structures, and the member countries (except Italy), as well as several countries hopeful of membership, had either complied or were planning to.

West Germany switched over to VAT at the beginning of 1968, and Sweden and the Netherlands in 1969. In the Netherlands the changeover touched off a price explosion, as sellers marked up prices by more than costs, requiring the authorities to institute price controls. Norway enacted a 20% VAT to go into effect at the beginning of 1970. The authorities in Belgium, where the VAT changeover was also scheduled for the beginning of 1970, were moved by the Netherlands experience first to scale down the proposed rates and later to postpone the change until 1971. (W. Le.)

See also Economic Planning; Economics; Payments and Reserves, International.

Greece

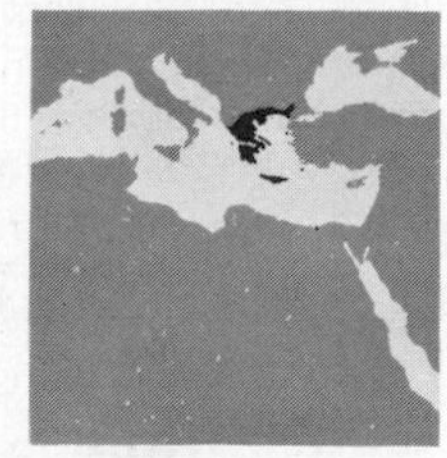

A constitutional monarchy of Europe, Greece occupies the southern part of the Balkan Peninsula. Area: 50,944 sq.mi. (131,944 sq.km.), of which the mainland accounts for 41,277 sq.mi. Pop. (1968 est.): 8,803,000. Cap. and largest city: Athens (pop., 1961, 627,564). Language: Greek. Religion: Orthodox. King, Constantine II, in exile since Dec. 14, 1967; regent in 1969, Lieut. Gen. Georgios Zoitakis; prime minister, Georgios Papadopoulos.

Domestic Affairs. During 1969 the leaders of the 1967 military coup continued to insist that they would restore full constitutional rule when—but only when—the Greek people had acquired "sufficient maturity" to preclude a relapse into prerevolutionary political manners and mores. They firmly refused to bind themselves to a timetable for parliamentary elections and kept the country under martial law. Although the new constitution had been put in force on Nov. 15, 1968, the structural legislation required to make its provisions fully operative was still in the drafting stage. The constitutional guarantees of civil and political liberties remained in abeyance at the regime's discretion.

This lack of speed inevitably raised questions about the regime's ultimate intentions. Doubts were increased by the peremptory manner in which the regime handled a crisis involving the Council of the Nation, the supreme administrative tribunal that rules on the legality of the government's actions. The crisis erupted when the council quashed (June 24) a massive dismissal of senior judges regarded as hostile to the regime. The regime declared the ruling illegal and the president of the tribunal, Michael Stasinopoulos, was asked to resign. When he refused, the regime issued (June 27) a decree accepting his resignation and nominating a successor. Three prominent lawyers who had successfully defended the appeal of the dismissed judges were arrested and deported from Athens.

The institutional reforms introduced in 1969 were clearly aimed at strengthening the control of the executive over most aspects of public life. The most significant was the promulgation of a new charter for the Orthodox Church of Greece (February 17), granting it a wide measure of autonomy from the state under an Assembly of Bishops. However, the charter transferred all the powers of this assembly to the regime for a period of three years.

Labour legislation was passed (May 11) to eliminate professionalism among trade-union officials by disqualifying those who were not otherwise employed. The regime also appointed (May 22) retired army generals as government commissioners to all Greek universities and graduate schools. Another army general, the chief of the National Security Department, was appointed (July 1) ombudsman, with special authority to probe into the private lives of civil servants. Generals were nominated as ambassadors to Paris and London (July 10). A press code introducing government selection of journalists was rejected by all Greek press unions.

Resistance to the military government increased, but it was still hardly on a scale that could threaten the regime's survival. A series of trials held before special military courts in May and June led to the conviction, on grounds of subversion, of more than 100 persons, mostly of the left. More arrests followed in July.

While the regime appeared to have effectively dismembered most leftist and centre underground groups, the emergence of a militant right-wing resistance was a new factor in 1969. Two organizations seemed to be particularly active: the Free Greeks, believed to consist of ousted royalist officers, and the National Resistance Movement (KEA), whose leader used the pseudonym "General Akritas." Both organizations declared their loyalty to King Constantine. Arrests of retired generals and senior officers—all known royalists—suggested that the regime had decided to crack down on the right-wing underground, which was potentially dangerous because of its possible influence within the armed forces. The regime publicly accused King Constantine of failing to discourage a known conspiracy, and the censored Athens newspapers launched a campaign warning the king that his throne was in danger unless he disassociated himself from these organizations.

The underground appeared to be working in two directions: to undermine the regime's claim that it had established law and order, and to induce the United States to apply more pressure against it. U.S. automobiles with "foreign mission" plates became favourite bomb targets throughout the summer, and the KEA, which claimed credit for most of the explosions, warned the Americans that their officials and diplomats would be kidnapped and even executed unless Washington revised its policy.

Foreign Relations. What Washington's policy toward the Greek regime actually was, was anybody's guess. The Greek leaders, who had regarded as a major victory the partial resumption of U.S. military equipment deliveries by the Johnson administration in October 1968, had nursed high hopes that the Nixon

UPI COMPIX

Lieut. Gen. Georgios Zoitakis, regent of Greece, reviews military parade in Athens, Oct. 28, 1969.

GREECE

Education. (1965–66) Primary, pupils 963,846, teachers 27,872; secondary, pupils 368,884, teachers 14,140; vocational, pupils 53,252; teacher training, students 4,350, teachers 261; higher (including 4 universities), students 55,334, teaching staff 1,826.

Finance. Monetary unit: drachma, with a par value of 30 drachmas to U.S. $1 (72 drachmas = £1 sterling). Gold and foreign exchange, central bank: (June 1969) U.S. $243.1 million; (June 1968) U.S. $228 million. Budget (1969 est.): revenue 51.1 billion drachmas; expenditure 48.6 billion drachmas. Gross national product: (1967) 211 billion drachmas; (1966) 196.9 billion drachmas. Money supply: (May 1969) 43,460,000,000 drachmas; (May 1968) 41,330,000,000 drachmas. Cost of living (1963 = 100): (June 1969) 114; (June 1968) 111.

Foreign Trade. (1968) Imports 41,795,000,000 drachmas; exports 14,033,000,000 drachmas. Import sources: EEC 44% (West Germany 18%, Italy 10%, France 8%); U.K. 10%; U.S. 8%; Japan 5%. Export destinations: EEC 48% (West Germany 20%, Italy 13%, France 7%); U.S. 10%; U.S.S.R. 5%; Yugoslavia 5%. Main exports: tobacco 21%; dried fruit (raisins, currants) 8%; cotton 7%; aluminum 7%; chemicals 7%; fresh fruit 6%; vegetable oils 6%. Tourism (1967): visitors 849,000; gross receipts U.S. $126.8 million.

Transport and Communications. Roads (1968) 34,358 km. (including 11 km. expressways). Motor vehicles in use (1968): passenger 169,139; commercial 87,134. Railways (1967): 2,572 km.; traffic 1,150,000,000 passenger-km., freight 563 million net ton-km. Air traffic (1968): 1,250,800,000 passenger-km.; freight 28,065,000 net ton-km. Shipping (1968): merchant vessels 100 gross tons and over 1,634; gross tonnage 7,415,984. Telephones (Dec. 1967) 660,129. Radio receivers (Dec. 1967) 994,000.

Agriculture. Production (in 000; metric tons; 1968; 1967 in parentheses): wheat *c.* 1,519 (1,848); barley 659 (839); oats *c.* 108 (165); corn 375 (338); potatoes 648 (721); rice 108 (91); tomatoes (1967) 679, (1966) 611; tobacco 88 (102); oranges 356 (211); lemons 69 (94); cotton, lint *c.* 86 (96); olive oil 155 (194); wine (1967) 395, (1966) 384; raisins (1967) 147, (1966) 186; currants and sultanas (1966) 183, (1965) 177; figs (1967) *c.* 120, (1966) *c.* 110. Livestock (in 000; Dec. 1967): sheep 7,874; cattle 1,094; goats (Dec. 1966) 3,945; horses 276; mules 208; asses 413; pigs 640; chickens (Dec. 1966) 25,017.

Industry. Production (in 000; metric tons; 1968): lignite 5,580; manufactured gas (cu.m.) 9,600; electricity (excluding most industrial production; kw-hr.) 6,950,000; petroleum products 3,897; bauxite 1,767; magnesite (1966) 338; cement 4,054; cotton yarn 37.

CAMERA PRESS—PIX FROM PUBLIX

Greek Army tanks rolling through the streets of Athens in a display of armed might. Members of the Greek government reviewed the parade.

administration would do even better. However, beyond the delivery of a few fighter aircraft in February, no heavy military equipment was sent to Greece. Furthermore, the U.S. ambassador's post in Athens was left vacant for most of 1969. Greek leaders who had felt secure in the affections of the U.S. military were left in doubt about the likelihood of securing cooperation from Washington.

The passive U.S. attitude was rooted in the failure to visualize a peaceful alternative to the regime. Meanwhile, however, most of the deposed Greek politicians appeared to have tacitly agreed that the only man who could rally the nation was Konstantinos Karamanlis, the former conservative prime minister (1955–63), who lived in Paris. In a strongly worded statement made on September 30, Karamanlis agreed to play this role.

The regime's relations with other Western European countries deteriorated. There was a move to suspend Greece from the Council of Europe for having abolished parliamentary democracy, as well as on grounds of torture of political prisoners, but at the December meeting of the Council's Consultative Assembly in Paris, Greece withdrew from the Council rather than waiting to be ousted.

The Economy. This uncertain situation was clearly reflected in the Greek economy which, for the third year in succession, suffered seriously from a lack of foreign investment capital. Combined with the lavish credits granted in previous years to combat the effects of domestic recession, this created a state of high liquidity and posed serious risks for the balance of payments.

The regime's effort to attain an 8.5% economic growth rate in 1969 (compared with rates as low as 4% in 1967 and 1968) resulted in an increase in spending for imports that was hardly matched by the slower rise in exports. Faced with a balance of payments deficit of some $300 million, the regime obtained high-interest bank loans abroad and also attempted to inhibit imports by imposing equalization levies and time-consuming controls on import invoices. Tight controls on domestic prices protected monetary stability and averted labour unrest.

(Mo. M.)

ENCYCLOPÆDIA BRITANNICA FILMS. *People of Greece* (1955); *The Mediterranean World* (1961).

Guatemala

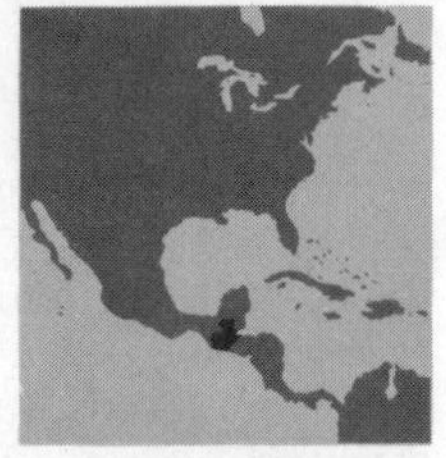

A republic of Central America, Guatemala is bounded by Mexico, British Honduras, Honduras, El Salvador, the Caribbean Sea, and the Pacific Ocean. Area: 42,042 sq.mi. (108,889 sq.km.). Pop. (1968 est.): 4,863,520. Cap. and largest city: Guatemala City (pop., 1967 est., 652,934). Language: Spanish, with some Indian dialects. Religion: predominantly Roman Catholic. President in 1969, Julio César Méndez Montenegro.

A return to political normalcy and an improvement in economic activity, which characterized the latter half of 1968, continued into 1969. Although the nation's attention was turned to a bitter campaign for the national elections in 1970, this did not lead to a renewal of terrorist activity. The economic state of affairs became somewhat clouded as a consequence of two events that occurred during the latter half of 1969. The July conflict between El Salvador and Honduras and its disruptive effect upon Guatemala and the Central American Common Market (CACM) had yet to be fully measured by the year's end. Also, a severe storm in late September and early October caused considerable damage and loss of life throughout the nation.

Political events of the year were focused upon the national elections, which were scheduled for the first Sunday in March of 1970. At that time, all 55 deputies in the Congress as well as the president were to be chosen. In February the right-wing National Liberation Movement (MLN) selected Col. Carlos Arana Osorio as its candidate. The following month Mario Fuentes Pieruccini, until recently the minister of finance, was chosen as the candidate of the ruling Revolutionary Party (PR). The Christian Democratic Party (PDC) nominated its first presidential candidate, Jorge Lucas Caballeros.

What violence did occur was associated with the campaign of Colonel Arana. In June left-wing elements were accused of having assassinated several leaders of the MLN, which in turn was accused of the attempted assassination of Irma Flaquer, a journalist and secretary to President Méndez' wife. In October the Institutional Democratic Party (PID), another right-wing group, joined in support of Colonel Arana, placing him in a strong position as a presidential aspirant. An extremist left-wing group known as the Rebel Armed Forces (FAR) condemned Colonel Arana to death, but terrorist activity remained relatively subdued. The comparative calm was indicated by the fact that the national "state of alarm," which had been imposed at the time of the assassination of the U.S. ambassador to Guatemala, J. Gordon Mein, in August 1968 and lifted later in that year, was not reinstituted.

In May Nelson Rockefeller visited Guatemala on his fact-finding mission throughout Latin America for U.S. Pres. Richard Nixon. After reading a brief statement at the airport, Rockefeller conferred with President Méndez in the National Palace. Because he remained in the country for only 3½ hours Rockefeller was criticized by much of the Guatemalan press. Businessmen also complained that he did not discuss the private sector of the economy with President Méndez.

Business and government activities continued to expand favourably, but a "wait and see" attitude might develop prior to the elections. In foreign trade, government restraint limited imports to their 1968 level, while income from exports appeared to have increased by nearly 25%. This contributed significantly to mitigating the nation's balance of payments problem. Federal expenditures for 1969 increased only slightly over the previous year's budget. A program of federal austerity and improved earnings provided the basis for economic stability and moderate economic gains during the year.

Continuing expansion in 1970, particularly in the sector of light industry, was expected to depend upon the maintenance of CACM trade, which had been disrupted by the midyear hostilities between Honduras and El Salvador. Storms, which occurred in September and October in the aftermath of Hurricane Francelia, severely damaged Guatemala's transportation system and inflicted particularly heavy losses on plantings of cotton.

On October 6 the ground crews and office personnel of Pan American World Airways in Guatemala went on strike. All Pan American flights to Guatemala were suspended until the strike was settled on October 14. During the week of the suspension there was an estimated 80% decrease in air freight to Guatemala and a decline in the tourist trade of about 75%. Despite these adversities, and the political uncertainties, it was anticipated that the economy would be maintained at the 1969 level during 1970. (O. H. H.)

See also Dependent States.

ENCYCLOPÆDIA BRITANNICA FILMS. *Guatemala—Nation of Central America* (1961).

GUATEMALA

Education. (1965–66) Primary, pupils 421,446, teachers 12,251; secondary, pupils 35,541, teachers 1,216; vocational, pupils 6,794, teachers 985; teacher training, students 6,798, teachers 1,197; higher (at 3 universities), students 8,171, teaching staff 705.

Finance. Monetary unit: quetzal, at par with the U.S. dollar (2.40 quetzales = £1 sterling). Gold and foreign exchange, central bank: (June 1969) U.S. $74.5 million; (June 1968) U.S. $84.5 million. Budget (1969 est.) balanced at 198 million quetzales. Gross national product: (1967) 1,417,000,000 quetzales; (1966) 1,379,000,000 quetzales. Money supply: (May 1969) 155.3 million quetzales; (May 1968) 158.9 million quetzales. Cost of living (Guatemala City; 1963 = 100): (May 1969) 103; (May 1968) 105.

Foreign Trade. (1968) Imports 247 million quetzales; exports 222 million quetzales. Import sources (1967): U.S. 41%; El Salvador 12%; West Germany 10%; Japan 9%. Export destinations (1967): U.S. 35%; El Salvador 14%; West Germany 12%; Japan 9%. Main exports (1967): coffee 35%; cotton 16%.

Transport and Communications. Roads (1965) 11,230 km. (including 830 km. of Pan-American Highway). Motor vehicles in use (1967): passenger 33,400; commercial (including buses) 19,400. Railways (1967): 1,160 km.; freight 120 million net ton-km. Air traffic: (1968) 77.4 million passenger-km.; freight (1967) 3,650,000 net ton-km. Telephones (Jan. 1968) 35,103. Radio receivers (Dec. 1968) *c.* 215,000. Television receivers (Dec. 1967) 75,000.

Agriculture. Production (in 000; metric tons; 1968; 1967 in parentheses): corn *c.* 690 (690); cotton, lint *c.* 79 (*c.* 76); cane sugar, raw value (1968–69) 154, (1967–68) *c.* 145; sugar, panela (1968–69) *c.* 27, (1967–68) *c.* 27; dry beans *c.* 69 (*c.* 69); coffee (1967) *c.* 108, (1966) *c.* 100; bananas (1967) *c.* 76, (1966) *c.* 74. Livestock (in 000; March 1967): cattle *c.* 1,350; sheep *c.* 820; pigs *c.* 580.

Industry. Production (in 000; metric tons; 1967): cement 205; petroleum products 600; lead ore (metal content) *c.* 0.6; zinc ore (metal content) *c.* 0.2; electricity (kw-hr.) 526,000.

Guinea

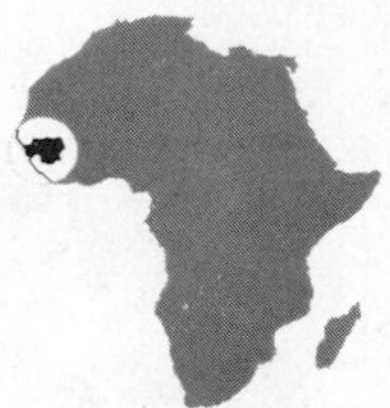

A republic on the west coast of Africa, Guinea is bounded by Portuguese Guinea, Senegal, Mali, Ivory Coast, Liberia, and Sierra Leone. Area: 94,925 sq.mi. (245,856 sq.km.). Pop. (1968 est.): 3,795,000, chiefly Fulani, Malinké, and Susu. Cap. and largest city: Conakry (pop., over 100,000). Language: French (official). Religion: mostly Muslim. President in 1969, Sékou Touré.

An unhappy atmosphere of permanent conspiracy prevailed in Guinea during 1969. In January "counterrevolutionary" demonstrations took place in Conakry, where the discovery of a new plot against President Touré was announced.

In March, Radio Conakry announced another conspiracy, among a company of parachutists stationed in Labé. The conspirators were alleged to have planned the assassination of the president and to have instigated regional secession on the lines of Biafra. Several officers and some other persons were arrested, including Col. Kaman Diaby, former army deputy chief of staff, and Fodeba Keita, secretary of state for rural economy, a once-influential dignitary who was best known as the founder of the Ballets Africains.

President Touré directly accused France of aiding the conspirators. Abdoulaye Touré, Guinean ambassador to the UN and successor of Achkar Marof, who had mysteriously disappeared, accused Marof of having entered into negotiations with the French government in order to overthrow the president. In March and April, Radio Conakry made violent personal attacks on French Pres. Charles de Gaulle and on the heads of state of Guinea's neighbours. President Touré later accused the Ivory Coast of harbouring and training foreign mercenaries whose intention was to overthrow his regime. The accusation was strongly denied.

In May the National Revolutionary Council of Guinea set up a special court and condemned to death 12 people, including Diaby and Keita. A score of others were condemned to hard labour. A thorough purge of the Guinean Army was undertaken, while an important ministerial reshuffle removed the portfolio of national defense from Gen. Lansana Diane and abolished the ministry.

During an official visit by Pres. Kenneth Kaunda of Zambia, a young Guinean, Keita Tidiane, made an abortive attempt on the life of President Touré.

GUINEA

Education. (1965–66) Primary, pupils 164,119, teachers 3,990; secondary, pupils 16,698, teachers 567; vocational, pupils 5,018, teachers 261; teacher training, students 822, teachers 52; higher, students 1,243, teachers 199.

Finance. Monetary unit: Guinea franc, with a par value of GFr. 246.85 to U.S. $1 (GFr. 592.45 = £1 sterling). Budget (1968–69 est.) balanced at GFr. 63 billion.

Foreign Trade. (1964) Imports GFr. 11,201,000,000; exports GFr. 16.1 billion. Import sources: U.S. 22%; U.S.S.R. 12%; China 10%. Export destinations: France 16%; U.S. 11%; Cameroon 10%; Poland 8%. Main exports (1962): aluminum 60%; bananas 10%; palm products 7%; coffee 6%; iron ore 6%.

Greek Orthodox Church: *see* Religion

Greenland: *see* Dependent States

Grenada: *see* Dependent States

Gross National Product: *see* Economy, World; Income, National

Guadeloupe: *see* Dependent States

Guam: *see* Dependent States

Guiana: *see* Dependent States; Guyana

Guided Missiles: *see* Defense

The assassin was hunted down and lynched by the crowd. A group of Guineans in exile in France (Regroupement des Guinéens en France) claimed responsibility for the attempt.

In July, Touré once again accused certain foreign ambassadors and societies of seeking to overthrow his government. In spite of this unfavourable atmosphere, the European Financial Society agreed in September to loan the Guinean Bauxite Company $10 million to finance construction work on the mining complex at Boké. (PH. D.)

Guyana

A parliamentary state and a realm of the Commonwealth of Nations, Guyana is situated between Venezuela, Brazil, and Surinam on the Atlantic Ocean. Area: 83,000 sq.mi. (214,970 sq.km.). Pop. (1969 est.): 741,978, including (1964) East Indian 50.2%; Negro 31.3%; mestizo and mulatto 11.9%; Amerindian 4.6%. Cap. and largest city: Georgetown (pop., 1969 est., 97,190). Language: English (official). Religion: Protestant and Roman Catholic. Queen, Elizabeth II; governor-general in 1969, Sir David Rose (d. November 10); prime minister, Forbes Burnham.

In 1969 Guyana's attention was engaged by the aftermath of a general election and by continuing border disputes with Venezuela and Surinam. In December 1968 the People's National Congress, led by Prime Minister Burnham, secured 30 seats in Parliament and 56% of the vote, compared with the 19 seats and 37% of the vote of Cheddi Jagan's People's Progressive Party. Burnham's victory was surrounded by the allegations of Cheddi Jagan of electoral fraud at home as well as in regard to the overseas vote. The prime minister countered that his party had won even if the overseas vote was discounted.

In spite of this beginning to his second term of office, Burnham could claim that during 1969 the People's National Congress became more firmly entrenched in public favour. There was no return to bitter racial strife, and Guyana's economic position showed signs of improvement. A $10 million loan from the U.K. as part of Guyana's 1966–72 development program was announced in July. Late in the year it was announced that Guyana would become a republic in February 1970.

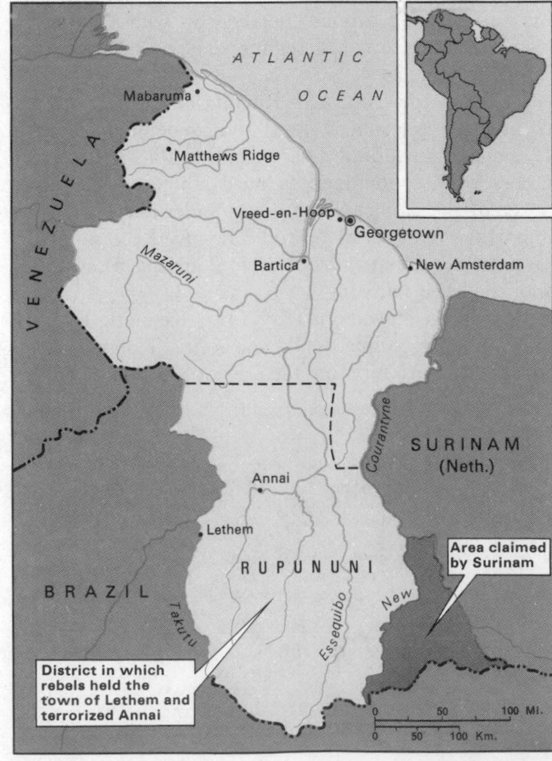

Border disputes between Guyana and neighbouring countries continued during 1969. Venezuela claimed a large area west of the Essequibo River but denied any connection with rebel activity in the area. Approximately 6,000 sq.mi. of territory was involved in a dispute with Surinam.

GUYANA

Education. (1967–68) Primary, pupils 167,909, teachers 5,255; secondary, pupils 16,656, teachers 620; vocational, pupils 1,334, teachers (1962–63) 56; teacher training, students 359, teachers 31.

Finance. Monetary unit: Guyanan dollar (Guy$2 = U.S. $1; Guy$4.80 = £1 sterling). Budget (1969 est.): revenue Guy$155,007,000; expenditure Guy-$146,924,000.

Foreign Trade. (1967) Imports Guy$225.3 million; exports Guy$197.5 million. Import sources: U.S. 28%; U.K. 26%; Canada 11%; Trinidad and Tobago 10%; West Germany 6%. Export destinations: U.K. 24%; U.S. 23%; Canada 19%; Trinidad and Tobago 9%; Norway 5%. Main exports: sugar 30%; bauxite 23%; alumina 16%; rice 13%.

Agriculture. Production (in 000; metric tons): sugar, raw value (1968–69) 366, (1967–68) 322; rice (1968) *c.* 180, (1967) 198; fish catch (1967) 14, (1966) 12. Livestock (in 000; 1967–68): cattle 306; sheep (1966–67) 83; pigs (1966–67) 68.

Industry. Production (in 000; metric tons; 1967): manganese ore (metal content) 63; bauxite (1965) 4,302; diamonds (metric carats) 97; electricity (kw-hr.) 240,000.

Guyana matched internal political improvement with increased prestige within the Caribbean Free Trade Area (CARIFTA), which maintained its secretariat in Georgetown. The benefits of this association were thought to be potentially greater in the long term, with short-term benefits to Guyana more likely to affect agriculture, particularly rice and beef exports.

In 1969 the dispute with Venezuela saw the involvement of Guyanan Amerindians. (*See* ANTHROPOLOGY: *Special Report.*) During January, at least seven people were killed in an attack on a police post in the remote Rupununi region. Rupununi formed part of a vast area of Guyana west of the Essequibo River claimed by Venezuela. Burnham accused hostile forces both inside and outside Guyana of forcing the Amerindians to participate and named the two leading Rupununi ranching families of Hart and Melville as the chief instigators of the armed revolt. The Venezuelan government denied any involvement and said that it would refuse an appeal for aid from Mrs. Valerie Hart, self-styled president of the provincial government of Rupununi. Nevertheless, Guyana protested to the UN against Venezuelan activities.

Surinam, meanwhile, had laid claim to approximately 6,000 sq.mi. of Guyanan territory. In August Guyanan troops clashed with Surinamese troops in the disputed southeast border region. Reports were that Surinam forces had been constructing an airstrip, which was taken over by the Guyanans. (RA. R.)

Guinea, Portuguese: *see* Dependent States

Gymnastics: *see* Sporting Record

Gynecology and Obstetrics: *see* Medicine

Haiti

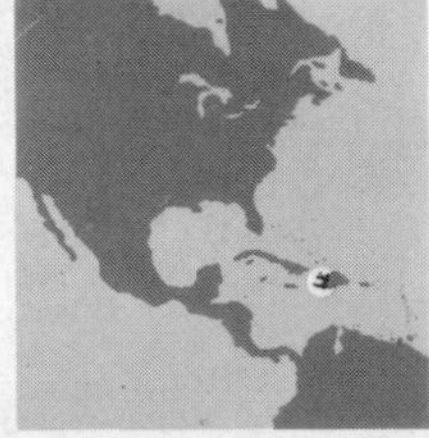

The Republic of Haiti occupies the western one-third of the Caribbean island of Hispaniola, which it shares with the Dominican Republic. Area: 10,714 sq.mi. (27,750 sq.km.). Pop. (1968 est.): 4,674,108, of whom 95% are Negro. Cap. and largest city: Port-au-Prince (pop., 1968 est., 340,175). Language: French and Creole. Religion: Roman Catholic; Voodooism practiced in rural areas. President in 1969, François Duvalier.

During 1969 political opposition to the Duvalier government increased and the economy continued to deteriorate. In February two underground opposition parties, the Parti d'Entente Populaire and the Parti Uni des Democrates Haïtiens, formed the Parti Unifié des Communistes Haïtien (PUCH), and for the first time a disciplined organization, using guerrilla tactics as its principal means of action, was established. The organization claimed to have the support of a progressive Roman Catholic group, Haiti Progrès, which included young priests. Terrorist activities, including bomb attacks in Port-au-Prince and attacks on villages, increasingly alarmed the government; in September it was reported that approximately 500 troops were searching for the guerrillas. In April an anti-Communist law was promulgated that also provided for penalties for priests convicted of helping terrorists; nine priests were deported for "Communist activities" in August. The government also abolished the national literacy agency and ruled that only qualified medical personnel could give treatment or prescriptions in country districts. About 20 people were killed in a gunfight in Port-au-Prince in June, including several leaders of PUCH; no major terrorist attacks were subsequently reported.

PUCH emerged as the most potent force in opposition. The traditional opposition groups, formed mainly by exiles in the U.S., were in disarray as a result of repeated failures and personal dissension. The Coalition Haïtienne split into two groups and one, led by a former army officer, Col. René J. Léon, and based in Miami, Fla., organized an air raid on Port-au-Prince aimed at the presidential palace, which caused only light damage.

Duvalier continued to suffer from ill health, and in May it was rumoured he had a severe heart attack. During his illness his daughter Marie Denise was reported to be prominent in government affairs; he was subsequently reported to have recovered and to have reassumed full control. There was, however, increased speculation about the succession. It was reported in May that the Army was grooming three officers to assume presidential powers on Duvalier's death; such a move was likely to be challenged by the Tonton Macoute, the secret police. The U.S. government was said to be looking for a successor within the ranks of the administration and the Army, and to be pressing for the merging of the Tonton Macoute with the Army.

CAMERA PRESS—PIX FROM PUBLIX

Pres. François Duvalier rides through Port-au-Prince in his bulletproof limousine. During 1969 he faced increasing political opposition and a deteriorating economy.

Duvalier used the increased opposition to his rule to press for a restoration of U.S. economic and military aid when Nelson Rockefeller visited Haiti early in July as part of his fact-finding mission to Latin America for U.S. Pres. Richard Nixon. In March Haiti attacked the Alliance for Progress for not granting economic assistance for the past five years.

The government experienced mounting economic difficulties and was able to pay the Tonton Macoute only irregularly. A report published by the Inter-American Development Bank stated that per capita income fell to $25 during the year. A French economic survey in April established that exports had fallen by 20% between 1962 and 1967; the road network had fallen into disrepair and would have to be entirely rebuilt; fertile areas such as the Artibonite Valley were becoming wastelands; and industrial production had fallen sharply in the previous three years.

There was, however, a small measure of foreign assistance for the economy. In July the International Monetary Fund granted Haiti a standby credit of $1.5 million to help alleviate balance of payments problems. (Rn. C.)

Encyclopædia Britannica Films. *The West Indies* (1965).

HAITI

Education. (1965–66) Primary, pupils 283,799, teachers 6,210; secondary, pupils 20,128, teachers 1,259; vocational, pupils 4,173, teachers 337; teacher training, students 213, teachers 46; higher (at University of Haiti), students 1,822, teaching staff 135.

Finance. Monetary unit: gourde, with a par value of 5 gourdes to U.S. $1 (12 gourdes = £1 sterling). Gold and foreign exchange, central bank: (June 1969) U.S. $3.9 million; (June 1968) U.S. $3.1 million. Budget (1967–68 est.) balanced at 140.2 million gourdes. Money supply: (Dec. 1968) 161.2 million gourdes; (Dec. 1967) 148.7 million gourdes. Cost of living (Port-au-Prince; 1963 = 100): (March 1969) 123; (March 1968) 114.

Foreign Trade. (1968) Imports 187.9 million gourdes; exports 178.2 million gourdes. Import sources (1967): U.S. 64%; Japan 7%; France 5%. Export destinations (1967): U.S. 53%; France 11%; Italy 9%; Japan 7%; Belgium-Luxembourg 6%. Main exports: coffee 38%; bauxite 12%; sugar 9%; sisal 5%.

Transport and Communications. Roads (1967) *c.* 3,000 km. (including *c.* 350 km. with improved surface). Motor vehicles in use: passenger (1967) 6,900; commercial (1966) 1,100. Railways (1967) 354 km. (used only for transporting sugarcane). Telephones (Jan. 1968) 4,335. Radio receivers (Dec. 1967) 75,000. Television receivers (Dec. 1966) *c.* 10,000.

Agriculture. Production (in 000; metric tons; 1967; 1966 in parentheses): coffee *c.* 30 (*c.* 28); sugar, raw value (1968–69) *c.* 65, (1967–68) *c.* 63; sisal *c.* 15 (*c.* 19). Livestock (in 000; 1966–67): cattle 769; pigs 1,504; goats 1,177; sheep 69.

Industry. Production (in 000; metric tons; 1967): cement 35; bauxite (exports) 370; electricity (kw-hr.) 78,000.

Heads of State

The following is a list of the names of those holding chief positions in their countries as of Dec. 31, 1969.

Country	Name and office	Accession
Afghanistan	Mohammad Zahir Shah, king	1933
	Noor Ahmad Etemadi, prime minister	1967
Albania	Enver Hoxha, first secretary of the Albanian (Communist) Party of Labour	1954
	Haxhi Leshi, president of the Presidium	1953
	Mehmet Shehu, chairman of the Council of Ministers	1954

Harbours:
see Transportation

Harness Racing:
see Horse Racing

Hats:
see Fashion and Dress

Hay:
see Agriculture

Heads of State

Country	Name and office	Accession
Algeria	Houari Boumédienne, president	1965
Andorra	Francesc Escudé-Ferrero, *sindic procurador general de les valls d'Andorra*	1967
Argentina	Juan Carlos Onganía, president	1966
Australia	Elizabeth II, queen	1952
	Sir Paul Hasluck, governor-general	1969
	John Grey Gorton, prime minister	1968
Austria	Franz Jonas, president	1965
	Josef Klaus, chancellor	1964
Barbados	Elizabeth II, queen	1952
	Sir John Stow, governor-general	1966
	Errol Walton Barrow, prime minister	1966
Belgium	Baudouin I, king	1951
	Gaston Eyskens, prime minister	1968
Bolivia	Gen. Alfredo Ovando Candía, head of the military government	1969
Botswana	Sir Seretse Khama, president	1966
Brazil	Gen. Emílio Garrastazú Médici, president	1969
Bulgaria	Todor Zhivkov, first secretary of the Bulgarian Communist Party (1954) and chairman of the Council of Ministers	1962
	Georgi Traikov, chairman of the Presidium	1964
Burma	Gen. Ne Win, chairman of the Revolutionary Council and prime minister	1962
Burundi	Michel Micombero, president	1966
Cambodia	Prince Norodom Sihanouk, chief of state	1960
	Gen. Lon Nol, premier	1969
Cameroon	Ahmadou Ahidjo, president	1960
Canada	Elizabeth II, queen	1952
	D. Roland Michener, governor-general	1967
	Pierre Elliott Trudeau, prime minister	1968
Central African Rep.	Jean Bedel Bokassa, president and premier	1966
Ceylon	Elizabeth II, queen	1952
	William Gopallawa, governor-general	1962
	Dudley Senanayake, prime minister	1965
Chad	François Tombalbaye, president (1960) and premier	1968
Chile	Eduardo Frei Montalva, president	1964
China, People's Rep.	Mao Tse-tung, chairman of the Communist Party	1949
	Chou En-lai, premier	1949
China, Rep. of (Taiwan)	Chiang Kai-shek, president	1943
	C. K. Yen, president of the Executive Yuan	1963
Colombia	Carlos Lleras Restrepo, president	1966
Congo, Dem. Rep.	Joseph Mobutu, president	1965
Congo, People's Rep. of the	Maj. Marien Ngouabi, president	1969
	Maj. Alfred Raoul, premier	1969
Costa Rica	José Joaquín Trejos Fernández, president	1966
Cuba	Osvaldo Dorticós Torrado, president	1959
	Fidel Castro, prime minister	1959
Cyprus	Archbishop Makarios III, president	1960
Czechoslovakia	Gustav Husak, first secretary of the Communist Party of Czechoslovakia	1969
	Ludvik Svoboda, president	1968
	Oldrich Cernik, premier	1968
Dahomey	Lieut. Col. Maurice Kouandete, head of the military government	1969
Denmark	Frederik IX, king	1947
	Hilmar Baunsgaard, prime minister	1968
Dominican Rep.	Joaquín Balaguer, president	1966
Ecuador	José María Velasco Ibarra, president	1968
El Salvador	Col. Fidel Sánchez Hernández, president	1967
Equatorial Guinea	Francisco Macías Nguma, president	1968
Ethiopia	Haile Selassie I, emperor	1930
	Akilu Habte Wold, prime minister	1961
Finland	Urho Kaleva Kekkonen, president	1956
	Mauno Koivisto, prime minister	1968
France	Georges Pompidou, president	1969
	Jacques Chaban-Delmas, premier	1969
Gabon	Albert Bernard Bongo, president	1967
Gambia, The	Elizabeth II, queen	1952
	Alhaji Sir Farimang Singhateh, governor-general	1966
	Sir Dawda Jawara, prime minister	1965
Germany, Federal Rep.	Gustav Heinemann, president	1969
	Willy Brandt, chancellor	1969
Germany, Dem. Rep.	Walter Ulbricht, first secretary of the Socialist Unity (Communist) Party of Germany (1946) and president	1960
	Willi Stoph, minister president	1964
Ghana	Brig. Akwasi A. Afrifa, J. W. K. Harlley, and Maj. Gen. A. K. Okran, members of three-man Presidential Commission	1969
	Kofi Busia, prime minister	1969
Greece	Constantine II, king	1964
	Lieut. Gen. Georgios Zoitakis, regent	1967
	Georgios Papadopoulos, prime minister	1967
Guatemala	Julio César Méndez Montenegro, president	1966
Guinea	Sékou Touré, president	1958
Guyana	Elizabeth II, queen	1952
	Governor-general, vacant	
	Forbes Burnham, prime minister	1966
Haiti	François Duvalier, president	1957
Honduras	Osvaldo López Arellano, president	1963
Hungary	Janos Kadar, first secretary of the Hungarian Socialist Workers' (Communist) Party	1956
	Pal Losonczi, president of the Presidential Council	1967
	Jeno Fock, president of the Council of Ministers	1967
Iceland	Kristjan Eldjarn, president	1968
	Bjarni Benediktsson, prime minister	1963
India	Varahagiri Venkata Giri, president	1969
	Mrs. Indira Gandhi, prime minister	1966
Indonesia	Suharto, president and prime minister	1968
Iran	Mohammad Reza Pahlavi, shah-in-shah	1941
	Amir Abbas Hoveida, prime minister	1965
Iraq	Ahmed Hassan al-Bakr, president	1968
Ireland	Eamon de Valera, president	1959
	John Lynch, prime minister	1966
Israel	Schneor Zalman Shazar, president	1963
	Mrs. Golda Meir, prime minister	1969
Italy	Giuseppe Saragat, president	1964
	Mariano Rumor, premier	1968
Ivory Coast	Félix Houphouët-Boigny, president and premier	1960
Jamaica	Elizabeth II, queen	1952
	Sir Clifford Campbell, governor-general	1962
	Hugh L. Shearer, prime minister	1967
Japan	Hirohito, emperor	1926
	Eisaku Sato, prime minister	1964
Jordan	Husain I, king	1952
	Bahjat al-Talhouni, prime minister	1967
Kenya	Jomo Kenyatta, president	1964
Korea, Rep.	Gen. Park Chung-hee, president	1963
	Gen. Chung Il Kwon, prime minister	1964
Korea, Dem. People's Rep.	Marshal Kim Il Sung, secretary-general of the Korean Workers' (Communist) Party and chairman of the Council of Ministers	1948
	Choi Yong Kun, president	1964
Kuwait	Sheikh Sabah as-Salim as-Sabah, amir	1965
	Crown Prince Sheikh Jabir as-Ahmed as-Jabir as-Sabah, prime minister	1965
Laos	Savang Vatthana, king	1959
	Prince Souvanna Phouma, premier	1962
Lebanon	Charles Helou, president	1964
	Rashid Karami, prime minister	1969
Lesotho	Moshoeshoe II, chief of state	1966
	Leabua Jonathan, prime minister	1966
Liberia	William V. S. Tubman, president	1944
Libya	Col. Muhammad al-Khadafy, leader of the Revolutionary Command Council	1969
	Mahmoud Soliman al-Maghreby, prime minister	1969
Liechtenstein	Francis Joseph II, sovereign prince	1938
	Gerard Batliner, chief of government	1962
Luxembourg	Jean, grand duke	1964
	Pierre Werner, prime minister	1959
Malagasy Rep.	Philibert Tsiranana, president	1960
Malawi	H. Kamuzu Banda, president	1966
Malaysia	Tuanku Ismail Nasiruddin Shah ibni al-Marhum Sultan Zainal Abidin, *yang di-pertuan agong*	1965
	Tunku Abdul Rahman, prime minister	1963
Maldives, Rep. of	Amir Muhammad Farid Didi, sultan	1948
	Ibrahim Nassir, president	1968
Mali	Lieut. Moussa Traore, head of military government	1969
Malta	Elizabeth II, queen	1952
	Sir Maurice Dorman, governor-general	1964
	George Borg Olivier, prime minister	1964
Mauritania	Mokhtar Ould Daddah, president	1960
Mauritius	Sir Leonard Williams, governor-general	1969
	Sir Seewoosagur Ramgoolam, prime minister	1968
Mexico	Gustavo Díaz Ordaz, president	1964
Monaco	Rainier III, prince	1949
	François-Didier Gregh, minister of state	1969
Mongolia	Yumzhagiyin Tsedenbal, first secretary of the Mongolian People's Revolutionary (Communist) Party (1958) and chairman of the Council of Ministers	1952
	Zhamsarangibin Sambuu, chairman of the Presidium of the Great People's Khural	1962
Morocco	Hassan II, king	1961
	Ahmed Laraki, prime minister	1969
Muscat and Oman	Sa'id bin Taimur, sultan	1932
Nauru	Hammer de Roburt, president	1968
Nepal	Mahendra Bir Bikram Shah Deva, king	1955
	Kirti Nidhi Bista, chairman of the Council of Ministers (prime minister)	1969
Netherlands	Juliana, queen	1948
	Piet J. S. de Jong, prime minister	1967
New Zealand	Elizabeth II, queen	1952
	Sir Arthur Porritt, governor-general	1967
	Keith J. Holyoake, prime minister	1960
Nicaragua	Anastasio Somoza Debayle, president	1967
Niger	Hamani Diori, president	1960
Nigeria	Yakubu Gowon, head of provisional military government	1966
Norway	Olav V, king	1957
	Per Borten, prime minister	1965
Pakistan	Gen. Agha Muhammad Yahya Khan, president	1969
Panama	Demetrios Lakas Bahas, provisional president	1969
Paraguay	Gen. Alfredo Stroessner, president	1954
Peru	Gen. Juan Velasco Alvarado, president of the military government	1968
Philippines	Ferdinand E. Marcos, president	1965
Poland	Wladyslaw Gomulka, first secretary of the Polish United Workers' (Communist) Party	1956
	Marian Spychalski, chairman of the Council of State	1968
	Jozef Cyrankiewicz, chairman of the Council of Ministers	1954

Heart and Circulatory Diseases: *see* Medicine

Hebrew Literature: *see* Literature

Hematology: *see* Medicine

Highways: *see* Engineering Projects; Transportation

Hinduism: *see* Religion

Country	Name and office	Accession
Portugal	Rear Adm. Américo Deus Rodrigues Tomás, president	1958
	Marcello José das Neves AlvesCaetano, premier	1968
Rhodesia	Ian D. Smith, prime minister	1964
Romania	Nicolae Ceausescu, general secretary of the Romanian Communist Party (1965) and president of the State Council	1967
	Ion Gheorghe Maurer, chairman of the Council of Ministers	1961
Rwanda	Grégoire Kayibanda, president	1961
Saudi Arabia	Faisal ibn 'Abd al-'Aziz ibn 'Abd al-Rahman Al Sa'ud, king and prime minister	1964
Senegal	Léopold Sédar Senghor, president	1960
Sierra Leone	Elizabeth II, queen	1952
	Banja Tejan-Sie, acting governor-general	1968
	Siaka Stevens, prime minister	1968
Singapore	Inche Yusof bin Ishak, president	1965
	Lee Kuan Yew, prime minister	1965
Somalia	Gen. Muhammad Siyad, chairman of the Supreme Revolutionary Council	1969
South Africa	Jacobus J. Fouché, president	1968
	Balthazar J. Vorster, prime minister	1966
Southern Yemen	Salem Ali Rubayyi, chairman of the Presidential Council	1969
	Muhammad Ali Haitham, prime minister	1969
Spain	Don Juan Carlos de Borbón y Borbón, prince	1969
	Gen. Francisco Franco Bahamonde, chief of state and premier	1939
Sudan	Maj. Gen. Gafaar Muhammad al-Nimeiry, president and prime minister	1969
Swaziland	Sobhuza II, king	1921
	Prince Makhosini Dlamini, prime minister	1968
Sweden	Gustaf VI Adolf, king	1950
	Olof Palme, prime minister	1969
Switzerland	Ludwig von Moos, president of the confederation	1969
Syria	Nureddin al-Attassi, chairman of the Presidency Council (1966) and premier	1968
Tanzania	Julius Nyerere, president	1964
Thailand	Bhumibol Adulyadej, king	1946
	Field Marshal Thanom Kittikachorn, prime minister	1963
Togo	Gen. Étienne Eyadema, president	1967
Trinidad and Tobago	Elizabeth II, queen	1952
	Sir Solomon Hochoy, governor-general	1962
	Eric Williams, prime minister	1962
Tunisia	Habib Bourguiba, president	1964
Turkey	Gen. Cevdet Sunay, president	1966
	Süleyman Demirel, prime minister	1965
Uganda	Apollo Milton Obote, president (1966) and prime minister	1962
U.S.S.R.	Leonid I. Brezhnev, general secretary of the Communist Party of the Soviet Union	1964
	Nikolai V. Podgorny, chairman of the Presidium of the Supreme Soviet	1965
	Aleksei N. Kosygin, chairman of the Council of Ministers	1964
United Arab Rep.	Gamal Abd-al-Nasser, president (1958) and prime minister	1967
United Kingdom	Elizabeth II, queen	1952
	Harold Wilson, prime minister	1964
United States	Richard M. Nixon, president	1969
Upper Volta	Gen. Sangoule Lamizana, president	1966
Uruguay	Jorge Pacheco Areco, president	1967
Vatican City State	Paul VI, pope	1963
Venezuela	Rafael Caldera, president	1969
Vietnam, Rep.	Nguyen Van Thieu, president	1967
	Tran Thien Khiem, premier	1969
Vietnam, Dem. Rep.	Ton Duc Thang, president	1969
	Pham Van Dong, premier	1955
Western Samoa	Malietoa Tanumafili II, head of state	1965
	Fiame Mata'afa Faumuina Mulinu'u II, prime minister	1962
Yemen, Rep.	Qadi Abdul Rahman al-Iryani, president	1967
	Abdullah Kurshumi, premier	1969
Yemen, Royalist	Muhammad al-Badr, imam	1962
Yugoslavia	Marshal Tito, president of the republic and secretary-general of the League of Communists	1953
	Mitja Ribicic, president of the Federal Executive Council	1969
Zambia	Kenneth Kaunda, president	1964

Historical Studies

Among numerous congresses held in 1969 was an interesting one on medieval Spain at Madrid, which included important papers by British, French, and other foreign scholars. Several conferences were meetings of commissions linked with the International Committee for Historical Sciences; they were concerned with ecclesiastical, economic, Byzantine, Slav, and parliamentary subjects, and most papers read were destined for publication, usually in the proceedings of the conference. Thus in 1969 appeared communications made to three *coloques internationals d'histoire maritime,* held at Venice, Italy, in 1962, at Beirut, Lebanon, in 1966, and at Seville, Spain, in 1967. Similarly, the voluminous *Actes du Colloque international,* held in Paris in 1964 to discuss *La Première Internationale,* were edited by E. Labrousse.

Under the sponsorship of the International Commission for the History of Towns, the first of several series intended to cover Europe up to 1800 began with *Historic Towns,* vol. i, edited by Mary D. Lobel. The tendency to widen the scope of history and link it with sociology was illustrated by the appearance of a new *Journal of Interdisciplinary History,* under the aegis of the Massachusetts Institute of Technology.

For the ancient world, an original contribution was J. I. Miller's *The Spice Trade of the Roman Empire.* A valuable new series on the Islamic world started with an English translation from the Italian by E. J. Costello of *Arab Historians of the Crusades.* Early European history was represented by biographies of *Otton III, empereur de l'an mille* by Alain Ollivier and *Frederick Barbarossa* by P. Munz. In commemoration of a thousand years of history since Mieszko I adopted Christianity in 966, two general works on Poland appeared: *Geschichte Polens* by R. Gotthold and a *History of Poland* for English readers jointly written by A. Gieysztor and four other Polish authors. R. Allen Brown made a fresh study of *The Normans and the Norman Conquest.*

The posthumous publication of *Essays in Czech History* by R. R. Betts showed the loss sustained by his untimely death. Nicolai Rubinstein, editor of the Medici papers, brought together 15 essays by U.S., British, and French scholars, *Florentine Studies: Politics and Society in Renaissance Florence.* There

Tintype of a woman in Victorian-style dress discovered by volunteer archaeologists searching for traces of Weeksville, a 19th-century community of free Negroes in what is now the Bedford-Stuyvesant area of Brooklyn, N.Y.

WIDE WORLD

also appeared a translation of a similar Italian collection: *The World of Renaissance Florence,* edited by G. Martinelli. Valuable for European history in general was N. R. Ker's *Medieval Manuscripts in British Libraries,* vol. i, devoted to those in London. A gap was filled in the series of *English Historical Documents* with vol. iv, 1327–1485, edited by A. R. Myers. Hermann Günther's *Der Eintritt der südlicher Hemisphäre in die europäische Geschichte* dealt with the opening up of the South African route to Asia. In *Spain Under the Hapsburgs,* vol. ii, John Lynch carried the story into the New World with *Spain and America, 1598–1700.*

Two more volumes for the later Tudors completed the massive collection of *Tudor Royal Proclamations* made by the U.S. scholars P. L. Hughes and James F. Larkin. Lady Antonia Fraser wrote a sympathetic biography of *Mary, Queen of Scots.* There was a general account by Claude Mettra of *Les Bourbons* and a survey of *Europe in the Age of Louis XIV* by Ragnhild Hatton. T. Besterman's *Voltaire* received a mixed welcome. J. M. Sherwig's *Guineas and Gunpowder* dealt with British foreign aid in the wars with France, 1793–1815. Two physicians, Ida MacAlpine and Richard Hunter, presented their findings concerning *George III and the Mad Business.* A detailed biography of *The Younger Pitt* by John Ehrman began with *The Years of Acclaim.* Similarly, Lady Longford called the first volume of her life of Wellington *The Years of the Sword.* Marking Napoleon's bicentenary, several English translations of French studies appeared, notably Georges Lefebvre's *Napoleon,* vol. i and ii. Among English works, R. F. Delderfield's *Imperial Sunset* dealt with the years 1813–14. *The Life of Joseph Chamberlain,* begun by J. L. Garvin more than 30 years before, was completed by Julian Amery. The best single volume on *Modern England* in a long time was the work of a U.S. professor, R. K. Webb.

Of studies in American history, particularly significant were an anthology of John C. Calhoun's writings edited by J. L. Thomas, based on the first three volumes of his *Papers; Franklin D. Roosevelt and Foreign Affairs,* vol. i–iii, January 1933–January 1937, edited by Edgar B. Nixon; and an analysis by Arthur M. Schlesinger, Jr., of *The Crisis of Confidence, Ideas, Power and Violence in America.* Two U.S. works of high quality were a *Modern History of Egypt* by P. J. Vatikiotis and a monograph on *Cotton and the Egyptian Economy, 1820–1914* by E. R. J. Owen. An attempt to evaluate the effect of European ideas on native cultures was made by John Hatch in his *History of the British in Africa.*

In France, G. Sautel's *Histoire des institutions publiques depuis la Révolution français,* G. Roux's biography of *Napoleon III,* and R. Poidevin's account of *Rélations économiques et financières entre la France et l'Allemagne de 1898 à 1914* were noteworthy. A German-American scholar, Hajo Holborn, completed his *History of Modern Germany* with vol. iii, 1840–1945. The origins of the *Führerprinzep* were skillfully traced in *Die deutsche Diktatur* by K. D. Bracher, and Nazi relations with other countries in *Nationalsozialistiche Aussenpolitik 1933–38* by H.-A. Jacobsen. (A. T. M.)

See also Literature.

ENCYCLOPÆDIA BRITANNICA FILMS. *India: Introduction to Its History* (1957); *Egypt: Cradle of Civilization* (1962); *The Mediterranean World* (1962); *Athens: The Golden Age* (Humanities Course) (1963); *Julius Caesar: Rise of the Roman Empire* (1964); *Life in Ancient Rome* (1964); *Middle Ages: Culture of Medieval Europe* (1965); *Middle Ages: Rise of Feudalism* (1965); *The Spirit of Rome* (1965); *The Medieval Mind* (1969); *Origin of Life—Chemical Evolution* (1969); *Reflections on Time* (1969); *Theories on the Origin of Life* (1969).

Historic Buildings

Throughout 1969, efforts to implement the "Recommendation on the Preservation of Cultural Property Endangered by Public and Private Works," unanimously adopted by the General Conference of UNESCO at the end of the previous year, continued. The principles elaborated in the recommendation, which was designed to encourage member states to take legislative and other steps to preserve their cultural heritage, included the advisability of establishing a national protective inventory; the carrying out of surveys on threatened cultural property well in advance of the start of public or private works; giving first priority to the preservation of sites and monuments in situ, together with their historic surroundings; planning for salvage or transfer of a threatened monument only when overriding economic or social conditions make it impossible to preserve it in place; and encouragement to private owners to maintain historically or artistically interesting structures through favourable tax rates and by furnishing technical advice.

The most important international project for the conservation of historic buildings was centred about Venice. Close cooperation was established between the Italian authorities and UNESCO and, for the first time, all of the disparate agencies and institutions concerned with the problem were working together. Legislative measures, considered for adoption by 1971, would provide for the adaptation of old buildings to meet modern health standards; measures to slow the lowering of the level of the land and the pollution of the canal system; a study of the lagoon; improved communications; and, finally, work to ensure the conservation of the most seriously threatened works of art.

A complete inventory was taken of historically or artistically interesting buildings (in addition to existing inventories of classified monuments). A study was under way on the socioeconomic factors that would preserve Venice, not as an open-air museum, but so

W. BRAUN—PIX FROM PUBLIX

that it might have a viable role in contemporary life.

UNESCO had sent two experts to Indonesia in January 1968 to examine the condition of the Buddhist monument of Borobudur, located near Jogjakarta in Central Java. Test borings had demonstrated that the monument was built on fill laid upon low hills. Infiltration of water during the rainy season had loosened the fill and caused settling of the lower terraces. Further, the high degree of moisture had contributed to weathering of the carved stone elements making up one of the longest and most detailed friezes known of the life of Gautama Buddha and of scenes from the visits of the Bodhisattva Sudhana to the great sages. UNESCO planned to assist the Indonesian government in seeking contributions for the restoration of the monument and to furnish experts. It was hoped that the restored Borobudur, together with nearby monuments such as Prambanan (a Hindu complex showing carved scenes of the Ramayana on the terrace of the principal temples) and the "Water Palace" of the sultan of Jogjakarta, would form the nucleus of a centre of cultural tourism.

The need to deal with urgent economic and social problems had led to the downgrading of cultural projects in many less developed countries. However, a monumental heritage capable of attracting tourists can be an important economic resource, not only directly but because the tourism infrastructure—hotels, improved communications, and so on—provides employment and investment opportunities. During 1969 other UNESCO projects were under way in Brazil for the conservation and development of Salvador de Bahía and Ouro Prêto; in Peru in the Machu Picchu-Cuzco area; on Easter Island and in Santiago, Chile; in Cambodia (the Khmer monuments); in the Tunis-Carthage area of Tunisia; and on the "historic route" of Ethiopia.

The International Council of Monuments and Sites (ICOMOS) continued to expand its activities. In its fourth year of existence it organized about 30 national committees and established international specialized subject committees to stimulate discussion and research. Noteworthy meetings took place on such problems as the preservation and development of historic quarters and the control of humidity in old buildings. The costs of many of these meetings were met through contributions from the local national committees and their respective governments. The French government contributed approximately $150,000 to adapt the coach house of the Hôtel de St. Aignan, built *c.* 1640 in the Marais section of Paris, for ICOMOS headquarters. The hôtel itself was purchased by the city of Paris and was being restored and adapted to serve as the city archive.

The second General Assembly of ICOMOS was held in Oxford, Eng., July 6–12. The major themes of the meeting were the preservation and development of monuments and sites and cultural tourism. P. Gazzola and R. Lemaire were reelected as president and secretary-general, respectively.

Although many outstanding buildings were sacrificed to "progress" during the year, increasing efforts were also being made to preserve man's monumental cultural heritage. An outstanding example of bilateral cooperation was the transfer of Christopher Wren's Church of St. Mary the Virgin, Aldermanbury (1667), which had been damaged by bombs in 1940, from London to Westminster College in Fulton, Mo. There it was installed as a memorial to the occasion in 1946 on which Sir Winston Churchill delivered his "iron curtain" speech.

In the United States the preservation of the French Quarter (Vieux Carré) of New Orleans, La., was ensured when federal funds for a proposed riverfront expressway were denied. Local organizations and the National Trust had worked strenuously to save the historic district. Urban renewal programs in several large American cities involved the incorporation and rehabilitation of older buildings. In Boston a $10 million plan to restore the historic Faneuil Hall markets district was announced. St. Louis, Mo., adopted a redevelopment plan that would save the more important half of the existing buildings at the Laclède's Landing area on the riverfront, the last surviving

COURTESY, JAPANESE TOURIST OFFICE

Famous avenue of cedars planted in 1648 was threatened by plans for a new road to Toshogu shrine in Nikko.

Rising waters of Venice are threatening to engulf city. Many first floors have had to be abandoned.

GAMMA—PIX FROM PUBLIX

Jewish Quarter of old Jerusalem (opposite page) being restored by the Israeli government as part of a program undertaken since the Six-Day War in 1967. Bas-relief (below) depicts an event from the life of Buddha on a terrace wall of the 9th-century Buddhist monument Borobudur near Jogjakarta, Indon. A worldwide campaign was planned to raise funds for restoration of the monument, which was crumbling from the effects of erosion.

WIDE WORLD

group of buildings of the 1865–75 period. New structures planned would conform to the character and scale of the older ones.

In England the National Trust succeeded in preserving Rainbow Wood Farm on the outskirts of Bath, which the city had attempted to take over for playing fields. On the debit side, the cobbled Regency courtyard of London's Carlton Mews, which linked Trafalgar Square with St. James's Park, was demolished in September to make room for offices and flats. Attempts to convert some of the squares around Mayfair into parking lots were defeated by conservationists, but Georgian Bloomsbury was less fortunate. Woburn Square, the first "square" in London, was to be swallowed up by extensions to London University, and other redevelopments threatening the character of the area were planned around the British Museum.

Anglican leaders expressed concern over the closing of many parish churches, some of which dated back to Norman times. A possible solution was the creation of "group ministries" in which several priests combined operations to serve depopulated parishes. The Civic Trust's report for 1968, published in February 1969, emphasized that conservation areas need not be frozen into museums, and that many historic buildings were being adapted to serve as offices, banks, and community centres. In accordance with this aim, consideration was being given to alternative uses for old church buildings. For example, the 15th-century churches of St. Saviour and St. Margaret at York were to be converted into hotels. The project to save the Corn Exchange in Bury St. Edmunds was another example of the adaptation of historically interesting buildings to new functions. The exchange—which held meetings once a week—was given quarters on the upper floor; five shops were installed and part of the premises was made available for recreational programs.

In the Netherlands a 20-year, $8.5 million program for the restoration of Delfshaven, the port from which the Pilgrims sailed for Massachusetts in 1620, was approved. This small port was the only old part of Rotterdam not razed by bombs in May 1940. The Zakkendraggershuis (the ancient headquarters of the stevedores' guild) was restored, as was the neighbouring "Kraahuis" where skilled craftsmen produced pewter objects for sale. The Pelgrimvaderskerk, where the English religious exiles worshiped before going to America, was restored to its 18th-century appearance.

In France the city council of Paris finally decided on the fate of Les Halles. The central market was first established in the reign of Philip II and took definitive form under Napoleon III. It had long been inadequate for the city of Paris and the surrounding area, but decisions concerning its transfer were delayed for many years. During this period a number of alternative uses for the area (totaling about 86 ac.) were discussed, among them the possibility of turning the land over to the University of Paris for classrooms; the creation of a cluster of modern buildings including conference halls, theatres, and stores; and use of the space for a series of parks and gardens. The final decision, based on the Capitant report, represented a victory for the conservationists. All the old market buildings would be razed except one, which —preserved as a witness to the past—would be adapted for recreational purposes. The central area (of 32 ac.) would be freed, and beneath it an underground city would be built with sports, business, and cultural centres. Gardens would set off buildings of architectural value, such as the Church of St. Eustache which had previously been obscured. The existing aspect of the surrounding area was to be preserved. Historically interesting buildings would be brought up to modern standards of hygiene and comfort, and many would be adapted for residential use.

Japan, which in recent years had experienced a rapid expansion of its industrial facilities, faced particular problems in the preservation of its cultural heritage. In the Tokyo-Osaka area especially, the surroundings of monuments were adversely affected and historically or artistically interesting buildings and sites were being sacrificed. The planned expansion of the highway leading to the Toshogu shrine in Nikko, for example, would have involved cutting down the famous avenue of cedars planted in 1648. The trees were spared temporarily, pending a government appeal to review the plan.

The former capital of Kyoto was threatened by urban redevelopment. Kyoto was modeled on the plan of Ch'ang-an, the capital of the Sui Dynasty (A.D. 589–618) in China. Originally it was a rectangular area measuring about 3.5 mi. from north to south and 3 mi. from east to west, surrounded by a moat and symmetrically divided by wide roads into squares which in turn were subdivided into smaller units by narrow lanes. During the course of its political ascendancy many outstanding shrines, temples, and palaces were built that became widely known for their harmonious proportions and beauty.

Kyoto's cultural importance caused it to be spared from bombing during World War II and, ironically, historic Kyoto was more seriously endangered by economic prosperity and expansion in 1969 than it had been by war. The low houses and other structures in old Kyoto were threatened with destruction and the more important buildings and monuments by removal and transfer outside the city where their associations would be lost. The Japanese UNESCO National Commission, with the aid of a grant from UNESCO, planned a study of the problems involved and of various alternatives that might be considered.

(H. Du.)

See also Museums and Galleries.

Hockey

Field Hockey. The season after an Olympic hockey tournament is invariably a time of reappraisal and reconstruction. In 1969 the process of change was more searching than usual, especially for Great Britain. At the Olympic Games in October 1968, Britain finished lower in world ranking than at any previous time, 12th out of 16. As England had a 70% stake in the Great Britain team, responsibility for this sorry performance rested heavily on English shoulders, and there was need for rapid action if England was to reestablish its standing at the European Cup Tournament to be held in Brussels in September 1970. The British selectors cast their net wider than usual and cast it especially among younger men. Only 5 of the 13 English players who went to the Olympics were included in the England trials five months later. A goalless draw against West Germany was followed by a 1–0 win against Wales; a 1–0 defeat by Scotland, which won the Home Countries' international championship; a 2–0 victory over the old enemy, Ireland; another goalless draw against South Africa; and a 2–1 defeat by the Netherlands. An aggregate score of 4 goals in 6 matches was hardly enough to keep any side on the road to success. Scotland beat Ireland 1–0; Ireland beat Wales 1–0; Wales drew with Scotland 0–0.

A visit to England by Pakistan, the Olympic champions, who brought eight of their winning team on a European tour in September, gave England an opportunity to take a fresh look at the team-building process and the resources available. Pakistan, however, won all their three games decisively, defeating England Under-23 8–0, an England XI 4–1, and England in a full international match 1–0. C. I. M. Jones, a former British Olympic halfback, asked to be relieved of his duties as England team manager for personal reasons and W. Vans Agnew, a former Scottish player, was appointed in his place.

Other international matches showed the following results: West Germany beat South Africa 2–0 and drew 1–1, and beat Switzerland 6–0; the Netherlands defeated South Africa 3–0, and drew with Ireland 1–1; Wales beat Belgium 3–1 and South Africa 2–0; South Africa won over France 2–0; Scotland defeated South Africa 1–0; and Belgium beat France 4–0.

At the end of October the International Hockey Federation announced it would organize a World Cup series every four years, starting in 1971.

The victory of Lancashire in the British county championships underlined the importance of careful preparation. Individually, the players were by no means the most talented in the competition but they spared no effort to make the most of themselves, grew in confidence and power as they won their way through successive rounds, and were worthy champions. They, like Berkshire, champions of the South, and Leicestershire, Midlands' champions, used a variation of the four-forward method, which suggested that there might be more in this formation than some of the traditionalists were prepared to admit.

On the other hand, Lincolnshire, which finished second to Lancashire, was strictly orthodox, fast, direct, determined, and uncomplicated. It forced Lancashire to a replay in the final, the first time it had been necessary to replay the final in the history of the competition.

The England women's team defeated the other three home countries, Ireland, Scotland, and Wales, but not without a struggle, especially against Wales at Wembley. If not up to the highest English standard, the team was gathering strength and confidence when it underwent a number of changes for the last match of the season against West Germany at Leverkusen. In this reorganization, the England captain, D. Parry, lost her place in the forward line and the much-changed team lost its unbeaten record, West Germany winning 3–2. (R. L. Hs.)

Amateur Ice Hockey. For a seventh successive season the world and European titles were won by the U.S.S.R., in Stockholm, Swed., on March 15–30. The outcome, however, was extremely close. Sweden, which finished second, and Czechoslovakia, third, tied with the Soviets on points, and so the medals were decided by goal average. The other competing teams were Canada, Finland, and the U.S.

NHL Final Standings

	Won	Lost	Tied	Goals	Goals against	Pts.
EASTERN DIVISION						
Montreal Canadiens	46	19	11	271	202	103
Boston Bruins	42	18	16	303	221	100
New York Rangers	41	26	9	231	196	91
Toronto Maple Leafs	35	26	15	234	217	85
Detroit Red Wings	33	31	12	239	221	78
Chicago Black Hawks	34	33	9	280	246	77
WESTERN DIVISION						
St. Louis Blues	37	25	14	204	157	88
Oakland Seals	29	36	11	219	251	69
Philadelphia Flyers	20	35	21	174	225	61
Los Angeles Kings	24	42	10	185	260	58
Pittsburgh Penguins	20	45	11	189	252	51
Minnesota North Stars	18	43	15	189	270	51

"MONTREAL STAR"

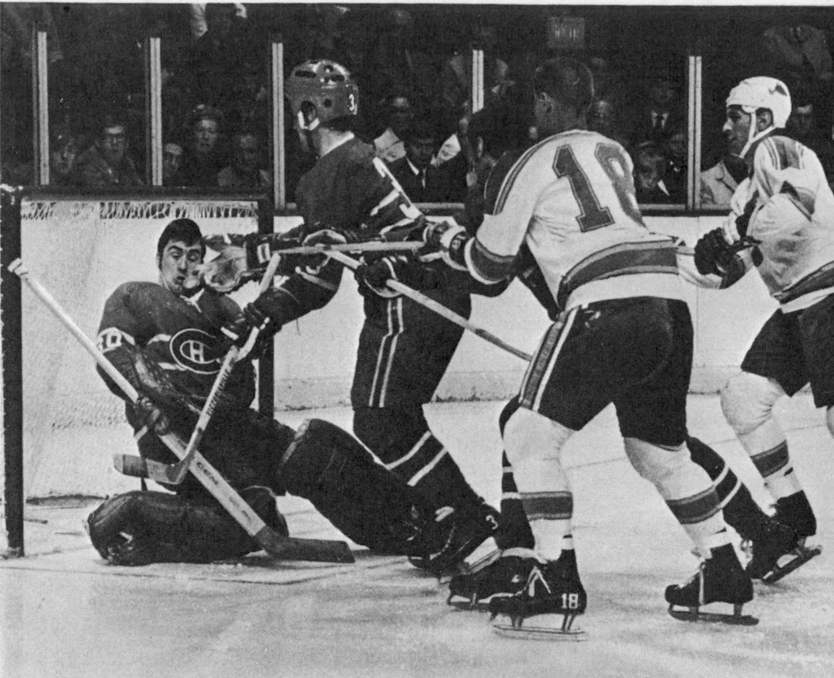

Montreal Canadien goalie Rogatien Vachon grimaces as puck flies past his face during Stanley Cup play-off action, April 27, 1969, with St. Louis Blues. Canadiens won 3–1.

A new development allowed only six countries to contest the Group A championship, each country playing the other five twice, whereas in previous seasons eight nations played each other once. The results were curious. Czechoslovakia beat the U.S.S.R. in each of their two encounters but failed to win the title because of losing twice to Sweden. The second Czechoslovak victory over the Soviet side precipitated anti-Soviet demonstrations in Prague, where political tension had been dangerously high.

Top scorers in the competition were Anatoli Firsov and Boris Mikhailov (U.S.S.R.), Ulf Sterner (Swed.), and Jaroslav Holik (Czech.), each with 14 points. The organizers named the three best players as Sterner and goalkeeper Leif Holmquist, both of Sweden, and the Czechoslovak defenseman Jan Suchy. The tournament was a setback for the U.S., the winners in 1960, which lost all of its ten games to suffer relegation to Group B, making way for the promotion of East Germany for the 1970 championships in Canada.

Another break with tradition was the separate playing of the Groups B and C competitions at other locations. Both were held in Yugoslavia, Group B at Ljubljana on February 28–March 9 and Group C at Skopje on February 24–March 2. Japan, which won the latter, demonstrated marked progress after being regarded only a few years previously as a "Cinderella" nation in this sport.

A proposal by Canada that future senior world championships be declared fully open to professionals was rejected by the International Ice Hockey Federation during its annual congress at Crans-sur-Sierre, Switz., on July 5–12. But the congress agreed to allow a maximum of nine professional players per team for a trial period. It was decided to let 16 teams compete in the 1972 Winter Olympics at Sapporo, Jap.

(H. B.)

Professional Ice Hockey. The Montreal Canadiens in 1969 won their fourth Stanley Cup in five seasons and their 16th in the 52-year history of the National Hockey League (NHL). The Canadiens swept through 14 play-off games with only 2 losses, both to the Boston Bruins in a tense 6-game final in the Eastern Division. They eliminated the New York Rangers in four games in a semifinal, beat Boston, and then won four in a row from the St. Louis Blues for the championship.

Montreal's conquest of the Blues represented the second consecutive season in which the Canadiens beat St. Louis in four successive games. The Montreal victory margins in 1969 were 3–1, 3–1, 4–0, and 2–1. The Blues romped through the Western Division and on their way to the championship finals eliminated the Philadelphia Flyers and the Los Angeles Kings in eight straight play-off victories. The Conn Smythe Trophy, awarded annually to the best player in the Stanley Cup tournament, was awarded to Serge Savard, a rangy 23-year-old Montreal defenseman.

Phil Esposito, a tall Boston centre, dominated the individual awards during the season. He won the Hart Trophy as the most valuable player and the Art Ross Trophy as leading scorer with a record 126 points. Esposito's precocious teammate Bobby Orr won the James Norris Memorial Trophy as the outstanding defenseman in the NHL for the second successive year.

Alex Delvecchio, an 18-year veteran with the Detroit Red Wings, won the Lady Byng Trophy as the player best combining talent with sportsmanlike conduct. It was the third time Delvecchio earned the award. Glenn Hall and Jacques Plante of St. Louis shared the Vezina Trophy as goalkeepers playing for the team that yielded the fewest goals. Danny Grant, a 23-year-old left wing for the Minnesota North Stars, won the Calder Trophy as the outstanding freshman in the NHL.

The all-star vote still indicated a strong preference for players in the established Eastern Division. Hall was the only Western Division player selected to either the first or second team. The first all-star team included: goalie, Hall; defense, Orr and Tim Horton (Toronto); centre, Esposito; right wing, Gordie Howe (Detroit); left wing, Bobby Hull (Chicago). Those elected to the second team were: goalie, Ed Giacomin (New York); defense, Ted Green (Boston) and Ted Harris (Montreal); centre, Jean Beliveau (Montreal); right wing, Yvan Cournoyer (Montreal); left wing, Frank Mahovlich (Detroit).

Esposito paced a year that saw 39 NHL records broken or tied. His mark for total points included a record number of assists, 77, and a record number of goals for centres, 49. Bobby Hull continued to be the league's supershooter, scoring 58 goals to break his former one-year standard of 54. As the 1969–70 season began, Hull refused to report to the Chicago Black Hawks until mid-November, claiming that the Hawks had reneged on certain fringe benefits contained in his four-year contract for $100,000 a year. He eventually withdrew his complaint.

Off the ice, the NHL governors voted to expand from 12 to 14 teams by 1970–71. The new franchises, Vancouver, B.C., and Buffalo, N.Y., would join the Eastern Division while the Chicago Black Hawks would move into the Western Division.

The Hershey (Pa.) Bears won the Calder Cup as champions of the American Hockey League, beating the Quebec Aces four games to one. The Vancouver Canucks dominated the Western Hockey League play-offs by drubbing the Seattle Totems and the Portland Buckaroos in eight straight play-off games. The Dallas Black Hawks required five games to beat the Oklahoma City Blazers for the championship of the Central Professional League. (R. H. BE.)

Hogs:
see Agriculture

Holland:
see Netherlands

Home Economics:
see Domestic Arts and Sciences

Honduras, British:
see Dependent States

Hong Kong:
see Dependent States

Honduras

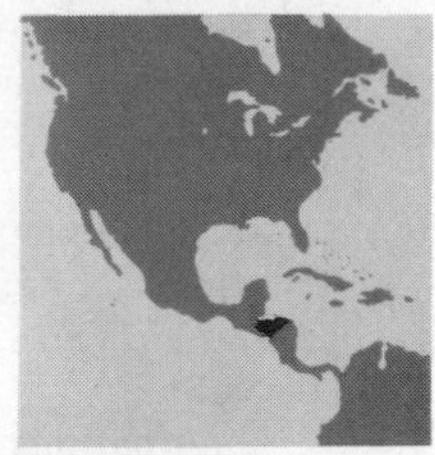

A republic of Central America, Honduras is bounded by Nicaragua, El Salvador, Guatemala, the Caribbean Sea, and the Pacific Ocean. Area: 43,277 sq.mi. (112,088 sq. km.). Pop. (1969 est.): 2,494,900, of which 90% is mestizo. Cap. and largest city: Tegucigalpa (pop., 1969 est., 218,510). Language: Spanish; some Indian dialects. Religion: Roman Catholic. President in 1969, Osvaldo López Arellano.

In July the 860-mi. undemarcated border common to Honduras and El Salvador became the focus of open warfare and hemisphere-wide concern. Border incidents between the two nations were not new, but in the past they had usually been localized and self-contained. The latest confrontation, however, grew into the most serious regional conflict in Central America in 60 years. The discord resulted from the fundamental territorial and demographic differences between the two agriculturally oriented nations. El Salvador, smallest of the Central American republics

HONDURAS

Education. (1965) Primary, pupils 283,606, teachers 9,862; secondary, pupils 17,980; vocational, pupils 2,450; teacher training, students 3,554; secondary, vocational, and teacher training, teachers (1964) 2,079; higher, students 2,578, teaching staff (1963) 302.

Finance. Monetary unit: lempira, with a par value of 2 lempiras to U.S. $1 (4.80 lempiras = £1 sterling). Gold and foreign exchange, central bank: (June 1969) U.S. $27,640,000; (June 1968) U.S. $33,390,000. Budget (1969 est.) balanced at 251.1 million lempiras. Gross national product: (1967) 1,153,000,000 lempiras; (1966) 1,085,000,000 lempiras. Money supply: (April 1969) 145,050,000 lempiras; (April 1968) 137,180,000 lempiras. Cost of living (Tegucigalpa; 1963 = 100): (May 1969) 121; (May 1968) 120.

Foreign Trade. (1968) Imports 370 million lempiras; exports 360.1 million lempiras. Import sources (1967): U.S. 48%; El Salvador 12%; Guatemala 7%; West Germany 5%. Export destinations (1967): U.S. 44%; West Germany 24%; El Salvador 7%; Italy 5%. Main exports: bananas 47%; coffee 12%; timber 8%; silver 5%.

Transport and Communications. Roads (1964) 3,347 km. (including 367 km. paved). Motor vehicles in use (1967): passenger 11,200; commercial (including buses) 11,500. Railways (1963) 1,152 km. (confined to northern plantation area). Air traffic (1967): 95,841,000 passenger-km.; freight 8,269,000 net ton-km. Shipping (1968): merchant vessels 100 gross tons and over 45; gross tonnage 68,958. Telephones (Jan. 1968) 10,161. Radio receivers (Dec. 1967) 136,000. Television receivers (Dec. 1966) *c.* 10,000.

Agriculture. Production (in 000; metric tons; 1968; 1967 in parentheses): corn *c.* 390 (*c.* 355); rice (1967) *c.* 25, (1966) *c.* 23; coffee (1967) *c.* 29, (1966) *c.* 20; sugar, raw value (1968–69) *c.* 45, (1967–68) *c.* 49; dry beans *c.* 55 (*c.* 51); bananas (1967) *c.* 1,100, (1966) *c.* 1,000; cottonseed *c.* 15 (*c.* 14); beef and veal (1967) *c.* 23, (1966) *c.* 23; timber (cu.m.; 1965) 3,800, (1964) 3,700. Livestock (in 000; 1966–67): cattle *c.* 1,750; pigs *c.* 920; chickens *c.* 6,400.

Industry. Production (in 000; metric tons; 1967): lead ore (metal content; exports) 12; zinc ore (metal content; exports) 13; silver (exports) 0.12; gold (troy oz.) 5.9; electricity (kw-hr.; 1966) 204,000.

(8,100 sq.mi.), had a population of 3.3 million, and thus was the most densely populated. All of its inhabitable territory was occupied. Honduras, with 43,277 sq.mi., was five times the size of its neighbour but, with fewer than 2.5 million people, had a population density only one-seventh that of El Salvador. Much of Honduras was thinly settled. Thus, Salvadorean farmers increasingly migrated to Honduras seeking land and livelihood, particularly in the districts nearest El Salvador, where the majority squatted on large tracts of Honduran government land. Also, in recent years growing numbers of semiskilled Salvadoreans moved from their native land into small Honduran provincial towns, where they obtained jobs at the expense of less skilled Hondurans. By 1969 perhaps as many as 300,000 Salvadoreans were living in Honduras, and the Hondurans were displaying increasing animosity toward them.

In April the government of Honduras decided to enforce the segment of its 1962 Agrarian Reform Law specifying that redistributed lands could be owned only by native-born Hondurans. The government lands nearest El Salvador were designated among the initial sites on which such redistribution procedures were to be implemented. This action struck directly at the Salvadoreans in the region, and by early June more than 11,000 had been ordered to leave Honduras. El Salvador charged that its people in Honduras were being persecuted and subjected to physical harm by Hondurans. Throughout June feelings increased as the two nations engaged in an impassioned three-game regional soccer play-off, a part of the World Cup soccer competition. El Salvador won the championship on June 27, and on that day Honduras severed diplomatic relations with El Salvador. On June 28 both countries accepted a mediation offer from Guatemala, Nicaragua, and Costa Rica, but tensions continued to mount.

Mediation efforts remained unsuccessful, confrontations between the two nations continued to escalate, and open warfare erupted in mid-July when Salvadorean forces invaded Honduras. Troops penetrated as far as 45 mi. into Honduras, directing their thrusts along the Pan-American Highway in the southern part of the nation, where the greatest resistance was encountered; across the central section of the border; and over the frontier near the Honduran provincial capital of Nueva Ocotepeque, which was captured. Salvadorean aircraft bombed several Honduran cities, including military installations near Tegucigalpa. In retaliation, Honduran aircraft bombed several Salvadorean port facilities as well as military sites on the outskirts of San Salvador. By July 17 the conflict had subsided. The next day a peace plan was accepted unanimously by the Council of the Organization of American States (OAS), with Honduras and El Salvador abstaining from the voting. The plan demanded that each side (1) accept a cease-fire, (2) permit neutral observers to patrol the frontier, (3) guarantee the rights and property of each other's nationals, and (4) return to the old frontiers that existed prior to July 14. The last of these four conditions was finally agreed to August 3 when El Salvador withdrew approximately 10,000 troops under threat of condemnation and possible sanctions by the OAS. In December, after several months of an uneasy truce, the Central American Common Market foreign ministers agreed on a formula whereby negotiations between Honduras and El Salvador would begin early in 1970.

On September 2 Hurricane Francelia moved across the Gulf of Honduras and buffeted the relatively well-populated north coast of Honduras west of Tela and the sparsely populated Bay Islands with 100-mph winds. Four thousand persons were evacuated from the coastal area to the nearby inland city of San Pedro Sula. Extensive flooding resulted from the hurricane. The railroad serving Puerto Cortés was washed out; floodwaters rendered coastal highways impassable; and banana plantations were inundated.

From the depressed economic conditions of 1967, Honduras in 1968 made a notable improvement in agricultural production and slowly began to institute or increase efforts in planning, agrarian reform, and transportation. The gross national product increased by more than 7% in 1968. In April 1969, Honduras became one of six Latin-American nations to participate in a $25 million program designed to stimulate trade in capital goods among Latin-American nations, financed jointly by the Chase Manhattan Bank of New York and the Deutsch-Südamerikanische Bank of West Germany. (A. D. Bu.)

Horse Racing

Thoroughbred Racing. *U.S.* Two outstanding features of the 1969 Thoroughbred racing season in the United States were the late-season performances of Arts and Letters, which gained the horse-of-the-year title with six consecutive stakes victories after defeats in the Kentucky Derby and Preakness, and the rise and fall in popularity of girl jockeys. Also of importance was the return of Thoroughbred racing to Pennsylvania, where it had been outlawed since colonial days, and the temporary stoppage of racing in California due to strikes by track employees.

During the first five months of the year, Arts and Letters, owned by financier Paul Mellon, of Upperville, Va., became the "bridesmaid" of the three-year-old division, having finished second to Majestic Prince in the Kentucky Derby and Preakness and second to Top Knight in the Flamingo Stakes and Florida Derby. However, just before experts classified Arts and Letters as "never a bride," the son of Ribot–All Beautiful, by Battlefield, came into his own at Aqueduct on Memorial Day when he defeated ten older horses, including Nodouble, Iron Ruler, and Vitriolic, in the Metropolitan Mile.

Jockey Diane Crump (centre), first girl ever to compete against men on a Florida racetrack, rides Bridle 'n Bit in the fourth race at Hialeah on Feb. 11, 1969. She finished fifth.

WIDE WORLD

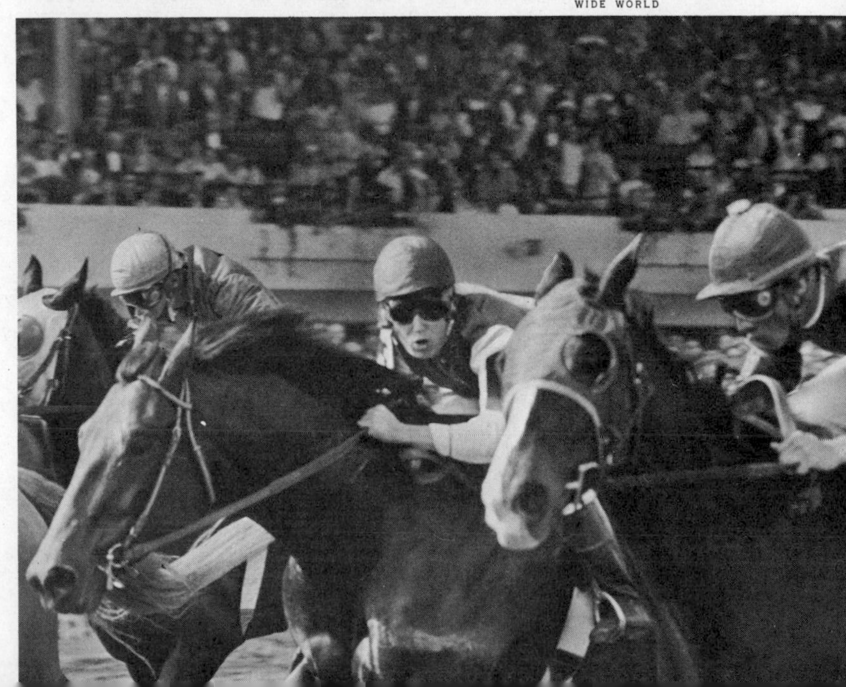

After that victory there was no stopping Arts and Letters, as he ran roughshod over all rivals for the horse-of-the-year title. The Virginia-bred chestnut colt won the Belmont Stakes by $5\frac{1}{2}$ lengths over his old nemesis, Majestic Prince. Arts and Letters then went to Saratoga Springs (N.Y.) to win the Jim Dandy and Travers stakes and then returned to Long Island to beat older stars again in the Woodward Stakes and the Jockey Club Gold Cup.

Normally, victories in the Kentucky Derby and the Preakness and a second in the Belmont Stakes—the three classics of the American Triple Crown—would have earned the three-year-old championship and horse-of-the-year title for Majestic Prince. These early-season successes, however, were overshadowed by Arts and Letters' complete domination of the three-year-old and handicap ranks during the final half of the year. By the season's end, Arts and Letters had won 8 (his last 6 in a row) of 14 starts to earn $555,604, while Majestic Prince won 7 of 8 starts to earn $408,700 in purses.

In the end-of-year polls for divisional championships, conducted by the *Daily Racing Form* and *Turf and Sport Digest,* Arts and Letters scored runaway victories in the voting for horse-of-the-year honours and, of course, for three-year-old leadership. In both polls, Silent Screen, winner of $397,966 through 5 wins in 6 outings, was selected best two-year-old colt or gelding; Gallant Bloom, which was unbeaten in 8 starts and won 7 stakes for earnings of $220,514, was selected best three-year-old filly; and Hawaii, a horse bred in South Africa which won 6 of 10 starts and $279,280, was voted best among the grass-course specialists. The *Racing Form* poll made Fast Attack, winner of 5 of 14 starts to earn $136,647, the best two-year-old filly, while Tudor Queen, which defeated colts, was picked for this honour by *Turf and Sport Digest.*

Also, the *Racing Form* experts made Arts and Letters handicap champion although he started but once under an assigned weight, 111 lb. in the Metropolitan. Meanwhile, Nodouble, winner of 4 of 12 starts, was selected handicap champion by the *Turf and Sport Digest.*

Majestic Prince, trained by former jockey great Johnny Longden and owned by Canadian businessman Frank M. McMahon, made his final start and suffered his lone defeat in the Belmont Stakes on June 7. Declaring that his charge had suffered a "mushy" ankle in the Belmont, Longden withdrew Majestic Prince from competition. As the year ended, Longden said that the horse would be mended and ready to renew competition with Arts and Letters in mid- or late 1970.

In 1968 New York sportsman David (Sonny) Werblin purchased a son of Prince John for $39,000 and gave the colt to trainer J. Bowes Bond for racing as a two-year-old. Named Silent Screen, the New York-bred colt was second in his first start at Saratoga in 1969 and then went undefeated in his next five outings, including the Arlington-Washington Futurity and the Champagne Stakes, to earn ten times his purchase price. Suffering a filled hindleg on the eve of the Garden State Stakes, when he could have clinched the juvenile title, Silent Screen was withdrawn by Bond and shipped to Hialeah Park. Forum won the $330,625 event by four lengths, but Silent Screen retained the juvenile crown and thus was the preseason favourite for the 1970 Triple Crown.

Thoroughbred racing suffered a loss in April with the death of trainer Max Hirsch at the age of 88. Prior to his death, however, the dean of U.S. trainers developed King Ranch's three-year-old filly Gallant Bloom, the only unbeaten champion of 1969. Gallant Bloom won eight straight races, all but one of them in stakes competition.

On February 22, Barbara Jo Rubin, a 19-year-old Miamian, broke an actual though undeclared boycott against female jockeys by becoming the first girl to ride a winner in a regular betting race at a U.S. pari-mutuel track. This was followed by a number of successes by a few girl jockeys throughout the country and, by midsummer, many believed that women were in the jockey ranks to stay. However, their popularity waned in later months so that they had only one winner in November and none in December.

The three Thoroughbred racetracks under construction in Pennsylvania at Philadelphia, Harrisburg, and Pittsburgh were not scheduled for completion until the summer of 1971. Nevertheless, Thoroughbreds invaded that state when the Pennsylvania Racing Board granted three associations permission to run at harness horse racing tracks.

During 1969, fewer Thoroughbred yearlings were reported sold at auction in North America than in 1968. Their average selling price was less than the record figure established in 1968. Of the 22,817 registered yearlings of 1969, only 3,242 were sold at the auctions, 169 fewer than during the previous year. The reported gross sales figure for all yearlings dropped $1,660,565 to $24,502,095, while the national yearling average price dropped $112 to $7,558. (W. B.)

Canada. The 110th consecutive running of the Queen's Plate, North America's oldest annual sporting fixture, was won by Jumpin Joseph, a three-year-old owned by Warren Beasley, of Toronto. Beasley's colt subsequently was selected as Canada's horse of the year. Jumpin Joseph's victory in the Queen's Plate earned Beasley $55,000 from a record purse of $84,650.

Other winners in Canada's widespread three-year-old racing division were: the Canadian Derby (Edmonton), Wyn d'Amour, owned by Frederick Mannix; the Quebec Derby (Montreal), Sharp-Eyed Quillo, owned by Jack Hood; the Manitoba Derby (Winnipeg), Fire N Desire, owned by Samuel Lima and Morris Rose; and the British Columbia Derby (Vancouver), Essence of Time, owned by Frank McMahon.

Regrettably, there were many casualties among the three-year-olds. Jumpin Joseph went wrong and was retired for the season after finishing third in the Prince of Wales Stakes on August 30. Fire N Desire broke down and was retired to stud shortly after his Manitoba Derby win. Grey Whiz was emerging as the late-season champion of the three-year-olds when he broke a leg in the Horometer Stakes at Toronto and had to be destroyed.

A new rider of considerable distinction appeared on Canada's tracks in 1970. Sanford Hawley rode 230 winners in 196 days of racing, to lead all other jockeys by a comfortable margin. George Gardiner was Canada's leading money-winning owner, while Lou Cavalaris was the leading conditioner of Thoroughbreds.

Canadian wagering continued to increase in 1970, but average daily attendance was static. The season's largest crowd, 32,806 at Woodbine on Queen's Plate Day, set a Canadian wagering record of $1,742,675 on the eight-race program. (JA. CO.)

Europe and Australia. National Hunt racing in England in 1968–69 suffered severely from frost and snow at the turn of the year. For the second season in a row the King George VI Steeplechase could not be run at Kempton Park in December 1968 (in 1967 foot-and-mouth disease had caused its cancellation), nor could the Schweppes Gold Trophy be run in February. At Cheltenham in March the Champion Hurdle was won for the second time by the superb hurdler Persian War. The Gold Cup Steeplechase was won by What a Myth after The Laird, the favourite, had been brought down. The Grand National Steeplechase at Aintree went to Highland Wedding, which won by 12 lengths from Steel Bridge with Rondetto third. Man of the West (at 20–1) beat the favourite Arcturus in the Hennessy Gold Cup Steeplechase at Newbury. Larbawn won the Whitbread Gold Cup, becoming the first horse to do so twice. R. Davies and T. Biddlecombe shared the National Hunt jockeys' championship.

In flat racing, two older horses were outstanding in Europe. The Irish six-year-old Levmoss not only took the two great endurance races, the Prix du Cadran at Longchamp, Paris, and the Ascot Gold Cup, but at the end of the season produced the speed to hold off Park Top and win the $1\frac{1}{2}$-mi. Prix de l'Arc de Triomphe at Longchamp, Europe's richest race; the other leader was the duke of Devonshire's five-year-old mare Park Top, which, in a busy season, took the Coronation Cup from Mount Athos and Connaught at Epsom, the Hardwicke Stakes from Chicago and the Italian Hogarth at Royal Ascot, and the King George VI and Queen Elizabeth Stakes from Crozier at Ascot. Prince Regent of France, a very fast-finishing third in the English Derby, won the Irish Sweeps Derby. The disappointment of the year was the luckless Ribofilio, which won no major race though he was second in the Irish Derby and in the St. Leger, which was won by Intermezzo. Right Tack, in winning the Two Thousand Guineas, the St. James's Palace Stakes, and the Irish Two Thousand Guineas, showed himself to be the best miler of his age on good or soft going. His stable companion, four-year-old Jimmy Reppin, also performed admirably, with victories in the Sussex Stakes at Goodwood, the Queen Elizabeth Stakes at Ascot, and the Prix Perth at St. Cloud, Paris. The One Thousand Guineas was won by Full Dress from Hecuba and Motionless, and the English Derby was won by Blakeney from Shoemaker and Prince Regent. Blakeney, bred, trained, and part-owned by A. Budgett, was later affected by the coughing epidemic that spread through English stables at midsummer and did not produce his Derby form again. Sleeping Partner, owned by Lord Rosebery, won the Oaks from Frontier Goddess and Myastrid, and her owner, a leading patron of the turf, had an outstanding season, being the most successful breeder and second only to D. Robinson among owners. The filly Lucyrowe, a brilliant miler, took the Coronation Stakes at Royal Ascot and the Nassau Stakes at Goodwood. The French filly Flossy unexpectedly beat Park Top in the Champion Stakes at Newmarket at the end of the season. Developing as the season went on, Karabas revealed himself as an outstanding colt whose victories included two at Longchamp and the Washington, D.C., International at Laurel Park, Md., in November.

In France, the Poule d'Essai des Poulains (French equivalent of the Two Thousand Guineas) was won by Don II from Le Mas Marvent, and the Poule

UPI COMPIX

Majestic Prince, with Bill Hartack up, charges across the finish line to win the Kentucky Derby on May 3, 1969. Arts and Letters (right), ridden by Braulio Baeza, was second.

d'Essai des Pouliches (One Thousand Guineas) by Koblenza from Princeline. The Prix Hocquart went to Beaugency, and the Prix Lupin to Prince Regent. The Prix du Jockey Club (Derby) was won by Goodly from Beaugency and Djakao. The Prix Jean Prat went to the English-trained, U.S.-bred Hill Run. The Prix de Diane (Oaks) was won by M. Boussac's Crepellana from Saraca, while Felicio II won the Grand Prix de Saint-Cloud from Goodly. Chaparral won the Grand Prix de Paris, and Le Chouan won the French St. Leger from Honeyville and Chaparral.

The Irish Two Thousand and One Thousand Guineas were won by Right Tack and Wenduyne, the Oaks by Gaia, and the St. Leger by Reindeer. The Italian Derby was won by Bonconte di Montefeltro, the favourite. The French filly Glaneuse won the Gran Premio del Jockey Club in Milan. Don Giovanni won the German Derby, and Four Socks the Danish Derby.

In December 1968 the Jockey Club and the National Hunt Committee merged, with the name of the new body to be the Jockey Club. This step was taken in order to streamline and bring up to date the administration of British racing.

In Australia, the Melbourne Cup, run over 2 mi., was won for the second year in succession by the five-year-old South Australian horse Rain Lover; second was Alsop of Victoria, and third the New Zealand champion, Ben Lomond. (R. M. Gn.)

Harness Racing. A new world champion trotter and an undefeated pacing champion wrote the brightest chapters in a brilliant year of accomplishment in U.S. harness racing in 1969. Nevele Pride, the trotting king, set new world marks for one mile while racing on 1-mi., $\frac{1}{2}$-mi., and $\frac{5}{8}$-mi. tracks, and was voted harness horse of the year for the third straight season, the first trotter to receive that honour three times. Nevele Pride's mile in 1 min. 54.8 sec. for trainer-driver Stanley Dancer over a 1-mi. track at Indianapolis, Ind., on August 31 was the fastest in 163 years of recorded harness racing history, and shattered the "unbreakable" mark set in 1938 by Greyhound at 1 min. 55¼ sec.

The four-year-old champion also trotted world record miles in 1 min. 56.8 sec. over the ½-mi. track at Saratoga Springs, N.Y., and in 1 min. 58 sec. over the ⅝-mi. strip at Laurel, Md. Late in the year, he was retired by his owners to stallion duty at Stoner Creek Stud in Kentucky with earnings of $871,738 and 57 victories in 67 starts over three seasons.

Overcall, a six-year-old owned by Mrs. Helen Buck of Far Hills, N.J., scored an unprecedented sweep of pacing's free-for-all division by winning all 21 races in which he competed in 1969. He closed out his career by winning the $100,000 American Classic at Hollywood Park for the second straight year, giving him 22 straight wins over two seasons. At the end of the year, he was retired to stud at Blue Chip Farm in New York after being syndicated for $1 million. Overcall retired with lifetime earnings of $786,448, and during his spectacular 1969 campaign for trainer-driver Del Insko he established a new world record of 3 min. 2.6 sec. for 1½ mi. on a half-mile track in the $50,000 International Pace at Yonkers Raceway. He also was the top money-earning harness horse of 1969, winning $375,650.

Insko, who drove Overcall in all of his races, set records of his own, dethroning for the first time in eight years the money-winning kingpins of U.S. drivers, Bill Haughton and Stanley Dancer, who had shared that honour evenly since 1960. Insko won more than $1.6 million in purses during 1969 and also placed second in North American standings in races won behind the world champion Herve Filion, who captured the title for the second straight year.

Most successful of all 32,000 harness horses that raced during the year, after Nevele Pride and Overcall, was the three-year-old trotting colt Lindy's Pride. He became the second horse ever to sweep the "big five" races for three-year-old trotters (Nevele Pride did it in 1968) by winning the $124,910 Hambletonian, the $173,456 Dexter Cup, the $100,000 Yonkers Futurity, the $101,670 Colonial, and the $64,757 Kentucky Futurity. Lindy's Pride's total earnings for the year were $323,998.

While Lindy's Pride dominated trotting's three-year-old ranks and Nevele Pride rewrote the sport's world records, a new international trotting star of major proportions rose on the scene. It was the superb six-year-old mare Fresh Yankee, purchased as a $900 yearling in 1964 by Duncan A. MacDonald of Sydney, N.S., and trained and driven by the veteran Joe O'Brien. Starting with an impressive victory in the Solvalla Elitlopp International mile in Stockholm in May, she won well over $200,000 during the season and defeated virtually every major trotting star in the sport during a long campaign that concluded with an easy victory in the $100,000 American Classic in California in December.

Pacing's "big four" events for three-year-olds—the $182,976 Messenger Stakes, the $109,731 Little Brown Jug, the $100,000 Cane Futurity at Yonkers, and the $88,970 Adios at The Meadows—were won by three horses. Laverne Hanover, champion of the division and winner of 21 of 28 starts and $290,668 during the season, captured the Little Brown Jug and the Adios; Kat Byrd, Laverne Hanover's most persistent rival all season long, won the Cane in November; and Bye Bye Sam won the Messenger, which was the second richest race in harness racing history. Laverne Hanover paced a mile in 1 min. 56.6 sec., the fastest race mile in the sport in 1969 at either gait, for trainer-driver Bill Haughton in July.

U.S. horses won two of the three international events held on the U.S. side of the Atlantic in 1969, with Overcall taking the $50,000 International pace and Snow Speed the $50,000 United Nations trot at Yonkers. Une de Mai of France won the $100,000 International trot at Roosevelt Raceway.

The top ten money earners of the year reflected the growing disparity between pacers and trotters. Trotting, once the dominant and most popular gait, continued to lose ground with fewer racing opportunities for trotters at the major pari-mutuel tracks. Of the ten leading money winners of the year, only three were trotters. In 1968, the top ten had been divided evenly between the two gaits. (St. F. B.)

Harness racing in Europe continued to improve through 1969, in regard to both performers and prize money. The speed and stamina of the French trotters was much in evidence, and after winning the Prix d'Amérique, Upsalin was sold to a leading Italian owner, Count Paolo Orsi-Mangelli. The famous French trotting mare Roquépine retired from racing with earnings of $950,000, which made her the world's top money-earning trotting mare. She was to be shipped to the U.S. and be mated with leading sire Stars Pride. Another top French trotter, Une de Mai, after winning the Roosevelt International, returned to Vincennes, Paris, to win the Prix d'Étoile of $51,000, bringing her earnings to a total of more than $500,000. She had also won the $48,000 Milan, Italy, Grand Prix.

In the United Kingdom on the occasion of Prince Charles's visit to Wales, a valuable 1¼-mi. cup race was held at Prestatyn and was won by Tryax Hall from Eastwood. The U.K. Trotting Association's two-year-old classic was won by Saunders Pearl. The National Pacing Derby went to Scots Silk, with Red Sails second, and the Trotters' Derby went to Yankee Doodle, with Zia Verna second.

In Australia the champion Brisbane pacer was Stormy Waters, which put up some remarkable performances during the season. In Sydney, the 1969 Miracle Mile was won by Victorian pacer Adaptor in 1 min. 59.2 sec., this being only the third sub-two-minute mile raced in Australia. Four-year-old Cocky Raider won the $10,000 Summer Cup from Adaptor, and James Darren set a new Australian two-year-old pacing record of 2 min. 2.6 sec. in the Edgar Tatlow Stakes at Harold Park. Champion trotter of the season was Intangible Command, winner of the Trotters' Cup and numerous free-for-all and invitation races.

The Inter-Dominion Championships were raced in Adelaide, and the final of the series was won by the Victorian mare Richmond Lass, with Adios Court second and Twinkle Hanover third. The $20,000 New Zealand Cup was won by the favourite, Humphrey. Top money winner of the year was four-year-old pacer Cardinal Garrison with $24,295, which won the Auckland Cup. Garçon Roux became the first three-year-old pacer in Oceania to break 2 minutes when he recorded 1 min. 59.6 sec. in a time trial at Hutt Park, Wellington, and Friendly Forbes established a three-year-old pacing record of 3 min. 10.2 sec. over 1½-mi. from a standing start. The new winning record for 2-year-old pacers over 1 mi. was set by Berkleigh in 2 min. 4.6 sec. Among the trotters the outstanding performance was a world record of 2 min. 53.6 sec. over 1⅜ mi. set by Mighty Hanover.

(N. Si.)

Horseshoe Pitching: *see* Sporting Record
Horticulture: *see* Gardening
Hospitals: *see* Medicine
Household Appliances: *see* Domestic Arts and Sciences

Housing

Throughout 1969, the housing situations in both developed and less developed countries showed trends similar to those in 1968: some progress was made in the developed countries, but there was little improvement in the less developed countries as a whole. Mass production techniques for building houses and for comprehensive housing and urban development programs were subjects of popular concern in the developed countries, but housing had not yet received proper recognition in the less developed nations.

In most of the less developed countries the population was increasing at an annual rate of 2 to 3%, while the rate of housing construction did not exceed two dwelling units per 1,000 inhabitants. This was far below the target recommended by the UN, which was ten dwelling units per 1,000 inhabitants per year. The UN Centre for Housing, Building and Planning estimated that about $12 billion in annual capital investment would be required to provide 24 million dwelling units throughout the world. It was also estimated that a minimum of 5% of national income each year would be required to achieve the projected goal. In 1969 most less developed countries allocated about 3.5% of their income to the housing sector.

Housing that was closely coordinated with regional development planning was being increasingly recognized as an essential tool to check accelerating urbanization, the population explosion, and growing unemployment. It was reported that the birthrate was much higher in slums or shantytowns than in communities with decent housing. Less developed countries were especially urged to formulate urban decentralization policies.

The formulation of long-range housing and building programs appeared to be essential to solving housing problems. In this connection, it was important to use effectively the existing housing stock through proper maintenance and modernization. The local policy on rents played an important role in this case. In places where rents were controlled by the government at a low level for a long time, landlords could not maintain or modernize dwellings properly. On the other hand, rent-paying ability of lower middle and low-income groups was rather limited even in the developed countries. Therefore, the likely solution seemed to be to extend some financial assistance (rent subsidy, housing allowance, etc.) to those income groups.

Rural housing in the less developed countries remained in a critical condition. For example, in India, nearly 34% of the households occupied only one room, and about 70% depended on tanks and ponds for drinking water; 94% had no bathroom. Because the cities in those countries could not give proper accommodation to any large number of rural migrants, it was important to improve conditions in the rural areas in order to persuade the inhabitants to continue living there.

Urban growth in Africa was likely to be faster than in any other region. It was estimated by the UN that the continent's urban population would increase from 36 million in 1960 to 89 million in 1980, with the larger cities rising from 25 million to 42 million. Aided self-help housing, in which about 30% of the cost of a dwelling was provided through the labour of owner-occupiers, was common in Africa. On the other hand, about 50% of the cost of an average building in Africa was for imported materials. Therefore, construction costs would be considerably reduced if increased use of indigenous materials could be achieved.

Despite the increasing urbanization, the population in rural districts and small towns in Africa continued to outnumber greatly the city dwellers. Rural housing posed problems that required differing solutions. Governments and local authorities provided assistance in such ways as roof-loan schemes (for example in Ghana), site and service schemes (Kenya), and rural cooperative housing.

A UN regional meeting on Technical and Social Problems of Urbanization with Emphasis on Financing of Housing was held in Addis Ababa, Eth., in January. Some of the main recommendations arising from the meeting were as follows: (1) the importance of controlling urbanization in relation to the existing housing situation in urban areas; (2) the necessity to establish and support saving and credit banks for the financing of housing for low- and middle-income groups.

The housing deficiencies in Latin America remained enormous in spite of the efforts made in recent years to wipe them out. Large masses of people continued to live in slums. For example, in Mexico City more than one-third of the population, 1.5 million people, lived in slumlike squatter settlements. In Brazil, only 45% of municipalities had water supplies and only 34% had sewage systems. In Chile, only 29% had sewage systems.

To tackle such gigantic problems, the second Inter-American Housing Congress was held in Caracas, Venez., in February. The main objectives of the congress were to place housing and urban development within the structural scheme that formed the social reality of countries and to put more emphasis on the conceptual content with special preference to its social and economic implications. It was noted that community development was an effective instrument to achieve the social integration of otherwise unaffiliated groups.

Housing problems in Asia were also serious. In Calcutta, 58% of all city dwellers lived in single rooms inhabited by more than five persons. The extremely high density of more than 12,000 persons per hectare was reported in slum areas of Hong Kong. Problems concerning the rapid growth of slum and squatter settlements were discussed at the Committee on Housing, Building, and Planning held at Bangkok, Thai., in September. It was suggested that the problem of squatters would be minimized by encouraging a more balanced distribution of development in both urban and rural areas and by redeveloping slum areas so that the worst were eradicated and the remainder improved.

A comparison of housing construction activities in European countries during the first half of 1969 with those during the same period of 1968 revealed the following: the number of newly completed houses increased in Spain (from 54,600 to 63,900 units), Norway (from 14,818 to 15,211 units), the Netherlands (from 55,500 to 55,600 units), Sweden (from 50,253 to 54,643 units), and Ireland (from 5,644 to 6,904 units). On the other hand, the following countries experienced a slowdown in construction activities: France (from 187,800 to 94,500 units), Italy (from 816,000 to 683,000 rooms), Switzerland (from 10,252 to 9,488 units), Yugoslavia (from 12,200 to 10,600 units), Poland (from 59,200 to 57,700 units), and Czechoslovakia (from 25,251 to 19,868 units). In

KEYSTONE

Squatters call to friends in the street from an empty house in Ilford, Eng., which they took over Feb. 9, 1969. The takeover was a part of the London Squatters' Campaign to dramatize the shortage of housing.

some of the latter countries, however (for example, Switzerland and Czechoslovakia), construction activities went up again in July and continued to rise. Based on the above-mentioned data and other statistical indicators, the number of completed houses in Europe in 1969 was expected to increase a little more than it did in 1968.

In Europe, though housing activities were widely different in various countries, some of the housing policies were the same throughout the continent. These included the encouraging of prefabricated housing construction, active concern with the maintenance and modernization of existing housing stocks on the one hand and with large-scale redevelopment of central areas on the other hand, new approaches to housing in relation to urban development, and governmental assistance in housing for low- and middle-income groups.

In the U.K. 412,715 houses were built in 1968, an increase of nearly 9,400 units over 1967. While the public sector built 191,722 houses, private industry achieved a postwar record total of 221,993. In England, the building of new dwellings reflected the pattern in Great Britain as a whole. Housing construction by the public sector had reached 159,022 units in 1967 but decreased to 149,220 in 1968. On the other hand, the private sector completed 183,718 units in 1967 and increased to 203,324 units in 1968. It was estimated in February 1967 that the number of unfit dwellings in England and Wales totaled 1.8 million, of which 1.1 million were in potential clearance areas.

UPI COMPIX

Beehive-style apartment house in Hamburg, W.Ger., completed in April 1969. Containing 345 units, the building was erected in ten months by using prefabricated sections.

Concerning the house-building cost yardstick in the U.K., there existed among those engaged in public housing programs a strong desire to revise it upward. According to a survey made by the National Housing and Planning Council, extreme difficulty in keeping within the yardstick was experienced by 111 local councils, some difficulty by 60, and no difficulty by 128 (mainly smaller authorities). On the other hand, many believed that the existing yardstick should be maintained. They argued that costs could be reduced by employing more efficient building techniques and improving the working conditions for construction labourers. Such measures, however, would take some time to become effective. By that time, there was a danger that local authorities and contractors would be obliged to keep costs down by lowering quality of the dwellings built.

In the U.S. the comprehensive housing policy formulated by the administration of Pres. Lyndon Johnson in 1968 was taken over by the administration of Pres. Richard Nixon without major changes in 1969. The new administration was, however, endeavouring to develop new concepts for more effective administration of existing urban aid programs. Some characteristics of its housing policy were as follows: (1) an aid program to rebuild cities hit hardest by civil disturbances; (2) reorganization of the administration of the Model Cities program; and (3) a "breakthrough" program for achieving low-cost, high-volume housing production for low- and middle-income groups.

According to the ten-year U.S. housing construction program, 26 million units of housing were required in the period 1969–78. This target was quite high compared with the actual housing production for 1959–68, which numbered 14.5 million units. To accelerate housing production there was a great need to mobilize resources effectively. For this purpose, it was being urged that a working partnership be established among government agencies, industry, and labour. To implement the "breakthrough" program, the federal government was providing financial assistance and technical advice to state and local governments and other interested groups. In this connection it was notable that the state governments were asked to play a major role in the program. As to the mass production system necessary for achieving the "breakthrough" program, the possibility of housing production on a large scale, such as 30,000 to 90,000 units a year, was being presented by the federal government to large industrial corporations in order to mobilize them. The state and local governments, with support from the federal government, were to be asked to undertake market surveys that would identify available land, sponsors, and the local demand for housing. Industry, labour, and consumer groups were to supplement this market information to the fullest extent possible.

The U.S. federal government spent $2,644,000,000 on housing programs in 1966, $2,616,000,000 in 1967, and $4,076,000,000 in 1968. The estimated outlays for 1969 and 1970 were $2,313,000,000 and $2,772,000,000, respectively. As to the 1970 outlays, they were to be used in three major fields: $1,216,000,000 for Concentrated Community Development (Model Cities program); $1,131,000,000 for low- and moderate-income housing; and $984 million for community environment. Under the Model Cities program, 150 communities were selected as participants, and some began to carry out their projects. Regarding low- and moderate-income housing, there were plans to build or repair 700,000 new dwelling units in 1969 and 1970. It was expected that the federal government would undertake 1,680 urban renewal projects with the funds of community environment. Late in December, in an effort to make more loan money available to home buyers, the federal government raised the maximum interest rate for Federal Housing Administration (FHA) and Veterans Administration home loan mortgages from 7.5% to 8.5%. (HI. S.)

See also Architecture; Cities and Urban Affairs; Economy, World; Industrial Review; Money and Banking.

ENCYCLOPÆDIA BRITANNICA FILMS. *The Living City* (1953); *Megalopolis: Cradle of the Future* (1962); *The House of Man, Part II—Our Crowded Environment* (1969).

Hovercraft: *see* Transportation

Hungary

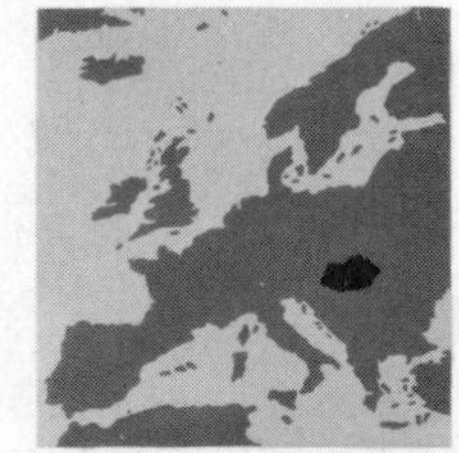

A people's republic of central Europe, Hungary is bordered by Czechoslovakia, the U.S.S.R., Romania, Yugoslavia, and Austria. Area: 35,920 sq.mi. (93,030 sq.km.). Pop. (1969 est.): 10,275,000, including (1956) Hungarian 97%; German 2.2%. Cap. and largest city: Budapest (pop., 1969 est., 2,010,000). Language (1960): Hungarian 98.2%. Religion (1956): Roman Catholic 67%; Protestant 27.3%; Orthodox 2.5%; Jewish 1.5%. First secretary of the Hungarian Socialist Workers' (Communist) Party in 1969, Janos Kadar; president of the Presidential Council (head of state), Pal Losonczi; president of the Council of Ministers (premier), Jeno Fock.

In a broadcast to the Hungarian people on Jan. 1, 1969, Premier Jeno Fock described 1968 as "a successful year" with regard to national unity. Nevertheless, he singled out for attention three groups of dissidents: those not interested in building socialism; the passive adversaries; and the active troublemakers. Trying to justify the invasion of Czechoslovakia, Fock said that the party and the government could not consult the people before the "event of Aug. 20, 1968," because it was not a Hungarian affair alone.

Janos Kadar stayed in Moscow for six days in February discussing with Soviet leaders the forthcoming Budapest meeting of the Warsaw Pact powers on European security. The meeting took place on March 17 and produced an appeal to all European countries to help in the convocation of a European conference to discuss security and peaceful cooperation.

On May 27 Fock arrived in Vienna, returning the visit to Budapest of Josef Klaus, the Austrian chancellor. The Hungarian premier conferred with Klaus and Kurt Waldheim, the Austrian foreign minister, on the proposed European security conference. Hungary, said Fock, set no preconditions and had no objection to the U.S. and Canada taking part in the conference. Waldheim expressed Austria's conviction that peace could only be preserved by improving relations between countries with different political and economic systems.

On September 26 Urho Kaleva Kekkonen, president of Finland, arrived in Budapest, the first time a Finnish head of state had ever visited Hungary. The main topic of discussion was achieving a détente in Europe. In December letters were exchanged between the Hungarian and Spanish governments establishing consular relations between the two countries.

Under the terms of the new agreement concluded between Hungary and the Vatican on January 23—following that of Sept. 15, 1964—eight ordinaries and two auxiliary bishops of Hungary's Roman Catholic hierarchy took the oath on the constitution before Pal Losonczi, president of the Presidential Council. Two new archbishops, Jozsef Ijjas and Pal Brezanoczy, and four new bishops were invested in leading sees. Also the administration of Hungary's primal see of Esztergom was unraveled, Imre Szabo, an auxiliary bishop in the archdiocese of Esztergom, being appointed apostolic administrator. The Vatican felt unable to elevate Szabo to archbishop of Esztergom because Jozsef Cardinal Mindszenty continued his refusal to resign from his position and to leave the self-imposed exile in the U.S. embassy that he had begun during the Hungarian revolt in 1956.

On March 21 the 50th anniversary of the first Hungarian Communist revolution was celebrated as a national holiday. Bela Kun's widow and other surviving veterans of the 133-day "Republic of the Soviets" took part at a rally in the central hall of Parliament. Gyula Kallai, chairman of the National Assembly, denounced as "a crude falsification of history" the allegation that after World War II the Soviet Army had forced the socialist system on Hungary. According to reliable sources in Budapest, Matyas Rakosi, whose death in the U.S.S.R. was reported in August 1963, was living at Tokmak, in Kirgizia, U.S.S.R. It was believed that Moscow was asking Kadar to allow the 77-year-old former dictator to return to Hungary.

In February work started on the construction of the 186.5-mi. second pipeline to carry Soviet crude oil from Uzhgorod in the Transcarpathian province of the Ukraine to Szazhalombatta, southwest of Budapest. The new 24-in.-diameter pipeline would have a yearly flow capacity of 10 million metric tons and was expected to be completed toward the end of 1972.

In June Premier Fock opened at Szazhalombatta a twin industrial plant of major importance to the country's power industry: the 3.5 million-ton-a-year Danube Oil Refinery and the 615 Mw. Danube Power Station. The refinery would supply about 60% of the oil

HUNGARY

Education. (1966–67) Primary, pupils 1,380,286, teachers 62,241; secondary, pupils 136,154, teachers 8,281; vocational, pupils 94,145, teachers 4,036; higher (including 14 universities), students 89,544, teaching staff 8,889.

Finance. Monetary unit: forint, with an official exchange rate of 11.74 forints to U.S. $1 (28.18 forints = £1 sterling) and a tourist rate (Oct. 1969) of 30 forints to U.S. $1 (72 forints = £1). Budget (1969 est.): revenue 154,219,000,000 forints; expenditure 155,929,000,000 forints. National income (net material product): (1968) 221.2 billion forints; (1967) 203.7 billion forints.

Foreign Trade. (1967) Imports 20,841,000,000 forints; exports 19,971,000,000 forints. Import sources: U.S.S.R. 33%; East Germany 11%; Czechoslovakia 9%; Poland 6%; West Germany 6%. Export destinations: U.S.S.R. 36%; East Germany 10%; Czechoslovakia 9%; Poland 6%; Italy 5%. Main exports (1966): machinery 19%; transport equipment 12%; chemicals 8%; fruit and vegetables 7%; iron and steel 6%; meat and products 5%; textiles 5%.

Transport and Communications. Roads (1968) 103,674 km. (including 53 km. expressways). Passenger vehicles in use (1968) 163,636. Railways: (1967) 8,808 km.; traffic (1968) 13,949,000,000 passenger-km., freight 17,558,000,000 net ton-km. Air traffic (1961): 2,355,000 passenger-km.; freight 1,311,000 net ton-km. Telephones (Dec. 1967) 634,527. Radio receivers (Dec. 1967) 2,479,000. Television receivers (Dec. 1967) 1,169,000.

Agriculture. Production (in 000; metric tons; 1968; 1967 in parentheses): corn 3,764 (3,580); wheat *c.* 3,137 (3,022); rye *c.* 238 (225); barley 902 (939); potatoes 1,336 (1,507); sugar, raw value (1968–69) 438, (1967–68) 441; tobacco 26 (24); sunflower seed (1967) 79, (1966) 102; dry peas (1967) 128, (1966) 105; apples (1967) 675, (1966) 396; wine (1967) 479, (1966) 337; beef and veal (1967) 158, (1966) 144; pork (1967) 297, (1966) 310. Livestock (in 000; March 1968): cattle 2,096; pigs 6,609; sheep 3,310; horses 274; chickens (March 1967) 53,378.

Industry. Index of production (1963 = 100): (1968) 131; (1967) 125. Production (in 000; metric tons; 1968): coal 4,242; lignite and brown coal 22,971; crude oil 1,806; natural gas (cu.m.) 2,692,000; electricity (kw-hr.) 13,155,000; iron ore (25% metal content) 638; pig iron 1,655; crude steel 2,902; bauxite 1,959; cement 2,800; sulfuric acid 446; nitrogenous fertilizers (nitrogen content; 1967) 188; superphosphates (1967) 151; cotton fabrics (sq.m.) 290,000; woolen fabrics (sq.m.) 30,000; pure silk fabrics (sq.m.; 1967) 192. New dwelling units completed (1967) 60,603.

products consumed nationally, while the power station accounted for a quarter of the national electric power capacity.

In April a consortium of eight Western banks, headed by the Bank of London and South America, signed an agreement with the National Bank of Hungary for a $15 million loan to the Hungarian State Aluminum Trust. Hungary would use this money to build its own aluminum-processing plant and thus eliminate its dependence on Poland and the U.S.S.R. for this work.

In June Bela Szalai, Hungarian deputy minister of foreign trade, visited London with the aim of increasing Anglo-Hungarian trade, which had tripled during the previous ten years. In 1968 Hungary supplied £10 million worth of exports to Great Britain, while British exports to Hungary totaled £12.7 million. In July Hungary formally applied to join GATT (General Agreement on Tariffs and Trade). (K. Sm.)

Encyclopædia Britannica Films. *Hungary and Communism—Eastern Europe in Change* (1964).

Iceland

Iceland is an island republic in the North Atlantic Ocean. Area: 39,777 sq.mi. (103,022 sq.km.). Pop. (1968): 202,191. Cap. and largest city: Reykjavik (pop., 1968, 81,026). Language: Icelandic (similar to Old Norse). Religion: 98% Lutheran. President in 1969, Kristjan Eldjarn; prime minister, Bjarni Benediktsson.

Following devaluation of the króna on Nov. 12, 1968, the balance of payments returned to surplus in 1969, and the recession caused by poor fish catches and declining export prices showed signs of slackening. However, the unemployment situation experienced in the winter was expected to recur. By 1969 almost 40% of Iceland's trade was with countries of the European Free Trade Association (EFTA). Iceland tabled a formal application for membership on January 24. On December 19 the EFTA Council stated that full agreement had been reached on the terms for Iceland's entry, which would probably take place in March 1970. Icelandic industrial products would immediately be free of duty within EFTA, while Iceland would have a ten-year period in which to lower its tariffs.

In September, Denmark, Finland, Norway, and Sweden decided to set up a fund to help Iceland to diversify its industries, which were almost entirely dependent on fish. Hopes centred on the export of meat, wool, and hides, and on making greater use of the country's hydroelectric and geothermal power resources.

An aluminum-smelting plant under construction south of Reykjavik since 1967 started production in September, with an initial capacity of 30,000 tons annually. The plant's electricity was supplied from a hydroelectric power station on the Thjorsa River. A projected seawater plant, designed to produce salt and other minerals, would make use of the hot springs located on Iceland's southwestern tip. A new scheme was also under consideration for a large hydroelectric power station in the east.

Early in 1969, Loftleidir (Icelandic Airlines) bought the stock of International Air Bahama, a competitor in low air fares. Loftleidir cooperated with the Scandinavian churches' relief organization, which had several planes flying medicines and foodstuffs to Biafra. (Va. K.)

ICELAND

Education. (1967–68) Primary, pupils 27,500, teachers 1,340; secondary, pupils 14,750, teachers 1,230; vocational, pupils 2,730, teachers (1966–67) 119; teacher training, students 670, teachers (1966–67) 27; higher (at Reykjavik University), students 1,200, teaching staff 135.

Finance. Monetary unit: króna, with a par value of 88 krónur to U.S. $1 (211.20 krónur = £1 sterling). Gold and foreign exchange, central bank: (June 1969) U.S. $32.3 million; (June 1968) U.S. $27.2 million. Budget (1968 est.): revenue 6,195,296,000 krónur; expenditure 6,120,431,000 krónur. Gross national product: (1967) 24 billion krónur; (1966) 24,050,000,000 krónur. Money supply: (June 1969) 3,505,000,000 krónur; (June 1968) 2,822,000,000 krónur. Cost of living (Reykjavik; 1963 = 100): (May 1969) 202; (May 1968) 166.

Foreign Trade. (1968) Imports 7,877,000,000 krónur; exports 4,680,000,000 krónur. Import sources: West Germany 15%; U.K. 13%; U.S. 11%; Denmark 10%; U.S.S.R. 8%; Norway 8%; Netherlands 6%; Sweden 6%. Export destinations: U.S. 26%; U.K. 13%; U.S.S.R. 11%; Sweden 9%; West Germany 8%; Italy 5%; Portugal 5%. Main exports: fish 73%; fish meal 9%.

Transport and Communications. Roads (1968) 11,100 km. Motor vehicles in use (1968): passenger 37,009; commercial 5,922. There are no railways. Air traffic (1968): 1,129,700,000 passenger-km.; freight 7,685,000 net ton-km. Shipping (1968): merchant vessels 100 gross tons and over 295; gross tonnage 133,162. Telephones (Dec. 1967) 62,698. Radio receivers (Dec. 1967) 59,000.

Agriculture. Production (in 000; metric tons; 1967; 1966 in parentheses): potatoes 8 (5); hay (1966) 342, (1965) 376; sheepskins 2.9 (2.6); mutton and lamb 13 (13); fish catch 896 (1,240). Livestock (in 000; Dec. 1966): cattle 55; sheep 847; horses (Dec. 1967) 36; chickens 120.

Industry. Electricity (public supply only; 1968) 719 million kw-hr.

Hurricanes: *see* Disasters; Meteorology

Hydroelectric Power: *see* Engineering Projects; Fuel and Power

Ice Hockey: *see* Hockey

Ifni: *see* Dependent States; Morocco

Immigration: *see* Migration, International

Immunology: *see* Medicine

Ice Skating

A feature of ice skating during 1969 was the trend toward dependence on artificially frozen ice. By using this, many mountain resorts maintained facilities throughout the summer months. Most leading figure skaters seldom performed outdoors on natural ice. Artificial ice for speed skating did not come into such general use because of the high maintenance costs of the courses.

The world ice figure and dance skating championships were held at the Broadmoor World Arena, Colorado Springs, Colo., from February 25 to March 1. Accidents during practice eliminated two prominent women contenders—Karen Magnussen, champion of Canada, fractured a leg, and Hana Maskova, the Czechoslovak champion, strained her back. Ninety-five skaters from 14 nations competed.

Tim Wood (U.S.) became the new men's champion, defeating Ondrej Nepela, the Czech runner-up, by a comfortable margin. Patrick Pera of France finished third. The first U.S. victor in ten years, Wood displayed a clear superiority in both figures and free skating. He included triple Salchow and triple toe Walley jumps, gaining three sixes for artistic impression.

Gabriele Seyfert (E.Ger.) captured the women's title with a brilliant freestyle performance after trailing in the figures behind Beatrix Schuba, the Austrian runner-up, who finished narrowly ahead of the third-placed Hungarian, Suzy Almassy. Any shortcomings Miss Seyfert had the previous season disappeared with the eight pounds she had since shed. Although no triple jump was attempted, every major double jump except one was confidently executed with spectacular height and clean landings.

Oleg and Ludmila Protopopov (U.S.S.R.), 36 and 33 years old, respectively, lost their pair skating crowns to their compatriots, Alek Ulanov and Irina Rodnina, who looked set for a long reign as they outshone the deposed masters with superbly timed flying camels and a skillful double twist lift. The Protopopovs finished third, fractionally behind Alek Mishin and Tamara Moskvina, in a Soviet grand slam.

Great Britain's Bernard Ford and Diane Towler won the ice dance championship for the fourth consecutive year. While admiration for technical finesse accompanied them all the way, the competitive interest switched to the struggle for second place. This was finally clinched by Alek Gorshkov and Ludmila Pakhomova of the U.S.S.R., who narrowly edged out James Sladky and Judy Schwomeyer of the U.S.

Ford and Miss Towler afterward changed status to win the 13th annual world professional ice dance title at Wembley, Eng., on April 18. Gary Visconti (U.S.) also forsook the amateur ranks to win the men's event, as did Walter Häffner and Gudrun Hauss (both W.Ger.) to gain the pairs. Wendy Jones (U.S.) was successful in the women's contest. Organized by the International Professional Skating Association, the four events were contested by 38 skaters from nine countries, with cash incentives for the contestants totaling £5,000.

The year's outstanding male speed skater in all events was Dag Fornæss (Nor.), but although he became overall world champion at Deventer, Neth., on February 15–16, he failed to finish first in any of the four distances. During the season Kees Verkerk (Neth.) won both the 1,500 m. and 5,000 m., and his fellow countryman Jan Bols outpaced everyone in the 10,000 m. The 500-m. sprint went to Keiichi Suzuki (Jap.), spearheading his country's clearly growing skating strength during the year.

Lasma Kauniste (U.S.S.R.) gained the world women's overall speed title at Grenoble, France, on February 1–2. She won the 1,000 m.; Kirsti Biermann (Nor.) took the 500 m.; and two Dutch racers, Stien Kaiser and Ans Schut, won the 1,500 m. and 3,000 m., respectively.

During the season new records were set or equaled for every world championship distance. Verkerk clocked new figures for the 1,500 m., 5,000 m., and 10,000 m. Fornæss raced the fastest 3,000 m., and Suzuki equaled the best 500 m. time. Miss Schut lowered the women's 1,500 m. and 3,000 m., and new figures were also set for the 500 m. and 1,000 m. by Ruth Schleiermacher (E.Ger.) and Elly van de Brom (Neth.), respectively.

The International Skating Union's biennial congress, at Maidenhead, Eng., on June 2–7, was the first to be held in the U.K. since 1899. Jacques Favart (France) was reelected president. National skating associations were granted permission to accept commercial sponsorship for future championships. It was also agreed to include women's events in European speed skating championships, hitherto restricted to men.

A motion to recognize separate titles for figures and free skating, in addition to the customary combined awards for overall ability, failed to gain sufficient support. A proposal to introduce four new skating figures in the international schedule, in order to suit modern changes in technique, was referred to a committee for ratification. (H. B.)

Income, National

The rate of growth of real gross national product (GNP) rose in the group of industrial countries to about $5\frac{1}{4}$–$5\frac{1}{2}$% in 1968, well above the increase of $3\frac{3}{4}$% in 1967 and in line with the increases for 1964–66. This rise was also comparable to, or somewhat above, those countries' average growth rate for the preceding decade. Growth rates picked up generally, noticeably in the United States, Canada, and the United Kingdom. In West Germany there was rapid expansion, but growth eased somewhat in France and Italy. The Scandinavian countries were following differing paths in 1968 as compared with 1967. Japan maintained its extraordinarily rapid but sustained growth during the year.

The latest indications from quarterly data showed that growth in the U.S. was declining through 1969 and that the Canadian economy might also be faltering. In West Germany growth still appeared rapid, with GNP in the first half of 1969 nearly 9% above the level of a year earlier. In the U.K. substantial differences among the three official indicators of real gross domestic product made interpretation difficult. It was clear, however, that the balance of payments

Table I. Levels and Growth of Gross National Product, 1968

Country	Currency	Gross national product: In national currency 1968	Percentage real increase: Average 1958–68	1967 over 1966	1968 over 1967
Industrial countries					
Austria	(billion schillings)	295.1	4.4	3½	4
Belgium	(BFr. billion)	1,044	4.3	3½	4
Canada	(Can.$billion)	67.30	4.8	3	4¾
Denmark	(billion kroner)	93.06	4.9	3¾	3¾
France	(Fr. billion)	625.1	5.0	4½	4¼
Germany, West	(DM. billion)	528.8	5.0	¼	7
Italy	(trillion lire)	46.74	6.0	6½	5¾
Japan	(trillion yen)	51.09	11.3	11¼	11½
Luxembourg	(LFr. million)	38.25	3.3	2	4
Netherlands	(billion guilders)	91.33	5.1	5½	5½
Norway	(billion kroner)	57.61	4.8	5¾	3¾
Sweden	(billion kronor)	132.3	4.5	2½	3¼
Switzerland	(SFr. billion)	73.18	4.8	1¾	4
United Kingdom	(£billion)	42.76	3.2	2	3
United States	($billion)	880.8	4.6	2¾	4¾
Other developed areas					
Australia*	(A$billion)	23.68	4.8	6¼	3¾
Finland	(billion markkaa)	33.66	5.1	3	2½
Greece	(billion drachmas)	226.7	6.6	5	6¼
Iceland	(billion Krónur)	25.50	3.0	−1½	−2¾
Ireland	(£million)	1,243	3.9	4	6
New Zealand*	(NZ$million)	4,280†	3.9	−1	1
Portugal	(billion escudos)	144.3	6.0	5½	5¾
South Africa‡	(R billion)	10.01	5.7	8	3½
Spain	(billion pesetas)	1,764	6.3	4¼	4½
Turkey	(billion lire)	103.57	5.1	6	6¼
Less developed areas					
Argentina	(billion pesos)	5,156§	2.6	2	4¾
Bolivia	(million pesos)	9,439	4.6	5½	5¼
Ceylon	(Crs. billion)	10.60	4.7	4½	8¼
Ecuador	(billion sucres)	26.51	5.0	5½	4¾
Ghana	(million new cedis)	2,035	3.9	1¾	1¾
Guatemala	(million quetzales)	1,530	4.8	4	5½
Honduras	(million lempiras)	1,255	4.3♀	5¼	..
Iran*	(billion rials)	603.0	7.0‖	11¼	10½
Israel	(I£billion)	14.02	8.4	1	12½
Jamaica	(£million)	395.7	4.6¶	..	..
Kenya	(£million)	456.9	4.2	3½	6¼
Korea, South	(billion won)	1,576	7.4	9	13
Mexico	(billion pesos)	334.3	6.3	6½	8
Morocco	(billion dirhams)	15.36	3.4	6¾	12½
Nicaragua	(million córdobas)	4,900	6.4	5¼	5
Pakistan*	(PakRs. billion)	61.61	5.1	5	7½
Philippines	(billion pesos)	28.11	4.4	½	..
Puerto Rico	(U.S. $million)	3,740	7.5	5½	8½
Rhodesia	(£million)	378	3.4♀	4¾	..
Taiwan	(NT$billion)	166.2	9.4	9¾	9½
Tunisia	(million dinars)	550.1	4.0	½	7¼
Uganda	(million shillings)	4,991	3.9	3½	3½
Venezuela	(billion bolivares)	38.25	4.0	5	..

*Financial year.
†Unofficial estimate.
‡South African national accounts include Botswana, Lesotho, South West Africa, and Swaziland.
§1967.
‖1959–60 to 1968–69.
¶1958 to 1966.
♀1958 to 1967.
Sources: Publications of United Nations; Organization for Economic Cooperation and Development; International Monetary Fund; official national sources.

surpluses of mid-1969 were associated with only a slow growth of the domestic economy.

In the group of other developed countries the rate of growth fell sharply in Australia and South Africa, while Iceland continued in recession. Ireland and Greece showed improved rates, while New Zealand seemed to have recovered to a certain extent from its recent recession.

Among the less developed countries there was, in general, some improvement over 1967, but experience differed widely. Recorded growth was particularly rapid in Ceylon, South Korea, and Taiwan in the Far East, and also in Iran, Israel, and Morocco. Output rose rapidly in Argentina, Guatemala, and Mexico in Latin America and also in Kenya, Pakistan, and Tunisia. (*See* Table I.)

Recent trends in expenditure of the GNP are analyzed for a large number of countries in Table II. The figures are not always completely comparable as between countries because of differences in national

Table II. Disposal of Gross National Product (%)

Country	Year	Private con-sumption	Public con-sumption	Gross fixed capital formation	Change in inven-tory	Inter-national surplus
Industrial countries						
Austria	1966	59.2	13.8	26.1	3.4	−2.6
	1967	59.2	14.7	25.0	2.8	−1.7
	1968	59.4	15.2	23.6	3.2	−1.3
Belgium	1966	65.0	13.1	21.5	0.9	−0.4
	1967	63.4	13.3	21.2	0.2	0.8
	1968	64.6	14.0	20.3	1.0	0.1
Canada	1966	60.1	14.8	26.0	1.6	−2.1
	1967	60.9	15.3	24.7	0.4	−1.0
	1968	60.9	15.3	23.2	1.0	−0.5
Denmark	1966	63.0	16.1	21.2	1.2	−1.5
	1967	63.2	16.8	21.3	0.7	−2.0
	1968	62.9	17.6	20.6	0.5	−1.6
France	1966	60.3	12.4	25.0	2.0	0.3
	1967	60.4	12.3	25.2	1.7	0.4
	1968	60.9	12.7	24.9	1.5	−0.0
Germany, West	1966	57.2	15.7	25.4	0.4	1.4
	1967	58.0	16.6	22.8	−0.7	3.3
	1968	56.2	15.7	23.1	1.6	3.5
Italy	1966	64.1	13.9	18.3	1.0	2.7
	1967	64.8	13.3	18.9	1.3	1.8
	1968	63.6	13.5	19.4	0.4	3.1
Japan	1966	55.7	9.1	31.0	2.8	1.4
	1967	53.8	8.7	32.3	5.2	−0.0
	1968	52.2	8.4	34.0	4.6	0.9
Netherlands	1966	57.9	15.8	25.7	1.3	−0.6
	1967	57.0	15.8	25.9	1.3	−0.1
	1968	56.1	15.4	26.5	1.5	0.5
Norway	1966	54.2	16.5	29.0	1.8	−2.0
	1967	54.0	17.2	30.8	0.4	−2.5
	1968	53.9	17.9	26.7	−0.2	1.8
Sweden	1966	55.8	19.8	23.9	1.2	−0.8
	1967	55.4	20.6	24.2	0.1	−0.3
	1968	55.3	21.9	23.6	−0.2	−0.6
Switzerland	1966	58.6	11.7	26.4	0.7	2.6
	1967	58.9	12.0	25.4	0.6	3.1
	1968	58.3	12.2	24.7	0.7	4.2
United Kingdom	1966	63.7	17.3	17.6	0.7	0.8
	1967	63.3	18.1	18.1	0.5	−0.1
	1968	63.3	18.0	18.2	0.5	−0.0
United States	1966	61.4	19.3*	17.1*	1.6	0.7
	1967	61.2	20.8*	16.6*	0.8	0.6
	1968	61.2	21.0*	16.6*	1.0	0.3
Other developed areas						
Australia	1965–66	63.1	11.6	27.7	1.1	−3.9
	1966–67	62.0	12.0	26.3	2.3	−2.5
	1967–68	63.4	12.8	27.0	1.3	−4.4
Finland	1966	57.4	15.3	25.8	3.7	−2.3
	1967	57.5	16.2	24.4	3.5	−1.6
	1968	55.9	16.7	23.2	3.4	0.8
Greece	1966	70.3	11.8	24.7	0.7	−7.6
	1967	69.9	12.9	22.9	0.5	−6.2
	1968	69.3	13.0	23.7	−0.4	−5.6
Iceland	1966	62.5	9.4	29.1	0.3	−1.3
	1967	65.6	10.4	33.5	0.3	−9.8
	1968	66.7	11.0	33.5	−0.9	−10.3
Ireland	1966	70.5	12.9	18.6	0.9	−3.0
	1967	68.6	13.0	19.1	−0.5	−0.1
	1968	68.3	13.2	20.5	1.0	−3.0
New Zealand	1966–67	60.9	14.5	24.6	3.5	−3.5
	1967–68	61.2	14.6	22.5	3.1	−1.4
	1968–69†	61.0	15.0	21.8	1.4	0.5

Country	Year	Private con-sumption	Public con-sumption	Gross fixed capital formation	Change in inven-tory	Inter-national surplus
Portugal	1966	74.1	12.4	19.0	−1.4	−4.1
	1967	70.1	13.2	19.3	−0.3	−2.2
	1968	74.2	12.8	16.0	...	−3.0
South Africa‡	1966	64.4	12.6	24.5	0.6	−0.9
	1967	62.5	12.1	23.8	5.5	−2.8
	1968	64.8	12.5	23.1	0.2	−0.2
Spain	1966	68.6	9.0	22.7	3.7	−4.0
	1967	69.8	10.2	21.3	2.0	−3.4
	1968	70.2	10.2	20.9	1.4	−2.8
Less developed areas						
Bolivia	1966	77.6	10.4	12.0	4.3	−4.3
	1967	78.6	10.3	15.1	1.0	−5.1
	1968	78.5	10.4	15.1	0.7	−4.7
Ceylon	1966	75.3	13.9	14.3	0.1	−3.9
	1967	74.1	13.6	15.1	0.1	−3.4
	1968	71.3	13.3	14.8	0.9	−3.5
Congo (Kinshasa)	1966	88.8		9.1	0.5	1.5
	1967	85.4		13.8	0.4	0.5
	1968	87.3		11.9	0.5	0.3
Ghana	1966	75.2	14.7	13.8	0.8	−4.5
	1967	73.2	17.5	12.1	0.3	−3.2
	1968	72.1	17.8	11.5	0.0	−1.4
Guatemala	1966	83.5	7.8	12.3	−1.3	−2.1
	1967	83.2	7.9	13.4	0.8	−5.3
	1968	82.2	7.5	14.1	0.0	−3.9
Honduras	1966	78.0	9.2	15.6	1.5	−4.3
	1967	78.0	9.3	17.1	1.4	−5.8
	1968	76.5	9.2	17.4	1.3	−4.4
Iran	1966–67	70.2	14.1	17.4	...	−1.7
	1967–68	69.0	13.8	19.8	...	−2.6
	1968–69	67.6	14.2	22.2	...	−4.0
Israel	1966	67.1	22.4	20.5	0.9	−10.9
	1967	68.0	27.9	15.6	−0.5	−10.9
	1968	65.8	27.7	19.0	1.1	−13.7
Kenya	1966	68.6	14.1	15.0	4.0	−1.7
	1967	67.5	14.9	20.2	1.6	−4.2
	1968	68.7	14.9	19.9	0.6	−4.1
Korea, South	1966	78.1	10.2	20.0	1.7	−8.5
	1967	78.4	10.6	21.2	0.7	−9.1
	1968	75.6	11.1	25.5	1.2	−11.7
Malaysia	1966	61.7	18.6	18.6		1.1
	1967	62.0	18.6	18.2		1.2
	1968	61.2	19.0	17.7		2.0
Mexico	1966	79.1	5.9	16.7	...	−1.7
	1967	79.1	5.9	17.6	...	−2.5
	1968	78.6	6.1	18.1	...	−2.7
Morocco	1966	74.8	14.6	11.9	−1.1	1.5
	1967	73.7	14.1	13.8	0.2	−0.1
	1968	70.6	13.9	12.8	4.0	0.3
Puerto Rico	1965–66	81.2	13.9	24.5	3.5	−23.1
	1966–67	77.6	14.8	26.9	1.0	−20.4
	1967–68	76.6	15.1	26.0	2.1	−19.9
Taiwan	1966	61.3	17.2	18.6	4.5	−1.0
	1967	60.2	17.6	20.4	4.0	−2.0
	1968	58.9	17.6	21.8	2.4	−0.3
Tunisia	1966	68.3	18.5	26.1	0.6	−13.6
	1967	70.3	19.6	24.8	0.0	−14.7
	1968	67.5	20.1	21.4	0.5	−9.5
Venezuela	1966	64.2	14.7	20.4	1.3	−0.6
	1967	66.4	15.0	22.1	1.9	−5.4
	1968	67.9	15.4	25.5	1.4	−10.2

*Public sector expenditure on equipment is included with public consumption.
†Research institute estimates.
‡South African national accounts include Botswana, Lesotho, South West Africa, and Swaziland.
Sources: UN, OECD, and IMF publications; official national sources.

accounting practices, but they do serve to show major differences. In some cases the original national accounts include a statistical discrepancy between the total and the sum of its components, so that the items shown do not necessarily add to a total of 100%.

While the share of private consumption expenditure had fallen since the late 1950s in virtually all countries, private consumption rose noticeably faster than the GNP in 1968 in Belgium, Australia, Iceland, Portugal, South Africa, Kenya, and Venezuela. It rose at a markedly slower rate than the GNP in West Germany, Italy, Japan, and Finland among the developed countries, and also in Ceylon, Taiwan, Iran, Israel, South Korea, Morocco, Tunisia, and several Latin-American countries.

Government expenditures generally took a higher share of the GNP in 1968 than in 1967, important exceptions being West Germany and Japan. Despite the continued slow rate of growth in the U.K., the pruning of public expenditure programs enabled the government's share to be cut back slightly there. During the 1960s the general tendency was for this category to rise faster than total expenditures in almost every country.

During 1968, the share of fixed investment did not respond to the generally faster rate of growth. In several advanced countries it fell noticeably. Among the less developed countries, as well as in most of the advanced ones, investment's share of the GNP generally rose during the 1960s, but in 1968 many reductions were to be found. Large increases were achieved, however, in Venezuela, Taiwan, Iran, Israel, and South Korea.

Inventory building was generally modest in the advanced countries. There seemed to have been a fairly general tendency toward adjustment, with those countries that devoted a large share of resources to inventory building in 1967 reducing their investment in 1968, and vice versa.

The international surplus as indicated in Table II includes all transactions in goods and services, and the net effect of factor incomes (payments such as dividends and interest arising in one country, which are paid to residents of another). Thus, the figures are comparable to the current account of the balance of international payments, excluding the effect of current international transfer payments. The largest relative surpluses were recorded in West Germany, Italy, and Switzerland; the largest deficits by Australia, Greece, Iceland, Israel, South Korea, Tunisia, and several Latin-American countries.

Table III shows the latest available figures on levels of national income, considered on both a total and a per capita basis, in more than 70 countries. The concept of national income is designed to measure the output of the national economy at the cost of producing that output less the value of the depreciation of the capital stock for that year. The table includes all countries for which data are available that had a national income of $1 billion or more in 1963. The national figures at current prices have been converted to U.S. dollars at current exchange rates. Thus, the figures are affected by changes in the price level

Table III. National Income and Income per Head

Country	National income in U.S. $000,000,000 1968	National income per head in U.S. $ 1958	1963	1968
Industrial countries				
Austria	8.4	590	830	1,145
Belgium	16.5	935	1,185	1,715
Canada	46.7	1,505	1,600	2,250
Denmark	9.5	890	1,335	1,960
France	96.2	1,005	1,270	1,925
Germany, West	100.6	840	1,255	1,670
Italy	60.6	480*	765*	1,150
Japan	112.2	285	560	1,110
Luxembourg	0.6	1,075*	1,340	1,750
Netherlands	20.4	695	995	1,605
Norway	6.9	870	1,200	1,805
Sweden	18.2†	1,200†	1,730†	2,300†
Switzerland	14.0	1,195	1,675	2,270
United Kingdom	79.9	1,015	1,300	1,445
United States	720.0	2,115	2,560	3,580
Other developed areas				
Australia‡	21.3§	1,125	1,485	1,785§
Finland	5.6	725	1,130	1,190
Greece	6.1	325	460	695
Iceland	0.2	965	1,270	1,075
Ireland	2.4	465	650	810
New Zealand‡	4.1†	1,170	1,505	1,490†
Portugal	4.3	215	300	455
South Africa‖	11.8	315	395	545
Spain	21.6	300*	440*	665
Turkey	10.6	180	225	315
Less developed areas				
Africa				
Algeria	2.3¶	235	205	...
Congo (Kinshasa)	0.9	70*	105	55
Ghana	1.8	140	190	215
Kenya	1.1	70	85	105
Libya	1.6§	110	430	925§
Morocco	2.7	160	165	185
Nigeria‡	3.6♀	45	60	60♀
Rhodesia	1.0	185	190	210
Sudan‡	1.2♂	80	90	90♂
Tanzania	0.7§	50*	60	70§
Tunisia	0.8	150	190	180
Uganda	0.7	60	65	85
United Arab Republic‡	4.8♀	110*	140	160♀
Zambia	0.9§	110	135	225§

Country	National income in U.S. $000,000,000 1968	National income per head in U.S. $ 1958	1963	1968
Caribbean and Latin America				
Argentina	14.7§	490	485	635§
Bolivia	0.7	85	120	145
Brazil	21.0♀	185	245	250♀
Chile	4.0§	325*	265	435§
Colombia	5.2§	190	265	270§
Costa Rica	0.6	320	325	385
Ecuador	1.0	155	160	180
El Salvador	0.8	210	215	245
Guatemala	1.2§	235	255	265§
Honduras	0.5§	170	189	220§
Jamaica	0.8	315	375	410
Mexico	24.2	270	350	510
Nicaragua	0.6	225	265	335
Peru	2.9♀	170	210	240♀
Puerto Rico‡	3.1§	540	825	1,140§
Uruguay	1.2♀	440	460	425♀
Venezuela	7.8	630*	605	800
Asia, East and Southeast				
Burma‡	1.5§	55*	60*	60§
Ceylon	1.3§	120*	130	110§
China (Taiwan)	3.3	100	150	245
Hong Kong	1.0¶	245	300	...
India‡	37.2§	65*	80	75
Indonesia	8.2¶	80	80	...
Iran‡	6.8	145*	180	250
Korea, South	4.7	125	130	155
Malaysia	2.4♀	195	225	250♀
Pakistan‡	12.3§	60	80	105§
Philippines	5.2§	185*	210	150§
Singapore	1.0♀	420	485	530♀
Thailand	4.2§	80	100	125§
Vietnam, South	1.7♀	90	80	105♀
Middle East				
Iraq	1.8♂	160	190	215♂
Israel	3.1	610	835	1,145
Jordan	0.5§	140	185	250§
Kuwait‡	1.8§	1,830	3,430	3,460§
Lebanon	0.9♂	210	295	360♂
Saudi Arabia‡	1.0¶	125	150	...
Syria	0.8♂	135	155	160♂

*Data not strictly comparable with later years.
†Unofficial estimates.
‡Financial year beginning in year shown.
§1967.
‖South African national accounts include Botswana, Lesotho, South West Africa, and Swaziland.
¶1963.
♀1966.
♂1965.
Sources: UN, OECD, and IMF publications; official national sources.

and do not indicate the growth of real per capita income.

Two important qualifications have to be made about the use of this procedure. First, the use of current exchange rates determined for foreign trade and payments purposes may not adequately reflect differences in the actual purchasing power of the various national currencies. Furthermore, devaluations and revaluations will distort the figures as between different years. Second, the figures in national currencies are themselves estimated in a variety of ways, and there are differences in the definitions used by the various countries. For these reasons, small differences in per capita national income should be regarded as insignificant.

Bearing these difficulties in mind, one may draw some conclusions from the data presented. About four-fifths of the aggregate income of the 77 listed countries was accounted for by the 15 industrial countries, while the 52 less developed countries represented between 10 and 15% of the total. The dominating size of the U.S. economy in relation to all other non-Communist countries is shown in Table III; it is roughly six or seven times the size of the two next largest, Japan and West Germany. It is likely, however, that a more sophisticated analysis that allowed for differences in the internal purchasing power of national currencies would show a somewhat different picture. The available evidence suggests that, in comparison with the U.S., real output in several Western European countries is relatively higher than suggested by the 1968 figures, particularly so in West Germany, Italy, and the U.K. Similarly, the gap in living standards between the advanced and the less developed countries is generally less than that suggested when current exchange rates are used to obtain per capita income figures.

In many countries much of the increase in per capita money income during the 1960s represents a rise in price level. Allowing for price changes, income per head probably rose by about 3½–4% in both the groups of developed countries and about 1½–2% for low-income countries. (M. F. F.)

See also Economy, World.

India

A federal republic of southern Asia and a member of the Commonwealth of Nations, India is situated on a peninsula extending into the Indian Ocean with the Arabian Sea to the west and the Bay of Bengal to the east. Area: 1,232,560 sq.mi. (3,192,184 sq.km.). Pop. (1968 est.): 524,080,000; Indo-Aryans and Dravidians are dominant, with Mongoloid, Negroid, and Australoid admixtures. Cap.: New Delhi (pop., 1968 est., 3,470,000). Largest city: Bombay (metro. pop., 1968 est., 5,368,000). Language falls into two main groups: Indo-Aryan, or northern, includes Hindi 30%; Dravidian, or southern, includes Telugu 10% and Tamil 8%. Hindi in the Devanagari script is the official language; English, an associate language, continued to be used. Religion (1961): Hindu 83.5%; Muslim 10.7%; Christian 2.4%; Sikh 1.8%; Jain 0.5%; Buddhist 0.7%; others 0.4%. Presidents in 1969, Zakir Husain to May 3 and, from August 16, Varahagiri Venkata Giri; prime minister, Mrs. Indira Gandhi.

Domestic Affairs. There were dramatic political developments in India in 1969. A president died. A deputy prime minister resigned. Major banks were nationalized. A power struggle within the Indian National Congress divided the party in two. Anti-Congress alliances were in difficulties in many states, and more than one ministry fell.

Elections in five states in February did not provide much comfort for the troubled Congress Party but, despite the radical group's attack on Deputy Prime Minister Morarji Desai, an outward semblance of unity was maintained at the party's annual session at Faridabad in April. Then the sudden death of the president of the republic, Zakir Husain (*see* OBITUARIES), on May 3 set off a series of events that shook both Congress and country. The election of a new president became the focal point of conflict between the prime minister and the conservatives in the Congress, generally referred to as "the syndicate."

A confrontation took place in July at Bangalore where the All-India Congress Committee met. Aware that the conservatives were moving to contain her, Mrs. Gandhi sprang a surprise on the meeting by submitting a radical economic program. The program was unanimously adopted, but the conservatives, who held the levers of the party machine, struck back by getting the Congress parliamentary board to adopt N. Sanjiva Reddy, speaker of the Lok Sabha (House of the People), as the official party candidate for the presidency against Mrs. Gandhi's wishes. V. V. Giri (*see* BIOGRAPHY), the vice-president who had been sworn in as acting president, announced his decision to contest the election as an independent candidate. Returning from Bangalore, Mrs. Gandhi divested Desai, one of the leaders of the conservative group, of the finance portfolio on the ground that she should assume direct responsibility for implementing the economic program, and Desai resigned from the government. In spite of efforts by several party leaders to bring about a reconciliation, the resignation was accepted on July 19. On the same day the government issued an ordinance nationalizing 14 leading banks, a move that assured Mrs. Gandhi of the support of the Congress left wing and of the leftist opposition groups.

Mrs. Gandhi's followers then moved to inflict a defeat on the organizational wing through the presidential election. Alleging that the head of the party, Congress Pres. S. Nijalingappa, had made deals with the right-wing Swatantra and Jan Sangh parties, they demanded a free vote, and Mrs. Gandhi declined Nijalingappa's suggestion that she instruct Congress members to vote for Reddy. Although the voting was confined to an electoral college consisting of members of Parliament and state assemblies, the election generated high popular excitement and there was an obvious polarization between left and right. Polling took place on August 12 and the results were announced on August 16, Giri securing 420,077 votes against Reddy's 405,427. Later in the month Gopal S. Pathak, the governor of Mysore, was elected vice-president, having been adopted unanimously as the Congress candidate.

The defeat of the official Congress candidate for president led to demands from the organizational wing that the prime minister and her associates be arraigned for defiance of the party mandate. A resolution of unity was adopted by the Congress working committee on August 25, but the truce was short-lived. The prime minister's group, which by then had the support of Y. B. Chavan, the home minister, started a move to summon the All-India Congress Committee to elect a new president of the party. Fighting for their survival, the conservatives ousted two of Mrs. Gandhi's supporters from the working committee, the party's highest executive, on the eve of its meeting on October 31. The prime minister retaliated by boycotting the meeting, and her supporters announced that they would hold a meeting of the All-India Congress Committee later in November. A split in the 84-year-old Congress Party appeared complete.

Mrs. Gandhi set up her own working committee, while the official committee met to censure her action and accused her of being a potential dictator. On November 12, in what some observers felt was the most historic political event since independence, Mrs. Gandhi was expelled from the party by the organizational members, comprising 11 of the 21 members of the working committee. Congress leaders directed Congress members of Parliament to take immediate steps to elect a new leader. The prime minister, however, announced that she did not recognize the official ruling. In spite of bitter clashes in Parliament, Mrs. Gandhi retained the support of a majority of Congress members of Parliament, and her position was secure at least for the time being. Nijalingappa was removed as party president by the All-India Congress Committee, although the organizational group claimed a majority of the delegates were not present.

Midterm elections took place in February in four states that had been under presidential rule. In West Bengal a united front of non-Congress parties trounced the Congress (which could win only 55 seats in an assembly of 280) and formed a ministry that was headed by Ajoy Mukherjee but was dominated by the Communist Party. In Bihar the Congress secured 118 seats out of 318 but formed a coalition government, which was voted out in June after 115 days. After a short-lived non-Congress government, the state again came under presidential rule in July. In Uttar Pradesh the Congress won 211 seats in a house of 425 and assumed office. In the Punjab, the Aklai Dal and Jan Sangh parties combined to form a coalition cabinet. In the Nagaland elections, the Naga Nationalist Organization was again victorious and H. Sema became chief minister. The union territory of Pondicherry chose a government of the Dravida Munnetra Kazhagam. In September the Manipur Cabinet fell, and the territory was placed under presidential rule. The united government of Kerala suffered a reverse in October, and the chief minister, E. M. S. Namboodiripad (Communist-Marxist), resigned. A new coalition government led by Achuta Menon (Communist Party of India) was sworn in.

Prime Minister Indira Gandhi (left) with newly elected Pres. V. V. Giri at the presidential palace after his election Aug. 20, 1969. Mrs. Gandhi backed Giri despite the fact that he was not the candidate chosen by her party.

RAGHUBIR SINGH FROM NANCY PALMER AGENCY

There was turmoil in Andhra Pradesh in the first half of the year because of a demand by people of the Telengana region for separate statehood. A scheme was announced by Mrs. Gandhi that would remove the economic and administrative grievances of the agitators and endow the Telengana regional committee with more powers. A bill amending the constitution to give special status to the hill regions of Assam was adopted by Parliament. Another bill passed by Parliament related to the appointment of an ombudsman who would investigate charges against ministers. The question of the future of the city of Chandigarh, one of the problems left unresolved when the state of Hariana was created in 1966, turned into a major controversy when Darshan Singh Pheruman, an 84-year-old Sikh political leader, undertook a fast demanding its inclusion in the Punjab. Pheruman died on October 27, the 74th day of the fast. There was widespread religious rioting in Gujarat in September in which the death toll was placed officially at 431. The National Integration Council called an all-party conference to formulate a campaign to strengthen secularism.

The country celebrated the centenary of the birth of Mohandas Gandhi and the quincentenary of the birth of Guru Nanak, the founder of the Sikh religion.

The Economy. The economic situation showed steady improvement. Food prices in October 1969 were 4.2% lower than in October 1968, but those of industrial raw materials were higher; the wholesale price index stood at 173.2 on Oct. 4, 1969, compared

INDIA

Education. (1965–66) Primary, pupils 49,639,000, teachers 1,570,000; secondary (1963–64), pupils 14,570,000, teachers 829,197; vocational, pupils 340,000, teachers 21,396; teacher training, students 140,000, teachers 9,477; higher (including 62 universities), students 1,145,554, teaching staff (1963–64) 80,247.

Finance. Monetary unit: rupee, with a par value of Rs. 7.50 to U.S. $1 (Rs. 18 = £1 sterling). Gold and foreign exchange, official: (June 1969) U.S. $838 million; (June 1968) U.S. $720 million. Budget (1968–69 est.): revenue Rs. 27,260,000,000; expenditure Rs. 25,950,000,000. National income: (1966–67) Rs. 242 billion; (1965–66) Rs. 211 billion. Money supply: (May 1969) Rs. 58.9 billion; (May 1968) Rs. 54,140,000,000. Cost of living (1963 = 100): (May 1969) 157; (May 1968) 158.

Foreign Trade. (1968) Imports Rs. 18,823,000,000; exports Rs. 13,153,000,000. Import sources: U.S. 35%; U.K. 7%; West Germany 7%; U.S.S.R. 7%; Japan 7%; Canada 5%. Export destinations: U.S. 17%; U.K. 16%; Japan 12%; U.S.S.R. 11%. Main exports: jute manufactures 15%; tea 13%; iron ore 7%; cotton fabrics 6%; iron and steel 6%; fruit and vegetables 5%; leather 5%.

Transport and Communications. Roads (1968) 928,200 km. (including 24,150 km. main roads). Motor vehicles in use (1968): passenger 550,305; commercial 290,800. Railways: (1967) 59,061 km.; traffic (1966–67) 102,564,000,000 passenger-km., freight 100,230,000,000 net ton-km. Air traffic (1967): 2,514,648,000 passenger-km.; freight 89,855,000 net ton-km. Shipping (1968): merchant vessels 100 gross tons and over 383; gross tonnage 1,945,037. Telephones (Dec. 1967) 1,017,990. Radio receivers (Dec. 1967) 7,579,000. Television receivers (Dec. 1967) 6,000.

Agriculture. Production (in 000; metric tons; 1968; 1967 in parentheses): wheat 16,567 (11,393); rice *c.* 58,500 (56,787); barley 3,469 (2,348); corn *c.* 6,500 (6,275); potatoes 4,233 (3,522); cassava (1967) 3,715, (1966) 3,361; tea (1967) 380, (1966) 376; chick-peas 6,042 (3,612); bananas (1966) 3,732, (1965) 2,693; sugar, raw value (1968–69) *c.* 2,715, (1967–68) 2,421; millet (1967) 9,074, (1966) 7,774; sorghum (1967) 10,107, (1966) 8,944; tobacco 344 (353); rapeseed and mustard seed 1,482 (1,228); linseed 398 (260); peanuts 4,476 (5,731); cotton, lint 1,084 (1,156); jute *c.* 900 (1,146). Livestock (in 000; 1966–67): cattle *c.* 176,000; sheep *c.* 42,100; buffaloes *c.* 53,220; goats *c.* 65,000; poultry *c.* 115,230.

Industry. Production (in 000; metric tons; 1968): iron ore (61% metal content) 27,361; pig iron 7,239; crude steel 6,445; coal (1967) 68,223; electricity (excluding most industrial production; kw-hr.) 43,809,000; aluminum 120; cement 11,911; cotton yarn 961; woven cotton fabrics (m.; 1967) 7,277,000; petroleum products (1967) 13,267; sulfuric acid 966; caustic soda 306; gold (troy oz.; 1967) 102; manganese ore (metal content; 1967) 640.

UPI COMPIX

Village farmers in Madras dig deep into a well in a desperate search for water. The spring of 1969 brought on one of the worst droughts in the area's history.

with 171.6 on Oct. 5, 1968 (1961–62 = 100). In a midyear assessment, the National Institute of Applied Economic Research placed the agricultural growth rate in 1969–70 at between 5 and 6% and the industrial growth rate at 7%. Exports in 1968–69 were 12.9% higher (at Rs. 13,355,000,000) than in the previous year. The union government's 1969–70 budget placed income at Rs. 35,190,000,000, including Rs. 1 billion obtained through revised taxation, and expenditure at Rs. 25,580,000,000. Together with the capital budget, the total allocation for development programs in the year was Rs. 17,380,000,000, including deficit financing of Rs. 2.5 billion.

The fourth five-year plan was launched on April 1. Its draft, as adopted by the National Development Council and presented to Parliament on April 21, envisaged public expenditure on development of Rs. 143,980,000,000 and private investment of Rs. 100 billion over a five-year period. Among the principal production targets to be achieved by March 1974 were: food production, 129 million metric tons; steel ingots, 10.8 million metric tons; machine tools, Rs. 650 million worth; iron ore, 53.4 million metric tons; coal, 93.5 million metric tons; cloth, 10,850,000,000 m.; and power, 82,000,000,000 kw-hr. Other targets included reducing foreign aid by half and raising the numbers of students and of practicing doctors.

A major structural change in the economy was effected when the 14 banks were brought under public ownership. The reasons given for nationalization, which appeared to some to have been motivated by political rather than economic arguments, were the removal of control by a few, prevention of the use of bank credit for speculation, and provision of more credit for agriculture and new entrepreneurs.

In February 1969 the first nuclear power station in India, at Tarapur in Maharashtra state, became operational when the second of its reactors became critical. Work on the satellite tracking station near Poona was nearing completion.

Foreign Affairs. In February, Mrs. Gandhi turned over the portfolio of external affairs to Dinesh Singh, formerly minister of commerce. In July, India and Pakistan settled their dispute over the Rann of Cutch, signing maps to show the border as fixed by the 1968 international tribunal. The government's decision to seek admission to the conference of Islamic powers at Rabat, Morocco, in September, where an Indian delegation was first heard and later excluded, led to adverse reaction in the country. It became a major issue in the battle between the parliamentary and organizational wings of the Congress. The Soviet Union's decision to offer military equipment to Pakistan caused dismay, and India gave a cool reception to the Soviet Union's proposals for Asian collective security.

Among important visitors to India was U.S. president Richard M. Nixon, with whom Mrs. Gandhi raised the question of U.S. arms supplies to Pakistan. Other visitors during 1969 were Soviet Premier Aleksei N. Kosygin, the shah of Iran, the presidents of Romania and Hungary, and the prime ministers of Bulgaria and New Zealand. Mrs. Gandhi attended the Commonwealth Prime Ministers' Conference in London in January and also visited Burma, Afghanistan, Japan, and Indonesia. (H. Y. S. P.)

ENCYCLOPÆDIA BRITANNICA FILMS. *Hindu Family* (1952); *India (Pakistan and the Union of India)* (1952); *Mahatma Gandhi* (1955); *Animals of the Indian Jungle* (1957); *India (Customs in the Village)* (1957); *India (Introduction to Its History)* (1957); *Ganges: Sacred River* (1965).

Starving cattle wander across the dried-up Vedanthangal Lake, a well-known bird sanctuary in Madras state, during the rainless months in south India early in 1969.

UPI COMPIX

Indonesia

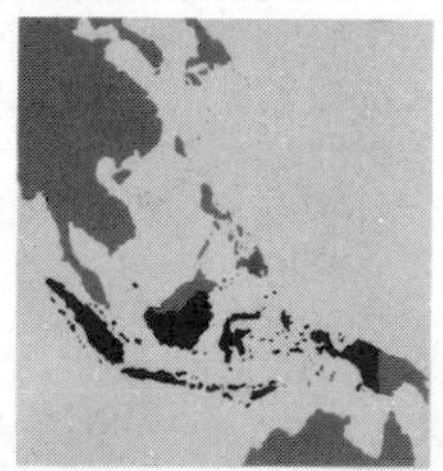

A republic of Southeast Asia, Indonesia consists of the major islands of Sumatra, Java, Kalimantan (Indonesian Borneo), Celebes, and Irian Barat (West New Guinea) and approximately 3,000 smaller islands and islets. Area: 735,268 sq.mi. (1,904,345 sq.km.). Pop. (1968 est.): 112 million. Cap. and largest city: Jakarta (pop., 1968 est., 4.5 million). Language: Bahasa Indonesia (official); Javanese; Sundanese; Madurese. Religion: mainly Muslim; some Christian, Buddhist, and Hindu. President and prime minister in 1969, General Suharto.

With the formal acquisition of Irian Barat in 1969, Indonesia for the first time encompassed a territory that stretched "from Sabang to Merauke," the area embraced by the revolutionary slogan that was raised with the Indonesian proclamation of independence in 1945. Thus, all the territories that once comprised the Netherlands East Indies empire from Sabang, at the northern tip of Sumatra, to Merauke, in the southeast corner of Irian Barat, had become Indonesian. International recognition of Indonesia's acquisition of Irian Barat followed a controversial plebiscite in the territory under the aegis of the UN.

Despite the historic significance of the acquisition of the territory, however, Indonesia in 1969 was preoccupied with rebuilding the country's shattered economy and restoring constitutional democracy in the aftermath of the disastrous Sukarno era. During the year, the economy continued to improve, but the pace of recovery slackened. An economic highlight was the launching of the country's five-year development plan (REPELITA). In July, three months after the plan was set in motion, the Indonesians were heartened when U.S. Pres. Richard Nixon, in the course of an Asian journey, visited Indonesia and had words of praise for the plan. It marked the first time that a U.S. president had come to the country.

In contrast to the overall economic improvement, less progress was recorded in the development of a viable political system. Although the Provisional People's Consultative Congress (MPRS) scheduled general elections for no later than July 7, 1971, the body had to struggle interminably with the election bills, and the delay became crucial since the government might require about 18 months to set up election machinery. In October, however, President Suharto met with party leaders, and on November 22 a general election bill was passed. The minister of the interior announced that elections would be held on July 5, 1971.

The bill provided for a parliament of 460 members, 100 of whom would be appointed and the remainder elected by a proportional list system on the basis of party preference. The appointees would include members of the armed forces (who were ineligible to vote or to run for election) and members of "functional groups" representing segments of society such as students and workers. A second body, the People's Consultative Congress, to be chosen later, would consist of 920 members, including Parliament. This body would elect a president in 1973. Principal objections to the bill stemmed from a provision that barred former members of any "outlawed" organization from voting.

Another political issue was the question of the fate of approximately 50,000 or more Communists held in detention, many of them since the abortive Communist coup in 1965. The government announced plans to resettle some of them on the underdeveloped island of Buru. However, there were also reports of a new massacre of Communists in the area of Purwodadi, Central Java, where the now illegal Indonesian Communist Party (PKI) had apparently sought to regroup itself. The government vigorously denied these reports.

Domestic Affairs. During the rise of Sukarno's "guided democracy," a euphemism for his personal dictatorship in collaboration with the PKI and "like-minded progressives," Sukarno dissolved the popularly elected national legislature and sought to govern ostensibly by the traditional village method of consultation (*musjawarah*). President Suharto, who crushed the 1965 coup as the commander of the Army's strategic reserve, pledged to restore representative government and civil liberties, and by 1969 he had moved in that direction. Indonesia, for the first time in years, had a popular, critical press, and with Suharto's open encouragement, a general election had been scheduled.

Among the critical problems being grappled with was the question of regional autonomy, a prickly issue in Indonesia, which is composed of wide-ranging ethnic, linguistic, and cultural blocs. These blocs occasionally produced small-scale revolts in Sumatra, Kalimantan, Sulawesi, and the Moluccas. In 1969 Suharto reiterated his desire for regional autonomy.

For the first time since the collapse of the 1965 coup some conflict arose within the armed forces. This stemmed from Suharto's decision in late 1969 to restructure the military. He reduced Indonesia's traditional four branches (Army, Navy, Air Force, and state police) to two, the armed forces and the state police. The Air Force and Navy, both of which had been heavily infiltrated by "progressive officers" during the Sukarno era, were unhappy with the plan, particularly the Navy. Suharto, however, held that the armed forces must develop into a "compact force possessing a single doctrine." Clearly, he was anxious to reduce interservice rivalries and forestall, with the restoration of constitutional democracy, the temptation of political parties to court favour with one or another military service. The reorganization was to take effect April 1, 1970.

Irian Barat. The formal incorporation of Irian Barat into the republic climaxed a 20-year campaign by Indonesia for the acquisition of the 161,000-sq.mi. area of largely impenetrable jungle, inaccessible mountains, and inhospitable escarpment. The area was inhabited by fewer than one million people scattered in small tribal units, some of them still possessing a Neolithic Age culture. Under the terms of the Round Table Agreement of 1949, which provided for the transfer of sovereignty from the Netherlands to Indonesia, both parties agreed to the exclusion of Irian Barat, pending negotiations. After years of unsuccessful intermittent negotiations within and outside the UN, Sukarno in January 1962 attacked the disputed territory. By astute diplomatic maneuvering, he secured the neutrality of the U.S. and the support of the Soviet Union and China. Confronted by this array of diplomatic opposition, the Dutch acceded to the Indonesian demand and on Aug. 15, 1962, at the UN, the two nations signed the New York Agreement. The accord stipulated that by 1969 the people of Irian Barat would be permitted an "act of free choice" to decide whether or not they wished to remain with Indonesia. In May 1963 Indonesia took over the administration of the territory.

Indonesian administration of the territory was marked by armed disturbances. The most serious occurred in late 1968 and early 1969 and were promoted by the Free Papua Organization, which sought independence for the territory. Although the UN representative in Irian Barat held that the "act of free choice" should be conducted on a "one man, one

INDONESIA

Education. (1967–68) Primary, pupils 12,574,820, teachers 288,146; secondary, pupils 1,148,502, teachers 64,576; vocational, pupils 352,235, teachers 24,512; teacher training, students 106,575, teachers 7,774; higher, students 110,677, teaching staff 1,902.

Finance. Monetary unit: rupiah, with a free rate (Oct. 1969) of 380 rupiah to U.S. $1 (910 rupiah = £1 sterling). Gold and foreign exchange, central bank: (Dec. 1963) U.S. $51 million; (Dec. 1962) U.S. $135 million. Budget (1968 est.) balanced at 97,186,000,000 rupiah. Gross national product: (1967) 921 billion rupiah; (1966) 323.7 billion rupiah. Cost of living (Jakarta; 1963 = 100): (June 1969) 64,839; (June 1968) 56,636.

Foreign Trade. (1967) Imports U.S. $649 million; exports U.S. $658 million. Import sources: Japan 25%; Hong Kong 18%; West Germany 12%; U.S. 11%; Netherlands 7%. Export destinations: U.S. 25%; Japan 24%; Netherlands 12%; West Germany 9%; Australia 9%. Main exports (1966): rubber 33%; petroleum and products 30%; palm oil 5%; coffee 5%; tin ore 5%.

Transport and Communications. Roads (1968) 84,268 km. Motor vehicles in use (1967): passenger 184,954; commercial 94,892. Railways (1967): 6,785 km.; traffic 4,947,000,000 passenger-km., freight 659 million net ton-km. Air traffic (1967): 526,326,000 passenger-km.; freight 13,239,000 net ton-km. Shipping (1968): merchant vessels 100 gross tons and over 479; gross tonnage 711,500. Telephones (Dec. 1967) 169,142. Radio receivers (Dec. 1967) *c.* 1.5 million. Television receivers (Dec. 1967) 54,000.

Agriculture. Production (in 000; metric tons; 1968; 1967 in parentheses): rice 15,249 (13,932); corn (1967) 2,527, (1966) 2,874; cassava (1967) 11,291, (1966) 12,100; sweet potatoes and yams (1967) *c.* 3,256, (1966) 2,308; sugar, raw value (1968–69) *c.* 600, (1967–68) 659; tea (1967) *c.* 78, (1966) *c.* 75; copra (1967) *c.* 495, (1966) *c.* 528; soybeans *c.* 455 (484); palm oil (estates only; 1967) 174, (1966) 151; peanuts (1967) 400, (1966) 488; coffee (1967) *c.* 150, (1966) *c.* 111; tobacco *c.* 110 (*c.* 95); pepper (exports; 1966) 20, (1965) 12; rubber (1967) *c.* 760, (1966) 716; fish catch (1966) 1,202, (1965) 1,067. Livestock (in 000; Dec. 1967): cattle 6,816; pigs 3,180; sheep (Sept. 1967) *c.* 2,400; horses 632; buffaloes (Dec. 1966) *c.* 2,900; goats (Dec. 1966) *c.* 11,200.

Industry. Production (in 000; metric tons; 1968): coal 176; crude oil (1967) 25,310; tin concentrates (metal content) 17; bauxite (1967) 912; electricity (excluding most industrial production; kw-hr.; 1967) *c.* 1,677,000.

vote" basis, this was rejected by Indonesia on the ground that the politically unsophisticated Papuans did not comprehend the meaning of regular balloting. Instead, Indonesia established consultative assemblies in Irian Barat's eight regencies and, through the process of *musjawarah,* 1,025 delegates were selected to vote on behalf of the people of the territory. The vote was completed on August 2. The delegates of each regency voted unanimously that Irian Barat should remain with Indonesia.

The unanimity of the vote confirmed the suspicions of many of Indonesia's critics, who believed that the whole performance was farcical. At the UN several member states, particularly those from Black Africa, were troubled by the world organization's failure to endorse the "one man, one vote" principle. Nonetheless, in November the UN General Assembly took formal note of the outcome of the plebiscite and the long-standing issue came to a close.

The Economy. Indonesia's overall economic performance continued to be generally satisfactory in 1969. The government concentrated on its economic stabilization and rehabilitation program, particularly the control of inflation. Index figures for the price of nine basic commodities (rice, salt, etc.) registered a decline of 13.8%. The budget was balanced. A bumper rice crop of ten million tons was harvested. Indonesia's balance of payments position improved moderately, primarily as the result of increased oil exports, but the country's foreign exchange reserves remained low. Some economists expressed concern that the stabilization measures were causing price declines, which resulted in depressed domestic production and caused sluggishness in economic activity.

Against this background, the Suharto Cabinet unfolded its five-year development plan. It called for an investment of $4 billion by the central government and upward of $600 million by private foreign enterprise. World Bank officials and others termed the plan realistic and in keeping with Indonesia's resources and financial possibilities. A primary objective of the plan was to make Indonesia self-sufficient in food. To do so, the country had to produce 15.4 million tons of rice annually by 1974, the last year of the plan. The plan's success was expected to depend in part on foreign aid, especially from Japan and the U.S. Although President Nixon mentioned no figure during his Indonesian visit, the impression there was that the U.S. might increase its current level of economic assistance, which consisted of $125 million in general economic aid and about $88 million in surplus food and other commodities. For the most part, however, the success of the plan would hinge on the ability of the Suharto government to combat corruption and smuggling and to trim the lethargic, oversized, and inefficient bureaucracy—problems left from the calamitous Sukarno era. (AR. C. B.)

ENCYCLOPÆDIA BRITANNICA FILMS. *Indonesia (New Nation of Asia)* (1959).

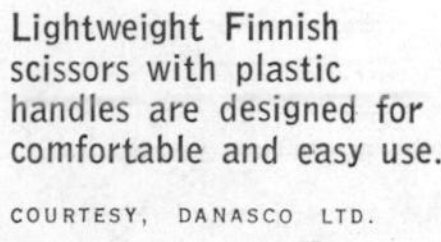

Lightweight Finnish scissors with plastic handles are designed for comfortable and easy use.

COURTESY, DANASCO LTD.

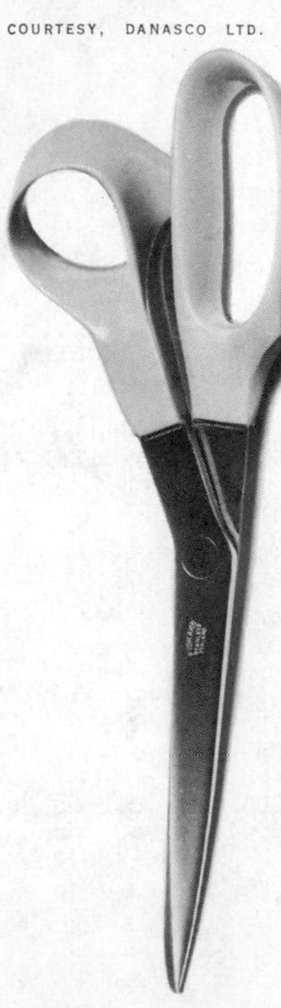

Industrial Design

Designers are never slow to get together at conferences where they worry collectively about the state of their craft and the contribution it could or should be making to the good of society. The year 1969 was altogether remarkable in this respect, however. There can have been few years in the relatively short history of design as an accepted profession when more designers and associates of designers spent more time and used more words to discuss the scope of their own activities.

COURTESY, BERNINI

Dondolo rocking chair designed by Cesare Leonardi and Franca Stagi, made from glass-reinforced polyester.

Some of the sternest words were spoken in the U.K., and came both from within the profession itself and from laymen. Prince Philip emphasized designers' obligations toward society at a meeting of Britain's Society of Industrial Artists and Designers (SIAD). He pointed out that what people see around them and the things they use in everyday life are not inevitable. They do not have to be hideous and they need not be inconvenient, unreliable, or inefficient. The trouble was that they would go on being hideous, inconvenient, unreliable, and inefficient as long as they were accepted as inevitable.

The same theme was amplified by the architect Sir Hugh Casson in a talk to the West London Architectural Society. Design, according to Sir Hugh, involved questioning the nature of accepted objects rather than merely trying to improve their style or materials. Technological problems could easily be overcome, but the chief contemporary problems were social, moral, and political. It was much easier to put a man on the moon than to solve the housing problem in Glasgow. He went on to attack what he called "scientism: the tremendous over-reverence for facts rather than ideas" and concluded that designers were good at analysis but not at synthesis.

More strictures along the same lines came from the ergonomist and educationalist John Christopher Jones, in a lecture to the Institute of Contemporary Arts significantly called "The Glass Box." He, too, put the moon trip into perspective. Man could circle and land on the moon, but he was still baffled by the problems of a city intersection. The modern designer was singularly ill-equipped to tackle the new kinds of problems that were likely to emerge within ten years. Society should be able to expect its designers to predict problems before they are swamped by them.

These attacks on present complacency and warnings of future difficulties were, not surprisingly, picked up in design conferences again and again in 1969. In the U.K. the Design and Industries Association's annual conference centred on the theme "Technology, Design and Society," and the SIAD's own annual conference devoted itself to "The Society Within Society." Most important, two major international conferences also devoted themselves to the future—the annual International Design Conference at Aspen, Colo., and the sixth international conference of the International Council of Societies of Industrial Design (ICSID), held at the Queen Elizabeth Hall, London, where 12 speakers from seven countries discussed "Design, Society and the Future."

The ICSID conference, at least, showed no sign of the reverence for facts criticized by Sir Hugh Casson. Speaker after speaker concentrated almost exclusively on theory and prediction, so that sometimes the effect was almost of a clean break with reality rather than an attempted extension from it. What did emerge, paradoxically enough, was an optimism about the future that was based on dissatisfaction with the present. The future, it seemed, was relatively rosy—largely because designers could hardly fail to learn from the mistakes they were currently making.

The most lucid—and consequently the most powerful—expression of this ambivalence came from Hasan Ozbekhan in a paper called "The Future as an Ethical Concept." In this paper Ozbekhan concluded that the technological battle was almost won, and designers must begin to face the victory. They had overcome the constraint of man's natural environment and must look beyond the goal of mere survival. There was a danger at this point that technique, not man, would become an end in itself. Energies had to be redirected toward human ends and, if humanity's chief aim was no longer survival amid scarcity, then new aims must be invented. If they were not found, man would be immured in a "perpetual present." If technology failed to lead toward a future that had relevance to what was human in man, we should be in that steady-state present from which there was no exit. Designers were so busy answering "yes" to any technological challenge that no one asked whether the question should be, "Ought I?" rather than "Can I?" and whether the aim ought to be a "willed future" resulting from judgments and choices formed with reference to the idea of the desirable.

Achievements. In a year when so many weighty statements were being made about design in the future, it was difficult to enthuse about the design of the present. Designs that actually sought to improve the quality of life now—let alone in 50 years' time—were few and far between, and hard to find among the acres of mere glossy styling. A can opener, a pair of scissors, a bottle cap—oddly enough, it was the tiny, everyday, easy-to-overlook things that for once seemed to be getting worthwhile attention from designers. There were, fortunately, at least two major projects that made a serious effort to design for flexibility, and hence for the future.

Two structures—one in the Netherlands, one in Japan—took, in the words of Britain's *Design* magazine, the form not of "buildings in the accepted sense of the word, but rather enclosed areas within which people may create their own environment." The designer of the town centre at Dronten, Neth., the engineer F. van Klingeren, was in fact quoted as saying: "For me architecture is not to make a building but to make a tool with which people can work." His steel structure was designed for a new town with a population of 10,000 that was expected to double by 1970. Measuring 50 by 70 m., it provided shelter for a wide range of activities, both organized and unorganized. There were no barriers between different areas: bowling alley, committee rooms, café, restaurant, theatre, and movie screen were all at least partly open to the unobstructed empty space in the middle, where anything from a market to a mass meeting could go on.

In contrast, Summerland, a new leisure area just outside Tokyo, provided precisely selected activities in clearly indicated zones. It was similar to the Dutch project in its desire to provide a sheltered, closed space that had as many of the advantages of an open space as possible, and in its attempt to provide, under one roof, the maximum variety of activity. The huge plastic dome, 162 by 81 m., housed restaurants, offices, terraces, and a swimming pool, among other things. The dome itself was the centre of a huge, wooded sports park incorporating natural areas and camping sites, as well as a motel, transport stations, and organized sports facilities.

Meanwhile, domestic life was getting a little assistance. Here, designers were not so much looking to the future as putting right some tedious errors of the present that no one had bothered to rectify.

A simple locking device for bottles or other round containers, invented by Eugene Treanor and known as the Cap-tiv, was welcomed in the U.K. by the government, the British Medical Association, and the Royal Society for the Prevention of Accidents. Put into production in the U.K., Canada, and the U.S., it was expected to reduce substantially the number of poisoning accidents to children, which had been growing considerably as pills for everyday use became more attractive. Instead of threads, the bottle neck had sets of teeth that formed a ratchet. Gaps between each set of teeth enabled the cap of the bottle to engage its own teeth, and lock into position. A sprung ring inside the bottle cap prevented unlocking unless the cap was simultaneously depressed and turned—a motion that was too complex to be performed by a small child.

The Finnish firm Fiskars pleased housewives by developing a new design for general purpose scissors that represented a considerable improvement in ease of use over most other kinds currently available. The molded nylon handles were designed to provide a comfortable grip with much less chance of the user's hand slipping during cutting. The blades themselves, of chromed steel with a high carbon content, were permanently set and needed no adjustment. This attention to detail resulted in a further gain in that the scissors were much lighter than conventional types.

A domestic design that promised to please both children and housewives demonstrated the benefit of carrying out user trials during a product's development. The aim had been to produce a baby carriage that was light, easy to collapse, and needed little storage space. The Baby Buggy—designed by aircraft engineer O. F. Maclaren for the British firm of Andrews Maclaren Ltd.—underwent extensive user trials at the department of ergonomics and cybernetics at Loughborough University of Technology. The finished design weighed only 6 lb., measured just 41 x 6 x 6 in. when collapsed, and could be erected and collapsed with one hand. The child passenger was also prevented from reaching the brake or from jamming his fingers in the wheels.

Child-size versions of modern furniture classics shown in 1969 include the molded plastic cylinder chair and table set (left) and an inflatable chair and ottoman (right).

THE NEW YORK TIMES STUDIO

The year's most dramatically designed product owed nothing to the moral glow that attends socially beneficial design. Its effect came from the sheer aesthetic pleasure of an utterly simple solution to a minor design problem carried out with irresistible boldness and panache. The Dondolo rocking chair, designed by the architects Cesare Leonardi and Franca Stagi for the Italian firm of Bernini, was made from one continuous strip of hollow, fluted, glass-reinforced polyester. With a length of 7 ft. 1 in., it was likely to overwhelm the average domestic interior, but its visual qualities were the most sheerly startling to be seen in domestic design in some years.

In a way, a measure of the slow progress of design was provided by an exhibition in New York proclaiming the virtues of a design creed as apparently well established as honesty in materials. Yet the Museum of Contemporary Crafts of the American Craftsmen's Council put on an extensive display called "Plastic as Plastic," emphasizing how customary it had become over the years to disguise plastics as wood, leather, marble—anything, in fact, but plastics. If nothing in the show seemed to have the wit of the Bernini rocking chair, certainly the sum of the exhibits added up to a convincing vindication of plastics as a material with a look of its own—as in tough but lightweight children's furniture in fibre-glass–reinforced polyester, designed by Gunter Beltzig for the West German firm of Brüder Beltzig. The pieces were water- and sun-proof so as to be suitable for indoor or outdoor use, and had the added refinement of a curved or lipped edge that would not damage floors or lawns. Whether it was really necessary to go to such lengths to vindicate what ought to be a well-established material was, of course, another matter, one that would demand attention in the future.

Design Schools and Industry. A new venture in the Netherlands gave promise of keeping industry in better touch with new, young thinking in design. The Dutch Institute of Industrial Design started a series of publications called "Between Design School and Practice." It came in the form of a small portfolio containing details of the content of the students' training, together with individual sheets prepared by the designers themselves to illustrate examples of their own work.

Two other countries began looking to design to improve their industrial efficiency. The State Committee of the Council of Ministers for Science and Technology of the U.S.S.R. was given the task of coordinating the introduction of design into the Soviet national economy, while the Ministry of Higher and Secondary Professional Education was given responsibility for improving the quality and quantity of industrial designers. *Izvestia* reported that industrial design requirements would be included in state standards, in briefs for the design and development of industrial products, and in all forms of construction products, and that design centres would be opened up for different branches of industry and would be responsible for recommending the discontinuation of items that were "outdated, ugly, and inconvenient in use."

At almost the same time, a U.S. consultant called in to advise the Israeli government on the future of design in Israel deplored the absence of a true link between designers and manufacturers. He warned that the economy of the country might be seriously affected within five years if Israel failed to put its house in order, and indicated that Israel needed a design centre and a school capable of training designers to degree level.

Design and the Public. In a year when what designers did tended to be overshadowed by what they said—especially by what they said about their own future—it would be inappropriate not to conclude with some further warnings. More than once during 1969 there were suggestions that the designer's role, both as conceiver of practicable ideas and as commercial middleman between consumer and manufacturer, was being gradually eroded.

British design critic Reyner Banham pointed out that the buying public was now intervening in the productive process—if only to the extent of selecting and assembling interchangeable, prefabricated components—and was therefore exercising a degree of personal choice and even of original craftsmanship. Similarly, a new British magazine called *What?* started publication as an outlet for the inventiveness of the public. It quickly proved itself to be not simply a platform for criticism ("bottles of sauce and mayonnaise should be redesigned") but also a journal in which the inventiveness normally felt to be the province of designers was displayed.

This tacit emphasis on the nonpassive elements among the public gave added point to a firmly worded statement made to the ICSID conference by Kenneth E. Boulding of the Institute of Behavioral Science, Colorado. Boulding declared that one of the problems of planning was that individuals were more often planned against than planners, more often designed against than designers. The sovereignty of the individual was of paramount importance. Every society designed its children to grow up and become members of it, but there must be strong limits on the extent to which adults can be designed. The problem of how to design without "having designs on" was one of the major unsolved problems of the human race. There were some partial solutions, but men still lived in a world in which too many people were pushed around and in which there was too sharp a distinction between the planners and the planned. (DE. C.)

See also Industrial Review.

Industrial Review

The trend of industrial growth in the 1960s (about 6% a year from 1960–66) was resumed again in 1968, following a period of considerably slower progress in 1967. Although the rise in activity was shared by all countries, the trebling of the growth rate was mainly due to an upturn in exactly those nations that had been in a state of stagnation a year earlier: the United States, West Germany, and the United Kingdom. The advance was well maintained during the first half of 1969; some decline in the rate of progress seemed likely toward the end of the year as a reaction to measures that had the effect of restricting demand in a number of countries.

The increase in industrial activity was much the same in industrial and less industrialized countries. The latter accounted for about one-eighth of world industrial output in 1963 and this had not changed more than marginally by 1968; nevertheless, this share was significantly higher than in 1958 when it was about 9%.

Productivity, as measured by output per man-hour in manufacturing, continued to increase rapidly. The advance was in line with that achieved in 1967, with the exception of the United Kingdom, where it accelerated.

The considerable rise of manufacturing output in the U.S. was mainly due to high consumer spending and to residential investment. Private demand for durable consumer goods rose about 11%, and for other goods rose just over 4%; and private fixed investment in dwellings was 15% higher than in 1967. The expansion was particularly marked in the first half of 1968. Various restrictive measures, such as the 10% federal income tax surcharge, tended to start depressing demand and output in the second half; in 1969, however, new stimulus came from higher business spending on plant and equipment. Developments in Canada were similar except that exports were a major stimulant to the growth of Canadian output.

Manufacturing production in Japan increased somewhat more slowly in 1968 than in the year before, but its rise, 18%, remained spectacular. In particular, requirements for investment goods increased rapidly (outlays for investment were more than 25% higher in the fiscal year ending March 1969 than a year before). Exports and private spending also showed strength.

West Germany's recovery from its 1967 recession was rapid: manufacturing output in 1968 was about one-eighth higher than a year earlier, and this rate of expansion continued into 1969. The recovery was led by a high level of new investment and an unusually large increase of exports (automobile exports, for example, exceeded the 1967 level by one-third). As a consequence of reflationary measures, output in France was about 5% higher in the early months of 1968 than in the same period in 1967; the nationwide strikes in May and June, however, caused a loss of production equal to two weeks of national output. By August activity had recovered, and in January–April 1969 it was approximately 10% above the prestrike level.

The Italian manufacturing industries increased their output by more than 6% in 1968, somewhat less than in 1967. The main stimulus came from exports, which expanded far ahead of domestic demand. The upswing continued into 1969 despite industrial troubles, and in the first six months output was approximately 8% higher than a year earlier. The Netherlands enjoyed a boom year in 1968. Manufacturing activity was 10% higher than in 1967 and about the same rate continued into 1969. Similar advances, though at a lower rate, were achieved in both years in Belgium.

After the mild recession in 1967 manufacturing in Britain advanced briskly in 1968, at a rate exceeding 5%, and reached a plateau of much slower advance in 1969. The recovery was led by exports, supported by the devaluation of the pound sterling in November 1967; investments picked up toward the middle of 1968, but private consumption was sluggish as a result of severe deflationary measures.

The development of manufacturing activity in 1968 was not uniform in the smaller European industrial countries. In the cases of Austria and Ireland the rate of growth exceeded 10%; it was somewhat lower, between 5 and 7%, in Sweden, Switzerland, Yugoslavia, and Portugal; while in Finland, Norway, and Greece the advance was not more than 3–4%.

The manufacturing output in the less industrialized nations expanded at a somewhat slower rate than in their more developed neighbours. In some countries, such as Mexico, the advance was very fast, but in most it remained more moderate. The larger members of this group (India, Pakistan, Australia, South Africa) achieved a growth rate of about 5 to 6%.

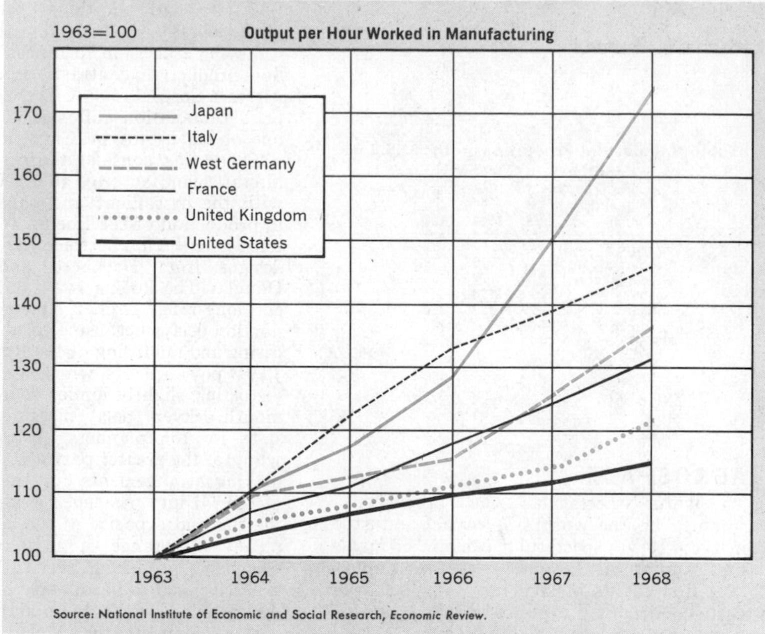

Source: National Institute of Economic and Social Research, *Economic Review.*

Industrial output rose in 1968 just above 8% in the U.S.S.R., slightly less rapidly than in 1967. This pattern of somewhat slower, though still rapid, advance was reflected in the other Eastern European countries as well, with the exception of Poland, which maintained its previous fast pace. The Soviet intervention in Czechoslovakia and the introduction of the "new economic mechanism" in Hungary might have partially accounted for the slowdown. (G. F. R.)

Table I. Index Numbers of World Production, Employment, and Productivity in Manufacturing Industries

1963 = 100

Area	Relative importance 1963	1968	Production 1966	1967	1968	Employment 1966	1967	1968	Productivity* 1966	1967	1968
World†	1,000	1,000	123	126	135	...	...	...	...	...	...
Industrialized countries	876	875	123	126	135	...	...	...	...	...	...
Less industrialized countries	124	125	125	129	136	...	...	...	...	...	...
North America‡	480	476	127	128	134	...	...	...	...	...	...
Canada	28	28	127	129	135	116	116	115	109	111	122
United States	452	448	127	128	134	113	114	116	112	112	116
Latin America§	49	49	123	127	135	...	...	...	...	...	...
Mexico	8	9	135	147	159	...	...	...	...	...	...
East and Southeast Asia‖	88	112	132	151	172	...	...	...	...	...	...
India	16	14	114	116	121	...	...	...	...	...	...
Japan	55	79	137	164	193	107	112	116	128	146	166
Pakistan	3	3	151	144	151	...	...	...	...	...	...
Europe¶	350	329	116	117	127	...	...	...	...	...	...
Austria	7	6	115	113	125	99	96	95	116	118	132
Belgium	11	10	113	114	123	103	101	99	110	113	124
Finland	4	4	120	123	127	102	103	102	118	119	125
France	51	48	117	121	128	99	98	96	118	123	133
Germany, West	89	85	117	115	129	102	97	98	115	119	132
Greece	2	2	138	142	147	110	108	106	125	131	139
Ireland	1	1	116	125	139	103	103	106	113	121	131
Italy	36	36	118	128	136	95	99	100	124	129	136
Netherlands	12	12	122	126	138	100	98	97	121	129	142
Norway	4	4	122	126	129	105	106	105	116	119	123
Portugal	2	2	127	135	143	...	...	...	...	...	...
Sweden	14	14	124	126	134	103	98	95	120	129	141
United Kingdom	73	64	113	112	118	103	100	99	110	111	119
Yugoslavia	13	14	135	134	142	111	111	110	122	121	129
Rest of the world♀	33	34	...	...	...	...	...	...	...	...	...
Australia	14	13	115	120	125	109	111	114	106	108	110
South Africa	5	5	130	138	145	129	134	138	101	103	105

*This is 100 times the production index divided by the employment index, giving a rough indication of changes in output per person employed.

†Excluding Albania, Bulgaria, China, Czechoslovakia, East Germany, Hungary, Mongolia, North Korea, North Vietnam, Poland, Romania, and the U.S.S.R.

‡Canada and the United States.

§South and Central America (including Mexico) and the Caribbean islands.

‖Afghanistan, Brunei, Burma, Ceylon, Hong Kong, India, Indonesia, Iran, Japan, Malaysia, Pakistan, Philippines, South Korea, South Vietnam, Taiwan, Thailand, and Singapore.

¶Excluding Albania, Bulgaria, Czechoslovakia, East Germany, Hungary, Poland, Romania, and the U.S.S.R.

♀Africa, the Middle East, and Oceania.

Sources: UN *Monthly Bulletin of Statistics;* U.K. National Institute of Economic and Social Research, *Economic Review.*

Table II. Industrial Production in the U.S.S.R. and Eastern Europe
1963 = 100

Country	1966	1967	1968
Bulgaria	143	162	181
Czechoslovakia	122	130	138
Germany, East	120	129	136
Hungary	124	134	141
Poland	129	139	150
Romania	144	164	189
U.S.S.R.	127	140	152

Source: UN *Monthly Bulletin of Statistics.*

AEROSPACE

The words "spectacular" and "prosperous" summed up the world's aerospace industry in 1969. It was spectacular because of man's first landing on the moon and two important first flights in civil air transport: the British Aircraft Corporation (BAC)/Sud-Aviation Concorde and the Boeing 747. Its prosperity could be gauged from the fact that the backlog of orders in the U.S. industry alone totaled $31 billion at the beginning of the year.

Sales in the U.S. of aircraft, spacecraft, and engines were expected to reach more than $15 billion during 1969, of which $5.8 billion were civil transports—a decline of about 9% from 1968. The $800 million increase in the total figure came from increased sales of military and private aircraft. In addition, sales of components in the aerospace field were expected to rise to more than $12 billion, an 8% increase.

Other major aircraft-producing nations, Britain, Canada, and France, had similar increases. West Germany remained the country with the fastest growing industry, with a rise of more than 20% over 1968.

Despite a continued decrease in its commitment in Vietnam, the U.S. maintained considerable development activity in military aircraft in 1969. It was concerned mainly with aircraft that would in the 1970s replace the current military types. These planes included the F-14A, a supersonic, swing-wing, carrier-based air-superiority fighter to be developed by the Grumman Aircraft Engineering Corp. to replace the F-111. The 50,000-lb. plane was to use TF30 engines, built by Pratt & Whitney Inc., and the U.S. Navy was expected to order several hundred of them. Other variants were to be the F-14B and C, which would use the same airframe but would have an unspecified "advanced technology" engine.

The McDonnell Douglas Corp. F-4 Phantom series remained in quantity production throughout the year; more than 3,400 were delivered, and export orders were placed by Britain, West Germany, and Spain. The first batch of F-4s for Israel were delivered in September, and a total of 50 was expected to be delivered before September 1970.

Another best seller from the U.S. was the Ling-Temco-Vought, Inc., A-7 Corsair 2, of which more than 1,650 were ordered in various configurations by the U.S. Air Force, Army, and Navy. Production of all versions ran at approximately three units per month during 1969, but a considerable step-up was anticipated in 1970 and 1971.

Another primarily military contractor, Bell Aerospace Corp., secured further orders for 600 OH-58A light observation helicopters, valued at $32.6 million. Total orders for this helicopter stood at more than 1,200. Bell also had additional orders for 170 HueyCobras (AH-1G) from the U.S. Army following a decision to cancel the $875 million production contract for the Lockheed Aircraft Corp. AH-56A Cheyenne. The surprise cancellation followed an accident to one of ten prototype Cheyennes in March.

There was considerable activity in civil aircraft manufacturing in the United States, with the first flight and subsequent delay in production of the Boeing 747, and the intense competition between the rival "airbus" designs from Lockheed and McDonnell Douglas. The Boeing 747, a 350–500-passenger, long-range airliner, suffered serious production delays because of problems with the casing and mounting of the Pratt & Whitney JT9D power plants, which were found to be distorting slightly under load. The three-month delivery delay meant a welcome respite for the planners of several airlines, who, for the greater part of 1969, were busy making arrangements for the introduction of the 747 into passenger service. Because of the size and capacity of the aircraft a completely new range of auxiliary equipment was being produced. Service with the 747 was scheduled to begin early in 1970 on Pan American's New York–London run.

Production of the McDonnell Douglas DC-10 began during the year. Powered by three General Electric CF6 engines of 40,000-lb. thrust (or by Pratt & Whitney JT-9D's), more than 100 DC-10s had been ordered by the end of 1969. Production of the Lockheed L-1011 TriStar (three Rolls-Royce RB.211 engines) was also begun. More than 180 were ordered, in various configurations, and the first flight was due in 1970.

In the supersonic field the Soviet Tu-144 was first in the air, with the BAC-Sud Concorde a close second. First shown to the public on May 21 in Moscow, the Tu-144 was expected to go into service in 1971 on internal Soviet routes and on services to New York and New Delhi. An additional 18 Tu-144s were said to be under construction.

The two Concorde prototype aircraft were heavily engaged in flight-test trials following the first flight in March. A developed version of the Rolls-Royce Olympus 593 engine was due to be installed in early 1970 for flight testing at speeds greater than Mach 2. Costs for the development of the Concorde reached more than $1,750,000,000 and by the end of the year no firm decision on Anglo-French governmental production funding had been announced.

In regard to the U.S. supersonic transport, Pres. Richard Nixon asked for development funding of $662 million, which was considered sufficient for Boeing to have two prototypes flying by the end of 1972. General Electric was to provide the engines, with other major subcontractors being Aerojet-General Corp., Aeronca, Inc., Avco Corp., Fairchild Hiller Corp., Ling-Temco-Vought, North American Rockwell Corp., Northrop Corp., and Rohr Corp. The involvement of so many major companies in one project reflected the increasing trend in aerospace to subcontract major parts of a project, for both political and economic reasons.

Outside the U.S. the major examples of such collaboration between competitors were between Britain and Europe—mainly West Germany and France—and included the Concorde, Jaguar (the Anglo-French trainer/strike aircraft), the European airbus project (designated the A-300B), and the SA 341 helicopter.

In the autumn the French government, as part of defense budget cuts, canceled a major part of another collaborative contract—the WG.13—which was to have been a joint arrangement between Sud-Aviation and Westland (U.K.) on the lines of the SA 341 agreement.

British industry, with the exception of Handley Page, Ltd., which had financial problems during the summer until the Cravens Corporation of America rescued it, continued to forge ahead steadily. In the first nine months of 1969 British aerospace exports reached more than £227 million ($540 million), as compared with £200 million ($480 million) for the same period in 1968. Exports to the U.S. accounted for more than £50 million ($120 million) of the total, thus maintaining the position of the U.S. as Britain's leading aerospace customer.

Production of the antisubmarine aircraft Nimrod by the Hawker Siddeley Group, Ltd., was well under way, with the first delivery of the aircraft to the Royal Air Force (RAF) in October. Hawker Siddeley Harriers were also being produced for the RAF, and an order for 12 of these vertical takeoff and landing (VTOL) ground-support aircraft was placed during the year by the U.S. Marine Corps.

West Germany was also active in the VTOL field. Three competitive designs were published by Dornier, Messerschmidt-Bölkow-Blohm, and Hamburger Flugzeugbau in response to a joint civil/military requirement for an 80–100-seat transport aircraft. (J. B. BE.)

AUTOMOBILES

The enterprising and highly competitive character of the automobile industry was well illustrated by the engineering and commercial advances made by car manufacturers of many nationalities during 1969. Car and truck production followed an upward trend in North America, Europe, and Japan, and the demand for motor vehicles continued to show a more rapid growth in many markets outside America than in the United States. International monetary problems, including the sudden devaluation of the franc in August, the vagaries of the West German mark, and the severe deflationary measures taken in Great Britain, were negative factors in an otherwise mainly favourable year. However, the British motor industry countered an artificially restricted home market by record-breaking exports which, in the first eight months, showed an 18.8% gain over 1968.

Various familiar factors caused a general rise in prices coincident with the introduction of the 1970 models in the fall, among which the increased cost of materials, higher wages for labour, and the specification changes required to meet safety regulations and exhaust emission requirements were of major importance. In Europe and to some extent in the U.S. there was an increasing tendency to make midseason announcements of entirely new models, although September continued to be the recognized period for changes and additions to existing model lines. European examples were the Ford Capri in January and the Austin Maxi, Fiat 128, and Opel "K-A-D" series in April. In the U.S. Ford also chose April to introduce the Maverick.

The U.S. Federal Safety Standards continued to influence engineering, commercial, and political thinking in Europe and elsewhere during 1969. The initial impact made by these standards in 1967 was due to the importance of the U.S. as an export market for European and Japanese car manufacturers. Later, however, the governments of countries where cars are used in large numbers began enacting their own safety measures and also became increasingly concerned about exhaust emissions.

The process of designing for greater safety was accompanied (both in the U.S. and in

Table III. Production and Exports of Motor Vehicles by the Principal Producing Countries
In 000 units

Country	1966 Passenger cars	1966 Commercial vehicles	1967 Passenger cars	1967 Commercial vehicles	1968 Passenger cars	1968 Commercial vehicles
Production						
United States	8,598.3	1,731.1	7,436.7	1,539.4	8,848.6	1,971.8
Germany, West	2,830.0	220.7	2,295.7	186.6	2,862.2	244.8
France	1,785.9	238.6	1,776.5	233.2	1,833.0	242.6
United Kingdom	1,603.7	438.7	1,552.1	385.1	1,815.9	409.3
Japan	877.7	1,408.7	1,375.8	1,770.7	2,055.8	2,030.0
Italy	1,282.4	81.5	1,439.2	103.5	1,544.9	118.7
Canada	701.5	200.5	720.8	226.4	900.9	279.1
Australia	280.1	64.0	313.6	76.5	345.0	73.4
Sweden	173.5	26.4	194.0	20.6	223.3	21.4
U.S.S.R.*	675.0		728.8		801.0	
Other countries*	1,234.6		1,313.5		1,529.3	
World total	24,453.0		23,688.7		28,151.0	
Exports						
Germany, West	1,475.5	105.7	1,350.8	104.8	1,801.6	145.6
United Kingdom	556.0	165.9	502.6	135.2	676.6	142.0
France	501.0	41.6	547.0	42.7	628.6	47.5
Italy	371.6	21.9	404.4	22.5	557.7	29.5
United States	177.6†	78.9†	280.6†	82.6†	330.5	92.2
Sweden	104.7	16.6	123.0	15.4	138.8	15.4
Japan	153.1	102.6	223.5	138.8	406.3	206.2
Canada	189.5	63.5	342.4	111.8	522.1	155.0

*In the case of the U.S.S.R. and "Other countries," a reliable breakdown between cars and commercial vehicles was not available.
†Excludes unassembled vehicles now recorded only by value.
Source: British Society of Motor Manufacturers and Traders, *The Motor Industry of Great Britain.*

Europe) by a continued proliferation of engine options that provided the user with greater power, higher maximum speeds, and livelier acceleration. While performance and safety were by no means incompatible, light cars with disproportionately large engines made extra demands upon skill and self-control that not all drivers were capable of meeting.

The use of fuel injection (in place of carburetion) as a means for getting increased power accompanied by a cleaner exhaust received increased attention in Europe. This was due in part to the availability of electronically controlled injection systems (Bosch in West Germany and AE-Brico in the U.K.) which metered the fuel more accurately in relation to varying road conditions than was possible with earlier mechanical systems. However, increased cost remained a serious deterrent.

Car designers in the United States succeeded in meeting the tighter exhaust emission requirements that were scheduled to become obligatory in 1970 by the concentrated refinement of carburetor engines. An example was the transmission control of vacuum spark advance developed by General Motors. Special equipment was also perfected to enable cars to meet the stringent restrictions upon evaporation from the fuel tank and carburetor that were demanded by the state of California. Engineers also made good use of the lull in new safety legislation to refine and perfect a number of automobile body details such as safety belts, defoggers for rear windows, and the automatic release of tipping seats (in two-door models) when the doors are opened.

Of the entirely new U.S. models the Ford Maverick was a compact two-door sedan styled with the long hood made popular by the Mustang. At the other end of the scale of size and power, a new Lincoln Continental appeared in the fall with conventional separation and insulation between body and frame; an interesting reversion after long experience with an integral body-frame structure.

Chevrolet's principal innovation for the 1970 model year was the Monte Carlo luxury two-door hardtop coupe, notable for a very long hood obtained by an unusually bold extension ahead of the front wheels. Publicized as "an elegant prestige car," it was offered with a choice of four V-8 engines.

Chrysler Corp. introduced a new model in the Dodge Challenger, with a unified body-frame structure and many safety features, including side-impact beams in the doors. A novel Chrysler development was a practical elaboration of the headlight delay system that gave the user the option of either using or canceling a 90-second period during which the headlights remained "on" after he had switched them off and left the car.

A new "polyglass" tire of bias-belted construction became widely used on U.S. 1970-season models. A number of important advantages were claimed for it, including better traction and cornering power, longer tread life, and higher resistance to punctures. It was generally considered to represent a major advance in safety.

European manufacturers continued to build a wide range of car sizes, of which those in greatest demand were in the "lower-medium" class with engines ranging from 1.1 to 1.6 litres in capacity. These accounted for more than half the total sales in many European countries. Entirely new models in this category were the Austin Maxi, the Fiat 128, and the Renault 12; all were front-drive cars but differed widely in design and styling features. The Fiat and Renault were four-door sedans, while the Austin had a five-door body in which the features of a sedan and a station wagon were combined in a highly practical manner. Fiat also brought out a new "top-of-the-line" model 130 (replacing the 2300 series), which had a conventional rear-drive configuration with a new V-6 engine at the front; twin overhead camshafts driven by belts were a novel feature.

Ford's major European announcement came early in the year when the Capri was launched; like the smaller Escort of 1968, it went into production in both the U.K. and West Germany. It was a medium-sized two-door sedan, styled and planned to appeal to sports-minded young people with families, and could be had with a variety of engine options.

Of the two General Motors subsidiaries in Europe, Opel (in West Germany) announced new models of the Kapitän-Admiral-Diplomat series in April, notable for the adoption of the DeDion type of rear suspension which had never previously been used in any GM-sponsored automobile. Vauxhall (in the U.K.) reintroduced its "VX4/90" label in the fall for a new high-performance version of the four-cylinder Victor.

Mercedes Benz, the first to offer Bosch electronic fuel injection as a six-cylinder option in 1968, used the same system on a new 3½-litre V-8 engine introduced in September 1969. Almost concurrently, the Bosch system was offered as an option on certain models by Citroën, Opel, and Saab. The rival (British) AE-Brico electronic injection system was adopted by Aston Martin.

Volkswagen and Porsche collaborated in the design and production of a new and unusual mid-engined two-seater sports coupe which first appeared at the Frankfurt (W.Ger.) motor show in September. At the same exhibition Mercedes Benz displayed an experimental mid-engined model of advanced design and outstanding performance (the "C-III") in which a new three-rotor Wankel engine was used, but this was not made available to the public at large. Series

Right, Porsche 917 racer, first shown at the Geneva Motor Show in spring 1969, has a 12-cylinder engine developing 520 hp with a top speed over 320 km. per hour (200 mph). Below, Ford Capri 3000 GT XLR was introduced at the 1969 London Motor Show.

AUTHENTICATED NEWS INTERNATIONAL

COURTESY, FORD MOTOR COMPANY LTD.

Right, the Dodge Challenger, a new model introduced for 1970 by Chrysler Corp.

COURTESY, CHRYSLER INTERNATIONAL S.A.

production of the Wankel engine in moderate numbers was maintained by NSU in West Germany and by Toyo Kogyo in Japan, but no additional car makers adopted this interesting though controversial type of power unit.

Honda, having obtained a footing in the automobile business with the diminutive N-series car, announced a new 1300 model early in the year to compete in the "lower-medium" category. The original and interesting design was notable for a transversely mounted, four-cylinder, air-cooled engine (largely built of light alloys); front-wheel drive; and independent rear suspension. In Australia, a new Holden range of passenger cars was introduced in midyear in which a V-8 engine of local design and manufacture was used for the first time. (M. PL.)

BUILDING AND CONSTRUCTION

The U.S. Department of Commerce reported that during the first seven months of 1969 the value of new construction in the U.S. amounted to $50.3 billion. On a seasonally adjusted basis, this figure was equal to an annual outlay of $91.1 billion. If this level of construction continued until the end of 1969, it would constitute a gain of 7.5% over the value of construction in 1968. As a general rule, such a percentage gain in the total dollar value of construction is a welcome stimulus to the national economy, but in 1969 U.S. Pres. Richard Nixon and other national leaders viewed this gain with concern because there were serious inflationary developments in the construction industry. A comparison of some of the major price indexes revealed this to be true. In July 1969, the consumer price index stood at 128.2, compared with an average of 121.2 in 1968 and 116.3 in 1967; the wholesale price index was at 113.3, compared with an average of 108.7 in 1968 and 106.8 in 1967; while the composite construction cost index had reached 142, compared with 131 in 1968 and 125 in 1967. (For all of these indexes 1957–59 = 100.)

On September 4 President Nixon, as a direct anti-inflation measure, ordered all U.S. federal agencies to immediately put into effect a 75% reduction in new contracts for government construction. The president hoped that this action would reduce the heavy demands that were being made on the construction industry and that resources would be diverted to home building. He was confronted with the vexing problem of finding a way to keep the construction of housing moving ahead while seeking to curtail all other types of construction. In a statement issued on the same date, President Nixon said, "The cost of building a home or an apartment house has become exorbitant. The Housing Act of 1968 sets as a goal 26 million houses in the next decade. Unless fundamental action is taken now to reduce the rise in housing prices, the nation will fall far short of that goal." The president also urged state and local governments and businessmen to follow the example of the federal government by cutting back temporarily on their own construction plans.

The cost components that were contributing to the inflationary condition in the construction industry were materials, labour, and funds to finance construction. The president viewed the shortage of skilled labour in the construction field as one significant contributor to these pressures. In order to achieve an increase in the needed skilled labour, Nixon ordered the secretaries of labour and of health, education, and welfare to move promptly to provide for manpower training and vocational education.

The U.S. Department of Housing and Urban Development embarked in June upon "Operation Breakthrough," an effort to meet the nation's housing requirements. This program revealed a recognition by the department that the magnitude of the housing problem required the large-scale involvement of private industry in addition to the government's existing housing programs. The purpose of the program was to involve private industry in the design, testing, evaluation, and construction of prototype housing that used innovative concepts now available to the construction industry. Contracts were to be awarded to private firms to begin a three-phase program: (1) design and development; (2) prototype housing construction; and (3) actual production of housing.

In Canada, according to the official report of the Dominion Bureau of Statistics, the outlook for construction in 1969 was favourable. The forecast was for total construction outlays of $13.3 billion, up sharply from the level of activity in 1968. Gains in all types of construction were expected, with nonresidential construction registering greater gains than the industry as a whole. Expected contributors to the gains in nonresidential building were office buildings, retail outlets, and hotels. However, it was expected that other construction gains would include housing, up 12%, and also roads, municipal works, transportation facilities, and power projects.

In Western Europe, as in the U.S., interest rates in 1969 moved to high levels. This was due in part to the demand pressure on real resources and to the strain on capital markets. Expectations of continuing price inflation appeared to help maintain the rate of fixed investment despite the high level of interest rates. The outlook for building construction was somewhat mixed, as it had been in 1968. In the United Kingdom investment in dwellings was expected to decline 3.9%, with private investment in dwellings showing a greater decline than public investment. In France the government's program in 1968 to increase output had resulted in an average monthly addition of 46,624 new dwelling units, compared with 39,116 in 1967. The government was subsidizing about 90% of the housing construction. The output of the building and construction industry stood at 162 in 1968 (1958 = 100).

In West Germany the output of the building and construction industry had dropped to 106 (1958 = 100) in 1968, lower than in 1966 or 1967. The average number of new dwelling units being built monthly in 1968 was 43,221. This figure was also lower than that reported for 1967. In Italy the monthly average number of new dwelling units built in 1968 was 22,579, which was slightly above the average in 1967. It was anticipated that the number of dwelling units added in 1969 would be equal to or greater than the number added in 1968.

In Czechoslovakia, Greece, Sweden, and Turkey, the reported number of new dwelling units built in 1968 revealed a higher level of activity than in 1967. In Denmark, East Germany, and Poland the reported number of new dwelling units was lower in 1968 than in 1967.

In Japan there was a continuing increase in the output of the building and construction industry. The monthly average number of new dwelling units built moved from 85,596 in 1967 to 100,140 in 1968. In Taiwan the output of the building and construction industry continued to show rapid expansion. Based on 1958 = 100, the index stood at 665 in 1967 and a record 840 in 1968. In Australia the national output rose in 1968, and the outlook for building construction continued to be good. The monthly average number of new dwelling units built in 1968 was reported to be 10,342. The economic recovery in New Zealand appeared to be soundly based, and industrial expansion was expected to continue throughout 1969. The number of houses and flats authorized per month was higher in 1968 than in 1967. In July and August of 1968 the monthly figure was more than 2,000, and the future outlook was favourable. (C. C. O.)

CHEMICALS

For large segments of the chemical industry 1969 was a year of progress liberally interspersed with problems. The progress was amply evidenced by figures for the first half of the year compiled by the Office of Business Economics of the U.S. Department of Commerce. Nonseasonally adjusted shipments of chemicals and allied products for the first six months of 1969 came to $24,629,000,000, 6.8% higher than the $23,067,000,000 worth of shipments made in the first six months of 1968. A high level of activity through the third quarter of the year indicated figures for the full year of 1969 would show an increase over the $46,465,000,000 value of shipments for the full year of 1968.

Inflation was contributing little if anything to the growth figures. The U.S. Federal Reserve Index of Quantity Output for chemicals and allied products rose from 203.8 (1957–59 = 100) in 1967 to 221.6 in 1968. It continued to climb during 1969, reaching 240.6 for the month of August. The U.S. Department of Labor's Index of Wholesale Prices for chemicals and allied products, on the other hand, dropped from 98.4 (1957–59 = 100) in 1967 to 98.2 in 1968 and continued to decline during the first half of 1969.

A survey by the U.S. Office of Business Economics and the Securities and Exchange Commission pointed to continued growth. The two agencies studied the amounts of money spent for new plant and equipment projects. They reported that the U.S. chemical industry spent $3,370,000,000 on starts for new projects in 1966; $2,460,000,000 in 1967; and $2,850,000,000 in 1968. In the first half of 1969, the industry spent $1,740,000,000.

The world chemical industry almost doubled its production during the first eight years of the 1960s, according to Norbert Platzer of the Monsanto Co. Using an estimate of $73 billion for 1960, Platzer said that the figure reached $115 billion in 1965 and $150 billion in 1968. The U.S. chemical industry accounted for $52.5 billion in 1968, 35% of the total. The Soviet Union was

Table IV. Value of World's Chemical Production, 196

Country	Production in $000,000,000
United States	52.5
U.S.S.R.	15.8
Japan	12
West Germany	11.3
Great Britain	10.5
France	8.3
Italy	7.5
Rest of Western Europe	9.6
Rest of Eastern Europe	9
Canada	2.3
Latin America	3
Rest of world	8.2
Total	150

Source: Norbert Platzer, Monsanto Co., at the 158th National Meeting of the American Chemical Society, September 1969.

second with $15.8 billion, while total Western European (including British) chemical production was $47 billion.

Although the U.S. industry was the largest and was continuing to grow, it was not growing as fast as those in other industrialized countries. Platzer reported that over the preceding ten years, the U.S. industry grew at an annual rate of more than 8.5%. Western Europe, however, grew at a better than 10% annual rate, and Japan at 15%.

The vital force that the chemical industry had become was illustrated by Platzer's estimates of world production figures for plastics and synthetic fibres. In 1968, production of resins totaled 41 billion lb. Included in that were 11 billion lb. of polyethylene, 10 billion lb. of polyvinyl chloride; and 4.5 billion lb. of resins derived from styrene. Production of man-made fibres (excluding cellulosics) in 1968 was estimated at 8.4 billion lb. The addition of 7.6 billion lb. of cellulosics (rayon, cellulose acetate, and triacetate) put the total for synthetic fibres at 16 billion lb., or more than 37% of the 42.7 billion lb. of fibres of all types produced in the world during 1968. Significantly, the total for the leading synthetic fibre, nylon, was the same as that for wool, 3.6 billion lb. Only cotton, with a production of 23 billion lb., surpassed the synthetics.

The older inorganic products were not growing at the rate that the synthetics were, but they continued to be the volume leaders. Production of sulfuric acid in the U.S. during 1968, for example, was 56.8 billion lb. valued at $229 million. Production of other large-volume products in the U.S. in 1968 in pounds (with dollar value in parentheses) was: oxygen, 25.8 billion ($189 million); ammonia, 24.2 billion ($337 million); sodium hydroxide, 17.6 billion ($172 million); and chlorine gas, 16.9 billion ($163 million).

The problems that the world chemical industry was experiencing came from several directions. The industry's response to the threatened population explosion had been a dramatic buildup in fertilizer capacity. The theory behind this was that more fertilizer meant more crop per acre and more total food production. Expansion of fertilizer capacity ran well ahead of demand, however, and U.S. fertilizer companies in particular were experiencing profit difficulties. Inflation during 1969 was a problem for the U.S. economy, but the chemical industry was being hit particularly hard because, although costs of doing business and of expansion were rising, competitive pressures were keeping selling prices down. The result was a dwindling of profit margins.

Table V. Deliveries and Exports of Electrical Machinery and Apparatus in 1967

Country	Total deliveries Value in U.S. $000,000	Total deliveries Percent increase over 1966	Exports Value in U.S. $000,000	Exports Percent increase over 1966
Germany, West	5,552	−5	1,761	9
Belgium	608	5	262*	2
France	3,349	7	591	6
Italy	1,530†	9	594	20
Netherlands	1,205	2	663	6
Austria	293	1	113	3
Denmark	320†	6	121	11
United Kingdom	5,022	0	951	−2
Switzerland	555†	8	249	9
Spain	637	5	16	...
Japan	9,600	28	1,156	10
United States	n.a.‡	...	2,097§	10

*Including Luxembourg.
†Provisional.
‡Not available; 40,834 in 1966.
§Excluding special category goods.
Source: Organization for Economic Cooperation and Development.

As with most industries, chemicals were feeling pressures to reduce drastically contributions to air and water pollution. A number of chemical products, moreover, were the subject of severe criticism. DDT, the powerful insecticide, drew fire from a number of groups. The product had made significant contributions in improving health and crop yields through eliminating insects but its continued, long-term use, many said, was causing irreversible damage to the environment. On November 20, the U.S. government ordered a ban on the use of DDT in residential areas within 30 days and a virtual halt to its use under any circumstances by 1971. At the same time, it announced that action regarding other persistent pesticides would be taken in 1970.

In October, the U.S. government ordered that all diet drinks artificially sweetened with cyclamates be banned as of Jan. 1, 1970, and that other diet foods containing cyclamates be removed from the shelves by February 1. The reason for the decision was that research showed a correlation between bladder cancer in rats and massive doses of cyclamate. The level of dosage producing this result was equivalent to 2,500 mg. per kilogram of body weight per day—equal to 500 ten-ounce bottles of diet soda drunk by an adult. The restriction on cyclamate-sweetened diet foods was subsequently eased. Nevertheless, the U.S. action triggered reactions in other countries, including Sweden, the U.K., and Japan, which imposed similar bans.

Within a week of the ban on cyclamates, another chemical product used in food became the focus of attention. A study by John W. Olney of Washington University of St. Louis showed that monosodium glutamate (MSG), a popular flavour enhancer, induced brain damage in animals when injected at levels only five times those an infant would receive in a typical baby food. Three large baby-food makers (who accounted for an estimated 80% of the U.S. market) promptly announced that they would withdraw the product from their formulations. Producers in the U.S. and in Japan (a major supplier of MSG) pointed out that MSG is merely the sodium salt of glutamic acid, and glutamic acid is an amino acid produced in large quantities by the human body itself. In Japan, it was said, average consumption was 2 grams a day, only 0.1% of the glumatic acid contained in an adult human. In addition, MSG had been shown safe to consume through an extended period of research and actual experience. Nevertheless, pressure was mounting for a closer look at all products used in food. The Food and Drug Administration, the U.S. agency charged with protecting the public interest in such matters, promised a review of the whole GRAS ("generally recognized as safe") list of food additives. Included on the list were such products as saccharin, the other big synthetic sweetener; chemical preservatives; and table salt, vinegar, and baking powder. (D. P. B.)

ELECTRICAL

The overall average annual growth rate in sales of electrical machinery and apparatus recovered from the slight fall in 1968 to surpass 8% in 1969. One of the most remarkable performances in the last few years was the phenomenal growth of the Japanese electrical industry. In 1966 production of electrical machinery and apparatus in Japan showed an 11% increase over the previous year and in 1967 the increase was 28%. As an exporter of electrical goods, Japan ranked third but, with a 32% (provisional) increase in exports in 1968 (36% in 1966 and 10% in 1967), it was possible that it might oust West Germany from second place in 1970 or 1971. Labour productivity in Japan's electrical industry was higher than in most other industrialized countries, partly due to the emphasis given in Japan to the manufacture of mass-produced goods.

COURTESY, WESTINGHOUSE ELECTRIC CORP.

A 100,000-lb. generator rotor is lowered into the new Westinghouse test facility at East Pittsburgh, Pa., which permits testing at speeds over 3,600 rpm.

A high level of productivity was also achieved in the U.S. where the output of the electrical engineering industry was almost double that of all Western Europe although 40% less labour was employed. Sales per employee in 1968 in the larger U.S. electrical companies averaged $20,000. The industry was benefiting from a large home market with a strong and continuing demand for mass-produced goods.

European industry was structured mainly at smaller national levels with less emphasis on mass production. It was also marked by a considerable unproductive effort devoted to designing and selling equipment in export markets. However, many electrical manufacturers in Europe were reporting much fuller order books than they had enjoyed in recent years, following organizational changes that had been made to improve efficiency. Some rationalization of the industry also took place in Europe, particularly in Britain where, in 1968, 25 large companies spent $1.3 billion in acquiring 38 other companies. Two of the top five electrical companies in Europe in terms of turnover, General Electric Co.–English Electric and Thomson-Brandt (France), were the results of recent mergers. Although the full benefits of these regroupings were not yet being felt, it was becoming accepted that if the industry in Europe was to continue to prosper, more such moves were inevitable.

In the meantime, the accent was on cooperative links between companies. An agreement covering collaboration in manufacturing and sales was signed early in 1969 by Allmäna Svenska Elektriska Aktiebolaget (ASEA) of Sweden and Brown Boveri of Switzerland. Jointly owned companies to manufacture and market domestic electrical appliances were formed by Phillips of the Netherlands and Ignis of Italy, and also by Allgemeine Elektrizitäts-Gesellschaft of West Germany and Zanussi of Italy. With these cooperative agreements and more mergers to come, the electrical industry in Europe was developing on the model of the U.S. industry, with a few large vertically integrated companies served by a large number of small component manufacturers.

To meet the needs of the utilities for large electric generating and transmission facilities extensive research and development programs had to be maintained, and these were tending to exceed the resources of even the largest manufacturing companies. It was particularly difficult to design a new high-voltage transmission system without undertaking full-scale development, and early in 1969 American Electric Power and the Ohio Brass Co. in the U.S. announced an $8 million joint research program with ASEA of Sweden to study the technical and economic feasibility of electric power transmission at voltages of 1,000 to 2,000 kv. The investigations and eventual design of commercial production facilities were to be carried out in both countries over eight years.

Because of the increasing complexity of the technical problems associated with the short-circuit testing of electrical apparatus, the Italian, Dutch, West German, and British testing authorities set up a joint committee to establish uniformity of testing methods.

Long-term developments aimed at reducing the cost of bulk transmission of electric power from large generators to urban load centres were being actively pursued in many countries. A "total energy" pipeline carrying liquid natural gas and containing cryoresistive or superconducting (very low temperature) cables was proposed in the U.S. Natural gas liquefies at about —160° C, and at that temperature the resistivity of copper is about 25% that at normal temperatures. Further refrigeration down to —269° C would be required for superconducting cable systems, although attempts were being made to find materials that exhibit superconductivity at higher temperatures. The University of California and Bell Telephone Laboratories, Inc., developed an alloy that remained superconducting at —252° C, but the commercial significance of the material had yet to be tested.

The contract for the first commercial direct-current transmission system to employ solid-state convertors was awarded to General Electric Co. in April 1969. The project, which was associated with a hydroelectric power station in Alaska, was to be rated at 80 Mw., but the voltage at which the thyristor convertors would be expected to operate was left to the manufacturer's choice.

The high cost of land in city centres led to the development of extra-high-voltage, metal-clad switchgear that would occupy one-tenth of the area needed by existing equipment. The first substations of this type, rated at 245 kv. and using sulfurhexafluoride gas insulation, were commissioned in Paris and Lyons, France, and in Zürich, Switz., toward the end of 1969. There was considerable interest in this development, and such equipment was likely to be installed in the near future in London and many cities in the United States, and also in areas of high atmospheric pollution. (T. C. J. C.)

GLASS

The year was one in which the productive capacity of the world glass industry expanded. It was estimated that the total sales of glass and glassware in Great Britain for the year were £172.2 million with exports running at 17.6% (£30.3 million) and imports £21.1 million. The principal producer of glass and glassware in Europe continued to be West Germany with 2,780,000 metric tons, followed closely by the United Kingdom (2,690,000 tons) and France (2,080,000 tons). West Germany and the U.K. produced about 47% of the total tonnage of glass and glassware in Europe and, combined with France and Italy, accounted for 76%. Taking 1962 as a basis, the index of production in the Common Market rose to 131% in 1968 and to 107% in the European Free Trade Area countries in the same year.

The Glass Container Manufacturers Institute of New York announced that shipments of U.S.-produced glass containers amounted to approximately 31.9 billion units in 1968. This was the second highest total for any year despite a 51-day strike in February and March that affected most glass container plants in the U.S. The estimated dollar value of the sales of glass containers in the U.S. amounted to a record $1,344,000,000.

Raymon H. Mulford, the chairman and chief executive officer of Owens-Illinois, Inc., the largest glass container manufacturers in the world, addressed the congress of the European Glass Federations, which was held in London in September. Mulford stressed the importance of research on glass and stated that his company's findings to date had merely whetted its appetite. Indeed, he said, "Our research has opened our eyes to the unique properties of glass and its plasticity to take on new properties in the hands of the chemist and physicist." Mulford stated that the U.S. was exhilarated by the outlook unfolding in many parts of the world and that the magnitude of the opportunities challenged the imagination. As an illustration of new uses of glass, two scientists from the Corning Glass Works reported that photochromic glasses fulfilled the basic requirements for information storage and display as new computer parts.

Various companies announced plans for expansion of production, notably in the U.S., Australia, and the Netherlands. The industry also increased its efficiency by means of company mergers in various parts of the world. An example of new production capacity and a new use for glass was the trebling of capacity in the North Carolina plant of PPG Industries, Inc., in order to deal with the anticipated demand for fibre glass in the manufacturing of automobile tires. (D. L. R.)

IRON AND STEEL

World crude steel production rose in 1969 to 565 million tons, an increase of 6.9% over the total for the previous year. This, in itself, was a small increase in the rate of growth, which had been 6.7% for the year before. However, it masked an underlying change in the entire production and trade situation. Whereas the growth in 1968 had been confined mainly to the U.S. and to its supplying countries, it was shared in 1969 by steel producers in all countries. The year, in fact, witnessed a boom in steel-market conditions virtually unprecedented since the immediate aftermath of World War II.

The causes of this were not altogether clear. The boom had been triggered by a threatened steel strike in the U.S. during 1968, which had led to higher stockpiling by U.S. consumers and, consequently, to higher output and imports in that country. It became clear in the course of 1968, however, that the boom was continuing for independent reasons. A significant factor was that in late 1968 and early 1969 there was, perhaps for the first time since World War II, simultaneous growth in the domestic economies of all major steel-making countries. There was rapid economic growth in the EEC during 1968; industrial production increased 7% and the rise continued in 1969. In the U.K. industrial production grew 5% in 1968 and the rise continued in the following year. The Japanese economy grew rapidly in 1968, and industrial production rose by more than 15% in fiscal 1969. In the U.S. real output grew by approximately 5% in 1968 and by a similar amount in the early part of 1969.

The effect of this worldwide development in steel-market conditions was to efface entirely, for the time being at least, the overcapacity problems that had beset steel industries for at least the previous ten years. There was some discussion as to whether the capacity surplus, which had been approximately 50–60 million tons before the onset of the boom, was, in fact, the hazard that most had thought it to be. Certainly it represented not more than 10% of the total production potential, a margin that might not on general grounds be thought overlarge. The key to the difficulties in earlier times of slower economic growth was, perhaps, that an underutilization of steelmaking capacity had tended to be concentrated in specific regions, principally the advanced steelmaking countries, and this had exerted more than proportional leverage on trade and prices. Certainly, the lesson of the crisis and the changeover to boom seemed to be that the health of the steel industry and of national economies were inseparable.

Output in the U.S. in 1969 was approximately 127 million tons, a growth of nearly 7% over the previous year. There were, however, some signs in the last quarter of a possible downturn. Both imports and exports improved during the year, imports falling to 6.6 million tons in the first half, as compared with 8.2 million tons during the same period of 1968. Exports were higher than they had been since the early 1950s. Profit levels in the first half year remained poor; United States Steel Corp. saw a drop of 40% in relation to the previous year. Price increases occurred at the end of July, led by United States Steel: cold-rolled sheet was raised $8 per ton, hot-rolled sheet by $6 per ton, and galvanized and other coated steel, $9.50 per ton. The combination of the price rises and higher production was expected to lead to better profits in the second half of 1969.

Raw materials presented a problem throughout the year. Owing to strikes, nickel and coal were in short supply. There were also shortages of scrap and iron ore.

The voluntary agreement on the limitation of exports to the U.S., operated by the European Coal and Steel Community (ECSC) and Japan, became largely formal, since those two suppliers fell short of their quotas by 60 and 45%, respectively. However, powerful lobbies in favour of the legal restriction of imports remained in the U.S. Congress.

Japanese output rose by 15% to 77 million tons. Demand in both the home and export markets was heavy, and investment continued at a high level. All major producers revised their export targets upward. There were problems in regard to coal supplies owing to the strike in the U.S. The Japanese Fair Trade Commission approved the proposed Fuji-Yawata merger in late October.

Output increased substantially in the ECSC, but steel shortages remained. These were met in part by deflecting exports into the domestic market and by increasing imports, some from Eastern Europe. Import duties were suspended in the autumn on ingots, slabs, billets, bars, coil, and plate. New investment rose rapidly, amounting in 1969 to about $1.1 billion, as compared with $822 million in 1968 and $730 million in 1967.

In the U.K., after considerable public discussion, a price rise was authorized by the government in mid-June. Demand remained strong, and this, combined with a number of strikes, led to increased imports, mainly of ingots, slabs, and coil. Import duties were suspended on those items and also on cold-rolled sheet and tinplate. Exports were estimated to be slightly under 5 million tons.

An interesting feature of the year was the report that GKN (Guest Keen and Nettlefold Ltd.), one of the British steel industry's major customers, was planning to build a new steelworks in Australia in conjunction with Broken Hill Proprietary Co. An indication of the increasing trend toward internationalization came with the announcement later in the year of studies between the British Steel Corporation and a number of U.S. firms, including Bethlehem, Armco, and Kaiser, for a joint plant in Australia with an output matching that of Broken Hill. In the U.S. the trend toward diversification into other industries continued; Republic Steel Corp., in particular, formed a subsidiary company especially for that purpose.

Production in the Soviet Union and Eastern Europe continued on the whole in line with existing trends. Output in the U.S.S.R. itself rose to 109 million tons, an increase slightly below that of the previous year. There were small increases in Poland and Czechoslovakia of 1.8 and 1.6%, respectively. In Romania the previous year's growth of 6.4% was surpassed by an increase in 1969 of 9.9%, while East Germany showed a strong gain from a rate of 2.9% to one of 16.5%. (W. A. P. M.)

MACHINERY AND MACHINE TOOLS

The first nine months of 1969 found orders for metal-cutting and metal-forming machine tools in the U.S. $360 million ahead of the same period in 1968 for a total of $1,371,150,000. Shipments of these tools were down by $120 million during this same period for a total of $1,167,100,000. The surge by purchasers in April brought orders to the highest level in 27 years, and continued ordering reflected the concern of companies to place orders before Congress canceled the investment tax credit. For several months during the period, spokesmen for the industry believed that the orders were inflated by the prospect of tax credit legislation, which was finally passed at year's end.

The export market was favourable for the U.S. in 1969. The economies of European countries continued to expand, and this market aided U.S. manufacturers. Production of machine tools in Western European countries continued to remain at a high level, but companies there were not able to meet the demand of the rapidly expanding automotive industry, which resulted in an increase of orders from the U.S.

There was some concern among U.S. machine-tool manufacturers in the last quarter of 1969 because orders were lagging. Prospective customers were waiting for a better view of the economy in 1970 before starting to purchase equipment for new tooling-up of factories. Many uncertainties faced industry at the end of the year. Policies to slow down the economy, the high interest rates, Vietnam, tight money, and the pending investment tax credit bill were the major factors that slowed purchases.

Numerical control (NC) equipment continued to be the fastest growing area of the machine-tool industry. Industry reports indicated that in mid-1969 there were about 18,000 NC units in the U.S., 4,500 in Western Europe, and approximately 1,000 in Japan. Milling and drilling operations were the most common NC applications, followed by turning operations. Many other NC systems were used in wire manufacturing, flame cutting, gas and arc welding, electron beam welding, plating, metal grinding, glass cutting, metal bending, drafting, inspection, wire harness making, electrical discharge machining, induction hardening, and complex metal contouring.

Manufacturers were faced with increased hourly labour costs and believed that they must reduce their costs with laboursaving equipment. This pressure greatly influenced the sale of NC equipment, and plant expansion in the direction of completely automated factories was expected to increase in 1970.

Another problem facing manufacturers of production machinery of all types was the reduction of noise levels that damage the hearing of workers. The recently enacted Walsh-Healey Act in the U.S. set regulations for mechanical noise in plants that contract with the federal government. The government would investigate those plants for excessive noise on the production line and take necessary action for correction of violations. In the future, machinery manufacturers were expected to engineer noise out of machines. Workmen's compensation claims for hearing losses were increasing rapidly, and the U.S. national average for each such claim was between $2,500 and $3,000.

Advanced techniques of machining and forming, such as plasma spraying and cutting, magnetic forming, electrochemical machining, and electrical discharge machining were continuing to furnish industry with efficient means of processing materials for certain applications. More recently, lasers have been used for such applications as hole punching, spot welding, drilling, and cutting. Lasers appeared to be well suited for automated operations, since the light beam replaced cutting tools that needed maintenance. Electrospark forming and ultrasonic cutting were two additional advanced machining techniques that were also being put

Table VI. World Production of Pig Iron and Blast Furnace Ferroalloys

In 000 metric tons

Country	1964	1965	1966	1967	1968
World	306,471	324,985	335,771	351,593	376,241
U.S.	78,210	80,612	83,594	78,911	80,042
U.S.S.R.	62,377	66,200	70,264	74,812	78,777
Japan*	23,778	27,502	32,018	40,095	46,397
Germany, West	24,182	26,990	25,413	27,366	30,305
United Kingdom	17,551	17,740	15,962	15,394	16,695
France	15,863	15,770	15,590	15,711	16,449
China†	12,000	14,000	14,000	15,000	15,500
Belgium	8,047	8,366	8,230	8,902	10,370
Italy*	3,498	5,490	6,259	7,294	7,826
Canada‡	5,943	6,422	6,547	6,306	7,605
India	6,593	6,952	7,041	6,889	7,000
Czechoslovakia	5,716	5,869	6,269	6,822	6,920
Poland	5,268	5,375	5,611	5,327	6,840
Australia*§	3,824	3,999	4,450	4,971	5,571
Luxembourg	4,191	4,145	3,963	3,960	4,308
South Africa	2,669	3,322	3,464	3,472	3,773
Brazil	2,487	2,538	2,889	2,963	3,359
Romania	1,924	2,019	2,198	2,456	2,992
Netherlands	1,947	2,364	2,209	2,579	2,821
Spain	1,901	2,328	2,095	2,679	2,779
Sweden	2,173	2,280	2,224	2,358	2,476
Austria	2,204	2,200	2,195	2,140	2,474
Germany, East	2,262	2,338	2,448	2,525	2,332
Korea, North	1,206	1,600	1,800	1,799	1,798
Hungary	1,494	1,583	1,635	1,659	1,655
Mexico	926	946	1,137	1,286	1,599
Yugoslavia	1,026	1,115	1,143	1,177	1,201
Bulgaria	449	696	875	1,028	1,111
Finland	592	934	934	1,017	1,105
Norway	434	524	630	637	680

*Pig iron only.
†Estimated.
‡Includes remelt iron produced in the smelting of titanium ores.
§Years ended May 31.
Source: British Iron and Steel Federation, Statistics Department.

Table VII. World Production of Crude Steel

In 000 metric tons

Country	1964	1965	1966	1967	1968	1969 Year to date	1969 No. of months	1969 Annual rate	Percent change 1969–68
World	433,356	456,461	472,993	495,693	528,531	...	...	564,600	+ 6.9
U.S.*	115,282	119,261	121,655	115,406	119,261	84,805	8	127,208	+ 6.7
U.S.S.R.	85,034	91,000	96,907	102,235	106,495	54,400	6	108,800	+ 2.2
Japan	39,799	41,161	47,784	62,154	66,893	45,113	7	77,340	+15.6
Germany, West	37,339	36,821	35,316	36,744	41,159	29,869	8	44,804	+ 8.9
United Kingdom	26,651	27,440	24,706	24,278	26,277	18,134	8	27,206	+ 3.5
France	19,780	19,604	19,585	19,655	20,394	14,527	8	21,791	+ 6.9
Italy	9,793	12,681	13,639	15,890	16,964	11,726	8	14,589	+ 3.7
China†	9,000	12,000	13,000	14,000	15,000	...	...	...	...
Belgium	8,726	9,162	8,911	9,711	11,571	8,322	8	12,483	+ 7.9
Poland	8,573	9,088	9,850	10,412	11,006	4,669	5	11,208	+ 1.8
Czechoslovakia	8,377	8,598	9,128	10,003	10,554	3,575	4	10,725	+ 1.6
Canada	8,281	9,134	9,090	8,427	10,204	11,537	5	10,889	+ 6.7
India	6,033	6,413	6,608	6,331	6,540	1,133	2	6,798	+ 3.9
Australia‡	4,889	5,274	5,716	6,290	6,502	2,870	5	6,888	+ 5.9
Sweden	4,444	4,724	4,764	4,768	5,068	2,746	6	5,492	+ 8.4
Spain	3,150	3,515	3,847	4,512	4,940	1,851	4	5,553	+12.4
Luxembourg	4,559	4,585	4,390	4,481	4,834	3,611	8	5,417	+12.1
Romania	3,039	3,425	3,670	4,089	4,751	1,740	4	5,220	+ 9.9
Brazil	3,073	3,017	3,713	3,665	4,434	1,184	3	4,736	+ 6.1
Germany, East	4,310	4,366	4,541	4,647	4,373	2,123	5	5,095	+16.5
South Africa§	3,002	3,287	3,291	3,702	4,051	2,260	6	4,520	+11.6
Netherlands	2,646	3,138	3,256	3,407	3,707	3,012	8	4,518	+21.9
Austria	3,194	3,221	3,193	3,023	3,468	2,283	7	3,912	+12.8
Mexico	2,327	2,455	2,788	3,040	3,258	1,683	6	3,366	+ 3.3
Hungary	2,364	2,520	2,648	2,739	2,902	1,262	5	3,029	+ 4.4
Yugoslavia	1,677	1,769	1,859	1,832	1,997	1,324	7	2,268	+13.6
Argentina	1,265	1,368	1,267	1,326	1,552	831	6	1,662	+ 7.1
Bulgaria	471	588	700	1,239	1,461	637	5	1,529	+ 4.7

*Excludes production of independent foundries.
†Estimated.
‡Years ended May 31.
§Up to 1964 steel ingots only.
Source: British Iron and Steel Federation, Statistics Department.

to wide practical use in manufacturing.

Internationally, West Germany continued to be a Western European leader in the manufacture of machine tools, while Japan was improving its position as an important world producer. The Soviet Union and Czechoslovakia continued as the Eastern European leaders. (O. K.)

PAINTS AND VARNISHES

Paint production generally continued to increase in 1969. The figures for 1968 showed that the U.K. had a record year, with an increase of 6% in volume and somewhat more than 8% in value. Exports in particular, benefiting from devaluation of the pound sterling, increased by 16½% in volume and 23% in value in 1968. This increase continued in 1969, with an additional rise of 4% as compared with the same period in 1968. Output in the U.S. also increased, the greatest gain there taking place in the sale of industrial finishes. Another country to show a remarkable increase in exports in 1968 was the Netherlands, with a gain of 15% over 1967.

The Soviet Union and other Eastern European nations continued to import considerable amounts of paint, mainly from Western Europe. It seemed likely that it would be some years before they could satisfy fully their own paint requirements.

Seldom is it possible to report any radical new development in paint, but in 1969 the British Paint Research Association developed a paint that conducts electricity. The paint takes the form of an inorganic silicate binder, pigmented with graphite, but the secret of its conductivity lies in the method of manufacture. These new coatings were expected to find use in providing large areas of low-temperature radiation heating for such purposes as space heating of buildings and the deicing of airport runways, certain areas of ships' superstructures, and even aircraft. The low resistance of such paint allows outputs of 40 w. per sq.ft. at voltages not exceeding 40 which should be well within acceptable safety margins.

Scientists at the Paint Research Station, Teddington, Eng., test an electricity-conducting paint. Future applications may include use as a heating system.

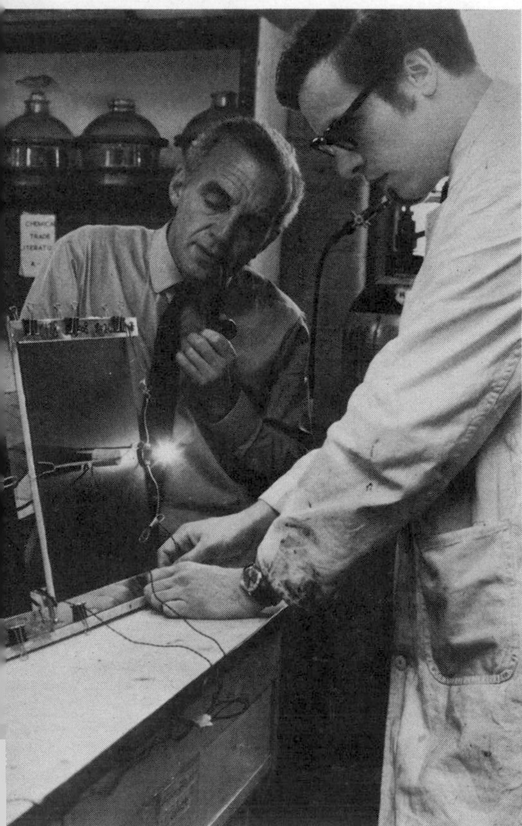

KEYSTONE

Other paint developments were largely centred on anticorrosive uses, and most interest was shown in metallic zinc pigmented silicate primers. Claims were made of improved corrosion resistance, even in the presence of some surface rust, for zinc-rich primers in which the metallic zinc has been replaced by metallic manganese dust. Recent claims suggested that polyamide-cured epoxides might have rust-inhibitive properties in their own right regardless of their pigmentation.

Monoamides were said to be useful as corrosion inhibitors for use in clear films such as those provided by alkyds. Another development in anticorrosive films was reputed to be based on the use of a cation exchanger incorporated into liquid paint; it formed insoluble salts at the metal interface, accepting iron cations and preventing the formation of additional corrosive salts.

While epoxy and coal-tar epoxy paints were increasingly used for the protection of large steel structures such as ships, oil installations, and the like, no low-temperature curing agent had been developed. Thus for painting carried out under very low temperature conditions the tendency was to use the more recently developed chlorinated rubber systems of the high-build type to replace cured epoxies and to use coal-tar vinyl combinations as a replacement for coal-tar epoxies.

Interest continued in powder coatings, and new developments were reported from the U.S. based on polyester and alkyd powders used separately or blended. These new powder coatings were claimed to cost less than the powders previously available and yet to give equally good results.

The expansion in coil coatings continued and recent developments suggested that the future lay in coatings based on fluorocarbon polymers. These substances were likely to produce suitable coatings of the greatest durability and colour stability. Polyester silicones were also favoured.

In the field of application methods electron-beam curing became an established process in the U.S. automobile industry; although research on this process continued in Europe it seemed unlikely that any commercial unit had yet been installed. For polymerizable coatings on flat surfaces, ultraviolet curing was reported to be gaining favour.

New production methods included an improvement to the vibratory-type ball mill, in which the principle was the replacement of balls by a series of concentric cylinders. New production units were largely restricted in their main machinery to high-speed or cavitation mixers, sand mills, and agitated vertical ball mills. This resulted in ample production capacity in a relatively small space.

Especially in Europe a tendency continued to form large groups by mergers, and the future paint industry seemed likely to be restricted to relatively few large companies operating on a worldwide basis. One surprise, however, was the withdrawal from the British scene of the American Celanese Corp. by the disposal of its subsidiary, British Paints, back into British hands. (A. D. C. H.)

PAPER AND PULP

World demand for paper and paperboard increased substantially in 1968, and total production was approximately 127 million short tons. The rise of almost 7 million tons or 5.5% from 1967 coincided almost exactly with the average annual world increase that had been recorded in the preceding decade. Newsprint production for the year was 22 million tons, up 2 million from 1967; printing and writing papers totaled 25 million tons, also up 2 million; and paperboard and other papers, 80 million tons, up 3 million.

The gain in world output in 1968 was larger than had generally been expected, and this strength in demand continued through 1969. It meant that much of the new capacity for manufacturing pulp and paper that was completed in Canada, the U.S., and other leading producing nations during a period of very rapid expansion, 1965–68, was required sooner than had been expected. This, in turn, dispelled much of the gloom of overcapacity that, as recently as the spring of 1968, had gripped some portions of the industry, especially the large exporters of newsprint and wood pulp. Indeed, by late 1969, world supply and demand in some grades appeared to be approximately in balance.

The increase in world production of paper and paperboard during 1968 was caused by rapid economic growth in a number of the largest consuming nations, especially the U.S., Japan, and West Germany. It was achieved largely by means of an increase in the manufacture of wood pulp, the chief raw material. World wood pulp output for the year totaled about 104 million tons. The increase from 1967 amounted to more than 5 million tons, more than three-quarters of which was shared by the six largest producing nations, the U.S., Canada, Sweden, Japan, the Soviet Union, and Finland. Those six already accounted for nearly 80% of the total world production of paper and paperboard, the other 20% being divided among approximately 65 other countries.

In terms of regions, North America in 1968 produced about 48% of the total world supply of paper and paperboard; Europe produced 34%, Asia 14%, Latin America 3%, and Africa 1%. Consumption of paper and paperboard followed roughly this same pattern.

International trade in pulp and paper continued to increase during 1968, total exports rising to approximately 34 million tons, as compared with 31 million tons in 1967. About 80% of this total was in newsprint and wood pulp, the products that, traditionally, moved duty-free into many of the major markets of the world. The other 20% comprised paperboard, printing and writing papers, tissues, kraft wrapping papers, and other papers; these products generally faced tariff barriers in most countries. Tariffs were, however, gradually being lowered in a number of the leading industrial nations.

As in previous years, Canada in 1968 was by far the leading pulp and paper exporting nation, accounting for 13 million tons, or nearly 40% of total world trade in those products. Canadian exports were chiefly to the U.S., but large and rapidly growing quantities moved to Europe and Japan, with smaller tonnages to Latin America, Australia, and other areas of the world. Other important trade flows in pulp and paper were from Scandinavia throughout Western Europe; from the U.S. to Western Europe and Japan; and from the U.S.S.R. to Eastern Europe.

Forecasts of future demand for pulp and paper products were made periodically by bodies such as the Food and Agriculture Organization of the United Nations. Such forecasts indicated that world requirements, which had been doubling about every 15 years, would continue to increase rapidly. Thus, it was estimated that world demand for paper and paperboard by 1975 would increase to approximately 180 million tons, and by 1980 to 225 million tons, as compared with the 124 million tons manufactured in 1968.

One element of future world demand that was impossible to estimate with any precision was the relatively new field of throwaway products made from paper and other materials. Product development work in this sphere was centred generally on nonwoven fabrics, that is, clothlike materials that emerge from a forming machine rather than a loom. Many were made by bonding layers of cellulose tissue to both sides of a nylon mesh or scrim. The fabrics could be produced in white or colours and could be sewn or glued, treated chemically for fire resistance, and coated with polyethylene for water resistance. Though there was some possibility of washing them a few times, they generally were meant to be discarded when soiled.

Paper fabrics were finding a variety of uses, for example, in sheets and pillowcases, overalls, aprons, graduation gowns, and various novelty products. One of the most promising markets was in hospitals, where nonwoven disposables were being used increasingly for bed linen, surgical drapes and gowns, emergency blankets, laboratory coats, operating-room hats and masks, and other purposes. The amount of research being focused on the development of new products in fields such as the above was increasing rapidly.

Expansion of pulp and paper manufacturing facilities, to serve both the traditional and the new uses for cellulose, was occurring in various parts of the world. However, the pace of such growth was considerably slower than in the 1965–68 period. In the U.S. the 1969–70 growth of productive capacity was chiefly in book and writing papers and tissue papers, whereas growth in paperboard had highlighted the earlier period. In Canada, the new productive capacity was chiefly for newsprint and kraft pulp. In Scandinavia, a considerable addition to newsprint capacity was being made.

The industry in the Soviet Union continued to grow, and that nation became the world's fifth largest producer of wood pulp and fourth largest manufacturer of paper and paperboard. All but a very small proportion of its output was used domestically, exports still being of only minor importance.

(Go. M.)

PETROLEUM PRODUCTS

The petroleum industry, on a worldwide basis, had another good but not outstanding year, despite the continued tension in the Middle East and tougher terms by concession countries for exploration and production privileges. The Middle East remained unstable, threatening to erupt into a conflagration many times greater than the lightning Six-Day War of 1967. And with this threat the prospect of disrupted crude oil supplies hung over the heads of both producers and dependent countries. International oil companies also lost another slice of their profit margin as many foreign countries demanded—and got—higher bounties for allowing companies the privilege of searching for hydrocarbons on their territory.

The U.S. petroleum industry enjoyed another successful and profitable year despite spiraling inflation and political attacks. Operations moved to record levels during the

Table VIII. World Petroleum Statistics for 1968

Area	Production of petroleum liquids (000 bbl. daily)	Refining capacity (000 bbl. daily)	Estimated proved reserves: Oil (000 bbl. daily)	Natural gas (000,000,000 cu. ft.)
Asia-Pacific	918.4	4,919.8	13,720,200	52,724
Europe	382.6	12,884.3	1,937,000	141,176
Middle East	11,384.9	2,296.5	270,760,000	223,775
Africa	3,864.9	756.1	44,568,800	168,345
Western Hemisphere	15,218.0	17,948.2	71,182,775	403,700
Soviet Union and other Communist areas	6,684.1	n.a.*	55,877,000	343,000
World total	38,452.9	38,804.9	458,045,775	1,332,720

*Not available
Source: *The Oil and Gas Journal.*

first half of 1969, though easing somewhat during the second half of the year. Total demand for oil during the first six months averaged 14,094,000 bbl. per day, while total demand for the entire year was forecast at about 13,867,000 bbl. per day, a 4.2% increase over 1968.

On the supply side, U.S. domestic production suffered somewhat because of increased imports of crude oil and products. Yet production for the year was expected to average 9,244,000 bbl. per day, up 1.5% over 1968. Drilling activity also had a good year, with 32,000 wells drilled for a 4.5% jump over the previous year.

The North Slope of Alaska (between the Brooks Range and the Arctic Ocean), with reserves estimated at between 50,000,000,000–100,000,000,000 bbl., continued to be the nation's beehive of interest and speculation. Many hopes and suspicions were revealed early in September when companies bid a record $900,220,590 for leases on 450,858 ac. on the slope. Average price per acre was $1,998.

With a booming processing industry and production at an all-time high, Latin America was also the scene of an exploration surge in 1969. Wildcatting campaigns, on and offshore, were under way in Mexico, most of Central America, and in several South American countries.

Venezuela, Latin America's major oil country, continued to be the world's third largest oil producer and the world's largest exporter. In 1968, 899,955,660 bbl. of Venezuelan crude were exported to 36 countries. The country's production slumped to 3,552,000 bbl. per day during the first half of 1969 but was expected to gain in the last half.

Across the Atlantic, Western Europe, one of the world's largest consuming areas, remained woefully low on the production side of the scale. Natural gas, however, was abundant, particularly in the North Sea off Britain and in the Netherlands.

Libya paced Africa's petroleum industry during 1969. The overthrow of King Idris I in early September caused many anxious moments for companies producing there, but the revolutionary junta later assured all firms that their concessions and agreements would be honoured. In May 1968 Libya's crude-oil production finally climbed over the 3-million bbl.-per-day mark. In passing that figure, the country vaulted into the third-place slot among Western producers for May, behind the U.S. and Venezuela. Iran, however, maintained the third-place position in the yearly averages.

The Middle East's oil industry was bristling with activity and, as usual, much of it was politically oriented. Saudi Arabia, the area's leading producer, had another banner year. Its reserves jumped a staggering 8.4 billion bbl., 4½ times the oil in the U.S. Production also continued to rise, averaging 2.8 million bbl. per day during the first half of 1969. Drilling and seismic work also continued at a good clip.

In the Communist world, the Soviet Union's oil and gas industries displayed both gains and losses in 1968 and in the first half of 1969. Hydrocarbon output gains lagged behind growth rates for Soviet industry as a whole. Pipelining and refining showed little progress; drilling footage was down considerably; and Soviet officials began to fret publicly about a declining reserves/production ratio for oil. The brightest spot by far for the Soviets was the continued sharp rise in proved gas reserves, now totaling more than 350 trillion cu.ft. That amount gave the U.S.S.R. a 55-year supply at present production rates. Soviet crude oil output for 1968 was set at 6,530,000 bbl. per day. Exports during 1968 were 1,174,000 bbl. per day.

(Mi. G. M.)

PLASTICS

There was in 1969 no slackening of the headlong expansion of plastics production and usage throughout the world that had been characteristic of the post–World War II period. Total output was estimated to have exceeded 25 million metric tons as against 22 million metric tons in 1968. This was consistent with the 12–15% average annual growth that was expected to be

Eight-story-high bubble of seamless polyethylene film at Union Carbide's Lindsay, Ont., plant. Demand for the film jumped 15% in 1969.

maintained at least throughout the 1970s.

Expansion was greatest in countries where activity as a whole was most intense, notably in West Germany, where production rose by 25% in 1969. However, even in the U.K., where the overall economy had not expanded much, plastics comfortably outstripped other industries, output having grown by about 12%.

The U.S., with production at approximately 8.3 million metric tons in 1968, remained by far the largest single manufacturing nation, but Western Europe taken as an area, led by West Germany with 4.1 million metric tons in 1969, was steadily increasing its lead and was up from 8.4 million metric tons in 1968 to an estimated 9.8 million metric tons. In 1968, West Germany and Japan, each with 3,250,000 metric tons, tied as world's second largest producers, but it was probable that in 1969 the Japanese growth, although continuing to be rapid, did not quite match up to that of West Germany. Behind these three came, in the West, Italy (1.6 million metric tons in 1969), the U.K. (1,350,000 metric tons), and France (1 million metric tons). In the East, the plastics industry of the U.S.S.R. began to expand more rapidly, and in 1969 it probably approached the Italian figure with about 1.5 million tons.

On the whole, 1969 confirmed a trend toward the consolidation of usage of existing plastics materials rather than the introduction of completely new ones. Although the level of research activity by large international chemical concerns continued unabated, much of this was devoted to the modification of known plastics and to improving ways of processing and using them. Additions to the roll of commercially valuable polymers seemed likely to be at a slower rate in the future, although specialized materials would continue to emerge from time to time. For instance, at Interplas in London, which was the major European plastics exhibition for 1969, the only completely new polymer shown was polyaryl ether from Uniroyal, Inc., in the U.S. It featured high heat resistance and impact strength, combined with ease of processing. In Japan, Showa Denko announced ACS resin, a terpolymer in which acrylonitrile and styrene are graft-polymerized onto chlorinated polythene to produce a thermoplastic offering resistance to weather, heat, and impact. A general move toward higher heat resistance in new materials was also seen in polyaryl sulfone, available from the Minnesota Mining & Manufacturing Co. of the U.S. However, although plastics with unique property combinations such as the above and their predecessors of the preceding decade were of immense value in solving complex design engineering problems effectively and economically, they tended to be high-priced specialty materials with limited tonnage potential.

The overwhelming proportion of growth in 1969 remained with the three established groups of "commodity" thermoplastics—the polyolefins, polyvinyl chloride, and the styrene plastics. Large new projects to produce the basic petrochemical components of these materials, as well as to make the actual plastics, were under way in many parts of the world. The capital sums involved were vast, and manufacturers found that their returns on certain materials, notably low-density polythene, had, with continually falling prices, become decidedly unattractive. Partly because of the hesitation that this situation caused and partly because of the difficulties of starting up the large plants that involved new engineering techniques, several materials were in distinctly short supply in 1969, especially polypropylene and, most important, ethylene monomer, on which the manufacture of all the commodity plastics depended. The result of this was a general increase in world plastics prices in 1969, to the relief of the producers.

Much of the effort of the plastics processing machinery manufacturers in 1969 continued to be aimed at enabling even larger components to be produced by such methods as injection molding and rotational casting. Improved methods of control programming and solid-state control were features of the injection-molding scene, and techniques for injection molding thermosetting plastics materials also made considerable headway. In the extrusion field, twin-screw types of machines became more prominent, and there was a tendency toward the use of longer screws with a higher ratio of length to diameter. With heightened interest in very large thermoformings for applications in such areas as the automotive and boat industries, a demand for ever-wider extruded sheet also made itself felt.

New applications were as prolific as ever, but particular progress was recorded during 1969 in the use of plastics in the automobile industry. In the U.S., it was estimated that 1970 models contained an average of 100 lb. of plastics per car, an increase of 15 lb. over those of 1969. Even in a year when car sales dropped in the U.S., this represented an increased usage of plastics approaching 50,000 tons. In Britain, the comparable figure was already about 70 lb. per car. Mechanical parts were currently the main areas of growth, but the expected movement toward mass-produced plastics panels and thence complete automobile bodies was gathering momentum. In 1969 Citroën increased output of its popular Mehari runabout to 100 cars per day at a new factory in Rennes, France; this was the first car in the world with a thermoplastic body to achieve mass production.

The furniture industry was also worthy of special mention as a comparatively new area for plastics applications in the form of molded units, while packaging showed renewed vigour as a major outlet for flexible wrappings and rigid or semirigid containers. The huge growth in disposable plastics packs resulted in 1969 in much public debate on the litter problem caused by their nondestructibility. In the form of collected refuse, these problems were probably not too difficult to surmount, but when discarded casually they became more complex; the incorporation of a biodegradable ingredient was one suggestion being pursued by industrial research. (R. C. Pe.)

PRINTING

After appearing on the scene only a few years earlier, "instant printing" began to make a real impact in 1969. In the U.S. one company started selling completely equipped franchises as a package deal so that compact printing operations could be set up by an inexperienced operator. These miniature printing works were equipped with typewriter composition facilities, a direct platemaking camera, a small offset machine, and simple stapling and gluing equipment. They were able to offer customers a finished product within a few hours after receiving an order. Usually only text matter and simple illustrations were handled, and colour reproductions did not fit into the standard fixed price per unit pattern. A few printers in the U.S. and Britain also opened such instant print shops, designed for urgent printing of company and legal work.

The Soviet Union held its first truly international printing machinery show at Moscow in July. It attracted a large number of visitors, especially from the Eastern European countries, and was reported as highly successful by most Western exhibitors. The U.S. was not represented in a national pavilion, but Western European sales agents and subsidiaries reported excellent sales, especially of business-form presses and high-speed metal and phototypesetting machines. The Soviet Union, too, surprised observers by the introduction of new typesetting, colour scanning, and printing presses of solid construction.

The major international printing exhibition of the year was GEC 69 at Milan, Italy, with the accent on web-fed offset and photogravure processes, as well as on new letterpress plates. Newspapers in particular carefully watched the progress of the West German BASF Nyloprint relief plate, a photopolymer plate on metal backing that offered fine detail printing and long life. In the U.S. the Grace Letterflex plate, extensively tested by the *South Bend* (Ind.) *Tribune,* was put on the market; it was announced that high-speed processing would make this plate competitive in production time with conventional platemaking methods, thus giving newspaper printers renewed impetus to retain their letterpress equipment rather than shifting to web-fed offset. The latter, however, continued to gain ground, and several large-circulation newspapers, especially in West Germany, placed orders for extra-wide presses.

The process that showed the most growth during the year was rotogravure. At their annual conference at Baden-Baden, W.Ger., the gravure printers of West Germany were told that the process was outstripping any other in growth. An indication of this success was the announcement that West German gravure giants Burda Druck and Verlag were to embark on a joint multimillion-dollar project with Meredith Corp. of Des Moines, Ia., to print part of the *Better Homes and Gardens* magazine by rotogravure. Most European mass-circulation quality magazines were printed by this process, but few U.S. magazines had been.

Computer-assisted phototypesetting was gaining ground on high-speed machines. The Spanish telephone authorities, as well as postal authorities in other countries, ordered Digiset/RCA cathode-ray tube phototypesetting machines to set their directories. Her Majesty's Stationery Office started using the British-made Linotron 505 for directory setting via computer compilation.

In sheet-fed offset lithography, Japanese and European printers (particularly those in Italy and Britain) ordered the extra-large U.S.-made Miehle multicolour machines, intended for high-quality, very long-run book and catalog printing. A Swiss company, Wifag, introduced a newspaper counting and stacking machine capable of handling 80,000 newspapers an hour. The number of copies required in a bundle could be preprogrammed on cards or tape. Advanced newspaper computer-controlled publishing rooms were announced for the *Chicago Tribune* and *Arbetet* in Malmö, Swed.

Computerized production control reached some of the largest printers in Europe before being introduced on an equal scale in the U.S. A small British printing company, Colour Reproductions Ltd., developed a computerized estimating and costing system for sale to other printers who could link up through a computer service bureau. Automated book warehouses were set up by publishers in the U.S., Italy, Britain, and West

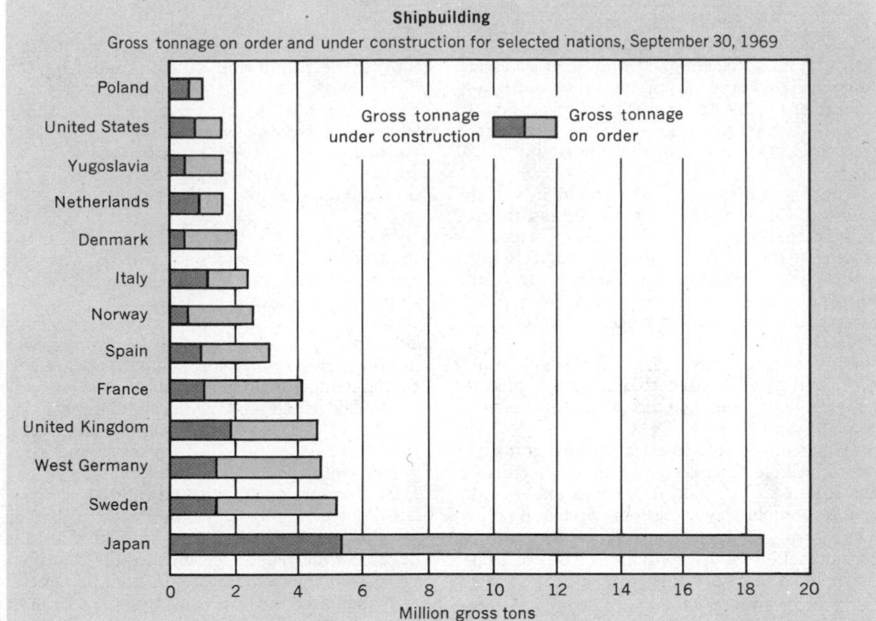

Germany to facilitate storage and shipping.

In October the International Congress of Master Printers was held in Madrid. The main concern of speakers and delegates focused on management development and training for the future of the graphic arts industry with its now-pronounced shift from a craft to a technological industry.

(W. P. JA.)

SHIPBUILDING

It was another boom year for the shipbuilding industry, with bulging order books and a record output of around 17 million gross registered tons (grt). Japan continued to dominate the industry, with about 9 million grt launched from its huge and highly efficient yards. West Germany, where a remarkably resurgent shipbuilding industry had almost cornered the market in the new deep-sea container ships, came second with over 1.5 million grt. Sweden was third with about 1.3 million grt, and Britain was fourth with about 1.2 million grt. All were substantially above the previous year.

There were, however, signs that could be interpreted as heralding a slowdown after several years of rapid growth. The increase in output was marginal compared with the previous five years, when it rose by nearly 70%. Moreover, shipowners' orders, after a frantic burst during the first half of the year, slowed down markedly in the second half in the face of sharply increased prices from the yards and the growing spectre—at least in some people's eyes—of overtonnaging and slump conditions during the early 1970s.

Technically the industry continued to forge ahead, with advances in welding techniques and computer designs that made important contributions to productivity. The buckling in very large tankers that had caused such problems the previous year seemed to have been solved. With 200,000–250,000-tonners pouring from the yards in increasing numbers, the upward march in bulk carriers for both wet and dry cargoes was resumed.

The six 326,000-tonners built for Gulf's Middle East-to-Bantry Bay, Ire., service were completed, and work started on a second series at El Ferrol in Spain. Yards that had just sunk millions into facilities for building ships of the 250,000-ton class were at first reluctant to take another big jump, but resistance weakened as the year wore on. Tokyo Tanker ordered a 370,000-tonner in Japan and was reported to be negotiating for a 450,000-tonner. At least one Japanese yard announced its intention to build a dock for million-ton ships and a British yard expressed a willingness to do the same. Others, more cautious in the face of the huge capital investment required for permanent building docks of this size, were exploring ways of meeting prospective demand by building pieces of larger ships to be welded together afloat. The rationalization measures begun some years before in Japan, Sweden, and Britain were carried a stage further with mergers between leading yards in the Netherlands and Japan.

In Britain the trials of the last great express liner, Cunard's "Queen Elizabeth 2," attracted much attention. Though brilliantly designed and decorated, the 65,000-ton ship encountered turbine troubles and was four months late in delivery. The heavy cost in both money and management resources nearly brought Upper Clyde Shipbuilders, Ltd., to its knees, and substantial infusions of government funds were needed to stave off liquidation.

Two underlying trends became increasingly apparent in the course of the year: standardization and diversification. In the case of basic ship types sufficiently in demand to justify series production—the 200,000-ton tanker, the 150,000-ton bulk carrier, the 28,000-ton container ship, and the various replacements for the war-built Liberty ship—the trend toward standardization continued. Individual owners were buying up to a dozen at a time, and others joined in to buy "off the shelf." At the same time, ships of growing complexity and technical sophistication—chemical, gas, and ammonia carriers, barge ships, combined container and roll-on vessels, even underwater craft for the expanding fields of marine geology and biology—were increasingly occupying the attention of specialist builders.

(M. BY.)

TEXTILES AND FIBRES

Textile Industry. World production of animal, vegetable, and man-made fibres generally increased in 1969, and employment was reasonably full with a minimum of labour unrest. Research and technical developments continued at high levels in promoting new synthetic fibres, shorter processes, fewer working hours, and many new fabrics and finishes. The University of Manchester Institute of Science and Technology signed a research contract with the International Institute for Cotton for a study of "the mechanism of fracture of cotton fibres." Efforts to develop more acceptable fire-retardant finishes were intensified by the prospect of stricter legislative requirements for fire-resistance. Considerable attention was given to improved processes employing phosphorous compounds in the U.K., U.S., and Japan.

British achievements included the discovery (in the research laboratories of J. and P. Coats) of a method for increasing the strength of cellulose materials. Stretching them 10 to 30% over their original length and treating them with liquid ammonia produced an increase in their tensile strength of up to 40% and considerably enhanced their lustre. Another new British process for urethane transfer coatings had almost limitless applications in garment manufacture, protective and industrial clothing, and in footwear manufacture. Several new developments appeared in manufacturing equipment to achieve better control over sizing, mercerizing, finishing, dyeing, printing, and foam backing. Remote control in dyeing techniques attained high efficiencies. Designed by the British Wool Industries Research Association, a high-efficiency wool scouring set was capable of running a full week with no stoppages for scouring-fluid changes.

A Scottish company spent more than £250,000 on a unit for weaving polypropylene tapes and capable of producing 10 million sq.yd. of fabric on a four-shift basis. To meet the steadily increasing demand for fibre glass in all industries, the most modern glass marble making tank in Europe was lit at Pilkington Bros. in Glasgow. The U.K. Ministry of Technology supported two new machines having tremendous possibilities. Contracts were given out for the purchase of open-end spinning machines and a new conception in weaving. Open-end spinning offered the advantages of greatly increased output per spinning element, elimination of clearer winding, and the ability to spin coarser materials. The "Sensamatic" weaving machine provided multiple-width cloth production at high speeds with minimum attention required by the operator and simple one-gauge setting. In knitting, a new electronic device immediately stopped circular machines in the event they were broken or damaged.

Exhibits at an international exhibition in Greenville, S.C., revealed further progress in machinery design to ensure more efficient production of better quality textiles. No revolutionary developments were seen. Higher speeds, more mechanization of processes, and many refinements in control of machines and operations were the main factors interesting many of the 35,000 visitors from more than 40 countries. Significant advances in electrostatic yarn-spinning were also announced by a prominent U.S. firm. Some yarns could be produced at twice the speed that they could by ring spinners. New ring-spinner drafting elements by another firm handled all staples within 1½ to 3 in. The U.S. National Bureau of Standards conducted studies to determine the effects of rates of strain in yarns under very-high-speed impact.

A new Swiss high-speed loom employed several small shuttles (less than the length of a match) moving continuously as a column through the warp shed. Another Swiss firm erected the largest open-width dyeing range ever to be built in Brazil.

Work by Soviet scientists threw new light on the methods suitable for permanent creasing and pleating of wool and wool-mixture fabrics. Soviet research on nylon-6 also showed that with a sufficiently high concentration of semicarbazide, a fairly high reaction temperature, and extended reaction time, the fibre apparently becomes cross-linked. A new Soviet ring and traveler for ring spinners was equally suitable for spinning wool, cotton, man-made, or blended yarns. (A. Dr.)

Natural Fibres. *Cotton.* At the end of the 1968–69 cotton season in July world production and consumption were roughly in balance for the first time in many years. This achievement was largely the result of acreage diversification requirements in the U.S. being further relaxed in an effort to restore equilibrium after two successive seasons of heavily curtailed crops. The burdensome surplus that had accumulated was accordingly cleared, leaving stocks at a lower level than at any time in the preceding decade.

World use of cotton continued at near-record levels but consumption failed to make any real headway. This emphasized the strong challenge being made to raw cotton by the man-made fibres. In 1968 it was estimated that world man-made fibre consumption on a cotton equivalent basis amounted to nearly 47% of the total fibre market, as compared with 42% in the previous year and only 27% in 1958.

Quality distribution of supply was better balanced than in other recent seasons, but world trade in cotton was lower, and as prices declined export earnings tended to fall. World output in 1968–69 was 52.7 million bales, as compared with the abnormally low crop of 47.7 million bales in the previous season. Growers in the U.S. produced 10.9 million bales; in the U.S.S.R., China, and Eastern Europe 16.3 million bales; and elsewhere, 25.5 million bales, mainly in Brazil, India, Pakistan, Mexico, and the United Arab Republic. Plantings generally expanded by nearly 4 million ac. under the stimulus of higher prices in the previous season. Growing conditions improved in many countries, raising the global average yield to a near-record level.

Prices later showed a tendency to decline in the face of limited demand and the sharp recovery in production of medium- and long-staple varieties of cotton. In May a new contract for cotton futures was introduced, with London as the site of trading instead of Liverpool. This international quotation, based on U.S. cents per pound, received reasonable support in early dealings, the December 1969 position being quoted at around 28.5 cents and October 1970 at 28 cents. In subsequent months the turnover dwindled, and prices drifted to lower rates of 27.5 cents for December and 27.3 cents for October.

World cotton stocks at the outset of the current season in August were equivalent to barely five months of consumption. Output in the U.S. was originally expected to reach nearly 12 million bales, but hurricane damage in the growing areas cut the forecast to 11 million. Yield prospects were not as favourable as in recent seasons. Varying projections were made about crop prospects in other countries. Overall anticipations indicated a rise of perhaps 750,000 bales; harvests were expected to exceed consumption. (A. Tl.)

Silk. The normally volatile raw-silk market remained remarkably static during the year. Japan continued to supplement its own production with imports, and its domestic price, isolated from supply and demand considerations abroad, moved between 5,900 and 7,200 yen per kilo—a relatively modest range when set against past fluctuations.

There was little or no abatement in world demand. Consumption of raw silk had fallen only in the U.S., and that tendency was arrested in the early months of 1969. Being denied the comparatively cheap source of supply from China, Americans were forced to pay the uneconomic prices prevailing in Japan.

Chinese prices rose during the year, however, and it was feared that they too might reach a level that would adversely affect consumption.

It was impossible to guess production figures in China, but certainly there had been an advance. The major increase in world production, however, was in South Korea, where output had doubled within three years. In 1969 South Korea moved into first place as a source of supply for the U.S. Since the American market was protected from Chinese competition, good prices were obtainable.

Meanwhile, research continued. Silk cocoons have traditionally been a catch crop confined to the season of mulberry leafage. To breed silkworms throughout the year was the target of researchers everywhere, and the Japanese were especially active in this area. Such a breakthrough would be needed to meet the 50% increase projected for world silk consumption in the next ten years. (P. W. Ga.)

Wool. Wool consumption rose in 1968 and the trend continued during 1969. Recovery from the recession of 1967 was complete, in the sense that consumption rates were now comparable to those recorded before the recession developed.

World wool production in the 1967–68 season amounted to some 5,935,000,000 lb. (greasy basis), according to the Commonwealth Secretariat. There was a further rise in 1968–69 to a total of 6,098,000,000 lb., and 6,177,000,000 lb. was expected for 1969–70. In addition to absorbing current production at slightly improved prices, the world's wool textile industries also absorbed part of the stock bought by the New Zealand Wool Commission under its floor price scheme and subsequently reoffered at sales during the 1968–69 and 1969–70 seasons.

Prices were relatively stable during the year. The main trend was very gradually downward; in the closing months prices were close to those reached toward the end of 1967, but there was no real weakness in the market. Price stability in wool at a relatively low level, partly due to competition from man-made fibres, was also partly attributable to high world interest rates, which militated against stockholding. The monetary crises of 1968 had led to higher prices and buying activity brought on by fears of devaluation, but the recurring crises in 1969 had less effect.

No major wool marketing changes were effected or even widely discussed in Australia and New Zealand, although there were moves to make relatively minor adjustments and improvements. The most important alteration was that by the New Zealand Wool Commission. Its floor price for growers, an average 22¼ cents per pound, was left unchanged. The 1968–69 buying-in floor price of 16¼ cents per pound was no longer applied, however. The commission stated that it would "not have a fixed buy-in level but will operate on a level that may vary up to but not exceeding the grower level of 22¼ cents."

The International Wool Secretariat's worldwide promotion scheme, based on the "Woolmark," entered its sixth year. Its aim was to establish wool as a distinctive quality fibre, and create a demand for wool that could not be met by substitute fibres. The support given to the scheme by growers indicated recognition of its success. (H. M. F. M.)

Man-Made Fibres. In 1969, the man-made-fibre industry continued to grow in most countries, and although the fully synthetic fibres showed a faster rate of expansion than the cellulosic types, there was considerable evidence of growth in the high wet modulus types of viscose, which appeared to be replacing cotton in a number of end products. Added to the widening demand for blends of polyester fibres with cotton, a trend spreading rapidly in Europe and elsewhere following major developments in the U.S., there was a substantial interest in similar blends of polyester fibre with high wet modulus rayon. The term high wet modulus became widely used to embrace the modified viscose fibres that tended to complement if not displace the polynosic types, though both types could be regarded as high wet modulus.

There was a notable expansion in demand for acrylic fibres in several countries and, in the U.K. particularly, the development of spun acrylic yarns on a modified cotton system to compete directly with worsted spun yarns for double jersey knitting was a major factor.

In several countries there appeared to be some overproduction of false-twist nylon yarns for stretch materials, and in the U.K. the overtaking of demand by supply followed very rapid growth in the previous two years. This situation appeared to be a temporary phase as there was believed to be scope for a much wider use of nylon and indeed polyester yarns in this form. In the polyester-stabilized false twist section, the promotion of jersey fabrics for men's suitings gained considerable momentum during the year.

Gradually more was being heard of second-generation synthetic fibres. Nylon with an outer skin of low melting point which did not require any spinning, weaving, or similar techniques began to be used for floor coverings. So far this development seemed to be confined to relatively rigid materials. Several bicomponent acrylic fibres were gradually finding a place in the fashioned knitting industry.

Development of carbon fibres, first produced in the U.K. and subsequently used for a revolutionary plastic material for aircraft and precision engineering, began to evolve on an international scale. The materials, described as a quarter the weight and four times the strength of steel, seemed likely to become more generally available, with large-scale production gradually reducing their very high basic cost. (P. M. Re.)

See also Advertising; Alcoholic Beverages; Cooperatives; Economy, World; Electronics; Employment, Wages, and Hours; Fisheries; Food; Fuel and Power; Housing; Industrial Design; Labour Unions; Merchandising; Metallurgy; Mining; Nuclear Energy; Prices; Rubber; Television and Radio; Timber; Tobacco; Tourism; Toys and Games; Trade, International.

Encyclopædia Britannica Films. *The Living City* (1953); *The Basic Elements of Production* (1954); *Glass—From the Old to the New Through Research* (1954); *You and the Aerospace Future* (1966); *The Industrial Revolution* (1968); *Midwest—Heartland of the Nation* (1968); *The Rise of Labor* (1968); *The Industrial City* (1969); *The Industrial Worker* (1969).

Information Science and Technology

Information science and technology is concerned with the structure and properties of scientific information, the techniques for information handling, the characteristics of information processing devices, and the design and operation of information handling systems. For some years this area has been of concern to an increasing segment of the population, in part because of the outpouring of potentially useful information—the production of printed materials, for example, is thought to increase at a rate of about 10% per year—in part because of the ever mounting costs of information generation and information handling, and in part because of the increasing technical difficulties in distributing selectively a large volume of information to a large number of users.

Two projects that were potentially far-reaching from a practical point of view related to the U.S. government's interest in furnishing common, centrally prepared information products to individual libraries and information centres. Under the National Program for Acquisitions and Cataloging, the Library of Congress was charged with the acquisition and cataloging throughout the world of all library materials of current interest. If this program were to become fully operational, individual information centres could be relieved of a great deal of effort currently devoted to the acquisition and classification of library materials. A companion project also conducted at the Library of Congress was Project MARC (Machine-Readable Cataloging); this consisted of recording catalog data on magnetic tapes in a standard format and selling them to participating libraries. These tapes could then be used by the receiving institutions to prepare acquisition records, catalog data, and related listings. These efforts were expected to prove of major consequence when the coverage became large enough to satisfy a large proportion of the requirements of individual information centres.

More visible, but conceivably of less practical importance, were the many experiments under way in on-line text processing. These were usually based on a mechanized store of texts, books, abstracts, and documents. To manipulate the stored information, they generally comprised a keyboard input system and typewriter or graphic display output consoles. Relatively sophisticated text editing systems were thus in existence that could be used to compose text and prepare it for printing or typesetting. The operations normally provided included browsing in a text by going forward or backward a line or a page at a time; implementing structural changes among various text portions by redefining the arrangement between paragraphs or sections; and editing text by the insertion, deletion, or substitution of words or phrases.

Several dozen on-line retrieval projects were also of interest. These were often based on stored, manually indexed information items, using a preconstructed vocabulary of allowable information identifiers. Less often, the information content analysis was also mechanized, and information identifiers were automatically assigned to stored items. The retrieval process usually included query negotiation procedures whereby a user suggested certain search terms that were then supplemented by information supplied by the system in the form of stored dictionaries or lists of related terms. When a satisfactory search formulation was on hand, selected documents could be retrieved and displayed for the user. These documents could then be accepted or, alternatively, they could be used for further search negotiation and for adjustment of the query formulation until satisfactory output products could be obtained.

As the research and development of new information handling devices continued, more attention was being paid to the social problems connected with large information stores. Thus, a number of studies were made of problems concerning the copyright and patent protection of the stored and easily reproducible information. The greatest concern, however, was voiced in connection with the protection of privacy of stored information.

While large information networks provided useful information sharing and often permitted rapid fulfillment of individual user requirements, as in automatic ticket reservation systems or automatic credit certification, adequate safeguards for the protection of sensitive information were not generally provided. Before mechanized information networks could come into more widespread use, it would be necessary to create protective devices that would prevent unauthorized access to the information. Some methods developed for this purpose included special techniques based on user passwords before access is obtained, reversible encoding to conceal stored information, monitoring techniques to keep track of each file access, and processing restrictions limiting access of certain consoles to only certain files. Additional legal safeguards were expected to be created to ensure fair use of stored information files. (GD. SN.)

See also Electronics.

Insurance

Private insurance maintained its growth during 1969 in most nations of the non-Communist world. Total sales approximated $100 billion for the year, although there was great variation between different countries and regions. For example, the U.S. had more than 60% of the total premium volume, Canada 4%, Australia and New Zealand 2%, Western Europe 25%, and all Asia, Africa, and South America less than 10%. A similar disparity was apparent in the ratios of life insurance in force to national income. Canada, where life insurance in force amounted to almost twice as much as national income, had the highest ratio.

Life and Health Insurance. U.S. life insurance companies reached another milestone early in the year when total life insurance in force passed one and a quarter trillion dollars ($1,250 billion). By year's end the amount was more than $1,350 billion, reflecting an annual growth rate of approximately 9%. Average life insurance protection per family was $19,000, with group life insurance accounting for 43% of the aggregate. Income of U.S. life insurers rose to $45 billion, of which an estimated $34 billion was from policyholder premiums and the remainder from investment and other income. Approximately 30% of premium income was from health insurance, 60% from life insurance, and 9% from annuities. Benefits paid by U.S. life insurance companies exceeded $15 billion, of which death payments accounted for about 43%.

Company assets amounted to over $192 billion at midyear. More than 42% was invested in bonds, 37%

Bowler-hatted insurance men form elegant picket line to protest refusal of the London Royal Exchange to recognize their union.

KEYSTONE

Inland Waterways: *see* Transportation

in mortgages, 6% in stocks, 6% in policy loans, 3% in real estate, and 5% in miscellaneous assets. The largest relative change occurred in the stock holdings, which rose approximately 14%. It was expected that the net rate of return before U.S. income taxes in 1969 would be above 5% for the first time since 1930. One of the major changes in life insurance during 1969 was the rapid affiliation of life insurers with related financial services such as mutual funds and variable annuities.

Health insurance in the U.S. also grew rapidly during 1969. Rising medical costs were a definite factor, as well as broadened group health insurance coverage. Medicare payments for persons 65 and over rose correspondingly, both for the basic hospital and nursing benefits paid by social security taxes (Part A) and for the supplementary optional program for physicians' and miscellaneous medical costs (Part B). Total health benefits paid by private insurers amounted to more than $15 billion; somewhat less than one-half came from the Blue Cross-Blue Shield type of association and the remainder from other insuring organizations.

Despite the steady pressure on personal incomes, demand for life insurance in the U.K. remained buoyant in 1968, and the industry broke all previous records. New ordinary and industrial (home service) insurance totaled £8,340 million, compared with £7,131 million in 1967. Of the new business, £7,602 million was written in the ordinary branch and £738 million in the industrial section. New premiums necessary to secure the new benefits were £385 million, compared with £346 million in the previous year. A gross investment yield of 9% was general throughout the industry, and bonus distributions to policyholders were at or above previous levels.

Property and Liability Insurance. Sales in the U.S. in 1969 rose almost 8% to approximately $30 billion, more than 40% of which was automobile insurance. The ratio of losses and expenses to premiums was expected to be about the same as in 1968, or slightly more than 100. Homeowners' and commercial multiple-peril insurance premiums rose to $3 billion, and in most states revised contracts emphasized such features as increased use of deductibles and endorsements that automatically raised the coverage to keep pace with inflation. Indications were that fire losses would increase by 7 to 10% in 1969. Fire damage was approaching $2 billion per year, and windstorm damage, after a slight decrease in 1968, was approximately $1.5 billion.

Proposed solutions for the problem of rising automobile accident costs ranged from minor revisions of the existing tort liability laws to a complete shift to compensation plans that would pay injured parties regardless of fault. Major changes were not likely, however, until the results of a Department of Transportation study were released in 1970.

Accessibility of insurance coverage to the public was increased in 1969 with the inauguration of Fair Access to Insurance Requirements (FAIR) plans in most states. These plans were being adjusted to become eligible for federal riot reinsurance. Flood insurance, also backed by federal reinsurance, became available to property owners in a few selected areas in mid-1969, with 40 regions scheduled for eligibility as the system matured.

The major disaster in the U.S. in 1969 was Hurricane Camille, which caused an estimated $500 million to $1 billion damage in Mississippi, Louisiana, Alabama, and Virginia. The insured loss was predicted at $100 million–$200 million. Spring floods and summer tornadoes in the Midwest were additional causes of loss. Riot damage in U.S. cities and campuses amounted to $15 million, much less than had been anticipated.

The worldwide premium income of member companies of the British Insurance Association (BIA) rose 11.6% in 1968 to £3,099 million, of which automobile insurance accounted for £603 million, fire for £495 million, and accident (nonmotor) for £459 million. The 0.8% underwriting loss of £12.9 million was the largest since BIA statistics were first compiled in 1965. Only miscellaneous accident insurance remained profitable, and even in this area profits declined. The companies netted a record £991.6 million in premiums on overseas fire, motor, and miscellaneous business in 1968, an increase of 15% that included some benefit from the 1967 sterling devaluation. Half of this total was earned in the U.S., where difficult underwriting conditions and inflation were offset by revenue on invested funds and reserves. The trading accounts of Lloyd's Underwriters on a three-year basis reflected the closure of the 1966 account with an underwriting loss of £18.5 million, compared with a £38 million loss in 1965. Only the life, automobile, and aviation sectors of the market showed a profit.

For marine insurers 1968 was slightly improved, but major casualties continued at a high level. Following disastrous years in 1964 and 1965 and only marginal results in 1966, a firmer approach was taken to hull and cargo renewals. Marine premiums of BIA members rose 24% in 1967, a high proportion of this coming from overseas. During 1968, 157 vessels, with an aggregate gross tonnage of 675,054, were totally lost, compared with 163 vessels with 746,834 gross tonnage in 1967. Ships sailing under Greek, Liberian, and Panamanian flags accounted for nearly half the number and more than half the tonnage.

The London aviation insurance market was involved in a loss of £7,250,000 by the destruction or near-destruction of 13 aircraft as the result of the Israeli attack on Beirut international airport in 1968. The incident served to highlight the problems of political and war risks. The loss of an Aer Lingus Viscount over the Irish Sea, followed by the crash of a British Eagle Viscount over West Germany, was of added concern to underwriters in view of the imminent introduction of jumbo jets. With jumbo jet hull values estimated at $20 million each, and some 400 people on board with a possible liability of $75,000 to $100,000 per person, the potential charge for one incident reached the staggering sum of $50 million to $100 million.

An unprecedented series of weather catastrophes in the U.K. in 1968—from Glasgow storms in January to the southeastern floods in September—cost insurance companies over £20 million. Fire damage rose 11% to reach £100 million for the first time. The upsurge in crime continued; burglary premium rates rose sharply, but were hardly sufficient to end the unprofitability of this account. BIA member companies paid out £16.3 million in crime losses, compared with £15.9 million in 1967.

At the end of 1968, the tariff rating system for automobile, employers' liability, and fidelity guarantee business came to an end, and each member company became free to apply its own premium schedules and to decide on its own coverage. The biggest effect was on automobile insurance, and the outcome was a reduction in the price of coverage for the good driver while all other motor costs continued to rise.

(D. L. Bi.; P. Ss.)

See also Cooperatives; Disasters; Industrial Review; Social Services.

Encyclopædia Britannica Films. *Casualty Insurance* (1954).

Intelligence Operations

Espionage continued throughout 1969, and counter-espionage produced its usual sporadic crop of arrests. The year was notable for the agreement between the U.K. and the U.S.S.R. under which the Soviet spies Helen and Peter Kroger were exchanged for the British lecturer Gerald Brooke. In one of the year's most curious spy cases, Hannsheinz Porst, West German millionaire and East German spy, received a mild sentence for his espionage activities.

Morris Cohen, alias Peter Kroger, and Leona Petka, alias Helen Kroger, both U.S. citizens and members of the U.S. Communist Party since the mid-1930s, began their work with the Soviet spy network operating in the United States under Rudolf Abel. They vanished from New York in 1950 within hours of the arrest of David Greenglass, who had been detained on charges of stealing atomic secrets and who had denounced his sister Ethel and her husband, Julius Rosenberg. The Krogers reappeared under that name in London in 1954 with forged New Zealand passports. They bought a suburban house in Ruislip, near London, and opened an antiquarian bookshop in the Strand. Their home was equipped with a powerful radio transmitter, which was used by the head of a Soviet spy ring, Konon Trofimovich Molody, alias Gordon Lonsdale, who possessed a forged Canadian passport.

The main task of this spy ring was to obtain secret information about ships of the Royal Navy and particularly about the work going on at the Admiralty Underwater Detection Establishment at Portland, Dorset. The three spies, with their two English aides, Harry Houghton and Ethel Gee, were arrested on Jan. 7, 1961. On March 22 Lonsdale was sentenced to 25 years' imprisonment, and the Krogers to 20 years each.

Abel, sentenced in New York on Nov. 15, 1957, to 30 years' imprisonment, was swapped on Feb. 10, 1962, in West Berlin, for the U.S. pilot Francis Gary Powers. Lonsdale was exchanged on April 22, 1964, for Greville Maynard Wynne, British businessman and secret agent. The Soviet Committee for State Security (KGB or Komitet Gosudarstvennoi Bezopasnosti) had arrested Gerald Brooke in Moscow on April 25, 1965. Brooke, a London lecturer, had acted as a courier for an anti-Soviet emigré group, carrying coding instructions concealed in a postcard album and a dressing case. He was sentenced on July 23, 1965, to a year in jail and four years' detention in a labour colony for anti-Soviet activities.

Almost immediately after Brooke's trial, feelers were put out from Moscow about the possibility of swapping Brooke for the Krogers. The British government, aware of the implications of such a deal, showed no interest until more sinister hints were dropped that Brooke could be tried again on new charges and sentenced to another 10–15 years. This time, on humanitarian grounds, the British government opened discussions with the U.S.S.R., and it was agreed to release the Krogers for Brooke and two other prisoners. In addition, four Britons received permission to marry their Soviet fiancées as part of the deal. On July 24, 1969, Brooke returned to London. On October 24 the Krogers left London by air for Warsaw—and supposedly a home in Lublin—under the pretense that they were Polish citizens. The Polish press ignored this event, which was of some significance since as a result of it there were no major Soviet spies in British or U.S. prisons, or British or U.S. agents in Soviet hands.

Hannsheinz Porst, 46, a Nürnberg millionaire whose camera shops were on almost every main street in West Germany, agreed in 1953 to work for the East German security service. Two years later he secretly joined the East German Socialist (Communist) Unity Party and, more openly, the West German Free Democratic Party (FDP). Porst became friendly with Erich Mende, then leader of the FDP and vice-chancellor of the West German coalition government. Porst was arrested in October 1967 and was released on bail of DM. 1 million. At his trial, which began in May 1969 before the Federal Court at Karlsruhe, the prosecution uncovered Porst's relations with the East German Ministry of State Security, to whom he had passed confidential political information. On July 8 Porst was sentenced to two years and nine months in jail and fined DM. 10,000.

On Oct. 10, 1967, Evgeni Runge, 39, a Soviet citizen of German nationality and an important agent of the KGB working in West Germany under many aliases, presented himself in West Berlin to the local representative of the Central Intelligence Agency (CIA) and the next day was flown to Langley, Va. An officer of the CIA informed Hubert Schrübbers, president of the Federal Office for the Protection of the Constitution (Bundesamt für Verfassungsschutz), that Runge had betrayed four of the West German members of his spy ring. Two of them were Heinz Sütterlin, a Bonn press photographer, aged 45, and his wife Leonore, 39, née Heinz. Both were arrested, but Leonore, a secretary at the West German Foreign Ministry, committed suicide in prison three days later after she had discovered that Sütterlin had married her on KGB orders. Heinz Sütterlin was sentenced on November 28 by a Cologne court to seven years' imprisonment. He had passed to the U.S.S.R. photographs of confidential documents to which his wife had had access since 1962. She had taken home the documents in a false-bottomed handbag, which her husband had provided. Runge was not allowed by the CIA to be present in court in Cologne, but gave evidence at a special hearing in the U.S.

On April 12, Rupert Sigl, 44, an Austrian-born member of the Soviet KGB, defected to the CIA in West Berlin. According to a West German newspaper, Sigl brought with him the names of as many as 250 Soviet agents working in West Germany.

Yuri Loginov, 36, a Soviet spy arrested in South Africa in September 1967, was flown from Pretoria to London and from there to West Berlin to be exchanged in July for ten West German agents detained in East Germany.

On February 25 Yuri Vorontsov, 45-year-old head of the political section of the Soviet Embassy at Bonn, was killed in an automobile accident. The West German magazine *Der Spiegel* alleged on March 24 that Vorontsov was a KGB officer with the rank of colonel and head of a group of 80 out of 100 secret service staff employed at the embassy and at the Soviet trade mission in Cologne. West German officials admitted that the Federal Intelligence Service (BND or Bundesnachrichtendienst) had been trailing Vorontsov for 2½ years.

The Soviet press retaliated. On May 23 *Izvestia* published an article denouncing the West German embassy in Moscow as a "nest of spies," and attacking Horst Gröpper, the former ambassador, and many high-ranking diplomats in the political and economic sections of the embassy. *Komsomolskaya Pravda* had earlier accused Ludwig Lerner, a third secretary who had been posted to Moscow in 1965, of being the head of a spy network and a well-trained agent of the BND. Shortly afterward Lerner left Moscow.

On May 3 a West German Army major, Hans Joachim Kruse, appeared on East German television and explained that he had been instructor of tactics at the officers' training college in Hamburg. According to Kruse, when he discovered that during one year the number of active neo-Nazi National Democratic Party (NPD) members in the Bundeswehr jumped from 400 to 1,000, he had become convinced that the policy of the West German government "did not serve peace," and had decided to escape to East Germany.

On August 13 French police charged Francis Roussilhe, 40, a French interpreter at NATO headquarters in Brussels, with working for Romania against French military, diplomatic, and economic interests. At the same time a Romanian diplomat disappeared from Paris and three others were expelled. Lieut. Col. Charles de Jurquet de la Salle d'Anfreville, one of the last survivors of the Normandie-Niemen fighter squadron that fought with the Soviets in World War II, committed suicide. Lieut. Col. Bernard Marie du Cheyrou de Beaumont d'Abzac de la Douze, head of the Eastern European section of the Ministry of Defense, died while returning from a visit to Bucharest when his car hit a military truck on the wide road leading to Bucharest airport. The commanding officer of the French Deuxième Bureau said in his funeral oration, "Du Cheyrou accepted the risk of making the supreme sacrifice."

Six Frenchmen, including two minor Quai d'Orsay officials and members of the counterespionage organization, and a Romanian, Atanese Mihai, were detained on espionage charges. It was understood that the French counterespionage service received a tip-off from a defecting Romanian UNESCO employee, Ion Iacobescu.

In September the Swiss government announced the arrest of an aircraft engineer, Alfred Frauenknecht, on charges of sending secret blueprints of jet fighter engines to Israel. It was alleged that the plans, prepared for the French firm SNECMA, which supplied engines for the Mirage fighter, had been smuggled to Israel via West Germany. The French arms embargo prevented Israel from getting spare parts for its Mirages from France.

U.S. intelligence operations in Vietnam were a cause of public controversy in 1969 as a result of the alleged murder by members of the U.S. Special Forces (Green Berets) of a Vietnamese double agent. (*See* DEFENSE.) In South Vietnam in August about 100 persons were arrested and charged with "liaison with the enemy" in what was described as a Communist intelligence network. Saigon police sources said that the group had contacts in Cambodia, Hong Kong, Laos, and France. (K. SM.)

Inter-American Affairs

Relations between the Latin-American republics and the U.S. were strained in 1969, although there were some improvements in mutual understanding among the Latin Americans themselves. The most significant development was a clarification of Latin-American grievances over economic aid and foreign trade in general and over financial relations with the U.S. in particular.

The election of Richard M. Nixon to the U.S. presidency aroused little enthusiasm and some anxiety in Latin America, partly because of recollections of the hostility that greeted him on his visit as vice-president in 1958, and partly because he had made it clear in his campaign speeches that he gave Latin America's problems low priority.

Both the Andean group of Pacific coast countries and those nations involved in the Río de la Plata Basin scheme owed their modest advancement to the growing skepticism engendered by the Latin American Free Trade Association (LAFTA), which proved unwieldy and geographically diffuse.

The progress of the Central American Common Market (CACM) was checked in 1969 not only by immediate threats from Costa Rica and Nicaragua to suspend concessions previously negotiated but also more dramatically by a small-scale war between El Salvador and Honduras.

There was hesitant progress in the development of the Caribbean Free Trade Association (CARIFTA), which included former British territories in the area and might later embrace former French and Dutch colonies and perhaps the Dominican Republic.

The kidnapping in September of the U.S. ambassador to Brazil, Charles Burke Elbrick, and his release in exchange for 15 political prisoners had no repercussions as both governments remained calm.

Relations with the U.S. In his dealings with Latin America President Nixon showed considerable caution, which was widely (though probably wrongly) interpreted in the region as indifference. It was not until April that he addressed a meeting of the Organization of American States (OAS); although he deplored the failure of the Alliance for Progress to achieve the social improvements in Latin America that were its main objective, he was not able to state that sufficient U.S. aid would be available to meet

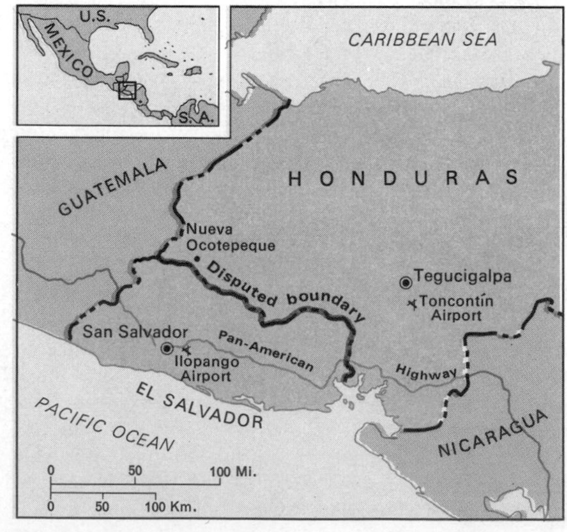

Latin America's development needs. His policy was to encourage investment of U.S. private capital in Latin America, in the hope that this would compensate for deficiencies in assistance from the government. The implication that official funds at low interest rates would be replaced by private capital demanding a much higher return was not welcomed in Latin America.

As if to stress the importance of private enterprise in U.S. financial relations with Latin America, Nixon announced in March the appointment as assistant secretary of state for Inter-American Affairs of Charles A. Meyer, a chain store executive with business experience in Latin America.

In June Nixon asked the U.S. Congress for aid appropriations for Latin America of slightly above $600 million, which was less than the $765 million applied for by Pres. Lyndon Johnson but more than the $420 million authorized for 1968–69. Nixon's plans were, perhaps, less radically different from those of his predecessors than had been assumed, and the accusation of indifference to Latin America's problems was certainly unjust. There was, however, a continuing element of bad luck in his dealings with Latin America.

Nixon announced in February that he had asked Gov. Nelson Rockefeller of New York to lead a fact-finding mission to Latin America. This was followed by a further deterioration in relations between the U.S. and Peru, which prompted the Peruvian military junta to state that Rockefeller's visit would be inopportune and pointless. Moreover, the timing of the mission for May–June gave the impression that Nixon was ignoring the meeting of the Comisión Especial de Coordinación Latinoamericana (CECLA) in Viña del Mar, Chile, on May 15–17; the idea of a special mission implied that nothing would be learned from the CECLA meeting (of foreign ministers), and also appeared to belittle the considered comments on U.S. financial relations with Latin America made by the secretary-general of the OAS, Galo Plaza Lasso, by the Committee for International Aid (sponsored by the World Bank), and by other well-informed bodies.

Other Latin-American governments followed the Peruvian example of declining to receive Rockefeller; in countries the mission did visit there were violent demonstrations of hostility. These reactions were reminiscent of those experienced by Nixon himself in 1958, but it was never clear—perhaps not even in the demonstrators' own minds—whether the expressions of antagonism were directed against Nixon, or Rockefeller, or Uncle Sam, or were merely additional evidence of the increasing frustration felt in Latin America at inadequate economic growth, unemployment, and an almost universal lack of opportunity.

Galo Plaza pointed out in November 1968 that the failure of the Alliance for Progress and indeed of the whole principle of bilateral official aid was in part the result of bureaucratic restrictions, such as the requirement that aid funds be used to buy U.S. products that would not otherwise be imported. Moreover, aid funds were loans which, though at low rates of interest, had to be repaid. It was claimed that in 1968 approximately 75% of the Alliance for Progress funds were used to repay earlier loans, and the Committee for International Aid found that the balance of loans, repayments, and related U.S. exports under the heading of "aid" resulted in a net inflow from Latin America into the U.S. of $175 million.

These and related subjects—especially the question of the barriers preventing access of Latin-American industrial products to the U.S. and other rich markets—were discussed at the CECLA meeting in Viña del Mar and incorporated into a report that the Chilean foreign minister, Gabriel Valdés, presented to Nixon in Washington in June. The report was also adopted as a basic document for the meeting of the OAS Inter-American Economic and Social Council in Port-of-Spain, Trinidad, June 14–23. Soon after this meeting Pres. Carlos Lleras Restrepo of Colombia stressed the importance of the CECLA report in his conversations with Nixon, and urged him to take suitable action.

The failure of the Rockefeller mission was due in part to its timing; it seemed to sensitive Latin-American feelings to show a lack of tact, particularly in light of the dispute between the military junta governing Peru and the International Petroleum Company (IPC)—a subsidiary of Standard Oil Co. (New Jersey). The junta introduced a strong element of nationalism into a traditionally liberal economy and decided to resolve a long-standing legal and fiscal dispute by expropriating all the assets of IPC in Peru. No payment for the expropriation was offered at first, in view of a claim for unpaid taxes that greatly exceeded the value of the assets expropriated. This placed the Nixon administration in the embarrassing position of being constitutionally obliged to apply the 1962 Hickenlooper amendment requiring the cessation of economic and military aid after a specified period of warning. In August, Nixon sent a special envoy to Lima, John Irwin (the ambassador having been recalled), who persuaded the junta to deposit a compensation payment in favour of IPC, thus eliminating the need to apply the amendment, even though the deposit was embargoed against the tax claim. This dispute was most embittered at the time when the Rockefeller mission would have visited Lima.

Concurrently with these negotiations, the question of U.S. fishing vessels in waters claimed by Peru as territorial—a matter that had not previously been given much attention—was used by the junta as another means of embittering relations with Washington (*see* below). It was to Irwin's credit that he not only avoided a breakdown of relations between Peru and the U.S. but persuaded the U.S. administration to increase Peru's sugar quota and the Peruvian junta to accept a new U.S. ambassador.

Rockefeller's report on his findings was made public in November. Urging that the "special relationship" between the U.S. and Latin America be maintained, he recommended a number of economic reforms, including preferential treatment of Latin-American exports, generous refinancing of debts owed to the U.S., and elimination of the provision that aid money be spent for U.S. goods. He also urged that military and democratic regimes receive equal treatment, that recognition not be used as a means of expressing approval or disapproval, and that more military aid be provided to counter insurgency, although the Latin-American nations should be discouraged from buying sophisticated weaponry. It was clear from President Nixon's October 31 statement on Latin America, however, that the administration did not intend to accept the full scope of Rockefeller's recommendations.

Territorial Waters. In March the Chilean foreign minister began conversations with the other Pacific coast countries with a view to drawing up a formal

PICTORIAL PARADE

U.S. ambassador to Brazil, Charles Burke Elbrick, who was abducted in September 1969 by Brazilian terrorists, was released in exchange for 15 political prisoners held by the Brazilian government.

collective declaration on territorial waters. At a conference in Buenos Aires in August, Chile, Ecuador, and Peru discussed with the U.S. their 17-year-old claim to 200 mi. of offshore waters as the "maritime zone." The concept of the continental shelf and the waters covering it as an extension of national territory had been enunciated for the U.S. by Pres. Harry S. Truman in 1945; the Pacific coast countries of South America, having virtually no continental shelf on which to base a claim, chose the mean width of the Humboldt Current, which had the same importance as a continental shelf in providing their offshore marine wealth. The shoals of anchovies in the Humboldt Current, for example, enabled Peru to become the world's major fishing nation. After the conference in Buenos Aires, Argentina and four Central American countries joined the Pacific group with declarations of jurisdiction extending 200 mi. off their shores.

Regional Integration. The Latin American Free Trade Association (LAFTA) held its eighth annual meeting in Montevideo at the end of 1968 and made good progress with the addition of tariff concessions to member countries' national lists. The enlargement of the common list of goods with such concessions by an additional 25% of regional trade, so as to include virtually the whole of regional trade by 1973, proved unattainable, however, since it would have meant including wheat and petroleum. Unanimous agreement on these important products was not obtainable, and the timetable for complete trade liberalization established in the Treaty of Montevideo had, therefore, to be abandoned. The plan to create a Latin-American Common Market to include LAFTA and the CACM appeared unattainable in the near future. The LAFTA secretariat was, however, arranging a series of meetings to reconsider the whole concept as defined in the Treaty of Montevideo.

The LAFTA proved to be a difficult association to make cohesive, involving as it did countries of different levels of economic development and disparate national interests, in an area of little geographical unity that lacked effective transport services, payments mechanisms, and common economic and monetary policies. Because of these difficulties, hopes were raised for more effective forms of integration in less unwieldy subregional groups.

The Andean group was first conceived in 1967 as an association of countries forming a geographical unit having common interests and reasonably similar levels of development. Bolivia, Chile, Colombia, Ecuador, Peru, and Venezuela after several inconclusive meetings finally achieved a treaty on May 26 in Bogotá, though Venezuela did not immediately sign it. This limited success was largely the result of the enthusiasm of Pres. Carlos Lleras Restrepo of Colombia and was seen as the first step toward an Andean customs union with internal trade liberalization and a common external tariff, to be achieved by 1980, and a common market, by 1990. Venezuela's reluctance to join—exactly as with LAFTA—was said to be due to its high cost structure and consequent vulnerability to competition. In July the Andean group treaty was approved by the LAFTA council as "compatible," and after ratification by Chile, Colombia, Ecuador, and Peru, it came into force on November 24, with Lima as the group's headquarters.

The Río de la Plata Basin group, consisting of Argentina, Bolivia, Brazil, Paraguay, and Uruguay—that is, countries with territory in the Paraná-Paraguay River system—was based on a geographical concept only, since there were great economic disparities among the members. Essentially the scheme was for the joint exploration and development of the area's resources. The plan was later enlarged to include economic integration and development of industries that would complement rather than compete with one another. The enthusiasm for the Río de la Plata Basin idea survived disputes between Argentina and Brazil over the latter's use of the waters of the upper Paraná, and between Argentina and Uruguay over demarcation in the Río de la Plata estuary. A treaty giving formal existence to the group was signed in Brasília on April 23, and the Inter-Governmental Coordinating Committee, first set up in February 1967, was made the permanent executive body. Argentina subsequently suggested to Uruguay that petroleum in the Río de la Plata estuary be exploited jointly, and the boundary dispute was not allowed to become serious.

The Central American Common Market, which had earlier been outstandingly successful in increasing trade both internally and externally for its five members (Costa Rica, El Salvador, Guatemala, Honduras, and Nicaragua), made some progress technically, but politically it was in danger of disintegrating. Costa Rica and Nicaragua had for two years faced balance of payments difficulties because of excessive imports. A protocol signed in July 1968 authorized the Common Market secretariat to increase external tariffs by 30%, but no action was taken. Pres. Anastasio Somoza Debayle of Nicaragua accused the Common Market of being the cause of his country's payments difficulties, and Costa Rica imposed restrictions on trade within the CACM, against which the other members retaliated.

More significant was the small war that broke out in July between El Salvador and Honduras. For some years Salvadoran peasant farmers had found it easier to obtain land in Honduras than in their own country. The government of Honduras, faced with an accumulated illegal immigration of about 300,000 Salvadorans, when its own population was only 2.5 million, attempted to halt the flow and to regulate land tenure. The government of El Salvador sought to protect the interests of its nationals in Honduras. A soccer match between the two countries led to excitement and violence and eventually to armed conflict. The OAS achieved a cease-fire, but trade between the two countries was more or less at a standstill. Toward the end of the year the CACM foreign ministers met in an attempt to break the deadlock, and it was announced that negotiations between the two countries would begin early in 1970.

Cuba. Fidel Castro desisted from his attempts to export the Cuban revolution to the South American continent and seemed disposed to renew relations with any country willing to repudiate the OAS decision of 1962 to ostracize Cuba. This decision, reflecting U.S. determination to impose a commercial and diplomatic embargo on Cuba, had been adopted by all OAS members except Mexico. Chile and Venezuela expressed the view that the ostracism of Cuba was irrelevant and should be ended. Other Latin-American governments were likely to adopt this view, if only to show their independence of the U.S. (DD. H.)

ENCYCLOPÆDIA BRITANNICA FILMS. *The Amazon—People and Resources of Northern Brazil* (1957); *Argentina—People of the Pampa* (1957); *Brazil—People of the Highlands* (1957); *Peru: People of the Andes* (1959); *Colombia and Venezuela* (1961); *Guatemala—Nation of Central America* (1961); *Puerto Rico: Past, Present, and Promise* (1965); *The West Indies* (1965).

Interior Decoration: *see* Domestic Arts and Sciences

International Bank for Reconstruction and Development: *see* Development, Economic

International Court of Justice: *see* Law

International Criminal Police Organization: *see* Police

International Development Association: *see* Development, Economic

International Finance Corporation: *see* Development, Economic

International Labour Organization: *see* Labour Unions

International Law: *see* Law

International Monetary Fund: *see* Payments and Reserves, International

International Organizations

The accompanying table shows the membership of the world's sovereign states in various international organizations as of Sept. 30, 1969. The growing realization that political and economic problems transcended international boundaries led to a proliferation of international organizations after World War II. Of these, the UN and its specialized agencies (some of which, such as the ILO and the UPU, antedated the

Membership in International Organizations

As of Sept. 30, 1969

SEE KEY ON PAGE 434

Country	UN 1	FAO 2	IMCO 3	IAEA 4	ICAO 5	ILO 6	IBRD 7	IDA 8	IFC 9	IMF 10	ITU 11	UNESCO 12	UPU 13	WHO 14	WMO 15	GATT 16	CE 17	AL 18	OAS 19	WEU 20	OCAS 21	C-Plan 22	Comecon 23	Euratom 24	ECSC 25	EEC 26	EFTA 27	IDB 28	LAFTA 29	OECD 30	ANZUS 31	CENTO 32	NATO 33	SEATO 34	WTO 35	Antarctic treaty 36	OAU 37	SPC 38
Afghanistan	●	●		●	●	●	●	●	●	●	●	●	●	●	●							●															
Albania	●			●		●					●	●	●	●	●								●												●			
Algeria	●	●	●	●	●	●	●	●		●	●	●	●	●	●			●																			●	
Argentina	●	●	●	●	●	●	●	●	●	●	●	●	●	●	●	●			●									●	●							●		
Australia	●	●	●	●	●	●	●	●	●	●	●	●	●	●	●	●						●									●			●		●		●
Austria	●	●		●	●	●	●	●	●	●	●	●	●	●	●	●	●										●			●							
Barbados	●				●	●					●		●	●		●			●																		
Belgium	●	●	●	●	●	●	●	●	●	●	●	●	●	●	●	●	●			●				●	●	●				●			●			●		
Belorussia	●			●		●					●	●	●	●	●																						
Bolivia	●	●		●	●	●	●	●	●	●	●	●	●	●	●				●									●	●								
Botswana	●	●					●	●		●	●		●																								●	
Brazil	●	●	●	●	●	●	●	●	●	●	●	●	●	●	●	●			●									●	●									
Bulgaria	●		●	●	●	●					●	●	●	●	●								●												●			
Burma	●	●	●	●	●	●	●	●	●	●	●	●	●	●	●	●						●															
Burundi	●	●				●	●	●		●	●	●	●	●	●	●																					●	
Cambodia	●	●	●	●	●						●	●	●	●	●							●															
Cameroon	●	●	●	●	●	●	●	●		●	●	●	●	●	●	●																					●	
Canada	●	●	●	●	●	●	●	●	●	●	●	●	●	●	●	●						●								●			●				
Central African Rep.	●	●			●	●	●	●		●	●	●	●	●	●	●																					●	
Ceylon	●	●		●	●	●	●	●	●	●	●	●	●	●	●	●						●															
Chad	●	●			●	●	●	●		●	●	●	●	●	●	●																					●	
Chile	●	●		●	●	●	●	●	●	●	●	●	●	●	●	●			●									●	●							●		
Colombia	●	●		●	●	●	●	●	●	●	●	●	●	●	●				●									●	●									
Congo (Brazzaville)	●	●			●	●	●	●		●	●	●	●	●	●	●																					●	
Congo (Kinshasa)	●	●		●	●	●	●	●		●	●	●	●	●	●																						●	
Costa Rica	●	●		●	●	●	●	●	●	●	●	●	●	●	●				●		●							●										
Cuba	●	●	●	●	●	●					●	●	●	●	●	●			●																				
Cyprus	●	●		●	●	●	●	●	●	●	●	●	●	●	●	●	●																						
Czechoslovakia	●		●	●	●	●					●	●	●	●	●	●							●												●	●		
Dahomey	●	●			●	●	●	●		●	●	●	●	●	●	●																					●	
Denmark	●	●	●	●	●	●	●	●	●	●	●	●	●	●	●	●	●										●			●			●			●		
Dominican Rep.	●	●	●	●	●	●	●	●	●	●	●	●	●	●	●	●			●									●										
Ecuador	●	●	●	●	●	●	●	●	●	●	●	●	●	●	●				●									●	●									
El Salvador	●	●		●	●	●	●	●	●	●	●	●	●	●	●				●		●							●										
Equatorial Guinea	●																																					
Ethiopia	●	●		●	●	●	●	●	●	●	●	●	●	●																								●	
Finland	●	●	●	●	●	●	●	●	●	●	●	●	●	●	●	●														●							
France	●	●	●	●	●	●	●	●	●	●	●	●	●	●	●	●	●			●				●	●	●				●			●	●		●		●
Gabon	●	●		●	●	●	●	●		●	●	●	●	●	●	●																					●	
Gambia, The	●	●					●	●		●						●																					●	
Germany, East																							●												●			
Germany, West		●	●	●	●	●	●	●	●	●	●	●	●	●	●	●	●			●				●	●	●				●			●					
Ghana	●	●	●	●	●	●	●	●	●	●	●	●	●	●	●	●																					●	
Greece	●	●	●	●	●	●	●	●	●	●	●	●	●	●	●	●	●													●			●					
Guatemala	●	●		●	●	●	●	●	●	●	●	●	●	●	●				●		●							●										
Guinea	●	●			●	●	●			●	●	●	●	●	●																						●	
Guyana	●	●			●	●	●	●	●	●	●	●	●	●	●	●																							
Haiti	●	●	●	●	●	●	●	●	●	●	●	●	●	●	●	●			●									●										
Honduras	●	●	●		●	●	●	●	●	●	●	●	●	●	●				●		●							●										
Hungary	●			●		●					●	●	●	●	●								●												●			
Iceland	●	●	●	●	●	●	●	●	●	●	●	●	●	●	●	●	●													●			●					
India	●	●	●	●	●	●	●	●	●	●	●	●	●	●	●	●						●															
Indonesia	●	●	●	●	●	●	●	●	●	●	●	●	●	●	●	●						●															
Iran	●	●	●	●	●	●	●	●	●	●	●	●	●	●	●							●										●						
Iraq	●	●		●	●	●	●	●	●	●	●	●	●	●	●			●																			
Ireland	●	●	●		●	●	●	●	●	●	●	●	●	●	●	●	●													●							
Israel	●	●	●	●	●	●	●	●	●	●	●	●	●	●	●	●																					
Italy	●	●	●	●	●	●	●	●	●	●	●	●	●	●	●	●	●			●				●	●	●				●			●					
Ivory Coast	●	●	●	●	●	●	●	●	●	●	●	●	●	●	●	●																					●	
Jamaica	●	●		●	●	●	●		●	●	●	●	●	●	●	●			●																		
Japan	●	●	●	●	●	●	●	●	●	●	●	●	●	●	●	●						●								●						●		
Jordan	●	●		●	●	●	●	●	●	●	●	●	●	●	●			●																			
Kenya	●	●		●	●	●	●	●	●	●	●	●	●	●	●	●																					●	
Korea, South		●	●	●	●		●	●	●	●	●	●	●	●	●	●						●															
Kuwait	●	●	●	●	●	●	●	●	●	●	●	●	●	●	●	●		●																			
Laos	●	●			●	●	●	●		●	●	●	●	●	●							●															
Lebanon	●	●	●	●	●	●	●	●	●	●	●	●	●	●	●			●																			
Lesotho	●	●				●	●	●		●	●	●	●	●																								●	
Liberia	●	●	●	●	●	●	●	●	●	●	●	●	●	●																								●	
Libya	●	●		●	●	●	●	●	●	●	●	●	●	●	●			●																			●	
Liechtenstein											●		●																								
Luxembourg	●	●		●	●	●	●	●	●	●	●	●	●	●	●	●	●			●				●	●	●				●			●					
Malagasy Rep.	●	●	●	●	●	●	●	●	●	●	●	●	●	●	●	●																					●	
Malawi	●	●			●	●	●	●	●	●	●	●	●	●	●	●																					●	
Malaysia	●	●			●	●	●	●	●	●	●	●	●	●	●	●						●															
Maldives	●		●									●		●	●								●															
Mali	●	●		●	●	●	●	●		●	●	●	●	●	●																						●	
Malta	●	●	●		●	●				●	●	●	●	●		●	●																						

war) aimed at least theoretically at universality. The World Bank, originally established to provide help to war-devastated nations, turned more and more in succeeding years toward concentration on the problems of economic development. Organizations with more restricted membership included regional political groupings (OAS, OAU), military alliances (NATO, the Warsaw Pact), and organizations with a primarily economic orientation (EEC, Comecon). Such groupings as the Colombo Plan and the Alliance for Progress were chiefly vehicles for channeling aid from the developed to the less developed countries.

Membership in International Organizations

As of Sept. 30, 1969

Country	UN 1	FAO 2	IMCO 3	IAEA 4	ICAO 5	ILO 6	IBRD 7	IDA 8	IFC 9	IMF 10	ITU 11	UNESCO 12	UPU 13	WHO 14	WMO 15	GATT 16	CE 17	AL 18	OAS 19	WEU 20	OCAS 21	C-Plan 22	Comecon 23	Euratom 24	ECSC 25	EEC 26	EFTA 27	IDB 28	LAFTA 29	OECD 30	ANZUS 31	CENTO 32	NATO 33	SEATO 34	WTO 35	Antarctic treaty 36	OAU 37	SPC 38
Mauritania	●	●	●		●	●	●	●	●	●	●	●	●	●	●	●																					●	
Mauritius	●						●	●	●	●																											●	
Mexico	●	●	●	●	●	●	●	●	●	●	●	●	●	●	●				●									●	●									
Monaco				●							●	●	●	●																								
Mongolia	●					●					●	●	●	●	●																							
Morocco	●	●	●	●	●	●	●	●	●	●	●	●	●	●	●			●																			●	
Nepal	●	●			●	●	●	●	●	●	●	●	●	●	●							●																
Netherlands	●	●	●	●	●	●	●	●	●	●	●	●	●	●	●	●	●			●				●	●	●				●			●			●		
New Zealand	●	●	●	●	●	●	●		●	●	●	●	●	●	●	●						●									●			●		●		●
Nicaragua	●	●		●	●	●	●	●	●	●	●	●	●	●	●	●			●		●							●										
Niger	●	●			●	●	●	●		●	●	●	●	●	●	●																					●	
Nigeria	●	●	●	●	●	●	●	●	●	●	●	●	●	●	●	●																					●	
Norway	●	●	●	●	●	●	●	●	●	●	●	●	●	●	●	●	●										●			●			●			●		
Pakistan	●	●	●	●	●	●	●	●	●	●	●	●	●	●	●	●						●										●		●				
Panama	●	●	●	●	●	●	●	●	●	●	●	●	●	●	●				●									●										
Paraguay	●	●		●	●	●	●	●	●	●	●	●	●	●	●				●									●	●									
Peru	●	●	●	●	●	●	●	●	●	●	●	●	●	●	●	●			●									●	●									
Philippines	●	●	●	●	●	●	●	●	●	●	●	●	●	●	●							●												●				
Poland	●	●	●	●	●	●					●	●	●	●	●	●							●												●	●		
Portugal	●	●		●	●	●	●		●	●	●	●	●	●	●												●			●			●					
Rhodesia											●					●																						
Romania	●	●	●	●	●	●					●	●	●	●	●								●												●			
Rwanda	●	●			●	●	●	●		●	●	●	●	●	●	●																					●	
San Marino													●																									
Saudi Arabia	●	●		●	●		●	●	●	●	●	●	●	●	●			●																				
Senegal	●	●	●	●	●	●	●	●	●	●	●	●	●	●	●	●																					●	
Sierra Leone	●	●		●	●	●	●	●	●	●	●	●	●	●	●	●																					●	
Singapore	●		●	●	●	●	●		●	●	●	●	●	●	●							●																
Somalia	●	●			●	●	●	●	●	●	●	●	●	●	●																						●	
South Africa	●			●	●		●	●	●	●	●		●	●	●	●																				●		
Southern Yemen	●												●	●				●																				
Spain	●	●	●	●	●	●	●	●	●	●	●	●	●	●	●	●														●								
Sudan	●	●		●	●	●	●	●	●	●	●	●	●	●	●			●																			●	
Swaziland	●									●																											●	
Sweden	●	●	●	●	●	●	●	●	●	●	●	●	●	●	●	●	●										●			●								
Switzerland		●	●	●	●	●					●	●	●	●	●	●	●										●			●								
Syria	●	●	●	●	●	●	●	●	●	●	●	●	●	●	●			●																				
Taiwan	●		●	●	●	●	●	●		●	●	●	●	●	●																							
Tanzania	●	●			●	●	●	●	●	●	●	●	●	●	●	●																					●	
Thailand	●	●		●	●	●	●	●	●	●	●	●	●	●	●							●												●				
Togo	●	●			●	●	●	●	●	●	●	●	●	●	●	●																					●	
Trinidad and Tobago	●	●	●		●	●	●			●	●	●	●	●	●	●			●									●										
Tunisia	●	●	●	●	●	●	●	●	●	●	●	●	●	●	●			●																			●	
Turkey	●	●	●	●	●	●	●	●	●	●	●	●	●	●	●	●	●													●		●	●					
Uganda	●	●		●	●	●	●	●	●	●	●	●	●	●	●	●																					●	
Ukraine	●			●		●					●	●	●	●	●																							
United Arab Republic	●	●	●	●	●	●	●	●	●	●	●	●	●	●	●			●																			●	
United Kingdom	●	●	●	●	●	●	●	●	●	●	●	●	●	●	●	●	●			●		●					●			●		●	●	●		●		●
United States	●	●	●	●	●	●	●	●	●	●	●	●	●	●	●	●			●			●						●		●	●		●	●		●		●
Upper Volta	●	●			●	●	●	●		●	●	●	●	●	●	●																					●	
Uruguay	●	●	●	●	●	●	●		●	●	●	●	●	●	●	●			●									●	●									
U.S.S.R.	●		●	●		●					●	●	●	●	●								●												●	●		
Vatican City				●							●		●																									
Venezuela	●	●		●	●	●	●		●	●	●	●	●	●	●				●									●	●									
Vietnam, South		●		●	●	●	●	●	●	●	●	●	●	●	●							●																
Western Samoa														●																								●
Yemen	●	●			●	●					●	●	●	●				●																				
Yugoslavia	●	●	●	●	●	●	●	●	●	●	●	●	●	●	●	●							●															
Zambia	●	●			●	●	●	●	●	●	●	●	●	●	●																						●	

KEY

UN **1** United Nations.
FAO **2** Food and Agriculture Organization of the United Nations.
IMCO **3** Intergovernmental Maritime Consultative Organization.
IAEA **4** International Atomic Energy Agency.
ICAO **5** International Civil Aviation Organization.
ILO **6** International Labour Organization.
IBRD **7** International Bank for Reconstruction and Development.
IDA **8** International Development Association.
IFC **9** International Finance Corporation.
IMF **10** International Monetary Fund.
ITU **11** International Telecommunication Union.
UNESCO **12** United Nations Educational, Scientific and Cultural Organization.
UPU **13** Universal Postal Union.
WHO **14** World Health Organization.
WMO **15** World Meteorological Organization.
GATT **16** General Agreement on Tariffs and Trade.
CE **17** Council of Europe.
AL **18** Arab League.
OAS **19** Organization of American States.
WEU **20** Western European Union.
OCAS **21** Organization of Central American States.
C-Plan **22** Colombo Plan for Co-operative Economic Development in South and South-East Asia.
Comecon **23** Council for Mutual Economic Assistance.
Euratom **24** European Atomic Energy Community.
ECSC **25** European Coal and Steel Community.
EEC **26** European Economic Community.
EFTA **27** European Free Trade Association.
IDB **28** Inter-American Development Bank.
LAFTA **29** Latin American Free Trade Association.
OECD **30** Organization for Economic Cooperation and Development.
ANZUS **31** Security treaty between Australia, New Zealand, and the United States.
CENTO **32** Central Treaty Organization.
NATO **33** North Atlantic Treaty Organization.
SEATO **34** Southeast Asia Treaty Organization.
WTO **35** Warsaw Treaty Organization.
36 Antarctic Treaty.
OAU **37** Organization of African Unity.
SPC **38** South Pacific Commission.

Investment, International

The main features of the international investment scene in 1968 and 1969 were the increased outflow of domestic capital from countries of the European Economic Community (EEC) and the increased inflow of foreign capital into the U.S., Japan, and Canada. The main forces at work were the underlying monetary conditions in various economies. Differences in interest rates and stock market conditions played a considerable role in influencing capital flows. The United States in an attempt to prevent its overall balance of payments position from further deterioration maintained curbs on international investment by U.S. companies. On the other hand, the West German authorities, embarrassed by a large current account surplus, maintained low interest rates and generally encouraged foreign investment.

It was becoming increasingly noticeable that many investors, particularly institutional investors, in many countries were showing a greater desire to build up their foreign portfolio holdings. This, added to the general growth in the international new issue market, was tending steadily to increase international portfolio investment.

United States. A major influence on international investment by U.S. corporations in 1968 and 1969 was the Foreign Direct Investment Program aimed at curbing the outflow of funds at a time when the nation's current account balance was deteriorating. Early in 1968, the curbs were tightened and made mandatory, which resulted in the increased use of reinvested earnings to finance investment and higher borrowing abroad by U.S. companies. The total rate of investment did not fall, but its effect on the U.S. balance of payments was eased.

The total value of U.S. foreign assets continued to increase, and the growth in value in 1968 of $7.2 billion was one of the largest in recent years. The total value amounted to $89 billion, of which 73% was accounted for by direct investments. (*See* Table I.)

Despite the various restrictions, the rate of direct investment rose in 1968 about 10% above 1967 to reach a level only fractionally below the 1966 record. (*See* Table II.) There was in 1968, however, a further decrease in the outflow of funds, and a much higher proportion than in previous years was financed by plowing back profits earned abroad. In the first half of 1969 there was a sharp increase in the outflow to a level 35% higher than a year earlier. In the second quarter of 1969 direct investment reached a level that had only been exceeded twice in the past—in the first quarter of 1965 and the third quarter of 1968.

A regional analysis of U.S. direct investments, given in Table IV, shows the importance of U.S. assets in Canada and Latin America, although the relative importance of European assets had risen steadily in recent years. In 1968 about one-quarter of U.S. direct investment was in Canada and a slightly larger proportion was in Europe. About two-thirds of the investment in 1968 was in industrial countries, compared with about 80% in 1967; this reflected the effect of the official curbs on investment abroad, which placed fewer restrictions on investment in less developed economies. Investment in Europe fell by $250 million in 1968 despite a $170 million increase in investment in the U.K. The flow of funds to West Germany, France, and, to a lesser extent, Italy fell back sharply. Investment in Canada (exempt from the restrictions) increased by $350 million, and there was a similar increase in investment in Latin America. Investment in Africa increased by $180 million, largely due to the development of petroleum facilities in Libya.

Manufacturing industries accounted for about 40% of U.S. international investment in 1968; the rate of investment was $2.2 billion, compared with $2.1 billion in 1967. The outflow of new funds was reduced from $1.3 billion to $1 billion with a rise in reinvested earnings from $800 million to $1.2 billion. Investment in Europe increased by $100 million to $1 billion with a particularly large increase in investment in the United Kingdom. The flow of funds to West Germany dropped sharply but was partly offset by higher reinvested earnings. Investment in manufacturing industries in Latin America increased by 50% with par-

Table I. U.S. Foreign Assets

In $000,000,000 at end of year

Item	1950	1960	1965	1966	1967	1968
Book value of direct investments	11.8	31.9	49.5	54.8	59.5	64.8
Portfolio investments*	5.7	12.5	21.5	21.0	22.2	24.1
Total	17.5	44.4	71.0	75.8	81.7	88.9

*Book value of foreign bonds and shares held by U.S. residents and U.S. banking claims.
Source: U.S. Department of Commerce, *Survey of Current Business*.

Table II. U.S. Investment Abroad

In $000,000

Item	1964	1965	1966	1967	1968	1st half 1969*
Direct investment						
New funds	2,416	3,418	3,543	3,154	3,025	4,058
Reinvested profits	1,431	1,542	1,739	1,555	2,245	...
Total	3,847	4,960	5,282	4,709	5,270	...
Portfolio investment	1,961	1,078	261	1,292	1,083	1,162
Total	5,808	6,038	5,741	6,001	6,353	...

*Seasonally adjusted; at annual rate.
Source: U.S. Department of Commerce, *Survey of Current Business*.

Table III. U.S. Investment Earnings

In $000,000

Item	1960	1965	1966	1967	1968	1st half 1969*
Direct investment						
Repatriated profits	2,355	3,963	4,045	4,518	4,985	5,450
Reinvested profits†	1,266	1,497	1,657	1,516	2,025	...
Total	3,621	5,460	5,702	6,034	7,010	...
Portfolio investment						
Total income	646	1,428	1,605	1,717	1,949	2,120
Total earnings	4,267	6,888	7,307	7,751	8,959	...

*Seasonally adjusted; at annual rate.
†Excluding interest but before deducting foreign withholding taxes.
Source: U.S. Department of Commerce, *Survey of Current Business*.

Table IV. U.S. Direct Investment and Earnings by Region, 1968

In $000,000

Area	Total value of assets at end of year	Net investment: Reinvested profits	Net investment: New funds	Net investment: Total	Earnings: Repatriated profits	Earnings: Total
Canada	19,488	797	594	1,391	849	1,478
Latin America	11,010	284	461	745	1,063	1,367
Other Western Hemisphere	1,979	89	111	200	169	219
EEC	8,992	123	425	548	438	540
United Kingdom	6,703	215	375	590	281	506
Other European countries	3,691	128	194	322	195	319
Africa	2,673	92	308	400	583	571
Asia	4,693	170	234	404	1,282	1,473
Oceania	2,821	137	164	301	85	208
International shipping	2,705	211	158	369	39	229
Total	64,756	2,245	3,025	5,270	4,985	7,010

Source: U.S. Department of Commerce, *Survey of Current Business*.

International Telecommunication Union:
see Telecommunications

Investment:
see Investment, International; Savings and Investment; Stock Exchanges

AUTHENTICATED NEWS INTERNATIONAL

Robert S. McNamara (right), president of the World Bank, and Muhammad Nassim Kochman (left), executive director of the World Bank for the Ivory Coast, visit oil palm plantation at Ehania, Ivory Coast. The World Bank loaned the Ivory Coast $17.1 million on June 13, 1969, to finance completion of the oil palm program.

ticularly large increases in Argentina, Brazil, Mexico, and Venezuela.

The petroleum industry accounted for a larger share of U.S. international investment in 1968 than in 1967, and all except about $200 million of the $1.4 billion investment was in the form of new capital flows. The expansion of refining and marketing facilities in Canada attracted $300 million of U.S. capital. After several years during which little or no new investment had taken place, the U.S. petroleum industry invested $200 million in Latin America, especially in Bolivia, Colombia, Ecuador, and Panama. Intensive development of offshore oil and natural gas resources increased investment by petroleum companies in the U.K. and the Netherlands.

Earnings of U.S. direct investments increased in 1968 by $1 billion to a record $7 billion. (*See* Table III.) The main factor causing this was the fairly rapid growth in economic activity in many countries where U.S. companies had assets. These improved trading conditions resulted in an increase in the rate of return on all investments from 11% to only a little less than 12%, thus almost reaching the rate that had prevailed throughout the early 1960s. Almost half the increase in earnings went toward increasing the level of repatriated profits and thus toward improving the balance of payments. Data for the first half of the year suggested that the increase in 1969 would be at least as great as in 1968.

The largest increase in earnings was on assets in Africa. About 70% of these earnings was accounted for by the petroleum industry, and most of the growth in 1968 reflected the very large increase in earnings from oil and gas production in Libya. Earnings in Canada continued to increase, with manufacturing industry contributing about half the total. Booming conditions for pulp and paper and larger exports of motor vehicles and their components increased the earnings of U.S. companies in Canada. In Latin America earnings recovered as the high level of investment in manufacturing began to yield productive results. European earnings increased, and the improved economic climate helped to offset the losses associated with gas and oil exploration in the North Sea.

Portfolio investment declined a little in 1968 from its high level of 1967. Purchases of newly issued foreign securities amounted to $1.7 billion in 1968, a little higher than in 1967, though redemptions of outstanding issues increased at a somewhat higher rate. Almost all the new issues were exempt from the interest equalization tax. New Canadian issues amounted to $1 billion and included the first Canadian government issue in the U.S. since 1963. Purchases of existing foreign securities (as opposed to new issues), which had amounted to only $100 million in the whole of 1968, increased sharply to $271 million in the second quarter of 1969. This was due partly to the reduction of the interest equalization tax in April and partly to the depressed state of U.S. stock markets. Earnings on portfolio investments increased quite sharply in 1968 and continued to rise rapidly during 1969.

United Kingdom. The value of British overseas investments at the end of 1969 was a little more than £15 billion, representing a considerable increase over the £8 billion value in 1962. About one-third of this increase was accounted for by the revaluation of existing assets, but the remainder, about £4.5 billion, represented new investments during those years. Investment was undertaken at particularly high levels in 1968 and 1969. Provisional estimates suggested that the rate of investment in 1969, at £630 million, was approximately £100 million below that in 1968, but even this level was 80% higher than the average for the years 1964–66.

The increase in investment in 1968 was divided almost equally between direct and portfolio investments, with investment by oil companies recording a sharp fall. (*See* Table V.) In 1969 direct investment continued to rise, not quite so rapidly as in the previous year, but enough to reach a record level of about £500 million. Portfolio investment, on the other hand, fell back sharply from the very high level reached in 1968, reflecting to a large extent the reduced purchases of shares in Australian companies.

Direct investment in 1968–69 was almost 70% higher than in 1966–67. To a certain extent this could be attributed to the devaluation of the pound sterling in 1967. (A given project overseas would cost more in terms of sterling than previously, and its sterling earnings would be correspondingly increased.) Also, this increase almost certainly reflected doubts about the future buoyancy of profitability of the domestic

Table V. U.K. Investment Abroad

In £000,000

Item	1960	1965	1966	1967	1968	1969*
Direct investment†						
New funds	165	141	93	91	135	n.a.
Reinvested profits	85	167	183	190	294	n.a.
Total	250	308	276	281	429	505
Portfolio investment‡	−37	−94	−82	52	218	50
Oil and miscellaneous	109	140	110	124	89	75
Total	322	354	304	457	736	630

n.a.—Not available.
*Estimate based on first half of year.
†Excluding oil and before 1963 insurance.
‡Net disinvestment in 1960, 1965, and 1966.
Sources: *U.K. Balance of Payments, 1969; Economic Trends.*

Table VI. U.K. Investment Earnings

In £000,000

Item	1960	1965	1966	1967	1968	1969*
Direct investment†						
Repatriated profits	173	233	246	248	287	n.a.
Reinvested profits	85	167	183	190	294	n.a.
Total	258	400	429	438	581	615
Portfolio investment	125	157	153	145	164	160
Oil and miscellaneous	286	467	412	436	428	540
Total	669	1,024	994	1,019	1,173	1,315

n.a.—Not available.
*Estimate based on first half of year.
†Excluding oil and before 1963 insurance.
Sources: *U.K. Balance of Payments, 1969; Economic Trends.*

economy and the increasingly international outlook of U.K. companies. As in previous years, about two-thirds of the new investment was financed by reinvesting profits, U.K. companies having been asked by the government to avoid financing investment in nonsterling-area countries in ways damaging to the current position of the U.K.

The latest available statistics of the regional pattern of U.K. investments are shown in Table VII. Direct investment was almost equally divided in 1967 and 1968 between the sterling and nonsterling areas, in contrast to the early 1960s when the sterling area received 60% or more of U.K. investment. This change was thought to reflect the greater buoyancy and profit potential and, in some cases, political stability of the nonsterling-area economies. The flow of investment to North America continued to increase, reaching a level three to four times that of the early 1960s. The negative figure for the European Free Trade Area (EFTA) in 1967 was due to a large reduction in assets in Portugal; in other countries investment continued at levels similar to those in previous years. In the sterling area, investment in both Australia and New Zealand was falling away from its peak level in 1963–64.

The proportion of U.K. overseas investment that was directed to less developed economies was 21–22% in 1966–68, somewhat below the figures for earlier years. In recent years only a small proportion of this amount was new funds, the bulk being reinvested profits. In 1966 and 1967, the latest years for which statistics were available, U.K. repatriated earnings from less developed economies exceeded U.K. investment by £38 million and £24 million, respectively, whereas in advanced countries investment exceeded repatriated earnings by £68 million and £57 million and by £160 million in 1968.

Portfolio investment declined to a more normal level in 1969 after the exceptionally large amount in 1968. A large part of the gain in 1968 was accounted for by increased investment in Australian company securities; there was also increased interest shown by British investors in other sterling-area companies, especially in South Africa. In the first half of 1969 the purchase of Australian securities was much reduced, and there were also considerable sales of nonsterling securities.

Earnings on U.K. investments rose considerably in both 1968 and 1969 although about half the increase in 1968 was due to the effect of devaluation. (*See* Table VI.) Earnings from direct investments increased by one-third between 1967 and 1968 and showed an additional small increase in 1969. Earnings on portfolio investments in 1969 were similar to 1968, but were well above those of earlier years. The pattern of earnings for oil and other investments was partly obscured by payments delayed from the latter part of 1968 to early 1969, but provisional figures suggested a definite increase. The regional pattern of earnings on U.K. direct investments showed little change from the previous years, with about 55% of the total coming from the sterling area. (*See* Table VII.) The proportion of earnings reinvested increased sharply to a little more than half in 1968, compared with 43% in previous years.

Other Industrial Nations. The main developments in other industrial nations in 1968 were the substantial increase in the outflow of long-term capital from EEC countries and the increased net inflows of foreign capital into Canada and Japan. In both cases portfolio investment changed more than direct investment since it is more sensitive to differentials in interest rates. (*See* Table VIII.)

Table VII. U.K. Direct Investment and Earnings by Region, 1965–68*

In £000,000

Area	Investment 1965	Investment 1966	Investment 1967	Investment 1968	Earnings 1965	Earnings 1966	Earnings 1967	Earnings 1968
North America	41	61	85	n.a.	85	108	113	n.a.
Latin America	18	11	8	n.a.	20	25	24	n.a.
EFTA	15	11	8	n.a.	8	8	10	n.a.
EEC	32	51	30	n.a.	19	25	25	n.a.
Other nonsterling areas†	16	23	24	n.a.	17	26	29	n.a.
Total nonsterling areas	122	157	139	214	149	192	201	266
India and Pakistan	20	3	12	n.a.	29	23	24	n.a.
Australia and New Zealand	67	57	52	n.a.	73	67	71	n.a.
South Africa	45	35	47	n.a.	57	60	65	n.a.
Other African states†	16	1	0	n.a.	30	25	22	n.a.
Other	38	23	31	n.a.	62	62	55	n.a.
Total sterling area	186	119	142	215	251	237	237	315
Total	308	276	281	429	400	429	438	581
Of which less developed countries (included above)	95	61	63	90				

n.a.—Not available.
*Excluding oil companies.
†Rhodesia is classified in the sterling area in 1965 and thereafter in the nonsterling area.
Sources: *U.K. Board of Trade Journal; U.K. Balance of Payments, 1969.*

Canada. The main feature of Canadian international investment in 1968 was the increase of $540 million in foreign portfolio investment in Canada. Canadian bonds issued overseas amounted to a little more than $1.4 billion, and there were small sales of existing Canadian bonds. Much of the increase in 1968 reflected increased Canadian borrowing in Europe. Canadian direct investment abroad increased sharply, and there was a slight reduction in foreign direct investment in Canada.

West Germany. The large surplus on current account increased domestic liquidity and kept interest rates low, thus encouraging West German investors to look abroad for outlets for their funds. In 1968, West German residents purchased $1.4 billion of foreign securities including $900 million of mark-denominated bonds issued by foreigners on West German capital markets. West German direct investment

Table VIII. Other Industrial Countries' International Investment, 1967–68

In $000,000

Country	1967 Direct	1967 Portfolio	1967 Total	1968 Direct	1968 Portfolio	1968 Total
Belgium						
Outflow	50	110	160	30	270	300
Inflow	230	60	290	230	−10	220
Net	−180	50	−130	−200	280	80
Canada						
Outflow	80	390	470	160	430	590
Inflow	570	850	1,420	540	1,390	1,930
Net	−490	−460	−950	−380	−960	−1,340
France						
Outflow	200	60	260	n.a.	n.a.	n.a.
Inflow	320	160	480	n.a.	n.a.	n.a.
Net	−120	−100	−220	n.a.	n.a.	600
West Germany						
Outflow	250	350	600	390	1,410	1,800
Inflow	700	−160	540	380	0	380
Net	−450	510	60	10	1,410	1,420
Italy						
Outflow	230	870	1,100	230	1,410	1,640
Inflow	260	60	320	330	50	380
Net	−30	810	780	−100	1,360	1,260
Japan						
Outflow	120	0	120	220	0	220
Inflow	50	60	110	80	350	430
Net	70	−60	10	140	−350	−210
Netherlands						
Outflow	210	40	250	220	270	490
Inflow	50	40	90	130	300	430
Net	160	0	160	90	−30	60

n.a.—Not available.
Source: OECD, *Economic Outlook*, No. 5, July 1969.

abroad increased quite considerably from $250 million to $390 million. There was also a marked reduction in foreign investment in West Germany.

Italy. In 1968 monetary policy was aimed at stimulating domestic demand. The resulting relatively low interest rates encouraged the outflow of capital from Italy, which helped to offset the large current account surplus. Italian direct investment abroad was unchanged in 1968, but portfolio investment increased by more than $500 million to $1.4 billion. At the same time, there was an increase in foreign direct investment in Italy.

Japan. The main features of Japanese international investment in 1968 were a sharp increase in Japanese direct investment and a very large rise in foreign portfolio investment in Japan. The latter partly reflected increased Japanese borrowing in European capital markets, where interest rates were not so high, but mostly resulted from increased foreign purchases of Japanese bonds because of their high yields and the booming condition of the nation's economy.

Netherlands. There were large increases in 1968 in both the inflow and outflow of portfolio capital. The increased outflow was principally due to Dutch purchases of U.S. securities. The increased foreign purchase of Dutch securities was chiefly accounted for by new issues in foreign markets. (A. G. A.)

See also Development, Economic; Payments and Reserves, International; Trade, International.

Iran

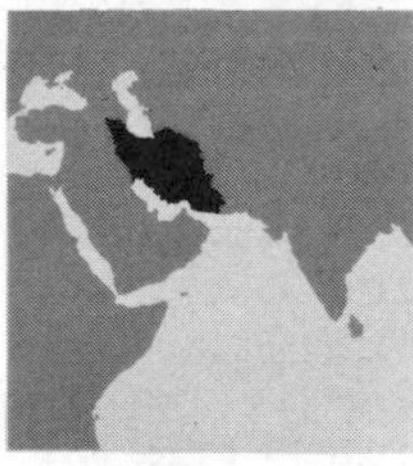

A constitutional monarchy of western Asia, Iran is bounded by the U.S.S.R., Afghanistan, Pakistan, Iraq, and Turkey and the Caspian Sea, the Arabian Sea, and the Persian Gulf. Area: 636,292 sq.mi. (1,648,000 sq.km.). Pop. (1969): 28,165,837. Cap. and largest city: Teheran (metro. pop., 1969 est., 2,980,041). Language: Farsi (Persian). Religion: Muslim; Christian, Jewish, and Zoroastrian minorities. Shah-in-shah, Mohammad Reza Pahlavi; prime minister in 1969, Amir Abbas Hoveida.

The growth rate of 10% that had marked the last year of the highly successful third five-year plan improved during the first year of the fourth plan, ending March 1969. The Plan Organization, a body directly responsible to the prime minister, continued to supervise the details of foreign aid and to approve particular projects. Among the more important of these was the establishment of Iran's first steel plant near Ahwaz, originally sponsored by a consortium of private investors and two financial corporations—an encouraging sign of the success of the government's policy of encouraging investment from the private sector—and later supported by the International Finance Corporation, the Bank of America, and five European groups. From the government side, participation came from the Plan Organization, Iran Insurance, and the Social Services Organization. The total investment involved was more than $18 million, and the plant's annual output was expected to be 140,000 tons of steel strip and 40,000 tons of pipe. In addition to such major projects, the fourth plan included the execution of separate development plans for each of the provinces, drawn up locally and approved by the Plan Organization, which was charged with giving priority to water supply, electric power, and communications.

The steady technical and industrial progress of Iran allowed the country to continue to occupy a key position in the Regional Cooperation for Development (RCD), in which Turkey and Pakistan also participated. The RCD made marked progress during 1968–69. In December 1968, the shah attended an RCD summit conference in Karachi along with Pres. Muhammad Ayub Khan of Pakistan and Prime Minister Suleyman Demirel of Turkey, in the course of which the reports of the ministerial and specialist meetings were reviewed, and the plans for future progress laid down. In order to strengthen cooperation in economic development among the three partners, it was agreed to implement the shah's suggestion for the establishment of a common market, which was approved in principle. Throughout 1969 satisfactory progress was made in tripartite cooperation in a number of fields, including banking, postal services, shipping, communications, tourism, and cultural exchanges. The new government of Pakistan that came into being in March showed itself as keenly interested as its predecessor in the promotion and extension of RCD, and in May Prime Minister Hoveida paid an official visit to Pakistan for a meeting of the RCD ministerial council, which Pakistani Pres. Agha Yahya Khan opened.

Iran continued to maintain friendly relations with the U.S.S.R. and other Communist countries, while its traditional friendship with the Western democracies remained unaffected. But while Iran took a full

IRAN

Education. (1966–67) Primary, pupils 2,411,505, teachers 75,502; secondary, pupils 636,819, teachers 21,771; vocational, pupils 15,956, teachers 1,159; teacher training, students 5,692, teachers 463; higher (including 8 universities), students 36,742, teaching staff 2,772.

Finance. Monetary unit: rial, with a par value of 75.75 rials to U.S. $1 (181.80 rials = £1 sterling). Gold and foreign exchange, central bank: (June 1969) U.S. $295 million; (June 1968) U.S. $310 million. Budget (1968–69) balanced at 274,579,000,000 rials. Money supply: (June 1969) 85,380,000,000 rials; (June 1968) 76,080,000,000 rials. Cost of living (1963 = 100): (June 1969) 112; (June 1968) 108.

Foreign Trade. (1968) Imports 105,030,000,000 rials; exports 142,370,000,000 rials. Import sources: West Germany 22%; U.S. 17%; U.K. 12%; Japan 9%; France 6%; Italy 6%. Export destinations: Japan 31%; U.K. 17%; India 6%; South Africa 5%. Main export crude oil 90%.

Transport and Communications. Roads (1967) *c.* 34,000 km. (including *c.* 20,000 km. all-weather). Motor vehicles in use (1967): passenger *c.* 164,200; commercial (including buses) *c.* 59,700. Railways: (1966) 3,569 km.; traffic (1967) 1,154,000,000 passenger-km., freight 1,884,000,000 net ton-km. Air traffic (1967): 387,779,000 passenger-km.; freight 3,774,000 net ton-km. Shipping (1968): merchant vessels 100 gross tons and over 37; gross tonnage 74,448. Telephones (Jan. 1968) 220,100. Radio receivers (Dec. 1967) 1,790,000. Television receivers (Dec. 1967) 131,000.

Agriculture. Production (in 000; metric tons; 1968; 1967 in parentheses): wheat *c.* 4,400 (*c.* 4,000); barley *c.* 1,160 (*c.* 1,020); cotton, lint *c.* 150 (*c.* 118); rice 957 (*c.* 954); sugar, raw value (1968–69) *c.* 445, (1967–68) *c.* 411; dates *c.* 281 (*c.* 281); grapes (1967) *c.* 260, (1966) *c.* 265; tobacco 18 (*c.* 22); tea (1967) *c.* 18, (1966) *c.* 18. Livestock (in 000; Oct. 1966): cattle *c.* 6,185; sheep *c.* 28,000; goats *c.* 18,200; asses (March 1968) *c.* 2,200.

Industry. Production (in 000; metric tons; 1967–68): coal *c.* 300; iron ore (metal content) *c.* 40; crude oil (1968) 140,521; lead concentrates (metal content; 1966–67) *c.* 20; chrome ore (oxide content; 1966–67) 67; cement (1967) 1,538; electricity (kw-hr.) 4,500,000.

part in UN activities, as exemplified in its interest in the Convention on Human Rights springing from the Teheran Declaration of April–May 1968 and support for the convention on outer space, there became apparent in 1969 a tendency for foreign policy to concentrate upon problems connected with Iran's geographic position in the Middle East. The success of RCD in the economic field led naturally to closer cooperation among the partners in the sphere of foreign policy; and although the attitude of Iran toward Israel and toward much of the Arab world differed from that of Pakistan, Iran gave support to Pakistan over the Kashmir question while Pakistan endorsed Iran's stand in its dispute with Iraq (*see* below). There was cautious exploration, possibly encouraged by Premier A. N. Kosygin of the U.S.S.R., of the prospects of enlarging RCD into a wider regional grouping to include India and Afghanistan, but the difficulties were formidable, and the offer that the shah made in the course of his visit to India in January to use his good offices to create a détente between that country and Pakistan, although welcomed by Pakistan, elicited little response from India. But a beginning was made to economic cooperation between Iran and India; a joint commission set up for this purpose held its inaugural meeting in Teheran in June.

The anxieties felt by Iran over the plans—encouraged by Iraq—of the Trucial States along the Persian Gulf to federate in preparation for Britain's withdrawal from them in 1971 were overshadowed in 1969 by a bitter dispute with Iraq over navigational rights on the Shatt al Arab. Iran, asserting that Iraq had consistently violated the treaty of 1937 that partitioned those rights, denounced it in April and claimed that the boundary with Iraq should follow a median line on the stream. Iraq then expelled large numbers of Iranians living in Iraqi territory, border clashes occurred, and relations continued strained throughout the remainder of the year. (L. F. R. W.)

ENCYCLOPÆDIA BRITANNICA FILMS. *The Middle East* (1955); *The Mediterranean World* (1961).

Iraq

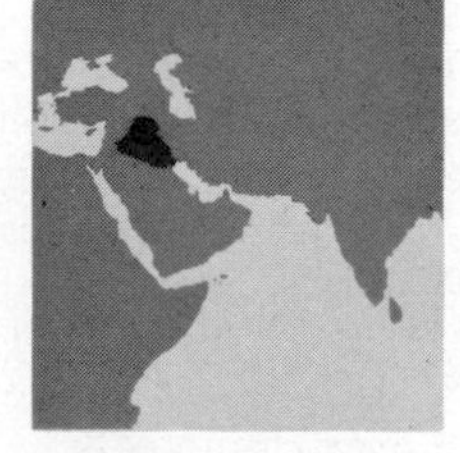

A republic of western Asia, Iraq is bounded by Turkey, Iran, Kuwait, Saudi Arabia, Jordan, Syria, and the Persian Gulf. Area: 169,284 sq.mi. (438,446 sq.km.). Pop. (1969 est.): 8,765,915, including Arabs, Kurds, Turks, Assyrians, Iranians, and others. Cap. and largest city: Baghdad (metro. pop., 1968 est., 1,884,151). Language: Arabic. Religion: mainly Muslim, some Christian. President and (until November) prime minister in 1969, Gen. Ahmed Hassan al-Bakr.

In 1969 the Baathist regime of President al-Bakr remained in power despite growing opposition and the prospect of renewed hostilities with the Kurdish minority. In July the president admitted that the Baath Party's efforts to obtain the collaboration of nationalists and progressives had failed "for reasons which concern them."

The government was at all times concerned with protecting its position by maintaining Baathists in key posts. Since the Baathist coup in July 1968 the post of commander in chief of the Air Force had remained vacant. On July 29 the appointment to the post of Col. Hussein Halawi was announced. The position of prime minister was abolished by constitutional amendment in November.

On January 27 there were strong international reactions to the public execution of 14 Iraqis, including 9 Jews, accused of spying for Israel. There were 31 additional executions during the year. Israel used every means to mobilize world opinion against Iraq, and the U.S. Department of State expressed the hope that the "bloodbath" would cease.

On February 4 President al-Bakr announced that his government had put into effect most provisions of the so-called June 29, 1966, statement proposing a solution to the Kurdish problem. There were, however, increasing reports of clashes between Iraqi regular forces and Kurdish partisan followers of Mustafa al-Barzani. The government announced that it was sending technical commissions to northern Iraq to carry out a scheme sponsored by the UN Food and Agriculture Organization for reconstruction in the Kurdish areas.

The Iraqi Baath Party held a ten-day conference in Baghdad in February that recommended a "scientific reform" of the government to eliminate corruption, called for the full implementation of the 1966 statement on the Kurds, and stressed the need of preserving the Arab character of the Persian Gulf. Wherever possible the government emphasized nationalism.

Relations with the left-wing Baathist regime in Syria were cool. Damascus Radio referred to the Iraqi rulers as a "criminal gang" and accused them of savage persecution of genuine Baathists. The two governments also exchanged accusations that the other was persecuting the Palestinian guerrillas. Despite this, military cooperation between the two countries was extended and in July a Syrian-Iraqi defense pact was signed. In May a new Iraqi draft law was announced, setting the minimum age at 19 with 23 months' service, to be modified according to educational qualifications. In April the government entered into an acrimonious dispute with Iran following the latter's denunciation

IRAQ

Education. (1965–66) Primary, pupils 964,327, teachers 42,878; secondary, pupils 241,065, teachers 6,935; vocational, students 7,626, teachers 729; teacher training, students 5,760, teachers 328; higher (including 4 universities), students 28,410, teaching staff 1,002.

Finance. Monetary unit: Iraqi dinar, with a par value of 0.36 dinars to U.S. $1 (0.86 dinars = £1 sterling). Gold and foreign exchange, central bank: (June 1969) U.S. $431.5 million; (June 1968) U.S. $432.6 million. Budget (1967–68 est.): revenue 337 million dinars; expenditure 424 million dinars. Money supply: (Dec. 1968) 176.5 million dinars; (Dec. 1967) 163.9 million dinars. Cost of living (Baghdad; 1963 = 100): (March 1969) 113; (March 1968) 104.

Foreign Trade. (1968) Imports 144.2 million dinars; exports 372.6 million dinars. Import sources (1967): U.K. 13%; West Germany 10%; U.S. 9%; U.S.S.R. 8%; Japan 6%; Italy 5%. Export destinations (1967): France 24%; Italy 14%; Netherlands 8%; Spain 6%; U.K. 5%. Main export crude oil 93%.

Transport and Communications. Roads (1968) 17,893 km. (including 4,271 km. main roads). Motor vehicles in use (1968): passenger 75,800; commercial 46,500. Railways: (1965) 1,635 km.; traffic (1965–66) 444 million passenger-km., freight 1,009,000,000 net ton-km. Air traffic (1968): 124,080,000 passenger-km.; freight 1,464,000 net ton-km. Telephones (Jan. 1968) *c.* 77,500. Radio receivers (Dec. 1966) *c.* 1 million. Television receivers (Dec. 1966) 180,000.

Agriculture. Production (in 000; metric tons; 1968; 1967 in parentheses): wheat 1,359 (866); barley 931 (860); rice 325 (308); dates (1967) *c.* 265, (1966) 380; oranges (1966) *c.* 44, (1965) *c.* 45; sesame 12 (12); linseed 12 (13); cotton, lint (1967) 12, (1966) 11; tobacco *c.* 14 (14). Livestock (in 000; 1967–68): sheep 11,040; cattle 1,455; horses 122; asses 542; goats *c.* 1,845.

Industry. Production (in 000): crude oil (metric tons; 1968) 73,848; electricity (excluding most industrial production; kw-hr.; 1967) 1,431,000.

UPI COMPIX

Bodies of two Iraqi Jews (top) hang in public square in Baghdad, Jan. 27, 1969, after execution of 14 persons charged with spying for Israel. Jews in Rome (above) protest the executions.

of the 1937 treaty governing the use of the Shatt al Arab waterway. Iran accused Iraq of expelling Iranian citizens resident in Iraq.

In March the minister of planning, Jawad Hashem, announced a new five-year economic and social plan at a cost of 973 million dinars. The government banned the employment of foreign consultants by Iraqi firms except in cases of extreme necessity. In early July the deputy prime minister, Gen. Saleh Mahdi Ammash, visited Moscow with a delegation and announced on his return a $72 million Soviet-Iraqi agreement to provide oil equipment and to develop the North Rumaylah oil field in southern Iraq. Other agreements with the U.S.S.R. covered the building of a series of dams, an iron and steel mill, and development of natural gas resources in Iraq. In July it was announced that East Germany, which Iraq had been the first Arab country to recognize, was providing $96 million on easy terms for large industrial projects in Iraq. As a reaction to Romania's raising its diplomatic representative in Israel to the rank of ambassador, Iraq withdrew its chargé d'affaires from Bucharest in August, declaring Romania's action to be "an arrogant defiance of the rights of the Palestinian people."

General Ammash visited Cairo in August with a delegation to coordinate military policy with the U.A.R. and again in early September to attend the "little summit" meeting of Sudan, Syria, Iraq, the U.A.R., and Jordan. From Cairo he went on to Libya to congratulate the new regime there that had just overthrown the monarchy. Iraq participated in the Arab summit held in December in Rabat, Mor., where it was among the "progressive" states voicing criticism of the rich, oil-producing countries for failing to provide more support for the Arab cause.

On August 30 the government ordered 15,000 Iraqis vacationing in Lebanon to return to their country in 24 hours because certain Lebanese newspapers had been continually attacking the Iraqi regime. The measure was rescinded a month later "in the interests of inter-Arab friendship." (P. Md.)

Encyclopædia Britannica Films. *The Middle East* (1955).

Ireland

Separated from Great Britain by the North Channel, the Irish Sea, and St. George's Channel, the Republic of Ireland shares its island with Northern Ireland to the northeast. Area: 27,136 sq.mi. (70,283 sq.km.), or 83% of the island. Pop. (1969): 2,921,000. Cap. and largest city: Dublin (pop., 1967, 568,772). Language: English (80%) and Gaelic. Religion: predominantly Roman Catholic (95%). President in 1969, Eamon de Valera; prime minister, John Lynch.

The Dail, which celebrated its 50th anniversary in January, was dissolved by the president on May 21, and a general election was called for June 18. This followed prolonged speculation and preparation by the two opposition parties, Fine Gael and the Labour Party, and defeat for the government party, Fianna Fail, after 12 years in office, was widely predicted. The election was fought in constituencies redrawn as a result of the 1968 defeat of the government referendum on proportional representation. The unwillingness of the Labour Party to make any kind of preelection coalition agreement with Fine Gael effectively eliminated the electorate's belief in the possibility of a strong, united alternative to the ruling party, and was the main factor contributing to Fianna Fail's reelection.

The outgoing Dail consisted of 74 Fianna Fail deputies, 46 Fine Gael deputies, 18 Labour deputies, and 3 Independents, with 3 seats vacant. The June election returned to the house 75 Fianna Fail deputies, 50 Fine Gael, and 18 Labour. Frank Aiken, deputy prime minister and minister for external affairs, left the Cabinet and became a backbencher. As de Valera's right-hand man through much of the period of Fianna Fail rule, Aiken was the last representative within the government of the old civil war tradition.

Among the successful Labour Party candidates were Conor Cruise O'Brien and a number of young members who brought to the party a more radical, left-wing image. This gained support in the urban centres, particularly Dublin, but lost the party much of its backing in the rural areas. For Prime Minister Lynch his first general election was a personal triumph, with victory coming at a time of party unpopularity and almost a year before an election was constitutionally obligatory.

The other dominant issues were the situation in Northern Ireland and the republic's economic problems, particularly the sharp upward trends in prices and wages. Following the prolonged troubles in Northern Ireland, which culminated in the rioting in Belfast in early August, Prime Minister Lynch called for a UN force in the province and for early talks on the constitutional position of the Ulster government. Army reserves were called up, field hospitals were established along the border with Northern Ireland, and camps for refugees from Belfast and other trouble spots were opened. The suggestion of UN intervention was rejected by both the British and the Ulster governments, but the minister for external affairs, Patrick J. Hillery, continued to press for a Security Council discussion of the problem.

The subsequent meeting of the Security Council was adjourned without having reached any decision on the Irish request for a peace-keeping force. Although the Irish position received considerable sympathy, the matter was not placed on the agenda. The prime minister stressed his condemnation of the use of force as a solution to the Irish border division, but made it clear that the republic regarded the troubles in Northern Ireland as its direct concern and not as a purely internal matter for the U.K. He also raised the question of a federal structure as a possible long-term solution of the Irish question. In spite of outspoken fears in Northern Ireland and threats in the republic, little serious activity by the Irish Republican Army was apparent. The prime minister declared that the government would not see its power usurped by any other organization. There were, however, charges that extremist Protestant organizations in Northern Ireland had made attacks on the Dublin television station, the Wolfe Tone memorial outside the city, and a power station in the northwest, all of which were damaged by explosions. (*See* UNITED KINGDOM.)

The economy suffered from continued inflation and from one of the worst strikes in the republic's history. The strike by maintenance workers, which lasted from January to March, brought large sections of industry to a halt, caused shortages of food and other essentials, seriously reduced exports, and gravely damaged industrial relations. The dispute revealed serious weaknesses within the organizations representing both management and labour and the 20% wage increase finally granted to the workers was well in excess of what economic growth could allow. Building workers received a comparable increase, and these two awards were likely to establish the basis for future pay negotiations. During 1969 prices rose more than 8%, and this was coupled with an adverse balance of payments, aggravated by the maintenance stoppage. Charles Haughey, minister for finance, warned of the dangers to the economy, but his preelection budget was a mild one, with a strong emphasis on social welfare and benefits for lower-paid workers. In the autumn he again warned of trends damaging to the future of the economy, and said that the tendency toward wage awards higher than could be met by national growth would be reflected in tougher measures in the 1970 budget.

In his 1969 budget, the minister released artists from payment of income tax on earnings from creative work; toward the end of the year the first foreign painter (from Spain) settled in Dublin in order to make use of the concession. The Dublin Theatre Festival was a failure, however, and the censorship controversy continued at the Cork Film Festival. The minister gave a generous grant to the Gate Theatre and, after a long absence, Hilton Edwards and Micheal Mac Liammoir, two of the major figures in 20th-century Irish theatre, returned to manage it. The proposal to merge Trinity College and University College was dropped in favour of other, more pressing, educational reforms. (B. AR.)

ENCYCLOPÆDIA BRITANNICA FILMS. *British Isles—The Land and the People* (1962).

IRELAND

Education. (1965–66) Primary, pupils 506,129, teachers 14,614; secondary, pupils 98,667, teachers 6,795; vocational, pupils 105,742, teachers 4,626; teacher training, students 1,736; higher, students 21,280, teaching staff (1962–63) 1,208.

Finance. Monetary unit: Irish pound, at par with the pound sterling (U.S. $2.40 = £1). Gold and foreign exchange, official: (May 1969) U.S. $488 million; (May 1968) U.S. $356 million. Budget (1968 69 est.) balanced at £332,690,000. Gross national product: (1968) £1,243 million; (1967) £1,126 million. Money supply: (May 1969) £353.2 million; (May 1968) £330.7 million. Cost of living (1963 = 100): (May 1969) 133; (May 1968) 125.

Foreign Trade. (1968) Imports £489.5 million; exports £332.5 million. Import sources: U.K. 51%; U.S. 7%; West Germany 7%. Export destinations: U.K. 69%; U.S. 10%. Main exports: meat 18%; livestock 17%; textiles and clothing 9%; dairy produce 7%; machinery 6%. Tourism (1967): visitors 1,812,000; gross receipts U.S. $194.4 million.

Transport and Communications. Roads (1966) 52,987 km. Motor vehicles in use (1967): passenger 314,434; commercial 45,575. Railways: (1967) 2,146 km.; traffic (1968) 524 million passenger-km., freight 470 million net ton-km. Air traffic (1968): 1,293,100,000 passenger-km.; freight 38,845,000 net ton-km. Shipping (1968): merchant vessels 100 gross tons and over 89; gross tonnage 172,582. Telephones (Dec. 1967) 253,446. Radio receivers (Dec. 1966) 816,000. Television receivers (March 1967) 308,000.

Agriculture. Production (in 000; metric tons; 1968; 1967 in parentheses): oats *c.* 271 (294); barley 740 (677); wheat 406 (293); potatoes 1,625 (1,748); sugar, raw value (1968–69) *c.* 167, (1967–68) 144; milk *c.* 3,726 (3,471); butter 78 (73); cheese 23 (25); meat (1967) 539, (1966) 473; fish catch (1967) 50, (1966) 40. Livestock (in 000; June 1968): cattle 5,546; sheep (June 1967) 4,239; horses 135; pigs 1,055; poultry (June 1967) 10,593.

Industry. Index of industrial production (excluding power; 1963 = 100): (1968) 143; (1967) 128. Unemployment: (1968) 6.7%; (1967) 6.7%. Production (in 000; metric tons; 1968): coal 172; cement 1,246; electricity (excluding most industrial production; kw-hr.) 4,543,000; manufactured gas (cu.m.) 186,000; beer (hl.; 1966–67) 3,481; woolen fabrics (sq.m.) 7,900; rayon and acetate fabrics (sq.m.) 8,500.

Israel

A republic of the Middle East, Israel is bounded by Lebanon, Syria, Jordan, the U.A.R., and the Mediterranean Sea. Area (not including territory occupied in the June 1967 war): 7,993 sq.mi. (20,700 sq.km.). Pop. (1969 est.): 2,841,100. Cap.: Jerusalem (pop., 1969 est., 269,100). Largest city: Tel Aviv-Jaffa (pop., 1969 est., 384,070). Language: Hebrew and Arabic. Religion: predominantly Jewish. President in 1969, Schneor Zalman Shazar; prime ministers, Levi Eshkol to February 26, Yigal Allon (interim), and, from March 17, Mrs. Golda Meir.

Although it was not always immediately apparent, 1969 was a year of considerable adjustment and profound change. Familiar figures had passed from the political scene, a reevaluation of national leaders was under way, an almost unperceived industrial revolution had changed the economic base of the country, and a regrouping of political parties produced a greatly simplified electoral alignment in the October general election.

In late 1968 the familiar tensions were relieved by faint rays of hope. Defense Minister Moshe Dayan's occupation policy combined firmness in the face of terrorism with moderation and tolerance where life continued undisturbed. The "open bridges" policy, which allowed Arab citizens of the occupied territories to travel in Jordan and other Arab countries and return home, was maintained; it also permitted visits from over 20,000 Arab citizens of other countries to

Ireland, Northern: *see* United Kingdom
Iron and Steel: *see* Industrial Review; Mining
Islam: *see* Religion

GAMMA—PIX FROM PUBLIX

Young Israelis celebrate the 21st anniversary of the state of Israel at a rock concert in Jerusalem. Because of political tension the celebration was nonmilitary.

Jerusalem supermarket shattered by an Arab terrorist's bomb on Feb. 21, 1969. Two persons were killed and nine injured in the explosion.

KEYSTONE

the occupied areas of the west bank and a relatively free exchange of goods and produce across the frontier with Jordan.

In the last days of 1968, there was a sudden increase in tension. First, on December 26, two members of the Popular Front for the Liberation of Palestine (the PFLP) attacked a Boeing 707 belonging to El Al, the Israeli airline, as it was about to take off from Athens. On the following day the U.S. Department of State announced that Pres. Lyndon B. Johnson had approved the sale of 50 Phantom F-4 interceptors and strike-bombers to the Israeli government. On December 28, an Israeli helicopter commando force raided Beirut airport, in Lebanon, and destroyed 13 airliners belonging to the Middle East and other airlines.

The UN Security Council condemned the raid and French Pres. Charles de Gaulle ordered a total embargo on all war equipment and strategic goods that the Israeli government had bought or intended to buy in France. After exchanges with Moscow, the French government proposed four-power consultations on the Middle East between France, the U.K., the U.S.S.R., and the U.S. On February 18, a second attack on an El Al airliner, this time at Kloten Airport in Zürich, Switz., resulted in the deaths of an Israeli pilot and an Arab nationalist.

Meanwhile the prime minister, Levi Eshkol, who had been ill, suffered another heart attack and died on February 26. Mrs. Golda Meir emerged as Israel's most powerful party politician (*see* BIOGRAPHY), and on March 17 she was sworn in as prime minister.

Mrs. Meir's assumption of office was reflected in the sharper tone of Israel's policy declarations. On March 17 she "rejected" the concept of great power mediation as reflected in the four-power talks. On April 10 she dismissed six peace proposals made by King Husain of Jordan in Washington as "not genuine," since they were starkly at variance with answers given at the same time by the Jordanian and U.A.R. governments to questions put to them by Gunnar Jarring, the UN mediator.

In June, Mrs. Meir went to the U.K. for talks in London with Prime Minister Harold Wilson and for the Congress of the Socialist International in Eastbourne, which was also attended by U.A.R. and Lebanese observers. Mrs. Meir had a much more fruitful journey to the U.S. at the end of September and early October, when the U.S. reiterated its insistence on a peace settlement prior to any Israeli withdrawal.

This was reassuring to the Israelis after earlier doubt about the policy of the Nixon administration. There was now also a distinct hardening of the situation on the borders as the prospect of an early settlement faded. This showed itself in increasing Israeli casualties, the majority of which were due to the mounting conflict along the Suez Canal. Following the first U.A.R. massed-artillery attack on the Israeli canal positions in October 1968, the Israeli fortification system had been substantially developed and modernized. When the U.A.R. assaults resumed in the early spring, the Israelis were able to keep the front positions with less than 7,000 troops confronting ten times their number.

In September, the Israelis began to fly almost daily sorties against U.A.R. canal fortifications. Israeli commandos also attacked positions and on September 9 stayed for ten hours in the area between El Hafayir and Ras Zafarana. By the end of October, Dayan expressed his satisfaction that the U.A.R. forces had been effectively contained and that the Israelis had destroyed virtually all their local Soviet-constructed missile launchers.

These pressures on the country helped to produce a broad consensus of political solidarity in the preparations for the general election on October 28. The Labour Front was consolidated into a United Labour Party made up of the Mapai, Ahdut Avoda, and Rafi parties, with which the leftist party, Mapam, was electorally aligned. As a result, the election was fought in effect between three major groups—Labour, which took 56 of the 120 seats in the Knesset (63 in 1965),

ISRAEL

Education. (1966–67) Primary, pupils 450,359, teachers 23,729; secondary, pupils 71,401, teachers 6,694; vocational, pupils 42,730, teachers 4,274; teacher training, students 4,408, teachers 411; higher (including 4 universities), students 39,126, teaching staff 5,-227.

Finance. Monetary unit: Israeli pound, with a par value of I£3.5 to U.S. $1 (I£8.40 = £1 sterling). Gold and foreign exchange, central bank: (June 1969) U.S. $542.5 million; (June 1968) U.S. $744.6 million. Budget (1968–69 est.) balanced at I£5,898 million. Gross national product: (1967) I£12,171 million; (1966) I£11,773 million. Money supply: (May 1969) I£3,047 million; (May 1968) I£2,824 million. Cost of living (1963 = 100): (May 1969) 130; (May 1968) 128.

Foreign Trade. (1968) Imports I£3,783.5 million; exports I£2,240.7 million. Import sources: U.S. 31%; U.K. 27%; West Germany 14%; Italy 7%; France 7%; Netherlands 6%. Export destinations: U.S. 19%; U.K. 11%; West Germany 9%; Belgium-Luxembourg 6%; Netherlands 5%; France 5%; Switzerland 5%. Main exports: diamonds 34%; oranges 10%; chemicals 9%; textile yarns and fabrics 5%; clothing 5%.

Transport and Communications. Roads (1968) 9,110 km. (including 1,689 km. main roads). Motor vehicles in use (1968): passenger 114,472; commercial 50,900. Railways: (1967) 746 km.; traffic (1968) 349 million passenger-km., freight 383 million net ton-km. Air traffic (1967): 1,531,656,000 passenger-km.; freight 48,113,000 net ton-km. Shipping (1968): merchant vessels 100 gross tons and over 111; gross tonnage 722,951. Telephones (Dec. 1967) 344,487. Radio receivers (Dec. 1967) 774,000. Television receivers (Dec. 1967) 26,000.

Agriculture. Production (in 000; metric tons; 1968; 1967 in parentheses): oranges 965 (812); grapefruit 220 (226); grapes (1967) 82, (1966) 76; wheat (1967) 222, (1966) 101; sorghum (1967) 24, (1966) 13; potatoes (1967) 93, (1966) 104; cotton, lint *c.* 33 (29); tomatoes (1967) 115, (1966) 112; olives (1967) *c.* 16, (1966) 25; bananas (1967) 51, (1966) 54; fish catch (1967) 22, (1966) 24. Livestock (in 000; Dec. 1967): cattle 225; sheep and goats 344; poultry 6,950.

Industry. Index of production (1963 = 100): (1968) 159; (1967) 123. Production (in 000; metric tons; 1968): cement 1,106; electricity (kw-hr.) 5,508,-000; salt (1967) 57; potash (oxide content; 1967–68) 300. New dwelling units completed (1968) 22,200.

BEN ROTH AGENCY

"Oh be careful. . . .it's so dangerous!!"—Behrendt, "Het Parool," Amsterdam.

the conservative Gahal Party, which took 26 (22), and the religious bloc, which took 18 (17). Eight other parties held the 20 remaining seats.

The results indicated a slight shift to the right in the national elections, a greater emphasis on independents in the municipal voting, and an impressive turnout of Arab voters in Jerusalem and elsewhere on the west bank, despite warnings and urgings against participation from the fedayeen (guerrillas) and the Jordanian government. Those voting represented 82% of the electorate, as against 83% in the previous and hotly contested election of 1965. Neither of the extreme groups, calling for either a peace settlement by surrender of all occupied territory or for retention of all occupied territory, received enough votes to qualify for a Knesset seat. Mrs. Meir's new Cabinet, presented to the Knesset on December 15, was younger than its predecessor but contained few surprises: Dayan, Deputy Prime Minister Yigal Allon, and Foreign Minister Abba Eban retained their posts.

While there was a broad national consensus on foreign and security policy, the new government faced a serious economic situation that required stringent control measures. One reason for the problem was the remarkable industrial transformation that had taken place since France had imposed its embargo on Israel two years before. A crash program to develop a self-sufficient aircraft and electronics industry that could meet Israel's principal defense requirements was strikingly successful and, by October 1969, was employing over 10,000 skilled men.

This had called for exceptional expenditure and imports, and had produced in 1969 a balance of payments deficit of $800 million and a drop in Israel's foreign currency reserves from $1 billion in August 1967 to $500 million in October 1969. The defense budget amounted to $829 million, $201 million more than in the previous year. This was more than 16% of the gross national product (GNP) at market prices, proportionally the highest national defense expenditure in the world. In an address to the Knesset on December 29, Mrs. Meir warned that even more economic sacrifice might be in the offing. Speaking of the U.S. peace proposals made earlier in the month, which she saw as a "grave danger to our security," she indicated that Israel must prepare to face a prolonged struggle on its own. Of the U.S. proposals, Israel took particular exception to those calling for withdrawal from the occupied territories, joint Israeli–Jordanian administration of Jerusalem, and repatriation of all Palestinian refugees choosing to return—a plan that, to Israelis, raised the spectre of an Arab fifth column and threatened the integrity of the Israeli state itself. Meanwhile, a boost was given to Israeli morale when five gunboats built in France for Israel but impounded because of the French arms embargo slipped out of Cherbourg Harbour on December 25 and arrived in Haifa on December 31. (J. K.)

ENCYCLOPÆDIA BRITANNICA FILMS. *Major Religions of the World (Development and Rituals)* (1954); *The Middle East* (1955); *Planning Our Foreign Policy (Problems of the Middle East)* (1955); *The Mediterranean World* (1961).

Italy

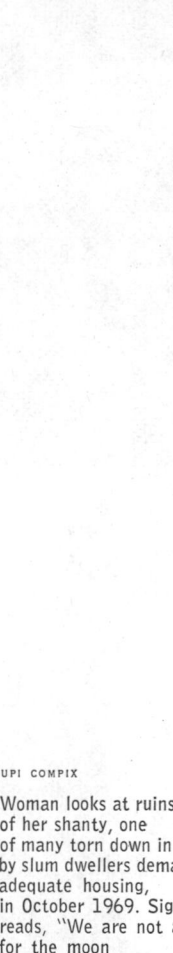

A republic of southern Europe, Italy occupies the Apennine Peninsula, Sicily, Sardinia, and a number of smaller islands. On the north it borders France, Switzerland, Austria, and Yugoslavia. Area: 116,316 sq.mi. (301,257 sq.km.). Pop. (1969 est.): 54,089,530. Cap. and largest city: Rome (pop., 1969 est., 2,707,159). Language: Italian. Religion: predominantly Roman Catholic. President in 1969, Giuseppe Saragat; premier, Mariano Rumor.

Domestic Affairs. In July 1969 the centre-left coalition, which had governed Italy since 1963, came to an end because of a schism within the Socialist Party, which was the major partner of the coalition. Contrary to the 1966 charter uniting the Socialist left- and right-wing factions, Deputy Premier Francesco de Martino and his left-wing group campaigned for cooperation with the Communist Party, contending that Socialist losses and Communist gains in the 1968 elections were due to the party's moderate course and that continued political boycott was no longer realistic. As a last minute effort to avoid the split, the party president and foreign minister, Pietro Nenni, submitted to the Socialist Party Central Committee a compromise motion calling for the reaffirmation of the principles of the unification charter. When the motion was rejected on July 4, Nenni resigned his post and the right-wing faction, together with many former Social Democrats, formed the Unitarian Socialist Party on July 5.

Unable to guarantee the support of their party, three Socialist ministers resigned, forcing Rumor (*see* BIOGRAPHY) to offer his own resignation to President Saragat. Whereas the Christian Democrats and So-

UPI COMPIX

Woman looks at ruins of her shanty, one of many torn down in Rome by slum dwellers demanding adequate housing, in October 1969. Sign reads, "We are not asking for the moon but for decent housing at a fair price."

Italian Literature: *see* Literature

ROMA PRESS—PIX FROM PUBLIX

Left-wing students protest U.S. Pres. Richard Nixon's visit to Rome in February 1969. Police clashed with crowd of 5,000.

cialists were prepared to enter a new coalition agreement, both the Unitarian Socialist Party and the Republican Party declined, worsening Rumor's chances of forming a new Cabinet. It took exactly a month, until August 5, for Rumor to solve this crisis. The end result was a one-party Christian Democratic government that expressed unconditional faith in the centre-left policy, and could therefore count on the support of the Socialists and the Unitarian Socialists and on the voting abstention of the Republican Party.

The minority government was clearly destined to feel every rocking of the Italian political boat. This was proved later in the year, when workers' unrest, especially in Turin, Milan, and other industrial cities of the north, showed up the government's inability to deal effectively with disorder. The country was repeatedly paralyzed by strikes and random 24- and 48-hour stoppages, and the disorders culminated in December when 14 persons were killed and about 100 injured in bombings in Rome and Milan, allegedly perpetrated by a group of young students and workers. The government was able, however, to warrant its acceptance by the two chambers and to survive all parliamentary obstacles, although not without straining the limits of compromise.

Local elections were held on June 8 in the provinces of Bolzano and Trento, where for the first time in years a relative peace was achieved between the Italian- and German-speaking populations (*see* below). The Christian Democrats gained 33.4% of the votes (a vast improvement over the 23.3% achieved in the previous local elections), whereas the Socialists got only 15% (previously 18%), and the Communists improved slightly from 6.8 to 7.1%. The Popular South Tyrol Party held its strong position, collecting 26.4% of the votes. Elections held on June 15–16 in Sardinia for the renewal of the regional council showed a general decline of the centre-left parties: the Christian Democrats, Socialists, and Republicans had 44.6, 11.9, and 3% of the votes, as compared with the previous figures of 43.4, 12.1, and 6.4%. The Communists also lost some ground: from 20.5 to 19.7%. Right-wing parties, however, had a slight improvement.

Two new bills were laid before Parliament on June 20. The first dealt with a complete review and reform of existing taxation laws to reduce the great number of taxable items and simplify fiscal procedures in accordance with similar steps taken in other countries of the European Economic Community. The second bill granted more incisive powers to unions in industry and made it unlawful to discriminate against workers with a record of union, political, or religious activity.

Foreign Affairs. Intense international activity followed an incident in May 1969 in which 10 Italian oilmen were killed and 14 taken prisoner by Biafran forces. On the night of May 9, the 24 Italians, 3 Germans, 1 Lebanese, and 1 Jordanian, all employees of the Italian state petroleum consortium (ENI), were attacked by surprise at their camp near Kwale, Nigeria, by troops of the secessionist state of Biafra. Diplomatic channels were opened to rescue the prisoners, who were sentenced to death by a special Biafran tribunal. The direct intervention of Pope Paul VI and Presidents Albert Bongo of Gabon and Félix Houphouët-Boigny of the Ivory Coast prevented the sentences from being carried out and, after a series of talks, the oilmen were reprieved and set free.

Foreign Undersecretary Mario Pedini flew to Biafra to meet the men in response to a personal decision of Foreign Minister Nenni, who declared at the time that he was well aware that such a move meant de facto political acceptance of the Biafran government. Formal recognition by Rome, however, continued to be denied. Two months after the incident the Italian government seemed ready to resume sending famine relief to the region. A communiqué released on August 25 invited all organizations dealing in this matter to expedite the shipment of food and medicines.

The Italian government reaffirmed its belief in the necessity of a united Europe capable of contributing to the process of détente already started by the great powers. Both Nenni and his successor, former Premier Aldo Moro, declared their desire for a dialogue with Eastern European countries and for the necessity of armaments control as specified at the June 1968 NATO meeting in Reykjavik, Ice., before the Soviet invasion of Czechoslovakia. Moro renewed Italy's pledge to NATO, that Italy's policy was open to new horizons within the scope of the alliance. Following press speculation, Moro conceded that Italy was considering official recognition of Communist China and acting toward that aim.

With regard to EEC policy, Italy expressed once more the feeling that British entry, as well as the entry

ITALY

Education. (1966–67) Primary, pupils 4,525,111, teachers 206,135; secondary, pupils 2,142,900, teachers 183,474; vocational, pupils 809,503, teachers 65,510; teacher training, students 246,489, teachers 17,391; higher (including 31 universities), students 342,478, teaching staff 27,233.

Finance. Monetary unit: lira, with a par value of 625 lire to U.S. $1 (1,500 lire = £1 sterling). Gold and foreign exchange, official: (June 1969) U.S. $4,417,000,000; (June 1968) U.S. $4,281,000,000. Budget (1968 est.): revenue 8,826,996,000,000 lire; expenditure 9,976,786,000,000 lire. Gross national product: (1967) 41,849,000,000,000 lire; (1966) 38,493,000,000,000 lire. Money supply: (May 1969) 21,156,000,000,000 lire; (May 1968) 18,405,000,000,000 lire. Cost of living (1963 = 100): (June 1969) 122; (June 1968) 119.

Foreign Trade. (1968) Imports 6,408,000,000,000 lire; exports 6,365,000,000,000 lire. Import sources: EEC 36% (West Germany 18%, France 11%); U.S. 12%. Export destinations: EEC 40% (West Germany 19%, France 13%, Netherlands 5%); U.S. 11%. Main exports: machinery 24%; motor vehicles 9%; textile yarns and fabrics 8%; chemicals 8%; clothing 6%; petroleum products 6%; fruit and vegetables 6%. Tourism (1967): visitors 12.6 million; gross receipts U.S. $1,424,000,000.

Transport and Communications. Roads (1968) 283,958 km. (including 2,664 km. expressways). Motor vehicles in use (1968): passenger 8,178,505; commercial 750,802. Railways: state (1967) 15,888 km.; private (1965) 4,963 km.; traffic (1968) 28,880,000,000 passenger-km., freight 17,129,000,000 net ton-km. Air traffic (1968): 5,798,000,000 passenger-km.; freight 227.9 million net ton-km. Shipping (1968): merchant vessels 100 gross tons and over 1,490; gross tonnage 6,623,643. Telephones (Dec. 1967) 7,057,187. Radio licenses (Dec. 1967) 11,621,000. Television licenses (Dec. 1967) 7,669,000.

Agriculture. Production (in 000; metric tons; 1968; 1967 in parentheses): wheat 9,590 (9,596); corn 3,988 (3,860); barley 258 (295); oats 390 (556); potatoes 3,960 (4,010); rice 639 (745); broad beans 324 (408); onions (1967) 480, (1966) 436; sugar, raw value (1968–69) *c.* 1,293, (1967–68) 1,661; tomatoes 3,258 (3,459); tobacco 72 (87); olives 1,950 (2,712); oranges 1,590 (1,439); lemons 740 (721); wine 6,600 (7,473); apples 1,923 (1,932); pears 1,369 (1,317); peaches (1967) 1,125, (1966) 1,419; figs 220 (237); cheese *c.* 470 (466); eggs (1967) 468, (1966) 480; beef and veal 784 (712); pork (1967) 356, (1966) 337. Livestock (in 000; Jan. 1968): cattle 9,794; sheep (Jan. 1967) 8,212; pigs 5,300; goats (Jan. 1967) 1,140; horses, mules, and asses 900; poultry *c.* 110,000.

Industry. Index of production (1963 = 100): (1968) 136; (1967) 128. Unemployment: (1968) 3.5%; (1967) 3.5%. Fuel and power (in 000; metric tons; 1968): lignite 1,729; coal 365; crude oil 1,512; natural gas (cu.m.) 10,407,000; manufactured gas (cu.m.) 2,811,000; electricity (kw-hr.) 105,100,000. Production (in 000; metric tons; 1968): iron ore (50% metal content) 708; pig iron 8,042; crude steel 16,951; zinc 112; lead 58; aluminum 142; cement 29,537; cotton yarn 180; rayon filament yarn 92; rayon staple fibre 95; nylon filament yarn 90; nylon fibres 105; nitrogenous fertilizers (1967–68) 1,096; sulfuric acid 3,313; petroleum products 79,633; passenger cars (units) 1,544; commercial vehicles (units) 118. Merchant vessels launched (100 gross tons and over; 1968) 499,000 gross tons. New dwelling units completed (1968) 271,000.

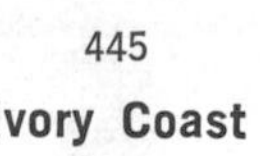

WIDE WORLD

Protesting a drop in the price of citrus fruits, orchard workers at Fondi, Italy, blocked the main rail line between Naples and Rome for several hours on Feb. 3, 1969.

of northern European countries, would be advisable. It further maintained the necessity for strengthening of supranational structures and for the election of a European Parliament. As far as the Middle East was concerned, the Italian government reaffirmed the necessity of action toward peace—a policy dictated by Italy's geographic position on the Mediterranean and its economic interests in the area.

Diplomatic activity included a visit to Rome, on January 16, by Canadian Prime Minister Pierre Elliott Trudeau; in February, Willy Brandt, then West German foreign minister, paid a visit to his Italian counterpart, Nenni; and March saw U.S. Pres. Richard M. Nixon in Rome, followed by Netherlands Foreign Minister Joseph Luns. Premier Rumor was a guest of President Nixon on the occasion of former U.S. Pres. Dwight D. Eisenhower's funeral. On April 22 President Saragat began a nine-day official visit to the U.K., where he was the first foreign head of state in 60 years to be a guest of Queen Elizabeth II at her Windsor residence. He was accompanied by Foreign Minister Nenni. In May UN Secretary-General U Thant and Belgian Prime Minister Gaston Eyskens were in Rome. Nenni went to Yugoslavia at the end of May, and in June Rumor visited Turkey. Ivory Coast President Houphouët-Boigny was in Rome on July 21. On September 1 Willy Brandt met Foreign Minister Moro in Rome.

On January 28 Italy signed the treaty for the nonproliferation of nuclear arms. On November 30 it was announced that the Italian and Austrian foreign ministers had reached agreement on the long-standing dispute over the Alto Adige, where a large German-speaking group lived under Italian rule. The accord would give German speakers more self-government and would include provision for referring disputes to the International Court of Justice.

The Economy. Labour unrest caused uncertainty in many sectors of the Italian economy in 1969 and one of the most serious effects was an enormous outflow of capital. The balance of payments in the first seven months of the year showed a deficit of $854.6 billion, compared with a surplus of $175.3 billion in the same period of 1968. The outflow of $1,805,700,000 more than did away with the original surplus of $951.1 billion. The trade balance, on the contrary, had shown a favourable trend. In the first six months exports had reached 3,716,000,000,000 lire and imports 3,770,000,000,000 lire, with a total deficit of 54,000,000,000,000 lire. Industrial production increased by 7.7% in the first six months of the year as compared with the same period in 1968. It had increased by 23.4% since 1966.

On July 1 the bank rate was raised from 3.5 to 5%. This change, the first in ten years, was taken in order to favour the growth of investment without causing setbacks to vital sections of the economy.

The trend was toward an unsettled year in 1970. Labour unrest at the end of 1969 did not calm the situation, and the preventive budget also raised some fears. A deficit of nearly $3 billion was forecast. One of the healthier sectors in the economy was the automobile industry, mainly represented by Fiat. In the first six months of the year the Turin firm produced 840,000 cars, an improvement of 70,000 over the same period in 1968. (F. G.)

ENCYCLOPÆDIA BRITANNICA FILMS. *Italy—Peninsula of Contrasts* (1952); *The Mediterranean World* (1961).

Ivory Coast

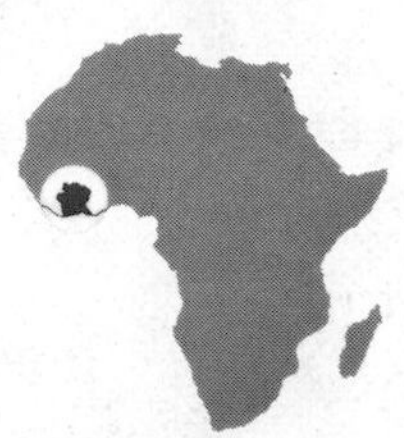

A republic on the Gulf of Guinea, West Africa, the Ivory Coast is bounded by Liberia, Guinea, Mali, Upper Volta, and Ghana. Area: 123,485 sq.mi. (319,822 sq.km.). Pop. (1968 est.): 4,100,000, including about 15,000 Europeans. Cap. and largest city: Abidjan (pop., 1963 est., 285,000). Language: French and local dialects. Religion: pagan 65%; Muslim 25%; Christian 10%. President and premier in 1969, Félix Houphouët-Boigny.

Following an exceptional economic expansion, little affected by a considerable decline in coffee production, the Ivory Coast in 1969 experienced some difficulties with a section of its intellectual elite. In May troops were used to evict militant students from the University of Abidjan, where there had been a week-long strike. The university was closed (though opened again in June), and the government decided that henceforth the student movement would be integrated into the Democratic Party of the Ivory Coast (the government party). This meant that financial grants would only be forthcoming to those students who showed themselves willing to cooperate with government policy. Disputes on the matter continued

IVORY COAST

Education. (1966–67) Primary, pupils 381,452, teachers 8,275; secondary, pupils 32,590, teachers (1965–66) 1,087; vocational, pupils 2,522, teachers 279; teacher training, pupils 717, teachers 39; higher, students (1964–65) 1,566.

Finance. Monetary unit: CFA franc, with a parity of CFA Fr. 50 to the French franc (CFA Fr. 277.71 = U.S. $1; CFA Fr. 666.50 = £1 sterling). Gold and foreign exchange, central bank: (June 1969) U.S. $82 million; (June 1968) U.S. $74 million. Budget (1968 est.) balanced at CFA Fr. 43.2 billion. Money supply: (March 1969) CFA Fr. 65,390,000,000; (March 1968) CFA Fr. 59,390,000,000.

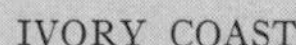

Foreign Trade. (1968) Imports CFA Fr. 77,630,000,000 (50% from France, 7% from West Germany, 6% from U.S., 5% from Italy, 5% from Netherlands); exports CFA Fr. 104,890,000,000 (35% to France, 15% to U.S., 10% to Netherlands, 9% to West Germany, 8% to Italy). Main exports: coffee 34%; timber 25%; cocoa 20%.

Agriculture. Production (in 000; metric tons; 1967; 1966 in parentheses): corn *c.* 205 (194); sweet potatoes 1,900 (1,916); cassava *c.* 1,100 (1,044); coffee *c.* 258 (130); cocoa 147 (150); bananas (1966) 179, (1966) 184; peanuts *c.* 29 (29); cottonseed *c.* 30 (17); timber (cu.m.) *c.* 8,800 (*c.* 8,300). Livestock (in 000; 1966–67): cattle 340; pigs 120; sheep 714; goats 790.

Trucks bearing logs wait for entry into the port of Abidjan, Ivory Coast, in 1969. Increased exports and diversified economic planning were expected to end the country's dependence on coffee and cocoa.

DR. GEORG GERSTER FROM RAPHO GUILLUMETTE

throughout the year between the newly formed, officially recognized Movement of Pupils and Students of the Ivory Coast (MEECI) and the disbanded but still active National Union of Students. At the end of the year the Army was reported to have put down a separatist revolt in the Sanwi region.

Having recalled the members of its mission in Moscow, in May the government suspended diplomatic relations (opened 18 months previously) with the Soviet Union on receiving evidence of Soviet involvement in student strikes. According to Moscow, however, the evidence was false.

On the economic front a Regional Development Commission was established to study and advise the government on development plans for the decade 1970–80. It was hoped to increase the annual national growth rate from 6.8 to 8.4% by 1975. On January 2, the country's second palm-oil plant began production at Toumangouie. Six more such plants were planned to begin operating by 1972 at a total cost of CFA Fr. 10 billion. (PH. D.)

Jamaica

A parliamentary state within the Commonwealth of Nations, Jamaica is an island in the Caribbean Sea about 90 mi. S of Cuba. Area: 4,244 sq.mi. (10,992 sq.km.). Pop. (1969 est.): 1,939,649, predominantly Negro, but including Europeans, Chinese, Indians, and persons of mixed race. Cap. and largest city: City of Kingston (pop., 1969 est., 542,432). Language: English. Religion: Christian, with Anglicans and Baptists in the majority. Queen, Elizabeth II; governor-general in 1969, Sir Clifford Campbell; prime minister, Hugh Lawson Shearer.

Wider cooperation both on a regional and on an international level was a feature of government policy during 1969. The economic benefits to be gained from participation in the Caribbean Free Trade Area (CARIFTA) stimulated industry and commerce as well as government. Jamaica agreed to join the Regional Development Bank and was admitted to membership in the Organization of American States, but this in no way lessened the nation's concern to protect its special interests should the U.K. join the EEC.

JAMAICA

Education. (1965–66) Primary (including preprimary), pupils 333,000, teachers 5,831; secondary, pupils 34,594, teachers 1,429; vocational, pupils 3,524, teachers 218; teacher training, students 212, teachers 10; higher (at University College of Mona), students 1,902.

Finance. Monetary unit: Jamaica dollar (new decimal unit introduced Sept. 8, 1969, equal to 10 shillings of old currency), with a par value of Jam$0.83 to U.S. $1 (Jam$2 = £1 sterling). Budget (1968–69 est.): revenue Jam$182,658,270; expenditure Jam$186,713,-300.

Foreign Trade. (1968) Imports Jam$319,360,000; exports Jam$182,720,000. Import sources: U.S. 39%; U.K. 20%; Canada 10%. Export destinations: U.S. 39%; U.K. 24%; Canada 14%; Norway 8%. Main exports: alumina 28%; bauxite 21%; sugar 20%; bananas 8%.

Agriculture. Production (in 000; metric tons; 1967; 1966 in parentheses): sweet potatoes *c.* 205 (*c.* 216); cassava *c.* 10 (*c.* 10); sugar, raw value (1968–69) 495, (1967–68) 452; bananas *c.* 300 (*c.* 330); oranges 72 (87); grapefruit 23 (19); copra 18 (17). Livestock (in 000; 1966–67): cattle 240; horses, mules, and asses *c.* 55; pigs 150; sheep *c.* 10.

Industry. Production (in 000; metric tons; 1967): bauxite 9,396; gypsum 167; cement 335; petroleum products 1,240; electricity (public service only; kw-hr.) 603,000.

Prime Minister Shearer visited a number of EEC and African countries with a view to closer collaboration.

The principal export crops, sugar and bananas, had a difficult year. The rising cost of sugar production, coupled with government failure to permit mechanization on a scale that would reduce costs, brought the largest producers to the point of closing down. Some smaller factories did close, and others were the subject of rescue operations. Strikes at leading ports, the uneven quality of the fruit, and poor prices hit the banana industry hard. However, the boom in the building industry showed no sign of abating. A new suburb of Kingston was growing up in the previously inaccessible Hellshire Hills, now linked to the city by a causeway.

Norman Manley, head of the People's National Party (PNP) since its foundation, retired from active politics early in 1969. His son Michael was elected to succeed him. The elder Manley's death in September was the occasion for national mourning. (*See* OBITUARIES.)

Parish council elections took place in March. The results revealed little change in strength between the two major parties. The PNP attracted slightly more of the popular vote, while the Jamaica Labour Party gained a narrow majority of seats. (G. C. CU.)

ENCYCLOPÆDIA BRITANNICA FILMS. *The West Indies* (1965).

Japan

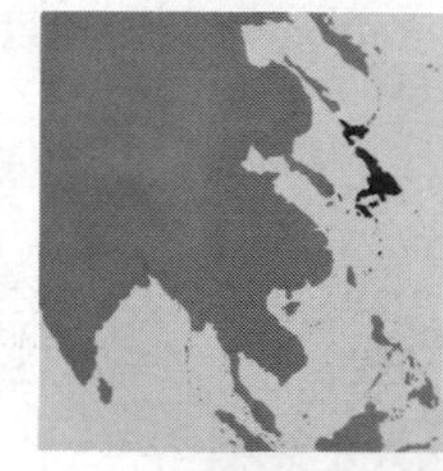

A constitutional monarchy in the northwestern Pacific Ocean, Japan is an archipelago composed of four major islands (Hokkaido, Honshu, Kyushu, and Shikoku) and minor adjacent islands. Area: 145,707 sq.mi. (377,-382 sq.km.). Pop. (1969 est.): 101,690,000. Cap. and largest city: Tokyo (pop., 1969 est., 9,035,000). Language: Japanese. Religion: primarily Shinto and Buddhist; Christianity 1.6%. Emperor, Hirohito; prime minister in 1969, Eisaku Sato.

Domestic Affairs. After Prime Minister Sato had been reelected president of the majority Liberal-Democratic Party (November 1968), he carried out a reorganization of his Cabinet. Key posts were assigned to Shigeru Hori (chief Cabinet secretary); former Foreign Minister Masayoshi Ohira (international trade and industry); Takeo Fukuda (finance); Kiichi Aichi (foreign affairs), to handle sensitive issues concerned with the U.S.-Japan Security Treaty and Okinawa; and Michita Sakata (education), to deal with widespread campus disorders.

The 61st regular session of the Diet, organized on Dec. 27, 1968, was reconvened on Jan. 27, 1969, for its 222-day sitting. Its deliberations centred on the question of Okinawa's reversion from U.S. to Japanese control, the U.S.-Japan Security Treaty, university disputes, and rising commodity prices. Party standings in the Diet were: (lower) House of Representatives: Liberal-Democrats (LDP) 276, Japan Socialists (JSP) 137, Democratic Socialists (DSP) 31, Komeito (KMT) 25, Japan Communists (JCP) 4, independents 2, vacancies 11 (total, 486), (upper) House of Councillors: LDP 139, JSP 64, KMT 24, DSP 10, JCP 7, independents 5, vacancies 1 (total, 250). In his opening policy speech,

Jammu and Kashmir: *see* India; Pakistan

Sato singled out three issues: his proposed visit to the U.S. in 1969 to set the timing for Okinawa's reversion; a more flexible stand toward Communist China; and the need for a stiff stand on university problems and campus disorders. Deeply split between distrustful governing and opposition parties from the start, the Diet ended its extended session on August 5 after having passed only 63 of 113 bills introduced by the government.

Despite some decline in national popularity ratings, the ruling LDP made a strong comeback in the Tokyo Metropolitan Assembly elections, held on July 13. The LDP garnered 54 seats; JSP, only 24 (a disastrous drop from the previous 45), ranking it behind the KMT with 25; the JCP, 18 (double its previous holdings); and the DSP, 4. Tokyo Gov. Ryokichi Minobe, although shocked by the crushing defeat of the Socialists who had helped elect him in 1967, announced "no change in posture."

By mid-1969, when the Cabinet decided to take stern action, campus disorders had spread throughout Japan with 34 national, 4 municipal, and 8 private universities in dispute. The National Police Agency announced on August 1 that a total of 5,984 persons had been arrested during the previous six months (double the figure recorded for the first half of 1968). Symbolic of the widespread unrest was the situation at prestigious Tokyo University where, in November 1968, Pres. Kazuo Okochi had tendered his resignation. On January 19 radical students barricaded in Tokyo's Yasuda Auditorium withstood a ten-hour siege by riot police, who used pressurized water cannons and helicopters to drop tear gas. The students hurled Molotov cocktails, bottles of acid, and slabs of concrete at the police. During a clearing of the Hongo campus 370 students were arrested, 35 persons were injured, and damage was reported at 170 million yen. Late in March in an election held off campus to avoid disruption, acting Pres. Ichiro Kato was elected 19th president of Tokyo University. He accepted the post early in April and promptly set about reordering the university decision-making process.

On April 28 students in Tokyo marked "Okinawa Day" (the 17th anniversary of the U.S. occupation of Okinawa) by virtually bringing to a halt all passenger train service. Approximately 50,000 attended a central rally at Yoyogi Park. By midnight about 800 had been arrested and more than 100 injured.

The Sato government introduced a bill on May 24 to restore order in strife-torn universities. It called for concentration of administrative power in the hands of the university president; penalties for students, staff, and faculty who attempt to hinder normalization; suspension of educational and research activities (including a 30% pay cut for personnel); and, if a suspension lasts more than three months, abolition of the institution in protracted trouble. On August 3 the LDP, by means of a surprise move in the upper house, forced a "university normalization" bill through the Diet. Opposition parties boycotted further legislative proceedings. Tokyo University's President Kato called the move "an outrageous act tantamount to the denial of minimum rules of parliamentary democracy" and predicted that the bill would make solutions even more difficult. Bearing out this prediction, on September 21, 2,000 riot police had to invade the campus of Kyoto University, clear barricades, and arrest self-styled student "revolutionaries." The administration then resumed classes, suspended since January, under riot police guard. One of the largest demonstrations in recent years took place on October 21, designated in Japan as "international antiwar day." More than 70,000 riot policemen, 25,000 in Tokyo alone, had to be called out to stop the violent disorders that broke out in many parts of the country.

On December 2, in the wake of his successful trip

KEYSTONE

Pavilions under construction at the site of Expo 70 in Osaka. The world's fair, Asia's first, was to run from March 15 to Sept. 13, 1970, and was expected to attract 50 million visitors.

JAPAN

Education. (1965–66) Primary, pupils 9,775,-532, teachers 347,326; secondary, pupils 8,964,-354; vocational, pupils 2,060,158; secondary and vocational, teachers 473,026; higher (including 69 universities), students 1,116,430, teaching staff 106,412.

Finance. Monetary unit: yen, with a par value of 360 yen to U.S. $1 (864 yen = £1 sterling). Gold and foreign exchange, official: (June 1969) U.S. $2,748,000,000; (June 1968) U.S. $1,730,-000,000. Budget (1968–69 est.) balanced at 5,-818,598,000,000 yen. Gross national product: (1968) 51,092,000,000,000 yen; (1967) 43,039,-000,000,000 yen. Money supply: (June 1969) 15,633,000,000,000 yen; (June 1968) 13,442,-000,000,000 yen. Cost of living (1963 = 100): (May 1969) 133; (May 1968) 127.

Foreign Trade. (1968) Imports 4,675,400,-000,000 yen; exports 4,669,800,000,000 yen. Import sources: U.S. 27%; Australia 7%; Canada 5%; Iran 5%; Saudi Arabia 5%. Export destinations: U.S. 32%; South Korea 5%. Main exports: machinery 21%; iron and steel 13%; textile yarns and fabrics 11%; ships 8%; motor vehicles 8%; chemicals 6%.

Transport and Communications. Roads (1968) 995,282 km. (including 608 km. expressways). Motor vehicles in use (1968): passenger 5,209,324; commercial 7,508,321. Railways: (1966) 27,949 km.; traffic (1968) 275,738,000,-000 passenger-km., freight 60,155,000,000 net ton-km. Air traffic (1968): 6,010,000,000 passenger-km.; freight 234.4 million net ton-km. Shipping (1968): merchant vessels 100 gross tons and over 6,877; gross tonnage 19,586,902. Telephones (Dec. 1967) 18,216,767. Radio receivers (Dec. 1966) 24,787,000. Television receivers (Dec. 1966) 19,002,000.

Agriculture. Production (in 000; metric tons; 1968; 1967 in parentheses): rice 18,765 (18,-770); wheat *c.* 1,012 (997); barley 1,011 (1,-032); sweet potatoes (1967) 4,031, (1966) 4,810; potatoes 4,056 (3,636); tea (1967) 85, (1966) 83; onions (1967) 1,541, (1966) 1,625; apples *c.* 1,100 (1,125); oranges 2,435 (1,850); tobacco 193 (209); timber (cu.m.; 1966) 59,600, (1965) 59,300; fish catch (1967) 7,814, (1966) 7,102; whale and sperm oil (1967–68) 29, (1966–67) 81. Livestock (in 000; Feb. 1968): cattle 3,155; sheep (Feb. 1967) 113; pigs 5,535; horses 216; goats (Feb. 1967) 246; chickens (Feb. 1967) 126,043.

Industry. Index of production (1963 = 100): (1968) 190; (1967) 162. Fuel and power (in 000; metric tons; 1968): coal 46,569; crude oil 781; natural gas (cu.m.) 2,311,000; electricity (kw-hr.) 263,500,000. Production (in 000; metric tons; 1968): iron ore (55% metal content) 2,-170; pig iron 47,463; crude steel 66,893; petroleum products 101,403; cement 47,678; cotton yarn 551; woven cotton fabrics (sq.m.) 2,743,-000; rayon filament yarn 143; rayon staple fibre 366; nylon filament yarn 305; nylon fibre 388; sulfuric acid 6,587; cameras (units) 4,063; radio receivers (units) 30,189; television receivers (units) 9,140; passenger cars (units) 2,056; commercial vehicles (units) 2,052; motorcycles (units) 2,226. Merchant vessels launched (100 gross tons and over; 1968) 8,664,000 gross tons.

WIDE WORLD

Radical leftist students battle riot police with sticks and stones in Ito, June 8, 1969. Rioters were protesting the opening of the nine-nation Asian and Pacific Council, which they feared would become an anti-Communist alliance.

to the U.S. where he had obtained a definite promise concerning the reversion of Okinawa (*see* below), Sato dissolved the Diet and called for elections to the House of Representatives on December 27. The result was a resounding victory for the ruling LDP, giving Sato's government a strong majority. The KMT and the JCP improved their standings, chiefly at the expense of the JSP. (*See* POLITICAL PARTIES.)

During fiscal 1968 (April 1, 1968–March 31, 1969), according to the Economic Planning Agency, Japan's gross national product (GNP) totaled 52,906,700,000,000 yen ($146,960,000,000), with national income per capita at $1,122. The GNP figures confirmed Japan's rank as second in the non-Communist world (behind the U.S.), but the country remained 20th in the world in per capita income. In fiscal 1968 the economy's growth rate was 18.3% in nominal terms (14% in real terms, the second highest on record). The production of automobiles, iron and steel, machine tools, and cement recorded historic highs.

Foreign Relations. The volume of traffic in high-level officials between Tokyo and Washington, D.C., was a clear indicator of the significance to both capitals of key issues needing decision in 1969–70. Although U.S. Pres. Richard Nixon did not choose to visit Japan during his summer world tour, Secretary of State William P. Rogers was in Tokyo during late July, and the U.S. saw to it that Japan received an experienced ambassador (if largely unknown in Japan), Armin H. Meyer. The former ambassador, U. Alexis Johnson, had left Tokyo to become deputy undersecretary of state.

The "American presence" in the form of military forces in eastern Asia and specifically of bases on Japanese soil offered a serious issue. On Dec. 23, 1968, the U.S. had presented a plan for the returning to Japan or relocating of 50 facilities and areas in Japan used by U.S. forces under the Status of Forces Agreement.

On May 3, after North Korea had downed a U.S. intelligence-gathering aircraft on April 15, Foreign Minister Aichi stated that Japan had the right under the "prior consultation" clause of the Security Treaty to refuse use of a Japanese port as base for U.S. Task Force 71 operating in the Sea of Japan. Prime Minister Sato added, however, that it was "unreasonable" to place the entire blame on the U.S. for tense developments in the area.

Most serious during 1969 and promising to carry over into 1970, when the Security Treaty would be subject to review, was the issue of the future status of Okinawa. In October 1968 the U.S. and Japan had agreed for the first time to allow elected Okinawan representatives to sit as observers in the Diet in Tokyo. Nevertheless, continued uneasiness on the island had resulted in the election, on Nov. 10, 1968, of Chobyo Yara as the first popularly selected governor of the Ryukyu Islands (of which Okinawa is the chief). Yara had been backed jointly by the opposition parties, and his election was a severe blow to the government and LDP. On Dec. 9, 1968, Yara met Prime Minister Sato in Tokyo and appealed for "an all-out effort to achieve an immediate, unconditional, and total reversion of Okinawa." He demanded treatment of Okinawa as a prefecture.

The Okinawa Base Problems Study Committee submitted its report in March to Sato and to U.S. officials. Since its first meeting in February 1968, the committee had studied the future status of U.S. bases after reversion of Okinawa. Administrative control should be returned to Japan, said the committee, by 1972 at the latest. The Security Treaty and Status of Forces Agreement should be applied to Okinawa, including the "prior consultation" clause (that is, bases on Okinawa would be placed under the same restrictions as those on the main islands). The Japanese Self-Defense Forces should assume the responsibility for the defense of the island. By March 22 Sato seemed to have shifted his position toward agreement with the report's *hondo-nami* ("same-as-mainland") formula: he promised to enter into negotiations with the U.S. demanding the same restrictions—including non-nuclear status—as held for bases in Japan.

Although a general strike in Okinawa was averted in February and again in June, teachers, students, and the 20,000-member Okinawa Military Employees Union protested aspects of the American presence on Okinawa. On June 5, U.S. military police carrying carbines with fixed bayonets forcibly removed some pickets, whereupon sharp protests were heard in the Diet.

Despite sporadic, occasionally bloody demonstrations on the eve of his departure, Sato left for the U.S. to meet with President Nixon on November 19–21. For the first time the two leaders formally agreed to "maintain indefinitely" the mutual security treaty. The U.S. promised to return Okinawa to Japan by 1972, but, at the same time, U.S. forces obtained greater flexibility of movement both on Okinawa (after 1972) and on the main islands. All uses of bases were to be subject to "prior consultation" with Japan, and nuclear weapons were to be removed from Okinawa.

Japan's other territorial claim was with the Soviet Union and was bound up with Soviet notions of its security. In the 1968 UN General Assembly, Takeo Miki had denounced the Soviet invasion of Czechoslovakia as "indisputably an act incompatible with the spirit and letter of the UN Charter." Possibly because of Japan's attitude, in Moscow on September 1 Soviet Premier Aleksei N. Kosygin made painfully clear to Foreign Minister Aichi that the U.S.S.R. had no intention of altering national boundaries defined at the end of World War II. As a result, a small group of islands at the southern tip of the Kuriles, territory that had always been a part of Japan, apparently was to remain in Soviet hands indefinitely. (A. W. Bs.)

ENCYCLOPÆDIA BRITANNICA FILMS. *Japan—Harvesting the Land and the Sea* (1963); *Japan—Miracle in Asia* (1963).

Jazz:
see Music

Jehovah's Witnesses:
see Religion

Jewish Literature:
see Literature

Jewry:
see Religion

Jordan

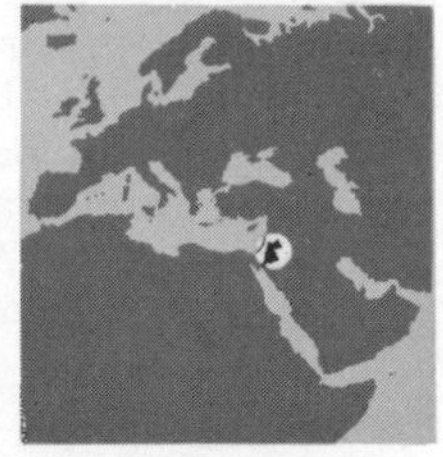

A constitutional monarchy in southwest Asia, Jordan is bounded north by Syria, northeast by Iraq, east and south by Saudi Arabia, and west by Israel. Area (including territory occupied by Israel in the June 1967 war): 37,737 sq.mi. (97,740 sq.km.). Pop. (1968 est.): 2,133,000. Cap. and largest city: Amman (pop., 1967 est., 330,220). Language: Arabic. Religion: Muslim 88%; Christian 12%. King, Husain I; prime ministers in 1969, Bahjat al-Talhouni to March 24, Abdel Monem Rifai, and, from August 12, al-Talhouni.

There was no lessening of Jordan's internal difficulties during 1969 as the west bank remained under Israeli occupation and the east bank was under constant Israeli bombardment. The government reached an understanding with the chief Palestinian guerrilla organizations largely as a consequence of its loss of faith in a political solution to the Middle East crisis.

Early in the year King Husain still believed that such a solution was possible, especially since the new U.S. administration had declared that it intended to pursue a more "evenhanded" policy in the Middle East. On March 24 Prime Minister Bahjat al-Talhouni, strongly in favour of the Palestinian guerrillas, resigned and was replaced by Abdel Monem Rifai. The king's uncle, Sherif Nasser ibn Jamil, who was unpopular with the Palestinians, became commander in chief of the armed forces. On April 10, after a guerrilla attack on the Israeli port of Eilat, the king announced that those responsible had been arrested. These moves were interpreted in the Middle East as preparations for a political settlement with Israel. In April the king went on a three-week visit to Washington, London, and Paris, but his hopes of favourable intervention by the great powers gradually receded. On August 12 he brought back al-Talhouni as prime minister, with Rifai remaining as deputy prime minister and foreign secretary. Israel reported that the Jordanian Army was increasingly cooperating with the Palestinian Al Fatah guerrillas.

Both the king and his ministers became openly critical of U.S. policy in the Middle East. In October Husain said that U.S. arms supplies to Israel had given it superiority over the Arabs and that, although Jordan's supplies were now adequate, it would look elsewhere than the West if necessary. In January Britain had supplied Jordan with £6 million worth of Tigercat surface-to-air missiles. On October 6 a plot by Muslim extremists to dethrone Husain was reported foiled.

The king continued to press for an Arab summit, but when it was finally held, in Rabat, Mor., in December it served only to widen the divisions within the Arab world. Husain continued to attempt to coordinate military policy with his Arab neighbours. Iraq maintained 12,000 troops in Jordan and in August Syria moved some troops into Jordanian territory. (P. Md.)

Encyclopædia Britannica Films. *The Middle East* (1955).

GAMMA—PIX FROM PUBLIX

Red Cross and UN relief agencies during 1969 were supplying food and supplies to 40,000 Arab refugees in tent camp near Amman, Jordan.

JORDAN

Education. (1966–67) Primary, pupils 318,122, teachers 8,140; secondary, pupils 103,791, teachers 4,318; vocational, pupils 3,382, teachers 237; teacher training, students 1,781, teachers 109; higher (including University of Jordan), students 2,628, teaching staff 133.

Finance. Monetary unit: Jordanian dinar, with a par value of 0.36 dinars to U.S. $1 (0.86 dinars = £1 sterling). Gold and foreign exchange, central bank: (June 1969) U.S. $259.3 million; (June 1968) U.S. $246.2 million. Budget (1968 est.): revenue 72,947,680 dinars; expenditure 84,651,030 dinars. Gross national product: (1967) 205.4 million dinars; (1966) 185.7 million dinars. Money supply: (June 1969) 93,290,000 dinars; (June 1968) 84,690,000 dinars.

Foreign Trade. (1968) Imports 56,610,000 dinars; exports 14,260,000 dinars. Import sources: U.K. 12%; West Germany 10%; U.S. 10%; Lebanon 6%; Syria 5%. Export destinations: Kuwait 17%; India 13%; Iraq 13%; Saudi Arabia 11%; Lebanon 8%; Yugoslavia 7%; Syria 6%. Main exports: phosphates 29%; vegetables 26% (tomatoes 16%); fruit 9%.

Transport and Communications. Roads (1967) 3,055 km. (excluding local roads). Motor vehicles in use (1967): passenger 16,400; commercial (including buses) 6,700. Railways (1967) 366 km. Air traffic (1968): 124.1 million passenger-km.; freight 1,054,000 net ton-km. Telephones (Jan. 1968) *c.* 33,000. Radio receivers (Dec. 1965) *c.* 269,000.

Agriculture. Production (in 000; metric tons; 1967; 1966 in parentheses): barley *c.* 80 (23); wheat (1968) *c.* 173, (1967) *c.* 226; cucumbers (1966) 40, (1965) 61; onions *c.* 22 (22); tomatoes *c.* 150 (145); olives *c.* 103 (33); oranges *c.* 40 (*c.* 45); grapefruit (1966) *c.* 12, (1965) 11; figs *c.* 20 (16); grapes *c.* 65 (62); bananas *c.* 17 (17). Livestock (in 000; 1966–67): sheep 1,136; cattle 78; goats 766; camels 17; asses *c.* 95; chickens *c.* 2,100.

Industry. Production (in 000; metric tons; 1967): phosphate rock 1,082; cement 321; electricity (kw-hr.) 157,000.

Kenya

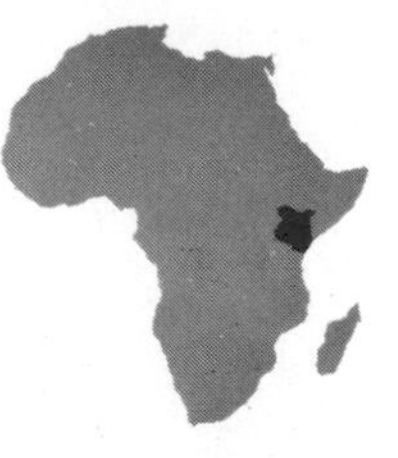

A republic and a member of the Commonwealth of Nations, Kenya is bordered on the north by Sudan and Ethiopia, east by the Somali Democratic Republic, south by Tanzania, and west by Uganda. Area: 224,960 sq.mi. (582,647 sq.km.), including 5,171 sq.mi. of inland water. Pop. (1969 est.): 10,504,000, including (1962) African and Somali 96.9%; Asian 2%. Cap. and largest city: Nairobi (pop., 1969 est., 506,000). Language: English (official); Bantu, especially Swahili; Nilotic. Religion: pagan; Christian and Muslim minorities. President in 1969, Jomo Kenyatta.

Kenya's Trade Licencing Act, which barred non-Kenyans from trading in a large number of basic commodities and from operating transport companies, came into force on January 1. Widespread concern about the likely effects of the act upon the Asian population were in no way allayed by the announcement of the minister of commerce and industry, Mwai Kibaki, that during the first six months of 1969 the government intended to refuse licenses to more than

Journalism: *see* Publishing

Judaism: *see* Israel; Religion

Judo: *see* Sporting Record

Karate: *see* Sporting Record

Karting: *see* Sporting Record

Kashmir: *see* India; Pakistan

CAMERA PRESS—PIX FROM PUBLIX

Mourners file past the open coffin of Tom Mboya, July 12, 1969. Widespread rioting by Mboya's Luo tribe and the dominant Kikuyus followed the assassination of the popular minister for economic planning and development.

3,000 Asian traders who were already in business in Kenya. On January 8, a number of Europeans were also told to wind up their businesses in accordance with the licensing laws. The Kenya government, with other East African governments, asked Britain to make it clear that the problems of Asians with British passports was distinct from that of British immigration policy in general, and that Britain accept full responsibility for those Asians who wished to leave East Africa. As the provisions of the act began to be felt more fully in April, it was noted that approximately 40% of Asians seeking to leave Kenya wished to go to India rather than to Britain, in contrast with only 20% in 1968. Of a rather different character was the expulsion in April of a Soviet diplomat and a journalist, whom the government required to leave the country without stating any official reason for their deportation.

KENYA

Education. (1968) Primary, pupils 1,133,179, teachers 30,000; secondary and vocational, pupils 90,690, teachers 3,000; teacher training, students 5,897, teachers 400; higher (1965), students 2,795.

Finance. Monetary unit: Kenyan shilling, with a par value of 7.14 Kenyan shillings to U.S. $1 (17.14 Kenyan shillings = £1 sterling). Budget (1968–69 est.): revenue 1,300,360,000 Kenyan shillings; expenditure 1,225,040,000 Kenyan shillings. Gross domestic product: (1967) 8,652,000,000 Kenyan shillings; (1966) 8,205,000,000 Kenyan shillings. Cost of living (Nairobi; 1963 = 100): (June 1969) 111; (June 1968) 110.

Foreign Trade. (Excluding trade with Tanzania and Uganda; 1968) Imports 2,293,000,000 Kenyan shillings; exports 1,248,000,000 Kenyan shillings. Import sources: U.K. 31%; West Germany 8%; Iran 8%; Japan 7%; U.S. 7%. Export destinations: U.K. 25%; West Germany 9%; U.S. 7%; Netherlands 5%; Zambia 5%. Main exports: coffee 21%; tea 18%; petroleum products 12%; corn 8%; meat and meat products 5%.

Transport and Communications. Roads (1968) 41,675 km. (including 6,162 km. main roads). Motor vehicles in use (1967): passenger 47,970; commercial 49,610. Railways: (1967) 2,050 km. (operated under East African Railways Corporation, serving Kenya, mainland Tanzania, and Uganda with a total of 5,870 km.); traffic (total East African; 1966) 4,529,000,000 passenger-km., freight (1967) 3,844,000,000 net ton-km. Ships entered (1966) vessels totaling 5,235,000 net registered tons; goods loaded (1967) 2,104,000 metric tons, unloaded 2,879,000 metric tons. Telephones (Jan. 1968) 60,691. Radio receivers (Dec. 1965) 350,000. Television receivers (Dec. 1967) 14,000.

Agriculture. Production (in 000; metric tons; 1967; 1966 in parentheses): corn (on farms and estates) *c.* 140 (144); wheat (on farms and estates; 1968) 159, (1967) 128; coffee 49 (52); tea 29 (20); sugar, raw value (1968–69) *c.* 106, (1967) *c.* 65; sisal 52 (57); cottonseed 9 (9); fish catch 28 (28). Livestock (in 000; May 1968): cattle *c.* 7,750; sheep (1966–67) *c.* 6,900; pigs *c.* 27; goats (on farms and estates; Aug. 1967) *c.* 6,500; camels (1966–67) *c.* 179; poultry (on farms and estates; 1966–67) 208.

Industry. Production (in 000; metric tons; 1967): salt 25; magnesite 0.4; soda ash 105; gold (troy oz.) 33; limestone 19; cement (1968) 544; electricity (kw-hr.; 1968) 380,000.

On January 27 President Kenyatta ordered the University College in Nairobi to be closed after students had boycotted lectures in protest against the government's refusal to permit the opposition leader, Oginga Odinga, to address them. All but five of the students were subsequently readmitted to the college after signing an apology to the government and pledging total obedience to official rules.

In March the government announced a five-year, £3 million housing development program. Nairobi would benefit most from the scheme, but £1 million was to be spent in Mombasa, and there were to be pilot projects in rural areas in an attempt to curb mass migration to towns. The budget introduced in June by James Gichuru, minister of finance, contained no remarkable features. Oginga Odinga branded it as an election budget since most of the changes envisaged appeared likely to reduce the incidence of taxation on poorer citizens while there were no startling measures to offset these minor concessions. To raise £1 million over and above the increased revenue arising from the normal expansion of the economy, estimated at £3.2 million, Gichuru proposed to move forward the dates on which the corporation tax and surtax were payable. To finance development he hoped to raise £14 million from overseas.

Tom Mboya, minister for economic planning and development, warned of deteriorating prospects for some of Kenya's main export crops, and while Gichuru was optimistic about the future of corn (maize) exports Mboya forecast a substantial loss on them for 1969–70; he also admitted that wheat production must aim to meet the needs of East Africa only since it would be impossible to compete in wider markets. Mboya's remedy was to concentrate on developing commodities of higher value, such as beef and dairy produce. These products, however, called for greater farming skills involving the further education of farmers.

On July 5 Mboya was shot dead in Nairobi (*see* OBITUARIES). There were immediate fears of tribal conflict since many Luo (the tribe of Mboya) suspected the politically powerful Kikuyu tribe of responsibility for Mboya's death. Vice-Pres. Daniel Arap Moi declared that the assassination was in his view politically motivated and, although he refused to offer any firm suggestion as to who was responsible, his statement that Western nations were not implicated led some to think that he suspected Maoists of being involved. On July 21, however, a Kikuyu, Nahashon Isaac Njenga Njoroge, was charged with the murder. In September he was found guilty and was later executed. No evidence was forthcoming concerning accomplices, and no clear motive for the crime was discovered.

The seriousness of the loss to the government caused by the death of Mboya was quickly demonstrated when highly critical members of the National Assembly defeated the government on July 17 on two votes during a debate in which 52 ministers and assistant ministers were accused of illegally appropriating a gratuity of 20% of their salaries dating back to

1962. Earlier attacks of a similar nature had been defeated by Mboya's eloquence.

In the National Assembly in August, Oginga Odinga called upon the government to deny or confirm that Kikuyu oath-taking ceremonies had taken place in President Kenyatta's house. Rumours of the revival of oath-taking had circulated in Nairobi since Mboya's death. The oaths were said to demand loyalty to the president and to the Kenya African National Union (KANU). Although Arap Moi denied that the oath-taking ceremonies were taking place, Oginga Odinga chose to regard the reports as evidence that KANU recognized its own failure to provide the country with adequate leadership. This opinion he expressed in September at the first full-scale conference of the opposition Kenya People's Union (KPU) that had been permitted by the government in two years. KANU leaders in the Western Province joined the chorus of criticism, and accusations that oath-taking was spreading to Kenya citizens in London were made by Gideon Mutiso, assistant minister for education. Arap Moi, on instructions from Kenyatta, had issued a statement condemning forcible and illegal oath-taking, but this, Mutiso said, had failed to stop the ceremonies.

In October Kenyatta was the centre of violent demonstrations in Kisumu, the home of Oginga Odinga, during which 11 persons were killed. With other opposition leaders, Odinga was placed under house arrest, and on October 30 the government banned the KPU, accusing the party of sedition and the fomenting of intertribal strife. Thus all 600 candidates for the 158 National Assembly seats contested in the December election ran on the KANU ticket. Nonetheless, the voters expressed some dissatisfaction with the existing government. More than 70 incumbents, including five government ministers and five junior officials, lost their seats. Since 22 incumbents did not seek reelection, a large majority of the next National Assembly would consist of new members.

On December 12, shortly before the election, President Kenyatta announced the second five-year plan at a rally in Nairobi. The plan aimed to raise agricultural output by more than a third and industrial production by 75%. (K. I.)

Encyclopædia Britannica Films. *East Africa (Kenya, Tanganyika, Uganda)* (1962).

Korea

A country of eastern Asia, Korea is bounded by China, the Sea of Japan, the Straits of Korea, and the Yellow Sea. It is divided into two parts at the 38th parallel.

Republic of Korea (South Korea). Area: 38,022 sq.mi. (98,477 sq.km.). Pop. (1969 est.): 31,139,000. Cap. and largest city: Seoul (pop., 1967 est., 3,972,000). Language: Korean. Religion: Buddhist; Confucian; Tonghak (Chutokyo). President in 1969, Gen. Park Chung-hee; prime minister, Gen. Chung Il Kwon.

Political turmoil at home and Communist threats from the north kept South Korea on tenterhooks for most of 1969. Apparently to consolidate his position, President Park reorganized the Cabinet on February 15, creating three new ministers and a new portfolio called the Unification Research Board. A storm broke, however, when he asked the ruling Democratic Republican Party to push through a constitutional amendment removing the legal barrier that prevented him from seeking a third term as president; his second four-year term was to end in 1971. The original amendment barring a third term was Park's own doing. He had enacted it soon after his 1961 coup in order to prevent another long reign like the 13 years of his predecessor, Syngman Rhee.

By June student rioting sparked by Park's constitutional amendment drive had assumed serious proportions. Approximately 300 opposition leaders formed the Pan-National Struggle Committee in July, arguing that the proposed amendment and Park's reelection would lead to perpetual dictatorship. Support for the president came from 250 retired military leaders, who said that the country needed strong leadership. On July 25 the president made a surprise announcement that he would order a national referendum and, if the verdict went against the idea of amending the constitution, resign immediately. But public opinion was not assuaged. In August opposition members of the National Assembly went on strike in a desperate attempt to block the amendment bill. The speaker thereupon bypassed the formal introduction and sent the bill to the Cabinet for a 30-day public notice as required under the constitution. On September 7, the day before the notice period was to expire, the opposition New Democratic Party dissolved itself in the hope of depriving three rebel members of their seats. The climax to this strange drama came on September 14 when the National Assembly held a session at 2:15 A.M. in an annex. Opposition members staging a sit-in strike in the main assembly hall were unaware of the meeting until it had passed the controversial bill. A rampage followed in which chairs and tables in the assembly hall were destroyed and the government imposed a curfew. Students rioted again and the National Assembly speaker resigned "to assume the responsibility" for the parliamentary crisis. The government's proposed referendum finally took place on October 17, and resulted in 65.1% support for President Park's proposal to seek reelection. Three days later Park made further extensive Cabinet changes.

Some observers were inclined to believe that the political crisis at home made President Park and his administration overplay the Communist threat from the north. The South Korean Central Intelligence Agency claimed a Viet Cong-style National Unifica-

WIDE WORLD

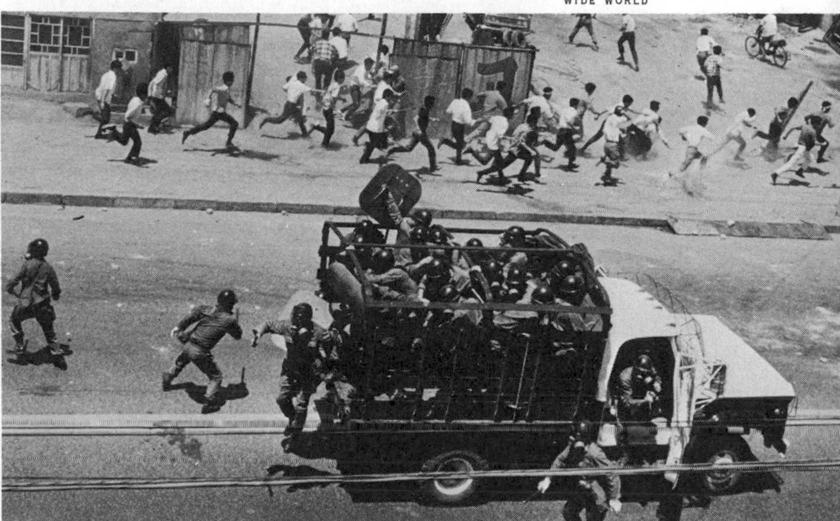

South Korean riot police pursue university students in Seoul on July 4, 1969. Students were protesting a proposed constitutional amendment to allow Pres. Park Chung-hee to run for a third term.

tion Liberation Front was being secretly organized by North Korean agents. In one week in July two prominent agents were executed in Seoul. In September a 12-man spy ring was said to have been smashed.

Visiting U.S. Pres. Richard Nixon in California on August 20, President Park said that North Korea had completed preparations for another war in line with Communist leader Kim Il Sung's pledge to unify the country by 1970. He warned that any weakening of the U.S. anti-Communist defense line in Asia could risk another Korean conflict. Earlier he had invited the U.S. to use Cheju Island either as a replacement for Okinawa or as a new naval and air base. President Nixon renewed the U.S. pledge to support South Korea. It was reported that military aid would continue at about $160 million a year. There was no immediate response to the South Korean request for $100 million supplementary military aid that the U.S. had promised after the seizure by North Korea of the U.S. ship "Pueblo" in 1968. South Korea was particularly eager to increase its air and naval power; its 620,000-strong land army was reputedly the fourth largest in the world. A three-man U.S. Defense Department team visited Seoul in June with plans to establish a production facility for M-16 rifles. The U.S. also transferred several thousand carbines to the 2.5 million-strong home reserve force as part of a plan to modernize the antiguerrilla equipment. In March about 700 U.S. paratroopers had been airlifted directly from the U.S. for "the longest airborne assault exercise in history" 40 mi. S of Seoul.

Meanwhile, the government was expecting the economy to slow down in 1970 after a period of impressive growth. The director of the Bank of Korea reported that the economic growth rate in 1968 was 13.1%, which was 1.1% higher than anticipated. The per capita gross national product (GNP) increased from $143.20 in 1967 to $164.40 in 1968. This he attributed to the "highest investment rate, of 24.5%, since 1954." However, Deputy Prime Minister Kim Hak Yul said in July that the GNP growth rate would decelerate in 1970 to 11% in real terms against 1969's estimated 15%.

Democratic People's Republic of Korea (North Korea). Area: 46,557 sq.mi. (120,583 sq.km.). Pop. (1969 est.): 13.7 million. Cap.: P'yongyang (pop., 1960 est., 653,100). Language: Korean. Religion: Buddhist; Confucian, Tonghak (Chutokyo). Secretary-general of the Korean Workers' (Communist) Party and chairman of the Council of Ministers (premier) in 1969, Marshal Kim Il Sung; president, Choi Yong Kun.

Diligently pursuing its policy of *juche*—economic, political, and cultural independence—North Korea in 1969 tangled with not only its traditional enemy, the U.S., but also with its ideological partners, the U.S.S.R. and China. With the Soviet Union there was no open clash, but neither was there any question of allowing friendship to be taken for granted. No North Korean fraternal delegation went to Moscow for the world conference of Communist parties in June, though Soviet Pres. Nikolai V. Podgorny had journeyed all the way to P'yongyang in May apparently to persuade the North Koreans to attend. Reflecting North Korean disapproval of Moscow's warmth toward the U.S., the president of the North Korean Supreme People's Assembly said to Podgorny that it was the Korean people who were "defending the western outpost of the socialist camp under difficult conditions in which they stand face to face with U.S. imperialism."

With China, North Korean border troops had at least two clashes, first in December 1968 and again in March 1969, but both sides played down the incidents. South Korean intelligence sources reported in June that, according to evidence they had collected, North Korea would eventually turn to China rather than to the U.S.S.R. for support in its plan to take over the South.

With the U.S. the struggle was as bitter as in the "Year of the 'Pueblo'." Indeed, North Korea achieved a repeat performance with the shooting down, on April 15, of an American EC-121 spy plane with a crew of 31 and six tons of sophisticated electronic equipment on board. It happened on Kim Il Sung's 57th birthday. President Nixon immediately announced that surveillance flights would continue and that in the future the planes would be protected, which provoked the North Koreans to issue a lengthy statement warning of "another total war in Korea." On August 17 they shot down an unarmed U.S. helicopter with a crew of three that had strayed into

KOREA: Republic

Education. (1966–67) Primary, pupils 5,382,500, teachers 89,277; secondary, pupils 1,171,022, teachers 29,626; vocational, students 198,199, teachers 8,005; higher (including 16 universities), students 166,061, teaching staff 7,985.

Finance. Monetary unit: won, with an official exchange rate (November 1969) of 305.10 won to U.S. $1 (732.24 won = £1 sterling). Gold and foreign exchange, central bank: (June 1969) U.S. $433 million; (June 1968) U.S. $379.5 million. Budget (1969 est.) balanced at 324.4 billion won (including defense expenditure 60.3 billion won). Gross national product: (1968) 1,570,000,000,000 won; (1967) 1,245,100,000,000 won. Money supply: (May 1969) 165,620,000,000 won; (May 1968) 139,510,000,000 won. Cost of living (1965 = 100): (May 1969) 150; (May 1968) 135.

Foreign Trade. (1968) Imports 377,360,000,000 won (including 12,040,000,000 won official aid); exports 126,030,000,000 won. Import sources: Japan 42%; U.S. 31%; West Germany 5%. Export destinations: U.S. 52%; Japan 22%. Main exports (1967): clothing 18%; textile yarns and fabrics 15%; plywood 11%; fish and fish products 8%; metal ores 7%; silk 5%.

Transport and Communications. Roads (1967) 34,476 km. Motor vehicles in use (1967): passenger 23,200; commercial (including buses) 37,500. Railways (1967): 5,103 km.; traffic 9,577,000,000 passenger-km., freight (1968) 6,592,000,000 net ton-km. Air traffic (1967): 63,755,000 passenger-km.; freight 305,000 net ton-km. Shipping (1968): merchant vessels 100 gross tons and over 232; gross tonnage 473,991. Telephones (Dec. 1967) 343,743. Radio receivers (Dec. 1966) 2,632,000. Television receivers (Dec. 1967) 78,000.

Agriculture. Production (in 000; metric tons; 1968; 1967 in parentheses): rice 4,286 (4,869); wheat *c.* 301 (310); potatoes 617 (566); barley *c.* 2,084 (1,916); sweet potatoes and yams (1967) 1,671, (1966) 2,690; soybeans *c.* 222 (201); tobacco 70 (66); fish catch (1967) 749, (1966) 701. Livestock (in 000; Dec. 1967): cattle 1,255; pigs 1,296; horses 25; goats (Dec. 1966) 161; poultry 17,079.

Industry. Production (in 000; metric tons; 1968): coal 10,242; iron ore (*c.* 50% metal content) 829; steel 366; cement 3,572; tungsten concentrate (oxide content; 1967) 2.8; graphite (1967) 64; kaolin (1967) 103; fluorspar (1967) 57; limestone (1967) 3,916; gold (troy oz.; 1967) 63; silver (1967) 0.018; electricity (excluding most industrial production; kw-hr.) 6,000,000.

KOREA: People's Democratic Republic

Education. (1964–65) Primary, pupils 1,113,000, teachers 25,221; secondary, pupils 704,000, teachers 27,162; vocational, pupils 441,000, teachers 17,176; higher (including 3 universities), students 186,000, teaching staff 9,013.

Finance and Trade. Monetary unit: won, with an official exchange rate of 2.57 won to U.S. $1 (6.17 won = £1 sterling). Budget (1968 est.) balanced at 5,215,000,000 won. Trade is almost entirely with China and the U.S.S.R. Main exports (1964): metals 50%; minerals 12%; farm produce 11%.

Transport. Motor vehicles in use (1961): passenger 3,226; commercial 1,600. Railways: (1967) *c.* 10,500 km.; freight traffic (1961) 9,823,000,000 net ton-km.

Agriculture. Production (in 000; metric tons; 1967; 1966 in parentheses): rice *c.* 2,500 (*c.* 2,500); corn *c.* 1,600 (*c.* 1,600); barley *c.* 250 (*c.* 250); potatoes *c.* 955 (*c.* 955); fish catch (1964) 770, (1963) 640. Livestock (in 000; Dec. 1967): cattle *c.* 700; pigs *c.* 1,280; sheep (Dec. 1966) *c.* 160; goats (Dec. 1966) *c.* 167.

Industry. Production (in 000; metric tons; 1967): coal *c.* 17,000; iron ore (metal content) *c.* 3,250; pig iron *c.* 1,750; steel *c.* 1,450; lead *c.* 55; zinc *c.* 80; magnesite *c.* 1,000; cement *c.* 2,500; electricity (kw-hr.; 1965) 13,300,000.

North Korean airspace; the men were released "in good condition" in December.

Reports of increased North Korean infiltration into South Korea kept war scare at a high pitch for most of the year. What Western sources described as the largest single Communist infiltration since the end of the war took place in November 1968. A month later the top North Korean strategist in guerrilla warfare, Gen. Choe Hyon, was named defense minister. It was also reported that the 1969 budget had considerably raised the defense allocation. (T. J. S. G.)

Kuwait

An independent Arab sheikhdom, Kuwait is on the northwestern coast of the Persian Gulf between Iraq and Saudi Arabia. Area: 7,450 sq.mi. (18,850 sq.km.). Pop. (1968 est.): 531,581. Cap. and largest city: Kuwait (pop., 1968 est., 106,197). Language: Arabic. Religion: Muslim. Amir in 1969, Sheikh Sabah as-Salim as-Sabah; prime minister, Crown Prince Sheikh Jabir as-Ahmed as-Jabir as-Sabah.

In 1969 Kuwait continued to play its important financial role in the Arab world, contributing $132 million to Jordan and the United Arab Republic in addition to loans to Syria and Lebanon through the Kuwait Fund for Arab Economic Development. Despite these heavy expenditures, rising oil revenues enabled the budget of 302.5 million dinars to show a surplus of 68 million dinars. In May the Kuwait government warned oil companies that if the expected increases in Iranian oil output were made at Kuwait's expense, Kuwait would have to revise its attitude toward those companies' concessions. The visit of the Kuwaiti defense minister to Paris and the return visit of the French armed forces minister indicated Kuwait's intention to buy French arms. In April the crown prince made an official visit to Paris.

Although continuing to express vigorous support for the Arab cause, the Kuwait government became alarmed at the sharp increase in the non-Kuwaiti Arab population, estimated at 200,000 since the 1967 war; many of them were without employment. As a consequence new restrictions on entering the country were imposed in March.

The government was confident that Kuwait could defend its independence after the British withdrawal from the Persian Gulf region in 1971. Of greater concern was the Libyan coup in September, which removed one of the few remaining pro-Western regimes in the Arab world. Libya was associated with Kuwait and Saudi Arabia in the Arab Oil Exporters Association. (P. Md.)

KUWAIT

Education. (1966–67) Primary, pupils 51,987, teachers 2,346; secondary, pupils 34,965, teachers 2,282; vocational, pupils 1,059, teachers 175; teacher training, students 1,750, teachers 224; higher, students 418, teaching staff 49.

Finance. Monetary unit: Kuwaiti dinar, with a par value of 0.36 dinars to U.S. $1 (0.86 dinars = £1 sterling). Gold and foreign exchange, official: (June 1969) U.S. $165.2 million; (June 1968) U.S. $167.7 million. Budget (1969–70 est.): revenue 302.5 million dinars; expenditure 234.5 million dinars. Money supply (March 1969) 130.7 million dinars.

Foreign Trade. (1968) Imports 218.3 million dinars; exports 496.7 million dinars. Import sources (1967): U.S. 22%; U.K. 12%; West Germany 9%; Italy 5%. Export destinations (1967): Italy 25%; Japan 20%; U.K. 13%; France 10%; Netherlands 9%. Main exports petroleum and products 97%.

Industry. Crude oil production (1968) 122,018,000 metric tons.

Labour Unions

The pattern of labour activity that had characterized the year 1968 remained basically unchanged during 1969. There was a high level of collective consciousness that resulted in widespread and intensive strike action, often involving governments. The main impulse continued to come from workers in their places of work rather than from the official union bodies. Frequently the unions had to accept the initiative of the workers in order to maintain their authority as workers' representatives. Also, as in 1968, the most intensive area of labour activity was Western Europe. The situation in France was relatively quiet, but in Britain and Italy it was at a continually high pitch. The most notable change occurred in West Germany where, in September, the country's postwar record as a relatively strike-free economy was broken by an outbreak of unofficial strikes. Another common element in the patterns for the two years was the involvement of governments in labour affairs.

It is important to note that in all industrialized areas of the world, labour has a continuing relationship with employers and governments in which day-to-day problems arise and are frequently settled in a quiet, unobtrusive manner. Even in countries marked by widespread open conflict between labour and employers, the vast majority of industrial disputes are settled inconspicuously. Therefore, a description of the publicized conflicts should not be taken as evidence of generalized open conflict. There are occasions, as in France in 1968 and in Britain in 1969, when labour unions are united in a conflict, but usually the disputes are sectional and sporadic. The important questions in any one year concern, on the one hand, the pressures that transform latent conflict into open hostility and, on the other, the reasons for variations between countries.

KEYSTONE

Striking Italian workers march through the streets of Rome, Feb. 5, 1969. Millions of workers staged a 24-hour strike to force the government to implement long-promised pension reforms.

Western Industrialized Countries. One of the comparatively few instances of a dispute spreading over a number of years concerned the California grape industry. In September 1965 the United Farm Workers Organizing Committee had called a strike against the California grape growers to establish the right to have a trade union and to bargain collectively. The farm workers did not have the organizing and collective bargaining protection given to workers in manufacturing industry by U.S. legislation. They experienced degrading working conditions and received less than half the average wage of manufacturing workers. The strike was supported by a boycott of California grapes led by the AFL-CIO, the Canadian Labour Congress, and the International Confederation of Free Trade Unions (ICFTU).

After two years, agreement was reached between the workers' representatives and the major California wine grape growers, but the dispute with the table grape growers continued. In October 1968 the Confederation of Mexican Workers announced it would take steps to halt the sale of grapes in Baja California and prevent their shipment to other parts of Mexico. Early in 1969 a number of European unions concerned with agriculture and transport endorsed the embargo

JACK DYKINGA, "CHICAGO SUN-TIMES"

White construction workers in Chicago climb on Picasso statue during demonstration in September against blacks who demanded training and placement in skilled union jobs.

on grapes. Following an appeal by the International Transport Workers' Federation in February 1969, the boycott was supported by unions in Sweden (the biggest European importer of California grapes in 1968) and Norway. In August it was estimated that 50,000 farm workers were connected with the United Farm Workers Organizing Committee, while in October it was claimed that the consumer boycott in the U.S. had forced growers to put almost 40% of their crop into cold storage.

Other continuing labour issues occurred in Spain and Japan, but open disputes were sporadic. Each year for many years the coal miners of the Asturias region of Spain had struck in defiance of a legal ban, and each year the strike leaders were arrested and imprisoned. In October 1968 the International Labour Organization (ILO) appointed a study group to investigate the situation. A strike of 1,500 miners began in the Asturias on Oct. 10, 1968, which was later supported by another 8,000 miners. By November 3, 8,000 miners were still on strike despite a government threat of severe retaliatory measures. Almost 20,000 miners took part in a protest strike on November 27.

The new year began with a miners' strike against poor safety measures. Strikes occurred in other industries, and on January 24 a state of emergency was declared. Official sources stated that 200 arrests were made, but unofficial sources calculated the number of arrests at 1,500. The state of emergency was lifted on March 25 but the strikes continued: 2,000 miners went on strike in May despite a threat of mass dismissals, and in June they engaged in lightning sitdown strikes against a management decision to stop allocations to the widows of miners killed in pit accidents.

The continuing issue in Japan concerned freedom to strike. Under the Local Public Service Law, it was illegal for public employees to strike, but the unions of both teachers and postal workers had continued to challenge this law and in the process had clarified its application. On April 2, 1969, the Supreme Court, in a case involving officials of the Municipal Teachers' Union of Tokyo, ruled that industrial action by public employees is exempt from penal responsibility unless it is specifically of an illegal character. The ruling tended to protect union officials from repressive action, but not the actual strikers. The National Railway authorities penalized more than 1,800 employees for participating in a strike on March 18. The Ministry of Postal Services disciplined 6,962 members of Zentai (Japan Postal Workers' Union) for striking for wage increases and annual paid vacations in April.

The pattern of collective bargaining contracts meant that few major contracts came up for renewal in the U.S. in 1969. There was no national bargaining in the aluminum, automobile, communications, rubber, steel, or trucking industries. The most significant contracts for the year, with General Electric, Westinghouse, and similar electrical manufacturing firms, were renewable in the autumn. The first of these contracts concerned General Electric and came up for renewal on October 26. GE pursued a policy of making what it considered to be a realistic offer and refusing to modify it. The offer, made on October 7, was rejected by the unions, and a strike of 147,000 GE production workers began on October 27. At the same time, the unions went to court on the ground that the GE policy of refusing to bargain was a violation of the National Labor Relations Act in that the company refused to "bargain in good faith." The U.S. Court of Appeals decided in October that General Electric was indeed violating the act and the company appealed to the Supreme Court.

The intention of the AFL-CIO to fight for a national minimum hourly wage of $2 was supported by the outgoing secretary of labour early in the year when he stated that, while the number of persons living in poverty in the U.S. was currently estimated at between 22 million and 26 million, unemployment was only 2 to 3 million, pointing to the conclusion that poverty in most cases was due to inadequate income rather than the absence of income. In mid-March the Oil, Chemical and Atomic Workers International Union initiated a boycott of the products of the Shell Oil and Shell Chemical companies because of the companies' refusal to grant fair labour contracts to 2,000 employees in California and for victimizing some of the workers. The AFL-CIO took a dramatic decision on February 20 when it disaffiliated from the International Confederation of Free Trade Unions, mainly because ICFTU was considering an application for affiliation from the United Automobile Workers, which had broken from the AFL-CIO in 1968.

Trade-union affairs dominated the political and industrial scene in Great Britain. The report and recommendations of the Royal Commission on Trade Unions and Employers' Associations, published in June 1968, had generated much debate in the labour movement. In January 1969, however, the government published its White Paper *In Place of Strife,* which rejected the main proposals of the royal commission. The White Paper proposed that there should be compulsory ballots before strikes in certain cases and that a compulsory conciliation pause should be enforced. The General Council of the Trades Union Congress (TUC) had not been consulted about the preparation of the White Paper, and on January 17 it published its own statement rejecting the notion of legal compulsion. On April 15 the chancellor of the exchequer announced that the government intended to introduce legislation on the lines outlined in the White Paper. On the following day the minister for employment and productivity described the government's proposals, which included a legally enforced conciliation pause of 28 days during which time it would be illegal to strike.

Feeling about penalty clauses had already been tested in Britain during a labour dispute involving the Ford Motor Co. Negotiations on a productivity agreement began in November 1968 and ended on March 18, 1969. They concerned a wage increase, fringe benefits, and penalty clauses for unconstitutional action. The National Joint Negotiating Committee at Ford accepted an offer made on February 11, but mass meetings at various Ford plants rejected it and on February 21 an unofficial strike began which by the 25th involved 35,000 out of Ford's 46,000 employees. The two largest unions involved, the Transport and General Workers' Union and the Amalgamated Union of Engineering and Foundry Workers, declared the strike official, and the company sought a High Court injunction to restrain them from doing so. The High Court refused to continue an injunction, and on March 11 the company withdrew its court action. The strike ended on March 18 with a compromise settlement.

On May 1 there were token strikes against the White Paper involving more than 250,000 workers. Tension continued to mount until June 18, when the government announced that it was not going ahead with antistrike legislation and that it had reached an agreement with the TUC under which the TUC would use its influence to reduce the incidence of strikes.

In the midst of the debate in Britain, a similar issue flared up in Australia. Since 1950 the Australian Federal Industrial Court had had power to enforce at law the rulings of the Arbitration Court. It could fine trade unions up to A$1,000 a day for defying the commission's ban on strikes or limitations of overtime. During May, Clarence O'Shea, the secretary of the Victorian tramways union, refused to produce union books or to be examined himself in connection with the nonpayment of A$8,100 in earlier fines on the ground that he was protecting the interests of his union members. O'Shea was imprisoned, and a wave of rolling strikes began throughout Australia. The fines were paid by a businessman on May 20, and the union leader was released. Nonetheless, the next day about 500,000 workers were on strike. The series of strikes continued until May 26, when the unions received assurances from the government. Melbourne port workers were on strike for 15 days and gas and electricity supplies were affected.

Both Italy and France experienced a series of general strikes that began early in 1969 and continued intermittently throughout the year. A total of 18 million workers were involved in a 24-hour general strike over a pension dispute in Italy on February 5. More than a million civil servants supported a 24-hour strike on April 19 for a wage increase. There was a 24-hour general strike in France on March 11 over a demand for an increase in real wages. In both countries the grievances culminated early in September. The French railway system was halted by a sudden strike on September 11. More than one million Italian metalworkers struck for a new collective bargaining contract on September 11 and they were followed by building, chemical, and public transport workers. Even farmers went on strike for an increase in the price of milk. Altogether, two million workers were on strike in Italy during the week beginning September 14. A lockout of 12,000 workers on September 24 at the Pirelli works in Milan precipitated a series of strikes and demonstrations. The agitation continued into October with a demonstration of 100,000 metal and mechanical workers in Milan on October 7 and staggered strikes thereafter. Workers in many other industries also continued their agitation.

Strike action was commonplace in Western Europe during the second half of the year. Despite the TUC's efforts, the London garbage collectors struck for a wage increase late in September, and on October 13 a strike of coal miners began that involved half of the industry's labour force. By December, when the government presented plans for limiting pay increases, strikes of schoolteachers, truck drivers, and stevedores were in progress. But it was in West Germany that the real surprise occurred. From 1964 to 1966 inclusive fewer than ten working days per 1,000 employees had been lost through strikes in West Germany and no large strikes had occurred. Then early in September a wave of wildcat strikes afflicted the steel and mining industries. There were steel strikes in Bremen and Osnabrück, coal strikes in the Saar, and shipyard strikes in Kiel and Lübeck. The success of some of the strikes encouraged many other groups, including 30,000 workers in the Bavarian brewing industry and garbage collectors in Bielefeld, to make wage demands and threaten strike action. On September 24 public service workers in three West German towns staged wildcat strikes.

In Ireland 50,000 workers were involved in a strike of 3,000 maintenance workers on February 5 for a wage increase. After five weeks the employers conceded to the workers' demands. Although strikes were illegal in Portugal, the workers at the General Motors and Ford assembly plants at Azambuja went on strike against low wages on February 10. A two-day general strike took place throughout Iceland on April 10–11 against the government decision to end the system of tying wages to the consumer price index. The workers at three Reykjavik factories continued their strike, the employers locked them out, and widespread sympathy strikes developed into a general strike. Agreement was reached on May 19, when the employers agreed to restore a permanent cost-of-living allowance. A long and bitter strike in the Canadian nickel industry began on July 10, and by the time it was settled in November had had international repercussions on the world nickel market.

Attempts were made during the year to coordinate the activities of unions in international firms. The International Federation of Chemical and General Workers' Unions called a meeting in Geneva on March 29 to organize international action for the 70,000 glass workers employed by the Saint-Gobain company, which had 143 factories in 12 countries. The European Metalworkers' Committee, which groups the metalworkers' unions in the EEC countries, adopted an action program at the end of February. The Consultative Council for Latin America and the Caribbean of the International Metalworkers' Federation urged its members to take practical steps of solidarity, and plans for the coordination and reinforcement of collective bargaining, training, and strike solidarity programs were formulated at a meeting of representatives of nearly 400,000 General Electric employees from all over the world at Bogotá, Colombia, in April. A resolution concerning the defense of workers' interests against multinational corporations was passed by the ICFTU congress in July.

Less Developed Countries. In general, labour unions in less developed countries had relatively little industrial power but did have significant political influence. For this reason they frequently came into conflict with governments. There was continuing strife on Okinawa between Kenrokyo, the All-Okinawa Prefectural Council of Trade Unions, and the U.S. administration. Kenrokyo called a 24-hour general strike on February 4 to protest against the presence of nuclear weapons on the Ryukyu Islands and to demand the withdrawal of B-52 bombers and an end to visits by nuclear-powered submarines. After worldwide protests, the Argentinian dockers' leader, Eustaquio Tolosa, was released from prison on parole on January 21. He had been arrested in December 1966 after voting for an international boycott of Argentinian ships. Early in the year there was a 48-hour strike by Kuwait oil workers in protest against the nonimplementation of labour laws passed in 1968. In Turkey, at the end of January, the textile workers' union called 30,000 workers in 25 textile plants out on strike because of the refusal of the biggest state-owned enterprise in Turkey, Sumerbank, to accept terms formulated by an impartial conciliation board.

Strike action in Pakistan played a crucial part in forcing the resignation of Pres. Muhammad Ayub Khan. Beginning in February, prolonged strike action continued in all sectors of the economy until the institution of military rule, the declaration of martial law, and the resignation of President Ayub on March 25. A government-sponsored labour conference in Karachi on May 17 proposed uniform labour laws for both West and East Pakistan, which would give all wage-earners the right to join unions and to strike. The government responded on July 5 by announcing a new labour policy that included the right to strike, a new minimum wage, and guaranteed freedom of association for all workers except members of the armed forces.

When the London-based Lonrho Co. took over control of the Ashanti Goldfields Corp. in Ghana, the Ghana Mineworkers' Union sought assurances that the miners would not lose benefits under their collective agreement. Most of the miners and the ground staff went on strike early in March over the issue; a riot began, about 6,000 strikers attempted to storm the police station, and three miners were shot dead by the police. After the bloodless coup in the Sudan on May 25, workers were warned that they would face the death penalty if they went on strike. Although government repression had occurred in Senegal at an earlier period, there was none when the postal workers struck for a revision of wage schemes in May. This was followed by a 72-hour strike by petroleum workers and a ten-day strike by bank workers. Curaçao in the Netherlands Antilles was the scene of rioting and political disturbances when the Curaçao Federation of Workers demonstrated in support of pay raises. Dutch Marines were brought from the Netherlands to assist the police. There was violence in Gwelo, Rhodesia, when the Hides, Shoe and Leather Workers' Union called a strike in June. Under Rhodesian law unregistered unions cannot carry out union functions, and the Hides, Shoe and Leather Workers' Union, though registered in other parts of Rhodesia, was not registered in Gwelo. Two of its officials were arrested under the Industrial Conciliation Act for "unlawful incitement, declaring or taking part in a strike."

A dispute between the General Confederation of Labour and the Argentinian government over government repression and pay demands came to a head at the end of August. The government had imposed a state of siege throughout the country on June 30 and had appointed an official trustee to negotiate with the unions. On August 12 a meeting of the leaders of 57 unions decided that the negotiations had failed and announced a general strike for the 27th. The government declared the strike illegal, ordered the police to take appropriate security measures, and invoked the 1967 Civil Defense Law. Nonetheless, about 50,000 railwaymen went on strike in September. The government placed the railway workers under military law on September 15 and ordered the arrest of their leader, Antonio Scipione. There were 36-hour sympathetic strikes in the provincial trade-union centres of Cordóba and Rosaria; violence flared in Rosaria and a number of persons were killed. In imposing military rule, the Argentinian government was following the example of Uruguay where, early in August, Pres. Jorge Pacheco Areco imposed the militarization of 2,100 striking bank clerks, thus classifying them as deserters subject to court-martial.

Communist Countries. As in 1968, attention was focused on Czechoslovakia. At the seventh congress of Czechoslovak trade unions held in Prague in March, the principle of the right to strike was incorporated into the new charter for unions. Legitimate strikes

KEYSTONE

Workman sprays carbolic powder on a 35-yd.-long rubbish pile during strike of garbage collectors in London in September 1969.

had to be endorsed by a trade-union organization; all other stoppages were illegal. The congress called for the continuation of the liberalization policies started by the Czechoslovak Communist Party in January 1968 and authorized its Central Council to examine, with the government, the proposed bill on state enterprises. Some dissatisfaction with the Central Council over its refusal to take account of the workers' criticisms was expressed on June 23 by metalworkers in about 20 large plants in Prague. The attitude of the Central Council to the liberalization policy altered on August 25, when the council expressed its approval of measures taken by the government, through the Army and the police, to prevent passive protests against the presence of Soviet troops.

A number of short work stoppages occurred in Yugoslavia, the only Communist country to publicize them. A two-day strike took place in the Jesenice foundry in Slovenia in April over low wages. On May 7 a group of workers in the Rakovica motor plant in Serbia struck over the nonpayment of personal incomes for four days. The most serious occurrence was in the port of Rijeka, Croatia, on June 2, when about 4,500 workers demonstrated against a wage cut. Some of the demonstrators attacked the port administration buildings and clashed with senior members of the management. (V. L. A.)

The ILO. The winner of the 1969 Nobel Peace Prize was the 50-year-old International Labour Organization. Founded under terms of the Treaty of Versailles in 1919, it was established to bring about basic humanitarian improvements in working conditions for people around the world. Following World War II it became a specialized agency working under the aegis of the United Nations.

The ILO had 45 member nations when it was organized. In 1969 it had 121 member nations, 2,700 officers of 100 nationalities, and 30 field offices around the world. Each national delegation comprised representatives of unions, management, and government officials, all of whom had voting power.

The selection of the ILO as Peace Prize winner was announced in Oslo on October 20 by Mrs. Aase Lionæs, a Labour member of the Storting (parliament) and chairman of the five-member Nobel Peace Prize Committee. She said:

> It is the international activity of ILO through 50 years that in my opinion makes it a worthy Peace Prize winner. Until World War II, ILO concentrated its activities on reducing social barriers between peoples in an effort to make nations work together in peace. After World War II, ILO had a wider perspective and has become a global institution in the work of peace. The organization is now deeply engaged in the enormous problem of solving unemployment in the poor world. . . . This is a gigantic challenge to ILO and a task that calls for a concentrated effort of all its talents and powers.

The ILO's director general since 1948 had been David A. Morse, a 62-year-old lawyer who had been a U.S. Labor Department official and acting secretary of labour during the Truman administration.

The ILO was the tenth organization to receive the Peace Prize since it was first conferred in 1901. Other organizations so honoured included the International Red Cross, the Office of the United Nations High Commissioner for Refugees, and the UN Children's Fund (UNICEF). (Ph. K.)

See also Education; Employment, Wages, and Hours; Police; Race Relations.

ENCYCLOPÆDIA BRITANNICA FILMS. *Working Together* (1952); *Walter P. Reuther* ("Dialogue for This Decade") (1962); *The Rise of Labor* (1968); *The Industrial Worker* (1969).

Laos

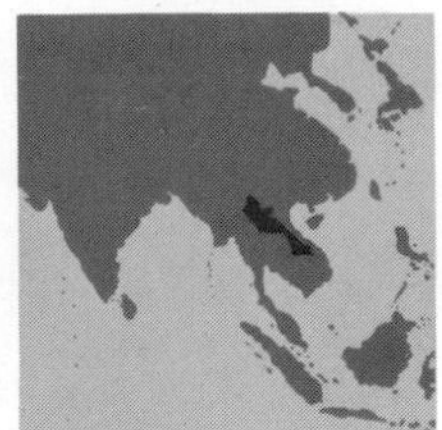

A constitutional monarchy of southeast Asia, Laos is bounded by China, North and South Vietnam, Cambodia, Thailand, and Burma. Area: 91,400 sq.mi. (236,800 sq.km.). Pop. (1968 est.): 2,825,000. Administrative cap. and largest city: Vientiane (pop., 1968 est., 140,000). Royal cap.: Luang Prabang (pop., 1968 est., 25,000). Language: Lao (official); French and English. Religion: Buddhist; tribal. King, Savang Vatthana; premier in 1969, Prince Souvanna Phouma.

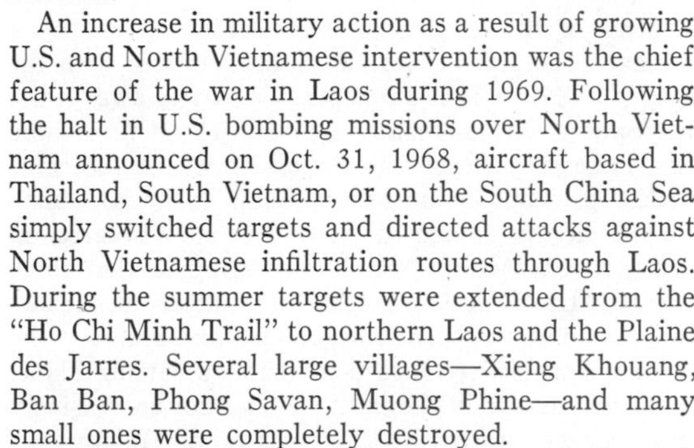

An increase in military action as a result of growing U.S. and North Vietnamese intervention was the chief feature of the war in Laos during 1969. Following the halt in U.S. bombing missions over North Vietnam announced on Oct. 31, 1968, aircraft based in Thailand, South Vietnam, or on the South China Sea simply switched targets and directed attacks against North Vietnamese infiltration routes through Laos. During the summer targets were extended from the "Ho Chi Minh Trail" to northern Laos and the Plaine des Jarres. Several large villages—Xieng Khouang, Ban Ban, Phong Savan, Muong Phine—and many small ones were completely destroyed.

At the same time U.S. logistic support to the Royal Laotian Army and to the Special Forces (an army composed primarily of Montagnard guerrillas) was stepped up by the issuing of U.S. M-16 rifles and the generalized use of helicopters piloted by U.S. civilian volunteers. In addition, Thai volunteers were recruited to fight in the Special Forces.

These measures came at a time when the attrition policy used since 1963 by the forces of the Neo Lao Hak Sat (Laotian extreme left-wing party) and by those of North Vietnam operating clandestinely in Laos had become a serious threat to the government. These forces in January blew up a large munitions depot 21 km. from Vientiane. In March, they overran the Na Khang base, the main fortress of the Special Forces in northern Laos. In April, they took Thateng, a strategic stronghold of the Royal Laotian Army, and at the same time managed to cut off all ground traffic

LAOS

Education. (1966–67) Primary, pupils 177,288, teachers 4,861; secondary, pupils 6,946, teachers 277; vocational, pupils 1,300, teachers 162; teacher training, students 2,171, teachers 185; higher, students 235, teaching staff 15.

Finance and Trade. Monetary unit: kip, with an official exchange rate of 240 kips to U.S. $1 (576 kips = £1 sterling) and a free rate (Oct. 1969) of 500 kips to U.S. $1 (1,200 kips = £1). Budget (1967–68 est.): revenue (excluding foreign aid) 6,391,000,000 kips; expenditure 15,310,000,000 kips (including military expenditure 8,345,000,000 kips). Foreign trade (1968): imports 12,878,558,000 kips (26% from Thailand, 21% from Japan, 14% from U.S., 8% from France, 7% from U.K.); exports 1,448,096,000 kips (56% to Malaysia, 28% to Thailand, 8% to Hong Kong, 7% to Singapore). Main exports (1967): tin ore 43%; timber 32%; coffee 18%.

Transport. Roads (1966) 5,623 km. (including 2,941 km. main roads). Motor vehicles in use (1966): passenger 6,800; commercial (including buses) 2,200. Air traffic (1967): 19,627,000 passenger-km.; freight 598,000 net ton-km. Inland waterways (main Mekong River routes only; 1967) 1,614 km.

Agriculture and Industry. Production (in 000; metric tons): rice (1968) 932, (1967) 784; coffee (1967) *c.* 3.5, (1966) *c.* 3.5; corn (1967) *c.* 22, (1966) *c.* 20; tobacco (1967) *c.* 3, (1966) *c.* 3; tin concentrates (1967) *c.* 0.3; electricity (excluding most industrial production; kw-hr.; 1967) 24,700.

Lacrosse: *see* Sporting Record

between the government-controlled towns in the Mekong Valley: Luang Prabang, Vientiane, Pak Sane, Thakhek, Savannakhet, and Pakse.

The Special Forces retaliated by taking Xieng Khouang, in the centre of the country, which had just been destroyed by bombing after remaining for five years the largest population centre occupied by the Neo Lao Hak Sat. This success was short-lived, as a North Vietnamese counterattack compelled the Special Forces to abandon the ruins in the following month. In June the Vietnamese achieved a major success in the same region when they took Muong Soui, the chief base of the neutralist forces allied to the Royal Laotian Army.

Most of these successes were later reversed by a violent counterattack of the Special Forces with the help of U.S. planes. In September, after five years, the Special Forces regained control of all the Plaine des Jarres and drove their enemies out of the ruins of Xieng Khouang and Muong Soui. At the same time they took the village of Muong Phine (situated on the "Ho Chi Minh Trail"), where, up to that time, the Neo Lao Hak Sat had had its military headquarters for all of southern Laos. In October, however, the Special Forces were forced to abandon Muong Phine.

Developments in the military situation increasingly drove peace efforts into the background. In May Le Van Hien, titular ambassador of North Vietnam to Laos, held talks in Vientiane with the king of Laos and with Prince Souvanna Phouma. But the military escalation hardened the positions of the various parties.

In the U.S. the stepping up of military involvement in Laos met with increased opposition, and led in October to an inquiry by a Senate subcommittee. Prince Souvanna Phouma nonetheless asked Pres. Richard M. Nixon, at their meeting in the U.S., for an increase in logistical support for the government forces. (M. CT.)

Law

Court Decisions and Related Developments. Many similar problems were resolved, sometimes differently, by courts and legislatures throughout the world in 1969. These problems mainly involved the matters of freedom of speech and expression, the right of privacy, the application of military law, equality of the sexes, and the legal implications of various medical developments.

Freedom of Speech and Expression. Important cases involving obscenity were decided in 1969 in Denmark and the U.S. In one case the Danish newspaper *Ekstra-bladet* was convicted by a Danish court of publishing obscene pictures. Following this conviction, the first of its kind in Denmark, a bill was passed by the Folketing abolishing the offense of publishing visual pornography. This new law supplemented an earlier one that removed obscene literature from the reach of criminal sanctions.

In the other case, the U.S. Supreme Court ruled in *Stanley* v. *Georgia* (394 U.S. 557, 89 S.Ct. 1243) that a state statute making private possession of obscene materials a crime was unconstitutional. In handing down the decision, the court reaffirmed its holding of *Roth* v. *U.S.* that obscenity is not protected by the First Amendment to the Constitution. But the decision held that this doctrine did not permit the states or the federal government to make the mere private possession of obscene material a crime.

Film censorship did not come before the courts in 1969 in any significant case, but the legislatures of some of the Scandinavian countries wrestled with it and came to conclusions based on adult-child distinctions that might well serve as models in other countries. In Denmark legislation effective July 1 abolished film censorship for adults. In Norway the Justice Committee of the Storting issued a report proposing retention of film censorship for those under 18. Similarly, the Film Censorship Committee of Sweden recommended abolition of censorship for adults, retention of censorship for children under 15, and the establishment of rules on legal liability for the content of films along the lines of recent legislation on broadcasting. (*See* CINEMA: *Special Report.*)

Censorship of the press resulted in three court decisions by the Federal Constitutional Court in West Germany. One case involved the review of a sentence under which a journalist was forbidden to write as part of his punishment for publishing material in contravention of the ban on the former Communist Party. The court held that the punishment of disqualification from following a profession, even the profession of journalism, is not contrary to the basic freedoms announced in the *Grundgesetz* (Basic Law). In a second case, the court delivered a judgment in favour of the pro-Communist weekly *Blinkfeuer* against the Axel Springer publishing house and *Die Welt,* which had promoted a boycott by newspaper distributors against *Blinkfeuer* because it published the programs of East Berlin radio stations. This decision, reversing a lower court judgment, held that anyone who promotes a boycott of the press on political grounds infringes upon the freedom of expression guaranteed by art. 5(2) of the *Grundgesetz.* In the third case, the court sustained the complaint of a journalist who was fined DM. 500 for refusing to reveal the source of his information. The court held that this punishment violated art. 5(1) of the *Grundgesetz* dealing with freedom of the press.

Legislative developments concerning press censorship showed both liberal and conservative tendencies. In Portugal the director of information announced that a new press law, abolishing most instances of precensorship, was being prepared. A similar liberal tendency appeared to have occurred in Nigeria, where the federal government established a committee to make recommendations on measures required for the freedom, independence, and viability of the press. On the other hand, a new press law in Iraq prohibited publication of anything derogatory to the president or members of his government or "harmful to the revolution." In Brazil a decree of March 21 placed the press under the jurisdiction of military courts.

The U.S. Supreme Court decided two unique cases on freedom of expression in 1969. In *Brandenburg* v. *Ohio* (395 U.S. 444, 89 S.Ct. 1827), the court reversed the conviction of a Ku Klux Klan leader who had been found guilty of violating Ohio's Criminal Syndicalism Act. This act made it a crime to "advocate or teach the duty, necessity, or propriety" of violence "as a means of accomplishing industrial or political reform." The court said that the states cannot make it a crime for a person merely to advocate, in the abstract, the use of force and violence, though they may prohibit his "incitement to imminent lawless action." In *Tinker* v. *Des Moines Independent Community School District* (393 U.S. 503, 89 S.Ct. 733),

Latin America:
see Inter-American Affairs; *articles on the various countries*

Latin American Free Trade Association:
see Commercial Policies; Inter-American Affairs

Latin-American Literature:
see Literature

Latter-day Saints:
see Religion

the court upheld the right of high school students to protest the war in Vietnam by wearing black armbands as long as such action had no disrupting effect on the administration of the school.

In *Red Lion Broadcasting Co.* v. *F.C.C.* (395 U.S. 367, 89 S.Ct. 1794), the court upheld a Federal Communications Commission order requiring a broadcaster to offer an opportunity for reply to an author who was personally attacked in another broadcast. The court said the "personal attack" rule was an application of the long-standing "fairness" doctrine, which previously had been invoked only to provide equal time for political candidates.

Right of Privacy. In a remarkable case, *Alderman* v. *United States* (394 U.S. 165, 89 S.Ct. 961), the U.S. Supreme Court held that the government may, in a criminal case, use the evidence it obtains by unlawful electronic surveillance against any defendant who does not have "standing to complain"; that a defendant has standing to complain only if he was a party to the overheard conversation or if it took place on his premises; and that when a defendant has standing to complain, illegally obtained surveillance records must be submitted to him so that their relevance to his trial may be determined in adversary proceedings. The Italian Tribuna di Roma held that the interception of a telephone conversation, if made without the reasoned authorization of a magistrate, cannot be used in evidence in criminal cases. In Sweden the minister of justice stated that limited telephone tapping was necessary to a successful fight against narcotics. Accordingly, he introduced a bill to permit phone tapping upon the issuance of a court order, valid for a maximum period of one month in each case.

In *Chimel* v. *California* (395 U.S. 752, 89 S.Ct. 2034), the U.S. Supreme Court defined the area of permissible search incidental to a valid arrest made without a warrant. The court's definition rejected a view, believed to be widely accepted in police circles, that it is permissible to search a man's house when he is validly arrested in it. In the case, the defendant was properly arrested in his home on charges of burglary. The arresting officers had no warrant to search the home, but they insisted they had this right as an incident to the lawful arrest. In searching the home over the protest of the defendant, the arresting officers discovered evidence of the burglary for which they had charged the defendant, and this evidence subsequently was used at the trial, where the defendant was convicted. The court reversed the conviction, holding that a police officer may search a person arrested in order to remove any weapons and to seize evidence on his person and may also search the area within the immediate control of the accused, meaning the area from within which he might gain possession of a weapon or destroy evidence.

Military Law. Important cases concerning conscription were decided in 1969 in France, Australia, the U.S., and by the European Commission of Human Rights. In France the Cour d'Appel d'Orléans confirmed a sentence of imprisonment (later suspended), fine, and five-year deprivation of civil rights imposed on two priests and a professor of philosophy for refusing induction into the armed services. The defendants had returned their army papers after their applications for classification as conscientious objectors had been dismissed on the sole ground that they had been submitted "too late."

The European Commission of Human Rights rejected the contention of a British conscript that military service was oppressive and tantamount to involuntary servitude.

In construing sec. 29A(1) of the National Service Act of 1951–65, the High Court of Australia held that a person whose conscientious beliefs do not allow him to engage in any form of military service in the prosecution of the war in Vietnam is not entitled to exemption from national service unless he is a total pacifist. The defendant had asserted that his beliefs would not allow him to engage in any form of military service that might assist in the prosecution of the Vietnam war, including service as a noncombatant on the Australian mainland. At the same time, the defendant admitted that he would be prepared to bear arms in defense of Australian territory. Because of this, the High Court found that the defendant was not a "total pacifist" and therefore was not entitled to an exemption.

In the U.S. two significant decisions involving the Selective Service law were handed down. In the first, *Oestereich* v. *Selective Service Board* (393 U.S. 233, 89 S.Ct. 414), sec. 10(b)(3) of the Military Selective Service Act of 1967 was interpreted by the court.

Abbie Hoffman, defendant in U.S. conspiracy trial, does a handspring on arrival at federal court in Chicago, Sept. 25, 1969. He and seven others were charged with intent to incite riots during Democratic Party convention in 1968.

WIDE WORLD

BEN ROTH AGENCY

"How About This—We Hold These Truths to Be Self Evident That All Men Are Subject to Wiretapping"
—Graham, "Arkansas Gazette."

This section provides that "No judicial review shall be made of the classification or processing of any registrant by local boards, appeal boards, or the President, except as a defense to a criminal prosecution. . . ." Under this section, it was thought that the only recourse open to one who claimed he was wrongfully classified was to resist induction and then use the allegedly erroneous classification as a defense to the criminal action for refusing induction. The court rejected this interpretation.

Oestereich was enrolled at a theological school and was preparing for the ministry. Accordingly, he was classified IV-D by his Selective Service board, pursuant to a section of the Selective Service law exempting divinity students from military service. He returned his draft card to the government as a means of protesting against the war in Vietnam. Shortly thereafter, his board declared him delinquent for failure to have a draft card in his possession and reclassified him I-A, making him liable for immediate induction. He lost an administrative appeal and was ordered to report for induction. At that point he brought suit to restrain induction, but the federal district court held that it had no power to review the classification because of sec. 10(b)(3). The Court of Appeals affirmed this decision, but the Supreme Court reversed it. In the majority opinion, Justice William O. Douglas pointed out that nothing in the Selective Service statute authorized the local board to reclassify Oestereich because he had surrendered his draft card. Since Oestereich had established that he was entitled to an exemption as a divinity student, it would be harsh to require him to test the validity of the reclassification in a criminal proceeding. Accordingly, a preinduction review should be permitted.

A dissenting opinion, written by Justice Potter Stewart and supported by Justices William J. Brennan, Jr., and Byron White, alleged that the majority had casually disregarded sec. 10(b)(3) because it felt that this section would lead to unnecessary harshness. "But if the statute is constitutional, we have no power to disregard it simply because we think it is harsh. That is a judgment for Congress, not for us."

In a potentially far-reaching decision, the federal district court of Massachusetts in *U.S.* v. *Sisson* (297 F.Supp. 902 [D.C. Mass. 1969]) held that no valid distinction could be drawn between religious and nonreligious conscientious objectors. Sisson claimed to be a conscientious objector to military duty but freely admitted that his objections did not rest on a religious base. His draft board took the view that the concept of conscientious objection was limited to cases in which the objection was made on religious grounds, and it drafted Sisson. The federal district court held that the government cannot draft a sincere, reasonable, though not religious, conscientious objector, and statutory law to the contrary was held to be in violation of "the establishment [of religion] clause" of the First Amendment to the Constitution. The U.S. government announced that it would appeal the decision to the Supreme Court.

The judge advocate general of the U.S. Navy held that the crew of the USS "Pueblo," captured by North Korea in 1968, were "illegal detainees" and not prisoners of war. As a result of this holding, the "confessions" of crew members while in the hands of the North Koreans did not render them liable to disciplinary measures applicable to U.S. servicemen held as prisoners of war. (*See* DEFENSE: *Special Report.*) In Israel the Military Court of Ram Allah (West Jordan) held that a terrorist who does not belong to a recognized military unit, wears no military uniform, and performs acts not usually associated with regular soldiers does not qualify as a "prisoner of war" for purposes of obtaining the protection of the Geneva Convention.

In the case of *O'Callahan* v. *Parker* (395 U.S. 258, 89 S.Ct. 1683), the U.S. Supreme Court decided that the armed forces cannot court-martial servicemen for crimes that are in no way service connected. A strong dissenting opinion was written by Justices John Marshall Harlan, Stewart, and White. The case involved an assault and attempted rape committed off a military base by a soldier while on an evening pass and dressed in civilian clothes. The soldier was arrested by city police who turned him over to military authorities, and he was subsequently convicted by a military court. The Supreme Court reversed this conviction on the ground that the soldier was entitled to be tried by a civilian court.

Equality of the Sexes. In 1969 the Australian Arbitral Commission adopted the principle of equal pay for equal work for women. New pay rates, to be introduced gradually over the period from Oct. 1, 1969 (85% of male rate), to Jan. 1, 1972, would eventually cover all women employed in Australian industries that do business with the federal government.

In Italy the Constitutional Court decided that former legal distinctions between males and females with regard to adultery are unconstitutional. The former rule provided that a wife was ipso facto guilty of an offense upon proof that she had committed adultery, whereas a husband was guilty only upon proof that he had established a permanent relationship with his mistress. A follow-up decision in December in effect eliminated adultery as a criminal offense.

In West Germany the Equal Rights Law was held to bar a husband's tort claim for the services of his deceased wife. The High Court held that the damages a husband may recover on account of his wife's death are limited to his own out-of-pocket expenses. It denied recovery for his claim for the loss of her services in the household because the Equal Rights Law freed her from the obligation to perform these services.

Drugs and Medical Developments. In England the House of Lords, in the case of *Sweet* v. *Parsley,* ruled that the defendant was not guilty of violating sec. 5(b) of the Dangerous Drugs Act of 1965 as a person "concerned in the management of any premises used" for the purpose of smoking cannabis, because there was no proof that she knew the premises were being used for that purpose.

The U.S. Supreme Court, in the case of *Leary* v. *U.S.* (395 U.S. 6, 89 S.Ct. 1532), reversed the conviction of Timothy Leary for violating the federal marijuana tax act. This act required that the names of all those who paid the tax be turned over to law enforcement officials in states where possession, use, or sale of marijuana are crimes. The court said that compliance with this part of the tax statute resulted in a form of self-incrimination, in violation of the Fifth Amendment to the Constitution.

The legal implications of organ transplants continued to be considered. In the U.S. the National Conference of Commissions on Uniform State Laws drafted a model law concerning the donation of human organs for transplantation. The draft was approved by the American Bar Association and enacted, in some cases with variations, in Kansas, Louisiana, and Maryland. The Committee of National Health and Medical Research Council of Australia drew up an elaborate proposal for the conduct of organ transplant operations. One interesting feature of this proposal was the requirement that two medical teams be involved—one for deciding when further medical treatment of the donor has become useless and a second for carrying out the operation.

In England a voluntary euthanasia bill was defeated by the House of Lords. In West Germany the Bundestag passed a law allowing castration of convicted sex criminals under limited circumstances. The castration could be performed only if the sex criminal was found likely to repeat his crime, was at least 25 years old, and consented to the operation, and if the crime was found to be directly attributable to exceptional sexual urges that could be eliminated by castration. (W. D. ID.)

The report concerning former Suffolk County Judge Floyd Sarisohn, appearing on page 254 in the 1968 *Britannica Book of the Year,* should not have been placed under the heading of "Major Crimes." No charge of any crime was ever made against former Judge Sarisohn. Further, the charge regarding Judge Sarisohn advising a prostitute was dismissed on appeal.

International Law. *Boundaries and Territorial Disputes.* A large number of boundary adjustments were made peacefully by negotiations during 1969. An 800-sq.km. tract of territory in the Chaco was transferred from Bolivia to Paraguay. An agreement signed by Venezuela and Brazil defined the common border and added about 1,000 sq.km. to Venezuela. After a century of dispute between the U.S. and Mexico, the island of El Chamizal in the Rio Grande was transferred to Mexico. An agreement signed in Moscow redefined part of the common frontier between Norway and the U.S.S.R.; the old line had become partly obsolete following construction of a dam and the consequent formation of a lake on the border. India and Pakistan agreed on the complete demarcation of the Rann of Cutch region of Gujarat and West Pakistan. A new dispute arose, however, between Iran and Iraq when Iran denounced the treaty of 1937 concerning the common frontier along the Shatt al Arab.

Spain's claim to Gibraltar reached a more serious stage with the closing of the land frontier and the cutting of telecommunications links. The UN resolution demanding termination of the colonial situation in Gibraltar by October 1 was rejected by Britain as unacceptable and unrealistic. The attempt of the UN General Assembly to terminate South Africa's mandate over South West Africa proved fruitless, and South Africa continued to administer the territory. In *S.* v. *Tuhadeleni* 1969 (1) S.A.153 (A.D.), the Appellate Division held that the South African courts had no power to review legislation that purported to extend to South West Africa, and that the South Africa Constitution Act of 1961, which denied them the power to inquire into the validity of any statute, also prevented them from testing statutes against the terms of the mandate.

Sanctions against Rhodesia had no greater success during 1969 than previously, in spite of occasional prosecutions of businessmen for exporting goods to Rhodesia via South Africa. In October a bill was introduced into the Rhodesian legislature for the enactment of a new constitution that would increase racial separatism and sever the final links with the British crown by declaring a republic.

In West New Guinea (Irian Barat), the "act of choice" (which the UN had required as a condition of handing the territory over to Indonesia) was held and declared in favour of continued association with Indonesia. The latter thereupon claimed the dependency as an integral part of Indonesian national territory. The "act" was not a plebiscite, but a taking of opinion from representatives of the population chosen by the administrators.

The success of the U.S. icebreaking tanker "Manhattan" in forcing the Northwest Passage around the northern coasts of Canada to the newly discovered

Al Fatah terrorists patrol the banks of the Jordan in 1969. An Israeli military court held that captured terrorists were not entitled to protection as prisoners of war under the terms of the Geneva Convention.

BLACK STAR

UPI COMPIX

RFK must be
be be disposed of
d d d
disposed
disposed d of
disposed
disposed of properly
Robert Fitzgerald
Kennedy must soon die
die die die die
die die die die die

Page from Sirhan B. Sirhan's diary was part of copy introduced as evidence on Feb. 25, 1969, at Sirhan's trial for the murder of Robert F. Kennedy.

Alaskan oil fields led to some concern that Canadian sovereignty over the Arctic territories and waters might be disputed. Legislation was prepared to reinforce Canadian jurisdiction in the area.

Even more activity took place in the field of maritime and water boundaries. This applied particularly to the continental shelf, but also to Lake Constance, where West Germany, Switzerland, and Austria began negotiations on their common boundaries. Interstate continental shelf boundaries were agreed between the U.S.S.R. and Poland (Baltic Sea and Gulf of Gdansk), Iran and Qatar (Persian Gulf), Brazil and Uruguay (South Atlantic), and Sweden and Norway (Skagerrak/Kattegat). Negotiations to the same end were opened between the U.S. and Canada.

The dispute over the continental shelf boundaries between West Germany on the one hand and Denmark and the Netherlands on the other was the subject of an inconclusive judgment by the International Court of Justice in February (*North Sea Continental Shelf Cases*). Under the widely adopted equidistance principle contained in art. 6 of the Geneva Convention on the Continental Shelf, 1958, West Germany, which has a concave coastline, would have only a small area of the North Sea as compared with the convex Netherlands. The court held that the equidistance principle was not binding on West Germany (which was not a party to the convention), but neither did the principle that "each coastal state is entitled to a just and equitable share" apply. No single principle did apply, and the parties were told to renegotiate on the basis of equitable principles, all relevant circumstances, and the principle of natural prolongation of land territory.

The trend toward a 12-mi. belt of territorial waters was continued by, among others, Kenya, The Gambia, Spain, Brazil, and Uruguay. Those Latin-American states that claimed a 200-mi. belt came into open conflict with the U.S., and negotiations were opened to try to find a satisfactory modus vivendi. (*See* INTER-AMERICAN AFFAIRS.) Canada promulgated an order in council delimiting its 3-mi. territorial belt and a further 9-mi. exclusive fishing zone off Nova Scotia, Vancouver Island, and the Queen Charlotte Islands.

Wars and Interventions. The war in Vietnam continued; some U.S. troops were withdrawn, but this and other signs of a battlefield slowdown seemed to have little effect on the Paris peace negotiations.

The civil war in Nigeria also continued, as the federal blockade of Biafra called down condemnation from many countries on humanitarian grounds. Civil war broke out in Chad, and the government called on France to send troops under the Franco-Chad mutual assistance treaty.

The Soviet occupation of Czechoslovakia gave rise to a new Soviet theory of "limited sovereignty," which appeared to apply to any state that fell within the sphere of influence of a major power.

A war that broke out in June between Honduras and El Salvador (the so-called "soccer war") ended in a cease-fire after strenuous mediation by the Organization of American States. Under pressure from the Central American Common Market, talks between the two countries were scheduled for early 1970.

The Arab-Israeli conflict intensified, with border skirmishes increasing in frequency and scale. The Palestinian terrorist organizations took the war to other countries by hijacking aircraft, bombing aircraft on foreign soil, and bombing buildings in several Western European countries.

The Sea. Perhaps the biggest topic of discussion in international law circles was the question of jurisdiction and sovereignty over the seabed and its resources outside the limits of the continental shelf. Conferences, discussions, draft proposals, learned articles, and books proliferated. The main dispute was between the protagonists of national jurisdiction (by an extension of the continental shelf rules—which can indeed be spelled out of the existing definition of the continental shelf in the 1958 Geneva Convention) and those favouring international jurisdiction (in trust for mankind as a whole; *i.e.*, in effect, the poor countries). The UN committee on the peaceful uses of the seabed and ocean floor beyond the limits of national jurisdiction adopted its report to the General Assembly. Meanwhile, exploration of the deep-sea bed took place despite the uncertainty over its legal status. Saudi Arabia specifically claimed rights over the ocean floor resources in the Red Sea.

Encroachment on the freedom of the high seas and its character as res nullius took other forms. The construction of artificial harbours for supertankers in international waters was projected in a number of countries, and the harbour off Kuwait was opened during 1969. A similar development was the positioning at sea of giant oil storage tanks to facilitate tanker loading, as was done in the Persian Gulf.

Of great concern was the problem of pollution. The 1954 convention on pollution of the sea was largely ineffectual, and states were unwilling to incur the expense of regular air patrols of the sea-lanes to detect unauthorized discharges of oil. A number of studies had been initiated, and the International Maritime Committee produced two conventions on liability for oil spillage at sea that were to be discussed at an international conference in 1970. The major oil tanker firms agreed on a scheme for meeting the damage caused by unlawful oil spillage up to a maximum of some $9.6 million. Both Sweden and the U.S.S.R. took initiatives to convene conferences of Baltic states to discuss cooperative efforts to prevent or minimize oil pollution in the Baltic. The North Sea states signed an agreement to exchange information on combating oil pollution. The U.S. introduced stringent regulations governing oil exploration within its jurisdiction (primarily as a result of oil seepage from a rig off the California coast), and a bill before the Senate provided for unlimited liability in cases of negligence.

Oil, however, was not the only potential source of pollution. The proposal of the U.S. authorities to transport large quantities of surplus poison gas cross-country and dump them in the sea caused a public outcry and drastic modification of plans. A ripple of apprehension also followed a report that the concrete canisters surrounding large quantities of poison that Sweden had dumped in the Baltic in the early 1930s were crumbling, and that if they released their contents there was enough to poison practically the whole of the Baltic.

In the field of marine fisheries, there was increasing concern about the new habit of netting salmon in the open sea. Salmon countries complained that they risked losing much of their salmon if the young fish were caught at sea before breeding.

International Adjudication. The International Court of Justice found itself out of work when it gave judgment in its last remaining cases, the *North Sea Continental Shelf Cases* and *Concerning the Barcelona Traction, Light and Power Company Ltd.* There was a flurry of speculation on the future of the court. The European Court of Human Rights, on the other hand, seemed at last to have picked up steam, and although it did not deliver any judgments during 1969, it had several cases on hand. In at least one of them, involving Belgium, it was expected to give judgment early in 1970.

Other events included the final adoption of the Vienna Convention on the law of treaties; the coming into force of the Tokyo Convention of 1963 on offenses and certain other acts committed on board aircraft and the growing agitation for even stronger rules to prevent or punish aircraft hijacking; the further consideration by the International Law Commission of its draft articles for a convention on the subject of relations between states and international organizations; the continuing work of the UN working party on direct broadcasting satellites; the legal principles worked out by the UN legal subcommittee on the peaceful uses of outer space, relating to compensation for damage caused by objects launched into outer space; and proposals that a special UN membership category be created for "microstates."

International Organizations. Two Latin-American groupings of potential importance appeared: the Andean Common Market (Colombia, Chile, Ecuador, Peru, and Bolivia—Venezuela for the time being standing aloof) and the Río de la Plata Basin Treaty (Argentina, Bolivia, Brazil, Paraguay, and Uruguay).

The Council of Europe continued its usual activities, in particular establishment of a convention on the protection of water from pollution. More important was the controversy over the membership of Greece. The action brought against Greece before the European Commission of Human Rights by the

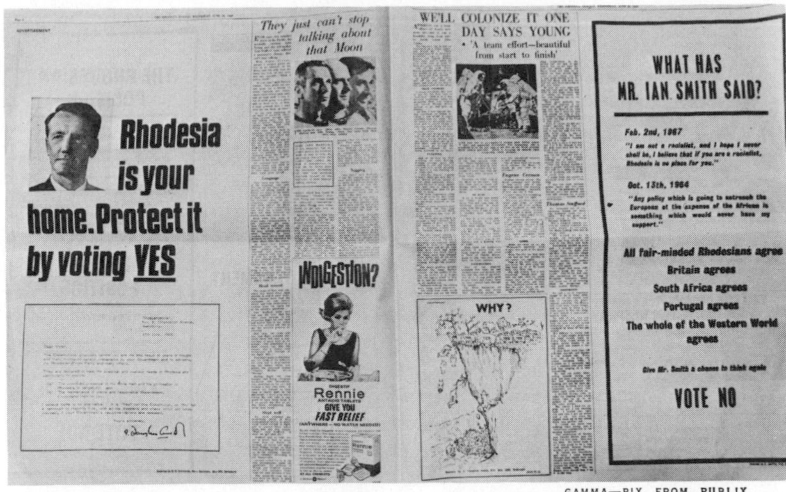

GAMMA—PIX FROM PUBLIX

Conflicting advertisements in June 18, 1969, issue of "Rhodesia Herald" oppose and support proposals for new constitution to ensure minority rule by whites.

Scandinavian states and the Netherlands reached its conclusion and the commission's report was published in November. It accused the Greek government of various undemocratic practices, including the torture of political prisoners. Facing almost certain expulsion, Greece withdrew from the Council.

In December 1968 the Nordic countries (excluding Iceland) produced a report on closer economic co-operation (Nordek), which was considered at a prime ministers' meeting in Stockholm on January 18–19. A further committee of experts prepared a second report and draft treaty by July, and this was the subject of extensive public discussion.

Expansion of the European Communities became a practical possibility with the resignation of French Pres. Charles de Gaulle. The European Commission produced an updated favourable report on admission of the existing applicants—the U.K., Ireland, Denmark, and Norway. Negotiations were expected to begin in 1970. (*See* EUROPEAN UNITY.)

Despite a number of traumatic breaches of the Community spirit by national governments (*e.g.,* French negotiation of a trade treaty with the U.S.S.R. without involving the Commission, West German unilateral imposition of import duties on agricultural produce after floating the mark, Belgian and Italian refusal to implement the directive requiring the value-added tax to be introduced in 1970), many advances were made. The convention on recognition and enforcement of foreign judgments in civil and commercial matters and a first-draft directive on freedom to supply services within the legal profession were major legal steps. The Commission for the first time imposed fines on high-ranking businesses for cartel policies violating art. 85 and 86 of the Rome Treaty (the quinine and the aniline dyes cases, respectively). In the aniline dyes case, the Commission went further and imposed fines on four foreign (non-EEC) companies. This attempt to exercise extraterritorial jurisdiction was resisted, and the matter was expected to be taken to the Court of Justice at Luxembourg.

Family Law. The most revolutionary development was the Swedish governmental proposal, embodied in the terms of reference of a committee set up to consider reform of the marriage laws, to abolish in practice the differences between the married and the unmarried state. Thus, the same laws of inheritance, distribution of property, and maintenance would apply whether children were legitimate or illegitimate and whether a union was or was not registered as a marriage.

In the U.K. the bill to reform the divorce law by allegedly making breakdown of marriage the sole ground (but in effect retaining the old matrimonial offenses under a new name and merely adding divorce by consent after two years and unilateral divorce after five) received the royal assent in October, after the Law Commission had produced its proposals for dealing with the property aspects of divorce. The bill would not come into force until January 1971 when, it was assumed, the more fundamental changes recommended by the commission would also be law.

A report on marriage and divorce was published in Kenya, which recommended breakdown of marriage as the sole ground for divorce and which had important things to say about the equality of husband and wife, the position of polygamous marriages, and consent in marriage. This report coped with the problems of a pluralist and African society and was expected to have considerable influence.

Consumer Protection. The effects were felt of two legislative events of major importance: the U.K. Trade Descriptions Act, 1968, and the U.S. Truth in Lending Act, 1968, both of which imposed strict standards on traders when selling goods or services to customers. Many other efforts were made toward consumer protection—an area of increasing concern to law reformers—including the Australian Uniform Packaging Code, the New South Wales Consumer Protection Act, and Canadian proposals for a series of statutes on consumer protection.

Censorship. The most far-reaching consideration of film censorship took place in the Scandinavian countries (see *Court Decisions and Related Developments,* above). An Indian report on film censorship recommended considerable liberalization of censors' practices, particularly by allowing kissing in Indian films and even, in certain cases, the portrayal of nudity. In the U.K., a report issued under the auspices of (but not by) the Arts Council recommended abolition of the offense of publishing obscene matter, but the home secretary stated that he would not support such an initiative. In West Germany, the Federal High Court held that *Fanny Hill* was not obscene since, to be punishable, literary descriptions of sexual intercourse must be gross and perverse.

In Finland a press council was set up, which would embrace radio and television broadcasting as well. A "press ombudsman" was instituted in Sweden (in addition to the existing press council) to handle complaints from the public and, where appropriate, initiate proceedings against newspapers.

Administrative Law. The institution of an ombudsman was officially proposed for the Netherlands, Ireland, and some other countries. The British ombudsman was also appointed to the new post of ombudsman for Northern Ireland. The government intended to extend his jurisdiction to cover local authorities as well as the central administration, to which he was at first restricted. In Sweden the first report was issued of the new combined and expanded ombudsman office; in Norway, the first report of the ombudsman since his jurisdiction was extended to include local authorities was published. Also in Norway, the new Administrative Law Statute was ordered by the Storting to come into force on Jan. 1, 1970. New principles of tortious liability of civil servants were contained in a Swedish government proposal. The principle of publicity in administration, an essential part of Swedish and Finnish administrative law, was embodied in government bills in both Norway and Denmark. It had been introduced in the U.S. two years earlier.

Serious concern was felt in many countries at the inability of the judicial machine to cope with the demands being put upon it. In Italy the machinery was breaking down. Far-reaching reforms were being worked out in France and the U.K., and in Sweden a thoroughgoing reorganization of the court structure was under way. (N. M. H.)

See also Crime; Defense; Police; Race Relations.

ENCYCLOPÆDIA BRITANNICA FILMS. *Understanding the Law—Equal Justice for All* (1953); *The Congress* (1954); *The Supreme Court* (1954); *The Bill of Rights of the United States* (1956); *The Constitution of the United States* (1956); *Magna Carta, Part I (Rise of the English Monarchy)* (1959); *Magna Carta, Part II (Revolt of the Nobles and the Signing of the Charter)* (1959); *Justice Under Law (Gideon Case)* (1966); *Equality Under Law—The Lost Generation of Prince Edward County* (1967); *Freedom to Speak (N.Y. v. Feiner)* (1967); *Equality Under Law—California Fair Housing Case* (1969); *Free Press vs. Fair Trial by Jury—The Sheppard Case* (1969).

Lebanon

A republic of the Middle East, Lebanon is bounded by Syria, Israel, and the Mediterranean Sea. Area: 4,015 sq.mi. (10,400 sq.km.). Pop. (1968 est.): 2,580,000. Cap. and largest city: Beirut (pop., 1961 est., 298,129). Language: Arabic. Religion: approximately 50% Christian, 34% Muslim. President in 1969, Charles Helou; prime ministers, Abdullah Yafi to January 8 and, from January 15, Rashid Karami.

Lebanon was gravely disturbed in 1969 by internal disunity over the Palestine problem and the Palestinian guerrillas. In January Lebanese and Arab nationalists among the Lebanese were united in criticism of the government for its total failure to defend Beirut airport against the Israeli raid on Dec. 28, 1968, and 25,000 students of all political persuasions demonstrated demanding the introduction of conscription

Lebanese mans a machine gun Nov. 2, 1969, in rebel-held section of Tripoli. The city was the scene of fighting in the Lebanese-guerrilla warfare brought about by the government's decision to prohibit guerrilla activity.

UPI COMPIX

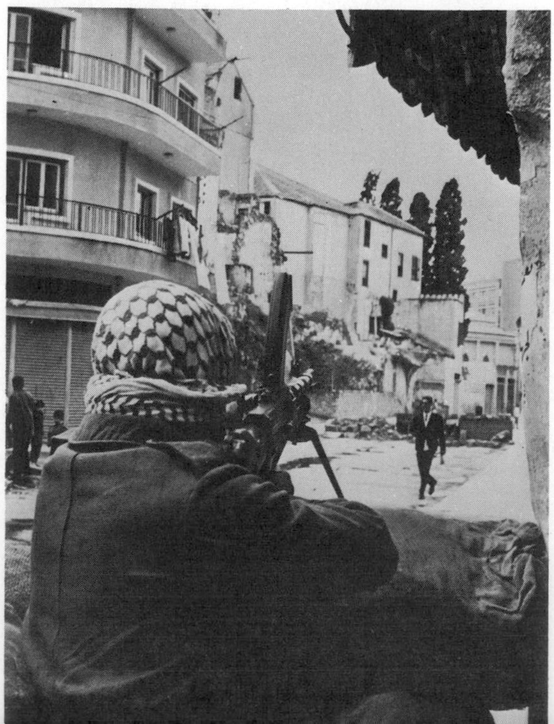

and a more vigorous defense policy. On January 8 the resignation of the government of Abdullah Yafi was accepted, and on January 15 Rashid Karami returned to power. The Maronite Christian leaders, Pierre Gemayel and Raymond Eddé, immediately resigned because their ally in the right-wing Triple Alliance, former Pres. Camille Sham'un (Chamoun), had not been invited to join the new government.

The Karami government was increasingly embarrassed by the presence of Palestinian guerrillas in southern Lebanon and especially by members of Al Saiqah, the Baathist group supported by the Syrians. In April, after a clash between the Lebanese Army and Al Saiqah, there was serious rioting. Curfews were imposed for a week and on April 24 Karami resigned, saying that he would not take office again until a common policy concerning the Palestinian problem had been worked out. This proved impossible. The Al Fatah guerrilla leader, Yasir Arafat (*see* BIOGRAPHY), came to Beirut for talks which were inconclusive despite mediation by the United Arab Republic. To avoid forcing the issue President Helou retained Karami as the head of a caretaker government. Israel launched several attacks on alleged guerrilla bases in Lebanon and during October 21–November 13 Syria closed its border with Lebanon in retaliation for Lebanese attacks on guerrillas. Karami resigned once more, but later agreed to remain in office.

Armed clashes between the guerrillas and Lebanese troops occurred frequently in late October, with the guerrillas establishing strongholds in southern and eastern Lebanon. Negotiations to end the conflict were begun in Cairo, and on November 2 a cease-fire was arranged. Lebanon endorsed the presence of guerrillas on its territory in return for a pledge by the guerrillas to "cooperate" with the Lebanese Army.

The Lebanese service-based economy was harmfully affected by the political uncertainty. Industrial exports rose sharply and transit trade was up because of closure of the Suez Canal but the banking, tourism, and building sectors were depressed. (P. MD.)

ENCYCLOPÆDIA BRITANNICA FILMS. *The Middle East* (1955); *The Mediterranean World* (1961).

LEBANON

Education. (1966–67) Primary, pupils 365,403; secondary, pupils 96,482; primary and secondary, teachers 25,008; vocational, pupils 1,482, teachers 446; teacher training, students 1,936, teachers 356; higher (including 4 universities), students 23,475, teaching staff (1965–66) 1,434.

Finance. Monetary unit: Lebanese pound, with an official rate of L£3.08 to U.S. $1 (L£7.40 = £1 sterling) and a free rate (Oct. 1969) of L£3.23 to U.S. $1 (L£7.70 = £1). Gold and foreign exchange, central bank: (June 1969) U.S. $321.8 million; (June 1968) U.S. $318.2 million. Budget (1968 est.) balanced at L£716 million. National income: (1965) L£3,154 million; (1964) L£2,861 million. Money supply: (May 1969) L£1,778 million; (May 1968) L£1,648 million.

Foreign Trade. (1967) Imports L£1,782 million; exports L£453 million; transit trade (through the free port of Beirut) L£957.7 million. Import sources: Syria 11%; U.S. 10%; West Germany 9%; France 9%; Italy 8%; U.K. 6%. Export destinations: Saudi Arabia 20%; Kuwait 11%; Jordan 8%; Iraq 7%; Syria 6%; U.S. 5%; U.K. 5%; Libya 5%. Main exports: fruit and vegetables 24%; precious stones and metals 20%; textiles and clothing 8%; livestock and meat 8%; machinery 6%.

Transport and Communications. Roads (1967) 7,108 km. (including 1,990 km. main roads). Motor vehicles in use (1967): passenger 114,242; commercial 12,763. Railways: (1967) 417 km.; traffic (1968) 6.7 million passenger-km., freight 36 million net ton-km. Air traffic (1967): 695,567,000 passenger-km.; freight 65,034,000 net ton-km. Shipping (1968): vessels 100 gross tons and over 122; gross tonnage 443,881. Telephones (Jan. 1968) *c.* 130,000. Radio receivers (Dec. 1967) 451,000. Television receivers (Dec. 1967) 150,000.

Agriculture. Production (in 000; metric tons; 1968; 1967 in parentheses): grapes 84 (88); wheat *c.* 45 (68); dry onions (1967) 44, (1966) 32; olive oil *c.* 6 (*c.* 13); figs 13 (13); bananas (1967) 27, (1966) 30; oranges 175 (168); lemons 61 (70); apples (1967) 157, (1966) 104; tobacco (1967) 6.4, (1966) 6.3. Livestock (in 000; 1966–67): cattle 97; asses 30; goats 431; sheep 198; poultry 14,980.

Industry. Production (in 000; metric tons; 1967): petroleum products 1,664; cement (1968) 906; electricity (kw-hr.) 907,000.

Lesotho

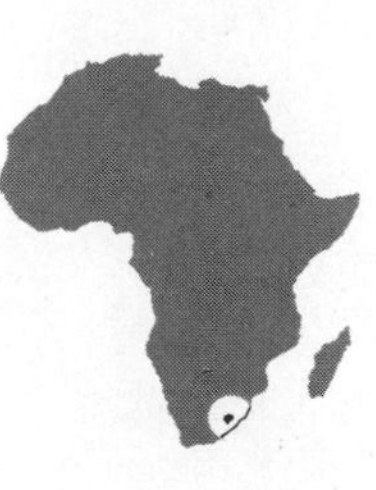

A constitutional monarchy of southern Africa, Lesotho is completely surrounded by South Africa. Area: 11,716 sq.mi. (30,344 sq.km.). Pop. (1968): 1,018,135, almost 99% African. Cap. and largest city: Maseru (pop., 1966, 14,000). Language: English (official) and Sesotho. Religion: about 70% Christian. Chief of state in 1969, Paramount Chief Moshoeshoe II; prime minister, Chief Leabua Jonathan.

Progress was made in all sectors of the economy in 1969. Agriculture still accounted for more than 70% of Lesotho's gross domestic product, followed by the output from small industries in the west and diamond exploitation in the Maluti Mountains. In spite of continuing drought which necessitated some famine relief, record wheat, wool, and cattle exports were achieved in 1968; and irrigation and conservation schemes progressed despite traditional land tenure problems. Farmers from Taiwan demonstrated methods of growing vegetables, and in August the prime minister, Chief Leabua Jonathan, visited Taiwan and signed a cooperative agricultural agreement. A $2.8 million agreement with Lonrho, a private firm, for mining and prospecting in the Mokhotlong area gave fresh impetus to the potentially vitally important diamond industry.

British aid, mainly budgetary and development grants, totaled more than £4 million for 1969–70 and led to the provision of a variety of voluntary agencies. The main hope for achieving a viable economy in Lesotho, the Oxbow hydroelectric scheme in the Maluti Mountains, reached the stage of final feasibility tests financed by the UN Development Program. South Africa, with which Lesotho maintained a currency and customs union, agreed to act as main power and water purchaser. The Lesotho National

LESOTHO

Education. (1966) Primary, pupils 167,169, teachers 2,799; secondary, pupils 2,825, teachers 120; vocational, pupils 173, teachers 29; teacher training, students 530, teachers 57; higher (University of Botswana, Lesotho, and Swaziland), students 344, teaching staff (1964) 38.

Finance and Trade. Monetary unit: South African rand, with a par value of R 0.71 to U.S. $1 (R 1.71 = £1 sterling). Budget (1969–70 est.) balanced at R 11,322,650 (including R 4,970,600 U.K. grant). Foreign trade (1967): imports R 23.8 million; exports R 4,168,000. Main exports: cattle 29%; diamonds 24%; wool 21%; peas and beans 11%; mohair 9%. The adverse trade balance is partly offset by receipts from labour working in South Africa (R 2,450,000 in 1968–69).

Agriculture. Production (in 000; metric tons; 1967; 1966 in parentheses): corn *c.* 110 (109); wheat *c.* 50 (58); sorghum (1966) 54, (1963) *c.* 54; wool (1966) *c.* 2.2, (1965) *c.* 2.2; meat *c.* 22 (*c.* 22). Livestock (in 000; 1967): cattle 376; sheep 1,526; goats 891.

Lawn Bowls:
see Bowling and Lawn Bowls

Lawn Tennis:
see Tennis

Lead:
see Mining

Leeward Islands:
see Dependent States

Development Corporation continued to promote small industries. South Africa maintained a supply of technical and practical aid and remained Lesotho's main source of revenue. About 60,000 Basuto working in South Africa earned more than R 10 million ($7 million) in 1969. In an effort to increase savings in Lesotho, a National Development Bank was established.

The first elections since independence, due in 1970, provoked a resurgence of political activity, with squabbles splintering the left-wing opposition parties. Chief Jonathan enhanced his stature at the Commonwealth Prime Ministers' Conference with his realistic views on economic cooperation and the problems of landlocked countries. He revealed that Lesotho had approached South Africa to allow easy access for tourists bound for Lesotho. (M. Mr.)

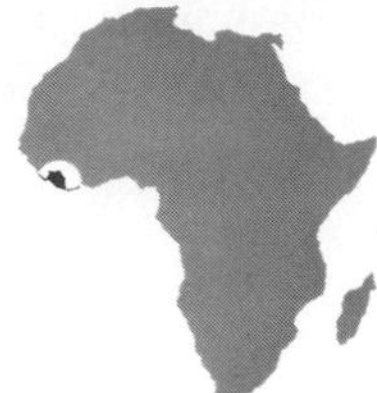

Liberia

A republic on the west coast of Africa, Liberia is bordered by Sierra Leone, Guinea, and Ivory Coast. Area: 43,000 sq.mi. (111,370 sq.km.). Pop. (1968 est.): 1,130,000. Cap. and largest city: Monrovia (pop., 1962, 80,992). Language: English and tribal dialects. President in 1969, William V. S. Tubman.

The first four days of January were devoted to a national celebration of William V. S. Tubman's 25th anniversary as president of Liberia. Gen. Joseph A. Ankrah, the only foreign head of state to attend the festivities, came from Ghana for his first visit. He told reporters that "relations between Liberia and Ghana have been very cordial and brotherly since the National Liberation Council came to power [in Ghana]," and he thanked Tubman for being the first head of state to recognize his government after the February 1966 coup d'etat. Ankrah was given Liberia's highest decoration, the Venerable Grand Order of Pioneers.

In a special silver jubilee gesture, Tubman announced on January 4 an "amnesty to all political prisoners . . . except those that have already been convicted." The amnesty decree did not apply to former Liberian ambassador Henry Fahnbulleh, who had been sentenced to 20 years in prison on treason charges in July 1968. The Supreme Court dismissed Fahnbulleh's appeal for release from confinement on February 7. Controversy over the Fahnbulleh case continued, however. In a nationwide broadcast on Nov. 8, 1968, Tubman had denounced the writers of anonymous letters calling for his resignation. In November 1969 Congress granted emergency powers to President Tubman following the murder of the American Episcopal missionary bishop of Liberia, the Right Rev. Dillard H. Brown.

Liberia showed encouraging signs of economic growth in 1969, although the country's large foreign debt remained a troublesome burden. In a review of economic and other achievements of Tubman's regime, Agence France-Presse reported on the last day of 1968 that Liberia's national budget had increased from less than $1 million in 1944 to more than $60 million for 1969. The report noted that since 1948 exports had risen from $15 million to $158 million, while imports had climbed from $9 million to $125 million. It also pointed out that Liberia's education budget had grown from $84,000 in 1944 to $13.5 million in 1967, with a corresponding rise in the number of schoolchildren from 19,000 to 122,000.

Liberia solidified its position as the world's foremost nation in terms of registered shipping tonnage. Lloyd's *Register of Shipping Statistics* reported late in 1968 that, in the year ending June 30, 1968, Liberia had added 3.1 million tons of new shipping for a total of 25.7 million tons. (Ri. W.)

LIBERIA

Education. (1966–67) Primary, pupils 110,251, teachers 3,137; secondary, pupils 11,324, teachers 521; vocational, students 856, teachers (1964–65) 39; teacher training, pupils 279, teachers 31; higher, students 797, teaching staff 129.

Finance. Monetary unit: Liberian dollar, at par with the U.S. dollar (L$2.40 = £1 sterling). Budget (1969 est.): revenue L$58 million; expenditure L$60.1 million.

Foreign Trade. (1968) Imports L$118 million; exports L$169 million. Import sources (1967): U.S. 44%; West Germany 12%; Japan 7%; U.K. 7%. Export destinations: U.S. 30%; West Germany 28%; Italy 11%; U.K. 9%; Belgium-Luxembourg 7%; France 5%; Netherlands 5%. Main exports (1967): iron ore 73%; rubber 17%.

Transport and Communications. Roads (1967) *c.* 3,200 km. Motor vehicles in use (1967): passenger *c.* 8,300; commercial (including buses) *c.* 5,100. Railways (1967) 420 km. Shipping (1968): merchant vessels 100 gross tons and over 1,613 (mostly owned by U.S. and other foreign interests); gross tonnage 25,719,642. Telephones (Jan. 1968) *c.* 3,500. Radio receivers (Dec. 1966) 152,000. Television receivers (Dec. 1967) 4,600.

Agriculture. Production (in 000; metric tons; 1967; 1966 in parentheses): rice *c.* 152 (*c.* 150); cassava *c.* 430 (*c.* 430); rubber (exports) 62 (53); palm kernels (exports) 14 (13); cocoa 1.9 (1.8); coffee *c.* 3.4 (*c.* 3). Livestock (in 000; Aug. 1967): cattle *c.* 29; pigs *c.* 31; sheep c. 12; goats *c.* 57.

Industry. Production (in 000; 1967): iron ore (metal content) 12,575 metric tons; diamonds (exports) *c.* 550 metric carats; electricity (1966) 339,000,000 kw-hr.

Libraries

The International Federation of Library Associations (IFLA) held its annual session in August 1969 at the Royal School of Librarianship, Copenhagen. The main theme, presented to 400 participants from 38 countries, was "Library Education and Research in Librarianship." Sir Frank Francis, formerly director of the British Museum, completed his two terms as president (1963–69), and his place was taken by H. Liebaers of Brussels for 1969–72; R. Malek of Prague was elected as one of the six vice-presidents.

UNESCO Department of Documentation, Libraries, and Archives. During 1968–69 UNESCO signed contracts with the IFLA and the International Federation for Documentation (FID) for studies on the national planning of library services; the standardization of bibliographical data in catalog entries; a ten-year trilingual supplement to the Universal Decimal Classification; an audio-visual course in librarianship in Spanish and French; and manuals on library legislation and library statistics. The development of library services was promoted by the establishment of a pilot project in school library service in Honduras, to serve as a model for Latin America; a pilot project on public and school libraries in Ceylon; and by continued support for training courses at Makerere University College, Uganda, and elsewhere. UNESCO also sent library experts on mission to 17 countries outside Europe.

Europe. *Austria.* In the summer of 1969 the National Library in Vienna held, in the famous "Prunksaal," an outstanding exhibition of Austrian portraits

continued on page 468

Lesser Eastern Churches: *see* Religion

THE AMERICAN LIBRARY IN PARIS

By Robert Faherty

In its 50th year, the American Library in Paris, Inc., could demonstrate forcefully the logic of its existence: it could prove that it was needed and show the value of its services. And so it maintained the faith of the many persons who had lent it a helping hand since it was chartered on May 20, 1920, as an offshoot of the War Service Libraries, a legitimate child of the American Library Association (ALA) of Chicago.

All through 1969, extraordinary evidences of the validity of the library's mission were seen in the pleasant rooms of its modest masonry building (wholly owned) at 10, rue Camou, in a quiet quarter of the Left Bank, a few blocks from the Eiffel Tower. Its 1969–70 term brought a peak in membership, creation of the Dillon Wing, and timely planning for the future.

The development of the American College, near at hand, founded in 1963 on the premises of the American Church on the Quai d'Orsay, assured a continuous march of U.S. students and professors into the library to consult the college's own 5,000 books that are given shelf space there and to use other books and periodicals. The reform of French education, which had followed the student revolt of May and June 1968, allowed students hours for broadened individual research and precipitated an influx into the rue Camou of French students avid for study of 20th-century American literature and American civilization. These French could be grateful that they had easy access to the largest English-language library on the European continent and the largest American library outside the U.S.—one with 150,000 books plus 700 periodical titles—and that they had the benefit of American library methods, which make books more visible and reachable than has been customary in Europe.

A considerable superstructure was needed for the library's extensive work, and this was strengthened during the year. The board of 23 trustees—elected every March for one year—was headed by John E. Fobes of UNESCO, who was first elected president of the library in 1968. The officer list included Robert H. Blake, Mrs. Johnson Garrett, Mrs. Benjamin T. Pierce, John E. Utter, and Theodore A. Steinert. The trustees were chosen by the "corporate body" composed of donors. In his 13th year with the library, Harry Goldberg, the chief librarian, planned for and supervised manifold work including the circulation of about 200,000 volumes, the supplying of many magazines for the periodical room, the functions of a Department for the Blind that distributed audio-records of books to many countries, the operation of a photoduplication service, and much activity related to the continual quest for funds.

The approach of the half-century anniversary occasioned a conference in Paris in October of sympathetic spirits, including David H. Clift of the ALA, to plan for the observance, for the future, and especially for the activities of a new U.S. Committee organized with the collaboration of trustee Foster E. Mohrhardt of the ALA. C. Douglas Dillon, former U.S. secretary of the treasury and ambassador to France, was honorary chairman of the U.S. Committee and Theodore Waller was chairman; the committee's headquarters was Waller's office in New York at the Grolier Educational Corp.

The work of the library was multiplying. The number of card-carrying members had grown to more than 3,000. The number of students and professors enrolled had increased 50% in one year to around 1,500, and then up to 1,625. More than 100 children carried cards to draw books from the juveniles' room. The library's collections on American civilization were unique in France. They drew many researchers—to the periodicals collection of more than 40,000 volumes that included issues of the 19th century, to the historical collection, with writings of statesmen, and to the literature collection, including biographies and critiques. In all, the library averaged some 5,000 visitors each month.

The American Library in Paris frankly asks and gratefully receives any assistance. It accepted 25,000 books from the Benjamin Franklin Library of the U.S. Information Service (USIS) in the Place de l'Odéon. A valuable painting was received and turned into cash. The American Council of Learned Societies gave $10,000 for the purchase of books on American studies. Shelves were cleared to receive from William Benton a donation of his personal Paris collection of copies of all the works published by the Encyclopædia Britannica. The Junior Guild of the American Cathedral collaborated in the work for the blind, for which the Library of Congress and the American Printing House for the Blind gave 150 talking books. Thirty-five U.S. publishers donated books regularly.

A large sum of money given by C. Douglas Dillon enabled the library first to accommodate the USIS books, and then to put stonemasons to work creating the Dillon Wing, a centre of American studies scheduled to be opened in 1970. Soon after that, Thayer Lindsley of New York wrote a check for $100,000 to endorse the library's endeavour to establish a substantial endowment fund.

The library has always been a symbol and a realization of the mutual interest and regard between France and the U.S. France did not oppose but, in fact, welcomed the transformation of the War Service Libraries (set up in France by the ALA in 1918) into the American Library in Paris, Inc. This was done on the ALA's site at 19, rue de l'Elysée with the cooperation of French teachers and students. Charles L. Seeger led the operation, giving money earned by the poems of his son, Alan Seeger, lost in the war, and the ALA gave books, cash, shelves, and chairs and helped to get the charter under the laws of Delaware. The desire of American librarians, and particularly of the ALA, to show U.S. library techniques in Europe helped to draw needed financial support to the enterprise. In the 1920s the Paris Library School was based there.

But the depression brought hard times, and the library barely survived. In 1936 it moved to 9, rue de Téhéran with 60,000 books. During World War II, the library provided books for French and British soldiers in Paris and in the field, but it needed money desperately. In 1940, the countess of Chambrun, the former Clara Longworth of Cincinnati, began to help the library's director, Dorothy Reeder. Later, under the German occupation, she headed the board of trustees, keeping the Germans at bay by negotiations and ruses so that the library survived. After the war the library was used by many French eager to read about the U.S. In 1947, Ian Forbes Fraser, a French-Canadian scholar, became the director, and he carried the library through a dozen years of growth-despite-struggle, including years in commodious quarters at 129, Avenue des Champs-Elysées before the move to the rue Camou building.

Lest it be forgotten that the library's existence today has a basis in the fraternal sentiments of Americans and French during the 1914–18 war fought on French soil, there is a bronze tablet on a wall in the library inscribed as follows: "The Home Service for American Soldiers Abroad dedicates this tablet to the memory of American volunteers in the Foreign Legion of France killed in 1915 and 1916 and the members of the society who gave their lives in the World War." There are 45 names; one of them is that of the poet Alan Seeger.

continued from page 466

and pictures from the end of the 19th century. At the end of 1968 the University Library, Salzburg, published a catalog of its older bookstock.

Belgium. On Feb. 17, 1969, the Royal Library in Brussels was inaugurated by King Baudouin. The inaugural visit was conducted by the director, H. Liebaers, and was followed by an open house. The next day an international symposium on national libraries was addressed by Étienne Dennery (Paris), Cornelis Reedijk (The Hague), Robert G. Vosper (Los Angeles), Ivan P. Kondakov (Moscow), and Sir Frank Francis (London). A technical advance was made at the library of the State University at Liège, where from January 1969 all acquisitions were recorded on punched cards and a computer was used to print-out lists and catalogs. The same library established a list of European theses received since Jan. 1, 1969. At the Bibliothèque Centrale du Centre Universitaire, Mons, some incunabula unique in Belgium were discovered, as well as a page of a Gutenberg Bible on vellum. A new draft on public libraries was submitted to experts for examination; many plans for new public library buildings were approved in the Flemish part of Belgium, while in the French-speaking part the unification of cataloging rules in the large public libraries was begun.

Bulgaria. The third International Conference on Library Building, Conservation, and Restoration of Library Materials was held in the autumn of 1968 at the National Library, Sofia. In 1969 the Bulgarian Library Council developed plans for the improvement of library service in villages.

Finland. By the end of 1968 the number of home loans from public libraries in Finland (pop. 4.6 million) had risen to 27.4 million. The number of active library users was nearly 1.2 million. A small new public library was completed at the end of 1968 at Mänttä, and a competition for a new library at Kouvola (pop. 25,000) was won by the architect J. Kivikoski. A branch in Helsinki, designed by Aarne Ervi, was to be opened in 1970. In the field of research libraries, the outstanding event was the publication of two reports of the Committee for the Development of Research Libraries, set up by the Ministry of Education in 1966. One report proposed the establishment of a bibliographical institute connected with Helsinki University Library, and the other proposed the coordination of bookstock through central libraries for different subjects.

France. Following the 1968 report on public libraries and reading, which had pointed up the low readership in France as compared with other countries, there were some important developments: new public libraries were opened at Coutances, Troyes, and La Roche-sur-Yon, and a children's library was opened at Bar-le-Duc. In the Parisian region the Municipal Library at St.-Denis opened its remodeled and modernized general reading room, and the Bibliothèque Historique de la Ville de Paris was inaugurated once again in the Hôtel Lamoignon, its original home in 1763, with a remodeled and rebuilt interior. An impressive demonstration took place at Lillers on Dec. 14, 1968, at which seven bookmobiles of the Pas-de-Calais Central Library were shown to the public. New libraries for science, law, and literature opened at the University of Saint-Martin d'Hères (Grenoble), and new libraries for medicine and pharmacy went into operation at Grenoble and Clermont-Ferrand.

West Germany. The 59th Deutscher Bibliothekartag (the annual conference of research librarians) was held at Kiel in May. A notable recommendation at the conference encouraged the supply of photocopies instead of loans in order to reduce the lending of originals; it was discovered that 30% of all loans from German academic libraries were already in this form. During the year the German Research Association gave financial support to three projects to promote access to specialized literature: a union catalog of German periodicals from the 17th to the 20th century in West German libraries; an index of 16th-century works published in German-speaking countries; and an information centre (at the Institut für Zeitgeschichte, Munich) on the literature of the German emigration, 1933–45. In 1968 the association had spent DM. 4.1 million on support for research libraries. In July plans were publicized for a new university library at Bremen, to contain some 1.6 million volumes. The outstanding event in the public library field was the publication by the Deutscher Büchereiverband and the Verein der Bibliothekare an öffentlichen Bibliotheken of *Bibliotheksplan,* a project for a complete network of public libraries in West Germany.

Hungary. The most important achievement was the inauguration, at the end of 1968, of the new national plan for acquisitions, under which groups of libraries, called "cooperative circles," became responsible for collecting the literature on 33 different subjects. In 1969 these circles were extended to include technology, agriculture, and geography, thus covering the whole field of knowledge.

Netherlands. For research libraries, the outstanding event was the publication in April by the State Advisory Committee on Library Affairs of the *De wetenschappelijke bibliotheken in Nederland; programma voor en beleid op lange termijn* (long-term program for research libraries), which included an urgent program for 1968–72. At the end of 1968 public libraries numbered 361, with 399 branches, 22 county libraries, and 35 mobile libraries—still rather low for the population of 13 million.

Poland. Following the passing of the new Library Act in April 1968, the Association of Polish Librarians quickly began to promote the rationalization and modernization of libraries. The new 22-member State Library Council held its first meeting on May 5, 1969. A new statute defining the tasks of the National Library in Warsaw was approved by the minister of culture and arts on April 15. At the end of 1968 Poland had 8,451 public libraries, with a total of about 50 million volumes, or 1.53 books per inhabitant; readers totaled over 6 million, or nearly 19% of the population.

Spain. The outstanding event was the opening of a new school of librarianship at Pamplona. The reconstruction and modernization of the National Library in Madrid continued; five new floors of bookstacks would be provided, as well as a new periodicals reading room and new premises for the special collections of maps, music, theatre, and rare books. The plan for a new library for the old University of Madrid was approved.

United Kingdom. The long-awaited *Report of the National Libraries Committee* (the "Dainton Report") was published in June 1969. It recommended that the library departments of the British Museum, including the National Reference Library for Science and Invention, the National Central Library, the

National Lending Library for Science and Technology, and the British National Bibliography, should be brought under a unified National Libraries Authority. It also recommended that the British Museum Library, including the Department of Prints and Drawings, redesignated as the National Reference Library, should remain in central London, and that the National Lending Library for Science and Technology at Boston Spa, Yorkshire, should take over the lending stock from the National Central Library. Library activity increased steadily, reaching record figures in all fields: the Library Association had 16,628 members at the end of 1968, and there were 2,406 full-time students in schools of librarianship. The College of Librarianship, Aberystwyth, Wales, instituted an honours degree. Among important new buildings were the Newcastle Central Library, designed by Sir Basil Spence; new county libraries for Merioneth and for Brecknock County, Wales; and a circular library at Fulwell Cross in the London borough of Redbridge. Expenditure on public libraries in 1968–69 rose by about £3 million to nearly £47 million. At the Public Libraries Conference of the Library Association, held at Southport in September, papers were presented on public library standards, cooperation with the British Museum, and the effect of the *Report of the Royal Commission on Local Government in England.*

Yugoslavia. Construction continued on two new national libraries, at Belgrade and at Skopje. Plans for the new building of the National and University Library at Zagreb were approved.

Other Countries. *Japan.* The Japan Library Association, with 3,941 members in 1968–69, held its 55th conference for all Japanese librarians in 1969; about two thousand persons were in attendance. At the end of 1968 there were 825 public libraries in Japan; the largest—in Tokyo—had half a million volumes. There were 382 libraries in 377 universities and colleges, with a total stock of nearly 50 million volumes.

South Korea. At the end of 1968 a national bibliographical centre was inaugurated as part of the Korean Library Association, with the support of the government. The Korean Library Association and the U.S. Information Service sponsored the Asia-Pacific Conference on Libraries and National Development, held at Seoul on May 28–30, 1969.

United States. The American Library Association was especially active, both at home and abroad. In conjunction with the U.S. Agency for International Development (AID), surveys were made in Asia and Latin America of the needs for books and libraries. The ALA administered grants from the Ford Foundation to assist the libraries of the University of Algiers and the University of Brasília. A committee for liaison with Japanese librarians continued its work, and was responsible for U.S. participation in a conference in Japan in May on the role of libraries in higher education and research. A *Foreign Service Directory of American Librarians* was published. ALA's Children's Service Division published *1968 Children's Books of International Interest,* which had been prepared for distribution at the IFLA annual session at Copenhagen in August, and sponsored a program on "library service to children in other countries" at the 1969 ALA annual conference. Ten Asian students attended U.S. library schools under an Asia Foundation Grant, and 13 Asian librarians in their home countries were awarded membership in the ALA. The report of the National Advisory Committee on Libraries, published late in 1968, made five basic recommendations: (1) to set up a National Commission on Libraries and Information Science; (2) to strengthen the Library of Congress as a national library; (3) to set up a federal Institute of Library and Information Science for research; (4) to recognize the vital role of the U.S. Office of Education in library service; and (5) to strengthen state library agencies. (A. Th.)

Encyclopædia Britannica Films. *The Library Story* (1952); *The Library: A Place for Discovery* (1965); *Library of Congress* (1969).

Libya

A socialist republic on the north coast of Africa, Libya is bounded by the United Arab Republic, Sudan, Tunisia, Algeria, Niger, and Chad. Area: 680,000 sq.mi. (1,760,000 sq.km.). Pop. (1969 est.): 1,869,000. Co-capitals and largest cities: Tripoli (pop., 1967 est., 273,000) and Bengasi (pop., 1967 est., 152,000). Language: Arabic. Religion: predominantly Muslim. King, Idris I (deposed); leader of the Revolutionary Command Council from Sept. 1, 1969, Col. Muhammad al-Khadafy; prime ministers, Wanis al-Gaddafi and, after September 1, Mahmoud Soliman al-Maghreby.

A brilliantly successful military coup made Libya a republic on September 1. The 79-year-old King Idris I, ruler since the country achieved independence in 1951, was deposed while in Turkey for medical treatment. Wanis al-Gaddafi, prime minister until September 1, was jailed along with his Cabinet and more than 1,000 former administrators, political leaders, and most former prime ministers. Mahmoud Soliman al-Maghreby, a 35-year-old lawyer previously imprisoned for his activities during the June 1967 war crisis, was appointed prime minister by the Revolutionary Command Council shortly after the coup. The new regime was received with popular demon-

WIDE WORLD

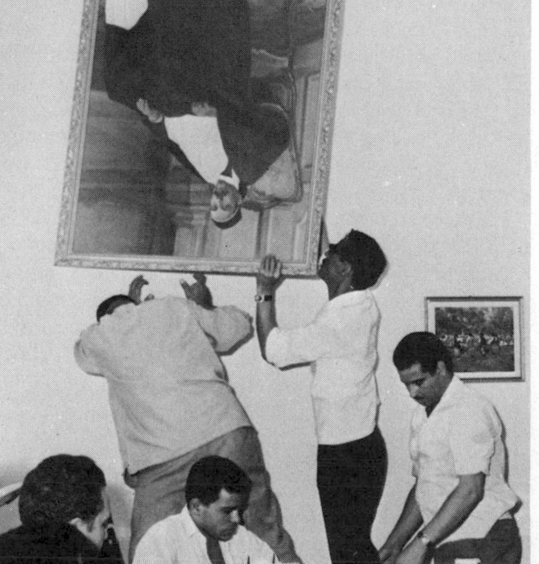

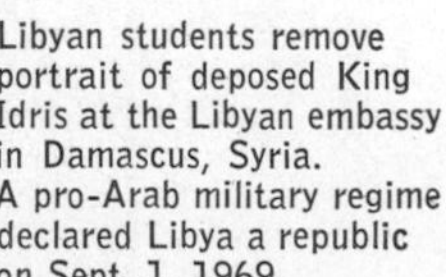

Libyan students remove portrait of deposed King Idris at the Libyan embassy in Damascus, Syria. A pro-Arab military regime declared Libya a republic on Sept. 1, 1969.

LIBYA

Education. (1966–67) Primary, pupils 215,841, teachers 7,278; secondary, pupils 26,846, teachers 1,807; vocational, pupils 1,064, teachers 121; teacher training, students 4,681, teachers 405; higher (at University of Libya), students 2,215, teaching staff 252.

Finance. Monetary unit: Libyan pound, with a par value of Lib£0.36 to U.S. $1 (Lib£0.86 = £1 sterling). Gold and foreign exchange, central bank: (June 1969) U.S. $919.1 million; (June 1968) U.S. $690.8 million. Budget (1968–69 est.) balanced at Lib£345 million. Gross national product: (1967) Lib£665.9 million; (1966) Lib£557.4 million. Money supply: (May 1969) Lib£179,340,000; (May 1968) Lib£142,430,000. Cost of living (Tripoli; 1964 = 100): (June 1969) 133; (June 1968) 124.

Foreign Trade. (1968) Imports Lib£230,210,000; exports Lib£669,020,000. Import sources: Italy 25%; U.S. 17%; U.K. 11%; West Germany 8%; Netherlands 5%; France 5%. Export destinations: West Germany 26%; Italy 20%; U.K. 19%; France 8%; Netherlands 8%; Spain 6%; U.S. 6%. Main export crude oil 99%.

Transport and Communications. Roads (with improved surface; 1966) *c.* 5,200 km. Motor vehicles in use (1967): passenger 63,200; commercial (including buses) 29,600. Railways (1967) 165 km. Ships entered (1967) vessels totaling 4,506,000 net registered tons; goods loaded (1967) 82,778,000 metric tons, unloaded 2,629,000 metric tons. Telephones (Dec. 1967) 24,690. Radio receivers (Dec. 1967) 75,000.

Agriculture. Production (in 000; metric tons; 1967; 1966 in parentheses): wheat 62 (58); barley 110 (99); olive oil 27 (18); dates 55 (56). Livestock (in 000; 1966–67): sheep 1,628; cattle 116; goats 1,405; camels 256; asses 129.

Industry. Production (in 000; metric tons; 1967): salt 25; crude oil (1968) 125,697; electricity (excluding industrial and small settlements; kw-hr.) 212,000.

strations throughout Libya. Its initial policies were essentially improvised and unclear. The arabization of public signs and notices proceeded, and the teaching of English in primary schools was forbidden. Although business concerns were to be 100% owned by Libyan nationals, assurances were given to foreign oil companies and banks that there would be no state interference, and oil exports were not affected. The new republican government declared that henceforth oil revenues would be more equitably distributed. It demonstrated its wish to identify with ideas of Arab unity by allocating $2.8 million to Al Fatah, the Palestinian guerrilla organization, but the Libyans remained understandably wary of their more powerful but less wealthy neighbours. The government also announced that the U.S. and U.K. military bases were to be closed on the expiration of agreements, and both countries agreed to pull out in 1970. In December an attempted coup by a group of army officers was thwarted.

Libya continued as one of the leading Middle East exporters of crude oil and in 1969 went ahead of Kuwait and Saudi Arabia with more than 125 million metric tons a year. Construction and road building were booming, and commercial activity was vigorous. (Jo. A. A.)

ENCYCLOPÆDIA BRITANNICA FILMS. *Oasis* (1965).

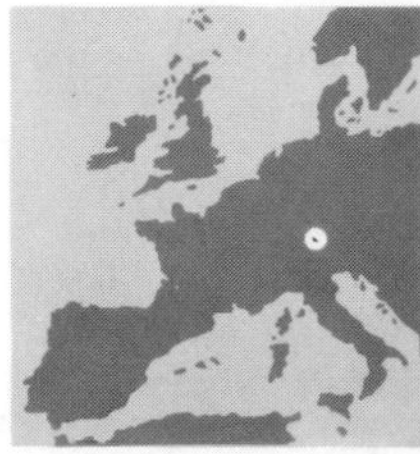

Liechtenstein

An independent principality between Switzerland and Austria, Liechtenstein is united with Switzerland by a customs and monetary union. Area: 62 sq.mi. (160 sq.km.). Pop. (1968 est.): 21,237. Cap. and largest city: Vaduz (pop., 1967 est., 3,966). Language: German. Religion: 92.3% Roman Catholic. Sovereign prince, Francis Joseph II; chief of government in 1969, Gerard Batliner.

The year 1969 marked the 250th anniversary of the founding of the principality of Liechtenstein. A gala series of celebrations was held during July.

On June 12, 1969, the quadrennial national elections were held in the principality. All former members of the government were reelected with the exception of one deputy member who retired to private life.

The demographic statistics for Dec. 1, 1967, were released in September 1969. The population of Liechtenstein was 20,433, including 10,216 males and 10,217 females; 13,893 (67.9%) were citizens of the principality. The annual increase in population was 517, of which 253 represented the excess of births over deaths while 264 came from immigration.

A total of 10,987 persons (42.6% of the population) were employed in the work force. Agricultural employment had decreased by 5.3% since 1960, while industrial and construction showed slight gains. The most important industries (textiles, precision instruments, ceramics, pharmaceuticals, and canned foods) involved products destined primarily for export. All parts of the economy continued to prosper, requiring the continued import of foreign labour. (R. D. Ho.)

Fireworks over the castle of Vaduz, residence of the prince of Liechtenstein, on July 13, 1969, celebrating the 250th anniversary of the principality.

KEYSTONE

LIECHTENSTEIN

Education. (1966–67) Primary, pupils 2,245, teachers 75; secondary, pupils 726, teachers 51; vocational, pupils 106, teachers 19.

Finance and Trade. Monetary unit: Swiss franc (SFr. 4.33 = U.S. $1; SFr. 10.39 = £1 sterling). Budget (1969 est.): revenue SFr. 45,773,000; expenditure SFr. 45,745,000. Exports (home produce; 1967) SFr. 196,700,074. Main export destination Switzerland 41%. Main exports: corn, vegetables, fruit, wine, livestock products, light manufactures. Tourism (1967): visitors 59,969; gross receipts *c.* SFr. 6 million.

Agriculture. Livestock (in 000; April 1967): cattle 6.1; sheep 1.1; pigs 4.3; chickens 14.6.

Literature

The 1969 Nobel Prize for Literature went to Samuel Beckett, the Irish-French dramatist, poet, and novelist. (*See* BIOGRAPHY.)

AMERICAN

At a time of civic soul-searching occasioned by the Vietnam war, turbulence in the streets and schools, and a change of government, American literature in 1969 produced little imaginative writing of merit but was replete—tormentedly so—with topical works, side by side with reminiscences of calmer days.

Fiction. *Portnoy's Complaint* by Philip Roth, a superb craftsman, was the most talked-about novel of the year: the story of an acutely intelligent and "successful" Jew who pours out his hang-ups to a psychoanalyst. Many critics thought it excellent, and one or two described it as "great" or "a masterpiece"; only a very few (and at least two of them were women) regarded it as thoroughly unpalatable. Some readers found the book uproariously funny; others found it unpleasant—even anti-Semitic. A Jewish novelist (not Roth) reported that his mother asked what *Portnoy* was about, and that he replied: "It's the story of a Jewish boy whose father and mother ruined his life" (an obvious oversimplification). The mother thought the statement over for a moment or so, then said firmly: "He shouldn't have let them." And that may have been the best of all *Portnoy* reviews.

A rival best seller was Mario Puzo's fast-moving *The Godfather.* This story about a Mafia family managed to make the murderous protagonist understandable if not exactly lovable. *Ada* by Vladimir Nabokov was called an erotic masterpiece but was received rather coolly and perplexedly by the general public. (See *English,* below.) *Slaughterhouse-Five* by Kurt Vonnegut, Jr., was a work of fiction based on the experiences of Vonnegut, who had been a prisoner of war in Dresden when the German city was bombed by British and U.S. planes and more than 100,000 civilians were killed by explosives and the subsequent fire storm. The reviewer Robert Scholes said: "This is what the book keeps whispering to us in its quietest voice: Be kind. Don't hurt. Death is coming for all of us anyway, and it is better to be Lot's wife looking back through salty eyes than the Deity that destroyed those cities of the plain in order to save them."

Surely the most curious novel of the year was *Naked Came the Stranger,* a golden jest by "Penelope Ashe." The actual creators of this deliberately meretricious novel were some 24 writers from *Newsday,* a Long Island, N.Y., newspaper. The man who dreamed up the hoax even sent back some of the chapters he had farmed out to his mob of authors to be redone because they were "too competent" to fit in with the rest! Despite the speedy exposure of this bit of literary legerdemain, the novel, as sex-drenched as the title was intended to suggest, not only sprang onto the best-seller list, but was peddled to Hollywood for a sizable sum. This also was the year's most revealing indication of the national taste in fiction.

Biography and Memoirs. Peter Maas offered a kind of accompaniment to Mario Puzo's fiction with *The Valachi Papers,* in which Joe Valachi, one of the few canaries ever to sing convincingly about the Mafia, revealed a great many verifiable facts about that sprawling criminal organization. Maas's book, said to have been published despite pressure to keep it from seeing print, was virtually a reference work for students of the underworld.

David Randall, director of Lilly Library at Indiana University, became a bookman after quitting Harvard Law School in 1929 for a job clerking at $17.50 a week. In *Dukedom Large Enough,* this civilized and amusing man told his own story, along with delicious anecdotes of many of the collectors, authors, and other book people he knew between 1929 and 1955, when he quit Scribner's for a quieter life among the Hoosiers. Another praiseworthy volume was Carlos Baker's *Ernest Hemingway: A Life Story.* Although some reviewers faulted Baker for putting in too much detail and too little of his own estimate of Hemingway's life and character, it was generally appreciated for its accuracy and completeness.

Life stories of stage figures were unusually plentiful and exceptionally good. In *Notes on a Cowardly Lion* John Lahr remembered his father, the comedian Bert Lahr (1895–1967), with love—love clear-eyed and professionally frank, making the book both entertaining and convincing. Lahr played parts ranging from burlesque to Shakespeare and, when he was asked (by Bosley Crowther) how he liked the movies, he replied: "I like anything as long as I'm making money." Other outstanding studies of the theatre were *The Season,* William Goldman's account of Broadway during the 1967–68 season (when he personally sat through more than 200 plays), and Lillian Hellman's *An Unfinished Woman.* Goldman, himself a playwright and screenwriter, covered all aspects of the Broadway scene, from ticket-scalping to play-doctoring and from homosexuality in the theatre to the farewell performance of Judy Garland. The book was racy and absorbing reading, and was certain to please most theatregoers while enraging most theatre critics—at least those in New York, whom Goldman finds, with very few exceptions, incompetent. Miss Hellman, a leading playwright since 1934, told much about the theatre but perhaps more about her life away from it—notably her friendship with Dashiell Hammett, the writer of mystery novels. Many reviewers complained that, although she opened doors permitting glimpses of her private life, she also kept a great many closed and thus created annoying gaps.

Politics and World Affairs. Dean Acheson's *Present at the Creation: My Years at the State Department* and the late Robert F. Kennedy's *Thirteen Days* were more than important in their own right: they exemplified the highly personal nature of the year's best writing on America's vexatious recent past. Acheson gave an uninhibited picture of the Truman era as he saw it from the vantage point of secretary of state. Wallace Carroll, former Washington news editor of the *New York Times,* said in his review: "As autobiography it is enthralling, as history indispensable, as manual on government and diplomacy invaluable." The Kennedy-on-Kennedy book—the senator's account of the president's handling of the Cuban missile crisis (October 1962)—evoked the grimness of days when the world was perhaps closer to nuclear war than at any time before or since. With clarity and enough detail to leave the reader once again tossing and turning in his sleep, the book disclosed, for example, that when all the presidential advisers except Robert McNamara and Robert Ken-

KEYSTONE

Samuel Beckett, recipient of the 1969 Nobel Prize for Literature.

Life Insurance: *see* Insurance

Liquors, Alcoholic: *see* Alcoholic Beverages

nedy himself were urging an immediate attack to destroy the missile sites in Cuba, President Kennedy replied by ordering the defusing of all American missiles armed with atomic warheads—to prevent the possibility of erring on the side of enthusiasm.

Two other books that may be mentioned together—though completely different in treatment and feeling—were *The Making of the President 1968* by Theodore H. White and *The Selling of the President 1968* by Joseph McGinnis. White's skillful study of the campaigns in behalf of Richard Nixon and Hubert Humphrey was, as readers of his 1964 and 1960 analyses rightly expected, both masterful and fair-minded. But Republicans must have found McGinnis' book about as unpalatable as anything they had tasted since the Goldwater vote of 1964. In the author's defense it should be said that he undoubtedly could, and would, have written an equally damning work about the Democrats and their image-creating job on Humphrey—except that when the young newspaperman approached the old pros in that party he was told, more or less politely, to get lost. He succeeded, however, in sweet-talking the Republicans into letting him observe what he came to regard as the "packaging" of Nixon for sale to the American voter. The resulting document was so revealing and so starkly etched that it should—but probably would not—lead to change in the uses of television during presidential campaigns. Another reportorial job on the 1968 race, but combining pictures and text, was *U.S.A.*, the photographer David Douglas Duncan's coverage of the two conventions. In this task he was aided greatly by his longtime friendship with Richard Nixon and by a telephoto lens of amazing spy-quality, which permitted Duncan to examine faces that would otherwise have been completely out of reach. This was one of the year's truly collectible books.

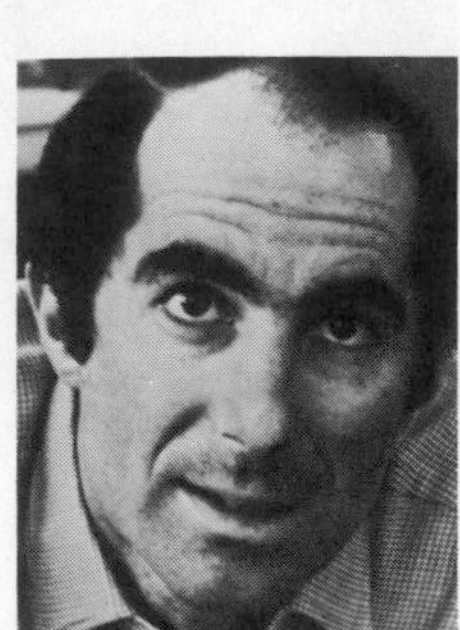

JUDY FEIFFER, COURTESY, RANDOM HOUSE

Philip Roth, whose controversial novel "Portnoy's Complaint" was published in 1969.

From the White House of other days, and by way of Eric Goldman, cultural adviser to President Johnson, came *The Tragedy of Lyndon Johnson,* an anecdotal book described by Max Frankel as "good reading but not satisfying history."

History. Foreign correspondents were responsible for three of the year's better books on recent European history. William L. Shirer's 1,000-page *The Collapse of the Third Republic* covered the fall of France—of which he had been a part-witness—in much the same manner as his memorable *The Rise and Fall of the Third Reich.* Harrison Salisbury in *The 900 Days* provided a gripping study of the siege of Leningrad, where as many as one million persons may have died of hunger. *A Long Row of Candles* by C. L. Sulzberger, a colleague of Salisbury's on the *New York Times,* described the romantic life of the foreign correspondent as he lived it, up to and during World War II: those were the days when being a newspaperman abroad was the next best thing to being footloose, fancy-free, and a millionaire.

WIDE WORLD

"Penelope Ashe," alleged author of the novel "Naked Came the Stranger," a deliberately bad book written by a committee of 24 persons. The part of Penelope Ashe was played by a relative of the perpetrator of the hoax.

The *New York Times* itself was closely examined, from its beginnings to the recent struggle for power among highly placed staff members, in *The Kingdom and the Power* by Gay Talese, a former *Times*man, who did a conscientious and loving job of depicting a great paper. The whole country, from 1587 to 1914, came under the scrutiny of the social historian J. C. Furnas in *The Americans.* Furnas said his book would focus on "who Americans were, what they were doing and sometimes why, where they were going and how, what they ate, drank, wore, hoped. . . .and on things—covered bridges, and flasks of whisky, muckraking and the Morgan horse." Clifton Fadiman said that "it shines with good sense, dressed in quiet, well-mannered English."

Other Nonfiction. Two books seemed poles apart, yet between them they spanned the troubles of the times. One was reportage, hot from the courtroom and the author's indignant heart: Jessica Mitford's *The Trial of Dr. Spock,* which examined a conspiracy charge (for urging young men to resist conscription) brought against a group of men who barely knew each other before they were indicted. The other was *The Inland Island* by Josephine Johnson (who, some 30 years earlier, won a Pulitzer Prize for a novel). Her slim book, about a tract of country near Cincinnati, O., described the birds and animals, the trees and streams—with here and there a quiet, Quakerish word about the war in Vietnam, the Pentagon, and pollution. (R. A. Cr.)

CANADIAN

English Language. The year was a good one for Canadian poetry. Distinguished books of verse included Phyllis Gotlieb's *Ordinary, Moving* and Tom Marshall's *The Silences of Fire.* Irving Layton wrote *The Whole Bloody Bird,* an entertaining potpourri of verse and prose observations on life in the Middle East and in Canada; the second section, a collection of pithy aphorisms, reflected Layton's usual vigorous style, as did the poems comprising the third section. Ralph Gustafson in *Ixion's Wheel* covered the sights and sounds of this same part of the world, touching the tourist attractions with his own particular vision. Toronto city life was represented by Raymond Souster in *So Far So Good* with simplicity and a directness that bespoke the warmth of the poet's feelings for the streets and the people. The poems in Alden Nowlan's *The Mysterious Naked Man* relied heavily on the poet's experiences and possessed a leisurely, conversational pace. Gwendolyn MacEwen in *The Shadow Maker* explored the world of dreams and nightmares—the necessary shadows in which we see ourselves. George Bowering produced *The Gangs of Kosmos,* a book of quietly personal poems, tightly controlled; they succeeded as more than one man's exercise in retrospection. Miriam Waddington's *Say Yes* consisted of her icons: simple images in which she can believe, centred on nature. The new poems in Milton Acorn's *I've Tasted My Blood* were as vigorous, as pungent, and as rich in image as any in his earlier collection, and some achieved a new richness of texture.

Several of the poets also distinguished themselves by producing enjoyable novels. Margaret Atwood in *The Edible Woman* showed what happens when a member of the North American consuming society identifies herself with the things consumed. Phyllis Gotlieb wrote *Why Should I Have All the Grief,* in which the central figure, Heinz, nightly relives horrors of which he cannot speak: he is unable to maintain communication between himself and his wife, and he cannot escape memories that go back to Auschwitz and earlier. Margaret Laurence's *The Fire Dwellers* displayed with remarkable insight the exchanges between a husband and wife in lower-middle-class Vancouver, B.C. The wife, unable to find someone to whom she can express her fears of losing her identity, lives in an ever shifting world of doubts and small successes—described here with poetry, irony, and humour. David Helwig was a well-known poet with a growing reputation as a writer of stories; these, collected in *The Streets of Summer,* were among the best published in 1969. *Cape Breton Is the Thought-Control Centre of Canada* by Ray Smith was another collection of Canadian short stories that proved to be entertaining and perceptive.

Percy Janes's *The House of Hate,* a first novel, told of a poor Irish family buffeted by events and by the people around them; set in Newfoundland, this work could be called a modern Canadian epic. James Bacque's *The Lonely Ones* was a novel based on the personal involvement of four people in the conflicts of the Quebec separatist movement; imaginary incidents, central to the plot, are an abortive raid on a broadcasting station in Montreal and the killing of the prime minister. In a very different vein, Farley Mowat provided an entertaining account of Newfoundland and its people in *The Boat Who Wouldn't Float.*

Graeme Gibson's *Five Legs* was a highly interesting and significant work from a new publisher, House of Anansi. The author describes the torments and the conflicting but often amusing interludes in the lives of some dwellers in North America's cities. The same publisher provided a series of short first novels by Canadian writers; among the most interesting were *The Telephone Pole* by Russell Marois and *Perte de Temps* by Pierre Gravel.

A New Encounter with Canada, prepared by Andy Wainwright, contained contributions from 38 leading English-Canadian writers who revealed their concern for Canadian traditions and institutions. George Grant's *Technology and Empire: Perspectives on North America* was a collection of his recently published articles on the future of Canada and the United States. The author was chairman of the department of religion at McMaster University, Hamilton, Ont.

Conspirators in Silence by Patrick Watson was a carefully documented account of the Canadian school system, mass media, and political life; in it the author challenged those responsible for directing and leading these Canadian institutions. Ramsay Cook edited *French-Canadian Nationalism,* a collection of 25 essays providing a background to current dissent in French Canada. The work consisted of two parts, the first interpreting the sense of identity shared by French Canadians and the second presenting statements by individuals involved, as they see it, in a struggle for French-Canadian survival.

Canadian writers were turning increasingly to the subject of the Canadian Indian. Sheila Burnford's *Without Reserve* was about the Crees and Ojibways living on the widely scattered reserves of northern Ontario, between Lake Superior and Hudson Bay. The author is not blind to the difficulties of Indian integration, and her book solved no problems, but it was written in a friendly and personal manner. George Clutesi in *Potlatch* revealed longhouse ceremonies and tribal mysteries of British Columbia Indians. The author, a Vancouver Island Indian who attended the feasts as a young man, told of the richly symbolic stories, dances, songs, and gift-givings that make up the potlatch.

Student Power and the Campus by Tim Reid analyzed and documented the struggles that took place among faculties and students in Canadian universities and high schools during 1968–69.

The Dictionary of Canadian Biography, vol. 2, edited by David M. Hayne and André Vachon, was a notable addition to Canadian scholarship. It dealt with the years 1701 to 1740, a formative period in Canadian history.

Lawren Harris, with an introduction by Northrop Frye, was edited by Beth Harris and R. G. P. Colgrove from the noted artist's works, both written and pictorial. The book traced Harris' work as a member of the Group of Seven and explored his early writings, as well as his paintings. Arnold Walter prepared *Aspects of Music in Canada,* a volume of essays (sponsored by the Canadian Music Council) appreciative of the writing and performance of music in present-day Canada. *The Awkward Stage,* a report of the Province of Ontario Council for the Arts, dealt in a comprehensive way with live theatre in Canada and its relation to other media, as well as to education and politics.

The year was notable for the production of books for young readers. Two Indian legends were retold by William Toye and strikingly illustrated, in colour, by Elizabeth Cleaver. One, *The Mountain Goats of Temlahan,* was about the retribution suffered by an Indian tribe in British Columbia when some of its members fail to obey their own laws of the goat hunt: the power of the supernatural permeates the tale. A companion volume, *How Summer Came to Canada,* presented a legend of the Micmac Indians of eastern Canada. *The Blind Boy and the Loon* by Ramona Maker contained 11 stories used in Eskimo families to entertain children and acquaint them with life. The book was illustrated with reproductions of Eskimo artwork.

Ruth Nichols' *A Walk Out of the World,* written when she was 18, was an important contribution to Canadian fantasy for children. In a very different style was *The Last Voyage of the Unicorn,* a realistic account by Delbert A. Young. (H. C. Cl.)

French Language. Well-known novelists who published books in 1969 included: Réjean Ducharme, with *La Fille de Christophe Colomb,* a novel in verse (see *French,* below); Marie Claire Blais, *Les Voyageurs sacrés* and *Vivre! Vivre!;* Jacques Ferron, *Le Ciel de Québec;* and Yves Thériault, *Tayaout* and two short novels. Other novels worthy of mention were *Non Monsieur* by Jovette Bernier, who won with this love story the prize of Le Cercle du Livre de France; *Faire Sa Mort comme faire l'amour* by the 25-year-old Pierre Turgeon; *Race de Monde* by Victor-Lévy Beaulieu; and *Jimmy* by Jacques Poulin.

The jury for the prizes of the province of Quebec did not give any prize in poetry in 1969—though quite a few good books of verse appeared, including one by Gemma Tremblay, *Les Seins gorgés.* Jean-Guy Pilon republished in Paris all of his previous books of poetry in one volume entitled *Comme Eau retenue* and produced a new one entitled *Saison pour la continuelle.* Guy Robert published five books of poems within the year. Among works by new poets were *Soleil de bivouac* by Pierre Chatillon, *Sens unique* by André Saint-Germain, and *Poèmes pour durer* by André Major.

The first book on Albert Laberge appeared: *Albert Laberge, sa vie son oeuvre* by Jacques Brunet. Réginald Hamel published the *Correspondance* of Charles Gill. An excellent book was *Deux Études sur la préhistoire du surréalisme* by Roymond Joly. Clément Moisan of Laval University, Quebec City, with *L'Age de la littérature canadienne* opened a new field, the comparative study of French and English expression in Canada. Of the many theses that were published, probably the most important were *La Religieuse dans la littérature française* by Jeanne Ponton and *Montréal dans le roman canadien* by Antoine Sirois. The

Irving Layton, whose verse and prose collection "The Whole Bloody Bird" was published in 1969.

COURTESY, MACMILLAN OF CANADA

Gwendolyn MacEwen, author of the collection of verse "The Shadow Maker," published in 1969.

JAC-GUY

Jean-Guy Pilon, who published two volumes of poetry in 1969—"Comme Eau retenue," a single volume containing all his previous books of poetry, and "Saison pour la continuelle," a collection of new poems.

group of "La Barre du Jour" published *Les Automatistes,* a study of Borduas and the people who helped him write his manifesto. Finally, the revue *Europe* titled its February–March 1969 issue *Littérature du Québec;* it contained many excellent articles on distinguished French-Canadian writers.

A few years earlier very few plays were being published in French Canada. In 1968 over 20 appeared, and in 1969 about the same number. Dramatists included Marcel Dubé, Françoise Loranger, Hubert Aquin, and Michel Tremblay, whose *Les Belles Soeurs* was a big hit on the stage in 1968 and who reinterpreted *Lysistrata* with the help of André Brassard.

Impressive works of history were *Les La Vérendry et le poste de l'ouest* by Antoine Champagne, *Les Canadiens après la conquête* by Michel Brunet, and *Le Canada* by Louis-Edmond Hamelin; in the social sciences, *Fin d'une réligion: monographie d'une paroisse canadienne-française* by Colette Moreux and *Vers un nouveau pouvoir* by Jacques Grand'Maison; and in philosophy, *La Philosophie dans la cité technique* by Roger Ebacher and *L'Action humaine dans l'oeuvre de Teilhard de Chardin* by Philippe Bergeron.
(AD. T.)

DANISH

The critical consensus was that 1969 was a particularly rich year for Danish literature. It saw writers of widely different generations and tendencies working side by side and attracting equal attention.

Two writers well advanced in age published new books during the year. Albert Dam's essays, poetic-historical myths, and autobiographical sketches displayed power and originality of thought and language. Johannes Wulff returned after a silence of several decades with a collection of frank, thoughtful, often erotically tinged verse. The leading woman poet of the 1930s and '40s, Tove Ditlevsen, struck a new harsh, self-mocking note with *De voksne.*

Klaus Rifbjerg, who more than anyone had set his mark on the Danish literary renaissance of the 1960s, published a new novel, *Anna (jeg) Anna,* a long monologue by a Danish diplomat's wife in her mid-30s who, involved in a young man's flight from the police, is driven radically to revise her standards and values. Straightforward realism was represented by Tage Skou-Hansen, whose novel about a returning peace corps volunteer conveyed much social criticism. Christian Kampmann produced his best novel of marital psychology, *Nærved og næsten,* while Henrik Stangerup made a notable debut with a novel about a journalist's moral decline.

The more fantastically inclined, symbolic writing that had made its first impact in the early 1960s was carried forward in 1969 by Sven Holm, whose "absurd" stories and fables had become increasingly political in tone, in *Rex,* and Ulla Ryum, who further explored the fantastic in *Tusindskove.* Jørgen Gustava Brandt, one of the Rifbjerg generation's leading poets, published a first novel, *Lüneburg hede.*

The year's most remarkable achievement was, however, the young poet Inger Christensen's *Det,* for which she was awarded the critics' prize. A massive work whose subdivisions follow an ingenious arithmetic pattern, *Det* could be described as a sort of meta-poetry, concerned at once with reality and the description of reality. Besides reflecting, as a purely linguistic construction, its own process of creation, it is also a catalog of contemporary phenomena.

Other interesting experiments by writers employing similar techniques included Vagn Lundbye's Pop novel *Nico* and Svend Åge Madsen's crime novel *Tredje gang så ta'r vi ham. . . .* Per Højholt produced his first prose work, a collection of sketches on the lines of diary entries by an abstract figure. Poet Kirsten Thorup's collection, *Love from Trieste,* was also characterized by the absence of any identifiable "I."
(NI. B.)

ENGLISH

Prose. In 1969 there was a sense of pause. The year brought endings and revisings, some revulsion from experiment, and a reshuffling of old ideas, but few signs of what might lie ahead in the 1970s.

Of the endings, the most notable were the final installment of *The Autobiography of Bertrand Russell* and the fifth volume of the memoirs of Leonard Woolf, *The Journey Not the Arrival Matters,* which appeared two months after his death in August. Russell's volume dealt firmly with the life of the aging public man—the campaigner for nuclear disarmament and founder of the War Crimes Tribunal. Woolf looked back to World War II and to his wife's suicide, and he elaborated still further on the stoical pessimism that pervaded his life after 1914, the year that extinguished for him the possibility of rational optimism. (*See* OBITUARIES.)

Christopher Booker, a repentant satirist, in *The Neophiliacs* also echoed this sense of ending. Its thesis was that the developed world generally, and Britain in particular, had been swept by a "psychic epidemic" whose symptoms were a Gadarene rush from reality and the promotion of social, sexual, and cultural fantasies on an unprecedented scale. Finally, however, the dominant 20th-century dream, of freedom without limit and of technology as a cornucopia, was breaking down: man had seen the future and found that it did not work out like that. Down with human self-assertiveness and back to God! cried Christopher Booker in his wilderness. Reviewers divided more or less evenly between those who dismissed his book as just another outburst of the new "Inside Right," as Marghanita Laski's *Times* review was headed, and those who thought it carried a certain warning resonance. Parts of this argument were deployed in *Growth: The Price We Pay* by E. J. Mishan, who developed the thesis that "everything is purchased at the price of something worse" from the point of view of a specialist in welfare economics.

Fiction. A more formidable warning voice was that of Doris Lessing, who ended her "Children of Violence" cycle with a fifth volume, *The Four-Gated City,* which brought her heroine, Martha Quest, to London at the end of the 1940s, carried her through the postwar decades, and deposited her, in a future not far distant, on a Scottish island with other survivors of our long-expected Armageddon. No one who knew Doris Lessing's work would expect this to be a simply fashionable essay in apocalyptics, though some reviewers found its accumulation of disaster too much for their nerves or their powers of credulity. "We did not know," wrote Martha with the benefit of hindsight, "how badly the world had hurt itself"; but we might have understood more readily, she argued at length, if we had listened to the "mad" instead of locking away or blocking with drugs their intimations of our diseased reality. The review in the *Times Literary Supplement* was representative: while regretting "that Mrs. Lessing writes with an almost wilful rejection of ease," the reviewer respected her ambition and seriousness. "It is difficult to accept the book but reject the views," the review concluded, "but that is what most readers are likely to do."

The end of an even more ambitious cycle, *The Gale of the World,* the 15th and last book of Henry Williamson's "Chronicle of Ancient Sunlight," brought not so much uneasiness as plain embarrassment to all but his most constant readers. Some of the admired pastoral notes were sounded once more, but here Williamson set his romantic near-Fascist politics and his admiration of Hitler and Oswald Mosley unambiguously in the centre of his picture, the action turning on a bizarre attempt to rescue Rudolf Hess from Spandau by glider.

Something to Answer For by P. H. Newby (*see* BIOGRAPHY) was a subtle and passionate comedy hinged on the Suez crisis of 1956; it was chosen in April as the first winner of the new £5,000 Booker Prize. The judges spoke of Forster and Conrad, thought the novel showed a considerable extension of Newby's powers, and preferred it to Iris Murdoch's *The Nice and the Good,* among other works shortlisted. *Bruno's Dream,* Iris Murdoch's next offering in 1969, however, was thought by many critics to be one of the best things she had done. This bold representation of the interplay between love and death, centred on a dying, disfigured old man, contained some of the author's most memorable images and was less compromised by freakishness than other recent works, though not without eruptions of characteristically black fantasy. The first two-thirds of it at least, P. J. Kavanagh thought, showed "evidence of a moral imagination in the *Middlemarch* class."

Reaction differed to Kingsley Amis' death-obsessed erotic ghost story *The Green Man,* which created fantasies almost at the Murdoch level and provided one of the most perceptive modern studies of hypochondria. Hypochondria and an itching groin were also the marks of Yarr, another formidable monster, grown out of the sour soil of small-town Ulster, in the novel *Poor Lazarus* by Maurice Leitch, of whom most critics hoped to hear more.

There were signs during the year of a reaction against the more demonstratively elaborate kinds of novel. The "turning-worm" syndrome was detectable in several reviews of Vladimir Nabokov's *Ada.* "Nabokov's Waterloo," was the heading of the *Times Literary Supplement*'s review, which concluded equivocally that "if literature was invented for critics to practise on, *Ada,* like *Finnegans Wake,* might crown the arch of European writing." True Nabokovians might find it his masterpiece: David Lodge in the *Guardian,* commenting that Nabokov's art "resists reductive interpretation," described *Ada* as "a feat of astonishing virtuosity." In *The Listener,* D. J. Enright invoked the law of diminishing returns. "To me," he declared, "it seems further evidence that great gifts can be put to small uses, a mountain of words give birth to a mousse." Brigid Brophy's strenuous variations on fashionable sexual themes provoked similar responses, as did B. S. Johnson's *The Unfortunates,* a cut-and-shuffle pack of ruminations in 27 sections, unbound, to be dealt at the reader's leisure. Michael Moorcock was thought to have bitten off more than he could chew in *The Stealer of Souls,* a sci-fi trip to Bethlehem, which discovered Jesus as a simple idiot; and Jerzy Peterkiewicz' *Green Flows the Bile* was admired a little distantly for the skills that concealed the machinery of its complexity.

Of the more traditional talents, Elizabeth Bowen created in *Eva Trout* a creature large and extravagant enough to split a seam or two of her neo-Jamesian style, and her aesthetic kinsman L. P. Hartley added to his list a self-indulgent comedy called *The Love-Adept.* Olivia Manning's return to native ground in *The Play Room* was greeted with restrained enthusiasm. Margaret Drabble's *The Waterfall* showed her settling into an attractive predictability—perhaps, as one reviewer suggested, as "a kind of sexier Jane Austen." *The Beastly Beatitudes of Balthazar B* by J. P. Donleavy (*see* BIOGRAPHY) was not altogether unexpected either: like Nabokov, Donleavy has tended more and more to ambiguous self-parody. Robert Shaw's ambiguities in *A Card from Morocco* were a good deal more purposeful. Clive Barry, back in Africa once more in *Fly Jamskoni,* remained original, transmitting with peculiar directness his hilarious discovering of reality. William Trevor set his new novel, *Mrs. Eckdorf in O'Neill's Hotel,* in Dublin, where his mannered style was seen to be quite at home at last.

CAMERA PRESS—PIX FROM PUBLIX

J. P. Donleavy, author of the novel "The Beastly Beatitudes of Balthazar B" which was published in 1969.

Two old masters of the short story were on view: V. S. Pritchett in the collection *Blind Love* and Frank O'Connor in *Collection 3,* the final collection of his work.

Of several unusual novels set in the past, the strangest in its pale, flat seriousness was Edward Upward's *The Rotten Elements,* continuing the testament of Christopher Isherwood's Marxist school friend. Dealing with the agonies of his break with the Communist Party in the late 1940s, it left in its wake a trail of respectful critics baffled by a work of evident integrity written apparently so plainly against the grain of the spiky and difficult sensibility reflected in Upward's early stories. *The French Lieutenant's Woman* by John Fowles was a more likely sort of modern experiment with history: a Victorian love story planted with symbols and allegory, with alternative endings and frequent author's interventions. Peter Vansittart's *Pastimes of a Red Summer* was notable for the richness of its evocation of time and place, in this case a French country house, transfigured by revolution. James Plunkett's *Strumpet City* was an imaginative first novel of massive proportions, a work of social history, dealing with the birth pains of trade unionism in Ireland.

History, Biography, Letters. "We are noted for our eccentricities," wrote a Harmsworth kinsman, reviewing *Strictly Personal,* the memoirs of the deposed press magnate Cecil Harmsworth King: "He has gone just that little too far." Readers less intimately involved were probably more indulgent—it was not often that so public a man had toyed in print with the notion that his mother was "an evil woman, determined to destroy me"—but regretted his reticence about other matters, such as just how he was toppled from his throne at the International Publishing Corporation.

The first two volumes of the *Whitehall Diary* of Thomas Jones presented the harder stuff of politics and history. They dealt with the last years of World War I, Ireland, and the General Strike. These notes direct from the Cabinet Room, where "T. J." served as secretary, not only gave vivid glimpses of Stanley Baldwin, Andrew Bonar Law, Lord Curzon, and Jones's first and most fascinating master, Lloyd George, but constituted, in the words of Asa Briggs, "a major contribution to our knowledge of 20th-century people, problems, and procedures."

COURTESY, GEORGE, ALLEN & UNWIN

Poet Brian Patten, whose book of poems, "Notes to the Hurrying Man," was published in 1969.

Baldwin by Keith Middlemas (editor of the *White-*

hall Diary) and John Barnes was a considerable effort at rehabilitation. There was effort in the reading as well as the writing, but the book certainly altered the outline of the received portrait of Baldwin as the arch-appeaser: it dwelt on his humane handling of the abdication crisis. Curzon, who appeared rather as a figure of fun in the *Diary,* was treated in a largely anecdotal way in Kenneth Rose's *Superior Person* and more usefully, in his proconsular role, by David Dilks in the first volume of *Curzon in India.*

Harold Macmillan, who employed David Dilks as a "ghost," produced the third volume of his memoirs. *Tides of Fortune* covered the years in opposition, the first failure to negotiate with Europe, and Churchill's immensely reluctant withdrawal from power. This portion of the memoirs ended, in the words of Anthony Howard, "as a cliff-hanger for the coming volume, the one we all want to read"—the volume dealing with Suez.

The year produced two outstanding volumes of social history, one popular, the other scholarly. The chronicler was Angus Calder, whose study of Britain in World War II, *The People's War,* did some useful demythologizing and traced the social forces leading to a revolution that never quite came off. The scholars were E. J. Hobsbawm and George Rudé, who traced in detail the last labourers' revolt, that of 1830. Their book, *Captain Swing,* filled out a complementary scene of rural poverty and degradation in Regency England to match the more familiar picture of the towns and dark satanic mills. "It reveals," wrote Edward Thompson, "at least through the distorting lens of repression, a whole layer of English society that had previously been hidden from historical awareness."

COURTESY, MACMILLAN & CO. LTD.

Alan Brownjohn, whose volume of poetry "Sandgrains on a Tray" was published in 1969.

Another "smashing book," as Peter Laslett was allowed to describe it in his *Guardian* review, was *A Second Identity,* a collection of essays by the boisterous Balliol historian of the French Revolution, Richard Cobb. The long introductory essay was a hilarious piece of autobiography, sprinkled with notes on the use of French archives, which set a high standard in carrying learning lightly. Weighty was a more appropriate description of C. A. Macartney's *The Habsburg Empire 1790–1918,* the heavy fruit of a life's work by a historian old enough to have known personally several of the actors in his history. The year also saw the publication of another installment of E. H. Carr's magisterial history of Soviet Russia, *Foundations of a Planned Economy 1926–29,* written with R. W. Davies. As a result no doubt of the Soviet invasion of Czechoslovakia, a growing interest in the U.S.S.R. was sensed by publishers. One part of the response was E. H. Carr's own collection of essays and book reviews *1917, Before and After.*

It was not an outstanding year for criticism or literary biography. Theodore Besterman's *Voltaire* depressed more than one reviewer with its turgid style and obsessively proprietorial air. *Henry James at Home,* written from James's home at Rye, in Sussex, by H. Montgomery Hyde, was an informal conducted tour *cum* biography that revealed little new of importance. Neither Charles Norman's *Ezra Pound* nor Phillippe Jullian's *Oscar Wilde* much altered the general view of their subjects.

Criticism, typically, came in collections of reviews rather than in books entire in themselves. There was another volume from Frank Kermode, *Continuities,* which carried forward some of his arguments from his last collection—notably against the prevalent modern myth of apocalypse. The subjects of Geoffrey Grigson's *Poems and Poets* were mostly Romantic, mad, and pastoral; this collection was admired by, among others, Philip Larkin. The prize essayists were undoubtedly Graham Greene and J. B. Priestley; the latter celebrated his 70th birthday with a handsome illustrated volume, *The Prince of Pleasure and His Regency,* and a collection, *Essays of Five Decades.* The year's best writing on contemporary theatre was Ronald Bryden's *The Unfinished Hero,* and the most stimulating pieces of art criticism were to be found among John Berger's essays in *The Moment of Cubism.* All these essayists would probably have read with pleasure, profit, and pangs of recognition John Gross's intelligent and well-written study of literary opinion makers, *The Rise and Fall of the Man of Letters.*

Finally, two wordbooks should be mentioned: an updated edition of Eric Partridge's fascinating *Dictionary of Slang and Unconventional English from the 15th Century to the Present Day* and—worthy successor to *The Language and Lore of Schoolchildren*—Iona and Peter Opie's *Children's Games in Street and Playground.* (W. L. WE.)

Poetry. Poetry was in a far more flourishing state at the end of the 1960s than it had been at the beginning—to judge by the astonishing number of verse collections made available during 1969, the public interest displayed in "performances" ranging from Royal Festival Hall recitals and poetry-and-jazz sessions in pubs to all-night poetry-reading marathons at the Roundhouse, and the poetry workshops and poetry-writing groups that sprang up, each with its own medium of communication, throughout the country. As the decade advanced, more and more verse was written, by young and old alike; more little presses were set up and more magazines (most of them cheaply duplicated) were launched to cater to the increasing demand; more people were reading or listening to poetry; more competitions were held (including several for children); and more poetry festivals were sponsored by local authorities. A 12-year-old secondary-modern schoolboy, John Dedman, leapt into prominence by winning first prize in the junior section of a competition organized for National Library Week with a remarkable poem about Vietnam entitled "Paints of My Own," which was published in the *Daily Express* and read at a National Theatre recital. In these broad circumstances, much that passed for poetry was not of a very high standard, but at least poetry began to have relevance for a greater number of people.

Though there was no obvious "book of the year" or violent eruption of genius, many competent and stimulating collections of poetry were published. The rich diversity of individual talents—determined to follow their own lines of development, exhibiting a wide variety in style, approach, technique, and use of language—made it an unusually interesting year. Plenty of groups were in evidence, each advocating a particular style or method of expression; but despite the publicity given to more sensational activities, no single group could effectively dominate a free-for-all scene in which even the most vociferous of the Pop poets, with their unsophisticated and often overemotional protest verse, could command an enthusiastic audience.

One interesting feature was the extension of the Faber "Introduction" series, previously confined to prose writers, to new poets whose work had appeared only in magazines. *Poetry: Introduction 1* contained substantial selections from the works of nine young poets, the most impressive of whom were Douglas Dunn, David Harsent, and Ian Hamilton (who had already gained a reputation as a reliable critic). Almost immediately afterward, two of these poets followed up the introductory anthology with volumes of their own that attracted favourable comment: Dunn with *Terry Street* and Harsent with *A Violent Country.* Other first volumes of note were *Moonsearch* by Barry Cole, *To Make Me Grieve* by Molly Holden, *North Bank Night* by Edward Storey, and *Out on a Limb* by David Sutton.

The Pop poets tended to receive more than their fair share of attention, for it seemed that Roger McGough's *Watchwords,* Adrian Henri's *Tonight at Noon,* Christopher Logue's *Numbers,* and Anselm Hollo's *The Coherences,* though containing a few striking phrases and colourful images, all relied too heavily upon gimmicky wordplay, facile puns, and slick typography for their effects. By far the best poet working in this genre was Brian Patten, whose meaningful *Notes to the Hurrying Man,* with its controlled lyricism and sense of direction, was a marked improvement upon his first book, *Little Johnny's Confession,* and promised a great deal for the author's future development.

Among the outstanding books of the year were *Sandgrains on a Tray* by Alan Brownjohn, *Door into the Dark* by Seamus Heaney, and *Root and Branch* by Jon Stallworthy. They were offered keen competition by such excellent collections as W. H. Auden's *City Without Walls,* Iain Crichton Smith's *From Bourgeois Land,* Sydney Tremayne's *The Turning Sky,* Laurence Lerner's *Selves,* and Elizabeth Jennings' *The Animals' Arrival,* to say nothing of the *Collected Poems* of Basil Bunting, John Hewitt, and Roy Fisher.

(Ho. S.)

FRENCH

Nonfiction. Writers, some of them very well known, seemed almost to have made an agreement to publish their memoirs simultaneously in 1969—providing an honest though incomplete picture of the literary period they had helped to shape. All of them were living except Roger Vailland, whose *Écrits intimes* documented in monumental form the personality of a deeply committed writer, who died in 1965 after involvement with drugs and with Communism. *Moi je* by Claude Roy was not without self-satisfaction: the autobiography included an attempt at Freudian psychoanalysis, and it was of further interest for its portraits of other writers, many of whom were Communists. The primary aim of *Dieu existe, je l'ai rencontré* by A. Frossard, essayist and humorist and the son of a militant Communist, was to describe his conversion to Catholicism; but the real substance of the book was its captivating narrative of his childhood. In *Mon Village et moi* the historian Pierre Gaxotte told of his childhood in Lorraine. Under the title *Tendre Bestiaire* Maurice Genevoix retold his "inner memoirs"; the animals in this book were often an excuse for fables and stories with morals, expressed in the richest style. J. L. Curtis in *Un Miroir le long du chemin* painted portraits worthy of La Bruyère and ironically mocked contemporary intellectual fashions; at the same time he published *Le Thé sous les cyprès,* a collection of stories reminiscent of Henry James. With three works, *Images, reportages, Le Jeu du roi,* and *Instants de Vérité,* the brilliant reporter J. Kessel revealed not only fascinating narratives but also the source of many of his novels. The publisher E. Buchet recalled in *Auteurs de ma vie* his contacts and relationships with French and foreign writers. Also of note were *Le Petit Journal* by J. Dutourd, which was lively and disillusioned; *Le Vif du sujet* by E. Morin, moving in its search for truth; and *Un Champ de solitude* by G. Picon. Bertrand Poirot-Delpech's *Finie La Comédie* was an exceedingly virulent pamphlet against intellectuals as a class and against the snobbism of obscurity—an attack against the New Criticism and the antinovel, which were defended by Claude Mauriac in a new edition of *L'Alittérature contemporaine.*

J. Romains in *Marc-Aurèle* described the private life of the philosopher Marcus Aurelius, setting the emperor against an accurate historical background. Camus's teacher and friend J. Grenier published *Albert Camus,* drawing on private documents to throw light on the writer's philosophy. M. Toesca's enormous and exhaustive *Lamartine* took the poet through all the stages of his passionate life, in both love and politics. In *Gustave Flaubert écrivain,* M. Nadeau portrayed Flaubert as he was revealed in his work, his correspondence, and his life.

Books about the events of May 1968 continued to appear, but their importance had lessened; an exception was *Le Mois de Mai du général* by R. Tournoux. *Par Le Sang versé* by P. Bonnecarrere was a story told with unbearable emotion, but with a sense of humour, about the discipline and heroism of the Foreign Legion. *Mémoires d'un architecte,* written by F. Pouillon after his escape from prison, *Papillon* by H. Carrière, a convict who escaped from Cayenne, and *Piaf,* a biography of Edith Piaf by her half sister S. Berteaut, also reached the top of the best-seller lists.

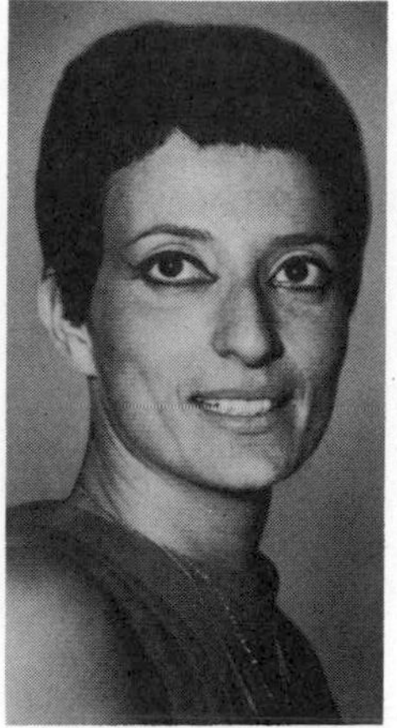

UPI COMPIX

Hélène Cixous won the 1969 Prix Médicis for her novel "Dedans."

Fiction. The award of the Nobel Prize to Samuel Beckett (*see* BIOGRAPHY) attracted more or less enthusiastic interest on the avant-garde. *Le Libera* by R. Pinget, giving an old man's description of the inhabitants of a village and creating suspense with the death of a young boy, was an unquestioned success. Nathalie Sarraute advised the reader not to look for characters in *Entre La Vie et la mort. Nombres* by Phillippe Sollers, "a book about nothing, written by no one," discouraged even his most faithful admirers. The critics who admitted the importance of *La Bataille de Pharsale,* by C. Simon, and had praised it, pointed out that the plot "falls to pieces, ceasing to give any internal coherence to the text." A new arrival on the scene, Hélène Cixous, made a name for herself with a collection of short stories; a thesis on Joyce; and *Dedans,* described as a novel, which won the Prix Médicis. One of her strongest admirers said that *Dedans* was "a rich and beautiful work, disconcerting insofar as it is like no other because we are unable to penetrate all its secrets." *La Promenade en barque* was an extremely obscure detective story, and not the best book, by the excellent writer P. Silvain. P. Bourgeade, author of three earlier erotic novels, looked to America for his most scandalous scenes in *New York Party.*

UPI COMPIX

Novelist and playwright F. Marceau, recipient of the Prix Goncourt in 1969.

Writers who do not owe their reputations to the avant-garde can nonetheless use comparable methods, as J. Cayrol did in *Je l'entends encore:* the life and death of a man were reflected in fragments by his grown-up son, who was brought up in a concentration camp. This was the work of a poet, who had also published *Poésie-Journal.* Jorge Semprun, a Spaniard writing in French and a former Communist, won the Prix Fémina for *La Deuxième Mort de Ramon Mercader,* an international spy novel that brought in the history of the Communist movement, together

A.F.P. FROM PICTORIAL PARADE

Jean Rousselot, whose 1969 publications included a translation of Shakespeare's sonnets and "Hors d'Eau," a work in prose and free verse, was awarded the prize of the Ville de Paris.

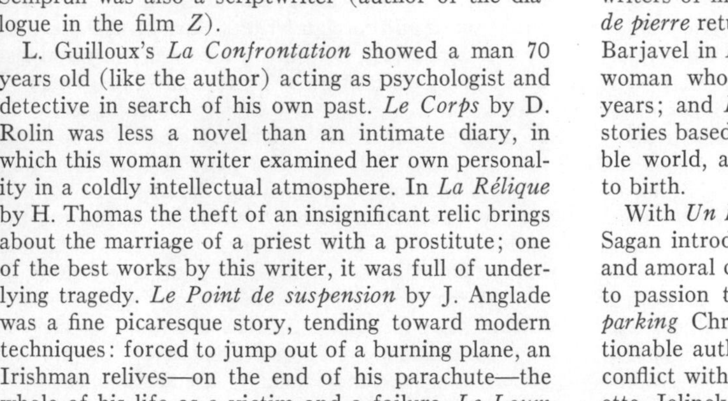

with psychological meditations reminiscent of Proust. Semprun was also a scriptwriter (author of the dialogue in the film *Z*).

L. Guilloux's *La Confrontation* showed a man 70 years old (like the author) acting as psychologist and detective in search of his own past. *Le Corps* by D. Rolin was less a novel than an intimate diary, in which this woman writer examined her own personality in a coldly intellectual atmosphere. In *La Rélique* by H. Thomas the theft of an insignificant relic brings about the marriage of a priest with a prostitute; one of the best works by this writer, it was full of underlying tragedy. *Le Point de suspension* by J. Anglade was a fine picaresque story, tending toward modern techniques: forced to jump out of a burning plane, an Irishman relives—on the end of his parachute—the whole of his life as a victim and a failure. *Le Loum* by R. P. Pilhes rejected both decency and coherence: exaggeration, obscenity, and incest had free rein in this novel with its disarmingly cynical and candid tone. *La Fille de Christophe Colomb* by the Canadian writer R. Ducharme was written in irregular verse that occasionally rhymed and had a certain verbal strength; it was the comic story of the daughter of the great explorer whom the author presented as being alive today. Jean-Marie Le Clezio in *Le Livre des fuites,* described as an "adventure novel" but having no story or characters, told of a voyage around the world, with rich descriptions, but it was not clear what was being fled or where it would all end up.

Traditional novelists allowed readers to get their feet back on the ground. *Un Adolescent d'autrefois,* the first novel for some years by François Mauriac, did not deviate from the psychological, social, and religious themes that had won him his vast reputation over the years. Autobiographical elements were to be found in it, as in *Les Garçons* by Henry de Montherlant, the first part of which was made up of the admirable play *La Ville dont le prince est un enfant,* the story of an excessive friendship between two schoolboys; the second part, a character study of the mother, was both less intense and of wider scope than was the play. Publication of *La Menteuse,* one of the earliest manuscripts of Jean Giraudoux (1882–1944), showed all of his grace and ease already present, though the story, of a woman and her lovers, was commonplace enough. *La Surprise de vivre* by J. Galzy was a social study of a great Protestant family of the south of France—a rich and absorbing novel, of which the second part was devoted to the relationship of two lesbians. *L'Amour et la vie d'une femme* by R. André was the saga of an insignificant former provincial family living in Paris; Juliette, apparently the most mediocre of them, helps her relations out of trouble by two prosperous marriages. The novel was closely worked and absorbing but perhaps overlong (like some others mentioned here). The monumental *L'Éternité plus un jour* by G. E. Clancier was really three novels in one. Under a title suggested by a tag from Shakespeare ("forever and a day"), this was the saga of two families of the provincial middle class, and the young people in the first part were reminiscent of those in *Le Grand Meaulnes* by Alain-Fournier, an accomplished work by a poet-novelist. Still popular, P. Vialar remained faithful to the world of horses and hunting with *La Cravache d'or* and *Les Invités de la chasse.* Guy des Cars's *La Vipère* was the most consistent best-seller of the year; it centred on the activities of a Chinese woman, an international spy in Paris in May 1968.

UPI COMPIX

M. Olivier-Lacamp received the Prix Renaudot in 1969 for his historical drama "Les Feux de la colère."

Fantasy continued to be exploited successfully by writers of high quality: M. Schneider in *Le Guerrier de pierre* returned to a legendary medieval time; René Barjavel in *La Nuit des temps* brought back to life a woman who had been imprisoned in ice for 9,000 years; and *Les Chimères* by P. Gascar consisted of stories based on myths of salt, blood, and the vegetable world, and of the magic that they had brought to birth.

With *Un Peu de soleil dans l'eau froide,* Françoise Sagan introduced into the little world of her spoiled and amoral characters a woman who abandons herself to passion to the point of death. In *Printemps au parking* Christiane Rochefort presented, with questionable authenticity, the personality of a student in conflict with his family. *La Vie de famille,* by Henriette Jelinek, was a realistic tale, in Maupassant's manner, of peasant avarice. In his third novel, *Une Fille cousue de fil blanc,* the young C. Gallois recreated, with a skillful balance of light and shade, the sad and comic story of a young girl who is the victim of a stupid accident. *La Vive* by R. Jean was one of the best novels by an accomplished writer: a provincial woman, unhappily married, has a number of affairs, then remarries. *Une Colère blanche* by M. Bataille examined the conscience of a painter faced with the commercialization of his work. *Le Tour de ville* by R. Bordier recreated the drama of a little village in decline and of a woman of 40 who is briefly infatuated with an adolescent.

P. Modiano made his name, in a single year, with *La Place de l'étoile*—the title referred to the yellow star forcibly worn by Jews during the German occupation—and *La Ronde de nuit,* the story, from the same period, of a traitor who divides his activities between the Resistance and the Gestapo. R. Sabatier was less unwonted and more populistic than before in *Les Allumettes suédoises,* the story of an orphan in Montmartre in Paris.

La Paroi, the third novel of P. Moustiers, won the French Academy's Grand Prix for fiction: it was the story of a mountain climb by two men belonging to different, and conflicting, generations. F. Marceau—whose career as a playwright appeared to be superseding his career as a novelist (*Le Babour* had a very successful run at the Théâtre de l'Atelier)—won the Prix Goncourt for *Creezy:* his story of the love of a parliamentary deputy for a fashion model was at once realistic, absurd, and charmingly humorous. M. Olivier-Lacamp, an outstanding journalist, won the Prix Renaudot for *Les Feux de la colère,* a historical drama about the Camisards (Protestant rebels in the south of France in the early 18th century) that was very finely told. With the publication of *Les Cerises d'Icherridène,* the third volume of his tetralogy on Algeria, Jules Roy won the Grand Prix des Lettres for the whole of his work, which bore the imprint of an active life. The Prix Interallié went to P. Schoendoerffer for his *L'Adieu au roi,* set in Borneo, where a white man, in flight from civilization, becomes king of a tribe.

Poetry. Two significant anthologies were published simultaneously: *La Nouvelle Poésie française* by Marc Alyn and *Un Certain Choix de poèmes* by J. Loisy. Each included about 40 poets—only four of whom appeared in both books. This was a clear indication of the difficulties of choice at a time when poetry hesitated between classical prosody and the greatest possible freedom.

Les Matins et les soirs by Philippe Chabaneix was

an accomplished example of the kind of classical poetry that can be immediately moving and of lasting interest. The same could be said of *Amour en profil perdu* by R. Houdelot, in which prose and poetry were mingled in a more melancholy mood. Equally nostalgic and passionate was *La Rose ardente* by M. Beguey. *La Route du feu* by G. Belloni was inspired by Christian themes. *Les Chemins perdus* by S. de Ricard was carried by its delightful rhythms. Much greater freedom was to be found in *Isabelle* by M. Berry. P. Dumaine's *Inscriptions* consisted of maxims and reflections that were concise and measured. Luc Bérimont's *Un Feu vivant* combined the abstract and the concrete in a captivating lyricism. In *La Pluie giboyeuse* by the well-known René Char, obscurity, preciosity, and precision went hand in hand. The novelist and poet Andrée Chedid, in *Contre-chat* and *Seul le Visage,* was obsessed by faces and by the earth.

Les Poisons délectables and *Les Châteaux des millions d'années,* remarkable for their decasyllables, assonances, and fantasy, won Robert Sabatier the Grand Prix de Poésie of the French Academy. The prize of the Ville de Paris went to Jean Rousselot, who published simultaneously an exceptional translation of Shakespeare's sonnets and *Hors d'Eau,* a work in prose and free verse, full of bitterness and richness. J. C. Renard, one of the most important French poets, offered a rather difficult metaphysics in *La Braise et la rivière,* where prose and poetry lay very close to one another. Loys Masson, born in 1915, and like Belloni a Christian poet, had just died when his book *La Croix de rose rouge* was published. (AE. B.)

GERMAN

Has the novel a future? This was a question as much discussed in Germany as elsewhere—and books published in 1969 by leading German novelists provided little ammunition for the optimists.

Anna Seghers, the most important writer domiciled in East Germany, published her long-awaited novel *Das Vertrauen,* the action of which was set in 1953 in both East and West Germany and in the U.S. Seeking by means of the most elementary literary devices and at the very lowest intellectual level to glorify the German Democratic Republic, even paying homage to Stalin, the book amounted to a declaration of bankruptcy by its once distinguished author.

Equally disappointing was the new book of Günter Grass, the most successful West German author. His novel *Örtlich betäubt* was concerned to a greater extent than any of his previous books with political and social motifs. Its central character, a 40-year-old West Berlin teacher, is a rationalist whose resigned attitude is intended to be typical of his generation of West German intellectuals. But instead of real people only shadows appeared, instead of an epic vision there was only wearisome artificiality, and Grass's language had none of its former tautness and strength.

Siegfried Lenz's novel *Deutschstunde,* while unusually successful with the public, met with a very mixed reception from the critics. Its theme was the conflict between art and authority, exemplified in the story of a painter in Nazi Germany whose work is unacceptable to the regime and who is prohibited from painting. However questionable the stylization of the narrative in the manner of a Nordic saga might at times seem, nevertheless Lenz was convincing in a number of masterly passages, particularly in the second part of the book.

Hans Erich Nossack's novel *Dem unbekannten Sieger,* an occasionally amusing but altogether unassuming little book, dealt with the relationship between historical writing and objective reality. Similar in theme was Peter Härtling's *Das Familienfest oder Das Ende der Geschichte,* set chiefly in the 1850s; its hero, an ambitious historian, finally capitulates in his search for the truth. Characteristic of this book—and indeed of other recent German novels; for example Dieter Wellershof's *Schattengrenze*—was its twisted, warped, pseudopoetical language, which served only to camouflage the author's failings.

The most important novel of the year—Christa Wolf's *Nachdenken über Christa T.*—came from East Germany. It was concerned with those intellectuals in the Democratic Republic who in their youth (*c.* 1945) had enthusiastically embraced Communism, but who with the passing of time had become disappointed and embittered. Personifying this disenchanted and disillusioned generation, the heroine of Christa Wolf's book is a sensitive Germanist who refuses to adapt herself to conditions in the Democratic Republic and for whom the only solution in the end is a retreat into her private and family life. The skillfully handled account of the heroine's decline and death in 1963 was in effect an indictment of East German bureaucracy, although conveyed without a word of anti-Communism. Particularly noteworthy was the sure-handed and natural use Christa Wolf made, in this elegiac defense of the individual, of various techniques and modes of expression employed by contemporary West German novelists.

AUTHENTICATED NEWS INTERNATIONAL

Günter Grass, whose political novel, "Örtlich betäubt," was published in 1969.

Also set in East Berlin was the novel *Maria Morzeck oder Das Kaninchen bin ich* by the satirist Manfred Bieler, who moved from East to West Germany in 1968. This was a love story, told realistically and with strong elements of social criticism; the first part was distinguished by its humour and accurately recorded slang dialogue. Among the year's lighter novels the experienced Hans Habe's *Das Netz,* about the murder of an Austrian call girl in Rome, scored a great success.

The most noteworthy collection of short stories published in 1969 was *Otto der Akrobat* by Mario Szenessy, a Hungarian living in West Germany and writing in German. Stylistically brilliant, Szenessy's seemingly realistic stories turn out to be also ironic parables. A Swiss author, Peter Bichsel, published a small volume of tales, *Kindergeschichten,* that were equally suitable for children and adults and reflected a fertile imagination. Among the year's numerous debutants in the short-story genre only the 26-year-old Wolf Wondratschek stood out: his collection of laconic miniatures, *Früher begann der Tag mit einer Schusswunde,* conveyed pointed and significant criticism of social conditions in the German Federal Republic.

The year's most important theatrical event was Tancred Dorst's *Toller.* Built around the German Expressionist poet and dramatist Ernst Toller and the uprising in Bavaria shortly after World War I, its theme was the relationship of intellectuals with power and politics. Dorst's loosely connected sequence of scenes, somewhat reminiscent of political revue, was considered by many critics a successful attempt to revive the German agitation-theatre of the 1920s. But the critics unanimously rejected Günter Grass's play *Davor,* and it failed completely.

The leading German lyricists were silent in 1969, but a little-known poet, the Swiss Kurt Marti, achieved a well-deserved success with his collection

Leichenreden, consisting of witty verse variations of conventional funeral orations and obituaries.

Particularly noteworthy among belletristic works was Walter Jens's *Von deutscher Rede,* a collection of eulogies and essays devoted mainly to great artists; these pieces were remarkable for their polished rhetoric and masterly characterization. Horst Krüger's *Deutsche Augenblicke* comprised sketches, travel notes, and essays that cast a sharply critical light on everyday life in East and West Germany.

Ludwig Marcuse, at the age of 76, published a remarkable book, *Nachruf auf Ludwig Marcuse*—spirited, unsentimental, and far exceeding the merely autobiographical in its deep insight into the nature of our epoch. (M. R.-R.)

ITALIAN

Once again, in 1969 some "new" books were in fact reprints of works that first appeared during the lean postwar years or else were posthumous "discoveries." Cesare Pavese's *Ciau Masino,* Beppe Fenoglio's *La paga del sabato,* and Elio Vittorini's *Le città del mondo,* unpublished in the authors' lifetimes, did not add much to their reputations. Corrado Alvaro's *Domani* occasionally rose to the level of his best novels of the "Rinaldo Diacono" cycle, with which it shared a moralizing and misogynistic outlook.

Among new novels by established writers, the near-octogenarian Riccardo Bacchelli's *L'Afrodite* rehearsed a familiar blend of frustrated eroticism and titillated conscience. The title was the name of a yacht in which wealthy Imelde Lesi, while cruising with her lover, is raped by a cabin boy and enjoys it. Doubt as to whether she should bear alone the guilt of such an involuntary pleasure or atone for it by confessing to her lover torments her (and the reader) until the end. Although style, like spirits, mellows with age, one feels that eroticism, like meat, should be fresh to be tasty.

There was no love interest in *L'Airone* by Giorgio Bassani. As in previous novels, he took his cue from his unrivaled knowledge of Ferrara's Jewry; but it was pointless to try to spot the "real" people behind his characters, for what matters most in his works is not documentary truth but aesthetic evidence. In this book the winter's day in 1947 when Edgardo Limentani decides to go hunting resembles one of those nightmares in which all one's efforts are hindered by a malignant force, and the flow of the dream is disturbed by the fleeting awareness of one's motionless body shrouded in the bedclothes. Edgardo's life flow appears similarly obstructed by his sluggish mental and bodily functions. The only way to wake up from his nightmare is to choose death: once this decision is taken, he can at last make sense of and be reconciled with life, in a concluding vision of great beauty.

Luciano Bianciardi's *Aprire il fuoco* telescoped into the unified perspective of his entertaining story, about an imaginary uprising in Milan, the separate historical planes of the Risorgimento and the Resistance. He succeeded not only in creating the new fictional dimension of a contemporary revolution but also in suggesting, under the pretence of explaining why it failed, the reasons for the failure of the earlier movements.

Italian writers, on the whole, are better at writing short stories than novels. Piero Chiara showed himself an accomplished storyteller in *L'uovo al cianuro,* and Giovanni Arpino's *Ventisette racconti* deserved more than a passing mention.

It was not a vintage year for poetry. Guido Ceronetti's *Poesie, frammenti, poesie separate,* 20 years in the making, lacked neither depth nor forcefulness, but its impact was weakened by the poet's declared faith in the dogma of the absolute word and his consequent rejection of creative ambiguity. The concise, but not reticent, poems in *Controbuio* by Giuseppe Favati had a pleasing epigrammatic quality. Dialect poetry was well represented by *Eccò 'a morte* (Why Death?), written by Albino Pierro in the language of Tursi (Lucania).

Some new work defied classification. Lalla Romano's *Le parole tra noi leggere* was much more than a biography of her obscure but not unremarkable son. It showed how young people abound in genius, poetry, and creativity, and how education, conformity, and moneymaking soon warp and stunt their natural attributes beyond repair. This compelling book did not pretend to explain intelligence, freedom, or the generation gap, but it did throw more light on these questions than its unpretentiousness appeared to promise. *La zona immobile* by Giorgio Chiesura was a verse story that took as its central theme the experience of concentration camps as a concrete metaphor of the human condition. "A nonexistent character in search of a story" might be the subtitle of Tommaso Landolfi's *Faust 67,* a Pirandellian divertissement that was, as usual, urbane, witty, and enjoyable.

Alberto Moravia's "play" *La vita è gioco* was really a philosophical dialogue, a form used previously by Moravia as a vehicle for his ideas. This time the idea was that social and moral conventions are rules unrelated to any enjoyable game, and that complete freedom might be like a game not bound by any rules: perhaps a more satisfying way of playing at life, but dangerous, since the stake is life itself. In *Marcel ritrovato* Giuliano Gramigna was apparently concerned with the disappearance of Marcel (who, we discover, has opted out of the rat race—but wisely, in relative comfort, among the fleshpots of Paris); he seemed, however, more interested in the mechanics of writing his novel, which he obscured by means of long footnotes, than in the vagaries of his characters. Giuliano Manganelli reiterated his attacks on literature in *Nuovo commento,* a long commentary upon a nonexistent text—the commentary itself being commented upon through pedantic methodological digressions: some of it read like run-of-the-mill Italian literary criticism.

Alberto Arbasino in *Off off* indulged in some erudite and caustic debunking of contemporary cultural trends. A useful survey of modern Italian literary criticism was Italo Viola's *Critica letteraria del Novecento;* and, of contemporary writing, Gian Carlo Ferretti's *La letteratura del rifiuto. Eugenio Montale* was an informative biography of the poet lovingly compiled by Giulio Nascimbeni. *Settecento riformatore* was the first of two volumes that Franco Venturi had worked on for over 20 years: a 750-page history of enlightened reform in Italy, from Muratori to Beccaria, that was surely destined to become the standard work on this subject for the present generation. Venturi was a man dedicated to the idea of reform as a means of changing society in general and university education in particular; nevertheless—and this is a tribute to Venturi's scholarship—the reader reached the end of the book with his faith in reform badly shaken. It emerged vividly that the untiring efforts of an intellectual elite, devoted to changing society in a predominantly intellectual way, were effectively blocked and almost nullified by the political and economic powers of the time. (G. C.)

JEWISH

Hebrew. In spite of the uncertainty and stress that marked daily life in Israel, Hebrew writers produced some valuable works of fiction and nonfiction.

Y. Hendel's *he-Hatzer Shel Mumo ha-Gedola* again confirmed her narrative ability. The writing team of Y. and A. Sand contributed the voluminous *ha-Nisayon ha-Nosaf*. Y. Kaniuk's *Adam Ben Kelev* (translated by the author as *Son of Dog*) was a novel with Surrealist undertones. War stories by G. Telpaz were entitled *la-Pahad Ain Tzeva;* topically somewhat similar was M. Shamir's *Ness Lo Kara Lanu*. Simply told was M. Taviv's *Masa la-Eretz ha-Gedola*.

The eighth volume—essays—of Shin Shalom's collected *Ketavim* appeared, along with *Masot u-Reshimot* by Sh. Zemach, consisting of studies of modern Hebrew literature, and I. Cohan's *Espaklariot*. Quaintly fascinating was A. M. Haberman's disquisition *Shaarai Sefarim Ivrim*. Y. Don's *Torat ha-Sod Shel Hasidai Ashkenaz* provoked some attention, as did A. Mirsky's scholarly work *Mahutan Shel Tzurot ha-Piyut*. A volume dealing with the archaeology of Jerusalem was *Yerushalayim le-Doroteaa* edited by Y. Aviram. Of contemporary historical significance were D. Ben-Gurion's *Medinat Yisrael ha-Mehudeshet* and L. Eshkol's *Brit Adama*.

The works of a 17th-century Italian Hebrew poet were introduced and annotated by P. Naveh in *Kol Shirai Yaakov Frances*. Reproduced in manuscript form was *Shirai Rachel u-Michtaveha;* an influential lyric poet, she died prematurely some decades earlier. *Mivhar Shirim* by A. Broides and *ba-Et u-Veona* by D. Chomsky represented an older "school" of poetry; K. A. Bertini's *Bakbuk Al Pnai ha-Mayim* was cast in a more modern mold. A keen, contemporary poetic statement was *Ahshav be-Raash* by Y. Amichai. The poems by the late Y. Mar in *Panim le-Kan* were moving. D. Ravikovich published a volume of lyric responses, *ha-Sefer ha-Shelishi*.

In the U.S., Hebrew literary activity was at a low point. Nevertheless, there appeared such volumes as *Otzar ha-Safa ha-Ivrit*, compiled by N. Stuchkoff; *Ofkai Mahshava* by G. Churgin; and R. Ben-Yosef's *Derech Eretz*, poems by an American-born Jew living in Israel. (G. P.)

Yiddish. Prose writings of the year emphasized a trend that had become conspicuous in Yiddish letters of the postwar era: reminiscences, recreating the world erased from the map by the Nazi onslaught, dominated all other kinds of writing.

To the category of memoirs and autobiographical novels belonged the works of some established writers, such as Fishl Bimko with a five-volume series *On the Way to Life* (all titles are given here in English translation) and L. Olitski with *Yeshiva People*, as well as quite successful attempts by little-known aspirants, notably B. Manitsh with *The Power of Faith* and Yankl Perlman with *The Boy from Krochmalna Street*. The reminiscences of childhood and youth in the prewar era were tinged with warmth and admiration for the values of traditional Jewish life, but the writings on the traumatic experiences of World War II dealt with a subject familiar in contemporary letters: man's inhumanity to man. The books of Yekhiel Hofer, Leon Leneman, and Yoel Perl were human documents telling the story of needless cruelty and senseless suffering in the Soviet slave labour camps. Political and social novels—I. D. Berkovitsh's *The Dawn*, B. Epshteyn's *The Sun Set in the South*, and B. Shlevin's *Lipe Kamashnmakher*—revealed facets of Jewish experience in Israel, South America, and Europe. An anthology, *Stories of Soviet-Yiddish Writers*, comprising a half-century of Yiddish writings in the U.S.S.R., appeared as a contribution to events marking the anniversary of the October Revolution.

The role of Yiddish poetry in present times was redefined in an essay by Yankev Glatshteyn: the poet, he said, should be a spokesman for his generation, and his poetry should be a poetry of involvement. Avrom Sutskever in *Poems from the Dead Sea* and Khayim Grade in *On My Way to You* epitomized this idea by giving poetic expression of unique quality and force to the basic, ambivalent Jewish experience of the postwar era: the feeling of irreparable loss caused by the annihilation of the six million, and the joy of rebirth in the Old-New Land of Israel. The theme reverberated also in new collections by Moyshe Knaphcys, Leyb Morgentory, Kh. L. Fuks, I. Emiot, L. Kusman, J. A. Rontsh, and M. M. Shafir. The Israeli group made up of I. Papernikov, Y. Z. Shargel, A. Shamri, M. Yungman, A. Shpigelblat, and L. Olitski added new dimensions to Yiddish poetry, revealing deep roots in the Israeli landscape, an ever-present awareness of the biblical tradition, and a feeling of miraculous transformation from dream to reality. The women poets—Pesye Pomerants-Honigboym, Malke Li, Reyzl Zhykhlinski, Brokhe Kopsheteyn, Mina Bordo-Rivkin, Shifre Verber, and Perl Halter—displayed talents ranging in expression from the harmonious and lucid to the direct, intimate, and unconventional. Yiddish poetry in the U.S.S.R. was represented by the late master Dovid Hofshteyn, one of the group of Yiddish writers destroyed by Stalinist purges, and by two younger contemporaries: a poet of sensitiveness and grace, Sh. Driz, and a spokesman for a generation of warriors and astronauts, Arn Vergelis.

UPI COMPIX

Former Prime Minister David Ben-Gurion published "Medinat Yisrael ha-Mehudeshet" in 1969.

The contributions of Eastern European Jewry to Jewish life and the present state of Yiddish culture the world over were assessed in a collection of essays, *Jewish Dialogues*, published by the World Jewish Congress. The fascinating subject of the Yiddish theatre was dealt with in a collective work, *Yiddish Theatre in Europe Between Two World Wars*, and in the sixth volume of Z. Zylbertsvayg's *Lexicon of the Yiddish Theatre*. (D. Az.)

LATIN-AMERICAN

By the end of the 1960s it had become clear that there was no longer an "Ibero-American literature." There were as many literatures as national realities; and although Spanish remained a common language, its written and spoken features in each country were those of a distinct language—just as, in Brazil, Portuguese had become Brazilian. Yet for the first time since Modernism, at the turn of the century, a new movement had emerged on a continental scale. The "new Latin-American novel" instigated a renovation of Spanish prose as far-reaching as the changes in Spanish verse fostered by Rubén Darío and his contemporaries.

The movement contained its own interpreters: exegesis of the new novel was not the province of scholars or reviewers but of the artists themselves. Carlos Fuentes in *La nueva novela hispanoamericana* and Julio Ortega in *La contemplación y la fiesta* wrote admirable interpretative essays using a Structuralist model; and, by allowing themselves considerable freedom, they avoided the sectarianism that coloured Severo Sarduy's *Escrito sobre un cuerpo*. This does not detract, however, from the lucidity of Sarduy's analyses, for example, in the essay on the Baroque in José Lezama Lima.

Hardly a week passed in which a young Argentinian writer did not offer a good new work to the public; at the same time the modern classics, like Jorge Luis Borges, continued and extended their work. Borges added some of his most intense recent poems to a *Nueva antología personal,* offered a moving *Elogio de las sombras,* and looked back over his 70 years of life in conversations with Victoria Ocampo recorded in *Diálogo con Borges*. Eduardo Mallea brought together 64 of his stories in *La red,* and Adolfo Bioy Casares published his most original novel, *Diario de la guerra del cerdo*. Ernesto Sábato considered modern literature through the work of Alain Robbe-Grillet, Jean-Paul Sartre, and Borges in *Tres aproximaciones a la literatura de nuestro tiempo*. Manuel Mujica Láinez traced the fictional life of a South American city from its origins to the year 4000. H. A. Murena embarked, with *Epitalámica,* on a cycle of Goyan inspiration called "El sueño de la razón."

Once again, however, the dominant figure in Argentinian letters was Julio Cortázar, who cast his increasingly influential gaze on the world and literature in *62: modelo para armar* and *El último Round;* defended in the pages of *Life* the characteristic political radicalism of Latin-American intellectuals; and demonstrated conclusively to his Cuban friends that Heberto Padilla's fine poetry in *Fuera del juego* was anything but counterrevolutionary. The importance and influence of Cortázar had found its confirmation in the five books and the 100 or more essays dedicated so far to the study of his work.

The work of poets as different as A. Pizarnik in *Extracción de la piedra de la locura* and F. Urondo in *Adolecer* was further testimony to the extraordinary vitality of Argentinian letters—whose major manifestation, however, as in most Latin-American countries, was in the novel. Manuel Puig's *Boquitas pintadas* combined the *feuilleton* and the newest in experimental literature; Néstor Sánchez amplified his mythology of the middle class in *El amor, los Orsinis y la muerte;* and Sara Gallardo's *Los galgos, los galgos* and A. di Benedetto's *Los suicidas* explored other levels of memory and experience. Among the youngest group of writers, E. Gudiño Kieffer with *Para comerte mejor* and Héctor Libertella with *El camino de los hiperbóreos* promised much for the future.

The major literary event of the year in Brazil was James Amado's edition of Gregorio de Matos' *Obras Completas*. De Matos (1633–96), a great Baroque poet, transformed a European style into an American expression full of indigenous and black elements. Among Brazilian contemporary poets Decio Pignatari claims first attention here with *Exercicio Findo,* which included the visual text "Mallarmé Vietcong," both an homage and an ironic challenge to the patron of the modern artistic adventure. *Uma Aprendizagem ou O Livro dos Prazeres* marked a new development in the introspective narrative of Clarice Lispector, whose prose was sometimes close to the *nouveau roman* and the lyricism of Virginia Woolf. Haroldo de Campos, mentor of the continent's most radical literary vanguard, included under the title *A Arte no Horizonte do Provável* artistic and literary essays, a theory of translation, and a plan for the synchronic revision of Brazilian literary historiography in the manner of Ezra Pound or the Structuralist project of Roman Jakobson.

R. Prada Oropeza's *Los fundadores del alba,* from Bolivia, was the best novel so far written on the theme of the rural guerrilla. In Colombia, the bitter short stories of *Esta mañana del mundo* by Oscar Collazos were outstanding. The *gamines,* the urchins abandoned in the night of Bogotá, populated M. Zapata Olivella's novel *Detrás del rostro*. The essay tradition was maintained by Francisco Psada with *Lukacs, Brecht y la situación actual del realismo socialista* and by J. Mejía Duque with *Literatura y realidad*. Germán Arciniegas represented the good journalistic prose of the pre-Garcia Marquez generation with *Nuevo diario de Noé*.

The literary development of socialist Cuba continued its encouraging trend with Reynaldo Arenas' extraordinary antihistorical novel *El mundo alucinante,* which evoked in the light of magical realism the life of a Mexican priest who has rebelled against both the ecclesiastical hierarchy and the Spanish empire. Miguel Barnet's *Canción de Rachel,* the biography of a Cuban vedette, underlined the unlimited artistic possibilities that the Cuban reality offers. Another field of huge potential was opened by the collective work *Che Comandante,* a biographical montage of a revolutionary.

Pablo Neruda celebrated his 65th birthday by accepting the Chilean presidential candidacy and publishing his latest poems under the title *Fin de mundo*. Once again, passages of inert rhetoric stood against examples of the most prodigious verbal gift that the Spanish language has known since Quevedo. Enrique Lihn's *Escrito en Cuba,* also chaotic at times, emphasized the overwhelming lyrical strength that had made Lihn the finest poet of the 1950 generation. Fernando Alegría in *Los días contados* described the life of a boxer in the poorer districts of Santiago; this novel confirmed the narrative dexterity that had come to be his mark. The year also saw the publication of fine volumes of short stories: Antonio Skármeta's *Desnudo en el tejado* and Christian Huneeus's *La casa en Algarrobo*. Nonetheless, Chilean narrative fiction still gave an impression of traditionalism in comparison with developments in poetry.

Miguel Angel Asturias published his first book since receiving the 1967 Nobel Prize: *Maladrón,* the story of a group of Conquistadores in search of unity between two oceans and of a new faith to replace beliefs lost in the shock of contact between two cultures. The best of Guatemala's poets, Luis Cardoza y Aragón, commemorated with beautiful images his childhood and adolescence in *Dibujos de ciego,* whose style seemed naked in relation to the Mayan Surrealism and neo-Baroque imagery of Asturias.

It was an exceptional year for Mexican poetry. *Ladera Este* was a collection of poems written by Octavio Paz during his six-year spell in India. The book proved that Paz had found there a new creative power—in an open poetic form introducing into Spanish both the possibility of a hitherto unknown musical quality and a rhythmic alternative to conventional verse. R. Bonifaz Nuño in *El ala del tigre* and Rosario Castellanos in *Materia memorable* testified that form is not an external obstacle but the visible manifestation of what the poetry is saying internally. Altogether, the range and quality of poetry published in 1969 confirmed the constant variety of the Mexican poetic tradition: apart from an *Antología* of the work of Carlos Pellicer, Mexico's first great modern poet, collections were offered by Efraín Huerta, M. Michelena, and M. Guardia, and new work was published by Gabriel Zaid, Homero Aridjis, M. A. Montes de Oca, Juan Bañuelos, and José Emilio Pacheco. In narrative prose, J. V. Melo with *La obediencia nocturna* and Gustavo Sáinz with *Obsesivos días circulares* continued their search for innovations in fiction.

The world of the young reappeared in José Agustín's strange McLuhanite dialogue-novel *Abolición de la propiedad.* The short story recovered its rightful place with books by Salvador Elizondo, J. M. Torres, and René Avilés Fabila; Juan García Ponce's *La presencia lejana* and *La cabaña* explored, on different levels, the mysterious and opaque qualities of human relationships. In *Maten al león* Jorge Ibarbengioitia drew a hilarious satirical sketch of the military dictators. The best contributions to the essay came from Fernando Benitez with *Los indios de Mexico,* Carlos Fuentes with *La nueva novela,* and Ramon Xirau with *Palabra y silencio.*

Ernesto Cardenal in *Homenaje a los indios americanos* and P. A. Cuadra in *Poesía escogida* underlined anew the extraordinary quality of Nicaraguan lyric poetry. Paraguay's literary stagnation found one explanation in Roque Vallejo's *La literatura paraguaya como expresión nacional:* he contended it was a result of the continuing atmosphere of repression in his landlocked country.

In Peru, the most important book was César Vellejo's *Obra poética completa,* a definitive edition correcting and superseding all others. Mario Vargas Llosa's third great novel, *Conversación en la catedral,* set both in Lima and in the jungle and mountains of Peru, recounted masterfully the concentric lives of characters from irreconcilable levels of the society. Julio Ortega, Milko Lauer, and Winston Orrillo were outstanding among Peru's new poets.

The Puerto Rican novelist P. J. Soto set his work *El francotirador* in the opposing ambits of Cuba and his native island. Images of Central America and Prague, Czech., were intermingled in *Taberna y otros lugares* by El Salvador's finest poet, Roque Dalton.

In Uruguay, as always, criticism took first place in literary activity. Emir Rodríguez Monegal presented the fruits of several decades of work: the monumental *El otro Andrés Bello;* studies of Delmira Agustini in *Sexo y poesía en el 900;* and interviews with new novelists in *El arte de Narrar.* Mario Benedetti produced both an excellent collection of short stories, *La muerte y otras sorpresas,* and a volume of critical articles, *Sobre artes y oficios,* which revindicated the artistic possibilities of the review. Angel Rama collated the results of fundamental research in *Los poetas modernistas y el mercado económico.* All the short stories and novels of Juan Carlos Onetti had now been collected in two volumes; and his son Jorge put Pop culture at the service of the narrative imagination in *Contramutis.* Casa de las Americas, Havana, published a collection of key articles on the elder Onetti in the series *Valoración múltiple,* which had already included a similar collection on the Mexican Juan Rulfo.

In Venezuela, A. González León's *País portátil* described with stylistic and structural richness a day in the life of an urban guerrilla. Salvador Garmendia in *La mala vida* painted an expressionistic picture of the gray antiheroes who inhabit the decaying sections of the huge but not yet great city of Caracas. Baica Dávalos, an Argentinian living in Venezuela, offered a number of books, of which the best-written and most imaginative was *Interregno.* (J. E. PA.; M. A. G.)

NORWEGIAN

In 1969 a novel of only 65 pages, *Omgivelser,* placed Kjell Askildsen above all other experimenters in modern Norwegian prose. With economy of expression and a virtuoso shifting of perspectives, the novel explored the tense, sex-laden, claustrophobic atmosphere on a small island, with the agonists a lighthouse keeper and his wife, their grown-up daughter, and a visiting writer.

A newcomer, Reidar Thomassen, showed mature epic mastery in *Konfrontasjonen,* centred on a writer's confrontation with a former leading Nazi. *Gemini* by Finn Alnaes incorporated contemporary scientific knowledge into a comprehensive philosophical system, tearing the solid ground from beneath the reader's feet and placing him in his cosmic context. A profound pessimism coloured Finn Havrevold's *Blårytter,* which explored the deranged sexual fantasies suffered by an intellectual after an air crash. Paal-Helge Haugen's mininovel *Anne* was an interesting experiment in collage technique. Ragnhild Magerøy's *Mens nornene spinner* was an uneven historical novel set in the early 12th century. *De skjulte tjenester* by Haavard Haavardsholm dealt with spying on private citizens in the name of national security, and its demoralizing effect on the spy himself.

The characters in Johan Borgen's short-story collection *Trœcer alene i skogen* were seeming nonentities; Gunnar Lunde's *Svart latter* was largely centred on psychopathic cases. *Probok* by Tor Åge Bringsværd successfully combined science fiction and social satire. Charm and elegance characterized Richard Herrmann's *Paradisveien,* a humorous presentation of the life and people of a suburban London street. Bjørg Vik's collection *Det grådige hjerte* revealed a mastery of detailed erotic description.

Jens Bjørneboe's play *Semmelweis* was a documentary dealing with the opposition to Ignaz Philipp Semmelweis' fight to overcome puerperal fever by antiseptic methods in the mid-19th century. Stein Mehren's poetic play *Narren og hans hertug* was set in Burgundy in the 1470s and had the court fool Hans van Niklashausen as its central figure. Both plays carried, however, strong contemporary overtones.

Norsk lyrikk nå, an anthology edited by Paal Brekke, contained a selection of Norwegian poetry from the 1960s. The collected poems of Tarjei Vesaas and of Georg Johannessen appeared as paperbacks. *Efterklang* by Herman Wildenvey was a collection of his articles and broadcasts, edited by the poet's widow. *Sandemoses ansikter,* a collection of articles and letters by a number of Scandinavian writers, gave a multifaceted picture of the work of Aksel Sandemose.

Critical works that appeared in 1969 included Einar Østvedt's *Henrik Ibsen: Miljø og mennesker,* which contained sympathetic portraits of Ibsen's much-maligned father and of his wife and mother-in-law. *Bjørnson og kristendommen 1832–1875* by Per Amdam was a copiously documented survey of Bjørnstjerne Bjørnson's attitude to Christianity from childhood to the period of his religious crisis, in the 1870s. In *Knut Hamsuns Mysterier* Gregory Nybø traced the thriller elements in Hamsun's novels. *Den plettfrie,* by a Japanese, Masahiko Inadomi, analyzed Sigurd Hoel's novel *Møte ved milepelen. Dikternes verden* by John Nome was a collection of ten literary essays on leading Norwegian writers from Holberg to Hoel.

In *Fra 40-tall til 60-tall* Willy Dahl gave a concise survey of Norwegian fiction during the preceding three decades. (To. S.)

SOVIET

In 1968–69 Soviet literature presented two faces to the world: one looking outward and forward, the other back to the stories of the 1917 Revolution and the "Great Patriotic War" or inward to the daily lives of Soviet citizens or the life of the countryside—"the homeland." The division was not along a straight line, between the growing "literature in exile"—published, of necessity, in the West, if not written abroad —and literature in the Soviet Union. Poets, in particular, by publishing mainly in periodicals or ephemeral "underground" popular broadsheets or by reading their work on television and radio, gained wide audiences for works of protest, in styles less traditional than that of the more "established" masters. Science fiction satirized the regime with apparent informality. Editors of liberal journals provided an outlet for, and encouraged the work of, "unpatriotic renegades": the editors might be dismissed but the journals continued. To Western critics, however, the creative writing published in the West seemed to belong most truly to the great Russian literary traditions. Indeed, the novelist Aleksandr Solzhenitsyn—none of whose major works had been published in the Soviet Union, but famous abroad for *The First Circle* (1968) and *Cancer Ward* (part i., 1968; ii, 1969)—was being compared with Tolstoi in depth and range of characterization and analysis of society.

Much Soviet literature followed established patterns, though it did not necessarily toe the party line. Novelists seemed disinclined toward new subjects or styles; literary historians continued to extol the founders of Communism and the Soviet state; memoirs of war heroes and others naturally looked back. Soviet writers continued to claim international respect —but, in 1968–69, more for subject than for style. In the U.S.S.R. there was no lack of interest in translations of works by Western authors, those by Thomas Mann, Iris Murdoch, and Robert Penn Warren being permitted and popular.

Biographies and critical works included a further flurry of preliminary fanfares for the centenary, in 1970, of Lenin's birth. The indefatigable Marietta Shaginian reached *Christmas in Sorrento* in her researches into his background and the years of exile. Sergei Antonov in *A Light from Afar* exhaustively chronicled a single year, 1920, and H. G. Wells's visit to Lenin in Moscow. Mikhail Sholokhov's misfiring *Sparks* studied Lenin and his dynamic influence. Among other literary studies were M. O. Mendelson's *Walt Whitman;* E. P. Lyubareva's *Soviet Lyric Poetry;* and *Faces from the Past,* a comparative survey of the work of Franz Kafka, Stefan Zweig, Lion Feuchtwanger, and other writers of German, by B. L. Suchkov.

Marshal Georgi Zhukov's *Memoirs* (1969; trans. 1969–70) was perhaps the most interesting of the year's output of reminiscences and reflections, partly because it contained not only a detailed and illuminating account of battles and military strategy but also a survey and analysis, with much new material, of his even more important years as defense minister. The circumstances of its publication were unusual. The British publishers, MacDonald & Co., had paid Novosti, the Soviet press agency, a six-figure sum for exclusive rights, and in March 1969 published a Russian-language edition to ensure international copyright. The first blow fell when MacDonald's translator recognized much of the "exclusive" material as having already appeared in Soviet military journals; the second, when a U.S. firm, Harper & Row, announced an English version of the first part as *Marshal Zhukov's Greatest Battles.* Novosti was cleared of deliberate duplicity, and a compromise was reached: the U.S. translation was published in Britain in 1969 as the first volume of the *Memoirs,* with the last two volumes to be published by the two firms jointly in 1970.

Other memoirs by war heroes included Adm. N. G. Kuznetsov's *The War Years* and Marshal N. I. Krylov's *The Defense of Odessa.* Boris Polevoi, editor of the liberal literary journal *Yunost* ("Youth"), gave an eyewitness account of the Nürnberg trials in *In the Long Run.* Aleksandr Deitch in *Today and Yesterday* remembered A. V. Lunarcharski and meetings with Soviet, German, and French writers and politicians. Vladimir Andreev, son of the early 20th-century novelist and playwright Leonid Andreev, who opposed the Revolution, described in *Return to Life* the experiences of Russian immigrants in the 1920s.

That the Revolution and its effects, and the events of World War II, still kept their hold on the popular imagination was shown by the number—and quality— of novels on them. Two novels treating the effects of the Revolution on neglected or remote communities were Leonid Gurunts' *Fathers* and Alim Keshokov's *Green Half-Moon,* the latter about the revolutionary fighting in Kabardino-Balkarskaya in the Caucasus, and the benefits of the Revolution to a primitive community, to which it brought education, freedom from superstition, and organized work for a reasonable wage in place of the struggle for mere existence of a nomad people. An outstanding work about World War II was the second volume of Aleksandr Chakovsky's *Blockade,* a gripping story of the siege of Leningrad. In *The Lieutenant* Sergei Krutilin described the feelings, as well as the heroic actions, of a young officer; and in *A Special Unit* Vadim Kozhevnikov told the story of a handpicked group on a secret mission.

Novels of contemporary life included Wil Lipatov's *Country Constable,* a sympathetic character study of a country policeman; Vladimir Orlov's *One Fine Day,* describing with insight the friendships, loves, and work of ordinary people; and Vladimir Amlinski's *The Life of Ernst Shatelov,* a psychological portrayal of a man whose life is made up of the usual anxieties, joys, and sorrows.

By far the most original novel of the year was *The Inherited Island* by the Strugatsky brothers, Arkadi and Boris, who had successfully used science fiction before for thinly veiled satire of Soviet society and institutions. By placing the action on another planet and disguising the Presidium and the Central Committee of the Communist Party as the "Unknown Fathers"—benevolent despots ruling a classless "Just Society," where the majority starve while the minority live on the fat of the land—they analyzed with pinpoint sharpness and clarity of aim the Soviet state, the struggles preceding its establishment, and its method of keeping itself in power. In their astronaut-discovered "paradise" (a variation on the old dystopian theme), propaganda convinces the masses that they live in the best of all possible states—but not "The Freaks," members of an intelligent underground, whose experiences at "phoney trials, rehearsed beforehand" and in concentration camps or remote uninhabited deserts strongly resemble those suffered by the "enemies" of the Soviet. Wit and a genuine skepticism prevented the satire from becoming too crude. This space allegory of life on earth was praised by *Novy Mir,* the most influential liberal Soviet journal.

In poetry, four established masters published collections: Evgeni Vinokurov, paratrooper and geologist, whose *Selected Poems* contained work of refinement and polish; Vladimir Sokolov, whose *Snow in September* was in the style of the older school of Soviet poetry; Konstantin Vanshenkin with the retrospective *Experience;* and Aleksandr Tvardovski with *Lyrical Poems.* Tvardovski, editor of *Novy Mir,* had been under attack and threat of dismissal during the year for "spreading cosmopolitan ideas," "mocking the Soviet peoples' most sacred feelings," and "denigrating Soviet patriotism." He had answered attackers by claiming that he was the "real patriot" and that none could doubt his love of his country, but he was determinedly opposed to "reactionary, nationalistic, neo-Slavophil" literary trends. Like his journalism, his poetry was courageous and sometimes surprisingly gay, and it showed an affinity with that of earlier patriotic Soviet poets: a poetry without bombast, and sincere in concern for the good of all the people.

One of the most brilliant of the "new" poets, Andrei Voznesensky, whose popularity was a measure of the mood of young people especially, published in the broadsheet *Phoenix* a poem with the revealing title "I Can't Write." "The cranes can sing in a chorus, but not the swan," he declared. Its mood of frustration was even more pungently expressed by the well-known Robert Rozhdestvenski in his long "Poem About Different Points of View" (published in *Yunost*), denouncing political inertia and philistinism, and asking ". . . on this tormented, torn-up, bloody earth . . . Why do I live?"—a question answered by a factory worker in a counterattack (published in the "Newspaper of the Russian Republic"): "Every Soviet citizen knows why he lives—to build Communism."

Evgeni Yevtushenko's only published work in a year or so was a long poem-cycle, which appeared in a literary journal in 1968, after his return from the U.S. Unusually enigmatic, with a bitter taste, it could be variously regarded as to form; but it was difficult to take one poem, "The Caged Fox," as other than allegorical, in its assertion that "the animal conceived in a cage is he who yearns for the cage."

This may be said to pinpoint the problem of the Soviet writer in relation to the regime and to the West. Some wholeheartedly supported the party, some found a way of living with it; some kept silent, some fought; some tried to leave and were imprisoned; some succeeded in becoming "Westerners." For the preservation of a genuine Soviet literature it was hard to say which response was most important: Yevtushenko was criticized in the West for failure to speak out in defense of imprisoned liberal intellectuals, but perhaps he feared the effects on his poetic inspiration of permanently leaving the "cage." One 1969 defection was a front-page news story: that of the controversial novelist Anatoli Kuznetsov, author of *Babii Yar* (1966). His disappearance on an official visit to London; the diplomatic embarrassments and exchanges preceding permission to stay in the West; his statements in newspapers and on television that he had left the Soviet Union because he could no longer "breathe, sleep, eat, or work" there and because everything he wrote was distorted by "editors" (he gave his London publisher, MacGibbon & Kee, ten original "unedited" manuscripts); his descriptions of the sufferings of liberal writers left behind, in prison or technically free—all this lifted the corner of a curtain. But the fact that writers in the West shared the dilemma of many in the Soviet Union was shown by the refusal of Arthur Miller, as president of the PEN International Congress at Merton, London, to read in full session Kuznetsov's appeal, in case delegates from Eastern Europe might walk out. The appeal had urged the PEN delegates to concern themselves urgently with the fate of Soviet literature, of liberal writers forced to publish abroad (a criminal offense), expelled from the Writers' Union, deprived of their jobs, denigrated, imprisoned.

The cases of the famous novelist Solzhenitsyn and the young unknown liberal intellectual Anatoli Marchenko gave the appeal added point and poignancy. Solzhenitsyn, threatened since 1964 with expulsion from the Writers' Union, accused of "unforgivable treachery" and of being "a conscious agent of his country's enemies," is widely regarded as the greatest living Soviet novelist. To have his novels known in translation is a deprivation, for linguistic purity is one of his greatest stylistic gifts. Finally, after many assertions and denials, in November 1969 he was expelled from the union for "painting a black picture of Soviet society" and failing to denounce publication of his works abroad. In answer, he appealed for freedom of expression. All he got was freedom "to go where anti-Soviet works are received with . . . delight." Marchenko, on the other hand, was not a writer, though experience made him one. Imprisoned on seemingly inadequate charges since 1960, in one camp he had become a friend of Yuri Daniel (sentenced, with Andrei Sinyavski, in 1967). His *My Testimony,* published in Britain in autumn 1969, did for contemporary Soviet camps what Solzhenitsyn and others had done for the Stalinist camps, and the more horrifyingly for its lack of conscious stylistic artistry.

"LONDON DAILY EXPRESS" FROM PICTORIAL PARADE

Soviet novelist Anatoli Kuznetsov defected to the West during a visit to London in 1969.

Whether the future of Soviet literature would depend ultimately on the "literature in exile" or on writers in the Soviet Union remained uncertain, therefore. During 1968–69 something of a crossroads seemed to have been reached. Of active and influential liberals only Tvardovski remained, uncertainly, at his post. Could the "literature in exile" maintain its strength when no longer rooted in immediate Soviet experience? Could literature in the Soviet Union broaden its outlook, without being driven, itself, into exile? (X.)

SPANISH

The Premio Planeta, the most famous Spanish literary award, worth 1.1 million pesetas, went in 1969 to the exiled Ramón J. Sender for a novel, *La vida de Ignacio Morel,* whose prepublication résumé sounded like the synopsis of a Hollywood scenario (Sender lived in Los Angeles). It was the second time Sender had won a literary contest in the country he refused to inhabit. He had already published in Spain during the year *Tres ejemplos de amor y una teoria,* an incisive study of the stormy loves of Goethe, Balzac, and Tolstoi. Sender postulated "a facilitating aesthetic and a rectifying ethic" in love; he also found that, generally speaking, love, unlike a warrior, "dies in bed." A finalist in the Planeta competition (with his novel *Penelope*), the Cuban exile Pedro Entenza, professor at the University of Maryland, was murdered in the U.S. on the eve of the award; only 37, he had already won the 1969 Villa de Torelló prize for a novel of the Cuban Revolution, *No hay aceras.* A good survey of contemporary Cuban writing issued in Spain was J. M. Caballero Bonald's *Narrativa cubana de la revolución.*

Already a classic, *Cien años de soledad* by Gabriel García Márquez went through three further editions during the year. The author, who brought back to Spain perhaps the best Castilian to come out of Hispanic America in decades, returned himself, to settle in Barcelona. A critical study of his work was published by M. Fernández Braso. A good collection of sociopolitical writings was *Simón Bolívar: Escritos políticos,* selected and introduced by Graciela Soriano; it contained the revolutionary's final judgment on America. "America," he wrote, "is ungovernable; to serve a revolution is to plow in the sea; the best thing to do in America is to emigrate."

Camilo José Cela, whose philological essay on one word, vol. i of *Diccionario secreto,* continued to sell widely, finished a long novel "not *of* the Spanish Civil War but *in* that war," where he alleged that the Inquisition on one side and the burning of convents and monasteries on the other were two sides of the same coin. Its title, *San Camilo, 1936,* referred to the saint's day on which the Civil War erupted. A phrase from the 19th-century Portuguese novelist Eca de Queiros served J. A. Zunzunegui for the title of his novel *Esta oscura desbandada;* the dark rout of humanity in post-Civil War Madrid.

Miguel Delibes' *Paráboladdel náufrago* satirized among other things the conscious and literary destruction of language. A novel by Francisco Ayala, *Muertes de perro,* was an investigation into a quintessential Hispanic dictatorship. A densely documented study of Goya and the sociopolitical structure of his times served as warp and woof of the biography *Goya y su Espana* by Gaspar Gómez de la Serna; in addition to its brilliant writing, the book was enhanced by a comprehensive and chronological appendix of Goya's works and their present ownership and whereabouts. A solid historical study of a key city in the history of Spanish liberalism was *El Cádiz de las Cortes* by Ramón Solís; its clarifying subtitle was "La vida en la ciudad en los años 1810 a 1813," during which period the Napoleonic siege was resisted and the constitution of 1812 was promulgated. An original study of the legal basis of property was *La función social de la posesión* by A. Hernández Gil. The search for an a la mode religion animated *La crisis del catolicismo* by J. L. L. Aranguren, a survey of the latest (largely American) tendencies of the "theology" of the "God is dead" movement.

In the strictly scholarly field, mention should be made of the appearance of the definitive edition to date, in any language, of a large volume of Miguel de Unamuno's poetry. *Poesie,* edited by Roberto Paoli, contained a rich and compact introductory survey of the verse, an extensive selection of the originals in Spanish with Italian translations, a detailed study of the style and antecedents of the individual poems, and a summary of the bibliography in the field (incomplete only as regards the U.S.). (AY. K.)

SWEDISH

Broadly speaking, the older, established writers ("the classics") continued to publish works in their traditional style while the young generation of writers tended, with some exceptions, to regard an aesthetic approach to literature as immoral and devoted their energies to producing socially and politically committed essays, documentary novels, and poems of protest. This generalization would not, however, quite fit the poet Artur Lundkvist—member of the Swedish Academy and a founder of the Modernist movement of the late 1920s: he was concerned with the agonies of the modern world in his poems *Besvärjelser till tröst,* but he conveyed an air of universality which set his work apart from the overtly left-wing involvement of many younger writers. Lundkvist also published short stories and, in collaboration with Gun Bergman, translations of Léopold Senghor's *Elegies.*

As for some other established writers, the 74-year-old Tage Aurell published one of his rare collections of short stories, characterized by a remarkable economy of style, and was collaborating on a new translation of the *Revelation of St. John.* The latter was part of the new Swedish Bible translation project, on which a special commission of experts was at work; a massive and interesting government report on this was published in 1968. The 68-year-old Ivar Lo-Johansson published *Girigbukarna,* another volume in his series exploring the human passions; this time the stories centred around avarice. No survey of this generation would be complete without mention of Olle Hedberg, who had succeeded in publishing a novel each year since 1930, all elegantly written and eminently readable, with a hard core of religious allusion under the polished surface.

The younger, politically and ideologically committed writers Sara Lidman, Göran Palm, and Jan Myrdal, all passionately concerned with the less developed countries and with the moral responsibility and guilt of Western society, published only articles and nonfiction in 1969. *Drakdödaren,* promising first novel of engineer and ornithologist Christer Persson, centred on the destruction of countryside and birdlife by modern society; it combined good writing with specialist knowledge. Other novels of a semidocumentary kind were Birgitta Stenberg's *Rapport,* being the experiences of a drug addict; *Tack vare Lamco* by Busk Rut Jonsson, a critical account of the way of life of Swedish technical experts in Liberia; and Ronnie Busk's *Änglaskuggor,* a young homosexual prisoner's experiences in a Swedish prison. Then there were the poets who defied categorization: the young Lars Norén, prizewinning author of violent, psychedelic verse, who published a collection called *Revolver;* Majken Johansson, erstwhile bohemian intellectual, whose slim volume *Omtal* combined faith with style; and Elsa Grave and Reidar Ekner, the authors, respectively, of *Vid nödläge* and *Andhämtning, bilder,* both of them lucid, low-keyed, personal, and very pleasing.

Finally, much amusement was occasioned by the roman à clef and thriller *Harpsundsmordet* by "Bo Balderson." The protagonists all belonged to the inner circles of government, and the authenticity of milieu and dialogue pointed to authorship by a very well-informed insider. (K. R. P.)

See also Libraries; Philosophy; Theatre.

ENCYCLOPÆDIA BRITANNICA FILMS. *Chaucer's England—With a Special Presentation of The Pardoner's Tale* (1958); *The Theater—One of the Humanities* (Humanities Course) (1959); *Early Victorian England and Charles Dickens* (Humanities Course) (1962); *Great Expectations I: The Story* (Humanities Course) (1962); *Great Expectations II: The Story Interpreted* (Humanities Course) (1962); *The Novel: What It Is, What It's About, What It Does* (Humanities Course) (1962); *Morning on the Lièvre* (1964); *Huckleberry Finn I* (1965); *Huckleberry Finn II* (1965); *Huckleberry Finn III* (1965); *The Odyssey I—The Structure of the Epic* (1965); *The Odyssey II—Return of Odysseus* (1965); *The Odyssey III—Central Themes* (1965); *Magic Prison* (1969).

Livestock and Animal Products: *see* Agriculture
Lumber: *see* Timber
Lutherans: *see* Religion

Luxembourg

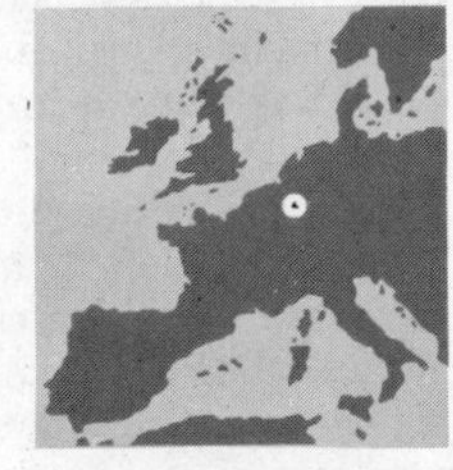

A constitutional monarchy, the Benelux country of Luxembourg is bounded on the east by Germany, on the south by France, and on the west and north by Belgium. Area: 999 sq.mi. (2,587 sq.km.). Pop. (1969 est.): 336,500. Cap. and largest city: Luxembourg (pop., 1969 est., 77,-458). Language: French and German. Religion: 97% Roman Catholic. Grand duke, Jean; prime minister in 1969, Pierre Werner.

The Christian Socialist-Socialist coalition government headed by Pierre Werner had fallen on Oct. 29, 1968, when the parties could not meet Socialist trade union demands for increased wages and pension benefits. In the Dec. 15, 1968, elections, the opposition Liberal (Democratic) Party had been the major winner, raising its total parliamentary delegation to 11. The Christian Socialists lost a seat but retained 21, while the Socialists fell from 21 to 18. The Communist Party gained one seat to total six in the new Parliament.

After protracted negotiations, the grand duke asked Werner to form a coalition government with the Liberals. The Christian Socialists were traditionally the nation's strongest party, drawing voting strength from farmers, Catholic labour circles, and other conservative groups, while the Liberals' support stemmed from professionals, merchants, and other elements of the urban middle class. In the new government, Christian Socialists held four Cabinet posts and Liberals, three. The government's program included measures to stimulate the economy through new employment facilities and new industry; restrictions on state indebtedness; and participation by workers in state-controlled enterprises.

The Benelux Economic Union made significant progress during the year. On April 29 the prime ministers of the three countries agreed to abolish virtually all border controls by Nov. 1, 1970. In addition, excise taxes and methods of collection were to be standardized; public administration harmonized; judicial practices closely coordinated; and economic, social, transport, energy, tourist, and industrial policies brought into line.

Luxembourg's estimated 1968 gross national product totaled LFr. 38.3 billion ($766 million), a rise of 4%. Per capita income averaged LFr. 114,000 ($2,280), the equivalent of a $100 increase in a year.

(R. D. Ho.)

LUXEMBOURG

Education. (1967–68) Primary, pupils 35,173, teachers 1,511; secondary, pupils 6,336, teachers 512; vocational, pupils 4,814, teachers 345; teacher training, students 194, teachers 47.

Finance. Monetary unit: Luxembourg franc, at par with the Belgian franc (LFr. 50 = U.S. $1; LFr. 120 = £1 sterling). Dollar assets reported by U.S.: (Dec. 1967) U.S. $32 million; (Dec. 1966) U.S. $25 million. Budget (1968 est.): revenue LFr. 10,647,431,000; expenditure LFr. 10,905,378,000. Gross national product: (1968) LFr. 38,251,000,000; (1967) LFr. 36,-052,000,000. Cost of living (1963 = 100): (June 1969) 118; (June 1968) 115.

Foreign Trade. *See* BELGIUM.

Transport and Communications. Roads (1968) 4,440 km. Motor vehicles in use (1968): passenger 74,329; commercial 14,795. Railways: (1967) 328 km.; traffic (1968) 314 million passenger-km., freight 641 million net ton-km. Air traffic (1968): 40,020,000 passenger-km.; freight 354,000 net ton-km. Telephones (Dec. 1967) 93,767. Radio licenses (Dec. 1967) 133,-000. Television receivers (Dec. 1967) 44,000.

Agriculture. Production (in 000; metric tons; 1968; 1967 in parentheses): oats 38 (45); wheat (1967) 49, (1966) 34; rye 8 (10); potatoes (1967) 91, (1966) 65. Livestock (in 000; May 1968): cattle 187; sheep 4; pigs 105; poultry 385.

Industry. Production (in 000; metric tons; 1968): iron ore (30% metal content) 6,398; pig iron 4,308; crude steel 4,833; electricity (kw-hr.) 2,042,000; manufactured gas (cu.m.; 1967) 15,240.

Malagasy Republic

The Malagasy Republic occupies the island of Madagascar and minor adjacent islands in the Indian Ocean off the southeast coast of Africa. Area: 226,657 sq.mi. (587,041 sq.km.). Pop. (1968 est.): 7,011,563. Cap. and largest city: Tananarive (pop., 1968 est., 332,-855). Language: French and Malagasy. Religion: Christian (approximately 50%) and traditional tribal beliefs. President in 1969, Philibert Tsiranana.

Malagasy's political malaise, spawned by persistent economic difficulties, continued into 1969. The publication of a tract entitled *Ten Years of the Malagasy Republic,* which made serious charges against the government, led to the arrest of several persons, including a French technical assistant, in February. One of the questions dealt with in this critique concerned the agreement concluded between the Malagasy government and a large French financial consortium, led by Jacques Mimran, which had obtained a number of commercial monopolies in return for a promise to develop the abundant timber resources in the northeast. Many ministers thought the advantages granted to Mimran were excessive, but he was supported by the president.

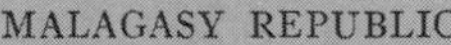

Apart from its effect on public opinion, the Mimran controversy led to a behind-the-scenes struggle among different groups within the ruling Social Democratic Party (PSD). The opposition remained passive, though it showed definite interest in the conflict. In

MALAGASY REPUBLIC

Education. (1965–66) Primary, pupils 672,100, teachers 9,475; secondary, pupils 55,439, teachers 2,404; vocational, pupils 7,715, teachers 539; teacher training, students 2,079, teachers (1964–65) 118; higher (including University of Madagascar), students 3,082.

Finance. Monetary unit: Malagasy franc, at par with the CFA franc (MalFr. 277.71 = U.S. $1; MalFr. 666.50 = £1 sterling). Budget (1968 est.): revenue MalFr. 30 billion; expenditure MalFr. 42,-925,000,000.

Foreign Trade. (1968) Imports MalFr. 42,020,-000,000 (63% from France, 6% from West Germany, 5% from U.S.); exports MalFr. 28,610,000,000 (34% to France, 23% to U.S., 12% to Réunion). Main exports: coffee 31%; rice 11%; vanilla 9%; sugar 6%.

Transport and Communications. Roads (1967) *c.* 40,000 km. (including 2,000 km. with improved surface). Motor vehicles in use (1967): passenger 38,100; commercial (including buses) 26,000. Railways: (1967) 864 km.; traffic (1968) 181 million passenger-km., freight 218 million net ton-km. Air traffic (1968): 198.1 million passenger-km.; freight 7,271,000 net ton-km. Telephones (Dec. 1967) 22,701. Radio receivers (Dec. 1967) 350,000.

Agriculture. Production (in 000; metric tons; 1967; 1966 in parentheses): cassava 900 (870); rice (1968) 1,400, (1967) 1,700; corn 97 (90); sweet potatoes 320 (300); potatoes 100 (85); bananas 165 (170); peanuts *c.* 39 (*c.* 45); sugar, raw value (1968–69) *c.* 112, (1967–68) 96; coffee (1966) 58, (1965) 55; tobacco 4.4 (4.8); pepper (1966) 2.2, (1965) 1.8; sisal *c.* 28 (30). Livestock (in 000; Dec. 1967): cattle 9,707; sheep (Dec. 1966) 490; pigs (Dec. 1966) 55; goats (Dec. 1966) 654; chickens *c.* 14,000.

Macao:
see Dependent States

Machinery and Machine Tools:
see Industrial Review

Madagascar:
see Malagasy Republic

Magazines:
see Publishing

September the government finally decided to cancel the Mimran agreement of November 1967, thus ending the most important private investment ever to have been made in Malagasy. This measure, supported by the majority within the government, contributed to a weakening of the moral authority of the president. Early in December, he dissolved the Cabinet which had functioned since 1965, and began consultations on the formation of a new one.

In April, President Tsiranana visited Malawi for talks with Pres. H. Kamuzu Banda. A joint communiqué expressed their mutual desire for the pursuit of "realistic policies" in the face of the superior forces possessed by the white minority regimes in South Africa, Rhodesia, and Mozambique. (PH. D.)

Malawi

A republic in east central Africa, Malawi is bounded by Tanzania, Mozambique, and Zambia. Area: 45,725 sq.mi. (118,428 sq.km.). Pop. (1968): 4,285,000, nearly all of whom are Africans. Cap.: Zomba (pop., 1966, 19,666). Largest city: Blantyre-Limbe (pop., 1966, 109,461). Language: English and Nyanja. Religion: predominantly traditional beliefs. President in 1969, H. Kamuzu Banda.

President Banda rounded off 1968 with further Cabinet changes. John Tembo, minister of finance for 4½ years, was transferred to the Ministry of Trade, Industry, and Development, while Aleke Banda became minister of finance and also minister of information and tourism, two departments formerly within the Ministry of Trade and Industry. These appointments took effect from January 1. In February, David van der Spuy, a senior officer in the South African information department, was appointed head of Malawi's information services. The continuing rapport between Malawi and South Africa was reflected in the 12-day visit paid by six South African members of Parliament at the invitation of the Malawi branch of the Commonwealth Parliamentary Association.

MALAWI

Education. (1966) Primary, pupils 286,753, teachers 8,778; secondary, pupils 6,718, teachers 416; vocational, pupils 886, teachers 109; teacher training, students 1,240, teachers 125; higher, students 436, teaching staff 70.

Finance. Monetary unit: Malawi pound, at par with the pound sterling (Mal£1 = U.S. $2.40). Budget (1969 est.): revenue Mal£14,220,000 (including Mal£2.8 million U.K. aid); expenditure Mal£17,620,000. Gold and foreign exchange, official: (June 1969) U.S. $21,880,000; (June 1968) U.S. $19,020,000.

Foreign Trade. (1968) Imports Mal£29.6 million (30% from U.K., 18% from Rhodesia, 11% from South Africa, 5% from U.S., 5% from Japan); exports Mal£20,278,000 (51% to U.K., 5% to U.S., 5% to Rhodesia). Main exports: tobacco 26%; tea 24%; peanuts 11%.

Transport and Communications. Roads (1968) 10,488 km. Motor vehicles in use (1968): passenger 8,893; commercial 6,240. Railways: (1967) 820 km.; traffic (1963) 49 million passenger-km., freight (1968) 206.4 million net ton-km. Air traffic (1968): 12,850,000 passenger-km.; freight 407,000 net ton-km. Telephones (Dec. 1967) 9,127. Radio receivers (Dec. 1966) 85,000.

Agriculture. Production (in 000; metric tons; 1967; 1966 in parentheses): corn *c.* 1,300 (*c.* 1,200); cassava (1966) *c.* 140, (1965) *c.* 140; sweet potatoes (1966) *c.* 45, (1965) *c.* 43; tobacco (1968) 15, (1967) 16; cottonseed 6 (8); peanuts 60 (60); tea 17 (15). Livestock (in 000; 1966–67): sheep 81; cattle 464; goats 668; pigs 149; poultry (on farms and estates) *c.* 2,600.

Industry. Production (in 000): electricity (public supply; kw-hr.; 1968) 98,000; cement (metric tons; 1967) 41.

This was the first delegation from the South African Parliament to visit a black African state, and a proposal was made for a return visit by members of the Malawi Parliament. The South Africans' visit was of an informal nature, but it was thought likely that further cooperation between the two countries would be discussed. The Dutch Reformed Church in South Africa launched a campaign to raise money to build six churches in Malawi, including one in the proposed new capital of Lilongwe.

President Banda's isolation from the leaders of other independent African states was underlined at the Commonwealth Prime Ministers' Conference in London in January when he aligned himself with the prime ministers of Malaysia, Australia, and Singapore in hoping that the subject of the minority white regime in Rhodesia would not dominate the proceedings of the conference. Other African leaders, including Presidents Kenneth Kaunda of Zambia and Milton Obote of Uganda, emphasized the need for a detailed consideration of the Rhodesian situation by the conference. Banda argued, as on previous occasions, against the use of force in Rhodesia, reiterating his view that the black African countries lacked the military resources to fight Rhodesia. He also objected to Malawi being used as the base for an attack on Rhodesia and said that he was unwilling to expose his country to the reprisals that such a line of action would undoubtedly bring in its wake. He was in favour of retaining the proposals made by the British prime minister, Harold Wilson, on board HMS "Fearless" in 1968 as a basis for future agreement.

In February, two Britons, employees of the state-controlled Farmers' Marketing Board, were deported to Rhodesia. In March Banda told a youth meeting in Lilongwe that expatriate teachers would be deported if their teachings ran contrary to government policy. British businessmen were also warned that Malawi's former colonial status would not prevent them from being deported if the government thought it desirable, and in June a British businessman and an Asian holding a British passport were served with deportation notices after being convicted of infringing export regulations.

On March 29 eight men convicted of treason were hanged in Blantyre-Limbe. They had been captured in October 1967 after entering Malawi from Tanzania with the alleged intention of killing Banda and overthrowing the government.

Intimidation of the public by officials of the Malawi Congress Party was strongly criticized by the president in September. A standing committee was set up to investigate allegations against party officials. (K. I.)

Malaysia

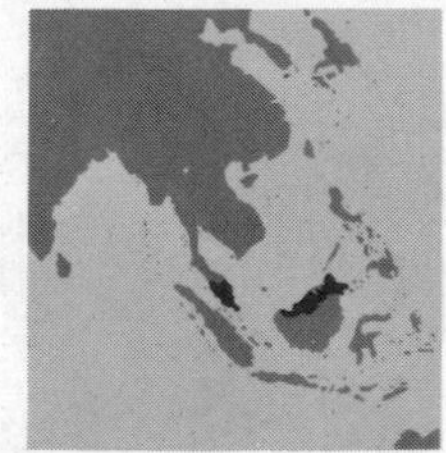

A federation within the Commonwealth of Nations comprising the 11 states of the former Federation of Malaya (known as West Malaysia) and Sabah (formerly North Borneo) and Sarawak (together known as East Malaysia), Malaysia is a federal constitutional monarchy situated in Southeast Asia at the southern end of the Malay Peninsula (excluding Singapore) and on the northern part of the island of Borneo. Area: 127,581 sq.mi. (330,435 sq.km.). Pop. (1968 est.): 10,-

MALAYSIA

Education. *West Malaysia.* (1966) Primary, pupils 1,260,197, teachers 45,960; secondary, pupils 402,432, teachers 17,457; vocational, pupils 9,980, teachers 347; higher (including University of Malaya), students 14,834, teaching staff 1,689. *East Malaysia: Sabah.* (1966) Primary, pupils 99,450, teachers 3,212; secondary, pupils 14,150, teachers 533; vocational, pupils 283, teachers 14; teacher training, students 457, teachers 49. *East Malaysia: Sarawak.* (1967) Primary, pupils 140,466, teachers (1966) 4,151; secondary, pupils 32,947, teachers 1,316; vocational, pupils 338, teachers 20; teacher training, students 436, teachers 57; higher, students 227, teaching staff (1965) 11.

Finance. Monetary unit: Malaysian dollar, with a par value of M$3.06 to U.S. $1 (M$7.35 = £1 sterling). Gold and foreign exchange, official: (May 1969) U.S. $559 million; (May 1968) U.S. $433 million. Budget (1968 est.): revenue M$1,882,020,000; expenditure M$1,932,180,000. Gross national product: (1967) M$9,713,000,000; (1966) M$9,344,000,000. Money supply: (May 1969) M$1,778,000,000; (May 1968) M$1,477,000,000. Cost of living (West Malaysia; 1963 = 100): (April 1969) 103; (April 1968) 107.

Foreign Trade. (1968) Imports M$3,548,000,000; exports M$4,109,000,000. Import sources (West Malaysia only): U.K. 15%; Japan 15%; Australia 8%; Singapore 7%; Thailand 7%; China 6%; U.S. 6%; West Germany 5%. Export destinations: (West Malaysia only): U.S. 19%; Singapore 19%; Japan 13%; U.K. 7%; U.S.S.R. 6%. Main exports: rubber 33%; tin 20%; timber 17%.

Transport and Communications. Roads (1967) 21,424 km. Motor vehicles in use (1967): passenger 212,800; commercial (including buses) 57,100. Railways (1968): 1,821 km.; traffic (including Singapore) 580 million passenger-km., freight 1,080,000,000 net ton-km. Air traffic (Malaysia-Singapore Airlines; 1968): 674.7 million passenger-km.; freight 10,105,000 net ton-km. Shipping (1968): merchant vessels 100 gross tons and over 85; gross tonnage 40,465. Ships entered (excluding Sabah; 1967) vessels totaling 26,934,000 net registered tons; goods loaded (1967) 18,824,000 metric tons, unloaded 8,470,000 metric tons. Telephones (Jan. 1968) 145,425. Radio receivers (Dec. 1967) 530,000. Television receivers (July 1966) 67,000.

Agriculture. Production (in 000; metric tons; 1967; 1966 in parentheses): rice 1,061 (1,106); rubber (1968) *c.* 1,107, (1967) 993; copra 180 (176); palm oil (West Malaysia; estates only) 217 (186); tea (West Malaysia only) *c.* 3.6 (3.5); bananas (excluding Sarawak) *c.* 339 (*c.* 339); pineapples (West Malaysia only) 350 (317); pepper (Sarawak only; 1966) 15, (1965) 18; timber (cu.m.) *c.* 14,000 (13,500); fish catch 367 (296). Livestock (in 000; 1966–67): cattle 311; pigs 927; goats 333; sheep (West Malaysia only) 37; buffaloes 326; poultry *c.* 24,000.

Industry. Production (in 000; metric tons; 1968): tin concentrates (metal content) 76; bauxite 799; cement (West Malaysia only) 954; iron ore (West Malaysia only; 60% metal content) 5,167; crude oil (East Malaysia: Sarawak only; 1967) 46; gold (troy oz.; 1967) 3.8; electricity (excluding Sabah; kw-hr.) 3,004,000.

169,179. Cap. and largest city: Kuala Lumpur (pop., 1968 est., 592,785). Official language: Malay. Religion: Malays are Muslim; Indians mainly Hindu; Chinese mainly Buddhist, Confucian, and Taoist. Supreme head of state in 1969, with the title of *yang dipertuan agong,* Tuanku Ismail Nasiruddin Shah ibni al-Marhum Sultan Zainal Abidin; prime minister, Tunku Abdul Rahman.

On May 13 Malaysia was shaken by unprecedented racial disturbances. Official figures gave the number killed as 196, including 123 Chinese, 22 Malays, and 12 Indians. Another 439 were injured, and six months later 39 people were still missing. Suspension of constitutional government followed the proclamation of a state of emergency throughout the country, and a National Operations Council with near-dictatorial powers was set up with the deputy prime minister, Tun Abdul Razak, as director of operations. A caretaker Cabinet was also established. More than six months passed before Prime Minister Rahman (*see* BIOGRAPHY) could announce on December 29 that he had resumed full political control.

The racial violence followed the general election in which the Alliance Party, made up of a coalition of the United Malays National Organization (UMNO), the Malaysian Chinese Association (MCA), and the Malaysian Indian Congress (MIC), fared rather badly in contrast to its landslide victory in 1964. The party won 66 seats in West Malaysia and 10 in Sabah, giving it a simple majority in the 144-member House of Representatives. The opposition parties consisted mainly of Chinese, thereby setting the stage for the subsequent rioting. Because of the declaration of emergency the remaining elections were suspended, leaving 24 seats in Sarawak, 6 in Sabah, and 1 in Malacca state still to be decided.

During the year, a Capital Investment Committee, under the chairmanship of Tun Tan Siew Sin, former finance minister, was set up to provide a top-level review of the country's industrial development policies and programs, both those of the central government and those of the states, with a view to coordinating them into a stronger, more consistent and integrated development strategy.

The Communist menace continued throughout the year, and Malaysia decided to create another nine new battalions. In November 1968 the government published a White Paper on "The Path of Violence to Absolute Power" that described the threat posed by the Communist Party of Malaya and its United Front to the security and public order of the country. This coincided with the arrest of 140 Communist militants in surprise swoops throughout Malaysia. The White Paper quoted extensively from captured Communist documents to show that the Communist United Front had abandoned the parliamentary struggle and that the Malayan Communist Party intended to return to an armed fight. It revealed the magnitude of the Communist infiltration into a number of social and political bodies in the country and the clandestine preparation that had been made to create conditions suitable for waging an armed struggle.

The Malaysian economy continued to expand, and at the end of 1968 the country had an overall balance of payments deficit of M$27 million, compared with a deficit of M$247 million the previous year. Gold and foreign exchange reserves at the end of the year stood at M$1,998,000,000.

The 1969 budget provided for ordinary expenditure of M$1,925,000,000 and revenue of M$1,962,000,000. With development expenditure estimates at M$720 million, an overall deficit of M$683 million was anticipated, to be financed by foreign grants (M$23 million) and loans (M$298 million), domestic loans (M$350 million), and accumulated assets.

The Employment Restriction Bill which was passed in the latter part of 1968 came into force in August. For the first time it required noncitizens to take out employment permits, which were issued for periods of three months, six months, one year, and two years depending on the type of skills—unskilled, semiskilled, skilled, and highly skilled, respectively. Overtime for skilled and unskilled workers was limited to 32 hours a month, a move that was expected to result in the creation of 100,000 new jobs.

A five-power defense meeting held in Kuala Lumpur in November and attended by representatives of the U.K., Australia, New Zealand, Malaysia, and Singapore to discuss the defense of the region after the British military withdrawal in 1971, decided that the proposed integrated air defense system for the Malaysia-Singapore area would be based at Butterworth in Penang state, where the Royal Australian Air Force had a base. (M. S. R.)

ENCYCLOPÆDIA BRITANNICA FILMS. *Malaya, Land of Tin and Rubber* (1957).

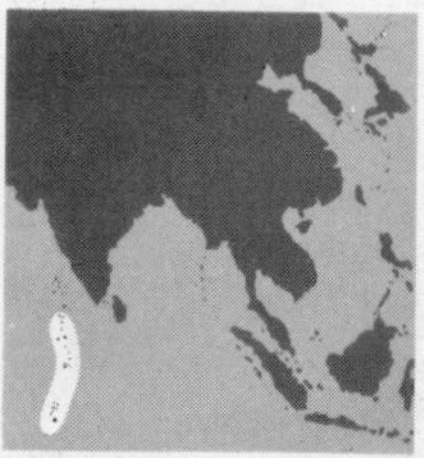

Maldives, Republic of

The Republic of Maldives lies in the Indian Ocean southwest of the southern tip of India. Area: 115 sq.mi. (298 sq.km.). Pop. (1968): 106,969. Cap. and largest city: Male (pop., 1968, 12,097). Language: Maldivian. Religion: Muslim. Sultan, Amir Muhammad Farid Didi; president in 1969, Ibrahim Nassir.

The Maldive Islands became a republic on Nov. 1, 1968, with Ibrahim Nassir as president and head of state. The change of name of the UN's smallest member state to Republic of Maldives was reported by the UN's protocol section in April 1969. The economy of the republic continued largely on a subsistence fishing and farming level. Trade, almost wholly with Ceylon, showed a continued improvement in 1968, with exports totaling MRs. 15 million and imports MRs. 13 million. The population continued to increase at a rate of 3% in 1968, and the government claimed a literacy rate of 97%.

The U.K. continued to develop Gan Island as a Royal Air Force staging post and a centre of Commonwealth military communications. During 1968–69 there were approximately 560 military personnel on Gan and 40 civilians. About 7,000 passengers a month on flights between Singapore and London were handled on the island, along with more than one million pounds of cargo. The island was also used as a ground station for Britain's Skynet satellite communications system, in the final stages of development in 1969. (M. Mr.)

MALDIVES, REPUBLIC OF

Education. (1964–65) Primary, pupils 4,864, teachers 315; secondary, pupils 762, teachers 32.

Finance. Monetary unit: Maldivian rupee, with a par value of MRs. 4.76 to U.S. $1 (MRs. 11.43 = £1 sterling). Budget (1965) expenditure MRs. 19,646,-830. U.K. grant for development from 1960 £850,000, of which *c.* £300,000 paid by mid-1965.

Foreign Trade. Mainly with Ceylon. Main exports (metric tons; 1967): fish 3,400; cowrie shells 7; copra 18. Fishing accounts for *c.* 95% of exports.

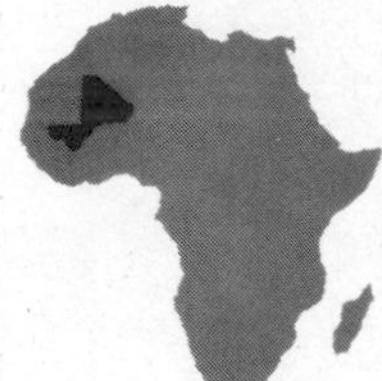

Mali

A republic of West Africa, Mali is bordered by Algeria, Niger, Upper Volta, Ivory Coast, Guinea, Senegal, and Mauritania. Area: 479,000 sq.mi. (1,240,000 sq.km.). Pop. (1967 est.): 4,740,800. Cap. and largest city: Bamako (metro. pop., 1967 est., 175,000). Language: French (official); Hamito-Semitic and various tribal dialects. Religion: Muslim 63%; animist 36%. Head of military government in 1969, Lieut. Moussa Traore.

Three ministerial reshuffles and an abortive coup d'etat on August 12 were evidence of the menacing instability that persisted in Mali throughout 1969. Those responsible for the attempted coup were political friends of the former president, Modibo Keita, who was under detention awaiting trial. Chiefly concerned was the former aide-de-camp of the ousted president, Captain Ouolouguem, who took advantage of the absence of the minister of defense on an official visit to the U.S.S.R. to attempt to reestablish the former regime.

During September the divisions within Mali's new leadership were brought into the open. Capt. Yoro Diakité, then president of the Military Committee of National Liberation (CMLN), expelled Foreign Minister Jean-Marie Kone from the government. Some days later, deciding to put an end to a two-headed regime, Lieut. Moussa Traore ousted, in his turn, Captain Diakité, who was, however, allowed to remain in the Cabinet as minister of transport, telecommunications, and tourism. Traore was henceforth to hold the office of president of the Military Committee of National Liberation as well as that of head of state which he already occupied. At the same time he proceeded with a ministerial reshuffle that enabled him to transfer portfolios from several of Diakité's friends to his own supporters.

From June 1 to 3 Mauritania and Mali held discussions in Bamako on delineating their common boundary, previously a source of conflict between them. In August Pres. Sékou Touré of Guinea sent a message to Bamako, hoping for an end to the deterioration in relations between the two countries following the fall of President Keita and urging the normalization of activities of the Organization of Senegal River States (OERS).

But one year after the military coup it was the economic situation that principally preoccupied Mali's leaders. A budgetary deficit, an empty treasury, external debt, and a deficit on the balance of payments seemed insoluble problems, even with French help. (Ph. D.)

MALI

Education. (1965–66) Primary, pupils 161,605, teachers 3,826; secondary, pupils 1,011, teachers 114; vocational, pupils 1,417, teachers 196; teacher training, students 748, teachers 36; higher, students 222, teaching staff 58.

Finance. Monetary unit: Mali franc, with a par value of MFr. 555.42 to U.S. $1 (MFr. 1,333 = £1 sterling). Budget (1967–68 est.): revenue MFr. 21.2 billion; expenditure MFr. 24.7 billion. Money supply: (May 1969) MFr. 24,590,000,000; (May 1968) MFr. 24,880,000,000.

Foreign Trade. (1968) Imports MFr. 22,770,000,-000; exports MFr. 9,010,000,000. Import sources (1967): France 30%; China 23%; U.S.S.R. 11%; Ivory Coast 7%; U.K. 6%. Export destinations (1967): Senegal 32%; Ivory Coast 28%; Ghana 15%; France 9%. Main exports: cotton 33%; fish 13%; peanuts 8%.

Agriculture. Production (in 000; metric tons; 1967; 1966 in parentheses): millet and sorghum 909 (837); rice *c.* 140 (158); corn *c.* 75 (76); peanuts *c.* 160 (160); sweet potatoes (1966) *c.* 70, (1965) *c.* 70; cassava (1966) *c.* 150, (1965) *c.* 150; cotton, lint (1966) *c.* 90, (1965) *c.* 90. Livestock (in 000; 1967–68): cattle *c.* 4,650; sheep (1966–67) *c.* 4,900; horses 174; asses 528.

Malta

An island in the Mediterranean Sea, between Sicily and Tunisia, Malta is a parliamentary state and a member of the Commonwealth of Nations. Area: 122 sq.mi. (316 sq.km.), including Malta, Gozo, and Comino. Pop. (1969 est.): 320,764. Cap.: Valletta (pop., 1968 est., 15,430). Largest city: Sliema (pop., 1968 est., 21,-572). Language: English and Maltese. Religion: mainly Roman Catholic. Queen, Elizabeth II; governor-general in 1969, Sir Maurice Dorman; prime minister, George Borg Olivier.

In March 1969 Malta's second five-year plan came to an end. Despite the decreasing size of British

MALTA
Education. (1966–67) Primary, pupils 45,000, teachers 2,012; secondary, pupils 7,666, teachers 508; vocational, pupils 1,692, teachers 114; teacher training, students 387, teachers 40; higher (including Royal University of Malta), students 970, teaching staff 72.
Finance and Trade. Monetary unit: Maltese pound, at par with the pound sterling (M£1 = U.S. $2.40). Budget (1968–69): revenue M£28,628,331; expenditure M£28,244,567. Foreign trade (1968): imports £51,399,000 (44% from U.K., 16% from Italy); exports £14,144,000 (35% to U.K., 10% to Italy, 6% to Libya, 5% to U.S., 16% as ship's stores). Main domestic exports: clothing 17%; textile yarns and fabrics 14%; petroleum products 11%; rubber products 6%; textile fibres 6%; beverages 5%; fruit and vegetables 5%. Tourism (1967): visitors 97,500; gross receipts U.S. $14 million.
Transport and Communications. Roads (1967) 1,110 km. Motor vehicles in use (1967): passenger 27,400; commercial (including buses) 8,500. There are no railways. Air traffic (1968): 170 million passenger-km.; freight 2,009,000 net ton-km. Shipping (1968): merchant vessels 100 gross tons and over 24; gross tonnage 67,742. Ships entered (1967) vessels totaling 1,761,000 net registered tons; goods loaded (1967) 68,000 metric tons, unloaded 778,000 metric tons. Telephones (Jan. 1968) *c.* 28,100. Radio receivers (Dec. 1967) 87,000. Television receivers (Dec. 1967) 35,000.

defense establishments, unemployment was contained within manageable limits, emigration was reduced, and the standard of living continued to rise. This wave of prosperity was sustained by the general expansion of tourism and by an unprecedented boom in the construction industry. The latter was brought about by a considerable inflow of new residents, mostly British, attracted by income tax benefits and the climate.

The budget for 1969–70, inaugurating the third five-year plan, provided for an investment program of M£13.5 million. Almost half this sum was to be covered by U.K. aid. However, after protracted discussions between the Maltese and U.K. governments, no agreement was reached on how much of this aid should be in the form of loans and how much should be grants. Pending the outcome of these negotiations, the U.K. government withheld all funds. The budget estimated ordinary expenditure at M£23.4 million, an excess of M£1 million over revenue. Stamp duties, miscellaneous fees, and postage rates were increased, and draft legislation was presented to Parliament for the introduction of taxes on property improvements and land gains. As a result, real estate transactions declined substantially. At about the same time, the absence of a double taxation relief agreement between the U.K. and Malta regarding death duties on estates of new residents became a prominent issue, complicating matters still further.

Work was started on a new industrial development of 225 ac. situated between the Grand Harbour and the projected free port zone. An outline physical development plan for Gozo, as well as the building of a small industrial zone there, received government approval.

Prime Minister Borg Olivier paid goodwill visits to Taiwan, Japan, India, and Singapore in November 1968 to discuss technical aid and investments in Malta. A commercial agreement was signed with Japan.

A long-standing political problem showed signs of improvement in April when a joint statement by the Roman Catholic Church authorities and the Malta Labour Party, led by Dom Mintoff, declared that relations between them had improved considerably and expressed the hope of a future entente. (A. G.)

Mathematics

The year 1969 saw a fundamental advance in the theory of manifolds. Manifolds are objects of primary interest in present-day topology. They are spaces built by pasting together pieces that look like ordinary Euclidean space. If the dimension of the Euclidean space is n, the manifold is called n-dimensional. One way to study a manifold is to try to break it into simple pieces resembling triangles; if the procedure is successful, it is said that the manifold has been triangulated. Up to 1969 the following question had remained unsettled: Can every manifold be triangulated? In the dimensions 2 and 3 it had been shown that the answer was "yes," by T. Rado in 1924 and E. Moise in 1952, respectively. Now a 5-dimensional manifold was discovered for which the answer was "no." In fact, the method also yielded such an example for every dimension represented by an integer greater than 5. Thus, the only dimension for which the question still needed to be settled was 4. The expectation was that the answer also would be "no" for dimension 4; this was enhanced by the fact that the investigation showed that the vanishing of a certain 4-dimensional cohomology class was the exact condition needed for triangulability.

Along with the question of triangulating a manifold there was a companion problem of uniqueness: Are two different triangulations of a manifold necessarily equivalent in a certain natural sense? This question carried the imposing German name *Hauptvermutung* (that is, the principal conjecture) of algebraic topology. Again the answer was found to be "no." The manifold for which failure occurred was extraordinarily simple; it is the product of a 3-dimensional sphere and two circles.

The basic work leading to these two advances was done by R. Kirby of UCLA, with a large number of other mathematicians contributing significantly.

In the field of rings of operators there was an important development in 1969. The basic building block for rings of operators is a special object called a factor of Type II_1, and a crucial question was to determine how many such factors existed. By 1968, after a generation of work, the number had slowly grown to 4. Then there was a rapid sequence of developments: S. Sakai increased the number to 5; J. Dixmier and E. Lance to 7; G. Zeller-Meier to 9; and, finally, D. McDuff to infinity.

In the field of minimal surfaces, a classical problem posed by S. Bernstein received a definitive answer. A minimal surface is one that has the smallest possible area among all surfaces bounded by a given curve. Soap films can be used to construct models of such minimal surfaces, using a piece of appropriately shaped wire for each bounding curve. In effect Bernstein had asked whether such a soap bubble could go all the way out to infinity. After this was answered in the negative, mathematicians considered the same question in higher dimensions. A sequence of memoirs culminated in the mathematical proof by J. Simons that the answer is negative up to dimension 8. Nevertheless, in the May 1969 issue of *Inventiones Mathematicae*, E. Bombieri, E. DiGiorgi, and E. Giusti mathematically proved on the contrary that the answer is affirmative starting at dimension 9.

An algebraic problem posed in 1916 by E. Noether was settled by R. Swan. Let $x_1, \ldots, x_n$ be independent

Manganese:
see Mining
Man-Made Fibres:
see Industrial Review
Manufacturing:
see Economy, World; Employment, Wages, and Hours; Industrial Review
Mariana Islands:
see Dependent States
Marine Biology:
see Biological Sciences
Marine Corps:
see Defense
Marriage:
see Vital Statistics
Marshall Islands:
see Dependent States
Martinique:
see Dependent States

variables over a field K. Let a group G permute the x variables and let L be the subfield of $K(x_1, \ldots, x_n)$ fixed under G. Noether questioned whether or not L is a purely transcendental extension of K. Despite numerous special cases for which this had turned out to be so, Swan found that it might not always be the case. For instance L is not a purely transcendental extension of K when $n = 47$ and G is the group that simply permutes the x variables cyclically.

Thus there were repeated instances for which the results turned out to be more complex than anticipated, leading some mathematicians to speculate that more than ever this would be the case in the future. But some discoveries simplified the outlook. An example was the proof by G. Nöbeling that the additive group of all bounded sequences of integers is free. E. Specker had shown this in 1950 on the basis of assuming the validity of the continuum hypothesis. Now K. Gödel and P. Cohen had shown that the truth or falsity of the continuum hypothesis was undecidable on the basis of the current foundations of mathematics. This left Specker's theorem in the position of being either true or undecidable, an odd fate for such a "concrete" problem. Nöbeling's result reinforced the conviction of some mathematicians that no down-to-earth problem would turn out to be undecidable.

In 1968–69 there appeared a long-awaited three-volume report on the state of mathematics, entitled *The Mathematical Sciences*. Sponsored by the U.S. National Academy of Sciences, it was prepared by COSRIMS (Committee on Support of Research in the Mathematical Sciences). Among its highlights are a thorough documentation of the assumption of mathematical leadership in the U.S. since World War II, a review of the new applications of mathematics opening up in the biological and social sciences, an analysis of today's mathematical community, and a forecast of tomorrow's needs. One volume contains 22 essays by leading experts, edited in collaboration with G. Boehm. The COSRIMS report notes in detail the remarkable growth of mathematics in the last generation, but realistically foresees that such growth cannot continue indefinitely.

Despite some signs of a leveling off in the growth of mathematics, the problem of keeping informed remained vexing for mathematicians. There was a widespread feeling that new methods of communication were needed. The American Mathematical Society launched an experimental Mathematical Offprint Service. Subscribers to this service placed standing orders for reprints in fields that interested them. By a scheme intended ultimately to be fully automatic, journals were scanned and orders filled. In some cases the reprints arrived before the journal itself was published. The success or failure of this experiment was being watched as a signpost for the future. (I. KA.)

Mauritania

The Islamic Republic of Mauritania is on the Atlantic coast of West Africa, adjoining Spanish Sahara, Algeria, Mali, and Senegal. Area: 397,683 sq.mi. (1,030,000 sq.km.). Pop. (1968 est.): 1,120,000. Cap.: Nouakchott (pop., 1967 est., 15,000). Language: Arabic (national); French (official). Religion: Muslim. President in 1969, Mokhtar Ould Daddah.

The Islamic summit conference held in Rabat, Mor., in September 1969 was an event of major importance to Mauritania. Nine years after its proclamation of independence and its entry into the UN, Mauritania finally made a significant appearance on the international scene. The meeting between Pres. Mokhtar Ould Daddah and King Hassan II of Morocco was a just reward for the former's perseverance. A normalization of relations between Mauritania and Morocco was in progress, following the de facto recognition of the former, whose legal existence had previously been contested by the Moroccans.

On June 27 an agreement was signed with the European Investment Bank for a loan of $2,754,000 for enlarging the wharf installations at Nouakchott. A trade agreement with the Congo (Brazzaville) was signed in September, and the UN Food and Agriculture Organization agreed to provide 1,800 tons of millet to aid Mauritania's drought victims in August.

Pres. William V. S. Tubman of Liberia visited Mauritania in March and signed a treaty of cooperation and a cultural agreement. Mauritania and Mali held discussions in June to settle the delineation of their common boundary. (PH. D.)

MAURITANIA

Education. (1967–68) Primary, pupils 23,635, teachers (1964–65) 1,161; secondary, pupils 2,168, teachers (1963–64) 61; vocational (1964–65), pupils 197; teacher training (1964–65), students 107.

Finance. Monetary unit: CFA franc, with a parity of CFA Fr. 50 to the French franc (CFA Fr. 277.71 = U.S. $1; CFA Fr. 666.50 = £1 sterling). Currency reserves, central bank: (June 1969) U.S. $6.1 million; (June 1968) U.S. $6.9 million. Budget (1969 est.): revenue CFA Fr. 6,549,000,000; expenditure CFA Fr. 6,649,000,000.

Foreign Trade. (1968) Imports CFA Fr. 9,333,000,000; exports CFA Fr. 17,920,000,000. Import sources (1966): France 53%; U.S. 17%; West Germany 6%. Export destinations (1966): France 21%; U.K. 20%; Italy 18%; West Germany 16%; Belgium-Luxembourg 10%. Main export iron ore 76%.

Mauritius

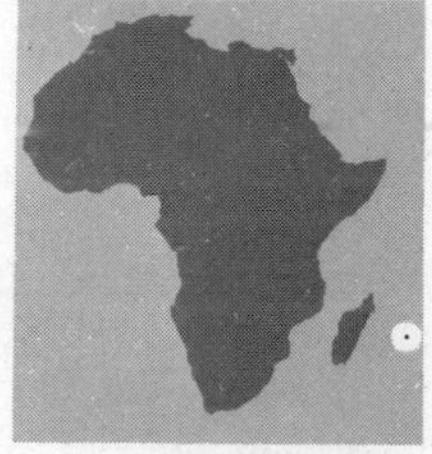

The parliamentary state of Mauritius, a member of the Commonwealth of Nations, lies about 500 mi. E of the Malagasy Republic in the Indian Ocean. Area: 720 sq.mi. (1,865 sq.km.). Pop. (1969 est.): 794,750, including Indian and Pakistani 67%; Creoles (mixed French and African) 29%; Chinese 3.5%; British and French 0.5%. Cap. and largest city: Port Louis (pop., 1969

MAURITIUS

Education. (1967–68) Primary, pupils 140,495, teachers 4,203; secondary, pupils 38,508, teachers 1,645; vocational, pupils 741, teachers 60; teacher training, students 568, teachers 31; higher, students 80, teaching staff 34.

Finance and Trade. Monetary unit: Mauritian rupee, with a par value of MauRs. 5.54 to U.S. $1 (MauRs. 13.30 = £1 sterling). Budget (1967–68 est.): revenue MauRs. 204,624,000; expenditure MauRs. 210,687,990. Foreign trade (1967): imports MauRs. 371,081,000 (21% from U.K., 8% from South Africa, 8% from Australia, 7% from Burma); exports MauRs. 304,882,000 (88% to U.K., 5% to U.S.). Main export sugar 94%. Tourism (1967): visitors 14,800; gross receipts U.S. $3 million.

Agriculture. Production (in 000; metric tons): sugar (1968–69) 597, (1967–68) 638; tea (1967) 2.1, (1966) 2; tobacco (1967) 0.6, (1966) 0.5. Livestock (in 000; April 1967): cattle 46; pigs 3; sheep *c.* 3; goats 66; chickens 385.

est., 137,650). Governor-general in 1969, Sir Leonard Williams; prime minister, Sir Seewoosagur Ramgoolam.

The first year of Mauritian independence passed without incident. The political situation in 1969 improved under Sir Seewoosagur Ramgoolam's Independence Party government (mainly Hindu-Muslim), which achieved a modus vivendi with the Parti Mauricien Social-Démocrate (African Creole and white Franco-Mauritian) to the extent of discussing the possibility of coalition. Political and economic problems remained inextricable among a people divided by race, colour, language, and religion. The situation was made worse by the density of the population (1,100 per sq.mi.), which was increasing because of diminishing emigration and continuing hostility to birth control. The result was increased fear by the minorities that they would be swamped by the Indians.

The economy remained dependent on the sugar industry (94% of exports) which, although efficient, showed signs of reaching a ceiling despite the Commonwealth Sugar Agreement by which Britain took 75% of the crop at £47 10*s*. a ton (world price £33). Political agitation for nationalization and the loss of stable markets should Britain join the EEC increased attempts to diversify the economy with such crops as tea and tobacco and with tourism. In December it was announced that Mauritius was to join the African and Malagasy Common Organization, uniting 14 French-speaking states. Until independence Mauritius had received more than £7 million under the Commonwealth Development and Welfare Acts. In addition to £3 million in development aid for 1968–69, there was £200,000 in technical assistance and an additional £6 million in the form of an interest-free development loan. Although no garrison was kept on the island, Britain continued to maintain a defense treaty, and Mauritius remained a valuable staging point in Commonwealth telecommunications. (M. Mr.)

Medicine

With the death of the world's longest surviving heart transplant patient (see *Surgery,* below), attention in the field of medicine and surgery was focused on areas other than cardiac transplantation, principally on drugs: the development of new therapeutic agents, the abuse of narcotics and neurogenic chemicals, and the action against use of agents thought to be harmful.

L-Dopa (see *Neurology,* below) was found to be effective against Parkinson's disease, and during 1969 clinical trials were conducted in 24 medical centres throughout the U.S. The drug had not been released for prescription use by the Food and Drug Administration, however, as of the end of the year.

Asparaginase, an enzyme produced by bacteria, caused temporary remissions in 50% of patients with certain types of acute leukemia. Expensive to produce, it presumably had an advantage over the commonly used cytotoxic drugs in that it destroyed only cancer cells, which require asparagine for growth while normal cells do not. This was disputed later in the year.

Chalones, naturally occurring growth inhibitors, were also effective in animals, but the large quantities required to suppress cell growth tended to inhibit also the cells responsible for the body's defenses, just as did immunosuppressive drugs.

Lidocaine, a well-known local anesthetic, when promptly injected, was found to be effective in stabilizing the heartbeat in arrhythmia. Phenytoin, an anticonvulsant, was also effective but tended to cause a fall in blood pressure. Glucagon, a hormone secreted by the alpha islet cells of the pancreas, appeared to improve cardiac output by direct action on the heart. Intensive treatment of coronary attacks by these and other means have reduced mortality probability during the acute episode by almost 50%.

DENNIS GALLOWAY FROM "MEDICAL WORLD NEWS"

Howard medical student Ewart Brown, representative for the militant Black Caucus, speaks at the National Medical Association convention at San Francisco in August 1969. He presented a list of 19 demands calling for more response to black people's needs and a more complete effort in recruiting black medical students. Sixteen demands were accepted.

Propanolol is a new preparation that has been used experimentally to reduce blood pressure in a patient in either the erect or supine position. It also reduces cardiac output and alters blood flow, however, and so its use is recommended only when other drugs have failed. Among the newer antihypertensive agents are guanethidine, methyldopa, debrisoquine, and guanoxan.

Isosorbide dinitrate, a drug having the same effect as the nitrites in the treatment of angina pectoris, taken sublingually begins to act in two to five minutes and its action lasts four to six hours.

The antibiotic rifamycin was shown to inhibit the trachoma agent and pox viruses in experimental animals. Its action was on the enzyme RNA-polymerase, essential to the production of RNA by the cell from the DNA-coded genetic material. The advantage of rifamycin over currently available antiviral drugs is that it inhibits viral or bacterial RNA-polymerase without affecting the enzyme of the host cell. (See *Pharmacology,* below.)

A more controversial aspect of the "drug scene" in 1969 was a source of alarm among parents, public health officials, and educators—the greatly increased incidence of drug use by college and high school students, and even among preteen-agers. Among the drugs most frequently used were marijuana ("grass"), LSD ("acid"), methedrine ("speed"), dexedrine ("hearts"), and nembutal ("yellow-jacks").

The chief of psychiatric service at Harvard University reported that high school students take drugs ostensibly to prove their courage, defy authority, get

Meat:
see Agriculture; Food
Medical Education:
see Medicine

WIDE WORLD

Young medical students, doctors, and nurses leave the 1969 summer session of the American Medical Association in New York City after charging the AMA with a lack of social consciousness.

a thrill, increase sexual desire and performance, and, vaguely, to find the meaning of life. College students turn to drugs presumably to have the experience (*i.e.*, that of their peers), reinforce drastic decisions (*e.g.*, to drop out), improve ability to communicate, demonstrate the irrationality of the drug laws and defy the "Establishment," and find a cure for emotional hang-ups.

The drug laws and their enforcement were a source of heated controversy. Proponents pointed out that marijuana, though nonaddictive, dulled the mind, was a depressant, and, consequently, a cause of automobile and other types of accidents. Those opposed to the laws claimed that if the supply of marijuana to the youngsters was cut off, they would be driven to the use of harder drugs—addictive narcotics—for their kicks. The arguments raged, and, meanwhile, the U.S. government put teeth into drug law enforcement. The Mexican government effected a search and destroy operation—seeking and burning all sources of the "weed." The enthusiasm of border guards at all entries from Mexico enforcing Operation Intercept, a search procedure, resulted in monumental tie-ups of vehicular and pedestrian traffic. Only after loud and long protests from both sides of the border was vigilance relaxed. As the source of "grass" dwindled, pushers on campuses sold all sorts of substitutes as marijuana, some of them injurious to the health of the user. As predicted, some of the youngsters turned to heroin and morphine. Others, however, decided it was not worth the effort and risk and returned to the "normal" life.

Sociologists, educators, psychologists, and public health physicians held one opinion in common: parents, to be able to cope with the situation, must be completely informed; they must know more about the commonly used drugs—the addictive qualities, physiology, short- and long-term effects, etc.—than their children. To be ignorant of the properties of drugs while berating the children for using them is sheer folly, it was pointed out.

Robert H. Finch, secretary of the U.S. Health, Education, and Welfare Department, in November softened his ban on the artificial sweetener cyclamate and approved its use in foods and as a sugar substitute in tablet or liquid form. After attention was called to research indicating the presence of tumours in animals administered large quantities of cyclamate, the secretary, on October 18, issued an order that removed cyclamate-sweetened products from the market for general use. Although the November announcement was intended to make cyclamate-sweetened foods available to diabetics, it meant that they would remain on the market. The sale of beverages containing the sweetener, however, was banned after Jan. 1, 1970.

The Chinese restaurant syndrome—a burning sensation in the neck and chest, tightness of face muscles, palpitations, and a feeling of faintness—had been experienced and reported upon by a number of people, worldwide. The symptoms appeared about 30 minutes after eating a Chinese meal, but fortunately disappeared rapidly and left no serious or lasting effects. A search for the cause implicated the food additive monosodium glutamate, used as a taste-enhancer. When MSG was fed to volunteers the severity of the reported symptoms varied with the dose and with individual susceptibility. Although no official action was taken against MSG, both U.S. and Canadian manufacturers of baby foods announced they would discontinue sale of MSG-flavoured products.

Saccharin also was given detailed study in Canada and the U.S. to determine whether it produces any harmful effects in living organisms. As of the end of the year none were definitely established.

Total starvation was ruled out as a method of treating obesity after reports of sudden death among patients on starvation therapy. Death was found to be caused by heart failure, and histological examination showed fragmentation of cardiac muscle fibres. Apart from the serious danger involved, there seemed to be no advantage in this type of regimen over one containing up to 500 calories per day.

Massive starvation, however, was forecast for the world by 1975 by a Northwestern University (Evanston, Ill.) biologist in November. R. C. Gesteland pointed out that one-third of the world is adequately fed and two-thirds are not, while a large percentage of the U.S. population is obese and wastes food. Short-term solutions, he said, include the development of modified and synthetic foods, rationing, and population control. Permanent prevention of worldwide famine will require much scientific research, engineering development, and close international cooperation.

Meanwhile, progress toward the ideal contraceptive pill continued. A mini-pill with a low progesterone content was introduced after extensive trials in the U.S., U.K., and Mexico. Claimed to have removed the threat of thrombosis, the pill was tested in 76 women and no clotting tendency was observed. Some promising tests of a male contraceptive were reported by R. E. Whalen and W. G. Luttge (California). Daily injections of cyproterone acetate abolished fertility in male rats after seven weeks without affecting sexual drive. Unfortunately the drug has been used in man for a number of conditions, and specifically for reducing libido, so it was doubtful if the results of the rat experiments were applicable. It appears likely, however, according to investigators in the field, that the effects of such hormonelike substances on fertility and libido could eventually be separated.

Slowly but surely medicine appears to be approaching a stage of automation. There is no thought, of course, that any machines, no matter how sophisticated, will ever replace the physician. They are, however, rendering him valuable assistance. Medical telemetry during the Apollo flights, discussed in all the media, made the average citizen aware of some of the miracles being accomplished in this field. Others include radio pill systems which, after being swallowed, transmit information on the pH of the intestinal contents and the pressure in the intestinal tract; artificial pacemakers and kidneys; laser ophthalmoscopes; electrosurgical knives; and a wide variety of medical computer systems that, although still in the experimental stage, may monitor a patient, assist in physical examinations, read X rays and electrocardiograms, confirm a physician's diagnosis, and perform a host of so-called physician-assistance functions. They may, indeed, modify the course of medical science in the future.

The 1969 Nobel Prize for Physiology or Medicine was shared by Max Delbrück, Salvador E. Luria, and Alfred D. Hershey for their "discoveries concerning the replication mechanism and genetic structure of viruses." (*See* BIOGRAPHY.) (X.)

ANESTHESIOLOGY

The fourth World Congress of Anesthesiologists was held in London in September 1968 and was the largest in its history with an attendance of 4,132. Sir Geoffrey Organe, retiring president, emphasized the rapid expansion of the specialty and the importance of better training. The new president, Francis Foldes, would preside over the next world congress in Japan in 1972. In 1970 the European congress was to be held in Prague and the Australian congress in Melbourne.

In 1969 progress was made toward establishing a uniform level of training in the specialty throughout the world. A measure of reciprocity was proposed between the American specialist examination and the Australasian, the English, and the Irish fellowships.

The greater demand for anesthetic services has caused a shortage of specialized personnel throughout the world, due in part to increased time-consuming surgery, demands of intensive care units and pain clinics, and use of the anesthetist in the treatment of patients suffering from ventilatory failure. The shortage has been met in different ways. In the U.S., where the role of the nurse anesthetist is well established, about two-thirds of all the anesthetics administered are given by nurse anesthetists. Scandinavian and Eastern European countries adopt a similar solution. In the U.K. and Australia, however, there has been resolute opposition to the use of nonphysician personnel in the administration of anesthetics.

Halothane (Fluothane) remains by far the most extensively used volatile anesthesia; methoxyflurane (Penthrane) has failed to make appreciable inroads as an alternative. Several new drugs have come under examination as possible substitutes. Of these a new halogenated agent, fluroxene, is under test in the U.S., where concern over the possibility of liver damage following the administration of halothane still exists despite results of the National Halothane Study which reported, after an examination of almost one million anesthetics, extremely low incidence of liver necrosis —actually no higher than that from any other anesthetic agent. There is evidence, however, from clinical reports that there may be a direct relationship between the administration of this drug and the very rare occurrence of fatal postoperative liver failure. The inability to reproduce this condition in experimental animals suggests that there may be an individual patient susceptibility. One theory, supported by some evidence, is that halothane may undergo a chemical change in the body and produce a substance toxic to the liver in susceptible individuals.

In an effort to meet the need of patients for a sleeplike state and to keep them from becoming too deeply anesthetized, several techniques of basal sedation have been tried. In these circumstances the introduction of diazepam (Valium), a potent tranquilizing agent that makes patients sleepy and unaware of the passage of time, has found ready acceptance.

Procaine and lidocaine (Xylocaine) have long been the most popular local anesthetics. The recent introduction of bipivacaine (Marcain) promises to meet the major disadvantage of the older drugs, *i.e.*, the short duration of their action, which limited the operating time to about one hour. Bipivacaine is effective for three to four hours and has an acceptably low incidence of side effects. It is at present undergoing clinical trial in the U.S.

The introduction in 1968 of a new steroid muscle relaxant, pancuronium (Pavulon), occasioned considerable interest. This drug has two quaternary ammonium side chains on a steroid nucleus. It was used widely in the U.K. and no untoward side effects have been reported. Major advantages have been claimed for this drug over presently accepted nonsteroid muscle relaxants such as curare. Detailed pharmacological studies, however, have not been made. Research continues for a short-acting muscle relaxant of the curare type, and to this end several other steroid compounds have been investigated. A new short-acting muscle relaxant (Dacuronium) is being tested.

Hypoxemia (too little oxygen in the blood) is a common postoperative condition, the cause of which has been attributed to the effects of anesthetic drugs, the occurrence of small areas of "collapse" in the lungs, the depressant effects of anesthetics upon the heart, and an increased utilization of oxygen by the body during recovery. Close supervision of the patient in special recovery areas is essential during this period, and the routine use of oxygen therapy has been advocated.

Recording arterial and venous blood pressure, oxygen and carbon dioxide tension, hydrogen ion concentration, temperature, and hematocrit are now commonly regarded as essential in the monitoring of gravely ill patients or those with grossly disturbed body processes. Such patients are usually treated by anesthetists in the intensive care units of hospitals. In many medical care facilities this monitoring is carried out by computers and related electronic instrumentation. As a result of the important part played by these devices, departments of clinical measurement have been established in the U.K. In recognition of the need for anesthetists to appreciate the functions of these machines and to be able to interpret their results, the specialist examination in the U.K. (FFARCS diploma) now requires the candidate to study clinical measurement and clinical chemistry as part of his curriculum. (S. A. F.)

CANCER

Studies of basic mechanisms concerned in immune responses and of the role of viruses in the causation of cancer continue to provide the most solid basis for advance in both the treatment and prevention of the disease.

Some of the most interesting new developments in this area have stemmed from the use of cell-fusion techniques by Henry Harris and his colleagues at Oxford. They reported the suppression of the malignant behaviour of a line of mouse cancer cells by fusing them (with the aid of the Sendai virus) to non-malignant hamster-derived cells of the A9 line. Also reported was the suppression of histocompatibility antigens.

Empirical treatment of cancer with growth-inhibitory drugs has to some extent given way to attempts to treat cancer by boosting the body's supposed or actual immunological reaction to cancers arising within it. The relatively long survival period of a few recipients of transplanted organs, despite the prediction on theoretical grounds of early rejection of the transplant tissues, and the grave nature of cancer as a disease process, justified attempts by clinicians to treat cancer by methods not fully tested previously in laboratory animals. Georges Mathé and co-workers have claimed encouraging results in the treatment of leukemia by nonspecific stimulation of immunity by repeated BCG vaccination and other means. Others have met with less success in similar attempts. At present the large-scale treatment of cancer by transplantation surgery or nonspecific immunotherapy still seems unfeasible. The most specific form of immunotherapy entails the injection into the patient of lymphocytes from another animal that has been exposed to tumour tissue from the patient. Such lymphocytes may be specifically reactive against the cancer cells in question, and destroy them. At least four lymphocytes are needed to destroy one cancer cell, however, so that for immunotherapy of this kind to be effective most of the cancerous tissue in a patient must first be removed by surgery or destroyed by drugs or radiotherapy, leaving relatively few cells to be destroyed by the injected lymphocytes.

COURTESY, DR. M. GOTO, KYUSHU UNIVERSITY SCHOOL OF MEDICINE

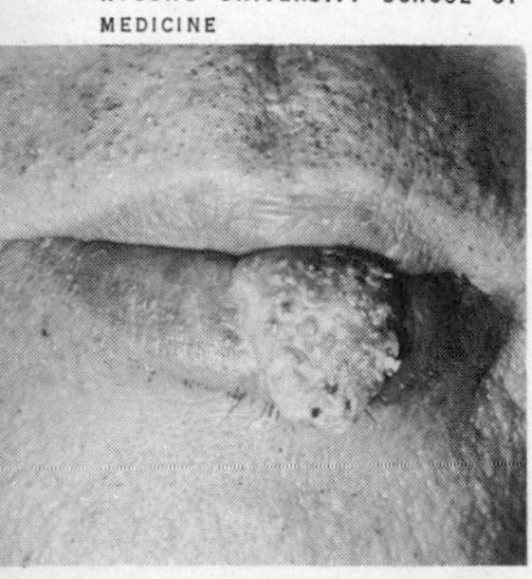

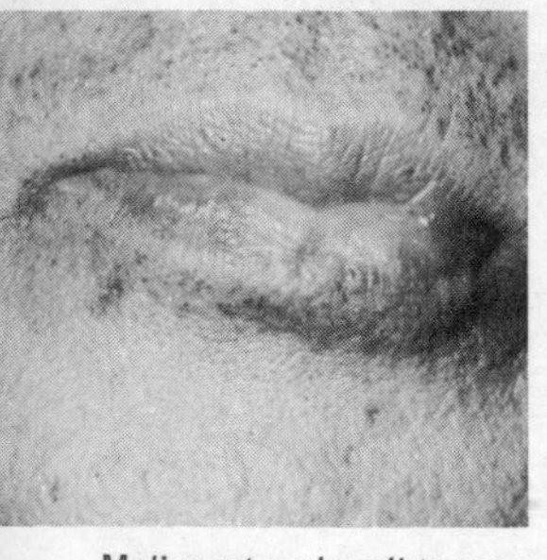

Malignant scaly cell tumour (top) on lip of patient was treated in a Japanese clinic with the antibiotic bleomycin by M. Goto. Tumour shrank by fifth day and disappeared by 37th day (above) of treatment. Bleomycin, effective with certain other cancers, has been available in Japan since February 1969 and was expected to be available in the U.S. in a few years.

A sinister complication of the prolonged drug-induced or antilymphocyte serum-induced immunosuppression necessary if organs or tissues are to survive usefully after homograft transplantation is that otherwise suppressed virus-induced cancers may be permitted to grow. This is the most likely explanation for the raised incidence of reticulum-cell sarcoma among recipients of kidney transplants, as it is of the increased risk of development of polyoma virus-induced cancers in mice following treatment with antilymphocyte serum.

A report by D. L. Morton, R. A. Malmgren, and their colleagues suggested that osteogenic and some soft-tissue sarcomas share common antigens, and may be caused by viruses. Whether or not this is true, it is becoming increasingly clear both that viruses and chemical agents capable of inducing cancer are widespread in nature, and that a wide variety of agents, including drugs, other chemicals, and viruses, may impair immune responsiveness. These facts make it difficult to distinguish between carcinogens and cocarcinogens (*i.e.*, agents that enhance the effect of carcinogens), and they make more likely the possibility that cancer development is as dependent on exposure to cocarcinogenic factors (including immune suppressants) and on the capacity of the body to rid itself of abnormal cells or repair them as it is on exposure to true carcinogens.

Despite these changes in concept of cancer causation, the identification of dimethylnitrosamine (DMN), a potent carcinogen, in an alcoholic beverage consumed in a locality in Africa where cancer of the esophagus is prevalent may have opened a new chapter in our understanding of important causes of cancer in man. Nitrosamines, such as DMN, may be formed by the interaction of secondary amines and nitrites. Secondary amines are present in many foodstuffs so that the advisability of using nitrites for preserving food has now come into question, as has their use as fertilizers and the safety of consuming foods naturally high in nitrate or nitrite content. Under present conditions, the abandonment of the use of nitrites to preserve meat products would greatly increase the risk of growth of *Clostridium botulinum* and consequently of rapidly fatal botulism. Nevertheless, if the presence of nitrosamines in nitrite-preserved foodstuffs is unequivocally demonstrated, there may have to be a complete revolution in food-preservative (especially meat- and cheese-preservative) methodology.

(F. J. C. R.)

DERMATOLOGY

Examination of the skin is frequently the key to a correct diagnosis in multisystem disease. Among the earliest signs of tuberous sclerosis—a disease characterized by mental retardation, seizures, and adenoma sebaceum of the face—are leaf-shaped hypopigmented macules. Patients may have from four to one hundred lesions which may be so subtle as to require differential examination under ultraviolet light. Another cutaneous marker of systemic abnormality may be congenital wartlike nevi, which appear to correlate with skeletal and central nervous system malformations.

Xeroderma pigmentosum is a genetic disease characterized by photosensitivity and the formation of numerous cutaneous cancers. Cells from patients with this condition are incapable of repairing solar-damaged DNA. There is now great interest as to how this alteration in DNA metabolism might account for the propensity to cancer formation.

The basis by which certain chemicals sensitize skin to sunlight remains unknown. The observation that 4,5′,8-trimethylpsoralen, a known photosensitizer, is bound to DNA in vivo suggests a possible molecular mechanism for this phenomenon.

Collagen is the major structural protein in the body. Cultures of human dermal connective tissue produce an enzyme capable of degrading this protein under physiologic conditions. This enzyme, collagenase, probably accounts for the normal degradation of collagen in skin and, in addition, may be the mechanism of connective tissue destruction in certain genetic blistering diseases.

The utilization of immunologic techniques in the study of skin disease has been effective. In bullous pemphigoid and in pemphigus vulgaris, there are antibodies circulating to the basement membrane and to the epithelial cells, respectively. The presence of an antibody in pemphigus suggests that interference with the immune mechanism might be appropriate therapy. A small series of patients has been treated with immunosuppressive drugs with considerable success, but this form of therapy remains highly experimental.

Malignant melanoma, the black cancer of pigment cells, can be biopsied without deleterious effect on prognosis. This finding emphasizes the fact that all questionable pigmented lesions should be biopsied early. A useful technique in identifying distant spread of tumour in melanoma patients is injection of radioactive iodoquine followed by total-body scanning. The melanoma tissue selectively concentrates the tagged iodoquine, indicating the areas of metastases by the increase in radioactivity.

Porphyria cutanea tarda is a disease characterized by blistering of the skin after exposure to the sun and by increased excretion of uroporphyrin and coproporphyrin in the urine. An effective mode of therapy

"LONDON DAILY EXPRESS" FROM PICTORIAL PARADE

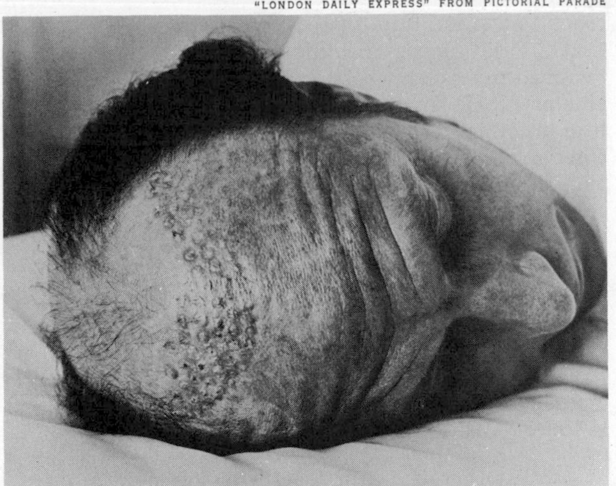

Balding patient in Melbourne, Austr., prepared for second grafting operation to restore his hair. Curve of welts on top shows where plugs of hair-root-containing tissue were transplanted.

for this condition appears to be systematic bleeding of patients. Removal of from 5 to 17 pints of blood over a period of months resulted in a clinical remission and a marked reduction in urinary uroporphyrins.

The development of cirrhosis of the liver in patients receiving methotrexate therapy for psoriasis has been reported. Although these patients were apparently treated too vigorously with the drug, caution is imperative, inasmuch as lower doses may also cause cirrhosis.

Sunburn, suntan, and the photosensitivity reaction in lupus erythematosus are caused by ultraviolet light in the wavelength range of 280 to 310 nanometres. An effective sunscreen for these wavelengths is 5% para-aminobenzoic acid in ethyl alcohol (70–95%). This solution is aesthetically agreeable and offers some protection even after swimming or perspiring. Patients with lupus erythematosus, xeroderma pigmentosum, fair skin, albinism, and a propensity to solar-induced skin cancers will probably find this preparation of value. (GE. S. L.; T. B. F.)

EAR, NOSE, AND THROAT DISEASES

Sir Norman Gregg noted in 1941 that German measles, when occurring in the first trimester of pregnancy, may cause deformities, blindness, and mild to profound hearing loss in the newborn. Recent observations indicate that the danger period may extend into the second trimester even when the presence of rubella in the mother is positive by laboratory tests but not clinically evident. A significant occurrence of hearing impairment was found by Maurice H. Miller and associates in 58% of 252 children with histories of maternal rubella. Adverse fetal outcome following maternal rubella after the first trimester of pregnancy (expanded rubella syndrome) has been reported from the Johns Hopkins Medical Institutions by Janet B. Hardy and co-workers. As yet no easy way, clinical or laboratory, is available to identify those infants with the more subtle manifestations of congenital rubella. Suitable screening tests during infancy and preschool years and prolonged follow-up are indicated when the maternal history is suggestive, or when the child is born in the wake of a major epidemic. C. S. Karmody found numerous instances in which deafness was the sole apparent congenital abnormality and in which the maternal rubella was asymptomatic. The vaccine of the live attenuated rubella virus was developed by Harry M. Meyer, Jr., and Paul Parkman of the National Institutes of Health and is being offered as immunization for children of age one to puberty, with a first priority suggested for those aged 5 to 9. Routine immunization of women of childbearing age is not recommended because conception may have occurred previously with consequent risk to the fetus. A single dose of the vaccine appears to be permanent, and it appears that this scourge of defects in the newborn can be completely eliminated.

More than one and one-half million people annually fly in the troposphere (the first division of the earth's atmosphere) on U.S. scheduled airlines. While most of these aircraft are pressurized, cabin "altitudes" of 3,200 to 7,500 ft. (at flight levels of 30,000 to 40,000 ft.) are still sufficient to produce significant ear and sinus problems in susceptible persons, especially on descent. Those with nasal blockage as the result of head colds, allergy, or anatomical obstructions may develop fluid in the ear (aero-otitis) or in the sinuses (aerosinusitis). Because hearing can be affected by repeated experiences, the warning of reducing such exposures must be heeded. The frequency of corrective surgical procedures for conductive types of hearing loss, with patients flying soon after surgery, is of great concern because of the possibility of a prosthesis being dislodged by changes in ambient pressure.

U.S. Navy physicians F. J. Stucker and W. B. Echols warned that any compressible space in the body is vulnerable to compression injury in deep underwater activities. This includes not only the ear and sinuses but also the tracheobronchial tree. The protective reflex closure mechanism can be triggered by a few drops of water, secretions, or regurgitation of gastric contents, so that a spasm may occur. If a swimmer becomes frightened or is suddenly subjected to painful stimulus, unless the respiratory centre overrides the suppression, death may ensue. As in flight, when the eustachian tube is obstructed, the eardrum retracts until ultimately hemorrhage or rupture occurs. A phenomenon of "cochlear bends," assumed to be caused by small air emboli occluding terminal arterial branches, may lead to sudden and prolonged sensorineural hearing loss.

At the Congress on Environmental Health Problems held in Chicago, D. H. Eldredge presented proof that exposure to excessive levels (short, high level and longer, lower levels) and durations of noise can injure the organs of hearing. This has been demonstrated empirically and by controlled experimentation. The observation by J. Sataloff of 200 iron-ore miners subjected to very loud intermittent drilling noise while working underground is of interest. When this exposure activity was interrupted briefly about 40 times daily, the damaging effect was substantially lowered. Although many workers in the field of environmental health look upon noise as an occupational hazard (as well as a public nuisance), much remains to be learned about the effects of noise on man. In the meantime, the general public is cautioned about high-volume rock 'n' roll music and the noises from mass transportation and construction equipment, in addition to industrial, military, and even household noises. A. Cohen, chief of the U.S. Public Health Service National Noise Study, suggested the word "sociocusis" as the term for the loss of hearing caused by noise from such sources.

Complete airway obstruction leads to cerebral anoxia, asphyxia, and cardiac arrest within five to ten minutes. Partial or increased airway resistance may result in increased work of breathing, hypoventilation, cerebral and pulmonary edema, cardiovascular disturbances, and a number of other life-threatening conditions. In a discussion of the recognition and management of airway obstruction, Peter Safar maintained that a patent or open airway is the key to resuscitation and life support. Complete airway obstruction is recognized by inability to hear or feel airflow at the mouth or nose, and by seeing inspiratory retraction of the supraclavicular or intercostal area when observing the chest. Where there is partial obstruction, retraction is present but the airflow is noisy. Snoring suggests that the back of the tongue is obstructing the throat; crowing is evidence of a spasm of the larynx; gurgling, the presence of foreign matter; and wheezing suggests bronchial obstruction. Safar outlined seven successful steps, some of which can be applied by nonmedical persons: tilt the head in a backward position, displace the lower jaw forward, open the mouth, suck out the secretions if such equipment is available, and insert a tube into the pharynx. Intermittent positive pressure ventilation (*e.g.*, with a self-refilling bag valve unit and 100% oxygen) then becomes a necessity. Other steps, *e.g.*, placing a tube into the lumen of the trachea (windpipe), require the services of more experienced personnel. The last, called tracheotomy, was the basis of a report by neurosurgical residents at the University of Pennsylvania who reported a fast (one minute) method which they advisedly stated was "simple and safe." "Not so easy," was the warning by a number of physicians who pointed out that there are many fatal mistakes an inexperienced surgeon can make, and that the procedure should be performed in an operating room for optimum results. Reports of complications by many observers attest to the fact that tracheotomy, while a lifesaving procedure, is neither simple surgery nor is it devoid of complications.

Finally, it has been pointed out by F. M. Key, Jr., and E. B. Mendel that prompt diagnosis and treatment of bilateral closure or atresia of the posterior nostrils (choanae) in newborns may avert death due to asphyxiation. Cyanosis and difficulty in breathing are apparent when the infant tries to breathe through the nose. An oral airway can be inserted until the obstruction in the back of the nose is relieved by surgical correction. (F. L. Lr.)

ENDOCRINOLOGY

Prostaglandin (PG) was discovered in crude form in 1930 in human seminal plasma and material from sheep seminal vesicles. Various PG's have since been found in almost every tissue. They all have the same basic atomic framework of prostanoic acid, and as little as one-thousandth of a microgram has biologic activity. There are 16 naturally occurring PG's; at least five of them have now been synthesized in the laboratory. Depending on which one of the hormones is used and where, the versatile new compounds can be muscle stimulants or relaxants, vasodilators or vasoconstrictors. Experimental studies are being carried on in the treatment of high blood pressure, in nasal decongestion, in management of peptic ulcer, induction of labour, and against male sterility. Prostaglandin $F_2\alpha$ has afforded a potentially new approach to contraception by its lytic effect on the corpus luteum ultimately resulting in menstruation.

D. D. Adams and colleagues at Dunedin, N.Z., compared the thyroid-stimulating hormone (TSH) content of serum from thyrotoxic and euthyroid patients. Their findings helped end the concept that thyrotoxicosis is caused by excessive stimulation by pituitary TSH. Thyrotoxic patients tested showed less than a normal amount of TSH in their serum. The observation is in accord with the view that the common form of thyrotoxicosis is an autoimmune disorder, the thyroid overactivity being due to stimulation by a specific thyroid antibody, called long-acting thyroid stimulator (LATS). It has been believed that psychological disturbances may play an etiological role in thyrotoxicosis. The new evidence points to the reverse—the thyrotoxic condition predisposes to psychological disturbance.

Barely six years after the discovery of calcitonin (thyrocalcitonin), its total synthesis has been reported. The hormone, at first thought to be produced by the parathyroids, then the thyroid, is produced primarily by the ultimobranchial body which is embryologically related to both the thyroid and parathyroid glands. The hormone accelerates calcium deposition and inhibits calcium resorption in bone.

A new approach to stimulation of luteinizing hormone (LH) release and possible ovulation has commanded considerable attention. A. Kastin and A. V. Schally, of New Orleans, La., in association with co-workers in Mexico and Ann Arbor, Mich., claimed that the administration to human males and females of an LH releasing hormone (LRH) purified from porcine hypothalamic tissue caused a 3.7-fold increase in serum-LH levels within a half hour. The administration of porcine LRH can induce release of LH in both men and women; the substance is not sex specific. LRH in proper dosage may eliminate the occurrence of multiple births and overstimulation of the ovaries frequently encountered when either clomiphene or human gonadotropins are employed.

C. A. Strott and M. Lipsett, of Bethesda, Md., claimed that a more accurate index of Leydig cell function of the testes could be obtained by measuring plasma 17-hydroxyprogesterone (HP) than plasma testosterone. After using suppressive doses of glucocorticoids to rule out an adrenal source of HP, they showed that 90% of the HP originated from the Leydig cells. They also found that plasma HP levels of males were twice those of females in the follicular phase of the cycle, and this suggested that the Leydig cell is a major source of the steroid.

Evidence of elevated ovarian progesterone production before ovulation in various research animals has accumulated in recent years. Elof Johansson, Sweden, studied the plasma content of progesterone and LH in the same plasma sample near the time of ovulation and concluded that there is evidence to support the idea that the elevated levels of progesterone found in the plasma on the day of the LH peak represent preovulatory progesterone in women. In the U.S. this concept was challenged by C. M. Cargille and co-workers, who also studied plasma follicle-stimulating hormone (FSH), LH, and progesterone in the same sample. A progesterone rise did not precede the FSH or LH midcycle peak, and they felt that progesterone was not the stimulus for these two events. Presently the evidence seems to point to rising levels of estrogen as primarily responsible for triggering the ovulatory surge of gonadotropins.

The association of Addison's disease with five cases of ovarian failure in women ranging in age from adolescence to 26 years suggested to a group of British workers, headed by W. J. Irvine of Edinburgh, that an autoimmune disturbance had taken place in the ovary. This suspicion was confirmed by the finding of antibodies reactive to the theca interna of the ovary in these patients. (R. B. Gt.)

GASTROENTEROLOGY

Improved fibre-optic equipment included a flexible tube containing both a miniature camera for photographing the interior of the stomach and a compartment for direct washing of suspicious areas for cancer diagnosis.

Vagotomy, separating the vagus nerves to the stomach, plus a drainage procedure, continued to be the most popular operative combination for peptic ulcer patients requiring surgery.

Medium-chain triglycerides (MCT) are neutral fats absorbed directly into the portal vein circulation and thence to the liver, rather than via usual intestinal lymphatic pathways. It was demonstrated that MCT could provide readily absorbable calories for the nutritional support of a variety of disorders including celiac disease, pancreatic insufficiency, bile salt deficiency, bacterial overgrowth, cystic fibrosis, regional enteritis, and postoperative complications after removal of the small intestine.

In the U.S. the incidence of colonic cancer has been increasing, while that of stomach cancer has been declining. With the exception of cancer of the lung, cancer of the large bowel was responsible for more deaths than cancer of any other site, including the breast and cervix. Approximately 50% of the tumours were within reach of the sigmoidoscope, a readily available and highly useful instrument, but, apparently, not used frequently enough.

Colon enlargement (toxic dilatation) during ulcerative colitis is an ominous development characterized by tender, distended abdomen, fever, toxemia, and severe diarrhea. Medical treatment includes tube decompression of the gastrointestinal tract, correction of fluid, protein, red cell, and electrolyte deficiencies, and administration of broad-spectrum antibiotics plus ACTH or steroids. Surgery may also be required. Delay in diagnosis and treatment may lead to perforation of the colon and subsequent peritonitis.

Acute inflammation of the pancreas (pancreatitis) was relatively common and serious. Causes included alcoholism, gallstones, bile duct disease, infections, metabolic derangements, nutritional disorders, injury, and hereditary influences. Diagnosis was substantiated by abnormalities in serum pancreatic enzymes (amylase, lipase), direct measurement of pancreatic secretion, and improved X-ray and scanning techniques. The condition often required surgery, including sphincterotomy, resection of diseased pancreatic tissue, drainage of associated pancreatic cysts and abscesses, and transduodenal or transpancreatic decompression of pancreatic ducts.

Removal of the gallbladder was advocated for patients with "silent gallstones" or a single large gallstone, to avoid obstruction of the bile duct and impairment of liver function.

The incidence of viral hepatitis increased in 1969 as anticipated. Factors in spread of the disease were the communal use of unsterilized needles and syringes for administration of drugs ("hippie hepatitis"), use of infected blood by blood banks, and, in a Connecticut outbreak, the ingestion of raw clams. An epidemic of viral hepatitis developed among patients receiving maintenance hemodialysis, and cases were reported following anesthesia.

There appeared to be a close relationship of the "Australia antigen" to the serum hepatitis virus, the antigen disappearing with clinical improvement. This antigen was first observed when the serum of a transfused hemophilia patient was tested against serum from an Australian aborigine. Tens of millions of asymptomatic people carry the Australia antigen chronically. It has occurred frequently in the serum of apparently healthy people living in the tropics and Southeast Asia, but only rarely in the normal North American and European communities. The antigen was detected more frequently in the blood of multitransfused patients, in the serum of approximately 20% of patients with viral hepatitis, in patients with Down's syndrome, among whom the incidence of hepatitis was very high, and in some forms of leukemia. The antigen was not found in the serum of patients suffering from various other liver diseases, indicating that it was not merely an end product of damaged liver cells. Additional studies suggested that the Australia antigen is the hepatitis virus itself.

Chronic active hepatitis was a disease of unknown cause, with variable but unremitting course, characterized by clinical, laboratory, and histological changes of acute and chronic hepatitis, punctuated by recurrent episodes of active liver disease. The chief cause of death was liver cell failure, with jaundice, ascites, and hepatic coma. (J. B. Kr.)

GENETICS

In the decade since the first discovery of an extra chromosome (21) in mongolism, or Down's syndrome, identifiable chromosome change has been related to: (1) abnormalities of sexual development (*e.g.*, in the XO Turner syndrome and XXY Klinefelter syndrome); (2) malformations (*e.g.*, trisomy 13 syndrome); (3) mental retardation (*e.g.*, *cri du chat* syndrome); (4) malignant neoplasma (*e.g.*, the Philadelphia chromosome in chronic myeloid leukemia); (5) behavioural disturbances (*e.g.*, the XYY syndrome); and (6) spontaneous abortions.

Characteristic malformations have been related to deletion of part of specific chromosomes. These "deletion syndromes" include absence of the short arm of chromosome 4 (Wolf syndrome), of the short arm of chromosome 5 (*cri du chat* syndrome), of the long arm of chromosome 13, of the short arm of chromosome 18, and of the long arm of chromosome 18.

An interesting group of Mendelian disorders inherited in an autosomal (nonsex-linked) manner have been found to have an exaggerated propensity to chromosomal breakage. "Chromosome breakage syndromes" include Fanconi's anemia, Bloom's syndrome, and ataxia-telangiectasia. It is plausible that the tendency to malignancy in these conditions is a consequence of the breakage tendency.

The effects of chemicals on the chromosomes, when added to cell culture or ingested by the subject, have attracted attention. Increased chromosome breakage by LSD has been claimed but disputed. Malformation in the babies of LSD users and an increased frequency of leukemia in such persons, secondary to chromosome breakage, have been suggested but await proof. Chromosome breakage is claimed to occur in cultured cells exposed to the artificial sweetener cyclamate.

Somatic cell genetics involves the study of body cells, usually fibroblasts, in cell culture. It permits the application to human genetics of techniques used by the microbiologist. Identification at the cellular level of the basic defect in many hereditary disorders has already been achieved by either biochemical (*e.g.*, in Tay-Sachs disease) or morphologic (*e.g.*, in cystic fibrosis) means. The finding that two different types of cells may fuse to form a hybrid cell when grown together in vitro has been used in the study of the human genetic makeup. Facilitation of this hybridization process by the Sendai virus permits fusion of the cells of man and mouse and of even more disparate species. Transformation of human cells in culture by treatment with foreign DNA is a promising advance.

Biochemical genetics encompasses both the chemistry of heredity (*i.e.*, the DNA-RNA-protein synthesis mechanism) and the molecular basis of variation, normal and pathologic. DNA-RNA hybridization (note the double use of the term hybridization) has been used to investigate in man as in other mammals the makeup of the chromosomes. About 30% of man's DNA appears to be present in multiple copies, about 10% of the genetic material being present in several million copies.

The discovery that DNA is not limited to the chromosomes in the nucleus but also occurs in the mitochondria of the cytoplasm opens the possibility that some disorders of man are due to mutation in mitochondrial DNA. Such disorders would be expected to show maternal transmission.

In the study of the inborn errors of metabolism, progress with the lysosomal diseases, the vitamin-dependent disorders, and the disorders of end-organ unresponsiveness deserve particular attention. Genetic disorders have been found to be related to deficiency of one or another of some 40 "digestive" enzymes contained in the lysosome. These are "storage" diseases related to resultant chemical failure. Indeed, a disorder resulting from deficiency of each of at least ten of the enzymes is now known. The discovery by John S. O'Brien and his associates of one such defect in Tay-Sachs disease is an important advance.

Some inborn errors of metabolism have been found to be the result of a defective enzyme, but the administration of large amounts of the coenzyme, *e.g.*, vitamin B_6 or vitamin B_{12}, sometimes permits the crippled enzyme to function adequately.

Organ transplantation has brought urgency to the problem of the genetics of histocompatibility. A main approach has been typing of white blood cells by methods analogous to those used for the last 70 years for typing red blood cells and also by new methods, particularly MLC (mixed leukocyte culture).

Genetic linkage studies aim to discover what genes are on the same chromosome and which specific chromosome carries specific genes. Analysis of pedigree data, families in which many members have been tested for various blood groups, has been computer assisted. About a dozen pairs of gene loci are now known which are on the same autosome (nonsex chromosome) and one triplet of loci is known to be on the same chromosome. By cytologic methods, either alone or in combination with family studies, the specific autosome that carries specific genes is known in three instances: the gene for the Duffy blood group is on chromosome 1, the gene for the blood protein haptoglobin is on chromosome 16, and the gene for the enzyme thymidine kinase is on chromosome 17.

Linkage must not be confused with association. People of blood type O have an increased propensity to peptic ulcer. This is blood-group-and-disease association, not genetic linkage. The phenomenon is based on a physiologic peculiarity of the type O person, not on location of two genes on the same chromosome. Women who are of a blood type other than type A have an increased risk of developing thrombosis in the veins; this risk is particularly striking if the woman is pregnant or is taking the current type of oral contraceptive. In the latter case the risk is more than three times that in women who are of blood type A.

An important factor in diagnosis is genetic heterogeneity. Study of what previously appeared to be a single entity has frequently revealed the existence of two or more simulating but fundamentally distinct disorders. The importance here is that the mode of inheritance is often different so that appropriate genetic counseling is different, and the prognosis and management may also be different. Examples of genetic heterogeneity are Marfan's syndrome and homocystinuria (a dominant and a recessive disorder, respectively), the several achondroplasia-like conditions, and the many types of congenital deafness.

Genetic counseling has been aided in prenatal diagnosis by amniocentesis. Withdrawal of a small amount of fluid from the amniotic sac which surrounds the fetus is safely performed during the 14th week of pregnancy or earlier. Chromosome abnormalities can be detected in the fetal cells in the fluid, and biochemical defects (*e.g.*, the enzyme defect of Tay-Sachs disease) can be demonstrated. This technical advance coupled with liberalized abortion laws permits the clinical geneticist to prevent parents who are carriers of a genetic disorder from producing defective children. (V. A. McK.)

GERONTOLOGY

Preventive geriatrics continues to search for the earliest manifestation of tissue breakdown, incipient organ failure, and altered behaviour, and then apply effective corrective measures. More knowledge is sought about the connection between physical disease and emotional states as well as the psychological reactions to physical changes incidental to aging.

In the U.S., only about 4% of those over 65 are permanently in medical institutions. Preretirement planning must be encouraged not only for economic situations but also for social, psychological, and medical needs, with emphasis on the dangers of both physical and mental inactivity, overweight, and prolonged fatigue. Too many elderly people are temporarily institutionalized for their need of personal care and attention rather than for medical care. Most of the needs of the aged are of the personal and "self-help" variety rather than medical, and these can best be met with the assistance of a trained home visitor.

The most discouraging development of the year to the gerontologist in the U.S. was the cutback in governmental appropriations for research in biological sciences. Only about a third of U.S. medical schools have departments of preventive medicine and even fewer teach clinical gerontology or geriatrics. Health insurance coverage does not yet include payment for periodic health evaluations on an out-hospital basis, nor provision for follow-up care plus counseling services for health maintenance. (B. B. Mo.)

GYNECOLOGY AND OBSTETRICS

Cigarette smoking by women during pregnancy was blamed by C. S. Russell for restricting the growth of the fetus. With R. Taylor and C. E. Law he showed that smokers gave birth to babies who were on average about 6 oz. (170 g.) lighter than those born to nonsmokers. Abortion, stillbirth, and neonatal death were 3.8% higher among smoking women than among nonsmokers. This reduction in birth weight and increased fetal mortality could not be accounted for by differences in age, education, diet, or work done by mothers during pregnancy. An explanation for these findings was given by C. R. Lowe who suggested that the nicotine in tobacco restricts the flow of blood to the placenta and thereby reduces the supply of nutrients to the fetus.

H. Frederiksen used the data collected by M. P. Vessey and R. Doll to show also a potentiating effect of cigarettes on the tendency for oral contraceptives to cause thrombosis or embolism. The risk of thromboembolism was increased 7 times by the taking of oral contraceptives alone, but it was increased 23 times by their use in women who smoked more than 15 cigarettes a day, he pointed out.

M. R. Melamed and his co-workers reported on the results of cervical cytology in the screening of nearly 40,000 women who were attending Planned Parenthood centres in New York. They found that among women who were taking oral contraceptives (9.8 per 1,000) more than twice as many had a carcinoma in situ on the cervix than did those who were using a diaphragm (4.1 per 1,000). It was not clear whether this difference was due to a direct effect of the steroids on the cervical epithelium, to the diaphragm acting as a protective barrier against the theoretically damaging effect on the cervix of smegma or spermatozoa, or, as suggested by G. I. M. Swyer, because the women on oral contraceptives were more susceptible to carcinoma.

Following the report from Mexico that J. Martinez-Manautou had successfully prevented pregnancy with continuous daily low-dosage progestogen, several trials of similar steroids were held elsewhere in the hope of avoiding the adverse thrombogenic and metabolic effects believed to be due to the estrogen component of the conventional combined contraceptive pill. G. Foss and E. Mears reported on results obtained with daily doses of 0.05 mg. norgestrel, and Mears and associates reported on the use of 0.5 mg. chlormadinone acetate daily. These drugs were well tolerated and simple to use. The results obtained in British trials were less satisfactory than in those elsewhere and a method-failure of about 6 pregnancies per 100 woman-years was reported. Unfortunately in several trials between one-quarter and one-half of the patients withdrew because of irregular, heavy, or prolonged bleeding.

Prolongation of the first stage of labour for more than 24 hours had long been recognized in the primigravida as entailing an increased risk of fetal death and maternal morbidity. By convention, attempts to stimulate uterine contractions in such cases were withheld because of the fear of an underlying disproportion or occipitoposterior and a belief that fetal anoxia or rupture of the uterus might be the result. K. O'Driscoll and his colleagues in Dublin published the details of labour in 1,000 consecutive primigravidae, in only one of whom was labour allowed to go on for more than 24 hours. The cervix was slow to dilate in 119 cases so they ruptured the membranes. Progress then became satisfactory in 84 cases but in the remaining 35 labour was hastened with an infusion of oxytocin. The only limiting factor was fetal distress. Forceps or ventouse deliveries took place in 19%, caesarean section in 4%, and the perinatal mortality was 2.5%. There were no uterine ruptures.

During 1969 the number of legal operations performed in Great Britain under the Abortion Act of 1967 exceeded 40,000, more than half on single, divorced, or widowed women. About 45% took place outside the National Health Service in approved private nursing homes. Approximately one-fifth of patients operated on privately came from abroad. The chief medical officer of the Department of Health and Social Security, Sir George Godber, said that if the large number of legal terminations of pregnancy was accompanied by a diminution in the number of illegally procured abortions there would be a real reduction in the loss of maternal lives, abortion being a leading cause of maternal deaths. In 1968, however, when therapeutic abortions were increasing rapidly, the number of deaths from "spontaneous" abortion showed no reduction. A report in the U.S. showed that in two Eastern European countries readily available legal abortion had not reduced criminal abortions, nor, according to L. Huldt, had it done so in Sweden. Many authorities, pointing out that unwanted pregnancies should be prevented rather than terminated, stressed the need for wider dissemination of birth-control information and the establishment of easily accessible contraceptive clinics. (T. L. T. L.)

"LONDON DAILY EXPRESS" FROM PICTORIAL PARADE

Staff at University College Hospital, London, monitor growth and development of unborn child. The research equipment was expected to help physicians correct developing defects.

HEART AND CIRCULATORY DISEASES

The surgeon, assisted by refined diagnostic methods, has been able to improve or to cure a majority of infant heart conditions, permitting survival beyond the first few weeks of life. Because of the possi-

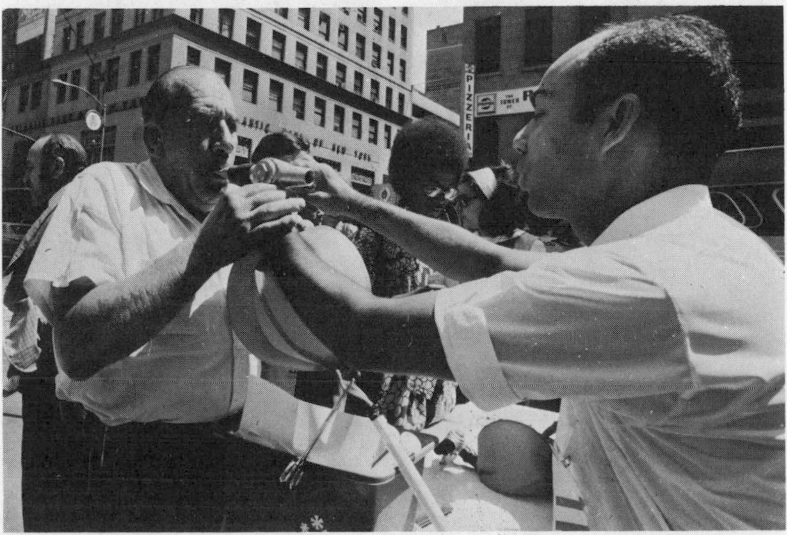

JOE BAKER FROM "MEDICAL WORLD NEWS"

New York City researchers sample pedestrian's breath on Manhattan street to determine the amount of carbon monoxide in bloodstream.

AUTHENTICATED NEWS INTERNATIONAL

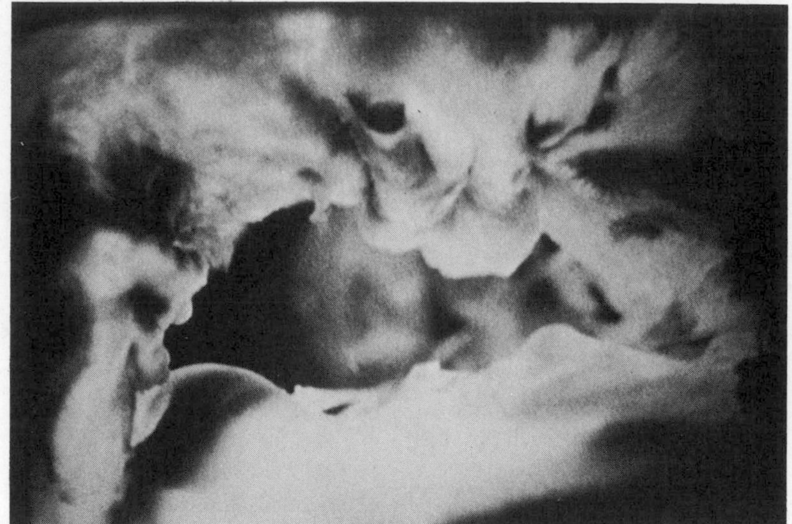

Frame from a film photographed inside a human heart shows scarring and shortening of the mitral valve cusps viewed from the left atrium. Made by Smith Kline & French Laboratories, the film was available to members of the medical profession.

COURTESY, HAMILTON STANDARD DIVISION OF UNITED AIRCRAFT CORP.

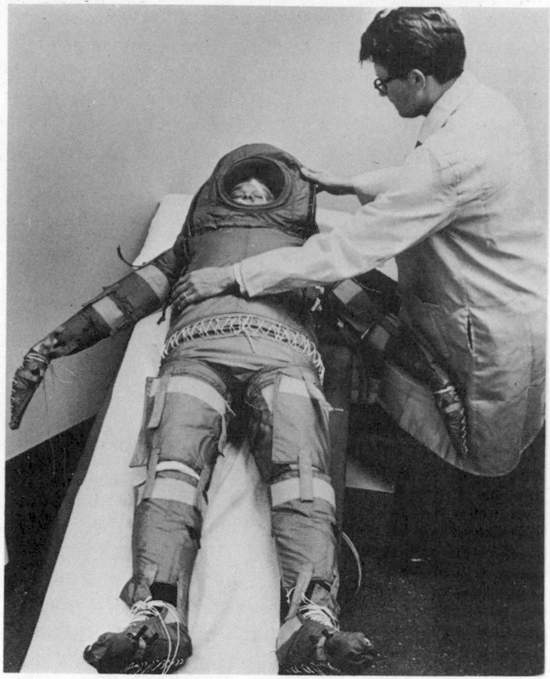

Styled after space suits, this pressure suit is used in heart research at the University of Texas Southwestern Medical School. In tests on animals it has achieved up to 30% increase in cardiac output.

bility of spontaneous improvement in certain small babies, operation has often been deferred to await the optimal time for intervention. Openings inside the heart (septal defects) have been known to close with the passage of time without the assistance of the surgeon. Recent studies have suggested that as many as 25% of the openings between the two lower chambers (ventricular septal defects) may close spontaneously in infancy and childhood. M. D. Li and his associates reported that 90% of such closures occur by the age of 8 years.

During 1969 interest intensified in the relationship between alcohol intake and heart disease. The exact nature of the effect on the heart was uncertain but it was considered that alcohol acted as a type of toxin actually damaging the heart. The features of this process were not specific, and were duplicated by certain other ill-defined forms of heart disease, usually grouped in the category of cardiomyopathies. If detected early, this form of heart disease due to alcohol might be reversible if the use of alcohol were stopped and a period of rest provided. When it was seen in its fully advanced form, however, treatment was unsatisfactory. Some physicians noted that alcoholic heart disease was not conspicuous where it might have been expected most—that is in institutions designed specifically to care for patients suffering from chronic alcoholism.

Natural rubber artificial heart (below) was designed by W. J. Kolff and C. S. Kwan-Gett at the University of Utah. It uses a heparin lining to prevent blood clots. Sac-type polyurethane heart (below right) was developed by S. F. Redo of Cornell University. It is powered by compressed air and water. Neither is ready for clinical use in humans.

COURTESY, DR. S. F. REDO, CORNELL UNIVERSITY SCHOOL OF MEDICINE AND DR. W. J. KOLFF, UNIVERSITY OF UTAH SCHOOL OF MEDICINE

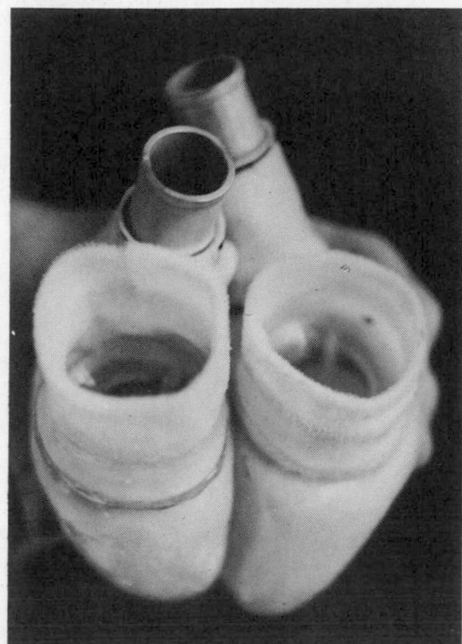

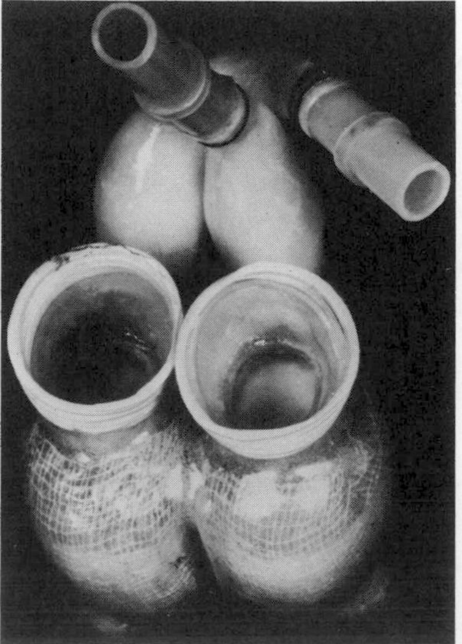

The thesis that hardening, or atherosclerosis, of the small blood vessels feeding the heart muscle (coronary arteries) was due to several factors which might operate singly or in combination was generally accepted. The factors most clearly implicated as prime offenders were elevations of blood cholesterol, high blood pressure, the use of cigarettes, and diabetes mellitus.

Scientists continued to uncover evidence that people living in regions with a soft water supply appeared to have a higher mortality from coronary heart trouble than residents of hard water areas. A recent report by J. R. Tiller and his associates also revealed that male workers exposed to carbon disulfide in viscose rayon factories had almost twice as many deaths from coronary heart disease as workers of the same age in other types of plants. All this seemed to reaffirm that the artery wall may deteriorate from a number of influences.

Methods of rescuing more people who suffered heart attacks outside a health care facility were studied. Mobile teams skilled in resuscitation, including the use of electric shock to terminate heartbeat irregularities, were being promoted. A. A. J. Adgey and co-workers reported in 1969 that 55 of 126 cardiac arrest cases outside a hospital were reached by a resuscitation unit within an estimated four minutes. Twenty-seven of these survived to leave the hospital to which they had been taken. The economics of this approach needed further study, and the answer for the future appeared to depend upon the detailed training of nonprofessional personnel to take the place of physicians.

The enthusiasm for transplantations of the heart waned late in 1969. Early successes were not followed by longer term good results; tissue typing was not a clear and simple answer to success; no new antiserum to prevent rejection had been found reliable; the reactions to the drugs used to prevent rejection were formidable; and the patients and their relatives became wary. The medical profession and the public also became distrustful and in some cases ordered restraints. The existence of even short-term success and the knowledge of the hopeless state of the recipients prompted a small group of dedicated workers to continue the study of the problem. The technical aspects of transplantation of the heart had been found to be surmountable. The recovery from the operation itself had been achieved many times. The issue was the one long known to science—that of maintaining acceptance by the body of an organ from another human. The issue had been joined but not resolved.

High blood pressure, or hypertension, is a recognized risk factor in coronary heart disease; even mild elevations of the blood pressure are of significance in increasing the likelihood of death. Recent studies demonstrated that not only was death from coronary disease more common among persons with hypertension, but so were other manifestations of coronary heart disease such as acute chest discomfort (angina pectoris) and heart attacks with survival. This association of high blood pressure with coronary disease exists in both sexes and in all adult groups. A. B. Baker and his co-workers showed that the patients with high blood pressure also had more extensive and severe hardening of the cerebral arteries than did those with normal blood pressures. (O. PL.)

HEMATOLOGY

A change in the treatment of iron-deficiency anemia was the increasing use of slow-release oral tablets or capsules of iron compounds. Investigation has shown that they are effective in about one-half of the conventional dose, and unpleasant side effects are much reduced. Two types of patients with iron-deficiency anemia, however, respond poorly or very slowly to all forms of oral iron therapy. In the first there is some defect in the ability of the red blood cell to use the iron that it takes up. The iron accumulates in the cytoplasm and can be stained there in the form of granules. This defect is sometimes familial and may be effectively treated with pyridoxine. In the second type the cause of the poor response is that the patient's iron stores are depleted and the iron that is absorbed goes into the store and not to the bone marrow for incorporation into hemoglobin. The physiological limitation of the rate of iron absorption may require many months of oral therapy to fill the store. This difficulty has been overcome by giving iron intravenously.

When a patient fails to absorb the necessary amount of iron from the food to cover normal loss, it is the iron stores in the liver and the muscles that become depleted first. Only when these stores are empty does the iron deficiency affect hemoglobin formation and lead to detectable anemia. There is now good evidence that this state of iron deficiency without anemia has a recognizable clinical picture with symptoms that will respond to iron treatment. The patients are mostly women who complain of fatigue, lack of energy, occasional sore tongue, and loss of appetite. If the condition is suspected the diagnosis can be confirmed by estimating the iron content of the serum, a routine laboratory procedure.

Blood platelets are the subject of much current research. It has been found that they play an essential part in stopping loss of blood from an injured blood vessel. When such an injury occurs, collagen fibres are exposed and passing platelets adhere to the fibres; these adherent platelets release a substance, adenosine diphosphate (ADP), that causes other platelets to aggregate on top of those already adhering to the damaged surface. These aggregated platelets release more ADP in their turn so that a chain reaction occurs that eventually blocks the tear. At the same time blood coagulation processes cause the formation of a clot. In patients subject to excessive bleeding, it has been found that both adhesiveness and aggregation may be defective, and that the defect can be inherited. It has long been known that the bleeding tendency could be inherited (hemophilia; Christmas disease). There are at least 13 known factors concerned with blood clotting, and rare cases of inherited defects have been found for each. There are other bleeders who may bleed for an unduly long time from small cuts. It is this group of bleeders who have defects of platelet function. One of these diseases is the inherited von Willebrand's disease which affects both sexes; patients may bleed excessively after such minor surgery as tooth extraction, but not spontaneously, and involvement of joints, the main disability of the hemophiliac, is rare. The bleeding time is always prolonged; there may be a low level of antihemophilic factor in the blood, but at least 10% of normal is present whereas true hemophiliacs have less than 10%. These patients have defective platelet adhesiveness, but platelet aggregation tests are normal. An important discovery was that the cryoprecipitate preparations for the treatment of hemophilia also correct the defects in von Willebrand's disease including the platelet adhesiveness. A similar syndrome is Glanzmann's thrombasthenia in which both platelet adhesiveness and aggregation are abnormal. The platelets fail to aggregate when exposed to ADP or collagen material. There is no defect of antihemophilic factor in this disease. Cryoprecipitate preparations are ineffective and no systemic technique for stopping the bleeding has been found.

A somewhat surprising discovery was that aspirin can cause defective platelet aggregation in some persons. Aspirin has been known for some time to cause stomach bleeding; the cause appears to be an interrelationship among local irritation, the platelet effect, and clotting factor VII.

Increasing attention is now being paid to the treatment of blood clots that form in blood vessels. Administration of anticoagulant drugs prevents the occurrence of fresh clots but cannot remove those already formed. Normally a blood clot is dissolved by the action of the fibrinolytic enzyme plasmin which is formed from an inactive precursor known as plasminogen. Activators of plasminogen are known to be urokinase (which occurs in human urine) and streptokinase (derived from streptococcal bacteria). Streptokinase therapy for thrombosis is especially valuable in the treatment of peripheral venous thrombosis and may be applicable as well to the early treatment of coronary thrombosis, pulmonary embolism, and in some other types of arterial thromboses. The treatment should be started as soon as possible after the presence of a clot is verified. If an overdose of streptokinase is administered, E-aminocaproic acid can be used as an antidote.

Streptokinase is unsuitable for long-term use, but several drugs are known to act as activators of fibrinolysis and several others have been tried. Recently a combination of phenformin, a drug actually developed as an antidiabetic agent, and ethylestrenol was given a thorough trial over a three-year period with satisfactory results; some salicylic acid derivatives also show promise. So far none of these methods has

D.P.A. FROM PICTORIAL PARADE

German clinic for diagnosis being built in Wiesbaden, W.Ger., to be the first of its kind in Europe. Scheduled for completion in April 1970, the facility was to include a diagnostic clinic, sick rooms for 90 patients, a guest-patient hotel with 260 beds, and apartment houses for nurses and physicians.

proved of value in the important group of cerebral thromboses. (M. C. G. I.)

HOSPITALS

The progress attained in the practice of medicine led to an increased tendency of teaching hospitals to select cases that would benefit from the more sophisticated methods of diagnosis and treatment. The opinion was held that they did not correctly fulfill their task of training medical students for day-to-day practice in which the common diseases are by far the most frequent.

Some changes in the concept of the teaching hospital have been implemented, the most revolutionary probably being that in the teaching hospital in Brasília. There a full integration of preventive and curative medicine was achieved through the administering of health centres by the medical school and its hospital in order to offer students a full range of social medical problems. The extension of this concept to the new medical school and teaching hospital in Yaoundé, Cameroon, was under consideration by the World Health Organization and the French bilateral assistance organization.

The other extreme was represented by the first achievements in the French reform concerning the University Hospital Centre. The combination of all medical disciplines, each of them with an average of 60 to 90 hospital beds, led to a large and complex hospital with from 1,500 to 2,000 beds, difficult to plan, manage, and adapt to changing circumstances. In order to extend the spectrum of medical care, the French University Hospital Centre collaborated with general hospitals in the various regions for intern training of medical students.

The need for planning new teaching hospitals was also recognized in other countries. In Belgium the separation of Flemish- and French-speaking universities necessitated the construction of new hospitals in Brussels, Liège, and Louvain.

In Italy a law was passed in 1968 creating regional hospital boards but its implementation was under discussion with local authorities and private voluntary bodies. In the U.S. it was noteworthy that in the majority of states legalities regarding the regionalization of hospitals were under discussion. Despite very careful wording in the proposals, many of these projects were rejected or delayed.

The implementation of the U.S. Medicare and Medicaid programs also faced various difficulties because some states were refusing to cover their 30% share.

Elderly patients picket in front of the Department of Health headquarters in London in September 1969. The oldsters asked to keep their homey 23-bed War Memorial Hospital in Ongar open despite the hospital board's charge that it is uneconomical and outdated.

"LONDON DAILY EXPRESS" FROM PICTORIAL PARADE

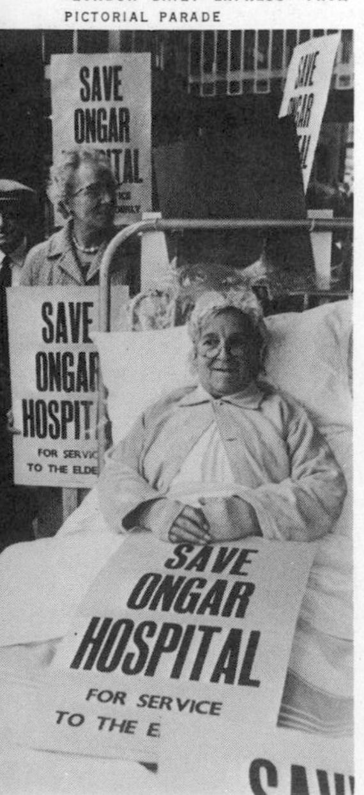

An event of considerable magnitude was the approval by the International Labour Conference, held in Geneva in June, of the list of revised conventions providing for an extended coverage of health expenditure by social security schemes. In addition to the traditional benefits, the cost of personal preventive care and rehabilitation was to be considered as an activity reimbursable by social security funds.

Financing of hospital systems required drastic revision. When projects were suggested in less developed countries, private hospital building firms were inclined to make tenders exceeding by four or five times the amount of the cost for a similar hospital in Europe, due to transportation, insurance, and the assembly of imported parts.

In developed countries severe cuts had been made in hospital building budgets. At the same time there was a steep increase in the cost of specialized equipment, in the requirement for necessary qualified personnel, and in the cost of medical care.

In the U.S. the per diem cost of hospitalization rose alarmingly, a subject for much discussion at the annual meetings of the various health and medical care associations. One West Coast hospital showed a drastic cut in costs by using disposables throughout the institution—even for linens and dishes. Another, in Louisiana, cut diet kitchen costs almost in half by computerized menu planning. More and more hospitals, in the U.S. and Sweden particularly, were computerizing many of their functions—not only business office activities, but also laboratory, medical records, patient monitoring, and numerous others. (R. F. Br.)

IMMUNOLOGY

Resistance to infection, according to the 80-year-old discovery of Elie Metchnikoff, is brought about by the ability of the phagocytic cells of the body to engulf the invading microorganisms and to destroy them with intracellular materials which he called cytases. Shortly after Metchnikoff's discovery came the observation that the body also synthesized substances, termed antibodies, which were present in the serum.

The work of Z. Cohn revealed that the cytases of Metchnikoff are real and the macrophages have a number of hydrolytic enzymes enclosed within lyso-

Schoolchildren in Jamaica receive the Cendehill strain of rubella (German measles) vaccine in clinical trials under direction of Louis Grant, head of the microbiology department at University of West Indies. The vaccine was first granted a license by health authorities in Switzerland in 1969.

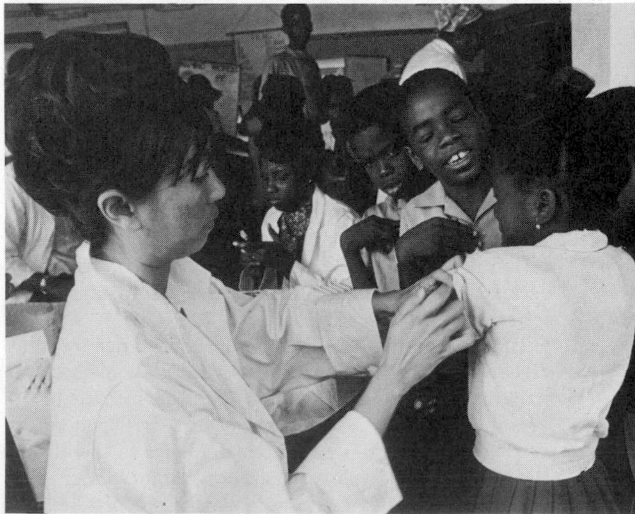

AUTHENTICATED NEWS INTERNATIONAL

somes. The latter rupture during the phagocytic process, and in many cases the released enzymes are capable of killing the microorganisms.

Some years ago it was shown that natural resistance to Arbor B viruses in two inbred strains of mice could be attributed to the presence of a single dominant gene in the genotypes of these mice. Both in vivo and in vitro experiments demonstrated that the phenotypic expression of the dominant gene for virus resistance was present in the macrophage cells of the genetically resistant mice. Tissue cultures of peritoneal macrophages prepared from individual mice of the eighth generation of backcrossing between virus-resistant hybrids and virus-susceptible mice were exposed to virus. Half of the cultures failed to support virus multiplication while the remaining cultures yielded the infectious virus. Thus the distribution of immunity and susceptibility in macrophage cultures reflected the cellular level genes segregating for virus immunity and susceptibility of the whole animal level.

Mouse typhoid is a naturally occurring infection that provides an excellent experimental model of the generalized salmonella infections of man. Living vaccines protect against virulent challenge whereas vaccines prepared from organisms killed by a variety of methods do little more than prolong microbial survival time. Passive transfer of serum from the actively infected or live-vaccinated animals increased the capacity of the host to clear organisms from its blood but in no way could it interfere with their subsequent multiplication in other tissues.

It could be shown that the mice exposed to living organisms had present on the surface of their macrophages a 7S gamma globulin. Moreover, RNA extracts from such immune macrophages when transferred to normal, nonimmune macrophages induced them to synthesize this 7S gamma globulin and manifest immune activity against the challenging infectious organism. Although these macrophages have arrived at this state by exposure to organism A, they are equally capable of phagocytizing organisms B and C. One possible explanation for this phenomenon is that as a consequence of contact with the macrophage, the living microorganism induces the macrophage to synthesize the 7S gamma globulin, which, in turn, activates the macrophage for nonspecific increased phagocytosis and killing potential. It has been shown that such macrophages kill over 95% of the ingested microorganisms within four minutes. To illustrate that the situation is not confined to the *Salmonella*, macrophages made immune to *Brucella* handle *Mycobacterium tuberculosis* equally as well. The reverse is also true.

There is present in humans a condition called chronic granulomatous disease of childhood. Afflicted children are repeatedly infected, usually by staphylococci, although other bacteria can be involved. What is known about these patients is that their lack of immunity is not due to the inability to form antibodies, but rather that the polymorphonuclear leukocytes (PMN's) are defective in bactericidal activity. Thus, although the PMN's are capable of phagocytosis, the killing capacity is absent.

An additional example of the lack of immunity related to possible metabolic blockage of killing capacity exists in the Chediak-Higashi syndrome. Children with this condition have repeated cutaneous infections, unexplained pyrexic episodes, recurrent oral ulcers, and pneumonia. (A. S. M.)

"TORONTO STAR"

"Whole body counter," connected to a data machine that details findings for doctors, scans a patient for radioactivity. The $320,000 counter was unveiled at Toronto General Hospital March 12, 1969.

INSTRUMENTATION

Although the computer has not yet acquired the position in medicine it occupies in commerce and industry, more and more biomedical computer applications are being employed each year. In addition to hospital business office and administrative functions, it is involved in laboratory analyses, chromosome mapping, electrocardiogram and electroencephalogram analyses, pulmonary function studies, and numerous others.

In radiotherapy, on the basis of critical doses in excess of which destruction of tissue occurs, the physician can use the computer to establish an irradiation schedule to ensure that the critical doses are exceeded only at sites where malignant tissues are localized.

The computer is also used to establish factors of importance for diagnostic evaluation (*e.g.*, heart rate) on the basis of the electrocardiogram. Comparison with pathological electrocardiograms stored in its memory enables the computer to diagnose the condition in question. A computer print-out of the values measured is almost immediately available to the physician. The diagnostic reliability has proved to be 99%. In most cases these data will merely serve as corroboration of the physician's conclusion.

A different situation, however, prevails in population surveys. Results made available in 1969 show that 41% of normal humans produced some sort of abnor-

Utilizing tiny camera mounted on a glass-fibre tube and introduced into patient's stomach, colour television is used in diagnosis and for benefit of medical students at Erlangen University Clinic in West Germany.

PICTORIAL PARADE

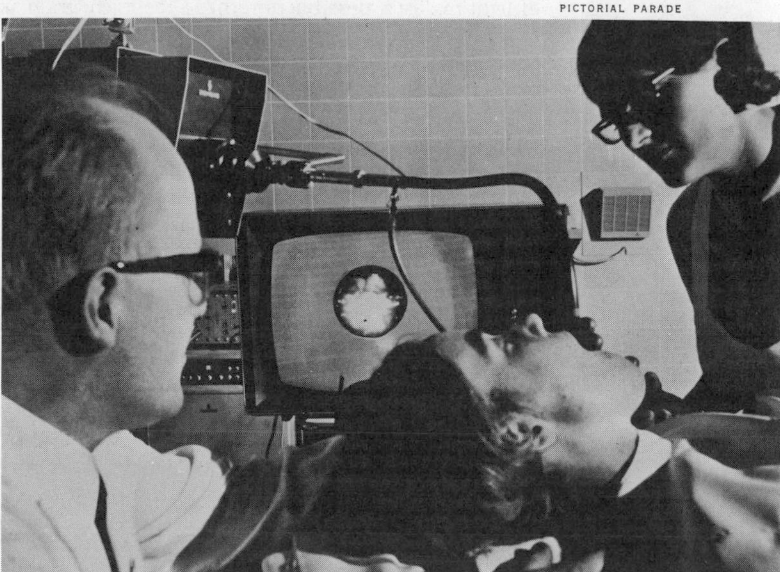

mality in the ECG that made them potential cardiac patients. Surveys of this type can be carried out only with the aid of the computer, however, because a classical procedure would require an impossible amount of manpower and time.

Another possible application is the surveillance of critically ill patients (patient monitoring) who can be watched continuously, and dangerous situations signaled immediately. The attending physician can read, at any time, a print-out of important physiological measurements (pulse, heart rate, etc.) taken on an hourly basis—an impossibility without computer assistance.

In a neonatal ward, the respiration of newborns was monitored by a computer. In 85% of the computer alarms, the nursing staff had been unaware of the occurrence of a respiratory disturbance (dyspnea). In 55% of these cases artificial respiration was necessary.

The ultrasonic Doppler effect, named after its discoverer and based on the change in frequency of sound waves transmitted through a moving medium, was successfully used in 1969 to measure flow rates of blood and to study heart contractions. Fetal heart movements can now be recorded with great accuracy; it is also possible to study heart movements that are important to the diagnosis of arrhythmia.

New possibilities for continuously charging pacemakers are being explored. A bio-autofuel cell has been developed which, deriving its energy from the extracellular fluid, supplies the power for the electronic impulse generator of the instrument. For defects in atrioventricular conduction, a pacemaker has been developed that automatically stimulates the ventricle after each atrial contraction.

A measuring device for estimating the length of time implanted pacemakers can function without disturbance has been designed and a radiographic technique evolved for the control of the charges of mercury cells in implanted pacemakers. A new heart-assist device, the intra-aortic balloon pump, was recently introduced. A balloon is inserted into the aorta with an arterial probe and is periodically inflated at the command of the ECG by means of an external pressure source. Arterial blood pressure is thus increased enhancing the efficiency of the heart and the blood flow to the tissues.

An interesting device for holographic reproduction of X-ray images was described. The undular character of light makes it possible to record a roentgenogram as an interference pattern on a special photographic (hologram) plate in a special arrangement. By rotating the plate in this arrangement, for example, successive images can be recorded on the same plate. This principle is known as holographic multiplexing. Applied to X rays obtained by means of an apparatus in which roentgen tube and film camera orbit around the patient, holographic multiplexing makes it possible to obtain spatial X-ray images that permit more detailed interpretation.

For tetraplegics (those incapable of movement at any level below the neck), a voice-operated typewriter has been designed. Orders are given in Morse code and converted into type by the machine.

Improved hearing aids are available for auditory defectives in which the traumatic effect of pulsating sounds is suppressed. (G. P. M. H.)

MEDICAL EDUCATION

In the U.S. the shortage of manpower continued to prevail in every phase of medical service during 1969. The Association of American Medical Colleges assumed an increasingly important role in medical education, and was concerned as well with standardization, publicity, and public relations in the field.

In 1968, 99 medical schools were accredited. The following table indicates the estimated number of medical schools and students enrolled annually through 1974:

Year	Number of students*	Number of schools
1969–70	10,264	101
1970–71	10,578	102
1971–72	11,031	107
1972–73	11,651	107
1973–74	12,088	107

*First year enrollments.

Additional schools established in 1969 were the Louisiana State University Medical School at Shreveport and the Medical College of Ohio at Toledo. In 1970–71, the University of Massachusetts at Worcester would accept its first class of students. In 1971–72, five additional schools would enroll freshman classes: University of South Florida at Tampa, University of Missouri at Kansas City, University of Nevada at Reno, State University of New York at Stony Brook, and the University of Texas at Houston.

Approved schools giving only the first two years of medicine were the University of Hawaii School of Medicine at Honolulu; Dartmouth Medical School at Hanover, N.H.; Rutgers at New Brunswick, N.J.; the University of North Dakota at Grand Forks; Brown University at Providence, R.I.; and the University of South Dakota at Vermillion.

Medical schools under development, some of which had already started early classes, were: University of Arizona College of Medicine at Tucson; University of California School of Medicine at Davis; University of California School of Medicine at San Diego; University of Connecticut School of Medicine at Farmington; Michigan State University College of Human Medicine at East Lansing; Mount Sinai School of Medicine at New York City; Pennsylvania State University College of Medicine, Milton S. Hershey Medical Center at Hershey; University of Texas Medical School at San Antonio.

The need for postgraduate medical education was becoming more apparent. The *Journal of the American Medical Association* published a list of all of the training courses available in this field. (M. Fi.)

MICROBIOLOGY

Pasteur realized that some relations between man and certain microbial agents might be mutually beneficial types of symbiosis. The presence of bacteria in the intestinal tract, for example, might actually be beneficial to man or animal, rather than harmful. Many of the bacteria that inhabit the lower portion of the small intestine produce vitamins of the B complex as a part of their normal metabolic process. The primary site of absorption of these vitamins, however, is in the upper intestine, not in that portion where the bacteria are most plentiful. Thus, it is not certain that this represents any real beneficial effect of the presence of bacteria. With the development of means of growing animals in a germ-free (gnotobiotic) environment, further investigation of the role of bacteria in the life of animals has become possible. Recently, further investigation of gnotobiotic rats and mice has revealed that in the intestine of such animals there is an accumulation of at least two substances, one of which is a toxin and the other, one that exerts significant effects on muscles, especially smooth muscle. This latter substance, called muscle active substance (MAS), appears to accumulate in the tissues and in the cecal content. The animal tends to develop a greatly enlarged cecum with thickened, irregular walls and may suffer from considerable digestive irregularity. Significantly, MAS is neutralized by the bacteria in the intestine. Thus, the normal bacterial flora of the intestine seem to play a role in preventing the ill effects of the accumulation of MAS. This is most suggestive evidence for a beneficial effect of bacteria living in close association with an animal.

A promising vaccine against rubella (German measles) has been developed; this disease can be almost eliminated or, at least, reduced to a low prevalence.

In another, and to a degree unrelated, field, microbiology has been playing a major role in one of the most exciting series of observations of recent years. Molecular biologists have been unraveling the mysteries of the genetic code. Recently two groups of investigators (University of Wisconsin and Massachusetts Institute of Technology) have independently crystallized the first nucleic acid. It was a molecule of transfer-RNA, one of several species of RNA, which are involved in the directing of protein synthesis. This molecule was crystallized from the bacterium *Escherichia coli*. The crystallization will now make it possible, for the first time, for biochemists to study the three-dimensional structure of this RNA molecule. Such studies will help explain the whole mechanism of protein synthesis at the molecular level.

Information on the problem of initiation of protein synthesis has recently been provided from work also done with *E. coli*. Whether this work is applicable to mammalian cells has yet to be elucidated. Proteins are synthesized under the direction of DNA and RNA on subcellular particles called ribosomes. These ribosomes are made of two subunits. The initiation of protein synthesis begins by the dissociation of the two subunits. One special type of initiating amino acid hooks up to one of these subunits. This, in turn, hooks up to the other subunit, and protein synthesis begins. Observations like this will eventually lead to a more complete understanding of the mechanisms of disease as well as to a better understanding of phenomena in what may seem a totally unrelated field such as genetics. (JA. G. S.)

NEUROLOGY

The treatment of parkinsonism with L-dopa (L-3,4-dihydroxyphenylalanine) continued to attract general attention throughout the year. There is no doubt that this drug, administered in comparatively large doses, offers substantial relief from the symptoms of Parkinson's disease, particularly the inertia, rigidity, and, to a lesser extent, tremor. To avoid nausea the dose has to be built up gradually; side effects, sometimes unpleasant, take the form of different types of involuntary movements. The overall cost of the drug, because of the large doses necessary, remains high, but there is prospect of the development of another drug that reduces the peripheral decarboxylation of L-dopa, possibly allowing the use of smaller doses. A woman with severe parkinsonism who was taking amantadine hydrochloride as an antiviral agent (for A2 [Asian] influenza) reported that her parkinsonism was a great deal better during this therapy. This information led to a large trial of amantadine in other sufferers from parkinsonism. Published results show that two-thirds of the patients benefited, and the side effects encountered so far, in about one-fifth, were not serious and disappeared within 36 hours after cessation of the amantadine therapy. At the end of 1969 L-dopa was still not released for prescription use.

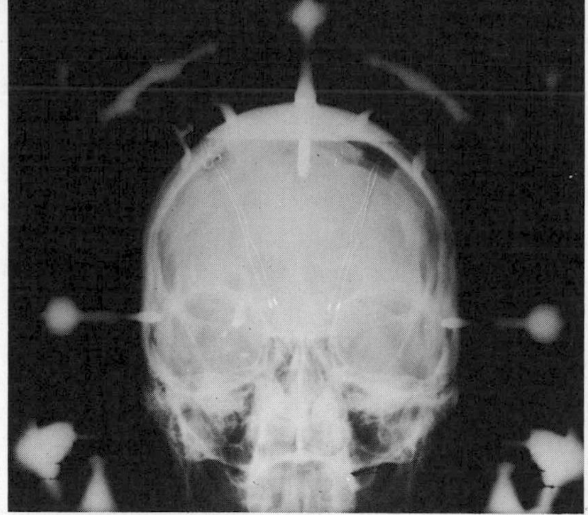

COURTESY, DR. BERTRAM FEINSTEIN, MT. ZION HOSPITAL, SAN FRANCISCO

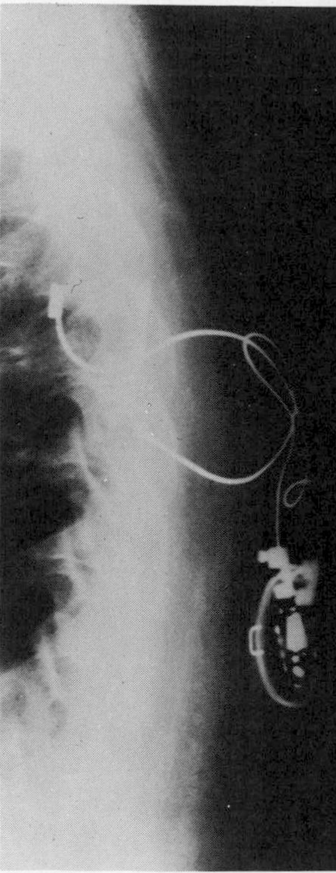

COURTESY, DR. NORMAN SHEALY, LACROSSE, WIS.

X-ray stereotaxic brain map (above left) of patient with movement disorder. Treatment developed by Bertram Feinstein of Mount Zion Hospital, San Francisco, included inserting thin probes to produce brain lesion with radiofrequency energy. X ray (above) of electrode implanted in spinal column of patient suffering intense chronic pain. Controlled by tiny adjustable radio transmitter, the electrode relieves pain by jamming the pain messages sent to brain. Device was developed by C. N. Shealy of the Gunderson Clinic in LaCrosse, Wis.

One by-product of the excitement over organ transplant surgery has been the controversy over the definition of death. Until recent years the belief that death occurs when the heart stops had gone unchallenged. What has happened recently is that critically ill patients have been given assisted respiration (which ensures adequate oxygen supply) and the heart has continued beating when other tissues, and particularly the brain, have been irreversibly damaged. Under these circumstances recovery is impossible. The need of the transplant surgeon is for organs that are still viable when irreversible brain damage has occurred, and for the earliest possible recognition of the type of brain damage that is considered irrevocable. Severe head injury with marked brain damage, severe brain hemorrhage, and malignant tumour of the brain in its terminal stages all lead to coma and finally to the cessation of spontaneous respiration. If these patients are placed in a respirator the criterion of cessation of respiration which would lead to cardiac arrest is invalidated, for the machine will go on working until it is switched off. An electroencephalogram (EEG) may help in demonstrating the absence of any electrical activity of the brain, and a repeat record a few hours later will add conviction to the belief that brain activity has ceased. That even this safeguard is insufficient is exemplified by the report that intoxication with barbiturates may give a so-called flat EEG record repeatedly and yet recovery can still take place. Obviously there is no room for error in clinical judgment here, for the switching off of the machine, and extending an invitation to the transplant surgeon to seek the permission of the relatives for the removal of organs, is quite irrevocable. The only possible criterion is that the degree of brain damage is so gross that there can be no doubt that recovery is impossible. Those who have this neurological responsibility of declaring the brain damage to be lethal must exercise extreme caution. Under some circumstances other organs also will have lost their viability and consequently their possible use to a transplant surgeon. This cannot be helped, for the needs of donor and recipient are necessarily exclusive of one another. If all the safeguards are taken and every attempt is made to resuscitate the donor, then the public at large can only gain in reassurance and organ transplant surgery in general acceptance.

Less controversial and more enlightening are the developing techniques of histochemical study of muscle diseases, and particularly the muscular dystrophies.

It is now known that some forms of congenital muscular dystrophy are comparatively benign, and consistent with a long life span. These pathological studies of a muscle biopsy, together with biochemical and enzyme measurements, as well as electromyographic examination, all help in the clarification of the clinical picture. Although the prognosis may be immeasurably better in some forms than in others, and hence the importance of an exact classified diagnosis, there is still no rational treatment for muscular dystrophy.

(K. J. Z.)

NURSING

An outstanding event in nursing in 1969 was the Quadrennial Congress of the International Council of Nurses (ICN), held in Montreal in June and attended by 10,000 nurses from more than 80 countries. The overall theme of "Focus on the Future" reflected the trends, problems, and hopes of 1969 and involved more than 250 international speakers. A new plan for "Nursing Abroad" through sponsorship of ICN member associations was approved; attention was drawn to the trend to form regional groups of nurses' associations; and the question of auxiliary nursing personnel was debated. A $6,000 nursing fellowship, financed by the Medical Products Division of Minnesota Mining and Manufacturing Co., to be administered by ICN, was announced.

In Detroit over 3,000 members of the National Student Nurses' Association gathered to discuss "nursing at the turn of the century." Nursing students in many countries were taking an increasingly active part in their educational programs.

Advances in education were under discussion and criticism. At the international level the World Health Organization (WHO) document "Guide Lines for the Development of Post-Basic Education for Nurses" attracted interest. At the national level in the U.S., the American Nurses' Association's (ANA) "Statement on Graduate Education in Nursing" would no doubt provoke as much discussion as its predecessor on basic nursing education. The General Nursing Council for England and Wales published its revised syllabus for basic nursing education. In the Canadian province of Quebec the transfer of all hospital schools of nursing into the colleges of general and professional education was completed.

The trend to university education at basic, postbasic, and postgraduate level continued. Of the 314 schools of nursing known to exist in the Latin-American and Caribbean areas of the region covered by the Pan American Health Organization (PAHO, regional office of WHO), only 13 had programs leading to a basic university degree, but there was increasing interest in the establishment of programs on the university level. In South Africa six universities had introduced basic four-year courses by 1969. In the U.K. a bachelor of nursing degree replaced the diploma in community nursing at the University of Manchester.

Focus was on legislation for nursing education and practice, with a publication from ICN, already widely distributed, to be used for an international seminar.

Nurses themselves were concerned about maintenance and improvement of standards of practice in the face of increased demand for nursing services and rapid technological change. The American Nurses' Association's Congress for Nursing Practice had responsibility to define, develop, and implement a program for the improvement of the practice of nursing, while staff and committees were exploring the nature of clinical practice in various areas to establish standards by which practice could be assessed.

There was increasing interest to improve psychiatric nursing services and include this course in basic educational programs, and the trend toward considering midwifery as postbasic to nursing was especially noticeable in Latin-American countries.

National planning of the nursing component of health services and the development of national systems of nursing personnel received attention. In November an intercountry workshop was sponsored by WHO's Regional Office for South-East Asia in Delhi, and in Mexico PAHO/WHO held a workshop for a group of 25 nurses. Studies of some aspects of utilization of nursing manpower resources were being carried out in Argentina, the Dominican Republic, Guatemala, and Guyana.

A recent WHO symposium in Budapest, Hung., on health manpower requirements noted the importance of nursing personnel in Europe, while in Switzerland a report on the utilization of nursing personnel in Swiss hospitals was published after three years of study. (S. M. Q.)

NUTRITION

Despite claims and counterclaims regarding the nutritional status of population groups in the U.S., precise data have not been available on the prevalence of malnutrition. Arnold Schaefer described the initial phase of a National Nutrition Survey planned to identify the incidence, magnitude, and location of malnutrition and related health problems within low income areas of ten states.

The survey was structured to include four types of information: (1) general household socioeconomic data; (2) dietary intake data; (3) physical examinations; and (4) laboratory analysis.

Early reports indicated that in areas where the survey had been completed, malnutrition did exist in the United States and in 10–25% of the sample. The National Nutrition Survey should point the way to appropriate programs for relieving areas where nutritive intake is less than that considered necessary for optimal health.

The Food and Nutrition Board of the National Research Council published the seventh revision of its well-known *Recommended Dietary Allowances* (RDA). These allowances are intended to serve as goals for planning food supplies and as guides for the interpretation of food consumption records of people. The actual nutritional status of groups of healthy individuals or groups of people must be judged on the basis of physical, biochemical, and clinical observations combined with observations of food or nutrient intakes. The RDA are not to be interpreted as nutritional requirements for individuals. If the RDA are used as reference standards for interpreting records of food consumption, it should not be assumed that malnutrition will occur whenever the recommendations are not completely met.

In the revision there are recommendations for the intake of seven nutrients not previously included: phosphorus, iodine, magnesium, vitamin B_6, vitamin E, vitamin B_{12}, and folacin. Some changes were made in the recommendations for other nutrients. For the purpose of estimating calorie allowances, a "reference" man and woman were used and described as 22 years of age and weighing 154 and 128 lb., respectively. Calorie allowances were reduced to 2,800 for the reference man and 2,000 for the reference woman.

Statistical data indicated that the most favourable health expectations are associated with conditions under which weight as normally achieved by age 22 is maintained throughout life. Energy requirements decline progressively after the years of early adulthood because of a decrease in resting metabolic rate, as well as lessened physical activity. In the diets of females, 18 mg. of iron daily was recommended. This is an increase over the previous RDA and was recommended because of widespread occurrence of iron-deficiency anemia in the U.S. (See *Hematology,* above.) A slight reduction in the amount of protein, vitamin C, and niacin and a slight increase in thiamine appeared in the new recommendations.

A revised statement by the American Heart Association on "Diet and Heart Disease" notes that "coronary heart disease is the result of many factors. Diets rich in saturated fat and cholesterol represent one important risk factor which can be safely modified." The following recommendations are for relatively healthy individuals to reduce dietary risk factors. They are particularly applicable to those with increased blood levels of cholesterol and other lipids or who have other characteristics that make them more susceptible to coronary heart disease: (1) A caloric intake adjusted to achieve and maintain desirable weight. Correction of obesity may reduce elevated serum lipid concentrations. (2) A decrease in the ingestion of saturated fats with a corresponding increase in polyunsaturated fats. An intake of somewhat less than 40% of calories from fat is considered desirable, and of this total, polyunsaturated fats should comprise at least the same quantity as saturated fats, preferably more, with the balance coming from monounsaturated fats. (3) A substantial reduction in dietary cholesterol. The average daily diet in the U.S. contains approximately 600 mg. cholesterol. Reduction in dietary cholesterol will help reduce the concentration of serum cholesterol in most people. In hypercholesterolemic individuals, reduction of dietary cholesterol to less than 300 mg. daily is recommended.

These changes, it was pointed out, can readily be made in the diet and will lessen the chances of developing coronary heart disease. (F. J. Se.; Je. Wi.)

OCCUPATIONAL MEDICINE

The choice of "Health, Labour, and Productivity" as the theme for World Health Day, 1969, indicated the importance placed on occupational health at an international level. In contrast to the similarity in legislative protection of workers against specific toxic and other physical hazards found in almost every country of the world, there were wide national and international differences in the provision and scope of health services for various occupational groups. In Britain the subject was excluded from the National Health Service, and although the legislative framework of the appointed factory doctor service was about to be recast, it was likely, for the time being, to remain outside the mainstream of medicine. In the European Economic Community such a health service, geared almost exclusively to prevention, was likely to become mandatory; in Communist countries a comprehensive service was provided by the state.

One sign of the growth of occupational medicine and its related discipline of occupational hygiene has been the recent significant expansion of university departments. With demands for time on the undergraduate medical curriculum greater than ever before, virtually all medical schools now included some basic training in this subject, a marked contrast to the situation only a few years earlier. The establishment of two new institutes of occupational health within the universities of London and Edinburgh brought Britain into line with similar developments in other countries. The London institute was establishing an occupational hygiene service to assess and control environmental hazards. The need for occupational health care of hospital staff had been accepted in the National Health Service and a number of such units were being developed.

Defined populations and adequate employment records have enabled some occupational groups to be utilized for valuable epidemiological research. Although national mortality data from the registrar general has long been used to assess the degree of risk in relation to occupation, the validity of some of this information is open to serious question. R. S. F. Schilling's investigation into the mortality of trawler fishermen has now established that this occupation has a 17-fold risk of death from accidents at work and that death rates from lung cancer, hypertension, and bronchitis among trawler fishermen are also higher than expected.

The recent finding that rayon spinners exposed to carbon disulfide 20 years ago had an excess mortality from coronary heart disease suggests that hazards at work may reveal themselves by an increased susceptibility to general medical conditions. L. E. Hinkle's observation that coronary heart disease is less frequent among managers and executives than in foremen and workers of the Bell Telephone System raised doubts about the popular view of coronary-prone executives.

Interest in the role of occupational factors in the etiology of chronic bronchitis was renewed by the results of careful studies reported by C. R. Lowe and his colleagues in South Wales and also from investigations among flax spinners in Northern Ireland. The evidence now suggests that, after allowing for smoking habits, continued exposure to dusty environments may well be an important cause.

It has become possible to measure the risk of developing asbestosis in relation to the degree and length of exposure to the dust in one large factory, but unfortunately relatively few organizations keep the necessary information. The value of linked medical records with computer analysis has been clearly demonstrated by the finding that a rare malignant tumour of the nasal cavity or sinuses is many times more prevalent in woodworkers of the furniture industry.

Black lung is a form of pneumoconiosis, a chronic lung inflammation caused by inhaling coal dust over long periods of time. Tissue changes ensue, frequently accompanied by bronchitis, emphysema, or cancer. As a result, soft-coal miners in the U.S. have death rates twice as high as the general population. At the end of 1969, after considerable popular agitation concerning black lung and other mine hazards, the U.S. Congress overwhelmingly approved the Federal Coal Mine Safety Act, the strongest coal mine health and safety measure in history. (P. J. T.)

OPHTHALMOLOGY

Diabetic retinopathy, the third most frequent cause of blindness in the U.S. and Great Britain, has been receiving increased attention. Approximately 80% of patients who have had diabetes mellitus for more than 25 years develop abnormal dilations (aneurysms) in the walls of the capillaries of the retina. Diabetes

Francis L'Esperance uses laser beam to treat eye disorders at Columbia-Presbyterian Medical Center in New York City. Beam was successfully used during 1969 to seal faulty retinal arteries.

JOHN SENZER FROM "MEDICAL WORLD NEWS"

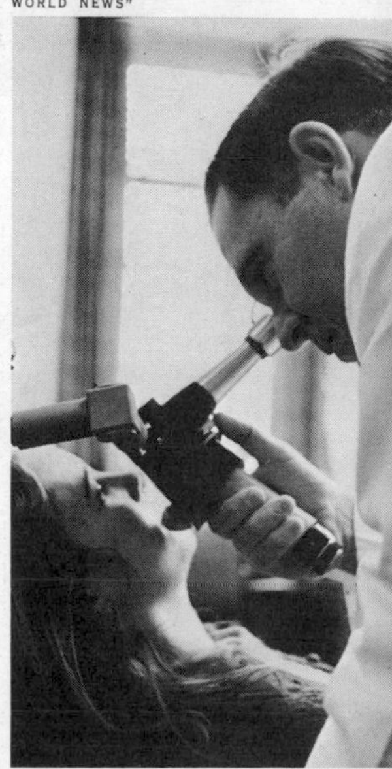

does not cause similar capillary aneurysms elsewhere in the body. These outpouchings on the vessel wall may be associated with bleeding into the retina and into the interior of the eye, and there may be an accumulation of fatty products in the retina. An overgrowth of retinal blood vessels occurs in a small percentage of patients, and these may extend into locations within the eye that are normally transparent.

Treatment of these blood vessel abnormalities has been unsatisfactory. For many years the only method was careful control of the diabetes mellitus by means of diet and insulin. A large number of patients have been treated since 1965 by a number of methods devised to decrease pituitary secretion. Pituitary gland removal prevents further deterioration of the retina in about 60% of the patients. More recently, areas of capillary proliferation in the retina have been coagulated by means of a xenon arc or laser. Controlled studies are extremely difficult, and the technique is indicated only in selected cases because it requires that the optic media of the eye be transparent so that the interior may be seen.

When the eye is stimulated with light, a characteristic pattern of electrical waves arises in the brain, the visually evoked response. This response is affected by "attention" or mental state. Thus the brain activity arising when the eye is stimulated with light is decreased when the person carries out simple arithmetic problems. Such studies provide the first solid reproducible experiments whereby "thinking" can be detected by an objective measuring device.

Fluorescein is a dye that has been used in the diagnosis of superficial conditions of the eye for many years. Since about 1950, the dye has been injected into the body to measure the secretion and flow of fluids within the eye. In 1961 photographic techniques were developed to record the passage of fluorescein in the retinal blood vessels. Such photographs have proved of value in a number of ocular conditions. Ordinarily, the back of the eye is studied by means of white light and sometimes with red, green, or blue light. In fluorescein studies, the interior eye is illuminated by means of ultraviolet light which causes fluorescein to emit green light.

Following injection of the fluorescein, it is possible to measure the transit time of dye through the eye and observe its slowing during disease processes. Even in conditions in which blood vessels appear not to carry blood, study with fluorescein may indicate that the vessels indeed are open, but that their walls are opaque. Such studies, which are becoming extremely widespread, have led to a much better understanding of a number of diseases of the eye, together with effective therapy of conditions that were previously unresponsive to treatment. (F. W. N.)

University of California surgeon W. R. Murray holds a two-part prosthesis of the type that his surgery team has used in total hip joint replacement. Successful results were reported by Murray in 1969.

DENNIS GALLOWAY FROM "MEDICAL WORLD NEWS"

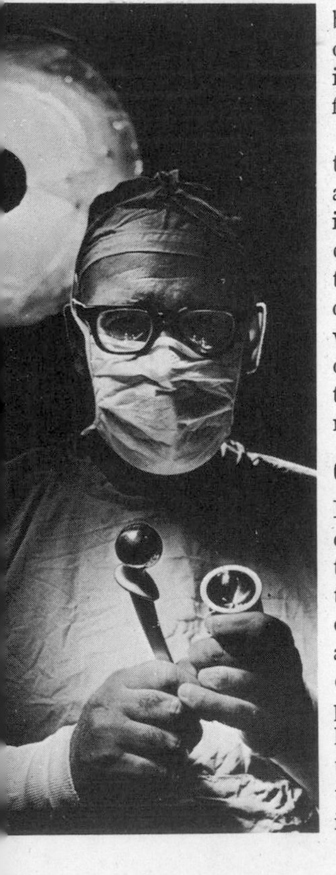

ORTHOPEDICS

In medically advanced countries the commonest form of spinal deformity, an angular hump, was a result of tuberculosis. Spinal tuberculosis has now become rare, though it is still common in countries with a low standard of living. What was the second commonest form, a lateral curvature, scoliosis, has now become first. It can be caused by disturbed muscle function, as in poliomyelitis, but in most cases the cause is still unknown in spite of much experimental work, notably that of I. V. Ponseti (U.S.), with chemicals that upset the composition of bone and produce the deformity in animals. A new approach, admittedly concerned with the effects rather than the cause of scoliosis, has been that of P. Zorab and his colleagues (London), who have studied the effects of deformity of the spine and thorax on function of the heart and lungs. In severe deformity both are defective. Thus there is a covert threat to life which lends urgency to discovering the cause of scoliosis and, meanwhile, to the prompt application of surgical measures available for correcting the deformity and maintaining the correction by one or another of the methods available for internal fixation of the affected vertebrae. Unfortunately, correction is not followed by any improvement in pulmonary function. Indeed, at least one type of operation is followed by further, though not progressive, impairment (H. D. Westgate and J. H. Moe, U.S.). This is not an argument against correction but rather one in favour of tackling progressive deformity early.

There is a group of anemic disorders stemming from genetically determined abnormalities of hemoglobin. As a consequence of the blocking of blood vessels in bone, some very crippling skeletal disorders can occur. The head of the femur, for example, and, in consequence, the hip joint, can be badly damaged. There is no remedy available. The main significance of these findings, reported from many countries, is diagnostic, though something can be done for the secondary bone infection which is often caused by bacteria of the genus *Salmonella*.

In 1967 reference was made to the activation of power-driven prostheses by currents picked up during the contraction of normal muscle. Surface electrodes have disadvantages because they tend to be activated by more than one muscle. Implanted electrodes would be more satisfactory; the problem is to find a sufficiently small and durable device that will not provoke an untoward reaction in the muscle in which it is embedded. F. R. Tucker and R. N. Scott (Canada) have overcome the latter problem by placing the electronic device in the marrow cavity of the bone in the amputation stump, the electrode attached to it lying on the surface of the bone beneath the muscle that provides the signals. This method is still experimental. A Scandinavian team has used an intramuscular device, a plastic-covered capsule 11 mm. long, in volunteers and in below-elbow amputees. All were removed after periods of up to 15 months to permit study of the implants and of the tissue reaction they provoked. Their electrical performance was mostly good. Signals could be picked up several metres away, though the normal position of the recording device was on the surface of the limb. The main electrical supply caused only negligible disturbance. The capsules showed structural defects, but it could reasonably be anticipated that this ingenious method of activating a powered artificial limb would soon be thoroughly effective. Myoelectrically controlled hand prostheses, operated by surface electrodes, were already available in Austria, Italy, and the U.S.S.R.

Hyperbaric oxygen has several uses in medicine; the dangers inherent in its employment are well known and can be avoided. A number of patients with gas gangrene (caused by the anaerobic *Clostridium welchii*) have now been successfully treated by exposure, in an appropriate chamber, to pure oxygen at a pressure of 2 atm. Under these conditions the partial pressure of oxygen in plasma is increased 16-fold. The duration of exposure is two hours with frequent repetitions until, and for a short period after, remission has become apparent. Some success has also been achieved in the treatment of chronic osteomyelitis although the causative organism is the aerobic *Staphylococcus pyogenes*. It may be that in this disease high oxygenation acts chiefly on the bone, which in chronic osteomyelitis is poorly vascularized and for this reason defective in its powers of repair. It is certain that under laboratory conditions bone formation is stimulated in an atmosphere containing 35% oxygen. (HE. SE.)

OSTEOPATHIC MEDICINE

During the first half of 1969 the osteopathic profession achieved full practice rights in Idaho, North Dakota, and both the Carolinas, making 46 U.S. states in which doctors of osteopathy were licensed as physicians and surgeons. Only Arkansas, Louisiana, Mississippi, and Montana still placed restrictions on the scope of osteopathic practice. In both Arkansas and Montana the legislatures established special commissions to study the possibility of granting unlimited licenses to osteopathic physicians.

A sixth osteopathic college was opened at Pontiac, Mich. In Pennsylvania, the legislature allocated $5.2 million toward an expansion project of the Philadelphia College of Osteopathic Medicine. At the federal level, osteopathic colleges received over $1 million in basic improvement grants from the Department of Health, Education, and Welfare. Under the Health Professions Educational Assistance Act, the Des Moines College of Osteopathic Medicine and Surgery was awarded $8.5 million in matching funds for development of a new campus. In 1969, 1,871 students were enrolled in and 427 graduated from osteopathic colleges in the United States.

Canada's provincial osteopathic societies formally disaffiliated from the American Osteopathic Association to become an independent Canadian Osteopathic Association.

In 1969 the AOA numbered 13,604 osteopathic physicians, and the American Osteopathic Hospital Association listed 266 hospitals with a total of 19,000 available beds. As of June 30, 80 osteopathic projects costing more than $79 million had received federal support of more than $24 million for construction under the Hill-Burton program. (R. A. KL.)

PEDIATRICS

Research on the detection of hereditary disorders in the unborn child was conducted in several centres during 1969. This was made possible by the culture of fetal cells shed into the amniotic fluid. Amniocentesis can be safely performed through the mother's abdominal wall to obtain a sample of the amniotic fluid. In addition to the older determination of erythroblastosis, cells in the fluid can now be studied with special stains that may permit identification of the sex of the fetus. Cells can also be grown in tissue culture and then studied for chromosomal abnormalities. This will permit, for example, the diagnosis of mongolism (Down's syndrome). Other inherited disorders characterized by chromosome abnormalities or enzyme deficiencies may be similarly identified. Galactosemia, for example, produces brain and liver damage because of a deficiency of an enzyme important in the milk metabolism. Recognition of a low level of the fetal enzyme will permit reduction of the mother's intake of milk throughout the period of pregnancy.

As of 1969, the detection of some 35 inherited disorders was possible before the birth of the infant. Although many of these had no specific treatment as yet, future research might well disclose therapy that would prevent damage.

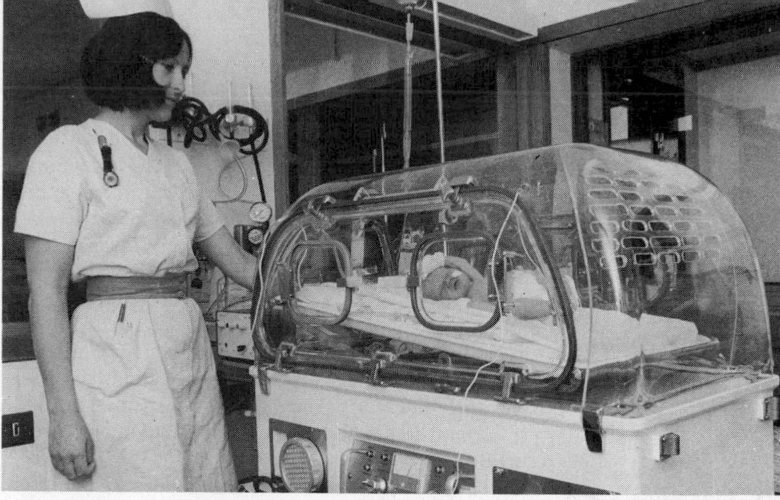

"LONDON DAILY EXPRESS" FROM PICTORIAL PARADE

Nurse tends premature baby lying on a ripple mattress, designed by John Lewin of London's National Institute for Medical Research. Mattress registers movement of baby by monitoring the flow of air in the ripples. If the baby stops breathing, the air stops flowing and an electrical device sounds the alarm.

The same techniques that allow diagnosis of disease or abnormality in the unborn child are proving to be of great diagnostic value for parents who may be carriers of some abnormalities. In cystic fibrosis, for instance, culture of cells from minute samples of the skin of the parents will enable the physician to determine the carrier state of the parent. If there is a history of cystic fibrosis in either of the families of a young married couple, it will be possible to determine if they are carriers of the gene.

Obstetricians and pediatricians are studying the weight gain of the expectant mother during pregnancy relative to the birth weight and subsequent growth and development of her infant. Results indicate a higher birth weight in the offspring of mothers with high weight gain during pregnancy. The increased weight gain has also been associated with improved growth and performance in the first year of the baby's life. Heretofore, weight gain during pregnancy was kept to a minimum; further research may indicate that this is undesirable.

Throughout the U.S. during 1969 many nurseries were equipped with light cradles containing 10–12 fluorescent bulbs placed over incubators containing premature babies. A great many newborn infants develop jaundice (yellow discoloration of the skin and whites of the eyes) during the first few days of life. Occasionally the pigmentation may be sufficiently severe to cause brain damage. Exposure of the infant to increased light bleaches the pigment and seems to lessen the risk of brain damage. The procedure is still experimental. Several centres are testing the efficacy of merely increasing the light source in ceiling lights.

A similar effect of diminishing jaundice has been noted in offspring of women who have been receiving phenobarbital during pregnancy. This appears to have a stimulating effect on the function of the liver of the fetus and the newborn infant.

During 1969 new information was obtained on a rare but important inherited childhood disorder characterized by severe abscesses of the skin and lymph glands. In these children, most of whom are males, antibody production by the blood is normal, and there has been no explanation for the inability to cope with infections. Investigators have shown that the white blood cells of these children function normally in ingesting bacteria but are then unable to destroy the organisms because of an inherited enzymatic deficiency in the white cells. (See *Immunology*, above.)

(S. S. G.)

PHARMACOLOGY

General. Basic research in pharmacology has been increasingly concerned with molecular pharmacology—the mode of action of drugs on cells and subcellular structures and components. Molecular pharmacological investigators prefer the methods and principles of this science in the search for new drugs in preference to more classical screening methods on isolated organs and on the whole animal. The bulk of new drug discoveries, however, have come, and are still coming, as a result of established research methods that are constantly being improved and supplemented with the use of biochemical, enzymatic, and other new procedures.

The U.S. Food and Drug Administration initiated a systematic review of the effectiveness of many drugs already on the market. Drug combinations, especially antibacterial medications, often appear to lack the advantages originally claimed for them, and several have been removed from the market.

New Drugs. It had been found a few years earlier that persons with Parkinson's disease have a deficiency, in certain areas of the brain, of the norepinephrine precursor dopamine. Attempts to correct this deficiency by administration of L-dopa (see *Neurology,* above) which is locally converted into dopamine have yielded excellent therapeutic results.

An interesting development in the treatment of manic-depressive conditions is the apparent effectiveness of lithium salts. These simple drugs were in regular use in several countries but were not yet generally available in the U.S. Since the therapeutic margin of lithium is not great, careful clinical and laboratory controls must accompany its administration.

Two new agents for the treatment of tuberculosis became available: the synthetic drug ethambutol hydrochloride and the antibiotic rifamycin. These medications are intended to be used in combination with other, established drugs, one of the advantages being that development of resistance of the bacteria against other chemotherapeutic agents can be delayed. The new antibiotic gentamycin appears to be an effective agent against gram-negative bacteria including pseudomonas, which often cause serious infections of the urinary tract and was also a potential threat to burn victims. There have been promising results with the topical use of this antibiotic as well as with the new sulfonamide derivative mafenide hydrochloride and with silver nitrate solutions.

One of the limitations of the useful group of chlorothiazide type diuretic and antihypertensive drugs is the tendency to produce an undesirable loss of potassium in the urine. A new pyrazinoyl guanidine derivative, amiloride, which was under clinical investigation, was found to be moderately diuretic itself and could be useful together with chlorothiazide diuretics since it tends to counteract the potassium-depleting action.

Though several fairly active antihypertensive drugs were in use, a new one called Catapres, already available in Europe and in clinical trials in the U.S., could become of interest because it appears to act by centrally inhibiting the vasoconstrictor mechanism. The introduction of propanolol as a new type of antiarrhythmic cardiac drug, with possible usefulness in coronary heart disease, has given rise to extensive research. Similar, perhaps more specific and effective agents of this type of beta-adrenergic blocking agents would no doubt become available in the future.

An exchange resin, cholestyramine, has yielded encouraging results in reducing elevated plasma cholesterol levels in many cases of atherosclerosis. Recently the new analgesic pentazocine was introduced with the claim that it would be free of the addicting properties of the morphine group. There is some evidence, however, that this is not the case. A possible new approach to the treatment of asthma may be realized with disodium cromoglycate, which seems to act by preventing the release of bronchoconstrictor substances from the tissues rather than counteracting their effect through a bronchodilator mechanism as most antiasthma drugs do. (See *Introduction,* above.) (R. K. R.)

Narcotics. Latest available figures on the production of opium in those countries that report to the United Nations show a decline to 778 tons in 1967 from 782 tons in 1966. India, the U.S.S.R., and Turkey accounted for 60.8, 23.3, and 14.8%, respectively, of this output—the U.S.S.R. and Turkey somewhat less than in the previous year, and India a little more. Some 366 tons of the opium went into the manufacture of morphine. The 143 tons of morphine manufactured from opium (67.6%) and from poppy straw (or its concentrate) compared with 149 tons manufactured the previous year. As usual, most of the morphine was converted into codeine.

Bolivia and Peru continued to be the main producers of coca leaves, with harvests in 1967 of 5,058 tons and 8,505 tons, respectively. Most of the product was used for chewing. In both countries the amount represented a reduction from the previous year's production—of 4.2 and 6.4%, respectively.

The increasing trend noted in previous years for the manufacture of pethidine, a widely used synthetic drug, was reversed in 1967 when 16.5 tons were produced, compared with 20.6 tons in 1966.

Southeast Asia and the Middle East remained the chief areas of illicit production of opium, morphine, and heroin; South America, of coca leaf and cocaine; and Africa and the Middle East, of cannabis. Total seizure of all these drugs in 1967 amounted to some 1,428 tons, compared with 416 in 1966. The amount of raw opium seized was 35 tons, compared with 52 tons in 1966, and of cannabis, 1,389 tons, compared with 361.7 tons in 1966. Those countries that had a significant problem of illicit opium poppy or cannabis cultivation continued to give economic and social assistance to the areas concerned, and to pursue programs of crop replacement.

During 1968 international collaboration in the United Nations' research programs was broadened and more scientists were nominated by the governments of Belgium, Canada, Denmark, Italy, New Zealand, Spain, the U.K., and the U.S. to participate in the research. A laboratory was also designated for this purpose by the government of Sweden. Collaborating scientists showed particular interest in the cannabis program, and important research in this field was being carried out in many countries. As in previous years, technical assistance in the form of training was provided by the United Nations' laboratory, which received fellowship holders from Afghanistan, Laos, Peru, and the U.A.R. (Pe. B.)

PHYSIOLOGY

For several decades it has been apparent that the neurological basis of learning and memory cannot be fully explained in terms of a highly localized telephonelike circuitry of nerve cells. A large body of evidence indicates information becomes coded into brain proteins. Learning can be inhibited and memory can be masked by puromycin and other compounds that block the synthesis of proteins. Recent studies indicate that in mice the hippocampal area of the brain contains the memory trace of recently learned maze behaviour and that with time the trace is found in the neocortex. Saline injections into the frontal cortex three days after training did not release the puromycin blockage of memory in the hippocampal area but injections of saline into the frontal cortex six and seven days after training did, thereby indicating that the memory trace extends widely into the cortex after the initial learning.

Psychological stress in human subjects and electrical stimulation of the hypothalamus of rabbits cause rises in plasma cholesterol. The neurogenic rise of plasma cholesterol in animals could be produced by giving a low-cholesterol diet. These results support the view that psychological factors can play a role in the development of cholesterolemia and possibly atherosclerosis.

Growth hormone of the anterior pituitary gland is secreted in the adult after skeletal growth has stopped. The rate of secretion is not constant but is affected by a number of stress stimuli such as exercise, insulin injection, or exposure to cold or heat. There is good evidence for a growth-hormone-releasing factor in the hypothalamus of several species. Probably this hormone is more than a growth promoting factor; it apparently plays an important homeostatic role in the economy of the body by its metabolic effects on the utilization and synthesis of proteins.

Investigation of the elasticity of the human lung in relation to age showed that the static recoil pressures are reduced throughout the age range studied, 20 to 60 years. There is no evidence that the lung surface material is altered with age but it is probable that the tissue components are. Some investigators have reported that there is a progressive increase in the elastin content of the aging lung but this may have been inferred incorrectly from artifacts of procedure.

The clinical syndrome of acute pulmonary edema of high altitude has been known for more than 30 years; several hundred cases have been recorded. An experimental model of early pulmonary edema has been induced in young rats breathing 8% oxygen, either at rest for 45–180 minutes or during swimming for 10 minutes. The earliest signs of edema were eosinophilic cuffs in the periarterial, perivenous, and peribronchial spaces, but the procedures failed to produce massive alveolar edema or death from pulmonary edema. There were no thromboses as occur in man where the syndrome develops after 12–36 hours at high altitude. (D. J. I.)

PSYCHIATRY

Abnormal anxiety was the subject of a symposium held in London by the World Psychiatric Association jointly with the Royal Medico-Psychological Association. Learning theory was brought to bear on the problems of pathological anxiety, which was regarded as a conditioned fear response to pain; *i.e.,* a secondary drive. Pavlov's laws relating to drives enabled the problem to be studied experimentally, whereby not only potential anxiety-provoking stimuli but also the personalities subjected to them could be varied.

The study of the physiological changes associated with anxiety revealed that there were two varieties, the passive, accompanied by a temporary cessation of respiration, slowing down of the pulse rate, and sometimes a transitory paralysis of movement; and the active, accompanied by increased muscle tension and acceleration of pulse and breathing. The former was regarded as a reaction of flight, the latter as a reaction of defense. Studies in the Soviet Union suggested that in mental disorders with anxiety there was an excessive loss of brain tissue and the appearance of antibodies in the blood. Anxiety was also found to be associated with certain endocrine and other biochemical reactions that could cause psychosomatic disease.

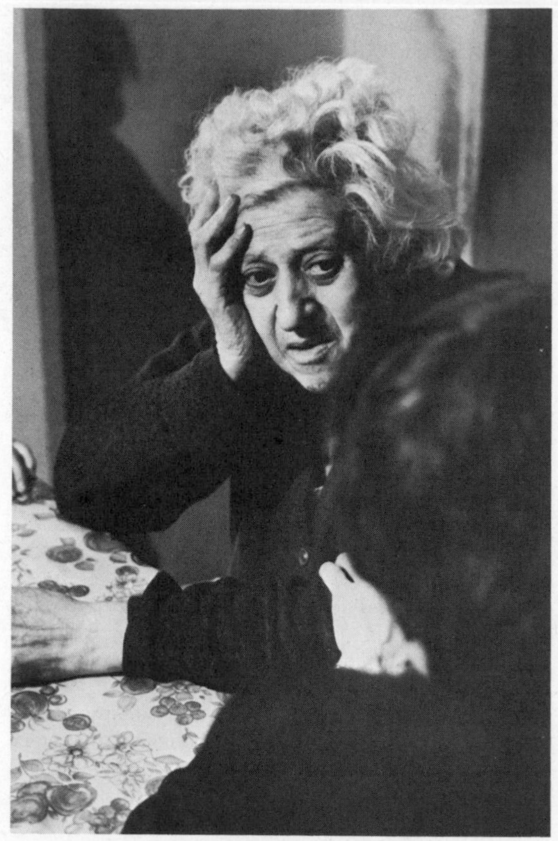

LEONARD MCCOMBE, "LIFE" MAGAZINE © TIME INC.

This 76-year-old woman was among the patients receiving psychiatric help at home from a team of specialists from New York's Gouverneur Hospital. The unique service was provided without charge to residents of the lower East Side as part of an experiment to prevent needless commitments to mental institutions.

Tests of adaptability showed that anxious patients adjusted to changing physiological stimulations more slowly than did normals. The somatic accompaniments of anxiety suggested that it was largely a physical phenomenon based on a central cerebral mechanism. J. J. Lopez Ibor of Madrid called it "vital anxiety" over which the psychodynamic structure of the anxiety neurosis was superimposed. It followed a phasic course similar to that of endogenous depression of which that type of anxiety was a part.

The role of heredity in anxiety neurosis was examined with the help of the twin method. There was evidence for the presence of hereditary factors determining the predisposition to abnormal anxiety states that were found to develop as the result of environmental influences.

Rating scales applied to the subjective and objective manifestations of abnormal anxiety showed three dimensions: the first of a general kind, the second related to bodily symptoms, and the third to certain constellations of symptoms.

The psychological factors in the origin of abnormal anxiety were reexamined. John Bowlby, following up the Freudian observations, regarded it as the result of disturbances in the relationship of a person with some other human being. Children with an unsettled home life were more anxiety-prone than children from settled homes. This applied particularly to girls, whereas boys tended to become abnormally excitable and aggressive. Bowlby believed that the drive to bonding preceded attachment behaviour based on the need for food and sex. Pathological anxiety arose from separation anxiety which led to behaviour patterns signifying a search for the lost object. Chronic pathological anxiety was also observed as the result of prolonged exposure to a threatening environment in adult life such as that experienced by concentration camp survivors. Abnormal anxiety was found to respond well to sedatives, especially to barbiturates which had been the main therapeutic standby for many years. Recently, antidepressant drugs, especially the monoamino-oxidase inhibitors, were found to damp down the somatic symptoms of anxiety and to reduce or abolish abnormal feelings of panic.

Behaviour therapy based on learning theory continued to receive much attention. Systematic desensitization, in which patients were gradually reexposed to a graded series of anxiety-provoking stimuli, proved useful in anxiety states. It was more successful in cases of phobia (abnormal fears of specific objects or situations) than in states of general anxiety. Although desensitization often had a beneficial effect on symptoms, psychotherapy tended to improve interpersonal relations. Various forms of relaxation therapy proved effective in pathological anxiety states. Neurosurgery was used only in exceptional cases when all other treatments had failed. The operations consisted of excision of carefully selected small areas of the brain, especially of the frontal lobes.

A sociological study by Jerome K. Myers and Lee L. Bean, in collaboration with Max P. Pepper, in New Haven, Conn., threw new light on the influence of social class upon the long-range outcome of psychiatric treatment and the adjustment of former patients in the community. The treatment status of 1,563 inpatients and outpatients was reexamined after a period of ten years. The population was divided into five socioeconomic classes, categories I to III comprising the upper and middle classes. Lower-class patients tended to remain in treatment longer than those in classes I to III. Class IV patients were less likely to be discharged and more likely to be readmitted than others. These differentials led to a piling-up process of I to III class patients in the outpatient clinics. Social adjustment in the community was more difficult for patients belonging to classes IV and V than for I to III class patients. Mental illness tended to be catastrophic for the lower-class patients and their families. This follow-up study explained earlier findings which made it appear that mental illness, especially the more severe types, was more common in the lower than in the middle and upper classes. It became clear that social variables influenced the therapist, the patient, and their relationship, as well as institutions and agencies that affected medical intervention and outcome of therapy. Employers' attitudes regarding the prospects of recovery from mental illness played an important part in readjustment. Continued treatment in the community irrespective of class was essential, but to make this possible the community had to be appropriately educated. (E. ST.)

PUBLIC HEALTH

Environmental Services. In 1969 worldwide concern for the quality of man's environment grew. Industry increased its efforts to meet regulatory and public demands. Espousal of causes was dramatic: oil spills,

LUIGI PELLEXFIERI

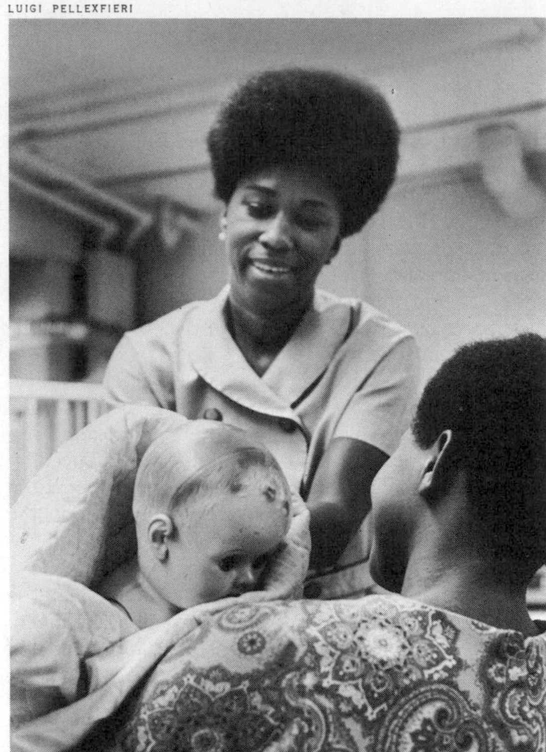

Unwed pregnant teen-ager receives instruction in child care in Project Teen Aid, accredited by board of education in Brooklyn, N.Y.

DDT residuals, thermal loads from power generator condensers on receiving waters, noise and air pollution from jet aircraft, radioactive releases from nuclear explosions, transport accidents releasing toxic substances requiring the evacuation of whole communities, and the threat of spills from the transport of surplus stocks of war gases for disposal.

The use of DDT-type pesticides was the subject of considerable debate during the year. In November the U.S. government ordered an end to the use of DDT in residential areas within 30 days and an almost complete ban by 1971. Similar action was taken by other countries, including Sweden and Denmark. DDT and its analogs are stable in the environment and accumulate in fatty tissue of all animals. In July, at the World Health Assembly in Boston, M. G. Candau, director general of the World Health Organization (WHO), expressed concern that DDT bans would be inimical to the Global Malaria Eradication Campaign, which as of 1969 protected over one billion people in formerly malarious areas.

Positive actions included: (1) The UN General Assembly unanimously agreed to a UN Conference on the Human Environment in 1972 in Stockholm. (2) Pres. Richard Nixon created an Environmental Quality Council made up of the secretaries of six departments. (3) The National Environmental Policy Act, creating a permanent three-member Council on Environmental Quality in the Executive Office of the President, was passed by the U.S. Congress. A bill that would establish an Office of Environmental Quality was still pending when the congressional session ended. (4) The Federal Water Pollution Control Administration approved the water quality standards of the 50 states, the District of Columbia, Guam, Puerto Rico, and the Virgin Islands. The approvals had reservations for 28 states, on which negotiations continued. (5) In February the U.S. National Air Pollution Control Administration issued air quality criteria for suspended particles and sulfur oxides. By October, NAPCA had designated 19 of the 57 air pollution control regions of the continental U.S., Puerto Rico, and the Virgin Islands, and had completed consultations on 22 others. The first 17 regions covered 50% of the total U.S. urban population. July 1970 was the goal for designating all 57 regions.

In South and Central America, the goal of the Continental Water Supply Program of the Alliance for Progress and the Pan American Health Organization in the decade 1961 to 1971 is that 70% of the urban population and 50% of the rural population have ample and accessible safe water. By 1969, 68% of the urban people were served by house connections or readily accessible public taps.

In the U.S., the chemical and petroleum industries' interest in protecting environmental quality was increasing. Examples are: (1) Shell, Velsicol, and Montrose joined in financing a study of the behaviour of pesticide residues in Lake Michigan. (2) The Dow Chemical Co. contracted to operate Cleveland's Westerly Sewage Treatment Plant using anionics and ferric chloride for phosphate removal to slow the eutrophication of Lake Erie. (3) The Manufacturing Chemists' Association reported that the chemical industry's cumulative capital expenditures for pollution control equipment rose from $475 million in 1962 to $673 million in 1967, and that the annual spending for operation and research rose from $82 million in 1962 to $120 million in 1967. The equivalent of 4,800 full-time people manage, operate, and investigate water, air, and solid waste control in the chemical industry in the U.S. (4) The American Petroleum Institute reported that in 1968 U.S. oil companies spent $382 million for air and water conservation with $231 million for capital equipment and $26 million for research.

As a reference bench mark, the appropriations of the two major U.S. federal agencies responsible for control of air and water pollution and solid wastes and general environmental sanitation, including operations, research, training, and grants for construction and demonstration projects, totaled $450 million in fiscal 1969. For fiscal 1970, the Bureau of the Budget recommended a total of $478.4 million for the air, water, solid waste, and general environmental control activities of the Consumer Protection and Environmental Health Service, for the water pollution control activities and plant construction grants of the Federal Water Pollution Control Administration of the Interior Department, and for fundamental research by the National Institute of Environmental Health Sciences. (E. T. CH.)

Epidemics. Smallpox incidence continued to decline in 1968, primarily because of the intensive program of eradication that started in 1967. During 1968, 79,539 cases with 12,877 deaths were reported from all parts of the world (against 119,095 cases in 1967). In Africa, 10,951 cases were reported from 25 countries, and in Asia, 64,739 cases from 7 countries, mainly India (35,165), Pakistan (11,091), and Indonesia (17,311). South America had 3,844 cases confined to Brazil. Only 3 cases of smallpox were imported into Europe (United Kingdom and Belgium).

Cholera in 1968 was reported from 10 countries, all of them in Asia (28,941 with 4,146 deaths). The principal endemic countries were India (18,076), Pakistan (2,852 in East and 4,483 in West Pakistan), and the Philippines (2,787), mainly caused by El Tor vibrio.

Yellow fever (jungle type) was reported from 5 countries in South America (Bolivia, Brazil, Colombia, Peru, and Surinam) with a total of 45 cases and 29 deaths. No cases of yellow fever were reported during 1968 in Africa.

Plague in 1968 was reported from 4 countries in Africa, 5 countries in the Americas, and 4 countries in Asia. Of a world total of 1,318 cases and 160 deaths, 973 cases with 90 deaths occurred in Asia. Vietnam with 780 confirmed cases was responsible, for the second successive year, for more than half the world's total. In 1968 not a single case of plague was reported in India, once the most affected country. No large outbreaks occurred either in Africa (Congo [Kinshasa], Lesotho, Malagasy Republic, and Tanzania), with a total of only 145 cases and 38 deaths, or in the Americas, where only 200 cases and 32 deaths (Bolivia, Brazil, Ecuador, Peru, and the U.S.) were reported.

Louse-borne typhus was reported from Algeria, Burundi, Ethiopia, and South Africa (7,954 cases), from Bolivia, Ecuador, Mexico, and Peru (199 cases), from Afghanistan and Malaysia (7 cases), and 1 case in Yugoslavia and 1 imported case in the U.K. The highest incidence was in Ethiopia (3,515 cases) and in Burundi (4,265 cases). The world total was 8,186 cases.

Louse-borne relapsing fever was reported in 1968 only from Ethiopia (3,729 cases) and the Sudan (1,948 cases). The reporting of this disease from other parts of the world is not considered reliable because it is not clearly differentiated from the tick-borne variety of relapsing fever.

Mosquito-borne hemorrhagic fever was reported from 58 provinces of Thailand (6,030 cases and 65 deaths), the Philippines (311 cases and 22 deaths), and from India (5 cases).

Influenza in the form of a major epidemic was reported in July 1968 from Hong Kong. It was caused by an A2 variant, antigenically different from A2 influenza viruses isolated in previous years. During August and September 1968, the Hong Kong strains of influenza virus spread rapidly to Singapore, Taiwan, the Philippines, Japan, Australia, Iran, Thailand, and India, and into the U.S. in early September. Before the end of December 1968 a relatively high mortality, due solely to pneumonia influenza, was observed. During the last months of 1968 influenza spread to Europe and continued to spread during the first half of 1969. An ailment known variously as Asian flu, Mao flu, and Hong Kong grippe spread through Europe in December 1969 in almost epidemic fashion. In Rome 800,000 of the city's 2.5 million persons were ill and 375 deaths were attributed to the disease. It was estimated that more than 25 million Italians were affected. In Britain the government reported that 294 persons died of the disease in the week before Christmas and 52 the week before that. British scientists said the flu was spreading at an average rate of 20 mph.

Poliomyelitis continues to be a severe health problem in several less developed countries in the world, where systematic immunization campaigns have not yet been started. An increased number of paralytic cases was reported from the Ivory Coast (167), Cameroon (108), Ethiopia (134), and Mali (388). In Venezuela 484 cases, mainly caused by type I, were reported in 1968, in comparison with 67 in 1967. In Ceylon 1,001 cases were registered. In Turkey, with 814 cases in 1967, 1,949 were reported in 1968. The high incidence continued into 1969 and late in the year 1,999 cases had been reported. A serious outbreak of type III poliomyelitis (458 cases) occurred in Poland.

Salmonella infections and intoxications were under continuous surveillance in Europe and other parts of the world, a firm indication of their increasing importance in public health and economics. The number of reported individual cases, as well as smaller or larger outbreaks, was increasing; the number of different salmonella serotypes causing these infections and intoxications was also climbing. (K. RA.)

RADIOLOGY

The first Glyn Evans Memorial Lecture was presented by Sir Brian Windeyer at Cardiff in October 1968. The speaker traced the growth of diagnostic and therapeutic radiology in Great Britain from its beginnings to the present day, emphasizing that the separation into two disciplines started in 1935 with separate diplomas for diagnostic and therapeutic radiology. There has been, nevertheless, an overall unity of both in the faculty of radiologists, he pointed out, and this has been a great focus for medical radiology, not only in Great Britain but internationally. The discussion then concentrated on the future, and, although both disciplines had to maintain extensive and growing service commitments in the hospital service, it was pointed out that more time in the future must be given to teaching at the undergraduate as well as postgraduate levels. Research in both diagnostic and therapeutic radiology must be extended to wider fields: in diagnosis, to more fundamental investigations undertaken with colleagues in other disciplines; in therapy, to more extensive collaborative studies with radiobiologists. This academic extension of radiodiagnosis and radiotherapy must be headed by university professors provided with sufficient time, technical staff, and budget to undertake investigative work. More personnel are required to extend better senior staffing in diagnostic departments at the district hospital level, and to implement radiotherapeutic services.

Undergraduate courses, particularly the basic medical sciences such as anatomy and physiology, should entail much more involvement with radiology—both diagnosis and therapy, according to Sir Brian.

Automatic processing of medical X-ray films is now sufficiently advanced that its use is becoming widespread, even in small radiological departments. One important advantage is the saving in time of personnel. Darkroom technicians using the old manual development technique were doing a time-consuming task, the results were subject to variable human judgment and care in procedure, and the work was tedious.

Automatic processing improves results in the final radiographic examination because of the constants involved: time for the films to pass through the various baths, drying, and the automatic replenishment of developer, hypo, and other chemicals.

One of the greatest advantages is, of course, the shortened processing time—only 2 minutes from the time the film enters the darkroom, as compared with 5–15 or more with manual techniques.

The tendency has been to install automatic processors in large X-ray departments, but it is now becoming obvious that in smaller departments, even those staffed by one or two radiographers, processing time saved by automation can be used for other tasks.

A methodology has also been developed for computer-assisted roentgenogram interpretation, but due to the present state of the art and the current high cost, the procedure is only slowly being adopted, and then only for research purposes.

THE "NEW YORK TIMES"

Teacher at the Lexington School for the Deaf in New York mimes meaning of a word to children born handicapped as a result of the 1964 rubella epidemic. Most of the 30,000 survivors reached school age in 1969.

The International Commission on Radiological Protection is one of the commissions maintained by the International Congress of Radiology, with a great public responsibility in that it concerns all protection problems for patients and staff. At a meeting of this commission and its committee in Oxford April 11–18, task groups were established to report to the commission on such matters as relative biological effectiveness of neutrons with respect to mutagenesis, the balance between genetic effects in the first generation versus later effects, respiratory absorption and elimination mechanisms, and methods of handling emergency and accidental radiation exposures. Recommendations were considered at the International Congress of Radiology held in Tokyo in October and would be put in final form and reported on in 1970. (Jo. W. McL.)

REHABILITATION

A record 241,390 disabled Americans were rehabilitated into gainful employment during the fiscal year ended June 30, 1969. This new record represents an increase of 16% over the previous year's total of 207,918. For the eighth consecutive year Pennsylvania led the nation in the number of disabled persons rehabilitated with 16,544. California ranked second with 14,450, followed by Illinois with 13,410. Ranked in terms of state population, the District of Columbia was first with 339 per 100,000, West Virginia, second with 323, followed by South Carolina with 290. The state-federal program of vocational rehabilitation, 50 years old in June 1970, had thus far rehabilitated more than 2.3 million physically and mentally handicapped persons into employment.

continued on page 519

COLD AS A TREATMENT FOR DISEASE

By Sir James Fraser

The controlled application of a very low temperature to living tissue to produce a complete and unselective destruction of all the cells within the affected area for therapeutic purposes is known as cryosurgery. Cold as a treatment for disease and for the relief of pain was probably fairly widely recognized in the 19th century, but the first documented report on its use was made in 1851 by a surgeon from the Middlesex Hospital, James Arnott, who had been at one time medical superintendent on St. Helena. Arnott described the use of a salt-ice mixture at about −20° C (−4° F) in the treatment of a wide range of conditions including patients with advanced breast cancer and cancer of the cervix of the uterus. His account indicated that although the disease was not cured there was a dramatic reduction in the discharge and bleeding from the surface of the tumour and a temporary regression in its total size.

This publication unfortunately did not stimulate the interest within the profession that it deserved. Local surface cooling, in the form of the ethyl chloride spray, was used as an anesthetic and solid carbon dioxide was used to treat warts and small skin tumours, but there was a delay of over 100 years after Arnott's report before the full potential of local freezing was again recognized.

The reason for this delay was undoubtedly the difficulty experienced in handling the very cold materials, and it was not until the research undertaken in the aeronautic and astronautic industries overcame these technical problems that interest in therapeutic freezing was again stimulated. In 1961 a New York neurosurgeon, Irving S. Cooper, in conjunction with the Union Carbide Corporation, developed a practical cryosurgery unit in which liquid nitrogen was used as the freezing agent and which could be used for local tissue destruction. The apparatus consisted of a metal probe through which the liquid nitrogen circulated and which was vacuum insulated except for its tip. The temperature could be controlled by interrupting the flow of the cooling agent and it could be accurately maintained at any temperature from 0° down to −196° C.

In the succeeding years other similar instruments were developed. Most used liquid nitrogen but Freon and liquid argon, although less effective as freezing agents, were more easily controlled and required less sophisticated equipment. An alternative instrument employed the Joule-Thomson effect in which a compressed gas is allowed to expand suddenly through a small aperture and is accompanied by a considerable drop in environmental temperature. By a system of precooling of the compressed gas it was possible to reach a very low temperature comparable to that of liquid nitrogen.

The significance of the introduction of this cryosurgical equipment was that cold could be safely and accurately applied to any part of the body to which the tip of the probe could be introduced, and the tissue surrounding the probe could be independently frozen and destroyed. Furthermore, the cold could be applied for any length of time and its temperature could be controlled with remarkable accuracy.

Cooper introduced his equipment for use in neurosurgery. It was soon recognized, however, that its special properties made it eminently suitable for use in other surgical fields as an alternative to surgical excision or electrocoagulation. It produced an absolute and unselective tissue destruction followed by an aseptic necrosis, an absorption of the dead tissue, and a rapid coverage of the defect by overgrowth of the surrounding cells. There was virtually no bleeding within the area that was treated; there was relative anesthesia within the treated area; and there was a discrete boundary between the destroyed tissue and the surrounding normal tissue, which was totally unaffected. The area of destruction could also be predicted with considerable accuracy provided the temperature and the duration of application were known.

Mechanisms of Freezing. The mechanism of cell death following freezing injury had been extensively studied by 1969 but most of the work had been undertaken on cell suspensions, principally with the purpose of demonstrating cell preservation rather than cell destruction. Several theories were proposed to explain this phenomenon.

1. Extracellular ice crystals develop within the extracellular phase and are produced when the rate of freezing is slow. They are large and their effect on living cells is a mechanical destruction in which the cell membrane is perforated by the sharp points of the crystals. Intracellular crystals appear when the freezing is rapid and to a low temperature. They seldom appear above a temperature of −80° C and destroy the cell by disorganization of the intracellular mechanisms.

2. The water content of the tissue, and especially the extracellular water, is utilized to form the ice crystals. This has the effect of concentrating the remaining solution within the cell, its osmotic tension rising with subsequent protein denaturation and cell death.

3. There was also the possibility that an alteration occurs in the intracellular pH, a measure used to express alkalinity or acidity, that is incompatible with life.

4. The most likely explanation, however, was that the freezing injures small blood vessels and by a combination of vascular stasis and thrombosis totally obliterates the local blood supply. The cause of death is, therefore, local anoxia.

Evidence in favour of one of these causes of death in preference to the others remained indefinite. Crystallization could be demonstrated in a suitable histological preparation, and there was little doubt that both the intracellular osmotic tension and pH were altered. There was also adequate evidence to suggest that the temperature produced during local freezing varied greatly within the zone of cell destruction and although it was at −196° C in the centre, it fell off rapidly and was unlikely to be less than −6° C (21.2° F) when recorded at the periphery of the zone. However, by comparing the radius of destruction seen on histological preparations with the temperature gradient within this area, one could also demonstrate that cell death took place exactly at the ice-water boundary and that the area was totally reproducible.

This last observation was of the utmost importance to the surgeon practicing cryosurgery. He could assume that the zone of destruction would duplicate within a few millimetres the dimensions of the iceball formed around the tip of the probe and that the amount of tissue destroyed at an operation could be determined by the block of ice that he could see or feel. The fact that death takes place at or close to the tissue freezing point was also of value in predicting the size of the iceball in circumstances where the dimensions could not be visibly or palpably determined. Many factors would obviously influence the rate with which the ice-water boundary expands around the point of freezing but provided these were known for a specific tissue, it was possible by altering the temperature of the probe and the duration of freezing to predict with considerable accuracy the ultimate dimensions. This degree of predictability was not found in any other method of tissue destruction.

Clinical Applications. Since cryosurgical equipment was first designed for use in neurosurgery, it was obviously in this field that most of the pioneer work on cryogenic techniques was undertaken. Cryosurgery's peculiar properties of accuracy of control, hemostasis, and the creation of a hard iceball in soft friable tissue made it eminently suitable for brain surgery. In soft friable brain tumours, the iceball is allowed to grow until it encompasses the tumour growth, which is then separated without difficulty from the soft, normal, surrounding brain tissue. Alternatively, since it is known that the frozen tissue will die, the tumour can be allowed to thaw in situ.

An additional attraction is the possibility of making an initial reversible lesion in which the probe is first applied at a temperature cold enough to paralyze the affected nerve cells but well above their freezing point. In parkinsonism and choreoathetosis, which are conditions associated with tremor and uncontrollable involuntary movements, the specific cells within the brain responsible for these movements can be identified by inserting the probe under local anesthesia. The brain tissue can then be cooled and the subsequent visual effect on the patient's symptoms will indicate whether the probe is correctly situated. If the effect is not exactly correct, the probe can be repositioned without permanent injury. When the position has been confirmed, the surgeon can reduce the temperature to a lethal degree and destroy with great accuracy the relevant, small group of pathological cells. A similar technique can be used to destroy the pain-carrying nerves in the spinal cord in patients with painful, irremovable cancers within the pelvis. In the treatment of all these conditions the stereotaxic "three dimensional procedure" helps the surgeon to reach deep areas of the brain that are not readily accessible by an open operation.

Pituitary destruction by freezing is known as cryohypophysectomy and is used in patients with tumours of the pituitary, in patients with breast cancer, and in certain cases of diabetes mellitus in which it is known that pituitary ablation will influence, and sometimes produce, a regression of associated retinal disease. To carry out this procedure the probe is inserted into the skull through the nasopharynx and passed into the pituitary fossa through a fine trocar and cannula. The position of the cannula is controlled by continuous monitoring with X rays. Although the pituitary can be destroyed without difficulty, great care must be taken to avoid damage to important neighbouring structures such as the optic nerves. Obviously, in these circumstances some means of predicting the size of the iceball is essential, since it is not possible either visually or by palpation to determine the size of the cryolesion.

The ability to destroy all tissue regardless of its type means that freezing is particularly indicated in the treatment of tumours that lie on one of the body surfaces. The technique is used for primary skin growths or metastatic deposits disseminated from a cancer elsewhere, but it can also treat surface tumours within the alimentary tract or the bladder. A small skin tumour up to four or five centimetres in diameter can be completely removed and the result in terms of the cosmetic appearance is unequaled by other methods. Unfortunately, when the probe is applied to a surface the resultant iceball will take the form of a hemisphere, while the malignant tumour with its deep extension is more comparable in shape to an iceberg. For this reason it is usually necessary to freeze a large area of skin to encompass the entire growth.

In ear, nose, and throat surgery the same principle can be used. In cryogenic tonsillectomy, the enlarged tonsil is frozen and allowed to shrink rather than removed as in the conventional operation. When complete removal of a naso- or oropharyngeal tumour is not possible, or where inaccessibility makes a conventional operation difficult or impracticable, cryosurgery can provide excellent palliation, often with a dramatic relief of symptoms. It is a fortunate feature of the technique that the presence of a large blood vessel or of bone is of little significance since both of these structures are functionally unharmed by freezing.

In place of the more usual probe whose tip is noninsulated, special-purpose probes have been designed for use in specific operative procedures. One of these has a curved end with a preterminal, noninsulated segment. This instrument can be inserted into the prostatic urethra and used to freeze the prostate gland. It produces a lemon-shaped iceball and, therefore, a zone of tissue destruction the size of which can be determined by the temperature and the duration for which the cold is applied.

This operation, cryoprostatectomy, is a relatively minor procedure and is in no way uncomfortable; in ill patients it can be carried out with minimal anesthesia. The frozen segment of the prostate gland undergoes an ischemic necrosis and gradually disappears within about three weeks. The technique may be used to treat any prostatic disease, but it is especially indicated for conditions, such as prostatic carcinoma, that are not amenable to the usual operation. Cryoprostatectomy is probably no better than the standard operative procedure for the fit patient with a simple enlarged gland, but it is especially indicated for those who are suffering from some other associated disease or who are under treatment with drugs such as anticoagulants, which greatly increase the risks of routine surgery.

The property of intense cold that is used in ophthalmology is one well known to Arctic explorers, namely, that any metal object will, when frozen, adhere firmly and permanently to all living tissues. The removal of the opaque lens from the eye in a cataract operation is a delicate procedure and any attempt to grasp the lens by forceps may rupture it. If a small cryoprobe is placed in contact with the periphery of the lens, a bond is formed that is quite strong enough to allow a gentle but controlled manipulation and extraction.

This is now a proven and highly successful technique and is probably one of the commonest indications for the cryoprobe. In other ophthalmological diseases, local freezing may also be of great value, for example, to produce a minute point of tissue coagulation within the eyeball as part of the fixation of a detached retina, or to control one of the inflammatory diseases.

The Future of Cryosurgery. The cryoprobe, with the exception of its use in the extraction of a cataract, should be regarded as a sophisticated instrument of destruction that has an undoubted value in its own particular field. It was likely that in the future its use would be widened to include new sites within the body and the treatment of a wider range of disease. There would be an improvement in its efficiency so that larger volumes of tissue could be destroyed and there would be greater refinement of the means by which it is possible to predict the volume of destruction.

A further property, and one that might prove to be of greatest significance to the surgeon, was the ability to stimulate an immune response to the tissue that is being frozen. It was well known that the body has the ability to produce antibodies against foreign protein and on occasions, in the so-called "autoimmune" disease, to produce antibodies to its own tissues. It was demonstrated recently that when some part of the body is destroyed by freezing, and especially after cryoprostatectomy, the destroyed tissue is in some way altered so that it stimulates the production of such antibodies. These antibodies appeared to react specifically not only against the frozen cells but also against the remaining normal tissue. Initially this response is not great, but if the freezing stimulus is repeated, it has the effect of increasing dramatically the antibody level. This phenomenon is of little consequence when the cryoprobe is used in benign disease but in cancer surgery the effect may be a suppression and even an eradication of remaining malignant tissue, whether local or disseminated throughout the body.

There is no doubt that an antibody response to frozen tissue does occur and there have been cases in which metastatic cancer regressed after cryoprostatectomy. The phenomenon had not yet been demonstrated in other cancers but if it should be confirmed, it would be one of the more dramatic contributions in the treatment of cancer and could well open a new era in the management of this disease.

continued from page 516

The curtailment of both federal and state funds for services to handicapped persons seriously hampered the expansion of public programs of vocational rehabilitation, medical rehabilitation centres, and sheltered workshops from which the state agencies purchased services on behalf of their clients. Federal funds available for research and training of professional personnel were also cut. The lack of qualified personnel continued to be a major problem.

The National Citizens Conference on Rehabilitation of the Disabled and Disadvantaged was held in Washington, D.C., in June. Reports showed that millions of Americans who were handicapped vocationally as a result of being disabled or disadvantaged were not receiving rehabilitation services.

The 11th World Congress of the International Society for Rehabilitation of the Disabled was held in Dublin in September. Conferees were told that a survey of 83 nations with 65% of the world's population revealed inadequate rehabilitation services for the handicapped.

The coveted Lasker Awards in international rehabilitation were presented to Raden Soeharso and his wife, of Indonesia, André Trannoy of France, and G. Gingras of Canada.

The Soeharsos were the founders and directors of the National Rehabilitation Centre at Oslo. Trannoy, himself a paraplegic, founded and organized rehabilitation services in France. Gingras was medical director of the Montreal Institute for Rehabilitation which had provided professional training for many rehabilitation workers from Latin America and Asia.

A special Albert Lasker Award was given to the International Labour Organization for its 50 years of contribution to vocational rehabilitation of the handicapped. In October, the International Labour Organization also had the signal honour of being awarded the 1969 Nobel Peace Prize. (H. A. Ru.)

RESPIRATORY DISEASES

In mid-July 1968 an extensive epidemic due to a strain of A2 virus differing from previous ones occurred in Hong Kong and spread rapidly (see *Public Health: Epidemics,* above).

Secondary bacterial infections were uncommon (6%) in previously healthy persons infected with *Mycoplasma pneumoniae.* For a previous outbreak, however, nonbacterial infections of the middle ear and nonbacterial meningitis were reported. In these cases *M. pneumoniae* could not be isolated from blood or cerebrospinal fluid.

Chronic heart and lung diseases were the most common illnesses predisposing to infection with *M. pneumoniae;* these occurred in 77% of 87 patients who had chronic illnesses.

In October 1967 the World Health Organization convened a Scientific Group on Respiratory Viruses and their report became available as WHO *Technical Report Series,* 1969, no. 408. The report contains recent information that has been accumulated about the importance and distribution of an increasing number of pathogenic agents; effective immunological control of diseases caused by a few of them now seemed attainable.

The report contains summaries, in tabular form, of the biophysical, serological, and biological properties and the various host systems (types of cells and animal species) of viruses associated with respiratory tract diseases. There is also a table listing the occurrence of diseases caused by enteroviruses and reoviruses and an assessment of the evidence of their ability to cause respiratory disease in man.

For Coxsackie A21 and B3, evidence is considered conclusive for causative relationship to colds, pharyngitis, simple upper respiratory infections, and, occasionally, lower respiratory disease and pneumonia. Echovirus 19 was clearly shown to be the cause of epidemics of upper respiratory infections among groups of children. Evidence for a causative relation of Coxsackie A1-10, A23, B1, 4, 5, and 6, and most of the other types of Echovirus to a variety of respiratory illness was published but in each instance was considered inconclusive.

Progress toward immunologic protection against viral respiratory infections has been slow. No marked changes have been made in the commercial methods of producing influenza virus vaccines. Experimentally, however, vaccines of reduced toxicity (by using split antigens) and increased potency without clinically evident toxicity (by employing metabolizable adjuvants) have shown considerable promise. Against parainfluenza viruses types 1, 2, and 3, which are agents of lower respiratory tract illness and croup in children, some progress has been made in the development of killed vaccines that produce good antibody levels, but their protective efficacy remains to be established. Respiratory syncytial virus is the most important cause of viral respiratory disease, especially in infants. Progress toward developing an effective vaccine against this virus has been slow; resistance apparently develops, however, after one or more natural infections.

The greatest progress in the 1960s has been in the elucidation of the role of rhinoviruses in the etiology of the common cold. More than 50 distinct serotypes have been clearly established and at least as many more candidate types have been proposed. Although this helps explain why common colds are so frequent and prevalent, it does nothing to provide a basis for effective control, particularly because there does not appear to be any small group of predominant types. Oral feedings in enteric-coated capsules fail to induce antibody production.

One of the most serious chronic conditions, particularly in middle-aged males, is the obstructive emphysema associated with chronic bronchitis. Although the attention of most investigators has been focused on the relentless deterioration in the later stages of the bronchitis when complicated by emphysema and its secondary effects on the heart, D. Reid (London) felt that this engenders a fatalism about the possibilities for effective prevention. He called attention, however, to circumstantial evidence from various studies pointing to events during early life that may be important in determining the development of serious bronchitis in middle age, when it takes its greatest toll. Repeated respiratory infections in childhood, he pointed out, predispose to adult bronchitis. In geographic areas where bronchitis is a common cause of hospitalization, there also are high rates of hospitalization of children for upper respiratory tract and related infections such as otitis. Based upon these and many similar observations Reid and his co-workers were of the opinion that investigations should be focused on the causes of respiratory illness in general at all ages, rather than merely on bronchitis in adults.

Evidence that gave promise of being useful in planning preventive measures came from studies of

British and Norwegian migrants to the U.S. and to South Africa. When they move, particularly in childhood, to the more favourable conditions, they smoke no less, but their death rates from chronic lung disease fall markedly, indicating that the higher standard of living is associated with a reduced tendency to die from respiratory illness. Finally, a survey among schoolchildren indicated that those who smoked had more respiratory symptoms than those who did not. Antismoking propaganda had little effect on the smoking habits, but changes in smoking habits resulted in appreciable changes in symptoms. (M. Fd.)

RHEUMATOLOGY

Arthritis and rheumatism include almost 100 diseases that affect the joints and connective tissue. Of these the most common and disabling are rheumatoid arthritis, osteoarthritis, rheumatic fever, gout, and systemic lupus erythematosus. In the U.S., with a population of 200 million, almost 17 million persons were afflicted by some form of arthritis. Nearly half of them were partly or totally disabled. Each year 250,000 more persons became victims. Arthritis appeared in one out of five families. The figures for other countries were proportionally similar. Arthritis sufferers in the U.S. lost 12.2 million workdays a year, a figure equivalent to 47,000 persons out of work for the entire year.

Rheumatoid arthritis, although it hits all ages, strikes principally at the 20–45-year age group, crippling in the prime-of-life years. Its victims numbered some five million, including even children, in the U.S. and almost 100 million throughout the world. For some reason it afflicts women three times more frequently than men. On the other hand, 90% of the gout and rheumatoid spondylitis patients are men. An estimated 15% of those afflicted with rheumatoid arthritis recover completely after one or a few attacks, 20% develop a serious disability, and 65% have some permanent discomfort with periodic flare-ups.

Investigators studying rheumatic diseases have discovered many changes in body chemistry that take place in joints inflamed by arthritis. An important research advance has been the disclosure that sacs containing enzymes break open and help bring about the pain and damage in arthritic joints.

Experts in arthritis therapeutic research have developed care programs involving a combination of medication, exercises, rest, heat, posture training, and methods for protecting inflamed joints. Surgery for joints damaged by arthritis is increasingly successful.

Effective drugs for various rheumatic diseases include aspirin, phenylbutazone, indomethacin, corticosteroids, organic gold salts, probenecid, and colchicine and allopurinol for gout. (W. S. Cl.)

SURGERY

When Philip Blaiberg, who survived for more than 19 months with a transplanted heart, finally succumbed on August 17 (*see* Obituaries), the intense enthusiasm for cardiac transplantation appeared to die with him. Although heart surgery and repair continued, transplants, if performed at all late in 1969, received no publicity.

A technique for myocardial revascularization was developed early in the year. The procedure involved triple implantation of systemic arteries and was used in 31 patients. One died of coronary thrombosis within 24 hours after surgery. Recovery was prompt with no major complications in most of the rest.

Diseased aortic valves in 70 patients were replaced with homograft valves. The technique can be used instead of insertion of Starr Edwards ball-valve prostheses. Hospital mortality was 4.3% and there were no instances of infection, thromboembolism, or late deaths. Fourteen percent had diastolic murmurs at postoperative evaluation, but the leakage was clinically significant in only one patient.

Modified bovine carotid artery heterografts were employed as femoral or popliteal artery replacements in 12 patients with favourable preliminary results.

Although, as mentioned previously, heart transplant surgery lost its popularity late in 1969, transplantation of other organs and tissues continued. Experience gained from 13 liver transplant operations was described in the *British Medical Journal* in July. Particular reference was made to the findings in nine patients who survived the immediate operative period. Infection was the major problem. Five patients were able to go home and were alive and well 14 or 20 weeks after the operation.

In the U.S., four-year-old Randy Bennett was the longest living liver transplant patient in the world. He received his new liver in February 1968 and in November he made one of his periodic visits to a Denver hospital for a routine checkup.

Skin loss from burns and extensive traumatic avulsions were treated in 41 infants and children (New Orleans, La.) by temporary cutaneous allografts of adult cadaver or fetal origin. Use of this material avoided immunologic difficulties and the grafts functioned as physiological dressings until wound closure was accomplished by healing or by autograft procedures.

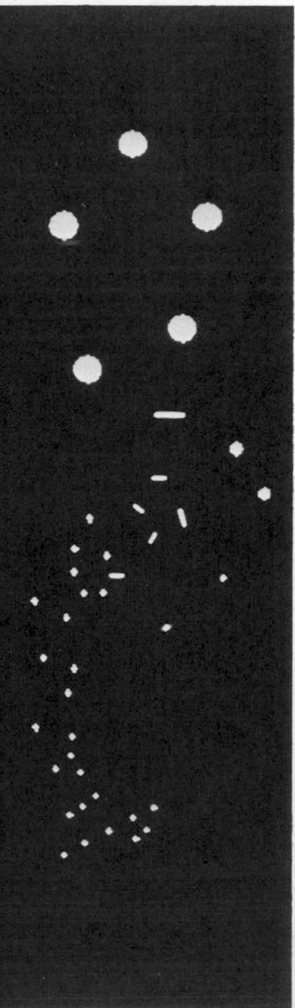

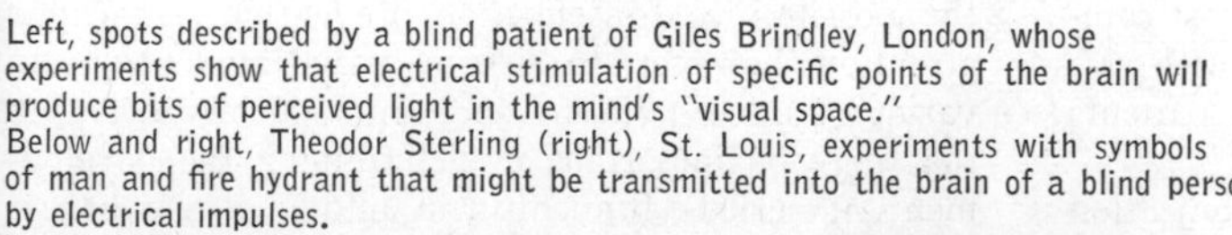

Left, spots described by a blind patient of Giles Brindley, London, whose experiments show that electrical stimulation of specific points of the brain will produce bits of perceived light in the mind's "visual space."
Below and right, Theodor Sterling (right), St. Louis, experiments with symbols of man and fire hydrant that might be transmitted into the brain of a blind person by electrical impulses.

GEORGE TAMES, "MEDICAL WORLD NEWS"

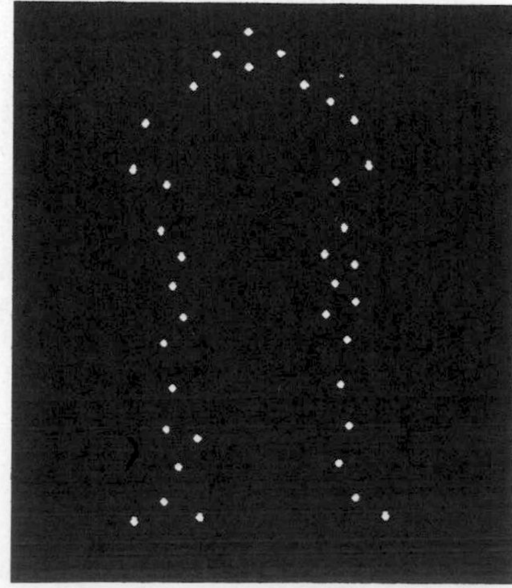

A report from Royal Victoria Hospital in Montreal in August revealed that the survival rate among 93 patients who received 108 cadaver kidney allografts was 42%. Follow-up continued from two weeks to 4.7 years.

The world's first transplant of a larynx, complete with vocal cords and surrounding tissues, was reported to *The Times* (London) from Ghent, Belg., in February. The operation, performed on a 62-year-old male cancer patient, was reported to be satisfactory, but details were unavailable.

As with heart transplants, the major problems encountered with other major transplant surgery were those of rejection and infection, the latter due primarily to reduced resistance as a result of immunosuppressive drug administration. (X.)

TROPICAL MEDICINE

Plague in Vietnam was cause for concern during the year (see *Public Health: Epidemics,* above), and American personnel were infected. The number of provinces in Vietnam reporting plague increased from 1 in 1961 to 24 in the first six months of 1966, and during this period the number of cases increased from 8 to 2,649. Plague also reappeared in Hue and Da Nang after being absent for 15 years. Infection was thought to be spread by rats carried in food trucks and in coastal shipments of rice.

An increase in plague was also reported from Central America. Several hundred cases appeared in Ecuador where the disease invaded coastal urban areas, causing a number of deaths.

Fortunately potent treatment for plague is now available. Among the older antibiotics streptomycin, chloramphenicol, and tetracycline are effective, as are kanamycin, neomycin, framycetin, and colistin among those more recently introduced.

Leprosy was encountered among immigrants to Britain and there were fears that transmission of the disease in temperate regions might reoccur. In the Netherlands one of some 300 patients being treated for leprosy was proved to have contracted the disease there. Among immigrants to the Netherlands from the West Indies, 1% had leprosy. Fears concerning transmission in temperate regions may be exaggerated, but the number of cases reported in tropical regions was astonishing. In Peru the population was increasing by 2% annually but the incidence of leprosy was increasing by 6.5%. In some districts the rate of increase was as much as 13% annually. A World Health Organization leprosy advisory team found that the cases of leprosy per 100 inhabitants were 12.37 in northeastern Thailand, 25.84 in Cameroon, and 28.73 in northern Nigeria.

Several ongoing studies indicate that inoculation with BCG (Bacillus Calmette-Guérin, vaccination), normally used for prophylaxis of tuberculosis, affords considerable protection against leprosy, but sulfones still remain the most widely used drugs for the treatment of the disease.

Gastrointestinal disorders are affecting more and more individuals as air travel to the tropics increases. A working party set up by the Medical Research Council, London, excluded as causes mere change in the richness or quality of food eaten overseas and the chemical constituents of drinking water and placed most of the blame on contaminated food and water. The etiology is typified by the findings of S. Bell in southern India where 15% of 166 nurses were found to harbour amebic cysts and three out of five food handlers were carriers of the infection. In West Africa amebic dysentery has a high mortality rate. Among the newer drugs tried against both the intestinal and hepatic form of the disease, metronidazole has been found to be effective.

Onchocerciasis, a filarial infection, is one of the most disabling of tropical diseases that cause blindness. In northeastern Tanzania the disease was found to be associated with ocular disorders, and more recently it was discovered in southern Tanzania. It now seems probable that onchocerciasis is prevalent over wide areas of Africa and in Central and South America where new endemic areas were reported in Venezuela and Colombia. In the tropics it is highly probable that there exist many disabling diseases which have been tolerated for generations but which go unreported. (A. W. Wo.)

WORLD HEALTH ORGANIZATION

The health manpower situation and medical education were among the preoccupations of the 22nd World Health Assembly, held in Boston in July. The assembly brought together delegates from most of WHO's 131 member and associate-member states and adopted a working budget of $67,650,000 for 1970, an increase of $5,528,300 over that for 1969.

A new approach to malaria eradication was adopted that would permit more flexibility in planning projects better adapted to locally prevailing health, economic, and social conditions.

The smallpox eradication program made progress in 1968. The total number of cases in the world was about 67,000, a 40% decrease from that of the preceding year. The reduction, achieved despite improved reporting, may reflect cyclical variations in the disease.

The assembly adopted the new International Health Regulations which, tentatively, will replace the International Sanitary Regulations on Jan. 1, 1971.

Fluoridation of community water supplies was recommended to WHO member states by the World Health Assembly in places where fluoride intake is below optimal levels, as a "practical, safe, and efficient public health measure." Dental caries is one of man's most prevalent diseases, affecting people of all ages in all countries.

Twenty-four countries were participating in WHO's program of population dynamics and family planning. The organization also supported laboratory and clinical research to test various approaches to family planning care.

The expanded medical research program now covered virtually all aspects of public health. It was of fundamental importance to WHO's work and an essential for the prevention or control of major communicable diseases, nutritional disorders, cancer, cardiovascular diseases, mental illness, and other problems.

There appeared to be no possibility of providing a sufficient number of physicians to practice in the less developed countries for at least a generation. The assembly requested the economically developed countries to assist in the establishment and operation of medical schools in the less developed countries. It was the opinion that the training of physicians in their own countries and regions prepared them to deal with local health problems and encouraged them to stay and serve their own people. Appeal was made to physicians native to the less developed countries but trained elsewhere to return home to practice.

(WHO)

See also Dentistry; Insurance; Molecular Biology; Psychology; Social Services; Vital Statistics.

Encyclopædia Britannica Films. *Alcoholism* (1952); *Allergies* (1952); *Antibiotics* (1952); *Drug Addiction* (1952); *Mental Health (Keeping Mentally Fit)* (1952); *Cancer* (1953); *The Skeleton* (1953); *Bacteria—Friend or Foe* (1954); *First Aid on the Spot* (1954); *Heart Disease—Its Major Causes* (1955); *The Human Brain* (1955); *Immunization* (1955); *The Spinal Column* (1956); *Tuberculosis* (1956); *Work of the Blood* (1957); *The Housefly* (1958); *Health in Our Community* (1959); *DNA—Molecule of Heredity* (1960); *The Blood* (1961); *Mitosis* (1961); *Bacteria* (1962); *Meiosis: Sex Cell Formation* (1962); *Eyes and Vision* (1963); *Gene Action* (1963); *Laws of Heredity* (1963); *Natural Selection* (1963); *The Digestive System* (1965); *The Hospital* (1966); *Chromosomes of Man* (1967); *The Eyes and Seeing* (1968); *The Work of the Heart* (1968); *Ears and Hearing* (1969); *Muscle: Chemistry of Contraction* (1969); *Muscle: Dynamics of Contraction* (1969); *Radioisotopes: Tools of Discovery* (1969); *Respiration in Man* (1969).

Merchandising

Most of the industrialized world continued its strong growth in 1969. Gross national product (GNP) figures reached new highs, and spending—in both the business and the private sector—continued unabated. The general economic background in Europe was one of continued strength of the West German mark and weakness of sterling and the French franc. This led to the devaluation of the franc in August, and to the revaluation of the mark in October. The respective countries' internal policies had to be seen in this light. The decision of the Common Market countries to harmonize on a value-added tax and of Britain to increase the selective employment tax resulted in upward pressure on prices. High interest rates resulted in further pressure on retail margins.

While the trend toward international activities in manufacturing was accelerating, the trend in merchandising lagged behind. There were signs in Europe that increased leisure was leading to more flexibility in opening hours, which in turn had a feedback on shopping habits, but the process was slow. There was also some evidence of the leveling off of prices, at least of textiles and clothing, which had increased most in the Netherlands where the overall level of prices was lowest.

However, severe strains on food prices and policies appeared in the Common Market countries, accentuated by a surplus of 400,000 metric tons of butter. The French were allowed to withdraw from the common policy when the franc was devalued and special protective measures were taken by West Germany when the mark was allowed to float. Almost certainly the agricultural policy would have to be reworked.

Automatic dispensers of bank notes, where a plastic credit-type card was inserted in a machine, were spreading in France and the United Kingdom. In both the U.K. and Sweden, shops selling clothes suitable for either sex has begun. If "unisex" clothes turned out to be a long-term trend, rather than a passing fad, considerable upheaval in the clothing trade could be expected. (*See* Fashion and Dress: *Special Report*.) Another trend, at the luxury end of the market, was for shops to colour-match home decorations, furniture, accessories, and even clothes so that purchase as a unit was possible. The growth of garden centres, particularly in France and the U.K., where qualified staff sold trees, shrubs, plants, seeds, bulbs, and gardening equipment, was likely to spread and affect the traditional nurseryman and seedsman.

Mental Health: *see* Medicine; Psychology

In the United States, the Nixon administration battled its foremost problem, inflation, but there was little evidence of a slowdown. Consumer spending was the only area in which the increases were not spectacular. Although retail sales reached all-time highs during each quarter of 1969, the major reason for this steady climb was the increase in prices, rather than rising volume. The continuation of the surtax made buyers more conservative in their purchases, and the Hong Kong flu epidemic, which hit the U.S. in the first part of the year, kept people out of stores.

Spending was highest for nondurables. In the first quarter, according to Commerce Department figures, apparel and department store sales jumped by 7% and drugstore sales rose 12%. Food prices soared at an annual rate of 9% between February and July, according to the Department of Commerce. Spending for durables was up slightly in the first half, but dropped 0.3% in the second half of the year. Late in the second quarter, the consumer appeared to be more optimistic. Data gathered by the Survey Research Center of the University of Michigan showed some improvement in consumer attitude. The index of consumer sentiment rose to 95.1% from a low of 92.1% in October 1968. The Canadian economy grew at a rate of 4% during 1969. Consumer demand picked up momentum in the second half of 1968 and continued through 1969. Increased sales of household appliances and furnishings partly reflected a pickup in housing starts.

Young people were spending a large amount of the consumer dollar; many were spending all they earned and taking great advantage of installment credit. Installment credit outstanding rose to more than $91 billion in the second quarter. The costs of medical, maintenance, and other services rose sharply; and the consumer paid the higher prices rather than cutting down spending in those areas. A major development in the U.S. was the growing importance of integrated marketing systems in virtually all lines of trade. These systems were professionally managed, centrally programmed networks designed to achieve operating economies and maximum market impact and were rapidly becoming the dominant distribution mechanisms in the U.S.

In the U.K. the share of trade of different types of outlet continued along familiar lines, with the multiples (chain stores) gaining at the expense of independent shops. Department stores showed a very mixed performance. The conversion of British currency to a decimal system on Feb. 15, 1971, was expected to cause a number of small shopkeepers to retire earlier than they would have otherwise and was, therefore, likely to accelerate the trend to multiples. A scheme by Securicor to set up check-cashing kiosks in large food stores was discontinued in August, after a short trial period. According to a Nielson survey of 18 products, nearly 30% of sales by value, representing over 35% by volume, were private label rather than national brands. The biggest enigma was still posed by the cooperative movement in which reforms had not been sufficient to stop a relative decline. A party was studying the Swedish Cooperation Förbundet in Stockholm.

There was a rapid development in cash and carry wholesaling. The largest group of users was still the independent grocers, but butchers, druggists, baked-goods shops, and packaged liquor outlets (off-licenses) were also using them. There was a long and acrimonious debate in the trade press about their use by the public. The idea of selling to "captive customers" occurred to British European Airways, which, in conjunction with Impress International Merchandising, began a mail-order operation in June known as the BEA Sky Shop. The aim was to give passengers the opportunity of buying goods associated with travel or the gift trade, mostly either of an exclusive nature or at special prices. Clairol, an American company, was selling its nail enamel and lipstick in Britain in a novel way. It supplied interested hairdressers with do-it-yourself manicure units that fit over the client's knees while she was sitting under a hair dryer.

Shopping centres were not having the success that was predicted, partly because of some overambitious schemes and lack of growth in retail trade. The U.S. pattern of shopping once a week by car was not being followed; a survey showed nearly 70% of shopping was done on foot several times a week with average spending on each occasion being only 14*s*. The U.S. trend toward small movie theatres fitted into shop and office developments or of the conversion of large cinemas into smaller units where a number of films can be shown simultaneously appeared to be spreading to Britain. A Cinecenta opened in January in London off Leicester Square.

A Monopolies Commission report found that the practice of manufacturer-recommended prices had grown rapidly since the resale price maintenance system had been abandoned. Particularly where there was a monopoly supplier, or where outlets were restricted, the general level of prices was likely to be higher with recommended prices. The report suggested that the government should have the power to prohibit the practice where it was shown to be against the public interest. Action was not expected until the commission reported on the more serious matter of stopping supplies to a retailer who is disliked by a manufacturer. The major phonograph manufacturers withdrew their case from the Restrictive Practices Court in June 1969. Consequently, discs and recording tape were no longer price-maintained and were expected to be sold more widely by supermarkets, which had been denied supplies unless they were sold at list prices.

A year after the ending of resale price maintenance on cigarettes, the number of small tobacco retailers forced out of business was not as high as had been forecast. After the first heady rush of price cutting by multiple shops, selling and stocking costs had been assessed and prices appeared to have settled at about 1*d*. off a packet of 20 cigarettes. In September Carreras announced it would give 20 Green Shield trading stamps with each pack of 20 cigarettes as a sales incentive for a new brand called Cambridge. Those multiples already using Green Shield stamps welcomed the move in the hope that if more people were induced to collect stamps then more people would go to those shops offering them. The powerful non-stamp-giving chains threatened a boycott of all Carreras products.

The Monopolies Commission also found that fees charged by real estate agents in Britain compared favourably with those in most other countries, but recommended that the practice of charging standard fees should go. A new venture called National Property Supermarkets, with 70 offices already opened and 100 more due before 1971, advertised a property locally for a fee of five guineas or nationally for ten guineas. The organization's suggestion that agents use its services had so far met with hostility.

In the U.S., more than 110 bills to protect buyers were introduced in the 91st Congress, which opened in January. A bill to set up a Cabinet-level Department of Consumer Affairs was sponsored by more than 100 members of the House of Representatives. On August 10, a task force of the Democratic Study Group in the House came out for a separate consumer agency in the government and endorsed 30 kinds of new protective measures. On August 12, the Federal Trade Commission ruled that gasoline stations and food stores must tell their customers more about their chances of winning in promotional games.

CENTRAL PRESS FROM PICTORIAL PARADE

Passers-by stare at nude models featured in the window display for the grand opening of a boutique in London's Carnaby Street in May 1969. Police arrested the shop owner for obstructing the highway.

Businesses became worried and frustrated over the potential for regulation. Pending warranty legislation was strict and, in the opinion of many industry leaders, almost impossible to live with. It included not only the requirement for a full parts and labour warranty if any guarantee of product performance was offered at all, but also compulsory arbitration of warranty grievances. Other areas of apprehension included industry-wide production standards and product certification.

After eight years of debate in Congress, the Consumer Credit Protection Act (Truth-in-Lending) became law during the first week of July. Few people expected that the new law would modify the borrowing patterns of the U.S. consumer. A survey published by the Federal Reserve Bank of Boston found that the ability to meet the periodic payment remained the consumer's primary concern.

In the U.S. auto market, 11 out of every 100 new car customers purchased an imported car—the highest percentage in history. Hoping to meet this challenge, in late March the Ford Motor Company introduced the Maverick, which had a basic sticker price of $1,995 and put Ford within $200 of Volkswagen, the most troublesome competition. In September, American Motors announced plans to introduce the first of the domestic subcompacts (now code-named the Gremlin) in early 1970. General Motors still debated about the debut date for its subcompact, the Chevrolet XP-887. The battle of the imports was expected to spread to the medium-priced lines. In April, Volkswagen of America, Inc., announced it would import the Audi, an over-$3,000 car, and combine it with the sporty, high-priced Porsche in a separate dealer organization.

The high cost of building and financing caused many thousands of families to turn toward a new style of living—the mobile home park. Most mobile units sold for less than $10,000 but luxury models might sell for over $25,000. Sales broke records month after month in 1969 and, overall, were estimated to be 400,000 units, up from 300,000 in 1968. Industry experts predicted mobile homes would soon account for one-third of all the new single-family houses sold in the U.S. Nearly six million persons were already living in them. It was understood that Sears, Roebuck & Co. would be marketing trailers in the '70s.

Antitrust policy was one of the three priorities set by the Justice Department. The department challenged the take-over of the food vending giant Canteen Corporation by International Telephone & Telegraph Corporation on the ground of potential reciprocity and served notice in June that it intended to challenge attempts by patent holders to fix licensees' prices in situations where the licensee was simply a retailer. In the Consolidated Foods case, the Supreme Court ruled that the food company must divest itself of Gentry, Inc., a seasonings manufacturer, because the mere potential for reciprocal dealing existed.

To counteract the decrease in the volume of cigarette sales, tobacco companies increased their promotional efforts in the first half of the year. Liggett & Myers introduced its Chesterfield Club coupons nationally on all packages of its Chesterfield brand, while Lorillard put its Old Gold 100s, which carry Five Star coupons, into additional markets. American Tobacco gave away two packs with the purchase of a carton. Lorillard engaged in cash giveaways keyed to the performance of local major league baseball teams.

The fastest growing business in the U.S. in 1969 was leisure. It was estimated that one million snowmobiles would be in use in the U.S. and Canada by the end of 1969, at an average cost of $1,000. More than $27 million was spent on rackets, balls, and accessories by nine million tennis players, and four million snow skiers spent $900 million for their equipment, lodging, and entertainment. In addition, a total of 1.7 million Americans owned second homes. Sales of recreational housing, typically single-story, four-room structures valued at $7,800, were expected to hit $1.4 billion in 1969.

The acceptance of women's trousers in 1969 gave a big boost to women's apparel sales and took accessories and a sagging sportswear business along with it. Manufacturers of women's pants reported 50% increases in sales in 1969 and new firms entering the field called their sales fantastic.

There was a drop in TV sales in the first half of 1969. Sales of colour sets ran 15–20% lower than in 1968, while black-and-white sales were down 5–10%. Consumers appeared to be waiting for the prices to go down or were confused by too many different sizes in picture tubes. Buyers of 1970 models in the second half of the year appeared to be more interested in portables and table sets than in the big console models.

During 1969, Ford of Europe, Inc., introduced the Capri, which was designed and built jointly by Ford's British and German subsidiaries. It was the first European car to offer a full range of engine options and, it was hoped, would change European car-buying tastes. In the U.K., Leyland Motor Corporation was merged with British Motor Holding to form the last major bulwark against complete U.S. ownership of the British auto industry. The company was expected to introduce a new Austin, aimed at the engineering-conscious British buyer, and a Morris for the more style-conscious Capri buyers.

The aftermath of the strikes of 1968 continued to dominate the French economy. The run on the franc in November 1968 was accompanied by the dropping of the $4\frac{1}{2}$% payroll tax and an increase in the value-added tax from $16\frac{2}{3}$ to 19% in an attempt to make exports more competitive. These measures resulted in a great upsurge in consumer purchases of both durable and nondurable goods in an attempt to beat price increases. Retail prices increased sharply early in 1969, and the spending spree leveled off and was not expected to resume for some time.

France's small businessman proved very militant in 1969, fighting a forlorn rearguard battle against the spread of multiple shops, supermarkets, and taxation. In February 20,000 demonstrated at Grenoble and in April a municipal building was dynamited at Quimper in Brittany. Also in April thousands of files were taken as "hostages" from a taxation office at La Tour-du-Pin and 5,000 cars were used to block roads in the area; the riot police used gas against the protesters. Gerand Nicoud, the leader, took to the hills. In September brief "kidnappings" of a mayor and two policemen occurred. Farmers in some places gave their produce away in protest against low prices.

In West Germany the growth of "hypermarkets" or large stores continued. It was estimated in October 1968 that there were 333 new stores with an average of 6,000 sq.m. of selling space. Fourteen companies operated over one-third of the stores. Frankfurt's shopping centre, faced with reluctance of shoppers to change their ways, staged a 99-day promotion campaign with puppet shows, an army band, and two special 16-day promotions. One had an Italian theme; the other, a Wild West scene, culminating in a "bank robbery" by five cowboys and the distribution of chocolate money among the children.

Small retailers in Sweden adopted the idea of renting space or having a shop within a department store. After forming an association to acquire premises, each trader rented his own space and a store manager took care of administration, advertising, and other communal matters. The idea started in 1960 and by 1969 there were 15 of these joint department stores ranging in size from 65,000 to over 100,000 sq.ft. These stores increased sales in 1967 by 15%, which, although less than the chain store figure of 18–20%, was considerably above the average of 8% for Swedish retail trade as a whole. A more puzzling development was the opening of a shop in Stockholm that sold clothes in partial exchange for other clothes.

Travel agents in the Netherlands appeared to be in for a tough time with the announcement that one of the country's two big banks, Algemene Bank Nederland, was linking with ANWB, the Dutch automobile association, to provide package tours. The bank saw this as a method of winning new customers and a logical extension of its existing services such as the provision of foreign currency and insurance.

In Zambia moves against non-Zambian traders were expected to have large-scale repercussions on trade. As of January 1969, non-Zambians were barred from retail trading outside the business centres of ten major towns, unless they were dealing in certain specialized goods. Wholesaling licenses were still being granted but this was a limited field. It was estimated that about 800 Asian traders were put out of business as one-third of the country's shops closed down.

In July, a joint venture, Gold Bond Japan Ltd., was announced between the Gold Bond Stamp Company and Mitsubishi Shoji, one of the most powerful general trading companies in Japan. Indications were that the firm planned to go from stamps into manufacturers' coupons, incentive motivation programs, direct-mail marketing, and merchandising via credit cards—all projects pioneered by Gold Bond in the U.S. over the preceding 30 years.

It was predicted that the 1970 sales target of Japan's supermarket industry would significantly surpass department store grosses forecast for the same period. Japanese department stores were subject to legislation that set limits on business hours and days, established sales-floor-space requirements, and set guidelines for mass media advertising. Supermarkets could escape compliance with these regulations by leasing blocks of floor space to different owners, thus avoiding the official classification of a department store.

(A. F. D.; G. C. Ho.)

See also Advertising; Consumer Expenditures; Industrial Review; Prices.

Metallurgy

The most notable event in metallurgy during 1969 was probably the nickel shortage that developed from a combination of chronic undersupply and a long strike involving much of the non-Communist world's production capacity. In the United States the "gray market" price reached more than three times the quoted price. Since they could not use scrap, electroplaters were particularly hurt. For decorative plating, copper directly under chromium was being used. The high-nickel-content superalloys for high-temperature service were mostly used in government projects and so had high priority, but the types of stainless and high-alloy steels in which manganese was being substituted for much of the nickel were being used in many places where they caused difficulty in the forming operations and gave less satisfactory service. The shortage quickly made apparent industry's dependence on the unique properties of nickel.

The entire field of powder metallurgy was widely believed to be on the verge of rapid expansion. A variety of metals and alloys were available in powder form, and numerous techniques for producing mill shapes and finished parts, many with unique properties, had been developed. The economic situation also favoured the savings in capital investment and labour that production by powder metallurgy allowed. The major difficulties in forming aluminum by powder metallurgy were surmounted, and suitable powders of aluminum and some alloys became available. Production capacity for iron powders exceeded demand and encouraged their use; titanium parts such as pipe fittings were being made by powder metallurgy; and new uses for beryllium (usually fabricated by powder metallurgy) were promising to expand as rapidly as supplies of this rather rare metal would allow. Hot pressing of sintered metal preforms was producing parts with mechanical properties equal to forgings and sized and finished so that little machining was necessary. Porous powder metallurgical repair parts for human bones were shown to be advantageous because they could be impregnated with antibiotics to reduce antagonism to the body, and growing tissue would penetrate the pores to hold the repair firmly in place.

Titanium seemed to be at a stage where its steadily increasing application was assured. Most of the metal-forming processes had been adapted to titanium, and standard and special shapes could be produced at reasonable cost. Alloys had been developed that made a fair range of properties available, although the potential existed for much greater development. A new beta-phase alloy was said to have the cold formability of other alloys when soft but to be heat-treatable to a tensile strength of 200,000 lb. per sq.in., which is comparable to high-strength steel. To overcome one barrier to the wider use of titanium, a large contract was let for a search for economical methods of reclaiming scrap. The only method in use was remelting clean scrap of known alloy composition, and this left a large amount of unsegregated material unreclaimable. Extrusions of titanium as well as other hard-to-work metals such as age-hardening stainless steel were being accurately sized and straightened by drawing through a sizing die with back tension as great as 70% of the yield strength. Trimming of the flash from titanium forgings was being done with the plasma torch as the very-high-temperature flame burned through the flash before much heat was conducted to the body of the forging. This process eliminated both overheating and the danger of cracking that exists with mechanical trimming.

Fatigue and fracture continued to be the subjects of some of the most active research in metallurgy. The onset of fracture remained quite unpredictable, and crack propagation could be very rapid. In the numerous situations where cracking could not be absolutely prevented, it became desirable to develop means of predicting when and where a crack might start and of being able to slow its growth so that there would be a chance to find it before failure occurred. The scanning electron microscope, a relatively new research tool, was being used to good advantage for direct observation of fracture surfaces to learn where and why cracks start and how they grow.

Testing and reliability continued to attract much attention. Among the most interesting test methods developed was ultrasonic holography. Two sets of ultrasonic waves, one of which passes through the specimen, can form an interference pattern of water waves on the surface of a bath in which the test assembly is submerged. A photograph of this wave pattern viewed by the light from a laser gives a view of the specimen and any defects capable of scattering the sound waves.

High-energy-rate forming was being widely used for producing large parts, such as 4½-ft.-diameter hemispheres of alloy steel shaped by using explosives, and also for difficult-to-form materials, especially where close-dimensional tolerance was required. The British development of a liquid-fueled, high-energy-rate machine capable of continuous operation with a short cycle time brought closer the commercial application of such high production rates. The cost of the machine was expected to be less than for the slower electric discharge or compressed gas machines.

The long-standing problem of brazing aluminum alloys efficiently was solved for many applications by cladding a base alloy with an aluminum alloy that had a lower melting point. Parts made of the clad material were assembled and heated in a vacuum to melt the cladding and join the assembly together. No flux was needed.

Several new alumina plants and new mills beneficiating iron ore came into use in connection with the development of new sources of ore, especially in Australia. A large part of the new iron ore production was contracted for by Japanese companies, though Australia was developing its own steel industry. A 5,000-ton-per-day blast furnace went into production in the U.S.; one of the most difficult problems in designing the furnace plant was handling the tremendous amount of liquid iron.

(D. F. C.)

See also Industrial Review; Mining; Physics.

Encyclopædia Britannica Films. *The Miner* (1967).

Merchant Marine:
see Transportation

Metals:
see Industrial Review; Metallurgy; Mining

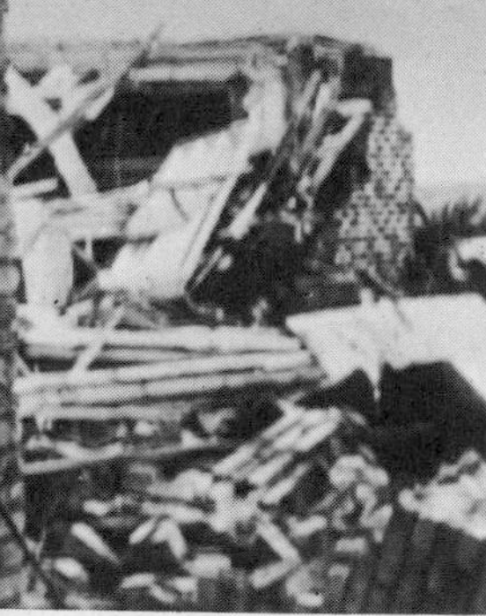

WIDE WORLD

Series of pictures of an approaching tornado photographed by a resident of Ripley, Okla., moments before his home was destroyed (bottom) by the storm in late June 1969.

Meteorology

Extremes and vagaries of weather and climate occurred during 1969, but none of the world's more than 100,000 climatological stations reported any atmospheric conditions that distinguished the weather as a whole from that of other years. In contrast, the science of the atmosphere was redoubling its attack on unsolved meteorological problems.

Indications of the scope and tone of meteorological activities during the year could be seen in the January 1969 *Bulletin* of the World Meteorological Organization (WMO). Among the subjects covered in the *Bulletin* were the development of space satellites; the growing utilization of data on air/sea relationships, especially from the tropical oceans; the first Global Atmospheric Research Program (GARP) experiment; the World Weather Watch (WWW); the costs of meteorological services; the development of hydrometeorology, including the forecasting of floods; and experiments in weather modification.

Atmospheric Exploration by Remote Probes. This subject, which was examined in a 700-page report by the National Academy of Sciences in January, was and continued to be the key to progress in meteorology. From its beginnings meteorology had been hampered by inadequate samplings of the vast ocean of air that makes up the earth's atmosphere. Even with the manifold increases in available data that had occurred since 1900, meteorologists estimated that they had only about one-fifth of the information that they needed. In a few countries of Western Europe, most of North America outside the Arctic regions, and in limited areas of other continents the facilities for observation and measurement of significant atmospheric parameters were perhaps greater than 50% of theoretical minimum requirements, but for most of the globe—especially over the oceans—data were scarce or entirely lacking.

Thus it was clear why meteorologists gave so much importance to the satellite infrared spectrometer (SIRS), which provided a method for almost continuous remote sensing of air temperatures from the top to the bottom of the atmosphere. SIRS had limitations; for example, it could not penetrate cloud layers to sense the temperatures of the air beneath. However, data telemetered through SIRS for the clear air up to heights of more than 100,000 ft. were practically identical with the measurements obtained by conventional radiosondes at comparable times and places. SIRS made it possible to increase upper air temperature measurements by several orders of magnitude and to obtain data from the oceans and polar regions.

A popular account of the evolution of SIRS from its first design in 1959 was published in *ESSA World* (U.S. Department of Commerce) in July 1969. The first operating model was carried on the Nimbus 3 satellite launched by the National Aeronautics and Space Administration (NASA) on April 14. Its success was described as "fantastic." For example, it transmitted some 5,000 temperature soundings per day from over the Southern Hemisphere, whereas the conventional radiosonde methods could provide only about 70 per day. SIRS was a 91-lb. instrument that measured the infrared radiation from the air on seven of the wavelengths in the 15-micron absorption band of carbon dioxide. The air temperatures at various levels were derived from these measurements through techniques developed by the ESSA Satellite Experiment Laboratory, Suitland, Md.

Emphasis on remote sensing extended to other, related spheres of geophysics. In a preliminary report by a National Academy of Sciences committee on solar-terrestrial research, scientists were reminded of the complexities of the sun-earth system. For example, a sun flare can release abnormal X-ray, ultraviolet, and cosmic radiation amounting roughly to 100 nonillion ergs (one nonillion has 30 zeros in the French and U.S. systems, 54 in the British and German systems). The consequences of such variations in solar output for the atmospheric elements that constitute weather and climate were the subject of speculation rather than knowledge in 1969, but it was quite possible that remote sensing and eventual understanding of the parameters in the sun-earth system might solve the mysteries of such secular changes in climate as the appearance of ice ages.

In the report, the committee's panel on atmospheric exploration by remote probes examined every promising method, including use of microwave line-of-sight propagation, optical line of sight propagation, radar, microwave radiometry, crossed beam correlation techniques, acoustic beams and waves, and lidar, a rather recent development defined as an optical radar-like technique using laser energy.

In September 1968 the monthly *Astronautics & Aeronautics* had published a committee statement on exploiting the explosive increase in atmospheric measurements. A host of sounding rockets and space satellites were transmitting floods of data of many different kinds. (Especially noteworthy during 1969 were profiles and vertical-column soundings of cloud masses, water vapour, and atmospheric ozone telemetered through satellites.) While the U.S. and the U.S.S.R. were the leading operators, several other countries financed launchings entirely or in part.

In February 1969 the *Bulletin* of the American Meteorological Society published photographs and analyses of Hurricane Gladys near Cuba and Florida and Typhoon Gloria over the western Pacific, as seen from Apollo 7 the preceding October. These were two of hundreds of thousands of such photographs that contributed essential knowledge of the structure and behaviour of tropical cyclones and improved the accuracy and effectiveness of storm warnings. Incomplete reports from the U.S.S.R. implied that Cosmos 243, among other satellites in the Cosmos series, carried devices for measuring temperatures, humidities, and ozone in the air column from top to bottom regardless of clouds. Scientists of the Meteorological Research Institute, Tokyo, the Japan Meteorological Agency, and the University of Chicago cooperated in designing and studying special time-lapse pictures derived through NASA satellite ATS-1, in stationary orbit over the mid-Pacific. From these they made further studies of typhoon formation and development and the extent and patterns of organized cloud systems over the Pacific.

In some cases special photographs for use in specific storm warnings were obtained by command; *e.g.*, during March Essa 8 and ATS-3 were used to derive better analyses of frontal systems over the Gulf of Mexico and lower Mississippi Valley when tornado-breeding factors began to appear on weather maps. By chance, the orbit of Apollo 9 crossed the suspected region at an opportune time, and the astronauts aboard that spacecraft could view the cloud systems

UPI COMPIX

Cyclonic storm system sighted about 1,200 mi. N of Hawaii. Photograph was taken by Apollo 9 astronauts on the 124th revolution of their space flight and displayed at the post-flight news conference on March 25, 1969.

involved. By virtue of a cooperative tornado surveillance program previously readied by ESSA, the U.S. Weather Bureau, NASA, and affiliated weather analysis centrals, the data obtained by the various satellites and by radar, radiosonde, and other methods were gathered and exchanged on a real-time basis and fed into the daily warning service system for broadcast to the public.

Other data inputs for the general worldwide synoptic weather reporting system, which in 1962–63 came to be known as the WWW, were still in the experimental stage. One of these, the GHOST (global horizontal sounding technique) balloon, had given a phenomenal performance by remaining in operation over the Southern Hemisphere for more than a year at an altitude of about 52,000 ft., circumnavigating the globe over the general latitudes of Australia and southern South America more than 30 times. Still another data source was the NOMAD ocean buoy moored in the Gulf of Mexico, where for several years it had automatically measured and transmitted by radio several weather elements vital to early detection of incipient hurricanes and other, less severe tropical cyclones.

BOMEX, GARP, and WWW. These were the interrelated components of the most basic and ambitious attempt ever made to solve the major problems of meteorology: the general circulation of the atmosphere and its detailed smaller mechanisms, and the predictability and controllability of atmospheric phenomena. BOMEX, the Barbados Oceanographic and Meteorological Experiment, was essentially a gigantic effort to solve these problems for a small segment of the atmosphere in the subtropics, the cube of atmosphere over a 90,000-sq.mi. area in the Atlantic east of Barbados. Since 1960 scientists had given considerable attention to the atmosphere over the tropics because the vast zones on both sides of the Equator are the chief source of energy for the "heat engine" that constitutes the general circulation of the atmosphere.

The operational phase of BOMEX was completed in July, but years of difficult analysis of data would be needed to determine how successful the experiment had been. BOMEX was made possible by cooperation among 7 federal agencies, 22 universities, 6 industrial laboratories, and the government of Barbados. Some 1,500 to 2,000 persons participated, and the facilities used included 17 aircraft, 12 ships, and 10 ocean buoys, all specially equipped for oceanographic or atmospheric measurements or observations. A unique craft among surface ships was the U.S. survey vessel "Flip," which was capable of being upended at sea to provide a floating laboratory instrument platform. The outputs from orbiting satellites that passed over the BOMEX area and from an elaborate array of scientific instruments installed on contiguous islands were tied into the data-gathering network. Indicative of the fantastic complexity of the concept were the 1,316 soundings of ocean temperature and salt content made by the 5 primary ships and the 2,367 air soundings made by balloons up to 100,000 ft., obtained by participating units of the U.S. Air Force. Broad-ranging aircraft reconnaissance was used to assist research into the convective processes in the trade winds and the possibility of a relationship between these and the formation of tropical cyclones.

Preliminary reports by the BOMEX scientists indicated that many accepted concepts on physical interactions at the air/sea interface needed modification. Oceanographers found some places with strong currents from the west where navigational charts had long shown westward drift. Radiation data indicated that possibly twice as much radiant energy from the sun was being absorbed by the atmosphere as had previously been thought, which meant that much less radiation was taken up by the ocean.

"Flip" obtained measurements from which the researchers confirmed a previously suspected but undocumented relation between local discontinuities in temperature, humidity, and cloud rows in the tropics. Aircraft pilots had noticed these frontal cloud patterns in the 1930s or earlier, but accurate data from fixed observation points at sea were lacking. Using the new data, scientists identified them as vestigial remnants of air mass intrusions from higher latitudes, in which the drier air had not yet thoroughly mixed with the warm, moist, tropical atmosphere. Another tentative conclusion was that many cloud clusters photographed by Tiros, ESSA, and other space satellites were dense cirrus forms rather than convective clouds and therefore were not major factors in the heat budget in the intertropical convergence zone between the northeast and southeast trade winds. BOMEX would serve as a trial run for GARP, so that plans for that more general program could be appraised and refined. Eventually the augmented weather reports required for GARP would be supplied by the WWW, which was expected to reach its full operating stage in the mid-1970s.

Weather and Its Modification. Floods induced by atmospheric disturbances caused death and destruction in scores of countries in 1969. Among the most catastrophic occurrences was the mud slide that began in mid-January as the result of record-breaking rains from coastal storms off southern California.

Table I. Selected Weather Headlines, 1969

Place	Date	Weather event	Unusual features
Boulder, Colo.	Jan. 6–8	Foehn winds ("chinook")	Gusts to 125 mph; property damage "freakish"
Southern California	Jan 15–26	Mountain mud slides from prolonged heavy rain	Houses buried in mud, 91 deaths; $1 billion in property losses
N. Pacific Ocean	March	Enormous cyclone covering most of the ocean	Photo from Apollo 7 gave great span and details
Berlin, N.H.	March 1	Snowfall to depth of 39 ft. following "endless days of snowing"	Northern New England covered with snow depths 200 in. or more
Western Europe	April	Late winter-type cyclones	Early weeks of spring stormy, cold, and wet
Great Britain	May	Dull, wet, and "thundery" throughout	Most localities had 30–50% subnormal sunshine
Taiwan and nearby islands	June	Typhoons; floods	Extremely heavy rains and high tides; huge loss
Australia	June–Sept.	Damaging droughts in many localities	Abnormal storm tracks caused subnormal rainfall
Biloxi, Miss.	Aug. 14–21	Hurricane Camille from Caribbean to Virginia	139 deaths; "the most intense hurricane ever to hit U.S."
Nelson County, etc., Va.	Aug. 19	30 in. rainfall, mostly within 8 hr.	186 deaths; unbelievably heavy rain flooded valleys; heavy loss
Chili, Equador, Peru	May–October	Drought prolonged; many places had no rain for years	Influence of erratic ocean currents reduced precipitation
Swan Island, Caribbean	September	Central "eye" Hurricane Francelia passed over	Radiosonde to 50,000 ft.; one of four ever made in "eye"
Canada and Lake Superior area of Michigan	mid-October	Temperatures below 0° F (near −19° C)	Early autumn outbreak of Arctic air set new record

Table II. Representative Hail Suppression Tests During 1959–69

Place	Purpose	Method	Quantity seeding	Estimate of results
Argentina	Research test	AgI seeding by ground generator	Moderate amounts of AgI	Uncertain; some reduction in hail reported
Iowa, Nebraska	Not research	Seeding by aircraft	Heavy AgI seeding	Reports favourable
Switzerland	Research	By ground generator	Light amount AgI	Five years' tests negative
U.S.S.R. (Ukraine)	Research and applied operations	By exploding shells fired by guns from ground	Moderate to heavy	Hail suppressed under selected circumstances

Note: The above cases illustrate the conflicting results of tests. Commercial operators claimed success in suppressing hail by seeding from aircraft, usually with silver iodide (AgI) smoke or pulverized crystals, but claims were controversial.

Houses in choice residential suburbs were buried or swept down the mountainside; highways were covered by mud to depths of 25 ft. or were scoured out into gullies; 91 persons died and property damage was estimated at more than $1 billion. Warnings and coordinated rescue operations kept losses fairly low, but the best available meteorological and geological knowledge had not been sufficient to permit prediction of the heavy rainfall or the extent of the slides. A few months later residents of the U.S. upper plains states benefited from perhaps the most farsighted and effective flood warning ever achieved. Deep snow accumulations over the plains had alerted hydrometeorologists to the flood potential, and warnings enabled civic organizations and individuals to take preventive measures and kept losses to a minimum. Even so, in some places, such as Minot, N.D., rivers overflowed even the highest emergency levees and destruction was heavy.

Several typhoons struck in the western Pacific, causing floods, loss of life, and property damage in Taiwan, Japan, the Philippines, and China. Despite the catastrophic damage in the affected localities, however, overall damage seemed to be less than usual in the region as a whole. In contrast, Hurricane Camille, which struck the coasts of Louisiana and Mississippi on August 17, was widely publicized as the most intense tropical cyclone to hit the U.S. since record keeping began. Because many victims were carried away in floodwaters or buried in debris, the casualties could only be estimated, but they almost surely reached several hundred. Winds at times exceeded 200 mph and tides in some places reached 20 ft. above normal high tide. Rainfall during the storm ranged from 10 to 20 in. over wide areas, and the remnant of the cyclone, by some combination of upper air conditions not yet understood, produced 30 in. or more at some points in western Virginia.

At about the same time, Hurricane Debbie had formed and moved to a region some 500 mi. S of Bermuda, where for the first time in many years Project Stormfury was able to seed the clouds near the hurricane centre in an effort to modify its forces. In December scientists announced that analysis of the results suggested the storm had been weakened, although this was by no means certain. Results of other weather modification experiments were also speculative. Soviet meteorologists reported success in hail suppression under specific circumstances, but except for unquestioned success in clearing fog by artificial means, weather modification continued to be a controversial subject. (*See* Table II.) Meanwhile, unintentional modification of climate by air pollution was receiving long overdue attention. (F. W. Rr.)

See also Astronautics; Conservation; Disasters; Oceanography.

Encyclopædia Britannica Films. *The Climates of North America* (1963); *Origins of Weather* (1963); *Weather Forecasting by Satellite* (1964); *Weather Satellites* (1965); *What Makes Clouds?* (1965); *What Makes the Wind Blow?* (1965); *Whatever the Weather* (1967).

Methodists:
see Religion

Mexico

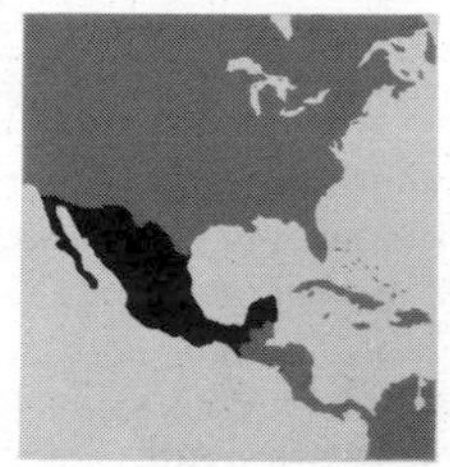

A federal republic of Middle America, Mexico is bounded by the U.S., British Honduras, and Guatemala. Area: 761,601 sq.mi. (1,972,547 sq.km.). Pop. (1969 est.): 48,933,000, including about 70% mestizo and 28% Indian. Cap. and largest city: Mexico City (pop., 1969 est., 3,483,649). Language: Spanish. Religion: predominantly Roman Catholic. President in 1969, Gustavo Díaz Ordaz.

Although Mexico's presidential elections were not due until July 1970, the country's political life in 1969 was considerably influenced by the preliminary activities surrounding the choice of a candidate to represent the Partido Revolucionario Institucional (PRI). No one in Mexico doubted that the official party's choice, as with each of the nine successive candidates put up by the PRI since its foundation, would in due course be elected to become Mexico's president for the 1970–76 term. In accordance with well-established practice, the selection was made by the president in office after consultations with former presidents, high-ranking members of the PRI, and a wide range of influential groups. For many months the identity of *El Tapado* ("the covered one") was the most debated political issue in the country. Finally, at the PRI's national convention, held in November, the name of Luis Echevarría Alvarez, secretary of the interior, was proposed, and the presidential choice received the necessary endorsement from the party delegates.

Popular interest, which normally died out once the name of the virtual new president was revealed, was kept alive by a discernible change of attitudes toward the PRI, particularly among the younger generation, a fact of some import since out of Mexico's estimated population of 47.3 million at the beginning of 1969, almost two-thirds were under 24. Interest centred on whether Congress would pass in time for the 1970 elections a bill proposed earlier in the year by Pres. Díaz Ordaz to lower the voting age from 21 to 18 years. There was no question of this factor alone altering the established pattern, but it was thought it might have an effect on the "universality" or otherwise of the PRI candidate. Many in the party feared that the 1970 polls would show a growing estrangement of the nation from the PRI and not necessarily along generation lines only.

The government, on the other hand, appeared to be relying on its authority to change the country's mood. A stricter control of public order by the armed forces after the violent disturbances of 1968 and the significant failure of workers and peasants to side with the students were probably explanations for the much less conciliatory tone used by Pres. Díaz Ordaz in his fifth annual "state of the nation" address on September 1. In contrast to his promises of reform in 1968, he declared that there were already sufficient legal channels for dissidents to express their views and that young rebels should analyze the realities of Mexico's position before rejecting the existing system.

Many Mexicans mourned the untimely death of Carlos Madrazo (*see* OBITUARIES), chairman of the PRI from 1964 until 1968 and known to favour a thorough democratization of Mexican politics; also regretted was the death on September 22 of Adolfo López Mateos, one of the most progressive of Mexico's presidents (*see* OBITUARIES). It was clear that political reforms could only emanate from within the PRI. Of the three other registered parties, the Partido Acción Nacional (PAN) was likely to confine itself to its role of loyal opposition, the Partido Popular Socialista (PPS) was in disarray following the death of its leader, Vicente Lombardo Toledano, in November 1968, and the Partido Auténtico de la Revolución Mexicano (PARM) was too small to pose any real threat.

Fears that the aftermath of the 19th Olympic Games and increased political tension might slow down economic activity proved groundless. Despite unfavourable international conditions, particularly in the U.S., economic progress continued uninterrupted, and the peso was as firm as ever 15 years after its last devaluation. In 1968 the gross national product grew by 7.1% or, in real terms, by 121.1 billion pesos (to exceed those of Australia and Sweden), bringing the total increase in the full four years of the administration to an impressive 25.6%. Moreover, the gain was achieved against a background of comparatively stable prices (the general cost of living in Mexico City rising by 1.9%), which augmented the average income per head to $564 a year, despite an annual population growth of 3½%.

As usual, manufacturing led the way, but agriculture made more substantial progress than in previous years. Exports rose by 7.7% to $1,189,000,000, but this was more than offset by a rise of 12.1% in imports to $1,960,000,000. The trade deficit of $771 million, which exceeded by $166 million that of 1967, was, however, easily absorbed by the other balance of payments components, and the country had an overall payments surplus of $49 million.

Pessimistic forecasts that unemployment in Mexico City would follow the Olympic construction boom found no confirmation. Some surplus labour was absorbed by the building of the capital's first underground railway. Constructed with French financial and technical aid, the Metro consisted of a first line of 10.3 mi. inaugurated in September and of two more lines that would add a further 15.9 mi. to relieve the serious transport problems of Mexico City.

Throughout 1969 the government was engaged in preparing measures to avoid the temporary slowdown that had accompanied changes of administration in the past, and indications were that the pace of economic activity would continue well into 1970. Two developments announced in 1969 were expected to help generate a good deal of activity and employment in the immediate future. One was the establishment of an important steel plant, the Siderúrgica las Truchas, in the state of Michoacán to develop iron-ore deposits reported to be sufficient to feed the plant for 40 years. The other was the discovery of a substantial oil field some 20 mi. off the mouth of the Panuco River, in the state of Tamaulipas. A pipeline was to be laid from the field to the Madero refinery.

Apart from these favourable announcements, the business community was somewhat concerned by the new federal labour law, scheduled to go into effect in January 1970, which would replace the one in force since 1931. Under the new law, minimum wages were to increase an average of 14.5% in urban areas and 13.7% in the countryside. The cheapness of labour had been one of the factors enabling the authorities to count on the creation of almost half a million new jobs every year, and businessmen were concerned about the effects of the new law on production costs. Equally doubtful were the consequences of a value-added tax being considered as a replacement for the commercial revenue tax. As in some European countries, the tax would be levied on imports and would be deductible on exports. (M. PU.)

ENCYCLOPÆDIA BRITANNICA FILMS. *Arts and Crafts of Mexico:* Part I, *Pottery and Weaving* (1961), Part II, *Basketry, Stone, Wood, and Metals* (1961); *Mexico—The Land and the People* (1961).

MEXICO

Education. (1967–68) Primary, pupils 7,772,-257, teachers 158,736; secondary and vocational, pupils 1,063,900, teachers 76,069; teacher training, students 57,845, teachers (1966–67) 6,553; higher (including 36 universities), students 154,-289, teaching staff (1966–67) 16,203.

Finance. Monetary unit: peso, with a par value of 12.50 pesos to U.S. $1 (30 pesos = £1 sterling). Gold and foreign exchange, central bank: (May 1969) U.S. $577 million; (May 1968) U.S. $525 million. Budget (1969 est.) balanced at 26,512,000,000 pesos. Gross national product: (1967) 301.4 billion pesos; (1966) 272.1 billion pesos. Money supply: (March 1969) 40,810,-000,000 pesos; (March 1968) 35,490,000,000 pesos. Cost of living (Mexico City; 1963 = 100): (June 1969) 119; (June 1968) 116.

Foreign Trade. (1968) Imports 24,501,000,-000 pesos; exports 15,674,000,000 pesos. Import sources: U.S. 63%; West Germany 8%. Export destinations: U.S. 57%; Japan 6%. Main exports: cotton 14%; sugar 8%; coffee 6%. Tourism (1967): visitors 1,445,000; gross receipts U.S. $958 million.

Transport and Communications. Roads (1966) *c.* 180,000 km. (including 66,591 km. highways and 254 km. expressways). Motor vehicles in use (1967): passenger 917,300; commercial (including buses) 440,200. Railways: (1966) 23,826 km.; traffic (1967) 4,252,000,000 passenger-km., freight 19,732,000,000 net ton-km. Air traffic (1967): 2,012,513,000 passenger-km.; freight 37,268,000 net ton-km. Shipping (1968): merchant vessels 100 gross tons and over 114; gross tonnage 403,573. Telephones (Dec. 1967) 1,045,506. Radio receivers (Dec. 1967) 10,932,-000. Television receivers (Dec. 1967) 1,792,000.

Agriculture. Production (in 000; metric tons; 1968; 1967 in parentheses): wheat 1,894 (2,-058); corn 9,360 (8,943); rice 455 (430); coffee (1967) 180, (1966) 185; cotton, lint (1967) 514, (1966) 552; dry beans *c.* 1,014 (1,008); bananas (1967) 441, (1966) 435; oranges 892 (882); lemons 145 (170); sugar, raw value (1968–69) *c.* 2,377, (1967–68) *c.* 2,299; *piloncillo* sugar, raw value (1966–67) 350, (1965–66) 350; tobacco 62 (69); sisal (1967) 147, (1966) 176; fish catch (1967) 350, (1966) 286. Livestock (in 000; Dec. 1967): cattle *c.* 35,000; sheep (1966–67) 6,695; pigs *c.* 14,950; horses *c.* 5,300; mules *c.* 2,010; asses *c.* 3,600; poultry (1965–66) *c.* 90,000.

Industry. Production (in 000; metric tons; 1968): crude oil 20,773; coal (1967) 1,424; natural gas (cu.m.) 16,336; electricity (kw-hr.) 22,798,000; cement 6,152; iron ore (60% metal content) 3,669; pig iron 1,599; steel 3,269; sulfuric acid 731; nitrogenous fertilizers (1967–68) 190; superphosphates (1967) 43; lead 166; zinc 84; copper, smelter 50; aluminum 23; manganese ore (metal content; 1967) 33; antimony ore (metal content; 1967) 3.8; silver (1967) 1.2; gold (troy oz.; 1967) 183.

Middle East

The Middle East situation remained dangerously explosive throughout 1969, although increasing violence did not lead to a new all-out Arab-Israeli war. The possibility of a political settlement of the Arab-Israeli conflict seemed as far away as ever, with the Israelis insisting on direct negotiations leading to a signed peace treaty and the Arabs rejecting these as tantamount to surrender and insisting on the prior withdrawal of Israeli forces from occupied Arab territories. Left-wing coups in Sudan and Libya strengthened the pro-Palestinian forces in the Arab world. Four-power talks on the Middle East and bilateral U.S.-Soviet discussions were generally welcomed by Arab governments (although not by the Palestinian guerrilla organizations) in the hope that they might lead to an enforced Israeli withdrawal from Arab territories; for the same reason they were disliked by the Israelis. A major U.S. peace initiative late in the year, in which Washington attempted an "even-handed" approach to the problem, pleased no one.

In September some faint hopes of a "Rhodes-type solution" (*i.e.,* indirect negotiations through a UN mediator leading to direct agreement between the two parties in the final stage, as occurred after the first Arab-Israeli war of 1948) were raised by remarks made by the United Arab Republic (U.A.R.) foreign minister at the UN. But most observers remained pessimistic, and the overall trend was for Arab-Israeli clashes across the cease-fire lines to cause increasing casualties and damages especially in Jordan and the U.A.R. The 12,000 Iraqi troops in Jordan saw little action, and the Golan Heights area of Israeli-occupied Syria was relatively quiet although there were signs of increased Syrian-backed guerrilla activity during the summer. Lebanon endeavoured to keep its frontier with Israel quiet, but its attempt to control the guerrillas led to brief hostilities and a government crisis.

BLACK STAR

Young Jordanian plunges through a fiery obstacle course barricade during training at an Al Fatah guerrilla camp near Amman in March 1969.

Attempts to Negotiate Peace. As the year opened, the Middle East was still affected by the consequences of the spectacular Israeli raid on Beirut airport on the night of Dec. 28, 1968, in which 13 planes worth about $56 million were destroyed. The Israelis described the raid as a reprisal for the attack on an El Al plane in Athens airport on December 26. The UN Security Council voted unanimously to condemn "Israel for its premeditated action" and called upon it to pay compensation, but a more significant consequence of the raid was the French government's decision to impose a total arms embargo on Israel instead of the partial one in force since 1967.

Microbiology:
see Medicine; Molecular Biology

In January reports of a Soviet Middle East peace plan appeared in the Middle East press. This provided for the two parties to confirm their acceptance of the November 1967 UN Security Council resolution and state their willingness to work with the UN mediator, Gunnar Jarring, on a timetable for its execution. The Israelis would then withdraw from the occupied territories, and both Israel and the Arabs would sign documents recognizing the independence and sovereignty of all states. The agreement would also provide for guaranteed freedom of navigation in international waterways and a just solution to the refugee problem. The Soviets were also reported to favour the demilitarization of certain areas and the formation of a UN peace-keeping force.

On January 17 France officially proposed that the U.S., U.S.S.R., U.K., and France should meet to discuss "establishing a just and lasting peace in the Middle East." The meeting would not impose a settlement but would work with the UN secretary-general to "define the conditions in which the November 1967 resolution would be carried out." On February 1 U.S. Pres. Richard Nixon decided to accept the French proposal.

On January 20 Pres. Gamal Abd-al-Nasser of the U.A.R. said in a speech that he would fight rather than cede any territory to Israel and that he would never sit down and negotiate with an enemy occupying Arab territory. He also paid tribute to the commandos "at whose disposal the U.A.R. unconditionally places all its resources." However, in February the U.S. magazine *Newsweek* published an interview with Nasser in which he strongly reaffirmed the U.A.R.'s acceptance of the UN Security Council resolution and said that in return for an Israeli withdrawal the U.A.R. offered a declaration of nonbelligerence and the recognition of the right of all Middle East states to live in peace and security. All the Palestinian organizations continued to reject these terms outright. At the opening session of the Palestine National Assembly in Cairo, Yasir Arafat (head of Al Fatah, the principal Palestinian organization; *see* BIOGRAPHY) was elected chairman of the new Palestine Liberation Organization (PLO) executive committee. The left-wing Popular Front for the Liberation of Palestine (PFLP) was the only significant Palestinian organization to remain outside the PLO.

In a *Newsweek* interview published in February, Israeli Prime Minister Levi Eshkol said that Israel remained flexible on the return of the occupied territories except for the Golan Heights of Syria and eastern Jerusalem. This apparent offer to return the West Bank to Jordan raised a political storm in Israel, but Eshkol survived a vote of confidence in the national legislature on the issue. A week later Eshkol died of a heart attack and was succeeded by Mrs. Golda Meir (*see* BIOGRAPHY).

On March 5 the Israeli defense minister, Moshe Dayan, called for a series of Israeli settlements along the west bank. He also proposed the replacement by Israeli law of Jordanian and U.A.R. law in the occupied areas and suggested that the Arabs in those areas be economically integrated with Israel. The Jewish Agency's Settlement Department announced that 22 new Israeli settlements had been established since the 1967 war and that 20 more would be established in two years. This policy received the enthusiastic support of the deputy prime minister, Yigal Allon.

Israeli ministers expressed strong criticism of the holding of four-power talks on the Middle East despite President Nixon's disclaimer that there was any question of imposing a settlement. Arab hopes were raised by U.S. irritation with the apparently increased rigidity of the new Israeli government. During a visit to the U.S. in April, King Husain of Jordan, who said he was speaking with the personal authority of President Nasser, proposed a six-point peace plan. Its terms were substantially those of the UN Security Council resolution, but it was the first time that an Arab leader had stated them so unequivocally. The proposals were rejected by Israeli spokesmen as "not genuine" (as also by the Palestinian guerrillas), but King Husain returned from his visit more hopeful than before of obtaining U.S. and other Western support in achieving a settlement.

The Jordanian monarch's optimism did not last long. The four-power talks were inconclusive and on May 4 the UN secretary-general said that if the members of the Security Council could not agree on "substantive issues," the deteriorating situation in the Middle East might get out of hand. Israeli hopes of a reversion of the French arms boycott following the resignation of Pres. Charles de Gaulle were dashed when the newly elected Pres. Georges Pompidou affirmed the continuation of de Gaulle's policy.

On April 30 Iraq recognized East Germany, to be followed later in the year by the Sudan, Syria, and the U.A.R. As the year progressed the majority of Arab states became increasingly disillusioned in their earlier hopes that the Nixon administration would be substantially less pro-Israel than its predecessor, but they also felt that the Soviet government was preparing to go too far to meet the U.S. point of view.

Israel was obliged to place increasingly heavy reliance on the U.S. as a source of arms. Following the boycott by France (formerly Israel's chief supplier), Israel's request for Chieftain tanks from Britain, which aroused widespread Arab criticism when first reported, was postponed indefinitely as the result of Arab diplomatic pressure. On the other hand, despite bitter Arab opposition, President Nixon announced that the supply to Israel of 50 Phantom jet fighters that had been promised in the last days of the Johnson administration would go ahead as planned. Mrs. Meir visited Washington, D.C., in September and asked for more fighters and bombers as well as substantial economic aid to be spread over several years.

At the end of June the Cairo newspaper *Al Ahram* published the outline of the 13-point U.S. peace plan that had been considered during the visit of the Soviet foreign minister, Andrei A. Gromyko, to the U.A.R. This called for free navigation in the Straits of Tiran and the Suez Canal, an end to the state of war, an Israeli withdrawal from U.A.R. territory that would be demilitarized, and an end to belligerent propaganda and support for the fedayeen (commandos). The U.A.R. view was that this—together with the delivery of Phantom fighters—showed that the U.S. was still fully supporting Israel.

On July 1 the big four talks on the Middle East adjourned indefinitely in New York after the 15th meeting, but it was agreed that informal discussions would continue. The Israeli foreign minister said that the talks had reached a complete impasse because of blind Soviet acceptance of the Arab position, but there were several signs that the U.A.R. government for one was dissatisfied with the Soviet attitude. In his address to the UN General Assembly on September 18, President Nixon proposed putting the whole Middle East into military quarantine through international agreement. In his reply the Soviet foreign minister insisted that there should be evacuation first and an arms embargo afterward.

When Gromyko held several meetings with U.S. Secretary of State William Rogers in September, it was apparent that the Soviet Union had relaxed its attitude on several points—notably its demand that the Israeli withdrawal from the occupied territories should precede the application of other provisions of the 1967 Security Council resolution and its rejection of all frontier readjustments. Improved Franco-U.S. relations following the resignation of de Gaulle and the announcement of a visit to the U.S. by President Pompidou in early 1970 eased the way toward U.S. acceptance of renewed big four talks in October.

Late in December a U.S. peace plan was presented to the four-power meeting; although this was the first time it had been made public, parts had been revealed to the Soviet Union as early as October and much of it had been contained in a December 9 speech by Secretary Rogers. Its principal points were that Israel should pull back from the Sinai and the west bank, in return for commitments to peace and recognition of Israeli sovereignty by the U.A.R. and Jordan; the U.A.R. should permit Israeli shipping through the Suez Canal and the Straits of Tiran; the administration of the Gaza Strip and the delineation of demilitarized zones, as well as minor border adjustments,

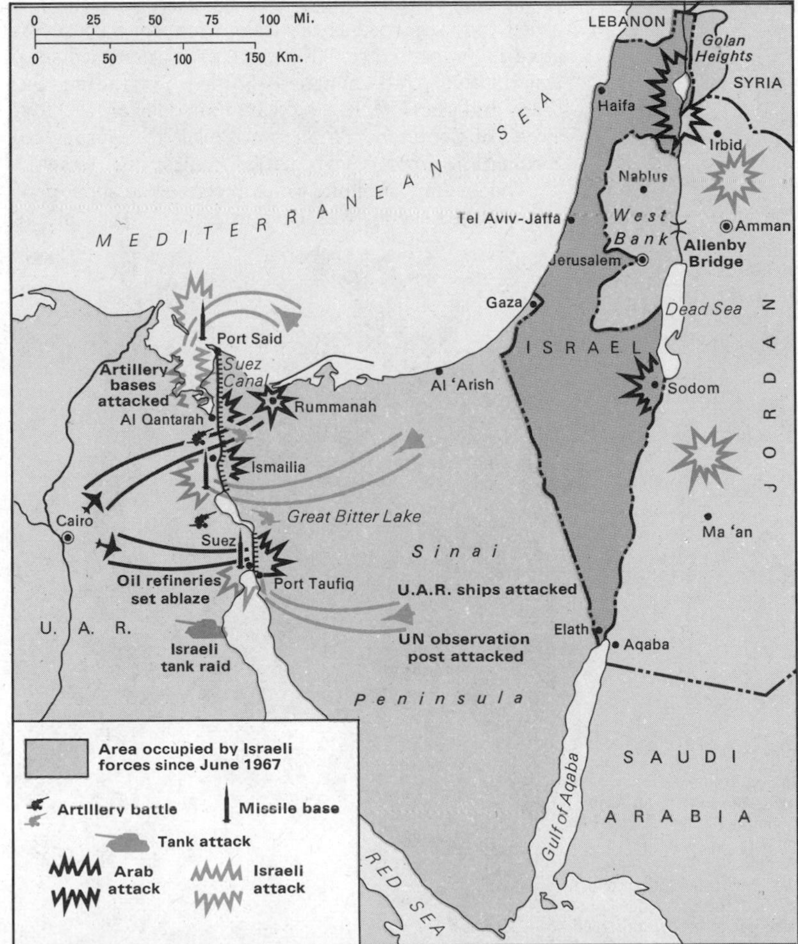

should be settled by negotiation; Jerusalem should be a unified city governed jointly by Israel and Jordan; Jordan should assume responsibility for controlling guerrilla raids; and refugees should be given the choice of resettling or reentering Israel.

The plan appeared to represent a shift in the U.S. stance—from being Israel's advocate (as against Soviet support for the Arabs) to impartiality. The Israeli reaction was intense; the plan was denounced point by point, with particular stress on the prior commitment to withdrawal from the occupied territories, the admission of all refugees who wished to return rather than a token number, and the proposed arrangements for Jerusalem. However, the plan also failed to please the Arabs, and the Soviet Union, in replying negatively, appeared to be hardening its position.

Arab Efforts to Achieve Unity. On August 21 the Middle East situation was further exacerbated by the partial destruction by fire of Al Aqsa Mosque in Jerusalem, one of the holiest places in Islam. The Arabs held Israel responsible, and there were widespread calls for a holy war from Arab and Muslim leaders. The Israelis' first reaction was that it had been an accident, but the next day their police arrested and charged with the crime a young Australian member of an extreme minority Christian sect who had been living and working in Israel. This did little to appease Arab opinion, and King Faisal of Saudi Arabia proposed the holding of an Islamic summit meeting. This was an alternative to the Arab summit which King Husain had long been asking for and for which President Nasser had declared his support. The Saudi monarch was unenthusiastic about a meeting that would be dominated by the more liberal Arab nations, just as the Arab progressives were suspicious of what they regarded as an attempt to form a conservative Islamic alliance. The result was a restricted summit of five Arab countries—Jordan, Syria, Iraq, Sudan, and the U.A.R.—held in Cairo during the first week of September. Plans were made to improve coordination among Arab armies confronting Israel.

The Islamic summit, which received the support of the Arab League, was held in Rabat, Mor., in the last week of September under the chairmanship of King Hassan of Morocco. The meeting succeeded in achieving unanimity on resolutions expressing support for the Palestinians and calling upon the big powers to hasten Israeli evacuation. But the Arab progressives at the meeting, Algeria, Sudan, the U.A.R., and Libya (Syria and Iraq were not represented), regarded the resolutions as weak, and they failed in their efforts to persuade Turkey, Iran, and other non-Arab Muslim states to break all contact with Israel. They did succeed in preventing the conclusion of any form of Islamic pact. It was decided instead that there would be a meeting of Muslim foreign ministers in Jidda, Saudi Arabia, in March 1970 to discuss the establishment of a permanent secretariat.

A full Arab summit was held in Rabat in December, but it ended in failure and open disagreement. Nasser walked out of one session following an argument over the refusal of Saudi Arabia and Kuwait to increase their financial support to the Arab forces facing Israel, and Syria, Iraq, and Southern Yemen boycotted the closing ceremonies. At year's end it was reported that the U.A.R., Syria, Jordan, and Iraq planned to hold their own summit in Cairo early in 1970.

Military Action. Throughout the year the military stalemate continued, with rising violence and increasing casualties on both sides. After each incident Israeli and Arab communiqués invariably conflicted widely. By the end of July Israel claimed to have shot down 25 U.A.R. planes since the 1967 war with the loss during the same period of only two of its own Mirages. Israel undoubtedly enjoyed air superiority, but in August the U.A.R. Air Force made its first bombing sorties over Israeli-held territory and the Israelis admitted some improvement in the U.A.R.'s performance. The Israelis responded with almost daily raids on the Suez Canal area. During the year the Israelis made commando attacks, using helicopters, on targets in Upper Egypt. Some of the Israeli claims for the success of these raids proved to be exaggerated, but they demonstrated Israel's ability to strike deep into U.A.R. territory. The U.A.R. troops also made frequent commando attacks on a smaller scale across the Suez Canal into Sinai.

On the Jordanian front a similar situation existed, with Israeli planes making frequent sorties against Jordanian Army positions and alleged Palestinian guerrilla camps in Syria and Lebanon as well as Jordan. In September General Dayan said that Israel's strategy was to force the U.A.R. to disperse its troops more widely (it had 60,000 to 70,000 concentrated in the Suez Canal area, compared with Israel's 4,000 to 6,000) and to make it increasingly costly for the commandos to cross the cease-fire line. He claimed that the latter policy was already partially successful.

Official Israeli figures at the end of September gave 435 soldiers and civilians killed and 1,763 wounded through all types of action by Arab regular forces and guerrillas since the end of the June 1967 conflict, as compared with 778 killed and 2,558 wounded in the war itself.

The Israelis claimed that guerrilla action presented no serious security threat and denied most of the frequent communiqués published by Al Fatah giving details of attacks inside Israeli-occupied territory. Al Fatah claimed that it only attacked civilian targets in response to Israeli attacks on Arab civilians. The left-wing PFLP claimed responsibility for most of the bomb explosions in Israeli cities. An explosion that wrecked oil installations in Haifa Port and another in

WIDE WORLD

Israeli soldier kicks aside the door of an Arab home in the Gaza area on Aug. 11, 1969. A house-to-house search was undertaken in an effort to find the guerrillas who had attacked an Israeli patrol a few days earlier.

"ISRAEL SUN"—PIX FROM PUBLIX

Israeli oil pipeline at the entrance to Kishon Harbour, Haifa, burns after an explosion on June 24, 1969. Sabotage by Arab guerrillas was suspected.

a Tel Aviv thoroughfare indicated that the commandos were for the first time receiving some help from Arab Israelis. Strikes and demonstrations on the west bank—especially by schoolchildren—were frequent during the year, but they did not present any serious security problem to the Israelis. Their greatest difficulty remained in Gaza, where hostility was most marked and reprisals were taken by the Arabs against anyone suspected of cooperating with the Israelis. Israel continued to expel from the west bank anyone suspected of helping the guerrillas.

The year ended on a bizarre note. Five gunboats, built in France for Israel but not delivered because of the French arms embargo, were sold to what purported to be a Norwegian company for use in offshore drilling operations. The Norwegian government later said it had no record of the company, which was apparently based in Panama. Before this came to light, however, the five ships, with Israeli crews aboard, slipped out of Cherbourg Harbour on Christmas Day and docked in Haifa on December 31. (P. Md.)

See also Defense; Migration, International; Refugees; also articles on the various political units.

Encyclopædia Britannica Films. *Egypt and the Nile* (1954); *The Middle East* (1955); *Planning Our Foreign Policy (Problems of the Middle East)* (1955); *Iran—Between Two Worlds* (1957); *The Mediterranean World* (1962); *The Nile Valley and Its People* (1962); *The Suez Canal—Gateway to World Trade* (1962); *Turkey—Emergence of a Modern Nation* (1963).

Migration, International

Voluntary migration in 1969 continued to be motivated by the desire of people to improve their living conditions and to escape from economic and social hardship. The international movement of workers to meet labour demands, particularly in Western Europe, was not achieved without serious tensions. Studies of international migratory movements were handicapped by a shortage of reliable comparative statistics, the result of the relative infrequency of national censuses.

The 1969 Commonwealth Prime Ministers' Conference in London was prefaced by a three-point plan produced by the Committee on United Kingdom Citizenship and designed to amend the Commonwealth Immigrants Act, 1968. The proposal to establish an inter-Commonwealth migration system suitable to all member countries and to seek a reexamination of citizenship was a reaction against the growth of unilateral legislation on immigration by Commonwealth members. Immigration was brought to the fore during the conference itself by the situation of Asians forced to leave East Africa, particularly Kenya and Uganda, as a result of local policies, especially legislation refusing trading permits to Asians. Many of these Asians were British citizens but the British government indicated that it was unwilling to increase the special quota of 1,500 work vouchers a year allotted in March 1968 for the entry of Kenya Asians into the U.K. The Indian government, while confirming that it regarded the matter as primarily one of British responsibility, announced that it was willing to receive Indian immigrants from East Africa. For its part, the Kenya government reiterated that Asians in Kenya had the opportunity of taking Kenya citizenship if they so wished.

The numbers of East African Asians seeking to enter Britain in fact showed a drop from 1968. Nevertheless, the situation in East Africa increased the pressure on would-be migrants from the West Indies, India, and Pakistan; the British government had made it clear that total annual immigration from the Commonwealth would not be allowed to increase. Anxiety over unilateral action on migration by Commonwealth states was not eased by the abruptness with which African governments, understandably anxious to see early africanization, particularly in service industries, introduced measures to bring this about. In January Asian traders at Monze in Zambia were given a week to hand over their shops to Zambians. During the year Hong Kong proposed changes in its immigration laws, under which Commonwealth citizens would be liable to the same restrictions as aliens. This was felt to be a reaction to the immigration laws of other Commonwealth states, such as Australia.

The U.K.'s immigration policy remained a thorny and emotional issue during the year. In May the home secretary announced that dependents of Commonwealth immigrants coming to Britain would have to obtain entry certificates before leaving their home country. Leaders of immigrant organizations in Britain criticized the move as a further concealed restriction. Further evidence came to light regarding the illegal methods used to smuggle immigrants, mainly Asians, into Britain across the Channel and countermeasures were tightened. In October the Joint Council for the Welfare of Immigrants announced that it would give free advice to prospective immigrants, whose greatest difficulty was usually the lack of personal documents. A report authorized by the British government recommended that advice to prospective immigrants should be given by British high commissions, whose staffs should be expanded to undertake this.

Figures released in September showed that in the period 1964–68 the U.K. had received 312,000 immigrants while 293,000 emigrants had left the country. Monthly figures for the numbers of Commonwealth citizens entering Britain showed a decrease of 16% in the first eight months of 1969 as compared with the same period in 1968. This drop was attributed to the compulsory entry permit system introduced in July 1968 and to hesitancy induced by awareness of well-publicized tendencies in the race relations climate in the U.K.

The number of voucher-holders entering the country for permanent settlement in 1968 was 4,691 (compared with 4,978 in 1967), the lowest since controls were imposed in 1962. The number of dependents joining heads of families or accompanying those admitted was 43,879 in 1968 (52,183 in 1967). These figures did not include holders of British passports controlled since 1968 under the special voucher system. In other categories 4,499 Commonwealth citizens were admitted for settlement, compared with 3,586 in 1967. This figure included 3,519 persons coming for marriage. In June the government announced that the granting of work vouchers to employers wishing to take on immigrant labour would be conditional on there being no suitable local labour available.

Statistics released by the government in Rhodesia in April showed that the number of European immigrants had fallen by nearly 25% compared with 1968, while the number of people leaving the country rose by almost 6%.

Australia was one of the most impressive examples of the contribution of selective mass voluntary immigration to economic development. Since the end of World War II the percentage of the population that was Australian-born had steadily decreased from 90.2% in 1947 to 81% in 1966. The number of immigrants in 1969 was expected to be the largest since 1963, but the proportion of immigrants from the U.K. continued to decrease, falling to below 42%.

In Western Europe the movement of large numbers of jobless men from the Mediterranean area to the chronically labour-hungry industrial countries of northern and western Europe was stimulated by the rising degree of economic interinvolvement in Europe. The EEC Commission reported that in the five EEC receiving countries an increase of about 100,000 foreign workers was to be expected in 1969.

The movement of foreign workers within Europe was not without national repercussions. In Switzerland, which was heavily dependent on imported labour, the government set up a working party to study new measures to counter what was termed "overalienization." The force of popular manifestations of animosity toward immigrant workers was shown by the success of a campaign for a national referendum, due in 1970. Swiss dislike was directed mainly against the Italians (60% of the total), and Spaniards. The proportion of foreigners increased in 1968 to 15.6% of the total population. Following a cut in the quota of foreign workers in 1968, the government imposed further restrictions on industrial firms.

In West Germany the government tightened its control over foreign workers who entered the country in the guise of tourists. The Ministry of the Interior calculated that between 1,000 and 2,000 persons were being turned away each month. Frontier officials were alerted to keep a special watch on Turks, Greeks, Yugoslavs, Spaniards, and "Orientals," presumably including Indians and Pakistanis. The authorities were concerned about the illegal networks for importing foreign labour that were known to have developed, and also about the possibility of illegal immigrants bringing infectious diseases into the country. The Turkish government ran a campaign to warn potential migrants of the dangers posed by the middlemen involved in illegal smuggling operations. The number of foreign workers in West Germany was estimated at about 1.3 million, some 5% of the total labour force.

In February a report by the French Economic and Social Council indicated that France would soon have to adopt a policy of selective immigration. The number of immigrants was estimated at over 3 million, of whom more than 2 million were Europeans. Unemployment and economic and social hardship were highest among those immigrants least able to assimilate easily into French society, notably those from North Africa.

The proportion of immigrants in Sweden was put at one in 16 persons. The 500,000 foreigners, attracted by the high-wage economy, were mainly Finns, Danes, Norwegians, Yugoslavs, Greeks, Italians, and Germans. The Swedish government formed a State Immigration Office to attract and keep the right kind of settlers by helping them to adjust to the Swedish way of life. Difficulties in assimilation were described as being caused by clashes of temperament rather than nationality.

During the summer the Danish authorities reported that an average of 100 Polish Jews were arriving in Denmark every week. Israeli officials were said to be taking a keen interest in the migrants, who were mainly former civil servants, intellectuals, and professional people. Emigration of Jews from Poland had reached a peak in 1968 during an anti-Zionist purge of the government and Communist Party. It was reported from Poland that from September 1 special regulations allowing Polish Jews easy emigration to Israel would be abolished. These regulations dated from the time of the 1967 Six-Day War, and over 5,000 Jews were reported to have left Poland between July 1967 and May 1969. (G. O. K. B.; X.)

In the U.S., the new immigration laws, in effect since July 1, 1968, were reviewed and evaluated in 1969. Radical shifts in the pattern of immigration were noted and unexpected backlogs in certain "preference" categories occurred. Much of the criticism was against the limitation of Western Hemisphere entries to 120,000 in fiscal 1969.

The shifting pattern of origin for immigrants to the U.S. solidified in fiscal 1969. Of the non-Western Hemisphere countries Italy ranked first with 24,465 visas issued, followed by the Philippines with 23,335, China with 21,811, Greece with 19,448, Portugal with 17,567, Great Britain with 10,994, Yugoslavia with 9,469, Germany with 8,695, India with 6,823, and Korea with 6,469. The ranking in fiscal 1965, the last year of the previous system, had been Great Britain, Germany, Italy, Poland, Ireland, France, the Netherlands, Japan, the U.S.S.R., and China.

In the Western Hemisphere, Canada had 15,722 emigrants to the U.S., a drop from 29,536 in fiscal 1968. Although the Cuban refugee airlift to the U.S. continued unabated and illegal entries through Mexico became an increasing problem, the number of visas issued to Cubans declined to 8,952 from 103,850 in fiscal 1968 when many of the refugees from previous years obtained immigrant status prior to the imposition of the new laws. Other Western Hemisphere totals and rankings remained roughly unchanged.

Although emigration figures from the U.S. were not kept, it was generally believed that Canada and Australia ranked among the top recipients. In the first six months of calendar 1969, immigration into Canada from the U.S. increased to 8,595 from 6,820 in 1968. Approximately 3,000 Americans emigrated to Australia in 1968.

Canada's overall immigration in the first half of 1969 fell to 71,121 from 85,339 in 1968. The number of Italian, Dutch, German, and French immigrants was half that of the previous year and English immigration dropped, though not as sharply. Immigration from Jamaica, Barbados, Trinidad and Tobago, and Guyana rose sharply and the figure from Asia held steady at just over 10,000.

Congressional reviews of the new U.S. laws and their effects included aspects of the Mutual Educational and Cultural Exchange Act (1961), which enabled doctors and other medical professionals to enter the country temporarily and the similar temporary admission of skilled workers and business executives, and the effect of the 1965 law on Western Hemisphere immigration. Additional areas of concern were declining immigration from Ireland caused by restrictions against unskilled workers, mounting backlogs of relatives of U.S. citizens, the possible redistribution of unused visas in certain preferences to others of high demand, and the speeding of entry by refugees. The U.S. Senate in 1969 passed and sent to the House a bill to exempt executives and other managerial personnel of Western Hemisphere businesses from being charged to the Western Hemisphere immigration quota. The bill had been sought by companies operating throughout the hemisphere, especially in both the U.S. and Canada. (D. Fo.)

See also Refugees.

Mining

The rising demand for minerals in 1969 stimulated an intensive worldwide search for new mines and the development of additional productive capacity. Nationalization policies in some countries in South America and Africa had an important effect on the mineral industries. Numerous minor work stoppages restricted output, and a major nickel industry strike in Canada severely crippled consumers of that metal. There was growing public concern about current and potential environmental damage from mining and mineral processing, and also about the health and safety of miners.

The mineral market was irregular. Because of abundant supply, many mineral prices were soft despite monetary inflation. Defense requirements helped to firm the markets, however, particularly for metals. Gold and silver prices reacted to speculation, tending downward but with silver gaining strength toward the end of the year. Although copper rose to high price levels in a fragmented world market, demand remained strong and there was little apparent substitution. The nickel price soared because a strike in Canada cut back mine and plant production, and antimony moved sharply upward when supply from China essentially stopped. Lead, zinc, and aluminum prices rose in an orderly market. An oversupply of potash brought prices down and led to a retraction of the U.S. industry. Inflation and high interest rates cut back construction and the demand for construction minerals. The U.S. federal government also curtailed its new construction programs, and other government projects were stretched out or postponed, partly because of high interest rates but also as anti-inflationary measures. The effect of these actions upon the mining of aggregates, clays, cement rock, and other construction minerals was uncertain even late in the year, but it was possibly offset by the vigorousness of general economic activity.

Strategic stockpile acquisitions and disposals by the U.S. government were less significant market factors in 1969 than during the previous three-year period. An overall review of the stockpile position was made by the Office of Emergency Planning, and objectives for a number of minerals were changed. Purchases to reach objectives and sales of surpluses were made with restraint in order to mitigate the effect on the market. Sales of mercury (U.S. Atomic Energy Commission surplus), tungsten, and silver (U.S. Department of the Treasury stocks) stabilized prices. Consumers were not able to obtain nickel, which was in critical supply, but late in the year an executive order was readied to allow nickel releases for defense orders. In October cobalt releases were raised from one to two million pounds a week for use as a nickel substitute. Aluminum and magnesium accounted for most of the value of mineral disposals from the U.S. stockpile.

The upward trend in U.S. and world mineral production persisted in 1969. Total value of output rose more than volume because of higher prices. Despite the record mine production there was also increased reclamation of scrap materials.

Industry Developments. Events affecting copper mining and a crippling strike against Canadian nickel producers dominated mineral industry news in 1969. Both Zambia and Chile, second- and third-ranking non-Communist copper mine producers, announced programs to establish direct government participation in the ownership of copper mining. In Peru the military government expropriated oil properties of International Petroleum Corp. and aroused fear that nationalization would be extended to mining. The influence of the nationalization programs on the world copper situation was difficult to assess. It was clear, however, that they had introduced additional uncertainty to an already tight market situation and thus contributed to the strong 25–30% price rise witnessed in 1969.

The non-Communist world added about 300,000 tons of annual copper production in 1969, and projects adding about 1.8 million tons per year over the period 1970–73 were relatively firm. South of Tucson, Ariz., the Duval Sierrita Corp. and the Anaconda Co. Twin Buttes large open-pit projects started producing late in 1969. At Tyrone, N.M., Phelps Dodge Corp. began producing 50,000 tons of copper a year. Another major new copper source was the 24,000-ton-a-year Kennecott Copper Corp. leaching plant at Ray, Ariz. In August and again in October the Anaconda Co. increased ore production at its Butte, Mont., mines.

Three copper projects designed to deliver more than 75,000 tons of copper a year were under way in Chile. The huge Exotica open-pit project was expected to start producing in 1970 at a 100,000-ton-a-year rate from a supply of 7.8 million tons of ore. Work was ahead of schedule at El Teniente, where output was to be raised by 280,000 tons a year by 1970. The renowned Chuquicamata pit production rate was being raised by 75,000 tons of metal a year.

In Peru the U.S.-owned Southern Peru Copper Corp. and the government signed an agreement under which the large Cuajone copper deposit would be brought into production. The 500 million-ton deposit was adequate for a copper output of 150,000 tons a year, and $355 million was to be invested in the project.

Another of the major world copper developments was in an entirely new copper region on Bougainville

Military Affairs: *see* Defense

Mineralogy: *see* Geology

Island of the Solomon group, a United Nations Trust Territory. Truly international in scope, the $350 million Panguna mine project was financed largely by an international group and contracts were negotiated for concentrate shipments to Japan, West Germany, and Spain. Plans called for a 30 million-ton-per-year open-pit mine and mill. The ore contains 0.47% copper and 0.02 oz. of gold per ton. Exploration on the nearby island of New Guinea-Papua-West Irian showed evidence of similar copper deposits.

Expanded output was scheduled at molybdenum mines, in addition to that from the many worldwide copper-molybdenum projects. Climax Molybdenum Co., operators of the Climax mine, largest underground mine in the U.S., was developing the equally large Henderson mine at Empire, Colo. The 300 million-ton body of ore lay at a depth of 2,000 ft. Initial ore production was to start in 1970 at a rate of 30,000 tons per day and reportedly might be increased later. In New Mexico the Molybdenum Corporation of America was increasing annual capacity at its Questa mine from 4,600 to 7,000 tons.

A strike closing most Canadian nickel mine and plant production began on July 10 and was not settled until November 15. The resultant worldwide nickel shortage forced the price to more than $6 a pound for specialty uses and caused a scramble for the scarce supply. The strike had a wide effect throughout industry because of the extensive use of nickel in stainless and other alloy steels and in plating and nonferrous alloys. The almost chronic nickel shortage of recent years, intensified by the strike, stimulated investigation of nickel deposits throughout the world. New mines were being developed in several countries, broadening the geographic base of the nickel supply; expansion plans in Canada, however, gave assurance that it would continue in its role as the leading world producer.

Nickel prospects were favourable in Indonesia, the Dominican Republic, the Philippines, Botswana, and several other areas, but the most notable new developments were in Australia. Western Mining Corp. planned to achieve a nickel output of 30,000 tons per year in 1970 from its Kambalda mine near Kalgoorlie. Reserves of 15 million tons of sulfide ore containing more than 3.4% nickel had been established and the potential was much greater. Wide-ranging prospecting disclosed other nickeliferous areas, and two other mines were being planned.

AUTHENTICATED NEWS INTERNATIONAL

Sir Robert Grieve, chairman of the Highlands and Islands Development Board, cuts a lump of coal from a new field discovered at Brora, Scot. The field, which went into production in 1969, was believed to hold eight million tons of coal and to have an estimated working life of 400 years.

The global pattern of iron ore production continued to enlarge, with the principal developments under way or expansion plans under scrutiny in Latin America, Africa, India, and Australia. The first shipment in April of iron ore to Japan from the vast Mt. Newman, Western Australia, deposits marked an important advance in the rapidly growing Western Australia iron ore industry. An initial shipment rate of 5.5 million tons a year was to be doubled by 1975.

Following adoption of the "two-tier" gold marketing system in 1968, gold producers realized about $41 an ounce for their outputs, compared with an official monetary price of $35. A substantial part of the large South African gold output apparently was not marketed, however, thus restricting supply and supporting a higher price for both industrial consumers and speculators. Some new South African gold appeared to have gone into monetary stocks through currency transactions, but the marketing pattern was not clear. In October the first allocation of $3.5 billion in Special Drawing Rights (SDR's), or so-called "paper gold," was approved by national representatives to the International Monetary Fund (IMF). The system was designed gradually to displace gold as a monetary metal. This and other events during 1969 tended to soften the free-market gold price which, having peaked at about $43.70 in June, slipped below the official $35 an ounce in December. Late in 1969 an international agreement was reached for sales of newly mined South African gold at $35 per ounce for monetary reserves. The world gold mining pattern was relatively unchanged. New developments in South Africa replaced older mines, but the 1968 record production level of nearly 31 million oz. was not reached in 1969. In the U.S. the Cortez open-pit gold mine in Nevada went into operation in January.

The irregular silver price performance apparent since demonetization in 1967 continued in 1969. Market behaviour was influenced more by governmental actions and speculative trading than by industry actions. In May the U.S. Department of the Treasury reversed previous policies and accepted recommendations of the Joint Commission on the Coinage to lift the ban on melting and on exporting U.S. silver coins, to reduce government silver sales from 2 million to 1.5 million oz. per week, and to ask Congress to authorize minting of silverless dollars and half-dollars and to authorize the sale of 2.9 million old silver dollars to high bidders.

There was vigorous and widespread search for uranium in 1969, along with revived expectation that nuclear energy generation would create a large demand by the mid-1970s. The U.S. Atomic Energy Commission reported that U.S. exploration would total about 30 million ft. drilled, 25% more than in 1968.

There were several unusual mineral developments in North America in 1969. The first large-scale beryllium mine treating nonpegmatitic-type ore was being prepared for production in the Spor Mountain area of Utah. A special hydrometallurgical process had to be contrived to extract the beryllium. In Canada the first large North American tantalum mine began production in August. Near Hot Springs, Ark., an open-pit vanadium mine started operation. A complex hydrometallurgical method was used to treat the unusual type of low-grade vanadium ore.

In 1969 the U.S. adopted the Coal Mine Health and Safety Act, the most stringent federal mine-safety legislation in the country's history. Impetus for passage had come from the death of 78 miners in a West Virginia explosion and fire at the end of 1968, as well as from the increasing incidence among miners of "black lung disease," resulting from excessive exposure to coal dust.

Technological Developments. Availability of superior materials, better equipment design, improved controls, and more attention to total mining systems were once again the principal factors in advancing mining technology. The superior materials included such diverse items as high-strength steels to lighten mobile equipment, far better tires giving longer life and fewer shutdowns, and harder and stronger cutting materials to speed drilling and boring. Much of the improvement in equipment design stemmed from on-the-job experience with the current equipment. Similarly, mining systems designs were improved as engineers' acquaintance with modern mechanized equipment enabled them to take better advantage of its capabilities.

The continual increase in mining equipment size was highlighted in 1969 by the "Big Muskie," the world's largest dragline, which was placed in operation for stripping overburden at an Ohio coal mine. The 13,000-ton, $20 million machine could scoop up 325 tons and shift its load more than 600 ft. in one pass. It was 490 ft. long and 220 ft. high.

A huge boring-type, continuous-mining machine installed in Canada could mine 15 tons of potash per minute. It could cut entries as large as 12 ft. high by 20 ft. wide. Near Grants, N.M., a 16.5-ft.-diameter uranium mine shaft was to be drilled to a depth of 775 ft. The deepest single-lift vertical shaft in the Western Hemisphere, the 21-ft. diameter, 7,137-ft.-deep Creighton No. 9 shaft, was sunk in the Sudbury district of Ontario.

Development of improved shaft and tunnel boring machines was notable, but conventional drill jumbos continued to be preferred for the hardest types of rock. Improved design of hydraulically operated jumbos increased their efficiency, avoided lost time, and reduced manpower requirements. Laser beams helped to position the jumbos, and better design enabled the big drill rigs to be moved in and out of the heading quickly to speed the drilling-breaking-hauling cycle. (P. F. Y.)

Production. World mineral production continued to increase and reached a new high in 1968. Of 68 minerals and mineral products that comprised by far the bulk of production, 56 registered gains ranging from 31% (beryl) to 0.2% (anthracite coal) above 1967 production for an average increase of 7.9%. Thirty-one metals, 17 nonmetals, and 8 fuel minerals contributed to the increase, the several groups rising by an average of 7.9, 8.4, and 3.8%, respectively. Cobalt (−2.4%), columbium-tantalum (−5.1%),

continued on page 540

Table I. Mineral and Metal Prices in 1969

New York market				London market								
January $	September $	Units	Grade	Commodity	Grade	Units	January £	January s.	January d.	September £	September s.	September d.
0.2645	0.270	Pound	99.5% ingot	Aluminum	99.5%	Long ton	247	6	6	247	6	6
5.80	9.73	S.T. unit	60% Sb	Antimony, ore	50–55% Sb	L.T. unit	...	56	...	...	90	...
0.425	0.62	Pound	Domestic, bulk	Antimony	Domestic, 99%	Long ton	372	10	...	472	10	...
4.00	5.125	Pound	Ton lots	Bismuth	Ton lots	Pound	...	33	4	...	40	...
2.80	3.50	"	Commercial sticks—ton lots	Cadmium	99.95%	"	...	23	3	...	29	...
35.00	38.50	Short ton	48–50% Cr_2O_3, 3½ Cr: 1 Fe	Chromium, ore	Rhodesian, 1st grade	Long ton		‡			‡	
0.96	0.96	Pound	98.5%, spot-aluminothermic	Metal	98–99%	Pound	...	7	3	...	7	3
0.201	0.212	"	67–71% Cr*	Ferroalloy	4–6% C, 60% Cr	Long ton	77	...	...	86	...	...
1.85	1.85	"	99% Co-500-lb. lots	Cobalt		Pound	...	15	6	...	15	6
0.43498	0.51359	"	Domestic (refinery)	Copper	Wire bars (cash)	Long ton	531	4	1	668	2	3
0.52086	0.68525	"	Export (refinery)	"	Wire bars (3 months)	"	521	10	...	660	5	11
42.76	41.28	Ounce†	Engelhard selling	Gold	Official	Ounce†	$42.30	...	...	$40.873	...	...
2.50	2.50	"	99.97% In (small lots)	Indium		"	...	19	2	...	19	2
190.00	170.00	"	Sponge, powder	Iridium	Sponge and powder	"	79	...	...	73	...	...
10.55	10.55	Long ton	Mesabi, non-Bessemer	Iron, ore				‡			‡	
‡	‡	Short ton	80%, Joplin, Mo.	Lead, ore	70–80%	Metric ton	$20	...	...	$20	...	...
0.134	0.155	Pound	New York	Metal	99.97%	Long ton	107	10	2	127	19	1
0.3525	0.3525	"	99.8% car lots	Magnesium, ingots		Pound	...	2	7	...	3	...
‡	‡	"		sticks	Bars	"	...	3	2	...	4	...
‡	0.57	L.T. unit	48% Atlantic ports	Manganese, ore	48% Mn	L.T. unit	...	...	56	...	...	56
0.2885	0.290	Pound	99.9% Mn (f.o.b.-ton lots)	Metal	99.9% Mn-(electro)	Long ton	235	...	...	250	...	...
164.50	164.50	Long ton	74–76%	Ferroalloy	78% Mn (standard)	"	51	5	...	52	15	...
89.00	89.00	Long ton	19–21% Mn	Spiegel	20% Mn	"	34	5	...	34	5	...
528.182	491.095	(76 lb.) Flask		Mercury		(76 lb.) Flask	223	...	...	223	...	...
1.62	1.72	Pound	Mo, Climax, Colo.§	Molybdenum, ore	85% MoS_2	Pound	...	13	6	...	14	4
3.75	4.00	"	99.95% Mo	Metal	Powder	"	...	40	...	...	40	...
2.17	2.27	"	58–64% Mo* powder	Ferroalloy	65–70% Mo*	"	...	18	1	...	19	...
1.03	1.03	"	Cathodes	Nickel	Refined	Long ton	986	...	...	986♀	...	...
45.00	34.00	Ounce†		Palladium		Ounce†	19	10	...	17	...	...
120.00	120.00	Ounce†	Wholesale	Platinum	U.K. and empire, refined	"	52	...	...	52	...	...
250.00	230.00	"		Rhodium		"	104	...	...	98	...	...
6.00	6.75	Pound	High purity	Selenium	99.5%	Pound	...	37	6	...	45	10
‖	‖	"	98% Si, spot (lump)	Silicon	98% Si	Long ton	142	...	...	150	...	...
0.138	0.141	"	50% Si*	Ferroalloy	45% Si	"	50	...	...	53	...	...
1.97886	1.78548	Ounce†	New York	Silver	.999 fine	Ounce†	...	...	201.001	...	...	179.917
‡	‡	Pound	60% Ta_2O_5-Cb_2O_5*	Tantalum, ore	60% Ta_2O_5	L.T. unit	...	1,590	...	...	$7.50♂	...
60.00	60.00	"	Sheet, high-grade	Metal	Powder	Pound		‡			‡	
6.00	6.00	"	Powder, 100-lb. lots	Tellurium	99% Lump, powder	"	...	50	...	...	50	...
1.62750	1.65655	"	Straits	Tin	99%+	Long ton	1,366	14	7	1,468	14	9
1.35	1.35	Short ton	25–40% Ti* Low carbon	Titanium, ferroalloy	20–25% Ti	"	230	...	...	230	...	...
21.00	21.00	Long ton	54% TiO_2	" , ilmenite	52–54% TiO_2, Malayan	"	9	10	...	9	10	...
126.00	160.00	Short ton	96% TiO_2	" , rutile	95–97% TiO_2, Australian	"	51	10	...	74	...	...
43.00	43.00	S.T. unit	Wolfram-65% WO_3	Tungsten, ore	65% Wolframite	L.T. unit	...	430	6	...	440	...
43.00	43.00	"	Scheelite-65% WO_3	"	65% Scheelite, Korean	"		‡			‡	
3.71	3.86	Pound	70–80% W* (UCAR)	Ferroalloy	80–85% W*	Pound	...	27	7	...	28	3
2.75	2.75	"	98.8% W, 1,000-lb. lots	Powder	98–99% W*	"	...	32	5	...	33	2
1.30	1.54	"	Domestic¶	Vanadium, ore	98% Fused oxide¶	"	...	7	6	...	10	3
2.90	3.12	"	57% V* (Standard)	Ferroalloy	50–60% V*	"	...	19	7	...	25	...
88.00	100.00	Short ton	60%, Joplin, Mo.	Zinc, ore	52–55% Zn (sulfide)	Metric ton	$48	...	...	$48	...	...
0.1384	0.14857	Pound	E. St. Louis	Metal		Long ton	113	19	1	126	12	9

*Per pound of base metal contained.
†Troy ounces.
‡Not quoted.
§Per pound of contained Mo, f.o.b. Climax, plus cost of containers.
‖Contracts negotiated.
¶Per pound of V_2O_5 contained.
♀Free market price at £5,000–£5,500 per long ton.
♂Per pound contained Ta_2O_5.

Source: *Metals Week* incorporating *E. & M. J. Metal and Mineral Markets* (New York); *Metal Bulletin* (London).

(F. H. Sk.)

Table II.—Select World Mineral and Metal Production in 1968

Metric tons unless otherwise specified; Th. indicates thousands, and Mi. millions of units

Country	Aluminum (Th.)	Bauxite (Th.)	Antimony*	Arsenic †	Asbestos (Th.)	Barite (Th.)	Beryl	Bismuth	Cadmium‡	Cement hydraulic (Th.)	Chromite (Th.)
North America											
Canada	893.6	—	510	314	1,447.9	124.9	—	290	950	7,511	—
Central America	—	—	274	—	—	—	—	—	—	766	—
Mexico	22.5	—	3,464	13,531	—	246.5	—	525	202	6,126	—
United States	2,952.9	1,691.4	777	W	109.5	240.7	152	W	4,831	67,806	—
West Indies	—	9,565.5	—	—	—	—	—	—	—	4,981	NA
South America											
Argentina	—	—	—	—	NA	e> 18.0	593	NA	—	4,211	—
Bolivia+	—	—	11,055	—	p	—	1	575	NA	71	—
Brazil	e>41.5	e> 306.0?	—	312	4.4	43.1	2,078*	—	—	7,281	e> 15.5
Chile	—	—	—	—	—	4.0	—	—	—	1,251	—
Colombia	—	—	—	—	—	7.6	—	—	—	2,367	—
Ecuador	—	—	—	—	—	—	—	—	—	434	—
Guyana	—	e> 2,800.0?	—	—	—	—	—	—	—	—	—
Peru	—	—	816	1,227	—	66.6	—	797	171	1,098	—
Surinam	+43.6	5,572.0	—	—	—	—	—	—	—	—	—
Venezuela	10.0	—	—	—	—	—	—	—	—	2,438	—
Europe											
Austria	85.9	—	161	NA	—	1.5	—	—	19	4,553	—
Belgium	—	—	—	NA	—	—	—	—	861	6,000	—
Bulgaria	—	—	—	—	e> 1.8	—	—	—	—	e>3,400	NA
Czechoslovakia	e> 65.0	—	1,100	NA	—	e> 5.0	—	—	—	6,416	—
Finland	—	—	—	NA	13.1	—	—	—	—	e>1,480	36.2
France	365.6	2,800.0	NA	e>13,600	NA	e> 100.0	—	60	565	e>15,300	—
Germany, East	e> 80.0	—	—	NA	—	30.0	—	—	e> 12	7,550	—
Germany, West	257.0	NA	—	80.0	—	455.9	—	e> 150	342	33,443	—
Greece	76.0	e>1,750.0	—	—	—	65.0	—	—	—	4,000	e> 13.0
Hungary	63.1	1,959.0	—	NA	—	—	—	—	—	2,801	—
Ireland	—	—	—	—	—	143.0	—	—	—	1,352	—
Italy	142.3	216.2	785	—	104.0	204.0	—	NA	245	29,536	—
Luxembourg	—	—	—	—	—	—	—	—	—	e> 180	—
Netherlands	49.0	—	—	—	—	—	—	—	e> 100	3,436	—
Norway	470.1	—	—	—	—	—	—	—	87	2,299	—
Poland	93.5	—	—	—	—	e> 47.0	—	—	e> 440	11,600	—
Portugal	—	—	50	e> 200	p	p	e> 104	—	—	1,861	—
Romania	76.3	e> 20.0	—	—	—	e> 55.0	—	—	—	7,026	NA
Spain	89.0	NA	133	130	—	55.0	—	p	60	e>15,100	—
Sweden	55.8	—	—	21,100	—	—	—	NA	—	3,912	—
Switzerland	76.9	—	—	—	—	—	—	—	—	4,321	—
U.S.S.R.	e>1,000.0	5,000.0	6,400	e>7,000	e> 800.0	e> 260.0	e> 1,200	40	2,200	87,500	1,650.0
United Kingdom	38.2	—	—	NA	—	e> 70.0	—	—	207	17,820	—
Yugoslavia	48.1	2,072.0	1,755	NA	10.4	e> 86.0	—	86	e> 150	3,765	e> 47.0
Africa											
Algeria	p	—	e> 112	—	—	e> 32.0	—	—	—	730	—
Angola	—	—	—	—	—	—	—	—	—	312	—
Congo (Kinshasa)	—	—	—	—	—	—	—	—	136	NA	—
Ethiopia	—	—	—	—	—	—	—	—	—	174	—
Gabon	—	—	—	—	—	—	—	—	—	—	—
Ghana	109.0	284.7	—	—	—	—	—	—	—	230	—
Kenya	—	—	—	—	NA	p	NA	—	—	545	—
Liberia	—	—	—	—	—	—	—	—	—	100	—
Malagasy Republic	—	—	—	—	—	—	77	—	—	68	—
Morocco	—	—	1,212	—	—	78.2	—	—	—	996	—
Nigeria	—	—	—	—	—	—	—	—	—	574	—
Rhodesia	—	e> 2.0	NA	NA	e> 120.0	e> 2.0	NA	—	—	NA	e> 275.0
Sierra Leone	—	350.0	—	—	—	—	—	—	—	—	—
South Africa	—	—	16,798	—	236.4	.5	308	2	—	e>4,100	1,152.9
South West Africa	—	—	—	484	—	—	NA	NA	168	—	—
Tanzania	—	—	—	—	—	—	—	—	—	156	—
Tunisia	—	—	—	—	—	—	—	—	—	e> 470	—
Uganda	—	—	—	—	—	—	361	1	—	156	—
United Arab Republic	NA	—	—	—	e> 2.5	.4	—	—	—	NA	—
Zambia	—	—	—	—	—	—	—	—	11	280	—
Asia											
Burma	—	—	40	—	—	10.1	—	—	—	170	—
China e>	90.0	380.0	12,000	NA	150.0	120.0	—	250	—	9,000	—
Cyprus	—	—	—	—	19.3	—	—	—	—	241	25.1
India	120.1	936.3	—	—	9.1	51.7	e>1,300	—	41	11,940	205.7
Indonesia	—	879.3	—	—	—	—	—	—	—	411	—
Iran	—	—	—	—	—	95.0	—	—	—	1,400	e> 160.0
Israel	—	—	—	—	—	—	—	—	—	e>1,200	—
Japan	482.9	—	19	686	22.0	55.4	—	724	2,195	48,009	27.9
Jordan	—	—	—	—	—	—	—	—	—	381	—
Korea, South	—	—	31	—	3.3	p	—	102	—	3,572	—
Malaysia	—	798.7	—	—	—	—	—	—	—	900	—
Pakistan	—	.9	84	—	—	15.3	—	—	—	2,437	26.0
Philippines	—	—	—	—	NA	NA	—	—	—	2,566	439.2
Taiwan	20.0	—	—	—	e> 1.2	—	—	—	—	3,993	—
Thailand	—	—	e> 189	—	—	p	—	—	—	2,365	—
Turkey	—	NA	3,126	—	3.2	20.3	—	—	—	4,733	603.1
Vietnam, South	—	—	—	—	—	—	—	—	—	145	—
Oceania											
Australia	97.3	4,958.1	844	—	.8	16.0	e> 30	388	459	3,938	—
New Caledonia	—	—	—	—	—	—	—	—	—	—	—
New Guinea	—	—	—	—	—	—	—	—	—	—	—
New Zealand	—	—	—	—	—	—	—	—	—	e> 764	—
Pacific Islands	—	—	—	—	—	—	—	—	—	51	—
World Total (estimate)	8,061.0	44,863.0	61,800	59,384	3,098.0	3,502.0	6,446	3,790	14,557	510,138	5,025.0

Country	Coal (Mi.)	Coke (Mi.)	Cobalt	Copper (in ore) (Th.)	Copper (smelter) (Th.)	Diamonds (Th. carats)	Feldspar (Th.)	Fluorspar (Th.)	Gold (Th. troy oz.)	Graphite (Th.)	Gypsum (Th.)	Ilmenite (Th.)	Iron Ore (Th.)	Pig Iron (Th.)	Steel (Th.)
North America															
Canada	9.99	4.8	1,582	551.9	476.2	—	9.7	e> 89.0	2,688.0	—	5,575	610.4	44,791	7,756	10,207
Central America	—	—	—	11.5	—	—	1.9	—	199.7	—	22	—	4	—	—
Mexico	2.6	1.2	—	61.1	59.8	—	80.3	926.0	177.0	53.0	1,235	—	3,202	2,021	3,285
United States	509.4	57.9	W	1,092.8	1,148.2	—	678.4	229.0	1,478.3	W	9,089	887.7	87,248	82,867	119,260
West Indies	—	—	1,100	8.1	—	—	—	—	p	—	313	—	—	—	—
South America															
Argentina	.5	.4	—	e> .4	—	—	e> 19.0	NA	p	NA	270	—	NA	565	1.552
Bolivia+	—	—	—	6.9	—	—	NA	—	68.3	—	2	—	—	—	—
Brazil	2.4	1.6	—	NA	e> 3.5	320	—	NA	170.1	2.3	80	17.9	e>24,200	3,405	4,436
Chile	1.6	e> .4	—	661.8	627.5	—	.9	NA	53.1	—	119	—	11,917	442	570
Colombia	3.0	p	—	—	—	—	21.8	—	237.5	—	80	—	1,075	199	265
Ecuador	—	—	—	.4	—	—	—	—	8.7	—	—	—	—	—	—
Guyana	—	—	—	—	—	66	—	—	4.1	—	—	—	—	—	—
Peru	e> .3	p	—	213.5	186.1	—	1.9	—	82.5	—	65	—	8,544	NA	105
Surinam	—	—	—	—	—	—	—	—	4.7	—	—	—	—	—	—
Venezuela	p	—	—	—	—	114	—	—	20.6	—	e> 99	—	16,190	614	747
Europe															
Austria	4.2	1.9	—	2.1	18.1	—	2.2	—	—	25.5	698	—	3,473	2,479	3,467
Belgium	14.8	7.2	—	—	—	—	—	—	—	—	74	—	e> 83	10,374	11,486
Bulgaria	e> 29.5	e> .8	NA	32.0	28.0	—	—	NA	NA	—	e> 170	NA	e> 2,700	950	750
Czechoslovakia	e> 95.8	e> 11.1	—	e> 10.0	—	—	NA	—	NA	NA	e> 375	NA	1,540	6,900	e>10,500
Finland	—	p	1,700	e> 29.8	35.9	—	e> 50.0	—	21.4	—	—	140.0	e> 851	1,047	700
France	45.1	12.5	—	e> .4	—	—	e> 180.0	280.0	e> 52.0	—	5,000	—	55,300	16,700	20,410
Germany, East	248.3	e> 9.9	NA	e> 20.0	e> 40.0	—	—	e> 80.0	NA	—	e> 280	NA	e> 1,450	2,333	4,374
Germany, West	214.4	38.5	e> 800	1.3	436.0	—	e> 270.0	102.0	e> 1.0	e> 12.0	1,100	—	7,714	30,305	41,159
Greece	5.7	NA	—	—	—	—	—	—	—	—	e> 215	—	12	NA	218
Hungary	27.2	e> 1.1	—	—	—	—	—	—	NA	—	—	NA	628	1,638	2,903
Ireland	p	p	—	6.5	—	—	—	—	—	—	220	—	—	—	e> 67
Italy	2.1	6.7	—	2.3	—	—	168.4	224.9	—	1.4	e>3,300	—	e>1,058	7,994	16,964
Luxembourg	—	p	—	—	—	—	—	—	—	—	10	—	6,398	e>4,000	e> 4,829
Netherlands	6.7	2.9	—	—	—	—	—	—	—	—	—	—	—	2,821	3,707
Norway	p	p	—	16.6	23.5	—	e> 105.0	—	—	8.2	—	427.4	3,699	1,381	824
Poland	155.5	e> 15.7	NA	17.0	43.6	—	e> 28.0	—	—	—	780	NA	3,050	6,839	11,007
Portugal	p	p	—	3.6	3.9	—	e> 21.2	—	18.7	—	105	.6	e> 204	288	313
Romania	NA	e> 1.1	—	—	—	—	NA	—	NA	—	NA	NA	e> 2,564	2,992	4,751
Spain	15.0	3.4	—	9.1	45.6	—	e> 50.0	256.0	NA	—	e>3,350	39.5	6,185	2,876	5,019
Sweden	p	e> 1.0	—	e> 18.2	46.0	—	27.3	—	49.7	NA	—	—	32,420	2,725	5,095
Switzerland	—	p	—	—	—	—	—	—	—	—	e> 100	—	—	28	453
U.S.S.R.	e> 594.0	71.5	1,400	e> 800.0	e> 800.0	e> 700	e> 240.0	380.0	6,040.0	e> 70.0	e> 4,850	NA	177,600	78,800	107,000
United Kingdom	166.4	28.2	—	—	—	—	e> 31.0	198.0	—	—	4,798	—	13,948	16,695	26,274
Yugoslavia	26.7	e> 1.2	—	e> 64.0	59.4	—	e> 35.0	—	e> 70.0	—	e> 171	—	2,720	1,286	1,997
Africa															
Algeria	p	p	—	e> 1.0	—	—	—	—	—	—	175	—	e> 2,700	e> 10	e> 17
Angola	—	—	—	—	—	1,667	NA	—	p	—	NA	—	3,218	—	—
Congo (Kinshasa)	p	—	e>10,000	320.6	320.6	11,904	—	—	170.0	—	—	—	—	—	—
Ethiopia	—	—	—	—	—	—	7.1	—	38.8	—	NA	—	—	—	—
Gabon	—	—	—	—	—	—	—	—	16.7	—	—	—	—	—	—
Ghana	—	—	—	—	—	e>2,447	—	—	727.1	—	—	—	—	—	—
Kenya	—	—	—	p	—	—	.5	—	32.0	—	41	—	—	—	—
Liberia	—	—	—	—	—	750	—	—	2.2	—	—	—	19,571	—	—
Malagasy Republic	—	—	—	—	—	—	—	—	.5	16.4	—	—	—	—	—
Morocco	p	—	1,518	3.0	—	—	—	—	—	—	e> 90	—	809	—	—
Nigeria	—	—	—	—	—	—	—	—	.2	—	—	—	—	—	—
Rhodesia	3.0	NA	—	e> 18.1	NA	—	—	p	e> 500.0	—	—	—	NA	NA	NA
Sierra Leone	—	—	—	—	—	e>1,410	—	—	—	—	—	—	3,000	—	—
South Africa	51.7	e> 3.4	—	128.2	128.2	7,433	20.0	108.6	31,094.5	.7	316	—	8,233	4,124	4,019
South West Africa	—	—	—	e> 37.0	32.0	1,722	NA	—	—	NA	—	—	38	—	—
Tanzania	p	—	—	—	—	702	—	—	17.5	—	.4	—	—	—	—
Tunisia	—	—	—	—	—	—	—	5.4	—	—	e> 10	—	1,016	128	80
Uganda	—	—	NA	18.7	15.6	—	—	—	—	—	—	—	—	—	—
United Arab Republic	—	NA	—	—	—	—	1.7	—	—	—	406	NA	447	NA	NA
Zambia	.6	—	1,199	665.1	665.7	—	—	—	e> 5.0	—	1	—	—	—	—
Asia															
Burma	p	—	—	p	—	—	—	—	e> .2	—	.4	—	NA	—	NA
China e>	300.0	15.0	—	90.0	100.0	—	NA	250.0	50.0	30.0	500	NA	38,000	19,000	15,000
Cyprus	—	—	—	17.0	—	—	—	—	—	—	20	—	—	—	—
India	73.4	e> 11.0	—	9.3	9.3	9	33.5	1.2	115.4	NA	1,321	58.7	27,433	e>7,322	e> 6,412
Indonesia	p	—	—	—	—	35	—	—	6.0	—	—	—	—	—	—
Iran	p	p	—	e> 12.0	—	—	—	—	—	—	982	—	e> 3	—	—
Israel	—	—	—	7.7	—	—	—	—	—	—	70	—	—	—	—
Japan	46.9	29.6	—	119.7	548.4	—	66.1	15.7	238.3	1.5	562	4.2	2,171	47,451	66,892
Jordan	—	—	—	—	—	—	—	—	—	—	—	—	—	—	—
Korea, South	10.2	—	—	1.2	4.6	—	21.0	46.6	62.4	129.8	—	—	830	17	364
Malaysia	—	NA	—	p	—	—	—	—	4.2	—	—	125.8	5,167	—	—
Pakistan	e> 1.5	—	—	—	—	—	—	—	—	—	46	—	—	—	e> 100
Philippines	p	—	—	113.9	—	—	42.3	—	527.4	—	8	—	1,353	—	—
Taiwan	5.0	p	—	e> 2.3	2.5	—	—	—	21.0	—	6	—	NA	76	e> 250
Thailand	p	—	—	—	—	—	—	245.1	NA	—	128	—	500	e> 40	NA
Turkey	13.9	1.4	—	28.8	23.6	—	—	2.0	—	—	e> 220	—	1,989	910	1,109
Vietnam, South	—	—	—	—	—	—	—	—	—	—	—	—	—	—	—
Oceania															
Australia	64.4	e> 4.6	200	106.8	93.0	—	e> 4.5	NA	796.6	—	833	558.9	26,400	5,571	6,437
New Caledonia	—	—	—	—	—	—	—	—	—	—	—	—	172	—	—
New Guinea	—	—	—	—	—	—	—	—	26.1	—	—	—	—	—	—
New Zealand	7.3	p	—	—	—	—	—	—	8.6	—	—	—	3	—	—
Pacific Islands	—	—	—	p	—	—	—	—	.2	—	—	—	—	—	—
World Total (estimate)	2,784.0	343.0	19,497	5,362.0	6,044.0	36,387	2,221.0	3,530.0	46,191.0	437.0	48,925	2,946.0	681,000	386,091	527,552

In addition, the following significant mineral production originates from the countries indicated: aluminum, Cameroon (45.4), Ghana (108.9); bauxite, Guinea (2,118), Surinam (5,300); graphite, Ceylon (10.8); iron ore, Mauritania (7,500); magnesite, North Korea (1,250); petroleum (crude), Bahrain (27.6), Brunei (44.7), Iraq (550.1), Kuwait (886.1), Libya (948.6), Muscat and Oman (87.9), Neutral Zone (156.7), Qatar (124.2), Saudi Arabia (1,035.8), Trucial States (181.8); phosphate rock, Senegal (1,145), Togo (1,374); tungsten, North Korea (e> 2,000).

Country	Lead (in ore) (Th.)	Lead (smelter) (Th.)	Crude Magnesite (Th.)	Magnesium	Manganese Ore (Th.)	Mercury (Flasks)	Mica Incl. scrap	Molybdenum	Nickel (Th.)
North America									
Canada	327.6	183.3	—	8,961	—	e>5,000	—	9,075	239.1
Central America	13.6	p	—	—	—	—	—	—	—
Mexico	174.2	172.3	—	—	86.1	17,195	737	80	—
United States	325.8	423.9	W	89,244	10.3	28,874	113,698	42,400	13.7
West Indies	—	—	—	—	NA	—	—	—	e>27.5
South America									
Argentina	30.9	25.0	—	—	NA	—	NA	—	—
Bolivia	22.3	NA	—	—	—	134	—	NA	—
Brazil	27.0	16.2	109.0	—	1,426.0	—	e>1,000	—	1.1
Chile	1.0	—	—	—	23.5	513	—	3,865	—
Colombia	.7	—	NA	—	—	285	3,275	—	—
Ecuador	NA	—	—	—	—	—	—	—	—
Guyana	—	—	—	—	130.8	—	—	—	—
Peru	167.8	83.4	—	—	7.2	3,119	—	809	—
Surinam	—	—	—	—	—	—	—	—	—
Venezuela	—	—	—	—	—	—	—	—	—
Europe									
Austria	e>5.6	7.1	1,546.7	—	NA	—	—	—	—
Belgium	—	95.5	—	—	—	—	—	—	—
Bulgaria	106.0	97.0	—	—	e>30.0	—	—	NA	—
Czechoslovakia	e>15.0	e>20.0	e>1,800.0	—	—	e>900	—	—	—
Finland	4.5	—	—	—	—	—	—	—	3.5
France	e>27.0	99.9	—	4,500	NA	—	e>250	—	—
Germany, East	e>12.0	e>25.0	—	—	—	—	—	NA	NA
Germany, West	52.5	120.0	—	—	—	—	—	—	—
Greece	e>9.8	8.9	400.0	—	8.0	—	—	—	3.7
Hungary	NA	NA	—	—	209.0	—	—	—	—
Ireland	62.0	—	—	—	—	—	—	—	—
Italy	36.5	57.6	NA	6,593	50.8	53,317	—	—	—
Luxembourg	—	—	—	—	—	—	—	—	—
Netherlands	—	17.0	—	—	—	—	—	—	—
Norway	e>3.7	—	—	e>31,340	—	—	+4,814	e>250	—
Poland	48.7	42.0	e>42.0	—	—	—	—	—	e>*1.5
Portugal	2.4	1.2	—	—	9.7	—	1,600	—	—
Romania	40.0	e>40.0	—	—	e>80.0	e>203	NA	—	—
Spain	71.3	63.7	e>100.0	—	12.9	57,262	—	NA	—
Sweden	72.0	41.9	—	—	—	—	NA	—	—
Switzerland	—	—	—	—	—	—	—	—	—
U.S.S.R.	400.0	e>400.0	e>3,000.0	e>40,000	e>7,500.0	45,000	36,000	7,000	95.0
United Kingdom	—	31.9	—	NA	—	—	—	—	—
Yugoslavia	e>110.0	94.8	400.3	—	NA	14,794	NA	NA	—
Africa									
Algeria	e>3.4	—	—	—	—	—	—	—	—
Angola	—	—	—	—	9.2	—	—	—	—
Congo (Kinshasa)	—	—	—	—	321.8	—	—	—	—
Ethiopia	—	—	—	—	—	—	—	—	—
Gabon	—	—	—	—	1,220.9	—	—	—	—
Ghana	—	—	—	—	413.3	—	—	—	—
Kenya	—	—	p	—	—	—	—	—	—
Liberia	—	—	—	—	—	—	—	—	—
Malagasy Republic	—	—	—	—	—	—	906	—	—
Morocco	72.4	24.2	—	—	160.2	—	—	—	e>.3
Nigeria	—	—	—	—	—	—	—	NA	—
Rhodesia	—	—	NA	—	NA	—	—	—	NA
Sierra Leone	—	—	—	—	—	—	—	—	—
South Africa	—	—	59.8	—	1,971.7	—	7,927	—	e>5.5
South West Africa	e>60.0	61.2	—	—	e>30.0	—	NA	NA	—
Tanzania	—	—	1.4	—	—	—	311	—	—
Tunisia	e>14.5	14.0	—	—	—	e>300	—	—	—
Uganda	—	—	—	—	—	—	—	—	—
United Arab Republic	NA	—	—	—	4.0	—	NA	—	—
Zambia	24.1	21.9	—	—	25.3	—	—	—	—
Asia									
Burma	11.0	8.5	—	—	—	—	—	—	p
China e>	100.0	100.0	900.0	1,000	900.2	20,000	NA	1,500	—
Cyprus	—	—	—	—	—	—	—	—	—
India	2.6	e>1.4	253.0	—	1,602.0	—	22,172	—	—
Indonesia	NA	—	—	—	1.0	—	—	—	7.9
Iran	e>15.0	.4	6.3	—	e>43.0	—	—	—	—
Israel	—	—	—	—	—	—	—	—	—
Japan	62.8	164.6	—	5,657	323.0	5,047	—	286	—
Jordan	—	—	—	—	—	—	—	—	—
Korea, South	17.3	3.1	—	—	4.2	—	—	192	NA
Malaysia	—	—	—	—	45.1	—	—	—	—
Pakistan	—	—	1.6	—	—	—	NA	—	—
Philippines	p	—	—	—	46.0	3,544	—	43	—
Taiwan	—	—	—	—	—	—	—	—	—
Thailand	2.7	—	—	—	41.1	—	—	—	—
Turkey	2.2	e>2.0	117.7	—	25.4	4,320	—	—	—
Vietnam, South	—	—	—	—	—	—	—	—	—
Oceania									
Australia	387.9	286.3	e>24.0	—	749.4	—	NA	—	4.6
New Caledonia	—	—	—	—	—	—	—	—	79.8
New Guinea	—	—	—	—	—	—	—	—	—
New Zealand	—	—	.8	—	—	—	—	—	—
Pacific Islands	—	—	—	—	e>63.6	—	—	—	—
World Total (estimate)	3,016.0	2,920.0	10,019.0	187,295	17,730.0	259,807	193,026	65,500	483.0

Country	Nitrogen§ e> (Th.)	Peat (Th.)	Petroleum (Mi. bbl.)	Phosphate Rock (Th.)	Platinum‖ (Th. troy oz.)	Potash¶ (Th.)	Pyrite (Th.)	Salt (Th.)
North America								
Canada	550.0	261	435.9	—	464.4	2,623	290	4,434
Central America	10.0	—	—	—	—	—	—	e>56
Mexico	190.0	—	160.5	26	—	—	—	3,500
United States	6,152.0	562	3,329.0	37,422	14.8	2,469	886	37,472
West Indies	90.0	—	67.7	93	—	—	—	e>900
South America								
Argentina	10.7	NA	125.5	NA	—	—	—	740
Bolivia	—	—	15.0	—	—	—	—	NA
Brazil	7.9	—	59.8	147	—	—	—	1,536
Chile	120.0	—	13.7	22	—	—	—	841
Colombia	40.0	—	63.4	—	15.1	—	—	500
Ecuador	—	—	1.8	—	—	—	—	NA
Guyana	—	—	—	—	—	—	—	—
Peru	63.0	—	27.1	e>75	—	—	—	132
Surinam	—	—	—	—	—	—	—	—
Venezuela	—	—	1,319.3	e>60	—	—	—	126
Europe								
Austria	245.0	—	e>18.0	—	—	—	—	442
Belgium	350.0	—	—	e>20	—	—	—	—
Bulgaria	353.9	—	4.0	—	—	—	150	e>115
Czechoslovakia	245.0	—	e>1.5	—	—	—	NA	e>205
Finland	121.5	e>225	—	—	—	—	774	—
France	1,300.0	NA	19.6	e>30	—	1,719	82	4,120
Germany, East	336.0	—	—	—	—	e>2,200	e>140	e>2,000
Germany, West	1,559.1	1,500	57.7	—	—	2,220	615	7,540
Greece	116.7	—	—	—	—	—	210	99
Hungary	188.0	NA	114.4	—	—	—	—	—
Ireland	37.0	5,779	—	—	—	—	—	—
Italy	1,095.8	—	10.3	—	—	e>266	1,406	3,926
Luxembourg	—	—	—	—	—	—	—	—
Netherlands	849.3	e>400	14.6	—	—	—	—	2,414
Norway	358.8	e>12	—	—	—	—	688	—
Poland	593.6	e>35	3.5	e>95	—	—	e>240	2,634
Portugal	119.6	—	—	—	—	—	553	e>451
Romania	372.3	—	99.0	—	—	—	e>360	e>2,100
Spain	371.7	NA	e>1.1	—	—	e>592	2,403	e>1,800
Sweden	139.4	e>125	—	—	—	—	474	—
Switzerland	38.0	—	—	—	—	—	—	255
U.S.S.R.	3,753.0	e>190,000	e>252.5	17,700	2,000.0	e>3,150	e>3,500	e>11,000
United Kingdom	855.0	—	.6	—	—	—	—	7,677
Yugoslavia	101.1	—	18.5	—	—	—	e>274	179
Africa								
Algeria	—	—	325.1	e>200	—	—	e>60	e>120
Angola	—	—	5.4	—	—	—	—	—
Congo (Kinshasa)	—	—	—	—	—	—	—	NA
Ethiopia	—	—	—	—	.3	—	—	262
Gabon	—	—	33.6	—	—	—	—	—
Ghana	—	—	—	—	—	—	—	e>29
Kenya	—	—	—	—	—	—	—	61
Liberia	—	—	—	—	—	—	—	—
Malagasy Republic	—	—	—	—	—	—	—	17
Morocco	—	—	.6	10,512	—	—	418	41
Nigeria	—	—	52.9	—	—	—	—	—
Rhodesia	NA	—	—	—	—	—	—	—
Sierra Leone	—	—	—	—	—	—	—	—
South Africa	105.0	—	—	1,565	e>864.0	—	704	342
South West Africa	—	—	—	—	—	—	—	e>110
Tanzania	—	—	—	—	—	—	—	30
Tunisia	—	—	23.5	3,444	—	—	—	360
Uganda	—	—	—	e>142	—	—	—	—
United Arab Republic	132.0	—	e>52.3	e>1,441	—	—	—	622
Zambia	NA	—	—	—	—	—	—	—
Asia								
Burma	—	—	NA	—	—	—	—	137
China e>	1,655.3	—	100.0	1,000	—	—	1,500	15,000
Cyprus	—	—	—	—	—	—	874	5
India	402.6	—	43.6	▲7	—	—	—	5,044
Indonesia	41.0	—	219.9	e>10	—	—	—	e>79
Iran	27.0	—	1,039.4	—	—	—	—	275
Israel	25.9	e>20	14.8□	777	—	310	—	73
Japan	2,041.8	70	5.5	—	6.8	—	4,475	967
Jordan	—	—	—	1,162	—	—	—	16
Korea, South	147.7	e>30	—	—	—	—	NA	561
Malaysia	—	—	1.5	—	—	—	—	—
Pakistan	100.0	—	3.8	—	—	—	—	898
Philippines	35.5	—	—	1	—	—	182	187
Taiwan	162.6	—	.4	—	—	—	39	311
Thailand	7.0	—	p	—	—	—	—	e>150
Turkey	32.2	—	22.2	—	—	—	137	567
Vietnam, South	—	—	—	—	—	—	—	e>160
Oceania								
Australia	55.0	—	13.9	6	—	—	e>170	e>800
New Caledonia	—	—	—	—	—	—	—	—
New Guinea	—	—	—	—	—	—	—	—
New Zealand	—	—	p	—	—	—	—	56
Pacific Islands	—	—	—	3,913	—	—	—	—
World Total (estimate)	54,400.0	199,024	14,168.0	83,743	3,365.0	15,549	22,104	125,976

Country	Silver (Th. troy oz.)	Sulfur (elemental) (Th.)	Talc (Th.)	Tantalum♀ (Th.)	Tin (in ore) (Long tons)	Tin (smelter) (Long tons)	Tungsten Conc.♂	Vanadium	Zinc (in ore) (Th.)	Zinc (smelter) (Th.)
North America										
Canada	45,621	2,345.5	70.1	1.9	150	—	1,295	—	1,155.1	387.3
Central America	4,813	—	—	—	—	—	6	—	e>14.8	—
Mexico	40,031	1,684.9	.6	—	519	317	266	—	240.0	80.0
United States	32,729	8,955.5	869.3	W	W	3,453	4,621	5,881	480.3	926.1
West Indies	e>13	e>33.4	—	—	—	—	—	—	—	—
South America										
Argentina	2,422	e>33.0	e>28.0	—	723	—	185	—	e>27.0	e>21.0
Bolivia	5,180	35.4	—	—	28,576	e>60	1,811	—	11.8	—
Brazil	464	6.9	e>64.0	◇5.3	2,240	1,251	435	—	NA	e>4.8
Chile	3,757	62.5	2.8	—	—	—	—	—	1.3	—
Colombia	100	28.8	NA	—	—	—	—	—	e>.6	—
Ecuador	136	.1	—	—	—	—	—	—	.1	—
Guyana	—	—	—	—	—	—	—	—	—	—
Peru	36,020	—	.3	—	99	—	509	—	309.1	68.0
Surinam	—	—	—	NA	—	—	—	—	—	—
Venezuela	—	—	—	—	—	—	—	—	—	—
Europe										
Austria	161	31.9	84.6	—	—	—	e>107	—	9.0	15.3
Belgium	—	e>5.0	—	—	—	4,799	—	—	—	254.3
Bulgaria	—	10.0	—	NA	—	—	—	NA	e>80.0	e>73.0
Czechoslovakia	NA	—	—	NA	e>155	—	—	NA	—	NA
Finland	677	125.2	e>6.0	—	—	—	—	1,198	65.4	—
France	e>2,000	1,617.0	e>210.0	—	e>475	—	—	—	23.0	207.3
Germany, East	e>4,800	e>125.0	—	—	e>1,000	e>1,200	—	NA	e>12.0	e>14.0
Germany, West	e>2,000	127.0	e>42.0	NA	—	1,502	—	—	117.0	122.0
Greece	261	—	4.5	—	—	—	—	—	10.6	—
Hungary	—	e>3.0	—	NA	—	—	—	NA	NA	—
Ireland	1,913	—	—	—	—	—	—	—	53.0	—
Italy	1,156	e>99.5	115.9	—	—	—	NA	—	139.8	112.3
Luxembourg	—	—	—	—	—	—	—	—	—	—
Netherlands	—	e>47.0	—	—	—	7,983	—	—	—	43.1
Norway	—	—	e>80.0	—	—	—	—	e>850	e>11.6	60.0
Poland	e>160	1,316.0	—	NA	—	—	—	NA	e>158.0	202.5
Portugal	300	e>.4	1.1	p	624	619	1,313	—	.5	—
Romania	e>800	—	e>130.0	NA	—	—	—	NA	—	NA
Spain	e>2,400	28.3	e>28.0	p	118	2,169	111	—	75.7	75.4
Sweden	3,524	—	23.5	—	—	NA	NA	—	81.3	—
Switzerland	—	—	—	—	—	—	—	—	—	—
U.S.S.R.	e>35,000	500.0	e>370.0	NA	26,000	26,000	e>6,200	NA	e>540.0	e>540.0
United Kingdom	—	e>50.0	e>10.0	—	1,798	24,933	—	—	—	142.9
Yugoslavia	2,577	—	—	—	—	—	—	—	e>100.0	79.0
Africa										
Algeria	e>100	—	—	—	—	—	—	—	e>10.0	—
Angola	—	—	—	—	—	—	—	—	—	—
Congo (Kinshasa)	2,139	—	—	p	6,895	1,892	39	—	126.5	62.6
Ethiopia	—	—	—	—	—	—	—	—	—	—
Gabon	—	—	—	—	—	—	—	—	—	—
Ghana	—	—	—	—	—	—	—	—	—	—
Kenya	3	—	—	—	—	—	—	—	—	—
Liberia	—	—	—	—	—	—	—	—	—	—
Malagasy Republic	—	—	—	p	—	—	—	—	—	—
Morocco	920	—	—	—	19	e>15	—	—	31.8	—
Nigeria	—	—	—	1.1	9,644	9,778	NA	—	—	—
Rhodesia	NA	—	NA	NA	NA	NA	NA	—	—	—
Sierra Leone	—	—	—	—	—	—	—	—	—	—
South Africa	3,337	e>6.0	9.1	p	1,837	686	25	2,266	—	—
South West Africa	1,350	—	—	NA	e>700	—	e>85	660	e>60.0	—
Tanzania	—	—	—	—	286	—	9	—	—	—
Tunisia	e>46	—	—	—	—	—	—	—	e>5.1	—
Uganda	—	—	—	p	228	—	44	—	—	—
United Arab Republic	—	3.2	e>32.0	—	—	—	—	—	NA	—
Zambia	e>768	—	—	—	—	—	—	—	53.8	53.1
Asia										
Burma	780	—	—	—	500	—	e>160	—	4.1	—
China e>	700	250.0	150.0	NA	20,000	20,000	8,000	NA	100.0	90.0
Cyprus	—	—	—	—	—	—	—	—	—	—
India	81	—	175.6	—	—	—	20	—	7.0	20.7
Indonesia	309	e>1.2	—	—	16,563	4,885	—	—	—	—
Iran	—	38.0	—	—	—	—	—	—	e>25.0	—
Israel	—	—	—	—	—	—	—	—	—	—
Japan	10,713	334.3	1,689.8	—	927	1,857	529	—	264.3	605.6
Jordan	—	—	—	—	—	—	—	—	—	—
Korea, South	611	—	149.4	—	44	—	2,092	—	19.3	2.5
Malaysia	—	—	—	p	75,069	88,318	65	—	—	—
Pakistan	—	NA	2.6	—	—	—	—	—	—	—
Philippines	1,575	p	.5	—	—	—	—	—	2.2	—
Taiwan	85	e>6.0	29.1	—	—	—	—	—	—	—
Thailand	—	—	3.4	p	23,678	24,662	482	—	—	—
Turkey	—	24.2	—	—	—	—	—	—	4.9	—
Vietnam, South	—	—	—	—	—	—	—	—	—	—
Oceania										
Australia	21,618	—	e>40.0	.1	6,623	3,692	1,148	—	420.4	208.8
New Caledonia	—	—	—	—	—	—	—	—	—	—
New Guinea	18	—	—	—	—	—	—	—	—	—
New Zealand	4	—	—	—	—	—	NA	—	—	—
Pacific Islands	55	—	—	—	—	—	—	—	—	—
World Total (estimate)	274,929	18,941.0	4,485.0	9.1	227,581	230,071	32,019	10,855	4,967.0	4,552.0

NOTES: NA not available; e> estimate; "p" indicates small production, unknown or less than the minimum base of the table; "W" indicates withheld to avoid disclosing individual U.S. company confidential data.
*Metal content of ore. †White arsenic. ‡To avoid duplication of figures, cadmium exported in concentrates, flue dust, etc., is excluded from the total. §Nitrogen content of fertilizer compounds not including nitrogen for industrial uses. (Fiscal year ending June 30, 1967.) Source: *United Nations Statistical Yearbook 1968*. ‖Includes all platinum-group metals ¶K_2O equivalent of salts produced (marketable). ♀Tantalum and columbium combined concentrates. ♂Contained tungsten. □Includes estimated production from occupied Egyptian oil fields. ◇Of which 4.9 th. were pyrochlore. ▲Apatite. +Exports. Source: U.S Department of the Interior, Bureau of Mines.

(F. H. Sk.)

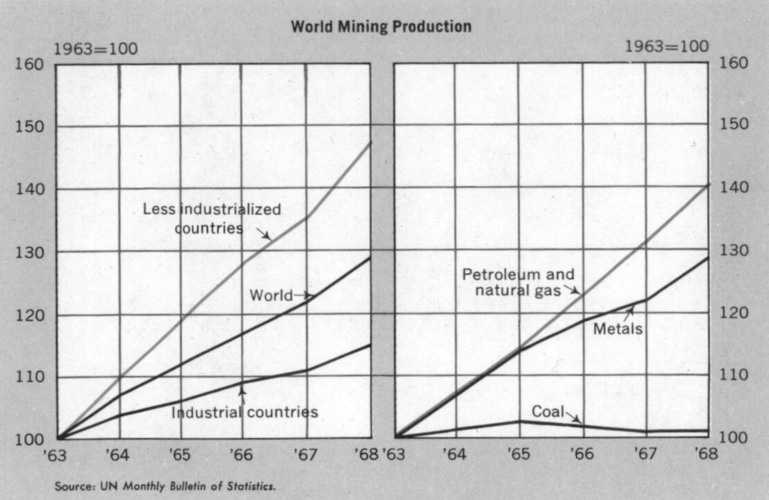

continued from page 537

molybdenum (−0.5%), and tellurium (−8%) were the four metals with declining outputs, while arsenic showed no change from the previous year. Decreased production was seen in five nonmetallic minerals: industrial diamonds (−18.9%), diatomite (−10.6%), magnesite (−2.6%), pumice (−3.4%), and pyrite (−0.5%), as well as in two fuels, nonmetallurgical coke (−8.9%) and fuel briquettes (−3.9%).

To the extent that worldwide figures were available, the U.S. led the world in 1968 production of 24 minerals or mineral commodities, including aluminum, copper, crude oil, natural gas, molybdenum, and phosphate. The Soviet Union led in 11, including lead, cement, chromite, coal, iron ore, and potash, but was second in many other minerals. Canada led in six, among which were nickel, asbestos, and silver, while South Africa's four included gem diamonds, gold, and platinum.

In the aggregate, it appeared that mineral prices also increased in response to a number of factors, including accelerating annual rates of growth in demand, increased capital investment requirements for mineral development, the rising cost of finance, and, predictably, the general pressure of inflation. Copper prices increased in 1968 and seemed to be confirming an upward trend that had persisted since the late 1950s. Aluminum and perhaps silver appeared to be following a similar course. Sulfur prices, on the other hand, fell slightly in 1968 from the near-record levels of the two or three preceding years.

As the demand for minerals and the technology for their exploration, development, and production changed, the geographic pattern of mineral production and consumption changed too. Fiji, for example joined the ranks of the copper producers in 1968; Honduras began to produce antimony; Iceland, diatomite; and Ceylon, rutile. This kind of change, however, required time. Perhaps the most notable example in the 1960s was the rise of Australia from relative obscurity to a place among the world's leading producers.

In general, mineral production expanded in the less developed countries at a greater rate than in the developed nations. Consequently, the value of the mineral component of international trade in 1968 undoubtedly exceeded that of the previous year as the flow of crude and partially processed minerals from the less developed to the more industrialized countries increased. This was also true of the reverse movement of processed mineral products from the developed to the less industrialized nations. In sum, the worldwide demand for larger quantities of an increasing variety of minerals and mineral products continued to grow in 1968 and caused mineral production to reach new highs.

Aluminum. In 1968 world production of primary aluminum reached a new high of 8,061,000 metric tons, an increase of 6.4% over 1967. The U.S. continued to be the world's leading producer, accounting for 36.6% of the total output, a slight drop from the previous year's 39.8% share. Maintaining their 1967 sequence, the Soviet Union (12.4%), Canada (11.1%), Japan (6%), Norway (5.8%), France (3.2%), and West Germany (1.8%) followed the U.S. These seven countries together provided 77% of 1968 production, leaving the remaining 23% to be shared among the other 28 producing countries. World demand increased to 6,808,000 metric tons in 1968, up 11.6% from 1967.

Antimony. The 1968 output of antimony was 61,800 metric tons, an increase of 6.9% over 1967 but still below the 1964 and 1965 output. Four countries accounted for 75% of world output. Retaining the same order they held in 1967, these were South Africa (16,793 metric tons), China (est. 12,000), Bolivia (11,055), and the Soviet Union (est. 6,400). World demand was increasing at slightly more than 3% per year, but in the more industrialized countries the demand was shifting away from metal to the oxide.

Asbestos. World production of asbestos reached a new high of 3,098,020 metric tons in 1968, a gain of 4.7% over 1967 output. The three largest producers accounted for 90% of world production. Maintaining the same relative ranking they had achieved for the past five years or more, these were Canada, with a new record of 1.45 million metric tons in 1968 for 46.7% of the world total; the Soviet Union with 800,000 metric tons (25.8%); and South Africa with 236,350 metric tons (7.6%).

Bauxite. At 44,863,000 metric tons, 1968 world bauxite production increased only 0.8% over the 1967 level. With no change from the 1967 national rankings, the leading producers in 1968 were Jamaica with 8,525,000 metric tons (accounting for 19% of the total), Surinam with 5,572,000 metric tons (12.4%), the Soviet Union estimated at 5 million (11.1%), Australia with 4,958;000 (11.1%), and Guyana and France, each with 2.8 million and 6.2% of total output. Reduced production in Jamaica (down 8% from 1967), France (−0.5%), Guyana (−17.2%), and Yugoslavia (−2.8%) was compensated for by other producers, particularly Australia. The latter country, in which no commercial bauxite deposits were known to exist in the mid-1950s, increased its production 16.8% over 1967 levels to a 1968 high of 4,958,000 metric tons. Perhaps the most significant development of 1968, however, was the successful financing and beginning of development of the new Boké bauxite deposit in Guinea with a planned initial productive capacity of 4.7 million metric tons per year by 1972.

Cement. World output of hydraulic cement increased 5.5% to reach 510.1 million metric tons in 1968. As it had since 1965, when it supplanted the U.S., the Soviet Union continued to lead as a producer with 87.5 million metric tons (17.2% of the world total) in 1968, followed by the U.S. with 67.8 million (13.3%), Japan, West Germany, and Italy. Although output reached record highs, the U.S. industry remained plagued by problems of overcapacity exacerbated by the marketing characteristics of the commodity, particularly the importance of transportation costs. As a result, despite efforts to increase prices in response to increases in the cost of almost all factors of production such as coal and labour, U.S. prices finished little if any above their starting point.

Chromium. Despite the continuation of UN sanctions against Rhodesian chromite, world production increased 5.1% in 1968 to a total of 5,025,379 metric tons. The Soviet Union, which produced 32.8% of the 1968 world total, continued in first place with 1,650,000 metric tons (23% of the total). The sanctions against Rhodesian ore created an artificial shortage of high-grade metallurgical chromite which could not be met from the alternative sources, Turkey and Iran. The non-Communist countries thus became increasingly dependent upon the Soviet Union for this commodity.

Cobalt. At 19,497 metric tons, 1968 world production of cobalt declined 2.4% below 1967 levels. Consumption in the U.S. declined for the second year in a row, a trend apparent throughout the rest of the world for most of the year. As usual, the Congo (Kinshasa) far outstripped all other producers. Its estimated 1968 production of 10,000 metric tons accounted for 51.3% of the world output.

Copper. Increasing by 6.9% to a total of 5,361,966 metric tons, world mine production of copper recovered from the decline of 1967 to establish a new record. The U.S., with 1,090,000 metric tons (20% of the world output) and the Soviet Union with an estimated 800,000 metric tons (14.9%) remained as they had long been, the largest and second largest producers. For the second time in five years, Zambia edged ahead of Chile for the number three spot with 665,072 metric tons (12.4%) to Chile's 661,841 metric tons (12.4%). The U.S. copper strike that began in July 1967 and was largely responsible for the marked 1967 drop in world output continued until the end of March 1968. A reasonably strong demand, concurrent with shortages due to the strike, resulted in significant price increases.

Diamonds. Total world production of diamonds declined 12% to 26.4 million carats in 1968 (29% gem diamonds, 71% industrial). The loss was in industrial diamond output (down 18.9% to 15.8 million carats), as gem diamond production rose by 10% to 10.6 million carats. Largest producer both overall and of industrial diamonds was the Congo (Kinshasa) with a total of 11,904,000 carats (32.7% of the world output), of which 11.4 million carats were industrial stones. South Africa, world's leading producer of gem diamonds (3.4 million carats comprising 32% of the world gem diamond output), was second in aggregate production with 7,433,000 carats (20.4% of world output). The Soviet Union, with an estimated 7 million carats, was third, and Ghana (2.4 million carats) was fourth with 6.7% of the world total. The apparent downturn in world production was due in part to depleted deposits, as in Tanzania, but probably more to illicit mining and sales. The Congo (Brazzaville), for example, had no mines but reported exports amounting to nearly 6 million carats in 1968. It was believed that most of the country's diamonds came illicitly from the Congo (Kinshasa).

Gold. In 1968 gold production increased 1.1% over the previous year to 46.2 million troy oz., a level below that of several previous years. The increase was due to gains by the two leading producers: South Africa was up 2.3% to 31,094,000 troy oz. (67% of world production) and the U.S.S.R. gained 5.3% to 6,040,000 troy oz. (13% of world output). The decline of 6.2% in U.S. production was attributed largely to the continuation of the copper strike to the end of March 1968, because most U.S. gold production was a by-product of copper mining.

Iron and Steel. World iron ore production of 681 million metric tons in 1968 was 9.2% above 1967 levels for a new record. In the order they had maintained for many years, the three largest producers were the Soviet Union with 177.6 million metric tons (26% of world output), the U.S. with 87,248,000 metric tons (12.8%), and France with 55.3 million metric tons (8.1%). Of note was Australia's remarkable climb from 17th place in 1963 (1.1% of world production) to 8th place in 1968 (3.8%). World steel production increased 7.2% in 1968 to 527.5 million metric tons. As it had throughout the century, the U.S. remained in first place with 119.3 million metric tons, 22.6% of world output, but the U.S.S.R. continued to gain, producing 107 million metric tons (20%). Japan with 66.9 million metric tons and West Germany with 41.2 million were third and fourth, accounting for 12.7% and 8% of the world total, respectively.

Lead. The record production of 3,016,000 metric tons of lead in 1968 was 4.9% above that of 1967. In their recent jockeying for first place, the U.S.S.R. nosed out Australia in 1968, 400,000 metric tons to 388,000 (13.7% of the world output to 12.9%). Canada was third and the U.S. fourth with 328,000 metric tons (10.9%) and 326,000 (10.8%), respectively. Heightened world demand, up approximately 5.3%, outstripped production but was met from producers' stockpiles, which were reduced to less than one month's supply.

Manganese. World production of manganese ore rose 6.3% to 17.7 million metric tons in 1968. The U.S.S.R., by far the largest producer, provided 42.3% of the total, followed by South Africa (11.1%), India (9%), Brazil (8%), and Gabon (7%), the latter having risen from tenth place in 1962, its first year of production. Manganese consumption was almost entirely dependent upon the steel industry, which used it primarily as a deoxidizer and a sulfur scavenger. Despite a 7.2% increase in steel production, the manganese market remained depressed and prices continued the decline of 1967, due largely to aggressive sales competition among producers.

Mercury. For the first time in two years, world mercury production increased, up 11.6% to 260,000 76-lb. flasks, a level below that of several earlier years. As usual, Spain was the leader with 57,262 flasks (22.1% of the world total) closely trailed by Italy with 52,215 flasks (21.5%). The U.S.S.R. produced an estimated 45,000 flasks for third place (19.3%), and the U.S. was fourth with 28,874 flasks (11.1%). Demand and supply were well balanced during 1968 with no surplus either way.

Molybdenum. World production declined 0.5% in 1968 to 65,500 metric tons. Output in the U.S., long the world's largest producer (64.7% of total), actually increased despite a marked decline in by-product molybdenum from copper mining, usually about 25% of the total national output, due to the continued copper strike. Canada's notable rise from sixth largest (with 378 metric tons in 1963) to being the second largest producer since 1966 was not seriously compromised by a small decrease in 1968 production to 9,075 metric tons due to labour difficulties. For the second consecutive year, world production exceeded consumption.

Nickel. World nickel output increased 9% in 1968 to 483,275 metric tons. Of the total, 49.5% came from Canada (239,082 metric tons), 19.7% from the U.S.S.R. (est. 95,000 metric tons), 16.5% from New Caledonia (79,849 metric tons), and the remaining 14.3% from the other 12 producing countries. Anticipated Canadian production was not realized, largely because of a serious shortage of both the mine labour and skilled construction labour required to complete the construction of new and the expansion of old mines and plants on schedule. The nickel shortage that had been developing for several years was, if anything, exacerbated by the lack of any new sales from the U.S. government stockpile, from which less than 4,500 metric tons were released, all under old contracts. Despite the shortage and the resulting price increases there was no noticeable effort toward substitution.

Phosphates. For the 11th consecutive year, world phosphate rock production increased. Up 7.2%, the output in 1968 was 83,743,000 metric tons. Nearly half the production (44.7%) came from the U.S., and almost 75% of that 37.4 million metric tons was mined in Florida. Other significant producers were the Soviet Union (21.1%), Morocco (12.6%), and Tunisia (4.1%). The increase in production, however, was not matched by consumption, particularly in the U.S., where a 9% decline in consumption was attributed to a bad year for fertilizer due to adverse weather.

Platinum-Group Metals. World production of platinum-group metals reached 3.4 million troy oz. in 1968, 6.2% above the 1967 level. The Soviet Union accounted for an estimated 59.4% of the total with approximately 2 million troy oz., followed, in the usual order, by South Africa with an estimated 864,000 troy oz. (25.7%) and Canada with 464,400 troy oz. (13.8%). Despite the increased production, a tightness in supply was shown by the unusually large gap (as much as $150 per ounce) between the producer (South African and Canadian) and the dealer (Soviet Union and small producer) prices for platinum.

Potash. In 1968 world potash production increased 1.7% to 15.5 million metric tons. At an estimated 85–90% of capacity, this output nevertheless exceeded apparent demand in non-Communist countries by about 3 million metric tons. For the second consecutive year U.S. production declined, and the 1968 output of 2.5 million metric tons (16.1% of the world total) dropped the U.S. from its customary first to third place. The Soviet Union took the lead with an estimated 3.2 million metric tons (20%) followed by Canada with 2.6 million. As a result of general excess capacity, prices weakened.

Salt. At 126 million metric tons, world salt production in 1968 was 5.5% above that in 1967. The 37.5 million metric tons produced in the U.S. kept that country well in the forefront as usual. It accounted for 30% of 1968 world production. Next in order were China (12.3%) and the Soviet Union (8.7%).

Silver. World silver production increased 5.4% to the highest level since 1940, reaching 274.9 million troy oz. Approximately 70% of the output was evenly divided among the top five producers. Canada (16.6% of the total) took the lead from Mexico (14.6%). These were followed by Peru (13.1%), the U.S.S.R. with an estimated 12.7%, and the U.S. with 11.9%. In 1968, for the first time since the 1930s, silver prices were not under a U.S. Treasury ceiling. They fluctuated wildly in the New York market, beginning the year at $2.15 per ounce, falling to $1.81 by February, rising to $2.565 in June, and ending the year at $1.90.

Sulfur. World production of elemental sulfur from all sources increased 5.7% to 18.9 million metric tons. The U.S. maintained its customary lead with 8.96 million metric tons (47.3% of world output) followed by Canada with 2.3 million (12.4%). For the first time since 1962 world production exceeded consumption, in part because of increased productive capacity but also because of a lessening in the rate of growth of demand.

Tin. World mine production of tin increased 5.8% to 227,581 long tons. In their customary order, the largest producers were Malaysia (33% of world total), Bolivia (12.6%), the Soviet Union (11.4%), and Thailand (10.4%). For the second consecutive year, tin production exceeded consumption and by the autumn had reached a level that led the International Tin Council to reintroduce mild export controls upon its producing-nation members in September. Prices, which had been weakening all year firmed and then increased in the last quarter in response to the pressure of hedge buying in anticipation of a U.S. East Coast dock strike, which materialized in December.

Tungsten. World tungsten production turned upward by 11.9% after declining in 1967, although the 1968 output of 32,019 metric tons of contained tungsten in ores and concentrates was by no means a record. As was customary, China led with an estimated 8,000 metric tons (25% of the total) followed by the U.S.S.R. and the U.S. The price in non-Communist countries remained stable, about $43 per short ton unit. The higher and stable price brought 35 new or reopened mines into production in the U.S.

Uranium. Production of uranium in the non-Communist nations increased 18.9% to 20,474 metric tons of uranium oxide. The U.S. remained the largest producer with 11,193 metric tons (54.7% of the total), but South Africa with 3,514 metric tons (17.1%) supplanted Canada (16.4%) in second place. Existing and anticipated increases in nuclear power plant capacity engendered an intensive exploration program that reached new heights of activity in the U.S., Canada, parts of Africa, and Australia. Substantial new deposits were found in three central African countries, Gabon, Niger, and the Central African Republic.

Zinc. World mine production of zinc increased 2.7% to 4,967,000 metric tons in 1968. Canada continued to lead with 1.2 million metric tons, accounting for 23.3% of the world output. The Soviet Union was second, having supplanted the U.S. in that position in 1967, with a 1968 output of 540,000 metric tons (10.9%). The U.S. accounted for 9.7%, and Australia 8.5%. Prices held stable throughout the year with a minor rise on the London Metal Exchange in December.

(F. H. Sk.)

See also Fuel and Power; Geology; Industrial Review; Metallurgy.

Missiles: *see* Defense

Molecular Biology

The accomplishment of the next logical step in the series of discoveries that had been revolutionizing molecular biology for the past 25 years was announced in November 1969. A team of Harvard Medical School scientists isolated one of the 3,000 genes on the chromosome of the intestinal bacterium *Escherichia coli* (*E. coli*) in an elegant experiment. The achievement would make possible a detailed study of the theory of the mechanisms of gene control proposed by French scientists François Jacob and Jacques Monod.

The team, headed by Jonathan Beckwith, used two bacteriophages (viruses) known to pick up the gene that controls lactose metabolism from the *E. coli* cells they infect. The double-stranded deoxyribonucleic acid (DNA) picked up by the two phages differs in that the sequence of chemical units for the lactose gene face in opposite directions. When single, separated, complementary strands of DNA from each phage were brought together in a test tube, the lactose genes immediately formed a new double strand. Other unwanted gene segments in the solution found no complements and were dissolved by an enzyme that breaks down only single-stranded DNA.

Biochemistry. Using a new ultracentrifugation technique, in 1969 Northwestern University's Hans Noll identified a 60S configuration of microbial ribosomes in *E. coli.* Svedberg units measure sedimentation and reflect configuration and molecular structure; thus while a ribosome consists of a 30S and 50S subunit, the normal configuration of a ribosome is 70S. Noll inferred that microbial ribosomes alternate from the 70S to the 60S form in polypeptide synthesis.

Studying mucins in the gland cells of cattle, W. Ward Pigman of New York Medical College identified isolated polypeptides of 20–28 amino acids produced by these glands. On the basis of this research and the findings of John M. Shackelford of the University of Alabama, Pigman proposed that the ribosomes perform only the first step in the two-part process of protein synthesis. He suggested that protein particles found by Shackelford near the membranes of Golgi bodies were completed glycoprotein molecules and that the second step in protein synthesis is assembly of finished proteins from polypeptide subunits on Golgi body membranes.

Electron micrographs of DNA made by California Institute of Technology scientists and shown at the 1969 Biophysical Society meeting. Left, white mass in centre believed to be enzymes attached to strands of DNA. Right, what appears to be the twisted, double spiral structure of DNA captured on film for the first time.

WIDE WORLD

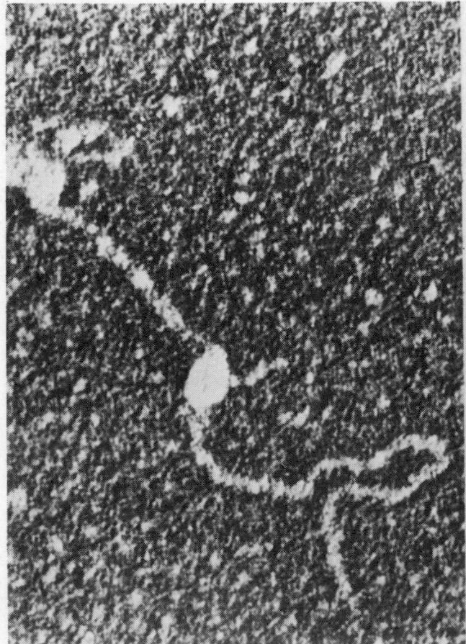

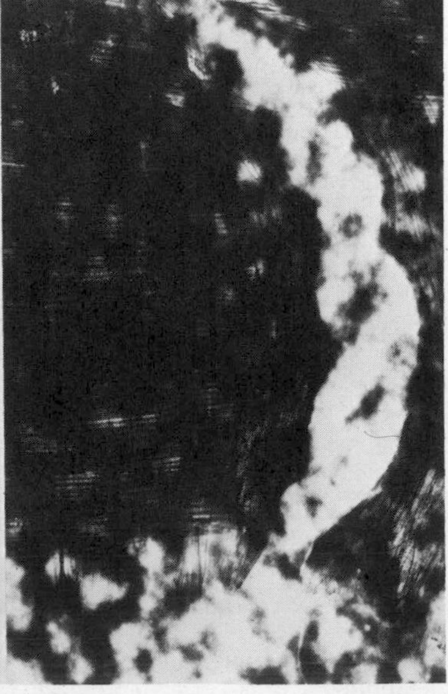

Protein research in 1969 centred around work with enzymes. A highly important development was the first total synthesis of an enzyme, ribonuclease, which breaks down ribonucleic acid (RNA), by teams at the Rockefeller University, New York, and Merck, Sharp & Dohme Research Laboratories. The Rockefeller team, led by Robert B. Merrifield and Bernd Gutte, bound the 124 amino acids of RNA-ase one at a time to a small polystyrene bead, using a process and technical devices developed by them that required 369 chemical reactions. Robert G. Denkewalter, Ralph F. Hirschmann, and associates of the Merck team prepared peptide fragments of 6–17 amino acids each and assembled them in a 104-amino-acid fragment known as S-protein and a 20-amino-acid fragment known as S-peptide. The two fragments were joined to produce a chemically active form of RNA-ase.

Further important research in 1969 involved gamma globulin, the protein molecule of immunity. Gerald M. Edelman and associates of the Rockefeller University described the complete sequence of 1,320 amino acids making up one gamma globulin antibody molecule. The molecule contained 19,996 atoms and had a molecular weight of 150,000. Antibodies were shown to have "variable" and "constant" regions.

Battelle Memorial Institute (Columbus, O.), scientists in 1969 reported the development of a new type of polymer-enzyme "micro-pill" by molecular biological means. Jackson Lynn and Richard D. Falb linked several enzymes of the glycolysis series to polymers. Techniques used in creating the experimental polymer-enzyme systems might be used to provide sufferers from kidney diseases with a daily supply of needed enzymes such as urease, aspartase, and fumaric acid. (J. S. Sw.)

Biophysics. Radioactive tracers and advanced physical concepts for instrumentation served to provide breakthroughs in 1969 in the understanding of the structure and functioning of the cell. Major accomplishments included the synthesis of important cellular components. Masayasu Nomura and Peter Traub of the University of Wisconsin produced biologically active ribosomes from a spontaneous reaction between RNA and proteins from *E. coli.* In approaching the problem of defining the functions of the variety of proteins in ribosomes, Nomura also succeeded in preparing a series of ribosome derivatives, each deficient in a specific ribosomal protein. When the properties of these particles were compared to those of normal ribosomes the role of a given ribosomal protein could be defined.

The first single crystals of transfer-RNA (tRNA) were made by Arnold Hempel and Robert Bock of the University of Wisconsin and Sung Hou Kim and Alexander Rich of the Massachusetts Institute of Technology. Now that crystals of tRNA were available, the way was open to probe its three-dimensional structure by X-ray diffractions and determine its active sites.

Progress in cracking the genetic code, at least in regard to the nucleotide base sequence in DNA, was undoubtedly aided by synthesis carried out by a research team at the Salk Institute for Biological Studies, San Diego, Calif. They were able to produce high yields of betacytidylic acid and uridylic acid by electrically sparking a mixture of nitrogen methane gases, formaldehyde, cyanide, cyanoacetylene, and phosphoric acid. Ultraviolet irradiation of the mixture converted the cytidylic acid from the biologically inactive alpha form to the biologically active beta form. *E. coli* fed on the latter, but rejected the former. At the Swiss Federal Institute of Technology, Zürich, Robert Schwyzer, who had previously synthesized two polypeptide hormones—angiotensin and adrenocorticotropic hormone (ACTH)—made significant progress in cracking the amino acid sequence code into words of a hormonal sentence defining various biochemical and cellular functions.

Crystallography remained essential to learning the structure of biological materials and simplifying their synthesis. British Nobel Prize winner Dorothy Hodgkin announced her discovery of the crystalline structure of insulin.

In addition to the preparation of artificial cell components, progress continued to be made in the analysis and identification of natural components. The discovery of many new RNA's led to the suggestion that there are two classes of RNA, one that moves freely between nucleus and cytoplasm, and another that is restricted to the nucleus. Harris Busch of the Baylor University College of Medicine, Houston, Tex., identified ten different types of nucleolar RNA in hepatoma (liver cancer), including a new low-molecular-weight species that displayed a unique labeling pattern and was the only species of RNA that remained in the nucleolus after its structure had been broken down with actinomycin-D or by radiation. All RNA species with a known function were critical elements for the translation of genetic information into protein synthesis. Therefore, the discovery of a new kind of RNA influenced considerably the interpretation of protein relationships.

Richard Burgess and Andrew Travers of Harvard discovered a protein, known as sigma, whose sole function is to stimulate the synthesis of RNA chains. In other words, sigma is the silent partner of the enzyme RNA polymerase that catalyzes RNA synthesis.

Ilan Sela of the Hebrew University of Jerusalem and Paul Kaesberg of the University of Wisconsin synthesized the protein of infectious tobacco mosaic virus by combining tRNA, ribosomes, and amino acids extracted from healthy tobacco leaves with adenosine triphosphate (ATP) and viral RNA.

Paul Mandel and Monique Jacob of the French Centre de Neurochimie, Strasbourg, continued their studies of RNA metabolism in brain cells. They showed that 1.2% of the information coded in DNA is expressed in various forms of messenger RNA (mRNA), two-thirds cytoplasmic and one-third nuclear, and proposed that this forms a level of regulation of the decoding process while the genetic information is on its way from the DNA to the ribosomal site of protein synthesis. Vincent Allfrey of the Rockefeller University and others reported experiments that suggested that histone acetylation cancels the gene-blocking effects of RNA-bound histones and is an essential part of the gene-regulating mechanism.

Charles Ehret and John Wille of Argonne (Ill.) National Laboratory suggested that mRNA in DNA may also be the basis for the timing cycle that regulates cell activity. They isolated unique classes of protozoan mRNA whose concentrations varied periodically. Cells in culture were synchronized by light pulses into a persistent rhythm of cell divisions with a free running period of about 21 hours. They suggested that the timekeeping mechanism has a sequential transpiration polycistronic component and a recycling component.

An exciting development in 1969 was the dramatic confirmation of G. N. Ling's theory of membrane transport. Freeman W. Cope of the U.S. Naval Air Development Center, Warminster, Pa., and a group at the Baylor University College of Medicine employed nuclear magnetic resonance spectroscopy to prove that tissue water is crystalline, *i.e.*, analogous to ice. Catalytic activities of enzymes might also be explained by proton transfer in such a medium. Jui Wang of Yale pointed out that protons transfer from an original location to a neighbour 70 times faster in ice than they do in liquid water. Hagai Rottenberg (Brooklyn) studied the mechanism of ATP synthesis and showed that the driving energy is an electric membrane potential produced by proton flow. It seemed to be an astounding coincidence that "polywater" was confirmed in 1969 as an unmistakable stable polymer of water. This began an exciting race to determine if this form of water is the same as postulated for tissues.

The year saw a number of innovations and developments of complex tools for the molecular biologists. New electron microscopes included the world's biggest, 3 MeV, and the first lensless as well as scanning version capable of 3.5 Å resolution, 20 times better than its predecessors. The fine structure of human red blood cells was revealed in London. An ultraviolet laser was being used to focus separately on chromosomes and nucleoli. An on-line computer system at the University of Chicago was programmed to distinguish between UV-absorption patterns produced by normal and cancerous cells. An ion microanalyzer provided instant photomicrographs of a specimen's chemical distribution by combining a mass spectrometer with an ion-emission microscope. The synthesis of protein molecules was now carried out at high speed by an automatic machine developed by Arnold Margolin and Robert Merrifield. High-speed analysis of proteins was also facilitated by Robert McKay of the University of Hawaii through a marriage of a computer and a spectrofluorometer.

(JB. K.)

Genetics. Among all enzymes the one to receive considerable attention in 1969 was the only known enzyme that had the necessary properties to be the replicating enzyme inside the cell. This enzyme was being studied in detail as a result of an ample supply of the purified, homogeneous enzyme isolated from 200 lb. of *E. coli.* Its properties, other than catalyzing the addition of mononucleotide bases to the 3′ hydroxy terminus of a primer DNA chain, included hydrolysis of a DNA chain from either the 3′ or 5′ hydroxy end, pyrophosphorolysis of a DNA chain from the 3′ end, and exchange of inorganic pyrophosphate with the terminal pyrophosphate group of a deoxyribonucleoside triphosphate. The studies showed that the DNA polymerase molecule binds to single-stranded DNA or to double-stranded DNA with nicks or single stranded regions. Closed double helices were essentially inert to the polymerase action. The enzyme also has a single binding site for the four nucleotide triphosphates. This property was also reported for a DNA polymerase isolated from mammalian tissue.

A new scheme to account for DNA replication by this enzyme was proposed. The DNA polymerase molecule would bind at the nicked position on a closed double helical DNA molecule and proceed to extend the 3′ hydroxy end of the DNA chain by covalent addition of mononucleotide units. The 5′ end of the DNA chain might be partially degraded by the 5′ to

COURTESY, O. L. MILLER AND BARBARA R. BEATTY, OAK RIDGE NATIONAL LABORATORY

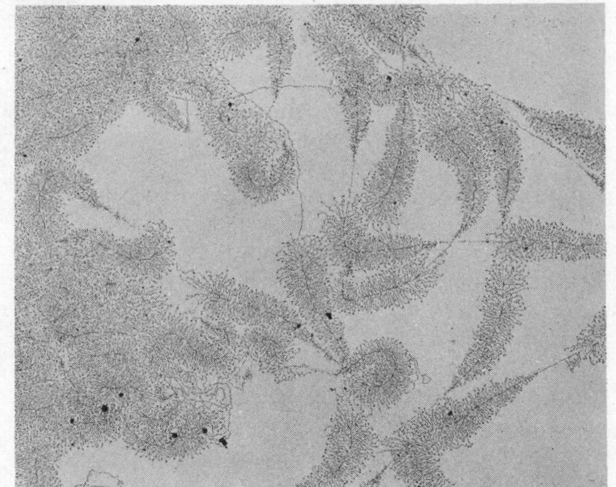

Electron micrograph released with a research report in May 1969 shows for the first time genes in the process of making identifiable RNA.

3′ nuclease action of this enzyme and eventually displaced with its free end attached to a membrane site. Replication would proceed for some distance and then switch over to the displaced strand. This would produce a closed fork, which was then cleaved by an endonuclease. This process would be repeated, leading to the production of small pieces of DNA located near the replication fork. (Discontinuous DNA synthesis was reported in 1969.) These segments would be joined by the action of another enzyme, ligase. If correct, this scheme would explain how one enzyme, known to extend the DNA molecule in only the 5′ to the 3′ direction, could copy the two parental strands of opposite polarity almost simultaneously.

Further work detailing the initiation event in *E. coli* reported that the initiation process was separated into three physiologically distinct steps based on sensitivity to the drugs chloramphenicol and phenethyl alcohol. One step required amino acids and was inhibited by high concentrations of chloramphenicol but not by lower concentrations. This process was completed approximately 15 minutes before initiation took place. The second step was inhibited by low concentrations of chloramphenicol and was completed about 30 minutes before initiation occurred. A third requirement for initiation was suggested by the observation that initiation did not occur immediately by the time necessary protein synthesis was completed.

Other results reported with the microorganism *Bacillus subtilis* showed that chromosome replication need not always go to completion once it has been started, but may pause or stop at intermediate positions. It was proposed that chromosome replication was regulated by at least two control circuits. One involved the initiation process and could act like an on-off switch. The other control circuits operated through the relationship of the amount of DNA to cell mass. This second regulatory circuit tended to modulate replication activity and served to entrain it with other events during the cell cycle such as growth and division.

A concerted effort was being made to determine the function of extrachromosomal mitochondrial DNA (M-DNA) and to describe its biogenesis. Recent evidence indicated that the M-DNA increases by a semiconservative replicative process that proceeds independently of nuclear DNA synthesis. Other evidence of this was the isolation and purification of a DNA polymerase from mitochondria of rat liver cells. The mitochondrial enzyme was shown to be distinct from the enzyme isolated from the nuclei. It was now clear that M-DNA represented a second genetic system in complex cells. Evidence suggested that mitochondria were autonomous, self-replicating organelles, even though they contained only some of the genetic information directing their organization and function.

Exciting electron micrographs showed the transcription of genes coding for ribosomal RNA in DNA isolated from the extrachromosomal nucleoli of amphibian oocytes. The transcription process involved an enzyme, RNA polymerase, which utilized the DNA molecule as a template on which to build complementary RNA molecules. Specifically, the electron micrograph showing that many precursor RNA molecules are synthesized simultaneously on each gene demonstrated pictorally what had been proposed for the transcription process. (JA. C. C.)

See also Biological Sciences; Medicine.

Monaco

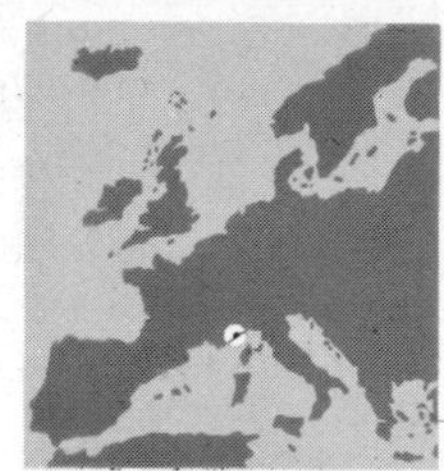

A sovereign principality on the northern Mediterranean coast, Monaco is bounded on all land sides by the French *département* of Alpes-Maritimes. Area: 0.579 sq.mi. (1.51 sq.km.). Pop. (1967 est.): 23,700. Language: French. Religion: Roman Catholic. Prince, Rainier III; ministers of state in 1969, Paul Demange and, from April 1, François-Didier Gregh.

On April 1 Prince Rainier issued a royal ordinance appointing François-Didier Gregh as minister of state in place of Paul Demange. By agreement, the minister of state is a senior French civil servant selected by the president of France with the approval of the prince. On his most recent assignment, Gregh, son of the poet Fernand Gregh, had headed the French delegation to UNESCO.

In an effort to raise the famed Monte Carlo casino from its economic doldrums, Prince Rainier in 1967 had bought out the holdings of the Greek shipping magnate Aristotle Onassis and in 1968 installed a U.S.-trained management under Wilfred Groote. The casino corporation, the Société des Bains de Mer (SBM), had lost $18 million during the 1966–67 season. Groote introduced modern purchasing and accounting methods, reorganized the company, and refurbished or replaced much of the antiquated equipment. Most of the 2,000 SBM employees adapted to the new systems, but certain key personnel resigned.

The main thrust of the changes was to appeal to wealthy Americans, and in the summer of 1969 almost three-quarters of the registered guests at the Hotel de Paris were American. While the SBM was operating in the black, some local elements feared that the increased "americanization" would cause Monaco to lose its individuality. In an effort to forestall criticism, the SBM made a large promotional effort in nearby Italian cities, in hopes that Italians would serve as a natural counterweight to Americans. (R. D. Ho.)

MONACO

Education. (1964–65) Primary, pupils 1,476, teachers 87; secondary, pupils 967, teachers 45; vocational, pupils 160, teachers 9.

Finance. Monetary unit: French franc, with a par value of Fr. 5.7 to U.S. $1 (Fr. 13.3 = £1 sterling). Budget (1968 est.): revenue Fr. 155,409,000; expenditure Fr. 155,407,000. Tourism: visitors (1967) 78,-300; gross receipts (1966) U.S. $6.1 million.

Money and Banking

The year 1969 might be remembered mainly as the one in which the speculators were proved right: the two major countries whose currencies had been under consistent pressure from the speculators for well over a year finally opted to change the exchange parities of those currencies—though in opposite directions. Depending on what the future brought, 1969 might also be remembered as the year of record interest rates. There were fewer financial and monetary crises than in 1968, but crisis never seemed far below the surface, and there was little to suggest that a real end to the general mood of unease was imminent.

The authorities in countries already committed to a tight monetary policy were, almost without exception, obliged to retain those policies through 1969. In the U.S. the persistence of a strong economic expansion, combined with pressures in the labour markets, perpetuated the rapid rate of price increase and forced the Federal Reserve to be even more stringent in the use of monetary instruments. In the U.K. the response of the trade account to the November 1967 devaluation remained disappointing until midyear. Thereafter, as the balance of payments position began to look stronger, official pronouncements made frequent references to the enormous burden of the nation's external debt, giving little hope that either fiscal or monetary policy could become significantly easier until a trade surplus sufficiently long-lived to permit repayment of this debt had been more or less guaranteed. In Canada four increases in the discount rate were the major instruments of monetary policy following the modest relaxation in the third quarter of 1968.

In France the speculation against the franc that had begun with the political disturbances of May and June 1968, compelling French policy in a restrictive direction, persisted after the international currency crisis of mid-November and Pres. Charles de Gaulle's 11th-hour decision not to devalue. Though devaluation was widely anticipated following the election of a new president, its timing was completely unexpected. Coming as it did at a relatively calm moment, it had the advantage, as compared with the British devaluation, of being unheralded by vast anticipatory speculation. Perhaps for this reason, its immediate effect on international currency markets was somewhat less marked than that of several lesser events of the preceding 18 months. The further tightening of French policy that necessarily accompanied it did add to the general restrictiveness of the world monetary situation, however.

Japan was the only major industrial nation in which a generally restrictive monetary policy in 1968 gave way to an easier policy in 1969. This was possible because, for the first time, the continuing high growth rate was unequivocally accompanied by a strong external payments position.

In the two major easy money countries of 1968—Italy and West Germany—policy makers were forced to think more seriously about tightening up than had been necessary for some time. In West Germany signs that the rapid growth of domestic demand was excessive, in the face of a diminishing surplus of unused resources, presented the policy makers with a difficult dilemma. In the event, priority was given to correction of the overheating of the economy. Modestly restrictive policies, including three increases in the discount rate, were introduced, despite the difficulties that these policies were likely to put in the way of a satisfactory adjustment of the external surplus. The ultimate policy for dealing with the latter problem, namely revaluation, was adopted on October 24 and was preceded by a period of about three weeks during which West Germany temporarily suspended its obligations to the International Monetary Fund (IMF) and allowed the exchange rate for the mark to float. In Italy the external payments position was weakened as capital outflows continued heavy and imports rose sharply in the face of buoyant home demand.

With an exceptionally large proportion of the major nations simultaneously applying restraint, it was scarcely surprising that the general level of interest rates—already high before the year began—moved even higher. The main influence on this movement originated in the U.S., where the interest rate record book had to be rewritten several times during the year. By June the yield on corporate bonds had reached levels that were said to be unsurpassed since the Civil War. The average issuing rate on nine-month Treasury bills reached a record 7.4%, while the rate for trading in federal funds attained an incredible level of over 11%. More modestly, the Federal Reserve discount rate moved to 6%—higher than had obtained for more than 40 years.

The main propelling force behind these developments was increasingly stringent Federal Reserve action to restrict credit—which, in turn, compelled several increases in the prime lending rate of the commercial banks. The rate moved in five jumps from $6\frac{1}{4}\%$ in December 1968 to $8\frac{1}{2}\%$ in June 1969. Unaided, as they had been in 1968, by any increase in the rates they were permitted to pay on certificates of deposit (CD's), the banks sustained a large liquidation of these deposits. They resorted to heavy borrowing from their European branches, at increasingly high rates, and to increases in the rates at which they were prepared to lend.

Though less spectacular, interest rate increases in

Selected Interest Rates

Country		1967	1968			1969		
		June	June	Sept.	Dec.	March	June	Sept.
Belgium	A	4.50	3.75	3.75	4.50	5.00	6.00	7.50
	B[1]	3.52	2.64	2.80	3.36	3.47	4.29	7.48
	C	5.92	5.50	5.49	5.56	5.66	5.94	6.00
France	A	3.50	3.50	5.00	6.00	6.00	7.00	7.00
	B[1]	4.29	5.76	6.76	8.22	8.18	9.46	9.39
	C	5.95	5.94	5.95	6.00	6.21	6.37	6.68
Germany, West	A	3.00	3.00	3.00	3.00	3.00	5.00	6.00
	B[2]	2.75	2.75	2.75	2.75	2.75	4.75	5.75
	C	6.90	6.40	6.30	6.30	6.40	6.70	6.90
Italy	A	3.50	3.50	3.50	3.50	3.50	3.50	4.00
	B	...	...	...	...	...	...	...
	C	5.62	5.66	5.64	5.62	5.62	5.65	5.90
Netherlands	A	4.50	4.50	4.50	5.00	5.00	5.50	6.00
	B[2]	4.68	4.56	4.39	4.65	5.00	5.50	6.00
	C	5.97	6.24	6.25	6.34	6.61	6.83	7.42
Switzerland	A	3.50	3.00	3.00	3.00	3.00	3.00	3.75
	B[1]	2.82	2.69	2.63	2.25	4.25	3.50	...
	C	4.75	4.34	4.34	4.33	4.60	4.69	5.37
United Kingdom	A	5.50	7.50	7.00	7.00	8.00	8.00	8.00
	B[2]	5.27	7.21	6.76	6.80	7.78	7.89	7.81
	C	6.87	7.46	7.43	7.99	8.62	9.46	...
United States	A	4.00	5.50	5.25	5.50	5.50	6.00	6.00
	B[2]	3.48	5.54	5.20	5.92	6.08	6.49	7.05
	C	4.86	5.23	5.09	5.65	6.05	6.06	6.41
Canada	A	4.50	7.50	6.00	6.50	7.00	7.50	8.00
	B[2]	4.34	6.75	5.62	5.96	6.64	7.03	...
	C	5.87	6.77	6.60	7.34	7.43	7.68	...
Japan	A	5.48	6.21	5.84	5.84	5.84	5.84	6.25
	B[1]	5.84	7.67	7.67	7.30	7.30	6.57	...
	C	6.80	6.90	6.90	6.90	6.90	6.90	...

A=Central bank's discount rate.
B=Money market rate.
B[1]=Day-to-day money.
B[2]=90-day Treasury bills.
C=Long-term government bond yield.

"French Stylist"
—Pierotti.

BEN ROTH AGENCY

other major countries were numerous. France, which had increased its discount rate from 5 to 6% in November 1968, increased it by a further 1% in mid-June 1969, and by a similar amount in October. Canada and West Germany both increased their discount rates three times during the year; Belgium raised its six times, Denmark twice (once by a massive 2%), and the Netherlands three times. In the U.K. the difficulties of curbing bank lending by putting ceilings on advances led to an increase in the bank rate from 7 to 8% in February.

Eurocurrency and Eurobond Markets. Two factors dominated the Eurocurrency market in the 12 months to September 1969: the heavy borrowing demands from the U.S. banks and the repeated speculation in favour of the mark. In November 1968 the main pressure came from withdrawals for conversion into marks, but thereafter the importance of this factor declined relative to heavy borrowings by U.S. banks, whose first-quarter borrowings exceeded the total growth of the Eurocurrency market in all of 1967. From a level of 6.16% in August 1968, the rate on three-month Eurodollar deposits in London reached 8.56% by April 1969.

In the same month, the possibilities of a new regime taking over in France revived speculation against the franc and in favour of the mark. Once again the funds for this speculation were either withdrawn or borrowed from Eurocurrency markets, and the rate rose by almost two points in little more than a week. The rate of 13% reached at one point in June was soon shown to be a temporary aberration, but rates remained near 10.5% in the face of continuing heavy demands from the U.S. and in spite of a partial retreat on the part of the speculators. They moved very much higher in August and September following the franc devaluation and the abandonment of the fixed parity applying to the mark. However, the West German revaluation was expected to be a strong influence for reduction.

With the Eurodollar markets expanding so rapidly, it was inevitable that some form of control should be brought to bear. The June measures of the U.S. Federal Reserve discussed below represented the first steps in this direction. There was little doubt that these originated as much from the anxieties of European central bankers as from those of the Americans themselves.

Meanwhile, the volume of new issue activity in Eurobond markets was somewhat reduced. The amounts involved in the first two quarters were $987 million and $635 million, compared with $1.1 billion and $1,011,000,000 in the preceding two quarters. The restrictions on the activities of Italian banks in international capital markets, the introduction of waiting lists for new issues in West Germany, and the postponement of issues in the hope of reduced rates in the future were the major factors involved. Calls on the market by private U.S. firms were substantially lower, both in absolute terms and as a proportion of the total, and the previous year's trend toward greater use of the convertible bond was sharply reversed.

United States. The enactment of the income tax surcharge in June 1968 and the expenditure cuts that accompanied it produced far less deceleration in the growth of economic activity than might reasonably have been expected. Though the growth of output was reduced below what would have been permitted by available capacity, and unemployment rose slightly from its extremely low level of December 1968, demand pressures remained strong and prices were forced even higher. The retail price index had risen 4.7% in the 12 months to December 1968, and the rate of inflation in the early months of 1969 was even more rapid. Monetary policy was already tight, but it clearly had to be made even tighter in the face of the inadequacy of existing fiscal measures and the difficulty of enacting new ones rapidly.

Dealers in bond and bill markets had begun to anticipate this in early December, and their presumptions were reinforced by an increase in the commercial banks' prime lending rate to 6½%. The first official moves came on December 17, when the discount rate of nine of the Federal Reserve banks was raised to 5½% (the discount rates of the other three reserve banks followed three days later). Though the increase was only ¼%, its effect was compounded by the fact that it was not accompanied by any rise in the ceiling rates of interest that commercial banks were permitted to pay on CD's. Since many banks were already paying the ceiling rates, the rise in the discount rate put CD's at a considerable disadvantage as compared with other instruments, and heavy net withdrawals occurred. The immediate response of the banks was to push their prime lending rate up by another ¼% to a new record level of 6¾%.

During the next six months the reserve positions of the banks deteriorated sharply. Their net borrowed reserves, which give a good indication of the ease of tightness of the reserve position, increased from $200 million in early November to $1 billion at the end of April and to $1.2 billion in June, after which they declined to about $1.1 billion by the end of August. At this point, net borrowed reserves were considerably in excess of the approximately $800 million reached in the credit squeeze of 1966. In early 1968, in a broadly similar situation of tightening monetary policy, the banks had been helped by an increase in the ceiling rate of interest on CD's, as permitted under Regulation Q. No such assistance was forthcoming on this occasion, and by the end of March the volume of

CD's outstanding was already $5 billion below the October peak.

In April the pressure on the banks was intensified by an increase of ½% in reserve requirements against demand deposits, effective from the period beginning on April 17. This was expected to increase the funds that member banks would have to set aside to reserves by some $650 million. The new top reserve requirement of 17½%, which applied to deposits of over $5 million at reserve city banks, was the highest rate since 1960. These increases followed a similar but less general increase that had taken effect in the first days of 1968.

The banks reacted to this deterioration in their reserve position in a way that had become familiar; by borrowing heavily from their branches in Europe. This form of borrowing has an advantage in that the rates that can be paid are not governed by the ceilings imposed by Regulation Q. In the first quarter of the year the total Eurodollar borrowing of the U.S. banks amounted to a massive $3.9 billion, enough to compensate for a substantial proportion of the CD attrition in the same period. The fact that these funds were costing the banks anything up to 13% did not seem to hinder the flow, and the total liabilities of the banks to their overseas branches rose by over $6 billion in the first half of the year. On June 26 the governors of the Federal Reserve announced their first attempt to exert some control over this form of borrowing, which, they argued, could have a distorting effect on credit flows in the U.S. and abroad. Borrowings by member banks from their overseas branches in excess of the borrowings in some base period would henceforward be subject to a 10% reserve requirement, as would credit extended to U.S. residents by an overseas branch of a member bank.

The net effect of these various developments was to curtail the expansion of bank credit significantly. The annual growth rate of total credit in the first quarter of 1969 was only 2%, compared with 19 and 9% in the previous two quarters. The growth of bank credit in the first three quarters of the year was at an annual rate of 3½%. Within this total increase, however, loans to business and consumers expanded rapidly as the inflationary climate persisted, while investments in government securities were run down in the first quarter at a faster rate than had been experienced for two decades. This rundown persisted in the subsequent months, though at a much reduced rate.

The demand for credit remained strong, especially from the business sector where expectations of a continuing rapid expansion of economic activity reacted only slowly to official attempts to prevent it. More specifically, the continuing high level of investment demand could be explained in terms of a desire to economize on manpower in the face of the persistent tightness of the labour market and of attempts to hedge against expected future increases in the price of equipment. With demands for consumer and inventory loans also expanding strongly, the banks were forced to raise their lending rates, both as a means of rationing credit and in order to cover the high cost of borrowing in the Eurodollar market. As already mentioned, the first increase took place early in December and was followed by a further increase on December 18 after the increase in the discount rate. The prime lending rate was subsequently moved to 7% on January 7, to 7½% on March 17, and to 8½% in June.

Prices and yields of government and corporate securities reacted to these developments in a fairly predictable way. In particular, the heavy selling of investments by the banks was a powerful influence behind the widespread price declines that occurred. In addition, a number of expectational factors exerted an important influence on the markets. A varying climate of opinion about the prospects for peace in Vietnam and doubt about the willingness of Congress to be sufficiently stern in the use of its fiscal weapons were particularly significant in this respect. More specifically, many security prices rose temporarily in November and January when the prospects for peace began to look rather brighter. Pessimism was compounded in the spring when it appeared possible that Congress would not renew the 10% tax surcharge, due for reenactment at the end of June. Finally, many prices recovered in April when the administration proposed a repeal of the 7% investment tax credit allowable against machinery and equipment and an extension of the income tax surcharge at 10% until the end of 1969 and at 5% for the following six months.

The inflow of funds to mutual savings banks and savings and loan associations was slowed somewhat as competing interest rates moved upward. However, mortgage debt outstanding was permitted to increase by virtue of increased borrowings from Federal Home Loan Banks and the sale of securities. By August the amount outstanding was some $8 billion above the December level, approximately the same sort of growth as in 1968. The growth of nonbank consumer credit was also at a rate comparable to that applying in 1968.

United Kingdom. An extremely stringent monetary and fiscal policy was continued throughout 1969. This was mainly because of the slow response of the balance of payments to the November 1967 devaluation, but it was also attributable in part to the fact that sterling was a marginal victim of the succession of mark/franc speculations. Restraint was continued even when the external payments position began to look stronger at the end of the year. The £50 travel allowance limit and the import deposit scheme, both of which seemed likely to be withdrawn, were in fact maintained.

"What's wrong with the one we've got?" —Waite, "The Sun," London.

BEN ROTH AGENCY

The main vehicle for restraint continued to be ceilings on bank and finance-house lending, introduced at the time of devaluation and successively tightened thereafter. The year saw a number of "clashes" between the banks and the authorities as advances remained obstinately above the ceilings. In both January and February, letters from the Bank of England reminded the banks of their obligations, but the banks nevertheless failed to meet their mid-March "target" and advances rose sharply again in May. This moved the authorities to put some teeth into their request, and on May 3 they announced that the rate of interest payable on the special deposits made by the clearing banks with the Bank of England would be halved until such time as compliance with the ceiling had been achieved. Some improvement followed, but the banks collectively remained above the ceiling until October, when the Bank of England seemed to be adopting a far more sympathetic view of their difficulties.

During the year there was a significant shift toward consideration of the money supply or, more correctly, "domestic credit expansion" (growth of the money supply adjusted for balance of payments surpluses or deficits) as an important variable of monetary policy. This was emphasized in the letter of intent to the IMF on May 22, when the two main objectives stated were a £300 million balance of payments surplus in the year to March 1970 and a domestic credit expansion of not more than £400 million in the same period. Accompanying the new emphasis on control of the money supply were signs of a much more limited official support of government securities markets.

WIDE WORLD

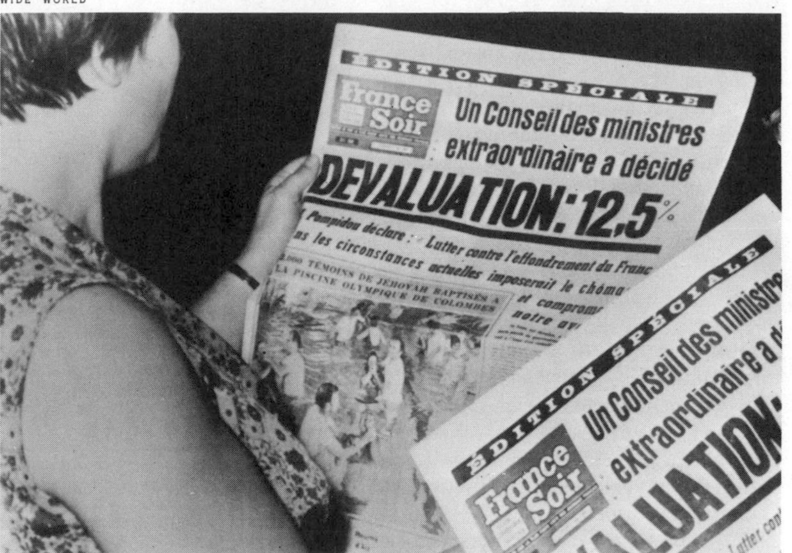

Front page of "France-Soir" of Aug. 8, 1969, announces devaluation of the French franc.

Partly for this reason, no doubt, but also partly because of international uncertainties and a generally pessimistic outlook regarding relief of credit restraint, security prices continued to fall to the end of July. In January, when expectations of a bank rate change were strong and the trade figures were poor, yields on long-dated government securities moved as high as 8%. There was a useful improvement following the chancellor of the exchequer's announcement in his budget of April 15 that sales of government securities would no longer be subject to capital gains tax, but the general tendency throughout the rest of the year was for prices to continue to fall.

At the shorter end of the market, the Treasury bill rate was considerably lower at the end of 1968 than it had been during the crisis months of May and June, but it rose slightly from September as the discount houses increased the tender rate. Following the increase in the bank rate at the end of February 1969, the houses reduced their bid substantially and forced the rate up by almost a full point to 7.8%. Thereafter, further slight reductions in the bid took place, in the face of continuing poor trade returns and the uncertain state of foreign exchange markets. The rate climbed to about 7.8% and stabilized at that level.

More stringent ceilings for lending by installment-credit finance houses were introduced in November 1968; the "target" of 100% of the October 1967 figure was reduced to 98%. Although the amount of new credit extended fell, the total outstanding continued to rise, and by the end of the year the houses were collectively about 5% above the ceiling. The slackness of business after December and the absence of any prebudget spending spree led to a fall in credit extensions sufficient to pull down the total of credit outstanding, and by August the houses were only fractionally above their ceilings. Business remained slack and the need for funds was therefore only modest, but the extreme tightness of credit forced the houses to pay very high rates for those funds that they did need; their three-month deposit rate rose from 7.4% in October 1968 to 10.2% a year later.

The building societies (similar to savings and loan associations in the U.S.) had another difficult period, as is generally the case when interest rates are rising. After the bank rate increase in February, the depleted inflow of funds proved inadequate to meet the demand for mortgages, and it was quickly announced that the borrowing rate for share investors would be raised to 5% from April 1. At the same time, the lending rate was raised by almost a full point to 8½%, thereby increasing the margins available to cover rises in tax rates. The shortage of funds, and the reduction in the number of eligible borrowers caused by the interest rate increase, nevertheless meant that mortgage lending was considerably lower than it had been in the preceding year.

EEC Countries. In 1968 the West German boom had not encountered any serious shortage of capacity and, as a result, the price increases associated with it were modest. By mid-1969, however, plant and equipment were being used at very near to capacity, signs of labour shortages were all too abundant, and prices were rising at the high rate—by German standards—of 3% per annum. At the same time, the current balance of payments situation remained extremely healthy, in spite of the border tax on exports and other measures that had been introduced in November 1968 to curtail it. Large capital exports were achieved to offset the current account surplus, with outflows of speculative short-term funds accumulated during the November currency crisis proving particularly important in the first part of the year. A speculative crisis that began at the end of April reversed this flow, and its effect persisted until June.

Despite the continuing dilemma over the external payments position, both fiscal and monetary policy became increasingly restrictive in an effort to deal with the internal overheating. As part of this policy, the discount rate was moved to 4% in April, to 5% in June, and to 6% in September.

Speculation in favour of a mark revaluation receded after May in response to firm denials by the government of any intention to revalue. As the disagreements between Christian Democrat and Social Democrat members of the governing coalition became more apparent, however, speculators increasingly inclined to the view that revaluation was unlikely before the election at the end of September. Speculation intensified as this point approached, and the foreign exchange market was closed in the last two days before the election because of the very real prospect of a frightening inflow of funds during that period. On the following Monday the market was opened, but so great was the inflow of foreign funds that it was closed again within a few minutes. The West Germans then announced a temporary suspension of their commitment to a fixed parity, and allowed the mark to find its own level. This succeeded in quelling speculation, avoided heavy losses of reserves on the part of Britain and other vulnerable countries, and led to a de facto revaluation of the mark. The restoration of the fixed parity took place about three weeks later, on October 24, at a higher rate. Though it was not greeted with anything like universal enthusiasm, the success of the West German "floating" experiment indicated that greater flexibility in exchange parities might prove to be an important way of dealing with international currency crises.

In France the monetary and fiscal measures taken in November 1968 proved inadequate to halt the rapid loss of reserves, and the additional loss between November and August was about $1.9 billion. At the same time, both consumer demand and business investment were booming, and some further measures of restraint were clearly called for. In May the ceilings on short-term bank loans were extended and restrictions on installment-credit lending were intensified. This was followed by a 1% increase in the discount rate in mid-June and by increases in the prime lending rates of the banks by 1½%. Nevertheless, lack of faith in the permanence of the existing parity persisted and was naturally accentuated by the departure of President de Gaulle.

The only surprising thing about the French devaluation on August 8 was its timing. Few, however, saw it as a guaranteed solution to France's economic problems, especially in view of increasing signs of capacity shortages, and many considered the change to be too small. Devaluation was accompanied by an immediate price freeze on all goods until September 15 and was followed three weeks later by a package of deflationary measures that were widely criticized for being insufficiently stringent. The existing commitment to reduce the budget deficit and the strong squeeze on credit were supplemented by a number of new incentives for higher saving, a speed-up of corporation tax payments, and cuts in government spending. Nevertheless, it was not until the mark revaluation that further pressures against the franc subsided. Two weeks before the West German action, a further 1% increase in the discount rate was needed as French reserves continued to dwindle.

In Italy the rate of economic growth remained high and the external balance on current account remained favourable. However, the enormity of the capital outflow began to cause concern, especially in view of the pressing developmental needs of certain parts of the country. The policy measures that were taken were aimed mainly at slowing this outflow. The modestly restrictive measures adopted between February and August included a new differential discount rate of 5% to apply in certain circumstances, though the basic rate, unchanged since 1958, remained at 3.5% until mid-August when it was increased to 4%.

In Belgium the margin of underutilized capacity was rapidly depleted as expansion proceeded, and prices and costs both rose sharply. Interest rates rose in response to this inflationary internal situation and to external pressures, and the year saw six upward adjustments of the discount rate to a new level of 7.5%.

Canada. The growth of output continued at a high rate during the first part of the year, mainly in response to buoyant consumption and to business and housing investment, and the rise of prices and costs accelerated. Monetary policy became increasingly restrictive after September 1968, both in an attempt to deal with the inflationary domestic situation and as a reflection of developments south of the border. It was complemented by stringent fiscal policy. The bank rate was raised to 6½% in December 1968 and by further ½% increments in March, June, and July. In April, paralleling the move in the U.S., a 1% increase in the secondary reserve requirements of the banks was announced and had the effect of reducing the availability of bank credit below the level then being demanded. Consumer loans were especially hard hit by this reduction of credit, but consumer loans from nonbank sources increased so that the relative importance of bank loans in the total declined severely.

The rapid rise of prices persisted until the end of the year, but by October, paralleling sentiments in the U.S., many commentators had begun to urge the need for some relaxation of policies in order to avoid plunging the economy into recession.

Japan. The Japanese economy had an extremely good year in 1969. A continuing high rate of economic growth was accompanied for the first time in many years by an unquestionably strong external payments position. The yen was seen by many commentators as

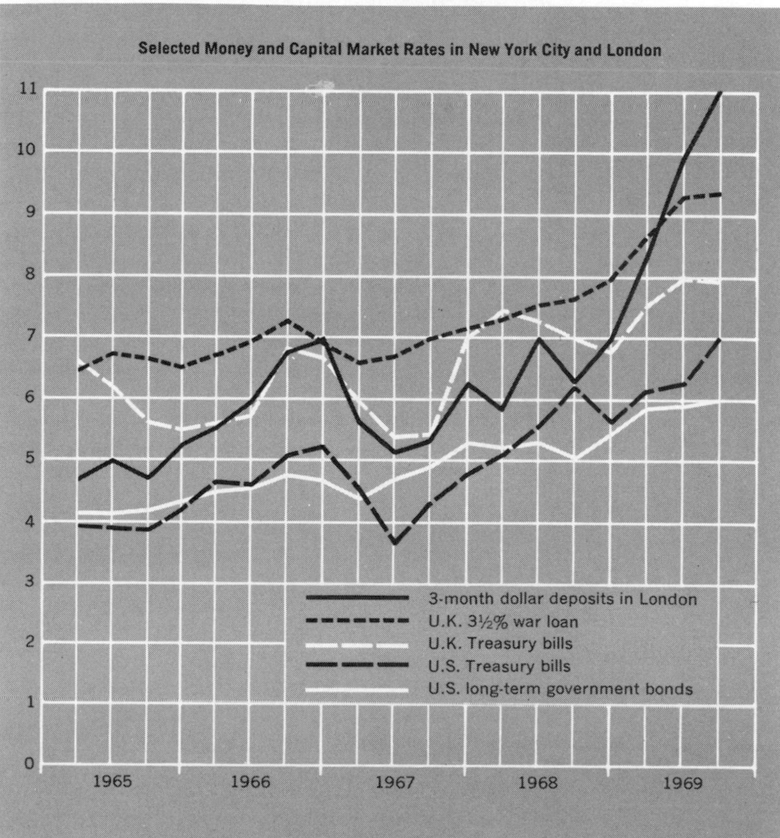

a strong candidate for revaluation, and this became increasingly true after the mark revaluation in October.

However, the rate of the rise in prices, especially wholesale prices, began to give some cause for concern later in the year, and a modest increase in the discount rate took effect in early September. Although foreign exchange reserves continued to rise rapidly, the official view persisted that these reserves were still inadequate and that the case for a yen revaluation was therefore rather poor. (A. R. R.)

See also Cooperatives; Economics; Economy, World; Government Finance; Housing; Investment, International; Merchandising; Payments and Reserves, International; Stock Exchanges.

Mongolia

A people's republic of Asia lying between the U.S.S.R. and China, Mongolia occupies the geographical area known as Outer Mongolia. Area: 604,247 sq.mi. (1,565,000 sq.km.). Pop. (1968 est.): 1,210,000. Cap. and largest city: Ulan Bator (pop., 1966 est., 250,000). Language: Mongolian. Religion: Lamaistic Buddhism. First secretary of the Mongolian People's Revolutionary (Communist) Party and chairman of the Council of Ministers (premier) in 1969, Yumzhagiyin Tsedenbal; chairman of the Presidium of the Great People's Khural, Zhamsarangibin Sambuu.

The major event of 1969 was the increase in Soviet forces stationed in Mongolia, following the signature on Jan. 15, 1966, of a 20-year treaty of Soviet-Mongolian alliance. In his book *The Coming War Between Russia and China,* Harrison E. Salisbury affirmed that the buildup of Soviet troops was turning that country into an armed camp with the most sophisticated modern weapons.

In a speech at the Moscow world conference of Communist parties in June, Tsedenbal claimed that China was out to reannex Mongolia. On October 20 a Soviet military mission headed by Marshal Vasili Chuikov arrived at Ulan Bator. In December closer relations with the U.K. were established by the appointment of an ambassador to the Court of St. James's.

The national economic plan for 1966–70 was nearing completion. Industrial output, which had been practically zero in the early 1950s, in 1969 was expected to increase by 18.7% over 1968.

The United Bloc of Communists and Non-Party People won 99.99% of the vote in elections to the Great People's Khural (Assembly) of June 22. Zhamsarangibin Sambuu was reelected chairman of the Presidium, and Yumzhagiyin Tsedenbal once more was asked to form a government. (K. Sm.)

MONGOLIA

Education. (1965–66) Primary and secondary, pupils 164,400, teachers 5,721; vocational, pupils 9,200; higher (including University of Ulan Bator), students 10,700.

Finance. Monetary unit: tugrik, with an official parity of 4 tugriks to U.S. $1 (9.60 tugriks = £1 sterling) and a tourist rate of 6 tugriks to U.S. $1 (14.40 tugriks = £1). Budget (1967 est.): revenue 1,670,000,000 tugriks; expenditure 1,660,000,000 tugriks.

Foreign Trade. (1962) Imports 102.6 million tugriks; exports 68.5 million tugriks. Import sources (1960): U.S.S.R. 62%; China 23%; Czechoslovakia 5%. Export destinations: (1960) U.S.S.R. 75%; Czechoslovakia 8%; China 5%. Main exports (1960): wool 44%; cattle 34%; butter and meat 8%; hides 6%.

Transport and Communications. Roads (1965) *c.* 75,000 km. (including *c.* 8,600 km. motorable). Railways (1967) 2,067 km. Telephones (Jan. 1968) 14,720. Radio receivers (Dec. 1968) 90,900.

Agriculture. Production (in 000; metric tons; 1967; 1966 in parentheses): wheat *c.* 325 (*c.* 253); potatoes *c.* 25 (*c.* 24). Livestock (in 000; Dec. 1966): cattle *c.* 2,074; sheep 13,065; goats (Dec. 1965) 4,786; horses (Dec. 1965) 2,433; camels (Dec. 1965) 685.

Industry. Production (in 000; metric tons; 1965): coal 45; crude oil (1966) 12; electricity (kw-hr.) 199,000.

Monophysite Churches: *see* Religion

Montserrat: *see* Dependent States

Mormons: *see* Religion

Motion Pictures: *see* Cinema

Motorboating: *see* Motor Sports

Motor Industry: *see* Industrial Review

Morocco

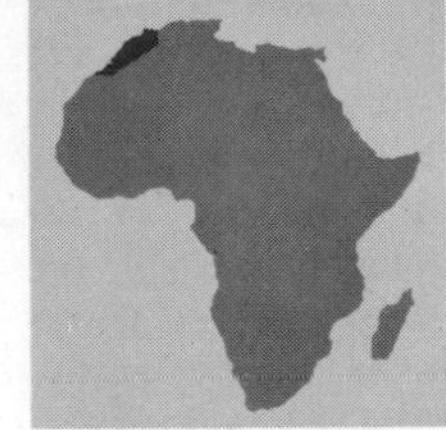

A constitutional monarchy of northwestern Africa, on the Atlantic Ocean and the Mediterranean Sea, Morocco is bordered by Algeria and Spanish Sahara. Area: 174,471 sq.mi. (451,880 sq.km.). Pop. (1968 est.): 14,634,000. Cap.: Rabat (pop., 1960, 227,445). Largest city: Casablanca (pop., 1960, 965,277). Language: Arabic; Berber. Religion: Muslim. King, Hassan II; prime ministers in 1969, Muhammad Benhima and, from October 7, Ahmed Laraki.

Morocco made peace with its neighbours Algeria and Mauritania in 1969, and the resultant relaxation in tension was expected to make it possible to devote more domestic energy to economic development. The year was also notable for continued financial cooperation with France, the Islamic and Arab summit conferences held in Rabat, and the holding of the first elections in six years.

The position of the monarchy appeared stable, a fact reflected in the continuity of the system in which legislative and executive powers remained concentrated in the hands of King Hassan II and in those of his appointed Cabinet, which had been in power since the king dissolved Parliament in June 1965. In October the foreign minister, Ahmed Laraki, became prime minister.

The opposition, led by the Istiqlal Party and the National Union of Popular Forces (NUPF), continued to demand legislative elections and a new constitution, but the only real threat to authority was a series of student strikes and demonstrations by leftist groups. The communal and municipal elections held on October 3 to renew councils elected in 1963 were boycotted by the NUPF and leftists, while the Istiqlal Party accused the authorities of falsifying results and urged its members to vote for "nonofficial" candidates.

King Hassan and Pres. Houari Boumédienne of Algeria concluded a treaty of friendship and solidarity in January, thus putting an end to a period of strained relations dating from 1963, when the two countries were involved in armed clashes on their frontier. The conflict arose out of Moroccan claims to vast tracts of Algeria in an area where the border had never been clearly defined.

In September Pres. Mokhtar Ould Daddah of Mauritania accepted an invitation to attend the Islamic summit conference in Rabat, after which he had a series of talks with King Hassan. It was the first direct contact between the two since 1960, when Mauritania became independent. At that time Morocco refused to recognize Mauritania's right to a separate existence. Later King Hassan indicated he preferred to sign a treaty of friendship with Mauritania, implying de facto recognition and a virtual renunciation of Moroccan territorial claims.

The Islamic summit assembled leaders of 25 Muslim states from Africa, Asia, and the Middle East who declared their support for the Palestine liberation movement, protested against Israeli occupation of Arab lands, and made a plea for the return of Jerusalem to its pre-June 1967 status. The conference established King Hassan as a moderating influence in the Middle East issue, and it enhanced Morocco's prestige because its diplomacy had made it possible to assemble many disparate and in some cases hostile elements at very short notice and get them to adopt a joint attitude on an extremely sensitive issue. The fifth summit conference of Arab heads of state, held in December, served only to emphasize Arab disunity.

In June Spain evacuated the desert enclave of Ifni in southern Morocco, which it had occupied since 1934, and Morocco assumed control of the area.

On the economic front a major development was the conclusion of an association agreement with the European Economic Community (EEC) which went into effect in September. Certain EEC products, mainly manufactured goods, were to be given tariff and quota concessions in Morocco, while Moroccan agricultural produce would have preferential treatment in the EEC countries.

Two of the EEC countries continued to give Morocco substantial financial aid. France granted credits totaling Fr. 110 million (after Fr. 268 million in 1968) and was expected to give more credits later in the year. West Germany granted Morocco credits of DM. 50 million. The second good harvest in succession, which eliminated the need for large grain imports such as had been necessary in the 1966–67 drought years, combined with financial aid, helped to redress the foreign exchange situation. Tourism progressed by about 25%, but industrial growth was slow and the mining industry was depressed. (Sn. H.)

MOROCCO

Education. (1965–66) Primary, pupils 1,115,645, teachers 27,594; secondary, pupils 195,169, teachers 7,214; vocational, pupils 14,705, teachers 886; teacher training, students 1,057, teachers (1964–65) 88; higher (including 3 universities), students 8,996, teaching staff 437.

Finance. Monetary unit: dirham, with a par value of 5.06 dirhams to U.S. $1 (12.15 dirhams = £1 sterling). Gold and foreign exchange, central bank: (June 1969) U.S. $128 million; (June 1968) U.S. $83 million. Budget (1968 est.): revenue 2,365,000,000 dirhams; expenditure 2,486,000,000 dirhams. Money supply. (March 1969) 4,751,000,000 dirhams; (March 1968) 4,212,000,000 dirhams. Cost of living (Casablanca; 1963 = 100): (June 1969) 109; (June 1968) 105.

Foreign Trade. (1968) Imports 2,790,000,000 dirhams; exports 2,279,000,000 dirhams. Main import sources (1967): France 37%; U.S. 10%; West Germany 9%. Main export destinations (1967): France 41%; West Germany 8%; U.K. 6%. Main exports (1967): phosphates 25%; citrus fruit 16%; tomatoes 8%; fish 5%. Tourism (1967): visitors 400,100; gross receipts U.S. $79.2 million.

Transport and Communications. Roads (1968) 24,337 (including 14 km. expressways). Motor vehicles in use (1967): passenger 178,388; commercial 63,781. Railways: (1966) 1,786 km. (including 732 km. electrified); traffic (1967) 408 million passenger-km., freight 2,334,000,000 net ton-km. Air traffic (1968): 313.5 million passenger-km.; freight 3,525,000 net ton-km. Shipping (1968): merchant vessels 100 gross tons and over 38; gross tonnage 70,066. Telephones (Dec. 1967) 144,863. Radio receivers (Dec. 1967) 800,000. Television receivers (Dec. 1967) 61,000.

Agriculture. Production (in 000; metric tons; 1968; 1967 in parentheses): wheat 2,556 (1,090); barley 3,215 (1,100); corn *c.* 240 (255); potatoes 160 (*c.* 260); oranges 775 (614); dry peas *c.* 43 (32); dry broad beans (1967) 52, (1966) 54; chick-peas (1967) 67, (1966) 41; wine (1967) *c.* 130, (1966) *c.* 210; olive oil *c.* 47 (*c.* 20); figs (1967) *c.* 70, (1966) 59; dates (1967) 147, (1966) 90; tomatoes (1967) *c.* 300, (1966) 303; linseed (1967) *c.* 8, (1966) 8; fish catch (1967) 258, (1966) 303. Livestock (in 000; 1966–67): cattle 2,850; sheep 10,600; goats 6,000; asses 910; horses and mules 721; camels 220.

Industry. Production (in 000; metric tons; 1968): coal 451; crude oil 89; cement 880; iron ore (55–60% metal content) 810; phosphate rock (1967) 9,922; manganese ore (metal content; 1967) 120; lead concentrates (metal content) 80; zinc concentrates (metal content) 32; electricity (kw-hr.) 1,538,000.

Motor Sports

Automobiles. Automobile racing continued to flourish during the 1969 season, and Formula One racing, for Grand Prix honours counting toward the World Drivers' Championship, remained the highest form of the sport. The far greater monetary rewards in U.S. racing, however, might diminish the primacy of Formula One events in the future.

The Grand Prix season was marked by the rise to supremacy of the French Matra cars and the winning of the world championship by Scotsman Jackie Stewart, driving for this team. The Matra organization, however, relied on Cosworth-Ford V-8 engines, like so many others. BRM, the British Racing Motor, sponsored by the Owen Organization, had a bad year, with one engine unsuccessful and the other unready; drastic changes were made within that organization.

Airfoils, used to give greater traction to the enormously wide tires used on modern road-racing cars, were declared dangerous to both drivers and spectators during the season and were banned in their more extreme forms. Safety in motor racing was emphasized considerably, the Grand Prix Drivers Association inspecting the courses over which their members would be required to race and refusing to allow competition on the famous Spa circuit in Belgium until such time as improvements were carried out. Almost at the end of the Grand Prix season former world champion Graham Hill of the U.K. suffered leg injuries when his Lotus overturned after a tire deflation. A Belgian driver, Lucien Bianchi, was killed during practice in his 3-litre Alfa Romeo.

Grand Prix racing continued to be for cars with engine sizes not exceeding 3,000 cc. and using normal gasoline as fuel. A significant development was the appearance of four-wheel-drive cars, but they did not match up to the performance available from conventional rear-wheel-driven chassis.

The Grand Prix season opened at Kyalami in South Africa, where Stewart proved himself the master, winning in the Matra-Cosworth from Graham Hill's Lotus-Cosworth. Former world champion Denis Hulme of New Zealand finished third in a McLaren-Cosworth. The second Matra-Cosworth, driven by the Frenchman J.-P. Beltoise, finished sixth, and out of 18 cars that filled the starting grid, only eight were listed as finishers. Stewart made the fastest lap.

The Spanish Grand Prix at the Montjuich Park circuit saw Stewart again the victor, with New Zealander Bruce McLaren second in a car of his own make using the popular Cosworth-Ford V-8 engine, and third place going to Beltoise for Matra International. Fastest lap, however, was accomplished by a young Austrian driver, Jochen Rindt, driving for the Lotus team. Stewart continued his domination of Grand Prix racing in the French Grand Prix at Clermont-Ferrand, with his teammate Beltoise in second place, ahead of another promising newcomer, Jackie Ickx from Belgium, driving a Brabham-Cosworth V-8. Stewart also had fastest lap. In this race 13 cars started and 10 fin-

Belgian driver Jackie Ickx crosses the finish line in a Ford GT-40 100 yd. ahead of a favoured Porsche in one of the closest finishes in the history of Le Mans, June 15, 1969.

GERRY CRANHAM, "SPORTS ILLUSTRATED" © TIME INC.

WIDE WORLD

Mario Andretti (right) passes Lloyd Ruby on first turn of the 86th lap in the Indianapolis 500, May 30, 1969. Andretti won the event with record speed of 156.867 mph.

ished, whereas at Montjuich Park only 5 had reached home out of 14 starters.

In the Monaco Grand Prix there were only 7 finishers from a field of 16. This was the race from which elaborate "wings," or movable airfoils, were banned. It was won by Hill, for Lotus, from Piers Courage in a Brabham-Cosworth. The British Grand Prix returned to the Silverstone circuit, and in warm, overcast weather Stewart won from Ickx and McLaren; Stewart and McLaren used MS-80 Cosworth engines, but Ickx drove with a BT-26 Cosworth power unit.

Nothing could stop Stewart, who triumphed in the Dutch Grand Prix at Zandvoort, second place being taken by Jo Siffert's Lotus-Cosworth and third place by the New Zealand driver Chris Amon in a Ferrari V-12. Generally throughout the season Ferraris performed far below their efforts in previous seasons.

The German Grand Prix over the difficult Nürburgring proved the merits of the top drivers, Stewart, Rindt, and Ickx all being on the front row of the starting grid. It was Ickx's Brabham-Cosworth that took the checkered flag, with Stewart second and McLaren third, Rindt having retired due to ignition trouble. Ickx clinched his rise toward supremacy by driving the fastest lap. Only 4 cars finished, although 13 had left the starting line. The Italian Grand Prix at Monza saw Stewart back in winning form, in a race from which only 4 cars dropped out, after 15 had started. Rindt and Beltoise finished second and third, respectively.

The 11th U.S. Grand Prix at Watkins Glen, N.Y., gained Rindt his first Grand Prix victory, from Courage's Brabham-Cosworth, with John Surtees finishing third in a BRM V-12-P139. Seventeen cars contested this event, and 10 failed to complete the course. Before this there had been the Canadian Grand Prix at Mosport Park. The race went to Ickx's Brabham-Cosworth, with Jack Brabham second and Rindt third in the Gold Leaf Team Lotus entry. Twenty started, and 8 finished. The final round of the 1969 Grand Prix season took place in Mexico, when Hulme's McLaren won at Mexico City from Ickx and Brabham, with Stewart fourth, in a race of 16 runners and 11 finishers. The season demonstrated the overwhelming superiority of the Ford-sponsored British Cosworth racing Formula One engine and saw Stewart take the place once occupied by the late Jim Clark, with Ickx and Rindt proving of great merit. The absence of Cooper and Honda cars and the poor showing of Ferrari and BRM reduced interest in intermake rivalry, and new blood was badly needed in Grand Prix racing.

In the United States the Indianapolis 500-mi. race was won by Mario Andretti in Andy Granatelli's (*see* BIOGRAPHY) turbo-powered Ford-Brawner Hawk. Dan Gurney finished second in an Eagle-Ford, and Bobbie Unser was third in a Lola-Offenhauser, the race being won at the record speed of 156.867 mph. Andretti also won the U.S. Auto Club (USAC) championship, clinching his title by winning the Trenton, N.J., 300 on September 24.

McLaren and Hulme completely dominated the Sports Car Club of America's premier series, the $1 million Canadian-American Challenge Cup for Group 7 cars (two-seaters with unlimited engine size). They won all 11 races in the series, with McLaren's triumph at the new Texas International Speedway at College Station enough to assure him the individual championship. McLaren won $158,700 during the series, while Hulme netted $146,000. Third in the series standings was Chuck Parsons, a veteran driver from California with $77,000, while Siffert of Switzerland finished fourth with earnings of $50,200. Even though McLaren and Hulme dominated this competition so completely, ten drivers won $20,000 or more.

In the National Association for Stock Car Auto Racing (NASCAR), 1969 was the year of the drivers' strike and, because of it, a newcomer, Richard Brickhouse, won the Talladega (Ala.) 500. The members of the newly formed Professional Drivers Association (PDA), including NASCAR's new champion, David Pearson, and Richard Petty, only active driver to win 100 Grand Nationals, were on the sidelines at Talladega for the opening of NASCAR president Bill France's new "fastest superspeedway in the world." Meanwhile, Brickhouse averaged 153.778 mph in beating a last-minute collection of Grand Touring circuit cars (supposedly ineligible), drivers from other associations, rookies, and a few regulars. The fastest qualifier, PDA member Charlie Glotzbach, in a Dodge, did not compete after winning the pole at 199.446 mph. By their numerous pit stops the competitors proved PDA fears that the tires available would not stand the new track surface at such speeds.

In other major championships Mark Donohue from Media, Pa., and car-owner Roger Pensko won the Trans-American Sedan crown for Chevrolet Camaro over Ford, but had to withdraw from Can-Am racing to concentrate on the task. In the Continental Championship, the A class was won on the final race of the season, December 28 at Sebring, Fla., by Tony Adamowicz of Wilton, Conn. In B class Mike Eyerly, Salem, Ore., won easily in a Brabham-Ford. In USAC stock cars Roger McCluskey in a Plymouth was the winner. In the NASCAR Grand Touring circuit an exciting all-season contest found Ken Rush of Winston-Salem, N.C., the new champion.

The most significant factor in U.S. automobile racing, however, was the fact that it moved further into the realm of big business. Larry LoPatin, a Detroit entrepreneur with little previous interest in the sport, assembled a chain of modern race facilities from coast to coast, some new, some existing, under his American Raceways Inc. banner. Beginning with the new $5 million Michigan International Speedway, LoPatin and colleagues acquired interests in the existing Riverside, Calif., and Atlanta, Ga., International Speedways. He completed Texas International Speedway and announced plans for a multimillion-dollar facility near the New Jersey Turnpike.

Porsche won the sports car championship but not the most important endurance race in the world, the 24 Hours of Le Mans. One of the most exciting finishes ever unfolded as the Porsches, which had led easily for 21 hours, suddenly found their huge entry diminished by crashes and clutch trouble. In a desperate attempt to overtake Ickx and Jackie Oliver, the eventual winners, in a John Wyer Ford GT-40, West Germany's Hans Herrmann managed to catch the three-time winning car on the five-mile straightaway in the final lap. But Herrmann could not hold off Ickx. Ickx/Oliver's speed was 129.923 mph for the 24 hours.

Earlier the same twosome had embarrassed Porsche by winning the 12-hour Sebring Grand Prix with an average speed of 103.363 mph. In the opening of the sports car series at Daytona Beach, Fla., both the GT-40s and the Porsches succumbed late in the race to mechanical woes. Mark Donohue and Chuck Parsons in a Lola Chevrolet won, followed by another Lola Chevrolet, a Pontiac Firebird, and two Porsches.

The stock car counterpart of the Indianapolis 500, the Daytona 500, turned into a last-lap thriller as Lee Roy Yarbrough moved his Ford around Charlie Glotzbach's Dodge in the final lap to win $38,950. The two had battled the final 95 mi. of the race as if it were a sprint. The average speed of 157.950 mph was a new record. Yarbrough also won Daytona's Firecracker 400.

Formula Two racing maintained its popularity, contested by Ferrari, Lotus, Matra, Brabham, and other makes, again with much reliance on Cosworth engines. Close racing was seen between Ford-powered Formula-Three machines, and in Britain all classes of racing were staged, including special events for racing cars nowadays regarded as historic. Formula Two and Three cars are scaled-down versions of the Formula One machines.

The European long-distance sports car contests included the age-old Targa Florio, which was a Porsche monopoly; the Belgian 1,000-km. race in which the winning Porsche was challenged by a 3-litre V-12 Ferrari 312P; a similar race at Monza in Italy, won by the Siffert/B. Redman Porsche 908, with another of those cars second, driven by Herrmann/K. Ahrens, and a Porsche 907 third; and the German Nürburgring 1,000-km. race which was an absolute Porsche-908 walkover. At the newly opened Zeltwig circuit in Austria another 1,000-km. race was a victory for the new big 4½-litre V-12 Porsche 917 handled by Siffert and Ahrens, with a 7-litre Lola T-70 Chevrolet second.

In the U.K. the race-going public was able to see such races as the Brands Hatch Race of Champions, which marked the beginning of the year's exhibition of prowess by Stewart and Matra International; the *Daily Express* International Trophy Race at Silverstone, won by Brabham from Rindt and Stewart; and the BOAC 500 sports car event at Brands Hatch, in which three Porsche 908s ran away from Amon's Ferrari 312P.

International rallies attracted much public following. Of the traditional type of rally, the winter Monte Carlo Rally was a success for Porsche, their B. Waldegaard/L. Helmer car taking top honours from another Porsche. Porsche scored again, with a 911L, in the Swedish Rally, but the San Remo Rally was won by Lancia, Fulvia HF's taking the first three places. Of great importance was the East African Safari, which in 1969 went to Ford, although Japanese Datsun cars took the coveted Team Prize. The Rallye du Maroc was won convincingly by Citröen and the Welsh International Rally by a twin-cam Ford Escort, as was also the Dutch Tulip Rally. A Porsche 911S took first place in the Acropolis Rally; Scotland's International fixture was a victory for a Saab V-4 from a Hillman Imp driven by crewmen who drove the winning Marathon car; and Ford with a twin-cam Escort took the Finnish Rally of the Thousand Lakes. The Alpine Rally was dominated by French Alpine-Renaults and the Autumn in Portugal Rally was won by a Citröen DS-21 from two Datsuns. The Royal Automobile Club International Rally of Great Britain was won by Swedish drivers H. Kallström and G. Häggbom (Lancia Fulvia), with Saabs in second and third places. (W. C. Bo.; R. J. Fe.)

Motorcycles. In motorcycle competition, scrambling (moto cross) and road racing continued to attract reasonable crowds, although in road racing the traditionally most important classes—for 350 cc. and 500 cc.—tended to be tame affairs after the 1968 retirement of Mike Hailwood, with his Japanese Honda machines, left the field open to his most consistent adversary, the Italian Giacomo Agostini, riding MV Agusta three-cylinder machines. Agostini won both titles, the 350 cc. as early in the season as the Czechoslovakian Grand Prix at Brno on July 20. In the 125-cc. class the Englishman D. A. Simmonds, riding a Japanese Kawasaki, emerged as champion. The 50-cc. class, in which the tiny machines, being driven near the limit of reliability, were invariably plagued by mechanical troubles, was finally won by a Spaniard, A. Nieto, riding a Spanish Derbi, when his chief opponent, A. Toersen (Neth.), retired in the Yugoslav Grand Prix (September 14) with a crank failure in his Kreidler. The most exciting racing in the series was seen in the 250-cc. class where, as late as the Yugoslav Grand Prix, there were three riders with a chance of winning the title: K. Andersson (Yamaha) of Sweden, K. Carruthers (Benelli) of Australia, and S. Herrero (Ossa) of Spain. Carruthers won the race, Herrero retired, and Andersson finished third; and so the world title went to Carruthers.

In the Isle of Man competition, winners of the various classes were as follows: 750-cc. sidecar, S. Schauzu (BMW); 500-cc. sidecar, K. Enders (BMW); 250 cc., Carruthers (Benelli); 350 cc., Agostini (MV Agusta); 500 cc., Agostini; 125 cc., Simmonds (Kawasaki). Winners of the September races on the Isle of Man, the Manx Grand Prix, were: lightweight (250 cc.), A. J. S. George (Yamaha); junior (350 cc.), R. G. Duffty (Aermacchi); senior (500 cc.), G. J. Daniels (Matchless).

In international moto cross Joel Robert (CZ) of Belgium won the 250-cc. class, beating his countryman Sylvain Geboers, whose CZ developed front-fork trouble in the crucial Finnish Grand Prix meeting.

German sidecar team of Klaus Enders and Rolf Englehardt won the 1969 world championship at Hockheim, W.Ger., May 11. The pair had been champions in 1967.

AUTHENTICATED NEWS INTERNATIONAL

1969 U.S. National Motorboat Racing Champions

Inboard

Class/Driver

7 Litre
George W. Babcock
Seattle, Wash.
280 Hydro
Walter J. Struzek
Norristown, Pa.
266 Hydro
Ron Larsen
Long Beach, Calif.
225 Hydro
Danny Walls
Belleview, Ky.
150 Hydro
Tom D'Eath
St. Petersburg, Fla.
145 Hydro
Billy Brown
Richmond, Va.
91 Hydro
Jack Sellers
St. Petersburg, Fla.
44 Hydro
James Campbell
Danville, Pa.
44 Runabout
William R. Overby
Metairie, La.
850 Hydro
Wesley Nickens
Prairieville, La.
Cracker Box
Bob Clune
Long Beach, Calif.
Jersey Speed Skiff
J. Chris Ziegler
Long Branch, N.J.
Ski Racing Runabout
Douglas Bouden
Lacombe, La.
Super Stock
Ed F. Johnson
Newport Beach, Calif.
B Racing Runabout
Jeff Walsh
Pleasant Hill, Calif.
E Racing Runabout
Bud Murphy
Whittier, Calif.
E Service Runabout
Ted Neuweiler
Miami, Fla.
F. Service Runabout
Mona Daily
Miami, Fla.
K Racing Runabout
Jim O'Leary
Long Beach, Calif.

Outboard

Class/Driver

M Hydro
not available
A Hydro
Jerry Waldman
Milwaukee, Wis.
B Hydro
Bob Hering
Sheboygan, Wis.
C Hydro
John Schubert
Clifton, N.J.
D Hydro
Jerry Waldman
Milwaukee, Wis.
F Hydro
Bob Viera
Oakland, Calif.
C Service Hydro
Bob Murphy
Springfield, Ill.
A Racing Runabout
Ralph Donald
Marietta, Ga.
B Racing Runabout
Ted May
Long Beach, Calif.
C Racing Runabout
Jerry Simison
Fergus Falls, Minn.
D Racing Runabout
Bill Seebold, Jr.
St. Louis, Mo.
F Racing Runabout
William Fales
Northport, N.Y.
C Service Runabout
Rocky Stone
Wilamina, Ore.

UPI COMPIX

Jim Merton pilots his Switzer wing to a record-setting win in the outboard division of the Parker, Ariz., nine-hour Enduro in March 1969.

John Banks of England, riding a BSA four-stroke in a field dominated by non-British-made two-strokes, appeared to have an excellent chance of winning the title; then, partly because of mechanical troubles, he dropped out of the running, and Bengt Åberg of Sweden, riding a native Husqvarna, went ahead and confirmed his hold on the title. The most important event of the season, the Trophée des Nations, was won by the powerful Belgian team, with Sweden second and Czechoslovakia third. (C. J. Ay.)

Motorboating. The prestigious Gold Cup race at San Diego, Calif., September 28, climaxed an unlimited hydroplane racing season in which there were no fatalities and only minor accidents. Bill Sterett of Owensboro, Ky., added the Gold Cup to three previous victories in the seven-race unlimited schedule to win the season boat and driver championships. His steady driving under pressure, in which he finished 20 of 22 heats, earned his $41,100 in prize money.

A rash of fatal accidents in previous seasons brought about the introduction in 1969 of a new life-support system for drivers of the unlimiteds, fastest group of watercraft in the world. Essentially a small parachute called a decelerator, it was designed to open automatically any time a driver was hurled from his cockpit in a flip or other violent maneuver. Tests showed it would function within a 5½-ft. vertical or 84-ft. horizontal distance.

Seven unlimited drivers wore the decelerator during the 1969 season, but fortunately it was never needed. First to don it was Tommy Fults, who wore it during a preseason effort to set a new world record for propeller-driven boats. The existing straightaway record speed was 200.419 mph, set by Roy Duby in 1962 at Guntersville, Ala. Fults missed by a substantial margin, but the owner of the boat, Dave Heerensperger, promised to try again.

Also new in 1969 was a turbine-powered unlimited hydroplane owned by Dave Edwards of Los Angeles. Edwards did not solve all his engineering problems and the novel craft never got into competition, but it was expected to appear on the 1970 circuit. So was a revolutionary tunnel-wing boat with a stern-drive engine—an inboard engine with an outboard drive unit. It was built by Los Angeles lumberman-racer Bill Cooper and Seattle industrialist Dave Puckett.

The only other major unlimited race of the season was the annual world championship at Detroit, won for the second year in a row by Bill Muncey. Dean Chenoweth won the Governor's Cup race at Madison, Ind., July 6, and the Atomic Cup at Pasco, Wash., July 20. In addition to the Gold Cup, Sterett won the season-opening Dixie Cup at Guntersville June 8; the Kentucky Governor's Cup at his home town June 15; and the Seattle Seafair Trophy August 3.

The Union of International Motorboating (UIM) world championship in offshore racing was won in 1969 by Don Aronow, who also held the title in 1967. A Miami boatbuilder, Aronow campaigned three identical boats, one based in Europe and two in the U.S. All were 32-ft. Carys and were fitted with twin 475-hp MerCruiser stern-drive engines.

The use of two boats solved a serious logistics problem in making the world circuit of approved races. Aronow dramatically demonstrated its value, despite the high cost, when he won the Long Beach Hennessy Cup Race in California August 23 and then flew immediately to Britain to win the Cowes-Torquay race a week later.

Winning the Cowes-Torquay wrapped up the UIM world championship for Aronow. His chief competition up to that point had come from two Italian sportsmen: Vincenzo Balestrieri, who had won the international title in 1968 and was trying for his second straight year; and Francisco Cosentino, who had raced in Balestrieri's crew and was attempting to win the world title on his own.

The U.S. offshore outboard driving champion was Pat Duffy of Mount Clemens, Mich. (Ja. E. M.)

Mountaineering

A striking feature of the year 1968–69 was the growing use as commercial tourist attractions of high mountain areas previously visited only by full-scale mountaineering expeditions. These tourist parties generally employed the services of Sherpas or other porters and of well-known mountaineers with much expedition experience as leaders. Thus all that was expected of the tourist was that he be reasonably fit and capable of walking in rough country. Such tours were organized in various parts of the Himalayas (a typical one being from Kathmandu, Nepal, to the Mt. Everest base camp area and back) and in the Andes in South America; even Greenland and Antarctica were no longer untouched by commercial development.

In the Alps the first winter ascents were made of the northeast faces of the Ober Gabelhorn and the Bishorn, the north face of Mont Collon, and the southeast face of the Lenzspitze; numerous strong parties got into position for the north face of the Droites, but this plum of winter ascents remained unpicked. During the summer this latter route was climbed solo by R. Messner; Jean Juges made a guided ascent of the Walker Spur of the Grandes Jorasses. A Japanese party made a "direct" route on the Eigerwand; a new route up the Pilier d'Angle of Mont Blanc de Courmayeur was accomplished by the Poles.

In Norway difficult climbing on the Trolltinder continued, with two new routes being achieved on Søndre Trolltind. In Greenland the Japanese crossed the ice cap from east to west in 1968, and a British Army party climbed many peaks in the Kristians Glacier area. In 1969 another British Army party was in northern Peary Land, and other British expeditions climbed in the Watkins Mountains and around the Kristians Glacier. A Scottish attempt on Einar Mikkelsen Fjell, the highest unclimbed peak in Greenland, failed. An Anglo-Danish expedition carried out mountain surveying, and an Irish party climbed on Upernavik Island. In New Zealand during the 1968–69 summer one of the last unclimbed named peaks, Lloyd's Peak, was climbed, and the Arrowsmith Range was traversed from East Horn to Jagged Peak.

In the U.S.S.R. new routes in 1968 in the Caucasus were the south face of Ushba by the "mirror," by a group from the Ukraine; the central bastion of Chanchakhi-Khokh by a party led by L. Popov; Krunkol from the north (by A. Timofeyev); and Kirpich by the south face. Important climbs in the Pamirs in 1968 were the central wall of OGPU Peak and the east rib of Communism Peak from the Bivachny Glacier by Spartak parties, the south face of Engels Peak by a *Trud* party, a new route on Tadzhikistan Peak by a party from Leningrad, and Revolution Peak from the Yazgulyem-Dar Glacier (led by S. Artyukhin). Other new routes were on Bodkhon, and on the southwest face of Communism Peak by a party from the Mountaineering Federation of the U.S.S.R.

In the Himalayas climbing got under way slowly in 1969 in Nepal after the lifting of the ban on expeditions in 1968. The German Alpine Club centenary expedition failed on Annapurna I but climbed several lesser peaks. The U.S. expedition to Dhaulagiri I ended in disaster, with the killing of five Americans and two Sherpas. Swiss climbers ascended Tukuche Peak (22,703 ft.) in the Dhaulagiri area. A Japanese party reconnoitred the southwest face of Everest, and other Japanese reached the South Col on skis.

In Garhwal in 1968 Indian parties climbed Bandarpunch I, Bhagirathi II, Santopath, and Trisul. An unsuccessful German attempt was made in 1968 on the Rupal face of Nanga Parbat. Japanese women climbed Kailas Parbat in Kulu. In the same area in 1969 Scots climbed Ali Ratni Tibba, while an Italian group was successful on the highest peak of Parbati. An Indo-British expedition was active in the Chamba area (Phabrang and Baihili Jot); another British party visited the Kitshtwar region in eastern Kashmir; and Indian women climbed Hanuman Tibba.

In the Karakoram in 1968 Austrians climbed Minapin (Diran, 23,861 ft.; the only 23,000-ft. peak climbed in 1968) on an unofficial visit. A Manchester expedition attempted Malubiting from the south, one member being killed. In 1969 an international expedition was active in the Hispar-Biafo area.

The Hindu Kush continued in popularity in late 1968; Wakhan was popular in 1969. A U.S.-Austrian ascent of Noshaq by the west ridge was made. A British Army party climbed Tirich Mir, and another British group explored the Thui peaks of the Hindu Raj.

In Alaska in 1968 ascents were made of Mt. Thor (Chugach), Mt. Kiliak, Mt. Ascension in the Kenai area, and several peaks in the Boundary Range between Skagway and Juneau. The fourth ascent of Mt. Foraker was achieved (by a new route on the south face). Japanese parties climbed Mt. Steele and the south peak of Mt. Vancouver in the Yukon, three being killed by an avalanche on the latter peak. A dozen first ascents by a U.S. party in the Brooks Range included Mts. Igikpak, Chitiok, and Papiok.

In 1969 several U.S. parties climbed Mt. McKinley by a new route from the east. First ascents were made of Mt. Kimbatt (East Alaska Range) and Paradise Peak (Kenai Peninsula), and also of peaks in the Cathedral (Kichatna) Spires. G. Hoeman climbed Mt. Wickersham (Chugach Mountains) solo. In Canada Mt. Robson was climbed by the north face, and the first winter ascent of Mt. Waddington was made.

South America continued to be the major area for expeditions. In 1968 in Peru Huascarán was climbed three times. British and Argentinian attempts on Huandoy Sar south face failed. New routes or peaks included Aquilpo, Pisco, Salcantay (north face and south ridge), Soray (Humantay—south ridge), Chainapuerto (Cordillera Urubamba), and peaks in the Alpamayo-Tayapampa area. In 1969 first ascents were made of Pumahuacanca, the southeast ridge of Chopicalqui, west ridge of Huascarán, east ridge of Jirishanca, and northeast spur of Yerupaja. An attempt on the north face of Huascarán ended fatally. The northeast face of Yerupaja was repeated. An Australian expedition visited the Pumasillo group, and the east ridge of Alpamayo was climbed by Germans. A French expedition to Huandoy was abandoned. In Bolivia a German expedition climbed 16 peaks in the Cordillera Apolobamba in 1968, and a Japanese party ascended seven peaks in the Cordillera Quimsa Cruz. Another Japanese expedition, to Patagonia in 1969, made a new crossing of the Hielo Continental from west to east. The third ascent of Cerro Fitzroy, by a new route up the southeast buttress, was accomplished by a U.S. expedition.

Seven blind Africans, with their guides, climbed Kilimanjaro, Africa's highest mountain at 19,340 ft., in February 1969. (Jo. N.)

FOX PHOTOS FROM PICTORIAL PARADE

Pupils at St. Peter's Preparatory School in Seaford, Sussex, scale a replica of the Matterhorn on their school grounds.

Muscat and Oman

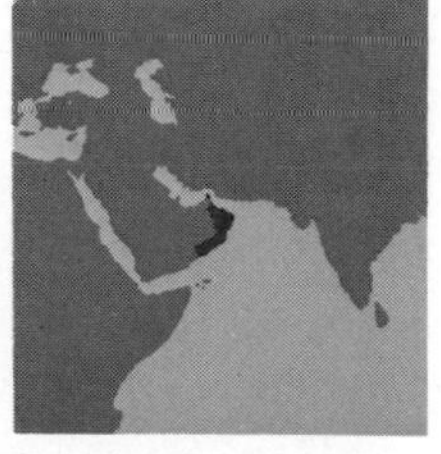

An independent sultanate, Muscat and Oman occupies the southeastern part of the Arabian Peninsula and is bounded by the Trucial States, Saudi Arabia, the Gulf of Oman, and the Arabian Sea. The exclave of Oman is surrounded by the Trucial States and the Gulf of Oman. Area: 82,000 sq.mi. (212,000 sq.km.). Pop. (1968 est.): 565,000. Cap.: Muscat (pop., 1960, 6,208). Largest city: Matrah (pop., 1960, 14,119). Language: Arabic. Religion: Muslim. Sultan in 1969, Sa'id bin Taimur.

MUSCAT AND OMAN

Finance and Trade. Monetary units: Persian Gulf rupee (official), valued at 1*s*. 9*d*. sterling (21 cents U.S.); Maria Theresa dollar or thaler (common medium of exchange; value varies between PGRs. 3.45 and PGRs. 3.75); and (in Dhofar province) half dollar; in interior generally, baiza (64 baizas = PGR. 1). A new currency, the Saudi riyal (with a par value equal to £1 sterling), was to be introduced. Budget (excluding oil revenue; 1967 est.) revenue *c*. £3 million. Foreign trade (1967): imports (excluding government and oil company imports of *c*. £2.5 million in 1966) £3,589,480 (mainly from India and U.K.); exports (excluding oil) *c*. £800,000. Main exports (1961–62): dates 48%; fruit and vegetables 24%; fish and fish products 9%.

Industry. Crude oil production (1968) 12,042,000 metric tons.

Motor Vehicles:
see Disasters; Industrial Review; Motor Sports; Transportation

Mozambique:
see Dependent States

Muhammadanism:
see Religion

Municipal Government:
see Cities and Urban Affairs

Munitions:
see Defense

Politically, 1969 was relatively inactive for Muscat and Oman. The sultanate maintained its long-standing tradition of isolation, belonging to no international organizations, having no diplomatic relations with any state other than Britain, and in general discouraging visits from outsiders. The British, whose protective relationship with the small Arab states in the area began in the 19th century, were due to leave the region by 1971. Perhaps as a result of their imminent departure, the sultan was reported to be exploring certain cooperative arrangements with Abu Dhabi (one of the Trucial States).

Some economic discontent in the sultanate resulted from the fact that, while the burden of taxation fell on the people, they did not expect to benefit from the oil resources, discovered in commercially exploitable quantities in 1964. A national liberation front was said to be operating against the sultan in the southern province of Dhofar, for the purpose of establishing a socialist revolutionary regime.

AUTHENTICATED NEWS INTERNATIONAL

Kinetic fountain by the Belgian sculptor Pol Bury commissioned for the University of Iowa Museum of Art which opened in 1969.

Museums and Galleries

International cooperation between museums and galleries in 1969, as furthered by seminars, conferences, and discussions organized by international and national institutions, came at a time when previously held conceptions about the role of museums and galleries were being questioned. The 15th general conference of UNESCO adopted a resolution authorizing the promotion of "the adaptation of museums to the needs of the contemporary world." And at an international symposium convened at UNESCO headquarters in November, representatives of museums, scholars, art critics, artists, sociologists, educationalists, and documentalists from more than 20 countries were invited to discuss this aim.

While UNESCO continued its international campaign for Florence and Venice in close cooperation with the Italian authorities, a sharper line of division was drawn between work to restore cultural property damaged as a result of the 1966 floods and the long-term effort to safeguard Venice and develop it as a cultural centre. In 1968 assistance was concentrated in Venice, especially on damp control in certain churches and experiments with preservation methods. In Florence, UNESCO's assistance was mainly on behalf of the state archives.

In August 1969 UNESCO published the preliminary report on the draft convention concerning the means of prohibiting and preventing the illicit import, export, and transfer of ownership of cultural property. The final version of the convention was to be voted on at the General Conference of UNESCO in Paris in 1970.

Other programs under UNESCO sponsorship included an international symposium on museum architecture, access, and circulation organized by the International Council of Museums (ICOM) in December 1968 in Mexico City. The West German national commission for UNESCO, in cooperation with the Folkwang Museum, Essen, organized the third in a series of international seminars in January 1969, this one on "Museums and Television." An international seminar on museums and anthropological research was organized in October 1968 in Dar es Salaam, Tanzania, for museum directors in English-speaking countries of Africa. Continuing a series of international meetings on museums and education, U.K. authorities organized one in 1969 on the training of museum educationalists. Other international seminars were held in Havana (on general museographical problems), in Marseilles, France, in London (on documentation of museum collections), and in New Delhi, India.

U.S. museums were concerned during the year by proposed changes in the federal tax laws, especially one that would have permitted donors of works of art to deduct only the purchase price of a gift from their federal income tax rather than the current market value. This provision was not included in the tax reform law as passed, however.

A major museum controversy erupted in Canada when the Royal Ontario Museum, Toronto, requested from the federal government both national status and an annual grant of $1 million. Intense reaction from the personnel of other museums pointed up the great lacks of their respective institutions and the need for a national reform in museum maintenance and operation. It was hoped that the National Museums Act, passed in 1968, would bring about more than a reorganization.

Museum Collections. The most important art museum acquisition, not only of 1969 but perhaps of the century, was the bequest by Robert Lehman to the Metropolitan Museum of Art, New York City, of about 3,000 items, which permitted the museum to nearly double its European art collection. The famous treasures included the "Portrait of Suzanne de Bourbon" by the Maitre de Moulins, "Annunciation" by Memling, "The Legend of St. Eloi" by Petrus

Exhibition in the Richard Kaselowsky art gallery, Bielefeld, W.Ger., which opened in 1969.

H. G. GESSNER

Christus, a self-portrait by Dürer, the "Annunciation" by Botticelli, portrait of Gérard de Lairesse by Rembrandt, "Saint Jerome as a Cardinal" by El Greco, a self-portrait by Goya, and works by Renoir, Degas, Gauguin, Monet, Seurat, Matisse, Van Gogh, Modigliani, and Picasso. The collection, considered one of the most important private collections in the world, was started in 1911 by the donor's father, Philip Lehman.

The Metropolitan was also presented with the Nelson A. Rockefeller collection of primitive art, which was to be housed in a new wing named after the New York governor's son Michael. Portions of the collection were displayed by the Metropolitan during the year. Announced in 1968 was author James Michener's gift to the University of Texas of 253 paintings by major 20th-century American artists.

In 1968 the National Gallery, London, purchased an outstanding work by Duccio di Buoninsegna entitled "The Virgin and Child with Four Angels," and works by Bernini, Velázquez, Andrea Sacchi, Monet, and Cézanne. In June 1969 the National Gallery purchased a ceiling painting by Tiepolo discovered in the United Arab Republic's London embassy. (*See* ART SALES.) The year also saw the opening in London of the National Postal Museum containing a collection of Victorian stamps and world stamps received from the Universal Postal Union since 1878.

In France the government established a National Centre of Contemporary Art (CNAC) to collect modern art and to serve as a kind of "banking house of contemporary French and 'France-born' art" for all museums in France. In Italy, where art objects feed many more foreign galleries than Italian, *Musei e Gallerie d'Italia* maintained an inventory of Italian art objects purchased by both European and non-European countries.

A new art museum opened in São Paulo, Braz., in 1969 was designed by the architect Lina Bo for the collection of F. Assis de Chateaubriand, who died in March 1969. The collection included paintings by Titian, Raphael, Mantegna, Massys, Velázquez, and an excellent choice of 19th- and 20th-century painters. The national museum in New Delhi received from Alice and Nasli Heeramaneck a collection of almost 400 objects representing the principal cultures of pre-Columbian America. This was the most important pre-Columbian collection in any Asian museum.

In October the permanent home of the Gulbenkian Foundation was opened in Lisbon. The centre included a museum, exhibition gallery, library, auditoriums, and conference facilities.

The problem of thefts still plagued museums and private collections. The French press reported 440 pictures stolen in France in the first eight months of 1969. The Izmir (Turkey) Archaeological Museum was robbed in July of 118 pieces from its Greek and Roman collection, worth an estimated £2 million. Sections in professional art reviews entitled "reported stolen" made pessimistic reading.

In the U.S. the year was marked by the initiation of centennial anniversaries by three of the largest museums. The Metropolitan announced a series of five important exhibitions beginning with a highly controversial show, "New York Painting and Sculpture 1940–1970." In Boston, the Museum of Fine Arts displayed one of the greatest Rembrandt etching exhibits ever shown in the U.S. The Philadelphia Museum of Art held an arresting exhibition of one of the 20th century's most influential sculptors—Constantin Brancusi—based on its Arensberg collection, the largest collection of Brancusi's works in the U.S.

THE "NEW YORK TIMES" FROM WIDE WORLD

The Metropolitan Museum of Art in August 1969 exhibited more than 1,000 pieces of primitive art of Oceania, Africa, and the Americas. Included were pieces from the Nelson Rockefeller collection, donated during the year to the museum.

In Dayton, O., the Art Institute presented "Fifty Treasures" of the museum, one for each of its years. By judicious buying during the 1960s, this smaller museum had achieved a fine, balanced collection. The oldest public art museum in the U.S., the Wadsworth Atheneum founded in Hartford, Conn., in 1842, reopened its galleries after a $5 million rebuilding and reinstallation program. In Washington, D.C., ground was broken in January for the Joseph H. Hirshhorn Museum, which would house the largest private art collection in the world. Meanwhile, the oldest and the newest major art galleries in Washington—the Corcoran Gallery of Art and the Washington Gallery of Modern Art—concluded plans to combine staffs, resources, and membership.

Museum Personnel. The sixth training course for African museum technicians at the UNESCO Regional Centre in Jos, Nigeria, terminated in November 1969. During 1963–69 courses at the Jos Centre had benefited 71 African museum technicians. Some of them, after advanced studies in Europe and the U.S., had become curators and keepers of their national museums.

The second training course at the regional American Centre in Mexico City for the study of the conservation and restoration of cultural property ended in December 1969. Eighteen laboratory technicians were trained in techniques for the preservation of pre-Columbian, Spanish colonial, and contemporary materials. The International Centre for the Study of the Preservation and the Restoration of Cultural Property in Rome trained architects and laboratory specialists in 1969. The Asia Pacific Museum training program of the Bishop Museum and Honolulu Academy of Arts, Honolulu, was awarded fellowships through the Institute for Technical Interchange of the East-West Center for its study programs.

UNESCO aided the organization of an international

BERND KIRTZ, ABCV

Sculpture is displayed both indoors and outdoors at the Wilhelm Lehmbruck gallery, Duisberg, W.Ger., which opened in 1969. The gallery was constructed with no internal columns for maximum flexibility.

postgraduate pilot course for the scientific staff of museums. The Institute Royal du Patrimoine Artistique in Brussels, the Musée du Louvre, Paris, and the Musée Ethnographique and the Institut d'Ethnologie in Neuchâtel, Switz., cooperated in the program. Leading European specialists in different fields of museography gave courses to 20 trainees from several European countries.

An international seminar on the training of scientific personnel for museums, organized by ICOM in cooperation with the French national committee of ICOM, was held at the Louvre from Jan. 20 to Feb. 28, 1969. ICOM also initiated a new formula for raising standards through national seminars to which internationally known museum specialists would be sent. Georges-Henri Rivière, permanent adviser to ICOM, visited three countries in North Africa to conduct national seminars and meetings and prepare further recommendations. UNESCO, in cooperation with the government of India, planned a new regional training centre in collaboration with the National Museum Laboratory, New Delhi. This and a training centre for the Arab states would complete world coverage by UNESCO programs for museography.

Museums continued to proliferate in the U.S. and future staff needs were anticipated in the grant given by the Ford Foundation to the museum training program at New York University's Institute of Fine Arts and the Metropolitan Museum. There was also the possibility that present needs might be remedied by the expansion of museum training courses offered at the undergraduate level at colleges and universities. The University of Iowa, for example, would be able to expand its training program and exhibitions in an elegant new building opened in the spring of 1969.

New Concepts. In Canada the Ontario Science Centre in Toronto, designed by Canadian architect Raymond Noriyama, was opened to the public on Sept. 27, 1969. Consisting of three main buildings on a 20-ac. site, the centre contained displays relating to basic science, man-the-controller, man-the-explorer, Canadian resources, life, communication, engineering, and transportation. The centre's exhibition policy was to give 20% coverage to historical objects, 70% to contemporary, and 10% to the examination of future problems.

In the U.K., the government announced plans to make available to the Tate Gallery additional land on an adjoining site. Earlier plans to extend the gallery on its existing site and to remove the portico had caused considerable public outcry. (*See* ARCHITECTURE.) Interest was aroused by the design for a new building to house the Pitt-Rivers Museum of Oxford University. The design by Pier Luigi Nervi in cooperation with Powell and Moya of London embraced the concept that living ecological exhibits could be planned as part of a single organically conceived structure. The museum would house tropical and subtropical plants and the exhibits were to be arranged in concentric circles, with each sector devoted to different cultures.

It was ironic that, in the U.S., the same year in which museums were threatened by financial problems because of proposed tax revisions also saw the appearance of *America's Museums: The Belmont Report,* a federally sponsored study of the state of U.S. museums and their relationship to other educational and cultural institutions. The report urged that the National Museum Act of 1966 be funded immediately with at least $1 million and concluded that there was no future alternative to federal support for the U.S. museums.

In 1969 less than 1% of the operating revenues of U.S. museums came from the federal government, and in 1967–68 less than 2% of the funds of private foundations went to museums. In contrast to the European tradition of government financing for museums, the U.S. museum had always had private support, and as a result had generally been more available to and aware of the community at large than its more aloof European counterpart. This situation was the background both for the financial plight of the U.S. museums and for their other current dilemma: the need to choose between the concept of the "open" museum, an up-to-date community service centre for all artistic manifestations, and the traditional "object oriented" museum, a repository of art and other objects of the past and present.

In 1969, as in previous years, it was Thomas Hoving, director of the Metropolitan (who, incidentally, announced his pending retirement in 1969), who provoked argument with his advocacy of an open policy when he presented "Harlem on My Mind" early in the year. The opening of this multimedia exhibition, a sociopsychological survey of the Negro community in upper Manhattan, was marked, for a complexity of reasons, by three days of picketing outside the museum and the marking of several major paintings within the museum with the letter "H."

Creation of a new type of museum without collections or permanent exhibitions, the Museum of the Media, was announced in New York. The museum would differ from other museums in that audiovisual means would replace exhibition programs of three-dimensional objects. The Bedford Lincoln Neighborhood Museum in Brooklyn set up a community centre in which children and adults could play and participate in the museum's departments.

Two major figures of Pop Art, Roy Lichtenstein and Claes Oldenburg, were honoured by large exhibitions in New York City. With Pop artists already being accorded museum retrospectives, the avant-garde appeared to be elsewhere, presumably in "process" or "concept" art in which the artist was involved only in ideas of works, the execution being left undone or to others, or in works whose realization left no objects behind. Examples ranged from ideas for huge, building-sized tubes to scattering a field with trash and removing a few papers each day.

It was, perhaps, remarkable that museums had already begun to document such art. Both the Solomon R. Guggenheim Museum and the Whitney Museum of American Art in New York, as well as smaller museums such as the Seattle (Wash.) Art Museum, gave such works "museum status." In New York City, an "antidealer" was established who published a catalog of works available only in the form of the photograph in the catalog. The Museum of Contemporary Art in Chicago organized "Art by Telephone" by constructing works according to concepts called in by the artists. In the show, negative and Dada-like works jostled more technologically oriented concepts. During the year, this same museum also staged a comprehensive exhibition of the works of Laszlo Moholy-Nagy, who had urged the formation of an impersonal, machine-oriented art in the decades between World Wars I and II.

Almost in contrast to this type of art was another strain of the avant-garde that encouraged outright acceptance of the new materials offered by technology.

Exhibitions in this category in 1969 included "Laser Light: A New Visual Art" at the Cincinnati (O.) Art Museum, "Art and Plastic" at the Milwaukee (Wis.) Art Center, and "Inflatable Sculpture" at New York's Jewish Museum. In Canada the Dan Flavin exhibition of "light situations" at the National Gallery in Ottawa pointed to the continuance of the museum's liberal exhibition policy. Meanwhile, the Vancouver (B.C.) Museum imported Seattle's concept art show and titled it "955,000," the population of Vancouver.

(A. S.; J. Kı.)

See also Art Exhibitions; Historic Buildings.

Music

At the end of 1968, Gilbert Amy, director of France's Domaine Musical, conducted a concert in London (November 20) with the BBC Symphony Orchestra in which he included several works of the French avant-garde—his own *Trajectoires,* Gérard Masson's *Dans le deuil des Vagues II,* and Jean Barraqué's Concerto for clarinet, vibraphone, and six instrumental groups. Two works had their London premieres in December—Hans Werner Henze's Second Piano Concerto (December 5) and Roberto Gerhard's Fourth Symphony. Also in December, the Cologne Course for New Music, a refresher course for composers very strongly influenced by Karlheinz Stockhausen, took place for the last time. At Athens the third Hellenic Week of Contemporary Music (December 15–22) included 16 premieres in its 12 programs, as well as many musical "happenings." Among the outstanding new works presented were Theodor Antoniou's *Climate of Absence* and *Katharsi* and Jani Christou's *Epicycle.*

The first performance of Stockhausen's *Stimmung,* a work for six voices, was given in Paris on December 9. The singers sat shoeless and cross-legged in a circle surrounded by the audience. The work included a part for tape recorder, audible only to the performers, which formed the base for 51 different "models," or pitch material, that succeeded one another in response to the composer's own "form-plan." The singers used a special type of voice production throughout. In addition to the models, the singers had a list of "magic names" which they intoned from time to time and integrated into the vowel patterns being made by the models.

In New York on Oct. 10, 1968, the New York Philharmonic gave the first performance of Luciano Berio's *Sinfonia,* conducted by the composer. The orchestra was joined by Les Swingles from Paris and by an electronic harpsichord and an electronic organ. The work used various texts in a colouristic and incantatory way, and there were also quotations from Bach and Beethoven and from Berio's contemporaries Stockhausen and Henri Pousseur. In November Colin Davis conducted the orchestra in a program of British music, including Elgar's First Symphony.

The first Dublin Festival of 20th-century music took place at the beginning of January 1969. Premieres included Gerard Schürmann's *Seven Studies of Francis Bacon,* Gerard Victory's *Kriegslieder,* a setting of six antiwar poems by August Stramm (a German poet killed in World War I), and Se'oirse Bodley's *String Quartet.* On January 14 the Royal Philharmonic Orchestra gave the first performance of William Mathias' First Symphony at London's Festival Hall.

MARC & EVELYNE BERNHEIM FROM RAPHO GUILLUMETTE

Above, new Juilliard School in Lincoln Center for the Performing Arts, New York City. Top, orchestra rehearses in the school's Alice Tully Hall for the dedicatory concert held Oct. 26, 1969.

An unusual event was held in January in Lebanon. At Jeita, near Beirut, an ancient gallery in the mountains, recently rediscovered, was opened to the public by a concert of electronic, concrete, and live music in the loftiest of several "halls." The most important work to be given was François Bayle's three-movement *Nadir* for three singers, three instruments (ondes martenot, bass clarinet, electric guitar), and tape.

On February 14, Hans Werner Henze was in London to conduct the first performance of his *Versuch über Schweinen,* a topical, occasional piece provoked by the reception of his previous work, *The Raft of Medusa.* A setting of a text by Gaston Salvatore, a young Chilean living in Berlin (the *"Schweinen"* of the title were rioting students, proudly flaunting the abusive epithet attached to them by police and bourgeoisie), it was composed for the English Chamber Orchestra, the Philip Jones Brass Ensemble, and Roy Hart, an extraordinary singer with a voice reputed to cover eight octaves. At the same concert, Henze's *Double-Bass Concerto* had its European premiere.

On February 5 in London's Festival Hall, Thea Musgrave's single-movement *Clarinet Concerto* was

LYNN PELHAM FROM RAPHO-GUILLUMETTE

Pablo Casals conducts a rehearsal at the 13th annual Festival Casals, held in Puerto Rico in June 1969.

"Schütz in the Round," a concert of three long settings of the Psalms, is performed by four choirs and four orchestras in St. Paul's Cathedral, London, Feb. 20, 1969.

"THE TIMES" (LONDON) FROM PICTORIAL PARADE

given its first performance by the BBC Symphony Orchestra, conducted by Colin Davis. Gervase de Peyer was soloist. Also in February, Harrison Birtwistle's *Verses for Ensembles* received its first performance, in the Queen Elizabeth Hall, from the London Sinfonietta, as did Oliver Knussen's *Pantomime* from the Melos Ensemble. At the Commonwealth Institute, Michael Ranta, from Illinois, introduced music by Harry Partch, a little-known U.S. composer.

At Palermo, Italy, the Settimana introduced several new works, among them Luigi Nono's *Contrappunto Dialettico,* Franco Donatoni's *Black and White No. 2,* Edison Denisov's *Ode,* Francesco Pennisi's *Choralis cum figuris,* John Cage's *Winter Music,* and Morton Feldman's *False Relationships and the Extended Ending.* In Detroit Ulysses Kay's *Scherzi Musicali* was given its premiere by the Princeton Chamber Orchestra.

Pierre Boulez (*see* BIOGRAPHY) conducted a series of 16 concerts with the New York Philharmonic in March (four programs each performed four times), including both classical and 20th-century works. On March 6 Hilde Somer gave the first performance of Alberto Ginastera's Piano Concerto no. 2 with the Indianapolis Symphony under Izler Solomon and, on March 11 in New York, Carlos Chávez conducted the Little Orchestra of New York in the premiere of his suite *Fuego Olimpico.*

Roger Smalley's *Transformations I* for piano and sine-wave generator was first performed in March at the City Music Society in London, and the Park Lane Group gave a concert of Roberto Gerhard's music to celebrate his 70th birthday. A concert marking Elliott Carter's 60th birthday was given in New York by Charles Rosen and a chamber group. Groupe de Recherches Musicales of the French Office de Radiodiffusion-Télévision Française (ORTF) gave two of the many electronic music concerts in London on March 5 and 7. The John Alldis Choir gave Justin Connolly's *Verse* its first performance in the Purcell Room on March 21. In New York the American Symphony Orchestra under Leopold Stokowski offered the first performance of Gian Carlo Menotti's *Triple Concerto* on March 10.

In April the ninth Easter Chamber Music Festival was held in Mittagong, near Sydney, Austr. The Sydney Symphony Orchestra, under Moshe Atzmon, gave a concert of modern music including new works by Nigel Butterley (*Pentad* for 27 wind instruments), Turo Takemitsu, and Peter Sculthorpe.

In April, London heard the first modern performance in public of Elgar's long-lost *Concert Allegro,* a substantial addition to the small Elgar piano literature, given by John Ogdon. There was a retrospective "exhibition" of John Cage's music in the Purcell Room (April 16). The centenary of Albert Roussel's birth was celebrated by a concert of his works for smaller groups at the Wigmore Hall, and Wilfred Josephs' Third Symphony had its premiere at the Festival Hall.

On May 2, Mayor John Lindsay of New York was the narrator in the first performance of Peter Mennin's *Pied Piper of Hamelin* at the Cincinnati May Festival. Leonard Bernstein ended his tenure as conductor of the New York Philharmonic on May 17 with a performance of Mahler's Third Symphony.

More than 150 works by 120 composers from some 24 countries were performed at the Zagreb, Yugos., Muzicki Biennale (May 7–18). The emphasis was on experiment and, in addition to local groups, there were contributions from the U.K.'s Pierrot Players, France's Domaine Musical, and the U.S. Sonic Arts group. The Cork International Choral Festival (April 30–May 4) included new pieces by A. J. Potter, Boris Blacher, and Malcolm Williamson. At London's Camden Festival, also in May, first performances included pieces by György Ligeti, Tim Souster, and Brian Dennis. Alexander Goehr's attractive *Konzertstück* for piano and orchestra had its first performance at the Brighton Festival. His *Naboth's Vineyard* was given by Music Theatre Ensemble in the same program as Walton's *Façade* and a new work by Birtwistle on May 8. In London, Benjamin Britten's *The Children's Crusade,* a setting of a poem by Bertolt Brecht, was given its first performance (St. Paul's Cathedral, May 19) by the Wandsworth School Boys' Choir. During May, Pierre Boulez conducted the London Symphony Orchestra at the Festival Hall in a series of five programs devoted to music by the second Viennese school: Mahler, Schoenberg, Berg, and Webern. He also directed the BBC Symphony Orchestra, of which he was conductor-elect, in a revised version of his own *Pli Selon Pli.*

The highlight of the Gulbenkian Festival at Lisbon in May and June was the first performance, on June 7, of Olivier Messiaen's full-scale oratorio *The Transfiguration,* a setting of Old and New Testament texts for a large orchestra and 100-voice choir. The seventh English Bach Festival (June–July)—something of a misnomer in view of the music presented—included works by the neglected Greek composer Nikos Skalkottas. The festival also included works by Berio, Peter Maxwell Davies, and Iannis Xenakis. The Bath Festival (June 12–29), under new management, held a series of "composer's choice" programs. The Aldeburgh Festival in June included the first performances of Gordon Crosse's opera *The Grace of Todd; The World Is Charged with the Grandeur of God* by Sir Arthur Bliss; Oliver Knussen's *Fire,* a capriccio for flute and string trio; and Britten's *Tit for Tat,* settings of poems by Walter de la Mare. At the York Festival (June 20–July 13) there were new pieces from Maxwell Davies, Wilfrid Mellers, and Richard Orton, as well as an evening of experimental works by Cornelius Cardew, Morton Feldman, and Earle Browne.

The Holland Festival (June 15–July 9) featured the premiere of the semiopera *Reconstruction* with contributions from no less than five composers. On June 10, at the Vienna Festival, Josef Krips directed a performance of Schoenberg's *Gurrelieder.* London premieres during June included Roger Smalley's *Pulses 5 & 4,* Robert Sherlaw Johnson's *The Resur-*

rection of Feng-Huang, and Roberto Gerhard's *Audiomobile no. 2.* At the Cheltenham Festival (July 4–13) there were new works by Alun Hoddinott, Maxwell Davies, and Lennox Berkeley. On July 16, at London's Festival Hall, the London Sinfonietta presented the first performance of John Tavener's *Celtic Requiem,* based on the Requiem Mass, Irish poetry, and children's singing games.

The 23rd Edinburgh Festival (August 24–September 13) concentrated on modern Italian music by Gian Francesco Malipiero, Goffredo Petrassi, Luigi Nono, Luigi Dallapiccola, Niccolo Castaglione, and Franco Donatoni. At the 43rd annual Festival of the International Society for Contemporary Music in Hamburg, W.Ger., 33 works from 14 countries were given, including Heinz Holliger's *Siebengesang,* Kazimierz Serocki's *Continuum,* and Mauricio Kagel's *Halleluja.* South Bank Summer Music at London's Queen Elizabeth Hall in August included a survey of Schoenberg's chamber works, as well as lieder programs with Dietrich Fischer-Dieskau and Janet Baker and classical chamber music. Daniel Barenboim masterminded the season and appeared in most of the programs.

At the Promenade Concerts at London's Albert Hall in August and September, new works included Hugh Wood's Cello Concerto and Maxwell Davies' *Worldes Blis* (a motet for orchestra based on a 13th-century English monody). The season began with Berlioz' *Requiem* conducted by Colin Davis, who also directed a concert performance of the same composer's *Béatrice et Bénédict*—all part of the celebrations of the centenary of Berlioz' death.

Other festivals of importance included those at Dubrovnik, Yugos. (July 10–August 25), Lucerne, Switz. (August 13–September 7; mostly regular repertory), Barcelona (September 26–November 1; new music), Montreux, France (August 29–October 5), Israel (August 3–September 1), and Shiraz-Persepolis, Iran (August 28–September 8).

Opera. Administrative changes during 1969 included the appointment of Wolfgang Sawallisch as musical director of the Bavarian State Opera; Vaclav Neumann as musical director and Wolfgang Windgassen as artistic director of the Würtemburg (W.Ger.) State Opera; Herbert Kegel as musical director of the Dresden (E.Ger.) State Opera; Heinrich Reif-Gintl as director of the Vienna State Opera; and John Pritchard as musical director of Glyndebourne, Eng. The 1969–70 season of the Metropolitan Opera, New York, was delayed for three months by a strike.

United States. In November 1968, D. F. E. Auber's *Fra Diavolo* was produced at San Francisco and Wagner's *Das Rheingold,* conducted and produced by Herbert von Karajan, at the Metropolitan. The New York City Opera produced Borodin's *Prince Igor* in February 1969. On September 26 the Chicago Lyric Opera opened its season with a new production of Mussorgsky's *Khovanshchina,* with Nicholai Ghiaurov as Prince Ivan. The New York City Opera began with new productions of Arrigo Boito's *Mefistofele* and *Lucia di Lammermoor.* At the San Francisco Opera on October 11 there was a new production of *Götterdämmerung.*

United Kingdom. In January, *Die Meistersinger von Nürnberg* was produced at the Royal Opera House, Covent Garden, in London. Humphrey Searle's *Hamlet* received its first performance in the U.K. at Covent Garden on April 18. Unfortunately it was not repeated because of the indisposition of the Canadian baritone Victor Braun, who was singing the main role. On May 3 at Glasgow, the first complete performance of Berlioz' *Les Troyens* ever given was performed by Scottish Opera. Janet Baker caused a sensation in the role of Dido. Birgit Nilsson returned to Covent Garden on May 8 to sing the title role in Richard Strauss's *Elektra,* with Georg Solti conducting.

Elena Suliotis appeared at Covent Garden in Verdi's *Macbeth* (June 26), with Kostas Paskalis in the title role. The Glyndebourne Festival (May 25–August 10) included a new production of *Così fan tutte* and an outstanding revival of Debussy's *Pelléas et Mélisande.* At the Aldeburgh Festival, Mozart's *Idomeneo* was staged in a makeshift performance in Blythburgh Church, with Britten conducting, after fire destroyed the Maltings. In August, Sadler's Wells presented Michael Geliot's new production of Berlioz' *The Damnation of Faust,* conducted by Charles Mackerras, who was appointed musical director of Sadler's Wells during the year. On September 17, Covent Garden unveiled Minos Volanakis' lavish new production of *Les Troyens,* conducted by Colin Davis.

West Germany. At Düsseldorf the Deutsche Opera am Rhein presented Verdi's *Les Vêpres Siciliennes*

MICHAEL MOUCHETTE

Scene from the opera "The Devils of Loudun" by Krzysztof Penderecki, performed for the first time in the U.S. in 1969 by the Santa Fe Opera Company.

(December 1968). Another new production was *Der Ring des Nibelungen* by Günther Rennert at the National Theatre, Munich. In March 1969 the Hamburg State Opera gave the first performance of Lars Johan Werle's *Die Reise.* Bernd Alois Zimmermann's *Die Soldaten,* an avant-garde work, received its most successful production to that time on March 23 at Munich. George Balanchine was in charge of a new production of Glinka's *Ruslan and Ludmila,* presented at the Hamburg State Opera on March 30 with Charles Mackerras conducting. At Frankfurt on May 10, Anja Silja sang Renata in a new production of Prokofiev's *The Fiery Angel.* The Hamburg State Opera gave the first performance of Krzysztof Penderecki's *The Devils of Loudun* on June 21, but most commentators preferred Rennert's Stuttgart production given two days later. At the Munich Festival (July 12–August 5), *Les Vêpres Siciliennes* had its Munich premiere in a German translation. Rennert also produced Richard Strauss's *Adriadne auf Naxos.*

At Bayreuth (July 25–August 28) the new production was August Everding's *Der fliegende Holländer,* the first production by a nonmember of the Wagner family since 1951. The outstanding performances, however, were those of Birgit Nilsson and Wolfgang Windgassen in *Tristan und Isolde*.

In September the Cologne Opera gave a new production of Mozart's *La clemenza di Tito,* which was subsequently seen in London at Sadler's Wells during the Cologne company's week-long season there. The Berlin Festival opened on September 25 with Boris Blacher's new opera, *Zweihunderttausen Taler,* conducted by Lorin Maazel.

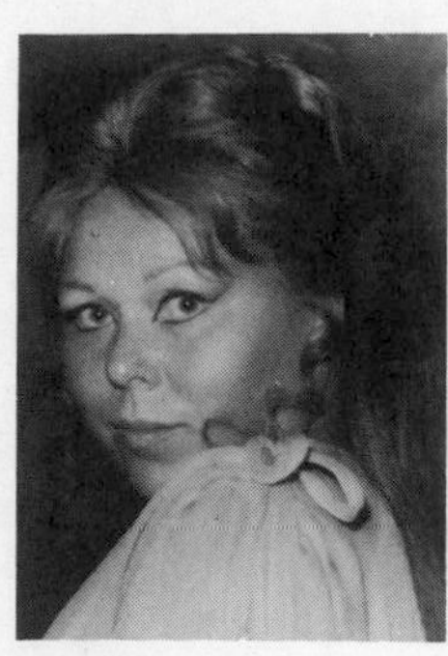

Renata Scotto as Gilda in the Edinburgh Festival performance of Verdi's "Rigoletto" in September 1969.

Austria. Alban Berg's *Lulu* was produced at the Vienna State Opera in December 1968, with Anja Silja in the title role. At Vienna in February 1969, the Volksoper produced *Fra Diavolo* and the Kammeroper gave Puccini's *La Rondine.* Luchino Visconti's new production of Verdi's *Simon Boccanegra* at the Vienna State Opera (March 28) was considered eccentric. On March 30 *Siegfried* was produced at the Salzburg Easter Festival. The centenary celebrations of the Vienna State Opera ended on May 26 with Mozart's *Don Giovanni,* conducted by Joseph Krips. At the Salzburg Festival (July 26–August 30) Böhm conducted *Der Rosenkavalier,* produced by Rudolf Hartmann. Jean-Pierre Ponnelle produced *Così fan tutte* and Herbert Graf resuscitated Emilio de'Cavalieri's sacred drama *La Rappresentazione di anima e di corpo* (1600). The Vienna State Opera gave a new production of *Dalibor* on October 19, with Leonie Rysanek and Ludovic Spiess.

Italy. In December 1968 there was a new production of *Ernani* at La Scala, Milan. Renata Scotto inaugurated the 1968–69 Teatro Massimo season at Palermo with a fine performance in Bellini's rarely performed *La Straniera.* She had a further success at the Edinburgh Festival in September when she appeared with the Florence Opera company as Gilda in *Rigoletto*—a success equal to that of her *Lucia di Lammermoor* in the Scala company's 1964 Moscow season at the Bolshoi. She was described by one distinguished British critic as being "unique among the younger generation of Italian operatic sopranos."

In January, Luigi Dallapiccola's *Ulisse* had its Italian premiere at La Scala. Also in January, Wagner's *Rienzi* was produced at the Teatro dell'Opera, Rome, and in February, Gian Francisco Malipiero's new opera, *Gli Eroi di Bonaventura,* had its premiere at the Piccola Scala. Ildebrando Pizzetti's *Clitennestra* was revived at Rome. Franco Mannino's *Luisella* had its premiere at Palermo in February. At La Scala, on April 11, Rossini's *L'assedio di Corinto* was given a new production, with Beverly Sills (*see* BIOGRAPHY) and Marilyn Horne in the main roles. The conductor was another American, Thomas Schippers. The Maggio Musicale at Florence (May 2–June 28) included a new production of *Fidelio* with Sena Jurinac and Verdi's *Aida* with Virginia Zeani, both conducted by Zubin Mehta. Georg Reinhardt produced Schoenberg's *Moses und Aron,* the third production of the opera in Italy.

Don Carlo was produced by Jean Vilar at the 47th Verona Summer Festival (July 16–August 17). There were also productions of *Turandot* (with Nilsson) and *Aida.* Besides *Rigoletto,* the Florence Opera brought three programs to the Edinburgh Festival (August 24–September 13): Malipiero's *Setto Canzoni* in a double bill with Dallapiccola's *Il Prigionero,* Donizetti's *Maria Stuarda* (with Leyla Gencer and Shirley Verrett), and Puccini's *Gianni Schicchi,* produced by Tito Gobbi with himself in the title role.

France. In December 1968 the Paris Opéra gave *La Damnation de Faust,* in Maurice Béjart's famous production. On Oct. 3, 1969, the Opéra-Comique in Paris gave the first performance of Henri Sauguet's one-act *La Gageure imprévue.*

Other Operatic Events. At the Teatro Colón, Buenos Aires, Arg., there was a new production of *Norma* on June 21, with Joan Sutherland. A complete cycle of Janacek's operas was presented at the Prague (Czech.) Festival in the spring. Henri Rabaud's *Marouf* was produced in January at La Monnaie in Brussels. (A. G. BL.)

Jazz. Without question, the 1960s had been the most crucial and revolutionary decade in jazz history. Many times in the past, particularly in the 1940s, the music had undergone convulsions that threatened to destroy its coherence, but only in the past few years had the music experienced the wholesale rejection of formal logic practiced by the new generation of improvisers. For some years the realization that making variations on a given set of harmonies was a finite art had nagged at the jazz soloist, but the free-form movement of the 1960s was less a solution than the denial of a need for one.

Whereas in all previous eras the jazz musician followed, however deviously, the iron laws of discord and resolution, by 1969 this practice had been replaced among the younger players by the "freakout," a process whereby each member of an ensemble played whatever came into his head and under his fingers, in the hope that the accumulative results might win for the music a new innocence. The fact that this approach was in some ways the musical equivalent of the six monkeys at the six typewriters did not deter its practitioners, who brought to their new methods a fierce dialectical justification that had the all too predictable effect of splitting the already fissiparous jazz world into even tinier splinters.

An added complication was the fact that much of the new jazz was so deeply involved with the philosophy of self-assertion, symbolized by the Black Power movement, that there were moments when criticism of the music was interpreted, quite wrongly, as a criticism of the political attitudes of the players. The problem was, of course, new only insofar as jazz was concerned. The spectacle of the committed artist was common enough, and the "new thing" in jazz only underlined the truth that art committed to a worthy cause is not necessarily worthy art.

It was this situation of violent turmoil and destructive reasoning that caused older musicians and commentators to wonder whether they were not perhaps witnessing the dissolution of the music, and to cling to the steadily decreasing examples of conventional mastery with renewed fervour. Because jazz was still a comparatively new art form, many of its founding fathers had remained active throughout its history, and the fate through 1969 of its three most dominant figures, Duke Ellington, Louis Armstrong, and Coleman Hawkins, perhaps served as an allegory of the future of the music itself.

By 1969 it was no longer possible to pretend that Louis Armstrong still retained the powers of genius that had enabled him to enrich the jazz tradition so prolifically. Reduced in effectiveness by illness and age, Armstrong in 1969 bore little resemblance to the trumpeter of even ten years before. He spent prolonged periods of the year in the hospital, and in spite of a popular vocal triumph with "Wonderful World," could no longer be regarded as an effective force.

Coleman Hawkins, who had literally invented the processes of playing jazz on the tenor saxophone, was perhaps an even more potent symbol than Armstrong, because he had retained much of his old resource into the 1960s. His physical decline horrified the jazz world, however, and it was no surprise when, after a lifetime of barnstorming all over the world playing superlative jazz, Hawkins died in New York City in May at the age of 65. (*See* OBITUARIES.) Perhaps the most eloquent testimony to his greatness was the fact that his recorded masterpieces of the 1930s, "Stardust," "Body and Soul," "Out of Nowhere," and dozens of others, still stood as magnificent examples of the jazz art, classical form draped in the dazzling colours of Hawkins' highly subjective, passionate romanticism.

For Duke Ellington, 1969 was the year of apotheosis as a remarkable career entered its sixth decade. In April, Ellington's 70th birthday was marked by tributes and celebratory concerts all over the world, a reception at the White House, and a bland denial by Ellington that he was old at all. For the moment the Ellington orchestra remained what it had been since 1927, an exquisite musical keyboard on which its leader produced fragments of impressionistic music that might yet oblige posterity to measure their intrinsic worth by standards broader than those associated with the tight little island of jazz.

The year saw many other important successes of a conventional kind. The rapid advance of the European-based and multinational Kenny Clarke-Francy Boland band was impressive proof that jazz in 1969 was less a local American dialect than an international musical language. The vibraphonist Gary Burton, still in his 20s, continued to flit back and forth between jazz and pop without ever diluting the intensity of his jazz gifts, while the older modernists, especially Miles Davis, showed no diminution of their ability. Perhaps the greatest shock of the year was the sudden apostasy of the saxophonist Stan Getz. For many years the supreme master of romantic improvisation, executed through a staggering technique and an ice-cool brain, Getz in his 1969 performances served notice that he intended to follow the younger players in their rejection of conventional methods.

Perhaps the crowning irony in a year of bewildering turbulence was the fact that the Newport Jazz Festival, for many years the great state occasion of jazz, was replaced as the most important event in the calendar by London's "Jazz Expo." While Newport succumbed more and more to the pressures of pop music, "Jazz Expo"—extended to eight days and involving more than 120 musicians, most of them American—demonstrated that an enormous body of people believed jazz to be one of the most vital and stimulating of all musical forms. (B. GR.)

Popular. If 1968 was the year of rock 'n' roll and revivals, 1969 followed with splits, supergroups, and self-consciousness. The noisy infant born in 1954 and christened rock 'n' roll was now 15 years old and changed almost beyond recognition.

For many of the British boom groups, 1969 marked the end of the line. Splits occurred everywhere: the Hollies lost Graham Nash, the Bee Gees decreased by degrees from five to two, and many other groups disbanded altogether. Even the Rolling Stones were affected, replacing Brian Jones with Mick Taylor; but this had nothing to do with the tragedy of a few weeks later, when Brian Jones was drowned in his swimming pool.

Mass disbandment led to ex-group members joining up in what were popularly termed supergroups. A typical example was Blind Faith, consisting of Stevie Winwood (ex-Traffic), Eric Clapton and Ginger Baker (ex-Cream), and Rick Grech (ex-Family). This was a true "supergroup," since its members were excellent musicians. However, the term came to be used to describe almost any re-formed group, such as Humble Pie which tried its best to reject it.

THE "NEW YORK TIMES" FROM WIDE WORLD

A crowd of 300,000 swarms around the stage at the Woodstock Music and Art Fair near Bethel, N.Y., on Aug. 16, 1969. Massive traffic jams, rain, food and water shortages accompanied performances by Joan Baez, Ravi Shankar, Jimi Hendrix, and the Jefferson Airplane.

Blind Faith made its much-publicized debut in June, in London's Hyde Park, where 150,000 people heard it for free. Free concerts in the park had been launched the previous year by Blackhill Enterprises; 1969 saw them well established, with Blind Faith and later the Rolling Stones drawing audiences of nearly half a million. The music heard at these concerts was of the "underground" genre. Originated on the U.S. West Coast, it was highly experimental and sought to transcend popular appeal and bring pop to the status of art. Beginning as the music of the hippies, it soon emerged into the daylight and became a huge commercial success. At worst it was pretentious and obscure, but the best was very fine indeed. Groups such as Deep Purple displayed genuine musicianship, and audiences, instead of rushing the stage, sat still and listened—a far cry from the days of Beatlemania.

Experiments in combining styles led to the breaking of musical barriers, and groups became more individual in style, making classification difficult. A favourite term was "heavy," used to describe the music of groups such as Led Zeppelin: simple in form, slow in pace, and massive in volume.

While the underground was preoccupied with experiment, the more commercial groups were returning to simple rock, led by the Beatles' April single, "Get Back." Despite the teething troubles of their Apple organization, the Beatles remained trend setters, and their double album became a best seller despite lukewarm reviews. John Lennon married Japanese artist Yoko Ono, and their story was told from the chart tops in "The Ballad of John and Yoko." There were rumours of the Beatles' giving a live show, but this never materialized; instead they produced another LP, "Abbey Road" (named after the location of EMI's studios). A macabre aftermath was the widespread rumour that Paul McCartney was dead and that "Abbey Road" contained clues to this fact, but McCartney vigorously denied it.

On the business side, the pattern of record sales

KEN REGAN—CAMERA 5

Returning to personal appearances for the first time since a motorcycle accident in 1966, Bob Dylan appeared in the Isle of Wight pop festival in August 1969.

was changing: singles were selling less, while album figures rose rapidly. Increasing emphasis was being placed on the LP, which was a natural medium for pop song cycles (The Moody Blues), works for group and orchestra (Deep Purple), and jazz-like extemporization. Still, good singles did appear: "Get Back," the Stones' "Honky Tonk Women," and Joe South's "Games People Play." Many of the year's most successful singles were rereleases. Tamla Motown did particularly well in this line, headed by the Isley Brothers' "This Old Heart of Mine" (first released in 1966).

Of the newcomers, one of the most promising was Peter Sarstedt, whose "Where Do You Go To, My Lovely" held the British number one position for most of March. On the female side the brightest new star was Mary Hopkin, the Beatles' Welsh protegée, who made a 1930s song, "Those Were the Days," a 1960s standard. She was nominated as the U.K. entrant in the 1970 Eurovision Song Contest. The 1969 contest in Madrid ended with four countries, France, the Netherlands, Spain, and the U.K.—represented by Lulu with "Boom bang-a-bang" (a song calculated to break through language barriers)—sharing first place. Another chart-topper that broke the language barrier was Jane Birkin's and Serge Gainsbourg's "Je t'aime . . . moi non plus," which gained notoriety by having its lyrics banned by the BBC.

Irish singer Clodagh Rogers and the Scottish group Marmalade made the charts after a long struggle, and U.S. artists Glen Campbell and the Fifth Dimension found British success. Tom Jones drew capacity audiences in cabarets in the U.S. Elvis Presley and Bob Dylan returned to live performance—Presley in Las Vegas, Dylan at the Isle of Wight pop festival.

Of considerable importance was the invasion of the theatre by pop, in the shape of the musical *Hair* and its numerous imitators. Premiered in New York City in 1968 and coming to Britain in the autumn, *Hair* was a great success on both sides of the Atlantic. Cast LP's became best sellers, and songs from the show provided hits for numerous artists.

Hair apart, 1969 saw a great calming down of pop; musicians were mellowed by experience, and fans had also matured. Pop had at last become respectable—a fact that, inevitably, meant the beginning of the end; pop was growing away from entertainment toward art. Whether it would retain its individuality was uncertain; pop and jazz were becoming increasingly interactive. Only one thing seemed sure: rock had run its course, and all the pop scene could do was wait until something completely new appeared to begin the cycle all over again. (H. R. Mo.)

Folk Music. An important event of 1969 was the 20th Conference of the International Folk Music Council, held at Edinburgh, August 6–13, by invitation of the School of Scottish Studies of the University of Edinburgh. Delegates from more than 30 countries attended. The themes of the conference were "Folk Music in a Bilingual Community," "Folk Music in Twentieth Century Composition," and "The Contribution of Films in the Study and Practice of Folk Dance and Instrumental Folk Music." In addition, there were meetings of representatives of radio and television organizations in which profitable discussions took place on methods of increasing interest in folk music among young people.

The academic study of folk music continued to develop in many countries, particularly in the U.S. where some 40 universities and colleges were offering courses in folk music or ethnomusicology. An *International Film Catalogue of Folk Music and Dance and Associated Customs* was compiled by the International Folk Music Council under the auspices of UNESCO. The cataloging and indexing of folk music collections, both manuscripts and recordings, played a prominent part in the work of many national institutions. Particularly noteworthy were the Romanian Institute of Ethnography and Folklore, the Irish Folklore Commission, and the School of Scottish Studies at Edinburgh, all of which had large collections. Many national and regional surveys were compiled and published, notably in the Eastern European countries.

Most important of all was the great increase in fieldwork being carried out in many parts of the world. UNESCO sponsored a much needed expedition to record peasant melodies in India, where little research had been done. Side by side with the collecting, there was an increase in the number of records and films published. The International Folk Music Council began a World Anthology of Folk Music Records, of which the first was *The Folk Music of Scotland.*

The countries of Africa showed an increasing appreciation of their rich heritage of folk music and dance. In Ghana the Arts Council organized national and regional folk-music events, while in Zambia the Cultural Services and Arts Trust were responsible for the formation of folk-music clubs in all parts of the country. A series of lectures on African music was organized by the Royal Anthropological Institute of Great Britain and Ireland.

The growing practice of folk song and dance was carried on in private circles, in clubs, and in public festivals. Radio and television were an important factor in encouraging knowledge and appreciation of folk music.

Publications included *Hebridean Folksongs: A Collection of Waulking Songs* by J. L. Campbell; *Anglo-American Folksong Style* by Roger A. Abrahams and George Foss; *Dance and Song Rituals of Six Nations Reserve, Ontario* by Gertrude Prokosch Kurath; and *Music in Aztec and Inca Territory* by Robert Stevenson. (Ma. Ka.)

See also Cinema; Dance; Television and Radio; Theatre.

Encyclopædia Britannica Films. *Listening to Good Music (The String Quartet)* (1955); *Playing Good Music (The String Quartet)* (1955); *The Brass Choir* (1956); *Conducting Good Music* (1956); *The Percussion Group* (1956); *The String Choir* (1956); *The Symphony Orchestra* (1956); *The Woodwind Choir* (1956); *Casals Conducts, 1964* (1965).

Narcotics: *see* Medicine

National Guard: *see* Defense

National Incomes: *see* Income, National

National Parks: *see* Parks

Natural Fibres: *see* Agriculture; Industrial Review

Naturalization: *see* Migration, International

Nauru

An island republic in the Pacific Ocean, Nauru lies about 1,200 mi. E of New Guinea. Area: 8.2 sq.mi. (21 sq.km.). Pop. (1969 est.): 6,516. President in 1969, Hammer de Roburt.

Late in 1968 Nauru became a member of the Commonwealth of Nations in a new associate category, which conferred full membership benefits except membership in the Prime Ministers' Conference. Nauru was also promised membership in the South Pacific Commission. Commenting on the nation's first year of independence, Pres. Hammer de Roburt said that merely to survive, without major difficulties, was progress.

NAURU
Education. (1966) Primary, pupils 1,298, teachers 79; secondary, pupils 317, teachers 19; teacher training (1965), students 15, teachers 1.
Finance and Trade. Monetary unit: Australian dollar (A$0.89 = U.S. $1; A$2.14 = £1 sterling). Budget (1965–66): revenue A$940,704; expenditure A$1,778,214. Foreign trade (1965–66): imports A$6,366,248 (82% from Australia, 7% from U.K., 7% from New Zealand); exports (phosphates) A$8,659,472 (54% to Australia, 34% to New Zealand, 12% to U.K., by tonnage).
Industry. Production (in 000): phosphate rock (metric tons; 1966–67) 1,806; electricity (kw-hr.; 1967) 17,300.

The republic's greatest difficulties concerned phosphate development. After independence the Nauru Phosphate Corporation (NPC) was set up to take over from the British Phosphate Commission (BPC). In June de Robúrt led discussions on Nauru's claim that it ought to sell phosphate directly to Australian manufacturers, in addition to renewing a contract with BPC, which handled the importation of Australian phosphate under a pool marketing arrangement. The 1969 BPC price for phosphate was A$11 ($9.80) a ton, but during the year Nauru was able to sell 300,000 tons to Japan at A$14 ($12.40) a ton.

By an agreement signed in Canberra, Austr., on September 17, the Australian airline, Qantas, was to operate from Australia to Nauru, while the Nauruan airline would fly between Nauru and Brisbane.

(A. R. G. G.)

Nepal

A constitutional monarchy of Asia, Nepal is in the Himalayas between India and Tibet. Area: 54,362 sq.mi. (140,797 sq.km.). Pop. (1968 est.): 10,651,626. Cap. and largest city: Kathmandu (pop., 1968, 137,400). Language: Nepali (official); also Newari and Bhutia. Religion: Hindu 85%; Buddhist 8%; Muslim 2%. King, Mahendra Bir Bikram Shah Deva; chairmen of the Council of Ministers (prime ministers) in 1969, Surya Bahadur Thapa and, from April 7, Kirti Nidhi Bista.

Locked between India and China geographically, strategically, and economically, Nepal was relying greatly on its improved communications. In 1969 for the first time jets flew twice a week between Kathmandu and Thailand. Progress was made on the Asian Highway linking Afghanistan and Nepal. The Mahendra Highway across Nepal, being built by the U.S.S.R., the U.S., the U.K., and India, was nearing completion; it would permit trade, for the first time, to remain on the trans-Nepalese route without making use of Indian railways. In December 1968, India agreed to undertake a survey for the improvement of the 60-km. railway between Raxaul and Hithoda. Chinese engineers, after completing the road from Kathmandu to Kodari, were building a 176-km. mountain road linking Kathmandu with Pokhara.

In the face of pressure from both India and China, Nepal remained sensitive about its neutrality. When India's minister of external affairs, Dinesh Singh, visited Kathmandu in June he stressed Nepal's "special relationship" with India. The Nepalese government promptly reasserted its sovereignty by demanding the withdrawal of Indian radio operators from checkpoints on the Tibetan border and of the 23-man Indian military liaison group. Nepal also announced that it had canceled its 1965 arms agreement with India. During this period of diplomatic coolness between the two countries, the Chinese ambassador, who had been recalled in June 1967, returned to Kathmandu. India agreed in September to the withdrawal of Indian contingents, but reports indicated that talks aimed at providing new arrangements had been inconclusive.

In March new rules for mountaineering expeditions were announced, placing greater emphasis on the maintenance of Nepalese security. In April unrest was reported from western villages. Reports indicated that as many as 50 peasants were killed in disturbances occasioned by the maladministration of land taxes intended to improve farming methods.

The release from detention in October 1968 of B. P. Koirala and other Nepali Congress Party leaders did not bring political stability. The king still considered the system of building democracy from the village council (*panchayat*) level indispensable, despite some student dissatisfaction. Kirti Nidhi Bista, who succeeded Surya Bahadur Thapa as prime minister on April 7, strengthened the royalist membership of the Cabinet and suspended the controversial land taxes. Student disturbances in Kathmandu and Biratnagar indicated that Nepal's feudalistic society was feeling the stresses of its slow but inevitable entry into the modern world.

(D. Wn.)

NEPAL
Education. (1965–66) Primary, pupils 386,100, teachers 13,400; secondary, pupils 57,440, teachers 3,280; vocational (1964–65), pupils 1,785, teachers 70; teacher training (1964–65), students 428, teachers 55; higher (including 1 university), students 8,100, teaching staff 565.
Finance. Monetary unit: Nepalese rupee, with a par value of NRs. 10.12 to U.S. $1 (NRs. 24.30 = £1 sterling; NRs. 1.35 = Indian Rs. 1). Gold and foreign exchange, central bank: (June 1969) U.S. $74.3 million; (June 1968) U.S. $58.4 million. Budget (1968–69): revenue NRs. 641 million (including NRs. 276 million foreign aid); expenditure NRs. 667 million (including NRs. 458.4 million development expenditure).
Foreign Trade. (1968) Imports NRs. 395 million (88% from India in 1963–64); exports NRs. 290.6 million (93% to India in 1963–64). Main exports (1964–65): food and livestock 59%; crude materials (including timber and jute) 26%; manufactures 11%.
Agriculture. Production (in 000; metric tons): rice (1968) 2,322, (1967) 2,217; jute (1967) *c.* 38, (1966) 38. Livestock (in 000; 1966–67): cattle *c.* 2,910; pigs *c.* 190; sheep 2,000; goats 2,250.

Netherlands

A kingdom of northwest Europe on the North Sea, the Netherlands, a Benelux country, is bounded by Belgium on the south and West Germany on the east. Overseas parts of the realm comprise the Netherlands Antilles and Surinam. Area: 14,139 sq.mi. (36,621 sq.km.). Pop. (1969 est.): 12,798,346. Cap. and largest city: Amsterdam (pop., 1969 est., 845,821). Language: Netherlandic (Dutch). Religion (1960): Roman Catholic 40.4%; Dutch Reformed 28.3%; Reformed Churches 9.3%. Queen, Juliana; prime minister in 1969, Piet J. S. de Jong.

The composition of the government in 1969 remained at six members of the Catholic People's Party, three members of the People's Party for Freedom and Democracy (Liberals), three members of the Anti-

Navies: *see* Defense

COURTESY, N.V. NEDERLANDS CONGRESGEBOUW

Main hall of the 11-ac. convention and civic centre, Nederland Congresgebouw, which opened officially in The Hague on March 14, 1969. Every other row of seats in the front area of the main hall can be converted to tables for large conferences.

revolutionary Party, and two members of the Christian Historical Union. Thirteen parties were represented in Parliament. On July 2 the upper house was elected by the members of the provincial states. The new house was composed as follows: Catholic People's Party, 24; Labour Party, 20; People's Party for Freedom and Democracy, 8; Antirevolutionary Party, 7; Christian Historical Union, 8; Pacifist Socialist Party, 3; Farmers' Party, 3; Communists, 1; and Political Party Radicals, 1.

Queen Juliana opened the new session of Parliament on September 16. In her speech from the throne she said that the government would promote democratization of education, of culture, and of enterprise. The budget for 1970, presented by the finance minister, Hendrik J. Witteveen, estimated an income of 26,772,000,000 guilders. Total expenditure in 1970, 6% higher than in 1969, was estimated at 28,965,000,000 guilders. Aid to less developed countries was to be increased by 135 million guilders to 767 million guilders, of which 175 million guilders were to go to Surinam and the Netherlands Antilles.

Economic developments in early 1969 were rather unbalanced. The introduction on January 1 of a new system of purchase tax, the value-added tax, caused a rapid rise in prices. At the end of March the price index for family consumption had risen by 5.5%. On April 8 the government announced a general price freeze, which was revoked on September 4, The Central Planbureau announced in its March 14 report that it expected further price and wage rises in 1969 and 1970.

The general economic situation was analyzed by the president of the Netherlands Bank, Jelle Zijlstra, in his report of April 29. Although he considered the improvement in productivity and employment gratifying, he warned of the danger of continued inflation. Productivity had risen by 10% and wages by 7% over 1968. The running account of the balance of payments showed a surplus of 253 million guilders. The 1968 export volume was 15.5% higher than in 1967 and the import volume, 12.5% higher.

New industrial mergers took place in 1969, most attention being drawn to that between AKU (General Rayon Union) and Koninklijke Zout-Organon (chemicals). In late October it was announced that a rich potassium deposit had been discovered in the province of Groningen. Some years previously one of the world's greatest natural gas fields had been discovered in the same area and exploited commercially.

The execution of the Delta Project (the closing of the sea arms in the southwestern part of the country) continued throughout 1969. On April 28 the Volkerak, a sea arm between the isle of Overflakkee and the province of Noordbrabant, was closed. On July 22 the opening of a tunnel under the Oude Maas River near Heineoord completed a high road across the Delta area from Rotterdam to Zealand. In the northern part of the country a new project of land reclamation that would add about 23,000 ac. to the Netherlands was started by the closing of the Lauwers Zee. The last of 25 caissons were sunk in the presence of Queen Juliana on May 23. These caissons had a total length of 900 m., a record for this method of dike building.

On July 28 the Netherlands withdrew from the multi-role combat aircraft 75 (MRCA-75) project, in which West Germany, Italy, and the U.K. were also participating in order to develop an aircraft to replace the Starfighter F-104G. Defense Minister Willem den Toom said the MRCA-75 did not satisfy Dutch operational demands and was too expensive. In reaction to the August 1968 invasion of Czechoslovakia by the U.S.S.R., the government decided in November 1968 to increase military expenditures for 1969–72 by 225 million guilders. In March the govern-

NETHERLANDS

Education. (1966–67) Primary, pupils 1,418,665, teachers 45,634; secondary, pupils 537,306, teachers (1965–66) 27,954; vocational, pupils 562,363; teacher training, students 12,780; higher (including 9 universities), students 163,213.

Finance. Monetary unit: guilder or florin, with a par value of 3.62 guilders to U.S. $1 (8.69 guilders = £1 sterling). Gold and foreign exchange, central bank: (June 1969) U.S. $1,965,000,000; (June 1968) U.S. $1,922,000,000. Budget (1969 est.): revenue 27,363,000,000 guilders; expenditure 30,101,000,000 guilders. Gross national product: (1968) 91,330,000,000 guilders; (1967) 82,970,000,000 guilders. Money supply: (May 1969) 23,080,000,000 guilders; (May 1968) 20,920,000,000 guilders. Cost of living (1963 = 100): (June 1969) 134; (June 1968) 124.

Foreign Trade. (1968) Imports 33,639,000,000 guilders; exports 30,199,000,000 guilders. Import sources: EEC 55% (West Germany 26%, Belgium-Luxembourg 18%, France 6%, Italy 5%); U.S. 11%; U.K. 5%. Export destinations: EEC 57% (West Germany 28%, Belgium-Luxembourg 14%, France 11%, Italy 5%); U.K. 9%; U.S. 5%. Main exports: chemicals 13%; electrical machinery 9%; machinery (nonelectrical) 7%; textile yarns and fabrics 7%; meat products 6%; petroleum products 6%.

Transport and Communications. Roads (1968) 75,163 km. (including 790 km. expressways). Motor vehicles in use (1968): passenger 2,073,450; commercial 311,522. Railways: (1967) 3,227 km. (including 1,642 km. electrified): traffic (1968) 7,337,000,000 passenger-km., freight 3,273,000,000 net ton-km. Air traffic (1967): 4,310,616,000 passenger-km.; freight 260,556,000 net ton-km. Navigable inland waterways (1967) 6,017 km. (including 2,491 km. for ships of 1,000 tons and over); freight traffic 28,395,000,000 ton-km. Shipping (1968): merchant vessels 100 gross tons and over 1,721; gross tonnage 5,267,681. Ships entered (1967) vessels totaling 93,187,000 net registered tons; goods loaded (1968) 40,687,000 metric tons, unloaded 150,310,000 metric tons. Telephones (Dec. 1967) 2,718,792. Radio receivers (Dec. 1967) 3,154,000. Television receivers (June 1967) 2,481,000.

Agriculture. Production (in 000; metric tons; 1968; 1967 in parentheses): wheat 679 (739); rye 239 (239); barley 389 (447); oats 321 (356); potatoes 5,045 (4,840); tomatoes 343 (346); apples *c.* 359 (480); sugar, raw value (1968–69) 720, (1967–68) 750; dry peas 36 (48); rapeseed 18 (15); linseed 14 (11); flax fibre 19 (13); beef and veal 284 (275); pork 593 (529); cow's milk 7,791 (7,535); butter *c.* 119 (99); cheese *c.* 246 (269); hen eggs 223 (217); fish catch (1967) 315, (1966) 353. Livestock (in 000; May 1968): pigs 4,683; cattle 4,116; sheep 550; horses used in agriculture 115; chickens (May 1967) 44,511.

Industry. Index of production (1963 = 100): (1968) 143; (1967) 129. Production (in 000; metric tons; 1968): coal 6,662; crude oil 2,145; natural gas (deliveries; cu.m.) 14,510,000; manufactured gas (cu.m.) 1,361,000; electricity (kw-hr.) 33,621,000; pig iron 2,821; crude steel 3,707; zinc 43; tin 8.1; cement 3,437; cotton yarn 58; wool yarn 16; rayon filament yarn 36. Merchant vessels launched (100 gross tons and over; 1968) 293,000 gross tons. New dwellings completed (1968) 122,800.

ment reached agreement in principle with the governments of West Germany and the U.K. on the common production of enriched uranium by means of ultracentrifugal processing.

On January 24, Liao Ho-shu, the acting Chinese chargé d'affaires in The Hague, resigned his post and asked to remain in the Netherlands. He later requested political asylum in the U.S.

The reform of the structure of scientific education drew much attention in 1969. On April 28 students of the Tilburg Economic High School occupied the university building and stayed there for nine days. For several days in mid-May Amsterdam students occupied the Maagdenhuis, the administrative centre of the University of Amsterdam. In other university cities, too, students took action to enforce their demands for greater participation in organizational and educational affairs.

Much public concern was aroused in January by a television program that alleged that the Netherlands Army, while in Indonesia during 1945–50, had committed war crimes. The government established an official research committee to comb out governmental and military archives. On June 2 Prime Minister de Jong sent the report of the committee to Parliament. He declared that the government deplored that excesses had taken place, but also stated that the evidence showed that there was no question of systematic cruelty having been committed.

At the end of June the nation was alarmed by a very serious poisoning of the Rhine River by industrial waste. Hasty measures had to be taken to protect the drinking water of large areas of the country.

From January 23 to January 30, Queen Juliana, Prince Bernhard, Crown Princess Beatrix, and Prince Claus paid a state visit to Ethiopia. On May 27 and 28 Prime Minister de Jong and Foreign Minister Joseph M. A. H. Luns visited Pres. Richard M. Nixon of the U.S. The Belgian prime minister, Gaston Eyskens, and foreign minister, Pierre Harmel, paid an official visit to the Netherlands on February 4.

On October 11 the third son of Crown Princess Beatrix and Prince Claus was born. He was named Constantijn Christof Frederik Aschwin. (G. H. v. E.)

See also Dependent States.

ENCYCLOPÆDIA BRITANNICA FILMS. *People of the Netherlands* (1957); *Holland: Hold Back the Sea* (1967).

New Zealand

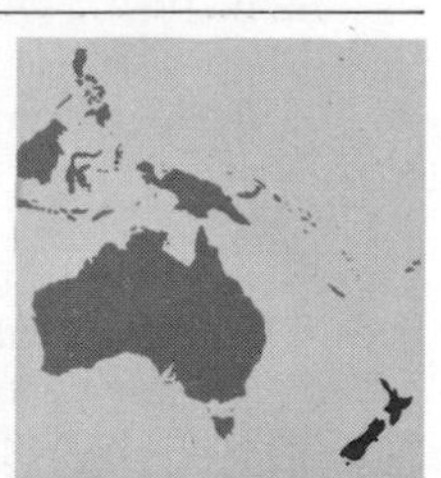

The Dominion of New Zealand, a parliamentary state and member of the Commonwealth of Nations, is in the South Pacific Ocean, separated from southeastern Australia and Tasmania by the Tasman Sea. The country proper consists of North and South islands and Stewart, Chatham, and other minor islands. Area: 103,736 sq.mi. (268,686 sq.km.). Pop. (1969 est.): 2,780,839. Cap.: Wellington (pop., 1969 est., 134,400). Largest city: Christchurch (pop., 1969 est., 165,700). Largest urban area: Auckland (pop., 1969 est., 588,400). Language: English; also Maori. Religion (1966): Church of England 33.7%; Presbyterian 21.8%; Roman Catholic 15.9%. Queen, Elizabeth II; governor-general in 1969, Sir Arthur Porritt; prime minister, Keith J. Holyoake.

In the general elections of Nov. 29, 1969, the National Party government resisted a strong challenge from the Labour Party and was returned with a 45-seat majority in the 84-seat Parliament.

Economic recovery from a slump in export receipts (mainly wool) two years previously continued in 1969, and unemployment, which reached 8,665 in mid-1968, was down to 3,358 by mid-1969 and was still falling. The improvement was assisted by the return of immigrants to their home countries and by the emigration of New Zealanders to Australia and other countries in such numbers that in the six months to the end of September 13,000 more people left the country than entered it. The government doubled its intake of assisted British migrants, retaining its preference for skilled workers. In spite of the healthier national finances, the preference of so many younger New Zealanders for the opportunities of other countries had an adverse effect on the national morale.

The brightest economic development was the discovery of oil offshore that looked promising enough for a Sedco 135F rig to be towed to the South Pacific to explore the field fully. In December it was reported that light crude oil and gas had been found in significant quantities off the Taranaki coast. Hydrocarbon-bearing sand was found in an Auckland district shore well in April, and gas at Hokianga in May. Arrangements went ahead during the year for the piping of natural gas to metropolitan areas from Kapuni. A NZ$100 million contract for Manapouri power for a Comalco smelter at Bluff was signed in September.

NEW ZEALAND

Education. (1967) Primary, pupils 500,898, teachers 17,983; secondary, pupils 168,534, teachers 8,356; vocational, pupils 87,374, teachers 633; teacher training, students 6,155, teachers 426; higher (at 7 universities), students 26,331, teaching staff 1,605.

Finance. Monetary unit: New Zealand dollar, with a par value of NZ$0.89 to U.S. $1 (NZ$2.14 = £1 sterling). Gold and foreign exchange, central bank: (June 1969) U.S. $165 million; (June 1968) U.S. $169 million. Budget (1967–68 rev. est.): revenue NZ$1,160,300,000; expenditure NZ$1,161,000,000. Gross national product: (1967–68) NZ$4,043,000,000; (1966–67) NZ$3,911,000,000. Money supply: (June 1969) NZ$762.1 million; (June 1968) NZ$729.2 million. Cost of living (1963 = 100): (2nd quarter 1969) 127; (2nd quarter 1968) 121.

Foreign Trade. (1968) Imports NZ$799.1 million; exports NZ$901.6 million. Import sources: U.K. 31%; Australia 20%; U.S. 12%; Japan 8%. Export destinations: U.K. 46%; U.S. 12%; Japan 9%; Australia 8%. Main exports: wool 20%; lamb and mutton 18%; butter 12%.

Transport and Communications. Roads (1968) 93,806 km. Motor vehicles in use (1968): passenger 826,155; commercial 163,249. Railways (state; 1968): 5,018 km.; traffic 564 million passenger-km., freight 2,497,000,000 net ton-km. Air traffic (1968): 1,266,300,000 passenger-km.; freight 33,590,000 net ton-km. Shipping (1968): merchant vessels 100 gross tons and over 127; gross tonnage 191,618. Telephones (Dec. 1967) 1,119,422. Radio receivers (Dec. 1968) 657,000. Television receivers (Dec. 1968) 604,000.

Agriculture. Production (in 000; metric tons; 1968; 1967 in parentheses): wheat 442 (348); barley 219 (135); oats 42 (28); potatoes 236 (250); dry peas 36 (32); apples (1967) 105, (1966) 119; mutton and lamb 578 (536); beef and veal 347 (318); milk 6,204 (6,242); butter 252 (260); cheese 112 (112); wool, greasy 330 (322); timber (cu.m.; 1967) 6,800, (1966) 6,600; fish catch (1966) 56, (1965) 48. Livestock (in 000; Jan. 1968): cattle 8,217; sheep (June 1968) 66,474; horses *c.* 84; pigs 612; chickens (April 1966) *c.* 4,600.

Industry. Fuel and power (in 000; metric tons; 1968): coal 588; lignite 1,709; manufactured gas (cu.m.) 167,000; electricity (excluding most industrial production; kw-hr.) 12,084,000. Production (in 000; metric tons; 1968): cement 762; superphosphates (1967) 1,358; mechanical wood pulp (1967–68) 225; chemical wood pulp (1967–68) 256; newsprint 195.

Netherlands Antilles: *see* Dependent States

Netherlands Overseas Territories: *see* Dependent States

Neurology: *see* Medicine

New Caledonia: *see* Dependent States

New Guinea: *see* Dependent States; Indonesia

New Hebrides: *see* Dependent States

Newspapers: *see* Publishing

Final approval for the development of Wellington and Auckland as container ports was given in October following the Molyneaux (March), Metra (April), Transport Commission (June), and Ports Authority (October) recommendations. A roll-on/roll-off ferry for trans-Tasman freighting (the Union Steam Ship Co.'s "Maheno") opened this era in May. In internal freighting the government confirmed the success of interisland road-rail ferrying by asking bids for a third Wellington-Picton ferry. The Union Steam Ship Co., which provided the news story of the previous year through the disastrous stranding of its Wellington-Lyttelton ferry, "Wahine," in a gale, ordered a replacement, to be called "Rangitira." A storm in May reminiscent of the previous year's April 10 hurricane shifted the wreck of the "Wahine" inside the Wellington Harbour heads, broke it to pieces, and delayed the work of a salvage team preparing it for foam treatment and removal into deeper waters. Maritime tragedies in 1969 were centred on the outlying, exposed Chatham Islands, where fishing boats hunting crayfish or running between the islands and the mainland seemed always to be sinking.

Crayfish exports became a big earner with 214,750 cwt. packed the previous year. But the grasslands continued to sustain the economy, with wool and meat continuing to earn well: September receipts for exports of meat were up NZ$66.1 million, and for wool up NZ$51.3 million. Total export receipts rose by NZ$174 million to NZ$1,061,500,000, to give an overall trade balance that was the highest yet: a current account surplus of NZ$72.2 million. Import payments also continued to rise; at NZ$797.2 million they were NZ$136.5 million above the previous year to September, a rise of 20.7% but only 7.4% over the predevaluation high year of 1965–66. The most notable payment increases were in travel and items associated with trade promotion. Repayment of official overseas debt was mainly responsible for a net capital outflow of NZ$47 million, financed by the current account surplus and leaving an overall balance of NZ$25.2 million.

Meat exports to the U.S. provoked an international incident when Prime Minister Holyoake in June warned U.S. Pres. Richard Nixon that government quotas on meat imports could have such a harmful effect on a primary industry trader like New Zealand that it would have to review its relations with any country shutting it out. Nixon in July replied that most serious efforts would be made to ensure that New Zealand's interests in the U.S. were advanced rather than harmed in "all decisions related to our mutual affairs." Visits by U.S. Secretary of State William Rogers to New Zealand in August and by Prime Minister Holyoake to the U.S. in September confirmed the inclusion of freer trade in the partnership. New Zealand dairy farmers, hit by surpluses in importing countries, were urged to move more into beef production, and the annual budget made special provision for these farmers. Wool growers who saw their reserves running out by the mid-1970s failed to obtain direct government assistance in paying their levy to the International Wool Secretariat.

The government planned much larger expenditures for university education and smaller classes for primary and secondary education, and refused to "auction" with the Labour Party opposition in the general elections in November on the amount of increased aid it would give private schools. It revised security legislation by defining "sedition" and providing for appeal against recommendations of the Security Service, after the Labour Party annual conference had suggested irregularities in the operation of the service.

The divorce rate increased in 1969 as a result of speeding up the enforcement of the Matrimonial Amendment Act of the previous year. A commission, starting with the Wellington district, began the reorganization of New Zealand's local government structure. The government decided in February that New Zealand troops would remain in Malaysia and Singapore after the British withdrawal in 1971. A new Broadcasting Authority had a troubled year caused by the need to replace its ailing chairman and reversals of attitude on procedure in calling for and deciding on applications for New Zealand's first independent (noncorporation) radio and TV stations. The voting and liquor-drinking age was reduced from 21 to 20.

(Jo. A. K.)

See also Dependent States.

Nicaragua

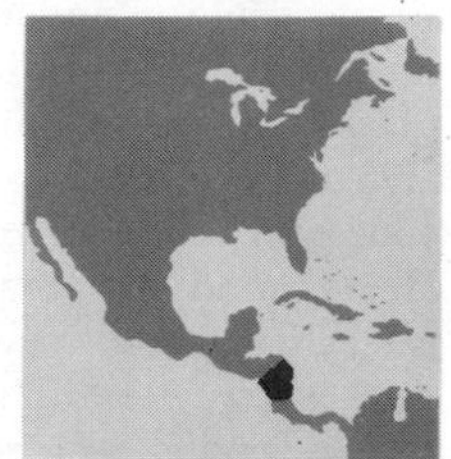

The largest country of Central America, Nicaragua is a republic bounded by Honduras, Costa Rica, the Caribbean Sea, and the Pacific Ocean. Area: 49,173 sq.mi. (127,358 sq.km.). Pop. (1968 est.): 1,809,477, including mestizo 70%; white 17%; Negro 9%; Indian 4%. Cap. and largest city: Managua (pop., 1968 est., 380,966). Language: Spanish. Religion: Roman Catholic. President in 1969, Brig. Gen. Anastasio Somoza Debayle.

The booming economy that characterized the first year of Pres. Anastasio Somoza Debayle's administration (May 1967–May 1968) tapered off to a standstill during the second year. The annual growth rate of the gross national product dropped from 6–8% to less than 1%. Cotton, the chief export and principal indicator of the nation's economy, was produced in good quantity after three dry years, but unfortunately this advantage was offset by a two-to-three-cent drop in price due to foreign competition. The cotton sector of the economy was further complicated by the fact that 20% of the cotton land was taken out of production in 1969. Not only did this cut the supply for the all-important export market, but the resultant layoffs of farm workers also threw many into the already swollen ranks of the unemployed.

Coffee, the second most important export, also enjoyed a good production year, both locally and worldwide. Nicaragua's international export quota was reduced 7½% by the International Coffee Council, and this cut, accompanied by a 30% drop in price, definitely affected the nation's economy. The meat industry grew 4½% and ranked as the nation's third most important export, but it too had its frustrations as the U.S. cut its quota of imported Nicaraguan beef. Because of these decreases in exports and a dwindling international reserve fund, there was a corresponding reduction in imports.

Because of a heavy trade deficit, Nicaragua became somewhat disillusioned about its position in the Central American Common Market. Nicaragua bought heavily of manufactured goods from its Central American neighbours, goods that could not carry an import duty according to terms of the Common Market agreement; in line with its hope of becoming the breadbasket of Central America, Nicaragua expected to pay for these imports with agricultural goods. There was, however, no Common Market policy on agricultural produce, and as a result Nicaragua could not maintain a favourable balance of trade.

The main goals of the government continued to be modernization and diversification of agriculture, and expansion of educational and health activities, at least partially through the support of outside loans. The attempt to diversify agriculture and become less dependent on cotton and coffee continued. Much investment was going into grain production, and centres for drying and storing grain were being constructed throughout the country. A $23 million loan was arranged with the U.S. Agency for International Development (AID) to be spent for rural electrification, rural health centres, and a basic grains program concentrated on insecticides and fertilizers.

Construction continued strong throughout the year: two luxury hotels, a national theatre, a textile plant, a kenaf bag factory, a chemical plant, and the enlargement of an oil refinery and cement facilities were either finished or were nearing completion. Industries tending to use local products were given priority. A shrimp freezing plant on the east coast offered good potential for a major new industry.

The austerity program presented by the president to cope with the recession found few friends. Belt-tightening tactics such as increased taxes, cuts in imports, limitation or elimination of numerous social and economic programs, and the firing of 5,000 government employees including the minister of economy pleased few. The cost of living increased sharply, while the standard of living dropped. In August the government schools were closed by a teacher strike.

(A. W. O.)

NICARAGUA
Education. (1965–66) Primary, pupils 206,349, teachers (including preprimary) 6,066; secondary, pupils 18,754, teachers 1,118, vocational, pupils 3,001, teachers 184; teacher training, students 4,822, teachers 351; higher (including 2 universities), students 3,343, teaching staff 430.
Finance. Monetary unit: córdoba, with a par value of 7 córdobas to U.S. $1 (16.80 córdobas = £1 sterling). Gold and convertible currency, central bank: (Feb. 1969) U.S. $55,240,000; (Feb. 1968) U.S. $34.9 million. Budget (1969 est.) balanced at 659 million córdobas. Gross national product: (1967) 4,485,000,000 córdobas; (1966) 4,201,000,000 córdobas. Money supply: (Feb. 1969) 546.2 million córdobas; (Feb. 1968) 600 million córdobas. Cost of living (Managua; 1963 = 100): (Dec. 1967) 113; (Dec. 1966) 113.
Foreign Trade. (1968) Imports 1,292,500,000 córdobas; exports 1,101,000,000 córdobas. Import sources: (1967): U.S. 43%; West Germany 7%; Costa Rica 7%; El Salvador 7%; Japan 7%; Guatemala 6%. Export destinations (1967): Japan 30%; U.S. 28%; West Germany 14%; Costa Rica 5%. Main exports: cotton 38%; coffee 14%; meat 10%.
Transport and Communications. Roads (1967) *c.* 7,000 km. (including 368 km. of Pan-American Highway). Motor vehicles in use: passenger (1966) 12,800; commercial (including buses; 1965) 5,000. Railways (1967): 349 km.; traffic 41 million passenger-km., freight 14 million net ton-km. Air traffic (1967): 46,160,000 passenger-km.; freight 905,000 net ton-km. Telephones (Jan. 1968) *c.* 13,200. Radio receivers (Dec. 1966) 105,000. Television receivers (Dec. 1967) 25,000.
Agriculture. Production (in 000; metric tons; 1968; 1967 in parentheses): rice *c.* 65 (*c.* 60); corn *c.* 180 (*c.* 174); sorghum (1967) *c.* 56, (1966) *c.* 54; dry beans *c.* 44 (*c.* 38); cotton, lint *c.* 92 (*c.* 102); coffee (1967) *c.* 33, (1966) *c.* 29; sugar, raw value (1968–69) *c.* 113, (1967–68) *c.* 107. Livestock (in 000; 1966–67): cattle *c.* 1,850; pigs *c.* 475.
Industry. Production (in 000; metric tons; 1966): cement 79; gold (troy oz.; 1967) 178; electricity (kw-hr.) 335,000.

Niger

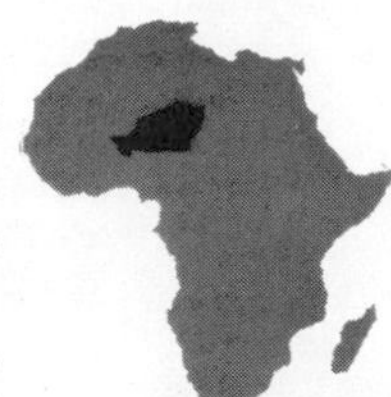

A republic of north central Africa, Niger is bounded by Algeria, Libya, Chad, Nigeria, Dahomey, Upper Volta, and Mali. Area: 458,993 sq.mi. (1,188,794 sq.km.). Pop. (1969 est.): 3,909,372, including (1962) Hausa 49%; Djerma 16%; Peuls 11%; Tuareg 9%. Cap. and largest city: Niamey (pop., 1969 est., 78,991). Language: French and Sudanic dialects. Religion (1960 est.): 1.8 million Muslims; 725,000 animists; 10,000 Christians. President in 1969, Hamani Diori.

Throughout 1969 President Diori maintained an intense level of diplomatic activity, as much in the name of Niger as in that of the African and Malagasy Common Organization (OCAM), of which he was re-elected president on January 27.

In February, Niger welcomed the first international conference of French-speaking states, attended by delegations from Africa, Asia, Europe, and, notably, Quebec (as part of Canada's delegation). André Malraux represented France at the sessions, at the end of which an Agency for Cultural and Technical Co-operation was created with President Diori as its provisional head. Informed sources stated that France had offered to pay 45% of the initial costs of setting up the agency.

Problems facing Niger's economy in 1969 included a decline in peanut prices; the consequences of the devaluation of the French franc; tax evasion; the lack of highly trained executives; high transport costs; the loss of customs duties through fraud; and the growth of population. In addition, the effects of the prolonged 1968 drought had been catastrophic. In the Sahel region 50% of the livestock, a major source of income, had been wiped out, and in the extreme east the figure was 75%. The financial loss was estimated at between CFA Fr. 4 billion and 5 billion. To restore the number of livestock to its former level would take at least ten years. The U.S. provided 5,000 tons of millet and the World Food Program 2,250 tons of sorghum as drought relief. New markets for meat exports in Ghana, Togo, and the Ivory Coast in 1969 helped somewhat to alleviate the CFA Fr. 3 billion decline in net income in 1968.

On July 18 the European Development Fund granted CFA Fr. 98 million for a flour mill at Zinder,

NIGER
Education. (1966–67) Primary, pupils 70,657, teachers 1,601; secondary, pupils 3,068, teachers 161; vocational, pupils 848, teachers 95; teacher training, students 557, teachers 27.
Finance. Monetary unit: CFA franc, with a parity of CFA Fr. 50 to the French franc (CFA Fr. 277.71 = U.S. $1; CFA Fr. 666.50 = £1 sterling). Budget (1968–69 est.) balanced at CFA Fr. 9,954,000,000.
Foreign Trade. (1967) Imports CFA Fr. 11,352,000,000; exports CFA Fr. 8,226,000,000. Import sources: France 49%; China 6%; Ivory Coast 6%; U.S. 5%; Japan 5%. Export destinations: France 69%; Nigeria 21%. Main exports: peanuts 69%; livestock 13%; peanut oil 8%.
Transport and Communications. Roads (1968) 6,753 km. Motor vehicles in use (1968): passenger 6,493; commercial 2,029. Telephones (Jan. 1968) *c.* 2,900. Radio receivers (Dec. 1967) 75,000.
Agriculture. Production (in 000; metric tons; 1967; 1966 in parentheses): millet 1,000 (842); sorghum 342 (277); cassava 169 (148); peanuts 298 (312); rice 33 (20); dates *c.* 5 (*c.* 5). Livestock (in 000; 1966–67): cattle *c.* 4,000; sheep *c.* 2,200; goats *c.* 5,900.

Nickel:
see Mining

$1,620,000 to finance water supply, and CFA Fr. 789 million to modernize the Niamey–Zinder road. Plans for industrial expansion included a large textile complex, a brewery, and a plant for the extraction and processing of the Arlit uranium deposits. In September, President Diori paid an official visit to Canada, and there signed an agreement which provided Niger with financial aid of Can$2.5 million. (Ph. D.)

Nigeria

A federal republic and a member of the Commonwealth of Nations, Nigeria is located in Africa on the north coast of the Gulf of Guinea, bounded by Dahomey, Niger, Chad, and Cameroon. Area: 356,669 sq.mi. (923,774 sq.km.). Pop. (1969 est.): 64.6 million, including (1963 est.): Hausa 18%; Ibo 16%; Yoruba 14%; Fulani 10%. Cap. and largest city: Lagos (pop., 1969, 841,000). Language: English (official). Religion: Muslim 48%; Christian 23%. Head of provisional military government in 1969, Maj. Gen. Yakubu Gowon.

In 1969, the third year of the Nigerian civil war, gradual advances by federal government forces reduced the territory controlled by Ibo secessionists to about 3,000 sq.mi. (as compared with 30,000 sq.mi. in 1967). Resistance by the Ibos in their breakaway state of Biafra continued, however, and by the end of the year there were stalemates on the military and diplomatic fronts. Biafran resistance depended largely on holding the Uli airstrip as a lifeline to outside aid. Arms supplies, routed through Gabon and the Ivory Coast, were unofficially reported to be coming from France, Czechoslovakia (both of whom were also supplying the federal government), Portugal, South Africa, and China. The U.K. and the U.S.S.R. continued to provide their military aid to the federal government.

Since the federal government refused to consider negotiations based upon a recognition of Biafran sovereignty, a condition on which the Biafran leader Gen. Odumegwu Ojukwu insisted, there was no basis for peace terms. General Gowon emphasized that the war was to prevent the disintegration of Nigeria and assured the Ibos of security within the nation's 12-state system. In February Gowon rejected a peace plan submitted by Nnamdi Azikiwe, Nigeria's first president and former prime minister of the Eastern (Ibo) Region. Azikiwe proposed an arms embargo, a plebiscite to decide Biafran sovereignty, and the involvement of a UN peace-keeping force. Recalling Katanga's attempted secession from the Congo (Kinshasa), UN Secretary-General U Thant confirmed that the UN could not support the secession of part of a member state.

CAMERA PIX—PIX FROM PUBLIX

Starving 15-year-old Biafran orphan begs by the roadside. War continued to bring suffering and starvation to the rebelling Biafrans in 1969 as federal government tightened its blockade of food and supplies.

Attempts by the Organization of African Unity (OAU) to mediate in the war were unsuccessful, as were those of British Prime Minister Harold Wilson, who visited Lagos on March 27–31. In April the OAU

NIGERIA

Education. (1966–67) Primary, pupils 3,025,981, teachers 91,049; secondary, pupils 202,638, teachers 11,055; vocational, pupils 26,092, teachers 1,378; teacher training, students 28,673, teaching staff 1,482.

Finance. Monetary unit: Nigerian pound, with a par value of N£0.36 to U.S. $1 (N£0.86 = £1 sterling). Gold and foreign exchange, official: (June 1969) U.S. $124 million; (June 1968) U.S. $116 million. Federal budget (1968–69 est.): revenue N£152 million; expenditure N£150 million. Gross domestic product: (1966–67 N£1,702 million; (1965–66) N£1,647 million. Money supply: (April 1969) N£169.1 million; (April 1968) N£129.8 million. Cost of living (Lagos; 1963 = 100): (June 1969) 127; (June 1968) 113.

Foreign Trade. (1968) Imports N£193,185,000; exports N£211,085,000. Import sources: U.K. 31%; U.S. 12%; West Germany 11%; Italy 7%. Export destinations: U.K. 29%; Netherlands 13%; West Germany 9%; U.S. 8%; Italy 6%; France 5%. Main exports: cocoa 25%; peanuts 18%; crude oil 18%; tin 6%; palm kernels 5%.

Transport and Communications. Roads (1967) *c.* 80,000 km. (including *c.* 16,000 km. with improved surface). Motor vehicles in use (1967): passenger 73,000; commercial (including buses) 31,000. Railways: (1966) 3,505 km.; traffic (1968) 521.3 million passenger-km., freight 1,745,000,000 net ton-km. Air traffic (1968): 148.8 million passenger-km.; freight 5,538,000 net ton-km. Shipping (1968): merchant vessels 100 gross tons and over 36; gross tonnage 70,615. Telephones (Jan. 1968) 77,883. Radio receivers (Nov. 1967) 1,250,000. Television receivers (Nov. 1967) 52,000.

Agriculture. Production (in 000; metric tons; 1967; 1966 in parentheses): millet and sorghum *c.* 6,600 (*c.* 6,600); corn *c.* 1,067 (*c.* 1,219); sweet potatoes (1966) *c.* 13,600, (1965) *c.* 13,600; cassava (1966) *c.* 6,500, (1965) *c.* 7,500; peanuts (1968) *c.* 1,542, (1967) 1,252; palm oil *c.* 325 (*c.* 508); cocoa 235 (267); cotton, lint *c.* 27 (50); rubber (exports) 48 (71). Livestock (in 000; 1966–67): cattle *c.* 7,590; sheep *c.* 5,090; pigs *c.* 700; horses (Northern Region only) 345.

Industry. Production (in 000; metric tons; 1968): crude oil 7,023; tin 10; electricity (kw-hr.) 1,109,000.

consultative committee met in Monrovia, Liberia, and issued a special declaration asking both sides to "accept in the supreme interests of Africa a united Nigeria."

The bombing of Biafra by the federal Air Force continued throughout the year. In April federal ground forces captured Umuahia, the administrative capital of Biafra. This victory culminated an offensive which also captured Enugu, Calabar, Onitsha, Port Harcourt, Aba, and Owerri. The Biafrans recaptured Owerri and in May pushed into the Mid-West state of Nigeria across the Niger River. During a Biafran attack near Kwale, 11 oil technicians, 10 of whom were Italians and one a Jordanian, were killed, and 18 were captured. The men were later released, but disruption of oil operations in the east was caused by Biafran bombing of wells and pumping stations. A rudimentary Biafran Air Force was formed, consisting of Swedish-made Minicon light aircraft brought to Nigeria by Count Carl Gustav von Rosen (*see* BIOGRAPHY), who was reported to have led Swedish and Biafran pilots in attacks on federal airfields. The federal Air Force replaced the United Arab Republic pilots of its MiG fighters, mainly with East Germans.

International disquiet concerning the conduct of the war continued. In January a report of the international observers invited by the federal government to investigate Biafran charges of genocide concluded that the accusations were unfounded. The plight of the starving Ibo people worsened, however, as disagreements bedeviled the efforts of the Red Cross and other agencies to airlift food and medical supplies to the stricken regions. The federal government maintained that illegal airlifts intruded on Nigerian sovereignty and that there was no guarantee that relief flights might not be used to supply the Biafran forces. Biafra refused to accept control from Lagos of any airlift and feared the use of a land corridor as a threat to its security.

Further attempts at mediation, by Pope Paul VI during his visit to Uganda in July and by African leaders following the OAU summit meeting in September, were no more productive. In August Azikiwe presented a second peace formula, in which he accepted the principle of a united Nigeria, a move welcomed by federal supporters. Biafran determination to continue the struggle seemed based on the hope that economic and political tensions within Nigeria as the war dragged on might lead to a willingness to compromise. Local riots in the Western state in September were ascribed by the governor to Yoruba sectionalism, which also represented a threat to Nigerian unity.

Nigeria's economic resilience under the impact of war and a slow campaign of attrition against Biafra was attributed to the skill of the federal finance minister, Chief Obafemi Awolowo, in implementing government emergency measures. Foreign exchange reserves, which had stood at about $200 million at the end of 1966, stabilized at approximately $105 million, and by May the government was able to lift embargoes on profits and dividends. The largely self-supporting agricultural and mining economy of Nigeria was less vulnerable than an advanced industrial economy to the effects of a war that left most of the country physically unscathed. Manufacturing output in 1968 exceeded that of 1966, and the upward trend continued in 1969. The balance of trade remained favourable, and major export crops recovered to their prewar level. The important cocoa and peanut crops showed an increase.

The Kainji Dam, opened on February 15 by General Gowon, was a measure of external and internal confidence. The £100 million project was backed by an international consortium of the U.K., the U.S., Canada, the Netherlands, and Italy and was supported by a World Bank loan amounting to 40% of the total cost. In 1969 the World Bank made an additional loan of about $5 million to the Nigerian Industrial Development Board, and the U.K. contributed approximately $25 million to a telecommunications project.

BEN ROTH AGENCY

"I'm getting a bit worried about the effect of all this violence being shown on TV!"—Garland, "Daily Telegraph," London.

Oil remained basic to the Nigerian economy. In 1969 production regained its prewar level at about 480,000 bbl. a day (statistics were classified). Disruption by Biafran air attacks was, however, likely to reduce the 1970 estimate of 1 million bbl. a day. Despite the threat to production activities, particularly in the east (the Mid-West and offshore fields were less affected by the war), Shell Oil Co. tripled its investment expenditure to about $120 million for 1969. Oil revenues were potentially far in excess of the total current federal budget and remained a major internal political issue. With oil revenues for 1970 estimated at N£600 million (as against a federal budget of N£190 million), the revenue allocation committee set up in August 1968 proposed that the government retain 90% for itself.

Although the 12 states replacing the former four regions of Nigeria were established in 1967, their administrative existence dated from April 1968 and practical organization began only in 1969. Although officially equal, this artificial parity began to disappear beneath population and resource differentials. The revenue allocation committee reported in April on the political and economic problems caused by interstate imbalances. The 1969 state budgets varied from £41 million for the Western state to £7 million for Benue. In a speech in October marking the ninth anniversary of Nigerian independence, General Gowon suggested that the 12-state system might be reexamined and also announced an amnesty for detainees who were no longer considered security risks. One of those released was the author Wole Soyinka. (M. MR.)

ENCYCLOPÆDIA BRITANNICA FILMS. *West Africa (Nigeria)* (1963).

Non-Chalcedonian Eastern Churches: *see* Religion

North Atlantic Treaty Organization: *see* Defense

Northern Ireland: *see* United Kingdom

Norway

A constitutional monarchy of northern Europe, Norway is bordered by Sweden, Finland, and the U.S.S.R.; its coastlines are on the North Sea, the Norwegian Sea, and the Arctic Ocean. Area: 125,181 sq.mi. (324,219 sq.km.), excluding the Svalbard Archipelago,

23,957 sq.mi., and Jan Mayen Island, 144 sq.mi. Pop. (1969 est.): 3,835,000. Cap. and largest city: Oslo (metro. pop., 1969 est., 598,515). Language: Norwegian. Religion: Lutheran (96.2%). King, Olav V; prime minister in 1969, Per Borten.

The parliamentary elections on September 7–8, in which 80.9% of the electorate participated, resulted in the return to power of the four non-Socialist coalition parties (Conservative, Liberal, Centre, and Christian People's), although with a reduced majority compared with the 1965 elections. The distribution of seats was: Conservative, 29 (31 in 1965); Liberal, 13 (18); Centre, 20 (18); Christian People's, 14 (13); Labour, 74 (68); Socialist People's, 0 (2).

While the coalition lost four seats, the Labour Party gained six and also increased its share of the total votes more than any other party, from 43.1 to 46.7%. Two of the new seats came at the expense of the left-wing Socialist People's Party, which lost its entire representation in the Storting (parliament).

Even with its overall majority in the Storting reduced from ten to two seats, the coalition government, which had been formed in 1965 after the Labour Party's three decades in power, was able to continue in office, and with no change in the allocation of portfolios among the four parties. The Centre Party leader, Per Borten, continued as prime minister.

Important economic measures were announced soon after the coalition parties resumed power. A price freeze on a wide range of consumer goods was decreed, fixing prices at the September 22 level, to counteract the tendency for prices to rise before a new value-added tax went into effect on Jan. 1, 1970. The new tax was to be 20%, compared with the 13.64% of the previous turnover tax.

To compensate needy sections of the community for the price rise, the 1970 budget presented to the Storting on October 10 proposed large increases in social benefits, particularly in children's allowances. Total expenditure was budgeted at 18.6% more than in 1969, and the finance minister, Ole Myrvoll, proposed that the increase should be met mainly through loans. While the value-added tax would increase indirect taxes by about 3 billion kroner, direct taxes on income and property would be reduced by about 1.6 billion kroner.

The new government also acted quickly in announcing (September 26) an increase in interest rates, to compensate in part for the growing divergence between interest rate levels in Norway and abroad. The Bank of Norway raised the discount rate, previously unchanged for 14 years, from 3.5 to 4.5%. Lending rates generally were adjusted accordingly. As the result of higher interest rates prevailing abroad, Norway's gold and currency holdings dropped by 60 million kroner from January to July, compared with a large increase in 1968. However, the current balance of payments was even more favourable in 1969 than in 1968 (the first surplus in ten years), with a surplus equivalent to $170.4 million from January to August, compared with $100.8 million in the corresponding period of 1968.

The balance of payments surplus was largely due to reduced imports of new ships and increased exports of secondhand tonnage. Net freight earnings were also running at a high level, due in part to the continued closing of the Suez Canal. Commodity exports also continued to increase, with particularly satisfactory results recorded by paper and pulp products, mineral oils and fuels, and the metal industry.

In the first six months of 1969 Norway had the fastest growth of exports of all EFTA countries, with an increase of 19% over the same period in 1968. Imports during the period increased by only 0.5% over the 1968 figure. Exports to EFTA increased by 17% while imports from EFTA decreased by 3.7%. Manufacturing rose 5%, mining 10%, and power 2%. Total production was 4% higher than in 1968. Exports to EEC countries increased by 23% in the first eight months of 1969.

In spite of the increased production and the recovery in demand for consumer and investment goods, the boom was considered temporary and not the result of any fundamental improvement in the structure of the economy. There was a steep rise in imports of such items as vehicles, chemical products, metal goods, and machinery. Norway's unit labour costs were rising faster than those of its rivals. The prospect of the increasing use of nuclear power abroad threatened to diminish the country's advantage in cheap hydroelectric power. There was also the threat from the British government's decision to subsidize its own aluminum industry (Norway was second only to Canada in 1968 as an aluminum exporter, and was the fourth largest producer). Norway was also involved in a protracted dispute over Britain's 10% import duty on frozen fish fillets, although at negotiations in Oslo in October a minimum price system was agreed upon.

Throughout the year, proposals for closer economic cooperation in Scandinavia, including a Nordic customs union, were a main topic of debate. The provisional report of a committee of government experts, presented in Stockholm in January, recommended broader cooperation between Denmark, Finland, Norway, and Sweden in a number of economic fields, but

NORWAY

Education. (1966–67) Primary, pupils 407,055, teachers 19,481; secondary, pupils 201,509, teachers 15,645; vocational, pupils 67,755, teachers 10,020; teacher training, students 7,908, teachers 911; higher (including 3 universities), students 21,001, teaching staff 2,189.

Finance. Monetary unit: Norwegian krone, with a par value of 7.14 kroner to U.S. $1 (17.14 kroner = £1 sterling). Gold and foreign exchange, central bank: (June 1969) U.S. $575.5 million; (June 1968) U.S. $622.2 million. Budget (1969 est.): revenue 15,044,000,000 kroner; expenditure 14,854,000,000 kroner. Gross national product: (1967) 59,460,000,000 kroner; (1966) 54,260,000,000 kroner. Money supply: (June 1969) 14,020,000,000 kroner; (June 1968) 12.3 billion kroner. Cost of living (1963 = 100): (June 1969) 127; (June 1968) 122.

Foreign Trade. (1968) Imports 19,325,000,000 kroner; exports 13,840,000,000 kroner. Import sources: Sweden 19%; West Germany 14%; U.K. 12%; U.S. 8%; Denmark 7%; Japan 6%. Export destinations: U.K. 19%; Sweden 15%; West Germany 13%; U.S. 8%; Denmark 7%. Main exports: ships 15%; aluminum 11%; chemicals 8%; paper 8%; fish 7%; machinery 7%; iron and steel 7%.

Transport and Communications. Roads (1968) 69,606 km. Motor vehicles in use (1968): passenger 619,039; commercial 135,456. Railways: (state only; 1967) 4,242 km. (including 2,185 km. electrified); traffic (1968) 1,640,000,000 passenger-km., freight 2,590,000,000 net ton-km. Air traffic (including Norwegian apportionment of international operation of Scandinavian Airlines System; 1968): 1,608,300,000 passenger-km.; freight 58,528,000 net ton-km. Shipping (1968): merchant vessels 100 gross tons and over 2,881; gross tonnage 19,667,441. Ships entered (1967) vessels totaling 13,930,000 net registered tons; goods loaded (1968) 35,876,000 metric tons, unloaded 16,993,000 metric tons. Telephones (Dec. 1967) 987,264. Radio receivers (Dec. 1967) 1,135,000. Television receivers (Dec. 1967) 662,000.

Agriculture. Production (in 000; metric tons; 1968; 1967 in parentheses): barley 621 (485); oats 176 (123); potatoes 912 (807); apples *c.* 59 (49); milk *c.* 1,805 (1,735); butter *c.* 22 (20); cheese *c.* 46 (50); beef and veal (1967) 54, (1966) 57; pork (1967) 58, (1966) 57; timber (cu.m.; 1966–67) 7,500, (1965–66) 6,800; fish catch (1967) 3,214, (1966) 2,865; whale oil (1967–68) 6, (1966–67) 18. Livestock (in 000; June 1968): cattle 1,010; sheep (June 1967) 2,067; horses 47; pigs 611; goats (June 1967) 108; chickens (June 1967) 5,112.

Industry. Fuel and power (in 000; 1968): coal (Svalbard mines) 330 metric tons; manufactured gas 29,300 cu.m.; electricity 60,123,000 kw-hr. Production (in 000; metric tons; 1968): iron ore (65% metal content) 3,701; pig iron 1,396; crude steel 824; zinc 60; copper 18; aluminum 470; cement 2,298; nitrogenous fertilizers (N content; 1967–68) 359; mechahical wood pulp (1967) 955; chemical wood pulp (1967) 845; newsprint 474; other paper (1967) 725. Merchant vessels launched (100 gross tons and over; 1968) 500,000 gross tons. Dwelling units completed (1967) 31,290.

complete agreement was not reached on customs, agriculture, fisheries, and financial policy.

In July a new report including a draft convention on Nordic economic cooperation (Nordek) was presented. The committee proposed a customs union, to be implemented from Jan. 1, 1970; preferential arrangements for agricultural produce from Nordic countries; abolition of restrictions on the inter-Nordic fish trade; stabilization of base prices; agricultural and fisheries funds; and a Nordic investment bank. Finland's sudden withdrawal from the Nordek talks in December led to their postponement, however, probably until after the Finnish elections in 1970.

Reaction to the proposed customs union in industrial, commercial, and shipping circles in Norway was largely unfavourable, and it was stressed also by government spokesmen that the country's prime aim must be to achieve membership in the EEC in order to obtain access to a greatly enlarged nontariff market.

Norway was one of the chief backers of the move to suspend Greece from the Council of Europe, which ended in Greece's withdrawal from that organization in December. (O. F. K.)

ENCYCLOPÆDIA BRITANNICA FILMS. *Scandinavia—Norway, Sweden, Denmark* (1962).

Nuclear Energy

The most important event of the year was the long-delayed beginning of nuclear arms limitation talks between the U.S. and the Soviet Union. Never before had the two countries actually met in formal session to discuss means of bringing their nuclear arms competition to an end. That the circumstances were favourable, perhaps more favourable than they would ever be again, was obvious and was implicitly acknowledged by both sides. Yet it was far from clear that any positive results, let alone a broad and effective agreement, would be achieved.

While both countries stressed that the first phase of the negotiations, begun in Helsinki, Fin., in November 1969, would be only preliminary, there was some faint hope that it might produce an agreement to halt the deployment and even the development of new nuclear weapons and delivery systems while the talks continued. That hope was disappointed: if such a moratorium was proposed by either side, word of it never reached the public. When the talks were temporarily suspended in December, the most hopeful sign was that the atmosphere of restrained goodwill and highly cautious optimism in which they had begun had not evaporated.

While the nominal objectives of the negotiators were clearly implied by the popular acronym SALT (for Strategic Arms Limitation Talks), nothing was known of either side's specific aims nor was it clear that either had defined its purposes in detail. In particular, it remained to be seen whether either was prepared to forgo installing a new, advanced strategic weapon whose impending advent threatened to push them both into an intense new nuclear arms competition.

That weapon was an intercontinental missile capable of delivering several thermonuclear warheads simultaneously. According to the U.S. concept, christened MIRV (multiple independently targeted reentry vehicle), each warhead could be aimed at a separate preselected target. Although the exact status of progress on MIRV was classified, it was no secret that the Department of Defense hoped to complete development of both land-based and submarine-launched versions in 1970.

Concerning the Soviet version, little reliable information was available, and U.S. intelligence agencies differed sharply in their estimates of its status. Accepting the most alarming assessment (by the Department of Defense), the U.S.S.R. probably would soon be in a position to use it in a full-scale attack, relying on its extremely large SS-9 intercontinental missile as the prime vehicle.

Such weapons would not only multiply each side's already enormous striking power but might open the way for the aggressor to destroy at a blow most of the other's ability to retaliate. For example, one or two might be enough to wipe out a complex containing a number of widely dispersed missile-launching sites. Moreover, the multiple warheads would be able, by sheer numbers, to overwhelm any foreseeable antimissile defenses.

Thus the new weapons promised to upset the "balance of terror" between the two countries: the temporary near-equilibrium of their capacities for mutual destruction. U.S. military authorities warned of the consequences of permitting the Soviet Union to win a long lead, and there was also evidence that the U.S.S.R. was under heavy pressure to keep abreast of the U.S. Failing an agreement to stop short, it seemed all but certain that both governments would soon be drawn, however reluctantly, into a new, incalculably dangerous and costly competition, with no end in sight and no reason to believe that either would be even as secure as when the race began. These grim prospects were made still more forbidding by the virtual certainty that the advent of the new offensive weapons would spur both sides to counter with ever more elaborate and costly antimissile defenses.

Worse still, it seemed obvious that if a new "balance of terror" were someday achieved at a higher level, both countries would find it harder than ever to work out an arms limitation agreement. One practical reason for this was that without mutual on-the-spot inspections, which the Soviet Union had never shown any willingness to accept, it would be impossible to determine whether a given site in either country was equipped to fire ordinary missiles or the multiple-warhead versions.

Citing that problem, many observers in the U.S. held that the SALT negotiations had probably begun far too late, and few were willing to speculate on the chances that the talks would permit the two countries to escape the heightened dangers that confronted them. Given the complexity of the negotiators' task and the many unresolved conflicts and deep suspicions that lay between their nations, the only certainty was that progress would be painfully slow at best. Meanwhile, it was taken for granted that without a temporary moratorium faithfully observed by both sides the development and deployment of new weapons would continue.

Those who took the most hopeful view of the SALT prospects could point out that the negotiations were the culmination of a series of U.S.-Soviet achievements reflecting a steady willingness to cooperate. Among them were the limited nuclear test-ban treaty of 1963 and the nuclear nonproliferation treaty of 1968.

The most impressive result of their cooperation, the nonproliferation treaty, passed a crucial obstacle in November, when the government of Chancellor Willy

Norwegian Literature: *see* Literature

Brandt committed West Germany to signing it. This move broke a long and embarrassing impasse: the U.S.S.R., which had long since signed the treaty, had been unwilling to ratify it until West Germany acted, and the U.S., in a position to ratify since early in the year, had held back until the Soviet Union was ready. Meanwhile, as the treaty's two main architects marked time, little progress was made toward meeting the requirement that 43 nations must ratify it before it could come into force. Even so, at the year's end more than half of the necessary ratifications had been achieved.

Several of the countries best equipped to acquire nuclear arsenals showed no inclination to adhere to the treaty. Heading the list were Israel and India, each capable of assembling a nuclear weapon in a matter of months if not of weeks. In Australia, there was much talk, difficult to evaluate, of the need for an independent national nuclear force to discourage any Chinese aggression. Japan, also reluctant to accept the treaty, was more concerned that it would hamper development of its commercial nuclear energy industry.

COURTESY, SANDIA LABORATORIES

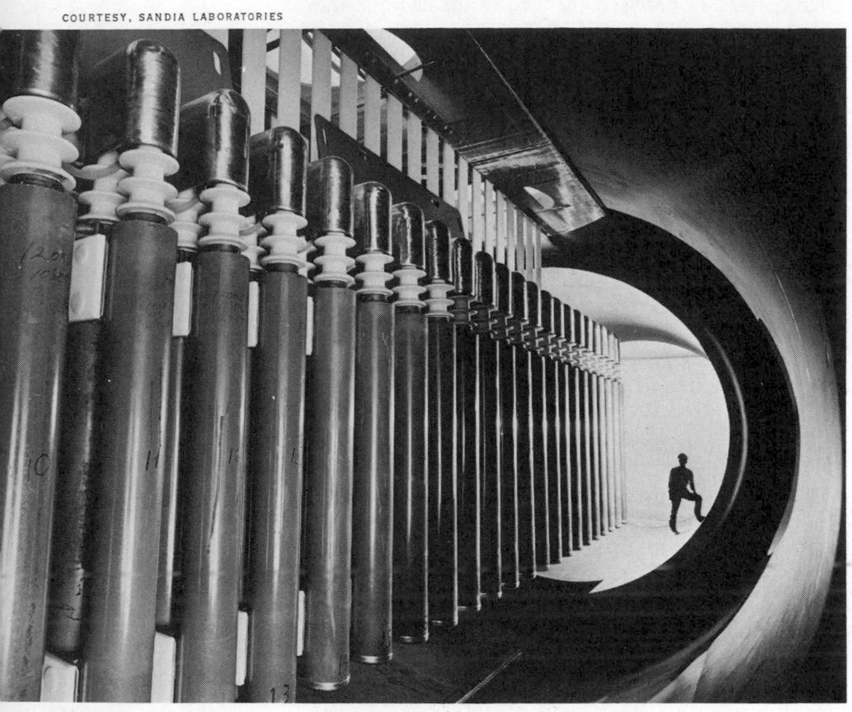

Hermes II, a giant generator at Sandia Laboratories in Albuquerque, N.M., which was used to simulate gamma radiation in tests by the Atomic Energy Commission. It produced bursts of energy of five trillion watts lasting 70 billionths of a second each.

Weapons and Weapons Tests. As the SALT negotiations began, U.S. and Soviet arsenals of long-range thermonuclear weapons systems were generally believed to be more or less in balance, in that either country, if attacked, could be fairly confident of being able to strike a devastating counterblow. Those arsenals, as described by the U.S. Department of Defense and U.S. intelligence agencies, consisted of:

1. Land-based missiles—In the U.S., 1,064, of which 1,000 were of the solid-fueled Minuteman type and the rest liquid-fueled Atlas missiles. The U.S.S.R.'s total was put at 1,300–1,400, of which about 300 were said to be of the SS-9 type, believed capable of carrying a much more powerful warhead than any U.S. missile.

2. Submarine-launched missiles—From U.S. submarines, 656 Polaris missiles. From Soviet submarines, about 200.

3. Long-range aircraft—Approximately 500 in the U.S. and 150 in the Soviet Union, all subsonic. Each was capable of carrying several large weapons.

The number of U.S. land-based intercontinental missiles had remained the same since 1966, as had the number of Polaris-launching submarines since 1967. The long-range bomber force had been steadily reduced since the mid-1960s. On the other hand, the long-range missile figures given for the U.S.S.R. were said to reflect a dramatic and continuing expansion—more than 500% in land-based missiles since 1966 and about 200% in submarine-launched missiles since 1968. No recent change in numbers of Soviet long-range bombers was reported.

In addition to these weapons, both the Soviet Union and the North Atlantic Treaty Organization (NATO) had installed large numbers of intermediate-range missiles in Europe. Whether any or all of these must be considered "strategic" and so subject to limitation was one of the many complex questions with which the SALT negotiators presumably would have to deal. Its implications were far from being merely academic, for NATO, faced with the need to compensate for a relative loss of strength in conventional arms, had adopted a policy of relying increasingly on "tactical" nuclear weapons—including intermediate-range missiles—to counter any aggression from the East.

In the U.S. there was abundant evidence that planning for the wide deployment of multiple-warhead strategic missiles—the land-based Minuteman III and the submarine-based Poseidon—was far advanced. The U.S.S.R.'s plans were another matter, and estimates from various sources differed sharply.

The conflicting opinions on Soviet plans figured importantly in the hard-fought, wide-ranging U.S. Senate debates precipitated by the government's proposal to begin deploying the nuclear-armed Safeguard anti-ballistic missile (ABM) system. Under fire from Congress, the Department of Defense quickly abandoned its first position, that the system would protect cities from a possible Chinese attack in the mid-1970s, and instead took the line that Safeguard would merely counterbalance Soviet ABM's already installed. To buttress its arguments, it cited its own intelligence estimates suggesting that the U.S.S.R.'s ABM's and its fast-growing strategic missile force together might soon give it a decisive offensive-defensive margin. Basic to this argument was the contention that Soviet multiple-warhead missiles were being developed and would be installed for the specific purpose of destroying U.S. strategic missile sites in an overwhelming first strike.

Senatorial critics quickly established that neither the U.S. Department of State nor the Central Intelligence Agency accepted this interpretation of Soviet motives. They were able, too, to find many in the scientific and technical communities who doubted the Safeguard system's ability to cope with a major attack, especially the multiple-warhead strike that the Department of Defense said it feared. The critics contended, moreover, that deploying Safeguard might well arouse Soviet suspicions of U.S. motives, opening the way for a new phase of nuclear weapons competition and practically ruling out any chance that arms limitation negotiations could succeed.

After weeks of debate touching on almost every aspect of U.S. defense policy, from the war in Vietnam to the Selective Service System, the administration prevailed and an authorization to install Safeguard at two strategic missile sites was granted. However, the tenacity of the opposition and the narrow margin of the victory left little room for doubt that the battle would be refought in 1970.

Britain's nuclear striking force consisted of a growing but still small flotilla of submarines equipped to fire the Polaris missile and a small, obsolescent force of medium-range aircraft. The U.K. had long since suspended virtually all nuclear weapons development efforts in favour of relying on U.S. technology. France, obliged to look entirely to its own resources, apparently needed at least one more series of weapons tests, to be held in Polynesia in 1970, to complete development of a submarine-launched thermonuclear weapon comparable to the Polaris. Meanwhile, its nuclear striking force consisted entirely of attack aircraft. During the year it advanced and later abandoned a proposal to Britain to create a joint force that would be independent of NATO.

To the outside world, the only solid evidence of China's nuclear weapons development efforts consisted of two tests in September at the Lop Nor test site in Sinkiang. One, obviously of a thermonuclear weapon or weapon prototype, produced an extremely powerful detonation, estimated by the U.S. Atomic Energy Commission (AEC) at the equivalent of three megatons of TNT. Contrary to its practice following the two earlier Chinese high-yield tests, the AEC did not identify the weapon's active components. The other test, the first that China conducted underground, was of a smaller weapon, described by the AEC as in the 20-200 kiloton range.

Again according to the AEC, nine underground nuclear explosions occurred in the Soviet Union during the year. The AEC itself reported having carried out more than 20 "weapons-related" tests, all underground. By far the largest and most controversial was the first at a new site, on Amchitka Island in Alaska. Opposed by some geologists and conservationists, who were concerned that it might cause severe ecological damage or even precipitate a major earthquake, it was conducted without incident.

Nuclear-Electric Power. For the nuclear power industry, 1969 was an uneven year, in some ways disappointing but never dull. Among the few clearly encouraging developments was a continued quickening of interest in nuclear-electric generation in countries that had had no experience with it. South Korea and Taiwan placed orders for their first nuclear power units, and Finland became the first non-Communist country to buy a Soviet-designed and manufactured plant. Others at or near the point of placing their first orders included Australia, Austria, Mexico, South Africa, Thailand, and Turkey.

An arrangement under which Greece was to buy its first nuclear power unit from Britain, paying for it with tobacco or other products, came to nothing when Britain failed to support Greece's efforts to retain membership in the Council of Europe. Both Romania and Czechoslovakia solicited nuclear power equipment bids from European and Canadian manufacturers.

In Britain, the power authorities found that they needed to buy little generating capacity of any kind and put off new orders until 1970. Meanwhile, government and industry were making the final moves in a broad reorganization aimed at creating a sounder nuclear-industrial structure that would combine private ownership with some government control. While efforts to sell British power reactor equipment to other countries met with no success, sales of nuclear fuel processing and manufacturing services reached significant levels.

Of all the heavily industrialized nations, France alone was not in a position to manufacture an economically attractive nuclear power system for domestic use, let alone for export. These humiliating realities were belatedly acknowledged in the autumn, when the government formally abandoned the line of natural uranium-fueled, gas-cooled reactors that had been the keystone of the national atomic power program under the de Gaulle regime and announced that it would look abroad for a viable alternative—primarily the water-cooled, enriched-uranium reactors first developed in the U.S.

The West German nuclear power industry clearly emerged as the most potent in Europe. Highly integrated, thanks largely to government encouragement, and technically proficient, it had proved itself fully capable of holding its own in international competition with General Electric Co. and Westinghouse Electric Corp., the huge U.S. reactor manufacturers. Its growth was hampered, however, by the slowness of West German utilities in placing new orders. Mostly small organizations, these utilities could seldom justify buying nuclear units of economic size without setting up cooperative arrangements among themselves, and this they found difficult.

As might be expected, Japan, too, emerged as a factor to be reckoned with. As in West Germany, the development of its nuclear power industry was based primarily on licensing arrangements with the two big U.S. manufacturers and on the resources of a highly developed industrial infrastructure. One clear indication of its coming of age was the first appearance of a Japanese firm as a competitor for contracting a nuclear power facility in another country.

In Sweden, where utilities were firmly committed to intensive use of nuclear power, two large plants were ordered from a domestic manufacturer. Canada, the only nation committed exclusively to power reactors fueled with natural (unenriched) uranium, encountered a serious if temporary problem: an acute worldwide shortage of the heavy water such units require. Italy's state power board after long delays contracted to buy its fourth nuclear unit, the first to be manufactured mostly by domestic firms. The Soviet Union announced no major new nuclear power construction plans and gave no indication that national policies favouring the generation of power by fossil fuels were soon likely to be changed.

In the U.S., nuclear power orders by utilities, which had fallen off sharply in 1968, continued to decline. At the end of 1969 they represented generating capacity of approximately 10 million kw., little more than the total for all other non-Communist countries combined and only about 40% of what U.S. utilities had bought in 1967. Even so, the new U.S. orders represented capital commitments of at least $2 billion. All called for the construction of enriched uranium-fueled, water-cooled reactors.

Heading the list of reasons why U.S. utilities turned away from nuclear power were the relatively high cost of building a nuclear plant—particularly significant at a time when costs of borrowing were extremely high—and the relatively long time required to complete it, amounting to at least one year longer than for a comparable fossil-fueled plant. Because of the latter difference, a number of utilities, under heavy pressure to install new generating capacity as fast as possible, found that they had little choice but to order coal-, gas-, or oil-fired units.

From the point of view of public policy, however, the most significant deterrent was the high probability that any new nuclear power project anywhere was likely to encounter determined opposition from groups who believed that it would endanger human life or degrade the environment. Essentially, these fears were a reflection of rising public concern about the effects of pollutants discharged by industrial installations of all kinds, and it was often apparent that those who opposed a given nuclear project would have been as disturbed if a fossil-fueled plant had been proposed in its place. From this point of view, the problem was merely an aspect of a dilemma that almost all utilities faced: confronted with a sharply rising demand for low-cost electricity, they often found that it was almost impossible to put in a noncontroversial plant of any kind at a noncontroversial site. However, nuclear power construction proposals were especially vulnerable to opposition of all kinds for they alone were always subject to elaborate federal licensing proceedings, including public hearings.

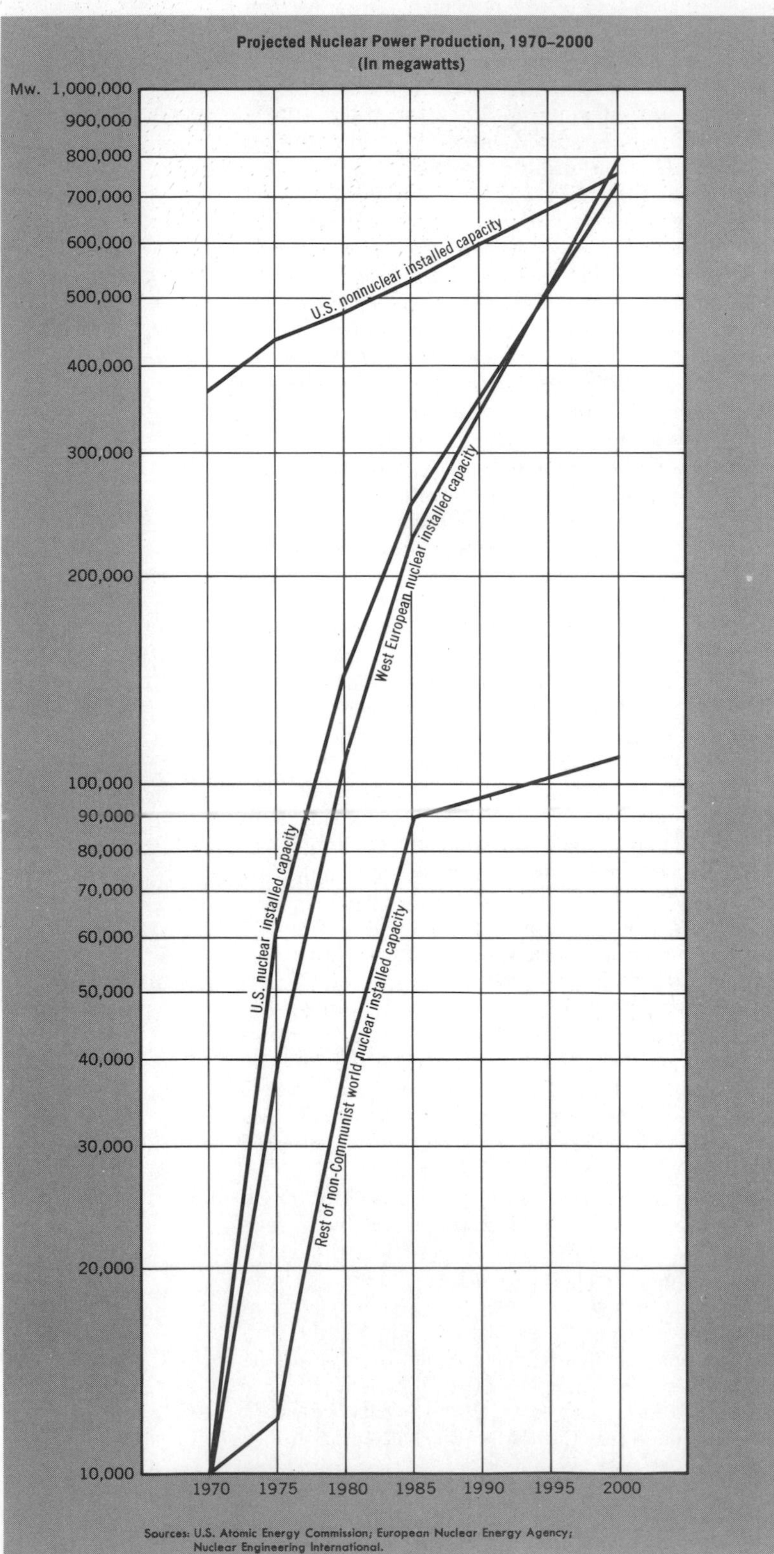

Sources: U.S. Atomic Energy Commission; European Nuclear Energy Agency; Nuclear Engineering International.

Much antinuclear-power sentiment stemmed from the belief, still widely held, that a power reactor might explode at any moment, bringing death to all in the area. Sophisticated opponents, however, usually concentrated their fire on two features common to all nuclear power plants of the types being built commercially throughout the world: the fact that they discharged large quantities of water heated by passage through their condensers, and the fact that they made small, controlled releases of radioactivity in liquid and gaseous effluents. Conceding that the radioactive discharges were consistent with internationally established limits and in practice were usually well below the limits of safety, critics often insisted that they were still excessive.

Broadly, the problem of cooling water discharges raised much the same kind of question. In this case, the immediate issue was "thermal pollution." Again and again, proposed nuclear power plants were challenged by conservation groups and state or local governments on the ground that their operation would —or might—degrade the ecology of the body of water into which the heated water was returned. Utilities often found themselves under pressure to install special equipment or take other costly steps to prevent the problem from arising, and in a few cases they were obliged to abandon otherwise satisfactory sites. Their difficulties were compounded because water quality standards and lines of regulatory authority were seldom clear and also because it was seldom possible to determine what action was really justified to make a given plant acceptable at a given site.

Generally, observers in the U.S. agreed that these and other problems discouraging new nuclear power commitments would be solved case by case, and that public confidence would rise as more and more large nuclear units proved themselves in performance. Meanwhile, the effect of the depression was severe, particularly for nuclear power equipment manufacturers that had incurred heavy losses in the past and had expected to recoup from new orders.

Even the uranium mining and milling sector of the industry, perhaps the only one that had been consistently profitable, found itself in a weak position. Beginning about 1966, scores of minerals companies, representing almost every industrialized country, had joined a new worldwide hunt for uranium, hoping to profit from the high prices then widely predicted for the near future. As it became increasingly clear that many had been successful in discovering low-cost deposits, they found themselves faced with the certainty that requirements for nuclear fuel would be disappointingly small, at least through the mid-1970s. Everywhere uranium prices were depressed, and there were unmistakable signs that enthusiasm for new exploration was fast evaporating. Internationally, the development that aroused the greatest interest—and in some quarters the greatest apprehension—was the progress of planning by Britain, the Netherlands, and West Germany for a novel venture: the cooperative construction of plants to produce slightly enriched uranium by the gas centrifuge process. The product, uranium containing a somewhat higher proportion of the isotope uranium-235 than is found in nature, was required by almost all of the nuclear power plants being built for commercial use. For their operators everywhere the prime source of the material, indeed, almost the only source, had been the U.S. Atomic Energy Commission, which produced it in large quantities at three huge installations originally built to supply highly enriched uranium (more than 90% uranium-235) for certain nuclear weapons. While similar plants, all using the gaseous diffusion process, were operated in the Soviet Union, Britain, France, and China, only the relatively small one in Britain had ever supplied enriched uranium commercially. The U.S., thus, had been for all practical purposes the sole world supplier of uranium enrichment services, a potent political advantage. Although it served all customers on the same terms, foreign nuclear power interests and their governments never happily accepted total dependence on the U.S., and the British-German-Dutch plan, first discussed by the three countries in 1968, was clearly a move to break the monopoly.

Its significance was greatly heightened by the fact that the three proposed to use the gas centrifuge process, which each had been developing independently. The AEC had long since declared that because the process could be used in small, easily concealed installations to produce material for weapons it must be considered especially sensitive. It had gone to great lengths to discourage other countries from developing the gas centrifuge and, failing in this, had induced most to treat the technology as highly secret. Domestically, it had taken the unprecedented step of forcing several companies to abandon gas centrifuge work already under way and had limited development efforts to its own laboratories and a handful of its own contractors.

Thus, the three countries' plans to build two small centrifuge-enrichment plants, one in the Netherlands and the other in Britain, were doubly unwelcome to the U.S. government. Undeterred, the three successfully concluded their basic negotiations in November.

Other Nonmilitary Uses. Confirming trends apparent in earlier years, the commercial use of radiopharmaceuticals and radiochemicals expanded rapidly in all advanced countries, and generally the same was true of the use of isotopic and accelerator radiation sources to process a wide variety of products. For the year, world demand for radiopharmaceuticals alone represented a market valued at approximately $60 million, largely supplied by private firms. About 25 fully commercial radiation processing plants equipped with cobalt-60 sources were in operation throughout the world. These were chiefly for the sterilization of medical supplies but increasingly were being used for other purposes, such as the production of enzymes for detergent compounds, cosmetic sterilization, and the irradiation of plastic-impregnated wood. A notable breakthrough was the purchase of almost ten acres of irradiated wood parquetry for a U.S. airport terminal.

In at least four countries—Britain, Canada, France, and the U.S.—efforts were continued to develop high-performance, isotope-fueled thermoelectric generators for such uses as power sources for navigation beacons and at untended weather stations. Many successful demonstrations were completed without apparently improving the chances that these devices would soon be economically feasible. On the other hand, the prospect that similar generators would at last find relatively wide use in the U.S. space program was enhanced by the good performance of the unit used to power the scientific instrument package that the Apollo 12 astronauts left behind on the moon. Reports of efforts in several countries to develop extremely small isotopic power sources for implantable heart pacers were encouraging.

Installed Capacity and Production of Nuclear-Electric Power in Selected Countries

Country	Capacity installed at Jan. 1, 1969 (000 kw.)	Production in 1968 (000,000 kw-hr.)	Cumulative nuclear-electric production (000,000 kw-hr.)
United Kingdom	4,780	28,000	119,700
United States	2,830	13,700	46,400
France	1,094	3,500	11,200
West Germany	860	2,000	3,900
Italy	622	2,400	15,600
Other countries	650	1,900	4,300
Total	10,836	41,500	201,100

Source: UNIPEDE.

In the major U.S. program to develop the technology of using nuclear explosives for nonmilitary purposes, a single test was held. It involved the detonation of a 40-kiloton explosive to fracture a tight natural gas formation in western Colorado. While preliminary technical results were satisfactory, the experiment aroused considerable opposition, not so much from local residents as from conservation groups and scientists concerned that such operations would trigger seismic disturbances or release dangerous quantities of radioactivity to the environment. These reactions, together with the U.S. government's evident inclination to go slow in this field, pointed to the likelihood that the value of the new technology for the recovery of minerals would be established much more slowly than its proponents wished. Its use for excavation evidently was still further off. Reports that the Soviet Union had a parallel program under way remained unconfirmed.

There were few signs of a significant rise of interest anywhere in the use of reactor-powered steam plants to power merchant ships. The first such vessel, the NS "Savannah," continued to operate in regular service chiefly because the U.S. Maritime Administration could think of nothing else to do with it. There was little reason to suppose that anything would come of the agency's tentative plans to underwrite construction of a small fleet of fast nuclear container-type ships.

West Germany's "Otto Hahn," designed as an ore carrier, completed a series of long, successful cruises but found itself shut out of all foreign ports for want of satisfactory international agreements governing its entry. Construction of Japan's small nuclear-powered freighter, due to be completed in 1972, continued steadily on schedule. Unconfirmed reports suggested that the Soviet Union had dropped plans to build a fleet of nuclear icebreakers as successors to the powerful but uneconomical "Lenin."

Nuclex 69, the second international exhibition of nuclear technology, was held in Basel, Switz., from October 6 to October 11, with the participation of 317 exhibitors from 21 countries including (for the first time) the U.S.S.R. The program included nine conferences attended by experts and officials from numerous countries. A third Nuclex was to be held in Basel in 1972. (Jo. H. S.)

See also Defense; Fuel and Power; Physics.

ENCYCLOPÆDIA BRITANNICA FILMS. *Atomic Radiation* (1953); *Carbon Fourteen* (1953); *Atomic Energy—Inside the Atom* (1961); *Electrons at Work* (1961); *Evidence for Molecules and Atoms* (1961).

Numismatics:
see Philately and Numismatics

Nursing:
see Medicine

Nutrition:
see Domestic Arts and Sciences; Medicine

Nuts:
see Agriculture

Obituaries 1969

The following is a selected list of prominent men and women who died during the year 1969.

ALEXANDER, BEN, U.S. actor (b. Goldfield, Nev., May 26, 1911—d. Hollywood, Calif., d. reported July 5, 1969), who played in many motion pictures before co-starring with Jack Webb in the "Dragnet" radio and television series of the 1950s. In the late 1960s he appeared in "Felony Squad," a TV series.

ALEXANDER OF TUNIS, HAROLD RUPERT LEOFRIC GEORGE ALEXANDER, 1st Earl, field marshal (ret.), British Army (b. London, Eng., Dec. 10, 1891—d. Slough, Buckinghamshire, Eng., June 16, 1969), one of the most distinguished military commanders in World War II, was commissioned in the Irish Guards in 1911. In World War I he won the DSO and MC and was three times wounded. A major general on the outbreak of World War II, he commanded the British rear guard at Dunkirk and later extricated British and Indian forces from Burma. In 1942 he was appointed commander in chief of the British Armies in the Middle East, and in 1943 brought about the surrender of German forces in Tunisia. As Gen. Dwight D. Eisenhower's deputy commander, he was in charge of the invasion of Sicily and Italy (1943). In 1944 he was made field marshal and supreme commander of the Allied Forces in the Mediterranean Theatre. During 1946–52 he was governor-general of Canada and from 1952 to 1954, minister of defense in Sir Winston Churchill's Conservative government. His *The Alexander Memoirs, 1940–45* was published in 1962.

ALLAIN, MARCEL, French writer (b. Paris, France, Sept. 15, 1885—d. Saint-Germain-en-Laye, France, Aug. 25, 1969), was one of the creators of Fantomas, an evil character widely known in France who gave his name to a long series of popular thrillers. Of a total of 45 *Fantomas* books, Allain, whose stories began to appear in 1905, wrote 33 in collaboration with Pierre Souvestre (d. 1914) and 12 on his own. They were translated into some 40 languages and many were adapted for motion pictures.

ALLEN, TERRY DE LA MESA ("Terrible Terry"), general (ret.), U.S. Army (b. Fort Douglas, Utah, April 1, 1888—d. El Paso, Tex., Sept. 12, 1969), World War II commander of the 1st Infantry Division in the North Africa and Sicily campaigns (1942–43), and of the 104th Infantry Division in the drive into Germany (October 1944–April 1945). Allen retired in 1946.

ALMEIDA, GUILHERME DE, Brazilian poet (b. 1891—d. São Paulo, Braz., July 11, 1969), known as the "prince of Brazilian poetry," whose works included *A Danca das Horas* ("Dance of the Hours") and *Era uma Vez* ("There Was a Time"). He was elected to the 40-member Brazilian Academy of Letters in 1942.

ANGELI, HELEN MARIA MADOX ROSSETTI, British-Italian author (b. London, Eng., Nov. 10, 1879—d. Sept. 11, 1969), daughter of the pre-Raphaelite W. M. Rossetti, acquired Italian nationality by her marriage in 1903 to Gastone Angeli. From the age of 13 she regularly attended anarchist meetings and with her sister, Olivia, ran an anarchist newspaper, *The Torch.* In later years Mrs. Angeli became interested in the arts; in 1949 she published *Dante Gabriel Rossetti: His Friends and Enemies,* and in 1954 *Pre-Raphelite Twilight: the Story of Charles Augustus Howell.*

ANNADURAI, CONJEEVARAM NATARAJAN, Indian politician (b. Sept. 15, 1909—d. Madras, India, Feb. 3, 1969), founded the Tamil nationalist Dravidian Progressive Forum (Dravida Munnetra Khazagam—DMK) in 1949, and as its leader became chief minister of Tamilnadu (Madras) when the DMK unexpectedly came to power in the state legislature following the Indian general elections of 1967. Previously a journalist, he founded the weekly *Dravidanadu* in 1942, and edited the Tamil weekly *Kanchi* until 1967.

ANSERMET, ERNEST, Swiss conductor (b. Vaud Canton, Switz., Nov. 11, 1883—d. Geneva, Switz., Feb. 20, 1969), was the founder (1918) of the 115-member Orchestre de la Suisse Romande, one of the world's finest symphony assemblies, which he conducted until his retirement in 1967.

ANSLOW, GLADYS AMELIA, U.S. physicist (b. Springfield, Mass., May 22, 1892—d. Brookline, Mass., March 31, 1969), who was an authority on mass spectroscopy, became professor of physics in 1936 (emeritus, 1960) at Smith College, Northampton, Mass., having been associated with that institution from 1914. Her work included a spectrochemical study of the structure of proteins and antibiotics, which was of importance in the production of synthetic foods and drugs. Her knowledge of mass spectroscopy led to her being the first woman to work on the cyclotron at the University of California.

ARENALES CATALÁN, EMILIO, Guatemalan diplomat (b. Guatemala City, Guat., May 10, 1922—d. Guatemala City, April 17, 1969), representative to the United Nations, and president of the UN General Assembly 1968–69. He was also his country's foreign minister from 1966 until the time of his death.

ARMSTRONG, CHARLOTTE, U.S. mystery writer (b. Vulcan, Mich., 1905—d. Glendale, Calif., July 18, 1969), author of more than a score of mystery books, including *Lay On, MacDuff,* her first (1942); *Mischief* (1950; made into a movie, *Don't Bother to Knock,* 1952); *A Dram of Poison* (1956, winner of the Edgar Allan Poe Award); *The Witch's House* (1963); *I See You* (1966); *Lemon in the Basket* (1967); and *The Balloon Man* (1968).

ARNOLD, TOM (Thomas Charles Arnold), British impresario (b. Yorkshire, Eng., 1897—d. London, Eng., Feb. 2, 1969), was a successful promoter of many types of public entertainment, ranging from musical comedy through ice shows, pantomime, rodeo, and films to Shakespearean drama. He brought the *Folies Bergère* to London in 1925 and was associated with Ivor Novello in some of the latter's best-known successes, such as *The Dancing Years* and *King's Rhapsody.*

ARROYO DEL RIO, CARLOS, Ecuadorian political leader (b. 1893—d. Guayaquil, Ec., Oct. 31, 1969), the president of Ecuador (1940–44), who leased military bases to the United States after the Japanese attack on Pearl Harbor at the beginning of World War II.

ASQUITH OF YARNBURY, HELEN VIOLET BONHAM CARTER, Baroness, British public figure and supporter of the Liberal Party (b. April 15, 1887—d. London, Eng., Feb. 19, 1969), was the daughter of H. H. Asquith, Liberal prime minister (1908–16), and actively helped her father's cause when he contested Paisley in the elections of 1920, 1922, 1923, and 1924. Badly defeated at Wells in the 1945 election, she nearly won Colne Valley in 1951. President (1944–45) of the Liberal Party, she was a governor of the BBC (1941–46), and president of the Royal Institute of International Affairs from 1964. She was created a Dame of the British Empire in 1953 and a life peeress in 1964.

Earl Alexander of Tunis

Conjeevaram Natarajan Annadurai

Tom Arnold

René Barrientos y Ortuño

KEYSTONE

CAMERA PRESS—PIX FROM PUBLIX

CAMERA PRESS—PIX FROM PUBLIX

WIDE WORLD

AUGENSTEIN, LEROY G., U.S. biophysicist (b. Decatur, Ill., March 6, 1928—d. near Charlotte, Mich., Nov. 8, 1969), who researched in genetics and brain function, was chairman of the biophysics department of Michigan State University (from 1962), and author of a study in genetic manipulation, *Let Us Play God* (1969).

AZHARI, ISMAIL AL-, Sudanese political leader (b. 1900—d. Khartoum, Sudan, Aug. 26, 1969), president of the Supreme Council of the Sudan from 1965 until deposed by a military coup on May 25, 1969, came into power with his National Unity Party in the Sudan's first national election in 1953. He served as the first prime minister and minister of the interior from 1954 until 1956. He proclaimed Sudanese independence in December 1955, rejecting a proposal to unite with the U.A.R., and thus broke the Anglo-Egyptian condominium that had existed from 1899.

BACCALONI, SALVATORE, U.S. opera singer (b. Italy, April 14, 1900—d. New York, N.Y., Dec. 31, 1969), was with the Metropolitan Opera Company from 1940 until 1962, singing the basso buffo roles of Don Pasquale, Leporello, Doctor Bartolo, Osmin, and others.

BACKHAUS, WILHELM, Swiss pianist (b. Leipzig, Ger., March 26, 1884—d. Villach, Aus., July 5, 1969), an exponent of the classical German musical tradition, studied at the Leipzig Conservatoire and later under Eugène d'Albert at Frankfurt am Main; made his first concert tour in 1910. He became professor of piano at Manchester Royal College of Music and also taught for a time at the Curtis Institute in Philadelphia.

BAER, ARTHUR ("Bugs"), U.S. humorist and columnist (b. Philadelphia, Pa., 1886—d. New York, N.Y., May 17, 1969), wrote "One Word Led to Another," which was syndicated by King Features and appeared in hundreds of dailies for almost half a century.

BARRIENTOS Y ORTUÑO, RENÉ, president of Bolivia (b. Tunary, Cochabamba, Bol., May 30, 1919—d. near Tocopaya, Bol., April 27, 1969), was killed when his helicopter struck a high-tension wire and crashed. He had been head of the Bolivian Air Force from the latter 1950s until 1964 when he led a military coup that deposed Pres. Víctor Paz Estenssoro. After serving as co-president with Gen. Alfredo Ovando Candía, Barrientos became sole president in 1964.

BARRY, SIR JOHN (VINCENT WILLIAM), Australian judge and criminologist (b. Albury, Austr., June 13, 1903—d. Melbourne, Austr., Nov. 8, 1969), was senior puisne judge of the Supreme Court of Victoria from 1947. Admitted as a barrister in 1926 in Victoria, and in 1946 in New South Wales, he was a leading law reformer and specialist in divorce proceedings. Barry was Australia's senior representative at UN congresses on crime prevention and also lectured on crime in Japan at the UN's request. Since 1951 he had been chairman of the Department of Criminology, Melbourne University.

BASALDELLA, MIRKO, U.S. sculptor (b. 1910—d. Boston, Mass., Nov. 24, 1969), director of the design workshop at Harvard University from 1957, designed the memorial bronze gates to the Ardeatine Caves in Rome (1949–50). He was accorded a number of honours, including election to the American Academy of Arts (1962) and the Order of Merit of the Republic of Italy (1969).

BERAN, JOSEF CARDINAL, Czechoslovak prelate of the Roman Catholic Church (b. Pilsen, Bohemia, Dec. 29, 1888—d. Rome, Italy, May 17, 1969), exiled archbishop of Prague and primate of Czechoslovakia, who had spent 17 years in Nazi and Communist prisons. Beran was arrested by the Nazis in 1942 and released from Dachau in 1945. The following year he was named archbishop of Prague. He was outspoken against restrictions of freedom after the Communist seizure of the Czechoslovak government in 1948 and an especially critical sermon brought house arrest in June 1949. Transferred to Rozelov prison in 1951, he was to remain there for 12 years until 1963. At that time he was not permitted to return to his see, but was permitted finally to go to Rome in February 1965. He was immediately made cardinal, although barred from taking up his duties in his homeland.

BLAIBERG, PHILIP, South African dentist (b. Uniondale, S.Af., May 24, 1909—d. Cape Town, S.Af., Aug. 17, 1969), received a heart transplanted from a 24-year-old donor in an operation performed by Christiaan Barnard at the Groote Schuur Hospital, Cape Town, on Jan. 1, 1968, when Blaiberg was in the last stages of heart failure. Not the world's first heart transplant patient, he survived the longest (19 months), overcoming a critical liver infection and a lung condition, thought to be the result of rejection reactions.

BOEHM, EDWARD MARSHALL, U.S. sculptor (b. Baltimore, Md., 1913—d. Trenton, N.J., Jan. 29, 1969), whose lifelike porcelain birds have been acquired for permanent display by many major museums, including the Metropolitan Museum of Art in New York City and the Smithsonian Institution of Washington, D.C. His work was exhibited in the White House, Buckingham Palace, and the Vatican. Many pieces were in private collections, such as a pair of song swallows valued at $18,000.

BOËTHIUS, (CARL) AXEL, Swedish archaeologist (b. Arvika, Swed., July 18, 1889—d. Rome, Italy, May 7, 1969), authority on Roman topography and architecture, was educated at Uppsala University, Berlin University, and the British School in Athens. He became in 1926 the first director of the Swedish Institute of Classical Studies in Rome. He was professor of classical archaeology at Göteborg University (1934–55) and its rector (1946–51). Among his publications were *The Golden House of Nero* (1960) and *The Etruscan Centuries in Italy* (1962).

BOLES, JOHN, U.S. actor (b. Greenville, Tex., Oct. 27, 1895—d. San Angelo, Tex., Feb. 27, 1969), who made more than a score of motion pictures, including *Desert Song* (1944), and last appeared in *Babes in Bagdad* (1952), also had roles in several Broadway plays, such as *One Touch of Venus* (1943).

BOOTH, MARY, British Salvation Army leader (b. Hadley Wood, Barnet, Hertfordshire, Eng., April 22, 1885—d. Finchampstead, Berkshire, Eng., Aug. 31, 1969), was a granddaughter of Gen. William Booth, founder of the Salvation Army. With the rank of colonel, she commanded sections of the Salvation Army in Great Britain, Germany, Belgium, and the West Indies. During World War I, she organized hospital visitations, and in World War II was interned in Belgium.

BOSTON, SIR HENRY (JOSIAH) LIGHTFOOT, Sierra Leonean statesman (b. Freetown, Sierra Leone, Aug. 19, 1898—d. London, Eng., Jan. 11, 1969), was governor-general of Sierra Leone from 1962 until 1967. He studied law in England and was called to the bar in Lincoln's Inn in 1926. After 20 years' private practice in Sierra Leone, he became a magistrate (1946) and later (1957) a judge of the Supreme Court. In the latter year he became speaker of the House of Representatives, and in 1962 was appointed governor-general—the first Sierra Leonean to hold that office, which he retained until the military coup of 1967.

BREEN, DAN, Irish patriot (b. 1894—d. Dublin, Ire., Dec. 27, 1969), was an Irish Republican Army commandant in the Irish War of Independence, 1918–21. He wrote of his service in *My Fight for Irish Freedom.*

BRISCOE, ROBERT, Irish politician (b. Dublin, Ire., Sept. 25, 1894—d. Dublin, May 30, 1969), the first Jewish lord mayor of Dublin (1956–57), became a member of the Sinn Fein Irish Nationalist movement in 1917 and carried out many exploits against the British. After the Irish Free State was recognized in 1921, Briscoe helped found the Fianna Fail Party (1926) and served in the Dail Eireann from 1927 until 1965.

BROWN, JOHN MASON, U.S. drama and literary critic (b. Louisville, Ky., July 3, 1900—d. New York, N.Y., March 16, 1969), was drama critic for the *New York Post* and the *World-Telegram* before going to the *Saturday Review* in 1944. After several years of writing his column "Seeing Things," he also took on the duties of the magazine's editor at large and held that post until his death. Besides the column which he wrote from 1944 until 1964, Brown published several books including the first volume of *The Worlds of Robert E. Sherwood: Mirror to His Times* (1965); the second was unfinished.

BYRNE, JOHN, British trade unionist (b. Scotland, Jan. 24, 1903—d. Glasgow, Scot., Dec. 4, 1969), played a large part in ending election rigging and Communist control of the Electrical Trades Union, of which he was general secretary from 1961 to 1966. Once an electrical fitter on Clydeside, he was Glasgow area secretary of the ETU in 1956 when he was awarded the OBE. In 1959 he contested the results of the union election, and after two years of litigation, was finally vindicated.

CAMPBELL, JOHN R., British Communist (b. Paisley, Scot., Oct. 15, 1894—d. London, Eng., Sept. 18, 1969), was editor of the *Daily Worker* from 1949 to 1959. He joined the British Socialist Party in 1912 and became a founder member of the British Communist Party in 1920.

CANNON, BERRY LOUIS, U.S. aquanaut (b. March 22, 1935—d. near San Clemente Island, Calif., Feb. 17, 1969), died while working 600 ft. beneath the Pacific Ocean in connection with the U.S. Navy's Sealab III Project. An electronics engineer, one of the first U.S. aquanauts, and a veteran of the 1965 Sealab II experiment, Cannon was at the site of the Sealab III habitat for a final check of the structure before the first-team divers were to enter it for an 80-day study of the effects of prolonged underwater life upon man.

CARRON, WILLIAM JOHN CARRON, BARON, British trade unionist (b. Hull, Eng., Nov. 19, 1902—d. London, Eng., Dec. 3, 1969), president of the one-million-strong Amalgamated Engineering Union from 1956 to 1967, was a member of numerous government committees. He was made a trustee of Churchill College, Cambridge, in 1958, and was a visiting fellow of Nuffield College, Oxford. He was a member of the National Economic Development Council, a director of Fairfield Shipyards and of the Bank of England, and became a life peer in 1967, on his retirement.

CASTLE, IRENE, U.S. dancer (b. New Rochelle, N.Y., 1894—d. Eureka Springs, Ark., Jan. 25, 1969), who, with her husband Vernon Castle (d. 1918), was internationally known for introducing the "Castle Walk" and other ballroom steps of the World War I era. She was also credited with having started the bobbed-hair craze of the 1920s. After retiring from her dancing career, Irene Castle became interested in animal welfare and founded the Orphans of the Storm animal shelter near Chicago, Ill.

CATROUX, GEORGES, French soldier, administrator, and diplomat (b. Limoges, France, Jan. 29, 1877—d. Paris, France, Dec. 21, 1969), spent much of his youth in the Middle East. He was wounded and captured during World War I, when he first met Charles de Gaulle, and later served in Algeria and Syria. Governor-general of Indochina in 1940, he joined de Gaulle in London. He commanded the French forces in Syria in 1941 and was active in the Middle East until the end of World War II. From 1945 to 1948 he was French ambassador in Moscow. A confidant of de Gaulle during the latter's retirement from politics (1953–58), he was appointed governor-general of Algeria in 1956; this provoked an outcry from European reactionaries and he resigned. He presided over the inquiry into the Indochina war in 1954, and in 1961 over the military court that condemned the rebel Algerian Army generals. He was grand chancellor of the Legion of Honour from 1954 to 1968.

CHEESMAN, (LUCY) EVELYN, British entomologist, author, and lecturer (b. Westwell, near Ashford, Kent, Eng., 1881—d. Chelmsford, Essex, Eng., April 15, 1969), was curator of the Insect House at the London Zoo (1920–26), and official entomologist on the St. George Expedition to the Pacific (1924–25). She subsequently divided her time between expeditions to the South Pacific and writing books on her discoveries.

CHEVALLIER, GABRIEL, French novelist (b. Lyons, France, May 3, 1895—d. Cannes, France, April 4, 1969), was best known as the author of *Clochemerle* (1934), a farcical Rabelaisian story of a small provincial town and its scandals. The novel, translated into many languages, had sold nearly 3 million copies by the 1960s. He wrote several other novels of a similar burlesque nature, including *Propre à Rien* (1936), *Sainte-Colline* (1937), and three sequels to *Clochemerle.*

CHUKOVSKY, KORNEI IVANOVICH, Soviet children's writer (b. St. Petersburg, Russia, 1882—d. Moscow, U.S.S.R., Oct. 28, 1969), was known to millions of Russian children as "Uncle Chukasha." Perhaps his best-known book was *From Two to Five* (1925), a collection of amusing children's remarks. He also wrote critical works, notably *The Mastery of Nekrasov* (1952).

CIANNELLI, EDUARDO, U.S. actor (b. Ischia, Italy, Aug. 30, 1889—d. Rome, Italy, Oct. 8, 1969), who achieved his greatest success as Trock Estrella in the 1935 Broadway play *Winterset* (film version, 1936), also appeared in dozens of motion pictures during his 45-year career, of which his last two, *The Secret of Santa Vittoria* and *The Brotherhood,* were released in 1969.

CLEMENT, FRANK GOAD, U.S. politician (b. Dickson, Tenn., June 2, 1920—d. Nashville, Tenn., Nov. 4, 1969), who became the youngest U.S. governor when in 1952 at age 32 he was elected governor of Tennessee. Reelected to a four-year term in 1954, but prohibited from succeeding himself, he again ran successfully in 1962.

COLLYER, BUD (CLAYTON JOHNSON HEERMANCE, JR.), U.S. television personality (b. New York, N.Y., 1908—d. Greenwich, Conn., Sept. 8, 1969), master of ceremonies for TV's "Beat the Clock" and "To Tell the Truth" programs, had also worked in many radio shows including "Truth or Consequences," "Road of Life" and many other soap operas.

COMPTON-BURNETT, IVY, British novelist (b. Pinner, Middlesex, Eng., June 5, 1884—d. London, Eng., Aug. 27, 1969), whose novels represent one of the most accomplished, idiosyncratic contributions to English fiction in the period 1930–60. From *Pastors and Masters,* her second novel but the first to reveal her distinctive talent (1925), to *A God and His Gifts* (1960) all follow one pattern: analysis of personal relationships in the middle-class Edwardian family, its servants and dependents. Tension is often resolved in melodramatic crime—incest (*Brothers and Sisters,* 1929), matricide (*Men and Wives,* 1931), suicide (*The Present and the Past,* 1953)—or by disclosure of hidden resentment in family life, as in *A House and Its Head* (1935), *Elders and Betters* (1944), *Manservant and Maidservant* (1947), *Two Worlds and Their Ways* (1949), *A Heritage and Its History* (1950), and *Mother and Son* (1955). *A Conversation,* her only nonfictional work, appeared in 1945. In 1951 Ivy Compton-Burnett was made Commander and, in 1967, Dame of the British Empire.

CONNOLLY, MAUREEN (MRS. NORMAN BRINKER), U.S. tennis champion (b. San Diego, Calif., Sept. 17, 1934—d. Dallas, Tex., June 21, 1969), who was known as "Little Mo," held the world's title in women's tennis from 1951 until 1954. She was the first woman to win the grand slam of tennis—the U.S., British, French, and Australian championships. Twice she successfully defended her U.S. championship, and had won her third singles championship at Wimbledon when, in July 1954, a horseback riding accident ended her tennis career.

Philip Blaiberg Evelyn Cheesman

WIDE WORLD CAMERA PRESS—PIX FROM PUBLIX

COSTA e SILVA, ARTUR, da, marshal (ret.), Brazilian Army (b. Taquari, Braz., Oct. 3, 1902—d. Rio de Janeiro, Braz., Dec. 17, 1969), president of Brazil from March 1967 until Aug. 31, 1969, when illness forced his retirement. He was leader of a military coup that ousted Pres. João Goulart in April 1964 and brought about the election of Humberto Castelo Branco as president. In the election of Oct. 3, 1966, Costa e Silva himself was elected president and took office the following spring. His announced plans for social reform were reaching slow realization at the time of his incapacitation.

COTTON, BILLY, British entertainer and broadcaster (b. London, Eng., May 6, 1899—d. London, March 25, 1969), the last surviving exponent of the 1930-style big-band comedy show, made his first radio broadcast as bandleader in 1928. His first TV shows were screened in 1956 and attracted large audiences for over seven years.

CREED, SIR THOMAS PERCIVAL, British educator (b. Farthinghoe, Northamptonshire, Eng., Jan. 29, 1897—d. Kensington, London, Eng., May 11, 1969), vice-chancellor of the University of London (1964–67), was also principal of Queen Mary College, London (1952–67). He entered the academic profession relatively late in life after a long legal career. He joined the Sudan Political Service in 1922 and from 1936 to 1941 was chief justice of the High Court of Sudan. In 1941 he became legal secretary to the Sudan government.

CRIST, BAINBRIDGE, U.S. composer (b. Lawrenceburg, Ind., Feb. 13, 1883—d. Hyannis, Mass., Feb. 7, 1969), whose symphonic and choral works included the tone poem "American Epic: 1620" (1943).

CROMPTON, RICHMAL (RICHMAL CROMPTON LAMBURN), British writer (b. Bury, Lancashire, Eng., Nov. 15, 1890—d. Jan. 11, 1969), created William Brown, a typical 11-year-old schoolboy, whose adventures filled numerous books, from *Just William* (1922) onward. The "William" books sold nearly nine million copies in English editions and were translated into several other languages; they were also filmed, dramatized, and serialized on radio and television. Miss Crompton, originally a teacher, also wrote about 40 adult novels.

DAHLGRÜN, ROLF, West German politician (b. Hanover, Ger., May 19, 1908—d. Hamburg, W.Ger., Dec. 19, 1969), was finance minister (1962–66) in the Christian Socialist-Free Democratic coalition governments. Following his law studies he rose to become chief legal adviser to a large Hamburg rubber factory. He entered the Bundestag as a Free Democrat in 1957 and soon became chairman of the Economic Committee. He left the Erhard government in 1966 following a dispute over the budget.

DAO, S. Y., Nationalist Chinese economist (b. Shanghai, China, 1919—d. New York, N.Y., Sept. 27, 1969), who was minister of economic affairs (from June 1969) in the government of Nationalist China, previously had been secretary-general of the Council for International Economic Co-operation and Development.

DAURAT, DIDIER, French aviator and administrator (b. Monteuil-sous-Bois, France, Jan. 2, 1891—d. Toulouse, France, Dec. 2, 1969), a pilot in World War I, entered civil aviation in 1919, joining the famous Latécoère airline company which later became Aéropostale and developed a mail service from France to South America via North Africa. After World War II he became personnel training director for Air France and later head of operations at Orly Airport. Antoine de Saint-Exupéry, in his *Vol de nuit* (*Night Flight*), portrayed Daurat in the character of Rivière, the airline manager who demanded and inspired complete devotion to duty in his pilots.

Billy Cotton Sir Thomas Percival Creed

CAMERA PRESS—PIX FROM PUBLIX CAMERA PRESS—PIX FROM PUBLIX

DAVENPORT, HAROLD, British mathematician (b. Accrington, Lancashire, Eng., Oct. 30, 1907—d. Cambridge, Eng., June 9, 1969), was prominent in his work on the geometry of numbers and analytic number theory. Educated at Manchester University and Trinity College, Cambridge, he was elected fellow of the Royal Society in 1940, and, in 1958, became the third Rouse Ball professor of mathematics at Cambridge.

DAVID-NEEL, ALEXANDRA EUGÉNIE MARIE LOUISE, French explorer and scholar (b. Saint-Mandé, France, Oct. 24, 1868—d. Digne, France, Sept. 8, 1969), won worldwide fame early in the century for her wanderings through central Asia. In 1924, dressed as a mendicant pilgrim, she became the first European woman to enter the forbidden city of Lhasa. She stayed in Tibet for 14 years, and as a Buddhist attained the rank of lama. She wrote 17 works in several languages; the major books in English were *My Journey to Lhasa, Magic and Mystery in Tibet,* and *Initiations and Initiates in Tibet.*

DEMPSEY, SIR MILES, general (ret.), British Army (b. Dec. 15, 1896—d. Yattendon, Berkshire, Eng., June 5, 1969), commanded the 13th Infantry Brigade in 1940 that fought a delaying action in the retreat to Dunkirk; he commanded the 13th Army Corps of the 8th Army in its way through Sicily and into Italy (1943), and the 2nd British Army that took part in the invasion of Normandy (1944).

DE VILMORIN, LOUISE LEVEQUE, French author (b. Verrières-le-Buisson, France, April 4, 1902—d. Verrières-le-Buisson, Dec. 26, 1969), several of whose books, which included the best seller *Madame de . . . , Sainte-Unefois, La Fin de Villavide, Le Retour d'Erica, Julietta,* and *La Lettre dans un Taxi,* were successfully filmed.

DIECKMANN, JOHANNES, German politician (b. Fischerhude, Ger., Jan. 19, 1893—d. East Berlin, Ger., Feb. 22, 1969), president of the East German Volkskammer (parliament) from 1949, was a co-founder (1945) of the Liberal-Democratic Party. Before that he had served as general secretary of the German Peoples Party (1919–33), and held a seat in the Diet of Saxony (1928–33). In 1960 he became deputy president of the State Council of the German Democratic Republic, and in 1963, president of the Society for German-Soviet Friendship—posts he still held at the time of his death.

DIRKSEN, EVERETT McKINLEY, U.S. senator from Illinois (b. Pekin, Ill., Jan. 4, 1896—d. Washington, D.C., Sept. 7, 1969), Republican Party leader in the U.S. Senate from 1945, won election in 1932 to the 73rd Congress. After eight consecutive terms as a representative he did not seek reelection in 1948 because of an eye ailment; however, in 1950 he made a successful run for the Senate. He became minority whip in 1957 and minority leader in 1959. In 1952 Dirksen nominated Sen. Robert Taft, who lost out to Gen. Dwight D. Eisenhower, as the Republican candidate for the presidency. Dirksen frequently reversed his stand on top legislation—during the 1960s three reversals were of note: the UN bond issue of 1962, the nuclear test-ban treaty of 1963, and the Civil Rights Act of 1964. Having been opposed to all three issues at the outset, he later came out in full support of each measure.

DORNIER, CLAUDE, German aircraft designer (b. Kempten, Allgäu, Ger., May 14, 1884—d. Zug, Switz., Dec. 5, 1969), pioneer designer of seaplanes, was for 50 years director of a factory that supplied bombers to the German Luftwaffe during World War II. In 1929 he designed and built the giant 12-engined Do-X transatlantic flying boat capable of carrying 170 passengers.

DOUGLAS OF KIRTLESIDE, WILLIAM SHOLTO DOUGLAS, 1ST BARON, marshal of the Royal Air Force (b. Headington, Oxfordshire, Eng., Dec. 23, 1893—d. Northampton, Eng., Oct. 29, 1969), commanded fighter squadrons during World War I and was by 1938 assistant chief of the Air Staff. In World War II he took over the Fighter Command following the Battle of Britain, and later organized attacks on Rommel's main sea supply line between Italy and Tunisia. In 1946 he followed Montgomery as commander of British Forces and military governor of the British zone of Germany. He joined the board of the British Overseas Airways Corporation in 1948, but left in 1949 to become chairman of British European Airways (BEA), a post that he held until 1964.

DUKE, VERNON (VLADIMIR DUKELSKY), U.S. composer (b. Pskov, Russia, Oct. 10, 1903—d. Santa Monica, Calif., Jan. 17, 1969), was the composer of the Broadway musicals *Walk a Little Faster* (1932) and *Cabin in the Sky* (1940), which included the popular songs "April in Paris," "Taking a Chance on Love," "Love Me Tomorrow," "Honey in the Honeycomb," and "Autumn in New York." Under his real name he also wrote a number of symphonies, ballets, concertos, and cantatas.

DULLES, ALLEN WELSH, U.S. lawyer and diplomat (b. Watertown, N.Y., April 7, 1893—d. Georgetown, D.C., Jan. 29, 1969), head of the U.S. Office of Strategic Services in Switzerland during World War II, became director of the U.S. Central Intelligence Agency in 1953, and served until 1961. As leader of the CIA his successes were unpublicized but his failures received worldwide attention, especially the Soviet capture of a U-2 reconnaissance plane in 1960, the almost successful attempt of the U.S.S.R. to establish missile bases in Cuba, and the Cuban Bay of Pigs fiasco in 1961. Dulles was the author of *Germany's Underground* (1947), *The Craft of Intelligence* (1963), and *The Secret Surrender* (1966).

DUPUY, PIERRE, Canadian diplomat (b. Montreal, Que., July 9, 1896—d. Cannes, France, May 21, 1969), who was ambassador to France from 1958 until 1963 when he retired from the diplomatic service to become commissioner general of Canada's world's fair, Expo 67.

EASTMAN, MAX FORRESTER, U.S. poet and editor (b. Canandaigua, N.Y., Jan. 12, 1883—d. Bridgetown, Barbados, March 25, 1969), was an authority on Communism, and a prominent radical during World War I and the 1920s. In 1918 he was indicted under the Sedition Act for advocating resistance to U.S. entry into World War I, which, as editor, he expressed in *The Masses,* a left-wing magazine. From 1941 Eastman was a roving reporter for *Reader's Digest.* His writings on the U.S.S.R. included *Marx and Lenin: The Science of Revolution* (1926) and *Stalin's Russia and the Crisis in Socialism* (1939). Besides his published poems he also wrote *The Enjoyment of Poetry* (1913; 23rd rev. ed., 1948), and two autobiographies.

EISENHOWER, DWIGHT DAVID, 34th president of the U.S. (b. Denison, Tex., Oct. 14, 1890—d. Washington, D.C., March 28, 1969), held the permanent rank of five-star general of the U.S. Army. He entered the U.S. Military Academy at West Point in 1911, graduated in 1915, and during World War I commanded a tank training centre. In 1926 he finished first in a class of 275 at the Army's Command and General Staff School, and in 1928 graduated from the Army War College. Stationed in Washington, D.C., he was in the office of the chief of staff, Gen. Douglas MacArthur, from 1933 until 1935, when he accompanied MacArthur to the Philippines.

At the start of World War II, Eisenhower returned to the U.S. and after the attack on Pearl Harbor he became chief of staff of the war plans

Everett McKinley Dirksen Dwight David Eisenhower

UPI COMPIX © KARSH, OTTAWA FROM RAPHO GUILLUMETTE

division of the Army General Staff. In June 1942 he was named commanding general of the European Theatre, and the following November he assumed command of the Allied Forces in North Africa. In December 1943 he was made Supreme Commander of Allied Expeditionary Forces for the invasion of western Europe, and on June 6, 1944, directed the landings on the Normandy beaches of France. In December of that year Eisenhower was promoted to the five-star rank of general of the army. In May 1945 he received Germany's unconditional surrender, and in November returned to Washington as army chief of staff. He resigned from active duty Feb. 7, 1948, to become president of Columbia University. In December 1950 he was appointed commander of the supreme headquarters of NATO, but in mid-1952 he resigned from the Army to accept the Republican nomination for the U.S. presidency. He defeated the Democrat Adlai E. Stevenson in the November election and was inaugurated Jan. 20, 1953.

Although his first term was marked by a severe heart attack and a major operation, Eisenhower was reelected for a second term, again defeating Stevenson. During his terms Eisenhower was concerned with ending the war in Korea (accomplished in July 1953), and with keeping peace throughout the world. His proposals for the latter resulted in the creation of the International Atomic Energy Agency to deal with peaceful uses of the atom, and in the formation of alliances, such as the South East Asia Treaty Organization (SEATO).

After leaving the White House, Eisenhower retired to his farm in Gettysburg, Pa., and returned to his writing, having already published his war memoirs, *Crusade in Europe,* in 1948. His further works included *Mandate for Change* (1962), *Waging Peace* (1965), *The White House Years,* and *At Ease: Stories I Tell My Friends* (1967).

ESHKOL, LEVI (LEVI SHKOLNIK), Israeli statesman (b. Oratovo, Kiev district, Ukraine, Oct. 25, 1895—d. Jerusalem, Israel, Feb. 26, 1969), was prime minister of Israel from 1963 until the time of his death. He went to Israel in 1914 and worked as a labourer; later he became interested in the Zionist Labour Party, and was one of the founders of Histadrut (General Federation of Labour). After Israel became an independent nation in 1948 he held several important government posts, including that of minister of finance (1952–63). In 1963, when David Ben-Gurion announced his retirement, Eshkol succeeded him as prime minister. Two years later Ben-Gurion again sought the leadership but Eshkol easily won the election. In the summer of 1967 he met the crisis of the Six-Day War. During his period of leadership Eshkol was successful in unifying the three major labour parties into the Israel Labour Party which, with the left-wing Mapam, became the first faction to hold a majority in Parliament.

EVERITT, HELEN, U.S. publishing executive (b. 1901—d. Boston, Mass., Oct. 28, 1969), editor in chief and director of Gambit, Inc., Boston publishers, was associate editor of the *Ladies Home Journal* from 1953 until 1962 when she became the first editor of Encyclopædia Britannica Press.

FIELD, WINSTON JOSEPH, Rhodesian statesman (b. Bromsgrove, Worcestershire, Eng., June 6, 1904—d. Salisbury, Rhod., March 17, 1969), who was prime minister of Southern Rhodesia from 1962 until 1964, became leader of the Dominion Party in 1956, and the following year headed the opposition in the federal Assembly. In December 1962, as leader of the new rightist Rhodesian Front Party, he was chosen as prime minister and served until 1964 when he lost his post to Ian Smith. Field retired from active politics in 1965.

FLEISCHMANN, RAOUL HERBERT, U.S. publisher (b. Ischi, Aus., Aug. 17, 1885—d. New York, N.Y., May 11, 1969), who with Harold Ross started *The New Yorker* magazine, putting out the first issue in February 1925. Fleischmann served variously as vice-president, president, chairman, and publisher.

FLEURE, HERBERT JOHN, British geographer, anthropologist, and archaeologist (b. Guernsey, Channel Islands, June 6, 1877—d. Cheam, Surrey, Eng., July 1, 1969), was professor of geography and anthropology at the University College of Wales (1917–30) and professor of geography at Manchester University (1930–44). His published works included *A Natural History of Man in Britain* (1951).

FLINT, SIR WILLIAM RUSSELL, British painter (b. Edinburgh, Scot., April 4, 1880—d. London, Eng., Dec. 27, 1969), was known for his technical skill as a water colourist, specializing in landscapes, costume studies, and nudes in a markedly individual style; he also did book illustrations and lithographs. He first exhibited at the Royal Academy in 1905 and became a full Academician in 1933. He was knighted in 1947.

FOSDICK, THE REV. HARRY EMERSON, U.S. clergyman and author (b. Buffalo, N.Y., May 24, 1878—d. Bronxville, N.Y., Oct. 5, 1969), was founder (1927) and pastor of the interdenominational Riverside Church in New York City until his retirement in 1946. During the same years his National Vespers radio program was heard by millions of listeners every Sunday afternoon. Fosdick was ordained as a Baptist minister on Nov. 18, 1903, and given a post at First Baptist Church in Montclair, N.J. In 1918, after duty with World War I troops in Europe, he went to First Presbyterian Church in Manhattan, N.Y. Because of his theological liberalism he created something of a furor among the Fundamentalists and was forced to resign from this pastorate in March 1925. He then accepted a post at the Park Avenue Baptist Church (New York City), which in 1927 evolved into Riverside Church. Fosdick was the author of several books, including *The Modern Use of the Bible* (1924), *A Faith for Tough Times* (1952), his autobiography, *The Living of These Days* (1956), and a number of hymns.

FOULKES, CHARLES, general (ret.), Canadian Army (b. Stockton-on-Tees, Durham, Eng., 1903—d. Ottawa, Ont., Sept. 12, 1969), who served as chairman of Canada's Chiefs of Staff Committee from 1951 until 1960, was leader of Canadian Forces on the Western and Italian fronts during World War II.

FRIEDMAN, WILLIAM F., lieutenant colonel (ret.), U.S. Army, and cryptologist (b. Kishinev, Russia, 1891—d. Washington, D.C., Nov. 2, 1969), headed the U.S. task force that worked on cracking the Japanese "purple" code from 1938 until September 1940, when it was finally solved shortly before the U.S. entered World War II. Friedman retired in 1955, having been awarded many honours for his work. He was a contributor to *Encyclopædia Britannica.*

GALLEGOS, RÓMULO, Venezuelan statesman and author (b. Caracas, Venez., Aug. 2, 1884—d. Caracas, April 4, 1969), was the first popularly elected president of Venezuela. He held the post only a few months—February through October 1948—when he was ousted by the military coup of Gen. Marcos Pérez Jiménez and sent into exile. Gallego returned to Venezuela in 1958 and was voted life membership in the senate. He attained literary success in 1920 with the novel *El último Solar,* followed by his best known, *Doña Bárbara,* which was translated into several languages, including English (1931). Other works included *El Forastero* (1942) and *Sobre la misma tierra* (1943).

GANDHI, RAMDAS MOHANDAS, Indian political worker (b. Johannesburg, S.Af., 1896—d. Bombay, India, April 14, 1969), last surviving son of Mohandas Gandhi, spent the first 24 years of his life in South Africa. He went to India in 1920 and joined in the struggle for independence. For some time he edited *Navjiwan Weekly* and later was manager of the Bardoli *ashram* (religious retreat). In 1952 he went to live in the Sevagram *ashram* founded by his father.

GARLAND, JUDY (FRANCES GUMM), U.S. actress (b. Grand Rapids, Minn., June 10, 1922—d. London, Eng., June 22, 1969), who appeared on the stage before she was three years old, also achieved success in films as a child star. Among her early hits were the *Andy Hardy* series (with Mickey Rooney), and especially *The Wizard of Oz* (released in 1939), from which she took her lifelong theme song "Over the Rainbow." A number of screen musicals followed: *Meet Me in St. Louis, The Pirate* (with Gene Kelly), *Easter Parade* (with Fred Astaire), after which she returned to the stage in vaudeville and singing shows. In 1954 she made another important film, *A Star Is Born,* but by the late 1950s she was plagued by illness and semiretired. However, in 1960 Judy Garland made a spectacular comeback with performances in London's Palladium and Carnegie Hall in New York. Later she worked in television, undertook several overseas appearances, and was nominated for an Oscar for her supporting role in *Judgment at Nuremburg* (1962).

Levi Eshkol Judy Garland

KEYSTONE WIDE WORLD

GENOVESE, VITO, U.S. underword figure and racketeer (b. Rosiglino, Italy, Nov. 27, 1897—d. Medical Center for Federal Prisoners, Springfield, Mo., Feb. 14, 1969), "Boss of All Bosses" of the Mafia (or Cosa Nostra), died while serving a 15-year prison term for narcotics smuggling.

GEORGIEV, KIMON, Bulgarian politician (b. Pazardzhik, Bulg., 1882—d. Sofia, Bulg., Sept. 28, 1969), premier of Bulgaria in 1934–35, and again, as leader of the coup that led the country into Communism, in 1944; he was defeated in an election in 1946.

GIMBEL, ADAM, U.S. merchandising executive (b. Milwaukee, Wis., Dec. 21, 1893—d. New York, N.Y., Sept. 9, 1969), was head of the Saks Fifth Avenue stores from 1926 until February 1969.

GIOVANNINI, ALBERTO, Italian politician and journalist (b. 1882—d. Bologna, Italy, April 20, 1969), a prominent liberal, was founder of the newspaper *La Libertà economica.* Entering Parliament in 1921, Giovannini signed in 1925 the motion of protest against Mussolini's assumption of dictatorial powers. Later his paper was suppressed, and Giovannini gave up political life. During World War II he fought with the Italian resistance forces against the Germans. After the war he became editor in chief of the Florentine daily newspaper *La Patria.* Returning to Parliament in 1948, he became minister without portfolio under Aristide De Gasperi.

GOETZ, WILLIAM, U.S. motion-picture producer and executive (b. New York, N.Y., 1903—d. Holmby Hills, Calif., Aug. 15, 1969), in the 1930s was founder and vice-president of Twentieth Century-Fox, then founder (1943) and head of production of Universal-International before he founded William Goetz Productions in 1953. Among his more than 100 film releases were *Sayonara, Song of Bernadette, The Glenn Miller Story, The Man from Laramie,* and his last, *Assault on a Queen* (1966).

GOMBROWICZ, WITOLD, Polish writer and playwright (b. Maloszyce, Pol., Aug. 4, 1904—d. Vence, France, July 25, 1969), started writing in the early 1930s, but his first novel, *Ferdydurke,* appeared in 1937. His best-known books are *Trans-Atlantyk* (1953), *Pornografia* (1960), and *Kosmos* (1963); his plays *Iwona księżniczka Burgunda* ("Yvonne, Princess of Burgundy") and *Ślub* ("The Vow") were produced in Paris.

GORCEY, LEO, U.S. motion-picture actor (b. New York, N.Y., 1917—d. Oakland, Calif., June 7, 1969), played "Spit" in the original *Dead End,* filmed between 1938 and 1942. Later he helped create the Bowery Boys, whose comical adventures were on the screen until the early 1950s.

GREEN, MITZI, U.S. actress (b. Bronx, N.Y., Oct. 22, 1920—d. Huntington Beach, Calif., May 24, 1969), as a child star appeared in about 15 films including *Tom Sawyer* (1929), *Huckleberry Finn* (1931), *Girl Crazy,* and *Little Orphan Annie* (1932). In 1937 she was in the Broadway show *Babes in Arms,* and during the next decade she toured the nightclub circuit and worked in television.

GROPIUS, WALTER ADOLF, German-U.S. architect (b. Berlin, Ger., May 19, 1883—d. Boston, Mass., July 5, 1969), founder of the Bauhaus

School of Design, studied at Charlottenburg-Berlin and Munich universities (1903–07), then began his career in the firm of Peter Behrens. One of his early designs was for the Fagus Building, a factory at Alfeld in Germany. In 1919 Gropius opened the Bauhaus School in Weimar, the first major school to unite art with industrial living. In 1925 the school was moved to Dessau, and in 1933 it was closed by the Nazis as "degenerate." Gropius left Germany, spent three years in England, then went to the U.S. as head of the architecture department of the Harvard Graduate School of Design. Retiring from Harvard in 1952, he organized his own firm, Architects' Collaborative. His later work included the architectural designs for the University of Baghdad and the U.S. embassy in Athens; he also was consultant on the design for the Pan Am Building in New York City.

GRUNITZKY, NICOLAS, Togolese statesman (b. near Lome, Togo, April 5, 1913—d. Paris, France, Sept. 27, 1969), the second president of Togo, served from 1963 until 1967 when he was ousted by a military coup. Before his country's independence in 1960 he was premier of the territory, known as French Togoland, during 1956–58.

GUARDIA, RICARDO A., de la, Panamanian statesman (b. March 14, 1899—d. Panama City, Pan., Dec. 29, 1969), who, as president of Panama during 1941–45, eliminated the 5% "political tax" on salaries, suspended gambling, established a practical price ceiling on food, and enlarged the education and health programs.

HAGEN, WALTER ("The Haig"), U.S. golf champion (b. Rochester, N.Y., Dec. 21, 1892—d. Traverse City, Mich., Oct. 5, 1969), was winner of 17 major titles, including the U.S. Open in 1914 and 1919, the PGA title five times (1921 and 1924 through 1927), and four British Opens (1922, 1924, 1928, and 1929). When he retired from competition in 1929, his earnings had reached more than $1 million. His autobiography, *The Walter Hagen Story,* was published in 1956.

HANAN, JOSIAH RALPH, New Zealand lawyer and politician (b. Invercargill, N.Z., June 13, 1909—d. Cairns, Queensland, Austr., July 23, 1969), as attorney general and minister of justice was largely responsible for a series of reforms, including the abolition of capital punishment (1962) and the alteration of the licensing hours (1967). National member of Parliament for Invercargill from 1946, he was minister of health (1954–57), minister of Maori affairs (1960–69), and of island territories (1963–69).

HARARI, MANYA, British publisher and translator (b. St. Petersburg, Russia, April 8, 1906—d. London, Eng., Sept. 24, 1969), was educated in Great Britain and lived in Cairo, Egypt, until 1939, when she returned to London. After World War II she founded the Harvill Press and published numerous works of modern Russian literature, she herself translating many of them. Among the authors was Boris Pasternak, whose *Dr. Zhivago* she translated with Marc Hayward.

HARTLEY, FRED A., JR., U.S. congressman (1929–50) from New Jersey (b. Harrison, N.J., Feb. 22, 1902—d. Linwood, N.J., May 11, 1969), was co-author of the Taft-Hartley (Labor-Management Relations) Act of 1947, outlawing the closed shop.

HAWKINS, COLEMAN ("Bean"), U.S. jazz musician (b. St. Joseph, Mo., 1905—d. New York, N.Y., May 19, 1969), known as the "father of the tenor saxophone," began his career in the early 1920s with Mamie Smith's Jazz Hounds and Fletcher Henderson's Band. He formed a small group in 1939 and made his famous "Body and Soul" recording. In later years he appeared in jazz concerts.

HAWKINS, ERIC W., British journalist (b. London, Eng., Nov. 24, 1888—d. Paris, France, Aug. 18, 1969), was editor of the *International Herald Tribune* in Paris from 1924 to 1960, when he became "editor emeritus." Hawkins, who had joined the old Paris *Herald* in 1915, was a well-known figure in international journalism. During the Nazi occupation of Paris he went to London and his activity there on behalf of France was mentioned in the memoirs of Charles de Gaulle.

HAWLEY, CAMERON, U.S. novelist (b. Howard, S.D., Sept. 19, 1905—d. Marathon, Fla., Feb. 9, 1969), was the author of *Executive Suite* (1952), *Cash McCall* (1955), *The Lincoln Lords* (1960), and *The Hurricane Years* (1968).

HAYES, GABBY (George Francis), U.S. cowboy actor (b. Wellesville, N.Y., May 7, 1885—d. Burbank, Calif., Feb. 9, 1969), made about 200 Western films but was best known for his role as "Windy" in the *Hopalong Cassidy* motion picture and television series of the 1930s and 1940s. Later he appeared in a number of other television series.

HEARNE, JOHN JOSEPH, Irish lawyer and diplomat (b. Waterford, Ire., 1893—d. Dublin, Ire., March 29, 1969), the Republic of Ireland's first ambassador to the U.S. (1950–60), had helped draft the constitution that created the republic from the Irish Free State in 1937.

HEILBRUNN, OTTO, German-British author (b. Frankfurt am Main, Ger., 1906—d. Gerrards Cross, Eng., Jan. 6, 1969), was a leading expert on Communist insurgency tactics. His publications included *Communist Guerilla Warfare* (with C. A. Dixon; 1954), *The Soviet Secret Services* (1956), *Partisan Warfare* (1962), *Warfare in the Enemy's Rear* (1963), and *Conventional Warfare in the Nuclear Age* (1965). He served as a U.S. assistant counsel at the Nürnberg War Crimes trials after World War II. Subsequently he became a British subject.

HENIE, SONJA, Norwegian skating champion and actress (b. Oslo, Nor., April 8, 1912—d. en route from Paris, France, to Oslo, Oct. 12, 1969), who won most of the world's major skating titles from 1927 through 1936 when she became a professional. After winning the junior figure skating championship of Oslo at age 8 and the Norwegian title at 11, she entered her first Olympics (1924) and finished third in the free skating. In Oslo in 1927 she won the first of her ten consecutive world championships. Her three Olympic gold medals were won at St. Moritz, Switz., in 1928, at Lake Placid, N.Y., in 1932, and at Garmisch-Partenkirchen, Ger., in 1936. As a professional, Sonja Henie toured the U.S. with her colourful and impressive ice show, and quickly signed for her first skating film, *One in a Million* (1939). A dozen other pictures followed, reportedly grossing $25 million. After her retirement from skating she became interested in modern art and, with her third husband, Niels Onstad, in 1968 presented to the people of Norway the Høvikodden Art Centre and 250 paintings, together valued at around $3.5 million.

HERBER, ARNIE, U.S. football player (b. Green Bay, Wis., 1910—d. Green Bay, Oct. 14, 1969), one of the earliest passers in the pro game, was with the Green Bay Packers from 1930 until 1940 when he retired. He led the NFL in passing in 1932, 1934, and in 1936 when he completed 77 passes for 1,239 yd. Herber was named to football's Hall of Fame in 1966.

HEYNS, GARRETT, U.S. penologist (b. Allendale, Mich., 1891—d. Olympia, Wash., Nov. 3, 1969), state institution director of Michigan (1916–57) and of Washington (1957–67), whose philosophy of penology stressed the possibility of probation and parole rather than strict adherence to traditional punishment. From 1967 he was executive director of the Joint Commission on Correctional Manpower and Training.

HILL OF WIVENHOE, EDWARD JAMES HILL, Baron, British trade unionist (b. London, Eng., Aug. 20, 1899—d. Colchester, Eng., Dec. 14, 1969), one of the most influential figures in the British trade union movement, was president of the Amalgamated Society of Boilermakers, Shipwrights, Blacksmiths and Structural Workers, 1963–65. He joined the United Society of Boilermakers in 1916, becoming shop steward, branch secretary, London district organizer; he was chairman of the London District Committee for ten years before promotion to general secretary of the Boilermakers' Union in 1949, a post he held until 1963. He was made a life peer in 1967.

HIRSCH, MAX, U.S. horseman (b. Fredericksburg, Tex., July 30, 1880—d. New Hyde Park, N.Y., April 3, 1969), who was considered the leading race horse trainer in the U.S., developed hundreds of Thoroughbreds, including three Kentucky Derby winners: Bold Venture (1936), Assault (Triple Crown holder, 1946), and Middleground (1950).

HLASKO, MAREK, Polish writer (b. Warsaw, Pol., Jan. 14, 1934—d. Wiesbaden, W.Ger., June 14, 1969), the literary hero of his country following the Polish political upheavals of 1956, published his collection of short stories, *Pierwszy krok w chmurach* ("First Step in the Clouds"), that same year. For his novel *Osmy dzien tygodnia* ("The Eighth Day of the Week") he received the literary prize of the Polish Publishers Association in 1957. A film based on the book was made, but both book and film were banned in Poland. Hlasko made his first trip abroad about that time, and when in West Germany asked for asylum. For a time he lived in Israel but settled in West Germany in 1962. His last two books were *The Graveyard* (1959) and *Next Stop—Paradise* (1960).

HOAK, DONALD ALBERT (Don), U.S. baseball player (b. Roulette, Pa., Feb. 5, 1928—d. Pittsburgh, Pa., Oct. 9, 1969), third baseman for the Pittsburgh Pirates (1958–63), had for his nine years (1954–63) with the National League a lifetime average of .265.

HO CHI MINH (Nguyen That Thanh), president of North Vietnam (b. Kim-Lien, Nghe-An Prov., Indochina, May 19, 1890—d. Hanoi, N.Viet., Sept. 3, 1969), who became a Communist organizer in Southeast Asia as early as 1923, was constantly attempting to free his country from foreign domination and to gain control over a unified Vietnam, first against the French and later against the involvement of the U.S. In 1945, as head of the Democratic Republic of Vietnam and seeking to establish the independence of the new country, Ho issued a proclamation over the objections of the French colonials. Although the French were driven out, Ho was compelled to accept the 17th-parallel partition of Vietnam, as outlined by the Geneva Conference of 1954. He set about consolidating the North, and by 1956 was engaging in guerrilla warfare against the South, where the regime of Pres. Ngo Dinh Diem was soon to be bolstered by a buildup of U.S. aid. In 1964 Ho launched a full-scale war against South Vietnam and its ally, the U.S. Even as peace talks dragged on in Paris, Ho was, at the time of death, still confident of victory.

HOGAN, PATRICK, Irish member of Parliament (b. 1886—d. Dublin, Ire., Jan. 24, 1969), was speaker of the Dail from 1951 until 1967.

HOLLAND, SIR EDWARD MILNER, British advocate (b. Sutton, Eng., Sept. 8, 1902—d. Hove, Eng., Nov. 2, 1969), was attorney general of the Duchy of Lancaster from 1951, and chairman of the committee appointed in 1963 to report on rented housing in London.

HOOVER, HERBERT CLARK, JR., U.S. engineer (b. London, Eng., Aug. 4, 1903—d. Pasadena, Calif., July 9, 1969), son of the 31st president of the U.S., served as U.S. undersecretary of state from 1954 to 1957.

HORNE, (CHARLES) KENNETH, British entertainer and broadcaster (b. London, Eng., Feb. 27, 1907—d. London, Feb. 14, 1969), made his name in the radio comedy series "Much Binding in the Marsh," centred on a mythical RAF airfield. He launched the radio series "Beyond Our Ken" and "Round the Horn" and had a comedy series "Horne a' Plenty" on Independent Television.

HORSBRUGH, FLORENCE HORSBRUGH, Baroness, British politician (b. Scotland, Oct. 13, 1889—d. reported Dec. 6, 1969), minister of education from 1951 to 1954, was the first woman in a Conservative government to be a member of the Cabinet, to which she was promoted by Winston Churchill in 1953. After 23 years in the House of Commons, in 1959 she was made a life peeress.

Gabby Hayes Sonja Henie

WIDE WORLD UPI COMPIX

HROMADKA, JOSEF L., Czechoslovak theologian (b. Hodslavice, Moravia, Austria-Hungary, June 8, 1889—d. Prague, Czech., Dec. 26, 1969), was founder (1958) and president (1958–69) of the Christian Conference for Peace, considered a spearhead for Christian-Marxist dialogue. After collaborating with his friend Thomas Masaryk in the birth of the first Czechoslovak republic, he was the sole Christian leader of his country to join the Communists in 1936 in their support for the Spanish Republic. After the Nazi take-over of his country (March 1939) he spent seven years teaching in the U.S. before returning to Czechoslovakia in 1947. Hromadka received the Lenin Peace Prize in 1958.

HUGHES, EMRYS, British politician (b. Tonypandy, Wales, July 10, 1894—d. Ayrshire, Scot., Oct. 18, 1969), who, representing the Scottish constituency of South Ayrshire from 1946, was an enthusiastic supporter of the Labour movement and a close associate of Kier Hardie, its founder. Hughes's independent left-wing extremism and pacifism (for which he spent three years in prison during World War I) frequently left him isolated from the bulk of his party. He was editor of *Forward,* the Scottish Socialist newspaper (1931–46), and of a Scottish edition of *Tribune* after World War II.

HUNT, MARTITA, British actress (b. Argentina, Jan. 30, 1900—d. London, Eng., June 13, 1969), began her stage career in 1921 with the Liverpool Repertory Company and from 1923 was seen, mostly in London, in parts differing as widely as polished socialites, Rosalind, the Queen in *Hamlet* for the Old Vic Company (1929), and Angelica in *Hotel Paradiso* (1956). She achieved acclaim as Aurelia in *The Mad Woman of Chaillot,* played in New York and on tour (1949–51). Her film roles included Miss Havisham in *Great Expectations.*

HUSAIN, ZAKIR, Indian scholar and statesman (b. Hyderabad, Deccan, India, Feb. 8, 1897—d. New Delhi, India, May 3, 1969), president of India from 1967 to 1969, was the first Muslim to attain that office. He was educated at Aligarh Muslim University where he became a staunch follower of Mohandas Gandhi. He was, in succession, vice-chancellor of the Jamia Millia Islamia and Aligarh Muslim universities. After a five-year term as governor of Bihar (1957–62), he served as vice-president of India from 1962 to 1967 and, as the nominee of the Congress Party, succeeded to the presidency in 1967.

HYMAN, LIBBIE, U.S. zoologist (b. Des Moines, Ia., Dec. 6, 1888—d. New York, N.Y., Aug. 3, 1969), research associate at the American Museum of Natural History (New York City) from 1937, whose study *The Invertebrates* (vol. 1 published in 1931, vol. 6 in 1968), a classic reference on the subject, was to be carried through volume 10 by other scientists, was the author of a number of college manuals, 150 papers on invertebrates (1914–66), and the editor of *Systematic Zoology* (1959–63). She received the Gold Medal of the Linnaean Society of London in 1960 and the Gold Medal for distinguished achievement from the American Museum of Natural History in 1969.

INGRAM, REX, U.S. actor (b. on the Mississippi River, 1896—d. Hollywood, Calif., Sept. 19, 1969), who, although holding a medical degree, spent 50 years on the stage and screen. He played such diverse roles as a native in the original Tarzan pictures of the 1920s, the Emperor in the stage production *Emperor Jones,* and "De Lawd" in *The Green Pastures,* an all-Negro film of 1936. In the 1960s Ingram appeared in a number of television series.

ITURBI, AMPARO, Spanish-U.S. pianist (b. Valencia, Spain, March 12, 1899—d. Beverly Hills, Calif., April 21, 1969), who sometimes joined her brother José in duo-piano concerts, but generally followed an independent career, having played with the New York Philharmonic, the Los Angeles Philharmonic, and the Lamoureux of Paris. Her last concert was given in New York City in November 1968.

JASPERS, KARL, German existentialist philosopher (b. Oldenburg, Ger., Feb. 23, 1883—d. Basel, Switz., Feb. 26, 1969), was professor of philosophy at Heidelberg (1920–37) and at Basel (from 1948). Educated at Heidelberg, Munich, Berlin, and Göttingen, he worked in a psychiatric clinic in Heidelberg (1910–16), and was professor of pathology there (1916–20) before being made extraordinary (1920) and then ordinary (1921) professor of philosophy. Removed by the Nazis (1937), he was reinstated in 1945. He was chiefly influenced by Kierkegaard, Kant, Nietzsche, and Max Weber. His works include *Allgemeine Psychopathologie* (1913; 6th ed., 1953), *Vermunst und Existenz* (1935; Eng. trans., *Reason and Existence,* 1956), *Philosophie,* 3 vol. (1932), and *Einführung in die Philosophie* (1950).

JENSEN, EILER, Danish trade unionist (b. Copenhagen, Den., April 14, 1894—d. Copenhagen, Dec. 23, 1969), chairman and secretary-general of the Danish Trade Union Congress from 1943 to 1967, was a Social-Democratic member of the Danish Parliament from 1945 to 1953, and in addition played an active part in the international trade union movement, being for many years vice-chairman of the International Confederation of Free Trade Unions.

JONES, (LEWIS) BRIAN, British guitarist (b. Cheltenham, Gloucestershire, Eng., Feb. 28, 1944—d. Hartfield, Sussex, Eng., July 3, 1969), one of the best-known figures in the field of contemporary popular music, was with the Rolling Stones, having joined the group at its outset in 1962.

JONES, THOMAS HUDSON, U.S. sculptor (b. Buffalo, N.Y., July 24, 1892—d. Hyannis, Mass., Nov. 4, 1969), designed the Tomb of the Unknowns, erected in 1931 at Arlington National Cemetery in Washington, D.C.

JORDAN, THE REV. CLARENCE L., U.S. clergyman (b. Talbotton, Ga., 1912—d. Koinonia Farm, Ga., Oct. 29, 1969), Southern Baptist minister, who founded (1942) a 1,400-ac. interracial farm near Americus, Ga., gained national attention in 1957 when the farm was subjected to nightly attacks. Jordan was the author of *Cotton Patch Version of Paul's Epistles* (1968).

JUNDI, COL. ABD-AL KARIM AL-, colonel, Syrian Army, and political leader (b. As Salamiyah, Hamah Prov., Syria, 1932—d. Damascus, Syria, March 2, 1969), was a supporter of the Baath Party and chief of Syrian national security at the time of his death by suicide. After following a military career he had become minister of agrarian reform and acting minister of the interior in 1964.

KABIR, HUMAYUN, Indian educator and author (b. West Bengal, India, Feb. 22, 1906—d. New Delhi, India, Aug. 18, 1969), member of the Indian Parliament, was education secretary in the Indian government during 1948–56; later he became minister of civil aviation and minister for scientific and cultural affairs. Among his publications were several volumes of poems in Bengali, *Education in New India* (1956), and *Britain and India* (1967).

KARLOFF, BORIS (William Henry Pratt), British-U.S. actor (b. London, Eng., Nov. 23, 1887—d. Midhurst, Sussex, Eng., Feb. 2, 1969), was famous for his portrayal of horrific parts in films. Originally intended for a diplomatic career, he ran away at the age of 21 to Canada and the U.S., adopting his maternal grandfather's name of Karloff. After ten years' acting in stock companies he turned to films and in 1931 won fame as the monster in *Frankenstein,* the first of a long series of films with titles like *Grip of the Strangler, The Body Snatchers, The Walking Dead, The Mummy,* and *The Cat People.* He was also successful on the stage, particularly in *Arsenic and Old Lace* in 1941 and as Captain Hook in *Peter Pan* in 1951.

KASAVUBU, JOSEPH, first president of the Democratic Republic of the Congo (b. Tshela, Léopoldville, Belgian Congo, 1917[?]—d. Boma, Republic of the Congo, March 24, 1969), one of the first Congolese leaders to demand independence from the Belgians, studied 11 years for the priesthood but entered the Belgian administration (1942) where he worked in the Treasury. In 1954 he became president of Abako, a cultural association of the Bakongo tribe which he organized as a political front, and in 1957, when the Belgians permitted elections for the major urban councils, became mayor of Dendale, a Léopoldville commune. On independence (June 30, 1960) he became president with Patrice Lumumba as prime minister. Both were ousted by Gen. Joseph D. Mobutu in his first coup (September 1960) but Kasavubu was reinstated and remained as head of state until Mobutu's second coup in November 1965.

KAY, VIRGINIA, U.S. columnist (b. Chicago, Ill., 1927—d. Chicago, April 9, 1969), wrote "Dateline: Chicago" for the *Chicago Daily News* from 1965.

KENNEDY, JOSEPH PATRICK, U.S. financier and diplomat (b. Boston, Mass., Sept. 6, 1888—d. Hyannis Port, Mass., Nov. 18, 1969), who served as U.S. ambassador to the United Kingdom from 1938 through 1940, after having amassed a huge fortune through many diverse business enterprises. In 1928 he bought the Keith-Albee-Orpheum theatre chain and quickly realized $5 million in the movie business. In the early 1930s he secured a franchise for Scotch whiskey, later selling the franchise for about $8 million in profit. In the late 1940s he bought Chicago's Merchandise Mart, world's largest commercial building, and properties in New York and Palm Beach, Fla., transactions that were to bring him many more millions. In the political field, Kennedy was the first chairman of the Securities and Exchange Commission (1932–35) and served as chairman of the Maritime Commission before taking the post of ambassador.

Joseph P. Kennedy was the father of four sons, each of whom served his country in the highest tradition: Joseph P. Kennedy, Jr., World War II Navy flier, who was killed over England in 1944; John F. Kennedy, U.S. senator from Massachusetts, 1952–60, and 35th president of the U.S., who was assassinated in 1963; Robert F. Kennedy, U.S. attorney general, 1960–64, and U.S. senator from New York, 1964 until his assassination in 1968; and Edward M. Kennedy, U.S. senator from Massachusetts from 1962.

Ho Chi Minh

A.F.P. FROM PICTORIAL PARADE

Kenneth Horne

CAMERA PRESS—PIX FROM PUBLIX

Brian Jones

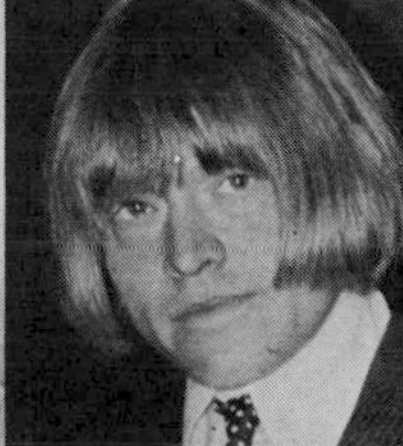

KEYSTONE

Boris Karloff

CAMERA PRESS—PIX FROM PUBLIX

Joseph Kasavubu

KEYSTONE

Joseph Patrick Kennedy

WIDE WORLD

KEROUAC, JACK, U.S. author (b. Lowell, Mass., March 12, 1922—d. St. Petersburg, Fla., Oct. 21, 1969), proponent of the "beat generation" of the 1950s, who wrote *On the Road,* the autobiographical account of his wanderings across the United States, and a voicing of his rejection of materialism (published in 1957). This work was the most successful of his 11 novels, which included *The Dharma Bums* (1958), *The Subterraneans* (1958), *Big Sur* (1962), and *Desolation Angels* (1965); a volume of poems, *Mexico City Blues,* appeared in 1959.

KERR, ANDREW ("ANDY"), U.S. football coach (b. Cheyenne, Wyo., Oct. 7, 1878—d. Tucson, Ariz., Feb. 16, 1969), as head coach at Colgate University from 1929 until 1946 led the Red Raiders to a record of 95 victories, 50 defeats, and 7 ties.

KING, FRANK, U.S. cartoonist (b. Cashon, Wis., 1883—d. Winter Park, Fla., June 24, 1969), in 1918 created "Gasoline Alley," a strip he continued to draw until 1951, when it was taken over by other artists; in 1969 it was still enjoyed by millions of newspaper readers.

KOPECHNE, MARY JO, U.S. political worker (b. Wilkes-Barre, Pa., July 26, 1940—d. near Edgartown, Mass., July 19, 1969), presumably drowned when a car driven by Sen. Edward M. Kennedy, and in which she was a passenger, plunged off a narrow bridge into a tidal pond. Miss Kopechne was one of a 12-member group participating in a reunion on Chappaquiddick Island off Martha's Vineyard. Along with others at the gathering, she had worked for Sen. Robert F. Kennedy during his campaign for the presidential nomination of the Democratic Party in 1968. After Senator Kennedy's assassination in June 1968, she accepted a position with Matt Reese Associates of Washington, D.C., a firm engaged in setting up campaign headquarters for politicians.

KOROTCHENKO, DEMYAN SERGEEVICH, Ukrainian politician (b. Pogrebki, Ukraine, 1894—d. Kiev, U.S.S.R., April 7, 1969), president of the Ukraine Republic, was a partisan leader in the Russian Revolution and World War II. He was also a deputy president of the Soviet Union, a hero of the Soviet Union, and held seven Orders of Lenin.

KOSTRZEWSKI, JOZEF, Polish archaeologist and anthropologist (b. Weglewo, Pol., Feb. 25, 1885—d. Poznan, Pol., Oct. 19, 1969), was one of the founders of the Poznan Polish University in 1919, and for almost five decades its professor of prehistory. He discovered a prehistoric Slavonic marsh dwelling at Biskupin, near Znin. He published over 700 works and studies, including *Die ostgermanische Kultur der Spätlatenezeit* (2 vol., 1919) and *The Prehistory of Polish Pomerania* (1936).

LA ROQUE, ROD, U.S. actor (b. Chicago, Ill., Nov. 29, 1898—d. Beverly Hills, Calif., Oct. 15, 1969), star of the silent screen, played in more than 30 pictures ranging through *The Ten Commandments, Gigolo, Captain Swagger, Our Dancing Daughters, One Romantic Night,* and into the sound era of the 1930s with *Till We Meet Again* and *The Hunchback of Notre Dame.*

LEE, EDWARD L., U.S. billiards champion (b. 1906—d. New York, N.Y., May 18, 1969), only American ever to hold the world title (1936) in amateur three-cushion billiards, won more championships (including 20 annual national titles, 1931–64) than any other player.

LEHMAN, ROBERT, U.S. banker and art collector (b. New York, N.Y., Sept. 29, 1891—d. Sands Point, N.Y., Aug. 9, 1969), senior partner of the investment firm of Lehman Brothers, whose art collection included the finest old masters and modern works. In addition to more than a thousand paintings, he owned tapestries, jewelry, bronzes, and glass. Lehman in 1963 endowed a chair in the history of art at Yale University, and in 1967 gave to New York University $1 million for its Institute of Fine Art.

LEIPER, ROBERT THOMSON, British physician (b. Kilmarnock, Ayrshire, Scot., April 17, 1881—d. Wheathampstead, Hertfordshire, Eng., May 21, 1969), a pioneer in tropical medicine, was best known for his discoveries in parasitology. His expert knowledge was acquired by travel and study in Europe, America, Africa, and Asia between 1905 and 1938, while he was helminthologist to the London School of Tropical Medicine (1905–24), and director of its Department of Parasitology (1924–46). He was emeritus professor of helminthology at the University of London.

LETTRICH, JOZEF, Slovak political leader (b. Diviaky, Austria-Hungary, June 17, 1905—d. New York, N.Y., Nov. 29, 1969), was dedicated to freeing Central European nations from Soviet domination. He organized young democratic forces in the underground during World War II, and was a leader in the 1944 Slovak uprising against the Nazis. After the war, with the reuniting of Czechoslovakia, he was president of the Slovak National Council and a co-founder of the Democratic Party of Slovakia. In 1948, with the Communist take-over in Czechoslovakia, Lettrich fled to the U.S. He became chairman of the Central Committee of the Council for a Free Czechoslovakia, and chairman of the Czechoslovak delegation to the Assembly of Captive Nations, serving as chairman of the assembly in 1968. He published *History of Slovakia* in 1955.

LEWIS, DOMINIC BEVAN WYNDHAM, British writer (b. Liverpool, Eng., 1891—d. Altea, Spain, Nov. 21, 1969), best known as a humorous columnist, was also a biographer and authority on French history and literature. After serving in the Welch Regiment during 1914–18, Wyndham Lewis became literary editor of the *Daily Express.* From 1925 to 1930 he wrote humorous columns for the *Daily Mail.* After a time in Paris he returned to the *Mail* in 1933, but later moved to the *News Chronicle.* In 1954, with Ronald Searle, he wrote *The Terror of St. Trinians.* He also published biographies and, in collaboration with Charles Lee, compiled an anthology of bad verse, *The Stuffed Owl* (1930).

LEWIS, JOHN L(EWELLYN), U.S. labour leader (b. Lucas, Ia., Feb. 12, 1880—d. Washington, D.C., June 11, 1969), for 40 years president of the United Mine Workers of America, started working in the mines at age 12. In 1909 he was elected legislative agent of the UMW; in 1917 he became vice-president, and in 1920, president of the union. Lewis was critical of the American Federation of Labor's method of organizing workers by craft and skill, wanting instead to lump workers in each of the big industries into special single unions. His idea was voted down at the 1935 AF of L convention in Atlantic City, N.J. Within a few weeks Lewis formed the Committee for Industrial Organization to sign up new unions in the auto and other open-shop industries. The UMW was withdrawn from the CIO in 1942 and by 1946 was back in the AF of L only to leave it again in 1948 over Lewis' refusal to sign the non-Communist affidavit, a requirement under the Taft-Hartley Act, with which he wholeheartedly disagreed. Lewis retired as president of the UMW on Jan. 14, 1960. In 1964 he was awarded a Presidential Medal of Freedom.

LEY, WILLY, German-U.S. science writer (b. Berlin, Ger., Oct. 2, 1906—d. New York, N.Y., June 24, 1969), chief popularizer of the rocket age, was the author of more than 30 books in German and English. In 1927, with a few German colleagues, he founded the Verein für Raumschiffahrt (Society for Space Travel), and among his recruits was Wernher Von Braun with whom he later collaborated on several books, including *The Exploration of Mars* (1956). Running afoul of the Nazis in 1935 over his rocket research, Ley went to England and then to the U.S., where he turned out a score of science-fiction books. He was science editor of the newspaper *PM* from 1940 until 1944, when he became a U.S. citizen and took up full-time writing and lecturing. One of his major works, *Man and the Moon,* was completed shortly before his death. Other of his later books were *Watchers of the Skies* (1963) and *Beyond the Solar System* (1964).

LINDSAY, NORMAN ALFRED WILLIAM, Australian artist and writer (b. Creswick, Victoria, Austr., Feb. 23, 1879—d. Sydney, Austr., Nov. 21, 1969), joined the art staff of the *Sydney Bulletin* in 1901 and was for many years the paper's chief cartoonist. Living in the Blue Mountains, he produced an abundance of paintings in oils and watercolour, sculptures, etchings, and line drawings, and illustrated Boccaccio, Casanova, Theocritus, and Petronius. His numerous novels, in which he often offended Australian moral attitudes of the day, included *Redheap, Saturdee, The Cautious Amorist,* and *The Age of Consent* (which was filmed with James Mason). He also wrote philosophical works, such as *Creative Effort.*

LI TSUNG-JEN, Chinese soldier and political figure (b. Kwangsi Prov., China, 1891—d. Peking, China, Jan. 30, 1969), vice-president of Nationalist China (1948–54), was, with Gen. Chiang Kai-shek, one of the leaders of the Kuomintang. Later he broke with Chiang but in 1937 the two generals united again to combat the Japanese invaders. In 1941 Li was elected vice-president of Nationalist China, and in 1949, when Chiang left the mainland for Taiwan, he was named acting president. The same year illness forced Li's hospitalization in New York City. Refusing to return to Taiwan, he was dismissed from his post in 1954. In 1966, however, after a 16-year self-imposed exile, Li defected to Communist China and settled in Peking.

LLOYD, MARION (MRS. JOSEPH VINCE), U.S. fencing champion (b. 1905—d. Beverly Hills, Calif., Nov. 2, 1969), who was national junior champion in 1926, went on to become U.S. women's foils champion in 1928 and 1931. She was a member of the U.S. Olympic teams of 1928, 1932, and 1936.

LOESSER, FRANK, U.S. composer (b. New York, N.Y., June 29, 1910—d. New York, July 28, 1969), whose many Broadway shows included *Where's Charley?* (Tony Award, 1948), *Guys and Dolls* (Tony Award, 1950), *The Most Happy Fella* (New York Drama Critics Circle Award, 1956), and *How to Succeed in Business Without Really Trying* (Pulitzer Prize, 1962). Among the more than 1,500 songs he wrote were "Baby, It's Cold Outside" (Academy Award, 1948), "Praise the Lord and Pass the Ammunition," "Once in Love with Amy," "Two Sleepy People," and "On a Slow Boat to China."

LOGAN, ELLA, U.S. musical comedy star (b. Scotland, 1913—d. Burlingame, Calif., May 1, 1969), best remembered for the role of Sharon McLonergan in the Broadway hit *Finian's Rainbow* (1947).

LÓPEZ MATEOS, ADOLFO, Mexican statesman (b. near Mexico City, Mex., May 26, 1910—d. Mexico City, Sept. 22, 1969), who served as president of Mexico from 1958 until 1964, entered national politics in 1946 as a member of the Partido Revolucionario Institucional and won a six-year term in the Senate. As president he nationalized the electric industry, worked at solving the El Chamizal border dispute with the U.S., endeavoured to make Latin America a nuclear-free zone, and encouraged the growth of the economy which, during his presidency, grew by 6% annually.

Jack Kerouac — Demyan Sergeevich Korotchenko — John L. Lewis — Willy Ley

WIDE WORLD — CAMERA PRESS—PIX FROM PUBLIX — WIDE WORLD — SEYMOUR—PIX FROM PUBLIX

LUKE, SIR HARRY CHARLES, British administrator (b. London, Eng., Dec. 4, 1884—d. Cyprus, May 11, 1969), was a member of the British Colonial Service (1908–43). He was acting high commissioner of Jerusalem (1928–29); lieutenant governor of Malta (1930–38); and governor of Fiji and high commissioner for the Western Pacific (1938–43). A traveler and writer with a particular interest in the Middle East, he was Bailiff of Egle (1961–69) and Bailiff Grand Cross (1960–69) of the Most Venerable Order of St. John of Jerusalem, and was a contributor to *Encyclopædia Britannica.*

MABANE, WILLIAM MABANE, 1st Baron, British politician (b. Leeds, Eng., Jan. 12, 1895—d. London, Eng., Nov. 16, 1969), was member of Parliament for Huddersfield from 1931 until 1945, holding a number of parliamentary secretaryships during that time. In 1944 he became a member of the Privy Council, and in 1945 was one of the British delegation to the founding conference of the United Nations in San Francisco. He was chairman of the Civil Defense Commission in 1951, was knighted in 1954, and raised to the peerage in 1962. From 1960 to 1963 he was chairman of the British Travel Association, and subsequently its president.

McCAREY, LEO, U.S. film director (b. Los Angeles, Calif., 1898—d. Santa Monica, Calif., July 5, 1969), won Academy Awards for directing *The Awful Truth* (1937), and for writing and directing *Going My Way* (1944).

McCOWN, THEODORE DONEY, U.S. anthropologist and educator (b. Macomb, Ill., June 18, 1908—d. Berkeley, Calif., Aug. 17, 1969), an authority on human fossils, joined the staff of the University of California at Berkeley in 1929 upon his graduation, and became a full professor of physical anthropology in 1951. One of his major finds was made in 1931 on Mt. Carmel in Palestine, when he unearthed the skeleton of a three-year-old child dating from the Mousterian period of the Stone Age. McCown was the author of *The Stone Age at Mt. Carmel* (with Arthur Keith, vol. ii, 1939). (*See* Anthropology.)

McGILL, RALPH EMERSON, U.S. publisher (b. Soddy, Tenn., Feb. 5, 1898—d. Atlanta, Ga., Feb. 3, 1969), a Southern liberal and longtime champion of civil rights, was winner of the 1958 Pulitzer Prize for his editorial writing covering the year 1958, and especially for "A Church, A School . . . ," that dealt with the bombings of a synagogue in Atlanta, Ga., and a school in Clinton, Tenn., terming it the work of "rabid, mad dog minds." As publisher and columnist of the *Atlanta Constitution* he attacked injustice in all forms. He upheld rapid desegregation of schools in the South, strove to better living conditions of the Southern poor, and, not confining himself to local problems, spoke out on world affairs as well. McGill had joined the *Atlanta Constitution* in 1929 as sports editor, then, after a study trip to Europe, returned as editor in 1942, becoming publisher in 1960. In 1963 he wrote *The South and the Southerner,* a significant contribution to an understanding of the region. McGill was awarded the Presidential Medal of Freedom in 1964.

McHUGH, JAMES F. (Jimmy), U.S. composer (b. 1895—d. Beverly Hills, Calif., May 23, 1969), wrote about 500 popular tunes including "The Sunny Side of the Street," "I'm in the Mood for Love," "Coming in on a Wing and a Prayer," "I Can't Give You Anything but Love, Baby," and "Lovely to Look At." He also wrote scores for some 55 screen plays and many Broadway hits.

Sir Harry Charles Luke   Miles Malleson

CAMERA PRESS—PIX FROM PUBLIX   CAMERA PRESS—PIX FROM PUBLIX

MACMICHAEL, SIR HAROLD ALFRED, British colonial administrator (b. Oct. 15, 1882—d. Folkestone, Eng., Sept. 19, 1969), was appointed assistant civil secretary to the Sudan in 1919, and later promoted to civil secretary. In 1933 he became governor of Tanganyika, and from 1939 to 1944 was high commissioner for Palestine and Trans-Jordan. He retired from regular service on leaving Palestine, but in 1945 visited Malaya to study problems of postwar reconstruction. From 1946 to 1947 he was constitutional commissioner in Malta.

McMILLAN, DONALD, U.S. Salvation Army officer (b. Middlesbrough, Eng., June 8, 1887—d. New York, N.Y., Dec. 3, 1969), was U.S. national commander of the Salvation Army from 1953 to 1957. During World War II he served as national secretary, and as vice-president of United Service Organizations (USO). He was appointed eastern territorial commander in 1947.

MacNALTY, SIR ARTHUR (SALUSBURY), British physician (b. Glenridding, Westmorland, Eng., Oct. 20, 1880—d. Epsom, Surrey, Eng., April 17, 1969), medical investigator, public health worker, and medical historian, whose first appointment on the preventive side of medicine was as medical inspector at the U.K. Local Government Board in 1913. From 1919 to 1932 he was deputy senior medical officer at the Ministry of Health, becoming chief medical officer in 1935. On his retirement in 1941 he was appointed editor in chief of the official medical history of World War II. MacNalty wrote several books and was a contributor to *Encyclopædia Britannica.*

MADRAZO, CARLOS, Mexican political leader (b. Tabasco State, Mex., June 7, 1915—d. near Monterrey, Mex., June 4, 1969), head of the Partido Revolucionario Institucional from December 1964 until November 1965, when he was forced to resign because of his desire to introduce broad reform within the party. Madrazo had served as governor of the state of Tabasco for six years (1958–64).

MALLESON, (WILLIAM) MILES, British actor and dramatist (b. Croydon, Surrey, Eng., May 25, 1888—d. London, Eng., March 15, 1969), best known for his interpretations of Shakespearean comic characters, first appeared on the stage in 1912 at the Liverpool Playhouse and made his début in London in 1913 at the Royalty Theatre. World War I gave him inspiration for such plays as *D. Company* and *Black 'Ell,* and in 1927 one of his most memorable works, *The Fanatics,* was produced. After World War II he appeared frequently with the Old Vic and National Theatre companies. Two of his plays, *The Fanatics* and *Six Men of Dorset,* were revived on television in the 1960s.

MANLEY, NORMAN WASHINGTON, Jamaican politician and barrister (b. Roxburgh, Jamaica, July 4, 1893—d. St. Andrew, Jamaica, Sept. 2, 1969), began his political career after the Jamaican labour riots of 1938 by founding the People's National Party. Giving up a career as an advocate, he took the post of chief minister in 1955, after his party's first electoral victory. He became the first premier of Jamaica in 1959 and served until 1962 when he became leader of the opposition. He campaigned again in Jamaica's first post-independence election, in 1967, but was unsuccessful. Manly retired from politics early in 1969.

MANN, ERIKA, German writer (b. Munich, Ger., Nov. 9, 1905—d. Zürich, Switz., Aug. 27, 1969), eldest daughter of Thomas Mann, studied for the stage under Max Reinhardt and in 1925 played a leading part in her brother Klaus's first play. In Munich in 1933 she staged her own satirical review *Die Pfeffermühle* ("The Peppermill"), which after Hitler's rise to power was much performed outside Germany. In 1936, in order to obtain a British passport, she married the poet W. H. Auden and went to the U.S., returning to Europe with her father in 1952. Her books include *School for Barbarians* (1938), *The Lights Go Down* (1940), and *A Gang of Ten* (1942).

MARCELLO, CLAUDIO, Italian civil engineer (b. Forli, Italy, Feb. 24, 1901—d. Milan, Italy, Jan. 9, 1969), an international authority on dam construction, gave his name to a type of gravity dam lightened by hollow elements, of which 15 had been built in Italy and elsewhere up to 1969. In 1937 he became director of the hydroelectric installation division of the Italian Edison group. In 1949 he was nominated president of the Committee of Studies for Hydroelectric Production of the International Union of Producers and Distributors of Electric Energy (UNIPEDE). From 1961 to 1964 he was president of the International Commission on Large Dams, and afterward honorary president. He was a contributor to *Encyclopædia Britannica.*

MARCIANO, ROCKY (Rocco Francis Marchegiano), U.S. boxer (b. Brockton, Mass., Sept. 1, 1923—d. near Des Moines, Ia., Aug. 31, 1969), undefeated world heavyweight champion, held the title from 1952 until 1956. Becoming a professional in 1947, he scored 12 knockouts in 1948 and 4 more in 1949. On Oct. 26, 1951, he met former champion Joe Louis and won the clash in the eighth round. By the next year Marciano earned the right to box the heavyweight champion, Jersey Joe Wolcott, and scored a knockout in the 13th round of the fight, held in Philadelphia on Sept. 23, 1952. In defense of his title, Marciano had a return match with Wolcott (May 1953), two bouts with Roland LaStarza (September 1953 and March 1955), two with Ezzard Charles (both in 1954), one with Don Cockell of England (1955), and one with Archie Moore (Sept. 21, 1955), his last. Marciano's record stood at 49 victories, 43 of them KO's, in 49 professional fights.

MARSHALL, GEORGE PRESTON, U.S. sports promoter (b. Charleston, W.Va., Oct. 11, 1896—d. Georgetown, D.C., Aug. 9, 1969), owner and president of the Washington Redskins of the National Football League, started his team in Boston in 1932, then moved it to Washington in 1937. Marshall was credited with originating the title play-off game and the Pro Bowl.

MARTIN, (BASIL) KINGSLEY, British journalist (b. Hereford, Eng., July 28, 1897—d. Cairo, U.A.R., Feb. 16, 1969), editor (1930–60) of the *New Statesman,* decisively influenced the intellectual opinion of the period from the mid-1930s to the mid-1950s. He served an apprenticeship (1927–30) on the *Manchester Guardian.* He turned the *New Statesman,* a near-bankrupt Liberal-imperialist journal, into the widest selling, most profitable weekly of its kind in the world; required reading in many countries for Cabinet ministers and university teachers and students. It reflected his own ideas and ideals; it also showed his ability to gather and nurture diverse and distinguished talents, and he was as concerned with upholding literary standards as with molding political opinions. Martin wrote many books, from the early historical studies (revised in retirement) to the acute analyses of *The Magic of the Monarchy* (1937), *The Press the Public Wants* (1947), *The Crown and the Establishment* (1962), and the autobiographical *Father Figures* (1967) and *Editor* (1968).

MARTIN, THE REV. WILLIAM KEBLE, British clergyman and botanist (b. Radley, Eng., July 9, 1877—d. Woodbury, Eng., Nov. 26, 1969), author of a best-selling book on British wild flowers (published when he was 87), studied botany at Oxford, where he took his master's degree in 1907, having been ordained in 1902. Over a long lifetime he painstakingly and with great skill built up a collection of coloured illustrations of 1,486 British plant species, which was published in 1965 as the *Concise British Flora in Colour.* It sold 100,000 copies within a year and had doubled that number within four years. The University of Exeter conferred on Keble Martin an honorary D.Sc., and some of his drawings were used on postage stamps issued in 1967.

MARTINELLI, GIOVANNI, U.S. operatic singer (b. Montagnana, Italy, Oct. 25, 1885—d. New York, N.Y., Feb. 2, 1969), was the Metropolitan Opera Company's leading dramatic tenor for 33 years, from 1913 until his retirement in 1945. He made his debut in Rome in 1910 in *The Girl of the Golden West.* His London debut in 1911 was followed by his first appearance at the Met in New York City in 1913 in *La Boheme.* His most important roles were in *Otello, Aida,* and *Norma.*

MASCHWITZ, ERIC, British theatrical producer, librettist, and broadcasting executive (b. Birmingham, Eng., June 10, 1901—d. Ascot, Eng., Oct. 27, 1969), wrote and produced several highly successful musical comedies, such as *Balalaika* (1936), *Carissima* (1948), *Belinda Fair* (1949), *Zip Goes a Million* (1951), and *Love from Judy* (1952). He also wrote some memorable song lyrics, including "Good Night Vienna," "These Foolish Things," and "A Nightingale Sang in Berkeley Square." Maschwitz worked with the British Broadcasting Corporation from 1926 to 1937 and again from 1958 to 1963 and was director of variety programs (1933–37) and assistant and adviser to the controller of television programs (1961–63). In 1963 he was appointed producer (special projects) to Rediffusion Television. His autobiography, *No Chip on My Shoulder,* appeared in 1957.

MAXWELL, GAVIN, Scottish author and naturalist (b. Scotland, 1914—d. Inverness, Scot., Sept. 7, 1969), was best known for his book about his two otters, *Ring of Bright Water* (1960). During World War II Maxwell served as a major in the Scots Guards. He spent his later years traveling and writing on wildlife from his cottage in the Western Highlands. His other books included *Harpoon Venture,* his first (1952), *People of the Reeds,* and *The Ten Pains of Death* (1960); also *The Rock Remains* (1963) and *Raven Seek Thy Brother* (1969), which completed the *Ring of Bright Water* trilogy.

MBOYA, THOMAS JOSEPH ("Tom"), Kenyan politician and Pan-Africanist (b. Kilima Mbago, Machakos District, Eastern Prov., Kenya, Aug. 15, 1930—d. Nairobi, Kenya, July 5, 1969), member of the Luo tribe, considered a possible successor to Jomo Kenyatta as president of Kenya, was assassinated in Nairobi. Mboya was one of eight Africans who were first elected to the former Legislative Council in 1957. Returned to power as member for Nairobi East in the general elections of 1961, and for Nairobi Central in 1963, he became minister for justice and constitutional affairs when Kenya became self-governing on June 1, 1963. After independence in December 1964 he was appointed minister for economic planning and development. Mboya was secretary-general of the Kenya African National Union (KANU), the ruling party.

MERLOT, JOSEPH JEAN, Belgian politician (b. Seraing, Belg., April 27, 1913—d. Liège, Belg., Jan. 21, 1969), was leader of the Walloon Socialists in the Social Christian-Socialist coalition government formed in June 1968 under Gaston Eyskens, and held the positions of deputy prime minister and minister of economic affairs. Previously he had been minister of public works but resigned in 1962 over the linguistic issue.

MERTON, SIR THOMAS (RALPH), British physicist (b. Jan. 12, 1888—d. Oct. 10, 1969), in 1916 succeeded in reproducing spectral features of hydrogen and helium, previously seen only in starlight. He later demonstrated the influence of impurities in gas spectroscopy. In 1935 he invented a cheap method of copying diffraction gratings, and in 1948 devised a new way of ruling them. He was elected to the Royal Society in 1920.

MIES VAN DER ROHE, LUDWIG, German-U.S. architect (b. Aachen, Ger., March 27, 1886—d. Chicago, Ill., Aug. 17, 1969), acclaimed for his uncompromisingly spare design, began his career in 1909 as an apprentice to Peter Behrens, the industrial architect, with whom Walter Gropius (*q.v.*) and Le Corbusier also worked. In the 1920s Mies developed his radically different designs for tall office buildings and apartments, using great amounts of steel and glass. For a time in the early 1930s he was director of the Bauhaus in Berlin, then in 1937 he left Germany for the U.S. to become head of the architecture department at the Illinois Institute of Technology. There he designed 20 buildings, including Crown Hall, for the 100-ac. campus. In 1951 he completed his dramatic 26-story, all-glass-facaded apartment towers on Chicago's lakefront—buildings that exemplified his concept of objective architecture based on technology. Mies was awarded the Presidential Medal of Freedom in 1963, and held gold medals from the Royal Institute of British Architects and the American Institute of Architects.

Thomas Joseph Mboya — Ludwig Mies van der Rohe

WIDE WORLD — UPI COMPIX

MILLIKAN, MAX, U.S. economist (b. Chicago, Ill., Dec. 12, 1913—d. Boston, Mass., Dec. 14, 1969), director of the Center for International Studies, Massachusetts Institute of Technology, from the time of its founding in 1952; was president of the World Peace Foundation from 1956.

MIRZA, SYED ISKANDER, Pakistani statesman (b. Bombay, India, Nov. 13, 1899—d. London, Eng., Nov. 12, 1969), was the first president of Pakistan upon its becoming a republic in February 1956. In 1926 he was selected for the Political Service and in 1938 became political agent in the Khyber. Three years later he became deputy commissioner of Peshawar and by 1946 was joint secretary in the Ministry of Defense, New Delhi. With partition of India in 1947, Mirza chose Pakistan and helped reorganize its Army. In 1954 he became minister of the interior, states, and frontier regions, and was responsible for forming West Pakistan into a single province. In October 1955 he became governor-general and was elected president the following year. Pakistan's increasing poverty and corruption, and the threat of a coup by young army officers, led to Mirza's turning over the government to Gen. Muhammad Ayub Khan in 1958. He spent his political retirement in London.

MODY, SIR HOMI, Indian politician and industrialist (b. Bombay, India, Sept. 23, 1881—d. Bombay, March 9, 1969), was governor of Uttar Pradesh (formerly the United Provinces), 1949–52. From 1927 to 1934 he was chairman of the Bombay Millowners' Association, being primarily responsible for the unification of the Indian textile industry. He was a member of the Indian Legislative Assembly from 1929 to 1943, when he resigned in protest against the government's treatment of Mohandas Gandhi. In September 1947 he acted as governor of Bombay before being returned to the Constituent Assembly (1948–49) following independence.

MONDLANE, EDUARDO CHIVAMBO, African guerrilla leader (b. southern Mozambique, 1920—d. Dar es Salaam, Tanzania, Feb. 3, 1969), killed in a bomb blast, was head of the Front for the Liberation of Mozambique (FRELIMO). Described as one of Portugal's most wanted men, he had set up an institute at Dar es Salaam to train future African political leaders, technicians, and administrators. After being expelled as a "foreign native" from the University of Witwatersrand, S.Af., he studied in Portugal and in the United States, where he obtained a doctorate in sociology from Northwestern University. After a period of teaching he became an official of the UN Trusteeship Council before returning to Africa to reorganize the splintered liberation movement in Mozambique.

MORGAN, RUSS, U.S. orchestra leader (b. Scranton, Pa., April 29, 1904–d. Las Vegas, Nev., Aug. 7, 1969), whose "big band sound" was popular in the 1930s and 1940s, formed his first group in the early 1920s. In 1936 he organized an orchestra to play for the Rudy Vallee radio show, and continued in radio and on television for many years. From 1964 Morgan led his orchestra at the Dunes Hotel in Las Vegas.

MOWBRAY, (CEDRIC) ALAN, U.S. actor (b. London, Eng., 1897—d. Hollywood, Calif., March 25, 1969), played character roles in more than 400 films, including *The King and I* (1956). He appeared in several Broadway shows, the last being *Enter Laughing* in 1964, and in the early 1950s had his own TV series, *Colonel Humphrey Flack.*

MURCHISON, CLINTON WILLIAMS, U.S. oil tycoon (b. Athens, Tex., Oct. 17, 1885—d. Athens, June 20, 1969), one of the world's richest men, at one time owned simultaneously 115 companies, including a controlling interest in the New York Central Railroad.

MUS, PAUL, French orientalist (b. Bourges, France, June 1, 1902—d. Murs, Vaucluse, France, Aug. 9, 1969), was professor of Far Eastern civilizations at the Collège de France. Educated at Hanoi, Indochina, and later in Paris, where he was a pupil of Alain (É. A. Chartier), he began early to study Far Eastern religions and philosophies. During World II he joined British parachutists and was dropped twice in Indochina, later becoming political adviser to Gen. Jacques Leclerc and taking part in the first negotiations with Ho Chi Minh. A large part of his published work concerns Vietnam.

MUTESA II, SIR EDWARD FREDERICK WILLIAM WALUGEMBE MUTEBI LUWANGULA MUTESA, 36th kabaka of Buganda (b. Mengo, Kampala, Uganda, Nov. 19, 1924—d. London, Eng., Nov. 21, 1969), was the first president of Uganda (1963–66). His education included two years at Cambridge University after his installation as kabaka in 1942. His reign coincided with the protectorate government's policy of unifying Uganda by means of a popularly elected assembly and his opposition to what appeared a threat to his own position as monarch, and to the independence of Buganda, led to his deportation by the British in 1953. He returned in 1955 and took a leading part in the subsequent constitutional conferences, being elected president of Uganda in 1963. His hostility to left-wing and Pan-African ideas, however, isolated him, and in 1966 he was overthrown.

NAUDÉ, JOZUA FRANÇOIS ("Tom"), South African politician (b. Middelburg, Cape Prov., S.Af., April 15, 1889—d. Cape Town, S.Af., May 31, 1969), represented Pietersburg from 1919 to 1960. A supporter of the James Hertzog-Jan C. Smuts coalition of 1933, he followed Hertzog when he broke with Smuts over the war issue in 1939. When Daniel Malan's Nationalist Party came to power in 1948 he was elected speaker, joining the Cabinet in 1950. He resigned his parliamentary seat in 1960 and in 1961 became president of the Senate. After a brief term as acting state president in 1967 he returned to his office as president of the Senate on April 10, 1968.

O'DANIEL, W(ILBERT) LEE ("Pappy"), U.S. senator (1941–48) from Texas (b. Malta, O., March 11, 1890—d. Dallas, Tex., May 11, 1969), was the owner of a flour mill who won the governorship of Texas after running on the slogan "Pass the biscuits, Pappy." He served one term (1939–41) before he was elected to the U.S. Senate.

O'DOUL, FRANK JOSEPH ("Lefty"), U.S. baseball player (b. San Francisco, Calif., March 4, 1897—d. San Francisco, Dec. 7, 1969), twice won the National League batting title: in 1929 with a .398 average while with the Philadelphia Phillies, and again in 1932 when he hit .368 while playing as an outfielder for Brooklyn. His lifetime average was .349—gained during 16 years (1919–35) of major league ball.

ORAM, SIR MATTHEW HENRY, New Zealand member (1943–57) of Parliament (b. Christchurch, N.Z., June 2, 1885—d. Jan. 22, 1969), was speaker of the House from 1950 to 1957.

ORLICH BOLMARCICH, FRANCISCO JOSÉ, Costa Rican politician (b. San Ramón, Costa Rica, March 10, 1907—d. San Jose, Costa Rica, Oct. 29, 1969), was president of Costa Rica from 1962 through 1966. He was strongly anti-Communist and strove to advance friendly relations with the U.S.

OSBORN, FAIRFIELD, U.S. naturalist and conservationist (b. Princeton, N.J., Jan. 15, 1887—d. New York, N.Y., Sept. 16, 1969), president of the New York Zoological Society from 1940 until 1968, was the author of *Our Plundered Planet* (1948) and *The Limits of the Earth* (1953).

OSTROVITYANOV, KONSTANTIN V., Soviet economist (b. Tambov Prov., Russia, 1892—d. Moscow, U.S.S.R., Feb. 9, 1969), advanced the Soviet economic theory that politics supersedes economics. He attained full membership in the Academy of Sciences in 1953, and served as its vice-president from 1953 until 1962.

OSUNA, RAFAEL, Mexican tennis champion (b. 1938?—d. near Monterrey, Mex., June 4, 1969), was killed in a plane crash a month after leading the Mexican Davis Cup team to a victory over

Australia in the American Zone semifinals. Osuna was winner of the U.S. singles title in 1963, shared in the U.S. doubles crown in 1962 and in the doubles at Wimbledon in 1960 and 1963.

OTANI, SADAO, U.S. pathologist (b. Japan, 1894—d. New York, N.Y., March 7, 1969), discovered two diseases: eosinophilic granuloma, a bone disease, and the glomus jugulare tumour (called Otani's tumour) of the middle ear.

OVERLIN, KEN, U.S. boxer (b. Decatur, Ill., 1910—d. Reno, Nev., d. reported July 24, 1969), middleweight champion of the world in 1940, retired in 1944 with a record of 127 victories, 13 defeats, and 7 draws.

PANHARD, PAUL, French automobile manufacturer (b. Versailles, France, Aug. 1, 1881—d. Neuilly, France, March 26, 1969), joined the Panhard-Levassor Company (founded by his uncle René Panhard in 1872 as a coachbuilding company) in 1904 and served as managing director from 1955 to 1965, when the firm merged with Citroën.

PAPEN, FRANZ VON, German statesman (b. Werl, Westphalia, Oct. 29, 1879—d. Obersasbach, W.Ger., May 2, 1969), whose intrigues helped Hitler seize power, began his career in the Army, and in World War I was military attaché at the German embassy in Washington, but had to leave the U.S. in 1915 because of espionage activities. He later became chief of staff with the Turkish Army in Palestine, and in 1921 entered the Prussian Landtag as an extreme right-wing member of the Centre (Catholic) Party. In 1932 he was chancellor for a few months and in 1933, believing that a coalition would restrain the Nazis, he became vice-chancellor under Hitler. In 1934 he was dismissed and appointed ambassador to Austria. After World War II, during which he was ambassador to Turkey, Papen was acquitted at the Nürnberg Tribunal but sentenced by a German court. On his appeal, however, he was released. His memoirs appeared in 1952.

PARKIN, BENJAMIN THEAKER, British Labour politician (b. 1906—d. Barnes, London, Eng., June 3, 1969), represented North Paddington, London, in Parliament from 1953, and was prominent in exposing Peter Rachman, the Paddington property racketeer, in 1963. He first entered Parliament in 1945, representing Stroud in Gloucestershire, but lost in 1950; he then won Paddington North in a 1953 by-election.

PASTOR, TONY (Antonio Pestritto), U.S. bandleader (b. Middletown, Conn., 1907—d. New London, Conn., Oct. 31, 1969), singer and saxophonist, in 1940 formed his own group, which continued as one of the last of the big bands until 1957.

PAYNE, JACK, British bandleader (b. 1899—d. Kent, Eng., Dec. 4, 1969), popular star of early radio, in 1928 joined the BBC as a radio bandleader and in the late 1930s set up a theatrical agency. In 1939 he formed another band and began entertaining the troops.

PEARSON, DREW (Andrew Russell), U.S. political columnist (b. Evanston, Ill., Dec. 13, 1897—d. Washington, D.C., Sept. 1, 1969), who launched his controversial column "Washington Merry-Go-Round" in 1932, shared its writing with Jack Anderson from 1959. Pearson, first to report the New Deal plan to "pack" the Supreme Court, often aroused the ire of presidents and other high officials. A Quaker, Pearson sponsored many humanitarian causes, and after World War II was the organizer of the Friendship Train to collect food for the people of Europe. With Robert S. Allen, an early co-author of the column, Pearson wrote several books, including *Washington Merry-Go-Round* (1931); with Anderson, he wrote *The Case Against Congress* (1968).

PECHNER, GERHARD, U.S. operatic singer (b. Berlin, Ger., 1903—d. New York, N.Y., Oct. 22, 1969), who sang more than 30 bass roles with the Metropolitan Opera Company (1941–66), made his U.S. debut in 1940.

PEGLER, (JAMES) WESTBROOK, U.S. columnist (b. Minneapolis, Minn., Aug. 2, 1894—d. Tucson, Ariz., June 24, 1969), who won a Pulitzer Prize in 1941 for his exposé of corruption in labour unions, began his column "Fair Enough" in 1933, writing for United Features Syndicate; in 1944 he switched to Hearst's King Features and retitled his column "As Pegler Sees It." He made constant caustic attacks on public figures—especially on those in the administrations in Washington during the 1930s, 1940s, and 1950s. In 1962 Pegler left the newspaper field, but wrote occasionally for the John Birch Society's publication *American Opinion.*

PERLSTEIN, MEYER AARON, U.S. neurologist (b. Chicago, Ill., April 6, 1902—d. San Jose, Calif., Oct. 29, 1969), professor of pediatric neurology at Northwestern University Medical School, Chicago, Ill., for many years, helped found the American Academy for Cerebral Palsy in 1949. He was the author of more than 200 papers on neuromuscular diseases in children.

PICKLES, WILLIAM NORMAN, British "country doctor" (b. Leeds, Eng., March 6, 1885—d. Northallerton, Yorkshire, Eng., March 2, 1969), noted for research into epidemiology and infectious diseases through his intimate contact with small communities. His principal publication, *Epidemiology in Country Practice* (1939), became a classic.

PIKE, JAMES ALBERT, U.S. churchman (b. Oklahoma City, Okla., Feb. 14, 1913—d. Judean Hills, Israeli-occupied Jordan, Sept. 3[?], 1969), perished near the Dead Sea after his car broke down during a trip into the desert. Pike studied for the Roman Catholic priesthood before he turned to law (J.S.D., Yale Law School, 1938). In 1944 he joined the Episcopal Church, and two years later, having earned a divinity degree, was ordained. In 1952 he was appointed dean of the Cathedral of St. John the Divine, New York City, and shortly began his Sunday afternoon radio talks on the "Dean Pike Show." Chosen bishop coadjutor of the diocese of California in 1958, he was to create a furor over an article he wrote (1960) for *Christian Century,* questioning the virgin birth, and again over his book *A Time for Christian Candor* (1963). Following the death of his son James by suicide in 1966, Pike left the active ministry and joined the Center for the Study of Democratic Institutions, Santa Barbara, Calif. Also in 1966 he was threatened with a heresy trial but was, instead, censured for his controversial statements. Because of his son's death Pike became interested in spiritualism and related certain of his psychic experiences in *The Other Side* (1968). In April 1969, he announced his decision to leave his church.

PIRE, DOMINIQUE-GEORGES, Belgian Roman Catholic priest (b. Dinant, Belg., Feb. 10, 1910—d. Louvain, Belg., Jan. 30, 1969), who in 1958 won the Nobel Peace Prize for his work for displaced persons, entered the Dominican priory of La Sorte at Huy (1928), and was ordained priest in 1934. He studied and taught philosophy and sociology and built up organizations to help needy families and give children vacations. During World War II he was an intelligence officer and chaplain in the Resistance. Immediately afterward he began helping the displaced, founding for them a number of "European villages" in Belgium, West Germany, and Norway. With his Peace Prize money he established at Huy a "University of Peace," where international groups could study world problems.

Franz von Papen   Drew Pearson   James Albert Pike   Dominique-Georges Pire

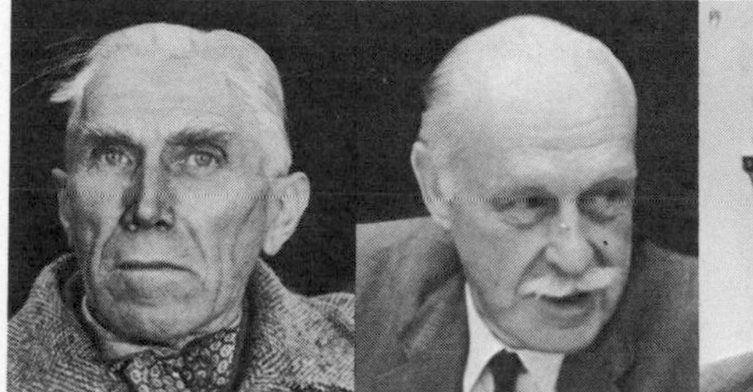

CAMERA PRESS—PIX FROM PUBLIX   WIDE WORLD   WIDE WORLD   KEYSTONE

PIRIE-GORDON, HARRY, British scholar, author, and genealogist (b. 1883—d. Dec. 8, 1969), had a career in journalism and in naval intelligence during World Wars I and II. He joined the foreign department of *The Times* in 1912, and in 1914 was sent as a naval intelligence officer to the eastern Mediterranean. After a period as deputy British commissioner to the Baltic provinces, he returned to *The Times* in 1919, later acting as special correspondent in Turkey, Palestine, and Mexico. In World War II and after he again served in naval intelligence. A founder and fellow of the Society of Genealogists, he was associated with Frederick William Rolfe, with whom he collaborated on several literary works.

POPE, ARTHUR UPHAM, U.S. archaeologist (b. Phoenix, R.I., Feb. 7, 1881—d. Shiraz, Iran, Sept. 3, 1969), authority on ancient Persian civilization, was director of the Asia Institute, Pahlavi University, from 1932 until 1952. He wrote *Survey of Persian Art* (1938) and was a contributor to *Encyclopædia Britannica.*

POPE, MERRITT, U.S. agronomist (b. Odeli, Ill., 1883—d. Memphis, Tenn., Oct. 28, 1969), discovered the fertilization process in cereal grains. He wrote many papers and contributed to *Encyclopædia Britannica.*

POPOV, MARKIAN MIKHAILOVICH, general (ret.), Soviet Army (b. Russia, 1902—d. U.S.S.R., April 22, 1969), played a leading military role in World War II when he commanded Soviet troops on the Leningrad front and served as deputy commander at Stalingrad.

PORTMAN, ERIC, British actor (b. Yorkshire, Eng., July 13, 1903—d. Cornwall, Eng., Dec. 7, 1969), known on stage, film, and television, commenced his acting career by joining Robert Courtneidge's Shakespeare Company, and had his first speaking part in 1924. In 1927 he joined the Old Vic and in 1929 had a great success as Undershaft in Shaw's *Major Barbara.* He played numerous leads in both contemporary and classical drama, in London and New York, later successes being in Graham Greene's *The Living Room* and Terence Rattigan's *The Browning Version* and *Separate Tables.* He also made a number of films, including *One of Our Aircraft Is Missing, The Colditz Story, The Prince and the Pauper,* and *The Whisperers.* He retired in 1968.

POTTER, STEPHEN, British humorist (b. Feb. 1, 1900—d. London, Eng., Dec. 2, 1969), was the inventor and author of *Gamesmanship* (1947), *Lifemanship* (1950), *One-upmanship* (1952), and *Supermanship* (1958), various methods of implanting doubt and uncertainty in the minds of rivals. After graduating from Oxford in 1923, Potter spent three years as secretary to playwright Henry Arthur Jones, and then took up a lectureship in English literature at London University. After publishing several books of criticism, he joined the British Broadcasting Corporation as a writer-producer in 1938, and became chairman of the BBC's literary committee.

POWELL, CECIL FRANK, British physicist (b. Tonbridge, Eng., Dec. 5, 1903—d. near Milan, Italy, Aug. 9, 1969), was awarded the 1950 Nobel Prize for Physics "for his development of the photographic method in the study of nuclear processes and for his discoveries concerning mesons." After a Cambridge University education and research work at the Cavendish Laboratory, he joined in 1928 the Wills Physical Laboratory at Bristol University, becoming subsequently (1948–63) Melville Wills professor of physics. An outstanding authority on subnuclear particles and cosmic radiation, Powell was also known for his work in promoting international cooperation in science, being elected in 1962 president of the World Federation of Scientific Workers. In 1967 he was awarded the Lomonosov Gold Medal, the highest award of the Soviet Academy of Sciences.

QUIRK, JAMES T., U.S. publisher (b. Philadelphia, Pa., 1912—d. Philadelphia, Jan. 18, 1969), who published *TV Guide* magazine since its inception in 1953.

RAGO, HENRY, U.S. poet and editor (b. Chicago, Ill., 1916—d. Chicago, May 26, 1969), joined *Poetry* magazine in 1954 as an associate editor, and became editor the following year.

REES, JOHN RAWLINGS, British psychiatrist (b. June 25, 1890—d. London, Eng., April 11, 1969), pioneered the development of social science psychiatry and group psychology mainly through his work as consulting psychiatrist to the British Army during World War II. He was director of the World Federation for Mental Health from 1949 to 1962. Among his numerous books were *The Health of the Mind* and *The Shaping of Psychiatry by War.*

RIAD, MUHAMMAD ABDEL MONEIM, general, U.A.R. Army (b. Tanta, Gharbia Governorate, Egypt, Oct. 22, 1919—d. Suez Canal zone, U.A.R., March 9, 1969), chief of staff of the U.A.R. armed forces from June 1967, died in an artillery clash with Israeli forces. A lifelong soldier, he played a prominent part in the Arab-Israeli war of 1967 as general chief of staff to the joint military command of the U.A.R. and Jordan and following the war was primarily responsible for the reequipment of the U.A.R. armed forces, heading a military delegation to Moscow in July 1967.

RICHARDSON, VICTOR, Australian cricketer (b. Adelaide, Austr., Sept. 7, 1894—d. Adelaide, Oct. 30, 1969), was an all-round athlete, and one of Australia's most popular sports personalities. A brilliant fielder and prolific scorer for South Australia in the Sheffield Shield contests during the 1920s and 1930s, he played 19 times for his country, captaining its team in 1935–36. After his retirement he was a cricket commentator with the Australian Broadcasting Company.

RITTER, THELMA, U.S. character actress (b. Brooklyn, N.Y., Feb. 14, 1905—d. New York, N.Y., Feb. 4, 1969), who first appeared in films as a Macy's customer in *Miracle on 34th Street* (1946), received nominations for Academy Awards for her roles in *All About Eve* (1950), *The Mating Season* and *Pillow Talk* (1959), and *Birdman of Alcatraz* (1962). She did receive television's Emmy Award for her work in *The Catered Affair* (1955), and was the winner of a Tony Award for Marthy in the Broadway musical *New Girl in Town* (1957).

ROLFE, ROBERT A. ("RED"), U.S. baseball player (b. Penacook, N.H., Oct. 17, 1908—d. Governor's Island, N.H., July 8, 1969), in 1969 named all-time third baseman of the New York Yankees, was a regular at third for that club from 1935 until retiring as a player in 1941. After a stint as head baseball and basketball coach at Yale (1942–45), he coached the Yankees (1946) and Toronto (1946–47). Going to the Detroit Tigers in 1948, he was manager during 1949–52. From 1954 to 1967 he was athletic director at Dartmouth. Rolfe's lifetime average was .289 (.329 in 1939).

ROSE, SIR DAVID, Guyanese administrator (b. 1923—d. London, Eng., Nov. 10, 1969), governor-general of Guyana, was killed when scaffolding collapsed and crashed into his parked limousine. Sir David, the first Guyanese to become governor-general of his country, had served the British government in the Caribbean for 20 years.

ROWLAND, CLARENCE ("PANTS"), U.S. baseball figure (b. Platteville, Wis., 1878—d. Chicago, Ill., May 17, 1969), became manager of the Chicago White Sox in 1914 and led the club to the American League pennant and a World Series victory in 1917. He was an American League umpire (1923–27), president of the Pacific Coast League (1944–54), and executive vice-president of the Chicago Cubs from 1954.

ROWLEY, THE REV. HAROLD HENRY, British biblical scholar (b. Leicester, Eng., March 24, 1890—d. Cheltenham, Eng., Oct. 4, 1969), was emeritus professor of Hebrew language and literature at Manchester University. After joining the Baptist Mission in China in 1922, where he became associate professor of the Old Testament at the Christian College, Shantung, he lectured in Semitic languages from 1930 to 1959 at the universities of Cardiff, Bangor, and Manchester. He was a fellow of the British Academy, president of the Baptist Union and of the Society for the Study of the Old Testament, and twice chairman of the Baptist Missionary Society. Rowley was a contributor to the *Encyclopædia Britannica.*

RUSSELL, CHARLES ("PEE WEE"), U.S. jazz clarinetist (b. 1907—d. Alexandria, Va., Feb. 15, 1969), played with many leading Dixieland groups, including the Red Nichols band.

SAINTHILL, LOUDON, Australian stage designer (b. Tasmania, Austr., Jan. 9, 1919—d. London, Eng., June 9, 1969), came to Britain after World War II and became a successful designer for productions for the Old Vic Theatre, Royal Shakespeare Theatre, Royal Opera House, Sadler's Wells Ballet, and West End theatres during the 1950s and 1960s. His costumes for *The Canterbury Tales* won a New York Tony Award.

ST. LEGER, DOUGLAS FRANCIS, U.S. musician (b. India, 1890—d. Bloomington, Ind., Dec. 26, 1969), was associated with the Metropolitan Opera Company in various capacities, including that of conductor, from 1939 until 1950. He became professor of music at Indiana University in 1953, and emeritus in 1963.

SAKHAROV, VLADIMIR, Soviet classical geneticist (b. 1903—d. Moscow, U.S.S.R., Jan. 10, 1969), a pioneer in the study of the mutation processes in plants and animals, who demonstrated in 1932 that chemicals could produce mutations in germ cells.

SALMON, ANDRÉ, French poet, critic, and novelist (b. Paris, France, Oct. 4, 1881—d. Sanary, France, March 12, 1969), was identified with Symbolist innovations in art and literature at the beginning of the century. He was one of the circle of writers and artists that grew up around Pablo Picasso in Montmartre. His principal collections of poetry are *Créances* (1926) and *Carreaux* (1928). In 1964 he was awarded the Grand Prix for poetry by the Académie française.

SARDI, VINCENT, SR., U.S. restaurateur (b. San Marzano Oliveto, Italy, Dec. 23, 1885—d. Saranac Lake, N.Y., Nov. 19, 1969), founder of Sardi's Restaurant, New York meeting place of theatrical people for almost 50 years.

SAUD (SA'UD IBN 'ABD AL-AZIZ), Saudi Arabian ruler (b. Kuwait, Jan. 15, 1901—d. Athens, Greece, Feb. 23, 1969), was king of Saudi Arabia from 1953 to 1964. Succeeding his father, King Ibn Saud, in 1953 and inheriting vast oil revenues, Saud, nevertheless, had twice to call on his brother Crown Prince Faisal to put the country's finances in order before he was finally deposed in favour of his brother in 1964. He suffered much from ill health and after his deposition he lived abroad, mainly in the U.A.R. and Greece.

Muhammad Abdel Moneim Riad — Thelma Ritter — Saud — Sir Lawrence Roger Lumley Scarbrough

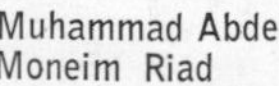

UPI COMPIX — WIDE WORLD — KEYSTONE — KEYSTONE

SCARBROUGH, SIR LAWRENCE ROGER LUMLEY, 11TH EARL of, British politician and public figure (b. July 27, 1896—d. Sandbeck Park, Rotherham, Yorkshire, Eng., June 29, 1969), was governor of Bombay (1937–43) and undersecretary for India and Burma in Winston Churchill's caretaker government (May–July 1945). He was Conservative M.P. for Hull East (1922–29) and for York (1931–37). Succeeding his uncle in 1945, he was created a Knight of the Garter (1948). As lord chamberlain (1952–63) he was responsible for stage censorship—abolished in 1968 following the report of a parliamentary committee of which he was a member.

SCHENCK, NICHOLAS M., U.S. motion-picture executive (b. Rybinsk, Russia, Nov. 14, 1881—d. Miami Beach, Fla., March 3, 1969), was a founder and president (1933–55) of Metro-Goldwyn-Mayer.

SCHERRER, PAUL, Swiss atomic scientist (b. Sankt Gallen, Switz., Feb. 3, 1890—d. Zürich, Switz., Sept. 25, 1969), the discoverer of a photoelectric effect in heavy nuclei, was professor of physics at the Swiss Federal Institute of Technology from 1920 to 1960. As a result of his efforts the institute was one of the first in Europe to have its own cyclotron. In 1946 he became head of the Swiss Atomic Energy Research Commission and later helped in the establishment of the European Nuclear Research Centre (CERN) in Geneva.

SCHMITT, BERNADOTTE EVERLY, U.S. historian (b. Strasburg, Va., May 19, 1886—d. Alexandria, Va., March 22, 1969), who received a Pulitzer Prize in 1931 for his major work, *The Coming of the War, 1914,* was Andrew MacLeish distinguished service professor at the University of Chicago from 1939 until 1946, when he became emeritus. Later works included *The Origin of the First World War* (1958) and *The Fashion and Future of History* (1961).

SCOBIE, SIR RONALD MacKENZIE, general (ret.), British Army (b. June 8, 1893—d. Mattingley, Hampshire, Eng., Feb. 23, 1969), who, as commander of the Tobruk fortress at the time of its relief in 1941, made an important contribution to the German defeat in North Africa. Also, as commander of British Forces in Greece (1944–46), he played an outstanding part in defeating the threatened take-over by Communist guerrilla forces in 1944.

SETON, SIR BRUCE LOVAT, Scottish character actor (b. May 29, 1909—d. Sept. 28, 1969), well known to British television and cinema audiences, especially in the title role of the series "Fabian of the Yard." Among the films in which he played was *Whisky Galore* (1949).

SHAHN, BEN, U.S. painter (b. Kaunas, Lith., Sept. 12, 1898—d. New York, N.Y., March 14, 1969), used his art for the social and political causes he believed in, as, for example, his series "The Passion of Sacco and Vanzetti" (23 small gouaches and two large panels, 1931–32). After several years spent working on murals, Shahn completed (1939) "Seurat's Lunch," "Vacant Lot," and "Handball," which were exhibited at his retrospective at the Museum of Modern Art in 1947. At the 1954 Venice Biennale, 34 of his paintings were hung, including "The Red Stairway" and "Spring." In 1961 a series on nuclear warfare, "The Saga of the Lucky Dragon," was shown at the Downtown Gallery in New York City. Shahn, also a fine commercial artist and poster designer, held the gold medal of the American Institute of Graphic Arts.

SHALIT, AMOS de-, Israeli nuclear physicist (b. Jerusalem, Palestine, 1927—d. Rehovoth, Israel, Sept. 2, 1969), an authority on the magnetic properties of atomic nuclear particles, was director of the Weizmann Institute of Science from 1966 to 1968. He joined the institute in 1954 as head of the nuclear research department; he was also Herbert H. Lehman professor of theoretical physics and head of the department of science teaching. In 1965 he was awarded the Israeli Prize for the Exact Sciences.

SHERMARKE, ABD-I-RASHID ALI, president of the Somali Republic (b. Somalia, Oct. 16, 1919—

d. Las Anod, Somalia, Oct. 15, 1969), felled by an assassin as he toured a drought-stricken area, was an architect of his country's post-independence neutralist policy. During 1948–51 he was secretary of the Somali Youth League; in 1953 he went to Italy, and the following year he was posted to the juridical department in Mogadishu (now Mozadiscio). He entered the Ministry of Finance in 1956, and later returned to Italy with a scholarship to Rome University, where he obtained a doctorate in political science in 1958. Only a year after his election to Parliament in 1959 he became prime minister. He lost the 1964 elections but was elected to the presidency in 1966.

SHORIKI, MATSUTARO, Japanese publisher (b. 1885—d. Tokyo, Jap., Oct. 9, 1969), chairman of Japan's Atomic Energy Commission from 1956, was the publisher of *Yomiuri Shimbun*, a Tokyo daily with a circulation of more than five million. Also a sports promoter, Shoriki introduced professional baseball to Japan in 1931 when he booked a team of U.S. major league players for an exhibition tour of his country.

SHORT, HUGH OSWALD, British aircraft designer (b. Derbyshire, Eng., Jan. 16, 1883—d. Hazelmere, Eng., Dec. 4, 1969), was honorary life president of Short Brothers and Harland Ltd. After building a balloon for J. T. C. Moore-Brabazon in 1903, Oswald and his brothers, Horace and Eustace, arranged to build aircraft under license to the Wright brothers. Moore-Brabazon won a *Daily Mail* prize in one of their planes, following which Short Brothers Ltd. was launched. The company was a pioneer in the use of aluminum alloys and stressed-skin construction. Famous designs included the Calcutta, Empire, Golden Hind, and Sunderland, flown by the RAF during World War II and in service until 1960.

SIERPINSKI, WACLAW, Polish mathematician (b. Warsaw, Pol., March 14, 1882—d. Warsaw, Oct. 19, 1969), founder of the Warsaw mathematical school, was doctor *honoris causa* of ten universities (including Paris and Moscow), and member of numerous foreign scientific academies and societies. He was professor of mathematics at the universities of Lwow (1910–18) and Warsaw (1918–60). He wrote over 700 works, studies, and articles, including *Leçons sur les nombres transfinis* (1928), *Cardinal and Ordinal Numbers* (1958), and *Elementary Theory of Numbers* (1964).

SIMPSON, THE REV. CUTHBERT ALKMAN, Canadian-U.S. Anglican clergyman and scholar (b. Charlottetown, P.E.I., May 24, 1892—d. Oxford, Eng., June 30, 1969), was professor of Old Testament at the General Theological Seminary in New York (1940–54), and regius professor of Hebrew at Oxford University (1954–59). The first U.S. citizen to be made dean of a Church of England cathedral, he served in that post at Christ Church, Oxford, from 1959. A Rhodes scholar at Oxford and ordained in 1921, he was rector of St. Alban's, Woodside, N.S. (1922–28). He became a naturalized U.S. citizen in 1937, but later reverted to Canadian nationality.

SITWELL, SIR (FRANCIS) OSBERT (SACHEVERELL), British man of letters (b. London, Eng., Dec. 6, 1892—d. Florence, Italy, May 4, 1969), was known, with his sister Edith (1887–1964) and brother Sacheverell (1897–   ), as a tilter at Establishment windmills in literature and the arts. He was a satirical poet: *Twentieth-Century Harlequinade* (with Edith, 1916), *Collected Poems and Satires* (1931), and *Mrs. Kimber* (1937). His short stories and novels included *Collected Short Stories* (1953) and *Before the Bombardment,* a portrayal of Scarborough society before World War I (1929). Much of his fame depended on the autobiographical series *Left Hand, Right Hand!* (1945), *The Scarlet Tree* (1946), *Great Morning* (1948), *Laughter in the Next Room* (1949), and *Noble Essences* (1950). With *Tales My Father Taught Me* (1962), he recreated the atmosphere of prewar life in an aristocratic intellectual milieu, such as childhood at the family seat, Renishaw Hall, near Sheffield, Yorkshire, and at Scarborough; schooldays at Eton; service in the Grenadier Guards. Sir Osbert was made a Companion of Honour in 1958, and in 1965 settled in Italy.

Ben Shahn   Mongi Slim

WIDE WORLD   WIDE WORLD

SLIM, MONGI, Tunisian diplomat (b. Tunis, Tun., Sept. 15, 1908—d. Tunis, Oct. 23, 1969), who served as his country's foreign minister (1956–64) and secretary of state for justice (from 1966), was ambassador to the U.S. from 1956 until 1961. Tunisia's permanent representative to the United Nations, Slim was president of the General Assembly in 1961–62.

SLIPHER, VESTO MELVIN, U.S. astronomer (b. Clinton County, Ind., Nov. 11, 1875—d. Flagstaff, Ariz., Nov. 8, 1969), who went to Lowell Observatory, Flagstaff, Ariz., in 1901, was director from 1926 until 1952. During that time he supervised the studies that led to the discovery of the planet Pluto in 1930. He was credited with the discovery of the rapid rotation and enormous space velocities of spiral nebulas that gave the observational basis for the expanding universe theory. In 1919 he received the Lalande Prize and gold medal of the Paris Academy of Sciences, and in 1932, the gold medal of the Royal Astronomical Society.

SMITH, SIR SYDNEY ALFRED, British medical authority (b. Wellington, N.Z., 1884—d. Edinburgh, Scot., May 8, 1969), emeritus professor of forensic medicine, was rector of Edinburgh University (1954–57). His career took him from New Zealand, via Egypt, to Edinburgh; he was often called to assist in murder investigations. In 1928 he became regius professor of forensic medicine at Edinburgh and was a member of the General Medical Council, 1931–56. His memoirs, *Mostly Murder,* were published in 1960.

SOBEL, HELEN (Mrs. Stanley Smith), U.S. bridge champion (b. Philadelphia, Pa., 1910—d. New York, N.Y., Sept. 11, 1969), whose career began in 1934 when she won her first title, played in the first world championships in 1937 and, teamed with Charles Vogelhofer and the Culbertsons, reached the finals. In national competition Helen Sobel held 33 titles, twice winning the Vanderbilt Cup and five times the Spingold Trophy. In 1944 she won the McKenny Trophy for the most master points earned by any player. Her third world championship appearance was in 1960 when her team was defeated in the final game by the Italian Blue team.

SOUTHWORTH, BILLY, U.S. baseball manager (b. Harvard, Neb., March 9, 1893—d. Columbus, O., Nov. 15, 1969), led the St. Louis Cardinals to World Series victories in 1942 and 1944. He was an outfielder with five major league clubs (1913–29) before assuming his managerial duties. His lifetime batting average was .298.

SPARGO, TONY (Anthony Sbarbaro), U.S. jazz musician (b. New Orleans, La., 1897—d. New York, N.Y., Oct. 30, 1969), last surviving member of the Original Dixieland Jazz Band, with which he played the drums from 1916 until the band broke up in 1925.

SPEAKMAN, JOHN BAMBER, British textile chemist (b. Manchester, Eng., Oct. 23, 1897—d. Leeds, Eng., July 5, 1969), was one of the founders of modern wool chemistry. During his 39 years at Leeds University, where he was lecturer (1924–39) and professor of textile industries (1939–63), he built up a department internationally famous for research and teaching. Among the processes for which his work was responsible was the permanent creasing of wool fibres.

SPRUANCE, RAYMOND AMOS, admiral (ret.), U.S. Navy (b. Baltimore, Md., July 3, 1886—d. Pebble Beach, Calif., Dec. 13, 1969), considered one of the best naval tacticians of World War II, was leader of the U.S. fleet during the Battle of Midway in June 1942. Spruance was appointed commander in chief of the Pacific Fleet in 1945 and retired in 1948. He served as U.S. ambassador to the Philippines from 1952 until 1955.

STECHKIN, BORIS SERGEEVICH, Soviet aviation pioneer (b. Trufanov, Russia, Aug. 5, 1891—d. Moscow, U.S.S.R., April 2, 1969), one of the founders of the Soviet School of Aviation Engineering, was a professor at the Moscow Air Force Engineering Academy for 47 years and in his last years produced several works on the theory of jet propulsion.

STEINBERG, SIGFRID HENRY, German-British historian (b. Goslar, Ger., Aug. 3, 1899—d. Ewell, Surrey, Eng., Jan. 28, 1969), editor in chief of *The Statesman's Year-Book* from 1946 to 1969, emigrated to England in 1935 and received a fellowship at the Courtauld Institute. He taught at Sedbergh School from 1941 to 1944; was on the editorial staff of *Chambers's Encyclopaedia* from 1945 to 1949 and also edited *Cassell's Encyclopaedia of Literature* (1953). His most successful books in English were *Historical Tables* and *500 Years of Printing.* He was a contributor to *Encyclopædia Britannica.*

STERN, OTTO, German-U.S. physicist (b. Sorau, Ger. [now Zary, Pol.], Feb. 17, 1888—d. Berkeley, Calif., Aug. 17, 1969), winner of the 1943 Nobel Prize for Physics, received his doctorate at the University of Breslau in 1912, then worked with Albert Einstein at the Universities of Prague and Zürich. In 1923 he was appointed professor of physical chemistry at the University of Hamburg. Stern went to the U.S. in 1933 as a research professor of physics at Carnegie Institute of Technology in Pittsburgh; he became emeritus professor in 1945. Stern was awarded the Nobel Prize for his work in the development of the molecular-ray method of detecting the magnetic momentum of protons.

STERNBERG, JOSEF von, U.S. film director (b. Vienna, Aus., 1894—d. Hollywood, Calif., Dec. 22, 1969), who discovered Marlene Dietrich and directed her in seven pictures beginning with *The Blue Angel* in 1930. His last major picture was *The Shanghai Gesture* (with Gene Tierney) in 1941. His autobiography, *Fun in a Chinese Laundry,* was published in 1965.

STONE, LEW, British dance-band leader (b. London, Eng., 1899—d. London, Feb. 13, 1969), became famous in the big-band era of the 1930s with such hits as "Isle of Capri" and "Red Sails in the Sunset."

STREUVELS, STIJN (Frank Lateur), Belgian short-story writer and novelist (b. Heule, Belg., Oct. 3, 1871—d. Ingooigem, Belg., Aug. 15, 1969), presented through portrayal of peasant life in a corner of his native southwest Flanders an epic view of man and his destiny, in a prose style blending poetic vision and realism. Works included his first stories, in *Lenteleven* (1899; *The Path of Life,* 1915); his first novel, *Langs de Wegen* (1902; *Old Jan,* 1936); and the more famous *De Vlaaschard* (1907), and *Werkmensen* (1926).

STULGINSKIS, ALEKSANDRAS, Lithuanian statesman (b. 1885—d. Kaunas, Lith., Sept. 22, 1969), was a signer of the Lithuanian Declaration of Independence (from Poland) in 1918, and president of the short-lived Republic of Lithuania from 1922 until 1926.

SULLIVAN, BRIAN (Harry Joseph), U.S. opera singer (b. Oakland, Calif., Aug. 9, 1919—d. Lake Geneva, Switz., d. reported June 17, 1969), sang tenor roles with the New York Metropolitan Opera for 16 years (1948–64).

SWARTHOUT, GLADYS, U.S. operatic mezzo-soprano (b. Deepwater, Mo., Dec. 25, 1904—d. Florence, Italy, July 7, 1969), famous for her starring role in *Carmen,* first sang for the Chicago Civic Opera Company (1924–26) and the Ravinia Opera (1927–28) before making her Metropolitan Opera debut in 1929 as La Cieca in *La Gioconda.* She created the part of Cathos in the U.S. premiere of *La Preziose Ridicole,* and excelled in her roles in *Romeo and Juliet, Lakmé, Faust,* and *Norma,* as well as in many others. Between operatic performances she made several motion pictures, innumerable concert tours, and appeared on radio. She retired from the Met in 1945, having missed but two seasons. She continued to make her concert tours, and in 1950 sang her well-loved role of Carmen in the first opera ever staged exclusively for television.

SWINGLER, STEPHEN THOMAS, British Labour politician (b. Nottingham, Eng., March 2, 1915—d. London, Eng., Feb. 19, 1969), M.P. for Newcastle-under-Lyme from 1951, was minister of state at the Department of Health and Social Security. During the 1950s he was a founder of the Campaign for Nuclear Disarmament and chairman of the "Victory for Socialism" group. His administrative capabilities led to his rapid promotion from parliamentary secretary to the Ministry of Transport in the 1964 Labour government to minister of state by 1968.

SZABO, FERENC, Hungarian composer (b. Budapest, Austria-Hungary, Dec. 27, 1902—d. Budapest, Hung., Nov. 4, 1969), was professor of composition at the Academy of Music, Budapest, from 1945. Once a pupil of Zoltan Kodaly, he studied violin, viola, and piano and for a time conducted an orchestra at Kispest. During 1932–45 he lived in the U.S.S.R. His music included orchestral, choral, piano, and chamber compositions.

TAYLOR, ROBERT (SPANGLER ARLINGTON BRUGH), U.S. film actor (b. Filley, Neb., Aug. 5, 1911—d. Santa Monica, Calif., June 8, 1969), who played in more than 70 films during his 30-year career, made his first picture, *Handy Andy,* in 1934. The following year he attained stardom in *Magnificent Obsession* with Irene Dunn. He gave other fine performances in *Camille* with Greta Garbo in 1937, *The Crowd Roars* (1938), *Billy the Kid* and *Waterloo Bridge* (1940), and *Johnny Eager* (1941). After service with the U.S. Navy in World War II, Taylor returned to Hollywood picture-making during the 1950s, but in 1961 launched his own television show, "The Detectives."

TESTA, GUSTAVO CARDINAL, Italian prelate of the Roman Catholic Church (b. Boltiere, Italy, July 18, 1886—d. Rome, Italy, Feb. 28, 1969), who spent most of his life in the Vatican's diplomatic corps, was ordained in 1910. His first diplomatic assignments, in the 1920s, were in Vienna and in the Ruhr and Saar regions of Germany. After the Lateran Treaty was signed in 1929, he became counselor to the first apostolic nuncio to Italy, and in 1934, having been made archbishop, he went as an apostolic delegate to Egypt and Palestine. He remained in the Middle East until going to Switzerland in 1953. Pope John XXIII elevated him to cardinal in December 1959, and recalled him to Rome, where he served as secretary, then prefect, of the Congregation for the Eastern Church until resigning in 1967.

THOMPSON, HENRY ("HANK"), U.S. baseball player (b. Oklahoma City, Okla., Dec. 8, 1925—d. Fresno, Calif., Sept. 30, 1969), third baseman with the New York Giants during the 1950s, had a lifetime average of .267 with 129 major league home runs.

TOBIN, JAMES ("JIM"), U.S. baseball player (b. Oakland, Calif., Dec. 27, 1912—d. Oakland, May 19, 1969), who pitched (1937–45) for the Pittsburgh Pirates, the Boston Braves, and the Detroit Tigers, held a 105–112 win-loss record. In one 1942 game he hit three homers in a row, a pitcher's record that stood until 1955.

TOLUSH, ALEXANDER, Soviet chess champion (b. 1911—d. Leningrad, U.S.S.R., March 3, 1969), became an international master in 1950 and an international grand master in 1955.

Stephen Thomas Swingler Robert Taylor

CAMERA PRESS—PIX FROM PUBLIX WIDE WORLD

TRAVEN, B. (TRAVEN TORSVAN[?]), U.S. writer (b. Chicago, Ill., March 5, 1890[?]—d. Mexico City, Mex., March 26, 1969), who maintained a mysterious silence concerning his background, was the author of *The Treasure of the Sierra Madre* (1934), an adventure novel that in its adaptation for the screen won an Academy Award in 1948. Some of his other works were *The Bridge in the Jungle* (1938), *The Death Ship,* and *White Rose.*

TRUJILLO, RAFAEL LEONIDAS, JR. ("RAMFIS"), lieutenant general, Dominican Army (b. 1929—d. Madrid, Spain, Dec. 27, 1969), son of the onetime Dominican dictator, was head of the Dominican Republic's armed forces for a short time from about May 27 (the time of his father's assassination) until Nov. 18, 1961, when he resigned and left the country to live in exile.

TSHOMBE, MOISE-KAPENDA, Congolese political leader (b. near Elisabethville [now Lubumbashi], Katanga Prov., Belgian Congo, Nov. 10, 1919—d. Algiers, Alg., June 29, 1969), was head of Katanga Province's secession from the newly independent Republic of the Congo in June 1960. He served as Katanga's president from that time until 1963, when resistance in the province was broken by UN troops. Tshombe fled to Spain but returned in a few months and became premier of the united Congo. In October 1965 he was dismissed from the post and again went into exile in Spain. Eighteen months later, as he plotted his second return to the Congo, he was kidnapped while on a plane trip, taken to Algiers, and imprisoned.

URBANI, GIOVANNI CARDINAL, Italian prelate of the Roman Catholic Church (b. Venice, Italy, March 26, 1900—d. Venice, Sept. 17, 1969), president of the Italian Bishops Conference from 1966, succeeded Angelo Cardinal Roncalli as patriarch of Venice when Roncalli became Pope John XXIII in 1958; in the same year he was elevated to cardinal.

URE, PETER, British scholar (b. 1919—d. Newcastle upon Tyne, Eng., June 30, 1969), was from 1960 professor of English literature in the University of Newcastle upon Tyne. After serving in the Friends' Ambulance Unit (1942–46) and as an UNRRA officer in Greece (1946), he lectured at Newcastle on English language and literature. A contributor to the *Encyclopædia Britannica,* his books included *Shakespeare and the Inward Self of the Tragic Hero* (1961) and works on W. B. Yeats.

VANDOR, AUGUSTO, Argentinian labour leader (b. 1920—d. Buenos Aires, Arg., June 30, 1969), head of the Metal Workers Union, was slain by unidentified assassins shortly after he had refused to endorse a general strike against the Onganía government. Led by an oppositionist labour faction, the strike was slated as a protest against a visit by Nelson Rockefeller of the United States.

VICTORIA ALICE ELIZABETH JULIA MARIE (PRINCESS ANDREW OF GREECE), mother of Prince Philip (b. Windsor, Eng., Feb. 25, 1885—d. London, Eng., Dec. 5, 1969), was the sister of Earl Mountbatten of Burma. Her marriage to Prince Andrew of Greece (d. 1944), then an officer in the Greek Army, took place in 1903. In 1949 she founded the Christian Sisterhood of Martha and Mary and devoted herself to caring for the sick and aged.

VICTORIA EUGENIE CRISTINA ("ENA"), member of the Spanish royal family (b. Balmoral, Scot., Oct. 24, 1887—d. Lausanne, Switz., April 15, 1969), a granddaughter of Queen Victoria, was the widow of King Alfonso XIII. The daughter of Prince Henry of Battenberg, and of the English Princess Beatrice, her marriage to Alfonso took place on May 31, 1906, on which occasion an attempt was made to assassinate them. In April 1931, after the proclamation of the Spanish Republic, they left Spain. After Alfonso's death in Rome (1941), the queen resided at Lausanne. Her visit to Spain (February 1968) for the christening of her great grandson aroused great enthusiasm among monarchists.

VIVIAN, VALENTINE PATRICK TERREL, lieutenant colonel (ret.), British Army (b. March 17, 1886—d. Lymington, Hampshire, Eng., April 15, 1969), was head of the counter-espionage section of the British Secret Intelligence Service during World War II. His early career was in the Indian Police Service (1906–25). It was his misfortune to have appointed (in good faith) to the Secret Service the notorious Kim Philby who betrayed his confidence and defected to the Soviet Union.

VOROSHILOV, KLIMENTI YEFRIMOVITCH, marshal of the Soviet Union (b. Verkhne, Dnepropetrovsk, Russia, Feb. 4, 1881—d. Moscow, U.S.S.R., Dec. 3, 1969), was president of the U.S.S.R. from 1953 to 1960. His military career began after the October Revolution with the defense of Petrograd; he was made commander in chief of defenses and commander of the 10th Army, and in 1919 was sent to stem Anton Denikin's advance on Moscow. Shortly after capturing Orel and Kursk, Voroshilov was appointed commissar for home affairs of the Ukraine Soviet Republic. He took part in the Polish-Russian war in 1920 and in 1921 crushed the Kronstadt rising, fought in the Far East, and was elected to the executive committee of the Communist Party. On Lenin's death in 1924 he was appointed to the command of the Moscow area. In 1925 he became people's commissar for naval and military affairs and chairman of the Revolutionary Committee. Shortly afterward he was elected to the Politburo and from 1934 to 1940 was people's commissar for defense. In May 1940 Voroshilov was appointed deputy premier and chairman of the Committee on Defense. When Germany attacked the U.S.S.R., Voroshilov was sent to the Leningrad front; his next post was organizing reserves in the Urals and from there he went to head the Asian armies against the Japanese. After the war he was chief of the Control Commission in Hungary until 1947. On Stalin's death in 1953 he became chairman of the Presidium of the Supreme Soviet—effectively president. He was replaced in 1960 by Leonid I. Brezhnev, but was reelected to the Presidium in 1962.

VVEDENSKY, BORIS A., Soviet editor and scientist (d. June 1, 1969), chief editor of the second edition of *Bolshaya Sovietskaya Entsiklopediya* ("Big Soviet Encyclopaedia"), was a radiophysics expert, especially in ultrashort waves.

WARBURG, JAMES PAUL, U.S. financier and writer (b. Hamburg, Ger., Aug. 18, 1896—d. Greenwich, Conn., June 3, 1969), president and director of many large banking firms, was an early supporter of the New Deal. He served as monetary adviser to the U.S. delegation at the London Economic Conference in 1933, but two years later broke with Pres. Franklin D. Roosevelt over monetary policy and became an equally ardent dissenter to governmental foreign and financial policies. Most of his 30 or more books were concerned with his arguments for peace, conciliation, and disarmament, as in *How to Co-Exist* (1952) and *Disarmament: Challenge of the 1960s* (1961). He was also a contributor to *Encyclopædia Britannica.*

WARDE, BEATRICE L., U.S. authority on typography (b. New York, N.Y., Sept. 20, 1900—d. Epsom, Surrey, Eng., Sept. 14, 1969), was director of publicity and later consultant for the Monotype Corporation, Ltd., of England. She was the author of *The Crystal Goblet: Sixteen Essays on Typography* (1956) and contributed to *Encyclopædia Britannica.*

WATSON, IVORY ("DEEK"), U.S. singer (b. Mounds, Ill., 1909—d. Washington, D.C., Nov. 4, 1969), was an original member, and the tenor, of the Ink Spots, popular jive quartet of the 1930s and early 1940s. The group attained national recognition in 1939 with the recording "If I Didn't Care." Watson later sang with various groups until retiring in 1969.

WEILL, ARMAND ("AL"), U.S. fight manager (b. Gebweiler, Alsace, Dec. 28, 1893—d. Miami, Fla., Oct. 20, 1969), guided four boxers to championships: heavyweight Rocky Marciano (*q.v.*); Joey Archibald, featherweight; Lew Ambers, lightweight; and Marty Servo, welterweight.

WEINSTOCK, JACK, U.S. urologist and playwright (b. New York, N.Y., 1907—d. New York, May 23, 1969), medical director of the U.S. Life Insurance Company, was co-author (with Willie Gilbert) of the Broadway musical *How to Succeed in Business Without Really Trying,* which won a 1961 Pulitzer Prize, the Drama Critics Circle Award, and seven Tony Awards. Later plays by the team included *Hot Spot* (1963) and *Catch Me If You Can* (1965).

WEISENBORN, GÜNTHER, German playwright (b. Velbert, Ger., July 10, 1902—d. West Berlin, Ger., March 26, 1969), was closely associated with Bertolt Brecht and the theatre of the Weimar Republic. A convinced pacifist and left-winger, he spent three years in Nazi prisons during World War II. Among his many plays was *Die Illegalen* (1946), about the German resistance movement.

WELCH, THE REV. HERBERT, U.S. churchman (b. New York, N.Y., Nov. 7, 1862—d. New York, April 4, 1969), senior bishop of the United Methodist Church, had served as president of Ohio Wesleyan University from 1905 until 1916 when he became a bishop. He was resident bishop in Japan and Korea, 1916–28, before returning to the U.S. to head the Pittsburgh area. In 1932 he was assigned as missionary bishop in Shanghai, then was interim bishop of the Boston area until taking the post of executive chairman of the Methodist Committee for Overseas Relief in 1941. He retired in 1949 at the age of 86.

WERTH, ALEXANDER, British author and journalist (b. St. Petersburg, Russia, Feb. 4, 1901—d. Paris, France, March 5, 1969), wrote numerous books on French and Soviet affairs, including *Russia at War, 1941–45* (1964), based on his experiences as a correspondent on the Eastern Front, and *France, 1940–45* (1956). He was Moscow correspondent (1941–46) for the *Manchester Guardian,* Paris correspondent (1949–53) for the *New Statesman* and the New York *Nation,* holding the same post for the *Nation* from 1957 until the time of his death.

WHITE, JOSH, U.S. folk singer (b. Greenville, S.C., 1908—d. Manhasset, N.Y., Sept. 5, 1969), who gained national fame with his first album, *Chain Gang,* brought out in the early 1940s, started his career in New York around 1932 with the Southernaires, a folk-song group. His best-loved songs included "One Meatball," which sold a million copies, "Outskirts of Town," "Hard-Time Blues," and "John Henry." In 1940 White appeared in the play *John Henry;* he was also in *Blue Holiday* (1945) and *A Long Way from Home* (1948). During the 1950s and 1960s, he appeared on the concert stage.

WHITE, RUTH, U.S. character actress (b. Perth Amboy, N.J., April 24, 1914—d. Perth Amboy, Dec. 3, 1969), who made her Broadway debut in 1949 in *The Ivy Green,* attained her first real success in *The Ponder Heart* in 1956. Other plays of the late 1950s and 1960s included *The Happiest Millionaire, Big Fish, Little Fish* (for which she received a Drama Critics Circle Award), and *The Birthday Party* (1967). In 1961 she won an Obie Award for her success in the off-Broadway production *Happy Days.* Ruth White also appeared in films, including *The Nun's Story* (1959), *To Kill a Mockingbird* (1963), and *Midnight Cowboy* (1969); also in 1969 she completed *The Reivers* and *The Pursuit of Happiness* shortly before her death. In television, she was the winner of an Emmy for her work in "Little Moon of Alban."

WIEDEMANN, GUILLERMO EGON, Colombian painter (b. Munich, Ger., 1906—d. Key Biscayne, Fla., Jan. 25, 1969), who, as a neo-Impressionist and member of the New Secession group, held four one-man shows of his oils and watercolours during 1946. In the 1950s he turned to abstracts and exhibited widely in Latin America, the U.S., and Europe.

WIERZYNSKI, KAZIMIERZ, Polish poet (b. Drohobycz, Pol., Aug. 27, 1894—d. London, Eng., Feb. 19, 1969), wrote a volume of carefree, juvenile optimism entitled *Wiosna i wino* ("Spring and Wine"). After World War I he lived in Warsaw where he became one of the pillars of the "Skamander" group of poets. In 1928, in Amsterdam, he was awarded the Olympic gold medal for his poem *Laur olimpijski* ("Olympic Laurel"). Among his best postwar works are *Wolnosc tragiczna* ("Tragic Freedom") and *Krzyze i miecze* ("Crosses and Swords").

Moise-Kapenda Tshombe Victoria Eugenie Cristina

WIDE WORLD WIDE WORLD

WILGRESS, (LEOLYN) DANA, Canadian diplomat (b. Vancouver, B.C., Oct. 20, 1892—d. Ottawa, Ont., July 21, 1969), began his career in 1914 in the Department of Trade and Commerce, and over the next 20 years served in various trade capacities abroad. Canada's first ambassador to the U.S.S.R., he remained in Moscow through World War II. After the war he was envoy to Switzerland (1947–49), then Canadian high commissioner in Britain (1949–52). Returning to Ottawa, he was undersecretary of state for external affairs (1952–53) and permanent representative to the NATO Council in Paris (1953–58). In 1959 he became chairman of the Canada-U.S. Permanent Joint Defense Board, a post he held until his retirement in 1966.

WILLIAMS, HUGH ANTHONY GLANMOR, British actor-playwright (b. Bexhill-on-Sea, Eng., March 6, 1904—d. London, Eng., Dec. 7, 1969), was seen regularly on the London stage from the 1930s onward. After several years at the Liverpool Playhouse and later tours in Australia and the U.S., Williams' success led to West End engagements. After World War II he took up writing (in collaboration with his wife, the actress Margaret Vyner), later acting in some of his own plays. These included *Plaintiff in a Pretty Hat, The Happy Man, The Grass is Greener, The Irregular Verb to Love, Past Imperfect, Charlie Girl,* and others.

WILSON, JOHN DOVER, British Shakespearean scholar and educator (b. London, Eng., July 13, 1881—d. Balerno, Midlothian, Scot., Jan. 15, 1969), who made an important contribution to Shakespearean studies by bold elucidation of textual obscurities and stimulating, if controversial, interpretation of the plays, was professor of education at King's College, London, from 1924 until 1935 when he became regius professor of rhetoric and English literature at Edinburgh University, remaining there until 1945. His first work was *Life in Shakespeare's England* (1911), but he became widely known for his part in *Shakespeare's Hand in the Play of Sir Thomas More* (1923), a landmark in textual criticism. Other works were *The Essential Shakespeare* (1932), *What Happens in Hamlet* (1935), *The Fortunes of Falstaff* (1943), and *Shakespeare's Sonnets: An Introduction for Historians and Others* (1963).

WILSON, THOMAS J., U.S. editor (b. Chapel Hill, N.C., Oct. 25, 1902—d. New York, N.Y., June 27, 1969), director of the Harvard University Press from 1947 until 1967, when he became director and senior editor at Atheneum Publishers.

WINIARSKI, BOHDAN, Polish jurist (b. Bohdanow, Pol., April 27, 1884—d. Poznan, Pol., Dec. 4, 1969), was adviser to the Polish delegation at the Paris Peace Conference (1919–20), professor at the University of Poznan (1921–39), deputy to the Sejm (1928–35), and judge of the International Court of Justice (1946–66). He wrote many books, including *Les Institutions politiques en Pologne au XIXe siècle* (1921), *Security, Arbitration, Disarmament* (1928), and *International Law of Communications* (1938).

WOOD, ROBERT ELKINGTON, brigadier general (ret.), U.S. Army, and merchandising executive (b. Kansas City, Mo., June 13, 1879—d. Lake Forest, Ill., Nov. 6, 1969), chosen in 1968 as the first honorary chairman of Sears, Roebuck & Company, had served the company from 1924, as president (1928–39) and chairman (1939–54). After his retirement in 1954 he continued as a director until receiving his honorary title. He guided the company from a strictly mail-order operation to the world's largest merchandising company and the first retailer to record a single month's sales of more than $1 billion (December 1967). His military career included service in Panama (1905–15) and in World War I, when he attained his rank of brigadier.

WOOLF, LEONARD SIDNEY, British man of letters, publisher, political worker, writer, journalist, and internationalist (b. London, Eng., Nov. 25, 1880—d. Rodmell, Sussex, Eng., Aug. 14, 1969), influenced literary and political life and thought more by his personality than by any one achievement, and may well be remembered for his autobiography, an expression of the toughness of moral fibre and quality of mind and spirit that made him one of the outstanding men of his time. Its first three volumes, *Sowing* (1960), *Growing* (1961), and *Beginning Again* (1964), recreate the world of intellectual liberal Jewry into which he was born, the excitement of Edwardian Cambridge, the experience (1904–11) as civil servant in Ceylon that made him an anti-imperialist, and the atmosphere of the Bloomsbury group, in which he and his wife, Virginia Woolf (whom he married in 1912), played a formative part. Their Hogarth Press (founded 1917) and their discerning understanding encouraged such writers as T. S. Eliot and E. M. Forster. The last volumes of the autobiography (*Downhill All the Way,* 1967; *The Journey Not the Arrival Matters,* 1969) span 1919–69, years of political influence, through editorial activity on left-wing and internationalist journals and writings that helped to lay the foundations of League of Nations and UN policy and the welfare state. His support for his wife during the mental illness that ended in suicide (1941) made possible her creative achievement.

WORBOYS, SIR WALTER (JOHN), British businessman (b. Cottesloe, Western Australia, Feb. 22, 1900—d. Kensington, London, Eng., March 17, 1969), chairman of the British Printing Corporation, was also executive chairman of B.T.R. Industries Ltd., chairman of the Royal Society of Arts, and chairman of the Council of Industrial Design (1953–60).

WRENN, CHARLES LESLIE, British scholar (b. Westcliffe-on-Sea, Essex, Eng., Dec. 30, 1895—d. Oxford, Eng., May 31, 1969), was Rawlinson and Bosworth professor of Anglo-Saxon at Oxford University (1946–63). After lecturing at Durham, Madras, Dacca, Leeds, and Oxford, he became professor of English language and literature, University of London (1939–46), before his appointment to the chair at Oxford. A notable philologist, he was founder of the International Conference of University Professors of English.

WYMAN, WILLARD GORDON, general (ret.), U.S. Army (b. Augusta, Me., March 21, 1898—d. Washington, D.C., March 29, 1969), World War II commander of the 1st Division and a leader of the Normandy beachhead invasion on June 6, 1944, later commanded the 71st Infantry Division in the U.S. linkup with the Soviet Army on the Enns River in Germany. In the Korean War he commanded the IX Corps, after which he was commander of NATO forces in Southeastern Europe (1952–54), head of the 6th Army (1954–55), and commander of the Continental Army (1955–58).

ZACHARY, TOM, U.S. baseball player (b. 1897—d. Graham, N.C., Jan. 24, 1969), the Washington Senator pitcher who threw the low, fast ball that Babe Ruth slammed for his 60th homer of the 1927 season. Zachary's lifetime record for his 19 years in the majors was 186 wins and 191 losses; as a relief pitcher for the New York Yankees in 1928 he won 12 games and lost none.

ZAWIEYSKI, JERZY, Polish novelist, playwright, and Catholic leader (b. Lodz, Pol., Oct. 2, 1902—d. Warsaw, Pol., June 18, 1969), began writing in the 1930s, but came into prominence after World War II. Forced from print and stage during the Stalinist repression, he resumed writing in 1956. As a liberal Catholic he was elected to the Sejm in 1957, becoming also a member of the Council of State, and for 11 years tried to establish a modus vivendi between the church and the state. He resigned his mandate in protest against repressive measures following the student riots in March 1968.

ZOMOSA, MAXIMILIANO, U.S.-Chilean ballet dancer (b. Valparaíso, Chile, Feb. 28, 1937—d. Woodbridge, N.J., Jan. 9, 1969), who danced the principal role in the New York City Center Joffrey Ballet's world premiere of the ballet *Astarte,* was soloist with the Chilean National Ballet from 1959 until joining the Joffrey in 1966.

Oceanography

The results of the U.S. National Science Foundation's Deep Sea Drilling Project provided the most interesting developments of 1969 in the field of oceanography. The project's research vessel "Glomar Challenger," which began work in 1968, completed its first four legs in the Atlantic in late March 1969 and the second of five planned legs in the Pacific in August. Its purpose was to drill and obtain cores of the sediments of the deep ocean basins down to the underlying basement.

The work in the western Pacific revealed ancient formations containing sediments more than 140 million years old, perhaps the oldest in the world. The rocks are progressively younger to the east. This finding suggests that the East Pacific Rise (extending from California past New Zealand) is the source of the sea floor's growth. According to the continental drift (or sea-floor spreading) hypothesis, young rocks are formed from the mantle, move upward toward the earth's surface at the rises, and spread outward, carried away by the moving sea floor. The results also indicate that the oceans as they now exist are relatively young (the North Atlantic began to form about 200 million years ago). The northwestern Pacific is an area of very old oceanic sedimentation, and must be a remnant of an ocean basin that existed at a time when the Atlantic Ocean either did not exist at all or was only a small feature in a large continental mass before America, Europe, and Africa began to drift apart.

COURTESY, U.S. NAVY

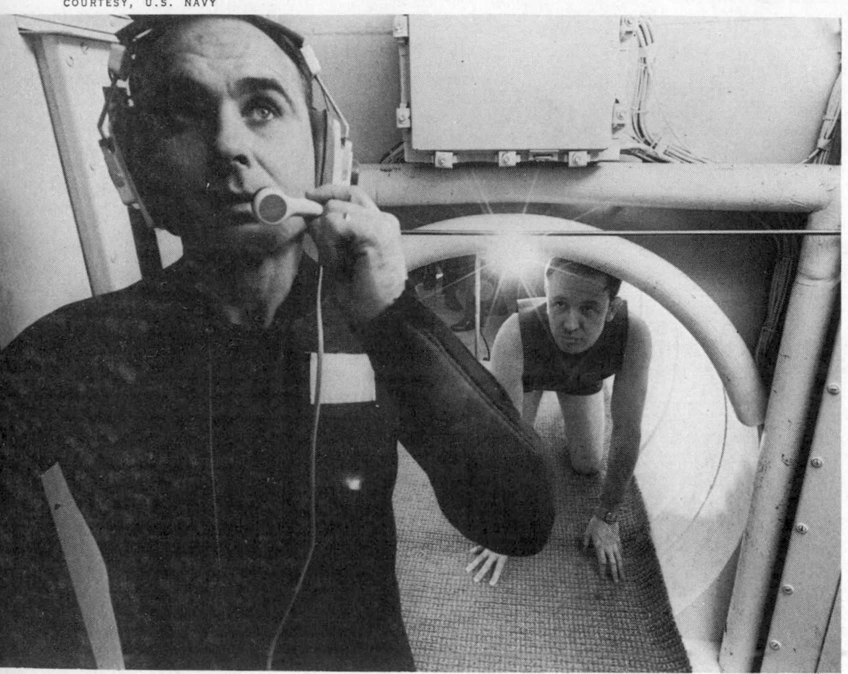

Two aquanauts check equipment in their underseas laboratory Tektite I in which four marine scientists lived on the ocean floor near the Virgin Islands from Feb. 15 to April 15, 1969.

Occupational Medicine: *see* Medicine

Oil: *see* Fuel and Power; Industrial Review

Oilseeds: *see* Agriculture

Opera: *see* Music

Ophthalmology: *see* Medicine

Organization for Economic Cooperation and Development: *see* Development, Economic

Organization of American States: *see* Inter-American Affairs

Continuing the study of the Weddell Sea begun in 1968, the U.S. Coast Guard cutter "Glacier" left Chile on Feb. 13, 1969, to take part in the second International Weddell Sea Expedition, and returned on March 25. Studies in physical oceanography, biology, and geophysics were carried out, though more severe ice conditions in 1969 limited the work to the area east of 35° W longitude; in the previous year work had extended as far as 50° W.

In the latter part of January measurements of water characteristics and speed were made in the Drake Passage, between the Antarctic continent and South America. Average daily speeds at the bottom of the Drake Passage varied from one-twentieth to one-third of a mile per hour. The width of the passage is about 300 mi. and the average depth a little over 2 mi. The total transport of water through the passage was estimated to be about 270 million tons per second, about twice the values estimated previously, without current meters, and approximately three times the estimated transport of the Gulf Stream.

BOMEX (Barbados Oceanographic and Meteorological Experiment) began its work in May. Designed to improve the accuracy of weather forecasts, it consisted of more than 80 independent research projects. The area being studied covered more than 90,000 sq.mi., just east of Barbados, where hurricanes form and pass. The energy received by the earth in the form of short-wave radiation is stored primarily in the upper layers of the ocean, and the tropical oceans, particularly in the western areas, have the greatest store of very warm water. The net gain in the tropics and loss in polar latitudes maintains a poleward energy flux carried mainly by the atmospheric circulation. The transfer takes place in several steps: first the energy from the upper tropical ocean moves into the lowest mile, the boundary layer, of the atmosphere; then convection moves it into the overlying troposphere; and finally the poleward transport takes place. BOMEX was studying the first two steps. Ten ships and a dozen buoys gathered data on the first step in May and June, and the second, convective, step was studied in July with aircraft and satellites.

In another program on the effect of air-sea interchange upon the deep ocean, seven research vessels from France, the U.K., Italy, NATO, and the U.S. worked together and in sequence during January–April in the area north and west of Corsica. The studies involved air-sea exchange processes (cooling and evaporation) and their effect in making the density of the surface water great enough to sink and mix with the underlying water to form the deep saline water that characterizes the Mediterranean.

On September 21 the 1,005-ft.-long tanker SS "Manhattan," which had left Pennsylvania on August 24, arrived at Prudhoe Bay on the north coast of Alaska after negotiating the Northwest Passage. Her mission was to find whether this route, through Baffin Bay and the Canadian Arctic, could be used to bring oil from the new discoveries on the northern coast of Alaska to the U.S. east coast. The vessel was modified to withstand and penetrate the sea ice that blocks this route, and carried various instruments to record ice thickness and pressure, water temperature and salinity, the depth beneath the keel, and the atmospheric data required to evaluate the possibility of regular and profitable voyages. Another voyage was planned for the spring of 1970, when the ice conditions would be much more severe.

The first, trial-run year of moored buoys in the North Pacific for air-sea interaction studies was completed. Previous studies of surface temperature had shown that there are large-scale, long-term temperature variations superimposed on the normal seasonal variation, and that these anomalies, usually covering about one-fifth of the North Pacific and enduring as long as 30 months, may be associated with the distribution of ocean life and with the weather over the ocean and the continental U.S. In order to study the associated subsurface temperature and its relation to the atmosphere, small catamaran-type buoys were moored in an area where the water is 12,000 to 18,000 ft. deep, about 1,000 mi. N of the Hawaiian Islands, and were equipped to measure and record the temperature of the air and of the water at various depths, winds and atmospheric pressure, solar radiation, and relative humidity. A larger "monster buoy," also moored in the area, could measure and transmit this and other information by radio.

In July and August 1969 the research submersible "Ben Franklin" drifted 1,500 mi. in 30 days at depths of from 600 to 2,000 ft. Its purpose was to study biological and acoustical aspects of the Gulf Stream. Launched off Florida, the vessel drifted with the Gulf Stream for the first 12 days, until it was spun off in an eddy. It was towed back into midstream and remained in the Gulf Stream until the end of the experiment, rising to the surface only 300 mi. off the coast of Halifax, Nova Scotia. Unlike other research submersibles, which are designed for great depth, speed, and maneuverability, the "Ben Franklin" had limited mobility and depth but high endurance. Scientist in charge was Jacques Piccard (*see* BIOGRAPHY).

The CSS "Hudson," a Canadian hydrographic survey vessel, began a circumnavigation of the American continents. Working southward from Nova Scotia and along the east coast of South America to Cape Horn, she would then move westward into the Pacific, northward to Alaska through Bering Strait, and eastward through the Canadian Archipelago (the Northwest Passage) to the Atlantic. The "Hudson" left Halifax in November 1969 and it was expected that she would complete her voyage in October 1970. Scientific work would include biological, chemical, and physical oceanography, underwater acoustics, geodesy, geophysics, geology, and hydrography.

An oil spill from an offshore well near Santa Barbara, Calif., early in the year, although much less intense than the spill from the tanker "Torrey Canyon" off England in 1967, was the largest single oil pollution incident in U.S. coastal waters since the end of World War II. Since the spill was from the drill hole in the ocean bottom, not from a container of known capacity, the amount could not be measured directly. Estimates were as high as 16,000 bbl. per day during the first few days, and by the end of May perhaps as much as three million gallons had poured into the ocean. The incident attracted interest as an area for research into control of released oil, surveillance of oil slicks, effects on beaches and harbours, and effects on living organisms.

Another deep-water salvage operation was carried out when the research submersible "Alvin," which had sunk in 4,500 ft. of water about 120 mi. SE of Cape Cod, Mass., was recovered in August. The sinking, which involved no injury or loss of life, occurred in October 1968 when a cable broke as the "Alvin" was being lowered from her mother ship. A second submarine, the "Aluminaut," located the vessel on the bottom and attached a cable. A salvage ship then hauled her out of the mud and towed her to a point off Martha's Vineyard, Mass., where she could be hauled aboard. After effects of corrosion on the vessel were studied, she was to be refitted for further dives.

On October 7, when the Lockheed research submarine "Deep Quest" dived to the bottom in 442 ft. of water off San Diego, Calif., a plastic mooring line attached to a heavy weight became entangled in her propeller and she was held about eight feet above the bottom. The oxygen supply was adequate for 48 hours for the four-man crew. Though she might have been able to pull free under her own power, there would have been danger of damage to the vessel, so another minisub, the General Oceanographic Company's "Nekton," was brought from Los Angeles and dived to the "Deep Quest" 's aid, about 12 hours after the entanglement occurred. The "Nekton" located the "Deep Quest" in about half an hour and cut the cable with a knife attached to her operating arm. Both vessels then returned safely to the surface. (J. L. RE.)

UPI COMPIX

These starfish under study in a U.S. Navy oceanography laboratory are typical of the species threatening destruction of Pacific coral reefs. The onslaught has puzzled scientists.

See also Antarctica; Biological Sciences; Geography; Geology; Law; Meteorology; Seismology.

ENCYCLOPÆDIA BRITANNICA FILMS. *Ocean Tides (The Bay of Fundy)* (1956); *The Marine Biologist* (1963); *Plankton —Pastures of the Ocean* (1965); *Waves on Water* (1965).

Pakistan

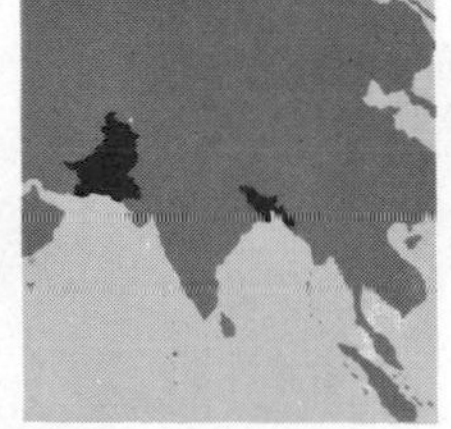

A federal republic and member of the Commonwealth of Nations, Pakistan is divided into two parts, separated by India. West Pakistan, the main part of the country, is bordered on the south by the Arabian Sea and on the west by Afghanistan and Iran; East Pakistan lies on the Bay of Bengal. Total area: 365,600 sq.mi. (946,900 sq.km.), excluding the Pakistani-controlled section of Kashmir. Pop. (1969 est.): 113,220,000. Cap.: Islamabad (pop., 1967 est., 226,000); legislative cap.: Ayubnagar (pop., 1968 est., 459,861). Largest city: Karachi (metro. pop., 1969 est., 3,060,400). Language: officially Urdu, Bengali, English. Religion (1961): Muslim 88.1%; Hindu 10.7%; Christian and Buddhist minorities. Presidents in 1969, Field Marshal Muhammad Ayub Khan to March 25 and, from March 31, Gen. Agha Muhammad Yahya Khan.

Domestic Affairs. The serious domestic upheaval that developed during the last three months of 1968 attained increased momentum between January and March 1969. Student unrest in West Pakistan touched off riots in Lahore, Rawalpindi, and Peshawar. More vigorous rioting then occurred in East Pakistan, where the student community, acting as the spearhead of general discontent, virtually displaced the governmental authorities. President Ayub Khan offered to negotiate with the opposition parties, made concessions to the student community, and on February 21 announced that he would not stand for reelection. But processions and demonstrations by employees of governmental and private enterprises grew more formi-

Ornithology: *see* Biological Sciences

Orthodox Churches: *see* Religion

Orthopedics: *see* Medicine

Osteopathy: *see* Medicine

Outer Mongolia: *see* Mongolia

Pacific Islands: *see* Dependent States

Packaging: *see* Merchandising

Painting: *see* Art Exhibitions; Art Sales; Museums and Galleries

Paints and Varnishes: *see* Industrial Review

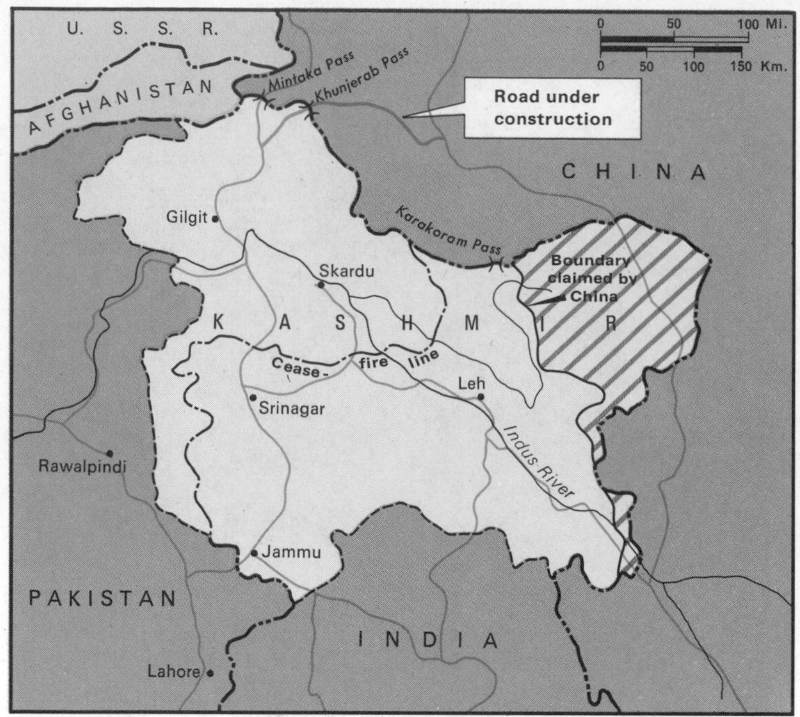

Highway under construction in 1969 links China's Sinkiang-Tibet highway with a major north-south artery in the Pakistan-controlled section of Kashmir. India protested the construction of the road.

dable; widespread strikes occurred among all classes; economic life was paralyzed; officials were powerless; and law and order were threatened in towns and countryside alike. In East Pakistan the situation grew increasingly unmanageable. On March 25 President Ayub Khan resigned, calling on the armed forces under the command of Gen. Agha Muhammad Yahya Khan (*see* BIOGRAPHY) to take control. Martial law was proclaimed immediately, and Yahya Khan became president on March 31.

The new president announced that his aim was to narrow the gaps separating various sections of the community and to remove the variations in income levels in different parts of Pakistan. Although public meetings were banned, political activity was not suppressed, and the president held conferences with political leaders. He announced that a new constitution would be framed by elected representatives of the people, and appointed Abdus Sattar as head of an election commission to delimit constituencies and prepare new electoral rolls in preparation for a return to civilian rule. A reorganization of the civil service gave East Pakistan effective representation in the form of six of the central secretaries; and when on August 4 seven civilian members were appointed to the president's Council of Ministers, four came from East Pakistan. Army recruitment from East Pakistan was also stepped up. With the proclamation of martial law, disturbances ceased, and the president's manifest determination to look into grievances and to reform abuses quickly restored national confidence. In December elections for the General Assembly were set for Oct. 5, 1970.

The remarkable economic progress of the country was hardly checked by the unrest in the early months of 1969. The gross national product showed a growth of 5.2% in 1968–69 as against 7.5% in 1967–68, and per capita gross income increased by 6.9% as against 3%. Self-sufficiency was attained in wheat, rice, and other food grains. Thanks to the success of the family planning campaign, population growth was held steady, while productivity continued to increase. The revenue budget for 1969–70, presented in June, showed an estimated surplus of income over expenditure of PakRs. 1.4 million. The capital budget provided for special allocations for education, low-cost housing, health, and other social welfare advances. In an effort to narrow economic disparities between East and West Pakistan, the total allocations were heavily weighted in favour of East Pakistan. The World Bank, meeting in Paris, noted that exports were up by 10%, agricultural production by 5%, and industrial production by 8%. The members of the Aid to Pakistan Consortium concurred that the country could effectively utilize external aid to a total of $500 million. In August a mission from the World Bank visited Pakistan, and it was agreed that during the forthcoming fourth plan period emphasis should be placed upon capital goods industries to reduce dependence upon imported machinery. Among loans received were $20 million from the U.S. for fertilizer and PakRs. 200 million from China. Work was begun on the great Tarbela Dam on the Indus River, and a steel mill was set up in Chittagong.

Foreign Relations. The continuity that marked economic development extended into the sphere of foreign relations. Treaties of economic and cultural cooperation were concluded with China, Indonesia, and Tunisia; and cordial relations were retained simultaneously with China, the U.S.S.R., U.S., and U.K. U.S. Pres. Richard Nixon's visit in August revitalized Pakistan's friendship with the U.S.

The closest ties remained those linking Paki-

PAKISTAN

Education. (1965–66) Primary, pupils 6,813,622, teachers 170,615; secondary, pupils 2,448,606, teachers 90,965; vocational, pupils 20,148; teacher training, students 15,989, teachers 1,050; higher, students 265,588, teaching staff 11,037.

Finance. Monetary unit: Pakistan rupee, with a par value of PakRs. 4.76 to U.S. $1 (PakRs. 11.43 = £1 sterling). Gold and foreign exchange, central bank: (June 1969) U.S. $316 million; (June 1968) U.S. $195 million. Budget (1968–69 est.): revenue PakRs. 6,889,300,000; expenditure PakRs. 5,842,100,000. National income: (1967–68) PakRs. 58,480,000,000; (1966–67) PakRs. 54,150,000,000. Money supply: (June 1969) PakRs. 11,459,000,000; (June 1968) PakRs. 10,014,000,000. Cost of living: (Karachi; 1963 = 100): (June 1969) 130; (June 1968) 128.

Foreign Trade. (1968) Imports PakRs. 4,741,000,000; exports PakRs. 3,429,000,000. Import sources: U.S. 30%; U.K. 12%; Japan 11%; West Germany 9%. Export destinations: U.K. 12%; U.S. 9%; Japan 7%; Hong Kong 7%; Singapore 5%. Main exports: textile yarns and fabrics 27%; jute 22%; cotton 14%.

Transport and Communications. Roads (1968) *c.* 200,000 km. (including 42,789 km. with improved surface). Motor vehicles in use (1968): passenger 80,813; commercial 26,790. Railways (1966–67): 11,339 km.; traffic 13,216,000,000 passenger-km., freight 9,574,000,000 net ton-km. Air traffic (1968): 1,459,500,000 passenger-km.; freight 63,595,000 net ton-km. Shipping (1968): merchant vessels 100 gross tons and over 170; gross tonnage 540,551. Telephones (Dec. 1967) 162,642. Radio receivers (Dec. 1966) 1,014,000. Television receivers (Dec. 1967) 20,000.

Agriculture. Production (in 000; metric tons; 1968; 1967 in parentheses): rice 19,515 (19,005); wheat 6,477 (4,393); barley 124 (104); corn 629 (795); millet 330 (414); sorghum 264 (291); chick-peas 606 (578); rapeseed and mustard seed 396 (307); onions 411 (397); sugar, raw value (1968–69) *c.* 428, (1967–68) 432; gur (indigenous raw sugar; 1967–68) 1,881, (1966–67) 1,911; tobacco 169 (178); bananas (1966) 821, (1965) 670; dates (1967) *c.* 150, (1966) *c.* 140; tea (1967) 30, (1966) 29; jute 1,044 (1,220); cotton, lint 532 (520); fish catch (1967) 417, (1966) 412. Livestock (in 000; 1966–67): cattle *c.* 35,700; sheep *c.* 11,000; goats *c.* 11,400; buffaloes *c.* 8,690; horses 497; asses 925; buffaloes *c.* 8,730; camels 601.

Industry. Production (in 000; metric tons; 1968): cement 2,324; crude oil (1967) 425; coal and lignite (1967) *c.* 1,400; natural gas (cu.m.; 1967) *c.* 2,012,000; electricity (kw-hr.; 1966) 3,903,000; chrome ore (oxide content; 1967) 13; jute manufactures (1967) 490.

stan to its Regional Cooperation for Development (RCD) partners, Iran and Turkey. At the beginning of 1969, the shah of Iran and the prime minister of Turkey visited Pakistan to review the progress made in economic and political cooperation among the three countries. The change of regime in Pakistan did not interrupt this process; the RCD ministerial body met in Islamabad in June, and President Yahya Khan inaugurated the conference, at which the foreign ministers of Iran and Turkey were present. A long communiqué registered the positive achievements of RCD and outlined even closer cooperation in the future, while specifying the joint projects that were to be set up in each of the three countries.

A slight breeze ruffled relations with Afghanistan when the three West Pakistan frontier states of Dir, Chitral, and Swat were incorporated into West Pakistan; but relations between Kabul and Islamabad, if not exactly cordial, remained correct. Only with India was there real antagonism, inflamed by the Kashmir quarrel and by Hindu-Muslim outbreaks in the Indian state of Gujarat. Even so, the partition of the Rann of Cutch was completed in July. The shah of Iran offered his help in bringing about better relations between the two countries. Pakistan accepted, but India did not take kindly to the idea. Ties with other Islamic countries were strengthened, and President Yahya Khan attended the Islamic summit conference at Rabat, Mor., in September. (L. F. R. W.)

ENCYCLOPÆDIA BRITANNICA FILMS. *India (Pakistan and the Union of India)* (1952); *Pakistan* (1955).

Panama

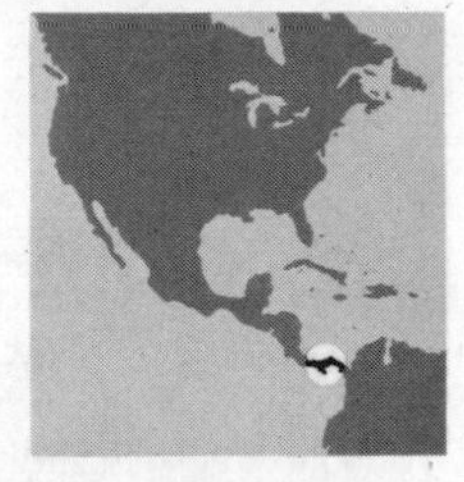

A republic of Central America, bisected by the Panama Canal Zone, Panama is bounded by the Caribbean Sea, Colombia, the Pacific Ocean, and Costa Rica. Area: 29,210 sq.mi. (75,650 sq.km.). Pop. (1969 est.): 1,417,100. Cap. and largest city: Panama (pop., 1969 est., 389,000). Language: Spanish. Religion: Roman Catholic 93%. Provisional presidents of the civilian-military government in 1969, Col. José M. Pinilla and, from December 18, Demetrios Lakas Bahas.

After the seizure of power on Oct. 11, 1968, by the National Guard and a governing junta of its officers, the Panamanian people found their activities restricted by a curfew and the suspension of their constitutional rights. The prices of the necessities of life were frozen, and those newspapers and radio programs controlled by the adherents of the former president were no longer available. These evidences of rule by military men were received, if not with equanimity, with but little resistance by the populace. They were unwilling to act in support of the appeals of former Pres. Arnulfo Arias for armed resistance.

During the first days of the new regime Col. José M. Pinilla, as provisional president, and Col. Bolívar Urrutia appeared to be at the forefront, but, by degrees Col. Omar Torrijos and Col. Boris Martinez emerged as the controlling figures in government. (Martinez later went into exile after refusing appointment as Panama's representative on the Inter-American Defense Board.) They tried to relieve popular anxieties by emphasizing the temporary character of the military control, by promising elections and electoral reforms, and by installing a civilian Cabinet. A drive to discredit the Arias government was launched by attributing Communist sympathies to it and by charging corruption, particularly in the form of padded government payrolls. At the same time, an infusion of National Guard officers in civilian government agencies was accomplished. Their intrusion in other quarters was felt, resulting in many political arrests and imprisonments.

The authoritarian methods and the long-continued restrictions on personal freedom led to internal friction in the government. Early in January five of the eight civilian Cabinet ministers, headed by the minister of foreign affairs, Carlos A. Lopez Guevara, resigned in protest. The military junta announced that they had been dismissed, speedily appointed replacements, and added a new officer, a minister of labour. An attempted coup against Torrijos on December 16, in which Pinilla and Urrutia were allegedly involved, resulted in the nomination of Demetrios Lakas as provisional president.

Opposition to the rule of the colonels remained focused in the remote province of Chiriqui, a rugged area on the boundary of Costa Rica. Partisans of Arias found a refuge and a centre for guerrilla activity there. In February, for a time, Panama closed the boundary.

The political upheaval and subsequent severe administration provided businessmen with uneasy moments. The government sought to offset this uncertainty by advertising its favourable attitude toward private initiative. The new minister of finance pointed to the multimillion dollar expansion plans of the United Fruit Company and of the Intercontinental Hotel Corporation.

The tonnage of oil, coal, ores, and grain carried on the Panama Canal continued to rise. The size of

PANAMA

Education. (1966–67) Primary, pupils 210,628, teachers 7,074; secondary, pupils 37,652, teachers 2,070; vocational, pupils 21,273, teachers 853; teacher training, students 1,313, teachers 56; higher (at 2 universities; 1967–68), students 9,156, teaching staff 376.

Finance. Monetary unit: balboa, at par with the U.S. dollar (2.40 balboas = £1 sterling). Total reported dollar assets: (June 1969) U.S. $150.4 million; (June 1968) U.S. $150.1 million. Budget (1969 est.): revenue 126.7 million balboas; expenditure 130 million balboas. Gross national product: (1967) 772.6 million balboas; (1966) 697.8 million balboas. Money supply (deposits only): (March 1969) 80.3 million balboas; (March 1968) 69.8 million balboas. Cost of living (Panama City; 1963 = 100): (2nd quarter 1969) 108; (2nd quarter 1968) 106.

Foreign Trade. (1968) Imports 243,350,000 balboas; exports 95,220,000 balboas. Net service receipts from Canal Zone (1968) 97.6 million balboas. Main import sources: U.S. 39%; Venezuela 21%. Main export destinations: U.S. 79%; Panama Canal Zone 5%. Main exports: bananas 58%; refined petroleum 19%; shrimps 10%.

Transport and Communications. Roads (1967) 6,712 km. Motor vehicles in use (1967): passenger 35,000; commercial (including buses) 11,600. Railways (1966) 684 km. (including 169 km. state controlled). Shipping (1968): merchant vessels 100 gross tons and over 798 (mostly owned by U.S. and other foreign interests); gross tonnage 5,096,956. Telephones (Jan. 1968) 57,759. Radio receivers (Dec. 1965) *c.* 500,000. Television receivers (Dec. 1966) 77,000.

Agriculture. Production (in 000; metric tons; 1967; 1966 in parentheses): rice 151 (140); sugar, raw value (1968–69) *c.* 64, (1967–68) *c.* 69; bananas *c.* 600 (*c.* 590); oranges 41 (41); coffee (1966) 5.1, (1965) 4.4; cocoa (1967–68) 0.5, (1966–67) 0.5. Livestock (in 000; 1966–67): cattle 1,037; pigs 169; horses *c.* 160.

Industry. Production (in 000; 1968): electricity (Panama and Colón; kw-hr.) 485,000; manufactured gas (cu.m.) 19,700; cement (metric tons; 1967) *c.* 150.

Palestine:
see Israel; Jordan

the tankers and carriers was up, and the tolls increased. But the canal was a source of worry also, as when a tanker broke in two and spilled oil into the channel off Cristóbal. Panamanians speculated on the possibility of the construction of a new canal far to the south. The report of the Atlantic-Pacific Inter-Oceanic Canal Study Commission on the feasibility of the various routes did not eliminate that possibility and did not allay their anxieties. Nor did the joint report of their own government and Colombia in September, suggesting for study an alternative route near the boundary of the two countries. With regard to the canal the new regime adopted the position of its predecessors: that the proposed treaties with the U.S. on canal and defense matters did not offer Panama sufficient concessions. (A. R. W.)

ENCYCLOPÆDIA BRITANNICA FILMS. *The Panama Canal: Gateway to the World* (1961).

Paraguay

A landlocked republic of South America, Paraguay is bounded by Brazil, Argentina, and Bolivia. Area: 157,-047 sq.mi. (406,752 sq.km.). Pop. (1968 est.): 2,243,-400. Cap. and largest city: Asunción (pop., 1968 est., 411,500). Language: Spanish (official), though Guaraní is the language of the majority of the people. Religion: Roman Catholic. President in 1969, Gen. Alfredo Stroessner.

During the 1968 presidential election campaign, "restricted democracy" had been heralded when President Stroessner allowed four opposition parties to participate, largely in compensation for his having changed the constitution in order to succeed to a further five-year term. This apparent political liberalization was reversed early in 1969, when opposition radio broadcasts were prohibited following the "Farias affair" in which a political detainee died while undergoing police interrogation.

New York Gov. Nelson Rockefeller's reception in June was the least stormy of his South American tour, with only minor student demonstrations—a reflection of Paraguay's severe security measures. Under a 1953 law Stroessner had regularly renewed the "state of siege" in the capital and certain frontier districts every 90 days to prevent partisan activity within the country and infiltration by exiled militant groups. In August an even stricter "Law for the Defense of Democracy" was put before Parliament. With the opposition already cowed into silence, only the church, at the annual national conference of Roman Catholic bishops, dared voice criticism of the new measure.

The political stability led to a significant inflow of foreign capital in 1969. However, the trade gap widened even further because, although export earnings increased, imports, facilitated by "shopping list" credits, rose even faster. A severe recession in meat-packing, Paraguay's foremost export industry, continued all year, but increased exports of cotton, tobacco, and coffee offset the decline in meat export earnings. Timber exports also rose as a result of recovery in the Argentinian construction industry.

In August an international commission redefined the northwest frontier, giving Paraguay over 300 sq.mi. of Chaco territory. (J. J. SM.)

PARAGUAY

Education. (1967) Primary, pupils 385,075, teachers 12,382; secondary, pupils (1965) 30,404, teachers (1964) 2,674; vocational (1964), pupils 3,054, teachers 529; teacher training (1965), students 3,285; higher (at National University and Catholic University), students 5,406, teaching staff 879.

Finance. Monetary unit: guaraní, with a free rate (October 1969) of 126 guaranies to U.S. $1 (297.50 guaranies = £1 sterling). Gold and foreign exchange, central bank: (May 1969) U.S. $7,360,000; (May 1968) U.S. $8,890,000. Budget (1969 est.): revenue 8,782,000,000 guaranies; expenditure 9.9 billion guaranies. Gross national product: (1967) 61,050,-000,000 guaranies; (1966) 57,950,000,000 guaranies. Money supply: (May 1969) 5,725,000,000 guaranies; (May 1968) 5,261,000,000 guaranies. Cost of living (Asunción; 1964 = 100): (June 1969) 111; (June 1968) 109.

Foreign Trade. (1968) Imports 7,730,600,000 guaranies; exports 5,778,100,000 guaranies. Import sources: U.S. 25%; Argentina 20%; West Germany 14%; Italy 7%; U.K. 6%. Export destinations: Argentina 27%; U.S. 24%; U.K. 11%; Netherlands 7%; France 5%. Main exports: meat 29%; timber 17%; oilseeds 10%; tobacco 10%.

Transport and Communications. Roads (1966) *c.* 12,500 km. (including *c.* 4,600 km. highways). Motor vehicles in use (1967): passenger 6,400; commercial (including buses) 6,500. Railways: (1966) 1,147 km.; traffic (1967) 14 million passenger-km., freight 17 million net ton-km. Navigable inland waterways (including Paraguay-Paraná River system; 1966) *c.* 3,000 km. Telephones (Jan. 1968) 16,048. Radio receivers (Dec. 1968) 164,000.

Agriculture. Production (in 000; metric tons; 1968; 1967 in parentheses): corn 180 (225); peanuts 18 (21); cassava 1,504 (1,460); sweet potatoes (1967) 90, (1966) 90; sugar, raw value (1968–69) *c.* 37, (1967–68) 40; tobacco 22 (13); oranges 216 (210); bananas (1966) 251, (1965) 232; cotton, lint 10 (9). Livestock (in 000; 1966–67): cattle 5,542; sheep 441; horses 710; pigs *c.* 900; chickens 6,399.

Industry. Production: cement (1967) 14,000 metric tons; electricity (1966) 205 million kw-hr.

Panama Canal Zone: *see* Dependent States; Panama

Paper Industry: *see* Industrial Review; Timber

Papua-New Guinea: *see* Dependent States

Parks

Europe. In the United Kingdom in 1969, a committee for Wales was appointed by the Countryside Commission, under the Countryside Act of 1968. The first National Park Centre, at Brockhole on Lake Windermere in the Lake District National Park, was opened on June 26, 1969. Standing in 32 ac. of beautiful grounds and commanding fine views across the lake, the property was purchased in 1966 for £65,000 by the Lake District Planning Board with the aid of a grant from the Countryside Commission. It was subsequently improved, again with the aid of a grant, to provide exhibition rooms, an information counter, a bookshop, a lecture theatre, and a cafeteria; outdoor facilities included a 300-vehicle parking lot, two pairs of toilet blocks, and a large picnic area. The centre, which had a permanent staff of eight headed by a director and was designed to introduce to newcomers the wealth of interesting features in the park, attracted large numbers of visitors. The board also acquired, on a 20-year lease, the islands of Liny Holme, Grass Holme, and Silver Holme in Lake Windermere.

In December 1968 the £56,000 restoration scheme for the Monmouthshire and Brecon Canal in the Brecon Beacons National Park was launched. The work of improving this picturesque 32-mi. section of the canal to pleasure-cruising standard was being undertaken by the British Waterways Board and the cost, with grant aid, was being borne by the English and Welsh national park authorities. Once restoration works were carried out, the government would be asked to make an order adding the canal to the cruising waterways as defined in the Transport Holding Act of 1968. With the help and advice of the Field Studies Council, the Countryside Commission established a countryside unit in the Pembrokeshire Coast National

Park. Conducted field tours and lectures formed part of the unit's special education and information services to visitors. In April 1969 the first permanent information centre in the Yorkshire Dales National Park was opened at Clapham in the West Riding area. The Cleveland Way, extending nearly 100 mi. along the borders of the North York Moors National Park, was officially opened in May; it was the second long-distance footpath to be completed. Approval was given to the North Downs Way long-distance footpath, stretching 141 mi. along the crest of the North Downs and coinciding in part with the medieval Pilgrim's Way from Winchester to Canterbury.

At a press conference held on May 1, 1969, the future role of country parks was outlined, the Countryside Commission's new country parks and picnic sites policy paper was introduced, and the country park symbol was displayed. The commission, acting as the central source for advice and reference on setting up these recreational areas, recommended 15 proposed schemes to the minister of housing and local government.

In Northern Ireland, Castlewellan Forest Park was opened to the public in March 1969. Service areas at Ness Wood, County Londonderry, and Crawfordsburn, County Down, though not officially opened, were used by the public.

Three nature reserves were established in Belgium: Rochers de Champalle (over 86 ac.), comprising limestone cliffs of geologic and botanical interest, and Lande de Sarcrave (37 ac.) and À la petite Champha (over 54 ac.), both moorland areas of botanical interest. In the Parc National de Port-Cros, France, the administrative council instituted port rights for passage and pleasure boats anchoring at Port-Cros Bay; approved in principle the construction of an autonomous station to supply electricity to the village of Port-Cros, the cost to be borne by the Ministry of Agriculture, Electricité de France, the local authorities, and the national park authority; erected a botanical path of about 656 yd. that permitted visitors to view the flora represented in the park; and set up a unit for the desalinization of seawater by the electric dialysis process to ensure the supply of drinking water for the village. Various port works were planned to facilitate connections with the mainland. Visitors to the park numbered 30,000. More than 62 mi. of pathways and four shelters were constructed in the Parc National des Pyrénées-Occidentales. Hunting was completely prohibited and game increased; fishing was free in the lakes and streams. Ten new shelters opened to the public in the Vanoise National Park were well patronized by excursionists and visitors.

Italy's Gran Paradiso park authority instituted an official "guides to nature" service operated by university students who explained the natural scientific features of the park to groups of visitors. In Spain new pathways and visitor shelters were built in the Montana de Covadonga National Park; a road was constructed from the Valleta Seca to the Valle de Monasterio in Algues Tortes and Lake San Mauricio Park; and in Ordesa Park, tables, benches, rustic writing benches, and outside toilets were installed. Visitors to the five national parks totaled approximately 220,000. A new bridge erected in Sweden's Padjelanta National Park, across the passage of the river at Vuojatätno of the Kvikkjokk-Vaisaluokta tourist path, replaced the former boat crossing of the watercourse. The total estimated number of visitors to the 16 national parks was 80,100. In the Netherlands the approximate number of visitors to De Hoge Veluwe was 520,000, to Kennemerduinen Park 200,000, and to Naardermeer Park 2,500.

North America. In Canada, Kejimkujik National Park (145 sq.mi.), the 19th in Canada's national park system, was formally opened on Aug. 9, 1969, after having been under development for several years. Situated in the counties of Annapolis, Digby, and Queens in south central Nova Scotia, its gently rolling wilderness landscape is cut by numerous rivers and dotted with about 35 shallow lakes. About 100 species of birds nested in the Kejimkujik Lake area. Services included a 250-site campground, a 50-site group-camping area, a supervised swimming beach, boating and sanitary facilities, a canteen, three picnic areas, and three hiking trails. University-trained naturalists carried out an active interpretation program, designed to explain the park's human and natural history to visitors; it included conducted hikes and slide-illustrated lectures. In Quebec's Gaspé region, an outstandingly beautiful part of the Forillon Peninsula was acquired for the province's first national park. The new David Thompson Highway, providing Banff National Park with an easy link with central Alberta, and a new chairlift at the Mount Temple Whitehorn ski area near Lake Louise were officially opened. Visitors to all the parks totaled approximately 11,850,000.

In the United States, more than 4,300 ac. of land on the island of Maui, Hawaii, were added to Haleakala National Park as the result of gifts from Laurance S. Rockefeller and the Nature Conservancy. Lying on the eastern slopes of the extinct Haleakala volcano, the donated area stretched from the edge of the crater to the Pacific Ocean and included the Seven Sacred Pools, once venerated in connection with the cult of the demigod Maui. Only the lower slopes were to be developed as recreational areas; the upper slopes, consisting of almost inaccessible rain forest, would be preserved for scientific purposes.

In his last official act before leaving office, Pres. Lyndon B. Johnson added 384,500 ac. to the National Park System—far less than the 7.5 million ac. that had been urged by his secretary of the interior, Stewart L. Udall. By presidential proclamation, Johnson added 49,000 ac. to the Arches National Monument and 215,000 ac. to the Capitol Reef Monument, both in Utah, and 94,000 ac. to the Katmai National Monument in Alaska. He also created the Marble Canyon National Monument, consisting of a strip of land connecting the Glen Canyon National Recreation Area and Grand Canyon National Park. Two anniversaries were observed in ceremonies at Grand Canyon National Park during the year: the 50th anniversary of the establishment of the park and the centenary of the first expedition down the Colorado River through the canyon, led by Maj. John Wesley Powell.

In June the new secretary of the interior, Walter J. Hickel, issued an 11-point policy directive for the National Park System, emphasizing the need for preserving natural areas while at the same time meeting the increasing needs of urban dwellers for recreation. The number of visitors to National Park System lands had been growing at the rate of about 7% annually, creating considerable pressure on facilities and danger to the parks themselves, especially in the more popular ones such as Yosemite. In November, Secretary Hickel announced a cooperative agreement between the National Park Service and the Boy Scouts of America that was expected to result in a considerable expansion of scouting activities in national park areas.

AUTHENTICATED NEWS INTERNATIONAL

Mather Gorge on the Potomac River at Great Falls, Va., was dedicated April 17, 1969, in honour of Stephen T. Mather, first National Park Service director.

Delays continued to surround the setting up of the Redwood National Park in northern California, established by act of Congress in 1968, principally because of difficulty in obtaining the transfer of three state parks to the federal government. In August, Pres. Richard Nixon journeyed to the Redwood park to dedicate the Ladybird Johnson Grove, named after the former first lady. In Yosemite National Park the famous Wawona redwood tunnel tree, 234 ft. tall and approximately 2,000 years old, toppled, presumably as a result of natural deterioration.

Two especially noteworthy national historic sites were dedicated during the year: the Saugus Iron Works at Saugus, Mass., a reconstruction of the first well-established ironworks in America; and the birthplace of Pres. John F. Kennedy at Brookline, Mass.

Africa. Progress was made in Tanzania's national parks in the building of roads, hotels, a museum, administrative buildings, water-supply systems, and bridges. A 40-minute, 16-mm. colour film with the sound track in Swahili was produced. Under the aegis of the national park educational project, 6,900 local people visited the parks, bringing the total attendance figure, excluding Sunday excursion flights to Serengeti, to more than 88,000.

In South Africa construction started on the massive Engelhard Dam on the Letaba River in the Kruger National Park, for which project U.S. mining millionaire Charles Engelhard donated R 120,000 (about $167,000) to the National Parks Board. Visitors to the eight parks numbered 539,000.

Improvements in the Dindir National Park in Sudan included the construction of an airstrip, providing regular Sudan Airways service twice weekly from December to May. More access roads were built to animal concentration areas, and a pumping set was installed to lift clean well water for drinking and domestic use at the campsite. The Nimule and Southern national parks were deserted because of security conditions, but it was expected that the park authorities' activities would be resumed in the near future.

Oceania. In New South Wales, Austr., nearly 71 sq.mi. were added to existing national and state parks and 308 sq.mi. to nature reserves, increasing the amount of land held by the National Parks and Wildlife Service by over 11%. Major construction included the erection of entrance stations at Kosciuske and Kuring-gai Chase national parks. The creation of 20 new ranger positions raised the total ranger force strength to approximately 100. The estimated number of visitors to all parks was 4,026,000.

Seven new national parks were established in Queensland. In the north, Park 645 (21.5 sq.mi.), opened in October 1968 in the parish of Pitt, south of Cardwell, was an area of unique biological complexity at the southern limit of the wet tropics of Australia. Park 1334 (4.5 sq.mi.), opened in November 1968 in the parish of Glady, embraced much of the well-known Eubenangee Swamp about 10 mi. NW of Innisfail. In November 1968, Park 647 (2 sq.mi.) in the parish of Rockingham was opened. Situated east of Tully between Hull River and the Tully-Mission Beach Roads, it represented a typical area of lowland vegetation on granite soils of the wet coastal plain and supported more than 20 species of rain forest birds. Park 135 (21 sq.mi.) in the parish of Curlewis, opened in June 1969, was located halfway between Bowen and Ayr and covered the northern section of Cape Upstart (named by Captain Cook). Park 1356 (about 1.75 sq.mi.) in the parish of Bellenden Ker, at the mouth of the Russell River north of Babinda, provided a mangrove habitat in a high rainfall zone with tea tree and vine swamps. In southern Queensland, Park 76 (13 sq.mi.) in the parishes of Mellish and Pyramid was proclaimed in June. Located north of Injune and formerly part of Lonesome Holding, the area preserved in its natural condition a large sample of the Brigalow scrub that was being cleared under the Fitzroy Basin development scheme. In southeast Queensland, Park 1161 (1.75 sq.mi.) in the parish of Noosa, established in November 1968, preserved a good sample of typical undisturbed wallum land supporting flora and fauna associated with such country.

Under the Forestry Act Amendment Act of 1968, reserves under 1,000 ac., previously termed scenic reserves, were given national park status. The act also provided for specialized management within the parks of areas declared as primitive, primitive and recreation, recreation, scientific, or historic. By altering the definition of "forest products," the amending legislation ensured the protection of all forms of animal life in the parks. Interest in the parks continued to increase, and the total number of visitors exceeded 1.5 million.

The National Parks Commission in South Australia was responsible for the care and control of 39 national parks, 1 wilderness park, and 12 national park reserves, covering 4,245 sq.mi. in all. In Tasmania, South West National Park (nearly 740 sq.mi.), which absorbed Lake Pedder Park, was proclaimed in October 1968 and became the largest in the state. With the completion of certain hydroelectric schemes, the park would contain the largest lake in Australia. Preliminary plans indicated that the lake shores would probably receive fairly intensive development, while the southern part of the park, extending to Tasmania's rugged south coast and consisting mainly of mountainous terrain, would remain undeveloped. The total area of parks and scenic reserves reached about 1,598 sq.mi. or 6.1% of the state's total area, by far the highest percentage of any Australian state.

One new park was established in Victoria: Little Desert (4.5 sq.mi.), situated in the northwest, 220 mi. from Melbourne. A landscape of extensive open country with high rainfall and poor soil, its special feature was the sanctuary of the Lowan or Mallee fowl. Developments in Wilson's Promontory National Park included the erection of two dwellings at Tidal River for staff residences and improvements to the water supply. Visitors to all parks numbered about 418,600.

A new national park, Torndirrup (nearly 14 sq.mi.),

was proclaimed in Western Australia. The area, southwest of the township of Albany, contained attractive coastal scenery with rugged rocky cliffs and small sandy bays, as well as undulating country inland. The 14 sq.mi. added to Nambung Park contained interesting features including a number of caves, and it was anticipated that these would eventually be opened to the public. In the Hamilla Hill area 2 sq.mi. were added to the Stirling Range National Park, primarily to protect the spectacular cranbrook bell (*Darwinia meeboldii*). Yanchep, which was given national park status, was increased to over 10 sq.mi. Firebreaks and access tracks for fire control continued to be provided, particularly in the larger parks. A vehicular track was constructed in the Kalbarri National Park to give access to the spectacular Murchison River gorge scenery, and a good road was provided to the fine coastal scenery south of Red Bluff. A biological survey was made of Kalbarri National Park, with staff assistance from the Department of Agriculture and the Western Australian Museum.

In New Zealand, park rangers previously employed by the individual park boards were transferred to the public service and provision was made for a separate occupation class for park rangers. The ten national parks received a total of 1,356,000 visitors.

Other Countries. Japan added 13 quasi-national parks to the national park system. Developments included the provision of camping and skiing grounds, picnic areas, access roads, and visitor centres. The construction of a new long-distance trail of about 808 mi. between Tokyo and Osaka was announced by the National Parks Bureau. Attendance figures for the 23 national parks exceeded 218 million and for the quasi-national parks, over 137 million. As a result of the large increase in visitors, the protection of the natural environment of the parks was becoming a serious problem.

Three new national parks were established in Israel. Jerusalem Park (about 500 ac.) comprised a greenbelt surrounding and protecting the Old City. Its special features included the valleys of Kidron and Hinnon, Mount Zion and the Mount of Olives, an old village of unique beauty, olive orchards, and pine groves. The park boundaries had yet to be made final. Mount Carmel National Park (40 sq.mi.) extended over the highest and most interesting parts of the oak groves. Achziv Park (about 110 ac.) was situated on a small hill on the shores of the Mediterranean near the site of an ancient Phoenician port. Special features of the park, which was being planned as a recreation area, were the picturesque arches remaining from the old village. (M. F. B. B.)

See also Conservation; Tourism.

Payments and Reserves, International

Against the background of the inflationary strains and stresses and the shortcomings in national policies in the principal countries reviewed under ECONOMY, WORLD, international trade and payments were—not too surprisingly—marked in 1969 by severe imbalances and the international monetary system passed through recurrent tensions and disturbances. Yet, what appeared on the surface to be international crises were, fundamentally, crises of national economies of several of the large industrial countries that were trying to live above their means or, in the case of the U.S., seeking to invest or otherwise spend abroad well in excess of international receipts.

For the international monetary system merely absorbs the shocks that spread from one domestic economy to another. At the same time, however, tensions and disturbances in international payments and in the world monetary system are themselves a sign that nations are unwilling to accept imprisonment within domestic boundaries. As nations have become increasingly interdependent and, specifically, as output and investment have become more and more international, the challenge to the world's payment and reserve arrangements and practices is obvious. The search for the most effective ways of meeting this challenge is—against the background of trends, developments, and policies during 1969—the main topic of this survey.

World trade in 1969 continued the rapid expansion it experienced in 1968—13%, the fourth highest rate of growth in the past two decades and more than double that of 1967 (Chart 2). Exports of industrial countries were about 20% higher in value than a year earlier. Because of rising prices for many commodities, the primary producing countries fared well and many of them were able to build up their monetary reserves. But the strong growth of trade was not well balanced because much of it over the last two years stemmed from a surge of imports sucked by inflation into three countries—the U.S., the U.K., and France; this surge was in turn instrumental in bringing about large trade surpluses for a few other countries, chiefly West Germany, Japan, and Canada.

The large trade surpluses and deficits of the industrial countries thus reflected principally the differences among them in the pressures of domestic demand and in the intensity and pervasiveness of inflation. Furthermore, differences in domestic monetary conditions, in policies to combat inflation, and in instruments actually used by central banks led to unusually large capital movements out of many currencies into high-interest earning dollars held on deposit in banks outside the U.S. ("Eurodollars"). Factors of confidence were also crucial. To defend corporate cash and to build up balances to meet future commitments, treasurers and others responsible for administering large amounts of money converted French francs, sterling, dollars, and other currencies into German marks.

Given all the circumstances, there also occurred, understandably, an outburst of speculation. The first storm gathered in March but was dispelled as political leaders in France rejected a devaluation of the franc as the "ultimate absurdity" and those of West Germany proclaimed the mark's parity to be "fixed for eternity." Once again, however, official avowals on currency matters failed to be corroborated by subsequent events. The French franc was quietly devalued in August and the German mark was allowed to appreciate in late September.

The devaluation of the French franc was carried out on August 10 with great skill and sangfroid (Table I). The new president and government decided to devalue early in their term because, as was revealed at the time of devaluation, French reserves had fallen—as a result of a trade gap and outflows of capital—from nearly $7 billion at the beginning of 1968 to $1.2 billion, a net figure after deduction of short-term borrowings. After sales totaling $1.7 billion, and although heavily mortgaged, France's $3.6 billion gold stock at the time of the devaluation remained the third largest in the world—exceeded only by those of the U.S. and West Germany (Chart 1).

The overvaluation of the franc could not have been corrected simply by restraining demand, for austerity measures required to redress the imbalance would have entailed, as the president of France stated, "unbearable sacrifices and massive unemployment." Realities had to be recognized; but to back up the devaluation, measures were taken to prevent an undue expansion of demand—thus, no doubt, trying to avoid the danger of slipping back into old ways (13 devaluations in 41 years).

The upvaluation of the German mark was widely anticipated. For one thing, West Germany began to experience renewed price-cost inflation (though, by international standards, a mild one) and, accordingly, an upvaluation of the currency—a move that, among other advantages, makes imports cheaper and tends to dampen exports—appealed to the defenders of German monetary stability against the dragon of imported inflation. And, for another thing, West Germany—because of its competitive strength but also because of the vigorous demand for German goods in countries experiencing greater inflation—built up a very large merchandise export surplus. True, West Germany also succeeded in exporting substantial amounts of long-term capital and, as a result, its "basic" balance of payments (*i.e.*, current and long-term capital account) was in deficit. But short-term capital inflows flooded the country with such force that official gold and foreign exchange reserves rose substantially.

In September, for the first time in any nation's monetary history, the exchange value of the currency became the subject of an election campaign; and, on the morrow of the elections, September 29, the outgoing Christian Democratic-Social Democratic coalition decided not to hold the exchange rate. The decision, however, was not the dawn of a new era hailed by advocates of "floating" exchange rates, for the mark floated under the monetary authorities' guidance and, on October 26, was stabilized by the new Social Democratic-Free Democratic government at a new fixed level (Table I).

In appraising the net effect of the upvaluation on German competitiveness in export markets, it should be recalled that West Germany's border tax changes in January 1968 resulting from the introduction of the value-added tax were tantamount to a mark devaluation of 3–4%. Since this devaluation was offset by opposite changes in the border taxes in November 1968, which were eliminated in October 1969, the change since the end of 1967 was a net upvaluation of about 5%—practically the same as the upvaluation in March 1961, which had no lasting effect on Germany's foreign trade.

CHART 1.

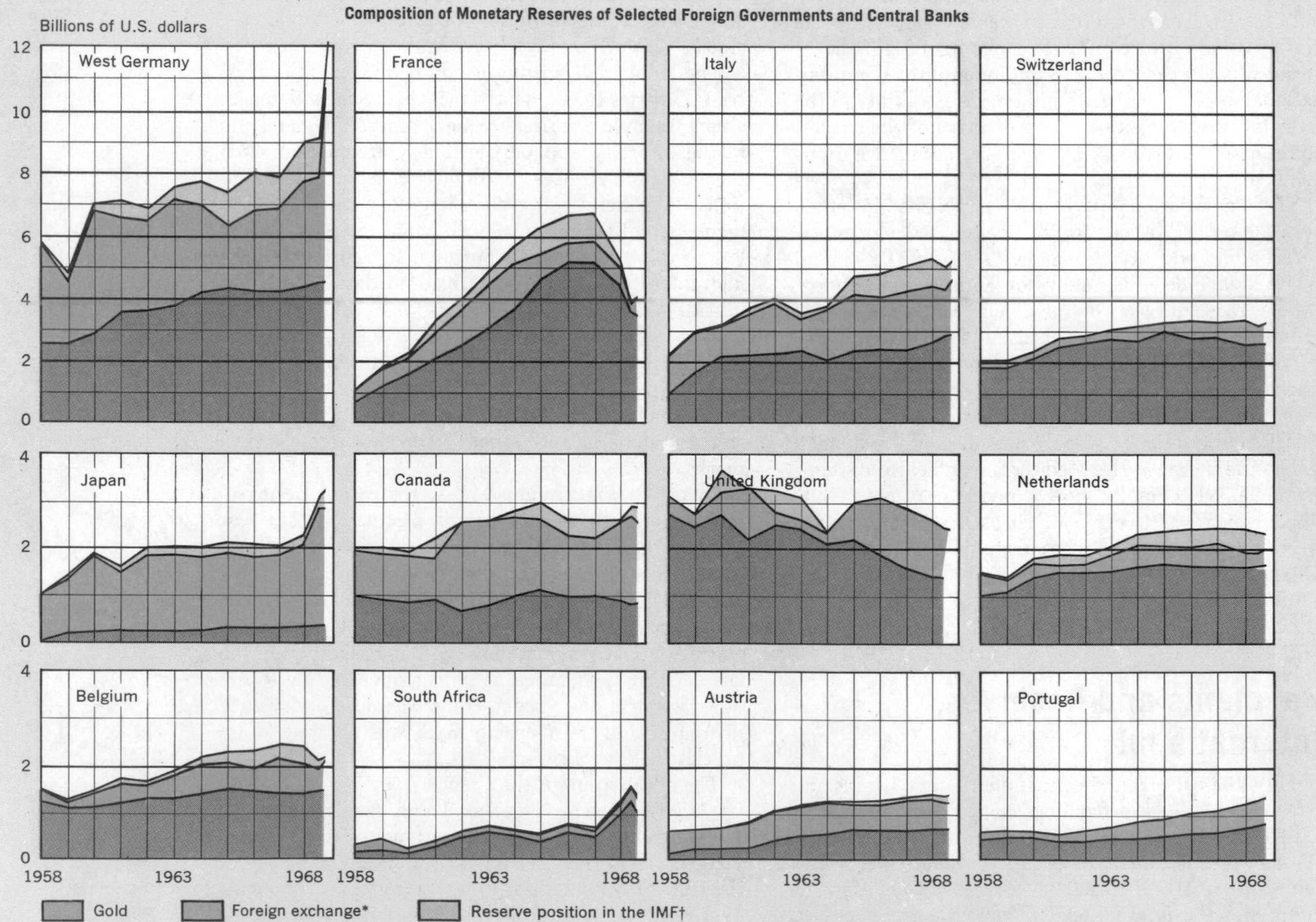

*Includes assets acquired as a result of support operations in foreign exchange markets or under other special intercentral bank arrangements.

†Amounts that can be drawn "essentially automatically" from the IMF, corresponding to members' gold subscriptions *plus* amounts of their currencies sold by the Fund to other members (net) *plus* outstanding lendings to the Fund.

Note: The countries included are those holding the largest monetary reserves with the exception of Australia, whose reserves consist predominantly of sterling.

Following the upvaluation, funds flowed out of marks into other currencies, with the result that Germany's monetary reserves fell markedly. Toward the year's end, the reserve of readily usable dollars declined to a point where Germany drew on the International Monetary Fund (IMF), liquidated a part of its holdings of medium-term U.S. Treasury securities, and sold $500 million of gold to the U.S. While foreign exchange markets were calmed, it remained to be seen how quickly the upvaluation—together with such other factors as the strong push of wage costs—would help reduce the German payments surplus.

Like West Germany, Italy and Japan also had heavy surpluses on current account. This similarity was, however, superficial for the underlying conditions were altogether different. The Italian lira—while strong because of the country's large current account surplus since the mid-1960s—is the currency of a nation that experienced, in 1969, increasing political turmoil and social discontent. As a result, the chronic drain of capital flowing abroad rose greatly and, for the first time in many years, the overall balance of payments moved into deficit. Italy's combination of current-account surpluses—entailing a transfer of real resources abroad, principally to other industrial nations—and long-term capital deficits—entailing a low propensity toward productive investment at home—appeared to be increasingly out of tune with the nation's political and social realities.

The Japanese yen was under pressure for upvaluation because of a sharp rise in the nation's monetary reserves during 1968–69. For, despite an ebullient boom, Japan did not run into balance of payments difficulties; on the contrary, the surplus on current external account and capital inflows, largely for investment in Japanese corporate stocks, reached a record level. To slow down the buildup of official reserves, the authorities encouraged a "yen shift"—a reduction in U.S. dollar financing of Japanese imports in favour of yen financing—and repayments of foreign debt. The governments of other industrial nations urged Japan to accelerate the dismantling of import restrictions and obstacles to capital exports.

The fortunes of the pound sterling improved as 1969 was coming to a close. For the first time since 1962, the U.K. had a surplus in its balance of payments. The trade deficit turned into a small surplus during the third quarter; and, with income from invisibles (interest and dividends, tourism, etc.), the current account balance of payments showed a surplus equivalent, on an annual basis, of $1.3 billion. Britain's monetary reserves rose even after large repayments on debts incurred in earlier years to help rescue the pound.

To some extent, of course, the improvement in Britain's balance of payments reflected reflows of funds out of German marks as well as long-term borrowings abroad. While the payments balance was undoubtedly better, it was still beset by a number of complications. To repay Britain's external debt, a continuous surplus would be needed for several years ahead. Furthermore, Britain's comeback took place at a time when the value of world trade was still expanding vigorously; but a slowdown would once again make Britain's export performance less assured.

The U.S. balance of payments, as portrayed in Table II, suffered a deterioration in 1969. The trade surplus, which had averaged nearly $5.5 billion for the first half of the 1960s but declined sharply later on, remained low in 1969; if $3 billion of exports financed by U.S. government aid is excluded, there was actually a large trade deficit. In an environment of inflation, the U.S. greatly increased its imports in the last two years; its export performance failed—notwithstanding a notable expansion of sales abroad—to match the growth of export markets outside the U.S. Defense outlays remained large. U.S. private capital flowing into investment abroad increased; foreign private investments in the U.S. declined from the very high levels recorded in 1968. Official policy aimed at restoring a substantial trade surplus through checking inflation in order to slow down the rate of growth of imports and provide conditions helpful for the competitiveness of U.S. exports.

The international position of the dollar was greatly eased by the fact that central banks of the surplus countries pushed dollars out of their reserves into private holdings. Dollars were sought by private traders and investors, for they yielded extraordinarily high interest rates in the Eurodollar market or, when invested in U.S. stock markets, offered for the long run a promise of capital growth unparalleled in other parts of the world. The channeling of dollars into private holdings had, from the point of view of foreign monetary authorities, the advantage of reducing the accumulation of unwanted dollars in their own reserves. From the U.S. point of view, it had the advantage of making less conspicuous the deterioration in the international liquidity position of the U.S.—the ratio of gold to U.S. liabilities to foreign governments and central banks (Chart 3).

As a result, the U.S. balance of payments on the "official settlements basis" (as measured by changes in U.S. reserves and liabilities to official institutions abroad) recorded a substantial surplus in 1969. But, for political as well as economic reasons, the principal countries outside the U.S.—while ready to add reasonable amounts of dollars to their reserves year in, year out—no longer wish to rely on the U.S. balance of payments deficit as the mechanism for the creation of international reserves. For this reason—and also because, after the establishment of the

Table I. How to Measure the Degree of French Franc Devaluation and West German Mark Upvaluation in 1969

	Gold parity	Exchange rate	
Currency	In terms of grams of fine gold per unit of currency	In terms of U.S. dollars per unit of local currency	In terms of units of local currency per U.S. dollar
French franc (August 10)			
Previous	0.180000 grams	$0.202550	Fr. 4.937060
New	0.160000	0.180044	5.554190
Change	0.020000 grams	$0.022506	Fr. 0.617131
Fraction of devaluation	0.020000 grams / 0.180000 grams	$0.022506 / $0.202550	Fr. 0.617131 / Fr. 4.937060
Percent of devaluation	11.1%	11.1%	12.5%
West German mark (October 26)			
Previous	0.222168 grams	$0.250000	DM. 4.000000
New	0.242806	0.273224	3.660000
Change	0.020638 grams	$0.023224	DM. 0.340000
Fraction of upvaluation	0.020638 grams / 0.222168 grams	$0.023224 / $0.250000	DM. 0.340000 / DM. 4.000000
Percent of upvaluation	9.3%	9.3%	8.5%

The French franc and German mark are legally defined in terms of gold. The change in the gold parity brings about a corresponding modification of the exchange rate in terms of the U.S. dollar, which is defined by legislation in terms of a fixed weight of gold. For holders of currencies, the degree of devaluation and upvaluation differs depending on whether it is calculated from the standpoint of exchanging dollars for the local currency or exchanging the local currency into dollars. Thus, after the devaluation of the French franc, holders of dollars who wish to acquire francs pay $0.022506 less per franc—or 11.1%. On the other hand, holders of francs who wish to acquire dollars pay Fr. 0.61713 more per dollar—or 12.5%. As a result of the upvaluation of the German mark, holders of dollars pay $0.23224 more per mark—or 9.5%. On the other hand, holders of marks pay DM. 0.3400 less per dollar—or 8.5%.

so-called two-tier gold system in March 1968, little gold was added out of new production to official monetary stocks of countries other than South Africa (Table III)—the governments decided to activate in 1970 a new international monetary facility in the form of special drawing rights ("paper gold").

Special Drawing Rights. Unlike gold and dollars, which (except for newly mined gold) can be acquired only through balance of payments surpluses, the SDR's will be distributed to governments freely in proportion to their IMF quotas; the governments are in turn obligated to accept SDR's from one another up to specified limits. (The word "special" is to distinguish the new instrument from the drawing rights on the Fund's ordinary resources.) The holdings of SDR's are, in effect, internationally acceptable assets that, like gold, are a claim on the world's resources. Like gold, the rights are usable automatically and unconditionally among central banks.

These attributes of paper gold do not mean that there are no limits to the willingness of governments of nations with balance of payments surpluses to build up their holdings of this untried asset. The SDR's are but entries in an international ledger—entries for which (disregarding initial distribution, which is free) the surplus nations will have to surrender to the deficit nations their own goods, services, and capital assets for an unspecified period or even "for good."

Understandably, therefore, the SDR facility is limited. First, the arrangement provides for partial repayment. Furthermore, important decisions regarding SDR's require 85% of the total voting power. Besides, no government is obligated to accept as payment from other participants more than twice the equivalent of its own drawing rights initially received. In addition, governments have the right to withdraw from the scheme. Finally, the SDR's are endowed with an absolute gold clause—absolute in that, unlike the clause applicable to ordinary Fund positions, it cannot be rescinded by a vote of IMF directors in the event of a uniform rise in the monetary price of gold. Making SDR's as much "goldlike" as possible enhances their desirability relative to reserves in the form of dollars, which enjoy no gold guarantee.

Table II. U.S. Trade and the Overall Balance of Payments

In $000,000,000

Period	Merchandise trade			Overall deficit (−) or surplus (+) as measured on	
	Exports	Imports	Balance	Liquidity basis	Official settlements basis
Annual					
1966	29.4	25.5	3.9	−1.4	0.3
1967	30.7	26.8	3.9	−3.5	−3.4
1968	33.6	33.0	0.6	0.2	1.6
Quarterly*					
1968 I	7.9	7.8	0.1	−0.6	−0.4
II	8.4	8.1	0.3	—	1.6
III	8.9	8.6	0.3	−0.1	0.1
IV	8.4	8.5	−0.1	0.9	0.4
1969 I	7.5	7.6	−0.1	−1.7	1.1
II	9.6	9.6	—	−3.9	1.2
III	9.6	9.2	0.3	−2.5	−0.9
IV	9.9	9.4	0.5	1.5	1.1

*Seasonally adjusted.

CHART 2.

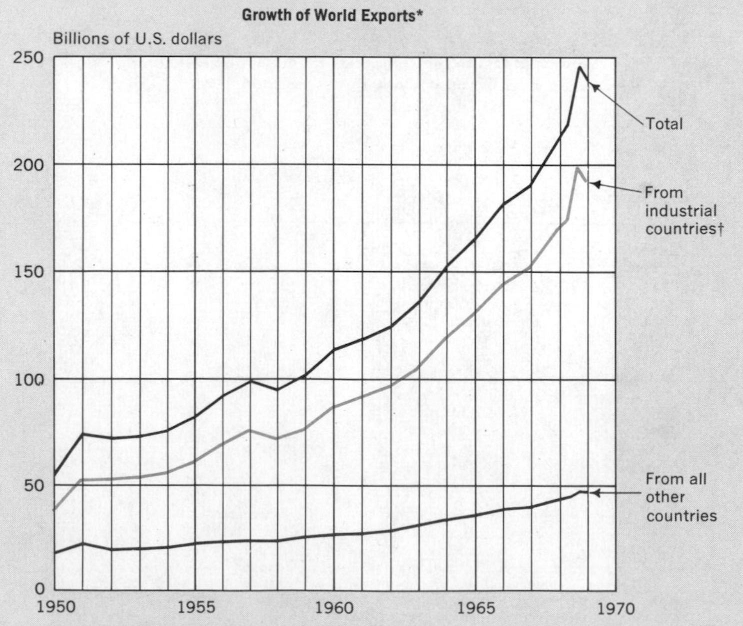

*Excluding exports of the U.S.S.R., other Eastern European countries, China, etc.

†United States, Canada, Western Europe, Australia, New Zealand, South Africa, and Japan.

Source: International Monetary Fund.

When the SDR facility was first negotiated, it was to supplement, not to supplant, gold. With relatively little new gold added to reserves of countries other than South Africa, the SDR's began to be regarded as a substitute for new gold as well as for dollars that, prior to the mid-1960s, had been the main source of growth of the world's monetary reserves but had actually declined in importance in the past few years in relative as well as in absolute terms. The much greater weight thus assigned to SDR's naturally led to a substantial increase in the amount that would be created. The initial basic period for annual allocations was to cover three years. For the first year, 1970, the issue of SDR's would amount to $3.5 billion; for each of the following two years, it was to be held down to $3 billion. Even the $3.5 billion figure is not, however, large when the aggregate is distributed among the more than a hundred participants (Table IV). Thus, the first year's allotment for the U.S. would be about $850 million—a small figure relative to past balance of payments deficits.

As the future was shaping up, three aspects of SDR's were crucial. The first was one of confidence. In a world in which there are several forms of international assets held as reserves—gold and such instruments as dollars, reserve positions in the IMF, and SDR's, each of which is linked to gold in a different way—instability can result from shifts from one kind of asset into another. Rules have, therefore, been devised to prevent switches from SDR's into gold; but switches from dollars into gold are not banned and the SDR's—endowed as they are with an absolute gold guarantee—may well be preferred to dollars, which enjoy no gold guarantee. To prevent shifts from one asset into another, proposals have accordingly been made to blend gold, dollars, and SDR's in fixed proportions; to take dollars out of official reserves by having them turned into entries on the books of an international institution; or to crown SDR's as the only reserve asset.

Proposals like these have found little support outside narrow circles. Historically, it may be recalled, governments and central banks chose freely to hold sterling or dollars in monetary reserves because they found it safe, profitable, and convenient to do so, and because they were confident that they could at any time, without having to give any explanation, shift from one currency to another or into gold. To-

Table III. Estimated Sources and Uses of Gold*
In U.S. $000,000

Period	Sources Out-put	Sources Sales by U.S.S.R.	Sources Total	Uses Recorded flows into official stocks	Uses All other
1955–64 average	1,157	271	1,428	607	821
1965	1,440	550	1,990	220	1,620†
1966	1,440	—	1,440	−45	1,410†
January–September 1967	1,068	—	1,068	−230	1,298
October 1967–March 1968	696	27	723	−2,720	3,143†
April 1968–December 1968	1,061	—	1,061	670	391
January 1969–September 1969	1,055	—	1,055	−10	1,065

*Excluding the U.S.S.R., other Eastern European countries, China, etc.

†Excludes purchases by governments of Eastern European countries and China, estimated at $150 million for 1965, $75 million for 1966, $300 million for October 1967–March 1968.

day, they are not ready to relinquish this freedom of choice.

The second aspect concerned the future of gold. It revolved around the thought that governments will become so used to the new international monetary facility that they will begin to prefer SDR's to gold and that, as a result, the importance of gold will rapidly diminish.

The thought that the growth of monetary reserves could come almost entirely from SDR's rests on the assumption that governments may be ready to give up gold, which is the principal form of reserves for most of the large countries (Chart 4). It overlooks that influential governments and central banks do not act as if they believed that gold demonetization today would represent an improvement in the international monetary system. In the recent past, they seized the opportunities to add to their gold stocks out of the substantial amounts sold by France ($1,683,000,000 from April 1968 through June 1969) and the IMF ($597 million); the Fund, to accommodate the British and French drawings, not only had to use its own resources and borrow currencies, but also had to raise funds by selling gold, out of its already reduced supply, to 16 countries. The U.S., which itself bought somewhat over one half of the French gold ($925 million), in turn sold gold to a number of countries throughout the world ($591 million net).

The gold problem was thus by no means disposed of at the Washington conference in March 1968 when the representatives of seven nations "felt" that, in view of the prospective activation of SDR's, central banks had sufficient gold and that there was no need to buy gold from the market. In the wake of the decline in the market price—on a thin volume—from the high of $43.65 a fine ounce in May 1969 to $35, the monetary price, in early December, the U.S. Treasury announced on December 16 "a basis for a satisfactory mutual understanding" on the handling of South African gold. The understanding followed discussions among governments and central banks of the major countries and was further elaborated by deliberations "in the framework of the IMF." It provided that South Africa may dispose of some of its gold to monetary authorities at $35. The view thus prevailed that additions from new gold output to official stocks at $35—without, therefore, denuding the U.S. gold stock—would be a stabilizing development. For the governments of the major nations of continental Europe that had increased their gold stocks fourfold in 15 years to a level representing almost half of the world's monetary stock could obviously not disinterest themselves in matters concerning the price of gold.

Some students of international liquidity regard the convertibility of dollars into gold as a fiction maintained only to reassure continental Europe and to comply with certain provisions of the IMF charter. They see the international monetary system gradually evolving toward a dollar standard—a system in which the growth of international reserves would take place through acceptance by foreign governments of dollars stemming from deficits in the U.S. balance of payments or from special operations to finance the deficits of other countries. The prospect of a dollar standard does not, however, appeal to other major countries, since such a standard would involve abandonment of autonomy and independence in their own domestic monetary conditions and policies.

The thought that the U.S. gold window could be closed formally so that the U.S. could escape from "the constraints of gold" thus fails to give weight to the dilemma in which the outside world would find itself in such a contingency. It underestimates the possibility that other important countries could form a currency bloc of their own independent from the dollar bloc. Needless to say, this would be the end—until a new order was achieved—of a common monetary system among Western nations.

The third aspect of the shape of things to come

CHART 3.

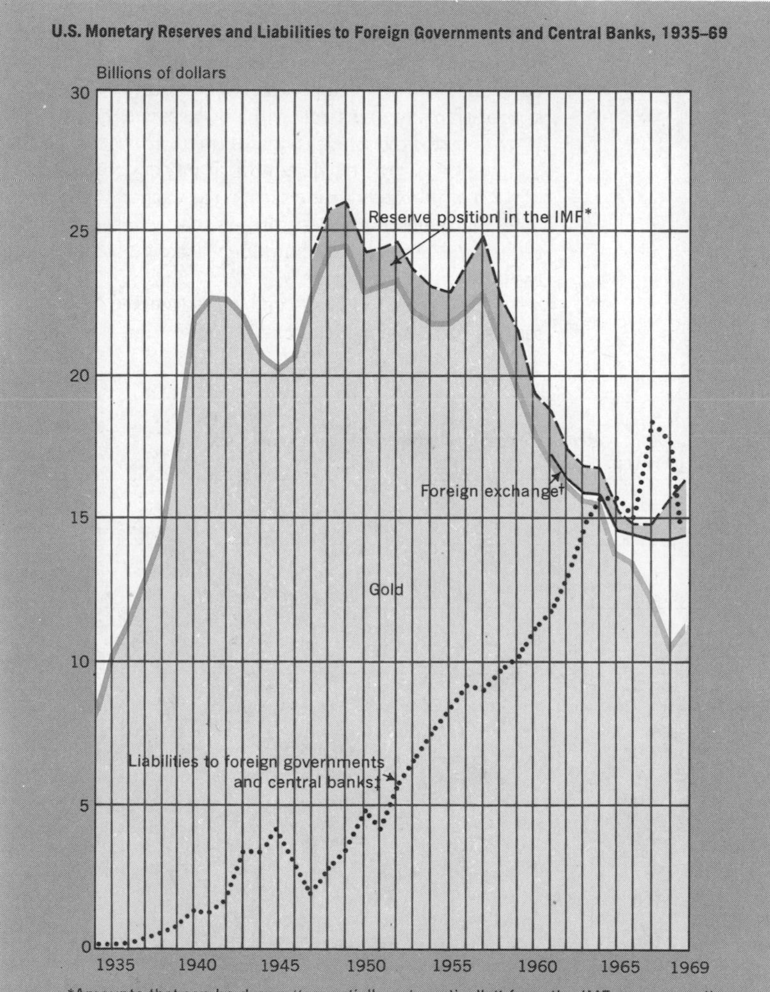

U.S. Monetary Reserves and Liabilities to Foreign Governments and Central Banks, 1935–69

*Amounts that can be drawn "essentially automatically" from the IMF, corresponding to the U.S. gold subscription and amounts of U.S. dollars sold by the Fund to other members (net).

†Largely assets acquired as a result of general support in foreign exchange markets for other currencies such as sterling. The United States can, therefore, use such holdings only for bilateral settlements.

‡Deposits, short-term money market instruments, and U.S. government notes and bonds, including special nonmarketable Treasury securities.

Source: *Federal Reserve Bulletin.*

was whether or not the allocation of SDR's would, by itself, help the process of adjustment in the balances of payments among the surplus and the deficit countries. The adjustment process comes, of course, through the workings of price, cost, and interest rate mechanisms—helped or hindered, as the case may be, by government policies or lack of policies—and through devaluations or upvaluations of exchange rates that have become inappropriate. Since the problem is political in nature and since, as experience shows, there is a wide gap between understanding and practice, the probable effect of SDR allocation on the balance of payments discipline of the world might well be to postpone rather than to speed up the painful and unpalatable measures necessary to deal with the balance of payments disequilibriums.

Exchange Rate Flexibility. Understandably, therefore, the thought emerged that SDR's alone cannot make the international monetary system once again workable. Further innovations should be sought to help smooth the process of adjustment through greater flexibility in exchange rates. In the aftermath of the five monetary crises between November 1967 and September 1969, this search, initiated mainly by nonofficial monetary doctors, did not come as a surprise. For in a dynamic world, the pace and the patterns of production and productivity change continuously, and prices and costs get out of line because of disparities among countries in the degree and pervasiveness of inflation. Exchange rate relationships appropriate at one time will not necessarily fit later. If they are nevertheless maintained, they accentuate balance of payments disequilibriums, encourage speculation, and exacerbate crises in the exchange markets. The real question, therefore, is not whether an unrealistic exchange rate should be changed, but when, by how much, and how.

Various possibilities have been suggested. The most radical and, theoretically, attractive idea is to abandon the present system of fixed parities, which—except for adjustments necessary to deal with "fundamental" (*i.e.*, persistent and serious) disequilibriums —offers but limited freedom for market rates. The drawback is that freely floating rates would be determined not only by the forces of trade and investment —which reflect, among other things, changes in purchasing power relationships among currencies—but also by gossip, guesswork, and mass psychology. Furthermore, governments cannot be expected to disinterest themselves in so vital a price as the exchange rate, which automatically and powerfully influences general prices, incomes, and the terms of trade. As the governor of the Bank of England, Sir Leslie O'Brien, remarked, "It seems to me Utopian to talk of taking the exchange rate out of politics: one might just as well talk of taking tax rates out of politics." Governments can thus let the day-to-day determination of actual trading be handled by the market; but they do not want to leave the entire process to be determined by market forces.

In view of the widespread doubts about the workability of a floating rate system among major industrial countries, emphasis is placed on a limited, circumscribed, and internationally agreed upon flexibility within the framework of a fixed-rate system. One version suggests the widening of exchange rate margins beyond the present permitted spread of 1% on either side of parity. Another version proposes crawling or gliding parities. At the IMF and World Bank annual meetings in late September and early October, the finance ministers expressed readiness to reexamine the appropriate role for adjustments in exchange rates in order to help deal with strains and disruptions in the world's exchange rate structure. This reexamination would also review the possibilities of making more active and intensive use of existing IMF arrangements and rules for keeping exchange rates realistic.

For the Fund, while wedded to the principle of exchange rate stability, has been since its very establishment pragmatic enough to have supported a measure of flexibility whenever circumstances made this desirable or unavoidable, as at one time or another in certain Latin-American and Asian countries, and in Canada from 1950 to 1962. During its entire existence, the Fund has endorsed some 60 devaluations. Of these, however, 13 occurred in September 1949 after it had been recognized that the prewar rates for sterling and other currencies had become unrealistic. During the subsequent 20 years, only eight devaluations took place in industrial countries, of which three were in France. There were only three upvaluations of currencies during these 20

Table IV. Initial Amounts of Special Drawing Rights Allotted out of the First $3.5 Billion Creation*

In $000,000

United States	851	Other Europe	229
United Kingdom	403	Australia, New Zealand, South Africa	141
West Germany	198	Developed countries	2,524
France	162		
Italy	103		
Netherlands	86	Asia other than Japan	381
Belgium, Luxembourg	73	Latin America	322
Canada	122	Africa other than South Africa	163
Japan	119		
Sweden	37	Middle East	110
Group of Ten	2,154	Less developed countries	976
		Grand total	3,500

*Assumes participation of all IMF members on the basis of present quotas.

CHART 4.

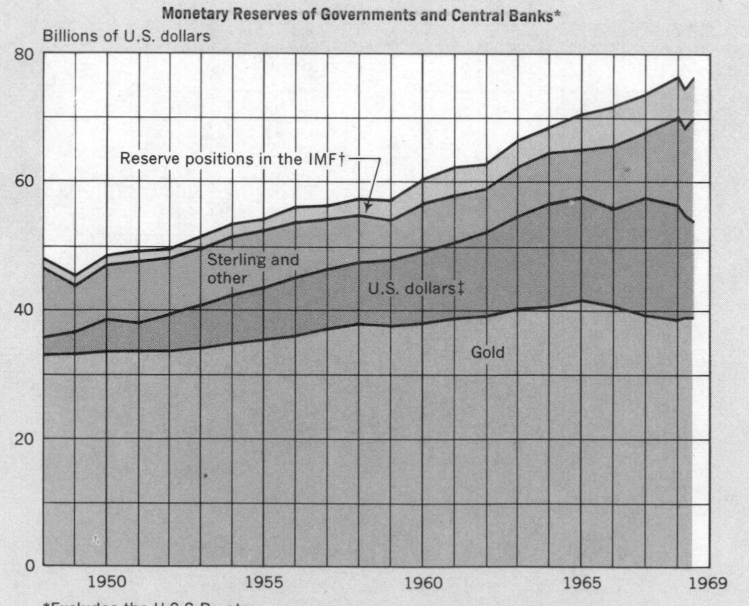

*Excludes the U.S.S.R., etc.

†Amounts that can be drawn "essentially automatically" from the IMF, corresponding to members' gold subscriptions *plus* amounts of their currencies sold by the Fund to other members (net) *plus* outstanding lendings to the Fund.

‡Includes special nonmarketable U.S. Treasury bonds sold to foreign governments and central banks.

Source: International Monetary Fund.

Table V. Parity Changes in the Major Industrial Countries, October 1949*–October 1969

Currency	Date of change	Percent change from previous rate	Percent change from October 1949 rate
Upvaluations			
Netherlands guilder	March 1961	5.0	5.0
West German mark	March 1961	5.0	5.0
	Oct. 1969	9.3	14.8
Devaluations			
French franc	Aug. 1957	−16.7	−16.7
	Dec. 1958	−14.9	−29.1
	Aug. 1969	−11.1	−37.0
New Zealand dollar	Nov. 1967	−19.5	−19.5
Austrian schilling	May 1953	−17.8	−17.8
Pound sterling	Nov. 1967	−14.3	−14.3
Canadian dollar	May 1962	− 8.1†	− 8.1†
Danish krone	Nov. 1967	− 7.9	− 7.9

*Following the devaluations of sterling and other currencies in September 1949—adjustments that marked the end of the immediate post-World War II period.

†Based on the average rate prevailing during the period of the floating Canadian dollar from September 1950 to May 1962 when a new parity was fixed.

years—two in West Germany and one in the Netherlands. Movements upward were even stickier than movements downward (Table V).

Changes in the values of currencies are, of course, effected in terms of the U.S. dollar, which is assumed to "stand still" as the centre currency fixed in terms of gold—at $35 an ounce. Unlike other countries, the U.S. does not intervene in exchange markets; it has only to be prepared to buy and sell gold at $35. In a fundamental sense, the dollar's exchange rate is the price of gold; but, in an operational sense, it is the composite result of the rates established by other countries at their own initiative for the dollar.

Understandably, therefore, exchange rate flexibility for other industrial nations raises the question of the necessary safeguards and protection for the U.S. As Secretary of the Treasury David M. Kennedy remarked at the IMF meeting: "We must guard against the possibility of encouraging a bias toward devaluations." The thought has also been expressed that the U.S. should encourage a bias toward upvaluation of other currencies. This is, however, easier said than done, for acceptance by other industrial nations of an upvaluation bias would presuppose a degree of readiness to help increase the competitiveness of U.S. exports and help decrease the competitiveness of their own exports to the U.S. and in third markets—a readiness they give little evidence of possessing.

In reexamining exchange rate arrangements, practices, and policies, there is an overwhelming need to draw a line between exchange rate realism and the risk of bringing about disorderliness in the markets. Many practitioners regard a small widening of the bands within which exchange rates are allowed to fluctuate as an innovation worth considering. Such a widening could provide a little more elbowroom and give the authorities a useful degree of flexibility in day-to-day operations. We live in a world of currency convertibility in which large amounts of funds move continuously through the exchange markets—a world that differs from the framework visualized after World War II when convertibility was envisaged for current transactions but not for capital transfers; these were expected to be suppressed through controls rather than financed.

Limited exchange rate flexibility within internationally agreed upon but modest limits may, of course, help to cope with exchange rate divergences and discrepancies of a minor sort. It would be less than helpful when inflationary patterns push exchange rates visibly and flagrantly out of line. Once currencies are out of balance, exchange rate changes are, sooner or later, necessary. Such changes are an integral part of the process of balance of payments adjustment and should not be hampered by matters of prestige or political sensitivity. Greater flexibility thus means greater willingness of the governments in the major industrial countries to change exchange rates more frequently and by smaller amounts that do not send shock waves through the international monetary system.

In breaking down the rigidities and inhibitions to orderly change, if change is necessary, it is essential that the adjustment remain orderly. For exchange rate changes cannot provide an easy way out by somehow making it unnecessary for nations to keep their economic and financial houses in order. Exchange flexibility is not a "sort of monetary LSD"—to use the words of the French finance minister, Valéry Giscard d'Estaing, at the IMF meeting. Devaluations and upvaluations are not a substitute for, but a complement to, other policies.

Furthermore, the fixing of rates of exchange for each currency is a matter of international concern. This remains as true as it was when the present IMF arrangements governing exchange matters were established to spare nations a repetition of the competitive exchange depreciations of the 1930s following the breakdown of the gold standard. The safeguards and protection provided by the IMF must be preserved. (M. A. K.)

See also Commercial Policies; Commodities, Primary; Economics; Economy, World; Investment, International; Money and Banking; Prices; Trade, International.

Peace Movements

Divergent trends marked the activities of world peace movements in 1969. In the U.S. eight months of relatively subdued protest yielded to markedly higher levels of demonstrations as impatience mounted over the halting pace of Vietnam peace negotiations. Peace leaders attempted with some success to graft the mass constituencies attracted by simple "end-the-war" politics onto a more radical core of "anti-imperialist" politics. They also sought to relate to the developing "culture of opposition," marked by experimentation with alternate life styles, communal efforts, and such graphic examples of the new youth culture as the Woodstock Music and Art Fair.

Ironically, just as a truly national end-the-war coalition was emerging, the radical New Left organizations, particularly the Students for a Democratic Society (SDS), split into sectarian factions. At its Chicago convention, SDS fragmented into the Revolutionary Youth Movement (which later divided into RYM I—also called the "Weatherman" group—and the less-violent RYM II) and the Worker-Student Alliance, dominated by the Progressive Labor Party.

Meanwhile, the heightened demands of traditional peace organizations were typified by SANE's call in September for immediate unilateral withdrawal of all U.S. forces from Vietnam and removal of support from the Thieu-Ky regime in Saigon. In the October 15 Moratorium, which had begun as a campus movement, thousands of citizens all over the country—including many government and business leaders—joined students and faculty members in demonstrating opposition to the war. In November the Moratorium's leaders joined forces with the New Mobiliza-

BEN ROTH AGENCY

"Spurned in Vietnam, ignored in Biafra, ridiculed in China. I don't know what keeps him going. . ." —Cookson, "London Daily Mail."

KEYSTONE

Cards bearing the names of dead U.S. servicemen are dropped into a coffin outside the U.S. embassy in London on Nov. 15, 1969, to demonstrate opposition to the war in Vietnam.

DAVID GAHR

New York City residents crowd Wall Street to show their support for the Oct. 15, 1969, Moratorium.

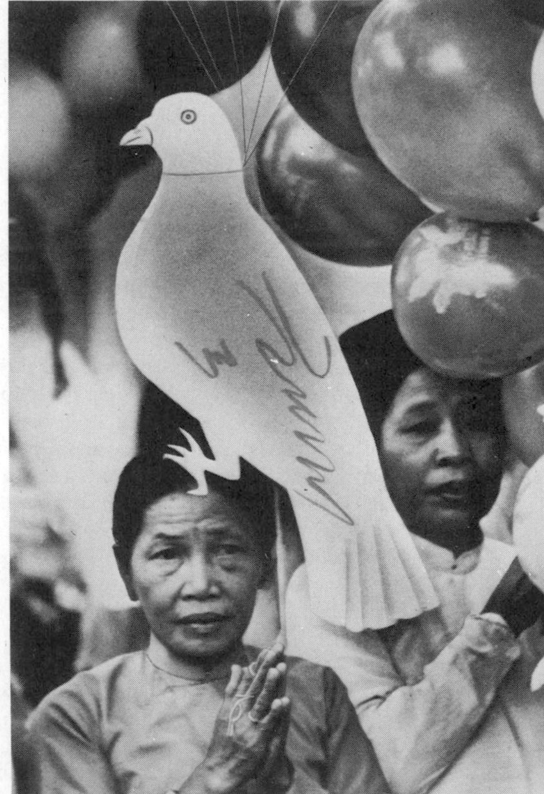

WIDE WORLD

Above, South Vietnamese women pray for peace during a Buddhist religious procession in January 1969.

"LONDON DAILY EXPRESS" FROM PICTORIAL PARADE

Left, young demonstrators in Bern protest Gen. William C. Westmoreland's presence in Switzerland.

tion Committee to End the War in Vietnam (successor to the National Mobilization Committee that had organized the 1967 march on the Pentagon) in sponsoring a massive march on Washington. The Moratorium group planned to continue its efforts each month until the war ended, but the December Moratorium was chiefly local and received comparatively little publicity.

Such activity marked a decisive shift in focus from the first six months of the year, when attention centred on the ABM (antiballistic missile) controversy. While the Nixon administration's "Safeguard" funds were voted by a narrow 51–50 tally in the Senate, the debate marked one of the few instances in 20 years of an intense evaluation of a major weapons system. Increased attention was also given chemical, biological, and radiological warfare, and passage of the "National Commitments Resolution" by a vote of 70–16 in June suggested Senate disenchantment with executive dominance in foreign policy.

Outside Congress, the Coalition on National Priorities and Military Policy succeeded the Arms Control and Disarmament Council, a Washington-based body founded in 1968. Designed to coordinate the efforts of over 20 religious, peace, liberal, and scientific groups, the Coalition sought a dramatic reduction in military spending and a redirection of resources.

Peace leaders counted at least a partial victory on July 11 when the U.S. Court of Appeals (1st Circuit) reversed the convictions of Benjamin Spock, William Sloane Coffin, Jr., Mitchell Goodman, and Michael Ferber. One year earlier, they had been found guilty of conspiring to counsel, aid, and abet evasion of the draft. Spock and Ferber were released, but the court indicated that Goodman and Coffin were vulnerable to retrial. In Chicago, eight key leaders of demonstrations at the 1968 Democratic convention were charged with conspiracy to incite a riot and brought to trial. The defendants, representing important if diverse sectors of the radical antiwar movement, included David Dellinger, Rennie Davis, Abbie Hoffman, John Froines, Tom Hayden, Lee Weiner, Jerry Rubin, and Bobby Seale. (Seale, a leader of the Black Panthers, was later severed from the trial and sentenced to four years for contempt.)

The transition of the nuclear disarmament campaigns (CND's) that dominated world peace movements in the late 1950s and early 1960s continued. Several organizations ceased to exist in this form, including those in Denmark, Sweden, Norway, Canada, and Australia. CND persisted in Britain, extending its interests to Vietnam and chemical and biological weaponry. In West Germany the organization became the Campaign for Democracy and Disarmament, fighting the emergency laws and participating in the Opposition Outside Parliament (APO). The French Mouvement contre l'Armement Atomique changed its name to Mouvement pour le Désarmement, la Paix et la Liberté and stressed opposition to the *force de frappe* and NATO.

The Japanese peace movements remained fragmented, although with the modification of the Japanese Communist Party's anti-Soviet line, the Congress and the Council Against A and H Bombs (Gensuikin and Gesuiko) moved somewhat closer together. The Japan Committee for Peace in Vietnam sponsored an August "Expo 69" for peace groups in Osaka.

The initial list of signatures to the Stockholm Appeal, composed at the Emergency Action Conference in Sweden in May, was presented to the U.S. delegation to the Vietnam peace talks in Paris on July 23 (the 15th anniversary of the Geneva accords). The Appeal called for self-determination in South Vietnam and for "the complete withdrawal of all U.S. and Allied troops without any conditions whatsoever."

Peace spokesmen were more frustrated in their attempts to respond fruitfully to the Nigeria-Biafra conflict and to the Middle East situation. The centenary of Gandhi's birth stimulated renewed interest in nonviolent resistance, with observers appraising the very limited successes of such tactics in Czechoslovakia. Furthermore, the aftermath of the Soviet intervention there severely compromised plans for détente in Europe. After many delays strategic arms limitation talks (SALT) between the U.S. and the U.S.S.R. began in Helsinki on November 17, but their progress seemed likely to be halting. Peace leaders welcomed ratification of the nuclear nonproliferation treaty by the U.S. and the U.S.S.R., but noted that ratification by numerous other countries was required before the treaty could take effect. (R. Hy.)

Peru

A republic on the west coast of South America, Peru is bounded by Ecuador, Colombia, Brazil, Bolivia, Chile, and the Pacific Ocean. Area: 496,222 sq.mi. (1,285,216 sq.km.). Pop. (1969 est.): 13,171,800, including approximately 52% whites and mestizos and 46% Indians. Cap. and largest city: Lima (pop., 1969 est., 2,415,700). Language: Spanish; Indians speak Quechuan or Aymaran. Religion: Roman Catholic. President of the military government in 1969, Maj. Gen. Juan Velasco Alvarado.

The military government that took power under the leadership of Gen. Juan Velasco Alvarado (*see* Biography) on Oct. 3, 1968, immediately began to implement a series of reforms that it regarded as fundamental for the future development of the country. The first significant act was to expropriate the installations and assets belonging to the International Petroleum Co. (IPC), a subsidiary of Standard Oil Co. (New Jersey), on the ground that the company owed Peru about $690 million in back taxes. This immediately caused U.S.-Peruvian relations to deteriorate; the U.S. Department of State threatened to apply the 1962 Hickenlooper amendment, by the terms of which all economic aid to Peru, and the U.S. sugar quota, would be canceled. The U.S. government also suspended military aid. Application of the Hickenlooper amendment was twice postponed while negotiations continued toward reaching a settlement over the IPC. Meanwhile, Peru attempted to enforce its 200-mi. offshore fishing limit and arrested two U.S. tuna-fishing boats within the claimed waters (*see* Inter-American Affairs). Relations mellowed substantially as the year progressed, particularly with the appointment of a new U.S. ambassador, Taylor Garrison Belcher, who was not associated with any existing U.S. interests in Peru. All of the installations of IPC were placed under the administration of Petroperú, the state petroleum agency (formerly Empresa Petrolera Fiscal).

The government outlined an extensive series of reforms, some of which would require a long period of time for their completion. The main reforms were to restructure the government bureaucracy by centralizing the government departments under fewer ministries; to reorganize banking procedures by introducing a system of selective credits to aid certain economic

Pediatrics:
see Medicine

Penology:
see Prisons and Penology

Pentathlon, Modern:
see Sporting Record

Persia:
see Iran

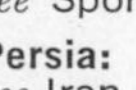

UPI COMPIX

Peruvian police block path of 7,000 copper miners and their families at Chicla, Sept. 15, 1969. Miners intended to march 120 mi. to Lima to dramatize their demand for six cents a day more than companies had offered in contract talks.

sectors and by limiting foreign participation and control; to nationalize communications and water sources; to amend the constitution, the laws under which companies operate, and the tax structure; and to introduce the most radical agrarian reform program seen in Latin America since the Cuban example of 1959. The agrarian reform law expropriated large landholdings for distribution among peasants, mainly in the coastal and central regions of the country, and provided for compensation payment partly in cash and bonds. This law was expected to go far toward reversing one of the world's most inequitable land distribution systems and toward incorporating the Indians, who formed about 50% of the total population, into the money economy. Reform was opposed by the landed oligarchy, but the government's determination to accomplish it was shown by the decision in June to replace the minister of agriculture, Gen. José Benavides, with Gen. Jorge Barandiarán Pagador, who was regarded as being more favourably disposed toward the agrarian policy. The government also planned to supervise closely the mining and fishing sectors, while encouraging foreign investment. Observers believed that it was significant that a military government, traditionally the opponent of change in Latin America, should combine in its approach to politics both nationalism and a desire to change the social structure.

The Peruvian revolution seemed unhindered except for the problem of repaying the enormous foreign debt. Aware of the need to refinance the debt, Manuel Ulloa, minister of finance under former Pres. Fernando Belaúnde Terry, had postponed part of the heavy debt repayments due in 1968 and 1969 to the early 1970s. Peru, however, still had a total of $847 million to repay between the beginning of 1970 and the end of 1975. Negotiations with creditor countries were held in an attempt to reschedule this debt over a ten-year period.

Economically, Peru had benefited from the devaluation of the sol in September 1967 and from the deflationary measures introduced in the first half of 1968. Exports in 1968 reached a record of $866 million, compared with $757 million in 1967. A record two million tons of fish meal were exported. There was a favourable trade balance of $142 million in the first half of 1969, $41 million above the figure for the same period in 1968. In May, the exchange reserves of the Banco Central were $112 million, the highest level experienced in the country since April 1967.

However, the gross national product at constant prices rose by only 1.7% in 1968, compared with increases of 4.6% in 1967 and an average of 6% between 1961 and 1966; the total output of manufacturing industry rose by 5.1% in 1968, slightly below the growth registered in 1967. But industrial electric power sales in June 1969 were still 17% above those registered the year before. The cost of living rose by only 3.2% in the first eight months of 1969, and the exchange rate remained quite stable during the year.

Foreign investment, although officially encouraged, was slow to materialize, possibly because the existing state of affairs was regarded as unstable. The main area offering advantages to foreign investors was mining. The government showed its concern for this sector by requiring that all mining companies whose concessions were valid on June 18, 1965, should sign firm contracts with the government by Dec. 31, 1969, and provide at the same time a five-year schedule of investment proposals. A $355 million investment agreement signed by Southern Peru Copper Corp. in December represented the first substantial foreign investment in Peru since the military government came to power. Peru, together with Chile, Colombia, and Ecuador, ratified the Andean Subregional Integration Agreement, which came into force on November 24.

(D. J. Ro.)

ENCYCLOPÆDIA BRITANNICA FILMS. *Peru: People of the Andes* (1959).

PERU

Education. (1966) Primary, pupils 2,157,246, teachers (1964) 52,390; secondary, pupils 362,551, teachers (1964) 16,069; vocational, pupils 72,718, teachers (1964) 6,645; teacher training, students 16,464; higher (1963), students 46,334.

Finance. Monetary unit: sol, with a free exchange rate (Oct. 1969) of 43 soles to U.S. $1 (102.50 soles = £1 sterling). Gold and foreign exchange, central bank: (June 1969) U.S. $154.6 million; (June 1968) U.S. $90.9 million. Budget (1969 est.) balanced at 41,844,000,000 soles. Gross national product: (1967) 153,810,000,000 soles; (1966) 134,020,000,000 soles. Money supply: (Nov. 1968) 17,150,000,000 soles; (Dec. 1967) 16,530,000,000 soles. Cost of living (Lima and Callao; 1966 = 100): (June 1969) 140; (June 1968) 132.

Foreign Trade. (1968) Imports 24,373,000,000 soles; exports 33,474,000,000 soles. Import sources: U.S. 34%; West Germany 11%; Argentina 10%; Japan 6%; U.K. 5%. Export destinations: U.S. 39%; Japan 15%; West Germany 11%; Belgium-Luxembourg 7%; Netherlands 6%. Main exports: copper 27%; fish meal 18%; silver 8%; iron ore 7%; sugar 7%; cotton 6%.

Transport and Communications. Roads (1965) 42,818 km. (including 10,635 km. with improved surface). Motor vehicles in use (1967): passenger 195,100; commercial (including buses) 111,800. Railways (1965): 3,345 km.; traffic 236 million passenger-km., freight 646 million net ton-km. Air traffic (1967): 622,322,000 passenger-km.; freight 12,790,000 net ton-km. Shipping (1968): merchant vessels 100 gross tons and over 275; gross tonnage 287,843. Telephones (Jan. 1968) 152,136. Radio receivers (Dec. 1968) *c.* 1,815,000. Television receivers (Dec. 1968) 310,000.

Agriculture. Production (in 000; metric tons; 1968; 1967 in parentheses): wheat *c.* 150 (152); rice 400 (461); barley *c.* 170 (172); corn 590 (591); potatoes 1,700 (1,711); cassava *c.* 500 (507); dry beans *c.* 44 (*c.* 49); sugar, raw value (1968–69) *c.* 650, (1967–68) *c.* 752; citrus fruit (1967) 270, (1966) 248; cotton, lint 87 (98); fish catch (1967) 10,110, (1966) 8,789. Livestock (in 000; 1967–68): cattle *c.* 3,800; sheep (1966–67) 15,500; horses *c.* 600; pigs *c.* 1,920; goats (1966–67) *c.* 4,000; poultry (1966–67) *c.* 22,000.

Industry. Fuel and power (in 000; metric tons; 1967): coal 175; crude oil 3,453; electricity (kw-hr.) 4,583,000. Production (in 000; metric tons; 1967): cement 1,087; iron ore (metal content) 4,809; pig iron 31; steel 62; lead (1968) 86; zinc (1968) 71; copper (1968) 42; tungsten concentrates (oxide content; 1966) 0.5; silver 1.12; gold (troy oz.) 96; fish meal 1,816.

Petroleum Industry: *see* Fuel and Power; Industrial Review

Pharmacology: *see* Medicine

Philately and Numismatics

Philately. Two boxes of 10-cent airmail stamps shipped by air from Finland and scheduled for sale by the United Nations on March 14, 1969, were missing for nine weeks. On February 26, about two months after the stamps were lost, the UN Postal Administration, over the signature of Robert Maxwell, postal chief, sent telegrams to all important philatelic publications notifying them of the loss and promising to reprint the "lost stamps" in different colours if they were not found. On March 4 another set of telegrams from the UN Postal Administration reported that the missing stamps had been found and would be released for sale on April 21.

The Foreign Assets Control Section of the U.S. Department of the Treasury banned the future importation of all Rhodesian postage stamps into the U.S. This brought to five the number of nations whose stamps could not be imported into the United States, the others being North Korea, China, Cuba, and North Vietnam.

For the first time in philatelic history, Sofia, Bulg., was chosen as the site for the major international philatelic exhibition of the year. The Grand Prix International was won by an Italian collector who entered a collection of Italian stamps. British participation was the strongest among non-Communist countries, and the awards to British collectors included three gold medals. George Photiades, the internationally known Greek philatelist, died suddenly while in Sofia for the exhibition.

The 1969 signatories to the Roll of the Distinguished Philatelists at the Diamond Jubilee meetings of the Philatelic Congress of Great Britain were: B. Leslie Barker, C. H. C. Harmer, and William A. Townsend of Great Britain; Col. John F. Rider of the U.S.; and Hugh M. Campbell of Australia.

At its international congress in Tokyo late in 1969, the Universal Postal Union (UPU) planned to consider dealing with the problem of postage stamps that some nations issue mainly for revenue purposes. Although the UPU opposed such types of "exploitative" issues, it had not tried to dictate postage-issuing policies to any of its member nations. In South and Central America, Panama, Ecuador, and Paraguay were accused of a lack of postal integrity, and collectors in El Salvador protested some of the practices of their own postal authorities. The American Philatelic Society continued to publish "black blot" ratings for any new issues that appeared to be guilty of one of the following: (1) a limited printing, or limited "on sale" time in country of origin; (2) an excessively extended issue; (3) unwarranted high values; (4) no direct relationship to the issuing country; (5) oddities intentionally included with the issue.

Although the stamp market remained depressed, scarce philatelic items and valuable collections continued to sell at high prices. The sales for the Josiah K. Lilly collection reached a single collection high of $3,145,298.50. By late 1969 the Dale-Lichtenstein collection had realized $1,514,219, all profits having been donated to the philanthropic societies that Mrs. Louise Boyd Dale named in her will. One of the 1918 airmail inverts that sold for $15,500 in 1964 went for $31,000 in 1969, and a block of four of those stamps sold for $115,000. An 1858 cover with a pair of 6-penny scarlet vermilion Newfoundland stamps of the 1857 series was sold in 1969 for $11,000.

Man's landing on the moon was commemorated by an outsized U.S. 10-cent airmail stamp in September. The Apollo 11 lunar flight carried a "moon letter," which contained a die proof of the commemorative stamp. Aboard the spacecraft also was an engraved die that was used to produce the stamp.

(R. F. MI.; K. F. C.)

Numismatics. The U.S. coin market was strong during 1969, as prices continued to climb. Common-date gold coins, commemoratives, proof sets, and type sets in choice condition led the way, according to the standard 1970 edition of *A Guide Book of United States Coins.*

Seekers after commemorative coins found that some countries were producing them. Some examples: Czechoslovakia, 50 koruny, 0.900 fine silver, 50th anniversary of the republic, 1918–68; West Germany, 10 marks, silver, 500th anniversary of the death of Johann Gutenberg; West Germany, 5 marks, 0.625 fine silver, 150th anniversary of the birth of Friedrich Wilhelm Raiffeisen; Israel, I£10, silver, 25th anniversary of the nation; Malaysia, M$1, copper nickel, 10th anniversary of the independence of the country; Bulgaria, 2 leva, copper nickel, 1,050th anniversary of the death of St. Clement; United Arab Republic (U.A.R.), 5 piastres, copper nickel, Cairo International Fair for industry; U.A.R., E£1, silver, marking the start of Aswan Dam operations; Nepal, NRs. 10, silver alloy, 10th anniversary of the UN Food and Agriculture Organization (FAO); Philippines, 1 peso, silver, 100th anniversary of the birth of Gen. Emilio Aguinaldo; Austria, 50 schillings, 0.900 fine silver, 450th anniversary of the death of Emperor Maximilian I; New Zealand, NZ$1, copper nickel, bicentenary of Capt. James Cook's death.

U.S. mints struck the following coins for other governments: Canada, 10 cents; Costa Rica, 1 colón, 50 centimos, 5 centimos; El Salvador, 10 centavos, 1 centavo; Liberia, 25 cents; Panama, 5 centemos, proof sets, proof coins, 50 centemos, 25 centemos, 5 centesimos, 1 centesimo; Philippines, 50 centavos, 25 centavos, 10 centavos, 5 centavos, 1 centavo.

COURTESY, AUSTRALIAN NEWS AND INFORMATION BUREAU

UPI COMPIX

S & G FROM PICTORIAL PARADE

AUTHENTICATED NEWS INTERNATIONAL

Stamp celebrating the third South Pacific Games in 1969 (top). Figure of St. George (above, left), one of six stamps issued by the Austrian Post Office commemorating the establishment of the Vienna diocese in 1469. Stamp (above, right) marking the tenth anniversary of the European Conference of Postal and Telecommunications Administrations. Special stamp (right) issued by the German Federal Post Office on Oct. 2, 1969, to honour the 100th anniversary of Mohandas Gandhi's birth.

S & G FROM PICTORIAL PARADE

Commemorative medal by Michael Rizzello has Welsh inscriptions: obverse, top, "Investiture of Charles Prince of Wales, Caernarvon, 1969"; reverse, above, "The Red Dragon Leads the Way."

The FAO suggested that governments throughout the world strike coins that would illustrate world food and agriculture development. The American Numismatic Association joined in the FAO's efforts by using the same theme for National Coin Week. A number of countries began issuing such coins. Some of them were: Uganda, five shillings, copper nickel; Vatican City, 8 denominations in aluminum, bronze, Ackmonital, and silver; South Vietnam, 20 dong, nickel-clad steel.

Although many countries continued to strike commemorative coins, the U.S. maintained its "no commemorative" policy. The way was cleared, however, for U.S. collectors of gold coins. By order of the U.S. Department of the Treasury, gold coins minted before 1934 could be imported into the U.S. without a license. Gold pieces dated from 1934 to 1960, if of sufficient numismatic interest, could be brought in under license. In another action, U.S. silver coins were allowed to be melted for their silver content. U.S. Secretary of the Treasury David Kennedy announced that he would urge Congress to pass legislation authorizing the striking of a nonsilver half dollar and a nonsilver dollar. Under a plan recommended by a U.S. joint commission on the coinage, 2.9 million rare silver dollars held in the Treasury vaults would be sold.

The new Philadelphia mint was officially opened August 14. Built at a cost of $39.4 million, it had a production capacity of more than 10,000 coins per minute. It was the fourth mint constructed in Philadelphia, the first having been built in 1792. The 1969 event was memorialized in a bronze medal available for purchase at the mint.

UPI COMPIX

Commemorative medal 2½ in. in diameter in silver or bronze of the Apollo 11 moon landing, designed by Ralph J. Menconi and released by the U.S. in September 1969.

The new Fiji bank notes were scheduled to be issued in 20-, 10-, 2-, 1-, and ½-dollar denominations. Malawi's decimal currency was to be introduced in March 1971. The new unit, the kwacha, would be divided into 100 tambolas. The new Argentine peso was to be equivalent to 100 of the old "peso moneda nacional." The release date was expected to be around Jan. 1, 1970. The bills were to be in denominations of 100, 50, 20, 10, 5, and 1, with coins having values of 50, 20, 10, 5, 2, and 1 centavos. The old-type Italian large-size 10,000-, 5,000-, and 1,000-lire notes ceased to be legal tender on June 30. Jamaica adopted the dollar-decimal system on September 8. The dollar was worth 10 shillings sterling of the old currency. Gold coins issued by the Bahamas, Bhutan, Tonga, and other governments were being reproduced on postage stamps for collectors unable to obtain the actual coins. (EL. G. B.)

See also Postal Services.

COURTESY, BRITISH INFORMATION SERVICES

Reverse side design of Britain's 50 new pence coin, the sixth in decimal series replacing present currency. The figure Britannia was designed by Christopher Ironside.

Philippines

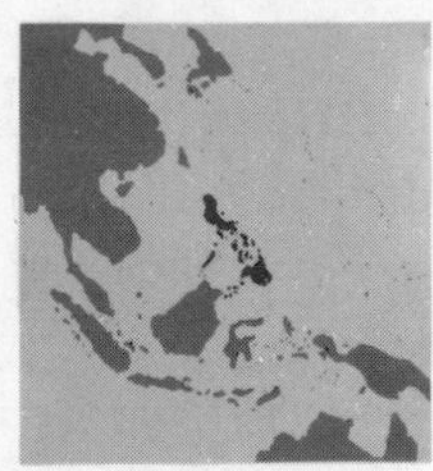

Situated in the western Pacific Ocean off the southeast coast of Asia, the Republic of the Philippines consists of an archipelago of about 7,100 islands. Area: 115,830 sq.mi. (300,000 sq.km.). Pop. (1968 est.): 35,883,000. Administrative capital and largest city: Manila (pop., 1968 est., 1,499,000). Legal capital: Quezon (pop., 1965 est., 545,500). Language: Tagalog or Filipino (official), English, Spanish, and many dialects. Religion: Roman Catholic 84%; Aglipayan 5%; Muslim 5%; Protestant 3%. President in 1969, Ferdinand E. Marcos.

The Philippines faced the year 1969 with a deficit in the budget, domestically as a result of heavy government spending on roads, schools, dams, and similar items, and internationally largely because of an upsurge in imports of capital goods. Imports during the previous year had risen 12%, while exports had gained by only 5%. The balance of payments deficit at the end of 1968 was $45 million.

In an effort to halt the resulting inflation, stringent import restrictions were imposed, as well as measures to encourage exports, tighten credit, and decrease the rate of dollar outflow. An agreement with the United States for the Philippine government to supply all the

PHILIPPINES

Education. (1966–67) Primary, pupils 5,815,675, teachers 184,938; secondary and vocational, pupils 1,172,695, teachers 31,668; higher (including 34 universities), students 527,284, teaching staff 26,020.

Finance. Monetary unit: peso, with a par value of 3.90 pesos to U.S. $1 (9.36 pesos = £1 sterling). Gold and foreign exchange, central bank: (June 1969) U.S. $138 million; (June 1968) U.S. $187 million. Budget (1968–69 est.): revenue 3,156,000,000 pesos; expenditure 3,013,000,000 pesos. Gross national product: (1968) 28,110,000,000 pesos; (1967) 25,420,000,000 pesos. Money supply: (April 1969) 3,423,000,000 pesos; (April 1968) 3,271,000,000 pesos. Cost of living (Manila; 1963 = 100): (June 1969) 125; (June 1968) 124.

Foreign Trade. (1968) Imports 5,031,000,000 pesos; exports 3,306,000,000 pesos. Import sources: U.S. 32%; Japan 28%; West Germany 6%. Export destinations: U.S. 46%; Japan 34%; Netherlands 5%. Main exports: coconut products 28%; timber 26%; sugar 17%.

Transport and Communications. Roads (1967) 56,180 km. Motor vehicles in use (1967): passenger 182,900; commercial (including buses) 149,700. Railways: (state; 1966) 1,026 km.; traffic (1967) 1,015,000,000 passenger-km., freight 146 million net ton-km. Air traffic (1968): 1,121,000,000 passenger-km.; freight 27,060,000 net ton-km. Shipping (1968): merchant vessels 100 gross tons and over 278; gross tonnage 854,256. Telephones (Jan. 1968) 207,593. Radio receivers (Dec. 1966) 639,000. Television receivers (Dec. 1967) 190,000.

Agriculture. Production (in 000; metric tons; 1968; 1967 in parentheses): rice 4,832 (4,561); corn 1,619 (1,517); sweet potatoes and yams (1967) 681, (1966) 687; cassava 496 (590); copra (1967) 1,333, (1966) 1,607; sugar, raw value (1968–69) *c.* 1,592, (1967–68) 1,595; abaca (1967) 81, (1966) 95; bananas (1966) 765, (1965) 683; tobacco 62 (51); pork (1967) 279, (1966) 241; timber (cu.m.; 1966–67) *c.* 10,300, (1965–66) *c.* 7,700; fish catch (1967) 769, (1966) 726. Livestock (in 000; March 1968): pigs *c.* 5,500; cattle 1,600; buffaloes (March 1967) 3,926; goats (March 1967) 599; horses *c.* 242; chickens (March 1967) 66,489.

Industry. Production (in 000; metric tons; 1968): cement 2,212; coal (1967) 65; chrome ore (oxide content; 1967) 156; manganese ore (metal content; 1967) 25; copper ore (metal content) 95; iron ore (55–60% metal content) 1,340; silver (1967) 0.04; gold (troy oz.; 1967) 500; electricity (kw-hr.) *c.* 5,500,000.

pesos needed by American bases in the Philippines was expected to conserve about $300 million a year in the Philippine reserves. The effect of the curb on imports, however, was felt by local industries that depended on imported goods. Furthermore, the major export products of copra and coconut were being adversely affected by low world prices.

While efforts such as the above were being made to help remedy the financial problem in the Philippines, tens of millions of dollars were still lost annually to the government treasury as a result of the continued presence of corruption in the government, tax evasion, nonpayment of customs duties, and smuggling. These were recurrent themes in the opposition party's campaign against the administration in the election year of 1969. The incumbent president, Ferdinand E. Marcos, had ordered government cutbacks totaling $50 million and had called for more careful spending among the citizens.

The widespread belief among the voters of the presence of corruption in the government under any administration was capitalized on by the opposition Liberal Party's presidential candidate, Sergio Osmeña, Jr., whose running mate, Genaro F. Magsaysay, was the brother of the late president Ramón Magsaysay. President Marcos, whose running mate was Fernando Lopez, in turn accused Osmeña of collaborating with the Japanese during World War II.

The election took place in November. Marcos and his running mate each won decisive victories. Marcos thus became the first president to be reelected since the Philippines gained independence. Violence flared in some sections of the country, especially on Luzon Island northwest of Manila, and approximately 60 people were killed.

In his campaign for reelection President Marcos had promised to seek a renegotiation of all major treaties with the U.S., to withdraw the controversial noncombat Philippine Civic Action Group from South Vietnam, and to continue to encourage trade with Communist countries. Minimizing the threat of external Communist aggression, he said, "Our real problem is the growth of internal Communism arising from urgent economic problems."

In October, Foreign Affairs Secretary Carlos P. Romulo proposed a discussion of four major U.S.-Philippine military and economic treaties: the Mutual Defense Pact of 1951, the Military Bases Agreement of 1947, the Military Assistance Pact of 1947, and the Laurel-Langley Agreement of 1955, which provided preferential tariff treatment on trade between the two nations. President Marcos had previously indicated a desire to enter into negotiations with the U.S. "to correct whatever inequities and imperfections may exist in the bases agreement." (In 1969 there were about 30,000 U.S. military personnel in the Philippines.) While he officially stated that the bases were needed for about five to ten years until the Philippines developed itself economically within the protective American "umbrella," he wanted the same rights enjoyed by other countries that had U.S. military bases, such as Japan and Spain, especially in regard to offenses committed by United States servicemen. Filipinos had been angered by the exoneration by a U.S. military court of a U.S. Navy petty officer in the fatal shooting of a Filipino worker at Subic Naval Base in June. They had asked that the now-retired sailor be returned for retrial in a Philippine court, but the U.S. refused, claiming that compliance with the request would result in a case of double jeopardy.

In accordance with an announcement by President Marcos in October, the Philippines' 1,500-man noncombat force was withdrawn from South Vietnam in December. The team was sent in 1966 to help improve the standard of living in the South Vietnamese countryside through civic action programs. Its presence in Vietnam had been the cause of several antiwar demonstrations in Manila.

In October Marcos also indicated a continuation of a cautious open-door policy on trade and cultural relations with the Soviet Union and China, if he was reelected. Philippine trade with European Communist countries had been initiated on an experimental basis in an effort to increase Philippine markets and to diversify them.

The opposition Liberal Party, in the meantime, was accusing the administration of being "soft" on Communism in the presence of a Communist-inspired Huk uprising in central Luzon. In early November 1968, Marcos had withdrawn constabulary and army troops from anti-Huk operations and had let civil authorities deal with the problem. The Supreme Court in 1969 cut to ten years or less the life imprisonment and/or death sentences imposed on 14 Huk leaders who led the uprising in the 1950s. Mounting assassinations and terrorism in central Luzon prompted Marcos to end his demilitarization policy, however, and, on August 8 the government began intensifying the campaign against the Huk movement. (Ra. Pa.)

Encyclopædia Britannica Films. *The Philippines: Land and People* (1960).

Philosophy

The social unrest of 1969 encouraged increasing interest in value philosophy and its relevance to concrete issues in social experience. The literature exhibited much concern for the theoretical meaning and practical nature of freedom and justice, of authority and law, and of punishment and accountability. Ethical problems were often pursued with a practical urgency that reflected more than simply academic interest.

Among works on moral and social philosophy, *Values and Imperatives,* papers of the late C. I. Lewis edited by John Lange, was mainly an argument for the primacy of reason in moral judgment. In *Moral Knowledge and Its Methodology in Aristotle,* Father J. Donald Monan found that, in the *Eudemian Ethics,* Aristotle's method was remarkably suggestive of today's techniques of moral analysis.

Robert D. Cumming's study of liberal political thought was published in two volumes as *Human Nature and History.* Tracing the development of liberalism to John Stuart Mill and the Utilitarians, Cumming concentrated on Mill's thought in analyzing the relation of political theory to moral theory and practical politics and in defining the relation of the individual to the state. In *The Logic of Leviathan,* David P. Gauthier of the University of Toronto analyzed the moral and political theory of Thomas Hobbes as "an attempt to construct a political order on the least favorable assumptions." *Soviet Ethics and Morality* by Richard T. De George was a critical analysis of the foundations of Soviet moral philosophy. De George held that Soviet morality is "incompatible with a global morality tolerant of different aims and values."

The apparent moral deterioration of society elicited an increased interest in the problem of moral values in the philosophy of education. The Farmington Trust

Research Unit of Oxford, which also established a new journal, *Moral Education,* sponsored an international conference on the subject as related to the British schools. *Approaches to Education for Character,* edited by Clarence H. Faust and Jessica Feingold, was a diversified compendium of 23 writers published by the Conference on Science, Philosophy and Religion.

The growing interest in the philosophy of law was evidenced by *Essays in Legal Philosophy,* edited by Robert S. Summers, in which ten British and American philosophers and lawyers examined the philosophical foundations of such legal concepts as justice, punishment, and liberty and the rational justification of legal policy and decision.

In the field of logic, theory of knowledge, and methodology, the first English version of Hans Reichenbach's classic analysis of space-time theory, *Axiomatik der relativistischen Raum-Zeit-Lehre,* was published as *Axiomatization of the Theory of Relativity.* In *Geometry and Chronometry in Philosophical Perspective,* Adolf Grünbaum examined the relation of convention to fact by attacking the question, "In what sense and to what extent can the ascription of a particular metric geometry to physical space and the chronometry ingredient in physical theory be held to have an empirical warrant?"

In *Mind, History, and Dialectic,* Louis O. Mink traced the dialectical method of R. G. Collingwood through his writings on art, history, and the philosophy of mind. Roy Wood Sellars' *Reflections on American Philosophy from Within* was a critique of 20th-century philosophy by one of the creators of critical realism.

In *Studies in Phenomenology,* Debabrata Sinha of Calcutta examined Edmund Husserl's methodology, especially as a connecting link between metaphysics and contemporary empirioanalytic techniques. *Knowing and Being,* edited by Marjorie Grene, was a collection of Michael Polanyi's essays opposing the traditional conception of knowledge as ignoring the nature of mind and the living things that are the knowers. In *Genetic Epistemology,* translated by Eleanor Duckworth, the Swiss psychologist Jean Piaget argued on experimental grounds that human thinking has its roots in the infant's perception of general coordination of actions rather than in symbolic functions.

Through an analysis of the *Theaetetus* and the *Sophistes,* Kenneth M. Sayre, in *Plato's Analytic Method,* advanced the view that Plato's analytical powers, as exhibited in both his methodological procedures and the logic of his argument, exceeded even his great talents in rhetoric and drama.

In metaphysics and the philosophy of religion and art, an English translation, by E. B. Ashton, of vol. i of Karl Jaspers' major work *Philosophie* was published as *Philosophy.* This volume, concerned especially with "philosophical world orientation," was the first part of Jaspers' existentialist inquiry into the world, the soul, and God. *East-West Studies on the Problem of the Self,* edited by P. T. Raju and Alburey Castell, was a collection of papers presented at the Conference on Comparative Philosophy and Culture at the College of Wooster (O.); it included the last public statement of Paul Tillich. Yves Simon's *Freedom of Choice,* edited by Peter Wolff, was published posthumously.

In *Studies in Religious Philosophy and Mysticism,* Alexander Altmann presented 12 essays on Arabic and Judeo-Arabic philosophy, Jewish mysticism, and modern Jewish thought. Altmann was especially concerned with the problem of anthropomorphism and with the claim of unity with God in the mystic experience. The effect of Platonism on Christian thought received specialized treatment in E. P. Meijering's *Orthodoxy and Platonism in Athanasius: Synthesis or Antithesis.*

The philosophy of the idealist Josiah Royce was given new visibility by the publication of *The Basic Writings of Josiah Royce,* edited in two volumes by John J. McDermott, and of Royce's *The Problem of Christianity,* with an introduction by John E. Smith. Horace M. Kallen's *Liberty, Laughter, and Tears* was a study of the role of tragedy and comedy in the cultivation and preservation of liberty. Comparative analyses of Oriental and Occidental aesthetic theories and art forms were published in *Philosophy East and West.*

Under the direction of Alastair McKinnon of McGill University, Montreal, a machine-readable version of Sören Kierkegaard's *Samlede Værker* was constructed with correlations to the standard English, French, and German translations. A massive enterprise undertaken in Belgium involved publication of facsimile reprints of the scattered critical and polemical literature produced in the wake of Immanuel Kant's work during the first 40-year period. More than 300 volumes were planned.

A new journal for philosophy and methodology of the social sciences, *Theory and Decision,* was announced in the Netherlands. The first volume of *Analecta Anselmiana* was published in Germany under the editorship of the Benedictine monk F. S. Schmitt. *Apeiron,* a new journal of ancient science and philosophy, was published in Australia. The first issue of the *Journal of the British Society for Phenomenology* was published at the Victoria University of Manchester.

An international congress was held in October in Rotterdam, Neth., to commemorate the quincentenary of the birth of Erasmus. A national Erasmus commemoration was also held in Belgium, with scholarly programs in several cities. The Academy of Sciences of the Socialist Republic of Romania and the Association of Scientists in Romania held a colloquium in Brasov on "Judgment Modality in Aristotle and Modern Logic." The Royal Institute of Philosophy and the British Society for Phenomenology sponsored a conference for European philosophers at the University of Southampton on a variety of subjects including the person, good and evil, and freedom and determinism. (S. M. Mc.)

ENCYCLOPÆDIA BRITANNICA FILMS. *Aristotle's Ethics: The Theory of Happiness* (1963); *Athens—The Golden Age* (1963); *Plato's Apology: The Life and Teachings of Socrates* (1963); *Emperor and Slave: The Philosophy of Roman Stoicism* (1965); *The Spirit of Rome* (1965); *The Medieval Mind* (1969).

Photography

The trend in pictorial photography in 1969 continued to be toward pictures with novelty and instant impact, instead of relying on traditional subjects and impeccable print quality. The majority of entries for the exhibitions were still in monochrome, though some colour prints were produced—especially for the exhibitions of the Royal Photographic Society and the London Salon of Photography. A few years earlier any colour print of high technical quality would have had a good chance of being hung. By 1969 evidence of picture-making ability was required, both in colour and in monochrome.

Derivative prints were especially popular and many different techniques were used. In essence, all these processes reduced the amount of detail and definition in the picture compared with a normal or straight print. High contrast was one such device; a picture that normally had a continuous range of tones through all the grays was rendered as almost pure whites and blacks. The easiest way to produce this effect was by printing a normal negative onto a high-contrast or "lith" material. If two consecutive copying stages were used, the print would be a normal positive, with shadows shown as dark, though of enhanced contrast. When only a single stage was employed, the tones were reversed, white objects being shown as black and the converse. However, after this reversal device became popular on the television screen it was seen less frequently on the exhibition wall. When grain (the broken or mealy appearance in pictures from high-speed film) was difficult to avoid, it was considered a fault; with the improvement in this aspect of modern films, however, it was sometimes introduced deliberately for artistic effect. Other ways of breaking up a normal image utilized texture screens, but in 1969 the familiar effects of steel etching or nylon-mesh texture appeared less frequently. The trend was toward the production of photographs that could stand on their own merit, rather than as imitations of paintings.

In colour printing there were also more derivations than previously, when the aim had been to produce correctly balanced colour prints resembling the original subject as closely as possible. The idea of breaking up the image with hammered glass or texture screens, inherited from black-and-white, now became popular in colour. The favourite method used in recent exhibitions was bas-relief in colour. This was done by having a negative and a positive transparency placed together but out of register. Contrast was reduced where the two overlapped, but there was an edge effect, giving a "shadow" on one side of an object and a "highlight" on the other, with reversed colours enhancing the outline. Another idea was the colour negative print (with red reproduced as cyan, yellow translated into blue, and so on), but this was generally regarded as insufficiently subtle and the number of such prints exhibited showed a sharp decline.

Colour transparencies were difficult to exhibit. In particular, the popular 35-mm. transparency could not be shown properly without projection (though the Royal Photographic Society had a successful system for the viewing of stereoscopic transparencies). Fairly large transparencies could be displayed with lighting from the rear, but much of their inherent quality was wasted and most exhibitions did not have the requisite facilities. Hence, despite the high number of colour transparencies taken each year, exhibitions showed mainly large prints, with the greatest number still in monochrome.

The greater availability of interchangeable lenses resulted in the use of different focal lengths for pictorial purposes, as distinct from the utilitarian one of filling the frame. Indeed, some ideas were fast becoming overworked clichés, such as the silhouetting of human figures against the red disk of the setting sun, using a lens of extreme focal length to make that disk relatively large. Curiously enough, wide-angle lenses were little used pictorially, and the fish-eye lenses (which reduced image scale toward the edges and allowed curvilinear distortion) had not yet been absorbed into the armoury of the pictorialists. Zoom lenses were mainly a technical convenience with few effects peculiar to their construction, but a few exhibition pictures were made with the lens zooming on a rapidly moving object during a fairly long exposure (such as 1/10 sec.). The result was that the centre image, where the main subject was placed, altered little in scale, but outside it a blur formed radially, giving an impression of speed or expansion.

Pictures of the internal structure of a stopwatch (left) and a flower (below) made by a process called neutrography in which the object is placed in a high-intensity beam of neutrons generated by a reactor. A neutrograph is able to detect parts made of materials such as plastic, nylon, and rubber because they are rich in hydrogen and relatively opaque to the neutron beam but transparent to X rays.

COURTESY, GENERAL ELECTRIC COMPANY

Technical excellence became commonplace on the general pictorial scene, so that novelty was achieved mainly by intentional departure from the sharp print with a full range of tones. The position was more stable than with painting, sculpture, and other art forms, but the main emphasis was on experimentation and free expression within the limits of the process. Some conventions were frequently broken. For example, the old cliché of having the main subject near a line dividing the print into three (an inexact and clumsy adaptation of the "golden mean" guide) aroused so strong a reaction in some photographers that central subject placing threatened to become a cliché in itself.

Processes and Equipment. Some of the older processes, often described as pictorial because of the opportunities they offered for manual control, became obsolete or at least comparatively rare. Examples were the trichrome Carbro print and the bromoil monochrome print. No new "hand-control" process was introduced in 1969, and the trend was toward the elimination of variable factors.

The next stage was to have the light-sensing cell on the camera instead of the flashgun, but as yet this was still in the developmental stage. Another increasingly used electronic device was the slave release or trigger. When a flash was fired, the slave cell responded by firing the second flash, to which it was connected. Devices of this type with large expendable flashbulbs had long been used for professional work, but it was new to have them especially built into the flashgun for amateur equipment. Radio impulse remote releases also became available for amateur use, but difficulties connected with radio transmission licenses threatened to prevent their widespread adoption.

Another area in which electronic devices were becoming more common was enlarging. Timers tended to be electronic rather than clockwork and were frequently combined with meters. Such measuring devices usually had a photoconductive cell (such as CdS type) of small dimensions on a lead, and measurements were made of the light falling on the baseboards. This involved intelligent selection of the area to be measured, and there was also the variable factor of paper emulsion speed to be considered. The latest type of enlarging paper, Ilfobrom, had a speed that was sufficiently constant from box to box and also through most of the contrast grades. This was an appreciable help in using electronic meters.

Photographic chemicals had not altered in principle over the previous year or so, but there was a definite swing toward the liquid kinds, which were much quicker and easier to prepare than solution from powders. The older practice of weighing out separate ingredients was virtually obsolete, and "ready-made" proprietary products dominated the field. In the search for simplification, colour-print-processing chemicals were altered (mainly by the use of sequestrenes to prevent precipitation) so that three solutions could be used instead of seven. Despite this, very little home processing of colour was done. Such work remained almost exclusively in the hands of professional printing houses.

Young girl views a large photograph of an early-20th-century Harlem street scene at the "Harlem on My Mind" exhibition presented at New York's Metropolitan Museum in 1969.

UPI COMPIX

One interesting development in the colour printing field was the Ciba paper. This was a bleach reversal process, in which colours were produced by subtraction from black rather than by addition to white. Positive prints were made directly from transparencies, and the process had the virtue of producing more stable hues than development methods could provide, as well as purer colours. The main reason for this was that a wider choice of dyes was available, since there was no necessity for them to couple with developing agents.

In motion-picture photography, the introduction of Super 8, the cartridge-loading amateur film, resulted in the virtual death of the former double or standard-8 system. Except in the Soviet bloc, almost all new equipment was for Super 8 and, although much of the film used was standard 8, the balance was slowly but inevitably swinging toward the newer and larger format. The Japanese single-8 system, which in theory had certain technical advantages over Super 8, made little impact, mainly because of the market dominance of Kodachrome cine film, which was available only in standard and Super 8. By the beginning of 1969, for the first time, more than 50% of the motion-picture film used by amateurs in the U.K. was Super 8.

On the financial front, events followed the familiar pattern of amalgamation between firms, generally by stock purchase. The amalgamation of Agfa and Gevaert (including Perutz) united the major continental film manufacturers, while Zeiss Ikon took over Voigtländer, Braun was purchased by Gillette, Ferrania by 3M Co., Adox by du Pont, and Ilford Ltd. became a wholly owned subsidiary of Ciba. Inevitably these changes in control were followed by a period of reorganization and "rationalization," involving a curtailment of diversity of products and concentration on the most profitable lines. However, the balancing factor of greater financial help for research could lead to improved products.

The main result of technical progress was to make photography easier for the tyro. Some advances were produced in lens design and in film manufacture, all conducive to the attainment of a higher standard, but generally the trend was toward greater automation.

An interesting phenomenon was the meteoric rise of the 126 "instant-loading" film cassette. While this size had an inherent weakness making it unsuitable for the production of large prints (the lack of a pressure plate created uncertainty in register), the foolproof loading made it attractive to the consumer. Furthermore, the characteristics of constant frame size with unvarying perforation location made it extremely popular with commercial printing houses, who could process at high speed without resetting printing masks and making other adjustments. Comparatively cheap colour prints could thus be produced automatically by machines using a bare minimum of human judgment. While such colour prints could not always match the original subject, and reprints usually differed slightly from the first set, the statistical percentage of acceptable prints proved sufficiently high. The latest figures showed that as much colour negative film (for prints) was sold during 1969 as colour transparency film (for slides), indicating a definite change in consumer habits.

There were also changes in the relative proportions of the various film sizes used. The overall or average figures showed that users of 5 $\times$ 4-in. film (mostly professional) tended to change to roll film ($2\frac{1}{4} \times 2\frac{1}{4}$ in. or closely related sizes), that many amateurs had moved from roll film to 35 mm., and that new photographers were likely to start with 126 (28 $\times$ 28-mm. frames). The net result was about 40% 126, 40% 35 mm., 15% 120 roll film, and the rest assorted. Of course, individual laboratories could show widely different balances, and the professional firms would, on analysis, reveal very different proportions from those catering to amateurs. Nevertheless, the basic trends were clearly toward the use of more colour, especially for prints, and toward the smaller formats with 126 as the lower popular limit. The half frame (24 $\times$ 18 mm. on 35-mm. film) diminished sharply in popularity, partly because processors were reluctant to mount transparencies in this size.

Camera design did not alter greatly, but electronic shutters became more common and it seemed likely that they would dominate the field eventually. As the cost of mechanical shutters rose and that of electronic ones fell, the crossover point was being approached. The ease of coupling a CdS photoconductive cell to an electronically timed shutter heralded the even wider availability of automatic exposure control.

Photographic manufacturers were eager to persuade more photographers to use flash, thus extending the season and keeping the processing houses fully occupied during the slack winter period. Flashbulbs were being partly replaced by flashcubes, which were basically four bulbs in expendable reflectors, the cube turning after each shot. Even the cheapest cameras had some means whereby flashbulbs could be used or cubes could be plugged directly into the camera.

Some of the more complicated cameras had iris diaphragms that could be linked to the focusing ring. Thus, as the camera was focused, the aperture altered automatically to give the right exposure for that distance. Even more ingenious was the automatic flash metering method used with some of the latest electronic flash units. Light emitted from the gun was reflected from the subject, and some of this reflected light was then measured by a cell on the flashgun. When sufficient light had been emitted, the cell actuated a relay that diverted any remaining energy in the condensers of the electronic flash, thus cutting off the light. The surprising factor about this method was the speed of reaction. Normally the flash duration was about 1/700 second (fast enough for all normal purposes), but with this automatic measuring and cutoff, the duration could fall to 1/10,000 second or even less. This was the most accurate method yet devised, since it took into account the light-reflecting powers of the subject and surroundings.

Holography. At the end of 1968, scientists at the Bell Telephone Laboratories in New Jersey announced the discovery of a new material for holographic storage. A single crystal of lithium niobate showed promise of providing up to 1,000 times more storage capacity for digital or pictorial information than conventional holographic materials. By freeing enough electrons within the crystal, a laser beam of sufficient intensity set up an internal electric field that caused changes in the refractive index (the speed of light) within the crystal. Since the refractive index change varied with the intensity of laser light hitting the crystal, variations on a reference beam interfering with an object beam could be recorded. The unique quality of lithium niobate as a holographic material was that since it recorded semipermanently instead of permanently, the records could be erased by heating the crystal to 170° C. The same crystal could thus be used again and again. (V. G. C. B.)

COURTESY, NEW JERSEY STATE MUSEUM, TRENTON

"Anemone," a study in contrast and design, by Naomi Savage from the exhibition "Two Generations of Photographs: Man Ray and Naomi Savage," at the New Jersey State Museum's Cultural Center in Trenton, December 1968–February 1969.

See also Astronautics; Cinema.

Physics

Solid State Physics. In 1969 solid state physics saw more than its share of advances. S. R. Ovshinsky reported finding a reversible electrical threshold switching behaviour in a broad range of amorphous materials (*Phys. Rev. Lett.*, vol. 21, p. 1450, 1968). According to Ovshinsky, these glassy semiconductors (in particular, a chalcogenide containing 48% Te, 30% As, 12% Si, and 10% Ge) can be used as memory devices with at least a five-year retention and can be switched 10^{12} times. Ovshinsky's report was front-page news because of the potential commercial applications. It even was stated that the chalcogenide glasses would replace transistors; but performance reliability seemed to need considerable improvement before this could happen.

KEYSTONE

Murray Gell-Mann of California Institute of Technology was winner of the 1969 Nobel Prize for Physics for his work on classification of elementary particles.

K. H. J. Buschow, W. Luiten, W. A. Nastepad, and F. F. Westendorp produced a permanently magnetizable material ($CoSm_5$) with an energy product $(BH)_{max}$ of 18.5 $\times$ 10^6 G-oe (*Philips Tech. Rev.*, vol. 29, p. 336, 1968). This measure of excellence from the $CoSm_5$ magnet is about five times greater than that previously obtained with iron-cobalt alloys. By using compounds corresponding to the cobalt-rich part of the $CoSm_5$ homogeneity region, Westendorp and Buschow have increased this energy product to more than 20 $\times$ 10^{15} G-oe (*Solid State Comm.*, vol. 7, p. 639, 1969). This increase in $(BH)_{max}$ would allow a considerable reduction in the size of permanent magnets required for specific applications.

R. Birgeneau, H. Guggenheim, and G. Shirane have

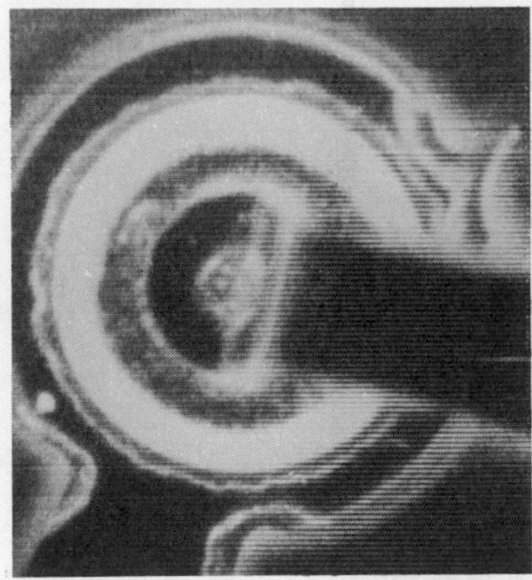

COURTESY, BARNES ENGINEERING COMPANY

Thermomicrogram (left) taken by an infrared microscope camera of a five-ampere power transistor dissipating two watts. The instrument, patented in 1969, is capable of measuring temperature differences of less than one degree in areas smaller than the diameter of a human hair. Highest temperatures show up white in the picture, and areas of progressively lower temperatures are darker. Photograph (right) of the same transistor.

reported that a single crystal of K_2NiF_4 behaves like a two-dimensional antiferromagnet above 97.1° K. (*Phys. Rev. Lett.*, vol. 22, p. 720, 1969). Neutron-diffraction experiments reveal that above the critical temperature the magnetic moments are arranged antiferromagnetically for distances of 1,000 atoms or more, but that there is no correlation from one plane to the next. The exchange coupling in the planes must be very large compared with the interaction between nearest neighbour planes.

Particle Physics. Great interest was aroused in 1964 when the Ω^- particle was discovered, completing the $3/2^+$ decuplet. The feat has now been emulated by the discovery of the Ξ^* particle which completes the $5/2^-$ octet. This cascade particle has strangeness -2 and a mass of $1{,}930 \pm 20$ Mev. The discovery was reported by J. Alliti and co-workers (*Phys. Rev. Lett.*, vol. 21, p. 1119, 1968).

By bombarding californium-249 with carbon ions, A. Ghiorso, M. Nurmia, J. Harris, K. Eskola, and P. Eskola at the University of California (Berkeley) have produced at least two and possibly three isotopes of element 104. This discovery was reported at the American Chemical Society's Mendeleev Centennial Symposium in 1969. The element was named kurchatovium by G. N. Flerov when he reported much less conclusive results in 1964.

The story of the violation of CP symmetry continues. C refers to charge conjugation (interchange of the signs of all electric charges), and P means parity (reversal of space coordinates). The value for $|\eta_{00}|^2$, the ratio of the two-neutral-pion decay rate of $K_2{}^0$ to that of a similar decay rate of $K_1{}^0$, is still under discussion. Recent measurements by M. Banner, J. W. Cronin, J. K. Liu, and J. E. Pilcher (*Phys. Rev. Lett.*, vol. 21, p. 1107, 1968) indicate a value of $5.1 \pm 1.2 \times 10^6$ for $|\eta_{00}|^2$. At least two independent values for $|\eta_{00}|^2$ are consistent with the value for $|\eta_{+-}|^2$ (the ratio of the two-charged-pion decay rate of $K_2{}^0$ to the two-neutral-pion decay rate of $K_1{}^0$). If η_{00} and η_{+-} are equal then the structure of $K_2{}^0$ is the only cause of CP violation.

K. O. Nielsen and W. M. Gibson measured the lifetime of a compound nucleus directly (cited in *Physics Today*, p. 67, July 1969). They used a time-of-flight technique with a flight path of less than 0.01 nanometers and time of 10^{-16} sec. They obtained a partial fission lifetime of 2×10^{-16} sec. for the excited Np^{238} nucleus at approximately 7.3 Mev average excitation. This agreed well with theoretical predictions.

Lasers. The rotation-vibration transition in methane at 3.39 microns is being used by R. L. Barger and J. J. Hall as a length standard (*Phys. Rev. Lett.*, vol. 22, p. 4, 1969). They have locked two lasers independently to the transition with a reproducibility of $\pm 1 \times 10^{11}$. This is two orders of magnitude better than the present standard, the 0.6056 micron line of Kr^{86}.

B. Byer, K. Oshman, J. Young, and S. Harris reported (*App. Phys. Lett.*, Aug. 1, 1968) that they had constructed a continuous-wave parametric oscillator with several novel features. The oscillator uses the output of a continuous argon laser at 0.5145 micron as pump and lithium niobate as nonlinear crystal. The output is in the visible and tunable range from 0.6800 to 0.7050 micron. Tuning is continuous, by changing the crystal temperature, and occurs without any noticeable variations on the output power of 1.5 mw. The bandwidth of the oscillator, about three wave numbers, is an order of magnitude less than previous oscillators, since a long crystal is used and the oscillator is operated well away from degeneracy.

General. The discovery in 1965 of anomalous water by B. V. Deryagin, M. V. Talaev, and N. N. Fedyakin (*Proc. Acad. Sci. U.S.S.R. Phys. Chem.*, vol. 165, p. 807, 1965) has been confirmed by other investigators. Anomalous water has a high density, high viscosity, low melting point, and low vapour pressure. The Soviet work has been repeated by E. Willis, G. K. Rennie, C. Smart, and B. A. Pethica (*Nature*, vol. 222, p. 159, 1969) and by E. R. Lippincott and co-workers (*Chem. Inds, Lond.*, p. 686, May 1969). The latter also have gone a step further and proposed that the substance is a polymer with formula $(H_2O)_n$ (*Science*, vol. 164, p. 1482, 1969). Using infrared and Raman spectroscopy the group proposes two possible structures: one a layered hexagon, the other a highly branched polymer chain.

B. N. Taylor and W. H. Parker have obtained more accurate values for the fundamental constants: the electron charge e, electron mass m, Planck's constant h, and Avogadro's number N (*Rev. Mod. Phys.*, vol. 41, p. 375, 1969). Their error is quoted as one-third that of E. R. Cohen and J. W. M. DuMond (*Rev. Mod. Phys.*, vol. 37, p. 537, 1965) and the values themselves have changed by several standard deviations. The constants were calculated mainly from measurements of the ac Josephson effect.

Gravitational waves, first postulated by Albert Einstein (*Annln Phys.*, vol. 49, p. 769, 1916), have been observed by J. Weber (*Phys. Rev. Lett.*, vol. 22, p. 1320, 1969). His measurements were made using detectors tuned to 1,660 Hz and spread over a 1,000-km. baseline. On a single day he observed 2 three-detection co-incidences that have a probability of occurring accidentally once every 70 million years. The results are said to indicate that the gravitational radiation is being emitted by sources in the earth's own galaxy such as supernovas or a pair of spiraling neutron stars. Further experiments using the earth and moon as co-incidence detectors are planned.

If the photon has a mass, then, from Maxwell's equations, a constant component should be added to the earth's magnetic field. A. S. Goldhaber and M. M. Nieto compared values of the earth's magnetic field from laboratory and satellite measurements to fields produced by external components and concluded that the mass must be less than 4.0×10^{-48} gm. (*Phys. Rev. Lett.*, vol. 21, p. 567, 1968). (S. B. P.)

See also Astronautics; Astronomy; Chemistry; Electronics; Nuclear Energy.

ENCYCLOPÆDIA BRITANNICA FILMS. *Laws of Motion* (1952); *Archimedes' Principle* (1953); *Atomic Radiation*

Physiology:
see Medicine

Pipelines:
see Fuel and Power; Transportation

Planning, Economic:
see Economic Planning

Plastics Industry:
see Industrial Review

Poetry:
see Literature

(1953); *Magnetism* (1953); *Atmospheric Pressure* (1955); *The Speed of Light* (1955); *Fuels—Their Nature and Use* (1958); *Electrons at Work* (1961); *Energy and Work* (1961); *Evidence for Molecules and Atoms* (1961); *Forces* (1961); *How to Bend Light* (1961); *How to Measure Time* (1961); *How to Produce Electric Current with Magnets* (1961); *Light and Color* (1961); *Magnetic, Electric and Gravitational Fields* (1961); *Vibrations* (1961); *Waves and Energy* (1961); *What Is Electric Current?* (1961); *What Is Space?* (1961); *What Is Uniform Motion?* (1961); *Molecular Theory of Matter* (1965).

Poland

A people's republic of Eastern Europe, Poland is bordered by the Baltic Sea, the U.S.S.R., Czechoslovakia, and East Germany. Area: 120,481 sq.mi. (312,046 sq.km.). Pop. (1969 est.): 32,555,000, including (1963 est.) Poles 30.7 million; Ukrainians 180,000; Belorussians 165,000; Jews 31,000; Slovaks 21,000; Russians 19,000; Lithuanians 10,000; Germans 3,000; Czechs 2,000; others 22,000. Cap. and largest city: Warsaw (pop., 1969 est., 1,279,000). Language: Polish. Religion: predominantly Roman Catholic; Orthodox and Lutheran minorities. First secretary of the Polish United Workers' (Communist) Party in 1969, Wladyslaw Gomulka; chairman of the Council of State, Marshal Marian Spychalski; chairman of the Council of Ministers (premier), Jozef Cyrankiewicz.

In 1969 Poland solemnly commemorated the 30th anniversary of the outbreak of World War II; it celebrated the 25th anniversary of the foundation of the people's republic; a new Sejm (Parliament) was elected and a new government constituted; a new five-year development plan was outlined; and in the field of foreign policy Poland took the initiative toward a rapprochement with West Germany.

On September 1 sirens sounded in Warsaw, Danzig, Katowice, and other towns in tribute to those who had fallen on the first day of World War II. Huge meetings were held, especially at Westerplatte near Danzig, where the first shots had been fired. In speeches and press articles homage was paid to the heroism of the Polish nation and its armed forces, including, as one periodical pointedly underlined, "the overwhelming majority of Polish generals," 40 of whom had died or were captured. Pres. Ludvik Svoboda of Czechoslovakia attended the Warsaw commemorative rally; as a lieutenant colonel, he took refuge in Poland after the dismemberment of his country and organized a Czechoslovak Legion that took part in the Polish campaign. The Soviet-Nazi pacts of 1939 were glossed over, but many indirect references to that collaboration appeared in the Polish press. In a book published shortly before the anniversary and entitled *History of the German Reich 1871–1945*, Jerzy Krasuski was allowed to summarize the two Ribbentrop-Molotov secret agreements, which until then had been ignored even in Polish collections of documents relating to World War II.

The celebrations of the 25th anniversary of "People's Poland" took place on July 22, the anniversary of the publication in 1944 at Lublin of a manifesto of the Polish Committee of National Liberation, considered a cornerstone of the Polish People's Republic. On the eve of the anniversary a special session of the Sejm was held at which Wladyslaw Gomulka, in a two-hour speech, condemned once more the leaders of pre-1939 Poland and glorified the Soviet victory over Nazi Germany.

Leonid I. Brezhnev, general secretary of the Communist Party of the U.S.S.R., proclaimed that for the Soviet people "the Soviet-Polish friendship is sacred." Gustav Husak, the first secretary of the Communist Party of Czechoslovakia, spoke warmly of the "brotherly collaboration and alliance" between his country and Poland. Willi Stoph, chairman of the Council of Ministers of the German Democratic Republic, proclaimed that the Oder-Neisse frontier was final, and added that that frontier was defended "west of the Elbe and Werra rivers."

Elections to the Sejm were held on June 1. There were 622 candidates in 80 constituencies. As only 460 deputies could be elected the electors had some opportunity to show their preference. Out of 20,635,000 valid votes (97.6% of the total electorate), 20,473,114 votes (99.2%) were cast on the lists of the National Unity Front. The political composition of the Sejm was as follows: Polish United Workers' Party (PZPR), 255; United Peasant Party, 117; Democratic Party, 39; nonparty members, 49. Of the 460 deputies, 191 were newly elected, 263 served a second consecutive term, and only 6 were old-timers of three or more terms. Among the nonparty deputies there were 14 Catholics.

On June 27 the new Sejm elected a new Council of State that included six new members, the most sig-

POLAND

Education. (1966–67) Primary, pupils 5,527,986, teachers 201,379; secondary, pupils 322,706, teachers 18,289; vocational, pupils 1,253,572, teachers 117,879; teacher training, pupils 68,667, teachers 7,685; higher (including 17 universities), students 274,471, teaching staff 24,411.

Finance. Monetary unit: zloty, with an official parity of 4 zlotys to U.S. $1 (9.60 zlotys = £1 sterling) and a tourist rate of 24 zlotys to U.S. $1 (57.60 zlotys = £1). Budget (1967 rev. est.): revenue 326.7 billion zlotys; expenditure 321.6 billion zlotys. National income (net material product): (1968) 665.4 billion zlotys; (1967) 605.6 billion zlotys. Cost of living (1963 = 100): (2nd quarter 1969) 109; (2nd quarter 1968) 108.

Foreign Trade. (1968) Imports 11,412,400,000 zlotys; exports 11,431,200,000 zlotys. Import sources: U.S.S.R. 35%; East Germany 10%; Czechoslovakia 8%; U.K. 6%. Export destinations: U.S.S.R. 36%; Czechoslovakia 9%; East Germany 8%; U.K. 5%. Main exports: machinery 28%; coal and coke 12%; transport equipment 9%; iron and steel 7%.

Transport and Communications. Roads (1968) 307,262 km. (including 139 km. expressways). Motor vehicles in use (1968): passenger 374,557; commercial 229,537. Railways: (1967) 26,638 km. (including 2,900 km. electrified); traffic (1968) 35,870,000,000 passenger-km., freight 92,636,000,000 net ton-km. Air traffic (1968): 450.6 million passenger-km.; freight 6,176,000 net ton-km. Shipping (1968): merchant vessels 100 gross tons and over 446; gross tonnage 1,341,665. Telephones (Dec. 1967) 1,530,479. Radio receivers (Dec. 1967) 5,539,000.

Agriculture. Production (in 000; metric tons; 1968; 1967 in parentheses): wheat 4,655 (3,934); rye 8,523 (7,694); barley 1,500 (1,412); oats (1967) 2,818, (1966) 2,625; potatoes 50,783 (48,620); sugar, raw value (1968–69) *c.* 1,707, (1967–68) 1,913; rapeseed *c.* 735 (651); linseed (1967) 73, (1966) 72; dry peas (1967) 83, (1966) 94; apples (1967) 537, (1966) 794; onions (1967) 306, (1966) 320; tobacco 81 (78); flax fibre (1967) 71, (1966) 55; hemp fibre (1967) 20, (1966) 20; butter *c.* 199 (194); cheese *c.* 215 (209); beef and veal 540 (489); pork 1,287 (1,315); fish catch (1967) 339, (1966) 335; timber (cu.m.; 1966–67) 17,400, (1965–66) 16,800. Livestock (in 000; June 1968): horses 2,673; cattle 10,940; pigs 13,911; sheep 3,328; chickens (June 1966) *c.* 132,500.

Industry. Index of industrial production (1963 = 100): (1968) 152; (1967) 140. Production (in 000; metric tons; 1968): coal 128,633; brown coal 26,878; coke (1967) 13,924; crude oil 475; natural gas (cu.m.) 2,557,000; electricity (kw-hr.) 55,503,000; manufactured gas (cu.m.; 1967) 6,444,000; iron ore (30% metal content) 3,050; pig iron 6,840; crude steel 11,007; zinc 203; copper 44; lead 49; cement 11,594; sulfuric acid 1,315; nitrogenous fertilizers (N content; 1967) 594; superphosphates (1967) 1,569; passenger cars (units) 40; commercial vehicles (units) 40; cotton fabrics (m.) 835,000; woolen fabrics (m.) 94,000; rayon and synthetic fabrics (m.) 118,000. Merchant vessels launched (100 gross tons and over; 1968) 416,000 gross tons. New dwellings completed (1967) 185,700.

CAMERA PRESS—PIX FROM PUBLIX

Leonid I. Brezhnev, general secretary of the Communist Party in U.S.S.R., calls for unity in the "Socialist Commonwealth" at the fifth congress of the Polish United Workers' Party held in 1969.

nificant among them being Zygmunt Moskwa, leader of the Democratic Party, and Mieczyslaw Moczar, a former minister of the interior and from November 1968 a secretary of the Central Committee of the PZPR.

Jozef Cyrankiewicz was once more asked to form a government. He retained two of the former three deputy premiers—Piotr Jaroszewicz, Poland's representative to the Council for Mutual Economic Assistance (Comecon), and Eugeniusz Szyr, a former fighter in the International Brigade in Spain and an old Communist of Jewish extraction—and made three new appointments—Stanislaw Majewski, Marian Olewinski, and Zdzislaw Tomal—for a new total of five. Most of the ministers retained their posts in the new government with three exceptions: Jozef Trendota became minister of finance to succeed Stanislaw Majewski; Edward Kowalczyk succeeded Moskwa as minister of communications; and Andrzej Giersz was appointed minister of building and building materials to succeed Marian Olewinski. In September Piotr Lewinski, minister of transport, was relieved of his post for inefficiency and replaced by Mieczyslaw Zajfryd.

The plenary meeting of the Central Committee of the PZPR discussed on November 14 and 15 the need for technological progress in order to ensure the success of the 1971–75 development plan. Jan Kaczmarek, chairman of the new Committee for Science and Technology of the Council of Ministers, declared that the country's industrialization had already attained such a level that it was necessary to enter a new phase of intensive and selective growth. It was decided in Moscow in April that a higher degree of economic integration within was essential, but this did not exclude economic and technological collaboration with the West. (*See* ECONOMIC PLANNING.)

In a speech in Warsaw on May 17 Gomulka dwelt on the German problem. Referring to the Budapest appeal for an all-European conference on collective security, he stated that, so far, successive West German governments had blocked every initiative aimed at détente. With pending West German elections in mind, Gomulka remarked that Willy Brandt, leader of the Social Democratic Party and then vice-chancellor in the coalition government, had made a realistic assessment of the German and European situation in Nürnberg on March 16, 1968. He had said, for instance, that he regarded it as necessary to recognize, or respect, the Oder-Neisse frontier.

When, after the elections of September 28, Brandt became head of the new West German government, he announced in the Bundestag on October 28 that he would propose to the Polish government the opening of bilateral negotiations on issues touched upon by Gomulka. On December 22, Warsaw, replying to a November 25 note from Bonn, indicated its willingness to begin talks on a number of issues. (K. SM.)

Police

Membership of the International Criminal Police Organization (Interpol) in 1969 numbered 105 countries. Reports to the General Assembly, held in Mexico City in October, concerned international drug traffic, measures to prevent the hijacking of aircraft, police powers of detention prior to arrest, and the use of firearms by police when making arrests. The General Secretariat also drew up a form for the identification of disaster victims. Throughout 1969, 16 laboratories in ten countries were engaged in a research program on the uses of electronic data processing in police work. The third African regional conference was held in Addis Ababa, Eth., in February. Interpol was also represented at the conference on illicit drug traffic held in Geneva in January, and submitted its annual report on the topic to the UN. Regular participation in the criminal work of the Council of Europe continued.

The most difficult situation confronting a police force in 1969 was probably that in Northern Ireland, where disturbances springing from alleged discrimination against the Roman Catholic minority almost reached the proportions of civil war. The 3,000-strong force of the Royal Ulster Constabulary (90% Protestant) was quite inadequate to deal with the series of violent outbursts that continued throughout the year, and the call-up of 8,400 B Special reservists (exclusively Protestant) only exacerbated the situation, leading to allegations of police partiality and brutality. These allegations were partly substantiated, and 16 policemen faced charges for misconduct in the January riots. With the building of barricades, the extensive burning of property, attacks on post offices and police stations, the use of gasoline bombs and machine guns by civilians, the death of at least 11 persons, and the wounding of hundreds, including 540 policemen, by mid-August the Northern Ireland government was forced to call in the British Army, which enforced an uneasy "peace line" between rival factions. An inquiry into the role of the B Specials led to their disbandment and to the disarming of the Royal Ulster Constabulary.

Student Protests. The spate of student protests that had erupted in 1968 continued. In London, following the student occupation of the London School of Economics in January and the subsequent erection of control gates by the authorities, busloads of police surrounded the site and clashed with militants, who succeeded in smashing the gates before being evicted. Later in the year police dealt firmly, but with minimal violence, with the "London Street Commune," groups of squatters, including hippies who had occupied a mansion in Piccadilly and a school in Holborn.

After the troubles of May 1968, French universities were relatively quiet, although students and police did clash at the Sorbonne, Vincennes, and in the Latin Quarter of Paris. In March there were three days of fighting between police and demonstrators in Louvain, Belg. Police used truncheons, tear gas, and water hoses; many of their opponents came prepared with crash helmets. In Rome police clashed with students and Communist demonstrators during U.S. Pres. Richard M. Nixon's visit in February. In March about 3,000 policemen raided the barricaded campus of Rome University and found dozens of Molotov cocktails, fused and ready for action.

In the U.S. police had to use tear gas three nights running to disperse rioting students at the University of Wisconsin in February. Five policemen were injured in a gun battle at an agricultural college in Greensboro, N.C. Shotguns, helicopters, and riot gas were used against students at Berkeley, Calif., in disturbances growing out of the closing of a "people's park" established by hippies on university-owned property. Other student uprisings that presented major police problems occurred in January at the San Francisco State College, in February at Duke University, Durham, N.C., in April at Harvard and Queens

College in New York, and in May at Brooklyn and City colleges in New York, Dartmouth College, Hanover, N.H., and Howard University in Washington, D.C. In May, the Federal Bureau of Investigation (FBI) was asked to look into reported connections between student militancy and Arab activists working on behalf of Al Fatah on U.S. campuses.

In Addis Ababa truckloads of police arrested more than 1,000 students in 24 hours in April after a month of agitation for educational reforms had led to a student's death. In India in January the universities of Hyderabad were closed indefinitely, following student demands for autonomy for the Telengana region, a Communist stronghold. Police used tear gas and batons to disperse demonstrators, and in Shamshad injured six students with gunfire. In September, rioting in Ahmedabad after the desecration of a Hindu temple resulted in at least 400 deaths. In South Africa, the inconclusive meetings between students and the minister of the interior and police, S. L. Muller, over the deportation of students, withdrawal of passports, and suspension of African students at Fort Hare, were followed by demonstrations in Cape Town, Johannesburg, and Natal.

After an admission that calling in police to disperse students in January had been rash, the Tokyo University authorities, one week later, proceeded to call in a greater show of force against demonstrators than had been witnessed since World War II. Six hundred students were arrested and nearly 200 police injured. Police were also called to the Kanda area, where barricades had gone up around two other universities. A few days later police tore up 50,000 paving stones in an attempt to deny weapons to the militants; 2,600 weapons were confiscated. In March, 2,300 police fought pitched battles with demonstrators at Kyoto University, 90 police and 140 civilians were injured. A six-month blockade of Hiroshima University ended August 18, when 1,200 policemen stormed the administration building. By August about one third of Japan's 327 universities had been involved in student strikes and all 20 major buildings at Tokyo University had been occupied.

North America. *United States.* Police strength in the U.S. increased for the second consecutive year. According to the FBI Uniform Crime Reports for 1968, the average number of police employees per 1,000 inhabitants in 1968 was 2.1, as compared with 2 in 1967, an increase of 5%. In cities of over 250,000 population, the average rate was 2.9, or an increase of 7% over the 1967 rate of 2.7; the rate remained at 1.5 in suburban areas. The increase stemmed from the greater utilization of civilian employees, particularly by the big police departments, to release sworn personnel for active police duties. In 1968 an average of 12.2% of all city police employees were civilians, as compared with 11.8% in 1967. This represented an increase of 3.4% in the ratio of civilian employees to total police personnel. When considering sworn personnel only, the average rate for cities in 1968 was 1.8 per 1,000 population, the same as in 1967. There were 50,640 employees in state police and state highway patrol organizations in 1968, or an increase of 9% over 1967.

There were 64 law enforcement officers killed by criminal action in 1968. Of the 626 offenders involved in the killing of 475 officers in 1960–68, 76% had been arrested previously. Assaults on police increased 17% in 1968 over 1967. Nationally there were 15.8 assaults per 100 officers in 1968, as compared with 13.5 in 1967 and 12.2 in 1966. The *Municipal Year Book 1969* reported that as of Jan. 1, 1969, the highest median maximum salary for policemen was $8,819 per annum in cities of 250,000–500,000 population, which was 37% higher than the highest median maximum salary reported ten years earlier. The right of policemen to organize, bargain collectively, and strike remained at issue. Nothing of the magnitude of the Montreal strike (*see* below) occurred in the U.S., but in many areas police, forbidden by law to strike, stayed away from work, claiming to be sick in epidemics of what the press called the "blue flu."

Civil disorders stemming from racial tensions continued to present critical problems for police throughout the U.S. in 1969. On March 29, in Detroit, one policeman was killed and another officer and four civilians wounded during a shoot-out between police and a black separatist group called the Republic of New Africa. In August, 45 persons including 12 policemen were injured in Pittsburgh, Pa. In September, a policeman was shot during a confrontation with a crowd of 150 blacks in Sarasota, Fla., and in Kokomo, Ind., two policemen were shot during disturbances following a high-school football game and three more policemen were wounded several hours later. In October, in Las Vegas, Nev., two persons were killed and over 50 injured during racial violence. During the summer there were serious racial troubles in Cairo, Ill., Charleston, S.C., and other localities. The year was punctuated by violence involving police and members of the Black Panther organization. Five Chicago policemen were shot in a confrontation in July and, in December, two Panther leaders were killed in a raid on a Chicago apartment and three policemen and three others were wounded in a shoot-out in Los Angeles. Claiming that 28 members had been killed by police since January 1968, the Panthers said they were being subjected to a concerted campaign of police harassment, but the allegation was denied by police sources. The Chicago deaths were under investigation by several groups as the year ended.

The need for greater representation from minority groups in police departments was being stressed. A 1968 report of the National Advisory Commission on Civil Disorders had stated that out of 80,621 sworn police personnel in 28 major cities, only 7,046 were nonwhite. By September 1969, however, blacks on the police force in Washington, D.C., had increased from 21 to 30%, in Detroit, from 5 to 9%, in St. Louis from 10 to 15%, and in New York City from 5 to 7%. In Baltimore, Md., one-third of the police force of 3,502 was black; in Chicago, blacks comprised one-fourth of the force; in Philadelphia, one-fifth; and in Newark, N.J., 150 of 1,500 policemen were black.

In August a report that during the past several years the New York City Police Department had appointed 62 men who had been charged with crimes ranging from homicide to burglary resulted in widespread concern among policemen over the flexibility in the department's hiring standards. On the other hand, six former convicts were working as full-time nonuniformed employees in the Los Angeles Police Department's community relations division.

Within the last two years, almost every major department in the U.S. had experienced hostility between black and white policemen. In several cities, blacks had withdrawn from traditional police organizations and formed their own. In September, the Chicago Afro-American Patrolmen's League an-

UPI COMPIX

Uniformed off-duty policeman pickets town hall in Weymouth, Mass., on Jan. 24, 1969. Police, seeking a 10% pay raise, protested the town's alleged refusal to bargain collectively for the raise.

nounced that its members would not be used as strike breakers against black pickets at construction sites. One source of friction was the question of whether black areas should be patrolled by black policemen. While blacks and Puerto Ricans graduating from the New York City police academy in September complained of their assignment to outside communities, in Boston, during disturbances in Roxbury, black officers turned down a suggestion that they be assigned to the slums. As a result of a complaint filed by a New York City police lieutenant, the State Division of Human Rights ruled that grammar questions on a written promotional test discriminated against competitors who had received inferior educations.

As of May 1969, the Law Enforcement Assistance Act had awarded over $1 million to finance the participation of law enforcement agencies in the National Crime Information Center, created in 1967 by the FBI. The centre, equipped to provide almost instantaneous information regarding wanted persons and stolen property, was servicing an average of 1,900 identifications a week. The New York City Police Department announced it was installing an electronic "war room," in which commanding officers could view major crowd-gathering events on television.

Department announced it was using video tape cameras to record police actions at demonstrations and provide photographic coverage for intelligence work. The American Civil Liberties Union, however, charged that such action might intimidate people from expressing themselves and thus abridge their rights of free speech and assembly.

Canada. On October 7, policemen in Montreal went on a strike over a salary dispute. During the one day, ten banks were robbed, nine other commercial establishments were held up, and 3 persons were slain and 12 wounded in a taxi drivers' riot. Several hundred youths smashed windows and looted stores along downtown streets. The only police patrolling were 200 senior municipal officers and provincial police, which were augmented to about 800 by nightfall. Early on October 8 the Policemen's Brotherhood ordered the 3,700 striking policemen back to work.

In September the Canadian Government vetoed plans to create a super antisubversion agency. The Royal Canadian Mounted Police would continue to handle intelligence investigations for the Canadian government, in spite of the recommendation by a royal commission study that a separate civilian-controlled security service be developed.

UPI COMPIX

Policemen patrol Main Street in the North End section of Hartford, Conn., on Sept. 2, 1969, amid debris left by rioters and looters. At least 160 persons were arrested during two days of civil disturbances.

On July 16, the San Francisco Police Department installed a computer-card ticket system designed to free officers from custodial chores and to allow them to spend more time on patrol. Under the new system, an officer could issue a ticket without taking a suspect into custody in cases involving minor crimes. The system did not apply to felony cases, sex crimes, narcotics, drunkenness requiring physical examination, prostitution, or cases in which the violator was armed or offered resistance. Every computer-card ticket issued there was estimated to save five hours of police work. The New York City Police Department announced that during the first five months of full operation, its Traffic Court Alert Project had kept 3,564 policemen on patrol who would otherwise have been appearing in court as witnesses. Under this project, policemen involved in Traffic Court cases remained on their normal patrol assignments and checked with the court each hour to see if their presence was needed. The effectiveness of helicopters during civil disorders had spurred police departments to establish aerial patrols, often with the aid of federal funds. In New York City, helicopters equipped with a high-intensity light called Spectro Night Sun were being utilized to pinpoint bands of youths congregating in a heavily foliated section of Central Park. The Detroit Police

Europe. *United Kingdom.* During 1969 the Home Office ran a crime prevention campaign in the Midlands with the object of encouraging the public to protect their property and to cooperate with the police. By the end of 1969 more than 50 panels enlisting local effort and enthusiasm for the prevention of crime had been set up throughout the country. The number of indictable offenses reported in 1968 was 1,289,000, an increase over 1967 of 6.8%. All of the new and enlarged forces called for under police amalgamation plans announced in May 1966 were in operation by October 1969. There were now 47 police forces in England and Wales and 20 in Scotland.

Increases in police manpower were again restricted, though not as severely as in 1968. By the end of 1969 the overall police strength in England and Wales was approaching 93,000. On September 30 Scotland Yard conceded it had been unsuccessful in its efforts to get black policemen to serve on the force, apparently because blacks were afraid of being shunned by their fellows. Among approximately 90,000 policemen in England and Wales, only 15 were nonwhite. In January, demonstrators and police shoved each other as about 5,000 persons marched in central London to protest Britain's alleged discrimination against nonwhite immigrants.

Strength of Scottish forces was approximately 10,-000. Although retirement was high and there was a fall in recruitment, total available manpower increased because more civilians were being employed as clerks, technicians, or traffic wardens. The use of more flexible methods of policing was extended to additional urban and rural areas. The Scottish Crime Squad, which assisted all Scottish police forces in investigation and intelligence work, became operational on May 16, 1969.

France. The Council of Ministers decided, on September 17, to abolish the General Secretariat of Police, created at the end of 1967, in an effort to introduce unity into the administrative and executive aspects of police duties. The active services of the Prefecture of Police, which remained united under the authority of the prefect of police, incorporated the volunteer services under the same title as the regional services and provincial police departments. All received their technical instruction from the central departments of the Interior Ministry. As in the past, the maintenance of order rested on the competence of the prefects, under the authority of the minister of the interior. Reorganization of the Department of Public Security involved the reestablishment of republican security corps distinct from the urban police and the establishment alongside each departmental prefect of a service chief charged with activating and coordinating department services. Deficiencies in the urban police force were increased by demographic movement, urbanization, and a rising crime rate. From 1966 to 1968 the number of individuals brought to justice in the principal sectors within police jurisdiction increased by 12%, while the number of criminal acts increased by 25%.

West Germany. Increased political activity for the federal parliamentary elections in September led to clashes between extreme right- and left-wing groups, and the understaffed police force (117,000) found it difficult to maintain order. Owing to booming economic conditions, police work remained unattractive. Delinquency in 1968 increased 4.5% over the previous year; 2,259,000 offenses were reported, while 1,118,-000 cases were solved. The Federal Border Guard (16,000) was equipped with helicopters to provide greater mobility and its strength was to be increased by recruiting men liable to compulsory military service. A federal weapons law was passed governing the manufacture, purchase and sale, importation, and test-firing of weapons. New regulations concerning issuance of firearms certificates and purchasing licenses were pending.

Scandinavia. The Danish police, with a total strength in 1969 of 7,771—in itself an adequate number—were considerably reduced in effectiveness by a high average age: retirement age remained 70 years for senior officers. In 1968, 195,000 crimes were reported, an increase of 12% over 1967. Crime rates for all but sexual offenses increased. Following the legitimization of pornographic literature in 1967, pictorial pornography was legalized and film censorship repealed in 1969. Violence between left-wing students and motorcycle gangs occurred several nights running outside a Copenhagen cinema showing John Wayne's *The Green Berets.*

A satisfactory year of recruitment left Norway's total police strength at approximately 5,000. In 1968 the number of cases investigated was 51,800, 73% of which were larcenies. While the number of traffic offenses was about equal to that of 1967, there was an 18% increase in convictions for drunken driving. There was a sharp decrease in offenses against public order.

BLOCK—PIX FROM PUBLIX

University of Wisconsin students battle police during demonstration on campus in support of black student demands.

U.S.S.R. The Ministry of Public Order was renamed the Ministry of Internal Affairs, and its various departments were made more accountable to local governmental bodies. Militiamen at city and district levels and the newly introduced district inspectors were henceforth obliged to have their nominations for enrollment endorsed by executive committees of the Soviets of Working People's Deputies, into which their departments were incorporated. The introduction of scientific techniques of criminal investigation led to an increase in initial training periods. The People's Brigade (civilian volunteer militia) numbered seven million in 1969; a recruitment drive was in progress and a network of training centres and refresher courses was set up.

Oceania. *Australia.* Public disquiet, particularly concerning conscription and the Vietnam war, resulted in a number of violent confrontations with police in Australia in 1969. Police tactics in controlling meetings and assemblies came under considerable criticism. Partly in response to these demands, several forces established crowd-control squads. Police difficulties were exacerbated by a continuing rise in the incidence of serious crime. It was hoped that a number of applications for substantial increases in police pay would, if granted, attract more recruits and reduce the current high resignation rate. The much-publicized siege by New South Wales officers of a house in Sydney where a heavily armed man held a woman and child hostage for several days, and a later incident in which two New South Wales police were killed when seeking to apprehend burglars, led to calls for more rigorous gun-control laws.

Other Countries. Troubles plagued Santiago, Chile, police searching for two bank robbers who had stolen $25,000. When the bandits escaped a police trap at a hotel, the detective in charge was summarily dismissed. A short time later, three detectives shot a man they believed to be a suspect in the robbery. He turned out to be a government agriculture department official who had fled because he believed the unshaven detectives were muggers and he sued the police. Still later, at Concepción, detectives boarded an airliner and dragged off a passenger as a suspect who turned out to be Judge Gabriel Fernández of Arauco Province.

The police of Lima, Peru, initiated a program of taking photographs to prove traffic violations; the fine imposed on violators included the cost of the pictures. Tokyo policemen began placing parking tickets on automobiles with a locked chain removable only at a police station. Too many motorists were throwing parking tickets away.

Nicola Scire, deputy police chief of Rome and Italy's most famous law enforcement officer, was jailed on June 1, accused of having accepted payoffs to protect gambling dens. The police of Brazil continued their efforts to track down and wipe out a "death squad," believed to be a clandestine group of policemen, which had killed more than 1,000 petty criminals in three years. The Cuban national network initiated a series of programs intended to glamorize the country's secret police and counterintelligence service. Appropriations for the Ministry of the Interior and Regional Organizations, which controlled the uniformed and secret political police, were believed to exceed $40 million. Ceylon's law enforcement agencies were being confronted with a new, growing problem—young men and women dressed in mod attire, many with more than a minimum of education, indulged in major criminal acts more for thrills than for pecuniary gain. (V. W. P.; X.)

See also Crime; Law; Prisons and Penology; Race Relations; United States.

ENCYCLOPÆDIA BRITANNICA FILMS. *Canada's Royal Canadian Mounted Police* (1960); *The Policeman* (Third Edition, 1966).

Political Parties

The following table is intended to provide a general world guide to political parties. All countries that were independent on Dec. 1, 1969, are included, but there are a number for which no analysis of political activities is given. Some of these cases are explained in the notes at the foot of the table.

Parties are included in most instances only if represented in parliaments (in the lower house in bicameral legislatures), but the figures in the last column of the table do not necessarily add up to the total number of seats in parliament because independents and certain small political groupings are sometimes omitted. The date of the most recent general election follows the name of the country.

The code letters in the affiliation column show the relative political position of the parties within each country; there is, therefore, no entry in this column for single-party states. There are obvious difficulties involved in labeling parties within the political spectrum of a given country. The key chosen is as follows: F—fascist; ER—extreme right; R—right; CR—centre right; C—centre; L—non-Marxist left; SD—social-democratic; S—socialist; EL—extreme left; and K—communist.

The percentages in the column "Voting strength" indicate proportions of the valid votes cast for the respective parties, or the number of registered voters who went to the polls in single-party states.

COUNTRY AND NAME OF PARTY	Affiliation	Voting strength	Parliamentary representation
Afghanistan (1969)			
Royal government with an elected House of the People (Wolesi Jirga)	—	—	216
Albania (1966)			
Albanian Labour (Communist)	—	99.99%	214
Algeria			
Military government since June 19, 1965	—	—	—
Andorra			
No parties*	—	—	24
Argentina			
Military government since June 28, 1966	—	—	—
Australia (1969)			
Country (Conservative)	R	...	20
Liberal	CR	...	46
Democratic Labor (DLP)	C	...	—
Australian Labor (ALP)	L	...	59
Austria (1966)			
Freiheitliche Partei Österreichs	R	5.4%	6
Österreichische Volkspartei	C	48.4%	85
Sozialistische Partei Österreichs†	SD	42.6%	74
Barbados (1966)			
Barbados National Party	R	...	2
Democratic Labour Party	C	...	14
Barbados Labour Party	L	...	8
Belgium (1968)			
Volksunie (Flemish)	R	9.8%	20
Parti pour la Liberté et le Progrès	CR	20.9%	47
Parti Social-Chrétien	C	31.7%	69
Parti Socialiste Belge	SD	28.0%	59
Parti Communiste Belge	K	3.3%	5
Bhutan			
No parties‡	—	—	130
Bolivia (1966)			
Frente de la Revolución Boliviana	R	79.7%	82
Comunidad Demócrata Cristiana	C	16.2%	19
Movimiento Revolucionario Paz-Estenssorista	L	...	1
Botswana (1965)			
Botswana Democratic Party	C	...	28
Botswana People's Party	L	...	3
Brazil (1966)			
Aliança Renovadora Nacional§	—	...	409
Bulgaria (1966)			
Bulgarian Communist, Agrarian Union, Nonparty } Fatherland Front	—	99.8%	416
Burma			
Military government since March 2, 1962	—	—	—
Burundi			
Military government since Nov. 28, 1966	—	—	—
Cambodia			
Royal government with a single party	—	...	77
Cameroon (1965)			
Uníon Nationale Camérounaise	—	...	50
Canada (1968)			
Social Credit	R	0.7%	—
Progressive Conservative	CR	31.4%	72
Liberal	C	45.5%	155
Rassemblement des Créditistes	C	4.8%	14
New Democratic	L	16.7%	22
Central African Republic			
Military government since Jan. 1, 1966	—	—	—
Ceylon (1965)			
United National	R	41.1%	66
Sri Lanka Freedom	CR	31.4%	41
Federal (Tamil)	C	5.6%	14
Lanka Sama Samaja (Trotskiist)	SD	8.2%	10
Mahajana Eksath Peramuna	S	3.0%	2
Communist	K	2.8%	4
Chad (1963)			
Union pour le Progrès du Tchad	—	99%	75
Chile (1969)			
Partido Nacional	R	20.9%	34
Partido Radical	C	13.4%	24
Partido Demócrata-Cristiano	C	31.1%	55
Partido Socialista Chileno	S	12.8%	15
Partido Comunista de Chile	K	16.6%	22
China, People's Republic of			
Communist (Kungchan-tang)	—	—	—
China (Taiwan), Republic of			
Nationalist (Kuomintang)	—	—	773
Colombia (1968)			
Alianza Nacional Popular	R	...	38
Partido Conservador Partido Liberal	R C	...	141
Congo (Kinshasa),			
Military government since Nov. 25, 1965	—	—	—
Congo (Brazzaville),			
Military government since September 1968	—	—	—
Costa Rica (1966)			
Partido de Liberación Nacional	R	...	28
Partido de Unificación Nacional	C	...	27
Unión Civica Revolucionaria	L	...	2
Cuba			
Partido Comunista de Cuba	—	—	—

COUNTRY AND NAME OF PARTY	Affiliation	Voting strength	Parliamentary representation
Cyprus			
Civil war since December 1963	—	—	—
Czechoslovakia (1964)			
Communist, Socialist, People's } National Front	—	99.9%	300
Dahomey			
On July 28, 1968, a referendum approved the appointment of a civilian president; military government was resumed after a coup on Dec. 10, 1969	—	—	—
Denmark (1968)			
Conservative	R	20.4%	37
De Uafhaengige (Independents)	R	0.5%	—
Venstre (Agrarian)	C	18.6%	34
Centre (Liberal)	C	1.3%	—
Radical-Liberal	C	15.0%	27
Social Democratic	SD	34.0%	62
Socialist People's	S	6.1%	11
Communist	K	1.0%	—
Left Socialists	—	2.0%	4
Dominican Republic (1966)			
Partido Reformista	R	...	48
Partido Revolucionario Dominicano	C	...	26
Ecuador (1968)			
Alianza Popular	R	...	...
Izquierda Democrática	L	...	...
El Salvador (1966)			
Partido de Conciliacion Nacional	R	60.0%	31
Partido Demócrata Cristiano	C	28.8%	15
Partido Acción Renovadora	C	7.7%	4
Partido Popular Salvadoreño	L	1.8%	1
Equatorial Guinea (1968)			
Movimiento por Unión Nacional de Guiné Ecuadorial (MUNGE); Idea Popular de Guiné Ecuadorial (IPGE); Movimiento Nacional por Liberación de Guiné Ecuadorial (MONALIGE)	—	...	35
Ethiopia (1965)			
Imperial government with an elected Yeheg Memria (lower chamber)	—	—	250
Finland (1966)			
Kansallinen Kokoomus Poulue (Cons.)	R	13.8%	26
Svenskapartiet (Swedish Party)	R	6.0%	12
Keskusliitto (Centre)	C	21.1%	49
Kansan Poulue (Liberal)	C	6.5%	9
Sosialidemokraatinen Poulue	SD	27.7%	55
Communist-controlled SKDL‖	K	21.1%	41
France (1968)			
Extreme right	ER	0.2%	—
Gaullists¶	CR	38.1%	292
Independent Republicans	CR	5.1%	61
Centre Démocrate♀	C	10.8%	33
Fédération de la Gauche Démocrate et Socialiste	L	18.0%	57
Parti Socialiste Unifié	EL	4.1%	10
Parti Communiste Français	K	22.1%	34
Gabon (1964)			
Bloc Démocratique Gabonais	—	—	31
Opposition (2 parties)	—	—	16
Gambia, The (1966)			
People's Progressive Party	C	...	24
United Party	L	...	8
German Democratic Republic (1967)			
Sozialistische Einheitspartei, Christlich-Demokratische Union, National-Demokratische Partei, Liberal-Demokratische Partei, Demokratische Bauernpartei } National Front	—	98.82%	434
Germany, Federal Republic of (1969)			
Christlich-Demokratische Union♂	R	46.1%	242
Freie Demokratische Partei	C	5.8%	30
Sozialdemokratische Partei Deutschlands	SD	42.7%	224
Ghana (1969)			
People's Action Party	R	...	2
National Alliance of Liberals	CR	...	29
Progress Party (Busia)	C	...	105
United Nationalist Party	...	...	2
Greece			
Military government since April 21, 1967	—	—	—
Guatemala (1966)			
Movimiento de Liberación Nacional	R	...	...
Partido Revolucionario	C	54%	30
Partido Institucional Democrático	C	...	...
Guinea (1968)			
Parti Démocratique de Guinée	—	—	75
Guyana (1968)			
People's National Congress	C	...	30
United Force	L	...	4
People's Progressive Party	EL	...	19
Haiti			
Presidential dictatorship since 1957	—	—	—
Honduras (1965)			
Partido Nacional	R	...	35
Partido Liberal	C	...	29
Hungary (1967)			
Hungarian Socialist Workers', National Peasant Party, Smallholders' Party } Patriotic People's Front	—	99.7%	349

COUNTRY AND NAME OF PARTY	Affiliation	Voting strength	Parliamentary representation
Iceland (1967)			
Independence (Conservative)	R	37.5%	23
Progressive	C	28.1%	18
Social-Democratic	SD	15.7%	9
United People's Socialist	K	17.6%	10
India (1967)			
Jan Sangh (Hindu Nationalist)	ER	...	35
Swatantra (Freedom)	R	...	42
Dravida Munnetra Kazhagam□	R	...	25
Indian National Congress	C	...	281
Praja Socialist	SD	...	13
Samyukta Socialist	S	...	23
Communist (pro-Soviet)	K	...	23
Communist (pro-Chinese)	K	...	19
Indonesia			
Military government since Oct. 1, 1965	—	—	—
Iran (1967)			
Iran Novin (New Iran)	R	...	180
Mardom (People's) Party	C	...	20
Pan-Iranian Party	C	...	5
Iraq			
Military governments since 1958	—	—	—
Ireland (1969)			
Fianna Fail (Sons of Destiny)	C	...	75
Fine Gael (United Ireland)	C	...	50
Labour	L	...	18
Israel (1969)			
Free Centre	ER	1.2%	2
Gahal (Herut-Liberal Alignment)	R	21.7%	26
National Religious	C	9.7%	12
Agudat Israel	C	3.2%	4
Poalei Agudat Israel	C	1.8%	2
Independent Liberal	C	3.2%	4
State List (Ben-Gurion)	L	3.1%	4
Maarakh (Labour Alignment)	L	46.2%	56
Two Arab lists	L	...	4
Haolam Hazé (Avnery)	L	1.2%	2
Communist (Maki or pro-Israel)	K	1.2%	1
Communist (Rakah or pro-Arab)	K	2.8%	3
Italy (1968)			
Movimento Sociale Italiano	F	4.5%	24
Partito Democratico Italiano di Unitá Monarchica	R	1.3%	6
Partito Liberale Italiano	CR	5.8%	31
Partito Democrazia Cristiana	C	39.1%	266
Partito Socialista Italiano	SD	14.5%	91
Partito Socialista Italiano di Unitá Proletaria◇	EL	4.5%	23
Partito Comunista Italiano	K	26.9%	177
Südtiroler Volkspartei	—	...	3
Ivory Coast (1960)			
Parti Démocratique de la Côte d'Ivoire	—	...	85
Jamaica (1967)			
Jamaica Labour Party	L	...	33
People's National Party	L	...	20
Japan (1969)			
Komeito▲	CR	10.91%	47
Liberal-Democratic	CR	47.63%	288
Democratic Socialist	SD	7.74%	31
Socialist	S	21.44%	90
Communist	K	6.81%	14
Jordan			
Royal government, no parties	—	—	60
Kenya (1969)			
Kenya African National Union	—	—	171
Korea, Republic of (1967)			
Democratic Republican Party	R	...	130
New Korea Party	C	...	44
Taejung Dang (Party of the Masses)	EL	...	1
Korea, People's Democratic Republic of (1967)			
Korean Workers' (Communist) Party	...	100%	300
Kuwait			
Princely government	—	—	30
Laos (1965)+			
Independents	R	...	27
Neutralist Party	C	...	13
Social Democrats	L	...	11
Rally of the Lao Party	EL	...	8
Lebanon (1969)			
Chamber of Deputies elected by universal suffrage according to the proportional division between Christians and Muslims	—	—	99
Lesotho (1965)			
Lesotho National Party	CR	41.6%	31
Lesotho Congress Party	C	39.6%	25
Marematlou Freedom Party	L	16.4%	4
Liberia (1968)			
True Whig Party	—	...	41
Libya			
Military Government since Sept. 1, 1969	—	—	—
Liechtenstein (1966)			
Vaterländische Union	CR	42.6%	7
Fortschrittliche Bürgerpartei	C	48.5%	8
Christlich-Soziale Partei	C	8.9%	—
Luxembourg (1968)			
Parti Chrétien-Social	CR	35.3%	21
Parti Libéral	C	16.6%	11
Parti Ouvrier Socialiste	SD	32.3%	18
Parti Communiste	K	15.5%	6
Malagasy Republic (1965)			
Parti Social-Démocrate	C	...	104
Malagasy Independence Party	L	...	3

Political Parties

COUNTRY AND NAME OF PARTY	Affili-ation	Voting strength	Parlia-mentary represen-tation
Malawi (1964)			
Malawi Congress Party	CR	...	50
Malawi Constitutional Party	L	...	3
Malaysia			
Republican constitution adopted following plebiscite in March 1968			
Maldives, Republic of the (1965)			
Government by the Didi family	—	...	54
Mali			
Military government since Nov. 19, 1968	—	—	—
Malta (1966)			
Nationalist Party	R	...	28
Malta Labour Party	SD	...	22
Mauritania (1965)			
Parti du Peuple Mauritanien	—	92%	40
Mauritius (1967)			
Independence Party (Indian-dominated)	C	...	39
Parti Mauricien Social-Démocrate	L	...	23
Mexico (1967)			
Partido Acción Nacional	CR	...	12
Partido Revolucionario Institucional	L	90%	189
Partido Auténtico de la Révolución Mexicana	L	...	3
Partido Popular Socialista	S	...	6
Monaco (1968)			
Union Nationale et Démocratique	—	...	18
Mongolia (1967)			
Mongolian People's Revolutionary Party	—	99%	295
Morocco			
Royal government since June 8, 1965	—	—	—
Nauru (1968)			
No political parties	—	...	18
Nepal			
Royal government since December 1960	—	—	—
Netherlands (1967)			
Staatkundig Gereformeerde Partij	R	2.01%	3
Boerenpartij (Farmers' Party)	R	4.77%	7
Anti-Revolutionaire Partij	CR	9.90%	15
Christelijk Historische Unie	CR	8.15%	12
Katholieke Volkspartij	C	26.51%	42
"Democraten '66"	C	4.46%	7
Volkspartij voor Vrijheid en Democratie	C	10.74%	17
Partij van de Arbeid	SD	23.55%	37
Pacifistisch Socialistische Partij	S	2.68%	4
Communistische Partij	K	3.61%	5
New Zealand (1969)			
National (Conservative)	CR	...	44
Labour Party	L	...	40
Nicaragua (1967)			
Partido Liberal Nacionalista (Somoza)	R	...	36
Partido Conservador Tradicionalista	R	...	15
Partido Demócrata Cristiano	C	...	2
Partido Liberal Independenta	C	...	1
Niger (1965)			
Parti Progressiste Nigérien	—	...	50
Nigeria			
Military governments since Jan. 15, 1966; civil war since May 30, 1967	—	—	—
Norway (1965)			
Høyre (Conservative)	R	20.1%	31
Kristelig Folkeparti	CR	7.8%	13
Senterpartiet (Agrarian)	CR	9.4%	18
Venstre (Liberal)	C	10.1%	18
Arbeiderpartiet (Labour)	SD	43.3%	68
Sosialistisk Folkeparti	S	6.0%	2
Norges Kommunistiske Parti	K	1.4%	—
Pakistan (1965)			
Conventionist Muslim League	—	...	118
Combined opposition	—	...	32
Panama			
Presidential elections in May 1968 were followed by a military coup			
Paraguay (1967)			
Partido Colorado (Stroessner)	R	69.4%	80
Partido Liberal Radical	C	21.5%	29
Partido Liberal	C	6.2%	8
Partido Revolucionario (Febrerista)	SD	2.8%	3
Peru (1963)			
Unión Nacional Odriista	R	...	23
Partido Acción Popular	C	...	48
Partido Demócrata-Cristiano	C		
Partido del Pueblo⊕	L	...	57
Philippines (1965)			
Partido Nacionalista	R	...	65
Partido Liberal	CR	...	39
Poland (1969)			
Polska Zjednoczona Partia Robotnicza (Front of National Unity)	—	97.6%	255
Zjednoczone Stronnictwo Ludowe (Front of National Unity)			117
Stronnictwo Demokratyczne (Front of National Unity)			39
Nonparty (Front of National Unity)			49**
Portugal (1965)			
União Nacional	—	...	130
Romania (1969)			
Partidul Comunist Romîn (People's Front)	—	99.75%	465
Nonparty (People's Front)			
Rwanda (1965)			
Parmehutu Party	—	...	47
San Marino (1964)			
Partito Democratico-Cristiano	C	...	29
Partito Social-Democratico	SD	...	10
Partito Socialista	S	...	6
Partito Comunista	K	...	14

COUNTRY AND NAME OF PARTY	Affili-ation	Voting strength	Parlia-mentary represen-tation
Saudi Arabia			
Royal government	—	—	—
Senegal (1968)			
Union Progressiste Sénégalaise	—	...	80
Sierra Leone (1962)			
Peoples' Party	C	...	48
All Peoples' Congress	L	...	14
Singapore (1968)			
People's Action Party	C	...	58
United People's Party	EL	...	—
Somalia			
Military government since Oct. 21, 1969	—	—	—
South Africa (1966)			
Nationalist Party	R	...	126
United Party	C	...	39
Progressive Party	L	...	1
Southern Yemen, Rep. of			
National Liberation Front	—	—	—
Spain (1967)			
Movimiento Nacional (nonparty and Falange†† Party members, the latter in minority)	—	...	564
Sudan			
Military government since May 25, 1969	—	—	—
Swaziland (1968)			
Imbokodvo Party	...	...	...
Sweden (1968)			
Högerpartiet (Conservative)	R	13.7%	32
Centerpartiet (Agrarian)	CR	16.1%	39
Folkpartiet (Liberal)	C	15.0%	34
Socialdemokratiska Arbetarepartiet	SD	50.9%	125
Vänsterpartiet-Kommunisterna	K	3.0%	3
Switzerland (1967)			
Conservative Christian-Social	R	...	45
Evangelical People's	R	...	3
Liberal Democratic	CR	...	6
Farmers, Artisans, and Middle Class	C	...	21
Radical Democratic	C	...	49
Independents	C	...	16
Social Democratic	SD	...	51
Communist (Partei der Arbeit)	K	...	5
Syria			
Baath and military government	—	—	—
Tanzania (1965)			
Tanganyika African National Union	C	...	107
Zanzibar Afro-Shirazi Party	L	...	52
Thailand			
Royal and military government	—	—	—
Togo			
Military government since Jan. 13, 1967	—	—	—
Trinidad and Tobago (1966)			
People's National Movement	C	...	24
Democratic Labour Party	L	...	12
Tunisia (1969)			
Destourian Socialist Party	—	—	101
Turkey (1969)			
Turkish Justice	R	56.9%	257
Republican Nation's	R	1.3%	6
Republican People's	C	31.8%	144
Reliance (breakaway from RPP)	C	3.3%	15
Union		1.8%	8
New Turkey	C	1.3%	6
Nationalist Action (Peasants)	L	0.2%	1
Turkish Workers'	EL	0.4%	2
Uganda			
Uganda People's Congress	—	...	...
Union of Soviet Socialist Republics (1966)			
Communist Party of the Soviet Union	—	99.7%	767
United Arab Republic (1968)			
Arab Socialist Union	—	...	350
United Kingdom (1966)			
Conservative and Unionist	R	41.9%	253
Liberal‡‡	C	8.5%	12
Labour	L	48.1%	364
Communist§§	K	0.2%	—
United States (1968)			
American Independent	R	13.5%	—
Republican	CR	43.5%	192
Democratic	C	43.0%	243
Upper Volta			
Military government since Jan. 3, 1966	—	—	—
Uruguay (1967)			
Partido Nacional (Blanco)	R	39.6%	41
Partido Colorado	C	49.8%	50
Partido Demócrata Cristiano	C	3.0%	3
Frente Izquierdista de Liberación	K	5.7%	5
Venezuela (1968)			
Cruzada Cívica Nacional‖‖	ER	11.4%	21
Unión Republicana Democrática	R	9.6%	17
Frente Nacional Democrático	R	2.6%	5
Fuerza Democrática Popular	C	5.5%	10
Social Christians (COPEI)¶¶	C	25.4%	57
Acción Democrática	C	28.0%	68
Movimiento Electoral del Pueblo	L	14.5%	27
Unión para Avanzar (Communist)♀♀	K	2.8%	5
Vietnam, North (1964)			
Lao Dong (Communist Party)	—	...	366
Vietnam, South (1967)			
National coalition	—	...	137
Western Samoa (1967)			
No political parties	—	...	45

COUNTRY AND NAME OF PARTY	Affiliation	Voting strength	Parliamentary representation
Yemen			
Civil war since Sept. 27, 1962	—	—	—
Yugoslavia (1969)			
League of Communists of Yugoslavia / Socialist Alliance of the Working People	—	...	670
Zambia (1968)			
United National Independence Party	—	...	81
African National Congress	—	...	23
Independents	—	...	1

*Council General elected by heads of families of the six parishes.
†The Kommunistische Partei Österreichs presented in 1966 only one (unsuccessful) candidate in Vienna; in all other constituencies it supported Socialist candidates.
‡The National Assembly (Tsongdu) meets once a year.
§In October 1965 all political parties were banned, but two months later an official party, the Aliança Renovadora Nacional, was created, and an official opposition, the Movimento Democratico Brasileiro, was authorized. The latter declared that it would not participate in any indirect elections.
||Suomen Kansan Demokraatinen Liitto or Finland's People's Democratic League.
¶After the 1968 election the Gaullists took the name of Union des Démocrates pour la République.
♀After the 1968 election the Centre Démocrate took the name of Progrès et Démocratie Moderne.
♂Including members of the Bavarian Christlich-Soziale Union.
□A right-wing opposition party based mainly in the Tamil-speaking Madras State.
◇A breakaway group from the Socialist Party formed in December 1963; it opposes the centre-left coalition government.
▲Komeito, a "Clean Government Party," was formed in November 1964; it is a political arm of the Soka Gakkai Buddhist movement.
+Theoretically Laos has a coalition government; in fact, it is a divided country with a pro-Communist Neo Lao Hak Sat party controlling territory bordering North Vietnam.
⊕ Formerly Alianza Popular Revolucionaria Americana founded in 1924 by Víctor Raúl Haya de la Torre.
**Including 14 Catholic deputies, of whom 5 were from "Pax" and 5 from "Znak."
††The full name of this only allowed political party is: Falange Española Tradicionalista y de las Juntas de Ofensiva Nacional-Sindicalistas.
‡‡Out of 630 constituencies, the Liberals contested only 311, forfeiting their deposits in 104.
§§The Communist Party of Great Britain presented its candidates in 57 constituencies only, forfeiting deposits in all of them. A candidate forfeits his deposit of £150 if he fails to poll more than one-eighth of the total votes cast.
||||New party formed by former dictator Marcos Pérez Jiménez.
¶¶Comitado Organización Política Electoral Independiente.
♀♀Partido Comunista Venezuelano was declared illegal in 1963.

(K. Sm.)

Political Science

The interest in methodological problems and investigating techniques shown by so many political scientists in previous years gave no sign of abating in 1969, but in many countries political circumstances and urgent problems substantially affected the direction of thinking, teaching, and research.

The trends that had first reached fruition in the United States in the early 1960s, a new preoccupation with theory as well as increasingly refined and meaningful empirical research—systems analysis, structural-functional and developmental studies, and the more rigorous and general use of quantitative data and automatic retrieval of information—continued to prevail in the more "advanced" countries and to influence many younger political scientists in the rest of the world. The strengthening of comparative studies, various plans for new or improved national and cross-national data banks and research centres, joint or national efforts to gather more and more adequate information about the processes of political socialization, legislative behaviour, models of decision making, and the like, clearly reflected these emphases.

The newly developed conceptual tools and techniques for data gathering were beginning to find their way into political science courses and textbooks, despite the resistance of the more traditionally minded scholars. It appeared from the proceedings of various international conferences that the fear of an ever widening gap between the "advanced" English-speaking countries and the rest of the world had perhaps been excessive. In many countries previously considered "backward," there existed political scientists well informed about the prevailing trends and fashions—even though, because of intellectual objections or lack of opportunity, this familiarity seldom showed in their own work.

Adverse political conditions continued to hamper the progress of political science in countries with authoritarian regimes, and in extreme cases made teaching and research virtually impossible. Scholars were intimidated, silenced, or dismissed from academic positions in Greece and Spain, as well as in Brazil and various other Latin-American countries. After the invasion of Czechoslovakia by the Warsaw Pact forces in August 1968, the slow development of political science was arrested in several of the Communist countries. The Soviet, Polish, and Czechoslovak political science associations gradually reduced their activity, and international contacts were made increasingly difficult for the practitioners of a potentially subversive discipline.

Even in nonauthoritarian countries, political scientists found it very difficult to remain aloof from current events. In France the consequences of the 1968 student uprising continued to be felt. Political scientists tried to avail themselves of the opportunities provided by the granting of autonomy to the component units of each university, and to improve academic structures and methods. The French Political Science Association suggested the adoption of new means of training and recruiting political scientists, independent of the law school examinations, and devoted a day-long session in March 1969 to an appraisal of weaknesses in French teaching and research and to seeking means of overcoming them. Other countries had to cope with more immediate, less scholarly problems. Outbursts of violence in the United Kingdom (especially at the London School of Economics and Political Science), Italy, Japan, and the United States (especially at Cornell, New York University, and Harvard) taxed the political scientists' powers of analysis as well as their political capacities. Willingly or not, scholars found themselves involved in university or nationwide crises and were compelled to take stands on issues of immediate policy, as individuals and as scholars.

In the United States the climate of political science studies was greatly changed not only by the surge of black student militancy and the activities of student radicals, but also by the continuation of the war in Vietnam—the occasion, if not the cause, of student agitation in many other countries. A substantial number of political scientists were increasingly outspoken in their opposition to Pres. Richard M. Nixon's policy and took an active part in the October 15 Vietnam Moratorium and other antiwar demonstrations. The view of the U.S. political system thus tended to be less complacent than it had been in the past. Many felt that stability might not be a virtue when it allowed a major power to "drift" into a war.

Some members of the profession, gathered in the "caucus for a new political science," criticized political science in general and the American Political Science Association (APSA) in particular for having invested energies "primarily in celebrating and supporting the economic, social, and political status quo." The caucus wished to encourage the development of "a *new* political science, devoted to radical social criticism and fundamental social change," and presented its own slate of candidates for APSA's various elective offices. A majority of U.S. political scientists, however, were clearly hostile to converting the association into a political action group and to blurring the traditional distinction between professional roles and citizens' concerns.

This did not mean that the profession was impervious to political considerations and to radical criticism. In his presidential address to APSA, David Easton of the University of Chicago spoke in September of "the new revolution in political science," which he christened the "post-behavioural revolution." He called for a temporary reallocation of resources as between basic and applied research in favour of the latter, in order to answer needs for relevant knowledge and action.

Whether responses to these challenges could be found—either in the United States or in the many other countries where political science was a lively discipline—was a subject that preoccupied the authorities of the International Political Science Association as they prepared for the eighth World Congress of Political Science, to be held in London from Aug. 31 to Sept. 5, 1970. The program of the congress was to include four topics for plenary sessions: quantitative and mathematical methods in political science (general reporter: Karl Deutsch, Harvard); governmental organization and elite formation in Europe (general reporter: Klaus von Beyme, University of Tübingen, W.Ger.); the church as a political institution (general reporter: Leo Moulin, College of Europe, Bruges, Belg.); and models and methods in the comparative study of nation-building (general reporter: Stein Rokkan, University of Bergen, Nor.).

In addition, there would be 14 specialist meetings: on European integration; the comparative study of local politics; food and politics; psychology and politics; recent trends in political theory; political finance; biology and politics; the theory of international relations; comparative political recruitment; the history of political thought from Hegel to Lenin; new approaches to the study of social structure and voting behaviour; political attitudes and opinions of young people; political opposition; and political decision making. (SE. H.)

ENCYCLOPÆDIA BRITANNICA FILMS. *Political Parties* (1952); *Presidential Elections* (1952).

Populations and Areas

World population continued to grow by about 2% annually during 1969, with the estimated number of people reaching 3,551,000,000 by July 1. The gain was roughly 2.2 persons per second, 132 per minute, 190,000 per day, and 1.3 million per week.

Fastest rates of growth continued to be recorded in the less developed nations of Latin America, Asia, and Africa, as the result of extremely high birthrates of 40–57 per 1,000 and declining death rates. Already these nations held 2.6 billion of the world's people. That constituted 73%.

In Latin America, where improved health standards and preventive medicine were forcing a decline in the death rate, the population was growing at more than 3% annually. Should this pattern continue the continent would double its 276 million people in 24 years. In Costa Rica, where the birthrate remained steady at 45 and the death rate was a low 7, doubling its 1.6 million people would only require 18 years, because the growth rate was 4%.

Slow growth, on the other hand, was recorded among the 900 million people in the industrially developed nations of Europe and North America, as well as in the countries of Australia, New Zealand, and Japan. In marked contrast to the less developed nations, the degree of literacy was high, and per capita income was above $600 annually. Birthrates in the more developed nations ranged between 14.6 and 25 and death rates between 6 and 13. The annual growth rate fell generally below the 2% mark. In most of these nations it was actually under 1%.

For several years, Romania, because abortions were permitted by law, claimed the lowest birthrate in the world: 14.3. In an attempt to spark lagging population increases, however, the government outlawed abortions. The result was a substantial, but probably temporary, jump in the birthrate to 27.1.

Slowest growth was reported in three European countries: Belgium, East Germany, and Luxembourg. All reported annual increases of 0.1%, which meant it would take 700 years to double their populations. At the other end of the scale was the oil-rich country of Kuwait, which added about 7.6% to its existing population of 531,581. Its high birthrate, 52, and low death rate, 6, ensured a doubling of the population in nine years.

If the population of Latin America was increasing most rapidly, Africa was certainly the continent with the highest potential for extremely fast population growth. Birthrates averaged in the high 40s. The figure in the Ivory Coast was 56, followed by Togo and Guinea, each with 55. What had been a brake on the overall increase was the high incidence of death, particularly among infants. Contributing factors were disease, hunger, malnutrition, and the narrow limits of available medical facilities. In Zambia, for example, fully one-quarter of the babies died within a year. In most African countries the infant death toll ran between 10 and 20%.

High birthrates and declining death rates were but one factor in establishing the growth potential of different countries. The percentage of the young was another. In slow-growing Europe, future parents, or those under 15, constituted only 25% of the population. In North America their proportion was 30%. But in the less developed nations that component was well over 40%. In Brazil, for example, 43% of its 91 million people were under 15. Its population was increasing at a rate three times as fast as that of the United States. It would double its population in 25 years. In Honduras 51% of the population was under 15. Such a situation placed tremendous demands

continued on page 630

Table I. The Ten Largest Nations by Area and by Population*

Rank		Area in sq.mi.	Rank		Population
1	U.S.S.R.	8,649,489	1	China	750,000,000
2	Canada	3,851,809	2	India	524,080,000†
3	China	3,691,501	3	U.S.S.R.	237,808,000†
4	United States	3,615,210‡	4	United States	203,200,000
5	Brazil	3,286,470	5	Pakistan	113,220,000
6	Australia	2,967,877	6	Indonesia	112,311,000†
7	India	1,232,560	7	Japan	101,690,000
8	Argentina	1,072,156	8	Brazil	93,000,000
9	Sudan	967,491	9	Nigeria	64,560,000
10	Algeria	919,590	10	Germany, West	60,463,000

*Based on independent countries, Dec. 31, 1969. Areas are latest official data available; populations are 1969 estimates.
†1968 estimate.
‡Excludes Great Lakes waters and territorial sea, 94,485 sq.mi.

Political Security: *see* Intelligence Operations
Polo: *see* Sporting Record

Table II. Populations and Areas of the Countries of the World

Continent and state	Area in sq.mi.	Population in 000	Persons per sq.mi.
World total	57,889,148	3,568,116	68.1*
AFRICA	11,662,077	390,393	33.5
Algeria	919,590	12,943	14.1
Botswana	220,000	623	2.8
British island dependencies	307	56	—
Burundi	10,759	3,475	350.4
Cameroon	183,591	5,562	30.5
Central African Republic	240,376	1,518	6.8
Chad	495,750	3,500	7.3
Congo (Brazzaville)	134,749	870	6.6
Congo (Kinshasa)	905,559	16,586	18.3
Dahomey	43,483	2,577	59.2
Equatorial Guinea	10,830	286	26.4
Ethiopia	471,776	23,900	50.6
French dependencies	10,688	846	—
Gabon	102,317	480	4.7
Gambia, The	4,361	357	81.9
Ghana	92,100	8,376	90.9
Guinea	94,925	3,795	39.9
Ivory Coast	123,485	4,100	33.2
Kenya	224,960	10,504	46.6
Lesotho	11,716	1,018	86.9
Liberia	43,000	1,130	26.2
Libya	680,000	1,869	2.7
Malagasy Republic	226,657	7,012	30.9
Malawi	45,747	4,285	117.9
Mali	478,652	4,832	10.1
Mauritania	397,683	1,120	2.8
Mauritius	720	795	1,103.8
Morocco	174,471	14,634	83.9
Niger	458,993	3,909	8.5
Nigeria	356,669	64,560	181.0
Portuguese dependencies	800,350	13,706	—
Rhodesia	150,820	5,090	33.7
Rwanda	10,169	3,405	334.8
Senegal	76,124	3,685	48.4
Sierra Leone	27,699	2,475	89.3
Somalia	246,155	3,000	12.2
South Africa	471,445	19,167	40.6
South West Africa (Namibia)	317,827	605	1.9
Spanish dependencies	102,703	48,607	—
Sudan	967,491	14,979	15.3
Swaziland	6,704	409	60.9
Tanzania	362,821	12,926	37.8
Togo	21,900	1,791	81.7
Tunisia	63,170	5,027	80.0
Uganda	91,076	8,133	89.2
United Arab Republic	385,237	32,501	84.4
Upper Volta	105,886	5,226	49.4
Zambia	290,586	4,143	14.6
ANTARCTICA	5,500,000†	0.2	—
Australian dependencies	2,472,000	—	—
British Antarctic Territory‡	650,000	0.1	—
French Southern and Antarctic Lands	157,874	0.1	—
Norwegian dependencies	96§	—	—
Ross Dependency (New Zealand)	160,000	—	—
ASIA (exclusive of U.S.S.R.)	10,646,960	1,965,335	184.6
Afghanistan	252,000	16,516	65.6
Australian dependencies	58	4	—
Bahrain‖	256	216	843.7
Bhutan (Indian protected state)	18,000	1,000	55.5
British dependencies	400	3,988	—
Brunei‖	2,226	116	52.0
Burma	261,789	26,980	103.0
Cambodia	69,898	6,557	93.8
Ceylon	25,332	11,964	478.6
China	3,691,501	750,000	203.1
Cyprus	3,572	622	174.1
India (incl. Kashmir)	1,232,560	524,080	425.2
Indonesia	735,268	112,311	152.7
Iran	636,293	28,166	44.3
Iraq¶	169,284	8,766	51.8
Israel	7,993	2,882	360.1
Japan	145,707	101,690	697.9
Jordan	36,500	2,133	58.7
Korea, North	46,557	13,700	294.3
Korea, South	38,022	31,139	819.0
Kuwait	7,450	532	713.5
Laos	91,400	2,825	31.0
Lebanon	4,015	2,580	642.6
Malaysia	127,581	10,169	79.7
Maldives	115	107	930.2
Mongolia	604,247	1,210	2.0
Muscat and Oman	82,000	750	9.1
Nepal	54,362	10,652	195.9
Pakistan	365,600	113,220	309.6
Philippines	115,830	36,944	318.9
Portuguese dependencies	5,769	880	—
Qatar‖	4,400	100	22.3
Ryukyu Islands (United States)	848	972	1,146.2
Saudi Arabia¶	873,972	7,100	8.1
Sikkim (Indian protected state)	2,744	191	69.6
Singapore	224	2,004	9,149.8
Southern Yemen	112,000	1,369	12.2
Syria	71,498	5,738	80.2
Taiwan	13,885	13,957	100.5
Thailand	198,455	34,738	175.8
Trucial States‖	32,278	133	4.1
Turkey	301,380	34,375	115.4
Vietnam, North	61,293	20,700	337.7
Vietnam, South	67,108	16,259	242.3
Yemen	75,290	5,000	66.4
AUSTRALIA and OCEANIA	3,290,091	19,185	5.8
Australia	2,967,877	12,295	4.1
Australian dependencies	183,145	2,310	—
British dependencies	18,960	714	—
British-French condominium	5,700	80	14.1
French dependencies	8,988	199	—
Nauru	8.2	7	794.6
New Zealand	103,736	2,781	26.8
New Zealand dependencies	192	28	—
Tonga‖	261	79	302.7
United States dependencies	100	181	—
United States-British condominium	27	370	13.7
Western Samoa	1,097	141	129.0
EUROPE (exclusive of U.S.S.R.)	1,904,037	456,574	239.7
Albania	11,100	1,965	177.3
Andorra	175	18	104.2
Austria	32,374	7,349	227.7
Belgium	11,781	9,632	817.6
British dependencies	291	186	—
Bulgaria	42,823	8,301	193.8
Czechoslovakia	49,370	14,418	292.0
Denmark (incl. Faeroe Islands)	17,143	4,911	—
Finland	130,128	4,699	39.8
France	211,209	50,223	239.1
Germany, East	41,766	17,084	409.0
Germany, West (incl. W. Berlin)	95,964	60,463	630.0
Greece	50,944	8,803	172.8
Hungary	35,920	10,275	286.0
Iceland	39,777	202	5.2
Ireland	27,136	2,921	110.1
Italy	116,312	54,090	465.0
Liechtenstein	62	21	342.5
Luxembourg	999	336	336.8
Malta	122	321	2,629.2
Monaco	0.6	24	40,000.0
Netherlands	14,139	12,798	980.5
Norway (incl. Svalbard and Jan Mayen Land)	149,282	3,838	—
Poland	120,481	32,555	270.2
Portugal	35,553	9,496	267.1
Romania	91,700	19,721	215.1
San Marino	24	19	781.6
Spain	194,884	32,411	167.7
Sweden	173,649	7,942	50.0
Switzerland	15,941	6,115	396.6
United Kingdom of Great Britain and Northern Ireland	94,222	55,282	594.0
Vatican City	0.2	0.9	5,029.4
Yugoslavia	98,766	20,154	204.5
NORTH AMERICA	9,351,321	312,985	33.4
Barbados	166	253	1,523.5
British dependencies	14,794	853	—
Canada	3,851,809	21,061	5.5
Costa Rica	19,650	1,615	82.2
Cuba	42,827	7,937	185.3
Dominican Republic	18,720	4,174	223.1
El Salvador	8,100	3,266	403.3
French dependencies	1,203	357	—
Greenland (Danish)	840,000	44	.05
Guatemala	42,042	4,864	115.7
Haiti	10,714	4,674	439.6
Honduras	43,277	2,495	57.6
Jamaica	4,244	1,940	457.0
Mexico	761,601	48,933	64.4
Netherlands Antilles	394	211	535.5
Nicaragua	49,173	1,809	39.6
Panama (excl. Canal Zone)	21,210	1,417	48.5
Trinidad and Tobago	1,980	1,030	520.2
United States	3,615,210	203,200	56.2
United States dependencies	4,206	2,852	—
SOUTH AMERICA	6,885,173	185,836	26.9
Argentina	1,072,156	23,983	22.4
Bolivia	424,162	4,500	10.6
Brazil	3,286,470	93,000	28.5
Chile	292,257	9,566	32.7
Colombia	439,735	19,929	45.1
Ecuador	109,483	5,776	52.8
Falkland Islands (British)	6,198	2	.3
French Guiana	34,700	44	1.3
Guyana	83,000	742	8.9
Paraguay	157,047	2,243	14.3
Peru	496,222	13,172	26.5
Surinam (Netherlands)	63,064	375	5.9
Uruguay	68,536	2,818	41.1
Venezuela	352,143	9,686	27.5
U.S.S.R.	8,649,489	237,808	27.4

Note: A dash (—) indicates none or negligible.

*In computing the world density the area of Antarctica is omitted.

†Estimated area, including some unclaimed territory.

‡Includes some territory claimed by Argentina and Chile.

§Insular dependencies only. Norwegian claims to continental Antarctica are undefined.

‖British protected state.

¶Excluding Iraq-Saudi Arabia neutral zone of 7,000 sq.mi.

Table III. World Census Data

POLITICAL UNIT	Year of census	ENUMERATED POPULATION Total	Male	Percent urban*	AGE DISTRIBUTION 0 to 15	16 to 45	46 and over	ECONOMICALLY ACTIVE Total	Agriculture	Mining and manufacturing
Albania	1960	1,626,315	834,384	30.9	...	...	...	730,800	...	...
Algeria	1966	11,833,126	6,079,900	...	5,947,800	4,387,700	1,744,800	2,335,200	1,300,000	183,500
American Samoa	1960	20,051	10,164	24.5	9,946	7,731	2,374	5,889	2,840	...
Angola	1960	4,830,449†	2,459,015	10.6	2,011,378‡	2,177,631‡	641,440‡	1,421,966	944,716	26,508
Antigua	1960	54,060†	25,230	60.1	23,154	20,964	9,942	16,873	12,564	4,084
Argentina	1960	20,008,945	10,034,544	...	5,772,043§	10,486,674§	3,663,094§	7,599,071	1,460,541	1,959,041
Australia	1966	11,550,462	5,816,359	83.2	3,392,488	4,873,899	3,284,073	4,856,455	...	1,368,468
Austria	1961	7,073,807	3,296,400	50.1	1,660,615	2,729,599	2,683,593	3,369,815	767,604	1,093,046
Bahama Islands	1963	130,220†	63,485	24.0‖	57,452¶	51,924¶	20,844¶	51,948	5,882	...
Bahrain	1965	182,203†	99,384	20.1	83,667	80,589	17,947	50,935	4,348	7,185
Barbados	1960	232,327	105,519	40.3	88,882‡	88,636‡	54,809‡	85,040	22,440	13,468
Belgium	1961	9,189,741	4,496,860	66.4	2,333,846	3,543,729	3,312,166	3,512,463	253,922	1,326,732
Bermuda	1960	42,640	21,233	9.6	14,199	18,179	9,470	19,498	309	322
Botswana	1964	543,105	264,535	...	242,424	204,797	80,198	250,678	227,009	1,800‖
Brazil	1960	70,119,071†	35,010,717	46.3	29,931,481¶	32,976,869¶	7,210,721¶	22,651,263	11,697,798	3,364,232
British Honduras	1960	90,505	44,659	53.7	40,369	34,615	15,521	26,029	8,833	3,329
British Solomon Islands	1959	124,076	65,550	2.3	64,940	43,960	16,140	8,000	3,061	2,508
British Virgin Islands	1960	7,338	3,930	12.1	3,793	2,737	808	2,128	629	107
Brunei	1960	83,877	43,676	43.6	39,109‡	33,059‡	11,709‡	24,830	8,317	5,171
Bulgaria	1965	8,227,866	4,114,167	46.4	2,112,364	3,789,130	2,326,372	4,267,793	1,891,398	1,124,885
Cambodia	1962	5,740,115	2,880,780	16.0	2,513,300‡	2,381,215‡	845,600‡	...	...	...
Canada	1966	20,014,880	10,054,344	73.6	6,591,757‡	8,325,686‡	5,097,437‡	6,458,156	648,910	1,101,553
Canal Zone	1960	42,122†	23,278	31.9	15,204¶	19,888¶	7,030¶	17,085	336	...
Cape Verde Islands	1960	199,661	94,027	23.2	99,023♀	69,816♀	29,358♀	105,570	42,387	1,294
Cayman Islands	1960	8,511†	3,974	41.4	3,020	3,515	1,976	3,132	...	...
Ceylon	1963	10,624,507	5,503,000	18.8	4,616,920	4,408,550	1,564,590	2,542,920	1,272,800δ	258,170
Channel Islands										
Guernsey	1961	47,099	22,718	33.3	11,262‡	17,410‡	18,427‡	...	...	...
Jersey	1961	63,550	30,715	...	12,534	25,643	25,373	30,696	3,259	2,028
Chile	1960	7,374,115	3,612,807	68.2	3,075,036	3,062,143	1,236,936	2,388,667	662,379	519,974
Christmas Island (Australian)	1966	3,381	2,151	...	...	...	...	...	...	...
Colombia	1964	17,484,508	8,614,652	52.8	8,155,529□	7,022,627□	2,306,508□	5,134,059	2,427,059	81,279
Costa Rica	1963	1,336,274†	668,957	34.5	636,665‡	516,395‡	183,214‡	395,273	194,309	46,459
Cyprus	1960	573,566†	281,983	35.9	221,656‡	226,612‡	125,298‡	241,823	93,287	37,718
Czechoslovakia	1961	13,745,577†	6,704,674	47.6	3,960,752	5,370,682	4,414,143	...	...	...
Denmark	1965	4,767,597	2,362,000‖	77.1	1,215,000‖	1,957,000‖	1,596,000‖	2,251,000‖	608,000‖	1,282,000‖
Dominica	1960	59,916	28,167	25.6	26,802‡	21,599‡	11,515‡	22,477	11,693	2,553
Dominican Republic	1960	3,047,070	1,535,820	30.1	1,440,900‡	1,218,440‡	387,730‡	820,710	504,820	58,890
Ecuador	1962	4,476,007	2,236,476	36.0	2,014,505	1,838,160	623,342	1,442,591	800,390	215,617
El Salvador	1961	2,510,984	1,236,728	38.5	1,176,744	1,011,819	322,421	807,092	486,213	104,227
Equatorial Guinea	1960	245,989	132,293	...	...	...	...	...	...	...
Faeroe Islands	1965	37,122	...	...	...	...	...	...	...	...
Falkland Islands	1962	2,172	1,195	49.4	568◇	1,134◇	470◇	930	359	...
Fiji	1966	476,727	242,747	33.4	232,826	190,543	53,112	125,809	656,921	10,451
Finland	1960	4,446,222†	2,142,263	38.4	1,338,991	1,831,849	1,275,382	2,033,268	720,817	444,516
France	1962	46,520,271†	22,595,000	63.0	14,967,160▲	25,654,380▲	5,834,720▲	18,956,380	3,849,700	5,666,460
French Guiana	1961	33,295†	16,288	75.1	12,127¶	14,296¶	6,872¶	11,981	3,273	...
French Polynesia	1962	84,550	43,106	...	45,232	34,591	3,643	25,593	9,484	5,715
French Somaliland	1964	82,100	...	57.4	...	...	...	...	...	...
Gabon	1960–61	444,264†	204,698	16.7	135,574	210,611	98,079	311,959	153, 414	21,512
Gambia, The	1963	315,486	160,849	8.8	118,586‡	155,834‡	41,066‡	160,000‖	135,000‖	2,500‖
Germany, East	1964	17,011,931†	7,751,862	72.9	4,262,941	6,338,075	6,410,915	7,657,786	1,267,257	3,140,721
Germany, West	1961	56,174,826†	26,413,362	77.8	12,184,784	22,935,570	21,054,478	26,527,328	3,587,000	12,908,000
Ghana	1960	6,726,815	3,400,270	23.1	2,996,506‡	2,894,238‡	836,071‡	2,723,026	1,581,331	282,168
Gibraltar	1961	21,785†	10,436	100.0	5,456	9,336	6,993	9,292	...	783
Gilbert and Ellice Islands	1963	48,780	23,927	5.4	22,521	18,192	8,067	11,884	8,272	902
Greece	1961	8,388,553	4,091,894	43.3	2,392,514	3,710,437	2,285,602	3,638,601	1,960,446	510,087
Greenland	1965	39,600	20,354	...	19,091	15,752	4,757	13,248	3,651	300
Grenada	1960	88,677	40,660	8.2	42,268‡	30,472‡	15,937‡	15,219	10,895	2,657
Guadeloupe	1961	283,222†	138,435	38.8	119,950‡	110,508‡	52,764‡	97,494	46,959	12,311
Guam	1960	67,044	39,211	...	28,014	31,709	7,321	26,304	411	535
Guatemala	1964	4,287,328	2,174,077	33.5	2,032,540	1,680,180	574,608	1,362,944	861,140	151,180
Guyana	1960	560,330	279,128	15.5	259,228‡	215,228‡	85,874‡	174,730	59,790	32,371
Honduras	1961	1,884,765	939,029	23.2	940,827	730,153	213,785	567,988	379,125	45,779
Hong Kong	1966	3,716,400	1,880,870	86.9	1,571,440	1,493,630	643,850	1,454,730	27,970	557,300
Hungary	1961	9,961,044	4,804,043	39.7	2,691,036	4,096,392	3,173,616	5,312,831	1,872,730	1,378,987
Iceland	1966	196,933	...	...	...	...	...	...	...	...
India	1961	439,234,771†	226,293,201	18.0	188,500,020	192,142,333	58,294,565	188,675,500	131,142,816	18,561,671
Indonesia	1961	96,318,829	47,493,854	14.8	40,544,678	42,458,049	13,316,102	34,578,234	23,516,197	1,943,546
Iran	1966	25,078,923	12,981,665	38.1	11,639,200✦	9,861,700✦	3,642,800✦	7,584,085	3,168,515	1,293,912
Iraq	1965	8,261,527	4,205,201	44.1	...	...	...	...	...	...
Ireland	1966	2,884,002	1,449,032	49.2	...	...	...	1,106,000	330,000δ	277,000
Isle of Man	1966	50,423	23,226	56.0	10,385	16,450	23,588	13,837	1,829	...
Israel	1961	2,179,491†	1,106,069	77.9	786,196‡	869,045‡	524,250‡	751,230	96,420	168,895
Italy	1961	50,623,569†	24,791,683	47.7	11,549,626□	22,903,305□	16,170,638□	20,096,693	5,657,446	7,886,181⊕
Jamaica	1960	1,609,814†	773,439	32.0	662,508‡	646,281‡	301,025‡	677,003	229,718	94,172
Japan	1965	98,274,961†	48,244,445	68.9	27,390,062	48,894,840	21,990,059	48,268,767	10,866,693	12,018,479
Jordan	1961	1,706,226	867,597	47.4	815,910**	638,732**	251,584**	389,978	137,757	41,932
Kenya	1962	8,636,263	4,276,963	7.8	3,975,500‡	3,530,300‡	1,130,400‡	...	...	...
Korea, South	1966	29,207,856	14,700,966	33.5	12,851,456‡	11,975,220‡	4,381,178‡	9,325,000	4,826,000	940,000
Kuwait	1965	467,339	286,312	71.0	184,967	247,905	34,467	179,284	1,983	31,925
Lesotho	1966	969,634	465,784	...	370,390‡	306,208‡	172,756‡	...	...	...
Liberia	1962	1,016,443	503,588	19.7	394,509	471,553	150,381	411,794	298,404	22,913
Libya	1964	1,564,369†	813,386	...	683,431‡	630,379‡	249,160‡	405,258	146,709δ	43,636
Liechtenstein	1960	16,628	8,130	...	4,792	6,267	5,569	7,575	962	3,273
Luxembourg	1966	334,790	164,575	...	75,450‡	138,781‡	120,559‡	164,575	14,554	45,864
Macao	1960	169,299†	83,897	95.2	68,556	60,472	40,271	37,905	1,717	22,000††
Malaysia										
West Malaysia	1957	6,278,758	3,237,579	26.5	2,752,208‡	2,576,252‡	950,298‡	2,164,861	468,317	58,499
East Malaysia	1960	1,198,950	612,462	15.0‖	197,826‡	199,091‡	57,504‡	470,911	381,941	7,451
Maldive Islands	1965	97,743	51,964	...	49,124▲	48,619▲		...	...	...
Malta	1967	318,806	150,467	...	100,671	134,601	82,833	94,303	...	...

Table III. World Census Data *(Continued)*

POLITICAL UNIT	Year of census	ENUMERATED POPULATION Total	Male	Percent urban*	AGE DISTRIBUTION 0 to 15	16 to 45	46 and over	ECONOMICALLY ACTIVE Total	Agriculture	Mining and manufacturing
Martinique	1961	290,679†	140,011	29.1	122,340‡	112,124‡	56,215‡	100,000‖	33,000‖	...
Mauritius	1962	681,619	342,306	34.2	323,007	258,285	100,327	187,401	70,866	27,560
Mexico	1960	34,923,129	17,415,320	50.7	16,205,849	13,999,075	4,718,205	11,332,016	6,144,930	2,147,963
Monaco	1961	22,297	9,933	...	2,742‡‡	14,962‡‡	4,570‡‡	10,580	9	1,700
Mongolia	1963	1,018,800†	508,800	39.5	411,300	378,100	227,700	483,400	279,200	41,900
Montserrat	1960	12,167†	5,407	16.0	5,198	3,946	3,023	4,282	1,881	...
Morocco	1960	11,626,232†	5,809,172	29.3	5,307,824	4,738,350	1,580,058	3,290,950	1,721,000‖	...
Mozambique	1960	6,578,604†	3,149,270	...	...	...	...	...	...	...
Nauru	1966	6,048	3,696	...	...	...	...	...	...	...
Nepal	1961	9,387,661	4,619,973	2.8	3,684,000‖	4,258,000‖	1,445,000‖	...	...	...
Netherlands	1960	11,461,964†	5,706,874	55.4	3,516,623‡‡	6,952,166‡‡	993,175‡‡	4,168,626	446,695	1,306,480
Netherlands Antilles	1960	192,538†	94,811	...	79,683‡	77,069‡	35,786‡	59,806	1,029	16,059
New Caledonia	1963	86,519	45,640	43.1	41,657▲	39,878▲	4,984▲	30,471	11,213	4,906
New Guinea, Territory of	1966	1,578,650	821,899	47.3	694,633	700,669	183,348	889,287	818,739	9,023
New Zealand	1966	2,676,919	1,343,858	62.4	...	...	...	...	...	...
Nicaragua	1963	1,535,588	757,922	40.9	740,729	603,072	191,787	474,960	283,106	59,644
Nigeria	1963	55,670,046	28,112,118	16.1	25,514,354	25,980,055	4,175,637	18,267,669	10,209,122	2,205,476
Norway	1960	3,591,234†	1,789,406	32.1	989,927	1,396,484	1,204,823	1,406,358	188,431	367,296
Pakistan⁺	1961	93,831,982†	49,308,645	13.1	40,178,518	36,322,838	13,781,318	30,205,981	22,441,788	...
Panama	1960	1,075,541	545,774	41.5	491,102	435,207	149,232	336,969	155,690	25,964
Papua	1966	606,336	318,460	87.7	274,873	270,698	60,765	312,748	269,076	4,375
Paraguay	1962	1,816,890	895,551	36.1	866,052	684,563	266,275	596,555	312,647	91,077
Peru	1961	10,420,351§§	4,925,518	47.4	4,290,084¶	4,143,473¶	1,468,200¶	3,124,579	1,555,560	477,393
Philippines	1960	27,087,685†	13,662,869	29.9	12,377,240□	11,310,181□	3,400,264□	10,692,000‖	5,768,000‖	1,120,000‖
Poland⁺	1960	29,775,508	14,404,218	47.7	9,935,779‡	11,871,906‡	7,598,044‡	13,907,442	6,636,632δ	3,237,814
Portugal	1960	8,889,392†	4,254,373	22.6	2,757,895	3,792,171	2,339,326	3,316,472	1,393,624	717,117
Portuguese Guinea	1960	521,336	260,650	...	...	...	...	...	...	...
Portuguese Timor	1960	517,079	267,783	...	...	...	...	...	...	...
Puerto Rico	1960	2,349,544	1,386,968	44.2	1,058,750	863,849	426,945	551,688	135,100	95,504
Réunion	1961	349,282	170,046	...	155,803‡	137,625‡	52,832‡	88,340	38,195	50,145
Rhodesia	1961–62	3,857,470	1,984,050	21.6	1,866,850	1,990,620		713,640	247,030	147,710
Romania	1966	19,105,056	9,356,715	38.2	...	...	...	...	...	...
Rwanda	1965	3,744,723†	1,493,963	...	1,397,928□	1,235,648□	487,147□	1,136,378	...	...
Ryukyu Islands	1960	883,122†	422,843	...	367,553‡	355,641‡	159,799‡	356,249	152,041	20,474
St. Helena	1966	4,649	2,233	...	1,944¶	1,501¶	1,204¶	1,562	...	...
St. Kitts-Nevis and Anguilla	1960	56,693†	26,149	32.9	25,920	19,378	11,395	32,023	8,565	2,078
St. Lucia	1960	86,108	40,693	24.9	38,109	33,122	14,877	28,544	15,144	3,485
St. Vincent	1960	79,948	37,561	...	39,305‡	28,267‡	12,376‡	23,310	9,954	2,868
São Tomé and Príncipe	1960	63,485†	35,259	...	...	...	...	...	...	...
Seychelles	1960	41,425	20,289	25.4	15,934	16,491	9,000	17,665	5,910	2,151
Sierra Leone	1963	2,180,355	1,081,123	...	800,404‡	1,016,240‡	363,711‡	...	682,588	88,846
Sikkim	1961	162,189	85,285	4.2	68,019	73,748	20,422	2,728	249	64
South Africa	1960	16,002,797	8,043,493	46.7	6,418,492‡	6,945,380‡	2,638,925‡	5,696,060	1,700,958	1,285,113
South West Africa	1960	526,004	265,312	21.9	217,541	227,238	81,225	203,271	118,996	18,647
Spain	1960	30,430,698	14,763,388	42.5	8,365,000	13,506,800	8,652,900	11,634,214	4,803,316	2,749,419
Spanish Sahara	1960	23,793	13,070	...	...	...	...	...	...	...
Surinam⁺	1964	324,211	161,855	40.1	147,927‡⁺	122,897‡⁺	46,668‡⁺	80,199§§	19,922§§	12,713§§
Swaziland	1966	374,571	178,795	12.5	174,455	145,618	54,498	121,063	85,103	23,480
Sweden	1960	7,495,316†	3,738,881	72.8	1,648,906‡	3,035,606‡	2,810,804‡	3,244,084	446,952	1,167,877
Switzerland	1960	5,429,061†	2,663,432	42.0	1,361,210	2,302,312	1,765,539	2,512,411	280,191	1,006,038
Syria	1960	4,565,121	2,344,224	41.9	2,014,509	1,656,452	680,094	1,016,347	518,933	128,954
Taiwan	1966	13,512,143	7,159,850	...	...	...	...	...	...	...
Tanzania	1967	12,231,342	5,969,107	53.8	...	...	...	...	...	...
Thailand	1960	26,257,916	13,154,149	12.5	11,023,535	10,949,932	3,484,393	13,836,984	11,334,382	500,595
Togo	1958–60	1,439,772	689,556	9.6	695,411	558,839	185,550	566,868	452,889	...
Tonga	1966	77,429	39,157	...	...	...	...	...	...	...
Trinidad and Tobago	1960	827,957	411,580	17.0	351,050‡	336,730‡	140,177‡	262,570	52,528	53,617
Trust Territory of the Pacific	1960	75,836†	38,721	...	33,332	27,139	15,092	...	...	...
Tunisia	1966	4,533,351	2,314,419	40.1	2,191,088	1,678,465	663,798	1,093,735	448,296	103,582
Turkey	1965	31,391,207	15,945,768	...	13,844,128	12,775,996	4,771,083	13,591,822	9,764,652	1,025,022
Turks and Caicos Islands	1960	5,668†	2,667	...	2,557	1,975	1,136	2,034	393	...
Uganda	1959	6,536,616	3,283,230	4.8	2,846,000	2,796,000	895,000	...	...	...
Union of Soviet Socialist Republics	1959	208,826,650	94,050,303	47.9	63,495,768**	94,205,904**	51,116,616**	99,130,212	38,425,967	36,575,187
United Arab Republic	1966	30,053,861	15,168,000	40.5	...	...	...	...	...	...
United Kingdom	1961	52,708,934	25,480,791	79.0	12,335,703‡	20,784,033‡	19,589,198‡	23,616,620	865,129	6,975,166
United States	1960	179,323,175	88,331,494	69.9	55,786,173‡	70,919,666‡	52,617,336‡	64,639,252	4,256,734	18,167,092
Uruguay	1963	2,592,563	1,289,454	...	721,500‡	1,143,600‡	727,500‡	1,015,500	181,800	213,600
Venezuela	1961	7,523,999§§	3,823,569	62.5	3,538,949	3,022,725	962,325	2,406,725	773,650	1,633,075
Vietnam, North	1960	15,916,955	7,687,814	9.5	7,055,544⦀	7,556,129⦀	1,305,282⦀	8,119,286	6,377,024	537,761
Virgin Islands of the United States	1960	32,099	15,930	57.9	12,768‡	12,510‡	6,821‡	10,845	610	894
Western Samoa	1966	131,379	67,809	19.2	...	...	...	...	...	...
Yugoslavia	1961	18,549,291†	9,043,424	28.8	5,770,817‡	8,168,259‡	4,610,215‡	8,340,400	4,674,856	1,137,848
Zambia	1961–63	3,493,590	1,734,860	21.3	1,492,150	3,092,400	401,190	693,000	220,000	72,000
DEMOGRAPHIC AND/OR SAMPLE SURVEYS										
Burundi	1962	2,319,540	1,104,266	...	...	...	...	...	...	...
Central African Republic	1959–60	1,177,000	577,000	6.8	429,000‡	661,000‡	81,000‡	610,000	461,000	52,000
Chad	1964	3,254,000	1,567,000	7.8	...	...	...	950,000	600,000	60,000
Congo (Brazzaville)	1960–61	794,400†	...	...	...	...	...	...	...	...
Cuba	1965	7,630,700	2,895,155	53.0	2,808,190¶¶	4,009,110¶¶	813,400¶¶	2,546,000	838,000	390,000
Dahomey	1961	2,106,000	...	...	...	...	...	...	...	...
Malagasy	1966	6,200,000	3,049,000	...	2,882,000‡	2,326,000‡	992,000‡	2,733,000	2,396,000	337,000
Malawi	1963	3,753,000†	...	...	...	...	...	...	...	...
Mali	1960–61	4,100,000	...	...	1,763,000	2,127,900	209,100	...	...	...
Niger	1959–60	2,556,211	...	...	...	...	...	1,506,490	703,610	4,510
Senegal	1960–61	3,109,840†	1,531,760	23.7	1,320,680	1,641,420	147,720	1,317,580	1,087,020	73,800
Upper Volta	1960–61	4,400,000	2,208,800	4.6	1,830,400	1,892,000	677,600	2,627,000	1,300,000	...

Note: Data reflect results of enumerations conducted 1957 to 1967, as available.

*That population defined as urban by the political unit.

†De jure population.

‡0–14, 15–44, 45 and over.

§0–13, 14–49, 50 and over.

‖Estimate.

¶0–14, 15–49, 50 and over.

♀0–19, 20–49, 50 and over.

δIncludes forestry, hunting, and fishing.

□0–14, 15–45, 46 and over.

°0–15, 16–49, 50 and over.

▲0–19, 20–64, 65 and over.

⁺Age distribution excludes unknown. Iran 474,322; Pakistan 3,437,939; Poland 369,779; Surinam 6,719.

⊕Includes public utilities and construction.

**0–15, 16–44, 45 and over.

††Includes transportation.

‡‡0–14, 15–64, 65 and over.

§§Excludes Amerindian.

⦀0–15, 16–55, 56 and over.

¶¶0–14, 15–54, 55 and over.

continued from page 626

on a society to build schools and health centres, which many less developed nations could not afford.

There were few signs of changes in this trend. Of the 331,000 births in the world each day, 51,000 occurred in the industrialized nations, and five times as many occurred in the "have not," less developed nations.

The pressure of population growth had become so extreme that, increasingly, world leaders were coming to view the relentless addition of huge numbers of people, particularly in the poorer countries, as a threat to security, to the economy, to resources, and to the future of mankind. Robert McNamara, president of the World Bank and a strong advocate of population policy, said: "The misery of the underdeveloped world is today a dynamic misery continuously broadened and deepened by a population growth that is unprecedented in history." He noted that the severely overtaxed economies of nations with low economic productivity were finding "capital projects overwhelmed by a tidal wave of population."

In his special message on population growth, sent to Congress July 18, U.S. Pres. Richard M. Nixon commented on the domestic pressures in this way: "I believe that many of our present social problems may be related to the fact that we have had only 50 years in which to accommodate the second hundred million Americans. In fact, since 1945 alone some 90 million babies have been born in this country. We have thus had to accomplish in a very few decades an adjustment to population growth which was once spread over centuries. And it now appears that we will have to provide for a third hundred million Americans in a period of just 30 years."

Nixon suggested preparing cities, education, and employment to meet the population challenge. He also raised the question of natural resources. In this sense he gave official sanction to continuing the dialogue on population policy. As of 1969, however, the U.S. government was spending $30 million on domestic population programs.

Alarm over world population increase stemmed from the recognition that most of the increase had occurred in the last 200 years. It required 600,000 years for world population to pass the one billion mark, around 1800. The next billion was added in 130 years, around 1930. In 1975, a span of only 45 years, the world would be inhabited by four billion people.

In the United States concern focused mostly on the quality of life. It was related to items discussed by President Nixon, as well as to conservation, pollution, and poverty. Compared with the less developed nations, population growth in the U.S. was slow, following a trend that had emerged in the 1950s. The birthrate declined from the high of colonial days, estimated to be around 50–60, to a low in the depression of the 1930s. The baby boom after World War II forced a rise in the birthrate, but this had continued to decline in the decade preceding 1969. In 1969 the U.S. birthrate dipped to 17.4. The death rate remained steady at 9.6, and the rate of growth remained at 1% annually, the same as that of the U.S.S.R. In effect it would require 70 years for the United States to double its present 203.2 million people. The country had increased by 23.2 million persons from the 1960 census figure of 180 million. This was an increase of 12.9%. The black population constituted 22.7 million persons, an increase of 20.5% in nine years.

Approximately 57% of the U.S. population lived in the 100 largest metropolitan areas, led by New York (including northern New Jersey) with 15,950,000 persons. In second place was Los Angeles with 7.17 million, followed by Chicago with 6.97 million. There were 28 metropolitan areas in the U.S. that claimed in excess of one million residents.

In ranking the states, California was first with an estimated 19.4 million persons, New York second with 18.3 million, and Pennsylvania third with 11.8 million. Nevada was the nation's fastest growing state, increasing its population by 60.2% from 1960 to 1969 to 457,000 persons. (W. Ei.)

The accompanying table of World Census Data reflects the principal results of population censuses held between 1959 and 1967. In the case of political units holding more than one enumeration during that period, the latest available data have been included.

See also **Food; Heads of State; Migration, International; Vital Statistics;** articles on individual political units.

Portugal

A unitary corporative republic of southwestern Europe, Portugal shares the Iberian Peninsula with Spain. Area: 35,553 sq.mi. (92,082 sq.km.), including the Azores (893 sq.mi.) and Madeira (308 sq.mi.). Pop. (1968 est.): 9,496,800. Cap. and largest city: Lisbon (pop., 1968 est., 828,000). Language: Portuguese. Religion: Roman Catholic. Portugal has seven overseas provinces (*see* Dependent States). President in 1969, Rear Adm. Américo Deus Rodrigues Tomás; premier, Marcello José das Neves Alves Caetano.

During 1969 Portugal enjoyed political stability and made some economic progress. The new premier, Marcello José das Neves Alves Caetano (*see* Biography), who took office in September 1968 following the illness of António Salazar, succeeded in introducing political reforms that led to some liberalization. He showed a more outgoing style of leadership than his predecessor and established a popular image, especially by making speeches on television; he visited Angola, Mozambique, and Portuguese Guinea in April (the first time that a Portuguese premier had done so), and later the United States and Brazil. He sponsored measures to liberalize press censorship; reform the leadership of trade unions and professional societies; abolish the secret police; allow prominent exiles to return to Portugal; reform the electoral law; and allow the opposition more freedom of expression.

The official party, the National Union, was reorganized, and many officials and parliamentary representatives were replaced; Caetano appointed several young technocrats including João Augusto Dias Rosas as minister of finance and economy and Xavier Pintado as minister of commerce. He succeeded in maintaining the support of business and military circles and of prominent Salazar appointees in the Cabinet, including the minister of the interior, António Manuel Gonçalves Rapazote.

The political scene during the year was dominated by the elections for 130 deputies in the National Assembly, held on October 26; during the following session deputies would enjoy power to change the constitution, an opportunity that occurred only once in ten years. The National Union won all the seats, as it had in elections during the preceding 50 years. The campaign, which began on September 27, was lively; opposition groups of socialists and Catholics were granted equal opportunities to campaign, but they were not allowed to function as political parties. The elections, however, were closely supervised.

The opposition groups that contested the election did not withdraw at the last moment as they had in previous years; their campaign, however, did not attract much public support except in large cities. Only 60% of the 1.8 million registered electors voted. There were several instances of violence during the campaign; armed attacks were made on the headquarters of opposition groups and their workers were assaulted. The most important innovation in the campaign was that for the first time public debate was allowed on Portuguese policy toward the overseas provinces; the opposition made the independence of these provinces the central issue of their platform. Caetano urged support for the government's policy of "continuity and evolution," but stated that there would be no departure from existing policy toward the overseas territories.

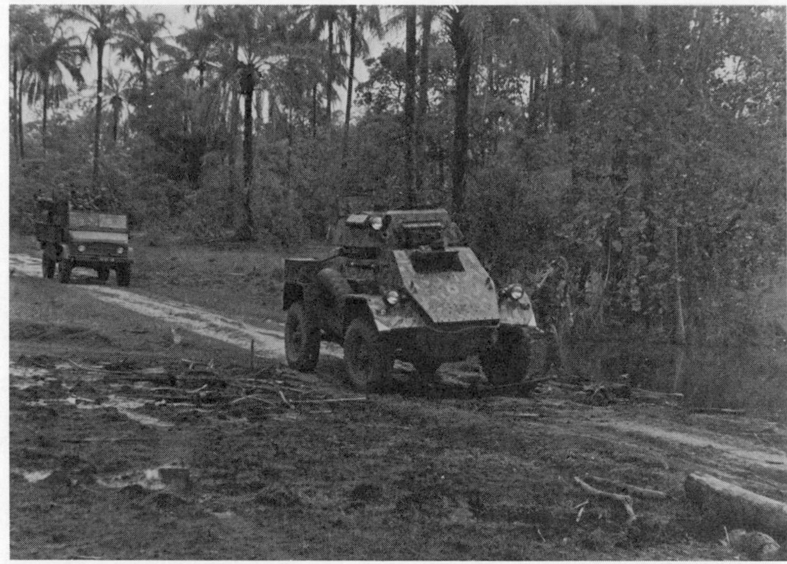

"LONDON DAILY EXPRESS" FROM PICTORIAL PARADE

Portuguese Army unit patrols road near Bafata, Guinea. An estimated 7,000 guerrillas continued attacks from neighbouring republics in an attempt to free Guinea from Portuguese rule.

The resignation of the minister of foreign affairs, Alberto Franco Nogueira, on October 4, brought into the open a conflict within the National Union between hard line Salazaristas and pro-Caetano moderates. No official reason was given for the resignation, and Caetano assumed responsibility for the portfolio. Nogueira had been foreign minister since 1961 and was well known as a strong advocate of Portugal's policy toward the overseas territories. He was elected to a seat in the National Assembly and was expected to assume the leadership of a pro-Salazarista bloc.

The most important political event in the overseas provinces was the assassination in February of the leader of the Mozambique Liberation Front (FRELIMO), Eduardo Mondlane (*see* OBITUARIES). Mondlane was a leader equally acceptable to Western and Communist countries, and was regarded as the unifying force behind the movement. There were contradictory reports that his assassination had been organized by the Portuguese secret police or by his rivals within FRELIMO. His death was a windfall to the Portuguese, and the military threat from the guerrillas in northern Mozambique declined perceptibly during the year. Further progress was made in containing the guerrilla threat in Angola, though the military situation in Guinea continued to be precarious. Portugal had some 122,000 troops engaged in security operations in its African territories, and was devoting 40% of its annual budget to defense.

The Portuguese Ministry of Foreign Affairs asked the U.S. in August for payment for the use of the military air base at Lajes, on the island of Terceira in the Azores. A note was also sent to the U.S. administration requesting talks on the renegotiation of the 1962 agreement for the base. Previously Portugal had refused to renew the agreement, mainly because Salazar had been displeased with the lack of U.S. support for Portuguese policy toward the overseas provinces.

The government continued to pursue highly cautious financial and economic policies aimed at maintaining a balanced budget and a strong external payments position. Steps were taken, however, to extend the terms and scope of medium-term credits granted by banks and other financial institutions; this alleviated the chronic shortage of investment funds at the disposal of many Portuguese firms. The establishment

PORTUGAL

Education. (1966–67) Primary, pupils 891,082, teachers 27,666; secondary, pupils 162,561, teachers 7,266; vocational, pupils 167,652, teachers 8,789; teacher training, students 2,867, teachers 323; higher (including 4 universities), students 36,332, teaching staff 2,158.

Finance. Monetary unit: escudo, with a par value of 28.75 escudos to U.S. $1 (69 escudos = £1 sterling). Gold and foreign exchange, official: (April 1969) U.S. $1,326,000,000; (April 1968) U.S. $1,197,000,000. Budget (1969 est.): revenue 20 billion escudos; expenditure 25.3 billion escudos. Gross national product: (1967) 132.8 billion escudos; (1966) 117.8 billion escudos. Money supply: (April 1969) 80,950,000,000 escudos; (April 1968) 73.8 billion escudos. Cost of living (Lisbon; 1963 = 100): (June 1969) 134; (June 1968) 124.

Foreign Trade. (1968) Imports 29,880,000,000 escudos; exports 21,051,000,000 escudos. Import sources: West Germany 16%; U.K. 13%; Angola 9%; France 7%; U.S. 6%; Italy 6%; Mozambique 6%. Export destinations: U.K. 20%; Angola 14%; U.S. 11%; Mozambique 9%; West Germany 6%; Sweden 5%; France 5%. Main exports: textile yarns and fabrics 28%; wine 7%; cork 6%; fish 5%. Tourism (1967): visitors 2,516,700; gross receipts U.S. $269 million.

Transport and Communications. Roads: continent (1967) 29,440 km.; islands (1961) 2,058 km. Motor vehicles in use (1967): passenger 316,000; commercial (including buses) 92,500. Railways: (continent; 1967) 3,591 km.; traffic (1968) 3,309,000,000 passenger-km., freight 976 million net ton-km. Air traffic (1967): 1,160,207,000 passenger-km.; freight 18,827,000 net ton-km. Shipping (1968): merchant vessels 100 gross tons and over 348; gross tonnage 771,643. Telephones (Dec. 1967) 615,965. Radio receivers (Dec. 1967) 1,345,000. Television receivers (Dec. 1967) 271,000.

Agriculture. Production (in 000; metric tons; 1968; 1967 in parentheses): wheat 797 (637); barley 95 (73); oats 143 (112); rye 197 (175); corn 529 (577); rice 153 (146); potatoes 1,041 (1,296); dry broad beans 35 (32); other dry beans 47 (55); chickpeas (1967) 35, (1966) 23; wine 1,090 (974); figs (1967) *c.* 365, (1966) *c.* 365; oranges 117 (140); olive oil 63 (81); apples (1966) 86, (1965) *c.* 90; pears (1966) 43, (1965) *c.* 55; meat (1967) 176, (1966) 178; timber (cu.m.; 1967) 5,900, (1966) 6,100; fish catch (1966) 506, (1965) 554. Livestock (in 000; 1966–67): cattle *c.* 1,100; sheep *c.* 5,790; pigs *c.* 1,724; horses *c.* 77; mules *c.* 140; asses *c.* 212; goats *c.* 600; chickens *c.* 8,100.

Industry. Fuel and power (in 000; metric tons; 1968): coal 397; lignite 31; electricity (kw-hr.) 6,200,000; manufactured gas (Lisbon only; cu.m.) 98,000. Production (in 000; metric tons; 1968): iron ore (50% metal content) 204; sulfur (1967) 239; cement 1,862; tin concentrates (metal content) 0.6; manganese ore (metal content; 1967) 3.6; tungsten concentrates (oxide content; 1967) 1.4; gold (troy oz.; 1967) 27; cotton yarn 74; woven cotton fabrics 45; preserved sardines (1967) 49; cork products (1967) 324.

in October of a state-backed company to supervise foreign investment projects confirmed that the government was seeking to increase foreign investment and its ties with Europe. The economies of the overseas provinces continued to expand; iron ore and petroleum production increased in Angola, and in Mozambique work was in progress on the large Cahorabassa hydroelectric scheme. (Rn. C.)

See also Dependent States.

Postal Services

With the admission of Qatar, Bhutan, Nauru, and Mauritius to the Universal Postal Union (UPU) in 1969, the number of member countries rose to 141. At its annual meeting in Bern, Switz., the executive council examined various matters connected with international cooperation to be discussed at the Universal Postal Congress, held at Tokyo from October 1 to November 14. During the congress the UPU expelled South Africa from its session because of its apartheid policies. A further proposal to remove South Africa from the union failed to achieve the required two-thirds majority. The problems of younger member states were again in the forefront of UPU discussions, and participation in the UN Development Program (UNDP) again increased. Aid allocations for 1968–69 to the UPU for the program within the UNDP totaled $1,037,975. Voluntary contributions to the UPU special fund, begun in 1967, amounted to $60,000.

In New Zealand, Post Office revenue increased from NZ$109 million in 1968 to NZ$115 million in 1969 and net profit for the year ended March 31, 1969, amounted to NZ$6.2 million. Increased traffic was recorded in all sectors of Post Office business; notable increases occurred in telephone installations, overseas toll calls, general mail, and vehicle licenses. In the June budget the minister of finance announced that eight-year-term National Development Bonds were to be issued. Incentive Savings Bonds would also be introduced with automatic random selection of prizewinners. In July the government announced that a consultant survey of the organizational structure of the Post Office would begin in August. With the bringing into service of the international exchange in Auckland, telephone subscribers were able to establish direct calls with subscribers on automatic exchanges in the U.K., the U.S., Australia, Canada, and the Far East. A satellite receiving station—to be erected north of Auckland—was planned to become operational toward the end of 1970.

The French postal services dealt with more than 10,000,000,000 items of correspondence in 1969. The amount handled daily exceeded 34 million, continuing a steady rise in business. A revised system of classification of mail was introduced following a revision of postal tariffs in January. This was aimed at regulating Post Office activity by achieving a more equal balance between urgent letter post (handled at night) and less urgent parcel and printed-matter post (handled by day). Following the changes the proportion of nonurgent mail increased from 15 to 30% and a better round-the-clock use of installations and plant was achieved. Modernization of post offices, stamp machines, and mail-handling equipment in sorting offices continued. The replacement of DC-3 aircraft in the postal air fleet by Fokker aircraft was completed and the remaining DC-4s were scheduled for replacement. More motorized rounds were introduced with an additional 1,000 urban rounds and 400 rural rounds.

During 1968 the West German Post Office handled about 9,800,000,000 letter items and 300 million parcels; 5,600,000,000 local telephone calls and 2.6 billion trunk calls were made; and 18 million telegrams were dealt with. At the end of 1968 the number of television broadcasting licenses issued totaled 19 million. Total revenues for 1968 rose to DM. 12,433,-600,000 and profit for the year amounted to DM. 505 million. In telephony the subscriber trunk dialing service accounted for 99.3% of inland traffic and 88.7% of traffic with foreign countries (934,321 new main stations were installed in 1968). In 1968 rationalization efforts based on profitability calculations, which had made the West German Post Office the largest user of commercial electronic data-processing systems in Europe, led to the elimination of 4,789 jobs; following the extension of the subscriber trunk dialing service, from which only 4 out of 500 group centres were excluded, 18 manual trunk exchanges were closed in 1968.

In Italy a two-day strike of postmen caused stacks of unsorted mail to pile up in May and some 70,000 telegrams to be undelivered in the Rome area. The government assigned an additional $8,160,000 to the Ministry of Posts and Telecommunications to pay overtime to postmen for the rest of the year; $1,680,-000 was earmarked for overtime payments to clear the backlog of mail. The postal workers claimed that they were working in conditions of extreme discomfort and further strikes in October again brought postal services to a halt.

In Pakistan the expansion of postal services, especially in rural areas, continued according to the national development plan. In 1969 the opening of 5,000 new post offices (457 in rural areas) brought the total to 13,536. The policy of establishing closer postal relations with other countries was extended and inland postage rates were applied for surface mails to and from Kuwait and Syria. Similar arrangements already existed with Ceylon, India, Indonesia, Iran, Iraq, Lebanon, Jordan, Nepal, Saudi Arabia, Turkey, and the U.A.R. The exchange of mail between East and West Pakistan was speeded up by utilizing all the available sailings. Good progress continued to be made with mechanization of mail handling. Emphasis was placed on the construction of new office buildings and residential accommodation for staff. New ventures for the Post Office in 1969 included the provision of group life insurance cover to government employees and the taking over of responsibility from the inland revenue authorities for the issuance of gun licenses and driving licenses and the collection of vehicle taxes.

In Sweden, where it was estimated that only 5% of letters did not arrive in time for the morning delivery, the Post Office abolished the second daily delivery throughout the country and the third delivery in central Stockholm. The five-digit postal code system, introduced in 1968, was reported to be used on 80% of all letters. Data-processing systems enabled the Swedish Post Office to offer a computerized banking and accounting service, as well as a new service to landlords for the payment of rents and auditing.

In the United Kingdom the total correspondence posted during 1968–69 was 11,300,000,000 items, a drop of 200 million from 1967–68. The number of parcels handled fell to 212.3 million from 216.6 million in the previous year. The postal service incurred

Portuguese Overseas Provinces:
see Dependent States

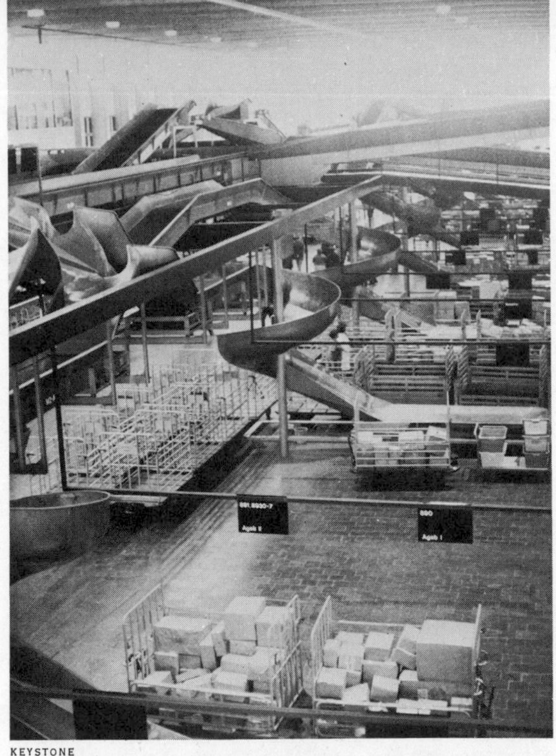

KEYSTONE

New Munich post office equipped to handle 420,000 parcels daily was opened in 1969. The complete operation covers an area seven times the size of a soccer field.

a loss of £5.8 million. Although revenue increased by £17.9 million to a total of £377.8 million, expenditure rose by £27.7 million, mainly as a result of pay increases (£14 million) and higher prices for goods and services (£5 million). In March it was reported that the first class (*5d.*) mail had gained its aimed-for share of 32% of the two-tier system, and that 94% was reaching its destination the day after posting. By the end of March the two-tier service showed a profit of some £3.5 million. The fast developing telecommunications services showed a surplus of £50 million in 1968–69.

Efforts to improve productivity were maintained. A new management and control system and a computerized routing system were both undergoing trials. Mechanized sorting centres for the parcel post continued to be developed and a new-style pilot scheme was in preparation. Subscriber trunk dialing extended to over 80% of subscribers and the coding of addresses covered a third of the country. The National Data-Processing Service was increasing its computer centres from three to five in an attempt to capture a significant share of the computer bureau market.

On October 1 the Post Office, which had been a government department since the inauguration of a public postal service in 1657, became a public corporation. The office of postmaster general was abolished, and the Ministry of Posts and Telecommunications was established with responsibility for both the Post Office and public broadcasting. The reformed Post Office was headed by an executive board under the chairmanship of Lord Hall, a leading industrialist. The Post Office Savings Bank became the National Savings Bank and was transferred to Treasury control. A more flexible form of control with greater commercial freedom for the management was considered appropriate for the rapidly developing enterprises of the Post Office.

In the U.S.S.R. the postal service was estimated to handle about 40% of the country's communications; over 50 million people used the service daily. In 1969 the Post Office delivered over 7,000,000,000 letters and 330 million telegrams. Upward of 600 million money orders and pensions were delivered. In addition 160 million parcels and over 30,000,000,000 newspapers and magazines were handled. To cope with the steady increase in the volume of business the Ministry of Communications opened 2,000 additional post offices in 1968 and the first half of 1969, bringing the total number to over 78,000. The distance covered by postal routes was over 3 million km. and in 1968 air freight alone carried some 350,000 tons of mail and printed matter. The emphasis on automation increased. Complete mechanization of mail handling was being introduced in the larger post offices, and priority was being given to automatic loaders and conveyor systems. To deal with the complete automation of mail processing, an automated system that would process letters with a standard six-digit code was under development. There were over 60,000 mail processing machines in operation.

Post offices in the U.S.S.R. also handled telephone subscriptions, the receipts of railway booking offices, which were transmitted to the State Bank, and citizens' savings where there was a post office savings bank. In rural areas the service also included receiving the takings of cooperative stores and, as of 1969, accepting payment of electricity bills from rural dwellers. Newspapers and magazines were also sold, and subscriptions handled. (X.)

In the U.S., Pres. Richard M. Nixon moved to implement comprehensive proposals to take the creaking postal system "out of politics" and place it on a businesslike "pay as you go" basis. Nixon asked Congress to establish a postal corporation, to be called the United States Postal Service, to take the place of the Post Office Department. Congress would continue to set policy, but management of the $8 billion-a-year enterprise would rest in the hands of presidentially appointed directors. The new corporation would assume such powers now held by Congress as setting rates and determining the wages of postal employees, who numbered 725,000 in 1969.

Even before the reform measure was submitted, Nixon asked the Senate to end its historic prerogative of confirming nominations of postmasters and rural letter carriers. The Senate, without debate, consented to the recommendation that, henceforth, postmasters in first-, second-, and third-class post offices would be chosen on the basis of civil service examinations. The move would eventually affect 25,000 of the nation's 32,200 postmasters and 31,000 rural letter carriers.

The sweeping Postal Service Act of 1969 was introduced in the House of Representatives on May 28. Key provisions included authorization to issue up to $10 billion in bonds to finance capital improvements, and authority to set mail rates and employee wages and to negotiate directly with employee unions. Employees would not have the right to strike, but labour disputes at an impasse would be referred to binding arbitration. A board of seven part-time directors nominated by the president, subject to Senate confirmation, would serve seven-year terms. The seven men, in turn, would select an eighth to serve as chief executive officer, and he would select a ninth director to serve as the chief operating officer.

The new corporation would handle its own funds, financing operations out of revenues and loans. The only monies it could receive from Congress would be those financing such public categories of mail and services as classroom publications, charity appeals,

London post office workers rally in Hyde Park, Jan. 30, 1969. Thousands demonstrated in support of one-day strike for wage increases and improved working conditions.

KEYSTONE

and materials from book and record clubs, which Congress had said did not have to pay their own way. Changes in rates and services would be considered by a three-member rate commission appointed by the board from a special civil service register. Their recommendations—after hearings were held on any objections—would be forwarded to the nine-member board, which could adopt, reject, or alter them. The board then would send its recommendations to Congress. Unless both houses vetoed the recommendations within 60 days, they would go into effect.

The new arrangement would put an end to long-standing but time-consuming practices requiring postal officials to go before Congress for approval of practically everything from rates and services to construction of new facilities. One of the chief problems under the current setup was that rates and wages were set by Congress and, historically, employees and large users lobbied extensively with key members of the House Committee on Post Office and Civil Service instead of with officials charged with operating the cumbersome service.

Despite widespread support, including that of Postmaster General Winton M. Blount, and a belief that Congress would be happy to be rid of the pressures generated practically every session by demands placed by and against the department, the proposal was not uniformly welcomed. Some members of Congress wished to retain ultimate control of the department, and leaders of the postal employees' unions feared the changes in labour-management relations that could develop. Rep. Thaddeus J. Dulski (Dem., N.Y.), chairman of the House Committee on Post Office and Civil Service, submitted his own reform measure which, while adopting many of the administration proposals, would keep the postal service as a government agency. Ultimately, Dulski's committee split 13–13 over the presidential measure.

As if to point up the need for reform, the Post Office Department issued a report in September of the first large-scale study ever undertaken on the efficiency of mail distribution. Contrary to popular expectations, the average first-class letter took a day and a half to reach its destination, while an airmail letter took two days, despite its theoretical priority status. Officials said they learned that putting an airmail stamp on a letter that was going 250 mi. or less actually delayed it, because of the special handling required. The department was striving to attain overnight delivery services throughout the continental U.S., but the survey disclosed that only 64% of first-class mail and 26% of airmail reached its destination in one day; 10% of first-class mail and 20% of the airmail actually took three days. The study followed 250,000 pieces of mail through 559 post offices from January through March 1968.

The Nixon administration also moved to clamp down further on the distribution of pornographic materials through the mails. Complaints to postal officials over obscene mailings had nearly doubled since 1964; 140,000 letters of protest were received during the nine-month period between August 1968 and April 1969. The proposed legislation would broaden a current law under which 170,000 householders had notified the Post Office not to forward mail from specific senders that they considered unwholesome. A second proposal would make it a federal crime to use the mails to deliver obscene materials to persons under the age of 18. A third measure would forbid literature advertising pornographic or obscene materials.

The year also was marked by further mechanization of the postal systems and efforts to utilize electronic equipment to speed delivery of the mails. In July, the Post Office and Western Union began a six-month test of an experiment to send telegrams via the mails. The wires would go via Western Union to the post office of the destination city, where they would be written out and delivered through the regular mails. Experiments were also undertaken in the use of laser beams to transmit messages from one point to another. In April, the first computer-directed mail sorter, which cost $350,000, began handling 36,000 pieces of mail an hour in New York, compared with about 1,000 pieces an hour handled manually.

As the cost squeeze tightened, the Post Office announced that deliveries to major businesses in the largest cities would be cut from three to two a day, providing a hoped-for savings of $4 million annually. Nixon also asked Congress to raise the cost of a first-class letter from six to seven cents an ounce. In this, he disregarded a proposal by former Pres. Lyndon B. Johnson that the first-class and airmail categories be merged into a single category, with a flat rate of seven cents an ounce. Appropriations for fiscal 1970 came to $7,678,000,000 while revenues were $6.5 billion, leaving a deficit of nearly $1.2 billion. Mail volume came to over 84,000,000,000 pieces. (JY. L.)

See also Philately and Numismatics; Telecommunications.

ENCYCLOPÆDIA BRITANNICA FILMS. *Our Post Office* (1965).

Prices

One of the main features of the world economic scene in 1969 was, undoubtedly, the continuous and growing problem of rising prices experienced by most of the industrial countries. In developed market economies the cost of living increased, on the average, by 4.1% in 1969, compared with 3.9% in 1968 and 3.5% for the period 1960–66. The comparable figures for the less developed countries (excluding Brazil, Chile, Argentina, and Peru, where price rises either had been exceptionally large in recent years or continued to be so) were 3.7% in 1969, 3.1% in 1968, and 3.5% in 1960–66.

As usual, the increases in wholesale prices were more moderate, although again the situation deterio-

Brazilian government inspector checks food market scale for accuracy. Tight controls on food sales came with government's anti-inflationary price freeze initiated in January 1969.

"MANCHETE" FROM PICTORIAL PARADE

Poultry:
see Agriculture

Power:
see Engineering Projects; Fuel and Power; Industrial Review; Nuclear Energy

Presbyterians:
see Religion

Presidents:
see Heads of State

BEN ROTH AGENCY

"Hold it ma'am—that's just for the BEEF!"—Yardley Jones, "Toronto Telegram."

rated in most developed market economies. On the other hand, there were improvements—often significant ones—in many less developed countries. On the average, wholesale prices went up in the advanced countries by 2.7% in 1969 and 1.9% in 1968. In less developed countries the average (excluding Brazil and Chile) declined from 1.6% in 1968 to 1.4% in 1969.

Consumer Prices. As can be seen from Table I, between 1968 and 1969 most industrial countries were going through a period of unusually rapid increases in the cost of living, caused in the majority of cases by very high levels of economic activity. There were, in fact, only four countries that experienced price rises of less than 3%: Italy (1.7%), Sweden (2.4%), Switzerland (2.5%), and West Germany (2.6%). In Italy the rise was quite moderate and resulted mainly from higher prices of foodstuffs and housing. In both Sweden and Switzerland the authorities introduced tighter credit controls: in the former chiefly to arrest the outflow of foreign exchange; in the latter to prevent further overheating of the economy. Similar measures, in a mild form, were applied in West Germany, where at midyear unemployment was down to 0.5% of the labour force and the level of capacity utilization in industry was higher than at the peaks of the previous two booms. It was quite remarkable, therefore, that West German prices remained among the most stable in the industrialized world and might have been even more so if higher rents had not pushed up the cost of living. The main reason for the stability was, of course, that productivity increases in West German industry were so substantial that they prevented significant rises in labour and other unit costs.

The biggest increases, over the period, took place in the Netherlands (8.1%), France (6.1%), the U.K. (5.9%), and the U.S. (5.4%). A sizable proportion of the rise in the Netherlands was caused by the switch on Jan. 1, 1969, to the value-added tax system, as part of the fiscal harmonization policy within the EEC. The problem with changes of this kind is that they may lead to unintended repercussions on wages and other costs that in turn tend to push prices up by a greater amount than is justified by the tax changes. This was apparently what happened in the Netherlands, mainly in the first few months of the year. The worst increases took place in medical supplies, recreation, clothing, and rents. In mid-April the government was forced to introduce a price freeze, after which prices remained more or less stable. However, the freeze was relaxed a few months later because of increases in the prices of raw materials and other imported commodities.

The French economy, on the other hand, never quite managed to recover from the shocks it had received in 1968. Consequently, the sharp rise in the cost of living in 1969 was at least partly due to the delayed effects of the large increases in costs the year before. Devaluation of the franc in August 1969 made a further contribution to the already strong upward trend. Similarly, the U.K. was still feeling the delayed effects of its own devaluation at the end of 1967, although increases in indirect taxes and the selective employment tax were responsible for the unusually large rise in the cost of living. At the same time, because of a whole host of deflationary measures including a severe credit squeeze, the pressure on resources was rather low throughout the year. Output increased very slowly, mainly in response to the demand for

Table I. Cost of Living—Selected Countries

Country	Index (1963 = 100)			Annual percentage changes over preceding year			
	1967	1968	1969*	1960–66 Average	1967	1968	1969†
Developed market economies							
Finland	127	138	141	4.9	5.8	8.7	3.7
Denmark‡	126	136	140	5.6	6.8	7.9	3.7
Netherlands	120	124	133	3.6	3.4	3.3	8.1
Japan	121	128	132	5.7	4.3	5.8	4.8
Norway	119	123	126	4.0	4.4	3.4	3.3
U.K.	115	121	126	3.5	2.7	5.2	5.9
New Zealand	117	122	126	2.7	6.4	4.3	4.1
Sweden	121	123	125	4.1	4.3	1.6	2.4
Belgium‡	116	119	123	2.8	2.6	2.6	3.4
Austria	116	119	122	3.6	4.5	2.6	3.4
France	112	117	122	2.9	2.8	4.5	6.1
Italy	118	119	121	4.5	4.4	0.8	1.7
Switzerland	116	119	121	3.5	3.6	2.6	2.5
Canada	112	117	120	2.0	3.7	4.5	4.3
Australia	113	116	119	2.1	2.7	2.6	3.5
U.S.	109	114	118	1.5	2.8	4.6	5.4
Germany, West	111	113	116	3.0	0.9	1.8	2.6
Centrally planned economies							
Yugoslavia	197	210	226	14.9	7.1	6.6	6.6
Hungary	107	107	107	1.0	0.9	0.0	1.9
Poland	105	107	105	1.2	1.9	1.9	0.0
Less developed countries							
Brazil	576	715	835	59.5	29.7	24.1	23.2
Chile	273	346	428	26.3	18.2	26.7	31.3
Argentina	268	311	328	24.7	29.5	16.0	7.2
Korea, South	182	194	219	14.7	11.0	6.6	11.2
Peru	155	185	195	9.2	9.9	19.4	8.3
Colombia	158	167	179	13.6	8.2	5.7	7.8
India	156	160	159	6.9	13.9	2.6	−0.6
Zambia‡	129	143	148	3.7	4.9	10.8	5.0
Spain	137	144	146	7.0	6.2	5.1	2.1
Turkey	131	138	144	4.8	13.9	5.3	5.9
Portugal	119	126	134	3.0	6.2	5.9	7.2
Ireland	119	125	132	4.0	3.5	5.0	6.4
Israel	124	127	129	7.3	1.6	2.4	1.6
Pakistan	126	126	128	3.3	6.8	0.0	2.4
Tunisia	119	122	126	2.4	3.5	2.5	4.1
Nigeria	111	113	122	4.1	−4.3	1.8	9.9
Cambodia	105	111	118	3.4	0.0	5.7	8.3
South Africa§	114	116	118	2.3	3.6	1.8	2.6
Mexico	114	116	118	2.1	3.6	1.8	1.7
Ceylon	106	112	118	1.4	2.9	5.7	7.3
Taiwan	105	114	116	2.3	2.9	8.6	5.4
Thailand	111	113	115	1.8	3.7	1.8	1.8
Greece	111	111	114	2.1	1.8	0.0	2.7
Iran	107	108	112	1.7	0.9	0.9	2.8
Iraq	101	103	112	0.9	2.0	1.9	8.7
Kenya‡	110	111	110	2.3	1.8	0.9	0.0
Costa Rica	104	108	110	1.9	1.0	3.8	2.8
Morocco	106	106	109	3.3	−0.9	0.0	2.8
Malta	105	107	109	1.7	1.0	1.9	1.9
Venezuela	106	107	109	1.7	0.0	0.9	2.8
Cyprus	101	105	107	0.3	1.0	4.0	2.9
Malaysia, West	105	105	104	0.7	4.0	0.0	−2.8
El Salvador	103	105	104	0.0	2.0	1.9	−1.0
Guatemala	100	102	103	0.3	0.0	2.0	1.0
Dominican Republic	102	102	102	2.3	1.0	0.0	0.0

*January–June (average).
†First half 1969 over first half 1968.
‡Excluding rent.
§White population only.
Sources: International Monetary Fund, *International Financial Statistics;* United Nations, *Monthly Bulletin of Statistics;* International Labour Office, *Bulletin of Labour Statistics.*

exports. In the U.S., where price increases gathered even more momentum in 1969, the curbing of inflation became one of the major tasks of the new administration. The authorities ruled out any direct controls over wages and prices and decided to rely mainly on tighter monetary measures to achieve the desired effect.

Very close to these countries, in terms of price increases, was Japan, where the cost of living went up by 4.8%. This was less than the year before or the average for 1960–66, but, chiefly for internal reasons, the problem of rising prices emerged as a major policy issue. The problem was thought to be largely structural and to require, therefore, longer-term policies, designed to raise the level of productivity in the less efficient sectors of the economy as well as to encourage labour mobility. At the same time, the authorities took precautionary monetary measures in order to slow down increases in bank lending and prices. A number of other industrial countries also resorted to tighter monetary controls. On the other hand, the revival of economic activity that began in Austria in 1968 continued undisturbed into 1969. For most of the year neither costs and prices nor the balance of payments presented a constraint on growth. However, the cost of living started to rise in the second half of the year.

Table II. Indices of Food Prices in Relation to Cost of Living Index

(1963 = 100)

Country	1966	1967	1968	1969*
Developed market economies				
Finland	103	102	104	104
Japan	101	102	103	103†
Australia	102	103	103	102‡
Denmark	99	100	100	102‡
Belgium	102	102	101	101
New Zealand	101	102	101	101‡
Norway	100	100	100	101
Sweden	102	101	100	100‡
Austria	101	101	99	100
U.S.	102	101	100	99
Canada	102	100	100	99
U.K.	98	98	97	98
Netherlands	101	99	98	97
France	100	99	98	97
Italy	100	98	97	97
Germany, West	100	98	96	96
Centrally planned economies				
Hungary	105	105	105	104‡
Yugoslavia	104	100	100	101
Poland	98	98	99	99‡
Less developed countries				
Thailand	105	108	109	109†
India	103	105	105	109‡
Puerto Rico	102	103	104	105‡
Costa Rica	102	102	103	105‡
Ceylon	103	104	105	104
South Africa§	104	104	104	104‡
Pakistan	104	105	104	103
Kenya	104	104	104	103
Iran	102	103	102	103
Tunisia	102	102	102	103
El Salvador	99	102	104	103‡
Dominican Republic	100	99	103	102
Malta	101	100	102	102
Greece	102	101	101	102‡
Nigeria	106	98	94	102‡
Zambia	103	104	101	101†
Cyprus	101	101	102	101
Mexico	101	101	101	101
Guatemala	100	99	101	100
Morocco	100	100	99	100‡
Portugal	105	101	100	99
Chile	103	100	99	99
Malaysia, West	99	100	99	99†
Colombia	103	100	98	98‡
Ireland	98	97	98	97†
Venezuela	98	97	96	97‡
Israel	94	95	96	97
Argentina	98	98	98	96
Spain	99	96	96	96‡
Korea, South	97	95	94	96‡
Cambodia	91	89	91	95‡
Brazil	98	94	91	90†

*January–July (average) except where stated otherwise.
†January–May (average).
‡January–June (average).
§White population only.
Sources: United Nations, *Monthly Bulletin of Statistics*; International Labour Office, *Bulletin of Labour Statistics*.

Finally, two of the advanced countries that had devalued toward the end of 1967 managed to stabilize their price levels considerably. In Finland the cost of living went up by only 3.7% in the period 1968–69, compared with well over 8% a year earlier. Moreover, the change for the better took place at a time of widespread improvement in the level of economic activity. In Denmark a number of factors combined to bring about a substantially lower increase in prices than in recent years. Among the most significant were easing in demand pressure; increased productivity in industry, which made it easier to absorb wage and other costs; as well as the ceiling imposed on profit margins in domestic trade.

Among the less developed countries, South America continued to be the area of exceptionally severe inflationary pressures. Brazil and Chile remained the two worst hit countries, while a remarkable improvement took place in Argentina. In Peru, after the heavy rise in 1968, price increases in 1969 were more in line with the country's past experience. At the opposite end, Venezuela's rise of only 2.8%, while considerably greater than in recent years, was still a notable exception on the continent. The cost of living continued to be rather stable in Central America. In El Salvador it even declined slightly.

In Asia price increases were noticeably higher in a number of countries. The worst rises were experienced by South Korea (11.2%), Iraq (8.7%), and Cambodia (8.3%). The cost of living declined somewhat in India, and Pakistan's rise of 2.4% was rather below the average for the first half of the 1960s. In Africa, the experience was mixed. By far the worst increase took place in Nigeria, largely because of the

Table III. Wholesale Prices for Selected Countries

Country	Index (1963 = 100) 1967	1968	1969*	Annual percentage changes over preceding year 1960–66 Average	1967	1968	1969†
Developed market economies							
Finland	118	131	134	3.4	2.6	11.0	3.1
New Zealand	107	115	120	1.6	0.0	7.5	6.2
U.K.‡	111	115	119	2.7	0.9	3.6	2.6
Sweden	112	113	116	3.1	0.0	0.9	2.3
Denmark	110	114	116	2.9	0.9	3.6	1.8
Austria	113	114	116	2.7	2.7	0.9	1.8
Australia§	115	116	116	1.1	2.7	0.9	0.0
Netherlands	115	116	115	2.7	0.0	0.9	0.0
Norway	112	113	115	2.1	1.8	0.9	2.7
Canada	108	110	115	2.0	1.9	1.8	4.5
France	105	106	113	2.2	0.0	1.0	7.6
U.S.	106	108	112	1.0	0.0	1.9	3.7
Belgium	107	107	111	1.8	−0.9	0.0	4.7
Italy	106	107	109	2.5	−0.9	0.9	1.9
Japan	105	106	107	0.7	1.9	1.0	0.9
Switzerland	104	104	106	1.9	0.0	0.0	1.9
Germany, West	104	99	100	1.3	−1.0	−4.8	1.0
Less developed countries							
Brazil‖	496	611	685	56.2	26.5	23.2	17.9
Chile	274	358	456	25.1	19.1	30.6	31.8
Argentina	236	258	266	22.7	25.5	9.3	4.3
Korea, South	172	186	197	15.9	6.2	8.1	7.1
India	160	158	160	6.8	15.9	−1.2	2.6
Yugoslavia¶	137	137	140	5.9	2.2	0.0	2.2
Tunisia	127	131	133	4.6	4.1	3.1	0.8
Pakistan	128	123	128	2.8	14.3	−3.9	6.7
Spain	117	120	124	4.5	0.9	2.6	1.6
Portugal	112	117	121	1.5	3.7	4.5	3.4
Philippines	117	120	119	5.1	4.5	2.6	−2.5
South Africa	112	114	116	2.3	1.8	1.8	2.6
Greece	112	111	114	3.0	0.0	−0.9	2.7
Mexico	111	113	114	1.8	2.8	1.8	1.8
Thailand	119	114	113	3.0	7.2	−4.2	−0.8
Dominican Republic	104	114	110	2.7	−2.8	9.6	−3.5
Iran	106	107	110	1.3	0.0	0.9	1.8
Costa Rica	104	107	108	1.2	3.0	2.9	1.9
Morocco	116	106	105	4.1	2.6	−8.6	−5.4
El Salvador	106	105	104	0.5	1.0	−0.9	−1.0
Taiwan	102	105	103	2.0	3.0	2.9	1.0

*January–June (average).
†First half 1969 over first half 1968.
‡Prices of finished goods only.
§Domestic goods.
‖Excluding coffee.
¶Producers' prices of industrial products.
Sources: International Monetary Fund, *International Financial Statistics*; United Nations, *Monthly Bulletin of Statistics*.

sharp upward movement in the price of food. The most favourable situation appeared to have been in Kenya, where prices were reported to have remained very stable.

Unlike Table I, which shows the changes in consumer prices in general, Table II indicates whether —and, roughly, to what extent—food prices went up at a higher (or lower) rate than the prices of all goods and services together. Since the figures in Table II are calculated by dividing the index of food prices by the aggregate cost of living index, the numbers over 100 indicate that prices of food rose faster than those of all goods and services. The importance of food prices for the standard of living, especially in the case of less developed countries, can best be appreciated from the fact that in India, for instance, about 60% of all consumer expenditure goes to foodstuffs, compared with around 30% in most of the developed market economies. Unfortunately, as the table shows, food prices went up faster in more than half of the less developed countries. In a number of cases the increase was substantial. At the same time, this happened in only 7 out of 16 developed market economies during the year.

Wholesale Prices. As can be seen from Table III, wholesale prices tended to be generally much more stable. Moreover, there were very few clear trends or dramatic changes. Among industrial countries, only six experienced increases of more than 3%, four of these appreciably so: France (7.6%), New Zealand (6.2%), Belgium (4.7%), and Canada (4.5%). It was noteworthy that the U.S., which until recently had had an extremely stable level of wholesale prices, was not far behind with a rise of 3.7%.

Quite a few improvements took place among less developed countries, however. (Yugoslavia was included in this group in Table III because of the lack of data for other centrally planned economies.) The most remarkable improvement was achieved by Argentina. South Korea, India, and Yugoslavia also managed to stabilize the increases in their wholesale prices at rates considerably below those experienced in the first half of the 1960s. This left Chile and Brazil as the only two countries with abnormally large increases in wholesale prices. (M. PAN.)

See also Commodities, Primary; Economy, World; Employment, Wages, and Hours; Income, National; Industrial Review; Investment, International; Merchandising; Money and Banking; Payments and Reserves, International; Stock Exchanges; Trade, International.

Prisons and Penology

A basic difference in legal systems underlay some of the differences in the type of prisoners kept in custody throughout the world in 1969. Under the accusatorial system, which existed in the United States, the United Kingdom, and Commonwealth countries, it was usual to assume that an accused was innocent until proven otherwise. Only after conviction were inquiries made about his background, previous social and medical history, and so on. It might take several days, or even a week or two, to collect this information after the guilt of the accused was established. The sentence would then take these factors into account. In most European countries, in Latin America, and in African countries with legal systems akin to those of the French or Portuguese, the inquisitorial system was the norm. All the information about the accused was collected before the trial, usually by an examining magistrate and under proper legal safeguards. Conviction and sentence could not be split into two parts, and the sentence closely reflected such matters as motive, provocation, or degree of responsibility, all of which were carefully inquired into by the examining magistrate.

WIDE WORLD

Rioting convicts stand on jail roof in Milan, Italy, in demand of prison reforms. After one-day demonstration April 14, 1969, prisoners surrendered to police.

The result was that in countries with an accusatorial system the vast majority of those in custody were convicted, whereas in countries with an inquisitorial system as many as 50% might be unconvicted and awaiting trial. (This was the case in Italy, where the resultant overcrowding, combined with inadequate accommodations, food, and sanitary arrangements, led to a series of riots in 1969. The system could be maintained only by the regular palliative of amnesties.) But one system was not necessarily better than the other. It was striking that in countries with inquisitorial systems and with ministries of justice, judges tended to know more about prisons and penology than in countries with accusatorial systems.

Moreover, prison populations (in proportion to total population) did not vary greatly among countries having the two different legal systems. Sweden, one of the most advanced countries of the world penologically, had a prison population of 5,170 for a total population of nearly 8 million in 1968. Belgium kept 6,350 in custody out of a total population of more than 9.5 million. England and Wales, with a population of 48 million, kept nearly 35,000 under lock and key. All three countries showed roughly the same proportion. There were, of course, exceptions to this rule —for example, the U.S.S.R. and South Africa, both of which kept a much higher proportion of persons in prisons.

On the whole, the period 1968–69 was one of consolidation rather than innovation in the field of penology. Despite prison-building programs, especially in such countries as France and the U.K. where the jails were old, overcrowding got worse. Modern industrial work in prisons was on the increase, and was most highly developed in the U.S. federal prison system. Work for prisoners and security were still two of the main preoccupations of penal administrators everywhere, but they also considered such questions as the problem of sexuality in prisons and the relationship between penal administrations and the public—as-

Primary Commodities: *see* Commodities, Primary

Printing: *see* Industrial Review

KEYSTONE

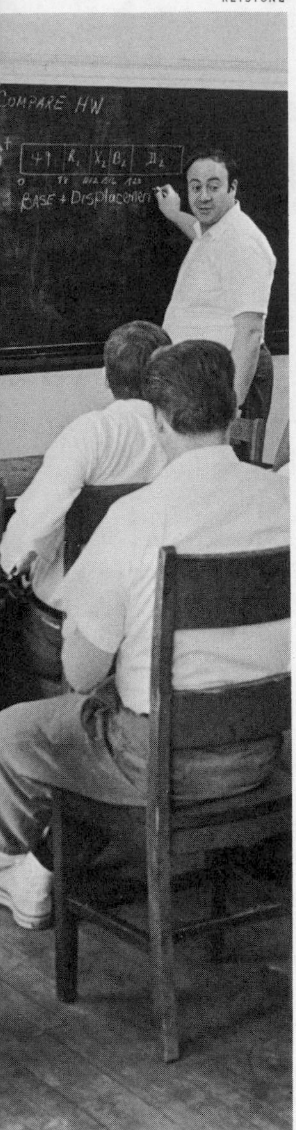

Prisoner-students at Sing Sing, New York, study computer programming in classes offered to inmates.

pects that received attention in the 1969 report of the International Penal and Penitentiary Foundation. At an international meeting of prison directors held in Lisbon in September 1969, the Portuguese minister of justice announced that a whole chain of small local jails with unsatisfactory conditions was to be replaced by a smaller number of modern regional prisons.

A number of hopeful and important new experiments were begun in 1969. In Austria, for example, psychodrama was successfully used in a prison for dangerous and unstable offenders (Mittersteig, Vienna). This was the first time such a method had been attempted in a closed prison of this type. Potentially explosive inmates acted out, in the form of a socially acceptable play, their discontent with treatment, food, or discipline; rivalries between individual inmates or groups; important incidents in their lives; and their fears and hopes for the future. Nothing was censored. Experience showed that revolutions threatened in psychodramas never materialized. Prison officers, who at first felt threatened, began to understand prisoners better, and prisoners felt they could communicate their problems. Not only was calm maintained in the institution, but real progress was made in achieving insight and greater realism. Some practical problems were solved. Long-term prisoners who had tended to become apathetic regained interest. The skill and truthfulness of some of the episodes gained recognition for the prisoners involved and increased their (usually low) self-respect. Psychodrama at Mittersteig led to a change in climate in the institutional treatment of offenders in Austria.

Normal group therapy was probably most advanced in the Grendon psychiatric prison in the U.K. Every prisoner was involved, and the whole prison could be considered as a therapeutic institute, with free communication between prisoners, all levels of staff, and specialists such as psychiatrists and psychologists. Nevertheless, the prison was secure. The Henderson Hospital, also in the U.K., was run on similar lines, but it was open, and there was an even higher degree of inmate self-administration. In the Netherlands, the Van den Hoeven Kliniek proved to be an outstanding example of a therapeutic community for offenders.

A different kind of experiment was carried out at some open prisons in Sweden. A number of long-term prisoners were given what amounted to a three-week holiday, with no obligation to work and with the possibility of having wife and family, or a close friend, with them. The experiment was considered a success in terms of improving the morale of long-term prisoners and maintaining family contacts. Other methods were also tested. For example, a hotel was opened at the Ulriksfors institution which offered weekend board and lodging to visiting relatives. The most far-reaching effort to preserve family ties was introduced at Knutby, where two families of long-term prisoners remained with them throughout a whole year. A similar scheme had been in progress in Mexico for a considerable time.

The treatment of offenders with special problems such as drunkenness received a good deal of attention. Prisons can usually do little more than withhold alcohol. The underlying personality and social difficulties often remain untouched. At an international symposium on this subject, held in London in May 1968, there was general agreement that the alcoholic should be considered as sick, often with a whole combination of adverse factors working against him. The symposium noted that in a number of countries drunks were no longer even taken to court by the police, but were taken to such other places as sobering-up centres (Warsaw), a medical detention centre (Milan), a university psychiatric clinic (Vienna), or the police medical service (Paris). The U.S. Supreme Court went so far as to rule that it was a "cruel and unusual punishment" (and hence a violation of the Constitution) to convict an alcoholic for being publicly intoxicated.

The treatment of even seemingly intractable chronic alcoholics was no longer hopeless. Special nursing, intensive counseling, and other therapeutic activities could succeed with a quarter to a third of this group. The issue as to whether treatment should be compulsory or voluntary was still open—too little voluntary treatment had been tried to permit a definitive judgment. The main problem, however, was to remove the drunk from the judicial and penal arena altogether. There was a long way to go before this aim could become a reality. In the U.K., where police cells housed between 70,000 and 80,000 drunks annually, a Home Office commission recommended the establishment of "detoxification centres" such as those already existing in the U.S., Poland, and Czechoslovakia. These centres would provide full medical supervision, with a clinical approach aimed at a long-term cure. Similar recommendations were put forward in Sweden.

In the field of aftercare, hostels and halfway houses were being started in many countries. One of the most interesting halfway house programs in the U.S. was that of Crofton House in San Diego, Calif., named after Sir Walter Crofton, an early penal reformer. Inmates were carefully selected and the regimen differed from other halfway houses—for example, in West Germany or the U.K.—in that there was a strong emphasis on group counseling, with a trained supervisor and his wife on the premises. The accent was on open expression of feelings—"pulling off the covers" when a resident evaded or distorted the need to face problems—and, at the same time, continued acceptance and mutual support. Relations with the other residents, employment outside and house duties inside, past criminal behaviour, and family background were all discussed, and participation at these sessions was compulsory. Efforts were also made to relate to the neighbouring community, through such events as Christmas parties and open house visits.

Sewing class in New York state rehabilitation centre for drug addicts. The State Narcotic Addiction Control Commission came under fire during 1969 from critics who claimed the institutions differed little from prisons and served mainly to keep addicts off the streets.

"THE NEW YORK TIMES" FROM WIDE WORLD

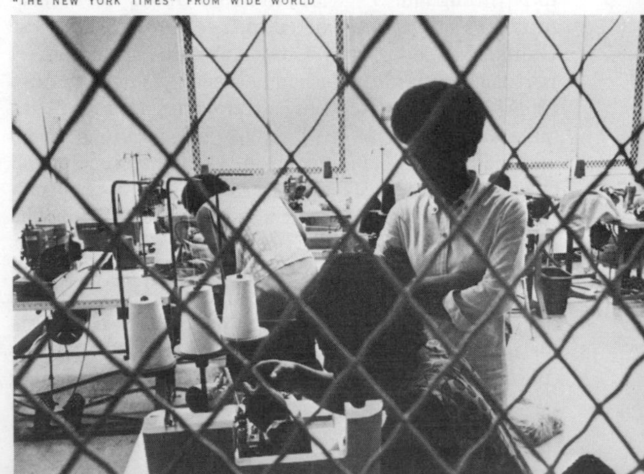

The participation of the public in such efforts was clearly important. It was selected as one of the main subjects for the UN Congress on the Treatment of Offenders and the Prevention of Crime, to be held in Kyoto, Jap., in 1970.

A useful piece of penological research in the U.K. was contained in *The Sentence of the Court,* a handbook for courts on the treatment of offenders, published in 1969. Apart from the detailed description of treatment methods, there were follow-up studies of the results of different sentences. For first offenders, fines proved the most effective (and clearly the most economical) sentence. The results had to be viewed in the light of the fact that the results of imprisonment—or even of probation—to some extent reflected the more serious nature of the offense involved. Nevertheless, there was sufficient variation in the practice of different courts to make the overall success rate of fines a factor worth serious consideration.

Finally, one of the most interesting penological developments of recent years, compensation of the victims of crimes of violence, was being extended. Usually the victim cannot claim recompense from the offender himself, who may be without means. Yet the victim may be seriously disabled by a criminal attack and may not be insured against this particular contingency. Compensation out of public funds already existed in the U.K. and in New Zealand; it was being discussed in Canada, and legislation for its introduction in the provinces of Ontario and Alberta was proposed early in 1969. (H. J. KL.)

See also Crime.

Profits

In most of the Western industrial countries, the stage for profit developments in 1969 was set by the interplay between the forces of expansion and inflation and the vigorous attempts by governments to subdue inflation. Timely information about profit trends around the world was scarce—surprisingly so since profits and the incentives they provide are the lifeblood of free enterprise economies. Such limited data as existed showed that in several important countries profit growth slowed in 1969. In at least one, the United States, profits actually began to decline late in 1968.

The current expansionary phase in the world economy followed on the heels of a general slowdown that began in 1966 and extended into 1967. This slowdown reflected the international repercussions of attempts by a number of governments, notably those of the U.S., U.K., and West Germany, to restore stability to their overheated economies. In Germany the slowdown actually turned into a recession that lasted from late 1966 through the middle of 1967.

The slowdown proved to be short-lived. Stimulated by rapidly rising output in West Germany and the U.S., the pace of activity in most industrial countries had accelerated by the end of 1967. A number of countries continued to enjoy increasing rates of growth through 1968. This was not true, however, for the U.S., where inflationary pressures had withstood the earlier slowdown and attempts to restrain demand had yielded slower real growth rates in 1968, though price increases continued to accelerate. In continental Europe, expansion was able to proceed without serious cost and price pressures until late in 1968, when governments intensified their anti-inflationary policies. By the first half of 1969, real growth slowed in the leading industrial countries. The only major exception was Italy, where inflation did not constitute an important threat.

West Germany. Profits were recorded in West Germany as part of a more general category, entrepreneurial and property income (EPI), but this was not published in a seasonally adjusted form. The data suggested that profit growth slowed significantly in the first half of 1969. (*See* Table I.) A peak was reached in the last half of 1968, when EPI reached DM. 80.3 billion. This was 19.8% higher than the second half of 1967 and substantially higher than the comparable 12.9% increase that occurred in national income. These record profits reflected the conjuncture of two unusual circumstances—an annual rate of growth of real gross national product (GNP), seasonally adjusted, that exceeded 10% in the second half of 1968 and a 3% decline in unit labour costs in manufacturing during all of 1968.

In the first half of 1969, EPI fell to DM. 69.7 billion, 9.7% higher than in the first half of the preceding year. In contrast, national income, which also declined from the level of the last half of 1968, showed a gain of 10.7% over the first half of 1968. The annual growth rate of real GNP, seasonally adjusted, fell by more than 50% from the last half of 1968. Reflecting these changes, the share of EPI in total national income fell to 33.7% in the first half of 1969, the lowest since the recession level of the first half of 1967.

In the absence of seasonally adjusted data, however, the implication of a downtrend in profits had to await later confirmation; lower second than first half-year results appeared to be the common seasonal pattern for EPI. Unpublished quarterly data made available by the Deutsches Institut für Wirtschaftsforschung suggested that the seasonally adjusted trend of EPI, though up during all of 1968, lost momentum as the year progressed. In the second half of 1969, continuing governmental efforts to curb price pressures and the effects of the revaluation of the mark could be expected to exert further moderating influences on the growth of profits. Investor confidence in the outlook remained high, however, as stock prices advanced without significant interruption.

United Kingdom. Profits before depreciation, income taxes, and adjustment for inventory profits maintained the moderately rising trend that began in the U.K. in mid-1967. After the beginning of 1968, however, the growth in profits resulted from increases in income from abroad and rent and nontrading income within the U.K., rather than from expanded gross trading profits arising from business. The latter, seasonally adjusted, maintained an essentially flat trend through the middle of 1969. (*See* Table II.)

Table I. West Germany: Profit and Income Developments

In DM. 000,000; without adjustment for seasonal variation

Period	National income	Entrepreneurial and property income: Before income taxes	Entrepreneurial and property income: Share of national income (%)	Change from previous corresponding period (%): National income	Change from previous corresponding period (%): Entrepreneurial and property income
1966: First half	172,390	56,090	32.6	7.0	2.8
Second half	192,360	65,690	34.2	4.4	1.0
1967: First half	170,650	53,280	31.1	−1.0	−5.0
Second half	193,030	67,030	34.7	0.3	2.0
1968: First half	186,930	63,510	34.0	9.5	19.2
Second half	217,980	80,310	37.0	12.9	19.8
1969: First half	207,000	69,650	33.7	10.7	9.7

Source: *Wirtschaft und Statistik,* 1969, No. 9.

Table II. United Kingdom: Gross Trading Profits, Seasonally Adjusted

In £000,000

Period	1967	1968	1969
First quarter	1,148	1,301	1,281
Second quarter	1,179	1,278	1,296
Third quarter	1,115	1,247	
Fourth quarter	1,195	1,291	

Source: *Financial Statistics* (October 1969).

Table III. Canada: Corporation Profits Before Taxes, Seasonally Adjusted

In Can $000,000

Period	All industries	Manufacturing
1967: First quarter	1,199	521
Second quarter	1,225	534
Third quarter	1,287	561
Fourth quarter	1,309	598
1968: First quarter	1,331	609
Second quarter	1,414	658
Third quarter	1,490	667
Fourth quarter	1,642	825
1969: First quarter	1,638	792
Second quarter	1,643	808

Source: *Canadian Statistical Review* (November 1969).

During 1968, profits were supported by greater growth than had been officially anticipated and by the favourable effect on earnings in the export industries of the devaluation of November 1967. The government, however, adopted increasingly restrictive monetary and fiscal measures in 1968 and 1969 in its continuing efforts to dampen inflation and strengthen Britain's international financial position by promoting a transfer of resources from production for domestic consumption into the export and import-competing industries. By the third quarter of 1969, these policies appeared to be bearing fruit. Price increases slowed after the first quarter and the trade balance improved significantly. The economy's rate of growth, however, was sharply curtailed and the index of U.K. stock prices plummeted 22% by July.

Canada. During the first and second quarters of 1969, Canadian corporate profits, adjusted for seasonal variation, remained at roughly the peak level reached in the final quarter of 1968. (*See* Table III.) This plateau followed a rapidly rising trend in corporate earnings that began after the first quarter of 1967. Significant gains in labour productivity contributed to this upsurge in profits. In an effort to moderate inflationary pressures, monetary policy was progressively tightened beginning in September 1968 and a more restrictive fiscal policy was adopted in October. These measures contributed to a slowing of inflation in 1969 and to a pronounced decline in the rate of real economic growth. Industrial production reached a peak in March 1969. Thereafter, at least through July, it remained on a plateau at a slightly lower level.

Table IV. United States Corporate Profits and Related Indicators

Period	Profits (in $000,000,000) Before taxes	Less inventory profits	After taxes	Profits per dollar of sales (cents)*	Ratio of profits to income originating in corporations (%)†	Ratio of price to unit labour cost index‡
1967: First quarter	78.4	78.3	46.1	5.0	11.9	101.7
Second quarter	79.1	78.3	46.4	5.0	11.9	100.6
Third quarter	79.5	79.1	47.0	4.9	11.7	100.0
Fourth quarter	84.4	81.1	49.9	5.1	12.1	100.4
1968: First quarter	87.9	82.5	47.9	5.1	11.5	99.8
Second quarter	90.7	88.2	49.7	5.0	11.4	99.8
Third quarter	91.5	90.6	50.0	5.1	11.2	99.4
Fourth quarter	94.5	90.3	51.6	5.1	11.4	98.7
1969: First quarter	95.5	89.5	52.2	5.0	11.3	99.8
Second quarter	95.4	89.2	51.8	4.9	11.1	99.9
Third quarter	92.4	88.7	50.0	—	10.5	99.8

*After taxes; all manufacturing.
†All industries.
‡Manufacturing; 1957–59=100.
Sources: *Survey of Current Business* (July and September 1969); *Business Conditions Digest* (October 1969).

United States. The growth of profits in the U.S. extended into 1969, but the underlying policy-induced slowdown in the economy took its toll. Faced with an acceleration of price increases, the government raised taxes in 1968 and progressively tightened its spending programs. Monetary policy became restrictive in the second half of 1967 and, after a period of relaxation in 1968, moved to an extremely tight posture in 1969. While price increases continued to mount, the economy's real growth declined sharply. By the third quarter of 1969, real growth fell to an annual rate of 2%.

The government's policy tended to place profits in a squeeze by aiming for a climate that would raise market resistance to price increases, including increases based on higher costs. On the other side, labour's drive to achieve larger gains in wages and fringe benefits was intensified, partly because inflation more than consumed past gains. In the first nine months of 1969, labour unions succeeded in winning median benefits of 8.1% per year over the lives of major contracts, compared with 6.6% for all of 1968.

A turning point in U.S. profits occurred in the first quarter of 1969 when profits before taxes for all corporations reached a record $95.5 billion and after-tax earnings a record $52.2 billion. (*See* Table IV.) If inventory profits were excluded, however, pre-tax profits peaked earlier—in the third quarter of 1968. Still, despite increases in all categories of corporate costs, profits gave ground only slowly. Corporations endeavoured to maintain margins by raising prices, while higher sales volume mitigated the effect of pinched margins on the aggregate level of profits. Thus, in the second and third quarters of 1969, pre-tax profits, after deducting inventory profits, were only 1.5 and 2.1%, respectively, below the peak reached in the third quarter of 1968.

The pressures on profits were unevenly distributed among industries. While total pre-tax profits, after adjustment for seasonal variation and inventory profits, turned down after the third quarter of 1968, financial institutions continued to enjoy profit growth at least through the third quarter of 1969. Quarterly data extending through the first half of 1969 showed that the profits of manufacturers of nondurable goods continued to grow. These data indicated that the profit decline occurred in the manufacture of durable goods—automobiles were especially hard hit—and in transportation, communication, and public utilities.

Developments through September 1969 gave indications that a further erosion of profits was likely to occur. After-tax profits per dollar of sales in manufacturing declined in the second quarter to a low point touched only once before during the preceding five years, and the ratio of profits to income originating in corporations continued its irregular downtrend of nearly four years' duration, reaching in the third quarter the lowest point since 1961. If the economy's growth rate decreased further, as was widely expected, there would be a somewhat sharper reduction in profits than was evident in the third quarter data. Changes in federal tax legislation were expected to affect after-tax profits in 1969. The combination of the surtax reduction and repeal of the investment tax credit would be adverse for after-tax profits in 1969, approximately neutral in the first half of 1970, and favourable in the second half. The trend of security prices in the U.S. also suggested that investors had anticipated lower earnings since the beginning of 1969. (G. A. Po.)

See also Stock Exchanges.

Propaganda

Propaganda of the deed and the event overshadowed propaganda of the word in 1969. Ho Chi Minh died, Charles de Gaulle passed from the political scene, and Alexander Dubcek was eclipsed. Richard Nixon, who in his first year as U.S. president was spared new international crises and a violent summer in the cities, visited Europe in February and the Far East in the summer, concluding with a visit to Communist Romania. The Sino-Soviet war of words escalated to military border clashes, and while a meeting between Soviet Premier Aleksei N. Kosygin and Chinese Premier Chou En-lai at the Peking airport was followed by extended talks between the two countries, there were no immediately visible results. Arabs and Israelis intensified their military operations, and a détente via diplomatic channels seemed increasingly unlikely. Soviet jamming of Voice of America broadcasts in mid-1969 was as severe as during Stalin's time. The U.S. put men on the moon and the U.S.S.R. put seven men in orbit simultaneously. Approval of a U.S. antiballistic missile (ABM) system was followed by resumption of Soviet tests of their space bomb delivery system, but the two superpowers did conduct the first round of strategic arms limitation talks (SALT) and reached agreement to discuss substantive arms-limitation issues in 1970.

Divisions in the Communist World. The quarrel between the Chinese and the Soviets, which had raged bloodlessly throughout most of the 1960s, suddenly erupted in March 1969 into military violence along the Ussuri River and, subsequently, at other points on the Sino-Soviet border. Each side blamed the other for starting it. In April, Peking produced a documentary film for saturation exposure to Chinese audiences entitled *Anti-China Atrocities of the New Tsars,* and followed this with a propaganda barrage that was both voluminous and remarkably sustained. The reason behind the unprovoked Soviet attacks, the Chinese maintained, was that the Soviet leaders had taken upon themselves the mantle of the old czars, but whereas the czars were guilty of out-and-out imperialism, the new Soviet breed had developed the policy of "social-imperialism." The Chinese charged that Marx, Engels, and Lenin had all harshly condemned the historical theft of Chinese territory by the czars, and these new Soviet revisionist renegades, in defending the actions of their imperialist ancestors, were showing the entire world where they stood in relation to the great Communist heroes of the past. Together with the United States, the Chinese said, the Soviet revisionists were the most ferocious enemies of national liberation in the world today. Chinese 20th-anniversary slogans warned against nuclear war triggered by the U.S. and the U.S.S.R. and urged people everywhere to prepare to fight such a war through worldwide revolution.

The Soviets countercharged that Chinese treachery was at the root of it all and alleged that the Chinese were stirring up trouble with the U.S.S.R. in preparation for direct talks with the United States. They then went on to accuse the Chinese of a long list of wrongdoings, including attacks against other socialist countries; slander of Communist parties in capitalist countries; and the driving of wedges in the national liberation movements in less developed countries.

In spite of all this, the Soviets insisted that "there is no Soviet hostility toward China" and that "the vital interests of the Soviet and Chinese people coincide." However, such practices as the Chinese initiation of border conflicts and the energetic exploitation of those conflicts by means of mass-distribution films certainly were not calculated to improve amity between the two nations. In a bitter turnabout, the Soviets found themselves in the unaccustomed role of complaining that "the film dishonestly exploits the lack of information of the Chinese people."

The purpose of the June World Conference of Communist and Workers' Parties in Moscow was advertised as discussing "the tasks of the war against imperialism in the present stage and the unity of action of communist and workers' parties and all anti-imperialist forces." The Soviets used the conference as a forum for savage blasts at the United States and China. The United States came in for censure as a result of its "dirty war" in Vietnam. China's foreign policy was scored by Leonid I. Brezhnev, the general secretary of the Soviet party, who charged that it had broken away from proletarian internationalism and had lost socialist class content. Soviet propaganda in general charged that Peking's opposition to the conference arose from its retrograde spirit of nationalism: "by taking the path of splitting the unity of the ranks of the democratic communist and workers' parties, Mao and his Tirana followers are becoming increasingly isolated"; they have shown their "true face . . . as enemies of the unity of forces of peace and democracy, as the tools of imperialism."

The French Turnover. Repercussions of de Gaulle's retirement and Georges Pompidou's election as president of France were felt in the nation's propaganda sector, as a result both of administrative changes and of subtle modifications in official policy that were reflected in propaganda tone and content. Administratively, the French government broadcasting organization, the Office de Radiodiffusion-Télévision Française (ORTF), which had briefly rebelled against its long-time role of government mouthpiece during the "troubles" of May 1968 and had suffered reprisals afterward, was removed from the control of the Ministry of Information. The ministry itself was abol-

Crowd in London's Trafalgar Square views the Apollo 11 moon walk on July 21, 1969. Complex satellite hookups enabled audiences around the world to watch the historic event.

"LONDON DAILY EXPRESS" FROM PICTORIAL PARADE

D.P.A. FROM PICTORIAL PARADE

Pres. Richard Nixon in Bucharest on Aug. 2, 1969, waves to crowds during his trip to Romania.

ished. The post of government spokesman was established as a voice of the government, and ORTF achieved a greater degree of independence. French propaganda content changed moderately in that it showed less hostility toward the U.S., reflected the government's policy of leaving the door ajar to possible British entry into the EEC, downplayed the question of greater independence for Quebec, and in general showed a reduced tendency to "ride the glory train."

The BBC, which had often found de Gaulle a difficult subject for comment, tended to keep its commentary on French external and domestic affairs factual and restrained. During the presidential election, the BBC took due note of any references by the candidates to better relations with Britain, but kept its comment on them cautious. After the election of Pompidou, the general line of BBC comment was that British membership in the EEC would become inevitable from France's point of view within the near future, particularly in view of the decision to hold an EEC summit meeting on the subject. This, however, was accompanied by a growing emphasis on the cost and difficulties for all the parties that would be involved in Britain's admission.

Czechoslovakia a Year Later. Another prominent figure to leave the spotlight in 1969 was Alexander Dubcek, who retired as first secretary of the Czechoslovak Communist Party in favour of the more conservative Gustav Husak. This was only one—albeit a dramatic—event in a long series that saw the Czechoslovaks being drawn back into subservience to Moscow after the August 1968 invasion. In his resignation speech Dubcek declared that because of the "exceptional situation in the country" there was an urgent need for reaffirmation of the Communist Party's leading role and the "acceleration of the normalization of friendly relations with the socialist countries."

The Soviets applauded the wisdom of Dubcek's decision and extended hearty congratulations to Comrade Husak, expressing the conviction that under his leadership the country would "do away with all the obstacles on the road toward socialism which had been put up by the right-wing forces." The Soviets also released virulent attacks against the BBC and the West German Deutsche Welle, claiming that the masters they served were experiencing "open irritation" because their hopes of "separating Czechoslovakia from the community of socialist countries and bringing it back to the path of capitalism" had been defeated.

Well in advance of the first anniversary of the invasion, the Soviets launched an intensive propaganda drive to justify the invasion's "necessity." A 65-minute documentary film entitled *Czechoslovakia: Year of Ordeal,* distributed to Soviet audiences on a wide scale, trumpeted the message that the invasion was the distasteful but imperative duty of true Communist progressives dedicated to protecting socialist Czechoslovakia from capitalist subversion. When the anniversary arrived, mass disorders broke out, first in Prague and subsequently in Brno, which were quelled only when the Czechoslovak authorities brought in soldiers with automatic rifles, armoured troop carriers, tanks, and tear gas. Soviet propaganda praised the Husak regime's "firm hand" and explained the disorders by saying that "the counterrevolutionary forces in Czechoslovakia, instigated by the West, have once again made a provocative sally in Prague."

Czechoslovak communications media, as of old totally in the service of the government, gave a detailed account of the violence, reporting that the crowds of protesters were "composed mainly of young people; . . . among them large numbers of various hostile, criminal and hooligan elements." They failed to state the announced motive of the protesters, which was to commemorate a "national day of shame." Instead, by labeling the protesters as "vandals," "antisocial elements," and the like, they tried to give the impression that the clashes were caused mainly by inveterate troublemakers, acting as the witting or unwitting dupes of right-wing antisocial forces spurred on by Western propaganda.

Chinese propaganda predicted that "whatever tricks [the Soviets and the Husak regime] may play, they cannot check the heroic struggle of the Czechoslovak people in defense of their national independence and the dignity of their motherland." The Chinese apparently chose to couch their argument in such terms as "national independence" and "the dignity of [the] motherland" because they had earlier denounced Dubcek as a Western-oriented revisionist. Thus they were unable to depict his supplantation by the Soviet-supported Husak as a fight between good Communists and bad Communists.

Nixon's First Year. The war in Vietnam continued to be the most controversial and divisive domestic issue in the U.S., contributing to an increasingly apparent polarization of American society. While the peace talks in Paris dragged on without much visible result, President Nixon attempted a different course. In June, after conferring with South Vietnamese Pres. Nguyen Van Thieu on Midway Island, he announced that he was authorizing the withdrawal of 25,000 U.S. troops from Vietnam and indicated that there would probably be more withdrawals in the future, especially if the Communists responded with meaningful concessions. Further withdrawals were, in fact, announced later in the year. After the conclusion of the Midway talks, Nixon traveled throughout the Far East, sounding the new theme that the U.S. would stand by its Asian commitments but that its future aid would involve more materiel than manpower.

While President Nixon was obviously gaining increased favour at home with his curtailment of the U.S. effort in Vietnam, he still had his vociferous detractors who said he was doing too little too late and that a timetable for the U.S. pullout should be announced. Two anti-Vietnam "Moratoriums"—in October and November—attracted considerable support. The report of an alleged massacre of Vietnamese civilians, including women and children, by U.S. soldiers in 1968 was cited by critics at home and abroad as further evidence that the "unjust war" was weakening America's moral fibre. Polls taken at the end of the year, however, revealed that most Americans either believed that the incident had not taken place or that there must have been extenuating circumstances.

In an attempt to improve U.S. relations with Latin America, President Nixon sent New York Gov. Nelson Rockefeller on a series of "fact-finding" missions to that part of the world. Both the Soviets and the Chinese gave lavish coverage to the savage hostility that Rockefeller encountered there. The Soviets said that "the peoples of Latin America will never greet with friendship an individual who represents imperialism and the great oil consortiums of the world." The Chinese agreed, but added the charge that the Soviets themselves viewed Latin America just as rapaciously as the U.S., having recently concluded a number of political, economic, and cultural agreements with Latin-American countries, and by so doing had "stretched their tentacles deeper and deeper into Latin America."

The Soviets also found rich food for commentary in the extremely difficult battle the Nixon administration had in getting Senate approval for its ABM system. They assiduously quoted the arguments of the ABM opposition forces, organizing their presentation in such a way as to imply that the U.S. was in a severe "guns-or-butter" dilemma and that past precedents indicated the nation's political leaders would heed the voices of the Pentagon and give priority to guns, as was witnessed by Vietnam. VOA pointed out that the Soviets had an ABM system already.

On the bright side for U.S. propagandists was the realization, by means of the Apollo 11 space flight, of man's age-old fantasies of a successful voyage to the moon. VOA claimed that it attracted the largest radio audience of all time for this event. An estimated 750 million people heard VOA's broadcasts, directly or through VOA pickups on their own national networks and domestic stations. Simultaneous specials in seven languages—English, Russian, Chinese, French, Arabic, Spanish, and Portuguese—were beamed around the world, with special feeds in many other languages.

By means of complex satellite hookups, television audiences the world over, including those of the Soviet Union and Eastern Europe (China blacked out the story), were treated to a "spectacular" of unprecedented scope and drama. As a contrast in propaganda styles, it was interesting to compare Nikita Khrushchev's gloating appraisal of Sputnik I, in October 1957, as hard proof of the superiority of Communism over capitalism with Neil Armstrong's words as he set foot on the moon's surface: "That's one small step for a man, one giant leap for mankind." (H. H. SA.)

Psychology

For the first time in its 77-year history the American Psychological Association (APA) annual meeting was "physically disrupted" (*Science,* vol. 165, pp. 1101–04, 1969). A group of black graduate students in psychology demanded, and were given, time to be heard by the APA council. A co-chairman of the Association of Black Psychologists criticized both black and white psychologists for using the ghetto as a "research plantation," charging that "psychologists and sociologists go into the black community and do research but refuse to specify and push major programs of improvement for the black community." Appropriately, the theme of the meeting was "Psychology and the Problems of Society," reflecting disagreement among psychologists as to how their skills can or should be used to deal with social distress. Psychologists were encouraged by some to be activists; to leave office practice or laboratory and get involved in the "real problems" of society. Others argued that psychologists have no expertise in resolving such difficulties; that they lack substantive, empirical knowledge on which to base decisions for social action. However, psychologists were moving into the community and, according to APA president George Miller, "More and more they're getting their noses rubbed in real problems."

So-called sensitivity training in groups was being increasingly used by professional organizations and businesses for such purposes as increasing communicative skills. However, the efficacy of what have come to be called T-groups or sensitivity groups has been questioned (*Psychological Bulletin,* vol. 70, pp. 73–104, 1968) because of failure to demonstrate transfer of communicative skills to actual, on-the-job situations.

Nude therapy groups represent a form of sensitivity training that has received substantial publicity but little in the way of investigative scrutiny. Such groups may meet continuously (usually throughout a weekend) with brief intervals for eating and sleeping. It is claimed that removal of clothing helps to lower normal social defenses (*Psychology Today,* pp. 25–28, June 1969) and that during this "trial by intimacy . . . masks and pretenses tend to peel away layer by layer revealing a more authentic self." Despite some enthusiastic testimonials, no systematic, rigorous research had been conducted to evaluate possible beneficial or deleterious effects.

Experimental studies with laboratory animals continued to suggest that many medically important psychosomatic (or bodily) symptoms may be learned (*Science,* vol. 163, pp. 434–445, 1969). For instance, if a child under stress repeatedly is rewarded for his queasy feeling in the stomach or his cardiovascular symptoms (*e.g.,* pallor and faintness) by being kept away from school, theoretically the reinforced symptom is more likely to occur in other instances of stress. It is further suggested that any symptom that is under control of the nervous system can be altered through appropriate reinforcement. Such new learning occurs with less interference in the laboratory when the animal is in a state of muscular relaxation. In this vein, one investigation with human subjects (*Journal of Abnormal and Social Psychology,* vol. 74, pp. 425–437, 1969) compared the effects of training in muscular relaxation and of hypnotic suggestion on physiological measures (*e.g.,* heart rate, skin conductance) considered to be indicators of anxiety. It was concluded that "progressive relaxation training is more effective than hypnotic suggestion in producing desired physiological changes."

While some evidence suggested that use in the U.S. of hallucinogens such as STP, LSD, and their derivatives was decreasing, the so-called green rebellion of marijuana continued. Despite social and legal taboos, one report (*Science,* vol. 162, pp. 1234–42, 1968) described marijuana as a "relatively mild intoxicant" with short-lived effects. Although other clinical investigations had indicated adverse marijuana reactions, no such reactions were reported in any of the subjects (eight who used the drug regularly and nine nonusers). All nonusers failed to identify the taste or smell of marijuana in the experimental cigarettes, but most guessed by the absence of effects when they had received inactive substitutes (placebos). No changes were reported in respiratory rate or blood glucose level in either group after smoking marijuana; (eye) pupil size also remained unaffected. Nonusers were significantly impaired in performance on simple psychological tests after smoking marijuana; however, they did not report the elation ("marijuana high") experienced by regular users. This suggests that set or expectancy may be important in determining subjective results; however, this does not rule out the possibility of true physiological sensitization.

In another study experienced users smoked sufficient marijuana to achieve "social marijuana high." These subjects showed significantly more speedometer errors in simulated automobile driving equipment than did control subjects. (Speedometer errors were a func-

Protected States:
see Dependent States

Protestant Episcopal Church:
see Religion

Psychiatry:
see Medicine

tion of the amount of time spent monitoring the speedometer.) There were no significant differences in accelerator, brake, signal, steering, and total errors. However, after intoxication by alcohol, the same subjects did accumulate significantly more accelerator, brake, signal, speedometer, and total errors than under normal sober conditions.

Other investigators (*Science,* vol. 163, p. 1359, 1969) reported that learning acquired under alcohol intoxication may be more readily recalled when the subject is again intoxicated than when he is sober. This effect may partially account for memory loss following a period of alcohol ingestion. For example, heavy drinkers sometimes are able to recall where they have hidden caches of alcohol only during subsequent drinking episodes.

Evidence has been offered that the psychiatric status of the mother affects the survival of the baby she delivers, depending on the infant's sex. In one study (*Science,* vol. 164, pp. 723–724, 1969), 13 pregnant women who developed symptoms of schizophrenia within one month after conception all delivered live females (suggesting that male infants failed to survive). Of another 13 mothers who became schizophrenic after delivery, only 2 gave birth to girls and 11 produced males. It was suggested ". . . that the male embryo and fetus are affected by the sudden development of the mother's prepartum schizophrenia . . ." and that this is ". . . consistent with a theory that schizophrenia is associated with plasma factors which interact with the fetus and provide the basis for a higher fetal mortality." Many women in the sample had been receiving treatment with a psychoactive drug. It has been observed that in such a study it may not be warranted to clearly ascribe causality without taking into account possible drug effects on the mortality of the unborn children. (J. T. G.)

See also Medicine.

Publishing

Merchant banker Jacob Rothschild votes at the Pergamon Press shareholders' meeting at the Connaught Rooms, London, Oct. 10, 1969. Rothschild represented the U.S. conglomerate Leasco Data Processing Equipment Corp. in its successful bid to oust Robert Maxwell as head of the Pergamon publishing empire.

KEYSTONE

Magazines. With few exceptions, optimism reigned among publishers of magazines in 1969. U.S. publishers, noting a 73% revenue gain over the past ten years, forecast a 6% revenue increase for the year. Odds for success seemed increasingly assured, particularly for the publication geared to a small, involved readership. The few remaining champions of mass magazines suffered a severe setback with the death of the 148-year-old *Saturday Evening Post* in February. Failure to find a loyal audience, coupled with rising costs and loss of advertising, proved an irresolvable problem. Other general, mass appeal publications that were either slipping or showing unspectacular revenue gains were *Life, Time, Look, McCall's, Ladies' Home Journal,* and *Good Housekeeping.*

In May *Life* appointed a new managing editor, Ralph Graves, and began to stress personalized journalism, social issues, and even anti-Establishment exposés. Losing ground to *Newsweek, Time* named a new top command in August, reversed itself on Vietnam, curbed the notorious Timestyle, and tried to shake its relatively conservative image. *Look* accused San Francisco Mayor Joseph L. Alioto of Mafia involvement and gained national publicity when the mayor denied the charges and sued the magazine for $12.5 million. *McCall's* named Shana Alexander its first female editor in 48 years.

The struggle for circulation and advertising revenue in Britain in 1969 was intensified by the credit squeeze, rising costs, labour troubles, and, most alarming perhaps, the invasion of the most profitable field, the popular weekly, by the *Daily Mirror,* which on October 4 launched its weekly colour magazine. Distributed free with Wednesday's issue of Britain's top-selling daily paper, *Mirror Magazine* claimed a guaranteed readership of some 14 million and clearly aimed to capture a substantial share of the women's weekly market. If successful, it could embarrass the International Publishing Corp. (IPC), the *Mirror's* own parent company, which, since setting up its separate magazines division in 1968, had developed an unrivaled range of magazines for women of all ages. IPC showed recognition of a danger of competition by offering advertisers preferential rates for joint insertions in *Mirror Magazine* and in others under its control.

IPC was also hit by labour troubles: an electrician's strike in March, followed in April by a pay dispute at Sun Printers. The *Sunday Times* colour supplement was also stopped by the strikes, and southern editions of the *TV Times,* the Independent Television Authority (ITA) weekly, came out without colour.

An outline of the future came from West Germany where editorial employees of the politically liberal weekly *Stern* threatened to strike when co-owner Richard Gruner planned to sell his interest to Henrich Bauer, the sensational publisher of *Quick.* The strike threat killed the sale and gave the editorial staff a major voice in *Stern's* editorial and economic future. In France 30 newspaper and magazine staffs grouped themselves into an association to protect their interests, particularly to gain a veto power in the choice of a new publisher and an important if yet limited voice in actual editorial content. Meanwhile, in the U.S., a writer observed in the May issue of *Media Scope* that efforts toward economic control of the periodical press by advertisers not only could kill a magazine, *e.g., The Saturday Evening Post,* but threatened freedom of the press.

The success of revised or new magazines, such as *Psychology Today, Redbook, Field and Stream,* and *Rotarian,* emphasized the need to satisfy readers first, advertisers second. Among the giants only *TV Guide* and *Reader's Digest* continued to report substantial gains, and both were more than aware of audience demands. At the business level, the split-run or regional edition supported the view of the importance of specialized, well-identified readers. Close to 250 U.S. magazines (in 1958 there were half as many) offered advertisers a part of their total circulation.

The only type of magazine to keep clear of the vicious circle caused by the credit squeeze in the U.K. was the "part-work," which carried no advertising and, once successfully launched, was sure of continued sales. First undertaken on a large scale in Britain in 1961 by Purnell, a subsidiary of the British Printing Corp. (BPC), the part-work is essentially a magazine method of book publication. A subject is chosen with the help of market research, and the two or more million-word work written on it by teams of international experts and editors is published over a period of a year or longer in magazine-length, lavishly illustrated weekly parts, at a price of 3*s.* 6*d.* to 4*s.* 6*d.*

Purnell's three most successful part-works, *The History of the Second World War* (launched in October 1966 and extended from 96 to 120 parts), *The History of the Twentieth Century* (launched in 1968), and *The History of the First World War* (launched in

1969), for which break-even sales of some 30,000 were forecast, all reached a weekly average of 120,-000–150,000 in Britain, with high overseas sales and translations into Dutch, French, German, and Italian.

A wry note was struck by the continually profitable *New Yorker*. After what editor William Shawn termed some 30 years of thinking it over, the sophisticate's magazine added a table of contents. There were other surprises. Clay Felker's *New York*, a city magazine with national aspirations, climbed out of the red, increasing circulation to 150,000. Success seemed due to a particular type of personalized journalism by such experts as Jimmy Breslin and Tom Wolfe, and a striking format. *Ramparts*, bankrupt, declared its muckraking days ended in February, but thanks to donations and a streamlined new business approach, survived. Hearst's *Eye*, a brilliant combination of graphics and somewhat weaker editorial content, gave up in May. A mild shock occurred when the conservative *National Review* and the liberal *New Republic* offered advertisers a combined 260,000 circulation at 10% discount. Salesmen could confidently claim there would be little or no readership overlap.

There were two interesting editorial changes in the U.K. during the year. On January 1, William Davis, financial editor of the *Guardian*, became editor of the humorous weekly *Punch;* and in August Geoffrey Cannon moved in to revitalize the *Radio Times*, the British Broadcasting Corporation (BBC) weekly television and radio program magazine. Some praised the changes that followed, some deplored them. Although the jokes in the new *Punch* seemed much the same, articles and general outlook became much more topical, often with several numbers devoted to one subject. Circulation trends suggested that the new formula was working.

The new-style *Radio Times*, begun in September, was certainly an improvement in general appearance. Many listeners complained, however, of the difficulty of reading program details for radio, which were tight-packed into one double-spread, while television listings luxuriated in a page or more. Among new magazines in the U.K., *Student* gave an accurate picture of the national and international swinging, politically oriented younger set. The glossy, well-produced magazine edited by an 18-year-old, Richard Branson, apparently would succeed where the U.S. counterpart, *Eye*, failed.

In the U.S., the highly successful music magazine *Rolling Stone* jumped its circulation to 80,000 in less than two years. The editor was 23 years old. Richard Goldstein, 24, saw the first issue of *US* off the press. The magazine in paperback format, supported by Bantam Books, was aimed at the under-30 market. Age, however, proved no sure formula for success. *Careers Today*, the brainchild of Nicholas H. Charney, 27, publisher of *Psychology Today*, failed after four issues.

Among children's magazines, the most ambitious project was the 25-cent quarterly *Wonderful World of Walt Disney*, distributed by service stations. The supermarket-distributed *Child's Day*, by publishers of *Woman's Day*, appeared to be doing equally well. The level of editorial content of children's magazines, however, remained relatively poor. Revenue for comic magazines reached a new high as comics became "in" reading for college students and were more in evidence at such places as the Newport Jazz Festival and the Woodstock rock gathering than any other type of reading matter.

Cover of the last issue of "The Saturday Evening Post," dated Feb. 8, 1969.

Never were publishers more aware of the power of an excellent design to help establish the unique character of a magazine. Samuel Antupit gave *Harper's* a face lifting and launched *Mayday* with a striking typographical design. Milton Glaser redesigned *New York*, and along with Peter Max continued to support the "now art" concept of colourful, pneumatic figures with imaginative background. Once parochial, dull trade magazines continued to forge a new image in 1969. The prestigious National Magazine Award went to McGraw-Hill's *American Machinist*, for a 48-page study on hard-core unemployment. Airlines now offered ten in-flight magazines in the U.S. and another half dozen overseas. The "city magazines," the once-staid chamber of commerce voices, gained publicity in many cities for muckraking, exposés, and new approaches to problems.

U.S. literary magazines showed modest, yet impressive gains in readership. After its 20th anniversary *Hudson Review* joined the *Partisan Review*, *Sewanee Review*, and the *Kenyon Review* as a leader in the field. New indexing and abstracting services popped up to try to bring order to the exploding scientific magazine field, which had increased to an estimated 1,500 worldwide in 1969. In terms of editorial adventure, minority groups offered the greatest challenge. At least two new magazines were willing to take a chance on support from readers rather than from advertisers. *New Lady*, with advice from *McCall's* and a $70,000 loan from the Ford Foundation, arrived at the end of the year to serve the upper-middle-class Negro woman, and *Time* experts lent

Public Health: *see* Medicine

Public Utilities: *see* Cooperatives; Fuel and Power; Industrial Review; Transportation

SYNDICATION INTERNATIONAL

Cover of the third issue of "Mirror Magazine," a new popular weekly launched on Oct. 4, 1969, by the "Daily Mirror" of London. The magazine entered the profitable women's weekly market already dominated by Britain's International Publishing Corp., owners of the "Daily Mirror."

assistance to another publication of the same type, *Sapphire.* The little magazines continued to grow in number, exceeding 600 in the U.S.

A cousin to the little magazine, the underground newspaper, showed equal growth in 1969. High school students discovered its potential power and organized HIPS (High School Independent Press Service). In the U.K., one of the most famous underground newspapers, *The International Times,* was raided by police in May. Using the Obscene Publications Acts as justification, the officers sought to challenge an Arts Council-sponsored report that called for repeal of the acts. (See *Books,* below.) In the U.S. publishers feared new pressures from the censor. Community attitudes were not always in sympathy with the liberal editorial policies of magazines and some newspapers. In New York the American Civil Liberties Union agreed to defend the editors of *Screw,* one of four underground newspapers devoted to sex that were being prosecuted at year's end.

Censorship of another sort played a minor role in Soviet-American relations during 1969. *Soviet Life,* the U.S.S.R. magazine distributed in the U.S., sought to run an article justifying its invasion of Czechoslovakia. The U.S. State Department, which sponsored a counterpart in the U.S.S.R., *American Illustrated,* refused to accept the notion. *Soviet Life* editors agreed to delete the story. Both magazines seemed safe for another year to plug away at noncontroversial cultural matters. (W. A. Ka.; X.)

Newspapers. "I don't mind a picture of a nude—provided the nude is pretty." The speaker, Rupert Murdoch, was the new owner of the *News of the World,* the largest-selling English-language Sunday paper. Certainly British journalism had left far behind the days when, early in the 1950s, the *Sunday Graphic* (then owned by Lord Kemsley) was in trouble for not removing the testicles from a picture of a prize bull.

Murdoch, the 38-year-old head of News (Australia) Ltd., was undoubtedly the most important new personality in Fleet Street in 1969. At first, however, it had seemed that the year's big "arrival" would be not Murdoch but Robert Maxwell (*see* BIOGRAPHY), wealthy Labour MP and owner of Pergamon Press, Ltd. Ironically, it was Maxwell's bid for the *News of the World* in 1968 that led to the arrival of Murdoch, called in by the owners, the Carr family, in December 1968 to save the paper from Maxwell.

Murdoch and Maxwell's names were in the headlines, on and off, all year. Much of Maxwell's publicity came from the Leasco-Pergamon take-over bid (see *Books,* below), but he was frustrated again by Murdoch in his bid for the *Sun,* an independent left-wing daily that in five years had cost its owners, IPC, nearly £9 million in losses. IPC gave warning that it might stop publication after January 1970, the date to which the paper had been guaranteed. Maxwell then put forward plans to run it as a nonprofit-making, small-circulation, 6*d.* paper supporting the Labour Party and guaranteed by an unidentified consortium of backers, headed by himself. In July, he began negotiations with the Society of Graphical and Allied Trades (Sogat), Britain's biggest printers' union, but a breakdown, for which each side blamed the other (September 3), caused him to withdraw and Murdoch entered the field. Murdoch quickly won IPC's confidence, and concluded negotiations with Sogat, who regarded his plans as more realistic than Maxwell's.

From mid-November the *Sun* was to be developed as a mass-circulation, politically independent, left-wing tabloid. Under IPC ownership it had lost the prestige acquired by its predecessor, the *Daily Herald,* as the first popular British daily to reach a two-million circulation, and had become known in Fleet Street as "King's Cross" after Cecil King, IPC chairman until May 1968. It was always a poor second to the *Daily Mirror,* IPC's top circulation daily, and if, under Murdoch, the *Sun* were to succeed, the *Mirror* would suffer. Perhaps in preparation for battle, the *Mirror* had launched a weekly colour magazine (see *Magazines,* above), and the *Daily Sketch,* a less successful right-wing tabloid, had appointed a new editor, David English, from the *Daily Express.*

During his first year in control of the *News of the World,* Murdoch set its circulation climbing swiftly by introducing more nudes and brasher exposés. His changes forced the IPC-owned rivals, the *People* and the *Sunday Mirror,* to follow its lead in order to maintain their five million and over circulations. Probably Murdoch's biggest circulation builder was the serialization of Christine Keeler's memoirs, for which the *News of the World* paid £21,000. The memoirs, disappointingly innocuous, raised far less heat than the decision to print them (before any book publisher had bought them). On October 17 the Press Council censured the proposed publication.

Before year's end Murdoch had plunged his finger into another publishing pie: the "giveaway" local weekly journal, packed with advertising and a minimum of local news, which, distributed free, competed successfully with the local weekly. In August he bought for the News of the World Organization Liverpool's *Observer,* Blackpool's *Journal,* and the southeast London and Kent *News Shopper.* In Australia Murdoch's News Ltd. group ran more than 30 giveaways, with a yearly revenue of A$750,000.

Except for the excitement Murdoch provided, it was a poor year for the British press. The credit squeeze hit advertising revenues, and circulations continued to fall. Circulations had also been hit, more effectively than was at first realized, by the 1968 price rises, and tighter money encouraged growing sales resistance, particularly to a second paper. Sunday papers had recovered more quickly, perhaps because readers preferred their magazine-type format and feature-article style.

Competition between *The Times,* the *Guardian,* and the *Daily Telegraph* for position as "top" quality daily grew keener with the tendency to drop a second paper, and led to speculation about the timing of new price rises. In February 1969 the *Guardian* was redesigned, and editorial changes were made in November. W. Harford Thomas, deputy editor since 1963, became managing editor.

The *Daily Telegraph,* financially safe as Lord Thomson's "second" daily, had lost less by price rise than other "popular" papers. Typographical improvements in February were followed in October by moving news to the front page in line with the *Guardian* and *The Times.* What might prove to be a general price rise began on October 18 when *The Times* went up to 8*d. The Times*'s circulation rise, begun in 1967 with Lord Thomson's ownership, continued but at a cost to him of more than £5 million in less than three years. During 1969 he stated in general terms the need for newspapers to sell at a more economic price. Soon after its price rise, however, *The Times* began a separate *Saturday Business News* to compete with the *Financial Times,* 8*d.* since July 1968, which, unlike other papers, had its highest sale on Saturday. Early in October the London *Evening Standard* was revamped, perhaps with an eye to increased home delivery.

Relations between managements and unions continued to be the industry's greatest problem. After a dispute about wage differentials between the National Graphical Association (NGA) and several managements (notably IPC), on September 22 the Newspaper Publishers Association (NPA) dismissed all NGA members. The *Daily Mirror* dispute, which had caused the loss of over nine million copies, had resulted from a claim by NGA machine-minders that separately negotiated productivity deals had eroded differentials between their pay and that of the operatives—members of Sogat. Sogat, meanwhile, gave warning that pay increases not related to productivity would put a stop to its productivity talks and necessitate renegotiation of existing settlements. By setting up an all-union meeting to discuss the printing industry's wage structure, the Trades Union Council averted a national strike, temporarily at least. (X.)

In the U.S. throughout most of the year it seemed as if the low-key approach to the presidency taken by Richard M. Nixon had carried over to activities involving the press. In mid-November, however, Vice-Pres. Spiro T. Agnew first charged that the three national television networks were abusing their power over public opinion and, a week later, extended the attack to include newspapers and the "concentration of more and more power over public opinion in fewer and fewer hands." He specifically named the *New York Times* and the *Washington Post,* whose parent company also published *Newsweek* magazine and owned radio and television stations in Washington, D.C.

While the White House maintained that Agnew was speaking for himself, it was generally known that the administration had not been happy with news media criticism of the president's November 3 policy statement on the Vietnam war. Fears that the attitudes expressed by Agnew could serve as a basis for restrictions on freedom of the press were expressed by all segments of the news media.

Concern over concentration of media ownership was apparent on several fronts during the year. A Supreme Court decision in March upheld an antitrust action against the joint operating arrangement of the newspapers in Tucson, Ariz. Action against newspapers in 21 other cities with similar arrangements was evidently being withheld pending a resolution of legislation that would exempt such newspapers from antitrust prosecution.

The Federal Communications Commission (FCC) started to show concern about newspaper owners who hold broadcast licenses. In January it transferred the license of WHDH-TV, owned by the Boston Herald-Traveler Corp., to another applicant, Boston Broadcasters, Inc. The FCC expressed concern about the actions of the parent newspaper in publishing an exclusive, significant story without sharing it with the television station. The decision also noted that the programming proposals of the rival applicant were better balanced than those of the owners, and that the rival better met the FCC criteria for diversification and integration. License renewals of two newspaper-owned stations were also held up pending an examination of charges of news distortion.

An agreement was reached in September between Times Mirror Co. of Los Angeles and the Times Herald Co. of Dallas, Tex., that would make the Los Angeles publisher the new owner of the *Dallas Times Herald* and its affiliated broadcasting stations. In another major purchase announced in October, Knight Newspapers, Inc., agreed to buy the *Philadelphia Inquirer* and the *Philadelphia Daily News* for a reported $55 million from Triangle Publications, headed by Walter H. Annenberg, the U.S. ambassador to Great Britain. The oldest Sunday newspaper supplement in the U.S., *This Week,* suspended publication late in 1969.

Pulitzer Prizes for journalistic efforts in the U.S. went to major publications with the exception of the editorial writing award, which was won by Paul Greenberg of the *Pine Bluff* (Ark.) *Commercial.* The *Los Angeles Times* won two prizes—meritorious public service and the international reporting award, which went to William Tuohy for his work in Vietnam.

Press control in other parts of the world included the return to prepublication censorship in Czechoslovakia and continued authoritarian reactions to the press in such countries as Greece, Spain, Brazil, South Vietnam, and South Africa. The Brazilian situation was probably the most serious. A pattern of censorship and prosecution of newsmen begun in 1968 carried through 1969.

In June the Greek government indicated that newsprint quotas would be adjusted up or down based on a newspaper's contribution to the nation's intellectual and moral standards. Spanish newspapers, free of prior censorship since January 1966, got a return taste of it in February and March 1969 when a "state of exception" was declared. By mid-1969 the South Vietnamese government had suspended over 30 newspapers for periods ranging from a few days to permanent suspension. The government also jailed several newspaper editors and publishers on charges unrelated to newspaper activities. South Africa opened itself up to new criticism by convicting the editor in chief and a reporter of the *Rand Daily Mail* for printing "false information" about prison conditions.

A more positive note was the abolishment in France of the Ministry of Information following the resignation of Pres. Charles de Gaulle. Hubert Beuve-Méry, founder-director of *Le Monde,* retired on the paper's 25th anniversary (December 23) and was succeeded by Jacques Fauvet. Also in Paris, the editors and staff of *Le Figaro* struck the newspaper in an effort to perpetuate an agreement that gave them a voice in the selection of the editor. Along a related line in the U.S., news media personnel in Chicago began publishing a critical review of their employers' journalistic efforts under the title of *Chicago Journalism Review.* (M. D. Bu.)

Books. The growing internationalism of publishing was evidenced in 1969 by international mergers, while technological improvements continued to benefit printing and packaging operations. Mergers increasingly involved companies and interests new to publishing. In July the Columbia Broadcasting System (CBS), which had earlier merged with the U.S. publishing house of Holt, Rinehart and Winston, entered the British market with its acquisition of Antony Blond Ltd. and Blond Educational Ltd. In May another U.S. firm, the International Textbook Co., which at the end of 1968 had acquired two New York companies, the John Day Co. and Ballantine Books Inc., acquired the British firm of Abelard-Schuman Ltd.; in both cases the British firms would continue under existing management.

The most discussed take-over in book publishing, as in newspapers, concerned Robert Maxwell. This time the Leasco Data Processing Equipment Corp. (New York) made an offer for Pergamon Press, Ltd., the British scientific and educational group headed by Maxwell. In August Leasco withdrew its £25 million bid for the share capital of Pergamon, expressing doubts about the position of related Maxwell holdings. There followed, amid mutual recriminations, an inquiry by the City take-over panel, and a fresh agreement in which five Leasco directors would join the Pergamon board. At an extraordinary meeting of the board in October Maxwell was voted off the reconstituted board and later resigned also as chairman of International Learning Systems Corp. (ILSC).

Also in the U.K. Hutchinson acquired a 48% interest in Constable, and the Granada Publishing Group acquired Weidenfeld and Nicolson (Educational) Ltd., incorporated from May 1 in the Rupert Hart-Davis educational list. Jonathan Cape and Chatto & Windus joined forces by forming a holding company, Chatto & Jonathan Cape Ltd., in which shareholders of each company had equal control.

In March the first Brussels Book Fair took place followed by the first International Book Festival at Nice, France (May 31–June 9). The organizers hoped these fairs would serve as half-year relays to the important Frankfurt (W.Ger.) Book Fair in October.

Publishers remained concerned over copyright legislation. The Intergovernmental Copyright Committee met with the Bern Union's permanent committee (Paris, February) to revise the so-called safeguard clause of the Universal Copyright Convention which, as a concession to less developed countries, had allowed transfer of membership from the Bern Union to the less restrictive Universal Convention.

The copyright revision bill introduced in January into the U.S. Senate would extend copyright to the life of the author plus 50 years, replacing the existing provision for an initial 28 years with 28-year renewal. The bill's passage was complicated by disputes about photocopying and cable television, and the duration of existing copyright protection was extended pending the bill's enactment.

THE CRISIS

A RECORD OF THE DARKER RACES

Volume One NOVEMBER, 1910 Number One

Edited by W. E. BURGHARDT DU BOIS, with the co-operation of Oswald Garrison Villard, J. Max Barber, Charles Edward Russell, Kelly Miller, W. S. Braithwaite and M. D. Maclean.

CONTENTS

PUBLISHED MONTHLY BY THE
National Association for the Advancement of Colored People
AT TWENTY VESEY STREET NEW YORK CITY

ONE DOLLAR A YEAR TEN CENTS A COPY

Cover of first issue of the NAACP monthly "The Crisis," edited by W. E. B. Du Bois. Arno Press in 1969 began publishing a 50-book facsimile edition of all the issues from 1910 to 1960.

Technological developments included the planned publication, announced in January, by Encyclopædia Britannica International Inc., of a series of comprehensive resource and research libraries in ultramicrofiche, a new medium that could contain up to 3,000 images on a small card. The first project, for publication in autumn 1970, would be *The Library of American Civilization, Beginnings to 1914,* representing 20,000 volumes.

The pattern of corporate mergers continued unabated in 1968. In December 1968, the U.S. Department of Commerce reported that, between 1963 and 1967, 637 major book publishing companies were acquired, half of them by other book publishers.

The principal book trade mergers in the U.S. in 1968 included the New York Times Co. purchase of 51% of Arno Press, publisher of facsimile reprints. Harcourt, Brace and World acquired Ojibway Press, publisher of 27 periodicals, and F. A. Owen Publishing, which published *Instructor* magazine in the education field, and expanded further into the trade magazine field. Crowell Collier and Macmillan bought 25 companies in 1968 including the rotogravure printer Publication Corp., Management Publishing Group, two publishers of Catholic books, P. J. Kenedy & Sons and Bruce Publishing, and G. Schirmer, a music publisher. Acquisitions in 1969 included Benziger Brothers, Inc., and Standard Rate and Data Service Inc. Litton Industries, one of the larger conglomerates, bought Chapman-Reinhold and D. Van Nostrand. David McKay Co. bought Ives Washburn and the firm that publishes the Fodor Travel Guides; Esquire, the magazine publisher, acquired the Globe Book Co. Capital Cities Broadcasting bought Fairchild Publications. National-

General Corp., a producer and exhibitor of films, purchased Grosset & Dunlap. Xerox Corp. added Ginn and Co. to its education division. Kraus Reprint was sold to U.K. press tycoon Lord Thomson. Columbia Broadcasting System entered the medical book field by acquiring W. B. Saunders Co. The Thomas Y. Crowell Co. was sold to Dun & Bradstreet, the financial publisher. Translation Publishing Co. became a part of Barnes and Noble. Viking Press bought Grossman Publishers. Farrar, Straus & Giroux bought Octagon Books. Arcata National bought Halliday Lithograph. Grolier bought Scarecrow Press.

In 1969 the Dell Publishing Co. completed its acquisition of Dial Press. Barnes and Noble became a subsidiary of Amtel; Harcourt Brace and World acquired Academic Press, owners of the Johnson Reprint Corp. Cass Canfield, Jr., vice-president of Harper and Row, set up a European affiliate, which was to be operated jointly by himself and Etas Kompass of Milan, Italy, for the publication of college-level works in the social and behavioural sciences. McGraw-Hill entered into a joint venture with Far Eastern Publishers Ltd. for printing and publishing in Singapore and Malaysia.

Time-Life Books announced a joint venture with Salvat Editores of Barcelona, Spain, for a book club to be known as Salvat Ediclub. A new group was set up to handle the company's relations with affiliated enterprises, which included Rowohlt books (West Germany), Editions Robert Laffont (France), and Organización Editorial Novaro (Mexico). In October Time-Life's acquisition of André Deutsch (U.K.) was announced.

In April Sir William Haley resigned as editor in chief of *Encyclopædia Britannica,* a post that he had taken in January 1968.

Censorship continued to be a headache in the U.S. The House Subcommittee on Postal Operations heard proposals to curb a reportedly increased flow of pornography through the mail. The Supreme Court ruled that states had the right to enact statutes imposing "variable censorship," *i.e.,* for adults and children. In the U.K. in July a conference on the obscenity laws adopted the report of a working party set up in 1968 by the Arts Council to investigate the operation of the Obscene Publications Acts of 1959 and 1964. The report advocated the repeal of all existing legislation, and the chairman explained that it was felt that the level of permissiveness controlled the obscenity laws.

The year was noteworthy for the publishing activity surrounding the successful journey of the Apollo 11 astronauts to the moon. The best-known project was the account of the moon landing by Norman Mailer (*see* BIOGRAPHY), for which Little, Brown and Co. paid an advance of $150,000 and *Life* magazine $100,000 for magazine rights. Both were owned by Time, Inc. A paperback co-published by Bantam Books and the *New York Times* entitled *We Reach the Moon* had been started two years earlier but the final chapter was written the day the astronauts splashed down in the Pacific. *The Times* of London prepared a book by its space team which was published in the U.S. by Doubleday.

In 1968 total U.S. output of books was 30,387, an increase of 5.6% over the previous year. The best-selling novel was *Airport* by Arthur Hailey with 250,000 copies. The *Better Homes and Gardens New Cook Book* was the top nonfiction work with 433,000 copies. Other best sellers in 1968 were:

Hardcover fiction: *Couples* by John Updike; *The Salzburg Connection* by Helen MacInnes; *A Small Town in Germany* by John Le Carré; *Testimony of Two Men* by Taylor Caldwell; *Preserve and Protect* by Allen Drury; *Myra Breckinridge* by Gore Vidal; *Vanished* by Fletcher Knebel; and *The Tower of Babel* by Morris L. West.

Hardcover nonfiction: *The Random House Dictionary of the English Language: College Edition,* Random House; *Listen to the Warm* by Rod McKuen; *Between Parent and Child* by Haim G. Ginott; *Lonesome Cities* by Rod McKuen; *The Doctor's Quick Weight Loss Diet* by Erwin M. Stillman and Samm Sinclair Baker; *The Money Game* by Adam Smith; *Stanyan Street and Other Sorrows* by Rod McKuen; *The Weight Watcher's Cook Book* by Jean Nidetch; *Better Homes and Gardens Eat and Stay Slim,* Meredith Press.

Paperback best sellers (all reprints of hardcover best sellers): *Rosemary's Baby* by Ira Levin; *Myra Breckinridge; The Arrangement* by Elia Kazan; and *The Exhibitionist* by Henry Sutton.

A novel, *The Chairman,* by Jay Richard Kennedy, achieved the curious distinction of appearing first as a film, then as a paperback, and finally in hardcover form. The author had written the screenplay first and had not completed the novel before the release of the film. Harold Robbins disclosed that he could earn more from book sales than from film rights, the reverse of the usual situation. He had received a $2.5 million advance for *The Inheritor,* while an independent Hollywood producer had paid only $1 million for the film rights. Publisher Lyle Stuart accepted a manuscript for a new sex-in-the-suburbs novel by "a demure Long Island housewife," Penelope Ashe. After 20,000 hardcover copies of *Naked Came the Stranger* had been sold, it was announced that the book had been written as an exercise in bad writing by 25 editors and reporters of *Newsday* newspaper.

In the U.K. the retirement of Sir Allen Lane, founder of Penguin Books, after 50 years in publishing, was a milestone. In 1968 British publishers produced 31,420 titles, the highest total ever. Although this exceeded the U.S. total output, U.S. publishers printed 23,321 new titles, compared with the U.K. figure of 22,642. The total British turnover was around £133 million, of which £59 million was earned in foreign exchange; exports accounted for 43% of output as against 6% for the U.S. This reflected a growth of 5% over the previous year. In 1968 an estimated 60 million paperbacks were sold in the U.K.

The number of paperback titles at all price levels issued in the U.S. in 1968 was substantially reduced from 1967 (1,432 from 1,613), reflecting a stabilization in this area of publishing. Publishers issuing paperbacks, however, reported a substantial increase in volume—from 10 to 20%, tending to follow the year's inflationary spiral in other businesses. U.S. total sales for 1968 approached $2,750,000,000, an increase over the $2,434,150,000 shown for 1967. A 1968 Gallup Poll reported a 3% rise in book readership between 1965 and 1969, but showed that 58% of the U.S. public did not read books at all. Sales of textbooks in 1968 totaled $782,430,000, an increase of 7.8% over 1967. Average book prices also rose; for novels, $5.82 in 1968 versus $4.32 in 1967; biography, $13.73 versus $8.39; and history, $9.95 versus $7.97.

In Australia the incidence of foreign take-overs remained high. Most significant during the year was the acquisition by the International Publishing Corp. of the Australian-owned half share of the Cheshire Group (F. W. Cheshire Publishing, Lansdowne Press, Jacarande Press, Landfall Press). IPC thus had control of the largest single slice of Australian publishing, with a claimed turnover in 1968–69 of A$14 million. During the year the federal government passed the Copyright Act 1968 making Australia a signatory to the Universal Copyright Convention. The Australian Book Publishers' Association joined with the Publishers Association of Great Britain to form a Joint Publishers' Committee to regulate trade matters in view of the Trade Practices Act. Australian branches of U.S. firms did not join, a decision regretted in Australia. In 1968 sales increased to A$11.2 million (1967: A$7.5 million). The number of books printed was 12.8 million (1967: 9.9 million), made up of 1,887 (1,420) titles and reprints. The Australian government ordered a tariff board inquiry into the book printing industry.

In the U.S.S.R. in 1968 more than 75,000 books and brochures, most of them original publications, were issued in 61 languages of the Soviet Union and in 37 foreign languages. Political and socioeconomic literature accounted for 15% of the total production and 13% of titles. Much activity was occasioned by the advent of the Lenin centenary in 1970. Production of scientific books increased by 15% over 1967. Works of fiction put out by the central and republican publishing houses in 1968 totaled 5,043.

Book production in West Germany rose from 30,683 titles in 1967 to a record 32,352 in 1968. Export figures for books and periodicals rose to DM. 490.5 million against DM. 434.2 million in 1967. Imports also rose, from DM. 143.5 million to DM. 153.8 million. In the Netherlands the most significant publishing event was the lifting of the ban on supplying books at discount prices to shops other than registered booksellers. Turnover in 1968 reached 1.2 million guilders (compared with 300,000 in 1966). Links were established between the Elsevier Publishing Co. and IPC. Book production in 1968 amounted to 11,174 titles (compared with 11,262 in 1967), of which 25% was fiction. A new purchase tax, together with inflationary trends, made the Dutch book, which had been the cheapest in Western Europe in 1965, the most expensive in 1969.

The growth of the home market in France remained slow. A survey reported that 57% of Frenchmen never bought a book. However, 17% of total book sales were said to be achieved by direct mail or door-to-door selling, which was on the increase in France. Production rose to around 23,000 titles in 1968 and exports rose by 23.5% to Fr. 320 million.

Italian book production amounted to 11,000 titles in 1968. An expanding market stimulated by the advance of popular education had led to the need for capital investment and to interest on the part of foreign publishers in take-overs of Italian publishing concerns.

In Switzerland book production in 1968 decreased slightly to 5,213 titles, compared with 5,270 in 1967. The number of new titles remained fairly constant at 4,560 (1967: 4,570). Production of travel books, however, rose by about 25%. Statistics also showed a considerable increase in books published in English (about 17%) in contrast to the overall decline in the number of works published in German and Romansh and the constant level of French and Italian titles.

In Spain 10,162 titles were printed in 1968 and total book production stood at 94 million. Austrian publishers produced 6,495 titles during the year, an increase of 3% over 1967. In Denmark 4,972 titles were published in 1968 (1967: 4,895); of these 1,650 were fiction, 382 children's books, and 959 paperbacks. (H. R. L.; P. B. St.; X.)

See also Law.

World Daily Newspapers and Circulations, 1968–69*

Country	Daily newspapers	Circulation per 1,000 of population
AFRICA		
Algeria	3	15
Angola	4	9
Cameroon	1	4
Central African Republic	2	0.6
Ceuta	1	58
Chad	1	0.4
Congo (Brazzaville)	3	1.3
Congo (Kinshasa)	7	2
Dahomey	3	1
Ethiopia	6	2
Gabon	1	1
Ghana	4	37
Guinea	1	†
Ivory Coast	1	3
Kenya	4	9
Liberia	1	9
Libya	8	5
Malagasy Republic	6	13
Mali	2	0.5
Mauritius	14	109
Melilla	1	60
Morocco	6	14
Mozambique	5	6
Niger	1	0.4
Nigeria	18	7
Portuguese Guinea	2	3
Réunion	1	61
Rhodesia	2	15
Senegal	1	6
Seychelles	2	48
Sierra Leone	2	10
Somalia	2	2
South Africa	21	57
South West Africa	2	12
Sudan	13	5
Tanzania	5	3
Togo	2	6
Tunisia	4	27
Uganda	5	8
United Arab Republic	8	15
Upper Volta	2	‡
Zambia	1	8
Total	179	
NORTH AMERICA		
Bahama Islands	2	114
Barbados	2	107
Bermuda	1	343
British Honduras	2	55
Canada	115	212
Costa Rica	5	59
Cuba	10	88
Dominican Republic	5	27
El Salvador	8	47
Guadeloupe	1	9
Guatemala	8	38
Haiti	5	5
Honduras	6	19
Jamaica	2	69
Leeward Islands	2	33
Martinique	1	67
Mexico	239	116
Netherlands Antilles	5	138
Nicaragua	6	49
Panama (incl. Canal Zone)	11	78
Puerto Rico	4	102
Trinidad and Tobago	2	102
United States	1,752	309
Virgin Islands (U.S.)	4	160
Windward Islands	1	8
Total	2,199	
SOUTH AMERICA		
Argentina	87	128
Bolivia	14	26
Brazil	73	34
Chile	36	118
Colombia	35	53
Ecuador	16	44
French Guiana	1	41
Guyana	4	191
Paraguay	5	37
Peru	72	47
Surinam	4	49
Uruguay	26	314
Venezuela	26	68
Total	399	
ASIA		
Afghanistan	15	6
Burma	8	9
Cambodia	18	11
Ceylon	9	44
China	392	19
Cyprus	11	103
Hong Kong	15	357
India	456	13
Indonesia	67	7
Iran	21	15
Iraq	6	12
Israel	20	188
Japan	116	465
Jordan	1	8
Korea, North	7	†
Korea, South	29	51
Kuwait	5	30
Laos	7	5
Lebanon	32	97
Macao	6	173
Malaysia	33	64
Mongolia	2	88
Nepal	16	3
Pakistan	93	18
Philippines	16	27
Ryukyu Islands	13	366
Saudi Arabia	5	8
Singapore	7	325
Syria	3	11
Taiwan	32	64
Thailand	18	22
Turkey	402	45
Vietnam, North	7	†
Vietnam, South	36	56
Yemen	5	18
Total	1,927	
EUROPE		
Albania	3	45
Austria	27	249
Belgium	59	285
Bulgaria	12	190
Czechoslovakia	24	283
Denmark	98	354
Finland	67	358
France	102	248
Germany, East	12	421
Germany, West	137	328
Gibraltar	1	120
Greece	94	125
Hungary	24	197
Iceland	5	435
Ireland	9	242
Italy	86	112
Luxembourg	6	477
Malta	7	‡
Netherlands	87	301
Norway	86	382
Poland	41	189
Portugal	20	69
Romania	9	164
Spain	62	159
Sweden	105	514
Switzerland	110	344
U.S.S.R.	616	295
United Kingdom	118	488
Vatican City (Holy See)	1	§
Yugoslavia	22	80
Total	2,050	
OCEANIA		
American Samoa	1	37
Australia	58	370
Cook Islands	1	37
Fiji Islands	1	20
French Polynesia	3	73
Guam	2	266
New Caledonia	1	65
New Zealand	37	380
Niue	1	60
Tonga	2	16
Total	107	
Grand total	6,861	

*Only newspapers issued four or more times weekly are included. Areas not listed had no known daily newspapers. †Total circulation less than 1 per 1,000 population. ‡Not available. §Circulation largely outside territory.

Sources: For numerical count: *Newspaper Press Directory 1969*, *Benn's Guide to Newspapers and Periodicals of the World*; for U.S. and Canada, *Editor & Publisher International Yearbook* (1969); other secondary sources. For circulation estimates: *UN Statistical Yearbook 1968* (1969).

(W. A. Ha.)

Race Relations

By 1969, W. E. B. Du Bois's prophecy that the problem of the 20th century would be the problem of the colour line had been overtaken by events. Despite widespread efforts by interested parties to perpetuate such a simplistic black and white presentation, it had become increasingly clear that many of the world's most intractable problems could not be interpreted adequately in terms of race or colour. Nationalism, not racialism, had so far proved the strongest political force of the 20th century, and though nationalism could become racialist, it could also be liberal, conservative, socialist, or revolutionary. Basic to this latter-day nationalism was the belief that ethnic groups were potential nations, with the right to form independent, sovereign, nationally homogeneous territorial states.

This nationalism, exported from its birthplace in Europe to the colonial territories ruled by the European powers, helped to break their rule. Because of arbitrarily drawn colonial boundaries, however, it was often uneasily superimposed on a group of otherwise disunited ethnic minorities, and once the main goal of independence was achieved, interethnic and intercommunal political rivalries were intensified. This was particularly true of Africa, with its persisting tribal loyalties and intertribal conflicts, its religious cleavages, its colonial legacy of white and Asian minorities, and even its imposed division between Francophile and Anglophile states. Indeed, the rivalry between and even within liberation movements grew increasingly bitter and violent. Many evolved from Pan-African or pan-national democratic or revolutionary parties into traditional and contending sectional parties, based on long-standing tribal rivalries or class antagonisms.

In most independent African states, ethnic or tribal rivalries also determined the course of political life. This was most tragically exemplified in Nigeria, but the assassination of Tom Mboya in Kenya and unease within Zambia's ruling coalition were symptoms of similar conflicts. So were the troubles reported from Ethiopia, Chad, and the Sudan.

The first Pan-African Cultural Festival, presented by the Organization of African Unity, was held in Algiers in July 1969. A number of African observers criticized it for being pan-Arab and political rather than pan-African and cultural, "a deliberate attempt to embarrass or belittle Black Africans, Anglophile Africans, Christian Africans, and Africans in sympathy with Israel." Among those present were representatives of the Palestinian Al Fatah and the U.S. Black Panther movement.

In the U.S. there was much less widespread violence than in 1968. The election of Richard M. Nixon was seen as a victory for the "forgotten" whites, descendants of European immigrants, lower-middle-class city dwellers caught between the wealthy WASP's (the popular acronym for white Anglo-Saxon Protestants —by extension, the Establishment) and liberals and the poor and black. Black militancy was most in evidence on the campuses and among the armed forces in Vietnam. Within the ghettoes, more constructive self-help and self-improvement programs were reported, with jobs and political power as the goals.

Elsewhere nationalism and ethnocentrism showed few signs of waning, although the gloomy prophecies about a resurgence of neo-Nazi voting strength in West Germany were not borne out by the election results. Great Russian and Chinese chauvinism were both stimulated by the confrontation on the Sino-Soviet border. However, the continuing existence of relics of "bourgeois nationalism" or "localism" was reported in some of the Soviet Union's own borderlands, notably Lithuania, the Transcarpathian district of the Ukraine, and Azerbaijan.

Among the most tragic happenings of 1969 was the acceleration of communal disorders in India, culminating in Gandhi's own state of Gujarat in the month of his birth centenary, October, with the most bloody Hindu-Muslim communal riots since his death.

South Africa. In a "Message to the People of South Africa," the South African Council of Churches reaffirmed its conviction that obedience to God came before loyalty to Caesar: "Christians betray their calling if they give their highest loyalty, which is due to Christ, to one group or tradition, especially where that group is demanding self-expression at the expense of other groups."

This message met with angry accusations of "meddling by 'political priests' " from B. J. Vorster's government, which in 1969 pushed through its omnibus General Law Amendment Act in the teeth of protests from judges, bar councils, professors of law, and the press. Particular criticism was focused on sec. 29, which authorized any Cabinet minister to prohibit the giving of evidence before a court or any statutory body if, in his opinion, this would be prejudicial to the interests of the public or the security of the state; and on sec. 10, which made it an offense to disclose any matter with which the newly founded Bureau of State Security (BOSS) was dealing. The total expenditure on secret services for 1969–70 was increased to more than R 5.3 million (some critics contrasted this with the figure for "Bantu education," which had remained at R 13 million for 12 years).

Between 30 and 40 persons were being held under the Terrorism Act (1967) after a single sweep in Pretoria, but the minister refused to give the total number held all over the country because it was "not in the national interest." In 1968, 32 persons were detained in the Transkei under Proclamation 400 of 1960, and a further 7 by May 1969; in the same period 11 persons were detained under the 180-day detention clause, 27 having been so detained in 1968. In August 1969 the Black Sash reported that at least 490 persons were living under banning orders, 42 were subject to house arrest, and 39 were subject to removal orders under the Bantu Administration Act; in 1968, 322 people had been refused passports, 69 had left on permanent exit permits, and 1,251 applications for visas to South Africa had been refused. Admissions to prison in 1967–68 were: 13,792 whites, 561,405 Bantu, 77,374 Coloureds, and 2,325 Asians.

The growing harshness of the security arrangements appeared to have silenced or obliterated any organized resistance or protest. Intergroup contacts, even on a totally nonpolitical level, became increasingly difficult. This was augmented by the continuing implementation of negative residential apartheid by means of such laws as the Group Areas Act, which had affected an estimated 109,000 Coloured people in Cape Town (where the traditionally Coloured "District Six" itself was to become "white") and another 102,000 Coloured people in the Transvaal, as well as over 80,000 Indians in the Transvaal and up to 140,000 in Durban.

Nearly 600,000 Coloured people, voting in the first elections for the Coloured Persons' Representative

Puerto Rico:
see Dependent States
Qatar:
see Dependent States
Quakers:
see Religion

Council in September 1969, gave the antiapartheid Labour Party a clear victory, only to have the government ensure a majority for itself by nominating 20 apartheid supporters to the 60-member council. In general the Coloured community suffered most from "petty apartheid" (beaches, transport, cultural facilities) and had potentially least to gain.

For over half a century of Afrikaner nationalist politics, there had been a steady progression toward extremism and "purified" nationalism, with each new leader gradually earning the description of "moderate" as his challenger or successor moved in. This happened to Prime Minister Vorster from 1966 on, because he combined his tough and illiberal internal policies with pragmatic attempts to unify the English- and Afrikaans-speaking whites into one South African nation, and to pursue Hendrik F. Verwoerd's outward-looking policy of making friends and influencing people in Black Africa. These policies were at the core of the long-simmering conflict between *verligtes* ("enlightened") and *verkramptes* ("cramped" or inward-looking) within the Nationalist Party (NP). The political and racialist thinking of many *verkramptes* was apparent not only in their well-known attitudes toward nonwhites, but in increasingly vituperative attacks on "the scum of Europe" (*i.e.,* recent Catholic immigrants), "liberalists, Jews, foreigners (including English) and profiteers."

At the Cape meeting of the NP in May 1969, the differences between *verligtes* and *verkramptes* were papered over, but they burst into the open again at the Transvaal Congress in September, where Albert Hertzog, the leading *verkrampte,* and ten others voted against Vorster's policy on sport and seven others abstained. This led to the expulsion of Hertzog and some supporters and the calling of a snap election for April 22, 1970, in the hope of isolating the *verkramptes* in a small "purified" opposition party and perhaps picking up considerable former United Party (UP) and English-speaking support for the new "pragmatic" outward-looking NP.

The majority of South African whites had always preferred the traditional policies of "segregation" and "baasskap" (white domination) to intellectual blueprints for the "separate development" of increasingly expensive and unrealistic Bantustans. The original blueprint had posited that the black tide to the "white" areas not only must, but would be checked, reversed, and finally stopped altogether. But 14 years after the Tomlinson report the number of Africans outside the homelands continued to grow, as did the dependence of South African industry on their labour. Meanwhile, the latest demographic statistics released by the Bureau of Standards showed a lowered white natural increase of 1.34% and an increased Coloured one of 2.7% in 1967. African figures were likely to be even more disturbing, and the black population was growing faster (an estimated 28 million by the year 2000) than the potential rate of development of the homelands; it was also becoming poorer relative to the white population. Erich Leistner of the Africa Institute estimated that the homelands would never be able to absorb more than 8 or 9 million in the next 30 years, leaving about 20 million Africans to be absorbed in white areas.

Development of the homelands—even as originally planned—had lagged badly (only R 40 million having been voted in 1969). Fewer than 1,000 new industrial jobs had been created in the Bantustans in 13 years; even in the "border areas" of industrial development, only 40,000 new jobs had been provided in the 8 years since this part of the scheme was launched. Nevertheless, the government pressed on. In February the minister of Bantu (African) administration, M. C. Botha, announced that under the new Bantu Homelands Citizenship Bill, all Africans would soon be issued "citizenship certificates" (called by the *Cape Times* a "passport to nowhere" for detribalized Africans). He also proposed to take powers giving him the unfettered right to introduce any form of job reservation without any safeguards or consultations at all.

Nongovernmental reactions to intensifying economic integration in the urban areas varied widely. Most employers took a liberal economic view, while many educators and others were perturbed about the consequences for the economy, the country, and the Africans themselves of the inferior quality and financing of "Bantu education." Only 8.7% of African manpower had gone even one stage beyond a primary education, there were particular weaknesses in mathematics and science teaching, and the dropout rate was high. Most Africans were thus unprepared to take part in economic life, while the white group's "know-how" and management skills were already overextended.

United Kingdom. Despite the reported passing of the "liberal hour" in British race relations, and a hardening of attitudes on both sides, the persistence or growth of a positive and pragmatic approach to race relations was discernible in 1969. There was also an increasing tendency to see the problems of coloured Commonwealth immigration in the wider context of bad housing, bad schooling, inadequate welfare services, and twilight neighbourhoods. Other issues, such as "law and order," drugs and dropouts, student power and left-wing fascism, the problem of such minority groups as the Gypsies, and, increasingly, the Protestant-Roman Catholic confrontation in Ulster (seemingly as intractable as any "racial" situation), attracted increasing attention. The issue of "voluntary" repatriation, propagated by MP Enoch Powell, retained a certain head of steam, despite its increasing impracticability as the number of immigrants who were registered U.K. citizens or British-born grew.

The total number of "new" Commonwealth immigrants (mostly but not all "coloured") admitted for settlement in 1968 was 50,150, compared with 57,648 in 1967. For the first eight months of 1969 the figure was 30,436. This decline could be attributed to the fact that most dependents had now joined the immigrants who had arrived when there were no immigration controls, or milder ones. About 236,000 was given as a maximum estimate of the number of dependents who might be expected to arrive in the ten years 1968–78 to join heads of households who had arrived before 1967 (David Eversley and Fred Sukdeo, *The Dependants of the Coloured Commonwealth Population of England and Wales,* Institute of Race Relations, London, Special Series, March 1969).

By the middle of 1969 it was estimated that there were up to 1,250,000 coloured Commonwealth immigrants and their British-born children (constituting about one-fifth of the total) in Britain. The number of immigrant pupils in maintained primary and secondary schools in England and Wales rose from 164,725, or 2.2% of total enrollment, in January 1967 to 200,742, or 2.78%, a year later. The main coloured groups were West Indians (mostly Jamaicans), who constituted over half the total, Indians (mostly Sikhs), and Pakistanis (the great majority from a few small areas). The 1969 report of the six-year Survey of Race

Relations in Britain (*Colour and Citizenship*, by E. J. B. Rose, Nicholas Deakin, and others for the Institute of Race Relations, London) estimated that the coloured population in Britain would be between 2 and 2.5 million in 1986.

This very comprehensive 250,000-word volume stressed that bad and overcrowded housing conditions and concentration in the twilight areas of the main conurbations were major handicaps for most immigrants, and that new and urgent housing policies were needed to prevent the development of U.S.-style ghettoes. Immigration had on balance been good for the economy and the standard of living of the native population, but despite their vital contribution to the economy, there was little sign that immigrants were breaking through into white-collar or professional work. This situation could become much more important in the second generation, when children born and educated in the U.K. would share the aspirations of their white counterparts.

The problems of coloured youth just out of school were also dealt with in the first report (September 1969) of the House of Commons Select Committee on Race Relations and Immigration. The committee saw the way in which these young people were treated as a test case, and agreed with the authors of *Colour and Citizenship* that race relations would be improved if the immigrants were more widely dispersed in the country. Such dispersal could be assisted by opening up a wider range of jobs for young British-educated immigrants. The committee came down firmly for "positive discrimination" where it was needed to provide equal opportunity.

An analysis of complaints received under the Race Relations Act, 1968, in the six months after it came into force (Nov. 26, 1968, to May 31, 1969) showed a total of 760 complaints, of which 366 concerned employment while 394 were chiefly concerned with such matters as places of public resort (54), police (30), and housing (80). Of the employment complaints, 46 were found to be outside the scope of the act; in 102 the opinion was "no discrimination"; while "discrimination" was judged in 18 cases. Of the nonemployment complaints, 89 were outside the scope of the act, 77 were not upheld, and 38 were upheld. In all cases but one (in which proceedings were taken), where unlawful discrimination was found, satisfactory assurances were obtained.

From the outset there had been considerable opposition to the inclusion in the Race Relations Act of the controversial sec. 6, which made it an offense to stir up hatred against people distinguished by colour, race, or ethnic origin by writing, distributing, or saying abusive things in a public place or meeting. In mid-October 1969 Mark Bonham Carter, chairman of the Race Relations Board, joined forces with Frank Cousins, chairman of the Community Relations Commission, to ask the home secretary to repeal this section, on the grounds that it was unnecessary, in view of the existence of the Public Order Act 1936, and probably did more harm than good. (SH. P.)

United States. After flight from legal prosecution and several years in hiding abroad, Robert Williams, a black militant, voluntarily asked in September 1969 to be repatriated, declaring that while armed self-defense was sometimes the black's best political instrument, America today still represented the "best chance ever" for social changes and racial justice. Disorders and violence, Williams said, had made the nation ripe for change. Perhaps the variable moods of the nation in 1969 were represented in this incident, based as it was on both a belief in the positive value of disorders and a concomitant persisting faith in the capacity of the nation to change and provide justice for all.

Several themes in race relations came into new prominence in 1969. The concept of community control of elementary and secondary schools became a major feature of both racial and class conflict in New York and other major cities. The idea was a development of the earlier theme of "maximum feasible participation" by the poor in decisions regarding their own communities, a theme that presidential assistant Daniel Moynihan and black intellectual leader Kenneth Clark both denounced as unsuccessful (the former at length in his book *Maximum Feasible Misunderstanding*).

The focal point of the battle over community control was the Ocean Hill-Brownsville school district in New York, where district supervisor Rhody McCoy, United Federation of Teachers president Albert Shanker, Mayor John Lindsay, and various leaders of ethnic community organizations became involved in a dispute that was still continuing at year's end. The dispute was an archetype of the demand from an increasing number of black militants and their supporters for some version of black self-determination. In direct contradiction to the earlier quest for full integration, "community control" unavoidably implied separate educational facilities. Without renouncing long-range hopes for a fully integrated society, the black community pressed for more control over their own lives and more of a share of public resources of all kinds on the explicit ground that they could not trust the white community to be sufficiently concerned with the well-being of black children or adults. Even so, two-thirds or more of the black community throughout the nation reported themselves as favouring integration.

Meanwhile, the Black Panthers, the one militant black movement that had developed a notion of the importance of a class struggle waged jointly by blacks and whites, was encountering serious difficulties. Fearing he would be killed in jail, Eldridge Cleaver (*see* BIOGRAPHY), under whose leadership the Panthers had come to increasing prominence, fled the country while on bail. Stokely Carmichael, who objected to the willingness of the Panthers to work with white sympathizers, had voluntarily exiled himself earlier to become involved in the Pan-African movement. Bobby Hutton was dead, Huey Newton in jail, and Bobby Seale awaiting trial. The Panthers' general

UPI COMPIX

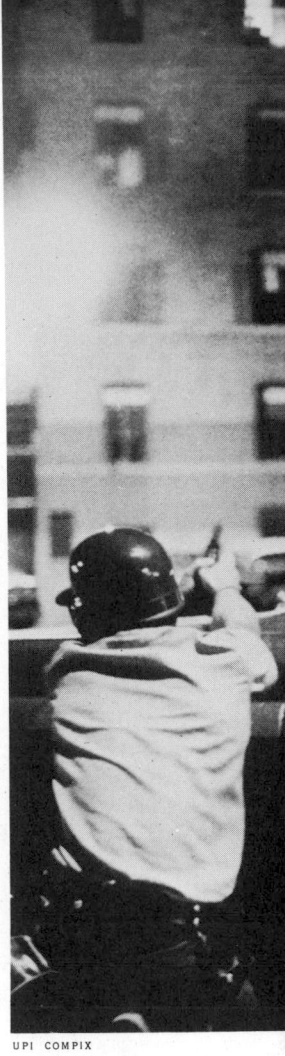

Policeman fires at sniper in a predominantly black neighbourhood of Indianapolis, Ind., on June 7, 1969. Two policemen were hurt and 70 persons arrested during racial disturbance.

Children hunt through debris of burned-out store in Omaha, Neb., black ghetto on June 26, 1969. Violence had started two nights before when a 14-year-old Negro girl was shot by a white policeman.

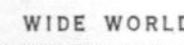
WIDE WORLD

counsel estimated that as many as 28 members had died in gunfights with the police since January 1968, and, following shoot-outs in Chicago and Los Angeles near the end of 1969, several groups undertook investigations to find whether there was a concerted effort by police to wipe out the organization.

Although 1969 was far more peaceful than 1968, violence broke out in various forms in several cities. A study of violent incidents in more than 20 locales conducted by the Lemberg Center for the Study of Violence at Brandeis University reported that these incidents revealed no central plan or conspiracy. Instead, it was indicated that the most frequent pattern was that of a single incident between one or two black individuals and one or two policemen, which then escalated as the response on each side mounted. Some of the disorders were expansive and relatively long-lived, while others were quickly brought to an end. Involved were such cities as San Francisco; Cairo, Ill.; Utica and Niagara Falls, N.Y.; Indianapolis, Evansville, and Kokomo, Ind.; Newark, Passaic, Red Bank, Lakewood, and Camden, N.J.; Middletown, Waterbury, and Hartford, Conn.; Harrisburg and York, Pa.; Columbus and Youngstown, O.; Forest City, Ark.; Fort Lauderdale, Fla.; Florence, S.C.; and Grand Rapids, Mich.

Perhaps even more disturbing were the varying forms of dissent on college campuses. Troubles at San Francisco State College continued throughout the year, though in differing degrees of intensity and without any decisive outcome. Those who claimed victory for the administration under Pres. S. I. Hayakawa (*see* BIOGRAPHY) pointed to a relative demoralization and scattering of the dissident element. On the other side, one could also point to demoralization of the faculty, backlash within the community, and reprisals by the state government. More attention was focused on Cornell University, largely because, in April, nationwide publicity was given to a photograph showing black students emerging from an occupied building with rifles in their hands. While earlier reports had made passing references to the series of events, including threats against lives, that had led the black students to arm themselves, the blacks' apparent readiness for a "shoot-out" brought great turmoil and resulted some months later in the resignation of Pres. James A. Perkins.

The core grievance in campus incidents usually referred to a demand by black students for black studies programs, separate black facilities—either dormitories or meeting places or both—and some added measure of control by black students over the courses and faculties to be involved in the black studies programs. In an increasing number of universities, students of other minority groups, particularly Puerto Ricans and Mexican-Americans, were joining with black students in these causes, sometimes under the aegis of a "third world" movement.

Elsewhere on the education front, the battle over desegregation and integration of primary and secondary schools continued. It came to a head at midyear when, with the date by which various school districts had been ordered to desegregate or lose federal support approaching, the Department of Health, Education, and Welfare and the Civil Rights Division of the Justice Department applied to the federal courts for permission to delay integration in districts where administrative or educational disorder might result. The request by the federal government for a delay in the implementation of its own orders proved politically embarrassing. There was an openly publicized rebellion among numerous staff lawyers attached to the Civil Rights Division, and considerable comment by observers on the probable influence of Sen. Strom Thurmond of South Carolina on the administration. Upon receiving the case, the Supreme Court, ironically now under President Nixon's appointee, Warren Burger, unanimously ordered the immediate desegregation of the schools, with no delays permitted beyond the previous due date.

The problem of persisting poverty in the midst of affluence continued to beset the country, resulting finally in two serious changes in government orientation toward the poor and the disadvantaged. The first concerned a proposal for a federal floor of $1,600 a year, uniform throughout the states, for family welfare benefits. This proposal was of special interest to the black community, since it was calculated that fully one-third of blacks lived below the poverty level. The inadequacy of such provisions, however, was revealed by the Bureau of Labor Statistics. Reporting on a study made in the spring of 1967, the bureau showed that, as a national average, it cost $5,915 a year for a family of four to maintain a low standard of living.

The second major change was a proposal by the President's Commission on Income Maintenance Programs to provide supplementary income to the "working poor"—those who, though at work, did not earn enough to rise out of the poverty bracket. This proposal had been hotly debated in the Cabinet, with the discussion centring around the possible consequences for "work incentives." Since substantial percentages of the official poor consisted of the old, the sick, the unemployable, and underage children and their mothers, the question seemed largely academic. Yet the fate of these proposals remained uncertain.

Interest and enthusiasm persisted for the development of a black entrepreneurial class. It was hoped that "black capitalism," with easy credit facilities and some training in business know-how, might make it possible for larger numbers of blacks to break into the business world. Support for these programs remained high despite the depressing rate of failure among small businesses ventured into by blacks during the preceding year. Another economic effort was seen in increased pressure throughout the business and professional world to recruit and train a larger number of black employees at all levels. While there were numerous jobs that clearly could be filled by skilled black employees, for many others, at lower levels of skill, some measure of compensatory training would have to be provided. The "old-line" craft unions continued to resist the admission of blacks to their ranks—a situation reflected in several cities by struggles between the black community and the building trades.

The continuing gains and persisting plight of the blacks in economic matters were both documented by various government reports during the year. Thus in March the Census Bureau, reporting on social and economic trends in 212 major metropolitan areas since 1960, cited gains in Negro family and Negro women's earnings and education, but also noted a rise in unemployment among Negro youths, in broken homes, and in the widening gap between Negro male adult and white male adult earnings.

The struggle for full enfranchisement of black voters, especially as promised in the Voting Rights Act of 1965, emerged into the spotlight in January when several congressmen opposed the five-year extension of the 1965 act beyond its scheduled expiration in August 1970. The administration at first supported a modified extension of the proposal, but urged new controls that opponents said would decrease the effectiveness of the act by putting the burden for vigilance on the Justice Department. When these modifications were attacked by leaders of both parties, the administration eased off, and at year's end it seemed reasonably sure that the existing act would be extended. The force of the black vote was dramatized in July when Negroes, who outnumbered whites by 10,000 to 3,500 in Eutaw and in Green County, Ala., won control over both the county government and the school board. In May Charles Evers (*see* BIOGRAPHY), field secretary of the National Association for the Advancement of Colored People, was elected mayor of Fayette, Miss.

The churches did not remain untouched by the conflict in race relations. Continuing demands upon all denominations to take more active roles in the struggle for racial equality were made from both within and without the churches throughout the year. The demands were dramatized by James Forman of the National Black Economic Development Conference, who demanded $500 million from Protestant churches as "reparations" due to American Negroes who had been "persecuted, exploited, and killed." (*See* RELIGION.)

The greatest development of "indigenous" effort by blacks occurred in the field of the arts, especially in the theatre and literature. A large array of writing by black authors, fictional and nonfictional, began appearing in bookstores throughout the country. At the same time, the notion grew that only blacks could interpret the black experience properly—evident in the nearly uniform denunciation of William Styron's *The Confessions of Nat Turner*. Black performers began to appear in much greater numbers in the theatre and several all-black companies were formed. Interviews revealed a wide range of definitions of "black art" and an equally variable set of conceptions of the obligations of the black artist—from the need for the artist to be artist above all to seeing the arts as primarily a political instrument.

Perhaps the most ironic note of the year was struck by the appearance, in the midst of the revival of black consciousness and militance, of a long article in the winter 1969 issue of the *Harvard Educational Review* by Arthur Jensen of the University of California. Jensen felt that compensatory educational programs, such as the Head Start program for underprivileged preschool children, had failed, and went on to suggest that probably the differences between black and white academic performance and ability reflected genuine genetic differences between the two "races." The unmistakable implication was that of the genetic inferiority of the black.

Two subsequent issues of the *Harvard Educational Review* (spring and summer 1969) contained full-scale critical evaluations of the Jensen report, along with his response to some of the critiques. The evaluations brought into serious question Jensen's assumptions, methods, samples, data, and conclusions. By then, however, the report had been so widely (and in some cases, irresponsibly) publicized that in many quarters it was believed that a "new" scientific look at the evidence indicated blacks were genetically inferior to whites in abilities relevant to academic and general mental performance.

The various critiques of the Jensen study collectively indicated that, in order to test whether there are genuine genetic differences between groups, certain conditions must be met, including: (1) two racial groups that are identifiably and measurably genetically distinct in certain important features that might be connected with the capabilities in question; (2) the presence of a test of native intelligence; and (3) total control over those environmental factors of opportunity and training that could result in important differences between various groups. None of these conditions had been met by any of the tests Jensen had used. It remained the conclusion of the majority of scientists that, in the present state of knowledge, nothing could be said about whether blacks were equal to, inferior to, or superior to whites in intelligence.

A follow-up report on the Kerner Commission report on civil rights in the United States indicated that one year after the report (February 1968) America still remained two communities, one black and one white, separate from each other in many important respects, and that little progress toward the reduction of that separateness had occurred. An apparent rise in crimes of violence in a number of urban areas, coupled with violent demonstrations in cities and on campuses, brought forth a significant measure of "backlash" from the white community, especially from the lower-middle-class members of various ethnic groups in urban areas. A number of candidates for local office evoked these fears during the year, but the results of the elections were indecisive, with victories for both sides. Meanwhile, throughout a growing portion of the black community it was coming to be felt that nonviolent methods of expressing dissent had little effect on local or national policy. The efforts of moderate leaders such as Roy Wilkins and Whitney Young to keep the Negro community on a forceful but nonviolent course of action, while still appealing to the majority of blacks, were running into increasing difficulty.

Meanwhile, a new area of racial conflict appeared in the military, which only a short time before had been heralded as the one place where blacks could find true equality. Black soldiers reenlisted at record rates, but there was evidence of considerable discontent, and claims were made that the traditional conditions of prejudice and discrimination had not been eliminated. Black servicemen joined together in various encampments in mass protests regarding their unfair treatment. It was somewhat encouraging to the black community, nevertheless, that military and civilian officials in the highest quarters were at least verbally indicating a concern for these matters and were making public avowals of their intention to promote greater justice and equality for black members of the armed services.

Black communities were not alone in their protests against racial prejudice and discrimination in 1969. Perhaps most salient was the rising rate of protest among Indians, especially with regard to conditions on reservations and the state of Indian education. Various public officials, including Sen. Edward Kennedy (Dem., Mass.), denounced the conditions of Indian life as a national disgrace. Commissioner of Indian Affairs Robert L. Bennett denied that the Indian Bureau's educational program was solely to blame for the Indian's plight, but continuous pressure brought his resignation in July. The appointment of an Indian as the new commissioner suggested some greater possibility of active interest in Indian affairs on the part of the administration. (M. M. TU.)

See also Crime; Education; Police; South Africa; United States.

UPI COMPIX

Black militant leader James Forman confronts Ernest T. Campbell, pastor of Riverside Church in New York City. Forman demanded that U.S. churches pay blacks $500 million as reparations for past exploitation.

Refugees

When the United Nations General Assembly in December 1968 adopted a resolution on the Annual Report of the High Commissioner for Refugees by acclamation, it reflected the growing acceptance by governments of the UNHCR's purely humanitarian and nonpolitical approach to refugee problems. By the end of 1969, 58 governments had ratified the 1951 convention on refugees' rights and status and 37 had ratified the 1967 protocol that complemented it. Furthermore, a convention governing specific aspects of refugee problems in Africa was adopted unanimously at the meeting of the Organization of African Unity (OAU) at Addis Ababa in September 1969. UNHCR and the OAU signed an agreement in June providing for close cooperation in all matters concerning refugee problems in Africa.

The High Commissioner's material assistance program comprised a great variety of projects including assistance to handicapped and aged refugees in Europe and Latin America, the promotion of migration, the pioneering of large-scale rural development programs in Africa, assistance to Tibetan refugees in Nepal, housing and social services for Chinese in Macao, and vocational training and education programs for refugees.

The number of refugees continued to increase during 1969. In Africa alone, the number of concern to UNHCR rose to over one million. In Europe, there were over 5,000 people in official reception and transit centres in Austria, Germany, and Italy at the end of 1969. Thanks to smoothly working resettlement machinery, the generosity of countries of immigration, the efforts of the Intergovernmental Committee for European Migration (ICEM), the support of voluntary agencies, and the work of UNHCR, refugee movements in Europe could be absorbed although some temporary overcrowding in transit centres occurred. A special problem in 1969 was the accumulation of individual refugee cases in African cities.

In 1969, over 70 governments, as against 67 in 1968, contributed approximately $4 million (against $3.5 million in 1968) toward a $6 million minimum target to finance UNHCR programs. More than half of the $5,769,400 approved for the High Commissioner's program for 1970 was to help refugees in Africa. Major projects were to be the consolidation of six settlements for Rwandese refugees in Uganda, the establishment of a rural community for Sudanese refugees in the Gambela area of Ethiopia, and settlements for Mozambique refugees in Tanzania and for Ethiopian refugees in the Sudan.

The 1969 Nansen Medal was awarded to H.R.H. Princess Princep Shah of Nepal, president of the Nepal Red Cross, in recognition of the exceptional services she had rendered in helping Tibetan refugees to settle in her country. (X.)

See also Migration, International.

Religion

Religion was much in the headlines in 1969, as the focal point of both hopeful and unhopeful events. Religious feeling already coloured such struggles as those between Israel and the Arab countries and between India and Pakistan. To these was added in 1969—in what seemed almost a throwback to the religious wars of the 17th century—the violent outbreak between Roman Catholics and Protestants in Northern Ireland. (*See* UNITED KINGDOM.) Ecumenical moves continued, with some setbacks and some successes. The Roman Catholic Church still attempted to come to terms with the aftermath of the second Vatican Council and, in the U.S. especially, churchmen of all faiths wrestled with conflicting demands regarding the church's role in social action.

For all the publicity, a Gallup poll taken during 1969 showed that 70% of those polled felt the influence of religion was declining, compared with only 14% in 1957. On the other hand, there were some indications that interest in religion was growing. College and university chaplains reported an increasing number of students enrolling in religion courses, and if interest in the formal, institutionalized expression of the church was waning, unorthodox religious expression—as in underground church movements, liturgical experimentation, and social activism of all kinds—seemed to be on the rise.

Perhaps the most explosive and traumatic event in American church life in 1969 occurred on Sunday, May 4, at Riverside Church, New York City, when James Forman (*see* BIOGRAPHY), former head of the Student Non-Violent Coordinating Committee (SNCC), interrupted the regularly scheduled church service to present the Black Manifesto. Not many church people had known of the Manifesto prior to that time, but before the week was out most Americans were painfully aware of it. The Manifesto was originally presented at the first National Black Economic Development Conference, held in Detroit late in April under the sponsorship of the Interreligious Foundation for Community Organization, funded by ten major religious agencies. Forman had led what he called a "seizure of power at this conference." The Manifesto was adopted at the meeting by a vote of 187–63, with many of the 600 delegates abstaining.

It was not until after Forman's Riverside Church appearance and subsequent appearances by him and his followers at various church conventions that church people learned the specific content of the Manifesto. It was based on the principle that the black man is entitled to reparations for damages from America's whites—specifically, $500 million from the churches. This money was to be used for a Southern land bank to secure land for black farmers; black-controlled publishing and broadcast enterprises; re-

Radio: *see* Television and Radio
Radiology: *see* Medicine
Railroads: *see* Transportation
Real Tennis: *see* Sporting Record
Reclamation: *see* Conservation
Recordings: *see* Music
Reformed Churches: *see* Religion
Rehabilitation: *see* Medicine
Relief: *see* Social Services

search and training centres devoted to the needs of black people; a black university to be located in the South; and a fund to develop cooperative businesses in the U.S. and Africa. The goal was later raised to $3 billion. The Lutheran Church in America was asked for $50 million in cash and 60% of revenues from assets. The demand for $200 million from U.S. Catholics was presented to New York archdiocesan officials. The American Baptist Convention was asked for $60 million and the investment of 60% of its financial holdings in black communities. Other major church bodies in the U.S. were asked for similar sums, depending in part on the size of the church body in question.

Reaction to the Manifesto varied from outright rejection to pleas for understanding. Orthodox rabbis voted unanimously to reject the demands "categorically." Bishop Stephen G. Spottswood, board chairman of the National Association for the Advancement of Colored People, approved the rejection by many churches. "In our long crusade," he said, "we have never subscribed to the reparations concept." The United Methodist Church Council of Bishops repudiated the ideology of the Black Manifesto and pointed out that the United Methodist Church had already set up a $20 million Fund for Reconciliation to aid minorities. (See *Methodists,* below.)

Most churches and their officials agreed that the Black Manifesto pointed up in a dramatic manner the existence of white racism and the depressed state of the blacks. One church leader declared that the Manifesto "makes us more painfully aware of the injustice, violence, and racism which black people know and experience. We acknowledge our involvement in and responsibility for the existence of these realities in our society." Whether the churches would or could raise $500 million, let alone the $3 billion, remained problematical, however.

The tax-exempt status of churches came under closer scrutiny during the year, both by the government and by the churches. Protestant publishing firms in Nashville, Tenn., lost their second round in a battle to maintain their tax-exempt status. The metropolitan government of Nashville-Davidson County's Board of Tax Equalization assessed some $35 million in church-owned property at the government's 40% formula, and submitted an annual tax bill for $742,-000. The decision was to be appealed to the U.S. Supreme Court.

The National Council of Churches, composed of 33 Protestant and Orthodox churches, and the U.S. Catholic Conference asked the federal government to end tax exemption for churches on income received from businesses unrelated to religion. The request to the government came after several months of negotiations involving Catholic and NCC leaders in consultation with the Synagogue Council of America.

Among significant church gatherings of 1969 was the first joint meeting of the Associated Church Press, largely Protestant, and the Catholic Press Association. Meeting in Atlanta, Ga., the two press groups, representing some 500 publications with over 50 million subscribers in the U.S. and Canada, noted a decline in subscribers to church journals during the past year.

At its triennial General Assembly, held in Detroit, the National Council of Churches elected Mrs. Theodore O. Wedel as its president. Mrs. Wedel, the candidate of the council's nominating committee, was opposed by Albert B. Cleague, Jr., militant black pastor of Detroit's Shrine of the Black Madonna. It was indicative of the times that, under these circumstances, the election of the first woman to hold the NCC presidency was considered in some quarters to be a retrogressive step.

The U.S. Congress on Evangelism attracted 5,000 delegates from 95 denominations to its meeting in

Estimated Membership of the Principal Religions of the World

Religions	North America*	South America	Europe†	Asia	Africa	Oceania‡	World
Total Christian	214,258,000	150,426,000	442,006,000	61,473,000	42,056,000	14,055,000	924,274,000
Roman Catholic	126,468,000	147,219,000	226,303,000	47,622,000	28,751,000	4,107,000	580,470,000
Eastern Orthodox	3,675,000	47,000	114,103,000	2,819,000	4,956,000	84,000	125,684,000
Protestant§	84,115,000	3,160,000	101,600,000	11,032,000	8,349,000	9,864,000	218,120,000
Jewish‖	6,035,000	705,000	4,025,000	2,460,000	238,000	74,000	13,537,000
Muslim¶	166,000	416,000	13,848,000	374,167,000	104,297,000	118,000	493,012,000
Zoroastrian♀	—	—	12,000	126,000	—	—	138,000
Shinto♁	31,000	116,000	2,000	69,513,000	—	—	69,662,000
Taoist□	16,000	19,000	12,000	54,277,000	—	—	54,324,000
Confucian□	96,000	109,000	55,000	371,261,000	9,000	57,000	371,587,000
Buddhist◊	187,000	157,000	8,000	176,568,000	—	—	176,920,000
Hindu▲	55,000	660,000	160,000	434,447,000	1,205,000	218,000	436,745,000
Totals	220,844,000	152,608,000	460,128,000	1,544,292,000	147,805,000	14,522,000	2,540,199,000
Population✢	304,439,000	174,246,000	636,993,000	1,907,481,000	328,134,000	18,127,000	3,369,420,000

*Includes Central America and the West Indies.

†Includes communicants claimed by established churches; includes also the U.S.S.R., in which the effect of a half-century of official Marxist ideology upon religious adherence is much disputed among specialists.

‡Includes New Zealand and Australia as well as islands of the South Pacific.

§Protestant statistics usually include "full members" rather than all baptized persons and are not comparable to those of ethnic religions or churches counting all adherents. The World Council of Churches in 1968 constituted a working committee to seek uniform nomenclature and reporting procedures.

‖Based on 1968 estimates of Jewish Statistical Bureau.

¶The chief base of Islam is still ethnic, and the statistics are largely derived from demographic studies. Evangelistic work is now carried on by Muslim renewal movements, and major gains have been made in Europe and the U.S. (viz. Black Muslims).

♀A declining number of Zoroastrians are found in Iran, Pakistan, and India.

♁A Japanese ethnic religion, Shinto's strength has declined since the emperor gave up claim to divinity (1947). Japanese religious statistics are highly problematical because adherents frequently are related to several different religions simultaneously. In 1968 the Japanese government instituted a statistical survey to clarify the status of different religions, cults, and movements, several of which claim millions of new adherents since World War II.

□Figures on China are highly speculative, including the number of remaining Muslims. The effect of Mao's Cultural Revolution upon Taoism and Confucianism is yet to be measured. Moreover, there is a long-standing dispute among scholars as to whether Confucianism should be counted as a "religion" at all.

◊Buddhism has several modern renewal movements which have won adherents in Europe and the U.S. The shift from an ethnic to a missionary base is evident in some areas not formerly ethnic-Buddhist.

▲Hinduism's strength in India has been enhanced by nationalism, and modern Hinduism has also developed renewal movements that have reached into Europe and the U.S. for converts.

✢Source: 1968 United Nations survey.

(F. H. Li.)

CAMERA PRESS—PIX FROM PUBLIX

Mrs. Coretta King, widow of Martin Luther King, Jr., preaches at St. Paul's Cathedral in London on Sunday, March 16, 1969. She was the first woman ever to speak from the pulpit of the cathedral.

Minneapolis, Minn. Sponsored by Billy Graham, Oswald C. J. Hoffmann, Leighton Ford, and other prominent evangelists, the congress studied ways and means to make the preaching of the gospel more relevant in an age in which the influence of Christianity was declining. The conservatively oriented congress heard several addresses urging Christians to respond to the physical as well as the spiritual needs of the minority poor; Ralph D. Abernathy, president of the Southern Christian Leadership Conference, urged the congress to solve the three great problems of the times—war, racism, and poverty. The congress attracted a largely white group. The 50 black delegates present issued a statement asking fellow conservative Protestants "to confess in word and action to the sins committed against black people."

Efforts to achieve a closer rapprochement between various Protestant bodies and the Roman Catholic Church continued. The Consultation on Church Union (COCU), involving the eventual merger of ten major Protestant bodies, continued in a series of conferences throughout the year. In the meantime, the first Baptist-Catholic dialogue in the U.S. was held at Wake Forest University's Ecumenical Institute; 19 Roman Catholics and 39 Southern Baptists adopted a resolution emphasizing the "overwhelming fact that we are brothers in Christ."

The Lutheran Council in the U.S.A. and the Episcopal Church began the first of what were expected to be semiannual theological discussions "to explore the problems which exist between our two communions as a step toward deeper dialogue." Lutheran discussions, with similar joint theological consultations, were also proceeding with the Roman Catholic and the Eastern Orthodox churches, as well as with Jewish theologians. In a historic first, Pope Paul VI spoke to a top-level delegation from the Lutheran World Federation and said that the differences between the Catholic Church and the Lutheran churches are deep and must not be passed over in silence. (See *Lutherans,* below.) Pope Paul's visit to the World Council of Churches headquarters at Geneva during August marked another major effort to increase understanding among the churches of Christendom.

The percentage of the U.S. population holding church membership fell by 1.2% in 1968, according to figures released in 1969. Total church membership was 126,445,110. Despite controversy within many churches over participation in civil rights activities and clerical support of activities opposing the war in Vietnam, there seemed to have been a slight increase in per-member contributions. The figure was difficult to determine, since church bodies used different reporting methods and followed different fiscal years, but the best available estimate was that contributions averaged $73.95 per member, an increase of $6.10 over the previous year's average. Religious construction during 1968 declined to $1,040,000,000 from $1,093,000,000 in 1967; a decline to $1 billion or less was projected for 1969. (A. P. Kl.)

PROTESTANT CHURCHES

Anglican Communion. In the aftermath of the 1968 Lambeth Conference, the decision to establish a permanent Anglican Consultative Council was defended by the bishop of Bangor (Wales) at the annual meeting of the Society for the Promotion of Christian Knowledge, held in London in March 1969. Speaking before this oldest of all Anglican societies, the bishop took the interesting position that the Anglican Communion had suffered in the past not from having too much bureaucracy, but from having too little. The only other event to suggest a central Anglican identity was the assumption of office by a new executive officer for the Anglican Communion: John Howe, bishop of St. Andrew's (Scotland), in succession to Ralph Dean, who returned to his Canadian see of Cariboo.

One indication of the way the communion, hitherto centred on Canterbury, might be regionalized was provided by the establishment of an Anglican Regional Council for North America at a meeting held in the Bahamas in February. Bishop Stephen Bayne of the U.S. had been one of the chief promoters of the council, which included the Anglican churches of Canada, the U.S., and the West Indies. The council determined that the three churches should act in concert in dealing with such issues as racial tension and the provision of external aid (especially to Latin America), and in pooling some personnel and publications.

The heartland of Anglicanism remained, however, in England and the Church of England. Statistics revealed a small but significant decline in the proportion of the population baptized and confirmed in the church and also in the number of Easter communicants; the fall in the number of new confirmations was drastic enough to cause anxiety. The lengthy process of reform in English Church government, initiated in 1947, reached some kind of goal with the publication in September of the collection of new Canons of the Church of England, the first complete revision of church rules and regulations since 1603, and with the final ratification of the new law establishing a general synod. Consisting of bishops with elected clergy and laity, the synod was to be the supreme governing body of the church from November 1970. It would thus take over the powers possessed for centuries by the purely clerical convocations.

In interchurch relations, the important event of 1969 was the failure of the Church of England to accept the official scheme for union with the Methodist Church. On July 8, described as "the most crucial day for English religion since the Reformation," the Anglican convocations of Canterbury and York refused to give the scheme the 75% majority required for approval. The majority was only 69% (in contrast to a 77% majority in the Methodist conference). Despite the fact that this result accurately reflected clerical opinion (in a secret referendum on the scheme, 9,642 Anglican clergymen voted in favour and 5,621 against), Michael Ramsey, archbishop of Canterbury, refused to accept it as a final rejection of a plan that he had striven to promote. In August he and Donald Coggan, archbishop of York, announced that they hoped to bring the scheme back for a second vote soon after the new general synod came into being, in the expectation that by then opposition would have lessened. In the meantime they appealed for close cooperation between Anglicans and Methodists at the local level, in order to further understanding and increase mutual confidence. (See *Methodists,* below.) Women made significant advances in Anglicanism. In England women were admitted as readers, with the right to preach and assist in administration of the sacraments, and the two leading Anglican missionary societies, the Church Missionary Society and the United Society for the Propagation of the Gospel, appointed women as their leaders for the first time.

In the U.S. the Episcopal Church met in a special general convention to complete unfinished business from its previous convention. The greater part of the sessions were devoted to the demands of the Black Manifesto and a consideration of the war in Vietnam. The delegates voted $200,000 to the National Committee of Black Churchmen, which was expected to serve as a pipeline to the Black Manifesto group. Two absent-without-leave U.S. servicemen presented themselves to the convention demanding sanctuary, which was granted. The accidental death of James A. Pike, former Episcopal bishop of San Francisco, while on a study mission in Israel brought to a dramatic end the career of a churchman whose writings and sermons had provoked controversy both within and outside the church (*see* OBITUARIES). (R. L. R.)

Baptists. The number of Baptists (baptized believers only) was increasing throughout the world faster than the birthrate. World population increased by 1.9% in 1968, while the number of Baptists rose by 2.25%—from 29,817,707 in May 1968 to 30,487,802 in May 1969. The greatest gain, 20.5%, was made in the southern Pacific.

One of the most important events for Baptists in 1969 was the European Baptist Congress, held at Vienna in August. At the opening of the congress representatives of all major branches of the church in Austria, including a representative of the cardinal archbishop of Vienna, welcomed the Baptists of Europe to the city. There were 2,500 registered delegates, of whom 1,000 came from Eastern Europe. Every European country except Bulgaria was represented.

The addresses demonstrated how far Baptists had advanced in their thinking during the previous ten years. Baptist leaders from the Soviet Union told the congress that their churches formed the largest Baptist national group in Europe. They remarked that "some brothers had differed from us in regard to the methods of our work, and decided upon a course of open infringement of the laws on religious cults"—a reference to the group of dissident Baptists often spoken of as the "initiatives," estimated by some to number about 16,000.

An appeal was made throughout Europe in 1969 for funds to build a new Baptist church in Bratislava. The Czechoslovak authorities had allocated a new site for the structure. Progress in Romania was encouraging. Baptist pastors and students were able to take up scholarships in West Germany and Switzerland, and Baptists were much freer to go about their evangelistic work.

In the U.K. the Baptist Men's Movement saw the fruition of plans launched in 1966, when a housing association was formed to provide accommodation for the elderly at reasonable rents. A block of apartments was opened and dedicated at the coastal resort of Worthing in Sussex, and two others were planned.

A report made in March 1969 by the ten general superintendents serving the churches of the Baptist Union of Great Britain and Ireland underlined the difficulty of effecting ministerial settlements. The report recorded frustration in the ministry, the result being that more and more ministers were seeking a part-time ministry and others were leaving pastoral work altogether.

More than 15,000 delegates attended the annual convention of the 11-million member Southern Baptist Convention in New Orleans, La. Prolonged debate centred around "social action," with conservatives declaring that those who favoured it ignored God's saving grace, while liberals asserted that the others neglected Christ's emphasis on moral, ethical, and social relationships. The Black Manifesto was rejected, although various resolutions encouraged Southern Baptists to become more involved in social issues.

The American Baptist Convention met in Seattle, Wash., in May. Thomas Kilgore, Jr., black pastor of the Second Baptist Church, Los Angeles, was elected president for 1969–70. Young American Baptist Churchmen (YABC) issued a daily mimeographed newsletter at the convention denouncing racism, poverty, hunger, antiballistic missiles, and the war in Vietnam.

Joseph Jackson of Chicago, president of the six million-member National Baptist Convention, U.S.A., Inc. (black), announced that the National Unity Program had purchased 479 ac. of land in Tennessee and was furnishing interest-free loans to families wishing to settle there; 100,000 ac. purchased in Liberia would be used to assist in the development of that country.

The Atlantic United Baptist Convention of Canada held two lay schools of theology in 1968—in February at Woodstock, N.B., and in March at Middleton, N.S. Forty churches were represented.

In Toronto, Leslie K. Tarr, editor of *Evangelical Baptist Magazine,* opposed tax exemptions for churches: "Evangelical churches should seize the initiative and declare themselves for the taxation of church property. Most opposition by churches to the tax is based on expediency, or the defense of special privilege." (R. E. E. H.; R. W. T.)

Christian Science. New programs in community relations marked 1969 for the Church of Christ, Scientist. The annual meeting in June, attended by more than 10,000 members, and the biennial Christian Science College Organization meeting in August, attended by more than 6,000 college students from 30 countries, were highlights of the year.

A Community Relations Office was established in 1969 under the direction of J. Buroughs Stokes, manager of committees on publication. The first class was enrolled at the Christian Science Nurses Training School, established May 1, 1968, at Chestnut Hill, Mass. Students from several countries were taking the one-year course for practical nurses and the three-year course for graduate nurses.

The First Church of Christ, Scientist, in Boston published and distributed over 75 million pieces of literature (including the *Christian Science Monitor*) in English and other languages. Advertising and sales of the Bible and the denominational textbook, *Science and Health with Key to the Scriptures* by Mary Baker Eddy, increased substantially. Books published included the second volume of *The Continuity of the Bible,* a compilation of a series appearing in the monthly *Christian Science Journal.*

Construction of the $30 million Christian Science Church Center, on a 16-ac. site adjacent to the First Church of Christ, Scientist, and the Christian Science Publishing Society building in the Back Bay area of Boston, was about 25% completed in 1969. The Church Center, comprising four structures including a 26-story administration building, would replace outdated facilities. (J. B. ST.)

Churches of Christ. In meetings among leaders of the Churches of Christ and the conservative Christian Church, stress was placed on holding these two groups close to the biblical pattern in worship, evangelism, church organization, and other doctrinal matters. Overall membership of the Churches of Christ in 1969 was estimated at 2.5 million. Churches outside the U.S. were estimated at more than 1,000, with the greatest growth in converts taking place in Brazil and

India. Evangelistic campaigns, using from 50 to 200 workers, were held in large centres in Africa, Europe, and America.

In the area of benevolence, a number of new establishments for homeless children were opened. The Lubbock, Tex., Children's Home arranged for the adoption of its 500th child and the Smithlawn Maternity Home was serving its 400th girl. Since Churches of Christ have no central organization, each of these works was under the direction of one congregation or under a separate board of trustees.

There was growing interest, especially among the young, in active participation in work with the poor and with deprived minorities. In New York City a number of subsistence-salaried workers from Camp Shiloh ministered to ghetto children. Day-care centres were opened for children of working mothers, and in some places space was rented in shopping areas where shoppers could rest and read Christian literature.

Campus Evangelism, a program to train college students to reach classmates with the gospel, conducted seminars across the U.S. Churches supported 100 campus centres near state colleges and universities which offered religion courses, many of them for credit. Over 150 summer youth and family camps were operated in the U.S., and new ones were purchased in West Germany, Belgium, and Brazil.

The nationwide radio and television program "Herald of Truth" shifted to a documentary format. The subject matter dealt with biblical applications to crime, racial tension, and illicit sex. (M. N. Y.)

Church of Jesus Christ of Latter-day Saints. Church membership in 1969 totaled approximately 2,750,000. There were about 13,000 full-time and 5,000 part-time missionaries serving in the missions and stakes of the church. Increased church membership made necessary the organization of stakes in São Paulo, Braz.; Pago Pago, Samoa; Dresden, E.Ger.; New Zealand; and a servicemen's stake in Europe, as well as numerous stakes in the U.S. The Southern Far East Mission was divided into two missions: the Hong Kong-Taiwan Mission and the Southeast Asia Mission. Additional missions were organized in California, Arizona, and the south central states. Ground was broken for the erection of three new temples, in Ogden and Provo, Utah, and Washington, D.C.

The first World Conference on Records was held in Salt Lake City, August 5–8, under the sponsorship of the Genealogical Society of the church. Archivists, historians, and librarians from 45 countries attended. A church library coordinating committee consisting of specialists in the various areas of church library activity was organized to coordinate procedures in all church libraries. A library facility was being developed in each meetinghouse to provide literature and audiovisual instructional materials and equipment for use in the curricula of church organizations.

The Young Women's Mutual Improvement Association with 370,000 members, organized in 1869 by Brigham Young, celebrated its centenary. The purpose of the organization is to prepare young women for their roles as wives and mothers through spiritual, cultural, recreational, and social activities. (Jo. A.)

Congregational Churches. During 1969 the International Congregational Council was largely concerned with the final steps toward union with the World Alliance of Reformed Churches. A joint meeting of executive committees in Beirut, Lebanon, planned the uniting council, to take place in Nairobi, Kenya, in August 1970. The united body would represent 60 million people in 129 churches in more than 70 countries. (See *Presbyterian and Reformed,* below.)

The union of the Congregational Church in England and Wales with the Presbyterian Church of England into the United Reformed Church made further progress at both assemblies. It was announced, however, that because of delay in the preparation of legal documents and the necessary act of Parliament, formal union could not take place until 1972. The approval of the Congregational Assembly was to be sought in 1971. This would have to be supported by the approval of a proportion of local churches, but this proportion was not immediately agreed upon. Its determination was a potential hazard to union since there were many small, independent congregations, some of which had expressed opposition to the inclusion in the scheme of an ordained eldership. The assemblies of the Church of Scotland and the Congregational Union of Scotland both approved a plan of union, which was expected to mature in 1970. This would merge the smaller denomination into the national church, but Congregational churches would retain their own system of internal government. With the merger of Western College into the Northern College, the number of distinctively Congregational theological seminaries in England was reduced to three.

Anniversaries of Congregational churches in 1969 included the 350th anniversary in May of the 25,000-member Remonstrant Brotherhood in the Netherlands and the 80th anniversary in June of the 9,000-member Free Church of Finland. (See *United Church of Canada; United Church of Christ,* below.) (R. F. G. C.)

Disciples of Christ (Christian Church). At its first General Assembly following reorganization as a "church" rather than a convention of congregations and agencies, the Christian Church (Disciples of Christ) took action to double the religious body's financial response to the race and poverty crisis. Meeting at Seattle, Wash., Aug. 15–20, 1969, the General Assembly, in a voice vote, doubled to $4 million and lengthened to four years, from two, the goal set a year earlier for funds to be raised in addition to regular church contributions. In so doing, the General Assembly implicitly endorsed a rejection by the church's General Board the previous May of the "ideology, methodology and language" of the Black Manifesto.

The action also committed church units to manpower and fund redeployment, and to employment and investment quotas with respect to assistance of minorities and the poor. It called for an Urban Affairs Commission to advise the church on sociological factors affecting its work.

The General Assembly was the first to be held on an every-other-year basis. Previously, the Disciples had held annual conventions. Up until 1967, these were on an everybody-come, everybody-vote basis. The church's new General Assembly had voting delegates from congregations, regions, and institutions.

The Christian Church set the following priorities for the period until 1975: leadership; evangelism and renewal; world order, justice, and peace; ecumenical involvement; and reconciliation in the urban crisis. A. Dale Fiers, who had been serving as general minister and president of the church since the restructure effort in 1968 brought the office into being, was elected to the first full six-year term as chief executive of the church. James M. Moudy, chancellor of Texas Christian University, was elected moderator, to serve until the fall of 1971. (R. L. F.)

Jehovah's Witnesses. This society of Christian ministers was active in 1969 in 203 countries, operating over 25,600 congregations organized under 94 branch offices. New ministers (members) baptized during the year totaled 120,905, a new high, bringing the membership to 1,336,112.

"Peace on Earth" international assemblies were held in 13 major cities of the U.S., Canada, England, and the European continent during the summer. Over 840,000 heard the featured talk on "The Approaching Peace of a Thousand Years." Appropriately, the "Peace on Earth" convention delegates set forth a declaration of their intention to live at peace with God and their fellow men and to maintain strict Christian neutrality toward the world's political controversies. At these assemblies a new book, *Is the Bible Really the Word of God?,* was released in English and ten other languages. Twelve more assemblies of this series were held later in the year in Japan, South Korea, Australia, New Zealand, Fiji, Mexico, and elsewhere.

A new office and residence building was completed, further expanding the Brooklyn, N.Y., headquarters

FOX PHOTOS FROM PICTORIAL PARADE

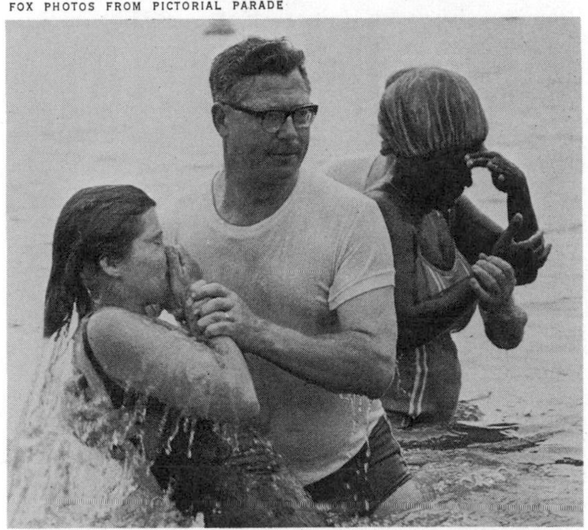

A Jehovah's Witness is baptized by total immersion at Ruislip Lido, Eng., on July 31, 1969. An estimated 70,000 Witnesses gathered to take part in a six-day convention that began at Wembley Stadium July 29.

facilities. The headquarters printing plant produced over 24 million bound books and Bibles and 194,780,200 magazines during the year. Circulation of the official journal of Jehovah's Witnesses, *The Watchtower,* was 5,850,000 in 72 languages in 1969. Its companion magazine, *Awake!,* reached a circulation of 5.7 million in 26 languages. (N. H. K.)

Lutherans. An increase of over 150,000 baptized members of Lutheran churches in 1969 brought the worldwide total to well over 75 million. The world figure represented more than 58 million members reported by Lutheran churches in 80 countries, plus 17 million Lutherans who belonged to United Churches in West Germany that also included some Reformed congregations.

The steady movement toward closer unity among the 9 million Lutherans in the U.S. gained major impetus in 1969. Despite organized opposition by a minority of traditionalists, the 2.8 million-member Lutheran Church-Missouri Synod voted at its 48th general convention to accept a proffer of pulpit and altar fellowship from the 2.6 million-member American Lutheran Church and to continue informal discussions on fellowship with the 3.2 million-member Lutheran Church in America, with which the American Lutheran Church had established such relations in 1968. (Churches in fellowship may practice intercommunion and their pastors may exchange pulpits.)

The Missouri Synod's favourable action surprised many. Earlier, delegates had unseated as president Oliver R. Harms, a staunch advocate of fellowship, and named in his stead Jacob Aall Ottesen Preus, a conservative theologian and an avowed foe of fellowship. For the second time in 17 years, the Missouri Synod rejected membership in the Lutheran World Federation (LWF); it also declined to act on affiliation with the World Council of Churches and authorized a study of the National Council of Churches.

In a precedent-setting action, it approved suffrage for women and election of women to boards and commissions of the church. Reversing its stand against selective conscientious objection, the Synod gave its support to those who refuse to serve in the armed forces in a specific war. Similar endorsement was voted by the Lutheran Church in America in 1968.

An agreement for formal merger in 1977 was approved by both the Missouri Synod and the 20,500-member Synod of Evangelical Lutheran Churches. The latter, meanwhile, had become the SELC District of the Missouri Synod. Another step toward unity was taken with the formation of the Lutheran Student Movement, which merged the Lutheran Student Association of America, comprising students of the American Lutheran Church and the Lutheran Church in America, and International Gamma Delta, serving students of the Missouri Synod.

Lutheran and Roman Catholic theologians completed their fifth year of doctrinal discussions. Their eighth and ninth meetings centred on efforts to harmonize existing differences in their respective traditions of ministerial service. The Lutherans also met for the second time with Eastern Orthodox churchmen and for the first time with the Conservative, Orthodox, and Reform branches of American Judaism and with the Episcopal Church.

Lutherans in the U.K. celebrated the 300th anniversary of the foundation of the first Lutheran congregation there. In a letter-patent dated June 17, 1669, Charles II had given instructions to the attorney general to prepare a bill for the royal signature granting permission for Lutherans in London to hold public services and build a church. The archbishop of Canterbury invested Dean Jask Taul with the Cross of St. Augustine during the year. The 64-year-old Lutheran church leader, head of the Lutheran Council of Great Britain since 1956, was honoured by the archbishop for meritorious service to the church in his native Estonia and for his efforts toward Christian unity.

A new chancery of the United Evangelical Lutheran Church in East Germany was constituted on Dec. 1, 1968. The presiding bishop was Niklot Beste of Schwerin. The 21st annual world gathering of Lutheran missions, held in Asmara, Eth., was attended by 150 participants from every continent. "Crosscurrents in Mission" was the theme of the meeting of the commission on world mission of the LWF.

In January the Tamil Evangelical Lutheran Church of India celebrated the 50th anniversary of its constitution as an autonomous body. The origins of the church, which in 1969 numbered around 66,000, could be traced to the work of the Protestant missionary Bartholomaeus Ziegenbalg, who landed in Tranquebar in 1709. Ceremonies also marked the 50th anniversary of the Gossner Evangelical Lutheran Church of India as an independent church. Numbering 273,000 adherents in 1969, the church had begun as a mission founded by the Gossner Missionary Society in 1845.

During his visit to Geneva, Pope Paul VI greeted the general secretary of the LWF, André Appel. Their meeting at the Ecumenical Centre followed an earlier one held in the pope's private library—the first official visit ever made to the Vatican by an LWF delegation. (E. W. M.; W. Vö.)

Methodists. In a year characterized by increasing cooperation between the churches, the British Methodist Conference voted decisively in favour of union with the Anglican Church. According to its constitution, the Methodist Church voted at three levels. In the circuit quarterly meetings in March, there was a majority vote in favour of proceeding on the basis of the final report of the Anglican-Methodist unity scheme. At the district synods held in May, only the three Welsh districts and Scotland had majorities against. The final and decisive vote was taken on July 8 in the annual conference, which met in Birmingham. The voting, which was by ballot, was 77.4% in favour of the scheme. On the same day the Anglican convocations meeting in London failed to reach the required 75% majority. (See *Anglican Communion*, above.)

In spite of this disappointment, hopes of unity were not dashed. On the local level there were many encouraging signs of much closer cooperation between the churches. Joint services and shared ministries ceased to be unusual, and in several places plans were approved for the joint use of buildings. A notable exchange took place during Christian Unity Week in January when John Cardinal Heenan, archbishop of Westminster, preached in Hinde Street Methodist Church, London, and the Rev. Gordon Wakefield, a Methodist minister, preached in Westminster Cathedral.

In the U.S. issues of race relations appeared to dominate the efforts of the United Methodist Church during 1969. Only one year old as a denomination, the church also was spending considerable time in attempts to reevaluate and revise the doctrines and structures of the two denominations that preceded it. Mergers of regional units of the former Methodist and Evangelical United Brethren churches were proceeding well ahead of expected schedules. Although annual conferences of the EUB Church had been authorized to maintain their separate identity for up to 12 years, 25 of the 32 conferences had completed mergers with former Methodist units by the end of 1969.

Major attempts to focus on racial problems came through the Commission on Religion and Race, established to accelerate the church's drive for racial inclusiveness, and the Fund for Reconciliation, aimed at overcoming racial, economic, and educational deprivation. Created primarily to answer the Black Power demand voiced in 1968, but also to meet the needs of other minorities within the church, the commission attempted to develop agreements that would permit merger of the last nine annual (regional) conferences of the church (out of the 17 extant in 1964), but also would assure equality of treatment, participation, and opportunity regardless of race. The Fund for Reconciliation, with a $20 million goal for 1968–72, used its first $2 million of income to finance projects across the U.S. Most of these stressed work with minority groups, especially in poverty areas.

The demands of the Black Manifesto first arrived within the denomination at the Board of Missions. After its New York headquarters was "occupied" for a day, the board's executive committee voted $300,000 for black economic development, to be administered by Negro members of the board and staff. Other responses to the Manifesto came from the leadership of church agencies, who urged United Methodists to "reorder their priorities" in order to make substantial funds available for development under black leadership, and from the Council of Bishops' executive committee, which "repudiated the ideology" of the Manifesto and rejected its demands. Black Methodists for Church Renewal called particularly upon the Boards of Evangelism and Education to revise their staffs and use their resources for greater racial equity.

During 1969 an office of the World Methodist Council (WMC) was opened in the World Council of Churches headquarters in Geneva. At the Executive Committee meeting in Geneva on September 22, Ole Borgen of Stockholm was appointed a full-time secretary of the WMC. A consultation between representatives of the WMC and the Vatican Secretariat for Promoting Christian Unity took place in Malta in September, the third such consultation to be held since 1967. Following the meeting of the Council of the European Methodist Conferences of Scandinavia, West Germany, and central and southern Europe, a consultation was held in Freudenstadt, W.Ger., in October. Representatives from 14 European countries were present.

A significant development in the church's conception of the ministry was approved by the British Methodist conference in July. Ralph E. Fennell was appointed secretary of a committee on "sector ministries." The "sectors" designated were industry, commerce, education, medicine, and the welfare services, and full consideration was to be given to the possibility of extending a pastoral ministry into these spheres.

During 1969 the Methodist Church in Belgium united with the Église Protestante Belgique to become one new church. (M. W. Wo.; W. H. Ta.)

Presbyterian and Reformed. During Aug. 1–6, 1969, the executive committee of the World Alliance of Reformed Churches (WARC) met jointly with the executive committee of the International Congregational Council (ICC) in Beirut, Lebanon, where both organizations had a member church. The meetings were chaired alternately by Wilhelm Niesel of West Germany, president of WARC, and Ashby E. Bladen of the U.S., moderator of the ICC. The principal occupation of the joint executive committee was the preparation for the assembly at Nairobi, Kenya, during Aug. 20–30, 1970, when WARC and the ICC would merge to become the new World Alliance of Reformed Churches (Presbyterian and Congregational). Most of this preparatory work was done in special subcommittees, which dealt separately with the content and form of the assembly, with finance and travel, and with information, publicity, and public relations.

If the proposed constitution and bylaws were adopted by the uniting council, the new WARC would have two principal departments apart from the general secretariat: a department of theology and a department of cooperation and witness. The latter would be chiefly responsible for the "life and work" of the alliance, and would serve to encourage and stimulate the member churches.

The joint executive committee took a unanimous decision to engage in bilateral conversations with the Roman Catholic Church. At the meeting, a telegram was read from Jan Cardinal Willebrands of the Secretariat for Promoting Christian Unity stating the pope's agreement to joint studies by the Reformed and Roman Catholic churches. The dialogue, scheduled to cover a three-year period, was to begin in the spring of 1970.

Two applications for membership in the alliance were approved. The entry of the Presbyterian Church of Burma (10,000 members) and of the Karo Batak Protestant Church in Indonesia brought the total membership of WARC to 112 churches.

Meetings of the North American Area Council of WARC, in Ocean City, N.J., in January and of the European Area's administrative committee in Vienna in September were attended for the last time by Marcel Pradervand, general secretary of the alliance, who was due to retire after the Nairobi assembly.

The Associate Presbyterian Church of North America and the Reformed Presbyterian Church of North America merged in June.

Conversations on a merger between the Presbyterian Church in the U.S. (approximately 957,000 members) and the Reformed Church in America (approximately 235,000 members), initiated in 1961, were rejected during the year when the merger plan failed to receive the approval of the Reformed Church's regional classes. Presbyteries in the Presbyterian Church in the U.S. had given the necessary three-fourths approval for the plan, but the Reformed Church classes' vote was far short of the two-thirds needed for approval. However, merger talks were initiated by action of the 109th General Assembly of the Presbyterian Church in the U.S. in Mobile, Ala., in April and endorsed the following month by the 181st General Assembly of the United Presbyterian Church, U.S.A., in San Antonio, Tex. The Interchurch Relations Committee of the Cumberland Presbyterian Church was also asked to communicate with these two churches with a view to possible participation in the study of union. The Orthodox Presbyterian Church voted to proceed in the direction of merger with the Reformed Presbyterian Church, Evangelical Synod. Plans for the union of the Presbyterian Church of England and the Congregational Church in England and Wales were approved by their respective assemblies in May. (See *Congregational Churches,* above.)

In the U.S. a unanimous Supreme Court decision, expected to have far-reaching implications among many denominations, was handed down during the year. In a case involving two Savannah, Ga., churches, the court declared that civil courts have no right to rule on church disputes when doctrine is at issue.

The quickest possible response to demands made by minority group spokesmen was promised by the governing bodies of the Presbyterian and Reformed judicatories in the U.S. The General Assembly of the United Presbyterian Church, U.S.A., also adopted a report on the status of women in society and in the church. (F. H. KA.; W. B. MI.)

Religious Society of Friends. The European Friends Conference, held in July at Birmingham, Eng., joined London Yearly Meeting in urging members to give 1% of their net income to "sharing the world's resources." Philadelphia Yearly Meeting and several other American bodies also adopted this goal. Friends United Meeting, at the triennial sessions in Richmond, Ind., urged members to give 1% to overseas development and a second 1% to meet domestic needs in urban centres. The international nature of the Friends United Meeting was emphasized by the presence of Joseph D. Otiende, minister for health in Kenya and a member of the East Africa Yearly Meeting, and of Thomas Lung'aho, the executive secretary of that 30,000-member Quaker body.

In 1969, Friends in both the U.S. and the U.K. began relief and rehabilitation work for the victims of the Nigerian civil war. On the Biafran side, Friends were cooperating with the Mennonites in medical care and food distribution. Friends in the U.K. urged the British government to initiate international action to stop the flow of arms to both sides.

The American Friends Service Committee launched a new effort to persuade the U.S. government to end the war in Vietnam with a silent witness before the White House on May 5–6. Some 1,300 Quakers shared in the demonstration. At the same time, the AFSC continued to send medical supplies to North Vietnam and conducted medical rehabilitation work with South Vietnamese civilians. The domestic program of AFSC emphasized work in the inner city and reorganization of youth activities to give the young a much larger share of responsibility.

Friends campaigned during the year against any restoration of the death penalty in the U.K. Irish Friends celebrated the tercentenary of the first national meeting of Quakers in Dublin.

(CD. H.; E. B. BR.)

Salvation Army. On July 23, 1969, the seventh High Council of the Salvation Army, comprised of 45 Salvationist leaders, elected Swedish Commissioner Erik Wickberg as general. Danish Commissioner

Quaker pickets take part in 21-hour vigil in front of the White House on May 5–6, 1969, to protest U.S. involvement in Vietnam.

LEN OWENS FROM PICTORIAL PARADE

Kaare Westergaard was the only other candidate to accept nomination. General Wickberg took office as the Army's ninth general on September 21, the 70th birthday of his predecessor, Gen. Frederick Coutts. To succeed him as chief of staff, a second-in-command position he had held since 1961, General Wickberg chose Canadian Commissioner Arnold Brown. Since 1964, Brown had served as secretary for public relations in London, where he had been responsible for the "For God's Sake Care" campaign.

Salvationist disaster relief included work among victims of earthquakes in the Philippines, bush fires in Australia, floods in South Africa and North America, and hurricanes and snowstorms in the U.S. Salvationist relief teams based on Abak in southeast Nigeria were responsible for 30 feeding stations. In Vietnam, Army relief workers included a doctor skilled in plastic surgery seconded as senior surgeon to a Saigon hospital. A team of U.S. Salvationists, appointed to medical and social rehabilitation work, gave priority to clinic facilities and care of refugee children.

The year was marked by an increase in international exchanges of personnel. The development of work among drug addicts continued—Prince Philip visited the Army's rehabilitation centre in Chelsea, London—and, in Canada, the first sheltered workshop exclusively for the mentally ill was established.

A new way of dramatizing Salvation Army services to man—via a collection of original paintings and sculpture—was used in the annual report of activities in the Greater New York area. After visiting Salvation Army installations, artists depicted the work of Army officers and soldiers, using a variety of styles and techniques from Pop Art posters to pictorial watercolours. Photographs of their works formed the basis of a special supplement to the *New York Times* of Nov. 10, 1968. (J. Gr.; W. P.)

Seventh-day Adventists. Zürich, Switz., was the site of the church's first worldwide youth congress, held July 22–27, 1969. Attendance totaled 12,000, with delegates from every continent. Reports indicated that in less than three years, youth of the church had won 111,333 converts.

Church growth in all countries accelerated in 1969. On March 27, 3,000 African youth were baptized, and on a single day, September 27, a total of more than 25,000 converts were baptized in the world. Membership in the denomination's 15,744 congregations increased to about 1.9 million.

In the U.S. the issue of federal aid to church-operated schools was debated on all levels of the church. The debate was crucial inasmuch as the denomination's school system in the U.S. was second largest among Protestant groups. At a special meeting of church administrators, held February 11–12 in Washington, D.C., the church's historic opposition to the use of tax funds for the support of parochial schools was reaffirmed.

Disaster and relief activities were given increased support. An offering given on one day by the churches of North America provided nearly $275,000 to rehabilitate institutions and provide aid for people in the Nigeria-Biafra area. Appropriations for missions and home-based programs voted at the church's annual Autumn Council, held in Washington, D.C., October 8–16, totaled $49,485,600.30, an increase of 5.32% over the previous year. (K. H. W.)

Unitarians and Universalists. The British General Assembly of Unitarian and Free Christian Churches met in Sheffield, April 10–13, 1969. The most important features of the meetings were the presentation of the Review Commission report and the recommendations for the reorganization of the council and departmental committees and the headquarters staff. The recommendations on staff were generally accepted by the assembly, but the proposals for the reorganization of the council and committees were referred back in order to enable the congregations to have more time to consider the matter and submit amendments.

The Review Commission spent the rest of the year considering the organization of the district associations of churches and the relations of the churches to the associations and to the assembly. The religious education department and the youth department were combined.

In the U.S. the Unitarian Universalist Association underwent a year of turbulent self-examination while confronted by radical efforts to gain changes and controls in its establishment. The design and corrections needed in a religious movement expected to deal effectively with society's current crises were debated across the continent by an unprecedented seven candidates for the association presidency. Robert Nelson West, minister of the First Unitarian Church in Rochester, N.Y., was elected by a clear majority. He succeeded Dana McLean Greeley, who became president of the International Association for Religious Freedom.

A Unitarian Universalist layman staged a six-day modified hunger strike in the denominational headquarters building in Boston to protest against UUA investments. He demanded that $2,250,000 in oil stocks be sold and reinvested in low-cost housing, and that investments in firms that exploit consumers and war, pollute natural resources, and perpetuate racist policies should be abandoned in favour of a "more humane and socially relevant" policy. A Social Implications Subcommittee was appointed to continue an ethical audit of the portfolio and search for more appropriate investment opportunities.

The eighth annual assembly of the Canadian Unitarian Council (CUC), held May 16–18 in Montreal, had as its theme: "Canadian Unitarians Now, Concern and Communications." Reflecting widespread discontent with inadequacies in the relationship between the UUA and the CUC, a resolution was introduced to separate the Canadian organization from the UUA and fund it entirely with Canadian societies' monies. The resolution was defeated, largely for economic reasons, by a narrow vote of 29–21.

The strategy of disruption and confrontation so apparent on world campuses also characterized minority power drives at the eighth annual General Assembly of the UUA, held in Boston, July 14–18, with over 1,785 delegates from 448 churches and 93 fellowships in the U.S. and Canada in attendance. Questions were raised concerning the efficacy of annual policy making by so large a body.

Currently, UUA programs on race were selected and administered by a Black Affairs Council (BAC), responsible to an all-black caucus. Unable to convince the assembly delegates to revise the agenda order of priorities in its behalf, BAC supporters seized the microphones and later staged a walkout. Returning the following morning, they persuaded the conference to deny $50,000 in funds to BAWA (Black and White Action), a group seeking greater white involvement in UUA programs to combat racism and increase equality and justice. The integration-emphasizing BAWA supporters, at a dinner attended by over 500 delegates, responded by announcing a separate drive among the churches for a $333,333 budget. The assembly voted down BAC demands that $6.5 million of UUA funds be placed in "reparations and social investments" under black control. Although irritation over BAC's tactics influenced this decision, there was also concern over possible shrinkage of investment income sorely needed for racial and denominational programs.

The International Association for Religious Freedom held its 20th congress in Boston, during July 12–21, combining with the annual assembly of the UUA. At the meetings the name of the association was changed by the omission of the words "for Liberal Christianity," thus retaining the initials IARF. The association appointed a fourth commission on human rights, justice, and peace to supplement the three commissions appointed in 1966. (J. N. B.; Jn. Ky.)

United Church of Canada. The election in 1968 of a layman as moderator for the first time in the history of the United Church heralded a series of tradition-shattering events in 1969. It became possible for a lay person to be president of a conference, an office previously held only by ministers. Since it is the president's duty to conduct the ordination service, the question arose to what extent a lay president could participate in that service; for example, could he lay his hands on an ordinand's head? The matter was referred to various authorities for an answer, but lay persons had taken part in the laying on of hands in ordination without protest, and such was the spirit of the times that a negative answer would not be popular. An attempt to open the chairmanship of the official board of a pastoral charge to the laity was unsuccessful.

An increased democratization of the church also was evident in 1969. A larger place was made for youth and laywomen in the governmental and administrative bodies of the church, and the right of the lower courts to elect rather than nominate representatives to the higher courts was recognized and acted on.

During the year an Interim Division of Ministry and Personnel was set up which devised a new plan of continuing education for ministers. The program would provide lectures, seminars, and clinics for three-week periods. Attendance of ministers was made possible by a ruling that provided for a three-week study leave annually. The same body set up an office to provide information concerning vacant positions and available personnel throughout the church.

Most far-reaching in its effects, perhaps, was the formation of the Toronto School of Theology, a cooperative federation of theological colleges of the Anglican, Presbyterian, Roman Catholic, and United churches. While each college remained autonomous and conferred its own degrees, there were common standards of admission and courses offered by each college would be open to the students of all the colleges. The school would operate at both the basic and the advanced degree levels.

The year saw the church more deeply committed than ever before to aiding the world's needy. A minimum of $1 million was guaranteed for development and relief programs overseas in 1969 and 1970. At home, in addition to ongoing programs, the church resolved to help alleviate the housing crisis, beginning with a pilot project that, it was hoped, would lead to a project for housing lower-income persons.

The way to union with the Anglican Church of Canada appeared to open up encouragingly. The General Synod of the Anglican Church decided to recommend to the diocesan bishops that they "permit Anglicans and members of other Christian Churches to share in Eucharistic practice with the full knowledge and consent of the proper authorities." The General Commission on Church Union continued to work on a basis of union which it hoped to present to the two churches by 1971. (A. G. R.)

United Church of Christ. When the United Church of Christ came into being in 1957, it brought together churches that, at the beginning of the 20th century, had belonged to four different communions. The Congregational and Christian Churches had united in 1931 and the Evangelical Synod of North America and the Reformed Church in the United States had merged in 1934. The membership of the united denominations in 1969 stood at 6,900 congregations and slightly more than two million members.

The meeting of the seventh General Synod of the church in Boston during the summer of 1969 made it clear that the United Church was facing the difficult issues of the times, especially the need to empower minorities.

It established a Commission for Racial Justice, stipulating that a majority of the members must be black and guaranteeing $500,000 for its programs in 1970. It also acted to ensure that at least 20% of the delegates to future meetings of the General Synod would be under the age of 30. At Boston less than 2% of the delegates were under 30.

As the most representative body of the denomination, the General Synod also went on record as calling for acceleration of the withdrawal of U.S. troops from Vietnam and for the licensing of gun users. It urged its national instrumentalities to give consideration to social justice as well as to security and yield in planning financial investments.

The United Church continued to understand itself as a "uniting" as well as a "united" body. It was a full participant in the Consultation on Church Union and was active in both the National and the World Council of Churches. In many local communities, United Church congregations were taking the initiative in forming clusters of congregations for ministry and in establishing ecumenical congregations. More than half of the work of the Boards for Homeland and World Ministries was done jointly with the agencies of other denominations.

Officers of the church in 1969 were Robert V. Moss (elected June 30), president; Joseph H. Evans, secretary; and Charles H. Lockyear, treasurer. (R. V. M.)

ROMAN CATHOLIC CHURCH

The year was marked by continued internal struggles over the reforms initiated by the second Vatican Council. Tension was reflected in the addresses of Pope Paul VI (*see* Biography). The Christmas call to Christians to "turn away from hope in human self-sufficiency" had by Easter become a plea for an end to the "crucifixion" of the church by criticism. On Maundy Thursday the pope spoke of the danger of schism, and critics of the encyclical *Humanae Vitae* ("Of Human Life"), which had upheld the church's traditional position on artificial means of contraception, were said to be "seeking the easy way." However, he denied that his speeches betokened any lack of confidence.

Roman Catholic priests Bernard L. Meyer (on curb) and Robert T. Begin after police evicted them from St. John's Cathedral in Cleveland, O., where they had attempted to conduct an unauthorized Mass.

WIDE WORLD

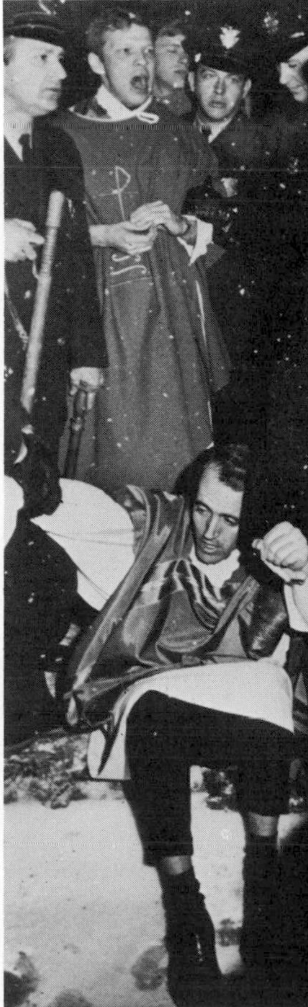

BEN ROTH AGENCY

"Yes, yes, Sister Rose, I'm all for the modern approach, but must you refer to 'Apologia Pro Vita Sua' as 'Newman's Complaint'?"—Gauerke, "National Review."

In 1969 the pope visited Geneva on the 50th anniversary of the International Labour Organization, and visited the headquarters of the World Council of Churches. The first papal visit to Africa, to preside at a meeting of African bishops in Uganda, was a great success. The increasing importance of the nonwhite world was also reflected in the inclusion of saints from Africa, Japan, and Oceania in the revised liturgical calendar, announced in May. This aspect of the revision was overshadowed, however, by the publicity given to the dropping of several well-known but possibly mythical saints, including St. Christopher and St. Nicholas.

Early in 1969 a group of theologians gathered by the international theological review *Concilium* signed a declaration that "the freedom of theologians and theology in the service of the church, regained by Vatican II, must not be lost again." The Holy Office, officially renamed the Congregation for the Doctrine of the Faith, had made various attempts to exercise control over theologians. Ivan Illich, head of an experimental community in Cuernavaca, Mex., and of considerable influence in South America, was interrogated and, although publication of the questions led to the dismissal of a few minor officials, resigned from the ministry. The International Theological Commission, recommended by the 1967 synod, was set up after Easter, and three signatories of the *Concilium* declaration were included.

It had been predicted that the future of the church would be decided in Latin America. The problems there were the problems of the whole church, more clearly defined and far more urgent. Within the Latin-American church the progressives were more progressive and the conservatives more conservative than elsewhere, a fact attributable to the immediacy of the problems.

In the Brazilian diocese of Botucatú, the clergy petitioned that a certain ultraconservative not be appointed bishop. At first they appeared to have succeeded, but later the conservative was appointed; as a result, 34 out of 39 secular priests in the diocese resigned. In Rosario, Arg., many resignations followed the local bishop's opposition to a program of pastoral and social renewal. Despite such difficulties, 1969 brought some improvements for Latin America. In Rome the newly created Committee for Human Development had a Brazilian chairman, and the *Populorum Progressio* fund was set up to further development in Latin America. Many local hierarchies showed cohesion and courage in the denunciation of dictatorial regimes, notably in Brazil, Argentina, and Peru.

The threatened celibacy crisis at last materialized, most seriously in Latin America and Western Europe, particularly the Netherlands. Clashes with authority in Latin America were often motivated and always complicated by this issue. In the Netherlands there was some slight relaxation and a large measure of sympathy for the priests involved, but the large numbers leaving the priesthood suggested that either the exceptions and sympathy were insufficient or the celibacy issue was merely a symptom. The psychological research department of the Catholic University of Nijmegen reported that those desiring some relaxation in the ruling were not so numerous as popularly supposed.

In the U.S. the resignation and marriage of Bishop James P. Shannon of Minneapolis–St. Paul was dramatic in its effect. A nationwide survey of the question of celibacy was ordered. In the U.S. church opinion polarized, with an aggressive right wing denouncing an equally aggressive left wing. The progressives had *The National Catholic Reporter* as their organ, and "underground churches," often starting from dissatisfaction with parish liturgies and deeply concerned about civil rights and the war in Vietnam, developed. Dissatisfaction was expressed with the way bishops were appointed—largely through the nomination of the apostolic delegate. A National Federation of Priests' Councils was formed which claimed to represent 38,000 priests.

Many of the problems of 1969 were discussed in a new book, *Coresponsibility in the Church* by Léon Josef Cardinal Suenens, archbishop of Malines-Brussels (*see* BIOGRAPHY). The much-publicized book called for an honest reappraisal of authority at all levels in the church, and particularly of the problem of the collegiality of the bishops. Despite his affirmations of loyalty to the Holy See, the cardinal was viewed with suspicion in many quarters. The pope himself referred to his critics in June, declaring that attacks on the Roman Curia were attacks upon himself, but that he would meditate upon the criticisms with "humility and sincere objectivity."

Willingly or not, Cardinal Suenens became the focus of dissent. When the European bishops met at Chur, Switz., in July, their meetings were interrupted by a group of dissident priests who chanted Suenens' name as he entered the hall. The same group also demonstrated in Rome during the synod that began on October 11.

The main questions on the synod's agenda were collegiality and relations between bishops and the Holy See. Without challenging the principle of papal authority, the bishops made quite clear their desire to function as the pope's chief advisers. Of their recommendations, the pope virtually accepted three: regular meetings of the synod every two years instead of at the pope's pleasure; establishment of a secretariat at Rome that would serve as a direct channel between bishops and pope; and the right of national conferences of bishops to propose issues to be discussed by the synod. Prospects for approval of a fourth proposal—that the pontiff would consult the bishops before issuing rulings affecting the entire church—appeared favourable. (P. A. H.)

EASTERN CHURCHES

The Orthodox Church. The preparation of the Great Council of the Orthodox Church, announced in 1968 at the Pan-Orthodox meeting in Chambéry, Switz., was furthered in 1969 when the Ecumenical Patriarchate appointed Archimandrite Damaskinos Papanderou as secretary of the preparatory commission.

Inter-Orthodox cooperation was also marked by official visits and celebrations. The newly elected patriarch of Alexandria, Nicholas, visited Athens; Belgrade, Yugos.; Sofia, Bulg.; Bucharest, Rom.; and Moscow. On May 11 a solemn commemoration of the 1,100th anniversary of the death of St. Cyril, the Byzantine missionary to the Slavs, took place in Sofia. The celebration was attended by the patriarchs of Constantinople and Alexandria, as well as by the archbishops of Athens and Prague, and the Roman Catholic Church was officially represented. Among the changes that occurred in the leadership of the autocephalous churches, the metropolitan of Warsaw, Steven, died on March 26 and a new archbishop of Sinai, Gregorios, was elected on January 4.

Information reaching the West seemed to indicate that direct administrative pressure against the Orthodox Church in the U.S.S.R. (as well as against the other religious groups) was less apparent. No massive closings of churches or religious institutions were reported, although the constant antireligious propaganda continued. There was, however, a general crackdown on intellectual dissent. The Orthodox free-lance religious writers Anatoly Levitin-Krasnov and Boris Talantov, whose articles and books circulated in manuscript and were frequently published in the West, were arrested in September. An appeal of Orthodox believers in the city of Gorki, directed to several international organizations, affirmed that the Soviet laws on religious freedom were being violated; in that city of some one million persons, only three small churches, able to accommodate no more than 4,000, were allowed to be open.

The events in Czechoslovakia placed the local Orthodox Church in an embarrassing position, especially in relation to the Roman Catholic Church. In 1950 the Orthodox Church had received a large number of "Greek Catholics" (Eastern rite Christians in communion with Rome), who returned to Rome in large numbers during the "liberalization." Rightly or wrongly, they accused the Orthodox Church of cooperation with the pre-January 1968 regime, and litigation on property rights and unfortunate excesses marked the change of allegiance in many areas of eastern Slovakia. A mixed commission of both churches was set up in an attempt to limit the moral damage.

A new charter for the Orthodox Church of Greece was promulgated by the military government on Feb. 17, 1969. The text had been prepared in cooperation with the archbishop of Athens, Hieronymos, with the synod of the hierarchy being invited to give its approval without the right to present amendments. The assembly met on March 1–10. The stormy character of the sessions prompted Archbishop Hieronymos to present his resignation, which was refused. The vote on the charter had to be postponed, and the assembly asked for the revision of several articles. The new charter gave the government the upper hand in selecting the archbishop of Athens, but it could also be called progressive in that it provided for lay participation in church administration and established the principle of the church's financial independence from the state. It practically suppressed the jurisdiction of the Ecumenical Patriarchate over the dioceses of northern Greece.

At their clergy-laity conventions, two national dioceses in the U.S.—the Romanian Episcopate and the Antiochian Archdiocese—expressed themselves formally as being in favour of a united and autocephalous Orthodox Church of America, without administrative ties with the mother churches abroad. The Russian Orthodox Church of America, a much larger body, had repeatedly favoured such a unification. In 1968 the clergy-laity congress of the Greek Archdiocese of America had also called for unification, but had envisaged it only under the jurisdiction of the Ecumenical Patriarchate.

The American-born Dimitri Royster was consecrated bishop of Berkeley, Calif., in the Russian Orthodox Church of America. That church officially decided to proceed with the canonization of the monk Herman, one of the first Orthodox missionaries among the Aleuts of Alaska, who died on Spruce Island, near Kodiak, in 1837.

Eastern Non-Chalcedonian Churches. During the year, several Non-Chalcedonian churches were visited by Orthodox delegations. The Syrian-Jacobite Church of India extended an invitation to the patriarch of Romania, Justinian, who inaugurated a new seminary building in Kottayam, Kerala. The same church also received a Russian Orthodox delegation, headed by the archbishop of Minsk. The Church of Ethiopia was visited by Patriarch Justinian, who was received in a formal ceremony as a state guest by Emperor Haile Selassie.

The Coptic Church, whose position as the largest non-Muslim religious body in the U.A.R. was, at times, a delicate one, repeatedly expressed its full solidarity with the U.A.R. position in the Middle East crisis. This attitude of loyalty appeared to have improved its standing in the eyes of the government, which had extended direct financial help toward the construction of the new Coptic cathedral in Cairo.

In April a delegation of high-ranking Coptic churchmen visited Rome and Venice. In the latter city, they participated in the celebration of the 1,900th anniversary of the death of St. Mark, the traditional founder of Christianity in Egypt. (J. Me.)

JUDAISM

The precarious position of Jews in the Arab countries, the U.S.S.R., Poland, and Czechoslovakia and the surprising eruption of black anti-Semitism in the U.S. headed the list on the agenda of Jewish collective concern in the year 1969 (5729–30, according to the Jewish calendar).

Some 75,000 Jews were still living within the Arab world. While no blatant anti-Jewish discrimination was noticeable in Morocco and Tunisia (estimated Jewish population 60,000), hundreds of Jews arrested in Syria (Jewish population 4,000), the U.A.R. (2,500), and Iraq (2,500) in June 1967 remained in prison. Others were virtual prisoners in their homes. Especially tragic was the plight of the remnants of the Jewish community in Iraq, which attracted worldwide attention in August 1969 following the public hanging of a group of Iraqi Jews accused of spying for Israel. Many Jews were arrested and kept incommunicado. No Jew was allowed to leave his town of residence or change his domicile without permission. Most Jewish employees had been dismissed, and Jewish merchants had their licenses withdrawn. Although Iraqi authorities had announced in May that Jews could apply for passports, only one of the 1,500 applications was answered. The 93-year-old chief rabbi

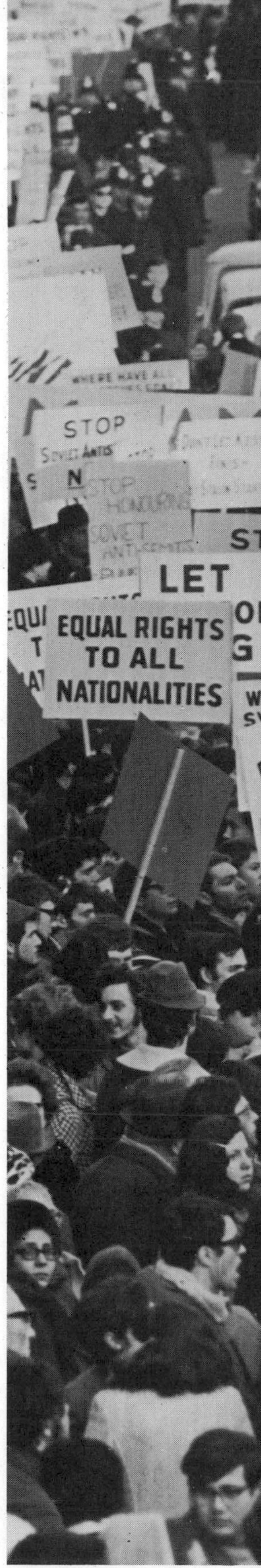

"THE TIMES" (LONDON) FROM PICTORIAL PARADE

English Jews march on the Soviet embassy in London on Feb. 2, 1969. Marchers presented Soviet First Secretary Aleksandr Kovalenko with a petition of 30,000 signatures accusing the Soviet Union of anti-Semitism.

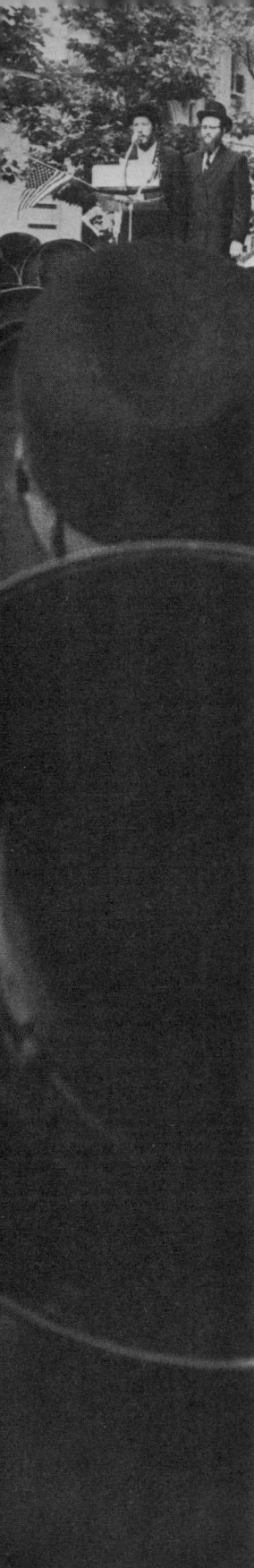

GAMMA—PIX FROM PUBLIX

Orthodox Jews gathered in front of the Israeli consulate in New York City to protest Israel's policy of forced autopsies, which they consider desecration of the dead.

of Iraq, Sasson Khadouri, whose own son was in prison, was forced to call a conference of Jewish leaders in Arab countries to denounce Zionism and Israel.

The religious aspects of the Arab-Israeli dispute—never truly separable from the political ones—were thrown into a frightening relief during the year by the fire that damaged a wing of the Al Aqsa Mosque in Jerusalem on August 21. Apparently set by a disturbed Australian Christian, Michael Rohan, the fire set off a tidal wave of bitterness in the Muslim world. While no Jew was to blame, the fears of Muslim people could be aroused by Arab propagandists on the ground that Jews might want to remove the two Muslim mosques on the site in order to rebuild the ancient Holy Temple.

Actually, only the Orthodox Jews would be interested in the reestablishment of a Holy Temple on the Temple Mount, and they believed that this task could be begun only after the coming of Elijah, the prophet and Messiah.

For non-Orthodox Jewry, the messianic dream had long been interpreted in universal terms: the focus of Jewish hope was not the person of the Messiah, but the messianic era of peace, justice, and happiness. Reform, Conservative, and Reconstructionist writers looked forward to the building of the heavenly Jerusalem in every land. It was in this sense that they interpreted the vision of Isaiah: "Out of Zion shall go forth teaching, and the word of God from Jerusalem" (Isa. 2:3). For a century the Jewish community was bitterly divided between Zionists and anti-Zionists, but in recent years a synthetic view that saw the fulfillment of the prophetic vision in both Israel and the diaspora had attained fairly general—although not universal—acceptance.

In the U.S.S.R. there was continued evidence of anti-Semitism and distrust of Jews. The discrimination was rarely physical, but consisted of a subtle combination of economic, cultural, and social pressures. Jews were barred from higher echelon jobs, and were not allowed to attain prestigious positions. They practically disappeared from the top ranks of the Communist Party, the armed forces, and the diplomatic service. Discrimination was also evident in education, especially on the higher levels.

Although Soviet propagandists and apologists were still careful to make a distinction between "Zionist imperialists" and "Jews," in practice this distinction became more and more blurred. The leading anti-Zionist "expert," Yuri Ivanov, author of the notorious pamphlet *Beware of Zionism!*, mentioned in one of his articles (*Molodoy Kommunist,* June) "such particularities of the Jewish religious complex as hatred of mankind, the preaching (in various forms and versions) of genocide, the nurturing of a love of power, and praise of criminal methods of achieving power."

In June the Polish authorities announced the tightening of existing emigration procedures for Jews in Poland. It was officially stated that since July 1967, 5,264 Jews had left Poland (although in all probability the number was much greater). Thousands were waiting for exit visas. The United Polish Workers' Party, the military establishment, the civil service, and institutions of higher learning became practically *Juderein* (the Nazi term), as hundreds of Jews were dismissed. Many Jewish cultural and social institutions were closed and some Jews were imprisoned or awaiting trial for "Zionist" offenses. Some of the most virulent "anti-Zionists" were dismissed from their posts, and anti-Jewish utterances by official spokesmen were largely discontinued, but the campaign against Israel and the Jews went on. It was estimated that about half of the 30,000 self-declared Jews in Poland had left—or were about to leave—a sad end to the thousand-year history of Jews in Poland.

Some 5,000 Jews also left Czechoslovakia following the Soviet invasion in May 1968. Certain conservative elements in the Czechoslovak Communist Party, backed by the Soviets, were reportedly pressing for an anti-Zionist show trial. Fortunately, this did not materialize. However, the celebration of the millennium of the Jewish settlement in Bohemia, originally planned for 1968 and rescheduled for 1969, was again canceled, possibly because of outside pressures.

It was in the U.S., however, that the most surprising development occurred. U.S. Jewry (estimated at some 5.8 million), the largest and most influential segment of the Jewish people, witnessed a sudden and unexpected eruption of black anti-Semitism. Both the source and the intensity were surprising. The majority of U.S. Jews, individually and collectively, had always sympathized with the Negro cause and had taken a prominent part in the fight for civil rights. The centre of the storm was in New York, where the 1968 teachers' strike—itself a reaction to Negro demands for more control of education in predominantly Negro areas where a high proportion of teachers were Jewish—had brought black anti-Semitism to the surface. It was bitterly expressed by a 16-year-old black high-school girl: "Behind every hurdle the Afro-American has yet to jump stands the Jew who has already cleared it. Blacks may find that anti-Jewish sentiments place them, for once, within a majority. Thus, our contempt for the Jews makes us feel more completely American in sharing a national prejudice." The emergence of black anti-Semitism left U.S. Jewry perplexed and worried. (J. B. A.; P. GL.)

BUDDHISM

By far the most important event for Buddhists in 1969 was the ninth general conference of the World Fellowship of Buddhists (WFB), held in Kuala Lumpur and Penang, Malaysia, April 12–21. It was attended by over 200 leaders representing WFB regional centres in Asia, Europe, North America, and Australia. The conference reelected Princess Poon Diskul of Thailand as president and elected 12 vice-presidents, including representatives from Asia, Europe, the U.S., and the U.S.S.R. The new regional centres of Brazil, Hungary, Ipoh (Malaysia), and Austria were admitted and a recommendation to establish the permanent headquarters of the WFB in Bangkok, Thailand, was unanimously adopted.

In India the Dalai Lama and his compatriots commemorated the tenth anniversary of the unsuccessful uprising of the Tibetans against the Peking regime. He was reported to have acquired 130 ac. of land in the Himalayan foothills with the hope of establishing a monastic university. Elsewhere in India, vigorous evangelistic activities were carried on by the so-called "New Buddhists," outcastes who had embraced Buddhism.

The year witnessed varied activities in the Theravada (Southern) Buddhist countries. In Ceylon the Sinhalese Buddhists promoted the formation of a Buddhist political party, the establishment of a Buddhist ecclesiastical court, and the appointment of a monk (*bhikku*) to the Cabinet. A group of monks broke away from the historic Syam Sect and formed a new sect called the Syamopali Vanawasa Sanghasabhawa. In Burma, Gen. Ne Win released 255 detainees, including a number of Buddhist monks (*pongyis*), from protective custody and assured the Buddhist leaders that the government was making the utmost efforts for the promotion of Buddhism. In Thailand the centenary of the death of the reformer-king Maha Mongkut (Rama IV), who spent 27 years as a monk before ascending the throne, was commemorated in October 1968. It was reported that 100,000 hill tribe people in northern Thailand had been converted from animism to Buddhism. In South Vietnam, where over 50 Buddhist temples had been destroyed in the war, Buddhists were split between moderate and militant wings. Early in 1969, near Saigon, a monk burned himself to death "for the sake of peace"—the 28th self-immolation since 1963.

There were few significant events in the Mahayana (Northern) Buddhist countries. In Japan some of the Buddhist-related "new religions" seemed to be taking their Buddhist heritage more seriously. South Korean Pres. Park Chung-hee unveiled a statue of Samyongdang, a 16th-century patriotic Buddhist monk. The first South Korean Buddhist army chaplains, five in number, were commissioned. Buddhist activities were at the lowest ebb in China.

Buddhism continued to make headway in the West. A new temple was built in Munich, W.Ger., with a Mongolian (Kalmyk) monk in charge. A Tibetan monastic institute was opened in Rikon, Switz. New Buddhist centres were also established in East London, S.Af., and Montreal, Que. Two American-born priests were installed as bishops—Bishop Kenryu Tsuji for the Buddhist Churches in America and Bishop Newton Ishiura for the Buddhist Churches in Canada.

Important Buddhist relics, dating from the 1st to the 5th century A.D., were found in Gandhara in Pakistan. Soviet archaeologists unearthed the head of a giant Buddha statue in the ruins of a 6th–7th century monastery in Tadzhikistan. The Nepalese Archaeological Department announced the unearthing of an ancient stupa in the Lumbini area. (J. M. KA.)

ISLAM

Once again political tensions preoccupied Muslims in 1969 almost to the exclusion of other concerns. Most of the problems and conflicts of the recent past remained active. In some regions, the Middle East particularly, tensions rose to the crisis point.

Both political and religious tensions were involved when, on August 21, Al Aqsa Mosque, part of the Haram ash Sharif in Jerusalem, was burned and severely damaged. An Australian described as a religious extremist was subsequently arrested and charged with arson. The area of Haram ash Sharif, which is the Temple area, is generally acknowledged as the third holiest place for Muslims, after Mecca and Medina. The fire brought an avalanche of reaction throughout the Muslim world. It was most marked among Arabs, though a riot was provoked in Kashmir, where the predominantly Muslim population remained restless under Indian rule.

Since the Six-Day War of 1967, when Israel took control of Jerusalem's Old City, a number of Arab Muslims had expressed fears that the city's Muslim holy places might be damaged by sabotage, desecration, or archaeological investigations. Though news accounts indicated that there was no conspiracy to set the fire and there were no implications of Israeli involvement, nevertheless Muslim and particularly Arab frustration over the Arab-Israeli situation was brought to a head. A number of Muslim heads of state called for renewed efforts to expel Israel from Jerusalem and other territories, adding to their call an appeal to Muslim sacred duty.

NEWSPHOT FROM PICTORIAL PARADE

Burning interior of Al Aqsa Mosque in Old Jerusalem, one of Islam's holiest sites.
An Australian citizen was charged with arson for the fire, which heavily damaged the ancient structure on Aug. 21, 1969.

The Al Aqsa fire could also be viewed in terms of the increasing armed clashes between Israel and its Arab neighbours, and especially the rising prominence of Arab guerrilla activities. By fall these activities had brought on an internal crisis in Lebanon that threatened to upset the delicate political balance between the religious communities in that country. (*See* MIDDLE EAST.) A conference of Islamic leaders was convened in Rabat, Mor., in September to deal with the issues raised by the fire. It issued a declaration urging the major powers to work toward a "speedy withdrawal" of Israel from occupied territory and giving "full support" for the Palestinian people in their "struggle for national liberation." The conference also called for a meeting of the foreign ministers of Muslim countries in 1970 to organize a permanent Islamic secretariat.

Hindu-Muslim riots, which continued in India during the year, were partly coloured by the efforts of Prime Minister Indira Gandhi to seek Muslim support as a counterweight to the conservative group within the Congress Party. There had been suggestions that in recent years the Congress Party had neglected the interests of Indian Muslims in favour of the Hindus. Indian-Pakistani relations continued to be strained over the Kashmir-Jammu question, although the Rann of Cutch border problem was worked out in January.

In Pakistan the agitation against the government of Pres. Muhammad Ayub Khan, which led to his resignation in March, was not cast in religious terms to any important extent. (R. W. SM.)

RELIGIONS OF ASIA

Religious development in Asia immediately following World War II had been marked by jubilant optimism on the part of religious leaders, who felt that national independence authenticated their respective religious claims and beliefs. The so-called resurgence of Asian religions, then, was the manifestation of a hopeful self-assurance on the part of Hindu leaders in India, Muslim leaders in Pakistan, Indonesia, and the Federation of Malaya (later Malaysia), and Buddhist leaders in Southeast Asia and the Far East.

Two decades later, many leaders, both clerical and lay—despite the sanguine note of their public pro-

KEYSTONE

His Divine Grace Swami A. C. Bhaktivedanta, head of the International Society for Krishna Consciousness, at a meeting for his followers in a lounge after his arrival at London airport on Sept. 11, 1969.

nouncements—were keenly aware of the ambiguities surrounding them. To be sure, they still jealously guarded their prerogatives as architects of the national and regional communities. However, the practical necessity of maintaining their leadership role side by side with politicians, generals, bureaucrats, writers, artists, and businessmen compelled them to shift their priorities from the primarily spiritual and mythological to the more mundane institutional, political, and social dimensions of religion and morality. Such a shift, which had come to be tacitly accepted in many Asian religions, added fuel to the tension between national and religious communities.

In India, Hindus and non-Hindus alike were celebrating the centenary of the birth of Mohandas Gandhi. Ironically, a postage stamp depicting a portrait of Gandhi with the image of the Buddha in the background had to be withdrawn by the government because of strong protests by the Buddhists. Following the death in May of Zakir Husain (*see* OBITUARIES), the first Muslim to serve as president of India, the presidential candidacy of Jagjivan Ram, a member of the scheduled ("untouchable") caste, was defeated by the powerful conservative wing of the Congress Party, even though he was supported by Prime Minister Indira Gandhi. Mrs. Gandhi did succeed in installing V. V. Giri, a labour leader, as president over heavy conservative opposition.

Many Hindus were fearful that the rapid growth of Christianity among the 75 million members of the scheduled caste might lead to a demand for the creation of a "Christianistan." In 1968 the strong sense of separate identity among the people of the Assam Division had compelled the government to create a substate there; the number of Christians in Assam had risen by 67% between 1951 and 1961. It was feared that non-Hindu minorities in other areas, such as the Christians in Kerala and the Sikhs in Harayana and Punjab—to say nothing of the Muslims in various states—might also demand separate political status. India continued to suffer from domestic Hindu-Muslim and other intrareligious conflicts, as well as a strained relationship with its Muslim neighbour, Pakistan.

In Ceylon the Sinhalese Buddhists, who comprised 70% of the population, remained critical of the government for its alliance with the Federal Party, the party of the Hindu-Tamil minority. In 1968 the government had rejected the Hindu-Tamils' request to establish a sacred area around the Konneswaram Hindu Temple. Later the government assured the Buddhist leaders that only Poya (Buddhist Sabbath) days would remain holidays and that no other religious holidays, including Sundays, would be recognized.

Southeast Asia, the crossroads of religions, continued to be troubled by internal disunity along religious, ethnic, and ideological lines. With varying degrees of success the governments of Burma and Thailand depended on the cooperation of Buddhist communities to counteract the rebellions of minority groups and Communists. Islam remained the most cohesive power in Malaysia, which suffered heavily from Malay-Chinese rioting and Communist terrorist activities, and in Indonesia, which was trying to rebuild the national order and economy despite the presence of Communist guerrillas. In South Vietnam, Buddhist animosity against Catholics in general and against Pres. Nguyen Van Thieu, a Catholic, in particular was accentuated by the arrest of 160 Buddhist leaders and the sentencing of Thich Thien Minh, a leader of the Unified Vietnamese Buddhist Church, to ten years' hard labour.

On the more optimistic side, the committee for the restoration of the colossal 9th-century Buddhist sanctuary of Borobudur in Java was greatly encouraged by the support it was receiving from Buddhist groups in Asia, the Netherlands government, the cities of Bremen, W.Ger., and New York, and UNESCO. (*See* HISTORIC BUILDINGS.) (J. M. KA.)

ENCYCLOPÆDIA BRITANNICA FILMS. *Major Religions of the World (Development and Rituals)* (1954).

Rhodesia

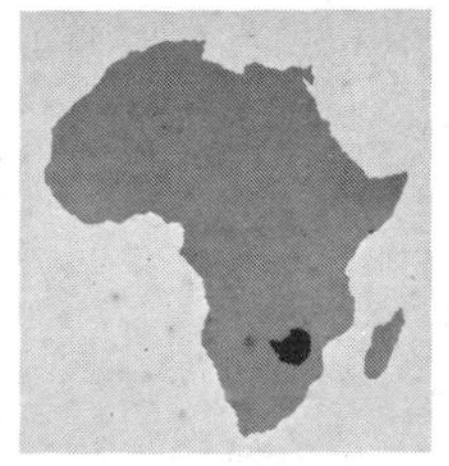

Though Southern Rhodesia declared its independence and assumed the name Rhodesia on Nov. 11, 1965, it remained a British colony in the eyes of many other nations. It is bounded by Zambia, Mozambique, South Africa, and Botswana. Area: 150,820 sq.mi. (389,622 sq.km.). Pop. (1969 est.): 5,090,000, of whom 94% are African and 5% white. Cap. and largest city: Salisbury (pop., 1969 est., 172,000). Language: English (official) and Bantu. Religion: predominantly traditional tribal beliefs; Christian minority. British governor to June 25, 1969, Sir Humphrey Gibbs; prime minister (not recognized by British government), Ian D. Smith.

Rhodesia's rejection of the constitutional proposals made at the meeting between Smith and British Prime Minister Harold Wilson aboard HMS "Fearless" in 1968 encouraged criticism of the government toward the end of 1968. T. H. P. Bashford, chairman of the Centre Party, accused Smith of wishing to introduce retrogressive changes into the country's policy, while both E. S. Newson, chairman of the Rhodesian Iron and Steel Corporation, and Evan Campbell, chairman of the Standard Bank in Rhodesia, wrote letters to the press emphasizing the disastrous effects of continuing sanctions on Rhodesia's economy. In December, Smith accused the two businessmen of divulging economic information in defiance of an understanding between the government and financial and industrial leaders. He also charged the Argus Press, which had printed their letters, with trying to prepare the country for a premature sellout to the Africans.

Grave dissatisfaction with the "Fearless" proposals was expressed at the Commonwealth Prime Ministers' Conference in London in January. Since the British government remained firmly opposed to the use of force, however, the majority of the Commonwealth leaders reluctantly agreed that the only method of maintaining pressure on Rhodesia was to continue and strengthen economic sanctions.

In February the Rhodesian government sent a memorandum on the "Fearless" proposals to Britain, with new constitutional proposals; it confirmed white domination of the legislature and rejected the Privy Council as the final court of appeal on the ground that this was inconsistent with the dignity of an independent state, as well as being unsuited to local conditions. This move to the right was thought by some to have been encouraged by the conviction that the worst effects of sanctions had already been felt. The British government argued that the memorandum merely reiterated the negative position previously adopted by Smith and his colleagues.

On June 20 the Rhodesian government held a referendum in which 54,724 voted for the adoption of the constitutional proposals, while 20,776 voted against. On the further question as to whether a republic should be declared, 61,130 were in favour while 14,372 were opposed. The electorate was 88,217, of whom 6,634 were Africans. On June 24 it was announced that Sir Humphrey Gibbs was resigning as governor.

Holding that there was no hope of renewed negotiations with Britain, Smith introduced the constitution bill into Parliament on October 2. The bill provided for the appointment of a president by the Cabinet to replace the existing officer administering the government. Opposition was widespread both among Rhodesian Africans and in the UN. Meetings arranged by the African Trades Union Congress to discuss the referendum were banned, but a number of tribal chiefs declared themselves dissatisfied with the constitutional proposals, especially with the proposal to break with the crown. At the UN in June there were demands that sanctions be strengthened, but a resolution by the African and Asian Security Council members urging Britain to take all necessary steps, including force, to end the rebellion and calling upon all states to give moral and material assistance to the national liberation movement failed to obtain the nine votes necessary for adoption.

In June and July it became clear that the agreements on sanctions were being broken. The British government, while maintaining that economic sanctions would assist political change in Rhodesia, admitted that economic activity in Rhodesia in real terms was higher than in 1965. However, the British government felt that this apparently satisfactory state of affairs was not wholly realistic. Comprehensive mandatory sanctions had seriously affected exports, while Rhodesia was attempting to hold imports to the minimum and was undergoing considerable economic strain in the process. Nevertheless, Rhodesia had contrived to sell £44 million worth of exports in 1968.

The Rhodesian minister of finance, John Wrathall, presented the budget on July 17. It was designed, he said, to encourage private enterprise and initiative; direct taxation would be substantially reduced, and the loss of revenue would be offset by increased indirect taxation. The adverse effects were most likely to be felt by Africans, for although the cost of basic foodstuffs was not affected, clothing and small luxuries would cost more.

The state of emergency was extended for a further 12 months on April 16. This was made possible by new legislation; formerly the maximum period for which a state of emergency could be declared without renewed legislation was three months. Leaders of the African nationalist movement suffered further setbacks. Joshua Nkomo had been served with a new order in December 1968 restricting him for five more years to the remote camp of Gonakudzingwa, where he had already been detained for four years without being charged or tried. Ndabaningi Sithole (*see* BIOGRAPHY) was sentenced to six years' hard labour in February on a charge of incitement to murder. Denying the allegation, Sithole said at the end of the trial that he disassociated himself from any terrorist activity and from any form of violence. On March 7 the Executive Council reprieved 49 Africans sentenced to death for entering the country carrying arms, and on August 19 a further 19 prisoners had their sentences commuted to life imprisonment. (K. I.)

RHODESIA

Education. (1968) African: primary, pupils 685,559; teachers 17,033; secondary, pupils 17,227, teachers 761; vocational and teacher training, students 2,565; teachers 177. Non-African: primary, pupils 38,699, teachers 1,551; secondary, pupils 24,844, teachers 1,452; African and non-African: higher (University College of Rhodesia), students 894, teaching staff 165.

Finance. Monetary unit: Rhodesian pound, with an exchange rate of R£0.36 to U.S. $1 (R£0.86 = £1 sterling). Budget (1969–70 est.): revenue R£99,240,000; expenditure R£101,970,000. Gross national product: (1967) R£387.4 million; (1966) R£357.7 million.

Foreign Trade. (1967): Imports R£93.5 million; exports R£100.6 million. Import sources (1965): U.K. 30%; South Africa 23%; U.S. 7%; Japan 6%. Export destinations (1965): Zambia 29%; U.K. 20%; South Africa 11%; West Germany 8%; Malawi 6%; Japan 5%. Main exports (1965): tobacco 29%; asbestos 7%.

Transport and Communications. Roads (1968) 78,470 km. (including 8,470 km. main roads). Motor vehicles in use (1967): passenger 111,000; commercial (including buses) 42,200. Railways: (1967) 3,330 km.; freight traffic (July 1967–May 1968, after separation of Rhodesian and Zambian lines) 5,454,000,000 net ton-km. Air traffic (apportionment of traffic of Central African Airways; 1966): 72,112,000 passenger-km.; freight 891,000 net ton-km. Telephones (Dec. 1967) 112,086. Radio receivers (June 1967) 105,078. Television receivers (Dec. 1967) 45,000.

Agriculture. Production (in 000; metric tons; 1968; 1967 in parentheses): tobacco *c.* 62 (*c.* 94); corn (1967) *c.* 640, (1966) 602; peanuts *c.* 37 (*c.* 79); tea (1966) 2.3, (1965) 1.6; sugar, raw value (1968–69) *c.* 147, (1967–68) *c.* 137; beef and veal (on farms and estates; 1967) *c.* 68, (1966) *c.* 68. Livestock (in 000; 1967–68): cattle *c.* 3,700; sheep (1966–67) *c.* 432; goats (1966–67) *c.* 643; pigs *c.* 142.

Industry. Production (in 000; metric tons; 1967): coal 2,739; chrome ore (oxide content; 1965) 281; asbestos *c.* 150; iron ore (metal content) *c.* 450; gold (troy oz.; 1966) 550; electricity (kw-hr.) 4,952,000.

Romania

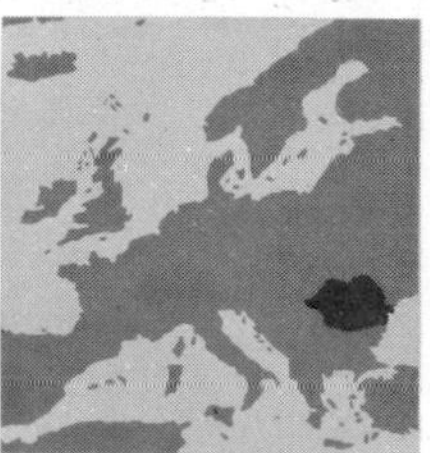

A socialist republic on the Balkan Peninsula in southeastern Europe, Romania is bordered by the U.S.S.R., the Black Sea, Bulgaria, Yugoslavia, and Hungary. Area: 91,699 sq.mi. (237,500 sq.km.). Pop. (1968 est.): 19,720,084, including (1968) Romanian 87.8%; Hungarian 8.4%. Cap. and largest city: Bucharest (pop., 1968 est., 1,431,993). Religion: Romanian Orthodox 70%; Greek Orthodox 10%. General secretary of the Romanian Communist Party and president

BEN ROTH AGENCY

"Limited Freedom" —Jusp, "Wir Bruckenbauer," Switzerland.

of the State Council in 1969, Nicolae Ceausescu; chairman of the Council of Ministers (premier), Ion Gheorghe Maurer.

During 1969, under the imaginative, genial, and firm leadership of Nicolae Ceausescu (*see* BIOGRAPHY), Romania made further progress on its difficult road toward socialism and national independence. At home, in the party and the government, the men of the old guard, steeped in Stalinist traditions, consistently lost ground. In its relations with the world at large, Romania expanded its political contacts and economic agreements with capitalist countries while remaining a member of the socialist community.

On March 2 a new Grand National Assembly was elected. Out of 13,577,143 valid votes, 13,543,499 (99.75%) were given to the candidates of the Socialist Unity Front. Among 465 deputies there were 41 Magyars, 12 Germans, and 9 of other nationalities. On March 13 the Assembly elected Stefan Voitec as its chairman and reelected Ceausescu as president of the State Council; it also elected four vice-presidents and 22 members of that supreme state body. Maurer was again invested by the Assembly as chairman of the Council of Ministers.

The tenth congress of the Romanian Communist Party (RCP) was held in Bucharest August 6–12. Addressing the 1,915 delegates, Ceausescu reaffirmed Romania's traditional policy of developing relations of friendship and many-sided cooperation with the U.S.S.R. As a European country Romania was particularly interested in European security and had joined the other Warsaw Treaty states in launching in March the Budapest appeal calling for the recognition of the "realities created after World War II," namely the two German states and the existing frontiers. Ceausescu also called for "strengthening the defensive capacity of Romania" and for perfecting the organization and the equipment of the armed forces.

The congress also approved the Central Committee's decision of April 1968 concerning political and legal rehabilitation of people unjustly persecuted under the government of the late Gheorghe Gheorghiu-Dej and the report, presented by Premier Maurer, on the directives concerning the 1971–75 plan and the guidelines for economic development in the 1976–80 period. It was proposed that in the five years beginning 1971 the output of industrial means of production would increase 9–10% yearly, and that of consumer goods 7–8%.

The most sensational event in the domain of Romania's foreign relations was the visit in Bucharest on August 2 of Richard Nixon, the first U.S. president to visit any Communist country in peacetime. Over a million people turned out to greet President Nixon who danced the hora with Romanian girls in a city square and had a 3½-hour talk with Ceausescu. Five days later, however, at the RCP congress, Konstantin Katushev, a Soviet delegate, warned Romanians about the "perfidious tactic of imperialism" in "building bridges" to divide the socialist countries.

During the year Ceausescu visited Turkey in March, Poland in May, Iran in September, and met with President Tito of Yugoslavia in February and September. In May Romanian troops took part in maneuvers in the Ukraine with Soviet, Bulgarian, and Hungarian ground forces. On August 17 Romania and Israel raised their diplomatic relations to ambassadorial level. As a result Syria and Sudan broke off diplomatic ties with Romania, the U.A.R. and Iraq recalled their heads of mission, and Algeria and Libya issued statements of protest. Premier Maurer and Foreign Minister Corneliu Manescu paid an official visit to the U.K. in November. (K. SM.)

ROMANIA

Education. (1966–67) Primary, pupils 2,907,943, teachers 130,068; secondary, pupils 216,476, teachers 11,713; vocational, pupils 295,836, teachers 19,163; teacher training, students 10,723, teachers 574; higher (including 11 universities), students 136,948, teaching staff 13,404.

Finance. Monetary unit: leu, with an official exchange rate of 6 lei to U.S. $1 (14.40 lei = £1 sterling) and a tourist rate of 18 lei = U.S. $1 (43.20 lei = £1 sterling). Budget (1968 est.): revenue 140 billion lei; expenditure 139 billion lei.

Foreign Trade. (1967) Imports 9,280,000,000 lei; exports 8,372,000,000 lei. Import sources: U.S.S.R. 26%; West Germany 17%; East Germany 6%; Czechoslovakia 6%; Italy 6%; France 5%. Export destinations: U.S.S.R. 31%; West Germany 7%; Italy 7%; Czechoslovakia 6%; East Germany 5%; U.K. 5%. Main exports: machinery 19%; foodstuffs 15%; raw materials (cereals, timber, etc.) 13%; petroleum products 9%; chemicals 6%.

Transport and Communications. Roads (1968) 77,019 km. (including 10,021 km. with improved surface). Motor vehicles in use: passenger (1965) *c.* 250,000; commercial (1967) 36,800. Railways (1968): 11,016 km.; traffic 16,142,000,000 passenger-km., freight 40,706,000,000 net ton-km. Air traffic (1968): 281.5 million passenger-km.; freight 7,614,000 net ton-km. Inland waterways in regular use (1967) 1,115 km. Shipping (1968): merchant vessels 100 gross tons and over 56; gross tonnage 324,999. Telephones (Dec. 1967) 551,820. Radio receivers (Dec. 1967) 3,019,000. Television receivers (Dec. 1967) 916,000.

Agriculture. Production (in 000; metric tons; 1968; 1967 in parentheses): wheat 4,848 (5,820); rye *c.* 70 (71); barley *c.* 425 (531); oats (1967) 163, (1966) 170; corn 7,105 (6,858); potatoes 3,697 (3,086); onions (1967) 248, (1966) 314; tomatoes (1967) 676, (1966) 647; sugar, raw value (1968–69) *c.* 406, (1967–68) 478; tobacco (1967) 35, (1966) 40; sunflower seed *c.* 730 (720); dry peas (1967) 183, (1966) 163; plums (1967) 670, (1966) 837; apples (1967) 234, (1966) 234; grapes (1967) 910, (1966) 954; cheese *c.* 52 (53). Livestock (in 000; Jan. 1968): cattle 5,332; pigs 5,752; sheep 14,380; horses 715; poultry 47,147.

Industry. Index of production (1963 = 100): (1968) 185; (1967) 163. Production (in 000; metric tons; 1968): coal 5,459; lignite 9,346; coke (1967) 1,131; crude oil 13,287; natural gas (cu.m.) 21,737; electricity (kw-hr.) 27,777,000; iron ore (30–35% metal content) 2,747; pig iron 2,992; crude steel 4,751; cement 7,024; sulfuric acid 773; superphosphates (1967) 165; nitrogenous fertilizers (1967) 372; cotton fabrics (sq.m.) 377,000; woolen fabrics (sq.m.) 52,000; newsprint 52; other paper (1965) 192; commercial motor vehicles (units) 28. New dwelling units completed (1967) 118,502.

Rowing

The rowing highlight of 1969 was the 55th European championships at Klagenfurt, Aus., in September, which attracted 102 entrants from 28 countries. Austria, East Germany, West Germany, Great Britain, the U.S.S.R., and the United States contested all 7 events, and 11 nations shared the medals. East Germany won medals in six events, including one gold, three silver, and two bronze. West Germany took a gold and two bronze medals but the U.S.S.R. collected only a gold and a bronze. The only double triumph was recorded by the U.S., and the other gold medals went to Argentina and Czechoslovakia.

The distribution of medals was wider than usual and included several surprises. L. Hough and A. Johnson (U.S.) avenged their Olympic defeat by East Germany by 0.34 sec. in the coxless pairs in the closest verdict on finals day. The second U.S. victory was scored in double sculls by J. Van Blom and T. McKibbon. In only the third race they had ever rowed together they beat Austria by more than 4 sec. The solitary Soviet success, in coxless fours, was also unexpected, and the winning West German coxed fours contained an oarsman who had only started serious rowing six months previously.

The standard was higher than in the 1968 Olympics, and none of the Mexico victors won again. In single sculls Olympic champion J. F. Wienese (Neth.) finished sixth, the winner being A. Demiddi (Arg.) with the Olympic silver and bronze medalists J. Böhmer (E.Ger.) and J. Meissner (W.Ger.) again placing second and third. In coxed pairs the Italian Olympic winners managed second place, but East Germany dropped to third in coxless fours.

West Germany did not repeat its Olympic triumph in eights. The European title went to an outstanding crew from East Germany which beat the U.S.S.R. by 2.1 sec. with the Olympic champions 0.04 sec. farther behind in third place. Other countries among the minor medal winners were Denmark, Hungary, Romania, and Switzerland.

The U.S.S.R. and East Germany claimed the principal honours in the Women's European championships, also held at Klagenfurt a week before the men's events. The Soviet Union triumphed in the coxed fours, quadruple sculls, and single sculls, while East Germany took the eights and double sculls. The Soviet oarswomen won a silver and a bronze medal and East Germany won two silver medals and one bronze. Other medal winners were Austria, Czechoslovakia, West Germany, and Romania.

West Germany won three of the seven events in the Féderation Internationale Sociétés d'Aviron (FISA) youth championships held in Naples, Italy, in August. The West Germans became junior world champions in coxed fours, coxless fours, and single sculls. France won the coxless pairs, the Netherlands the coxed pairs, Italy the double sculls, and Czechoslovakia the eights.

In the U.K. an important development was the introduction of a selective draw at the Henley Royal Regatta, which attracted a record 224 entrants. The Henley stewards also disclosed that active consideration was being given to the possibility of introducing four-lane racing with repechages (second trial heats in which losers of the first round are given a second chance to qualify for further competition). The overseas entry of 53 from 9 nations was another record, and non-British crews won eight of the ten events they contested. East Germany won the Grand Eights and Diamond Sculls; the Double Sculls and Silver Goblets went to Switzerland; the Netherlands achieved a triple triumph in the Ladies' Plate and the Stewards' and Prince Philip cups; and the sole U.S. victor was Washington Lee High School in the Princess Elizabeth Cup. In the 115th Boat Race between Oxford and Cambridge, the latter easily gained its 63rd victory in the 140-year-old series. (K. L. O.)

KEYSTONE

Start of the eights in the International Regatta at Lucerne, Switz., July 1969. Event was won by the crew representing East Germany (top).

Rubber

World production of natural rubber in 1968 was estimated at 2.6 million long tons, an increase of about 150,000 long tons over 1967. Production for the first six months of 1969 was estimated at 1,297,500 long tons, up 110,000 long tons compared with the corresponding period of 1968.

The management committee of the International Rubber Study Group (IRSG), meeting in London in July 1969, estimated world production of new rubber as follows: natural rubber supply, 2,820,000 long tons in 1969 and 2,910,000 long tons in 1970; synthetic rubber supply, 4,430,000 long tons in 1969 and 4,750,000 long tons in 1970. The U.S. government had discontinued sales of natural rubber from its stockpile, which stood at approximately 365,000 long tons. The committee estimated that the world would consume (*i.e.*, turn into manufactured goods) some 2,850,000 long tons of natural rubber and 4,310,000 long tons of synthetic rubber in 1969, and 2.9 million long tons of natural rubber and 4,570,000 long tons of synthetic rubber in 1970. The U.S.S.R., China, and some countries in Eastern Europe were not members of the IRSG.

The New York spot price for no. 1 ribbed smoked sheet bottomed out at 16½ cents per pound in March 1968; recovered to 21 cents at the end of September 1968; continued its uptrend to 31½ cents at the end of August 1969; and stood at about 28 cents at the end of September 1969. Strong demand, especially from the U.S. (which took 75,067 long tons of West Malaysian rubber in the first six months of 1969, 37% more than the year before), was probably the basic factor in the price rise.

Exports of natural rubber latex from producing

Table I. Natural Rubber Production
In 000 long tons

Country	1964	1965	1966	1967	1968
Malaysia	890	934	983	985	1,092
Indonesia	638	706	704	750*	740*
Thailand	218	213	204	211	255
Ceylon	110	116	129	141	146
Vietnam	73	60	48	40	29
Cambodia	45	48	51	53	51
India	44	49	52	62	68
Africa	—	—	—	—	156*
Brazil	28	29	24	21	23
Others	189*	187*	202*	189*	56*
Total	2,235*	2,342*	2,397*	2,452*	2,600*

*Estimate.

Table II. Synthetic Rubber Production
In 000 long tons

Country	1964	1965	1966	1967	1968
United States	1,765	1,814	1,970	1,912	2,131
Canada	197	203	200	197	194
United Kingdom	153	172	191	200	233
Germany, West	136	161	182	180	234
France	128	146	161	186	220
Japan	120	159	228	276	375
Italy	110*	118*	121*	116*	123*
Netherlands	90*	100*	111*	125*	161
Brazil	32	35	53	51	58
Czechoslovakia	20*	30*	30*	33*	35*
Australia	18	21	20	26	30
Belgium	15*	21*	20*	20*	25*
India	12	16	15	22	25
South Africa	6	16	18	24	25
Argentina	—	3	10	17	22
Spain	—	—	—	10*	26
Mexico	—	—	—	20*	34*
Total	2,802*	3,015*	3,330*	3,415*	3,951*

*Estimate.

Source: International Rubber Study Group.

countries totaled an estimated 231,750 long tons (dry basis) in 1968; world consumption in the same period was estimated at 232,500 long tons (dry basis). World consumption of synthetic latices in 1968 was estimated at 211,000 long tons (dry basis).

World production of all types of synthetic rubber for 1968 (excluding the Soviet Union and other countries not reporting) was 3,950,000 long tons (including latices), of which the U.S. produced 2,131,105 long tons (including oil content). World production of all types in the first six months of 1969 was estimated at 2,175,000 long tons, compared with 1,957,500 long tons for the corresponding period of 1968. Reported stocks (worldwide) of synthetic rubber at the end of May 1969 totaled 621,000 long tons.

Production of reclaimed rubber for 1968 was 368,482 long tons (this figure includes only the U.S., the U.K., West Germany, Australia, Canada, and Brazil). For the first six months of 1969, production was estimated at 187,000 long tons, compared with 195,000 long tons for the corresponding period of 1968. Consumption of reclaimed rubber in 1968 was reported at 390,360 long tons (France not reporting but included at 32,000 long tons). The figure was equivalent to 5.8% of total world consumption of new (natural and synthetic) rubber.

World consumption of new rubber in 1968 was again at a new high—6,685,000 long tons, of which 64.6% was synthetic. World consumption of new rubber in the first six months of 1969 was estimated at 3,577,500 long tons, of which 59.3% was synthetic.

In the U.S. the 1969 yearbook of the Tire and Rim Association carried new designations for the sidewall to better describe the load-bearing capacity of the tire and its shape, and these were adopted by the tire industry. For example, the sidewall marking 8.25-15 was replaced with G78-15. The letter G indicated that the tire had a load-bearing capacity of 1,380 lb. The number 78 indicated the aspect ratio; that is, in linear dimensions, the vertical cross section of this tire was 78% as great as the horizontal cross section. The number 15, as in the past, indicated the size of rim the tire was built to fit. If the tire was of radial construction, the letter R would follow the first letter; in this case, the designation would be GR78-15. Ply ratings, formerly molded on the sidewall, were replaced by letters; thus, load-range B replaced 4-ply rating; load-range D replaced 8-ply rating. Load-carrying capacities indicated by the first letters were as follows: F can carry 1,280 lb. (old size marking, 7.75 section width); G can carry 1,380 lb. (old size marking, 8.25 section width); H can carry 1,510 lb. (old size marking, 8.55 cross section width).

Two-ply bias tires were disappearing as original equipment on U.S. automobiles. Belted bias tires, which were replacing them, had a two-ply carcass with a two-ply overhead belt. In the usage of tire-cord fibre, nylon was first, polyester second, and rayon third. There were some indications that belted bias tires might in the immediate future go to all-rayon construction.

During 1969 a U.S. conglomerate company, Northwest Industries, Inc. (NWT), made a determined effort to take over control of the B. F. Goodrich Company of Akron, O. Falling stock prices, court decisions, and other matters forced NWT to desist and the matter was in abeyance at the end of the year. It was reported, however, that the conglomerate still controlled the block of stock it acquired during the fight. (E. B. Nn.)

Rwanda

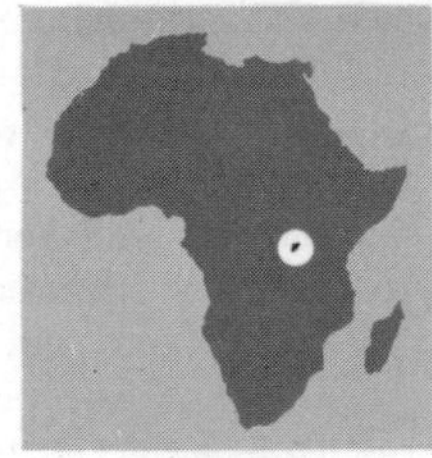

A republic in eastern Africa, Rwanda is bordered by the Congo (Kinshasa), Uganda, Tanzania, and Burundi. Area: 10,169 sq.mi. (26,338 sq.km.). Pop. (1968 est.): 3,405,000; composed of Tutsi (Watutsi), Hutu (Bahutu), and Twa (Batwa) tribes. Cap. and largest city: Kigali (pop., 1967 est., 20,000). Language: French (official); tribal dialects. Religion: traditional or tribal beliefs 50%; Roman Catholic. President in 1969, Grégoire Kayibanda.

Relations with the Congo (Kinshasa), broken off in 1968 after Rwanda's refusal to hand over European

RWANDA

Education. (1963–64) Primary, pupils 359,542, teachers 4,892; secondary, pupils 2,268; vocational, pupils 3,370, teachers 84; teacher training (state only), students 2,016, teachers 103; higher (1965–66), students 127.

Finance and Trade. Monetary unit: Rwanda franc, with a par value of RwFr. 100 to U.S. $1 (RwFr. 240 = £1 sterling) and a free market rate (Oct. 1969) of RwFr. 128 to U.S. $1 (RwFr. 305 = £1). Foreign exchange, central bank: (June 1969) U.S. $1,020,000; (June 1968) U.S. $4,610,000. Budget (1967 rev. est.): revenue RwFr. 1,251,000,000; expenditure RwFr. 1,375,000,000.

Foreign Trade. (1967) Imports RwFr. 2,022,200,000; exports RwFr. 1,403,900,000. Import sources (1966): Belgium-Luxembourg 30%; Japan 16%; Uganda 14%; West Germany 8%. Export destinations (1966): U.S. 57%; Belgium-Luxembourg 33%. Main exports: coffee 55%; tin 30%.

Agriculture. Production (in 000; metric tons; 1967; 1966 in parentheses): sorghum *c.* 140 (*c.* 135); dry beans *c.* 92 (*c.* 90); coffee *c.* 11.4 (8.8); potatoes *c.* 46 (*c.* 45); sweet potatoes *c.* 300 (*c.* 260); cassava *c.* 190 (*c.* 180). Livestock (in 000): cattle (July 1968) *c.* 630; sheep (July 1967) *c.* 135.

Rugby Football: *see* Football

Rulers: *see* Heads of State

Russia: *see* Union of Soviet Socialist Republics

Russian Literature: *see* Literature

Ryukyu Islands: *see* Dependent States

Sabah: *see* Malaysia

Sahara, Spanish: *see* Dependent States

mercenaries, improved in 1969. The border was reopened in February following a conciliation move at the meeting of heads of state of the African and Malagasy Common Organization (OCAM) in Kinshasa in January. The first Rwandan ambassador was accepted by Kinshasa in August. The most pressing difficulty remained refugees from Rwanda, of whom some 24,000 were reported in the Congo.

In June the foreign ministers of the Congo (Kinshasa), Rwanda, and Burundi met in Kinshasa to discuss a regional economic grouping to be called the Common Organization for Economic Cooperation in Central Africa (OCCEAC). Suggested projects included a joint power plant, exploitation of natural gas from Lake Kivu, and an increase in commercial exchanges. A summit meeting to discuss the organization took place in Gisenyi in December. (M. Mr.)

Sailing

Among the most evident signs of the still expanding public interest in water sports was the proliferation of boat shows and the growing attendance at those that had become established. The Paris Salon International de la Navigation de Plaisance proved to be the biggest boat show in the world in terms of its 615 exhibitors when it opened in January. In the same month the ninth London International Boat Show had 537 exhibitors and a record attendance of 328,023 visitors. In the United States the 59th New York National Boat Show was only one of the more than 20 held in various cities; and in the United Kingdom new shows in Birmingham, Southampton, and Belfast showed the spreading of interest. In Europe there were shows at Göteborg, Hamburg, Barcelona, and Genoa among other places.

A yachting year more than usually international in character brought from the U.S. to Europe a fleet of 21 yachts in a transatlantic race of 2,750 mi. from Newport, R.I., to Cork Harbour, Ire. This was promoted by the Cruising Club of America and the Royal Cork Yacht Club, the latter celebrating its 250th anniversary. Entries came from Canada, Argentina, Italy, Ireland, the Netherlands, and Finland, which sent one boat each, the balance being from the U.S. The race generally took place under overcast skies with light winds. The winners and the owners, all from the U.S., were: Class A, "Kialoa II," John B. Kilroy; Class B, "Carina," Richard S. Nye; Class C, "Aura," Wallace J. Stenhouse, Jr. The overall winner, "Kialoa II," received a Waterford glass bowl from the wife of Ireland's prime minister. This race led the U.S. fleet to the Fastnet race and the three others included in the Admiral's Cup series.

The increasing numbers of entries and intensity of competition for the Admiral's Cup demonstrated the growing international status of that event since its foundation in 1957, when only Britain and the U.S. competed. In 1967, when Australia won the cup, there were nine nations involved. In the 1969 series 11 nations entered 31 boats, and Australia approached the defense of the cup with a dedication that made the preliminary selection of its team rival the attention paid to the preparations for the 1971 America's Cup. With "Ragamuffin," "Koomooloo," and "Mercedes III," the Australians brought forward for their team two new boats built especially for the contest and one that had sailed in the victory of 1967. In the first offshore event of the series, the Channel race, and in the second Cowes Week inshore race, the New York Yacht Club Cup, Australia gained more points than any other team. Australia then finished second only to Britain in the Cowes Britannia Cup. With only the Fastnet race, which carried the most points in the series, yet to be sailed, the leaders were Australia 317, U.K. 273, Italy 250, U.S. 244. Australia's position thus appeared safe.

The Fastnet was a slow, light-wind performance ruled to an unusual extent by chance, equally unsatisfactory for the 31 yachts of the Admiral's Cup teams and the 150 other competitors, and fatal in its whims to the well-placed Australian team. Struggling in light airs and calms, the U.S. team was able to add enough points to its score to overtake both Australia and Britain. The final standings were: U.S. 496 points; Australia 482 points; U.K. 471 points; Italy 451 points. The results of the Fastnet race itself were unsatisfactory owing to uncertainties in the timings of the leading yachts. The overall prize was awarded to "Red Rooster" (R. E. Carter) of the U.S. team, which on corrected time was 68 disputed seconds ahead of "Crusade" (Sir Max Aitken of the U.K.), the timekeepers on the shore and on the latter yacht disagreeing with each other.

The international organization of yachting underwent a crucial change in the course of 1969 as the result of an agreement between the Cruising Club of America and the Royal Ocean Racing Club to adopt

CAMERA PRESS—PIX FROM PUBLIX

Lone yachtsman Robin Knox-Johnston sails into Falmouth Harbour, England, in his 32-ft. ketch "Suhaili" on April 22, 1969, after a ten-month nonstop voyage around the world to win a race sponsored by the "Sunday Times."

JOE HOURIGAN, CANADIAN PRESS

U.S.-owned "Niagara" (right) comes up on the Canadian yacht "Manitou" to win the second race in the Canada's Cup from the defending champion at Toronto, Sept. 8, 1969.

a common international rule of measurement for offshore racing yachts. Since the use of these rules had become worldwide (being adopted for short-distance handicap racing as well as for ocean racing), the effect of the change, coming into effect in 1970, would be far-reaching. The new rule was formulated by an international technical committee, most of whose members belonged also to the British Royal Ocean Racing Club, and was headed by the U.S. naval architect Olin Stephens. The technical and creative side of yachting suffered a loss in February by the death of the naval architect J. Laurent Giles.

The continuing growth of interest in racing under time allowance in seagoing yachts, for which the new international rule would cater, was shown by the attention being focused on the sport in the Mediterranean. The Greek yacht clubs ran a program during the year over courses in the Aegean and Ionian seas that totaled 1,000 mi. In the last days of 1968 the first Middle Sea race took place. Organized by the Royal Malta Yacht Club, it covered a distance of 580 mi., starting and finishing at Malta and encircling Sicily, Lampedusa, Pantellaria, Favignana, Levanzo, and Stromboli. The winner was "Josian" sailed by John Ripard. A second Middle Sea race was organized in November 1969, and it was hoped it would in time join the three classics of offshore racing, the Bermuda, Fastnet, and Sydney-Hobart.

Preparations for an America's Cup challenge proceeded during the year in Australia and France, the rules for the contest now allowing prior international competition for the selection of a challenger. It was made clear in April that Britain would not be competing against Australia and France in the selection trials. What was never more than a fragile possibility was eliminated by a statement from the Royal Dorset Yacht Club in April, the cause of the withdrawal being, it would seem, less financial than a lack of general interest in what formerly had been regarded as an exclusively Anglo-American competition.

Robin Knox-Johnston, returning to Falmouth in April, earned the *Sunday Times* (London) Golden Globe by becoming the first person to sail around the world single-handed and nonstop. The 32-ft. ketch "Suhaili," in which he achieved this, was essentially a simple, rather old-fashioned yacht, but nevertheless beautifully balanced; this enabled it to be handled efficiently by one man when the self-steering gear failed. Knox-Johnston was the only entrant to complete the course in this endurance test of sailing, and there was some anxiety when for about four months no news was received of him. Cmdr. W. L. King sailing "Galway Blazer II," a new yacht of advanced design, had been forced out of the race in 1968, but in September 1969 he sailed again from Plymouth, Eng., with the object of achieving another single-handed nonstop circumnavigation. The Frenchman Bernard Moitessier chose, when it appeared that he might win the race, to continue sailing, again around the world, though no longer nonstop. Lieut. Cmdr. Nigel Tetley, Royal Navy, sailing the trimaran "Victress," had his craft break up in heavy seas, having already achieved the longest nonstop voyage in a multihull boat. He also became, when he crossed his outward-bound course before sinking, the first man to circumnavigate the world in a trimaran and to sail south of Cape Horn in such a craft. The contest led to the loss, under tragic and partly mysterious circumstances, of Donald Crowhurst in the trimaran "Teignmouth Electron."

"Flyway," a 40-ft. yawl owned by Ogden Reid of New York, won the 811-mi. Miami-Montego Bay race in March. The 330-mi. Marblehead-Halifax race in July was won by "Summertime," a 39-ft. sloop owned by Irwin Tyson. Graham Hall of Larchmont, N.Y., won the Mallory Cup, emblematic of the North American men's sailing championship. In the Canada's Cup race the Canadian "Manitou" won from the U.S. challenger "Niagara."

During the year the selection by the International Yacht Racing Union of classes for the 1972 Olympic Games encountered severe criticism, the types of boat chosen being less acceptable in Britain than they might be in other countries. The classes chosen were Dragon, Star, Soling, Tempest, Flying Dutchman, Finn. That the first four of these were keelboats was one source of objection, and the Dragons and Stars were regarded as obsolete or obsolescent.

At the end of 1969 the Sydney-Hobart race included a team of three Royal Ocean Racing Club yachts with, as reserve, "Morning Cloud," belonging to Edward Heath, leader of the Conservative Party opposition in Great Britain. "Morning Cloud," a 32-ft. sloop skippered by Heath, won the 640-mi. race on handicap. Sir Max Aitken's "Crusade" was first across the finish line. (D. H. C. P.-B.)

St. Helena: *see* Dependent States

St. Kitts-Nevis and Anguilla: *see* Dependent States

St. Lucia: *see* Dependent States

St. Pierre and Miquelon: *see* Dependent States

St. Vincent: *see* Dependent States

Salt: *see* Mining

Salvador, El: *see* El Salvador

Salvation Army: *see* Religion

Samoa: *see* Dependent States; Western Samoa

San Marino

A small republic, San Marino is an enclave in northeastern Italy, 14 mi. SW of Rimini. Area: 24 sq.mi. (61 sq.km.). Pop. (1969 est.): 18,758. Cap. and largest city: San Marino (metro. pop., 1969 est., 3,985). Language: Italian. Religion: Roman Catholic. San Marino is united with Italy by a customs union. The country is governed by two *capitani reggenti,* or coregents, appointed every six months by a Grand and General Council.

SAN MARINO

Education. (1966–67) Primary, pupils 1,388, teachers 78; secondary, pupils 740, teachers 45.

Finance. Monetary unit: Italian lira (625 lire = U.S. $1; 1,500 lire = £1 sterling). Budget (1968–69 est.) balanced at 5,325,000,000 lire. Tourism (1967) 2,206,459 visitors.

Transport and Communications. Roads (1965) *c.* 100 km. Electric funicular railway 32 km. Telephones (Jan. 1968) 1,802. Radio receivers (Dec. 1967) 3,000. Television receivers (Dec. 1967) 1,900.

Capitani reggenti in 1969 were Aldo Zavoli and Pietro Giancecchi to March 31; Ferruccio Piva and Stelio Montironi from April 1 to September 30; and, from October 1, Alvaro Casali and Giancarlo Ghironzi.

Quadrennial elections for the Grand and General Council were held on September 7. Under San Marino's constitution, any native-born person remains a citizen and a voter for life. In past elections absentee balloting, mostly by mail, had been legal, but a 1966 change forbade absentee balloting from outside Europe—an action designed to reduce conservative voting strength. The ruling Christian Democrats chartered aircraft to fly approximately 450 American supporters to San Marino, at a cost estimated at between $65,000 and $100,000.

Six parties, including a newly formed pro-Chinese Communist group, entered candidates for the 60 council seats. Of 16,720 qualified voters, including 7,419 living abroad, 13,314 cast votes and 12,966 ballots were judged valid. The Christian Socialists won 27 seats (−2) and their coalition partners, the Social Democrats 11(+1), giving the government an 8-vote majority. The 22-man opposition included 14 Communists, 7 left-wing Socialists, and 1 other.

(R. D. Ho.)

Saudi Arabia

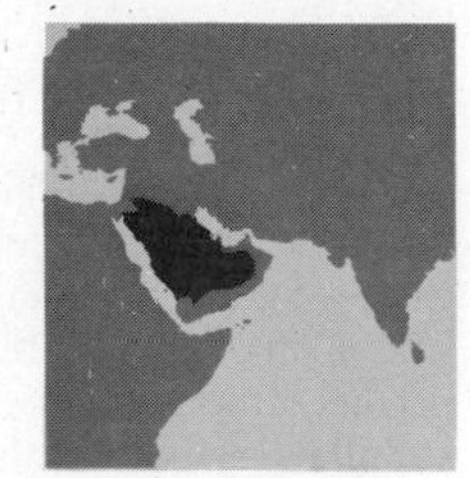

A kingdom occupying four-fifths of the Arabian Peninsula, Saudi Arabia has an area of 873,972 sq.mi. (2,263,587 sq.km.). Pop. (1968 est.): 7.1 million. Cap. and largest city: Riyadh (pop., 1963, 170,000). Language: Arabic. Religion: Muslim. King and prime minister, Faisal ibn 'Abd al-'Aziz ibn 'Abd al-Rahman Al Sa'ud.

SAUDI ARABIA

Education. (1965–66) Primary, pupils 260,586, teachers 11,585; secondary, pupils 24,429, teachers 1,323; vocational, pupils 2,713, teachers 388; teacher training, students 6,406, teachers 449; higher, students 1,831, teaching staff 199.

Finance. Monetary unit: riyal, with a par value of 4.50 riyals to U.S. $1 (10.80 riyals = £1 sterling). Gold and foreign exchange, official: (June 1969) U.S. $727 million; (June 1968) U.S. $740 million. Budget (1968–69 est.) balanced at 5,530,000,000 riyals. Money supply: (Feb. 1969) 2,260,000,000 riyals; (Feb. 1968) 2,003,000,000 riyals.

Foreign Trade. (1968) Imports 3,258,000,000 riyals; exports 8,752,000,000 riyals. Import sources: (1967) U.S. 32%; Japan 11%; West Germany 9%; U.K. 9%; Italy 6%. Export destinations: Japan 27%; Italy 13%; West Germany 11%; U.K. 9%; Spain 7%; Netherlands 5%. Main exports: (1967–68) crude oil 81%; petroleum products 13%.

Transport and Communications. Roads (1968) *c.* 22,000 km. (including 9,412 km. with improved surface). Motor vehicles in use (1968): passenger 35,736; commercial 25,992. Railways (1967): Dammam–Riyadh line 584 km., Jordan–Medina line (under reconstruction) 567 km. Shipping (1968): merchant vessels 100 gross tons and over 39; gross tonnage 49,625. Telephones (Jan. 1968) *c.* 29,000. Radio receivers (Dec. 1964) *c.* 77,000. Television receivers (Dec. 1964) 30,000.

Agriculture. Production (in 000; metric tons; 1967; 1966 in parentheses): wheat *c.* 150 (149); barley *c.* 34 (34); millet *c.* 16 (*c.* 16); sorghum 52 (50); dates *c.* 380 (375). Livestock (in 000; 1966–67): cattle 150; sheep 3,800; goats 2,900; camels 355; asses *c.* 125.

Industry. Production: crude oil (1968) 140,844,000 metric tons; electricity (excluding most industrial production; 1966) 377 million kw-hr.

In 1969 the Saudi government of King Faisal continued to pursue conservative Islamic and strongly anti-Communist policies. Relations with the U.A.R. and the other socialist Arab states were cool but correct. The king scored a diplomatic success when the Islamic summit meeting was held in Rabat, Mor., in September as an alternative to an Arab summit meeting following the Al Aqsa Mosque fire in Jerusalem. At the same time, Saudi relations with the U.S. were endangered by continuing U.S. support and arms supplies for Israel and the consequent unpopularity of the U.S. in the Arab world. Before visiting Washington in October, the king's brother and vice-premier, Prince Fahd, expressed the hope that the U.S. would adopt a more evenhanded policy toward the Arab-Israeli conflict. Economic relations with France were strengthened. At least part of the failure of the December Arab summit meeting was attributable to Saudi Arabia's refusal to increase its financial support for the Arab nations directly confronting Israel as much as those countries desired.

The Saudi government took a keen interest in efforts to form a federation of Persian Gulf sheikhdoms. Despite mediation efforts at the first Rabat summit meeting, Saudi Arabia did not normalize its relations with the Yemeni Republic on the ground that no settlement had been achieved between republicans and royalists. Nor did it recognize Southern Yemen which, according to Prince Fahd, "threatened the security of Arabia."

The Saudi government was alarmed at the spread of left-wing influences in the Arabian Peninsula. In June and September there were unsuccessful coups against the regime by left-wing Baathist and Arab nationalist elements in the armed forces and civil service. The government denied reports emanating from the so-called Saudi Liberation Front in Aden that 30 suspects had been tortured and summarily executed in September.

The Saudi Monetary Agency reported that oil revenues in 1968 had risen to $926 million—a 1.9% increase over 1967. The budget for 1969–70 amounted to $1,325,800,000, representing a 7.8% increase over 1968–69. Oil revenues for 1968–69 were less than had been estimated—partly because of the blowing up of the Tapline pipeline in Syria by Palestinian commandos. Oil revenues for 1969–70 were estimated at $1,155,000,000—a 24% increase over the previous year.

(P. Md.)

Encyclopædia Britannica Films. *The Middle East* (1955).

SIPAHIOGLU—PIX FROM PUBLIX

King Faisal of Saudi Arabia at the Islamic summit conference in Rabat, Mor. Representatives from 25 Muslim nations attended the three-day meeting, Sept. 22–25, 1969, at which discussion centred on Arab unity.

Savings and Investment

In 1969 there were important changes in the behaviour of savings and investment in most countries. These changes were accompanied by significant developments in financial markets, domestic and international, and could be attributed to a large extent to policies adopted by the authorities that were designed expressly to influence the cost and availability of external funds required for investment.

As a rule, periods of rapid increases in domestic investment, which generate additional savings, are periods of expansion in total output and are associated with strong cyclical upswings. During such periods, sooner or later, the generation of additional savings lags behind the additional investment, forcing the authorities to adopt measures that slow down the

São Tomé and Príncipe: *see* Dependent States

Sarawak: *see* Malaysia

Satellites, Space: *see* Astronautics

Table I. Changes in Gross National Product, Fixed Domestic Investment, Stock Building, and Foreign Balance in Selected Countries

Country	Year	Percent increase in GNP	Change in total fixed domestic investment	Change in stock building	Change in foreign balance
U.S.	1967	2.4	−1.4	−1.7	−0.7
	1968	5.0	6.6	0.2	−0.4
	1969*	(3.25)	(5.25)	(—)	(0)
Canada	1967	3.1	−1.0	−1.5	0.9
	1968	4.7	−1.8	0.8	1.0
	1969	(5)	(5.5)	(0.5)	(−0.5)
U.K.†	1967	1.8	6.8	−0.2	−1.2
	1968	3.1	−3.0	0.2	0.7
	1969	(1.75)	(2.75)	(0.25)	(0.5)
West Germany†	1967	0	−7.3	−1.1	2.1
	1968	6.7	8.8	2.4	0.4
	1969	(6.5)	(14.5)	(. . .)	(−1.5)
France	1967	4.5	6.0	−0.3	−0.1
	1968	4.2	−5.6	−0.2	−0.3
	1969	(8)	(9)	(1.5)	−0.5
Italy†	1967	6.5	10.2	0.4	−0.8
	1968	5.4	−7.5	−0.9	1.4
	1969	(7.25)	(10)	(0.75)	(−0.25)
Japan	1967	12.9	17.1	3.2	−1.4
	1968	14.4	22.7	0.4	1.0
	1969	(12.5)	(19.0)	(−1)	(1)

*All 1969 figures are estimates.
†Gross domestic product.
Source: Organization for Economic Cooperation and Development, *Economic Outlook*, July 1969.

pace of expansion and, in the process, limit the volume of investment. In contrast, periods when domestic investment slows down markedly tend to be periods of stagnation and recession. At such a time, the authorities try to increase investment to the extent that will utilize the full productive potential of the economy and also increase the amount of savings.

In 1968 domestic investment had increased substantially in only three major industrial countries, the U.S., West Germany, and Japan, and had shown marked signs of hesitation in Canada, the U.K., France, and Italy. In 1969, however, it moved up rapidly in all these countries and also other industrial countries, except in the U.S., where its advance began to lose momentum.

The appreciable increase in 1968 in the U.S. in fixed domestic investment, covering both productive investment and housing as well as additions to inventories (*see* Table I), was accompanied by acute pressure on the balance of payments and prices which caused the government to adopt a number of restrictive measures. The result of these measures was to slow down the pace of expansion, first by reducing additions to inventories and then by cutting investment in housing. This process continued throughout 1969 and began to affect productive investment.

In contrast to the developments in the U.S., the rate of fixed investment in Canada, which fell in 1967, declined again in 1968. There was, however, an increase in inventories, and since national savings fell less, there was an improvement in foreign balance. These trends were reversed in 1969, when there was a strong recovery in housing accompanied by expansion in productive investment and modest additions to inventories. This increase in domestic investment was greater than in national savings, so that the balance of payments current account deteriorated.

In West Germany, a sharp decline in fixed domestic investment and also in inventories in 1967 was followed by a strong upsurge in spending on plant and equipment as well as on housing and inventories in 1968. These increases were instrumental in initiating strong cyclical expansion which continued in 1969, with the rate of increase in fixed domestic investment, and especially investment in machinery and equipment, showing further acceleration. The 1968–69 investment boom was not, however, accompanied by a corresponding rise in national savings. As a result, there was a decline in current account surplus in 1968, followed by another one in 1969.

The three major industrial countries that experienced a slowing down in domestic investment in 1968 but where recovery set in in 1969 were France, Italy, and the U.K. The progress of the French economy was affected in 1968 by political difficulties. These principally affected inventories; housing, which was very slack during the politically turbulent first half of the year, improved in the second half, with productive investment showing relatively little change. There was, however, further deterioration in the nation's external balance of trade, reflecting the pressure on consumption and insufficient expansion in savings. The policy measures taken in 1969 did not restore an equilibrium. While productive investment continued to rise, expansion in housing activity was modest, inventories were being built up, and the foreign balance did not improve sufficiently to bring savings into line with domestic investment.

The Italian economy experienced a significant decline in investment at home in 1968, but at the same time showed a marked improvement in foreign balance. This position changed fundamentally in 1969 when productive investment, spurred partly by special tax allowances and residential construction, showed marked signs of acceleration. The expansion in domestic investment and total output was not accompanied by a corresponding advance in national savings. Consequently, there was a deterioration in the balance of payments current account.

Following the devaluation of the pound sterling in the late autumn of 1967, fixed domestic investment in the U.K. declined in 1968 chiefly as a result of restrictive government policies intended to shift resources into exports. These measures primarily affected housing and public spending on capital account but did bring about some improvement in the balance of payments. The improvement gathered momentum in 1969 and was accompanied by an appreciable advance in productive investment with national savings increasing at a rate adequate to cover not only domestic investment but also to provide a surplus on the balance of payments current account.

In Japan, the large upsurge in domestic investment that started in 1966 and was responsible for a strong boom continued uninterrupted in 1968 and 1969. The generation of savings during the 1966–69 upswing more than kept pace with rises in addition to capital stock at home and enabled Japan to raise its surplus on current external account to a record level.

Vigorous cyclical expansion in the major industrial countries in 1968 and 1969 had favourable effects on the growth of total income and investment and savings in other countries in Europe as well as on other continents. The two elements of investment that contributed to the rise in demand in 1968 in most of the smaller European countries were net foreign balance and inventories. The rise of the former reflected an upsurge in exports; that in the latter was associated with the increase in imports and consumption. Fixed investment and, above all, private productive investment did not begin to advance until the closing months of 1968 but moved ahead very rapidly after that time.

In Belgium, Sweden, and Switzerland, domestic fixed investment in 1968 rose less than total output,

Scandinavian Literature: *see* Literature

Scholarships: *see* Education

Schools: *see* Education

Scotland: *see* United Kingdom

Sculpture: *see* Art Exhibitions; Art Sales; Museums and Galleries

Secondary Metals: *see* Mining

Securities: *see* Savings and Investment; Stock Exchanges

Table II. Savings and Investment in U.S., U.K., West Germany, and Japan in 1968

Item	Households	Enterprises	Public sector	Banking and financial institutions	Foreign sector	Total
U.S. (in $000,000,000)						
Gross saving	+141.6	+82.2	−11.7	+2.5	+0.8	+214.6
Gross physical investment	−107.9	−101.1	—	−1.2	—	−210.2
Capital transfers and adjustments	−8.3	−1.4	+1.9	−0.8	+0.3	−5.5*
Net financial saving	+25.4	−20.3	−9.8	+0.5	+1.1	−1.1
Financial assets	−60.2	−30.8	−25.0	−92.4	−8.1	−7.0
Indebtedness	+34.8	+51.1	+34.8	+91.9	+7.0	+8.1
U.K. (in £000,000)						
Gross saving	+2,079	+2,522	+3,005	+260	+265	+7,866
Gross physical investment	−1,203	−2,576	−3,868	−355		−8,002
Capital transfers and adjustment	+723	−522	−249	−295	+214	−343
Net financial savings	+1,599	−576	−1,112	−390	+479	−479
Financial assets	−2,687	−1,007	−1,841	−6,070	−3,837	15,442
Indebtedness	+1,088	+1,538	+2,953	+6,460	+3,358	15,442
West Germany (in DM. 000,000,000)†						
Gross saving	+40.8	+70.9	+25.5	+6.3	−12.0	+131.5
Gross physical investment	—	−108.5	−20.5	−2.5	—	−131.5
Capital transfers and adjustments	−5.5	+15.4	−10.1	−0.4	+0.6	—
Net financial saving	+35.3	−22.3	−5.1	+3.4	−11.4	—
Financial assets	−38.5	−16.6	−7.8	−78.3	−12.4	153.5
Indebtedness	+3.2	+38.9	+12.9	+74.9	+23.8	153.5
Japan (in 000,000,000 yen)						
Gross saving	+8,147	+7,321	+3,740	—	+496	+19,704
Gross physical investment	−4,738	−10,215	−4,751	—	—	−19,704
Capital transfers and adjustment	+1,259	−17	−369	—	−873	—
Net financial savings	+4,668	−2,911	−1,380	—	−377	—
Financial assets	−7,521	−6,072	−2,443	−9,134	−599	−25,769
Indebtedness	+2,853	−8,983	−4,823	+9,134	+976	−25,769

Note: For gross national saving, gross physical investment, and capital transfers and adjustments, + means receipts and — means expenditure; for financial assets, — means spending on assets; for indebtedness, + means increase in indebtedness.
*Including discrepancies unallocated to individual sectors.
†Enterprises including housing.
Sources: *Federal Reserve Bulletin;* Bank of England, *Quarterly Review; Monthly Report* of the Deutsche Bundesbank; *Annual Report on National Income and National Income Statistics; Flow of Funds Accounts.*

and in Austria, Denmark, Norway, and Finland it declined. Only in the Netherlands and Ireland (and, as mentioned before, in West Germany, France, and Italy) was the rise larger than that of the gross national product. The recovery that gathered momentum in 1969 comprised both private spending on productive investment and additions to inventories.

Among the rich non-European countries, Australia experienced a large increase in private fixed investment in 1968, associated mainly with the rapid expansion of the mining sector. This continued in 1969. National savings, however, did not increase correspondingly and, consequently, the net foreign balance deteriorated. In contrast, in New Zealand and South Africa fixed investment and inventories did not rise in 1968, but exports improved.

The less developed countries of Asia, Africa, and Latin America benefited from the expansion of output in industrial countries. This resulted in an increase in the volume of the less developed countries' imports and higher prices for their primary commodities, which made it possible to maintain and, indeed, raise domestic investment.

In the planned economies of Eastern Europe and the U.S.S.R., domestic investment continued to grow in 1968 and such evidence as was available suggested that this growth was maintained in 1969. The rise, which increased still further the share of national resources so used, was a result of government policies. However, it was also helped by the reform of economic planning and management and a partial, though modest, decentralization of investment decisions.

Differences in coverage, methods, and institutional organizations prevented a full comparison of savings and investment in the flow-of-funds framework for even the major industrial countries. A simplified form of such accounts for four large industrial countries —the U.S., the U.K., West Germany, and Japan— in 1968 is shown in Table II. It shows that the pressures on balance of payments and financial markets in the U.S., which grew in intensity in 1969, were associated with large deficits in the public and the business sectors, which were greater than the surplus in the household sector. This development caused the monetary authorities to tighten their policy in 1969 in order to reduce the pressures on resources, but in doing so they pushed up interest rates to record-high levels. (T. M. R.)

See also Money and Banking; Profits; Stock Exchanges.

Seismology

The field of seismology entered a new phase in 1969 with the placement of seismometers on the moon by the Apollo 11 and 12 astronauts. During the few weeks that the Apollo 11 seismometer operated, signals from several seismic disturbances were transmitted back to

Devastated homes in village near Alaşehir, Turk. The area was at the centre of an earthquake that struck on March 28, 1969, killing 64 people and injuring 350.

KEYSTONE

"LONDON DAILY EXPRESS" FROM PICTORIAL PARADE

Turkish vehicle on road between Izmir and Denizli, Turk., after an earthquake on March 28, 1969, destroyed road surfaces in the area.

UPI COMPIX

Severely damaged buildings in Banja Luka, Yugos., after the third earthquake in two days hit the area on Oct. 27, 1969, killing 22 persons and injuring 700.

earth, but their source was not definitely determined. Experiments performed during Apollo 12 were designed to assist in interpreting these data. However, scientists were puzzled when the crash of the jettisoned lunar module caused seismic waves that lasted for 55 minutes—far longer than would have resulted from a similar impact on earth.

The first documented case of an earthquake on one fault causing movements on other faults was reported. The movement was associated with the southern California earthquake at Borrego Mountain in April 1968. The shock was magnitude 6.5 on the Richter scale and the area's largest earthquake in more than 15 years. According to the California Institute of Technology, recent studies revealed that the shock apparently triggered small displacements on other faults within 50 mi. of the earthquake's epicentre.

Examination of records from underground nuclear explosions at the Nevada test site of the U.S. Atomic Energy Commission (AEC) showed an increase in earthquake activity in nearby regions to a degree dependent on the size of the explosion. The earthquakes were usually one or two orders of magnitude lower than the initial explosion, somewhat analogous to the relationship between major earthquakes and aftershocks. Thousands of aftershocks occurred in the six-week period following the Boxcar underground nuclear test in April 1968. Most were found to be shallower than the hypocentres of natural earthquakes in the Nevada area. After Benham, a 1.1-megaton shot at NTS in December 1968, some 10,000 aftershocks were recorded within four weeks. According to the AEC, each shot caused linear fracturing and faulting for a distance of nearly five miles on Pahute Mesa, where the tests occurred, producing displacements similar to those caused by some earthquakes.

As California's population has increased, concern has grown over the possible effects of a large-magnitude event in this highly earthquake-prone area. Early in 1969, considerable publicity was given to the predictions of various southern California cultists that a severe earthquake would occur in April. Several dates were given, with April 4—Good Friday—most generally mentioned. Although the month passed without incident and the flurry of interest subsided, serious seismologists continued to express concern, especially with regard to the large and complex structures being built or planned in San Francisco and Los Angeles. For example, the new Los Angeles aqueduct system crosses the San Andreas Fault three times.

One effort to meet this problem was reported by the Los Angeles Building and Safety Department, which announced that it had programmed a computer to show how existing and planned buildings might react to earthquake forces. By analyzing the motion of a building as a whole and the motions of each floor, the computer could predict how proposed structures would react to a quake. The system could also provide enough detailed information to permit an objective decision on whether to raze or repair a damaged structure. Data on the natural sway of a building were fed into the computer, to be retrieved after a major quake occurred. The natural sway would then be measured again and, if there was a change, structural damage could be assumed to exist, even though it was not immediately visible.

In October the AEC conducted a calibration shot on Amchitka Island in the Aleutian chain off Alaska, to perfect a thermonuclear device. Since the shot was announced many weeks in advance, considerable political interest was evidenced by groups in the U.S., Canada, and Japan. Many feared that the explosion would set off a damaging earthquake or that a tsunami (seismic sea wave) might be generated and propagated across the Pacific Ocean. The explosion, a 1.2-megaton yield at 4,200 ft. below sea level, was detonated on October 2, with a computed magnitude of 6.5 as recorded by many seismograph stations around the world. No untoward effects were reported.

International seismologists convened in Madrid, September 1–12, for the International Union of Geodesy and Geophysics meetings. Scientists from the U.S., the U.S.S.R., and the U.K. took the leading roles, primarily as a result of their great efforts in the study of sea-floor spreading, seismotectonics, and convection theory in the earth's mantle. Studies relating to the sea-floor-spreading hypothesis were concentrated on zones of convergence in the lithosphere, largely because of recent contributions from branches of geophysics in the form of seismicity, focal mechanism, gravity and magnetic anomalies, and thermal gradients. (L. M. M.)

See also Disasters.

Senegal

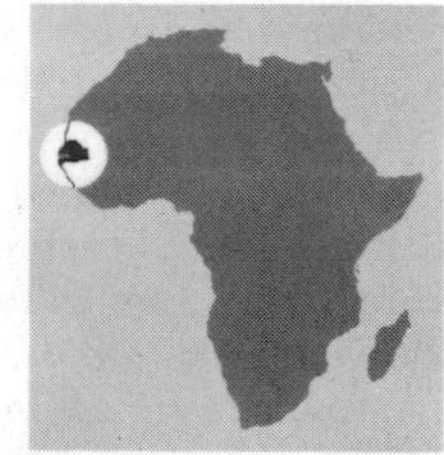

A republic of northwestern Africa, Senegal is bounded by Mauritania, Mali, Guinea, and Portuguese Guinea, and by the Atlantic Ocean. The independent nation of The Gambia forms an enclave within the country. Area: 76,124 sq.mi. (197,161 sq.km.). Pop. (1968 est.): 3,685,000. Cap. and largest city: Dakar (pop., 1965 est., 576,-

SENEGAL

Education. (1965–66) Primary, pupils 218,795, teachers 5,133; secondary, pupils 25,574, teachers 885; vocational, pupils 8,244, teachers (1964–65) 364; teacher training, students 826, teachers 80; higher (including University of Dakar), students 2,755, teaching staff 230.

Finance. Monetary unit: CFA franc, with a parity of CFA Fr. 50 to the French franc (CFA Fr. 277.71 = U.S. $1; CFA Fr. 666.50 = £1 sterling). Budget (1968–69 est.) current expenditure CFA Fr. 36,750,-000,000.

Foreign Trade. (1968) Imports CFA Fr. 44,680,-000,000; exports CFA Fr. 37.3 billion. Import sources (1967): France 48%; China 8%; Cambodia 6%; West Germany 5%. Export destination (1967) France 80%. Main exports (1967): peanuts and peanut oil 77%; phosphates 7%.

093). Language: French (official); Wolof; Peular (Fulani); other tribal dialects. Religion: Muslim; pagan, Christian minority. President in 1969, Léopold Sédar Senghor.

In spite of a difficult year, President Senghor decided on the progressive liberalization of the government in 1969. The economic situation was still troubling, and the severe financial crisis exposed the government to serious political risk.

A strike of schoolchildren and students that began on March 28 took on a political dimension. On several occasions clashes took place between police and students, and President Senghor blamed the troubles on subversion from abroad. In May student organizations called for a general strike, but the labour unions remained loyal to the government. The Army and police closed the University of Dakar on May 6 and cleared the student quarter.

Nonetheless, in June the unions in their turn did resort to political agitation, but they were not able to unify for effective action and their sporadic calls for a general strike were unsuccessful. The unions, victims of a trial of strength that they themselves had wished to provoke, then split apart. In August the National Union of Senegalese Workers lodged a complaint against the government with the International Labour Organization, accusing it of confiscating the union's goods and offices and of handing them over to a new, government-affiliated National Confederation of Senegalese Workers.

In accordance with President Senghor's decision to put into operation an important reform of Senegal's political structures, aimed at greater decentralization and a strengthening of the National Assembly, a new constitution providing for a prime minister responsible to the head of state and the National Assembly was drawn up and was to be submitted to a national referendum, tentatively in February 1970.

Joseph Mbaye, former minister of commerce in the Mamadou Dia government who was condemned to 20 years in prison in May 1963 for his part in an attempted coup, was pardoned in June. This was thought to herald the release of Dia and his friends.

On December 9–10 Senegalese forces took up positions along the border with Portuguese Guinea following the bombardment by Portuguese forces of Senegalese villages thought by them to be harbouring guerrillas. In accordance with treaty commitments, France provided logistic support to the Senegalese Army. On December 17 President Senghor visited French Pres. Georges Pompidou in Paris. (PH. D.)

Sierra Leone

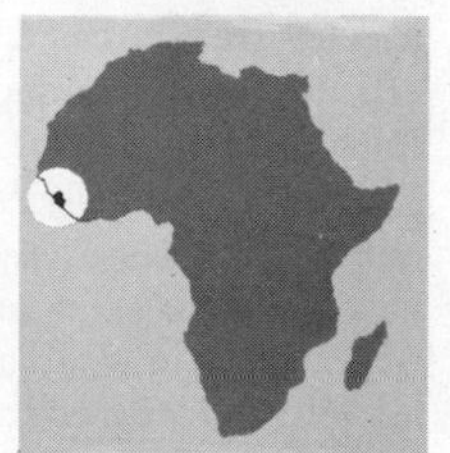

A parliamentary state within the Commonwealth of Nations, Sierra Leone is a West African nation located between Guinea and Liberia. Area: 27,699 sq.mi. (71,740 sq.km.). Pop. (1968 est.): 2,475,000, including (1962 est.) Mende and Temme tribes 60%; other tribes 38.5%; Creole 1.2%. Cap. and largest city: Freetown (pop., 1968 est., 163,000). Language: English (official); tribal dialects; Hausa. Religion: Christian; pagan; Muslim minority. Queen, Elizabeth II; acting governor-general in 1969, Banja Tejan-Sie; prime minister, Siaka Stevens.

The state of emergency imposed in November 1968 because of violence in some parts of the country was lifted in March 1969. By-elections took place in which the All People's Congress (APC) and the Sierra Leone People's Party (SLPP) each won five seats. This brought the division in Parliament to 48 seats for the APC, 12 for the SLPP, and 6 independents.

The minister of finance, M. S. Forna, presented his budget on June 25. No new taxes were proposed, but the agreements with the mining companies were revised to increase government revenue. Revenue for 1969–70 was estimated at 45.4 million leones, compared with an original forecast of 41.7 million leones for the previous year. Current expenditure at 42.6 million leones included public debt charges of 8.3 million leones. The increase over the original estimate of 40.7 million leones was chiefly accounted for by increased allocations for primary and secondary education and for the military and police forces. The minister said that the overall picture was heartening, with foreign exchange reserves standing at a record 29 million leones in May. However, recurrent government expenditure would be severely restricted.

The Consolidated African Selection Trust reported that illicit diamond mining was on the increase within leases granted by the Sierra Leone Selection Trust. The unchecked influx of thousands of outside dealers provided a ready market for stolen diamonds, and corruption was spreading. Both legitimate trading by the Selection Trust, and government revenues, were suffering as a result. Diamonds accounted for 60 to 70% of Sierra Leone's exports and approximately 15% of revenue. The Selection Trust paid about $6 million, and the government collected $1.6 million from small miners. Much revenue was lost by smuggling, mostly to Liberia. The smugglers bought cigarettes, liquor, and other goods for resale in Sierra Leone, and further losses resulted from cocoa and coffee smuggling.

A national oil refinery was completed toward the end of 1968 at a cost of 6 million leones. On Jan. 3, 1969, the government signed an agreement with five oil companies under which the government and the companies would each hold 50% of the shares. The refinery would be managed by British Petroleum.

Parliament had passed a constitutional reform bill under Sir Albert Margai's administration in February 1967, but after the overthrow of the National Reformation Council in April 1968 the old constitution had been restored. Prime Minister Siaka Stevens told a press conference in London in January that it was likely that a republican constitution would be adopted,

SIERRA LEONE

Education. (1966–67) Primary, pupils 123,287, teachers 3,729; secondary, pupils 20,247, teachers 879; vocational, pupils 814, teachers 58; teacher training, students 802, teachers 87; higher, students 930, teaching staff 158.

Finance and Trade. Monetary unit: leone, with a parity of 0.83 leones to U.S. $1 (2 leones = £1 sterling). Budget (1969–70 est.): revenue 45.4 million leones; expenditure 42.6 million leones. Foreign trade (1968): imports 75,474,000 leones; exports 79,719,000 leones. Import sources: U.K. 28%; Japan 12%; U.S. 9%; France 6%; West Germany 5%. Export destinations: U.K. 67%; Netherlands 12%; West Germany 8%. Main exports: diamonds 57%; iron ore 13%; palm kernels 11%.

Agriculture and Industry. Production (in 000; metric tons): palm kernels (1967) *c.* 57, (1966) 55; coffee (1967) *c.* 4.8, (1966) *c.* 3.9; iron ore (metal content; 1967) 1,259; diamonds (metric carats; 1967) 1,400.

Selective Service: *see* Defense
Seventh-day Adventists: *see* Religion
Seychelles: *see* Dependent States
Sheep: *see* Agriculture
Shinto: *see* Religion
Ships and Shipping: *see* Industrial Review; Transportation
Shipwrecks: *see* Disasters
Shoes: *see* Fashion and Dress
Shooting: *see* Sporting Record
Show Business: *see* Cinema; Dance; Fairs and Shows; Music; Television and Radio; Theatre

and in February, while touring Northern Province, he told a meeting in Tonkolili district that the government would appoint a committee to draw up such a constitution. Opening the new Parliament, just over a year after the government had taken office, the acting governor-general said in the speech from the throne that the question of establishing a republic would be considered. A committee of 28 members had, in fact, already been appointed but apparently made little progress. (W. H. Is.)

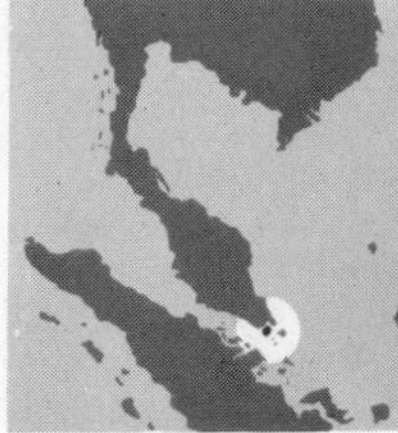

Singapore

The republic of Singapore occupies a group of islands, the largest of which is Singapore, at the southern extremity of the Malay Peninsula. Area: 224.5 sq.mi. (581.5 sq.km.). Pop. (1969 est.): 2,003,800, including approximately 80% Chinese, 12% Malays, and 7% Indians and Pakistanis. Cap. and largest city: Singapore (pop., 1965 est., 1,150,000). Language: official languages are Malay, Chinese, Tamil, and English. Religion: Malays are Muslim; Chinese, mainly Buddhist; Indians, mainly Hindu. President in 1969, Inche Yusof bin Ishak; prime minister, Lee Kuan Yew.

Singapore had another successful year in 1969, and the economy experienced growth in most fields. There was an 8.8% rise to Sing$1,992 in per capita income. Foreign trade was up by 16.6% to Sing$9,715,000,000; cargo handled at port by 11.9%; total revenue by 21.2%; bank deposits by 23.8%; and tourism by 22%. Approximately 15,000 more people got jobs, and an apartment was built every 36 minutes. Entrepôt trade, always important to the economic growth of the republic, after growing at a rate of only 1% in 1967 accelerated to 20.3% in 1968—the highest on record for the 1960s. Economic growth, up by 13%, was achieved in an atmosphere of monetary stability.

Lee Kuan Yew warned against complacency, however, and said that Singaporeans must put in five more years of intensive effort to overcome the problems posed by the British military withdrawal in 1971.

Singapore was expected to spend 10% of its gross national product in the next few years on the rapid buildup of its defense forces, including a small navy; a small but efficient air force equipped with Jet Provosts, Alouette helicopters, and two squadrons of interceptor Hawker Hunters; five operational battalions; four Peoples Defense Force battalions by 1971; an armoured unit; artillery engineers and ancillary units; and a reserve force through a national service system.

There was no shortage of foreign investments, and the industrialization program was paying dividends. From 554 industrial establishments in 1959, the figure had risen by 1969 to 1,563, ranging from simple industries to more sophisticated establishments in such industries as steel, shipbuilding, and electronics.

During the year the government-sponsored International Trading Company of Singapore, with an authorized capital of Sing$50 million, was formed to trade with countries whose foreign trade was a state monopoly. This was one of three institutional changes incorporated to give impetus to Singapore's industrialization program, the other two being the Development Bank of Singapore (capitalized at Sing$200 million) and the Jurong Town Corporation.

Singapore continued with its policy of political neutrality, geared to secure the maximum number of friends and the minimum of enemies. Starting from scratch in 1965 when it broke away from Malaysia, the nation's diplomatic representation in 1969 spanned the entire globe. It had 22 missions, the latest being in the Philippines.

Singapore celebrated the 150th-anniversary of its founding in 1969. (M. S. R.)

SINGAPORE

Education. (1966–67) Primary, pupils 364,846, teachers (including preprimary) 12,553; secondary, pupils 116,956, teachers 5,082; vocational, pupils 16,541, teachers 726; higher (including 3 universities), students 13,184, teaching staff 982.

Finance and Trade. Monetary unit: Singapore dollar, with a par value of Sing$3.06 to U.S. $1 (Sing$7.35 = £1 sterling). Budget (1968 est.): revenue Sing $646,730,000; expenditure Sing$616,450,000. Foreign trade (1967): imports Sing$4,406,400,000; exports Sing$3,490,500,000. Import sources: Malaysia 24%; Japan 12%; China 9%; U.K. 8%; U.S. 6%. Export destinations: Malaysia 31%; U.S. 7%; U.K. 6%. Main exports: rubber 22%; petroleum and products 19%; ships and aircraft stores 10%.

Transport and Communications. Roads (1968) 1,912 km. Motor vehicles in use (1968): passenger 121,106; commercial 27,435. Railways (1967) 45 km. Railway and air traffic: *see* MALAYSIA. Shipping (1968): merchant vessels 100 gross tons and over 73; gross tonnage 133,855. Shipping traffic (1968) goods loaded 14,190,000 metric tons, unloaded 22,030,000 metric tons. Telephones (Dec. 1967) 106,124. Radio receivers (Dec. 1964) 389,000. Television receivers (Dec. 1967) 98,000.

Sikkim:
see Dependent States

Silk:
see Industrial Review

Silver:
see Mining

Skating:
see Hockey; Ice Skating; Sporting Record

Skiing

An increase in the number of people who skied for pleasure was evident in 1969 from the travel and accommodation statistics concerning winter sports centres and from the demand for specialized clothing and equipment. This trend was observed in traditional skiing areas and in lands previously less associated with the sport.

Australia attracted more European and American instructors. More than 85,000 skiers used the newly developed Thredbo area on the slopes of Mt. Kosciusko, New South Wales. South American facilities expanded around Portillo, Chile, its ideal terrain above 10,000 ft. having drawn greater attention since the 1966 world championships were staged there. Japanese participation grew, notably around Sapporo, the site of the 1972 Winter Olympics. New resorts also drew more skiers to the Spanish Pyrenees.

In Switzerland and other long-established skiing regions the season was lengthened in several districts because additional, often spectacular, mechanized ascents transported skiers to previously less accessible altitudes where adequate snow was available for a longer time than at lower heights.

The Ski Industries of America Trade Show, held at Los Angeles in April, reflected equipment tendencies toward plastic boots and fibre-glass skis. The days of leather and wood appeared to be numbered. A more advanced transformation was a marked decrease in the popularity of bootlaces in favour of various kinds of clip fastenings. Further progress was also apparent in the greater efficiency of mechanical toe-release and heel-release safety devices designed to minimize injury when falling. Improved accessories ranged from ski wax in aerosol cans to goggles with adjustable ventilation.

An offshoot of skiing called ski bobbing, using a kind of wooden or metal bicycle frame with minia-

COURTESY, SWISS NATIONAL TOURIST OFFICE

Skier demonstrates ski bobbing, an increasingly popular sport in Europe where more than 100,000 ski bobs have been sold.

ture skis instead of wheels, became more popular. In Europe more than 100,000 ski bobs were sold. World ski bobbing championships were held at Montana, Switz., and combined winners of downhill and slalom were P. Bonvin (Switz.) and Miss G. Schiffkorn (Aus.).

Alpine Racing. The World Alpine Ski Cup tournament enjoyed a successful third season. At some 15 selected top international meetings at different places, the first ten skiers earned points. Each racer's highest aggregate score in any three downhill, slalom, and giant slalom events counted toward the result. The respective men's and women's winners were Karl Schranz and Gertrud Gabl, both of Austria, gaining the trophies undefended by Jean-Claude Killy (France) and Nancy Greene (Canada), who had both retired from amateur competition.

Emphasizing a resurgence of Austrian success following three seasons of French dominance, the same two racers took the combined titles in the 34th Arlberg-Kandahar competition, at St. Anton, Aus., on January 31–February 2. This tournament, still widely regarded as the major international meeting in a season between biennial world championships, provided Schranz with his fifth overall title in a remarkably consistent period spanning 13 years. No other racer had attained the honour more than three times. Schranz also gained his sixth downhill triumph, three more than anyone else in the competition's history, dating from 1928.

Compensating for her lesser skill in downhill racing, Miss Gabl demonstrated admirable technique in the slalom and giant slalom but lost a powerful rival early in the season when Annie Famose, the small but highly competent French racer, broke an ankle at a time when she impressively headed the Alpine Cup scorers. Second and third to Schranz in the World Cup were Jean-Noel Augert (France) and Reinhard Tritscher (Aus.). The women's runner-up to Miss Gabl was Florence Steurer (France), with Wiltrud Drexel (Aus.) third.

The fourth annual international Martini-Kandahar Citadin meeting, at Mürren, Switz., on January 15–19, widened the appeal and recognition of the special category of "citadin" races, restricted to skiers not living in mountain resorts. Thirteen nations competed, and the respective men's and women's international trophy winners were Pierre Poncet (Switz.) and Chloe Varley (U.K.).

The International Ski Federation, meeting in Barcelona on May 18–24, confirmed a relaxed interpretation of amateur status which permitted racers to receive various kinds of "broken-time" payments and commercial backing, provided they were not paid for actual racing. The International Olympic Committee, meeting afterward in Warsaw on June 6–10, dispelled considerable doubts by giving assurance that, despite its new rules, skiing would be allowed to continue in the Olympic Games program.

Nordic Events. In a season without world championships in cross-country racing, more attention switched to biathlon and jumping. The world biathlon championships, still held annually, remained under the domination of northern Europeans during competition at Zakopane, Pol., on February 22–March 3. The U.S.S.R. retained the team title and recaptured the individual award with the competent performances of Aleksandr Tikhonov.

Bjørn Wirkola of Norway retained esteem as an outstanding jumper when he captured the overall honours at the annual Four Hills tournament, held in January at Oberstdorf and Garmisch, W.Ger., and at Innsbruck and Bischofshofen, Aus. He placed first on all but the fourth hill, where he was narrowly defeated by his Czechoslovak rival, Jiri Raska, the eventual runner-up.

Wirkola became the first man to clear 156 m. at Planica, Yugos., on March 21; 160 m. still seemed a distant target but, only two days later at Planica, five jumpers all achieved that milestone within 24 hours, and a new world record of 165 m. (542 ft.) was set by an East German, Manfred Wolf. The other four were Raska, 164 m.; Wirkola, 162 m.; Horst Queck (E.Ger.), 161 m.; and Bohumil Dolezal (Czech.), 160 m. Plans to enlarge the jump hills at Oberstdorf, W.Ger., and Vikersund, Nor., suggested that it would not be long before those figures were bettered. (H. B.)

"PARIS MATCH" FROM PICTORIAL PARADE

Karl Schranz competes in the slalom at the 34th Arlberg-Kandahar events in 1969. Schranz won his fifth title in 13 years.

Snooker: *see* Sporting Record

Snow-Karting: *see* Sporting Record

Soccer: *see* Football

Social Services

Most new provisions in social security programs in 1969 continued to be concerned with improvements rather than innovations. In this the various international bodies helped considerably. At a Round Table convened by the International Social Security Association in Mexico, special consideration was given to the problems of the less developed countries in Asia, Africa, and Latin America. Since 1964 the International Labour Organization (ILO) had been engaged in bringing the prewar conventions up to date, and those on sickness insurance were still being revised. Studies were also undertaken in family allowances and in social security schemes for rural populations and self-employed workers. In these matters ILO continued to work closely with other international organizations.

The World Health Organization (WHO) and the Intergovernmental Maritime Consultative Organization cooperated in securing agreements between the four countries bordering on the Rhine (France, West Germany, the Netherlands, and Switzerland) and Belgium and Luxembourg in which national social security systems were applied to the 45,000 boatmen sailing on the river. Similar agreements were envisaged to cover boatmen on other great rivers. The UN Commission for Social Development was planning a five-year program to include social policies and income distribution and social planning.

In India the campaign to eradicate illiteracy continued to have good results, especially through the work of voluntary organizations. According to a report by UNESCO, however, illiteracy was on the increase throughout the less developed world. It was feared that in 1970 about 810 million of the world's 2,335,000,000 adults would be unable to read or write. Literacy drives were being hampered by lack of funds.

In all industrialized countries voluntary organizations continued to take an increasing part with the public authorities in meeting the needs of the elderly and the handicapped. Much of their expenditure, however, had to be met from voluntary sources. A full investigation undertaken in the U.K. by a working party appointed by the National Council of Social Service drew attention to the need for keeping down administrative expenditure through a system of budgetary control. The working party recommended setting minimum standards for fund-raising but did not feel that such a code could be legally enforced.

A survey undertaken by the British National Old People's Welfare Committee drew attention to the need for the increased training of voluntary workers, the organization on a bigger scale of voluntary visiting, and the provision of more services to enable old people to live in their own homes instead of having to seek admission to an institution.

In a Gerontological Congress in Washington, speakers from several countries stressed the value of encouraging meaningful activities by old people through clubs, centres, and other means. In the U.S. these were considered to be part of the preventive health program. About 5% of old people used such centres where they were available. The percentage in the U.K. was considered to be much higher. In Britain (and to a much lesser extent in other countries) much use was made of meals services by the elderly, either those provided in lunch clubs or those by delivery at the home.

The government-sponsored Social Science Research Council published a report dealing with research on poverty in Britain. The complexity of the subject was shown by the fact that any such inquiry must involve six different departments of government in England and Wales. It was suggested that the government should clarify the responsibilities and authority of the departments concerned or that there should be one official body, responsible to a minister of Cabinet rank, who would be permanently accountable for gathering, appraising, and publishing information about poverty, living standards, and income distribution. It was concluded that there could be no single definition of poverty but that "poverty policies" were an aspect of social policies, which were, in turn, a way of looking at all the actions of government.

United Kingdom. The Ministry of Social Security and the Ministry of Health were amalgamated into a new department—the Department of Health and Social Security—under a minister designated as secretary of state for social services. Among the first priorities of the new department was the integration of research and the development of central planning. The Supplementary Benefits Commission worked within the new department.

Family allowances were raised from 15*s.* to 18*s.* a week for the second child and from 17*s.* to 20*s.* a week for each subsequent child. The national insurance benefits for children were also adjusted. The increases in family allowances were linked with reductions in the amount of child tax allowances so that the actual advantage of the increased rates was confined to poorer families.

The standard weekly rates of flat-rate retirement and widows' pensions and of flat-rate unemployment and sickness benefits were increased from £4 10*s.* to £5 for a single person and from £7 6*s.* to £8 2*s.* for a married couple. The amount that a pensioner might earn without affecting his pension was altered from £6 10*s.* to £7 10*s.*

The flat-rate national insurance contributions for persons who were not contracted out of the graduated scheme were increased for an employed man from £1 6*s.* 9*d.* to £1 8*s.* 7*d.*, the increases being shared equally by the employer and the employee. The total joint contribution for a man in this position was thus raised to £4 8*s.* 5*d.*, of which the employee paid £1 0*s.* 1*d.* and his employer £3 8*s.* 4*d.* Supplementary benefit rates were increased by 5*s.* a week for a single householder and 8*s.* for a married couple.

The trend to earlier retirement continued and the proportion of those who claimed retirement pensions at the minimum age rose from nearly 50% in 1961 to about 70% in 1968, while the proportion of all men aged between 65 and 70 who had retired increased from under 70% in 1961 to over 80% in 1968.

The estimated proportion of national insurance beneficiaries receiving supplementary unemployment benefit at the end of 1968 was 20.2%, compared with 23% in 1967; 14.5% were receiving sickness benefit (13.5% in 1967); and 28.6%, retirement pension (28.3% in 1967). About 23,250,000 claims for benefits and allowances were made in 1968. Under national insurance benefits there were 663,000 claims for retirement pensions (compared with 643,000 in 1967); 63,000 for widows' pensions and widowed mothers' allowances (62,000 in 1967); 10,608,000 for sickness benefit (10,048,000); and 3,117,000 for unemployment benefit (3,275,000). In addition, 406,000 claims were made for supplementary pensions, compared with 428,000 in 1967, and 5,675,000 for supplementary allowances (4,509,000 in 1967).

As compared with the last full year of the National Assistance Board, continuing awards in 1968 increased by over 50%, immediate payments by almost 80%, and the number of callers at local offices by over 50%. These increases were no doubt due to the publicity for the new scheme on the abolition of the expression "national assistance." Family allowances were being paid at the end of 1968 to over 4 million families containing nearly 11 million children. About 59% were families with two children; 25% with three; 10% with four; 3.5% with five; and 2.5% with six or more.

The Department of Health and Social Security published a White Paper setting out proposals for fundamental changes whereby both contributions and benefits would be related to earnings. The new contributions would be required for 20 years before the first pension at the full rate would be payable to a person then reaching pension age.

It was claimed that the plan would remove one of the worst features of the prevailing system whereby two million old people had to rely on supplementary pensions because of inadequate personal resources and inability to join occupational pension schemes. Under the proposed scheme, employed women, whether single, married, or widowed, would contribute on the same basis as men and would earn pensions and other personal benefits in their own right.

At the start of the new scheme the contribution rate payable by employees would be 6.75% of earnings and by employers 6.75% of the total payroll. The minimum ages for pension would remain at 65 for men and 60 for women. Until age 70 for men and 65 for women, pensions would only be paid at the full rate to persons who had retired from regular employment—as under the old scheme. Those retiring after the minimum age would continue to earn extra pensions in respect of continued contributions. Rights to the full new pension would be built up gradually over the first 20 years and pensions of those who reached pension age during this period would be at intermediate rates. The government was expected to introduce the necessary legislation in the 1969–70 session of Parliament with a view to the scheme starting in April 1972.

The National Old People's Welfare Council decided to become an independent body instead of being an associated group of the National Council of Social Service. It was hoped that closer cooperation with other national bodies concerned with the welfare of the elderly would be achieved. The National Council of Social Service undertook a full review of its functions as the central body for voluntary activity on the national level.

Other European Countries. In Denmark where the pension was income-related and those with higher incomes had been receiving a minimum pension only, there was an alteration whereby in April 1970 all pensioners would receive the full amount irrespective of income. The payments would continue to be made through the social welfare office of the local authority, thus providing a direct link between the social security and welfare services. This arrangement, peculiar to Denmark, facilitated the provision of additional assistance by the local authority in. cases of need.

In Norway a research study of the circumstances of a sample of persons aged 80 and over showed that their attending health and welfare centres provided by the National Health Association was of value in preventing the need to apply for admission to residential homes. A longitudinal research project by the National Institute of Gerontology showed that some of the elderly were not prepared for retirement. The institute, in cooperation with another body, organized preretirement education courses.

WIDE WORLD

Elderly citizens attend a session held by the Senate Special Committee on Aging, April 29, 1969, to hear Social Security Commissioner Robert M. Ball.

In Sweden a new program was introduced, with the approval of the Trade Union Congress, to deal with social assistance for those on strike or subject to a lockout. Assistance would be payable to those with large families who could prove that their children were suffering. There were also improvements in the social security programs of the Netherlands.

In Poland the basis for calculation of pension was altered so as to be the average earnings during the last 12 months of employment or during 24 consecutive months chosen by the insured person from the last 12 years of employment. Another alteration made supplements payable to beneficiaries of retirement pensions who held high decorations awarded by the government, or were scientific workers or persons invalided through military service.

In Hungary the scope of the family allowances program was extended to members of agricultural cooperatives, and in Italy the scope of the insurance plan was extended to all workers who had contributed for 40 years and the percentage rates of pensions were raised. In Switzerland pension rates were increased by 33%.

North America. *Canada.* Development of the security program proved helpful both in meeting the needs of individuals and in relieving the provinces of expenditure. The age of eligibility for old-age security pension and the guaranteed income supplement was reduced to 66, making it unnecessary to apply for basic assistance under the shared federal-provincial program. At the end of 1968, 750,000 old-age security beneficiaries were receiving the supplement; more than 450,000 at the full rate. The further cost-of-living escalation of benefits brought the old-age security pension to Can$78 a month and the combined guaranteed income supplement to Can$109.20 a month.

The Canada and Quebec pension plans had begun to make a significant contribution in the field of income maintenance. In February 1968 benefits for survivors were paid for the first time and by the end of the year some 11,000 widows and orphans were receiving such benefits under the Canada Pension Plan alone—replacing mothers' allowance or general assistance. By the end of the year more than 37,000 persons were receiving such benefits which, in January 1969, reached a maximum of Can$32 a month. The maximum payment for persons retiring at the end of 1969 was Can$42 a month.

Newfoundland, Nova Scotia, Manitoba, Alberta, and Ontario joined the Canada national program for health insurance, bringing the number of provinces participating to seven.

There was increasing evidence of the effectiveness of the Canada Assistance Plan not only in integrating and improving existing assistance programs but also in enhancing the child-welfare services, providing support for health and welfare services, and providing for Indian welfare and work activity projects. Federal payments under the plan for 1969–70 were estimated at Can$500 million.

United States. A proposed revision of the public welfare system announced in 1969 by Pres. Richard M. Nixon introduced the concept of a minimum income for all U.S. families. At an estimated cost of $4 billion a year, the program would provide $1,600 a year for all families of four with no employment or other form of income. These payments were to be made by the federal government and supplemented from state funds. The chief instrument of welfare currently was the Aid to Families with Dependent Children Program, through which the states controlled all dispensations while providing only a fraction of the money. Payments varied; Mississippi paid only

Social Security Programs, by Country, 1969* and 1958

Type of program available

Country	Old age, invalidity, survivors		Health, sickness, maternity		Work injury		Unemployment		Family allowances	
	1969	1958	1969	1958	1969	1958	1969	1958	1969	1958
Afghanistan					X	X				
Albania	X	X	X	X	X	X			X	
Algeria†	X		X		X				X	
Argentina	X	X	X		X	X	X		X	X
Australia	X	X	X	X	X	X	X	X	X	X
Austria	X	X	X	X	X	X	X	X	X	X
Barbados†	X		X		X					
Belgium	X	X	X	X	X	X	X	X	X	X
Bolivia	X	X	X	X	X	X			X	X
Botswana†					X					
Brazil	X	X	X	X	X	X	X		X	X
Bulgaria	X	X	X	X	X	X	X	X	X	X
Burma			X	X	X	X				
Burundi†	X				X					
Cambodia†					X				X	
Cameroon			X		X				X	
Canada	X	X	X	X	X	X	X	X	X	X
Central African Rep.†	X		X		X				X	
Ceylon	X	X	X		X	X				
Chad†			X		X				X	
Chile	X	X	X	X	X	X	X	X	X	X
China	X	X	X	X	X	X				
Colombia	X		X	X	X	X			X	
Congo (Brazzaville)†	X		X		X				X	
Congo (Kinshasa)†	X		X		X				X	
Costa Rica	X	X	X	X	X	X				
Cuba	X	X	X	X	X	X				
Cyprus†	X		X		X		X			
Czechoslovakia	X	X	X	X	X	X			X	X
Dahomey†			X		X				X	
Denmark	X	X	X	X	X	X	X	X	X	X
Dominican Rep.	X	X	X	X	X	X				
Ecuador	X	X	X	X	X	X	X	X		
El Salvador			X	X	X	X				
Ethiopia†			X		X					
Finland	X	X	X		X	X	X	X	X	X
France	X	X	X	X	X	X	X	X	X	X
Gabon†	X				X				X	
Gambia, The†					X					
Germany, East	X	X	X	X	X	X	X	X	X	X
Germany, West	X	X	X	X	X	X	X	X	X	X
Ghana	X		X		X	X				
Greece	X	X	X	X	X	X	X	X	X	
Guatemala	X		X	X	X	X				
Guinea†	X		X		X				X	
Guyana†	X				X					
Haiti	X		X		X	X				
Honduras			X	X	X	X				
Hungary	X	X	X	X	X	X	X		X	X
Iceland	X	X	X	X	X	X	X		X	X
India	X	X	X	X	X	X				
Indonesia			X		X	X				
Iran	X	X	X	X	X	X			X	X
Iraq	X	X	X	X	X	X				
Ireland	X	X	X	X	X	X	X	X	X	X
Israel	X	X	X	X	X	X			X	
Italy	X	X	X	X	X	X	X	X	X	X
Ivory Coast†	X		X		X				X	
Jamaica†	X				X					
Japan	X	X	X	X	X	X	X	X		

Country	Old age, invalidity, survivors		Health, sickness		Work injury		Unemployment		Family allowances	
	1969	1958	1969	1958	1969	1958	1969	1958	1969	1958
Jordan					X	X				
Kenya†	X		X		X					
Korea, South					X					
Lebanon	X		X		X	X			X	
Liberia†	X				X					
Libya	X	X	X	X	X	X				
Luxembourg	X	X	X	X	X	X	X	X	X	X
Malagasy Rep.†			X		X				X	
Malawi†					X					
Malaysia	X	X	X		X	X				
Mali†	X		X		X				X	
Malta†	X		X		X		X			
Mauritania†	X		X		X				X	
Mexico	X	X	X	X	X	X				
Morocco	X		X		X	X			X	X
Netherlands	X	X	X	X	X	X	X	X	X	X
New Zealand	X	X	X	X	X	X	X	X	X	X
Nicaragua	X	X	X	X	X	X				
Niger†	X		X		X				X	
Nigeria†	X		X		X					
Norway	X	X	X	X	X	X	X	X	X	X
Pakistan			X		X	X				
Panama	X	X	X	X	X	X				
Paraguay	X	X	X	X	X	X				
Peru	X	X	X	X	X	X				
Philippines	X	X	X	X	X	X				
Poland	X	X	X	X	X	X			X	X
Portugal	X	X	X	X	X	X			X	X
Romania	X	X	X	X	X	X			X	X
Rwanda†	X				X					
Saudi Arabia†	X				X					
Senegal†			X		X				X	
Sierra Leone†					X					
Singapore†	X		X		X					
Somalia†					X					
South Africa†	X	X			X	X	X	X	X	X
Spain	X	X	X	X	X	X	X	X	X	X
Sudan†					X					
Sweden	X	X	X	X	X	X	X	X	X	X
Switzerland	X	X	X	X	X	X	X	X	X	X
Syria†	X				X					
Taiwan	X	X	X	X	X	X				
Tanzania†	X		X		X					
Thailand					X	X				
Togo†	X		X		X				X	
Trinidad and Tobago†	X				X					
Tunisia			X		X	X			X	X
Turkey	X	X	X	X	X	X				
Uganda†	X				X					
U.S.S.R.	X	X	X	X	X	X			X	X
U.A.R.	X	X	X		X	X	X			
United Kingdom	X	X	X	X	X	X	X	X	X	X
United States	X	X	X	X	X	X	X	X		
Upper Volta†	X		X		X				X	
Uruguay	X	X	X		X	X	X	X	X	X
Venezuela	X		X	X	X	X				
Vietnam, North	X		X		X	X			X	X
Vietnam, South			X		X	X			X	X
Yugoslavia	X	X	X	X	X	X	X	X	X	X
Zambia†	X				X					

*Data as of October 1969.
†Country not reported prior to 1964.
Source: U.S. Department of Health, Education, and Welfare, Social Security Administration, Office of Research and Statistics, *Social Security Programs Throughout the World.*

$39 a month to families of four whereas New Jersey paid $263. It was intended that, while removing some of the inefficiencies in the existing system, the new program would introduce an incentive to work by letting the wage-earner keep a diminishing proportion of the federal grant until his total income reached $3,920 a year. Special arrangements were to be made for families headed by a mother. The program was subject to the approval of Congress.

Also announced was a $2.5 billion program for the eradication of hunger by increasing the scope of the Food Stamp Program under which stamps purchased at a fraction of the value of groceries could be exchanged at food stores with the difference being met by the government. Families with incomes of $30 a month would receive food stamps at no cost while those on a higher income would pay proportionately. The federal government also started a food relief program under which certain surplus food could be given to needy families.

The Social Security Administration defined poverty as an income of $3,335 or less a year for a nonfarming family with four children; the median income for families of that size was $8,995. It was estimated that the number of people living in poverty declined from 40 million in 1960 to 26 million in 1967 and that by January 1969 the number was reduced further to 22 million. Although most of the poor were whites, the incidence of poverty was far higher among nonwhites—about one household in three compared with about one in seven among whites.

Social welfare expenditure, including employment, public assistance, health and medical programs, the veterans' program, education, housing, and other programs increased between 1965 and 1968 by $35.3 billion to a total of $112.4 billion. Social expenditure in 1968 amounted to 13.7% of the gross national product, as compared with 11.8% in 1965. The total government expenditure (federal, state, and local) for social welfare rose from 42.5% in 1965 to 43.7% in 1968. At the federal level the total outlay for social welfare rose from 32.7% in 1965 to 36.1% in 1968.

Monthly cash benefits were payable at the end of April 1969 to about 24.8 million persons under the Old Age, Survivors, Disability, and Health Insurance (OASDHI) program—823,000 more than at the end of April 1968. The number of beneficiaries under age 65 increased by more than 5%—more than twice the rate of increase for those 65 and over. In April 1968 the Social Security Administration received approximately 545,300 hospital admission notices for aged persons covered by the Medicare program. Since the beginning of the fiscal year the notices had totaled 4.9 million. The only major alteration in social security generally during the year was in improvement of the veterans' pension plan. The tax bill passed late in December provided for a 15% increase in social security payments effective in January 1970.

By the end of 1968 nearly one-fourth of the men aged 62–64 and more than 80% of those 65 and over were drawing retirement benefits under the social security program. About 30% of all men (and more than half of all women retirees) received benefits reduced by up to 20% because they had been claimed before age 65. Four-fifths of those receiving reduced benefit classified themselves as disabled (*i.e.*, more or less limited in their ability to work) and almost half said they were severely disabled. Nearly one-third of the men who claimed benefit at 62 had had earnings at or above the taxable limit and regular employment. Presumably most of them were also eligible for a private pension and had other resources.

Other Countries. In Australia old-age pensions granted under the Commonwealth scheme increased by 20% following liberalization of the income test. This was especially marked in the case of women. Over previous years there had been a change from payment of pensions at post offices to payment by check. A new reciprocal agreement was made with the U.K. in regard to invalid and widows' pensions.

In New Zealand family maintenance allowances were introduced to supplement the income-tested benefit of beneficiaries, other than widows and those receiving mother's allowance, who had dependent children. The rate was NZ$8.75 a week for the first dependent child plus NZ$1 for each additional child. The rates of sickness and unemployment benefits were increased by NZ$26 a year, with corresponding increases for dependent wives. A special survey of those receiving unemployment benefit in March 1969 showed that 52% were females aged 16 to 19 years.

In Ceylon, although the funds voted for public assistance had more than doubled in ten years, they were still inadequate to pay all who were eligible. A special problem was the relief of distress caused by widespread flooding. A beggar-rehabilitation scheme was in operation, including the provision of residential accommodation for the aged. Progress was also made with a government scheme to provide a house of detention for the rehabilitation of antisocial persons. The basis of grants to voluntary organizations was improved.

In India begging was considered a major industry in the cities. It was estimated that there were 33,000 beggars in the streets of Calcutta to whom over Rs. 33,000 was given daily. Consideration was being given to the establishment of a corporation to coordinate the activities of organizations helping in this problem and in the collection of funds for the purpose. In Pakistan relief of distress through flooding involved an expenditure of Rs. 125 million annually.

In Brazil provision was made for increases in the minimum wage to be applied to social security pensions through a computer operation. In Chile the coverage of work-accident and occupational disease insurance was extended and a new health insurance plan was authorized for salaried employees in the public and private sectors. In Togo a national assistance scheme was established for all wage and salaried workers subject to the labour code, and pension was payable at age 55. Improvements were also made in the social insurance schemes of Libya and Ivory Coast. In Bermuda a new contributory pensions scheme came into operation and in Jamaica the first full pensions under an act of 1966 became payable. This program covered only about 160,800 employed persons out of a total of 700,000. Plans were being made in Trinidad and Tobago for the introduction of a national insurance plan providing retirement benefits ranging from 50 to 73% of wages. (JN. M.)

See also Education; Housing; Insurance; Labour Unions; Medicine; Migration, International; Race Relations; Refugees.

Sociology

During 1969 numerous universities throughout the world suffered some degree of disruption from demonstrations by student activists. Invariably the departments of sociology in these universities shared in the turmoil. This was especially true at the University of Chicago, and the situation there is worth examining in detail as an example of the problems facing sociologists and other academics in many institutions.

Since their first chairman, Albion W. Small, took office in 1892, the members of the faculty of Chicago's department of sociology had concentrated on the objective analysis of society. All the department chairmen from Small to Morris Janowitz, who was chairman in 1969, had held that ideally sociologists should regard themselves as scientists. Nearly all sociologists were aware that for them many of the most cherished goals of pure science were unattainable. The sociologist does not have a laboratory in the sense that the physicist has one. Nevertheless, as researchers they had generally striven to achieve a high degree of emotional detachment and value neutrality.

In the last few years, a contrary view of the nature and goals of sociology had arisen among graduate students and young faculty members at a number of major universities. According to this new and rather revolutionary view, sociology was to be regarded as a social movement, the principal goal of which should be the restructuring of society to remove inequities and injustices. At the University of Chicago a collision between the older and the newer views occurred when, in accordance with long-established procedures, the tenured members of the sociology faculty were called upon to decide whether or not to recommend the reappointment of Marlene Dixon and Richard Flacks, two younger and nontenured members of the faculty. Mrs. Dixon and Flacks had vigorously espoused the new revolutionary view of sociology, while most of the tenured members held to the older, scientific one.

The case of Mrs. Dixon became quite complicated. She held a joint appointment as assistant professor in both the department of sociology and an interdisciplinary program called the Committee on Human Development. On the one hand, the tenured members of the department of sociology voted to recommend nonreappointment because her research and publishing activities had fallen below their expectation. On the other hand, the tenured members of the Committee on Human Development voted to recommend reappointment because she had met their expectations as a teacher. Mrs. Dixon, moreover, charged that the decision of the tenured members of the department of sociology was the result of political bias and prejudice against her as a woman. While the matter was being reviewed by the dean of faculties, a group of students seized and held the university administration building for 16 days, demanding, among other things, that Mrs. Dixon be reappointed and that henceforward students should be accorded 50% of the votes in regard to faculty appointments. These two demands were among those that university officials refused to meet. Mrs. Dixon was not reappointed.

As the tenured members of the sociology faculty were pondering the future of Richard Flacks, he was attacked by a stranger in his office and seriously injured. The assailant escaped. Flacks was offered reappointment as associate professor but, upon recovering from his injuries, chose to join the department of sociology at the University of California at Santa Barbara.

In September 1969 the American Sociological Association convened in San Francisco, where its 64th annual meeting was devoted to the theme "Group Conflict and Mutual Acceptance." Three dissident groups sought the attention of the delegates: the Black Caucus, organized by Tilman C. Cothran of Atlanta (Ga.) University; the Women's Caucus, sponsored by Alice Rossi of Johns Hopkins University; and the Sociology Liberation Movement Caucus, headed by Carol Brown of Columbia. The association's president, Ralph H. Turner of the University of California at Los Angeles, met with the leaders of these caucuses, gave them meeting rooms and lobby tables to display their literature, and accorded them time during the business meeting to present grievances.

In general, the association members present held that the representatives of the Black Caucus and the Women's Caucus made justified demands and called attention to them in legitimate and dignified ways. Although most of the association members were sympathetic to many of the demands of the Sociology Liberation Caucus—a group of students and young faculty members with views similar to those of Marlene Dixon and Richard Flacks—the manner in which representatives of this group harassed speakers during both the professional and business sessions caused them to lose the crucial backing of many moderate delegates.

Among the major disappointments of 1969 was the failure of exchanges to develop between sociologists in Eastern Europe and those elsewhere in the world. Following the Soviet invasion of Czechoslovakia in 1968, contacts had grown progressively weaker. In addition, promising sociological developments in Greece were suppressed by the military regime, and military governments in Latin-American countries could be expected to continue to discourage sociological research. In view of this increasingly unfavourable international climate, the International Sociological Association, whose secretariat was located in Milan, Italy, was petitioned by 106 of its more prominent members throughout the world to assume the task of seeking out, publicizing, and vigorously protesting against any and all attempts to suppress sociological inquiry. (J. E. McK.)

See also Anthropology; Psychology; Social Services.

ENCYCLOPÆDIA BRITANNICA FILMS. *The Living City* (1953); *Man and His Culture* (1954); *Megalopolis—Cradle of the Future* (1962); *Population Ecology* (1964); *Operation Bootstrap* (1968); *Heritage in Black* (1969).

Somalia

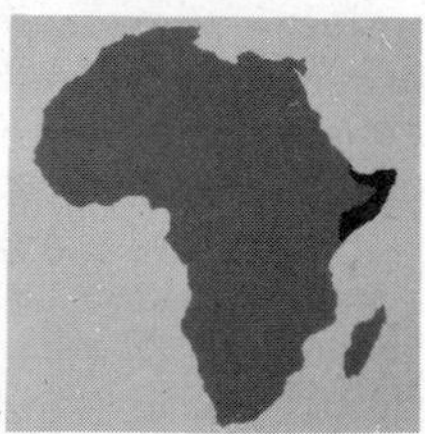

A republic of northeast Africa, the Somali Democratic Republic, or Somalia, is bounded by the Gulf of Aden, the Indian Ocean, Kenya, Ethiopia, and the French Territory of Afars and Issas. Area: 246,155 sq.mi. (637,541 sq.km.). Pop. (1969 est.): 3 million, predominantly Hamitic, with Arabic and other admixtures. Cap. and largest city: Mozadiscio (pop., 1969 est., 200,000). Language: Cushitic Somali with some Arabic influence. Religion: orthodox Muslim. President in 1969, Abd-i-Rashid Ali Shermarke until October 15; prime minister, Muhammad Haji Ibrahim Egal until October 21; chairman of the Supreme Revolutionary Council from October 22, Gen. Muhammad Siyad.

On October 15 President Shermarke, who had held office since 1967, was assassinated. His death occurred at a time of widespread public discontent following the results of the allegedly rigged elections of March,

Soil Conservation: *see* Conservation

SOMALIA

Education. (1965–66) Primary, pupils 28,890, teachers 1,124; secondary, pupils 7,104, teachers 438; vocational, pupils 2,627, teachers 135; teacher training, students 763, teachers 64; higher (at University Institute of Somalia), students 791, teaching staff 23.

Finance. Monetary unit: Somali shilling, with a par value of 7.14 Somali shillings to U.S. $1 (17.14 Somali shillings = £1 sterling). Budget (1968 est.) balanced at 281,624,000 Somali shillings. Money supply: (June 1969) 272.9 million Somali shillings; (June 1968) 246.6 million Somali shillings. Cost of living (Mozadiscio; 1966 = 100): (May 1969) 109; (May 1968) 103.

Foreign Trade. (1967) Imports 286.4 million Somali shillings; exports 286.4 million Somali shillings. Import sources (1966): Italy 31%; U.K. 8%; Japan 8%; U.S. 7%; West Germany 5%; Iran 5%. Export destinations (1966): Italy 45%; Saudi Arabia 32%; Southern Yemen 13%. Main exports: bananas 34%; hides and skins 5%.

Transport and Communications. Roads (1967) 17,750 km. (including 600 km. asphalted). Motor vehicles in use (1967): passenger *c.* 6,700; commercial (including buses) *c.* 7,800. There are no railways. Shipping (1968): merchant vessels 100 gross tons and over 15; gross tonnage 58,677. Telephones (Jan. 1968) *c.* 6,500. Radio receivers (Dec. 1967) 40,000.

Agriculture. Production (in 000; metric tons; 1967; 1966 in parentheses): bananas 184 (127); millet and sorghum *c.* 55 (*c.* 55); cassava *c.* 20 (*c.* 20). Livestock (in 000; 1966–67): cattle *c.* 850; sheep *c.* 3,900; goats *c.* 4,660; camels *c.* 2,825.

at which the Somali Youth League government party again proved its invincibility, winning 73 of the 124 seats in the National Assembly. On hearing of the president's death Prime Minister Egal returned from a visit to the U.S. to head a new government.

On October 21, the day following Shermarke's funeral, the Army and police staged a coup, thus ending Somalia's nearly ten years of democratic government. Prime Minister Egal and his Cabinet were arrested and charged with corruption. The constitution was abolished and the National Assembly dissolved. Rule by decree was introduced pending the drafting of a new constitution, and the name of the nation was changed to the Somali Democratic Republic.

The Supreme Revolutionary Council, led by Gen. Muhammad Siyad, commander in chief of the armed forces, declared its neutrality, its respect for existing treaties and interstate relations, and its desire for peaceful coexistence. It gave assurances of respect for human rights and individual liberty, and of noninterference in the internal affairs of other states. However, it also supported the "rightful causes of all liberation movements," and this was taken as a reference to Somalia's claims to disputed border areas controlled by Kenya, Ethiopia, and France (thus reversing Egal's policy of reconciliation with those neighbouring states). On November 1 a 14-man Cabinet was appointed, of which all but the minister of the interior were civilians. (I. M. L.)

South Africa

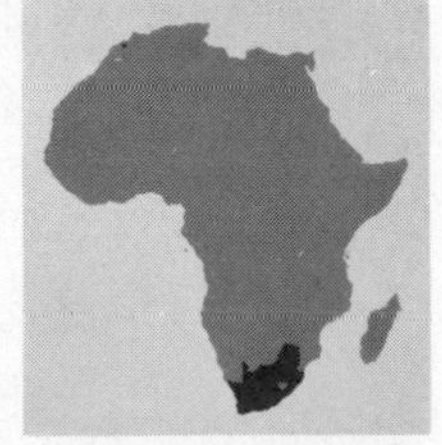

A republic occupying the southern tip of Africa, South Africa is bounded by South West Africa, Botswana, Rhodesia, Mozambique, and Swaziland. Lesotho forms an enclave within South African territory. Area: 471,445 sq.mi. (1,221,037 sq.km.), excluding Walvis Bay, 372 sq.mi. Pop. (1968 est.): 19,167,000, including Bantu 68.1%; white 19%; Coloured 9.9%; Asian 3%. Administrative cap.: Pretoria (metro. pop., 1967 est., 523,000); judicial cap.: Bloemfontein (pop., 1967 est., 197,000); legislative cap.: Cape Town (metro. pop., 1967 est., 758,000). Largest city: Johannesburg (metro. pop., 1967 est., 1,309,000). Language: Afrikaans and English. Religion: mainly Christian. State president in 1969, Jacobus J. Fouché; prime minister, Balthazar J. Vorster.

Domestic Affairs. A major political development, following dissension within the ruling National Party, was the formation of a new party, the Herstigte Nasionale Party (HNP, literally the Reconstituted National Party), headed by a former Cabinet minister, Albert Hertzog. He was joined by three other members of Parliament who were expelled or who resigned from the National Party. The HNP adopted a program to the right of the National Party on foreign relations, particularly with Black Africa; immigration; the prohibition of racially mixed sports tours in South Africa; and relations between Afrikaans-speaking and English-speaking South Africans. Other small political groups supported the new party. In September it was announced that the general election would be held on April 22, 1970, a year early. A new minister of national education, J. P. van der Spuy, was appointed to succeed J. de Klerk, who became president of the Senate on the death of J. F. Naudé.

In June a Bureau of State Security (BOSS) was established, with Gen. H. J. van den Bergh at its head. There was criticism by judges and others of the powers granted to the government and the bureau by a new General Law Amendment Act; these powers included the right to withhold evidence from the courts in the interests of public security. A judicial commission was set up to inquire into the national security structure, and an act was passed abolishing the jury system. A state legal aid bureau was also established.

Following the publication in the *Rand Daily Mail* of a series of articles on prison conditions in 1965, the editor in chief, Laurence Gandar, and a senior reporter, Benjamin Pogrund, were found guilty on charges under the Prisons Act. Gandar was fined, and a prison sentence of six months on Pogrund was conditionally suspended for three years.

The minister of defense, P. W. Botha, announced defense plans costing R 1,647,000,000 over five years. In the 1969 budget the defense allocation was increased from R 262 million to a record R 271 million. In December 1968 the first guided missile designed and developed in South Africa was test-launched from the missile range at St. Lucia Bay in Zululand. The South African Navy was to be equipped with guided missiles. In conjunction with France a low-level, ground-to-air missile defense system was developed and made available for foreign purchase. Saldanha Bay, near Cape Town, would become the third South African naval base in addition to Simonstown and Richard's Bay. South Africa's first two French-built submarines were launched in March and October, and a third was on order. The civil defense organization, previously under the Ministry of Justice, was placed under the Ministry of Defense, and provision was made for two civil defense training centres for girls.

Intensive oil exploration continued. Petroleum gas was found on the continental shelf near Plettenberg Bay. An oil refinery costing R 52 million was being established at Sasolburg, the site of an oil-from-coal plant. South Africa's third state-owned iron and steel project was to be at Newcastle, Natal. The other two

Sorghum Grains: *see* Agriculture

were in Pretoria and Vanderbijlpark, Transvaal. Details were announced in May concerning a hydroelectric installation, initially costing R 22.6 million, to be linked with the Orange River irrigation project. Final agreement was concluded between South Africa and Portugal on the R 218 million Cahorabassa hydroelectric project on the Zambezi River in northern Mozambique, and contracts for the first three stages were awarded in September to an international consortium headed by South Africa.

A Medical Research Council was established and provision made for the opening of three additional medical schools, the first in Bloemfontein. A new National Education Council was constituted to develop a coordinated national education policy.

Race Relations. The first general election by Coloured (racially mixed) voters to choose 40 members of the Coloured Persons' Representative Council was held in September. The antiapartheid (racial separation) Labour Party won 26 seats, and the Federal Party and smaller parties 14 seats. Under the council's constitution the government nominated 20 additional members, all belonging to the pro-apartheid Federal Party, which thus secured a majority and appointed the executive. The council was given limited legislative and administrative powers to deal with matters affecting the Coloured population.

Partial self-government, similar to that of the Transkei, was granted to various Bantu tribal authorities. During the year Bantu tribal communities in Natal and the Transvaal were removed to other areas. State aid was given to decentralized industries near the Bantu homelands. Other industrial development involving the employment of Bantus was subject to government control. Bantu artisans and technicians were to be trained for the industries in the homelands, which would be established by white agents of Bantu development corporations. A Bantu mining development corporation was to investigate and exploit the mineral potential of the homelands.

The Trade Union Council of South Africa, which had previously allowed Bantu labour unions, barred from legal registration, to become affiliated members, decided under pressure from some of its member bodies to reverse this decision. Later the council suggested that affiliated unions should, through their own machinery, help Bantu workers to obtain better wages and labour conditions.

Robert Mangaliso Sobukwe, former university lecturer and Pan-Africanist Congress leader, was released after six years' detention on Robben Island on charges of incitement to subversion, but remained under restriction in Kimberley. Eleven Bantu were found guilty in Pretoria of contravening the Terrorism Act and jailed for from 5 to 20 years. In October the trial began of 22 Bantu, charged under the Suppression of Communism Act, who had previously been held under the 180-day law. Among them was Winifred Mandela, wife of Nelson Mandela, former leader of the banned African National Congress, himself imprisoned on Robben Island on charges under the Suppression of Communism Act. (*See* RACE RELATIONS.)

Foreign Affairs. The apartheid policy and South Africa's administration of South West Africa continued under attack at the UN. With the major Western powers abstaining, the Security Council passed a resolution calling on South Africa to withdraw from South West Africa and hand over control to the UN by Oct. 4, 1969. South Africa rejected the demand. By 95 votes to 2 (South Africa and Portugal), with 6 abstentions, the UN General Assembly on October 31 adopted a resolution submitted by the Trusteeship Committee condemning South Africa and urging that measures be taken against the republic for disregarding the Security Council resolution.

Ministerial and naval visits and trade missions were exchanged between South Africa and Argentina, Brazil, and Australia. Tentative suggestions were made for the formation of a South Atlantic pact. In view of the closure of the Suez Canal, the British government's policy of withdrawal from the Indian Ocean, and the appearance of Soviet naval vessels in the area, the importance of protecting the Cape sea route was underlined by South Africa. Efforts to induce the United States and Britain to revoke the embargo on the supply of arms to South Africa were unsuccessful, however.

As part of the "outward policy" toward the newly independent black African states, financial and technical aid was given to Malawi. Aid was also given to Botswana, Lesotho, and Swaziland, South Africa concluding a revised customs agreement more favourable to those states. South Africa continued to maintain armed police in white-controlled Rhodesia to oppose guerrilla infiltration.

SOUTH AFRICA

Education. European (1966): primary, secondary, and vocational, pupils 810,266, teachers 68,824; teacher training, students 9,734, teachers 737. Non-European (1967): primary, secondary, and vocational, pupils 2,853,837, teachers 59,000; teacher training, students 8,173. Higher (including 11 universities), students 64,388 (including 57,211 European), teaching staff 4,493.

Finance. Monetary unit: rand, with a par value of R 0.71 to U.S. $1 (R 1.71 = £1 sterling). Gold and foreign exchange, official: (June 1969) U.S. $1,557,000,000; (June 1968) U.S. $1,122,000,000. Budget (1969–70 est.): revenue R 1,667,900,000; expenditure R 1,655,100,000. Gross national product: (1968) R 10,013,000,000; (1967) R 9,440,000,000. Money supply: (June 1969) R 2,099,000,000; (June 1968) R 1,782,000,000. Cost of living (1963 = 100): (June 1969) 119; (June 1968) 115.

Foreign Trade. (1968) Imports R 1,877,500,000; exports (excluding gold) R 1,503,500,000 (outflow of gold R 769 million). Import sources: U.K. 24%; U.S. 18%; West Germany 13%; Japan 7%. Export destinations (excluding gold): U.K. 32%; Japan 14%; U.S. 7%; West Germany 7%. Main exports: diamonds 13%; fruit and vegetables 8%; cereals 8%; nonferrous metals 9%; wool 7%; metal ores 5%; iron and steel 5%.

Transport and Communications. Roads (1967) *c.* 350,000 km. (including 10,030 km. main roads). Motor vehicles in use (1968): passenger 1,405,000; commercial 343,000. Railways (1967): 19,762 km. (excluding South West Africa; 2,340 km.); freight traffic (including South West Africa; 1968) 49,410,000,000 net ton-km. Air traffic (1968): 1,837,000,000 passenger-km.; freight 47,376,000 net ton-km. Shipping (1968): merchant vessels 100 gross tons and over 244; gross tonnage 470,078. Telephones (Dec. 1967) 1,322,101. Radio receivers (Dec. 1967) 2.7 million.

Agriculture. Production (in 000; metric tons; 1968; 1967 in parentheses): corn (on farms and estates only) 5,089 (9,299); wheat (on farms and estates only) 1,225 (1,089); sorghum 207 (844); oats *c.* 143 (170); peanuts 211 (429); sunflower seed 82 (101); potatoes (1967) *c.* 497, (1966) *c.* 303; sugar, raw value (1968–69) 1,505, (1967–68) 1,822; oranges (1967) *c.* 580, (1966) *c.* 510; wine (1967) 420, (1966) 425; tobacco 34 (28); wool, greasy (1967–68) 139, (1966–67) 132; meat (1967) 571, (1966) 571; milk *c.* 2,650, (*c.* 2,620); butter (1967–68) *c.* 49, (1966–67) 48; fish catch (1967) 904, (1966) 532; whaling catch (number; 1966–67) 2,692, (1965–66) 4,148; whale and sperm oil 11, (1965–66) 16. Livestock (in 000; June 1968): cattle *c.* 11,500; sheep (Aug. 1967) 35,570; horses *c.* 460; pigs *c.* 1,700; goats (Aug. 1967) *c.* 5,400; chickens (Aug. 1967) *c.* 11,500.

Industry. Index of manufacturing production (1963 = 100): (1968) 143; (1967) 138. Fuel and power (in 000; 1968): coal (metric tons) 51,650; electricity (kw-hr.) 40,948,000. Production (in 000; metric tons; 1968): iron ore (60–65% metal content) 7,220; pig iron 4,119; crude steel 4,001; copper ore (metal content) 133; cement 4,411; asbestos (1967) 244; chrome ore (oxide content; 1967) 514; antimony concentrate (metal content; 1967) 12; manganese ore (metal content; 1967) 828; gold (troy oz.) 31,116; diamonds (metric carats) 7,433. New dwelling units completed (private construction only in 18 principal urban areas; 1968) 14,200.

At various international gatherings South Africa's right to representation was challenged, and in some cases South African delegates were excluded or refused visas by the host countries. The question of permitting racially mixed sports teams to visit the country was the subject of political controversy, touched off by the proposed tour in 1970 by a New Zealand Rugby team that would include Maoris. A scheduled visit by a cricket team from the U.K. was canceled because of South African government objections to the inclusion of a Coloured player, a former South African. The visit of the South African Rugby team to the U.K. was disrupted by protests.

The Economy. Introducing the budget on March 26, the minister of finance, N. J. Diederichs, announced a shift from direct to indirect taxation. Personal income tax concessions were balanced by the imposition—for the first time in South Africa—of a sales tax on a wide range of commodities, estimated to yield R 100 million in 1969–70. Diederichs undertook to revise the tax later if it was found to operate harshly on the lower income groups. Direct taxes on companies and on marketable securities were raised, but Diederichs did not, for the time being, accept the Franszen commission's proposal for a capital gains tax.

After showing a substantial surplus in 1968, the balance of payments took a downward turn as a result of a bad agricultural season and a drop in exports. Gold sales were a major preoccupation in view of international speculation, the introduction of the two-tier gold price, and the system of Special Drawing Rights ("paper gold") that would supplement international exchange. South African negotiations to establish permanent international arrangements for the sale of gold on the free market and to the central banks were inconclusive. Unspecified quantities of gold were sold on the free market, yielding R 47 million in premiums for the gold mines to the end of September. Gold and foreign exchange assets held by the Reserve Bank reached a peak of R 1,174,000,000 in April and fell to R 914 million in October.

Credit restrictions on commercial banks to reduce liquidity were intensified, and new tax-free savings schemes were introduced. Prices of stocks, which had risen spectacularly in the first half of the year, dropped sharply during the second half. Widespread financial losses led to public agitation for the relaxation of the credit squeeze. Exchange control was eased to allow approved financial institutions, except banks, to invest in foreign exchanges. (L. H.)

See also Race Relations.

ENCYCLOPÆDIA BRITANNICA FILMS. *The Republic of South Africa* (1963).

Southeast Asia

A pervading atmosphere of instability and foreboding developed in Southeast Asia during the first half of 1969. The racial riots in Malaysia in May were perhaps the greatest single factor contributing to this. While other Southeast Asian states were analyzing the possible impact on their own peoples of the violent eruption of racial feeling in Malaysia, big-power interest in the area took on an unprecedented colour. The U.K. and the U.S. declared their intentions of progressively disengaging themselves from the region, while Soviet involvement assumed the proportions of an all-out campaign. Japan's emergence as an economic power and China's growing military might rendered the region's problems more complex.

UPI COMPIX

Malaysian Prime Minister Tunku Abdul Rahman (right) announces the formation of a new multiracial Cabinet to newsmen in Kuala Lumpur, Malaysia, on May 19, 1969. A week of racial violence between Malays and Chinese prompted the decision and the appointment of Deputy Prime Minister Tun Abdul Razak to head an emergency council to help restore order.

Relations with the U.S.S.R. and the West. The new element in Southeast Asia's politics was without doubt the U.S.S.R. Soviet efforts to strengthen relations with Southeast Asian countries were sustained and determined. The Soviet initiative for "a system of collective security for Asia," announced by Communist Party leader Leonid I. Brezhnev in June, indicated the extent of the U.S.S.R.'s newfound interest in the region. Asian governments as well as outside observers saw this interest as an offshoot of Soviet anxiety to contain China. The Chinese themselves virulently attacked the collective security idea as an example of Soviet aggression and accused several Southeast Asian governments of collusion with the U.S.S.R. But the political accusations did not seem to discourage the Soviet Union. In June, following the Brezhnev statement, Soviet ambassadors in Southeast Asia were called to Moscow for prolonged consultations.

Initially, Soviet activities in Southeast Asia seemed confined to trade. A trade fair was organized in Kuala Lumpur, Malaysia, in September. A similar show in Singapore in 1968 had made the U.S.S.R. a major supplier of such items as pharmaceuticals and cosmetics to that country. In Malaysia the U.S.S.R. bought approximately 200,000 tons of rubber annually and sold high-demand heavy machinery, such as excavators, at cut-rate prices. Going beyond trade relations the U.S.S.R. maintained a joint watch-manufacturing project with Singapore in that country. Soviet dancers and musicians were acclaimed there, and the Soviet newspaper *Izvestia* asked for permission to station a correspondent. The Tass news agency had had a man in Singapore for three years. Aeroflot inaugurated a scheduled air service to Singapore in May, and Soviet airline and tourism representatives visited Hong Kong and said they would welcome many more Asian tourists visiting the U.S.S.R. Two Soviet ships ran regular passenger services between Hong Kong and the Soviet port of Nakhodka.

The relentless campaign to build up goodwill in Southeast Asia extended to countries that the U.S.S.R. had previously abhorred; now they too were wooed with trade and culture, and seemed ready to return the compliment. The Philippine Chamber of Com-

continued on page 694

South Arabia: *see* Southern Yemen

SPECIAL REPORT

UNITED STATES FOREIGN POLICY IN EAST ASIA

By Hans J. Morgenthau

BEN ROTH AGENCY

"Waiting for the Towing Service"
—Behrendt, "Het Parool," Amsterdam.

Once the war in Vietnam has ended, the United States will have to come to terms with the basic issue from which its involvement in Vietnam arose: the U.S. interests in Asia and the policies serving them.

The United States has consistently pursued in Asia the same basic interest it has pursued in Europe: the maintenance of—or, if need be, the restoration of—the balance of power. The U.S. has started from the assumption that the dominance of any one nation in Europe or Asia would constitute a direct threat to its security in the Western Hemisphere. Thus, the United States has always opposed what appeared to be the most powerful nation on either continent and has supported the prospective victims of the latter's imperialistic designs.

The policies of the United States concerning Asia consistently served this interest. U.S. Secretary of State John Hay's "open door" policy for China was an attempt to prevent any one European or Asian nation from adding to its power the enormous power potential of China and thereby gaining a position of predominant power in Asia. Until World War II U.S. policies served the same purpose. During that war and its immediate aftermath, the United States looked to China as a counterweight against Japan. When the Communist victory in the Chinese civil war removed China as a possible ally of the United States, the U.S. embarked upon a policy of containing China; it was in implementing that policy that it overcommitted itself.

Limitations of Containment Policy. The United States thought that the policy of peripheral military containment that appeared to have worked so well against the Soviet Union in Europe would work equally well against China. However, the threat that faced Asia was different from the one that Western Europe had to deal with in the immediate aftermath of World War II. The latter threat was primarily military: that of the Soviet Army marching westward. In contrast, the risk that the Chinese armies were poised to conquer Asia was negligible. The issue China posed instead was that of political and cultural predominance. In dealing with this the U.S. could no more contain Chinese influence in Asia by arming Thailand and fighting in South Vietnam than China could contain American influence in the Western Hemisphere by arming, say, Nicaragua and fighting in Lower California. If the U.S. were convinced that it could not live with a China predominant on the mainland of Asia, then it would have to strike at the heart of Chinese power—that is, rather than try to contain the power of China by nibbling at the periphery of its empire the U.S. would have to try to destroy that power itself.

China remained largely immune to the specific types of power in which the superiority of the United States consisted—that is, nuclear, air, and naval power. Its very backwardness protected it; in order to be vulnerable to that type of power, a nation must possess large concentrations of industry and population upon which its viability depends. Certainly, the United States had the power to destroy the nuclear installations and the major industrial and population centres of China, but this destruction would not defeat China in its present backward state; it would only set back its development. To be defeated, China would have to be conquered.

Physical conquest would require the deployment of millions of U.S. soldiers on the mainland of Asia. No American military leader ever advocated a course of action so fraught with incalculable risks, so uncertain of outcome, requiring sacrifices so out of proportion to the interests at stake and the benefits to be expected. U.S. Pres. Dwight Eisenhower declared on Feb. 10, 1954, that he could "conceive of no greater tragedy than for the United States to become involved in an all-out war in Indochina." Gen. Douglas MacArthur, in the U.S. congressional hearings concerning his dismissal and in personal conversation with Pres. John F. Kennedy, emphatically warned against sending American foot soldiers to the Asian mainland to fight China.

If the United States did not want to set itself goals that could not be attained with the means it was willing to employ, it had to learn to accommodate itself to the political and cultural predominance of China on the Asian mainland. It was instructive to note that those Asian nations that had done just that, such as Burma and Cambodia, lived in relative peace in the shadow of the Chinese giant. On the other hand, those Asian nations that allowed themselves to be transformed into outposts of U.S. military power, such as Laos, South Vietnam, and Thailand, became the actual or prospective victims of Communist aggression and subversion. Thus, in the case of China it appeared that peripheral military containment was counterproductive. Challenged at its periphery by U.S. military power at its weakest—that is, by the proxy of such client states as Thailand—China or its proxies could respond with locally superior military and political power.

Even if the Chinese threat were primarily of a military nature, peripheral military containment would be ineffective in the long run in view of China's local military superiority. By believing otherwise, the United States fell heir to a misconception of its containment of the Soviet Union and of the reasons for its success. The Soviet Union was not contained by the armed forces that the United States was able to put in the field locally in Europe. Instead, it was contained by the near certainty that an attack upon those forces would be countered by nuclear retaliation from the U.S. If one were to assume that the Chinese armies stand, or one day would stand, poised to sweep over Asia, they, in turn, would not be contained by the armed forces that the United States or its allies could put into the field on the mainland of Asia. They would only be deterred by the near certainty that China would be destroyed through nuclear retaliation.

A Policy of Disengagement and Its Exceptions. Thus, the United States was overcommitted insofar as it had committed its military power on the mainland of Asia for the purpose of containing China at the periphery of its empire. It could correct this error by returning to the policy that Secretary of State Dean

BEN ROTH AGENCY

"Prospective New Fathers"—Wetzel.

Acheson formulated in his speech to the National Press Club on Jan. 12, 1950, and that it pursued before the outbreak of the Korean War: to limit its military commitments to the local defense of the island chain from Japan to the Philippines, supported by its retaliatory nuclear power.

The U.S. policy of disengagement from exposed military positions on the mainland of Asia was for the time being likely to suffer only two exceptions: South Korea and South Vietnam. The U.S. commitment to the defense of South Korea was predicated on the continuing threat from North Korea and the inability of South Korea to defend itself against that threat without the physical presence of U.S. troops. Once that threat had abated or that deficiency had been remedied, the armed forces of the United States would have no reason to continue their presence in South Korea.

As of 1969, the conditions of the future U.S. military presence in South Vietnam were less clearly defined. At one end of the spectrum, there was the possibility that the war might go on indefinitely and that, in view of the continuing inability of the government of South Vietnam to keep itself in power without a massive U.S. military presence, U.S. armed forces would be indefinitely involved, although probably on a reduced scale. At the other end of the spectrum, there was a possibility that the war would end and the fundamental issue over which the war had been fought—who should govern South Vietnam?—would be decided one way or another in the foreseeable future. The U.S. military presence in South Vietnam would then come to an end. Between those two extremes of the U.S. acting as a belligerent and of no military involvement whatsoever, one could visualize a number of intermediate situations that might require the continuation of a U.S. military presence. They might include logistic support and reconnaissance on behalf of the South Vietnamese government, advisers to that regime, or a guarantee of the Vietnam peace settlement.

However, even if the U.S. were to disengage its military forces completely from the mainland of Asia, it would still have to deal with the basic issue that for two decades has pitted the United States against China: the Nationalist Chinese regime in Taiwan. After his defeat by the Communists in the Chinese civil war, Chiang Kai-shek fled to Taiwan, which he and his Nationalist forces have ruled since that time. The government of mainland China has been prevented from extending its control to the island nation by the United States 7th Fleet, which patrols the Straits of Taiwan. However, both Mao Tse-tung and Chiang Kai-shek consider Taiwan to be an integral part of China. Regardless of its ideological commitment, no patriotic government of China could be expected to give up this claim, and any Chinese government that believed it had the power to recover Taiwan would try to do so. The issue of Taiwan indeed proved the main stumbling block in the Geneva and Warsaw negotiations between the U.S. and China, and it seemed bound to do so in the future. That it had not yet become a battleground was due to China's perhaps only temporary military weakness. If and when China realizes its military potential through the acquisition of the modern technologies of transportation, communications, and weaponry, the issue of the future of Taiwan, if it has not been settled in the meantime, will be the most likely cause of hostilities between the United States and China.

Limits of U.S. Control. While the issues thus far discussed were in considerable measure subject to U.S. control, there were three others that might be influenced by U.S. policy but could not be controlled by it: the power potential of China, the actuality of Japanese power, and the possibility of a Sino-Soviet war.

If and when China should become a highly developed modern nation, in full possession of the technologies of communications, transportation, and warfare, it would then be the most powerful nation on earth. To what purpose would it put that power? If one assumes China's superiority over all other nations, then its traditional ethnocentrism combined with the ability to destroy the world with nuclear weapons might well call forth utterly irrational policies that could indeed result in the destruction of the civilized world. On the other hand, while Chinese statesmen frequently have indulged in extremely irrational rhetoric, they have pursued their actual foreign policies with great caution, limiting their territorial aims to the traditional objects of China's national aspirations, such as Taiwan, Tibet, and the rectification of the frontier with India. They also have seemed fully aware of the actual distribution of power and, more particularly, of China's military weakness.

Thus, there is the hope that if and when China reaches those heights of power, it will be as aware as the United States and the Soviet Union that nuclear weapons are not instruments of rational foreign policies but are instead means of genocide and suicide. The relations between the United States and China would then be carried on by conventional means under the nuclear umbrella of mutual deterrence.

Japan's attitude toward the United States was ambivalent. On the one hand, it found U.S. responsibility for its defense most convenient: the U.S. bore all the political, military, and financial burdens, and Japan enjoyed the military and economic advantages. On the other hand, that arrangement was a continuous and visible insult to Japanese pride and could expose Japan to serious military risks, unwarranted by Japanese national interests, since it transformed Japan into a staging area for far-flung U.S. military operations.

United States policy must adapt itself to this Japanese ambivalence in three different ways. It must continue to shoulder the main burden of Japan's defense, for by doing so it is able to control to a marked degree the foreign policies of Japan. It must stop urging a reluctant Japan to increase its military expenditures, for a newly armed Japan might well strike out again on its own without regard for the interests of the U.S. Finally, the U.S. must make a concerted effort to cater to the national sensibilities of Japan.

In 1969 those sensibilities were focused on the status of Okinawa. Bowing to the inevitable, the United States agreed to return the island to Japan by 1972, although the exact conditions remained to be spelled out. Japan wished to change the status of the United States bases there to that of the U.S. bases on other Japanese islands.

A war between China and the Soviet Union would strengthen one or the other belligerent, according to who would win, or it would end in a stalemate likely to weaken both. Thus, since such a war would in one way or another affect the distribution of power in Asia, it would also affect the interests of the United States. But it would not necessarily require drastic changes in U.S. foreign policies. For regardless of the outcome of such a war, the U.S. would still have to try to maintain the balance of power in Asia by offsetting the power of whoever would be predominant on the mainland of Asia with its own power, based on Japan and the island chain off the coast of Asia.

continued from page 691

merce sent its top men on a tour of the U.S.S.R. and Eastern Europe, and a Soviet trade team later returned the visit. Government leaders in the Philippines began talking in terms of establishing diplomatic links with Communist countries. Thailand also sent a trade delegation to the Soviet Union. The results of these high-level visits were not immediately apparent in trade figures, but the local impression was that the U.S.S.R. was willing and able to increase its trade with Southeast Asian countries substantially, thereby helping their economic growth.

Cautious contacts were made between the U.S.S.R. and the anti-Communist administration of post-Sukarno Indonesia. In August a Soviet economic mission visited Jakarta to discuss possible rescheduling of Indonesia's $696.6 million debt to the U.S.S.R. The U.S.S.R. first took the stand that Indonesia should start repayment immediately. The deadlock that followed was broken by a decision to continue the talks in Moscow. Observers commented that the progress made by Western investors in Indonesia had disturbed the U.S.S.R., which was therefore trying to drive a hard bargain. During the talks in Jakarta, however, it became clear that both countries were interested in resuming economic relations.

Growing Soviet influence in Southeast Asia caused some concern in Australia, though other developed countries, including Japan, seemed to take it in their stride. There were reports that Soviet naval activity in the Indian Ocean had prompted Australian defense planners to give top priority to proposals for a powerful new naval base in Cockburn Sound, Western Australia, and that Australia was discussing with the U.S. its possible participation in the project. External Affairs Minister Gordon Freeth won Soviet approval—and much criticism at home—when he said it was natural for a world power like the U.S.S.R. to seek to promote its influence in such an important area as the Indian Ocean. Defense Minister Allen Fairhall was among those who attacked this line, warning that the U.S.S.R. was out to fill the power vacuum in the Indian Ocean created by Britain's decision to pull out its troops from Asia by 1971.

In Southeast Asia there was considerable talk about the power vacuum and the need for Asian countries to fill it. But during Indian Prime Minister Indira Gandhi's visit to Jakarta, Indon., in July, she

U.S. Pres. and Mrs. Richard Nixon wearing native formal dress join Philippine Pres. Marcos and his wife at a state dinner in Malacanang Palace, Manila, on July 26, 1969.

WIDE WORLD

UPI COMPIX

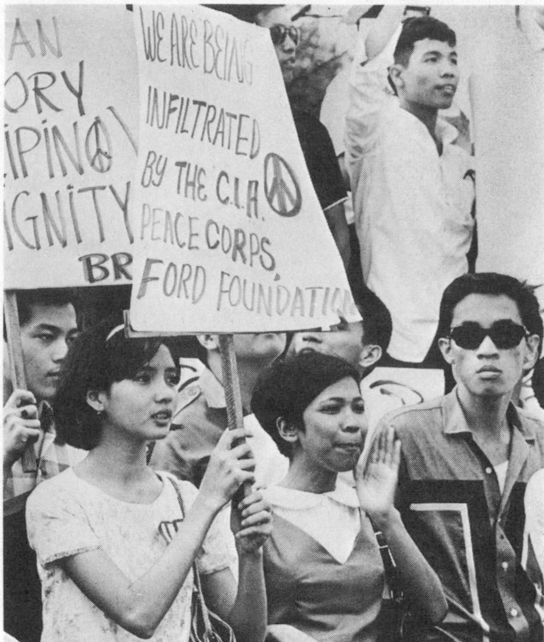

Philippine students protest against alleged U.S. control of the islands outside Congress on Jan. 27, 1969. Pres. Ferdinand Marcos was delivering a speech to Congress at the time.

was unenthusiastic about the Indonesian suggestion that as a first step naval units of non-Asian powers be denied berthing and fueling facilities in Asian ports. Some Singapore newspapers reported that, possibly by 1970, the Soviet Navy would begin goodwill visits to Singapore and Malaysia. Singapore was already a major point on Soviet merchant shipping schedules.

The U.K. repeatedly pointed out that its planned military withdrawal from the area would not mean desertion. British political and military spokesmen stressed that Britain would continue to work closely with Australian and New Zealand forces through joint exercises in Southeast Asia. However, an uncertain element was introduced by the British Conservative Party's claim that, if returned to power, it would continue to maintain a British presence in the region. Pointing to Britain's heavy economic stake in the area, former Prime Minister Sir Alec Douglas-Home estimated that the U.K.'s balance of payments derived annual benefits worth about £300 million from Southeast Asia and that the total value of British investments in the region was about £1,115,000,000.

The five-power Commonwealth Conference on Far East Defense in Canberra, Austr., June 19–20, was expected to work out the problems of Southeast Asian defense in the light of the developing situation. But it turned into a sour diplomatic confrontation, largely because of the Malaysian riots and the fears they generated in other countries. The conference found the U.K., Australia, and New Zealand, as well as Malaysia and Singapore, holding separate press conferences to explain why they could not make bigger contributions to regional defense. Australia was clearly anxious to keep its troops out of any possible Malaysian entanglement with the Philippines over Sabah or with Singapore over race relations.

Weary of the Vietnam war and of entanglement with Asia in general, the U.S. administration decided on a policy of disengagement and of encouraging "Asian solutions to Asian problems." At the same time it felt the need to reassure Southeast Asian countries that it was not abandoning the area or going back on its commitments. Pres. Richard M. Nixon made a personal tour of five Asian countries in July to explain his policy. At Guam at the start of his tour he said he would look to America's Asian allies to do more for themselves militarily in the future so that dependence on the U.S. should not lead to new Vietnams. In Manila he said that the U.S. would remain a Pacific power and offer assistance and cooperation to its Asian allies. He declared in Jakarta that the U.S. would not try to change Indonesia's nonaligned policy. In Bangkok he said "the U.S. will stand proudly with Thailand against those who might threaten it from abroad or from within," while in India and Pakistan he repeated that it was his desire not to thrust U.S. concepts on Asian countries. Nixon made it clear during his tour that the general policy for the region would be to let Asians manage their own affairs while maintaining a U.S. presence in some carefully located bases.

Southeast Asia Treaty Organization (SEATO). Though Nixon predictably pledged continuing U.S. support to SEATO, this kingpin of previous Western security arrangements for the region continued to decline. At its 14th Ministerial Council meeting held at Bangkok in May, delegates made the customary declaration that covert and overt Communist aggression remained a major threat in Southeast Asia, expressing determination that this aggression must not be allowed to succeed. The meeting reaffirmed the importance of the organization as a deterrent to Communist aggression and as a source of support to member nations encountering Communist subversion. All this sounded rather irrelevant, however, against the background of diminishing interest among member countries. For example, Pakistan's delegate wanted it to be recorded that he did not participate in the drafting of the council's communiqué and that what the council said did not necessarily reflect his government's position. France had withdrawn from the meeting in order to "remain neutral in the Vietnam war."

Ironically, the naval exercise SEATO organized in June turned out to be anything but the morale booster it was intended to be. During the exercise the U.S. destroyer "Frank E. Evans" collided with the Australian aircraft carrier "Melbourne" and was cut in two. More than 70 U.S. sailors died, and the exercise was called off.

Regional Organizations. The nonmilitary regional organizations also came in for a good deal of criticism, while managing to survive, if not to flourish. The most ambitious and potentially the most important of the groupings was the Association of Southeast Asian Nations (ASEAN), comprising the Philippines, Indonesia, Singapore, Malaysia, and Thailand. It took some serious knocks in quick succession—the dispute between Malaysia and the Philippines over Sabah, the quarrel between Singapore and Indonesia over Singapore's execution of two Indonesian Marines on terrorist charges, and the bitterness that grew between Malaysia and Singapore following the racial disturbances beginning in May. With each crisis the organization seemed about to go under, but apparently government leaders were eager to avert a total collapse. Thailand's foreign minister Thanat Khoman summed up the situation when he said in August that although it took ten years to lay the groundwork for ASEAN, its formation in 1967 had not made it any easier for member countries to cooperate with each other. He said that while the quarrels among members were a serious obstacle to development, Communist circles were out to make ASEAN appear like a military grouping because the organization stood in the way of their influence spreading in the region.

WIDE WORLD

Leftist students demanding the return of Okinawa to Japanese rule clash with riot police in Tokyo, April 28, 1969.

This was evidently a reference to the U.S.S.R.'s surprising faux pas at the 25th session of the UN Economic Commission for Asia and the Far East (ECAFE) in April; objecting to an ECAFE secretariat suggestion to study economic cooperation and development in the ASEAN area, the Soviet representative had called ASEAN a military alliance. This false note on a sensitive point seemed inexplicable in view of the Soviet effort in the region. ASEAN countries took strong objection to the Soviet stand and asked Moscow to leave ASEAN alone. Toward the end of the ECAFE session, the Soviet delegate said ASEAN projects could be economic and cultural and that the U.S.S.R. would change its attitude if convinced that ASEAN was not military.

Making some attempts to push its hopes for economic cooperation, ASEAN organized a meeting of the heads of its national secretariats in May. The meeting announced plans to set up a series of permanent committees: for food in Jakarta, for air traffic services and meteorology in Kuala Lumpur; for civil aviation in Singapore; for shipping in Bangkok; and for commerce and industry in Manila. At the secretariat level the committees were expected to make some headway, but there were few illusions that real progress could take place in the absence of understanding and cooperation among the members at the political level.

ECAFE itself received a barrage of criticism from some Southeast Asian countries, but its programs maintained their usual pace. At the 25th session in Singapore, Indonesia wanted ECAFE to work for the harmonization of tourism development plans in Malaysia, the Philippines, Thailand, and Indonesia. The Philippines called for an overhaul of ECAFE and for a committee to review the present and assess the future of the organization, suggesting that subregional groupings like ASEAN and the Ministerial Conference for Economic Development of Southeast Asia gave the impression that ECAFE was too thinly spread out to give effective leadership. (T. J. S. G.)

See also articles on the various political units.

ENCYCLOPÆDIA BRITANNICA FILMS. *Burma, People of the River* (1957); *Malaya, Land of Tin and Rubber* (1957); *Thailand, Land of Rice* (1957); *Indonesia—New Nation of Asia* (1959); *The Philippines: Land and People* (1960).

Southern Rhodesia: *see* Rhodesia

Southern Yemen

A people's republic in the southern coastal region of the Arabian Peninsula, Southern Yemen is bordered by Yemen, Saudi Arabia, and Muscat and Oman. Area: 121,000 sq.mi. (290,000 sq.km.). Pop. (1968 est.): 1,369,500. Cap. and largest city: Aden (pop., 1968 est., 300,000); administrative cap.: Madinat ash Sha'b. Language: Arabic. Religion: Islâm. President in 1969, Qahtan Muhammad al-Shaabi to June 22; chairman of the Presidential Council from June 22, Salem Ali Rubayyi; prime ministers, Qahtan Muhammad al-Shaabi, Faisal Abdul Latif al-Shaabi from April 6, and, from June 24, Muhammad Ali Haitham.

In 1969 Southern Yemen continued to suffer acute economic difficulties owing to the continued closure of the Suez Canal and the general decline of Aden. In February, Faisal Abdul Latif al-Shaabi was appointed foreign minister, and on April 6, after a meeting of the National Liberation Front General Command, he became prime minister as well. In June Pres. Qahtan al-Shaabi visited Damascus but shortly after his return, on June 22, he resigned and was replaced by a five-man Presidential Council headed by Salem Ali Rubayyi. Another member was Muhammad Ali Haitham who had recently been dismissed from the post of minister of the interior by former President al-Shaabi. Haitham was named prime minister in the new government. These changes indicated a further move to the left.

In foreign policy the government pursued a left-wing revolutionary line. In January Soviet warships paid a goodwill visit to Aden, and during the following month President al-Shaabi made an 11-day visit to the U.S.S.R. Relations with Yemen deteriorated sharply, with Southern Yemen accusing the Yemeni republican government of aiding Southern Yemeni dissidents. Late in the year fighting was reported on the Southern Yemen-Saudi Arabian border.

On March 5 President al-Shaabi accused Britain of continuing to violate Southern Yemeni airspace. In October the government broke off diplomatic relations with the U.S., alleging the latter's continued favouritism for Israel against the Arabs. (P. MD.)

SOUTHERN YEMEN

Education. (1967–68) Primary, pupils 50,101, teachers 1,440; secondary, pupils 16,113, teachers 795; vocational (1966–67), pupils 445, teachers 29; teacher training, students 363, teachers 43.

Finance and Trade. Monetary unit: South Arabian dinar, at par with the pound sterling (1 dinar = U.S. $2.40). Budgets (former Aden and Federated States; 1967–68 est.): revenue 31,790,352 dinars; expenditure 33,034,847 dinars (revenue included British aid of 22,872,176 dinars; this ceased in May 1968). Foreign trade (1967): imports 72.2 million dinars; exports 50.5 million dinars. Import sources: Kuwait 16%; Japan 13%; Iran 12%; U.K. 9%. Export destinations: U.K. 16%; South Africa 7%; Australia 6%; Yemen 5%. Main export: petroleum products 62%.

Transport. Roads (1967) *c.* 4,500 km. (including 225 km. in Aden). Motor vehicles in use (1967): passenger 13,600; commercial (including buses) 3,200. There are no railways. Ships entered (1966) vessels totaling 28,844,000 net registered tons; goods loaded (1966) 4,202,000 metric tons, unloaded 8,669,000 metric tons.

Agriculture and Industry. Production (in 000; metric tons): millet and sorghum (1967) *c.* 35, (1966) 30; cotton, lint (1967) 5, (1966) 4; dates (1967) *c.* 8, (1966) 8; salt (1967) 72; petroleum products (1967) 5,254.

South West Africa: *see* Dependent States; South Africa

Sovereigns: *see* Heads of State

Soviet Literature: *see* Literature

Soviet Union: *see* Union of Soviet Socialist Republics

Soybeans: *see* Agriculture

Spacecraft: *see* Astronautics

Space Exploration: *see* Astronautics

Spanish-American Literature: *see* Literature

Spanish Literature: *see* Literature

Spanish Overseas Territories: *see* Dependent States

Speedway: *see* Sporting Record

Spain

A nominal monarchy of southwest Europe, Spain is bounded by Portugal, with which it shares the Iberian Peninsula, and by France. Area: 194,884 sq.mi. (504,750 sq.km.), including the Balearic and Canary islands. Pop. (1969 est.): 32,685,061, including the Balearics and Canaries. Cap. and largest city: Madrid (pop., 1969 est., 3,241,054). Language: Spanish. Religion: Roman Catholic. Prince of Spain, Don Juan Carlos de Borbón y Borbón; chief of state and premier in 1969, Gen. Francisco Franco Bahamonde.

Political developments were dramatic in 1969. On January 24 the government reinstated press censorship and imposed a three-month "state of exception" throughout the country (part of the Basque region, where considerable unrest continued, had been under a "state of exception" since the previous August). With five articles of Spain's Bill of Rights suspended for three months, the police had powers to carry out house searches without warrants and to detain suspects indefinitely without trial. Hundreds of arrests followed, and many university teachers and prominent people were exiled to remote villages.

The official explanation that the state of emergency had been made necessary by the militant attitude of

A member of an underground Basque youth movement carries burning effigy of Franco through Spanish village street in demonstration for Biscayan independence. Marcher's face was blotted out by photographer.

CAMERA PRESS—PIX FROM PUBLIX

students was considered by many as merely a pretext to silence mounting criticism from journalists, teachers, businessmen, and lawyers. Whatever the reasons, it soon became clear that insufficient attention had been paid to the economic consequences of reverting to hard-line politics, at a time when the economy was highly dependent on foreign investment and tourism. On March 25, a month early, both the "state of exception" and press censorship were lifted as suddenly as they had been introduced and, in addition, a general amnesty for all acts committed during the Civil War was declared to mark the 30th anniversary of its conclusion.

In line with the basic legislation to institutionalize the regime, gradually implemented over the previous three years, Franco took a new step in July that aroused more comment abroad than in Spain. The Cortes was convened to a plenary session and a law was passed proclaiming Don Juan Carlos de Borbón y Borbón (*see* BIOGRAPHY) as prince of Spain, to become king when the present office of head of state was vacated by Franco. On the following day the future king was sworn to adhere to the principles of the National Movement, in the expectation that he would provide the necessary continuity for the regime's basic institutions. Although the 31-year-old prince had previously protested that his father, the pretender Don Juan, had first claim to the crown, earlier in the year he had made it known that he now accepted the principles of the new succession law, bypassing under art. 9 ("anyone of royal lineage and over 30 years of age may be chosen") the principle of dynastic rights. Apart from embittering family relations, this incident did nothing to endear the prince to the Spanish people, who greeted his proclamation with marked apathy.

Public reaction to press disclosures in August of what was probably the most serious fraud ever recorded in Spain was far from apathetic, however. Maquinaria Textil del Norte de Espãna S.A. (MATESA), a textile-machine manufacturing company, had been so successful in the export field that the company had been granted official credits and tax refunds equivalent to $143 million. Textile machinery was, in fact, exported not to foreign buyers, but to the company's subsidiaries abroad, where much of the machinery remained in stock while the funds were used by MATESA to buy shares in foreign companies. How this was accomplished without arousing the suspicions of the official credit institutions remained unexplained. Six executives of MATESA were jailed, a senior official resigned, and the press took the unprecedented step of demanding Cabinet resignations.

If the material damage was substantial, the harm in terms of loss of confidence was immeasurable, especially at a time when the business community needed assistance from the government to increase exports. Reluctant though Franco was to yield to pressures, he had no choice but to dissociate himself from a team responsible for the peseta devaluation of 1967, the economic recession of the two preceding years, and, in international affairs, the difficulties involved in the negotiations about U.S. military bases in Spain and the failure to make headway on the Gibraltar question. In addition, yet another African possession was lost through the cession of Ifni to Morocco in June. On October 29, Franco dismissed all but 4 of the 18 Cabinet members in the most comprehensive reshuffle of his more than three decades of rule. To what extent these changes would restore confidence remained a matter for speculation.

One of the most pressing problems facing the new administration was the need to relieve pressure on Spain's balance of payments. Assisted by the marked buoyancy of world trade, satisfactory agricultural yields, and a high level of public investment, the Spanish economy showed considerable gains from the second half of 1968. National income in 1968 rose by 4.4% in real terms, while the stable cost of living was partly accounted for by a freeze on prices and wages, prolonged until the end of 1969. The rate of economic growth was expected to be greater in 1969, and the increase in the cost of living marginally higher.

Foreign trade was the main beneficiary of the peseta devaluation in November 1967: exports rose in 1968 by 14.8% to $1,589,000,000, while imports increased only 1.1% to $3,522,000,000, reflecting the slackness of the economy in the first half of that year. The export trend was maintained and even increased in 1969, but imports rose again and statistics for the first three quarters pointed to a probable deficit some $230 million larger than in 1968. (M. PU.)

ENCYCLOPÆDIA BRITANNICA FILMS. *People of Spain* (1955); *Spanish Children* (1964).

LIAISON

Don Juan Carlos, proclaimed prince of Spain in July 1969, was to become king when General Franco ceased to be chief of state.

SPAIN

Education. (1965–66) Primary, pupils 3,357,-813, teachers (1964–65) 107,627; secondary, pupils 834,290, teachers (1964–65) 25,725; vocational: pupils 311,614, teachers 22,415; teacher training, students 63,116, teachers 2,429; higher (including 16 universities), students 131,766, teaching staff 7,820.

Finance. Monetary unit: peseta, with a par value of 70 pesetas to U.S. $1 (168 pesetas = £1 sterling). Gold and convertible currencies, official: (June 1969) U.S. $915 million; (June 1968) U.S. $958 million. Budget (1968–69) balanced at 224 billion pesetas. Gross national product: (1967) 1,616,000,000,000 pesetas; (1966) 1,477,000,-000,000 pesetas. Money supply: (May 1969) 624.3 billion pesetas; (May 1968) 546.6 billion pesetas. Cost of living (1963 = 100): (June 1969) 145; (June 1968) 144.

Foreign Trade. (1968) Imports 244.8 billion pesetas; exports 111.2 billion pesetas. Import sources: EEC 34% (West Germany 13%, France 10%, Italy 6%); U.S. 17%; U.K. 8%; Saudi Arabia 5%. Export destinations: EEC 29% (West Germany 10%, France 9%, Netherlands 5%); U.S. 18%; U.K. 10%. Main exports: fruit 13% (citrus 7%); machinery 9%; vegetables 8%; petroleum products 8%; chemicals 6%. Tourism (1967): visitors 16,399,100; receipts U.S. $1,120,000,000.

Transport and Communications. Roads (1967) 140,220 km. (including 220 km. expressways). Motor vehicles in use (1967): passenger 1,301,900; commercial 561,900. Railways: (1967) 17,361 km. (including 3,835 km. electrified); traffic (state system only; 1968) 11,836,-000,000 passenger-km., freight 8,230,000,000 net ton-km. Air traffic (1968): 3,880,000,000 passenger-km.; freight 77,260,000 net ton-km. Shipping (1968): merchant vessels 100 gross tons and over 2,046; gross tonnage 2,820,784. Telephones (Dec. 1967) 3,359,029. Radio receivers (Dec. 1967) 7,150,000. Television receivers (Dec. 1967) 2,685,000.

Agriculture. Production (in 000; metric tons; 1968; 1967 in parentheses): wheat 5,480 (5,-654); barley 3,441 (2,567); oats 539 (492); rye 364 (336); corn 1,473 (1,195); potatoes 4,570 (4,508); rice 363 (366); chick-peas (1967) 149, (1966) 127; lentils 32 (40); dry broad beans 124 (130); other dry beans *c.* 113 (121); tomatoes (1967) 1,390, (1966) 1,323; apples 428 (320); pears 218 (110); oranges 1,815 (2,031); lemons 82 (113); sugar, raw value (1968–69) *c.* 680, (1967–68) 582; olive oil 420 (269); wine 2,468 (2,344); onions (1967) 843, (1966) 819; bananas (1967) 410, (1966) 350; dates (1967) *c.* 20, (1966) *c.* 20; figs (1967) 149, (1966) 133; tobacco 30 (31); cotton, lint 61 (65); meat (1967) 801, (1966) 698; fish catch (1967) 1,-431, (1966) 1,363. Livestock (in 000; 1967–68): cattle 4,000; horses 316; mules 686; asses 458; pigs 5,662; sheep 18,642; goats (1966–67) 2,-649; chickens (Sept. 1967) 44,991.

Industry. Index of industrial production (1963 = 100): (1968) 153; (1967) 146. Fuel and power (in 000; metric tons; 1968): coal 12,-283; lignite 2,809; electricity (kw-hr.) 45,180,-000; manufactured gas (cu.m.) 632,000. Production (in 000; metric tons; 1968): iron ore (50% metal content) 6,186; pig iron 2,968; crude steel 4,939; manganese ore (metal content; 1967) 3; zinc 75; copper 79; lead 64; cement 14,650; potash (oxide content; 1967) 550; sulfur (1967) 1,130; cotton yarn 85; cotton fabrics 83; wool yarn 33; rayon filament yarn 17; rayon staple fibre 30; nylon filament yarn 20; nylon fibre 19. Merchant vessels launched (100 gross tons and over; 1968) 505,000 gross tons.

Speleology

New exploration in the Flint Ridge cave system in Kentucky brought its length to 72.7 mi. The second longest cave in the world was still the Hölloch (Switzerland), where the winter expedition of 1968–69 extended its known length to 64.6 mi. In Cuba discoveries in the Sistema de Cuyaguateja made it the fourth longest in the world at 32.75 mi. Further explorations in Jewel Cave (South Dakota) brought its total mapped length to over 30 mi. and it thus became the fifth longest. Blue Spring Cave, Indiana, with 18.9 mi. mapped, was the longest in the state and the ninth longest in the world.

The world's deepest cave was still the Gouffre de la Pierre Saint-Martin on the Franco-Spanish border, where a descent late in 1968 reached the new record of 3,872 ft. A combined French, British, Belgian, Spanish, and Italian team continued exploration elsewhere in the system during 1969. Gouffre Berger, the next deepest, remained at 3,755 ft. In May, Italian explorers reached 2,648 ft. in the Grotta di Montecucco, near Perugia, and it thus became the fifth deepest cave in the world. In August a British expedition discovered a completely new series of passages in another part of the cave. There were two British expeditions to the 2,642-ft.-deep Antro della Corchia in Italy; they explored farther in the mile-long gallery they had discovered the year before and also found other passages. The Cueva de Río Iglesia was surpassed by the Sotano del San Agustín (also in Mexico) as the deepest cave in the Western Hemisphere at 2,008 ft. Anna Taparkova of Bulgaria was the first woman to achieve 3,681 ft. when she reached the sump in the Gouffre Berger.

The deepest sheer drop in a single pitch remained the 1,298 ft. of the Proventina entrance shaft in Greece, but the next deepest was found in Le Pot II in the Vercors (France), where the 1,106-ft.-pitch was first explored in the second half of 1968 by a 15-year-old boy, Jean-Marie Burlet (compare the height of the Eiffel Tower: 1,052 ft. with its TV antennae). The new record for the United States was in Ellison's Cave (Georgia), which contains one free-fall drop, deep in the cave, of 510 ft. and another of 440 ft.

A 300-ft.-long underwater sump was passed in the Koppenbrullerhöhle (Austria), leading to new passages. J. Eyre and a British team explored the Epos Chasm (Greece) to the final lake at a depth of 1,500 ft.; 1,340 ft. of the descent was made by rope ladder. Other British expeditions went to Romania, Spain, and North Africa. Papoose Cave (Idaho) was still being surveyed; measurements reached a depth of 690 ft. out of what was expected to be about 900 ft. An expedition from the University of Papua and New Guinea studied the caves of Vakuta, one of the Trobriand Islands.

Philippe Englender climbs out of Ollivier Cave near Nice, France, on Jan. 15, 1969. He and another speleologist, Jacques Chabert, had remained in the cave for a voluntary five-month experiment to study biological and psychological reactions by humans subjected to a timeless environment in which days were not measured and work, sleep, and recreation were not regulated.

A.F.P. FROM PICTORIAL PARADE

In January two Frenchmen, Jacques Chabert and Philippe Englender, returned to the surface after spending nearly five months (separately) in the Ollivier Cave near Nice. Away from all normal restraints of time, they woke and slept in "days" lasting 48 hours, and during each period they slept for only 12 hours—results that were of direct application to space travel.

Frits Went of Nevada University showed that the stalactites of Lehman Caves all had a thread-like fungus at the tip, which he believed acted as a nucleus for crystallization and ensured that the stalactite would grow straight downward. In New Zealand the effect of earthquake movements on dripstone formations was studied.

Using an electronic detector, John Hooper continued his researches into the recognition of individual cave bat species from the pattern of ultrasounds they emit. Converted electronically to audible sounds, these patterns can be identified in the same way as birdsongs, and this is particularly useful when the bats are flying in darkness. British cave-dwelling greater horseshoe bats were shown to live to an age of at least 19¼ years. Zoologists from nine European countries attended a colloquium on the study of the cavern-dwelling crustacean *Niphargus*. The cave fungus that causes the lung disease histoplasmosis was found in Europe for the first time, in bat guano in the Topolnita Cave (Romania); previously it had been known only in America and Africa.

Control of the fungus that had been attacking the Paleolithic paintings in Lascaux Cave progressed, and the French government allowed ten visitors a day to enter the cave. Important Paleolithic wall paintings were discovered in a cave near Ribadesella on the coast of northern Spain; others were found in the Ojoguarena Cave in Burgos province. The prehistoric human occupation of Salts Cave in Kentucky was studied by a National Geographic Society expedition, and human footprints of about 2,400 years ago were found.

Caves continued to be threatened by quarrying. In New South Wales a determined attempt was being made to protect those in the Colong Caves Reserve.

The year marked the 50th jubilee of the University of Bristol Spelaeological Society. Formed in March 1919 with a nucleus of members from the former Bristol Spelaeological Research Society, it had long been one of the more eminent exploration and research groups in Britain. Another anniversary was the centenary of the birth of H. E. Balch, for many years the doyen of speleologists in Mendip (England).

The *Manual of Caving Techniques*, published during the year by the Cave Research Group of Great Britain, was the most comprehensive book on its subject and became the standard work. The history of cave research was the subject of serious study; the *Journal of Spelean History* completed its second year of publication in the United States. (T. R. Sh.)

Sporting Record

ARCHERY

Event	Winner	Country
WORLD CHAMPIONS—TARGET		
Men's individual	H. Ward	U.S.
Men's team		U.S.
Women's individual	D. Lidstone	Canada
Women's team		U.S.S.R.
WORLD CHAMPIONS—FIELD		
Men	R. Branstetter	U.S.
Women	E. Danielssen	Sweden

BADMINTON

Event	Winner	Country
ASIAN CHAMPIONS		
Men's singles	Muljadi	Indonesia
Men's doubles	P. Gunalan, Ng Boon Bee	Malaysia
Women's singles	Pang Yuet Mui	Hong Kong
EUROPEAN JUNIOR CHAMPIONS		
Men's singles	F. Delfs	Denmark
Men's doubles	K. Arthur, R. Stevens	U.K.
Women's singles	A. Berglund	Denmark
Women's doubles	J. van Bessekom, M. Luesken	Netherlands
DUTCH OPEN CHAMPIONS		
Men's singles	Oon Chong Hau	Malaysia
Women's singles	G. Perrin	U.K.
ALL-ENGLAND CHAMPIONS		
Men's singles	R. Hartono	Indonesia
Men's doubles	H. Borch, E. Kops	Denmark
Women's singles	H. Yuki	Japan
Women's doubles	M. Boxall, S. Whetnall	U.K.
Mixed doubles	R. Mills, G. Perrin	U.K.
U.S. CHAMPIONS		
Men's singles	R. Hartono	Indonesia
Men's doubles	Ng Boon Bee, P. Gunalan	Malaysia
Women's singles	M. Minarni	Indonesia
Women's doubles	M. Minarni, R. Koestijah	Indonesia
Mixed doubles	E. Kops, P. Moelgaard-Hansen	Denmark
SWEDISH OPEN CHAMPIONS		
Men's singles	S. Andersen	Denmark
Men's doubles	S. Andersen, E. Kops	Denmark
Women's singles	G. Perrin	U.K.
Women's doubles	M. Boxall, S. Whetnall	U.K.
Mixed doubles	R. Mills, G. Perrin	U.K.
WEST GERMAN OPEN CHAMPIONS		
Men's singles	S. Andersen	Denmark
Men's doubles	J. Mortensen, H. Borch	Denmark
Women's singles	A. Flindt	Denmark
Women's doubles	A. Flindt, P. Moelgaard-Hansen	Denmark
Mixed doubles	A. Jordan, S. Whetnall	U.K.
UBER CUP (world team championship, women)		Japan

BIATHLON

Event	Winner	Country
WORLD CHAMPIONS		
Individual	A. Tikhonov	U.S.S.R.
Relay	A. Tikhonov, V. Mamatov, V. Gundartsev, R. Sofian	U.S.S.R.

BILLIARDS AND SNOOKER

Event	Winner	Country
BILLIARDS		
World professional championship	L. Dielis	Belgium
World 3-cushion championship	R. Ceulemans	Belgium
World 47/1 championship	T. Schrauwen	Belgium
European professional championship	H. Scholte	Netherlands
European 47/1 championship	D. Müller	West Germany
European 71/2 championship	J. Marty	France
World amateur championship	J. Karnehm	U.K.
SNOOKER		
World professional championship	J. Spencer	U.K.
U.K. amateur championship	R. Edmonds	

BOBSLEDDING

Event	Winner	Country
World two-man champions	N. De Zordo, A. Frassinelli	Italy
World four-man champions	W. Zimmerer, S. Geisreiter, W. Steinbauer, P. Utzschneider	West Germany
European two-man champions	E. Thaler, R. Durnthaler	Austria
European four-man champions	A. Frigo, A. Brancaccio, L. de Paolis, A. Basuino	Italy

CANOEING

Event		Winner	Country
WORLD CHAMPIONS—MEN			
Kayak singles	500 m.	A. Tishenko	U.S.S.R.
	1,000 m.	A. Schaparenko	U.S.S.R.
	10,000 m.	V. Tsarev	U.S.S.R.
Kayak pairs	500 m.	A. Vernescu, A. Sciotnic	Romania
	1,000 m.	A. Schaparenko, V. Morozov	U.S.S.R.
	10,000 m.	J. Szaba, I. Timar	Hungary
Kayak fours	1,000 m.	East Germany	
	10,000 m.	Norway	
Kayak relay	4 x 500 m.	U.S.S.R.	
Canadian singles	1,000 m.	T. Wichman	Hungary
	10,000 m.	T. Wichman	Hungary
Canadian pairs	1,000 m.	I. Patzaichin, S. Covaliev	Romania
	10,000 m.	S. Szerna, J. Hingl	Hungary
WORLD CHAMPIONS—WOMEN			
Kayak singles	500 m.	A. Zhimanaskaya	U.S.S.R.
Kayak pairs	500 m.	Z. Lyaushko, A. Zhimanaskaya	U.S.S.R.
Kayak fours	500 m.	U.S.S.R.	
WORLD SLALOM CHAMPIONSHIPS—MEN			
Canadian singles		W. Peters	West Germany
Canadian pairs		J. Olry, M. Olry	France
Canadian singles, team		West Germany	
Canadian pairs, team		West Germany	
Canadian pairs, mixed		V. Svoboda, L. Taplova	Czechoslovakia
Kayak singles		R. Peschier	France
Kayak singles, team		France	
WORLD SLALOM CHAMPIONSHIPS—WOMEN			
Kayak singles		L. Polesna	Czechoslovakia
Kayak singles, team		West Germany	
WORLD WILD WATER CHAMPIONSHIPS—MEN			
Canadian singles		J. Boudehen	France
Canadian singles, team		West Germany	
Canadian pairs		G. Chapuis, J. Feuillette	France
Canadian pairs, team		France	
Canadian pairs, mixed		H. Spitz, M. Ramelov	Austria
Canadian pairs, mixed team		France	
Kayak singles		J. Burny	Belgium
Kayak singles, team		West Germany	
WORLD WILD WATER CHAMPIONSHIPS—WOMEN			
Kayak singles		L. Polesna	Czechoslovakia
Kayak singles, team		Czechoslovakia	

CROSS-COUNTRY

Event	Winner	Country
INTERNATIONAL CHAMPIONS		
Senior, individual	G. Roelants	Belgium
Senior, team	England	
Junior, individual	D. Bedford	England
Junior, team	England	
Women	D. Brown	U.S.
Women's team	U.S.	
NATIONAL CHAMPIONS		
Australia	K. O'Brien	
Belgium	G. Roelants	
France	N. Tijou	
Ireland	S. O'Sullivan	
Northern Ireland	D. Graham	
Scotland	R. Wedlock	
Spain	M. Haro	
U.K.	M. Tagg	
U.S. (AAU)	J. Mason	
U.S.S.R.	N. Sviridov	
Wales	A. Simmons	
NATIONAL CHAMPIONS—WOMEN		
U.K.	R. Lincoln	
U.S. (AAU)	D. Brown	
U.S.S.R.	L. Bragina	

CURLING

Event	Country
WORLD CHAMPIONS	Canada

CYCLING

Event	Winner	Country
MAJOR RACE WINNERS		
Tour of France	E. Merckx	Belgium
Tour of Italy	F. Gimondi	Italy
Tour of Spain	R. Pingeon	France
Tour of Belgium	E. de Vlaeminck	Belgium
Flèche Wallonne	J. Huysmans	Belgium
Liège-Bastogne-Liège	E. Merckx	Belgium
Tour of Britain	F. den Hartog	Netherlands
Tour of Switzerland	V. Adorni	Italy
Tour of Luxembourg	D. Boifava	Italy
Paris–Luxembourg	E. Merckx	Belgium
Bordeaux-Paris	W. Godefroot	Belgium
Tour de l'Avenir	J. Zoetemelk	Netherlands
Paris–Tours	H. van Springel	Belgium
Tour of Lombardy	G. Karstens	Netherlands
Milan–San Remo	E. Merckx	Belgium
Tour of Flanders	E. Merckx	Belgium
Paris–Nice	E. Merckx	Belgium
Paris–Roubaix	W. Godefroot	Belgium

Spices:
see Agriculture

Spirits:
see Alcoholic Beverages

Event	Winner	Country
WORLD CHAMPIONS—AMATEUR		
Sprint	D. Morelon	France
Individual pursuit	X. Kurmann	Switzerland
Individual time trial	G. Sartori	Italy
Tandem sprint	W. Otto, J. Geschke	East Germany
Team pursuit	U.S.S.R.	
Motor-paced	A. Broom	Netherlands
Team time trial, road	Sweden	
Individual road race	L. Mortensen	Denmark
Women's sprint	G. Careva	U.S.S.R.
Women's individual pursuit	R. Obodovskaya	U.S.S.R.
Women's road race	A. McElmury	U.S.
WORLD CHAMPIONS—PROFESSIONAL		
Sprint	P. Sercu	Belgium
Individual pursuit	F. Bracke	Belgium
Motor-paced	J. Oudkerk	Netherlands
Individual road race	H. Ottenbros	Netherlands
NATIONAL ROAD-RACE CHAMPIONS		
Belgium	R. de Vlaeminck	
France	R. Delisle	
Italy	V. Adorni	
Luxembourg	G. Schutz	
Netherlands	J. Frijters	
Switzerland	B. Vifian	
West Germany	P. Giemser	
U.K.	W. Lawrie	Australia
CYCLO-CROSS WORLD CHAMPIONS		
Professional, individual	E. de Vlaeminck	Belgium
Professional, team	Belgium	
Amateur, individual	R. Declercq	Belgium
Amateur, team	Belgium	

EQUESTRIAN SPORTS

Event	Winner	Country
European men's show jumping championship	D. Broome	U.K.
European women's show jumping championship	I. Kellett	Ireland
European three-day event champion	M. Gordon-Watson	U.K.
European three-day event champion, team	U.K.	
Badminton three-day event	R. Walker	U.K.

FENCING

Event	Winner	Country
WORLD CHAMPIONS		
Men's foil	F. Wessel	West Germany
Men's épée	B. Andrejewski	Poland
Men's sabre	V. Sydiak	U.S.S.R.
Men's team foil	U.S.S.R.	
Men's team épeé	U.S.S.R.	
Men's team sabre	U.S.S.R.	
Women's foil	E. Novikova	U.S.S.R.
Women's team foil	Romania	
WORLD JUNIOR CHAMPIONS		
Men's foil	L. Kozijewski	Poland
Men's épeé	D. Giger	Switzerland
Men's sabre	P. Reskiy	U.S.S.R.
Women's foil	T. Kanurkhina	U.S.S.R.

FISHING

Event	Winner	Country
WORLD CHAMPIONS		
Individual	R. Harris	U.K.
Team	Netherlands	

FOOTBALL

Event	Winner	Country
ASSOCIATION FOOTBALL INTERNATIONAL CUP WINNERS		
European Champions' Cup	AC Milan	Italy
European Cup-winners' Cup	Slovan Bratislava	Czechoslovakia
Inter-Cities Fairs' Cup	Newcastle United	U.K.
South American Champion Clubs' Cup	Estudiantes de la Plata	Argentina
Inter-Continental Champion Clubs' Cup	AC Milan	Italy
NATIONAL LEAGUE CHAMPIONS		
Argentina	Boca Juniors (Section A) Racing Club (Section B)	
Austria	FC Austria Vienna	
Belgium	Standard Liège	
Bolivia	Bolivar	
Brazil	Santos (National League) Fluminense (Rio League)	
Bulgaria	CSKA Sofia	
Chile	Valparaiso Wanderers	
Colombia	Union Magdalena	
Cyprus	Olympiakos Nicosia	
Czechoslovakia	Spartak Trnava	
Denmark	KB Copenhagen	
East Germany	ASK Vorwärts	
Ecuador	Deportivo Quito	
England	Leeds United	
Finland	Palloseura Turku	
France	St. Étienne	
Greece	Panathinaikos	
Hungary	Ferencvaros	
Ireland	Waterford	

Event	Winner
Italy	Fiorentina
Luxembourg	Avenir Beggen
Malta	Pawla Hibernians
Netherlands	Feijenoord
Northern Ireland	Linfield
Norway	Lyn Oslo
Peru	Sporting Cristal
Poland	Legia Warsaw
Portugal	Benfica
Romania	UT Arad
Scotland	Glasgow Celtic
Spain	Real Madrid
Sweden	Oster Växjö
Switzerland	FC Basle
Turkey	Galatasaray
Uruguay	Penarol
U.S.S.R.	Dynamo Kiev
West Germany	Bayern Munich
Yugoslavia	Red Star Belgrade
NATIONAL CUP WINNERS	
Albania	Dinamo Tirana
Austria	Rapid Vienna
Belgium	Lierse S.K.
Bulgaria	CSKA Sofia
Cyprus	Apoel Nicosia
Czechoslovakia	Dukla Prague
Denmark	KB Copenhagen
East Germany	FC Magdeburg
England	Manchester City
Finland	Palleoseura Kuopio
France	Olympique Marseille
Hungary	MTK Budapest
Iceland	IBV Reykjavik
Ireland	Shamrock Rovers
Italy	AS Roma
Luxembourg	Union Sportif Luxembourg
Malta	Sliema Wanderers
Netherlands	Feijenoord
Northern Ireland	Ards
Norway	Lyn Oslo
Poland	Gornik Zabrze
Portugal	Benfica
Romania	Steaua Bucharest
Scotland	Glasgow Celtic
Spain	Atletico Bilbao
Sweden	IFK Norrköping
Switzerland	St. Gallen
Turkey	Göztepe Izmir
U.S.S.R.	Torpedo Moscow
Wales	Cardiff City
West Germany	Bayern Munich
Yugoslavia	Dynamo Zagreb

GYMNASTICS

Event	Winner	Country
EUROPEAN CHAMPIONS—MEN		
Pommeled horse	M. Cerar	Yugoslavia
Horse vault	V. Klimenko	U.S.S.R.
Parallel bars	M. Voronin	U.S.S.R.
Rings	M. Voronin	U.S.S.R.
Horizontal bar	V. Lisitzki	U.S.S.R.
Floor exercises	R. Khristov	Bulgaria
Combined exercises	M. Voronin	U.S.S.R.
EUROPEAN CHAMPIONS—WOMEN		
Horse vault	K. Janz	East Germany
Asymmetrical bars	K. Janz	East Germany
Beam	K. Janz	East Germany
Floor exercises	O. Karasyeva	U.S.S.R.
Combined exercises	K. Janz	East Germany
JAPANESE CHAMPIONS		
Men	A. Nakayama	
Women	M. Kandori	
U.S. CHAMPIONS		
Men	S. Hug	
U.K. CHAMPIONS		
Men	S. Wild	
Women	M. Bell	
U.S.S.R. CHAMPIONS		
Men	M. Voronin	
Women	L. Turisheva	

HANDBALL

Event	Winner
U.S. HANDBALL ASSOCIATION 4-WALL CHAMPIONS	
Singles	P. Haber
Doubles	L. Kramberg, L. Russo
Masters singles	J. Scopis
Masters doubles	K. Schneider, G. Lewis
AAU CHAMPIONS	
Singles	S. Sandler
Doubles	S. Sandler, M. Decatur
Masters doubles	A. Goldstein, N. Schifter

JUDO

Event	Winner	Country
WORLD CHAMPIONS		
Lightweight	Y. Sonada	Japan

continued on page 703

DO AMATEURS EXIST IN SPORTS?

By William Barry Furlong

Amateurism is a thing of the spirit. It's inside a person. The devotion of the true amateur athlete is the same devotion that makes an artist starve in his garret rather than commercialize his work. If a man has the ability to succeed in any other field, he has no business taking part in professional athletics.

Avery Brundage, President,
International Olympic Committee

For more than half a century, Avery Brundage has been struggling to uphold the highest ideals of amateurism—first as a competitor (he was in the 1912 Olympic Games) and later as head of the United States and the international Olympic organizations. The fight against professionalism was as heated as ever in 1969, and there were signs that Brundage, more than 80 years old but unflaggingly vigorous, might be losing ground.

The issue he faced in 1969 was the growing commercialism of amateur sports, particularly amateur skiing. During the Winter Olympics at Grenoble, France, in 1968, Brundage grumbled about the open commercialism of the games. "We had 'Olympic' butter, 'Olympic' liquor, 'Olympic' petrol," he said. And he brooded over the brazen efforts of many medal-winning skiers to get the trademarks of the equipment they used into news photographs and television scenes. Many believed that the athletes were being paid by the equipment makers. "If I had my way, we wouldn't have given them any medals," said Brundage. "I didn't go to any of those events in Alpine skiing. It was the only thing I could do—stay away."

By early 1969 he was trying to do more. He sent a letter to the Fédération Internationale de Ski (FIS) demanding that medal winners in the Alpine skiing events at Grenoble return their Olympic medallions. ("Come and try to get them," said Jean-Claude Killy of France, a triple gold-medal winner.) Brundage suggested that Alpine skiing would not be welcome in the 1972 Winter Olympics in Japan. "It seems that sliding down mountains is not the most important sport in the world, and it is doubtful if it should be on the Olympic program," he said.

But the skiers defied Brundage. They adopted a rule that allowed "amateurs" to be paid for appearing in advertisements and for the time that they were away from their jobs, as much as nine months a year, they asserted. Then, as the struggle approached a climax, the skiers backed down a bit. They agreed that the income from product endorsements should go not to the individual but to the national federation that regulated skiing. The International Olympic Committee (IOC) accepted the changes, but established some additional regulations. It would have to give prior approval to all income contracts set up by the skiers; it would restrict "compensated time" payments to one month rather than nine; and it insisted that "all national associations work under the same rules . . . in all sports." The last regulation appeared to contradict the others, for the rules of other Olympic sports did not permit what the skiers demanded. In any case, the IOC was being firm but not militant: "In the light of this," the apparent agreement on FIS rules, "no action is being taken on medals or any pending matter at this time." It seems that "amateur" skiers could keep the medals but not the money they earned through their sport.

Growth of Commercialism in Sports. The thicket of details and legalism surrounding this controversy could not obscure the growing trend toward commercialism of amateur sports. It was affecting virtually every sport. "Bird-watching remains unsullied so far," said Brundage, "but sooner or later, I suppose, they'll find a way to commercialize that, too." It was also affecting virtually every country. In West Germany certain athletes were getting help from their national Olympic association. In Pakistan many members of the Olympic field hockey team worked for an international airline that made certain they had the time and opportunity to practice. The members of the crack women's volleyball team in Japan all worked, coincidentally, in the same textile plant near Osaka, where they could practice together every day. In certain African countries an "amateur" athlete who had sufficient skill might be employed by the military police or the army and spend up to 90% of his time practicing his sport. The best athletes in the Soviet Union and other Communist-bloc countries were employed by the state in "cover" jobs that provided them with a very comfortable standard of living while they spent most of their time polishing and honing their athletic skills. Finally, in the United States, the system of compensating "amateur" athletes by providing them with everything from jobs to jackets, from tuition to television sets was reaching from college down through high school to the preteen level: in a suburb of Chicago, officials of two "amateur" football leagues reached the fist-fight stage over claims they had on boys who were eight and nine years old.

Perhaps the most significant revelation was that 85% of the medal winners in the track-and-field events of the 1968 Olympics had been paid by a company in West Germany that made track shoes. Also, another 10% had been paid by a rival company. Payments to individual athletes were said to range as high as $10,000 as some competitors bargained with the two companies in order to get them to raise their cash bids. Altogether, it was said, the two companies paid more than $100,000 in cash and gave more than $35,000 in equipment to "amateur" athletes during the Olympic year of 1968. Information and evidence on the accusations were delivered to amateur and Olympic officials, but no immediate action against the individuals was taken.

Origins in Ancient Olympics. In one sense, all this fits into the Olympic tradition. At the outset, in ancient Greece, the Olympics were conceived as a quadrennial celebration of mind *and* body: there were cultural competitions that were every bit as important as the athletic contests. So profound was the influence of the Olympics on the civilization of that time that wars were put aside for the period of the games; indeed, Sparta was fined for violating the sacred truce of the Olympic Games during the Peloponnesian Wars. But athletic contests, being, perhaps, more dramatic than cultural competition, attracted the greatest attention. And so the people of the various city-states began rewarding their triumphant athletes. At first, the rewards were symbolic: a three-time winner had a statue erected to him in his home community. Then the rewards became more materialistic. The winners were entertained lavishly at public expense. They were made exempt from paying taxes and were given a free home. They often received free meals for the rest of their lives.

Eventually the Greek city-states decided to import good athletes and reward them handsomely to represent them in the Olympics. This corruption of the Olympic ideal became more common as Greece was conquered by foreign invaders. To rebuild their fading image in the world, and their self-respect, the Greeks hungered for athletic success; thus they became bolder and bolder in recruiting professional athletes and sending them to the Olympics as "amateurs." The Romans, their conquerors, responded in kind and eventually the Olympics degenerated into a long squabble over professionalism. This corruption of the Olympic ideals, along with a raid upon the Olympic site by marauding Goths, led to a decree by the Roman emperor Theodosius I ending the Olympics in A.D. 393.

The Olympics were revived in 1894, and almost ever since they have been immersed in charges and countercharges about professionalism. No matter what the country, or the political or economic system, there developed a system of compensating successful athletes. The techniques varied, as they did in ancient Greece. In the Western countries, or any nation where the economy was not completely regulated by the state, compensation came by means of the profit system: the athlete received his reward, secretly or otherwise, in return for the potential profits that might be developed from his success. In Communist countries, or any place with a state-controlled economy, compensation was arranged by the political system: the athlete received his reward from the state, generally a state-provided job and fringe benefits, in return for the political profit that might be made from his success. In both systems the effect was identical: the standard of living of the athlete was raised because of his athletic skills, not because of contribution to the economy. And this was generally achieved through a program of deceit and hypocrisy that denied the facts of the case.

Current Status of Amateurism. In 1969 the worldwide trend toward professionalism in all amateur competition was, perhaps, more candid than ever before. In track and field it was common in the 1950s and 1960s to engage in many deceitful practices in order to pay off athletes. For example, a meet official might make an absurd bet, that an athlete could not leap over a folded chair laid flat on the floor, and then when the athlete succeeded pay him $250 for winning the bet. Other officials would slip cash to athletes in envelopes or the folded pages of souvenir programs. Not infrequently, officials would pay a competitor his "expenses" of as much as $1,000 or $1,500.

In Europe, athletes competing in certain countries received as much as $2,000 a meet; as a result, some athletes in 1969 were hiring agents to book them into track meets in West Germany and Scandinavia. So potent was the trend that there developed several plans and proposals to form professional track associations where the athletes could compete openly for money. "I feel the amateurs are out of date," said Tommie Smith, 1968 Olympic 200-m. gold medalist. "Everybody is turning pro in one way or another. If track turns pro, it gives the athletes what they deserve." The attempt did not succeed in 1969, at least not at the outset.

In tennis the expectation of the "amateur" to be paid well was being met more openly than ever. For many years U.S. amateur tennis players had been allowed expense money of $28 a day and travel costs. But players frequently sought, and obtained, under-the-table payments that far exceeded their expenses. One prominent amateur was known to have received $1,200 to appear in a particular tournament in 1968. Even the United States Lawn Tennis Association (USLTA) got into the act: it was revealed in 1966 that it had been paying $7,000 to $9,000 to "amateurs" on the U.S. Davis Cup team. The USLTA claimed that it was compensating the players for salaries they lost while they were in training—the same attitude that the FIS decided to adopt for skiing in 1969. The fact remained, however, that the compensation for the "training period" exceeded the average family income for an entire year in the United States.

Despite the foregoing cases, many amateurs could see that becoming openly and candidly professional would bring greater rewards than could be achieved by remaining a clandestine "professional amateur." Rod Laver won $70,359 on a professional tennis tour in 1968, and Arthur Ashe turned down an offer of $500,000 to turn professional in 1969. Fearing that defections to the professional ranks of many of the game's best players would leave amateur tennis a skeletal affair, the officials who ran the sport took several steps to blunt that probability. "Open" tournaments, those allowing pros to compete against amateurs, were held for the British and U.S. championships for the first time in 1968. Then, in 1969, the USLTA approved a kind of competitor called a "player." Such an athlete could accept expense money, play for prize money, accept money for endorsements, and negotiate for guarantees simply to show up at a tournament. He could do all this and still be eligible for USLTA events, which had long been confined to "amateurs." The only kind of "professional" who could not qualify as a "player" was one who was under contract to one of the professional groups staging tournaments throughout the world. Thus, Arthur Ashe could be a "player" and so could former touring pros such as Tony Trabert. The idea was to deliver more power into the hands of the USLTA by trying to bring as many "name" players as possible under its jurisdiction. One of the main effects, however, was to blur further the difference between the "amateur" and the "professional" tennis player.

In college sports the system of deceit and hypocrisy had a long history. Seven members of the 1893 football team at the University of Michigan were not even enrolled at the university. In 1902 Yale University acquired a fine tackle named James Hogan by guaranteeing him free tuition, a ten-day trip to Cuba, a free suite in Vanderbilt Hall, and a monopoly on the sale of scorecards. Over the years such payoffs became institutionalized by making it "legal" to offer an athlete room, board, books, tuition, and fees, a package that in 1969 was worth $20,000 or more if the "amateur" athlete could stay in school for four years.

Some players received even more. One basketball player, who later became a professional, told in 1969 of the various sources of income given him by colleges that sought his services: he was given "expenses" to amateur tournaments by recruiters, he found $10 bills slipped into his napkin when he went to dinner with recruiters, and he encountered many job offers that would reward him handsomely—one college offered him a large weekly salary to keep its football field free of seaweed, though the nearest ocean was more than 1,000 mi. away. Many other athletes commented on the absurd deceits used to reward them: one reported that he was offered $110 a month to water the track occasionally, another was offered $50 a month to answer the coach's phone, while still another was offered $50 a month to "keep the coach's desk clean." The idea was that nobody really expected them to perform this work; it was all part of the deceit.

To the amateur athlete the justification for taking such payoffs was obvious. He could see that everybody was making money off his skills but himself. At many universities football was big business: at Ohio State, among others, it brought in more than $1 million a year in gate receipts. The television rights for college football were sold in 1969 for more than $24 million for two years, while the television rights for the 1972 Olympic Games were sold for $6.5 million. In all of this affluence, the performer was expected to want nothing and get nothing.

Effects on Athletes. Many men besides Avery Brundage have spoken out on the hypocrisy of "amateurism" and its significance in sports. The late A. Whitney Griswold, then president of Yale, once branded the handing out of athletic scholarships as "the greatest swindle ever perpetrated on American youth." Reuel Denny, a sociologist who collaborated with David Riesman on *The Lonely Crowd,* observed that in highly commercialized sports, the amateur athlete is "first turned into a robot, and then sometimes the robot becomes a burglar. I think the first stage, when the human being is turned into a robot, is far worse."

It is not simply the athlete who is corrupted by the deceit but also the institution. John Usher Monro, then dean of Harvard College, deplored the priorities that are fertilized in deceit with this statement several years ago:

> It does not matter how bad the high school, how poor the family, how dull the mind—the gifted athlete gets to college. We have to mobilize everybody for miles around to do it—coaches, schools, parents, neighbors, alumni, boosters' clubs, special tutors—no effort is too great. . . . Indeed, there is apt to be remuneration: the athlete expects it; it is part of his all-American birthright. The colleges have learned to care about athletes and our failure with merely able minds is a fantastic irony and a thoroughly unpleasant truth of American colleges and universities.

It is an unpleasant truth for many people in many countries. For the phenomenon is worldwide: it reflects an emphasis that is not only away from the mind but also away from the most cherished ideals of amateur sport. Sport today has become less a personal pleasure than a way to increase profits or to build prestige. And that is a distant shadow of the high ideals held by the great champions of amateur sport. Avery Brundage expressed these ideals succinctly: "Sport is a pastime and a diversion. The minute it becomes more than that, it's business or work."

continued from page 700

Event	Winner	Country
Light-middleweight	H. Minatoya	Japan
Middleweight	I. Sonoda	Japan
Light-heavyweight	F. Sasahara	Japan
Heavyweight	S. Suma	Japan
Unlimited weight	M. Shinomaki	Japan
EUROPEAN CHAMPIONS		
Lightweight	S. Feist	France
Light-middleweight	D. Rudman	U.S.S.R.
Middleweight	A. Bondarenko	U.S.S.R.
Light-heavyweight	P. Snijders	Netherlands
Heavyweight	W. Ruska	Netherlands
Unlimited weight	W. Ruska	Netherlands
Team	West Germany	
JAPANESE CHAMPION		
	I. Okano	

KARATE

Event	Winner	Country
EUROPEAN CHAMPIONS		
Individual	D. Valera	France
Team	France	

KARTING

Event	Winner	Country
World champion, individual	F. Goldstein	Belgium
European champions, team	West Germany	

LACROSSE

Event	Winner	Country
World championship, women	British Pioneers	U.K.
U.S. Intercollegiate Lacrosse Association champions	Johns Hopkins, Army	
U.S. club champions	Long Island Athletic Club	

MODERN PENTATHLON

Event	Winner	Country
WORLD CHAMPIONS		
Individual	A. Balczo	Hungary
Team	U.S.S.R.	

POLO

Event	Winner
Cowdray Gold Cup (Eng.)	Windsor Park
Copa de las Americas (U.S. *v.* Argentina)	Argentina
U.S. 20-goal champions	Oak Brook
U.S. open champions	Tulsa Green Hills

REAL (COURT) TENNIS

Event	Winner	Country
World open champion	P. Bostwick	U.S.
U.S. open champion	J. Bostwick	U.S.
U.K. amateur champion	H. Angus	U.K.

ROLLER HOCKEY

Events	Winner	Country
European champions	Spain	
European Champion Clubs' Cup	Reus Madrid	Spain

ROLLER SKATING

Event	Winner	Country
EUROPEAN FIGURE SKATING CHAMPIONS		
Men	M. Obrecht	West Germany
Women	C. Kreutzfeld	West Germany

SAILING

Event	Winner	Country
WORLD CHAMPIONS		
Flying Dutchman	R. Patisson	U.K.
5-0-5	J. Le Guillou	France
Soling	P. Elvstrøm	Denmark
O.K.	K. Carlsson	Sweden
Canoe	A. Emus	U.K.
420	Z. Karmel	Israel
Vaurien	J. Quevarec	France
Cadet	C. Winters	Belgium
Moth	D. McKay	Australia
Hornet	S. Lodge	Australia
Tempest	C. Norbury	U.K.
Star	P. Pettersson	Sweden
Dragon	R. Mosbacher	U.S.

SHOOTING

Event	Winner	Country
WORLD CHAMPIONS—MEN		
Olympic trench, individual	E. Matarelli	Italy
team	Italy	
Skeet, individual	Y. Tsuranov	U.S.S.R.
team	U.S.S.R.	
WORLD CHAMPIONS—WOMEN		
Olympic trench, individual	N. Avril	Italy
Skeet, individual	N. Ortiz	Mexico
EUROPEAN CHAMPIONS—MEN		
Free rifle, combined (individual)	V. Kornev	U.S.S.R.
(team)	U.S.S.R.	
Free rifle, prone (individual)	V. Kveliashvili	U.S.S.R.
Free rifle, kneeling (individual)	V. Kornev	U.S.S.R.
Free rifle, standing (individual)	H. Andersen	Denmark
Small-bore rifle, combined (individual)	O. Lapkin	U.S.S.R.
(team)	U.S.S.R.	
Small-bore rifle, prone (individual)	P. Gorewski	East Germany
(team)	Romania	
Small-bore rifle, kneeling (individual)	F. Donna	Italy
(team)	U.S.S.R.	
Small-bore rifle, standing (individual)	O. Lapkin	U.S.S.R.
(team)	U.S.S.R.	
Air rifle (individual)	P. Sandor	Romania
(team)	West Germany	
Service rifle (individual)	B. Melnyk	U.S.S.R.
(team)	U.S.S.R.	
Standard rifle (individual)	F. Donna	Italy
(team)	West Germany	
Free pistol (individual)	G. Kosykh	U.S.S.R.
(team)	U.S.S.R.	
Rapid-fire pistol (individual)	G. Liverzani	Italy
(team)	Czechoslovakia	
Air pistol (individual)	H. Mertel	West Germany
(team)	U S.S.R.	
Centre-fire pistol (individual)	L. Falta	Czechoslovakia
(team)	Czechoslovakia	
Standard pistol (individual)	L. Falta	Czechoslovakia
(team)	U.S.S.R.	
Olympic trench (individual)	J. Baud	France
(team)	Italy	
Skeet (individual)	I. Penot	France
(team)	U.S.S.R.	

Event	Winner and country	Performance
WORLD RECORDS—MEN		
Free rifle, kneeling	V. Kornev (U.S.S.R.)	392/400
Small-bore rifle, combined	G. Anderson (U.S.)	1,168/1,200
team	U.S.S.R.	4,632/4,800
Small-bore rifle, prone	P. Gorewski (East Germany)	598/600
team	Romania	2,380/2,400
Small-bore rifle, kneeling, team	U.S.S.R.	1,557/1,600
Small-bore rifle, standing	G. Anderson (U.S.)	380/400
team	U.S.S.R.	1,494/1,600
Air rifle	P. Sandor (Romania)	376/400
team	West Germany	1,474/1,600
Service rifle	B. Melnyk (U.S.S.R.)	566/600
team	U.S.S.R.	2,226/2,400
Standard rifle	F. Donna (Italy)	578/600
Free pistol	G. Kosykh (U.S.S.R.)	572/600
team	U.S.S.R.	2,240/2,400
Air pistol, team	U.S.S.R.	1,516/1,600
Centre-fire pistol, team	Czechoslovakia	2,276/2,400
Standard pistol	L. Falta (Czechoslovakia)	582/600

SNOW-KARTING

Event	Winner	Country
WORLD CHAMPIONS		
Men	L. Negrini	Italy
Women	S. Salice	Italy

SPEEDWAY

Event	Winner	Country
World champion, individual	I. Mauger	New Zealand
World champion, team	Poland	
World champion, pairs	I. Mauger, R. Andrews	New Zealand
European champion, individual	V. Klementiev	U.S.S.R.

SQUASH RACKETS

Event	Winner	Country
World championship	Australia	
U.K. amateur championship, men	J. Barrington	U.K.
U.K. open championship, men	G. Hunt	Australia
U.K. open championship, women	H. McKay	Australia
U.S. national championship	A. Nayar	India
U.S. veterans championship	H. Salaun	U.S.
U.S. seniors championship	E. Hahn	U.S.
U.S. doubles championship	S. Howe, R. Howe	U.S.
U.S. team championship	Ontario	Canada

TABLE TENNIS

Event	Winner	Country
WORLD CHAMPIONS		
Men's team	Japan	
Women's team	U.S.S.R.	
Men's singles	S. Ito	Japan
Men's doubles	H. Alser, K. Johansson	Sweden
Women's singles	T. Kowada	Japan
Women's doubles	Z. Rudnova, S. Grinberg	U.S.S.R.
Mixed doubles	N. Hasegawa, Y. Konno	Japan

TOBOGGANING

Event	Winner	Country
WORLD CHAMPIONS		
Men	J. Feistmantl	Austria
Women	P. Tierlich	West Germany
Men's pairs	I. Schmid, E. Walch	Austria

TRACK AND FIELD

Event	Winner and Affiliation	Performance
U.S. NATIONAL COLLEGIATE ATHLETIC ASSOCIATION CHAMPIONS (OUTDOORS)		
100 yd.	J. Carlos, San Jose State	9.2 sec.
220 yd.	J. Carlos, San Jose State	20.2 sec.
440 yd.	C. Mills, Texas A&M	44.7 sec.
880 yd.	B. Dyce, NYU	1 min. 45.9 sec.
1 mi.	M. Liquori, Villanova	3 min. 57.7 sec.
3 mi.	O. Oleson, Southern California	13 min. 41.9 sec.
6 mi.	F. Shorter, Yale	29 min. 00.2 sec.
Steeplechase	J. Barkley, Oregon State	8 min. 44.4 sec.
120-yd. high hurdles	E. Hall, Villanova	13.3 sec.
440-yd. hurdles	R. Mann, Brigham Young	49.6 sec.
High jump	R. Fosbury, Oregon State	7 ft. 2½ in.
Pole vault	R. Seagren, Southern California	17 ft. 7½ in.
Long jump	J. Proctor, Redlands	26 ft. 11¾ in.
Triple jump	P. Pousi, Brigham Young	52 ft. 1½ in.
Shot put	K. Salb, Kansas	64 ft. 9 in.
Discus throw	J. Van Reenan, Washington State	200 ft. 8 in.
Hammer throw	S. DeAutremont, Oregon State	190 ft. 5 in.
Javelin	M. Murro, Arizona State	265 ft. 9 in.
1-mi. relay	UCLA	3 min. 3.4 sec.
440-yd. relay	San Jose State	39.1 sec.
Team	San Jose State	48 pt.
U.S. NATIONAL COLLEGIATE ATHLETIC ASSOCIATION CHAMPIONS (INDOORS)		
60 yd.	J. Carlos, San Jose State	6.0 sec.
440 yd.	L. James, Villanova	47.3 sec.
600 yd.	W. Wehrwein, Michigan State	1 min. 9.8 sec.
880 yd.	F. Murphy, Villanova	1 min. 51.1 sec.
1,000 yd.	R. Arrington, Wisconsin	2 min. 8.0 sec.
1 mi.	J. Ryun, Kansas	4 min. 2.6 sec.
2 mi.	O. Oleson, Southern California	8 min. 45.2 sec.
60-yd. high hurdles	E. Hall, Villanova	7.0 sec.
High jump	R. Jourdan, Florida	7 ft. ¾ in.
Pole vault	L. Smith, Miami (Ohio)	16 ft. 6 in.
Long jump	R. Jessie, Kansas	25 ft. 2½ in.
Triple jump	L. Burgher, Nebraska	52 ft. ½ in.
Shot put	K. Salb, Kansas	66 ft. 8¾ in.
35-lb. weight	C. Ajootian, Harvard	61 ft. 8½ in.
1-mi. relay	Tennessee	3 min. 14.6 sec.
2-mi. relay	Kansas State	7 min. 32.2 sec.
Distance medley relay	Villanova	9 min. 45.8 sec.
Team	Kansas	41½ pt.
U.S. NATIONAL AAU MEN'S CHAMPIONS (OUTDOORS)		
100 yd.	I. Crockett, Southern Illinois	9.3 sec.
220 yd.	J. Carlos, unattached	20.2 sec.
440 yd.	L. Evans, San Jose State	45.6 sec.
880 yd.	B. Dyce, United Athletic Association	1 min. 46.6 sec.
1 mi.	M. Liquori, unattached	3 min. 59.5 sec.
3 mi.	T. Smith, Southern California Striders	13 min. 18.4 sec.
6 mi.	J. Bacheler, Florida Track Club	28 min. 12.2 sec.
Steeplechase	M. Manley, Southern California Striders	8 min. 36.6 sec.
120-yd. high hurdles	L. Coleman, Southern California Striders, W. Davenport, Houston Striders	13.3 sec.
440-yd. hurdles	R. Mann, Southern California Striders	50.1 sec.
High jump	O. Burrell, Southern California Striders	7 ft. 1 in.
Pole vault	R. Seagren, Southern California Striders	17 ft. 6 in.
Triple jump	J. Craft, Eastern Illinois	52 ft. 9¼ in.
Long jump	R. Beamon, unattached	26 ft. 11 in.
Shot put	N. Steinhauer, Pacific Coast Club	67 ft. 4 in.
Discus throw	J. Cole, Pacific Coast Club	208 ft. 10 in.
Hammer throw	T. Gage, New York Athletic Club	228 ft. 5 in.
Javelin	M. Murro, unattached	284 ft. 3 in.
2-mi. walk	R. Laird, New York Athletic Club	13 min. 31.6 sec.
Team	Southern California Striders	129 pt.
U.S. NATIONAL AAU MEN'S CHAMPIONS (INDOORS)		
60 yd.	C. Greene, Hushers Track Club	6.0 sec.
600 yd.	M. McGrady, unattached	1 min. 12.3 sec.
1,000 yd.	H. Germann, New York Athletic Club	2 min. 8.0 sec.
1 mi.	H. Szordykowski, Poland	4 min. 5.0 sec.
1-mi. walk	D. Romansky, unattached	6 min. 21.9 sec.
3 mi.	G. Young, unattached	13 min. 9.8 sec.
60-yd. high hurdles	W. Davenport, Houston Striders	7.0 sec.
High jump	J. Rambo, Pacific Coast Club	6 ft. 10 in.
Pole vault	P. Chen, Sports International	16 ft. 6 in.
Long jump	N. Tate, unattached	25 ft. 8 in.
Triple jump	N. Tate, unattached	53 ft. 1 in.
Shot put	G. Woods, Pacific Coast Club	63 ft. 11½ in.
35-lb. weight	Al Hall, unattached	70 ft. 9 in.
1-mi. relay	Sports International	3 min. 18.1 sec.
2-mi. relay	University of Chicago Track Club	7 min. 35.6 sec.
Sprint medley relay	Grand Street Boys Club	1 min. 55.7 sec.
Team	Pacific Coast Club	

Squash Rackets:
see Sporting Record

Stamp Collecting:
see Philately and Numismatics

Steel Industry:
see Industrial Review

TRAMPOLINE

Event	Winner	Country
EUROPEAN CHAMPIONS		
Men	P. Luxon	U.K.
Women	U. Czech	West Germany
Men's pairs	J. Treiter, J. Riehle	West Germany
Women's pairs	E. Jarosch, V. Jarosch	Czechoslovakia

VOLLEYBALL

Event	Winner	Country
World Cup, men	East Germany	
South American championship, men	Brazil	
European Champion Clubs' Cup, men	TSKA Sofia	Bulgaria
European Champion Clubs' Cup, women	Moscow Dynamo	U.S.S.R.
West European Cup, men	Belgium	
Inter-Continental Cup, men	East Germany	
AAU U.S. championship	Armed Forces All-Stars	

WATER POLO

Event	Winner	Country
European Champion Clubs' cup	Mladost Zagreb	Yugoslavia

WATER SKIING

Event	Winner	Country
WORLD CHAMPIONS		
Men's combined	M. Suyderhoud	U.S.
Men's jumping	W. Grimditch	U.S.
Men's slalom	V. Palomo	Spain
Men's tricks	B. Cockburn	Australia
Women's combined	E. Allan	U.S.
Women's jumping	E. Allan	U.S.
Women's slalom	E. Allan	U.S.
Women's tricks	E. Allan	U.S.
Team		U.S.
U.S. *v.* EUROPE (MEN)		
Men's combined	M. Suyderhoud	U.S.
Men's jumping	J. Potier	France
Men's slalom	M. Suyderhoud, J. Potier	U.S., France
Men's tricks	M. Suyderhoud	U.S.

WEIGHT LIFTING

Event	Winner and country	Performance
WORLD CHAMPIONS		
Flyweight	V. Krishinin (U.S.S.R.)	744 lb.
Bantamweight	M. Nassiri (Iran)	793 lb.
Featherweight	Yoshiyuki Miyake (Japan)	848 lb.
Lightweight	W. Baszanowski (Poland)	981 lb.
Middleweight	V. Kurentsov (U.S.S.R.)	1,030 lb.
Light-heavyweight	M. Ohuchi (Japan)	1,075 lb.
Middle-heavyweight	K. Kangasniemi (Finland)	1,135 lb.
Heavyweight	J. Talts (U.S.S.R.)	1,207 lb.
Super-heavyweight	J. Dube (U.S.)	1,273 lb.
EUROPEAN CHAMPIONS*		
Bantamweight	A. Kirov (Bulgaria)	766 lb.
Featherweight	M. Kutchev (Bulgaria)	848 lb.
Light-heavyweight	K. Bakos (Hungary)	1,075 lb.
Super-heavyweight	S. Reding (Belgium)	1,256 lb.

*Note: European champions at other weights are as given in World Champions table, above.

WRESTLING

Event	Winner	Country
WORLD FREESTYLE CHAMPIONS		
Light-flyweight	E. Javadi	Iran
Flyweight	R. Sanders	U.S.
Bantamweight	T. Tanaki	Japan
Featherweight	S. Abdulbekov	U.S.S.R.
Lightweight	A. Mohaved	Iran
Welterweight	Z. Beriashvili	U.S.S.R.
Middleweight	F. Fozzard	U.S.
Light-heavyweight	B. Gurevich	U.S.S.R.
Heavyweight	S. Lomidze	U.S.S.R.
Super-heavyweight	A. Medved	U.S.S.R.
WORLD GRECO-ROMAN CHAMPIONS		
Light-flyweight	G. Berceanu	Romania
Flyweight	F. Aluzadeh	Iran
Bantamweight	R. Kazakov	U.S.S.R.
Featherweight	R. Rurua	U.S.S.R.
Lightweight	S. Popescu	Romania
Welterweight	V. Igumenov	U.S.S.R.
Middleweight	P. Kroumov	Bulgaria
Light-heavyweight	A. Yurkevich	U.S.S.R.
Heavyweight	N. Yakovenko	U.S.S.R.
Super-heavyweight	A. Roshchin	U.S.S.R.

(D. K. R. P.)

See also Baseball; Basketball; Bowling and Lawn Bowls; Boxing; Chess; Contract Bridge; Cricket; Football; Golf; Hockey; Horse Racing; Ice Skating; Motor Sports; Rowing; Skiing; Swimming; Tennis; Track and Field Sports.

Stock Exchanges

Most major stock market indexes throughout the world scored gains in 1969. Ten of the 12 major world stock price indexes (excluding the U.S.) posted higher prices from the end of 1968 to the end of 1969. (*See* Table I.)

Western Europe. Stock markets throughout Western Europe were generally strong during 1969, with Great Britain the single most important exception. Among the countries for which the full year's data were available, bull markets were experienced by France, West Germany, Italy, Austria, Sweden, Switzerland, the Netherlands, and Belgium. Where only partial information on stock prices was available rising markets were in progress in Norway, Finland, Denmark, and Portugal, while Ireland experienced lower stock prices. The devaluation of the French franc and the upward revaluation of the West German mark were the most influential factors affecting stock price movements throughout Europe.

After rising 30% in 1968, the London Stock Exchange experienced a bear market in 1969. For the year as a whole, the average decline in the *Financial Times* index of 30 British industrials was 20%. Disappointment over the growth of corporate profits and dividends and the lack of improvement in Britain's balance of payments were the major contributing factors.

Equity prices declined almost 23% from January to June. The downward trend began in February when it became evident that overall corporate profits for 1968 would show a gain of 3–4%, substantially below the expected growth rate of 10%. Moreover, investors were probably anticipating the unfavourable economic news that was reported by government officials in March. On an annual basis, retail prices had risen by 7¼%, salaries by 8%, and effective weekly wages by 10%. These developments, coupled with a rise in the corporate tax rate from 42.5 to 45%, created a bearish atmosphere for a substantial part of the year.

The *Financial Times* industrial price index reached its lowest point in late July. Britain's balance of payments deficit for July had worsened to $89 million from a revised June figure of $60 million, and the news that the Bank of England had to intervene in the foreign-exchange market to support the pound also contributed to investor fears. The devaluation of the franc in early August caused equity prices to move sharply and nervously in both directions. Stock prices were relatively trendless during September. Although British officials publicly welcomed the revaluation of the mark in late October, the stock market reacted negatively. However, the government's announcement in early November that the dividend-restraint legislation, due to expire at the end of 1969, would not be renewed enabled equity prices to rebound. In mid-December the government reported a November trade surplus of nearly $29 million, the fourth consecutive month of improvement. The year ended with equity prices 14% above the July lows but 22% below the all-time high of January.

Beginning with the first trading session of 1969, the French stock market entered an upward phase of considerable proportions. Prices on the Paris Bourse at the end of December were 29% higher than at the beginning of the year. This was the second strongest bull market of any country for which the full year's data were available. The first quarter rise in stock prices amounted to 22%, despite enormous pressure on the franc in foreign-exchange markets. In addition, the country faced a series of general strikes that threatened to produce another bout of social disorder comparable to that of May 1968. However, investors chose to focus on predictions of favourable developments in the French economy that supposedly might occur as a result of government legislation. In addition, restrictions on investing capital outside France severely limited investors' choices.

Stock prices continued strong throughout April and May, with an all-time high recorded on June 2. The eclipse of Pres. Charles de Gaulle and the emergence of a new French president were interpreted by investors as increasing the possibility of devaluation, thereby renewing the competitiveness of French industry. After the election of Georges Pompidou on June 15, the stock market experienced considerable profit taking. From mid-June to the end of July, stock prices dropped 6%. However, the recovery that followed was particularly sharp. The devaluation of the franc on August 8 led to a sustained rally, with year-end prices less than 2% below the all-time high.

The West German stock markets turned in a strong performance for the second year in a row. The stock

New York Stock Exchange prices and average daily volume, 1969.

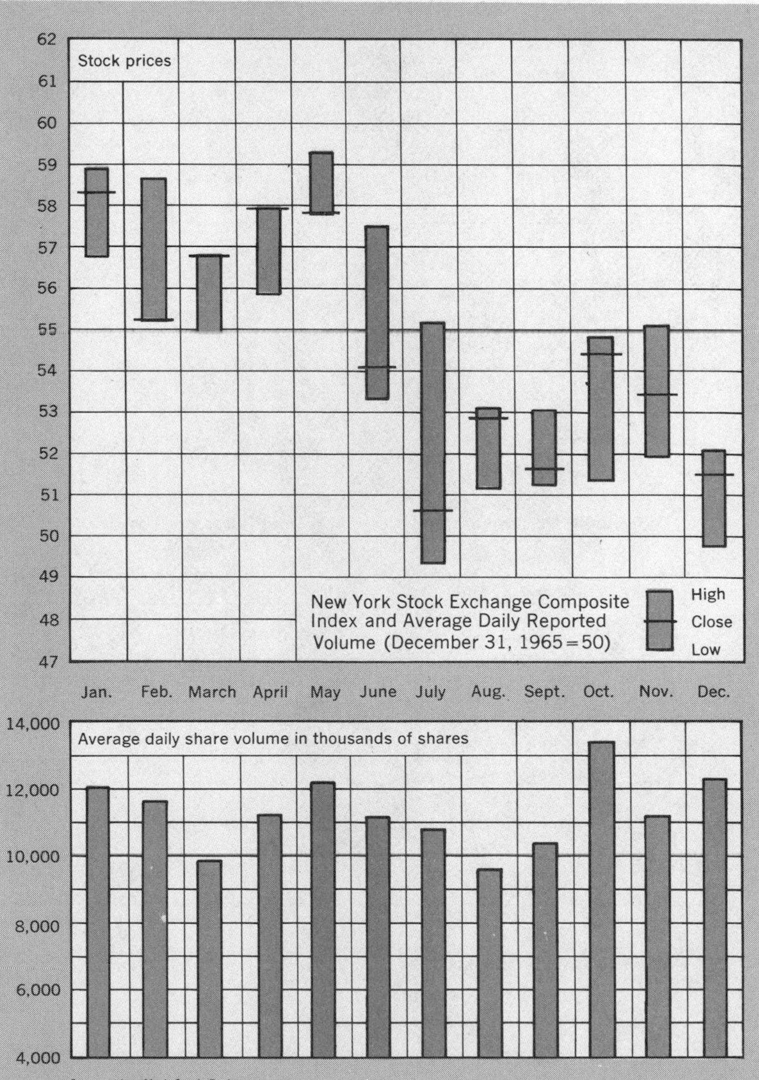

price index rose steadily throughout the year, except for periods of profit taking in July and December, finishing 1969 some 10% higher than the year before. The fact that this performance did not match the 1968 rise (13%) was due primarily to the government's desire to dampen some of the nation's economic expansion, as well as to uncertainty about the outcome of the fall elections and possible revaluation of the mark.

After a relatively modest rise during the first five months of 1969, West German equities rose somewhat faster in May and June, ending the first half with a 5% gain. This period was marked by cuts in government spending, an increase in the discount rate from 3 to 4%, and a rise in the prime rate from 4 to 5%. In the early part of July, with the average stock price level close to the year's high and the West German balance of payments in a new record surplus position, it became apparent to investors that international exchange rates would have to be readjusted. Possible revaluation of the mark, with its danger of altering the relationship between internal and external prices to the extent of considerably reducing corporate profitability, led to a 3% decline in equity prices over a three-week period. Prices rallied thereafter, picking up considerable momentum after France devalued the franc. By mid-October the stock price index had moved about 10% above the July low, despite an increase in the discount rate from 5 to 6% effective September 11. In late October, in its first major act, the new government announced an upward revaluation of the mark. Equity prices rallied during November, establishing the year's high on November 17. During December, the stock price index slid nearly 5%.

The Italian stock market also experienced a bull market in 1969 (+11%). In mid-February prices on the Milan Stock Exchange reached their lowest point, nearly 15% below the 1968 close. Stock prices then rallied throughout the summer to regain all of the year's earlier loss; by the end of September the average was up about 15%. Stock prices continued to rise following the revaluation of the mark, which paved the way for greater Italian sales to Germany. During November and December, however, investors chose to take some profits, causing prices on the Milan Stock Exchange to end 1969 7% below the year's highs.

The price index of shares traded on the Vienna Stock Exchange reversed a two-year decline. The increase of 9% from the end of 1968 to the end of 1969 was the fourth best in Western Europe. The first half of the year saw average share prices drop 2%, and the market remained in a relatively narrow range in August and September. The final three months of the year accounted for the year's entire gain. The increase was due mainly to investor expectations of greater economic activity in 1970 and the revaluation of the mark.

In 1968 stock prices in Sweden had enjoyed the largest increase among the major world stock market indexes, and the uptrend, triggered by a booming economy, continued well into 1969. By early June average share prices were 42% higher than in December 1968. The unprecedented rate of expansion of the Swedish economy led to substantial gains in wages, however. In addition, Sweden's central bank raised its discount rate to 7 from 6% in early July, limited the availability of credit to commercial banks, and placed special restrictions on commercial bank reserves. After establishing an all-time high on May 8, equity prices plunged 19% under the weight of these circumstances, reaching their lowest level on September 9. The subsequent rebound left year-end share prices 13% below the May highs and 8% above the September lows.

In Switzerland stock prices on the Zürich Stock Exchange rose 3% from the end of 1968 to the end of 1969. After reaching their high in May, equity prices declined on balance until mid-September. The market rallied following the devaluation of the mark, but prices were trending lower at the end of December. The Swiss economy operated at a very high level throughout 1969. However, government plans announced in October called for a much smaller growth in expenditures and a considerable increase in revenues during 1970.

Table I. Selected Major World Stock Market Price Indexes*

Country	1969 range High	1969 range Low	Year-end indexes 1968	Year-end indexes 1969	Percent change
Australia	654	545	600	654	+ 9%
Austria	2,054	1,747	1,789	1,956	+ 9
Belgium	102	90	91	92	+ 1
France	82	63	63	81	+29
West Germany	137	117	117	129	+10
Italy	75	60	63	70	+11
Japan	2,359	1,715	1,715	2,359	+38
Netherlands	129	107	120	122	+ 2
South Africa (gold stocks)	83	45	79	47	−41
Sweden	384	303	309	327	+ 6
Switzerland	388	318	337	347	+ 3
United Kingdom	520	357	506	407	−20

*Index numbers are rounded, and limited to countries for which full year's data were available.
Sources: *Barron's*, *The Economist*, *Financial Times*, *New York Times*, Swiss Bank Corporation.

Table II. U.S. Stock Market Prices and Yields

Month	Railroads (20 stocks) 1969	Railroads (20 stocks) 1968	Industrials (425 stocks) 1969	Industrials (425 stocks) 1968	Public utilities (55 stocks) 1969	Public utilities (55 stocks) 1968	Composite (500 stocks) 1969	Composite (500 stocks) 1968	Yield (200 stocks; %) 1969	Yield (200 stocks; %) 1968
January	54.11	43.38	110.97	103.11	68.65	68.02	102.04	95.04	3.24	3.40
February	54.78	42.35	110.15	98.33	69.24	65.61	101.46	90.75	3.39	3.49
March	50.46	41.68	108.20	96.77	66.07	62.62	99.30	89.09	3.28	3.47
April	49.53	44.79	110.68	104.42	65.63	63.66	101.26	95.67	3.22	3.22
May	49.97	48.00	114.53	107.02	66.91	62.92	104.62	97.87	3.23	3.22
June	46.43	51.72	108.59	109.73	63.29	65.21	99.14	100.53	3.41	3.16
July	43.00	51.01	103.68	109.16	61.32	67.55	94.71	100.30	3.62	3.21
August	42.04	48.80	103.39	106.77	59.20	66.60	94.18	98.11	3.48	3.20
September	42.03	51.11	103.97	110.53	57.84	66.77	94.51	101.34	3.58	3.18
October	41.75	54.26	105.07	113.29	58.80	66.93	95.52	103.76	3.44	3.17
November	40.63	53.74	105.86	114.77	59.46	70.59	96.21	105.40	3.58	3.12
December		55.19		116.01		70.54		106.48		3.27

Source: U.S. Department of Commerce, *Survey of Current Business*. Prices are Standard and Poor's monthly averages of daily closing prices with 1941–43=10. Yield figures are Moody's index of 200 stocks.

Table III. U.S. Government Long-Term Bond Prices and Yields
Average price in dollars per $100 bond

Month	Average 1969	Average 1968	Yield (%) 1969	Yield (%) 1968	Month	Average 1969	Average 1968	Yield (%) 1969	Yield (%) 1968
January	67.61	73.09	5.74	5.18	July	64.75	73.99	6.07	5.09
February	66.55	73.30	5.86	5.16	August	65.18	74.48	6.02	5.04
March	64.90	70.98	6.05	5.39	September	62.64	73.95	6.32	5.09
April	67.73	72.06	5.84	5.28	October	63.05	72.44	6.27	5.24
May	66.68	70.89	5.85	5.40	November	61.08	71.27	6.51	5.36
June	64.84	72.58	6.06	5.23	December		68.47		5.65

Source: U.S. Department of Commerce, *Survey of Current Business*. Average prices are derived from average yields on the basis of an assumed 3% 20-year taxable U.S. Treasury bond. Yields are for U.S. Treasury bonds that are taxable and due or callable in ten years or more.

Table IV. U.S. Corporate Bond Prices and Yields
Average price in dollars per $100 bond

Month	Average 1969	Average 1968	Yield (%) 1969	Yield (%) 1968	Month	Average 1969	Average 1968	Yield (%) 1969	Yield (%) 1968
January	72.5	77.2	6.59	6.17	July	68.7	76.1	7.08	6.24
February	72.1	77.5	6.66	6.10	August	68.4	78.1	6.97	6.02
March	71.0	76.9	6.85	6.11	September	67.2	78.4	7.14	5.97
April	70.1	76.2	6.89	6.21	October	66.5	77.0	7.33	6.09
May	70.2	75.3	6.79	6.27	November	65.6	75.7	7.35	6.19
June	68.8	75.6	6.98	6.28	December		73.0		6.45

Source: U.S. Department of Commerce, *Survey of Current Business*. Average prices are based on Standard and Poor's composite index of A1+ issues. Yields are based on Moody's Aaa domestic corporate bond index.

The Dutch stock market finished 1969 with a gain of 2%, after rising 23% in 1968. Inflationary pressures pushed price indexes up by an annual rate of slightly more than 4%. The value-added tax system, which was adopted by the country at the beginning of 1969, led businessmen to raise prices and, as a result, the government postponed until the beginning of 1971 a rate increase originally scheduled for 1970. Nevertheless, the threat of new fiscal measures to reduce the pace of economic activity seemed to dampen investor enthusiasm. The Belgian central bank raised its discount rate in September. The half-point rise to 7.5% was designed to moderate the business boom in Belgium, which was creating fears of runaway inflation. During the year industrial share prices on the Brussels Stock Exchange increased 1%, continuing a rise begun in 1967.

Norway also reflected a bull market through the end of October. Average share prices in October were 40% higher than in December 1968. However, investor optimism might cool as a result of government plans to impose a 20% value-added tax, effective Jan. 1, 1970.

On the average, stock prices in Denmark rose 14% between the fourth quarter of 1968 and the second quarter of 1969, but dropped 6% during the next three months. In Ireland stock prices on the Dublin Stock Exchange dropped 8% on average from the end of 1968 through October. Nearly all of the decline occurred after mid-July, following the outbreak of riots in Northern Ireland. (R. H. Tr.)

United States. The bull market of the 1960s came to an end on May 14, 1969, when most major averages of securities prices reached their 1969 peak and began a rapid descent in response to the tight money restraints imposed by the Federal Reserve Board. Between Dec. 31, 1968, and Dec. 31, 1969, all major indexes reflected significant price declines. The Standard and Poor's 425 industrials were off 10.20%; the 20 rails were off 31.36%; the 55 utilities, 19.51%; and the 500 stock composite was off 11.36%. The Dow Jones industrial averages, which closed 1968 at 943.75, ended 1969 at 800.36, a drop of about 15%. At its low point in the year, 769.93 on December 17, the market was off 18%. On the over-the-counter market, where the highest growth rates were shown in 1967 and 1968, the averages dipped 0.76% in 1969.

The conversion from a long-term bull to a bear market manifested itself early in 1969, as the 1968 year-end levels came under attack due to a major shift in economic policy from one of monetary expansion and growth to one of inflation control. From a relatively high level in the first weeks of 1969, the market was depressed by an increase in the prime rate to 7% in January and a further increase to 7½% by March. The Federal Reserve discount rate jumped to 6% in April. Strong rumours of imminent peace in Vietnam raised the prices of the blue chips to 1969 record levels on May 14, but realization that the peace rumours lacked substance and continued monetary restraint drove prices down sharply during the last half of May. The prime rate went to a record 8½% in June and the House of Representatives voted to extend the surtax on incomes for an additional year. At the end of August the Federal Reserve Board took additional measures to contract the money supply. By the third and fourth quarters it was clear that corporate earnings would not sustain their long-term average growth rates, and profits would be erratic because of uncertainties about a possible recession.

BEN ROTH AGENCY

"... and you be thankful I'm not down there losing my shirt."
—Norris, "Vancouver Sun."

Mutual funds measured their 1969 performances in terms of how little was lost rather than in terms of growth. Of 376 mutual funds followed by one service, only 19 showed any gain over 1968; the rest showed losses that in some instances exceeded 25%. The average loss of the 376 funds was 14.5%. Many of the most glamorous "go-go" funds lost most of their 1968 gains in 1969.

The average prices of industrial stocks in the Standard and Poor's index, which rose steadily during the last half of 1968, reversed course in 1969. (*See* Table II.) Beginning at a level of 110.97 in January 1969, they dropped during February and March, then rose in April and May before falling off to levels well below the corresponding months of the previous year. The high for the year was 116.24 and the low, 97.75. Standard and Poor's 425 industrials reflected smaller fluctuations than the Dow Jones industrials because of a broader base and because some of the individual components of the Dow recorded very poor price performances. Public utilities, confronted with rapidly rising money costs, were depressed during 1969; from an average level of 68.65 in January and following a slight rise during February, they fell away to a low in September of 57.84 and a year-end low in December. The year's high was 70.74 and the low, 54.33. From year end to year end the drop was 19.51%.

Railroad prices were off more sharply than either utilities or industrials, declining from a high of 54.78 in February 1969 to a November level of 40.63, with a brief interruption of the trend during May. On a year-to-year basis, the Standard and Poor's index showed a drop of 31.36% and the Dow index a drop of 35.07%. Because of the rapidly declining interest in rails as an investment category, index services planned to broaden the lists in 1970 to include trucking and airlines.

Average yields on common stocks rose to the highest levels since 1966. From a January 1969 low of 3.24% and after irregularity during the early months of the year, a climb began in April that, with brief interruptions, culminated in average levels of about 3.5% in November. Nevertheless, the disparity between stock and bond yields grew more during 1969 than in any previous year, with a reverse ratio of more than 2 to 1. While total payments in 1969 increased, fewer companies raised their rates than in any of the preceding six years. Moody's Investors Service tallied 1,283 dividend increases in the first 51 weeks of 1969, down from 1,530 in 1968, and 943 extras in the period, down from 1,009.

U.S. government long-term bond prices, as seen in Table III, declined irregularly in 1969. From an average price per $100 bond of $67.61 in January, the index fell back to a November low of $61.08. Yields rose correspondingly from a January low of 5.74 to an all-time November high of 6.51%. Rates on government securities of all maturities rose to record levels during the third quarter as a response to tight money conditions. Rates on most Treasury bills recorded their sharpest rises of the year in November and swept to new all-time high levels by year's end. Yields on intermediate and long-term Treasury coupon issues also rose to record highs in November. The pressures generated by the large volume of federal agency and corporate new issue flotations were an important contributing factor. Fastest rising yields were on local government bond issues, which moved from an average of about 65% of the Treasury bond yield level in normal years to 77% in 1969.

U.S. corporate bond prices, as seen in Table IV, slipped steadily from a January average of 72.5 to a November low of 65.6. Straight debt financing became so expensive during 1969, with a prime rate of 8½% and average yields on quality issues in some instances climbing above 9%, that "kickers" in the form of warrants and convertible issues came to be used increasingly as part of the financing mix. General Public Utilities Corp. sold a $50 million issue of five-year debentures with a 10¼% coupon rate, said to be the highest ever for a U.S. corporate bond issue,

Index of industrial ordinary share prices on the London Stock Exchange, 1948–69.

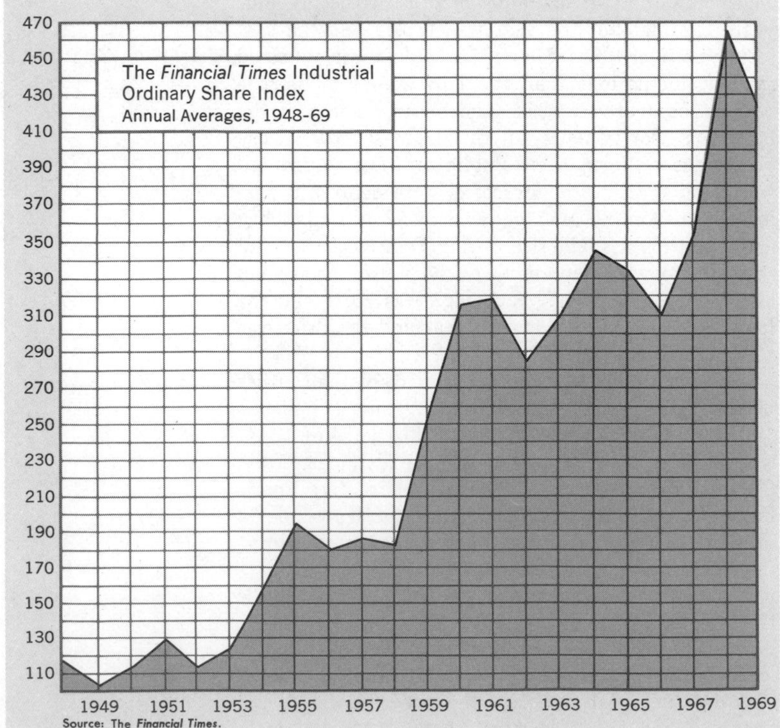

Source: The *Financial Times*.

during December 1969. The net new volume of straight debt corporate bonds, which reached a peak of $12.5 billion in 1967, averaged only about $9.7 billion in 1968 and 1969. In contrast the net volume of convertible bond offerings—bonds that can be exchanged for common stock—increased sharply, climbing from a few hundred million in the early 1960s to $4.6 billion in 1968 and 1969. The net volume of convertibles accounted for approximately 32% of the total net volume of corporate bond offerings in 1969, up from 4% in 1960 and 11% in 1965. Average yields on high-grade corporate bonds rose fairly steadily from a January 1969 low of 6.59 to a November high of 7.35.

The two dominant themes affecting the behaviour of investors in 1969 were uncertainties about the federal government's commitment to inflation control and foreign military expenditures. Inflation was more severe in 1969 than in any of the previous five years. Overall prices rose about 5%, while consumer prices increased 5.6%. After an expansive monetary policy in 1968, the government determined to break the psychology of inflation expectations by a policy of control through monetary and fiscal means. A budget surplus was planned for the first time in several years, restrictive monetary supply programs were introduced, and stock margin requirements were held at the 80% level. By mid-1969 it was clear that the controls were beginning to take hold, so that real economic growth had come to a halt by the last quarter of the year. By year's end most economic indicators began to suggest that an economic recession was in the making. Nevertheless, inflationary expectations continued. Congressional zeal to cut taxes and proceed with domestic spending programs was expected to conflict with monetary policy efforts. Gross national product in 1969 was at an annual rate of $933 billion, up some 7.8% from 1968. Pretax corporate profits declined. The rate of unemployment, which hit the lowest levels in a decade at the beginning of the year, climbed by year's end. Housing starts were off 25% between the first and last quarters of the year, and 1969 automobile production fell 6.8% below 1968.

In a year of severe monetary restraint, with total bank credit expansion smaller than in any other year of the 1960s, credit growth showed little visible decline in the first three quarters of 1969. Bank loans and investments in the first nine months were equivalent to only 7% of the total new credit extended. The average over five years was 37%, and even in 1966 it was 27%. Interest rates had been driven so high by year's end that the Treasury Department was obliged to pay 8.101% on six-month bills and 8.096% on three-month bills, the highest interest rates on record. Among the contributing factors were the recognition that the unusually low level of housing starts was creating a demand backlog that would have to be filled, and the general recognition of problems of the environment that would call for heavy deployment of capital in the next decade.

On the New York Stock Exchange the volume of transactions was 2,850,784,841 shares, an average of 11,403,139 throughout the 250 trading days. In 1968 volume was 2,921,555,941 shares, an average of 12,971,486 in 226 trading days. This was the first year in some time in which there was no year-to-year increase in share volume. The drop in activity resulted in a sharp retrenchment on Wall Street, with some brokers disposing of branch offices and cutting commissions on their sales, as well as selling exchange seats. The price of a seat on the New York Exchange fell by about 50%, from a level of $515,000 in January to $270,000 near the year's end. Bond volume on the New York Stock Exchange was off as well. In 1969 bond sales on the Big Board aggregated $3,646,159,200, compared with $3,814,239,550 in 1968.

During 1969 the board of governors of the New York Stock Exchange approved public stock offerings by member firms, with the issue being forced by Donaldson, Lufkin & Jenrette, a New York brokerage firm that filed for a public issue with the Securities and Exchange Commission. The board also authorized a new block automation system, to cost $1 million, and a movement of the exchange from its location at Broad and Wall streets to a new building at the east end of Wall Street. The exchange added $5 million to its special trust fund, used to help customers of financially troubled member firms. On two occasions during 1969 the fund was tapped to cover the liquidation of firms in financial difficulty.

On the American Stock Exchange, volume in 1969 was 1,240,742,012 shares, for a daily average of 5 million. This compared with 1,435,597,381 shares in 1968, or 4.9 million per trading day. The Amex ended the year with an all-time record daily trading volume on December 31—11,360,000 shares. The rapid growth of the Amex during the 1960s was indicated by the fact that trading volume rose from 374 million shares in 1959 to 1.2 billion in 1969; daily turnover rose to 5 million from 1.5 million during the same period, and listings grew to 1,360 issues with 2.6 billion shares outstanding at a value of $67 billion in 1969, compared with 930 issues, 1.5 billion shares, and a market value of about $26 billion ten years earlier. The price of a seat on the Amex fell from an all-time high of $350,000 in June 1969 to $150,000 in December.

Regional exchanges responded to the loss of nonmember "give-ups," a brokerage fee-splitting arrangement banned in 1968, by an aggressive set of moves to increase their services and volume. The Midwest Stock Exchange board of governors approved changes in the exchange's rules that would allow members to sell their shares to the public. Under the new rules, mutual funds could become members under certain conditions. While most markets recorded a drop in volume in 1969, turnover on the Pacific Coast Stock Exchange rose 20% to 172 million shares.

Other Countries. The Canadian securities markets followed patterns similar to those in the U.S. in 1969. The inflationary psychosis hit the bond market, causing investors to protect themselves against erosion of the purchasing power of the dollar by avoiding investments in straight long-term bonds except at very high rates. As a result, bond prices spiraled steadily downward during the year, forcing most borrowers on the market to use extendable or redeemable issues or offerings with equity features in order to attract buyers. In addition, the Bank of Canada maintained a constant restrictive policy of tight credit. Yield on long-term Government of Canada bonds moved from 7% to about 8.15% over the year, and the longest maturity for a straight new issue was nine years. Provincial yields on top-quality issues increased approximately 1.25%, to about 9–9.25%, with borrowings generally confined to extendable issues. The municipal market was hardest hit, with yields running to 9½–10%. The corporate sector was

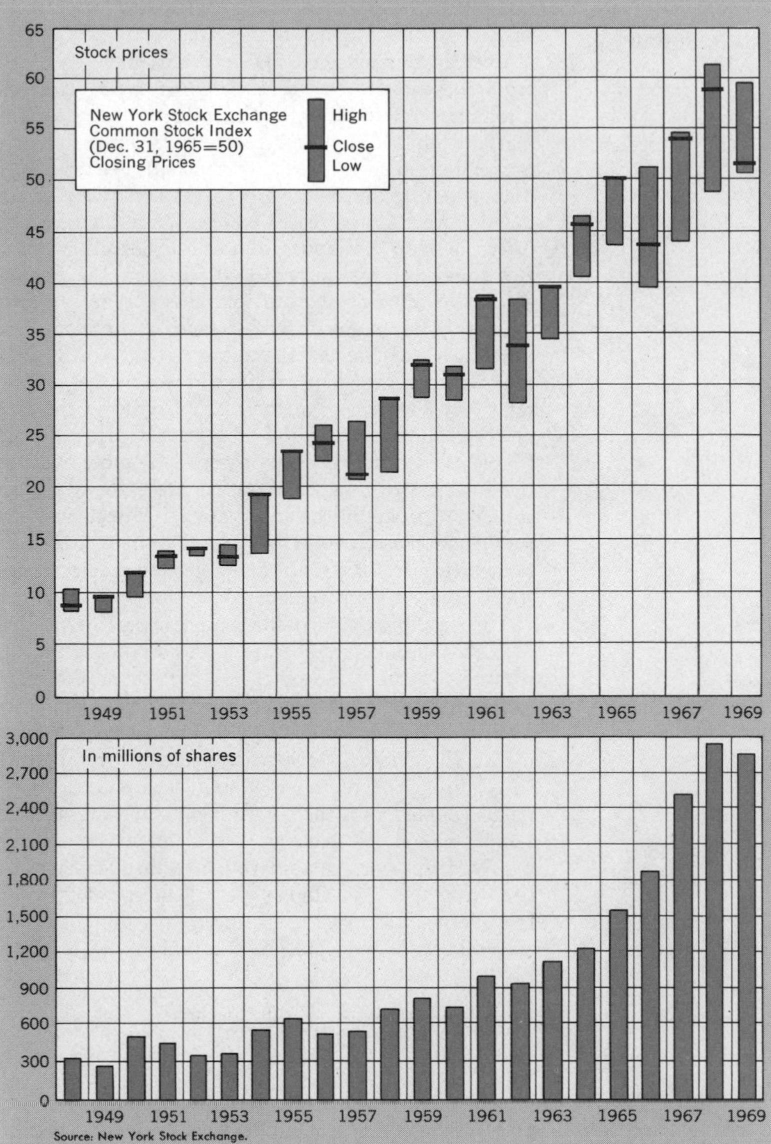

Stock trading on the New York Stock Exchange: yearly range of prices and number of shares sold, 1948–69.

hurt least, since borrowers were better able to tailor their offerings to meet lenders' demands. (I. PR.)

The Japanese stock market experienced the largest increase in equity prices in 1969 (+38%) among the major world stock market indexes. An unprecedented surge of foreign interest pushed the 225-stock index of the Tokyo Stock Exchange to all-time high levels, and in early June the index broke the 2,000 yen barrier for the first time. For the fiscal year ended March 31, net foreign buying of Japanese equities totaled more than $320 million, nearly six times the level for fiscal 1968. After the stock price index pierced the 2,000 yen level, prices drifted slightly lower during the next three months. A strong rally developed in the final week of September, and prices rose virtually without pause to a record high level at year's end.

Diverse stock price trends prevailed in the Philippines and Ceylon. Mining shares on the Manila Stock Exchange showed spectacular gains, with average prices in September 1969 112% above December 1968 levels. Sugar shares, however, dropped 6% on average during the same period. In Ceylon, shares of rubber plantations showed an average rise of 5% from December 1968 to June 1969, while shares of tea plantations experienced a 15% decline. The stock market in India through September was 18% higher than in the final month of 1968.

The Australian stock market on average rose 9% from the end of 1968 to the end of 1969. After an initial rise in the first four months of the year, the market fell sharply and reached its lows in early September. The subsequent rebound began slowly but picked up steam toward the end of the year, so that the year's final prices were all-time highs. Stock prices in New Zealand also were higher on balance. Prices on average gained 12% through the end of August, continuing the bull market of 1968.

South African gold stocks (traded in London) had the largest decline of the major world stock price indexes. The 41% decline for the year reflected the relatively sharp drop in the price of gold in the free market. The return of the free market price of gold to the $35-an-ounce level in mid-December marked the lowest price in 21 months. Also, the year-end agreement whereby the International Monetary Fund would purchase gold from South Africa near the monetary price of $35 an ounce tended to discourage speculation in gold stocks.

The economies of Chile, Venezuela, Peru, and Mexico continued to operate at relatively high levels throughout 1969. However, both Peru and Mexico experienced bear markets, mainly because of government policies that tended to discourage foreign investment. The Chilean stock price index on average rose 73% through September. Rapid economic development, coupled with the government's unsuccessful attempt to control inflation, were the major factors involved. In Venezuela share prices through September were up 8%. Higher petroleum production, a relatively stable price level, and a favourable balance of trade were the chief forces behind the market's rise. (R. H. Tr.)

See also Economy, World; Investment, International; Money and Banking; Savings and Investment.

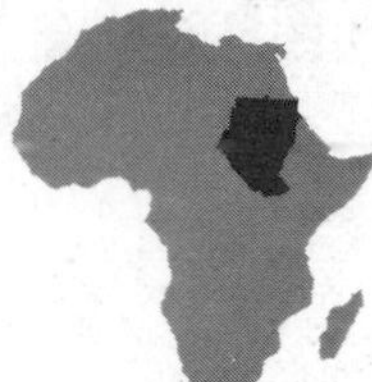

Sudan

A republic of northeast Africa, the Sudan is bounded by the U.A.R., the Red Sea, Ethiopia, Kenya, Uganda, the Congo (Kinshasa), the Central African Republic, Chad, and Libya. Area: 967,491 sq.mi. (2,505,805 sq.km.). Pop. (1968 est.): 14,979,000, including Arabs in the north and Negroes in the south. Cap.: Khartoum (pop., 1967 est., 188,000). Largest city: Omdurman (pop., 1967 est., 203,000). Language: Arabic; various tribal languages in the south. Religion: Muslim in the north; predominantly pagan in the south. Presidents in 1969, Ismail al-Azhari and, from May 25, Maj. Gen. Gafaar Muhammad al-Nimeiry; prime ministers, Muhammad Ahmed Mahgoub, Abubakr Awadallah from May 25, and, from October 28, General al-Nimeiry.

The political system that had been in effect in Sudan during most of the years since independence in 1956 was suddenly disrupted on May 25, 1969, when a group of radical socialist army officers seized power. The Supreme Council and Constituent Assembly (parliament) were dissolved, all political parties were banned, and leading political figures, including the president of the Supreme Council, Ismail al-Azhari (who died in August; *see* Obituaries), were detained. Senior army officers and ministerial officials were dismissed on the recommendation of "purge" committees.

The nine officers who organized the coup formed a Revolutionary Council, with Maj. Gen. Gafaar Muhammad al-Nimeiry as its president and as commander in chief of the armed forces. The council appointed Abubakr Awadallah, a former chief justice known for his radical leanings, as prime minister in a mainly civilian Cabinet, which included three members of the Sudan Communist Party (SCP) and seven or more sympathizers with that party. Differences on policy within the Cabinet, between the Communist-minded and those with more moderate Arab nationalist views, early became apparent, and in October General al-Nimeiry took over himself as prime minister. Awadallah was relegated to the portfolios of foreign affairs and justice.

Apart from the stated desire of the new revolutionary leaders for radical reform, the coup resulted from widespread dissatisfaction with the political and economic mismanagement of the government headed by Muhammad Ahmed Mahgoub. He returned to the country at the end of February after three months' illness abroad but proved unable to hold his coalition government together and in late April offered his resignation. The country's heavy foreign indebtedness was added to by increased government borrowing internally from the commercial banks. The final decisive factor that prompted the timing of the coup was, however, an agreement in early May between the main political parties, the Democratic Unionist Party and the reunified Umma Party, on the draft of a permanent constitution, to be submitted to a popular referendum.

The new regime was much preoccupied in its first six months with reorganization of the government machinery at the central and local levels, with at-

SUDAN

Education. (1965–66) Primary, pupils 492,085, teachers 10,895; secondary, pupils 92,407, teachers 4,453; vocational, pupils 6,391, teachers 479; teacher training, students 1,680, teachers 174; higher (including 3 universities), students 7,701, teaching staff 737.

Finance. Monetary unit: Sudanese pound, with a par value of Sud£0.35 to U.S. $1 (Sud£84 = £1 sterling). Foreign exchange, official: (June 1969) U.S. $48.2 million; (June 1968) U.S. $50.1 million. Budget (1968–69 est.): revenue Sud£113.5 million; expenditure Sud£100 million. Gross national product: (1965–66) Sud£473.6 million; (1964–65) Sud£483 million. Money supply: (June 1969) Sud£89,680,000; (June 1968) Sud£74,610,000. Cost of living (1963 = 100): (March 1969) 111; (March 1968) 103.

Foreign Trade. (1968) Imports Sud£68,030,000; exports Sud£85,150,000. Import sources (1967): U.K. 22%; India 11%; U.S. 9%; China 8%; Japan 6%; West Germany 6%. Export destinations (1967): West Germany 12%; Italy 12%; India 9%; U.K. 8%; Japan 8%; Netherlands 6%; U.S. 6%; France 5%. Main exports: cotton 60%; gum arabic 10%; peanuts 7%.

Transport and Communications. Roads (1966) *c.* 50,000 km. (mainly tracks, including *c.* 2,500 km. with improved surface). Motor vehicles in use: passenger (1967) 21,100; commercial (including buses; 1966) 17,600. Railways (1967): 4,749 km.; freight traffic 2,162,000,000 net ton-km. Air traffic (1967): 74,391,000 passenger-km.; freight 1,467,000 net ton-km. Telephones (Jan. 1968) 42,524. Radio receivers (Dec. 1968) *c.* 180,000. Television receivers (Dec. 1968) *c.* 20,000.

Agriculture. Production (in 000; metric tons; 1968; 1967 in parentheses): millet 300 (369); sorghum 1,300 (1,980); cotton, lint 184 (179); durra (1967) 880, (1966) 914; sesame (1967) *c.* 168, (1966) 134; dates (1967) *c.* 45, (1966) *c.* 45; bananas *c.* 10 (*c.* 10); peanuts *c.* 197 (*c.* 307). Livestock (in 000; 1966–67): cattle *c.* 7,600; sheep *c.* 8,670; goats *c.* 6,900; camels *c.* 2,000; horses *c.* 20; asses *c.* 590.

Industry. Production (in 000; 1967): salt (metric tons) 58; electricity (public supply only; kw-hr.) 318,000.

Strikes:
see Labour Unions

tempting to make ends meet financially, and in dealing with potential opponents. The system of local administration through tribal chiefs was abolished, and the three southern provinces, where clashes with rebel groups continued, were promised regional autonomy. Some sectors of both the import and the export trade were nationalized, but the regime showed itself wary of pressing foreign-owned firms and banks too far. Opposition to the new regime came mainly from Muslim groups; in December the government announced that it had foiled an attempted coup by right-wing Muslims.

In a swing toward the Arab world and Eastern Europe the new leaders pledged their full support to the Palestine Arab commandos. At the September meeting of Arab leaders in Cairo, General al-Nimeiry pressed for a more active coordinated Arab confrontation with Israel. (PR. K.)

ENCYCLOPÆDIA BRITANNICA FILMS. *The Nile Valley and Its People* (1964).

Swaziland

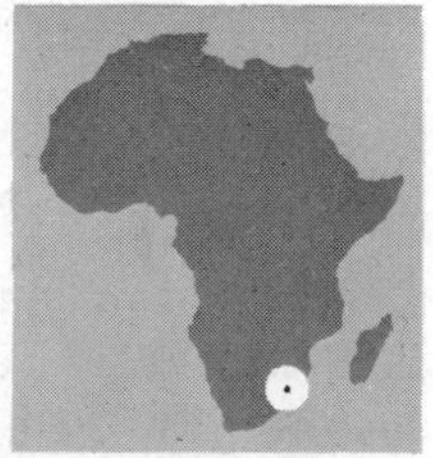

A landlocked constitutional monarchy of southern Africa, Swaziland is bounded by South Africa and Mozambique. Area: 6,704 sq.mi. (17,363 sq.km.). Pop. (1969 est.): 408,609. Cap. and largest city, Mbabane (pop., 1966 est., 13,803). Language: Swazi. Religion: Christian 60%. King, Sobhuza II; prime minister in 1969, Prince Makhosini Dlamini.

In 1969, the year following its accession to independence, Swaziland's economic situation remained satisfactory, and political stability was maintained. The trade surplus increased from $7.8 million in 1967 to $11.2 million in 1968. Exports rose to $58.4 million, while imports dropped to $48 million. Agricultural exports were hit by drought, and the World Food Program approved $373,000 worth of famine relief aid. Crop failure as a result of the drought was estimated for corn at between 60 and 80% of the average harvest. The fall in agricultural exports was compensated for by increases in exports of processed products and mineral ores. A close economic relationship was maintained with South Africa, with which the Usutu Basin hydroelectric project had been planned.

In his budget speech in March the minister of finance, Leo Lovell, indicated the main sources of revenue for 1969–70 as income tax (about 38%) and customs and excise (about 24%). He warned that amendments to the South African tax structure might lead to tax changes in Swaziland. The budget deficit for 1969–70 would be met almost completely by a U.K. grant-in-aid of $4.6 million. The minister said that if Swaziland obtained a more reasonable share of revenues from its customs union with South Africa, Botswana, and Lesotho, it would be able to balance the current budget without U.K. aid. Ministerial talks were held on the customs union in Pretoria, S.Af., in August, at which time an agreement in principle was reached.

With the population growing rapidly, the government was under increasing pressure to demand the return of land held by European settlers (approximately 50% of the total). During a visit to Kenya in June the prime minister, Prince Makhosini Dlamini, said that the transfer of land to African ownership in Swaziland would follow the Kenyan pattern. Businessmen from Swaziland would be sent to Kenya to study the methods used there to assist traders to establish their businesses. The prime minister also visited Uganda and Tanzania during his tour on June 2–11 and praised the good relations existing between Swaziland and its East African neighbours. Trade agreements, promising closer economic cooperation and increased trade, were signed with each of the three countries visited, and in Tanzania the prime minister expressed Swaziland's interest in joining the East African Community. He also visited Zambia in August. A Swaziland delegation attended the African Labour Ministers' Conference in Algiers in March, and three Cabinet ministers attended the third anniversary celebrations of the republic in Malawi in July. (M. MR.)

SWAZILAND

Education. (1967) Primary, pupils 59,287, teachers 1,539; secondary, pupils 3,792, teachers 232; vocational (1965), pupils 111, teachers 22; teacher training, students 195, teachers 29; higher (1968), students 69, teaching staff 15.

Finance and Trade. Monetary unit: South African rand (R 0.71 = U.S. $1; R 1.71 = £1 sterling). Budget (1969–70 est.): revenue R 14,477,000 (including U.K. grant-in-aid R 3,256,000); expenditure R 14,627,000. Foreign trade (1968): imports R 34,104,000; exports R 42,106,800. Main exports: iron ore 28%; timber and wood pulp 20%; sugar 18%; asbestos 14%; meat and products 5%.

Agriculture. Production (in 000; metric tons; 1967; 1966 in parentheses): corn c. 60 (63); rice 6 (7); sugar, raw value (1968–69) 154, (1967–68) 150; cotton, lint 2 (2). Livestock (in 000; 1966–67): cattle c. 505; sheep c. 36; pigs c. 9; goats c. 235; asses c. 15; chickens (Sept. 1967) 344.

Industry. Production (in 000; metric tons; 1967): coal 78; iron ore 1,098; asbestos 38.

Sweden

A constitutional monarchy of northern Europe lying on the eastern side of the Scandinavian Peninsula, Sweden has common borders with Finland and Norway. Area: 173,649 sq.mi. (449,750 sq.km.). Pop. (1969 est.): 7,941,561. Cap. and largest city: Stockholm (pop., 1969 est., 756,697). Language: Swedish, with some Finnish and Lappish in the north. Religion: predominantly Lutheran. King, Gustaf VI Adolf; prime ministers in 1969, Tage Fritiof Erlander until September 28 and, from October 14, Olof Palme.

In 1969 Sweden changed its leader for the first time in 23 years. Tage Erlander, 68, chairman of the Social Democratic Party and prime minister since 1946, retired and was succeeded by Olof Palme, 42 (*see* BIOGRAPHY). Palme took over at a time when his country's neutrality was being increasingly questioned. There appeared to be some difficulty abroad in understanding Sweden's attitude: that its intention to remain free from alliances during peacetime in order to maintain neutrality during war should not be confused with neutrality of opinion. Foreign Minister Torsten Nilsson said in March 1969 that an important object of Swedish foreign policy was to assert the ideals and evaluations of democracy in international deliberations with determination and consistency. In October, Prime Minister Palme observed that "being neutral does not mean we have to keep quiet."

In the U.S., in particular, reservations were expressed about Sweden's attitude. Relations between the two countries deteriorated markedly in 1969, and

Sugar: *see* Agriculture
Sulfur: *see* Mining
Surgery: *see* Medicine
Surinam: *see* Dependent States

SWEDEN

Education. (1966–67) Primary, pupils 622,336, teachers 27,700; secondary, pupils 395,479, teachers 38,660; vocational, pupils 205,558, teachers 15,157; teacher training, students 8,907; higher (including 8 universities), students 84,262, teaching staff (1964–65) 2,296.

Finance. Monetary unit: krona, with a par value of 5.17 kronor to U.S. $1 (12.42 kronor = £1 sterling). Gold and foreign exchange, central bank: (June 1969) U.S. $470 million; (June 1968) U.S. $763 million. Budget (1969–70 est.): revenue 40,605,000,000 kronor; expenditure 42,124,000,000 kronor. Gross national product: (1967) 123,770,000,000 kronor; (1966) 115,010,000,000 kronor. Money supply: (June 1969; new series not comparable with 1968 figures) 14,760,000,000 kronor; (June 1968) 16,560,000,000 kronor. Cost of living (1963 = 100): (June 1969) 126; (June 1968) 123.

Foreign Trade. (1968) Imports 26,496,000,000 kronor; exports 25,542,000,000 kronor. Import sources: West Germany 19%; U.K. 14%; U.S. 9%; Denmark 7%; Norway 6%; Netherlands 5%. Export destinations: U.K. 15%; West Germany 12%; Norway 10%; Denmark 9%; U.S. 8%; Finland 5%; France 5%; Netherlands 5%. Main exports: machinery 24%; paper 9%; iron and steel 9%; wood pulp 9%; motor vehicles 7%; timber 7%; ships and boats 5%.

Transport and Communications. Roads (1968) 172,495 km. (including 329 km. expressways). Motor vehicles in use (1968): passenger 2,071,303; commercial 138,800. Railways: (1967) 12,911 km. (including 7,546 km. electrified); traffic (state system only; 1968) 4,698,000,000 passenger-km., freight 13,691,000,000 net ton-km. Air traffic (including Swedish apportionment of international routes of Scandinavian Airlines System; 1968): 2,026,000,000 passenger-km.; freight 90,340,000 net ton-km. Shipping (1968): merchant vessels 100 gross tons and over 1,074; gross tonnage 4,865,365. Telephones (Dec. 1967) 3,757,495. Radio receivers (Dec. 1967) 2,928,000. Television receivers (Dec. 1967) 2,268,000.

Agriculture. Production (in 000; metric tons; 1968; 1967 in parentheses): wheat 1,059 (1,130); barley 1,776 (1,564); oats 1,523 (1,396); rye 207 (197); potatoes 1,424 (1,300); sugar, raw value (1968–69) 293, (1967–68) 260; rapeseed 256 (238); meat (1967) 398, (1966) 395; butter *c.* 66 (65); cheese 59 (60); timber (cu.m.; 1966–67) 54,000, (1965–66) 49,600; fish catch (1967) 338, (1966) 314. Livestock (in 000; June 1968): cattle 2,065; horses 69; sheep (June 1967) 272; pigs 2,043; chickens (June 1967) 8,578.

Industry. Index of industrial production (1963 = 100): (1968) 134; (1967) 126. Production (in 000; metric tons; 1968): iron ore (60% metal content) 32,821; coal (1967) 11; electricity (92% hydroelectric in 1967; kw-hr.) 56,324,000; pig iron 2,470; crude steel 5,060; cement 3,912; copper 47; lead (1967) 42; silver (1967) 0.11; gold (troy oz.; 1967) 60; mechanical wood pulp (1967) 1,260; chemical wood pulp (1967) 5,589; newsprint 809; other paper (1967) 2,592; cotton yarn 14; wool yarn 7.8. Merchant vessels launched (100 gross tons and over; 1968) 1,098,000 gross tons. New dwelling units completed (1968) 106,200.

there was some apprehension about the possibility of an economic backlash from the U.S. For most of 1969 there was no U.S. ambassador in Stockholm. There was concern over the opening of a National Liberation Front (Viet Cong political arm) information office in Stockholm; Sweden's establishment of diplomatic relations with North Vietnam; its decision to give aid worth 200 million kronor to North Vietnam after the cessation of hostilities; and its willingness to provide safe haven for U.S. deserters (325 by mid-November). Sweden also came under fire from Portugal when its decision to supply aid to freedom movements in Portuguese Guinea and Mozambique was revealed in October. On September 3 the Swedish heavy electrical engineering concern ASEA had announced its withdrawal from the South African-led consortium Zamco, which had obtained the £125 million contract to build the Cahorabassa Dam for Portugal in northern Mozambique. Reasons for the withdrawal were the fear of prosecution under Sweden's new sanction laws against Rhodesia (which hoped to supply cement and services for the project) and mounting opposition from Sweden's progressive forces. In August the Swedish Broadcasting Corporation decided not to cover the European athletics championships in Greece.

Sweden's gross national product rose 3.5% in 1968 (2% in 1967). Private investment, however, fell for the second year in succession and unemployment rose slightly. The rise in costs and prices was relatively slow. Exports increased, but not as much as imports, so the balance of payments deficit did not improve. The 1969 budget, presented in January, followed the policy of general restraint evident for the previous few years.

Expenditure was dominated by a continuation of reforms that had been launched in previous years and an expansion of employment and individual security programs. The budget revealed an increase in government spending of 3.2% over 1968. In terms of total expenditure, the ministries that received the largest appropriations were those dealing with social matters, education, and defense.

The Nordek proposals—which envisaged a customs and economic union between Sweden, Denmark, Norway, and Finland—continued to be discussed throughout 1969. Although there was a strong case for Scandinavian cooperation of this kind, it was felt in some quarters that Nordek was a little irrelevant and that all energies should be directed toward gaining entry into the EEC. Nevertheless, Nordek was important to Sweden because, if implemented, it would provide a useful fall-back position should any future effort to join the EEC run into trouble. In addition, Nordek would give the Scandinavian countries a common front at Brussels. However, Sweden's enthusiasm was not matched by its partners. In December, Finland withdrew from the Nordek talks, and the entire matter was postponed until after the 1970 Finnish elections.

State ownership of industry—a modest 5–6% at the beginning of the period under review—increased somewhat during 1969. Minister of Economics Krister Wickman announced the formation of a state holding company consisting of 20 government-controlled firms. The government purchased a large drug manufacturer and three machine tool companies. It also created, in collaboration with two private concerns, a company that would produce components for atomic energy plants, and acquired control of a nuclear development organization in which it had previously had only a half share. Wildcat strikes by Göteborg dockers (November) and by Kiruna miners (from early December and unsettled at year's end) disrupted Sweden's long stable labour relations.

Environmental protection had been the subject of a running debate in Sweden during the 1960s, and 1969 saw some significant developments in this area. A new law was approved directing that air and water pollution must be prevented where it was practical and economically possible. In addition, it was announced that the use of DDT would be banned from 1970 for a two-year research period. There was a suggestion that those who polluted the environment should pay an extra tax, the amount depending on the degree of contamination caused (it was stated that car owners were expected to contribute one-third of the 15 million kronor that it was estimated Sweden would spend on environmental protection during the coming decade). An opinion poll revealed that 54% of the Swedish people thought it was desirable to forgo some of the advantages of the rise in the standard of living in order to have a better environment. At the UN Sweden introduced a resolution, supported by 50 nations, which contained the proposal that an international conference should be held in 1972 to deal with the problem of environmental protection.

The misuse of narcotics received much publicity

Swedish Literature: *see* Literature

during 1969. It had been noted that the use of narcotics was increasing in Sweden, and there was heated debate on what should be done about it. The police decided on a program of strong action. Police personnel were instructed to give special attention to the problem and a campaign was launched to inform people of the dangers of narcotics. The campaign was especially aimed at schoolchildren, parents, military personnel, business, and trade unions. At its own expense, an advertising agency issued billboards in the form of death announcements: "Kerstin. Born Jan. 20, 1954, died Dec. 24, 1968. Killed by drugs."

The voice of Swedish youth was hardly silent during the year. There was a great deal of opposition to the war in Vietnam and strong support for aid to less developed countries. Christmas 1968 saw a new kind of initiative from the young in the form of demonstrations for the decommercialization of the festive season. The "alternative Christmas" put forward at meetings and protest marches entailed helping the poor and homeless, visiting the lonely, and making constructive moves to assist the needy. All this did not have much affect on sales, but it certainly led to some new thinking. Not all the actions of youth were so idealistic, however; in February 700 pupils in a school in north Sweden went on strike because their holidays were altered. (A. D. Wi.)

Encyclopædia Britannica Films. *Scandinavia—Norway, Sweden, Denmark* (1962).

Swimming

Post-Olympic years supposedly bring a letdown in swimming performances. Measured by the standard of world records, that was only half true in 1969. The men swam better than ever. Of the 13 world records for men's individual races, nine were broken, two equaled officially, and one tied unofficially. But the women, who had rewritten most of their record book annually for most of the decade, took a sabbatical. Only three of their 13 individual world records were bettered. One reason was the retirement of such teen-aged U.S. Olympic champions as Claudia Kolb, Catie Ball, and Lillian ("Pokey") Watson. Another was the lack of a large-scale college swimming program for U.S. women.

The best of the male swimmers were Gary Hall, Mike Burton, Mark Spitz, and Don Havens of the United States; Hans Fassnacht of West Germany; Roland Matthes of East Germany; and Nikolai Pankin of the Soviet Union. The leading women (actually, teen-aged girls) were Debbie Meyer and Susie Atwood of the United States, Karen Muir of South Africa, and Gabriella Wetzko of East Germany.

Swimming World magazine chose Hall and Miss Meyer as the swimmers of the year (Miss Meyer also was the leading woman swimmer of 1968). Fassnacht and Miss Wetzko were named as the best in Europe.

In the Amateur Athletic Union (AAU) national long-course (outdoor) championships, August 12–17 at Louisville, Ky., Hall broke three world records in four days. The 18-year-old high-school senior from Garden Grove, Calif., set the records in the 200-m. individual medley (2 min. 9.6 sec.), 400-m. individual medley (4 min. 33.9 sec.), and 200-m. backstroke (2 min. 6.6 sec., a record that stood only 15 days). In the AAU national short-course (indoor) championships, April 8–13 at Long Beach, Calif., Hall won two races, both in U.S.-record time.

World Records Set in 1969

Event	Name	Country	Time
MEN			
200-m. freestyle	Mark Spitz	U.S.	*1 min. 54.3 sec.
400-m. freestyle	Hans Fassnacht	West Germany	4 min. 4.0 sec.
800-m. freestyle	Mike Burton	U.S.	8 min. 28.8 sec.
1,500-m. freestyle	Mike Burton	U.S.	16 min. 4.5 sec.
100-m. breaststroke	Nikolai Pankin	U.S.S.R.	1 min. 5.8 sec.
200-m. breaststroke	Nikolai Pankin	U.S.S.R.	2 min. 25.4 sec.
100-m. butterfly	Mark Spitz	U.S.	*55.6 sec.
100-m. backstroke	Roland Matthes	East Germany	57.8 sec.
200-m. backstroke	Roland Matthes	East Germany	2 min. 6.4 sec.
200-m. individual medley	Gary Hall	U.S.	2 min. 9.6 sec.
400-m. individual medley	Gary Hall	U.S.	4 min. 33.9 sec.
WOMEN			
1,500-m. freestyle	Debbie Meyer	U.S.	17 min. 19.9 sec.
100-m. backstroke	Karen Muir	South Africa	1 min. 5.6 sec.
200-m. backstroke	Susie Atwood	U.S.	2 min. 21.5 sec.

*Equaled record.

Burton, from Carmichael, Calif., was a 5-ft. 9-in., 22-year-old former UCLA swimmer, now swimming for the Arden Hills Swim Club of Sacramento, Calif. For the fourth consecutive year he won the AAU 1,500-m. freestyle in world-record time, lowering his mark to 16 min. 4.5 sec.; he also set a world record en route of 8 min. 28.8 sec. for 800 m. Also for the fourth consecutive year, he won the AAU 1,650-yd. freestyle indoors in U.S.-record time, lowering his mark to 15 min. 40.1 sec. (the indoor meets were swum in 25-yd. pools; world records could be set only in 50-m. or 55-yd. pools).

Spitz, a 19-year-old Indiana University freshman from Santa Clara, Calif., tied two world records—his own 55.6 sec. for the 100-m. butterfly and the retired Don Schollander's 1 min. 54.3 sec. for the 200-m. freestyle. In the same meet, Spitz tied the U.S. record of 52.6 sec. for the 100-m. freestyle.

Spitz was the only triple winner in the National Collegiate Athletic Association (NCAA) championships, March 27–29 at Bloomington, Ind. (his Indiana team won overall honours). The following month he swam in several European meets, but was then so tired from that schedule that he did not enter the AAU outdoor and indoor championships.

Havens, a 6-ft. 5-in. senior at the University of Southern California, captured the AAU 100-yd. freestyle title indoors for the third straight year. With a

Hans Fassnacht of West Germany set a world record of 4 min. 4 sec. in the 400-m. freestyle at the AAU national championships at Louisville, Ky., in August 1969.

AUTHENTICATED NEWS INTERNATIONAL

WIDE WORLD

Gary Hall of California competes in the national AAU swimming and diving championships in Long Beach, Calif., on April 11, 1969. He won the 400-yd. individual medley with a time of 4 min. 0.8 sec. to set a new U.S. record.

flying start, he swam 100 yd. in a relay in 44.7 sec., the fastest time ever for this distance though not eligible for consideration as a record because of the relay start. Outdoors, he won the AAU 100-m. freestyle title, and a week later in an unofficial time trial he equaled the world record of 52.2 sec. for 100 m.

Fassnacht, only 5 ft. 8 in., was an 18-year-old freshman at Long Beach State College. He won the 200-m. and 400-m. freestyles in the AAU outdoor meet, setting a world record of 4 min. 4 sec. for 400 m. He also won those two freestyle races and both individual medley titles in the European Cup meet for men, August 23–24 at Würzburg, W.Ger.

The 18-year-old Matthes, winner of two Olympic titles in 1968, continued his domination of the backstroke. He set world records of 57.8 sec. for 100 m. and 2 min. 6.4 sec. for 200 m. He also captured both races in the European Cup meet. At 6 ft. 4 in. and 170 lb., he swam with a long, easy stroke of textbook beauty.

Although Soviet swimming had not made as much progress as expected, the U.S.S.R. did produce outstanding breaststrokers. The 20-year-old Pankin was the best, setting world records of 1 min. 5.8 sec. for 100 m. and 2 min. 25.4 sec. for 200 m. Like Matthes, he won two European Cup titles.

In 1968 the apple-cheeked Miss Meyer broke four women's world freestyle records, won three Olympic gold medals, and was voted the Sullivan Award as America's leading amateur athlete. The 17-year-old high-school junior from Sacramento was not as spectacular in 1969, but she won three AAU titles outdoors and one indoors, and was impressive in meets in France and West Germany.

The keenest women's rivalry of the year involved Miss Meyer and 16-year-old Vicky King, teammates on the Arden Hills Swim Club. In the AAU outdoor meet, when Miss Meyer lowered her world record in the 1,500-m. freestyle to 17 min. 19.9 sec., Miss King was only a tenth of a second behind her. In the Santa Clara invitation meet 1,500 m., Miss Meyer won by four-tenths of a second. In the AAU indoor 500-yd. freestyle, Miss King beat Miss Meyer by a tenth of a second.

In the past, Miss Meyer usually swam well ahead of the others. She enjoyed the new challenge. "It's very exciting having somebody swim next to you," she said. "After the Olympics, I asked myself, 'What's there to shoot for?' Now I've got her to shoot for."

The 16-year-old Susie Atwood, from Lakewood, Calif., won four AAU backstroke titles, two outdoors and two indoors. She set U.S. records in all four races and a world record of 2 min. 21.5 sec. for 200 m. outdoors. The 100-m. backstroke record fell to the slender 16-year-old Karen Muir in 1 min. 5.6 sec. She also had set world records at the ages of 12, 13, 14, and 15.

Gabriella Wetzko, a 15-year-old freestyler, was the star of the European Cup women's meet, August 23–24 at Budapest, Hung. She won the 100-m. final in 59.6 sec. and the 200-m. title in 2 min. 8.9 sec., both European records, and anchored the East German medley relay team to a European record.

Jim Henry, a 20-year-old Indiana University junior from Dallas, Tex., was America's outstanding diver. In the three major championships—AAU outdoor, AAU indoor, and National Collegiate Athletic Association (NCAA)—he won five of the eight diving titles and was never worse than fourth.

Cynthia Potter, an 18-year-old Indiana University freshman from Houston, Tex., captured three of the six AAU diving titles for women. Micki King, a 25-year-old Women's Air Force lieutenant, took two titles outdoors (she did not compete in the AAU indoor meet).

Overseas, the major competitions were the separate European Cup meets for men and women. In each, East Germany finished first and the Soviet Union second. The East Germans captured 6 of the 15 races for men and 9 of the 14 for women, and they established themselves as second in the world to the Americans. The East Germans, like the Americans, rose to prominence after establishing a mammoth program of age-group competition for youngsters.

The British men placed seventh among the eight teams in the European Cup competition and were relegated to Group B for the 1971 meet. The British women finished fourth among eight teams. Britain did well in one major meet, again winning the Six Nations competition, September 12–13 at Blackpool, Eng.

In the British Amateur Swimming Association championships, August 4–9 at Blackpool, 18-year-old Martyn Woodroffe of Wales tried for nine titles. He won five and twice finished second to Ron Jacks of Canada. Fourteen-year-old Donna Gurr of Canada won five titles for women.

In the Canadian outdoor championships, August 11–15 at Quebec, Angela Coughlan easily won all four freestyle races for women, two in Canadian-record time. George Smith and Jacks took three men's titles each. (F. L.)

Switzerland

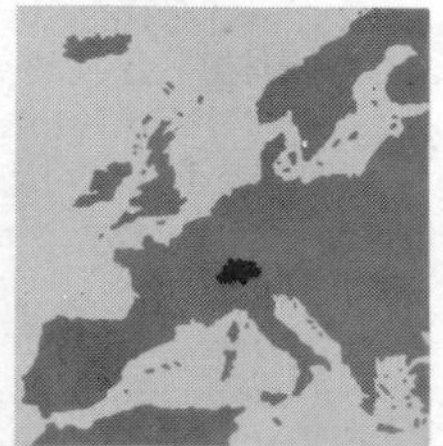

A federal republic in west central Europe consisting of a confederation of 22 cantons, Switzerland is bounded by Germany, Austria, Liechtenstein, Italy, and France. Area: 15,941 sq.mi. (41,288 sq.km.). Pop. (1969 est.): 6,115,000. Cap.: Bern (pop., 1969 est., 166,800). Largest city: Zürich (pop., 1969 est., 432,400). Language (1960): German 69.3%; French 18.9%; Italian 9.5%; Romansh 0.9%. Religion (1960): Protestant 52.6%; Roman Catholic 45.6%. President in 1969, Ludwig von Moos.

In 1969 the revision of the federal constitution, expected by 1974, its centenary year, continued to be discussed. In November the cantons, political parties, churches, and various interested organizations were invited by the federal government to answer, by May 1970, a five-point questionnaire concerning the abrogation or replacement of the anti-Catholic articles. Possible new clauses were proposed providing for religious freedom within the law. The cantons and the Confederation would be authorized to maintain public order among the diverse religious communities, while a federal decree might ban any groups permanently disturbing public order and religious peace.

Slow progress was made in the field of women's suffrage. By the end of November six cantons (Vaud, Neuchâtel, Geneva, Basel Town and Basel Country, and Ticino) had granted women the right to vote on both cantonal and local affairs. In three cantons (Zürich, Bern, and Graubünden) the communes were authorized to enfranchise women. In two cantons, however (Schaffhausen and Solothurn), a majority of the male citizens still voted against women's suffrage. Another plebiscite on women's suffrage in federal matters (rejected in 1959) was expected, but the outcome remained in doubt.

SWITZERLAND

Education. (1964–65) Primary, pupils 468,664, teachers (excluding craft teachers; 1961–62) 23,761; secondary, pupils 242,249, teachers (full time; 1961–62) 6,583; vocational, pupils 19,500 (excluding 131,897 in apprenticeship training schools); teacher training, students 10,410; higher (including 8 universities; 1966–67), students 33,579, teaching staff 2,304.

Finance. Monetary unit: Swiss franc, with a par value of SFr. 4.37 to U.S. $1 (SFr. 10.50 = £1 sterling). Gold and foreign exchange, central bank: (June 1969) U.S. $3,220,000,000; (June 1968) U.S. $3.4 billion. Budget (1968 rev. est.): revenue SFr. 6,310,000,000; expenditure SFr. 6,504,000,000. Gross national product: (1968) SFr. 73,175,000,000; (1967) SFr. 68,940,000,000. Money supply: (May 1969) SFr. 36,540,000,000; (May 1968) SFr. 33,810,000,000. Cost of living (1963 = 100): (June 1969) 122; (June 1968) 119.

Foreign Trade. (1968) Imports SFr. 19,394,000,000; exports SFr. 17,051,000,000. Import sources: EEC 59% (West Germany 30%, France 13%, Italy 10%); U.S. 9%; U.K. 7%. Export destinations: EEC 37% (West Germany 14%, Italy 9%, France 9%); U.S. 10%; U.K. 7%; Austria 5%. Main exports: machinery 30%; chemicals 21%; clocks and watches 14%; textile yarns and fabrics 7%. Tourism (1967): visitors 5,914,200; gross receipts U.S. $694 million.

Transport and Communications. Roads (1968) 58,358 km. Motor vehicles in use (1968): passenger 1,180,474; commercial 115,729. Railways: federal (1967) 2,934 km. (including 2,906 km. electrified); private (1966) 2,118 (including 2,109 km. electrified); traffic on federal railways (1968) 7,701,000,000 passenger-km., freight 5,706,000,000 net ton-km.; traffic on private railways (1967) 1,233,000,000 passenger-km., freight 386 million net ton-km. Air traffic (1968): 3,334,000,000 passenger-km.; freight 117.6 million net ton-km. Shipping (1968): merchant vessels 100 gross tons and over 33; gross tonnage 201,771. Telephones (Dec. 1967) 2,533,684. Radio receivers (Dec. 1967) 1,734,000. Television receivers (Dec. 1967) 868,000.

Agriculture. Production (in 000; metric tons; 1968; 1967 in parentheses): wheat (including spelt) 373 (424); barley 112 (117); oats (1967) 32, (1966) 33; rye 65 (65); potatoes 1,098 (1,125); apples (1967) 600, (1966) 360; pears *c.* 210 (270); sugar, raw value (1968–69) 68, (1967–68) 64; wine 90 (89); milk 3,344 (3,274); butter *c.* 37 (41); cheese *c.* 86 (86); meat 311 (276). Livestock (in 000; April 1968): cattle 1,855; horses 59; sheep (April 1967) 236; pigs 1,849; goats (April 1967) *c.* 73; chickens (April 1967) 5,433.

Industry. Index of industrial production (1963 = 100): (1968) 123; (1967) 116. Production (in 000; metric tons; 1968): cement 4,320; aluminum 77; rayon yarn 12; rayon staple fibre (1967) 10; cigarettes (pieces; 1967) 18,562,000; watches (units; 1967) 42,083; electricity (kw-hr.) 30,765,000; manufactured gas (cu.m.; 1966) 383,000.

WIDE WORLD

Swiss Protestants gather at the Wall of the Reformers in Geneva, June 8, 1969, to protest Pope Paul's visit to the city.

Some progress was made on the crucial issue of the autonomy-seeking, French-speaking, Catholic Jura region of the canton of Bern. The report commissioned by the federal government to find a compromise solution proposed a "Jura statute" allowing considerable autonomy, followed by plebiscites in the various districts to allow each one to decide either for the status quo, for greater autonomy within the canton of Bern, or for the establishment of a new canton. Bern in its own report adopted a similar line. The separatists, however, were dissatisfied with an "imposed" procedure and called for "mediation as between equal partners."

The resignation at the end of the year of two ministers, Hans Schaffner, minister of economics, and Willy Spühler, minister of foreign affairs, led to competition among political parties and the cantons for the vacant posts. Adhering to the time-honoured but increasingly criticized pattern of regional and party representation, the Federal Assembly in December elected Pierre Graber, Socialist of Neuchâtel, and Ernst Brugger, Radical of Zürich, to fill the vacancies. Federal Councillor Hans Peter Tschudi was elected president of the Confederation for 1970.

Switzerland continued to debate membership in the UN. The long-awaited report by the Federal Council, while taking a positive view of the UN, emphasized its many failures and considered the time was not ripe for Switzerland to join. In any event, membership would be possible only on condition that Switzerland be allowed to maintain its neutrality. The Federal Council favoured a campaign of public information to acquaint people with the merits of the UN and an intensification of Swiss cooperation with UN agencies.

Another manifestation of Switzerland's conservatism in foreign affairs was the rejection by the Council of States of the Federal Council's proposal that Switzerland sign the European Convention on Human Rights. In November the Federal Council decided to sign the nuclear nonproliferation treaty. Ratification, however, would be delayed until a "sufficient" number of other states had ratified the treaty.

Parliament approved the new law that provided for a systematic coordination of all national defense activities. Defense became a controversial issue when the federal government distributed to every household a "little red book" on civil defense that, in addition to technical and practical information, provided what seemed to many an uncalled-for definition of Swiss patriotism. Thousands of copies were returned.

In the autumn the Federal Council and the Assembly recommended rejection in a forthcoming plebiscite of the "second Schwarzenbach initiative" introduced in May, which demanded that the number of foreigners in each canton be limited to 10% of the population.

The balance of payments surplus in 1968 was $540

million (1967: $240 million), and the gross national product rose by 3.5%. Toward the year's end inflationary symptoms appeared and the government called for reduced spending. After the revaluation of the West German mark there was speculation whether the Swiss franc might follow suit. The government proposed a series of palliative measures instead. In the budget for 1970 federal expenditure amounted to only about one-third of total public expenditure. Swiss exports rose by over 14% in the first quarter of 1969. On the occasion of a visit to Bern by Jean Rey, president of the EEC Commission, the government declared itself eager to "enter into conversations" with the EEC but explained that this did not imply negotiations. (M. F. S.)

ENCYCLOPÆDIA BRITANNICA FILMS. *Switzerland: Life in a Mountain Village* (1963).

Syria

A republic in southwestern Asia on the Mediterranean Sea, Syria is bordered by Turkey, Iraq, Jordan, Israel, and Lebanon. Area: 71,498 sq.mi. (185,180 sq.km.). Pop. (1968 est.): 5,738,000. Cap. and largest city: Damascus (pop., 1966 est., 594,426). Language: Arabic (official); also Kurdish, Armenian, Turkish, and Circassian. Religion: predominantly Muslim. Chairman of the Presidency Council and premier in 1969, Nureddin al-Attassi.

In 1969 there were only minor changes in Syria's uncompromising, independent policies despite a restructuring of the regime and a broadening of the government's base. On January 4 the trial of 77 Syrian politicians ended with prison sentences ranging up to hard labour for life for 61, including the right-wing Baathist former premier, Salah al-Din Bitar. A struggle for power in which the defense minister, Gen. Hafez al-Assad, confronted President al-Attassi and the assistant secretary-general of the Syrian Baath Party, Gen. Salah Jadid, was not pressed to its conclusion although a compromise reached in March left General Assad in the ascendancy. The al-Attassi camp was weakened by the suicide on March 2 of the military intelligence chief, Col. Abdul Karim al-Jundi. An 11-day Baath Party congress ended on March 31 with a resolution calling for a relaxation in the political system and the issuing of a provisional constitution. General Jadid was reelected to the Baath national executive council. General al-Assad was reputed to favour a rapprochement with the moderate Baathist regime in Iraq and a scaling down of Syria's close relations with the U.S.S.R. At the end of March some Iraqi troops were stationed on Syrian territory at Syria's request. However, Damascus and Baghdad radios continued to exchange accusations, the Syrians claiming that the Iraqis were attempting to suppress the Palestinian organizations. Syria's left-wing Baathist regime feared a coup organized by the Iraqi Baathists in cooperation with exiled Syrian politicians.

On May 5 it was announced that President al-Attassi had postponed his planned visit to the Soviet Union. At the same time the Syrian military chief of staff, Gen. Mustafa Tlass, visited Peking and it was reported that China would be building missile sites for Syria. The Syrians were understood to be dissatisfied with the slow delivery of Soviet arms supplies. However, the slight cooling off between Syria and the U.S.S.R. did not last long. On June 4 Syria pleased Moscow by recognizing East Germany, and in July President al-Attassi paid his postponed visit to the U.S.S.R., during which he signed a new agreement for Soviet financial and technical aid.

In May there was a serious clash between the Lebanese Army and Al Saiquah, the Palestinian guerrilla organization supported by the Syrian Baathists. Throughout the Lebanese crisis, which continued during the summer and autumn, Syria strongly supported the right of the Palestinians to operate from Lebanese bases. Syria's own border with Israel was relatively quiet, but on July 8 the air forces of the two nations clashed over the occupied Golan Heights.

Despite Syria's cool relations with its Arab neighbours, some attempt was made to coordinate its defense policy with theirs. On July 30 an Iraqi-Syrian defense agreement was signed, and a few days later some Syrian troops were moved onto Jordanian territory with Jordan's approval. In August President al-Attassi and General al-Assad went to Cairo to revive the moribund Syrian-U.A.R. defense agreement.

On May 29 the long-awaited new Cabinet with a wider base was formed under President al-Attassi. It included Arab nationalists, unionists, and independents as well as Baathists, although the Baath retained all the key positions.

In August the hijacking of a Trans World Airlines plane to Damascus, and Syria's detention of two Israeli male passengers, caused a major international incident. In September Syria refused to attend the Islamic summit meeting in Rabat. The Syrian Baathists were unenthusiastic about Islamic solidarity, although the official reason for staying away was that Syria had no diplomatic relations with Morocco. A Syrian delegation attended the Arab summit in Rabat in December, however.

The Syrian economy improved in 1969. The 1968–69 cotton crop was a record one, and exports were up 15% over the previous season. The grain harvest was also well above recent years, and Syria's new but growing oil industry was producing 100,000 bbl. a day by the end of the year. (P. MD.)

ENCYCLOPÆDIA BRITANNICA FILMS. *The Middle East* (1955); *The Mediterranean World* (1961).

SYRIA

Education. (1966–67) Primary, pupils 742,681, teachers 20,658; secondary, pupils 201,977, teachers 7,029; vocational, pupils 5,256, teachers 509; teacher training, students 7,464, teachers 347; higher (including 2 universities), students 31,644, teaching staff (1965–66) 839.

Finance. Monetary unit: Syrian pound, with a par value of S£2.19 to U.S. $1 (S£5.26 = £1 sterling) and an approximate free rate (Oct. 1969) of S£4.20 to U.S. $1 (S£10 = £1). Budget (1968 est.) balanced at S£1,120 million. Money supply: (March 1968) S£1,514 million; (March 1967) S£1,228 million. Cost of living: (Damascus; 1963 = 100): (April 1969) 114; (April 1968) 117.

Foreign Trade. (1968) Imports S£1,262.7 million; exports S£673 million. Import sources: Czechoslovakia 12%; U.S.S.R. 9%; Italy 8%; France 8%; U.S. 7%; Iraq 6%; West Germany 6%; Lebanon 5%. Export destinations: Lebanon 21%; U.S.S.R. 11%; Italy 8%; Japan 7%; Kuwait 5%; France 5%. Main exports: cotton 37%; livestock 16%; fruit and vegetables 8%.

Transport and Communications. Roads (1968) 13,900 km. (including 9,700 km. with improved surface). Motor vehicles in use (1968): passenger 29,466; commercial 14,140. Railways: (1967) 844 km.; traffic (1968) 85 million passenger-km., freight 122 million net ton-km. Air traffic (1967): 93,341,000 passenger-km.; freight 1,110,000 net ton-km. Ships entered (1967) vessels totaling 10,451,000 net registered tons; goods loaded (1967) 21,256,000 metric tons, unloaded 1,590,000 metric tons. Telephones (Dec. 1967) 91,407. Radio receivers (Dec. 1965) 1,745,000. Television receivers (Dec. 1968) 92,500.

Agriculture. Production (in 000; metric tons; 1968; 1967 in parentheses): wheat 600 (1,049); barley 512 (590); millet and sorghum 37 (40); grapes (1967) 214, (1966) 206; raisins (1967) 8.8, (1966) 8.1; figs 52 (54); olive oil *c.* 16 (24); tobacco (1967) 6, (1966) 9.7; dry broad beans (1967) 14, (1966) 13; chick-peas (1967) 64, (1966) 16; lentils 50 (84); cotton, lint *c.* 154 (127); wool, greasy (1967) 13, (1966) 11. Livestock (in 000; 1967–68): cattle *c.* 460; sheep (1966–67) 5,569; horses *c.* 63; mules *c.* 63; asses *c.* 240; goats (1966–67) 757; chickens (Dec. 1966) 4,090.

Industry. Production (in 000; metric tons; 1967): petroleum products 1,050; cement (1968) 917; cotton yarn 19; electricity (kw-hr.) 676,000.

Taiwan

Taiwan, which consists of the islands of Formosa and Quemoy and other surrounding islands, is the seat of the Republic of China (Nationalist China). It is situated north of the Philippines, southwest of Japan and Okinawa, and east of Hong Kong. The island of Formosa has an area of 13,807 sq.mi. (35,760 sq.km.); including its 77 outlying islands (14 in the Taiwan group and 63 in the Pescadores group), the area of Taiwan totals 13,885 sq.mi. Pop. (1969 est.): 13,956,612, excluding armed forces and aliens. Cap. and largest city: T'ai-pei (pop., 1969 est., 1,645,794). President in 1969, Chiang Kai-shek; vice-president and premier (president of the Executive Yuan), C. K. Yen.

On October 10 the Republic of China celebrated its 58th anniversary, the 20th time that it had done so in exile on Taiwan. Although the recovery of the mainland and the construction of a new China were the declared policies of Taiwan's Nationalist government and the avowed aim of its president, the possibilities for accomplishing this remained remote. However, the deepening of the conflict between Communist China and the Soviet Union, and disunity and bitter factionalism within the Chinese Communist Party during and after the Cultural Revolution, gave considerable encouragement to the Nationalist cause. As a result of this the basic slogan of "Resisting Russia" was not in evidence during the year. It was also interesting that the foreign minister of the Soviet Union, Andrei A. Gromyko, when addressing the General Assembly of the UN on September 19, did not call for the admission of Communist China and the expulsion of Nationalist China in insulting terms. After former Communist Chinese Pres. Liu Shao-ch'i and his associates were denounced by the Maoists as revisionists and early collaborators with the Nationalists, President Chiang regarded Mao Tse-tung as the archenemy and evildoer in China and indicated his readiness to cooperate with any group on the mainland opposing Mao. Nevertheless, during the year the Formosa Strait was relatively quiet. The Nationalists asserted that their commando forces raided the Communist naval base in Fukien Province, and that their agents attacked Communist military posts in Yünnan and Kwangtung provinces and in Tibet.

The tenth National Congress of the ruling Kuomintang was convened on March 29 to improve the organization and operation of the party and to intensify preparation for the recovery of the mainland. More than 600 representatives from the party in Taiwan and in foreign countries attended the 12-day session. The congress adopted a party platform and a number of resolutions emphasizing the importance of preparation for the recovery of the mainland, economic and scientific progress, administrative efficiency, educational expansion, and social welfare. It elected an enlarged Central Committee of 99 members, which included many top managerial and technological persons in and outside of the government.

"PARIS MATCH" FROM PICTORIAL PARADE

Members of the Taiwan Women's Army Corps pass in review during training exercise in 1969. Mme Chiang Kai-shek directs the corps.

With the approval of the Standing Committee, President Chiang reshuffled his Cabinet ministers on June 25, appointing his son, Chiang Ching-kuo, as deputy premier. Huang Chieh, governor of Taiwan, replaced Chiang Ching-kuo as defense minister. Chen Ta-ching, commander in chief of the Army, became the new governor of Taiwan. The appointment of young Chiang was generally regarded as a move prompted by the eventuality of President Chiang's retirement in a few years. For several years supporters of young Chiang had been systematically put in key positions in the Kuomintang and the government. An election to fill vacant seats in the legislature—the first since the Nationalist government came to Taiwan—was held December 20. In T'ai-pei two independents, including one who had been highly critical of the government, were elected to seats for which the Kuomintang did not put up candidates.

The Nationalist government strengthened its good relations with anti-Communist countries in Asia as a result of an exchange of state visits. Japanese Prime

TAIWAN

Education. (1967–68) Primary, pupils 2,348,218, teachers 55,683; secondary (1965–66), pupils 543,019, teachers 19,882; vocational (1965–66), pupils 117,575, teachers 6,194; teacher training (1965–66), students 3,159, teachers 225; higher (including 10 universities), students 138,613, teaching staff 7,564.

Finance. Monetary unit: New Taiwan dollar (NT$40.10 = U.S. $1; NT$96.24 = £1 sterling). Gold and foreign exchange, official: (June 1969) U.S. $440 million; (June 1968) U.S. $416 million. Budget (1967–68 actual): revenue NT$31,291,000,000; expenditure NT$29,756,000,000. Gross national product: (1968) NT$166.2 billion; (1967) NT$144.1 billion. Money supply: (June 1969) NT$25,180,000,000; (June 1968) NT$24,160,000,000. Cost of living (1963 = 100): (June 1969) 116; (June 1968) 114.

Foreign Trade. (1968) Imports U.S. $903.3 million; exports U.S. $802.2 million. Import sources: Japan 40%; U.S. 27%. Export destinations: U.S. 36%; Japan 16%; Hong Kong 9%; West Germany 6%; South Vietnam 6%; Canada 5%. Main exports: plywood 7%; bananas 6%; sugar 6%.

Transport and Communications. Roads (1967) *c.* 18,500 km. Motor vehicles in use (1967): passenger 25,100; commercial (including buses) 24,500. Railways: (1967) 3,820 km.; traffic (1968) 5,543,000,000 passenger-km., freight 2,709,000,000 net ton-km. Air traffic (1968): 348 million passenger-km.; freight 4,227,000 net ton-km. Shipping (1968): merchant vessels 100 gross tons and over 187; gross tonnage 762,515. Telephones (Jan. 1968) 230,229. Radio receivers (Dec. 1967) 1,402,000. Television receivers (Dec. 1967) 164,000.

Agriculture. Production (in 000; metric tons; 1968; 1967 in parentheses): rice 3,275 (3,162); sweet potatoes 3,564 (3,720); cassava (1967) 299, (1966) 264; peanuts 99 (136); oranges *c.* 150 (135); tobacco 21 (18); tea (1967) 24, (1966) 21; sugar, raw value (1968–69) *c.* 784, (1967–68) 872; bananas (1967) 654, (1966) 528; jute 13 (10). Livestock (in 000; Dec. 1967): cattle 104; pigs 3,003; goats (Dec. 1966) 156; chickens (Dec. 1966) 10,886.

Industry. Production (in 000; metric tons; 1968): coal 5,013; natural gas (cu.m.) 704,000; electricity (kw-hr.) 9,802,000; cement 3,993; pig iron 76; salt (1967) 518; petroleum products (1966) 2,187; cotton yarn 68; paper (1966) 214.

Table Tennis: *see* Sporting Record

Minister Eisaku Sato's reiteration of Japan's one-China policy on March 5 heartened the Nationalists. Speaking to a budget committee of the Japanese Diet, Sato declared that since Japan had chosen the Nationalist regime as China's only legitimate government it could not change its original attitude, and that his government would continue to regard any change in China's representation in the UN as an important question requiring a two-thirds vote.

Nationalist China took an active part in the work of the fourth Asian and Pacific Council and expanded its programs of technical cooperation, largely with African countries. The number of countries maintaining diplomatic relations with Nationalist China increased by 2 to 68, including 22 of the 42 African countries. However, U.S. Pres. Richard Nixon's declared policy of reducing and avoiding U.S. involvement in post-Vietnam-war Asia and repeated U.S. overtures to Communist China caused general concern in Taiwan. On his tour of Asian-Pacific countries in connection with President Nixon's global journey, U.S. Secretary of State William P. Rogers visited Taiwan on August 1–3 with the reported purpose of reassuring President Chiang that the U.S. would maintain its commitment to defend Taiwan. At a press conference in T'ai-pei, however, Rogers affirmed U.S. willingness to have more friendly relations with all nations, including Communist China.

The fifth four-year economic development plan, with emphasis on acceleration of industrialization and the development of natural resources, began on January 1 after 16 years of continued economic progress. A major portion of the estimated $4.5 billion needed to carry out the plan was expected to come from foreign sources. The official report revealed that the gross national product in 1968 amounted to $4,160,000,000, with an increase in per capita income from $203 in 1967 to $237 in 1968. (H. T. Ch.)

See also China.

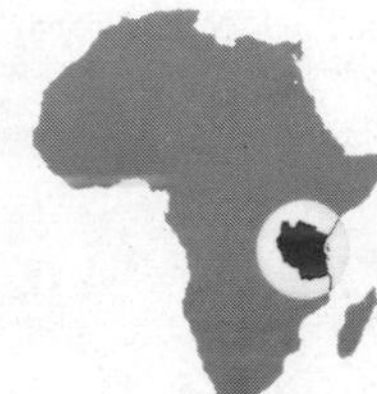

Tanzania

This republic, an East African member of the Commonwealth of Nations, consists of two parts: Tanganyika, on the Indian Ocean, bordered by Kenya, Uganda, Rwanda, Burundi, the Congo (Kinshasa), Zambia, Malawi, and Mozambique; and Zanzibar, just off the coast, including Zanzibar Island, Pemba Island, and small islets. Total area of the united republic: 362,821 sq.mi. (939,706 sq.km.). Total pop. (1969 est.): 12,926,000 (approximately 98% Africans and 1% Arabs). Cap. and largest city: Dar es Salaam (pop., 1967, 272,821), in Tanganyika. Language: primarily Bantu, of which Swahili serves as the lingua franca. Religion: predominantly pagan; many Muslims in coastal areas and in up-country settlements; Christian minority. President in 1969, Julius Nyerere.

At the Tanganyika African National Union (TANU) national conference in June, President Nyerere outlined Tanzania's second five-year development plan. It differed from its predecessor in its greater flexibility—the government was firmly committed only to those projects planned for the first two years of the scheme—and in the extent of the consultations that had gone into its preparation. The keynote was self-reliance, with 60% of government expenditure to be financed from within Tanzania itself, while the East African Community was expected to provide $69.6 million. The aim of the plan was to produce a 6.5% growth in the gross domestic product in each year. In spite of the long-term plans for industrial expansion, most of the country's economic growth would depend upon the rural workers.

CAMERA PRESS—PIX FROM PUBLIX

Pres. Julius Nyerere inspects honour guard at Heroes' Day parade in Dar es Salaam in 1969.

The farming community was already responding to the government's challenge. In the Rungwe district in the southern highlands nearly 2,000 small landholders growing tea formed themselves into a cooperative to transport their crop to nearby factories for processing. Seven hundred Masai families who had moved with their cattle to Lugoba, near Bagamoyo, raised about $5,000 toward the cost of constructing an adequate water supply.

TANZANIA

Education. (1966) Primary, pupils 740,991, teachers 14,809; secondary, pupils 23,836, teachers 1,171; vocational, pupils 2,499, teachers 68; teacher training, students 2,473, teachers 230; higher (at the Dar es Salaam University College; 1965), students 440.

Finance. Monetary unit: Tanzanian shilling, with a par value of TShs. 7.14 to U.S. $1 (TShs. 17.14 = £1 sterling). Budget (1968–69 est.): revenue TShs. 1,055,284,000; expenditure TShs. 1,051,414,000. National income (mainland only): (1967) TShs. 5,201,000,000; (1966) TShs. 5,003,000,000. Cost of living (Dar es Salaam; 1963 = 100): (June 1969) 120; (June 1968) 119.

Foreign Trade. (Excluding trade with Kenya and Uganda; 1968) Imports TShs. 1,532,000,000; exports TShs. 1,626,000,000. Import sources: U.K. 28%; Japan 9%; West Germany 7%; Italy 7%; Iran 6%; China 6%; U.S. 5%; Netherlands 5%. Export destinations: U.K. 24%; Zambia 11%; Hong Kong 8%; India 7%; Japan 7%; U.S. 6%; West Germany 5%. Main exports: cotton 18%; coffee 16%; sisal 10%; diamonds 8%.

Transport and Communications. Roads (1967) *c.* 35,000 km. (including *c.* 1,000 km. in Zanzibar and Pemba). Motor vehicles in use (1966): passenger *c.* 38,000; commercial (including buses) *c.* 12,500. Railways (1967) 2,970 km. (for traffic *see* KENYA). Shipping traffic (mainland only; 1967) goods loaded 1,254,000 metric tons, unloaded 1,633,000 metric tons. Telephones (Jan. 1968) 29,282. Radio receivers (Dec. 1967) 138,000.

Agriculture. Production (in 000; metric tons; 1968; 1967 in parentheses): cotton, lint (mainland) *c.* 54 (68); sisal (mainland) *c.* 197 (*c.* 220); corn (mainland; 1967) *c.* 800, (1966) 1,150; sweet potatoes (mainland; 1966) 248, (1965) 238; millet and sorghum (mainland; 1967) *c.* 1,100, (1966) *c.* 1,100; sugar, raw value (mainland; 1968–69) *c.* 117, (1967–68) *c.* 87; rice (1967) *c.* 125; (1966) *c.* 143; cassava (1967) *c.* 1,200, (1966) *c.* 1,180; timber (cu.m.; 1967) *c.* 11,800, (1966) *c.* 11,600; fish catch (1967) 118, (1966) 92. Livestock (in 000; 1967–68): cattle *c.* 11,060; sheep (mainland; 1966–67) 3,093; goats (1966–67) *c.* 4,694; asses (mainland) *c.* 160; pigs (mainland) *c.* 18.

Industry. Production (in 000; metric tons; 1967): salt *c.* 40; tin concentrates (metal content) 0.4; gold (troy oz.) 18; diamonds (exports; metric carats) 986; electricity (public supply; kw-hr.) 297,000.

In anticipation of the development plan 100 Soviet geologists arrived in Tanzania in February to speed prospecting and geologic investigations, while in June Italy agreed to lend $9.6 million to build an airport at the foot of Mt. Kilimanjaro. The survey for the Tanzania-Zambia railway to be built by Chinese engineers was nearing completion, and a joint agreement was signed by the three countries on November 15. A $7.5 million loan for roads was received from the International Development Association in December.

The rural workers were among the few to benefit directly from the tough budget announced late in June by the minister of finance, Amir Jamal. Faced with a recurrent expenditure of $180 million, the minister proposed a basic sales tax of 10% on all consumer goods, rising to 15 or 20% on luxury goods. For the benefit of agricultural workers the produce tax was abolished and the minimum wage was increased by TShs. 20 a month.

At the TANU national conference Nyerere was reelected unopposed as president of Tanzania and Rashidi Kawawa as second vice-president. By contrast, First Vice-Pres. Sheikh Abeid Karume announced that there would be no elections in Zanzibar because elections were unsuitable for any African country and had only been introduced by the colonialists to cause friction among Africans.

In a characteristic speech in December 1968, Nyerere reassured the Asians of Tanzania that they would be judged by performance and not by racial origins. Less characteristic was his decision to arrest Kassim Hanga, former vice-president of Zanzibar, Othman Shariff, formerly ambassador to the U.S., and Ali Mwange Tambwe, a junior minister, on charges of plotting against the Zanzibar government. The three men, all former members of the Zanzibar Revolutionary Council, were flown to the island in September and were later executed, while nine others, said to be fellow conspirators, were imprisoned. Shariff had previously left Zanzibar with Nyerere's assistance after being threatened with death for allegedly plotting against the revolutionary council and had only returned to Tanzania on receiving an assurance of safety from the president. Hanga also had returned from Guinea in 1967 on a similar understanding. These executions followed the arrest and imprisonment in January of A. Edarus Baalawy, minister of health and welfare in the sultan of Zanzibar's government; Salim Kombo Saleh, minister of home affairs, and Abadhar Juma Khalib, minister of agriculture. The three men, held in detention since 1964, were released in December 1968, on the mainland of Tanzania. They were then taken back to Zanzibar for a brief period of questioning before being told that they were free to go anywhere. Returning once again to the mainland, they were persuaded to go back to Zanzibar where their imprisonment followed almost at once. Concern about the situation in Zanzibar increased on the mainland.

The president was not without his own problems. During his absence on a visit to the U.S.S.R. and Hungary in October, Michael Kamaliza, a former trade union leader and minister of labour, and Bibi Titi Muhammad, a leader of the women's wing of TANU, were detained, along with four army officers, on charges of subversion. In December the oil pipeline to Zambia was bombed, but the identity of the saboteurs was unknown. (K. I.)

ENCYCLOPÆDIA BRITANNICA FILMS. *East Africa (Kenya, Tanganyika, Uganda)* (1962).

Telecommunications

As had no previous year, 1969 highlighted the contradictions of modern telecommunications. Millions sat at home and watched a telephone conversation between U.S. Pres. Richard Nixon and two men on the moon, while being far from sure that they would be able to put through a trouble-free call to their friends to talk about it afterward. An old, supposedly defunct communications satellite, Early Bird, burst into life again to give a bonus of extra service while a new one, 23,000 mi. over the Atlantic, broke down just when the world was looking to it to relay a historic event from Wales to a record audience in the U.S. Puzzled observers saw the U.S. and the U.K. take diametrically opposite decisions in the ordering of their internal telecommunications affairs. Meanwhile, the world, crowding to take part in the new age of global telecommunications made possible by U.S. expertise in satellite launching, remained opposed to U.S. domination of the management of the resulting network.

The fundamental problem of how to devise regulations that preserved the integrity of the telephone network without stifling innovation was tackled head-on in the U.S. and in Britain. The U.S. Federal Communications Commission (FCC) continued to redefine the terms of near monopoly under which the American Telephone and Telegraph Company (AT & T) operated the Bell Telephone system. In the U.K., the monopoly of the Post Office over telecommunications had to be restated before the Post Office, a government department, could become a public corporation in October. Speaking in the House of Commons, the postmaster general said, "We must ensure that possible technical developments are caught within the monopoly . . . before they are invented and before they become competitive with the monopoly." By contrast, a report by former U.S. Pres. Lyndon B. Johnson's task force on telecommunications policy, unratified but released in the spring, made the following statement: "The broad goal of public policy on telecommunications should be to release and encourage potentialities for innovation in technology and management, both within the public message telephone network and outside it, where such changes do not affect its basic integrity and viability."

Chances for a global satellite communications system linking all nations of the world without regard to political ideology brightened in 1969. Diplomats from member nations and "observer" representatives from the Soviet Union and the Eastern European socialist countries met in Washington, D.C., throughout 1969 and appeared near agreement on a new permanent charter for the commercial International Telecommunications Satellite Consortium (Intelsat) by the year's end. A successful conclusion of the talks would mean that the organization would be prepared to more fully exploit satellites for high-quality, low-cost communications services for all nations, rich or poor. Soviet-bloc participation, which by the end of 1969 seemed likely, would further enhance the system's efficiency and utility.

Under its six-year-old interim charter, Intelsat grew to include 69 nations in 1969, and at the end of the year nearly 40 ground stations for receiving signals were in use or in an advanced stage of construction. A new superpowerful Intelsat 3 satellite

AUTHENTICATED NEWS INTERNATIONAL

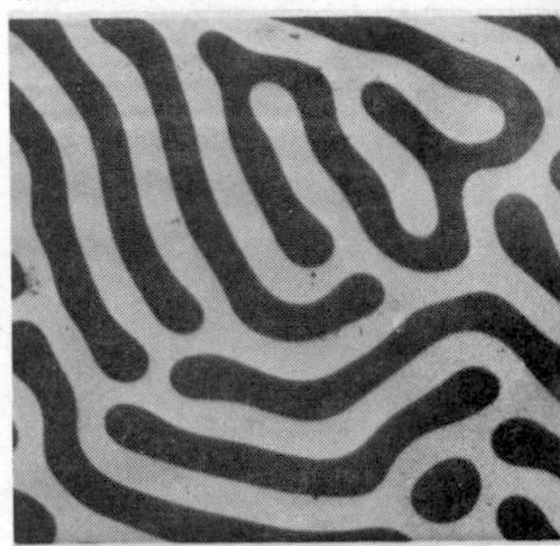

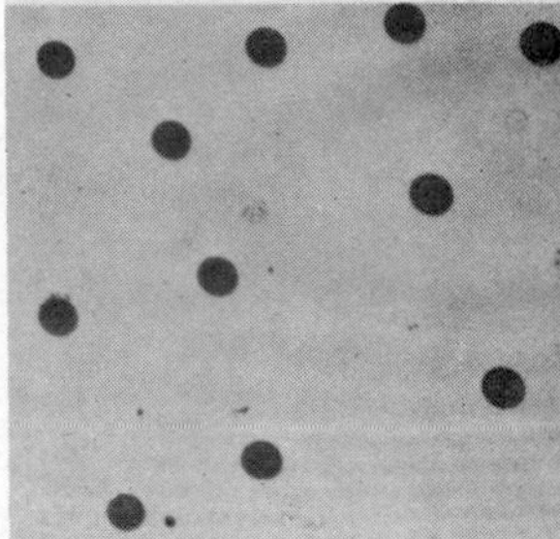

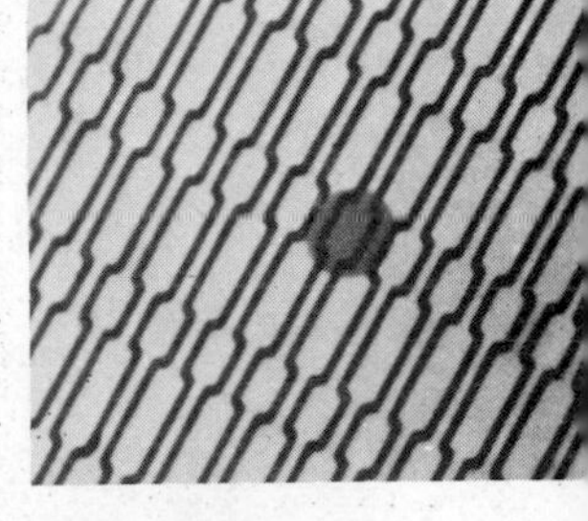

Magnetic memory "bubbles" developed by AT & T designed for use in communications switching systems and computers. Strip magnetic domains (top) are subjected to a bias field to form the bubbles (centre). Bubbles can be placed in a printed circuit conductor array (bottom) and moved at data rates of three million bits per second.

Tariffs: *see* Commercial Policies; Trade, International

Taxation: *see* Government Finance

Tea: *see* Agriculture

also went into operation. As a consequence of this progress, large portions of the world were able to watch on television sets such events as the U.S. Apollo astronauts setting foot on the moon, the inauguration and world tour of President Nixon, and the investiture of Prince Charles.

Satellites. Clearly, the most significant event in telecommunications was the progress toward a new permanent charter for Intelsat. When the meeting was started in February, nearly 100 nations were represented as shareholding members or observers who had expressed serious interest in becoming members.

The negotiations got off to a rocky start when the U.S. delegation took a tough stand by insisting that U.S. domination of the organization must be continued. Later, however, the U.S. softened its stand and the organization's future brightened. Specifically, the U.S. agreed to forgo some of the powers held by Comsat, its corporate representative in Intelsat. The compromise called for Comsat to give up its management responsibilities to an international secretariat but for it to continue serving as technical manager under a contract from Intelsat.

Furthermore, the U.S. agreed to a formula for curtailing its own voting strength. Since Intelsat ownership shares were based on the extent to which a country used international communications services, the U.S., with 53% ownership, could effectively veto decisions by the other members. The U.S. voting strength would be reduced under the new agreement.

The shift in the U.S. position was geared mainly to lessening the hostility that had grown up among the industrialized nations of Western Europe, Canada, and Japan. Those countries believed that their managers were able to operate the system as well as Comsat, and this factor became the main source of friction in the talks.

Fortunately, the same steps taken to ease the feelings of those nations were also appealing to the Soviet Union and its Eastern European allies. By the end of 1969 most of the stumbling blocks preventing Soviet-bloc membership in Intelsat had been cleared. Diplomats were still trying to work out ownership shares for the Communist nations, which thus far had used little in the way of international communications services.

Many diplomats grumbled, however, over the lack of a U.S. policy. They complained that it was difficult to negotiate an international satellite agreement when the U.S. had not even settled on a domestic satellite plan. One policy statement was, however, made in 1969. A task force on telecommunications policy appointed by President Johnson in 1967 had its work reported in the spring of 1969. This group recommended, in part, an immediate start on a domestic satellite system, an end to competition between cable and satellite technologies, a stronger government policy planning agency, and new frequency allocation procedures.

The report of the group failed to get the endorsement of President Johnson who commissioned it or of President Nixon who was in office when it was released. Instead, the White House announced a smaller task force to look into domestic satellite problems.

Elsewhere, progress was more tangible in 1969. Canada took a major step toward a domestic satellite system, and contracts with industrial companies were signed. With the completion of the system in late 1971, Canada expected to be able to provide television and telephone service to remote mining villages in the north. Officials believed that such facilities would help attract mine workers to the north.

In September India negotiated a deal with the U.S. National Aeronautics and Space Administration (NASA) to launch a satellite that would beam educational television programs to that country. It would be the first large-scale use of satellites to distribute television signals to small, inexpensive ground terminals. The program was to be designed to assist the Indian people in learning more about agriculture, family planning, and sanitation, as well as reading and writing. Brazil expressed interest in a similar system.

Britain's largest ground station, Goonhilly 2, came into operation at the beginning of the year and was designed to accept 400 telephone circuits and television mostly between Europe and stations in North America, using an Intelsat 3 satellite over the Atlantic. Meanwhile, the newly refurbished Goonhilly 1 was to be able to link the Middle and Far East using an Intelsat 3 over the Indian Ocean. The Atlantic Intelsat 3 was to have enabled Goonhilly 2 to carry more traffic than Goonhilly 1 and all the transatlantic submarine cables put together, but the Atlantic satellites underwent some difficulties. The first had to be dumped into the Atlantic when its booster rocket failed on launching. A replacement designed to last five years failed after a few months just before it was due to transmit to the U.S. live television broadcasts of the investiture of the prince of Wales, forcing transmission of the ceremony to be achieved via the Indian Ocean satellite. Another Intelsat 3 launched over the Atlantic in July went into an orbit 3,000 mi. too low and had to be abandoned. Fortunately, Intelsat 1 (Early Bird) was still in orbit and was able to take most of the Atlantic traffic. The satellite that failed later came back into service.

The military services were taking full advantage of the flexibility offered by satellite communications. Completed in 1969 and due for operation early in 1970 was Skynet, Britain's satellite-based communi-

Countries Having More Than 100,000 Telephones

Telephones in service, 1968

Country	Number of telephones	Percentage increase over 1958	Telephones per 100 population	Country	Number of telephones	Percentage increase over 1958	Telephones per 100 population
Algeria*	145,000	...	1.14	Lebanon*	130,000	223.1	5.10
Argentina	1,553,281	31.5	6.69	Malaysia	145,425	...	1.42
Australia	3,178,278	75.2	27.05	Mexico	1,044,415	152.9	2.25
Austria	1,163,194	96.4	15.85	Morocco*	145,000	14.8	1.01
Belgium	1,753,698	77.7	18.26	Netherlands	2,715,635	106.0	21.45
Brazil	1,472,677	66.3	1.70	New Zealand	1,119,422	85.0	40.63
Bulgaria	338,446	...	4.06	Norway	987,292	49.6	25.67
Canada	8,385,476	73.7	40.65	Pakistan	162,642	182.2	0 15
Chile	294,712	83.8	3.27	Peru	152,136	92.2	1.21
China†	244,028	...	0.05	Philippines	207,593	181.3	0.59
Colombia*	515,000	130.1	2.64	Poland	1,530,479	132.3	4.77
Cuba	238,224	57.3	2.92	Portugal	615,965	102.0	6.49
Czechoslovakia	1,678,717	99.1	11.71	Puerto Rico	239,528	236.6	8.83
Denmark	1,469,195	54.5	30.11	Rhodesia	112,086	80.8	2.45
Finland	949,976	81.1	20.32	Romania*	550,000	...	2.84
France	6,999,621	100.1	13.96	Singapore	106,124	126.7	5.37
Germany, East	1,780,319	58.5	10.42	South Africa	1,322,101	59.6	7.06
Germany, West	10,321,281	118.1	17.21	Spain	3,378,865	152.2	10.47
Greece	660,129	329.3	7.52	Sweden	3,934,694	63.3	49.84
Hong Kong	353,912	373.1	9.13	Switzerland	2,533,684	82.9	41.84
Hungary	634,527	69.3	6.20	Taiwan	230,229	346.9	1.73
India	993,590	201.4	0.19	Turkey	427,770	110.2	1.30
Indonesia	169,142	99.5	0.15	U.S.S.R.*	9,100,000	155.8	3.84
Iran	220,100	240.5	0.83	United Arab Republic*	335,000	85.2	1.07
Ireland	249,473	92.6	8.58	United Kingdom	12,099,000	64.5	21.87
Israel	342,455	328.1	12.74	United States	103,752,000	63.1	51.81
Italy	7,057,187	145.8	13.44	Uruguay*	195,000	51.3	6.96
Japan	18,216,767	321.5	18.07	Venezuela	327,038	133.9	3.44
Korea, South	421,091	653.7	1.41	Yugoslavia	506,039	155.5	2.52

*Estimate. †1948.

Source: American Telephone and Telegraph Co., *The World's Telephones, 1958* and *1968.*

cations system. Skynet comprised nine ground stations and two satellites, one operational and one standby, procured from and launched by the U.S. into a closely defined orbit over the Indian Ocean. Five ground stations would be fixed on land, two installed in assault ships, and two would be transported by air in emergencies. This network permitted military communication from the Atlantic to the Far East including Hong Kong. Skynet was complementary to the U.S. Initial Defense Satellite Communications System.

In February a consortium headed by Standard Electric Lorenz AG was awarded a DM. 100 million contract by NATO. A massive project, the system was to use 12 ground stations in conjunction with a NATO satellite. COMEST, a new European consortium, asked the European Space Research Organization to provide a European communications satellite that would carry sound and television programs within the Eurovision countries and Africa.

Cables and Radio. The twin failures of a new satellite and the most recent Anglo-American cable at the height of international communications concerning the investiture of the prince of Wales and the moon voyagers proved that diversity in telecommunications was still essential.

Once the subject of controversy because it was believed that Intelsat 3 would make it unnecessary, the TAT5 submarine cable carrying 720 high-quality speech circuits from Rhode Island to Spain had by 1969 become sorely needed. Via a microwave link to the Spanish Mediterranean coast, the cable, due for completion in March 1970, would have access to a projected cable, MAT1 (640 circuits), to Rome. Another microwave link northward to Lisbon would connect TAT5 with SAT1 (360 circuits), already open to South Africa. As a safeguard against damage by trawlers, the ends of TAT5 were to be plowed into the shore using a specially developed vehicle.

Tropospheric scatter radio equipment continued to provide economic links for low traffic. One eight-channel system was installed by Marconi to link southern Spain with northern Africa using ultrahigh frequency to bounce the signal over the intervening mountains. A similar system was used to bridge 400 mi. of the South China Sea from East to West Malaysia.

Telephones. Worldwide, the number of telephones in service in 1969 climbed to near the 225 million mark, with more than 114 million in the United States. The number of transoceanic telephone calls was increasing at an annual rate of 20%. More than 15 million overseas calls were completed in 1968, and nearly 140 million were expected to be completed in 1980.

AT & T, which serviced most of the telephones in the U.S., handled approximately 105 billion messages in 1968. Long-distance calls were up 11% to almost six billion. The company spent $4.7 billion on building new and improved facilities, bringing the investment in the Bell System's lines, equipment, and buildings to $45 billion.

AT & T said in 1969 that it planned to introduce intercontinental direct distance dialing between the U.S. and Great Britain, providing for overseas calls without the use of an overseas operator. This development would be accompanied by a 25% overall reduction in rates for the service. With the completion of the new submarine cable to Spain, all rates to Europe would be reduced about one-fourth.

The quality of telephone service in the U.S., always touted as the world's finest, came into serious question in 1969. Service complaints were widespread throughout the year. In some locations, notably the Wall Street section of New York, Chicago suburbs, and parts of Florida, service problems reached crisis proportions. Some businesses took full-page ads in newspapers to complain of bad service and to chide the telephone companies—mainly AT & T—for not correcting the faults. AT & T accelerated its spending program on the affected services and made other efforts to ease the difficulties.

Meanwhile, technology continued its unceasing, ever accelerating pace. The most dramatic news was an announcement by AT & T stating that the company had developed magnetic memory "bubbles" that could be used in the switching and computer systems of the future. The tiny, movable magnetic dots—each smaller than the diameter of a human hair—could be moved around in precise patterns to represent coded information, do computations, or switch signals. Because of their size, enormous amounts of information could be stored in one square inch.

In other research experiments the British Post Office worked on devising means of applying pulse code modulation—the technique that interweaves conversations to increase the capacity of an ordinary telephone line twelvefold—to satellite communication and to television. In the U.S. Bell Telephone began using stored program control on its newest exchanges; in this system one computer, with another as standby, directs the actions of the exchange—where to route calls when congestion builds up, for example. Such changes previously had had to be carried out manually.

Research in the U.S., the U.K., Japan, and elsewhere was directed at overcoming the major obstacle in the way of the picturephone. This was the large and uneconomical bandwidth needed to carry the picture information. By transmitting only the changes in picture information—lip and eye movements, for example—the Bell Laboratories cut the transmission facilities needed to one-third. In the Soviet Union speech was being transmitted experimentally over a laser beam from the Byurakan Astrophysical Laboratory in Armenia to the capital city of Yerevan, a distance of 17 mi. (W. D. Hı.; L. H. Jo.)

A new antenna (left) for use in transatlantic communications was put into operation in October 1969 at Raisting, W.Ger. The main reflector has a diameter of 28.5 m.

D.P.A. FROM PICTORIAL PARADE

COURTESY, STANDARD TELEPHONES AND CABLES LTD.

Technician performs mechanical stress tests on coaxial submarine cable at Southampton, Eng. The cable, scheduled to be in operation in March 1970, could carry 720 high-quality speech circuits.

International Telecommunication Union. The 24th session of the Administrative Council of the International Telecommunication Union (ITU) took place in May at ITU headquarters in Geneva. The council decided that a World Administrative Radio Conference for Space Telecommunications should be held in Geneva starting on June 7, 1971, and lasting for about six weeks. Included in the agenda were the following topics: (1) to consider, revise, and supplement as necessary existing administrative and technical provisions of the Radio Regulations, and adopt new provisions for radiocommunications services using space radio techniques, including those for manned space vehicles and for the radio astronomy services, so as to ensure the efficient use of the broadcasting spectrum; (2) to consider, revise, and supplement as necessary the Radio Regulations to provide for the use of space radio techniques by the aeronautical mobile and maritime mobile services, for communication as well as for radio determination purposes; (3) to consider, revise, and supplement as necessary the existing Table of Radio Frequency Allocations in the Radio Regulations for radiocommunications services, insofar as they may use space radio techniques, and the radio astronomy service; (4) to consider, revise, and supplement the existing provisions pertaining to the technical criteria and the procedures for frequency sharing between space and terrestrial services, and to establish technical criteria and procedures for frequency sharing between space systems; and (5) to consider the feasibility of coordinated frequency planning for radiocommunications satellites, including those placed in geostationary orbit.

In September the ITU's Regional Plan Committee for the Development of Telecommunication in Latin America and the Regional Working Party on International Tariffs for Latin America met in Asunción, Paraguay. The committee established a general plan for the Latin-American international telecommunications network based on short-term estimates until 1975 and long-term estimates until 1978. (ITU)

See also Industrial Review; Television and Radio.

ENCYCLOPÆDIA BRITANNICA FILMS. *Development of Communications (From Telegraph to TV)* (1955).

Television and Radio

With television service already established in more than 100 countries and with radio in even more, there was less room for growth in 1969. Expansion continued, but on a more modest scale than in earlier years. The latest official estimates, by the United States Information Agency on Jan. 1, 1966, put the number of television sets then in use throughout the world at 182 million and the number of radio sets at 543 million. By 1969, according to estimates compiled by *Broadcasting* magazine and *Broadcasting Yearbook,* the totals had reached 223 million television sets and 606 million radio sets.

Approximately 81 million, slightly more than one-third, of the world's 223 million television sets were in the U.S. According to *Broadcasting,* the U.S.S.R. had more than 25 million, Japan 21.3 million, the United Kingdom 20 million, West Germany 15 million, France 11 million, Italy 8.4 million, Canada 6.7 million, Poland 3.5 million, Spain 3 million, Australia 2.7 million, and Sweden 2.3 million. At the other extreme, *Broadcasting* found Uganda with 10,000 sets, Liberia with 5,000, and Sierra Leone with 3,000.

Television stations on the air or under construction throughout the world in 1969 totaled about 6,350. Western Europe had about 2,000, the Far East 2,100, the U.S. 1,042, Eastern Europe 905, South America 165, and Africa 30. In some areas of the world, viewers had little or no choice of programs to watch; in others they had many choices. In the U.S., it was estimated that 99% of the TV-equipped homes could receive programs from at least two stations, more than half (53%) could receive at least seven, and almost one-fourth (24%) could receive nine or more.

Approximately 12,700 radio stations were operating or being built throughout the world. Most were amplitude modulation (AM) stations; the rest were frequency modulation (FM) stations or the booster or relay units used in many countries to extend radio programming into remote areas. More than half of the 12,700 radio stations, or 6,957, were in the U.S., and of the U.S. total almost two out of every five were FM, according to a November count by *Broadcasting.* Slightly more than half of the world's 606 million radio sets, or 303.4 million, were in the U.S.; the rest were spread among other countries in densities that ranged from 1 set for every 2 persons to less than 1 set for every 100 persons.

Organization. The year's biggest achievement in organization was worldwide transmission of the Apollo 11 moon landing (July 20–21). Approximately 600 million viewers in 49 countries watched the broadcast live in a worldwide linkup that cost an estimated $55 billion; 40,000 technical and programming staff were on duty to keep image and sound running through a complex network of satellite and earth-station circuits, microwave links, and landlines. It had been planned to use, for the first time, three Intelsats 3 in synchronous orbit over the Atlantic, Pacific, and Indian oceans, but because of the last-minute failure of the Atlantic Intelsat 3, the moon walk, for example, reached Europe by going round the world "the wrong way." (*See* TELECOMMUNICATIONS.) Transmission of the Apollo 12 moon landing in November was unsuccessful because the television camera failed.

Transmission of the Apollo 11 moon mission, by showing the potentialities of global and interplanetary television, underlined the rapid evolution to be expected in transmission techniques in the 1970s. Acceleration of earth-station construction, with 23 stations in 15 countries in operation in January 1969 and plans for at least double that number by January 1970, also emphasized the pace of change.

Domestic and regional use of satellites was being discussed. In the U.S. the Communications Satellite Corp. (Comsat) and the National Central Television Association (NCTA) had proposed to the Federal Communications Commission (FCC) plans for a six-channel, nationwide service of specialized programming relayed by satellite to community antenna television (CATV) systems. Two channels would go to the Corporation for Public Broadcasting (CPB) and National Educational Television (NET), with one used for medical education and one to carry live and taped coverage of congressional sessions. The proposals had been supported by Pres. Lyndon B. Johnson's task force on telecommunications, but with Pres. Richard Nixon's impending transfer of the FCC's main powers to a White House-based office of telecommunications management, no decisions were immediately likely.

In Canada, plans went ahead to provide total radio and television coverage by a satellite-aided earth-station organization, Telesat. The cost was estimated at approximately $93 million.

In the Soviet Union the Orbita system, by which Central Television programs were transmitted from Moscow to remote areas by the Molniya 1 communications satellite series, was of growing importance. From the new Ostankino television centre in Moscow (fully operational by 1969) signals were transmitted to Orbita earth stations by the Molniya satellites, then relayed to television screens. The Orbita system was of high enough quality to relay signals successfully through up to ten time belts. For transmission within Eastern Europe, and to countries of the Middle East, Asia, Africa, and South and Central America, a newly designed range of Intersputnik satellites was planned.

At the opposite end of the scale from satellite transmission was the revitalization of radio. Adaptation to the situation created by mass television audiences had been slow, though in some parts of the world—Italy, Norway, Eastern Europe, the Middle East, Asia, Africa, Australia—for reasons ranging from cultural pride and the need of scattered rural communities for education and entertainment to lack of money, radio had never lost hold. But in Britain, where plans for radical changes in broadcasting in the 1970s were greeted by some with horror (*see* below), a long, last-ditch effort to popularize radio was reaping somewhat untimely rewards. Official figures showed that in 1969 listening had increased by nearly 70%, not all accounted for by the "pop" Radio 1.

In the U.S. the Radio Advertising Bureau's 1969 report stated that in 1968 industry's spending on radio advertising for the first time topped $1 billion, a 12% increase over 1967. President Nixon's announcement that, as a result of the success of his radio speeches in the election campaign, he planned to give some of his more important policy statements on radio, highlighted the tendency.

In television, colour continued to affect sales of sets and to have a serious effect on broadcasting organizations' investment planning. Newcomers and expected newcomers to colour were Hungary and Télé Monte-Carlo (1969); Sweden, Denmark, and Finland (1970); Belgium and Italy (1971); and Yugoslavia (1973).

United States. Colour had become an established television service by 1969. All three major networks—the American Broadcasting Company (ABC), the Columbia Broadcasting System (CBS), and the National Broadcasting Company (NBC)—were broadcasting almost exclusively in colour, and the proportion of local programming that individual stations presented in black and white was diminishing. By Oct. 1, 1969, the number of homes having colour television sets was estimated by NBC at 22.2 million, or 37.5% of all U.S. television homes, a gain of 27% in total colour sets in 12 months.

The issue of domestic satellites to relay television and radio programming appeared late in 1969 to be approaching a resolution. It came to a head when the American Telephone & Telegraph Co., which handled most network-program distribution by terrestrial means, announced rate increases that, effective in October, raised the television networks' program transmission costs by approximately $20 million to an annual total of $65 million. CBS responded by endorsing in principle earlier proposals of ABC and NBC that a separate domestic satellite system be established to relay network programs—including those of the NET network at no charge—to affiliated stations. Comsat followed with a plan to provide, through its own satellites, interconnection service to all the networks at rates that it said would be substantially less than those charged by AT & T.

The final decision would have to be made by the FCC, which had postponed action, first in 1967 when the president of the U.S. created a task force on communications policy, and again in 1969 after the presidency had changed hands and the White House requested time to review the issue.

Commercial broadcasters came increasingly under attack in 1969. The FCC rocked them in January by invoking a 1965 policy statement in order to revoke the license of station WHDH-TV in Boston, Mass., owned and operated by the owners of the *Boston Herald-Traveler* newspaper, and award it to Boston Broadcasters, Inc. In its decision, the commission made clear that a multimedia owner being challenged at license-renewal time (every three years) might need more than a satisfactory programming record to keep his license. The owners of WHDH-TV said they would take the case to court, but the decision had repercussions throughout the industry. *Broadcasting* magazine estimated that the FCC policy in the case could jeopardize broadcast holdings that, in the 50 biggest markets alone, were valued at $3 billion.

In June broadcasters were jolted again—and this time the FCC as well—by another court. In the last

Sales of Colour and Black-and-White Television Sets in the U.S.

Year	Total	Colour	Black and white
1967	11,564,000	5,563,000	6,001,000
1968	13,211,000	6,215,000*	6,996,000

*Includes 2,123 units that are both colour and black and white.
Source: Electronic Industries Association.

decision written by Judge Warren E. Burger before he became chief justice of the U.S., the U.S. Court of Appeals for the District of Columbia took away the license of station WLBT-TV in Jackson, Miss.—a station long involved in litigation over viewers' charges of racism in its programming—and ordered the FCC to invite new applicants for the license. The decision reprimanded the FCC for its attitude toward public interveners who had appeared in the case, and ordered it to treat such interveners in the future as "an ally," not "an opponent." The decision was widely construed as encouraging community groups to file protests or competing applications against license renewals for existing stations.

The U.S. Department of Justice continued its strong opposition to concentrations of control of mass media. Just before the start of 1969, it had filed suit to break up the radio-television-newspaper interests of the Gannett Co. in Rockford, Ill., on antitrust grounds, forcing Gannett to sell WREX-TV there. In another case, in 1969, it asked the FCC to require Frontier Broadcasting Co. of Cheyenne, Wyo., to sell KFBC-TV there because of Frontier's local broadcasting, newspaper, and CATV interests, though it reserved judgment on whether antitrust laws had been violated.

Television broadcasters also took their lumps in congressional hearings on sex and violence in programming, and in hearings before the National Commission on the Causes and Prevention of Violence. The latter issued a report concluding that TV violence had contributed to violence in real life and urging broadcasters to reduce violence in programs, especially those for children.

The most spectacular trouble broadcasters encountered, however, came from U.S. Vice-Pres. Spiro T. Agnew in a mid-November speech denouncing television network news as biased and unfair. Although he specifically disavowed implications of government censorship, he called upon the public to "register their complaints on bias through mail to the networks and phone calls to local stations." Mail and telephone response was overwhelmingly on his side, but network executives, many newspapers and news magazines, and a substantial number of private citizens called the attack an attempt to intimidate a news medium dependent upon government licensing for its existence.

Canada. The Canadian Radio-Television Commission (CRTC), formed in 1968 to replace the Board of Broadcast Governors as the regulatory authority for television and radio, propelled itself into controversy by a number of actions in 1969. In May it issued guidelines for CATV operations, banning advertising from CATV systems and forbidding CATV systems from linking themselves into networks. In July, in awarding franchises, it called for divestiture of ownership of CATV systems by broadcasters, newspapers, and other CATV operators. This produced strong protests by broadcasters who believed that the CRTC had exceeded the limits of the guidelines issued in May.

In another ruling, the CRTC held that CKLW-AM-FM-TV in Windsor, Ont., owned by RKO General Inc., a U.S. company, and serving audiences in Detroit, Mich., as well as Windsor, must give up its U.S. ownership. After an appeal that failed, RKO General sold the stations to Canadian publishers in the latter part of 1969. The CRTC also ruled that CATV systems, as well as radio and television broadcasting stations, must be controlled primarily (80% of the voting shares) by Canadians.

Mexico. Mexican broadcasters, threatened by a government take-over of 49% of their stock or 25% of their advertising revenues, devised a settlement that the government accepted in mid-1969. Under the agreement, the country's 482 radio and 47 television stations received 20-year license renewals on July 1, 1969, but agreed in return to give the government 12.5% of their air time each day for whatever use the government wished, without charge. The government indicated it planned to use the time basically for programs to teach peasants to read and write and to encourage good citizenship.

Europe. Changes in broadcasting structure and organization were in progress or planned in many European countries as they moved toward the 1970s. Partly this resulted from financial stress, with colour television as yet rarely repaying what was spent on it. Other reasons were greater efficiency, political necessity, and growing program specialization. In Czechoslovakia, where in June a former member of the Stalinist Novotny regime was made director of Prague Radio, considerable changes resulted, with staff dismissals and streamlining to place the new director in command of every aspect of organization and programming.

In France the delaying of the planned third channel to 1971 or later resulted from the post-devaluation austerity program. Otherwise, French television and radio, long stagnant, were on the upgrade, with 9 million television sets in use and advertising revenues from commercial television (introduced in 1968) encouragingly high.

Full television coverage was achieved in Norway in autumn 1969, when videotaped programs began to be taken twice daily by plane from Oslo to the small mining community at Longyearbyen, Vestspitsbergen. Radical reorganization in the Netherlands beginning May 29, when the new Broadcasting Act took effect, was aimed at coordination and expansion.

In Austria, change was caused by reforms that gave broadcasting political and economic independence. The one television and two radio stations were replaced by three radio and two television stations, with daily radio transmission of 93 hours and television of 11 hours. West Germany was preparing to raise television and radio license fees to cover the increasing cost of colour television. A problem remaining serious only in West Germany, "pirate" broadcasting, was met by restrictive legislation.

Eamonn Andrews of Thames Television's "Today" program interviews John Lennon and his wife Yoko in bed during the program on April 1, 1969. Lennon and his wife were staging a bed-in for peace.

KEYSTONE

That colour set ownership or rental was a key to broadcasting's future was highlighted by the statement of the BBC's new director general, Charles Curran, that unless colour television license holders rose to 2 million in Britain by 1974, the BBC would be in the red. Much of the planning for the future was affected by lack of money. Colour TV sales in Britain had been disappointing, and investment high. With set prices of up to £350–£400 and relatively few programming hours, the public inclined to a "wait-and-see" mood, hoping for lower prices, more up-to-date models, and more transmissions. This vicious circle—high investment costs, low sales with demand for more and better colour, leading to higher investment—cracked perceptibly under pressure from competition by the Japanese Sony Corp., which planned to sell a 13-in. colour set in quantity in Britain early in 1970 at less than £200.

The Soviet Union had cut colour set prices by 24% (from about $1,320 to $1,000) early in the year, and had raised average weekly colour program time from 7.5 hours in 1968 to 12 hours with two television centres, Kiev and Tbilisi, starting regular colour transmission in November.

The biggest organizational changes took place in Britain, where BBC, the Independent Television Authority (ITA), and the commercial programming companies (ITV) set up in 1968 were all in difficulties. The BBC's financial crisis was partially caused by license fee evasion (costing an estimated £7.5 million a year in revenue). A campaign against license evasion was launched in London in October, to become nationwide in 1970.

Related, but more serious in effect, was July publication of the BBC's blueprint for "Broadcasting in the Seventies." By early December details were still not clear, but in outline the plan, after modification resulting from consultation with the government and the postmaster general, provided for the replacement of four regional radio stations (North, Midland, South, West) by a structure of eight English regions (with Scottish, Welsh, and Northern Irish regional stations retained) for both radio and television. Within this framework would be the two BBC television channels (to be increased to three if money permitted and if ITV, also facing financial crisis, failed to press its claim) and the four radio programs, reorganized for specialization with a clear-cut division developing between Radio 1 (pop music) and Radio 2 (light music and "speech") and with classical music and "speech" gradually taking over Radios 3 and 4. The plan to confine Radio 3 to VHF (with loss to some 60 million listeners) was shelved. Public protest in press and in Parliament was directed at the sacrifice of quality by reduction of "serious" radio and television.

In Eastern Europe, most organizational developments arose from closer cooperation among countries of the Soviet bloc and between those countries, the Soviet Union, and the less developed countries of the Middle East (Lebanon, Iraq, the United Arab Republic, Cyprus, Turkey), the Far East (notably Burma and Ceylon), and Africa.

Australia. With two permanent earth stations and one temporary, and two under construction, Australia's role in world television transmission was increasingly important. To reach isolated communities in the interior the government encouraged extension of domestic television; and the national network's 39th transmission centre, operational from early 1967, formed part of the plan for achievement of total coverage during the 1970s.

New Zealand. The reorganization of broadcasting began, with the Broadcasting Authority Act, 1968, placing radio and television under the newly created New Zealand Broadcasting Authority (NZBA), with power to grant warrants to broadcasting companies (including the New Zealand Broadcasting Corporation—NZBC) and to control program content and bias in "newscasts."

Africa. Development of educational broadcasting organizations was still Africa's greatest need. In Tanzania radio had been used in schools since the early 1960s, but no authority was responsible for adult education. Private organizations, notably the Moshi Cooperative Education Centre, broadcast to cooperatives, with some 300 listening groups by 1969. An experiment in educational television in Dakar, Senegal, 1965–67, provided material for development of television teaching. Treating mainly hygiene and nutrition, basic programs were interspersed with a more general series, "Meeting-Point," which gained audience participation by inviting suggestions for programs and production methods. This was intended to form a model for African countries with television.

India-Pakistan. Apart from an earth station for satellite transmission, to be constructed near Poona by the Ahmedabad Research Centre, and an educational television station for Ahmedabad, with broadcasts transmitted by a synchronous satellite to be launched in 1972 by the U.S., developments depended on the possibility of large-scale manufacture of low-cost television receivers. Work on basic equipment continued, with new stations under construction in Bombay and Srinagar. Commercial radio was being extended to reach approximately 5,500 villages and serve a population of more than 10 million.

Japan. By March 1968 there were more than 20.2 million television receivers in use, including more than 1.5 million for colour. Plans were made in 1969 for a new tower for transmission of television broadcasts in Tokyo and its suburbs. At 1,800 ft., it would be the highest of its kind in the world. The decision for a nationwide switch from VHF to UHF television transmission during the 1970s made the tower's construction, planned in 1964 but postponed for financial reasons, a necessity.

(S. Tf.; R.W.Cr.; Ja.Ma.; X.)

COURTESY, WIDE WORLD

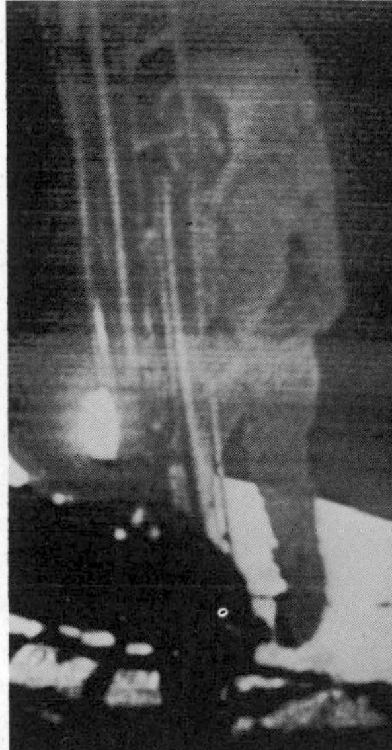

Apollo 11 astronaut Neil Armstrong descends the lunar module ladder to become the first human to set foot on the moon, July 20, 1969. The photo is from the live telecast of the event broadcast around the world.

Programming. News remained a primary service of television and radio broadcasters throughout the world in 1969. Live coverage of the Apollo 11 moon landing on July 20 was carried by stations linked in a global satellite network while live reports by radio carried the event into areas and homes not reached by television. Extensive TV and radio coverage was also provided for the Apollo 9 and 10 moon-orbiting flights earlier in the year and for the Apollo 12 moon landing in November; for the inauguration of President Nixon in January; and for the investiture of Prince Charles as prince of Wales in July.

Comedies, Westerns, and mysteries produced in the U.S. remained staples in most television countries, and U.S.-made motion pictures became increasingly popular. The movie trend had become evident in 1968, when American movie sales outside the U.S. increased by 100% over the 1967 total; in 1969, it became "the single most distinctive programming trend to emerge abroad," according to a study by *Broadcasting.* Audiences around the world also showed growing interest in taped music-variety programs, such

BEN ROTH AGENCY

"Your set is safe radiation-wise . . . have you checked the program they've been exposed to?" —Norris, "Vancouver Sun."

as the "Ed Sullivan Show," the "Carol Burnett Show," and "Kraft Music Hall," as well as in standards such as "Bonanza," a Western; "Bewitched," a fantasy-comedy; "My Three Sons," a family situation comedy; "Gunsmoke," a Western; and "Perry Mason," a detective series.

Also notable was the growing international market for British programs. British salesmen returned from the 1969 Cannes International Television Market with orders worth more than £1 million, and the BBC reported 1968–69 sales of 16,180 television series to 88 countries. Adventure and comedy series, especially made for television, were finding new markets: such old favourites as "Robin Hood" could be seen in Iceland and Algeria. They reached their destinations via the U.S., earning dollars that helped to peg prices to a level attractive to new companies' budgets. Thames Television's "Life and Times of Lord Mountbatten" and Granada TV's "The Avengers" (in colour) went to more than 20 countries. The BBC's "Forsyte Saga," based on John Galsworthy's novels, was seen in 1969 in many countries, including the U.S. and the Soviet Union.

Live coverage of sports remained a top favourite throughout the world. Sports events accounted for more than 85% of EBU (European Broadcasting Union) exchange programs.

U.S. Special events in the television spotlight in 1969, besides the moon landing, included the inauguration of President Nixon on January 20, the first such ceremony covered, with all of its allied events, completely in colour; and memorial programs and funeral rites for former Pres. Dwight D. Eisenhower over a five-day period from his death March 28 through his burial on April 2.

Although Vice-President Agnew's attack on network TV news indicated that the president had become dissatisfied with some television coverage, Nixon went to unusual lengths to use television by scheduling his first news conferences for live prime-time television coverage and, before that, in a move without precedent, by employing prime-time network television to announce his Cabinet appointments and introduce the appointees.

A widely publicized dispute involved the "Smothers Brothers Comedy Hour." On the ground that the Smothers brothers (*see* BIOGRAPHY) had failed to live up to an agreement to have tapes of their Sunday show available the previous Wednesday for viewing by affiliated stations, CBS announced early in the year that it would not renew the show for the 1969–70 season. Tom Smothers denied the validity of the agreement and claimed that CBS was obligated to broadcast 26 "Smothers Brothers" shows in 1969–70. The network stood firm, however, and the show was not aired during the new season.

Aside from the unusual events, routine day-to-day news remained one of the staples of broadcast programming. The extent to which TV news in particular had become a part of American life was demonstrated in March when a special study, conducted for the Television Information Office by Roper Research Associates, Inc., showed that, despite all the criticism that had been leveled against television, it remained the primary source of news for most people and also was considered the most credible news medium.

Entertainment programming in 1969 was marked by an almost total absence of violence and by a diminishing emphasis on sex, as broadcasters responded to widespread criticism of "sex and violence" on TV. No new Westerns were added to the network schedules, and some old ones were taken off despite good audience ratings. Stations as well as networks gave increased attention—and air time—to racial and social problems. Radio as well as television stations offered more and more programs designed to find jobs and training for unemployed minority-group members.

The three TV networks were spending approximately $275 million for the production of regularly scheduled nighttime programs for the 1969–70 season, approximately $15 million more than in 1968–69. Many of the most popular programs in the U.S. were also hits overseas. A *Broadcasting* study in mid-1969 found, for example, that "Bonanza," a Western going into its 11th year on U.S. network television, had been sold in 89 other countries. Others with exceptional sales records in other countries included "Beverly Hillbillies," "My Three Sons," "Gunsmoke," "Petticoat Junction," "This Is Tom Jones," "The Virginian," "Ironside," "Family Affair," and "Mod Squad."

Sports continued to attract big audiences and ever higher prices. *Broadcasting* reported that in 1969 television and radio networks and stations paid $37,190,000 for major-league baseball rights, up almost 20% from 1968; almost $53.2 million for professional and college football, about 1% more than the 1968 revised figure; and lesser but increasing sums for golf, basketball, and hockey.

In noncommercial broadcasting, some of the first fruits of the Corporation for Public Broadcasting's program grants became visible on television screens across the U.S. in 1969. These included "The Advocates," a 39-week series on public issues, cast in the format of a court trial, and the "Forsyte Saga," acquired from the BBC. Both projects were underwritten jointly by the Ford Foundation ($2.4 million) and the CPB ($1.2 million).

One of the most ambitious programs with which CPB was associated, "Sesame Street," described as the most intensive effort ever made to use television to reach and teach young children, was launched in November as a daily one-hour series on 170 noncommercial television stations. A two-year project of the Children's Television Workshop in New York City, "Sesame Street" used animation and other techniques designed to interest the nation's 12 million preschool children in words, numbers, and concepts.

Australia. In Australia a rise in popularity of home-produced programs boosted national pride. At least six Australian series were in the top ten in popularity ratings throughout the year. Of four new Australian-produced drama series, Channel 9's crime series, "Division 4," was in the top ten in most states; and in some states the pop music show, "Bandstand," held top place for several months. Talent quest programs gained high ratings as, more surprisingly, did the unusual "Spellbound," conducted by a hypnotist. Most popular single program was "Royal Family" from the U.K., and the most popular Australian TV personality was Graham Kennedy of Melbourne.

Europe. In many countries programming policy was linked to organization by growing specialization. New facilities were introduced to provide specialist-interest programs, or (as in Britain) existing networks were redeployed. In France, to attract attention and restore confidence after broadcasting's involvement in 1968's political crisis, André François, television's new director, reorganized transmissions and program networks. In Britain, radical restructuring of services scheduled for the 1970s was preceded by 1968's experiments in local radio and "independent" television companies. That local radio was judged a success could be deduced from its promised extension, and the smaller television companies, despite financial and management problems, had produced some good programs, so that restructuring could claim a clear go-ahead signal.

New policies guiding programming in Italy in 1968–69 were concern for adult education, with more attractive "popular culture" programs; and provision for a wider range of listeners and viewers. Radio, with increased hours, played a twofold part, providing "easy listening" and more "conversational" culture programs. The Terzo Programma kept up prestige with such notable broadcasts as Ludovico Ariosto's *Orlando Furioso,* with the novelist Italo Calvino as narrator. Music and evening variety shows proved popular. The new experimental cultural magazine program "Chiamate Roma 3131" achieved audiences of 300,000. In television drama, large audiences watched old favourites like "Commissaire Maigret" and new spectacular successes: a dramatized *Odyssey* had 16.6 million viewers.

Television in France continued disappointing. Colour and increased viewing time only highlighted the lack of inspiration. On the Première Programme the only work worth mention was Claude Goretta's "Vivre ici"—produced for Suisse-Romande Télévision and shown during its French fortnight. With so little creative work to praise, credit must go to real-life documentary series: "Les Femmes aussi" (with Eliane Victor); "La Bataille de Moscou" and "La Bataille de Normandie" (Henri Turenne, Jean-Louis Guiffand, Daniel Costelle). Daniel Le Comte's new "Ombre et Lumière" was outstanding, exploring creative artistic media. On the Deuxième Programme there was one "great occasion": Pierre Koralnik's film version of Oscar Wilde's play *Salomé,* in colours reminiscent of the richness of Baroque art.

In Britain, too, the year was neither distinguished in itself nor reassuring for the future. Commercial television was under fire, largely because the new companies' performance betrayed their promise. They had won their concessions in 1968 by describing their high cultural objectives, but with ratings falling and advertising revenue threatened, most were forced to emasculate their intentions. London Weekend Television in particular had proposed a raising of sights. An effort was made, but a decline in the audience forced a statement brutal in its commercial realism from a reshuffled board of directors, reinstating popularity as the criterion of success. Yet London Weekend, within its terms of reference, had not done too badly. Its comedy series (notably "Please Sir," an affectionate look at the lower end of state education) and its thrillers (such as "The Gold Robbers") were not below other companies' efforts, and the David Frost shows, while tending to confuse "trial-by-TV" with probing in the public interest, were consistently lively.

If the "independent" companies were under a cloud, so was the BBC. Though the BBC and commercial companies were under financial strain, this could not wholly explain the prevailing intellectual conformity. Despite notable programs—Sir Kenneth Clark's BBC-2 "Civilisation" series being outstanding—the impression remained that competitive pursuit of high ratings had supplanted the quest for quality. It was significant that BBC-1's "Wednesday Play," once a platform for brave experiment, played safe; and the showing, in a truncated form and at a late hour, of Tony Parker's remarkable study by interview of women in prison, "Five Women," was not reassuring. There were more hopeful signs in comedy. "Me Mammy," a series about a mother-dominated Irishman, was very funny; "Beachcomber" was back and so was the inventive Marty Feldman, star of "Marty" and, in autumn 1969, of BBC-2's "One Pair of Eyes."

If television caused concern, it was as nothing to the misgivings aroused by the BBC's attitude to radio. "The Critics," Radio 4's Sunday morning contribution to intelligent conversation on books, plays, films, broadcasting, and the arts, went off the air early in the year, while Radio 1 showed decreasing interest in serious "pop" music.

Neither West Germany nor Norway had much new to offer. Elections provided some exciting viewing and crime series were popular, Norway's most successful home-produced program being "Taxi" by the well-known writer André Bjerke. Norwegian television drama was criticized for being too avant-garde in choice of plays and production methods. West Germany, continuing to cater to wide audiences with popular new series such as "Menschen, Tieren, Sensationen" and "Der Kommissar," could not be accused of neglecting minority audiences, with excellent productions of such rarely seen works as the Eugene O'Neill play *Strange Interlude* and Zoltan Kodaly's neglected "little opera" *The Spinning Wheel.* Ulf von Mechow's well-written "Free Until Next Time," treat-

Princess Anne, Queen Elizabeth II, Prince Philip, and Prince Charles at lunch in Windsor Castle in a scene from a new 1¾-hour film about the private life of the royal family. The film was first shown on British television June 21, 1969.

CENTRAL PRESS FROM PICTORIAL PARADE

ing the fate of Gypsies in today's Germany, was imaginatively directed by Korbiman Kóberle and acted with moving sincerity, and provided an unforgettable experience.

The Netherlands was going forward, and fast. Radio came to the fore with specialized programming: up-to-the-minute road reports for motorists; background music for factories; experimental all-night programs. More important, radio was used to "create" a new medium, verbosonic drama. From the 1950s the Netherlands had acted as a research laboratory for experiments with music, voice (in the widest sense of "vocal chords"), and other means of sound production; with developments in electronics, linguistics as a science, and new musical instruments, it had "penetrated to the interior of sound." For the first verbosonic play recorded, Gerrit Pleiter's "De Hondmens," a "verbal score" allowed the author to use all possible means to create sounds in accurate detail and to arrange dialogue or monologue in planes in order to concentrate expression. Thus, speech and reaction could be simultaneously presented or overlaid in new patterns, with emphasis, emotional evocation, phonetic background, etc., added on a third plane. Sound patterns were used to plumb deeper levels of thought and feeling than did conventional techniques.

In Eastern Europe, some closing of the ranks was discernible, with emphasis on celebration of "politically acceptable" anniversaries—"liberation," Soviet-inspired achievement, and centenaries of revolutionaries and party members. With this went the usual themes—education; "Industrialization and Technical Progress" (title of two radio series, Czechoslovak and Bulgarian); competitions, especially for young people; village life; and regional culture. Specialized programming in the Soviet Union tackled mainly problems of distance or serving both urban and rural communities.

Notable programs begun in 1968–69 in the Soviet Union included "About You and for You," for women, based on listeners' letters; and television films produced by Central Television's new film studio, Screen (begun in 1968), such as "With Glory Let Us Rise!" (songs of the 1930s with Soviet history as background). Outstanding or popular programs elsewhere included Hungarian Television's "Dead Men Return," a play about a 1944 Budapest trial of fascist war criminals; the joint German Democratic Radio-Polish People's Republic Radio children's quiz "Neighbours, Get to Know One Another"; Radio Sofia's audience-participation "Musiclover's Radio Club," which aimed to turn all amateurs' societies into listeners' groups; and Polish Radio's new reviews "Sound," treating economic and social problems, and "Horizon," a popular program on science.

(S.Tf.; R.W.Cr.; Ge.Me.; X.)

Amateur Radio. In August Hurricane Camille, the fiercest ever to strike the U.S. mainland, destroyed or seriously overloaded all regular communications channels in much of the southeastern quarter of the U.S., particularly in Louisiana, Mississippi, and Virginia. Radio amateurs stepped into their traditional role as emergency communicators, handling damage reports and requests for supplies and personnel from radio stations in their cars or set up quickly in disaster areas. Amateurs prepare for such emergencies through two nationwide exercises, the Simulated Emergency Test in January and the Field Day in June. In 1969, about 25,000 people took part in these drills, sponsored by the American Radio Relay League, the national association of radio amateurs in the U.S. and Canada.

On the regulatory front, U.S. radio amateurs completed their first year under the new incentive licensing program instituted by the FCC in November 1968. During the year many amateurs seeking increased operating privileges upgraded their licenses, as the number of Extra Class licensees doubled and Advanced Class license holders became 25% more numerous. The second phase of the program, announced in late September, further expanded the higher class license voice privileges. The FCC made the Novice Class license available to former amateurs for the first time. Persons who had not held a license 12 months prior to application were eligible, but the simultaneous holding of Novice and Technician class licenses was no longer permitted.

A prominent radio amateur, Sen. Barry Goldwater (Rep., Ariz.), introduced a bill in the U.S. Senate to allow the FCC to issue amateur licenses to immigrants who had taken out first citizenship papers. By the end of 1969, the number of American radio amateurs stood at more than 260,000.

With the admission of Western Samoa, Hungary, and Trinidad and Tobago, membership in the International Amateur Radio Union (IARU) grew to 83 societies. Twenty-seven of these were represented at the triennial IARU conference of European and African societies in Brussels during May. Reciprocal licensing, encouragement of amateur radio in less developed countries, and representation at future intergovernmental radio communications conferences were among the subjects discussed. (R. M. My.)

See also Advertising; Astronautics; Cinema; Music; Telecommunications.

Encyclopædia Britannica Films. *Development of Communications (From Telegraph to TV)* (1955); *Getting the News* (1967).

Tennis

The first full year of open tournaments, with all major individual events open to all categories of players, made for a stimulating season, marked by a high standard of play among the men. The most prominent and successful players were Rod Laver (*see* Biography), the Queenslander whose left-handed skill made him open singles champion of Australia, South Africa, France, Wimbledon, and the United States, and Margaret Court, formerly Margaret Smith, another Australian, who became singles champion of Australia, France, and the U.S.

The various categories of players, differing from one nation to another, presented a confusing picture. However, the two broad classes of players were no longer amateur and professional but "contracted" professional and otherwise, a "contracted" professional being a player under specific contract to a promoter and to that extent beyond the authority of the national associations. "Contracted" professionals were barred from all the traditional events except those tournaments specifically designated as "open" by the management committee of the International Lawn Tennis Federation (ILTF).

Efforts to make the Davis Cup, the international men's team championship, open to all classes of player were unsuccessful. At the same time an increase in the number of open tournaments in 1970 was promised when the ILTF ruled that any tournament with prize money in excess of $15,000 was automatically open.

Disapproval of South Africa's racial policies by some nations brought controversy at the highest administrative level. At the annual meeting of the ILTF Sweden proposed a motion that, if passed, would have barred South Africans—and Rhodesians as well—from international participation as both teams and individuals. It failed to be passed, but the management committee was vested with power to exclude South Africans from international team events if they deemed such action prudent. In successive rounds of the European Zone of the Davis Cup, Poland and Czechoslovakia defaulted to South Africa in protest against its racial policies. In the case of Czechoslovakia the default was against the published wishes of the members of the Czechoslovak team.

Davis Cup. The United States retained the Davis Cup at Cleveland, O., in September without difficulty. Romania was, surprisingly, the challenger, when Arthur Ashe and Stan Smith in the singles and Smith and Bob Lutz in the doubles easily beat the two-man team of Ion Tiriac and Ilie Nastase by 5–0.

Australia failed to gain the challenge round for the first time since 1937. Competing in the American Zone, they were beaten 3–2 by Mexico in Mexico City with substantially the same team, Ray Ruffels and Bill Bowrey playing the singles, that conceded the cup to the United States in 1968. The outstanding Mexican player was Rafael Osuna, who was killed in an air crash not long afterward. With its team drastically weakened, Mexico, the first nation other than the U.S. to beat Australia since the U.K. in 1936, failed to go further. Brazil won the American Zone.

India easily won in the Eastern Zone, while Great Britain and Romania triumphed in the two sections in the European Zone. The British success was unexpected. After easy victories over Switzerland and Ireland, the British team met with strong competition from West Germany. The U.K. triumphed 3–2 in a tournament notable for producing the largest number of games ever played in the Davis Cup. In the doubles Wilhelm Bungert and Christian Kuhnke of West Germany beat Mark Cox and Peter Curtis 10–8, 17–19, 13–11, 3–6, 6–2, for a total of 95 games. The unexpected British success continued with a 3–2 victory over South Africa at Bristol, this competition being interrupted more than once by demonstrations against South African racial policy. Subsequently, Great Britain beat Brazil 3–2 in the interzone semifinal at Wimbledon, but in the next round Romania beat Great Britain 3–2 at Wimbledon to qualify for the challenge round. The major share of the British success was achieved by Graham Stilwell.

Tiriac and Nastase carried Romania through six rounds before their unsuccessful challenge against the United States. In the European Zone Romania beat the United Arab Republic 3–2, Israel 5–0, Spain 4–1, and the U.S.S.R. 4–1. Then a win 4–0 over India brought Romania to its match against Great Britain.

Men's Competition. *Singles.* In 1962 Laver became the first man since the U.S. player Don Budge in 1938 to win the Grand Slam, the championships of Australia, France, Wimbledon, and the United States. He also won the Italian and German championships that year. In 1969 Laver gained a unique place in the history of the game not only by winning the Grand Slam for the second time but by winning it in the increased competition of open tournaments. He won the South African title as well.

The Australian championships, staged in Brisbane, were the least successful of the open events. Laver, after beating Australians Roy Emerson and Fred Stolle, won a semifinal against Tony Roche, also of Australia, with difficulty, 7–5, 22–20, 9–11, 1–6, 6–3. It was his longest match of the season. In the final he defeated Andres Gimeno of Spain 6–3, 6–4, 7–5.

THE "NEW YORK TIMES" FROM WIDE WORLD

Rod Laver makes a return in the last set of his marathon five-set struggle with Dennis Ralston at the U.S. Open tennis championship, Sept. 1, 1969. Laver won 6–4, 4–6, 4–6, 6–2, 6–3 and went on to win the championship to complete his second Grand Slam.

The South African championships in Johannesburg brought success in the singles to Laver when he beat Bob Hewitt of South Africa in the quarterfinal, South African Cliff Drysdale in the semifinal, and Tom Okker of the Netherlands 6–3, 10–8, 6–3 in the final. Roche forfeited to Okker in the semifinal because of injury.

John Newcombe of Australia won the Italian championship in Rome. In the semifinal he beat the Czechoslovak Jan Kodes, an earlier victor over Ashe, and in the final defeated Roche (who had beaten Okker) 6–3, 4–6, 6–2, 5–7, 6–3.

Laver gained his third big title in the French championships in Paris. His quarterfinal victory was against Gimeno, his semifinal against Okker, and his final 6–4, 6–3, 6–4 against the defending champion Ken Rosewall of Australia.

At Wimbledon, Laver beat Drysdale in the quarterfinal and Ashe in the semifinal after a match of unusually hard hitting. In the final he beat Newcombe by 6–4, 5–7, 6–4, 6–4. Laver thus won the open Wimbledon title for the second year and the title as such for the fourth time, for he had been the amateur champion in 1961 and 1962.

After Wimbledon Laver remained unbeaten until after the U.S. Open championships at Forest Hills. Laver was hard pressed to beat Dennis Ralston of the U.S. in his hardest match. In the quarterfinal he beat Emerson, in the semifinal Ashe, and in the final, played a day late because of rain, Roche (who had beaten Newcombe) 7–9, 6–1, 6–2, 6–2.

Roche won the German title in Hamburg prior to the New York event. That and the Italian title taken by Newcombe were the only major singles not gained by Laver; he challenged for neither.

Doubles. Newcombe and Roche won at Wimbledon and also in France to make themselves the most notable partnership of the year. Emerson and Laver won in Australia and placed second in France. Okker and Marty Riessen of the U.S. were finalists at Wimbledon and winners in Germany. The U.S. Open title went to Rosewall and Stolle.

Women's Competition. *Singles.* Margaret Court initiated a conspicuously successful year by winning the Australian title for the eighth time. In the semifinal she beat her compatriot Kerry Melville, and in the final avenged her defeat in the same match the year before by triumphing over Billie Jean King of the U.S. 6–4, 6–1.

Mrs. King, the top woman player of 1968, had her only notable singles success in the South African title meeting. She beat Ann Jones of Britain 5–7, 6–3, 6–0 in the semifinal and Nancy Richey of the U.S. 6–3, 6–4 in the final.

The Italian championship, with an entry less strong than in some years, saw Mrs. King defeated in the quarterfinal by Miss Melville. Julie Heldman of the U.S., perhaps the most improved player of the season, beat Mrs. Jones in the semifinal and Miss Melville in the final 7–5, 6–3.

Mrs. Court dominated the French championship. The Australian Lesley Bowrey beat Mrs. King in the quarterfinals. In the semifinals Mrs. Jones defeated Mrs. Bowrey and Mrs. Court beat Miss Richey. Mrs. Court's final victory over Mrs. Jones was 6–1, 4–6, 6–3. The outcome of the Wimbledon championship stirred British patriotism with Mrs. Jones taking the title, the first home success since Angela Mortimer won in 1961. Her quarterfinal success was against Miss Richey. In the semifinal, when she played outstandingly good lawn tennis, she beat Mrs. Court, and in the final she defeated Mrs. King 3–6, 6–3, 6–2.

Mrs. Court resumed her invincibility on the grass courts in the United States. After taking the U.S. National title, held in Boston, her athletic skill dominated the U.S. Open at Forest Hills. She won over Virginia Wade, the British titleholder of the previous year, 7–5, 6–0 in the semifinal. Miss Richey, semifinal victor over Rosemary Casals 7–5, 6–3, was the other finalist. In the title match Mrs. Court beat her 6–2, 6–2. (Mrs. Jones did not compete.)

Doubles. Mrs. Jones and the French Françoise Durr, both contracted professionals, were champions of South Africa, France, and Italy. Mrs. Court won Australia and Wimbledon with Judy Tegart, another Australian. Miss Durr partnered Darlene Hard of the U.S., long absent from the game, to win the U.S. Open.

Wightman Cup. The United States beat Great Britain 5–2 to regain the trophy in Cleveland. Miss Heldman was the outstanding performer on the U.S. side, and her opening win against Miss Wade provided an impetus to the U.S. that was never lost. Miss Heldman was supported by Miss Richey, Jane ("Peaches") Bartkowicz, Mrs. Mary Ann Curtis, formerly Miss Eisel, and Valerie Ziegenfuss. With Miss Wade were Winnie Shaw, Christine Janes, and Nell Truman.

Federation Cup. Played in Athens, this was won for the fourth time by the United States, represented by Miss Heldman, Miss Richey, and Miss Bartkowicz. They beat Yugoslavia 3–0, Italy 3–0, the Netherlands 3–0, and, in the final, Australia 2–1. (L. O. T.)

Textiles:
see Industrial Review

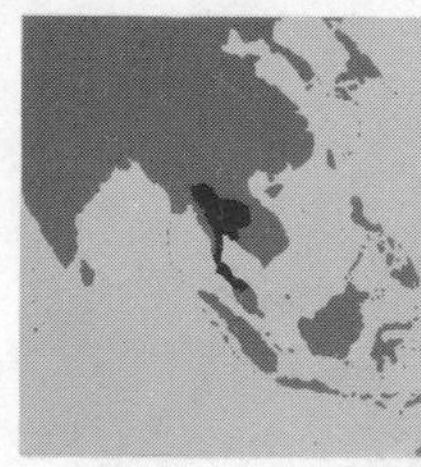

Thailand

A constitutional monarchy of Southeast Asia, Thailand is bordered by Burma, Laos, Cambodia, and Malaysia. Area: 198,455 sq.mi. (514,000 sq.km.). Pop. (1969 est.): 34,738,000. Cap. and largest city: Bangkok (pop., 1967 est., 2,136,432). Language: Thai. Religion (1964): Buddhist 93.7%; Muslim 3.9%. King, Bhumibol Adulyadej; prime minister in 1969, Field Marshal Thanom Kittikachorn.

A new era in politics opened for Thailand on Feb. 10, 1969, with the holding of the first general election in more than 11 years. Although less than 25% of the 15 million electorate voted, and the military regime had no intention of being ousted, for the first time polling was free from violence and from the threat of a military coup d'etat. Both the military government and opposition politicians agreed that the permanent constitution, proclaimed in June 1968, should be made to work, since it represented a moderate first step toward full democracy.

The military leaders formed their own political party, the United Thai People's Party (UTPP), and by effective campaigning in the rural areas they succeeded in getting the UTPP returned as the majority party in Parliament. The election was not without its warning for the military rulers, however. The major opposition party and the UTPP's only serious rival, the Democrats, led by a prominent lawyer and former prime minister, M. R. Seni Pramoj, captured all 21 seats in Bangkok and nearby Thonburi.

Marshal Thanom told Parliament in his first policy speech that Thailand considered Communism the greatest threat to its security and would continue to fight it with U.S. assistance. When U.S. Pres. Richard M. Nixon visited Thailand on July 28–31, however,

THAILAND

Education. (1965) Primary, pupils 4,630,424, teachers 126,813; secondary, pupils 316,736, teachers 17,490; vocational, pupils 35,011, teachers 3,460; teacher training, students 14,173, teachers 436; higher (including 6 universities), students 50,722, teaching staff 4,956.

Finance. Monetary unit: baht, with a par value of 20.80 baht to U.S. $1 (49.92 baht = £1 sterling). Gold and foreign exchange, official: (June 1969) U.S. $1 billion; (June 1968) U.S. $1,027,000,000. Budget (1967–68 est.) balanced at 21,262,000,000 baht. Gross national product: (1967) 105,630,000,000 baht; (1966) 96.8 billion baht. Money supply: (May 1969) 19,380,000,000 baht; (May 1968) 18.1 billion baht. Cost of living (Bangkok; 1963 = 100): (May 1969) 116; (May 1968) 115.

Foreign Trade. (1968) Imports 24,718,000,000 baht; exports 13,721,000,000 baht. Import sources (1967): U.S. 37%; Japan 26%; U.K. 6%; West Germany 6%. Export destinations (1967): Japan 22%; U.S. 14%; Malaysia 9%; Hong Kong 8%; Singapore 7%; India 5%. Main exports: rice 28%; rubber 13%; corn 11%; tin 11%; tapioca 6%; kenaf 5%.

Transport and Communications. Roads (1965) 12,275 km. (including 5,706 km. with improved surface). Motor vehicles in use (1967): passenger *c.* 110,000; commercial (including buses) *c.* 132,500. Railways (1967): 3,765 km.; traffic 3,666,000,000 passenger-km., freight 2,001,000,000 net ton-km. Air traffic (1968): 462.1 million passenger-km.; freight 5,930,000 net ton-km. Shipping (1968): merchant vessels 100 gross tons and over 49; gross tonnage 63,780. Shipping traffic (Bangkok only; 1967) goods loaded 5,225,000 metric tons, unloaded 8,038,000 metric tons. Telephones (Dec. 1967) 98,390. Radio receivers (Dec. 1966) 2,765,000. Television receivers (Dec. 1966) 210,000.

Agriculture. Production (in 000; metric tons; 1968; 1967 in parentheses): rice 10,895 (9,595); peanuts *c.* 150 (*c.* 130); sweet potatoes (1966) *c.* 180, (1965) 196; corn *c.* 1,300 (*c.* 1,200); rubber *c.* 260 (*c.* 214); soybeans (1966) 58, (1965) 19; cassava (1966) 2,323, (1965) 1,475; sesame (1967) *c.* 17, (1966) *c.* 18; sugar, raw value (1968–69) *c.* 527, (1967–68) *c.* 385; bananas (1966) *c.* 1,200, (1965) 1,243; tobacco 90 (*c.* 90); cotton, lint *c.* 35 (*c.* 27); kenaf (hard fibre; 1967) *c.* 280, (1966) *c.* 550; timber (cu.m.; 1967) 4,500, (1966) 3,900; fish catch (1967) 849, (1966) 708. Livestock (in 000; 1966–67): cattle 5,167; buffaloes 6,878; pigs 4,045; horses 175; chickens *c.* 37,000.

Industry. Production (in 000; metric tons; 1968): tin concentrates (metal content) 24; cement 2,170; tungsten concentrates (oxide content; 1967) 0.5; lead concentrates (metal content) 2.8; electricity (Bangkok and Thonburi only; kw-hr.) 2,492,000.

he made it clear that the U.S. would not like to be involved in any more land wars of the Vietnam type in Asia, that the bulk of U.S. forces stationed in Thailand would be withdrawn if there was progress toward a Vietnam settlement, and that Thailand itself should shoulder the major responsibility for defense against Communist subversion. The president assured Thai leaders that the U.S. would be prepared to supply the necessary arms and equipment. Thai leaders, who remained apprehensive of the power vacuum likely to be created in Southeast Asia after the planned withdrawal of British forces in 1971, were slightly jolted by President Nixon's statement. Attempts were made to obtain a commitment that at least a token force of U.S. troops would be based in Thailand after the Vietnam war, but without success. In September it was agreed that withdrawal of the over 48,000 U.S. troops in Thailand should depend on the course of the war in Vietnam. In early October it was announced that 6,000 U.S. troops, mainly engineers and advisers, would be withdrawn by July 1, 1970.

Communist terrorist activity in north and northeast Thailand declined in 1969 as compared with the previous year. In the southern region bordering Malaysia, however, Communist guerrillas boosted their strength from 500 in 1968 to 1,000 in mid-1969, partly with fresh recruits from the Chinese community in Malaysia following the Sino-Malay riots in May. A new threat to Thai sovereignty also loomed in the south in September, when fanatical Muslims stepped up their campaign to secede from Thailand and join Malaysia. Thai and Malaysian leaders met and agreed on measures to curb Communist subversion and Thai-Muslim separatism.

The Thai economy remained stable, although reduced agricultural exports and low world market prices forced the growth rate down to about 6% from the 7.2% recorded in the previous three years. Government and trade circles were concerned over the continuing trade deficit—over 10.5 billion baht (about $505 million) in 1968—and called for drastic measures to reduce imports and raise exports. Fears were expressed that withdrawal of U.S. forces and loss of the $250 million spent annually by the U.S. military could seriously affect the economy. The government budgeted for a total expenditure of 27.3 billion baht in the fiscal year beginning October 1969; revenue was estimated at 22.3 billion baht. (G. U.)

Theatre

Great Britain and Ireland. "Third time lucky" might have been the motto of Britain's National Theatre in 1969, when, on November 3, Jennie Lee, government minister responsible for the arts, helped break ground in London for the theatre's forthcoming permanent home. Meantime, urged on by the critical success of a brief tryout season at the Jeannetta Cochrane, a small London design-school theatre, the National embarked on the erection of a flexible 500-seat, studio-stage theatre alongside the Old Vic, to be named the Young Vic. A first "holiday play for young people from 7 to 70" by James Saunders, *The Travails of Sancho Panza,* was staged at the Old Vic as a token of things to come.

National Theatre highlights during the year included: *"H" or Monologues at Front of Burning Cities,* a semidocumentary by Charles Wood about Sir Henry Havelock's role in the Indian Mutiny; *The National Health,* by Peter Nichols, a bittersweet view of human life ebbing away in a welfare-state hospital; John Spurling's antiheroic *Macrune's Guevara (as realised by Edward Hotel)*; and Maureen Duffy's *Rites,* a modern variant of the *Bacchae* story. There were also revivals of *The Way of the World, The White Devil,* and George Bernard Shaw's five-play cycle *Back to Methuselah,* staged in two parts on consecutive nights for a limited season, and a visit from Paris of Jean-Louis Barrault's *Rabelais.*

Despite record box-office receipts and attendance (exceeding 1 million), the Royal Shakespeare Company, with playhouses in London and Stratford, chalked up a deficit of more than £160,000 to mar Trevor Nunn's first season as sole man in charge. Nonetheless, his own highly original productions at Stratford of *The Winter's Tale* and *Henry VIII* were widely acclaimed, second only to John Barton's *Twelfth Night,* Terry Hands's *Pericles,* and Thomas Middleton's *Women Beware Women.* The transfers from Stratford to London of *Much Ado About Nothing, Troilus and Cressida,* and Cyril Tourneur's *The Revengers Tragœdie* were able to vie in popularity with such of the year's highlights as Edward Albee's *A Delicate Balance,* the laconic Harold Pinter double bill of *Landscape* and *Silence, Bartholomew Fair,* and *The Silver Tassie,* not seen in London since its production in 1929. Simon Gray's black farce *Dutch Uncle* flopped badly at the Aldwych.

Peter Daubeny's World Theatre Season at the Aldwych was the best yet. Anna Magnani was outstanding in Giovanni Verga's *La Lupa,* while rave notices went to the Planchon company, the Prague Theatre Behind the Gate, the Negro Ensemble Company from New York (though the first of their two offerings, Peter Weiss's anticolonialist *The Song of the Lusitanian Bogey,* got a critical drubbing), and the Greek Art Theatre. In return, the RSC players won the highest praise in the U.S. for their *Dr. Faustus* and *Much Ado About Nothing* and in Europe for their *Troilus and Cressida.*

The Royal Court Theatre made world news with the award won by Edward Bond's (*see* BIOGRAPHY) *Saved* at the Belgrade Festival, the season of three Bond plays (from 1968) at home, and the scandal that followed the bid of the new triangular management (William Gaskill, Lindsay Anderson, Anthony Page) to forestall more adverse criticism in a weekly magazine by withholding press seats from its drama

Cast rehearses Bertolt Brecht's "Turandot" or "The Whitewashers Congress" for its premiere performance in Zürich, Switz., Feb. 8, 1969.

KEYSTONE

critic. The last-mentioned did little to help the cause of an otherwise well-ordered theatre that had given London two effective new proletarian dramas by David Story (*In Celebration* and *The Contractor*), a new studio stage (The Theatre Upstairs), and Frank Norman's candid dramatic guide to prison life, *Inside-out.*

Other nonprofit theatres—large and small—maintained an endless struggle against rising costs. Some, like the Arts Lab, which proved in Jane Arden's *Vagina Rex* that total nudity could be totally inoffensive, fell by the wayside, while others, like the Ambiance, started afresh in new premises. Outstanding at the Open Space was the Charles Marowitz collage of *Macbeth.* At the Hampstead Theatre Club there was a mixed bill on marriage by eight authors, which later was transferred to the West End as *Mixed Doubles.* The London premiere of Thomas Kilroy's *The Death and Resurrection of Mr. Roche* achieved success at the Cochrane. Other noteworthy productions were the National Youth Theatre's presentation of Peter Terson's student-revolt drama *Fuzz,* and Terence Frisby's hilarious satire of the exploited underdogs of the welfare state, *The Bandwagon.*

London's newest, the Greenwich Theatre, was unveiled on October 21 with the world premiere of Ewan Hooper's semidocumentary *Martin Luther King.* Offbeat experiments were staged at the theatre of the Institute of Contemporary Arts and at the Roundhouse; notable at the last-named were the open-stage *Hamlet,* starring Nicol Williamson (*see* BIOGRAPHY), a return visit of the U.S. Living Theatre, John Arden's musical about Nelson (*The Hero Rises Up*), and Dennis Potter's *The Son of Man,* the first modern drama portraying Christ to be seen in England in public.

Hits in London's West End included *The Price, Plaza Suite, Play It Again, Sam, Mame,* and *The Boys in the Band* from the U.S., and *Anne of Green Gables* from Canada. Other foreign successes were Bertolt Brecht's *The Resistible Rise of Arturo Ui,* starring Leonard Rossiter; *Lovers* by Brian Friel, from Dublin; and *The Au Pair Man,* whose ending Hugh Leonard had reshaped since its Dublin premiere. New English dramas of note were the late Joe Orton's farcical *What the Butler Saw;* Peter Barnes's *The Ruling Class,* a Gothic extravaganza; *Conduct Unbecoming* by Barry England, a glimpse of foul deeds in British India; and the witty *The Lionel Touch,* by George Hulme, which gave Rex Harrison a fitting vehicle for a London comeback. Other milestones were the Prospect Productions revival of *Edward II* and *Richard II* with Ian McKellen, John Mortimer's *Cat Among the Pigeons,* Roy Dotrice's one-man show *Brief Lives,* and, on October 1, the 7,000th performance of Agatha Christie's *The Mousetrap,* which entered its 18th year on November 25.

The Abbey Theatre's productions of *She Stoops to Conquer* and *Borstal Boy* won Ireland's National Theatre further renown at the Paris Festival, while Thomas Murphy's sprawling drama of social criticism, *A Crucial Week in the Life of a Grocer's Assistant,* competed for local accolades with Tyrone Guthrie's production of Eugene McCabe's play on Jonathan Swift, Hugh Hunt's of John Synge's *The Well of the Saints,* Alan Simpson's of *The Quare Fellow,* and Peter O'Toole's performance as Vladimir in *Waiting for Godot.* The world premiere of Conor Cruise O'Brien's literate drama of political expediency versus conscience, *King Herod Explains,* starring and directed by Milton Edwards at the Gate, stole the 1969 Dublin Festival thunder.

France. "The mess in the French theatre," to quote the critic of *Le Monde,* reached a new low mark despite the promising appointment of Edmond Michelet to succeed the outgoing cultural minister, André Malraux. Several regional directors were ousted, and both the commercial and subsidized stages displayed considerable timidity after the disorders of earlier years. The Comédie Française continued with its routine productions of Pirandello, Molière, Claudel, and Marivaux, though the quasi-documentary 17th-century backstage frolic *Les Italiens à Paris* had more life in it. Robert Hirsch, the company's great comic actor, excelled in *Arturo Ui,* not in his regular home but at the Théâtre National Populaire (TNP) as guest actor. The TNP's way of resisting government censorship was to confine itself to recent revivals. A pale and lifeless season was all that could be said of the Théâtre des Nations since it and the Théâtre de France had been deprived of their artistic director, Barrault, whose independently staged *Rabelais* had meantime repaid his private investment and thrilled audiences in London, Berlin, and Brussels, as well as in Paris. The unchallenged highlight of the year in Paris was Oskar Panizza's "celestial tragedy," *Le Concile d'Amour,* written 80 years earlier by a German and banned throughout the world until Lars Schmidt, the Swedish-born Parisian producer, engaged Jorge Lavelli to stage it at the Théâtre de Paris.

Nonconformism was also the prevailing sentiment in Fernando Arrabal's three latest dramas, *Le Jardin des Délices, Ils Passerènt des Menottes aux Fleurs,* and *Le Lai de Barabbas,* as well as in Eduardo Manet's *Les Nonnes,* a Cuban play written in French for a Paris producer that had a Haitian setting in which violence and superstition were uncomfortably close neighbours. The same might apply to *Pizarro,* as Jean Mercure, who staged it at the Théâtre de la Ville, called Peter Shaffer's *The Royal Hunt of the Sun,* and to Brecht's anticolonialist *Tambours et Trompettes* at the same theatre.

Memorable performances in the boulevard theatre were given by Claude Dauphin in *The Price,* Jean Marais in Cocteau's *Oedipe Roi,* Maria Casarès in *Mother Courage,* Pierre Fresnay in André Roussin's *On Ne Sait Jamais,* and Françoise Rosay as a *monstre sacré* in Jean Anouilh's smash-hit black comedy, *Cher Antoine.*

Other popular successes were Félicien Marceau's *Le Babour,* a modern satire in which the sexes exchanged roles with disastrous results; two political dramas by a newcomer, Remi Forlani; Pierre Barrilet and Jean Pierre Grédy's *Quatre Pièces sur Jardin;* sumptuous revivals of *Occupe-Toi d'Amélie* and *La Périchole,* with Jane Rhodes from the Opéra as guest star in the second; and a string of foreign hits, including *Hair, The Boys in the Band, Fiddler on the Roof, A Day in the Death of Joe Egg,* Natalia Ginzburg's *Teresa* (as *The Advertisement* was called in French), starring Suzanne Flon, Alberto Moravia's *The World Is What It Is,* and Pinter's *The Caretaker,* with Jacques Dufilho.

Switzerland, Germany, Austria, Belgium. The growing spirit of dissent found expression not only in the themes of new plays but also in administration. In Frankfurt, the concept of the arbitrary despotism of the "Intendant," or managing director, was challenged by demands for "shared responsibility," with the ensuing departure of the dissidents. In Basel, where Friedrich Dürrenmatt had peacefully collaborated with Werner Düggelin as co-manager, the former withdrew after differences with his colleagues, despite the resounding success of his adaptations of Shakespeare's *King John* and Strindberg's *Dance of Death;* the latter play, reduced to 90 minutes' playing time and three characters in-fighting as in a boxing ring, was taken up by dozens of theatres at home and abroad, and became the hit of the 1969 Dubrovnik Festival in Yugoslavia.

Peter Loeffler's return to Zürich as manager evoked accusations of radicalism that eventually resulted in his dismissal. The rowdy world premiere of *Prometheus* by the East German Heiner Müller and over-realistic handling of Bond's cannibalistic *Early Morning* had contributed to this. Munich's Residenz-Theater lost its brilliant director Heinz Lietzau to Hamburg, which claimed him as its new manager, a post well earned in the light of the success at the annual Berlin Drama Festival of his productions of *The Brigands* and Heiner Müller's rendition of *Philoctetes.* Changes of literary staff also affected the neighbouring Kammerspiele, where Peter Zadek continued to shock the bourgeois spectator with his radical re-evaluation of Bond's *Narrow Road to the Deep North.* At Bremen, the highlight was Peter Stein's inventive revision of *Torquato Tasso.* Other notable events were Peter Handke's play without words, *My Foot My Tutor,* at the third Frankfurt Experimenta, Hartmut Lange's translation of *Richard II* in Frankfurt, his own anti-Prussian *The Countess of Rathenow* in Cologne, Günter Grass's study of student problems, *Davor* (*Beforehand*), at the Berlin Schiller, the premiere of Arthur Schnitzler's 50-year-old posthumous *The Word* at the Vienna Josefstadt, and the emergence of a handful of promising Austrian playwrights, headed by Wolfgang Bauer.

In East Berlin, controversy also reigned. Benno Besson ushered in a new era at the Volksbühne with a revised version of a contemporary "socialist" drama, *Horizons,* in which several leading players, having left the Deutsches and the Berliner Ensemble to join Besson, gave performances of distinction. A wave of well-made "socialist" dramas, ranging from Helmut Baierl's *Joan of Döblen* at the Berliner Ensemble to Armin Stolper's *Contemporaries* in Halle, typified the latest developments throughout East Germany, where further managerial changes were forecast. The most notable events in Belgium were the discovery by the National Theatre of Georges Renoy, whose first play, *Mourir un peu,* was an antiwar satire set in the future, and Maurice Béjart's latest venture into "total theatre," using the text of Hermann Closson's *The Four Sons of Aymon.*

Italy. After resigning from the Piccolo in Milan and forming his own troupe, with whom he staged an unforgettably telling adaptation of Weiss's anti-colonialist musical under the title of *Il Mostro Lusitane,* Giorgio Strehler accepted the post of manager of the Rome City Theatre on specific artistic terms. When these were not fulfilled he withdrew, leaving the theatre without a policy, a company, a season, or a manager. Elsewhere, the theatre went its way undisturbed, though the use of nudity resulted in the expulsion of the Living Theatre from Italy. Outstanding events at drama festivals were: Luca Ronconi's staging of Ariosto's *Orlando Furioso* in Spoleto as a popular simultaneous entertainment on numerous movable stages throughout the town; the Milan Piccolo's revival of Ruzzante's *La Betia* in Venice under the direction of Gianfranco De Bosio; Swedish and British troupes at the fourth Florence Drama Festival; and the Aquila City Theatre's double triumph of Antonio Calenda's unusually evocative *Coriolanus* (starring Luigi Proietti) at the Turin and Verona festivals and, on the company's home ground, the same actor's performance in Moravia's symbolic anti-Nazi drama *God Kurt.*

MARTHA SWOPE

As Shakespeare's Henry V, Len Cariou is surrounded by dead soldiers in the opening performance of the American Shakespeare Festival at Stratford, Conn., in June 1969.

Eastern Europe. Yugoslavia was the first Eastern country to feel the shock of the nudity wave, first at the University Theatre Festival in Zagreb and later in the Belgrade premiere of *Hair.* Marshal Tito's banning of a play on political grounds and the performance of a new work, *Viktoria,* in which its Jewish author, Djordje Lebović, asked some awkward questions, brought into relief the two contradictory Yugoslav attitudes toward freedom of expression. Elsewhere in the East (East Germany included), the threat to freedom of expression remained a signal feature of theatrical activity. Czechoslovak authors who had supported the liberalization policy that had been reversed in 1968 fell silent, and the vanguard companies in Prague took refuge in the classics (*Lorenzaccio* at the Theatre Behind the Gate and *The Cherry Orchard* at the Cinoherni Klub, though the latter also staged a promising first play in the Pinteresque tradition by Pavel Landovsky entitled *Rooms by the Hour*).

Radu Beligan's Comedy Theatre in Bucharest, after suffering the departure of David Esrig and its two leading actors, lost its founder, Beligan, to Romania's National Theatre. Beligan's successor, Lucian Giurchescu, staged Brecht's *A Man's a Man* at the Comedy. Other highlights included Beate Fredanov in *Ghosts* at the "Lucia-Sturdza-Bulandra" and Andrei Sherban's exhilarating production of *The Good Woman of Setzuan* at the Youth Theatre in Piatra-Neamt. György Szabo's *Love Locked Out* in Budapest revealed a new absurdist dramatist in the tradition of Istvan Örkeny, whose *Tot Family* found producers in a growing number of European theatres.

Moscow theatres went on producing regardless of the ideological struggle, which got Yuri Liubimov into more trouble at the Taganka, first with his stage version of Boris Mozhayev's *From the Life of Fyodor Kuzhkin,* which was banned just before opening, and then with *Tartuffe* and Gorki's *Mother,* both attacked for being unorthodox. Aleksei Arbuzov's *Happy Days of an Unhappy Man,* eyed with suspicion by the authorities, nevertheless achieved two outstanding productions in Moscow and in Leningrad. Gorki's *The Old Man,* neglected for 40 years for its outspokenness, was revived simultaneously at the Maly, with Mikhail Tsaryov, and at the Mossviet, with Sergei Tseits. Two other much-debated productions were Leonid Heifits' of *Uncle Vanya* at the Central Army Theatre and Boris Livanov's of *The Seagull* at the Moscow Art Theatre, the latter radically reshaped and staged more like a film than a play.

Scandinavia. A new Finnish dramatist, the poet Paavo Haavikko, had a promising first play, an anti-Stalinist pseudohistorical drama called *Agricola and the Fox.* It was presented at the ultramodern Helsinki City Theatre, where, on the large stage, an original production of *Fiddler on the Roof* topped 350 performances. The Danish Odin Teatret with Peter Seeberg's *Ferai,* staged by Jerzy Grotowski's former assistant, Eugenio Barba, attracted some notice at the Paris and Venice festivals. The most sensational production was Ingmar Bergman's of Georg Büchner's *Woyzeck,* which he staged "in the round" at the Stockholm Royal Dramatic Theatre, not least because of an altercation with a critic at one of the rehearsals which cost the director a substantial fine "for disturbing the peace." Otherwise, protest, mostly political, was confined to an ever growing number of collectively conceived and staged dramas throughout the country. Of special interest were Nikolai Erdmann's *The Suicide,* in Göteborg, a forgotten and unperformed Soviet drama by a victim of Stalin; Alf Sjöberg's four-hour-long revival of *The Threepenny Opera* at the Royal Dramatic; and the debut as the City Theatre's new manager of Vivica Bandler from Finland. (O. Tr.)

U.S. and Canada. The breaking of barriers and changes in traditional arrangements, reflecting the same spirit in the outside world, marked the American theatrical scene during the year. The nudity fad, the emergence of black playwrights, the development of resident professional theatres, the renewed strength of off-Broadway, the decline of Broadway itself, had all been in evidence previously, but they seemed to dominate American theatre more than ever in 1969.

The trend toward sexual freedom in the theatre aroused a great deal of merely prurient interest, but it was also significant as a reflection, in however extreme and distorted a fashion, of some important changes in American life. The Broadway version of *Hair* (April 1968) had a brief and dimly lit nude scene. In *Sweet Eros* by Terrence McNally (produced off-Broadway in November 1968), an actress named Sally Kirkland performed nude during the entire length of a one-act play. In January 1969 came *Geese* by Gus Weill, a pair of off-Broadway one-acts featuring both boys and girls in the nude. In March 1969, an off-off-Broadway attraction called *Che!* by Lennox Raphael was raided by the police for using nudity and simulated sex acts as metaphors to represent the relations between the U.S. and Latin America; it later continued its run in a somewhat toned-down form.

The trend continued in May with two competing off-Broadway adaptations from the works of the Marquis de Sade; and finally in June came *Oh! Calcutta!,* devised by Kenneth Tynan and directed by Jacques Levy, with material written by (among others) Samuel Beckett, Jules Feiffer, and John Lennon. The sketches, songs, and dances that comprised *Oh! Calcutta!* were exclusively concerned with sex, and much of the show was performed in the nude; it was offered frankly as "elegant erotica." Though given bad reviews by some critics, it was a tremendous success and established a precedent by charging a top price of $25 a ticket. Significantly, *Oh! Calcutta!* was presented off-Broadway, though Broadway would have seemed the natural place for such a thoroughly commercial and highly profitable entertainment; the days when Broadway was the home of commercial entertainment, while off-Broadway was consecrated to high ideals and low budgets, clearly seemed to be ended.

MARTHA SWOPE

Howard Da Silva as Benjamin Franklin and William Daniels as John Adams ponder the Declaration of Independence in the musical "1776."

UPI COMPIX

Douglas Turner Ward of the Negro Ensemble Company does a typical old-time Harlem dance in a scene from "Ceremonies in Dark Old Men" by Lonne Elder III. The play was an off-Broadway hit in 1969.

A very different manifestation in the theatre of the recent changes in U.S. society was the emergence of new and talented black playwrights; this too was far more evident off-Broadway than on. The Negro Ensemble Company (NEC) had the greatest success of its career with *Ceremonies in Dark Old Men,* a realistic comedy-drama of Harlem life by Lonne Elder III; after Elder's play had concluded its run at the NEC's theatre in lower Manhattan, it was recast and presented successfully at a regular off-Broadway house by a commercial producer. During its 1968–69 season the NEC also offered *God Is a (Guess What?),* a satirical minstrel-show-in-reverse by Ray McIver; a triple bill of one-act plays by Alice Childress, Ted Shine, and Derek Walcott; and a Trinidadian musical called *Man Better Man* by Errol Hill. In September, *The Reckoning* by Douglas Turner Ward was presented "in cooperation" with the NEC, of which Ward was artistic director.

Other off-Broadway managements offered other works by black playwrights: *To Be Young, Gifted, and Black,* a compilation from the works of the late Lorraine Hansberry, and *A Black Quartet,* a bill of one-act plays by Ben Caldwell, Ronald Milner, Ed Bullins, and LeRoi Jones. And the Public Theatre of the New York Shakespeare Festival presented *No Place to Be Somebody,* a brilliant realistic-phantasmagoric comedy-melodrama set in a barroom in Greenwich Village and written by another new black playwright, Charles Gordone.

These black playwrights were united in expressing a sense of the difficulty of life for the black man in a predominantly white society, but in other respects it was hard to generalize about them; in style, they ranged from realistic to expressionistic to poetic, and in content, from apolitical to militant. It could be said, however, that in 1969 black theatre seemed mainly playwright-oriented: there seemed to be little interest in creating theatre pieces out of group improvisation, as was the tendency among the white avant-garde.

On the avant-garde front, the most important event of 1969 was the brief visit to New York City of the Polish Laboratory Theatre, headed by Jerzy Grotowski, whose exercises, methods, and pronouncements had had considerable influence on the Living Theatre, the Open Theatre, the Performance Group, and other similar U.S. companies. At Grotowski's insistence only 100 people, at most, were allowed to attend each performance; even those favoured few had difficulty, unless they knew Polish, in following the action, but the rigorous austerity and discipline of the company and the intensity and precision of their physical and vocal work were greatly admired.

Nothing produced in 1969 by the U.S. avant-garde proved as influential or as popular as the work of Richard Schechner, Tom O'Horgan, or the Living Theatre in previous years, though *The Serpent,* an account of the events in Eden presented by the Open Theatre with a text by Jean-Claude van Itallie, was favourably received. But the institutionalization of the avant-garde took a long step forward with the opening of the new headquarters of the Café La Mama. After years of being harried from loft to loft by the Department of Licenses, La Mama gained its own building in Manhattan, containing two theatres (the La Mama Repertory Theatre and the La Mama Experimental Theatre Club), bought and renovated with the aid of grants from several major foundations.

In 1969, as in the past two or three years, the avant-garde conducted most of its work off-Broadway, where costs were kept down by not paying salaries. Off-Broadway, after a few lean years, became increasingly popular and productive as a commercially viable alternative to Broadway. New off-Broadway theatres were springing up rapidly. Two factors were mainly responsible for off-Broadway's resurgence. First, the costs of Broadway production had increased tremendously, making off-Broadway a bargain by comparison; and second, a national market for off-Broadway-type material was discovered, so that the income from touring productions, movie sales, and record albums helped make off-Broadway production economically feasible.

Little Murders, Jules Feiffer's brilliant black comedy about violence and fear as they impinge upon the life of an "ordinary" New York family, was a quick Broadway failure in 1967; revived at the off-Broadway Circle in the Square in January, it seemed more timely than ever and was able to attract a substantial audience. Another of the season's off-Broadway successes was a pair of one-act comedies, *Adaptation* by Elaine May and *Next* by Terrence McNally. *Next,* an affair of nightmarish hilarity about a fat, middle-aged man who is somehow summoned by his draft board for a physical examination, was notable particularly for James Coco's virtuoso performance. But a new play by Tennessee Williams, entitled *In the Bar of a Tokyo Hotel,* proved to be a sad affair and vanished quickly.

The small-scale, off-Broadway musical became a genre all its own; there were a number of successful shows of this kind during the 1968–69 season. *Dames at Sea* (book and lyrics by George Haimsohn and Robin Miller, music by Jim Wise) was a parody of a Busby Berkeley film musical, with a cast of six. Two successful off-Broadway shows had musical scores by Al Carmines: *Peace,* an adaptation from Aristophanes with a book by Timothy Reynolds, and *Promenade,* with a book by Maria Irene Fornes. The first commercially successful off-Broadway musical of the 1969–70 season was *Salvation* by Peter Link and C. C. Courtney, an imitation of *Hair.*

Meanwhile, among the regional theatres, several tendencies were in evidence. Large new auditoriums,

MICHAEL CHILDERS—CAMERA 5

INGER MC ABE FROM RAPHO GUILLUMETTE

Nudity on stage was mark of several off-Broadway shows during 1969. "Oh! Calcutta!" (left) was still playing to capacity crowds at year's end. A political drama, "Che!," was closed by police after short run.

© BEATA BERGSTRÖM

Sigge Fürst (the Captain) and Tommy Berggren (Woyzeck) in Ingmar Bergman's production of Georg Büchner's "Woyzeck" at the Royal Dramatic Theatre, Stockholm.

built to house resident professional companies, opened in Atlanta (October 1968), Houston (November 1968), and Milwaukee (October 1969). On the other hand, regional theatres generally were having economic troubles; some had already gone out of business, and several others were shaky.

Both of these tendencies were discernible in Canada. In June the National Arts Center in Ottawa opened its doors. A controversial $46 million complex of three theatres, designed by Fred Lebensold, the Arts Center was to serve as a winter home for the Stratford Festival company, also known as the Stratford National Theatre of Canada; it was also to house a French-speaking theatre company and a variety of music, dance, and theatre attractions. On the other hand, Theatre Toronto, an ambitious attempt at creating a major resident professional theatre in that city, expired during its second season. However, Toronto's St. Lawrence Center for the Arts, which was scheduled to open in February 1970, was to have its own resident company. The rising tide of Canadian nationalism was also making itself felt in the theatre; there was increased interest in Canadian-written plays about Canadian subjects, both in English and in French.

The Repertory Theatre of Lincoln Center in New York City had probably its most successful season to date. Its most popular offering was *In the Matter of J. Robert Oppenheimer,* a documentary play by Heinar Kipphardt, which was given its U.S. premiere at the Mark Tapor Forum of the Center Theatre Group of Los Angeles; the Lincoln Center presentation was based on the Los Angeles production, with the same director (Gordon Davidson) and several of the same leading actors. In contrast, the APA-Phoenix Repertory Company, which had become a fixture on Broadway, proved unable to sustain itself financially in New York any longer, and at the end of its 1968–69 season it was forced to take to the road.

As for Broadway proper, it still retained a good measure of its old prestige and preeminence, but it originated little of any significance. It continued to turn out light comedies and musicals but did so in smaller numbers than formerly. During the 1968–69 season the most notable of the new musicals was *Promises, Promises,* a big, slick, well-crafted production adapted from the motion picture *The Apartment,* with a book by Neil Simon and music by Burt Bacharach. Harold Prince produced and directed *Zorba,* based on the novel and movie *Zorba the Greek;* and there was also *1776,* which succeeded in making a popular show-business occasion out of the events leading up to the signing of the Declaration of Independence. In the way of light comedy, the best Broadway could do during 1968–69 was *Jimmy Shine* by Murray Schisgal, a flimsy pretext for Dustin Hoffman's star performance; *Forty Carats* (adapted from the French) starring Julie Harris; and *Play It Again, Sam,* a vehicle for Woody Allen written by Allen himself. Good new comedies being scarce, there were revivals of old ones: *The Front Page* and *Three Men on a Horse* both returned to Broadway in 1969.

The few serious plays that appeared on Broadway in 1968–69 came almost entirely from Britain or from the U.S. regional theatres. From Britain came *The Man in the Glass Booth* by Robert Shaw, a play inspired by the Adolf Eichmann case with Donald Pleasence in the leading role; and *Hadrian VII,* adapted by Peter Luke from the novel by Frederick William Rolfe, starring Alec McCowen as a man who would be pope. To start the fall season of 1969 there was *A Patriot for Me,* John Osborne's chronicle of homosexuality under the Hapsburgs.

The regional theatres made their presence felt on Broadway in two ways. The Tyrone Guthrie Theatre of Minneapolis and the American Conservatory Theatre of San Francisco both played guest engagements on Broadway but their reception was disappointing. More important, for the moment at least, was the fact that during the 1968–69 season there were no less than eight Broadway productions of plays that had had previous productions in regional theatres; in several cases, the regional-theatre production itself was transferred to Broadway. The great dramatic success of the season was *The Great White Hope* by Howard Sackler; both play and production were imported to Broadway from the Arena Stage in Washington, D.C.

The success of *The Great White Hope* helped to induce more regional companies to take more chances with new plays; the Cleveland Play House, for instance, put on *The United States vs. Julius and Ethel Rosenberg,* a rather tendentious documentary play by Donald Freed; it was a huge success in Cleveland, and was optioned for Broadway production. And an early success of the 1969–70 Broadway season was *Indians* by Arthur Kopit, which examined Buffalo Bill as a prototypical white liberal; like *The Great White Hope,* this production was imported from the Arena Stage in Washington. (J. No.)

See also Dance; Literature; Music.

Encyclopædia Britannica Films. *The Age of Sophocles* (1959); *The Character of Oedipus* (1959); *Hamlet: The Age of Elizabeth* (1959); *Hamlet: The Poisoned Kingdom* (1959); *Hamlet: The Readiness Is All* (1959); *Oedipus Rex: Man and God* (1959); *Our Town and Ourselves* (1959); *The Recovery of Oedipus* (1959); *The Theatre: One of the Humanities* (1959); *Thornton Wilder: Our Town and Our Universe* (1959); *What Happens in Hamlet?* (1959); *Macbeth: The Politics of Power* (1964); *Macbeth: The Secret'st Man* (1964); *Macbeth: The Themes of Macbeth* (1964); *The Cherry Orchard I—Chekhov: Innovator of Modern Drama* (1967); *The Cherry Orchard II—Comedy or Tragedy?* (1967); *A Doll's House I—The Destruction of Illusion* (1967); *A Doll's House II—Ibsen's Themes* (1967).

Theology:
see Religion

Tibet:
see China

Timber

The value of the world's output of forest products increased by more than 25% in the first seven years of the 1960s. Estimates by the Forestry and Forest Industries Division of the UN Food and Agriculture Organization (FAO), based on reports from 180 countries, placed the total value of world production of forest products in 1967 (the latest year for which figures were available) at $43.1 billion, compared with $33.9 billion in 1960. The 1950 figure was $23.9 billion. Estimates were in terms of U.S. dollars based on constant 1960 prices.

Of the $43.1 billion value of world output in 1967, $15 billion represented sawn wood or lumber (including railway sleepers and boxboards). The value of wood pulp products (paper and paperboard) was $17.8 billion; of panel products (veneers, plywood, particle board, fibreboard), $4.9 billion; and of all other wood products, $5.4 billion. The production of panel products was much higher in the industrialized regions, but it was reported that output was growing rapidly in the less developed countries. The pulp and paper industries continued to expand in 1967, accounting for 41% of the total value of world output of forest products, compared with 36% in 1950 and 1960. World production of newsprint rose only marginally, however. Printing and writing papers showed a larger increase, but the greatest growth was in the category of noncultural paper and paperboard.

The total volume of roundwood cut from the world's forests in 1967 was estimated at 2,095,900,000 cu.m. (1 cu.m. = 35.31 cu.ft.). Of this 1,165,100,000 cu.m. was removed for industrial uses, the remainder being cut for fuel wood, charcoal, and other domestic or nonindustrial purposes. Estimated removals of industrial wood rose about 23% in the decade 1958–67. For all uses, removals of coniferous (softwood) and broad-leaved (hardwood) roundwood in 1967 were about equal. For industrial uses, however, coniferous roundwood accounted for nearly 80% of the total.

Sawn wood or lumber accounted for more than one-third of total removals. Although world production of sawn wood in 1967 was about 20% above the figure of ten years earlier, it showed a slight drop compared with 1966. Increases in the production of both coniferous and broad-leaved sawn wood occurred in Latin America and Asia. Broad-leaved sawn wood production declined considerably in North America and slightly in Africa and the Pacific area, but rose significantly in other regions.

The 1967 total of world sawn wood production was 370,916,000 cu.m. (1 cu.m. lumber measure = 424 bd-ft.). The FAO's revised estimate for 1966 was 372,864,000 cu.m. For both years, about 80% of the total was coniferous sawn wood. The temperate regions of the Northern Hemisphere accounted for approximately 90% of coniferous sawn wood production.

The U.S.S.R. ranked first in production of sawn wood in 1967, with a reported total of 109 million cu.m. This exceeded the combined total of 106 million cu.m. for the U.S. and Canada. Europe, excluding the U.S.S.R., produced 71.6 million cu.m.; Asia, 62.3 million cu.m.; South America, 10.7 million cu.m.; the Pacific area, 4.8 million cu.m.; Central America 3.1 million cu.m.; and Africa, 3.2 million cu.m.

Among individual nations, the U.S. ranked second to the U.S.S.R. in 1967 sawn wood production, with 81,645,000 cu.m. Japan's 1967 production was not reported, but in 1966 it ranked third with 35.3 million cu.m. Canada was fourth, with 24,451,000 cu.m. China's output was not reported, but its 1966 production was estimated by the FAO at 12 million cu.m. Sweden was first among European nations with a 1967 output of 9,549,000 cu.m. West Germany produced 8,753,000 cu.m.; France, 8,243,000 cu.m. in 1966 (1967 production not reported); Poland, 6,906,000 cu.m.; Finland, 5,788,000 cu.m.; Romania, 5,308,000 cu.m.; Austria, 4,879,000 cu.m.; Czechoslovakia, 3,702,000 cu.m.; Yugoslavia, 2,904,000 cu.m.; and Italy, 2,037,000 cu.m. Brazil's production of sawn wood in 1967 was reported at 6,618,000 cu.m. and Australia's at 3.1 million cu.m. Other countries producing more than one million cubic metres in 1967 were Bulgaria, East Germany, Norway, Portugal, Spain, Switzerland, Mexico, Turkey, Malaysia, Philippines, Thailand, and New Zealand.

Preliminary estimates of U.S. lumber production, based on information compiled by the National Forest Products Association, were available for 1968. The total 1968 output was 37,094,000,000 bd-ft., including 30,134,000,000 bd-ft. of softwood lumber and 6,960,000,000 of hardwood lumber. The combined output of softwood and hardwood lumber showed a substantial gain from the 35,275,000,000 bd-ft. (revised estimate) produced in 1967. The postwar high of 38.9 billion bd-ft. was reached in 1950. U.S. exports totaled 1,159,000,000 bd-ft. in 1968. Imports were 6,155,800,000 bd-ft. The wholesale price index of lumber at the end of 1968 was 142.2, up 27.2% from December 1967 (1957–59 = 100). By August 1969 it had dropped to 131.1.

Canadian production of lumber in 1967 was reported at 10,367,224,000 bd-ft., close to the 10,449,480,000 bd-ft. (revised figure) produced in the preceding year. About 95% of the total was softwood lumber. Canada exported about two-thirds of its lumber production.

The rapid expansion of world pulp production that had occurred since World War II slowed down in 1967. That year's total output was estimated by the FAO at 85.1 million metric tons, only a slight increase over the revised estimate of 84.7 million in 1966. The 1966 total, however, had shown a considerable gain over the 78.5 million produced in 1965. Chemical (including semichemical) pulp represented approximately 70% of world output, the remainder being mechanical wood pulp (about 24%) and pulp from materials other than wood (about 6%).

North America accounted for more than half of the 1967 world total of pulp production. The U.S. produced 32.2 million metric tons and Canada, 14.3 million. Among European producers, Sweden led with 6.8 million tons, followed by Finland (5.7 million), Norway (1.8 million), France (1.6 million), and West Germany (1.4 million). The U.S.S.R. reported 4.7 million tons. Japan's production was 6.2 million. Austria, Czechoslovakia, East Germany, Italy, Poland, Spain, Portugal, Yugoslavia, Mexico, Brazil, Chile, South Africa, China, New Zealand, and Australia were important producers, although none produced as much as one million tons.

World production of paper and paperboard in 1967 reached 106 million metric tons, according to the FAO. The 1966 output was 104.7 million tons. The U.S. led in 1967 with 39.8 million tons, followed by

Canada with 10.7 million tons. Other leading producers were Japan (9.1 million), the U.S.S.R. (5.7 million), the U.K. (4.4 million), West Germany (4.4 million), France (3.5 million), Finland (3.4 million), Sweden (3.3 million), China (3.1 million in 1966), Italy (2.8 million), the Netherlands (1.3 million), and Norway (1.1 million). The 1967 total included 18.4 million tons of newsprint, only an insignificant increase over 1966. More than half was produced in North America, with Canada accounting for 7.6 million metric tons and the U.S. for 2.1 million. Other leading newsprint producers were Japan, Finland, the U.S.S.R., the U.K., Sweden, France, Italy, Norway, China, New Zealand, West Germany, the Netherlands, Switzerland, Austria, Brazil, Chile, and Spain.

World production of plywood made a slight gain according to the FAO; 25,655,000 cu.m. were reported in 1967, compared with 25,333,000 cu.m. in 1966. The U.S. report to the FAO for 1967 was delayed, but in 1966 the U.S., with an output of 13,014,000 cu.m., accounted for more than half of the world total. Japan produced 3,101,000 cu.m. in 1966. Canada reported plywood production of 1,867,600 cu.m. for 1967; the U.S.S.R., 1,818,800 cu.m.; West Germany, 584,100 cu.m.; Finland, 575,000 cu.m.; France 498,000 cu.m.; Italy 300,000 cu.m.; and Romania 264,000 cu.m.

Plywood production in a number of Asian and African countries had risen significantly in recent years. South Korea produced 439,600 cu.m. in 1967; Taiwan, 334,000 cu.m.; and the Philippines, 285,000 cu.m. In Africa, Gabon (63,300 cu.m.) and Ghana (26,800 cu.m.) were the leading producers. Brazil ranked first among Latin-American countries with a 1966 output of 220,000 cu.m. (1967 not reported). Mexico produced 78,600 cu.m. in 1967 and Argentina, 63,500 cu.m. Australia's plywood production in 1967 was 107,300 cu.m.

In the U.S., heavy market demand for lumber for housing construction brought rapidly escalating prices and temporary shortages of softwood lumber and plywood in the early months of 1969. The timber holdings of forest industry companies were mostly covered with young, immature timber, while private forest lands in farm and other nonindustrial ownership were generally poorly managed and produced relatively little usable timber. Forest industry spokesmen therefore urged measures to increase the allowable annual cut from the national forests. Following hearings by the Senate and House Banking and Currency committees, bills were introduced aimed at giving the U.S. Forest Service long-term funding for intensified timber management on national forest lands. Later in the year, a slackening in the rate of housing construction reduced the demand and brought a rapid decline in softwood lumber and plywood prices, but the industry continued to press for intensified national forest management.

With the approval of the Board of Governors of the Chicago Mercantile Exchange, trading in plywood futures started on Oct. 1, 1969. The New York Mercantile Exchange opened trading in plywood futures on September 2. (C. E. R.)

See also Industrial Review.

ENCYCLOPÆDIA BRITANNICA FILMS. *The Temperate Deciduous Forest* (1962); *The Lumberman* (1965); *Trees and Their Importance* (1966); *Science Conserves Forests* (1967); *The Coniferous Forest Biome* (1969); *Problems of Conservation—Forest and Range* (1969).

Timor:
see Dependent States
Tin:
see Mining

Tobacco

Against a background of slowly rising world consumption of tobacco products in 1969, local difficulties rather than market saturation prevented several high-consumption countries from sharing in the general uplift.

According to a report presented in October 1969 to the committee on commodity problems of the UN Food and Agriculture Organization, cigarette sales throughout the world were increasing by 70 billion every year. World output of cigarettes in 1966 (the latest year for which complete figures were available) was more than 2.8 trillion, or 45% higher than the 1955–59 average. In any projection based on these figures, however, both mounting fiscal pressures on cigarette prices in many countries and the increasing activity of antismoking lobbies in the more developed countries would have to be taken into account. The report added that although more cigarettes were being smoked, the growing preference for filter tips and, in the U.K. particularly, for smaller cigarettes meant that less tobacco was being used.

The increasingly sophisticated methods of antismoking propagandists were having their greatest effect on the U.S. industry. Not content with an agreement from the tobacco manufacturers to phase out all radio and television advertising by September 1970, in mid-1969 the health lobby demanded a total ban of all forms of tobacco advertising. Cigarette consumption in the U.S. declined in 1968 for the first time since the release of the surgeon general's report in 1964. This decline continued in 1969 despite efforts to halt it with increased advertising. In the summer of 1968, the Federal Communications Commission had required TV and radio stations to grant as much time to antismoking commercials as they did to cigarette advertising, and in September 1968 several newspapers announced a ban on all cigarette advertising.

In Canada, too, rumblings of a similar campaign grew louder, while in Australia the four leading manufacturers answered threats to their advertising freedom by setting up a tobacco research foundation to examine the smoking and health question. With the government in the U.K. increasingly preoccupied with preelection tactics, tobacco manufacturers unexpectedly backed a growing conviction that restrictions on the industry were well down the list of priorities. They revived coupon brands, even though there had been a direct threat that this form of promotion would be banned.

First estimates of the total U.S. tobacco crop in 1969 stood at 1,799,447,000 lb. This was 444 million lb. below the annual average during the period 1962–64 when tobacco production was at its peak. Notable features of the 1969 tobacco sale were the all-time record price fetched by flue-cured leaf and the smaller-than-expected quantity of tobacco going into Commodity Credit Corporation stocks. Exports of unmanufactured tobacco from the U.S. were held up during January and most of February by a dockers' strike, but were resumed on a large scale in March, reaching a particularly high level in May when they amounted to 66.5 million lb. Nevertheless, the total of 160.9 million lb. for the first five months was still 37.7 million lb., or almost one-fifth, less than in the corresponding 1968 period.

Shipments to the U.K. amounted to no more than

26.1 million lb., or under three-fifths as much as in the first five months of 1968. Consignments to West Germany rose by two-fifths to reach 39.2 million lb., making that country by far the best customer of the U.S. There was a steep fall in exports to Japan and Thailand, and exports to the three Scandinavian countries, Australia and New Zealand, and Hong Kong were also markedly less in these first five months. Shipments to Switzerland, the Philippines, and France all enjoyed marked increases.

Imports into the U.K. during the first seven months of 1969, at 150.7 million lb., were 23.2 million lb. less than in the corresponding 1968 period. Arrivals from the U.S. accounted for only 28% of the total. Imports from Canada were up considerably at 48.7 million lb., while those from India, at 29.4 million lb., were nearly one-sixth lighter. Commonwealth sources accounted for only 45.4% of gross withdrawals of Rhodesian leaf tobacco from bond storage in the first half of 1969, as against 46.8% a year earlier and 52.5% in 1967. A remarkable feature of the U.K. market was the continued rise in cigarette exports. In the first seven months of 1969 these reached 23.2 million lb., or 9% more than the corresponding 1968 figure and 89% more than in 1964. Mainly responsible was the development of demand in Saudi Arabia and, to a lesser extent, the Sudan.

In Australia the 1968–69 crop was estimated at 31 million lb. harvested from some 25,200 ac., potentially the heaviest since the crop of 1963–64, which led to the Tobacco Industry Stabilization Plan and an annual domestic marketing quota of 26 million lb. (wet weight) for the next four years. The leaf marketing quota for the 1969–70 season was raised by a further 1 million lb. to 32 million lb. (green weight) following a review of the overall supply, consumption, and stock position. Consumption trends had been steadily upward whereas manufacturers' stocks had declined markedly since the earlier quota levels had been set. Prices at the Zambia and Malawi auctions were appreciably higher than a year earlier. At the Lusaka sales flue-cured amounted to 11.1 million lb. in place of the 14 million lb. originally hoped for, but the average price of 49.4*d.* a pound showed a rise of 6.6*d.* The U.K. provided the main market.

Canadian production figures for 1969 were not expected to differ much from the 219 million lb. harvested from 135,000 ac. in 1968. The quota acreage set for 1969 amounted to 120,408 ac., from which it was hoped to produce a crop of 200 million lb., nearly 6 million lb. heavier than that of the previous year.

First estimates from India put the area under tobacco in 1968–69 at 6% above the 1967–68 figure. Main reasons were favourable seasonal conditions at the time of sowing, good prices for Virginia leaf, and various development measures. Pakistan, too, estimated a small increase in the total area under the crop, to 255,000 ac.

Exports of unmanufactured tobacco from Turkey during the first five months of 1969 totaled 84 million lb., 7 million lb. more than for the same period in 1968. Consignments to the U.S., by far the country's biggest customer, accounted for 54% of the total but, at 45.2 million lb., were just under 2 million lb. lighter than a year earlier. This drop was more than balanced by an increase in exports to countries of the Soviet bloc. Production in Spain was unofficially reported to have amounted to some 62 million lb. in 1968, the menace of blue mold disease having been largely overcome. Exports of unmanufactured tobacco from Tanzania showed a rise in 1968 to 11.6 million lb., three-quarters of which went to the U.K.

BEN ROTH AGENCY

"Never mind about yer pot smokers mate, what about tobacco smokers?"
—Waite, "The Sun," London.

In the first half of the year exports from Greece, at 71 million lb., were appreciably higher. Exports of unmanufactured tobacco from Yugoslavia had declined from a peak of 51 million lb. in 1951 to 35 million lb. in 1968; in 1968 the outstanding feature of these figures was the steep fall in shipments to the U.S. and the marked rise in those to the Soviet Union.

The Rhodesian crop target for 1969–70 was again set at 132 million lb., and the average price was to continue at 25*d.* a pound. This was the first season since independence in which the government's financial support was not reduced. However, a Rhodesian Tobacco Association survey put the cost of producing this crop at 28.1*d.* a pound. (V. F. Ra.)

Togo

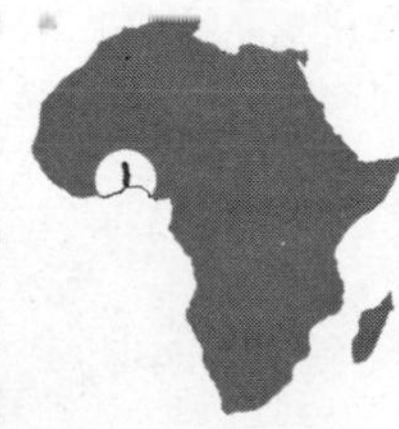

A West African republic, Togo is bordered by Ghana, Upper Volta, and Dahomey. Area: 21,900 sq.mi. (56,600 sq.km.). Pop. (1969 est.): 1,791,300. Cap. and largest city: Lomé (pop., 1969 est., 92,700). Language: French (official). Religion: pagan; Muslim and Christian minorities. President in 1969, Gen. Étienne Eyadema.

The death in Paris of former president Nicolas

TOGO

Education. (1966–67) Primary, pupils 157,548, teachers 3,031; secondary, pupils 12,589, teachers 497; vocational, pupils 1,303, teachers 102; teacher training, students 57, teachers 7; higher, students 85, teaching staff 8.

Finance. Monetary unit: CFA franc, with a parity of CFA Fr. 50 to the French franc (CFA Fr. 277.71 = U.S. $1; CFA Fr. 666.50 = £1 sterling). Budget (1968 est.) balanced at CFA Fr. 6,071,000,000.

Foreign Trade. (1968) Imports CFA Fr. 11,623,000,000; exports CFA Fr. 9,549,000,000. Import sources: France 32%; Japan 11%; U.K. 9%; West Germany 7%; Italy 5%; China 5%. Export destinations: France 39%; Netherlands 23%; West Germany 11%; Belgium-Luxembourg 7%; U.K. 5%. Main exports: phosphates 34%; cocoa 24%; coffee 17%; palm nuts 6%.

Tobogganing: *see* Sporting Record

Grunitzky on September 27, after injuries sustained in a road accident in the Ivory Coast (*see* OBITUARIES), marked a turning point in Togo's political development. Four years after the assassination of Sylvanus Olympio, the removal of his brother-in-law, Grunitzky, brought onto the scene a completely new generation. Although hardly a single former political activist showed interest in overthrowing the military regime, one exception was Bonito Herbert Olympio, son of the former president, who was expelled from Ghana for conspiring with a Togolese agent to overthrow Togo's government.

Although President Eyadema announced in January that political activities could once again be resumed, the decision was later reversed, and all such activities remained under ban, apparently with popular support. On September 21, Togo's traditional chiefs met to pledge unanimous support for Eyadema's policies, approving his plan for the foundation of a single party —the Movement of the Togolese National Rally (MRNT)—announced at the end of August.

Early in the year a convention was signed between Togo and France for financial aid of CFA Fr. 143 million for economic and social development projects, including a modernization of the telecommunications system and the introduction of light industry with help from Cameroon. (PH. D.)

COURTESY, CUNARD LINE, LTD.

Stern view of the new British superliner, "Queen Elizabeth 2," shows her two outdoor swimming pools and expansive deck space. After many delays she made her transatlantic maiden voyage, which ended triumphantly in New York Harbor on May 7, 1969.

Tourism

A significant landmark in the history of modern tourism was the convening in May 1969 of an Intergovernmental Conference on Tourism in Sofia, Bulg. The conference met to discuss the future of tourism. A majority of countries present at the conference endorsed a resolution acknowledging, "the vital contribution that international tourism is making towards the progress of mankind in the economic, cultural, social and educational fields, as well as in strengthening world peace." The delegates, "convinced that the establishment of an intergovernmental organization is the most appropriate and effective way to rationalize and strengthen efforts in the expanding field of tourism," invited the UN Economic and Social Council to approve guidelines for establishing an "International Tourism Organization" on UN lines.

Following the success of the 1967 "International Tourist Year," steps had been taken by many countries to prolong certain of the initiatives taken during that year into 1968. These included continuing relaxations of frontier and visa formalities. Toward the end of 1968 the African countries, conscious of the growing importance of tourism to their continent, took the initiative of proclaiming 1969 "International Year of African Tourism." A program to promote "tourist consciousness" among Africans was undertaken, as well as plans to facilitate cooperation between African governments. Many frontier formalities were relaxed, and the emphasis of the "International Year of African Tourism" was placed on encouraging tourists from other continents to visit Africa for the first time.

International Tourism. In the decade before 1967, world tourist arrivals and receipts had grown at an annual average rate of 10–12%. In 1967, international tourist arrivals grew by 6% and receipts by 7%. In 1968 the increase in arrivals was barely 2%, while receipts rose by only 4%. However, while the cause of tourism's slow progress in 1967 was stagnant world economic growth, the factors behind the unimpressive performance in 1968 were essentially political and of short duration. Nor was the overall picture a gloomy one, as tourism continued to grow rapidly in the less developed countries. Many countries, particularly those that had devalued their currencies in November 1967, experienced a remarkable boom in tourism in 1968. International tourism thus presented a more complex appearance in 1968.

The key to the fortunes of international tourism in 1968 was the decline—for the first time in more than 20 years—of U.S. expenditure on foreign travel. Receipts earned from the foreign travel of U.S. residents amounted to $3.9 billion, $100 million less than in 1967. Although it was clear that certain short-term factors were involved, such as U.S. Pres. Lyndon B. Johnson's call for restriction of nonessential travel outside the Western Hemisphere, there was also evidence of some redistribution of U.S. travel spending, mainly in favour of destinations nearer home such as Mexico, Central and South America, and the Caribbean. But the predominant factor was the decline in U.S. travel spending in Canada—U.S. travelers spent $250 million less in Canada during 1968 than during 1967 when a world's fair had opened in Montreal. While this factor more than accounted for the net decline of $100 million in spending, it should be observed that receipts from U.S. tourists declined in several European countries in 1968. Evidence of the seriousness with which President Johnson's warning was taken was the simultaneous decline in average U.S. tourist spending in Europe during 1968. In Western Europe, total spending amounted to $925 million, 2% below the 1967 figure of $944 million.

The effects of civil disturbances abroad seemed to have caused widespread cancellations of planned trips. Others were postponed, but could not be subsequently rescheduled for later in the year. In France, where total tourist arrivals fell by 10%, from 12 million to 10.8 million, arrivals of U.S. tourists were down by 20% compared with 1967. And as total arrivals in Greece

Tonga:
see Dependent States

Tornadoes:
see Disasters; Meteorology

slumped in 1968 in response to the unhealthy political climate, there were one-third fewer U.S. arrivals. In Czechoslovakia tourism saw its first setback in several years, as total arrivals dropped 10% to 4.2 million, a symptom of the August occupation by the Soviet Union.

With devaluation putting a competitive edge on prices, several countries, notably Cyprus, Ireland, Malta, Spain, and the United Kingdom, showed above-average growth of tourism in 1968. In Spain, where U.S. arrivals declined in 1968, total arrivals of foreign tourists grew from 17.8 million to 19.2 million. Receipts from tourism reached $1,221,000,000, worth more than 30% of Spain's exports. The U.K. showed an increase in tourist arrivals from 4.3 million to 4.8 million in 1968, while receipts from foreign tourism climbed from $652 million to $658 million in spite of the devaluation of the pound sterling. U.S. arrivals to the U.K. played an important part, rising by 9% in 1968. Total spending of U.S. travelers in Britain, at $200 million, amounted to more than 25% of total U.K. receipts from foreign tourism. Thanks to post-devaluation prices, holidays in Britain cost tourists 5% less per person than in 1967. Among the non-devaluing countries, West Germany succeeded in attracting 13% more U.S. tourists in 1968, although overall arrivals showed no change. Currently, West Germany was earning more than $900 million per year from foreign tourism.

Outside Europe, and on the doorstep of the U.S., Mexico saw tourist arrivals rise from 1.4 million in 1967 to 1.7 million in 1968. Total receipts from foreign tourism grew from $363 million to $424 million. A major factor in Mexico and in all of Latin America was the redistribution of U.S. travel spending referred to above. This brought the earnings of Central America and the Caribbean from U.S. travelers to $325 million in 1968, 10% higher than in 1967. U.S. spending in the Bahamas rose by 20% to exceed $100 million, while the increase in Jamaica was by 18% to $78 million. During the autumn of 1968 it was estimated that the Olympic Games brought an extra 30,000 foreign tourists to Mexico as spectators or participants.

In Israel, travel receipts jumped from $52 million to $96 million as tourists celebrated with nationals the 20th anniversary of the founding of the state of Israel. Of the 432,000 tourist arrivals recorded in 1968, approximately 133,000 came from the U.S. In Lebanon, receipts rose from $80 million to $110 million, and arrivals reached 710,000. But arrivals continued to fall off in most of the other Arab-speaking countries of the Middle East, notably in Jordan and the United Arab Republic.

Asia, Australasia, and Africa continued to experience high growth rates, reflecting the rapidly developing state of tourism in these regions. This was very much the result of strenuous promotional efforts by countries of those regions.

Domestic Tourism. While the volume and value of international tourism was easily measured, the growth rate of domestic tourism was harder to assess. This was due to the fact that no frontier crossings or exchange transactions were involved. Domestic tourism expenditure was, however, estimated to account for 75% of total world tourist expenditures.

For geographic reasons, as well as on account of its size, the U.S. was the largest single spender on domestic tourism. Receipts from interstate travel reached $30 billion in 1967. In other parts of the world, especially Europe, domestic tourism spending was rising, but there was little evidence that, even during periods of restraint, domestic travel was replacing international travel as far as main holidays were concerned.

Tourism in 1969. The travel trade, conscious of tourism's disappointing results in 1968, took a generally cautious outlook concerning 1969, anticipating that it would be the third year in succession when the number of tourist arrivals would rise only moderately. At the same time, it was predicted that the total number of tourist nights spent in accommodations would remain static or, in some cases, decline.

By the end of 1969, however, it appeared that the year would be a better one for tourism than the pundits had predicted. This was possible for a number of reasons, notably the absence of political unrest which had upset the tourism picture in 1968, the renewed travel of North Americans to Europe, and a spell of comparatively fine weather in Europe during the peak holiday months. In the first half of 1969 arrivals in Greece, Italy, Spain, and the U.K. were well above 1968 levels and, during August, London found itself with a temporary shortage of accommodations as foreign tourists arrived in numbers far exceeding forecasts. Outside Europe, there was an increase of about 20% in foreign visitors to the U.S. in 1969, a substantially higher rate of growth than in 1968. One factor in this increase was the liberalization of frontier formalities for tourists from Mexico, who were consequently expected in greater numbers.

Africa's tourism in 1969 responded well to the challenge set by the "International Year of African Tourism." The North African countries especially witnessed a continued rapid growth of arrivals, as a result of promotion aimed at the neighbouring European market. In Tunisia, arrivals were more than 30% higher in the first half of 1969 than in the comparable period of 1968. At the same time, the number of tourist nights recorded in the hotel industry there rose by more than 20%. In Kenya, the principal tourist country of East Africa, arrivals had already quadrupled between 1964 and 1968 to reach 264,000. During 1969 tourism in East Africa was expected to show a further increase of more than 15%.

Travel in Asia and Australasia was largely unaffected by the setbacks of 1968, and 1969 appeared to be another good year. Arrivals grew 17% between 1967 and 1968, and data for the first half of 1969 showed a similar or even better performance by most

Table I. International Tourist Arrivals, 1967–68

Region	Arrivals 1967	Arrivals 1968	Change Absolute	Change Percent
Europe	102,300,000	104,000,000	+1,700,000	+ 2
North America	25,600,000	24,300,000	−1,300,000	− 5
Latin America	4,700,000	5,300,000	+ 600,000	+13
Africa	1,600,000	1,900,000	+ 300,000	+18
Asia/Australia	2,900,000	3,400,000	+ 500,000	+17
Middle East	2,000,000	2,100,000	+ 100,000	+ 5
Total	139,100,000	141,000,000	+1,900,000	+ 1.5

Source: International Union of Official Travel Organizations, Geneva.

Table II. International Tourist Receipts, 1967–68

In $000,000

Region	Receipts 1967	Receipts 1968	Change Absolute	Change Percent
Europe	8,280	8,620	+340	+ 4
North America	2,850	2,700	−150	− 5
Latin America	1,110	1,270	+160	+14
Africa	300	350	+ 50	+17
Asia/Australia	700	860	+160	+23
Middle East	190	200*	+ 10	+ 5
Total	13,430	14,000	+570	+ 4

*Provisional figure.
Source: International Union of Official Travel Organizations, Geneva.

Asian countries, though tourism in India and Pakistan occupied the lower end of the growth scale. Australia and Japan were the principal generators of tourism within the region, and the relaxation of currency allowances by Japan was bound to add a further stimulus. Tourism in the Arab-speaking countries of the Middle East showed only a few signs of improvement.

Organization and Promotion. The authority and power of the national tourist organizations grew considerably during 1968–69. In August royal assent was given to a new tourism development law setting up a statutory British Tourist Authority. The new authority would have extensive responsibilities in the spheres of promotion and development, and was to come into full operation during 1970.

The rate of increase of spending on tourist promotion slowed down somewhat in 1968, total annual budgets of the world's national tourist organizations being 10% higher than in 1967. The 1967 figure had been nearly 17% more than that of 1966. More than $85 million was spent on promotional activities by the national tourist organizations alone. This was supplemented by the activities of airline companies, travel agents, and tour operators, who spent $190 million on promotion during 1968. (P. SH.)

See also Parks; Transportation.

Toys and Games

As for many other industries, 1969 was a tough year for the toy trade. But while world economics was against manufacturers, the success of one achievement *outside* the world gave a great boost to the industry in the middle of the year. The July 20 moon landing could be said to add the title "the greatest merchandising venture ever" to its list of other records. Virtually every manufacturer latched onto it as a major sales promotion device. There were many, of course, who had been making space toys for some years. They capitalized on their existing products plus some new models. Others entered the field for the first time.

One of the outstanding successes was Gemini Datakits. Strictly speaking, this was a publishing venture that fell into the anomalous category occupied by the hugely successful Jackdaw series, rather than a toy or game. The Datakit was created and assembled with the help of the U.S. National Aeronautics and Space Administration (NASA), and included a flight plan, briefing, lunar charts, and spacecraft diagrams.

Equally notable was Waddington's new game, "Blast Off," while, of course, sales soared for traditionally space-associated toys and models such as Mattel's Major Matt Mason. Even the producers of a series of press-out cardboard models made record sales with two products geared to the space venture.

The development of a toy industry based on cardboard, an old material but used in new ways, gained momentum during the year. The interesting aspect of this boom was not so much the use of heavy-duty cardboard for toys traditionally made of wood, such as playhouses and even rocking horses, but rather that it encouraged many firms whose experience was in the design field rather than in production to enter the toy industry. Cardboard Engineering's "rocking horse," for instance, was very much an abstract version that could be assembled by slotting together three sections of polythene-coated fibreboard. Polypops Products, a division of Polycell, was extensively involved in this field. Their line included a space station capable of housing about eight youngsters, and a lunar track (an articulated caterpillar track inside which a child could crawl).

The Planpit, a sandbox table billed as a pacifier for the tense executive or a conversation piece for home or office. The box has hand-sculptured combing tools of forged iron and cast bronze for tracing patterns in sand.

COURTESY, BIRCHALL-GOAD AND CO. LTD.

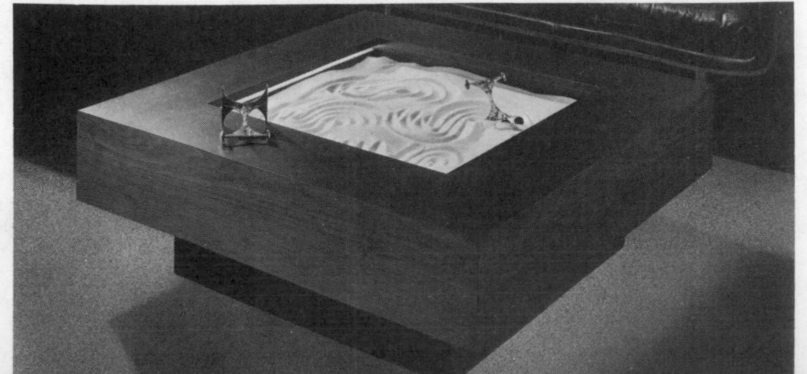

BEN ROTH AGENCY

—Dunnett, Canada.

In the same way that the material introduced new design elements to the trade, so the creators of the designs injected new colour ideas that were exciting and vivid. The design approach to toy making perhaps gained greatest publicity through the creation by the Denys Fisher organization of a "think tank." This produced some of the biggest successes of 1968–69, including Paint Wheels, which headed the British top ten for some months at the beginning of the year. In France and West Germany, a new approach to slotted-together building sets, called Fischertechnik, a winner for its simplicity, won Toy of the Year awards in both countries for the third consecutive year.

Two significant steps were taken during 1969 toward true internationalism in the toy industry. The European Toy Institute in Brussels at last tackled the perennial problem of safety and drew up 15 principles for application on a European level. These were still being discussed by member countries at the end of the year. However, the Institute had already contacted the Common Market Commission, which was expected to draft a law regarding toy safety.

The same institute also devised and published a detailed classification system applicable to all toys available in Europe. Toys were divided into groups, and each toy in each classification was given a number. It was intended that in the future that number would become the standard reference for the toy throughout Europe and, eventually, the world.

In the U.S., action was also taken in regard to the safety of toys. Pres. Richard Nixon signed a bill in November authorizing the secretary of health, education, and welfare to ban the sale of toys that present electrical, mechanical, or heat hazards. The law also allowed a buyer to return such a toy and receive a refund.

Market research undertaken during 1969 in Japan

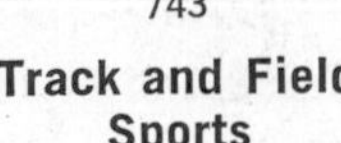

COURTESY KINETIC OBJECTS, INC.

Tork, a new scientific toy consisting of a weight attached to a steel spring and mounted on a wooden base, demonstrates varying kinds of motion depending on the amount and direction of the starting force.

contained a significant ray of hope for all other producers. The country's annual output during the year totaled approximately $200 million, of which approximately 60% was exported. However, as the standard of living in Japan continued to rise, it was thought that a considerable proportion of the total toy output would be diverted to home consumption.

The craze business is an annual if ephemeral affair. The late 1968 introduction, Ride-a-Roo, and its many related forms, lasted well into 1969. No worthy replacement appeared immediately, although Britain at least had the promised introduction of Yahtzee to look forward to. A game already well known in the U.S., Yahtzee was to be launched in the U.K. by the popularizer of modern Bingo. In the U.S. Skipsy Doodle, a 4-ft.-long plastic playground toy that resembled a large gravy boat, was gaining increased popularity.

(J. M. Th.)

Track and Field Sports

The year 1969 may have marked that long-awaited "inevitable year" of track and field competition—the year when the record breaking had at least to pause if not to stop. Except for Pam Kilborn of Australia in the 200-m. hurdles, not a single significant new world record was set at metric distances in the running events, though new ground was broken in 5 of the 13 scheduled men's and women's field events. Particularly surprising was the inability of any long (broad) jumper, including Bob Beamon himself, to approach even remotely Beamon's great Olympic Games leap of 29 ft. 2⅜ in. set at the 7,000-ft. altitude of Mexico City in 1968.

The two greatest feats of the year were the running of a marathon (26 mi. 385 yd.) at an average pace of 12.24 mph (4 min. 54.3 sec. for each mile) near Antwerp, Belg., on May 30 by an English-born Australian, Derek Clayton, and the prodigies of a Soviet woman shot putter, Nadyezhda Chizhova, whose put of 67 ft. ¼ in. was 6 ft. farther than the best of her famous compatriot Tamara Press.

International Tournaments. The year saw three major meets: the Commonwealth of Nations *v.* United States *v.* U.S.S.R. triangular match in Los Angeles on July 18–19; the Europe *v.* Western Hemisphere dual meet in Stuttgart, W.Ger., on July 30–31; and the IXth European Championships in Athens, Greece, on September 16–21.

The meeting in the Los Angeles Coliseum produced many very good but no great performances. The Soviet steeplechaser Aleksandr Morozov beat Australia's Kerry O'Brian by 4 yd. in 8 min. 26 sec., and Bob Seagren (U.S.) vaulted 17 ft. 6¾ in. The United States suffered a rare defeat from a Commonwealth quartet in the sprint relay, but their Olympic decathlon champion, Bill Toomey, left nothing to chance in compiling a score of 7,938 points over the ten events. The U.S. beat the U.S.S.R. 125–110 points and the Commonwealth 137–95. The United States' girls' team achieved their first victory ever over the Soviet women athletes (70–67) and also triumphed over the Commonwealth 81–56.

The Stuttgart meeting on an all-weather rubber composition track drew crowds of 30,000 both evenings, but was marred by an over compression of the program such that at one point five field events were being staged simultaneously with the track events. Europe won the men's match 113–97 and the women's match 81–54, with the outstanding performance among the losers being victories in the 100-m. and 200-m. dashes by John Carlos (U.S.) in 10.2 and 20.4 sec. into a head wind. Josef Plachy (Czech.) took the 800 m. in 1 min. 45.4 sec., while in a brilliant 400-m. run a French girl, Nicole Duclos, equaled the European record of 52 sec. U.S. dominance in the pole vault was upset when the world record holder, John Pennel of Florida, was unable to clear 17 ft. 1 in.

Contrary to the custom of staging the European Championships in the even years between celebrations of the Olympic Games, the IXth European Championships were held in Athens a year earlier so that the tenth edition could be accommodated in Helsinki in 1971, before the Munich Olympic Games of the following year.

The Athens meet was largely dominated by East Germany (pop. 16 million), with 11 gold and 14 other medals, whose team outshone that of the U.S.S.R. (pop. 238 million). The Soviet athletes took 9 of the 38 titles at stake. Great Britain was the next most successful with 17 medals of which 6 were gold, and was thus well ahead of France (3 gold) and Poland and Czechoslovakia, which each provided two champions.

The championships were marred by the withdrawal of the West German team, in protest over the refusal of the International Amateur Athletics Federation to allow a former East German, Jürgen May, to run on their team on the ground that this would, as previously warned, be contrary to the federation rules that placed time limits on switching "nationalities."

The five days of competition produced new championship records in 16 of the 24 men's events, including a world record in the hammer throw by the squat, immensely powerful Anatolyi Bondarchuk (U.S.S.R.), on whose shoulders there was a centrifugal strain of more than 450 lb. at the moment of release. Of the ten established women's events, there were records in six, while that for the high jump was equaled by Miloslava Rezkova of Czechoslovakia, who in clearing 6 ft. 0 in. (1.83 m.) lived up to her reputation for being able to clear the greatest height above her own stature (5 ft. 6⅜ in.). There was a new world record in the women's 400 m. of 51.7 sec. by the French pair, Nicole Duclos and the reigning Olympic 400-m. cham-

Town Planning: *see* Cities and Urban Affairs

pion, Colette Besson, but they were still half a second shy of the unofficial time set in 1964 by Sin Kim Dan of the then-suspended North Korea.

The 1,600 (4 × 400) m. relay was the most thrilling race ever witnessed in the 45 years of women's international athletics. France, with its two new co-holders of the world 400-m. record, was clearly the favourite. The first three British girls, Rosemary Stirling, Pat Lowe, and Janet Simpson, yielded nothing, so that on the anchor stage Colette Besson was only 1½ yd. clear of her arch rival, Lillian Board (U.K.), from whom she had snatched the Olympic 400-m. gold medal in the last few strides in Mexico City. The French girl covered the first 200 m. in a breathtaking 23.6 sec., with the London girl falling 9 yd. back. However, Miss Board closed remorselessly, and won by 4 in. in the last stride in a world record time of 3 min. 30.8 sec. for an average of 52.7 sec. per stage. (N. D. McW.)

"LONDON DAILY EXPRESS" FROM PICTORIAL PARADE

Britain's Dick Taylor wins the 5,000-m. event in the Great Britain-U.S. match at the White City, London, on Aug. 13, 1969. His time of 13 min. 29 sec. set a new British record.

U.S. Competition. In the U.S. several outstanding performers left the sport during the year. Three 1968 Olympic Games champions retired: Jim Hines (100 m.) and Tommie Smith (200 m.) to play professional football and Al Oerter (four-time discus winner) to wind up a 15-year career. Bronze medalists Tom Farrell (800-m.) and George Young (steeplechase) also ended long careers, as did hammer-thrower Ed Burke.

One of the most discussed events of 1969 was the retirement of Jim Ryun, world record holder at 880-yd., one mile, and 1,500 m. Besieged by injury, burdened by mounting pressures, and committed to a new career, Ryun was beaten in the collegiate championships and the next week stepped off the track less than halfway through the U.S. Amateur Athletic Union (AAU) title race. He announced his retirement for the season, and perhaps for all time. Only partly active, either through slackened interest or because of injury, were three Olympic winners: Bob Beamon (long jump), Dick Fosbury (high jump), and Randy Matson (shot put).

Among the competitors who distinguished themselves in 1969 was Willie Davenport, Olympic high-hurdle winner. At Zürich, Switz., he equaled the records of 13.2 sec. for the 120-yd. and 110-m. high-hurdle races. He also had a record-breaking year in indoor competition. Olympic decathlon king Bill Toomey came back better than ever, scoring 8,417 points for a new world record. He scored more than 8,000 points six more times (only one other athlete had managed 8,000 points more than twice during a full career) and tallied an all-time high of 4,123 points in the pentathlon, for which there was no official world record.

Javelin-thrower Mark Murro threw 292 ft. 8 in. for a new U.S. record. Olympic winner Lee Evans came within two-tenths of a second of a new 440-yd. record, while Bob Seagren, another Olympic titlist, won his important tests and flirted with pole vaulting's "magic number" of 18 ft. But both Evans and Seagren were upstaged by other U.S. athletes who carried off world records in their specialties. Evans was surprised in the NCAA (National Collegiate Athletic Association) title meet by Curtis Mills, a young sophomore from Texas A and M. Mills not only scored an upset victory but set a new international standard of 44.7 sec. Seagren's downfall was at the hands of an old rival, John Pennel, who achieved a world record with a vault of 17 ft. 10¼ in.

John Carlos equaled the world record when he dashed 100 yd. in 9.1 sec. Carlos, of San Jose State College, clearly dominated the U.S. and international sprint picture, losing only one race at any distance. Another mark was tied when Erv Hall of Villanova ran the 120-yd. high hurdles in 13.2 sec.

Matching the U.S. record in the 440-yd. hurdles was

Table I. World Outdoor Records—Men

Event	Competitor, country, date	Performance
100 yd.	J. Carlos, U.S., May 10	9.1 sec.*
440 yd.	C. Mills, U.S., June 21	44.7 sec.
120-yd. hurdles	E. Hall, U.S., June 19	13.2 sec.*
120-yd. hurdles	W. Davenport, U.S., July 4	13.2 sec.
110-m. hurdles	W. Davenport, U.S., July 4	13.2 sec.
3,000-m. steeplechase	V. Dudin, U.S.S.R., August 18	8 min. 22.2 sec.
Pole vault	J. Pennel, U.S., June 21	17 ft. 10¼ in. (5.44 m.)
Hammer throw	A. Bondarchuk, U.S.S.R., October 13	247 ft. 7 in. (74.48 m.)
Javelin	J. Kinnunen, Finland, June 18	304 ft. 1½ in. (92.70 m.)
20-km. walk	G. Agapov, U.S.S.R., April 4	1 hr. 26 min. 45.8 sec.
30-mi. walk	C. Höhne, East Germany, October 18	4 hr. 0 min. 6.2 sec.
50-km. walk	C. Höhne, East Germany, October 18	4 hr. 8 min. 5.0 sec.
Decathlon	W. Toomey, U.S., December 11	8,417 pt.

*Ties record.

Table II. World Outdoor Records—Women

Event	Competitor, country, date	Performance
400 m.	N. Duclos, France, September 18	51.7 sec.
	C. Besson, France, September 18	51.7 sec.
1,500 m.	J. Jehlickova, Czechoslovakia, September 20	4 min. 10.7 sec.
100-m. hurdles	K. Balzer, East Germany, September 5	12.9 sec.
200-m. hurdles	P. Kilborn, Australia, December 17	25.8 sec.
1 mi.	M. Gommers, Netherlands, June 14	4 min. 36.8 sec.
Shot put	N. Chizhova, U.S.S.R., September 16	67 ft. ¼ in. (20.43 m.)
Discus throw	L. Westermann, West Germany, September 27	209 ft. 10 in. (63.96 m.)
Pentathlon	L. Prokop, Austria, October 4–5	5,352 pt.
1,600-m. relay (4 x 400 m.)	U.K., September 20	3 min. 30.8 sec.
1,600-m. relay (4 x 400 m.)	France, September 20	3 min. 30.8 sec.

Table III. World's Best Indoor Performances*

Event	Competitor, country, date	Performance
MEN		
50 m.	A. Morozov, U.S.S.R., February 15	5.4 sec.†
60 yd.	J. Carlos, U.S., January 10	5.9 sec.†
70 yd.	M. Pender, U.S., February 15	6.8 sec.†
100 yd.	L. Miller, Jamaica, January 24	9.4 sec.
	J. Green, U.S., January 24	9.4 sec.
300 yd.	R. Allen, U.S., January 24	30.0 sec.‡
300 m.	J. Nallet, France, February 21	33.1 sec.
500 yd.	L. James, U.S., February 15	55.4 sec.
600 yd.	H. McAlhaney, U.S., January 25	1 min. 8.1 sec.‡
	W. Wehrwein, U.S., February 22	1 min. 8.6 sec.
800 m.	D. Fromm, East Germany, March 8	1 min. 46.6 sec.
880 yd.	R. Doubell, Australia, January 25	1 min. 47.9 sec.
1,000 yd.	R. Schultz, U.S., March 1	2 min. 6.0 sec.
3,000 m.	B. Diessner, East Germany, February 16	7 min. 47.8 sec.
2 mile	G. Young, U.S., February 22	8 min. 27.2 sec.†
3 mile	G. Young, U.S., March 1	13 min. 9.8 sec.
45-yd. high hurdles	W. Davenport, U.S., February 1	5.3 sec.
50-yd. high hurdles	W. Davenport, U.S., February 14	5.8 sec.
60-yd. high hurdles	W. Davenport, U.S., February 7	6.8 sec.†
70-yd. high hurdles	W. Davenport, U.S., February 15	7.8 sec.
120-yd. high hurdles	W. Davenport, U.S., January 24	13.5 sec.
1-mi. relay	University of Texas, January 24	3 min. 8.4 sec.‡
2-mi. relay	Villanova University, February 15	7 min. 22.8 sec.
Sprint medley relay	Kansas State Univ., January 24	3 min. 17.9 sec.‡
Pole vault	R. Seagren, U.S., February 8	17 ft. 6 in.
35-lb. weight	G. Frenn, U.S., February 1	73 ft. 3½ in.
WOMEN		
400 m.	C. Besson, France, March 8	54.0 sec.†
800 m.	B. Wieck, East Germany, March 9	2 min. 5.3 sec.
50-m. high hurdles	M. Rallins, U.S., March 20	7.0 sec.

*The International Amateur Athletic Federation does not officially recognize world indoor records but refers to them as "world best."
†Ties record.
‡Set on oversized track of 352 yd.

Table IV. European Championships

Event	Athens, Greece, September 16–21 Competitor, country	Performance
100 m.	V. Borzov, U.S.S.R.	10.4 sec.
200 m.	P. Clerc, Switzerland	20.6 sec.
400 m.	J. Werner, Poland	45.7 sec.
800 m.	D. Fromm, East Germany	1 min. 45.9 sec.
1,500 m.	J. Whetton, U.K.	3 min. 39.4 sec.
5,000 m.	I. Stewart, U.K.	13 min. 44.8 sec.
10,000 m.	J. Haase, East Germany	28 min. 41.6 sec.
3,000-m. steeplechase	M. Zhelev, Bulgaria	8 min. 25.0 sec.
Marathon	R. Hill, U.K.	2 hr. 16 min. 47.8 sec.
20,000-m. walk	P. Nihill, U.K.	1 hr. 30 min. 49.0 sec.
50,000-m. walk	C. Höhne, East Germany	4 hr. 13 min. 32.8 sec.
110-m. hurdles	E. Ottoz, Italy	13.5 sec.
400-m. hurdles	V. Skomorokhov, U.S.S.R.	49.7 sec.
400-m. relay	France	38.8 sec.
1,600-m. relay	France	3 min. 2.3 sec.
High jump	V. Gavrilov, U.S.S.R.	7 ft. 1½ in.
Pole vault	W. Nordwig, East Germany	17 ft. 4¾ in.
Long jump	I. Ter-Ovanesyan, U.S.S.R.	26 ft. 9¾ in.
Triple jump	V. Saneyev, U.S.S.R.	56 ft. 10¾ in.
Shot put	D. Hoffman, East Germany	66 ft. ¼ in.
Discus throw	H. Losch, East Germany	202 ft. 10 in.
Hammer throw	A. Bondarchuk, U.S.S.R.	245 ft. 0 in.
Javelin	J. Lusis, U.S.S.R.	300 ft. 3 in.
Decathlon	J. Kirst, East Germany	8,041 pt.

Table V. United States v. Soviet Union v. Commonwealth of Nations

Event	Los Angeles, July 18–19 Competitor, country	Performance
100 m.	J. Carlos, U.S.	10.3 sec.
200 m.	J. Carlos, U.S.	20.3 sec.
400 m.	L. Evans, U.S.	45.3 sec.
800 m.	J. Luzins, U.S.	1 min. 46.7 sec.
1,500 m.	M. Liquori, U.S.	3 min. 40.1 sec.
5,000 m.	R. Sharafutdinov, U.S.S.R.	13 min. 58.8 sec.
10,000 m.	R. Clarke, Australia	28 min. 35.4 sec.
Steeplechase	A. Morozov, U.S.S.R.	8 min. 26.0 sec.
110-m. hurdles	W. Davenport, U.S.	13.5 sec.
400-m. hurdles	N. Lee, U.S.	49.7 sec.
20,000-m. walk	P. Nihill, U.K.	1 hr. 31 min. 49.8 sec.
400-m. relay	Commonwealth	39.4 sec.
1,600-m. relay	U.S.	3 min. 3.1 sec.
High jump	V. Gavrilov, U.S.S.R.	7 ft. 3 in.
Long jump	S. Whitley, U.S.	26 ft. 8½ in.
Pole vault	R. Seagren, U.S.	17 ft. 6¾ in.
Triple jump	V. Saneyev, U.S.S.R.	55 ft. 5¾ in.
Shot put	K. Salb, U.S.	64 ft. 8 in.
Discus throw	V. Lyakhov, U.S.S.R.	202 ft. 1 in.
Hammer throw	A. Bondarchuk, U.S.S.R.	237 ft. 5 in.
Javelin	J. Lusis, U.S.S.R.	277 ft. 3 in.
Decathlon	W. Toomey, U.S.	7,938 pt.
Team points	U.S. 125, U.S.S.R. 110; U.S. 137, Comm. 95	

Table VI. Europe v. Western Hemisphere

Event	Stuttgart, W.Ger., July 30–31 Competitor, country	Performance
100 m.	J. Carlos, U.S.	10.2 sec.
200 m.	J. Carlos, U.S.	20.4 sec.
400 m.	L. Evans, U.S.	44.9 sec.
800 m.	J. Plachy, Czechoslovakia	1 min. 45.4 sec.
1,500 m.	M. Liquori, U.S.	3 min. 37.2 sec.
5,000 m.	G. Lindgren, U.S.	13 min. 38.4 sec.
10,000 m.	J. Haase, East Germany	28 min. 51.4 sec.
Steeplechase	M. Zhelev, Bulgaria	8 min. 33.0 sec.
110-m. hurdles	L. Coleman, U.S.	13.3 sec.
400-m. hurdles	G. Hennige, West Germany	50.0 sec.
400-m. relay	Western Hemisphere	38.8 sec.
1,600-m. relay	Western Hemisphere	3 min. 1.6 sec.
High jump	O. Burrell, U.S.	7 ft. 1 in.
Pole vault	R. Dionisi, Italy	17 ft. ¾ in.
Long jump	L. Davies, U.K.	26 ft. 7¼ in.
Triple jump	J. Drehmel, East Germany	53 ft. 3¾ in.
Shot put	H.-P. Gies, East Germany	67 ft. 5¾ in.
Discus throw	L. Danek, Czechoslovakia	209 ft. 9 in.
Hammer throw	R. Theimer, East Germany	233 ft. 6 in.
Javelin	P. Nevala, Finland	280 ft. 6 in.
Team points	Europe 113, Western Hemisphere 97	

Ralph Mann of Brigham Young University. His mark was made during the NCAA meet on the University of Tennessee's fast track, as were the records by Hall and Mills, as well as U.S. relay records at two distances. San Jose State, anchored by Carlos with contributions from Sam Davis, Kirk Clayton, and Ronnie Ray Smith, chopped the 440-yd. relay to 38.8 sec., while UCLA achieved a mile-relay record time of 3 min. 3.4 sec. from John Smith, Len Van Hofwegen, Andy Young, and Wayne Collett.

Team titles in the major U.S. outdoor meets were earned by San Jose State in the NCAA, the Southern California Striders in the AAU, and Prairie View A and M in the NAIA (National Association of Intercollegiate Athletics).

UPI COMPIX

Olympic champion Willie Davenport (left) competes in the 45-yd. high hurdles in the 80th Boston Athletic Association Track Meet at Boston Garden, Feb. 1, 1969. Davenport won the event with a time of 5.3 sec., a new world's indoor best performance.

Many more records were set in indoor competition than during the outdoor season. A number of Olympic athletes performed notably during the January-through-March indoor circuit but then did not compete in the outdoor campaign. Most conspicuous of these athletes was George Young, third in the Olympic steeplechase. He equaled the world's best mark (there are no official world records indoors) in the two-mile run with 8 min. 27.2 sec. and then retired after setting a new low of 13 min. 9.8 sec. for three miles. Villanova's Larry James covered 500 yd. in 55.4 sec.; Ralph Doubell, the Olympic 800-m. winner from Australia, ran 880 yd. in 1 min. 47.9 sec.; Villanova ran the two-mile relay in 7 min. 22.8 sec.; and Seagren vaulted 17 ft. 6 in., all the best performances ever indoors. Record-equaling marks were 5.9 sec. for 60 yd. by Carlos and 6.8 sec. for the 60-yd. high hurdles by Davenport. The latter also performed admirably in nonstandard events, turning in best-ever times for high-hurdle races at 45, 50, 70, and 120 yd. Indoor marks were also equaled or bettered in the 70-yd. dash, 100-yd. dash, 60-yd. low hurdles, 70-yd. low hurdles, and 35-lb. weight.

In women's track, the U.S. had to be content with three new national records outdoors. Eleanor Montgomery high-jumped 5 ft. 11 in., 17-year-old Kathy Hammond ran the 400 m. in 52.1 sec., and Doris Brown and Francie Larrieu covered 1,500 m. in 4 min. 16.8 sec. Indoors, Mamie Rallins achieved a world's best mark in a seldom-run new event, the 50-m. high hurdles, while Tennessee State University's Madeline Manning gained a U.S. record of 2 min. 7.9 sec. for the half-mile. Tennessee State won both the indoor and outdoor national women's AAU titles.

(Be. N.)

Trade, International

A period of rapid growth in world trade began with the revival of economic activity in the major industrial nations at the end of 1967. By the second quarter of 1969, the total value of world trade was 27% higher than in the same quarter of 1967; the average price of world exports had risen by only 2% in this period so the volume of trade had expanded by 25%. Although the value increase was not quite so rapid as in the 1964 boom, the rise in volume was a record. The expansion owed a great deal to increased imports by the U.S. and West Germany, which in 1968 accounted for almost half the total growth in world trade.

Imports of industrial countries from primary producing economies rose sharply early in 1968 and continued rising in 1969, although there were signs late in the year that the growth rate was slackening somewhat as industrial expansion eased. Provisional figures for 1969 suggest that, despite this slackening, the increase in the value of trade compared with 1968 was greater than that between 1967 and 1968; growth in the volume of trade was much the same in both years. The growth was widespread although, as in earlier years, the most rapidly expanding part of world trade was that between industrial countries. Sino-Soviet trade rose 9% in 1968, but much of this growth was in trade among the Sino-Soviet countries themselves; only modest increases were recorded in trade with capitalist economies.

Primary Producing Countries. The trading position of primary producing countries improved in 1968 and 1969, with exports increasing by 8%. After relatively slow growth in 1967, exports to industrial countries rose 11% in 1968 as economic activity in the major industrial economies expanded. The fortunes of individual countries were varied; those regions most dependent on U.S. demand (Africa, South and Southeast Asia) and on West German demand (African countries sent 60% of their exports to the EEC) fared best.

In addition to the cyclical upswing in the demand from industrial countries, export earnings of primary producers were improved by abnormal growth in the demand for—and prices of—certain commodities. Political tension in the Middle East increased demand and prices of petroleum products, while the U.S. copper strike resulted in very high copper prices. In general, demand for industrial materials was strengthened by political uncertainties following the Czechoslovak crisis and in anticipation of the U.S. dock strike. The market for agricultural materials was more stable in 1968. Exports of most tropical products rose markedly, but exports of many temperate zone products fell slightly.

The average export price of primary products rose a little in 1968, reversing the downward trend of recent years. Price movements of individual products varied considerably, and all the increase in the average price was attributable to higher prices of metals and minerals, especially copper. The price index of agricultural products fell slightly. In 1969 there was a marked increase in primary product export prices, with the copper price continuing to rise steeply. Coffee prices rose following the poor Brazilian harvest, and the price of industrial materials rose in the first half of the year but leveled off in the second half. In the third quarter the average price of primary product exports was some 10% above the 1968 average.

The trading positions of the main groups of primary producers are shown in Table II. The surplus in Latin America was almost halved to $500 million. Exports of Brazil, Mexico, Peru, and Uruguay expanded rapidly in 1968 but in the first two countries the growth in imports was greater and their trading balances worsened by $180 million and $100 million, respectively. The growth in Peruvian exports was helped by improved mining supply conditions; with imports falling 24% in the face of devaluation, import surcharges, and prohibitions, the balance of trade moved from a deficit of $50 million to a surplus of $180 million. Argentina and Venezuela both recorded reduced trading surpluses.

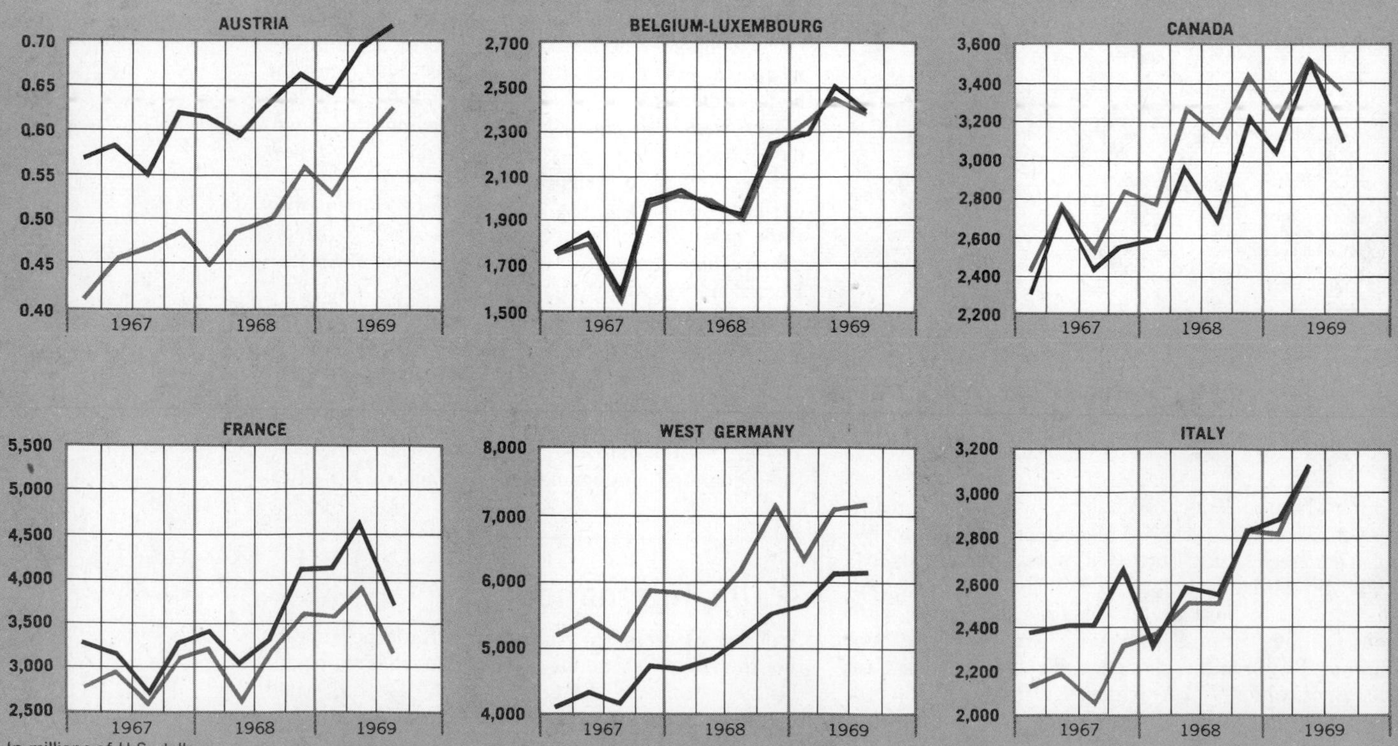

The overall trading deficit of Asian countries was reduced by $300 million in 1968, although demand in industrial countries was generally unfavourable, especially for jute and tea. There was a sharp increase in exports of oilseeds and vegetable oils, however, and exports of timber and fruit from the Far East continued to expand rapidly. Improved grain harvests in India and Pakistan enabled those countries to cut their grain imports, and Pakistan also enjoyed a growth in textile exports. The trading deficit of India was lowered by $500 million and that of Pakistan by $200 million. Although prices of the principal Malaysian exports fell, increased volume of trade brought higher earnings and a more favourable trading balance.

Middle Eastern oil production expanded sharply, and the trading balance of most oil producers improved considerably. The exception was Iran, where oil production had already risen sharply in 1967 and where imports rose 25%.

There was a large increase in the combined trading surplus of African countries. Export markets were very favourable for petroleum producers in North Africa and for African copper producers. The Libyan trading surplus rose from $600 million to $1.2 billion, and the Congo (Kinshasa) and Tunisia recorded improvements of $100 million and $50 million, respectively. Exports of tea, coffee, and cocoa were considerably higher than in 1967, but it was a poor year for West African exports of oilseeds and vegetable oils.

Industrial Countries. After slow growth in 1967, exports by industrial countries expanded rapidly in 1968 and this growth accelerated in 1969. The level of exports in 1968 was 13% above 1967 and a further increase of 16% was recorded in the first nine months of 1969. It is notable that the expansion in the value of industrial countries' exports in 1968 and 1969 was matched by increases in the volume of trade. The average price of their exports actually fell slightly in 1968 and rose by about 2% in 1969, while the growth in volume was much the same in both years—about 14%. As had been the case in previous years, the trade between industrial countries was the fastest

Table I. Growth in Value of World Trade

Percentage change from previous year

Exports from		Exports to: Industrial countries	Primary producing countries: More developed*	Primary producing countries: Less developed†	Sino-Soviet countries	World
Industrial countries‡	1965	11	15	7	22	10
	1966	11	4	9	22	11
	1967	7	5	2	7	6
	1968	15	3	12	8	13
Primary producing countries						
More developed*	1965	−1	8	10	23	4
	1966	12	10	19	−3	11
	1967	5	−3	10	15	6
	1968	8	1	1	−11	4
Less developed†	1965	6	9	−1	19	5
	1966	8	3	4	−1	6
	1967	3	4	1	−4	2
	1968	11	7	6	3	8
Sino-Soviet countries	1965	15	4	13	4	7
	1966	15	15	6	2	6
	1967	7	2	4	8	7
	1968	5	6	3	11	9
World	1965	9	13	6	9	9
	1966	11	5	8	4	9
	1967	6	5	3	7	5
	1968	13	4	10	8	11

*Australia, New Zealand, South Africa, and primary producing countries in Europe.
†All other primary producers.
‡Excludes U.S. military exports.
Source: International Monetary Fund, *Annual Report*.

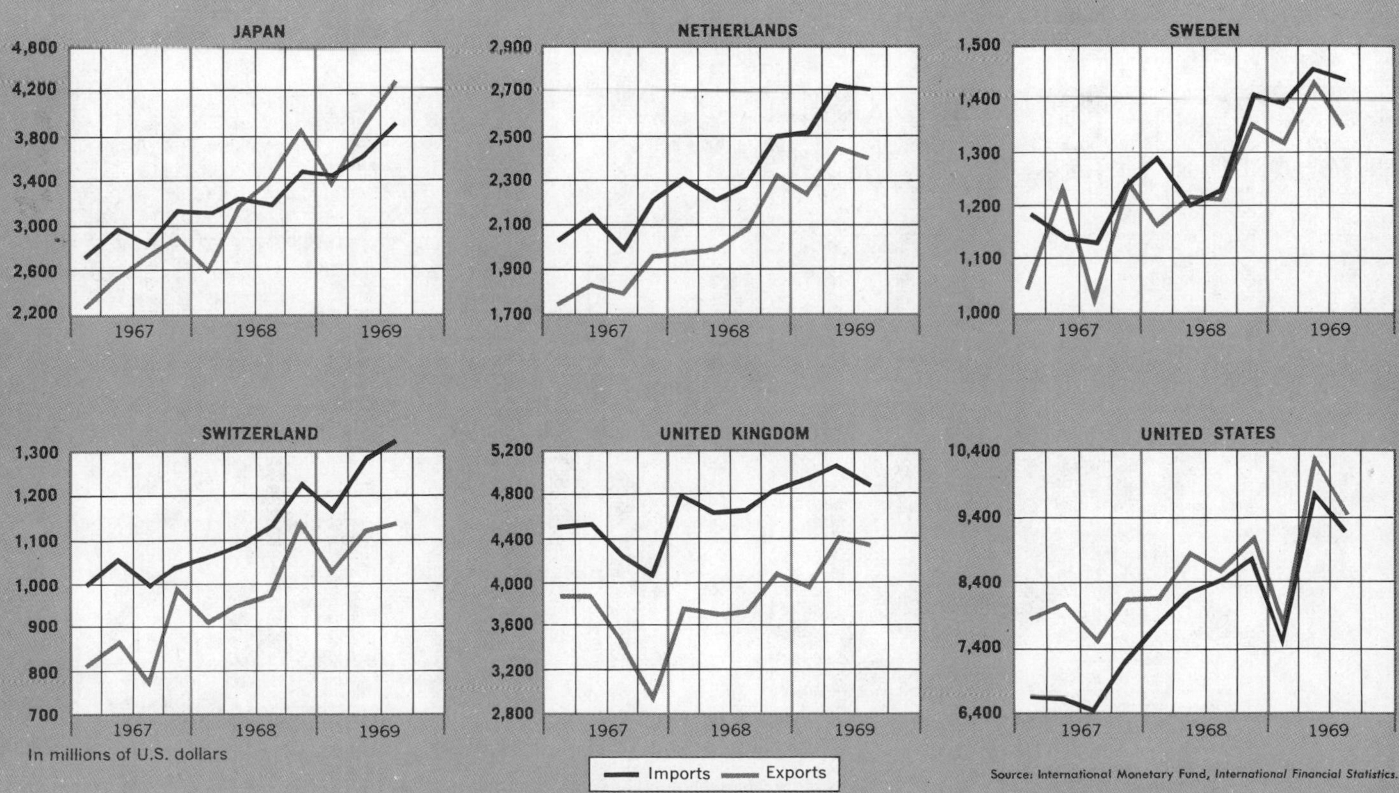

Table II. Primary Producing Countries' Foreign Trade

In $000,000

Area	1967 Exports	1967 Imports*	1967 Balance of trade	1968 Exports	1968 Imports*	1968 Balance of trade
More developed countries	14,107	17,756	−3,649	14,842	18,274	−3,432
Less developed countries						
Latin America	11,432	10,441	991	12,023	11,484	539
Asia	8,233	12,118	−3,885	9,113	12,685	−3,572
Middle East	5,244	4,104	1,140	6,055	4,835	1,220
Africa	4,743	4,097	646	5,705	4,313	1,392
	29,652	30,760	−1,108	32,896	33,317	−421
All primary producers	43,759	48,516	−4,757	47,738	51,591	−3,853

*Imports in most cases exclude freight and insurance charges.
Source: International Monetary Fund, *Annual Report.*

Table III. World Exports of Manufactured Goods

	Total value in $000,000,000*	Percent of total value: United States	United Kingdom	West Germany	France	Italy	Japan	Other†
1955	34.0	24.5	19.8	15.5	9.3	3.4	5.1	22.4
1960	52.4	21.6	16.3	19.3	9.7	5.1	6.9	21.0
1965	82.8	20.5	13.5	19.2	8.8	6.8	9.4	21.8
1966	92.4	20.2	12.9	19.5	8.6	6.9	9.8	22.1
1967	99.2	20.5	11.9	19.7	8.5	7.0	9.8	22.6
1968	114.0	20.2	11.1	19.5	8.3	7.3	10.7	22.9
1969‡	130.9	18.9	10.9	19.4	8.4	7.8	11.4	23.2

*Excluding arms.
†Belgium, Luxembourg, Canada, Netherlands, Sweden, and Switzerland.
‡First nine months (seasonally adjusted); value at annual rate.
Source: National Institute of Economic and Social Research, *Economic Review.*

growing element of world trade—the level in the first half of 1969 was 18% higher than in the same period of 1968 and about one-third higher than in 1967. Trade between the EEC countries grew 27% between the end of 1967 and the end of 1968, with the expansion of the West German economy being a major factor.

The relative performances of the main industrial countries in export markets for manufactured goods can be seen from Table III. After several years of stability, the U.S. share fell quite sharply in 1969. There were definite signs in 1969 that the long, steady decline in the U.K. share had been slowed down, if not halted. The provisional figure for the U.K. share in the third quarter of 1969 was 11.1%. Also worth noting was the continuation, and even the slight acceleration, in the increase of the Italian and Japanese shares. The fall in the price of Italian and Japanese exports over the preceding decade, associated with a rapid increase in the productivity of their industries, had enabled them steadily to increase their shares in the world market. Over this period world exports of manufactures rose 180%, while Italian exports increased fourfold and Japanese exports even faster. At the same time, the steadily rising prices of U.S. and U.K. exports reduced their competitive power and their market shares shrank accordingly. The sharp drop in U.K. export prices in 1968 reflects the devaluation of sterling at the end of 1967, the effects of which were beginning to be felt in the export share in 1969.

The combined trade balance of the industrial nations deteriorated in 1968 and 1969, but there were some more noteworthy changes in the balances of individual countries. There was a sharp reduction in the U.S. trade surplus in 1968 and a further deterioration in 1969. On the other hand, Canada, Italy, and Japan recorded marked improvements in 1968, and a further large improvement in the Japanese balance occurred in 1969. The large West German surplus rose a little in 1968 but was reduced somewhat in 1969. The U.K. trade balance deteriorated in 1968, as devaluation initially had more effect on the value of imports than on exports. A marked improvement occurred in 1969, and a surplus was recorded in the third quarter.

The expansion of domestic demand in the U.S. in 1968 brought with it a very sharp increase in imports, which reached a level 23% above 1967. The increase in exports was only 10%, and the trade balance was reduced by some $3.3 billion. Much of the increase in U.S. imports came from trade with other industrial nations, in particular West Germany, Japan, and Belgium. The favourable U.S. trading balance with Western Europe was reduced by $1.2 billion, and for the first time in 80 years the U.S.

Table IV. World Exports by Provenance and Destination, 1968

F.o.b. value in U.S. $000,000

Exports from ↓ / Exports to →	World*	Economic class I†	Economic class II‡	Economic class III§	United States	Canada	Latin America	Europe economic class I: Total‖¶	EEC¶	EFTA: Total	EFTA: United Kingdom	Northern Europe♀	Southern Europe♂
World*	238,150	165,290	45,890	25,380	32,010	10,850	12,010	104,820	59,280	35,250	16,790	2,680	7,600
Economic class I†	167,690	126,910	33,740	6,510	23,370	9,900	9,370	82,050	46,540	27,830	11,770	2,180	5,490
Economic class II‡	43,430	32,180	8,680	2,220	8,460	850	1,690	17,570	10,490	5,700	4,210	150	1,230
Economic class III§	27,030	6,200	3,470	16,650	180	90	950	5,200	2,260	1,710	820	345	880
United States	34,230	23,330	10,720	215		7,950	4,660	10,980	6,060	3,740	2,240	150	1,030
Canada**	12,560	11,480	800	280	8,530		370	2,120	710	1,330	1,130	18	67
Latin America	12,150	8,960	2,450	740	4,060	400	1,340	3,840	2,340	1,060	670	61	370
Europe economic class I‖¶	101,530	80,350	15,530	5,240	9,900	1,480	3,690	64,690	38,190	20,410	6,510	1,950	4,130
EEC¶	64,190	51,840	9,260	2,760	5,770	610	2,230	43,640	28,910	11,220	3,130	620	2,880
EFTA	31,030	23,960	5,540	1,470	3,450	830	1,150	17,340	7,600	7,350	2,220	1,300	1,080
United Kingdom	14,810	10,650	3,560	600	2,110	620	540	6,070	2,860	1,870		830	510
Northern Europe♀	2,490	2,020	125	330	195	14	58	1,770	485	1,220	890	20	44
Southern Europe♂	3,820	2,530	610	670	490	31	260	1,940	1,190	620	275	15	120
Eastern Europe and U.S.S.R.¶□	25,000	5,590	2,530	16,160	175	69	870	4,860	2,060	1,590	740	340	880
U.S.S.R.	10,630	2,420	1,490	6,620	43	20	650	1,960	760	580	365	255	365
South Africa**††	2,110	1,610	395	1	160	37	13	1,100	375	680	640	18	27
Africa economic class II	9,610	7,840	980	590	770	59	44	6,490	4,360	1,780	1,320	30	325
Northern Africa◊	3,850	3,190	240	435	150	2	20	3,000	2,220	570	440	11	195
Japan	12,970	6,800	5,580	580	4,130	345	600	1,670	690	760	365	35	190
Asia economic class II													
Asian Middle East▲	8,630	6,670	1,680	160	355	72	120	4,260	2,510	1,320	980	36	390
Other Asia	10,860	6,910	3,240	720	2,420	200	95	2,340	1,050	1,150	960	21	120
Asia economic class III+	2,030	620	930	...	2	21	85	335	200	125	76	8	2
Oceania economic class I‡‡	4,300	3,370	720	200	650	84	41	1,490	510	910	880	9	53
Rest of world⊕	2,170	1,790	330	2	860	125	90	640	225	395	285	4	25

Note: The data cover world trade with the exception of the trade with one another of: China, Mongolia, North Korea, and North Vietnam. For most countries they represent the official export figures, converted to U.S. dollars. Where official figures are not available, estimates, based on imports reported by partner countries and on other subsidiary data, are used. A dash (—) means magnitude nil or less than $500,000; (.) means not applicable.
*The figures for total exports include certain exports which, because their regions of destination could not be determined, are not included elsewhere in the table.
†United States, Canada, Europe economic class I, Australia, New Zealand, South Africa, Japan.
‡Sum of regions other than economic classes I and III.
§Eastern Europe and U.S.S.R., China, Mongolia, North Korea, and North Vietnam.
‖Includes Turkey and Yugoslavia.
¶The transactions between West Germany and East Germany have been omitted. Based on data reported by the sender, they were $359 million from West Germany to East Germany and $335 million from East Germany to West Germany.
♀Finland, Iceland, Ireland.

recorded a trading deficit with Canada. About one-eighth of the increase in imports could be attributed to higher imports of copper and steel resulting from actual or anticipated strikes. Of the remaining 20%, almost half was accounted for by higher imports of food, cars, and consumer goods. Imports of motor vehicles and components from countries other than Canada increased 65%, and imports of capital goods were 20% higher than in 1967, although domestic capital formation rose only 10%. Increases in exports were generally moderate, with aircraft exports accounting for one-fifth of the total rise.

During 1969 the growth in U.S. domestic demand slackened, and there was some improvement in the trading position. Between the first half of 1968 and the first half of 1969, imports rose by 8% and exports by 7%. Agricultural exports were $360 million lower, partly because of the U.S. dock strikes but also because of reduced demand for U.S. wheat as production increased in some importing countries. Exports of manufactured goods rose by only $150 million; machinery exports were up 10%, but this was less than the increase in 1968. Although still high, the growth in imports in 1969 was considerably below the growth rate in 1968; imports of food and industrial materials fell, as did steel imports after their strike-inflated level a year earlier. With the dampening of domestic activity, consumer goods imports fell in the third quarter.

The Canadian trading balance improved by $600 million in 1968 to a surplus of $1,130,000,000, the largest in many years. Exports rose by 18% and imports by 7%. Both flows were dominated by trade in motor vehicles, engines, and components. There were large increases in exports of timber and minerals, but wheat exports were lower despite increased shipments to China. The buoyancy of the West German and U.S. markets were important factors, and Canadian exports to these countries increased by 28 and 25%, respectively. In 1969 there was a sharp deterioration in the trading surplus. Imports in the first half of the year were 18% above the corresponding period in 1968, whereas exports were up only 10%. Reduced wheat exports and slackening demand in the U.S. were the main influences.

Table V. Trade of Industrial Countries

In U.S. $000,000,000

Country	1968 Exports	1968 Imports†	1968 Balance of trade	1969* Exports	1969* Imports†	1969* Balance of trade
United States	34.23	33.09	1.14	35.06	34.60	0.46
Canada	12.56	11.43	1.13	13.20	13.10	0.10
EEC	64.19	61.83	2.36	72.94	72.78	0.16
EFTA	31.05	37.52	−6.47	34.90	40.52	−5.62
Germany, West	24.82	20.15	4.67	27.16	23.84	3.32
France	12.68	13.94	−1.26	14.82	16.98	−2.16
Italy	10.18	10.25	−0.07	11.96	11.88	0.08
Netherlands	8.34	9.29	−0.95	9.42	10.52	−1.10
Belgium	8.15	8.20	−0.05	9.63	9.67	−0.04
United Kingdom	14.84	18.41	−3.57	16.32	18.69	−2.37
Japan	12.97	12.99	−0.02	15.40	13.78	1.62
Total	155.00	156.86	−1.86	171.50	174.78	−3.28

*First half of year (seasonally adjusted) at annual rate.
†Imports are valued c.i.f. except for U.S. and Canada; insurance and freight costs on U.S. and Canadian imports are approximately 7% of value of the goods.
Sources: National Institute of Economic and Social Research, *Economic Review*; United Nations, *Monthly Bulletin of Statistics*.

The combined trade surplus of the EEC countries rose from $1.2 billion to $2,360,000,000 between 1967 and 1968, but was sharply reduced in the first half of 1969. Much of the change was accounted for by changes in the West German trading balance and the large improvement in the Italian balance in 1968. All member countries shared in the 14% increase in exports, with Italian exports rising by 17%. The lowest export increase, that of France, was still as high as 12%. West Germany increased its already large trading surplus in 1968, but in 1969 the growth in West German imports exceeded the growth in exports, an important factor being the 4% export tax and the corresponding 4% rebate on imports. These border taxes were suspended in October 1969, after the fixed parity of the mark was abandoned. The subsequent revaluation was expected to reduce the large surplus that had been an embarrassment both to West Germany and to other industrial countries.

Eastern Europe and U.S.S.R.¶□			Africa economic class II			Asia economic class II		Asia economic class III+	Oceania economic class I		←Exports to / Exports from ↓
Total	U.S.S.R.	South Africa	Total	Northern Africa◊	Japan	Asian Middle East▲	Other Asia			Rest of world⊕	
22,980	9,070	2,550	8,930	3,080	10,770	6,050	15,540	2,400	4,290	3,350	World*
5,380	2,170	2,180	6,920	2,300	5,780	4,420	10,910	1,130	3,630	2,120	Economic class I†
1,900	1,020	365	1,250	260	4,310	1,100	3,420	320	610	1,230	Economic class II‡
15,700	5,880	—	770	520	680	540	1,200	950	51	3	Economic class III§
215	58	455	790	335	2,930	1,030	3,560	—	980	680	United States
125	83	65	44	16	560	34	240	150	205	110	Canada**
640	325	16	75	38	630	68	83	100	18	890	Latin America
4,710	1,800	1,450	4,940	1,900	1,110	2,850	3,060	530	1,700	990	Europe economic class I‖¶
2,380	800	670	3,340	1,530	640	1,550	1,630	385	520	510	EEC¶
1,340	460	760	1,440	245	425	1,170	1,330	130	1,150	465	EFTA
530	245	630	910	150	225	820	930	69	1,000	355	United Kingdom
320	260	13	20	11	10	24	14	12	21	7	Northern Europe♀
670	280	9	150	115	40	110	79	4	13	7	Southern Europeδ
15,220	5,650	—	650	480	455	480	540	950	20	1	Eastern Europe and U.S.S.R.¶□
5,640	.	—	330	260	390	225	295	580	2	—	U.S.S.R.
1	—	.	350	—	290	4	31	—	19	1	South Africa**††
520	260	135	560	68	365	135	200	72	30	38	Africa economic class II
400	200	1	95	37	37	40	66	38	3	19	Northern Africa◊
235	180	170	750	45		460	3,610	350	485	155	Japan
											Asia economic class II
145	72	150	280	78	1,640	600	610	15	195	71	Asian Middle East▲
590	365	62	300	68	1,590	290	2,500	135	315	59	Other Asia
...	...	—	125	45	225	55	670	.	31	2	Asia economic class III+
95	50	42	35	4	880	50	405	105	230	190	Oceania economic class I‡‡
2	1	4	27	7	93	4	37	—	58	170	Rest of world⊕

δGreece, Spain, Turkey, Yugoslavia.
□Albania, Bulgaria, Czechoslovakia, East Germany, Hungary, Poland, Romania, and U.S.S.R.
◊Algeria, Libya, Morocco, Tunisia, U.A.R.
▲Includes Cyprus and Iran.
+Estimates based on import data of trading partners. Exports of and to Mongolia, North Korea, and North Vietnam are included under this heading. The inter-trade of these countries and their trade with China are excluded.
⊕Consists mainly of islands in the Caribbean and the Pacific areas.
**General exports.
††1968 country distribution estimated from data for ten months.
‡‡Australia, general exports for 1966.
Source: United Nations, *Monthly Bulletin of Statistics*.

(B.N.D.)

There was a marked improvement in the Italian trading balance in 1968, with the $960 million deficit of 1967 being almost wiped out. This improvement continued into the first half of 1969 when a small surplus was recorded. Domestic demand in Italy in 1968 was relatively low, and this kept the rise in imports down to a mere 5% above 1967. Exports, on the other hand, rose 17%, with industrial exports expanding by one-fifth. While exports continued to grow rapidly in 1969, imports accelerated after the first quarter. A small surplus was recorded in the first half of the year, but the trading account moved sharply into deficit in the third quarter.

The large deficit of the EFTA countries was reduced slightly in 1968 and, with the improvement in the U.K. trading account, there was a sizable reduction in the deficit in 1969. Switzerland and Norway increased their exports in 1968 by 15 and 12%, and reduced their trading deficits by $120 million and $250 million, respectively.

The improvement expected in the U.K. trading balance following the devaluation of sterling in November 1967 did not appear for some time. The value of imports rose 21% in 1968; the price of imports rose by 11%, and the volume by 9%. Most of the volume increase was concentrated in the first quarter of the year, reflecting the rise in consumer demand and domestic activity before the announcement of the budget in March. Throughout the rest of 1968 the volume of imports remained fairly stable. Imports of food, beverages, and tobacco were 8% higher than in 1967, and imports of fuels were up 25%, largely because of higher prices resulting from devaluation. Imports of industrial materials rose by 28%, about half of this increase being accounted for by higher prices and half by a volume increase resulting from the expansion in industrial production and a high rate of inventory building.

U.K. exports in 1968 increased by 23%. The sterling price of exports rose 8% as a result of devaluation, and by the second half of the year devaluation was having a favourable effect on export volume, the foreign price of U.K. exports having fallen by some 6%. Exports to all major areas showed a substantial improvement. The largest increases were in exports to the U.S. (43%), Latin America (35%), and Eastern Europe and the U.S.S.R. (36%). Exports to Western Europe rose by 19%, with a 24% increase in sales to the EEC being offset by a modest increase in exports to fellow EFTA countries. In 1969 the favourable effect of devaluation on the U.K. competitive position and the continued restrictions on home demand resulted in marked improvement in the U.K. balance. Exports rose 16% and imports only 5%, and the deficit in the first half of 1969 was at an annual rate of $2,370,000,000, compared with $3,570,000,000 in 1968. (A. G. A.)

See also Commercial Policies; Commodities, Primary; Payments and Reserves, International.

ENCYCLOPÆDIA BRITANNICA FILMS. *World Trade for Better Living* (1951); *Round Trip: The U.S.A. in World Trade* (1952); *Food and People* (1956); *Britain: World Trader* (1964).

Trade Fairs: *see* Fairs and Shows
Trade Unions: *see* Labour Unions
Traffic Accidents: *see* Disasters

Transportation

An ever increasing desire throughout the world for greater mobility and speedier movement by all modes of transportation resulted in much technological experimentation and development during 1969. In the air, the Anglo-French Concorde supersonic airliner (SST) successfully cut through the sound barrier in October, as had the Soviet Tupolev Tu-144 approximately four months earlier. The U.S. government finally authorized construction of two even larger and faster SST prototypes. The jumbo jets, though further delayed, were preparing to carry their 362 to 490 passengers across the Atlantic early in 1970.

On the seas the size of ships continued to grow, with tankers of 350,000 tons deadweight and new types of specially constructed cargo ships carrying bulk and unit loads and containers to the world's ports. The ports, in turn, continued to expand and adapt their facilities to receive the new ships, thereby cutting down greatly on the amount of time a ship needed to be docked while unloading. Liverpool was already studying the requirements for handling ships of up to one million tons.

On land the railways, fighting a losing battle with the motor vehicle and airplane for passengers but making tactical gains with freight, sought to regain business by developing new forms of tractive power that would reach speeds of 250 to 500 mph. The railways turned to the dynamics of aeronautics, the computer, and automation to ensure the safe running of high-speed trains on existing tracks. Paradoxically, to defeat the air pollution created by its gasoline engine, the motor vehicle was looking backward to the steam engine as well as forward to the gas turbine and electric propulsion. Meanwhile, with traffic mounting, escape from congestion in urban areas was sought in completely new forms of transport, both above and below ground and on the surface. The most revolutionary was a U.S. design for a gravity rail system in which a train would operate in an evacuated underground tube, sloping downward for the first half and upward for the second half of the journey. As a train approached a station, slowed by the pull of gravity, it would trigger a valve that would close off the tube behind it and the station would be filled with air. The potential was considered by the U.S. government to justify a full-scale examination. Much experimentation was also under way on applying the air cushion principle, employed by ground-effect machines, to fast transport, and in the United Kingdom, France, and the United States experiments were under way for tracked air-cushion vehicles. While there may not have been any revolutionary advance in such new modes during 1969, sufficient progress was made to hold out the prospect of achievement in the early 1970s.

The year was also marked by governmental action on both the national and international levels to ensure the maintenance of essential transport services, particularly rail and mass transportation, where they were considered essential in the national interest for economic or social reasons. Railway systems were being subsidized on an increasing scale, and many urban transportation schemes were instituted, particularly in the U.S., to provide satisfactory public services as an alternative to using automobiles for the journey to work. Acceptance by governments of responsibility for transportation planning in relation to the urban environment was also increasingly noticeable. (E. A. J. D.)

AVIATION

The year was a worrisome one for the airlines, particularly those in the U.S. With little time left before the introduction of the really large-capacity jets, traffic growth was faltering and load factors (the ratio of available seats to passengers carried) were low on many trunk routes. The industry was afraid that the introduction of the 362–490-seat Boeing 747 into service in increasing numbers during 1970 and 1971 would produce a situation similar to, and much more serious than, the profit recession in the early 1960s when the first-generation jets entered service in large numbers and increased the available seat-mile capacity beyond any possible traffic growth.

For the U.S. carriers the profit margins were decreasing. The relatively small domestic fare increases approved early in the year by the U.S. Civil Aeronautics Board (CAB) were not enough to save the situation, yet the bigger increases being asked for by the airlines could be expected to slow the normal traffic growth. Further increases, based on airline costs and designed to improve revenues, were agreed to by the CAB early in September. The approval was, however, hedged about with special requirements and subject to reconsideration before the end of January 1970.

Heavy losses were reported by U.S. domestic trunk, regional, and international airlines during the first half of the year, and at least one major domestic carrier found it necessary at midyear to cancel important reequipment orders because suitable financing could not be arranged. The red light for the U.S. domestic airlines was already shining by the end of 1968, during which load factors fell dramatically because of a large increase in offered capacity—an increase equivalent to more than the total capacity that had been offered on such services as recently as ten years earlier. According to the International Civil Aviation Organization (ICAO) the average load factor of all the world's airlines (excluding those of the U.S.S.R. and China) had, in 1968, fallen below 50% for the first time since the jets were introduced in 1958 and to the lowest figure since 1946.

On the North Atlantic routes—generally considered to be the "thermometer" of airline traffic health, although not, as often assumed, the most remunerative of services—there was, however, a reasonably big growth in passengers during the first half of 1969. The airlines of the International Air Transport Association (IATA), which celebrated its 50th anniversary in August, showed an average growth of 13% over the same period of 1968. However, seat capacity was increased by an even greater amount, so that the passenger load factor fell below 50%, a fact that did not augur well for the era of the jumbo jets. By contrast, cargo tonnage increased by a phenomenal 61%, including a 71% increase on scheduled all-cargo services. It seemed that the long-prophesied freight breakthrough might be on the way at last—although it remained to be seen whether such a surge would be a profitable one for the airlines concerned.

The year was a relatively good one for safety. In the first eight months 450 passengers were killed in 14 accidents on scheduled services operated by airlines other than those of the U.S.S.R. and China. These were low numbers by previous standards, but there were, later in the year, several accidents involving heavy loss of life and these spoiled what might otherwise have been an exceptionally good year for safety. Stated baldly, the eight-month record looked poor, but the figures compared well with those for any previous year when related to the total number of passengers carried and passenger-miles flown. In the 12 months of 1968 there were 34 fatal accidents involving 976 passenger fatalities on scheduled services. In that year—the best so far in terms of relative passenger safety apart from 1967—approximately 192,000,000,000 passenger-miles were recorded by the ICAO and 3,750,000,000 mi. were flown. The fatality rate, thus, was 0.51 per 100 million passenger-miles (0.40 in 1967), and the number of fatal accidents per 100 million miles flown was 0.91 (the same as in 1967).

KEYSTONE

The Anglo-French "Concorde" supersonic airliner during its successful first test flight near Toulouse, France, March 2, 1969.

In matters of technical progress and civil aircraft development, one of the most significant events of the year was the first flight of the British Aircraft Corp./Sud-Aviation (BAC/Sud) Concorde SST prototype 001 at Toulouse, France, on March 2. This flight took place a little more than two months after that of the less sophisticated Soviet Tupolev Tu-144 SST, which had flown on the last day of 1968. The British-built Concorde 002 prototype flew from Filton, Bristol, on April 9, and landed at the Royal Air Force airfield at Fairford, where the flight-test program was to continue. The Tu-144 flew supersonically for the first time on June 5, and the Concorde 001, on October 1. The Concorde test program had, by all accounts, gone well during the previous six months, but the overall Concorde program was by then under criticism in Britain because of its substantial increase in cost, which had not been adequately reported to Parliament. These costs had risen from the original 1962 estimate of £150 million–170 million to £500 million in 1966 and £730 million in May 1969. The actual expenditure on the project up to March 31, 1969, had been about £330 million, divided between the British and French governments. In November pilots from Air France, BOAC, Pan American, and TWA flew in the Concorde 001 at Toulouse and expressed satisfaction with its handling qualities.

The situation over the proposed United States SST

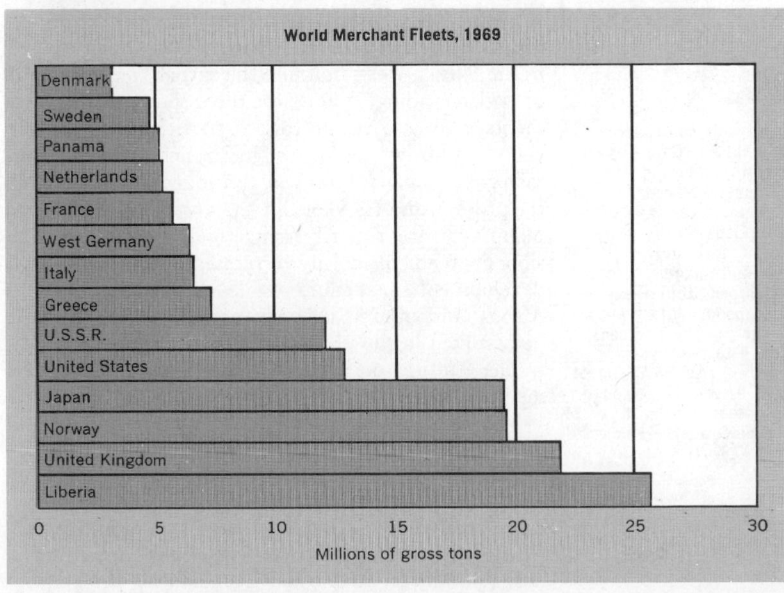

had remained static until September, though design and development work by Boeing and the aviation authorities continued. Late in 1968 the original variable-geometry (swing-wing) proposal had been dropped by Boeing and the U.S. Federal Aviation Administration (FAA), and had been replaced by a more conventional design with a fixed delta-shaped wing and tail plane. A decision to proceed with this revised design, and to start the building of two prototypes, was made by U.S. Pres. Richard Nixon on September 23, and he asked Congress to approve the annual appropriations necessary to keep the program on schedule. Although the initial sums were smaller than had been expected, Boeing considered that they were adequate, along with its own contributions, to enable the company to build two prototypes for flight tests beginning at the end of 1972, with entry into passenger service scheduled for 1978.

WIDE WORLD

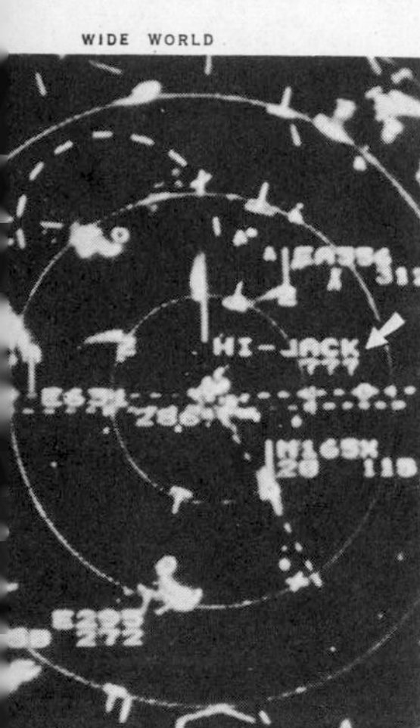

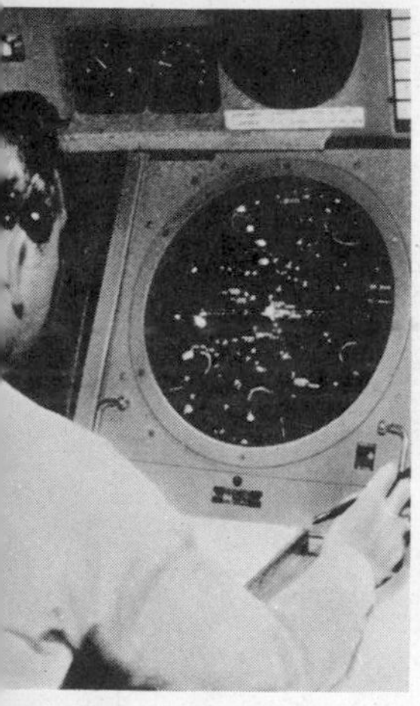

Air traffic controller at Atlanta (Ga.) Airport monitors a new computerized radar system that indicates each plane's directional path, speed, altitude, and flight number. Close-up of screen (top) shows transponder hijack alarm (near centre of screen) added to the system in 1969. All FAA control centres were expected to be equipped with the new radar equipment by 1973.

Meanwhile, the construction of the prototypes of the two U.S. medium-haul, large-capacity, wide-bodied trijets, the Lockheed 1011 and the McDonnell Douglas DC-10, had started. The first Boeing 747 long-haul jumbo jet made its initial flight on February 9 after delays caused by weather and technical problems. By the end of July all five 747s allocated to the test program were flying and, notwithstanding development problems and delays in the delivery of the fully developed power plants, the planned entry into North Atlantic service by mid-December was still hoped for at mid-August. Early in September, however, Boeing announced that, because of various delays, the first 747s would be up to eight weeks late in delivery to the airlines; Pan American Airways, the first customer, canceled its plans for North Atlantic services in December.

At the Paris Air Show in May and June orders for the DC-10 by a consortium of European airlines were announced. All four airlines in this consortium—the Netherlands' KLM; Swissair; the Scandinavian Airlines System (SAS); and the French independent airline, Union de Transports Aériens (UTA)—were operators of DC-8s and the choice, therefore, was not unnatural. Nevertheless, the order was a setback for Lockheed and for Rolls-Royce, whose RB.211 engines would power the Lockheed 1011; the decision might be expected also to have an effect on the sales prospects of the proposed European airbus.

Late in 1968 a revised, slightly smaller, version of the big-capacity, short-haul European airbus project, the A-300B, had been announced. This design change, in the British view, nullified the earlier "memorandum of understanding" among the three sponsoring governments, and as a result British participation was officially withdrawn in April. The French and West German governments, however, continued to cooperate on the project, and Hawker Siddeley, the British airframe manufacturer primarily concerned, reached a provisional agreement in July to remain within the A-300B development consortium with Sud-Aviation, Deutsche Airbus, and other European manufacturers likely to be involved in the project.

The future of Britain's "go-it-alone" short-to-medium haul, large-capacity project for the mid-1970s, the BAC's (British Aircraft Corporation's) Three-Eleven twin-jet, remained uncertain, with government backing and BAC go-ahead dependent on firm orders for a minimum of approximately 50 aircraft, preferably with at least one buyer from the U.S. A revised and improved version of the Three-Eleven based on known airline requirements following a vigorous sales campaign was being offered by midyear, and British European Airways had indicated that it was a prospective customer.

Among the major route-licensing questions during the year were those concerned with the South Pacific, on which a second U.S. carrier, in addition to Pan American, was to be nominated. A decision was made by the CAB that the route to Australia and New Zealand should go to Continental Airlines, a U.S. domestic trunk carrier with other Pacific interests. This was ratified by U.S. Pres. Lyndon Johnson late in 1968, but was rejected later by President Nixon. The case was therefore returned to the CAB, whose eventual nomination of American Airlines was approved in July. There were considerable misgivings in Australia about the effects of this increase in capacity over the South Pacific.

Trans-Siberia rights for Western Hemisphere airlines continued to be the subject of discussions. Japan Air Lines (JAL) was the only carrier then operating on the route, though with Soviet Aeroflot aircraft and flight crews. JAL expected to be using its own aircraft and crews in 1970, and KLM obtained provisional rights for the future.

The problems of congestion, in the air and on the ground, had, since the heavy delays of July 1968 in the U.S., been seen to be the result of a lack of forward thinking and coordination in aircraft and air traffic control planning and a lack of adequate resources. The measures taken by the FAA to restrict aircraft movements by category at the airports of New York City, Washington, D.C., and Chicago were reasonably successful during the peak months of 1969 and were to be extended elsewhere in the U.S.; however, the need for longer-term decisions was now accepted. Various temporary solutions, such as the development of short takeoff and landing (STOL) operations, were put forward during the year. The problem of gaining public acceptance for the locations of additional airports for major metropolitan areas such as those of New York and London was still unsolved.

Meanwhile, the Edwards Committee, set up in 1967 to recommend, in effect, the best form of British air transport organization, reported in great detail in May 1969. The committee recommended, among other things, the setting up of a Civil Aviation Authority, to be responsible for the economic and safety regulatory functions and the negotiation of traffic rights under a clearly stated government policy, and also a National Air Holdings Board that would have control over the two state airlines, the British Overseas Airways Corporation (BOAC) and British European Airways (BEA).

The report also recommended the merging of two or more major private carriers to form a "second-force" airline with a viable network of routes and with the government having a financial and management interest. In preparation for this, British United Airways (BUA)—recommended in the committee's report as a suitable major independent airline—applied in September to the British Air Transport Licensing Board for an extended route network.

As expected, there was strong resistance in some quarters to many of the proposals and recommendations of the Edwards Committee. By and large, however, they were accepted by the government in its White Paper published on November 12, although no positive legislative action was seriously expected before the general election in 1970.

World Transportation

Country	Railways: Route length in 000 km.	Railways Traffic: Passenger in 000,000 pass.-km.	Railways Traffic: Freight in 000,000 net ton-km.	Motor transport: Road length in 000 km.	Motor transport: Vehicles in use: Passenger in 000	Motor transport: Vehicles in use: Commercial in 000	Merchant shipping, Ships of 100 tons and over: Number of vessels	Merchant shipping: Gross reg. tons in 000	Air traffic: Total km. flown in 000	Air traffic: Passenger in 000 pass.-km.	Air traffic: Freight in 000 net ton-km.
EUROPE											
Austria	5.9*	5,934*	8,247*	93.3	1,053.3	107.4	3	1	9,005	312,000	4,309
Belgium	4.3*	7,908*	6,634*	91.8	1,806.5	270.0	218	933	36,132	1,977,000	125,000
Bulgaria	4.2	5,708	12,200	29.2†	9.3†	20.4†	112	548	...	506,677†	8,678†
Czechoslovakia	13.3	18,960	56,710	133.0†	521.2	165.2	8	74	18,674	776,000	13,600
Denmark	2.4*	3,224*	1,380*	61.6†	955.3	254.2	1,140	3,204	21,236‡	1,202,400‡	55,400‡
Finland	5.6*	2,153*	5,627*	71.0	581.0	97.1	399	1,128	15,662	439,200	7,588
France	37.3	35,730*	63,036*	784.5	11,210.0	1,748.0	1,495	5,796	165,715	10,151,980	321,406
Germany, East (excluding Berlin)	15.5	16,800	38,581	160.0	827.0	330.8	361	806	...	...	...
Germany, West (excluding Berlin)	34.7†	34,301	60,159	405.0	12,045.7§	1,025.4§	2,732	6,528	99,914	6,007,000	348,548
Greece	2.6	1,150	536	34.4	169.1	87.1	1,634	7,416	20,135	1,250,800	28,065
Hungary	8.8	13,949	17,558	103.7	163.6	42.0†	20	28	...	2,355†	1,311†
Ireland	2.1	524	470	53.0†	314.4	45.6	89	173	19,922	1,293,100	38,845
Italy	20.9†	28,880	17,129	284.0	8,178.5	750.8	1,490	6,624	99,108	5,798,000	227,900
Netherlands	3.2	7,337	3,273	75.2	2,073.4	311.5	1,721	5,268	74,579	4,310,616	260,556
Norway	4.2*	1,640*	2,590*	69.6	619.0	135.5	2,881	19,667	38,989‡	1,608,300‡	58,528‡
Poland	26.6	35,870	92,636	307.3	374.6	229.5	446	1,342	12,680	450,600	6,176
Portugal	3.6	3,309	976	31.5	316.0	92.5	348	772	24,342	1,160,207	18,827
Romania	11.0	16,142	40,706	77.0	250.0†	36.8	56	325	7,013	281,500	7,614
Spain	17.4	11,836*	8,230*	140.2	1,301.9	561.9	2,046	2,821	61,182	3,880,000	77,260
Sweden	12.9	4,698*	13,691*	172.5	2,071.3	138.8	1,074	4,865	38,992‡	2,026,000‡	90,340‡
Switzerland	2.9*	7,701*	5,706*	58.4	1,180.5	115.7	33	202	54,045	3,334,000	117,600
U.S.S.R.	133.3	234,429	2,160,528	1,363.5†	1,100.0†	4,500.0†	4,206	12,062	...	53,500,000	1,662,000
United Kingdom	21.2‖	29,111‖	23,720‖	350.7	11,078.0	1,606.6	4,020	21,921	265,597	14,095,000	491,417
Yugoslavia	11.4	10,285	16,371	79.9	439.9	99.1	337	1,267	10,890	459,800	4,608
ASIA											
Burma	4.3†	2,133	813	25.0†	27.9	27.3	31	42	3,682	98,560	1,720
Cambodia	0.6	142	66	10.8	21.7	10.6	3	4	1,645	50,880	1,152
Ceylon	1.5	2,560†	322†	21.0	84.7	28.2	26	9	2,613	97,100	2,900
China	36.0†	45,670†	265,260†	550.0†	50.0	300.0	239	766	...	63,882†	1,967†
India	59.1	102,564	100,230	928.2	550.3	290.8	383	1,945	56,087	2,514,648	89,855
Indonesia	6.8	4,947	659	84.3	185.0	94.9	479	711	13,874	526,326	13,239
Iran	3.6†	1,154	1,884	34.0	164.2	59.7	37	74	8,588	387,779	3,774
Iraq	1.6†	444†	1,009†	17.9	75.8	46.5	35	37	2,591	124,080	1,464
Israel	0.7	349	383	9.1	114.5	50.9	111	723	17,997	1,531,656	48,113
Japan	27.9†	275,738	60,155	995.3	5,209.3	7,508.3	6,877	19,587	118,704	6,010,000	234,400
Korea, South	5.1	9,577	6,592	34.5	23.2	37.5	232	474	2,835	63,755	305
Malaysia	1.8	580¶	1,080¶	21.4	212.8	57.1	85	40	7,109♀	337,300♀	5,052♀
Pakistan	11.3	13,216	9,574	c.200.0	80.8	26.8	170	541	24,348	1,459,500	63,595
Philippines	1.0*†	1,015	146	56.2	182.9	149.7	278	854	26,332	1,121,000	27,060
Syria	0.8	85	122	13.9	29.5	14.1	3	1	2,340	93,341	1,110
Taiwan	3.8	5,543	2,709	18.5	25.1	24.5	187	763	7,672	348,000	4,227
Thailand	3.8	3,666	2,001	12.3†	110.0	132.5	49	64	10,451	462,100	5,930
Turkey	8.1	4,301	5,062	c.70.0	128.9	105.9	298	648	10,147	310,479	3,165
Vietnam, South	1.3†	13	18	20.3†	42.3	44.9	23	16	9,307	474,800	4,040
AFRICA											
Algeria	3.9†	857	1,232	35.5†	98.0	80.2	6	16	7,610	293,364	3,570
Central African Republic	—	—	—	19.0	4.9	7.3	...	...	1,332δ	57,454δ	3,906δ
Chad	...	...	...	11.8†	3.7†	4.8†	...	...	1,612δ	61,074δ	4,041δ
Congo (Kinshasa)	5.2†	457	1,848	141.3	43.5	32.9†	5	12	10,342	358,700	12,260
Dahomey	0.6	67	73	6.9	9.9	6.0	...	...	1,202δ	56,154δ	3,896δ
Gabon	0.6	...	...	5.6	5.2	4.5	2	1	2,662δ	74,754δ	4,061δ
Ghana	1.3	425	276	31.0	29.2	18.8	57	120	4,062	122,704	5,060
Ivory Coast	0.7	479	325	34.6	38.6†	24.4†	20	18	1,567δ	59,787δ	3,980δ
Kenya	2.1	4,529†□	3,844□	41.7	48.0	49.6	16	13	4,656◊	184,386◊	6,818◊
Malawi	0.8	49†	206	10.5	8.9	6.2	...	...	660▲	12,850	407
Mali	0.6‖	66	116	12.1	4.5	4.9	...	...	2,272	47,981	2,944
Morocco	1.8†	408	2,334	24.3	178.4	63.8	38	70	5,705	313,500	3,525
Nigeria	3.5†	521	1,745	80.0	73.0	31.0	36	71	4,584	148,800	5,538
Rhodesia	3.3	...	8,671†+	78.5	111.0	42.2	...	...	2,834†▲	72,112†▲	891†▲
Senegal	1.2	249	188	10.6	32.6	16.8	13	9	1,402δ	61,939δ	3,906δ
South Africa	22.1⊕	...	49,410⊕	c.350.0	1,405.0	343.0	244	470	27,815	1,837,000	47,376
Tanzania	3.0	4,529†□	3,844□	35.0	38.0†	12.5†	7	18	4,656◊	184,386◊	6,818◊
Uganda	0.9	4,529†□	3,844□	24.2	29.2	8.8	...	...	4,656◊	184,386◊	6,818◊
United Arab Republic	4.5†	6,268	3,068	47.7‡	108.0	27.1	122	250	14,378	620,500	8,138
Zambia	1.0	...	8,671†+	34.1	49.7	20.0	...	...	2,602▲	66,239▲	825▲
NORTH AND CENTRAL AMERICA											
Canada	69.5	4,400	139,500	806.3	5,771.9	1,505.0	1,296	2,403	186,960	11,690,000	286,300
Costa Rica	0.7	26	28†	10.0†	29.8	15.9	7	8	3,538	110,600	8,570
El Salvador	0.7	...	...	8.4†	30.1	13.7	...	...	...	...	...
Guatemala	1.2	...	120	11.2†	33.4	19.4	2	4	3,541	77,400	3,650
Honduras	1.2†	...	...	3.3†	11.2	11.5	45	69	6,033	95,841	8,269
Mexico	23.8†	4,252	19,732	c.180.0†	c.850.0†	c.460.0†	114	404	46,705	2,012,513	37,268
Nicaragua	0.3	41	14	7.0	12.8†	5.0†	8	15	1,195	46,160	905
Panama	0.7†	...	...	6.7	35.0	11.6	798	5,097	...	...	...
United States	338.8	21,100	1,087,500	5,962.6	80,414.2	16,192.8	3,232	19,668	2,950,753	183,242,000	6,168,114
SOUTH AMERICA											
Argentina	41.2†	13,779	13,226	215.3	1,110.7	629.2	315	1,197	40,224	1,555,610	25,853
Bolivia	3.6	236†	300†	28.0†	21.7	6.3	...	...	3,690	61,880	1,400
Brazil	32.0†	13,517	19,893	803.1†	1,533.4	953.7	398	1,294	81,667	3,210,027	94,217
Chile	9.0	2,085	2,637	54.5	195.3	58.9	130	269	17,414	601,400	49,847
Colombia	3.5†	351	1,125	45.0	140.2	116.5	47	209	44,457	1,560,000	60,474
Ecuador	1.3†	53	66	18.3†	19.8	28.1	14	43	8,184	216,744	2,966
Paraguay	1.1†	14	17	12.5†	6.4	6.5	26	22	...	...	...
Peru	3.3†	236	646	42.8†	195.1	111.8	275	288	16,585	622,322	12,790
Uruguay	3.1	...	...	41.6	144.0	92.0	42	131	3,290	72,895	319
Venezuela	0.8	39	17	31.0	450.0	191.4	89	351	26,945	871,940	41,780
OCEANIA											
Australia	40.5*	3,504*†**	20,490*	911.0	3,383.5	908.9	314	818	149,637	6,412,970	193,124
New Zealand	5.0*	564*	2,497*	93.8	826.2	163.2	127	192	31,010	1,266,300	33,590

Note: Data are for 1967 or 1968 unless otherwise indicated.
. . . Indicates not known.
*State system only.
†Data given are the most recent available.
‡Including apportionment of traffic of Scandinavian Airlines System.
§Including West Berlin.
‖Excluding Northern Ireland.
¶Including Singapore.
♀Apportionment of traffic of Malaysia-Singapore Airlines.
δIncluding apportionment of traffic of Air Afrique.
□Total for Kenya, Tanzania, and Uganda (East African Railways Corporation).
◊Including apportionment of traffic of East African Airways Corp. and Caspair Ltd.
▲Including apportionment of traffic of Central African Airways Corp.
+Total for Rhodesia and Zambia.
⊕Including South West Africa (Namibia).
**Excluding New South Wales and Queensland.

Sources: UN, *Statistical Yearbook 1968; Monthly Bulletin of Statistics; Annual Bulletin of Transport Statistics for Europe* (1967); Lloyd's Register, *Statistical Tables* (1968); International Road Federation, *World Road Statistics 1969; Jahrbuch des Eisenbahnwesens 1968.*

(M. C. MacD.)

A cause of grave concern throughout the year was the growing frequency of airplane hijacking, emphasized by a number of spectacular incidents. Means of combating it were considered by the Interpol General Assembly in Mexico City in October, and the ICAO, IATA, and IFALPA (International Federation of Air Line Pilots' Associations) pressed for discussion of the matter in the UN Security Council. (H. A. TA.)

COMMERCIAL MOTOR TRANSPORTATION

For commercial motor transportation the year was marked by an increase in the proportion of total freight traffic carried by motor vehicles, technological advances in the development of the larger and heavier vehicles, experimentation with turbine power units, and increased state regulation of the construction and use of vehicles. Two major steps toward the internationalization and standardization of road traffic taken in 1968–69 were the final approval at the Vienna world conference in October 1968 of two UN conventions on road traffic and road signs and signals, and the coming into force on Jan. 1, 1969, of the common transport policy for road haulage of the six members of the European Economic Community (EEC). In addition to covering the road traffic rules, the first Vienna convention included conditions for the admission of motor vehicles and trailers to international traffic and the regulation and conditions of operation of international road traffic. The second convention established standard systems of traffic signs, but permitted use of both the U.S. and European systems.

The common transport policy of the EEC as provided for in the Treaty of Rome established a quota system which enabled truck operators in possession of an EEC license to transport goods between member countries entirely without restriction. This was unique in the liberalization of international road transport, because, in effect, the new license issued by the EEC Commission amounted to a Community passport for international road haulage purposes. The Commission placed EEC licenses at the disposal of the authorities concerned in the member states, who issued them to haulers established on their territory in accordance with the procedure of the country. An EEC license holder might transport goods for hire with the vehicle of his own choosing between any points in the member states. For all these operations, embracing several EEC countries and involving loads carried from one country to another, the road hauler in question needed one document only: an EEC license. Under a bilateral system of licenses a succession of operations such as this would not be possible. But this quota system was in addition to the existing procedure of bilateral licenses for which national governments were responsible and which allowed a varying degree of freedom of operation between the respective countries. During the year a number of such bilateral agreements were entered into between states outside the EEC and EEC states as well as between nonmembers of the EEC. The U.K., for instance, concluded road haulage agreements with France, Italy, West Germany, the Netherlands, and several non-EEC states.

To bring their national transport policies in line with the common transport policy of the EEC, several countries made changes in their previous procedures. In West Germany, following the abandonment of its declared policy of diverting long-distance road traffic to the railways, which was considered incompatible with the transport policies of other EEC members, a tax on road-freight traffic was introduced. This was to be an interim measure only and would be replaced in 1971 by a pricing system based on the regulations planned within the EEC framework. In France a special tax on certain types of road vehicles was introduced, the basis of the tax being total authorized laden weight and the amount varying according to the categories of vehicles as defined by their contribution to the wear and tear on road surfaces.

In the U.K., with the passing of the Transport Act, 1968, which was designed to achieve a more rational allocation of traffic between road and rail services, the road haulage industry faced considerable changes during 1969. Road transport services of the nationalized British Railways Board and the nationalized sector of road transport, the Transport Holding Corp., were merged into the National Freight Corp. (NFC), which then had 10% of the road haulage capacity in the U.K. The NFC jointly with British Railways would control and manage the freight services of container trains operating from special terminals between major cities and would provide a door-to-door service by the most suitable transport for parcels and merchandise, consignments by full trainload exempted.

The private sector of the commercial road transport industry was to be subject to a quantitative licensing system for long-distance haulage, the purpose of which was to maximize the economic use of rail transport by ensuring that the railways obtained all the traffic they could carry as efficiently as could road transport. A special license would be required for any freight-carrying vehicle with a gross weight of more than 16 tons engaged on hauls of more than 160 km. or in carrying special goods, such as coal and certain mineral ores, over shorter distances. There was to be no distinction between a commercial hauler and one carrying on own account. Introduction of this licensing system was postponed until the freightliner services were sufficiently developed to take the long-distance traffic so diverted.

Despite such measures taken by several countries to protect the railways against uncontrolled encroachment on their freight business by trucks, both the total amount of freight and the proportion of freight car-

"The sky above, the earth below."—Liederman, "Long Island Press," N.Y.

BEN ROTH AGENCY

ried by road continued to increase as compared with other transport modes, although in some countries, such as West Germany, at a somewhat slower pace. International traffic in particular rose substantially in Europe. Few statistics for total road movements were available and fewer still on a basis permitting comparison between countries. In the U.K. 1,550,000,000 tons of freight were carried by road in 1968, compared with 1,500,000,000 in 1967, the ton-mileage being 44 million against 40 million. In the U.S. the total motor vehicle mileage traveled was estimated to exceed 1,000,000,000 mi. in 1968, of which commercial road haulage (trucks and truck combinations) was responsible for 19%. The total of intercity ton-miles attributed to trucks in the U.S. represented only about 22% of the total for all modes—motor, rail, waterways, pipelines, and air. But if petroleum and coal products were excluded, the proportion of all intercity tonnage of manufactured products carried by road exceeded 50%. In the U.S.S.R. the tonnage of freight carried rose in 1969 by 1% to 1,693,000,000 tons as compared with the first six months of 1968.

Whereas during the year there was no reversal of the trend for travel by bus to decline, certain factors tended to reduce the rate at which this occurred. Closings of railway lines in a number of countries were accompanied by the substitution for them of bus services, frequently subsidized. Also, an increasing number of cities introduced traffic management measures to facilitate public transport movement, including reserved lanes for buses and exemptions from directional traffic controls and turning bans. Parking restrictions and traffic congestion itself also caused commuters to leave the private car at home, to the benefit of public transport. However, with few exceptions the numbers traveling by public road transportation continued to decline. Contrary to this general trend was the increase in international long-distance travel by bus.

The U.K. witnessed a major change in the organization of its road passenger system with the implementation of the Transport Act, 1968. The Passenger Transport Authorities for the four urban clusters outside London (Greater Manchester, Merseyside, West Midlands, and Tyneside) were set up during 1969 with responsibility for the planning, coordination, and provision of the full range of public services in the areas where transport needs were to be considered as a whole. To them were transferred the local bus services, and close cooperation with British Railways and the National Bus Corp. (NBC) was provided for. The NBC and the Scottish Transport Group became responsible for operating the nationalized sector of the road passenger industry, which represented about one-third of the U.K. buses, mostly engaged on interurban and rural services. The Transport (London) Act passed in 1969 provided for the transfer of the London Transport Board (LTB)—the public corporation operating London's underground rail and bus and coach services—to the Greater London Council (GLC). To ensure that the LTB was handed over to the GLC as a viable system on the scheduled day, Jan. 1, 1970, the government relieved the board of its total outstanding capital debt and fares were increased.

PIPELINES

Although experiments were being carried out for the transport of a variety of products, including solids and slurries, by pipelines, few actual systems for carrying other than liquids and gases, mainly crude oil and refined oil products, were operating. In the U.S. studies were being made concerning the feasibility of carrying natural gas by pipeline in liquefied form because of the high cost of transport in its natural state. Conventional gas lines were limited by economics to hauls of 2,500 mi., whereas it was estimated that liquefied natural gas could be transported in insulated pipelines at less than half the cost for up to 4,000 mi. or more. In Canada the Canadian Pacific Railway and Shell Canada undertook joint research on the transport of solids by pipeline. Similar research work was being carried out in the U.K. Among the solid or slurry materials proposed for such pipelines were iron ore; mixtures of limestone, chalk, and clay; sand and silt (dredged); and sewage sludge.

With more projects for the transport of natural gas completed or in progress, Europe's natural-gas pipeline system expanded to cover the greater part of the continent. In West Germany, for example, completion of the line from the Netherlands border to the Mannheim area extended its length to 371 km., while the pipeline network from the Ems estuary reached a total length of 1,200 km. In addition to the previously completed connections to Hamburg, Lübeck, Hanover, and Wolfsburg, a new line was laid southward toward the Rhine where it was linked with the existing Ruhrgas network. A 153-km., 10-in. ethylene pipeline with an annual capacity of 450,000 tons, completed by Ruhrgas to connect chemical plants in the Cologne, Frankfurt am Main, and Ludwigshafen areas, was also opened. It was proposed to extend the line to the Netherlands, ultimately as far as the Rotterdam-Amsterdam area, and also possibly to Lorraine in France. Gaz de France was constructing an 18-in., 38-mi. natural-gas pipeline in the Alsace-Vosges region as a branch of the Groningen–Paris line. In Yugoslavia work started on a major gas pipeline 200 km. long from the new Velebit oil and gas field near the Hungarian border to Belgrade. In the U.S.S.R. it was announced that the capacity of the existing gas lines from the Ukraine to Czechoslovakia was to be raised ultimately to 4,000,000,000 cu.m. a year. Work started in 1969 on a second 500-km. pipeline to the Czechoslovakian frontier with a capacity of up to 100,000,000,000 cu.m. a year; this capacity might be doubled in the mid-1970s when gas from Siberia reached the Ukrainian area.

The extension of several natural-gas pipelines in Canada was planned, the most ambitious being a 2,600-mi. system to supply the U.S. Middle West. The first stage would comprise 900 mi. from Alberta's Empress field to the Minnesota system at North Branch, and the second called for 1,710 mi. from the Northwest Territory Pointed Mountain to North Branch via Emerson, Man. The first was to be ready in 1971 and the second in 1975. The Interprovincial Pipeline Transcontinental Crude System was constructing a third Edmonton–Superior line and a second Superior–Sarnia line with 460 mi. of 34-in. and 30-in. diameter, respectively; the West Coast Transmission Co. was planning an extension to its natural-gas pipeline capacity with the construction of 160 mi. of 36-in. main line looping and of a 110-mi., 20-in. line connecting the Beaver River field with West Coast's Fort Nelson plant; permission was also being sought to build a 186-mi. pipeline from Cochrane, Alta. to Edmonton.

Relatively few new oil pipelines came into operation in Europe during the year. Work continued on the

418-km., 18-in. Adriatic–Vienna (AWP) pipeline, a spur from the existing Trans-Alpine (TAL) pipeline stretching from Trieste to southern Germany. Scheduled for completion in 1970, AWP would extend from Wurmlach in Kärnten to Schwechat near Vienna and would cost about $53 million. Work started on a 60-mi., 34-in. crude-oil pipeline linking Antwerp to Rotterdam Europoort and providing for an annual flow of 20 million tons; also, the Amsterdam–Rotterdam pipeline came into operation.

Sweden, with Europe's largest oil consumption per capita (3,366 l.), was planning construction of its first major oil pipeline system at a cost of approximately $29 million. It would consist of two parallel 150-km., 10-in. lines, one for white oils and the other for heavy fuel oil, and would extend from the important oil port and refinery centre of Göteborg on the southwest coast to Örebro on Lake Hjälmaren in central Sweden. In the U.K. the 245-mi. Thames–Mersey pipeline system came into full operation in March. This was the first coast-to-coast commercial pipeline in the U.K. and was one of the largest for the supply of white oil products in the whole European area.

With few exceptions pipeline flows in Europe continued to rise, particularly through the West German and French networks. The flow of 16.5 million tons in 1968 was a 12% rise over 1967 for the pipeline from Rotterdam to West Germany. The Rhine–Danube pipeline, however, continued to suffer from competition from the Central Europe (Genoa–Ingolstadt) line. In the U.S.S.R. record flows were recorded in 1968, and these increased further during the first half of 1969, rising to 153 million tons in the first six months.

With the development of the rich oil fields in northern Alaska, the three major companies with the biggest stakes in north Alaskan oil—British Petroleum, Atlantic Richfield, and Humble Oil—joined forces in a $900 million pipeline project to bring crude oil south from Alaska's North Slope to the Gulf of Alaska. This proposed trans-Alaskan pipeline system would be a 48-in. diameter, 800-mi. line and was scheduled for completion in 1972, with an initial capacity of about 500,000 bbl. a day. The proposed route was from Prudhoe Bay to Valdez. The biggest crude-oil pipeline in the U.S., Capline (from St. James, La., to Pakota, Ill.), was in full operation by the beginning of 1969 with a flow of 350,000 bbl. a day. The line was 640 mi. in length and had a diameter of 40 in. Flows through North American pipeline networks, which extended nearly 250,000 mi., rose during the year and represented more than 20% of total intercity transport by all modes as measured by ton-miles.

Danube River bridge of unique construction and design was completed in 1969 by Austrian firm.

AUTHENTICATED NEWS INTERNATIONAL

In South America, Argentina undertook the construction of a 240-km., 30-in. crude-oil pipeline from Cape San Antonio to refineries in La Plata and Buenos Aires. The second stage of the line from Luján de Cuyo to Cordoba and Buenos Aires was begun. The 625-km. Medanito–Allen–Puerto Rosales crude-oil pipeline neared completion. One of the oil industry's most spectacular projects, the trans-Andean pipeline from Orito to Tumaco in southern Colombia, was opened in May. This was the second pipeline across the Andes, the other being from Santa Cruz in Bolivia to Arica in the extreme north of Chile.

RAILWAYS

Technological development aimed at producing facilities competitive with other modes of transportation characterized the railway industry throughout the year. Although there was no startling breakthrough in developing new forms, sufficient progress was made for railway authorities to look forward with confidence to considerable advances in railway techniques by the mid-1970s. The few new systems coming into service experienced teething troubles. For example, the Turbotrain in Canada, introduced late in 1968, had to be withdrawn from service. Similarly, the Metroliner operating between New York City and Washington, D.C., proved to be little more than a conventional train traveling at high speeds. Progress on the freight side was more encouraging because, with the steady increase of unit load transportation methods, particularly containerization, movement of goods by rail tended to increase.

Modernization of existing systems throughout the world was concentrated mainly on replacing steam with electrification and dieselization and on the application of small on-line digital computers for rail-traffic operation and control. On the less developed systems modernization took the form of conversion from narrow to broad or standard gauge and the improvement of rolling stock. Closings of uneconomic lines generally occurred when there was no government subsidization to retain them. Apart from some less developed countries where the opening up of natural resources and industrial areas justified it, there was little new construction.

Technologically, the most promising railway research was in progress in Britain on the Advanced Passenger Train (APT) with a potential speed of 200 mph. This was to be a lightweight train powered by a gas turbine engine; it would achieve higher speeds not only by the conventional improvement of acceleration and braking rates but by drastic changes in the suspension system of the coaches that would enable trains to take curves safely at far higher speeds without the realignment of track. The principle was one of dynamics combined with the application to rail of lightweight construction techniques developed by the aircraft industry. A hydraulically operated tilting mechanism was designed to permit the banking of the body of the train up to 9° from the vertical on curves without any radial loss of speed. Dynamic loads on both vehicles and track would thus be reduced to an acceptable level to enable the forces acting between wheel and track to guide the train without making it dynamically unstable. The development of the train was to be spread over a five-year program.

Existing methods of signaling were considered suitable to cope with high-speed trains such as the APT up to 125 mph, but British Railways developed a system that would allow far higher speeds. This was a continuous communications system that would be able to control trains running at virtually any speed because it brought the signaling system right into the driver's cab and allowed for two-way communication between the driver and a central control office.

Meanwhile, the electric-powered Metroliner came into operation on the New York-Washington, D.C., run. It averaged 90 mph, with a top speed limited to 110 mph. The main feature of this high-speed train was the automatic control of acceleration and deceleration which enabled 120 mph to be reached in two minutes. The high-speed train operating between New York and Boston had its speed limited to 120 mph. The Toronto-Montreal Turbotrain service introduced in late 1968 had to be withdrawn, the suspension system presenting difficulties as did cold weather conditions and unsatisfactory auxiliaries. Japan undertook preliminary tests with gas-turbine power units, and full-scale trials were scheduled for 1970. Meanwhile, the second new Tokaido line was to use linear-motor traction between Tokyo and Osaka, and the prototype was being designed for speeds up to 500 mph.

France maintained a lead in the development of tracked air-cushion vehicles, with its aerotrain operating on an experimental six-mile-long track at 200 kph (125 mph). Another French experiment under way was the Rail Jet, which consisted of a conventional linear induction unit with the rail forming the armature. The accelerating and decelerating efforts were thus provided through direct induction in the rail, leaving to the wheel only the functions of support and guidance and thereby freeing the train from the major limitation of adherence. In Britain development continued of a government-sponsored experimental tracked air-cushion vehicle designed for 250 mph. The first three miles of track at Cambridge were expected to be completed by the spring of 1970, with a 30-ft. research vehicle in operation. In the U.S. the General Electric Co. designed a tracked ground-effect machine supported on four air cushions, to be propelled either by aircraft turbofan engines or by an electric linear induction motor. On the Long Island Railroad an experimental suburban railcar propelled by its own gas-turbine-generated electricity was being tested.

Meanwhile, electrification of more densely traveled routes continued. In the 18 countries represented in the European Conference of Ministers of Transport (ECMT) nearly 50,000 km. had been converted to electric traction by the end of 1968, with France, West Germany, Italy, and Sweden accounting for two-thirds of the total. For the remainder of the system conversion to diesel power continued, with steam traction rapidly disappearing.

New construction during the year included steady progress on the Kathua–Jammu line into Kashmir by the Northern Railway of India, completion being planned for 1972. Progress was made on the CENTO Turkey-to-Iran railway, the section from Mus to Tatvan being continued to the Iranian border at Qotur and thence to Harikar, and in southern India on the line from Trivandrum to Tirunelveli via Cape Cormorin. In Africa on the trans-Cameroon railway the section from Mbanga to Kumba was opened, and work began on the second section, helped by a $20 million loan from the EEC. Gabon proposed to construct a railway from Owendo to Belinga; progress was made in the planning of the Tanzania–Zambia (Tanzam) railway, with the survey between Kidatu and the Zambia border completed and the extension of the line to Dar es Salaam being surveyed by the Chinese. On November 14 China, Tanzania, and Zambia jointly signed an agreement committing themselves to the project.

In Australia the 156-mi. line between Port Hedland and Mount Newman in the north of Western Australia was completed, and work was started on a 136-mi. line to serve the new coalfield at Goonyella in Queensland and link with the new port at Hay Point. In Brazil the 108-km. branch of the Vitória a Minas iron-ore railway from Costa Laierda to Fábrica was finished, and in Argentina surveys were undertaken for a 120-km. line from San Antonio Oeste to the iron ore deposits at Sierra Grande, Patagonia. The U.S. federal government allocated funds for an engineering survey for an extension of the government-owned Alaskan railroad from Fairbanks to the North Slope with a branch to Kobuk. This was to meet transport demands arising from developments in the North Slope oil fields.

Closings of uneconomic lines continued on a considerable scale, although government policy in several countries kept those open that were considered of national importance for social or economic reasons. The United States especially witnessed a further decline of passenger services, with closings accelerated despite the Interstate Commerce Commission's (ICC) refusal of permission to abandon some. During the previous decade the number of regular intercity trains in the U.S. had declined more than 60%, and over 36% of the 1958 routes had been eliminated; 14 railroads had abandoned all intercity services. By 1969 barely 500 regular intercity trains were operating, and the ICC urged a federal study to ensure the preservation of a national rail passenger service, which recommendation the government accepted. Meanwhile, a number of rail mergers were concluded, particularly in the eastern states. The eastern railroads had been grouped into three major categories: (1) the Pennsylvania–New York Central system; (2) the Norfolk and Western system (including the Erie Lackawanna, the Delaware and Hudson, and the Boston and Maine railroads); and (3) the Chesapeake and Ohio-Baltimore and Ohio system. In Europe closings also continued on a considerable scale during the year: in West Germany 182 km. of lines were closed to both passenger and freight and 405 km. to passenger traffic only; 385 km. were closed in Spain; nearly 1,000 km. in France; 340 km. in Sweden; and more than 400 km. in the United Kingdom. In Canada, also, extensive shutdowns were planned, totaling 844 mi. on the Canadian National and 673 mi. on the Canadian Pacific.

The improved economic situation in the majority of industrial countries brought about a significant increase in rail freight traffic, while the deterioration of passenger traffic continued. In the 18 ECMT countries freight traffic experienced a marked recovery, with an increase of roughly 4% in the volume of traffic carried and of 3.2% in ton-kilometres. In 1968, 1,200,000,000 tons were carried, compared with 1,150,000,000 tons in 1967. The number of passengers declined by nearly 2% and of passenger-kilometres by 1.4%.

Passenger journeys on British Railways fell from 877 million in 1967 to 831 million in 1968, but freight carryings increased and the rise in net ton-miles was more than 1,000,000,000. Deficit financing ended in 1968 with a deficit of £147.4 million, a decrease in the loss of £5.6 million. British Railways subsequently had to operate without loss, and charges were consequently increased.

In North America the Canadian National Railway system recorded increases of 4.5% in freight revenues. The number of passengers carried declined by 19%, whereas freight tonnage increased 2.4%. Canadian Pacific, however, experienced a decline in both passenger and freight service. The number of passengers carried fell by 13.9% and passenger-miles by 8.2%; tons of freight carried declined 18.5% and ton-miles by 2.3%. In the United States total operating revenue increased by about 4%, freight traffic rising and passenger numbers declining except for commuters. (E. A. J. D.)

WATER TRANSPORTATION

Shipping. World shipping continued its striking growth in 1969, the merchant fleet having passed the 200-million-ton mark at the end of 1968. This represented a doubling of tonnage in only 14 years, compared with the 40 years—1914 to 1954—needed to grow from 50 to 100 million tons. The main stimulant was, of course, the huge increase in world oil consumption in the wake of industrialization. While the world fleet as a whole had doubled during the previous decade, the tanker fleet tripled in size, from 25 million tons to about 75 million tons, or nearly 40% of the tonnage afloat. The dry-cargo bulk carrier fleet also increased at a rapid rate, with demand for iron ore leading the way. Bulk carriers accounted for about 40 million tons of the world fleet at the year's end.

Along with the increase in fleets came a continuing increase in the size of individual ships. About 200 tankers of 200,000 tons deadweight and over were in service, under construction, and on order, along with about a dozen of 300,000 to 350,000 tons. Japanese owners were actively preparing for tankers of 450,000–500,000 tons and bulk carriers of up to 350,000 tons. On the general cargo side, ships were also getting bigger, with container ships of 20,000–30,000 tons replacing conventional cargo liners of about 13,000 tons.

More striking though were the increases in speed. Cargo-liner speeds had shifted noticeably only twice since World War II, from about 15 to 17 knots in the 1950s and from 17 to 20 knots in the '60s. Suddenly, the U.S. giant Sea-Land Service, Inc., pioneers of the containerization revolution, startled the shipping world in the spring of 1969 with orders for a fleet of 33-knot container ships, fast enough to knock several days off some of the longer trade routes. Clearly Sea-Land's intention was to obtain for itself the best cargo on Atlantic and Pacific routes, possibly on a round-the-world service, and its plan had the immediate effect of pushing up speeds from 22 to about 26 knots on subsequent orders by established lines. Sea-Land's move was typical of the new initiatives in the United States, where a formerly moribund shipping industry was drawing new life from container ships with their high productivity and low labour costs and was expanding on world trade routes for the first time for many years, in some cases without the help of subsidy. U.S. shipping had once more become a force to be reckoned with.

Fears that the rapid growth in carrying capacity would lead to a slump failed to materialize, partly because of the steady advance in world trade and partly because the Suez Canal remained closed, adding considerably to the distances of many routes. But with new orders still flowing into the shipyards, helped by favourable fiscal treatment for owners and cheap credit from builders, there was a growing feeling that the slump had merely been postponed for a year or two.

The last of the big passenger ships, Cunard's "Queen Elizabeth 2," entered service in May amid much publicity and with some initial difficulties. As she did so, passenger shipping, after a decade in the doldrums, began showing signs of improvement. Several cruise ships of modest size—mostly about 20,000 tons—were ordered by the Norwegians, primarily for use in the New York, Florida, and Caribbean trades.

The voyage of the 115,000-ton tanker "Manhattan" through the Northwest Passage during the latter part of the year had considerable implications for shipping interests and raised the possibility of a new pattern of world trade. (M. By.)

Hovercraft. Following the diversification of Hovercraft (air-cushion machines operating over water) operations in 1968, there was a substantial increase in both manufacturing and operating activity throughout the world in 1969, although technical and economic problems were still evident. The number of SR-N4 Mountbatten-class (165-ton craft carrying 250 passengers and 30 cars) Hovercraft operating between Britain and France increased to four and completed a summer schedule of regular services with an overall reliability of 94%. Crossing time between Dover and Boulogne was reduced to 35 minutes. It was announced in November that the British government was to sponsor research into the reliability, maintenance, and cost problems encountered by the SR-N4 operators. Other craft from the British Hovercraft Corp., of the Winchester and Warden classes, continued services on the much shorter routes between England and the Isle of Wight. Similar craft saw charter service in India, the Gulf of Arabia, Canada, and the Netherlands.

A breakthrough in the use to which Hovercraft could be put came in the seismographic exploration field. Pacific Hovercraft Ltd., a Vancouver, B.C., company, operated three Winchesters on the northern slopes of Alaska during the summer-long search for oil in the area. A similar search was conducted in the Netherlands. Both operations were said to have been successful.

In the United States two companies, Bell Aerosystems and Aerojet-General, received government contracts to build 100-ton models of proposed 1,000-ton "Surface Effect Ships." These were to be non-amphibious craft, driven by waterscrews and water-jets, respectively, and were expected to be operating by mid-1970. (J. B. Be.)

Docks and Harbours. Extension of facilities to accommodate both larger vessels and specialized bulk shipments and container roll-on/roll-off services marked development in ports throughout the seafaring countries during 1969. Imaginative plans were drawn for vast expansion to meet the possible increase in the size of ships from the current maximum of more than 300,000 tons deadweight. In the U.K., the Mersey Docks and Harbour Board conducted a preliminary feasibility study on the possible construction of a £45 million man-made island 11 mi. off the coast for tankers of one million tons. Rotterdam-Europoort, which held its lead as Europe's foremost port with seven dock areas comprising 46 dock basins, was building an eighth, the Maasvlakte, by reclaiming more than 6,000 ac. from the North Sea, and was planning construction of a container port on the right bank of the Maas, only 7 km. from the sea. The Port of London also looked ahead and began studying the practicability of dredging a deepwater approach to the outermost limits of the port and reclaiming 46 sq.mi. of land for construction of new port facilities off Foulness, Essex.

The Port of New York Authority was speeding up its vast expansion program by two years and began construction of the last five berths for the Port Elizabeth marine terminal to make it the world's largest container-ship facility. Work on this $30 million project began in the fall of 1969 with a completion target for 1973, when the facility would comprise 25 deep-sea-vessel berths. Singapore entered its bid to replace Yokohama, Jap., as the world's third largest port with a five-year program costing $55 million, half of which would be spent on a container terminal.

Meanwhile, many new facilities came into use or neared completion. In the U.K. the phased shutdown of some of London's inner docks continued with the extension of facilities downstream at Tilbury, where additional container and bulk-cargo facilities were provided, and farther down the Thames estuary, where berthing facilities were able to receive deep-draft tankers of more than 210,000 tons deadweight. At Port Talbot the new tidal harbour was ready to receive its first 100,000-ton iron-ore carriers by the end of the year, and a second berth with a built-in capacity of 175,000 tons deadweight was to be constructed. At Liverpool work started on the entrance channel to the new £33 million complex at Seaforth, which was to provide modern deepwater berths for general cargo and specialized accommodation with at least ten container berths, the first by 1971; in the existing port an additional container berth was to be provided.

In France, at Le Havre, a new deepwater entrance channel was in service providing for tankers of 200,000 tons deadweight, and the channel was to be extended from 3 to 7 nautical miles to permit 250,000-ton ships to enter. A new six-year (1970–75) plan included further improvements at the Port of Antwerp, and Hamburg was to build two more container berths at the Burchardkai terminal, the first by 1971, making six in all. In Sweden at Hälsingborg the new Scania container terminal was opened, and Torshamnen, the crude-oil harbour of Göteborg, had its entrance channel deepened and was able to receive tankers of 250,000 tons deadweight.

In North America, the ore pier complex at Baltimore, Md., to take ore carriers of up to 160,000 tons deadweight was scheduled to be operational by 1971; the second phase of a three-phase project to provide new dual-purpose facilities with four berths at the Locust Point marine terminal progressed, as did work at the Dundalk, Md., marine terminal where the $21 million expansion was to add six more container berths. The new deep-sea terminal at Skagway, Alaska, for handling concentrates from the developing Alaskan mines came into operation. In Canada, Vancouver's outer port of Roberts Bank, with facilities for handling several million tons of coal annually at berths 65 ft. deep at low water, was expected to be in use early in 1970, and the First Narrows entrance to the inner port was being dredged to 50 ft. at low water to enable large bulk carriers to use existing facilities.

Europe's major seaports experienced increased traffic during the year. Rotterdam-Europoort maintained the lead with international seaborne goods traffic passing through the port rising to the record figure of 156.9 million tons in 1968, compared with 141.4 million tons in 1967, of which 132.2 million and 118.8 million tons, respectively, represented bulk goods. In order of tonnage handled in millions of tons, Antwerp finished second with 72.4 (60 in 1967); London had 60.1 (traffic being practically unchanged compared with 1967); Marseilles 57 (62.5); Genoa 51.1 (45.5); Le Havre 43.4 (37.5); and Hamburg 38.3 (35.4). The Port of New York Authority handled just under 10 million tons of cargo at its six marine terminals during 1968, an increase over 1967 of 11.3%.

Inland Waterways. Although in the U.S. in 1967 there had been a decline in inland waterway traffic as measured by ton-miles compared with the previous year, during 1968 traffic was booming. Approximately 17,000 barges plied the 25,000 mi. of navigable water and carried nearly 10% of all intercity freight, double the amount transported 15 years before. This increase was attributed to the inherently low cost of water transportation and to the many technological advances in equipment, with more powerful tugs pushing longer strings of barges designed to carry a greater variety of products. The largest tug that came into service during the year, the "United States" of 9,000 hp., could push an integrated tow of more than 40 barges at 15 mph. Barge strings were longer than the largest ocean liner and carried more cargo than a seagoing freighter. Two 26,000-ton barges also came into use for moving phosphates, which could be unloaded by conveyors at 3,000 tons an hour. On the U.S. inland waterway system, several projects were under construction and scheduled for completion in the early 1970s, including the cross-Florida barge canal and the Arkansas and Ohio rivers redevelopment programs.

STUART LAKE FROM CANADIAN PRESS

Held in heavy ice, the U.S. oil tanker SS "Manhattan" (left) waits for help from Canadian icebreaker "Sir John A. MacDonald" before completing voyage through Northwest Passage to reach new Alaskan oil fields in 1969.

Traffic on the St. Lawrence Seaway reached new records during 1968 with general cargo tonnage rising by 32% on the Montreal–Lake Ontario section and by 42% on the Welland section; total figures reached 48 million tons (44 million in 1967) on the former and 58 million tons (53 million) on the latter. In 1968 the Seaway completed ten years of operation, during which traffic and ship movements had more than doubled on the Montreal–Lake Ontario section. On the Welland section tonnage rose from 27.5 million to 58 million and transits from 4,000 to 8,200 during the ten years. Technological improvement was reflected in a rise in average vessel capacity from 3,400 tons in 1958 to between 7,000 and 8,000 tons in 1968. On the Welland section a new 8.6-mi. channel was being constructed. Toronto, the largest of the Great Lakes ports, was spending $2.4 million on a new freight terminal to handle ocean freight containers.

During 1968 progress was made on improvements to the European waterways network. Development of the Dunkirk–Scheldt link and its international extensions proceeded, with completion of the Dunkirk–Denain section during 1968; work was in progress on the Denain–Valenciennes section, and was completed on the Oudenaarde bypass on the Belgian side and on the Ghent ring canal during 1968–69. With the installation of the Arzwiller–Saint Louis lock elevator, the canal from the Marne to the Rhine was open to ships drawing up to 2.30 m. This unique transversal inclined plane replaced 17 locks and was the first of its kind to be constructed. On the Rhine–Main–Danube link the 30-km. stretch between Bamberg and Forchheim was opened to navigation, and work on the Forchheim–Nürnberg section was expected to be completed by 1972. In northern West Germany development of the Elbe to provide a link from Hamburg to the waterways network of Western Europe, including the Mittelland Canal, proceeded, with construction nearing completion on the Bergeshövede–Minden section. The link with the Elbe near Artlenburg was expected to be established in 1969. The canalization of the Neckar between Stuttgart and Plochingen was opened to traffic, and work progressed to make the West German waterways network accessible to 1,350-ton craft.

Movement by inland water transport increased in most European countries during 1968; Rhine traffic at the West German-Netherlands frontier during the first six months of the year rose by about 28% upstream and 14% downstream. The Netherlands itself exceeded the record traffic registered in 1967, while in Belgium an increase of about 4% was estimated. In both cases international traffic was largely responsible, due to the continuing increase of shipping through the ports of Rotterdam-Europoort and Antwerp for transshipment via the Rhine. At Rotterdam the arrivals and departures by international inland shipping increased by about 10%, from 51.4 million tons in 1967 to about 57 million tons in 1968. At Antwerp navigation to and from the Rhine by inland waterway rose by 19 and 28%, respectively, during the year. In France, international traffic across the Belgian border and on the Moselle navigation rose, but internal traffic declined, as did traffic in Switzerland through the Basel ports. In the case of Basel the decline was largely due to a decrease in petroleum shipping arising from the full-scale production at the new refineries which received their crude oil by pipeline. In the U.S.S.R. ton-kilometres declined by 8% during the first six months of 1969 compared with 1968. Throughout 1969, its centenary year, the Suez Canal remained closed to shipping. The Panama Canal, on the other hand, established new highs for cargo tonnage and tolls in fiscal 1969, with approximately 108 million tons and about $96 million in tolls. The number of oceangoing commercial ships using the canal was 13,125, a slight decline from the record total of 13,199 in fiscal 1968. (E. A. J. D.)

See also Cities and Urban Affairs; Engineering Projects; Industrial Review.

ENCYCLOPÆDIA BRITANNICA FILMS. *The Living City* (1953); *Inland Waterways* (1956); *Development of Transportation* (1958); *The Gasoline Age* (1958); *The Steam Age* (1958); *The St. Lawrence Seaway* (1959); *The Panama Canal* (1961); *The Suez Canal* (1962); *Our Shrinking World—Jet Pilot* (1964).

Tropical Medicine: *see* Medicine

Trucial States: *see* Dependent States

Truck Farming: *see* Agriculture

Trucking Industry: *see* Transportation

Trust Territories: *see* Dependent States

Tunnels: *see* Engineering Projects

Trinidad and Tobago

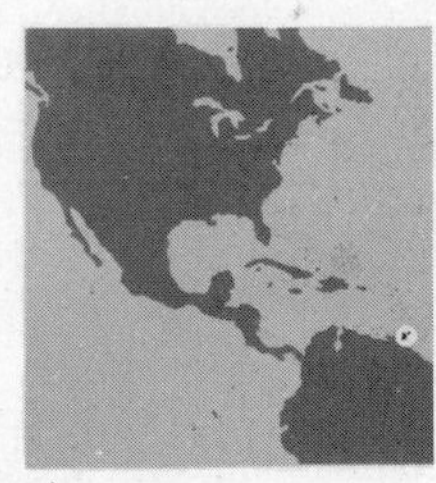

A parliamentary state and a member of the Commonwealth of Nations, Trinidad and Tobago consists of two islands off the coast of Venezuela, north of the Orinoco River delta. Area: 1,980 sq.mi. (5,128 sq.km.). Pop. (1968 est.): 1,030,000, including (1960) Negro 43.3%; East Indian 36.5%; mixed 16.3%. Cap. and largest city: Port-of-Spain (pop., 1965 est., 85,100). Language: English (official); Hindi, French, Spanish. Religion (1960): Christian 66%; Hindu 23%; Muslim 6%. Queen, Elizabeth II; governor-general in 1969, Sir Solomon Hochoy; prime minister, Eric Williams.

In his budget speech in November 1968 Prime Minister Williams indicated that the state would exercise increased control over the assets of the country. The third five-year plan (1969–73) called for priority in the development of agriculture, export industries, and tourism, and for increased participation by young people in national development. Public sector development expenditures over the period of the plan would be TT$375 million, of which TT$230 million (62%) would come from local sources.

In May the World Bank announced a loan of $2 million to the Trinidad and Tobago Electricity Commission for the improvement of power services. The government announced that it would make available to interested parties the results of a seismic and aeromagnetic survey for petroleum made off the north coast. On July 1, in partnership with Tesoro Petroleum Corp. (Tex.), the government acquired British Petroleum's local assets. The state also took control of the Port-of-Spain harbour, and completed its purchase of television and radio interests and the local

TRINIDAD AND TOBAGO

Education. (1966–67) Primary, pupils 219,679, teachers 6,311; secondary (1963–64), pupils 33,641, teachers 1,017; vocational (1963–64), pupils 1,051, teachers 122; higher (1965–66), students 910, teaching staff 120.

Finance and Trade. Monetary unit: Trinidad and Tobago dollar, with an exchange rate of TT$2 to U.S. $1 (TT$4.80 = £1 sterling). Budget (1969 est.): revenue TT$282.9 million; expenditure TT$346,750,-000. Foreign trade (1968): imports TT$840.1 million; exports TT$932.5 million. Import sources: Venezuela 44%; U.S. 15%; U.K. 15%. Export destinations: U.S. 46%; U.K. 11%; Sweden 8%. Main exports: petroleum and products 78%; sugar 5%.

Transport and Communications. Roads (1967) *c.* 4,100 km. Motor vehicles in use (1967): passenger 62,900; commercial (including buses) 17,400. Air traffic (1967): 381,308,000 passenger-km.; freight 4,155,-000 net ton-km. Shipping traffic (1967): goods loaded 18,660,000 metric tons, unloaded 12.3 million metric tons. Telephones (Jan. 1968) 46,089. Radio receivers (Dec. 1966) 200,000. Television receivers (Dec. 1967) 36,000.

Agriculture. Production (in 000; metric tons; 1967; 1966 in parentheses): rice *c.* 10 (*c.* 10); sweet potatoes *c.* 18 (*c.* 15); oranges (1968) 11, (1967) 9; grapefruit (1968) 16, (1967) 18; sugar, raw value (1968–69) 277, (1967–68) 247; copra *c.* 13 (*c.* 13). Livestock (in 000; 1966–67): cattle *c.* 58; pigs *c.* 45; sheep *c.* 5; goats *c.* 32; poultry *c.* 1,000.

Industry. Production (in 000; metric tons; 1968): crude oil 9,467; petroleum products 20,252; cement 210; asphalt (1967) 145; electricity (kw-hr.) 1,118,-000.

branch of Cable and Wireless Ltd. of the U.K. In November it was announced that the Trinidad and Tobago External Telecommunications Company, created by this merger, had placed an order with Marconi of the U.K. for a space communications ground station to be built at Matura.

Student unrest at the University of the West Indies led to the barring from the campus of the governor-general of Canada, a boycott of classes, and student participation in a strike by bus workers. A government commission was set up in November to investigate staff appointments of the university, one of the causes of the unrest. (RA. R.)

ENCYCLOPÆDIA BRITANNICA FILMS. *The West Indies* (1965).

Tunisia

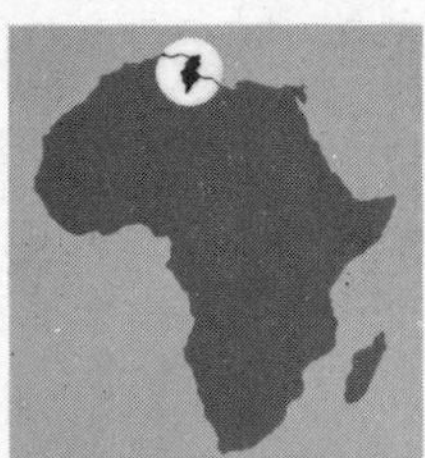

A republic of North Africa, lying on the Mediterranean Sea, Tunisia is bounded by Algeria and Libya. Area: 63,170 sq.mi. (163,610 sq.km.). Pop. (1969): 5,027,000. Cap. and largest city: Tunis (pop., 1966, 468,997). Language: Arabic (official). Religion: Muslim; Jewish and Christian minorities. President in 1969, Habib Bourguiba; prime minister, Bahi Ladgham.

Following the presidential elections of November 2, as a result of which Habib Bourguiba, the sole candidate, was reelected with 99.76% of votes cast, an important ministerial reshuffle reflected the president's aim of significantly strengthening state institutions and giving a new impetus to economic policy. Bahi Ladgham, secretary of state to the presidency, was given the newly created post of prime minister, while Ahmed Ben Salah, already dismissed from the government, was ejected from the Neo-Destour Socialist Party.

With the demotion of Ben Salah, known for his forceful socialist convictions, and the death in October of Mongi Slim (*see* OBITUARIES), a political personality of international repute, a chapter of Tunisia's history came to an end. The uneasiness aroused by former minister Ahmed Mestiri's public criticism of the regime, some weeks before the election, was quickly dissipated.

President Bourguiba saw no necessity to modify a policy that from September had demonstrated his opposition to Ben Salah's cooperativization of the agricultural sector, which the president regarded as ill-suited to Tunisian realities. Bourguiba had practically designated as his heir Ladgham, the man most resolutely determined to limit the agrarian reform in order to delay its application. Still feeling the effects of an illness from which he had hardly recovered—and which had totally interrupted his activities in May and June—the president was anxious to prepare for his succession.

The opening of a chemical complex near the new port of Gabès in the spring inaugurated a new emphasis on the industrialization of the poor and hitherto underprivileged southern region. French development loans amounted to more than $26 million, while the World Bank and the Swedish government provided $20 million to modernize the country's water system.

In the international field the two most important events were the signing of a cooperative agreement with Algeria in April, and the visit of Habib Bourguiba, Jr., secretary of state for foreign affairs, to France in February. The latter event marked the desire by France to wipe away the bad memories left by the Bizerta affair of 1961 and the nationalization of French colonial territories in 1964, and Tunisia's determination, in turn, to forget tactfully France's repressive measures at Bizerta and Tunisia's subsequent lengthy quarantine. The change was embodied in the immediate establishment of Franco-Tunisian cooperation, culminating in a visit by the French foreign minister, Maurice Schumann, in November and an official invitation to President Bourguiba to visit France in 1970; it also explained the massive aid given by the French government to the Tunisian authorities, who in September and November struggled against the disastrous ravages of floods that caused several hundred deaths. (PH. D.)

TUNISIA

Education. (1967–68) Primary, pupils 826,069, teachers (1965–66) 12,878; secondary (1965–66), pupils 103,339; vocational (1965–66), pupils 6,394; secondary and vocational (state only; 1965–66), teachers 1,293; teacher training (1965–66), students 4,745; higher (at University of Tunis), students 7,828.

Finance. Monetary unit: Tunisian dinar, with a parity of 0.52 dinars = U.S $1 (1.26 dinars = £1 sterling). Gold and foreign exchange, central bank: (June 1969) U.S. $29.9 million; (June 1968) U.S. $29.2 million. Budget (1969 est.) balanced at 130 million dinars. Gross national product: (1967) 511.1 million dinars; (1966) 493.2 million dinars. Money supply: (April 1969) 175,690,000 dinars; (April 1968) 158,130,000 dinars. Cost of living (1963 = 100): (June 1969) 128; (June 1968) 120.

Foreign Trade. (1968) Imports 114.5 million dinars; exports 82,830,000 dinars. Import sources (1967): France 32%; U.S. 25%; West Germany 8%; Italy 6%. Export destinations (1967): France 28%; Italy 12%; West Germany 8%; Libya 5%. Main exports: phosphates 27%; crude oil 17%; olive oil 14%.

Transport and Communications. Roads (1968) 17,292 km. Motor vehicles in use (1968): passenger 60,596; commercial 31,522. Railways: (1967) 2,021 km.; traffic (1968) 438 million passenger-km., freight 1,312,000,000 net ton-km. Air traffic (1968): 177.7 million passenger-km.; freight 1,776,000 net ton-km. Telephones (Dec. 1967) 58,321. Radio receivers (Dec. 1967) 375,000. Television receivers (Dec. 1967) 35,000.

Agriculture. Production (in 000; metric tons; 1968; 1967 in parentheses): wheat 383 (330); barley 130 (70); tomatoes (1967) 119, (1966) 149; wine *c.* 95 (93); dates (1967) 39, (1966) 42; figs (1967) 20, (1966) 24; olive oil 80 (53); oranges *c.* 65 (65); lemons (1967) 12, (1966) 15. Livestock (in 000; 1966–67): sheep 4,205; cattle 619; horses 89; asses 169; mules 56; goats 585; camels 214; poultry *c.* 5,700.

Industry. Production (in 000; metric tons; 1968): iron ore (55% metal content) 1,015; phosphate rock (1967) 2,810; lead 14; cement 514; electricity (public supply; kw-hr.) 545,000.

Turkey

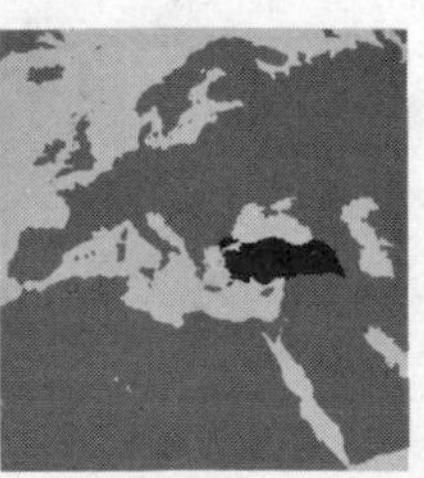

A republic of southeastern Europe and Asia Minor, Turkey is bounded by the Aegean Sea, the Black Sea, the U.S.S.R., Iran, Iraq, Syria, the Mediterranean Sea, Greece, and Bulgaria. Area: 301,380 sq.mi. (780,576 sq.km.), including 9,158 sq.mi. in Europe. Pop. (1969): 34,375,000. Cap.: Ankara (pop., 1969, 1,157,000). Largest city: Istanbul (pop., 1965, 1,750,642). Language: Turkish 90.7%; Kurdish 6.7%; Arabic 1.3%. Religion: predominantly Muslim. President in 1969, Gen. Cevdet Sunay; prime minister, Suleyman Demirel.

In 1969 a number of incidents involving students and other militants and a major political crisis in

May seemed to threaten stability and parliamentary rule. However, Suleyman Demirel's Justice Party (JP) administration rode out the storm and proceeded to win the general elections, held in an atmosphere of calm on October 12.

Violence first erupted on January 6, when students of the Middle East Technical University in Ankara burned the car of U.S. Ambassador Robert Komer, who was later recalled. On February 16, one man was killed and many injured in Istanbul, when right-wing militants attacked left-wingers who had been protesting against the presence in Istanbul of the U.S. 6th Fleet. The planned visit of the fleet to Izmir had to be canceled. In April student troubles in Ankara led to the closing of the Middle East Technical University, and there was a strike of Turkish civilian personnel at U.S. military bases.

A major threat to parliamentary rule developed in May when the leader of the opposition Republican People's Party (RPP), 85-year-old Ismet Inonu, staged a reconciliation with his rival (and contemporary) Celal Bayar, former leader of the Democratic Party, who had been removed from the presidency of the republic by the Army in a coup on May 27, 1960. As a result of this reconciliation the RPP's vote secured on May 15 the passage of a constitutional amendment, originally proposed by rank-and-file members of the JP, to remove the electoral disqualification imposed on leading members of the dissolved Democratic Party. However, the amendment was withdrawn from the Senate, at Prime Minister Demirel's insistence, when the armed forces declared their opposition to it. Demirel was immediately accused of being either in collusion with the military or too weak to resist their pressure, but he retorted that his major concern was to secure the holding of free elections in October. In order to prevent the automatic enactment of the amendment, without Senate approval, the session of Parliament was terminated on May 29. The delay that this caused in the implementation of measures for university reform and for better workers' pensions led to more student unrest, causing the postponement of examinations until the autumn. An attempt to reconvene Parliament failed on June 13, but as an orderly workers' protest rally in Ankara on August 24 showed, there was little desire in the country to depart from parliamentary rule.

The election was fought largely on the issue of the political rehabilitation of the former Democrats, ex-President Bayar coming out openly against Demirel, and the small New Turkey Party making a bid for Democratic support. Prime Minister Demirel, who had been for the previous four years assailed by the left wing, thus found himself also under attack from the right. Nevertheless, the results of the elections held on October 12 showed that not only had he succeeded in preserving the broad mass of his electoral support, but that interest in politics was decreasing (participation fell from 73 to 64% between 1965 and 1969). The JP won 47% of the votes (53% in 1965) and, thanks to a changed electoral law, 257 out of the 450 seats in the Assembly (240 in 1965). It was followed by the RPP with 27% of the poll (29% in 1965) and 144 seats (134), and by the new Reliance Party, a breakaway from the Republicans, with 7% of the votes and 15 seats. The remaining five parties all won fewer than the ten seats needed to form a parliamentary group, the New Turkey Party receiving only 2% of the votes cast, as compared with 4% in 1965. Of the two extremist parties, the Marxist Turkish Workers' Party's share of the poll fell by 0.3% to 2.7%, but under the new law this entitled it to only 2 seats (15 in 1965), while the right-wing militants of the Nationalist Action Party (formerly Republican Peasants and Nation Party) increased by 0.8% to 3% their share of the poll, but lost 10 of the 11 seats which they held in 1965. Eleven independents, mostly right-wing, were elected to the new Assembly.

On November 3, the prime minister announced his new Cabinet, in which the right wing of the JP (the so-called Bilgic group) was deprived of all representation. Nevertheless, the excluded faction supported the government on November 12 when the Assembly approved its program by 263 votes to 165. On the same day the electoral disqualifications of the old Democratic Party leaders were also finally removed.

The prime minister retained as his foreign minister Ihsan Sabri Caglayangil, the architect of Turkey's policy of maintaining friendly relations with all countries while preserving a basic reliance on the West. During 1969 this policy was expressed by visits to Turkey by the president of Romania, by the Italian prime minister, and by President Sunay's state visit to the Soviet Union in November. (A. J. A. M.)

See also Cyprus.

ENCYCLOPÆDIA BRITANNICA FILMS. *The Middle East* (1955); *Turkey: Emergence of a Modern Nation* (1963).

TURKEY

Education. (1966–67) Primary, pupils 4,273,-977, teachers 93,398; secondary, pupils 655,251, teachers 23,458; vocational, pupils 194,323, teachers 11,507; teacher training, students 54,-637, teachers 1,737; higher (including 7 universities), students 60,654, teaching staff 4,217.

Finance. Monetary unit: Turkish pound or lira, with a par value of 9 lire to U.S. $1 (21.60 lire = £1 sterling) and a tourist rate of 12 lire to U.S. $1 (28.80 lire = £1 sterling). Gold and foreign exchange, central bank: (June 1969) U.S. $149 million; (June 1968) U.S. $123 million. Budget (1968–69 rev. est.): revenue 20,712,211,-000 lire; expenditure 21,612,211,000 lire. Gross national product: (1967) 103,860,000,000 lire; (1966) 92,480,000,000 lire. Money supply: (May 1969) 12,750,000,000 lire; (May 1968) 11,070,-000,000 lire. Cost of living (Istanbul; 1963 = 100): (June 1969) 145; (June 1968) 139.

Foreign Trade. (1968) Imports 6,934,000,000 lire; exports 4,467,000,000 lire. Import sources: West Germany 20%; U.S. 16%; U.K. 13%; Italy 9%. Export destinations: West Germany 17%; U.S. 15%; U.K. 7%; U.S.S.R. 6%; Switzerland 5%; Italy 5%; Lebanon 5%. Main exports: cotton 27%; tobacco 19%; hazelnuts 15%; raisins 5%.

Transport and Communications. Roads (1968) *c.* 70,000 km. (including *c.* 32,000 km. main roads). Motor vehicles in use (1968): passenger 128,900; commercial 105,900. Railways (1967): 8,008 km.; traffic 4,301,000,000 passenger-km., freight 5,062,000,000 net ton-km. Air traffic (1967): 310,479,000 passenger-km.; freight 3,165,000 net ton-km. Shipping (1968): merchant vessels 100 gross tons and over 298; gross tonnage 648,171. Telephones (Dec. 1967) 427,770. Radio receivers (Dec. 1967) 2,789,000. Television receivers (Dec. 1966) 2,500.

Agriculture. Production (in 000; metric tons; 1968; 1967 in parentheses): wheat (including spelt) 9,602 (10,110); barley 3,560 (3,800); oats 450 (510); corn 1,000 (1,050); rye 820 (900); onions (1967) 550, (1966) 470; potatoes 1,805 (1,760); sunflower seed 230 (230); chick-peas (1967) 97, (1966) 89; dry beans *c.* 137 (142); lentils (1967) 106, (1966) 100; oranges 390 (451); lemons 99 (90); apples (1967) 640, (1966) 440; pears (1967) 165, (1966) 135; grapes (1967) 3,500, (1966) 3,100; raisins (1967) *c.* 270, (1966) 250; figs (1967) 232, (1966) 215; sugar, raw value (1968–69) *c.* 706, (1967–68) 791; olive oil 159 (80); tobacco 161 (182); cotton, lint *c.* 407 (396); meat (1967) 194, (1966) 190. Livestock (in 000; Dec. 1967): cattle 14,165; sheep 35,878; horses 1,183; mules 259; asses 1,965; buffaloes 1,248; goats 20,659; camels 43; chickens (Oct. 1966) 30,387.

Industry. Fuel and power (in 000; metric tons; 1968): crude oil 3,103; coal (1967) 5,031; lignite (1967) 3,416; electricity (kw-hr.) 6,890,000. Production (in 000; metric tons; 1968): iron ore (55–60% metal content) 1,902; pig iron 910; crude steel 1,109; copper (1967) 8; sulfur (1967) 85; sulfuric acid (1967) 28; cement 4,-893; superphosphates (1967) 205; manganese ore (metal content; 1967) 15; chrome ore (oxide content; 1967) 244; cotton yarn (1967) 127; woven cotton fabrics (m.; 1967) 710,000; wool yarn (1967) 24.

Uganda

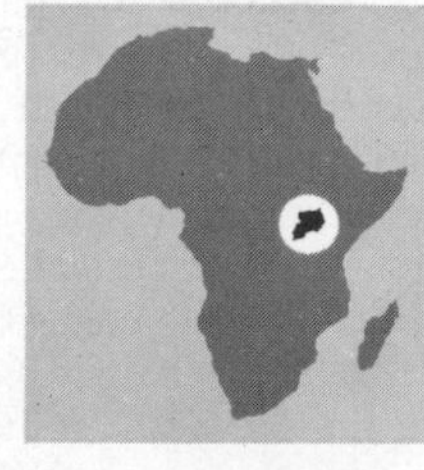

A federal parliamentary state and a member of the Commonwealth of Nations, Uganda is bounded by the Sudan, the Congo (Kinshasa), Rwanda, Tanzania, and Kenya. Area: 91,076 sq.mi. (235,886 sq.km.), including 16,364 sq.mi. of inland water. Pop. (1968 est.): 8,133,000, about 99% of whom are African. Cap. and largest city: Kampala (pop., 1965 est., 76,597). Language: Bantu, Nilotic, Nilo-Hamitic, and Sudanic. Religion: pagan, with Hindu, Muslim, and Christian minorities. President and prime minister in 1969, Apollo Milton Obote.

A year of political unrest culminated in December 1969 when President Obote was wounded by a would-be assassin. A number of important opponents and critics of the regime were detained under emergency regulations during the year. In January Princess Victoria, sister of the deposed kabaka of Buganda (who died on November 17; *see* OBITUARIES), was arrested. A few days later Rajat Neogy, a magazine editor, and Abu Mayanja, a member of Parliament, both of whom had been detained in October 1968, were tried on charges of sedition. The two were acquitted but were immediately reimprisoned under emergency regulations. Neogy was released on March 27, but Mayanja remained in detention uncharged. In September Benedicto Kiwanuka, Uganda's first prime minister and later the leader of the opposition, was also arrested on charges of sedition and criminal libel against President Obote. Meanwhile, the state of emergency in Buganda was twice extended for periods of six months from April and October. Challenged by the opposition Democratic Party to justify the October extension, the minister of internal affairs merely claimed that he was acting on police advice, a reply which led to allegations that the emergency regulations were being used as a political tool.

MARION KAPLAN

Pres. Milton Obote's government faced political unrest throughout most of 1969, and he narrowly escaped death by assassination in December.

Toward manifestations of student power President Obote adopted a firm line. He urged students to advance the African revolution and emphasized the need for schools and universities to produce men and women dedicated to the cause of African development, but he made it clear that student power did not mean the destruction of property.

In October Obote announced his Charter for the Common Man, which outlined Uganda's future development along socialist lines. The charter aimed at bridging the gap between rich and poor in order to avoid future conflict and to help in the development of the country's resources. It also laid down as a guiding economic principle that the means of production must be in the hands of the people as a whole. Cooperative banks were to be established, while all foreign and local investment was to be controlled and channeled into priority schemes. In keeping with this program Parliament passed a banking act on October 13 which required all foreign banks to become incorporated in Uganda and to have a minimum cash investment of $2,760,000 in such assets as the government might approve.

The assassination attempt against President Obote occurred on December 19, as he was leaving the annual meeting of the Uganda People's Congress in Kampala. Wounded in the face, he was taken immediately to Mulago Hospital, where it was later reported that his injuries were not serious. An armed man was arrested at the scene, but his identity was not immediately revealed. Vice-Pres. John K. Babiiha declared a state of emergency and the opposition Democratic Party was banned.

After the president had stated in January that the 40,000 Asians in Uganda who held British passports would have to leave, the Asian community was given some reassurance when the government announced on January 20 that Asians would only be replaced as qualified Ugandans became available, and that this would take at least five years. (K. I.)

ENCYCLOPÆDIA BRITANNICA FILMS. *East Africa (Kenya, Tanganyika, Uganda)* (1962).

UGANDA

Education. (1966) Primary, pupils 564,190, teachers 17,821; secondary, pupils 90,904, teachers 1,101; vocational, pupils 3,128, teachers 282; teacher training, students 4,097, teachers 281; higher (at the Makerere University College of the University of East Africa; 1965), students 1,240.

Finance. Monetary unit: Uganda shilling, with a par value of UShs. 7.14 to U.S. $1 (UShs. 17.14 = £1 sterling). Budget (1969–70 est.): revenue UShs. 1,026,000,000; expenditure UShs. 990 million. Gross domestic product: (1967) UShs. 4,958,000,000; (1966) UShs. 4,664,000,000. Cost of living (Kampala; 1963 = 100): (Feb. 1969) 130; (Feb. 1968) 116.

Foreign Trade. (Excluding trade with Kenya and Tanzania; 1968) Imports UShs. 876 million; exports UShs. 1,327,000,000. Import sources: U.K. 33%; West Germany 11%; Japan 11%; Italy 5%. Export destinations: U.S. 25%; U.K. 23%; Japan 12%; India 5%. Main exports: coffee 54%; cotton 22%; copper 8%; tea 6%.

Transport and Communications. Roads (1967) 24,173 (including 2,938 km. main roads). Motor vehicles in use (1967): passenger 29,163; commercial 8,829. Railways (1967) 850 km. (for traffic *see* KENYA). Telephones (Jan. 1968) 23,368. Radio receivers (Dec. 1965) 200,000. Television receivers (Dec. 1967) 7,500.

Agriculture. Production (in 000; metric tons; 1967; 1966 in parentheses): millet *c.* 400 (*c.* 430); sorghum *c.* 270 (271); sweet potatoes (1966) 2,644, (1965) *c.* 1,600; cassava (1966) *c.* 2,000, (1965) *c.* 1,480; peanuts *c.* 200 (217); dry beans (1966) 261, (1965) *c.* 160; cotton, lint (1968) *c.* 67, (1967) 73; coffee (1966) 170, (1965) 220; tea 11 (11); sugar, raw value (1968–69) *c.* 161, (1967–68) *c.* 152; sesame *c.* 20 (17); timber (cu.m.; 1966–67) *c.* 10,900, (1965–66) *c.* 10,800; fish catch 88 (83). Livestock (in 000; Dec. 1967): cattle 3,971; sheep (Jan. 1967) 784; goats (Jan. 1967) 1,900; pigs 43; chickens (1966–67) *c.* 10,300.

Industry. Production (in 000; metric tons; 1968): cement 155; copper, smelter 16; tin concentrates (metal content) 0.17; beryl (1967) 0.31; salt (1967) 5; phosphate rock (1967) 15; electricity (kw-hr.) 732,000.

Turks and Caicos Islands: *see* Dependent States

Unemployment: *see* Employment, Wages, and Hours; Social Services

UNESCO: *see* United Nations

Union of Soviet Socialist Republics

The Union of Soviet Socialist Republics is a federal state covering parts of eastern Europe and northern and central Asia. Area: 8,649,489 sq.mi. (22,402,-200 sq.km.). Pop. (1969 est.): 237,808,000, including Russians 55%; Ukrainians 18%; Belorussians 4%; Uzbeks 3%; Tatars 2%. Cap. and largest city: Moscow (pop., 1967 est., 6,507,000). Language: officially Russian, but many others are spoken. Religion: about 40 religions are represented in the U.S.S.R., the major ones being Christian denominations. General secretary of the Communist Party of the Soviet Union in 1969, Leonid I. Brezhnev; chairman of the Presidium of the Supreme Soviet (president), Nikolai V. Podgorny; chairman of the Council of Ministers (premier), Aleksei N. Kosygin.

Domestic Affairs. The resistance to change, the chief characteristic of Soviet politics since the removal from office of Nikita S. Khrushchev in 1964, continued to dominate both the foreign and internal policy of the Soviet Union throughout 1969. As in the past few years, any real criticism of the Soviet system was stifled, and official insistence on ideological conformity remained almost absolute. The case that attracted the most attention abroad involved the writer Aleksandr I. Solzhenitsyn, who had been criticized in 1968 not only for allegedly distorting reality by his descriptions of Soviet life and attitudes but also for playing into the hands of the U.S.S.R.'s enemies by allowing his works to be published abroad. In November 1969 Solzhenitsyn was expelled from the National Soviet Writers' Union and thus deprived of his professional status and of any opportunity to earn his living as a writer in the Soviet Union. He responded by circulating an open letter in which he attacked Soviet society as "sick." Solzhenitsyn's case aroused much indignation among intellectuals both within and outside the U.S.S.R.; the last word seemed to belong to Ekaterina Furtseva, the Soviet minister of culture, who, speaking in Paris in December, rejected appeals from abroad on Solzhenitsyn's behalf.

This affair perhaps received more than its fair share of publicity because of Solzhenitsyn's worldwide reputation as a writer. In the long term, the systematic use of the Soviet judicial machinery to grind down dissent was more typical of a social and political system dedicated to the maintenance of the status quo. This process culminated at the end of the year when on December 23 a Moscow court imposed a five-year term of exile on an economist, Viktor Krasin, a leading member of a small group of Moscow intellectuals who had been campaigning for civil rights in the U.S.S.R. In June Krasin had been among the signatories of a petition addressed to the United Nations Commission on Human Rights, which was signed by approximately 50 Soviet citizens and which asked for a UN investigation into "the repression of basic civil rights in the Soviet Union." The signatories of the petition included the wife and son of former Maj. Gen. Pyotr G. Grigorenko, who had become involved with the agitation for the return of the Crimean Tatars to their homeland, from which they had been expelled by Joseph Stalin during World War II. Grigorenko was arrested in May, and certified as insane in November. Some of the leaders of the Crimean Tatars were tried in Simferopol and sentenced to long terms of imprisonment in April.

Open dissent was expressed much more discreetly in statements by more established figures, such as the physicist Pyotr L. Kapitsa (who in February called for more discussion with intellectuals in the West) and in the attitudes of a few well-known writers, such as Aleksandr T. Tvardovsky.

The official reaction, apart from arrests and trials, was to insist that "Peaceful coexistence does not extend to the struggle of ideologies" (Brezhnev on June 7) and that therefore all dissent must be opposed as giving comfort to the ideological enemy.

While dissent and criticism must inevitably worry the authorities, they were in fact no more than marginal problems. The critics were a small minority even within the intellectual elite, and in relation to the country as a whole they were a very faint voice indeed. This did not make their dissent less honourable or less valid, but their relative isolation did illustrate the degree to which Soviet society seemed to be content with the status quo. A particularly dramatic incident that seemed to indicate discontent occurred in Moscow on January 23 when shots were fired by a man later described as a "schizophrenic" at the triumphal motorcade carrying the Soyuz 4 and Soyuz 5 cosmonauts to their official welcome in the Kremlin; this incident, however, seemed to have had little or no political significance.

The Soviet leaders were able to point to some successes in space exploration during the year. Although none of them had the dramatic impact of the U.S. manned landings on the moon, they represented a solid contribution to space technology and to the scientific exploration of outer space. In January, Soyuz 4 and Soyuz 5 completed a successful docking operation between two manned space vehicles. In May, two unmanned spacecraft, Venera 5 and Venera 6, began relaying information from within the atmosphere of the planet Venus. Closer to the earth, the Soviets registered another success when the Tupolev Tu-44 supersonic passenger airliner made its maiden flight at the end of 1968.

There was little change in the country's economic policies. Officially, there was considerable satisfaction with the economic progress achieved in the first four years of the current five-year plan (1966–1970). At a meeting of the Supreme Soviet, December 16–19, Nikolai K. Baibakov, the chairman of the

"I've got a good mind to send an unmanned rocket to Mao as well!" —Garland, "Daily Telegraph," London.

BEN ROTH AGENCY

CAMERA PRESS—PIX FROM PUBLIX

Soviet athletes march through Moscow's Red Square during the 1969 May Day celebrations. Instead of the usual display of tanks, soldiers, and intercontinental ballistic missiles, the celebration parade consisted of civilians, gymnasts and athletes, and a display of Soviet space achievements.

State Planning Committee, announced that the rise in real wages during the period 1966 to 1969 had exceeded the original planned target and that during 1970 the average pay of workers would be increased by 3% and that of collective farmers by 4.6%. He pointed out that consumption patterns in the U.S.S.R. were changing, and he quoted as an example the fact that the consumption of bread and potatoes decreased considerably in 1969, as the consumption of less starchy foods increased. On the other hand, Baibakov admitted that the demand for certain durable consumer goods, mainly furniture, refrigerators, and motorcars, had not been fully met, and he expected that the demand for such goods would continue to exceed the supply in 1970.

It also emerged from the discussions of the Supreme Soviet that many areas of the nation were suffering from a manpower shortage and that the rate of technological progress in industry remained unsatisfactory. In particular, it was stressed that for the U.S.S.R. as a whole the rise in labour productivity was not proceeding fast enough. Bad weather conditions in 1969 had an adverse effect on agriculture, and food production targets for the year were not reached. Total grain production in 1969 amounted to 160.5 million tons, compared with more than 171 million tons in 1968.

At the beginning of 1969 the new system of improved decentralized planning and the use of economic incentives to stimulate labour productivity were being applied to more than 25,000 enterprises, which represented roughly half the total volume of the nation's industrial output. By the end of the year nearly 75% of all industrial enterprises were working under the new system, and they accounted for more than 83% of profits in industry.

An internal issue of some significance during the year involved the central Asian Soviet republic of Tadzhikistan, a region bordering on Pakistan and China and far from Moscow. The U.S.S.R.'s Communist Party leaders in January charged the republic with corruption, agricultural failures, and toleration of such Muslim customs as child marriage. The officials in Tadzhikistan were given one year to make the necessary improvements. The apparent reason for Moscow's interest in the area was that it was soon to become the site of several large industrial projects.

Foreign Relations. Preoccupation with the status quo was also the dominant theme of Soviet foreign policy throughout 1969, with certain limited local exceptions. At the end of the year, a new approach to relations with West Germany appeared to herald new possibilities in central Europe, but this was due primarily to initiatives pursued by the new government in West Germany in its desire to explore fresh options in relation to Eastern Europe in general and East Germany in particular. The Soviet reaction was extremely cautious: West German Chancellor Willy Brandt's government was welcomed as an improvement over its predecessor, and Moscow did not reject its overtures for talks. On the other hand, the solution of the German problem was still seen in Moscow in the light of the Soviet Union's special relationship with East Germany, which formed an integral part of the Soviet system in central Europe.

The Soviet Union's attitude toward West Germany emerged without ambiguity during the Berlin crisis in February, which arose from the West German decision to hold its presidential election in West Berlin on March 5, following a precedent set in 1954. On February 9, the East Germans announced their intention to prevent travel by road to West Berlin of members of West Germany's Electoral Assembly, and in this they were backed by the Soviet government. In a note addressed to West Germany, the Soviet foreign minister insisted that West Berlin was not a part of the Federal Republic, but, on the contrary, was situated "within the territory of the other sovereign German state"; the U.S.S.R. concluded that the "West German president could not be elected on foreign territory." However, as access by air to West Berlin was not affected by the East German measures, the presidential election was carried out without difficulty. The crisis merely served as yet another opportunity for the Soviet Union to state its views on the partition of Germany. In July, Soviet Foreign Minister Andrei A. Gromyko restated his government's foreign policy in the following terms: "We shall not agree to any steps harming the legitimate interests of the German Democratic Republic [East Germany] and affecting the special status of West Berlin." By the end of the year, nothing had happened to indicate that the Soviet government might be prepared to abandon this position.

Soviet policy in the aftermath of the 1968 Czechoslovak crisis was in line with this unyielding determination to prevent change. The emphasis was on "normalization," and Alexander Dubcek's successors found it impossible to extract any worthwhile concessions from Moscow. In February, the Soviet Union made an effort to mend some of its fences in Eastern Europe, where after the subjection of Czechoslovakia, Romania seemed to stand out as the last remaining potential dissident within the Warsaw Pact.

At the Warsaw Pact summit meeting in Budapest in March, an attempt was made to meet some of

Soviet crowds demonstrate at the Chinese embassy in Moscow on March 7, 1969, against the reported brutality of Chinese troops during a border clash with Soviets. Many carried banners calling for the destruction of Mao Tse-tung.

"LONDON DAILY EXPRESS" FROM PICTORIAL PARADE

U.S.S.R.

Education. (1966–67) Primary, pupils 39,058,000, teachers (1965–66) 1,449,000; secondary, pupils 4,186,000, teachers (1965–66) 251,000; vocational (including teacher training), pupils 3,993,800, teachers (1965–66) 251,000; higher (including 45 universities), students 4,123,200, teaching staff (1965–66) 201,000.

Finance. Monetary unit: ruble, with an exchange rate of 0.90 rubles to U.S. $1 (2.16 rubles = £1 sterling). Budget (1969 est.): revenue 134,098,000,000 rubles; expenditure 133,898,000,000 rubles.

Foreign Trade. (1967) Imports 7,683,000,000 rubles; exports 8,684,000,000 rubles. Import sources: Sino-Soviet area 67% (East Germany 17%, Czechoslovakia 12%, Poland 11%, Bulgaria 9%, Hungary 7%, Romania 5%). Export destinations: Sino-Soviet area 63% (East Germany 15%, Czechoslovakia 10%, Poland 9%, Bulgaria 8%, Hungary 6%, Cuba 6%). Main exports: machinery 21%; crude oil 7%; iron and steel 6%; timber 5%; petroleum products 5%.

Transport and Communications. Roads (1965) 1,363,500 km. (including 379,000 km. surfaced). Motor vehicles in use (1965): passenger *c.* 1.1 million; commercial *c.* 4.5 million. Railways (1967): 133,300 km. (including 29,100 km. electrified); traffic 234,429,000,000 passenger-km., freight 2,160,528,000,000 net ton-km. Air traffic (1967): 53,500,000,000 passenger-km.; freight 1,662,000,000 net ton-km. Navigable inland waterways (1965) 142,700 km.; traffic (1967) 143,700,000,000 ton-km. Shipping (1968): merchant vessels 100 gross tons and over 4,206; gross tonnage 12,061,833. Telephones (Dec. 1967) 9,680,000. Radio receivers (Dec. 1967) *c.* 80.7 million. Television receivers (Dec. 1967) 22.7 million.

Agriculture. Production (in 000; metric tons; 1968; 1967 in parentheses): wheat 96,200 (77,419); barley 26,100 (24,662); oats (1967) 11,581, (1966) 9,199; rye *c.* 13,000 (12,986); corn 8,800 (9,163); rice 1,047 (895); millet 3,000 (3,218); potatoes 101,600 (95,464); sugar, raw value (1968–69) *c.* 9,709, (1967–68) *c.* 10,433; cotton, lint (1967) 2,052, (1966) 2,056; flax fibre (1967) 484, (1966) 461; tobacco 245 (260); sunflower seed 6,640 (6,608); dry peas (1967) 4,122, (1966) 4,738; soybeans *c.* 610 (543); tea (1967) 55, (1966) 55; wine (1967) 1,800, (1966) 1,586; wool, greasy (1967) 395, (1966) 371; eggs (1967) *c.* 1,860, (1966) *c.* 1,740; meat (1967) 8,510, (1966) 7,866; milk 82,100 (79,800); butter 1,190 (1,177); cheese 460 (444); timber (cu.m.; 1967) *c.* 383,100, (1966) *c.* 373,400; fish catch (1967) 5,777, (1966) 5,349. Livestock (in 000; Jan. 1968): cattle 97,167; pigs 50,867; sheep (Jan. 1967) 135,483; goats (Jan. 1967) 5,559; horses 8,025; poultry (Jan. 1967) 516,156.

Industry. Index of industrial production (1963 = 100): (1968) 151; (1967) 139. Fuel and power (in 000; metric tons; 1968): coal and lignite 594,000; crude oil 308,000; natural gas (cu.m.) 171,000,000; electricity (kw-hr.) 638,000,000. Production (in 000; metric tons; 1968): iron ore (60% metal content) 176,000; pig iron 78,777; steel 106,495; aluminum (1967) *c.* 965; copper (1967) *c.* 960; zinc (1967) *c.* 600; lead (1967) *c.* 400; gold (troy oz.; 1967) *c.* 5,700; silver (troy oz.; 1967) *c.* 35,000; manganese ore (metal content; 1967) *c.* 3,240; tungsten concentrates (oxide content; 1967) *c.* 7.8; magnesite (1967) *c.* 3,000; superphosphates (1967) 14,760; nitrogenous fertilizers (1967) 3,753; sulfuric acid 10,266; cement 87,502; newsprint (1967) 966; other paper (1967) 2,835; passenger cars (units) 281; commercial vehicles (units; 1967) 697; cotton fabrics (sq.m.) 6,112,000; woolen fabrics (sq.m.) 584,000; rayon and synthetic fabrics (sq.m.) 950,000.

Romania's objections to the Pact's system of command and control. Agreement was reached concerning new regulations on combined armed forces and joint commands, and a Defense Ministers' Committee was established to increase the weaker nations' participation in strategic decision-making. However, the Romanians did not prove entirely amenable to Soviet pressure: they refused to be part of a joint condemnation of China, and they opposed the East German proposals for closer integration of national military contingents. The U.S.S.R. did, however, get unanimous support from its Warsaw Pact allies for the proposal for a European security conference that would be based upon recognition of the position of the two German states and of the existing frontiers in Europe; *i.e.*, the status quo.

Both the U.S. and the Soviet Union seemed content during the year to continue their mutual respect for the other's position and to cooperate in seeking areas of mutual agreement. In his July review of the international scene before the Supreme Soviet (parliament), Gromyko said: "We want relations with the United States to be friendly," and nothing that happened in 1969 gave cause to doubt the sincerity of this statement. Early in the year, on January 20, a press statement issued by the Soviet Foreign Ministry affirmed the Soviet government's desire to begin talks with the U.S. on the limitation of strategic nuclear weapons "as soon as the Nixon administration declares its readiness to do so." The question of strategic arms limitation was among the most important common interests of both the U.S.S.R. and the U.S., stemming not only from their declared policy of minimizing the risks of nuclear war but also from their need to limit their growing burden of expenditure on arms. Preliminary talks on such limitations began in Helsinki, Fin., on November 17. U.S.-Soviet talks on the peaceful uses of nuclear explosions took place in Vienna in April, the first time that the U.S.S.R. had agreed to exchange information on this subject.

The Soviet Union's resolve to preserve the status quo in Europe had to be viewed in relation to its problems in the Far East, where during 1969 the military tension with China reached new heights. The long series of minor border incidents involving Soviet and Chinese troops along the Amur and Ussuri rivers blew up into a major military engagement in March over the possession of Damansky (Chenpao) Island in the Ussuri River. About 3,000 troops were committed on each side, and each suffered some fatal casualties. Immediately after the clashes, the Soviet news agency Tass announced that large contingents of young civilian volunteers were leaving the European part of the U.S.S.R. for "constructive work" in the Far East. Perhaps even more alarming to China were the economic negotiations under way between Japan and the Soviet Union about the development of Siberia. A Soviet-Japanese air agreement, allowing Japan Air Lines to operate an independent trans-Siberian service, was concluded in February. More significantly, the Damansky Island incident was followed within days by reports of ambitious schemes for Japanese participation in the development of Siberia.

The military buildup on the Soviet and Mongolian frontiers with China continued throughout the year, and the Damansky incident was by no means the last. At the beginning of July, there was another clash on Goldinsky Island, and in August, for the first time in many months, there were reports of serious trouble on the Sinkiang border.

Apart from the obvious military measures, the Soviet Union undertook serious diplomatic steps to cope with the situation. The attempt to use the international Communist movement to isolate China culminated in the long-deferred conference of the world's Communist parties, which opened in Moscow on June 5. It was hampered by the absence of 5 of the 14 parties that controlled their nations. Many delegations had misgivings about criticizing China, and 14 parties out of the 73 attending refused to sign the final document. The Soviets did succeed in getting a qualified endorsement for their policies from at least some of the other Communist parties, but this had little or no practical effect on China. In his speech to the conference, Brezhnev flew a new diplomatic kite in the form of a proposal for a collective security system in Asia. This was interpreted by some commentators as an attempt to maintain the status quo in Asia while the Soviet quarrel with China remained unsolved.

A more fruitful diplomatic approach to the Far Eastern problem developed from Premier Kosygin's

Unions:
see Labour Unions
Unitarians:
see Religion

CAMERA PRESS FROM PICTORIAL PARADE

Army recruits of the U.A.R. learn the techniques of tank operation from a Soviet diagram. During 1969 the Army continued to receive tanks and other military equipment from the U.S.S.R.

stopover in Peking on his way back from Ho Chi Minh's funeral in North Vietnam on September 11. At that time, Kosygin met China's premier, Chou En-lai. Their talks, described as "useful to both sides," were followed in October by the arrival in Peking of a Soviet delegation, led by Deputy Foreign Minister Vasily V. Kuznetsov, to begin talks on the border issue with China.

Another area where the Soviet Union had to cope with a fluid situation was the Middle East. The Soviet government tried to assure the Arab states of its support, while trying to restrain them from taking major military action. High-level visits proliferated during the year: Podgorny visited Algeria and Morocco in March; Gromyko went to Cairo in June; and in July, the president of Syria traveled to Moscow. The Soviet Union, however, was active in trying to promote agreement among the great powers to secure a settlement in the Middle East, conducted mainly by means of negotiations with U.S., British, and French representatives at the UN.

Finally, in Vietnam, the U.S.S.R. continued to give diplomatic support to North Vietnam and to the Viet Cong. Its attitude concerning the issue of war and peace there was best summarized by Gromyko in a foreign policy statement on July 10: "The Soviet Union would like to believe that a sober consideration of all aspects of the situation and possible consequences of the policy and actions of the United States will make the American Government end its war of aggression in Vietnam. This is a sure way to the success of the talks now being held by the sides concerned, and the Soviet Union is looking forward to this success." (OT. P.)

See also **Communist Movement; Propaganda.**

ENCYCLOPÆDIA BRITANNICA FILMS. *The Soviet Challenge (The Industrial Revolution in Russia)* (1962).

United Arab Republic

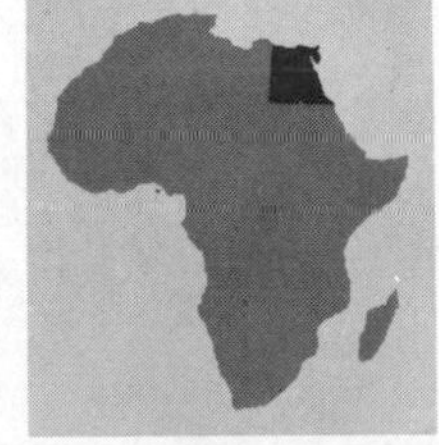

A republic of northeast Africa, the United Arab Republic (U.A.R.) is bounded by Israel, Sudan, Libya, the Mediterranean Sea, and the Red Sea. Area: 385,237 sq.mi. (997,765 sq.km.). Pop. (1969): 32,501,000. Cap. and largest city: Cairo (pop., 1969 est., 4,769,000). Language: Arabic 97%. Religion: Muslim 91%; Christian 8%. President and prime minister in 1969, Gamal Abd-al-Nasser.

The continued lack of progress toward a settlement with Israel cast a dark shadow over the U.A.R.'s future in 1969. At the beginning of the year the country was still feeling the effects of student violence in Cairo and Alexandria the previous November. The government announced in January that those arrested in connection with the riots would be released for disciplining by their universities, and after two months of being closed, all U.A.R. universities were allowed to reopen.

On January 8 elections were held for the National Assembly, which had been dissolved by presidential decree in November 1968. In the first round 319 candidates backed by the Arab Socialist Union (ASU) and 11 independents were elected. Runoff elections had to be held for 20 seats.

The minister of local administration declared a state of emergency on February 25 on the ground that the U.A.R. did not want the Israeli raid on Beirut, Lebanon, to be repeated against Cairo airport. Compulsory military training was introduced for all students.

Incidents with Israel continued throughout the year, varying only in intensity from week to week. On March 9 the U.A.R. chief of staff, Gen. Muhammad Abdel Moneim Riad (*see* OBITUARIES), was killed in an artillery clash on the Suez Canal; he was replaced by Gen. Ahmed Ismail Ali (who was replaced by Maj. Gen. Muhammad Sadek in September). According to U.S. military sources, the U.A.R. had 700 tanks, 800 heavy mortars, and 50,000 to 70,000 troops in the Canal area. In October large forces of U.A.R. com-

UNITED ARAB REPUBLIC

Education. (1966–67) Primary, pupils 3,414,232, teachers (1965–66) 87,390; secondary, pupils 900,379, teachers (1965–66) 34,819; vocational, pupils 136,486, teachers (1965–66) 9,975; teacher training, students 42,549, teachers (1965–66) 4,531; higher (including 5 universities), students (1965–66) 177,123, teaching staff (1964–65) 10,406.

Finance. Monetary unit: Egyptian pound, with a nominal par value of E£0.35 to U.S. $1 (E£0.84 = £1 sterling) and an effective exchange rate of E£0.43 to U.S. $1 (E£1.04 = £1 sterling). Gold and foreign exchange, central bank: (June 1969) U.S. $191 million; (June 1968) U.S. $175 million. Budget (1967–68 rev. est.): revenue E£1,363 million; expenditure E£1,158.1 million. Money supply: (June 1969) E£687.2 million; (June 1968) E£649.8 million. Cost of living (Cairo; 1963 = 100): (Jan. 1969) 137; (Jan. 1968) 130.

Foreign Trade. (1968) Imports E£300.9 million; exports E£270.3 million; Suez Canal dues, receipts (1966) E£95.3 million. Import sources: U.S.S.R. 16%; France 11%; West Germany 7%; Romania 6%; U.S. 6%; Italy 5%; East Germany 5%. Export destinations: U.S.S.R. 28%; India 8%; Czechoslovakia 5%. Main exports: cotton 61%; cereals 17%.

Transport and Communications. Roads (1964) *c.* 47,700 km. (including 17,058 km. with improved surface). Motor vehicles in use (1967): passenger 108,000; commercial (including buses) 27,100. Railways: (1965) 4,508 km.; traffic (1966–67) 6,268,000,000 passenger-km., freight 3,068,000,000 net ton-km. Air traffic (1968): 620.5 million passenger-km.; freight 8,138,000 net ton-km. Shipping (1968): merchant vessels 100 gross tons and over 122; gross tonnage 250,075. Telephones (Dec. 1967) 352,316. Radio receivers (Dec. 1965) 1,613,000. Television receivers (Dec. 1967) 399,000.

Agriculture. Production (in 000; metric tons; 1968; 1967 in parentheses): corn 2,297 (2,169); wheat 1,518 (1,293); barley *c.* 105 (100); sorghum 906 (881); potatoes 472 (278); sweet potatoes (1967) 68, (1966) 83; rice 2,586 (2,316); sugar, raw value (1968–69) *c.* 445, (1967–68) *c.* 383; tomatoes (1967) 1,230, (1966) 1,366; dry broad beans (1967) 189, (1966) 381; lentils (1967) 34, (1966) 44; cotton, lint *c.* 421 (437); dates (1967) 319, (1966) 317; oranges 495 (617); lemons 99 (88); bananas (1967) 66, (1966) 85; grapes (1967) 120, (1966) 118; onions (1967) 560, (1966) 724; cheese 264 (262); fish catch (1965) 94, (1964) 115. Livestock (in 000; 1966–67): horses 59; mules 11; asses 1,185; sheep 2,044; cattle 1,651; goats 794; buffaloes 1,675; camels 177; chickens 23,624.

Industry. Production (in 000; metric tons; 1968): crude oil 8,995; iron ore (metal content; 1967) 211; cement 3,253; phosphate rock (1967) 683; manganese ore (metal content; 1966) 47; salt (1967) 584; asbestos (1966) 1.9; cotton yarn 157; cotton fabrics (m.) 695,000; electricity (kw-hr.; 1966) 5,895,000.

"PARIS MATCH" FROM PICTORIAL PARADE

Flag-covered casket of Gen. Abdel Riad, U.A.R. Army chief of staff, is escorted by 250,000 persons during funeral procession in Cairo, March 10, 1969. Riad was killed by Israeli shelling on banks of Suez Canal.

mandos crossed the canal on several occasions, and in November they made two raids for the first time in daylight. On November 9 U.A.R. destroyers bombarded Israeli positions 12 mi. E of Port Said.

In July the Israelis launched a commando attack on a fortified island near the southern end of the Suez Canal, and in August they mortared U.A.R. Army headquarters at Mankabad in Upper Egypt. A strong Israeli force with tanks landed at Al Khafayer 25 mi. S of Suez on September 9 and drove 30 mi. S to Ras Zafarana before withdrawing several hours later. The Israeli Air Force flew hundreds of sorties against U.A.R. positions and claimed to have destroyed all missile sites in the Canal area.

As the year proceeded, the U.A.R. government became increasingly gloomy about the prospects for peace. On May 1 President Nasser said that Israel would have to be uprooted but warned against moves to push the U.A.R. precipitately into war. On July 23 he said that the best strategy was for the Arabs to conduct a war of attrition against Israel. He told the National Assembly on November 6 that the Arabs had no alternative but to liberate the occupied lands "over a sea of blood with horizons of fire." He said the U.A.R. then had 500,000 men under arms. The U.S.S.R. showed concern with President Nasser's renewed militancy, although there was doubt that he had irrevocably abandoned hope of a peaceful settlement. In September the U.A.R. foreign minister, Mahmoud Riad, said that if Israel withdrew to its 1948 frontiers the U.A.R. would recognize it.

Relations with the U.S. went from bad to worse. On July 9 Cairo accorded full diplomatic recognition to East Germany. In October the U.A.R. issued a strong protest about the alleged employment of hundreds of U.S. citizens in the Israeli armed forces, and in his November 6 speech President Nasser described the U.S. as an enemy of the Arab peoples. U.A.R. spokesmen described the latest U.S. proposals for a solution in the Middle East as worse than its previous proposals, alleging that they aimed to detach the U.A.R. from the other Arabs by encouraging it to sign a separate peace with Israel.

On September 18 President Nasser's visit to Moscow, planned for September 23, was canceled for health reasons. Although it was widely believed to be a "diplomatic illness," Nasser reported that he had severe influenza and he did not resume work for a month. In November he sent a high-powered delegation to Moscow for talks. In September Nasser had replaced Ali Sabry with Sharawi Gomaa in the key post of secretary of the ASU. The official reason was a customs violation by one of Ali Sabry's staff, but the change was widely interpreted as a move against the left in reaction against excessive Soviet influence. There were, however, no clear indications of any serious breach between Cairo and Moscow.

Nasser succeeded in his long-standing attempt to secure an Arab summit, against Saudi opposition, but the meeting, held in Rabat, Mor., in December, ended in dissension, largely over the size of Saudi and Kuwaiti financial support for the Arab cause. U.A.R. dependence on Saudi economic aid had been reduced by the offer of the new Libyan regime to increase its aid to the U.A.R. substantially. Nasser also welcomed Libyan and Sudanese support against the extreme line adopted by the Syrian Baathists in the dispute between Lebanon and the Palestinian guerrillas. He played a leading role in the subsequent agreement between the Lebanese Army and the Palestinians.

The loss of Suez Canal revenues continued to be compensated by aid from Kuwait, Saudi Arabia, and Libya totaling about $215 million a year. The 1969–70 budget presented in July totaled approximately $5,520,000,000—a 15% increase over the previous year. Of this, $1.2 billion was earmarked for defense and $790 million for new investment. In May the U.A.R. signed an agreement with the World Food Program for $45 million in aid for land resettlement and reclamation. While the cotton and rice harvests were satisfactory, the most hopeful development in the economy was in the oil industry. Total output, which had more than recovered from the loss of the Sinai oil fields, passed 300,000 bbl. a day by the middle of 1969 and was on schedule for the targets of 400,000 bbl. a day by the end of the year and 500,000 bbl. a day by the end of 1970. The main increase was in the Morgan field in the Red Sea, but prospects were also good in the Western Desert where preliminary surveys by U.A.R. and Soviet experts indicated that the rich Libyan oil fields might extend into U.A.R. territory. In September the U.S. independent Pan American Petroleum Co. extended its operations in the U.A.R. with an agreement for exploration in the Western Desert.

In July the U.A.R. contract for construction of a 42-in., 200-mi. Suez–Alexandria crude-oil pipeline was awarded to a consortium of French, Italian, and Spanish companies headed by the French firm, Socea.

(P. MD.)

See also Middle East.

ENCYCLOPÆDIA BRITANNICA FILMS. *Egypt and the Nile* (1954); *The Middle East* (1955); *The Suez Canal* (1962); *The Nile Valley and Its People* (1964).

United Church of Canada: *see* Religion

United Church of Christ: *see* Religion

United Kingdom

A constitutional monarchy in northwestern Europe, the United Kingdom comprises the island of Great Britain (England, Scotland, and Wales) and Northern Ireland, together with many small islands. Area: 94,222 sq. mi. (244,034 sq.km.), excluding 1,160 sq.mi. of inland water, the crown possession of the Isle of Man, and the crown dependencies of the Channel Islands. Pop. (1968 est.): 55,282,500. Cap. and largest city: London (pop. [Greater London], 1968 est., 7,763,-820). Language: English is spoken almost universally, but some Welsh and Gaelic are also used. Religion: mainly Protestant. Queen, Elizabeth II; prime minister in 1969, Harold Wilson.

Domestic Politics. In 1969, as throughout the decade, the by now obsessional concentration on the economic fever chart was Britain's primary domestic concern. To correct the balance of payments remained the central issue on which British policy turned; it determined the diminishing scale of overseas commitments and put the brake on economic growth, hence postponing much development and expansion at home. In his budget speech on April 15, the chancellor of the exchequer, Roy Jenkins, said that economic growth in 1968 had been 4% in real terms. New budget measures were intended to curb consumer spending further and to promote export-oriented industries. Increases were announced in the selective employment tax, corporation tax, and purchase tax, and in betting and gaming duties. Personal savings were to be encouraged by a "save as you earn" scheme for payroll deductions of up to £10 per month. Restraint on incomes and on personal borrowing from banks remained essential.

While the stringent economic policy at last showed signs of reward in better trade figures, the Labour Party continued to bear the brunt of public discontent. The assumption that there would be a general election in 1970 sharpened the party conflict. The five-year term of the Labour government extended to April 1971, but in practice British governments rarely held on until the last moment for fear of being forced into an election at an unfavourable time. Opinion polls and by-elections in 1969 were, therefore, followed with growing interest as pointers to the general election. The opinion polls suggested an unusually volatile state of public opinion. There were considerable differences between the leading polls, but they all showed a huge lead for the Conservatives in the early part of the year, going as high as 25% near midsummer, but then falling back abruptly in the autumn. The Gallup poll gave the Conservatives a 23-point lead in July, but this fell to only 2 points by mid-October. This apparent shift provided special interest concerning five by-elections on October 30. Labour retained four of these seats, at Glasgow (Gorbals), Islington North, Newcastle-under-Lyme, and Paddington North, but lost Swindon to the Conservatives. These five contests showed on the average a 10.5% swing to the Conservatives, similar to the trend in 1968 though less damaging to Labour than the results of three by-elections on March 27, which produced adverse swings

KEYSTONE

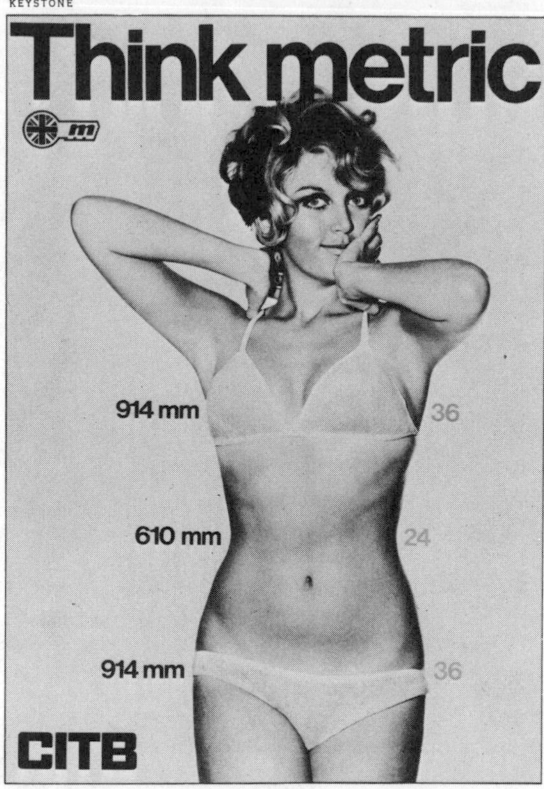

Instructional poster was issued by Construction Industry Training Board to help British public understand the metric system of measurement, to be introduced in the early 1970s.

UNITED KINGDOM

Education. (1965–66) Primary, pupils 5,416,-926; secondary, pupils 3,541,438; primary and secondary, teachers 431,776; vocational, pupils 205,971, teachers 41,042; higher (universities only), students 186,762, teaching staff 22,385.

Finance. Monetary unit: pound sterling, with a par value of £0.42 to U.S. $1 (£1 = $2.40). Gold and convertible currency, official: (June 1969) U.S. $2,443,000,000; (June 1968) U.S. $2,683,000,000. Budget (1969–70 est.): revenue £15,008 million; expenditure £12,551 million. Gross national product: (1968) £42,440 million; (1967) £39,710 million. Money supply: (March 1969) £15,236 million; (March 1968) £14,371 million. Cost of living (1963 = 100): (June 1969) 127; (June 1968) 121.

Foreign Trade. (1968) Imports £7,899 million; exports £6,394 million. Import sources: EEC 20% (West Germany 6%, Netherlands 5%); U.S. 13%; Canada 6%. Export destinations: EEC 20% (West Germany 6%); U.S. 14%; Australia 5%. Main exports: machinery 27%; motor vehicles 11%; chemicals 10%; textile yarns and fabrics 5%; precious stones 5%.

Transport and Communications. Roads (1968) 350,723 km. (including 951 km. expressways). Motor vehicles in use (1968): passenger 11,078,000; commercial 1,606,600. Railways (excluding Northern Ireland; 1967): 21,199 km.; traffic 29,111,000,000 passenger-km., freight (1968) 23,720,000,000 net ton-km. Air traffic (1968): 14,095,000,000 passenger-km.; freight 491,417,000 net ton-km. Shipping (1968): merchant vessels 100 gross tons and over 4,020; gross tonnage 21,920,980. Ships entered (1967) vessels totaling 118,727,000 net registered tons; goods loaded (1967) 35,152,000 metric tons, unloaded 167,548,000 metric tons. Telephones (Dec. 1967) 12,008,000. Radio licenses (Dec. 1968) 18,008,000. Television licenses (Dec. 1968) 15,-506,000.

Agriculture. Production (in 000; metric tons; 1968; 1967 in parentheses): wheat 3,571 (3,-903); barley 8,408 (9,215); oats 1,250 (1,386); potatoes 6,846 (7,201); sugar, raw value (1968–69) *c.* 975, (1967–68) 963; apples (1967) 337, (1966) 374; pears (1967) 27, (1966) 41; dry peas (1967) 65, (1966) 44; dry broad beans (1966) *c.* 80, (1965) *c.* 80; tomatoes 84 (86); onions (1967) 100, (1966) 87; hen eggs 896 (869); beef and veal 906 (921); mutton and lamb 246 (262); pork 835 (801); wool 36 (39); milk 12,478 (13,059); butter *c.* 42 (42); cheese *c.* 120 (122); fish catch (1967) 1,026, (1966) 1,068. Livestock (in 000; June 1968): cattle 12,151; sheep 28,004; pigs 7,387; chickens 121,-753.

Industry. Index of industrial production (1963 = 100): (1968) 117; (1967) 112. Fuel and power (in 000; 1968): coal (metric tons) 166,-100; natural gas (cu.m.) 1,713,000; manufactured gas (cu.m.) 26,732,000; electricity (kw-hr.) 221,444,000. Production (in 000; metric tons; 1968): iron ore (25–30% metal content) 13,930; pig iron 16,690; crude steel 26,280; superphosphates (1967) 142; nitrogenous fertilizers (1967–68) 855; cement 17,880; passenger cars (units) 1,816; commercial vehicles (units) 409; agricultural tractors (units) 179; cotton fabrics (m.) 619,000; woolen fabrics (sq.m.) 246,000; rayon and other synthetic fabrics (m.) 469,000. Merchant vessels launched (1968) 915,-000 gross tons. New dwellings completed (1968) 426,000.

WIDE WORLD

Queen Elizabeth II crowns Charles prince of Wales during the solemn investiture ceremony at Caernarvon Castle on July 1, 1969.

ranging from 14 to 18%. The Conservatives retained Weston-super-Mare and Brighton (Pavilion) with increased majorities and won Walthamstow East from Labour. The Conservative lead was further strengthened in December when the party retained Louth and captured Wellingborough, with swings of 14.3 and 9.7%, respectively.

By-elections, however, were notoriously unreliable guides to general election performance. On past experience, the party of the government in office was likely to improve by 3 or 4 points at a general election. Even with such a gain the results toward the year's end on that calculation indicated a comfortable general election victory for the Conservatives; a 4% swing would give them a small majority in Parliament, while a 10% swing would produce a majority of more than 200. Labour was faced with the prospect of reversing the trend in the last year before the election more dramatically than any government had done since the war.

Two of the earlier by-elections produced unusual results. In April Bernadette Devlin (*see* BIOGRAPHY), a 21-year-old student and leader of the Ulster civil rights movement, was elected as member for Mid-Ulster, and later made headlines when she took part in street fighting in Belfast. In June the Liberals won the Birmingham constituency of Ladywood with a strong local candidate, Wallace Lawler, who became the first Liberal to represent a Birmingham constituency since 1885 and the 13th Liberal member of Parliament in the Commons.

For the third consecutive year Labour suffered heavy losses in the local government elections, losing control of another 25 boroughs in England and Wales (although regaining control of Sheffield). After the elections Labour controlled only 28 of the 342 English and Welsh boroughs.

A major reorganization of the departmental structure of government was made in conjunction with a Cabinet reshuffle in October. Responsibility for industry and industrial development was concentrated in an enlarged Ministry of Technology under Anthony Wedgwood Benn (*see* BIOGRAPHY), which took in the Ministry of Power. A group of departments concerned with planning were brought together in a new Department of Local Government and Regional Planning under Anthony Crosland (*see* BIOGRAPHY). The scope of the Board of Trade was reduced to a primary concern with overseas trade and export promotion, though it retained responsibilities for domestic commerce (as distinct from industry). The Department of Economic Affairs was abolished, and its responsibilities redistributed between the Treasury and the Department of Employment and Productivity.

The enlarged Ministry of Technology embraced aerospace, nuclear energy, technological research, engineering, shipbuilding, electronics, the nationalized power industries, steel, chemicals, mineral development, and the regional distribution of industry. The department was reorganized into five groups, each headed by a minister: industrial, regional (location of industry), aviation, research, and economic.

The Department of Local Government and Regional Planning included separate departments for housing and transport (both with ministers, but no longer of Cabinet rank). It was to control the work of the regional economic planning councils, and was given newly defined responsibilities for dealing with pollution of the environment. Crosland was to take charge of the negotiations for the reform of the structure of local government.

Ministerial changes reduced the Cabinet from 23 to 21; the average age of the new ministers was 38. The major changes on October 5 led to the departure of three ministers: Richard Marsh (transport), Frederick Lee (chancellor of the duchy of Lancaster), and Kenneth Robinson (planning and land). New Cabinet appointments were George Thomson as chancellor of the duchy of Lancaster, responsible for European affairs; Roy Mason as president of the Board of Trade; Peter Shore as minister without portfolio; and Harold Lever as paymaster general. Judith Hart left the Cabinet on becoming minister of overseas development. Frederick Mulley, minister of transport, and Anthony Greenwood, who remained minister of housing, also left the Cabinet. The reorganization was completed on October 12 by a number of new junior ministerial changes.

Conservative "shadow cabinet" appointments in October also reflected these structural changes, with Peter Walker taking transport while remaining responsible for housing and local government, and Sir Keith Joseph combining technology and power. Sir Edward Boyle, who had been the "shadow" minister for education, retired from politics to become vice-chancellor of Leeds University, and his place was taken by Margaret Thatcher.

Industrial Relations. The government set out its policy on industrial relations in a White Paper, *In Place of Strife,* published on January 17. This went beyond the 1968 Donovan Commission's report on trade unions in proposing a 28-day conciliation pause, or cooling-off period, before strike action was taken in certain cases, and also a compulsory ballot of union members before strike action in certain cases where the public interest or the economy was threatened. The White Paper also announced the intention of setting up a Commission on Industrial Relations. It noted that the typical British strike was unofficial (accounting for 95% of strikes) and often unconstitutional in being in breach of agreed-upon procedure. The Commission on Industrial Relations would advise on the reform of industrial relations and on the improvement of procedure. The government did not think collective agreements should be made legally binding.

Trade union leaders at once criticized the White Paper for proposing powers of intervention by the state. The Confederation of British Industry, speaking for management, found the conciliation pause inadequate and said interference would weaken management. The White Paper was opposed by a substantial number of Labour members of Parliament with 55 voting against it in the House of Commons in March. The Conservatives wanted agreements between management and trade unions to be legally binding, and trade unions to be given corporate status and their rules registered.

In spite of opposition from the trade unions and within the Labour Party, the government went ahead with the preparation of a bill based on the White Paper, including financial penalties for trade unionists who refused an order to go back to work during a 28-day conciliation pause, but without powers to call for strike ballots. Prime Minister Wilson had said that the passage of the bill was "essential to the government's continuance in office," and prolonged negotiations with the Trades Union Council (TUC) continued through May and June. The TUC insisted that it could not accept legal procedures and penal sanctions in industrial relations, and presented a plan for it to intervene itself to resolve disputes and to improve procedures. The TUC adopted this program at a special congress on June 5. On June 19 Wilson announced the decision to abandon the bill in return for "a solemn and binding undertaking" by the TUC to intervene itself in serious unconstitutional stoppages.

Social Security. Far-reaching reform of the social security system was announced in a White Paper published in January. This was the first major overhaul of the welfare services, which were based on the Beveridge Report of 1942. The most important proposal was to relate pensions to earnings. A graduated scale of payments according to earnings would produce a pension of about 50% of earnings averaged over a lifetime's work. Average and higher paid workers would pay relatively more for their pensions than those with lower pay. There would also be earnings-related widows' pensions and unemployment and sickness benefits. Government pension rights and payments were to be geared into privately operated occupational pension schemes, and pensions were to be regularly adjusted to take account of inflation.

Legislation. Acts of Parliament passed during the 1968–69 session included the Representation of the People Act, which reduced the voting age to 18, and the Family Law Reform Act, which similarly reduced the legal age of majority from 21 to 18. The Immigration Appeals Act established an appeals procedure for immigrants against decisions taken under the provisions of the Commonwealth Immigrants Act and the Aliens Restriction Act. The Iron and Steel Act provided for the financial and structural reorganization of the nationalized iron and steel industry, while the Post Office Act transformed the Post Office from a government department into a corporation, as of October 1. The legislative framework for the transition to decimal currency beginning Feb. 15, 1971, was provided for by a second Decimal Currency Act. Legislation extending the rights of wives and dependents was introduced to complement the Divorce Reform Act, which was to become effective in 1971. Toward the end of the year the government's declared intention to make permanent the abolition of capital punishment revealed wide differences in public and party opinion, but was approved by Parliament.

Local Government. The royal commission on the reform of local government, under the chairmanship of Lord Redcliffe-Maud, presented its report in June. The Maud Report applied only to England (outside London). It proposed replacing the existing system of county boroughs (in large cities and towns) and county councils (in predominantly country areas) by all-purpose unitary authorities in all areas except the major conurbations. There would be 58 unitary authorities, taking in both urban and rural areas. As exceptions, there would be a two-tier system for the conurbation areas of Birmingham, Liverpool, and Manchester, which would be designated metropolitan authorities and subdivided into metropolitan districts. Eight provinces, with a nominated council, would exercise strategic planning powers. The commission commented that the fragmentation of England into 79 county boroughs and 45 counties, exercising independent authority and dividing town from country, had made the proper planning of development and transportation impossible.

The government accepted in principle the main recommendations of the report. While allowing time for comment before a final decision, it planned to introduce a bill into Parliament as soon as possible. A royal commission on local government reform in Scotland, reporting in September, came to an opposite conclusion on principle, favouring a two-tier system with administrative functions shared between 7 regional authorities and 37 district authorities, in place of the existing 430 Scottish local authorities. Proposals for the reorganization of local government in Wales had been made in July 1967. (*See* CITIES AND URBAN AFFAIRS.)

Royal Household. Prince Philip's remark, made on a U.S. television interview in November, to the effect that the royal household was in the red and the queen was being forced to use her private wealth to meet expenses caused considerable stir in Britain. Questions were asked in Parliament and the government promised to set up a special parliamentary committee to study the royal finances. Earlier in the year, on July 1, the investiture of Prince Charles (*see* BIOGRAPHY) as prince of Wales at Caernarvon Castle provided an occasion for a display of royal pageantry. TV coverage of the event, relayed by satellite, was viewed by millions around the world.

Foreign Policy. The central issue of British foreign policy remained the application for entry into the European Economic Community (EEC). Hopes of a successful application revived after the retirement of Pres. Charles de Gaulle of France, which was judged to promise a relaxation of French opposition and a tacit withdrawal of the French veto. At the meeting of EEC heads of government at The Hague, Neth., in December, it was agreed that negotiations with Britain would begin by the end of the first half of 1970. Popular enthusiasm for membership in Britain was reported, however, to have declined. In February Franco-British relations were exacerbated by the attempt to develop the Western European Union (WEU), in which the U.K. participated, into a forum for the coordination of a European foreign policy. This led to a French boycott of the WEU Council. Relations were further embittered by the alleged

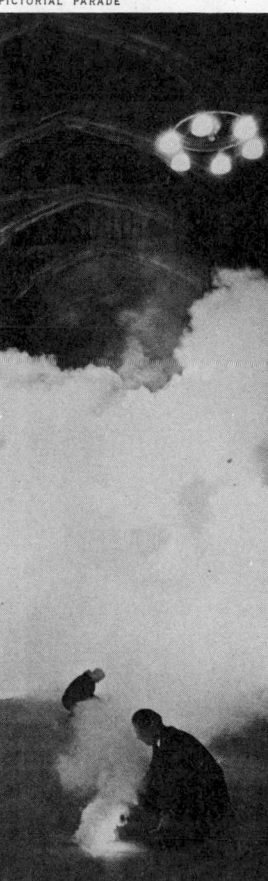

"THE TIMES," LONDON, FROM PICTORIAL PARADE

Exterminators release insecticidal smoke in Westminster Hall, London, in March 1969. The smoke was the second stage of an attempt by the Ministry of Public Buildings and Works to rid the historic hall of deathwatch beetles.

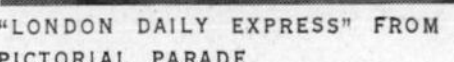
"LONDON DAILY EXPRESS" FROM PICTORIAL PARADE

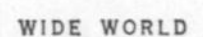
WIDE WORLD

Left, Bernadette Devlin, Independent Unity member of Parliament for Mid-Ulster, urges Roman Catholics to defend their homes during rioting in Northern Ireland in August 1969. Above, the Rev. Ian Paisley (centre), militant Protestant leader, heads a march in Belfast to demand the dismissal of Prime Minister Terence O'Neill.

leakage to the French press of proposals made by President de Gaulle to the British ambassador in Paris, Christopher Soames. The proposals were supposedly to replace the EEC with an economic association of European countries, including a four-power political association of France, West Germany, Italy, and Britain. The British government felt obliged to tell its WEU partners of these proposals, which were denied in an official French statement. This incident did not, however, disturb amicable relations for long.

The British response to the Nigerian civil war continued to cause political dispute at home. The government was criticized for continuing to supply arms to the Nigerian federal government and for failing to bring pressure to bear to secure relief supplies for Biafra. In Parliament in March Foreign Secretary Michael Stewart defended British policy on the grounds that the Biafran secession was a rebellion and that to cut off arms supplies to Nigeria would be tantamount to supporting the rebellion; it would also lead to greater Soviet influence in Nigeria, and the estrangement of Britain from Nigeria and other African countries. At the end of March Prime Minister Wilson visited Nigeria and Ethiopia in the hope of mediating in the war. He issued an invitation to the Biafran leader, Odumegwu Ojukwu, to a meeting outside Biafra, but the Biafran authorities complained that this was received only after the time limit for its acceptance had expired, and no meeting took place.

In March the government rejected a Rhodesian memorandum on the proposals made in a meeting between Prime Minister Wilson and Ian Smith of Rhodesia in October 1968. The resignation of Sir Humphrey Gibbs as governor in June followed Rhodesia's vote for a republic. Britain continued to rely on sanctions as the only practical means of bringing about political change in Rhodesia.

The dispute with Spain over Gibraltar worsened during the year. Gibraltar's new constitution declared that it remained "part of Her Majesty's dominions." Spanish pressure included the closing of the La Línea border post and the Algeciras ferry, thus cutting off the supply of Spanish labour. Spain also cut its telephone links with Gibraltar and stationed warships near the harbour. Britain repeated its promises of support to the people of Gibraltar, and there were indications, following Spain's government reshuffle in October, of a possible softening of Spanish attitudes.

The new republican government of Libya announced in September that the military agreement with Britain providing an air base at El Adem would not be renewed.

The detention of British subjects in Communist countries became a matter of worldwide interest. Gerald Brooke, sentenced by a Soviet court in 1965 to five years' imprisonment for anti-Soviet activities, was released in July in exchange for the release of the Soviet spies Helen and Peter Kroger, sentenced to 20 years' imprisonment in 1961 for espionage. Two other British subjects detained for drug smuggling in the U.S.S.R. were also released when the Krogers left Britain for Poland in October. In China Reuters correspondent Anthony Grey, who had been under house arrest since July 1967, in retaliation for the imprisonment of a number of Communist journalists in Hong Kong, was freed in October. A number of other British subjects detained in China were also released.

In March a detachment of British paratroops and a party of London police were sent to Anguilla in the Caribbean after the island announced its secession from the associated state of St. Kitts-Nevis-Anguilla in January (*see* DEPENDENT STATES: *Caribbean*). Later, British Army engineers were sent to replace the paratroops and carry out improvements on Anguilla. The affair emphasized the problems of the remaining small colonial territories, many of which were neither economically nor politically viable.

Defense. The defense budget for 1969–70 was reduced to less than 6% of the gross national product.

It was forecast that by April 1970 the strength of the armed forces would be down to about 375,000. This was in line with a program of streamlining and economizing conducted by Defense Minister Denis Healey in an unbroken tenure of office since October 1964. The 1969–70 defense White Paper noted that 1968 was the first year since 1962 when British forces were not fighting in a colonial or former colonial territory. The planned withdrawal from Asia emphasized the priority of commitment to Europe. Since the Soviet invasion of Czechoslovakia, Britain had increased its commitments to NATO. Meanwhile, British forces were still stationed in Hong Kong, Malaysia, Singapore, the Persian Gulf, and the Caribbean. In Parliament in March Healey said that by 1972–73 British defense expenditure would be down to about 5% of the gross national product, the average for European NATO countries. The Conservative opposition feared that this would be inadequate to maintain national and overseas interests, and stated that a Conservative government would maintain a military presence east of Suez.

The Economy. The year opened with the best set of trade figures for 18 months, a deficit in January of £10 million. Progress was erratic until, in the late summer, trade records were broken again, with an August surplus of £40 million. The monthly export-import figures had become distinctly suspect since the disclosure that exports had been underrecorded by something like £12 million a month, but allowing for the earnings of invisible trade, it was calculated that in the later part of the year the balance of payments was in surplus by about £40 million a month. By November the National Institute of Economic and Social Research was forecasting a record £850 million balance of payments surplus in 1970. Bearing in mind that 1968 had shown a deficit of £458 million (mainly incurred during the first half of that year), there had been, whatever the calculations, a very large switch of resources to exports.

Jenkins, since going to the Treasury in November 1967, had determined on a massive shift of resources from domestic consumption to foreign trade as the necessary cornerstone for resuming a program of growth and expansion. After the severe budget of 1968 Jenkins altered the emphasis of his financial policy to control of the money supply. The deflationary effect of taxation in 1968 had been to a large degree neutralized by an expansion of about £1,225 million in domestic credit in the financial year to March 1969. In November 1968, Jenkins had called on the clearing banks to reduce lending in the private sector by £150 million. Although bank credit was restrained, it was not quickly reduced, and Jenkins saw this as a factor behind the continuing growth of consumer spending. When, in February, bank credit showed a further rise to £200 million above the limit set by the chancellor, the bank rate was raised to 8% (it had been 7% since September 1968). Jenkins made an additional attack on bank credit in June by making a sharp cut in the interest rate paid to the banks on the special deposits they were required to make; by cutting the rate of interest on these deposits by half, he was in effect imposing a fine equivalent to about £8 million a year on the banks until they brought their lending back to the ceiling figure.

In a letter of intent on British economic policy, addressed to the International Monetary Fund and published on June 23, Jenkins forecast a £300 million balance of payments surplus during the year to March 1970, and noted that a limit of 1% increase had been put on public expenditure. The budget increased taxation by an estimated £340 million in a full year, spread over a number of relatively small tax increases. Jenkins emphasized that growth, estimated to be 3.5% in 1969–70, must be led by exports, and that therefore it was still necessary to restrain private consumption and the growth of incomes. Earnings continued to rise faster than the government would have wished, in spite of the prices and incomes policy; between the first and third quarters of the year earnings advanced by an average of about 3%. Trade union leaders hoped the government might abandon the official ceiling for wage increases, but a revised incomes policy for 1970 provided for norms varying between 2½ and 4½% for wage increases.

Northern Ireland. The sectarian feud between extremist Protestants and Roman Catholics deteriorated into a state approaching civil war. The Unionist government under Terence O'Neill was reelected in the general election of February 24. A vote of confidence in O'Neill encouraged him to go ahead with a reform program that included the appointment of an ombudsman, a special commission for the government of Londonderry, fairer allocation of housing, and the introduction of universal suffrage in local elections. The controversy surrounding these reforms led to clashes between the largely Catholic civil rights movement and Protestant extremist demonstrators, followers of the Rev. Ian Paisley (*see* BIOGRAPHY). There were serious riots in Londonderry and Belfast in April, when gasoline bombs were thrown. Loss of support in his own party forced O'Neill to resign on April 28. His successor as prime minister was James Chichester-Clark (*see* BIOGRAPHY). Though more middle-of-the-road than O'Neill, Chichester-Clark maintained the reform program after talks with Wilson and Home Secretary James Callaghan in London about a timetable for social reform.

Rioting broke out again in July and August and reached its peak in mid-August when barricades were set up in the worst affected parts of Londonderry and Belfast. Eight people were killed and 514 civilians and 226 police injured in the five days of street fighting, August 12–16. British troops were called in to relieve the police in Londonderry on August 14, and on the following day more British troops were moved to help restore law and order in Belfast. For several weeks these troops took over the duty of policing the worst affected areas of Belfast and Londonderry.

Further rioting occurred in October after an advisory committee headed by Lord Hunt recommended the disbandment of the controversial special constabulary, the B Specials, who were accused of Unionist-Protestant partiality, and the disarming of the Royal Ulster Constabulary. A weekend curfew on public houses helped dispel the disturbances, and by the end of October the barricades had been taken down in Londonderry and Belfast with troops holding the "peace line." To replace the B Specials, the British government proposed to establish an Ulster Defense Regiment, which would not be used for riot control, under regular British officers answerable to London. To back the reform program and relieve unemployment, the government advanced an extra £6 million in economic aid. (W. H. Ts.)

ENCYCLOPÆDIA BRITANNICA FILMS. *The British Isles—The Land and the People* (1963); *Britain—Searching for a New Role* (1964).

United Nations

UN Secretary-General U Thant on May 9 warned that UN members had "perhaps ten years left in which to subordinate their ancient quarrels and launch a global partnership to curb the arms race, to improve the human environment, to defuse the population explosion, and to supply the required momentum to world development efforts."

Middle East. The Security Council, at six meetings between March 27 and March 29, considered Jordanian and Israeli complaints about military incidents involving both of them. Jordan stated that Israeli jet fighters had "brutally attacked" Jordanian villages, rest houses, and winter resorts less than one mile from Salt, killing 17 civilians, many of them elderly women and children, and wounding 25, three seriously. Jordan had written the president of the Security Council that the Israelis were using napalm against Jordan and should be checked before they embarked upon more violations of the UN cease-fire resolution. Israel, in turn, asked on March 27 for an urgent meeting of the council to consider "grave and continual violations by Jordan of the cease-fire, the provisions of the United Nations Charter, and of international law" including "armed attacks, armed infiltration and acts of murder and violence by terrorist groups operating from Jordan territory" with official support.

At the seventh meeting of the council dealing with these charges (April 1), Pakistan introduced a draft resolution, which, as revised, condemned Israel's "recent premeditated air attacks" and warned Israel that such attacks, if repeated, would require the council to take "further more effective steps as envisaged in the Charter." Israel denounced the resolution, which was adopted 11–0, as "one-sided" and "incomprehensible" for failing to take account of the activities of "Arab terror organizations."

Along the Suez Canal, almost daily incidents in March and April reached "a virtual state of active war," according to a special report by the secretary-general on April 21. By May 2, UN observers were in such constant danger that Lieut. Gen. Odd Bull, chief of the UN Truce Supervision Organization (UNTSO), urged the need for neutral zones around UNTSO observation posts.

On July 3, the Security Council censured Israel again. A resolution, submitted jointly by Pakistan, Senegal, and Zambia, confirmed that legislative and administrative measures purporting to alter the status of occupied Jerusalem, including expropriation of land and properties, were invalid, and it urgently called on Israel to rescind all measures tending to change the status of the city. The vote was 14–0, with only the U.S. abstaining on the ground that Jerusalem's status was not an isolated problem to consider apart from the general situation in the Middle East.

On August 26, the council had occasion to condemn unanimously the "premeditated air attack by Israel on villages in southern Lebanon in violation of its obligations under the Charter and Security Council resolutions." This action capped a series of council meetings, beginning on August 13, at which the council considered Lebanese and Israeli complaints of armed attacks against each other.

Within Lebanon itself, fighting broke out in late October between Lebanese troops and Palestinian guerrillas who were operating against Israel from Lebanese territory. One of the results of the conflicts, which ended officially on November 3 under an agreement arranged in Cairo, was that 14 of the 15 refugee camps operated by the UN Relief and Works Agency for Palestine Refugees in the Near East (UNRWA) were taken over by the commandos.

Hopes for an overall settlement in the Middle East rested primarily in the hands of Gunnar Jarring, special representative of the secretary-general, but the only point on which the Middle Eastern states could agree was the potential value of his efforts. On substantive matters, the parties remained far apart, as revealed in answers they gave to a questionnaire Jarring distributed in March. Israel, for instance, reiterated that peace must be reached "by negotiation" and must be "juridically expressed, contractually defined and reciprocally binding." Jordan and the U.A.R. emphasized that Israel had to withdraw completely from occupied territories and asserted that the parties would have to sign separate instruments addressed to the Security Council.

Other Troubled Areas. The General Assembly, acting on a report from its Commission for the Unification and Rehabilitation of Korea, authorized for another year the presence of 55,000 U.S. troops serving in Korea under the UN flag. The commission pointed out in its annual report that it was unable to achieve its objectives because of the activities of North Korea. It believed, however, that its presence was important in maintaining peace.

On March 26, U Thant expressed his hope that all concerned would expedite the intercommunal talks between leaders of the Greek and Turkish communities on Cyprus. The secretary-general pointed out that additional time would not necessarily help resolve the problems. Meanwhile, the UN force in Cyprus was down to half its original (1964) strength.

On September 12, the secretary-general pointed out that the UN was not directly involved in searching for solutions to either the Vietnam or Biafran problems. He reaffirmed his belief that direct talks between the parties involved appeared to be the right step for solving the Vietnam situation and that the political aspects of the Nigerian civil war were properly left to the Organization of African Unity.

Arms Race. A decision in the spring to enlarge the Conference of the 18-Nation Committee on Disarmament led it to change its name August 26 to Conference of the Committee on Disarmament. The conference met March 18–May 23 and July 3–October 31. The new members were Argentina, Hungary, Japan, Mongolia, Morocco, the Netherlands, Pakistan, and Yugoslavia. France, one of the original members, continued not to take its seat.

Inscribed on the committee's agenda were measures for stopping the nuclear arms race, encouraging nuclear disarmament, avoiding chemical and biological warfare, preventing an arms race on the seabed, and promoting general and complete disarmament under strict and effective international control. At the spring meeting, the committee attempted to break the deadlock that had kept the U.S.S.R. and the U.S. from agreeing on the type of inspection system needed to ensure that neither was testing nuclear weapons underground. The U.S. had been asking for on-site inspection; the U.S.S.R. held national self-inspections sufficient.

At the spring conference meetings Sweden submitted a preliminary version of a comprehensive test-ban treaty. This draft provided that a state could invite outsiders to inspect its territory if it was challenged to show that any seismic phenomenon was not an underground nuclear explosion. Although neither the U.S. nor the U.S.S.R. abandoned its position in formal meetings, press reports in November suggested that the U.S. might have given up expecting the Soviets to agree to on-site inspection.

The summer meetings of the conference produced two draft treaties, a British text on germ warfare and a U.S.-U.S.S.R. draft designed to ban arms from the seabed. The seabed treaty draft, as amended in the conference and presented to the General Assembly, prohibited placing nuclear weapons and other weapons of mass destruction outside an imprecisely defined offshore zone, permitted parties to take disputes over verification to the Security Council, and allowed a government to withdraw from the treaty on three months' notice. On December 12, the assembly referred the treaty back to the conference for further discussions.

The year's initiatives relating to germ warfare began in mid-1968, when Britain submitted a working paper proposing a supplement to the Protocol for the Prohibition of the Use in War of Asphyxiating, Poisonous or Other Gases, and of Bacteriological Methods of Warfare, signed in Geneva on June 17, 1925. More than 60 states had ratified it over the years, including all major powers except Japan and the U.S. On November 25, U.S. Pres. Richard Nixon announced that he would ask the U.S. Senate to consent to his ratifying the 1925 Geneva Protocol and pledged further that the U.S. would never engage in germ warfare. The U.S. continued to maintain, however, that it would still be free to use tear gas and defoliants. Other nations believed that those two agents were proscribed under the Geneva Protocol, and the General Assembly on December 16 specifically proclaimed that view as authoritative (80–3 with 36 abstentions). The U.S. then denied the assembly's authority to pronounce on questions of international law.

Economic and Social Development. As part of the planning for the Second Development Decade (the 1970s), the board of the UN Industrial Development Organization (UNIDO) undertook at its third session (April 24–May 15 in Vienna) to assist the less developed countries to follow up and implement industrial growth targets set for the decade. In Geneva on July 9, UNIDO and the Food and Agriculture Organization signed an agreement under which they would cooperate in planning agricultural and industrial development, in developing production of industrial inputs in agriculture, and in implementing projects in industries based on agriculture. UNIDO also arranged during the year to increase the number of its industrial field advisers and brought to 30 the number of its national committees for UNIDO, which acted as advisory bodies to their respective governments.

On December 10, the International Labour Organization received the Nobel Peace Prize for 1969 for "translating into action the fundamental idea on which it is based." The Nobel Prize for Economics went to Jan Tinbergen (*see* BIOGRAPHY), chairman of the Committee for Development Planning, an international group of experts which advised the UN.

Dependent Peoples. Continued efforts to liquidate the vestiges of colonialism and discrimination against indigenous peoples were largely concentrated in southern Africa (South Africa, South West Africa [Namibia], Rhodesia, and the Portuguese colonies).

South Africa. On February 19, the General Assembly's Special Committee on the Policies of Apartheid appealed to nations to take special steps on March 21 to show their abhorrence of apartheid (racial separation). The March date, designated International Day for the Elimination of Racial Discrimination, commemorated the anniversary of the massacre in Sharpeville, S.Af., in 1960. The committee suggested special resolutions, publicity measures, diplomatic pressure, contributions to special UN aid programs for Africa, and an end to cultural exchanges with and immigration to South Africa.

On November 21, the General Assembly urged increased assistance to "the national movement of the oppressed people of South Africa," and directed its Special Committee on the Policies of Apartheid to encourage governments to supply funds, food, and clothing to assist anticolonial groups. The resolution invited states to take various means for economic and other disengagement from South Africa by stopping air and sea traffic to South Africa, denying facilities to air and shipping lines that continued serving South African ports, and heeding the arms embargo which the Security Council adopted against South Africa in 1963. The assembly drew the Security Council's attention to "the grave situation in South Africa, and in southern Africa as a whole," and recommended that the council urgently consider the apartheid question "with a view to adopting effective measures, including those under Chapter VII [enforcement measures] of the Charter, to eliminate the threat to international peace and security." The resolution was adopted, 80–5 (Australia, Portugal, South Africa, the U.K., the U.S.), with 23 abstentions.

Rhodesia. The Rhodesian question came before both the Security Council and the General Assembly in 1969. In June, 60 member states, mainly African and Asian, requested all states to "sever immediately all economic and other relations with the illegal racist minority regime in South Rhodesia"; to condemn the "so-called constitutional proposals [a reference to the June 20 referendum which approved a new constitution embracing apartheid and the idea of establishing Rhodesia as a republic outside the British Commonwealth] aimed at perpetuating [the regime's] power and sanctioning . . . apartheid"; and to censure South Africa and Portugal for supplying aid to Rhodesia. The resolution called for sanctions against South Africa and the Portuguese colony of Mozambique and urged the U.K., as administering power in Rhodesia, to take all necessary measures, including force, against the "rebellion." When the council voted, June 24, the draft resolution, which needed nine affirmative votes to pass, received only eight (Algeria, China, Hungary, Nepal, Pakistan, Senegal, the U.S.S.R., and Zambia). During the debate, the U.K., as in the past, opposed the idea of using force.

South West Africa. On March 20, the Security Council, by a vote of 13–0, with two abstentions (France, the U.K.), called on South Africa to withdraw its administration immediately from South West Africa and stated that if South Africa failed to comply, the council would meet immediately to determine future steps. The resolution recognized that the General Assembly had in 1966 terminated South Africa's mandate, granted by the League of Nations, and it characterized South Africa's continued presence as illegal, contrary to the principles of the UN Charter and UN decisions, and detrimental to the interests of the indigenous population and the international community. The Security Council called for South Africa to withdraw from South West Africa by October 4 and warned of further measures if it refused to do so.

The October 4 deadline passed unnoted by South Africa, and on October 31, the General Assembly called the Security Council's attention to the "deteriorating situation" in South West Africa resulting from South Africa's refusal to withdraw. The vote was 95–2 (South Africa and Portugal) with six abstentions (Australia, Botswana, France, Ivory Coast, Malawi, the U.K.).

Portuguese Colonies. In July, the Security Council considered a Zambian complaint that Portugal had attacked its territory along the Mozambique frontier. The council on July 28, by a vote of 11–0, with four abstentions (France, Spain, the U.K., the U.S.), censured Portugal for the alleged attacks and called on it "to desist forthwith from violating the territorial integrity and from carrying out unprovoked raids against Zambia." The council demanded that Portugal release and repatriate immediately all Zambian civilians "kidnapped by Portuguese military forces operating in the colonial territories of Angola and Mozambique" and requested that it return all property unlawfully taken from Zambian territory by those forces.

On November 21, the General Assembly, by a vote of 97–2 (Portugal, South Africa), with 18 abstentions, called on Portugal to help the colonies move to self-determination and independence, recommended that the Security Council take effective steps to get Portugal to implement assembly resolutions, called for increased moral and material assistance to peoples in the territories who were struggling for their freedom and independence, and urged all states to withhold assistance to Portugal.

Legal Matters. The Vienna Convention on the Law of Treaties was adopted by a vote of 79–1, with 19 abstentions; on May 23, 32 states actually signed the convention of 85 articles and an annex providing for conciliation commissions to resolve disputes between parties to a treaty who had exhausted all existing procedures for settling differences under the UN Charter. The convention was the product of work by the UN International Law Commission and the UN Conference on the Law of Treaties.

The International Court of Justice proposed amending art. 22 of its statute to allow it to meet at places other than The Hague. On October 27, the General Assembly and Security Council elected five new judges to sit on the court effective Feb. 6, 1970. Those chosen were Federico de Castro (Spain), Hardy C. Dillard (U.S.), Louis Ignacio-Pinto (Dahomey), Eduardo Jiménez de Aréchaga (Uruguay), and Planton D. Morozov (U.S.S.R.). They succeeded José Luis Bustamante y Rivero (Peru), president of the court; Vladimir M. Koretsky (U.S.S.R.), vice-president; Philip C. Jessup (U.S.); Gaetano Morelli (Italy); and Kotaro Tanaka (Japan). (*See* LAW.)

Organizational Matters. Angie E. Brooks (*see* BIOGRAPHY), assistant secretary of state of Liberia, was elected president of the 24th General Assembly at the first meeting of its 24th session (September 16–December 17). UN membership remained constant at 126 during 1969, and on August 29 the Security Council, acting on a U.S. suggestion, established a committee of experts, consisting of all council members, to consider the question of "microstates" and their relation with the UN.

On November 11, the assembly once again decided that any proposal to change Chinese representation required a two-thirds majority vote. It then went on to reject, 48–56–21, a resolution that sought to designate the People's Republic of (Communist)

Table I. Member States of the United Nations

Dec. 31, 1969

Afghanistan	Ecuador*	Lesotho	Senegal
Albania	El Salvador*	Liberia*	Sierra Leone
Algeria	Equatorial Guinea	Libya	Singapore
Argentina*	Ethiopia*	Luxembourg*	Somalia
Australia*	Finland	Malagasy Rep.	South Africa*
Austria	France*	Malawi	Southern Yemen
Barbados	Gabon	Malaysia	Spain
Belgium*	Gambia, The	Maldives	Sudan
Belorussia*	Ghana	Mali	Swaziland
Bolivia*	Greece*	Malta	Sweden
Botswana	Guatemala*	Mauritania	Syria*
Brazil*	Guinea	Mauritius	Taiwan*
Bulgaria	Guyana	Mexico*	Tanzania
Burma	Haiti*	Mongolia	Thailand
Burundi	Honduras*	Morocco	Togo
Cambodia	Hungary	Nepal	Trinidad and Tobago
Cameroon	Iceland	Netherlands*	Tunisia
Canada*	India*	New Zealand*	Turkey*
Central African Rep.	Indonesia	Nicaragua*	Uganda
Ceylon	Iran*	Niger	Ukraine*
Chad	Iraq*	Nigeria	U.S.S.R.*
Chile*	Ireland	Norway*	United Arab Republic
Colombia*	Israel	Pakistan	United Kingdom*
Congo (Kinshasa)	Italy	Panama*	United States*
Congo (Brazz.)	Ivory Coast	Paraguay*	Upper Volta
Costa Rica*	Jamaica	Peru*	Uruguay*
Cuba*	Japan	Philippines*	Venezuela*
Cyprus	Jordan	Poland*	Yemen
Czechoslovakia*	Kenya	Portugal	Yugoslavia*
Dahomey	Kuwait	Romania	Zambia
Denmark*	Laos	Rwanda	
Dominican Rep.*	Lebanon*	Saudi Arabia*	

*Signatories to original charter.

Table II. Council Membership

Years indicate date membership expires

Country	Security Council	Economic and Social Council	Trusteeship Council
France*	Permanent	1972†	Permanent
Taiwan	Permanent		Permanent
U.S.S.R.*‡	Permanent	1971	Permanent
United Kingdom*‡	Permanent	1971	Permanent§
United States*‡	Permanent	1970	Permanent§
Argentina*		1970	
Australia‡			§
Brazil*		1972	
Bulgaria*‡		1970	
Burundi	1971		
Ceylon		1972	
Chad		1970	
Colombia	1970		
Congo (Brazz.)		1970	
Finland‡	1970		
Ghana		1972	
Greece		1972	
India*‡		1970	
Indonesia		1971	
Ireland		1970	
Italy*‡		1972	
Jamaica		1971	
Japan*		1970	
Kenya		1972	
Nepal	1970		
Nicaragua	1971		
Norway		1971	
Pakistan*		1971	
Peru		1972	
Poland*‡	1971		
Sierra Leone‡	1971		
Spain	1970		
Sudan		1971	
Syria‡	1971		
Tunisia‡		1972	
Upper Volta		1970	
Uruguay		1971	
Yugoslavia*‡		1971	
Zambia	1970		

*Members of the Conference of the Committee on Disarmament in addition to: Burma, Canada, Czechoslovakia, Ethiopia, Hungary, Mexico, Mongolia, Morocco, the Netherlands, Nigeria, Romania, Sweden, and the U.A.R.

†Reelected.

‡Members of the Committee of 24 on decolonization in addition to: Afghanistan, Chile, Ethiopia, Honduras, Iran, Iraq, Ivory Coast, Malagasy Republic, Mali, Tanzania, and Venezuela.

§Administering authorities.

China as the only lawful Chinese government and, therefore, entitled to the seat occupied by the Republic of (Nationalist) China. The vote on a comparable resolution in 1968 was 44–58–23.

On August 29, the secretary-general proposed a UN budget of $164,123,000 for 1970, representing a 6% increase over funds budgeted for 1969. At individual pledging conferences, 98 states pledged $131.6 million for the UN Development Program (October 9), with expectations that late pledges would bring the amount to $238 million. On October 10, 26 nations pledged about $775,000 for the Capital Development Fund; and on November 11, UNIDO received $1.5 million in pledges. (R. N. S.)

UNESCO. In 1969, the UN Educational, Scientific, and Cultural Organization continued its programs in education, science, culture, and communications for the promotion of international cooperation and for the economic and social development of people in the less developed regions of the world. Many of its educational activities during the year centred on preparing for the International Education Year (IEY) in 1970. IEY was aimed at focusing world attention on the present crisis in education and on a number of major requirements needed for its expansion and development, both in quantity and—above all—in quality. Some idea of the crisis could be gathered from the fact that a survey showed that in approximately 200 countries and territories only about half the children attended school, and that about 40% of the world's adult population was illiterate.

The ferment of youth in many parts of the world caused UNESCO in 1969 to launch a large-scale inquiry into the problems of youth, carried out in collaboration with the UN, its specialized agencies, and various research institutions. (R. D. A. G.)

See also Defense; Southeast Asia.

United States

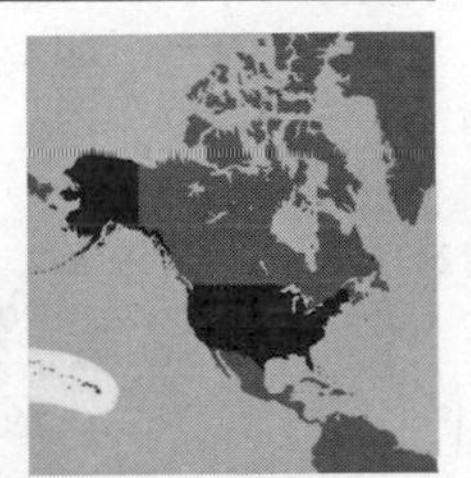

The United States of America is a federal republic composed of 50 states, 49 of which are in North America and one of which consists of the Hawaiian Islands. Area: 3,615,210 sq.mi. (9,363,405 sq.km.), including 66,237 sq.mi. of inland water but excluding the 60,306 sq.mi. of the Great Lakes that lie within U.S. boundaries. Pop. (1969 est.): 203.2 million, including (1960) white 88.6%; Negro 10.5%. Language: English. Religion (1963 est.): Protestant 64,435,000; Roman Catholic 42,877,000; Jewish 5,365,000; Orthodox 2.8 million. Cap.: Washington, D.C. (pop., 1969 est., 825,000). Largest city: New York (pop., 1968 est., 8,125,000). Presidents in 1969, Lyndon Baines Johnson and, from January 20, Richard Milhous Nixon.

The United States twice landed men on the moon in 1969, but foreign and domestic problems on earth continued to plague the country. Chief among these, as in several previous years, was the war in Vietnam. President Nixon (*see* BIOGRAPHY) declared in his inaugural address that "The greatest honor history can bestow is the title of peacemaker." The new president set out to claim that honour for himself by withdrawing some American troops from the war and by seeking—fruitlessly, as it turned out—a negotiated settlement in the peace talks at Paris.

The war also was responsible for many of the country's domestic difficulties. Massive antiwar demonstrations were held in Washington and other cities toward the end of the year, and they contributed to a growing political polarization. The demands of the war on the overheated U.S. economy helped to push inflation to its highest rate since the Korean War year of 1951. Prices soared despite the federal government's efforts to curb spending through a tight-money policy and a 10% surtax on incomes.

In Congress, 1969 was a relatively unproductive year. The president proposed little in the way of major legislation, while Congress dragged its feet even on such routine measures as appropriations bills. Nixon's major legislative requests included revamping of the welfare system, reorganization of the Post Office Department, and revenue-sharing with the states. None was enacted.

Much of Congress' time in 1969 was taken up by a wide-ranging tax reform and relief bill. As finally approved by the House of Representatives and Senate on December 22, the bill would provide tax cuts for everyone, increase Social Security benefits by 15%, and make scores of changes in special provisions of the federal tax laws, including a reduction in the oil depletion allowance from 27½ to 22%. The measure would provide tax relief by increasing the personal exemption and the standard deduction, by providing a special tax-free allowance for low-income individuals, and by taxing single persons at rates lower than those previously in force. It would provide no other reductions in tax rates, except for a special new maximum rate on "earned income," principally salaries and professional fees. The personal exemption, which had been $600, would rise to $650 on July 1, 1970, remain at that level through 1971, and then increase to $700 for 1972 and $750 for 1973. The standard deduction would increase in stages from the current 10% of income or $1,000, whichever is lower, to 15% or $2,000 in 1973.

The reform provisions of the legislation included a wholly new concept in federal tax law, a "minimum tax" designed to prohibit individuals or corporations from amassing large quantities of income completely free of federal taxation. But one major loophole, tax-exempt state and municipal bond interest, would not be affected. House Ways and Means Committee Chairman Wilbur Mills said that the bill would produce $6.4 billion in additional federal tax revenue in 1970 and $288 million in additional revenue in 1971. By 1972, however, the government would receive $1.7 billion less than present revenue, and the loss would grow to about $3.7 billion in 1973.

In related action, Congress approved and the president signed legislation to extend the surcharge on federal income taxes through June 30, 1970. The surcharge rate in 1969 was 10%, but the rate was reduced to 5% for the period Jan. 1–June 30, 1970—or, in effect, 2½% for the entire year. The surtax extension bill also provided for repeal of the 7% investment tax credit and for postponement until Dec. 31, 1970, of scheduled reductions in telephone and automobile excise taxes.

A major but narrow victory for the administration came when the Senate defeated, on a 50–50 tie vote, an amendment that would have permitted research on, but not deployment of, the Safeguard antiballistic missile (ABM) system. The long and acrimonious debate on the ABM issue epitomized growing dissatisfaction in Congress over the high cost of maintaining the military establishment. The extent of this feeling

UPI COMPIX

Deadly phosgene gas from the Rocky Mountain Arsenal moves by rail through Memphis, Tenn., on Aug. 15, 1969, en route to Geismar, La. Cross-country shipments of the gas were the subject of protests in many cities through which they passed.

Farm home and buildings near Drayton, N.D., surrounded by water from the flooding Red River in April 1969. Hundreds of farms from Grand Forks to the Canadian border were covered.

WIDE WORLD

was expressed in the fiscal 1970 defense appropriation bill, which provided $5 billion less than the Nixon administration had requested. Further evidence of skepticism toward the Department of Defense could be found in the Senate's national commitments resolution, which directed the president not to commit U.S. troops to foreign military engagements without the firm consent of Congress.

Nixon proposed in May that the Selective Service law be amended to permit a lottery system for choosing armed forces draftees, and Congress finally approved such legislation in mid-November. The first draft lottery was held at Selective Service headquarters in Washington, D.C., on December 1. There were two drawings—the first for each day (or birthdate) in the year and the second for each letter in the alphabet. The order in which the dates were drawn determined the order by which eligible men between the ages of 19 and 26 would be drafted in 1970. The second drawing was to determine the order of induction of those having the same birthdate, with the initial letter of the individual's last name providing the key.

Foreign Relations. The difficult task of terminating U.S. involvement in the Vietnam war preoccupied President Nixon throughout the year. While progress to that end was difficult to discern, fewer American troops were in the field at the end of 1969 than at the beginning, and more of the burden of combat had been assumed by South Vietnamese forces. In a major speech on May 14, the president proposed an eight-point peace plan for Vietnam that included provisions for mutual withdrawal of "the major portions" of U.S., allied, and North Vietnamese troops from South Vietnam and internationally supervised elections to ensure "each significant group in South Vietnam a real opportunity to participate in the political life of the nation." Nixon strongly hinted that he would order a partial withdrawal of U.S. combat troops from South Vietnam before an agreement with the Communists on a total withdrawal and regardless of developments at the Paris peace talks.

In a second, related address on Vietnam on November 3, Nixon said that his administration had adopted a plan of cooperation with the South Vietnamese for the complete withdrawal of all U.S. combat ground forces "on an orderly, scheduled timetable." But he declined to give details of the timetable on the ground that to do so would remove the enemy's incentive to negotiate. Nixon also disclosed that he had taken a secret peace initiative in a letter to the late North Vietnamese Pres. Ho Chi Minh, but that Ho had "flatly rejected" it.

The November 3 speech was notable for its appeal for national unity in support of the administration's efforts toward peace in Vietnam. "North Vietnam cannot defeat or humiliate the United States," the president said. "Only Americans can do that." He went on to direct a special plea to "the great silent majority of my fellow Americans" for support.

Two and one-half weeks after Nixon delivered his address, the Paris peace talks came to a virtual halt. Henry Cabot Lodge, head of the U.S. delegation at Paris, resigned his post, and so did Lawrence E. Walsh, Lodge's deputy. In his letter of resignation to Nixon, Lodge said that the president had "left no stone unturned" in efforts to find a peaceful solution to the war. It was "sad," he added, that the Communist negotiators had "flatly refused to reciprocate in any kind of meaningful way."

Nixon gave substance to his announced intention of reducing U.S. involvement in the war by ordering the withdrawal of some U.S. troops from Vietnam. The first withdrawal of 25,000 men was announced on June 8 after Nixon and South Vietnamese Pres. Nguyen Van Thieu had conferred on Midway Island. A second withdrawal, this time of 35,000 troops, was ordered on September 16. Three months later the president announced a third withdrawal of 50,000 troops to be completed by April 15, 1970. Secretary of Defense Melvin Laird said in December that draft calls for 1970 might be reduced by 25,000 men as a result of plans to remove troops from Vietnam and to cut the overall size of the armed forces.

One of Nixon's two major trips abroad in 1969 included a 5½-hour unannounced visit to South Vietnam on July 30. The president conferred with South Vietnamese leaders and addressed troops of the First Infantry Division near Saigon. Other stops on Nixon's nine-day midsummer trip included Indonesia, Thailand, India, Pakistan, Romania, and Britain. On his return, the president described his reception in Romania by huge crowds as "the most moving experience I have had in traveling to over 60 countries."

Nixon's first overseas journey as president took him to five Western European nations in late February and early March. He conferred with leaders in Brussels, London, Bonn, West Berlin, Rome, Paris, and the Vatican as well as with NATO officials and with the U.S. negotiating team at the Vietnam peace talks in Paris. In a statement issued prior to his trip, Nixon had emphasized that he wanted to create a "new spirit of consultation" and "confidence" between the U.S. and its European allies and to strengthen relations among the member countries of NATO.

Two significant steps toward international arms control were taken in 1969. President Nixon on November 24 completed action on the nuclear nonproliferation treaty by signing it eight months after Senate ratification. The signing ceremony coincided with ratification by the Presidium of the Supreme Soviet in Moscow and signature by Soviet Pres. Nikolai V. Podgorny. The Soviet Union and the U.S. became the 23rd and 24th nations to ratify the treaty; 43 ratifications were required before it could take effect. One week before the dual ratification ceremonies, U.S. and Soviet representatives opened pre-

continued on page 782

THE CONGLOMERATE PHENOMENON

By Joel E. Segall

In the financial literature of 1969, conglomerate mergers were being deplored because they might result in economic concentration; applauded because they might encourage efficient business operation; attacked for their unorthodox financing techniques and accounting treatment; and defended as a reflection of the creative vigour and iconoclasm of the times. It seemed clear that the conglomerate movement in the U.S. had fascinated the financial press, the investment community, and, of course, the antitrust authorities. This fascination was not surprising. The firms involved were frequently huge and well known, their products ludicrously diverse, the financial arrangements complicated and sometimes associated with proxy fights or other public contests for stockholder approval, and the stock price movements large and abrupt.

The attempt to classify corporate mergers had enlarged even if it had not enriched the vocabulary of business. A combination by common ownership of firms producing the same or similar products is called a horizontal merger. A combination of a firm with its supplier or customer is called a vertical merger. A combination of firms without horizontal or vertical elements is called a conglomerate merger. Conglomerate mergers are sometimes further classified into those involving firms related in production or distribution, as in the product extension mergers; those involving firms with similar products but different geographical locations, as in the market extension mergers; and those involving firms showing none of the preceding characteristics and called by some authorities pure conglomerate or agglomerate mergers. Other terms describing conglomerates but less well defined and less commonly used are circular, concentric, and congeneric. These apparently refer to conglomerate mergers with at least some common elements in managerial abilities, financing sources, production techniques, or some other dimension of the merging firms, and are not particularly useful in a general survey.

Conglomerate mergers were certainly more common than they had ever been. As the accompanying table shows, the proportion of horizontal to total large mergers has declined sharply and systematically since 1950; the proportion of vertical mergers rose through the '50s but declined during the '60s; and the proportion of conglomerate mergers has risen sharply and systematically since 1950.

Acquisitions of Mining and Manufacturing Companies with Assets Greater than $10 Million

Percent of total in each period

Type of merger	1951–54	1955–58	1959–62	1963–66	1967	1968*
Horizontal						
Number	37.0	28.0	16.7	14.8	7.1	7.3
Assets	39.6	34.4	19.3	14.1	12.8	4.1
Vertical						
Number	12.3	15.9	18.2	14.6	10.1	8.9
Assets	8.9	20.2	23.8	14.7	6.0	7.2
Conglomerate						
Number	50.6	56.1	65.2	70.6	82.8	83.9
Assets	51.5	45.4	56.9	71.2	81.1	88.6

*Preliminary figures.

Sources: U.S. Federal Trade Commission, Bureau of Economics, as reported in Mueller, Willard F., "The Celler-Kefauver Act: 16 Years of Enforcement," *The Journal of Reprints for Antitrust Law and Economics*, vol. I; U.S. Federal Trade Commission, *Current Trends in Merger Activity, 1968.*

The Rationale for Conglomerates. A careful explanation of the growth of conglomerate mergers should probably start with an economic explanation of merger movements generally. Unfortunately, economics does not offer a general theory of merger activity, but only some clues as to the conditions under which business firms may be expected to grow. Since merging is one way of growing, economics does yield some implications for merger activity. We may infer that firms grow to achieve monopoly (or oligopoly) positions, or to reach an optimum size, or to reduce risk through diversification. Growth for such reasons will improve the financial positions of the owners and is, therefore, consistent with the profit maximizing principle so critical to traditional economic theory. But monopoly and optimum size are essentially industry concepts and can at best explain only horizontal and, perhaps, vertical mergers, not conglomerates. In addition, it is difficult to reconcile the cyclical nature of merger activity with these goals. It seems unlikely that monopoly power becomes available, or that the optimum size increases, or that preference for risk-reduction increases at about the same time in the wide variety of industries in which mergers take place.

Diversification as a goal warrants additional consideration, since conglomeration, roughly speaking, implies diversification. But even if we beg the question of the cyclical nature of mergers, diversification has severely limited explanatory power for conglomerate mergers. A conglomerate merger may achieve perfect diversification if it combines firms of equal size whose profits have perfect negative correlation. The result would be one firm with perfectly stable profits, capitalized at a riskless rate; but it is difficult to find two firms whose profits have substantial, let alone perfect, negative correlation. The most likely candidates for diversification, then, are firms whose profits are relatively independent, uncorrelated. Such a merger combines independent risks so that the average profit per dollar invested is more stable for the two firms combined than for the two firms operating independently.

Yet there is absolutely no reason why the firm should perform such a diversification function for its stockholders. First, not all stockholders may want all the stability that a merger for diversification implies; some may prefer the possibility of a very large gain even at the risk of exposure to a very large loss. Second, and more important, stockholders can get all the diversification they want at a relatively low cost through adjustment of their personal portfolios. Nothing prevents a Gulf and Western stockholder from selling some of his Gulf and Western shares and putting the proceeds in another or several other firms, or in a mutual fund for that matter. In short, each stockholder may achieve exactly the degree of diversification suitable for his own preferences and his own portfolio all by himself. Diversification through merger seems unwieldy and inefficient. Economic theory, then, leaves us with little more than ad hoc explanations for mergers.

As a consequence, some scholars have turned away from profit-oriented motives for merger to management-oriented motives. It has been argued that managers seek the prestige, power, and excitement that comes with negotiating and managing combinations of firms with hundreds of millions of dollars in resources. Risk-reduction, too, is probably more relevant for managers than for stockholders since a manager's main source of income, his job, is tied to the stability and life of the firm. Indeed, it has been argued that managers' salaries depend more on sales than on profits. Still, managers do not have complete freedom to seek their personal interests at the expense of the stockholders' interests. Corporate raiders are not uncommon and deposed managements not unknown. In any event, the empirical evidence in support of management-oriented mergers remains sparse and the issue of management versus stockholder motives has to be regarded as unsettled.

It has also been argued that conglomerate mergers increased in popularity because horizontal and vertical mergers of large firms had become increasingly difficult in the current antitrust climate. This is probably correct—horizontal mergers have long been vulnerable to antitrust complaint, vertical mergers for a lesser time, and conglomerate mergers lesser still—but the argument presupposes a purpose to merging and does nothing to explain the purpose. It is probably correct to say that little is known about why mergers in general take place and even less is known about why conglomerate mergers take place.

The Financial Mechanics of Conglomerate Merging. There are almost no financial principles for the process of conglomerate merging. One or more firms may exchange cash or other assets, bonds, stocks, convertible securities, options, warrants, or some combination of these for all or part of the stock or assets of one or more other firms. These varied financing techniques make it possible for acquiring companies to record—at least temporarily—dramatic increases in earnings even without operating benefits from the merger. The techniques are available in all mergers, but they seemed especially common in the conglomerates.

Even in a simple stock-for-stock exchange, an acquiring company with a high price/earnings ratio will increase its earnings per share by acquiring a company with a low price/earnings ratio, as long as the exchange ratio is close to the relative market value of the stocks involved. In a bond-for-stock exchange based on market values, the acquiring company will show an increase in earnings per share regardless of the price/earnings ratios as long as the interest yield on the bonds does not exceed the earnings yield (reciprocal of price/earnings ratio) on the acquired company's stock; the earnings per share of the acquiring company will be greater still because of the tax-deductible nature of the interest payments on the bonds. In an option-for-stock exchange, the earnings of the acquiring company will be higher to the extent that the acquired company has any positive earnings at all—regardless of exchange ratios or price/earnings ratios. Hybrid securities that combine bond or stock features with option features, such as convertible debentures or convertible preferred stock, can secure for the acquiring firm almost any combination of the individual financing instruments.

By 1969, however, the Securities and Exchange Commission (SEC) had begun to require that the reporting of earnings be based on the assumption that all convertible securities are converted. This requirement was in addition to the normal reporting requirements and was designed to warn investors of the potential reduction of earnings per share inherent in the conversion feature. Accounting standards continued to lag behind financing techniques, though, and similar requirements did not exist for options.

Though firms may clearly increase reported earnings by their financing techniques, the effect on market value of the stock is much less clear. In financial theory, the market value of the stock should be unaffected by financing techniques except for any tax savings involved. The market value of a stock is taken to be a function of its expected earnings stream and the risk that investors perceive with that stream. A relatively low price/earnings ratio comes about because investors regard the earnings stream as involving a relatively high risk.

In such a circumstance, an exchange of stock with a firm with a low price/earnings ratio may increase the earnings per share of the acquirer, but should not increase the market value of the stock; the price/earnings ratio after the merger should be simply the weighted average of the price/earnings ratios before the merger. Similarly, with an exchange of bonds for stock, the circumstance that interest yields on bonds are lower than earnings yields on stocks reflects only the lower risk to bondholders associated with the interest payment stream; an exchange of bonds for stock may increase earnings per share, but, in theory at least, should not increase market price. The few empirical studies of the impact on market price generally support the theory. Stockholders of acquiring firms do not appear to achieve gains in market value and/or dividends as a result of acquisitions; and gains in earnings per share are of dubious value unless they are translated into gains in market price or dividends.

The accounting treatment of merged firms also provides flexibility in reporting earnings. A merger may be accounted for as a "purchase" or as a "pooling of interests." If it is treated as a purchase, the acquired firm is accounted for in the same way as any other asset. Any excess of purchase price over book value of net worth is considered "goodwill" and is amortized against future earnings. Reported earnings are lower, then, as a consequence of the amortization. If the SEC permits the merger to be treated as a pooling of interests, the book values of the constituent firms are simply added together and there is no goodwill to amortize. If purchase price exceeds book value, a pooling treatment will generally show higher reported earnings than a purchase treatment. Again, the value of higher reported earnings is dubious, but the consummation of many mergers has been said to depend on permission to use the pooling treatment. Pooling was under criticism, and it seemed likely that accounting rules would be changed to require amortization of the difference between purchase price and book value, except for some of the firms that merge through exchange of common stock only.

The use of complicated and unorthodox financing instruments generated concern about the welfare of the stockholders of acquired firms. Officials of the SEC, the New York Stock Exchange, and some congressmen speculated that warrants, options, and convertible securities (called "funny money" and "Confederate money" by some writers) are not readily evaluated by investors, and as a consequence recipients of such instruments may be misled about the true value of the financial consideration they receive.

It seems obvious that many investors are incapable of evaluating complex securities, just as many are incapable of evaluating straight stocks or bonds. However, accurate price determination in an efficient market does not require universal sophistication, but only substantial sophistication. Enough sophisticated investors will, through their bids and offers, ensure that complex securities trade at prices no less warranted than prices of simple securities. Recently, rates of return to stockholders who received funny money in exchange for their stock in acquired firms were found to be higher than the rates of return on a general stock market index and higher than on randomly selected stocks.

The Antitrust Status of Conglomerate Mergers. Antitrust complaints against conglomerate mergers came largely or entirely under sec. 7 of the Clayton Act as amended in 1950. Enforcement of the act had been directed primarily at large horizontal and vertical mergers, but in the last few years, complaints have been brought against conglomerate mergers of the market or product extension type. In the spring of 1969, the Justice Department initiated an expansion of the scope of the antitrust law by filing suits against two pure conglomerate mergers. This action marked a change in antitrust philosophy and reflected concern that conglomerate mergers would reduce the likelihood of independent entry into the industries involved, increase the likelihood of reciprocal buying, and increase the concentration of ownership of assets. There were other concerns, but these three seemed to be unique to conglomerate mergers.

There is some reason to question the soundness of the new philosophy. In its suit against the acquisition of Jones & Laughlin Steel Corp. (J & L) by Ling-Temco-Vought, Inc. (LTV), the Justice Department alleged that LTV and J & L "specifically considered" entering each other's industries and so the merger reduced "potential competition." But every growth-minded firm must consider entering many different industries, and it is difficult to assess the social harm arising from the loss of one particular potential competitor. The cost of preserving potential competition is in precluding the economic benefits, if any, expected to flow from the merger. For example, one firm may acquire another not because the acquiring firm has a profound interest in the industry of the acquired firm, but because the acquiring firm believes it can manage the assets of the acquired firm more efficiently. In such a case, inhibition of the merger protects inefficient management rather than potential competition. Similarly, a firm may prefer to enter an industry by acquisition rather than by internal expansion because acquisition may be quicker or cheaper. If entry by acquisition is blocked, the firm may find it too costly, in terms of time or money or both, to enter the industry at all. In any event, it is difficult to find documented cases of significant economic loss arising from mergers that reduce "potential competition."

Reciprocal buying takes place when a firm uses its economic power as a purchaser of supplies to induce suppliers to buy its products. In its suit to force International Telephone and Telegraph Corp. (IT & T) to divest itself of Canteen Corporation, the Justice Department was contending that the combined firm would benefit from reciprocity by inducing suppliers of IT & T to become buyers from Canteen. In the LTV–J & L suit, the department pointed out that LTV buys many automobiles for its National Car Rental System, Inc., subsidiary and could induce an automobile manufacturer to buy steel from J & L, another subsidiary, in order to secure LTV's automobile business.

Yet, the logic of such reciprocal buying is not entirely clear. If the automobile manufacturer does not ordinarily buy its steel requirements from J & L, it is because a competitive steel supplier provides the automobile manufacturer with something valuable, perhaps location, speed of delivery, convenience, or even a price concession. The automobile manufacturer will, therefore, sustain a loss from switching its purchases to J & L. For reciprocal buying to be profitable to the automobile manufacturer, the loss in switching steel suppliers must be more than made up in the profits from selling cars to National Car Rental. For LTV, reciprocal buying would be profitable only if the profits from selling steel to the automobile manufacturer more than made up for the loss in shifting car purchases away from the preferred supplier to the automobile manufacturer in question.

But the loss (to the automobile manufacturer) in shifting steel suppliers must be greater than the profits (to LTV) from selling steel to the automobile manufacturer because if that were not true, J & L could have profitably secured the automobile manufacturer's steel business by offering a price concession or other benefit in excess of the automobile manufacturer's loss from shifting suppliers. In such circumstances, the automobile manufacturer would have bought from J & L in the first place. Similarly, the loss to LTV in switching automobile suppliers must be greater than the gain (to the automobile manufacturer) from selling automobiles to LTV. Total losses will exceed total gains and a reciprocal buying arrangement will be unprofitable. Reciprocal buying arrangements may be profitable where there exist impediments to free pricing, but that circumstance must be uncommon and hardly fits the cases in which the Justice Department cited reciprocal buying as a danger.

Historically, antitrust concern about concentration had to do primarily with concentration in particular markets and industries. Concentration of ownership of assets is a more recent concern. The most commonly cited datum on concentration of ownership is the proportion of all manufacturing assets owned by the 200 largest firms. That proportion increased from less than 50% in 1948 to 54% in 1960 to about 60% in 1969. Mergers certainly played a large role in the increased concentration, but probably not as large as is frequently attributed to them; the period of rapid growth in concentration did not coincide with the period of rapid growth in mergers, and also mergers were found to contribute more to the growth of intermediate-sized firms than to the growth of the largest firms.

In 1969, the extent of concentration did seem frightening, and the frequency of mergers was unprecedented. A longer perspective suggests that this concern, too, may have received too much attention. The merger wave at the turn of the century was at least as important to the nation and much more important in terms of concentration. Though the number of mergers per year was very much lower than in more recent history, the number of firms available to merge was also very much lower. It was estimated that the total value of the merged firms in the early period amounted to about 30% of the annual gross national product (GNP). It was difficult to settle on corresponding estimates for the current merger wave, but it was highly unlikely that the 30% figure was being exceeded. The merger movement of the 1920s was not as important as either the current or the turn-of-the-century movement, but even then, according to S. R. Reid, 37 mergers alone accounted for a total of $5.4 billion in assets, or more than 5% of the 1929 GNP.

As for concentration, G. J. Stigler reports that in 1900, International Harvester produced 85% of harvesting machines and American Sugar Refining refined virtually all the sugar in the U.S. In 1901, American Can produced 90% of the industry production. In 1902, National Biscuit controlled 70% of biscuit output, American Smelting and Refining accounted for 85–95% of the copper refining, Corn Products had 80% of its industry's capacity, U.S. Leather accounted for more than 60% of the leather output, Distillers Securities produced more than 60% of the whiskey output, and International Paper produced 60% of all newsprint.

It is important to note that these data represent concentration within industries, a much more serious economic dimension than the concentration across industries with which concentration of ownership of assets is concerned. Indeed, it has yet to be demonstrated that concentration of ownership of corporate assets has any important economic effect. Fear of concentration of ownership is very close to fear of bigness per se. It may be that the frightening thing about the increasing concentration of ownership is the allegation that large political powers inhere in large aggregations of assets. This, too, has yet to be demonstrated.

The Future of Conglomerate Mergers. Since we do not know why conglomerate mergers take place, it is difficult to assess their future. There were, however, several factors likely to influence their future. First, there was a recent and apparently continuing attempt by the antitrust authorities to apply the law to all large conglomerate mergers and with a new set of arguments. These arguments seemed at least moderately unsound, but would probably prevail in at least some cases in the near term. The fear of antitrust activity so generated was likely to reduce the frequency of large conglomerate mergers. Second, the prospective change in accounting rules to restrict the use of pooling treatments would reduce the extent to which reported earnings per share could be represented as growing when in fact the growth resulted from the mechanics of the merger. To the extent that showing growth in earnings was relevant to the success of mergers, the frequency of mergers would be lowered as a result of this change. The restriction of pooling to firms that merge by exchange of common stock only (and some other conditions) would serve also to reduce the use of funny money in mergers. Third, there was already evidence that some conglomerates were experiencing operating difficulties. A few had, in fact, already sold previously acquired firms that were being operated as divisions.

The conglomerate movement was of recent origin and conglomerate firms, with their typically heavy debt burdens and small management teams, had not yet been widely tested in periods of stress. They might be less glamorous to investors in the future. Indeed, the stock price behaviour of conglomerate firms in 1969 suggested that some disenchantment had already set in.

BEN ROTH AGENCY

—Emmwood, "London Daily Mail."

continued from page 778

liminary talks in Helsinki on limitation of strategic armaments. After five weeks of what was termed "useful" discussion, both sides agreed to open formal negotiations in Vienna on April 16, 1970. The cordiality and seriousness of the preliminary exchange gave rise to the hope that a substantive agreement eventually would be reached.

The nations of Latin America received little attention from the U.S. during the year. Nixon's first policy statement on hemispheric relations was not delivered until October 31, and it seemed to represent at least partial abandonment of the goals of the eight-year-old Alliance for Progress. Calling for a "more mature" partnership of Western Hemisphere countries, Nixon said that social and economic progress in Latin America henceforth would depend less on the U.S. than on Latin-American initiatives. The president also said that "We must deal realistically with governments in the inter-American system as they are"—a statement that was taken to mean that the U.S. would accord equal treatment to democratic and dictatorial governments.

Domestic Affairs. The United States' greatest triumphs in 1969 occurred when American astronauts landed on the moon and returned safely to earth in two separate missions in July and November. The two landings climaxed an eight-year program set in motion by the late president John F. Kennedy on May 25, 1961, when he called on the U.S. to achieve the goal, "before this decade is out, of landing a man on the moon and returning him safely to the earth." Achievement of that objective within the allotted time led to suggestions that the country adopt new and more ambitious goals in outer space. A special Space Task Group proposed on September 17 that the U.S. undertake a manned mission to Mars before the end of the century. The proposal ran into opposition from many scientists, who contended that a manned flight to Mars would be a "stunt," and from many members of Congress, who objected to the great expense that would be entailed by such a project. (*See* ASTRONAUTICS.)

The Supreme Court underwent a tumultuous year that saw an associate justice resign under pressure, a new chief justice appointed, and a nominee to the court rejected by the Senate. Abe Fortas (*see* BIOGRAPHY) stepped down from the court effective May 14, ten days after the disclosure by *Life* magazine that he had accepted—and returned 11 months later—a $20,000 payment from the family foundation of financier Louis E. Wolfson, who was serving a one-year prison term for selling unregistered securities. Fortas had issued a statement denying any wrongdoing, but pressure for his resignation had been fed by congressional criticism of the propriety of his association with Wolfson and by the revelation that Attorney General John N. Mitchell had met secretly with Chief Justice Earl Warren to tell him of "far more serious" information about Fortas than had already been disclosed.

One week after the Fortas resignation, President Nixon appointed Warren E. Burger (*see* BIOGRAPHY), a judge of the U.S. Court of Appeals for the District of Columbia, to succeed Earl Warren as chief justice of the U.S. Warren, who had served since 1953, was scheduled to retire at the end of the spring term in June. Burger was considered a moderate on civil rights cases, an advocate of "law and order," and a critic of the Supreme Court's trend toward broadening the rights of criminal suspects. The new chief justice was confirmed by the Senate, 74 to 3, on

UNITED STATES

Education. (1966–67) Primary (including preprimary), pupils 32,527,000, teachers 1,176,000; secondary and vocational, pupils 17,328,000, teachers 864,000; higher (including junior colleges and teacher-training colleges), students 6,389,872, teaching staff 537,000.

Finance. Monetary unit: U.S. dollar ($2.40 = £1 sterling; $35 = 1 troy oz. of gold). Gold and foreign exchange, official: (June 1969) $14,510,000,000; (June 1968) $13,160,000,000. Federal administrative budget (1970 est.): revenue $198,686,000,000; expenditure $195,272,000,000. Gross national product: (1968) $865.7 billion; (1967) $789.7 billion. Money supply: (June 1969) $189 billion; (June 1968) $183.2 billion. Cost of living (1963 = 100): (June 1969) 120; (June 1968) 113.

Foreign Trade. (1968) Imports $33.252,000,000; exports (excluding military aid to the value of $573 million) $34,087,000,000. Import sources: Canada 27%; Japan 12%; West Germany 8%; U.K. 6%. Export destinations: Canada 24%; Japan 9%; U.K. 6%; West Germany 5%. Main exports: machinery 25%; motor vehicles 10%; chemicals 10%; cereals 7%.

Transport and Communications. Roads (Jan. 1, 1969) 3,684,085 mi. (including 2,869,883 mi. surfaced). Motor vehicles in use (1968): passenger 83,692,699; commercial 16,994,615; buses 351,799. Railways: railway mileage owned (Jan. 1, 1969) 208,111 mi.; traffic (1967) 15,264,000,000 passenger-mi., freight 1,498,000,000 revenue-tons originated. Air traffic (1968): 113,959,000,000 revenue passenger-mi. flown; freight 2,506,307,000 ton-miles flown. Inland waterways: freight traffic (1967) 281,392,000,000 ton-mi. (including 106,809,000,000 ton-mi. on Great Lakes system and 114,579,000,000 ton-mi. on Mississippi River system). Shipping (1968): merchant vessels 100 gross tons and over 3,232; gross tonnage 19,668,421. Ships entered (including Great Lakes international traffic; 1967) vessels totaling 162,613,000 net registered tons; goods loaded (1968) 195,675,000 short tons; unloaded 303,229,000 short tons. Telephones (Dec. 1967) 104,073,849. Radio receivers (Dec. 1967) 285 million. Television receivers (Dec. 1967) 78 million.

Agriculture. Production (in 000; short tons; 1968; 1967 in parentheses): corn 122,494 (133,281); wheat 47,113 (45,671); oats 14,872 (12,627); barley 10,035 (8,950); rye 650 (677); rice 5,266 (4,482); linseed 764 (561); sorghum 20,678 (21,167); dry beans 884 (780); soybeans 32,390 (29,282); dry peas 187 (181); peanuts 1,263 (1,237); potatoes 14,709 (15,270); sweet potatoes 689 (683); tobacco 856 (984); sugar, raw value (1968–69) 4,922, (1967–68) 5,322; apples 2,727 (2,713); pears 616 (463); oranges 8,459 (5,812); grapefruit 2,238 (1,781); lemons 759 (734); grapes 3,577 (3,069); cotton, lint 2,597 (1,790); wool 43 (50); beef and veal 10,689 (10,373); pork 6,437 (6,188); milk 58,649 (59,399); butter *c.* 590 (618); cheese *c.* 959 (957); hen eggs 4,508 (4,562); softwood timber (cu.ft.; 1967) 8,161,169, (1966) 8,267,113; hardwood timber (cu.ft.; 1967) 3,301,901, (1966) 3,354,873; fish catch (1967) 2,628, (1966) 2,803. Livestock (in 000; Jan. 1969): cattle 109,661; sheep and lambs 21,111; horses (Jan. 1968) *c.* 2,900; pigs 57,205; chickens 420,204.

Industry. Index of industrial production (1963 = 100): (1968) 133, (1967) 127; mining (1968) 117, (1967) 115; manufacturing (1968) 134, (1967) 128; electricity and gas (1968) 144, (1967) 132; construction (1968) 111, (1967) 105. Unemployment: (1968) 3.6%; (1967) 3.8%. Fuel and power (in 000; short tons; 1968): coal 551,734; crude oil 496,478; natural gas (cu.yd.) 716,206,000; electricity (kw-hr.) 1,433,000,000. Production (in 000; short tons; 1968): iron ore (50–55% metal content) 96,071; pig iron (1967) 89,479; crude steel 13,109; cement (shipments) 73,009; newsprint 2,797; sulfuric acid 28,376; caustic soda 8,799; superphosphates (1967) 2,938; nitrogenous fertilizers (N content; 1967–68) 6,781; plastics and resins 7,298; synthetic rubber 2,386; passenger cars (units) 8,823; commercial vehicles (units) 1,900. Merchant vessels launched (100 gross tons and over; 1968) 441,000 gross tons. New dwellings started (1968) 1,548,000.

June 9, and he was sworn in as Warren's successor two weeks later.

A quite different fate awaited Clement F. Haynsworth, Jr., of South Carolina (*see* BIOGRAPHY), Nixon's choice to succeed Fortas as an associate justice. Haynsworth, chief judge of the Fourth Circuit Court of Appeals, was nominated by the president on August 18 to fill the Fortas vacancy. Three months later, on November 21, the Senate rejected Haynsworth's nomination by the surprisingly large margin of 55–45. Opponents of the nomination said repeatedly that they did not question Haynsworth's honesty or integrity; they did, however, question his sensitivity to the appearance of ethical impropriety and his judgment regarding participation in cases where his financial interests could be said to be involved, even indirectly. Haynsworth also was opposed by labour and civil rights leaders.

President Nixon's year-long efforts to end U.S. participation in the Vietnam war failed to stem the tide of antiwar protest. A nationwide series of antiwar demonstrations, planned and coordinated by the Vietnam Moratorium Committee in Washington, D.C., was carried out on October 15. Moratorium Day activities included rallies, speeches, church and synagogue services, readings of the names of Vietnam war dead, tolling of bells, candlelight marches, teach-ins, seminars, folk-song concerts, vigils, wreath-layings, and door-to-door canvassing. Opponents of the Moratorium displayed the U.S. flag in front of their homes and drove their cars with headlights on during daylight hours. The extent of opposition to, like the extent of support of, the Moratorium was difficult to assess.

Another massive antiwar demonstration, organized by the New Mobilization Committee to End the War in Vietnam, was held on November 15. The two largest turnouts of protesters occurred in Washington, D.C., and San Francisco. About 250,000 persons took part in a march down Pennsylvania Avenue and/or attended a rally on the Washington Monument grounds in the nation's capital. But the most memorable feature of the Washington demonstration was a 40-hour March Against Death in which approximately 46,000 persons carried—from Arlington National Cemetery to the Capitol grounds—the name of a U.S. soldier killed in Vietnam or of a Vietnamese village allegedly destroyed by U.S. troops. In connection with the latter, the alleged "Pinkville" massacre of South Vietnamese civilians by U.S. troops, which had taken place in 1968 but did not come to light until late 1969, helped intensify antiwar sentiment.

The Nixon administration did not suffer criticism of its Vietnam war policy in silence. Vice-Pres. Spiro T. Agnew (*see* BIOGRAPHY) said on October 19 that the Moratorium Day activities had been "encouraged by an effete corps of impudent snobs who characterize themselves as intellectuals." Agnew warned that "hard-core dissidents and professional anarchists" within the antiwar movement were planning "wilder, more violent" demonstrations on November 15. And President Nixon, as noted, referred obliquely to Moratorium Day when he appealed to the "silent majority" of Americans for support of his Vietnam policies in his speech of November 3.

Agnew, whose "impudent snobs" remarks received wide press coverage, lashed out at the three commercial television networks in a speech at Des Moines, Ia., on November 13. He charged that network commentators were hostile to Nixon's November address on Vietnam; that television's immense power over public opinion was in the hands of "a small and unelected elite" of network producers, commentators, and newsmen; and that these men were often biased and, "to a man," reflected the "geographical and intellectual confines of Washington, D.C., or New York City." He added that "the views of the majority of this fraternity do not—and I repeat not—represent the views of America." One week later, in an address before the Alabama Chamber of Commerce, Agnew broadened his attack on the news media to include the press. He criticized in particular the *Washington Post* and the *New York Times*.

Off-year elections held in 1969 seemed on balance to enhance Republican prospects in the general elections scheduled for November 1970. Voters in New Jersey and Virginia elected Republican governors to succeed Democratic incumbents. In New York City, Mayor John V. Lindsay won reelection in a three-way race against Democratic and Republican-Conservative candidates. Lindsay, elected in 1965 on the Republican ticket, was forced to run as candidate of the Liberal Party in 1969 after having been defeated in the Republican primary by State Sen. John J. Marchi.

WIDE WORLD

American Indians in the main cell block of Alcatraz in San Francisco Bay on Nov. 19, 1969, after occupying the former prison. The Indians demanded that the government give the island to them as an Indian centre.

In other municipal election results, incumbent Los Angeles Mayor Sam W. Yorty defeated City Councilman Thomas Bradley, a Negro; police Lieut. Charles Stenvig was elected mayor of Minneapolis over City Council Pres. Dan Cohen; Wayne County Sheriff Roman S. Gribbs became mayor of Detroit by narrowly defeating County Auditor Richard H. Austin, a Negro; liberal Democrat Sam H. Massell, Jr., outpolled moderate Republican Rodney Cook in Atlanta's mayoral race; and Cleveland's Negro mayor, Carl Stokes, won a second term by defeating Republican Ralph Perk. Some of the foregoing results, especially the election of Stenvig, were interpreted as evidence of a rising tide of "law and order" sentiment in the nation's cities, but the outcome of other elections indicated no such thing.

The nation's racial problems appeared no nearer solution in 1969 than in previous years. Nevertheless, the country experienced less urban violence during the volatile summer months than it had in perhaps half a decade. In general, disorders were limited to small and medium-sized cities—Forrest City, Ark.; Hartford, Conn.; Fort Lauderdale, Fla.; Cairo, Ill.; Baton Rouge, La.; Youngstown, O.; Glassboro and Lakewood, N.J.; and Tacoma, Wash., among others. However, gun battles occurred in a number of cities between police and members of the Black Panther party, a militant Negro organization. The police-Panther shootouts in Los Angeles and Chicago toward the end of the year gave rise to charges that the FBI and the nation's police forces were engaged in a conspiracy to eliminate the party's leadership. One of the party's leaders, Bobby G. Seale, was a defendant in the trial of the so-called "Chicago Eight," a group of persons charged with conspiracy to incite a riot at the 1968 Democratic Party national convention. After several courtroom outbursts, Seale was sentenced to four years in prison on 16 counts of contempt of court and was severed from the trial, which thereafter became that of the "Chicago Seven."

There were few civil rights developments of national significance during the year. The most important was the unanimous Supreme Court decision of October 29 which held that school districts must end racial segregation "at once" and must "operate now and hereafter only unitary schools." The ruling, which rejected the Nixon administration's appeal for delay in desegregating 30 Mississippi school districts, abandoned the court's previous standard of allowing integration to proceed "with all deliberate speed." It was the first major decision delivered by the court under Chief Justice Burger.

The administration's efforts in behalf of minority rights were concentrated in the field of equal employment opportunity, particularly in the high-paying construction industry. Secretary of Labor George P. Shultz on September 23 ordered into effect the so-called Philadelphia Plan, which set forth specific hiring "goals" for contractors performing federally assisted construction work in the Philadelphia area.

Members of a military honour guard surround the casket of former U.S. Pres. Dwight D. Eisenhower as it lies in state in the rotunda of the Capitol on March 30, 1969.

UPI COMPIX

WIDE WORLD

National guardsmen enforce closure of a "people's park" in Berkeley, Calif., in May 1969. Thousands rioted in protest when the park was closed and surrounded with a steel mesh fence.

On such projects, the plan stipulated that by 1973 at least 26% of the work force in six largely white building trades be made up of minority-group members. Minority-group membership in the union locals that represented the six trades in the Philadelphia area currently was about 1%, according to the Labor Department. More than 30% of the population of the city of Philadelphia was black.

The Philadelphia Plan encountered stiff opposition in Congress and from labour unions. It was asserted that the plan was in clear violation of Title VII of the Civil Rights Act of 1964, which barred employment quotas based on the proportion of a minority group in the total population in a given area. Labour leaders contended that the real purpose of the plan was not to aid minority-group workers but to weaken or destroy the power of unions. The Senate voted to prohibit implementation of the Philadelphia Plan in an amendment to a supplemental appropriations bill. The House, however, voted to strip the amendment from the measure. Court challenges of the constitutionality of the plan—possibly ending in a Supreme Court decision—seemed almost certain to be undertaken. (RI. W.)

ENCYCLOPÆDIA BRITANNICA FILMS. *People Along the Mississippi* (1952); *Southwestern States* (1954); *Far Western States* (1955); *Northwestern States* (1956); *Southeastern States* (1956); *The Wheat Farmer* (1956); *Hawaii—The 50th State* (1959); *Alaska—The 49th State* (1960); *Corn Farmer* (1960); *Chicago—Midland Metropolis* (1963); *Our Changing Way of Life—The Cotton Farmer* (1963); *Our Changing Way of Life—Cattleman (A Rancher's Story)* (1964); *Our Changing Way of Life—The Dairy Farmer* (1965); *Our Changing Way of Life—The Lumberman* (1965); *Washington D.C.—Capital City U.S.A.* (1965); *The Great Plains—Land of Risk* (1966); *The Interior West—The Land Nobody Wanted* (1966); *Making the Desert Green* (1966); *New England Fisherman* (1967); *The Northeast: Gateway for a Nation* (1967); *The Northeast: Headquarters for a Nation* (1967); *The Northeast: Port of New York* (1967); *The Orange Grower* (1967); *The Sheep Rancher* (1967); *Midwest—Heartland of the Nation* (1968); *Problems of Conservation—Air* (1968); *Produce—From Farm to Market* (1968); *The House of Man, Part II—Our Crowded Environment* (1969); *The Pacific West* (1969); *Problems of Conservation—Forest and Range* (1969); *Problems of Conservation—Minerals* (1969); *Problems of Conservation—Water* (1969); *The South: Roots of the Urban Crisis* (1969).

Upper Volta

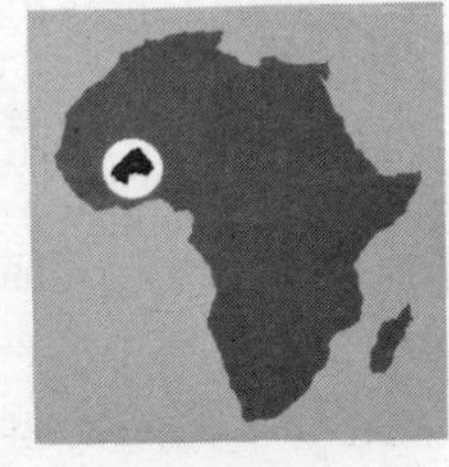

A republic of West Africa, Upper Volta is bordered by Mali, Niger, Dahomey, Togo, Ghana, and Ivory Coast. Area: 105,869 sq.mi. (274,200 sq.km.). Pop. (1969 est.): 5,226,000. Cap. and largest city: Ouagadougou (pop., 1968 est., 100,000). Language: French (official); various tribal languages and dialects. Religion: pagan; Muslim and Christian minorities. President in 1969, Gen. Sangoule Lamizana.

Undoubtedly influenced by events in neighbouring countries—especially in Dahomey and Ghana—in 1969 the military regime of Upper Volta evidently seriously considered restoring power to the civil authorities, from whom they had seized it in January 1966. President Lamizana even drew up a schedule, confirming in April that he and his colleagues would use the period from November 1969 to November 1970 for the progressive restoration of a civil regime.

On April 28 a former president, Maurice Yaméogo, was brought to trial. The special tribunal condemned him to five years' hard labour (later cut to two years) and imposed a heavy fine for the embezzlement of funds amounting to CFA Fr. 722 million.

In October another former president, Joseph Conombo, was in his turn tried on the same charge. One-time mayor of Ouagadougou, Conombo was one of the men who had dominated the political scene immediately after World War II. He was acquitted by the tribunal and was carried in triumph through the streets of the capital. After the death of Nazi Boni, former deputy of Upper Volta to France, in an automobile accident in May, Conombo appeared to be the sole traditional political leader whom the military would have to take into account when the time came for them to withdraw from power. (PH. D.)

UPPER VOLTA

Education. (1967–68) Primary, pupils 129,364, teachers (including preprimary; 1965–66) 1,714; secondary, pupils 10,145; vocational, pupils 2,157; teacher training, students 1,447; higher (1965–66), students 28; secondary, vocational, teacher training, and higher (1965–66), teachers 226.

Finance. Monetary unit: CFA franc, with a parity of CFA Fr. 50 to the French franc (CFA Fr. 277.71 = U.S. $1; CFA Fr. 666.50 = £1 sterling). Budget (1968 est.) balanced at CFA Fr. 8,564,000,000.

Foreign Trade. (1968) Imports CFA Fr. 10,120,000,000; exports CFA Fr. 5,290,000,000. Import sources: France 44%; Ivory Coast 16%. Export destinations: Ivory Coast 53%; France 14%; Ghana 10%; Japan 7%. Main exports (1967): livestock 51%; cotton 19%; peanuts 6%.

Uruguay

A republic of South America, Uruguay is on the Atlantic Ocean and is bounded by Brazil and Argentina. Area: 68,536 sq.mi. (177,508 sq.km.). Pop. (1968 est.): 2,818,000, including white 89%; mestizo 10%. Cap. and largest city: Montevideo (pop., 1967, 1,280,000). Language: Spanish. Religion: mainly Roman Catholic. President in 1969, Jorge Pacheco Areco.

The acute economic and political disorder experienced in Uruguay during 1968 continued into 1969, highlighted by a series of paralyzing strikes, periods of emergency rule, a further deterioration of the nation's economy, and the intensification of terrorist activities by the Tupamaro National Liberation Front (FLN). Reaction by labour to a determined government program to halt the country's runaway inflation and the strong political measures taken by the administration to ensure its success were largely responsible for the social unrest. Meanwhile, a British ban on Uruguayan meat imports slowed the nation's economic recovery. Together, these factors shook the foundations of Uruguay's economic stability and democratic tradition.

Labour problems plagued Uruguay throughout 1969. Although a nationwide strike called by the 500,000-member, Communist-dominated National Labour Federation (CNT) failed to materialize, a series of other strikes followed. Teachers walked out of schools in early January protesting the cancellation of Christmas bonuses; municipal and government employees struck after their mid-month paychecks were a week late; and secretaries and custodians took over the schools of veterinary medicine and agronomy at the National University during the following month. Most serious were the four-month strike by 14,000 meatpackers over termination of a daily gift of 4.4 lb. of meat, and a series of nationwide strikes called in sympathy with them. The meat strike ended in August but was followed by a strike of 2,000 bank clerks.

As a result of strikes, associated violence, and eco-

URUGUAY

Education. (1965–66) Primary, pupils 335,089, teachers (including preprimary) 9,152; secondary, pupils 91,371; vocational, pupils 26,298; teacher training, students 4,947; higher, students 17,087, teaching staff (1963–64) 2,182.

Finance. Monetary unit: peso, with an official rate of 250 pesos to U.S. $1 (600 pesos = £1 sterling). Gold and foreign exchange, central bank: (May 1969) U.S. $193 million; (May 1968) U.S. $179 million. Budget (1968 est.): revenue 46.1 billion pesos; expenditure 56.4 billion pesos. Money supply: (June 1968) 37,907,000,000 pesos; (June 1967) 17,509,000,000 pesos. Cost of living (Montevideo; 1963 = 100): (March 1969) 1,931; (March 1968) 1,440.

Foreign Trade. (1968) Imports U.S. $165 million; exports U.S. $179.1 million. Import sources (1967): U.S. 14%; Brazil 12%; West Germany 10%; U.K. 8%; Argentina 7%; Kuwait 6%. Export destinations: U.K. 21%; U.S. 12%; Italy 7%; Spain 7%; West Germany 7%; Greece 6%; Netherlands 6%. Main exports: wool 44%; meat 34%; hides and skins 9%.

Transport and Communications. Roads (1967) *c.* 41,600 km. (including *c.* 5,000 km. with improved surface). Motor vehicles in use (1967): passenger *c.* 144,000; commercial (including buses) *c.* 92,000. Railways (1967) 3,102 km. Air traffic (1967): 72,895,000 passenger-km.; freight 319,000 net ton-km. Shipping (1968): merchant vessels 100 gross tons and over 42; gross tonnage 131,123. Telephones (Jan. 1968) *c.* 195,000. Radio receivers (Dec. 1967) *c.* 1 million. Television receivers (Dec. 1965) 200,000.

Agriculture. Production (in 000; metric tons; 1968; 1967 in parentheses): wheat *c.* 250 (*c.* 147); barley *c.* 42 (*c.* 14); oats (1967) *c.* 33, (1966) 72; sweet potatoes (1967) *c.* 80, (1966) *c.* 81; corn *c.* 69 (*c.* 117); linseed *c.* 26 (40); sunflower seed (1967) 76, (1966) 99; rice (1967) 116, (1966) 107; sugar, raw value (1968–69) *c.* 64, (1967–68) *c.* 30; oranges (1966) *c.* 45, (1965) *c.* 42; wine (1967) *c.* 70, (1966) *c.* 85; wool, greasy (1967) *c.* 81, (1966) *c.* 80; beef and veal (1967) *c.* 238, (1966) *c.* 237; mutton and lamb (1967) *c.* 58, (1966) *c.* 58. Livestock (in 000; May 1968): cattle *c.* 8,800; sheep *c.* 21,700; horses *c.* 440; pigs *c.* 355.

Industry. Production (in 000; metric tons; 1967): cement 421; limestone 727; electricity (kw-hr.) 1,841,000.

United States Dependencies: *see* Dependent States

Universalist Church: *see* Religion

Universities: *see* Education

Uranium: *see* Mining; Nuclear Energy

Urban Affairs: *see* Cities and Urban Affairs

nomic disruption, Uruguay was placed under a state of emergency by President Pacheco on June 24. A distinct possibility existed that Uruguay's long tradition of democratic government might be in jeopardy for the first time since a short-lived military dictatorship ended in 1934. A fight for power involving the executive, with military backing, and the legislative branches of government emerged over the proper ways to bring order to the nation.

The economic picture darkened when the British Ministry of Agriculture announced its refusal to accept Uruguayan meat products after April 30. Although warned by the British five years earlier to make improvements in their meat-packing facilities, 9 of Uruguay's 14 slaughterhouses still failed to meet British or United States health standards. An estimated $10 million in foreign exchange was lost during 1969 because of the ban.

Terrorism by the Tupamaro FLN increased greatly in 1969. Its members were charged with stealing more than $250,000 from banks and casinos during the year. One of the country's leading bankers and publishers was kidnapped in September. A clandestine radio station was put into operation by the FLN to promote the overthrow of the Pacheco regime. A Gallup poll, however, showed that the Tupamaros enjoyed a high degree of support from the populace, which thought of them as "Robin Hoods." In December, President Pacheco forbade the news media to make any reference to them.

Despite the strikes, political difficulties, and terrorism, President Pacheco's stringent economic stabilization program seemed to be paying off. The cost of living, which had risen by almost 200% in 1967 and 1968, was held in check. During the first half of 1969 the rate of inflation was less than 10%, as compared with 63.7% a year earlier. Furthermore, the administration held the line on devaluation.

Uruguay received several loans during 1969 and concluded a trade pact with the Soviet Union. Loans of $30 million from Swiss banks to improve tourist facilities and of $23 million from the Inter-American Development Bank to extend the country's road system were expected to stimulate growth. (E. Gn.)

Vatican City State

This independent sovereignty, surrounded by but not part of Rome, came into being with the signing of the Lateran Treaty between the Holy See and the Italian government on Feb. 11, 1929. As a state with territorial limits, it is properly distinguished from the Holy See, which, being the pope together with the nine congregations of the Roman Curia, constitutes the worldwide administrative and legislative body for the Roman Catholic Church. The area of Vatican City is 108.7 ac. (44 ha.). Pop. (1968): 1,000. As sovereign pontiff, Paul VI is the head of state. Vatican City is administered by a pontifical commission of five cardinals, of which the secretary of state, Jean Cardinal Villot, is president.

Of considerable significance during 1969 was the nomination for the first time in 55 years of a non-Italian secretary of state. Jean Cardinal Villot, 63-year-old former archbishop of Lyons, France, was chosen less as an administrator than as a practicing man of the church, who would continue his pastoral duties. In this same spirit of a return to evangelical sources, the synod of bishops was charged with interpreting the principle of collegiality laid down by the second Vatican Council. (*See* Religion.)

In January, Vatican Radio lauded the suicides of young people reported from Czechoslovakia in the wake of the Soviet invasion. Two days later the pope said that he could not approve of the suicides but that he treasured the valour and self-sacrifice of the victims.

In March the pope announced that Vatican real estate in Paris was being sold to establish a fund to combat social injustice, poverty, hunger, and ignorance in Latin America. The fund was to be administered by the Inter-American Development Bank in consultation, where appropriate, with the Holy See.

Canadian Prime Minister Pierre Trudeau visited the Vatican in January and told the pope the Canadian government was considering opening diplomatic relations with the Vatican. U.S. Pres. Richard M. Nixon ended his European tour in March with a meeting with the pope. Subsequently, in July, the president announced that, for the present, it had been decided not to establish formal diplomatic relations. (Mx. B.; X.)

U.S.S.R.:
see Union of Soviet Socialist Republics

Utilities, Public:
see Cooperatives; Fuel and Power; Industrial Review; Transportation

Vegetables:
see Agriculture; Food; Gardening

Venezuela

A republic of northern South America, Venezuela is bounded by Colombia, Brazil, Guyana, and the Caribbean Sea. Area: 352,143 sq.mi. (912,050 sq. km.). Pop. (1968 est.): 9,686,486, including mestizo 69%; white 20%; Negro 9%; Indian 2%. Cap. and largest city: Caracas (metro. pop., 1966 est., 1,764,274). Language: Spanish. Religion: predominantly Roman Catholic. Presidents in 1969, Raúl Leoni and, from March 11, Rafael Caldera.

In 1969 Venezuela achieved its first legal transfer of power between presidents of different parties, from Raúl Leoni of Acción Democrática to Rafael Caldera of the Comitado Organización Politica Electoral Independiente (COPEI), who took office on March 11. President Caldera's program, however, was hindered by his lack of a legislative majority; in the elections for both houses of Congress his party finished second to Acción Democrática, with 16 against 19 senators and 59 against 66 deputies. This meant that to secure a majority COPEI had to form alliances with some of the smaller parties, but so dissimilar were their interests that a firm coalition was not possible. The Cabinet, for instance, included only six members of COPEI; the others were political independents.

To elect a member of COPEI as president of the Senate, it was necessary for its leaders to enlist the support of the Cruzada Cívica Nacional (4 senators, 21 deputies), the party of the former dictator Marcos Pérez Jiménez, who during his period of power had consistently persecuted COPEI. Pérez Jiménez' own election to the Senate in 1968 was annulled by the Supreme Court in April, on the ground that as a candidate he had not fulfilled the necessary legal conditions.

The effect of the change of government first became apparent in the sphere of foreign relations. President Caldera repudiated the "Betancourt Doctrine," under which for the previous ten years Venezuela had automatically suspended diplomatic relations with any

Latin-American country that suffered a change of government by coup d'etat. This doctrine, a holdover from 1959 when most Latin-American governments were constitutionally elected, was becoming less and less relevant to existing conditions. Diplomatic ties were established with the military regimes of Argentina, Panama, and Peru. A related step by the new government was the restoration in March of legal status to the Communist Party, which had been outlawed in 1962 because of its involvement with guerrilla movements.

Relations with Eastern European countries improved. In January talks on restoring formal relations, suspended at the time of the crisis in Czechoslovakia, were resumed, and several trade missions were later exchanged; diplomatic relations were resumed with the U.S.S.R., Hungary, and Romania.

The president's economic policy received two serious setbacks during the year. The first was the government's decision, taken at the last moment in opposition to Caldera's personal wishes, not to approve the agreement establishing the Andean Subregional Integration Group; this meant that the group comprised only Chile, Bolivia, Colombia, Ecuador, and Peru. Venezuela had, according to the agreement, a second chance to sign, as a founder-member of the group, by the end of 1970. Membership in the group was regarded with trepidation by the Venezuelan business community, because the degree of integration envisaged would put Venezuelan industry, which was mainly high-cost, at a disadvantage.

VENEZUELA

Education. (1965–66) Primary, pupils 1,453,310, teachers 42,623; secondary, pupils 189,583, teachers 9,045; vocational, pupils 93,120, teachers 4,738; teacher training, students 12,831, teachers 1,470; higher (including 7 universities), students 46,825, teaching staff 4,762.

Finance. Monetary unit: bolívar, with an official selling rate of 4.50 bolivares to U.S. $1 (10.80 bolivares = £1 sterling), a rate of 4.40 bolivares to U.S. $1 (10.56 bolivares = £1) for petroleum and iron ore exports, and a rate of 4.48 bolivares to U.S. $1 (10.75 bolivares = £1) for other exports. Gold and foreign exchange, central bank: (June 1969) U.S. $770 million; (June 1968) U.S. $758 million. Budget (1969 est.) balanced at 9,280,000,000 bolivares. Gross national product: (1967) 38,320,000,000 bolivares; (1966) 35,720,000,000 bolivares. Money supply: (May 1969) 5,984,000,000 bolivares; (May 1968) 4,921,000,000 bolivares. Cost of living (Caracas; 1963 = 100): (June 1969) 110; (June 1968) 106.

Foreign Trade. (1967) Imports (f.o.b.) 5,632,000,000 bolivares; exports 12,705,000,000 bolivares. Import sources: U.S. 50%; West Germany 9%; Japan 6%; Canada 5%; U.K. 5%; Italy 5%. Export destinations: U.S. 34%; Netherlands Antilles 21%; Canada 9%; U.K. 6%; Trinidad and Tobago 5%. Main exports: crude oil and refined petroleum products 92%; iron ore 5%.

Transport and Communications. Roads (1967) *c.* 31,000 km. (including *c.* 14,000 km. with improved surface). Motor vehicles in use (1967): passenger 450,000; commercial (including buses) 191,400. Railways (1967): 773 km.; traffic 39 million passenger-km., freight 17 million net ton-km. Air traffic (1967): 871,940,000 passenger-km.; freight 41,780,000 net ton-km. Shipping (1968): merchant vessels 100 gross tons and over 89; gross tonnage 350,591. Telephones (Jan. 1968) 327,038. Radio receivers (Dec. 1967) 1,676,000. Television receivers (Dec. 1965) 650,000.

Agriculture. Production (in 000; metric tons; 1967; 1966 in parentheses): corn 604 (557); sesame 80 (60); sweet potatoes 111 (107); cassava 328 (320); dry beans 50 (47); coffee 62 (61); tobacco (1968) 12, (1967) 10; cocoa 23 (24); bananas 1,276 (1,258); oranges 167 (159); sugar, raw value (1968–69) *c.* 447, (1967–68) *c.* 400; cotton, lint 19 (18); meat 223 (212). Livestock (in 000; 1967–68): horses 414; asses *c.* 480; cattle 6,911; pigs 1,989; sheep (1966–67) 98; poultry (1966–67) 14,169.

Industry. Production (in 000; metric tons; 1968): crude oil 189,204; natural gas (cu.m.) 7,754,000; petroleum products (1967) 58,820; iron ore (62% metal content) 15,503; cement (1967) 2,278; gold (troy oz.; 1967) 19; diamonds (metric carats; 1967) 70; electricity (kw-hr.; 1967) 9,479,000.

The second setback was probably even more serious. Partly because of overestimates in the 1969 budget of revenue from the petroleum, iron-ore, and income taxes, and partly because of overspending by the outgoing administration, the new government quickly found itself short of cash and applied to Congress for authorization to contract up to 2,025,000,000 bolivares in loans. After two months of discussion the majority in the Chamber of Deputies reduced this total to 780 million bolivares; the government later became deeply concerned about the execution of the 1970 budget, for which it sought authority to borrow an additional sum of 1 billion bolivares.

The new government's oil policies were based on expediting the allocation of service contracts covering the southern part of Lake Maracaibo, and persuading the U.S. authorities to grant Venezuelan oil the import privileges already granted to Canadian and Mexican oil. The timetable laid down for the service contracts required all bids for the five blocks offered in the southern part of Lake Maracaibo to be received by July 4. The bids then had to be discussed by Congress, and it was feared that political considerations might delay congressional approval.

Venezuela seemed by the end of the year to be close to success in its attempt to secure entry into the U.S. market for its oil on the preferential terms offered to Canadian and Mexican oil. The case was presented by the Venezuelan government, the National Pro-Petroleum Front set up in Venezuela earlier in the year, the U.S. Chamber of Commerce in Caracas, and the oil companies. If this proposal was accepted, Venezuelan exports to the U.S. were expected to show an increase of 300,000 bbl. a day over the 1968 level.

Meanwhile, investment in Venezuelan oil in 1969 was expected to reach about $370 million, the highest level since the boom years of 1957 and 1958 when the last round of concessions was granted. Part of this total was being spent on desulfurization plants, to render the oil acceptable in the U.S. market. During the first half of 1969, crude oil production showed a decline of 2.3% compared with January–June 1968, to 3.5 million bbl. a day.

Great attention was being paid to developing mineral resources. Apart from iron ore, long important (production rose in the first half of 1969 to 8,320,000 tons, 8.2% above January–June 1968), bauxite and manganese were being actively developed.

Again in 1969, considerable interest in Venezuela's development was shown by the international financing organizations. Among the principal loans received were $85 million to the government from a group of 18 U.S. and Canadian banks to repay government debts; $31 million from the World Bank to the Caroní electricity undertaking to buy a fourth 175-Mw. generator for the Guri hydroelectric complex; $20 million, also from the World Bank, to help finance the building of an expressway around Caracas; and $16 million from the Inter-American Development Bank to the Cadafe electricity agency to finance a hydroelectric plant on the Santo Domingo River.

One event in 1969 aroused concern among foreign investors. In July the central bank conditioned the granting of local bank loans to foreign-owned companies established in Venezuela on their retaining within Venezuela all their capital, loans from abroad, reserves, and retained earnings, and on their not making loans or investments abroad (unless such transactions helped to develop exports of Venezuelan manufactures). In August this regulation was modified to exclude those companies owned mainly by foreign individuals who lived in Venezuela. (J. C. G. B.)

ENCYCLOPÆDIA BRITANNICA FILMS. *Colombia and Venezuela* (1961).

Veterinary Medicine

There was relatively little change in the world animal disease situation during 1969, at least with regard to new outbreaks of epizootic proportions. The last such major problem had been the outbreak of foot-and-mouth disease that began in England during 1967, following importation of infected meat from South America, and that cost some £150 million before it was eradicated in 1968. This experience led government agencies in other developed countries to increase surveillance and review their methods of controlling diseases introduced from other countries.

Although naturally occurring foot-and-mouth disease had long been thought to involve only cloven-footed animals (cattle, sheep, swine, deer, etc.), one human case was reported during the British outbreak and, in 1969, several researchers and animal attendants at one experiment station in the U.S. became infected. A retrospective survey indicated that several children in a Baltimore, Md., orphanage had contracted the disease after drinking the milk of affected cows during a major outbreak in 1914.

Foot-and-mouth disease, rinderpest, and other enzootic diseases continued to be major deterrents to efficient food-animal production in many countries of South America, Asia, Africa, and Eastern Europe. Using expanded slaughter and/or vaccination programs, several nations made considerable progress toward reducing the economic drain imposed by these diseases. Thus, in Argentina, more than 90% of some 50 million cattle were vaccinated against foot-and-mouth disease, and in Uruguay a compulsory vaccination program instituted in 1968 was expected to include all cattle by the beginning of 1970.

In Europe the foot-and-mouth disease problem was confounded by the diversity of prevention and control measures. The overall incidence was reduced from about 12,850 farms affected in 1966 to 3,650 in 1968; in West Germany it was reduced from 4,689 to 68 and in the Netherlands from 2,194 to none. In Spain and Portugal, however, the incidence rose from 46 to 1,474 during the same period.

A significant stage in the ten-year program begun in 1962 to eradicate hog cholera (swine fever) in the U.S. was reached in July, when the U.S. Department of Agriculture prohibited interstate shipment of vaccine into the 43 states and Puerto Rico that had reached the "stamping-out" phase (*i.e.,* slaughter of all affected and in-contact animals). First used in the early 1900s, immunization with live or modified-live vaccine had long been the only means of saving the swine industry from destruction. In recent years, however, it had served to perpetuate the disease through a carrier state induced by vaccination. The disease had cost producers some $50 million annually, or about 20% of net profits, most of which represented the cost of vaccination rather than direct losses from disease. As of August 1969, 12 states were cholera-free and 29 others had nearly realized this goal.

Great Britain had been free of canine rabies since 1922, when a six-month quarantine was imposed on all dogs entering the country. In 1969, however, a pet dog brought to Camberley, near London, from West Germany developed rabies ten days after being released from quarantine. Hundreds of animals in the vicinity of Camberley were shot, and in December the quarantine was raised to eight months and a number of animals susceptible to rabies, other than those going to zoos or research establishments, were barred from the country. In Denmark, where vigorous reduction of the fox population had eliminated rabies after 1965, one case was recorded—in a fox that apparently had escaped through the buffer zone established on the German border where all wild carnivores and nonvaccinated dogs had been systematically destroyed.

Veterinarians in the U.S. continued to be active in such varied fields as laboratory animal medicine, aerospace research, and projects having primary application in human medicine, such as the implantation of nuclear-powered cardiac pacemakers in dogs. The search for animals in which rare human diseases could be simulated was intensified. A "sea-grant" program (so-named to distinguish it from traditional land-grant college programs) was instituted at the Texas A and M College of Veterinary Medicine for the study of fish diseases.

The first class from a new veterinary school in Saskatchewan, the third school in Canada, graduated in 1969. In the U.S. a faculty was appointed for a school in Louisiana and monies were appropriated for a school in Florida. A school in Connecticut, still in the planning stages, would bring the U.S. total to 21. Interest in specialization continued to increase, and in 1969 seven professionally recognized specialty boards in the U.S. had several hundred diplomates enrolled. (J. F. Ss.)

Vietnam

A country comprising the easternmost part of the Indochinese Peninsula, Vietnam, from July 21, 1954, was divided de facto into two republics.

Republic of Vietnam (South Vietnam). This is bordered by North Vietnam (along the 17th parallel), the South China Sea, Cambodia, and Laos. Area: 67,108 sq.mi. (173,809 sq. km.). Pop. (1968 est.): 16,259,334, including (1967 est.) Vietnamese 87%; Chinese 8%; Cambodian and Laotian 2%; others 3%. Cap. and largest city: Saigon (pop., 1968 est., 1,681,893). Language: Vietnamese. Religion: Buddhist; pagan; Confucian; Christian. President in 1969, Nguyen Van Thieu; premiers, Tran Van Huong until August 23 and, from September 1, Tran Thien Khiem.

The United States in 1969 moved to disengage itself from the Vietnamese conflict, which U.S. Pres. Richard Nixon acknowledged could not be won by "attempting to impose a purely military solution on the battlefield." America's first steps to withdraw were marked by a corresponding effort to "vietnamize" the war. On July 8, a group of 814 men of the U.S. 9th Infantry Division left South Vietnam. They were the first Americans to be pulled out, reversing a massive four-year U.S. troop buildup.

U.S. officials had consulted with President Thieu even prior to the inauguration of Nixon and had requested the withdrawal of limited numbers of American combat personnel. U.S. military strength reached its highest level ever on February 22 when the American military command announced the presence in South Vietnam of 542,500 troops. After that time the numbers steadily declined.

U.S. disengagement and greater efforts to turn the main burden of the fighting over to the armed forces of South Vietnam took place against the background of the stalemated Paris peace talks. Officials in Saigon shared the U.S. observation that the Viet Cong and North Vietnamese delegations were unyielding in their positions and that little progress could be expected at the bargaining sessions. On November 20 Henry Cabot Lodge and his chief deputy, Lawrence Walsh, resigned as U.S. delegates to the conference. In a final statement Lodge said that the only concrete progress achieved by the talks was agreement on the shape of the conference table.

Military Action. Following the announcement by the United States on Oct. 31, 1968, of a complete halt in the bombing of North Vietnam, action in South Vietnam was scattered and limited. Still unknown understandings were reached at that time that had the effect of restricting combat activity, particularly the indiscriminate shelling of cities and towns. On February 23, however, the Viet Cong and North Vietnamese launched a series of coordinated attacks on about 105 population centres, including Saigon, and military targets. In March, inexplicably, North Vietnamese infiltration into the South began decreasing appreciably. It was estimated that only 3,000 men per month were being moved southward, or 7,000 per month less than during 1968. During the period from August through October, North Vietnamese infiltration was less than 20% of what it was during the same period of 1968. A sustained battle lull followed for most of the year. In October, however, infiltration increased markedly and continued at a high rate during the remainder of the year. Action on the battlefield was also somewhat intensified during the last weeks of the year, and some officials believed that North Vietnam and the Viet Cong were building strength for a major offensive early in 1970.

The National Liberation Front, political arm of the Viet Cong, presented a ten-point peace plan in May. Most of the proposals had been previously stated by North Vietnam. On May 14 President Nixon countered with an eight-point plan. Among the proposals was one calling for mutual troop withdrawals over a 12-month period, coupled with an internationally supervised cease-fire. The NLF, which rejected Nixon's plan as "unjust and unreasonable," did not turn it down completely, but the areas of possible understanding in the two offers were too narrow to permit development of a basis for serious negotiation.

Presidents Thieu and Nixon met on Midway Island June 8 and announced a 25,000-man American troop withdrawal. Later, Nixon indicated his hope that most of the U.S. combat forces could be returned home by the end of 1970. While additional plans for withdrawal were delayed, primarily because of a brief resurgence of fighting in August, Nixon announced in September that 35,000 more U.S. military personnel would be pulled out by December 15. In December, Nixon announced an additional troop withdrawal of 50,000 to be accomplished by April 15, 1970.

Failing to win specific guarantees from the Viet Cong and the North Vietnamese for a military cease-fire and noting the lack of progress in Paris, the U.S. embarked in earnest on its program of "vietnamization." In March U.S. Secretary of Defense Melvin Laird first announced that additional funds would be requested for the plan to modernize the South Vietnamese forces. These troops, though numbering more than a million men, were still considered ill-equipped and unable to cope with battlefield situations in which they would find themselves as more American units withdrew. Regular military units and militia forces were to be equipped with advanced weaponry, including 750,000 individual and crew-served weapons, 500 heavy artillery pieces, 1,200 tanks and armoured personnel carriers, 25,000 jeeps and trucks, and 100 planes and helicopters.

U.S. military commanders in the field were instructed to keep casualties to "an absolute minimum, consistent with their mission to protect allied forces and the civilian population." President Nixon told Gen. Creighton Abrams in July that "the primary mission of our troops is to enable the South Vietnamese forces to assume the full responsibility for the security of South Vietnam." The number of U.S. casualties reflected the new orders. Losses were one-third lower for the first nine months of 1969 than they were for the same period of 1968, although they increased later in the year.

South Vietnamese officials, while expressing some apprehension about the U.S. withdrawal, publicly stated their hope that their forces would soon be able to carry the principal burden of the fighting. President Thieu, in a major address to the South Vietnamese National Assembly and Senate on November 5, said: "We, the Vietnamese people, are

VIETNAM: Republic

Education. (1965) Primary, pupils 1,660,968, teachers 28,803; secondary, pupils 370,668, teachers 9,903; vocational, pupils 8,015, teachers (full time) 444; teacher training, students 2,497, teachers 54; higher, students 27,282, teaching staff 932.

Finance. Monetary unit: piastre, with an official exchange rate of 80 piastres to U.S. $1 (192 piastres = £1 sterling) and a principal effective rate of 118 piastres to U.S. $1 (283.20 piastres = £1). Gold and foreign exchange, central bank: (June 1969) U.S. $214 million; (June 1968) U.S. $342 million. Budget (1967 rev. est.) balanced at 83 billion piastres. Money supply: (May 1969) 133,310,000,000 piastres; (May 1968) 111,260,000,000 piastres. Cost of living (Saigon; 1963 = 100): (June 1969) 420; (June 1968) 346.

Foreign Trade. (1968) Imports U.S. $466,160,000; exports U.S. $11,710,000. Import sources (1967): U.S. 32%; Japan 26%; Formosa 15%. Export destinations (1967): France 37%; U.K. 14%; Japan 14%; West Germany 14%; Italy 7%. Main export rubber 79%.

Transport and Communications. Roads (1966) 20,255 km. (including 6,371 km. main roads). Motor vehicles in use (1967): passenger 42,272; commercial (including buses) 44,941. Railways: (1966) 1,278 km.; traffic (1968) 13 million passenger-km., freight 18 million net ton-km. Air traffic (1968): 474.8 million passenger-km.; freight 4,040,000 net ton-km. Telephones (Jan. 1968) 27,082. Radio receivers (Dec. 1967) 1.3 million.

Agriculture. Production (in 000; metric tons; 1967; 1966 in parentheses): sweet potatoes 253 (246); cassava 262 (280); rice (1968) 4,366, (1967) 4,688; rubber (1968) 29, (1967) 42; tea 4.2 (5.2); coffee 3.3 (3.1); fish catch (1966) 380, (1965) 375. Livestock (in 000; 1966–67): cattle 1,033; buffaloes 665; pigs 3,185; horses *c.* 55.

Industry. Production (in 000; metric tons; 1967): cement 181; salt (1966) 87; cotton yarn 7.4; woven cotton fabrics (m.; 1966) 132,000; electricity (public supply; kw-hr.) 682,000.

VIETNAM: Democratic Republic

Education. (1965–66) Primary, pupils 2,270,000, teachers 34,730; vocational, pupils 49,600; higher (including University of Hanoi), students 15,900; vocational and higher, teaching staff 920.

Finance and Trade. Monetary unit: dong, with an official exchange rate of 3.50 dong to U.S. $1 (8.40 dong = £1 sterling). Budget (1963) balanced at 1,779,288,000 dong. Foreign trade, total turnover (1965) 780 million dong (85% with China, U.S.S.R. and other Eastern European countries).

Transport. Roads (1965) *c.* 9,000 km. Railways (1965) 937 km.

Agriculture. Production (in 000; metric tons; 1967; 1966 in parentheses): rice *c.* 4,700 (*c.* 4,500); corn *c.* 220 (*c.* 250); tobacco *c.* 4 (*c.* 5); sweet potatoes *c.* 800 (*c.* 800); tea *c.* 2.7 (*c.* 3); timber (cu.m.; 1964) 10,950; fish catch (1962) 289, (1961) 223. Livestock (in 000; 1966–67): buffaloes *c.* 1,700; cattle *c.* 825; pigs *c.* 6,000.

Industry. Production (in 000; metric tons; 1967): coal *c.* 2,800; apatite ore (1966) *c.* 1,000; salt *c.* 150; cement *c.* 750; cotton fabrics (m.; 1964) 105,200; paper (1964) 19; electricity (kw-hr.; 1964) 548,700.

determined to replace the bulk of the U.S. fighting units in 1970." He added, however: "As long as peace with guarantees has not yet been restored in Vietnam and a new Communist aggression is still threatening this part of the world, I think that under whatever form, the Free World Forces should remain on this land."

Of all the major battles in 1969, the one that commanded the most attention in the U.S. was the fight for Hamburger Hill, or Ap Bia Mountain, in the A Shau Valley. The peak was seized by U.S. forces of the 101st Airborne Division in a ten-day battle that resulted in 84 dead and 480 wounded Americans. It came at a time when U.S. commands were under orders to hold casualties to a minimum. The high ground was deemed important by field officers, who foresaw North Vietnamese forces attempting to filter through the valley in an effort to overrun the city of Hue, as they had done during the Tet offensive of 1968. Hamburger Hill was, however, abandoned by the Americans on May 27, and North Vietnamese forces eventually reoccupied it. U.S. Sen. Edward Kennedy described the effort as "senseless and irresponsible." To those who sought a rapid de-escalation of the war, it was a symbol of the military pursuing its activities without regard to political considerations.

Considerable criticism was also leveled at the military when it was alleged in November that an Army platoon had killed from 40 to 500 South Vietnamese civilians in the "Pinkville massacre" of March 1968. The Army charged one of its officers with multiple murder and an enlisted man with assault with intent to murder, and the incident was under investigation at the year's end.

The death of North Vietnamese Pres. Ho Chi Minh in September was followed by a Viet Cong proclamation of a 72-hour period of mourning, to be observed by a cease-fire. U.S. officials indicated their desire to agree to this in the hope of encouraging a significant, longer-term de-escalation. President Thieu and the Saigon government were insistent that to honour Ho in any way would be contrary to its principles. The clear split resulted in a face-saving formula permitting field commanders "to be influenced by the nature of enemy operations." U.S. B-52 raids were halted, and other air and artillery operations were also sharply curtailed.

South Vietnam's Approach to Peace. Initially, the South Vietnamese government was a reluctant partner in efforts to resolve the conflict through a negotiated settlement in Paris. Encouraged by the U.S. to assume a more constructive attitude, Saigon eventually became more flexible. On March 25 President Thieu stated his government's willingness to begin private bargaining sessions with the National Liberation Front (NLF) without preconditions of any kind. Even though the offer was rejected by North Vietnam and the NLF the next day, Thieu advanced a six-point peace plan on April 7 as a further means of breaking the stalemate. While it called for a policy of what was termed "national reconciliation," permitting full citizenship rights to all, including the Viet Cong, Thieu's proposal stated that the "Communists must abandon their war of aggression" and ruled out any possibility of a coalition government.

To some observers Thieu's approach matched the intransigence displayed by the NLF. A more significant offer was advanced by Thieu on July 11. He said: "The only way for the people of South Vietnam to exercise their right of self-determination, to participate in public affairs, and to determine the future of the country, is through elections in which they can genuinely express their choice, free from fear and coercion." To that end, Thieu proposed that the NLF, and all other political parties, join in the electoral process, with the balloting to be supervised by an international body. All parties were to accept the outcome, without reprisals or discrimination.

The government of South Vietnam on July 20 moved to start direct negotiations with the North Vietnamese, with Thieu later stating that "everything is negotiable." As it had before, however, the NLF reiterated its demands that the "puppet regime" in

Left and below, village of Tan Hiep near Bien Hoa air base in South Vietnam after an attack by U.S. and South Vietnamese forces using rockets and napalm to drive out an entrenched Viet Cong force. Every structure in the village was destroyed or hopelessly damaged during the battle.

GAMMA—PIX FROM PUBLIX

Saigon be dissolved before any further action could be taken.

In June, the NLF established a provisional revolutionary government, declaring itself to be the legitimate ruler of South Vietnam. Huyn Tan Phat, secretary-general of the NLF, was named head of the provisional government.

Political Developments. Aware of the NLF's efforts to expand its political base and to meet the challenge off the battlefield, President Thieu sought to improve his government's position among the people. His first step was the creation of the National Social Democratic Front, to bring together the deeply divided political elements in a non-Communist alliance. Thieu promised that the Front would not be "totalitarian or despotic." Final composition of the Front turned out to be disappointing, even to Thieu, who had hoped for broader representation. Eventually, only six major political groups were able to unite under Thieu's banner, primarily conservatives and strongly anti-Communist refugees from North Vietnam. Still, these allied parties had in the 1967 national elections collectively polled 48% of the total vote, and the willingness of some hitherto antagonistic groups to join in a pro-government alliance represented a step toward basic political unity which the South Vietnamese had not seen in years.

In an additional effort to command a stronger political following, Thieu announced on July 19 that a major reshuffle of the Cabinet would be undertaken. He noted that politicians of "real force" would be added to the government. Premier Huong had already been under heavy pressure from the legislature. A no-confidence motion was introduced by the National Assembly on June 16, and two weeks later 92 of the 135 deputies sent a letter to Thieu demanding Huong's removal. They charged the premier with ignoring the pressing economic problems confronting South Vietnam and with not displaying sufficient initiative in rooting out corruption.

Thieu's moves to reconstitute the Cabinet were thwarted by long-standing feuds and by a reluctance on the part of many politicians of stature to identify themselves with the government, particularly in non-prestigious posts. Finally, on September 1, Thieu announced the formation of a new 31-man Cabinet, the largest in the country's history. It included six members from the military and nine who had served in the old Cabinet. The new premier, Tran Thien Khiem, was elevated from deputy premier and interior minister. As a general, he had long occupied positions of power. Notably absent in the new administration were members from the Buddhist elements and representatives from the non-Communist opposition. The general conclusion was that Thieu's concerted efforts to establish a more representative, more popular government had failed.

Buddhist leaders were also critical of the new government. Their antigovernment attitudes hardened in March with the arrest of Thich Thien Minh, a ranking official in the religious hierarchy and a Buddhist youth leader, for antistate activities. Thien Minh was originally sentenced to ten years at hard labour. His prison term was reduced to three years, and he was then freed by Thieu in an amnesty to mark South Vietnam's National Day on November 1.

The Economy. Wartime necessities again dictated South Vietnam's meagre budgetary allotments, and the pinch of barely controllable inflation plunged the country into moves of desperation. South Vietnam was only able to sustain itself with large infusions of U.S. aid. Expenditures exceeded revenues by 65%, representing a deficit of $400 million.

UPI COMPIX

South Vietnamese children watch as a force of U.S. armoured personnel carriers patrols a road near Duc Pho in June 1969.

President Thieu's stated objectives to be attained by the government in 1969 emphasized military and military-related activities. He listed them as: "the development and modernization of the armed forces; the improvement of the village administration; the pushing forward of the Pacification and Reconstruction program; and the Land Reform program." Where competition for the limited resources of the country became manifest, the military goals were given priority consideration. More than 60% of the national budget was earmarked for national defense.

Rampant inflation sparked the midyear political crisis that led to the Cabinet reshuffle and the ouster of Premier Huong. According to the National Institute of Statistics, the consumer price index in July reached 388.6 for middle-class families and 421.8 for working-class families (with 100 representing the 1963 base). From July through September, the cost of living climbed 23%. Severe shortages of basic commodities, such as sugar and rice, were chiefly responsible for the spiraling costs.

Economic austerity was one of the first moves undertaken by the Khiem government. Drastically higher taxes were imposed on 1,523 imported items, mostly in the luxury category. The new revenues were expected to bring in the equivalent of $350 million annually, cutting the budget deficit by 70%.

U.S. economic aid remained vital to South Vietnam. Total assistance for the 1970 fiscal year was expected to reach $600 million. In the previous year it had been $447 million. In late spring, the U.S. exerted pressure on the South Vietnamese government to initiate economic reforms by withholding $40 million in aid.

The national legislature was still considering a land reform program at year's end. When the measure was first proposed by the government in 1969, about 800,000 landless peasants were to receive ownership of the properties they tilled, with the government compensating the absentee owners. It was estimated that the cost would be $400 million, with the U.S. contributing 10% of the amount. By the time the bill had been debated and amended in the National Assembly, the number of peasants to benefit was reduced to fewer than 300,000 and actual implementation would have been delayed to the point of losing the political impact for which the program was conceived. (Ro. Go.)

Members of U.S. 25th Infantry Division reconnaissance patrol use motorcycles to scout trails around Firebase Buell near the Cambodian border in April 1969.

WIDE WORLD

CAMERA PRESS—PIX FROM PUBLIX

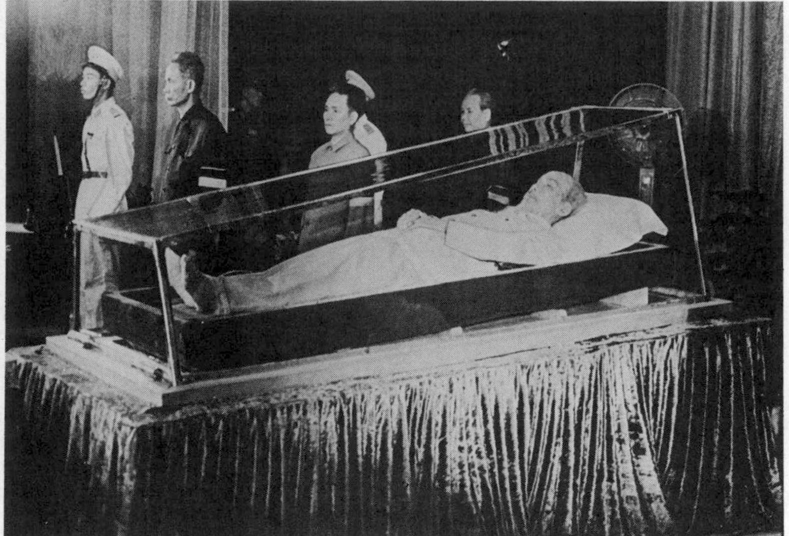

North Vietnamese officials form an honour guard around the coffin of Pres. Ho Chi Minh in the hall of the National Assembly, Hanoi, in September 1969.

Democratic Republic of Vietnam (North Vietnam). This is bordered by China, the Gulf of Tonkin, the South China Sea, South Vietnam, and Laos. Area: 61,293 sq.mi. (158,750 sq.km.). Pop. (1968 est.): 20.7 million, including (1960) Vietnamese 85.1%. Cap. and largest city: Hanoi (pop., 1965 est., 500,000). Language: Vietnamese. Religion: Buddhist; pagan; Confucian; Christian. Presidents in 1969: Ho Chi Minh until September 3 and, from September 24, Ton Duc Thang; premier, Pham Van Dong.

Pres. Ho Chi Minh's death (*see* OBITUARIES), announced on September 4, overshadowed the issues of war and peace in North Vietnam in 1969. At the funeral five days later, delegations from 34 countries heard the party first secretary read out the dead leader's last will in which he had made an impassioned appeal for unity in the world Communist movement. But Sino-Soviet rivalry was very much in evidence at the funeral. Within hours of the announcement of the death, a Chinese delegation led by Premier Chou En-lai flew into Hanoi. But it flew back the same evening, apparently on receipt of the news that Soviet Premier Aleksei N. Kosygin was also going to Hanoi. For the funeral itself China sent a second delegation headed by Vice-Premier Li Hsien-nien. However, the Soviet premier used the good offices of the North Vietnamese leaders to request a meeting with his Chinese counterpart. After leaving Hanoi on September 10 and flying through India into Soviet territory, Kosygin changed course and flew to Peking for talks "in the spirit of the Ho Chi Minh will."

The Vietnamese themselves seemed to take the passing of their patriarch calmly. On September 24 it was announced that Vice-Pres. Ton Duc Thang was elected president. It was generally understood that this was no more than a constitutional formality. Effective power was believed to be in the hands of a triumvirate: Le Duan, first secretary of the party and for many years listed as the number two man in Hanoi; Truong Chinh, chairman of the Standing Committee of the National Assembly and considered the party's chief theoretician; and Pham Van Dong, the premier. Le Duan appeared to be the chief political personality, and there was speculation elsewhere that a power struggle would eventually develop.

There was hardly any evidence after Ho's death of change in either the course of the war in Vietnam or the tactics of the peace talks at Paris. U.S. spokesmen, in fact, said that the Communist side had grown tougher if anything. Earlier, President Nixon's peace feelers had been greeted by Hanoi with an intensification of the fighting. By February–March the shelling of South Vietnamese cities had become continuous and heavy enough for the U.S. to threaten retaliation. To this Hanoi retorted by saying "We are not afraid of American bombings." After a 12-day offensive that almost wrecked the Paris peace talks, North Vietnam claimed staggering victories: "From the night of February 22 to March 30, 104,000 enemy troops wiped out or captured, among them 52,000 GI's; 1,600 aircraft and 1,440 tanks destroyed." For the first half of 1969 the figures claimed were 330,000 enemy casualties, 3,950 aircraft, and 6,000 tanks. Figures released by the U.S. also told a grim tale. In early March it was stated that total U.S. aircraft losses had crossed the 5,000 mark, with 2,593 fixed-wing planes and 2,409 helicopters lost. Military sources said a conservative estimate of the cost of the destroyed aircraft was $5 billion. From late March until October infiltration from the north into South Vietnam and battlefield action slowed down. Infiltration increased rapidly in October, however, and continued until the end of the year; at the same time, military activity was stepped up.

In June the NLF dramatically announced the formation of a provisional revolutionary government. It won immediate recognition from the Communist-bloc countries and thereafter from a number of nonaligned countries. This was the second development of the year that gave the Communist side fresh political strength. The first had occurred on January 10 when Sweden became the first Western government to extend diplomatic recognition to North Vietnam.

Conscious perhaps of the growing political status of the Communists, the U.S. established secret contacts with them outside the framework of the Paris conference. U.S. Sen. George McGovern reported that, in secret talks between himself and the Communists in Paris, the latter had only two basic points: unconditional U.S. troop withdrawal and an end to the support given to the "puppet" Thieu regime in Saigon. The day after McGovern's statement, North Vietnam announced the decision to release three U.S. prisoners of war in a Fourth of July gesture.

The goodwill gesture did not prevent Ho from strongly attacking Nixon by name in an appeal marking the 15th anniversary of the Geneva agreements on Vietnam on July 20. He accused the U.S. of stepping up the war and committing atrocities against the Vietnamese people with intensified B-52 attacks using toxic chemicals. By October the virulence of North Vietnamese propaganda attacks on Nixon had increased perceptibly. The official daily *Nhan Dan* repeatedly published commentaries "exposing the utter hypocrisy of U.S. President Nixon" and detailing the history of U.S. aggression since the end of World War II. Diplomatic observers were inclined to think that Hanoi's anger was the result of Nixon's call for a moratorium on domestic criticism against his Vietnam policy; this seemed to have upset Hanoi's calculation that continued pressure from the peace lobby would force Nixon to accept peace at any price.

Meanwhile, there were signs of accelerated economic planning in Hanoi. In January the first Japanese traders' team to be admitted into North Vietnam for two years held discussions in Hanoi. A second team followed in February. They reported that North Vietnam was in touch with France, Sweden, and other countries to promote various economic cooperation projects. On September 30 Sweden announced plans to give North Vietnam $40 million in relief and loans over a period of three years.

The most important sources of assistance, however, continued to be the U.S.S.R. and China. What was described as the country's first postwar budget was reportedly underwritten by the Soviet Union in an agreement signed in Moscow in December 1968. This program gave priority to roads, basic industrial plant, and agriculture. Comments from Communist sources suggested that the agreements with the U.S.S.R. and China were sufficient to convert North Vietnam into a socialist showpiece—provided there was an end to the war. (T. J. S. G.)

See also Defense.

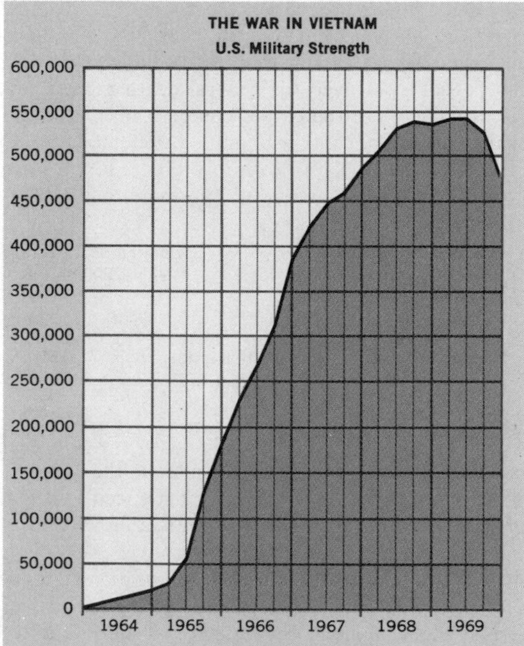

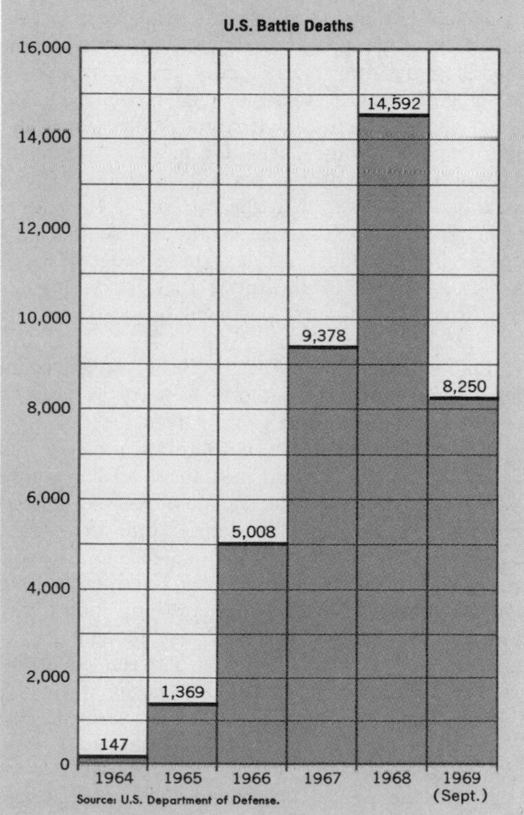

U.S. troop strength and battle deaths in Vietnam for the years 1964 to 1969. Estimated number of U.S. troops in Vietnam as of Nov. 30, 1969, was 478,800. Battle deaths for the six-year period totaled 38,744.

Vital Statistics

Two interregional seminars for vital statisticians and demographers of over a dozen nations were conducted in September 1969 under the auspices of the United Nations. One was held in cooperation with the Ukrainian government in Kiev, U.S.S.R. The other, in reality a workshop, was held in Copenhagen and was focused on the methodology of sample surveys that can provide substitute data for estimating birth and death rates. It was of particular value for representatives of less developed countries without centralized, nationwide systems for registration of births and deaths.

In June 1969 the U.S. National Committee on Vital and Health Statistics marked its 20th anniversary as an advisory committee to the surgeon general of the Public Health Service by a conference in which 45 experts in vital and health statistics and allied fields participated. Topics discussed by the conferees included the issues of invasion of privacy and breach of confidentiality that were of growing public concern in the U.S., not only with regard to birth and death records but also for population surveys and medical research. Popular misconceptions about the protection given to individual identities and lack of appreciation for the scientific value of statistical studies had jeopardized traditional programs for the collection of some vital data, such as those on race and legitimacy.

To help meet the acute need for trained vital and health statisticians, the Applied Statistics Training Institute had been organized by the National Center for Health Statistics of the Public Health Service in 1968 for the purpose of providing training for employees of state and local health departments. It became firmly established in 1969 at Research Triangle Park, N.C., where its practical one- and two-week courses attracted some 225 students.

Birth Statistics. Slightly more than 3.5 million births reportedly occurred in the U.S. in the 12 months ended August 1969. The provisional birthrate was 17.6 per 1,000 population, or 1% above the rate for the comparable period ended August 1968. Thus it appeared that the decline in the birthrate had been interrupted, if not ended, in 1969. Between 1957 and 1968 the rate had declined from 25.3 to 17.4, the lowest ever observed for the U.S. Births in 1968 numbered 3,470,000, 1% less than in 1967, when the birthrate was 17.8.

The fertility rate continued its decline into 1968, when it was 84.8 births per 1,000 women 15–44 years of age, 31% lower than the 1957 rate of 122.9 but only 3% below the 1967 rate of 87.6. This was, however, above the low levels of 76 to 79 observed during the years from 1933 to 1939, a period of notably low birth and fertility rates. Recent birthrates were much closer to the levels of the 1930s than recent fertility rates because the childbearing population (assumed to consist of women 15–44 years of age) constituted a smaller proportion of the total population in the 1960s than it did, for example, in 1936.

Between 1966 and 1967, birthrates for U.S. women

Virgin Islands: *see* Dependent States

in the age groups 35–39 and 40–44 years had the greatest declines; *i.e.*, about 9%. The smallest decline (4%) occurred in the age group 15–19. The birthrate for white women in 1967 was 16.8 per 1,000 population, compared with 25 for nonwhites. Both rates showed relatively the same decline from their values for 1966. In 1967 there were an estimated 40.2 million women 15–44 years of age, according to the U.S. Bureau of the Census. By 1975 the number of women of childbearing age was expected to reach 46.9 million, an increase of 17%. The projected increase in the age group 20–29 years, where childbearing is most heavily concentrated, was proportionately even larger, amounting to 35%. Thus, unless age-specific birthrates fell drastically, the number of births would rise in the next five years.

Birthrates for the European countries shown in Table I were in general quite similar to that for the U.S. The rate for the U.S.S.R. was nearly identical with that for the U.S. in 1968. Rates for the less developed countries of Asia were relatively high, but the highest rates were those reported by the Latin-American countries, which in some cases exceeded 40 births per 1,000 population. Provisional birthrates of 20 and 22.6 for Australia and New Zealand, respectively, in 1968 were near the levels of 1966 and 1967.

Death Statistics. In the U.S. the provisional death rate for the 12 months ended August 1969 was 9.6 per 1,000 population, or the same as for the corresponding period of 1967–68. There was widespread influenza activity in the U.S. during the 1968–69 influenza season; pneumonia-influenza mortality first exceeded the epidemic threshold during the week ended Dec. 7, 1968, after which the number of excess deaths rose sharply to a peak in mid-January 1969. Pneumonia-influenza mortality was paralleled by increases in the total number of deaths in major cities.

Excess mortality from influenza and pneumonia occurred in the U.S. at the beginning as well as the end of 1968, with the result that the estimated death rate was 9.6 per 1,000 population, compared with 9.4 for 1967. The most recent prior year in which the death rate was this high was 1963. Year-to-year fluctuations in the rate had been associated chiefly with the occurrence or absence of large-scale influenza outbreaks.

In several countries of Western Europe the death rates were higher than the U.S. rate. (*See* Table I.) Exceptions were the Netherlands, Norway, and Spain. Canada reported lower mortality, and Australia and New Zealand also experienced comparatively low death rates in 1968. Japan's rate continued at a level well below the rates for English-speaking countries. Factors that influenced the general death rate, in addition to age, were the ethnic composition of the national populations and economic development.

The leading causes of death in the U.S. in 1968 are shown below. Deaths from all causes totaled 1,923,000.

Cause of death	Estimated death rate per 100,000 population
All causes	962.2
Diseases of the heart	372.9
Malignant neoplasms, including neoplasms of the lymphatic and hematopoietic tissues	159.6
Cerebrovascular disease	104.8
Accidents	55.8
Influenza and pneumonia	34.9
All other causes	234.2

These rates follow the eighth revision of the International Classification of Diseases, introduced in 1968, and therefore are not precisely comparable with rates for various diseases for previous years.

Infant and Maternal Mortality. Infant mortality in the U.S. continued to decline in 1969; in each of the first eight months, the rate was lower than for the corresponding month a year earlier. Apparently this decline in the provisional rate, which was in contrast to the general death rate, was not attributable to significantly lower mortality for any major disease, but reflected small decreases for several conditions.

In 1968 there were 75,300 infant deaths (*i.e.*, those under one year of age), resulting in an estimated infant mortality rate of 21.7 per 1,000 live births. This was about 3% lower than the rate of 22.4 for 1967 and marked the sixth successive annual decrease. The rate for infants under 28 days old (neonatal rate) was 15.9, or 73% of the total; that for infants 28 days through 11 months (postneonatal rate) was 5.8. Both rates fell in 1968.

Infant mortality rates for the Scandinavian countries, France, and the Netherlands were lower than the rate for the U.S. The gap between the U.K. and the U.S. narrowed slightly in 1968. In Australia and New Zealand, where infant mortality had been notably low for many years, the decline of the rate was interrupted. The rate for Japan rose from 18.5 infant deaths per 1,000 live births in 1965 to 19.3 in 1966, then declined to about 15 in 1967. Differences in availability and recourse to prenatal and infant care under social insurance systems were thought to account for part of the differences between countries.

Maternal mortality in the U.S. declined slightly in 1968, from 28 maternal deaths per 100,000 live births in 1967 to 27.4 in 1968. (Maternal deaths were those assigned to complications of pregnancy, childbirth, and the period immediately following childbirth.) This continued the long downward trend that had accelerated in the mid-1940s; between 1945 and 1965 the rate dropped from 207.2 per 100,000 live births to 31.6. Among the factors that made child-

Table I. Birthrates and Death Rates per 1,000 Population and Infant Mortality per 1,000 Live Births in Selected Countries, 1967*

Country	Birth-rate	Death rate	Infant mortality
Africa			
Mauritius	30.4	8.5	64.2
South Africa (white)	22.8†	8.6†	25.9‡
United Arab Republic	39.3	14.3	83.2
Asia			
Ceylon	31.5	8.2	55.8
Cyprus	25.6	6.5	26.7
Hong Kong	23.0	5.1	25.6
Israel	24.8	6.6	25.3†
Japan	19.3	6.7	13.3
Jordan†	46.2	5.0	36.3
Malaysia, West†	37.3	7.6	50.0
Singapore	27.1	5.4	25.8†
Syria	32.1	4.5	28.1
Taiwan	28.5	5.5	20.2†
Europe			
Albania	34.0†	8.6†	86.8§
Austria	17.4	13.0	26.4
Belgium	15.2	12.2	23.7
Bulgaria†	15.0	9.0	32.9
Czechoslovakia†	15.6	10.0	23.7
Denmark†	18.4	10.3	16.9
Finland	16.5	9.4	15.0
France	16.8	10.8	17.1
Germany, East	14.8	13.2	21.2
Germany, West‖	17.3	11.2	23.5
Gibraltar†	23.8	8.2	11.8
Greece	18.5	8.3	34.7
Hungary	14.5	10.7	38.4
Iceland†	23.9	7.1	13.7
Ireland	21.1	10.7	24.4
Italy	18.1	9.7	34.3
Luxembourg	14.8	12.3	20.4
Malta	16.5	9.4	27.5
Netherlands	18.9	7.9	14.7
Norway	18.0	9.2	16.8
Poland	16.3	7.7	38.0
Portugal	21.1	10.0	59.3
Romania	27.1	9.3	46.8
Spain	21.1	8.7	33.2
Sweden	15.5	10.1	12.6
United Kingdom	17.5	11.2	18.8
England & Wales	17.2	11.2	19.0
N. Ireland	22.4	9.8	23.4
Scotland	18.6	11.5	21.0
Yugoslavia	19.5	8.7	61.3
North America			
Canada	18.0	7.3	23.1
Costa Rica	39.2	6.9	69.9†
El Salvador	44.2	9.2	62.0†
Guatemala†	44.2	16.6	91.5
Jamaica	35.4	7.0	35.4†
Mexico	42.7	8.9	62.9†
Panama	40.2	6.9	45.0†
Puerto Rico	26.2†	5.5†	36.7§
Trinidad & Tobago	30.2	7.1	35.3
United States	17.9	9.4	22.1
Virgin Islands (U.S.)	40.5	6.6	30.2
Oceania			
American Samoa†	36.5	5.5	36.1
Australia	19.5	8.8	18.2
Guam†	33.4	4.1	20.4
New Zealand	22.4	8.4	17.7
South America			
Argentina	22.5	8.8	58.3
Chile†	30.6	10.4	127.5
Ecuador†	41.5	11.2	90.4
Uruguay†	21.4	9.0	43.3
U.S.S.R.	17.4	7.6	26.0

*Registered births and deaths only.
†1966.
‡1965.
§1964.
‖Not including West Berlin.
Sources: United Nations, *Monthly Bulletin of Statistics* (October 1968), *Population and Vital Statistics Report* (July 1, 1968), *Demographic Yearbook* (1967).

bearing safer were increased prenatal care and hospitalization for delivery; the review of causes of maternal deaths by local medical societies and hospital staff; research on complications of pregnancy and childbirth; and the introduction of sulfonamides and antibiotics, together with the use of blood or its substitutes for treatment of hemorrhage.

Though maternal mortality rates in some small countries with homogeneous populations were lower than those for the U.S. as a whole, several states experienced rates comparable to or lower than those reported by Western European countries. In the 1960s the maternal death rate declined more rapidly for nonwhite mothers than for white, but the rate for nonwhites in 1967 was still about 3.6 times that for whites.

Expectation of Life. Life expectancy at birth is the measure of the average number of years that persons born in a given year would live if the age-specific death rates of that year prevailed throughout their lives. In the U.S. the estimated expectation of life at birth in 1968 was 70.2 years, or slightly less than the all-time high of 70.5 years reported for the total population in 1967. For males born in 1967 the average expectation of life was 67 years, compared with 74.2 for females. The longevity record of some European countries in the 1960s was even better than that of the U.S. In African countries life expectancy at birth was relatively low. Australia, New Zealand, and Japan achieved life expectancies very similar to one another. (*See* Table II.) (E. H. HA.)

Table II. Life Expectancy at Birth, in Years, for Selected Countries

Country	Period	Male	Female
Africa			
Gabon	1960–61	25.0	45.0
Mauritius	1961–63	58.7	61.9
United Arab Republic	1960	51.6	53.8
Upper Volta	1960–61	32.1	31.1
Asia			
Cambodia	1958–59	44.2	43.3
Hong Kong	1961	63.6	70.5
India	1951–60	41.9	40.6
Israel (Jewish population)	1966	70.9	73.7
Japan	1966	68.3	73.6
Korea, South	1955–60	51.1	53.7
Taiwan	1959–60	61.3	65.6
Western Malaysia	1956–58	55.8	58.2
Europe			
Albania	1960–61	63.7	66.0
Austria	1966	66.8	73.5
Belgium	1959–63	67.7	73.5
Bulgaria	1960–62	67.8	71.4
Czechoslovakia	1964	67.8	73.6
Denmark	1964–65	70.2	74.7
Finland	1956–60	64.9	71.6
France	1965	67.8	75.0
Germany, East	1963–64	68.3	73.3
Germany, West	1964–65	67.6	73.5
Greece	1960–62	67.5	70.7
Hungary	1964	67.0	71.8
Iceland	1961–65	70.8	76.2
Ireland	1960–62	68.1	71.9
Italy	1960–62	67.2	72.3
Malta	1964–66	67.5	71.1
Netherlands	1961–65	71.1	75.9
Norway	1961–65	71.0	76.0
Poland	1960–61	64.8	70.5
Portugal	1959–62	60.7	66.4
Romania	1963	65.4	70.3
Spain	1960	67.3	71.9
Sweden	1961–65	71.6	75.7
Switzerland	1958–63	68.7	74.1
United Kingdom			
England and Wales	1963–65	68.3	74.4
Northern Ireland	1964–66	67.8	73.0
Scotland	1964–66	66.6	72.6
Yugoslavia	1961–62	62.4	65.6
North America			
Canada	1960–62	68.4	74.2
El Salvador	1960–61	56.6	60.4
Guatemala	1963–65	48.3	49.7
Jamaica	1959–61	62.7	66.6
Mexico	1956	55.1	57.9
Puerto Rico	1959–61	67.1	71.9
Trinidad and Tobago	1959–61	62.2	66.3
United States	1966	66.7	73.8
Oceania			
Australia	1960–62	67.9	74.2
New Zealand	1960–62	68.4	73.8
South America			
Argentina	1960–65	63.7	69.5
Venezuela	1960	61.2	65.6
U.S.S.R.	1965–66	66.0	74.0

Source: United Nations, *Demographic Yearbook* (1967).

Marriage and Divorce. Generally, the marriage rates for the areas for which there were reported statistics in the UN *Monthly Bulletin of Statistics* remained fairly constant for 1968 as compared with 1967. The marriage rate during this period increased in a few more countries than it decreased. No rates were reported for India, China, and the Soviet Union, among others.

During 1968 the countries with the highest marriage rates per 1,000 population were the U.S. (10.3), Puerto Rico (9.6), Hungary (9.5), Japan (9.5), and the Netherlands (9.2); the countries with the lowest marriage rates were El Salvador (3.2), Panama (3.8), Jamaica (4.1), Mauritius (5), and Trinidad and Tobago (5.6). Data refer to the number of marriages performed, marriage licenses issued, or marriages registered. In countries where the number of consensual marriages is large, the rates based on recorded marriages are correspondingly low.

The marriage rates for all other reporting countries ranged between 6.5 and 8.9. Reporting areas with rates between 8 and 8.9 were Australia, Canada, Czechoslovakia, Finland, Israel, New Zealand, Poland, Portugal, Ryukyu Islands, the U.K., and Yugoslavia; with rates between 7 and 7.9 were Austria, Belgium, Taiwan, France, East Germany, West Germany, Greece, Italy, Mexico, Norway, Romania, Spain, and Switzerland; with rates between 6.5 and 6.9 were Ireland, Luxembourg, Malta, and Sweden.

From 1963 to 1968 the marriage rates of nine countries with populations of five million or more increased by at least 10% (Australia, Canada, Hungary, the Netherlands, New Zealand, Norway, Poland, the U.K., and the U.S.). They decreased 10% or more for East Germany, West Germany, Greece, Italy, and Romania. Changes in the marriage rates for other reporting countries of this size were less than 10%.

The marriage rate of 10.3 for the U.S. in 1968 was the highest since 1951 and marked the sixth successive annual rise. These increases followed a five-year period when the marriage rate (8.4 in 1958 and 8.5 in 1959–62) was lower than for any year in the 38-year period 1920–57 except for 1932.

Statistics on divorce were published by a number of countries, but frequently this information was not available until two or more years after the year in which the divorces occurred. A few countries reported the divorce rate per 1,000 population. For those countries not giving this figure, it could be approximated from the estimated population. Estimates of the divorce rates of several countries (for 1966 except where specified) were as follows: Australia 0.8, Belgium 0.6 (1965), Canada 0.5 (1967), Czechoslovakia 1.4, Denmark 1.4, France 0.6, West Germany 1, East Germany 1.6, Iceland 1, Mexico 0.6 (1965), the Netherlands 0.5, New Zealand 0.8, Poland 0.8, Portugal 0.1, Romania 1.4, Sweden 1.3, Switzerland 0.8 (1965), and the U.K. 0.8. The divorce rate of 2.9 for the U.S. in 1968 was the highest since 1949 and was exceeded only during the years 1945–47, immediately after World War II. (W. W. E.)

See also Populations and Areas.

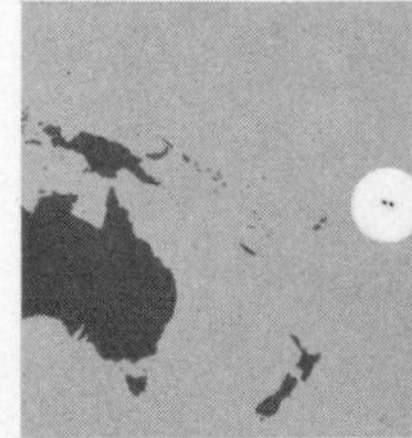

Western Samoa

An independent parliamentary state, Western Samoa is an island group in the South Pacific Ocean, about 1,600 mi. E of New Zealand and 2,200 mi. S of Hawaii. Area: 1,097 sq.mi. (2,842 sq.km.), with two major islands, Savai'i (662 sq.mi.) and Upolu (435 sq.mi.), and seven smaller islands. Pop. (1969 est.): 141,500. Cap. and largest city: Apia (pop., 1969 est., 27,400). Language: Samoan and English. Religion: about 80% Protestant, 20% Roman Catholic. Head of state (*O le Ao o le Malo*) in 1969, Malietoa Tanumafili II; prime minister, Fiame Mata'afa Faumuina Mulinu'u II.

A good recovery from the 1968 hurricane and an upsurge in agricultural production and export earnings brightened prospects for development. The national budget appropriated WS$403,080 for agricultural projects, extended public works, hydroelectricity, and tourism. A New Zealand loan was approved for new Parliament buildings, Australia gave aid to the banana industry, and the UN to agricultural research. Difficulties in opening the Asau Channel delayed the start of timber milling by Potlatch Forests Inc. A new WS$700,000 contract to complete the work by January 1970 was partly financed by an advance payment for timber from Potlatch. After prolonged negotiations, land was leased for a mill site and forestry operations.

Despite air transport difficulties, the tourist industry, worth $1 million in 1968, continued to boom, though insufficient local support for the Casino Hotel loan led to an agreement to sell to Travel Lodge of Australia. To upgrade Faleolo Airport and the road to Apia, a loan was sought from the Asian Development Bank. The fourth meeting of the Pacific Islands Producers' Association demonstrated growing awareness of the value of interterritorial cooperation, notably in the banana trade.

A motion to introduce universal suffrage for *matai* (titled heads of families) candidates was overwhelmingly defeated. To prevent the creation of new titleholders for electoral purposes, it was made illegal to confer a title on any person under 21 years old.

The Revised Samoan Bible was formally introduced for all three churches in the country—Christian Congregational Church (formerly London Missionary Society), Methodist, and Roman Catholic.

(My. B. B.)

WESTERN SAMOA

Education. (1966) Primary, pupils 26,134, teachers 789; secondary and vocational, pupils 8,188, teachers 329; teacher training, students 220, teachers 13.

Finance. Monetary unit: Western Samoan dollar (thaler), with a par value of WS$0.71 to U.S. $1 (WS$1.71 = £1 sterling). Budget (1966 rev. est.): revenue WS$4,670,000; expenditure WS$4,824,000.

Foreign Trade. (1966) Imports WS$5,728,000; exports WS$3,160,000. Import sources: New Zealand 30%; Australia 24%; U.K. 10%; Japan 7%; U.S. 5%. Export destinations: Netherlands 26%; New Zealand 25%; West Germany 19%; U.K. 12%; U.S. 6%; Denmark 5%. Main exports: copra 52%; cocoa 38%; bananas 5%.

Transport and Communications. Roads (1967) *c.* 770 km. (including 160 km. surfaced). Motor vehicles (1967): passenger 705; commercial (including buses) 588. Ships entered (1966) vessels totaling 305,000 net registered tons; goods loaded (1967) 20,000 metric tons, unloaded 45,000 metric tons. Telephones (Jan. 1965) 1,405. Radio receivers (Dec. 1967) 15,000.

West Indies:
see Barbados; Cuba; Dependent States; Dominican Republic; Haiti; Inter-American Affairs; Jamaica; Trinidad and Tobago

West Indies Associated States:
see Dependent States

West New Guinea:
see Indonesia

Wheat:
see Agriculture

Wildlife Conservation:
see Conservation

Windward Islands:
see Dependent States

Wines:
see Alcoholic Beverages

Wool:
see Agriculture; Industrial Review

Words and Meanings, New

The moon landing, the most dramatic event of 1969, brought many new terms into the language, some of which would undoubtedly survive. The **command module** of the three-man spacecraft Apollo 11 was named "Columbia." Its detachable **lunar module** called "Eagle" touched down on the Sea of Tranquillity on July 20. **Extraterrestrial exploration** went ahead, making it necessary to construct the **lunar receiving laboratory,** a special quarantine facility, at Houston, Tex.

The year closed with no proof that life existed outside the **biosphere** of earth. This "life globe" or realm of living organisms was limited to the earth's crust **(lithosphere),** waters **(hydrosphere),** and air blanket **(atmosphere).** Nevertheless, the terms **astrobiologist,** "student of life on stars," and **exobiologist,** "student of life outside earth," gained wide currency. **Selenologists,** students of the moon's physical characteristics, especially its surface features, began to speak of **mascons** and **astroblemes.** Mascons, discovered by orbiting spacecraft late in 1968, are **mas**sive **con**centration**s** of rock embedded beneath the moon's circular **maria.** Astroblemes, literally "star-wounds," are mysterious depressions, of which the Arizona crater is the best known. It was unfortunate that **lunanaut** was sometimes printed **lunarnaut** in reports. **Selenonaut** would have been unexceptionable as a neo-Hellenic compound. On the other hand, **moonquake** was the obvious counterpart of **earthquake.**

In the field of computer technology the distinction between **hardware** and **software** was modified by the introduction of the term **firmware** to denote "software designed as an integral part of hardware." A team of chemists at the University of Maryland isolated a polymer of ordinary water and called it **polywater.** It is heavier than water, freezes at −40° C, and remains stable up to 500° C. Zoologists succeeded in generating the **geep,** the offspring of a goat and a sheep.

Members of **YIP,** the Youth International Party, decided to christen themselves **yippies.** They regarded themselves as a cross between the hippies and the New Left. *Vox populi vox Dei,* written by Alcuin of York in a letter to Charlemagne in A.D. 800, was reduced to **vox pop** and became a slang term for a momentary observation on some burning question of the hour spoken into a proffered TV microphone by some casual passerby.

Portmanteau words or blends continued to multiply. Chemists spoke of **gox** (gaseous oxygen), as well as **lox** (liquid oxygen). Aviation electronics became **avionics** (construed as a singular). Similarly, biology electronics became **bionics.** A thermal transistor, whose action varied in its resistance with changes of temperature, became a **thermistor.** A television marathon, which went on for hours, became a **telethon.** The influence of English upon other world languages had assumed such considerable proportions that purists in Paris and Moscow began to deplore the emergence of **Franglais** and **Sovangliski.**

Word formation was conspicuously active. ISV, the International Scientific Vocabulary as defined and described in *Webster's Third New International Dictionary* of 1961, went more and more to neo-Hellenic sources for its new terms. The prefixes **macro-** ("long, large"), **micro-** ("small"), **para-** ("alongside"), and **poly-** ("many") were frequently used formatives. A valuable distinction was drawn between **macroeconomics,** concerned at the highest level with GNP or gross national product, and **microeconomics,** concerned with the price-cost relationships of individual undertakings. **Microcircuitry, microclimatology,** and **microengineering** denoted new spheres of invention and discovery. **Parabibliographical** studies were concerned with catalogs and collections of manuscripts. In a jocular mood, psychologists invented **parasynonyms** to denote those differing qualities ascribed by the speaker to his esteemed self, to the person addressed, and to the person spoken about: I am firm, you are obstinate, he is pigheaded.

The prefix **mini-** is strictly an abbreviation of Italian miniature, a manuscript illumination painted in minium or red lead, which, being small, became associated with the **min-** of Latin **minor** and **minimus.** In an overcrowded world mini formations flourished endlessly: **mini-bag, mini-beard, miniskirt,** and scores of others. The prefix **mini-** merely took the place of the old epithet small. Its opposite was **maxi-,** a clipped form of the Latin **maximus.**

The Greek adjectival suffix **-ac** had already been used to form substantives denoting persons affected by some disability—**amnesiac,** "one suffering from loss of memory," and **insomniac,** "one unable to sleep." It now acquired an additional derivative in **nostalgiac,** "one afflicted by nostalgia, homesickness, sentimental yearning for the past."

By far the most prolific of these formatives was **-ee,** an undergoer suffix deriving from the French past participle and corresponding to the agent suffix in **-er** or **-or.** Some were nonce words, as indeed Samuel Richardson's **lovee** and Laurence Sterne's **jestee** had turned out to be in the 18th century, but certainly **advisee, awardee, biographee, braindrainee,** and **murderee** were used in serious speech and writing.

Derivatives in **-wise** (influenced, no doubt, by German formations in *-weise* in such familiar expressions as *haufenweise,* "in crowds"), deprecated by purists, continued to multiply: **advertisementwise,** "by way of advertising"; **careerwise,** "relating to careers"; **fashionwise,** "with an eye to fashion"; **manpowerwise,** "in terms of manpower."

The Russian agent suffix **-nik** also continued its existence (at least informally) in **beatnik** ("member of the beat generation"), **peacenik** ("pacifist"), and even **Mitnik** ("transformational linguist trained at the Massachusetts Institute of Technology").

The adverb-preposition **in,** used as a suffix in the **sit-in** or **stay-in** strikes of the 19th century, had assumed new life during the protest movements of the 1960s, as with **teach-in** and **pray-in.** The jollification preceding the moon flight's blastoff on July 16 was called a **laugh-in,** which was also the name of a popular U.S. TV show. Wordplay, perhaps influenced by James Joyce and the crossword puzzle, became a kind of popular pastime. The first syllable of **safari** (from Arabic through Swahili; "hunting expedition") was modified to **seafari** ("long sea voyage of adventure") and **snowfari** ("polar expedition").

In the evolution of verbs the year saw a striking increase in the use of progressive forms consisting of some tense form of the verb **to be** + present participle—**I am going.** Progressive forms denote that an action or state is (1) actually in progress, (2) of short duration, or (3) vividly pictured in the speaker's mind. Until recently, many verbs expressing mental states and attitudes—**believe, forget, hate, hear, hope, imagine, know, like, love, mean, remember, seem, smell, taste,** and **understand**—had been seldom or never used in their progressive forms. This remained valid in principle, but of these 15 verbs only four—**believe, hate, know,** and **seem**—resisted the growing preference for **-ing** forms, although these forms were actually longer. (We really don't know) **what President Nixon is meaning** (by this document) was two syllables and four letters longer than **what President Nixon means,** but it somehow seemed more arresting and vivid. Perhaps it was only a transient fashion.

It would seem, however, that **going to** had come to stay. **Is it going to remain fine?** was everywhere more usual than **Will it remain fine?** although it was longer by three syllables. **Apollo 12 is going to cost $12 million** sounded more urgent, more definite, and at the same time more impressive than plain **will cost.**

The year also saw a marked increase in the choice of phrasal verbs like **break down** and **set up** instead of their classical synonyms **analyze** and **establish.** In a rapidly changing world, **phase out** became a special favourite. It was used both transitively, in the sense "to ease something gently out of service," and intransitively, meaning "to withdraw gradually." As a noun, **phaseout** suggested a less painful transition than **changeover** or **layoff.** So, too, **breakthrough** in the sense of "forceful advance," originally a military term, was applied to the sudden overcoming of an obstruction to progress in research, the unexpected move forward after a prolonged **buildup** of resources and power. Among the commonest nouns from phrasal verbs were **breakaway** and **getby.** The next stage was seen in the functional shift of these phrasal-verb nouns into attributive adjectives, as in **breakaway group, getby makeshift,** and **takeover bid.**

Vogue words, highly significant for students of psycholinguistics, were exceptionally interesting: **ambience,** "total environment, milieu"; **charisma,** "that special grace which gives its possessor power and influence over others"; **confrontation,** a solemn and ponderous word denoting "direct and open encounter between rival powers"; **dialogue** (in depth), more impressive than "negotiations" and more dignified than mere "talks."

Vogue adjectives included **rebarbative,** "repellent, evoking annoyance and irritation (like a prickly beard)" and **open-ended,** "permissive, not restrictive, allowing the broadest possible interpretation." Outstanding among vogue phrases were **areas of agreement,** especially in collective bargaining; **corridors of power,** echoing the title of C. P. Snow's novel; **golden handshake,** the formal dismissal (with a gift) of that unwanted chairman or aging director; **grassroot facts,** basic or fundamental realities, stated without embellishment or humbug; and **status symbol,** any object by which its possessor's position is judged by society. (St. P.)

The words, phrases, and some other forms listed below achieved some currency in the information media during 1969. Additional words and terms will be found and defined in the *Book of the Year* in articles in which they are pertinent. This list has been prepared by the permanent editorial staff of G. & C. Merriam Company, Springfield, Mass., publishers of *Webster's Third New International Dictionary* and a subsidiary of Encyclopædia Britannica, Inc.

accommodationist *n* : one who seeks accommodation with a conflicting point of view; *specif* : a Negro willing to cooperate with whites

Afram *adj* : AFRO-AMERICAN

agrichemical *or* **agrochemical** *n* : a chemical (as a fungicide, herbicide, or insecticide) used in agriculture

airshed *n* : a region having a common air supply

ambisextrous *adj* **1** : not distinguishable as male or female : common to males and females <*ambisextrous* clothing> **2** : involving males and females <an *ambisextrous* party>

archeomagnetism *n* : the residual magnetism exhibited by archaeological remains that is used for dating them and for determining the positions of the earth's magnetic pole in former times — **archeomagnetic** *adj*

backhander *n, Brit* : BRIBE

barbecue maneuver *n* : the rolling of a spacecraft about its long axis so that all sides are equally exposed to the heat of the sun and the cold of space — called also *barbecuing*

blindgating *n* : driving close enough behind another vehicle to be taken unawares by an obstacle that unexpectedly appears in front of and is avoided by the preceding vehicle

blip *vb, specif* : to remove recorded sound from a videotape so that in the received television program there is an interruption in the sound <a censor *blipped* the swearwords>

block parent *n* : one who offers his place of residence or business as a refuge for children in distress and far from help

bodyshirt *n* : a woman's fitted blouse often with a high collar and deep cuffs

bounceball *n* : volleyball played by two players or pairs of players on a trampoline

brain bank *n* : a pool of academic talent

branchheading *n* : the practice of speaking (as by a politician) in a folksy style characterized by ostensibly naïve mistakes in pronouncing polysyllabic words

cat suit *n* : a one-piece or two-piece form-fitting bell-bottomed woman's garment for casual wear <flowered cotton *cat suit*>

cherry sheet *n* : a report of the distribution of state tax revenue to the cities and towns of the state

Chinese restaurant syndrome *n* : a set of symptoms including numbness of the neck, arms, and back, headaches, dizziness, and palpitations that affects susceptible persons after eating Chinese food in a Chinese restaurant and that has been attributed to various causative agents including monosodium glutamate

Christmas-tree bill *n* : a legislative bill that includes various riders relating to pet projects of individual legislators

coffee-tabler *n* : an expensive, illustrated oversize book suitable for display on a coffee table

crunch *n, specif* **1** : pressure on banks and other financial institutions for cash as opposed to credit <a *crunch* cripples home mortgages and cuts employment as credit evaporates> 2 : a critical point in the buildup of pressure between opposing elements : CRISIS, SHOWDOWN, CONFRONTATION <to be prepared when the military *crunch* comes>

curdler *n* : a high-frequency noisemaker used to control unruly crowds

dashiki *or* **daishiki** *n* : a usually brightly colored pullover garment for men that hangs loose over the upper body and midriff

earthrise *n* : the apparent rising of the earth above the horizon of the moon as seen from the moon or its vicinity

equigravisphere *n* : the area between celestial bodies (as the moon and the earth) in which gravitational influence of the bodies is equal

falsie *n, specif* : a piece of false hair (as a moustache) worn on the face by men

fleshprinting *n* : the production of electrophoretic protein patterns of flesh (as of fish) for purposes of specific identification or analytic study

geezer *n* : an injected dose of a narcotic

giro *n* : a highly computerized low cost system of money transfer comparable to a checking account that is one of the national post office services in many European countries

G job *n* : a personal project carried on by a worker on company time with company machinery

hairweaving *n* : the covering of a bald spot with a wig whose nylon base is sewn to the wearer's remaining hair — **hairweave** *n* — **hair weaver** *n*

headhunter *n, specif* : a recruiter of senior personnel (as executives for a corporation)

hydrairport *n* : an airport designed as a floating structure (as on Long Island Sound)

hydrogasification *n* : gasification and hydrogenation of a substance (as coal or shale oil) for the production of fuel — **hydrogasifier** *n*

internationalite *n* : a person of international social prominence

jazzotheque *n* : a discotheque in which jazz music is played

jet belt *n* : a beltlike harness on which a jet engine is mounted to provide a wearer with aerial propulsion

kamagraphy *n* : a process for making multiple copies of a painting produced by an artist on a specially treated canvas in which the copies retain the texture of the brushstrokes of the original but the original is destroyed in the process — **kamagraph** *n* — **kamagrapher** *n* — **kamagraphic** *adj*

khiva *n* : an indoor lounging area furnished only with pillows

knockoff *n* : a copy (as of the design of a textile or apparel product) that sells for less than the original

[1]**loid** *n* : a strip of celluloid used (as by a burglar) to open a door

[2]**loid** *vb* : to unlock (a door) by using a strip of celluloid to retract the spring bolt

luminal art *n* : an art form created by electric lighting (as in projected still or moving patterns of colored light or an arrangement of flashing colored light bulbs) — called also *lumia* — **luminism** *n* — **luminist** *n*

magnetocardiograph *n* : an instrument for recording the changes in the magnetic field around the heart during the heartbeat that is used to supplement information given by an electrocardiograph — **magnetocardiogram** *n* — **magnetocardiographic** *adj*

magnicide *n* : the murder of a prominent leader or ruler

Malayan whip *n* : a bent tree limb or bamboo armed with spikes that is used as a booby trap

megaversity *n* : a multiversity with divisions at widely separate locations

mind-blowing *adj* **1** : PSYCHEDELIC; *also* : of, relating to, or causing a psychic state similar to that produced by a psychedelic drug **2** : mentally or emotionally stimulating : OVERWHELMING

mocamp *n* : a camp providing tourists with a protected area for tents and trailers and offering various conveniences and services

motique *n* : a vehicle from which merchandise (as women's clothing) is sold on suburban streets

negative income tax *n* : a government payment to individuals whose income falls below a prescribed level — called also *negative tax*

noise pollution *n* : pollution consisting of annoying noise <*noise pollution* caused by automobile traffic, a jet airplane, or a vacuum cleaner> — called also *sound pollution*

pacey *adj* : appropriate to the times : UP-TO-DATE — **paceyness** *n*

people sniffer *n* : a device for detecting concealed persons (as enemy troops) by bodily odors (as of ammonia) in the air

Phillips curve *n* : a curve formulated by the London economist A. W. Phillips indicating that the rate of unemployment increases as the rate of inflation decreases and vice versa

photoserigraph *n* : a serigraph made from a photograph

pokerism *n* : a tendency to keep future plans secret

proof-listen *vb* : to listen to and note mistakes in a recording made for the blind

pushout *n* : a student dropped from school for unsatisfactory performance

ranchero *n* : a casual necktie designed for wear with an open-collared or collarless shirt

rejective art *n* : a simplified and often depersonalized art (as painting or sculpture) based on the principle of the artist's rejecting various options open to him — called also *reductive art, reductivism, rejectivism*

sand surfing *n* : the sport of sliding down a sand slope while standing on a small board — **sand surfer** *n*

stagorium *n* : an establishment (as a resort hotel or a bar) that serves as a meeting place for unmarried men and women

starfish *vb* : to bend in the sides of a food container so as to make it hold less

starkers *adj, Brit* : STARK-NAKED

technetronic *adj* : of or being a society shaped by the impact of technology and electronics and especially of computers and communications on its structure, culture, psychology, and economics

ultramicrofiche *n* : a photographic reproduction of printed matter in greatly reduced form <a four-by-six inch *ultramicrofiche* card containing images of 3000 pages>

undergroundling *n* : a moviegoer especially interested in underground productions

[1]**unisex** *n* : a group of males and females not distinguishable (as by hair or clothing styles) as to sex

[2]**unisex** *adj* : AMBISEXTROUS <*unisex* fashions>

welting *n* : the practice of working only half the hours that one is paid for

Yemen

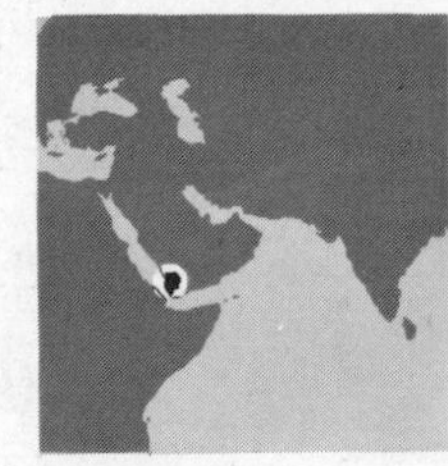

A country situated in the southwestern coastal region of the Arabian Peninsula, Yemen is bounded by Southern Yemen, Saudi Arabia, and the Red Sea. Although Yemen was largely republican controlled, the imam continued to rule in the remoter parts of the north, and his royalist government was recognized by some countries. Area: 75,290 sq.mi. (195,000 sq.km.). Pop. (1968 est.): 5 million. Cap. and largest city: San'a' (pop., 1960 est., 60,000). Language: Arabic. Religion: Muslim. Republican Yemen: president in 1969, Qadi Abdul Rahman al-Iryani; premiers, Maj. Gen. Hassan al-Amri until July 8 and, after September 2, Abdullah Kurshumi. Royalist Yemen: imam, Muhammad al-Badr.

After six years of intermittent civil war, 1969 was a time of relative peace and stability for Yemen. Economic activity increased as many businesses in Aden (Southern Yemen) moved to San'a'. However, the country suffered from a prolonged drought, and severe food shortages were feared at the end of the year.

Tribal skirmishing continued in the north where the former royalist stronghold of Sada repeatedly changed hands. The republic was not at first seriously concerned with the royalist threat, however, because King Faisal of Saudi Arabia had temporarily cut off his aid to the royalists. Despite mediation efforts at the Islamic summit meeting in Rabat, Mor., and peace overtures from the republicans, King Faisal continued to refuse recognition to the republic on the ground that he was awaiting the establishment of a government freely chosen by the Yemeni people. In November the Yemeni government accused Saudi Arabia of stirring up royalist tribes on the northern borders, but of greater concern to Yemen was internal opposition from Soviet-trained army officers and left-wing exiles in Aden and Cairo. In January a curfew was imposed in San'a' after clashes between right- and left-wing military factions.

In March the Republican Council resigned to make way for a new National Council to elect a president and premier. A new National Assembly was formed with 57 seats, of which 12 were left vacant for Southern Yemen. The government maintained that Yemen and Southern Yemen were being prevented from uniting only by the extremist intransigence of the latter's government.

YEMEN

Education. (1965–66) Primary, pupils 69,139, teachers 1,726; secondary, pupils 1,949, teachers 126; vocational, pupils 45, teachers (1963–64) 2; teacher training, students 125, teaching staff 5.

Finance and Trade. Monetary unit: riyal (Maria Theresa dollar), with a value of 1.07 riyal to U.S. $1 (2.57 riyals = £1 sterling). Budget (1967–68) balanced at 50,948,500 riyals. Foreign trade (with U.K. only; 1968): imports £315,000 (but most British goods enter via Southern Yemen); exports £8,000. Main exports: coffee, hides and skins, salt.

Agriculture. Production (in 000; metric tons; 1967; 1966 in parentheses): wheat *c.* 18 (*c.* 16); dates *c.* 60 (*c.* 60); coffee *c.* 3 (*c.* 3.6). Livestock (in 000; March 1967): cattle *c.* 1,270; sheep *c.* 11,800; camels *c.* 56; horses *c.* 3.

The National Assembly elected a three-man Republican Council consisting of President al-Iryani, former Premier Hassan al-Amri, and Muhammad Ali Uthman. Al-Amri formed a new government but resigned in July owing to left-wing opposition. It was two months before a successor was found in Abdullah Kurshumi, former minister of communications in the al-Amri government.

The al-Iryani regime made efforts to reduce its dependence on the Communist bloc. In July it succeeded in obtaining West German recognition and a $5 million loan. In November roving ambassador Muhammad Naaman visited London and Paris in an effort to obtain U.K. and French recognition, but without success. (P. Md.)

Yugoslavia

A federal socialist republic, Yugoslavia is bordered by Italy, Austria, Hungary, Romania, Bulgaria, Greece, and Albania. Area: 98,766 sq.mi. (255,804 sq.km.). Pop. (1968 est.): 20,154,000. Cap. and largest city: Belgrade (pop., 1967 est., 737,000). Language: Serbo-Croatian, Slovenian, and Macedonian. Religion (1953): Orthodox 41.4%; Roman Catholic 31.8%; Muslim 12.3%. President of the republic and secretary-general of the League of Communists in 1969, Marshal Tito (Josip Broz); presidents of the Federal Executive Council (premiers), Mika Spiljak and, from May 17, Mitja Ribicic.

Continued economic reform and changes in party organization were features of 1969, along with renewed curbs on artistic expression as divisions within the nation increased. The year was also marked by improved relations with the U.S.S.R.

In March the ninth Congress of the League of Communists adopted new statutes guaranteeing the right of party members to hold minority opinions. It also approved a Central Committee report calling for further curbs on bureaucracy, the extension of workers' self-management in industry, and a greater role in decision making for the Socialist Alliance, the trade unions, and other recognized social organizations. A new 15-member Executive Bureau consisting of President Tito, the two top political figures from each of the republics, and one from each of the two autonomous regions was established in place of the 11-man Executive Committee, and a new 52-member Presidium based on geographic representation replaced the Central Committee's former 35-man Presidium. The former Central Committee of 154 was abolished to make way for a 200-member annual League Conference.

In the elections of April–May more than 43,000 candidates campaigned for half as many seats in Parliament and local government, and there was a record number of independent candidates. In May Mirko Tepavac became secretary for foreign affairs, Mitja Ribicic was elected president of the Federal Executive Council, and Milentije Popovic, president of the Federal Assembly.

Between March and July the courts in the Kosmet autonomous region and the Macedonian Republic sentenced more than 30 people of Albanian origin for "fomenting national hatred." Some were accused of conspiring with Albanian officials to bring about the secession of certain Yugoslavian towns. In August President Tito made a bitter attack on "undisciplined party leaders" after the Slovenian Republic's govern-

World Bank: *see* Development, Economic
World Council of Churches: *see* Religion
World Health Organization: *see* Medicine
World's Fairs: *see* Fairs and Shows
Wrestling: *see* Sporting Record
Yachting: *see* Sailing
Yemen, People's Republic of Southern: *see* Southern Yemen
Yiddish Literature: *see* Literature

YUGOSLAVIA

Education. (1966–67) Primary, pupils 2,921,607, teachers 165,776; secondary, pupils 180,303, teachers 9,185; vocational, pupils 445,000, teachers 17,655; teacher training (1965–66), students 27,908, teachers 1,549; higher (including 7 universities; 1965–66), students 184,923, teaching staff 15,760.

Finance. Monetary unit: dinar, with a par value of 12.50 dinars to U.S. $1 (30 dinars = £1 sterling). Gold and foreign exchange, central bank: (June 1969) U.S. $175 million; (June 1968) U.S. $131 million. Budget (1967 est.): revenue 18,564,000,000 dinars; expenditure 18,427,000,000 dinars. Gross material product: (1966) 99.1 billion dinars; (1965) 79.5 billion dinars. Money supply: (April 1969) 29.3 billion dinars; (April 1968) 22,520,000,000 dinars. Cost of living (1963 = 100): (May 1969) 230; (May 1968) 216.

Foreign Trade. (1968) Imports 22,460,000,000 dinars; exports 15.8 billion dinars. Import sources: West Germany 18%; Italy 14%; U.S.S.R. 10%; Czechoslovakia 6%; U.S. 5%; U.K. 5%; Austria 5%. Export destinations: U.S.S.R. 16%; Italy 14%; West Germany 10%; U.S. 7%; U.K. 5%. Main exports: machinery 12%; nonferrous metals 9%; meat 8%; ships and boats 7%; clothing 6%.

Transport and Communications. Roads (1968) 79,938 km. (including 10,178 km. main roads). Motor vehicles in use (1968): passenger 439,892; commercial 99,053. Railways: (1967) 11,351 km.; traffic (1968) 10,285,000,000 passenger-km., freight 16,311,000,000 net ton-km. Air traffic (1968): 459.8 million passenger-km.; freight 4,608,000 net ton-km. Shipping (1968): merchant vessels 100 gross tons and over 337; gross tonnage 1,266,592. Telephones (Dec. 1967) 506,039. Radio receivers (Dec. 1967) 3,059,000. Television receivers (Dec. 1967) 1,002,000.

Agriculture. Production (in 000; metric tons; 1968; 1967 in parentheses): wheat (including spelt) 4,363 (4,823); barley 450 (606); oats 295 (363); rye 138 (171); corn 6,810 (7,200); rice 18 (20); hemp fibre 12 (42); potatoes 2,890 (2,810); sunflower seed 309 (250); sugar, raw value (1968–69) *c.* 389, (1967–68) 490; dry beans (1967) 200, (1966) 217; onions 203 (216); tomatoes 323 (322); plums (1967) 705, (1966) 723; apples *c.* 224 (289); pears 99 (87); olives (1967) 40, (1966) 30; figs 23 (26); wine 608 (523); tobacco 44 (54); beef and veal (1967) 256, (1966) 227; pork (1967) 309, (1966) 287; timber (cu.m.; 1967) 17,400, (1966) 18,100; fish catch (1967) 48, (1966) 45. Livestock (in 000; Jan. 1968): cattle 5,693; sheep 10,300; pigs 5,865; horses 1,126; chickens (Jan. 1967) 31,079.

Industry. Fuel and power (in 000; metric tons; 1968): coal 855; lignite 25,897; crude oil 2,494; electricity (kw-hr.) 20,642,000; natural gas (cu.m.) 584,000; manufactured gas (gasworks only; cu.m.) 75,000. Production (in 000; metric tons; 1968): iron ore (35% metal content) 2,720; pig iron 1,287; crude steel 1,998; bauxite 2,073; antimony ore (metal content; 1967) 3.1; chrome ore (oxide content; 1967) 15; manganese ore (metal content; 1967) 3; copper 70; lead 95; zinc 79; aluminum 48; cement 3,765; sulfuric acid 589; cotton yarn 102; wool yarn 30; wood pulp (1967) 482; newsprint 73; other paper (1967) 415.

ment had repeatedly challenged the federal government's decision to withhold from it foreign credits for highway modernization. In September the Slovenian government and party Central Committee formally endorsed the federal decision, but in November tension increased as the central authorities stepped in to discourage radical changes in the management of Slovenijales, the Slovenian furniture manufacturers.

In March Dragoljub Golubovic, a journalist employed by *Politika,* was expelled from the party for publishing a letter charging that he had been harassed for writing an article in 1966 that exposed high living on the part of some party officials. In June Tanjug News Agency editor Momcilo Pudar was forced to resign after printing an unauthorized article critical of the world Communist summit conference. At the end of August, shortly before the visit of the Soviet foreign minister, Andrei A. Gromyko, the literary paper *Knjizevne Novine* was banned for including an article condemning the behaviour of Soviet troops in Czechoslovakia. Its author, Zoran Gluscevic, was dismissed from his editorship of the paper and in October was given a six-month prison sentence.

The success of the motor firm Crvena Zastava in attracting bondholders in 1968 induced several other firms to follow suit, including Yugoslav Railways. In October Yugoslavian, U.S., and Western European bankers combined to establish the International Investment Corporation for Yugoslavia to help prospective foreign investors find suitable Yugoslavian partners for joint ventures and also to give financial help to Yugoslavian exporters. By October industrial production was 13.5% above the previous year's October level, but there were serious imbalances in the economy. In August 57% of Yugoslavia's enterprises were reported to be unable to meet their financial liabilities, while serious delays in the payment of salaries along with some wage cuts had caused several strikes. By October Yugoslavia's trade deficit was sufficiently grave to produce a government tightening of credit facilities. But there was optimism regarding trade with such countries as China, the U.S.S.R., Czechoslovakia, Hungary, Romania, and the countries of the EEC. In December the government's economic stabilization program for 1970 was approved by the Federal Assembly, after meeting with outspoken criticism of its vagueness and unjustified optimism.

During the first half of the year relations with the Soviet Union and its allies were strained. In January the Yugoslavian delegation walked out of the European Student Conference at Budapest after being accused of "subversion" by Soviet, Polish, and Hungarian participants. At the Italian Communist Congress in February, Yugoslavian speakers attacked the Soviet concept of "limited sovereignty," and although Yugoslavia was represented at the Comecon meeting in Moscow in April, it boycotted most of the other Soviet-sponsored multilateral gatherings. Yugoslavia did not attend the world Communist summit conference in Moscow in June or the meetings to prepare for it, and also shunned the congresses of Eastern European writers and artists in Budapest in March. The Yugoslavian Party Congress was, in turn, boycotted by all the Soviet-bloc countries except Romania.

Following a report in the Macedonian National Assembly that Bulgaria was intensifying its subversion of Macedonia, there was a large anti-Bulgarian demonstration in Skopje in March. In April the government strove to minimize Soviet influence in the Army by retiring nearly a dozen senior generals. Relations with Romania continued to improve. President Tito conferred with Romanian Pres. Nicolae Ceausescu in February and September, and a Romanian People's Army delegation was warmly received in Belgrade in June. There was little improvement in relations with Albania, even though in March the Albanian press pledged solidarity with Yugoslavia in the event of a conflict with the U.S.S.R. Relations with China, however, thawed after February when the two countries opened their first bilateral economic exchanges in nine years.

In May the Soviet press muted its criticisms of Yugoslavia, and the Yugoslavs were handed specific proposals for a Soviet-Yugoslavian détente. Although Yugoslavia made no immediate reply, Belgrade toned down its attacks on Moscow's policies, and in September the Soviet foreign minister visited Yugoslavia, agreeing to the principle of "noninterference."

In July the 51-nation consultative conference of the nonaligned nations was held in Belgrade. Yugoslavian officials were inclined to blame the Algerians for the failure of the conference to draw up a timetable for another nonaligned summit conference. President Tito's visit to Algiers in November was thought to have reduced existing frictions between the two countries, however, despite their failure to agree on an approach to the Middle East crisis. (G. H. St.)

Zambia

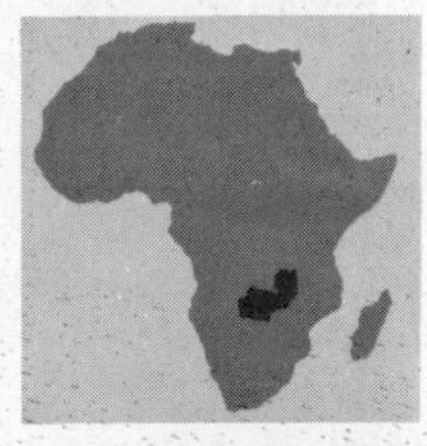

A republic and a member of the Commonwealth of Nations, Zambia is bounded by Tanzania, Malawi, Mozambique, Rhodesia, South West Africa, Angola, and the Congo (Kinshasa). Area: 290,587 sq.mi. (752,621 sq.km.). Pop. (1969 est.): 4,143,700, of whom 99% are Africans. Cap.: Lusaka (pop., 1969 est., 160,500). Language: English and Bantu. Religion: predominantly pagan beliefs; Europeans are Christian. President in 1969, Kenneth Kaunda.

President Kaunda was sworn in for a second term on Dec. 21, 1968, after the electoral victory of the United National Independence Party (UNIP). Polling was heavy, and UNIP won 81 seats to the 23 of the African National Congress (ANC), with one seat going to an independent. The ANC made gains in Barotse Province (renamed Western Province in August) where the Lozi resented the government ban on their working in South Africa. A successful candidate was the exiled Nalumino Mundia, leader of the banned United Party, many of whose followers voted for the ANC candidates. Kaunda appointed eight new ministers, responsible for individual provinces, to promote rural development. Robinson Nabulyato was appointed speaker of the second National Assembly and ruled that the ANC would not be recognized as the official opposition.

On January 30 the vice-president, Simon Kapwepwe (*see* BIOGRAPHY), introduced a stiff budget aimed at checking inflation and steadying the balance of payments position. The income tax was raised, and wives were to be taxed on the same basis as their husbands.

ZAMBIA

Education. (1966) Primary, pupils 473,432, teachers 9,325; secondary, pupils 24,005, teachers 1,290; vocational (1965), pupils 3,245, teachers 96; teacher training, students 1,510, teachers 147; higher, students 347, teaching staff 64.

Finance. Monetary unit: kwacha, with a par value of 0.71 kwachas to U.S. $1 (1.71 kwachas = £1 sterling). Gold and foreign exchange, central bank: (June 1969) U.S. $145.9 million; (June 1968) U.S. $95.9 million. Budget (1969 est.): revenue 296.9 million kwachas; expenditure 199.5 million kwachas. Gross national product: (1967) 838.7 million kwachas; (1966) 724.3 million kwachas. Cost of living (1963 = 100): (April 1969) 148; (April 1968) 141.

Foreign Trade. (1968) Imports 326,615,000 kwachas; exports 541,918,000 kwachas. Import sources: South Africa 23%; U.K. 23%; U.S. 10%; Rhodesia 7%; Japan 6%. Export destinations: U.K. 30%; Japan 21%; West Germany 13%. Main export copper 95%.

Transport and Communications. Roads (1967) 34,135 km. (including 9,270 km. with improved surface). Motor vehicles in use (1967): passenger 49,700; commercial (including buses) 20,000. Railways (1967) 1,046 km. (Zambian and Rhodesian railway operations were separated in 1967; a railway linking Zambia with Dar es Salaam in Tanzania was planned). Air traffic (including apportionment of traffic of Central African Airways; 1967): 66,239,000 passenger-km.; freight 825,000 net ton-km. Telephones (Jan. 1968) 43,267. Radio receivers (Dec. 1967) *c.* 80,000. Television receivers (Dec. 1967) 11,000.

Agriculture. Production (in 000; metric tons; 1967; 1966 in parentheses): corn *c.* 280 (*c.* 260); peanuts 20 (10); cassava *c.* 160 (*c.* 155); tobacco 5.3 (7.6). Livestock (in 000; 1966–67): cattle *c.* 1,300; sheep *c.* 38; goats *c.* 149; pigs *c.* 63.

Industry. Production (in 000; metric tons; 1968): copper 572; zinc 53; lead 22; manganese ore (metal content; 1967) 14; electricity (kw-hr.) 653,000.

Taxes on luxury goods were increased, while government expenditure was to be cut by nearly $120 million. In February a government White Paper on zambianization in the mining industry forecast that by 1972 more than 5,500 Zambians would have replaced workers from other countries. In April the World Bank announced a loan of $17.4 million for educational development, and in August it came to a preliminary arrangement with the U.K. and Zambian governments on a £20 million plan to end the Zambian copper industry's dependence upon power supplies from the Rhodesian side of the Kariba Dam. On November 14 Zambia, Tanzania, and China signed a joint agreement to proceed with construction of the Tanzam Railway.

Kaunda announced on August 11 that to safeguard Zambia's economic independence the copper industry was being nationalized. The mining companies were to consign 51% of their shares to the government and compensation would be paid out of future profits. New mining companies would be invited to cooperate with the state in mining development. At the same time the president announced a new mineral tax of 51% on gross profits.

In July Kaunda clashed with the white judiciary when he rebuked a judge, Ifor Evans, for quashing sentences on two Portuguese soldiers convicted of illegal entry into Zambia from Angola. Evans had earlier ruled elections for 13 seats invalid because UNIP supporters had physically prevented ANC candidates from handing in nomination papers. He was supported by Chief Justice James Skinner and the judiciary. Rioting youths ransacked the High Court in Lusaka, and both Evans and Skinner left the country and subsequently resigned. On November 3 Godfrey Muwo was sworn in as Zambia's first African High Court judge.

On August 25 Vice-President Kapwepwe resigned, claiming that he and his Bemba supporters had been abused and persecuted. Kaunda announced that he was taking personal control of UNIP and would rule the country as party secretary-general. He had been urged to adopt more extreme programs to win the support of the Bemba radicals, who were critical of Kaunda's policy and had sought to control UNIP. On August 27 Kapwepwe withdrew his resignation at the president's request. (K. I.)

Zoos and Botanical Gardens

Zoos. Zoos in many parts of the world continued to give aid to endangered species during 1969 by supporting the World Wildlife Fund. In 1968 the "panda" collecting boxes produced £12,841 in the U.K. and $2,897 in the U.S., and two wishing wells at Bristol, Eng., and Basel, Switz., made a considerable profit. In order to protect endangered species, many zoos placed a self-imposed ban on their importation. Frankfurt am Main, W.Ger., gave generously to the Serengeti National Park in Tanzania, aided the setting up of wildlife colleges in Africa, and bought an aircraft for the Tanzania Wildlife Division.

As zoos became larger, transporting huge numbers of visitors around them became of prime importance. Two U.S. zoos solved this problem in very similar ways. Philadelphia had a monorail tour of the zoo, and San Diego, Calif., had a "Skyfari" chairlift with four passenger chairs.

Zoo history was made when a 576-lb. male gorilla was transported uncaged by air from the Como

Zanzibar: *see* Tanzania
Zinc: *see* Mining
Zoology: *see* Biological Sciences

SYNDICATION INTERNATIONAL

Captain Flint, a penguin at the Hanover (W.Ger.) Zoo, demonstrates his gait on an artificial leg. Veterinarians amputated his leg because of severe infection.

(Switz.) Zoo to the Henry Doorly Zoo, Omaha, Neb. The animal was given tranquilizing drugs for the journey and was a model passenger.

Throughout the world, zoos were constructing more spacious and natural enclosures for their animals. At Bronx Zoo, New York City, a "World of Darkness" building was opened in which nocturnal animals inhabited lighted environmental enclosures while visitors stood in darkness. A new idea for giving reptiles more freedom in captivity was put into practice at Rapid City, S.D. Three huge underground viewing dens were constructed, connected to a one-acre paddock and surrounded by a snake- and rodent-proof fence. At Chester, Eng., a new ape house was opened to accommodate lowland gorillas and orangutans. Indoors the visitors viewed the apes through armour-plated glass windows where they were seen against a background of tropical vegetation; the animals had free access to outside moated islands. San Diego planned to open a wild animal park, 1,800 ac. in extent, at San Pasqual, the site having been chosen for its topographical similarity to the plains of East Africa. A $750,000 home was constructed for the five species of penguins at Detroit.

The breeding of many rare and endangered species in zoos met with increasing success. Antwerp, Belg., made zoo history by breeding the rare mountain gorilla in captivity for the first time. Duisberg, W.Ger., bred five bat-eared foxes; previously this species had been born in captivity at Rotterdam, Neth., but the offspring were not reared. Jersey, Channel Islands, bred the volcano rabbit for the first time, and a spectacled penguin hatched at Stuttgart, W.Ger., was also a first. Philadelphia bred American mergansers for the second time on record, and both Frankfurt and Edinburgh, Scot., bred cassowaries, a very rare occurrence.

Rarities received by zoos included three Cameroon bare-headed rock fowl (*Picathartes oreas*), which arrived at Frankfurt. Only one of this species had ever been in captivity before. The prime minister of New Zealand presented Washington, D.C., with two kiwis, the first at the zoo since 1925. San Diego was also presented with a pair of these birds as a gift to commemorate the city's 200th anniversary. (G. S. Mo.)

"LONDON DAILY EXPRESS" FROM PICTORIAL PARADE

Four young elephants at Windsor Safari Park Zoo, near London, wear earmuffs to protect them from noise of nearby jet airport. The animals had panicked on arrival in September 1969 at first sound of jets and stampeded out of the park.

Botanical Gardens. The Huntingdon Botanical Gardens, California, reported three consecutive nights during the winter of 1969 in which temperatures below freezing were recorded. This unusual cold spell caused considerable damage to the cacti in the desert garden. The winter of 1969 was also unusually wet, and this too had deleterious effects. At the Rancho Santa Ana Botanic Garden, California, the heavy rain did not cause as severe damage as it did to surrounding areas. Some trees were lost and there was other minor damage. During the previous year a record total of over 61,000 people had visited the garden. The Arnold Arboretum of Harvard University reported extensive winter damage from snow and ice storms. Repeated heavy wet snows broke trees, stripped branches, and caused weakening of structures. Development of an additional 15 ac. of land began with the installation of fences and roads on the Weld Walter trace in preparation for display plantings suitable for dry hillsides.

The Olu Pua Botanic Garden on Kauai Island, Hawaii, opened to the public in 1968, began to attract increasing numbers of visitors. A sanctuary was being created for the dwindling endemic plants of Hawaii, which had long been noted for the richness of its flora. At the same time many exotics were also being grown, especially plants from the Peruvian Andes and the Philippines.

Another new venture, the Chicago Botanic Garden, was being developed from the Skokie marsh, at one time famous for its wildlife. The marshes were being made into a 2,000-ac. recreational area that would also serve as a wildflower and wildlife preserve.

At the Royal Botanic Gardens, Kew, Eng., Queen Elizabeth II opened the new Queen's Garden, constructed near Kew Palace, on May 14, 1969. The garden was designed in the 17th-century style and planted with species and varieties grown at that period. On the same occasion the large extension to the herbarium and library was opened. Elsewhere at Kew, changes included reorganization of the shrub and flower beds to facilitate maintenance.

The botanic garden in Halle an der Saale reported on the excellent collection of cacti and succulents in its showhouse, the largest in East Germany. The Palmengarten, Frankfurt, integrated scientific botanical studies with recreational and cultural activities. A similar theme was the subject of the international symposium held at the Geneva Botanic Garden in 1968 and published in 1969 under the title *Les Multiples Fonctions d'un jardin botanique.*

The alpine garden at Lautaret in the French Alps, founded after World War I, continued to function as a research establishment with accommodations for scientific personnel. Half the garden was devoted to the cultivation of some 6,000 varieties, while the remainder was maintained as natural mountain grassland.

In Australia the Wagga Wagga Botanic Gardens, New South Wales, opened on Aug. 24, 1968, functioned as an advice centre, as well as concentrating on the cultivation of native Australian plants. Realization of the potential of native species and their threatened extinction in the wild also encouraged their cultivation at King's Park Botanic Garden, Perth. Similarly, native species were being grown at Christchurch Botanic Garden in New Zealand.

During 1969 the second edition of the important *International Directory of Botanical Gardens* was published, giving details of each institution.

(F. N. HE.)

Index

The black type entries are article headings in the *Book of the Year*. These black type article entries do not show page notations because they are to be found in their alphabetical position in the body of the book. They show the dates of the issues of the *Book of the Year* in which the articles appear. For example "Agriculture 70, 69, 68, 67, 66" indicates that the article "Agriculture" is to be found in the 1970, 1969, 1968, 1967 and 1966 *Book of the Year*.

The light type headings that are indented under black type article headings refer to material elsewhere in the text related to the subject under which they are listed. The light type headings that are not indented refer to information in the text not given a special article. Biographies and obituaries are listed as cross references to the articles "*Biography*" and "*Obituaries*" for the year in which they appear. References to illustrations are preceded by the abbreviation "il."

All headings, whether consisting of a single word or more, are treated for the purpose of alphabetization as single complete headings. Names beginning with "Mc" and "Mac" are alphabetized as "Mac"; "St." is treated as "Saint." All references below show the exact quarter of the page by means of the letters *a, b, c,* and *d,* signifying, respectively, the upper and lower halves of the first column and the upper and lower halves of the second column. Exceptions to this rule are tables, illustrations, and references from biographies and the articles "*Fuel and Power*" and "*Industrial Review.*"

A

C

D

E

H

I

J

K

L

Q

R

S

T

U

*In the 1969 edition of the Book of the Year the United Federation of Teachers was erroneously listed in the index as the Jewish United Federation of Teachers. The error was caused by a misreading of text and no harm or offense was meant to any party.

X

Y

Z

States Statistical Supplement

ENCYCLOPÆDIA BRITANNICA, INC.

Developments in the states in 1969

A slowing of the pace of governmental innovation was apparent in the U.S. as a whole in 1969, and the states were not immune to the general trend. Forty-seven legislatures assembled in regular session during the year. Governmental administrative reorganization was a major state concern as nine states expanded their efforts to improve delivery of public services and broaden their planning and coordination functions. At the same time, legislative improvements and state efforts to deal with urban problems proceeded apace.

Minnesota and New Jersey established Cabinet-level urban affairs councils similar to the one created by Pres. Richard M. Nixon. The first implementation of Model Cities plans was begun, though on a reduced scale due to federal funding reductions; 150 communities in 45 states were participating in the program. The role of the states in what was once to have been an exclusively federal-local program was enhanced as federal guidelines were redrawn to allow the states to coordinate planning grants. Thirty states received grants for increased planning staffs, and experimental programs were launched with four states to provide their cities with more technical assistance.

Under the new arrangements, states would be required to establish a system of priorities and then evaluate all local requests to see where they fell within that system. The states would receive the grants and transmit them to the appropriate localities. The first states to sign single contracts implementing the new arrangements were Minnesota, Missouri, and New Jersey. States chosen for pilot technical assistance programs were California, Connecticut, North Carolina, and Pennsylvania.

Improvements in state-federal coordination continued in numerous ways. Taking advantage of the option offered them by Pres. Lyndon B. Johnson, at least half of the states had established uniform intrastate administrative districts that were binding on federal as well as state agencies.

Thirty-six states raised taxes in 1969; total state tax collections were $42.1 billion in fiscal 1969, up from $36.4 billion in 1968. The tight money market affected state government in many ways but perhaps most significantly by interfering with sales of state and local revenue bonds. As interest rates soared and the tax-exempt status of the bonds was threatened, states reached their legal interstate ceilings and could not find buyers for their bonds at those rates. Motor fuel tax rates were raised in 15 states, the largest number since 1955.

One of the year's most notable features was the emergence of a trend toward the revival of state constitutional law as a meaningful element in American jurisprudence. In civil rights perhaps the major thrust was toward abandonment of 21 as the age at which persons received the rights of adults.

Improved law enforcement replaced poverty and civil rights as the most provocative public concern in 1969, continuing the trend begun earlier. All of the states qualified for federal aid under the Safe Streets Act of 1968 before the federal deadline, and many undertook to strengthen law enforcement procedures on their own. Perhaps most significant were the efforts to improve criminal justice procedures in the courts and corrections procedures in the prisons as well as to strengthen anticrime programs.

By the end of 1969, 40 states had ratified the Uniform Anatomical Gift Act, regulating human organ transplants, and the other ten were set to act early in 1970. Another case of cooperation developed as the states moved to harmonize their holiday calendars with the federal legislation providing three-day weekends.

Consumer protection issues continued to be of major importance as state actions on a wide variety of fronts limited insurance, credit, and mail-order abuses. The major setback to consumer protection came as state after state had to raise its interest rate ceiling to enable any lending activity at all to occur.

State aid to nonpublic schools continued to grow as an issue in the wake of Pennsylvania's enactment of a major aid bill in 1968.

State Government. The governor of Alabama instituted a code of ethics covering all state employees, and created a commission to enforce it. Arizona strengthened its laws against bribery and corruption. New Jersey and Pennsylvania became the first states to receive planning funds from the Department of Housing and Urban Development to help develop planning, programming, and budgeting (PPB) systems and the in-house staff capability to utilize them. Five other states were negotiating with HUD for similar assistance.

School decentralization became an issue in most big cities, and a number of state legislatures had to grapple with the problem. Campus disturbances led to considerable new state legislation to strengthen the hand of university administrators in dealing with student troublemakers.

In a continuing effort to reduce environmental pollution, the states took the lead in banning or severely limiting the use of DDT. By July, 14 states containing approximately half of the country's population had formally indicated that they intended to establish air quality standards under the 1967 Air Quality Control Act.

Abortion reform continued to be an issue in 1969. Among the states easing their abortion laws were Arkansas, Delaware, Kansas, Oregon, and New Mexico. The California Supreme Court held, in September, that the state's liberal law was unconstitutionally vague and denied women their fundamental rights by restricting their right to abortions in any way. Similar cases were pending in other states.

California replaced its divorce laws with a simplified "dissolution of marriage" procedure while New York's liberalized divorce law rapidly raised the number of divorces granted in that state. West Virginia added incurable insanity and voluntary separation for two years to the grounds for divorce in that state.

Direct involvement in the provision of housing by states for their citizens increased in 1969 with six more states establishing or expanding state-level housing agencies.

California established a policy to charge private consulting firms for the time and services of state employees who provide them with ideas and data and thereby enable them to make substantial profits on federal contracts.

Constitutional Revision. Texas voters approved the removal of obsolete sections of that state's constitution. The Illinois constitutional convention convened in the fall to begin work on revising or replacing that state's basic law. The Massachusetts Supreme Court held that the governor of that state had the power and the obligation to call a constitutional convention to decide which amendments would be placed on the November ballot.

Legislatures and Legislative Procedures. In the past three years, support for state legislatures increased 37.4%. Connecticut created a permanent Legislative Management Committee to handle all money appropriated for legislative expenses. Codes of ethics were adopted in Connecticut and Oklahoma. Legislators' salaries were increased in Florida (from $1,200 to $12,000), Idaho, Indiana, Maine, Massachusetts, South Dakota, and Tennessee. Hawaii established a Legislative Reapportionment Commission with apportionment advisory councils.

Administration. Several states embarked on major governmental reorganization programs. In an effort brought about by the adoption of a new constitution in 1968, Florida inaugurated the office of lieutenant governor and reorganized the entire state administrative structure, consolidating 200 agencies into 23 departments. Delaware created departments of Health and Social Services, Natural Resources and Environmental Control, and Transportation as part of a new Cabinet form of government. The 130 state agencies and commissions were to be merged into 12 departments.

Wisconsin entered into its first collective bargaining contract with its public employees. Limited in both application and scope, it represented a first step for the state's employees.

Wyoming inaugurated a major administrative reorganization. The governor's appointment and planning powers were enhanced, and he was authorized to participate in all meetings of nonconstitutional boards and commissions. A permanent state reorganization commission was established under joint gubernatorial-legislative control.

Illinois established a Bureau of the Budget to assist the governor in his capacity as chief executive, staffing it with a number of "bright young men." California activated its new Department of Human Resources Development, which combined a number of human development agencies.

Massachusetts enacted legislation establishing nine Cabinet-level departments that would absorb hundreds of existing state agencies. The governor of Rhode Island was given powers to reorganize the state's administration subject to legislative veto. Several measures enacted in Maryland initiated a larger administrative reorganization. New Hampshire established a task force to study state government reorganization.

A federal court in North Carolina held that state's ban on union activities among police and firemen unconstitutional but sustained another state law forbidding governmental units to negotiate with public-employee unions. Nevada and South Dakota prohibited strikes by public employees but allowed them to bargain collectively under certain circumstances. New York increased the penalties for strikes by public employees under the Taylor Law, established a code of unfair labor practices, and created an Office of Employee Relations. Vermont enacted labor relations acts for state employees and teachers.

Judiciary and Law Enforcement. Connecticut revised and codified its criminal statutes, substantially liberalizing the state's sex laws. Arkansas became the 49th state to institute a jury wheel system for the selection of all jurors in the state's circuit courts. Connecticut introduced selection of jurors by computer.

Idaho adopted a major reorganization of its lower court system that would substitute a uniform system of magistrate courts with appointed magistrates for the present justice, probate, and police courts. Oklahoma created an intermediate appellate court and provided for review of revocations of suspended sentences. Rhode Island consolidated its district and special courts into a single statewide system.

New Mexico became the 14th state to abolish at least partially the death penalty. The New Jersey Supreme Court ruled unconstitutional local criminal registration laws that required persons with criminal records to register with local police within 24 hours of their arrival in town, holding that such powers were reserved to the state. Arizona modified the U.S. Supreme Court ruling on informing suspects of their constitutional rights to widen possibilities for prosecution of defendants. Connecticut widened its search and seizure provisions and granted immunity from prosecution to witnesses testifying in cases of serious crimes. Tennessee lawmen were authorized to execute search warrants at night.

Penal laws relating to stolen or forged credit cards were strengthened in Massachusetts and New York. Florida instituted procedures for the revocation of the corporate charters of businesses discovered to be connected with organized crime. Maryland enacted a preventive detention act applicable to people who commit violent crimes while free on bail.

The Oregon Supreme Court upheld that state's implied consent law, under which the holder of a driver's license is considered to have consented to tests for drunkenness. The Massachusetts Supreme Court held that revocation of a driver's license could come only after a proper hearing except when the driver had "become an immediate threat to the general safety." Arizona, Indiana, Maine, Nevada, New Mexico, Tennessee, and Alaska enacted implied consent laws while Wyoming rejected one. Maryland's new law demanded "express consent" of applicants for driver's licenses.

New York established a new procedure whereby less serious traffic violations in

New York City would be handled by an administrative agency rather than in the courts. Crime-control "packages" were enacted in Florida, Indiana, Nevada, and Rhode Island.

Arkansas made it a felony to incite or engage in a riot and a misdemeanor to do the same on school campuses. Florida upgraded its riot-control capability and, along with New York and Utah, provided special penalties for campus rioters. Georgia and Idaho legislated penalties for school and college rioters. Maryland provided for the exchange of personnel and equipment with other states and the District of Columbia in time of emergency. Oklahoma provided for a similar interstate exchange, made incitement to riot a felony, and gave campus administrators greater disciplinary powers. Massachusetts enacted a campus disorder control "package." Vermont enacted a comprehensive antiriot act. Tennessee made it a felony for a nonstudent to incite or participate in a riot at any public school.

Court-regulated electronic surveillance was legalized in Florida, New Hampshire, and Rhode Island. New York changed its "eavesdropping" law to conform to the new federal enactment. Vermont brought its law on the interstate control of firearms into conformity with the federal statute but defeated a general gun-control measure. The New Jersey Supreme Court sustained a requirement that applicants for gun permits disclose any past membership in subversive organizations. New Mexico increased the penalty for crimes committed with firearms. Oklahoma made purchase of firearms by its residents subject to the provisions of federal law.

Drug-control laws were tightened in Florida, Indiana, Maine, Nevada, New Hampshire (which also instituted a drug-abuse program), and Wyoming. Massachusetts enacted a comprehensive drug-control and addict-rehabilitation program. Possession of marijuana was reduced from a felony to a misdemeanor in Connecticut. Hawaii gave judges discretionary powers in this matter when dealing with first offenses.

Obscenity- and pornography-control legislation was enacted in Georgia and Nevada. The California Supreme Court held that neither the state nor its subdivisions could prohibit "topless" or "bottomless" dancing without violating the right of free expression.

Finance and Taxation. New ways of raising additional revenue were sought by many states in 1969. New Jersey voters approved the institution of a state lottery, making theirs the third state to do so. Wisconsin voters eliminated the constitutional restrictions on state borrowing so that the state government would be able to borrow directly. Utah opened the door to investment of state funds in the stocks of private industry to improve earnings. Texas voters eliminated the constitutional interest-rate limitation on state bonds.

Illinois and Maine adopted state income taxes, bringing the number of states using this revenue source to 38. Illinois established a flat rate tax of $2\frac{1}{2}\%$ on individuals and 4% on corporations and included a revenue-sharing feature assuring cities and counties of one-twelfth of the revenue collected. Both states also increased cigarette and gasoline taxes. Illinois increased liquor, beer, and hotel taxes and vehicle license fees. In return, it lowered its sales tax from $4\frac{1}{4}$ to 4% and authorized cities and counties to levy the additional $\frac{1}{4}\%$, thus raising local sales taxes to as much as 1%.

Maine's personal income tax was graduated from 1 to 6% and its corporate rate was 4%. The state also raised its sales tax. The Vermont Supreme Court sustained a 1966 state law allowing Vermont to collect income tax on a nonresident's total earnings if part of his income was earned in Vermont. The decision was to be appealed to the U.S. Supreme Court.

Alaska benefited from what was very likely the greatest revenue windfall since the federal assumption of Revolutionary War debts in the 1790s. The leasing of oil lands on that state's Arctic North Slope virtually guaranteed the state enough revenue in the foreseeable future to obviate the necessity to levy other taxes.

Major tax-increase packages were enacted in Arkansas, Connecticut, Illinois, Maine, Massachusetts, Missouri, Montana, New Hampshire (though it continued to reject all broad-based taxes), New Mexico, North Carolina, North Dakota, Rhode Island, South Dakota, and Vermont. Georgia experienced a virtual stalemate in its efforts to raise additional revenues as fighting between the governor and the legislature continued. New York was forced to reduce its projected state aid to local governments for public assistance, Medicaid, and education to balance its budget.

Hawaii provided tax relief for homeowners and lower income groups. Indiana replaced the personal property tax on vehicles with an excise tax and provided that homeowners of low-value properties would not have to pay increased taxes as a result of home improvements. North Carolina levied its first cigarette tax, the last state to do so.

North Dakota eliminated all personal property taxes, replacing them with sales and excise taxes that would be distributed to local governments previously dependent upon the property tax. South Dakota committed 80% of revenues produced by tax increases enacted in 1969 to its local governments.

Politics and Elections. New Jersey and Virginia voters elected Republican governors in the most important elections of 1969. In Virginia, it was the first such Republican triumph since Reconstruction. Referenda generated mixed responses from voters. Texas voters rejected a package of legislative reforms and a proposed water resources development program.

Arkansas codified and reformed its election laws. Indiana liberalized its absentee voter provisions, required that polls stay open only 12 hours, and provided for culling of registration lists every two years. Maine lowered the voting age to 20. New Jersey and Ohio voters rejected proposals to lower the voting age to 18. New Mexico moved its primary date from August to June of even-numbered years. Tennessee enabled its residents who moved to other states to vote for president in Tennessee until they qualified as residents in their new states. In the aftermath of the 1968 elections, Ohio made it easier for third parties to get on the state ballot and provided space for write-ins.

Maine altered its "winner-take-all" allocation of its four electoral votes, providing that two would go to the statewide winner and the two others to the winners in each of the state's two congressional districts.

Massachusetts altered its presidential primary to provide, as in Oregon, for the placing of all generally recognized candidates on the ballot. New Mexico and Rhode Island instituted presidential primaries.

State-Federal Relations. The governor of California created an Office of Intergovernmental Management and designated the lieutenant governor as coordinator of all state activities requiring intergovernmental attention. Illinois expanded its Washington office to coordinate all activities between federal and state agencies as well as all state applications for federal funds.

The New York legislature established a Federal-State Liaison Office in the state Senate. To enhance state coordination of federal aid, North Carolina required State Department of Administration approval of all projects to be financed by nonstate funds. Approximately one-fourth of the states now had such a requirement.

In a major anti-inflation move, President Nixon ordered a 75% cutback in federally financed construction and requested the states and localities to take similar action. Not only did few respond positively but a task force of the National Governors' Conference called on the president to modify the cutback order.

The Bureau of the Budget began issuing regulations to implement the landmark Intergovernmental Cooperation Act of 1968 and other related legislation. Under the BOB rules, states would receive full information on all grants-in-aid flowing into their agencies for purposes of better program coordination.

The state-federal struggle over revision of the federal welfare regulations resulted in a moderation of the proposed change that would simplify to only a declaration of need the procedures required for a welfare applicant to qualify for assistance. The simplified procedure, if made mandatory, would be implemented on a staggered basis.

The states were to establish Technical Consultation Panels to evaluate the new method and report on its progress. HEW also required that the states continue to provide aid to persons they wished to remove from the rolls (or whose level of assistance they wished to reduce) during the hearing procedure.

The Department of Transportation replaced the very complex equal opportunity regulations for federal-aid highway construction issued in 1968 with simplified uniform standards. The Department of Labor reorganized the Manpower Administration, in consultation with state officials, to consolidate its administrative and field structure.

U.S. Legislation. In a relatively quiet year, Congress amended the Medicaid Act to ease the burden on the states, and the states and cities successfully turned back an effort to limit the tax exempt status of municipal bonds, though the uncertainty of the outcome of this effort during the year played havoc with bond sales. At the same time, Congress eliminated all funds for the state technical services program ("industrial extension") for fiscal year 1970. In 1969 all states except Florida, Maryland, and North Dakota were participating in the program. The Older Americans Act increased the state's role in programs for the aging.

The Supreme Court and the States. In its last year, the Warren Court continued its earlier trends with some slight moderation. In *Gaston County* v. *U.S.*, the court ruled that literacy tests for voting are unconstitutional when applied to blacks who have had separate and inferior schooling.

On criminal rights issues, the court reversed two earlier decisions to hold, under the Fourth Amendment, that law officers must have signed search warrants that describe "with particularity" what they are looking for, and that state officials may be required by prisoners to answer written questions concerning their cases in federal habeas corpus proceedings. The court also extended the Fifth Amendment prohibition of double jeopardy to the states.

Refusing to extend the "equal protection" doctrine in a radical new direction, the court ruled that it is not unconstitutional for the states or their subdivisions to allocate unequal amounts of money for education in different school districts.

In a long-predicted decision affecting 40 states and the District of Columbia, the court held welfare residency requirements to be unconstitutional. A decision that could have momentous consequences was the U.S. Court of Appeals ruling that a state may ban auto safety equipment it believes to be hazardous even though the same equipment meets minimum federal standards.

Reapportionment. A three-judge federal panel struck down Indiana's large multiple-member legislative districts on the ground that they deprived blacks of adequate representation. Hawaii was divided into two congressional districts and adopted the "one-voter, one-vote" approach, using only registered voters as the basis for apportionment to prevent skewing by the large number of nonvoting military families in the state. The U.S. Supreme Court held New York's congressional districts to be in violation of the "one-man, one-vote" doctrine and ordered their reapportionment before the 1970 election.

State Programs and Nationwide Concerns. *Antipoverty Programs.* The new administration took a number of important steps to expand the states' role in the antipoverty programs. Crucial to all this was implementation by the Office of Economic Opportunity of the 15 provisions for an active state role included in the antipoverty legislation, which OEO officials had generally ignored in the past. The effort was made at least partly in response to mounting state dissatisfaction with their exclusion and to increasing federal recognition that such dissatisfaction affected the program's success.

Business Regulation and Consumer Protection. Consumer protection issues continued to be of major importance during 1969. Alaska, Arkansas, Connecticut, Hawaii, Idaho, Massachusetts, Ohio, and West Virginia enacted legislation allowing their citizens to keep as gifts unsolicited merchandise sent them. Nevada outlawed service station games and contests. New York instituted regulation of retailers' promotional games. Arkansas, New Hampshire, New York, and Ohio adopted legislation regulating cancellation of auto insurance policies.

Church-State Relations. School issues continued to dominate the church-state scene, with tax exemption questions a close second. Connecticut authorized $6 million in state funds to assist nonpublic schools in their secular educational programs provided that the recipient schools agreed to admit Connecticut children regardless of their religion. The act provided for a quick court test.

Minnesota provided funds to reimburse school districts for home economics and shop shared-time programs involving parochial schools. Ohio broadened its nonpublic school aid program to provide what was, in effect, a general subsidy for secular subjects in parochial schools in return for state certification of teachers and increased state supervision. Nonpublic aid measures failed in Illinois, Michigan, North Dakota, and Vermont, among other states. In New York, Gov. Nelson A. Rockefeller vetoed, on constitutional grounds, a measure that would have provided state aid to church-related colleges.

Civil Rights. The New Jersey Supreme Court ruled unanimously that local communities have the right to adopt their own antiblockbusting ordinances stronger than the regulations of the State Real Estate Commission. New Mexico enacted a new antidiscrimination act covering employment, public accommodations, and housing and established a new commission with broad powers to enforce it. New York extended its antidiscrimination law to cover all rental housing, and banned blockbusting. Massachusetts prohibited discrimination in selling or leasing homes to veterans or members of the armed forces and invalidated restrictive covenants. Ohio extended its fair housing laws to cover all dwellings.

Education. Arkansas enacted a Quality Education Act that paved the way for the introduction of public kindergarten and adult education programs. The state also instituted a new aid formula offering across-the-board per capita grants to each school district plus equalization funds for poorer districts. Indiana revised and simplified its school aid formula and increased its amount. North Dakota and Vermont altered their school aid formulas. Wyoming reorganized its school districts and increased the amounts of state aid they were to receive.

Florida continued its efforts at statewide educational innovation through its Minimum Foundation Program for elementary and secondary schools. Among other things, school districts were authorized to institute year-round operations on a quarterly basis. Oklahoma created a Commission on Education to develop a long-range plan for educational improvement in the state. The New York legislature enacted a school decentralization plan for New York City and prohibited state action to initiate bussing in order to overcome segregated school patterns.

Connecticut forbade teachers' strikes. Oklahoma and South Dakota created professional standards boards to upgrade teacher certification standards. South Dakota introduced incentive pay scales as well.

Maryland reorganized its educational

structure: school boards were enlarged, uniform nonpartisan election methods were introduced, and a new state aid formula that increased funds to Baltimore inner-city schools was adopted. In a radical move, Rhode Island created a single Board of Regents to supervise all public education in the state from kindergarten through college and with the power to establish a department of education and auxiliary boards. Ohio established a State Board of School and College Registration.

Bilingual public education projects were instituted, with federal aid, in Arkansas, New Mexico, Oklahoma, and Texas to improve the education of Spanish-speaking children. At least five other states—California, Florida, Louisiana, New York, and Pennsylvania—provided some bilingual educational opportunities in their public education systems.

Texas voters approved an expanded student loan plan. Hawaii and West Virginia instituted student loan programs. Utah guaranteed repayment of federal student loans. Minnesota secured interim bank loans for students while the federal program was being revised.

Massachusetts opened the door to the appointment of students to the boards of trustees of its institutions of higher learning. Vocational and technical education programs were regionalized in Montana, expanded in Idaho, and given a separate department in Oklahoma. Utah created a single Board of Higher Education with absolute budgetary and appointment control over all colleges and universities. West Virginia altered the structure of its higher education governing board.

Environmental Management and Pollution Control. The assault on pesticide pollution took on new dimensions in 1969. Arizona, Florida, Illinois, Michigan, Pennsylvania, and Wisconsin took the lead by suspending, severely limiting, or banning the use of DDT, often at the initiative of their legislatures as well as their agricultural agencies.

Connecticut appropriated $300,000 for an inventory and survey of its tidal wetlands, the despoliation of which had become an issue in recent years. Maine established a Land Use Regulation Commission with powers to prevent undesirable development of certain wild lands and a Mining Commission to regulate reclamation and restoration of mined land. The Arkansas Soil and Water Conservation Commission began the development of a state water plan with a related land resources management program. Mining companies in Arkansas and Wyoming were required to restore land damaged in opencut mining.

Utah utilized its fiscal powers in an attempt to maintain agricultural open space by providing that land in farm use for at least five years would be taxed at its agricultural rather than its market value but that back taxes would have to be paid if the land was sold for nonagricultural use.

New York voters amended their constitution to establish a Conservation Bill of Rights and a State Nature and Historical Reserve, by a five-to-one margin. Illinois and Pennsylvania became the first two states to actually adopt air quality control standards.

Alaska enacted an air pollution control act establishing a commission to set and enforce air quality standards statewide with provision for localities to assume most of the task if they so choose. Arizona entrusted the task to its State Health Department under similar terms. Illinois enacted an antipollution package that gave its attorney general significant statewide powers to combat water and air pollution. Indiana's strengthened Air Quality Control Act established air quality control basins, outlawed open dumps, and initiated auto-emission regulation.

Oklahoma provided income tax credits on up to 20% of the total investment for installation of air pollution control equipment until total cost is recovered. The California Highway Patrol began experimenting with two steam-powered vehicles to test the potential of such vehicles in the state's war against smog. Vermont required utility companies to secure a state certificate of public good before construction of any nuclear power facilities, thereby strengthening state control in that field.

In efforts to control water pollution, Maine adopted federal standards for bacteria and acidity levels and provided for dealing with oil spills in state waters. Pennsylvania provided for a statewide computer network to monitor water pollution, which would parallel one under construction for monitoring air pollution. West Virginia amended its Water Pollution Control Act to give the chief of the Division of Water Resources powers to immediately close down polluting activities that presented a clear and present danger to public health. Hawaii empowered its state health department to seek court injunctions to stop violations of pure water standards. California established an interim regional planning agency to control pollution development in the Lake Tahoe area until the interstate compact would go into effect.

Three headline-grabbing environmental controversies involved the states and the federal government in tension as well as in tandem, and a fourth with headline potential emerged. The oil leak off the Santa Barbara coast of California, which had occurred while oil drilling was being conducted under federal standards that were substantially lower than those of the state, led to a massive public response, state intervention on behalf of higher standards, and a substantial federal capitulation.

The new Alaskan oil bonanza led to conflict between exploitation-oriented and preservation-oriented groups over the development of access routes to the oil fields, which divided both the state and federal authorities. So, too, did the controversy over a new airport in the Everglades of Florida. The decision went in favor of the conservationists when the governor of Florida threw his weight on their side. The new issue involved a controversy between the state of Minnesota and the federal Atomic Energy Commission in which the state wished to apply higher standards to the regulation of nuclear power plants than those demanded by the AEC.

Health and Welfare. The administrative unification of the health and welfare services proceeded in several states in 1969. The governor of Pennsylvania used his executive authority to transfer all health functions under the Public Welfare Department to the Health Department pending legislative action to merge the two departments into a new Department of Human Services.

Texas voters amended their constitution to increase the limit of state aid for public welfare programs from $60 million to $80 million. To improve the delivery of the state's social services, Kentucky established two coordinating groups, the Human Resources Coordinating Commission, consisting of eight state department heads, and the Human Resources Coordinating Council, consisting of laymen, professionals, and recipients of state social services.

Georgia enacted a mental health "bill of rights" to secure the civil rights of patients in state mental hospitals. New York opened the first of 15 transition centers designed to ease mental patients back into society. Vermont revised its mental patient commitment laws.

Massachusetts placed its Medicaid program, in operation since 1966, on the statute books and put a ceiling on state funds available for it. New Mexico cut back its payments under Medicaid by 25% after trying to reduce the scope of the program against federal opposition. Tennessee and Virginia approved state funding of the basic five services under the Medicaid program. Tennessee approved a $50 million program for the first year and Virginia a $54 million one.

New York tightened its welfare requirements, required all counties to participate in the federal Food Stamp Program, and provided funds for the establishment of day-care centers. Ohio placed its day-care centers under the regulation of the Department of Public Welfare and required the department to provide care for eligible children of low-income families.

Idaho required applicants for county assistance to make themselves available for work on county projects. Connecticut tightened its welfare operations, ending its open-ended welfare budget, creating a system of state medical examiners, and extending workmen's compensation coverage to victims of radioactivity exposure. Florida increased by 40% the aid from its general fund to support for health and welfare. Hawaii passed a welfare benefit improvement. North Dakota increased its welfare appropriations equally generously. Wyoming cut its welfare budget so drastically that the governor threatened to call a special legislative session.

Massachusetts enacted legislation to facilitate distribution of federal surplus foods and to help communities develop lunch programs for senior citizens. A state superior court also held that welfare clients are entitled to state reimbursement for legal assistance costs incurred in obtaining benefits, the first application of the right-to-counsel doctrine to a civil case.

The National Governors' Conference and a number of state legislatures called on Congress to assume all welfare payments and set uniform nationwide welfare standards, echoing a growing sentiment among the states.

West Virginia authorized family planning clinics to provide birth control information to unwed mothers and wives separated from their husbands.

Alaska initiated a new program to combat drug abuse and alcoholism. Hawaii launched a venereal disease reduction program. Maryland established a state center for control of narcotics users and a program for their rehabilitation. South Dakota made fluoridation of all water supplied in the state mandatory. Ohio mandated fluoridation in public water systems serving 5,000 or more persons, with the state reimbursing cities for the cost of equipment and installation.

The Oklahoma Department of Public Welfare was authorized to contract with counties and other public or private agencies to operate community mental retardation facilities. Tennessee authorized the issuance of $6 million in bonds for construction of mental health and correctional facilities. Wyoming created a board of nursing home administrators to license and regulate nursing homes.

Idaho recognized osteopaths as medical practitioners and added them to the state board of medicine. New York enacted legislation to encourage general practice in medicine by requiring each state university medical center to establish a department of general practice with appropriate staff and courses to develop a specialization in the field. Ohio made immunization against measles a prerequisite for school admission and required tuberculosis examinations for school employees and students.

Housing. Connecticut created a Mortgage Authority with $5 million in bonding funds to guarantee home mortgages of low- and moderate-income families. The state also adopted a statewide housing code, introduced regulation of the sale of out-of-state real estate, and provided that verbal agreements to lease housing carried an unwritten presumption that the house was inhabitable.

Delaware created a Department of Housing. Maine created a State Housing Authority with power to purchase up to $20 million in home mortgages and to sponsor federal housing projects. Maryland created a state authority to aid in the development of low-cost housing. Missouri created a State Housing Development Commission with power to issue revenue bonds to make low-interest loans to private developers of middle- and low-income housing.

New Jersey appropriated $12.5 million for construction or rehabilitation of homes for low- and moderate-income families. Oklahoma created a housing authority to develop low-income single- or two-family homes for sale around the state. Ohio gave temporary tax exemption to houses constructed or rehabilitated in areas of dilapidated property. Massachusetts enacted tenant protection laws.

Labor. Nevada established a mine advisory board to develop and administer mine safety regulations. West Virginia revamped its mine safety code and improved its enforcement. Wyoming established a commission to promulgate and enforce safety standards for industrial workers. Maryland created a State Department of Mediation and Conciliation to help settle labor disputes. Montana created an industrial safety board. Minnesota's newly enacted occupational safety laws were commended by the U.S. Department of Labor as the most progressive in the country.

Idaho provided that women were to receive pay equal to that of men. States raising their minimum wage included Hawaii, Maryland, South Dakota, and Vermont. New York established a minimum wage for farm workers.

Alaska raised unemployment benefits and extended them to some seasonal workers, as did Hawaii. Unemployment benefits were also raised in Georgia, Maryland, Montana, Nevada, and New Mexico. Workmen's compensation benefits were increased in Idaho and Maryland. New Mexico introduced vocational rehabilitation under the state's workmen's compensation law. Hawaii created an insurance system for workers injured off the job. West Virginia revised workmen's compensation laws and included broad coverage for black-lung disease. Ohio included black-lung disease under workmen's compensation.

Local Government and Urban Affairs. Wisconsin extended the county executive form of government throughout the state by constitutional amendment, thereby strengthening the governing capabilities of counties significantly. Montana gave its cities more home rule. New Mexico increased the possibilities for state technical assistance to localities by allowing state employees to work temporarily for cities or counties without losing their state retirement benefits. Utah transferred power to set salaries of elected county officials to the commissioner of each county and eliminated the state statutory maximum. The Montana legislature relinquished its right to set the salaries of mayors and aldermen and gave the power to city councils.

The urban affairs councils established by Minnesota and New Jersey would, among other things, facilitate federal aid programs for cities, particularly the Model Cities Program. Minnesota also created an Urban Action Center within the state planning agency to develop a state policy and coordinate state activities in the urban field.

New Jersey greatly increased the state's aid to its cities on a wide variety of fronts, concentrating on the six largest cities. The U.S. Department of Housing and Urban Development granted $75,000 to New Jersey to expand state services to Model Cities projects. The state Model Cities Program provided money and technical assistance to enable cities to plan for participation in the federal program and to initiate projects before federal funding was available.

The governor of New York created an Office for Community Affairs by executive order, consolidating three other offices. The new office would serve as the state's liaison with the federal Model Cities and Economic Opportunity programs and as a developer of creative approaches to urban problems. New Jersey passed the Hackensack Meadowlands and Reclamation Act, which inaugurated a 30-year land reclamation project to create a new town and industrial area.

North Dakota granted its cities broad home-rule powers contingent upon local voter approval. Charter provisions would supersede conflicting state laws within the city limits. West Virginia codified and clarified its municipal laws in a 700-page act.

Alaska inaugurated a multiple-purpose, state-local revenue-sharing arrangement. Arkansas authorized its local governments to levy a $5 motor vehicle tax, issue bonds to construct convention centers, or levy a 1% hotel-motel receipt tax to support an advertising commission. Connecticut provided $33.4 million in bond revenues for its Department of

Community Affairs. Local government taxing and bonding powers were increased in Idaho, which also delayed application for a 1965 property tax equalization requirement.

Indiana eliminated the maximum interest rate ceiling on local bonds. Missouri authorized cities of over 500 population to levy local sales taxes of ½ or 1% by local referendum with the state administering the tax collections. Montana gave its cities a greater share of the state tax revenues. Nevada cities and counties were allotted all the new revenue from state cigarette and liquor tax increases and authorized to increase their own sales and gasoline taxes by ½ and 1%, respectively.

New Mexico cities were authorized to levy a tax of up to 2% on hotel bills to raise funds for tourist promotion or civic building improvements. New Mexico prohibited its cities and counties from increasing their tax intake by more than 5% in any one year without permission from the State Department of Finance and Administration. The state also reassumed the entire gross-receipts levy with the proviso that it would distribute what was formerly the cities' share in the cities where the tax was collected.

South Dakota increased the revenue resources of its local governments by opening up all non-ad valorem taxes except the motor-fuel tax to its cities and by providing for the transfer of most of its tax increases to local government. On the other hand, the Utah legislature, meeting in special session, rejected various gubernatorial proposals to grant that state's cities greater taxing flexibility.

Utah authorized its cities to participate in two more federally funded programs but provided for no state role in either. Cities were authorized to establish public transit districts to acquire, develop, and operate mass transit systems with federal aid. The right to constitute themselves as neighborhood agencies and thereby become eligible for participation in federal redevelopment programs was extended to all cities and counties in the state. West Virginia gave the chief inspector of public offices power to provide for at least an annual inspection of the financial affairs of every local government office or political unit.

A new Arkansas law specified that cities could annex land only by majority vote within the city and in the territory to be annexed. Arkansas localities were given the option to decide by referendum whether to allow hotels, motels, and restaurants to serve mixed drinks. The Arkansas legislature reversed a state Supreme Court ruling arising out of an auto accident case that had made that state's cities liable in tort lawsuits but required all local subdivisions to carry motor vehicle liability insurance.

Georgia authorized its cities of over 3,000 population to bargain directly with the State Highway Department for road construction, bypassing their county officials. New York authorized its local governments to reapportion their governing bodies according to the "one-man, one-vote" principle.

In an unprecedented and far-reaching action, the Indiana legislature approved the consolidation of Indianapolis and the unincorporated parts of Marion County (its metropolitan hinterland) under a reorganized municipal government structure. Maine established procedures whereby two or more adjoining cities could consolidate by referendum, and authorized cities to form regional councils. Tennessee authorized smaller municipalities to annex adjacent unpopulated areas by ordinance rather than referendum. The Minnesota legislature strengthened the hand of the Twin Cities Metropolitan Council, giving it great planning and policy-making responsibilities.

Massachusetts established a state board to which nonprofit or limited-profit housing developers might appeal adverse local zoning decisions designed to keep out low- and moderate-income housing. The state board could override the local decisions within certain limits. Missouri authorized its cities to tear down derelict buildings and permitted its courts to force repair of slum property. Montana authorized its cities to acquire land for open-space use, renew blighted areas, and redevelop neighborhoods under the federal urban renewal program. Nevada required voter approval of urban renewal projects in some cities.

National and Civil Defense. Arkansas revised substantially its state military code for the first time in 40 years. New Mexico established a Department of Military Affairs. Seven states—Connecticut, Delaware, Illinois, Louisiana, Massachusetts, Pennsylvania, and South Dakota—authorized cash bonuses for their Vietnam veterans.

Parks and Recreation. Nevada established a Fish and Game Department. Indiana codified its fish and game laws and expanded the authority of its Department of Natural Resources in the regulation of the state's parks and streams. Minnesota established a state zoological garden under a state board to be located in the Twin Cities metropolitan area.

Transportation and Highways. Delaware established a Department of Transportation. To plan and coordinate its transportation development, Minnesota established an interdepartmental task force on transportation in the State Planning Agency. New Mexico established a State Railroad Authority. Idaho cities were empowered to hold revenue bond referenda to finance airport facilities.

Illinois increased taxation for highway construction purposes to provide both state and local governments with substantial additional funds. Indiana raised the gasoline tax by one-third. Gasoline tax increases and new bond issues were designed to give Louisiana and Mississippi substantial new highway construction funds. Utah raised the gasoline tax to raise revenues for city and county feeder roads. West Virginia authorized sale of $90 million in road bonds. Wyoming extended statewide its optional one-cent gasoline tax for local road construction.

The Washington Supreme Court ruled that gasoline tax money cannot be spent on rapid transit under the state constitution. New York provided its regional transportation authorities with additional funds by increasing the tax on recording mortgages. Oregon provided for metropolitan transit authorities with gubernatorially appointed directors. Maryland created a state transportation authority to acquire and develop rapid-transit facilities in the Baltimore area and to cooperate in the development of a Washington metropolitan regional system.

The New Jersey Department of Transportation inaugurated a demonstration project that bussed formerly unemployed residents of depressed central cities in the northern part of the state to jobs in the suburbs, which they would otherwise be unable to reach. The project was financed entirely within the state by utilizing state, county, and industry funds as well as users' fares.

Wyoming provided for state assistance to persons and businesses forced to relocate because of highway construction. Florida established a State Road Arbitration Board to settle contract disputes between the highway department and the contractors, and required governmental units responsible for road construction and maintenance to propose local five-year plans.

Maine enacted a billboard control measure conforming to federal standards. Vermont revised its billboard control act. Ohio authorized the provision of state matching funds for local airport construction and improvement. New Jersey put four helicopters into state highway patrol service to become the first state to have routine daily statewide aerial patrols.

DANIEL J. ELAZAR
Director
Center for the Study of Federalism
Temple University, Philadelphia

Area and Population

Area and population of the states

State	AREA in sq.mi. Total	Inland water*	RESIDENT POPULATION† April 1, 1960, census	July 1, 1969, estimate‡	Percent increase 1960-69
Alabama	51,609	549	3,266,740	3,531,000	8.1
Alaska	586,400	15,335	226,167	282,000	24.9
Arizona	113,909	334	1,302,161	1,693,000	30.0
Arkansas	53,104	605	1,786,272	1,995,000	11.7
California	158,693	2,120	15,717,204	19,443,000	23.7
Colorado	104,247	363	1,753,947	2,100,000	19.7
Connecticut	5,009	110	2,535,234	3,000,000	18.3
Delaware	2,057	79	446,292	540,000	21.0
District of Columbia	69	8	763,956	798,000	4.5
Florida	58,560	4,308	4,951,560	6,354,000	28.3
Georgia	58,876	602	3,943,116	4,641,000	17.7
Hawaii	6,424	9	632,772	794,000	25.4
Idaho	83,557	849	667,191	718,000	7.6
Illinois	56,400	470	10,081,158	11,047,000	9.6
Indiana	36,291	106	4,662,498	5,118,000	9.8
Iowa	56,290	258	2,757,537	2,781,000	0.8
Kansas	82,264	216	2,178,611	2,321,000	6.5
Kentucky	40,395	532	3,038,156	3,232,000	6.4
Louisiana	48,523	3,417	3,257,022	3,745,000	15.0
Maine	33,215	2,203	969,265	978,000	0.9
Maryland	10,577	703	3,100,689	3,765,000	21.4
Massachusetts	8,257	390	5,148,578	5,467,000	6.2
Michigan	58,216	1,197	7,823,194	8,766,000	12.1
Minnesota	84,068	4,059	3,413,864	3,700,000	8.4
Mississippi	47,716	493	2,178,141	2,360,000	8.4
Missouri	69,686	548	4,319,813	4,651,000	7.7
Montana	147,138	1,402	674,767	694,000	2.9
Nebraska	77,227	615	1,411,330	1,449,000	2.6
Nevada	110,540	752	285,278	457,000	60.2
New Hampshire	9,304	290	606,921	717,000	18.2
New Jersey	7,836	315	6,066,782	7,148,000	17.8
New Mexico	121,666	156	951,023	994,000	4.5
New York	49,576	1,637	16,782,304	18,321,000	9.2
North Carolina	52,712	3,645	4,556,155	5,205,000	14.2
North Dakota	70,665	1,208	632,446	615,000	−2.8
Ohio	41,222	250	9,706,397	10,740,000	10.7
Oklahoma	69,919	1,032	2,328,284	2,568,000	10.3
Oregon	96,981	733	1,768,687	2,032,000	14.9
Pennsylvania	45,333	326	11,319,366	11,803,000	4.3
Rhode Island	1,214	156	859,488	911,000	5.9
South Carolina	31,055	783	2,382,594	2,692,000	13.0
South Dakota	77,047	669	680,514	659,000	−3.2
Tennessee	42,244	482	3,567,089	3,985,000	11.7
Texas	267,338	4,499	9,579,677	11,187,000	16.8
Utah	84,916	2,577	890,627	1,045,000	17.4
Vermont	9,609	333	389,881	439,000	12.5
Virginia	40,815	977	3,966,949	4,669,000	17.7
Washington	68,192	1,483	2,853,214	3,402,000	19.2
West Virginia	24,181	102	1,860,421	1,819,000	−2.2
Wisconsin	56,154	1,449	3,951,777	4,233,000	7.1
Wyoming	97,914	503	330,066	320,000	−2.9
Total U.S.	3,615,210	66,237	179,323,175	201,921,000	12.6

*Does not include the Great Lakes and coastal waters. †1969 data not equal to total due to rounding. Percentages are based on unrounded numbers. ‡Provisional.
Source: U.S. Department of Commerce, Bureau of the Census.

Largest cities by area

July 1, 1969

Rank	City	Area in sq.mi.	Rank	City	Area in sq.mi.
1	Jacksonville, Fla.	840	11	Fort Worth, Tex.	210
2	Oklahoma City, Okla.	647	12	New Orleans, La.	199
3	Los Angeles, Cal.	464	13	Memphis, Tenn.	189
4	Houston, Tex.	454	14	San Antonio, Tex.	183
5	New York City, N.Y.	320	15	Detroit, Mich.	140
6	Kansas City, Mo.	316	16	Atlanta, Ga.	131
7	San Diego, Cal.	313	17	Philadelphia, Pa.	129
8	Dallas, Tex.	296	18	Columbus, Ohio	120
9	Phoenix, Ariz.	248	19	Denver, Col.	98
10	Chicago, Ill.	224	20	Milwaukee, Wis.	96

Source: City Planning Departments.

Largest metropolitan areas by population

Area	Population July 1, 1969, estimate	Area	Population July 1, 1969, estimate
Standard Consolidated Areas		Newark	1,959,100‡
New York–Northeastern New Jersey	15,953,141*	Houston	1,875,000
Chicago–Northwestern Indiana	7,600,000	Minneapolis–St. Paul	1,835,908
Standard Metropolitan Statistical Areas		Dallas	1,480,800§
New York	11,900,000	Milwaukee	1,462,000
Los Angeles–Long Beach	7,168,200	Cincinnati	1,431,462
Chicago	6,972,000	Anaheim–Santa Ana–Garden Grove	1,404,100
Philadelphia	4,850,000	Kansas City	1,390,000
Detroit	4,250,000	Seattle	1,378,500‖
Boston	3,205,000	San Diego	1,360,000
San Francisco	3,130,000†	Paterson–Clifton–Passaic	1,359,610¶
Washington, D.C.	2,981,263	Buffalo	1,350,000
St. Louis	2,606,700	Atlanta	1,302,000
Pittsburgh	2,360,000	Miami	1,259,840
Cleveland	2,221,000	Denver	1,210,000
Baltimore	2,000,000	San Bernardino–Riverside–Ontario	1,146,301
		New Orleans	1,140,000
		Indianapolis	1,016,000

*July 1, 1966. †July 1, 1968. ‡December 31, 1968. §January 1, 1969. ‖April 1, 1969. ¶July 1, 1967.
Source: City and state governments.

Largest cities by population

Rank in 1969	City	POPULATION April 1, 1960, census	July 1, 1969, estimate	Mayor in 1969
1	New York, N.Y.	7,781,984	8,000,000	John V. Lindsay (re-elected)
2	Chicago, Ill.	3,550,404	3,540,000	Richard J. Daley
3	Los Angeles, Cal.	2,481,595	2,940,000	Samuel W. Yorty
4	Philadelphia, Pa.	2,002,512	2,050,000	James H. J. Tate
5	Detroit, Mich.	1,670,144	1,570,000	Jerome P. Cavanagh (Roman S. Gribbs)
6	Houston, Tex.	938,219	1,257,000	Louie Welch (re-elected)
7	Baltimore, Md.	939,024	926,000	Thomas J. D'Alesandro III
8	Dallas, Tex.	679,684	870,000	J. Erik Jonsson
9	Washington, D.C.	763,956	825,000	Walter E. Washington
10	Cleveland, Ohio	876,050	781,000	Carl B. Stokes (re-elected)
11	Milwaukee, Wis.	741,324	779,000	Henry W. Maier
12	San Antonio, Tex.	587,718	753,552	Walter W. McAllister, Sr.
13	San Francisco, Cal.	740,316	748,700*	Joseph L. Alioto
14	New Orleans, La.	627,525	709,000	Victor H. Schiro
15	San Diego, Cal.	573,224	703,200	Frank E. Curran
16	St. Louis, Mo.	750,026	668,700	Alfonso J. Cervantes
17	Kansas City, Mo.	475,539	617,000	Ilus W. Davis
18	Boston, Mass.	698,080	616,326	Kevin H. White
19	Seattle, Wash.	557,087	591,000†	Floyd C. Miller (Wesley C. Uhlman)
20	Columbus, Ohio	471,316	589,555	M. E. Sensenbrenner
21	Memphis, Tenn.	497,524	567,300	Henry Loeb
22	Pittsburgh, Pa.	604,000	555,000	Joseph M. Barr (Peter F. Flaherty)
23	Phoenix, Ariz.	439,170	546,381	Milton H. Graham (John Driggs)
24	Jacksonville, Fla.	455,411‡	541,000	Hans G. Tanzler, Jr.
25	Denver, Col.	439,887	535,000	William H. McNichols, Jr.
26	Indianapolis, Ind.	476,258	525,000	Richard G. Lugar
27	Cincinnati, Ohio	502,550	510,017	Eugene P. Ruehlmann (re-elected)
28	Atlanta, Ga.	487,455	502,500	Ivan Allen, Sr. (Sam Massell)

Names in parentheses are winners of elections held in 1969.
*July 1, 1968. †April 1, 1969. ‡Adjusted to include all of Duval County, which became Jacksonville city proper on October 1, 1968.
Source: City and state governments.

Population change

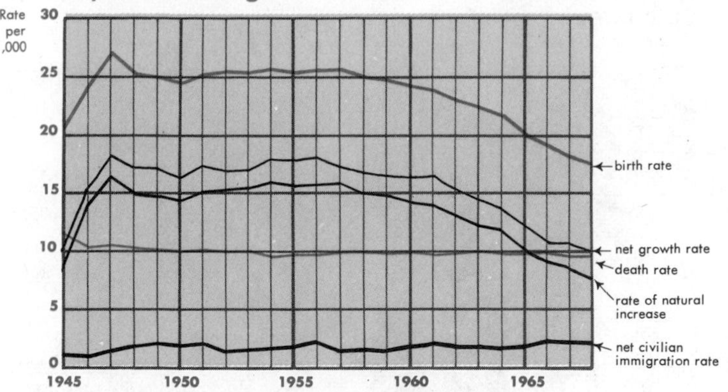

Source: U.S. Department of Commerce, Bureau of the Census.

Expectation of life at birth

in years

Year	TOTAL POPULATION Total	Male	Female	WHITE Total	Male	Female	NONWHITE Total	Male	Female
1920	54.1	53.6	54.6	54.9	54.4	55.6	45.3	45.5	45.2
1930	59.7	58.1	61.6	61.4	59.7	63.5	48.1	47.3	49.2
1940	62.9	60.8	65.2	64.2	62.1	66.6	53.1	51.5	54.9
1950	68.2	65.6	71.1	69.1	66.5	72.2	60.8	59.1	62.9
1960	69.7	66.6	73.1	70.6	67.4	74.1	63.6	61.1	66.3
1961	70.2	67.0	73.6	71.0	67.8	74.5	64.4	61.9	67.0
1962*	70.0	66.8	73.4	70.9	67.6	74.4	64.1	61.5	66.8
1963*	69.9	66.6	73.4	70.8	67.5	74.4	63.6	60.9	66.5
1964	70.2	66.9	73.7	71.0	67.7	74.6	64.1	61.1	67.2
1965	70.2	66.8	73.7	71.0	67.6	74.7	64.1	61.1	67.4
1966	70.1	66.7	73.8	71.0	67.6	74.7	64.0	60.7	67.4
1967	70.5	67.0	74.2	71.3	67.8	75.1	64.6	61.1	68.2
1968†	70.2	66.7	74.0	71.1	67.6	74.9	63.9	60.3	67.6

Prior to 1960, data exclude Alaska and Hawaii.
*Figures by color exclude data for New Jersey. †Provisional
Source: U.S. Department of Health, Education, and Welfare, Public Health Service, *Vital Statistics of the United States.*

Immigration and naturalization

year ending June 30, 1969

Country or region	Total immigrants admitted	Quota immigrants	NONQUOTA IMMIGRANTS Total	Families of U.S. citizens	Aliens naturalized
Europe*	120,086	94,811	25,275	23,046	51,847
Austria	758	522	236	206	688
France	2,024	1,252	772	736	1,416
Germany	9,289	3,919	5,370	5,275	10,618
Greece	17,724	15,534	2,190	2,120	3,029
Hungary	1,795	1,322	473	380	1,725
Ireland	1,989	1,579	410	285	2,626
Italy	23,617	18,494	5,123	4,926	8,773
Netherlands	1,303	882	421	386	1,930
Poland	4,052	3,253	799	702	3,643
Portugal	16,528	15,490	1,038	1,007	1,543
Spain	3,916	2,869	1,047	907	721
United Kingdom	15,014	11,326	3,688	3,443	7,979
Yugoslavia	8,868	7,850	1,018	553	1,808
Other Europe*	13,209	10,519	2,690	2,120	5,354
North America	132,426	111,944	20,482	16,898	24,831
Canada	18,582	14,954	3,628	2,778	6,387
Mexico	44,623	31,951	12,672	10,400	5,111
Cuba	13,751	13,286	465	435	9,654
Dominican Republic	10,670	9,933	737	612	522
Jamaica	16,947	16,266	681	620	481
Other North America	27,853	25,554	2,299	2,053	2,676
South America	23,927	22,295	1,632	1,324	3,758
Argentina	3,938	3,770	168	106	1,014
Brazil	1,713	1,510	203	183	366
Colombia	7,627	7,292	335	266	742
Ecuador	5,085	4,913	172	121	444
Other South America	5,564	4,810	754	648	1,192
Asia	73,621	55,328	18,293	17,084	15,362
China†	15,440	12,312	3,128	2,640	3,399
Hong Kong	5,453	4,946	507	468	—
India	5,963	5,532	431	384	384
Israel	2,049	1,724	325	304	1,836
Japan	3,957	1,588	2,369	2,307	2,067
Korea	6,045	2,904	3,141	3,106	1,646
Philippines	20,746	16,210	4,536	4,142	3,877
Other Asia	13,968	10,112	3,856	3,733	2,153
Africa	5,877	4,925	952	777	671
Australia and Oceania	2,639	1,691	948	885	384
Other countries	3	1	2	2	1,856
Total	358,579	290,995	67,584	60,016	98,709

Data are preliminary. Immigrants listed by country of birth; aliens naturalized by country of former allegiance. *Includes Turkey and the U.S.S.R. †Includes Taiwan.
Source: U.S. Department of Justice, Immigration and Naturalization Service.

Church membership

Religious body	Total clergy	Inclusive membership
Adventists, Seventh-day	3,443	396,097
Apostolic Overcoming Holy Church of God	350	75,000
Armenian Apostolic Church of America	35	125,000
Armenian Church of North America	64	300,000
Assemblies of God	11,459	626,660
Baptist Bodies		
American Baptist Association	3,309	782,902
American Baptist Convention	7,352	1,454,965
Baptist General Conference	1,006	100,000
Baptist Missionary Association of America	3,000	200,000
Conservative Baptist Association of America	...	300,000
Free Will Baptists	3,395	184,869
General Association of Regular Baptist Churches	...	190,000
General Baptists	837	65,000
National Baptist Convention of America	28,574	2,668,799
National Baptist Convention, U.S.A., Inc.	27,500	5,500,000
National Baptist Evangelical Life and Soul Saving Assembly of U.S.A.	137	57,674
National Primitive Baptist Convention, Inc.	623	1,465,000
North American Baptist General Conference	466	55,100
Primitive Baptists	...	72,000
Progressive National Baptist Convention, Inc.	863	521,692
Southern Baptist Convention	...	11,330,481
United Baptists	1,100	63,641
United Free Will Baptist Church	784	100,000
Brethen (German Baptists)		
Church of the Brethren	2,056	187,957
Buddhist Churches of America	100	100,000
Christian and Missionary Alliance	1,227	119,826
Christian Church (Disciples of Christ)	7,428	1,592,609
Church of God (Anderson, Ind.)	2,767	146,807
Church of God (Cleveland, Tenn.)	2,814	243,532
Church of God	2,648	74,171
Church of the Nazarene	6,386	364,789
Churches of Christ	6,200	2,400,000
Congregational Christian Churches, National Association of	...	110,000
Eastern Churches		
American Carpatho-Russian Orthodox Greek Catholic Church	61	104,500
Antiochian Orthodox Christian Archdiocese of New York and All North America	101	100,000
Bulgarian Eastern Orthodox Church	13	86,000
Exarchate of the Russian Orthodox Church in North and South America	98	152,973
Greek Orthodox Archdiocese of North and South America	586	1,875,000
Romanian Orthodox Episcopate of America	46	50,000
Russian Orthodox Church Outside Russia	168	55,000
Russian Orthodox Greek Catholic Church of America	355	1,000,000
Serbian Eastern Orthodox Diocese for the U.S.A. and Canada	64	65,000
Ukrainian Orthodox Church in America	131	87,475
Episcopal Church	11,010	3,373,890
Evangelical Covenant Church of America	676	66,021
Evangelical Free Church of America	762	59,041
Friends United Meeting	575	69,494
Independent Fundamental Churches of America	1,166	121,485
International Church of the Foursquare Gospel	2,690	89,215
Jehovah's Witnesses	...	333,672
Jewish Congregations	6,200	5,780,000
Latter-Day Saints		
Church of Jesus Christ of Latter-day Saints	...	2,180,064
Reorganized Church of Jesus Christ of Latter Day Saints	16,475	149,708
Lutherans		
American Lutheran Church	5,943	2,576,105
Lutheran Church in America	7,197	3,279,517
Lutheran Church—Missouri Synod	6,719	2,781,892
Wisconsin Evangelical Lutheran Synod	789	358,466
Mennonite Church	1,769	85,682
Methodist Bodies		
African Methodist Episcopal Church	7,089	1,166,301
African Methodist Episcopal Zion Church	4,800	870,421
Christian Methodist Episcopal Church	2,259	466,718
Free Methodist Church of North America	1,752	63,611
United Methodist Church*	33,236	10,990,720
Moravian Church in America (Unitas Fratrum)	215	59,898
North American Old Roman Catholic Church	111	59,389
Pentecostal Assemblies		
Pentecostal Church of God of America, Inc.	1,325	115,000
Pentecostal Holiness Church, Inc.	1,883	66,790
United Pentecostal Church, Inc.	2,273	225,000
Polish National Catholic Church of America	144	282,411
Presbyterian Bodies		
Cumberland Presbyterian Church	736	88,540
Presbyterian Church in the U.S.	4,338	961,767
The United Presbyterian Church in the U.S.A.	12,939	3,222,663
Reformed Bodies		
Christian Reformed Church	896	281,523
Reformed Church in America	1,285	383,166
Roman Catholic Church	59,950	47,873,238
Salvation Army	5,249	329,515
Spiritualists, International General Assembly of	190	164,072
Unitarian Universalist Association	968	282,307
United Church of Christ	9,058	2,032,648
The Wesleyan Church†	3,309	82,358

Table includes churches reporting a membership of 50,000 or more and represents the latest information available.
*Unofficial composite; formed in 1968 by a merger of The Methodist Church and the Evangelical United Brethren Church.
†Unofficial composite; formed in 1969 by a merger of The Wesleyan Methodist Church and the Pilgrim Holiness Church.
Source: National Council of Churches, *Yearbook of American Churches, 1970.* (C. H J.)

Illegitimate live births

in thousands, except as indicated

	1940	1950	1960	1967
Total	89.5	141.6	224.3	318.1
Percent of all births	3.5	3.9	5.3	9.0
Rate*	7.1	14.1	21.8	24.0
By age of mother				
Under 15 years	2.1	3.2	4.6	6.9
15–19	40.5	56.0	87.1	144.4
20–24	27.2	43.1	68.0	101.6
25–29	10.5	20.9	32.1	34.5
30–34	5.2	10.8	18.9	17.3
35–39	3.0	6.0	10.6	10.1
40 and over	1.0	1.7	3.0	3.3
By color of mother				
White	40.3	53.5	82.5	142.2
Nonwhite	49.2	88.1	141.8	175.8

Prior to 1960, data exclude Alaska and Hawaii.
*Rate per 1,000 unmarried (never married, widowed, and divorced) women aged 15–44 years.
Source: U.S. Department of Health, Education, and Welfare, Public Health Service, *Monthly Vital Statistics Report.*

Birth rates by age of mother

live births per 1,000 women in 1967 in specified age and color

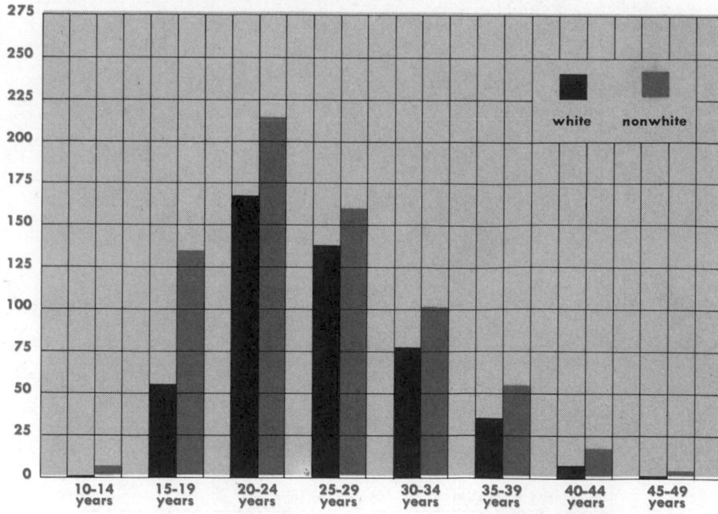

Source: U.S. Department of Health, Education, and Welfare, Public Health Service, *Monthly Vital Statistics Report.*

Median age at first marriage

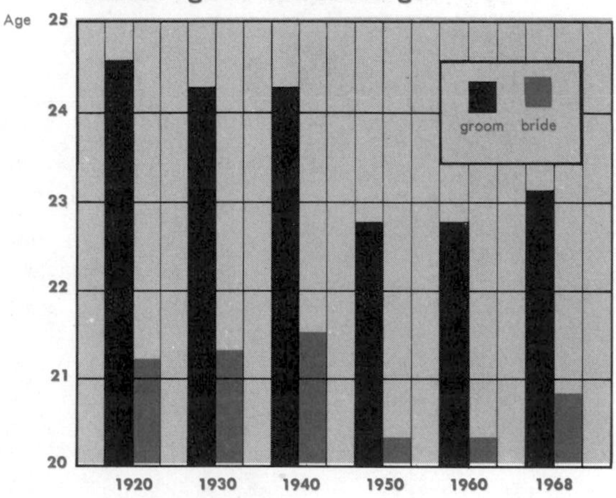

Source: U.S. Department of Health, Education, and Welfare, Public Health Service, *Monthly Vital Statistics Report.*

Marriage and divorce rates

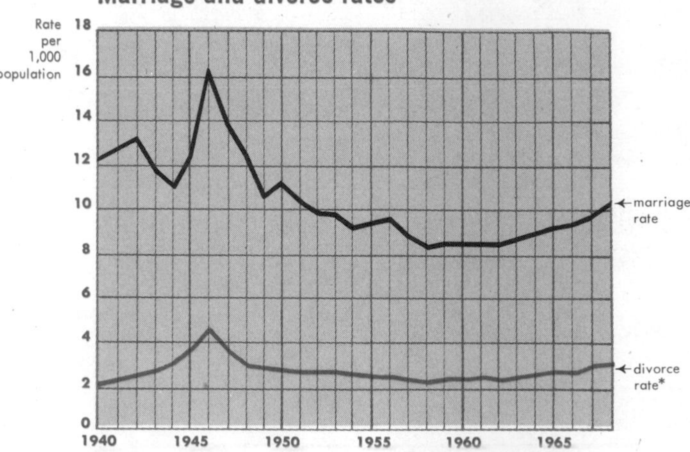

All rates are based on population excluding Armed Forces abroad, except 1941-46 divorce rates which include Armed Forces abroad.
*Includes annulments.
Source: U.S. Department of Health, Education, and Welfare, Public Health Service, *Monthly Vital Statistics Report.*

Death rate

rates per 1,000 population of specified groups

	1900	1920	1940	1960	1968
Sex and color					
Total	17.2	13.0	10.8	9.5	9.6
Male	17.9	13.4	12.0	11.0	11.1
Female	16.5	12.6	9.5	8.1	8.2
White	17.0	12.6	10.4	9.5	9.6
Male	17.7	13.0	11.6	11.0	11.0
Female	16.3	12.1	9.2	8.0	8.2
Nonwhite	25.0	17.7	13.8	10.1	9.9
Male	25.7	17.8	15.1	11.5	11.5
Female	24.4	17.5	12.6	8.7	8.4
Age					
Under 1 year	162.4	92.3	54.9	27.0	22.0
1 to 4	19.8	9.9	2.9	1.1	0.8
5 to 14	3.9	2.6	1.0	0.5	0.4
15 to 24	5.9	4.9	2.0	1.1	1.2
25 to 34	8.2	6.8	3.1	1.5	1.6
35 to 44	10.2	8.1	5.2	3.0	3.2
45 to 54	15.0	12.2	10.6	7.6	7.4
55 to 64	27.2	23.6	22.2	17.4	17.2
65 to 74	56.4	52.5	48.4	38.2	38.3
75 to 84	123.3	118.9	112.0	87.5	80.3
85 and over	260.9	248.3	235.7	198.6	196.6

Prior to 1960, rates exclude Alaska and Hawaii. All rates exclude fetal deaths.
Source: U.S. Department of Health, Education, and Welfare, Public Health Service, *Monthly Vital Statistics Report.*

Causes of deaths

death rates per 100,000 population

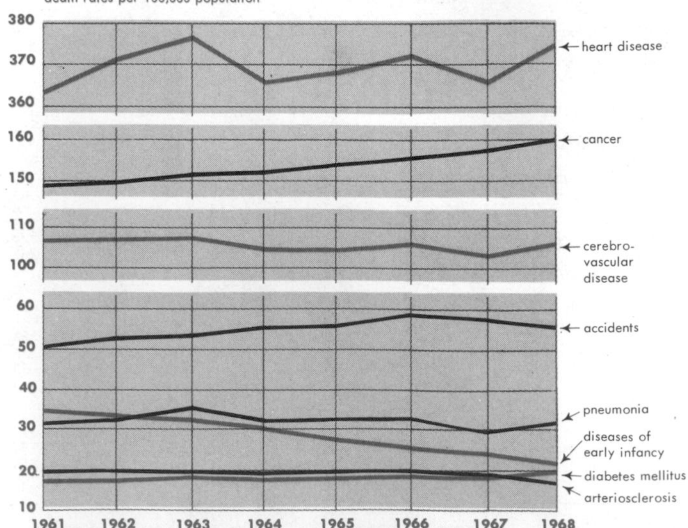

Source: U.S. Department of Health, Education, and Welfare, Public Health Service, *Monthly Vital Statistics Report.*

National Government

The national executive

December 31, 1969

Department, bureau, or office	Executive officer and official title
DEPARTMENT OF STATE	William P. Rogers, secretary
	Elliot L. Richardson, undersecretary
Political Affairs	U. Alexis Johnson, undersecretary
Public Affairs	Michael Collins, asst. secretary
Economic Affairs	Philip H. Trezise, asst. secretary
African Affairs	Joseph Palmer II, asst. secretary
Inter-American Affairs	Charles A. Meyer, asst. secretary
European Affairs	Martin J. Hillenbrand, asst. secy.
East Asian and Pacific Affairs	Marshall Green, asst. secretary
Near Eastern, South Asian Affairs	Joseph J. Sisco, asst. secretary
International Organization Affairs	Samuel DePalma. asst. secretary
Peace Corps	Joseph H. Blatchford, director
DEPARTMENT OF THE TREASURY	David M. Kennedy, secretary
	Charls E. Walker, undersecretary
Monetary Affairs	Paul A. Volcker, undersecretary
Bureau of Customs	(vacancy)
Bureau of Engraving and Printing	James A. Conlon, director
Bureau of the Mint	Eva Adams, director
Internal Revenue Service	Randolph W. Thrower, commissioner
U.S. Savings Bonds Division	Elmer L. Rustad, national director
U.S. Secret Service	James J. Rowley, director
DEPARTMENT OF DEFENSE	Melvin R. Laird, secretary
	David Packard, deputy secretary
Joint Chiefs of Staff	Gen. Earle G. Wheeler, chairman
Chief of Staff, U.S. Army	Gen. W. C. Westmoreland
Chief of Naval Operations	Adm. Thomas H. Moorer
Chief of Staff, U.S. Air Force	Gen. John P. McConnell
Commandant, Marine Corps	Gen. Leonard F. Chapman, Jr.
Department of the Army	Stanley R. Resor, secretary
	Thaddeus R. Beal, undersecretary
Department of the Navy	John H. Chafee, secretary
	John W. Warner, undersecretary
Marine Corps	Gen. L. F. Chapman, Jr., commandant
Department of the Air Force	Robert C. Seamans, Jr., secretary
	John L. McLucas, undersecretary
DEPARTMENT OF JUSTICE	John N. Mitchell, attorney general
	R. G. Kleindienst, deputy atty. gen.
Solicitor General	Erwin N. Griswold
Federal Bureau of Investigation	J. Edgar Hoover, director
Bureau of Prisons	Myrl E. Alexander, director
Narcotics, Dangerous Drugs	John E. Ingersoll, director
Immigration and Naturalization	Raymond F. Farrell, commissioner
POST OFFICE DEPARTMENT	W. M. Blount, postmaster general
	E. T. Klassen, deputy postmaster gen.
Bureau of Operations	Frank J. Nunlist, asst. post. gen.
Bureau of Personnel	Kenneth A. Housman, asst. post. gen.
Chief Postal Inspector	William J. Cotter
DEPARTMENT OF THE INTERIOR	Walter J. Hickel, secretary
	Russell E. Train, undersecretary
Fish and Wildlife, and Parks	Leslie L. Glasgow, asst. secretary
National Park Service	George B. Hartzog, Jr., director
Mineral Resources	Hollis Dole, asst. secretary
Bureau of Mines	John F. O'Leary, director
Geological Survey	William T. Pecora, director
Public Land Management	Harrison Loesch, asst. secretary
Indian Affairs	(vacancy)
Bureau of Outdoor Recreation	(vacancy)
Water and Power Development	James R. Smith, asst. secretary
Water Quality and Research	Carl L. Klein, asst. secretary
DEPARTMENT OF AGRICULTURE	Clifford M. Hardin, secretary
	J. Phil Campbell, undersecretary
Rural Development, Conservation	Thomas K. Cowden, asst. secretary
Farmer Co-op Service	David W. Angevine, administrator
Forest Service	Edward P. Cliff, chief
Rural Electrification	David W. Hamil, administrator
Soil Conservation Service	Kenneth E. Grant, administrator
International Affairs	C. D. Palmby, asst. secretary
Marketing and Consumer Services	Richard Lyng, asst. secretary
DEPARTMENT OF COMMERCE	Maurice H. Stans, secretary
	R. C. Siciliano, undersecretary
Economic Development	Robert A. Podesta, asst. secretary
Domestic, Internat'l Business	K. N. Davis, Jr., asst. secretary
Science and Technology	Myron Tribus, asst. secretary
Economic Affairs	W. H. Chartener, asst. secretary
Bureau of the Census	A. Ross Eckler, director
Environmental Science Services	Robert M. White, administrator
Maritime Administration	Andrew E. Gibson, administrator
National Bureau of Standards	Allen V. Astin, director
Patent Office	W. E. Schuyler, Jr., commissioner
U.S. Travel Service	C. L. Washburn, director
DEPARTMENT OF LABOR	George P. Shultz, secretary
	James D. Hodgson, undersecretary
Manpower	Arnold R. Weber, asst. secretary
Labor-Management Relations	W. J. Usery, Jr., asst. secretary
Wage and Labor Standards	A. A. Fletcher, asst. secretary
Women's Bureau	Elizabeth D. Koontz, director
Employees' Compensation	John Ekeberg, director
DEPARTMENT OF HEALTH, EDUCATION, AND WELFARE	Robert H. Finch, secretary
	John G. Veneman, undersecretary
Community and Field Services	Patricia Reilly Hitt, asst. secretary
Education	James E. Allen, Jr., asst. secretary
Health and Scientific Affairs	(vacancy)
Public Health Service	C. C. Johnson, Jr., administrator
Social Security Administration	Robert M. Ball, commissioner
DEPARTMENT OF HOUSING AND URBAN DEVELOPMENT	George W. Romney, secretary
	R. C. Van Dusen, undersecretary
Research and Technology	Harold B. Finger, asst. secretary
Metropolitan Development	Samuel C. Jackson, asst. secretary
Model Cities	Floyd H. Hyde, asst. secretary
Renewal and Housing Assistance	Lawrence M. Cox, asst. secretary
DEPARTMENT OF TRANSPORTATION	John A. Volpe, secretary
	James M. Beggs, undersecretary
U.S. Coast Guard	Adm. Willard J. Smith, commandant
Federal Aviation Administration	John H. Shaffer, administrator
Federal Highway Administration	F. C. Turner, administrator
Federal Railroad Administration	R. N. Whitman, administrator
Urban Mass Transportation	C. C. Villarreal, administrator
St. Lawrence Seaway	Brendon T. Jose, acting
National Transportation Safety	John H. Reed, board chairman
INDEPENDENT OFFICES AND ESTABLISHMENTS	
Atomic Energy Commission	Glenn T. Seaborg, chairman
Civil Aeronautics Board	John H. Crooker, Jr., chairman
Commission of Fine Arts	William Walton, chairman
District of Columbia	Walter E. Washington, commissioner
Equal Employment Opportunity Commission	William H. Brown III, chairman
Export-Import Bank of the U.S.	Henry Kearns, pres. and chairman
Federal Communications Commission	Rosa H. Hyde, chairman
Federal Deposit Insurance Corp.	K. A. Randall, chairman
Federal Maritime Commission	John Harllee, chairman
Federal Mediation and Conciliation Service	J. Curtis Counts, director
Federal Power Commission	John N. Nassikas, chairman
Federal Reserve System	William McC. Martin, Jr., chairman
Federal Trade Commission	Paul Rand Dixon, chairman
General Services Administration	Robert L. Kunzig, administrator
Interstate Commerce Commission	Virginia Mae Brown, chairman
National Aeronautics and Space Administration	Thomas O. Paine, administrator
National Labor Relations Board	F. W. McCulloch, chairman
National Science Foundation	Leland J. Haworth, director
Railroad Retirement Board	H. W. Habermeyer, chairman
Securities and Exchange Commission	Hamer H. Budge, chairman
Selective Service System	Lieut. Gen. Lewis B. Hershey, director
Small Business Administration	Hilary Sandoval, Jr., administrator
Smithsonian Institution	S. Dillon Ripley, secretary
Tennessee Valley Authority	Aubrey J. Wagner, chairman
U.S. Arms Control and Disarmament Agency	Gerard Smith, director
U.S. Civil Service Commission	Robert E. Hampton, chairman
U.S. Information Agency	Frank Shakespeare, director
U.S. Tariff Commission	(vacancy)
Veterans Administration	Donald E. Johnson, administrator
EXECUTIVE OFFICE OF THE PRESIDENT	
Assistant for Domestic Affairs	John D. Ehrlichman
Assistant for National Security Affairs	Henry A. Kissinger
Counselor, Political Affairs	Bryce N. Harlow
Assistant for Urban Affairs	Daniel P. Moynihan
Director, Bureau of the Budget	Robert P. Mayo
Director, Office of Economic Opportunity	Donald Rumsfeld
Director, Office of Emergency Preparedness	George A. Lincoln
Director, Office of Science and Technology	Lee A. DuBridge
QUASI-OFFICIAL AGENCIES	
American National Red Cross	E. Roland Harriman, chairman
National Academy of Sciences	Philip Handler, president
National Academy of Engineering	Eric A. Walker, president

House of Representatives

membership in 1969

State, district, name, and party	Residence
Ala.—1. Edwards, W. J. (R)	Mobile
2. Dickinson, W. L. (R)	Montgomery
3. Andrews, George W. (D)	Union Springs
4. Nichols, William (D)	Sylacauga
5. Flowers, W. W. (D)	Tuscaloosa
6. Buchanan, John H., Jr. (R)	Birmingham
7. Bevill, Tom (D)	Jasper
8. Jones, Robert E., Jr. (D)	Scottsboro
Alaska—Pollock, H. W. (R)	Anchorage
Ariz.—1. Rhodes, John J. (R)	Mesa
2. Udall, Morris K. (D)	Tucson
3. Steiger, Sam (R)	Prescott
Ark.—1. Alexander, Bill (D)	Osceola
2. Mills, Wilbur D. (D)	Kensett
3. Hammerschmidt, J. P. (R)	Harrison
4. Pryor, David (D)	Camden
Calif.—1. Clausen, Don H. (R)	Crescent City
2. Johnson, Harold T. (D)	Roseville
3. Moss, John E. (D)	Sacramento
4. Leggett, Robert L. (D)	Vallejo
5. Burton, Phillip (D)	San Francisco
6. Mailliard, William S. (R)	San Francisco
7. Cohelan, Jeffery (D)	Berkeley
8. Miller, George P. (D)	Alameda
9. Edwards, W. Donlon (D)	San Jose
10. Gubser, Charles S. (R)	Gilroy
11. McCloskey, Paul N., Jr. (R)	Portola Valley
12. Talcott, Burt L. (R)	Salinas
13. Teague, Charles M. (R)	Ojai
14. Waldie, Jerome R. (D)	Antioch
15. McFall, John J. (D)	Manteca
16. Sisk, B. F. (D)	Fresno
17. Anderson, Glenn M. (D)	Torrance
18. Mathias, Robert B. (R)	Visalia
19. Holifield, Chet (D)	Montebello
20. Smith, H. Allen (R)	Glendale
21. Hawkins, Augustus F. (D)	Los Angeles
22. Corman, James C. (D)	Van Nuys
23. Clawson, Del M. (R)	Compton
24. Lipscomb, Glenard P. (R)	Los Angeles
25. Wiggins, Charles (R)	El Monte
26. Rees, Thomas (D)	Beverly Hills
27. Goldwater, Barry, Jr. (R)	Burbank
28. Bell, Alphonzo (R)	Beverly Hills
29. Brown, George E., Jr. (D)	Monterey Park
30. Roybal, Edward R. (D)	Los Angeles
31. Wilson, Charles H. (D)	Los Angeles
32. Hosmer, Craig (R)	Long Beach
33. Pettis, Jerry (R)	Loma Linda
34. Hanna, Richard T. (D)	Fullerton
35. Utt, James B. (R)	Santa Ana
36. Wilson, Bob (R)	San Diego
37. Van Deerlin, Lionel (D)	San Diego
38. Tunney, John V. (D)	Riverside
Colo.—1. Rogers, Byron G. (D)	Denver
2. Brotzman, D. G. (R)	Boulder
3. Evans, Frank (D)	Pueblo
4. Aspinall, Wayne N. (D)	Palisade
Conn.—1. Daddario, Emilio Q. (D)	Hartford
2. St. Onge, William L. (D)	Putnam
3. Giaimo, Robert N. (D)	North Haven
4. Weicker, Lowell P., Jr. (R)	Greenwich
5. Monagan, John S. (D)	Waterbury
6. Meskill, Thomas J. (R)	New Britain
Del.—Roth, William V., Jr. (R)	Wilmington
Fla.—1. Sikes, Robert L. F. (D)	Crestview
2. Fuqua, Don (D)	Altha
3. Bennett, Charles E. (D)	Jacksonville
4. Chappell, William, Jr. (D)	Ocala
5. Frey, Louis, Jr. (R)	Winter Park
6. Gibbons, Sam (D)	Tampa
7. Haley, James A. (D)	Sarasota
8. Cramer, William C. (R)	St. Petersburg
9. Rogers, Paul G. (D)	West Palm Beach
10. Burke, J. Herbert (R)	Hollywood
11. Pepper, Claude (D)	Miami
12. Fascell, Dante B. (D)	Miami
Ga.—1. Hagan, G. Elliott (D)	Sylvania
2. O'Neal, M. (D)	Bainbridge
3. Brinkley, Jack (D)	Columbus
4. Blackburn, B. B. (R)	Atlanta
5. Thompson, S. F. (R)	East Point
6. Flynt, J. J., Jr. (D)	Griffin
7. Davis, John W. (D)	Summerville
8. Stuckey, W. S., Jr. (D)	Eastman
9. Landrum, Phil M. (D)	Jasper
10. Stephens, Robert G., Jr. (D)	Athens
Hawaii—1. Mink, Patsy (D)	Waipahu
2. Matsunaga, Spark M. (D)	Honolulu
Ida.—1. McClure, James A. (R)	Payette
2. Hansen, Orval (R)	Idaho Falls
Ill.—1. Dawson, William L. (D)	Chicago
2. Mikva, Abner (D)	Chicago
3. Murphy, William T. (D)	Chicago
4. Derwinski, Edward J. (R)	Chicago
5. Kluczynski, John C. (D)	Chicago
6. (vacancy)	
7. Annunzio, Frank (D)	Chicago
8. Rostenkowski, Dan (D)	Chicago
9. Yates, Sidney R. (D)	Chicago
10. Collier, Harold R. (R)	Berwyn
11. Pucinski, Roman C. (D)	Chicago
12. McClory, Robert (R)	Lake Bluff
13. Crane, Philip M. (R)	Arlington Heights
14. Erlenborn, J. N. (R)	Elmhurst
15. Reid, Charlotte T. (R)	Aurora
16. Anderson, John B. (R)	Rockford
17. Arends, Leslie C. (R)	Melvin
18. Michel, Robert H. (R)	Peoria
19. Railsback, Thomas F. (R)	Moline
20. Findley, Paul (R)	Pittsfield
21. Gray, Kenneth J. (D)	West Frankfort
22. Springer, William L. (R)	Champaign
23. Shipley, George E. (D)	Olney
24. Price, Melvin (D)	East St. Louis
Ind.—1. Madden, Ray J. (D)	Gary
2. Landgrebe, Earl F. (R)	Valparaiso
3. Brademas, John (D)	South Bend
4. Adair, E. Ross (R)	Fort Wayne
5. Roudebush, Richard L. (R)	Noblesville
6. Bray, William G. (R)	Martinsville
7. Myers, John (R)	Covington
8. Zion, Roger (R)	Evansville
9. Hamilton, L. H. (D)	Columbus
10. Dennis, David (R)	Richmond
11. Jacobs, A., Jr. (D)	Indianapolis
Iowa—1. Schwengel, Fred (R)	Davenport
2. Culver, J. C. (D)	Marion
3. Gross, H. R. (R)	Waterloo
4. Kyl, John H. (R)	Bloomfield
5. Smith, Neal (D)	Altoona
6. Mayne, Wiley (R)	Sioux City
7. Scherle, W. J. (R)	Henderson
Kan.—1. Sebelius, Keith G. (R)	Norton
2. Mize, C. L. (R)	Atchison
3. Winn, Larry, Jr. (R)	Leawood
4. Shriver, Garner E. (R)	Wichita
5. Skubitz, Joseph (R)	Pittsburg
Ky.—1. Stubblefield, Frank A. (D)	Murray
2. Natcher, William H. (D)	Bowling Green
3. Cowger, William O. (R)	Louisville
4. Snyder, Gene (R)	Jeffersontown
5. Carter, Tim L. (R)	Tompkinsville
6. Watts, John C. (D)	Nicholasville
7. Perkins, Carl D. (D)	Hindman
La.—1. Hébert, F. Edward (D)	New Orleans
2. Boggs, Hale (D)	New Orleans
3. Caffery, Patrick (D)	New Iberia
4. Waggonner, Joe D., Jr. (D)	Plain Dealing
5. Passman, Otto E. (D)	Monroe
6. Rarick, John R. (D)	St. Francisville
7. Edwards, Edwin W. (D)	Crowley
8. Long, Speedy O. (D)	Jena
Me.—1. Kyros, Peter (D)	Portland
2. Hathaway, W. D. (D)	Auburn
Md.—1. Morton, Rogers C. B. (R)	Easton
2. Long, Clarence D. (D)	Ruxton
3. Garmatz, Edward A. (D)	Baltimore
4. Fallon, George H. (D)	Baltimore
5. Hogan, Lawrence J. (R)	Hyattsville
6. Beall, J. Glenn, Jr. (R)	Frostburg
7. Friedel, Samuel N. (D)	Baltimore
8. Gude, Gilbert (R)	Bethesda
Mass.—1. Conte, Silvio O. (R)	Pittsfield
2. Boland, Edward P. (D)	Springfield
3. Philbin, Philip J. (D)	Clinton
4. Donohue, Harold D. (D)	Worcester
5. Morse, F. Bradford (R)	Lowell
6. Harrington, M. J. (D)	Beverly
7. Macdonald, Torbert H. (D)	Malden
8. O'Neill, Thomas P., Jr. (D)	Cambridge
9. McCormack, John W. (D)	Dorchester
10. Heckler, Margaret (R)	Wellesley Hills
11. Burke, James A. (D)	Milton
12. Keith, Hastings (R)	West Bridgewater
Mich.—1. Conyers, John, Jr. (D)	Detroit
2. Esch, Marvin (R)	Ann Arbor
3. Brown, Garry E. (R)	Schoolcraft
4. Hutchinson, Edward (R)	Fennville
5. Ford, Gerald R., Jr. (R)	Grand Rapids
6. Chamberlain, Charles E. (R)	East Lansing
7. Riegle, D. W., Jr. (R)	Flint
8. Harvey, James (R)	Saginaw
9. Vander Jagt, Guy (R)	Cadillac
10. Cederberg, Elford A. (R)	Bay City
11. Ruppe, Philip (R)	Houghton
12. O'Hara, James G. (D)	Utica
13. Diggs, Charles C., Jr. (D)	Detroit
14. Nedzi, Lucien N. (D)	Detroit
15. Ford, W. D. (D)	Taylor
16. Dingell, John D. (D)	Detroit
17. Griffiths, Martha W. (D)	Detroit
18. Broomfield, William S. (R)	Royal Oak
19. McDonald, J. H. (R)	Detroit
Minn.—1. Quie, Albert H. (R)	Dennison
2. Nelsen, Ancher (R)	Hutchinson
3. MacGregor, Clark (R)	Plymouth Village
4. Karth, Joseph E. (D)	St. Paul
5. Fraser, Donald M. (D)	Minneapolis
6. Zwach, John M. (R)	Walnut Grove
7. Langen, Odin (R)	Kennedy
8. Blatnik, John A. (D)	Chisholm
Miss.—1. Abernethy, Thomas G. (D)	Okolona
2. Whitten, Jamie L. (D)	Charleston
3. Griffin, Charles (D)	Utica
4. Montgomery, G. V. (D)	Meridian
5. Colmer, William M. (D)	Pascagoula
Mo.—1. Clay, William (D)	St. Louis
2. Symington, James W. (D)	Clayton
3. Sullivan, Leonor K. (D)	St. Louis
4. Randall, William J. (D)	Independence
5. Bolling, Richard (D)	Kansas City
6. Hull, W. R., Jr. (D)	Weston
7. Hall, Durward G. (R)	Springfield
8. Ichord, Richard H. (D)	Houston
9. Hungate, W. L. (D)	Troy
10. Burlison, Bill D. (D)	Cape Girardeau
Mont.—1. Olsen, Arnold (D)	Helena
2. Melcher, John (D)	Billings
Neb.—1. Denney, Robert V. (R)	Fairbury
2. Cunningham, Glenn (R)	Omaha
3. Martin, David (R)	Kearney
Nev.—Baring, Walter S. (D)	Reno
N.H.—1. Wyman, Louis C. (R)	Manchester
2. Cleveland, James C. (R)	New London
N.J.—1. Hunt, John E. (R)	Pitman
2. Sandman, Charles W., Jr. (R)	Cape May
3. Howard, J. J. (D)	Wall Township
4. Thompson, Frank, Jr. (D)	Trenton
5. Frelinghuysen, Peter, Jr. (R)	Morristown
6. Cahill, William T. (R)	Collingswood
7. Widnall, William B. (R)	Saddle River
8. Roe, Robert A. (D)	
9. Helstoski, Henry (D)	E. Rutherford
10. Rodino, Peter W., Jr. (D)	Newark
11. Minish, Joseph G. (D)	West Orange
12. Dwyer, Florence P. (R)	Elizabeth
13. Gallagher, Cornelius E. (D)	Bayonne
14. Daniels, Dominick V. (D)	Jersey City
15. Patten, Edward J. (D)	Perth Amboy
N.M.—1. Lujan, Manuel, Jr. (R)	Albuquerque
2. Foreman, Ed (R)	Las Cruces
N.Y.—1. Pike, Otis G. (D)	Riverhead
2. Grover, James R., Jr. (R)	Babylon
3. Wolff, L. L. (D)	Great Neck
4. Wydler, John W. (R)	Garden City
5. Lowenstein, A. K. (D)	Long Beach
6. Halpern, Seymour (R)	Forest Hills
7. Addabbo, Joseph P. (D)	Ozone Park
8. Rosenthal, Benjamin S. (D)	Elmhurst
9. Delaney, James J. (D)	Long Island City
10. Celler, Emanuel (D)	Brooklyn
11. Brasco, Frank J. (D)	Brooklyn
12 Chisholm, Shirley (D)	Brooklyn
13. Podell, B. L. (D)	Brooklyn
14. Rooney, John J. (D)	Brooklyn
15. Carey, Hugh L. (D)	Brooklyn
16. Murphy, John M. (D)	Staten Island
17. Koch, Edward I. (D)	New York City
18. Powell, Adam C. (D)	New York City
19. Farbstein, Leonard (D)	New York City
20. Ryan, William Fitts (D)	New York City
21. Scheuer, James (D)	Bronx
22. Gilbert, Jacob H. (D)	New York City
23. Bingham, J. B. (D)	Bronx
24. Biaggi, Mario (D)	Bronx
25. Ottinger, R. (D)	Pleasantville
26. Reid, Ogden R. (R)	Purchase
27. McKneally, M. B. (R)	Newburgh
28. Fish, Hamilton, Jr. (R)	Millbrook
29. Button, Daniel E., Jr. (R)	Albany
30. King, Carleton J. (R)	Saratoga Springs
31. McEwen, Robert (R)	Ogdensburg
32. Pirnie, Alexander (R)	New Hartford
33. Robison, Howard W. (R)	Oswego
34. Hanley, James M. (D)	Syracuse
35. Stratton, Samuel S. (D)	Amsterdam
36. Horton, Frank J. (R)	Rochester
37. Conable, B., Jr. (R)	Alexander
38. Hastings, James F. (R)	Allegany
39. McCarthy, R. D. (D)	Buffalo
40. Smith, H. P., III (R)	N. Tonawanda
41. Dulski, Thaddeus J. (D)	Buffalo
N.C.—1. Jones, Walter B. (D)	Farmville
2. Fountain, L. H. (D)	Tarboro
3. Henderson, David N. (D)	Wallace
4. Galifianakis, Nick (D)	Durham
5. Mizell, Wilmer (R)	Winston-Salem
6. Preyer, L. R. (D)	Greensboro
7. Lennon, Alton (D)	Wilmington
8. Ruth, Earl B. (R)	Salisbury
9. Jonas, Charles Raper (R)	Lincolnton
10. Broyhill, James T. (R)	Lenoir
11. Taylor, Roy A. (D)	Black Mountain

State, district, name, and party	Residence
N.D.—1. Andrews, Mark (R)	Mapleton
2. Kleppe, Thomas S. (R)	Bismarck
Ohio—1. Taft, Robert A., Jr. (R)	Cincinnati
2. Clancy, Donald D. (R)	Cincinnati
3. Whalen, Charles W., Jr. (R)	Dayton
4. McCulloch, William M. (R)	Piqua
5. Latta, Delbert L. (R)	Bowling Green
6. Harsha, William H., Jr. (R)	Portsmouth
7. Brown, Clarence J., Jr. (R)	Urbana
8. Betts, Jackson E. (R)	Findlay
9. Ashley, Thomas L. (D)	Waterville
10. Miller, Clarence E. (R)	Lancaster
11. Stanton, J. W. (R)	Painesville
12. Devine, Samuel L. (R)	Columbus
13. Mosher, Charles A. (R)	Oberlin
14. Ayres, William H. (R)	Akron
15. Wylie, Chalmers P. (R)	Columbus
16. Bow, Frank T. (R)	Canton
17. Ashbrook, John M. (R)	Johnstown
18. Hays, Wayne L. (D)	Flushing
19. Kirwan, Michael J. (D)	Youngstown
20. Feighan, Michael A. (D)	Cleveland
21. Stokes, Louis (D)	Shaker Heights
22. Vanik, Charles A. (D)	Cleveland
23. Minshall, William E. (R)	Cleveland
24. Lukens, Donald E. (R)	Middletown
Okla—1. Belcher, Page (R)	Enid
2. Edmondson, Ed (D)	Muskogee
3. Albert, Carl (D)	McAlester
4. Steed, Tom (D)	Shawnee
5. Jarman, John (D)	Oklahoma City
6. Camp, J. N. H. (R)	Waukomis
Ore.—1. Wyatt, Wendell (R)	Astoria
2. Ullman, Al (D)	Baker
3. Green, Edith (D)	Portland
4. Dellenback, John R. (R)	Medford
Penn.—1. Barrett, William A. (D)	Philadelphia
2. Nix, Robert N. C. (D)	Philadelphia
3. Byrne, James A. (D)	Philadelphia
4. Eilberg, Joshua (D)	Philadelphia
5. Green, William J., III (D)	Philadelphia
6. Yatron, Gus (D)	Reading
7. Williams, L. G. (R)	Springfield
8. Biester, E. G., Jr. (R)	Furlong
9. Watkins, G. R. (R)	West Chester
10. McDade, Joseph M. (R)	Scranton
11. Flood, Daniel J. (D)	Wilkes-Barre
12. Whalley, J. Irving (R)	Windber
13. Coughlin, R. L. (R)	Villanova
14. Moorhead, William S. (D)	Pittsburgh
15. Rooney, Fred B. (D)	Bethlehem
16. Eshleman, Edwin D. (R)	Lancaster
17. Schneebeli, Herman T. (R)	Williamsport
18. Corbett, Robert J. (R)	Pittsburgh
19. Goodling, George A. (R)	Loganville
20. Gaydos, Joseph (D)	McKeesport
21. Dent, John H. (D)	Jeannette
22. Saylor, John P. (R)	Johnstown
23. Johnson, Albert W. (R)	Smethport
24. Vigorito, J. P. (D)	Erie
25. Clark, Frank M. (D)	Bessemer
26. Morgan, Thomas E. (D)	Fredericktown
27. Fulton, James G. (R)	Pittsburgh
R.I.—1. St. Germain, Fernand J. (D)	Woonsocket
2. Tiernan, Robert O. (D)	Warwick
S.C.—1. Rivers, L. Mendel (D)	Charleston
2. Watson, Albert W. (R)	Columbia
3. Dorn, W. J. Bryan (D)	Greenwood
4. Mann, James R. (D)	Greenville
5. Gettys, Thomas S. (D)	Rock Hill
6. McMillan, John L. (D)	Florence
S.D.—1. Reifel, Ben (R)	Aberdeen
2. Berry, E. Y. (R)	McLaughlin
Tenn.—1. Quillen, James H. (R)	Kingsport
2. Duncan, John J. (R)	Knoxville
3. Brock, W. E., III (R)	Chattanooga
4. Evins, Joseph L. (D)	Smithville
5. Fulton, Richard (D)	Nashville
6. Anderson, W. R. (D)	Waverly
7. Blanton, Ray (D)	Adamsville
8. Jones, Edward (D)	Yorkville
9. Kuykendall, Dan (R)	Memphis
Tex.— 1. Patman, Wright (D)	Texarkana
2. Dowdy, John (D)	Athens
3. Collins, James M. (R)	Grand Prairie
4. Roberts, Ray (D)	McKinney
5. Cabell, Earle (D)	Dallas
6. Teague, Olin E. (D)	College Station
7. Bush, George (R)	Houston
8. Eckhardt, Robert C. (D)	Houston
9. Brooks, Jack (D)	Beaumont
10. Pickle, J. J. (D)	Austin
11. Poage, W. R. (D)	Waco
12. Wright, James C., Jr. (D)	Fort Worth
13. Purcell, Graham (D)	Wichita Falls
14. Young, John (D)	Corpus Christi
15. de la Garza, E. (D)	Mission
16. White, Richard C. (D)	El Paso
17. Burleson, Omar (D)	Anson
18. Price, Robert (R)	Pampa
19. Mahon, George (D)	Lubbock
20. Gonzalez, Henry B. (D)	San Antonio
21. Fisher, O. C. (D)	San Angelo
22. Casey, Robert R. (D)	Houston
23. Kazen, Abraham, Jr. (D)	Laredo
Utah—1. Burton, Laurence J. (R)	Ogden
2. Lloyd, Sherman P. (R)	Salt Lake City
Vt.—Stafford, Robert T. (R)	Rutland City
Va.—1. Downing, Thomas N. (D)	Newport News
2. Whitehurst, G. W. (R)	Norfolk
3. Satterfield, D. E., III (D)	Richmond
4. Abbitt, Watkins M. (D)	Appomattox
5. Daniel, W. C. (D)	Danville
6. Poff, Richard H. (R)	Radford
7. Marsh, John O., Jr. (D)	Strasburg
8. Scott, William L. (R)	Fairfax
9. Wampler, William C. (R)	Bristol
10. Broyhill, Joel T. (R)	Arlington
Wash.—1. Pelly, Thomas M. (R)	Seattle
2. Meeds, Lloyd (D)	Everett
3. Hansen, Julia Butler (D)	Cathlamet
4. May, Catherine (R)	Yakima
5. Foley, Thomas S. (D)	Spokane
6. Hicks, Floyd V. (D)	Tacoma
7. Adams, B. (D)	Seattle
W.Va.—1. Mollohan, R. H. (D)	Fairmont
2. Staggers, Harley O. (D)	Keyser
3. Slack, John M., Jr. (D)	Charleston
4. Hechler, Ken (D)	Huntington
5. Kee, James (D)	Bluefield
Wis.—1. Schadeberg, H. C. (R)	Burlington
2. Kastenmeier, Robert W. (D)	Watertown
3. Thomson, Vernon W. (R)	Richland Center
4. Zablocki, Clement J. (D)	Milwaukee
5. Reuss, Henry S. (D)	Milwaukee
6. Steiger, William A. (R)	Oshkosh
7. Obey, David R. (D)	Wausau
8. Byrnes, John W. (R)	Green Bay
9. Davis, Glenn R. (R)	New Berlin
10. O'Konski, Alvin E. (R)	Mercer
Wyo.—Wold, John (R)	Casper

Supreme Court

Chief Justice of the United States: Warren Earl Burger

Associate Justices:

Hugo L. Black	Potter Stewart
William O. Douglas	Byron R. White
John M. Harlan	Thurgood Marshall
William J. Brennan, Jr.	(vacancy)*

*Vacancy caused by the resignation of Abe Fortas, May 14, 1969.

Senate

membership in 1969

State, name, and party	Residence	Term expires
Ala.—Allen, James B. (D)	Gadsden	1975
Sparkman, John (D)	Huntsville	1973
Alaska—Gravel, Mike (D)	Anchorage	1975
Stevens, Theodore F. (R)	Anchorage	1971
Ariz.—Goldwater, Barry (R)	Phoenix	1975
Fannin, Paul J. (R)	Phoenix	1971
Ark.—Fulbright, J. W. (D)	Fayetteville	1975
McClellan, John (D)	Little Rock	1973
Calif.—Cranston, Alan (D)	Los Angeles	1975
Murphy, George (R)	Beverly Hills	1971
Colo.—Dominick, Peter (R)	Englewood	1975
Allott, Gordon (R)	Lamar	1973
Conn.—Ribicoff, Abraham (D)	Hartford	1975
Dodd, Thomas J. (D)	West Hartford	1971
Del.—Williams, John J. (R)	Millsboro	1971
Boggs, J. Caleb (R)	Wilmington	1973
Fla.—Gurney, Edward (R)	Winter Park	1975
Holland, Spessard L. (D)	Bartow	1971
Ga.—Talmadge, Herman (D)	Lovejoy	1975
Russell, Richard B. (D)	Winder	1973
Hawaii—Inouye, Daniel K. (D)	Honolulu	1975
Fong, Hiram L. (R)	Honolulu	1971
Ida.—Church, Frank (D)	Boise	1975
Jordan, Len B. (R)	Boise	1973
Ill.—*Smith, Ralph T. (R)	Alton	1971
Percy, Charles H. (R)	Kenilworth	1973
Ind.—Bayh, Birch E., Jr. (D)	Terre Haute	1975
Hartke, Vance (D)	Evansville	1971
Ia.—Hughes, Harold (D)	Ida Grove	1975
Miller, Jack R. (R)	Sioux City	1973
Kan.—Dole, Robert (R)	Russell	1975
Pearson, James B. (R)	Prairie Village	1973
Ky.—Cook, Marlow W. (R)	Louisville	1975
Cooper, John S. (R)	Somerset	1973
La.—Long, Russell (D)	Baton Rouge	1975
Ellender, Allen J. (D)	Houma	1973
Me.—Muskie, Edmund S. (D)	Waterville	1971
Smith, Margaret Chase (R)	Skowhegan	1973
Md.—Mathias, C. M., Jr. (R)	Frederick	1975
Tydings, Joseph D. (D)	Havre de Grace	1971
Mass.—Kennedy, Edward M. (D)	Boston	1971
Brooke, Edward W. (R)	Newton Center	1973
Mich.—Hart, Philip A. (D)	Mackinac Island	1971
Griffin, Robert P. (R)	Traverse City	1973
Minn.—McCarthy, Eugene (D)	St. Paul	1971
Mondale, Walter F. (D)	Minneapolis	1973
Miss.—Stennis, John (D)	DeKalb	1971
Eastland, James (D)	Doddsville	1973
Mo.—Eagleton, T. F. (D)	St. Louis	1975
Symington, Stuart (D)	St. Louis	1971
Mont.—Mansfield, Mike (D)	Missoula	1971
Metcalf, Lee (D)	Helena	1973
Neb.—Hruska, Roman L. (R)	Omaha	1971
Curtis, Carl T. (R)	Minden	1973
Nev.—Bible, Alan (D)	Reno	1975
Cannon, Howard W. (D)	Las Vegas	1971
N.H.—Cotton, Norris (R)	Lebanon	1975
McIntyre, Thomas J. (D)	Laconia	1973
N.J.—Williams, Harrison, Jr. (D)	Westfield	1971
Case, Clifford P. (R)	Rahway	1973
N.M.—Anderson, Clinton (D)	Albuquerque	1973
Montoya, Joseph M. (D)	Santa Fe	1971
N.Y.—Javits, Jacob K. (R)	New York City	1975
Goodell, Charles E. (R)	Jamestown	1971
N.C.—Ervin, Sam J., Jr. (D)	Morganton	1975
Jordan, B. Everett (D)	Saxapahaw	1973
N.D.—Young, Milton R. (R)	La Moure	1975
Burdick, Quentin N. (D)	Fargo	1971
Ohio—Saxbe, William (R)	Mechanicsburg	1975
Young, Stephen M. (D)	Shaker Heights	1971
Okla.—Bellmon, Henry (R)	Red Rock	1975
Harris, Fred R. (D)	Lawton	1973
Ore.—Packwood, Robert (R)	Portland	1975
Hatfield, Mark O. (R)	Salem	1973
Penn.—Schweiker, R. S. (R)	Worcester	1975
Scott, Hugh (R)	Philadelphia	1971
R. I.—Pastore, John O. (D)	Providence	1971
Pell, Claiborne (D)	Newport	1973
S.C.—Hollings, Ernest F. (D)	Charleston	1975
Thurmond, Strom (R)	Aiken	1973
S.D.—McGovern, George (D)	Mitchell	1975
Mundt, Karl E. (R)	Madison	1973
Tenn.—Gore, Albert (D)	Carthage	1971
Baker, Howard, Jr. (R)	Knoxville	1973
Tex.—Yarborough, Ralph (D)	Austin	1971
Tower, John G. (R)	Wichita Falls	1973
Utah—Bennett, Wallace (R)	Salt Lake City	1975
Moss, Frank E. (D)	Salt Lake City	1971
Vt.—Aiken, George D. (R)	Putney	1975
Prouty, Winston L. (R)	Newport	1971
Va.—Byrd, Harry F., Jr. (D)	Winchester	1971
Spong, William, Jr. (D)	Portsmouth	1973
Wash.—Magnuson, Warren (D)	Seattle	1975
Jackson, Henry M. (D)	Everett	1971
W.Va.—Byrd, Robert C. (D)	Sophia	1971
Randolph, Jennings (D)	Elkins	1973
Wis.—Nelson, Gaylord (D)	Madison	1975
Proxmire, William (D)	Madison	1971
Wyo.—McGee, Gale W. (D)	Laramie	1971
Hansen, Clifford P. (R)	Jackson	1973

*Appointed Sept. 17, 1969, to fill a vacancy created by the death of Everett M. Dirksen, Sept. 7, 1969.

Major legislation passed by Congress 1969

Act	House vote	Senate vote	Date of enactment
Debt Ceiling (Increased permanent national debt ceiling from $358 billion to $365 billion. Permitted additional temporary increase of $12 billion, through June 30, 1970.)	313–93 Yeas: D. 173, R. 140 Nays: D. 52, R. 41 (March 19)	67–18 Yeas: D. 36, R. 31 Nays: D. 14, R. 4 (March 26)	Signed April 7
Income Tax Surtax (Continued the 10% federal income tax surtax through December 31, 1969.)	237–170 Yeas: D. 85, R. 152 Nays: D. 144, R. 26 (Aug. 4.)	70–30 Yeas: D. 35, R. 35 Nays: D. 22, R. 8 (July 31)	Signed Aug. 7
Food Stamp Authorization (Increased from $340 million to $610 million the authorized federal spending for food stamps for the poor for fiscal 1970.)	Passed by voice vote (Nov. 5)	Passed by voice vote (Nov. 6)	Signed Nov. 13
Military Procurement Authorization (As part of $20.7 billion military purchasing authorization, provided $750 million for start of deployment of anti-ballistic missile system. Also included $28 million to begin work on simplified fighter plane.)	311–44 Yeas: D. 157, R. 154 Nays: D. 39, R. 5 (Oct. 3)	81–5 Yeas: D. 45, R. 36 Nays: D. 3, R. 2 (Sept. 18)	Signed Nov. 19
Nuclear Nonproliferation Treaty (Prohibited signing nations with nuclear weapons from turning any over to nonnuclear nations. Nuclear nations may transfer information about peaceful uses to the others. Prohibited nonnuclear signatories from obtaining nuclear weapons. Nonnuclear powers must submit to inspections to safeguard against the possibility of their making a nuclear weapon.)	Not needed	83–15 Yeas: D. 49, R. 34 Nays: D. 7, R. 8 (March 13)	Signed Nov. 24
Selective Service Reform (Amended Selective Service Act of 1967 to permit selection of draftees by lottery system.)	382–13 Yeas: D. 207, R. 175 Nays: D. 12, R. 1 (Oct. 30)	Passed by voice vote (Nov. 19)	Signed Nov. 26
Tax Reform Act of 1969 (Increased Social Security benefits 15%. Extended income surtax at 5% through June 30, 1970. By 1973 will increase personal exemption to $750. Repealed 7% investment credit. Reduced tax rate for single taxpayers. Provided additional $1,000 exemption for the poor. Reduced maximum tax on earned income to 50%, effective 1972. Instituted minimum tax of at least 10% on income over $30,000, except interest from state and municipal bonds. Decreased oil depletion allowance from 27½% to 22%. Instituted 4% tax on foundations' investment income.)	394–30 Yeas: D. 218, R. 176 Nays: D. 20, R. 10 (Aug. 7)	69–22 Yeas: D. 51, R.18 Nays: D. 2, R. 20 (Dec. 11)	Signed Dec. 30
Coal Mine Health and Safety Act of 1969 (Committed the Federal Government to support disability benefits of up to $272 a month for coal miners for at least seven years. A substitute system financed by the states and the mining industry is to take over then. Established first legal limit on amount of coal dust permissible in mine air. Tightened requirements for mine safety inspections. Provided compensation for miners with occupational "black lung" disease. Set up tighter controls over methane gas. Required that all electrical equipment and wiring be made sparkproof. Banned smoking and the use of flames in mines. Required reporting of all accidents and ignitions even if minor. Fixed expanded criminal penalties for willful violations. Established new controls over roof falls. Required improved mine lighting and at least two separate escapeways from each mine.)	389–4 Yeas: D. 217, R. 172 Nays: D. 0, R. 4 (Oct. 29)	73–0 Yeas: D. 40, R. 33 Nays: D. 0, R. 0 (Oct. 2)	Signed Dec. 30
Defense Appropriations Act of 1970 (Provided $69.6 billion for military expenditures in fiscal 1970—$5.6 billion below President Nixon's request. The appropriations allotted the Army and the Air Force $22 billion each, the Navy $20.8 billion, and other defense agencies $4.4 billion. Prohibited use of American ground combat troops in Laos or Thailand. Provided financing to convert four submarines to be armed with the Poseidon missile.)	330–33 Yeas: D. 173, R. 157 Nays: D. 29, R. 4 (Dec. 8)	85–4 Yeas: D. 47, R. 38 Nays: D. 2, R. 2 (Dec. 15)	Signed Dec. 30
Economic Opportunity Act of 1969 (Extended until June 30, 1971, the federal Office of Economic Opportunity.)	276–117 Yeas: D. 180, R. 96 Nays: D. 48, R. 69 (Dec. 12)	72–3 Yeas: D. 41, R. 31 Nays: D. 1, R. 2 (Oct. 14)	Signed Dec. 31
Foreign Aid Authorization (Authorized $1.97 billion in foreign aid for fiscal 1970—$1.62 billion in economic aid and $350 million in military aid. Authorized slightly smaller amount for fiscal 1971.)	176–163 Yeas: D. 105, R. 71 Nays: D. 86, R. 77 (Nov. 20)	52–31 Yeas: D. 28, R. 24 Nays: D. 19, R. 12 (Dec. 12)	Signed Dec. 31

(Ro. P. H.)

Ambassadors and envoys

Country	From the U.S.	To the U.S.
Afghanistan	Robert G. Neumann	Abdullah Malikyar
Algeria	(Embassy closed June 6, 1967)	
Argentina	John Davis Lodge	Alejandro Roca
Australia	Walter L. Rice	Sir Keith Waller
Austria	John P. Humes	Karl Gruber
Barbados	Eileen R. Donovan	Valerie T. McComie
Belgium	John S. D. Eisenhower	Baron Louis Scheyven
Bolivia	Ernest V. Siracusa	Julio Sanjines-Goytia
Botswana	†Charles H. Pletcher	Linchwe II Molefi Kgafela
Brazil	C. Burke Elbrick	Mario Gibson Barboza
Bulgaria	John M. McSweeney	Luben Nikolov Guerassimov
Burma	Arthur W. Hummel	U Hla Maung
Burundi	Thomas P. Melady	Terence Nsanze
Cambodia	*Lloyd M. Rives	*Thay Sok
Cameroon	Lewis Hoffacker	Joseph Owono
Canada	Adolph W. Schmidt	A. Edgar Ritchie
Central African Republic	Geoffrey W. Lewis	Michel Gallin-Douathe
Ceylon	Andrew V. Corry	Oliver Weerasinghe
Chad	Terence A. Todman	Lazare Massibe
Chile	Edward M. Korry	Domingo Santa Maria
China (Formosa)	Walter P. McConaughy	Chow Shu-kai
Colombia	Jack Hood Vaughan	Misael Pastrana-Borrero
Congo (Brazzaville)	(Embassy closed Aug. 13, 1965)	
Congo (Kinshasa)	Sheldon B. Vance	Justin-Marie Bomboko
Costa Rica	—	Luis Demetrio Tinoco
Cyprus	David H. Popper	Zenon Rossides
Czechoslovakia	Malcolm Toon	Ivan Rohal-Ilkiv
Dahomey	Matthew J. Looram, Jr.	Maxime-Leopold Zollner
Denmark	Guilford Dudley, Jr.	Torben Rønne
Dominican Republic	Francis E. Meloy, Jr.	Mario Read Vittini
Ecuador	Edson O. Sessions	Carlos Mantilla-Ortega
El Salvador	William G. Bowdler	Julio A. Rivera
Equatorial Guinea	Lewis Hoffacker	—
Estonia	(Legation at Tallinn closed)	†Ernst Jaakson
Ethiopia	William O. Hall	Minasse Haile
Finland	Val Peterson	Olavi Munkki
France	R. Sargent Shriver	Charles E. Lucet
Gabon	Richard Funkhouser	Leonard Antoine Badinga
Gambia	L. Dean Brown	—
Germany, West	Kenneth Rush	Rolf Pauls
Ghana	Thomas W. McElhiney	Ebenezer Moses Debrah
Greece	Henry J. Tasca	*John G. Gregoriades
Guatemala	Nathaniel Davis	Francisco Linares Aranda
Guinea	Robinson McIlvaine	Fadiala Keita
Guyana	Spencer M. King	Sir John Carter
Haiti	Clinton E. Knox	Arthur Bonhomme
Honduras	Hewson A. Ryan	Ricardo Midence Soto
Hungary	Alfred Puhan	János Nagy
Iceland	Luther I. Replogle	Magnus V. Magnusson
India	Kenneth B. Keating	Nawab Ali Yavar Jung
Indonesia	Francis J. Galbraith	R. M. Soedjatmoko
Iran	Douglas MacArthur II	Amir Aslan Afshar
Iraq	(Embassy closed June 7, 1967)	
Ireland	John D. J. Moore	William P. Fay
Israel	Walworth Barbour	Yitzhak Rabin
Italy	Graham A. Martin	Egidio Ortona
Ivory Coast	John F. Root	Timothée N'Guetta Ahoua
Jamaica	Vincent de Roulet	Sir Egerton R. Richardson
Japan	Armin H. Meyer	Takeso Shimoda
Jordan	Harrison M. Symmes	Abdul Hamid Sharaf
Kenya	Robinson McIlvaine	Leonard Oliver Kibinge
Korea, South	William J. Porter	Dong Jo Kim
Kuwait	John Patrick Walsh	Talat al-Ghoussein
Laos	G. McMurtrie Godley	Khamking Souvanlasy
Latvia	(Legation at Riga closed)	*Arnolds Spekke
Lebanon	Dwight J. Porter	Najati Kabbani
Lesotho	—	Mothusi T. Mashologu
Liberia	S. Z. Westerfield, Jr.	S. Edward Peal
Libya	Joseph Palmer II	Fathi Abidia
Lithuania	(Legation at Kaunas closed)	*Joseph Kajeckas
Luxembourg	Kingdon Gould, Jr.	Jean Wagner
Malagasy Republic	—	*René Gilbert Ralison
Malawi	Marshall P. Jones	Nyemba Wales Mbekeani
Malaysia	Jack W. Lydman	Tan Sri Ong Yoke Lin
Maldive Islands	Andrew V. Corry	Abdul Sattar
Mali	G. Edward Clark	Seydou Traore
Malta	John C. Pritzlaff, Jr.	Arvid Pardo
Mauritania	(Embassy closed June 8, 1967)	
Mauritius	—	Pierre G. G. Balancy
Mexico	Robert H. McBride	Hugo B. Margáin
Morocco	Henry J. Tasca	Ahmed Osman
Nepal	Carol C. Laise	Kul Shekhar Sharma
Netherlands	William J. Middendorf II	Baron R. B. Van Lynden
New Zealand	Kenneth Franzheim II	Frank Corner
Nicaragua	Kennedy Crockett	Guillermo Sevilla-Sacasa
Niger	Samuel C. Adams, Jr.	Adamou Mayaki
Nigeria	William C. Trueheart	Joe Iyalla
Norway	Philip K. Crowe	Arne Gunneng
Pakistan	Joseph S. Farland	Agha Hilaly
Panama	Robert M. Sayre	Roberto R. Aleman
Paraguay	J. Raymond Ylitalo	Roque J. Avila
Peru	Taylor G. Belcher	Fernando Berckemeyer
Philippines	Henry A. Byroade	Ernesto V. Lagdameo
Poland	Walter J. Stoessel, Jr.	Jerzy Michalowski
Portugal	Ridgway B. Knight	Vasco Vieira Garin
Romania	Leonard C. Meeker	Corneliu Bogdan
Rwanda	Leo G. Cyr	Fidèle Nkundabagenzi
Saudi Arabia	Hermann F. Eilts	Ibrahim al-Sowayel
Senegal	L. Dean Brown	Cheikh Ibrahima Fall
Sierra Leone	Robert G. Miner	John J. Akar
Singapore	Charles T. Cross	Ernest Steven Monteiro
Somali Republic	Fred L. Hadsel	Yusuf O. Azhari
South Africa	William M. Rountree	Harold L. T. Taswell
Southern Yemen	—	—
Spain	Robert C. Hill	Marquis de Merry del Val
Sudan	(Embassy closed June 7, 1967)	
Swaziland	—	Msindazwe Sukati
Sweden	—	Hubert de Besche
Switzerland	Shelby Davis	Felix Schnyder
Syria	(Embassy closed June 6, 1967)	
Tanzania	Claude G. Ross	Gosbert M. Rutabanzibwa
Thailand	Leonard Unger	Sunthorn Hongladarom
Togo	Albert W. Sherer, Jr.	Alexandre Ohin
Trinidad and Tobago	J. Fife Symington, Jr.	Sir Ellis E. I. Clarke
Tunisia	John A. Calhoun	Rachid Driss
Turkey	William J. Handley	Melih Esenbel
Uganda	—	E. Otema Allimadi
U.S.S.R.	Jacob D. Beam	Anatoliy F. Dobrynin
United Arab Republic	(Diplomatic relations severed June 6, 1967)	
United Kingdom	Walter H. Annenberg	John Freeman
Upper Volta	William E. Schaufele, Jr.	Paul Rouamba
Uruguay	Charles W. Adair, Jr.	Hector Luisi
Venezuela	—	Julio Sosa-Rodriguez
Vietnam, South	Ellsworth Bunker	Bui Diem
Yemen	(Embassy closed June 7, 1967)	
Yugoslavia	William Leonhart	Bogdan Crnobrnja
Zambia	Oliver L. Troxel, Jr.	Rupiah B. Banda

U.S. AMBASSADORS TO INTERNATIONAL ORGANIZATIONS

Ambassadors at Large	W. Averell Harriman
	George C. McGhee
International Atomic Energy Agency	Henry D. Smyth
North Atlantic Treaty Organization	Robert Ellsworth
Organization of American States	Joseph J. Jova
European Office of the UN and other International Organizations—Geneva	Idar Rimestad
European Communities	J. Robert Schaetzel
United Nations	Charles W. Yost

*Charge d'affaires. †Consul general.
Source: U.S. Department of State, *The Department of State Bulletin* and *Diplomatic List* (November 1969).

The federal government dollar

estimates for year ending June 30, 1970

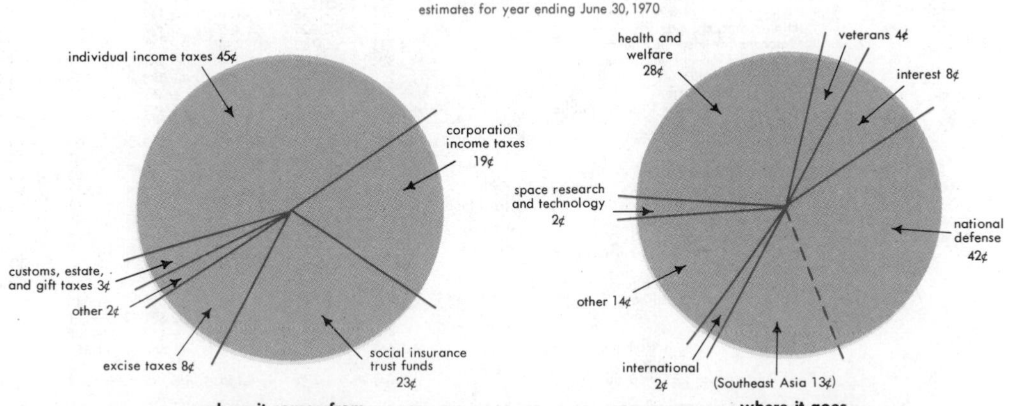

Data are based on federal administrative budget and trust fund receipts and expenditures.
Source: Executive Office of the President, Bureau of the Budget, *The Budget in Brief*.

The federal administrative budget

in millions of dollars

Source and function	1968	1969 estimate	1970 estimate
Budget receipts	153,676	186,092	198,686
Individual income taxes	68,726	84,400	90,400
Corporation income taxes	28,665	38,100	37,900
Excise taxes:			
Federal funds	9,700	10,325	10,737
Trust funds (highway)	4,379	4,475	4,963
Employment taxes and contributions	29,224	34,842	39,863
Unemployment insurance	3,346	3,300	3,575
Contributions for other insurance and retirement	2,051	2,366	2,431
Estate and gift taxes	3,051	3,200	3,400
Customs duties	2,038	2,300	2,300
Miscellaneous receipts	2,498	2,784	3,117
Budget expenditures*	178,862	183,701	195,272
National defense*	80,516	80,999	81,542
Department of Defense military functions	77,373	77,790	...
Military assistance	654	610	...
Atomic energy	2,466	2,451	...
Defense-related activities	139	282	...
International affairs and finance*	4,619	3,938	3,755
Conduct of foreign affairs	354	372	...
Economic and financial assistance	3,053	2,527	...
Foreign information and exchange activities	253	244	...
Food for Freedom	1,204	1,037	...
Space research and technology	4,721	4,247	3,947
Agriculture and agricultural resources*	5,944	5,448	5,181
Farm income stabilization	3,934	4,509	...
Financing farming and rural housing	779	−335	...
Financing rural electrification and rural telephones	304	351	...
Agricultural land and water resources	351	353	...
Research and other agricultural services	618	655	...
Natural resources*	1,702	1,898	1,891
Water resources and power	2,250	2,279	...
Land management	639	663	...
Mineral resources	85	87	...
Fish and wildlife resources	157	164	...
Recreation resources	229	321	...
General resource surveys and administration	618	655	...
Commerce and transportation*	8,076	8,048	8,969
Air transportation	951	1,144	...
Water transportation	844	885	...
Ground transportation	4,367	4,327	...
Postal service	1,080	929	...
Advancement of business	395	74	...
Area and regional development	501	706	...
Regulation of business	97	109	...
Housing and community development*	4,076	2,313	2,772
Concentrated community development	648	732	...
Community environment	486	801	...
Community facilities	106	192	...
Community planning and administration	37	60	...
Low and moderate income housing aids	948	935	...
Maintenance of housing mortgage market	1,863	−349	...
Health and welfare*	43,508	48,839	54,966
Health	9,743	11,379	...
Income security payments	32,827	36,275	...
Social and individual services	955	1,188	...
Education and manpower*	7,012	7,165	7,887
Elementary and secondary education	2,430	2,182	...
Higher education	1,392	1,368	...
Vocational education	265	252	...
Manpower training	1,263	1,511	...
Science education and basic research	449	480	...
Other aids	1,227	1,386	...
Veterans benefits and services*	6,882	7,692	7,724
Service-connected compensation	2,466	2,600	...
Nonservice-connected pensions	2,048	2,127	...
Readjustment benefits	673	881	...
Hospitals and medical care	1,469	1,582	...
Other veterans benefits and services	718	990	...
Interest*	13,744	15,171	15,958
Interest on the public debt	14,573	16,000	...
Interest on refunds of receipts	120	126	...
Interest on uninvested funds	10	11	...
General government*	2,632	2,948	3,275
Legislative functions	180	199	...
Judicial functions	94	105	...
Executive direction and management	27	33	...
Central fiscal operations	1,024	1,109	...
General property and records management	569	623	...
Central personnel management	211	209	...
Law enforcement and justice	452	539	...
National capital region	104	150	...
Other general government	243	275	...
Allowances for pay increase and contingencies	...	100	3,150
Undistributed intragovernment payments	−4,570	−5,105	−5,745
Total net lending	6,032	1,386	...
Total deficit (−)	−25,187	2,391	...

Data are for years ending June 30.
*Totals reflect interfund and intragovernmental transactions and applicable receipts not shown separately.

Source: U.S. Department of Commerce, Bureau of the Census, *Statistical Abstract of the United States*. Data compiled by the Executive Office of the President, Bureau of the Budget.

Federal trust fund receipts and expenditures

in millions of dollars

Description	1965	1966	1967	1968	1969 estimate	1970 estimate
Trust fund receipts	29,207	33,004	42,945	44,724	52,390	58,693
Federal OASI trust fund	16,413	18,451	23,370	23,641	27,842	32,385
Federal disability insurance trust fund	1,241	1,616	2,322	2,800	3,759	4,358
Federal hospital insurance trust fund	—	916	3,072	3,902	5,368	5,467
Federal supplementary medical insurance trust fund	—	—	1,285	1,353	1,910	1,864
Unemployment insurance fund	4,074	4,085	4,043	3,788	3,772	4,092
Railroad retirement funds	1,252	1,319	1,511	1,476	1,567	1,637
Federal employees retirement funds	2,675	2,836	3,106	3,449	3,791	4,006
Highway trust funds	3,670	3,925	4,455	4,427	4,530	5,036
Veterans life insurance funds	711	740	736	741	748	759
Advances, foreign military sales	824	708	1,078	961	978	952
Other trust funds	269	241	269	298	306	263
Interfund transactions	−460	−470	−540	−459	−497	−519
Proprietary receipts from the public	−1,461	−1,363	−1,763	−1,653	−1,684	−1,608
Trust fund expenditures	26,963	31,709	36,790	41,529	43,037	48,431
Federal OASI trust fund	15,962	18,769	19,842	21,510	24,641	27,138
Federal disability insurance trust fund	1,495	1,930	2,071	2,163	2,605	2,902
Federal hospital insurance trust fund	—	64	2,612	3,800	4,471	5,044
Federal supplementary medical insurance trust fund	—	—	798	1,532	1,751	1,807
Unemployment insurance fund	3,040	2,595	2,768	2,632	2,959	3,097
Railroad retirement funds	1,447	1,696	2,090	2,631	1,767	2,590
Federal employees retirement funds	1,447	1,696	2,090	2,631	1,767	2,590
Highway trust funds	4,026	3,966	3,973	4,171	3,958	4,815
Veterans life insurance funds	616	529	970	457	705	747
Advances, foreign military sales	745	751	1,070	1,015	1,040	930
Other trust funds	427	2,037	1,515	2,391	−171	−99
Interfund transactions	−460	−470	−540	−459	−497	−519
Proprietary receipts from the public	−1,461	−1,363	−1,763	−1,653	−1,684	−1,608
Trust fund surplus (+) or deficit(−)	+2,245	+1,295	+6,155	+3,195	+9,353	+10,262

Years ending June 30.
Source: U.S. Department of Commerce, Bureau of the Census, *Statistical Abstract of the United States*. Data compiled by the Executive Office of the President, Bureau of the Budget.

Budget expenditures of government agencies

in millions of dollars

Agency	1967	1968	1969 estimate
Legislative branch	240	255	298
The Judiciary	88	91	102
Executive Office of the President	28	28	33
Funds appropriated to the President	4,872	4,913	5,154
Department of Agriculture	5,828	7,308	7,650
Department of Commerce	738	807	872
Department of Defense			
Military	67,466	77,373	77,790
Civil	1,310	1,300	1,247
Department of Health, Education, and Welfare	35,153	40,576	46,259
Department of Housing and Urban Development	2,793	4,140	2,017
Department of the Interior	529	264	541
Department of Justice	409	430	516
Department of Labor	3,361	3,271	3,688
Post Office Department	1,141	1,080	929
Department of State	419	424	434
Department of Transportation	5,428	5,732	6,011
Department of the Treasury	13,098	14,655	16,272
Atomic Energy Commission	2,264	2,466	2,451
General Services Administration	131	413	453
National Aeronautics and Space Administration	5,423	4,721	4,247
Veterans Administration	6,846	6,858	7,719
Other independent agencies	4,870	6,328	4,018
Allowance for contingencies	—	—	100
Undistributed intragovernmental payments	—4,022	—4,570	—5,105
Total	158,414	178,862	183,701

Years ending June 30.
Source: U.S. Department of Commerce, Bureau of the Census, *Statistical Abstract of the United States*. Data Compiled by the Executive Office of the President, Bureau of the Budget.

Debt of the federal government

Year	DEBT OUTSTANDING* on June 30			INTEREST PAID on public debt for fiscal year	
	Total in $000,000†	Per capita	Gross public debt in $000,000	Total in $000,000	Percent of federal expenditures
1900	1,263.4	$ 16.60	1,263.4	40	7.7
1905	1,132.4	13.51	1,132.4	25	4.3
1910	1,146.9	12.41	1,146.9	21	3.1
1915	1,191.3	11.85	1,191.3	23	3.0
1920	24,299.3	228.23	24,299.3	1,020	15.9
1925	20,516.2	177.12	20,516.2	882	28.8
1930	16,185.3	131.51	16,185.3	659	19.2
1935	32,823.6	257.95	28,700.9	821	12.6
1940	48,496.6	367.08	42,967.5	1,041	11.5
1945	259,115.3	1,851.70	258,682.2	3,617	3.7
1950	257,376.9	1,696.80	257,357.4	5,750	14.5
1951	255,251.2	1,654.39	255,222.0	5,613	12.7
1952	259,150.7	1,651.13	259,105.2	5,859	9.0
1953	266,123.1	1,667.80	266,071.1	6,504	8.8
1954	271,341.0	1,670.91	271,259.6	6,382	9.4
1955	274,418.4	1,660.37	274,374.2	6,370	9.9
1956	272,824.7	1,621.82	272,750.8	6,787	10.2
1957	270,634.3	1,580.12	270,527.2	7,244	10.4
1958	276,444.4	1,587.47	276,343.2	7,607	10.6
1959	284,816.9	1,606.74	284,705.9	7,593	9.4
1960	286,470.6	1,585.48	286,330.8	9,180	11.9
1961	289,211.2	1,573.89	288,970.9	8,957	10.9
1962	298,645.0	1,599.98	298,200.8	9,120	10.3
1963	306,466.2	1,617.94	305,859.6	9,895	10.6
1964	312,525.9	1,626.72	311,712.9	10,666	10.9
1965	317,864.2	1,633.63	317,273.9	11,346	11.8
1966	320,368.6	1,627.54	319,907.1	12,014	11.2
1967	326,733.1	1,640.90	326,220.9	13,391	10.7
1968	348,147.0	1,730.77	347,578.4	14,573	. . .
1969	354,317.3	1,743.37	353,720.3	16,613‡	. . .

*Includes certain securities not subject to statutory limitation. †Gross public debt plus guaranteed debt of U.S. government agencies held outside the Treasury. ‡Preliminary
Source: U.S. Department of the Treasury, *Annual Report of the Secretary of the Treasury*.

Per capita federal aid to states

in dollars per fiscal year 1968

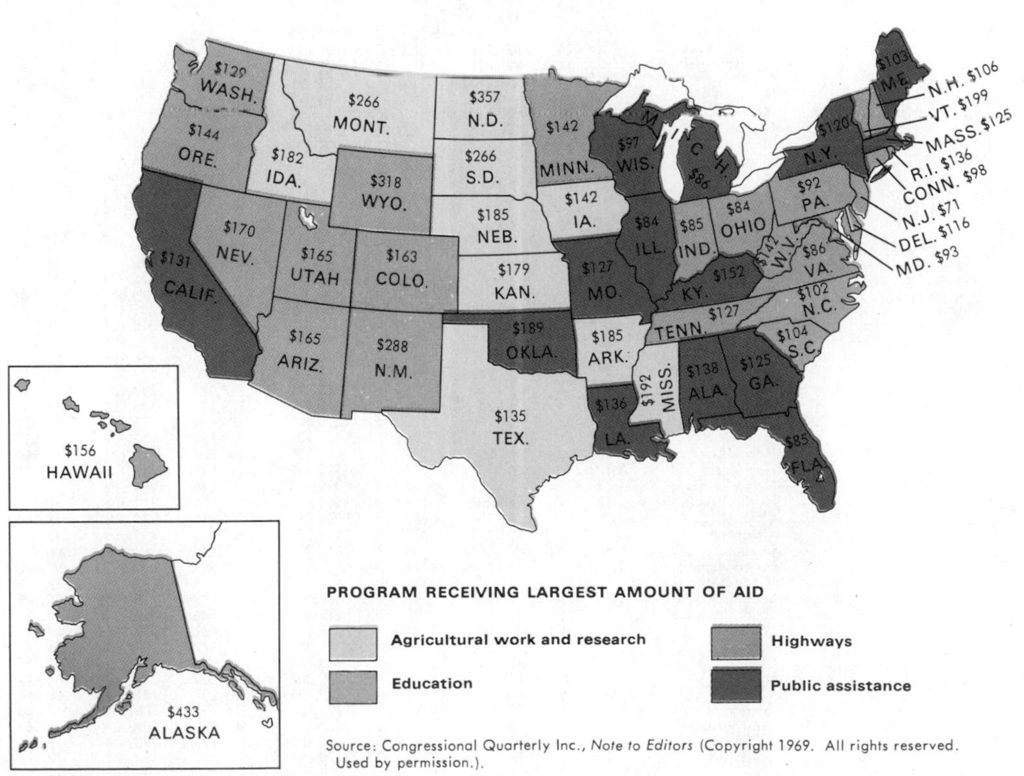

Source: Congressional Quarterly Inc., *Note to Editors* (Copyright 1969. All rights reserved. Used by permission.).

State Government

Executive officials

September 1, 1969

State	Governor	Lieutenant Governor	Secretary of State	Treasurer
Alabama	Albert P. Brewer (D)	(vacancy)	Mabel Amos (D)	Agnes Baggett (D)
Alaska	Keith H. Miller (R)	—	Robert W. Ward (R)	—
Arizona	Jack Williams (R)	—	Wesley Bolin (D)	Morris A. Herring (R)
Arkansas	Winthrop Rockefeller (R)	Maurice L. Britt (R)	Kelly Bryant (D)	Nancy Hall (D)
California	Ronald Reagan (R)	Ed Reinecke (R)	Frank M. Jordan (R)	Ivy Baker Priest (R)
Colorado	John A. Love (R)	Mark A. Hogan (D)	Byron A. Anderson (R)	Virginia N. Blue (R)
Connecticut	John N. Dempsey (D)	Attilio R. Frassinelli (D)	Ella T. Grasso (D)	Gerald A. Lamb (D)
Delaware	Russell W. Peterson (R)	Eugene D. Bookhammer (R)	Gene Bunting (R)	Daniel Ross (R)
Florida	Claude R. Kirk, Jr. (R)	Ray C. Osborne (R)	Tom Adams (D)	Broward Williams (D)
Georgia	Lester G. Maddox (D)	George T. Smith (D)	Ben W. Fortson, Jr. (D)	Jack B. Ray (R)
Hawaii	John A. Burns (D)	Thomas P. Gill (D)	—	—
Idaho	Don Samuelson (R)	Jack M. Murphy (R)	Pete T. Cenarrusa (R)	Marjorie R. Moon (D)
Illinois	Richard B. Ogilvie (R)	Paul Simon (D)	Paul Powell (D)	Adlai E. Stevenson III (D)
Indiana	Edgar D. Whitcomb (R)	Richard E. Folz (R)	William N. Salin (R)	John K. Snyder (R)
Iowa	Robert D. Ray (R)	Roger W. Jepsen (R)	Melvin D. Synhorst (R)	Maurice E. Baringer (R)
Kansas	Robert B. Docking (D)	James H. DeCoursey, Jr. (R)	Mrs. Elwill M. Shanahan (R)	Walter H. Peery (R)
Kentucky	Louie B. Nunn (R)	Wendell H. Ford (D)	Elmer Begley (R)	Thelma Stovall (D)
Louisiana	John J. McKeithen (D)	C. C. Aycock (D)	Wade O. Martin, Jr. (D)	Mary E. Parker (D)
Maine	Kenneth M. Curtis (D)	—	Joseph T. Edgar (R)	Norman K. Ferguson (R)
Maryland	Marvin Mandel (D)	—	Blair Lee III (D)	John A. Luetkemeyer (D)
Massachusetts	Francis W. Sargent (R)	(vacancy)	John F. X. Davoren (D)	Robert Q. Crane (D)
Michigan	William G. Milliken (R)	(vacancy)	James M. Hare (D)	Allison Green (R)
Minnesota	Harold LeVander (R)	James B. Goetz (R)	Joseph L. Donovan (DFL)	Val Bjornson (R)
Mississippi	John B. Williams (D)	Charles L. Sullivan (D)	Heber Ladner (D)	Evelyn Gandy (D)
Missouri	Warren E. Hearnes (D)	William S. Morris (D)	James E. Kirkpatrick (D)	William E. Robinson (D)

Party affiliations are indicated by (D) for Democrat, (R) for Republican, and (DFL) for Democratic Farmer Labor Party.
*In the only elections held in November 1969, William T. Cahill (R) was elected governor of New Jersey, and Linwood Holton (R) was elected governor and J. Sargeant Reynolds (D) lieutenant governor of Virginia.
Source: State governments.

State government revenue, expenditure, and debt

in thousands of dollars

State	FISCAL YEAR TOTALS: Revenue 1960	Revenue 1968	Expenditure 1960	Expenditure 1968	GENERAL REVENUE, FISCAL 1968: Total	State taxes	Intergov-ernmental	Charges and other	Liquor store revenue fiscal 1968
Alabama	543,686	1,078,364	565,342	1,117,439	954,546	530,662	316,195	107,689	62,215
Alaska	74,646	263,609	56,109	286,550	246,279	60,402	124,358	61,519	—
Arizona	296,060	660,955	261,986	602,337	562,405	315,916	167,708	78,781	—
Arkansas	278,621	552,906	261,687	556,109	518,897	289,644	188,527	40,726	—
California	3,752,919	9,133,093	3,583,197	8,583,253	7,524,580	4,664,275	2,282,872	577,433	—
Colorado	358,008	727,156	332,201	698,014	658,366	361,251	199,275	97,840	—
Connecticut	420,958	921,621	446,898	935,575	808,997	499,826	206,099	103,072	—
Delaware	113,116	239,073	120,107	256,240	233,041	144,789	46,657	41,595	—
Florida	812,496	1,564,937	764,831	1,499,181	1,442,733	973,130	341,490	128,113	—
Georgia	613,748	1,322,560	564,300	1,298,891	1,217,316	737,181	369,956	110,179	—
Hawaii	204,909	450,718	192,088	457,702	402,174	242,655	110,606	48,913	—
Idaho	140,271	271,953	131,137	236,446	229,881	136,790	68,680	24,411	17,823
Illinois	1,452,061	2,889,620	1,362,598	2,779,315	2,673,010	1,730,634	729,625	212,751	—
Indiana	683,221	1,434,052	668,466	1,448,030	1,328,114	819,152	288,159	220,803	—
Iowa	526,688	975,518	483,789	979,523	849,914	502,453	242,345	105,116	62,646
Kansas	353,168	645,936	335,321	607,684	606,954	357,045	163,710	86,199	—
Kentucky	431,776	1,002,605	439,419	1,090,818	931,655	509,316	322,276	100,063	—
Louisiana	815,037	1,442,978	829,944	1,449,964	1,348,814	740,679	357,791	250,344	—
Maine	187,742	313,210	181,352	311,171	249,913	146,145	68,842	34,926	34,926
Maryland	524,786	1,205,903	491,234	1,200,095	1,113,854	752,954	243,425	117,475	—
Massachusetts	852,001	1,791,015	914,283	1,775,269	1,608,463	1,034,864	431,720	141,879	—
Michigan	1,652,216	3,354,618	1,641,812	3,147,560	2,842,451	1,885,629	615,823	340,999	245,941
Minnesota	628,990	1,472,194	631,621	1,357,616	1,357,515	815,121	368,766	173,628	—
Mississippi	339,277	668,900	350,718	681,809	599,302	322,520	207,131	69,651	36,085
Missouri	587,514	1,169,165	561,443	1,111,382	1,076,966	656,967	322,124	97,875	—
Montana	165,614	279,938	159,118	268,976	228,690	104,973	86,388	37,329	21,376
Nebraska	182,125	381,355	176,582	345,570	367,079	193,977	119,753	53,349	—
Nevada	87,239	213,967	80,186	210,901	175,330	103,528	55,207	16,595	—
New Hampshire	128,109	227,700	122,774	220,503	154,809	75,261	54,396	25,152	52,752
New Jersey	811,011	1,943,783	698,699	1,661,131	1,559,752	953,954	392,331	213,467	—
New Mexico	240,940	489,287	221,381	454,401	457,902	217,137	151,587	89,178	—
New York	3,303,310	7,604,454	3,317,205	7,595,930	6,462,311	4,447,165	1,284,608	730,538	—
North Carolina	734,712	1,491,781	643,510	1,432,222	1,351,248	901,528	303,198	146,522	—
North Dakota	154,290	263,298	155,833	264,542	249,771	101,456	73,746	74,569	—
Ohio	1,841,221	3,149,451	1,686,780	2,907,693	2,251,310	1,370,216	580,582	300,512	284,374
Oklahoma	471,373	929,953	457,316	949,299	896,982	427,502	315,818	153,662	—
Oregon	485,498	808,219	443,697	812,338	631,750	324,797	200,124	106,829	71,650
Pennsylvania	2,065,941	3,796,160	2,131,883	3,753,871	2,970,223	2,003,822	725,380	241,021	323,813
Rhode Island	158,249	341,002	153,308	380,510	288,608	166,730	86,379	35,499	—
South Carolina	381,898	720,404	329,748	699,789	653,123	413,406	162,348	77,369	—
South Dakota	121,683	212,192	117,284	215,364	206,146	87,980	81,083	37,083	—
Tennessee	517,311	1,034,971	494,351	993,351	958,787	577,320	304,786	76,681	—
Texas	1,419,751	2,787,575	1,304,665	2,621,384	2,590,147	1,437,971	795,612	356,564	—
Utah	209,399	435,335	191,534	423,714	379,179	183,511	132,055	63,613	21,372
Vermont	92,315	207,461	94,239	232,303	175,222	88,172	65,811	21,239	17,995
Virginia	622,126	1,378,883	576,246	1,340,235	1,171,202	731,674	282,310	157,218	134,929
Washington	829,161	1,681,842	767,069	1,497,172	1,339,256	878,644	308,168	152,444	116,694
West Virginia	364,187	694,748	345,956	687,706	581,600	320,207	198,260	63,133	42,806
Wisconsin	686,891	1,644,232	645,248	1,637,403	1,477,198	990,548	317,537	169,113	—
Wyoming	119,391	189,289	109,260	179,894	168,599	68,671	73,315	26,613	9,356
All states	32,837,660	68,459,939	31,595,755	66,254,175	59,132,364	36,400,150	15,934,942	6,797,272	1,556,753

Source: U.S. Department of Commerce, Bureau of the Census, *State Government Finances.*

State	Governor	Lieutenant Governor	Secretary of State	Treasurer
Montana	Forrest H. Anderson(D)	Thomas L. Judge(D)	Frank Murray(D)	Alex Stephenson(R)
Nebraska	Norbert T. Tiemann(R)	John E. Everroad(R)	Frank Marsh(R)	Wayne R. Swanson(R)
Nevada	Paul Laxalt(R)	Ed Fike(R)	John Koontz(D)	Michael Mirabelli(D)
New Hampshire	Walter Peterson(R)	—	Robert L. Stark(R)	Robert W. Flanders(R)
New Jersey*	Richard J. Hughes(D)	—	Robert J. Burkhardt(D)	John A. Kervick(D)
New Mexico	David F. Cargo(R)	E. Lee Francis(R)	Ernestine D. Evans(D)	Jesse D. Kornegay(D)
New York	Nelson A. Rockefeller(R)	Malcolm Wilson(R)	John P. Lomenzo(R)	—
North Carolina	Robert W. Scott(D)	H. Patrick Taylor, Jr.(D)	Thad Eure(D)	Edwin Gill(D)
North Dakota	William L. Guy(D)	Richard F. Larsen(R)	Ben Meier(R)	Bernice Asbridge(R)
Ohio	James A. Rhodes(R)	John W. Brown(R)	Ted W. Brown(R)	John D. Herbert(R)
Oklahoma	Dewey F. Bartlett(R)	George Nigh(D)	John Rogers(D)	Leo Winters(D)
Oregon	Tom L. McCall(R)	—	Clay Myers(R)	Robert Straub(D)
Pennsylvania	Raymond P. Shafer(R)	Raymond J. Broderick(R)	Joseph J. Kelley, Jr.(R)	Grace M. Sloan(D)
Rhode Island	Frank Licht(D)	J. Joseph Garrahy(D)	August P. LaFrance(D)	Raymond H. Hawksley(D)
South Carolina	Robert E. McNair(D)	John C. West(D)	O. Frank Thornton(D)	Grady L. Patterson, Jr.(D)
South Dakota	Frank L. Farrar(R)	James Abdnor(R)	Alma Larson (R)	Neal Strand(R)
Tennessee	Buford Ellington(D)	Frank Gorrell(D)	Joe C. Carr(D)	Charles Worley(D)
Texas	Preston E. Smith(D)	Ben Barnes(D)	Martin Dies, Jr.(D)	Jesse James(D)
Utah	Calvin L. Rampton(D)	—	Clyde L. Miller(D)	Golden L. Allen(R)
Vermont	Deane C. Davis(R)	Thomas L. Hayes(R)	Richard C. Thomas(R)	Frank H. Davis(R)
Virginia*	Mills E. Godwin, Jr.(D)	Fred G. Pollard(D)	Martha B. Conway(D)	Lewis H. Vaden(D)
Washington	Daniel J. Evans(R)	John A. Cherberg(D)	A. Ludlow Kramer(R)	Robert S. O'Brien(D)
West Virginia	Arch A. Moore, Jr.(R)	—	John D. Rockefeller IV(D)	John H. Kelly(D)
Wisconsin	Warren P. Knowles(R)	Jack B. Olson(R)	Robert C. Zimmerman(D)	Harold W. Clemens(R)
Wyoming	Stanley K. Hathaway(R)	—	Thyra Thomson(R)	Minnie A. Mitchell(R)

GENERAL EXPENDITURES, FISCAL 1968					Liquor store expenditure fiscal 1968	INSURANCE TRUST FUND, FISCAL 1968				DEBT, FISCAL 1968		
							Expenditures					
Total	Education	Highways	Public welfare	Hospitals		Revenue	Total	Unemployment compensation	Employee retirement	Gross debt outstanding at end of year	Long-term debt issued	Long-term debt retired
1,020,576	478,212	213,476	141,426	44,781	56,574	61,603	40,289	23,118	17,165	608,755	72,852	26,878
276,724	66,672	89,955	9,567	5,627	—	17,330	9,826	8,375	1,421	176,850	39,178	2,933
557,468	248,998	135,929	38,546	10,835	—	98,550	44,869	12,224	8,126	82,969	12,805	1,197
531,596	211,745	128,425	91,424	26,105	—	34,009	24,513	13,471	11,033	116,772	9,912	8,346
7,546,602	2,507,068	1,218,133	1,601,042	250,891	—	1,608,513	1,036,621	419,286	304,577	5,253,923	702,768	175,189
663,425	301,156	123,923	101,396	44,566	—	68,790	34,589	7,535	14,557	149,372	30,288	6,907
860,926	268,242	177,070	128,958	77,905	—	112,624	74,649	47,016	27,533	1,444,568	117,300	58,694
248,990	115,616	42,536	21,755	13,012	—	6,032	7,250	6,580	654	366,049	50,908	21,506
1,431,307	675,254	270,089	134,306	69,349	—	122,204	67,874	21,937	45,358	823,965	16,795	87,593
1,256,036	602,271	224,856	166,353	79,782	—	105,244	42,855	18,957	23,898	837,117	145,796	36,806
432,485	184,072	42,840	29,854	18,687	—	48,544	25,217	8,713	16,504	343,406	83,545	14,993
210,564	74,597	57,783	21,738	6,932	13,602	24,249	12,280	7,347	3,324	18,515	3,820	1,580
2,588,990	1,034,191	552,241	452,322	190,371	—	216,610	190,325	94,131	96,098	1,267,183	97,915	69,694
1,378,330	696,004	321,688	63,838	78,561	—	105,938	69,700	34,364	35,284	561,287	22,120	14,356
903,880	377,769	239,143	99,233	45,789	45,593	62,958	30,050	13,798	16,249	89,443	12,525	3,909
585,988	259,781	119,475	73,395	41,148	—	38,982	21,696	10,551	11,099	236,369	3,270	22,927
1,047,999	393,044	303,257	141,686	35,428	—	70,950	42,819	21,426	18,835	1,119,486	149,768	25,490
1,388,877	548,732	243,616	233,826	90,544	—	94,164	61,087	30,742	30,345	737,110	39,275	20,564
265,562	95,510	65,046	36,520	13,500	23,244	28,371	22,365	8,582	13,783	175,272	19,265	12,002
1,151,413	420,650	194,521	151,099	79,821	—	92,049	48,682	27,214	18,856	926,660	106,420	71,473
1,614,636	365,852	215,652	333,581	143,533	—	182,552	160,633	93,072	67,495	1,800,603	54,710	90,415
2,772,481	1,336,809	436,818	364,790	161,717	190,272	266,226	184,807	118,529	57,139	972,940	62,677	71,970
1,302,077	548,529	261,333	128,999	75,592	—	114,679	55,539	26,361	28,993	356,641	65,787	19,060
634,468	263,530	141,139	84,053	27,887	30,088	33,513	17,253	8,432	8,808	445,259	155,807	16,575
1,059,402	438,669	227,439	167,340	74,629	—	92,199	51,980	35,906	15,950	145,849	9,520	6,169
233,082	92,388	71,168	20,100	8,837	17,376	29,872	18,518	5,295	9,024	84,776	14,215	10,523
325,314	109,014	92,029	44,863	25,151	—	14,276	20,256	6,146	14,102	55,512	270	875
186,661	67,507	50,675	15,496	3,884	—	38,637	24,240	9,839	6,730	30,371	13,685	1,223
174,639	57,069	52,763	15,050	11,036	39,785	20,139	6,079	2,423	3,656	146,863	100	9,954
1,401,046	490,865	332,180	170,999	94,569	—	384,031	260,085	128,934	94,686	1,145,972	1,970	55,250
436,204	231,997	82,538	48,774	10,546	—	31,385	18,197	7,529	10,668	135,104	1,730	8,999
7,010,176	2,686,897	755,215	1,297,032	516,483	—	1,142,143	585,754	302,090	203,362	5,663,618	665,564	141,876
1,382,078	694,090	273,653	104,618	84,691	—	140,533	50,144	26,799	23,332	493,781	83,494	46,789
254,163	89,586	67,169	24,208	8,509	—	13,527	10,379	3,953	2,143	31,767	2,340	1,643
2,327,495	881,313	650,554	300,664	113,874	226,344	613,767	353,854	63,931	175,546	1,282,622	44,575	85,755
921,562	320,672	199,272	230,087	38,981	—	32,971	27,737	12,353	12,383	665,734	25,307	6,889
703,997	287,596	153,579	67,784	30,813	43,649	104,819	64,692	27,946	10,374	494,632	47,240	35,099
3,202,272	1,306,611	771,341	389,990	206,797	266,662	502,124	284,937	112,296	132,740	2,427,497	414,555	106,892
340,785	90,581	85,820	63,080	24,759	—	52,394	39,725	14,971	10,737	308,685	43,900	7,017
670,237	321,933	123,536	40,598	38,428	—	67,281	29,552	15,601	13,033	313,809	25,895	22,939
211,912	74,653	70,656	21,400	8,532	—	6,046	3,452	2,915	537	28,250	7,495	444
948,919	419,067	220,688	109,453	50,342	—	76,184	44,432	30,753	13,557	363,119	70,600	15,668
2,523,502	1,238,387	533,859	356,553	124,937	—	197,428	97,882	26,769	71,094	853,482	164,618	32,780
387,453	210,369	81,182	36,707	13,268	15,748	34,784	20,513	10,661	6,328	110,638	9,780	6,738
207,543	70,264	71,371	21,250	6,627	17,532	14,244	7,228	4,635	2,593	139,900	48,110	7,295
1,193,633	525,274	324,723	55,435	88,643	118,969	72,752	27,633	9,027	18,606	258,878	9,795	16,414
1,286,754	606,834	265,787	152,937	45,565	85,108	225,892	125,310	39,524	35,192	636,911	91,155	39,632
605,976	248,898	180,136	68,966	24,227	33,341	70,342	48,389	14,330	15,748	439,126	71,718	15,928
1,563,431	584,487	225,641	168,923	81,925	—	167,034	73,972	43,684	29,111	445,280	61,930	6,298
165,691	59,261	66,162	7,030	4,863	8,708	11,334	5,495	1,783	1,642	53,538	—	1,242
60,395,357	24,278,586	11,848,080	8,649,044	3,373,279	1,232,595	7,770,822	4,626,223	2,041,854	1,810,008	35,666,228	4,005,067	1,571,388

State finance

Major sources of revenue

in billions of dollars

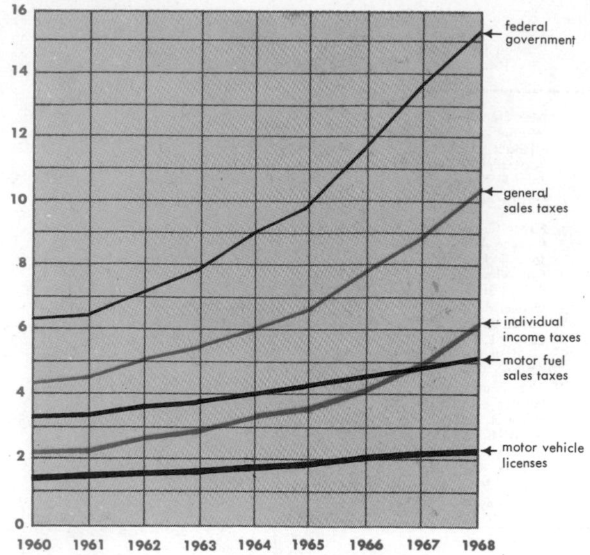

federal government
general sales taxes
individual income taxes
motor fuel sales taxes
motor vehicle licenses

0 2 4 6 8 10 12 14 16
1960 1961 1962 1963 1964 1965 1966 1967 1968

Major expenditures

in billions of dollars

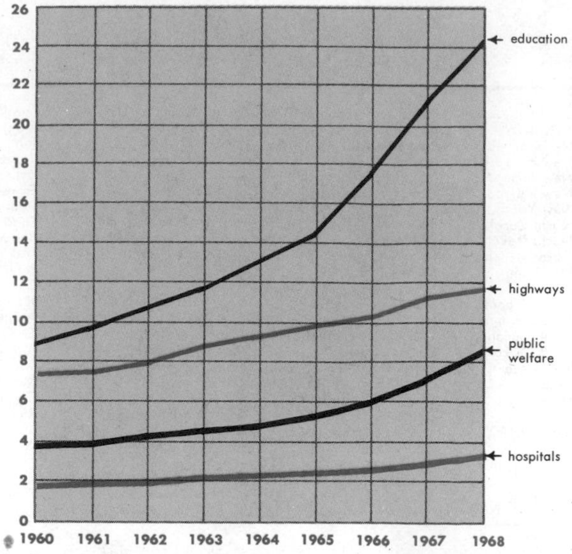

education
highways
public welfare
hospitals

0 2 4 6 8 10 12 14 16 18 20 22 24 26
1960 1961 1962 1963 1964 1965 1966 1967 1968

Source: U.S. Department of Commerce, Bureau of the Census, *State Government Finances.*

State legislatures

State	Name of house	September 1, 1969 composition: Total seats*	Demo-crats	Repub-licans
Alabama	Senate	35	33	1
	House of Representatives	105	103	1
Alaska	Senate	20	9	11
	House of Representatives	40	22	18
Arizona	Senate	30	13	17
	House of Representatives	60	26	34
Arkansas	Senate	35	34	1
	House of Representatives	100	96	4
California	Senate	40	19	21
	Assembly	80	39	41
Colorado	Senate	35	11	24
	House of Representatives	65	27	38
Connecticut	Senate	36	24	12
	House of Representatives	177	110	67
Delaware	Senate	19	6	13
	House of Representatives	39	14	25
Florida	Senate	48	32	16
	House of Representatives	119	77	42
Georgia	Senate	56	48	7
	House of Representatives	195	168	27
Hawaii	Senate	25	17	8
	House of Representatives	51	39	12
Idaho	Senate	35	14	21
	House of Representatives	70	32	38
Illinois	Senate	58	19	37
	House of Representatives	177	81	94
Indiana	Senate	50	15	35
	House of Representatives	100	27	73
Iowa	Senate	61	16	44
	House of Representatives	124	37	86
Kansas	Senate	40	8	32
	House of Representatives	125	38	87
Kentucky	Senate	38	24	14
	House of Representatives	100	56	42
Louisiana	Senate	39	39	0
	House of Representatives	105	105	0
Maine	Senate	32	14	18
	House of Representatives	151	66	85
Maryland	Senate	43	35	8
	House of Delegates	142	117	25
Massachusetts	Senate	40	27	13
	House of Representatives	240	172	68
Michigan	Senate	38	18	20
	House of Representatives	110	57	53
Minnesota†	Senate	67	—	—
	House of Representatives	135	—	—
Mississippi	Senate	52	49	3
	House of Representatives	122	119	2
Missouri	Senate	34	23	11
	House of Representatives	163	109	54
Montana	Senate	55	28	27
	House of Representatives	104	46	58
Nebraska†	Unicameral	49	—	—
Nevada	Senate	20	11	9
	Assembly	40	17	22
New Hampshire	Senate	24	9	14
	House of Representatives	400	144	255
New Jersey	Senate	40	9	31
	General Assembly	80	22	57
New Mexico	Senate	42	25	17
	House of Representatives	70	44	26
New York	Senate	57	24	33
	Assembly	150	71	78
North Carolina	Senate	50	38	12
	House of Representatives	120	88	29
North Dakota	Senate	49	6	43
	House of Representatives	98	18	77
Ohio	Senate	33	12	21
	House of Representatives	99	35	64
Oklahoma	Senate	48	39	9
	House of Representatives	99	74	25
Oregon	Senate	30	16	14
	House of Representatives	60	22	38
Pennsylvania	Senate	50	23	27
	House of Representatives	203	106	96
Rhode Island	Senate	50	37	13
	House of Representatives	100	76	24
South Carolina	Senate	46	43	3
	House of Representatives	124	118	5
South Dakota	Senate	35	8	27
	House of Representatives	75	16	59
Tennessee	Senate	33	21	12
	House of Representatives	99	49	49
Texas	Senate	31	29	2
	House of Representatives	150	142	8
Utah	Senate	28	8	20
	House of Representatives	69	21	48
Vermont	Senate	30	8	22
	House of Representatives	150	50	100
Virginia	Senate	40	33	7
	House of Delegates	100	85	14
Washington	Senate	49	27	22
	House of Representatives	99	43	56
West Virginia	Senate	34	22	12
	House of Delegates	100	63	37
Wisconsin	Senate	33	9	22
	Assembly	100	47	52
Wyoming	Senate	30	12	18
	House of Representatives	61	16	45

*The total number of seats is not always equal to the number of Democrats plus Republicans because of vacancies and seats held by independents. †Nonpartisan election.
Source: State governments.

Taxation

City taxes, 1967–68

in thousands of dollars for the 25 largest cities

City	Total	Property	TAX: General sales and gross receipts	Income taxes	Motor vehicle licenses
New York, New York	2,680,466	1,619,301	413,745	430,191	3,895
Chicago, Illinois	327,905	204,220	35,215	—	25,877
Los Angeles, California	257,550	140,627	62,279	—	2
Philadelphia, Pennsylvania	265,016	108,675	—	126,247	15
Detroit, Michigan	165,600	114,723	—	47,337	136
Houston, Texas	73,829	65,006	—	—	40
Baltimore, Maryland	176,886	131,362	—	30,211	—
Dallas, Texas	63,288	55,822	—	—	—
Washington, D.C.	304,157	110,842	45,995	70,350	7,979
Cleveland, Ohio	68,447	55,983	—	9,676	31
Milwaukee, Wisconsin	58,944	56,640	—	—	10
San Antonio, Texas	22,434	21,126	—	—	—
San Francisco, California	166,393	138,311	21,989	—	40
New Orleans, Louisiana	50,058	22,986	15,733	—	895
San Diego, California	39,273	21,446	11,656	—	32
St. Louis, Missouri	89,326	35,706	—	30,351	1,437
Kansas City, Missouri	45,345	18,132	—	11,531	1,499
Boston, Massachusetts	179,341	176,745	—	—	27
Seattle, Washington	36,011	19,593	—	—	24
Columbus, Ohio	25,467	5,825	—	18,282	26
Memphis, Tennessee	37,183	27,607	—	—	2,763
Pittsburgh, Pennsylvania	55,374	34,640	—	11,237	—
Jacksonville, Florida	...	...	...	...	...
Denver, Colorado	54,749	31,598	17,628	—	232
Phoenix, Arizona	30,792	13,602	13,929	—	—

Cities ranked by size of city proper population as of July 1, 1969.
Source: U.S. Department of Commerce, Bureau of the Census, *City Government Finances in 1967–68.*

State taxes

fiscal year 1968

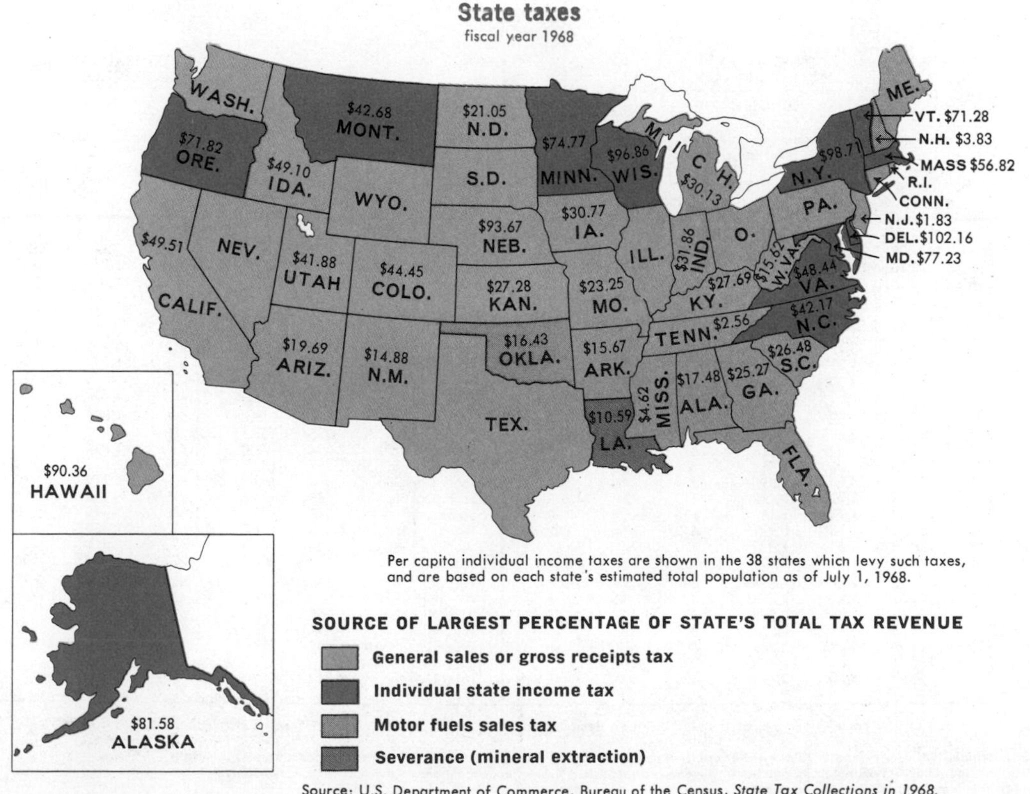

Per capita individual income taxes are shown in the 38 states which levy such taxes, and are based on each state's estimated total population as of July 1, 1968.

SOURCE OF LARGEST PERCENTAGE OF STATE'S TOTAL TAX REVENUE

- General sales or gross receipts tax
- Individual state income tax
- Motor fuels sales tax
- Severance (mineral extraction)

Source: U.S. Department of Commerce, Bureau of the Census, *State Tax Collections in 1968.*

Internal revenue collections

in millions of dollars

Type of tax	1968	1969
Corporation income tax	29,896	38,338
Individual income and employment taxes	106,338	130,509
Withheld	82,377	99,958
Not withheld	22,495	28,973
Railroad retirement	858	939
Unemployment insurance	607	640
Estate tax	2,710	3,137
Gift tax	372	393
Alcohol taxes	4,287	4,554
Distilled spirits	3,197	3,390
Wines	127	157
Beer	963	1,007
Tobacco taxes	2,122	2,138
Cigarettes	2,066	2,082
Cigars	55	54
Stamp taxes on documents, other instruments, and playing cards*	49	1
Manufacturers' excise taxes	5,714	6,501
Gasoline	3,031	3,186
Lubricating oils	92	97
Tires and tubes	462	604
Passenger cars, chassis, bodies, etc.	1,531	1,864
Trucks and buses, chassis, bodies, etc.	448	589
Parts and accessories for cars, trucks, etc.†	76	81
Fishing rods, creels, etc.	9	12
Firearms (except pistols and revolvers), shells, cartridges	31	33
Pistols and revolvers	5	6
Retailers' excise taxes‡	1	§
Miscellaneous excise taxes	1,859	2,147
Admissions taxes‖	1	§
Club dues and initiation fees‖	1	1
Telephone, wire, etc., and equipment services¶	1,105	1,316
Air transportation of persons	199	224
Sugar	102	108
Diesel and special motor fuels	202	225
Use tax on highway motor vehicles weighing over 26,000 lb.	109	124
Coin-operated gaming devices ♀	15	12
Narcotics and marijuana	2	2
Unclassified excise taxes	288	200
Total	153,637	187,920

Years ending June 30.

*Tax on playing cards and issues and transfers of stock repealed effective June 22, 1965, and January 1, 1966, respectively. †Tax on auto parts and accessories repealed effective January 1, 1966. ‡Repealed effective June 22, 1965.

§Less than $1,000,000. ‖Repealed effective noon December 31, 1965.

¶Tax on local and toll telephone and typewriter service reduced to 3% and tax on private communications services, telegraph service, and wire equipment service repealed effective January 1, 1966. Tax on general and toll telephone service and typewriter exchange service is increased from 3% to 10% on bills paid after April 1, 1966 for services rendered after January 31, 1966.

♀Repealed effective July 1, 1965.

Source: U.S. Department of the Treasury, Internal Revenue Service.

Tax collections

	STATE TAX COLLECTIONS fiscal 1968		FEDERAL TAX COLLECTIONS			LOCAL TAX COLLECTIONS fiscal 1968	
State	Total in $000,000	Per capita	Total in $000,000, fiscal 1969	Individual income and employment tax in $000,000, fiscal 1969	Per capita*, fiscal 1968	Total in $000,000	Per capita
Alabama	532	$149.09	1,333	1,040	$ 453	199	$ 57.10
Alaska	60	218.06	132	121	737	32	133.88
Arizona	316	189.17	717	620	587	239	145.99
Arkansas	290	143.96	652	524	422	112	56.77
California	4,663	242.62	16,777	13,051	850	4,724	251.40
Colorado	361	176.39	2,243	1,878	674	360	179.44
Connecticut	500	168.92	3,478	2,567	1,013	555	188.43
Delaware	145	271.14	1,319	648	1,150	41	78.43
District of Columbia	—	—	†	†	1,009	304	387.02
Florida	973	157.98	3,626	2,844	645	805	131.66
Georgia	737	160.68	2,615	1,905	533	385	86.32
Hawaii	243	311.90	527	413	697	85	117.97
Idaho	137	194.03	380	311	532	86	121.42
Illinois	1,731	157.70	14,286	9,990	899	1,892	173.62
Indiana	819	161.66	3,410	2,278	710	724	143.23
Iowa	502	182.84	1,442	1,136	666	475	171.40
Kansas	357	155.03	1,185	951	642	384	170.28
Kentucky	509	157.73	2,541	1,029	493	224	70.66
Louisiana	740	198.40	1,640	1,291	516	306	83.43
Maine	146	149.28	470	376	588	124	128.91
Maryland	771	205.31	5,425†	4,470†	836	590	162.06
Massachusetts	1,033	190.06	5,455	3,948	824	1,119	207.35
Michigan	1,886	215.75	13,872	7,374	809	1,319	152.45
Minnesota	815	223.57	3,196	2,341	663	613	167.58
Mississippi	323	137.71	620	492	359	156	67.27
Missouri	657	141.99	4,783	3,414	690	600	131.40
Montana	105	$151.48	273	227	$592	130	$189.40
Nebraska	194	134.99	1,032	796	668	272	189.29
Nevada	104	228.54	351	284	870	91	206.83
New Hampshire	75	107.21	448	371	688	115	163.86
New Jersey	954	134.78	6,670	4,592	877	1,515	216.49
New Mexico	217	213.93	368	322	542	69	70.99
New York	4,447	245.52	33,245	10,200	919	4,673	257.49
North Carolina	900	175.30	4,066	1,963	504	313	62.41
North Dakota	101	162.33	202	178	515	96	157.03
Ohio	1,370	129.38	12,407	2,407	764	1,562	147.50
Oklahoma	428	169.78	1,598	1,056	568	243	97.24
Oregon	325	161.75	1,288	1,029	680	316	157.80
Pennsylvania	2,004	171.07	11,111	1,667	747	1,492	127.20
Rhode Island	167	182.53	891	676	764	136	154.03
South Carolina	412	153.19	963	779	446	129	497.68
South Dakota	88	133.75	219	185	488	127	191.97
Tennessee	577	145.20	1,868	1,442	515	326	83.33
Texas	1,438	131.06	7,615	1,180	607	1,227	113.46
Utah	184	177.48	435	361	559	128	124.46
Vermont	88	208.94	212	174	583	60	138.93
Virginia	732	159.16	2,829	1,875	615	505	113.90
Washington	879	268.21	2,472	1,980	751	368	114.41
West Virginia	321	177.60	630	513	509	129	71.12
Wisconsin	991	235.12	3,354	2,364	697	635	150.88
Wyoming	69	218.00	145	119	681	59	184.95
Total U.S.	36,414‡	182.94	187,920§	130,509§	723	31,171‡	157.78

*Federal tax burden is estimated by Tax Foundation, Inc.,by a special formula designed for this purpose, since data on Federal tax collections do not accurately reflect the tax burden by state.

†District of Columbia included with Maryland. ‡Data not equal to total due to rounding. §Includes some collections not allocated by state.

Sources: Tax Foundation, Inc.,U.S. Department of Commerce, Bureau of the Census, *Governmental Finances* and *State Tax Collections*. U.S. Department of the Treasury, Internal Revenue Service.

Living Conditions

Income and Expenditures

Personal consumption expenditures

in billions of dollars

Type of expenditure	1960	1965	1968
Food, beverages, tobacco	87.5	107.2	124.7
Clothing, accessories, personal care	38.3	50.9	64.6
Housing	46.3	63.5	77.4
Household operation	46.9	61.8	75.9
Medical care expenses	19.1	28.1	38.6
Personal business	15.0	21.9	29.6
Transportation	43.1	58.1	72.2
Recreation	18.3	26.3	33.5
Private education and research	3.7	5.9	8.4
Religious and welfare activities	4.7	6.0	7.9
Foreign travel and other, net	2.2	3.1	3.8
Total	325.2	432.8	536.6

Source: U.S. Department of Commerce, Office of Business Economics, *Survey of Current Business.*

Disposition of personal income

in billions of dollars

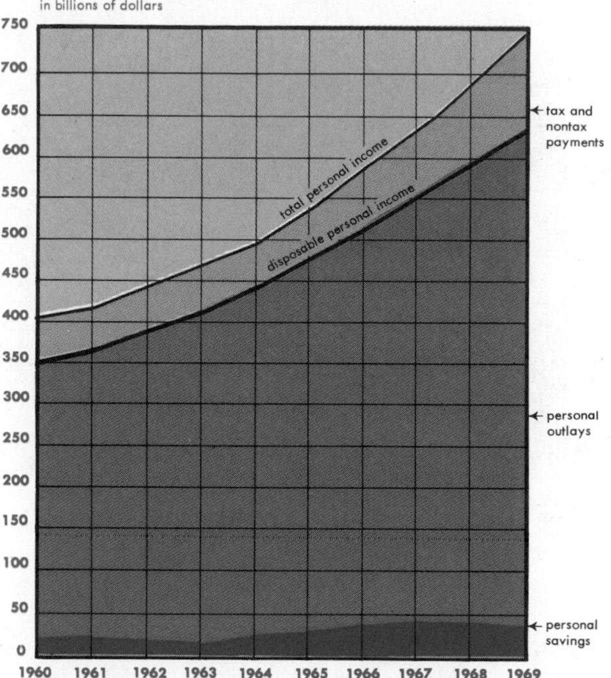

1969 data are for the second quarter, seasonally adjusted at annual rates.
Source: U.S. Department of Commerce, Office of Business Economics, *Survey of Current Business.*

Family income levels

by region

	North-east	North central	South	West	Total U.S.
	(Percent distribution)				
1968 INCOME LEVEL					
Under $1,000	1.3	1.3	2.8	1.5	1.8
$1,000 to $1,999	2.5	2.7	5.6	2.2	3.4
$2,000 to $2,999	4.3	4.4	6.8	4.1	5.1
$3,000 to $3,999	4.8	5.5	8.1	5.3	6.1
$4,000 to $4,999	5.4	5.6	7.4	5.2	6.0
$5,000 to $5,999	6.9	5.9	8.1	6.2	6.9
$6,000 to $6,999	7.5	7.2	8.0	7.5	7.6
$7,000 to $7,999	8.5	8.2	8.2	7.6	8.2
$8,000 to $8,999	8.1	8.4	7.4	7.6	7.9
$9,000 to $9,999	7.7	7.0	6.5	7.1	7.3
$10,000 to $11,999	13.1	13.9	10.4	13.2	12.5
$12,000 to $14,999	13.6	14.0	9.6	13.6	12.5
$15,000 to $24,999	13.1	12.7	9.3	15.0	12.1
$25,000 and over	3.1	2.4	1.9	3.8	2.6
MEDIAN INCOME	$9,089	$9,103	$7,384	$9,368	$8,632

Data do not total 100 percent, due to rounding.
Source: U.S. Department of Commerce, Bureau of the Census, *Current Population Reports.*

Median family income

by year of school completed by head of family, 1968

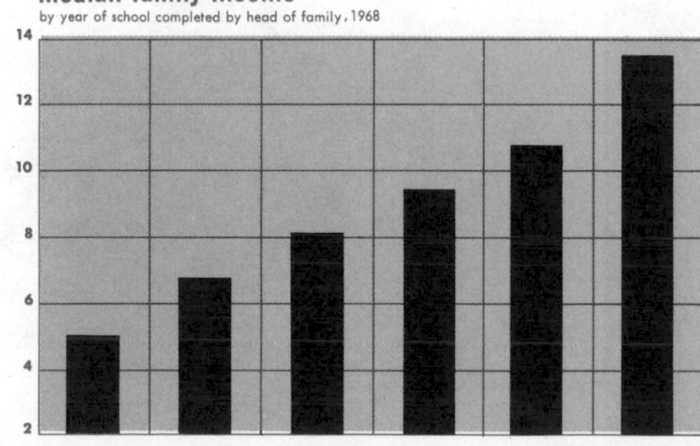

Data are for families with head 25 years old and over.
Source: U.S. Department of Commerce, Bureau of the Census, *Current Population Reports.*

Average employee earnings

September figures

Industry	AVERAGE WEEKLY EARNINGS 1968	1969	AVERAGE HOURLY EARNINGS 1968	1969
MANUFACTURING	$125.25	$132.84	$3.04	$3.24
Durable goods	135.01	143.45	3.23	3.44
Ordnance and accessories	137.85	141.29	3.29	3.48
Lumber and wood products	109.03	113.65	2.64	2.82
Furniture and fixtures	104.33	109.08	2.52	2.68
Stone, clay, and glass products	129.93	138.13	3.05	3.25
Primary metal industries	148.68	162.93	3.60	3.87
Fabricated metal products	136.43	142.38	3.21	3.39
Nonelectrical machinery	143.40	155.00	3.39	3.63
Electrical equipment and supplies	120.66	127.70	2.95	3.13
Transportation equipment	160.07	167.11	3.74	3.96
Instruments and related products	123.22	132.16	3.02	3.20
Nondurable goods	112.03	118.00	2.78	2.95
Food and kindred products	116.48	124.02	2.80	2.96
Tobacco manufactures	94.49	98.81	2.38	2.54
Textile mill products	94.02	98.16	2.26	2.40
Apparel and related products	82.26	84.37	2.26	2.35
Paper and allied products	135.60	142.99	3.11	3.31
Printing and publishing	137.35	144.75	3.54	3.75
Chemicals and allied products	138.60	146.37	3.30	3.51
Petroleum and coal products	162.49	174.15	3.77	4.05
Rubber and plastics products	125.46	129.58	2.98	3.13
Leather and leather products	85.43	87.58	2.26	2.38
NONMANUFACTURING				
Metal mining	153.30	160.70	3.50	3.72
Coal mining	152.31	163.94	3.77	4.14
Oil and gas extraction	140.28	150.77	3.27	3.45
Contract construction	173.76	192.57	4.49	4.90
Local and suburban transportation	124.98	136.40	2.99	3.24
Telephone communication	127.48	134.64	3.14	3.30
Electric, gas, and sanitary services	153.55	164.32	3.70	3.95
Wholesale trade	124.22	131.86	3.09	3.28
Retail trade	75.99	79.45	2.19	2.33
Hotels, tourist courts, and motels	59.29	64.73	1.67	1.86

Source: U.S. Department of Labor, Bureau of Labor Statistics, *Employment and Earnings.*

Employment

Trends in the labor force

in millions of persons

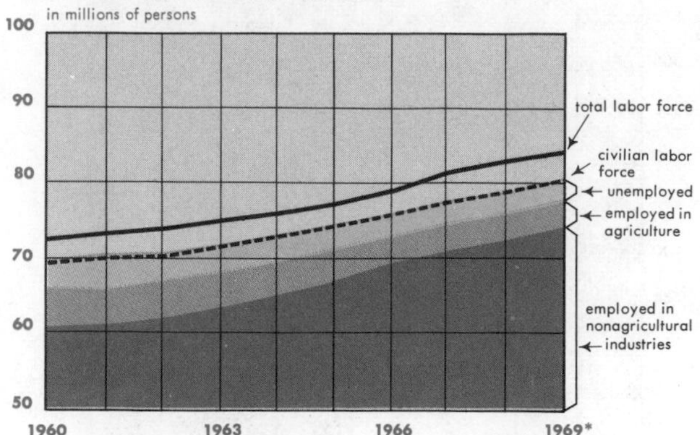

Graph includes persons 16 years of age and over.
*Average of first three quarters only.
Source: U.S. Department of Labor, Bureau of Labor Statistics, *Employment and Earnings*.

Work stoppages

Year	Number	Average duration (calendar days)	WORKERS INVOLVED: Number* (in 000)	WORKERS INVOLVED: Percent of total employed†	MAN-DAYS IDLE DURING YEAR: Number (in 000)	MAN-DAYS IDLE DURING YEAR: Percent of estimated working time‡	MAN-DAYS IDLE DURING YEAR: Per worker involved
1940	2,508	20.9	577	1.7	6,700	0.08	11.6
1945	4,750	9.9	3,470	8.2	38,000	0.31	11.0
1950	4,843	19.2	2,410	5.1	38,800	0.33	16.1
1955	4,320	18.5	2,650	5.2	28,200	0.22	10.7
1960	3,333	23.4	1,320	2.4	19,100	0.14	14.5
1962	3,614	24.6	1,230	2.2	18,600	0.13	15.0
1963	3,362	23.0	941	1.1	16,100	0.11	17.1
1964	3,655	22.9	1,640	2.7	22,900	0.15	14.0
1965	3,963	25.0	1,550	2.5	23,300	0.15	15.1
1966	4,405	22.2	1,960	3.0	25,400	0.18	12.9
1967	4,595	22.8	2,870	4.3	42,100	0.25	14.7
1968	5,045	24.5	2,649	3.8	49,018	0.32	18.5

Beginning date of stoppage determines year. Exclude work stoppages involving fewer than 6 workers or lasting less than one day. Prior to 1960, data exclude Alaska and Hawaii.
*Workers counted more than once if involved in more than one work stoppage during year. †Includes agricultural wage and salaried workers. ‡Estimated working time computed by multiplying average number of employed workers by number of days worked by most employees.
Source: U.S. Dept. of Commerce, Bureau of the Census, *Statistical Abstract of the United States*. Data compiled by U.S. Dept. of Labor, Bureau of Labor Statistics, *Monthly Labor Review*, and annual bulletin, *Analysis of Work Stoppages*.

Nonagricultural employment

in thousands, August 1969

State	Total	Mining	Contract construction	Manufacturing	Transportation and public utilities	Wholesale and retail trade	Finance, insurance, and real estate	Services	Government
Alabama	988	8	59	317	55	184	41	131	193
Alaska	96	4	10	11	9	14	3	11	34
Arizona	513	19	34	94	29	115	27	85	110
Arkansas	539	5	38	168	31	105	21	73	98
California	6,934	33	279	1,694	473	1,506	367	1,219	1,362
Colorado	715	13	38	115	52	171	37	125	163
Connecticut	1,162	*	57	461	51	210	69	171	142
Delaware	213	†	15	76	11	43	9	30	29
District of Columbia‡	704	†	18	20	32	87	32	138	376
Florida	1,969	8	169	305	146	509	121	354	356
Georgia	1,508	7	85	477	106	312	72	172	278
Hawaii	280	†	22	30	23	63	16	53	72
Idaho	204	3	11	40	14	49	8	32	47
Illinois	4,416	25	223	1,408	296	941	232	685	606
Indiana	1,871	8	105	743	100	358	75	208	274
Iowa	878	4	47	222	52	208	41	141	163
Kansas	677	11	43	138	53	156	30	98	147
Kentucky	894	28	62	244	62	184	35	125	155
Louisiana	1,061	53	90	181	97	231	48	153	206
Maine	335	†	17	119	18	64	12	44	61
Maryland§	1,288	2	91	286	79	294	69	234	233
Massachusetts	2,271	†	103	688	116	473	127	463	301
Michigan	3,026	13	124	1,156	153	579	116	399	486
Minnesota	1,310	17	77	331	88	309	63	205	221
Mississippi	564	6	36	180	29	103	20	64	126
Missouri	1,642	9	73	462	126	362	89	253	266
Montana	208	6	13	25	18	49	8	33	56
Nebraska	473	2	28	89	37	117	28	77	95
Nevada	197	4	12	8	14	37	7	80	35
New Hampshire	268	‖	14	99	11	50	10	52	31
New Jersey	2,582	3	120	899	173	522	116	399	348
New Mexico	288	18	18	20	20	61	12	56	84
New York	7,207	9	286	1,896	506	1,423	600	1,339	1,148
North Carolina	1,689	3	98	704	91	302	68	204	220
North Dakota	157	2	11	9	13	44	7	29	44
Ohio	3,911	20	202	1,470	229	759	156	547	527
Oklahoma	750	40	37	130	53	165	36	110	178
Oregon	718	2	37	192	51	160	35	108	134
Pennsylvania	4,356	40	215	1,581	275	807	186	668	584
Rhode Island	346	†	14	127	16	67	15	54	53
South Carolina	787	1	50	334	35	131	28	77	130
South Dakota	173	2	10	16	10	47	7	31	49
Tennessee	1,311	7	73	472	65	246	54	174	220
Texas	3,613	108	234	744	267	848	189	576	647
Utah	353	13	16	56	24	80	14	54	95
Vermont	153	1	11	45	8	28	5	31	24
Virginia§	1,426	14	104	365	97	289	66	208	282
Washington	1,130	1	64	286	75	250	59	170	234
West Virginia	514	47	27	133	42	92	15	63	93
Wisconsin	1,533	3	75	531	80	322	61	221	240
Wyoming	115	12	8	7	12	26	4	18	27
Total U.S.¶	70,607	647	3,707	20,435	4,533	14,660	3,642	11,253	11,730

*Combined with construction. †Combined with services. ‡Data as of July, 1969.
§Federal employment in Maryland and Virginia sectors of the Washington Standard Metropolitan Statistical Area is included in data for District of Columbia.
‖Less than 1,000.
¶Totals differ from the sum of the state figures because methods of computation vary.
Source: U.S. Department of Labor, Bureau of Labor Statistics, *Employment and Earnings*.

Women in the labor force

marital status in percentage

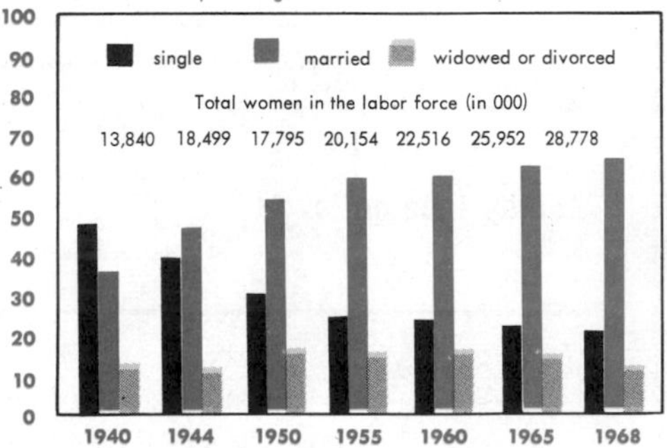

Persons 14 years old and over except 1968, persons 16 years old and over.
Prior to 1960, excludes Alaska and Hawaii.
Includes institutional population.
Source: U.S. Department of Commerce, Bureau of the Census, *Statistical Abstract of the United States*.

Unemployment trends

quarterly averages, seasonally adjusted

Percent

service workers

blue-collar workers

farm workers

white-collar workers

1 2 3 4 1966 · 1 2 3 4 1967 · 1 2 3 4 1968 · 1 2 3 1969

Source: U.S. Department of Labor, Bureau of Labor Statistics, *Monthly Labor Review*.

Prices

Purchasing power of the dollar

1957-59=$1.00

Year	Wholesale prices	Consumer prices
1940	$2.326	$2.048
1945	1.727	1.595
1950	1.152	1.194
1955	1.073	1.071
1960	.993	.971
1961	.997	.960
1962	.994	.949
1963	.997	.937
1964	.995	.925
1965	.976	.910
1966	.945	.884
1967	.943	.860
1968	.920	.825
1969*	.893	.794

Prior to 1961, wholesale prices exclude data for Alaska and Hawaii; prior to 1964, consumer prices exclude data for those states.
*Data are average of first six months only.
Source: U.S. Department of Commerce, Office of Business Economics, *Survey of Current Business.*

Retail food prices

in cents per pound, except as indicated

Commodity and unit	1940	1950	1960	1969*
Cereals and bakery products				
Flour, wheat	4.3	9.8	11.1	11.6
Corn flakes (12 oz.)	10.7	18.5	25.8	31.3
Bread, white	8.0	14.3	20.3	22.9
Meats, poultry, and fish				
Steak, round	36.4	93.6	105.5	119.0
Hamburger	...	56.6	52.4	58.0
Pork chops, center cut	27.9	75.4	85.8	104.7
Bacon, sliced	27.3	63.7	65.5	80.8
Frying chickens	...	59.5	42.7	41.1
Ocean perch, fillet, frozen	...	...	47.4	53.8
Dairy products				
Milk, fresh (grocery)	11.5	19.3	24.7	27.3
Butter	36.0	72.9	74.9	84.1
Cheese, Am. process	25.9	51.8	68.6	91.2
Fruits and vegetables				
Apples	5.2	12.0	16.2†	24.3
Oranges, size 200 (doz.)	29.1	49.3	74.8	82.9
Potatoes	2.4	4.6	7.2	7.8
Tomatoes	...	24.3	31.6	44.0
Peas, green, can	10.6	...	20.7	21.6
Other				
Eggs, Grade A, large (doz.)	33.1	60.4	57.3	60.1
Margarine	15.9	30.8	26.9	27.8
Sugar	5.2	9.7	11.6	12.3
Coffee‡	21.2	79.4	75.3	75.9

Prior to 1965, data exclude Alaska and Hawaii.
*March, 1969.
†11-month average. ‡Beginning 1960, vacuum-pack can only.
Source: U.S. Department of Commerce, Bureau of the Census, *Statistical Abstract of the United States.* Data compiled by the U.S. Department of Labor, Bureau of Labor Statistics, *Retail Food Prices by Cities* and *Estimated Retail Food Prices by Cities.*

Medical care prices

1957-59=100

	PROFESSIONAL SERVICES							
Year	Physicians' fees	Obstetrical case	Tonsillectomy and adenoidectomy	Dentists' fees	Optometric examination and eyeglasses	Drugs and prescriptions	Hospital daily service charges	Total medical care
1940	54.5	43.6	55.8	53.5	70.8	69.3	25.4	50.3
1945	63.3	54.3	65.5	63.3	77.8	73.2	32.5	57.5
1950	76.0	67.7	81.5	81.5	89.5	86.6	57.8	73.4
1955	90.0	90.8	92.7	93.1	93.8	92.7	83.0	88.6
1960	106.0	105.0	107.9	104.7	103.7	102.3	112.7	108.1
1961	108.7	107.3	110.0	105.2	107.0	101.1	121.3	111.3
1962	111.9	110.7	112.5	108.0	108.6	99.6	129.8	114.2
1963	114.4	112.5	115.3	111.1	109.3	98.7	138.0	117.0
1964	117.3	115.2	118.7	114.0	110.7	98.4	144.9	119.4
1965	121.5	117.8	122.2	117.6	113.0	98.1	153.3	122.3
1966	128.5	123.0	127.5	121.4	116.1	98.4	168.0	127.7
1967	137.6	132.3	134.3	127.5	121.8	97.9	200.1	136.7
1968	145.3	139.2	140.9	134.5	125.7	98.1	226.6	145.0

Prior to 1964, data exclude Alaska and Hawaii.
Source: U.S. Department of Commerce, Bureau of the Census, *Statistical Abstract of the United States.* Data compiled by the U.S. Department of Labor, Bureau of Labor Statistics, *Price Indexes for Selected Items and Groups, Annual Averages.*

Annual cost of living for a family of four, 1967

based on spring prices in dollars

			SHELTER				
Area	Total budget cost*	Food	Rental†	Homeownership‡	Transportation	Clothing and personal care	Medical care
Urban United States	9,076	2,105	1,271	1,903	872	985	477
Atlanta	8,328	1,988	1,125	1,418	856	961	443
Baltimore	8,685	1,992	1,358	1,536	846	954	458
Boston	9,973	2,272	1,397	2,514	869	978	476
Chicago§	9,334	2,105	1,503	2,273	812	1,002	494
Cincinnati	8,826	2,059	1,171	1,902	859	961	410
Cleveland	9,262	2,048	1,260	2,306	859	1,009	436
Detroit	8,981	2,138	1,126	1,783	855	1,011	472
Honolulu	10,902	2,489	1,796	2,408	1,034	960	474
Houston	8,301	2,020	1,086	1,441	913	902	487
Kansas City	8,965	2,088	1,269	1,725	925	1,003	451
Los Angeles-Long Beach	9,326	2,066	1,422	1,813	881	1,039	635
Milwaukee	9,544	2,032	1,323	2,235	870	996	450
Minneapolis-St. Paul	9,399	2,027	1,363	2,000	886	1,000	445
New York§	9,977	2,330	1,324	2,440	771	1,024	512
Philadelphia	9,079	2,264	1,070	1,859	788	992	467
Pittsburgh	8,764	2,169	1,104	1,639	846	980	459
St. Louis	9,140	2,156	1,266	1,912	898	1,001	446
San Diego	9,209	2,015	1,249	1,920	910	901	507
San Francisco-Oakland	9,774	2,163	1,617	2,025	923	1,093	555
Seattle	9,550	2,229	1,529	1,922	994	1,082	499
Washington, D.C.	9,273	2,118	1,357	1,976	871	972	469

Refers to annual cost of a moderate living standard for a family comprising a 38 year old employed husband, wife not employed outside home, 8 year old girl, and 13 year old boy.
*Includes personal income and social security taxes, occupational expenses, gifts and contributions and basic life insurance. †Average contract rent plus cost of heating fuel, gas, electricity, water, specified equipment, and insurance on household contents. ‡Interest and principal payments plus taxes, insurance on house and contents, and cost of refuse disposal, heating fuel, gas, electricity, water, specified equipment, and home repair and maintenance. §Standard Consolidated Area.
Source: U.S. Department of Labor, Bureau of Labor Statistics, *Monthly Labor Review.*

Consumer prices by commodity groups

1957-59=100

Commodity	1950	1955	1960	1965	1967	1968	1969*
Food	85.8	94.0	101.4	108.8	115.2	119.3	125.5
Food away from home	...	91.8	105.5	117.8	129.6	136.3	143.7
Food at home	85.8	94.4	100.6	107.2	112.3	115.9	121.8
Housing	83.2	94.1	103.1	108.5	114.3	119.1	126.3
Rent	79.1	94.8	103.1	108.9	112.4	115.1	118.5
Home ownership	...	92.6	103.7	111.4	120.2	127.0	138.7
Fuel and utilities	...	92.8	104.5	107.2	109.0	110.4	112.7
Household furnishings and operation	...	97.3	101.5	103.1	108.2	113.0	117.9
Apparel and upkeep	90.1	95.9	102.2	106.8	114.0	120.1	127.0
Transportation	79.0	89.7	103.8	111.1	115.9	119.6	124.6
Private	82.6	89.9	103.2	109.7	113.9	117.3	121.8
Public	64.6	89.0	107.0	121.4	132.1	138.2	149.1
Health and recreation	...	91.4	105.4	115.6	123.8	130.0	136.3
Medical care	73.4	88.6	108.1	122.3	136.7	145.0	155.2
Personal care	78.9	90.0	104.1	109.9	115.5	120.3	126.2
Reading and recreation	89.3	92.1	104.9	115.2	120.1	125.7	130.4
Other goods and services	82.6	94.3	103.8	111.4	118.2	123.6	154.3
All items	83.8	93.3	103.1	109.9	116.3	121.2	127.6

Prior to 1960, data exclude Alaska and Hawaii. *6-month average.
Sources: U.S. Dept. of Commerce, Bureau of the Census, *Statistical Abstract of the United States;* U.S. Dept. of Labor, Bureau of Labor Statistics, *Monthly Labor Review.*

Housing

Homes with selected electrical appliances

number of wired homes in millions

Product	1953 Number	1953 Percent	1960 Number	1960 Percent	1965 Number	1965 Percent	1968 Number	1968 Percent	1969 Number	1969 Percent
Total number of wired homes	42.3	100.0	50.6	100.0	56.4	100.0	60.1	100.0	61.3	100.0
Air conditioners, room	0.6	1.3	6.5	12.8	11.4	20.2	22.0	36.7	26.1	42.5
Bed coverings	3.6	8.6	10.8	21.3	18.3	32.4	25.4	42.3	28.0	45.6
Blenders	1.5	3.5	3.8	7.5	6.2	11.0	12.0	20.0	15.9	25.9
Can openers	...	...	...	...	11.1	19.7	20.7	34.5	24.2	39.4
Coffee makers	21.6	51.0	27.0	53.4	38.6	68.5	47.8	79.6	50.8	82.9
Dishwashers	1.3	3.0	3.2	6.3	6.7	11.8	10.9	18.1	12.7	20.8
Dryers, clothes*	1.5	3.6	9.0	17.8	13.7	24.2	20.8	34.6	23.8	38.8
Food disposers	1.4	3.3	4.8	9.5	7.6	13.5	10.8	18.0	12.6	20.5
Freezers	4.9	11.5	11.2	22.1	15.1	26.7	16.3	27.2	17.5	28.5
Fry pans	...	...	20.6	40.7	27.6	49.0	31.1	51.8	32.7	53.4
Irons	37.9	89.6	44.9	88.6	55.4	98.3	59.6	99.3	61.0	99.5
Mixers	12.6	29.7	27.0	53.4	39.7	70.4	47.1	78.5	49.3	80.5
Radios	43.7	96.2	50.0	96.1	55.2	97.9	59.8	99.5	61.1	99.7
Ranges										
Free-standing	10.2	24.1	15.3	30.3	18.0	31.9	20.5	34.1	22.2	36.2
Built-in			2.7	5.3	5.4	9.5	7.7	12.9	8.4	13.7
Refrigerators	37.8	89.2	49.6	98.0	56.0	99.3	59.9	99.7	61.1	99.8
Television										
Black and white	19.8	46.7	45.5	89.9	53.1	94.1	58.9	98.1	60.3	98.5
Color	—	—	...	...	2.9	5.1	15.7	26.2	21.9	35.7
Toasters	30.0	70.9	35.6	70.4	45.8	81.1	52.6	87.6	54.7	89.3
Vacuum cleaners	25.1	59.4	36.7	72.5	45.8	81.2	55.3	92.9	57.1	93.1
Washers, clothes	32.2	76.2	42.0	83.1	49.0	86.9	56.6	94.3	58.1	94.8

Data as of January 1. *Includes gas dryers.
Source: U.S. Department of Commerce, Bureau of the Census, *Statistical Abstract of the United States*.
Data from *Merchandising Week*, Billboard Publications, Inc., Copyright 1969.

Residential rents

1957-59=100, except as indicated

Standard Metropolitan Statistical Area	1950	1955	1960	1965	1968
Atlanta	82.6	97.0	102.3	105.2	111.3
Baltimore	81.4	93.7	103.7	108.7	113.3
Boston	75.1	87.4	108.4	121.3	129.4
Chicago*	66.9	92.3	102.5	105.8	110.4
Cincinnati	73.9	93.2	101.7	103.2	104.8
Cleveland	67.5	90.7	101.3	101.0	104.5
Detroit	72.6	96.4	97.1	95.9	104.9
Honolulu†	...	...	...	102.4	110.4
Houston	91.0	99.4	99.7	99.7	104.2
Kansas City	79.6	98.1	102.3	104.7	107.2
Los Angeles-Long Beach	78.3	95.8	102.4	110.2	114.9
Milwaukee	71.8	96.4	100.8	102.7	107.5
Minneapolis-St. Paul	72.1	93.1	103.2	108.6	114.1
New York*	82.0	92.9	105.9	117.3	124.8
Philadelphia	83.6	92.5	103.3	109.6	115.5
Pittsburgh	81.0	95.8	103.6	107.7	112.5
St. Louis	73.4	93.8	103.3	105.8	109.6
San Diego‡	...	...	...	100.0	108.2
San Francisco-Oakland	72.3	91.5	107.1	122.9	136.6
Seattle	75.2	94.6	103.9	108.5	122.4
Washington, D.C.	84.3	96.9	103.9	113.7	119.5

Through 1960, indexes applied only to families of 2 persons or more in urbanized area. Beginning 1964, indexes represent entire urban area
*Standard Consolidated Area. †Dec. 1963=100. ‡Feb. 1965=100.
Source: U.S. Department of Commerce, Bureau of the Census. *Statistical Abstract of the United States*. Data compiled by the U.S. Department of Labor, Bureau of Labor Statistics.

Mortgage loan interest rates

conventional mortgages on single-family homes

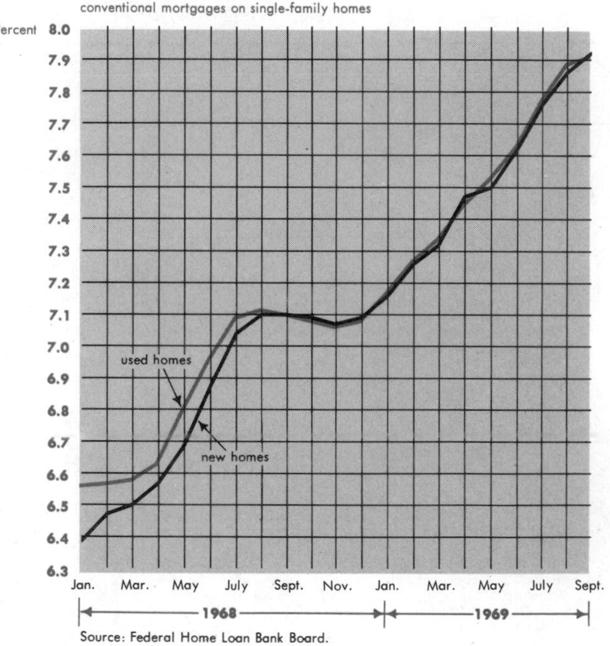

Source: Federal Home Loan Bank Board.

Housing starts

in thousands of units

Year and month	Total	TYPE OF STRUCTURE One-family	Two-family	Multi-family	OWNERSHIP Private	Public	LOCATION Metropolitan	Nonmetropolitan	GEOGRAPHIC REGION Northeast	North central	South	West
1968												
January	82.7	45.3	3.4	34.0	80.5	2.1	63.5	19.2	8.8	15.1	35.6	23.2
February	87.2	55.4	3.8	27.9	84.6	2.5	61.5	25.7	7.5	14.8	43.9	21.0
March	128.6	79.4	4.6	44.6	126.6	2.1	92.1	36.5	12.7	30.1	60.3	25.6
April	165.2	98.0	4.6	62.6	162.0	3.2	118.5	46.7	27.5	45.4	60.7	31.7
May	145.1	87.0	4.7	53.4	140.9	4.3	101.3	43.9	24.5	36.2	55.8	28.6
June	142.9	81.6	6.2	55.1	137.9	5.1	103.7	39.3	22.0	40.1	54.3	26.6
July	142.5	86.5	4.7	51.3	139.8	2.7	100.6	41.9	28.7	36.7	56.1	21.0
August	141.0	82.6	4.2	54.3	136.6	4.4	101.2	39.9	27.2	33.8	55.3	24.8
September	139.8	80.3	5.0	54.5	134.3	5.5	103.0	36.8	26.1	35.1	52.4	26.3
October	143.3	85.6	5.4	52.3	140.8	2.5	101.0	42.3	21.9	37.9	57.3	26.2
November	129.5	65.1	3.8	60.6	127.1	2.3	96.9	32.6	17.2	31.4	58.1	22.9
December	99.8	53.9	3.2	42.7	96.4	3.4	75.1	24.7	12.9	21.6	44.0	21.3
1969												
January	105.8	51.3	3.2	51.4	101.5	4.3	80.9	24.9	12.1	22.0	51.3	20.3
February	94.8	48.0	3.5	43.3	90.1	4.7	73.3	21.5	8.3	21.9	47.2	17.4
March	135.6	72.0	4.2	59.4	131.9	3.7	102.0	33.6	18.7	32.0	54.8	30.1
April	159.9	85.0	4.3	70.6	159.0	.9	117.8	42.0	28.6	40.6	55.0	35.7
May	157.7	91.4	4.8	61.5	155.5	2.1	114.5	43.2	27.4	38.4	58.0	34.0
June	150.8	82.9	4.1	63.8	147.3	3.6	109.1	41.7	26.4	34.1	59.4	31.0

Source: U.S. Department of Commerce, Business and Defense Services Administration, *Construction Review*.

Mobile homes and travel trailers

manufacturers' shipments

Year	NUMBER OF UNITS Mobile homes	Travel trailers	Mobile homes as a percent of total shipments
1960	103,700	40,300	72.0
1961	90,200	40,500	69.0
1962	118,000	57,000	67.4
1963	150,840	72,170	67.6
1964	191,320	90,370	67.9
1965	216,470	107,580	66.8
1966	217,300	122,700	63.9
1967	240,360	130,420	64.8
1968	317,950	158,300	66.8
1969*	189,870	114,240	62.4

*First six months only.
Source: U.S. Department of Commerce, Business and Defense Services Administration, *Construction Review*.

Recreation

Participation in selected outdoor activities, 1965

persons 12 years old and over

Activity	Number of participants in 000,000	Average number of days per participant
Picnicking	80.5	5.6
Driving for pleasure	77.7	12.1
Sightseeing	69.2	6.6
Swimming	67.8	14.3
Walking for pleasure	67.8	15.2
Playing outdoor games and sports	53.7	17.3
Fishing	42.4	7.6
Attending outdoor sports events	42.4	5.8
Boating	33.9	6.5
Bicycling	22.6	20.6
Nature walks	19.8	5.9
Sledding	18.4	...
Hunting	17.0	...
Attending outdoor concerts and plays	15.5	3.0
Camping	14.1	6.9
Ice skating	12.7	...
Horseback riding	11.3	6.8
Hiking	9.9	5.1
Water skiing	8.5	6.6
Bird watching	7.1	15.9
Snow skiing	5.7	...
Canoeing	4.2	4.5
Sailing	4.2	6.2
Wildlife and bird photography	2.8	5.9
Mountain climbing	1.4	3.1

Data pertain to the summer season only, with the exception of hunting and the three winter activities which are for the period September 1964 through May 1965.
Source: U.S. Department of Commerce, Bureau of the Census, *Statistical Abstract of the United States*. Data compiled by the U.S. Department of the Interior, Bureau of Outdoor Recreation.

Overseas travelers

travelers (residents of the U.S. and Puerto Rico) in thousands

	1929	1937	1947	1955	1965	1968*
Total†	517	435	435	1,075	2,623	3,885
Means of transport						
Sea	...	...	...	318	237	147
Air	...	...	...	757	2,386	3,738
Region of destination						
Europe and Mediterranean	350	248	149	482	1,405	1,937
West Indies and Central America	136	153	245	522	891	1,461
South America	8	9	27	34	127	223
Other	23	24	14	37	200	264

*Preliminary. †Excludes travel to Canada, Mexico, Puerto Rico, and the Virgin Islands, cruise travelers, military personnel and other government employees and their dependents stationed abroad.
Source: U.S. Department of Commerce, Bureau of the Census. *Statistical Abstract of the United States*. Data compiled by the U.S. Department of Commerce, Office of Business Economics, *Survey of Current Business*.

Expenditures for recreation

in millions of dollars

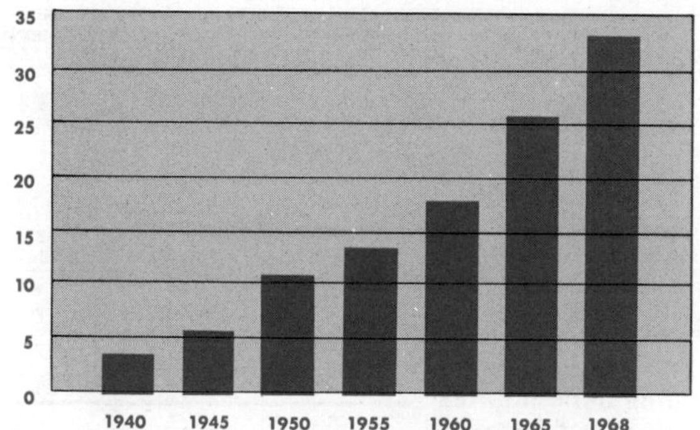

Represents market value of purchases of goods and services by individuals and nonprofit institutions. Prior to 1960, excludes Alaska and Hawaii.
Source: U.S. Department of Commerce, Bureau of the Census, *Statistical Abstract of the United States*.

The national park system

number of visits in thousands

Park	1967	1968
Acadia	2,102	2,303
Big Bend	173	192
Bryce Canyon	295	321
Canyonlands	23	26
Carlsbad Caverns	631	668
Crater Lake	499	578
Everglades	1,098	1,251
Glacier	844	964
Grand Canyon	1,805	1,986
Grand Teton	2,644	2,970
Great Smoky Mountains	6,710	6,667
Guadalupe Mountains*	—	—
Haleakala	103	133
Hawaii Volcanoes	786	918
Hot Springs	1,981	1,914
Isle Royale	9	10
Kings Canyon	910	1,064
Lassen Volcanic	358	443
Mammoth Cave	1,283	1,540
Mesa Verde	435	450
Mount McKinley	40	33
Mount Rainier	1,806	1,683
North Cascades†	...	...
Olympic	1,905	2,014
Petrified Forest	797	869
Platt	1,346	1,707
Rocky Mountain	1,915	2,188
Redwood†	...	...
Sequoia	746	874
Shenandoah	2,133	2,273
Virgin Islands	103	124
Wind Cave	882	962
Yellowstone	2,210	2,230
Yosemite	2,238	2,281
Zion	788	877

*Not open to the public.
†Established October 2, 1968.
Source: U.S. Department of the Interior, National Park Service.

State parks and related recreation areas, 1967

State	PARKS Number	PARKS Acres	Visits in 000
Alabama	53	43,111	2,863
Alaska	63	39,369	...
Arizona	10	25,000	642
Arkansas	29	17,790	8,007
California	197	796,441	35,668
Colorado	44	83,068	2,599
Connecticut	82	24,183	5,195
Delaware	9	5,991	1,888
Florida	70	155,779	6,714
Georgia	46	41,725	6,624
Hawaii	34	8,747	3,245
Idaho	19	22,359	363
Illinois	97	60,354	20,058
Indiana	35	60,041	6,034
Iowa	92	30,451	10,477
Kansas	28	21,625	3,996
Kentucky	35	49,147	18,751
Louisiana	25	13,287	2,310
Maine	44	518,302	1,391
Maryland	38	38,799	6,869
Massachusetts	58	218,255	1,971
Michigan	74	193,228	16,222
Minnesota	99	143,649	4,335
Mississippi	19	13,721	1,736
Missouri	46	77,326	11,287
Montana	34	19,160	500
Nebraska	82	97,000	5,525
Nevada	9	31,828	801
New Hampshire	65	23,749	3,443
New Jersey	86	222,389	6,566
New Mexico	22	15,180	3,642
New York	204	2,919,277	42,310
North Carolina	29	51,316	2,469
North Dakota	66	5,402	339
Ohio	113	130,554	28,316
Oklahoma	47	90,849	12,723
Oregon	210	74,500	18,580
Pennsylvania	217	275,200	24,438
Rhode Island	81	9,100	4,196
South Carolina	28	50,536	2,694
South Dakota	105	87,074	6,277
Tennessee	29	48,445	6,210
Texas	61	61,666	12,300
Utah	35	43,464	819
Vermont	34	11,532	1,442
Virginia	26	29,141	1,693
Washington	172	79,367	16,783
West Virginia	31	58,690	3,098
Wisconsin	58	88,555	6,252
Wyoming	12	126,600	397
Total	3,202	7,352,322	391,063*

The period covered for acreages is the calendar year of 1967. The period for attendance varies. Some states reported for the calendar year, others for the fiscal year.
*Data does not add to total due to rounding.
Source: U.S. Department of the Interior, Bureau of Outdoor Recreation, *1967 State Park Statistics*.

Health and Welfare

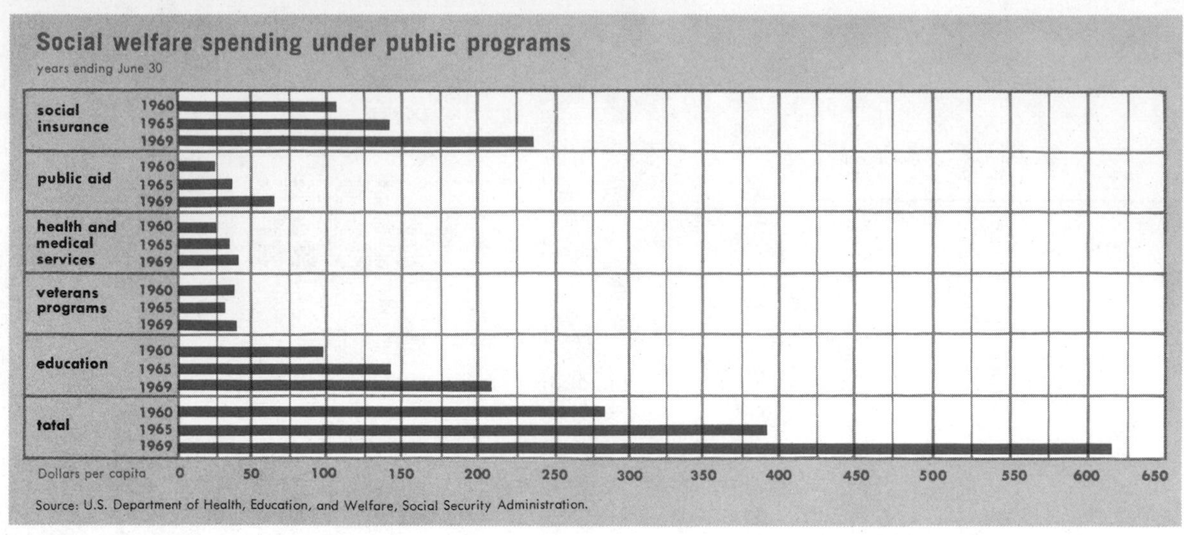

Social insurance beneficiaries and benefits

State	OLD-AGE AND SURVIVORS INSURANCE		DISABILITY INSURANCE			UNEMPLOYMENT INSURANCE State programs	
	Benefi-ciaries Jan. 1, 1969	Benefits for year ending Jan. 1, 1969 in $000	Benefi-ciaries Jan. 1, 1969	Benefits for year ending Jan. 1, 1969 in $000	Medicare enrollment* July 1, 1968	Benefi-ciaries† June 30, 1969	Benefits for year ending June 30, 1969 in $000
Alabama	371,911	310,780	60,269	51,887	314,676	8,880	21,589
Alaska	9,697	9,692	946	937	6,122	2,461	7,528
Arizona	171,451	173,005	22,735	23,016	140,990	2,810	8,588
Arkansas	258,916	205,602	40,899	33,209	230,169	5,522	11,568
California	1,892,680	2,018,119	204,364	226,300	1,721,949	136,651	394,399
Colorado	200,412	199,207	18,695	18,410	183,701	1,947	6,525
Connecticut	306,332	362,567	21,749	25,093	280,837	18,638	59,445
Delaware	50,510	53,623	5,205	5,381	43,616	2,141	6,162
District of Columbia	68,121	66,077	7,103	6,888	70,055	3,585	7,926
Florida	937,213	940,877	90,380	89,307	839,642	11,279	20,484
Georgia	410,227	347,289	74,682	62,325	353,338	7,151	14,237
Hawaii	54,519	52,575	5,296	5,304	41,510	2,600	6,550
Idaho	79,227	77,481	7,553	7,306	66,668	2,384	6,906
Illinois	1,174,251	1,308,192	91,562	102,384	1,086,461	30,762	86,165
Indiana	559,806	597,322	47,911	50,232	487,227	9,496	25,239
Iowa	378,487	379,109	23,807	23,840	352,867	5,407	15,241
Kansas	280,005	277,645	19,386	19,431	264,521	5,580	12,813
Kentucky	384,511	330,986	65,704	53,699	335,317	8,253	19,830
Louisiana	328,708	283,816	60,792	49,244	294,358	17,132	37,084
Maine	129,849	127,579	11,203	10,390	118,147	4,885	10,122
Maryland	318,279	330,725	29,078	30,869	280,933	10,424	30,083
Massachusetts	651,313	733,586	47,295	50,972	630,312	32,403	94,299
Michigan	897,612	992,958	84,301	93,624	747,803	35,945	109,508
Minnesota	446,040	437,806	28,382	28,059	407,409	5,550	23,200
Mississippi	257,111	188,366	42,667	32,512	218,269	3,932	7,564
Missouri	584,497	578,389	56,117	54,086	553,582	16,591	35,298
Montana	80,266	80,678	7,716	7,460	68,367	1,578	4,994
Nebraska	193,633	188,944	11,795	11,511	182,130	1,769	6,216
Nevada	32,872	36,234	3,489	3,909	28,013	2,820	8,378
New Hampshire	86,645	93,038	6,298	6,585	79,588	1,033	2,174
New Jersey	752,918	868,831	62,159	70,778	676,272	46,929	155,060
New Mexico	85,314	74,684	14,355	11,417	68,174	2,849	5,941
New York	2,110,786	2,446,266	182,311	203,915	1,947,537	103,305	288,662
North Carolina	505,386	427,130	75,723	64,952	396,303	14,761	21,951
North Dakota	77,275	70,771	5,641	4,731	66,488	737	4,053
Ohio	1,091,320	1,174,122	105,289	111,087	985,532	16,960	60,771
Oklahoma	302,172	280,221	39,692	35,986	288,168	6,549	11,029
Oregon	250,991	263,019	23,521	25,228	217,956	9,328	23,471
Pennsylvania	1,391,749	1,513,561	132,660	146,689	1,256,677	42,681	120,598
Rhode Island	111,219	122,478	9,879	10,434	102,327	5,769	16,693
South Carolina	239,047	198,038	44,851	37,862	185,060	6,526	12,573
South Dakota	91,238	84,288	6,453	5,642	80,610	511	3,620
Tennessee	429,894	362,538	59,492	51,453	373,329	15,307	27,148
Texas	1,055,845	963,496	117,147	105,797	943,504	14,802	26,418
Utah	86,540	89,992	7,527	7,630	73,281	3,317	9,158
Vermont	53,006	52,801	5,252	4,918	48,628	1,438	4,442
Virginia	415,677	377,278	61,819	55,014	352,202	4,672	8,297
Washington	352,985	377,291	29,074	31,575	313,830	17,001	43,559
West Virginia	235,699	219,187	54,578	49,755	195,646	5,917	12,926
Wisconsin	530,353	552,356	39,445	41,417	466,017	10,029	39,141
Wyoming	33,885	34,469	2,930	2,906	30,259	468	1,713
Total U.S.	22,225,240‡	22,642,180‡	2,335,134‡	2,294,256‡	19,819,390‡	729,465	1,997,339

*Includes hospital and/or medical insurance. †Weekly average. ‡Includes data for American Samoa, Guam, Puerto Rico, Virgin Islands, and for beneficiaries or enrollees living abroad.
Source: U.S. Department of Health, Education, and Welfare, Social Security Administration.

Public assistance

June 1969

States	NUMBER OF RECIPIENTS					AVERAGE MONEY PAYMENTS				
	Old-age assistance	Aid to dependent children*	Aid to the permanently and totally disabled	Aid to the blind	General assistance	Old-age assistance	Aid to dependent children, per recipient	Aid to the permanently and totally disabled	Aid to the blind	General assistance
Alabama	114,000	105,000	17,000	1,900	83	$61.90	$15.60	$50.00	$70.20	$13.25
Alaska	1,500	7,000	620	95	240	89.30	47.85	114.00	120.00	24.20
Arizona	11,800	45,400	6,200	560	5,100	55.50	28.60	65.35	73.35	21.95
Arkansas	60,700	40,700	11,200	1,800	690	53.60	19.60	60.55	67.45	4.40
California	308,000	1,004,000	149,000	12,900	65,000	106.00	49.85	123.00	146.40	46.65
Colorado	38,000	57,200	7,600	200	2,600	78.10	39.55	73.10	81.15	15.15
Connecticut	7,700	78,300	6,000	240	20,300†	90.65	60.10	113.50	93.15	33.55
Delaware	1,800	18,100	1,300	360	5,100	58.20	32.95	96.35	88.95	27.20
District of Columbia	2,400	33,000	4,800	190	1,600	75.60	41.85	88.60	85.75	81.75
Florida	69,400	178,000	20,400	2,300	19,400†	48.80	20.85	61.35	64.00	—
Georgia	90,700	161,000	31,000	3,200	3,900	50.80	24.55	60.60	62.25	17.45
Hawaii	2,000	21,400	1,600	66	3,800	90.00	47.80	123.55	108.10	53.50
Idaho	3,200	13,000	2,800	110	—	64.95	47.70	76.05	78.85	—
Illinois	37,500	337,000	36,800	1,700	58,100	64.50	47.60	86.80	86.70	50.25
Indiana	16,900	60,100	4,400	1,500	—	46.95	32.10	51.50	61.85	—
Iowa	23,400	58,600	2,700	1,000	8,300†	107.80	50.90	133.75	112.50	—
Kansas	14,200	46,900	5,600	370	6,100	78.35	47.20	94.35	82.30	48.40
Kentucky	64,200	123,000	15,000	2,100	—	53.65	29.25	69.95	69.60	—
Louisiana	120,000	178,000	22,000	2,400	7,600	69.30	24.10	53.50	76.60	47.40
Maine	10,200	29,300	3,200	220	5,900	59.80	32.55	85.35	84.25	12.50
Maryland	8,600	118,000	14,900	340	6,600	74.25	39.15	84.10	88.45	75.70
Massachusetts	49,600	181,000	15,400	2,600	24,800	89.60	63.60	106.90	148.05	58.90
Michigan	37,500	217,000	22,900	1,400	68,200	72.25	47.50	93.85	94.10	34.85
Minnesota	22,300	66,100	9,000	800	17,400	65.70	56.15	88.65	80.60	35.00
Mississippi	71,900	106,000	21,500	2,200	1,500	39.40	10.20	48.75	49.55	14.95
Missouri	90,100	124,000	18,100	3,800	12,800	72.20	26.75	74.05	86.65	53.20
Montana	3,600	11,400	1,800	160	2,200	63.30	37.50	77.60	80.30	17.45
Nebraska	8,000	26,500	3,700	340	—	57.65	37.65	67.00	85.30	—
Nevada	3,000	9,400	—	180	—	68.65	32.40	—	90.00	—
New Hampshire	4,200	7,700	750	230	2,000	116.25	44.00	103.70	116.65	24.45
New Jersey	14,700	221,000	11,300	910	8,800	79.70	66.40	102.20	98.90	106.80
New Mexico	9,200	44,800	7,100	370	190	55.60	31.30	70.15	75.00	26.50
New York	86,500	1,005,000	62,000	3,500	204,000	89.85	65.65	103.85	120.45	60.05
North Carolina	38,100	115,000	25,200	4,700	3,300	70.85	28.55	74.80	90.55	12.30
North Dakota	3,900	10,100	2,000	84	670	78.35	50.00	87.90	97.50	13.60
Ohio	58,800	248,000	28,700	2,700	50,400	59.45	39.60	72.15	72.95	37.90
Oklahoma	75,300	88,800	19,700	1,400	2,200	70.00	34.15	93.40	102.60	8.05
Oregon	7,200	52,000	4,800	470	5,000	63.10	43.05	88.25	93.35	31.55
Pennsylvania	44,900	376,000	26,500	8,900	70,800	83.70	52.05	89.60	110.30	72.95
Rhode Island	3,700	35,300	3,600	120	10,000	49.75	48.00	77.55	70.40	25.45
South Carolina	19,000	42,200	9,700	1,900	1,300	45.10	18.50	51.60	57.95	33.10
South Dakota	4,600	15,000	1,400	110	680	61.50	45.90	65.05	84.45	11.05
Tennessee	49,800	114,000	21,000	1,800	4,600	51.05	26.25	65.20	66.70	10.40
Texas	228,000	166,000	20,300	4,100	...	59.25	16.95	59.20	72.15	—
Utah	4,300	29,700	5,200	140	1,300	44.25	37.95	60.95	60.15	73.25
Vermont	4,300	11,500	1,700	100	...	71.55	49.95	89.30	89.65	—
Virginia	11,200	71,100	7,300	1,100	11,500	66.15	38.45	79.15	81.65	29.00
Washington	22,900	79,700	12,900	460	10,700	62.80	48.20	83.35	87.40	52.95
West Virginia	11,200	83,200	6,700	570	3,700	66.85	26.25	56.50	60.10	33.00
Wisconsin	18,200	82,600	6,600	650	14,800	88.45	55.95	74.15	86.35	35.15
Wyoming	2,000	4,500	820	41	400	80.60	38.00	73.40	...	22.90
Total U.S.§	2,036,000	6,558,000	755,000	80,200	769,000‡	70.55	43.85	85.65	95.35	47.65

*Includes children and parents or caretaker relatives in families in which these adults were included in determining amount of assistance. †Estimated.
‡Partly estimated. Excludes Idaho, Indiana, Kentucky, Nebraska, Nevada, Puerto Rico. §Includes Guam, Puerto Rico, and the Virgin Islands.
Source: U S. Department of Health, Education, and Welfare, Social Security Administration, *Social Security Bulletin*.

Low income counties

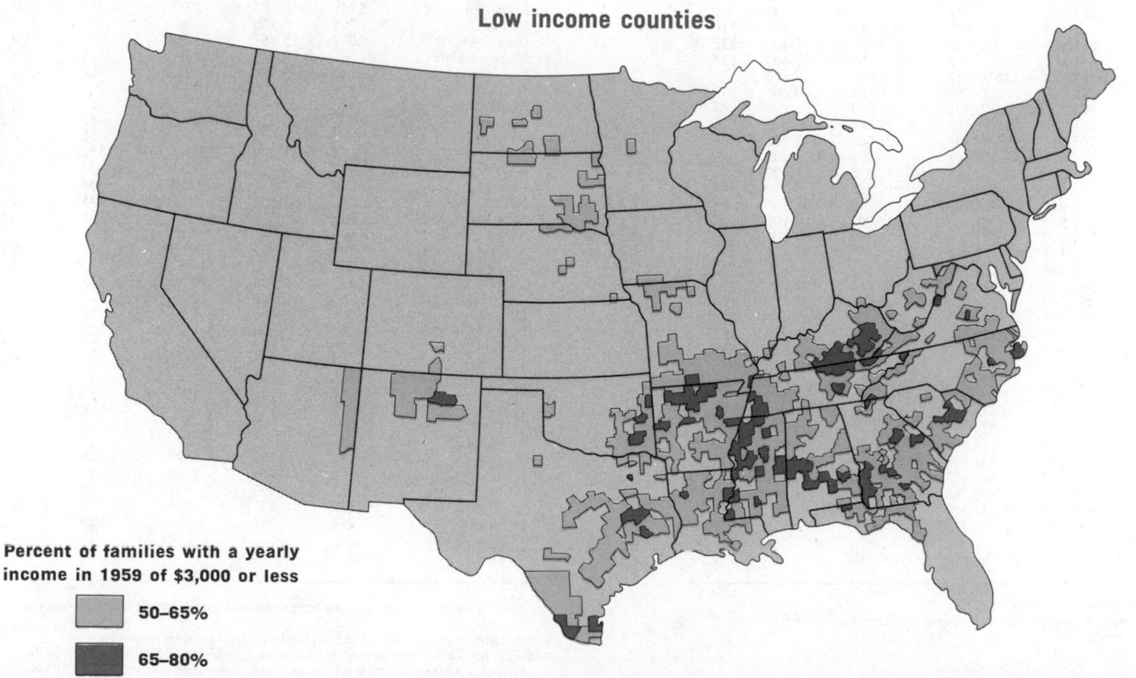

Source: U.S. Department of Commerce, Bureau of the Census, *County and City Data Book*.

Vocational rehabilitation

year ending June 30 ,1969

State	DISABLED PERSONS Number rehabilitated	Number in process of rehabilitation June 30	Total federal and state funds
Alabama	6,074	10,737	$ 15,215,418
Alaska	249	707	933,333
Arizona	1,454	2,685	4,350,445
Arkansas	5,320	9,497	10,164,961
California	14,450	28,038	32,509,672
Colorado	2,898	4,958	5,758,407
Connecticut	2,398	4,836	4,499,385
Delaware	706	1,491	1,361,111
District of Columbia	2,739	4,434	4,694,167
Florida	10,212	20,543	17,402,478
Georgia	10,212	15,292	18,945,872
Hawaii	644	2,109	1,880,000
Idaho	606	1,703	1,386,445
Illinois	13,410	14,725	19,382,622
Indiana	2,551	6,860	3,567,063
Iowa	3,920	10,849	7,804,243
Kansas	1,382	2,083	2,585,894
Kentucky	7,668	8,220	7,866,667
Louisiana	3,406	11,471	10,313,333
Maine	693	1,459	1,675,455
Maryland	6,934	10,299	8,725,806
Massachusetts	3,807	7,280	9,216,831
Michigan	5,499	14,571	15,554,634
Minnesota	3,908	9,863	10,563,418
Mississippi	3,474	5,648	7,061,671
Missouri	5,770	9,478	9,533,970
Montana	780	2,793	$ 1,550,106
Nebraska	1,395	3,638	2,501,110
Nevada	461	863	1,327,778
New Hampshire	420	880	874,667
New Jersey	8,050	9,559	11,987,799
New Mexico	660	1,154	1,547,778
New York	10,250	27,165	32,693,494
North Carolina	9,637	14,337	15,700,821
North Dakota	929	2,133	1,761,111
Ohio	6,869	11,100	12,496,639
Oklahoma	5,350	15,575	9,206,764
Oregon	1,862	4,620	5,134,793
Pennsylvania	16,544	35,894	31,951,232
Rhode Island	1,888	4,414	2,397,333
South Carolina	7,723	13,321	12,841,768
South Dakota	508	1,783	1,517,095
Tennessee	5,244	10,932	9,916,705
Texas	11,861	24,460	25,074,674
Utah	1,667	4,567	3,201,111
Vermont	494	1,004	1,511,222
Virginia	8,086	11,703	12,123,540
Washington	2,557	5,283	7,414,944
West Virginia	5,814	7,319	8,133,333
Wisconsin	8,801	17,572	12,535,322
Wyoming	417	807	1,042,445
Total U.S.*	241,390	461,905	$464,096,286

*Includes Guam, Puerto Rico, and the Virgin Islands.
Source: U.S. Department of Health, Education, and Welfare, Social and Rehabilitation Service.

Maternity and child welfare services

State	FEDERAL GRANTS year ending June 30, 1969: Maternal and child health services	Services for crippled children	Child welfare services	CHILDREN RECEIVING SERVICES March 31, 1968: Total	Rate per 10,000 children
Alabama	$ 977,061	$1,231,408	$1,082,471	11,000	73
Alaska	168,999	174,265	124,799	1,300	98
Arizona	345,465	413,529	487,643	4,200	57
Arkansas	585,553	748,950	621,899	2,000	24
California	2,160,076	2,460,380	3,186,518	58,300	76
Colorado	362,396	419,394	490,407	7,800	95
Connecticut	430,048	482,040	507,550	11,900	104
Delaware	188,996	202,656	158,662	2,800	126
District of Columbia	229,556	228,631	170,744	9,400	302
Florida	1,353,536	1,334,333	1,397,955	10,000	47
Georgia	1,319,346	1,489,794	1,280,397	13,200	68
Hawaii	220,101	232,558	223,760	1,300	40
Idaho	203,814	241,887	248,009	1,400	46
Illinois	1,317,776	1,504,926	1,867,121	17,300	40
Indiana	987,926	1,204,395	1,113,097	17,800	85
Iowa	607,473	765,835	665,078	5,600	51
Kansas	408,121	550,468	549,634	4,400	48
Kentucky	947,140	1,152,008	915,779	10,000	76
Louisiana	1,083,393	1,186,673	1,123,124	14,500	88
Maine	293,682	309,147	308,349	4,400	111
Maryland	838,465	715,448	784,821	21,400	139
Massachusetts	694,603	771,600	1,014,850	11,400	54
Michigan	1,453,924	1,704,257	1,798,690	5,700	16
Minnesota	782,088	933,507	876,176	30,600	201
Mississippi	925,660	1,073,481	832,334	8,900	83
Missouri	851,460	1,026,182	1,015,575	13,300	75
Montana	205,294	226,637	239,267	1,800	62
Nebraska	312,620	396,149	385,666	1,800	30
Nevada	182,272	192,689	142,325	1,200	61
New Hampshire	201,981	218,060	218,566	3,000	109
New Jersey	822,834	951,103	1,184,716	17,600	65
New Mexico	291,940	325,106	364,004	3,900	81
New York	2,142,892	2,211,199	2,853,965	82,800	120
North Carolina	1,526,191	1,915,582	1,424,622	15,600	73
North Dakota	202,875	250,577	237,511	4,800	175
Ohio	1,796,267	2,139,496	2,215,269	37,200	86
Oklahoma	496,724	644,705	646,020	5,700	60
Oregon	388,977	472,505	467,299	9,900	126
Pennsylvania	2,083,414	2,326,922	2,330,654	38,700	87
Rhode Island	225,643	237,692	238,967	3,800	111
South Carolina	932,191	1,090,297	860,784	6,400	55
South Dakota	206,652	257,717	250,633	2,300	81
Tennessee	1,012,463	1,278,322	1,090,940	9,100	58
Texas	2,084,408	2,551,731	2,778,954	17,200	37
Utah	295,188	282,092	348,604	3,100	64
Vermont	174,918	186,950	172,699	2,300	134
Virginia	986,181	1,204,330	1,140,324	18,300	98
Washington	571,045	647,917	666,183	13,600	110
West Virginia	519,183	673,280	531,738	8,600	121
Wisconsin	893,676	1,041,353	982,470	22,300	127
Wyoming	166,283	175,171	141,119	920	69
Total U.S.*	$50,000,000	$57,000,000	$46,000,000	656,000	80

*Includes Guam, Puerto Rico, and the Virgin Islands.
Source: U.S. Department of Health, Education, and Welfare, Social and Rehabilitation Service.

Physicians and hospital facilities

State	PRACTICING PHYSICIANS* Jan. 1, 1969: Total	Engaged in patient care	In other professional activity†	HOSPITALS 1968: Number	Beds
Alabama	2,766	2,619	147	139	28,399
Alaska	168	162	6	26	1,937
Arizona	1,841	1,790	51	80	10,238
Arkansas	1,585	1,505	80	92	11,297
California	31,928	30,204	1,724	639	134,909
Colorado	3,258	3,013	245	92	16,337
Connecticut	5,141	4,735	406	65	24,777
Delaware	656	635	24	14	5,113
District of Columbia	2,890	2,509	381	21	15,093
Florida	7,360	7,006	354	186	43,253
Georgia	4,314	4,034	280	162	34,134
Hawaii	935	898	37	32	6,290
Idaho	610	598	12	54	3,980
Illinois	14,160	13,313	842	314	102,407
Indiana	4,778	4,516	262	138	39,129
Iowa	2,763	2,566	197	144	20,568
Kansas	2,383	2,228	155	166	19,916
Kentucky	3,010	2,795	215	133	22,937
Louisiana	3,941	3,704	237	152	26,891
Maine	955	935	20	58	9,652
Maryland	6,093	5,466	627	84	33,259
Massachusetts	10,504	9,584	920	205	64,543
Michigan	10,180	9,590	590	251	71,415
Minnesota	5,136	4,802	334	206	34,115
Mississippi	1,687	1,603	84	104	16,479
Missouri	5,461	5,030	431	146	39,610
Montana	656	645	11	65	4,554
Nebraska	1,596	1,479	117	116	12,943
Nevada	423	415	8	22	2,756
New Hampshire	849	797	52	36	6,668
New Jersey	9,061	8,688	373	141	52,776
New Mexico	863	788	75	58	5,918
New York	38,829	36,044	2,785	432	204,190
North Carolina	4,937	4,484	453	164	35,567
North Dakota	554	535	19	65	6,238
Ohio	13,234	12,539	695	247	81,275
Oklahoma	2,365	2,240	125	145	15,888
Oregon	2,605	2,422	183	87	15,801
Pennsylvania	16,560	15,380	1,180	321	116,606
Rhode Island	1,289	1,255	34	24	8,700
South Carolina	2,000	1,906	94	84	19,002
South Dakota	507	503	4	61	6,320
Tennessee	4,278	3,946	332	160	32,886
Texas	11,279	10,644	635	558	74,614
Utah	1,298	1,188	110	39	4,772
Vermont	677	590	87	25	4,565
Virginia	4,887	4,538	349	130	38,275
Washington	4,271	3,973	298	130	18,866
West Virginia	1,683	1,590	93	89	15,926
Wisconsin	4,833	4,539	294	202	37,394
Wyoming	293	288	5	33	4,025
Total U.S.	264,330‡	247,256	17,072	7,137	1,663,203

*Excludes data for physicians temporarily abroad, or whose addresses are unknown.
†Includes medical school faculty, administration, and research.
‡Includes 24,015 physicians in government service not allocated by state.
Sources: American Hospital Association, American Medical Association.

Law Enforcement

Arrests, 1968

Offense charged	UNDER 18 Persons arrested	UNDER 18 Percent change from 1967	18 AND OVER Persons arrested	18 AND OVER Percent change from 1967	ALL AGES Persons arrested	ALL AGES Percent change from 1967
Murder and nonnegligent manslaughter	982	+24.1	8,883	+14.9	9,865	+15.7
Manslaughter by negligence	225	− 2.2	2,719	+ 4.7	2,944	+ 4.2
Forcible rape	2,448	+ 2.9	9,525	+ 1.3	11,973	+ 1.6
Robbery	22,479	+22.2	44,850	+15.4	67,329	+17.6
Aggravated assault	16,949	− 4.7	83,553	+ 1.6	100,502	+ 0.5
Other assaults	40,721	+12.9	189,443	+ 7.4	230,164	+ 8.3
Burglary—breaking or entering	133,687	+11.5	109,850	+ 6.4	243,537	+ 9.1
Larceny—theft	240,295	+ 3.0	202,894	+ 9.0	443,189	+ 5.7
Auto theft	72,797	+ 6.0	47,014	+12.7	119,811	+ 8.5
Arson	5,466	+13.6	3,152	+20.3	8,618	+16.0
Forgery and counterfeiting	3,902	+ 8.3	28,643	+ 8.4	32,545	+ 8.4
Fraud	2,437	+ 6.0	51,451	+ 4.9	53,888	+ 5.0
Embezzlement	237	− 4.4	5,029	− 9.1	5,266	− 8.9
Stolen property; buying, receiving, possessing	12,140	+28.6	23,176	+32.8	35,316	+31.3
Vandalism	78,302	− 0.5	26,113	+11.2	104,415	+ 2.2
Weapons; carrying, possessing, etc.	14,175	+16.4	66,060	+20.4	80,235	+19.7
Prostitution and commercialized vice	860	+ 6.6	41,267	+10.3	42,127	+10.2
Sex offenses (except forcible rape and prostitution)	10,829	−12.8	34,778	− 8.5	45,607	− 9.5
Narcotic drug laws	41,617	+104.1	115,526	+52.7	157,143	+63.6
Gambling	1,917	− 6.9	73,720	− 7.7	75,637	− 7.7
Offenses against family and children	528	−46.7	47,001	− 6.9	47,529	− 7.7
Driving while intoxicated	2,946	+11.1	287,688	+12.7	290,634	+12.6
Liquor law violations	62,905	+ 4.6	136,387	− 0.1	199,292	+ 1.4
Drunkenness	35,317	+ 8.7	1,313,974	− 3.8	1,349,291	− 3.5
Disorderly conduct	123,223	+17.9	444,192	+ 6.3	567,415	+ 8.6
Vagrancy	10,690	+20.0	84,470	− 2.5	95,160	− 0.4
All other offenses, except traffic	193,151	+ 7.6	415,106	− 4.5	608,257	− 1.0
Suspicion	21,165	+ 1.0	65,732	− 8.8	86,897	− 6.6
Curfew and loitering law violations	92,769	+ 4.6	—	—	92,769	+ 4.6
Runaways	140,748	+16.0	—	—	140,748	+16.0
Total arrests*	1,364,742	+ 9.7	3,896,464	+ 2.4	5,261,206	+ 4.2

Data are from 4,216 agencies reporting on estimated population of 136,780,000.
*Excludes arrests for suspicion.
Source: U.S. Department of Justice, Federal Bureau of Investigation, *Uniform Crime Reports*.

Rearrests

Age, and type of release	Within 30 months of 1963 release	Within 5 years of 1963 release
	Percent	
Age		
Under 20	65	72
20–24	64	69
25–29	59	67
30–39	55	63
40–49	46	54
50 and over	34	40
All ages	55	63
Type of release		
Fine and probation	30	36
Suspended sentence and probation	47	55
Parole	57	61
Fine	63	74
Mandatory release	67	74
Acquitted or dismissed	83	91

Source: U.S. Department of Justice, Federal Bureau of Investigation, *Uniform Crime Reports*.

Public expenditures and employment for law enforcement

Expenditure (in 000,000)	1955	1960	1965	1967
All governments	2,231	3,349	4,573	...
Police protection	1,359	2,030	2,792	3,332
Judicial	409	597	748	...
Correction*	463	722	1,033	1,119
Federal Government	206	291	377	429
Police protection	129	173	243	282
Judicial	49	74	75	87
Correction*	28	44	59	60
State governments	475	769	1,135	1,369
Police protection	139	245	348	441
Judicial	68	99	155	181
Correction*	268	425	632	747
Local governments	1,550	2,289	3,062	...
Police protection	1,091	1,612	2,201	2,609
Judicial	292	424	518	...
Correction*	167	253	343	392
Employees (in 000)				
Police protection, all governments	265	363	420	458
Federal	...	22	23	25
State	...	32	41	48
Local	244	309	357	385
Correction, all governments	...	...	117	129
Federal	...	...	3	5
State	...	...	71	77
Local	...	...	43	46

1955 and 1960 expenditures are for fiscal years closing during calendar year; 1965 and 1967 are for years closing during the 12 months ending June 30. Employees as of October.
*Includes capital outlay.
Source: U.S. Department of Commerce, Bureau of the Census, *Statistical Abstract of the United States*.

Deaths by firearms

1962 to 1967

State	Total number of murders	Percent by use of firearm
Alabama	2,166	63.5
Alaska	130	62.1
Arizona	531	66.3
Arkansas	855	69.1
California	4,857	52.3
Colorado	501	60.3
Connecticut	303	46.5
Delaware	170	57.4
District of Columbia	788	47.2
Florida	3,132	67.8
Georgia	2,811	68.7
Hawaii	109	48.6
Idaho	132	68.2
Illinois	3,721	57.0
Indiana	991	64.5
Iowa	222	64.7
Kansas	423	66.1
Kentucky	1,158	77.3
Louisiana	1,728	63.5
Maine	95	47.0
Maryland	1,402	51.3
Massachusetts	712	39.9
Michigan	2,073	52.4
Minnesota	312	58.6
Mississippi	1,197	69.1
Missouri	1,586	67.1
Montana	97	70.3
Nebraska	187	67.0
Nevada	221	67.6
New Hampshire	86	63.1
New Jersey	1,310	41.2
New Mexico	360	65.2
New York	4,835	34.9
North Carolina	2,385	70.2
North Dakota	46	29.0
Ohio	2,350	63.6
Oklahoma	776	62.8
Oregon	322	59.4
Pennsylvania	2,173	43.9
Rhode Island	82	34.1
South Carolina	1,539	74.1
South Dakota	88	61.5
Tennessee	1,642	67.1
Texas	5,104	70.7
Utah	124	74.1
Vermont	26	83.3
Virginia	1,763	63.1
Washington	460	55.4
West Virginia	459	64.0
Wisconsin	391	59.3
Wyoming	84	55.4
TOTAL U.S.	59,015	58.2

Source: U.S. Department of Justice, Federal Bureau of Investigation, *Uniform Crime Reports*.

Crime rates per 100,000 population

Unit	MURDER* 1960	MURDER* 1968	FORCIBLE RAPE 1960	FORCIBLE RAPE 1968	ROBBERY 1960	ROBBERY 1968	AGGRAVATED ASSAULT 1960	AGGRAVATED ASSAULT 1968	BURGLARY 1960	BURGLARY 1968	LARCENY† 1960	LARCENY† 1968	AUTO THEFT 1960	AUTO THEFT 1968
STATE														
Alabama	12.9	11.8	8.3	11.1	26.9	41.0	123.2	168.5	368.6	617.5	183.2	420.4	95.6	170.7
Alaska	10.2	10.5	**20.8**	21.7	28.3	52.7	45.1	90.6	332.1	747.3	352.4	778.7	242.3	482.3
Arizona	6.1	6.3	16.1	18.7	54.6	86.7	120.1	151.9	687.1	1,167.4	415.0	936.3	339.6	421.2
Arkansas	8.6	8.1	8.7	17.3	25.0	39.6	56.7	151.7	273.9	514.0	160.2	413.4	46.5	94.2
California	3.9	6.0	18.3	**29.9**	98.0	192.5	120.2	194.6	913.3	**1,644.5**	494.5	1,075.0	328.1	621.4
Colorado	4.2	5.4	13.3	26.1	80.0	96.5	41.0	135.0	579.7	917.0	317.3	800.7	217.5	420.6
Connecticut	1.7	2.5	4.2	8.0	9.5	45.0	21.9	73.7	330.7	964.4	179.0	606.9	131.1	376.1
Delaware	6.5	7.7	8.3	12.7	34.5	101.7	21.1	75.7	557.0	820.4	179.3	516.1	162.7	409.2
Florida	10.5	11.9	8.4	18.1	81.1	159.9	114.7	263.3	829.6	1,327.0	366.1	801.5	198.6	319.9
Georgia	12.0	**13.9**	7.6	13.5	26.6	47.5	98.9	141.0	408.1	660.8	179.4	447.5	153.7	236.4
Hawaii	2.4	2.8	3.3	7.2	10.9	22.6	5.2	52.4	525.9	1,363.8	284.9	796.1	269.9	505.8
Idaho	2.4	2.3	7.0	8.4	13.9	11.8	14.7	51.1	301.3	470.6	265.0	485.5	100.0	118.2
Illinois	5.1	8.1	12.4	16.4	**159.7**	211.5	94.2	172.0	521.4	683.6	340.1	492.0	307.5	441.0
Indiana	4.4	4.7	4.7	13.2	34.4	98.5	37.4	78.0	429.7	691.0	182.8	526.9	162.2	392.3
Iowa	0.6	1.7	3.7	6.8	11.2	25.0	8.7	35.0	233.5	474.1	181.9	431.2	77.1	164.6
Kansas	3.2	3.7	5.3	13.2	20.8	47.5	29.0	85.8	355.4	615.6	168.6	508.7	91.0	205.5
Kentucky	6.8	8.9	5.5	10.2	33.7	60.1	51.8	85.4	376.8	522.5	211.5	455.1	125.7	332.2
Louisiana	8.7	9.5	9.5	16.4	52.8	90.3	78.0	198.4	411.2	678.0	242.8	510.5	225.3	282.6
Maine	1.7	3.0	5.0	6.7	7.9	8.8	10.7	41.8	246.0	452.4	150.7	250.7	117.9	128.1
Maryland	5.5	9.3	7.3	26.0	37.9	**275.6**	90.1	**312.0**	366.8	1,310.2	239.7	764.5	184.3	605.0
Massachusetts	1.5	3.5	5.0	9.5	21.2	74.3	20.1	76.7	309.9	868.3	185.1	545.7	215.6	**806.6**
Michigan	4.3	7.3	12.4	26.5	73.7	210.7	96.0	168.9	592.1	1,106.0	273.9	753.0	178.5	425.5
Minnesota	1.3	2.2	2.5	10.9	29.4	81.2	10.8	45.9	360.1	801.8	218.0	576.1	141.8	351.1
Mississippi	10.0	9.9	5.1	7.6	15.0	13.2	66.0	114.3	205.3	313.7	89.8	180.7	48.4	72.0
Missouri	4.6	8.8	11.0	23.3	76.2	153.6	71.6	143.2	523.4	976.6	231.9	513.3	177.0	446.4
Montana	3.9	3.3	7.3	7.2	28.0	18.2	24.5	59.3	401.3	567.8	269.3	549.1	248.1	198.4
Nebraska	2.3	2.3	4.2	7.2	18.0	49.6	16.5	87.3	231.8	507.4	125.6	391.6	125.8	302.4
Nevada	8.8	5.5	12.6	17.4	74.0	142.8	50.5	112.6	**913.5**	1,282.1	**541.9**	1,010.6	**391.9**	449.7
New Hampshire	1.3	1.4	4.1	2.7	3.0	10.3	4.9	25.4	182.6	371.1	88.5	255.3	57.7	141.3
New Jersey	2.9	5.1	7.9	11.3	46.0	123.6	59.8	96.1	438.6	1,011.9	236.9	671.1	201.9	518.5
New Mexico	7.3	6.2	12.0	20.5	38.7	49.5	89.0	164.7	434.9	925.7	378.4	853.8	371.1	321.9
New York	2.9	6.5	6.3	13.7	44.1	328.4	73.8	187.6	336.3	1,332.4	403.3	**1,104.2**	178.2	571.7
North Carolina	10.1	9.7	7.3	11.0	17.0	35.3	**182.1**	288.4	258.2	499.4	140.2	364.3	78.2	137.6
North Dakota	0.5	1.1	2.2	4.6	6.3	5.8	5.2	16.2	199.2	239.0	93.4	286.7	68.5	80.6
Ohio	3.3	5.3	6.0	12.4	41.6	102.0	34.2	80.7	350.4	659.4	195.4	479.4	138.1	380.2
Oklahoma	7.5	6.4	12.8	15.2	40.2	48.5	36.0	103.1	536.7	689.8	261.0	533.5	199.4	212.2
Oregon	2.4	3.2	9.3	17.2	31.9	76.5	26.0	100.0	406.3	945.1	317.3	818.5	130.9	270.6
Pennsylvania	2.8	4.0	9.0	9.7	36.1	83.2	53.7	73.5	308.8	551.2	149.6	299.2	128.2	275.8
Rhode Island	1.0	2.4	2.3	3.7	14.5	49.3	19.8	81.9	517.3	1,089.6	419.2	646.9	317.3	765.5
South Carolina	**13.3**	13.6	9.4	14.3	20.4	42.8	102.2	146.0	371.4	629.6	205.4	371.2	104.7	176.2
South Dakota	2.1	3.8	5.4	10.2	9.1	19.3	16.0	52.4	247.9	430.1	198.8	359.8	86.6	103.5
Tennessee	8.5	8.7	5.2	11.6	27.8	71.2	50.4	129.0	469.4	719.7	153.5	390.3	132.2	267.4
Texas	8.7	10.6	9.3	14.6	32.8	81.4	111.8	160.9	613.8	932.7	233.1	561.1	168.1	302.9
Utah	1.6	2.9	9.5	11.1	28.1	33.7	34.5	68.5	517.7	741.3	320.1	703.5	207.3	255.2
Vermont	0.3	2.6	2.3	7.3	2.3	6.2	4.6	21.1	242.1	496.0	201.9	168.0	87.7	85.8
Virginia	10.0	8.3	7.3	14.0	25.3	63.5	102.1	149.7	346.3	692.7	212.0	449.3	120.0	248.5
Washington	2.1	3.6	5.9	17.1	31.5	98.4	15.5	93.7	488.7	1,019.5	331.5	843.7	158.0	297.1
West Virginia	4.4	5.5	4.4	4.4	13.5	25.5	35.5	73.2	239.0	349.8	198.4	236.3	71.5	92.0
Wisconsin	1.3	2.2	2.8	6.2	8.5	33.1	16.9	39.2	199.6	503.8	378.1	456.9	106.4	204.1
Wyoming	4.8	6.3	7.0	8.9	53.6	12.4	51.5	60.6	300.2	545.1	331.8	575.9	114.8	136.8
METROPOLITAN AREA														
Baltimore	7.2	13.6	8.5	37.9	56.5	454.5	132.1	**506.1**	424.7	1,675.9	319.2	974.4	245.6	786.8
Boston	1.8	4.4	5.2	10.2	29.4	96.5	28.4	83.4	313.5	831.8	203.0	572.2	262.8	935.7
Chicago	6.7	10.7	17.0	21.4	**237.5**	304.5	134.9	228.2	640.8	759.6	451.4	537.8	442.3	595.3
Cleveland	5.3	9.6	5.3	11.2	81.7	185.7	33.0	89.5	265.0	610.7	125.6	506.0	196.3	838.3
Detroit	5.1	11.3	14.6	34.5	130.6	377.5	159.6	192.7	746.3	1,403.0	303.8	918.5	256.1	674.3
Houston	**10.9**	**14.7**	16.1	21.4	53.7	232.3	149.9	202.3	877.8	1,321.7	312.3	687.0	261.7	542.2
Los Angeles–Long Beach	4.4	8.6	**29.0**	**45.0**	143.9	272.7	**199.1**	319.5	**1,200.9**	1,932.5	**657.3**	1,280.4	**444.3**	846.7
Minneapolis–St. Paul	1.8	3.8	3.9	19.6	62.5	167.0	19.0	81.7	585.7	1,254.3	345.2	867.7	258.2	639.9
Newark	3.8	8.2	12.7	19.7	95.4	266.2	121.0	176.5	663.5	1,455.3	411.9	868.5	332.7	725.6
New York	4.0	8.5	8.4	17.0	64.2	**485.1**	106.9	258.3	414.2	1,707.6	565.0	**1,485.3**	228.4	772.2
Philadelphia	4.8	6.7	16.5	13.5	62.3	115.4	119.4	114.2	430.3	653.2	184.7	337.3	135.9	328.6
Pittsburgh	2.4	2.9	10.6	12.7	47.9	149.9	34.0	88.0	354.9	730.3	212.6	532.8	261.4	589.4
St. Louis	5.7	11.8	17.4	26.8	152.8	220.3	133.0	177.0	785.9	1,238.3	350.7	535.7	279.7	689.8
San Francisco–Oakland	3.5	7.7	11.9	27.5	102.8	377.0	92.9	196.5	739.9	**2,118.6**	335.7	972.7	320.8	**966.2**
Washington, D.C.	6.9	9.5	10.2	21.0	67.3	378.9	183.6	187.8	455.1	1,357.6	270.8	735.8	192.6	725.8

Boldface type indicates highest rate for that crime among the states or the listed metropolitan areas.
*Includes nonnegligent manslaughter. †$50 and over.
Source: U.S. Department of Justice, Federal Bureau of Investigation, *Uniform Crime Reports*.

Prisoners

Year	PRISONERS PRESENT AT END OF YEAR: All institutions Number	Rate	Federal institutions Number	Rate	State institutions Number	Rate	PRISONERS RECEIVED FROM COURTS: All institutions Number	Rate	Federal institutions Number	Rate	State institutions Number	Rate
1940	173,706	132.0	19,260	14.6	154,446	117.3	73,104	55.5	15,109	11.5	57,995	44.1
1945	133,649	100.5	18,638	14.0	115,011	86.5	53,212	40.0	14,171	10.7	39,041	29.4
1950	166,123	110.3	17,134	11.4	148,989	98.9	69,473	46.1	14,237	9.5	55,236	36.7
1955	185,780	113.4	20,088	12.3	165,692	101.1	78,414	47.9	15,286	9.3	63,128	38.5
1960	212,957	118.6	23,218	12.9	189,739	105.7	88,575	49.3	13,723	7.6	74,852	41.7
1961	220,149	120.8	23,696	13.0	196,453	107.8	93,513	51.3	13,517	7.4	79,996	43.9
1962	218,830	118.3	23,944	12.9	194,886	105.3	89,082	48.1	13,514	7.3	75,568	40.8
1963	217,283	115.7	23,128	12.3	194,155	103.4	87,826	46.8	12,882	6.9	74,944	39.9
1964	214,336	112.6	21,709	11.4	192,627	101.2	87,578	46.0	12,482	6.6	75,096	39.4
1965	210,895	109.5	21,040	10.9	189,855	98.6	87,505	45.4	12,781	6.6	74,724	38.8
1966	199,654	102.7	19,245	9.9	180,409	92.8	77,857	40.0	11,508	5.9	66,349	34.1
1967	194,896	99.1	19,579	10.0	175,317	89.2	77,850	39.6	11,447	5.8	66,403	33.8

Rate per 100,000 estimated civilian population, excluding Alaska and, prior to 1960, Hawaii. Excludes state institutions in Alaska and, prior to 1960, those in Hawaii.
Source: U.S. Department of Justice, Bureau of Prisons, *National Prisoner Statistics*.

Education

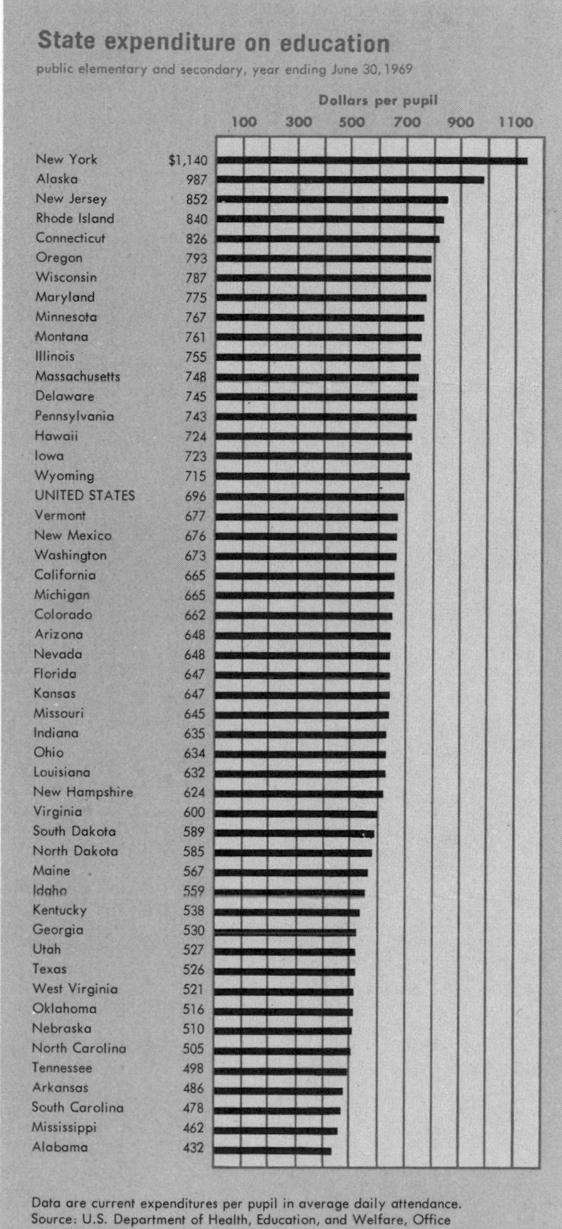

Data are current expenditures per pupil in average daily attendance.
Source: U.S. Department of Health, Education, and Welfare, Office of Education.

Vocational education

Type of program	NUMBER OF STUDENTS 1959–60	1964–65	1967–68
Agriculture	796,237	887,529	851,158
Distributive occupations	303,784	333,342	574,785
Home economics	1,588,109	2,098,520	2,283,338
Trades and industry	938,490	1,087,807	1,628,542
Health occupations	40,250	66,772	140,987
Technical education	101,279	225,737	269,832
Office occupations	—	730,904	1,735,997
Total	3,768,149	5,430,611	7,533,936

Data refer to vocational programs receiving federal aid.
Source: U.S. Department of Health, Education, and Welfare, Office of Education, *Digest of Educational Statistics*.

Federal funds supporting education

in thousands of dollars

Funds	Year ending June 30, 1960	Year ending June 30, 1969*	Year ending June 30, 1970*
Supporting education in educational institutions			
Grants, total	$1,512,329	$7,754,427	$8,559,128
Elementary-secondary education	507,170	2,765,875	3,009,761
Higher education	734,718	3,754,515	4,094,908
Adult, vocational technical, and continuing education (not classifiable by level)	270,441	1,234,037	1,454,459
Loans, total	222,305	569,027	548,766
Elementary-secondary education	394	—	—
Higher education	221,911	569,027	548,766
Vocational-technical and adult education	...	...	...
Other funds for education and related activities			
Research and development†	545,585	1,287,641	1,288,000
School services	307,926	622,913	653,466
Training of federal personnel	67,738	1,240,164	1,320,807
Library services	18,980	159,098	154,602
International education	53,359	323,318	330,481
Other	62,633	351,404	377,007

*Estimated data.
†Includes funds for applied research.
Source: U.S. Department of Health, Education, and Welfare, Office of Education, *Digest of Educational Statistics.*

Characteristics of high school graduates and dropouts

based on civilian noninstitutional population (16 to 21 yrs. old) as of Oct., 1968

	Graduates		Dropouts	
	Male	Female	Male	Female
Occupation group of employed	100%	100%	100%	100%
Professional, technical, and kindred workers	6.7	6.6	1.1	1.4
Clerical and kindred workers	10.7	54.4	4.5	14.3
Sales workers	3.5	5.3	1.2	5.7
Craftsmen, foremen, and kindred workers	17.0	—	12.7	—
Operatives and kindred workers	33.6	10.4	39.8	36.7
Service workers, including private household	6.0	16.2	7.6	35.1
Farm laborers and foremen	3.5	.5	10.7	3.5
Laborers, except farm and mine	13.6	—	21.5	—
Others	5.4	1.6	.8	3.3
	White	Nonwhite	White	Nonwhite
Annual family income*	100%	100%	100%	100%
Less than $3,000	5.9	22.4	20.6	41.0
$3,000 to $4,999	10.9	23.5	23.1	33.5
$5,000 to $7,499	22.4	26.9	24.7	17.6
$7,500 and over	60.7	27.2	31.6	7.9

Data for high school graduates relate to those not enrolled in college and include those who attended college prior to survey date; data for dropouts relate to persons not in regular school and not high school graduates.
*Includes only families of unmarried persons living with, and related to, head of household.
Source: U.S. Department of Labor, Bureau of Labor Statistics.

Enrollment in special education

programs for exceptional children

Type	1958	1963	1966 estimate
Visually handicapped	12,000	21,531	23,300
Deaf and hard of hearing	20,000	45,594	51,400
Speech impaired	490,000	802,197	989,500
Crippled and special health problems	52,000	64,842	69,400
Emotionally and socially maladjusted	29,000	79,587	87,900
Mentally retarded	223,000	431,890	540,100
Other handicapped conditions	12,000	22,039	32,500
Gifted	52,000	214,671	312,100
Total	890,000	1,682,351	2,106,200

Data are for February of years reported.
Beginning 1963, includes public and private residential schools; 1958 includes public day schools only.
Source: U.S. Department of Health, Education, and Welfare, Office of Education.

Public elementary and secondary schools

1969–70 estimates

State	Operating school districts	Instruction rooms in use*	ENROLLMENT Elementary	ENROLLMENT Secondary	High school graduates	INSTRUCTIONAL STAFF Total	Principals and supervisors	Teachers, elementary Total	Teachers, elementary Men	Teachers, secondary Total	Teachers, secondary Men	TEACHERS' AVERAGE ANNUAL SALARIES Ele-mentary	TEACHERS' AVERAGE ANNUAL SALARIES Secon-dary
Alabama	120	31,500	464,130	389,207	45,300	35,932	1,669	16,755	935	17,508	6,493	$ 6,745	$ 6,887
Alaska	28	2,880	62,345	27,346	3,220	3,889	194	2,154	476	1,360	729	10,598	10,499
Arizona	294	19,454	335,016	126,148	22,500	19,850	810	12,850	3,265	5,300	3,300	8,435	9,390
Arkansas	384	18,332	253,913	209,445	25,300	20,790	662	10,166	686	9,444	4,297	6,193	6,476
California	1,082	171,400	3,176,000	1,868,000	285,000	210,750	12,750	115,000	23,000	75,000	53,000	9,775	10,825
Colorado	181	21,552	325,000	240,000	30,800	26,550	1,700	12,400	2,000	11,000	6,000	7,400	7,800
Connecticut	173	25,830	436,000	240,000	34,000	35,638	2,567	17,720	3,796	13,035	7,592	8,900	9,320
Delaware	26	5,173	76,500	57,700	7,150	6,244	237	2,857	463	2,872	1,548	8,663	9,137
District of Columbia	1	4,851	99,000	59,000	5,400	8,990	600	4,150	500	3,560	1,270	...	...
Florida	67	47,541	852,974	682,185	72,000	70,600	3,170	32,930	3,790	29,200	14,310	8,180	8,440
Georgia	190	42,211	751,120	406,177	57,059	49,030	2,479	28,131	2,299	18,420	7,414	7,134	7,216
Hawaii	1	7,111	103,000	78,000	10,500	8,603	600	4,415	264	2,943	1,295	9,420	9,500
Idaho	115	7,435	98,000	92,000	12,400	8,567	513	3,808	495	4,159	2,342	6,480	7,240
Illinois	1,221	88,507	1,504,000	814,000	131,033	109,456	3,300	61,227	12,745	42,729	24,004	9,250	10,200
Indiana	322	45,120	716,400	560,000	71,824	56,810	3,700	25,610	4,010	25,000	14,500	8,891	9,402
Iowa	453	30,229	485,526	203,508	43,859	37,770	1,563	17,824	2,317	15,249	9,150	8,079	8,987
Kansas	311	25,869	402,383	161,681	33,646	26,799	1,396	12,328	1,365	11,838	6,904	7,485	7,745
Kentucky	193	25,500	519,000	200,000	37,700	32,478	1,600	17,978	2,467	10,900	4,900	7,220	7,880
Louisiana	66	36,839	559,650	350,350	46,500	42,050	2,050	22,300	2,650	17,700	7,350	6,810	7,220
Maine	239	9,505	173,500	65,500	12,500	11,895	585	7,335	1,520	3,725	2,250	7,380	7,950
Maryland	24	30,673	538,669	390,264	46,300	45,396	2,552	21,335	2,451	19,347	9,142	9,235	9,547
Massachusetts	377	44,148	648,000	487,000	65,300	54,400	3,111	26,137	3,737	22,552	13,000	8,600	8,800
Michigan	635	69,970	1,234,000	963,000	123,000	98,756	4,739	41,740	5,958	51,677	26,626	9,572	10,024
Minnesota	798	37,544	521,000	424,000	63,000	46,500	2,200	21,000	2,730	21,300	13,680	8,450	8,900
Mississippi	148	21,625	345,000	249,224	30,550	24,934	1,320	12,354	954	10,275	4,575	5,747	6,020
Missouri	644	38,221	789,000	279,000	55,300	47,991	2,941	29,719	5,647	13,175	7,440	7,745	7,917
Montana	704	8,387	115,000	66,000	11,000	9,300	410	5,400	900	3,060	1,930	7,300	8,150
Nebraska	1,200	16,586	201,000	139,000	21,100	17,334	720	8,989	500	7,400	3,900	7,074	8,052
Nevada	17	4,772	89,000	56,000	5,700	5,700	340	2,650	510	2,400	1,380	9,213	9,472
New Hampshire	158	6,360	95,400	61,970	8,790	7,687	345	3,720	540	2,981	1,697	7,617	7,837
New Jersey	575	53,954	996,200	500,500	87,200	78,800	4,366	39,700	8,300	27,300	15,600	8,950	9,330
New Mexico	89	11,540	165,000	133,000	15,700	13,346	965	6,355	1,176	5,416	3,087	7,840	7,820
New York	735	136,000	2,030,300	1,550,000	194,100	200,586	15,187	88,389	14,036	84,584	42,630	9,400	10,000
North Carolina	152	50,179	863,348	357,274	67,100	54,012	2,620	33,192	4,412	15,642	6,360	7,284	7,842
North Dakota	375	7,415	106,500	47,500	10,710	7,565	310	4,475	799	2,536	1,710	6,300	7,580
Ohio	641	90,200	1,544,900	926,870	146,300	107,100	5,600	53,500	7,800	42,900	24,000	7,680	8,100
Oklahoma	685	27,253	345,622	269,116	36,000	28,438	1,509	14,146	2,320	12,463	7,749	6,884	7,105
Oregon	345	21,112	298,079	198,720	33,134	25,750	1,550	12,300	2,800	9,500	5,700	8,500	9,100
Pennsylvania	600	83,755	1,280,200	1,089,000	151,200	117,600	5,700	52,000	9,600	53,000	30,600	8,600	8,000
Rhode Island	40	5,803	103,567	78,671	10,652	9,555	507	4,260	724	4,215	2,411	8,778	8,838
South Carolina	93	24,659	400,000	269,000	35,700	31,022	1,347	14,900	900	12,425	4,250	6,550	7,000
South Dakota	663	7,707	119,000	52,000	11,700	9,720	475	5,900	700	2,975	1,975	5,670	7,060
Tennessee	149	33,499	581,585	338,915	48,000	37,950	1,750	20,650	2,450	13,600	5,700	6,935	7,600
Texas	1,210	113,056	2,015,000	754,000	145,000	129,900	6,837	62,625	7,452	55,153	27,080	7,215	7,335
Utah	40	10,486	188,226	140,839	18,500	13,000	750	5,850	1,080	5,400	3,350	7,580	7,650
Vermont	274	4,200	67,867	39,746	5,400	6,430	422	3,053	422	2,501	1,417	7,680	8,320
Virginia	134	47,632	717,500	383,900	58,800	54,150	3,250	30,000	2,700	20,900	8,100	7,700	8,400
Washington	323	32,722	460,000	376,700	50,500	39,100	2,650	17,900	3,680	15,300	5,865	8,700	9,420
West Virginia	55	16,603	233,271	182,873	27,100	18,585	1,700	8,633	794	7,760	3,259	7,490	7,730
Wisconsin	455	37,061	617,440	411,627	64,697	50,743	3,747	25,424	4,831	21,572	13,375	8,750	9,200
Wyoming	156	4,548	48,000	41,000	5,114	4,974	295	2,260	351	2,191	1,389	8,108	8,380
Total U.S.	17,961	1,764,509	29,151,131	18,086,956	2,640,338	2,219,015§	122,360	1,106,494	170,297	892,442	477,625	$ 8,310	$ 8,831

Kindergartens are included in the elementary schools; junior high schools, in the secondary schools.
Enrollment data show cumulative count of pupils registered at any time during the school year in each state.
All dollar amounts for Alaska should be reduced by about one-fourth to make purchasing power generally more comparable to data reported for other areas.
*At the beginning of the 1968–69 school year. †Money received from loans, sales of bonds, sales of property purchased from capital funds, and insurance adjustments.
‡Includes summer schools, adult education, community services, and community colleges and vocational schools when operated by local school districts.
§Includes librarians, guidance and psychological personnel, and related instructional workers.
Sources: National Education Association, Research Division, *Estimates of School Statistics, 1969–70* (Copyright 1969. All rights reserved. Used by permission).
U.S. Department of Health, Education, and Welfare, Office of Education, *Fall 1968 Statistics of Public Schools.*

Private elementary and secondary day schools

fall 1969 estimates

State	ENROLLMENT Elementary	ENROLLMENT Secondary	CLASSROOM TEACHERS Elementary	CLASSROOM TEACHERS Secondary
Alabama	19,900	7,600	840	570
Alaska	1,300	900	70	90
Arizona	24,000	7,200	900	510
Arkansas	8,800	3,300	360	230
California	309,000	98,800	11,430	6,070
Colorado	30,600	10,400	1,400	860
Connecticut	75,900	37,900	2,910	2,920
Delaware	13,300	5,400	480	360
District of Columbia	13,400	7,900	600	640
Florida	67,600	17,200	2,770	1,270
Georgia	17,400	9,400	770	750
Hawaii	17,400	10,200	720	660
Idaho	6,900	1,400	230	100
Illinois	387,200	111,300	12,300	5,750
Indiana	100,800	26,700	3,370	1,480
Iowa	65,400	25,400	2,540	1,470
Kansas	34,700	11,700	1,230	720
Kentucky	62,300	22,400	2,100	1,400
Louisiana	98,400	30,600	3,640	1,780
Maine	17,000	11,900	580	890
Maryland	94,300	31,000	3,300	2,210
Massachusetts	161,100	73,200	5,600	4,670
Michigan	241,200	78,600	7,380	3,970
Minnesota	116,900	29,900	4,290	1,920
Mississippi	14,000	5,600	650	390
Missouri	121,400	37,700	4,210	2,470
Montana	13,000	4,300	490	260
Nebraska	39,500	14,200	1,470	890
Nevada	3,300	1,000	140	60
New Hampshire	21,800	10,800	810	820
New Jersey	231,900	63,500	7,260	3,940
New Mexico	17,000	5,200	670	410
New York	623,300	193,300	22,090	10,790
North Carolina	15,500	4,900	750	490
North Dakota	12,600	5,000	540	350
Ohio	260,000	85,000	8,170	4,440
Oklahoma	13,000	3,700	580	290
Oregon	24,200	7,700	930	550
Pennsylvania	406,500	137,800	12,130	7,260
Rhode Island	35,000	10,900	1,230	710
South Carolina	10,800	4,100	550	320
South Dakota	12,200	4,600	530	360
Tennessee	19,800	12,700	970	940
Texas	116,000	28,600	5,070	2,040
Utah	3,700	2,000	140	160
Vermont	8,500	7,200	320	550
Virginia	38,700	18,800	1,730	1,550
Washington	40,100	13,600	1,410	870
West Virginia	9,800	3,600	360	270
Wisconsin	200,800	43,100	6,870	2,460
Wyoming	2,800	800	120	70
Total U.S.	4,300,000	1,400,000	150,000	85,000

Data exclude subcollegiate departments of institutions of higher education and residential schools for exceptional children.
Source: U.S. Department of Health, Education, and Welfare, Office of Education, *Digest of Educational Statistics.*

Total in $000	Federal	State	Local	Non-revenue receipts† in $000	For day schools	For other programs‡	Capital outlay in $000
REVENUE RECEIPTS	Source of receipts percent of total				CURRENT EXPENDITURES in $000		
408,861	14.5	63.0	22.5	10,000	341,581	2,000	36,950
88,112	25.7	43.7	30.6	28,493	79,541	620	22,000
347,283	8.7	47.5	43.7	28,683	285,195	...	47,233
247,247	17.1	45.5	37.5	25,000	222,968	2,700	30,992
4,430,000	5.2	35.0	59.8	400,000	3,420,000	450,000	550,000
418,700	6.4	25.3	68.3	20,000	348,000	4,500	40,000
635,200	3.7	33.1	63.2	50,000	525,000	4,400	32,000
124,505	7.6	70.6	21.8	27,500	96,200	251	31,700
206,000	30.2	...	69.8	...	141,787	5,700	48,406
1,077,347	9.1	56.5	34.4	11,325	931,917	1,200	257,808
642,789	10.6	58.7	30.7	50,000	617,365	13,852	50,000
171,200	9.1	87.0	3.9	...	141,000	7,100	17,300
118,100	7.7	43.2	49.1	9,000	103,000	160	10,000
2,315,718	5.0	34.4	60.5	237,195	1,735,861	80,250	263,000
1,030,100	4.1	34.9	61.0	120,600	787,700	15,400	194,200
554,258	4.0	30.1	65.9	50,000	552,700	23,000	80,000
449,811	7.1	26.1	66.8	66,932	342,309	17,328	83,000
446,700	13.8	52.6	33.6	50,000	395,000	4,200	33,000
569,570	10.8	58.3	30.9	80,000	503,440	1,260	80,000
175,000	5.4	44.9	49.8	20,000	151,300	4,700	25,000
855,781	6.4	35.2	58.4	110,091	715,783	6,450	175,862
998,400	6.0	20.0	74.0	88,300	783,100	12,100	81,700
1,707,708	3.9	45.1	51.0	240,000	1,674,000	18,500	272,000
841,000	5.4	43.4	51.2	120,000	680,000	8,800	151,900
314,000	22.0	51.6	26.4	10,000	257,000	19,200	27,000
741,323	6.3	34.5	59.2	57,000	648,606	33,000	97,500
145,500	5.8	30.9	63.2	12,000	128,100	2,000	15,200
211,928	6.4	20.0	73.6	14,250	167,500	7,600	32,600
103,300	6.0	39.2	54.8	5,000	87,400	1,600	7,000
110,138	4.2	8.5	87.2	15,800	96,978	680	18,942
1,503,000	4.3	28.5	67.2	120,000	1,300,000	35,000	150,000
204,344	14.0	62.7	23.3	7,364	176,000	5,350	27,013
4,560,000	3.5	45.4	51.1	475,000	3,988,000	202,000	456,000
805,705	10.8	70.9	18.2	38,000	675,722	56,830	60,000
104,900	7.1	27.2	65.8	6,000	87,500	1,700	17,000
1,773,100	4.7	31.6	63.7	240,000	1,540,000	30,000	230,000
349,934	10.0	40.8	49.2	12,000	301,727	2,600	38,000
470,500	5.8	20.6	73.5	42,000	384,956	28,377	59,059
2,214,268	5.8	46.9	47.3	101,000	1,901,000	75,692	146,181
148,674	8.1	34.5	57.5	20,000	146,308	901	12,699
397,774	13.3	61.6	25.1	18,500	335,700	11,000	47,000
106,500	11.3	13.6	75.1	10,000	100,000	300	17,000
521,400	10.4	49.3	40.4	45,000	461,500	9,000	45,000
1,812,200	9.2	42.8	48.0	210,000	1,329,475	12,000	249,900
217,123	5.5	51.4	43.0	8,423	173,407	3,545	29,869
73,665	3.3	28.6	68.1	8,230	78,403	107	11,039
820,000	9.1	36.6	54.3	75,000	690,000	20,000	110,000
680,270	5.9	58.8	35.3	90,000	575,000	50,000	81,000
279,000	12.4	48.2	39.4	6,000	237,700	3,300	27,000
875,285	3.2	29.4	67.4	87,850	771,771	12,262	75,600
72,700	22.3	25.4	52.3	4,000	66,436	...	8,200
38,475,921	6.6	40.7	52.7	3,581,536	32,280,936	1,308,515	4,709,853

Earned degrees conferred, 1967–68

Field of study	Bachelor's degrees*	Master's degrees	Doctorates
Agriculture	6,742	1,492	561
Architecture	2,956	536	6
Biological sciences	32,055	5,517	2,786
Business and commerce	80,440	17,868	445
Computer science and systems analysis	459	548	36
Education	135,848	63,664	4,079
Engineering	37,614	15,188	2,932
English and journalism	52,489	8,654	1,009
Fine and applied arts	25,555	6,563	528
Foreign languages and literature	19,522	4,865	707
Forestry	1,586	315	87
Geography	2,624	549	96
Health professions	17,571	3,718	243
Home economics	7,420	966	71
Law	477	724	36
Library science	814	5,165	22
Mathematical subjects	23,625	5,533	947
Military science	2,029	—	—
Philosophy	5,768	657	278
Physical sciences	19,442	5,508	3,593
Psychology	23,972	3,482	1,268
Religion	4,575	2,724	401
Social sciences	121,643	20,426	2,821
Trade and industrial training	3,173	65	1
Miscellaneous	8,244	1,825	119
All fields	636,863	177,150	23,091

*Includes bachelor's degrees requiring four or five years.
Source: U.S. Department of Health, Education, and Welfare, Office of Education.

Cost of attending college

in dollars

	1959 Public	1959 Private	1964 Public	1964 Private	1969 Public	1969 Private
Tuition and required fees						
Total	192	729	234	1,012	298	1,436
2 year institution	81	392	97	642	121	992
4 year institution	198	734	254	1,031	339	1,477
Board rates						
Total	415	456	435	487	482	544
2 year institution	353	391	361	427	392	534
4 year institution	416	460	436	490	486	545
Charges for dormitory rooms						
Total	190	250	257	316	353	415
2 year institution	130	184	172	244	229	379
4 year institution	190	250	260	319	358	421

For entire academic year ending in year stated. Represents average charges per full-time resident degree-credit student; not adjusted for changes in purchasing power of the dollar.
Source: U.S. Department of Health, Education, and Welfare, Office of Education, *Digest of Educational Statistics.*

Universities and colleges

state statistics

State	Number of institutions fall, 1968 Total	Number of institutions fall, 1968 Public	Enrollment fall, 1968 Total	Enrollment fall, 1968 First-time students	Earned degrees conferred 1967–1968 Bachelor's and first professional	Master's, except first professional	Doctor's
Alabama	45	25	94,850	25,585	9,607	1,695	165
Alaska	3	1	7,193	2,638	204	118	6
Arizona	15	10	90,944	28,079	6,391	2,478	232
Arkansas	21	10	50,615	14,500	5,651	1,028	102
California	193	104	1,103,594	272,528	55,873	15,831	2,576
Colorado	29	19	102,822	24,979	9,572	3,010	549
Connecticut	47	17	106,234	24,896	8,782	3,522	396
Delaware	6	3	18,517	6,212	1,097	354	62
District of Columbia	23	3	69,532	9,573	7,106	3,789	394
Florida	60	34	201,914	55,597	14,868	3,837	496
Georgia	58	27	108,816	24,811	11,460	2,378	235
Hawaii	5	1	25,614	9,118	1,989	825	49
Idaho	11	6	27,789	9,184	2,254	378	42
Illinois	133	40	390,831	106,547	31,802	10,875	1,531
Indiana	42	5	175,904	40,816	18,543	7,531	962
Iowa	51	15	103,516	29,990	12,529	2,095	531
Kansas	51	24	92,486	25,767	10,027	2,657	265
Kentucky	36	7	94,020	22,912	10,297	1,875	134
Louisiana	24	13	115,332	25,302	10,911	2,401	300
Maine	15	2	27,336	6,600	3,489	470	10
Maryland	48	22	124,993	27,824	10,399	2,049	461
Massachusetts	108	29	269,785	68,229	27,444	9,074	1,339
Michigan	86	39	342,995	85,038	28,892	11,033	1,163
Minnesota	56	24	92,486	35,046	14,951	2,304	489
Mississippi	42	25	68,667	22,761	6,942	1,252	123
Missouri	66	19	165,178	40,921	16,324	4,279	457
Montana	12	9	25,560	7,026	2,863	456	44
Nebraska	27	11	60,950	14,789	7,262	1,139	160
Nevada	2	2	10,109	2,537	808	177	13
New Hampshire	21	6	27,061	6,908	1,114	498	32
New Jersey	55	21	170,072	41,339	16,956	4,296	498
New Mexico	12	8	38,326	8,294	3,088	1,121	110
New York	214	69	704,009	143,026	63,519	22,204	2,676
North Carolina	89	42	148,370	44,486	15,191	2,917	504
North Dakota	14	10	27,676	8,358	3,257	503	63
Ohio	87	17	336,921	89,621	34,602	7,203	882
Oklahoma	35	23	106,130	26,720	9,963	2,674	354
Oregon	39	20	96,333	28,405	8,421	2,559	354
Pennsylvania	143	30	372,259	83,197	41,066	9,406	1,125
Rhode Island	14	3	44,740	10,550	3,965	903	132
South Carolina	42	18	56,139	20,670	6,441	665	86
South Dakota	17	7	28,909	7,388	3,680	640	30
Tennessee	52	12	122,373	28,512	13,049	2,492	323
Texas	114	63	379,379	97,967	32,287	7,143	853
Utah	10	6	69,916	14,707	7,613	1,448	247
Vermont	18	5	17,787	5,652	2,319	569	16
Virginia	57	24	127,526	37,293	11,675	2,006	233
Washington	39	27	153,902	52,984	11,857	2,489	403
West Virginia	22	11	59,264	15,241	5,986	1,044	68
Wisconsin	60	29	172,239	43,133	16,141	3,978	762
Wyoming	7	7	13,816	4,493	1,034	325	49
Total U.S.	2,476	1,004	7,497,864	1,892,849	663,865	175,993	23,086

All totals exclude data for service academies.
Source: U.S. Department of Health, Education, and Welfare, Office of Education.

Universities and colleges

Selected list of accredited schools, 1969

A

Institution and location	Year founded	Total students	Faculty	Bound library volumes	Endowment fund
Abilene Christian Col., Abilene, Tex.	1906	2,847	181	140,000	$ 4,899,000
Abraham Baldwin Ag. Col. (Jr.), Tifton, Ga.	1933	1,286	86	37,000	—
Adams St. Col., Alamosa, Colo.	1921	3,449	150	130,000	—
Adelphi U., Garden City, N.Y.	1896	7,448	532	190,000	2,666,000
Adrian Col., Adrian, Mich.	1859	1,448	107	74,000	2,244,000
‡Agnes Scott Col., Decatur, Ga.	1889	744	85	111,000	12,000,000
Ag., Mech. & Normal Col., Pine Bluff, Ark.	1873	3,445	172	59,000	—
†Air Force Inst. of Tech., Wright-Patterson AFB, O.	1919	539	109	90,000	—
Akron, U. of, Akron, O.	1870	14,432	807	332,000	2,101,000
Alabama, U. of, University	1831	18,619	1,700	1,206,000	12,587,000
Alabama A. & M. Col., Norman	1875	1,288	121	...	—
Alabama St. Col., Montgomery	1874	2,169	87	...	—
Alaska, U. of, College	1917	2,045	205	200,000	1,823,000
Alaska Methodist U., Anchorage	1957	812	50	62,000	613,000
Albany St. Col., Albany, Ga.	1903	1,635	100	50,000	—
‡Albertus Magnus Col., New Haven, Conn.	1925	592	61	58,000	463,000
Albion Col., Albion, Mich.	1835	1,684	134	142,000	9,190,000
Albright Col., Reading, Pa.	1856	1,586	114	110,000	2,825,000
Albuquerque, U. of, Albuquerque, N.M.	1940	1,483	85	49,000	—
Alcorn A. & M. Col., Lorman, Miss.	1871	2,393	120	50,000	210,000
Alderson-Broaddus Col., Philippi, W.Va.	1871	896	64	44,000	238,000
Alfred U., Alfred, N.Y.	1857	1,689	173	155,000	5,073,000
Alice Lloyd Col. (Jr.), Pippa Passes, Ky.	1923	248	21	17,000	—
Allan Hancock Col. (Jr.), Santa Maria, Calif.	1920	3,829	183	27,000	—
Allegheny Col., Meadville, Pa.	1815	1,531	114	185,000	8,462,000
Alliance Col., Cambridge Springs, Pa.	1912	629	50	50,000	—
Alma Col., Alma, Mich.	1886	1,269	75	78,000	2,008,000
‡Alvernia Col., Reading, Pa.	1958	258	22	29,000	—
‡Alverno Col., Milwaukee, Wis.	1936	965	79	75,000	242,000
Alvin Jr. Col., Alvin, Tex.	1949	1,613	94	11,000	—
Amarillo Col. (Jr.), Amarillo, Tex.	1929	3,509	137	30,000	—
American International Col., Springfield, Mass.	1885	1,692	131	70,000	722,000
American River Col. (Jr.), Sacramento, Calif.	1955	10,968	241	35,000	—
American U., Washington, D.C.	1893	13,619	454	244,000	4,350,000
†Amherst Col., Amherst, Mass.	1821	1,205	141	402,000	57,000,000
Anderson Col., Anderson, Ind.	1917	1,507	101	123,000	535,000
Anderson Col., Anderson, S.C.	1911	821	48	13,000	285,000
Andrew Col. (Jr.), Cuthbert, Ga.	1854	426	25	18,000	280,000
Andrews U., Berrien Springs, Mich.	1874	2,061	142	195,000	373,000
Angelo St. Col., San Angelo, Tex.	1928	3,080	130	75,000	25,000
‡Anna Maria Col. for Women, Paxton, Mass.	1946	670	54	28,000	—
‡Annhurst Col., Woodstock, Conn.	1941	432	52	29,000	—
Antelope Valley Col., Lancaster, Calif.	1929	3,046	116	25,000	—
Antioch Col., Yellow Springs, O.	1852	1,825	125	166,000	6,241,000
Appalachian St. U., Boone, N.C.	1903	6,131	281	173,000	556,000
Aquinas Col., Grand Rapids, Mich.	1923	1,239	100	70,000	—
Aquinas Inst. Sch. of Philosophy, River Forest, Ill.; Sch. of Theology, Dubuque, Ill.	1939	283	34	60,000	—
Arizona, U. of, Tucson	1885	21,965	1,944	1,300,000	1,638,000
Arizona St. U., Tempe	1885	23,341	1,013	927,000	787,000
Arizona Western Col. (Jr.), Yuma	1963	1,889	82	24,000	—
Arkansas, St. Col. of, Conway	1907	4,012	190	116,000	—
Arkansas, U. of, Fayetteville	1871	10,600	780	560,000	—
Arkansas A. & M. Col., College Heights	1909	1,679	92	47,000	—
Arkansas Col., Batesville	1872	330	25	45,000	1,000,000
Arkansas Polytech. Col., Russellville	1909	2,252	107	53,000	—
Arkansas St. U., State University	1909	5,747	277	201,000	25,000
Armstrong Col., Berkeley, Calif.	1918	398	31	12,000	—
Armstrong St. Col., Savannah, Ga.	1935	1,714	100	54,000	—
Art Center Col. of Design, Los Angeles, Calif.	1930	1,180	95	6,000	548,000
Art Inst. of Chicago (Ill.), The School of The	1866	1,177	84	83,000	1,870,000
Asbury Col., Wilmore, Ky.	1890	957	66	72,000	5,000,000
Ashland Col., Ashland, O.	1878	2,701	153	110,000	1,500,000
†Assumption Col., Worcester, Mass.	1904	1,232	64	93,000	613,000
†Athenaeum of Ohio, Norwood, Cincinnati, O.	1829	416	55	86,000	3,970,000
Athens Col., Athens, Ala.	1822	1,105	69	40,000	1,500,000
Atlanta U., Atlanta, Ga.	1865	1,051	105	370,000	—
Atlantic Christian Col., Wilson, N.C.	1902	1,510	94	76,000	966,000
Atlantic Union Col., South Lancaster, Mass.	1882	754	63	66,000	—
Auburn U., Auburn, Ala.	1856	12,887	825	575,000	4,320,000
Augsburg Col., Minneapolis, Minn.	1869	1,727	117	95,000	503,000
Augusta Col., Augusta, Ga.	1925	2,306	119	77,000	—
Augustana Col., Rock Island, Ill.	1860	1,762	128	140,000	3,623,000
Augustana Col., Sioux Falls, S.D.	1860	1,971	137	90,000	817,000
Aurora Col., Aurora, Ill.	1893	1,212	94	65,000	244,000
Austin Col., Sherman, Tex.	1849	907	93	83,000	4,018,000
Austin Peay St. Col., Clarksville, Tenn.	1929	2,938	162	94,000	—
‡Averett Col. (Jr.), Danville, Va.	1859	553	37	20,000	96,000
Avila Col., Kansas City, Mo.	1916	471	47	51,000	50,000
Azusa Pacific Col., Azusa, Calif.	1899	1,021	55	50,000	476,000

B

Institution and location	Year founded	Total students	Faculty	Bound library volumes	Endowment fund
Babson Inst., Babson Park, Mass.	1919	1,262	67	50,000	5,000,000
Bacone Col. (Jr.), Bacone, Okla.	1880	770	31	21,000	854,000
Baker U., Baldwin City, Kan.	1858	875	75	57,000	3,119,000
Bakersfield Col. (Jr.), Bakersfield, Calif.	1913	9,254	238	39,000	—
Baldwin-Wallace Col., Berea, O.	1845	2,796	194	130,000	5,025,000
Ball St. U., Muncie, Ind.	1918	14,446	579	338,000	—
Bank Street Col. of Ed., New York, N.Y.	1916	827	60	35,000	899,000
‡Barat Col., Lake Forest, Ill.	1863	683	63	55,000	—
Barber-Scotia Col., Concord, N.C.	1867	315	30	23,000	713,000
Bard Col., Annandale-on-Hudson, N.Y.	1860	599	60	101,000	284,000
‡Barnard Col., New York, N.Y.	1889	1,900	186	110,000	16,459,000
Barrington Col., Barrington, R.I.	1900	630	54	42,000	870,000
‡Barry Col., Miami, Fla.	1940	1,189	119	69,000	48,000
Barstow Col. (Jr.), Barstow, Calif.	1960	1,253	25	16,000	—
Bates Col., Lewiston, Me.	1864	985	74	130,000	8,600,000
Baylor U., Waco, Tex.	1845	8,164	750	500,000	24,801,000
‡Bay Path Jr. Col., Longmeadow, Mass.	1897	500	28	20,000	750,000
‡Beaver Col., Glenside, Pa.	1853	821	84	63,000	232,000
Belhaven Col., Jackson, Miss.	1883	588	51	37,000	1,200,000
Bellarmine-Ursuline Col., Louisville, Ky.	1968	1,930	90	58,000	—
†Belmont Abbey Col., Belmont, N.C.	1878	780	53	65,000	600,000
Belleville Area Col., Belleville, Ill.	1946	3,391	190	15,000	—
Belmont Col., Nashville, Tenn.	1951	1,025	64	42,000	$ 600,000
Beloit Col., Beloit, Wis.	1846	1,563	125	200,000	6,816,000
Bemidji St. Col., Bemidji, Minn.	1913	4,492	250	85,000	—
Benedict Col., Columbia, S.C.	1870	975	56	32,000	517,000
‡Bennett Col., Greensboro, N.C.	1873	711	73	60,000	1,907,000
‡Bennett Col. (Jr.), Millbrook, N.Y.	1891	332	38	27,000	1,400,000
‡Bennington Col., Bennington, Vt.	1932	506	65	57,000	1,159,000
Bentley Col., Waltham, Mass.	1917	1,995	114	...	—
Berea Col., Berea, Ky.	1855	1,311	122	162,000	41,000,000
Berry Col., Mount Berry, Ga.	1926	1,116	71	65,000	11,007,000
Bethany Bible Col., Santa Cruz, Calif.	1919	507	27	23,000	—
Bethany Col., Bethany, W.Va.	1840	1,140	87	100,000	9,376,000
Bethany Col., Lindsborg, Kan.	1881	582	43	42,000	1,064,000
Bethany Nazarene Col., Bethany, Okla.	1899	1,570	80	72,000	—
Bethel Col., McKenzie, Tenn.	1842	851	52	48,000	966,000
Bethel Col., North Newton, Kan.	1887	532	58	61,000	993,000
Bethel Col., St. Paul, Minn.	1871	984	84	55,000	172,000
Bethune-Cookman Col., Daytona Beach, Fla.	1872	1,160	57	53,000	1,385,000
Biola Col., La Mirada, Calif.	1908	1,447	110	83,000	—
Birmingham-Southern Col., Birmingham, Ala.	1856	1,008	69	75,000	5,847,000
†Biscayne Col., Miami, Fla.	1961	360	32	35,000	50,000
Bishop Col., Dallas, Tex.	1881	1,787	131	69,000	598,000
Bismarck Jr. Col., Bismarck, N.D.	1939	945	48	18,000	—
Blackburn Col., Carlinville, Ill.	1837	573	39	52,000	4,110,000
Black Hawk Col., Moline, Ill.	1946	2,799	160	25,000	—
Black Hills St. Col., Spearfish, S.D.	1883	2,134	112	46,000	—
Blinn Col. (Jr.), Brenham, Tex.	1883	1,569	75	17,000	—
Bloomfield Col., Bloomfield, N.J.	1868	1,014	82	55,000	1,080,000
Bloomsburg St. Col., Bloomsburg, Pa.	1839	3,819	249	125,000	—
Bluefield Col. (Jr.), Bluefield, Va.	1922	378	29	22,000	118,000
Bluefield St. Col., Bluefield, W.Va.	1895	1,118	79	41,000	—
‡Blue Mountain Col., Blue Mountain, Miss.	1873	323	31	31,000	1,209,000
Bluffton Col., Bluffton, O.	1900	730	61	52,000	1,144,000
Boise St. Col., Boise, Ida.	1932	3,871	259	70,000	—
Borromeo Sem. of Ohio, Wickliffe, O.	1954	202	21	30,000	—
Boston Col., Chestnut Hill, Mass.	1863	9,729	959	688,000	8,685,000
Boston Con. of Music, Boston, Mass.	1867	445	62	15,000	—
Boston U., Boston, Mass.	1869	23,806	2,141	782,000	21,057,000
†Bowdoin Col., Brunswick, Me.	1794	932	129	400,000	31,000,000
Bowie St. Col., Bowie, Md.	1867	1,395	98	45,000	—
Bowling Green St. U., Bowling Green, O.	1910	12,396	924	538,000	—
‡Bradford Jr. Col., Bradford, Mass.	1803	409	51	37,000	776,000
Bradley U., Peoria, Ill.	1897	6,133	378	175,000	4,659,000
Brandeis U., Waltham, Mass.	1947	2,895	380	395,000	35,000,000
‡Brenau Col., Gainesville, Ga.	1878	518	54	31,000	1,800,000
Brescia Col., Owensboro, Ky.	1925	1,054	86	46,000	300,000
Brevard Col. (Jr.), Brevard, N.C.	1853	686	50	27,000	820,000
Brevard Jr. Col., Cocoa, Fla.	1960	6,090	186	40,000	—
Brewton Parker Col., Mt. Vernon, Ga.	1904	720	27	14,000	460,000
‡Briarcliff Col., Briarcliff Manor, N.Y.	1903	681	70	44,000	—
Briar Cliff Col., Sioux City, Ia.	1930	1,108	73	58,000	112,000
Bridgeport, U. of, Bridgeport, Conn.	1927	8,657	472	172,000	3,700,000
Bridgewater Col., Bridgewater, Va.	1880	830	66	67,000	1,208,000
Brigham Young U., Provo, Utah	1875	21,742	1,492	800,000	19,315,000
Brooklyn (N.Y.), Polytech. Inst. of	1854	4,749	351	175,000	5,760,000
Brooks Inst., Santa Barbara, Calif.	1945	535	31	2,000	—
†Broward Jr. Col., Fort Lauderdale, Fla.	1960	4,860	184	38,000	—
Brown U. (incl. ‡Pembroke Col.), Providence, R.I.	1764	5,126	1,137	1,235,000	98,293,000
Brunswick Col. (Jr.), Brunswick, Ga.	1964	664	26	15,000	—
Bryant Col., Providence, R.I.	1863	3,036	102	42,000	—
‡Bryn Mawr Col., Bryn Mawr, Pa.	1885	1,311	202	360,000	30,000
Bucknell U., Lewisburg, Pa.	1846	2,753	219	268,000	25,000,000
Buena Vista Col., Storm Lake, Iowa	1891	939	58	57,000	610,000
Butler U., Indianapolis, Ind.	1855	4,177	250	190,000	11,000,000

C

Institution and location	Year founded	Total students	Faculty	Bound library volumes	Endowment fund
Cabrillo Col. (Jr.), Aptos, Calif.	1959	3,977	123	25,000	—
‡Cabrini Col., Radnor, Pa.	1957	380	40	37,000	—
‡Caldwell Col. for Women, Caldwell, N.J.	1939	811	62	58,000	—
California, U. of (campuses at Berkeley, Davis, Irvine, Los Angeles, Riverside, San Diego, San Francisco, Santa Barbara, Santa Cruz)	1868	95,138	12,547	9,756,000	210,650,000
California Col. of Medicine, Los Angeles	1896	315	584	52,000	—
California Baptist Col., Riverside	1950	906	44	73,000	62,000
California Col. of Arts and Crafts, Oakland	1907	1,212	92	16,000	78,000
†California Inst. of Tech., Pasadena	1891	1,484	627	193,000	124,000,000
California Inst. of the Arts, Los Angeles	1962	806	70	12,000	—
California Lutheran Col., Thousand Oaks	1959	1,100	76	56,000	153,000
California St. Col., California, Pa.	1852	5,537	340	100,000	—
California St. Col., Dominguez Hills, Gardena	1962	1,268	75	55,000	—
California St. Col., Fullerton	1959	10,564	566	300,000	—
California St. Col., Hayward	1959	10,000	648	310,000	—
California St. Col., Long Beach	1949	25,205	1,452	361,000	—
California St. Col., Los Angeles	1947	20,830	1,200	400,000	—
California St. Col., San Bernardino	1967	1,310	91	105,000	—
California St. Polytech. Col., Kellogg-Voorhis, Pomona	1966	6,804	390	140,000	—
California St. Polytech. Col., San Luis Obispo	1901	9,280	617	230,000	—
Calvin Col., Grand Rapids, Mich.	1876	3,393	186	200,000	360,000
Cameron State Ag. Col., Lawton, Okla.	1909	3,506	145	35,000	—
Campbell Col., Buie's Creek, N.C.	1887	2,270	128	68,000	962,000
Campbellsville Col., Campbellsville, Ky.	1906	904	52	45,000	180,000
Canal Zone Col., Balboa Heights, C.Z.	1933	1,150	60	20,000	—
Canisius Col., Buffalo, N.Y.	1870	3,819	242	135,000	789,000
Capital U., Columbus, O.	1850	1,849	159	86,000	1,929,000
†Cardinal Glennon Col., St. Louis, Mo.	1900	198	30	49,000	—
‡Cardinal Stritch Col., Milwaukee, Wis.	1937	563	56	41,000	151,000
Carleton Col., Northfield, Minn.	1866	1,408	141	240,000	17,600,000
‡Carlow Col., Pittsburgh, Pa.	1929	1,204	102	80,000	350,000
Carnegie-Mellon U., Pittsburgh, Pa.	1967	5,228	493	309,000	100,179,000
Carroll Col., Helena, Mont.	1909	1,002	70	46,000	3,000,000
Carroll Col., Waukesha, Wis.	1846	1,100	95	88,000	2,077,000
Carson-Newman Col., Jefferson City, Tenn.	1851	1,754	116	96,000	1,533,000

†Men's schools, ‡women's schools; the others are coeducational.

Institution and location	Year found-ed	Total stu-dents	Faculty	Bound library volumes	Endowment fund
Carthage Col., Kenosha, Wis.	1847	2,200	115	77,000	$ 3,600,000
Case Western Reserve U., Cleveland, O.	1826	9,632	4,200	1,045,000	136,000,000
Casper Col., Casper, Wyo.	1945	2,555	133	27,000	100,000
Castleton St. Col., Castleton, Vt.	1867	1,088	80	32,000	—
Catawba Col., Salisbury, N.C.	1851	1,018	81	76,000	4,749,000
‡Catherine Spalding Col., Louisville, Ky.	1920	1,500	117	92,000	—
Catholic U. of America, Washington, D.C.	1887	6,591	825	730,000	7,207,000
Catholic U. of Puerto Rico, Ponce	1948	6,574	416	127,000	436,000
‡Cazenovia Col., Cazenovia, N.Y.	1824	542	48	23,000	287,000
‡Cedar Crest Col., Allentown, Pa.	1867	712	62	62,000	2,078,000
Centenary Col., Shreveport, La.	1825	1,140	98	89,000	6,549,000
‡Centenary Col. for Women, Hackettstown, N.J.	1867	673	70	33,000	332,000
Central Col., Pella, Ia.	1853	1,194	87	72,000	1,238,000
Central Connecticut St. Col., New Britain	1849	10,215	638	150,000	—
Central Florida Jr. Col., Ocala	1958	1,005	56	22,000	250,000
Centralia Col. (Jr.), Centralia, Wash.	1925	1,545	80	20,000	—
Central Methodist Col., Fayette, Mo.	1854	922	65	97,000	4,185,000
Central Michigan U., Mt. Pleasant	1892	10,865	523	302,000	125,000
Central Missouri St. Col., Warrensburg	1871	11,944	595	245,000	—
Central St. Col., Edmond, Okla.	1890	8,809	281	118,000	—
Central St. U., Wilberforce, O.	1887	2,626	175	87,000	—
Central Washington St. Col., Ellensburg	1891	6,208	403	137,000	—
Central Wesleyan Col., Central, S.C.	1906	258	25	23,000	215,000
Centre Col. of Kentucky, Danville	1819	705	60	81,000	5,500,000
Cerritos Col., Norwalk, Calif.	1955	10,997	273	41,000	—
Chabot Col. (Jr.), Hayward, Calif.	1961	4,922	187	37,000	—
Chadron St. Col., Chadron, Neb.	1911	1,888	97	90,000	—
Chaffey Col. (Jr.), Alta Loma, Calif.	1883	6,673	255	46,000	—
Chaminade Col. of Honolulu, Hawaii	1955	832	63	36,000	—
Chapman Col., Orange, Calif.	1861	3,519	270	77,000	1,120,000
Charleston, Col. of, Charleston, S.C.	1770	482	33	36,000	826,000
‡Chatham Col., Pittsburgh, Pa.	1869	662	74	78,000	12,000,000
‡Chestnut Hill Col., Philadelphia, Pa.	1871	1,038	78	79,000	601,000
Cheyney St. Col., Cheyney, Pa.	1837	1,900	149	105,000	—
Chicago, The U. of, Chicago, Ill.	1892	10,508	1,128	2,713,000	197,714,000
Chicago St. Col., Chicago, Ill.	1869	5,911	309	149,000	—
Chico St. Col., Chico, Calif.	1887	7,987	555	220,000	—
Chipola Jr. Col., Marianna, Fla.	1947	1,104	65	28,000	—
Chowan Col. (Jr.), Murfreesboro, N.C.	1848	1,204	77	30,000	275,000
†Christian Brothers Col., Memphis, Tenn.	1871	1,160	81	55,000	300,000
‡Christian Col. (Jr.), Columbia, Mo.	1851	537	38	23,000	117,000
Church Col. of Hawaii, Laie	1955	1,004	75	57,000	—
Cincinnati, U. of, Cincinnati, O.	1819	26,124	2,507	1,033,000	39,626,000
Cisco Jr. Col., Cisco, Tex.	1940	780	53	12,000	100,000
Citrus Jr. Col., Azusa, Calif.	1915	5,857	233	45,000	—
Claflin Col., Orangeburg, S.C.	1869	772	49	38,000	556,000
Claremont College System, Claremont, Calif.					
†Claremont Men's Col.	1946	785	82	622,000	10,000,000
Claremont U. Ctr.	. . .	968	. . .	506,000	—
Harvey Mudd Col.	1955	346	44	500,000	2,232,000
‡Pitzer Col.	1963	597	46	625,000	1,645,000
Pomona Col.	1887	1,272	123	650,000	20,330,000
‡Scripps Col.	1926	496	63	65,000	8,594,000
Clarion St. Col., Clarion, Pa.	1866	3,661	273	175,000	—
Clark Col., Atlanta, Ga.	1869	980	97	33,000	1,771,000
Clark Col. (Jr.), Vancouver, Wash.	1933	2,997	155	23,000	—
‡Clarke Col., Dubuque, Ia.	1843	1,106	114	72,000	641,000
Clarke Memorial Col. (Jr.), Newton, Miss.	1908	299	20	13,000	530,000
Clarkson Col. of Tech., Potsdam, N.Y.	1895	2,528	169	83,000	3,816,000
Clark U., Worcester, Mass.	1887	2,800	230	286,000	10,743,000
Clemson U., Clemson, S.C.	1889	6,839	392	394,000	620,000
Cleveland St. U., The, Cleveland, O.	1964	10,550	503	140,000	—
Coe Col., Cedar Rapids, Ia.	1851	996	100	125,000	5,740,000
‡Coker Col., Hartsville, S.C.	1908	337	32	46,000	4,000,000
Colby Col., Waterville, Me.	1813	1,532	129	260,000	22,000,000
‡Colby Jr. Col. for Women, New London, N.H.	1837	594	61	40,000	1,333,000
†Colgate U., Hamilton, N.Y.	1819	1,954	169	254,000	25,713,000
‡College Misericordia, Dallas, Pa.	1924	1,079	95	60,000	253,000
Colorado, U. of, Boulder and Denver	1876	29,250	2,450	1,202,000	7,150,000
Colorado Col., Colorado Springs	1874	1,666	146	233,000	11,565,000
Colorado School of Mines, Golden	1874	1,685	135	133,000	400,000
Colorado St. Col., Greeley	1890	8,568	344	290,000	—
Colorado St. U., Fort Collins	1870	15,361	949	455,000	1,067,000
Columbia Basin Col., Pasco, Wash.	1955	2,208	115	19,000	—
‡Columbia Col., Columbia, S.C.	1854	858	68	58,000	2,000,000
Columbia Union Col., Takoma Park, Md.	1904	1,064	106	75,000	—
Columbia U., New York, N.Y.	1754	17,040	4,723	4,000,000	227,000,000
Columbus Col., Columbus, Ga.	1958	1,599	75	32,000	35,000
Concord Col., Athens, W.Va.	1872	1,705	104	90,000	—
Concordia Col., Moorhead, Minn.	1891	2,182	155	118,000	987,000
Concordia Col., St. Paul, Minn.	1893	679	63	55,000	—
Concordia Col. (Jr.), Milwaukee, Wis.	1881	269	22	36,000	—
Concordia Col. (Jr.), Portland, Ore.	1950	131	17	23,000	223,000
Concordia Collegiate Inst., Bronxville, N.Y.	1881	417	45	27,000	164,000
Concordia Lutheran Col. (Jr.), Austin, Tex.	1926	182	23	13,000	—
Concordia Lutheran Jr. Col., Ann Arbor, Mich.	1962	479	39	23,000	—
†Concordia Senior Col., Fort Wayne, Ind.	1957	492	41	46,000	160,000
Concordia Tch. Col., River Forest, Ill.	1864	1,399	137	89,000	419,000
Concordia Tch. Col., Seward, Neb.	1894	1,447	104	54,000	116,000
Connecticut, U. of, Storrs	1881	19,351	1,078	770,000	1,432,000
Connecticut Col., New London	1911	1,558	170	243,000	6,525,000
Connors St. Col. (Jr.), Warner, Okla.	1908	616	30	30,000	—
Contra Costa Col. (Jr.), San Pablo, Calif.	1948	5,627	195	40,000	—
‡Converse Col., Spartanburg, S.C.	1889	820	92	78,000	1,799,000
Cooke County Jr. Col., Gainesville, Tex.	1924	1,279	66	17,000	190,000
Cooper Union, New York, N.Y.	1859	1,178	180	102,000	26,505,000
Copiah-Lincoln Jr. Col., Wesson, Miss.	1928	867	53	17,000	—
Coppin St. Col., Baltimore, Md.	1900	647	57	55,000	—
Cornell Col., Mount Vernon, Ia.	1853	982	100	150,000	6,900,000
Cornell U., Ithaca, N.Y.	1865	14,706	2,544	3,250,000	190,952,000
Corpus Christi, U. of, Corpus Christi, Tex.	1947	675	38	48,000	—
‡Cottey Col. (Jr.), Nevada, Mo.	1884	330	40	40,000	—
Cranbrook Acad. of Art, Bloomfield Hills, Mich.	1927	113	14	15,000	1,100,000
Creighton U., Omaha, Neb.	1878	4,180	667	261,000	5,426,000
Cuesta Col. (Jr.), San Luis Obispo, Calif.	1963	2,534	93	17,000	—
Culver-Stockton Col., Canton, Mo.	1853	865	58	83,000	959,000
Cumberland Col., Williamsburg, Ky.	1889	1,117	63	23,000	915,000
Cumberland Col. of Tennessee (Jr.), Lebanon	1842	397	26	20,000	—
Cypress Jr. Col., Cypress, Calif.	1964	3,244	99	22,000	—

Institution and location	Year found-ed	Total stu-dents	Faculty	Bound library volumes	Endowment fund

D

Institution and location	Year found-ed	Total stu-dents	Faculty	Bound library volumes	Endowment fund
Dakota St. Col., Madison, S.D.	1881	1,342	55	35,000	—
Dakota Wesleyan U., Mitchell, S.D.	1885	801	51	46,000	$ 1,177,000
Dallas, U. of, Irving, Tex.	1956	1,271	107	65,000	8,000,000
Dallas Baptist Col., Dallas, Tex.	1898	1,310	73	50,000	325,000
Dana Col., Blair, Neb.	1884	1,261	55	61,000	300,000
†Dartmouth Col., Hanover, N.H.	1769	3,736	485	1,000,000	128,881,000
David Lipscomb Col., Nashville, Tenn.	1891	2,205	111	80,000	2,153,000
†Davidson Col., Davidson, N.C.	1837	1,035	93	145,000	17,800,000
Davis and Elkins Col., Elkins, W.Va.	1904	821	61	52,000	646,000
Dayton, U. of, Dayton, O.	1850	10,118	542	235,000	3,000,000
Daytona Beach Jr. Col., Daytona Beach, Fla.	1958	2,338	83	35,000	—
Dean Jr. Col., Franklin, Mass.	1865	932	70	25,000	1,000,000
De Anza Col., Cupertino, Calif.	1967	6,898	323	30,000	—
†Deep Springs Col. (Jr.), Deep Springs, Calif.	1917	17	5	12,000	—
Defiance Col., The, Defiance, O.	1850	1,111	85	55,000	626,000
DeKalb Col. (Jr.), Clarkston, Ga.	1963	3,462	119	31,000	382,000
Delaware, U. of, Newark	1833	12,225	652	700,000	57,200,000
Delaware St. Col., Dover	1891	1,044	80	57,000	75,000
†Delaware Valley Col. of Sc. & Ag., Doylestown, Pa.	1896	1,168	74	42,000	2,291,000
Del Mar Col. (Jr.), Corpus Christi, Tex.	1935	3,796	190	59,000	—
Delta Col. (Jr.), University Center, Mich.	1957	4,005	209	55,000	—
Delta St. Col., Cleveland, Miss.	1924	2,535	117	75,000	—
Denison U., Granville, O.	1831	1,880	136	160,000	12,821,000
Denver, U. of, Denver, Colo.	1864	8,926	664	578,000	13,173,000
De Paul U., Chicago, Ill.	1898	8,869	524	260,000	2,161,000
De Pauw U., Greencastle, Ind.	1837	2,370	191	277,000	14,611,000
Desert, Col. of the (Jr.), Palm Desert, Calif.	1958	1,580	81	27,000	—
Detroit, U. of, Detroit, Mich.	1877	8,880	569	325,000	3,425,000
Detroit Inst. of Tech., Detroit, Mich.	1891	1,285	90	39,000	83,000
Diablo Valley Col. (Jr.), Pleasant Hill, Calif.	1948	10,375	319	48,000	—
Dickinson Col., Carlisle, Pa.	1773	1,546	124	167,000	9,939,000
Dickinson St. Col., Dickinson, N.D.	1916	1,639	83	58,000	—
Dillard U., New Orleans, La.	1869	944	86	83,000	6,503,000
District of Columbia Tch. Col., Washington	1851	2,711	146	95,000	—
Dixie Col. (Jr.), St. George, Utah	1911	1,069	45	25,000	—
Doane Col., Crete, Neb.	1872	741	48	56,000	4,047,000
‡Dominican Col., Houston, Tex.	1945	348	70	49,000	—
Dominican Col., Racine, Wis.	1935	630	54	35,000	—
‡Dominican Col. of San Rafael, Calif.	1890	941	81	60,000	—
Donnelly Col. (Jr.), Kansas City, Kan.	1949	926	40	18,000	—
Drake U., Des Moines, Ia.	1881	7,321	375	300,000	4,200,000
Drew U., Madison, N.J.	1866	1,510	153	286,000	13,966,000
Drexel Inst. of Tech., Philadelphia, Pa.	1891	10,357	708	270,000	14,783,000
Dropsie Col. for Hebrew & Cognate Learning, Philadelphia, Pa.	1907	160	22	100,000	1,073,000
Drury Col., Springfield, Mo.	1873	2,308	175	98,000	3,029,000
Dubuque, U. of, Dubuque, Ia.	1852	985	57	53,000	2,249,000
Duke U., Durham, N.C.	1838	7,666	1,034	1,940,000	63,914,000
‡Dunbarton Col. Holy Cross, Washington, D.C.	1935	543	59	51,000	41,000
DuPage, Col. of (Jr.), Naperville, Ill.	1966	2,500	227	. . .	—
Duquesne U., Pittsburgh, Pa.	1878	6,939	434	279,000	1,800,000
‡D'Youville Col., Buffalo, N.Y.	1908	1,329	116	72,000	210,000

E

Institution and location	Year found-ed	Total stu-dents	Faculty	Bound library volumes	Endowment fund
Earlham Col. (incl. Eastern Indiana Ctr.), Richmond, Ind.	1847	1,876	152	163,000	11,409,000
East Carolina U., Greenville, N.C.	1907	8,435	596	329,000	70,000
East Central Jr. Col., Decatur, Miss.	1928	769	44	11,000	—
East Central St. Col., Ada, Okla.	1909	2,725	108	86,000	—
Eastern Arizona Col. (Jr.), Thatcher	1888	1,299	55	18,000	—
Eastern Baptist Col., St. Davids, Pa.	1932	508	50	45,000	1,000,000
Eastern Baptist Theol. Sem., Philadelphia, Pa.	1925	182	20	71,000	5,273,000
Eastern Connecticut St. Col., Willimantic	1889	1,613	110	59,000	—
Eastern Illinois U., Charleston	1895	6,663	424	166,000	—
Eastern Kentucky U., Richmond	1906	8,634	450	214,000	—
Eastern Mennonite Col., Harrisonburg, Va.	1917	866	75	52,000	390,000
Eastern Michigan U., Ypsilanti	1849	16,670	990	200,000	70,000
Eastern Montana Col., Billings	1927	3,573	160	125,000	—
Eastern Nazarene Col., Wollaston, Mass.	1918	780	60	53,000	396,000
Eastern New Mexico U., Portales	1934	3,584	200	166,000	—
Eastern Oklahoma St. Col. (Jr.), Wilburton	1909	1,060	145	21,000	—
Eastern Oregon Col., La Grande	1929	1,695	104	70,000	—
Eastern Utah, Col. of, Price	1938	648	37	18,000	—
Eastern Washington St. Col., Cheney	1890	5,317	346	155,000	—
East Mississippi Jr. Col., Scooba	1928	397	29	13,000	—
East Stroudsburg St. Col., E. Stroudsburg, Pa.	1893	2,550	174	150,000	—
East Tennessee St. U., Johnson City	1911	8,966	607	215,000	—
East Texas Baptist Col., Marshall	1912	691	42	58,000	1,864,000
East Texas St. U., Commerce	1889	8,890	425	500,000	—
‡Edgecliff Col., Cincinnati, O.	1935	965	89	59,000	—
‡Edgewood Col., Madison, Wis.	1927	754	68	47,000	—
Edinboro St. Col., Edinboro, Pa.	1857	6,054	325	192,000	—
Eisenhower Col., Seneca Falls, N.Y.	1968	222	26	18,000	50,000
El Camino Col. (Jr.), El Camino College, Calif.	1946	15,457	351	54,000	—
El Centro Col. (Jr.), Dallas, Tex.	1965	7,102	175	25,000	—
Elizabeth City St. Col., Elizabeth City, N.C.	1891	1,011	72	62,000	—
‡Elizabeth Seton Col. (Jr.), Yonkers, N.Y.	1960	447	46	22,000	—
Elizabethtown Col., Elizabethtown, Pa.	1899	1,789	121	73,000	1,422,000
Elmhurst Col., Elmhurst, Ill.	1871	1,520	112	86,000	990,000
Elmira Col., Elmira, N.Y.	1855	1,183	79	103,000	3,300,000
Elon Col., Elon College, N.C.	1889	1,692	89	66,000	1,368,000
Embry-Riddle Aero. Inst., Daytona Beach, Fla.	1926	1,276	115	11,000	—
Emerson Col., Boston, Mass.	1880	1,300	115	35,000	284,000
†Emmanuel Col., Boston, Mass.	1919	1,489	141	75,000	—
Emory and Henry Col., Emory, Va.	1836	826	76	90,000	3,175,000
Emory U., Atlanta, Ga.	1836	5,241	1,622	867,000	76,600,000
Oxford Col. of Emory U., Oxford, Ga.	1836	422	30	20,000	—
Emporia, Col. of, Emporia, Kan.	1882	908	54	50,000	625,000
‡Endicott Jr. Col., Beverly, Mass.	1939	885	64	30,000	—
Erskine Col., Due West, S.C.	1839	724	64	47,000	1,597,000
Eureka Col., Eureka, Ill.	1855	525	45	53,000	1,330,000
Evangel Col., Springfield, Mo.	1955	833	66	53,000	29,000
Evansville, U. of, Evansville, Ind.	1854	4,665	195	92,000	2,096,000

F

Institution and location	Year found-ed	Total stu-dents	Faculty	Bound library volumes	Endowment fund
†Fairfield U., Fairfield, Conn.	1942	2,872	188	92,000	—
Fairleigh Dickinson U., Rutherford, N.J.	1941	19,042	1,100	369,000	$11,000,000
Fairmont St. Col., Fairmont, W.Va.	1867	2,796	154	82,000	—
Fashion Inst. of Tech. (Jr.), New York, N.Y.	1944	5,480	225	28,000	—
Fayetteville St. Col., Fayetteville, N.C.	1877	1,326	78	61,000	—
Ferris St. Col., Big Rapids, Mich.	1884	8,200	355	148,000	—
Ferrum Jr. Col., Ferrum, Va.	1913	1,190	52	30,000	445,000
‡Finch Col., New York, N.Y.	1900	403	50	55,000	—
Findlay Col., Findlay, O.	1882	1,312	87	48,000	660,000
Fisk U., Nashville, Tenn.	1867	1,126	119	167,000	8,945,000
Florence St. U., Florence, Ala.	1873	2,760	151	95,000	—
Florida, U. of, Gainesville	1853	17,750	2,300	1,300,000	3,500,000
Florida A. & M. U., Tallahassee	1887	3,507	261	162,000	—
Florida Atlantic U., Boca Raton	1961	3,751	265	172,000	—
Florida Col. (Jr.), Temple Terrace	1946	402	25	18,000	23,000
Florida Inst. of Tech., Melbourne	1958	1,929	138	28,000	—
Florida Keys Jr. Col., Key West	1965	561	67	6,000	—
Florida Memorial Col., St. Augustine	1892	850	45	50,000	500,000
Florida Presbyterian Col., St. Petersburg	1958	853	65	78,000	—
Florida Southern Col., Lakeland	1885	1,576	107	108,000	7,000,000
Florida St. U., Tallahassee	1857	14,595	1,373	807,000	360,000
‡Fontbonne Col., St. Louis, Mo.	1917	833	91	65,000	—
Foothill Col. (Jr.), Los Altos Hills, Calif.	1958	7,900	287	56,000	—
Fordham U., Bronx, N.Y.	1841	10,261	624	818,000	4,567,000
Forsyth Tech. Inst. (Jr.), Winston-Salem, N.C.	1960	1,029	228	6,000	—
Fort Hays Kansas St. Col., Hays	1902	5,459	270	275,000	531,000
Fort Lewis Col., Durango, Colo.	1911	1,723	86	64,000	200,000
Fort Valley St. Col., Fort Valley, Ga.	1895	1,654	85	60,000	82,000
‡Fort Wright Col. of the Holy Names, Spokane, Wash.	1907	345	51	44,000	125,000
Francis T. Nicholls St. Col., Thibodaux, La.	1948	4,371	172	92,000	—
Franklin Col. of Indiana, Franklin	1834	723	62	70,000	3,810,000
Franklin and Marshall Col., Lancaster, Pa.	1787	1,758	137	194,000	11,516,000
Franklin Pierce Col., Rindge, N.H.	1962	894	68	18,000	22,000
Frank Phillips Col. (Jr.), Borger, Tex.	1946	708	45	20,000	—
Freed-Hardeman Col. (Jr.), Henderson, Tenn.	1908	718	45	29,000	403,000
Fresno City Col. (Jr.), Fresno, Calif.	1910	9,689	196	31,000	—
Fresno St. Col., Fresno, Calif.	1911	11,489	716	268,000	—
Friends U., Wichita, Kan.	1898	946	52	43,000	950,000
Frostburg St. Col., Frostburg, Md.	1898	1,932	130	80,000	—
Fullerton Jr. Col., Fullerton, Calif.	1913	12,511	370	61,000	—
Furman U., Greenville, S.C.	1826	1,783	117	155,000	7,676,000

G

Institution and location	Year found-ed	Total stu-dents	Faculty	Bound library volumes	Endowment fund
Gadsden St. Jr. Col., Gadsden, Ala.	1963	2,343	112	28,000	—
Gainesville Jr. Col., Gainesville, Ga.	1965	720	28	12,000	—
Gallaudet Col., Washington, D.C.	1864	640	97	102,000	—
Gannon Col., Erie, Pa.	1944	2,947	160	83,000	565,000
Gardner-Webb Jr. Col., Boiling Springs, N.C.	1905	1,213	70	40,000	1,180,000
‡Garland Jr. Col., Boston, Mass.	1872	405	48	13,000	—
Gaston Col. (Jr.), Gastonia, N.C.	1952	1,691	109	24,000	—
Gavilan Col., Gilroy, Calif.	1919	1,175	43	14,000	—
General Motors Inst., Flint, Mich.	1919	2,610	234	38,000	—
Geneva Col., Beaver Falls, Pa.	1848	1,704	120	77,000	3,735,000
George Fox Col., Newberg, Ore.	1891	392	50	35,000	1,400,000
George Peabody Col. for Teachers, Nashville, Tenn.	1875	1,800	170	1,000,000	13,000,000
Georgetown Col., Georgetown, Ky.	1829	1,321	96	92,000	1,446,000
Georgetown U., Washington, D.C.	1789	7,730	1,796	704,000	15,019,000
George Washington U., The, Washington, D.C.	1821	13,065	1,683	461,000	13,000,000
George Williams Col., Downers Grove, Ill.	1890	865	52	43,000	743,000
Georgia, U. of, Athens	1785	23,103	2,050	1,000,000	3,800,000
Georgia Col. at Milledgeville	1889	1,561	92	100,000	425,000
Georgia Inst. of Tech., Atlanta	1885	7,113	469	560,000	2,329,000
†Georgia Mil. Col. (Jr.), Milledgeville	1879	229	22	15,000	—
‡Georgian Court Col., Lakewood, N.J.	1908	673	53	48,000	186,000
Georgia Southern Col., Statesboro	1908	4,320	276	135,000	—
Georgia Southwestern Col., Americus	1926	2,089	119	42,000	—
Georgia St. Col., Atlanta	1913	10,585	512	250,000	18,000
Gettysburg Col., Gettysburg, Pa.	1832	1,803	157	175,000	2,561,000
Glassboro St. Col., Glassboro, N.J.	1923	9,135	314	110,000	—
Glendale Col. (Jr.), Glendale, Calif.	1927	5,190	180	30,000	—
Glenville St. Col., Glenville, W.Va.	1872	1,670	88	44,000	—
Goddard Col., Plainfield, Vt.	1938	883	68	35,000	—
Golden Gate Col., San Francisco, Calif.	1901	3,099	150	54,000	502,000
Golden West Col. (Jr.), Huntington Beach, Calif.	1966	5,155	79	22,000	—
Gonzaga U., Spokane, Wash.	1887	2,549	213	297,000	781,000
‡Good Counsel Col., White Plains, N.Y.	1923	500	51	55,000	—
Gordon Col., Wenham, Mass.	1889	629	42	56,000	748,000
Gordon Military Col. (Jr.), Barnesville, Ga.	1852	550	28	13,000	—
Goshen Col., Goshen, Ind.	1894	1,269	140	104,000	397,000
‡Goucher Col., Baltimore, Md.	1885	1,088	118	140,000	9,261,000
Graceland Col., Lamoni, Ia.	1895	1,131	76	63,000	466,000
Grambling Col., Grambling, La.	1901	3,484	230	81,000	—
Grand Canyon Col., Phoenix, Ariz.	1949	736	39	49,000	173,000
Grand Rapids Jr. Col., Grand Rapids, Mich.	1914	4,893	180	25,000	—
Grand Valley St. Col., Allendale, Mich.	1960	2,220	85	83,000	—
Grand View Col. (Jr.), Des Moines, Ia.	1896	1,544	75	30,000	250,000
Grays Harbor Col. (Jr.), Aberdeen, Wash.	1930	1,772	100	30,000	—
Great Falls, Col. of, Great Falls, Mont.	1932	1,264	62	40,000	341,000
‡Green Mountain Col. (Jr.), Poultney, Vt.	1834	648	46	33,000	360,000
Greensboro Col., Greensboro, N.C.	1838	674	58	56,000	1,712,000
Greenville Col., Greenville, Ill.	1892	744	58	66,000	350,000
Greenville Tech. Ed. Ctr. (Jr.), Greenville, S.C.	1962	6,983	67	15,000	—
Grinnell Col., Grinnell, Ia.	1846	1,123	122	185,000	11,745,000
Grossmont Col. (Jr.), El Cajon, Calif.	1961	6,357	175	34,000	—
Grove City Col., Grove City, Pa.	1876	1,988	110	110,000	2,400,000
Guam, U. of, Agana, Guam	1952	1,386	101	68,000	8,000
Guilford Col., Greensboro, N.C.	1837	1,487	121	120,000	4,551,000
Gulf Coast Jr. Col., Panama City, Fla.	1957	1,359	70	21,000	—
‡Gulf Park Col. (Jr.), Long Beach, Miss.	1919	300	31	13,000	—
Gustavus Adolphus Col., St. Peter, Minn.	1862	1,756	126	119,000	1,532,000
‡Gwynedd-Mercy Col., Gwynedd Valley, Pa.	1948	1,055	109	35,000	—

H

Institution and location	Year found-ed	Total stu-dents	Faculty	Bound library volumes	Endowment fund
†Hamilton Col., Clinton, N.Y.	1793	828	79	287,000	$22,431,000
Hamline U., St. Paul, Minn.	1854	1,174	93	110,000	10,298,000
†Hampden-Sydney Col., Hampden-Sydney, Va.	1776	607	52	75,000	4,000,000
Hampton Inst., Hampton, Va.	1868	2,265	199	130,000	32,000,000
Hanover Col., Hanover, Ind.	1827	1,038	74	120,000	8,901,000
Harding Col., Searcy, Ark.	1924	1,872	96	88,000	13,000,000
Hardin-Simmons U., Abilene, Tex.	1891	1,676	108	110,000	4,670,000
Harris Tch. Col., St. Louis, Mo.	1857	1,458	65	45,000	—
Hartford, U. of, West Hartford, Conn.	1957	7,799	466	155,000	3,503,000
‡Hartford (Conn.) Col. for Women (Jr.)	1933	183	30	30,000	380,000
Hartnell Col. (Jr.), Salinas, Calif.	1920	3,179	128	41,000	33,000
Hartwick Col., Oneonta, N.Y.	1928	1,567	105	70,000	4,363,000
†Harvard U., Cambridge, Mass.	1636	16,641	7,357	7,920,000	665,940,000
‡Radcliffe Col.	1879	1,215		140,000	21,499,000
Hastings Col., Hastings, Neb.	1882	806	64	72,000	3,000,000
†Haverford Col., Haverford, Pa.	1833	613	76	270,000	26,853,000
Hawaii, U. of, Honolulu	1907	21,378	1,149	648,000	792,000
Hebrew Col., Brookline, Mass.	1921	122	13	52,000	340,000
†Hebrew Union Col.-Jewish Inst. of Religion, Cincinnati, O.	1875	257	26	310,000	6,932,000
Heidelberg Col., Tiffin, O.	1850	1,213	92	93,000	3,952,000
Henderson County Jr. Col., Athens, Tex.	1946	1,079	65	17,000	—
Henderson St. Col., Arkadelphia, Ark.	1929	3,350	140	90,000	—
Hendrix Col., Conway, Ark.	1884	902	50	75,000	7,100,000
Hesston Col. (Jr.), Hesston, Kan.	1909	418	35	20,000	31,000
Hibbing St. Jr. Col., Hibbing, Minn.	1916	819	40	17,000	—
Highland Park Col., Highland Park, Mich.	1918	4,211	151	26,000	—
Highline Col., Midway, Wash.	1961	5,317	293	30,000	—
High Point Col., High Point, N.C.	1924	1,214	71	73,000	2,303,000
Hillsdale Col., Hillsdale, Mich.	1844	1,167	65	44,000	4,111,000
Hinds Jr. Col., Raymond, Miss.	1917	2,645	130	25,000	—
Hiram Col., Hiram, O.	1850	1,052	90	101,000	6,885,000
Hiwassee Col. (Jr.), Madisonville, Tenn.	1849	532	32	29,000	382,000
†Hobart and ‡Wm. Smith Colleges, Geneva, N.Y.	1822	1,529	120	130,000	3,222,000
Hofstra U., Hempstead, N.Y.	1935	12,645	718	280,000	7,183,000
‡Hollins Col., Hollins College, Va.	1842	934	93	105,000	4,707,000
Holmes Jr. Col., Goodman, Miss.	1925	1,198	76	23,000	—
†Holy Cross, Col. of the, Worcester, Mass.	1843	2,373	186	248,000	5,053,000
‡Holy Family Col., Manitowoc, Wis.	1935	620	43	40,000	—
‡Holy Family Col., Philadelphia, Pa.	1954	630	50	55,000	—
‡Holy Names, Col. of, Oakland, Calif.	1880	1,084	106	84,000	201,000
‡Hood Col., Frederick, Md.	1893	767	76	86,000	3,292,000
Hope Col., Holland, Mich.	1866	1,980	131	125,000	2,379,000
Houghton Col., Houghton, N.Y.	1883	1,161	88	75,000	400,000
Houston, U. of, Houston, Tex.	1934	22,636	1,214	500,000	5,833,000
Houston Baptist Col., Houston, Tex.	. . .	769	68	40,000	—
Howard Payne Col., Brownwood, Tex.	1889	1,288	76	88,000	2,980,000
Howard U., Washington, D.C.	1867	8,852	1,169	575,000	8,074,000
Humboldt St. Col., Arcata, Calif.	1913	4,566	357	110,000	—
Huntingdon Col., Montgomery, Ala.	1854	850	68	71,000	2,570,000
Huntington Col., Huntington, Ind.	1897	519	42	39,000	545,000
Huron Col., Huron, S.D.	1883	585	48	45,000	2,000,000
Huston-Tillotson Col., Austin, Tex.	1876	723	63	46,000	249,000

I

Institution and location	Year found-ed	Total stu-dents	Faculty	Bound library volumes	Endowment fund
Idaho, Col. of, Caldwell	1891	890	89	75,000	1,520,000
Idaho, U. of, Moscow	1889	5,913	456	640,000	14,750,000
Idaho St. U., Pocatello	1901	5,704	352	167,000	17,000
Illinois, U. of, (3 campuses: Urbana-Champaign, Chicago Circle, Medical Center in Chicago), Urbana	1868	45,774	9,542	4,533,000	16,388,000
Illinois Col., Jacksonville	1829	799	53	61,000	3,800,000
Illinois Inst. of Tech., Chicago	1892	7,193	704	1,100,000	9,437,000
Illinois St. U., Normal	1857	12,735	950	350,000	—
Illinois Wesleyan U., Bloomington	1850	1,524	145	10,000	5,281,000
‡Immaculata Col., Immaculata, Pa.	1920	945	94	85,000	237,000
Immaculata Col. of Washington, D.C.	1904	270	36	27,000	—
†Immaculate Conception Sem., Conception, Mo.	1873	245	35	55,000	—
‡Immaculate Heart Col., Los Angeles, Calif.	1916	829	86	130,000	130,000
Imperial Valley Col. (Jr.), Imperial, Calif.	1922	2,000	84	16,000	—
‡Incarnate Word Col., San Antonio, Tex.	1881	1,209	112	73,000	1,082,000
Indiana Central Col., Indianapolis	1902	2,148	131	54,000	707,000
Indiana Inst. of Tech., Fort Wayne	1930	843	68	45,000	—
Indiana St. U., Terre Haute	1870	14,000	721	410,000	230,000
Indiana U., Bloomington	1820	49,310	6,157	2,626,000	10,100,000
Indiana U. of Pennsylvania, Indiana, Pa.	1875	9,062	500	350,000	—
Indian River Jr. Col., Fort Pierce, Fla.	1960	1,125	58	26,000	—
Inter American U. of Puerto Rico, San German	1912	8,437	275	110,000	830,000
†Iona Col., New Rochelle, N.Y.	1940	3,198	180	92,000	515,000
Iowa, U. of, Iowa City	1847	19,506	3,016	1,354,000	4,144,000
Iowa St. U., Ames	1858	18,083	984	640,000	2,752,000
Iowa Wesleyan Col., Mt. Pleasant	1842	1,090	65	54,000	1,160,000
Itawamba Jr. Col., Fulton, Miss.	1948	717	43	20,000	—
Ithaca Col., Ithaca, N.Y.	1892	3,545	280	130,000	377,000

J

Institution and location	Year found-ed	Total stu-dents	Faculty	Bound library volumes	Endowment fund
Jackson St. Col., Jackson, Miss.	1877	3,686	176	59,000	—
Jacksonville St. U., Jacksonville, Ala.	1883	4,907	196	150,000	—
Jacksonville U., Jacksonville, Fla.	1934	2,697	157	120,000	2,400,000
Jamestown Col., Jamestown, N.D.	1884	565	70	38,000	2,315,000
Jefferson St. Jr. Col., Birmingham, Ala.	1963	4,343	190	25,000	4,000
Jersey City (N.J.) St. Col.	1927	7,130	350	100,000	—
Jewish Theol. Sem. of America, New York, N.Y.	1887	567	98	150,000	17,261,000
John Brown U., Siloam Springs, Ark.	1919	753	49	42,000	12,000,000
John Carroll U., Cleveland, O.	1886	4,302	312	218,000	3,089,000
†Johns Hopkins U., Baltimore, Md.	1876	10,322	1,890	1,766,000	167,229,000
Johnson C. Smith U., Charlotte, N.C.	1867	1,428	94	78,000	1,346,000
Johnson St. Col., Johnson, Vt.	1867*	633	41	23,000	—
Jones County Jr. Col., Ellisville, Miss.	1927	3,252	93	28,000	—
Judson Col., Elgin, Ill.	1913	295	33	29,000	700,000
‡Judson Col., Marion, Ala.	1838	501	39	37,000	1,047,000
Juilliard Sch. of Music, New York, N.Y.	1905	955	156	35,000	—
Juniata Col., Huntingdon, Pa.	1876	1,132	90	103,000	3,373,000

Institution and location	Year found-ed	Total stu-dents	Faculty	Bound library volumes	Endowment fund
K					
Kalamazoo Col., Kalamazoo, Mich.	1833	1,215	102	150,000	$12,817,000
Kansas, U. of, Lawrence	1866	17,790	1,030	1,500,000	26,000,000
Kansas City (Mo.) Art Inst.	1885	514	43	30,000	—
Kansas St. Col. of Pittsburg	1903	5,645	438	295,000	331,000
Kansas St. Tch. Col., Emporia	1863	6,763	376	320,000	1,000,000
Kansas St. U. of Ag. & Applied Sc., Manhattan	1863	11,818	1,325	518,000	5,122,000
Kansas Wesleyan U., Salina	1886	731	50	56,000	1,430,000
Kaskaskia Col. (Jr.), Centralia, Ill.	1966	1,376	56	13,000	—
Kearney St. Col., Kearney, Neb.	1905	5,116	245	97,000	167,000
†Kemper Military Sch. & Col. (Jr.), Boonville, Mo.	1844	550	29	18,000	—
Kendall Col. (Jr.), Evanston, Ill.	1934	773	64	20,000	295,000
Kennesaw Jr. Col., Marietta, Ga.	1963	1,278	47	16,000	—
Kent St. U., Kent, O.	1910	24,599	1,225	562,000	—
Kentucky, U. of, Lexington	1865	14,224	1,330	1,000,000	639,000
Kentucky St. Col., Frankfort	1886	1,610	89	50,000	—
Kentucky Wesleyan Col., Owensboro	1858	1,183	64	48,000	895,000
Kenyon Col., Gambier, O.	1824	1,000	84	180,000	7,500,000
‡Keuka Col., Keuka Park, N.Y.	1892	791	70	55,000	1,271,000
Keystone Jr. Col., La Plume, Pa.	1868	791	48	18,000	599,000
Kilgore Col. (Jr.), Kilgore, Tex.	1935	2,435	125	40,000	—
King Col., Bristol, Tenn.	1867	346	36	51,000	1,400,000
King's Col., The, Briarcliff Manor, N.Y.	1938	659	64	53,000	—
†King's Col., Wilkes-Barre, Pa.	1946	1,906	125	94,000	540,000
Knox Col., Galesburg, Ill.	1837	1,317	97	138,000	10,670,000
Knoxville Col., Knoxville, Tenn.	1875	869	84	45,000	1,400,000
Kutztown St. Col., Kutztown, Pa.	1866	4,296	244	112,000	—
L					
‡Ladycliff Col., Highland Falls, N.Y.	1933	602	48	46,000	—
†Lafayette Col., Easton, Pa.	1826	2,008	170	234,000	26,500,000
LaGrange Col., LaGrange, Ga.	1831	532	46	43,000	4,509,000
Lake City Jr. Col. and Forest Ranger School, Lake City, Fla.	1962	858	39	21,000	—
‡Lake Erie Col., Painesville, O.	1856	611	56	60,000	1,881,000
Lake Forest Col., Lake Forest, Ill.	1857	1,266	99	105,000	6,844,000
Lakeland Col., Sheboygan, Wis.	1862	680	42	42,000	190,000
Lake Michigan Col., Benton Harbor, Mich.	1946	2,505	85	28,000	—
Lake-Sumter Jr. Col., Leesburg, Fla.	1962	900	42	54,000	—
Lamar St. Col. of Tech., Beaumont, Tex.	1923	9,396	429	138,000	278,000
Lambuth Col., Jackson, Tenn.	1843	833	62	51,000	3,226,000
Lander Col., Greenwood, S.C.	1872	591	48	55,000	—
Lane Col., Jackson, Tenn.	1882	1,036	53	45,000	403,000
Laney Col. (Jr.), Oakland, Calif.	1948	5,853	336	14,000	—
Langston U., Langston, Okla.	1897	1,386	85	110,000	—
Laredo Jr. Col., Laredo, Tex.	1947	1,357	42	29,000	—
†La Salle Col., Philadelphia, Pa.	1863	6,426	330	135,000	2,800,000
‡Lasell Jr. Col., Auburndale, Mass.	1851	897	81	26,000	113,000
Lassen Col. (Jr.), Susanville, Calif.	1925	846	38	8,000	—
La Verne Col., La Verne, Calif.	1891	662	46	36,000	1,105,000
Lawrence Inst. of Tech., Southfield, Mich.	1932	3,929	110	26,000	—
Lawrence U., Appleton, Wis.	1847	1,365	121	155,000	22,488,000
Lebanon Valley Col., Annville, Pa.	1866	1,204	82	95,000	2,434,000
Lee Col. (Jr.), Baytown, Tex.	1934	2,653	98	45,000	—
Lee Col., Cleveland, Tenn.	1918	1,127	66	43,000	—
Lees Jr. Col., Jackson, Ky.	1883	386	22	12,000	550,000
Lees-McRae Col. (Jr.), Banner Elk, N.C.	1900	687	41	33,000	750,000
†Lehigh U., Bethlehem, Pa.	1865	4,970	495	492,000	45,921,000
Leicester Jr. Col., Leicester, Mass.	1784	300	22	13,000	410,000
Le Moyne Col., Syracuse, N.Y.	1946	1,610	112	79,000	1,029,000
LeMoyne-Owen Col., Memphis, Tenn.	1870	850	45	58,000	310,000
Lenoir Rhyne Col., Hickory, N.C.	1891	1,279	106	66,000	1,782,000
‡Lesley Col., Cambridge, Mass.	1909	714	59	45,000	179,000
Lewis and Clark Col., Portland, Ore.	1867	1,884	131	80,000	2,700,000
Lewis-Clark Normal School, Lewiston, Ida.	1955	997	58	45,000	89,000
†Lewis Col., Lockport, Ill.	1930	2,020	103	50,000	159,000
‡Limestone Col., Gaffney, S.C.	1845	690	52	39,000	1,042,000
Lincoln Col. (Jr.), Lincoln, Ill.	1865	689	51	17,000	1,051,000
Lincoln Memorial U., Harrogate, Tenn.	1897	715	42	58,000	2,718,000
Lincoln U., Jefferson City, Mo.	1866	2,250	131	90,000	—
†Lincoln U., Lincoln University, Pa.	1854	911	115	100,000	1,707,000
Lindenwood Colleges, The, St. Charles, Mo.	1827	595	66	63,000	9,435,000
Lindsey Wilson Col. (Jr.), Columbia, Ky.	1904	462	32	16,000	170,000
Linfield Col., McMinnville, Ore.	1849	1,063	81	64,000	2,500,000
Little Rock U., Little Rock, Ark.	1927	3,054	164	75,000	6,000,000
Livingstone Col., Salisbury, N.C.	1879	838	66	66,000	518,000
Livingston U., Livingston, Ala.	1835	1,628	80	40,000	—
Lock Haven St. Col., Lock Haven, Pa.	1870	2,090	143	170,000	—
Loma Linda U., Loma Linda, Calif.	1905	2,922	1,200	282,000	2,894,000
Long Beach (Calif.) City Col. (Jr.)	1927	24,280	872	82,000	—
Long Island U. (incl. Brooklyn Center, C. W. Post Campus, Southampton Campus, and Brooklyn Col. of Pharmacy), Greenvale, N.Y.	1926	20,435	1,106	360,000	3,585,000
‡Longwood Col., Farmville, Va.	1884	1,696	130	105,000	—
Lon Morris Col. (Jr.), Jacksonville, Tex.	1873	340	25	19,000	1,025,000
†Loras Col., Dubuque, Ia.	1839	1,664	134	170,000	—
‡Loretto Heights Col., Denver, Colo.	1918	896	88	86,000	180,000
Los Angeles (Calif.) Col. of Optometry	1904	174	29	5,500	355,000
Louisburg Col. (Jr.), Louisburg, N.C.	1787	776	51	33,000	678,000
Louisiana Col., Pineville	1906	1,022	63	60,000	2,650,000
Louisiana Polytech. Inst., Ruston	1894	6,760	429	142,000	—
Louisiana St. U. & A. & M. Col., Baton Rouge,	1860	16,036	1,243	1,199,000	618,000
St. U. at Alexandria	1960	610	45	55,000	—
St. U. in New Orleans	1958	8,962	310	300,000	—
St. U. Medical Center, New Orleans	1931	704	226	75,000	—
Louisville, U. of, Louisville, Ky.	1798	7,999	500	520,000	8,575,000
‡Lourdes Jr. Col., Sylvania, O.	1958	128	19	44,000	125,000
Lowell Tech. Inst., Lowell, Mass.	1895	6,032	263	106,000	7,000
Lower Columbia Col. (Jr.), Longview, Wash.	1934	2,286	65	19,000	—
Loyola Col., Baltimore, Md.	1852	2,867	175	78,000	1,911,000
Loyola U., Chicago, Ill.	1870	13,548	1,484	485,000	14,537,000
†Bellarmine Sch. of Theol., North Aurora, Ill.	1934	139	29	100,000	—
†Loyola U. of Los Angeles, Calif.	1911	2,635	176	215,000	2,254,000
Marymount Col. (Jr.), Palos Verdes Est., Calif.	1932	165	17	50,000	300,000
Loyola U., New Orleans, La.	1912	4,446	354	235,000	. . .
Lubbock Christian Col. (Jr.), Lubbock, Texas	1957	646	30	26,000	$ 750,000
Luther Col., Decorah, Ia.	1861	1,980	139	160,000	1,293,000
Lycoming Col., Williamsport, Pa.	1812	1,481	110	80,000	1,250,000
Lynchburg Col., Lynchburg, Va.	1903	1,755	118	69,000	4,500,000
Lyndon St. Col., Lyndonville, Vt.	1911	602	41	30,000	—
M					
Macalester Col., St. Paul, Minn.	1885	1,897	161	175,000	27,732,000
MacMurray Col., Jacksonville, Ill.	1846	1,012	74	97,000	4,761,000
Madison Col., Harrisonburg, Va.	1908	3,857	225	136,000	—
‡Madonna Col., Livonia, Mich.	1947	727	56	52,000	—
Maine, U. of (incl. Portland and Augusta campuses), Orono	1865	13,743	748	472,000	5,101,000
Aroostook St. Col., Presque Isle	1903	450	28	. . .	—
Farmington St. Col., Farmington	1864	1,037	68	42,000	250,000
Ft. Kent St. Col., Ft. Kent	1878	260	20	. . .	—
Gorham St. Col., Gorham	1879	855	70	35,000	—
Washington St. Col., Machias	1909	300	26	. . .	—
Malone Col., Canton, O.	1892	1,077	65	49,000	592,000
Manatee Jr. Col., Bradenton, Fla.	1958	3,000	120	35,000	—
Manchester Col., North Manchester, Ind.	1889	1,369	82	91,000	1,467,000
†Manhattan Col., Bronx, N.Y.	1853	4,500	310	125,000	1,691,000
Manhattan School of Music, New York, N.Y.	1917	693	137	9,000	2,500,000
Manhattanville Col., Purchase, N.Y.	1841	1,461	135	180,000	2,835,000
Mankato St. Col., Mankato, Minn.	1867	11,699	575	265,000	—
Mansfield St. Col., Mansfield, Pa.	1857	2,625	203	86,000	—
Marian Col., Indianapolis, Ind.	1851	1,074	90	60,000	120,000
‡Marian Col. of Fond du Lac, Wis.	1936	476	49	38,000	—
Marietta Col., Marietta, O.	1835	1,857	118	164,000	4,709,000
‡Marillac Col., St. Louis, Mo.	1955	348	63	56,000	126,000
Marin, Col. of (Jr.), Kentfield, Calif.	1926	5,394	146	34,000	—
Marion Col., Marion, Ind.	1920	792	48	40,000	—
†Marion Inst. (Jr.), Marion, Ala.	1842	374	34	16,000	—
†Marist Col., Poughkeepsie, N.Y.	1929	1,860	98	61,000	—
Marlboro Col., Marlboro, Vt.	1946	169	31	26,000	20,000
Marquette U., Milwaukee, Wis.	1864	10,067	736	425,000	4,928,000
Marshalltown (Ia.) Comm. Col. (Jr.)	1927	1,147	54	18,000	—
Marshall U., Huntington, W.Va.	1837	8,041	375	165,000	—
Mars Hill Col., Mars Hill, N.C.	1856	1,351	93	75,000	750,000
Martin Col. (Jr.), Pulaski, Tenn.	1870	410	30	12,000	990,000
‡Mary Baldwin Col., Staunton, Va.	1842	718	51	82,000	2,250,000
‡Marycrest Col., Davenport, Ia.	1939	1,080	76	65,000	336,000
‡Marygrove Col. (incl. Monroe campus), Detroit, Mich.	1910	1,191	104	133,000	760,000
‡Mary Hardin-Baylor Col., Belton, Tex.	1845	859	62	64,000	4,000,000
‡Mary Immaculate Sem., Northampton, Pa.	1939	80	13	38,000	—
†Maryknoll Col., Glen Ellyn, Ill.	1949	186	34	42,000	—
Maryland, U. of, College Park	1807	32,544	3,148	1,000,000	9,133,000
Maryland St. Col. at Princess Anne	1886	717	65	55,000	—
‡Marylhurst Col., Marylhurst, Ore.	1893	550	70	74,000	228,000
‡Mary Manse Col., Toledo, O.	1922	1,012	73	67,000	—
Marymount Col., Salina, Kan.	1922	518	66	46,000	—
‡Marymount Col., Tarrytown, N.Y.	1918	1,060	97	70,000	—
‡Marymount Col. of Virginia (Jr.), Arlington	1950	721	50	26,000	—
‡Marymount Manhattan Col., New York, N.Y.	1936	525	72	35,000	245,000
‡Mary Rogers Col., Maryknoll, N.Y.	1931	182	29	50,000	—
Maryville Col., Maryville, Tenn.	1819	757	66	85,000	4,250,000
‡Maryville Col. of the Sacred Heart, St. Louis, Mo.	1872	465	50	60,000	—
‡Marywood Col., Scranton, Pa.	1915	2,000	129	89,000	272,000
Massachusetts, U. of, Amherst campus	1863	16,209	968	766,000	1,112,000
Boston campus	1863	3,370	204	65,000	1,000
Massachusetts Col. of Art, Boston	1873	474	44	21,000	—
Massachusetts Inst. of Tech., Cambridge	1861	7,764	1,714	1,134,000	142,417,000
Massachusetts State Colleges:					
Boston St. Col.	1852	7,313	355	63,000	—
Bridgewater St. Col.	1840	6,250	275	55,000	25,000
Fitchburg St. Col.	1894	3,293	166	60,000	—
Framingham St. Col.	1839	3,740	170	50,000	—
Lowell St. Col.	1894	1,855	159	60,000	—
North Adams St. Col.	1894	1,352	80	45,000	—
Salem St. Col.	1854	5,989	212	71,000	—
Westfield St. Col.	1839	3,257	142	50,000	—
Worcester St. Col.	1871	3,997	124	59,000	—
Mauna Olu Col., Paia, Hawaii	1861	127	25	14,000	20,000
Mayville St. Col., Mayville, N.D.	1889	880	46	66,000	—
McMurry Col., Abilene, Tex.	1922	1,611	89	80,000	2,925,000
McNeese St. Col., Lake Charles, La.	1939	4,533	229	97,000	—
McPherson Col., McPherson, Kan.	1887	768	48	41,000	1,198,000
Medaille Col., Buffalo, N.Y.	1937	435	35	56,000	—
Memphis Acad. of Arts, Memphis, Tenn.	1936	510	30	7,000	—
Memphis St. U., Memphis, Tenn.	1909	15,544	645	275,000	—
†Menlo Col., Menlo Park, Calif.	1915	537	52	30,000	—
Merced Col. (Jr.), Merced, Calif.	1963	3,050	57	19,000	—
Mercer U., Macon, Ga.	1833	1,908	118	140,000	10,000,000
‡Mercy Col., Dobbs Ferry, N.Y.	1950	640	69	49,000	—
Mercy Col. of Detroit, Mich.	1941	1,155	92	60,000	—
‡Mercyhurst Col., Erie, Pa.	1926	701	62	45,000	—
‡Meredith Col., Raleigh, N.C.	1891	859	69	52,000	1,201,000
Meridian Jr. Col., Meridian, Miss.	1937	1,425	81	14,000	—
Merrimack Col., North Andover, Mass.	1947	2,389	170	58,000	423,000
Merritt Col., Oakland, Calif.	1953	8,861	351	45,000	—
Mesa Jr. Col., Grand Junction, Colo.	1925	2,440	105	32,000	—
Mesabi St. Jr. Col., Virginia, Minn.	1966	687	35	25,000	—
Messiah Col., Grantham, Pa.	1909	494	45	50,000	468,000
Methodist Col., Fayetteville, N.C.	1956	994	56	38,000	—
Metropolitan Jr. Col., Kansas City, Mo.	1915	6,104	173	42,000	—
Miami, U. of, Coral Gables, Fla.	1925	14,647	672	854,000	26,533,000
Miami-Dade Jr. Col., Miami, Fla.	1960	24,098	1,050	114,000	—
Miami U., Oxford, O.	1809	10,655	696	500,000	1,675,000
Michigan, U. of, Ann Arbor	1817	38,021	2,356	3,889,000	53,868,000
Michigan St. U., East Lansing	1855	49,515	4,888	1,105,000	8,609,000
Michigan Tech. U., Houghton	1885	4,115	335	135,000	1,030,000
Lake Superior St. Col., Sault Ste. Marie	1946	1,299	72	25,000	—

Institution and location	Year founded	Total students	Faculty	Bound library volumes	Endowment fund
Middlebury Col., Middlebury, Vt.	1800	1,546	125	180,000	$17,445,000
Middle Georgia Col. (Jr.), Cochran	1928	1,821	93	35,000	—
Middle Tennessee St. U., Murfreesboro	1911	6,413	360	162,000	—
Midland Lutheran Col., Fremont, Neb.	1883	824	54	60,000	702,000
‡Midway Jr. Col., Midway, Ky.	1847	171	17	15,000	4,525,000
Midwestern U., Wichita Falls, Tex.	1922	3,633	173	115,000	—
Millersville St. Col., Millersville, Pa.	1855	4,487	304	145,000	—
Milligan Col., Milligan College, Tenn.	1882	837	53	50,000	—
Millikin U., Decatur, Ill.	1901	1,344	96	102,000	3,781,000
‡Mills Col., Oakland, Calif.	1852	792	89	148,000	15,295,000
‡Mills Col. of Education, New York, N.Y.	1909	525	42	38,000	225,000
Millsaps Col., Jackson, Miss.	1892	896	85	79,000	4,769,000
Milton Col., Milton, Wis.	1848	638	46	44,000	109,000
Milwaukee Tech. Col. (Jr.), Milwaukee, Wis.	1951	8,499	570	28,000	—
Minneapolis (Minn.) School of Art	1886	352	39	22,000	—
Minnesota, U. of, Minneapolis, St. Paul, Duluth, Morris, Crookston	1851	66,824	3,621	2,690,000	80,703,000
Minot St. Col., Minot, N.D.	1913	3,144	130	100,000	—
MiraCosta Col. (Jr.), Oceanside, Calif.	1934	2,126	84	16,000	—
Mississippi, U. of, University	1848	7,226	704	480,000	748,000
Mississippi Col., Clinton	1826	2,258	98	114,000	2,000,000
Mississippi Delta Jr. Col., Moorhead	1911	1,047	55	18,000	—
‡Mississippi St. Col. for Women, Columbus	1884	2,496	157	145,000	200,000
Mississippi St. U., State College	1878	7,983	729	300,000	414,000
Mississippi Valley St. Col., Itta Bena, Miss.	1946	2,497	158	43,000	—
Missouri, U. of,—Columbia	1839	18,883	2,673	1,382,000	5,800,000
Missouri, U. of,—Kansas City	1933	8,570	900	350,000	944,000
Missouri, U. of,—Rolla	1870	5,309	584	150,000	—
Missouri, U. of,—St. Louis	1963	8,082	277	73,000	—
Missouri Baptist Col. (Jr.), Hannibal	1858	645	44	26,000	32,000
Missouri Southern Col., Joplin	1937	2,662	124	65,000	—
Missouri Valley Col., Marshall	1888	825	48	61,000	1,983,000
Missouri Western Col., St. Joseph	1915	1,548	80	28,000	—
Mitchell Col. (Jr.), New London, Conn.	1938	1,550	82	31,000	94,000
Mitchell Col. (Jr.), Statesville, N.C.	1852	496	28	16,000	487,000
Mobile Col., Mobile, Ala.	1960	372	31	25,000	—
Modesto Jr. Col., Modesto, Calif.	1921	4,271	230	62,000	8,008,000
‡Molloy Catholic Col. for Women, Rockville Centre, N.Y.	1955	912	77	51,000	—
Monmouth Col., Monmouth, Ill.	1853	1,233	104	123,000	2,200,000
Monmouth Col., West Long Branch, N.J.	1933	5,179	284	100,000	1,226,000
Montana, U. of, Missoula	1893	7,218	510	450,000	1,218,000
Montana Col. of Min. Sc. & Tech., Butte	1893	693	42	36,000	1,600,000
Montana St. U., Bozeman	1893	6,505	643	465,000	3,380,000
Montclair St. Col., Upper Montclair, N.J.	1908	8,194	330	134,000	150,000
Monterey (Calif.) Inst. of Foreign Studies	1955	206	44	26,000	—
Monterey Peninsula Col., Monterey, Calif.	1947	2,816	98	38,000	—
Montevallo, U. of, Montevallo, Ala.	1896	2,150	115	105,000	—
‡Monticello Col. (Jr.), Godfrey, Ill.	1835	352	41	29,000	844,000
Montreat-Anderson Col. (Jr.), Montreat, N.C.	1916	415	30	30,000	377,000
‡Moore Col. of Art, Philadelphia, Pa.	1844	481	77	22,000	5,000,000
Moorhead St. Col., Moorhead, Minn.	1887	4,355	275	100,000	12,000
Moravian Col., Bethlehem, Pa.	1807	1,157	83	102,000	4,973,000
Morehead St. U., Morehead, Ky.	1922	5,922	295	151,000	—
†Morehouse Col., Atlanta, Ga.	1867	985	87	228,000	4,601,000
Morgan St. Col., Baltimore, Md.	1867	3,936	273	103,000	—
Morningside Col., Sioux City, Ia.	1894	1,312	99	99,000	2,479,000
Morris Brown Col., Atlanta, Ga.	1881	1,142	96	22,000	1,004,000
Morris Harvey Col., Charleston, W.Va.	1888	3,012	136	54,000	1,292,000
Morristown Col., Morristown, Tenn.	1881	171	18	13,000	228,000
Morton Col., Cicero, Ill.	1924	2,675	180	21,000	—
‡Mt. Aloysius Jr. Col., Cresson, Pa.	1939	431	49	25,000	—
Mt. Angel Col., Mt. Angel, Ore.	1887	331	50	46,000	39,000
†Mt. Angel Sem., St. Benedict, Ore.	1887/89	102	35	50,000	—
‡Mt. Holyoke Col., South Hadley, Mass.	1837	1,786	186	300,000	29,917,000
‡Mt. Marty Col., Yankton, S.D.	1936	439	62	35,000	—
‡Mt. Mary Col., Milwaukee, Wis.	1872	980	95	72,000	475,000
‡Mt. Mercy Col., Cedar Rapids, Ia.	1928	630	44	35	—
Mt. Olive Jr. Col., Mt. Olive, N.C.	1951	346	31	18,000	295,000
‡Mt. St. Agnes Col., Baltimore, Md.	1867	489	50	42,000	199,000
Mt. St. Clare Col. (Jr.), Clinton, Ia.	1918	314	38	24,000	—
‡Mt. St. Joseph on-the-Ohio, Col. of, Mt. St. Joseph, O.	1854	929	98	78,000	423,000
‡Mt. St. Mary Col., Hooksett, N.H.	1934	298	43	29,000	180,000
‡Mt. St. Mary Col., Newburgh, N.Y.	1959	471	65	38,000	—
†Mt. St. Mary's Col., Emmitsburg, Md.	1808	932	78	86,000	565,000
‡Mt. St. Mary's Col., Los Angeles, Calif.	1925	1,240	110	90,000	494,000
‡Mt. St. Scholastica Col., Atchison, Kan.	1863	917	68	60,000	—
‡Mt. St. Vincent, Col. of, Bronx, N.Y.	1910	999	90	50,000	475,000
Mt. San Antonio Col. (Jr.), Walnut, Calif.	1946	11,723	425	70,000	—
Mt. Union Col., Alliance, O.	1846	1,344	91	120,000	4,000,000
‡Mt. Vernon Jr. Col., Washington, D.C.	1875	275	32	17,000	350,000
Muhlenberg Col., Allentown, Pa.	1848	1,425	103	132,000	3,795,000
Multnomah Col. (Jr.), Portland, Ore.	1897	860	80	12,000	54,000
‡Mundelein Col., Chicago, Ill.	1930	1,243	98	76,000	241,000
Murray St. Col. of Ag. and Ap. Sc., Tishomingo, Okla.	1908	803	35	16,000	—
Murray St. U., Murray, Ky.	1922	6,737	400	160,000	—
Museum Art School, Portland, Ore.	1909	120	27	4,000	220,000
Muskingum Col., New Concord, O.	1837	1,399	112	110,000	6,840,000
N					
Napa Col. (Jr.), Napa, Calif.	1942	3,057	147	25,000	—
Nasson Col., Springvale, Me.	1912	877	64	45,000	915,000
National Col. of Ed., Evanston, Ill.	1886	1,720	102	56,000	541,000
Naval Postgrad. School, Monterey, Calif.	1909	1,400	253	241,000	—
Navarro Jr. Col., Corsicana, Tex.	1946	965	59	21,000	—
‡Nazareth Col., Kalamazoo, Mich.	1924	506	62	47,000	85,000
Nazareth Col. of Kentucky, Nazareth	1814	441	60	42,000	—
‡Nazareth Col. of Rochester, N.Y.	1924	1,380	119	100,000	—
Nebraska, U. of, Lincoln	1869	18,375	976	891,000	2,700,000
Nebraska, U. of, at Omaha	1908	10,010	389	261,000	296,000
Nebraska Wesleyan U., Lincoln	1887	1,458	110	80,000	3,800,000
Nevada, U. of, Reno	1874	6,539	412	360,000	3,580,000
Nevada Southern U., Las Vegas	1964	2,947	...	158,000	—
New Col., Sarasota, Fla.	1960	350	43	47,000	—
Newark Col. of Engineering, Newark, N.J.	1881	6,080	400	56,000	167,000
Newark St. Col., Union, N.J.	1855	10,934	273	100,000	—
New Church, Acad. of the, Bryn Athyn, Pa.	1876	120	34	73,000	$15,063,000
New England Col., Henniker, N.H.	1946	765	73	27,000	—
New England Cons. of Music, Boston, Mass.	1867	2,321	223	25,000	—
Newberry Col., Newberry, S.C.	1856	849	62	54,000	969,000
New Hampshire, U. of, Durham	1866	7,229	637	493,000	4,361,000
Keene St. Col., Keene	1909	1,649	108	65,000	—
Plymouth St. Col., Plymouth	1870	1,977	103	65,000	—
New Haven Col., West Haven, Conn.	1920	3,621	258	50,000	125,000
New Mexico, The U. of, Albuquerque	1889	13,639	741	600,000	10,395,000
New Mexico Highlands U., Las Vegas	1893	2,128	90	99,000	—
New Mexico Inst. of Mining & Tech., Socorro	1889	688	69	57,000	1,247,000
†New Mexico Military Inst. (Jr.), Roswell	1891	934	55	50,000	—
New Mexico St. U., Las Cruces	1889	7,356	359	237,000	2,054,000
New Orleans (La.) Baptist Theol. Sem.	1917	846	45	112,000	800,000
‡New Rochelle, Col. of, New Rochelle, N.Y.	1904	952	100	98,000	1,057,000
New School for Social Research, The New York, N.Y.	1919	13,873	464	60,000	—
‡Newton (Mass.) Col. of the Sacred Heart	1946	830	95	65,000	—
Newton Jr. Col., Newtonville, Mass.	1946	503	52	21,000	—
New York (N.Y.), City U. of (all campuses)	1847	159,625	12,279	2,100,000	13,200,000
Brooklyn Col., Brooklyn	1930	27,354	1,612	466,000	60,000
City Col., New York	1847	18,906	1,400	833,000	2,270,000
Hunter Col., New York	1870	18,968	1,000	310,000	1,300,000
Queens Col., Flushing	1937	23,844	1,154	282,000	138,000
New York, St. U. of, Albany	1948	105,513	7,044	4,694,000	—
St. U. at Albany	1844	10,141	633	368,000	—
St. U. at Binghamton	1946	4,588	317	322,000	—
St. U. at Buffalo (incl. Health Sciences Ctr.)	1846	22,344	1,329	1,009,000	—
St. U. at Old Westbury	1965	107	9	...	—
St. U. at Stony Brook	1957	6,739	460	275,000	—
Col. at Brockport	1867	5,514	290	154,000	—
Col. at Buffalo	1867	8,931	495	183,000	—
Col. at Cortland	1868	4,474	268	175,000	—
Col. at Fredonia	1867	3,742	201	146,000	—
Col. at Geneseo	1871	4,136	267	144,000	—
Col. at New Paltz	1885	5,952	359	175,000	—
Col. at Oneonta	1887	5,036	313	179,000	—
Col. at Oswego	1861	6,650	358	222,000	—
Col. at Plattsburgh	1889	4,321	229	152,000	—
Col. at Potsdam	1867	3,547	255	125,000	—
Downstate Health Science Ctr. at Brooklyn	1858	914	402	307,000	—
Upstate Health Science Ctr. at Syracuse	1834	616	381	90,000	—
Col. of Forestry at Syracuse U.	1911	1,516	101	69,000	—
†Maritime Col. at Ft. Schuyler	1874	724	52	48,000	—
Col. of Agriculture at Cornell U.	1904	3,146	142	374,000	—
Col. of Ceramics at Alfred U.	1900	528	37	43,000	—
Col. of Home Economics at Cornell U.	1925	1,052	85	374,000	—
School of Industrial and Labor Relations at Cornell U.	1944	501	31	87,000	—
Veterinary Col. at Cornell U.	1894	294	30	47,000	—
Niagara U., Niagara University, N.Y.	1856	2,803	195	98,000	211,000
†Nichols Col. of Bus. Adm., Dudley, Mass.	1815	673	41	25,000	437,000
Norman Col. (Jr.), Norman Park, Ga.	1900	200	16	14,000	694,000
North Carolina, U. of, Chapel Hill					
North Carolina St. U. at Raleigh	1887	11,153	1,600	430,000	1,503,000
North Carolina, U. of, at Asheville	1927	737	60	60,000	—
North Carolina, U. of, at Chapel Hill	1789	15,678	1,600	1,822,000	18,104,000
North Carolina, U. of, at Charlotte	1946	2,351	146	103,000	1,454,000
North Carolina, U. of, at Greensboro	1891	5,738	374	300,000	—
North Carolina A. & T. St. U., Greensboro	1891	4,011	280	264,000	—
North Carolina Col. at Durham	1910	3,042	255	191,000	—
North Carolina Wesleyan Col., Rocky Mount	1956	643	51	35,000	—
North Central Col., Naperville, Ill.	1861	833	67	100,000	2,988,000
North Dakota, U. of, Grand Forks	1883	7,010	452	342,000	1,200,000
North Dakota St. U., Fargo	1890	6,228	448	235,000	2,828,000
Northeastern Illinois St. Col., Chicago	1869	6,137	374	97,000	—
Northeastern Jr. Col., Sterling, Colo.	1941	1,428	93	29,000	—
Northeastern Oklahoma A. & M. Col. (Jr.), Miami	1919	2,114	78	23,000	—
Northeastern St. Col., Tahlequah, Okla.	1846	5,583	212	134,000	—
Northeastern U., Boston, Mass.	1898	35,447	1,860	211,000	22,000
Northeast Louisiana St. Col., Monroe	1931	6,820	334	123,000	—
Northeast Mississippi Jr. Col., Booneville	1948	918	60	16,000	—
Northeast Missouri St. Col., Kirksville	1867	5,321	218	159,000	—
Northern Arizona U., Flagstaff	1899	8,151	375	220,000	—
Northern Baptist Theol. Sem., Oakbrook, Ill.	1913	46	10	65,000	411,000
Northern Illinois U., DeKalb	1895	21,449	916	502,000	—
Northern Iowa, U. of, Cedar Falls	1876	8,450	485	310,000	—
Northern Michigan U., Marquette	1899	6,294	286	84,000	—
Northern Montana Col., Havre	1929	1,193	86	45,000	—
Northern Oklahoma Col., Tonkawa	1901	1,207	51	17,000	—
Northern St. Col., Aberdeen, S.D.	1901	3,201	150	115,000	—
North Florida Jr. Col., Madison	1958	1,039	63	23,000	—
North Georgia Col., Dahlonega	1873	1,032	56	75,000	—
North Greenville Jr. Col., Tigerville, S.C.	1934	497	31	16,000	126,000
North Idaho Jr. Col., Coeur d'Alene	1939	868	63	16,000	—
Northland Col., Ashland, Wis.	1892	681	57	40,000	1,196,000
North Park Col. and Theol. Sem., Chicago, Ill.	1891	1,722	112	104,000	1,449,000
Northrop Inst. of Tech., Inglewood, Calif.	1942	1,867	102	20,000	—
North Texas St. U., Denton	1890	14,511	887	680,000	—
Northwest Christian Col., Eugene, Ore.	1895	404	23	35,000	153,000
Northwestern Col., Orange City, Ia.	1928	734	62	42,000	450,000
Northwestern Michigan Col. (Jr.), Traverse City	1951	1,116	57	27,000	—
Northwestern St. Col., Alva, Okla.	1897	2,641	96	72,000	—
Northwestern St. Col. of Louisiana, Natchitoches	1884	5,512	300	170,000	—
Northwestern U., Evanston, Ill.	1851	16,734	2,313	1,936,000	253,870,000
Northwest Mississippi Jr. Col., Senatobia	1927	1,517	96	11,000	—
Northwest Missouri St. Col., Maryville	1905	4,365	230	110,000	—
Northwest Nazarene Col., Nampa, Ida.	1913	1,043	72	60,000	159,000
†Norwich U., Northfield, Vt.	1819	1,197	116	90,000	7,250,000
‡Notre Dame, Col. of, Belmont, Calif.	1851	1,364	90	68,000	—
‡Notre Dame of Maryland, Col. of, Baltimore	1873	1,232	82	55,000	—
†Notre Dame, U. of, Notre Dame, Ind.	1842	7,526	699	872,000	62,000,000
‡Notre Dame Col., Cleveland, O.	1922	621	62	47,000	—
‡Notre Dame Col., St. Louis, Mo.	1954	332	39	70,000	—
‡Notre Dame Col. of Staten Island, N.Y.	1931	500	43	38,000	—
†Notre Dame Sem., New Orleans, La.	1923	117	26	46,000	—
Nyack Missionary Col., Nyack, N.Y.	1882	651	49	43,000	—

Institution and location	Year founded	Total students	Faculty	Bound library volumes	Endowment fund

O

Institution and location	Year founded	Total students	Faculty	Bound library volumes	Endowment fund
Oakwood Col., Huntsville, Ala.	1896	513	48	45,000	$ 300,000
Oberlin Col., Oberlin, O.	1833	2,557	235	648,000	70,244,000
Occidental Col., Los Angeles, Calif.	1887	1,718	122	225,000	20,302,000
Odessa Col. (Jr.), Odessa, Tex.	1946	2,398	181	35,000	—
Oglethorpe Col., Atlanta, Ga.	1835	1,042	46	39,000	1,700,000
Ohio Dominican Col., Columbus, O.	1911	991	76	48,000	210,000
Ohio Northern U., Ada	1871	2,160	148	120,000	3,183,000
Ohio St. U., Columbus	1870	41,032	4,500	2,104,000	38,883,000
Ohio U., Athens	1804	16,998	822	475,000	1,000,000
Ohio Wesleyan U., Delaware	1842	2,562	160	320,000	9,479,000
Oklahoma, U. of, Norman	1890	19,055	1,720	1,800,000	25,565,000
Oklahoma Baptist U., Shawnee	1911	1,530	104	80,000	2,974,000
Oklahoma Christian Col., Oklahoma City	1950	1,039	43	55,000	—
Oklahoma City (Okla.) U.	1904	2,239	200	132,000	2,362,000
Oklahoma Col. of Liberal Arts, Chickasha	1908	913	65	64,000	—
Oklahoma Mil. Acad. (Jr.), Claremore	1919	634	34	17,000	—
Oklahoma Panhandle St. Col. of Ag. and App. Sc., Goodwell	1909	1,267	63	42,000	—
Oklahoma St. U., Stillwater	1890	16,562	1,255	918,000	10,254,000
Old Dominion Col., Norfolk, Va.	1930	8,648	386	135,000	1,320,000
Olivet Col., Olivet, Mich.	1844	778	56	53,000	486,000
Olivet Nazarene Col., Kankakee, Ill.	1907	1,831	106	63,000	400,000
Olympic Col. (Jr.), Bremerton, Wash.	1946	3,880	205	26,000	—
Orange Coast Col. (Jr.), Costa Mesa, Calif.	1947	15,798	482	65,000	—
Oregon, U. of, Eugene	1872	14,000	1,400	987,000	3,538,000
Oregon Col. of Ed., Monmouth	1856	3,257	240	85,000	—
Oregon St. U., Corvallis	1868	14,524	1,210	585,000	1,289,000
Oregon Tech. Inst., Klamath Falls	1947	1,120	110	26,000	—
Orlando, The Col. of (Jr.), Orlando, Fla.	1941	1,285	66	40,000	300,000
Otero Jr. Col., La Junta, Colo.	1941	1,046	45	18,000	—
Otis Art. Inst. of Los Angeles County, Los Angeles, Calif.	1918	416	30	8,000	—
Ottawa U., Ottawa, Kan.	1865	938	71	64,000	1,228,000
Otterbein Col., Westerville, O.	1847	1,417	101	60,000	2,164,000
Ottumwa Heights Col. (Jr.), Ottumwa, Ia.	1925	390	34	24,000	—
Ouachita Baptist U., Arkadelphia and Little Rock, Ark.	1886	1,637	83	88,000	2,553,000
†Our Lady of Hope Sem., Newburgh, N.Y.	1966	48	10	16,000	—
‡Our Lady of the Elms, Col. of, Chicopee, Mass.	1928	650	68	42,000	—
‡Our Lady of the Lake Col., San Antonio, Tex.	1911	1,668	105	82,000	1,091,000
Ozarks, The Col. of the, Clarksville, Ark.	1834	565	35	55,000	587,000
Ozarks, School of the, Point Lookout, Mo.	1906	766	45	62,000	23,000,000

P

Institution and location	Year founded	Total students	Faculty	Bound library volumes	Endowment fund
Pace Col. (incl. Westchester branch, Pleasantville), New York, N.Y.	1906	8,575	555	180,000	—
Pacific, U. of the, Stockton, Calif.	1851	4,021	570	190,000	4,580,000
Pacific Col., Fresno, Calif.	1944	380	36	50,000	48,000
Pacific Lutheran U., Tacoma, Wash.	1894	2,686	165	101,000	600,000
Pacific Oaks Col., Pasadena, Calif.	1945	274	13	14,000	141,000
Pacific Union Col., Angwin, Calif.	1882	1,807	118	78,000	—
Pacific U., Forest Grove, Ore.	1849	1,114	103	75,000	6,919,000
‡Packer Collegiate Inst. (Jr.), Brooklyn, N.Y.	1845	100	23	17,000	625,000
Paine Col., Augusta, Ga.	1883	754	53	41,000	387,000
Palm Beach Jr. Col., Lake Worth, Fla.	1933	4,700	189	58,000	—
Palomar Jr. Col., San Marcos, Calif.	1946	5,123	154	50,000	—
Palo Verde Col. (Jr.), Blythe, Calif.	1947	379	35	9,000	—
Pan American Col., Edinburg, Tex.	1927	4,009	149	75,000	—
Panola Col. (Jr.), Carthage, Tex.	1948	573	35	14,000	—
Paris Jr. Col., Paris, Tex.	1924	543	38	14,000	—
Park Col., Parkville, Mo.	1875	713	52	78,000	3,167,000
Parsons Col., Fairfield, Ia.	1875	1,590	87	121,000	—
Pasadena (Calif.) City Col. (Jr.)	1924	12,922	349	90,000	—
Pasadena (Calif.) Col.	1902	1,228	67	105,000	—
Pasadena (Calif.) Playhouse Col. of Theatre Arts	1928	128	35	22,000	—
Paterson St. Col., Wayne, N.J.	1855	6,775	269	114,000	—
Peabody Inst. of Baltimore, Md.	1857	466	77	275,000	—
‡Peace Col. (Jr.), Raleigh, N.C.	1857	474	26	20,000	1,000,000
Pearl River Jr. Col., Poplarville, Miss.	1912	952	63	20,000	—
Pembroke St. Col., Pembroke, N.C.	1887	1,564	103	55,000	—
Peninsula Col. (Jr.), Port Angeles, Wash.	1961	997	50	15,000	—
Pennsylvania, U. of, Philadelphia	1740	18,081	4,611	2,100,000	164,000,000
Pennsylvania Col. of Optometry, Philadelphia	1919	398	55	10,000	469,000
Pennsylvania St. U., University Park	1855	38,625	2,900	1,164,000	517,000
Pensacola Jr. Col., Pensacola, Fla.	1948	3,912	165	43,000	—
Pepperdine Col., Los Angeles, Calif.	1937	1,665	140	90,000	1,058,000
Perkinston Col. (Jr.), Perkinston, Miss.	1911	555	43	17,000	—
Peru St. Col., Peru, Neb.	1867	1,132	60	90,000	—
Pfeiffer Col., Misenheimer, N.C.	1885	958	72	54,000	1,800,000
Philadelphia (Pa.) Col. of Art	1876	919	104	28,000	1,010,000
Philadelphia (Pa.) Col. of Bible	1913	994	58	29,000	—
Philadelphia (Pa.) Col. of Pharm. & Science	1821	944	866	49,000	6,379,000
Philadelphia (Pa.) Col. of Textiles & Science	1884	1,511	74	30,000	2,184,000
Philander Smith Col., Little Rock, Ark.	1877	609	49	497,000	582,000
Phillips U., Enid, Okla.	1907	1,330	105	155,000	3,750,000
Piedmont Col., Demorest, Ga.	1897	629	37	56,000	1,800,000
Pikeville Col., Pikeville, Ky.	1889	1,209	60	58,000	970,000
‡Pine Manor Jr. Col., Chestnut Hill, Mass.	1911	499	54	19,000	12,000
Pittsburgh, U. of, Pittsburgh, Pa.	1787	25,024	1,572	1,189,000	81,717,000
PMC Colleges, The, Chester, Pa.	1821	2,836	255	63,000	825,000
Point Park Col., Pittsburgh, Pa.	1960	3,190	147	42,000	590,000
Polk Jr. Col., Bartow, Fla.	1964	3,275	137	28,000	—
Polytechnic Inst. of Brooklyn, N.Y.	1854	5,283	475	105,000	6,032,000
Porterville Col. (Jr.), Porterville, Calif.	1927	883	47	16,000	—
Portland, U. of, Portland, Ore.	1901	1,785	144	130,000	—
Portland St. U., Portland, Ore.	1955	9,020	734	239,000	—
Prairie St. Col. (Jr.), Chicago Heights, Ill.	1958	2,915	75	18,000	—
Pratt Inst., Brooklyn, N.Y.	1887	4,448	521	225,000	16,300,000
Presbyterian Col., Clinton, S.C.	1880	669	56	66,000	2,576,000
Presbyterian Sch. of Christian Ed., Richmond, Va.	1914	190	11	125,000	1,599,000
Princeton Theol. Sem., Princeton, N.J.	1812	640	58	287,000	21,044,000
Princeton U., Princeton, N.J.	1746	4,761	885	2,307,000	146,484,000
Principia Col., Elsah, Ill.	1910	697	62	96,000	12,000,000
†Providence Col., Providence, R.I.	1917	2,458	205	110,000	1,263,000
Puerto Rico, U. of, Rio Piedras, P.R.	1903	28,230	2,225	60,000	—
Puerto Rico Jr. Col., Rio Piedras, P. R.	1949	2,886	111	26,000	$ 75,000
Puget Sound, U. of, Tacoma, Wash.	1888	3,770	185	134,000	5,543,000
Purdue U., Lafayette, Ind.	1869	33,884	2,821	900,000	17,381,000

Q

Institution and location	Year founded	Total students	Faculty	Bound library volumes	Endowment fund
‡Queens Col., Charlotte, N.C.	1857	740	69	61,000	2,828,000
Quincy Col., Quincy, Ill.	1860	1,632	105	139,000	821,000
Quinnipiac Col., Hamden, Conn.	1929	2,438	200	55,000	—

R

Institution and location	Year founded	Total students	Faculty	Bound library volumes	Endowment fund
‡Radford Col., Radford, Va.	1910	3,464	220	92,000	—
†Randolph-Macon Col., Ashland, Va.	1830	860	67	77,000	3,518,000
‡Randolph-Macon Woman's Col., Lynchburg, Va.	1891	866	86	115,000	3,729,000
Ranger Jr. Col., Ranger, Tex.	1926	394	21	8,000	—
Redlands, U. of, Redlands, Calif.	1907	1,723	130	159,000	11,800,000
Redwoods, Col. of the (Jr.), Eureka, Calif.	1964	3,400	89	14,000	—
Reed Col., Portland, Ore.	1909	1,185	120	185,000	5,254,000
Reedley Col. (Jr.), Reedley, Calif.	1926	1,816	79	17,000	—
Regis Col., Denver, Colo.	1888	1,189	81	73,000	1,350,000
‡Regis Col., Weston, Mass.	1927	1,180	103	85,000	—
Reinhardt Col. (Jr.), Waleska, Ga.	1883	249	20	14,000	702,000
Rensselaer Polytech. Inst., Troy, N.Y.	1824	5,891	620	168,000	62,533,000
Rhode Island, U. of, Kingston	1892	6,138	613	340,000	70,000
Rhode Island Col., Providence	1854	5,810	213	108,000	—
Rhode Island School of Design, Providence	1877	1,063	101	39,000	14,074,000
Rice U., Houston, Tex.	1912	2,914	325	605,000	102,000,000
Richmond, U. of, Richmond, Va.	1830	5,146	296	194,000	10,494,000
Ricker Col., Houlton, Me.	1848	553	38	33,000	—
Ricks Col. (Jr.), Rexburg, Ida.	1888	3,974	200	58,000	—
Rider Col., Trenton, N.J.	1865	5,282	283	175,000	3,224,000
Rio Hondo Jr. Col., Whittier, Calif.	1963	5,600	450	29,000	—
Ripon Col., Ripon, Wis.	1850	951	84	86,000	2,416,000
Riverside City Col. (Jr.), Riverside, Calif.	1916	3,912	162	46,000	—
‡Rivier Col., Nashua, N.H.	1933	782	54	58,000	—
Roanoke Col., Salem, Va.	1842	1,095	70	74,000	1,818,000
Robert Morris Jr. Col., Pittsburgh, Pa.	1921	3,349	124	21,000	—
Roberts Wesleyan Col., North Chili, N.Y.	1866	766	78	46,000	—
Rochester, U. of, Rochester, N.Y.	1850	8,679	1,744	1,200,000	85,500,000
Rochester Inst. of Tech., Rochester, N.Y.	1829	9,402	722	95,000	22,000,000
Rochester St. Jr. Col., Rochester, Minn.	1915	1,700	103	19,000	—
Rockford Col., Rockford, Ill.	1847	1,396	114	63,000	2,750,000
†Rockhurst Col., Kansas City, Mo.	1910	1,943	131	75,000	—
Rocky Mountain Col., Billings, Mont.	1883	515	55	55,000	871,000
Rollins Col., Winter Park, Fla.	1885	2,730	137	147,000	8,000,000
Roosevelt U., Chicago, Ill.	1945	6,829	280	216,000	1,200,000
‡Rosary Col., River Forest, Ill.	1901	1,206	114	117,000	700,000
‡Rosary Hill Col., Buffalo, N.Y.	1948	1,299	117	58,000	53,000
‡Rosemont Col., Rosemont, Pa.	1921	671	80	98,000	—
†Rose Polytech. Inst., Terre Haute, Ind.	1874	959	65	36,000	4,400,000
‡Russell Col., Burlingame, Calif.	1966	160	...	23,000	—
‡Russell Sage Col., Troy, N.Y.	1916	1,449	100	100,000	4,540,000
Rutgers, The St. U., New Brunswick, N.J.	1766	25,852	2,963	1,367,000	25,766,000

S

Institution and location	Year founded	Total students	Faculty	Bound library volumes	Endowment fund
Sacramento (Calif.) City Col. (Jr.)	1916	7,310	282	64,000	—
Sacramento (Calif.) St. Col.	1947	12,800	733	250,000	—
‡Sacred Heart, Col. of the, Santurce, P. R.	1935	571	52	40,000	50,000
‡Sacred Heart Col., Belmont, N.C.	1892	467	40	22,000	—
Sacred Heart Col., Wichita, Kan.	1933	728	51	39,000	—
‡Sacred Heart Col. (Jr.), Cullman, Ala.	1940	186	30	13,000	—
†Sacred Heart Sem., Detroit, Mich.	1919	200	27	36,000	—
†St. Ambrose Col., Davenport, Ia.	1882	1,467	80	40,000	—
St. Andrews Presbyterian Col., Laurinburg, N.C.	1858	850	75	55,000	2,000,000
†St. Anselm's Col., Manchester, N.H.	1889	1,396	123	78,000	—
St. Augustine's Col., Raleigh, N.C.	1867	740	51	25,000	479,000
‡St. Benedict, Col. of, St. Joseph, Minn.	1913	616	53	67,000	205,000
†St. Benedict's Col., Atchison, Kan.	1858	1,099	72	170,000	—
St. Bernard Col., St. Bernard, Ala.	1892	833	56	56,000	195,000
St. Bonaventure U., St. Bonaventure, N.Y.	1859	2,565	185	140,000	390,000
St. Catharine Col. (Jr.), Springfield, Ky.	1931	186	17	15,000	—
‡St. Catherine, Col. of, St. Paul, Minn.	1905	1,304	140	162,000	1,643,000
St. Cloud St. Col., St. Cloud, Minn.	1869	8,842	400	210,000	12,000
St. Edward's U. and Maryhill Col., Austin, Tex.	1885	833	84	57,000	4,927,000
‡St. Elizabeth, Col. of, Convent Station, N.J.	1899	895	100	80,000	503,000
‡St. Francis, Col. of, Joliet, Ill.	1930	904	67	65,000	250,000
St. Francis Col., Biddeford, Me.	1953	608	37	31,000	—
†St. Francis Col., Brooklyn, N.Y.	1884	2,353	133	70,000	117,000
St. Francis Col., Fort Wayne, Ind.	1890	2,073	117	60,000	—
St. Francis Col., Loretto, Pa.	1847	1,630	100	97,000	—
†St. Francis Sem., Milwaukee, Wis.	1856	280	19	50,000	—
‡St. John Col. of Cleveland, O.	1928	1,146	97	45,000	—
†St. John Fisher Col., Inc., Rochester, N.Y.	1948	1,179	80	60,000	395,000
St. John's Col., Annapolis, Md. and Santa Fe, N.M.	1696	529	79	69,000	8,707,000
†St. John's Col., Camarillo, Calif.	1939	335	25	61,000	—
St. John's Col. (Jr.), Winfield, Kan.	1893	292	35	32,000	165,000
St. Johns River Jr. Col., Palatka, Fla.	1958	1,441	94	38,000	—
†St. John's U., Collegeville, Minn.	1857	1,521	135	183,000	5,245,000
St. John's U., Jamaica, N.Y.	1870	12,010	648	448,000	1,031,000
‡St. Joseph Col., Emmitsburg, Md.	1809	578	70	55,000	421,000
‡St. Joseph Col., West Hartford, Conn.	1932	986	85	60,000	293,000
‡St. Joseph's Col., North Windham, Me.	1915	188	30	29,000	—
†St. Joseph's Col., Philadelphia, Pa.	1851	6,592	262	88,000	736,000
†St. Joseph's Col., Rensselaer, Ind.	1889	1,427	87	130,000	775,000
‡St. Joseph's Col. for Women, Brooklyn, N.Y.	1916	617	72	64,000	54,000
†St. Joseph Sem. Col., St. Benedict, La.	1891	129	22	44,000	—
†St. Joseph's Sem. & Col., Yonkers, N.Y.	1833	149	42	72,000	—
†St. Joseph's Seminary of Washington, D.C.	1888	33	8	24,000	—
St. Leo Col., St. Leo, Fla.	1963	1,200	90	31,000	—
St. Lawrence U., Canton, N.Y.	1856	2,054	145	195,000	8,550,000
St. Louis U., St. Louis, Mo.	1818	10,769	1,678	750,000	21,713,000
St. Martin's Col., Olympia, Wash.	1895	868	79	66,000	1,055,000

Institution and location	Year found-ed	Total stu-dents	Faculty	Bound library volumes	Endowment fund
‡St. Mary, Col. of, Omaha, Neb.	1923	661	65	38,000	—
‡St. Mary Col., Xavier, Kan.	1860	574	63	101,000	—
St. Mary of the Plains Col., Dodge City, Kan.	1952	705	50	36,000	—
‡St. Mary-of-the-Woods Col., St. Mary-of-the-Woods, Ind.	1840	534	74	158,000	$ 1,500,000
‡St. Mary's Col., Notre Dame, Ind.	1844	1,473	131	102,000	905,000
†St. Mary's Col., St. Mary's College, Calif.	1863	910	87	81,000	2,000,000
St. Mary's Col., Winona, Minn.	1912	1,080	85	80,000	250,000
‡St. Mary's Dominican Col., New Orleans, La.	1910	568	64	62,000	709,000
St. Mary's Col. of O'Fallon, Mo.	1921	247	37	22,000	—
‡St. Mary's Jr. Col., Raleigh, N.C.	1842	473	37	17,000	530,000
St. Mary's Col. of Maryland, St. Mary's City	1839	428	32	23,000	21,000
†St. Mary's Sem. & U., Baltimore, Md.	1791	644	57	190,000	—
St. Mary's U. of San Antonio, Tex.	1852	3,896	350	171,000	557,000
†St. Meinrad Col., St. Meinrad, Ind.	1861	278	41	70,000	289,000
†St. Meinrad School of Theology, Meinrad, Ind.	1861	107	27	70,000	224
†St. Michael's Col., Winooski, Vt.	1903	1,521	103	63,000	550,000
St. Norbert Col., West De Pere, Wis.	1898	1,553	128	65,000	1,150,000
St. Olaf Col., Northfield, Minn.	1874	2,599	190	224,000	2,764,000
†St. Patrick's Col., Menlo Park, Calif.	1898	173	31	40,000	—
St. Paul's Col., Lawrenceville, Va.	1888	496	44	43,000	589,000
†St. Paul's Col., Washington, D.C.	1889	100	20	40,000	—
†St. Paul Sem., St. Paul, Minn.	1894	128	25	60,000	—
St. Petersburg Jr. Col. (incl. campus at Clearwater), St. Petersburg, Fla.	1927	9,884	341	100,000	—
St. Peter's Col., Jersey City, N.J.	1872	4,716	288	100,000	1,002,000
St. Philip's Col., San Antonio, Tex.	1898	1,545	78	15,000	—
St. Procopius Col., Lisle, Ill.	1887	792	91	75,000	—
‡St. Rose, Col. of, Albany, N.Y.	1920	1,343	100	62,000	364,000
St. Scholastica, Col. of, Duluth, Minn.	1912	541	70	62,000	—
†St. Stephen's Col., Dover, Mass.	1955	50	14	18,000	—
‡St. Teresa, Col. of, Winona, Minn.	1907	1,311	136	100,000	810,000
†St. Thomas, Col. of, St. Paul, Minn.	1885	2,238	136	160,000	6,400,000
St. Thomas, U. of, Houston, Tex.	1947	1,017	114	40,000	1,150,000
†St. Thomas Sem., Denver, Col.	1906	226	36	40,000	—
†St. Thomas Sem. (Jr.), Bloomfield, Conn.	1891	145	18	33,000	750,000
†St. Vincent Col., Latrobe, Pa.	1846	987	85	215,000	959,000
St. Xavier Col., Chicago, Ill.	1847	867	110	85,000	—
Salem Col., Salem, W. Va.	1888	1,586	89	56,000	939,000
‡Salem Col., Winston-Salem, N.C.	1772	542	67	73,000	3,151,000
Salisbury St. Col., Salisbury, Md.	1925	987	56	71,000	—
‡Salve Regina Col., Newport, R.I.	1934	885	78	45,000	90,000
Samford U., Birmingham, Ala.	1842	2,717	169	200,000	2,698,000
Sam Houston St. Tch. Col., Huntsville, Tex.	1879	7,600	350	275,000	—
San Antonio Col. (Jr.), San Antonio, Tex.	1925	12,201	490	80,000	—
San Diego (Calif.), U. of, Col. for Men	1949	655	80	72,000	—
San Diego (Calif.), U. of, Col. for Women	1949	647	55	70,000	—
San Diego (Calif.) St. Col.	1897	22,726	1,449	585,000	—
San Fernando Valley St. Col., Northridge, Calif.	1958	17,125	1,007	312,000	—
San Francisco (Calif.), U. of	1855	6,302	235	110,000	1,155,000
San Francisco (Calif.) Art Institute Col.	1871	812	64	24,000	460,000
‡San Francisco (Calif.) Col. for Women	1921	689	68	141,000	364,000
San Francico (Calif.) Cons. of Music	1917	118	67	32,000	550,000
San Francisco (Calif.) St. Col.	1899	16,500	1,250	320,000	—
San Jacinto Col. (Jr.), Pasadena, Tex.	1960	5,544	198	33,000	—
San Joaquin Delta Col., Stockton, Calif.	1935	5,115	188	39,000	—
San Jose (Calif.) St. Col.	1857	22,350	1,348	478,000	191,000
†San Luis Rey (Calif.) Col.	1929	133	10	30,000	—
San Mateo (Calif.), Col. of (Jr.)	1922	16,086	790	72,000	—
Santa Ana (Calif.) Col. (Jr.)	1915	6,542	210	37,000	—
Santa Clara (Calif.), U. of	1851	5,859	309	182,000	12,718,000
Santa Fe, Col. of, Santa Fe, N.M.	1947	1,264	72	65,000	—
Sante Fe Jr. Col., Gainesville, Fla.	1965	1,866	...	11,000	—
Santa Rosa (Calif.) Jr. Col.	1918	3,440	125	55,000	4,000,000
Sarah Lawrence Col., Bronxville, N.Y.	1926	653	95	103,000	2,025,000
Savannah St. Col., Savannah, Ga.	1890	1,875	109	77,000	—
Scarritt Col. for Christian Workers, Nashville, Tenn.	1892	203	25	25,000	2,296,000
Schoolcraft Col. (Jr.), Livonia, Mich.	1961	3,779	150	39,000	—
Schreiner Inst. (Jr.), Kerrville, Tex.	1923	381	35	13,000	2,809,000
†Scranton, U. of, Scranton, Pa.	1888	2,843	151	112,000	2,196,000
Seattle Pacific Col., Seattle, Wash.	1891	1,917	137	73,000	509,000
Seattle U., Seattle, Wash.	1891	3,677	228	118,000	—
Sequoias, Col. of the (Jr.), Visalia, Calif.	1925	2,536	113	44,000	—
Seton Hall U., South Orange, N.J.	1856	9,184	700	180,000	3,863,000
‡Seton Hill Col., Greensburg, Pa.	1883	957	72	65,000	—
Shasta Col. (Jr.), Redding, Calif.	1950	2,446	106	31,000	—
Shaw U., Raleigh, N.C.	1865	846	70	37,000	494,000
Shelton Jackson Col. (Jr.), Sitka, Alaska	1878	109	23	18,000	—
Shenandoah Col. (Jr.) and Shenandoah Conservatory of Music, Winchester, Va.	1875	549	61	18,000	130,000
Shepherd Col., Shepherdstown, W.Va.	1871	1,395	80	60,000	—
Sheridan Col. (Jr.), Sheridan, Wyo.	1948	3,112	173	27,000	—
Shimer Col., Mt. Carroll, Ill.	1853	381	34	30,000	328,000
Shippensburg St. Col., Shippensburg, Pa.	1871	3,253	240	200,000	—
Shorter Col., Rome, Ga.	1873	695	55	46,000	1,108,000
†Siena Col., Loudonville, N.Y.	1937	1,761	121	121,000	761,000
‡Siena Col., Memphis, Tenn.	1922	343	32	29,000	12,000
‡Siena Heights Col., Adrian, Mich.	1919	608	63	67,000	—
Sierra Col. (Jr.), Rocklin, Calif.	1936	2,615	68	30,000	—
‡Simmons Col., Boston, Mass.	1899	2,147	285	125,000	8,757,000
Simpson Bible Col., San Francisco, Calif.	1921	219	20	24,000	315,000
Simpson Col., Indianola, Ia.	1860	989	73	72,000	3,550,000
Sioux Falls Col., Sioux Falls, S.D.	1883	1,023	55	50,000	500,000
Siskiyous, Col. of the (Jr.), Weed, Calif.	1957	570	35	14,000	—
Skagit Valley Col., Mt. Vernon, Wash.	1926	2,345	75	26,000	—
‡Skidmore Col., Saratoga Springs, N.Y.	1911	1,663	162	140,000	2,419,000
Slippery Rock St. Col., Slippery Rock, Pa.	1889	4,427	310	142,000	—
‡Smith Col., Northampton, Mass.	1871	2,491	250	716,000	61,588,000
Snead St. Jr. Col., Boaz, Ala.	1935	522	28	15,000	200,000
Solano Col. (Jr.), Vallejo, Calif.	1945	5,101	178	15,000	—
Sonoma St. Col., Rohnert Park, Calif.	1960	2,936	185	97,000	—
†South, U. of the, Sewanee, Tenn.	1858	776	72	187,000	17,536,000
South Alabama, U. of, Mobile	1964	3,882	248	125,000	—
South Carolina, U. of, Columbia	1801	14,314	480	750,000	2,500,000
South Carolina St. Col., Orangeburg	1896	2,294	124	89,000	—
South Dakota, U. of, Vermillon, S.D.	1882	4,600	350	215,000	—
South Dakota Sch. of Mines & Tech., Rapid City	1885	1,665	125	60,000	250,000
South Dakota St. U., Brookings	1883	5,767	498	200,000	3,269,000

Institution and location	Year found-ed	Total stu-dents	Faculty	Bound library volumes	Endowment fund
Southeastern Christian Col. (Jr.), Winchester, Ky.	1949	184	14	12,000	—
Southeastern Massachusetts Tech. Inst., North Dartmouth	1895	2,852	198	100,000	$ 115,000
Southeastern St. Col., Durant, Okla.	1909	2,087	111	98,000	—
Southeast Missouri St. Col., Cape Girardeau	1873	6,491	343	128,000	—
Southern Baptist Col. (Jr.), Walnut Ridge, Ark.	1941	601	32	27,000	125,000
Southern Baptist Theol. Sem., Louisville, Ky.	1858	1,077	73	162,000	8,968,000
Southern California, U. of, Los Angeles	1880	19,598	2,518	1,291,000	25,487,000
Southern California Col., Costa Mesa	1920	602	31	28,000	100,000
Southern Colorado St. Col., Pueblo	1933	5,900	302	83,000	—
Southern Connecticut St. Col., New Haven	1893	10,269	511	200,000	—
Southern Idaho, Col. of (Jr.), Twin Falls	1964	1,517	43	10,000	—
Southern Illinois U., Carbondale	1869	30,557	2,932	1,000,000	—
Southern Louisiana Col., Hammond	1925	5,225	317	107,000	—
Southern Methodist U., Dallas, Tex.	1911	8,510	600	875,000	19,000,000
Southern Missionary Col., Collegedale, Tenn.	1892	1,270	120	53,000	—
Southern Mississippi, U. of, Hattiesburg	1910	9,225	399	243,000	—
Southern Oregon Col., Ashland	1926	3,650	225	95,000	—
‡Southern Sem. Jr. Col., Buena Vista, Va.	1867	350	35	14,000	500,000
Southern St. Col., Magnolia, Ark.	1909	2,755	115	51,000	—
Southern St. Col., Springfield, S.D.	1881	942	82	52,000	475,000
Southern U., Baton Rouge, La.	1880	6,814	435	209,000	—
Southern Utah St. Col., Cedar City	1897	1,763	88	50,000	—
South Florida, U. of, Tampa	1960	13,806	491	210,000	175,000
South Florida Jr. Col., Avon Park	1965	352	11	1,200	—
South Georgia Col. (Jr.), Douglas	1906	1,031	50	38,000	—
South Plains Col. (Jr.), Levelland, Tex.	1957	1,633	86	25,000	—
South Texas Jr. Col., Houston	1948	5,018	131	48,000	800,000
Southwest Baptist Col., Bolivar, Mo.	1878	1,167	65	47,000	108,000
Southwestern at Memphis, Tenn.	1848	955	91	100,000	5,487,000
Southwestern Col., Chula Vista, Calif.	1961	5,720	118	26,000	—
Southwestern Col., Winfield, Kan.	1885	651	58	60,000	3,755,000
Southwestern Louisiana, U. of, Lafayette	1898	9,066	526	325,000	—
Southwestern St. Col., Weatherford, Okla.	1901	4,861	181	100,000	—
Southwestern Union Col., Keene, Tex.	1916	405	41	38,000	—
Southwestern U., Georgetown, Tex.	1840	762	70	90,000	8,163,000
Southwest Mississippi Jr. Col., Summit	1929	693	30	21,000	—
Southwest Missouri St. Col., Springfield	1906	7,093	827	150,000	—
Southwest Texas Jr. Col., Uvalde	1946	942	41	18,000	—
Southwest Texas St. Col., San Marcos	1899	7,813	355	180,000	—
Spartanburg Jr. Col., Spartanburg, S.C.	1911	738	35	19,000	24,000
‡Spelman Col., Atlanta, Ga.	1881	780	71	18,000	5,008,000
Spring Arbor Col., Spring Arbor, Mich.	1873	634	47	30,000	32,000
Springfield Col., Springfield, Mass.	1885	2,396	102	92,000	3,834,000
Springfield Jr. Col. in Illinois, Springfield	1929	832	59	23,000	—
Spring Hill Col., Mobile, Ala.	1830	1,143	97	109,000	2,250,000
Stanford U., Stanford, Calif.	1885	10,608	1,241	3,100,000	224,846,000
Stanislaus St. Col., Turlock, Calif.	1960	1,778	91	70,000	—
Stephen F. Austin St. Col., Nacogdoches, Tex.	1923	7,999	358	225,000	54,000
‡Stephens Col., Columbia, Mo.	1833	1,867	174	80,000	1,700,000
Sterling Col., Sterling, Kan.	1887	566	40	60,000	1,766,000
Stetson U., DeLand, Fla.	1883	2,589	152	182,000	4,965,000
Steubenville, Col. of, Steubenville, O.	1946	1,243	70	56,000	75,000
†Stevens Inst. of Tech., Hoboken, N.J.	1870	2,650	196	73,000	42,000,000
Stillman Col., Tuscaloosa, Ala.	1876	839	49	40,000	1,283,000
Stonehill Col., North Easton, Mass.	1948	1,263	81	64,000	25,000
Stout St. U., Menomonie, Wis.	1893	4,117	288	87,000	112,000
‡Stratford Col., Danville, Va.	1852	562	48	33,000	385,000
Sue Bennett Col. (Jr.), London, Ky.	1896	344	24	25,000	—
Suffolk U., Boston, Mass.	1906	3,916	156	90,000	1,562,000
‡Sullins Col. (Jr.), Bristol, Va.	1870	365	37	31,000	1,300,000
†Sulpician Sem. of the Northwest, Kenmore, Wash.	1931	163	23	40,000	—
Sul Ross St. Col., Alpine, Tex.	1920	2,298	125	125,000	—
Susquehanna U., Selinsgrove, Pa.	1858	1,210	100	79,000	1,404,000
Swarthmore Col., Swarthmore, Pa.	1864	1,029	144	327,000	30,473,000
‡Sweet Briar Col., Sweet Briar, Va.	1901	731	78	131,000	5,977,000
Syracuse U. (incl. Utica Col.), Syracuse, N.Y.	1870	22,667	1,136	1,432,000	54,149,000

T

Institution and location	Year found-ed	Total stu-dents	Faculty	Bound library volumes	Endowment fund
Tabor Col., Hillsboro, Kan.	1908	385	42	35,000	250,000
Taft Col. (Jr.), Taft, Calif.	1922	1,048	54	17,000	—
Talladega Col., Talladega, Ala.	1867	397	33	47,000	1,730,000
Tampa, U. of, Tampa, Fla.	1931	2,219	102	89,000	750,000
Tarkio Col., Tarkio, Mo.	1883	720	38	52,000	498,000
Taylor U., Upland, Ind.	1846	1,358	85	76,000	593,000
‡Temple Buell Col., Denver, Colo.	1888	1,077	92	80,000	25,000,000
Temple Jr. Col., Temple, Tex.	1926	1,003	54	18,000	—
Temple U., Philadelphia, Pa.	1884	28,285	2,071	750,000	6,620,000
Tennessee, U. of (main branches at Martin, Memphis, Nashville), Knoxville	1794	30,771	2,879	1,075,000	4,646,000
Tennessee, U. of, at Chattanooga	1886	2,440	178	107,000	4,412,000
Tennessee A. & I. St. U., Nashville	1909	4,536	286	165,000	—
Tennessee Tech. U., Cookeville	1915	5,672	325	260,000	—
Tennessee Wesleyan Col., Athens	1857	762	59	50,000	—
Texarkana Col. (Jr.), Texarkana, Tex.	1927	1,619	77	27,000	—
Texas, U. of (incl. branches at Arlington, Dallas, El Paso, Galveston, Houston, San Antonio), at Austin	1881	56,974	4,074	2,881,000	560,236,000
Texas A&M University System:					
Prairie View A. & M. Col., Prairie View	1876	3,713	220	106,000	—
Tarleton St. Col., Stephenville	1899	2,289	121	94,000	—
†Texas A&M U., College Station	1876	12,053	1,025	500,000	3,295,000
Texas A&I U., Kingsville	1925	6,404	280	213,000	—
Texas Christian U., Fort Worth	1873	6,005	517	630,000	27,500,000
Jarvis Christian Col., Hawkins	1912	497	44	35,000	—
Texas Lutheran Col., Seguin	1891	674	55	65,000	699,000
Texas Southern U., Houston	1947	4,306	226	165,000	—
Texas Southmost Col. (Jr.), Brownsville	1926	1,493	57	65,000	—
Texas Tech. Col., Lubbock	1923	18,299	1,267	1,000,000	—
Texas Wesleyan Col., Fort Worth	1891	1,878	91	71,000	2,710,000
‡Texas Woman's U., Denton	1901	5,066	320	345,000	—
†The Citadel, Charleston, S.C.	1842	2,200	152	105,000	—
Thiel Col., Greenville, Pa.	1866	1,336	99	74,000	1,427,000
Thomas More Col., Ft. Mitchell, Ky.	1921	2,172	131	59,000	—
‡Tift Col., Forsyth, Ga.	1847	650	34	38,000	1,667,000

Institution and location	Year founded	Total students	Faculty	Bound library volumes	Endowment fund
Toledo, The U. of, Toledo, O.	1872	12,423	717	667,000	$ 592,000
Tougaloo Col., Tougaloo, Miss.	1869	715	51	50,000	522,000
Towson St. Col., Baltimore, Md.	1866	7,867	328	112,000	—
Transylvania Col., Lexington, Ky.	1790	815	70	68,000	1,110,000
Trenton St. Col., Trenton, N.J.	1855	8,773	264	147,000	—
Trinidad St. Jr. Col., Trinidad, Colo.	1925	1,533	68	25,000	—
‡Trinity Col., Burlington, Vt.	1925	474	43	36,000	—
†Trinity Col., Hartford, Conn.	1823	1,836	142	485,000	25,000,000
‡Trinity Col., Washington, D.C.	1897	913	123	108,000	1,394,000
Trinity U., San Antonio, Tex.	1869	2,463	205	290,000	41,400,000
Tri-State Col., Angola, Ind.	1884	1,762	100	40,000	250,000
Troy St. U., Troy, Ala.	1887	2,779	133	84,000	—
Tufts U. (incl. ‡Jackson Col.), Medford, Mass.	1852	5,188	1,650	400,000	23,998,000
Tulane U. (incl. ‡Newcomb Col.) of Louisiana, New Orleans	1834	7,931	785	1,000,000	40,516,000
Tulsa, U. of, Tulsa, Okla.	1894	6,567	318	350,000	9,000,000
Tusculum Col., Greeneville, Tenn.	1794	548	43	45,000	2,200,000
Tuskegee Inst., Tuskegee Institute, Ala.	1881	3,177	335	167,000	17,794,000
Tyler Jr. Col., Tyler, Tex.	1926	3,622	166	33,000	—

U

Institution and location	Year founded	Total students	Faculty	Bound library volumes	Endowment fund
Union Col., Barbourville, Ky.	1879	888	62	50,000	1,924,000
Union Col., Lincoln, Neb.	1891	1,029	87	78,000	—
Union Col., Cranford, N.J.	1933	1,734	94	30,000	12,000
Union Col. and U. System					
Albany Col. of Pharmacy, Albany, N.Y.	1881	454	22	5,000	—
Albany Law School, Albany, N.Y.	1851	298	17	70,000	800,000
Albany Medical Col., Albany, N.Y.	1839	304	335	64,000	1,300,000
†Union Col., Schenectady, N.Y.	1795	1,465	144	261,000	27,361,000
Union Theol. Sem., New York, N.Y.	1836	662	94	402,000	—
Union U., Jackson, Tenn.	1825	701	53	43,000	906,000
†U.S. Air Force Acad., Colorado Springs, Colo.	1954	3,270	599	270,000	—
†U.S. Coast Guard Acad., New London, Conn.	1876	900	110	76,000	—
U.S. Intern'l U. (incl. California Western U.), San Diego, Calif.	1924	1,970	130	145,000	1,125,000
†U.S. Merchant Marine Acad., Kings Point, N.Y.	1938	960	88	58,000	—
†U.S. Military Acad., West Point, N.Y.	1802	3,800	489	290,000	—
†U.S. Naval Acad., Annapolis, Md.	1845	4,000	639	210,000	—
Upper Iowa U., Fayette	1857	1,178	75	82,000	950,000
Upsala Col., East Orange, N.J.	1893	1,811	145	108,000	1,286,000
Ursinus Col., Collegeville, Pa.	1869	1,951	124	78,000	5,564,000
‡Ursuline Col., Cleveland, O.	1871	579	68	45,000	—
Utah, U. of, Salt Lake City	1850	19,684	1,835	1,058,000	1,700,000
Utah St. U. of Ag. & App. Sc., Logan	1888	7,712	472	541,000	956,000

V

Institution and location	Year founded	Total students	Faculty	Bound library volumes	Endowment fund
Valdosta St. Col., Valdosta, Ga.	1906	2,475	153	80,000	—
Valley City St. Col., Valley City, N.D.	1889	1,264	70	69,000	850,000
†Valley Forge Mil. Jr. Col., Wayne, Pa.	1928	250	35	32,000	1,500,000
Valparaiso U., Valparaiso, Ind.	1859	3,597	292	195,000	2,355,000
Vanderbilt U., Nashville, Tenn.	1872	5,529	1,185	1,112,000	80,081,000
‡Vassar Col., Poughkeepsie, N.Y.	1861	1,621	204	387,000	69,422,000
Ventura Col. (Jr.), Ventura, Calif.	1929	6,622	270	35,000	—
Vermilion St. Jr. Col., Ely, Minn.	1922	240	20	8,000	—
Vermont, U. of, Burlington	1791	5,789	686	461,000	13,592,000
‡Vermont Col. (Jr.), Montpelier	1834	521	48	22,000	225,000
Victoria Col. (Jr.), The, Victoria, Tex.	1925	1,381	60	22,000	—
Victor Valley Col. (Jr.), Victorville, Calif.	1961	1,604	51	24,000	—
‡Villa Julie Col. (Jr.), Stevenson, Md.	1947	213	39	12,300	—
‡Villa Maria Col., Erie, Pa.	1925	672	64	35,000	80,000
Villanova U., Villanova, Pa.	1842	7,857	586	344,000	7,202,000
Vincennes U. (Jr.), Vincennes, Ind.	1806	959	45	15,000	29,000
Virginia, The U. of, (incl. branches: Clinch Valley, George Mason, Patrick Henry, Eastern Shore) at Charlottesville, Va.	1819	11,355	1,175	1,445,000	51,777,000
‡Mary Washington Col., Fredericksburg	1908	2,010	176	193,000	12,000
Virginia Commonwealth U., Richmond	1917	10,588	466	100,000	300,000
‡Virginia Intermont Col. (Jr.), Bristol	1884	547	39	24,000	993,000
†Virginia Military Inst., Lexington	1839	1,223	130	153,000	4,764,000
Virginia Polytech. Inst., Blacksburg	1872	9,427	934	485,000	875,000
Virginia St. Col., Petersburg	1882	2,579	234	116,000	183,000
Virginia Union U., Richmond	1865	1,280	79	67,000	1,490,000
‡Viterbo Col., La Crosse, Wis.	1931	544	63	51,000	—
Voorhees Col., Denmark, S.C.	1897	725	53	33,000	137,000

W

Institution and location	Year founded	Total students	Faculty	Bound library volumes	Endowment fund
†Wabash Col., Crawfordsville, Ind.	1832	880	78	184,000	21,000,000
Wagner Col., Staten Island, N.Y.	1883	2,527	185	110,000	1,163,000
Wake Forest U., Winston-Salem	1834	3,062	481	358,000	19,700,000
Waldorf Col. (Jr.), Forest City, Ia.	1903	634	41	22,000	175,000
Walker Col. (Jr.), Jasper, Ala.	1938	790	47	16,000	425,000
Walla Walla Col., College Place, Wash.	1892	1,445	110	87,000	—
Warner Pacific Col., Portland, Ore.	1937	358	40	35,000	—
Warren Wilson Col., Swannanoa, N.C.	1894	378	44	32,000	—
Wartburg Col., Waverly, Ia.	1852	1,350	90	90,000	303,000
Washburn U. of Topeka, Kan.	1865	3,993	205	97,000	7,800,000
Washington, U. of, Seattle	1861	29,923	5,152	1,626,000	54,408,000
†Washington and Jefferson Col., Washington, Pa.	1781	861	84	140,000	10,500,000
†Washington and Lee U., Lexington, Va.	1749	1,471	136	249,000	13,981,000
Washington Col., Chesterton, Md.	1782	622	60	82,000	2,133,000
Washington St. U., Pullman, Wash.	1890	11,492	797	900,000	42,819,000
Washington U., St. Louis, Mo.	1853	11,908	2,944	1,009,000	68,965,000
Wayland Baptist Col., Plainview, Tex.	1908	618	49	50,000	3,340,000
Waynesburg Col., Waynesburg, Pa.	1849	1,052	78	72,000	1,952,000
Wayne St. Col., Wayne, Neb.	1891	2,577	129	99,000	—
Wayne St. U., Detroit, Mich.	1868	33,177	2,124	1,111,000	2,927,000
Weatherford Col. (Jr.), Weatherford, Tex.	1921	997	38	20,000	115,000
†Webb Inst. of Naval Arch., Glen Cove, N.Y.	1889	67	14	17,000	—
Weber St. Col., Ogden, Utah	1889	10,280	362	115,000	70,000
Webster Col., St. Louis, Mo.	1915	814	75	33,000	—
‡Wellesley Col., Wellesley, Mass.	1870	1,762	200	416,000	79,000,000
‡Wells Col., Aurora, N.Y.	1868	597	68	152,000	5,662,000
Wenonah St. Jr. Col., Birmington, Ala.	1963	752	57	15,000	—
†Wentworth Inst. (Jr.), Boston, Mass.	1904	1,955	151	23,000	—
†Wentworth Mil. Acad. and Jr. Col., Lexington, Mo.	1880	290	32	21,000	—
Wesley Col. (Jr.), Dover, Del.	1873	866	42	19,000	$ 280,000
‡Wesleyan Col., Macon, Ga.	1836	597	58	75,000	4,228,000
Wesleyan U., Middletown, Conn.	1831	1,568	270	620,000	115,802,000
‡Westbrook Jr. Col., Portland, Me.	1831	469	47	16,000	208,000
West Chester St. Col., West Chester, Pa.	1812	7,751	449	160,000	—
West Coast U., Los Angeles, Calif.	1909	1,605	70	8,000	—
Western Baptist Bible Col., El Cerrito, Calif.	1935	394	20	20,000	6,000
Western Carolina Col., Cullowhee, N.C.	1889	3,935	214	91,000	205,000
‡Western Col. for Women, Oxford, O.	1853	425	55	60,000	1,922,000
Western Connecticut St. Col., Danbury	1903	3,043	153	100,000	—
Western Illinois U., Macomb	1899	9,461	594	234,000	—
Western Kentucky U., Bowling Green	1906	9,888	501	350,000	211,000
Western Maryland Col., Westminster	1867	2,125	95	82,000	3,248,000
Western Michigan U., Kalamazoo	1903	18,071	858	496,000	26,000
Western Montana Col., Dillon	1893	913	42	42,000	—
Western New England Col., Springfield, Mass.	1919	3,044	132	38,000	783,000
Western New Mexico U., Silver City	1893	1,354	83	82,000	—
Western St. Col., Gunnison, Colo.	1901	2,916	138	106,000	—
Western Washington St. Col., Bellingham	1899	7,211	458	200,000	56,000
West Georgia Col., Carrollton	1933	3,208	175	62,000	—
West Hills Col. (Jr.), Coalinga, Calif.	1932	640	47	20,000	—
West Liberty St. Col., West Liberty, W.Va.	1837	3,815	204	75,000	—
Westmar Col., Le Mars, Ia.	1890	1,169	71	70,000	645,000
†Westminster Col., Fulton, Mo.	1851	774	68	67,000	3,253,000
Westminster Col., New Wilmington, Pa.	1852	1,941	108	102,000	4,450,000
Westminster Col., Salt Lake City, Utah	1875	881	44	27,000	243,000
†Westminster Theol. Sem., Philadelphia, Pa.	1929	153	17	52,000	300,000
Westmont Col., Santa Barbara, Calif.	1940	720	57	67,000	351,000
West Texas St. U., Canyon	1910	6,727	296	142,000	—
West Valley Col. (Jr.), Campbell, Calif.	1966	6,699	...	20,000	—
West Virginia Inst. of Tech., Montgomery	1895	2,141	143	58,000	—
West Virginia St. Col., Institute	1891	2,865	170	91,000	—
West Virginia U., Morgantown	1867	13,856	1,216	888,000	1,875,000
Potomac St. Col., Keyser	1901	816	48	25,000	—
West Virginia Wesleyan Col., Buckhannon	1890	1,754	118	83,000	1,800,000
Wharton County Jr. Col., Wharton, Tex.	1946	1,853	86	30,000	11,000
‡Wheaton Col., Norton, Mass.	1834	1,121	100	126,000	5,310,000
Wheaton Col., Wheaton, Ill.	1860	1,915	170	150,000	10,000,000
Wheeling Col., Wheeling, W.Va.	1954	810	64	64,000	29,000
‡Wheelock Col., Boston, Mass.	1889	669	56	40,000	227,000
Whitman Col., Walla Walla, Wash.	1859	1,037	87	143,000	13,994,000
Whittier Col., Whittier, Calif.	1901	1,995	125	80,000	4,700,000
Whitworth Col., Spokane, Wash.	1890	1,571	94	58,000	1,865,000
Wichita St. U., Wichita, Kan.	1895	11,568	384	304,000	2,416,000
Wilberforce U., Wilberforce, O.	1856	858	41	34,000	95,000
Wiley Col., Marshall, Tex.	1873	703	54	49,000	1,000,000
Wilkes Col., Wilkes Barre, Pa.	1933	3,050	175	90,000	3,835,000
Willamette U., Salem, Ore.	1842	1,570	123	113,000	9,312,000
William and Mary, Col. of, Williamsburg, Va.	1693	3,769	379	445,000	4,941,000
William Carey Col., Hattiesburg, Miss.	1906	881	56	40,000	563,000
William Jewell Col., Liberty, Mo.	1849	1,006	81	94,000	5,561,000
William Penn Col., Oskaloosa, Ia.	1873	950	61	60,000	550,000
‡William Woods Col., Fulton, Mo.	1870	932	50	103,000	1,250,000
†Williams Col., Williamstown, Mass.	1793	1,267	161	300,000	48,414,000
Wilmington Col., Wilmington, N.C.	1947	1,193	85	50,000	—
Wilmington Col., Wilmington, O.	1870	888	67	75,000	2,000,000
‡Wilson Col., Chambersburg, Pa.	1869	714	71	95,000	5,629,000
Windham Col., Putney, Vt.	1951	704	59	47,000	—
Wingate Col. (Jr.), Wingate, N.C.	1896	1,588	90	42,000	995,000
Winona St. Col., Winona, Minn.	1858	3,641	213	82,000	—
Winston-Salem St. Col., Winston-Salem, N.C.	1892	1,236	104	78,000	264,000
‡Winthrop Col., Rock Hill, S.C.	1886	3,521	180	237,000	—
Wisconsin, The U. of (all campuses)	1848	62,206	...	3,082,000	21,863,000
Wisconsin-Madison, U. of, Madison	1848	34,670		2,363,000	
Wisconsin-Milwaukee, U. of, Milwaukee	1956	16,768		440,000	
Wisconsin-Green Bay, U. of (campuses at Green Bay, Menasha, Manitowoc, Marinette)	1968	2,959		50,000	
Wisconsin-Parkside, U. of (campuses at Racine, Kenosha)	1968	1,796		41,000	
Wisconsin St. U.—Eau Claire	1916	6,705	400	160,000	—
Wisconsin St. U.—La Crosse	1909	6,850	375	225,000	—
Wisconsin St. U.—Oshkosh	1871	11,096	630	230,000	—
Wisconsin St. U.—Platteville	1866	5,024	335	145,000	—
Wisconsin St. U.—River Falls	1874	4,052	260	135,000	—
Wisconsin St. U.—Stevens Point	1894	6,319	405	160,000	—
Wisconsin St. U.—Superior	1896	3,140	218	127,000	309,000
Wisconsin St. U.—Whitewater	1868	8,664	591	160,000	125,000
Wittenberg U., Springfield, O.	1845	3,972	191	180,000	12,066,000
†Wofford Col., Spartanburg, S.C.	1854	958	72	93,000	2,420,000
Woodbury Col., Los Angeles, Calif.	1884	2,024	73	15,000	—
Wood Jr. Col., Mathiston, Miss.	1886	168	13	13,000	260,000
†Woodstock Col., Woodstock, Md.	1869	164	26	145,000	3,000,000
Wooster, The Col. of, Wooster, O.	1866	1,654	137	200,000	12,347,000
Worcester Jr. Col., Worcester, Mass.	1938	2,306	115	20,000	675,000
Worcester Polytech. Inst., Worcester, Mass.	1865	1,740	234	73,000	22,804,000
Wright St. U., Dayton, O.	1967	7,810	263	113,000	—
Wyoming, U. of, Laramie	1886	7,924	574	390,000	12,381,000

X

Institution and location	Year founded	Total students	Faculty	Bound library volumes	Endowment fund
†Xaverian Col. (Jr.), Silver Spring, Md.	1931	195	22	31,000	—
Xavier U., Cincinnati, O.	1831	6,003	277	161,000	2,773,000
Xavier U., New Orleans, La.	1925	1,207	87	98,000	—

Y

Institution and location	Year founded	Total students	Faculty	Bound library volumes	Endowment fund
Yakima Valley Col., Yakima, Wash.	1928	3,040	135	30,000	—
Yale U., New Haven, Conn.	1701	8,665	2,725	5,300,000	482,897,000
Yankton Col., Yankton, S.D.	1881	617	55	49,000	1,430,000
Yeshiva U., New York, N.Y.	1886	4,683	2,235	422,000	5,000,000
York Col. of Pennsylvania, York	1941	2,084	71	50,000	929,000
Young Harris Col. (Jr.), Young Harris, Ga.	1886	389	30	30,000	2,700,000
Youngstown St. U., Youngstown, O.	1908	14,115	750	190,000	—
Yuba Col. (Jr.), Marysville, Calif.	1927	4,747	183	30,000	—

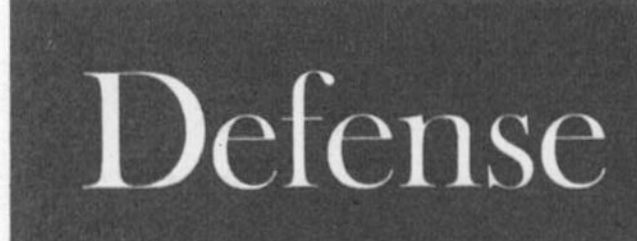

Army personnel

Military status	1960	1965	1969
Personnel on active duty	873,078	968,313	1,512,169*
Officers	101,236	111,541	172,590
Enlisted	771,842	856,772	1,337,047
Reserve personnel not on active duty†	703,000	641,000	699,898
National Guard	402,000	379,000	388,954
Officers	37,000	34,000	30,432
Enlisted	365,000	345,000	358,522
Army Reserve	301,000	262,000	310,944
Officers	50,000	40,000	45,240
Enlisted	251,000	221,000	265,704

Data are for June 30 of years reported.
*Includes cadets and officer candidates.
†Paid status only; excludes personnel in inactive reserve.
Source: U.S. Department of Defense.

Navy and Marine Corps personnel

Military status	1960	1965	1969
Personnel on active duty	788,605	861,196	1,085,640*
Navy	617,984	671,009	775,869
Officers	69,559	77,720	85,199
Enlisted	548,425	593,289	684,145
Marine Corps	170,621	190,187	309,771
Officers	16,203	17,234	25,698
Enlisted	154,418	172,953	284,073
Reserve personnel not on active duty†	165,000	169,000	186,579
Naval Reserve	120,000	123,000	136,660
Officers	26,000	23,000	22,406
Enlisted	94,000	100,000	114,254
Marine Corps Reserve	45,000	46,000	49,919
Officers	4,000	3,000	3,340
Enlisted	41,000	43,000	46,579

Data are for June 30 of years reported.
*Includes cadets and officer candidates.
†Paid status only; excludes personnel in inactive reserve.
Source: U.S. Department of Defense.

Air Force personnel

Military status	1960	1965	1969
Personnel on active duty	814,752	823,633	862,353*
Officers	129,689	131,141	135,476
Enlisted	685,063	692,492	722,936
Reserve personnel not on active duty†	129,000	123,000	130,940
Air National Guard	71,000	76,000	83,414
Officers	9,000	10,000	10,281
Enlisted	62,000	66,000	73,133
Air Force Reserve	58,000	46,000	47,526
Officers	22,000	11,000	12,333
Enlisted	37,000	36,000	35,193

Data are for June 30 of years reported.
*Includes cadets and officer candidates.
†Paid status only; excludes personnel in inactive reserve.
Source: U.S. Department of Defense.

Coast Guard personnel

Military status	1960	1965	1968
Personnel on active duty	31,406†	31,792†	37,482*
Officers	4,011	4,492	5,372
Enlisted	26,991	26,860	31,311
Reserve personnel not on active duty†	14,144	16,578	17,142
Officers	1,712	1,943	1,882
Enlisted	12,432	14,635	15,260

Data are for June 30 of years reported.
*Includes cadets.
†Paid status only; excludes personnel in inactive reserve.
Source: U.S. Department of Transportation, U.S. Coast Guard.

Summary of major conflicts

Item and branch of service	Civil War*	Spanish American War	World War I	World War II	Korean conflict
Personnel serving	2,213,363	306,760	4,743,826	16,353,659†	5,764,143‡
Army	2,128,948	280,564	4,057,101	11,260,000	2,834,000
Navy	84,415 (Navy and Marines)	22,875	599,051	4,183,466	1,177,000
Marines		3,321	78,839	669,100	424,000
Air Force	—	—	§	§	1,285,000
Coast Guard	—	—	8,835	241,093	44,143
Average duration of service (in months)	20	8	12	33	19
Officers	...	8	14	39	24
Enlisted	...	8	12	33	18
Casualties					
Battle deaths	140,414	385	53,402	291,557†	33,629‡
Army	138,154	369	50,510	234,874	27,704
Navy	2,112	10	431	36,950	458
Marines	148	6	2,461	19,733	4,267
Air Force	—	—	§	§	1,200
Wounds not mortal	281,881	1,662	204,002	670,846‡	103,284‡
Army	280,040	1,594	193,663	565,861	77,596
Navy	1,710	47	819	37,778	1,576
Marines	131	21	9,520	67,207	23,744
Air Force	—	—	§	§	368

*Union forces only. Estimates of the number serving in the Confederate forces range from 600,000 to 1,500,000. †Covers period Dec. 1, 1941 to Dec. 31, 1946. ‡Covers period June 25, 1950 to July 27, 1953. §Included in Army.
Source: U.S. Department of Commerce, Bureau of the Census, *Statistical Abstract of the United States*. Data compiled by the President's Commission on Veterans' Pensions, *Veterans' Benefits in the United States;* and Department of Defense, Office of the Secretary.

Budget outlays for Southeast Asia

in millions of dollars, except percent

	OUTLAYS						
		Military defense excluding Southeast Asia		Southeast Asia			
				Total			
Year	Total defense	Total	Percent of total defense	Amount	Percent of total defense	Military defense	Economic assistance
1965	49,578	46,070	92.9	103	0.2	103	—
1966	56,785	48,597	85.6	6,094	10.7	5,812	282
1967	70,081	47,333	67.5	20,557	29.3	20,133	424
1968	80,516	50,826	63.1	26,839	33.3	26,547	292
1969	80,999	48,978	60.5	29,192	36.0	28,812	380
1970	81,542	53,074	65.1	25,733	31.6	25,397	336

Data are for June 30 of years reported.
Source: U.S. Department of Commerce, Bureau of the Census. *Statistical Abstract of the United States*. Data compiled by the Executive Office of the President, Bureau of the Budget.

Vietnam

U.S. armed forces and casualties

	1961	1962	1963	1964	1965	1966	1967	1968	1969*
Military forces	3,200	11,300	16,300	23,300	184,300	385,300	485,600	536,100	478,800
Army	2,100	7,900	10,100	14,700	116,800	239,400	319,500	359,800	331,400
Navy†	100	500	800	1,100	8,400	23,300	31,700	36,100	31,400
Marine Corps	—	500	800	900	38,200	69,200	78,000	81,400	56,800
Air Force	1,000	2,400	4,600	6,600	20,600	52,900	55,900	58,400	58,700
Coast Guard	—	—	—	—	300	500	500	400	500
Casualties‡									
Battle deaths	11	31	78	147	1,369	5,008	9,378	14,592	8,250
Killed	1	19	53	112	1,130	4,179	7,482	12,588	7,188
Died of wounds	—	1	5	6	87	517	981	1,636	980
Died while missing	10	11	20	28	151	309	911	367	82
Died while captured	—	—	—	1	1	3	4	1	0
Wounded, nonfatal									
Hospital care required	2	41	218	522	3,308	16,526	32,371	46,799	28,739
Hospital care not required	1	37	193	517	2,806	13,567	29,654	46,021	32,438

Data are for December 31 of years reported, except as indicated. 1969 figures for military forces are preliminary.
*Military forces as of November 30; casualties as of September 30.
†Excludes personnel on ships off Vietnam's shores.
‡Represents casualties from enemy action. Deaths exclude servicemen who died in accidents or from disease.
Source: U.S. Department of Defense.

The Selective Service, 1969

State	Registrants subject to draft as of June 30	Registrants forwarded to Armed Forces year ending June 30*	Inductions year ending June 30	ENLISTMENTS† year ending June 30: Regular	ENLISTMENTS† year ending June 30: Reserves or National Guard
Alabama	461,990	21,775	5,392	10,678	2,843
Alaska	18,219	918	231	547	235
Arizona	164,288	8,168	1,821	4,302	789
Arkansas	251,465	12,164	2,656	6,530	1,555
California	1,777,926	77,809	21,665	41,593	7,935
Colorado	200,148	8,667	2,069	5,769	873
Connecticut	280,462	10,901	2,797	6,639	2,083
Delaware	49,068	2,267	724	1,330	560
District of Columbia	83,159	3,380	831	1,900	237
Florida	545,835	27,327	6,434	17,240	3,322
Georgia	520,962	25,888	7,270	12,837	2,470
Hawaii	76,938	2,687	587	3,504	449
Idaho	86,204	2,891	868	2,497	502
Illinois	1,064,675	59,958	14,161	23,369	4,293
Indiana	520,056	29,023	7,422	13,163	2,943
Iowa	309,995	13,805	4,157	8,729	1,671
Kansas	243,442	10,415	2,619	7,263	1,712
Kentucky	396,299	22,441	6,125	8,407	1,571
Louisiana	433,117	30,639	5,619	8,720	2,221
Maine	112,688	4,225	1,098	4,004	579
Maryland	356,993	19,643	4,283	8,892	2,264
Massachusetts	565,236	26,813	4,434	14,925	5,100
Michigan	895,246	44,642	15,020	19,208	3,211
Minnesota	388,691	17,672	5,839	9,781	2,443
Mississippi	314,340	16,642	3,258	5,991	1,640
Missouri	473,092	20,889	7,950	12,396	2,470
Montana	66,225	3,136	797	2,288	765
Nebraska	155,870	7,670	2,152	4,274	1,211
Nevada	35,559	1,431	530	1,042	217
New Hampshire	70,952	2,634	537	2,456	443
New Jersey	666,695	27,583	6,986	14,425	4,375
New Mexico	111,909	4,731	1,354	3,376	508
New York	1,804,529	81,267	16,973	35,578	9,459
North Carolina	618,274	34,270	8,274	15,637	1,981
North Dakota	76,730	3,604	1,137	1,818	562
Ohio	1,079,904	52,293	15,608	26,655	5,096
Oklahoma	283,827	8,823	3,335	8,972	2,166
Oregon	204,832	9,132	2,411	6,753	1,392
Pennsylvania	1,205,676	56,762	13,230	31,307	7,457
Rhode Island	86,163	3,685	963	2,459	826
South Carolina	325,326	18,674	5,032	8,409	1,901
South Dakota	84,442	2,749	764	2,148	704
Tennessee	474,838	26,106	8,017	11,327	2,151
Texas	1,194,766	56,649	13,625	29,533	4,683
Utah	115,111	6,352	1,535	2,351	1,378
Vermont	47,703	1,727	323	1,530	376
Virginia	482,899	20,373	6,507	12,695	2,502
Washington	334,019	13,702	3,041	10,518	1,993
West Virginia	244,168	9,850	3,359	7,368	943
Wisconsin	442,243	25,905	7,120	10,422	2,466
Wyoming	37,784	1,799	550	1,175	262
Total U.S.‡	21,268,941	1,022,958	262,646	517,175	112,655

*For preinduction examinations. †Estimated. ‡Includes Canal Zone, Guam, Puerto Rico, and Virgin Islands. Source: Selective Service System.

Production

Gross national product and national income

in billions of dollars

Item	1960	1965	1968	1969*
Gross national product	503.8	683.9	865.7	924.3
By type of expenditure				
Personal consumption expenditures	325.2	433.1	536.6	572.0
Durable goods	45.3	66.0	83.3	90.6
Nondurable goods	151.3	191.2	230.6	242.1
Services	128.7	175.9	222.8	240.1
Gross private domestic investment	74.8	107.4	126.3	137.4
Fixed investment	71.3	98.0	119.0	130.5
Changes in business inventories	3.6	9.4	7.3	6.9
Net exports of goods and services	4.1	6.9	2.5	1.6
Exports	27.2	39.1	50.6	57.1
Imports	23.2	32.2	48.1	55.5
Government purchases of goods and services	99.6	136.4	200.3	212.9
Federal	53.5	66.8	99.5	100.6
State and local	46.1	69.6	100.7	112.3
By major type of product				
Goods output	259.6	346.6	431.1	456.5
Durable goods	99.5	139.5	176.7	190.3
Nondurable goods	160.1	207.1	254.4	266.2
Services	187.3	262.9	347.5	373.4
Structures	56.8	74.4	87.1	94.8

Item	1960	1965	1968	1969*
National income	414.5	562.4	714.4	765.7
By type of income				
Compensation of employees	294.2	393.9	513.6	558.2
Proprietors' income	46.2	56.7	63.8	66.5
Rental income of persons	15.8	19.0	21.2	21.6
Corporate profits and inventory valuation adjustment	49.9	74.9	87.9	89.2
Net interest	8.4	17.9	28.0	30.3
By industry division				
Agriculture, forestry, and fisheries	16.9	21.0	21.9	24.2
Mining and construction	26.5	35.3	42.9	47.8
Manufacturing	125.8	171.8	215.4	228.9
Nondurable goods	52.2	66.3	82.9	88.3
Durable goods	73.6	105.5	132.5	140.5
Transportation	18.2	23.1	27.2	28.9
Communications and public utilities	17.1	22.6	27.9	29.8
Wholesale and retail trade	64.4	84.2	105.2	111.7
Finance, insurance, and real estate	45.9	61.3	78.2	84.4
Services	44.4	63.7	86.1	93.6
Government and government enterprises	52.9	75.2	105.0	112.5
Other	2.4	4.2	4.7	3.9

*Second quarter, seasonally adjusted at annual rates. Source: U.S. Department of Commerce, Office of Business Economics, *Survey of Current Business*.

Agriculture

Farming trends

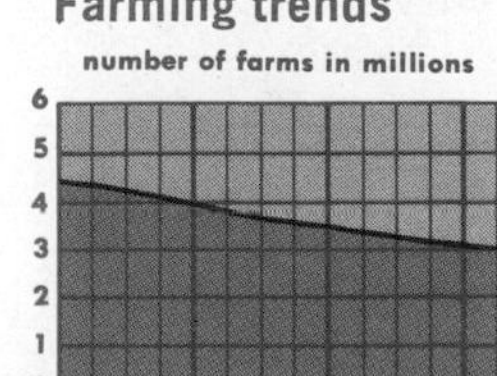

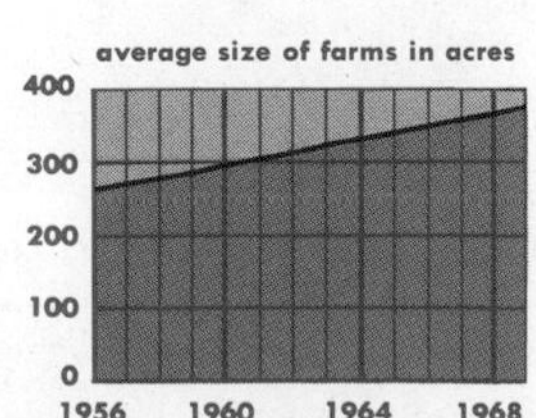

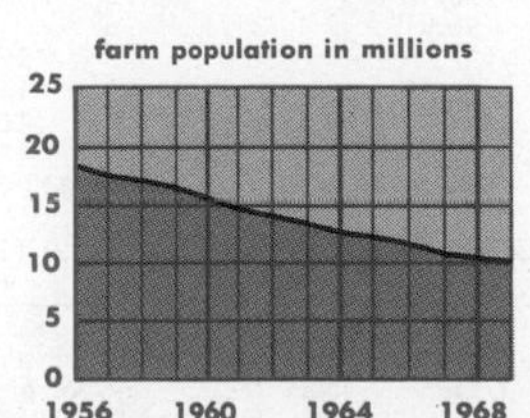

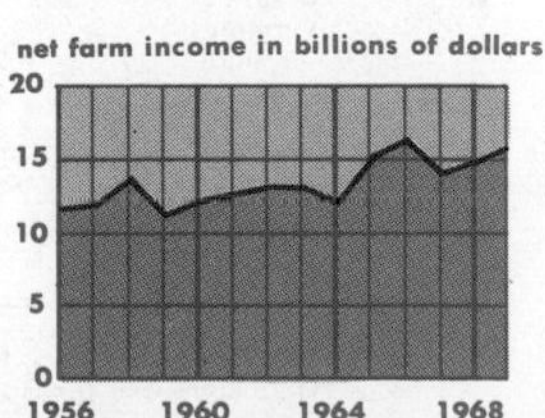

Sources: U.S. Department of Agriculture, Statistical Reporting Service, *Number of Farms and Land in Farms*; U.S. Department of Commerce, Bureau of the Census, Economic Research Service.

Farms and farm income

State	Number of farms 1969*	Land in farms 1969* in 000 acres	CASH INCOME, 1968, IN $000			Realized net income per farm 1968
			Farm marketings			
			Crops	Livestock and products	Government payments	
Alabama	90,000	15,000	194,632	465,055	84,605	$ 2,962
Alaska	310	1,900†	1,174	2,913	122	671
Arizona	6,000	43,400	301,536	285,651	44,656	26,564
Arkansas	75,000	17,900	512,828	473,577	80,838	5,023
California	59,000	37,000	2,669,203	1,604,851	100,731	17,118
Colorado	30,500	39,500	217,058	686,537	62,923	4,862
Connecticut	4,900	620	66,084	95,796	835	9,087
Delaware	3,700	710	39,655	85,863	2,048	9,695
Florida	34,000	16,200	895,952	336,591	19,872	14,756
Georgia	78,000	17,600	414,970	623,761	80,187	5,008
Hawaii	4,600	2,350	166,184	38,321	11,257	19,947
Idaho	28,900	15,400	294,358	251,790	39,884	5,487
Illinois	129,000	29,700	1,367,140	1,224,222	160,928	6,007
Indiana	96,000	17,300	607,001	745,472	120,206	4,735
Iowa	143,000	34,500	913,324	2,548,186	246,281	6,668
Kansas	88,000	50,000	533,878	1,002,036	228,176	5,294
Kentucky	130,000	16,900	379,610	445,201	47,619	3,036
Louisiana	54,000	12,100	399,084	229,659	50,693	5,388
Maine	10,300	2,400	70,457	139,350	2,044	4,654
Maryland	18,700	3,250	111,105	235,409	6,777	5,414
Massachusetts	6,500	750	73,754	87,272	716	6,212
Michigan	87,000	13,200	395,642	453,858	65,314	3,129
Minnesota	130,000	32,200	586,406	1,278,525	134,510	4,369
Mississippi	97,000	17,600	413,633	433,235	122,943	4,336
Missouri	145,000	33,300	446,763	955,452	141,281	3,444
Montana	26,700	67,100	193,321	316,184	74,129	6,666
Nebraska	74,000	48,200	484,227	1,273,329	185,260	$6,992
Nevada	2,100	8,800	11,098	46,124	1,985	2,773
New Hampshire	3,600	740	13,024	43,379	655	2,234
New Jersey	8,700	1,010	150,188	97,828	4,534	7,183
New Mexico	13,800	48,300	101,580	220,773	35,963	8,338
New York	58,000	11,600	293,963	748,029	22,176	5,605
North Carolina	163,000	16,100	733,554	505,066	61,592	3,356
North Dakota	43,000	42,000	453,316	266,998	140,243	5,616
Ohio	113,000	17,400	519,311	704,269	94,712	3,394
Oklahoma	92,000	37,200	267,678	578,305	108,414	2,626
Oregon	41,000	20,900	270,843	241,958	22,604	2,954
Pennsylvania	75,000	10,650	243,994	688,854	23,858	3,717
Rhode Island	900	92	9,700	10,578	74	2,647
South Carolina	52,000	8,400	228,787	145,393	52,989	2,696
South Dakota	47,500	45,500	205,034	753,001	88,760	7,032
Tennessee	128,000	15,500	250,864	372,586	70,093	2,027
Texas	191,000	145,000	1,254,916	1,414,115	465,425	4,973
Utah	14,500	13,300	45,809	151,712	10,869	3,270
Vermont	7,500	2,300	13,405	127,838	1,531	5,029
Virginia	73,000	11,600	230,132	290,287	17,853	2,294
Washington	46,000	18,100	522,267	291,031	52,647	7,020
West Virginia	30,000	5,200	24,848	75,417	4,009	624
Wisconsin	114,000	20,600	215,764	1,242,979	51,707	4,568
Wyoming	8,600	37,000	37,439	204,608	14,526	7,849
Total U.S.	2,976,310	1,123,372	18,846,493	25,539,242	3,462,054	4,841

*Preliminary. †Includes about 1,830,000 acres of grazing land leased from the U.S. government.
Source: U.S. Department of Agriculture, Economic Research Service, *Farm Income Situation;* Statistical Reporting Service, *Number of Farms and Land in Farms.*

Livestock on farms

State	AGGREGATE VALUE OF 5 SPECIES, IN $000		NUMBER, IN 000 HEAD, 1969					VALUE, IN $000, 1969				
	1960	1969	All cattle	Hogs and pigs	Sheep and lambs	Chickens	Turkeys	All cattle	Hogs and pigs	Sheep and lambs	Chickens	Turkeys
Alabama	188,198	270,976	1,896	937	7	18,895	44	227,520	23,331	83	19,840	202
Alaska	...	2,821	9	1	27	30	...	1,952	56	745	68	...
Arizona	138,231	193,940	1,206	51	500	1,474	5	182,106	1,357	8,901	1,548	28
Arkansas	158,292	242,473	1,719	259	8	22,510	131	213,156	6,268	142	22,285	622
California	733,873	1,009,217	4,954	172	1,356	50,335	1,499	901,628	6,330	35,504	57,885	7,870
Colorado	338,813	517,656	3,119	230	1,337	1,935	76	474,088	6,486	34,710	1,935	437
Connecticut	41,548	42,022	120	10	5	5,134	8	31,800	310	103	9,755	54
Delaware	11,199	9,101	32	38	2	834	7	6,720	1,140	35	1,168	38
Florida	184,463	286,133	1,804	328	6	17,333	22*	256,168	9,020	74	20,800	115*
Georgia	180,505	316,302	1,870	1,551	5	36,969	118	231,880	41,257	79	42,514	572
Hawaii	...	43,876	238	64	...	1,276	...	37,842	3,546	...	2,488	...
Idaho	212,296	287,575	1,668	119	852	1,053	22*	260,208	3,142	23,114	1,106	115*
Illinois	704,261	783,090	3,379	6,977	413	10,780	36	537,261	226,055	7,743	11,858	173
Indiana	397,221	452,767	1,841	4,278	282	18,049	56	289,037	135,613	5,265	22,561	291
Iowa	1,200,620	1,753,378	7,551	14,855	961	15,162	191	1,193,058	522,896	19,772	16,678	974
Kansas	586,828	875,697	5,564	1,711	386	4,966	40	812,344	49,619	8,792	4,718	224
Kentucky	305,185	453,371	2,748	1,361	112	4,067	20	406,704	40,558	2,229	3,782	98
Louisiana	201,423	219,926	1,722	196	26	5,340	5	208,362	5,076	320	6,141	27
Maine	39,353	43,185	147	9	17	7,267	1	30,282	276	267	12,354	6
Maryland	92,172	95,214	418	181	19	1,989	19	86,108	5,629	386	2,984	107
Massachusetts	44,421	33,757	121	91	11	3,023	17	30,855	3,039	205	5,441	114
Michigan	312,427	310,751	1,439	554	257	8,199	149	274,849	18,171	5,492	11,479	760
Minnesota	670,758	822,774	3,958	3,248	579	11,745	741	680,776	111,731	11,442	15,268	3,557
Mississippi	226,717	330,887	2,415	496	19	15,630	8	299,460	13,194	224	17,974	35
Missouri	603,332	860,710	4,748	4,257	306	7,982	247	721,696	125,156	5,661	7,024	1,173
Montana	354,483	538,466	2,984	162	1,225	1,297	22*	501,312	4,666	30,982	1,492	115*
Nebraska	732,337	1,110,619	6,266	3,134	393	5,638	58	996,294	100,601	8,535	4,905	284
Nevada	821,192	102,303	591	10	231	28	...	95,742	290	6,237	34	...
New Hampshire	21,937	21,847	74	13	6	2,140	12	17,390	426	100	3,852	79
New Jersey	75,553	50,713	135	124	8	5,111	13	37,935	4,625	158	7,922	73
New Mexico	181,582	214,457	1,346	48	840	963	22*	195,170	1,109	17,241	924	115*
New York	486,348	503,200	1,849	86	103	13,747	36	473,344	2,752	2,138	24,745	221
North Carolina	147,463	203,424	1,020	1,469	20	19,685	967	136,680	41,573	344	20,669	4,158
North Dakota	272,321	362,834	2,025	266	373	1,360	23	344,250	9,310	7,804	1,346	124
Ohio	416,831	453,684	2,094	2,485	744	11,632	166	347,604	75,792	14,760	14,540	988
Oklahoma	415,872	657,995	4,659	386	136	3,037	41	642,942	9,303	2,573	2,976	201
Oregon	207,397	263,719	1,577	117	569	3,258	204	241,281	3,288	14,128	3,910	1,112
Pennsylvania	436,839	471,312	1,799	506	170	17,973	181	420,966	17,255	3,230	28,757	1,104
Rhode Island	6,453	4,573	13	9	2	495	1	3,354	309	39	866	5
South Carolina	72,952	98,465	623	460	2	7,146	356	75,383	12,144	28	9,290	1,620
South Dakota	517,669	814,642	4,366	1,678	1,266	5,638	20	720,390	58,898	29,852	5,412	90
Tennessee	252,512	350,930	2,308	927	49	7,303	16	318,504	24,658	833	6,865	70
Texas	1,249,699	1,677,157	11,521	943	3,949	17,445	793	1,566,856	22,349	65,908	18,317	3,727
Utah	125,650	158,797	785	52	1,053	1,711	88	125,600	1,305	29,585	1,797	510
Vermont	81,388	90,131	351	6	6	751	1	88,452	171	113	1,389	6
Virginia	213,161	237,718	1,404	545	197	6,419	223	209,196	15,532	4,295	7,703	992
Washington	183,221	232,868	1,259	80	148	6,592	29	217,807	2,480	3,883	8,570	128
West Virginia	77,171	74,049	461	56	166	1,733	83	66,845	1,417	3,420	1,993	374
Wisconsin	812,721	962,697	4,076	1,644	179	6,916	168	896,720	52,772	3,644	8,645	916
Wyoming	209,784	272,347	1,389	25	1,782	209	22*	226,407	682	44,974	272	115*
Total U.S.	15,944,672	20,192,443	109,661	57,205	21,111	420,204	6,919	17,362,284	1,822,963	466,092	506,845	34,259

Data are for January 1 of years reported. Total may not equal the sum of the parts due to rounding.
*Data combined for Florida, Idaho, Montana, New Mexico, and Wyoming.
Source: U.S. Department of Agriculture, Statistical Reporting Service, *Livestock and Poultry Inventory.*

Principal crops

of the United States and each state

Crops (unit of production)	Amount produced in 000 1969	Acreage harvested in 000 acres 1969	VALUE OF PRODUCTION in $000 1968	1969
UNITED STATES				
Corn, grain (bu.)	4,577,864	54,573	4,763,061	5,178,781
Hay (tons)	127,127	61,838	2,896,858	2,806,035
Soybeans for beans (bu.)	1,116,876	40,857	2,679,210	2,580,029
Wheat (bu.)	1,458,872	47,555	1,950,462	1,786,156
Tobacco (lb.)	1,802,611	921	1,188,622	1,282,137
Cotton lint (bales)	10,080	11,094	1,212,045	1,075,700
Sorghum grain (bu.)	743,124	13,463	699,188	795,626
Potatoes (cwt.)	307,229	1,404	652,729	616,320
Oats (bu.)	949,874	18,003	569,114	552,923
Rice (cwt.)	91,303	2,128	520,888	449,162
Alabama				
Cotton lint (bales)	465	545	46,807	49,988
Peanuts harvested for nuts (lb.)	284,900	185	28,801	34,188
Soybeans for beans (bu.)	14,743	641	29,655	33,909
Corn, grain (bu.)	17,332	619	25,979	23,745
Hay (tons)	764	492	19,628	21,774
Alaska				
Hay (tons)	8	9	588	532
Potatoes (cwt.)	71	1	654	378
Silage (tons)	14	4	344	257
Barley (bu.)	34	1	117	59
Arizona				
Cotton lint (bales)	645	309	86,125	74,522
Hay (tons)	1,096	224	28,176	29,592
Sorghum grain (bu.)	15,522	199	20,804	20,644
Barley (bu.)	10,224	144	14,133	12,473
Cottonseed (tons)	270	...	16,118	10,800
Arkansas				
Soybeans for beans (bu.)	86,674	4,228	215,007	208,018
Rice (cwt.)	24,720	515	124,702	126,072
Cotton lint (bales)	1,135	1,055	123,672	122,012
Hay (tons)	1,124	705	31,234	25,290
Wheat (bu.)	9,030	301	16,472	10,384
California				
Grapes (tons)	3,570	...	197,254	221,895
Hay (tons)	7,496	1,842	196,850	206,140
Cotton lint (bales)	1,320	705	186,841	155,138
Rice (cwt.)	21,395	389	118,471	106,975
Peaches (bu.)*	47,292	...	107,810	106,031
Potatoes (cwt.)	28,976	94	83,559	71,277
Barley (bu.)	54,191	1,153	78,033	66,655
Colorado				
Hay (tons)	3,356	1,691	79,434	83,900
Wheat (bu.)	45,045	2,145	45,196	49,563
Sugar beets (tons)	3,428	194	38,904	...
Corn, grain (bu.)	25,753	283	25,792	31,161
Potatoes (cwt.)	11,643	50	18,833	20,943
Connecticut				
Tobacco (lb.)	8,455	5	21,916	19,525
Hay (bales)	207	104	7,810	7,556
Apples (bu.)†	1,157	...	3,928	3,985
Potatoes (cwt.)	1,215	5	3,010	2,916
Delaware				
Corn, grain (bu.)	13,260	170	9,887	16,310
Soybeans for beans (bu.)	4,698	162	7,114	10,805
Potatoes (cwt.)	1,680	8	3,309	3,696
Hay (tons)	82	37	2,380	2,993
Florida				
Oranges (tons)	5,836	...	281,408	351,947
Grapefruit (tons)	1,695	...	86,459	58,392
Sugarcane for sugar (tons)	5,062	153	52,392	50,620
Tobacco (lb.)	26,028	16	30,453	30,999
Corn, grain (bu.)	13,962	358	18,643	17,871
Georgia				
Peanuts harvested for nuts (lb.)	953,800	502	110,254	115,410
Tobacco (lb.)	97,890	61	77,305	75,483
Corn, grain (bu.)	47,058	1,426	68,094	63,999
Cotton lint (bales)	275	385	29,150	27,500
Soybeans for beans (bu.)	11,208	467	17,346	26,899
Hawaii				
Papayas (lb.)	19,150	...	2,260	2,470
Macadamia nuts (lb.)	10,478	...	2,434	2,282
Coffee (lb.)	5,500	...	1,548	1,518
Taro (lb.)	8,705	...	676	670
Bananas (lb.)	5,930	...	499	563
Idaho				
Potatoes (cwt.)	67,000	310	139,648	119,640
Hay (tons)	3,761	1,339	67,940	82,742
Wheat (bu.)	47,982	1,051	64,819	59,648
Sugar beets (tons)	3,383	187	47,347	...
Barley (bu.)	30,368	584	21,702	28,242
Illinois				
Corn, grain (bu.)	956,774	9,763	987,615	1,090,722
Soybeans for beans (bu.)	220,966	6,596	520,512	519,270
Hay (tons)	3,411	1,281	79,965	80,158
Wheat (bu.)	48,137	1,301	60,287	56,802
Oats (bu.)	43,798	718	29,938	25,403

Crops (unit of production)	Amount produced in 000 1969	Acreage harvested in 000 acres 1969	VALUE OF PRODUCTION in $000 1968	1969
Indiana				
Corn, grain (bu.)	446,016	4,646	427,508	490,618
Soybeans for beans (bu.)	104,896	3,278	249,293	241,261
Hay (tons)	2,156	927	54,586	51,744
Wheat (bu.)	35,061	899	38,298	39,970
Oats (bu.)	19,706	334	14,023	11,627
Iowa				
Corn, grain (bu.)	922,768	9,416	975,994	1,015,045
Soybeans for beans (bu.)	174,339	5,283	434,203	392,263
Hay (tons)	7,405	2,575	143,920	148,100
Oats (bu.)	92,000	1,840	67,055	54,280
Sorghum grain (bu.)	2,952	36	3,058	2,982
Kansas				
Wheat (bu.)	305,319	9,849	309,302	354,170
Sorghum grain (bu.)	182,896	3,266	148,626	186,554
Hay (tons)	5,112	2,387	99,141	107,352
Corn, grain (bu.)	91,464	1,236	90,153	105,184
Soybeans for beans (bu.)	19,596	852	55,028	43,111
Kentucky				
Tobacco (lb.)	429,700	173	297,674	290,838
Corn, grain (bu.)	76,846	998	81,158	96,058
Hay (tons)	3,116	1,607	79,461	85,960
Soybeans for beans (bu.)	13,580	485	29,514	31,234
Wheat (bu.)	6,222	183	7,613	7,466
Louisiana				
Rice (cwt.)	20,774	611	126,266	98,676
Soybeans for beans (bu.)	30,552	1,608	94,604	71,797
Sugarcane for sugar (tons)	5,900	236	66,614	55,342
Cotton lint (bales)	485	425	61,838	54,562
Sweet Potatoes (cwt.)	4,420	52	15,517	15,470
Maine				
Potatoes (cwt.)	35,100	156	67,386	56,160
Hay (tons)	419	294	10,900	10,684
Apples (bu.)†	1,452	...	5,075	4,874
Oats (bu.)	1,564	34	1,231	1,017
Maryland				
Corn, grain (bu.)	38,799	479	35,138	47,335
Tobacco (lb.)	31,500	30	22,301	21,987
Hay (tons)	665	328	21,568	21,945
Soybeans for beans (bu.)	6,765	205	12,488	15,560
Wheat (bu.)	4,563	117	4,815	5,521
Massachusetts				
Cranberries (bbl.)	755	11	10,956	12,533
Hay (tons)	245	133	8,810	8,330
Tobacco (lb.)	3,320	2	8,328	7,804
Apples (bu.)†	2,381	...	6,671	7,580
Potatoes (cwt.)	950	5	2,486	2,185
Michigan				
Corn, grain (bu.)	93,684	1,266	99,102	103,989
Hay (tons)	3,207	1,485	76,028	70,554
Beans, dry edible (cwt.)	8,119	671	50,320	52,774
Wheat (bu.)	25,120	628	34,090	28,386
Soybeans for beans (bu.)	11,822	514	28,771	27,191
Apples (bu.)†	16,191	...	29,082	27,064
Cherries (tons)	128	...	37,480	19,914
Minnesota				
Corn, grain (bu.)	355,640	4,184	375,756	352,084
Soybeans for beans (bu.)	76,008	3,167	172,072	171,018
Hay (tons)	7,939	3,185	158,486	166,719
Oats (bu.)	193,368	3,453	110,510	106,352
Wheat (bu.)	24,607	838	47,195	35,526
Mississippi				
Cotton lint (bales)	1,325	1,190	174,401	149,062
Soybeans for beans (bu.)	50,380	2,290	140,238	120,912
Hay (tons)	996	619	27,888	24,900
Cottonseed (tons)	568	...	33,476	24,424
Corn, grain (bu.)	9,858	318	17,893	13,407
Missouri				
Corn, grain (bu.)	182,210	2,603	267,610	218,652
Soybeans for beans (bu.)	81,900	3,150	246,154	188,370
Hay (tons)	5,620	2,838	119,826	120,830
Wheat (bu.)	33,120	1,035	50,187	38,419
Cotton lint (bales)	325	305	25,777	34,938
Montana				
Wheat (bu.)	96,794	3,645	146,008	116,819
Hay (tons)	3,882	2,419	80,662	97,050
Barley (bu.)	67,194	1,617	33,333	50,936
Sugar beets (tons)	1,215	67	15,510	...
Potatoes (cwt.)	1,388	7	5,917	4,303
Nebraska				
Corn, grain (bu.)	433,659	4,663	341,918	477,025
Hay (tons)	6,963	4,354	133,188	146,223
Sorghum grain (bu.)	114,608	1,508	89,524	111,170
Wheat (bu.)	85,586	2,717	118,273	96,712
Soybeans for beans (bu.)	26,829	813	43,737	59,024
Nevada				
Hay (tons)	882	428	15,557	22,491
Barley (bu.)	630	11	814	876
Wheat (bu.)	1,102	19	1,017	1,355
New Hampshire				
Hay (tons)	200	128	5,665	5,900
Apples (bu.)†	905	...	3,823	3,215
Potatoes (cwt.)	176	1	621	458

1969 figures are preliminary estimates; 1968 figures are revised estimates.
Boldface type indicates states which lead in the value of production for the ten leading crops in the United States.
*48 lb. equivalents. †42 lb. equivalents.
Source: U.S. Department of Agriculture, Statistical Reporting Service, Crop Reporting Board, *Crop Production* and *Crop Values*, December 1969.

Principal crops (continued)

Crops (unit of production)	Amount produced in 000 1969	Acreage harvested in 000 acres 1969	VALUE OF PRODUCTION in $000 1968	1969
New Jersey				
Hay (tons)	326	136	11,122	11,899
Peaches (bu.)*	2,396	...	8,241	8,280
Potatoes (cwt.)	3,250	13	7,818	7,898
Apples (bu.)†	2,786	...	6,482	6,634
Corn, grain (bu.)	4,941	61	4,368	6,473
New Mexico				
Hay (tons)	293	1,063	27,798	28,170
Cotton lint (bales)	165	147	21,831	21,391
Sorghum grain (bu.)	16,856	301	16,020	19,890
Wheat (bu.)	5,088	159	9,531	6,614
Cottonseed (tons)	70	...	3,915	3,150
New York				
Hay (tons)	5,523	2,590	129,344	138,075
Apples (bu.)†	22,024	...	49,883	41,625
Potatoes (cwt.)	16,974	69	40,271	39,823
Corn, grain (bu.)	18,525	247	20,304	24,268
Grapes (tons)	120	...	15,660	16,200
Oats (bu.)	20,440	365	17,346	14,921
North Carolina				
Tobacco (lb.)	716,123	385	444,481	515,410
Corn, grain (bu.)	89,828	1,321	90,586	114,980
Soybeans for beans (bu.)	24,258	933	41,504	57,006
Peanuts harvested for nuts (lb.)	342,350	167	42,969	43,821
Hay (tons)	600	407	18,755	19,800
North Dakota				
Wheat (bu.)	203,561	6,782	295,731	278,711
Barley (bu.)	92,650	2,180	85,082	69,488
Oats (bu.)	139,440	2,490	52,729	65,537
Hay (tons)	4,061	3,296	60,140	62,946
Flaxseed (bu.)	19,064	1,513	38,531	49,566
Ohio				
Corn, grain (bu.)	232,900	2,740	259,214	272,493
Soybeans for beans (bu.)	67,976	2,344	166,603	156,345
Hay (tons)	2,907	1,481	83,300	71,222
Wheat (bu.)	39,479	1,067	51,713	45,796
Oats (bu.)	32,480	560	26,145	19,163
Oklahoma				
Wheat (bu.)	118,275	4,150	152,979	141,930
Hay (tons)	3,037	1,674	64,522	69,851
Cotton lint (bales)	290	465	24,897	26,825
Peanuts harvested for nuts (lb.)	204,000	120	26,615	24,888
Sorghum grain (bu.)	25,474	542	24,850	28,021
Oregon				
Hay (tons)	2,354	1,141	51,332	61,204
Potatoes (cwt.)	13,115	49	23,472	25,832
Wheat (bu.)	30,030	788	38,607	38,138
Pears (tons)	188	...	13,570	19,248
Cherries (tons)	40	...	8,202	12,510
Pennsylvania				
Hay (tons)	4,146	1,969	112,338	116,088
Corn, grain (bu.)	76,188	907	70,875	98,283
Potatoes (cwt.)	7,810	35	19,721	21,087
Oats (bu.)	22,644	444	18,966	16,304
Wheat (bu.)	11,608	327	14,373	14,626
Rhode Island				
Potatoes (cwt.)	1,326	5	2,961	3,315
Hay (tons)	27	13	936	1,053
Apples (bu.)†	98	...	388	341
South Carolina				
Tobacco (lb.)	136,658	68	81,262	99,487
Corn, grain (bu.)	18,894	402	20,201	24,751
Soybeans for beans (bu.)	21,578	959	28,746	50,708
Cotton lint (bales)	205	287	30,659	22,550
Peaches (bu.)*	7,292	...	18,800	17,850
Hay (tons)	383	230	11,163	11,682
South Dakota				
Corn, grain (bu.)	139,479	2,447	114,768	142,269
Hay (tons)	5,330	4,156	99,976	103,935
Oats (bu.)	109,600	2,357	59,396	58,088
Wheat (bu.)	42,915	1,963	86,105	57,692
Flaxseed (bu.)	9,454	652	21,635	25,053
Tennessee				
Tobacco (lb.)	124,245	59	85,101	81,096
Soybeans for beans (bu.)	28,632	1,193	59,877	65,854
Hay (tons)	1,971	1,325	51,272	57,159
Cotton lint (bales)	425	405	39,149	45,688
Corn, grain (bu.)	27,830	605	36,493	37,014
Texas				
Sorghum grain (bu.)	309,800	6,196	323,741	340,780
Cotton lint (bales)	2,900	4,675	344,142	278,591
Rice (cwt.)	21,646	548	135,005	102,818
Hay (tons)	3,451	1,976	107,794	88,000
Wheat (bu.)	68,856	2,869	106,029	85,381
Cottonseed (tons)	1,228	...	75,245	49,734
Peanuts harvested for nuts (lb.)	408,375	297	49,877	48,188
Utah				
Hay (tons)	1,555	577	32,384	37,320
Wheat (bu.)	6,072	229	9,437	7,914
Barley (bu.)	6,912	128	7,036	7,396
Sugar beets (tons)	539	32	7,425	...
Potatoes (cwt.)	1,332	7	2,927	3,064
Vermont				
Hay (tons)	938	512	24,000	24,857
Apples (bu.)†	905	...	3,086	3,184
Maple sirup (gal.)	290	...	1,568	1,856
Potatoes (cwt.)	254	1	798	686
Virginia				
Tobacco (lb.)	132,835	73	74,229	93,371
Hay (tons)	1,749	1,045	61,446	58,592
Corn, grain (bu.)	33,264	432	34,671	42,245
Peanuts harvested for nuts (lb.)	234,600	102	28,633	30,263
Soybeans for beans (bu.)	9,025	361	17,246	21,209
Apples (bu.)†	10,833	...	19,907	18,064
Washington				
Wheat (bu.)	95,242	2,462	140,578	120,065
Hay (tons)	2,378	930	56,368	61,828
Apples (bu.)†	40,238	...	81,488	55,094
Potatoes (cwt.)	29,286	72	40,377	43,203
Pears (tons)	106	...	19,278	8,894
Sugar beets (tons)	1,628	65	19,639	...
West Virginia				
Hay (tons)	890	596	27,816	27,145
Apples (bu.)†	6,190	...	12,828	11,570
Corn, grain (bu.)	3,087	49	3,018	4,167
Tobacco (lb.)	3,705	2	2,413	2,519
Wheat (bu.)	420	14	561	529
Wisconsin				
Hay (tons)	10,949	4,022	194,094	191,608
Corn, grain (bu.)	139,772	1,684	176,172	159,340
Oats (bu.)	102,907	1,687	68,951	65,860
Potatoes (cwt.)	12,400	53	32,115	31,360
Soybeans for beans (bu.)	3,306	174	8,359	7,604
Wyoming				
Hay (tons)	1,679	1,147	33,600	39,456
Sugar beets (tons)	1,232	68	15,446	...
Barley (bu.)	5,916	116	4,568	5,798
Wheat (bu.)	4,884	242	8,551	5,260
Beans, dry edible (cwt.)	459	28	3,942	3,305

(H. R. Sh.)

Farm wage workers, 1968

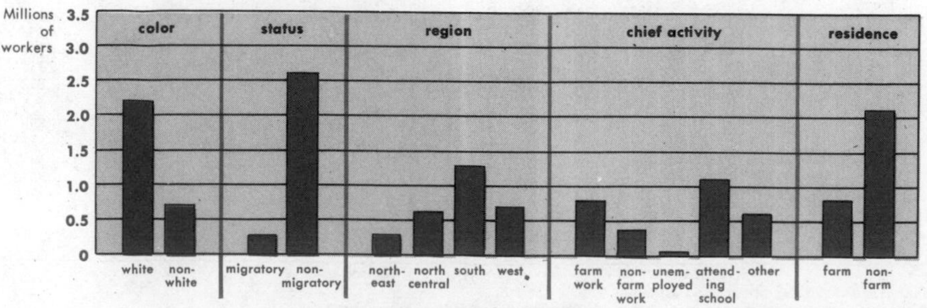

total workers: 2,919,000

Source: U.S. Department of Agriculture, Economic Research Service.

Mining

Principal minerals produced

in the United States and each state

Mineral (unit of production)	1960 Quantity	1960 Value in $000	1968 Quantity	1968 Value in $000
UNITED STATES		18,032,000		24,974,000
Mineral fuels		12,142,000		16,820,000
Petroleum, crude (000 42-gal. bbl.)	2,574,933	7,420,181	3,329,042	9,794,826
Natural gas (000,000 cu.ft.)	12,771,038	1,789,970	19,322,400	3,168,688
Coal (000 short tons)				
Bituminous and lignite*	415,512	1,950,425	545,245	2,546,340
Pennsylvania anthracite	18,817	147,116	11,461	97,245
Natural-gas liquids (000 gal.)				
Natural gasoline and cycle products	5,842,507	416,819	8,360,058	571,679
Liquefied petroleum gases	8,444,074	391,566	14,753,004	552,335
Nonmetallic minerals, except fuels		3,868,000		5,452,000
Cement				
Portland (000 376-lb. bbl.)	321,646	1,089,134	388,525	1,227,942
Masonry (000 280-lb. bbl.)			23,167	66,259
Naturalandslag (000376-lb.bbl.)			86	332
Stone† (000 short tons)	616,784	952,555	819,403	1,317,753
Sand and gravel (000 short tons)	709,792	720,432	917,739	1,020,336
Lime (000 short tons)	12,935	172,731	18,637	249,639
Salt (000 short tons)	25,479	161,140	41,274	272,275
Clays (000 short tons)	49,069	162,411	57,233	246,898
Phosphate rock (000 short tons)	19,620	117,041	41,251	250,692
Sulfur, Frasch-process mines (000 long tons)	5,003	115,494	6,645	268,146
Potassium salts, K_2O equivalent (000 short tons)	2,638	89,676	2,722	75,664
Bromine (000 lb.)	175,010	44,637	362,452	86,787
Boron minerals (000 short tons)	641	47,550	1,026	79,827
Metals		2,022,000		2,703,000
Copper, recoverable (000 short tons)	1,080	693,468	1,205	1,008,195
Iron ore, usable (000 long tons)	82,963	724,131	81,934	836,433
Zinc, recoverable (000 short tons)	435	112,365	529	142,950
Uranium (recoverable U_3O_8) (000 lb.)	7,970‡	152,188‡	24,139	182,698
Molybdenum, content of concentrate (000 lb.)	69,941	87,406	93,245	151,000
Lead, recoverable (000 short tons)	247	57,722	359	94,903
Gold (troy oz.)	1,666,772	58,336	1,478,292	58,038
Silver, recoverable (000 troy oz.)	30,766	27,846	32,729	70,191
Alabama [22]		221,802		259,621
Coal, bituminous (000 short tons)	13,011	92,439	16,440	115,815
Cement†				
Portland (000 376-lb. bbl.)	12,931	42,706	15,514	48,147
Masonry (000 280-lb. bbl.)			2,523	7,309
Stone (000 short tons)	13,503	19,970	20,643	33,847
Petroleum, crude (000 42-gal. bbl.)	7,329	§	7,635	20,385
Sand and gravel (000 short tons)	4,359	4,759	8,140	9,130
Iron ore, usable (000 long tons)	4,068	23,511	1,151	6,730
Alaska [25]		21,860		221,717
Petroleum, crude (000 42-gal. bbl.)	559	1,230	66,204	186,695
Sand and gravel (000 short tons)	6,013	5,483	18,013	20,366
Arizona [10]		417,225		617,541
Copper, recoverable (000 short tons)	346	345,784	628	525,566
Sand and gravel (000 short tons)	14,490	14,235	13,981	14,423
Molybdenum (000 lb.)	4,359	5,211	12,127	19,207
Silver, recoverable (000 troy oz.)	4,775	4,322	4,958	10,633
Stone (000 short tons)	4,249	5,107	5	1,469
Arkansas [28]		159,519		198,723
Petroleum, crude (000 42-gal. bbl.)	30,117	83,424	19,464	53,137
Stone (000 short tons)	10,939	13,555	16,322	22,256
Bauxite (000 long tons)	1,932	20,469	1,582	23,058
Bromine (000 lb.)	§	§	95,499	20,790
Sand and gravel (000 short tons)	8,192	10,262	12,997	14,643
Natural gas (000,000 cu.ft.)	55,451	6,599	156,627	24,456
California [3]		1,422,087		1,808,147
Petroleum, crude (000 42-gal. bbl.)	305,352	751,166	375,496	883,644
Natural gas (000,000 cu.ft.)	517,535	138,182	714,893	221,077
Cement (000 376-lb. bbl.)	39,712†	128,826†	47,595	151,961
Sand and gravel (000 short tons)	87,679	107,503	124,655	153,360
Natural-gas liquids (000 gal.)	1,203,035	83,978	923,664	61,712
Stone (000 short tons)	33,075	49,842	36,125	52,671
Boron minerals (000 short tons)	641	47,550	1,026	79,827
Mercury (76-lb. flasks)	18,764	3,955	568	9,301
Colorado [17]		345,418		359,458
Petroleum, crude (000 42-gal. bbl.)	47,469	137,660	31,937	94,215
Molybdenum (000 lb.)	51,615	65,448	61,684	100,296
Coal, bituminous (000 short tons)	3,607	21,090	5,558	26,785
Sand and gravel (000 short tons)	19,053	16,882	23,131	26,608
Zinc, recoverable (000 short tons)	31	8,070	50	13,570
Natural gas (000,000 cu.ft.)	107,404	12,781	121,424	16,392
Uranium (recoverable U_3O_8) (000 lb.)	1,150‡	23,462‡	2,706	20,009
Connecticut [45]		15,353		23,876
Stone (000 short tons)	5,057	8,313	6,383	12,729
Sand and gravel (000 short tons)	6,575	5,960	8,752	9,321
Delaware [50]		989		1,996
Sand and gravel (000 short tons)	1,084	907	1,596	1,483
Florida [18]		180,286		304,623
Phosphate rock (000 long tons)	12,321	82,530	§	§
Stone (000 short tons)	27,629†	37,419†	36,692†	46,563†
Clays (000 short tons)	252†	6,357†	808	11,699
Titanium concentrate (000 short tons)	286	7,489	§	§
Georgia [29]		92,305		173,090
Clays (000 short tons)	3,519	40,160	5,111	88,632
Stone (000 short tons)	14,297	37,033	26,903	56,177
Sand and gravel (000 short tons)	3,338	3,047	3,803	4,314
Hawaii [46]		9,367		23,225
Cement (000 376-lb. bbl.)	113	571	1,841	9,254
Stone (000 short tons)	3,535	6,443	5,211	11,273

Mineral (unit of production)	1960 Quantity	1960 Value in $000	1968 Quantity	1968 Value in $000
Idaho [32]		57,606		114,253
Silver, recoverable (000 troy oz.)	13,647	12,351	15,959	34,225
Lead, recoverable (000 short tons)	43	10,040	55	14,478
Zinc, recoverable (000 short tons)	37	9,495	57	15,457
Phosphate rock (000 long tons)	2,177	11,044	3,879	22,721
Sand and gravel (000 short tons)	7,088	6,594	8,224	9,133
Illinois [8]		589,874		647,543
Coal, bituminous (000 short tons)	45,977	184,087	62,441	250,685
Petroleum, crude (000 42-gal. bbl.)	77,341	228,929	56,391	173,120
Stone (000 short tons)	41,721	55,593	55,858	80,188
Sand and gravel (000 short tons)	33,138	36,255	45,609	52,943
Cement				
Portland (000 376-lb. bbl.)	9,139	30,732	9,372	32,475
Masonry (000 280-lb. bbl.)			602	2,097
Natural-gas liquids (000 gal.)	374,862	21,254	16,380‖	18,438‖
Fluorspar (000 short tons)	134,529	6,936	188,325	9,134
Indiana [23]		210,932		235,386
Coal, bituminous (000 short tons)	15,538	61,570	18,486	71,680
Cement (000 bbl.)	14,052	48,310	14,774†	48,096†
Stone (000 short tons)	18,956	34,920	26,307	46,790
Petroleum, crude (000 42-gal. bbl.)	12,054	35,439	8,692	26,511
Sand and gravel (000 short tons)	20,752	18,377	25,774	26,160
Iowa [31]		99,319		117,297
Cement				
Portland (000 376-lb. bbl.)	12,517	44,204	13,900	47,275
Masonry (000 280-lb. bbl.)			624	1,986
Stone (000 short tons)	23,185	30,321	26,150	40,397
Sand and gravel (000 short tons)	14,692	13,516	16,332	15,192
Gypsum (000 short tons)	1,283	5,428	1,351	5,838
Kansas [12]		486,534		568,701
Petroleum, crude (000 42-gal. bbl.)	113,453	329,014	94,505	285,405
Natural gas (000,000 cu.ft.)	634,410	74,226	835,555	115,307
Helium (000,000 cu.ft.)	21,696	350	3,041,400¶	40,900¶
Cement				
Portland (000 376-lb. bbl.)	8,162	26,373	9,680†	29,898†
Masonry (000 280-lb. bbl.)			383†	1,177†
Stone (000 short tons)	11,814†	15,031†	14,402	20,714
Natural-gas liquids (000 gal.)	127,270	6,343	864,024	36,804
Salt (000 short tons)	1,213	14,109	1,128δ	15,520δ
Kentucky [15]		414,553		534,863
Coal, bituminous (000 short tons)	66,846	282,395	101,156	395,039
Petroleum, crude (000 42-gal. bbl.)	21,147	60,268	14,036	41,125
Stone (000 short tons)	15,810	21,493	30,105	43,266
Natural gas (000,000 cu.ft.)	75,329	18,380	89,024	22,256
Sand and gravel (000 short tons)	5,113	5,763	7,478	8,081
Louisiana [2]		1,990,895		4,321,010
Petroleum, crude (000 42-gal. bbl.)	400,832	1,258,138	817,426	2,570,641
Natural gas (000,000 cu.ft.)	2,988,414	511,019	6,416,015	1,212,627
Natural-gas liquids				
Natural gasoline (000 gal.)	875,567	66,214	2,096,976	156,903
Petroleum gases, liquefied (000 gal.)	606,023	28,147	2,400,930	91,464
Sulfur, Frasch-process mines (000 long tons)	2,256	52,639	4,074	162,664
Salt (000 short tons)	4,792	21,959	10,908	53,854
Sand and gravel (000 short tons)	14,319	19,106	20,411	26,504
Maine [47]		14,108		17,810
Sand and gravel (000 short tons)	9,833	3,892	11,866	5,978
Stone (000 short tons)	1,012	3,851	1,187	3,205
Maryland [38]		57,697		71,844
Stone (000 short tons)	7,944	16,962	13,344	26,606
Sand and gravel (000 short tons)	10,076	13,221	11,719	17,157
Coal, bituminous (000 short tons)	748	2,799	1,447	5,318
Massachusetts [43]		28,245		43,340
Sand and gravel (000 short tons)	14,789	13,013	17,799	20,106
Stone (000 short tons)	5,247	12,782	6,917	19,501
Michigan [9]		437,598		627,075
Iron ore, usable (000 long tons)	10,792	95,791	12,699	148,890
Cement				
Portland (000 376-lb. bbl.)	22,361	77,694	31,375	99,158
Masonry (000 280-lb. bbl.)			2,006	5,527
Copper, recoverable (000 short tons)	56	36,199	75	62,607
Sand and gravel (000 short tons)	46,910	39,304	56,663	54,979
Petroleum, crude (000 42-gal. bbl.)	15,899	46,266	12,974	38,287
Stone (000 short tons)	31,256	32,274	37,279	41,092
Salt (000 short tons)	4,088	33,759	4,893	44,481
Magnesium compounds, MgO equivalent (000 short tons)	§	§	266	25,087
Lime (000 short tons)	1,177	15,730	1,630	19,870
Minnesota [13]		515,521		567,427
Iron ore, usable (000 long tons)	54,723	470,874	51,275	508,814
Sand and gravel (000 short tons)	30,302	24,611	44,674	36,414
Stone (000 short tons)	4,234	10,034	4,427	13,045
Manganiferous ore (000 short tons)	441	§	192	§
Mississippi [26]		199,210		220,955
Petroleum, crude (000 42-gal. bbl.)	51,673	146,235	58,708	164,396
Natural gas (000,000 cu.ft.)	172,478	32,426	135,051	22,601
Sand and gravel (000 short tons)	6,181	5,568	11,980	12,669
Missouri [21]		162,244		275,955
Stone (000 short tons)	27,180	37,878	38,763	58,522
Cement				
Portland (000 376-lb. bbl.)	12,183	42,330	20,081	71,206
Masonry (000 280-lb. bbl.)			405	1,312
Lead, recoverable (000 short tons)	112	26,196	213	56,180
Iron ore, usable (000 long tons)	365	3,760	1,648	23,585
Lime (000 short tons)	1,254	14,701	§	§
Sand and gravel (000 short tons)	10,207	11,601	10,649	14,204
Coal, bituminous (000 short tons)	2,890	12,450	3,205	13,460

Principal minerals produced (continued)

Mineral (unit of production)	1960 Quantity	1960 Value in $000	1968 Quantity	1968 Value in $000
Montana [24]		179,406		228,131
Petroleum, crude (000 42-gal. bbl.)	30,240	72,878	48,460	124,488
Copper, recoverable (000 short tons)	92	59,046	69	58,151
Sand and gravel (000 short tons)	12,589	11,657	8,762	7,754
Stone (000 short tons)	1,183	1,576	3,314	4,878
Silver, recoverable (000 troy oz.)	3,607	3,265	2,133	4,574
Nebraska [37]		103,942		74,837
Petroleum, crude (000 42-gal. bbl.)	23,825	68,378	13,183	36,781
Sand and gravel (000 short tons)	10,876	8,746	13,013	13,175
Stone (000 short tons)	3,336	5,651	4,416	7,435
Natural-gas liquids (000 gal.)	§	§	25,368	1,367
Natural gas (000,000 cu.ft.)	15,258	2,670	8,129	1,423
Nevada [30]		80,892		120,041
Copper, recoverable (000 short tons)	77	49,745	77	64,623
Sand and gravel (000 short tons)	4,085	5,224	7,812	10,442
Iron ore, usable (000 long tons)	740	3,683	569	2,917
Gold (troy oz.)	58,187	2,037	317,382	12,460△
Mercury (76-lb. flasks)	7,821	1,648	4,780	2,560
New Hampshire [48]		5,439		9,166
Sand and gravel (000 short tons)	6,621	3,687	7,742	5,698
Stone (000 short tons)	104	594	383	3,377
New Jersey [36]		56,469		77,466
Stone (000 short tons)	10,202	22,814	13,151	30,343
Sand and gravel (000 short tons)	11,594	19,511	20,306	33,570
Zinc, recoverable (000 short tons)	—	—	26	6,930
Clays (000 short tons)	664	1,597	373	1,008
New Mexico [7]		653,766		893,775
Petroleum, crude (000 42-gal. bbl.)	107,380	305,895	128,550	378,708
Potash, K_2O equivalent (000 short tons)	2,440	82,645	2,289	63,406
Natural gas (000,000 cu.ft.)	798,928	85,485	1,164,182	156,000
Copper, recoverable (000 short tons)	67	43,199	91	75,968
Natural-gas liquids (000 gal.)	966,783	49,200	1,372,140	58,093
Uranium (U_3O_8) (000 lb.)	3,793‡	61,827‡	12,282	95,144
Coal, bituminous (000 short tons)	295	1,747	3,429	13,507
New York [19]		260,922		299,636
Stone (000 short tons)	29,802	46,955	35,441	63,510
Sand and gravel (000 short tons)	30,687	35,152	43,439	45,812
Salt (000 short tons)	4,008	30,763	5,218	42,488
Zinc, recoverable (000 short tons)	66	17,122	66	17,872
North Carolina [34]		45,096		82,819
Stone (000 short tons)	14,721	23,296	24,543	42,429
Sand and gravel (000 short tons)	8,801	7,453	10,771	11,178
Feldspar (000 long tons)	271	2,781	317	4,340
Clays† (000 short tons)	2,476	1,548	3,310	2,148
Mica, scrap (000 short tons)	47	1,100	69	1,640
North Dakota [33]		78,378		98,036
Petroleum, crude (000 42-gal. bbl.)	21,992	59,598	25,040	66,106
Sand and gravel (000 short tons)	8,648	6,904	10,839	10,159
Natural gas (000,000 cu.ft.)	19,483	2,221	41,023	6,769
Coal, lignite (000 short tons)	2,525	5,790	4,487	7,986
Natural-gas liquids (000 gal.)	§	§	113,988	5,101
Ohio [14]		406,142		536,898
Coal, bituminous (000 short tons)	33,957	130,877	48,323	191,427
Stone (000 short tons)	35,856	59,479	48,057†	78,830†
Cement				
Portland (000 376-lb. bbl.)	17,480	61,478	15,222	49,814
Masonry (000 280-lb. bbl.)			1,063	3,155
Lime (000 short tons)	3,117	44,403	3,701	49,367
Petroleum, crude (000 42-gal. bbl.)	5,405	16,053	11,204	35,722
Sand and gravel (000 short tons)	37,943	44,979	46,734	57,671
Salt (000 short tons)	3,108	24,149	5,713	43,172
Clays (000 short tons)	5,165	14,325	4,750	15,216
Oklahoma [4]		782,579		1,016,832
Petroleum, crude (000 42-gal. bbl.)	192,913	563,306	223,623	668,202
Natural gas (000,000 cu.ft.)	824,266	98,088	1,390,884	197,506
Natural-gas liquids				
Natural gasoline (000 gal.)	531,995	33,074	584,010	38,829
Petroleum gases, liquefied (000 gal.)	762,258	32,409	1,070,874	39,520
Stone (000 short tons)	14,054†	16,098†	17,290	21,950
Helium (000 cu.ft.)	289,068	4,691	308,600♀	8,700♀
Oregon [40]		55,772		64,449
Sand and gravel (000 short tons)	17,673	16,170	18,260	21,457
Stone (000 short tons)	16,913	19,721	14,312	21,168
Nickel, content of ore (000 short tons)	13	5,246	17	§
Lime (000 short tons)		§	120	2,407
Pennsylvania [6]		838,146		904,044
Coal				
Bituminous (000 short tons)	65,425	345,971	76,200	408,982
Anthracite (000 short tons)	18,817	147,116	11,461	97,245
Cement				
Portland (000 376-lb. bbl.)	38,320	131,763	43,018	123,176
Masonry (000 280-lb. bbl.)			3,151	8,706
Stone (000 short tons)	42,136	74,168	62,812	108,151
Sand and gravel (000 short tons)	13,011	21,204	18,101	31,076
Natural gas (000,000 cu.ft.)	113,928	36,229	87,987	24,460
Petroleum, crude (000 42-gal. bbl.)	6,009	27,341	4,160	18,698
Pennsylvania (continued)				
Lime (000 short tons)	1,120	16,277	1,702	24,272
Clays† (000 short tons)	3,557	16,536	3,034	17,679
Rhode Island [49]		5,727		4,222
Sand and gravel (000 short tons)	1,535	1,355	2,291	2,546
Stone (000 short tons)	1,810	4,372	§	§
South Carolina [42]		30,987		51,858
Stone (000 short tons)	7,327	10,593	8,942	13,717
Clays (000 short tons)	1,297	6,201	1,936	8,923
Sand and gravel (000 short tons)	3,029	3,048	5,662	8,074
South Dakota [41]		47,675		54,086
Gold (troy oz.)	554,771	19,417	593,052	23,283△
Sand and gravel (000 short tons)	13,548	9,359	11,558	11,578
Cement				
Portland (000 376-lb. bbl.)	§	§	1,826	6,228
Masonry (000 280-lb. bbl.)	§	§	54	180
Stone (000 short tons)	3,149	7,909	1,860	9,687
Tennessee [27]		145,538		201,334
Stone (000 short tons)	20,074	29,942	32,083†	43,854†
Zinc, recoverable (000 short tons)	91	23,579	124,039	33,491
Cement				
Portland (000 376-lb. bbl.)	8,246	27,384	8,488	27,691
Masonry (000 280-lb. bbl.)			1,370	3,836
Coal, bituminous (000 short tons)	5,930	21,154	8,148	29,647
Phosphate rock (000 short tons)	2,172	15,424	3,149	23,628
Sand and gravel (000 short tons)	6,293	7,655	7,344	11,140
Copper, recoverable (000 short tons)	13	8,168	14	11,881
Texas [1]		4,126,419		5,505,831
Petroleum, crude (000 42-gal. bbl.)	927,479	2,748,735	1,133,380	3,450,707
Natural gas (000,000 cu.ft.)	5,892,704	665,876	7,495,414	1,011,881
Natural-gas liquids				
Natural gasoline (000 gal.)	2,880,906	207,583	4,077,150	269,182
Petroleum gases, liquefied (000 gal.)	4,476,142	200,478	7,944,804	278,068
Cement				
Portland (000 376-lb. bbl.)	23,365	76,577	34,499	107,532
Masonry (000 280-lb. bbl.)			1,059	3,371
Sulfur, Frasch-process mines (000 long tons)	2,747	62,855	2,571	105,482
Stone (000 short tons)	39,029	45,088	48,480	58,006
Sand and gravel (000 short tons)	29,844	30,754	31,843	41,546
Salt (000 short tons)	4,756	18,222	8,534	42,663
Lime (000 short tons)	821	9,087	1,564	21,154
Helium (000 cu.ft.)	120,921	2,044	1,400,800¶	20,500¶
Utah [16]		432,712		423,951
Copper, recoverable (000 short tons)	218	139,987	228	191,027
Petroleum, crude (000 42-gal. bbl.)	37,594	103,008	23,504	62,826
Coal, bituminous (000 short tons)	4,955	31,458	4,316	24,893
Uranium (U_3O_8) (000 lb.)	1,090‡	27,843‡	1,712	13,175
Iron ore, usable (000 long tons)	3,334	23,862	1,764	11,281
Silver, recoverable (000 troy oz.)	4,783	4,329	5,121	10,982
Lead, recoverable (000 short tons)	39	9,219	45	11,945
Gold (troy oz.)	368,255	12,889	344,419	13,129△
Vermont [44]		22,903		28,715
Stone (000 short tons)	2,114	17,444	2,536	21,401
Sand and gravel (000 short tons)	1,809	1,218	3,587	2,806
Virginia [20]		208,880		295,663
Coal, bituminous (000 short tons)	27,838	122,723	36,966	178,946
Stone (000 short tons)	19,358	33,019	31,217	53,533
Sand and gravel (000 short tons)	7,666	11,432	10,859	13,644
Lime (000 short tons)	711	8,028	919	11,138
Zinc, recoverable (000 short tons)	20	5,142	19	5,199
Washington [35]		72,404		81,385
Sand and gravel (000 short tons)	25,594	19,459	31,432	27,839
Cement				
Portland (000 376-lb. bbl.)	§	§	6,328	23,030
Masonry (000 280-lb. bbl.)	§	§	56	175
Stone (000 short tons)	13,897	15,796	14,331	16,690
Zinc, recoverable (000 short tons)	21	5,500	14	3,749
Lead, recoverable (000 short tons)	8	1,808	6	1,494
West Virginia [5]		722,628		917,708
Coal (000 short tons)	118,944	597,222	145,921	775,720
Natural gas (000,000 cu.ft.)	208,757	54,694	236,971	62,086
Natural-gas liquids (000 gal.)	353,085	18,040	288,288‖	14,290‖
Stone (000 short tons)	8,001	14,001	9,011†	16,789†
Petroleum, crude (000 42-gal. bbl.)	2,300	9,361	3,312	13,149
Sand and gravel (000 short tons)	4,506	9,802	5,657	11,900
Wisconsin [39]		78,760		71,695
Sand and gravel (000 short tons)	35,681	25,648	39,807	30,903
Stone (000 short tons)	16,486	22,302	17,000	25,223
Zinc, recoverable (000 short tons)	18	4,750	26	6,942
Wyoming [11]		439,256		576,190
Petroleum, crude (000 42-gal. bbl.)	133,910	336,114	144,250	380,589
Natural gas (000,000 cu.ft.)	181,610	21,793	248,481	36,278
Uranium (U_3O_8) (000 lb.)	1,357‡	27,387‡	5,928	44,343
Iron ore, usable (000 long tons)	§	§	1,967	19,452
Clays (000 short tons)	788	9,571	1,828	17,275
Coal, bituminous (000 short tons)	2,024	6,992	3,829	12,117

Figure in brackets is the rank of the state by value of 1968 mineral production.
Boldface type indicates the state that leads in value of production for that mineral.
Production is measured by mine shipments, sales, or marketable production (including consumption by producers).

*Includes small quantity of anthracite mined in states other than Pennsylvania. †Excludes certain varieties. ‡Short tons of uranium ore. §Figure withheld to avoid disclosing confidential data. ‖Estimate by Independent Petroleum Association of America. ¶Includes crude. ♀Grade A. ♁Excludes salt in brine. △Based on average treasury price ($35.00) January 1 through March 15, 1968 and New York selling price for remainder of year.
Source: U.S. Department of the Interior, Bureau of Mines.

(F. H. SK.)

Forestry and Fisheries

Forest land

State	Total forest land in 000 acres*	COMMERCIAL FOREST LAND* in 000 acres: Total	Federally owned or managed	State, county, municipal	Private	Number of national forests June 30, 1968
Alabama	21,770	21,742	799	202	20,741	4
Alaska	118,487	5,761	5,585	146	30	2
Arizona	19,902	3,870	3,701	34	135	7
Arkansas	21,591	21,530	2,641	205	18,684	3
California	42,541	17,391	9,153	194	8,044	22
Colorado	22,583	12,275	8,907	235	3,133	12
Connecticut	1,990	1,973	1	154	1,818	—
Delaware	392	391	1	8	382	—
Florida	19,904	18,474	1,640	580	16,254	3
Georgia	26,365	26,298	1,674	135	24,489	2
Hawaii	1,982	1,089	9	487	593	—
Idaho	21,815	15,823	11,817	940	3,066	15
Illinois	3,871	3,761	229	11	3,521	1
Indiana	4,018	3,960	177	117	3,666	1
Iowa	2,620	2,595	13	24	2,558	—
Kansas	1,668	1,664	1	—	1,663	—
Kentucky	10,891	10,840	575	77	10,188	2
Louisiana	16,576	16,512	704	181	15,627	1
Maine	17,425	17,169	66	139	16,964	1
Maryland	2,920	2,897	54	160	2,683	—
Massachusetts	3,288	3,259	29	370	2,860	—
Michigan	19,699	19,121	2,540	3,780	12,801	4
Minnesota	19,047	17,056	2,813	6,720	7,523	2
Mississippi	18,008	17,976	1,267	452	16,257	6
Missouri	15,296	14,977	1,361	224	13,392	2
Montana	22,048	17,300	11,801	639	4,860	11
Nebraska	1,162	1,140	66	12	1,062	1
Nevada	12,036	109	32	—	77	4
New Hampshire	5,019	4,907	579	118	4,210	1
New Jersey	2,229	2,120	17	237	1,866	—
New Mexico	18,807	6,083	4,118	161	1,804	7
New York	14,450	12,002	98	797	11,107	—
North Carolina	20,862	20,216	1,247	290	18,679	5
North Dakota	439	424	118	10	296	—
Ohio	5,171	5,121	88	272	4,761	1
Oklahoma	9,235	5,299	423	60	4,816	1
Oregon	30,739	26,613	15,379	923	10,311	15
Pennsylvania	15,186	15,089	485	2,815	11,789	1
Rhode Island	434	430	—	26	404	—
South Carolina	11,640	11,559	837	176	10,546	2
South Dakota	1,837	1,706	1,139	84	483	2
Tennessee	13,907	13,643	834	365	12,444	1
Texas	23,954	11,991	719	34	11,238	4
Utah	14,955	3,999	3,096	240	663	9
Vermont	3,730	3,713	231	98	3,384	1
Virginia	16,492	15,829	1,277	140	14,412	2
Washington	23,050	19,510	8,159	2,200	9,151	9
West Virginia	11,469	11,389	883	153	10,353	3
Wisconsin	15,588	15,396	1,910	3,156	10,330	2
Wyoming	9,777	4,853	3,883	111	859	9
Total U.S.	758,865	508,845	113,176	28,692	366,977	153†

*Data are for January 1, 1963. However, since change in forest land is slow, the data are generally indicative of the current situation.
†Total is less than the sum of the state figures because forests extending into two or more states are shown for each state.
Source: U.S. Department of Agriculture, Forest Service.

Lumber production

in millions of board feet

Kind of wood	1960	1965	1968*
Softwoods	26,672	29,295	27,874
Cedar	...	633	575
Douglas fir	8,832	8,783	8,180
Hemlock	2,032	2,576	2,353
Ponderosa pine	3,169	3,776	3,768
Redwood	1,000	1,087	939
Southern yellow pine	5,660	6,628	6,415
Spruce	471	641	686
Sugar pine	408	464	495
White fir	2,224	2,422	2,263
White pine	...	1,151	1,092
Other softwoods	675	1,134	1,117
Hardwoods†	6,254	7,467	7,401
Ash	125	141	149
Basswood	92	87	77
Beech	195	182	160
Birch	126	109	96
Cottonwood and aspen	206	198	202
Elm	195	206	200
Maple	602	786	702
Oak	2,789	3,356	3,421
Sweet (red and sap) gum	331	387	385
Tupelo and black gum	292	385	342
Yellow poplar	592	681	666
Other hardwoods†	709	788	1,001
Total	32,926	36,762	35,275

*Preliminary.
†Includes estimate for western hardwoods, not reported by species.
Source: U.S. Department of Commerce, Bureau of the Census, *Current Industrial Reports;* and U.S. Department of Agriculture, Forest Service.

Forest fires

in thousands of acres

Place and cause	1950	1960	1965	1968
Total fires	208,588	103,387	113,684	125,376
On protected areas	105,182	89,627	100,568	117,721
Percent of total	50.4	86.7	88.5	93.9
Lightning	6,518	11,068	8,730	9,066
Campfires	3,802	3,614	3,404	2,986
Smoking	18,287	16,030	16,517	17,162
Debris burning	18,768	21,870	22,882	31,192
Arson	40,127	21,162	26,860	32,417
Machine use	...	...	6,734	8,387
Miscellaneous	17,680	15,883	15,441	16,511

Source: U.S. Department of Commerce, Bureau of the Census, *Statistical Abstract of the United States.* Data compiled by the U.S. Department of Agriculture, Forest Service.

Commercial fishing

1968 catch, by states

State	Quantity in 000 lb.	Value in $000	State	Quantity in 000 lb.	Value in $000
Alabama	32,300	9,800	Missouri*	626	93
Alaska	433,700	71,600	Montana*	521	63
Arizona*	21	4	Nebraska*	349	43
Arkansas*	6,391	900	New Hampshire	1,300	800
California	446,100	53,300	New Jersey	124,800	10,200
Colorado	...	...	New Mexico*	41	9
Connecticut	5,300	1,800			
Delaware	700	300	New York	60,300	14,400
Florida	181,000	32,900	North Carolina	232,200	10,200
Georgia	14,338	6,210	North Dakota*	585	44
Hawaii	12,896	3,451	Ohio	10,500	1,100
			Oklahoma*	1,013	127
Idaho*	3,071	106	Oregon	94,498	16,692
Illinois*	7,271	776	Pennsylvania	478	63
Indiana*	3,380	389	Rhode Island	70,800	6,000
Iowa*	3,326	309	South Carolina	21,319	5,608
Kansas*	50	9	South Dakota*	4,268	319
Kentucky*	3,319	583			
Louisiana	747,500	40,600	Tennessee*	8,879	951
Maine	218,700	25,600	Texas	149,000	44,200
Maryland	54,800	15,300	Utah*	728	72
			Virginia	388,500	20,600
Massachusetts	337,400	41,600	Washington	125,037	20,517
Michigan	21,900	2,500	Wisconsin	39,400	2,200
Minnesota*	12,356	931			
Mississippi	242,400	8,700	Total U.S.	4,123,361	471,969

Data are preliminary.
*1967 catch.
Source: U.S. Department of the Interior, Fish and Wildlife Service.

Commercial fishing

principal species caught

Species	QUANTITY in 000 lb.: 1960	1965	1968*
Total	4,942,229	4,776,766	4,116,100
Menhaden	2,018,263	1,726,089	1,380,900
Salmon	235,447	326,871	301,400
Tuna	298,203	318,895	293,840
Shrimps	249,452	243,645	291,600
Crabs	221,681	335,407	245,524
Flounder	127,048	180,121	134,610
Herring, sea	239,018	110,293	107,500
Whitings	111,602	82,574	77,900
Ocean perch	150,275	111,960	76,926
Haddock	118,697	133,892	71,300
Clams	49,572	70,849	70,763
Cod	45,753	46,201	57,755
Jack mackerel	75,137	66,856	57,400
Oysters	60,010	54,688	55,600
Lobsters, Northern	31,168	30,246	32,300
Mullet	40,839	41,392	30,500
Halibut	51,202	40,825	25,700
Scup	49,229	35,870	14,500

*Preliminary.
Source: U.S. Department of the Interior, Fish and Wildlife Service.

Power

Mineral fuels and electricity production

in trillions of British thermal units

Year	Total production	MINERAL FUELS: Bituminous coal and lignite	Anthracite	Crude petroleum	Natural gas, wet (unprocessed)	ELECTRICITY*: Hydro-power	Nuclear power
1960	41,704	10,886	478	14,935	13,822	1,578	5
1961	42,499	10,558	443	15,185	14,691	1,605	17
1962	44,146	11,060	429	15,495	15,365	1,774	23
1963	46,274	12,024	464	15,741	16,271	1,741	33
1964	47,836	12,759	436	15,690	17,056	1,861	34
1965	49,467	13,417	378	15,930	17,652	2,051	39
1966	52,256	13,988	329	16,925	18,894	2,062	58
1967	55,400	14,479	311	18,098	20,087	2,344	81
1968†	57,304	14,279	291	18,880	21,372	2,352	130

The fuel equivalent of hydropower and nuclear power is calculated from the kilowatt-hours of power produced, converted to coal input equivalent, at the prevailing average pounds of coal per kilowatt-hour each year at central electric plants, using 12,000 BTU per pound.
*Includes installations owned by manufacturing plants and mines, as well as government and privately owned public utilities. †Preliminary.
Source: U.S. Department of the Interior, Bureau of Mines. (F. H. Sk.)

Electric utilities

State	Number of utilities	Number of plants*	Total capacity in kw.	SALES OF ELECTRIC ENERGY in 000 kw-hrs.: 1968	1969
Alabama	5	29	9,088,368	26,427,404	28,182,704
Alaska	27	53	320,772	749,826	842,247
Arizona	10	32	3,932,000	10,035,647	10,699,490
Arkansas	14	31	2,713,280	10,518,445	11,578,308
California	27	216	26,651,595	96,974,640	104,561,271
Colorado	31	74	2,758,391	8,213,014	9,039,350
Connecticut	10	41	3,506,468	12,635,914	13,818,177
Delaware	4	13	822,733	3,301,610	3,872,299
District of Columbia	2	4	1,114,550	†	†
Florida	27	71	10,561,998	34,967,000	39,716,115
Georgia	7	39	5,051,625	22,236,725	25,609,757
Hawaii	6	15	831,267	2,835,568	3,132,081
Idaho	10	42	1,260,570	8,885,121	9,863,484
Illinois	42	95	15,570,233	55,720,316	61,206,358
Indiana	21	53	9,427,823	30,055,877	33,187,166
Iowa	94	182	3,386,453	12,033,845	13,197,301
Kansas	80	125	3,391,879	10,800,801	11,895,690
Kentucky	10	27	6,680,674	26,732,303	28,322,251
Louisiana	30	63	5,994,706	20,642,067	24,025,994
Maine	15	66	886,223	4,157,398	4,459,407
Maryland	11	26	4,134,027	20,733,683†	22,959,102†
Massachusetts	23	65	5,104,047	19,584,897	21,250,915
Michigan	50	159	10,121,931	45,627,174	49,939,202
Minnesota	73	162	3,709,082	15,426,991	17,378,637
Mississippi	12	24	2,115,313	10,897,521	12,300,928
Missouri	62	94	4,984,441	20,328,650	22,345,190
Montana	8	29	1,851,130	6,596,007	7,433,147
Nebraska	66	96	2,000,258	6,092,704	6,777,808
Nevada	7	25	1,508,945	4,651,243	4,749,775
New Hampshire	7	27	1,126,612	2,681,501	3,028,745
New Jersey	8	31	7,418,622	30,055,343	32,600,535
New Mexico	16	27	1,913,732	4,450,669	4,771,017
New York	30	191	18,542,240	73,622,461	77,482,342
North Carolina	23	75	7,938,720	29,898,720	33,749,162
North Dakota	14	39	1,116,948	2,198,262	2,389,225
Ohio	37	89	14,383,314	71,943,428	77,273,583
Oklahoma	30	64	3,788,243	12,140,059	13,510,030
Oregon	11	68	4,212,047	21,340,104	22,857,588
Pennsylvania	20	86	13,803,373	60,562,048	66,167,918
Rhode Island	6	11	399,625	3,078,294	3,412,938
South Carolina	9	48	3,206,939	16,213,416	18,148,322
South Dakota	30	55	1,640,169	2,267,857	2,431,287
Tennessee	5	35	9,437,838	47,614,651	48,083,103
Texas	61	173	21,856,504	69,765,264	77,642,102
Utah	25	76	792,929	4,163,059	4,430,232
Vermont	11	60	303,265	1,671,514	2,059,077
Virginia	18	48	5,432,904	22,401,260	25,493,740
Washington	21	64	11,605,395	39,428,239	42,175,078
West Virginia	9	20	5,814,134	12,867,670	14,190,093
Wisconsin	46	157	5,029,155	19,873,973	21,641,395
Wyoming	15	44	1,121,944	3,036,324	3,261,661
Total U.S.	1,128‡	3,439	290,365,434	1,099,136,507	1,199,143,327

Data as of Jan. 1, 1969, except Jan. 1, 1968 where indicated. Figures for number of utilities and plants and total capacity are preliminary.
*Each prime mover at combination plants is counted as a plant. †District of Columbia included with Maryland. ‡Adjusted to exclude duplications because of utilities with generating plants in more than one state.
Source: Federal Power Commission.

Manufacturing

Business activity in manufacturing

Item	1960	1965	1967*
Number of businesses (in 000)			
Sole proprietorships	193	186	170
Active partnerships	47	37	34
Active corporations	166	186	197
Business receipts (in $000,000)			
Sole proprietorships	6,935	7,267	6,473
Active partnerships	7,372	5,596	5,640
Active corporations	364,612	502,982	576,570
Net profit (less loss) (in $000,000)			
Sole proprietorships	645	774	748
Active partnerships	602	589	562
Active corporations	22,145	39,852	40,329

Data cover accounting periods which ended between July 1 of the year shown and June 30 of the following year. *Preliminary.
Source: U.S. Department of the Treasury, Internal Revenue Service, *Statistics of Income, U.S. Business Tax Returns,* and *Corporation Income Tax Returns.*

Manufacturing activity in major industry groups, 1967

Industry group	ALL EMPLOYEES: Number in 000	Payroll in $000,000	PRODUCTION WORKERS: Number in 000	Man-hours in 000,000	Wages in $000,000	New capital expenditures in $000,000	Value added by manufacture in $000,000	Cost of materials* in $000,000	Value of shipments* in $000,000
Food and kindred products	1,654	10,012	1,118	2,255	5,988	1,601	26,352	56,602	81,705
Tobacco products	75	377	65	125	306	53	2,011	2,898	4,957
Textile mill products	931	4,394	831	1,693	3,548	710	8,003	11,765	19,767
Apparel and related products	1,363	5,249	1,202	2,197	4,250	198	9,693	11,057	20,750
Lumber and wood products	563	2,760	500	985	2,255	394	4,828	6,026	10,875
Furniture and fixtures	429	2,222	357	717	1,622	197	4,041	3,577	7,634
Paper and allied products	643	4,440	506	1,074	3,200	1,426	9,676	11,298	20,927
Printing and publishing	1,064	7,295	648	1,256	4,099	821	14,155	7,568	21,677
Chemicals and allied products	854	6,518	544	1,098	3,579	2,833	23,440	18,951	42,188
Petroleum and coal products	140	1,196	100	200	778	1,004	5,356	16,696	21,967
Rubber and plastics products†	504	3,193	397	788	2,229	605	6,474	5,868	12,362
Leather and leather products	332	1,468	294	553	1,150	61	2,577	2,543	4,877
Stone, clay, and glass products	605	3,877	476	967	2,805	722	8,408	6,105	14,769
Primary metal industries	1,283	9,837	1,041	2,080	7,450	2,968	20,148	27,329	47,023
Fabricated metal products	1,307	9,009	1,023	2,093	6,253	1,009	17,054	16,119	33,191
Nonelectrical machinery	1,872	14,300	1,345	2,813	9,236	1,739	27,697	21,715	49,077
Electrical machinery	1,884	12,936	1,338	2,630	7,571	1,462	24,855	19,369	43,606
Transportation equipment	1,890	15,602	1,380	2,805	10,187	1,717	28,901	41,731	70,539
Instruments and related products	377	2,684	255	501	1,503	359	6,063	3,434	9,503
Miscellaneous manufacturing	423	2,273	342	663	1,540	188	4,525	3,953	8,413
Ordnance and accessories‡	377	3,388	213	432	1,476	201	5,044	3,767	8,757
Total	19,398§	131,876§	13,975	27,925	81,025	20,231	259,301	298,371	555,863

Data are preliminary.
*Includes extensive duplication arising from shipments between establishments in the same industry classification.
†Excludes certain products included under other industry groups.
‡Excludes government-owned and operated establishments.
§Includes data for administrative offices and auxiliary units not allocated by industry group.
Source: U.S. Department of Commerce, Bureau of the Census, *1967 Census of Manufactures.*

Principal manufacturing industries

In the United States and each state

Industry	Employees 1963	Employees 1966	Value added by manufacture* in $000 1963	Value added by manufacture* in $000 1966
United States	16,960,983	19,024,041	192,103,102	250,880,137
Transportation equipment	1,601,158	1,891,711	22,765,674	29,308,079
Motor vehicles and equipment	693,821	859,940	12,780,577	16,144,274
Aircraft and parts	679,385	745,126	7,867,349	10,031,360
Nonelectrical machinery	1,459,377	1,803,746	17,310,599	27,034,936
Metalworking machinery	259,002	330,371	3,037,659	4,899,129
General industrial machinery	233,143	280,955	2,812,672	4,196,403
Construction machinery	210,959	261,312	2,732,269	3,963,846
Office and computing machines	137,138	184,224	1,633,690	3,649,696
Food and kindred products	1,643,111	1,642,145	21,825,516	24,895,940
Beverages	204,621	216,112	3,724,834	4,403,766
Canned and frozen foods	244,824	259,098	2,778,810	3,400,287
Bakery products	280,144	274,394	3,030,822	3,371,132
Dairy products	256,828	238,868	3,184,867	3,344,890
Meat products	299,576	297,516	2,882,580	3,209,366
Electrical machinery	1,511,819	1,810,989	17,010,665	23,481,676
Communication equipment	476,849	486,022	5,341,463	6,287,033
Electronic components	288,527	384,525	2,508,117	4,222,615
Electrical industrial apparatus	160,953	203,923	1,889,181	2,735,977
Chemicals and allied products	737,414	822,354	17,586,138	22,655,574
Industrial chemicals	236,652	245,107	6,171,182	7,549,557
Plastics materials and synthetics	144,713	177,413	2,865,399	3,998,422
Drugs	99,001	109,052	2,807,331	3,674,797
Cleaning and toilet goods	85,572	95,201	2,866,446	3,648,501
Primary metal industries	1,126,536	1,296,221	15,261,089	20,898,802
Blast furnace and basic steel products	568,849	637,799	8,617,266	10,917,475
Nonferrous rolling and drawing	167,005	194,318	2,127,688	3,480,770
Iron and steel foundries	199,635	237,912	1,959,949	2,796,364
Fabricated metal products	1,082,102	1,252,294	11,791,081	15,791,932
Structural metal products	325,470	371,619	3,219,813	4,370,295
Printing and publishing	913,243	1,017,581	10,476,433	13,264,493
Newspapers	306,439	333,490	3,201,872	4,012,212
Commercial printing	300,309	337,426	2,961,069	3,674,810
Paper and allied products	588,014	633,939	7,395,677	9,417,167
Apparel and related products	1,279,534	1,359,833	7,861,011	9,180,536
Women's and misses' outerwear	405,466	420,979	2,459,739	2,926,631
Stone, clay, and glass products	573,859	615,982	7,043,987	8,494,586
Textile mill products	863,246	927,339	6,122,982	8,028,374
Rubber and plastics products†	414,959	491,823	4,653,953	6,277,082
Instruments and related products	305,452	362,004	3,992,131	5,833,280
Lumber and wood products	563,135	571,759	4,020,600	4,791,202
Petroleum and coal products	153,486	139,765	3,713,231	4,753,750
Petroleum refining	119,297	105,548	3,137,603	4,099,214
Furniture and fixtures	376,548	428,625	3,068,287	3,989,882
Ordnance and accessories‡	245,934	300,528	2,882,521	4,091,858
Leather and leather products	327,489	341,078	2,078,572	2,480,757
Tobacco manufactures	77,330	72,363	1,680,594	1,871,980
Alabama	243,800	294,425	2,518,314	3,644,184
Primary metal industries	40,078	44,007	693,292	896,858
Steel rolling and finishing	21,774	22,971	494,292	577,074
Textile mill products	35,474	39,176	219,338	341,102
Chemicals and allied products	8,490	10,610	216,531	326,739
Paper and allied products	11,675	13,811	165,574	277,232
Food and kindred products	22,420	24,313	203,421	253,230
Alaska	5,809	7,106	84,954	131,060
Food and kindred products	2,860	3,417	39,819	65,872
Arizona	57,039	71,018	627,141	926,452
Electrical machinery	9,131	19,438	86,431	205,546
Electronic components	5,776	13,242	48,687	131,568
Nonelectrical machinery	5,771	12,679	51,324	195,590
Arkansas	113,658	135,953	960,886	1,409,827
Food and kindred products	17,878	19,968	155,929	224,431
Lumber and wood products	21,198	21,562	119,830	147,693
Paper and allied products	7,224	7,231	118,853	143,180
Electrical machinery	7,619	9,289	79,169	94,365
California	1,398,611	1,501,767	17,162,564	21,331,103
Transportation equipment	202,090	228,424	2,665,830	3,213,139
Food and kindred products	155,731	162,324	2,412,559	2,875,705
Canned and frozen foods	51,619	53,759	656,233	828,224
Electrical machinery	187,965	187,213	2,192,114	2,543,904
Communication equipment	96,738	84,291	1,166,416	1,215,535
Ordnance and accessories‡	136,447	138,340	1,743,355	2,238,788
Nonelectrical machinery	93,308	114,160	1,086,421	1,626,148
Fabricated metal products	88,535	100,965	1,036,525	1,355,355
Chemicals and allied products	35,703	41,511	809,488	1,097,089
Printing and publishing	74,407	83,204	846,820	1,031,806
Colorado	93,722	104,129	1,193,828	1,457,914
Nonelectrical machinery	5,172	9,932	65,722	312,053
Food and kindred products	18,597	18,389	252,251	272,100
Primary metal products	7,642	8,609	91,813	117,577
Electrical machinery	3,486	9,249	43,322	93,738
Connecticut	419,412	468,914	4,495,878	6,184,996
Transportation equipment	84,784	94,226	898,047	1,272,800
Aircraft and parts	65,193	73,091	706,556	1,036,679
Nonelectrical machinery	58,587	67,047	684,061	951,803
Electrical machinery	43,302	48,166	483,694	628,114
Fabricated metal products	40,334	48,199	422,235	587,478
Primary metal industries	25,865	28,682	321,769	569,227
Nonferrous rolling and drawing	15,250	16,799	192,859	379,794
Delaware	58,395	68,434	658,189	955,501
Food and kindred products	6,124	6,962	54,634	137,569
Fabricated metal products	1,617	2,366	20,768	32,521
Primary metal industries	2,282	2,172	19,371	18,896
District of Columbia	22,147	24,020	256,813	302,875
Printing and publishing	13,153	15,714	162,058	203,328
Newspapers	4,789	5,126	55,591	71,218

Industry	Employees 1963	Employees 1966	Value added by manufacture* in $000 1963	Value added by manufacture* in $000 1966
Florida	215,447	249,305	2,351,973	2,938,367
Food and kindred products	39,593	41,411	499,694	521,159
Chemicals and allied products	18,143	19,299	346,897	403,722
Paper and allied products	13,594	14,997	204,604	291,494
Electrical machinery	15,125	20,402	153,347	218,613
Fabricated metal products	14,459	18,998	137,556	213,400
Transportation equipment	16,667	21,394	132,541	209,063
Georgia	354,023	415,319	3,254,007	4,568,664
Textile mill products	93,482	105,342	618,226	976,183
Transportation equipment	30,357	43,006	514,266	804,930
Food and kindred products	41,949	44,317	441,953	547,439
Paper and allied products	20,484	22,416	339,327	458,016
Apparel and related products	57,145	66,356	323,163	388,870
Hawaii	25,144	24,839	261,147	310,763
Food and kindred products	15,231	13,946	166,986	180,287
Canned and frozen foods	7,502	7,085	63,012	66,536
Idaho	30,487	35,293	366,411	494,175
Food and kindred products	9,881	11,681	111,086	144,191
Lumber and wood products	10,288	10,884	88,581	119,577
Illinois	1,210,802	1,404,819	14,640,121	19,855,186
Nonelectrical machinery	178,573	220,794	2,264,672	3,322,842
Construction and like equipment	52,590	65,055	735,987	1,065,846
Electrical machinery	167,834	222,083	1,806,838	2,552,359
Food and kindred products	116,063	117,844	2,059,037	2,446,523
Fabricated metal products	121,879	137,740	1,366,458	1,868,109
Primary metal industries	97,851	110,833	1,176,747	1,707,657
Printing and publishing	95,476	109,542	1,197,739	1,536,759
Chemicals and allied products	47,468	53,290	1,218,465	1,490,602
Indiana	609,840	706,694	7,726,942	10,116,658
Primary metal industries	93,613	112,348	1,456,412	1,821,319
Steel rolling and finishing	59,295	68,274	1,056,396	1,189,349
Electrical machinery	91,105	123,078	1,125,703	1,650,824
Transportation equipment	91,203	98,981	1,119,585	1,455,965
Motor vehicles and equipment	60,226	63,593	775,522	955,062
Nonelectrical machinery	54,501	68,166	678,261	1,005,112
Chemicals and allied products	22,185	23,595	597,366	767,239
Iowa	178,199	205,602	2,287,001	3,030,559
Food and kindred products	50,356	48,042	653,155	742,126
Meat products	25,659	24,049	281,560	293,119
Nonelectrical machinery	35,496	44,871	476,926	731,839
Farm machinery and equipment	21,605	27,234	287,319	473,859
Electrical machinery	19,635	26,689	252,644	368,781
Kansas	114,288	135,548	1,460,374	1,955,579
Transportation equipment	34,610	43,040	446,673	606,650
Food and kindred products	21,225	19,104	239,227	249,047
Chemicals and allied products	6,224	8,791	179,704	246,895
Petroleum and coal products	3,954	3,677	115,621	158,315
Nonelectrical machinery	8,486	13,393	97,032	153,488
Kentucky	180,460	217,925	2,548,531	3,466,216
Food and kindred products	23,849	23,373	444,202	501,615
Beverages	10,003	10,657	288,516	339,092
Electrical machinery	21,319	31,885	350,172	494,007
Nonelectrical machinery	16,156	21,361	231,352	455,409
Chemicals and allied products	11,189	13,405	273,669	376,817
Louisiana	139,511	151,606	1,915,625	2,530,638
Chemicals and allied products	15,629	19,305	435,387	716,928
Basic chemicals	10,865	13,867	308,005	546,813
Food and kindred products	29,588	30,893	367,891	383,190
Petroleum and coal products	11,126	8,275	273,562	291,560
Petroleum refining	10,004	7,419	258,454	272,966
Maine	99,926	107,451	785,730	980,292
Paper and allied products	16,537	17,675	232,399	286,495
Paper mills, except building	13,526	14,326	190,688	233,560
Leather and leather products	24,699	27,546	135,204	181,096
Maryland	263,672	288,629	3,001,468	3,587,852
Primary metal industries	36,035	38,390	509,289	555,563
Food and kindred products	35,881	35,700	419,836	503,364
Chemicals and allied products	14,227	18,310	298,182	402,883
Transportation equipment	31,671	24,897	403,388	344,614
Electrical machinery	26,871	29,212	312,625	334,798
Massachusetts	674,023	705,244	6,403,789	8,378,212
Electrical machinery	96,183	101,753	985,805	1,265,771
Nonelectrical machinery	67,673	75,748	714,596	1,152,850
Fabricated metal products	39,608	44,579	450,999	629,430
Instruments and related products	28,431	30,626	343,078	565,956
Printing and publishing	40,578	44,870	439,640	562,191
Michigan	961,090	1,145,756	13,090,328	17,629,228
Transportation equipment	281,870	359,783	5,090,843	6,729,740
Motor vehicles and equipment	263,442	339,568	4,906,456	6,477,680
Nonelectrical machinery	134,256	160,921	1,794,126	2,751,731
Metalworking machinery	49,673	61,316	661,570	1,086,653
Primary metal industries	81,807	96,831	1,155,577	1,619,686
Fabricated metal products	86,619	110,859	1,025,281	1,499,328
Chemicals and allied products	33,595	35,915	761,996	955,659
Food and kindred products	52,472	51,239	729,211	835,151
Minnesota	245,931	281,201	2,806,116	3,823,620
Nonelectrical machinery	37,532	48,045	482,493	799,323
Food and kindred products	48,619	48,053	587,507	664,386
Electrical machinery	18,953	22,993	225,256	312,310
Printing and publishing	21,879	27,497	206,341	266,078
Paper and allied products	13,505	14,649	177,998	264,761
Stone, clay, and glass products	10,961	13,699	158,740	242,844
Chemicals and allied products	5,646	6,441	166,551	223,180

Principal manufacturing industries

(continued)

Industry	Employees 1963	Employees 1966	Value added by manufacture* in $000 1963	Value added by manufacture* in $000 1966
Mississippi	128,506	157,802	1,016,962	1,488,493
Lumber and wood products	20,914	23,332	130,696	174,653
Food and kindred products	14,641	15,170	130,946	165,103
Apparel and related products	31,435	34,459	131,465	153,387
Missouri	391,254	450,942	4,296,036	5,807,736
Transportation equipment	58,206	78,362	998,328	1,436,752
Motor vehicles and equipment	23,467	32,357	632,520	781,915
Food and kindred products	48,188	48,803	629,933	738,457
Chemicals and allied products	19,558	21,274	395,319	516,522
Nonelectrical machinery	26,449	32,236	275,562	439,927
Printing and publishing	27,643	29,826	286,952	383,921
Montana	20,247	21,898	236,230	304,189
Primary metal industries	3,261	3,910	47,795	79,677
Lumber and wood products	8,297	8,968	70,670	78,803
Nebraska	64,882	71,392	746,597	992,938
Food and kindred products	26,698	25,052	316,634	370,154
Meat products	12,613	11,893	115,537	137,281
Electrical machinery	5,348	7,540	64,379	92,704
Nevada	6,768	6,352	106,278	114,242
Chemicals and allied products	849	719	22,273	23,254
New Hampshire	84,107	96,336	636,088	866,114
Electrical machinery	11,508	14,243	100,912	139,518
Nonelectrical machinery	8,002	11,405	78,269	127,932
Leather and leather products	20,137	19,871	104,325	123,785
New Jersey	829,201	876,511	9,957,333	12,246,302
Chemicals and allied products	84,490	93,359	2,103,260	2,799,914
Basic chemicals	30,209	31,029	654,206	798,039
Drugs	16,775	18,835	539,611	784,639
Electrical machinery	127,564	131,967	1,315,329	1,671,922
Communication equipment	57,898	55,022	612,512	738,543
Food and kindred products	61,098	60,551	1,034,623	1,106,223
Nonelectrical machinery	57,384	65,310	703,081	974,011
Fabricated metal products	57,451	61,812	687,255	828,827
New Mexico	15,324	15,756	149,641	148,116
Food and kindred products	3,595	4,136	34,537	43,313
Stone, clay, and glass products	1,353	1,472	19,264	17,916
New York	1,853,050	1,933,538	19,559,120	24,588,259
Printing and publishing	171,593	189,466	2,576,592	3,192,027
Nonelectrical machinery	134,680	151,748	1,541,141	2,695,362
Office machines	36,466	41,724	324,940	1,143,910
Apparel and related products	316,522	299,536	2,472,531	2,586,075
Electrical machinery	185,978	205,519	1,964,932	2,533,403
Transportation equipment	99,811	110,568	1,342,730	1,982,019
Instruments and related products	75,499	84,008	1,259,704	1,955,127
Photographic equipment	39,401	46,243	882,624	1,521,195
Food and kindred products	128,774	114,119	1,846,827	1,824,501
Chemicals and allied products	61,352	64,232	1,373,598	1,628,824
Primary metal industries	68,539	74,990	916,516	1,126,194
North Carolina	530,646	611,851	4,566,547	6,132,997
Textile mill products	220,929	246,409	1,425,377	1,973,229
Knitting mills	68,203	75,705	385,621	542,380
Yarn and thread mills	47,992	56,424	312,216	474,184
Tobacco manufactures	29,187	26,043	849,989	897,492
Cigarettes	19,507	18,297	792,928	838,563
Furniture and fixtures	47,994	56,299	337,299	476,059
Household furniture	44,371	52,578	311,142	439,782
Electrical machinery	23,195	31,938	279,179	439,497
North Dakota	6,507	6,671	72,445	100,883
Food and kindred products	3,063	2,848	36,747	34,232
Ohio	1,239,515	1,411,058	15,506,118	20,132,127
Transportation equipment	164,408	191,905	2,459,304	3,059,396
Motor vehicles and equipment	112,368	132,536	1,895,276	2,270,345
Nonelectrical machinery	167,277	202,898	2,036,679	3,008,458
Primary metal industries	155,447	179,024	2,197,734	2,855,628
Steel rolling and finishing	92,152	103,656	1,441,640	1,812,305
Electrical machinery	117,182	139,387	1,547,622	2,003,955
Fabricated metal products	115,296	133,119	1,345,844	1,826,710
Chemicals and allied products	43,323	50,490	956,050	1,300,259
Rubber and plastics products†	80,471	88,970	968,715	1,235,889
Oklahoma	97,691	110,057	978,774	1,241,913
Food and kindred products	14,212	13,146	148,173	166,847
Nonelectrical machinery	11,032	12,725	120,244	160,383
Transportation equipment	7,801	13,735	67,542	145,684
Oregon	145,164	160,867	1,574,816	1,992,308
Lumber and wood products	69,975	71,824	700,535	804,393
Millwork and related products	27,982	29,880	284,488	323,360
Sawmills and planing mills	27,199	26,238	252,005	269,020
Food and kindred products	19,938	21,272	234,720	281,411
Pennsylvania	1,392,922	1,552,492	14,043,602	18,752,302
Primary metal products	210,388	239,047	2,663,777	3,758,875
Steel rolling and finishing	161,235	183,393	2,155,134	2,992,192
Electrical machinery	107,010	131,007	1,190,613	1,856,971
Nonelectrical machinery	112,607	135,071	1,257,664	1,832,812
Food and kindred products	107,508	108,529	1,355,664	1,501,892
Fabricated metal products	104,800	114,360	1,085,860	1,376,888
Chemicals and allied products	45,805	49,674	987,162	1,295,645
Transportation equipment	66,339	87,042	733,011	1,158,607
Apparel and related products	173,130	183,215	876,008	1,063,228
Rhode Island	113,940	127,130	958,575	1,354,881
Miscellaneous manufacturing	21,239	25,364	152,303	237,655
Jewelry and silverware	8,467	11,055	71,953	116,358
Textile mill products	22,863	22,382	155,023	183,366
Nonelectrical machinery	9,106	14,393	88,643	169,927
Primary metal industries	9,096	9,495	94,983	155,687
Nonferrous rolling and drawing	6,425	7,212	60,568	117,394
South Carolina	261,655	297,720	2,111,117	2,979,576
Textile mill products	130,371	139,304	941,238	1,271,709
Weaving mills, cotton	67,371	63,842	426,634	556,198
Weaving mills, synthetics	23,087	30,148	170,690	260,563
Chemicals and allied products	16,181	18,994	342,833	472,767
Fibers, plastics, rubbers	5,625	9,527	141,351	252,528
South Dakota	13,234	14,099	140,042	166,306
Food and kindred products	7,905	7,463	94,923	91,634
Meat products	4,922	4,746	59,676	56,939
Tennessee	339,108	405,660	3,302,688	4,627,832
Chemicals and allied products	39,820	48,262	826,807	1,073,920
Basic chemicals	16,299	15,969	403,979	479,440
Fibers, plastics, rubbers	16,582	22,383	300,809	409,982
Electrical machinery	17,530	26,494	230,442	449,860
Food and kindred products	31,928	31,802	349,348	437,864
Apparel and related products	52,140	63,940	251,859	363,537
Texas	513,802	607,556	7,086,283	9,725,369
Chemicals and allied products	43,538	48,351	1,644,714	2,156,052
Basic chemicals	27,130	29,738	1,215,258	1,573,067
Petroleum and coal products	35,963	34,094	1,016,211	1,313,884
Petroleum refining	33,700	31,325	986,911	1,283,402
Food and kindred products	75,351	74,867	929,542	1,137,371
Transportation equipment	50,099	70,195	615,617	1,046,496
Aircraft and parts	34,341	48,087	362,289	722,040
Utah	53,504	47,154	710,627	699,388
Food and kindred products	8,463	7,062	99,108	97,309
Nonelectrical machinery	3,150	4,305	33,689	48,912
Fabricated metal products	2,639	2,362	28,851	42,531
Vermont	33,740	42,274	309,253	514,191
Nonelectrical machinery	6,398	7,698	68,140	105,684
Electrical machinery	1,871	4,751	19,939	101,633
Virginia	302,084	335,638	3,046,268	3,938,350
Chemicals and allied products	35,106	40,074	609,341	794,075
Fibers, plastics, rubbers	21,888	26,717	395,447	550,571
Tobacco manufactures	13,740	13,279	308,014	368,345
Cigarettes	8,744	9,386	271,637	332,828
Food and kindred products	32,048	32,011	326,468	363,942
Textile mill products	35,961	40,297	260,606	347,121
Washington	224,375	251,610	3,028,577	3,289,275
Transportation equipment	72,402	93,329	1,058,202	942,900
Lumber and wood products	42,440	42,962	360,706	443,317
Food and kindred products	26,704	26,832	360,950	434,071
Paper and allied products	17,985	19,804	330,262	398,709
Primary metal industries	9,768	13,368	202,202	275,566
Primary nonferrous metal	4,234	5,049	138,061	175,573
West Virginia	117,026	124,581	1,887,148	2,146,937
Chemicals and allied products	22,573	22,987	783,235	856,973
Basic chemicals	14,915	14,373	606,027	630,442
Primary metal industries	21,652	24,029	389,749	441,614
Steel rolling and finishing	14,771	15,471	272,193	298,681
Wisconsin	461,807	515,211	5,363,153	6,831,674
Nonelectrical machinery	85,113	108,163	1,004,641	1,549,316
Food and kindred products	58,714	58,335	754,500	877,211
Electrical machinery	49,762	52,950	596,348	761,973
Paper and allied products	36,339	38,196	501,795	607,816
Transportation equipment	42,975	37,904	734,560	569,334
Motor vehicles and equipment	37,721	31,989	692,595	511,899
Wyoming	6,797	6,674	81,678	93,213
Petroleum and coal products	2,127	1,798	37,222	42,366

Sum of state totals may not add to United States total because figures were independently derived.
Boldface type indicates the state which leads in the value added by manufacture for that industry.
*Adjusted. Represents value of products shipped less cost of materials, supplies, fuel, electric energy, and contract work plus the net change in finished products and work-in-process inventories.
†Excludes certain products. ‡Excludes government owned and operated establishments.
Source: U.S. Department of Commerce, Bureau of the Census, *1963 Census of Manufactures* and *1966 Annual Survey of Manufactures*.

Distribution and Services

Services

Kind of service	NUMBER OF SERVICES* First quarter 1967	NUMBER OF SERVICES* First quarter 1968	EMPLOYEES Mid-March pay period 1967	EMPLOYEES Mid-March pay period 1968
Hotels and other lodging places	53,232	52,033	700,093	737,050
Hotels, tourist courts, and motels	36,855	35,527	589,414	617,173
Rooming and boarding houses	6,777	6,885	72,104	84,501
Personal services	184,800	184,255	1,025,260	1,037,043
Laundries and dry cleaning plants	49,714	48,928	644,828	540,703
Photographic studios	7,048	6,891	34,524	33,686
Beauty shops	66,423	69,275	250,086	271,346
Barber shops	30,745	29,158	65,902	62,654
Funeral services, crematories	13,620	13,435	63,188	64,945
Miscellaneous business services	80,014	83,569	1,271,868	1,365,505
Advertising	7,617	7,755	110,397	112,221
Credit reporting and collection	5,565	5,556	58,809	61,385
Duplicating, mailing, stenographic	4,964	5,024	67,768	61,971
Building services	13,413	14,107	218,921	241,302
Private employment agencies	3,949	4,344	39,586	38,925
Research and testing laboratories	2,893	1,823	123,314	80,828
Business consulting services	13,971	14,983	161,457	199,749
Detective agency and protective services	2,558	2,981	96,614	118,451
Auto repair, services, and garages	67,218	68,417	339,549	348,833
Auto rentals, without drivers	4,443	4,912	45,506	52,181
Auto parking	4,287	3,945	37,256	36,169
Auto repair shops	52,599	53,395	188,678	200,023
Miscellaneous repair services	37,838	37,795	188,293	196,360
Electrical repair shops	12,751	12,791	51,617	55,815
Motion pictures	10,967	10,880	168,544	177,688
Picture production, distribution	2,434	2,461	47,560	50,212
Motion picture theaters	8,083	7,949	111,001	113,608
Other amusement, recreation services	39,970	39,109	390,302	408,469
Producers, orchestras, entertainers	6,660	6,428	56,937	59,196
Bowling alleys, billiard parlors	11,037	10,374	97,693	96,128
Golf clubs, country clubs	4,131	4,454	73,891	80,774
Race tracks, stables	1,417	1,353	25,813	27,519
Medical and other health services	203,581	210,045	2,362,174	2,572,012
Physicians' and surgeons' offices	102,985	103,814	319,160	337,495
Dentists', dental surgeons' offices	60,766	62,028	130,471	140,840
Hospitals	5,223	5,215	1,479,698	1,586,502
Medical, dental laboratories	6,392	6,606	40,401	44,592
Legal services	67,191	67,899	202,994	214,671
Educational services	28,332	29,625	761,702	816,673
Elementary and secondary schools	20,043	20,971	245,798	268,570
Colleges and universities	1,726	1,765	426,538	451,406
Correspondence and vocational schools	3,011	3,148	43,463	46,894
Museums, botanical gardens, zoos	705	746	15,015	16,211
Nonprofit membership organizations	116,969	119,454	967,796	1,054,116
Business associations	11,645	11,841	67,236	69,619
Labor organizations	20,041	20,235	126,138	133,862
Civic and social organizations	28,083	28,344	226,107	235,687
Religious organizations	40,137	41,501	249,752	270,483
Charitable organizations	6,840	6,644	133,163	138,397
Miscellaneous services	56,412	56,901	503,771	517,015
Engineering, architectural services	21,260	21,171	250,465	242,785
Nonprofit research agencies	3,341	3,372	88,689	99,021
Accounting, auditing, bookkeeping	27,500	27,918	141,654	151,514
Total†	949,163	963,485	8,938,459	9,517,738

*Each business is counted as only one service in each county for each kind of service it performs, regardless of the number of establishments it operates.
†Includes administrative and auxiliary businesses not shown separately.
Source: U.S. Department of Commerce, Bureau of the Census, *County Business Patterns.*

Sales of merchant wholesalers

in millions of dollars

Kind of business	1960 total	1965 total	1968 total	1969 1st half
Durable goods	56,803	76,232	100,012	53,341
Motor vehicles, automotive equipment	7,883	10,945	16,696	9,138
Electrical goods	8,660	11,248	14,969	7,420
Furniture, home furnishings	2,910	3,392	4,905	2,563
Hardware, plumbing, heating equipment, supplies	6,422	7,947	9,804	5,213
Lumber, construction materials	6,680	7,747	10,427	5,921
Machinery, equipment, supplies	14,287	20,279	25,466	13,903
Metals, metalwork (except scrap)	5,708	8,796	10,998	5,653
Scrap, waste materials	3,296	4,590	4,708	2,561
Jewelry	960	1,294	...	...
Nondurable goods	80,477	101,354	119,930	60,488
Groceries and related products	27,661	36,478	44,131	22,991
Beer, wine, distilled alcoholic beverages	7,424	9,496	11,088	5,455
Drugs, chemicals, allied products	5,370	6,859	8,830	4,566
Tobacco, tobacco products	4,164	4,856	5,612	2,800
Dry goods, apparel	6,675	8,614	10,271	4,909
Paper, paper products (excluding wallpaper)	4,153	5,234	6,707	3,510
Farm products (raw materials)	11,683	12,808	13,364	6,177
Other nondurable goods	13,346	17,008	20,203	10,092
Total	137,281	177,587	219,943	113,828

Source: U.S. Department of Commerce, Bureau of the Census, *Monthly Wholesale Trade Report.*

Retail sales

in millions of dollars

Kind of business	1960 total	1965 total	1968 total	1969 1st half
Durable goods stores	70,733	93,718	110,245	56,007
Automotive group	39,509	56,266	65,261	34,169
Passenger car, other automotive dealers*	36,981	53,217	60,660	31,823
Tire, battery, accessory dealers	2,528	3,049	4,601	2,346
Furniture and appliance group	10,598	13,737	16,540	7,881
Furniture, home furnishings stores	6,770	8,538	10,227	5,058
Household-appliance, TV, radio stores	3,828	4,223	5,235	2,377
Lumber, building, hardware, farm-equipment group	14,819	16,274	19,129	9,326
Lumberyards, building-materials dealers†	8,618	9,302	10,984	5,440
Hardware stores	2,693	2,813	...	1,542
Nondurable goods stores	148,796	190,232	229,465	112,246
Apparel group	13,708	15,752	19,265	8,996
Men's, boys' wear stores‡	2,619	3,258	4,516	2,133
Women's apparel, accessory stores§	5,329	6,243	7,429	3,443
Family clothing stores	2,728	2,981	3,451	1,598
Shoe stores	2,450	2,571	3,196	1,520
Drug and proprietary stores	7,530	9,335	11,458	5,645
Eating and drinking places	16,096	21,423	25,285	12,387
Food group	53,837	66,920	73,267	37,045
Grocery stores	48,339	61,068	68,311	34,689
Meat and fish markets	1,560	1,552	1,920	911
Bakeries	1,034	1,142	1,106	515
Gasoline service stations	17,594	21,765	24,526	12,314
General merchandise group	24,007	35,840	54,493	25,090
Department stores and dry goods, general merchandise stores	16,994	27,939	39,887	18,301
Variety stores	3,899	5,320	6,152	15,463
Mail-order houses (department store merchandise)	1,857	2,581	3,256	1,472
Liquor stores	4,880	6,305	6,969	3,435
Total	219,529	283,950	339,710	168,253

*Includes both franchised and nonfranchised car dealers. †Includes lumberyards, building materials dealers; paint, plumbing, and electric stores. ‡Includes men's, boys' clothing, furnishings stores, and custom tailors. §Includes women's ready-to-wear; other apparel, accessory, specialty shops; and furriers.
Source: U.S. Department of Commerce, Bureau of the Census, *Monthly Retail Trade Report.*

Business activity in wholesaling, retailing, and services

Item	WHOLESALING 1960	WHOLESALING 1965	WHOLESALING 1967*	RETAILING 1960	RETAILING 1965	RETAILING 1967*	SERVICES 1960	SERVICES 1965	SERVICES 1967*
Number of businesses (in 000)									
Sole proprietorships	306	265	260	1,548	1,554	1,544	1,966	2,208	2,328
Active partnerships	41	32	31	238	202	187	159	169	166
Active corporations	117	147	143	217	288	316	121	188	221
Business receipts (in $000,000)									
Sole proprietorships	17,061	17,934	19,712	65,439	77,760	81,116	23,256	29,789	34,784
Active partnerships	12,712	10,879	10,796	24,787	23,244	23,294	9,281	12,442	14,744
Active corporations	130,637	171,414	182,687	125,787	183,925	216,341	22,106	36,547	45,211
Net profit (less loss) (in $000,000)									
Sole proprietorships	1,305	1,483	1,512	3,869	5,019	5,412	8,060	11,008	13,020
Active partnerships	587	548	558	1,612	1,654	1,684	3,056	4,402	5,315
Active corporations	2,130	3,288	3,705	2,225	4,052	5,144	849	1,505	1,983

Data cover accounting periods which ended between July 1 of the year shown and June 30 of the following year.
*Preliminary figures.
Source: U.S. Department of the Treasury, Internal Revenue Service, *Statistics of Income, U.S. Business Tax Returns* and *Corporation Income Tax Returns.*

Foreign Aid and Commerce

International investment position

in millions of dollars

Type of investment	January 1, 1968	January 1, 1969*
U.S. assets and investments abroad	134,739	146,134
Private investments	93,603	101,900
Long-term	81,700	88,930
Direct	59,486	64,756
Foreign dollar bonds	9,666	10,614
Other foreign bonds	1,113	1,088
Foreign corporate stocks	5,238	6,464
Banking claims	3,725	3,367
Short-term assets and claims	11,903	12,970
U.S. government credits and claims	26,306	28,524
Long-term credits†	23,643	25,940
Foreign currencies and short-term claims	2,663	2,584
IMF gold tranche position	420	1,290
Convertible currencies	2,345	3,528
Foreign assets and investments in the U.S.	69,720	81,121
Long-term	32,011	40,267
Direct	9,923	10,815
Corporate stocks	15,511	19,528
Corporate, U.S. Government agency, state, and municipal bonds	2,159	4,236
Short-term assets and U.S. government obligations	4,590	7,237
Private obligations	1,778	2,531
U.S. government obligations	2,812	4,706
Bills and certificates	9,325	7,260
Marketable or convertible bonds and notes	2,381	1,667

*Preliminary. †Excludes World War I debts not currently being serviced.
Source: U.S. Department of Commerce, Office of Business Economics, *Survey of Current Business.*

Major recipients of foreign assistance

in millions of dollars

Program and country	1962	1963	1964	1965	1966	1967	1968	1969*
Total	6,242	6,550	5,869	5,719	6,553	6,696	6,225	5,068
By program								
Economic assistance programs	4,715	4,564	4,332	4,410	5,147	5,216	4,754	4,010
Agency for International Development	2,509	2,300	2,141	2,033	2,554	2,253†	1,892†	1,449†
Loans	1,330	1,346	1,333	1,129	1,228	1,091	929	568
Grants	1,180	954	808	904	1,326	1,162	963	881
Food for Peace	1,406	1,482	1,544	1,410	1,646	1,010	1,408	1,296
Export-Import Bank long-term loans	340	289	349	396	398	1,399	857	774
Other economic programs‡	460	492	298	572	549	553	596	490
Military assistance programs	1,527	1,986	1,537	1,309	1,406	1,480	1,471	1,058
By country								
Africa								
Congo (Kinshasa)	83	73	43	27	39	47	37	13
Ethiopia	26	25	19	28	63	27	26	21‖
Ghana	130	3	3	3	9	37	29	43‖
Guinea	10	16	14	19	7	§	4	33‖
Liberia	12	44	15	42	11	11	9	14
Morocco	48	72	46	35	61	53	85	50
Nigeria	25	29	50	35	30	18	22	73‖
Tunisia	48	63	48	53	21	54	48	45‖
Asia								
Afghanistan	39	17	40	31	34	32	15	23
Ceylon	6	4	3	4	14	10	27	31
India	744	685‖	664‖	697‖	901‖	592	618	505
Indonesia	41	49	19	−1	20	60	106	249
Iran	100	111	53	91	114	182	128	166
Israel	80	74	38	70	39	14	77‖	76‖
Japan	136	149	75	91	52	124	97	109
Jordan	48	58	56	46	53	64	18‖	14‖
Korea, South	327	363	342	355	417	331	386	385
Laos	64	37‖	42‖	48‖	55‖	55‖	63‖	52‖
Pakistan	417‖	351‖	375‖	343‖	141‖	232	356	123
Philippines	44	116	28	45	39	66	47	57
Ryukyu Islands	25	11	11	17	15	39	14	18
Taiwan	157	163	171	133	136	92	124	70
Thailand	87	94	68	78	101	82	50¶	41¶
Vietnam, South	287	384	403	543	899	542¶	444¶	414¶
Canada	—	—	—	—	—	—	30	6
Europe								
Greece	81	141	108	131	78	46	45	66
Ireland	—	—	—	—	—	20	12	15
Italy	105	135	89	88	35	113	86	51
Spain	66	54	73	99	155	177	21	61
Turkey	341	335	271	311	262	270	201	196
United Kingdom	27	12	§	§	86	407	396	100
Yugoslavia	114	111	73	87	136	12	11	27
Latin America								
Argentina	60	134	13	16	34	12	46	78
Bolivia	39	65	79	14	39	31	24	38
Brazil	42	10	17	14	23	17	27	80
Chile	182	109	136	139	113	290	115	120
Colombia	83	134	131	38	104	148	120	142
Costa Rica	10	15	17	16	14	15	11	15
Dominican Republic	35	52	16	77	110	62	73	36
Ecuador	39	41	30	28	32	8	16	17
El Salvador	22	23	16	19	10	4	10	15
Guatemala	11	16	15	14	5	22	20	81
Guyana	1	1	—	12	7	10	8	18
Jamaica	2	13	8	7	7	5	8	18
Mexico	50	46	106	105	35	102	87	18
Panama	25	10	25	24	14	36	21	18
Paraguay	7	10	9	10	16	6	8	18
Peru	90	24	87	43	52	39	27	33
Oceania								
Australia	1	12	18	19	118	243	181	182
Trust Territory of the Pacific Islands	6	11	16	18	18	24	40	43
Nonregional	463	642	548	345	617	516	471	475

Years ending June 30. Economic assistance data on net obligation and loan authorization basis, rather than expenditure basis. Military assistance data represent value of goods delivered. A minus figure indicates deobligations in excess of new obligations.
*Preliminary. †Excludes $43 million reimbursements in 1967, $34 million in 1968, and $35 million in 1969 by Department of Defense for grants to Vietnam. ‡Principal programs include capital subscriptions to Inter-American Development Bank and International Development Association, Peace Corps, Philippines Rehabilitation, and Civilian Relief in Korea. §Less than $500,000. ‖Economic assistance only; military assistance data classified. Values are included in overall total. ¶Economic assistance only. Military assistance transferred to Department of Defense funding.
Source: U.S. Department of State, Agency for International Development.

Trade by commodity groups

in millions of dollars

Commodity group	EXPORTS 1961	1962	1963	1964	1965	1966	1967	1968	IMPORTS 1961	1962	1963	1964	1965	1966	1967	1968
Food and live animals	2,960	3,245	3,657	4,083	4,003	4,562	4,061	3,890	3,018	3,243	3,401	3,487	3,460	3,948	4,003	4,577
Beverages and tobacco	506	498	531	554	517	624	649	702	437	431	462	535	553	642	698	786
Crude materials, inedible, except fuels	2,794	2,227	2,494	2,970	2,856	3,071	3,284	3,541	2,487	2,706	2,726	2,880	3,103	3,310	2,997	3,347
Mineral fuels and related materials	797	828	978	953	947	976	1,104	1,056	1,738	1,887	1,924	2,030	2,221	2,262	2,248	2,529
Animal and vegetable oils and fats	272	301	303	414	472	357	338	274	93	98	105	119	116	146	122	158
Chemicals	1,789	1,876	2,009	2,364	2,402	2,675	2,802	3,289	726	760	701	702	769	955	963	1,135
Machinery and transport equipment	7,313	8,026	8,243	9,369	10,147	11,155	12,574	14,462	1,363	1,674	1,823	2,216	2,948	4,823	5,794	7,991
Other manufactured goods	3,646	3,766	4,046	4,795	4,890	5,388	5,468	6,085	4,420	5,215	5,546	6,188	7,528	8,668	9,004	11,508
Other transactions	675	676	841	794	954	1,187	959	929	435	450	518	591	730	866	1,065	1,221
Total	20,754	21,444	23,102	26,297	27,187	29,994	31,238	34,227	14,716	16,464	17,207	18,749	21,429	25,618	26,889	33,252

Export data exclude reexports.
Import data show commodities released for domestic consumption during each year.
Source: U.S. Department of Commerce, Bureau of the Census, *Statistical Abstract of the United States*.
Data compiled by U.S. Department of Commerce, Bureau of International Commerce.

Principal trading partners

by exports and imports, in millions of dollars

Country	EXPORTS 1955	1960	1965	1968
North America	5,160	5,506	7,742	10,645
Bahamas	15	49	107	165
Canada	3,404	3,810	5,643	8,058
Dominican Republic	64	42	76	115
Guatemala	59	64	96	93
Honduras	35	35	54	75
Jamaica	23	48	87	147
Mexico	719	831	1,106	1,365
Netherlands Antilles	65	65	75	89
Panama	78	90	125	136
South America	1,743	2,177	2,175	2,742
Argentina	155	359	268	281
Brazil	273	464	348	709
Chile	99	203	237	307
Colombia	354	253	198	319
Ecuador	51	57	80	98
Peru	135	147	282	196
Venezuela	577	567	626	655
Europe	5,126	7,399	9,364	11,151
Belgium and Luxembourg	407	467	650	797
Denmark	97	146	209	206
France	536	699	971	1,078
Germany, West	607	1,272	1,650	1,712
Greece	120	103	172	180
Ireland	42	43	69	87
Italy	473	715	891	1,120
Netherlands	581	817	1,088	1,370
Norway	129	108	130	140
Portugal	69	45	74	86
Spain	182	208	472	519
Sweden	165	332	336	439
Switzerland	166	263	369	558
Turkey	200	178	205	267
United Kingdom	1,006	1,487	1,615	2,180
Yugoslavia	198	88	149	90
Asia	2,581	4,186	6,012	7,580
Hong Kong	51	125	191	304
India	194	650	928	718
Indonesia	83	100	42	169
Iran	84	156	195	279
Israel	92	130	224	279
Japan	683	1,447	2,080	2,950
Korea, South	145	231	274	511
Kuwait	16	41	66	92
Lebanon	43	45	75	83
Pakistan	59	182	336	302
Philippines	373	307	349	436
Saudi Arabia	84	46	137	187
Singapore*	—	—	—	102
Taiwan	361	277	234	387
Thailand	73	71	107	186
Vietnam, South	...	...	...	271
Australia and Oceania	295	514	956	1,026
Australia	231	423	797	872
New Zealand and Western Samoa	56	78	133	114
Africa	642	793	1,229	1,269
Libya	6	43	65	115
South Africa	272	288	438	455
Total	15,547	20,575	27,478	34,413

Country	IMPORTS 1955	1960	1965	1968
North America	4,038	4,429	6,579	11,164
Canada	2,653	2,901	4,832	8,925
Costa Rica	28	35	57	88
Dominican Republic	62	110	111	156
Honduras	23	34	72	83
Jamaica	22	54	125	138
Mexico	397	443	638	893
Netherlands Antilles	217	265	319	330
Panama	20	24	60	78
Trinidad and Tobago	6	55	142	215
South America	2,224	2,435	2,624	2,880
Argentina	126	98	122	207
Brazil	633	570	512	670
Chile	201	193	209	203
Colombia	442	299	277	264
Ecuador	53	65	106	90
Peru	111	183	241	328
Venezuela	576	948	1,018	950
Europe	2,453	4,268	6,292	10,332
Austria	34	49	66	96
Belgium and Luxembourg	242	364	494	766
Denmark	58	98	147	220
Finland	44	52	84	103
France	202	396	615	842
Germany, West	366	897	1,341	2,720
Ireland	6	28	58	110
Italy	180	393	620	1,102
Netherlands	147	213	251	456
Norway	61	66	124	156
Poland	27	39	66	97
Portugal	27	35	56	88
Spain	59	88	133	308
Sweden	85	170	243	390
Switzerland	147	198	306	438
Turkey	57	60	83	99
United Kingdom	616	993	1,405	2,048
Yugoslavia	26	41	61	102
Asia	1,876	2,721	4,528	6,913
Hong Kong	15	139	343	637
India	221	228	348	312
Indonesia	212	216	165	174
Iran	34	51	88	83
Israel	17	27	62	117
Japan	432	1,149	2,414	4,057
Korea, South	6	5	54	199
Malaysia†	—	...	212	240
Philippines	253	307	369	435
Taiwan	6	20	93	270
Thailand	105	56	41	81
Australia and Oceania	174	266	453	624
Australia	126	142	311	485
New Zealand and Western Samoa	44	119	130	187
Africa	619	534	878	1,121
Ghana	50	52	59	78
Ivory Coast‡	—	—	46	79
Libya	§	§	30	90
South Africa	96	108	226	253
Total‖	11,384	14,654	21,366	33,114

For security reasons, exports of Special Category commodities are excluded from totals for certain countries. They are, however, included in the continent totals.
*Part of Malaysia prior to Aug. 1965. †Became independent Aug. 1957. ‡Became independent Aug. 1960.
§Less than $500,000. ‖Includes estimates for low-valued shipments from countries which could not be identified because of illegible reporting on import entries.
Source: U.S. Department of Commerce, Bureau of the Census, *Statistical Abstract of the United States*.

Major commodities traded, 1968

in millions of dollars

Item	Total	Canada	American republics	Western Europe*	Far East†	Other areas
EXPORTS						
Total‡	34,660	8,074	4,704	11,147	6,538	4,197
Agricultural commodities						
Grains and preparations§	2,463	131	241	634	1,144	313
Fruits, nuts, and vegetables§	464	208	40	144	44	28
Tobacco, unmanufactured	524	4	5	366	106	43
Soybeans	810	77	6	433	260	34
Cotton, excluding linters, waste	459	13	‖	95	312	39
Nonagricultural commodities						
Ores and scrap, metal	587	98	34	248	204	3
Coal, coke, and briquettes	524	154	40	154	172	4
Petroleum products	449	61	74	131	130	53
Chemicals	3,289	462	624	1,184	625	394
Machinery¶	8,822	2,221	1,509	2,603	1,239	1,250
Agricultural machines and tractors, and parts	874	307	186	153	87	141
Other nonelectrical machinery¶	5,662	1,370	948	1,706	808	830
Electrical apparatus	2,286	544	375	744	344	279
Road motor vehicles¶	3,057	2,081	429	164	109	274
Automobile parts, nonmilitary	1,529	1,203	151	70	29	76
Aircraft, civilian, and parts for all aircraft	1,904	270	219	876	212	327
Pulp, paper, and manufactures	824	105	155	337	124	103
Metals and manufactures	2,116	564	320	714	314	204
Iron and steel-mill products	582	185	107	82	131	77
Textile yarn, fabrics, and made-up articles	522	124	72	168	48	110
Other agricultural and nonagricultural exports, including re-exports and "Special Category" items	7,846	1,501	936	2,896	1,495	1,018
IMPORTS						
Total	33,252	9,007	4,308	10,142	6,556	3,239
Agricultural commodities						
Meat and preparations	746	48	174	186	3	335
Fruits, nuts, and vegetables	653	29	327	129	135	33
Coffee	1,140	—	769	‖	41	330
Sugar	640	‖	393	1	160	86
Nonagricultural commodities						
Alcoholic beverages	626	157	4	459	3	3
Pulp, paper, and manufactures	1,414	1,284	3	99	19	9
Ores and scrap, metal	1,008	485	220	19	26	258
Petroleum, crude and partly refined	1,308	433	507	4	52	312
Petroleum products	1,037	19	456	94	‖	468
Chemicals	1,135	292	76	523	103	141
Machinery	3,776	932	53	1,705	1,069	17
Transport equipment	4,215	2,352	2	1,527	330	4
Automobiles, new	2,782	1,349	‖	1,239	194	—
Iron and steel-mill products♀	1,962	192	45	884	815	26
Nonferrous base metals	1,812	629	325	484	224	150
Textile yarn, fabrics, and made-up articles	963	22	34	324	548	35
Fish, including shellfish	631	162	122	75	135	137
Other agricultural and nonagricultural imports	10,186	1,971	798	3,629	2,893	895

*Includes Greece and Turkey. †Asia, excluding the Near East.
‡Includes commodities classified as "Special Category" for security reasons.
§Includes shipments for relief by individuals and private agencies.
‖Less than $500,000. ¶Excludes "Special Category" commodities.
♀Excludes pig iron.
Source: U.S. Department of Commerce, Bureau of the Census, *Statistical Abstract of the United States*. Data compiled by the U.S. Department of Commerce, Bureau of International Commerce.

Components of surplus or deficit in the balance of payments

in billions of dollars

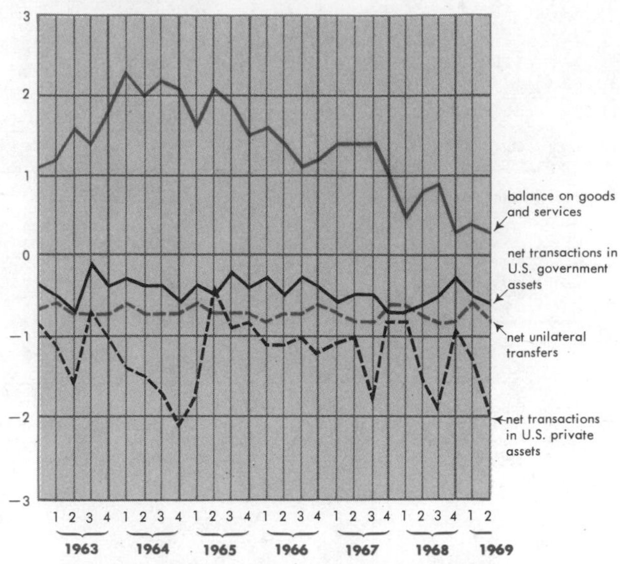

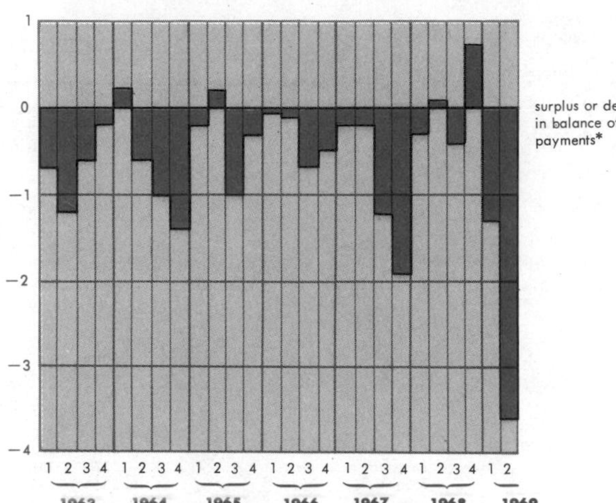

Data in top grid are seasonally adjusted and exclude military grant aid. Negative amounts are net increases in assets abroad and net unilateral transfers to foreigners.
*Measured by increase in U.S. official reserve assets and decrease in liquid liabilities to all foreigners.
Source: U.S. Department of Commerce, Office of Business Economics, *Survey of Current Business.*

Transactions in the balance of payments

in millions of dollars

Type of transaction	1960	1965	1966	1967	1968	1969 1st quarter	1969 2nd quarter
Exports of goods and services	29,253	41,027	44,362	47,093	51,432	11,852	14,800
Merchandise	19,650	26,447	29,389	30,681	33,598	7,445	9,885
Military transfers	2,100	2,458	1,831	2,145	2,265	568	618
Transportation	1,782	2,414	2,608	2,775	2,924	571	822
Travel	919	1,380	1,590	1,646	1,770	432	560
Miscellaneous services	1,454	2,436	2,693	2,973	2,177	775	809
Income on investments abroad	3,349	5,893	6,252	6,872	4,985	1,368	1,313
Imports of goods and services	−23,355	−32,278	−38,081	−41,011	−48,078	−10,967	−14,079
Merchandise	−14,744	−21,496	−25,463	−26,821	−32,972	−7,335	−9,736
Military expenditures	−3,087	−2,952	−3,764	−4,378	−4,530	−1,204	−1,217
Transportation	−1,943	−2,675	−2,922	−2,990	−3,248	−677	−940
Travel	−1,750	−2,438	−2,657	−3,195	−3,022	−542	−857
Miscellaneous services	−795	−989	−1,133	−1,266	−1,374	−316	−309
Income on foreign investments in U.S.	−1,063	−1,729	−2,142	−2,362	−2,933	−892	−1,021
Net unilateral transfers (to foreigners [−])	−4,025	−4,386	−3,835	−3,903	−3,703	−786	−1,058
Private remittances	−382	−581	−556	−755	−753	−161	−198
U.S. government transfers	−3,643	−3,805	−3,279	−3,148	−2,950	−625	−860
Net transactions in U.S. private assets (increase [−])	−3,878	−3,794	−4,310	−5,655	−5,157	−1,288	−2,059
Net transactions in U.S. government assets (increase [−])*	−1,104	−1,598	−1,534	−2,421	−2,249	−468	−703
Net transactions in U.S. official reserve assets (increase [−])	2,145	1,222	568	52	−880	−48	−299
Net transactions in foreign assets in the U.S. (increase [+])	2,120	383	3,320	6,852	9,277	2,957	4,095
Net errors and omissions	1,156	−576	−489	−1,007	−642	−1,253	−698

*Excluding transactions in official reserve assets.
Source: U.S. Department of Commerce, Office of Business Economics, *Survey of Current Business.*

Finance

Coin production

in millions of pieces; years ending June 30

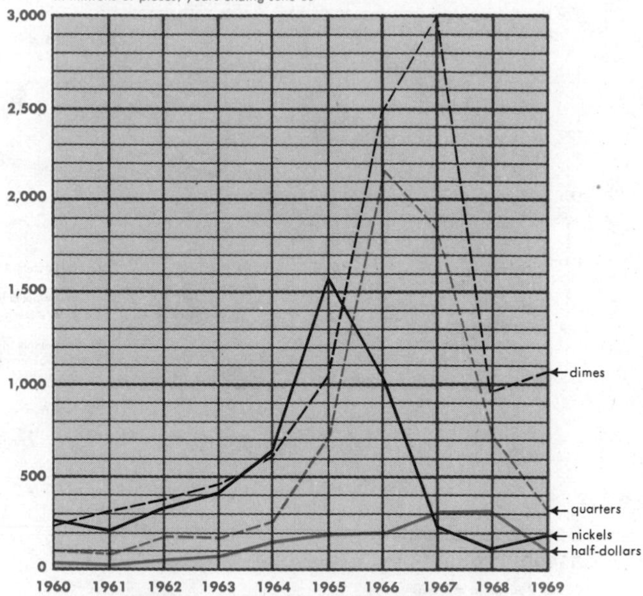

After July 1965, because of the silver shortage, dimes and quarters were minted of copper and cupronickel, and the silver in half-dollars was reduced to 40%.
Source: U.S. Department of the Treasury, Bureau of the Mint.

Money stock and money in circulation

in millions of dollars, except per capita

Year	Stock of money in U.S.*	MONEY HELD IN TREASURY: In trust against gold and silver certificates	MONEY HELD IN TREASURY: Treasury cash	MONEY HELD IN TREASURY: For federal reserve banks and agents	MONEY OUTSIDE OF TREASURY: Held by federal reserve banks and agents	MONEY OUTSIDE OF TREASURY: In circulation† Amount	MONEY OUTSIDE OF TREASURY: In circulation† Per capita
1960	53,071	(21,455)	395	16,213	4,398	32,065	177.46
1961	51,947	(19,662)	379	14,440	4,724	32,405	176.35
1962	52,195	(18,435)	379	13,342	4,705	33,770	180.92
1963	53,335	(17,585)	369	12,641	4,855	35,470	187.30
1964	55,451	(16,997)	391	12,369	4,957	37,734	196.46
1965	56,690	(14,559)	747	13,669	2,554	39,720	204.33
1966	60,362	(13,595)	1,049	12,992	3,768	42,554	213.99
1967	61,408	(13,006)	1,472	12,607	2,616	44,712	225.97
1968	61,506	(10,026)	838	10,024	3,003	47,640	238.37
1969	64,387	(10,027)	633	10,026	2,792	50,936	252.26

Data are for June 30 of each year.
*Does not include duplications, which are shown in parentheses.
†Includes any paper currency held outside the U.S. and currency and coin held by banks.
Source: Board of Governors of the Federal Reserve System, *Federal Reserve Bulletin*.

Banks

January 1, 1969

State	Number of banks*	Total assets or liabilities in $000,000	SELECTED ASSETS in $000,000: Loans†	SELECTED ASSETS: Investments	SELECTED ASSETS: Reserves, cash, and bank balances	SELECTED LIABILITIES in $000,000: Deposits: Total	Deposits: Interbank	Deposits: Other: Demand	Deposits: Other: Time	Capital accounts
Alabama	268	4,763	2,284	1,628	751	4,287	157	2,208	1,921	381
Alaska	14	473	251	150	52	430	3	196	230	32
Arizona	13	3,231	2,075	689	363	2,856	21	1,251	1,584	203
Arkansas	248	2,903	1,394	900	542	2,625	151	1,442	1,032	232
California	162	52,099	30,417	12,101	7,489	45,421	1,202	17,887	26,332	3,278
Colorado	257	4,363	2,406	1,048	781	3,885	205	1,856	1,824	323
Connecticut	135	10,389	6,950	2,312	925	9,328	117	2,682	6,529	825
Delaware	21	1,637	912	498	196	1,456	19	708	728	146
District of Columbia	14	3,009	1,512	922	608	2,704	83	1,547	1,074	230
Florida	461	12,780	5,699	4,536	2,200	11,542	684	5,523	5,335	869
Georgia	428	7,384	4,002	1,814	1,294	6,529	408	3,301	2,820	593
Hawaii	11	1,554	859	432	190	1,380	22	634	723	145
Idaho	26	1,259	719	347	160	1,146	5	558	582	86
Illinois	1,074	36,913	19,075	11,535	5,120	31,587	1,783	14,101	15,703	2,801
Indiana	419	10,766	5,377	3,389	1,807	9,603	284	4,642	4,677	726
Iowa	673	6,385	3,112	2,223	956	5,806	263	2,728	2,814	511
Kansas	601	4,891	2,269	1,833	708	4,412	177	2,261	1,974	429
Kentucky	346	5,139	2,509	1,645	902	4,652	293	2,482	1,877	402
Louisiana	229	6,365	2,966	2,021	1,255	5,708	444	2,964	2,300	496
Maine	75	2,105	1,293	576	195	1,862	19	518	1,325	185
Maryland	128	6,204	3,499	1,662	865	5,512	164	2,586	2,762	506
Massachusetts	332	22,997	14,491	5,845	2,159	20,006	786	6,075	13,144	1,880
Michigan	338	21,209	12,121	6,189	2,438	19,234	397	6,747	12,091	1,324
Minnesota	724	10,072	5,193	3,123	1,573	9,088	622	3,559	4,907	667
Mississippi	185	3,004	1,514	945	475	2,698	135	1,545	1,017	220
Missouri	667	12,341	5,908	4,088	2,118	10,933	980	5,397	4,556	982
Montana	135	1,555	777	537	205	1,400	35	641	724	108
Nebraska	441	3,445	1,701	1,085	596	3,094	225	1,618	1,251	282
Nevada	9	1,057	546	320	153	956	13	441	502	73
New Hampshire	109	2,099	1,475	447	145	1,855	16	401	1,438	185
New Jersey	250	17,547	9,864	5,374	1,949	15,776	158	6,302	9,317	1,259
New Mexico	63	1,344	691	407	208	1,217	24	655	539	98
New York	444	145,898	88,748	27,796	23,576	121,905	10,224	43,494	68,187	10,684
North Carolina	121	7,243	3,804	2,034	1,192	6,325	337	3,033	2,956	519
North Dakota	169	1,506	679	644	158	1,362	19	588	754	120
Ohio	526	22,577	11,962	7,063	3,122	20,094	537	8,672	10,884	1,745
Oklahoma	424	5,414	2,601	1,685	1,024	4,853	278	2,525	2,050	452
Oregon	51	4,390	2,451	1,199	564	3,969	45	1,523	2,401	267
Pennsylvania	516	33,761	19,355	9,415	4,219	29,648	1,070	11,448	17,129	2,744
Rhode Island	20	2,955	1,945	733	223	2,609	19	680	1,911	234
South Carolina	118	2,251	1,133	664	400	1,986	41	1,334	611	182
South Dakota	165	1,459	700	559	171	1,326	17	600	709	110
Tennessee	303	7,230	3,713	1,987	1,338	6,220	577	2,895	2,748	564
Texas	1,151	26,524	13,435	6,930	5,429	23,475	2,153	11,848	9,474	1,943
Utah	54	1,881	1,052	475	302	1,696	61	714	920	134
Vermont	51	1,091	761	233	81	994	3	260	731	80
Virginia	237	7,674	4,325	2,132	1,042	6,876	188	2,930	3,759	554
Washington	101	7,026	4,252	1,611	902	6,283	125	2,480	3,678	482
West Virginia	195	2,626	1,247	981	332	2,298	44	1,112	1,142	249
Wisconsin	606	9,379	4,830	3,068	1,263	8,490	306	3,480	4,704	659
Wyoming	70	784	390	249	127	703	20	326	356	63
Total U.S.‡	14,179	573,021	321,277	150,105	84,748	500,160	25,960	205,422	268,778	42,275

*Includes two banks for which asset and liability data are not available.
†Includes Federal Funds sold and securities purchased under agreement to resell. ‡Includes a member bank in the Virgin Islands.
Source: Board of Governors of the Federal Reserve System, *Federal Reserve Statistical Release*.

Assets of commercial banks

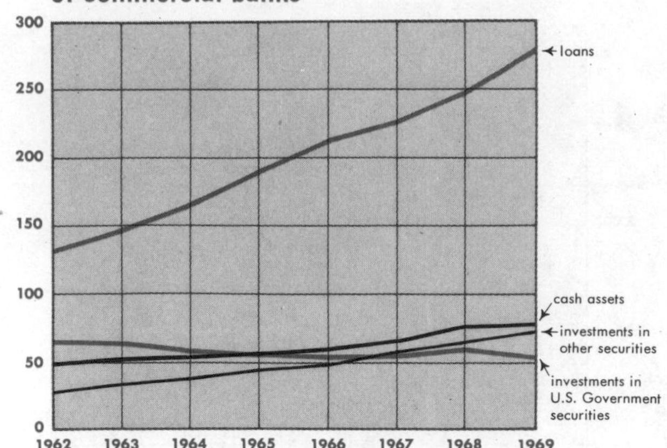

Data are for the end of June of years reported.
Source: Board of Governors of the Federal Reserve System, *Federal Reserve Bulletin*.

Credit unions

dollar figures in millions

Year	Number of active credit unions	Number of members	Savings*	Loans outstanding to members†	Reserves	Assets
1955	16,201	8,153,641	$ 2,447	$ 1,934	$110	$ 2,743
1956	17,256	9,061,339	2,914	2,326	137	3,271
1957	18,203	9,819,452	3,382	2,778	165	3,813
1958	18,838	10,431,606	3,870	3,078	198	4,346
1959	19,452	11,262,581	4,436	3,708	232	5,024
1960	20,047	12,037,533	4,975	4,377	272	5,653
1961	20,615	12,882,793	5,636	4,818	326	6,383
1962	20,951	13,762,047	6,331	5,477	381	7,186
1963	21,369	14,586,988	7,166	6,171	441	8,131
1964	21,807	15,619,210	8,242	7,046	510	9,361
1965	22,119	16,753,106	9,249	8,095	590	10,552
1966	22,692	17,897,351	10,106	9,003	678	11,609
1967	23,053	19,079,864	11,128	9,879	779	12,778
1968‡	23,563	20,338,750	12,298	11,261	885	14,099

*Shares and deposits.
†Includes some loans to other credit unions before 1960.
‡Preliminary.
Source: CUNA International, Inc.

Savings and loan associations

dollar figures in millions

State	NUMBER OF ASSOCIATIONS Total	NUMBER OF ASSOCIATIONS State	ASSETS Total	ASSETS State	Mortgage loans outstanding	Savings capital
Alabama	57	8	$ 1,107	$ 151	$ 946	$ 989
Alaska	3	0	61	0	52	52
Arizona	12	10	868	501	721	733
Arkansas	63	23	854	170	729	763
California	256	185	29,438	19,912	25,197	24,321
Colorado	55	35	1,954	984	1,670	1,622
Connecticut	39	21	1,325	350	1,140	1,149
Delaware	28	25	94	49	84	80
District of Columbia	23	14	2,318	1,680	2,049	2,005
Florida	135	6	7,409	138	6,282	6,561
Georgia	106	6	2,500	16	2,173	2,135
Hawaii	14	12	606	490	513	502
Idaho	12	4	278	33	241	245
Illinois	570	431	12,992	5,985	11,171	11,107
Indiana	206	103	3,403	799	2,893	3,041
Iowa	91	47	1,694	643	1,424	1,513
Kansas	100	71	1,841	781	1,622	1,591
Kentucky	134	45	1,714	198	1,477	1,527
Louisiana	106	70	2,026	1,532	1,764	1,776
Maine	28	19	202	130	173	175
Maryland	296	231	2,810	821	2,390	2,389
Massachusetts	189	154	3,769	2,033	3,219	3,295
Michigan	70	32	3,979	1,250	3,423	3,511
Minnesota	77	24	2,888	131	2,500	2,492
Mississippi	81	50	711	209	607	631
Missouri	140	95	3,634	1,984	3,138	3,160
Montana	16	7	$ 241	$ 44	$ 207	$ 217
Nebraska	47	26	1,133	668	961	986
Nevada	6	5	632	542	510	437
New Hampshire	25	18	313	89	275	271
New Jersey	369	343	5,787	4,943	4,976	5,131
New Mexico	37	27	455	228	377	395
New York	209	124	9,607	3,008	8,359	8,421
North Carolina	184	147	2,822	1,827	2,492	2,479
North Dakota	14	7	411	208	342	354
Ohio	531	393	11,949	6,969	9,790	10,396
Oklahoma	58	28	1,373	382	1,211	1,235
Oregon	32	14	1,266	425	1,101	1,075
Pennsylvania	685	551	7,054	2,846	6,110	6,084
Rhode Island	8	6	422	371	368	346
South Carolina	76	29	1,487	403	1,292	1,300
South Dakota	18	10	204	35	173	180
Tennessee	70	0	1,690	0	1,443	1,488
Texas	277	193	6,646	4,461	5,652	5,746
Utah	19	13	741	413	623	613
Vermont	8	6	82	14	73	69
Virginia	77	45	1,550	503	1,344	1,366
Washington	65	30	2,386	417	2,050	2,061
West Virginia	38	15	403	54	341	357
Wisconsin	144	101	3,472	2,124	2,994	2,997
Wyoming	12	3	159	25	136	142
TOTAL U.S.	5,916	3,862	152,760	71,969	130,798	131,511

Data are for January 1, 1969, for all federally chartered and state chartered savings and loan associations and cooperative banks.
Source: United States Savings and Loan League.

Consumer credit outstanding

in billions of dollars

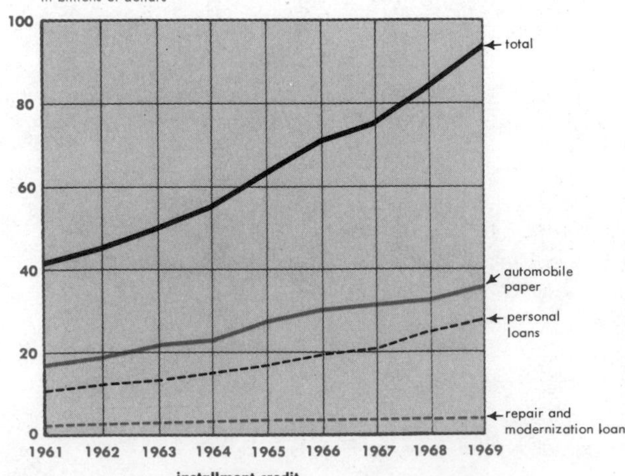

installment credit

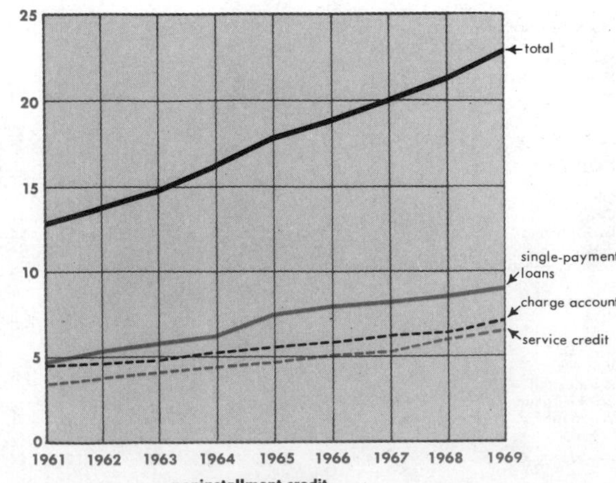

noninstallment credit

Graphs cover loans outstanding as of June 30 to individuals for household, family, and other personal expenditures, except real estate mortgage loans.
*Holdings of financial institutions only.
Source: Board of Governors of the Federal Reserve System, *Federal Reserve Bulletin*.

Health insurance

Item	1960	1965	1968
Premiums received (in $000,000)	7,485	12,130	14,985
Insurance companies	4,671	7,352	9,082
Other*	2,814	4,778	5,903
Benefit payments (in $000,000)	5,688	9,617	12,238
By type of insurer			
Insurance companies	3,069	5,160	6,717
Other*	2,619	4,457	5,521
By type of benefit			
Hospital expense†	3,207	5,695	7,069
Surgical and medical expense†	1,642	2,876	3,761
Loss of income	839	1,046	1,408
Number of persons covered, Dec. 31 (in 000)			
Insurance companies‡			
Hospital expense	78,885	97,042	104,408
Surgical expense	75,305	93,717	96,120
Regular medical expense	41,312	58,398	68,395
Blue Cross, Blue Shield, and Medical Society			
Hospital expense	58,050	64,495	71,288
Surgical expense	50,281	55,420	63,013
Regular medical expense	45,017	52,042	59,176
Independent plans§			
Hospital expense	5,542	7,376	7,660
Surgical expense	6,573	8,974	8,800
Regular medical expense	6,773	8,718	8,900

*Blue Cross, Blue Shield, and other insuring organizations.
†Includes benefits from major medical expense policies.
‡Persons covered by more than one insurance company are counted only once.
§Industrial plans, community plans, private group clinics, college health plans, and consumer-sponsored plans.
Source: Health Insurance Institute.

Life insurance

dollar figures in millions

Item	1960	1965	1967	1968	1969
Number of companies	1,442	1,610	1,726	1,758	1,812
Amount in force	$560,000	$849,000	$1,030,000	$1,140,000	$1,240,000
Value of purchases*	72,989	108,989	127,357	147,650	154,896
Ordinary	52,382	78,122	90,952	99,284	108,823
Group	13,706	23,506	29,339	41,513	39,557
Industrial	6,901	7,361	7,066	6,853	6,516
Benefit payments					
Death payments	3,253	4,643	5,446	5,976	6,478
Matured endowments	652	933	998	994	969
Policy dividends	1,541	2,416	2,796	2,995	3,265

Years ending June 30.
*Exclusive of revivals, increases, dividend additions, and reinsurance acquired.
Source: Institute of Life Insurance.

Sales of stocks and bonds

in millions

Year and month	Market value of all sales	STOCKS* Market value	STOCKS* Number of shares	BONDS† Market value	BONDS† Principal amount
1968					
October	$19,155	$18,560	479	$522	$534
November	16,786	16,165	411	501	474
December	19,639	18,864	508	587	556
1969					
January	18,613	17,957	515	498	517
February	15,710	15,187	407	400	409
March	13,762	13,234	366	388	426
April	14,427	13,911	379	407	446
May	18,729	18,189	502	422	438
June	15,313	14,860	420	370	410
July	13,069	12,685	359	330	393
August	12,766	12,392	367	316	376
September	12,753	12,429	355	271	338

*Includes voting trust certificates, certificates of deposit for stocks, American depository receipts for stocks; excludes rights and warrants.
Excludes U.S. Government bonds.
†Source: U.S. Securities and Exchange Commission, *Statistical Bulletin.*

Stock dividends

July data, at annual rates per share in dollars

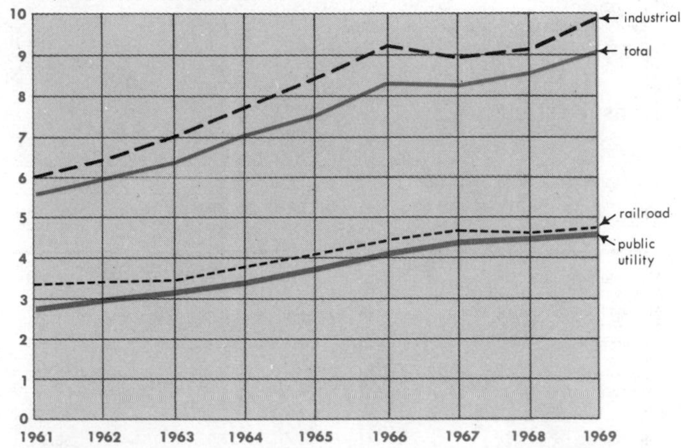

Source: U.S. Department of Commerce, Office of Business Economics, *Survey of Current Business.* Data compiled by Moody's Investors Service, Inc.

Stock market prices

1941-43=10

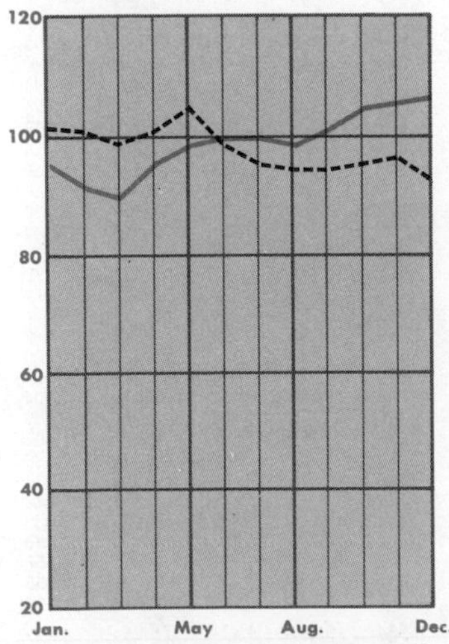

Composite (500 stocks)

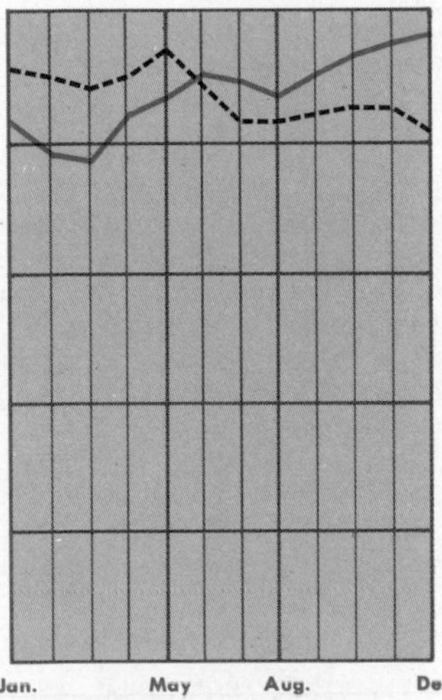

Industrials (425 stocks)

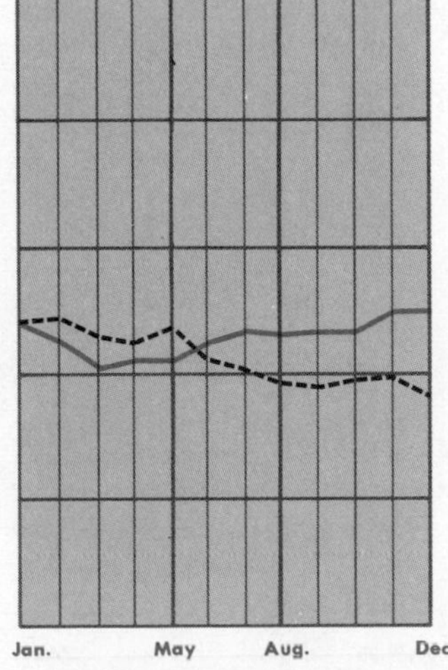

Public utilities (55 stocks)

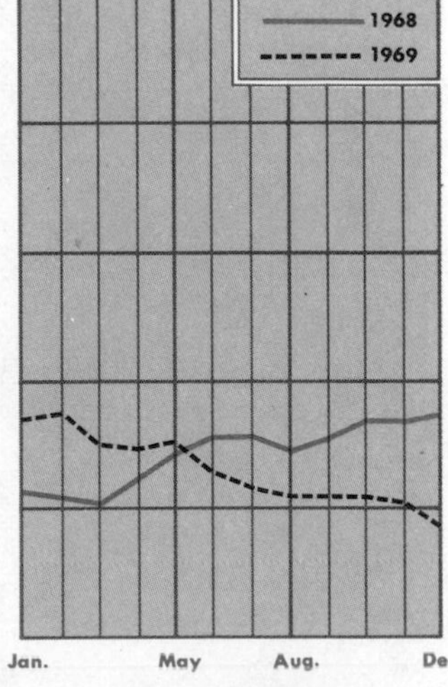

Railroads (20 stocks)

Monthly averages except December 1969 which is the closing price.
Source: U.S. Department of Commerce, Office of Business Economics, *Survey of Current Business.* Data compiled by Standard & Poor's Corporation.

Transport and Communications

Automobile ownership

Unit	1950	1955	1960	1965	1968
Total number of families in the U.S. (000,000)	45.2	49.1	53.4	58.4	61.2
Percent of families owning automobiles	59	70	77	79	79
Owning 1 automobile	52	60	62	55	53
Owning 2 or more automobiles	7	10	15	24	26
Age of automobiles owned, by percent					
Less than 2 years old	17	12	14	16	14
2 and 3 years old	19	22	20	21	24
4 to 7 years old	6	43	41	33	36
8 years old and over	58	23	25	30	26
Total automobiles purchased (000,000)	...	13.6	14.1	18.3	19.2
New cars (000,000)	...	4.4	5.2	7.2	6.9
Average price paid	...	$2,730	$3,140	$3,140	$3,290
Used cars (000,000)	...	9.2	9.1	11.1	12.3
Average price paid, gross	...	$ 780	$ 980	$ 920	$1,050
Method of financing purchases, by percent					
Full cash (including trade-in allowance)	47	38	38	48	42
Installment credit and other borrowing	52	60	62	52	58

Source: U.S. Department of Commerce, Bureau of the Census, *Statistical Abstract of the United States*. Data compiled by The University of Michigan, Survey Research Center, *Survey of Consumer Finances*.

Traffic accidents

Type of action	PERSONS KILLED 1950	1960	1965	1968	PERSONS INJURED 1950	1960	1965	1968
Driver action:								
Number	26,700	30,400	41,600	45,800	1,210,000	2,600,000	3,682,000	3,880,000
Percent distribution								
Speeding	49.8	36.1	41.1	40.8	39.3	38.5	42.2	20.9
Wrong side of road	17.8	17.0	16.4	14.2	8.7	6.7	6.8	5.6
No right-of-way	10.4	12.8	13.0	13.1	26.6	22.5	18.9	19.2
Drove off road	5.2	16.6	10.5	12.7	2.9	8.3	6.9	8.8
Reckless driving	8.5	12.5	14.9	14.7	9.0	13.5	19.2	39.7
Other*	8.3	5.0	4.1	4.5	13.5	10.5	6.0	5.8
Pedestrian action:								
Number	9,400	7,600	9,000	9,600	299,500	255,500	274,700	277,000
Percent distribution								
Crossing at intersection								
With signal	4.6	6.2	4.8	7.3	10.1	11.9	8.6	11.3
Against signal	6.3	7.1	8.6	8.3	9.4	8.5	9.5	11.4
No signal	13.5	15.9	7.4	9.4	13.6	12.3	8.1	10.2
Crossing between intersections	39.8	37.1	40.8	40.6	26.1	32.2	31.6	25.3
Children playing in street	5.8	5.3	3.3	3.1	16.6	6.6	6.3	5.0
At work in road	3.1	2.9	2.8	3.1	2.7	2.2	1.8	1.9
Coming from behind parked car	6.7	6.2	6.9	3.1	9.1	15.7	16.8	11.7
Walking on rural highway	13.0	10.0	15.6	14.1	2.3	2.4	7.6	6.9
Not on roadway	3.5	4.2	4.7	3.7	6.5	4.5	3.6	5.8
Other†	3.7	5.1	5.1	7.3	3.6	3.7	6.1	10.5

*Cutting in; improper passing; improper or no signalling; movement of driverless car; miscellaneous. †Standing on safety isle; getting on or off other vehicle; riding or hitching on vehicle; miscellaneous.
Source: U.S. Department of Commerce, Bureau of the Census, *Statistical Abstract of the United States*. Data compiled by The Travelers Insurance Companies, Hartford, Conn., annual report, *The Travelers Book of Street and Highway Accident Data*.

Transportation

State	ROAD AND STREET MILEAGE Jan. 1, 1969: Total*	Total surfaced	Municipal mileage	Rural mileage: State controlled	Rural mileage: Locally controlled	AUTOMOBILES, TRUCKS, AND BUSES registrations, in 000, 1968: Total	Private and commercial: Automobiles	Private and commercial: Trucks and buses	Publicly owned†	RAILROAD MILEAGE OWNED Jan. 1, 1969: Total	Class 1	AIRPORTS‡ Jan. 1, 1969: Total	Private	CIVIL AIRCRAFT Jan. 1, 1969: Total	Eligible
Alabama	78,097	71,281	11,385	19,913§	46,799	1,806	1,440	339	27	4,577	3,898	124	48	2,934	2,079
Alaska	6,850	3,215	526	4,310	1,477	123	87	31	4	20	—	667	184	3,324	2,046
Arizona	41,062	20,098	5,682	5,183	17,529	944	717	206	20	2,052	1,879	197	99	3,018	1,982
Arkansas	78,839	57,707	8,420	12,935	55,609	1,023	714	297	12	3,605	3,314	130	66	2,370	1,579
California	158,159	116,580	42,795	13,501	70,821	11,123	9,256	1,706	161	7,483	6,661	699	453	24,672	17,100
Colorado	81,517	48,011	6,499	8,222	66,745	1,300	987	289	23	3,737	3,620	174	108	2,914	2,159
Connecticut	18,116	17,966	12,803	1,513	3,800	1,626	1,440	168	18	695	640	76	64	1,522	1,080
Delaware	4,847	4,829	1,401	3,446§	—	283	237	42	4	292	—	22	17	669	541
District of Columbia	1,083	1,072	1,083	—	—	257	230	19	9	31	12	3	—	994	772
Florida	85,889	58,766	19,700	16,530	48,607	3,628	3,153	424	51	4,348	3,844	283	176	7,574	4,988
Georgia	98,241	66,615	14,029	15,641	68,231	2,324	1,867	431	26	5,449	3,809	171	73	3,590	2,657
Hawaii	3,442	3,275	943	883	1,525	355	312	36	6	—	—	43	27	378	210
Idaho	54,758	30,323	2,817	4,679	26,691	471	319	139	13	2,668	2,478	167	55	1,495	1,070
Illinois	129,419	122,619	26,811	13,140	89,468	4,990	4,340	595	55	10,917	9,134	483	407	7,845	5,580
Indiana	90,950	85,940	12,634	10,170	68,146	2,739	2,198	515	26	6,488	3,428	163	106	4,359	3,182
Iowa	112,349	105,138	12,689	9,164	90,490	1,703	1,329	345	29	8,225	7,964	230	132	3,092	2,399
Kansas	133,405	96,694	10,111	9,986	113,308	1,501	1,072	405	23	7,864	7,840	278	168	3,852	2,873
Kentucky	69,909	56,776	5,049	23,756	40,668	1,691	1,327	343	21	3,511	3,089	63	17	1,218	920
Louisiana	52,733	47,431	10,842	14,232§	27,373	1,662	1,311	330	20	3,803	3,492	210	143	2,929	2,043
Maine	21,311	19,627	2,352	10,954‖	7,845	480	384	90	6	1,679	1,523	135	93	806	557
Maryland	25,885	25,817	4,065	4,920	16,757	1,704	1,485	200	19	1,122	564	81	68	2,028	1,462
Massachusetts	27,805	26,239	20,313	1,098	6,365	2,336	2,094	211	31	1,495	1,291	114	88	2,459	1,748
Michigan	114,170	95,522	19,145	7,952	87,071	4,317	3,715	537	65	6,303	4,218	278	151	6,952	4,977
Minnesota	127,099	114,250	16,369	11,503	97,385	2,086	1,672	384	29	7,973	7,851	265	141	4,519	3,293
Mississippi	66,104	63,405	6,456	9,762	49,356	1,061	789	255	17	3,653	3,170	149	81	2,071	1,370
Missouri	114,596	106,560	14,785	30,017	69,142	2,345	1,853	469	23	6,414	5,785	275	184	4,485	3,294
Montana	76,437	40,364	2,258	11,682	51,518	463	302	151	10	4,926	4,889	189	73	1,930	1,426
Nebraska	103,464	71,410	6,247	9,457	87,198	909	660	234	15	5,499	5,499	262	181	2,271	1,698
Nevada	47,562	14,932	1,766	6,233§	39,562	303	226	66	11	1,635	1,474	89	45	1,359	974
New Hampshire	14,669	12,007	4,697	3,046	6,849	353	297	50	6	816	679	49	34	534	362
New Jersey	31,522	30,738	16,410	1,791	13,316	3,333	2,969	313	51	1,790	940	154	135	3,819	2,669
New Mexico	66,450	19,437	4,020	11,581	45,655	589	430	146	13	2,219	2,145	125	63	1,659	1,130
New York	102,327	92,015	16,849	13,750	71,693	6,310	5,616	596	98	5,670	4,751	371	311	8,340	5,902
North Carolina	85,029	76,824	13,192	70,019§	—	2,573	2,020	483	70	4,164	2,948	179	129	3,071	2,189
North Dakota	107,237	67,218	3,070	6,476	96,412	414	264	142	8	5,164	5,096	191	117	1,372	992
Ohio	108,360	106,589	23,177	16,676	68,507	5,442	4,831	558	53	7,954	4,644	416	324	7,535	5,319
Oklahoma	107,321	77,565	13,280	11,303	82,708	1,610	1,151	436	24	5,451	5,145	205	104	3,816	2,774
Oregon	90,810	56,866	6,034	8,895	34,980	1,242	1,000	216	26	3,081	2,780	183	98	3,553	2,562
Pennsylvania	113,911	93,928	23,325	44,067	46,302	5,547	4,828	660	58	8,456	5,600	447	381	5,601	4,070
Rhode Island	5,203	4,974	4,204	504	495	452	400	47	5	146	103	12	6	269	207
South Carolina	59,520	38,698	6,576	30,530	21,897	1,250	1,015	212	22	3,131	2,116	100	50	1,314	1,004
South Dakota	84,333	58,365	2,933	8,606	71,135	411	283	118	10	3,805	3,805	110	45	1,227	849
Tennessee	77,617	75,395	9,075	8,300	59,048	1,907	1,537	341	29	3,020	2,601	97	37	2,235	1,691
Texas	240,130	172,432	43,351	59,863	136,018	6,180	4,773	1,317	90	13,951	13,272	938	708	13,591	9,630
Utah	39,040	21,919	4,290	5,220	20,663	571	445	114	12	1,771	1,707	76	24	1,028	737
Vermont	14,208	12,217	935	2,391	10,751	207	170	33	4	771	326	41	29	357	268
Virginia	60,428	59,162	8,099	49,467§	787	2,048	1,711	299	37	3,951	3,297	147	103	2,278	1,635
Washington	73,955	60,909	10,067	11,364	39,522	1,987	1,548	403	36	4,932	4,816	212	118	4,532	3,146
West Virginia	35,850	26,364	3,550	31,336§	—	805	637	155	12	3,549	3,161	49	30	762	558
Wisconsin	101,729	96,130	13,682	10,698	77,273	2,027	1,685	304	38	6,007	5,695	233	135	3,229	2,353
Wyoming	40,338	17,669	1,247	5,615	20,998	226	145	74	6	1,848	1,841	87	45	813	596
Total U.S.	3,684,085	2,869,883	532,038	702,280	2,274,495	101,039¶	83,276¶	16,279¶	1,484¶	208,111	178,834	10,442	6,474	178,564	126,702

*Includes federally controlled rural roads. †Excludes vehicles owned by military services. ‡Includes seaplane bases, heliports, and military fields having joint civil-military use.
§Includes mileage of state-controlled county roads. ‖Includes the state-aid system. ¶Data not equal to total due to rounding.
Sources: Interstate Commerce Commission; U.S. Department of Transportation, Federal Aviation Administration; Federal Highway Administration, Bureau of Public Roads.

Transportation accident death rates

per 100,000,000 passenger-miles

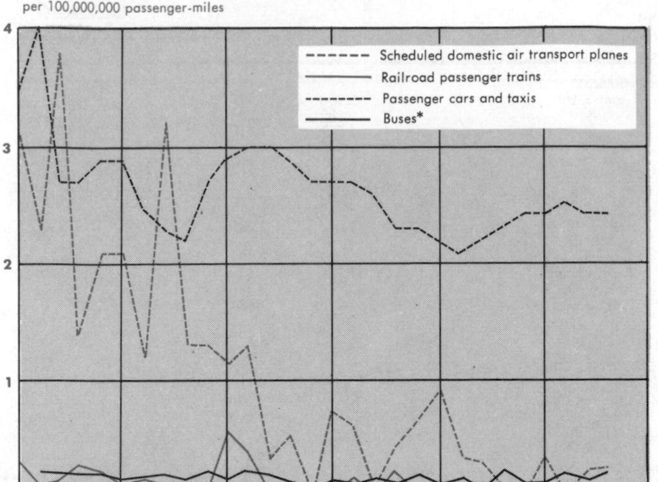

*1940 data included with passenger cars and taxis.
Source: National Safety Council.

Aviation

Item		1960	1968
CIVIL FLYING			
Total aircraft		111,580	166,598*
Hours flown†	(000)	13,121	23,972
Miles flown†	(000,000)	1,769	3,740
Aircraft accidents†		4,793	5,069
Aircraft accident fatalities†		787	1,374
Pilot licenses		348,062	691,695
SCHEDULED AIR CARRIERS			
Aircraft operating‡		1,822	2,129*
Fixed wing		1,797	2,129*
Four-engine		1,141	997*
Twin-engine		651	711*
Express and freight flown§	(000 ton-miles)	578,518	2,506,307
Mail flown	(000 ton-miles)	239,258	1,243,505
Domestic operations‖			
Number of operators§		39	36*
Route miles in operation¶		101,414	112,984*
Revenue passengers carried	(000)	56,352	145,774
Revenue passenger-miles flown	(000,000)	30,557	87,508
International operations‖			
Number of operators§		10	12*
Route miles in operation		148,303	150,036*
Revenue passengers carried	(000)	5,904	16,407
Revenue passenger-miles flown	(000,000)	8,306	26,451

*1967. †Excludes civil flying performed by public carriers.
‡Excludes aircraft used for crew training and general utility purposes, those held for disposal, and those operated by the scheduled all-cargo carriers.
§Excludes all-cargo operators. ‖Operations between conterminous U.S. and Hawaii and Alaska included with international. ¶Excludes intra-Alaska.
Source: U.S. Department of Commerce, Bureau of the Census, *Statistical Abstract of the United States.* Data compiled by U.S. Department of Transportation, Federal Aviation Administration, *FAA Statistical Handbook of Aviation.*

Railroads

years ending December 31

Item		1960	1965	1967
Number of operating companies*		407	372	370
Miles of road owned, first track†		217,552	211,384	209,292
Total miles operated		381,745	370,636	368,030
Number of locomotives in service		31,178	30,061	29,874
Number of passenger-train cars in service‡		25,746	20,022	17,822
Operating revenues	($000,000)	9,642	10,425	10,582
Operating expenses	($000,000)	7,657	8,003	8,359
Net income§	($000,000)	473	866	368‖
Passenger revenue	($000,000)	641	556	489
Passengers carried	(000,000)	327	306	304
Passenger-miles	(000,000)	21,284	17,454	15,264
Revenue per passenger-mile	(cents)	3.014	3.185	3.201
Average journey per passenger	(miles)	65.05	57.07	50.21
Freight revenue	($000,000)	8,152	9,037	9,329
Freight revenue-tons originated	(000,000)	1,301	1,479	1,498
Tons carried one mile	(000,000)	575,360	705,705	727,075
Revenue ton-miles per mile of road	(000)	2,497	3,121	3,238
Revenue per ton-mile	(cents)	1.417	1.281	1.283
Haul per ton				
U.S. as a system	(miles)	442.14	477.15	485.21
Individual railroad	(miles)	238.83	257.40	262.49
Revenue per ton				
U.S. as a system	(dollars)	6.26	6.11	6.23
Individual railroad	(dollars)	3.38	3.30	3.37
Average number of employees	(000)	793	655	624
Compensation of employees	($000,000)	4,957	4,887	5,026

All data are for Classes I and II.
*Includes unofficial companies.
†Includes lessors, proprietary and unofficial companies.
‡Includes switching and terminal companies.
§Includes lessors.
‖After extraordinary and prior period items.
Source: Interstate Commerce Commission.

U.S. postal service

Year ending June 30	Number of post offices	FINANCES in $000,000: Net revenue	FINANCES in $000,000: Obligations	Postage stamps issued, in 000	MONEY ORDERS ISSUED in $000,000: Domestic	MONEY ORDERS ISSUED in $000,000: International	Pieces of mail handled, in 000,000
1960	35,238	3,276.8	3,874.0	23,773,570	5,030.6	39.9	63,674.6
1961	34,955	3,423.1	4,249.4	23,001,808	4,957.6	35.3	64,932.9
1962	34,797	3,557.0	4,331.6	25,405,929	4,787.4	33.7	66,493.2
1963	34,498	3,879.1	4,698.5	31,669,175	4,709.1	33.4	67,852.7
1964	34,040	4,276.1	4,927.8	24,692,326	4,719.4	32.3	67,676.5
1965	33,624	4,420.8	5,274.8	22,652,248	4,519.7	31.8	71,628.0
1966	33,121	4,682.5	5,629.6	23,503,959	4,606.0	28.9	75,800.0
1967	32,626	4,962.7	6,133.4	26,320,662	4,697.3	26.2	79,165.0
1968	32,261	5,505.3	6,635.8	34,500,000*	4,614.5	26.8	81,500.0
1969	32,004	6,114.4	7,228.1	27,383,826	4,643.8	25.6	82,004.5

*Approximate.
Source: U.S. Post Office Department.

Sources of major air pollutants

in millions of tons per year

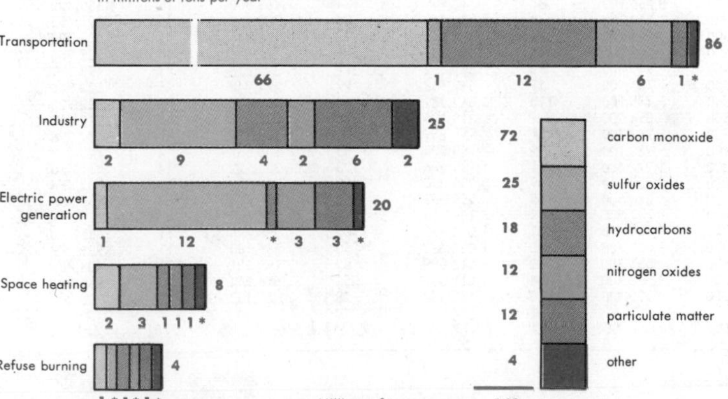

*Less than one million tons.
Source: U.S. Public Health Service.

Intercity freight traffic

in percent by year

1940
1945
1950
1955
1960
1965
1968

0 10 20 30 40 50 60 70 80 90 100

railroads
motor vehicles
waterways
oil pipelines

Air freight is not shown because it is less than one percent.
Source: Interstate Commerce Commission.

Commerce of selected ports

1968, in thousands of short tons (cargo)

Port	Imports	Exports	DOMESTIC COMMERCE* Receipts	Shipments
COASTAL PORTS				
Atlantic coast				
Portland, Me.	22,669	1	3,766	568
Salem, Mass.	524	—	955	5
Boston, Mass.	8,495	735	11,124	1,248
Providence, R.I.	1,770	197	6,295	584
New Haven, Conn.	2,796	207	6,354	1,630
Bridgeport, Conn.	1,137	63	1,815	360
Norwalk, Conn.	—	—	1,105	—
New York, N.Y. and N.J.	53,589	6,767	28,316	21,076
Hempstead, N.Y.	—	—	1,913	2,508
Port Jefferson, N.Y.	582	—	1,625	49
Albany, N.Y.	784	266	2,126	24
Delaware River ports†	50,405	3,084	28,912	8,017
Baltimore, Md.	19,069	5,290	3,645	1,403
Norfolk, Va.	3,562	27,742	1,945	2,314
Newport News, Va.	633	7,909	2	889
Wilmington, N.C.	1,383	196	1,939	146
Charleston, S.C.	2,103	915	2,777	97
Savannah, Ga.	2,317	1,147	1,904	123
Jacksonville, Fla.	3,650	1,540	3,854	515
Port Everglades, Fla.	2,205	206	5,306	262
Pacific coast				
Long Beach, Calif.	3,745	4,966	3,133	2,380
Los Angeles, Calif.	5,229	4,746	6,635	5,840
San Francisco Bay area, Calif.	6,117	5,898	15,340	8,317
Stockton, Calif.	173	890	115	45
Portland, Ore.	1,084	3,906	4,080	261
Longview, Wash.	227	2,814	572	67
Tacoma, Wash.	1,942	2,247	294	116
Seattle, Wash.	2,419	1,354	2,921	999
Honolulu, Hawaii	1,313	151	3,208	2,156

Port	Imports	Exports	DOMESTIC COMMERCE* Receipts	Shipments
Gulf coast				
Tampa, Fla.	2,050	10,525	10,463	3,383
Mobile, Ala.	8,885	2,236	159	1,601
New Orleans, La.	6,711	21,057	1,798	26,266
Baton Rouge, La.	6,247	4,981	839	9,991
Lake Charles, La.‡	172	1,210	196	2,420
Galveston, Tex.	353	2,018	173	45
Texas City, Tex.	30	335	760	4,593
Houston, Tex.	5,085	11,508	2,634	15,554
Corpus Christi, Tex.	2,866	2,285	155	11,675
Harbor Island, Tex.	—	—	51	4,095
Freeport, Tex.	89	1,209	66	829
Brazos Island, Tex.	1,839	601	1	1,641
Beaumont, Tex.	47	3,029	1,378	14,731
Port Arthur, Tex.	220	1,430	3,437	11,076

GREAT LAKES PORTS	ALL COMMERCE Receipts	Shipments
Ashtabula, Ohio	6,550	1,656
Buffalo, N.Y.	14,008	629
Chicago, Ill.	13,974	9,552
Cleveland, Ohio	22,515	557
Conneaut, Ohio	7,812	6,538
Detroit, Mich.	31,162	1,182
Duluth-Superior, Minn. and Wis.	3,590	34,132
Indiana Harbor, Ind.	13,419	4,609
Lorain, Ohio	5,060	5,206
Milwaukee, Wis.	4,479	1,822
Sandusky, Ohio	18	6,831
Toledo, Ohio	6,871	27,464

Data exclude purely local port traffic and commerce with ports on internal rivers and canals.
*Domestic commerce figures for coastal ports exclude commerce with Great Lakes ports.
†Includes tributaries. ‡Includes Calcasieu River and Pass.
Source: U.S. Department of the Army, Corps of Engineers, *Waterborne Commerce of the United States.*

Communication facilities

State	Post offices July 1, 1969	RADIO STATIONS Jan. 1, 1968 AM	FM	TV STATIONS Jan. 1, 1969 Commercial	Educational	TELEPHONES Jan. 1, 1969 Total	Residence	NEWSPAPERS Daily Number Feb. 1, 1969	Daily Circulation Oct. 1, 1968	Weekly July 11, 1969 Number	Weekly Circulation	Sunday Number Feb. 1, 1969	Sunday Circulation Oct. 1, 1968
Alabama	674	128	38	14	8	1,407,700	1,047,900	21	723,374	100	318,231	13	612,118
Alaska	203	18	3	7	—	74,000†	41,400†	7	66,824	6	6,224	3	21,646
Arizona	217	55	12	11	2	803,000	547,000	13	401,953	57	128,119	5	330,110
Arkansas	713	81	25	6	1	755,000	558,200	34	422,783	129	208,811	12	358,108
California	1,175	227	134	48	8	12,363,400	8,766,600	134	5,767,724	442	2,153,546	37	4,690,177
Colorado	428	67	22	11	1	1,212,900	840,800	26	677,094	129	267,051	9	713,478
Connecticut	256	37	16	5	3	1,912,000	1,404,300	28	939,381	46	169,831	7	701,940
Delaware	57	10	3	—	1	337,200	245,600	3	152,168	14	34,891	—	—
Dist. of Columbia	1	6	6	6	1	837,800	434,900	3	1,015,270	...	...	2	987,768
Florida	473	185	70	25	9	3,519,400	2,456,800	50	1,938,949	134	367,944	29	1,733,262
Georgia	662	168	45	14	10	2,075,000	1,497,500	31	990,477	187	498,814	11	892,280
Hawaii	80	25	3	10	2	364,700†	245,000†	5	221,866	2	13,248‖	2	177,608
Idaho	278	42	5	7	1	317,600	227,400	14	170,688	64	100,056	5	136,655
Illinois	1,299	121	84	21	5	6,566,800	4,742,000	85	3,962,802	609	2,296,865	20	3,045,435
Indiana	770	80	67	18	2	2,620,600	1,954,000	86	1,707,199	202	424,869	20	1,179,595
Iowa	975	70	28	12	1	1,496,400	1,146,400	44	1,005,019	362	673,915	9	869,198
Kansas	737	59	19	12	1	1,194,300	898,000	53	666,160	253	380,380‖	14	436,779
Kentucky	1,371	98	50	8	11	1,291,900	964,900	27	767,645	135	372,592	13	567,527
Louisiana	553	88	31	15	1	1,621,900	1,209,100	22	756,443	91	239,945	10	662,576
Maine	521	34	10	7	4	433,700	323,700	9	266,679	35	77,557	1	108,947
Maryland	435	51	30	5	—	2,193,600	1,605,300	12	756,482	68	401,968	4	722,088
Massachusetts	457	61	35	10	2	3,232,900	2,277,900	46	2,385,549	134	606,475	8	1,638,301
Michigan	889	122	67	19	4	4,711,400	3,512,800	54	2,434,953	284	1,211,031	12	2,084,883
Minnesota	893	83	24	13	4	2,000,600	1,495,800	30	1,137,919	329	623,791	8	1,057,189
Mississippi	494	90	22	9	—	781,300	589,300	20	307,840	102	156,152	7	181,402
Missouri	1,017	96	33	20	2	2,544,300	1,867,900	53	1,809,166	287	612,228	14	1,555,480
Montana	395	41	4	9	—	327,100	237,600	15	191,466	73	119,906	9	182,448
Nebraska	568	45	13	14	8	798,100	597,300	19	485,746	202	332,537	5	362,588
Nevada	100	19	7	7	1	275,200	168,300	7	138,363	16	22,120	4	124,422
New Hampshire	256	25	10	2	4	366,200	273,900	9	152,941	33	90,870	1	49,019
New Jersey	525	32	23	1	—	4,346,500	3,230,100	31	2,046,765	209	970,391	8	1,319,248
New Mexico	348	54	14	7	1	450,800	294,200	19	206,013	25	32,722	12	174,496
New York	1,654	151	82	28	7	11,706,400	8,066,900	81	7,742,439	434	1,465,680	15	6,635,490
North Carolina	799	187	65	17	6	2,055,200	1,518,700	48	1,286,248	136	233,950	18	891,753
North Dakota	484	25	5	11	1	304,600	221,900	10	153,615	99	158,541	2	64,322
Ohio	1,092	111	99	28	8	5,742,300	4,283,300	96	3,557,180	251	1,173,578	20	2,329,966
Oklahoma	668	61	31	10	3	1,323,400	949,800	52	851,452	211	346,857	41	795,391
Oregon	373	78	14	12	2	1,075,600	764,900	21	649,758	99	294,940	5	532,946
Pennsylvania	1,872	165	99	24	8	6,873,500	5,175,900	110	4,042,589	246	786,847	10	2,882,920
Rhode Island	59	15	6	3	1	485,500	354,200	7	319,106	13	53,050	2	219,213
South Carolina	404	96	31	11	5	1,009,300	743,700	17	551,859	76	129,225	7	432,296
South Dakota	438	28	2	10	2	306,100	230,100	12	169,595	145	176,661	4	120,313
Tennessee	610	139	52	15	3	1,739,300	1,292,600	31	1,139,676	123	355,522	14	911,470
Texas	1,585	279	107	52	5	5,555,300	3,930,000	109	3,202,850	495	729,542	80	3,032,754
Utah	231	31	7	3	5	535,400	384,500	5	259,057	50	108,634	4	255,700
Vermont	297	17	1	2	4	205,600	147,200	9	109,745	15	27,652	—	—
Virginia	981	121	48	13	5	2,189,700	1,565,500	31	1,053,898	109	336,796	11	685,470
Washington	505	92	31	13	6	1,816,800	1,303,400	23	1,032,672	150	862,160	11	939,579
West Virginia	1,089	58	20	9	—	710,600	534,400	32	513,099	82	195,621	11	404,858
Wisconsin	803	91	63	16	3	2,168,200	1,578,400	38	1,211,502	251	656,254	7	853,087
Wyoming	183	29	1	3	—	180,500	125,000	10	72,444	28	55,133	2	28,303
Total U.S.	32,064*	4,092	1,717	653	172	109,217,600	78,872,300	1,752‡	62,535,394‡	7,739§	22,138,708§	578‡	49,692,602‡

*Includes 117 post offices in U.S. territories. †Jan. 1, 1968.
‡Total has been adjusted to account for double listings of Covington, Ky. edition of Ohio newspaper.
§Excludes District of Columbia. ‖March 1967.
Sources: American Newspaper Representatives, Inc. American Telephone and Telegraph Co. Federal Communications Commission. Television Digest, Inc., *Television Factbook* (Copyright 1969. All rights reserved. Used by permission). The Editor & Publisher Co., Inc. *International Year Book* (Copyright 1969. All rights reserved. Used by permission). U.S. Post Office Department.

Printed in U.S.A. by R. R. Donnelley & Sons Company